Sports Illustrated 2008 Almanac

By the Editors of Sports Illustrated

SPORTS CALENDAR

BASEBALL

PRO FOOTBALL

COLLEGE FOOTBALL

PRO BASKETBALL

COLLEGE BASKETBALL

HOCKEY

TENNIS

GOLF

BOXING

HORSE RACING

MOTOR SPORTS

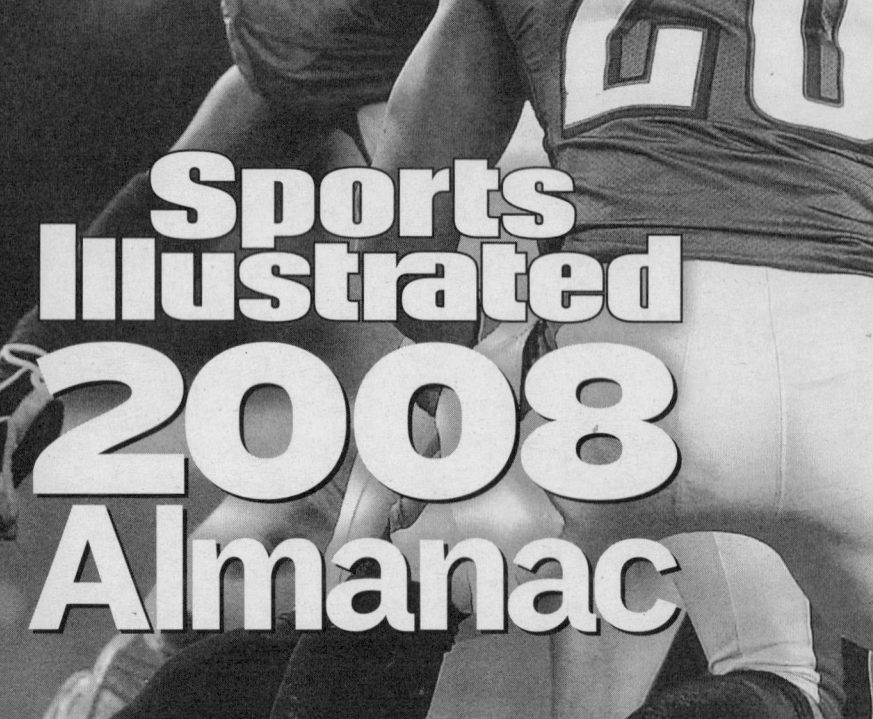

Sports Illustrated
2008
Almanac

First Edition
ISBN10: 1-933405-46-5
ISBN 13: 978-1-933405-46-9

SPORTS ILLUSTRATED 2008 Almanac was prepared by
Touchpoint Sports Publishing, of White Plains, N.Y.

Editorial Director: Morin Bishop   Managing Editor: Reed Richardson
Art Director: Barbara Chilenskas   Associate Editor: Max Berry
Photo Editor: John Blackmar   Editorial Intern: Monica Perschetz
Proofreaders: Erin Friar, Connor Ennis

Cover photography credits:
PEYTON MANNING: Al Tielemans/Sports Illustrated
ROGER FEDERER: Bob Martin
ALEX RODRIGUEZ: Chuck Solomon
TIGER WOODS: Fred Vuich/Sports Illustrated

Back cover photography credits:
SIDNEY CROSBY: Lou Capozzola
VENUS WILLIAMS: Bob Martin
TIM TEBOW: Heinz Kluetmeier

Spine photography credit: LEBRON JAMES: Greg Nelson

Title page photography credit: Evan Pinkus/WireImage.com

TIME INC. HOME ENTERTAINMENT

Publisher .... Richard Fraiman
General Manager .... Steven Sandonato
Executive Director, Marketing Services .... Carol Pittard
Director, Retail & Special Sales .... Tom Mifsud
Director, New Product Development .... Peter Harper
Assistant Director, Brand Marketing .... Laura Adam
Associate Counsel .... Helen Wan
Book Production Manager .... Jonathan Polsky
Design & Prepress Manager .... Anne-Michelle Gallero
Brand Manager .... Danielle Terwilliger

Special thanks: Bozena Bannett, Alexandra Bliss, Glenn Buonocore, Suzanne Janso, Robert Marasco,
Brooke Regert, Mary Sarro-Waite, Ilene Schreider, Adriana Tierno, Alex Voznesenskiy

We welcome your comments and suggestions about Sports Illustrated Books. Please write to us
at: Sports Illustrated Books, Attention: Book Editors, P.O. Box 11016, Des Moines, IA 50336-1016
If you would like to order any of our hardcover Collector's Edition books, please call us at
1-800-327-6388. (Monday through Friday, 7:00 a.m.- 8:00 p.m. or Saturday, 7:00 a.m.- 6:00 p.m.
Central Time)

CONTENTS

THE YEAR IN SPORTS by Hank Hersch 9

BASEBALL by Mark Bechtel 43

PRO FOOTBALL by Hank Hersch 121

COLLEGE FOOTBALL by B.J. Schecter 217

PRO BASKETBALL by Stephen Cannella 283

COLLEGE BASKETBALL by B.J. Schecter 321

HOCKEY by B.J. Schecter 363

TENNIS by B.J. Schecter 405

GOLF by Stephen Cannella 437

BOXING by Stephen Cannella 477

HORSE RACING by Stephen Cannella 499

MOTOR SPORTS by Mark Bechtel 539

SOCCER by Hank Hersch 565

NCAA SPORTS by Hank Hersch 585

OLYMPICS by Merrell Noden 635

TRACK AND FIELD by Merrell Noden 687

SWIMMING by Mark Bechtel 711

MISCELLANEOUS SPORTS by Merrell Noden 727

TRIVIA GUIDE 775

AWARDS 805

OBITUARIES 811

2008 MAJOR EVENTS 817

In compiling the Sports Illustrated 2008 Almanac, the editors would like to extend their gratitude to the media relations offices of the following organizations for their help in providing information and materials relating to their sports: Major League Baseball; Elias Sports Bureau, the Canadian Football League; the National Football League, Arena Football League; the National Collegiate Athletic Association; the National Basketball Association; the National Hockey League; the Association of Tennis Professionals; the Women's Tennis Association; the U.S. Tennis Association; the U.S. Golf Association; the Ladies Professional Golf Association; the Professional Golfers Association; National Thoroughbred Racing Association; the U.S. Trotting Association; the Breeders' Cup; Churchill Downs; the New York Racing Association, Inc.; the Jockey's Guild, Inc.; the Champ Car Auto Racing circuit; the National Hot Rod Association; the International Motor Sports Association; the National Association for Stock Car Auto Racing; the Professional Bowlers Association; the United Soccer Leagues; Major League Soccer; the Fédération Internationale de Futbol Association; the U.S. Soccer Federation; the U.S. Olympic Committee; USA Track & Field; U.S. Swimming; U.S. Diving; U.S. Skiing; U.S. Figure Skating Association; the U.S. Chess Federation; U.S. Curling; the Iditarod Trail Committee; the International Game Fish Association; USA Gymnastics; U.S. Handball Association; the Lacrosse Foundation; the American Power Boat Association; the Unlimited Hydroplane Racing Association; the Professional Rodeo Cowboys Association; U.S. Rowing; the American Amateur Softball Association; U.S. Speed Skating ; U.S. Rugby Football Union; USA Triathlon; the National Archery Association; USA Wrestling; the U.S. Squash Racquets Association; the U.S. Polo Association; ABC Sports; and the U.S. Volleyball Association.

SOURCES *(Cont.)*

The following sources were consulted in gathering information:

Baseball mlb.com, worldseries.com, baseballhalloffame.org, baseball-almanac.com, Associated Press (LCS, WS game recaps)

Pro Football nfl.com, superbowl.com, nfleurope.com arenafootball.com, arenabowl.com, profootballhof.com

College Football ncaasports.com, heisman.com, *Official 2007 NCAA Division I-A and I-AA Football Records Book, Official 2007 Division II and III Football Records Book*

Pro Basketball nba.com, hoophall.com

College Basketball ncaasports.com, *Official 2008 NCAA Division I Men's Basketball Records Book, Official 2008 NCAA Division I Women's Basketball Records Book, Official 2008 NCAA Division II and III Men's Basketball Records Book*

Hockey nhl.com, hhof.com, ushockeyhall.com

Tennis atptennis.com, sonyericssonwtatour.com, usopen.org, australianopen.com, wimbledon.org, rolandgarros.com, masters-cup.com, daviscup.com, fedcup.com, tennisfame.com

Golf pgatour.com, masters.org, usopen.org, usga.org, opengolf.com, pga.com, randa.org, lpga.com, knc.com, ussenioropen.com, usamateur.org, rydercup.com, walkercup.org, curtiscup.org, pinggolf.com

Boxing wbaonline.com, wbcboxing.com, ibf-usba-boxing.com, ibhof.com, thering-online.com, usaboxing.org, olympic.org

Horse Racing ntra.com, ustrotting.com, equibase.com, bloodhorse.com, kentuckyderby.com, belmontstakes.nyra.com, preakness.com

Motor Sports nascar.com, formula1.com, indycar.com, americanlemans.com, nhra.com, champcarworldseries.com, lemans.org, indy500.com, daytona24hr.com

Soccer fifa.com, fifaworldcup.yahoo.com, mlsnet.com, ussoccer.com, uefa.com, rsssf.com, premierleague.com, uslsoccer.com, soccernet.com

NCAA Sports ncaasports.com

Olympics torino2006.org, olympic.org, en.beijing2008.com, usoc.org

Track and Field iaaf.org, usatf.org, chicagomarathon.com, parismarathon.com, usoc.org, bostonmarathon.org, nycmarathon.org, maratonadiroma.it, london-marathon.co.uk, fortismarathonrotterdam.nl, asahi.com/tokyo-marathon, *Track and Field News*

Swimming fina.org, usaswimming.org, ishof.org, panpacs2006.com, usoc.org

Miscellaneous Sports letour.fr, usarchery.org, pba.com, fide.com, uschesschampionship.com, worldcurling.org, usacurl.org, usacycling.org, uci.ch, iditarod.com, igfa.org, usfigureskating.org, isu.org, usoc.org, fig-gymnastics.com, usa-gymnastics.org, ushandball.org, uscla.com, nll.com, littleleague.org, abrahydroplanes.com, us-polo.org, prorodeo.org, usrowing.org, usarugby.org, rugbyworldcup.com, amnrl.com, ussailing.org, americascup.com, issf-shooting.org, fis-ski.com, asasoftball.com, isu.org, us-squash.org, ironmanlive.com, usatriathlon.org, fivb.org, usavolleyball.org, themat.com

Sports Illustrated

AUGUST 13, 2007

HISTORY
Barry Bonds Hits Home Run No. 755

In 2007, sports history was made by the famous and infamous alike

The Year In Sports

Summer of Our Discontent

In 2007, incredible comebacks and unpredictable upsets bookended a sour summer filled with cheating scandals, felony convictions and one very controversial record

BY HANK HERSCH

I T WAS THE SECOND SUNDAY IN September, which, like almost any Sunday in any calendar year, was packed with sports events of various magnitudes, all accessible with a click of the remote control. Only on this Sunday, the acute channel flipper could feel as if he were the maestro of a philharmonic, summoning genius with every gesture he made. Movement upon movement, stroke upon stroke, the crescendo built through three events, and, more important, among three brilliant soloists, each in his prime, each exhibiting the skill, focus and precision that had already made him legendary. From Roger Federer's seizing his fourth straight U.S. Open title to Tiger Woods's final round 63 to win the BMW Open to Alex Rodriguez's homering in his fifth straight game, a September Sunday in 2007 afforded agile viewers at home a harmonic convergence of greatness.

The fan would have done well to let those soaring performances soak in, because only a few weeks earlier the notes sounded in the sports world had been far less than uplifting. In July, a federal grand jury indicted Atlanta Falcons quarterback Michael Vick, whose number 7 jersey was once the most popular in the NFL, on charges of sponsoring and wagering on dogfighting through his operation based in Surrey County, Va., and of treat-

ing his dogs with chilling cruelty. To wit: In running Bad Newz Kennels, Vick and his associates allegedly hanged, drowned, electrocuted and fatally slammed to the ground animals deemed insufficiently aggressive. The 27-year-old Vick would plead guilty to a felony dogfighting charge, while an arbitrator would rule that he had to repay the Falcons nearly $20 million in bonus money from the record 10-year, $130 million contract he signed in 2004. The highest total purse for any of the 30 Bad Newz fights mentioned in the indictment: $26,000.

As Vick's case played out, Tour de France officials were uncovering yet another cheating scandal amongst that sport's biggest names, while, here in the U.S., federal authorities were ensnaring a less familiar figure whose nefarious activities, according to one U.S. Congressman, could constitute "one of the most damaging scandals in the history of American sports." NBA referee Tim Donaghy, a 13-year veteran, pleaded guilty in August to two felonies for betting on games he officiated and giving inside information to gamblers. Allegedly, he told members of organized crime which three-ref crews would be working which games, information that isn't supposed to be available until officials arrive at the arena. Such knowledge can help a gambler decide which team to wager on or

Though an asterisk will not taint Bonds' career home run total in official record books, Ecko let fans decide that Bonds' historic 756th home run ball *will* carry such a mark.

AVIV SMALL/ZUMA PRESS

how to bet the over-under line; according to Covers.com, games that the by-the-book Donaghy worked "showed about a 60 percent lean toward the over" in the last two years. After entering his guilty plea, Donaghy was expected to cooperate with authorities looking into the betting patterns of NBA officials. "People are going to look at refs with raised eyebrows because one of us committed the ultimate sin," said one former NBA ref during the Donaghy investigation. "And that's going to be awfully tough to take."

San Francisco Giants slugger Barry Bonds did not cop a plea like Vick and Donaghy, but in the dog days of summer he remained under federal investigation on perjury and tax-evasion charges. Bonds had already been found in contempt by the court of public opinion after numerous reports in recent years linking him to the use of performance-enhancing drugs. No matter: On Aug. 7 at AT&T Park, off a 3–2 pitch from Washington Nationals lefthander Mike Bacsik, he deposited a ball 435 feet into the right centerfield seats for the 756th home run of his career, breaking the 33-year-old record set by Hank Aaron. "This record is not tainted," Bonds, 43, protested to reporters in his post-756 news conference. "At all. At all. Period. You guys can say whatever you want."

In an unofficial yet revealing referendum, fashion designer Marc Ecko, who bought the epic home run ball for $752,467 in an auction, asked online voters to decide if he should 1) donate it as is to the Hall of Fame, 2) brand it with an asterisk and give it to the Hall or 3) blast it into space on a rocket. The asterisk voters prevailed.

Voters and asterisks have often colored the end of the college football season, but the advent of the BCS has left less room for controversy. In the championship game at the University of Phoenix Stadium, Florida eliminated any uncertainty about who deserved to be No. 1, finishing off an unbeaten season with a 41–14 dismantling of Ohio State, which had won 19 straight. Under heavy pressure from the Gators'

defensive ends, Buckeyes quarterback Troy Smith, the Heisman Trophy winner, completed just four of 14 passes for an offense that amassed all of 82 yards. Oft-criticized Florida QB Chris Leak, meanwhile, connected on 25 of 36 passes to six different receivers and was named the game's MVP. "I can't tell you how proud I am of him," said Gators coach Urban Meyer. "I love a fighter, and he's a fighter."

Not to be outdone, the Florida basketball team did its own number on Ohio State to win a title, routing the Buckeyes 84–75 in the NCAA final at Atlanta's Georgia Dome. The victory marked the second straight championship for the four junior roommates who constituted the Gators' nucleus: shot-blocking dynamo Joakim Noah, low-post scorer Al Horford, dogged playmaker Taurean Green and silky wingman Corey Brewer, the Final Four's Most Outstanding Player. Only one other school in the last 33 seasons—Duke in 1991 and '92—had reigned supreme in back-to-back seasons. "I'd like this team to be remembered as the greatest team that ever played," said 41-year-old Florida coach Billy Donovan. "I'm not saying this team would beat the UNLVs [of the early 1990s] or the

PHOTO BY JOE MURPHY/NBAE VIA GETTY IMAGES

The post-season gambling revelations involving veteran referee Donaghy rocked the NBA and left both fans and players questioning the outcome of many games.

was showing any signs of needing to be supplanted. With more than a little help from point guard Tony Parker, the NBA Finals MVP, Duncan's San Antonio Spurs swept the Cleveland Cavaliers and their precocious leader, LeBron James, to win their fourth title in nine seasons. The Spurs' biggest postseason challenges came from the Phoenix Suns and Utah Jazz in the Western Conference playoffs, though they didn't have to tussle with the 67-win Dallas Mavericks. The No. 1 seed fell in the first round to the Golden State Warriors, whose six-game victory marked the greatest postseason series upset in league history.

The Indianapolis Colts made much better use of the home-field advantage, finally defeating their arch nemesis, the New England Patriots, in the AFC title game at the RCA Dome. Down 21–3 in the second quarter, the Colts rallied to win 38–34 after quarterback Peyton Manning led an 80-yard TD march in the final 2:17. Indy's workmanlike 29–17 win over the Chicago Bears at Dolphin Stadium in Super Bowl XLI will be remembered for the MVP performance of Manning, the erratic play of Chicago QB Rex Grossman and the first-time matchup of two black coaches: Tony Dungy of the Colts and Lovie Smith of the Bears. For a league in which two-thirds of the players are African-American, that last fact may have the most significant impact. "At first I didn't even realize that we could have two black head coaches in the Super Bowl," said Philadelphia Eagles cornerback Sheldon Brown. "But when I did, I knew this would be a huge deal."

The 2006–07 NHL season, likewise, may be remembered less for the rings earned by the Anaheim Ducks, who defeated the Ottawa Senators in five games to become the first California team to win the Stanley Cup, than for the hardware collected by 19-year-old Pittsburgh Penguins center Sidney Crosby, the scoring champion who became the league's youngest MVP since Wayne Gretzky in 1980. The two most compelling

UCLAs [of the John Wooden dynasty]. I'm not talking about wins and losses. I'm talking about the word *team*."

That cohesiveness was needed to throttle the inside-out attack of Ohio State. The out part, in particular, was off for the Buckeyes: They hit just four of 23 from beyond the arc, even as 7-foot freshman Greg Oden was putting up 25 points and 12 boards in the paint. A new age-minimum rule had denied Oden and others immediate entry to the NBA, giving rise to perhaps the greatest freshman class ever. Kevin Durant of Texas, a spindly 6'9" do-it-all forward, ranked fourth in the nation in scoring (25.8 points per game) and rebounding (11.1) and was named Player of the Year. And yet he went second in the NBA draft, to the Seattle SuperSonics, after the Portland Trail Blazers bagged Oden with the No. 1 pick. Any hope that Oden would right the reeling franchise as a rookie ended before the season started, however, when he underwent microfracture surgery on his right knee.

Oden would have to wait to become the next Tim Duncan—not that the current one boxers of their time tried to kindle interest in their sport, but Floyd Mayweather Jr.'s super welterweight decision over Oscar De La Hoya in Las Vegas failed to live up to its record $19 million gate. Soccer tried to get a similar boost from English superstar David Beckham, who signed a five-year contract potentially worth more than $200 million to play for the Los Angeles Galaxy. But because of ankle and knee injuries he played in only a handful of matches and his team failed to qualify for the MLS playoffs.

But then, it's hard to live up to the hype—unless you happen to be named Federer or Woods. Ranked No. 1 since Feb. 2, 2004, a record duration, the 26-year-old Federer, from Basel, Switzerland, merely won Wimbledon for the fifth consecutive time (tying Bjorn Borg's mark), claimed an unprecedented fourth straight U.S. Open title, became the first player to win at least three majors in three calendar years, appeared in a record 10th straight Grand Slam final and ran his majors victory total to 12, second only to Pete Sampras's 14.

Woods watchers have sensed his greatness ever since he turned pro as a 20-year-old in 1996. By his standards, 2007 wasn't a banner year in the majors—but only by his standards. After tying for second in both the Masters and the U.S. Open and finishing 12th at the British, he won the PGA at Southern Hills in Tulsa, Okla., by firing a second-round 63 to tie the lowest score in major-championship history. That 13th major came in the midst of one of the most breathtaking runs of Woods's incomparable career: four victories and one second-place finish in his final five tournaments, during which he was a total of 75 under par.

The last two of those triumphs—the BMW Open, the Tour Championship—were in the inaugural FedEx Cup playoffs, the PGA Tour's attempt, á la NASCARS's Chase for the Cup, to bring meaning and drama to the end of its season. Meaning, it may have achieved; drama, it didn't. Despite skipping one of the four playoff tournaments, Woods won the Cup handily, earning a $10 million bonus deposited tax-free into his retirement account in addition to his season prize money of $10,867,052.

Was the new format a letdown because of Woods's landslide win? Said Phil Mickelson, "I'm sure Tiger doesn't feel that way."

Of the three stars ascendant on that September Sunday, only the 32-year-old Rodriguez would have his glorious season end with a fizzle. In his fourth summer with the Yankees he finally seemed to have won the hearts of New York fans, first by belting a record-tying 14 home runs in April, then by becoming the youngest player in history to reach the 500 homer mark and finally by helping the team, which, near the end of May, was eight games under .500, to a 94–68 record and the AL wild card berth. But for the third straight year the Yankees could not advance past the first round of the playoffs, losing to the Cleveland Indians. Rodriguez, who batted .314 with 54 homers and 156 RBIs during the regular season, drove in one run in the four playoff games—or one more than he had in New York's two previous postseason flameouts.

But while the Yankees were fading, the Colorado Rockies were rolling: They finished the season by winning 13 of 14 games just to qualify for a single-game playoff with the San Diego Padres, which they took 9–8 in 13 innings. After that came sweeps of the Philadelphia Phillies and the Arizona Diamondbacks, putting Colorado on a 21–1 run entering the World Series. And after that came the Boston Red Sox, who had rallied from a 3–1 deficit in the ALCS against the Cleveland Indians. The team that until 2004 toiled under the 86-year-old Curse of the Bambino proceeded to sweep a World Series for the second time in four autumns, becoming the first outfit since the historically great 1998 Yankees to win the championship after having the best record in the regular season. Once lovable losers, the Sox have played 17 postseason elimination games since 2003. They have won 15.

As the World Series MVP, Boston third baseman Mike Lowell, put it after homering in a 4–3, title-clinching win in Denver, "With the Red Sox, people expect you to win." It was the fourth Sunday in October, and yet another chance for sports fans to appreciate greatness.

November 2006

NOV 1 Pittsburgh Penguins rookie center Evgeni Malkin sets a modern-day NHL record by scoring at least one goal in each of his first six games.

THEY SAID IT

Jon Spoelstra, former New Jersey Nets president, on his team's scrapes with the law in the mid-1990s: "One year we had six guys in jail. Not together, because that would have meant teamwork."

NOV 19 Jimmie Johnson seals the NASCAR Nextel Cup Series Championship after the final race of the season, the Ford 400.

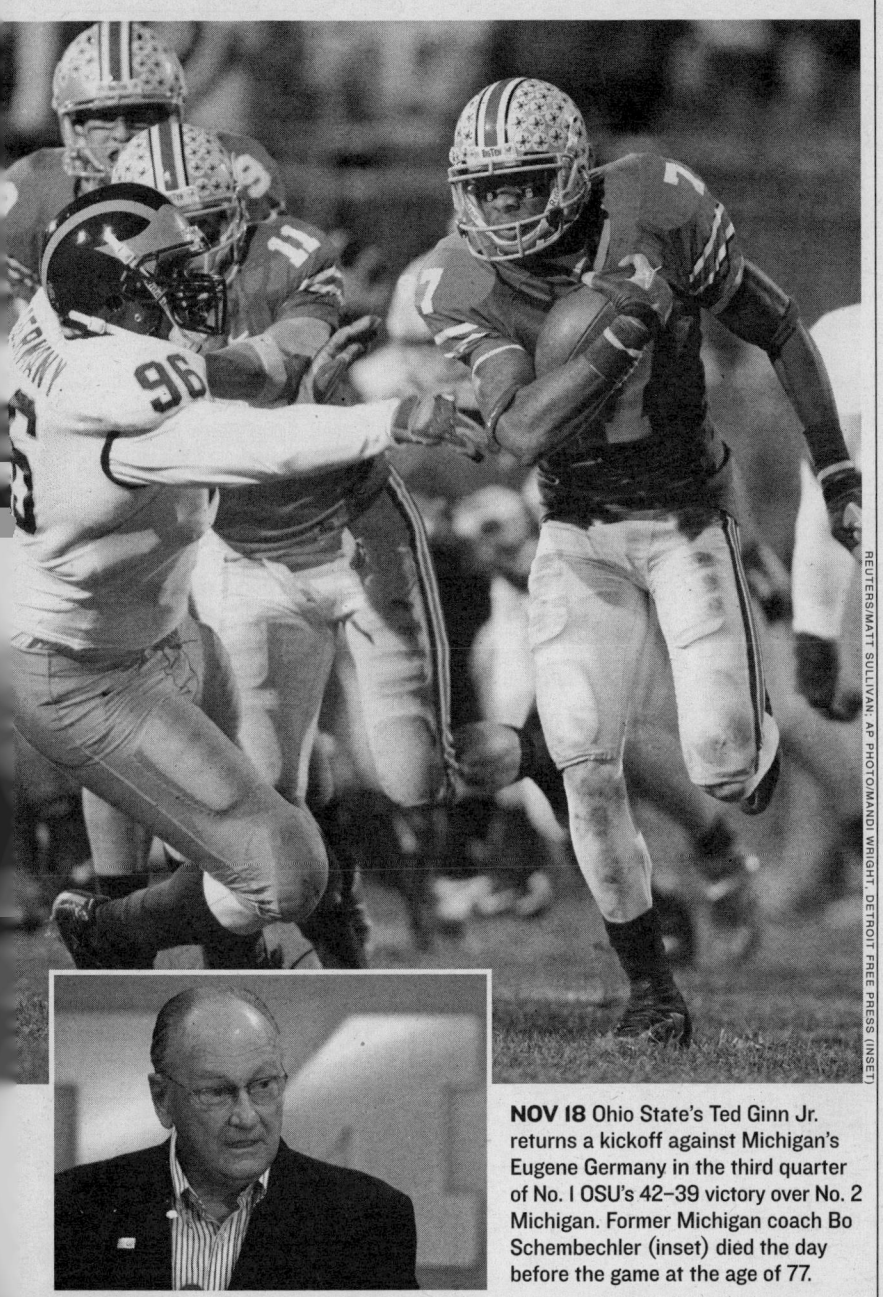

NOV 18 Ohio State's Ted Ginn Jr. returns a kickoff against Michigan's Eugene Germany in the third quarter of No. 1 OSU's 42–39 victory over No. 2 Michigan. Former Michigan coach Bo Schembechler (inset) died the day before the game at the age of 77.

December 2006

JUSTIN SULLIVAN/GETTY IMAGES

DEC 1 Jockey Russell Baze claims his 9,531st career win to surpass Laffit Pincay Jr. for the all-time thoroughbred horse-race winning record.

THEY SAID IT

Joey Porter, Steelers linebacker, apologizing for directing a homosexual slur at Cleveland's Kellen Winslow after a game: "I didn't mean to offend nobody but Kellen Winslow."

BOB ROSATO

DEC 23 In what would prove to be a foreshadowing of the 2007 men's NCAA championship game, Florida's Al Horford helps the Gators to an 86–60 victory over an Ohio State team that Greg Oden just recently returned to after a wrist injury.

January 2007

ROBERT BECK

JAN 8 Chris Leak (l.) completes 25 of 36 passes for 213 yards and one touchdown to lead the Florida Gators to a 41–14 victory over Ohio State in the BCS title game.

JAN 1 Texas Tech coach Bob Knight earns his 880th career win with a victory over New Mexico, surpassing Dean Smith for the most Division I men's basketball victories in NCAA history.

AP PHOTO/LM OTERO

GO FIGURE

1,264 Games it took Lakers coach Phil Jackson to reach 900 wins; no coach has reached the mark faster.

31.2 Turnovers per game in the NBA while the league used the synthetic ball it introduced last season.

28.8 Turnovers per game in 2007 after the NBA reinstated its leather ball.

JAN 27 Unseeded Serena Williams earns her eighth career Grand Slam title by defeating top-seeded Maria Sharapova 6–1, 6–2 in the Australian Open final.

THIS MONTH'S SIGN OF THE
APOCALYPSE

A New Zealand bride and groom played 18 holes of miniature golf to decide who would give up their surname.

FEB 4 Indianapolis QB Peyton Manning (r.) leads the Colts to a 29–17 victory at a rainy Superbowl XLI in Miami.

ROBERT BECK

FEB 11 Phil Mickelson ties Mark O'Meara's record-low score of 268 at the AT&T Pebble Beach Pro-Am, earning his 30th career PGA Tour title.

THEY SAID IT

Arthur Blank, 64-year-old owner of the Atlanta Falcons, on the benefits of winning the Super Bowl next year: "It would get my mother off my back."

March 2007

MARCH 4 A flagrant foul by Duke's Gerald Henderson leaves North Carolina's Dewey Burke with a bloodied nose in the final seconds of the Tar Heels' 86–72 victory.

MARCH 17 The Dallas Stars' Mike Modano (c.) scores his 503rd career goal to surpass Joe Mullen and become the top-scoring American-born player in NHL history.

KEVIN C. COX/WIREIMAGE.COM

AP PHOTO/JOHN RUSSELL

GO FIGURE

19 : 207 Age, in years and days, of the Penguins' Sidney Crosby when he became the youngest NHL player to reach 200 career points.

140 Days by which Crosby beat Wayne Gretzky, who had been the youngest to 200.

20,180 Crowd at the Inside Lacrosse Face-Off in Baltimore, an NCAA regular-season lax record.

4 Triple doubles by Massachusetts forward Stephane Lasme, tying the NCAA single-season record held by Cal's Jason Kidd (1994) and Drexel's Michael Anderson ('86).

MARCH 31 OSU's Greg Oden proves to be too much for Georgetown's Roy Hibbert (l.) as the Buckeyes defeat the Hoyas 67–60 in the NCAA men's Final Four semifinal.

April 2007

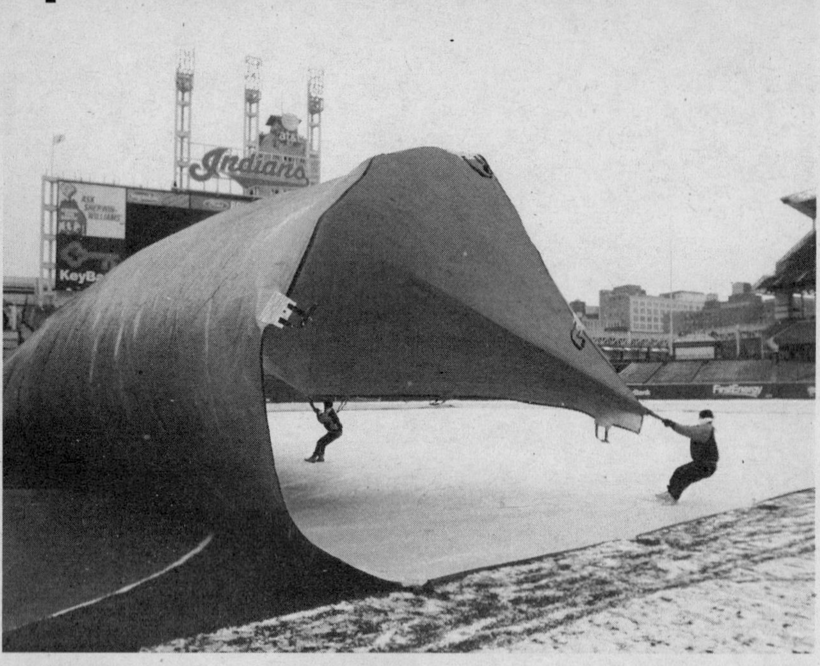

AP PHOTO/THE PLAIN DEALER, SCOTT SHAW

GENE J. PUSKAR/AP

APR 5 The Cleveland Indians grounds crew tries in vain to ready the field for the team's home opener at Jacobs Field during a snowy start to the MLB season. The series was eventually moved to Milwaukee.

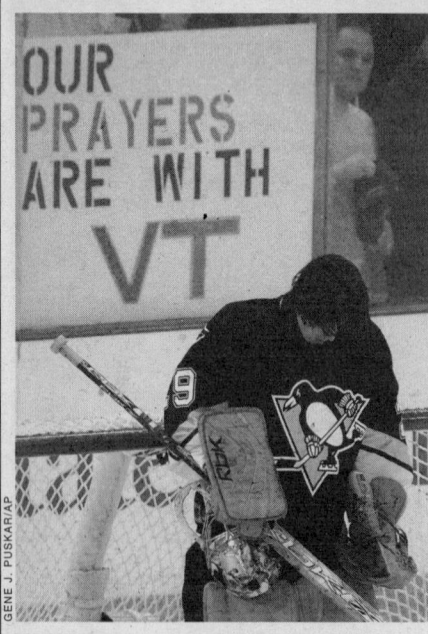

APR 17 Penguins goaltender Marc-Andre Fleury observes a moment of silence for the Virginia Tech shooting victims before playoff action against the Ottawa Senators.

APR 28 LSU QB JaMarcus Russell is chosen first overall by the Oakland Raiders in the 2007 NFL draft.

THEY SAID IT

Ichiro Suzuki, Mariners outfielder, on facing Red Sox pitcher Daisuke Matsuzaka (in Japanese): "I hope he arouses the fire that's dormant in the innermost recesses of my soul. I plan to face him with the zeal of a challenger."

May 2007

MAY 3 Rap star Snoop Dogg and some young fans look on as the No. 8 seed Golden State Warriors upset the top-seeded Dallas Mavericks 4–2 in the first round of the NBA Playoffs.

GO FIGURE

5 Home runs journeyman Jack Cust, who played for four teams between 2001 and '06, hit in 144 major league at bats before the '07 season.

6 Homers Cust hit in his first 26 at bats with the Athletics after being traded to Oakland by San Diego on May 3.

12 Consecutive wins by the Angels' Bartolo Colon against the Rangers, tying Pedro Martinez's 12–0 mark against Seattle from 1998 to 2004 for the longest winning streak by a pitcher against one team.

11 Three-pointers hit by the Warriors in the first half of their Game 3 win over the Jazz in the Western Conference Semifinals, an NBA playoff record for one half.

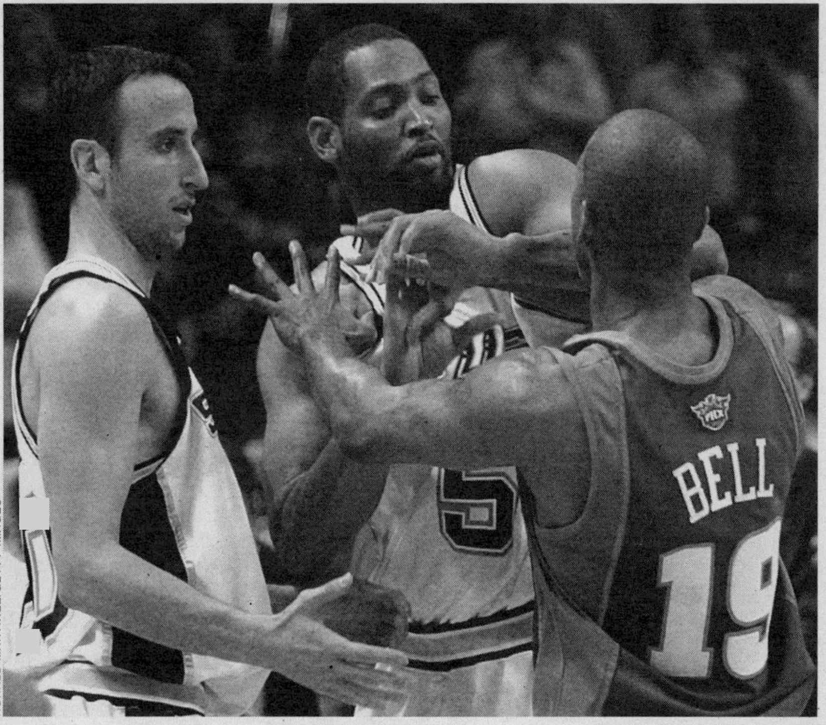

RONALD MARTINEZ/GETTY IMAGES

AP PHOTO/THE CITIZENS' VOICE, RALPH FRANCELLO

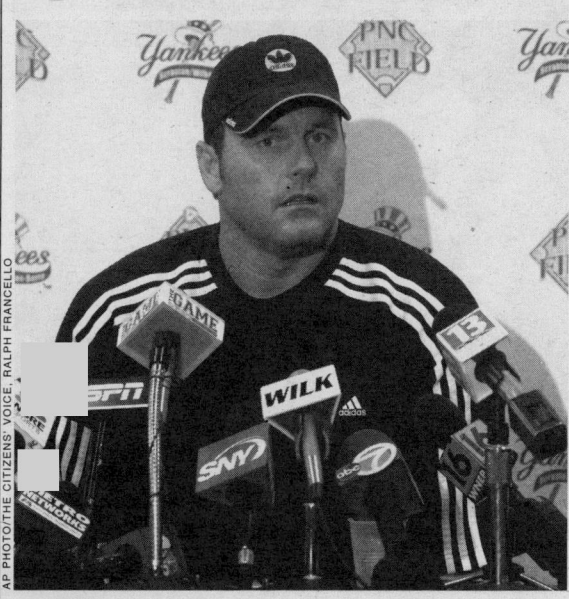

MAY 14 Pheonix's Raja Bell shoves Robert Horry after the Spurs forward's flagrant foul of Steve Nash in Game 4 of the NBA Western Conference Semifinals.

MAY 28 Roger Clemens pitches six shutout innings for the Triple-A Scranton/Wilkes Barre Yankees in his final minor league tuneup before rejoining the New York Yankees.

June 2007

BOB MARTIN

GO **FIGURE**

8,200 Maximum altitude, in feet, at which international soccer games can be played under a new FIFA directive; several teams complained that playing World Cup qualifiers at 11,180 feet in La Paz gave Bolivia an unfair advantage.

1 NFL stadium where the official soda is neither Coke nor Pepsi: Seattle's Qwest Field, after the Seahawks signed a deal with local soft-drink maker Jones Soda Co.

$39 million Revenue for Jones Soda in 2006.

$56.7 billion Combined revenue for Coke and Pepsi in 2006.

JUN 10 Spaniard Rafael Nadal, the world's No. 2 tennis player, defeats top-ranked Roger Federer in four sets for the second straight year to win his third straight French Open title.

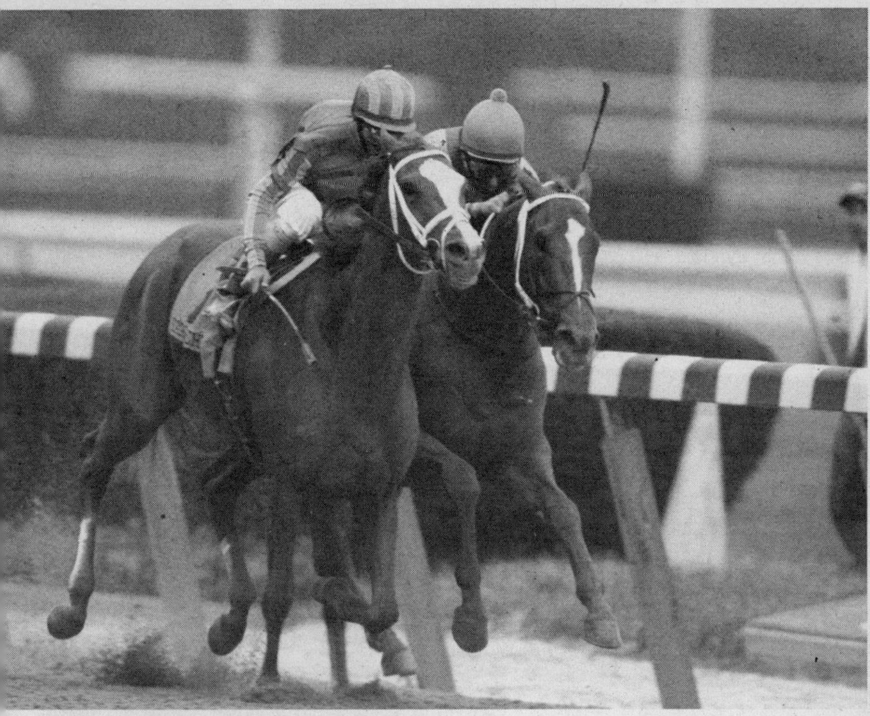

BILL FRAKES

AP PHOTO/OTTAWA CITIZEN,WAYNE CUDDINGTON

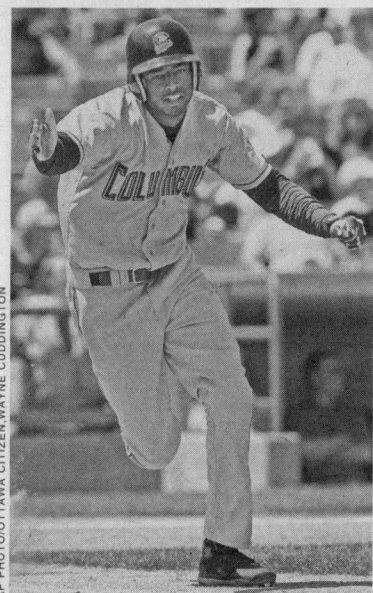

JUNE 9 Rags to Riches (l.), ridden by John Velazquez, becomes the first filly since 1905—and only the third in horse racing history—to win the Belmont Stakes.

THEY SAID IT

Ichiro Suzuki, Mariners outfielder, on Seattle's trip to face the Indians: "I'm not excited to go to Cleveland, but we have to. If I ever saw myself saying I'm excited going to Cleveland, I'd punch myself in the face because I'm lying."

JUNE 17 Brandon Watson, center fielder for the Triple-A Columbus Clippers, extends his hitting streak to 43 games, breaking Jack Lelivelt's 95-year-old Triple-A record. His streak would end the next day.

JUNE 17 Swimmer Kate Ziegler shatters the 1,500 meter freestyle world record by more than nine seconds at the TYR Meet of Champions, posting a time of 15:42.54 that easily bests Janet Evans' 1988 mark of 15:52.10.

AP PHOTO/KRISTEN BOISEN

THIS MONTH'S SIGN OF THE
APOCALYPSE

Redskins rookie LaRon Landry missed a pre-season practice after being shot in the groin during a team paintball outing.

BRANDON MALONE/ACTION IMAGES/ICO

JUNE 17 Eventual champion Angel Cabrera of Argentina enjoys a smoke during the fourth round of the U.S. Open Golf Championship.

JUNE 28 During a game against the Minnesota Twins at the Metrodome, Toronto's Frank Thomas connects on his 500th career home run.

THEY SAID IT

Phillip Wellman, manager of the Double-A Mississippi Braves, on his much-replayed meltdown in which he uprooted bases, crawled on the ground and lobbed a rosin bag as if it were a hand grenade: "Once again, my mother is very proud and my wife and kids are creeping around in disguise."

July 2007

JULY 1 Eventual champion Cristie Kerr birdies a putt on the 14th to give her a one-shot lead in the final round of the U.S. Women's Open Championship.

JULY 20 The *New York Post* breaks the story that veteran NBA referee Tim Donaghy placed bets on league games.

GO FIGURE

0 Japanese players who have appeared in an NFL game; in July 2007 the Falcons signed receiver-kick returner Noriaki Kinoshita from NFL Europa.

0 Times in their 46-year history that the Mets had opened a game with consecutive home runs before Jose Reyes and Ruben Gotay did it in the first inning against the Reds in July.

$54 Amount earned by a homeless man in Sao Paulo who confessed to sawing off the arms of a 36-year-old bronze statue of Pele and selling them for scrap metal; he was arrested and faces four years in prison.

JULY 10 All-Star Game MVP Ichiro Suzuki goes 3-for-3 and hits the event's first-ever inside-the-park home run.

JULY 17 The Philadelphia Phillies suffer the 10,000th defeat in the franchise's 124-year history as Ryan Howard strikes out in the ninth inning against St. Louis.

GO FIGURE

10 Times the Celtics will appear on national TV during the 2007–08 season.

0 Times the Celtics appeared on national TV during the 2006–07 season.

66,237 Attendence at Giants Stadium for August's Red Bulls—Galaxy game, in which David Beckham made his first MLS start.

11,573 The Red Bulls' average attendance for their 10 home games before Beckham's debut.

5 Penalty in yards NFL teams will face if their players spike the ball following a nonscoring play during the 2007 season.

AUG 1 New Boston Celtics forward Kevin Garnett throws out the first pitch before the Boston Red Sox game against the Baltimore Orioles at Fenway Park.

ROBERT BECK

THEY SAID IT

Hideki Matsui, Yankees leftfielder, after hitting two homers in a game in August while batting after Alex Rodriguez: "There was no pressure in my at bats. Everybody was in the bathroom."

AUG 7 Barry Bonds hits his 756th career home run, breaking the record set by Hank Aaron in April 1974. Bonds finished the season with 762 home runs.

HIENZ KLUETMEIER

August 2007 (Cont.)

AUGUST 27 Dalton Carriker hits a walk-off solo home run to help Georgia defeat Tokyo 3–2 in the championship game at the Little League World Series.

AP PHOTO/GENE J. PUSKAR

AUGUST 27 Atlanta Falcons quarterback Michael Vick pleads guilty to a federal dogfighting charge and is suspended without pay from the NFL indefinitely.

AP PHOTO/GERALD HERBERT

BOB MARTIN

AUGUST 26 Bernard Lagat wins the men's 1,500 meter run at the 2007 IAAF Athletics World Championships in Osaka, Japan. He later won the 5,000, making him the first athlete to become world champion in both events at the same meet.

THIS MONTH'S SIGN OF THE
APOCALYPSE

Titans cornerback Pacman Jones signed a contract to appear at pro wrestling events while he serves his season-long suspension.

September 2007

SEPT 1 The Appalachian State Mountaineers stun No. 5 Michigan 34–32, recording the first-ever win for an FCS (Div. I-AA) team over a ranked FBS (Div. I-A) team.

SEPT 1 Red Sox rookie pitcher Clay Buchholz pitches a no-hitter against the Orioles, making him the 11th pitcher to throw a no-hitter in Fenway Park history.

THIS MONTH'S SIGN OF THE
APOCALYPSE

A Florida man pleaded guilty to giving steroids to his 13-year-old son, who was training for a roller skating competition.

THEY SAID IT

Ron Artest, Sacramento Kings forward, on Michael Vick: "[He] lied and then came back and apologized to everybody. I felt that was classy."

SEPT 18 The Super Bowl champion Indianapolis Colts open their 2007 season at home with a 41–10 victory over the New Orleans Saints.

DUMMY CREDIT

AP PHOTO/DAVID J. PHILLIP

BRAD MANGIN

OCT 15 Rockies catcher Yorvit Torrealba and shortstop Troy Tulowitzki celebrate after the Rockies win Game 4 of the National League Championship series 6–4 to complete their sweep of the Arizona Diamondbacks and advance to the first World Series in franchise history.

GO FIGURE

25 Minutes it took to sell 42,000 tickets for the outdoor Pittsburgh Penguins-Buffalo Sabres game on New Year's Day.

95% Graduation rate for women's skiing according to an NCAA Division I study, the highest rate of any sport; fencing, gymnastics and lacrosse had the highest rate (88%) among men's sports.

THEY SAID IT

Mark Cuban, Mavericks owner, on how long it took him to get over Dallas' upset loss to the Warriors in the 2007 playoffs: "About three six-packs."

Late October 2006

DAVID E. KLUTHO

OCT 3 The Stanley Cup champion Anaheim Ducks open the 2007–08 NHL season against the Detroit Red Wings, losing in a shootout, 3–2.

OCT 19 Joe Torre announces that he has rejected a one-year, $5-million contract to return as manager for the New York Yankees in 2008, calling the incentive-laden deal an "insult." Eleven days later, former Yankees bench coach Joe Girardi would be named the new skipper.

AP PHOTO/JULIE JACOBSON

OCT 28 Only ten months after undergoing chemotherapy for lymphoma, 23-year-old Red Sox pitcher Jon Lester pitches 5⅔ shutout innings to win World Series Game 4.

Baseball

Red Sox closer
Jonathan Papelbon
celebrates after
striking out the
final batter of the
2007 World Series

Sweeps Weeks

After a near wire-to-wire run in the regular season, the Red Sox took home their second title in four years at the end of a postseason marked by series blowouts

BY MARK BECHTEL

THE BOSTON RED SOX WON their second World Series in four years with an impressive display of October teamwork: good starting pitching, timely hitting, solid bullpen work. "It took all 25 of us to get the job done," closer Jonathan Papelbon said. "It's just phenomenal." That stood in contrast to the regular season, when the focus for most of the year was on individual achievements. And no achievement got more attention than Barry Bonds's quest to become the greatest home run hitter the game has ever known.

The absurdity of the public's reaction to Barry Bonds's assault on Hank Aaron's career home run record was best articulated, somewhat improbably, by Padres outfielder Milton Bradley: "You say you hate him, and then you pay all this money to go see him?" Yes, that's what fans said, and yes, that's what fans did. The allure of seeing history made—albeit by a man in a black hat, literally and figuratively—proved too strong. The Giants leftfielder hit number 754 on July 27 to pull within one of Aaron's mark. And with that, the frenzy was on.

The Giants then hit the road, going to Los Angeles, where the normally late-arriving Dodgers fans beat an early path to Chavez Ravine, lest they miss a first inning at bat. It was so crowded on the freeways that the wife of Dodgers outfielder Luis Gonzalez left home at her usual time before the first game and didn't arrive until the fourth inning. After a fruitless series in L.A., Bonds and his traveling roadshow pulled in to San Diego, where he finally tied the record—ironically, off Clay Hensley, a pitcher who served a 15-game suspension for steroids in 2005.

Three days later he made history, sending a fastball from Washington's Mike Bacsik over the rightfield fence in San Francisco. The crowd of 43,154 roared, providing Bonds with enough support to offset the fact that both commissioner Bud Selig (in New York for a meeting with steroids czar George Mitchell) and Hank Aaron (asleep) skipped out on the event. (Aaron did send a videotaped message.) "This record is not tainted," Bonds said. "At all. At all. Period. You guys can say whatever you want."

As it turned out, not many of the people who were so captivated by Bonds's chase shared that opinion. Marc Ecko, the designer who bought the ball for more than $750,000, held an online vote to determine what should be done to the ball: donate it to the Hall of Fame, donate to the Hall but brand an asterisk onto it or blast it into space. The asterisk won. The Hall accepted

it, with its president saying, "Baseball belongs to the fans—it always has and always will. The asterisk represents the voice of the fans at this moment in time." Bonds, on the other hand, called the whole thing "stupid."

Bonds's achievement was the crowning milestone in a year in which several were reached. Craig Biggio got his 3,000th hit and Sammy Sosa hit his 600th homer. The 500-homer club got three new members: Frank Thomas, Jim Thome and its youngest member, Alex Rodriguez. Tom Glavine won his 300th game.

Of all the chases—Bonds aside, of course—A-Rod's was the most compelling. After a miserable postseason in which he was dropped to eighth in the batting order

In 2007, Mets starter Glavine became only the 23rd pitcher—and just the fifth lefthander—in major league history to reach the mark of 300 career wins.

for the Yankees' elimination game at the hands of the Tigers, Rodriguez burst out of the chute with perhaps the greatest April the game has ever seen.

It was apparent from Opening Day that the 2007 version of A-Rod was different from last year's. He dropped 15 pounds and lowered his body fat from 18 to 10 percent. He set up the game-winning run by stealing second on his own. "Last year? No way I even try," he said. "Because I would have been out by two feet." He also installed a hi-tech batting cage in his home and put in long hours there with the Yankees' new hitting coach, former journeyman player Kevin Long, who overhauled A-Rod's swing-from-the-heels cut. In the first month of the season, Rodriguez hit .355 with 14 homers—including a walkoff grand slam—and 34 RBIs.

Not even appearing in tabloid headline after tabloid headline could slow him down. In late May, the *New York Post* ran pictures of Rodriguez at a Toronto hotel with a blonde who was reportedly a former stripper. The tabs had a field day: "STRAY ROD" and "YANKEE DOODLE RANDY" were among the headlines, but two days after the story broke, the Yankees beat Boston to finally move out of the cellar.

Rodriguez didn't stop hitting until he got to career homer number 499, on July 25, at which point he went into a prolonged funk. He went 28 at bats without a homer, tying Mickey Mantle for the third-longest wait ever. Manager Joe Torre said he was "swinging at everything but the resin bag." Rodriguez finally got 500 on August 4 with a three-run shot off Kansas City's Kyle Davies. "To do it at home, wearing this beautiful uniform, it's special. You know, I've had my trials and tribulations here in New York. I've learned from them. I've had some great times and some tough times. But a day like this kind of brings it full circle and maybe there's a happy ending for me somewhere."

It didn't appear likely at the time. As well as A-Rod played, his teammates—especially the pitchers—were just as bad. In May, the Yankees announced they had signed Roger Clemens to join the rotation. By the time his debut rolled around, the Yanks were still 10½ games out of first place, with the Red Sox looking ready to run away with the AL East.

Boston made baseball's biggest offseason acquisition, investing $123 million in Japanese righty Daisuke Matsuzaka. (The Sox paid a $51.1 million posting fee and gave him a six-year, $52 million deal.) Armed—supposedly—with the mysterious gyroball, Dice-K at times lived up to the hype. He went 15-12 but he had plenty of help in the rotation, as Josh Beckett was baseball's only 20-game winner and Tim Wakefield won 17 games. But Boston's feared lineup showed signs of slowing down. Aging Manny Ramirez drove in just 87 runs and new signee J.D. Drew hit just 11 homers. When the Yankees bats woke up in the summer, Boston saw its lead slip to 1½ games on September 23.

In the last week of the season, the Yankees, who had been 21–29 on May 29, clinched their 12th consecutive playoff berth. "This has definitely been the hardest one," said shortstop Derek Jeter. "We scuffled early on, but everyone here knew we had a good team, we were just playing bad. A lot of people counted us out, but I think everyone sort of liked that. People like the challenge. It says a lot about the team that we didn't hang our heads and we continued to battle." Their quest to catch the Sox, however, came up two games short, sparing Boston the disgrace of blowing a seemingly insurmountable lead. That was an ignominy that another team would suffer.

Like New York's other team, the Mets celebrated an individual milestone in 2007 when Tom Glavine won his 300th game. But while Rodriguez's play spurred the Yankees to the postseason, Glavine's played a part in his team's collapse. With 17 games left in the season, the Mets led the Phillies by seven games in the NL East. But New York won just five more times, including losing six games in the season's final week, while the Phillies went 13–4, including a three-game sweep at Shea, giving Philadelphia its first division title in 14 years. (In a nice touch of irony, the Phils' return to the postseason came in the same year they became the first pro sports franchise to lose 10,000 games.) "It's embarrassing," Mets closer Billy Wagner said. "That's the big thing."

Despite their epic collapse, the Mets had a chance to salvage the division title on the final day of the season. The two teams entered the day tied. With Glavine on the hill, the Mets were playing the Marlins at home in a 1:10 start; the Phillies, with their own 40-something, soft-throwing lefty (Jamie Moyer) on the mound, were playing

HEINZ KLUETMEIER

snuck into the playoffs as the NL wild card winner by finishing the season on a 13–1 jag, including a 9–8, 13-inning win over the Padres in a one-game play-off. The Rockies swept Philadelphia and made short work of the Diamondbacks in the NLCS, meaning they entered their first World Series on a 21–1 run.

Boston's route to the Fall Classic was a little trickier. After disposing of the Angels, the Red Sox ran into the Indians in the ALCS. Cleveland knocked the Yankees out in the first round in a wild series highlighted by a plague of midges that flew in off Lake Erie and swarmed reliever Joba Chamberlain in the eighth inning of Game 2. Unnerved, the rookie gave up the tying run on a wild pitch, and the Indians won the game in 11 innings. None of that sat well with Yankees owner George Steinbrenner, who, as the series shifted back to New York, declared that if the Bombers didn't win the series he couldn't see manager Joe Torre keeping his job.

It was no idle threat designed to fire up a team of fiercely loyal players. Cleveland won the series in four games, and within a week Torre was out of a job. Steinbrenner didn't fire him, but the Yankees made it pretty clear that they weren't interested in seeing the 67-year-old return. Torre was offered a one-year deal with a base salary of $5 million—a substantial cut from his 2007 salary of $7 million. The deal had incentives that would have paid Torre an additional $3

the Nationals in a 1:35 start. By the time the first pitch was thrown in Philly, however, the Mets were already losing 7–0. Glavine got just one out, allowed five hits and walked two batters. All seven runners scored.

The Phillies, meanwhile, got a strong performance from Moyer, who gave up just one earned run in 5⅓ innings. The 6–1 win vindicated the preseason comments of Philadelphia second baseman Jimmy Rollins, who before the season ruffled some feathers in Queens by proclaiming that the Phils would win the division. Said Rollins, "I'm no prophet, just a baseball player." And a pretty good one at that. Rollins finished the season with 30 homers and 93 RBIs—not bad for a 160-pounder.

In the playoffs, though, the Phillies ran into the one team that finished the season hotter than they did: the Rockies. Colorado

Lowell (sliding), a "throw-in" to the 2005 trade the Red Sox made for Josh Beckett, was named the 2007 World Series MVP.

million for winning the World Series. Torre—who led the Yankees to the playoffs in all 12 of his seasons in the Bronx—didn't appreciate being told he had to prove himself. "I'd been there 12 years and did not feel motivation was needed," he said. "I didn't think it was the right thing for me or the right thing for my players. I expressed my dissatisfaction with the length of the contract. I explained that and the fact that the incentives, which to me I took as, you know, an insult— that [it implies that] we basically get to the postseason and then all of a sudden we're satisfied."

With the Yankees out of the picture, the battle for the AL pennant came down to Cleveland and Boston, who each finished the season with a major-league best 96 wins. Cleveland took a 3–1 lead, but as they did in 2004, when they won their first World Series in 86 years, the Red Sox battled back. With their season on the line, the

Sox outscored the Tribe 30–5 over the final three games, the first in Cleveland, the last two at Fenway. "We worked too hard all year long to have our season get cut short," said second baseman Dustin Pedroia. "Nobody wanted to go home, nobody wanted to say goodbye to everybody. So once we got that win in Cleveland, which brought us back here, we started to believe."

Their lumber finally awakened, the Red Sox had little trouble with the Rockies, who sat idle for nine days between the conclusion of their NLCS sweep and the first game of the World Series. In Game 1, Josh Beckett continued his remarkable postseason performance, holding Colorado to one run on six hits and lowering his career postseason ERA to 1.73. The Sox wrapped the Series up in Game 4 in Denver, thanks to Series MVP Mike Lowell, who homered, doubled and scored twice in a 4–3 win. Lowell came to the Red Sox with Beckett in a 2005 trade; Florida insisted on adding him into the deal because they wanted to dump his contract. "Pretty good 'throw-in,' I guess," Lowell said as he clutched his MVP trophy. "Icing on the cake."

FOR THE RECORD•2007

National League

EASTERN DIVISION

Team	Won	Lost	Pct	GB	Home	Away
Philadelphia....89	73	.549	--	47–34	42–39
NY Mets.........88	74	.543	1.0	41–40	47–34
Atlanta 84	78	.519	5.0	44–37	40–41
Washington.....73	89	.451	16.0	40–41	33–48
Florida.............71	91	.438	18.0	36–45	35–46

CENTRAL DIVISION

Team	Won	Lost	Pct	GB	Home	Away
Chi. Cubs.......85	77	.525	--	44–37	41–40
Milwaukee 83	79	.512	2.0	51–30	32–49
St. Louis 78	84	.481	7.0	43–38	35–46
Houston...........73	89	.451	12.0	42–39	31–50
Cincinnati 72	90	.444	13.0	39–42	33–48
Pittsburgh.......68	94	.420	17.0	37–44	31–50

WESTERN DIVISION

Team	Won	Lost	Pct	GB	Home	Away
Arizona...........90	72	.556	--	50–31	40–41
†*Colorado.....89	73	.549	1.0	50–31	39–42
*San Diego.....89	73	.549	1.0	47–34	42–49
LA Dodgers....82	80	.506	8.0	43–38	39–42
San Francisco..71	91	.438	19.0	39–42	32–49

*played one-game NL Wild Card tiebreaker

American League

EASTERN DIVISION

Team	Won	Lost	Pct	GB	Home	Away
Boston 96	66	.593	--	51–30	45–36
†NY Yankees...94	68	.580	2.0	52–29	42–39
Toronto............83	79	.512	13.0	49–32	34–47
Baltimore 69	93	.426	27.0	35–46	34–47
Tampa Bay 66	96	.407	30.0	37–44	29–52

CENTRAL DIVISION

Team	Won	Lost	Pct	GB	Home	Away
Cleveland.......96	66	.593	--	52–29	44–37
Detroit 88	74	.543	8.0	45–36	43–38
Minnesota 79	83	.488	17.0	41–40	38–43
Chi. White Sox..72	90	.444	24.0	38–43	34–47
Kansas City....69	93	.426	27.0	35–46	34–47

WESTERN DIVISION

Team	Won	Lost	Pct	GB	Home	Away
LA Angels 94	68	.580	--	54–27	40–41
Seattle............88	74	.543	6.0	49–32	39–42
Oakland 76	86	.469	18.0	40–41	36–45
Texas..............75	87	.463	19.0	47–34	28–53

†Wild-card team.

2007 Playoffs

National League Division Playoffs

Oct 3 ....Colorado 4 at Philadelphia 2
Oct 4 ....Colorado 10 at Philadelphia 5

Oct 6 .... Philadelphia 1 at Colorado 2

(Colorado won series 3–0)

Oct 3 ....Chicago 1 at Arizona 3
Oct 4 ....Chicago 4 at Arizona 8

Oct 6 ....Arizona 5 at Chicago 1

(Arizona won series 3–0)

National League Championship Series

Oct 11 ....Colorado 5 at Arizona 1
Oct 12 ....Colorado 3 at Arizona 2, (11 inn.)

Oct 14 ....Arizona 1 at Colorado 4
Oct 15 ....Arizona 4 at Colorado 6

(Colorado won series 4–0)

GAME 1

Colorado	0	1	3	0	0	0	1	0	0	**5**	**8**	**0**
Arizona	1	0	0	0	0	0	0	0	x	**1**	**9**	**1**

W—Col: Francis. **L**—Ariz: Webb. **LOB**—Col: 6; Ariz: 8.
2B—Ariz: Byrnes, Snyder. **SB**—Col: Taveras, Matsui.
RBI—Col: Matsui, Hawpe (2); Ariz: Byrnes. **GIDP**—
Col: Tulowitzki. **HBP**—Ariz: Reynolds. **E**—Ariz: Jackson.
T—3:12. **A**—48,142.

Recap: Neither a ruckus by the Arizona crowd nor a four-day layoff could slow Colorado down. Jeff Francis outpitched Brandon Webb, Brad Hawpe got the big hit and Colorado won the NLCS opener 5–1 in a game interrupted when fans angered by an umpire's disputed interference call threw objects onto the field. After several water bottles landed near Colorado players, umpires pulled the teams off the field in the bottom of the seventh inning. The wild-card Rockies escaped the jam and their superb bullpen did the rest. All seven hits Webb surrendered were singles.

GAME 2

Colorado	0	1	0	0	1	0	0	0	0	1	**3**	**7**	**I**
Arizona	0	0	1	0	0	0	0	0	1	0	**2**	**9**	**I**

W—Col: Corpas. **L**—Ariz: Valverde. **LOB**—Col: 11;
Ariz: 11. **2B**—Col: Taveras; Ariz: Clark, Davis.
CS—Ariz: Young. **RBI**—Col: Taveras, Helton,
Torrealba; Ariz: Young, Byrnes.**SF**—Col: Helton.
HBP—Ariz: Young. **E**—Col: Matsui; Ariz: Reynolds.
T—4:26. **A**—48,219.

Recap: The crazy run for Colorado continued as the Rockies joined the 1976 Cincinnati Reds as the only NL teams to win their first five games in the postseason. A bases-loaded walk to Willy Taveras in the 11th inning by Jose Valverde provided the margin of victory and propelled the Rockies to a 2–0 lead in the NLCS. The Rockies recovered after closer Manny Corpas blew a ninth-inning lead. Leading off the 11th, pinch-hitter Ryan Spilborghs reached on an infield single and Brad Hawpe and Jamey Carroll walked against Valverde.

National League Championship Series *(Cont.)*

GAME 3

Arizona	0	0	0	1	0	0	0	0	0	**1**	**8**	**0**
Colorado	1	0	0	0	0	3	0	0	X	**4**	**9**	**0**

W—Col: Fogg. **L**—Ariz: Hernandez. **SV**—Col: Corpas. **LOB**—Ariz 5; Col: 9. **HR**—Ariz: Reynolds; Col: Holliday, Torrealba. **RBI**—Ariz: Reynolds; Col: Holliday, Torrealba (3). **GIDP**—Col: Drew, Ojeda. **IBB**—Col: Atkins.
T—3:04. **A**—50,137.

Recap: With a cold rain falling, Josh Fogg shut down Arizona's bats in his first postseason start and Yorvit Torrealba hit a tiebreaking three-run homer to fuel the Rockies' 4–1 victory in Game 3 of the NLCS. MVP hopeful Matt Holliday also homered as the wild-card Rockies took a 3–0 series lead with their 20th win in 21 games, a streak that has taken Colorado from afterthoughts to the buzz of baseball. Torrealba connected in the sixth inning, three pitches after watching one of Livan Hernandez 's trademark "eephus" offerings poke across the plate for a strike—it was so slow it didn't register on the stadium scoreboard radar. Fogg, who won Game 2 of the NLDS in relief, scattered seven hits, including rookie Mark Reynolds' solo home run in the fourth, in six stellar innings. He didn't walk a batter and struck out three.

GAME 4

Arizona	0	0	1	0	0	0	0	3	0	**4**	**10**	**1**
Colorado	0	0	0	6	0	0	0	0	x	**6**	**6**	**1**

W—Col: Herges. **L**—Ariz: Owings. **SV**—Col: Corpas. **LOB**—Col: 5; Ariz: 8. **HR**—Ariz: Snyder; Col: Holliday. **3B**—Ariz: Upton. **2B**—Ariz: Young, Upton, Snyder; Col: Smith. **RBI**—Col: Matsui, Holliday (3), Smith (2); Ariz: Jackson, Snyder (3). **CS**—Ariz: Young. **HBP**—Col: Upton, Holliday. **E**—Ariz: Snyder; Col: Hawkins.
T—3:17. **A**—50,213.

Recap: Series MVP Matt Holliday hit a three-run homer into the pine-filled rock pile in center field that capped a six-run outburst in the fourth inning, and Colorado was on its way. Born as an expansion team in 1993, the wild-card Rockies are headed to their first World Series. The Rockies joined the 1976 Reds as the only teams to start the postseason with seven straight wins. Colorado has won 10 in row overall and lost only once since Sept. 16. Ahead 6–1, the Rockies withstood Chris Snyder's three-run homer in the eighth. Chris Young doubled with one out in the ninth off closer Manny Corpas, but Stephen Drew popped out on a 3–0 pitch. Eric Byrnes followed with a checked-swing grounder that shortstop Troy Tulowitzki charged. His throw beat Byr nes' headfirst dive, and the Rockies were NLCS champs.

American League Division Playoffs

Oct 3 ....Los Angeles 0 at Boston 4
Oct 5 ....Los Angeles 3 at Boston 6
Oct 7 ....Boston 9 at Los Angeles 1

(Boston won series 3–0)

Oct 4 ....New York 3 at Cleveland 12
Oct 5 ....New York 1 at Cleveland 2 (11 inn.)
Oct 7 ....Cleveland 4 at New York 8
Oct 8 ....Cleveland 6 at New York 4

(Cleveland won series 3–1)

American League Championship Series

Oct 12 ....Cleveland 3 at Boston 10
Oct 13 ....Cleveland 13 at Boston 6 (11 inn.)
Oct 15 ....Boston 2 at Cleveland 4
Oct 16 ....Boston 3 at Cleveland 7
Oct 18 ....Boston 7 at Cleveland 1
Oct 20 ....Cleveland 2 at Boston 12
Oct 21 ....Cleveland 2 at Boston 11

(Boston won series 4–3)

GAME 1

Cleveland	1	0	0	0	0	1	0	1	0	**3**	**8**	**0**
Boston	1	0	4	0	3	2	0	0	x	**10**	**12**	**0**

W—Bos: Beckett. **L**—Cle: Sabathia. **LOB**—Bos 9; Cle 7. **HR**—Cle: Hafner. **2B**—Bos: Ortiz, Varitek, Lowell, Crisp, Lugo; Cle: Lofton, Blake. **RBI**—Bos: Ramirez (3), Lowell (3), Varitek (2), Kielty (2); Cle: Cabrera (2), Hafner. **SF**—Cle: Cabrera. **GIDP**—Bos: Lowell; Cle: Peralta. **HBP**—Bos: Ortiz; Cle: Garko. **IBB**—Bos: Kielty.
T—3:35. **A**—36,986.

Recap: Josh Beckett threw six innings of four-hit ball to outpitch C.C. Sabathia, and David Ortiz and Manny Ramirez reached base all 10 times they came to the plate to lead the Boston Red Sox over the Indians 10–3. Ramirez went 2-for-2 with an RBI single and three walks—two of them with the bases loaded—and Ortiz went 2-for-2 with two walks and a hit-by-pitch. Beckett, who struck out seven while giving up two runs, a hit batter and a wild pitch, surrendered a first-inning homer to Travis Hafner before retiring 18 batters in a row. By the time the Indians got another run, Boston led 8–2, Sabathia was gone and the Red Sox were on their way to jumping ahead in the best-of-seven series.

GAME 2

Cleveland	1	0	0	3	1	1	0	0	0	7	**13**	**17**	**0**
Boston	0	0	3	0	3	0	Q	0	0	0	**6**	**10**	**0**

W—Cle: Mastny. **L**—Bos: Gagne. **LOB**—Bos: 6; Cle: 8. **HR**—Bos: Ramirez, Lowell; Cle: Sizemore, Peralta, Gutierrez. **2B**—Cle: Sizemore, Martinez, Peralta. **RBI**—Bos: Ramirez (3), Lowell (3); Cle: Sizemore, Nixon, Martinez, Garko, Peralta (4), Gutierrez (4). **GIDP**—Bos: Ramirez, Varitek, Lugo; Cle: Gutierrez. **IBB**—Cle: Sizemore, Martinez (2).
T—5:14. **A**—37,051.

Recap: Former Red Sox outfielder Trot Nixon's pinch-hit single snapped an extra-inning tie, and the Indians scored seven runs in the 11th—the most in a final inning in LCS history—to even the ALCS at a game apiece. The anticipated pitching matchup of postseason star Curt Schilling and 19-game winner Fausto Carmona fizzled into a stalemate that lasted 5 hours, 14 minutes. Manny Ramirez set a record with his 23rd postseason homer, and Mike Lowell followed with a shot that gave the Red Sox a 6–5 lead in the fifth. But after that, their big bats went quiet. Tom Mastny got the win by retiring David Ortiz, Ramirez and Lowell in order in the 10th.

American League Championship Series *(Cont.)*

GAME 3

Boston	0 0 0	0 0 0	2 0 0	**2**	**7**	**0**
Cleveland	0 2 0	0 2 0	0 0 x	**4**	**6**	**I**

W—Cle: Westbrook. **L**—Bos: Matsuzaka. **SV**—Cle: Borowski. **LOB**—Cle: 5; Bos: 5. **HR**—Cle: Lofton; Bos: Varitek. **2B**—Bos: Ortiz. **RBI**—Cle: Cabrera, Hafner, Lofton (2); Bos: Varitek (2). **GIDP**—Bos: Ortiz, Ramirez, Crisp. **E**—Cle: Garko.
T—3:28. **A**—44,402.

Recap: Jake Westbrook, often overlooked in Cleveland's top-heavy starting rotation, kept Boston grounded for nearly seven innings Monday night, leading the Indians to a 4–2 win over the Red Sox. Backed by an early homer from veteran Kenny Lofton, the right-hander took a shutout into the seventh inning. Boston grounded into three double plays, two by October's scariest twosome—David Ortiz and Manny Ramirez. The Red Sox couldn't do anything until the seventh, when Jason Varitek hit a two-run homer. Jensen Lewis relieved with a runner on and struck out rookie Dustin Pedroia to end the inning. Rafael Betancourt worked a perfect eighth and Borowski, the AL saves leader, pitched a rare 1-2-3 ninth.

GAME 4

Boston	0 0 0	0 0 3	0 0 0	**3**	**8**	**I**
Cleveland	0 0 0	0 7 0	0 0 x	**7**	**9**	**0**

W—Cle: Byrd. **L**—Bos: Wakefield. **LOB**—Cle: 7; Bos: 4. **HR**—Cle: Peralta, Blake; Bos: Youkilis, Ortiz, Martinez. **2B**—Cle: Peralta. **RBI**—Cle: Cabrera, Martinez, Peralta (3), Blake (2); Bos: Youkilis, Ortiz, Martinez. **SB**—Cle: Sizemore, Lofton. **GIDP**—Bos: Lugo. **HBP**—Cle: Shoppach. **E**—Bos: Youkilis.
T—3:12. **A**—44,008.

Recap: Pumping his arms with an old-school windup, Paul Byrd blanked Boston long enough as the Indians beat the Red Sox 7–3 for a 3–1 lead in the ALCS. Boston knuckleballer Tim Wakefield, who had Cleveland's hitters flailing at air for nearly four innings, stumbled in the fifth. Hurt by a dropped foul pop and a ball seemingly headed for an inning-ending double play that tipped off his glove, Wakefield saw the Indians score seven runs to blow the game open. The down time seemed to hurt Byrd as well, though, who gave up back-to-back homers in a seven-pitch span to Kevin Youkilis and David Ortiz to open the sixth. Jensen Lewis replaced Byrd and gave up a homer to Manny Ramirez, as the Red Sox became the first team in ALCS history to hit three straight homers.

GAME 5

Boston	1 0 1	0 0 0	2 3 0	**7**	**I2**	**I**
Cleveland	1 0 0	0 0 0	0 0 0	**I**	**6**	**I**

W—Bos: Beckett. **L**—Cle: Sabathia. **LOB**—Cle: 7; Bos: 10. **HR**—Bos: Youkilis. **3B**—Bos: Youkilis. **2B**—Cle: Sizemore, Garko; Bos: Pedroia, Ramirez, Drew. **RBI**—Bos: Youkilis (3), Ortiz (2), Ramirez. **GIDP**—Cle: Hafner; Bos: Youkilis, Lugo. **HBP**—Bos: Varitek, Lowell. **E**—Cle: Perez; Bos: Beckett.
T—3:46. **A**—44,588.

Recap: A day after he created a ruckus with remarks that winning the ALCS didn't mean everything, Manny Ramirez, Boston's laid-back cleanup hitter wound up with a 390-foot single instead of a two-run homer, but it turned out to be not so big a deal. Facing elimination, the Red Sox beat Cleveland 7–1 thanks to another gem by Red Sox ace, Josh Beckett, sending the best-of-seven series back to Boston for Game 6. In a repeat performance from Game 1, Beckett locked down the Indians hitters, striking out 11 and surrending only one run on five hits over eight innings. And, as in Game 1, the Red Sox were able to solve C.C. Sabathia, chasing him in the seventh with a leadoff double by Pedroia followed by a Youkilis triple. The Red Sox never looked back after that.

GAME 6

Cleveland	0 1 0	0 0 0	1 0 0	**2**	**6**	**2**
Boston	4 0 6	0 0 0	2 x	**12**	**13**	**0**

W—Bos: Schilling. **L**—Cle: Carmona. **LOB**—Bos: 8; Cle: 3. **HR**—Bos: Drew; Cle: Martinez. **3B**—Cle: Garko. **2B**—Bos: Pedroia, Ortiz, Lugo. **RBI**—Bos: Drew (5), Youkilis, Ramirez, Lowell, Ellsbury, Lugo (2); Cle: Martinez, Peralta. **SF**—Bos: Ramirez; Cle: Peralta. **GIDP**—Bos: Ortiz; Cle: Sizemore. **E**—Cle: Cabrera, Garko.
T—3:09. **A**—37,163.

Recap: Struggling Red Sox right fielder J.D. Drew drove in five runs, including a first-inning grand slam, backing yet another postseason gem from Curt Schilling as Boston battered Cleveland 12–2 to tie the ALCS at three games apiece. Fausto Carmona failed to get anybody out in the third inning, giving up seven runs on six hits and four walks. Schilling, on the other hand, gave up Victor Martinez 's solo homer in the second inning and otherwise held the Indians scoreless until Ryan Garko tripled and scored on Jhonny Peralta 's sacrifice fly in the seventh. But by that time, it was already 10–2 and the Red Sox were well on their way to Game 7.

GAME 7

Cleveland	0 0 0	1 1 0	0 0 0	**2**	**10**	**I**
Boston	1 1 1	0 0 0	2 6 x	**II**	**15**	**I**

W—Bos: Matsuzaka. **L**—Cle: Westbrook. **LOB**—Bos: 4; Cle: 7. **HR**—Bos: Pedroia, Youkilis. **2B**—Bos: Lowell, Youkilis, Pedroia, Varitek; Cle: Hafner, Garko. **RBI**—Bos: Pedroia (5), Youkilis (2), Ramirez, Lowell, Drew; Cle: Garko, Sizemore. **SF**—Bos: Lowell; Cle: Sizemore. **GIDP**—Bos: Pedroia, Drew, Lugo; Cle: Blake. **IBB**—Bos: Ramirez, Ellsbury. **E**—Bos: Lugo; Cle: Blake.
T—3:33. **A**—37,165.

Recap: Daisuke Matsuzaka pitched five solid innings, and Hideki Okajima and Jonathan Papelbon each threw two scoreless innings in relief. Boston also got some help when, with a chance to tie the game in the seventh inning, Cleveland third-base coach Joel Skinner inexplicably held up speedy Kenny Lofton as he rounded the bag after Franklin Gutierrez's base hit caromed off the photographer's box in foul territory and back in front of leftfielder Manny Ramirez. On the next at-bat, with runners at the corners and one out, Casey Blake grounded into an inning-ending double play. The Red Sox blew it open after that, scoring two runs in the seventh and six more in the eighth. Pedroia, who homered earlier, hit a three-run double and Kevin Youkilis launched a two-run homer off the giant Coke bottle above the Green Monster.

Oct 24 ....Colorado 1 at Boston 13
Oct 25 ....Colorado 1 at Boston 2

Oct 27 ....Boston 10 at Colorado 5
Oct 28 ....Boston 4 at Colorado 3

(Boston won series 4–0)

GAME 1

Colorado	0	1	0	0	0	0	0	0	0		1	6	0
Boston	3	1	0	2	7	0	0	x			13	17	0

W—Bos: Beckett. **L**—Col: Francis. **LOB**—Bos: 12; Col: 5. **HR**—Bos: Pedroia. **2B**—Bos: Youkilis (2), Ortiz (2), Ramirez, Lowell, Drew, Varitek; Col: Helton, Atkins, Tulowitzki (2). **RBI**—Bos: Pedroia (2), Youkilis, Ortiz (2), Ramirez (2), Varitek (2), Drew (2), Ellsbury, Lugo; Col: Tulowitzki. **GIDP**—Col: Holliday. **IBB**—Bos: Martinez, Lowell. **BK**—Col: Morales.
T—3:30. **A**—36,733.

Recap: Josh Beckett, Dustin Pedroia and the Boston Red Sox were revved up and ready. Not so the Colorado Rockies, who lurched into Beantown with all the zip of a creaky old stagecoach. Back in the World Series with no Bambino's curse to worry about, the Red Sox flattened the Rockies 13–1 in Game 1. Boston set a record for runs and victory margin in an opener and finished with 17 hits, becoming the first club with eight doubles in a Series game since 1925. After taking a 6–1 lead against Colorado ace Jeff Francis, the Red Sox piled on seven runs in the fifth, when Rockies reliever Ryan Speier walked four straight batters with the bases loaded—the first time that has happened in the Series. Boston's pitching dazzled, however, as 27-year-old Beckett blew away the Rockies with 95-97 mph fastballs the first time through the order, then started mixing in a 77 mph curve. He scattered six hits and one run over seven innings, struck out nine and walked one, improving to 4–0 with a 1.20 ERA in the postseason.

GAME 2

Colorado	1	0	0	0	0	0	0	0	0		1	5	0
Boston	0	0	0	1	1	0	0	0	X		2	6	1

W—Bos:Schilling. **L**—Col: Jimenez. **SV**—Bos: Papelbon. **LOB**—Bos: 12; Col: 5. **2B**—Bos: Lowell. **RBI**—Bos: Lowell, Varitek. Col: Helton. **SAC**—Bos: Lugo. Col: Torrealba. **SF**—Bos: Varitek. **SB**—Bos: Ellsbury. **GIDP**—Col: Torrealba. **HBP**—Bos: Drew; Col: Taveras. **E**—Bos: Lowell.
T—3:39. **A**—36,730.

Recap: Relying more on guile than gas, Curt Schilling, just twenty days shy of his 41st birthday, pitched Boston to a 2–1 victory and a 2–0 lead in the World Series over the suddenly stagnant Rockies. After allowing a run in the first, Schilling settled in, inducing an inning-ending double play in the second and striking out two in the third. He put the leadoff batter on in the next two innings, but pitched out of trouble. Nearly automatic in October, Schilling pitched 5⅓ solid innings and improved to 11–2 with a 2.23 ERA in 19 postseason starts, tipping his cap to the pulsing crowd as he walked off the mound—perhaps for the final time in a Red Sox uniform. Lowell hit a tiebreaking double in the fifth and the Red Sox got 3⅔ innings of shutout relief from Hideki Okajima and Jonathan Papelbon to win their sixth straight World Series game going back to 2004.

GAME 3

Boston	0	0	6	0	0	0	0	3	1		10	15	1
Colorado	0	0	0	0	2	0	3	0	0		5	10	1

W—Bos: Matsuzaka. **L**—Col: Fogg. **SV**—Bos: Papelbon. **LOB**—Col: 11; Bos: 7. **HR**—Col: Holliday. **3B**—Col: Hawpe. **2B**—Bos: Ortiz, Ellsbury (3), Drew, Pedroia, Lugo. **RBI**—Col: Hawpe, Torrealba, Holliday (3); Bos: Ellsbury (2), Pedroia (2), Matsuzaka (2), Ortiz, Lowell (2), Varitek. **SAC**—Bos: Cora. **SF**—Bos: Varitek. **SB**—Col: Matsui; Bos: Lowell. **IBB**—Bos: Ramirez. **HBP**—Col: Atkins. **E**—Bos: Drew.
T—4:19. **A**—49,983.

Recap: It was a night when rookies ruled. Jacoby Ellsbury and Dustin Pedroia sparked the Red Sox from the top of the order, going 7-for-10 with three runs scored and four RBIs, and Daisuke Matsuzaka pitched shutout ball into the sixth inning as Boston beat Colorado 10–5 to take a 3–0 Series lead. Ellsbury became the first rookie in 61 years with four hits in a Series game, getting three of Boston's seven doubles. Pedroia had three hits, including a bunt single that helped spark a six-run third against Josh Fogg, who allowed 12 of 19 batters to reach. Colorado was seemingly out of it but came back with two runs in the sixth. The Rockies then closed to 6–5 when Matt Holliday hit a three-run homer in the seventh off of Hideki Okajima's first pitch. But the Red Sox answered in the top of the eighth when Ellsbury lofted an RBI double down the right-field line off Brian Fuentes that just eluded Brad Hawpe's attempt at a sliding, backhand catch. Pedroia followed with a two-run double to start that made it 9–5. Jason Varitek added a sacrifice fly in the ninth inning of a game that took 4 hours, 19 minutes—the longest nine-inning game in Series history.

GAME 4

Boston	1	0	2	0	0	0	0	1	0		4	9	0
Colorado	0	0	0	1	0	0	2	0	0		3	7	0

W—Bos: Lester. **L**—Col: Cook. **LOB**—Bos: 3. Col: 7 **2B**—Bos: Ellsbury, Lowell. Col: Helton, Matsui. **RBI**—Bos: Ortiz, Varitek, Lowell, Kielty. Col: Hawpe, Atkins (2) **HR**—Bos: Lowell, Kielty. Col: Hawpe, Atkins. **GIDP**—Bos: Ramirez, Lugo, Pedroia.
T—3:39. **A**—50,041.

Recap: Lester, undergoing chemotherapy at this time last year for cancer, pitched shutout ball into the sixth inning and Jonathan Papelbon closed with his third save of the Series. Rookie Jacoby Ellsbury got it started again with a leadoff double and, even without big contributions from sluggers Manny Ramirez and Ortiz, Boston was too good. Bobby Kielty made the most of his first appearance in this Series, connecting for a pinch-hit home run in the eighth, giving Boston a 4–1 lead. That hit proved to be the difference after Garret Atkins connected for a two-run shot in the bottom of the eighth. Lowell, who hit a leadoff double in the fifth—he later scored—and a solo shot in the seventh, was named the MVP after batting .400, scoring six runs, stealing a base and driving in four in the Series. Overwhelming in every way, the Red Sox swept to their second World Series title in four years and the wild-card Rockies, who won a remarkable 21 of 22 games to get this far, were a mere afterthought by the end.

BOSTON

BATTING	AB	R	H	HR	RBI	Avg
Pedroia	18	2	5	1	4	.278
Ellsbury	16	4	7	0	3	.438
Ramirez	16	3	4	0	2	.250
Drew	15	1	5	0	2	.333
Lowell	15	6	6	1	4	.400
Ortiz	15	4	5	0	4	.333
Varitek	15	2	5	0	5	.333
Lugo	13	2	5	0	1	.385
Youkilis	9	3	2	0	1	.222
Crisp	2	1	1	0	0	.500
Hinske	1	0	0	0	0	.000
Kielty	1	1	1	1	1	1.000
Pitchers	5	0	1	0	2	.200
Totals	**141**	**29**	**47**	**3**	**29**	**.333**

PITCHING	G	IP	H	BB	SO	ERA
Beckett	1	7.0	6	1	9	1.29
Lester	1	5.2	3	3	3	0.00
Schilling	1	5.1	4	2	4	1.69
Matsuzaka	1	5.1	3	3	5	3.38
Papelbon	3	4.1	2	0	3	0.00
Okajima	3	3.2	4	0	6	7.36
Timlin	3	2.1	2	0	4	7.71
Delcarmen	2	1.1	3	1	1	6.75
Gagne	1	1.0	0	0	1	0.00
Lopez	1	0.0	2	0	0	—
Totals	**4**	**36.0**	**29**	**10**	**36**	**2.50**

COLORADO

BATTING	AB	R	H	HR	RBI	Avg
Holliday	17	1	5	1	3	.294
Matsui	17	1	5	0	0	.294
Hawpe	16	1	4	1	2	.250
Helton	15	2	5	0	1	.333
Torrealba	14	0	2	0	1	.143
Atkins	13	3	2	1	2	.154
Tulowitzki	13	1	3	0	1	.221
Spilborghs	10	0	0	0	0	.000
Taveras	8	1	0	0	0	.000
Sullivan	3	0	1	0	0	.333
S. Smith	2	0	1	0	0	.500
Carroll	1	0	0	0	0	.000
Baker	1	0	0	0	0	.000
Pitchers	3	0	1	0	0	.333
Totals	**133**	**10**	**29**	**3**	**10**	**.218**

PITCHING	G	IP	H	BB	SO	ERA
Cook	1	6.0	6	0	2	4.50
Jimenez	1	4.2	3	5	2	3.86
Francis	1	4.1	10	3	3	13.50
Fuentes	3	3.2	6	2	1	9.82
Herges	3	3.1	1	2	4	0.00
Affeldt	4	3.0	2	1	2	0.00
Morales	2	3.0	7	1	1	21.00
Fogg	1	2.2	10	2	2	20.25
Hawkins	2	2.0	1	0	2	4.50
Corpas	2	1.2	1	0	1	0.00
Speier	1	0.0	0	3	0	—
Totals	**4**	**34.0**	**47**	**19**	**20**	**7.68**

National League Batting

BATTING AVERAGE

Matt Holliday, Col	.340
Chipper Jones, Atl	.337
Hanley Ramirez, Fla	.332
Edgar Renteria, Atl	.332
Chase Utley, Phi	.332
Albert Pujols, StL	.327
David Wright, NYM	.325
Miguel Cabrera, Fla	.320
Todd Helton, Col	.320
Dmitri Young, Wash	.320

HITS

Matt Holliday, Col	216
Hanley Ramirez, Fla	212
Jimmy Rollins, Phi	212
Juan Pierre, Chc	196
David Wright, NYM	196
Jose Reyes, NYM	191
Carlos Lee, Hou	190
Aaron Rowand, Phi	189
Miguel Cabrera, Fla	188
Jeff Francoeur, Atl	188

DOUBLES

Matt Holliday, Col	50
Dan Uggla, Fla	49
Hanley Ramirez, Fla	48
Chase Utley, Phi	48
Adrian Gonzalez, SD	46
Aaron Rowand, Phi	45

TRIPLES

Jimmy Rollins, Phi	20
Jose Reyes, NYM	12
Kelly Johnson, Atl	10
Alfredo Amezaga, Fla	9
Corey Hart, Mil	9
Orlando Hudson, Ari	9

HOME RUNS

Prince Fielder, Mil	50
Ryan Howard, Phi	47
Adam Dunn, Cin	40
Matt Holliday, Col	36
Lance Berkman, Hou	34
Ryan Braun, Mil	34
Miguel Cabrera, Fla	34
Carlos Beltran, NYM	33
Alfonso Soriano, Chc	33
Carlos Lee, Hou	32

RUNS SCORED

Jimmy Rollins, Phi	139
Hanley Ramirez, Fla	125
Matt Holliday, Col	120
Jose Reyes, NYM	119
Dan Uggla, Fla	113
David Wright, NYM	113
Prince Fielder, Mil	109
Chipper Jones, Atl	108
Brandon Phillips, Cin	107
Aaron Rowand, Phi	105
Chase Utley, Phi	104

STOLEN BASES

Jose Reyes, NYM	78
Juan Pierre, Chc	64
Hanley Ramirez, Fla	51
Eric Byrnes, Ari	50
Jimmy Rollins, Phi	41

RUNS BATTED IN

Matt Holliday, Col	137
Ryan Howard, Phi	136
Miguel Cabrera, Fla	119
Prince Fielder, Mil	119
Carlos Lee, Hou	119
Brad Hawpe, Col	116
Carlos Beltran, NYM	112
Garrett Atkins, Col	111
David Wright, NYM	107
Adam Dunn, Cin	106

SLUGGING PERCENTAGE

Prince Fielder, Mil	.618
Matt Holliday, Col	.607
Chipper Jones, Atl	.604
Ryan Howard, Phi	.584
Albert Pujols, StL	.568

ON-BASE PERCENTAGE

Todd Helton, Col	.434
Albert Pujols, StL	.429
Chipper Jones, Atl	.425
David Wright, NYM	.416
Chase Utley, Phi	.410
Matt Holliday, Col	.405

BASES ON BALLS

Barry Bonds, SF	132
Todd Helton, Col	116
Pat Burrell, Phi	114
Ryan Howard, Phi	107
Adam Dunn, Cin	101

National League Pitching

EARNED RUN AVERAGE

Jake Peavy, SD	2.54
Brandon Webb, Ari	3.01
Brad Penny, LAD	3.03
John Smoltz, Atl	3.11
Chris R. Young, SD	3.12
Roy Oswalt, Hou	3.18
Tiim Hudson, Atl	3.33
Cole Hamels, Phi	3.39
Oliver Perez, NYM	3.56
Matt Cain, SF	3.65

SAVES

Jose Valverde, Ari	47
Francisco Cordero, MIL	44
Trevor Hoffman, SD	42
Takashi Saito, LAD	39
Chad Cordero, Wash	37
Billy Wagner, NYM	34
David Weathers, Cin	33
Kevin Gregg, Fla	32
Jason Isringhausen, StL	32

WINS

Jake Peavy, SD	19
Brandon Webb, Ari	18
Carlos Zambrano, Chc	18
Jeff Francis, Col	17
Aaron Harang, Cin	16
Tim Hudson, Atl	16

Four tied with 15.

GAMES PITCHED

Jon Rauch, Wash	88
Saul Rivera, Wash	85
Joe Beimel, LAD	83
Jonathan Broxton, LAD	83
Aaron Heilman, NYM	81
Heath Bell, SD	81

INNINGS PITCHED

Brandon Webb, Ari	236.1
Aaron Harang, Cin	231.2
Tim Hudson, Atl	224.1
Jake Peavy, SD	223.1
Carlos Zambrano, Chc	216.1

STRIKEOUTS

Jake Peavy, SD	240
Aaron Harang, Cin	218
John Smoltz, Atl	197
Brandon Webb, Ari	194
Rich Hill, Chc	183
John Maine, NYM	180
Cole Hamels, Phi	177
Ian Snell, Pit	177
Carlos Zambrano, Chc	177

COMPLETE GAMES

Brandon Webb, Ari	4
Derek Lowe, LAD	3
Matt Morris, Pit	3
Aaron Cook, Col	2
Cole Hamels, Phi	2

SHUTOUTS

Brandon Webb, Ari	3
J.D. Durbin, Phi	1
Jeff Francis, Col	1

American League Batting

BATTING AVERAGE

Magglio Ordonez, Det .... .363
Ichiro Suzuki, Sea .... .351
Placido Polanco, Det .... .341
Jorge Posada, NYY .... .338
David Ortiz, Bos .... .332
Chone Figgins, LAA .... .330
Vladimir Guerrero, LAA........ .324
Mike Lowell, Bos................... .324
Derek Jeter, NYY .... .322
Dustin Pedroia, Bos.............. .317

HITS

Ichiro Suzuki, Sea 238
Magglio Ordonez, Det 216
Derek Jeter, NYY 206
Michael Young, Tex................201
Placido Polanco, Det 200
Orlando Cabrera, LAA............192
Mike Lowell, Bos....................191
Nick Markakis, Bal 191
Alex Rios, Tor.........................191
Robinson Cano, NYY..............189

DOUBLES

Magglio Ordonez, Det 54
David Ortiz, Bos 52
Aaron Hill, Tor.........................47
Vladimir Guerrero, LAA............45
Torii Hunter, Min......................45
Nick Markakis, Bal...................43

TRIPLES

Curtis Granderson, Det 23
Akinori Iwamura, TB 10
Carl Crawford, TB......................9
David DeJesus, KC 9
Carlos Guillen, Det 9

HOME RUNS

Alex Rodriguez, NYY 54
Carlos Pena, TB.......................46
David Ortiz, Bos 35
Jim Thome, Chi.........................35
Paul Konerko, Chi....................31
Justin Morneau, Min 31
Jermaine Dye, CWS 28
Torii Hunter, Min 28
Magglio Ordonez, Det 28
Vladimir Guerrero, LAA............27

RUNS SCORED

Alex Rodriguez, NYY 143
Bobby Abreu, NYY 123
Curtis Granderson, Det 122
Grady Sizemore, Cle 118
Magglio Ordonez, Det 117
David Ortiz, Bos 116
Alex Rios, Tor.........................114
Ichiro Suzuki, Sea ....'...111
Gary Sheffield, Det 107
Placido Polanco, Det 105

STOLEN BASES

Carl Crawford, TB....................50
Brian Roberts, Bal 50
Chone Figgins, LAA 41
Corey Patterson, Bal................37
Ichiro Suzuki, Sea 37

RUNS BATTED IN

Alex Rodriguez, NYY 156
Magglio Ordonez, Det 139
Vladimir Guerrero, LAA...........125
Carlos Pena, TB.......................121
Mike Lowell, Bos.....................120
David Ortiz, Bos 117
Victor Martinez, Cle 114
Nick Markakis, Bal 112
Justin Morneau, Min 111
Torii Hunter, Min 107
Raul Ibanez, Sea 105

SLUGGING PERCENTAGE

Alex Rodriguez, NYY .... .645
Carlos Pena, TB...................... .627
David Ortiz, Bos .... .621
Magglio Ordonez, Det .... .595
Jim Thome, CWS .... .563

ON-BASE PERCENTAGE

David Ortiz, Bos .... .445
Magglio Ordonez, Det. .... .434
Jorge Posada, NYY .... .426
Alez Rodriguez, NYY .... .422
Carlos Pena, TB...................... .411

BASES ON BALLS

David Ortiz, Bos 111
Jack Cust, Oak 105
Carlos Pena, TB.......................103
Travis Hafner, Cle 102
Grady Sizemore, Cle 101

American League Pitching

EARNED RUN AVERAGE

John Lackey, LAA.................3.01
Fausto Camona, Cle.............3.06
Danny Haren, Oak................3.07
Erik Bedard, Bal...................3.16
C.C. Sabathia, Cle................3.21
Josh Beckett, Bos.................3.27
Johan Santana, Min..............3.33
Kelvim Escobar, LAA 3.40
Scott Kazmir, TB 3.48
Mark Buehrle, CWS 3.63

SAVES

Joe Borowski, Cle 45
Bobby Jenks, CWS..................40
J.J. Putz, Sea.........................40
Francisco Rodriguez, LAA 40
Todd Jones, Det 38
Joe Nathan, Min 37
Jonathan Papelbon, Bos 37
Jeremy Accardo, Tor 30
Mariano Rivera, NYY 30
Al Reyes, TB 26

WINS

Josh Beckett, Bos....................20
Fausto Carmona, Cle...............19
John Lackey, LAA....................19
C.C. Sabathia, Cle...................19
Chien-Ming Wang, NYY...........19
Kelvim Escobar, LAA 18
Justin Verlander, Det................18

GAMES PITCHED

Scott Downs, Tor......................81
Jamie Walker, Bal 81
Chad Bradford, Bal..................78
Luis Vizcaino, NYY...................77
Jimmy Gobble, KC 74
Pat Neshek, Min 74

INNINGS PITCHED

C.C. Sabathia, Cle...............241.0
Joe Blanton, Oak 230.0
Roy Halladay, Tor.................225.1
John Lackey, LAA.................224.0

SHUTOUTS

Paul Byrd, Cle...........................2
Jose Contreras, CWS 2
John Lackey, LAA.......................2
Jeff Weaver, Sea........................2

COMPLETE GAMES

Roy Halladay, Tor......................7
C.C. Sabathia, Cle.....................4

Four tied with 3.

STRIKEOUTS

Scott Kazmir, TB 239
Johan Santana, Min...............235
Erik Bedard, Bal......................221
Javier Vazquez, CWS 213
C.C. Sabathia, Cle..................209
Daisuke Matsuzaka, Bos 201
Josh Beckett, Bos...................194
Danny Haren, Oak...................192
James Shields, TB....."............184
Justin Verlander, Det...............183

National League

TEAM BATTING	G	AB	R	H	2B	3B	HR	TB	RBI	BA	OBP	SLG	OPS
*Colorado Rockies	163	5691	860	1591	313	36	171	2489	823	.280	.354	.437	.791
Los Angeles Dodgers	162	5613	735	1544	276	35	129	2277	706	.275	.337	.406	.743
New York Mets	162	5605	804	1543	294	27	177	2422	761	.275	.342	.432	.775
Atlanta Braves	162	5689	810	1562	328	27	176	2472	781	.275	.339	.435	.774
St. Louis Cardinals	162	5529	725	1513	279	13	141	2241	690	.274	.337	.405	.743
Philadelphia Phillies	162	5688	892	1558	326	41	213	2605	850	.274	.354	.458	.812
Chicago Cubs	162	5643	752	1530	340	28	151	2379	711	.271	.333	.422	.754
Cincinnati Reds	162	5607	783	1496	293	23	204	2447	747	.267	.335	.436	.772
Florida Marlins	162	5627	790	1504	340	38	201	2523	749	.267	.336	.448	.784
Pittsburgh Pirates	162	5569	724	1463	322	31	148	2291	694	.263	.325	.411	.736
Milwaukee Brewers	162	5554	801	1455	310	37	231	2532	774	.262	.329	.456	.785
Houston Astros	162	5605	723	1457	293	30	167	2311	700	.260	.330	.412	.742
Washington Nationals	162	5520	673	1415	309	31	123	2155	646	.256	.325	.390	.715
San Francisco Giants	162	5538	683	1407	267	37	131	2141	641	.254	.322	.387	.708
*San Diego Padres	163	5612	741	1408	322	31	171	2305	704	.251	.322	.411	.732
Arizona Diamondbacks	162	5398	712	1350	286	40	171	2229	687	.250	.321	.413	.734

TEAM PITCHING	GP	W	L	SV	SVO	CG	SHO	R	ERA	IP	Ks	BB
*San Diego Padres	163	89	74	45	67	1	20	666	3.70	1484.2	1136	474
Chicago Cubs	162	85	77	39	53	2	10	690	4.04	1446.2	1211	573
Atlanta Braves	162	84	78	36	51	1	6	733	4.11	1456.1	1106	537
Arizona Diamondbacks	162	90	72	51	66	7	12	732	4.13	1441.0	1088	546
San Francisco Giants	162	71	91	37	60	5	10	720	4.19	1453.2	1057	593
Los Angeles Dodgers	162	82	80	43	60	4	6	727	4.20	1450.0	1184	518
New York Mets	162	88	74	39	56	2	10	750	4.26	1452.1	1134	570
*Colorado Rockies	163	90	73	39	68	4	7	758	4.32	1472.0	967	504
Milwaukee Brewers	162	83	79	49	69	3	6	776	4.41	1444.1	1174	507
Washington Nationals	162	73	89	46	73	0	6	783	4.58	1446.2	931	580
St. Louis Cardinals	162	78	84	34	45	2	8	829	4.65	1435.2	945	509
Houston Astros	162	73	89	38	64	2	6	813	4.68	1464.2	1109	510
Philadelphia Phillies	162	89	73	42	63	5	5	821	4.73	1458.1	1050	558
Pittsburgh Pirates	162	68	94	32	51	4	5	846	4.93	1447.2	997	518
Cincinnati Reds	162	72	90	34	62	6	7	853	4.94	1449.2	1068	482
Florida Marlins	162	71	91	40	64	0	4	891	4.94	1443.2	1142	661

*includes NL Wild Card tiebreaker game

American League

TEAM BATTING	G	AB	R	H	2B	3B	HR	TB	RBI	BA	OBP	SLG	OPS
New York Yankees	162	5717	968	1656	326	32	201	2649	929	.290	.366	.463	.829
Detroit Tigers	162	5757	887	1652	352	50	177	2635	857	.287	.345	.458	.802
Seattle Mariners	162	5684	794	1629	284	22	153	2416	754	.287	.337	.425	.762
Los Angeles Angels	162	5554	822	1578	324	23	123	2317	776	.284	.345	.417	.762
Boston Red Sox	162	5589	867	1561	352	35	166	2481	829	.279	.362	.444	.806
Baltimore Orioles	162	5631	756	1529	306	30	142	2321	718	.272	.333	.412	.746
Cleveland Indians	162	5604	811	1504	305	27	178	2397	784	.268	.343	.428	.771
Tampa Bay Devil Rays	162	5593	782	1500	291	36	187	2424	750	.268	.336	.433	.769
Minnesota Twins	162	5522	718	1460	273	36	118	2159	671	.264	.330	.391	.721
Texas Rangers	162	5555	816	1460	298	36	179	2367	768	.263	.328	.426	.754
Kansas City Royals	162	5534	706	1447	300	46	102	2145	660	.261	.322	.388	.710
Toronto Blue Jays	162	5536	753	1434	344	24	165	2321	719	.259	.327	.419	.746
Oakland Athletics	162	5577	741	1430	295	16	171	2270	711	.256	.338	.407	.745
Chicago White Sox	162	5441	693	1341	249	20	190	2200	667	.246	.318	.404	.722

TEAM PITCHING	GP	W	L	SV	SVO	CG	SHO	R	ERA	IP	Ks	BB
Boston Red Sox	162	96	66	45	56	5	13	657	3.87	1438.2	1149	482
Toronto Blue Jays	162	83	79	44	69	11	9	699	4.00	1448.2	1067	479
Cleveland Indians	162	96	66	49	63	9	9	704	4.05	1462.2	1047	410
Minnesota Twins	162	79	83	38	52	5	8	725	4.15	1436.2	1094	420
Los Angeles Angels	162	94	68	43	57	5	9	731	4.23	1435.0	1156	477
Oakland Athletics	162	76	86	36	61	4	9	758	4.28	1448.0	1036	530
Kansas City Royals	162	69	93	36	54	2	6	778	4.48	1437.1	993	520
New York Yankees	162	94	68	34	55	1	5	777	4.49	1450.2	1009	578
Detroit Tigers	162	88	74	44	65	1	9	797	4.57	1447.1	1047	566
Seattle Mariners	162	88	74	43	58	6	12	813	4.73	1434.1	1020	546
Texas Rangers	162	75	87	42	56	0	6	844	4.75	1430.0	976	668
Chicago White Sox	162	72	90	42	65	9	9	839	4.77	1440.2	1015	499
Baltimore Orioles	162	69	93	30	55	4	9	868	5.17	1438.2	1087	696
Tampa Bay Devil Rays	162	66	96	28	49	2	2	944	5.53	1429.2	1194	568

Arizona Diamondbacks

BATTING	G	AB	R	H	2B	3B	HR	RBI	TB	BB	SO	SB	OBP	SLG	BA
Eric Byrnes................160	626	103	179	30	8	21	83	288	57	98	50	.353	.460	.286
Chris B. Young 148	569	85	135	29	3	32	68	266	43	141	27	.295	.467	.237
Stephen Drew 150	543	60	129	28	4	12	60	201	60	100	9	.313	.370	.238
Orlando Hudson...........139	517	69	152	28	9	10	63	228	70	87	10	.376	.441	.294
Conor Jackson...........130	415	56	118	29	1	15	60	194	53	50	2	.368	.467	.284
Mark Reynolds...........111	366	62	102	20	4	17	62	181	37	129	0	.349	.495	.279
Chris Snyder 110	326	37	82	20	0	13	47	141	40	67	0	.342	.433	.252
Carlos Quentin 81	229	29	49	16	0	5	31	80	18	54	2	.298	.349	.214
Chad Tracy.................76	227	30	60	18	2	7	35	103	29	43	0	.346	.454	.264
Tony Clark 113	221	31	55	5	1	17	51	113	21	59	0	.310	.511	.249
Miguel Montero 84	214	30	48	7	0	10	37	85	20	35	0	.292	.397	.224
Scott Hairston..............76	176	21	39	13	1	3	16	63	19	37	2	.301	.358	.222
Alberto Callaspo 56	144	10	31	8	0	0	7	39	9	14	1	.265	.271	.215
Justin Upton 43	140	17	31	8	3	2	11	51	11	37	2	.283	.364	.221
Augie Ojeda 57	113	16	31	2	2	1	12	40	15	13	1	.354	.354	.274

PITCHING	GP	GS	W–L	SV	SHO	R	ERA	IP	Ks	BB
Brandon Webb 34	34	18–10	0	3	91	3.01	236.1	194	72
Livan Hernandez 33	33	11–11	0	0	116	4.93	204.1	90	79
Doug Davis.....................33	33	13–12	0	0	100	4.25	192.2	144	95
Micah Owings...................29	27	8–8	0	1	81	4.30	152.2	106	50
Enrique Gonzalez 32	12	8–4	0	0	61	5.03	102.0	62	28
Tony Pena 75	0	5–4	2	0	36	3.27	85.1	63	31
Brandon Lyon 73	0	6–4	2	0	25	2.68	74.0	40	22
Jose Valverde 65	0	1–4	47	0	21	2.66	64.1	78	26
Juan Cruz 53	0	6–1	0	0	28	3.10	61.0	87	32
Yusmeiro Petit 14	10	3–4	0	0	30	4.58	57.0	40	18
Randy Johnson................10	10	4–3	0	0	26	3.81	56.2	72	13
Bob Wickman...................57	0	3–4	20	0	24	3.58	50.1	37	21
Dustin Nippert...............36	0	1–1	0	0	30	5.56	45.1	38	16
Doug Slaten....................61	0	3–2	0	0	15	2.72	36.1	28	14

Atlanta Braves

BATTING	G	AB	R	H	2B	3B	HR	RBI	TB	BB	SO	SB	OBP	SLG	BA
Jeff Francoeur...........162	642	84	188	40	0	19	105	285	42	129	5	.338	.444	.293
Andruw Jones...........154	572	83	127	27	2	26	94	236	70	138	5	.311	.413	.222
Kelly Johnson...........147	521	91	144	26	10	16	68	238	79	117	9	.375	.457	.276
Chipper Jones 134	513	108	173	42	4	29	102	310	82	75	5	.425	.604	.337
Brian McCann.............139	504	51	136	38	0	18	92	228	35	74	0	.320	.452	.270
Edgar Renteria..........124	494	87	164	30	1	12	57	232	46	77	11	.390	.470	.332
Matt Diaz..................135	358	44	121	21	0	12	45	178	16	63	4	.368	.497	.338
Walt Harris...............117	344	56	93	20	8	2	32	135	40	71	17	.349	.392	.270
Yunel Escobar............94	319	54	104	25	0	5	28	144	27	44	5	.385	.451	.326
Scott Thorman 120	287	37	62	18	0	11	36	113	14	70	1	.258	.394	.216
Mark Teixeira.............54	208	38	66	9	1	17	56	128	27	46	0	.404	.615	.317
Jarrod Saltalamacchia..47	141	11	40	6	0	4	12	58	10	28	0	.333	.411	.284
Chris Woodward 92	136	16	27	6	1	1	8	38	10	29	1	.252	.279	.199
Julio Franco 55	90	8	20	3	0	1	16	26	14	23	2	.321	.289	.222

PITCHING	GP	GS	W–L	SV	SHO	R	ERA	IP	Ks	BB
Tim Hudson 34	34	16–10	0	1	87	3.33	224.1	132	53
John Smoltz 32	32	14–8	0	0	78	3.11	205.2	197	47
Chuck James....................30	30	11–10	0	0	77	4.24	161.1	116	58
Buddy Carlyle...................22	20	8–7	0	0	67	5.21	107.0	74	32
Peter Moylan....................80	0	5–3	1	0	27	1.80	90.0	63	31
Kyle Davies......................17	17	4–8	0	0	61	5.76	86.0	59	44
Oscar Villarreal 51	0	2–2	1	0	40	4.24	76.1	58	32
Rafael Soriano 71	0	3–3	9	0	26	3.00	72.0	70	15
Tyler Yates 75	0	2–3	2	0	44	5.18	66.0	69	31
Jo-Jo Reyes.....................11	10	2–2	0	0	39	6.22	50.2	27	30
Lance Cormier..................10	9	2–6	0	0	38	7.09	45.2	27	22
Chad Paronto....................41	0	3–1	1	0	20	3.57	40.1	14	19
Ron Mahay......................30	0	1–0	0	0	8	2.25	28.0	23	16
Manny Acosta...................21	0	1–1	0	0	6	2.28	23.2	22	14
Royce Ring 26	0	1–0	0	0	8	2.70	20.0	21	17

Chicago Cubs

BATTING	G	AB	R	H	2B	3B	HR	RBI	TB	BB	SO	SB	OBP	SLG	BA
Alfonso Soriano	135	579	97	173	42	5	33	70	324	31	130	19	.337	.560	.299
Derek Lee	150	567	91	180	43	1	22	82	291	71	114	6	.400	.513	.317
Ryan Theriot	148	537	80	143	30	2	3	45	186	49	50	28	.326	.346	.266
Aramis Ramirez	132	506	72	157	35	4	26	101	278	43	66	0	.366	.549	.310
Mark DeRosa	149	502	64	147	28	3	10	72	211	58	93	1	.371	.420	.293
Jacque Jones	135	453	52	129	33	2	5	66	181	34	70	6	.335	.400	.285
Cliff Floyd	108	282	40	80	10	1	9	45	119	35	47	0	.373	.422	.284
Matt Murton	94	235	35	66	13	0	8	22	103	26	39	1	.352	.438	.281
Mike Fontenot	86	234	32	65	12	4	3	29	94	22	43	5	.336	.402	.278
Michael Barrett	57	211	23	54	9	0	9	29	90	17	36	2	.307	.427	.256
Cesar Izturis	65	191	15	47	11	0	0	8	58	13	16	3	.298	.304	.246
Felix Pie	87	177	26	38	9	3	2	20	59	14	43	8	.271	.333	.215
Jason Kendall	57	174	21	47	10	1	1	19	62	19	15	0	.362	.356	.270

PITCHING	GP	GS	W–L	SV	SHO	R	ERA	IP	Ks	BB
Carlos Zambrano	34	34	18–13	0	0	100	3.95	216.1	177	101
Ted Lilly	34	34	15–8	0	0	91	3.83	207.0	174	55
Rich Hill	32	32	11–8	0	0	89	3.92	195.0	183	63
Jason Marquis	34	33	12–9	0	1	111	4.60	191.2	109	76
Sean Marshall	21	19	7–8	0	0	52	3.92	103.1	67	35
Bob Howry	78	0	6–7	8	0	31	3.32	81.1	72	19
Michael Wuertz	73	0	2–3	0	0	30	3.48	72.1	79	35
Carlos Marmol	59	0	5–1	1	0	11	1.43	69.1	96	35
Ryan Dempster	66	0	2–7	28	0	36	4.73	66.2	55	30
Scott Eyre	55	0	2–1	0	0	26	4.13	52.1	45	35
Will Ohman	56	0	2–4	1	0	20	4.95	36.1	33	16
Angel Guzman	12	3	0–1	0	0	12	3.56	30.1	26	9
Kerry Wood	22	0	1–1	0	0	9	3.33	24.1	24	13
Steve Trachsel	4	4	1–3	0	0	16	8.31	17.1	11	7

Cincinnati Reds

BATTING	G	AB	R	H	2B	3B	HR	RBI	TB	BB	SO	SB	OBP	SLG	BA
Brandon Phillips	158	650	107	187	26	6	30	94	315	33	109	32	.331	.485	.288
Ken Griffey	144	528	78	146	24	1	30	93	262	85	99	6	.372	.496	.277
Adam Dunn	152	522	101	138	27	2	40	106	289	101	165	9	.386	.554	.264
Edwin Encarnacion	139	502	66	145	25	1	16	76	220	39	86	6	.356	.438	.289
Alex Gonzalez	110	393	55	107	27	1	16	55	184	24	75	0	.325	.468	.272
Scott Hatteberg	116	361	50	112	27	1	10	47	171	49	35	0	.394	.474	.310
David Ross	112	311	32	63	10	0	17	39	124	30	92	0	.271	.399	.203
Norris Hopper	121	307	51	101	14	2	0	14	119	20	33	14	.371	.388	.329
Josh Hamilton	90	298	52	87	17	2	19	47	165	33	65	3	.368	.554	.292
Ryan Freel	75	277	44	68	13	3	3	16	96	18	47	15	.308	.347	.245
Javier Valentin	97	243	19	67	21	0	2	34	94	19	25	0	.328	.387	.276
Jeff Keppinger	67	241	39	80	16	2	5	32	115	24	12	2	.400	.477	.332
Jeff Conine	80	215	23	57	11	1	6	32	88	20	28	4	.320	.409	.265
Juan Castro	54	89	5	16	5	0	0	5	21	4	21	0	.211	.236	.180

PITCHING	GP	GS	W–L	SV	SHO	R	ERA	IP	Ks	BB
Aaron Harang	34	34	16–6	0	1	100	3.73	231.2	218	52
Bronson Arroyo	34	34	9–15	0	0	109	4.23	210.2	156	63
Matt Belisle	30	30	8–9	0	0	111	5.32	177.2	125	43
Kyle Lohse	21	21	6–12	0	0	76	4.58	131.2	80	33
David Weathers	70	0	2–6	33	0	33	3.59	77.2	48	27
Mike Stanton	69	0	1–3	0	0	39	5.93	57.2	40	18
Bobby Livingston	10	10	3–3	0	0	35	5.27	56.1	27	8
Todd Coffey	58	0	2–1	0	0	36	5.82	51.0	43	19
Victor Santos	32	0	1–4	0	0	28	5.14	49.0	44	23
Homer Bailey	9	9	4–2	0	0	32	5.76	45.1	28	28
Jared Burton	47	0	4–2	0	0	15	2.51	43.0	36	22
Kirk Saarloos	34	3	1–5	0	0	36	7.17	42.2	27	19

Colorado Rockies

BATTING	G	AB	R	H	2B	3B	HR	RBI	TB	BB	SO	SB	OBP	SLG	BA
Mattt Holliday	158	636	120	216	50	6	36	137	386	63	126	11	.405	.607	.340
Troy Tulowitzki	155	609	104	177	33	5	24	99	292	57	130	7	.359	.479	.291
Garrett Atkins	157	605	83	182	35	1	25	111	294	67	96	3	.367	.486	.301
Todd Helton	154	557	86	178	42	2	17	91	275	116	74	0	.434	.494	.320
Brad Hawpe	152	516	80	150	33	4	29	116	278	81	137	0	.387	.539	.291
Kazuo Matsui	104	410	84	118	24	6	4	37	166	34	69	32	.342	.405	.288
Yorvit Torrealba	113	396	47	101	22	1	8	47	149	34	73	2	.323	.376	.255
Willy Taveras	97	372	64	119	13	2	2	24	142	21	55	33	.367	.382	.320
Ryan Spilborghs	97	264	40	79	14	1	11	51	128	28	45	4	.363	.485	.299
Jamey Carroll	108	227	45	51	9	1	2	22	68	28	34	6	.317	.300	.225
Chris Iannetta	67	197	22	43	8	3	4	27	69	29	58	0	.330	.350	.218
Jeff Baker	85	144	17	32	2	2	4	12	50	13	40	0	.296	.347	.222
Cory Sullivan	72	140	19	40	6	1	2	14	54	9	25	2	.336	.386	.286
Steve Finley	43	94	9	17	3	0	1	2	23	8	4	0	.245	.245	.181
Omar Quintanilla	27	70	6	16	4	0	0	5	20	5	15	0	.280	.286	.229

PITCHING	GP	GS	W–L	SV	SHO	R	ERA	IP	Ks	BB
Jeff Francis	34	34	17–9	0	1	103	4.22	215.1	165	63
Aaron Cook	25	25	8–7	0	0	87	4.12	166.0	61	44
Josh Fogg	30	29	10–9	0	0	99	4.94	165.2	94	59
Jason Hirsh	19	19	5–7	0	0	63	4.81	112.1	75	48
Taylor Buchholz	41	8	6–5	0	0	47	4.23	93.2	61	20
Ubaldo Jimenez	15	15	4–4	0	0	46	4.28	82.0	68	37
Rodrigo Lopez	14	14	5–4	0	0	43	4.42	79.1	43	21
Manny Corpas	78	0	4–2	19	0	20	2.08	78.0	58	20
Brian Fuentes	64	0	3–5	20	0	26	3.08	61.1	56	23
Jeremy Affeldt	75	0	4–3	0	0	26	3.51	59.0	46	33
LaTroy Hawkins	62	0	2–5	0	0	21	3.42	55.1	29	16
Jorge Julio	58	0	0–3	0	0	25	3.93	52.2	50	20
Matt Herges	35	0	5–1	0	0	17	2.96	48.2	30	15
Franklin Morales	8	8	3–2	0	0	15	3.43	39.1	26	14

Florida Marlins

BATTING	G	AB	R	H	2B	3B	HR	RBI	TB	BB	SO	SB	OBP	SLG	BA
Hanley Ramirez	154	639	125	212	48	6	29	81	359	52	95	51	.386	.562	.332
Dan Uggla	159	632	113	155	49	3	31	88	303	68	167	2	.326	.479	.245
Miguel Cabrera	157	588	91	188	38	2	34	119	332	79	127	2	.401	.565	.320
Josh Willingham	144	521	75	138	32	4	21	89	241	66	122	8	.364	.463	.265
Miguel Olivo	122	452	43	107	20	4	16	60	183	14	123	3	.262	.405	.237
Jeremy Hermida	123	429	54	127	32	1	18	63	215	47	105	3	.369	.501	.296
Mike Jacobs	114	426	57	113	27	2	17	54	195	31	101	1	.317	.458	.265
Alfredo Amezaga	133	400	46	105	14	9	2	30	143	35	52	13	.324	.358	.263
Aaron Boone	69	189	27	54	11	0	5	28	80	21	41	2	.388	.423	.286
Todd Linden	115	184	21	45	8	1	1	11	58	19	59	4	.319	.315	.245
Joe Borchard	85	179	20	35	9	0	4	19	56	21	60	4	.287	.313	.196
Cody Ross	66	173	35	58	19	0	12	39	113	20	38	2	.411	.653	.335
Matt Treanor	55	171	16	46	7	1	4	19	67	19	29	0	.357	.392	.269
Alejandro De Aza	45	144	14	33	8	2	0	8	45	6	37	2	.261	.313	.229

PITCHING	GP	GS	W–L	SV	SHO	R	ERA	IP	Ks	BB
Dontrelle Willis	35	35	10–15	0	0	131	5.17	205.1	146	87
Scott Olsen	33	33	10–15	0	0	134	5.81	176.2	133	85
Sergio Mitre	27	27	5–8	0	0	88	4.65	149.0	80	41
Byung-Hyun Kim	23	19	9–5	0	0	74	5.42	109.2	102	62
Kevin Gregg	74	0	0–5	32	0	34	3.54	84.0	87	40
Rick VandenHurk	18	17	4–6	0	0	63	6.83	81.2	82	48
Lee Gardner	62	0	3–4	2	0	19	1.94	74.1	52	18
Matt Lindstrom	71	0	3–4	0	0	27	3.09	67.0	62	21
Justin Miller	62	0	5–0	0	0	27	3.65	61.2	74	24
Wes Obermueller	18	7	2–3	0	0	49	6.56	59.0	35	36
Renyel Pinto	57	0	2–4	1	0	25	3.68	58.2	56	32
Taylor Tankersley	67	0	6–1	1	0	22	3.99	47.1	49	29

Houston Astros

BATTING	G	AB	R	H	2B	3B	HR	RBI	TB	BB	SO	SB	OBP	SLG	BA
Carlos Lee	162	627	93	190	43	1	32	119	331	53	63	10	.354	.528	.303
Lance Berkman	153	561	95	156	24	2	34	102	286	94	125	7	.386	.510	.278
Craig Biggio	141	517	68	130	31	3	10	50	197	23	112	4	.285	.381	.251
Mark Loretta	133	460	52	132	23	2	4	41	171	44	41	1	.352	.372	.287
Hunter Pence	108	456	57	147	30	9	17	69	246	26	95	11	.360	.539	.322
Luke Scott	132	369	49	94	28	5	18	64	186	53	95	3	.351	.504	.255
Brad Ausmus	117	349	38	82	16	3	3	25	113	37	74	6	.318	.324	.235
Chris Burke	111	319	39	73	19	2	6	28	114	27	52	9	.304	.357	.229
Mike Lamb	124	311	45	90	14	2	11	40	141	36	45	0	.366	.453	.289
Morgan Ensberg	85	224	36	52	10	0	8	31	86	31	48	0	.323	.384	.232
Adam Everett	66	220	18	51	11	1	2	15	70	14	31	4	.281	.318	.232
Jason Lane	68	169	18	30	5	0	8	27	59	16	30	1	.257	.349	.178
Ty Wigginton	50	169	24	48	12	0	6	18	78	13	40	2	.342	.462	.284
Eric Bruntlett	80	138	16	34	5	0	0	14	39	20	27	6	.346	.283	.246
Eric Munson	50	132	14	31	4	0	4	15	47	16	15	0	.313	.356	.235
Orlando Palmeiro	101	103	12	24	3	0	0	6	27	16	8	0	.342	.262	.233

PITCHING	GP	GS	W–L	SV	SHO	R	ERA	IP	Ks	BB
Roy Oswalt	33	32	14–7	0	0	80	3.18	212.0	154	60
Woody Williams	33	31	8–15	0	0	114	5.27	188.0	101	53
Wandy Rodriguez	31	31	9–13	0	1	102	4.58	182.2	158	62
Chris Sampson	24	19	7–8	0	0	64	4.59	121.2	51	30
Matt Albers	31	18	4–11	0	0	77	5.86	110.2	71	50
Jason Jennings	19	18	2–9	0	0	73	6.45	99.0	71	34
Chad Qualls	79	0	6–5	5	0	29	3.05	82.2	78	25
Dave Borkowski	64	0	5–3	1	0	46	5.15	71.2	63	34
Brad Lidge	66	0	5–3	19	0	29	3.36	67.0	88	30
Brian Moehler	42	0	1–4	1	0	29	4.07	59.2	36	17
Dan Wheeler	45	0	1–4	11	0	28	5.07	49.2	56	13
Trever Miller	76	0	0–0	0	0	26	4.86	46.1	46	23

Los Angeles Dodgers

BATTING	G	AB	R	H	2B	3B	HR	RBI	TB	BB	SO	SB	OBP	SLG	BA
Juan Pierre	162	668	96	196	24	8	0	41	236	33	37	64	.331	.353	.293
Rafael Furcal	138	581	87	157	23	4	6	47	206	55	68	25	.333	.355	.270
Russell Martin	151	540	87	158	32	3	19	87	253	67	89	21	.374	.469	.293
Jeff Kent	136	494	78	149	36	1	20	79	247	57	61	1	.375	.500	.302
Luis Gonzalez	139	464	70	129	23	2	15	68	201	56	56	6	.359	.433	.278
Andre Ethier	153	447	50	127	32	2	13	64	202	46	68	0	.350	.452	.284
Nomar Garciaparra	121	431	39	122	17	0	7	59	160	31	41	3	.328	.371	.283
James Loney	96	344	41	114	18	4	15	67	185	28	48	0	.381	.538	.331
Matt Kemp	98	292	47	100	12	5	10	42	152	16	66	10	.373	.521	.342
Tony Abreu	59	166	19	45	14	1	2	17	67	7	21	0	.309	.404	.271
Wilson Betemit	84	156	22	36	8	0	10	26	74	32	49	0	.359	.474	.231
Ramon Martinez	67	129	10	25	4	0	0	27	29	11	15	1	.248	.225	.194
Mark Sweeney	106	123	20	32	9	0	2	13	47	14	29	2	.350	.382	.260
Olmedo Saenz	92	110	9	21	5	0	4	18	38	16	25	0	.295	.345	.191
Andy LaRoche	35	93	16	21	5	0	1	10	29	20	24	2	.365	.312	.226
Mike Lieberthal	38	77	6	18	2	0	0	1	20	4	11	0	.280	.260	.234
Wilson Valdez	41	74	12	16	2	1	0	7	20	4	12	1	.263	.270	.216
Shea Hillenbrand	20	70	6	17	0	2	1	9	24	2	12	0	.257	.343	.243

PITCHING	GP	GS	W–L	SV	SHO	R	ERA	IP	Ks	BB
Brad Penny	33	33	16–4	0	0	75	3.03	208.0	135	73
Derek Lowe	33	32	12–14	0	0	100	3.88	199.1	147	59
Chad Billingsley	43	20	12–5	0	0	56	3.31	147.0	141	64
Mark Hendrickson	39	15	4–8	0	0	75	5.21	122.2	92	29
Brett Tomko	33	15	2–11	0	0	75	5.80	104.0	79	42
Randy Wolf	18	18	9–6	0	0	55	4.73	102.2	94	39
Jonathan Broxton	83	0	4–4	2	0	30	2.85	82.0	99	25
Rudy Seanez	73	0	6–3	1	0	33	3.79	76.0	73	27
Joe Beimel	83	0	4–2	1	0	30	3.88	67.1	39	24
Takashi Saito	63	0	2–1	39	0	10	1.40	64.1	78	13
Eric Stults	12	5	1–4	0	0	26	5.82	38.2	30	17
David Wells	7	7	4–1	0	0	23	5.12	38.2	19	9
Scott Proctor	31	0	3–0	0	0	14	3.38	32.0	27	15

Milwaukee Brewers

BATTING	G	AB	R	H	2B	3B	HR	RBI	TB	BB	SO	SB	OBP	SLG	BA
J.J. Hardy	151	592	89	164	30	1	26	80	274	40	73	2	.323	.463	.277
Prince Fielder	158	573	109	165	35	2	50	119	354	90	121	2	.395	.618	.288
Corey Hart	140	505	86	149	33	9	24	81	272	36	99	23	.353	.539	.295
Bill Hall	136	452	59	115	35	0	14	63	192	40	128	4	.315	.425	.254
Ryan Braun	113	451	91	146	26	6	34	97	286	29	112	15	.370	.634	.324
Johnny Estrada	120	442	40	123	25	0	10	54	178	12	43	0	.296	.403	.278
Geoff Jenkins	132	420	45	107	24	2	21	64	198	32	116	2	.319	.471	.255
Rickie Weeks	118	409	87	96	21	6	16	36	177	78	116	25	.374	.433	.235
Kevin Mench	101	288	39	77	20	3	8	37	127	16	21	3	.305	.441	.267
Craig Counsell	122	282	31	62	12	2	3	24	87	41	47	4	.323	.309	.220
Tony Graffanino	86	231	34	55	8	0	9	30	90	24	44	0	.315	.390	.238
Damian Miller	58	186	19	44	9	0	4	24	65	14	39	1	.296	.349	.237
Gabe Gross	93	183	28	43	12	2	7	24	80	25	37	3	.329	.437	.235
Tony Gwynn Jr.	69	123	13	32	3	2	0	10	39	12	24	8	.326	.317	.260

PITCHING	GP	GS	W–L	SV	SHO	R	ERA	IP	Ks	BB
Jeff Suppan	34	34	12–12	0	0	113	4.62	206.2	114	68
Dave Bush	33	31	12–10	0	0	110	5.12	186.1	134	44
Chris Capuano	29	25	5–12	0	0	93	5.10	150.0	132	54
Ben Sheets	24	24	12–5	0	0	62	3.82	141.1	106	37
Claudio Vargas	29	23	11–6	1	0	80	5.09	134.1	107	54
Carlos Villanueva	59	6	8–5	1	0	52	3.94	114.1	99	53
Yovani Gallardo	20	17	9–5	0	0	48	3.67	110.1	101	37
Scott Linebrink	71	0	5–6	1	0	33	3.71	70.1	50	25
Derrick Turnbow	77	0	4–5	1	0	36	4.63	68.0	84	46
Francisco Cordero	66	0	0–4	44	0	23	2.98	63.1	86	18
Matt Wise	56	0	3–2	1	0	30	4.19	53.2	43	17
Chris Spurling	49	0	2–1	0	0	31	4.68	50.0	28	14
Brian Shouse	73	0	1–1	1	0	19	3.02	47.2	32	14
Manny Parra	9	2	0–1	0	0	13	3.76	26.1	26	12
Scott Linebrink	27	0	2–3	0	0	14	3.55	25.1	25	11

New York Mets

BATTING	G	AB	R	H	2B	3B	HR	RBI	TB	BB	SO	SB	OBP	SLG	BA
Jose Reyes	160	681	119	191	36	12	12	57	287	77	78	78	.354	.421	.280
David Wright	160	604	113	196	42	1	30	107	330	94	115	34	.416	.546	.325
Carlos Beltran	144	554	93	153	33	3	33	112	291	69	111	23	.353	.525	.276
Carlos Delgado	139	538	71	139	30	0	24	87	241	52	118	4	.333	.448	.258
Shawn Green	130	446	62	130	30	1	10	46	192	37	62	11	.352	.430	.291
Paul Lo Duca	119	445	46	121	18	1	9	54	168	24	33	2	.311	.378	.272
Moises Alou	87	328	51	112	19	1	13	49	172	27	30	3	.392	.524	.341
Luis Castillo	50	199	37	59	8	2	1	20	74	24	17	10	.371	.372	.296
Damion Easley	76	193	24	54	6	0	10	26	90	19	35	0	.358	.466	.280
Ruben Gotay	98	190	25	56	12	0	4	24	80	16	42	3	.351	.421	.295
Lastings Milledge	59	184	27	50	9	1	7	29	82	13	42	3	.341	.446	.272
Jose Valentin	51	166	18	40	11	1	3	18	62	15	28	2	.302	.373	.241
Endy Chavez	71	150	20	43	7	2	1	17	57	9	16	5	.325	.380	.287
Ramon Castro	52	144	24	41	6	0	11	31	80	10	39	0	.331	.556	.285
Carlos Gomez	58	125	14	29	3	0	2	12	38	8	27	12	.288	.302	.232
David Newhan	56	74	9	15	1	1	1	6	21	8	19	2	.289	.284	.203

PITCHING	GP	GS	W–L	SV	SHO	R	ERA	IP	Ks	BB
Tom Glavine	34	34	13–8	0	1	102	4.45	200.1	89	64
John Maine	32	32	15–10	0	1	90	3.91	191.0	180	75
Oliver Perez	29	29	15–10	0	0	90	3.56	177.0	174	79
Orlando Hernandez	27	24	9–5	0	0	64	3.72	147.2	128	64
Jorge Sosa	42	14	9–8	0	0	58	4.47	112.2	69	41
Aaron Heilman	81	0	7–7	1	0	36	3.03	86.0	63	20
Mike Pelfrey	15	13	3–8	0	0	47	5.57	72.2	45	39
Billy Wagner	66	0	2–2	34	0	22	2.63	68.1	80	22
Pedro Feliciano	78	0	2–2	2	0	26	3.09	64.0	61	31
Guillermo Mota	52	0	2–2	0	0	39	5.76	59.1	47	18
Scott Schoeneweis	70	0	0–2	0	0	36	5.03	59.0	41	28
Aaron Sele	34	0	3–2	0	0	34	5.37	53.2	29	21
Joe Smith	54	0	3–2	0	0	18	3.45	44.1	45	21
Brian Lawrence	6	6	1–2	0	0	22	6.83	29.0	18	13
Pedro Martinez	5	5	3–1	0	0	11	2.57	28.0	32	7
Ambiorix Burgos	17	0	1–0	0	0	10	3.42	23.2	19	9

Philadelphia Phillies

BATTING	G	AB	R	H	2B	3B	HR	RBI	TB	BB	SO	SB	OBP	SLG	BA
Jimmy Rollins	162	716	139	212	38	20	30	94	380	49	85	41	.344	.531	.296
Aaron Rowand	161	612	105	189	45	0	27	89	315	47	119	6	.374	.515	.309
Chase Utley	132	530	104	176	48	5	22	103	300	50	89	9	.410	.566	.332
Ryan Howard	144	529	94	142	26	0	47	136	309	107	199	1	.392	.584	.268
Pat Burrell	155	472	77	121	26	0	30	97	237	114	120	0	.400	.502	.256
Shane Victorino	131	456	78	128	23	3	12	46	193	37	62	37	.347	.423	.281
Carlos Ruiz	115	374	42	97	29	2	6	54	148	42	49	6	.340	.396	.259
Greg Dobbs	142	324	45	88	20	4	10	55	146	29	67	3	.330	.451	.272
Wes Helms	112	280	21	69	19	0	5	39	103	19	62	0	.297	.368	.246
Jayson Werth	94	255	43	76	11	3	8	49	117	44	73	7	.404	.459	.298
Abraham Nunez	136	252	24	59	10	1	0	16	71	30	48	2	.318	.282	.234
Tadahito Iguchi	45	138	22	42	10	0	3	12	61	13	23	6	.361	.442	.304
Chris Coste	48	129	15	36	3	0	5	22	54	4	20	0	.311	.419	.279
Rod Barajas	48	122	16	28	8	0	4	10	48	21	24	0	.352	.393	.230
Michael Bourn	105	119	29	33	3	3	1	6	45	13	21	18	.348	.378	.277

PITCHING	GP	GS	W–L	SV	SHO	R	ERA	IP	Ks	BB
Jamie Moyer	33	33	14–12	0	0	118	5.01	199.1	133	66
Cole Hamels	28	28	15–5	0	0	72	3.39	183.1	177	43
Adam Eaton	30	30	10–10	0	0	117	6.29	161.2	97	71
Kyle Kendrick	20	20	10–4	0	0	53	3.87	121.0	49	25
Jon Lieber	14	12	3–6	0	1	44	4.73	78.0	54	22
Brett Myers	51	3	5–7	21	0	33	4.33	68.2	83	27
Geoff Geary	57	0	3–2	0	0	44	4.41	67.1	38	25
J.D. Durbin	18	10	6–5	1	1	42	5.15	64.2	39	36
Kyle Lohse	13	11	3–0	0	1	33	4.72	61.1	42	24
Freddy Garcia	11	11	1–5	0	0	39	5.90	58.0	50	19
Ryan Madson	38	0	2–2	0	0	19	3.05	56.0	43	23
Clay Condrey	39	0	5–0	0	0	30	5.04	50.0	27	16
Antonio Alfonseca	61	0	5–2	8	0	31	5.44	49.2	24	27
Tom Gordon	44	0	3–2	6	0	21	4.73	40.0	32	13

Pittsburgh Pirates

BATTING	G	AB	R	H	2B	3B	HR	RBI	TB	BB	SO	SB	OBP	SLG	BA
Freddy Sanchez	147	602	77	183	42	4	11	81	266	32	76	0	.343	.442	.304
Adam LaRoche	152	563	71	153	42	0	21	88	258	62	131	1	.345	.458	.272
Jason Bay	145	538	78	133	25	2	21	84	225	59	141	4	.327	.418	.247
Jose Bautista	142	532	75	135	36	2	15	63	220	68	101	6	.339	.414	.254
Jack Wilson	135	477	67	141	29	2	12	56	210	38	46	2	.350	.440	.296
Ronny Paulino	133	457	56	120	25	0	11	55	178	33	79	2	.314	.389	.263
Xavier Nady	125	431	55	120	23	1	20	72	205	23	101	3	.330	.476	.278
Nate McLouth	137	329	62	85	21	3	13	38	151	39	77	22	.351	.459	.258
Ryan Doumit	83	252	33	69	19	2	9	32	119	22	59	1	.341	.472	.274
Chris Duffy	70	241	31	60	11	3	3	22	86	21	43	13	.313	.357	.249
Jose Castillo	87	221	18	54	18	1	0	24	74	6	48	0	.270	.335	.244
Cesar Izturis	45	123	16	34	3	2	0	8	41	6	3	0	.310	.336	.276
Nyjer Morgan	28	107	15	32	3	4	1	7	46	9	19	7	.359	.430	.299
Matt Kata	47	88	9	22	7	1	1	10	34	0	15	0	.258	.386	.250
Josh Phelps	58	77	13	27	4	2	5	19	50	14	23	0	.463	.649	.351

PITCHING	GP	GS	W–L	SV	SHO	R	ERA	IP	Ks	BB
Ian Snell	32	32	9–12	0	0	94	3.76	208.0	177	68
Tom Gorzelanny	32	32	14–10	0	1	90	3.88	201.2	135	68
Matt Morris	32	32	10–11	0	0	123	4.89	198.2	102	61
Paul Maholm	29	29	10–15	0	1	110	5.02	177.2	105	49
Zach Duke	20	19	3–8	0	0	74	5.53	107.1	41	25
Tony Armas	31	15	4–5	0	0	68	6.03	97.0	73	38
Shawn Chacon	64	4	5–4	1	0	42	3.94	96.0	79	48
Matt Capps	76	0	4–7	18	0	22	2.28	79.0	64	16
Shane Youman	16	8	3–5	0	0	40	5.97	57.1	29	23
Salomon Torres	56	0	2–4	12	0	34	5.47	52.2	45	17
John Grabow	63	0	3–2	1	0	27	4.53	51.2	42	19
Damaso Marte	65	0	2–0	0	0	14	2.38	45.1	51	18

St. Louis Cardinals

BATTING

	G	AB	R	H	2B	3B	HR	RBI	TB	BB	SO	SB	OBP	SLG	BA
Albert Pujols	158	565	99	185	38	1	32	103	321	99	58	2	.429	.568	.327
David Eckstein	117	434	58	134	23	0	3	31	166	24	22	10	.356	.382	.309
Aaron Miles	133	414	55	120	16	1	2	32	144	25	40	2	.328	.348	.290
Scott Rolen	112	392	55	104	24	2	8	58	156	37	56	5	.331	.398	.265
Chris Duncan	127	375	51	97	20	0	21	70	180	55	123	2	.354	.480	.259
Jim Edmonds	117	365	39	92	15	2	12	53	147	41	75	0	.325	.403	.252
Yadier Molina	111	353	30	97	15	0	6	40	130	34	43	1	.340	.368	.275
So Taguchi	130	307	48	89	15	0	3	30	113	23	32	7	.350	.368	.290
Ryan Ludwick	120	303	42	81	22	0	14	52	145	26	72	4	.339	479	.267
Juan Encarnacion	78	283	43	80	17	1	9	47	126	18	43	2	.324	.445	.283
Ada, Kennedy	87	279	27	61	9	1	3	18	81	22	33	6	.282	.290	.219
Scott Spiezio	81	223	31	60	14	0	4	31	86	27	40	0	.354	.386	.269
Brendan Ryan	67	180	30	52	9	0	4	12	73	15	19	7	.347	.406	.289
Skip Schumaker	88	177	19	59	12	2	2	19	81	8	20	1	.358	.458	.333
Rick Ankiel	47	172	31	49	8	1	11	39	92	13	41	1	.328	.535	.285
Gary Bennett	59	155	12	39	7	0	2	17	52	8	16	1	.286	.335	.252

PITCHING

	GP	GS	W–L	SV	SHO	R	ERA	IP	Ks	BB
Adam Wainwright	32	32	14–12	0	0	93	3.70	202.0	136	70
Braden Looper	31	30	12–12	0	0	100	4.94	175.0	87	51
Kip Wells	34	26	7–17	0	0	116	5.70	162.2	122	78
Brad Thompson	44	17	8–6	0	0	76	4.73	129.1	53	40
Anthony Reyes	22	20	2–14	0	0	77	6.04	107.1	74	43
Ryan Franklin	69	0	4–4	1	0	28	3.04	80.0	44	11
Russ Springer	76	0	8–1	0	0	18	2.18	66.0	66	19
Jason Isringhausen	63	0	4–0	32	0	21	2.48	65.1	54	28
Joel Pineiro	11	11	6–4	0	0	29	3.96	63.2	40	12
Todd Wellemeyer	20	11	3–2	0	0	31	3.11	63.2	51	29
Randy Flores	70	0	3–0	1	0	31	4.25	55.0	47	15
Kelvin Jimenez	34	0	3-0	0	0	36	7.50	42.0	24	17
Troy Percival	34	1	3–0	0	0	8	1.80	40.0	36	10
Mike Maroth	14	7	0–5	0	0	56	10.66	38.0	23	17
Tyler Johnson	55	0	1–1	0	0	18	4.03	38.0	24	16

San Diego Padres

BATTING

	G	AB	R	H	2B	3B	HR	RBI	TB	BB	SO	SB	OBP	SLG	BA
Adrian Gonzalez	161	646	101	182	46	3	30	100	324	65	140	0	.347	.502	.282
Khalil Greene	153	611	89	155	44	3	27	97	286	32	128	4	.291	.468	.254
Mike Cameron	151	571	88	138	33	6	21	78	246	67	160	18	.328	.431	.242
Kevin Kouzmanoff	145	484	57	133	30	2	18	74	221	32	94	1	.329	.457	.275
Brian Giles	121	483	72	131	27	2	13	51	201	64	61	4	.361	.416	.271
Marcus Giles	116	420	52	96	19	3	4	39	133	44	82	10	.304	.317	.229
Josh Bard	118	389	42	111	27	2	5	51	157	50	58	0	.364	.404	.285
Geoff Blum	122	330	34	83	21	1	5	33	121	32	52	0	.319	.367	.252
Jose Cruz Jr.	91	256	37	60	12	3	6	21	96	31	65	6	.316	.375	.234
Terrmel Sledge	100	200	22	42	9	0	7	23	72	27	60	1	.310	.360	.210
Milton Bradley	42	144	31	45	5	1	11	30	85	23	27	3	.414	.590	.313
Michael Barrett	44	133	6	30	8	0	0	12	38	2	21	0	.235	.386	.226
Russell Branyan	61	122	16	24	5	1	7	19	52	21	48	1	.322	.426	.197
Scott Hairston	31	87	16	25	5	1	8	20	56	7	18	0	.337	.644	.287

PITCHING

	GP	GS	W–L	SV	SHO	R	ERA	IP	Ks	BB
Jake Peavy	34	34	19–6	0	0	67	2.54	223.1	240	68
Greg Maddux	34	34	14–11	0	0	92	4.14	198.0	104	25
Chris R. Young	30	30	9–8	0	0	66	3.12	173.0	167	72
Justin Germano	26	23	7–10	0	0	72	4.46	133.1	78	40
David Wells	22	22	5–8	0	0	74	5.54	118.2	63	33
Heath Bell	81	0	6–4	2	0	21	2.02	93.2	102	30
Cla Meredith	80	0	5–6	0	0	38	3.50	79.2	59	17
Doug Brocail	67	0	5–1	0	0	33	3.05	76.2	43	24
Kevin Cameron	48	0	2–0	0	0	24	2.79	58.0	50	36
Trevor Hoffman	61	0	4–5	42	0	21	2.98	57.1	44	15
Justin Hampson	39	0	2–3	0	0	17	2.70	53.1	34	16
Clay Hensley	13	9	2–3	0	0	40	6.84	50.0	30	32
Scott Linebrink	44	0	3–3	1	0	19	3.80	45.0	25	14
Brett Tomko	7	4	2–1	0	0	14	4.61	27.1	26	6

San Francisco Giants

BATTING	G	AB	R	H	2B	3B	HR	RBI	TB	BB	SO	SB	OBP	SLG	BA
Randy Winn..............155	593	73	178	42	1	14	65	264	44	85	15	.353	.445	.300
Pedro Feliz 150	557	61	141	28	2	20	72	233	29	70	2	.290	.418	.253
Omar Vizquel...........145	513	54	126	18	3	4	51	162	44	48	14	.305	.316	.246
Bengie Molina 134	497	38	137	19	1	19	81	215	15	53	0	.298	.433	.276
Ray Durham 138	464	56	101	21	2	11	71	159	53	75	10	.295	.343	.218
Dave Roberts 114	396	61	103	17	9	2	23	144	42	66	31	.331	.364	.260
Ryan Klesko 116	362	51	94	27	3	6	44	145	46	68	5	.344	.401	.260
Barry Bonds 126	340	75	94	14	0	28	66	192	132	54	5	.480	.565	.276
Rich Aurilia 99	329	40	83	19	2	5	33	121	22	45	0	.304	.368	.252
Kevin Frandsen 109	264	26	71	12	1	5	31	100	21	24	4	.331	.379	.269
Fred Lewis.................58	157	26	40	9	1	7	54	14	19	25	17	.363	.380	.282
Rajai Davis 51	142	34	45	6	2	3	9	71	21	28	22	.361	.374	.279
Nate Schierholtz.........39	112	9	34	5	3	0	10	45	2	19	3	.316	.402	.304
Mark Sweeney...........76	90	18	23	8	0	2	10	37	13	18	2	.368	.411	.256

PITCHING	GP	GS	W–L	SV	SHO	R	ERA	IP	Ks	BB
Matt Cain 32	32		7–16	0	0	84	3.65	200.0	163	79
Barry Zito 34	33		11–13	0	0	105	4.53	196.2	131	83
Noah Lowry 26	26		14–8	0	0	76	3.92	156.0	87	87
Tim Lincecum 24	24		7–5	0	0	70	4.00	146.1	150	65
Matt Morris........................21	21		7–7	0	0	79	4.35	136.2	73	39
Kevin Correia 59	8		4–7	0	0	39	3.45	101.2	80	40
Brad Hennessey.............69	0		4–5	19	0	26	3.42	68.1	40	23
Randy Messenger 60	0		2–4	1	0	30	4.20	64.1	34	21
Vinnie Chulk.....................57	0		5–4	0	0	22	3.57	53.0	41	14
Jonathan Sanchez...........33	4		1–5	0	0	34	5.88	52.0	62	28
Jack Taschner 63	0		3–1	0	0	31	5.40	50.0	51	29
Russ Ortiz 12	8		2–3	0	0	32	5.51	49.0	27	20
Steve Kline.......................68	0		1–2	2	0	25	4.70	46.0	17	18
Randy Messenger 37	0		1–3	1	0	23	5.09	40.2	22	12

Washington Nationals

BATTING	G	AB	R	H	2B	3B	HR	RBI	TB	BB	SO	SB	OBP	SLG	BA
Ryan Zimmerman.....162	653	99	174	43	5	24	91	299	61	125	4	.330	.458	.266
Felipe Lopez 154	603	70	148	25	6	9	50	212	53	109	24	.308	.332	.245
Austin Kearns 161	587	84	156	35	1	16	74	241	71	106	2	.355	.411	.266
Ronnie Belliard.........147	511	57	148	35	1	11	58	218	34	72	3	.332	.427	.290
Ryan Church 144	470	57	128	43	1	15	70	218	49	107	3	.349	.464	.272
Dmitri Young.............136	460	57	147	38	1	13	74	226	44	74	0	.378	.491	.320
Brian Schneider 129	408	33	96	21	1	6	54	137	56	56	0	.326	.336	.235
Nook Logan..............118	325	39	86	18	4	0	21	112	19	86	23	.304	.345	.265
Robert Fick...............118	197	24	46	6	1	2	16	60	19	42	0	.309	.305	.234
Jesus Flores 79	180	21	44	9	0	4	25	65	14	48	0	.310	.361	.244
Cristian Guzman 46	174	31	57	6	6	2	14	81	15	21	2	.380	.466	.328
Ryan Langerhans......103	162	24	32	6	2	6	22	60	22	63	3	.296	.370	.198
Wily Mo Pena 37	133	24	39	4	0	8	22	67	8	36	2	.352	.504	.293
D'Angelo Jimenez 73	102	14	25	7	0	2	10	38	21	22	2	.379	.373	.245
Tony Batista 80	101	10	26	3	0	2	16	35	12	14	0	.347	.347	.257

PITCHING	GP	GS	W–L	SV	SHO	R	ERA	IP	Ks	BB
Matt Chico 31	31		7–9	0	0	96	4.63	167.0	94	74
Mike Bacsik 29	20		5–8	0	0	73	5.11	118.0	45	29
Jason Bergmann 21	21		6–6	0	0	59	4.45	115.1	86	42
Shawn Hill 16	16		4–5	0	0	42	3.42	97.1	65	25
Saul Rivera 85	0		4–6	3	0	39	3.68	93.0	64	42
Jon Rauch 88	0		8–4	4	0	37	3.61	87.1	71	21
Tim Redding 15	15		3–6	0	0	35	3.64	84.0	47	38
Chad Cordero 76	0		3–3	37	0	31	3.36	75.0	62	29
Jason Simontacchi 13	13		6–7	0	0	53	6.37	70.2	42	23
Jesus Colome 61	0		5–1	1	0	30	3.82	66.0	43	27
Micah Bowie 30	8		4–3	0	0	30	4.55	57.1	42	27
Joel Hanrahan 12	11		5–3	0	0	35	6.00	51.0	43	38

Baltimore Orioles

BATTING

	G	AB	R	H	2B	3B	HR	RBI	TB	BB	SO	SB	OBP	SLG	BA
Nick Markakis	161	637	97	191	43	3	23	112	309	61	112	18	.362	.485	.300
Brian Roberts	156	621	103	180	42	5	12	57	268	89	99	50	.377	.432	.290
Aubrey Huff	151	550	68	154	34	5	15	72	243	48	87	1	.337	.442	.280
Miguel Tejada	133	514	72	152	19	1	18	81	227	41	55	2	.357	.442	.296
Kevin Millar	140	476	63	121	26	1	17	63	200	76	94	1	.365	.420	.254
Melvin Mora	126	467	67	128	23	1	14	58	195	47	83	9	.341	.418	.274
Corey Patterson	132	461	65	124	26	2	8	45	178	21	65	37	.304	.386	.269
Jay Payton	131	434	48	111	21	5	7	58	163	22	42	5	.292	.376	.256
Ramon Hernandez	106	364	40	94	18	0	9	62	139	36	59	1	.333	.382	.258
Jay Gibbons	84	270	28	62	14	0	6	28	94	15	52	0	.272	.348	.230
Chris Gomez	73	169	17	51	10	1	1	16	66	10	20	1	.339	.391	.302
Paul Bako	60	156	13	32	3	1	1	8	40	15	50	0	.277	.256	.205
Tike Redman	40	132	23	42	9	2	2	16	61	5	18	7	.341	.462	.318
Freddie Bynum	70	96	21	25	8	2	2	11	43	2	30	8	.290	.448	.260
Luis Hernandez	30	69	5	20	2	0	1	7	25	1	10	2	.300	.362	.290
Brandon Fahey	40	54	10	9	1	1	0	1	12	2	9	2	.196	.222	.16

PITCHING

	GP	GS	W–L	SV	SHO	R	ERA	IP	Ks	BB
Daniel Cabrera	34	34	9–18	0	0	133	5.55	204.1	166	108
Erik Bedard	28	28	13–5	0	1	66	3.16	182.0	221	57
Jeremy Guthrie	32	26	7–5	0	0	78	3.70	175.1	123	47
Steve Trachsel	25	25	6–8	0	0	73	4.48	140.2	45	69
Brian Burres	37	17	6–8	0	0	81	5.95	121.0	96	66
Chad Bradford	78	0	4–7	2	0	28	3.34	64.2	29	16
Jamie Walker	81	0	3–2	7	0	25	3.23	61.1	41	17
Rob Bell	30	0	4–3	0	0	37	5.94	53.0	28	24
Danys Baez	53	0	0–6	3	0	36	6.44	50.1	29	29
Chris Ray	43	0	5–6	16	0	22	4.43	42.2	44	18
John Parrish	45	0	2–2	0	0	26	5.40	41.2	36	33
Kurt Birkins	19	2	1–2	0	0	31	8.13	34.1	30	14
Garrett Olson	7	7	1–3	0	0	28	7.79	32.1	28	28
Jon Leicester	10	5	2–3	0	0	27	7.59	32.0	16	13
Adam Loewen	6	6	2–0	0	0	14	3.56	30.1	22	26

Boston Red Sox

BATTING

	G	AB	R	H	2B	3B	HR	RBI	TB	BB	SO	SB	OBP	SLG	BA
Mike Lowell	154	589	79	191	37	2	21	120	295	53	71	3	.378	.501	.324
Julio Lugo	147	570	71	135	36	2	8	73	199	48	82	33	.294	.349	.237
David Ortiz	149	549	116	182	52	1	35	117	341	111	103	3	.445	.621	.332
Kevin Youkilis	145	528	85	152	35	2	16	83	239	77	105	4	.390	.453	.288
Coco Crisp	145	526	85	141	28	7	6	60	201	50	84	28	.330	.382	.268
Dustin Pedroia	139	520	86	165	39	1	8	50	230	47	42	7	.380	.442	.317
Manny Ramirez	133	483	84	143	33	1	20	88	238	71	92	0	.388	.493	.296
J.D. Drew	140	466	84	126	30	4	11	64	197	79	100	4	.373	.423	.270
Jason Varitek	131	435	57	111	15	3	17	68	183	71	122	1	.367	.421	.255
Alex Cora	83	207	30	51	10	5	3	18	80	7	23	1	.298	.386	.246
Royce Clayton	77	195	24	48	14	0	1	12	65	14	53	2	.296	.333	.246
Eric Hinske	84	186	25	38	12	3	6	21	74	28	54	3	.317	.398	.204
Wily Mo Pena	73	156	18	34	9	1	5	17	60	14	58	0	.291	.385	.218
Jacoby Ellsbury	33	116	20	41	7	1	3	18	59	8	15	9	.394	.509	.353
Doug Mirabelli	48	114	9	23	3	0	5	16	41	11	41	0	.278	.360	.202
Bobby Kielty	20	52	6	12	2	0	1	9	17	5	17	0	.295	.327	.231

PITCHING

	GP	GS	W–L	SV	SHO	R	ERA	IP	Ks	BB
Daisuke Matsuzaka	32	32	15–12	0	0	100	4.40	204.2	201	80
Josh Beckett	30	30	20–7	0	0	76	3.27	200.2	194	40
Tim Wakefield	31	31	17–12	0	0	104	4.76	189.0	110	64
Curt Schilling	24	24	9–8	0	1	68	3.87	151.0	101	23
Julian Tavarez	34	23	7–11	0	0	89	5.15	134.2	77	51
Hideki Okajima	66	0	3–2	5	0	17	2.22	69.0	63	17
Jon Lester	12	11	4–0	0	0	33	4.57	63.0	50	31
Jonathan Papelbon	59	0	1–3	37	0	12	1.85	58.1	84	15
Mike Timlin	50	0	2–1	1	0	23	3.42	55.1	31	14
Kyle Snyder	46	0	2–3	0	0	29	3.81	54.1	41	32
Eric Gagne	54	0	4–2	16	0	22	3.81	52.0	51	21
Manny Delcarmen	44	0	0–0	1	0	11	2.05	44.0	41	17
Kason Gabbard	7	7	4–0	0	0	17	3.73	41.0	29	18
Javier Lopez	61	0	2–1	0	0	16	3.10	40.2	26	18

Chicago White Sox

BATTING	G	AB	R	H	2B	3B	HR	RBI	TB	BB	SO	SB	OBP	SLG	BA
Paul Konerko	151	549	71	142	34	0	31	90	269	78	102	0	.351	.490	.259
Juan Uribe	150	513	55	120	18	2	20	68	202	34	112	1	.284	.394	.234
Jermaine Dye	138	508	68	129	34	0	28	78	247	45	107	2	.317	.486	.254
A.J. Pierzynski	136	472	54	124	24	0	14	50	190	25	66	1	.309	.403	.263
Jim Thome	130	432	79	119	19	0	35	96	243	95	134	0	.410	.563	.275
Josh Fields	100	373	54	91	17	1	23	67	179	35	125	1	.308	.480	.244
Jerry Owens	93	356	44	95	9	2	1	17	111	27	63	32	.324	.312	.267
Tadahito Iguchi	90	327	45	82	17	4	6	31	125	44	65	8	.340	.382	.251
Darin Erstad	87	310	33	77	13	1	4	32	104	28	44	7	.310	.335	.248
Rob Mackowiak	85	237	34	66	11	2	6	36	99	23	53	3	.354	.418	.278
Scott Podsednik	62	214	30	52	13	4	2	11	79	13	36	12	.299	.369	.243
Andy Gonzalez	67	189	17	35	6	0	2	11	47	25	61	1	.280	.249	.185
Danny Richar	56	187	30	43	9	3	6	15	76	16	33	1	.289	.406	.230
Alex Cintron	68	185	23	45	7	1	2	19	60	9	35	2	.281	.324	.243
Joe Crede	47	167	13	36	5	0	4	22	53	10	24	0	.258	.317	.216

PITCHING	GP	GS	W-L	SV	SHO	R	ERA	IP	Ks	BB
Javier Vazquez	32	32	15–8	0	0	95	3.74	216.2	213	50
Jon Garland	32	32	10–13	0	1	114	4.23	208.1	98	57
Mark Buehrle	30	30	10–9	0	1	86	3.63	201.0	115	45
Jose Contreras	32	30	10–17	0	2	134	5.57	189.0	113	62
John Danks	26	26	6–13	0	0	92	5.50	139.0	109	54
Gavin Floyd	16	10	1–5	0	0	45	5.27	70.0	49	19
Bobby Jenks	66	0	3–5	40	0	20	2.77	65.0	56	13
Matt Thornton	68	0	4–4	2	0	31	4.79	56.1	55	26
Boone Logan	68	0	2–1	0	0	30	4.97	50.2	35	20
Mike MacDougal	54	0	2–5	0	0	37	6.80	42.1	39	33
Nick Masset	27	1	2–3	0	0	33	7.09	39.1	21	26
Ryan Bukvich	45	0	1–0	0	0	23	5.05	35.2	18	24
David Aardsma	25	0	2–1	0	0	24	6.40	32.1	36	17

Cleveland Indians

BATTING	G	AB	R	H	2B	3B	HR	RBI	TB	BB	SO	SB	OBP	SLG	BA
Grady Sizemore	162	628	118	174	34	5	24	78	290	101	155	33	.390	.462	.277
Casey Blake	156	588	81	159	36	4	18	78	257	54	123	4	.339	.437	.270
Jhonny Peralta	152	574	87	155	27	1	21	72	247	61	146	4	.341	.430	.270
Victor Martinez	147	562	78	169	40	0	25	114	284	62	76	0	.374	.505	.301
Travis Hafner	152	545	80	145	25	2	24	100	246	102	115	1	.385	.451	.266
Ryan Garko	138	482	62	140	29	1	21	61	234	34	94	0	.359	.483	.289
Josh Barfield	130	420	53	102	19	3	3	50	136	14	90	14	.270	.324	.243
Trot Nixon	99	307	30	77	17	0	3	31	103	44	59	0	.342	.336	.251
Franklin Gutierrez	100	271	41	72	13	2	13	36	128	21	77	8	.318	.472	.266
Jason Michaels	105	267	43	72	11	1	7	39	106	20	50	3	.324	.397	.270
David Dellucci	56	178	25	41	11	2	4	20	68	17	40	2	.296	.382	.230
Kenny Lofton	52	173	24	49	9	3	0	15	64	17	23	2	.344	.370	.283
Kelly Shoppach	59	161	26	42	13	0	7	30	76	11	56	0	.310	.472	.261
Asdrubal Cabrera	45	159	30	45	9	2	3	22	67	17	29	0	.354	.421	.283

PITCHING	GP	GS	W-L	SV	SHO	R	ERA	IP	Ks	BB
C.C. Sabathia	34	34	19–7	0	1	94	3.21	241.0	209	37
Fausto Carmona	32	32	19–8	0	1	78	3.06	215.0	137	61
Paul Byrd	31	31	15–8	0	2	107	4.59	192.1	88	28
Jake Westbrook	25	25	6–9	0	0	78	4.32	152.0	93	55
Cliff Lee	20	16	5–8	0	0	73	6.29	97.1	66	36
Rafael Betancourt	68	0	5–1	3	0	13	1.47	79.1	80	9
Jeremy Sowers	13	13	1–6	0	0	49	6.42	67.1	24	21
Joe Borowski	69	0	4–5	45	0	39	5.07	65.2	58	17
Rafael Perez	44	0	1–2	1	0	15	1.78	60.2	62	15
Tom Mastny	51	0	7–2	0	0	30	4.68	57.2	52	32
Aaron Laffey	9	9	4–2	0	0	26	4.56	49.1	25	12
Aaron Fultz	49	0	4–3	0	0	12	2.92	37.0	28	18
Fernando Cabrera	24	0	1–2	0	0	22	5.61	33.2	39	22
Jensen Lewis	26	0	1–1	0	0	8	2.15	29.1	34	10
Jason Stanford	8	2	1–1	0	0	15	4.78	26.1	16	1
Roberto Hernandez	28	0	3–1	0	0	21	6.23	26.0	18	0

Detroit Tigers

BATTING	G	AB	R	H	2B	3B	HR	RBI	TB	BB	SO	SB	OBP	SLG	BA
Curtis Granderson	158	612	122	185	38	23	23	74	338	52	141	26	.361	.552	.302
Magglio Ordonez	157	595	117	216	54	0	28	139	354	76	79	4	.434	.595	.363
Placido Polanco	142	587	105	200	36	3	9	67	269	37	30	7	.388	.458	.341
Carlos Guillen	151	564	86	167	35	9	21	102	283	55	93	13	.357	.502	.296
Brandon Inge	151	508	64	120	25	2	14	71	191	47	150	9	.312	.376	.236
Ivan Rodriguez	129	502	50	141	31	3	11	63	211	9	96	2	.294	.420	.281
Gary Sheffield	133	494	107	131	20	1	25	74	228	84	71	22	.378	.462	.265
Sean Casey	143	453	40	134	30	1	4	54	178	39	42	2	.353	.393	.296
Craig Monroe	99	343	47	76	19	0	11	55	128	20	94	0	.264	.373	.222
Marcus Thames	86	269	37	65	15	0	18	54	134	13	72	2	.278	.498	.242
Mike Rabelo	51	168	14	43	10	2	1	18	60	6	41	0	.300	.357	.256
Omar Infante	66	166	24	45	6	1	2	17	59	9	29	4	.307	.355	.271
Ryan Raburn	49	138	28	42	12	2	4	27	70	8	33	3	.340	.507	.304
Timo Perez	29	90	12	35	9	2	0	13	48	6	6	1	.427	.533	.389
Ramon Santiago	32	67	10	19	5	1	0	7	26	1	10	3	.324	.388	.284

PITCHING	GP	GS	W-L	SV	SHO	R	ERA	IP	Ks	BB
Justin Verlander	32	32	18-6	0	1	88	3.66	201.2	183	67
Nate Robertson	30	30	9-13	0	0	98	4.76	177.2	119	63
Jeremy Bonderman	28	28	11-9	0	0	105	5.01	174.1	145	48
Chad Durbin	36	19	8-7	1	0	71	4.72	127.2	66	49
Jason Grilli	57	0	5-3	0	0	46	4.74	79.2	62	32
Mike Maroth	13	13	5-2	0	0	47	5.06	78.1	28	33
Andrew Miller	13	13	5-5	0	0	43	5.63	64.0	56	39
Kenny Rogers	11	11	3-4	0	0	36	4.43	63.0	36	25
Todd Jones	63	0	1-4	38	0	29	4.26	61.1	33	23
Zach Miner	34	1	3-4	0	0	22	3.02	53.2	34	22
Fernando Rodney	48	0	2-6	1	0	27	4.26	50.2	54	21
Bobby Seay	58	0	3-0	1	0	12	2.33	46.1	38	15
Tim Byrdak	39	0	3-0	1	0	23	3.20	45.0	49	26
Wilfredo Ledezma	23	0	3-1	0	0	21	4.79	35.2	24	26
Joel Zumaya	28	0	2-3	1	0	16	4.28	33.2	27	17
Jair Jurrjens	7	7	3-1	0	0	16	4.70	30.2	13	11

Kansas City Royals

BATTING	G	AB	R	H	2B	3B	HR	RBI	TB	BB	SO	SB	OBP	SLG	BA
David DeJesus	157	605	101	157	29	9	7	58	225	64	83	10	.351	.372	.260
Mark Teahen	144	544	78	155	31	8	7	60	223	55	127	13	.353	.410	.285
Alex Gordon	151	543	60	134	36	4	15	60	223	41	137	14	.314	.411	.247
Tony Pena Jr.	152	509	58	136	25	7	2	47	181	10	78	5	.284	.356	.267
Mark Grudzielanek	116	453	70	137	32	3	6	51	193	23	60	1	.346	.426	.302
Emil Brown	113	366	44	94	13	1	6	62	127	24	71	12	.300	.347	.257
Esteban German	121	348	49	92	15	6	4	37	131	43	60	11	.351	.376	.264
John Buck	113	347	41	77	18	0	18	48	149	36	92	0	.308	.429	.222
Billy Butler	92	329	38	96	23	2	8	52	147	27	55	0	.347	.447	.292
Ross Gload	102	320	37	92	22	3	7	51	141	16	39	2	.318	.441	.288
Mike Sweeney	74	265	26	69	15	1	7	38	107	17	29	0	.315	.404	.260
Joey Gathright	74	228	28	70	8	0	0	19	78	20	36	9	.371	.342	.307
Ryan Shealy	52	172	18	38	6	0	3	21	53	13	53	0	.286	.308	.221
Jason LaRue	66	169	14	25	9	0	4	13	46	17	66	1	.240	.272	.148
Shane Costa	55	103	13	23	6	1	0	12	31	5	23	0	.257	.301	.223

PITCHING	GP	GS	W-L	SV	SHO	R	ERA	IP	Ks	BB
Gil Meche	34	34	9-13	0	0	98	3.67	216.0	156	62
Brian Bannister	27	27	12-9	0	0	76	3.87	165.0	77	44
Odalis Perez	26	26	8-11	0	0	90	5.57	137.1	64	50
Jorge De La Rosa	26	23	8-12	0	0	88	5.82	130.0	82	53
Zack Greinke	52	14	7-7	1	0	52	3.69	122.0	106	36
Joel Peralta	62	0	1-3	0	0	39	3.80	87.2	66	19
David Riske	65	0	1-4	4	0	19	2.45	69.2	52	27
Joakim Soria	62	0	2-3	17	0	20	2.48	69.0	75	19
Jimmy Gobble	74	0	4-1	1	0	23	3.02	53.2	50	23
Kyle Davies	11	11	3-7	0	0	41	6.66	50.0	40	26
Brandon Duckworth	26	3	3-5	1	0	30	4.63	46.2	21	23
Leo Nunez	13	6	2-4	0	0	21	3.92	43.2	37	10

Los Angeles Angels of Anaheim

BATTING	G	AB	R	H	2B	3B	HR	RBI	TB	BB	SO	SB	OBP	SLG	BA
Orlando Cabrera	155	638	101	192	35	1	8	86	253	44	64	20	.345	.397	.301
Vladimir Guerrero	150	574	89	186	45	1	27	125	314	71	62	2	.403	.547	.324
Gary Matthews Jr.	140	516	79	130	26	3	18	72	216	55	102	18	.323	.419	.252
Casey Kotchman	137	443	64	131	37	3	11	68	207	53	43	2	.372	.467	.296
Chone Figgins	115	442	81	146	24	6	3	58	191	51	81	41	.393	.432	.330
Reggie Willits	136	430	74	126	20	1	0	34	148	69	83	27	.391	.344	.293
Garret Anderson	108	417	67	124	31	1	16	80	205	27	54	1	.336	.492	.297
Howie Kendrick	88	338	55	109	24	2	5	39	152	9	61	5	.347	.450	.322
Maicer Izturis	102	336	47	97	17	2	6	51	136	33	39	7	.349	.405	.289
Mike Napoli	75	219	40	54	11	1	10	34	97	33	63	5	.351	.443	.247
Shea Hillenbrand	53	197	19	50	5	0	3	22	64	5	18	0	.275	.325	.254
Erick Aybar	79	194	18	46	5	1	1	19	56	10	32	4	.279	.289	.237
Robb Quinlan	79	178	21	44	9	0	3	21	62	14	27	3	.304	.348	.247
Jeff Mathis	59	171	24	36	12	0	4	23	60	15	49	0	.276	.351	.211
Jose Molina	40	125	9	8	80	0	0	10	36	3	30	2	.242	.288	.224
Kendry Morales	43	119	12	35	10	0	4	15	57	6	21	0	.333	.479	.294

PITCHING	GP	GS	W–L	SV	SHO	R	ERA	IP	Ks	BB
John Lackey	33	33	19–9	0	2	87	3.01	224.0	179	52
Kelvim Escobar	30	30	18–7	0	1	79	3.40	195.2	160	66
Jered Weaver	28	28	13–7	0	0	77	3.91	161.0	115	45
Ervin Santana	28	26	7–14	0	0	103	5.76	150.0	126	58
Joe Saunders	18	18	8–5	0	0	56	4.44	107.1	69	34
Bartolo Colon	19	18	6–8	0	0	74	6.34	99.1	76	29
Dustin Moseley	46	8	4–3	0	0	45	4.40	92.0	50	27
Chris Bootcheck	51	0	3–3	0	0	43	4.77	77.1	56	24
Scot Shields	71	0	4–5	2	0	36	3.86	77.0	77	33
Francisco Rodriguez	64	0	5–2	40	0	22	2.81	67.1	90	34
Darren Oliver	61	0	3–1	0	0	31	3.78	64.1	51	23
Justin Speier	51	0	2–3	0	0	17	2.88	50.0	47	12
Hector Carrasco	29	1	2–1	0	0	34	6.57	38.1	33	23

Minnesota Twins

BATTING	G	AB	R	H	2B	3B	HR	RBI	TB	BB	SO	SB	OBP	SLG	BA
Torii Hunter	160	600	94	172	45	1	28	107	303	40	101	18	.334	.505	.287
Justin Morneau	157	590	84	160	31	3	31	111	290	64	91	1	.343	.492	.271
Michael Cuddyer	144	547	87	151	28	5	16	81	237	64	107	5	.356	.433	.276
Jason Bartlett	140	510	75	135	20	7	5	43	184	50	73	23	.339	.361	.265
Nick Punto	150	472	53	99	18	4	1	25	128	55	90	16	.291	.271	.210
Jason Kubel	128	418	49	114	31	2	13	65	188	41	79	5	.335	.450	.273
Joe Mauer	109	406	62	119	27	3	7	60	173	57	51	7	.382	.426	.293
Luis Castillo	85	349	54	106	11	3	0	18	123	29	28	9	.356	.352	.304
Jason Tyner	114	304	42	87	14	2	1	22	108	16	26	8	.331	.355	.286
Mike Redmond	82	272	23	80	13	0	1	38	96	18	23	0	.346	.353	.294
Alexi Casilla	56	189	15	42	5	1	0	9	49	9	29	11	.256	.259	.222
Luis Rodriguez	68	155	18	34	5	1	2	12	47	12	14	1	.281	.303	.219
Jeff Cirillo	50	153	18	40	9	2	2	21	59	15	13	2	.327	.386	.261
Lew Ford	55	116	13	27	6	0	3	14	42	11	24	3	.315	.362	.233
Rondell White	38	109	8	19	4	0	4	20	35	6	19	0	.235	.321	.174
Brian Buscher	33	82	8	20	1	0	2	10	27	10	16	1	.323	.329	.244
Garrett Jones	41	77	7	16	2	1	2	5	26	6	20	1	.262	.338	.208

PITCHING	GP	GS	W–L	SV	SHO	R	ERA	IP	Ks	BB
Johan Santana	33	33	15–13	0	1	88	3.33	219.0	235	52
Carlos Silva	33	33	13–14	0	1	99	4.19	202.0	89	36
Boof Bonser	31	30	8–12	0	0	108	5.10	173.0	136	65
Scott Baker	24	23	9–9	0	1	70	4.26	143.2	102	29
Ramon Ortiz	28	10	4–4	0	0	54	5.14	91.0	44	15
Matt Guerrier	73	0	2–4	1	0	23	2.35	88.0	68	21
Matt Garza	16	15	5–7	0	0	44	3.69	83.0	67	32
Joe Nathan	68	0	4–2	37	0	15	1.88	71.2	77	19
Pat Neshek	74	0	7–2	0	0	25	2.94	70.1	74	27
Kevin Slowey	13	11	4–1	0	0	39	4.73	66.2	47	11
Juan Rincon	63	0	3–3	0	0	38	5.13	59.2	49	28
Sidney Ponson	7	7	2–5	0	0	31	6.93	37.2	23	17

New York Yankees

BATTING

	G	AB	R	H	2B	3B	HR	RBI	TB	BB	SO	SB	OBP	SLG	BA
Derek Jeter	156	639	102	206	39	4	12	73	289	56	100	15	.388	.452	.322
Robinson Cano	160	617	93	189	41	7	19	97	301	39	85	4	.353	.488	.306
Bobby Abreu	158	605	123	171	40	5	16	101	269	84	115	25	.369	.445	.283
Alex Rodriguez	158	583	143	183	31	0	54	156	376	95	120	24	.422	.645	.314
Hideki Matsui	143	547	100	156	28	4	25	103	267	73	73	4	.367	.488	.285
Melky Cabrera	150	545	66	149	24	8	8	73	213	43	68	13	.327	.391	.273
Johnny Damon	141	533	93	144	27	2	12	63	211	66	79	27	.351	.396	.270
Jorge Posada	144	506	91	171	42	1	20	90	275	74	98	2	.426	.543	.338
Jason Giambi	83	254	31	60	8	0	14	39	110	40	66	1	.356	.433	.236
Andy Phillips	61	185	27	54	7	1	2	25	69	12	26	0	.338	.373	.292
Doug Mientkiewicz	72	166	26	46	12	0	5	24	73	16	23	0	.349	.440	.277
Miguel Cairo	54	107	12	27	7	0	0	10	34	8	19	8	.308	.318	.252
Wilson Betemit	37	84	11	19	4	0	4	24	35	6	33	0	.278	.417	.226
Josh Phelps	36	80	8	21	2	0	2	12	29	6	19	0	.330	.363	.263
Shelley Duncan	34	74	6	19	1	0	7	17	41	8	20	0	.329	.554	.257

PITCHING

	GP	GS	W-L	SV	SHO	R	ERA	IP	Ks	BB
Andy Pettitte	36	34	15–9	0	0	106	4.05	215.1	141	69
Chien-Ming Wang	30	30	19–7	0	0	84	3.70	199.1	104	59
Mike Mussina	28	27	11–10	0	0	90	5.15	152.0	91	35
Roger Clemens	18	17	6–6	0	0	52	4.18	99.0	68	31
Luis Vizcaino	77	0	8–2	0	0	37	4.30	75.1	62	43
Phil Hughes	13	13	5–3	0	0	39	4.46	72.2	58	29
Mariano Rivera	67	0	3–4	30	0	25	3.15	71.1	74	12
Kei Igawa	14	12	2–3	0	0	48	6.25	67.2	53	37
Kyle Farnsworth	64	0	2–1	0	0	35	4.80	60.0	48	27
Scott Proctor	52	0	2–5	0	0	27	3.81	54.1	37	29
Brian Bruney	58	0	3–2	0	0	28	4.68	50.0	39	37
Ron Villone	37	0	0–0	0	0	20	4.25	42.1	25	18
Mike Myers	55	0	3–0	0	0	14	2.66	40.2	21	16
Sean Henn	29	1	2–2	0	0	32	7.12	36.2	28	27
Matt DeSalvo	7	6	1–3	0	0	20	6.18	27.2	10	18
Tyler Clippard	6	6	3–1	0	0	19	6.33	27.0	18	17
Darrel Rasner	6	6	1–3	0	0	14	4.01	24.2	11	8
Joba Chamberlain	19	0	2–0	1	0	2	0.38	24.0	34	6

Oakland Athletics

BATTING

	G	AB	R	H	2B	3B	HR	RBI	TB	BB	SO	SB	OBP	SLG	BA
Mark Ellis	150	583	84	161	33	3	19	76	257	44	94	9	.336	.411	.276
Shannon Stewart	146	576	79	167	22	1	12	48	227	47	60	11	.345	.394	.290
Nick Swisher	150	539	84	141	36	1	22	78	245	100	131	3	.381	.455	.262
Dan Johnson	117	416	53	98	20	1	18	62	174	72	77	0	.349	.418	.236
Jack Cust	124	395	61	101	18	1	26	82	199	105	164	0	.408	.504	.256
Bobby Crosby	93	349	40	79	16	0	8	31	119	23	62	10	.278	.341	.226
Eric Chavez	90	341	43	82	21	2	15	46	152	34	76	4	.306	.446	.240
Marco Scutaro	104	338	49	88	13	0	7	41	122	35	40	2	.332	.361	.260
Mike Piazza	83	309	33	85	17	1	8	44	128	18	61	0	.313	.414	.275
Jason Kendall	80	292	24	66	10	0	2	22	82	12	27	3	.261	.281	.226
Travis Buck	82	285	41	82	22	5	7	34	135	39	66	4	.377	.474	.288
Kurt Suzuki	68	213	27	53	13	0	7	39	87	24	39	0	.327	.408	.249
Mark Kotsay	56	206	20	44	14	0	1	20	61	19	20	1	.279	.296	.214
Jack Hannahan	41	144	16	40	12	0	3	24	61	21	39	1	.369	.424	.278
Donnie Murphy	42	118	21	26	8	0	6	21	52	10	35	1	.290	.441	.220

PITCHING

	GP	GS	W-L	SV	SHO	R	ERA	IP	Ks	BB
Joe Blanton	34	34	14–10	0	1	106	3.95	230.0	140	40
Darren Haren	34	34	15–9	0	0	91	3.07	222.2	192	55
Chad Gaudin	34	34	11–13	0	0	108	4.42	199.1	154	100
Lenny DiNardo	35	20	8–10	0	0	74	4.11	131.1	59	50
Joe Kennedy	27	16	3–9	0	0	48	4.37	101.0	42	48
Dallas Braden	20	14	1–8	0	0	59	6.72	72.1	55	26
Alan Embree	68	0	1–2	17	0	30	3.97	68.0	51	19
Santiago Casilla	46	0	3–1	2	0	25	4.44	50.2	52	23
Huston Street	48	0	5–2	16	0	20	2.88	50.0	63	12
Jay Marshall	51	0	1–2	0	0	33	6.43	42.0	18	22
Andrew Brown	33	0	3–3	0	0	21	4.54	41.2	43	17
Kiko Calero	46	0	1–5	1	0	26	5.75	40.2	31	21
Ruddy Lugo	27	0	4–0	0	0	18	4.30	37.2	26	24

Seattle Mariners

BATTING	G	AB	R	H	2B	3B	HR	RBI	TB	BB	SO	SB	OBP	SLG	BA
Ichiro Suzuki	161	678	111	238	22	7	6	68	292	49	77	37	.396	.431	.351
Adrian Beltre	149	595	87	164	41	2	26	99	287	38	104	14	.319	.482	.276
Jose Guillen	153	593	84	172	28	2	23	99	273	41	118	5	.353	.460	.290
Raul Ibanez	149	573	80	167	35	5	21	105	275	53	97	0	.351	.480	.291
Jose Vidro	147	548	78	172	26	0	6	59	216	63	57	0	.381	.394	.314
Yuniesky Betancourt	155	536	72	155	38	2	9	67	224	15	48	5	.308	.418	.289
Jose Lopez	149	524	58	132	17	2	11	62	186	20	64	2	.284	.355	.252
Kenji Johjima	135	485	52	139	29	0	14	61	210	15	41	0	.322	.433	.287
Richie Sexson	121	434	58	89	21	0	21	63	173	51	100	1	.295	.399	.205
Ben Broussard	99	240	27	66	10	0	7	29	97	17	50	2	.330	.404	.275
Willie Bloomquist	91	173	28	48	3	0	2	13	57	10	35	7	.321	.329	.277
Jamie Burke	50	113	19	34	8	0	1	12	45	7	17	0	.363	.398	.301
Adam Jones	41	65	16	16	2	1	2	4	26	4	21	2	.300	.400	.246
Jason Ellison	63	46	9	13	0	0	0	0	13	1	12	3	.298	.283	.283
Mike Morse	9	18	1	8	2	0	0	3	10	1	4	0	.500	.556	.444

PITCHING	GP	GS	W–L	SV	SHO	R	ERA	IP	Ks	BB
Jarrod Washburn	32	32	10–15	0	1	102	4.32	193.2	114	67
Miguel Batista	33	32	16–11	0	0	101	4.29	193.0	133	85
Felix Hernandez	30	30	14–7	0	1	88	3.92	190.1	165	53
Jeff Weaver	27	27	7–13	0	2	105	6.20	146.2	80	35
Horacio Ramirez	20	20	8–7	0	0	86	7.16	98.0	40	42
Cha Seung Baek	14	12	4–3	0	0	45	5.15	73.1	49	14
J.J. Putz	68	0	6–1	40	0	11	1.38	71.2	82	13
Sean Green	64	0	5–2	0	0	31	3.84	68.0	53	34
Brandon Morrow	60	0	3–4	0	0	29	4.12	63.1	66	50
Eric O'Flaherty	56	0	7–1	0	0	26	4.47	52.1	36	20
Ryan Feierabend	13	9	1–6	0	0	44	8.03	49.1	27	23
George Sherrill	73	0	2–0	3	0	12	2.36	45.2	56	17
Ryan Rowland-Smith	26	0	1–0	0	0	19	3.96	38.2	42	15
Sean White	15	0	1–1	0	0	24	5.60	35.1	16	20
Jason Davis	16	0	2–0	0	0	21	6.31	25.2	14	16

Tampa Bay Devil Rays

BATTING	G	AB	R	H	2B	3B	HR	RBI	TB	BB	SO	SB	OBP	SLG	BA
Delmon Young	162	645	65	186	38	0	13	93	263	26	127	10	.316	.408	.288
Carl Crawford	143	584	93	184	37	9	11	80	272	32	112	50	.355	.466	.315
Brendan Harris	137	521	72	149	35	3	12	59	226	42	96	4	.343	.434	.286
Akinori Iwamura	123	491	82	140	21	10	7	34	202	58	114	12	.359	.411	.285
Carlos Pena	148	490	99	138	29	1	46	121	307	103	142	1	.411	.627	.282
B.J. Upton	129	474	86	142	25	1	24	82	241	65	154	22	.386	.508	.300
Dioner Navarro	119	388	46	88	19	2	9	44	138	33	67	3	.286	.356	.227
Ty Wigginton	98	378	47	104	21	0	16	49	173	28	73	1	.329	.458	.275
Jonny Gomes	107	348	48	85	20	2	17	49	160	35	126	12	.322	.460	.244
Josh Wilson	90	263	25	66	15	3	2	24	93	12	51	6	.291	.354	.251
Greg Norton	75	202	25	49	9	0	4	23	70	37	55	1	.358	.347	.243
Elijah Dukes	52	184	27	35	3	2	10	21	72	33	44	2	.318	.391	.190
Rocco Baldelli	35	137	16	28	6	0	5	12	49	9	35	4	.268	.358	.204
Josh Paul	35	105	8	20	3	0	1	9	26	6	30	1	.234	.248	.190

PITCHING	GP	GS	W–L	SV	SHO	R	ERA	IP	Ks	BB
James Shields	31	31	12–8	0	0	98	3.85	215.0	184	36
Scott Kazmir	34	34	13–9	0	0	91	3.48	206.2	239	89
Edwin Jackson	32	31	5–15	0	1	116	5.76	161.0	128	88
Andy Sonnanstine	22	22	6–10	0	0	87	5.85	130.2	97	26
Jason Hammel	24	14	3–5	0	0	58	6.14	85.0	64	40
Gary Glover	67	0	6–5	2	0	44	4.89	77.1	51	27
Casey Fossum	40	10	5–8	0	0	71	7.70	76.0	53	27
Brian Stokes	59	0	2–7	0	0	49	7.07	62.1	35	25
Al Reyes	61	0	2–4	26	0	35	4.90	60.2	70	21
Jae Seo	11	10	3–4	0	0	53	8.13	52.0	28	16
J.P. Howell	10	10	1–6	0	0	45	7.59	51.0	49	21
Shawn Camp	50	0	0–3	0	0	33	7.20	40.0	36	18
Juan Salas	34	0	1–1	0	0	19	3.72	36.1	26	17
Scott Dohmann	31	0	3–0	0	0	13	3.31	32.2	26	18
Dan Wheeler	25	0	0–5	0	0	20	5.76	25.0	26	10

Texas Rangers

BATTING	G	AB	R	H	2B	3B	HR	RBI	TB	BB	SO	SB	OBP	SLG	BA
Michael Young	156	639	80	201	37	1	9	94	267	47	107	13	.366	.418	.315
Ian Kinsler	130	483	96	127	22	2	20	61	213	62	83	23	.355	.441	.263
Marlon Byrd	109	414	60	127	17	8	10	70	190	29	88	5	.355	.459	.307
Sammy Sosa	114	412	53	104	24	1	21	92	193	34	112	0	.311	.468	.252
Gerald Laird	120	407	48	91	18	3	9	47	142	30	103	6	.278	.349	.224
Brad Wilkerson	119	338	54	79	17	1	20	62	158	43	107	4	.319	.467	.234
Frank Catalanotto	103	331	52	86	20	4	11	44	147	28	37	2	.337	.444	.260
Kenny Lofton	84	317	62	96	16	3	7	23	139	39	28	21	.380	.438	.303
Nelson Cruz	96	307	35	72	15	2	9	34	118	21	87	2	.287	.384	.235
Ramon Vazquez	104	300	42	69	13	3	8	28	112	29	72	1	.300	.373	.230
Mark Teixeira	78	286	48	85	24	1	13	49	150	45	66	0	.397	.524	.297
Hank Blalock	58	208	32	61	16	3	10	33	113	21	38	4	.358	.543	.293
Jason Botts	48	167	19	40	8	1	2	14	56	19	59	1	.326	.335	.240
Jarrod Saltalamacchia	46	167	28	42	7	1	7	21	72	9	47	0	.290	.431	.251
Travis Metcalf	57	161	25	41	12	1	5	21	70	13	41	0	.307	.435	.255
Jerry Hairston Jr.	73	159	22	30	7	0	3	16	46	11	24	5	.249	.289	.189
Victor Diaz	37	104	13	25	4	0	9	25	56	1	33	0	.259	.538	.240

PITCHING	GP	GS	W–L	SV	SHO	R	ERA	IP	Ks	BB
Kevin Millwood	31	31	10–14	0	0	111	5.16	172.2	123	67
Kameron Loe	28	23	6–11	0	0	96	5.36	136.0	78	56
Vincente Padilla	23	23	6–10	0	0	88	5.76	120.1	71	50
B. McCarthy	23	22	5–10	0	0	62	4.87	101.2	59	48
Robinson Tejeda	19	19	5–9	0	0	78	6.61	95.1	69	60
Joaquin Benoit	70	0	7–4	6	0	28	2.85	82.0	87	28
Jamey Wright	20	9	4–5	0	0	35	3.62	77.0	39	41
C.J. Wilson	66	0	2–1	12	0	25	3.03	68.1	63	33
Willie Eyre	33	2	4–6	1	0	42	5.16	68.0	42	32
Frank Francisco	59	0	1–1	0	0	33	4.55	59.1	49	38
Mike Wood	21	4	3–0	0	0	36	5.33	50.2	25	15
John Rheinecker	23	7	4–3	0	0	38	5.36	50.1	40	28
Wes Littleton	35	0	3–2	2	0	23	4.31	48.0	24	16
Kason Gabbard	8	8	2–1	0	1	25	5.58	40.1	26	23
Scott Feldman	29	0	1–2	0	0	26	5.77	39.0	19	32
Ron Mahay	28	0	2–0	1	0	24	2.77	39.0	32	21

Toronto Blue Jays

BATTING	G	AB	R	H	2B	3B	HR	RBI	TB	BB	SO	SB	OBP	SLG	BA
Alex Rios	161	643	114	191	43	7	24	85	320	55	103	17	.354	.498	.297
Aaron Hill	160	608	87	177	47	2	17	78	279	41	102	4	.333	.459	.291
Vernon Wells	149	584	85	143	36	4	16	80	235	49	89	10	.304	.402	.245
Frank Thomas	155	531	63	147	30	0	26	95	255	81	94	0	.377	.480	.277
Lyle Overbay	122	425	49	102	30	2	10	44	166	47	78	2	.315	.391	.240
Troy Glaus	115	385	60	101	19	1	20	62	182	61	102	0	.366	.473	.262
Matt Stairs	125	357	58	103	28	1	21	64	196	44	66	2	.368	.549	.289
Gregg Zaun	110	331	43	80	24	1	10	52	136	51	55	0	.341	.411	.242
John McDonald	123	327	32	82	20	2	1	31	109	11	48	7	.279	.333	.251
Adam Lind	89	290	34	69	14	0	11	46	116	16	65	1	.278	.400	.238
Reed Johnson	79	275	31	65	13	2	2	14	88	16	56	4	.305	.320	.236
Royce Clayton	69	189	23	48	14	0	1	12	65	14	50	2	.304	.344	.254
Jason Phillips	55	144	11	30	7	0	1	12	40	10	21	0	.269	.278	.208
Curtis Thigpen	47	101	13	24	5	0	0	11	29	8	17	2	.294	.287	.238

PITCHING	GP	GS	W–L	SV	SHO	R	ERA	IP	Ks	BB
Roy Halladay	31	31	16–7	0	1	101	3.71	225.1	139	48
Dustin McGowan	27	27	12–10	0	1	80	4.08	169.2	144	61
A.J. Burnett	25	25	10–8	0	0	74	3.75	165.2	176	66
Shaun Marcum	38	25	12–6	1	0	76	4.13	159.0	122	49
J. Litsch	20	20	7–9	0	0	56	3.81	111.0	50	36
J. Kennedy	36	16	4–9	0	0	59	4.42	108.0	50	53
Josh Towers	25	15	5–10	0	0	73	5.38	107.0	76	22
Casey Janssen	70	0	2–3	6	0	22	2.35	72.2	39	20
Jeremy Accardo	64	0	4–4	30	0	19	2.14	67.1	57	24
Brian Tallet	48	0	2–4	0	0	26	3.47	62.1	54	28
Scott Downs	81	0	4–2	1	0	15	2.17	58.0	57	24
Jason Frasor	51	0	1–5	3	0	29	4.58	57.0	59	23
Tomo Ohka	10	10	2–5	0	0	39	5.79	56.0	21	22
Brian Wolfe	38	0	3–1	0	0	17	2.98	45.1	22	9

FOR THE RECORD • Year by Year

The World Series

Results

1903..............Boston (A) 5, Pittsburgh (N) 3	1956..............New York (A) 4, Brooklyn (N) 3
1904..............No series	1957..............Milwaukee (N) 4, New York (A) 3
1905..............New York (N) 4, Philadelphia (A) 1	1958..............New York (A) 4, Milwaukee (N) 3
1906..............Chicago (A) 4, Chicago (N) 2	1959..............Los Angeles (N) 4, Chicago (A) 2
1907..............Chicago (N) 4, Detroit (A) 0; 1 tie	1960..............Pittsburgh (N) 4, New York (A) 3
1908..............Chicago (N) 4, Detroit (A) 1	1961..............New York (A) 4, Cincinnati (N) 1
1909..............Pittsburgh (N) 4, Detroit (A) 3	1962..............New York (A) 4, San Francisco (N) 3
1910..............Philadelphia (A) 4, Chicago (N) 1	1963..............Los Angeles (N) 4, New York (A) 0
1911..............Philadelphia (A) 4, New York (N) 2	1964..............St. Louis (N) 4, New York (A) 3
1912..............Boston (A) 4, New York (N) 3; 1 tie	1965..............Los Angeles (N) 4, Minnesota (A) 3
1913..............Philadelphia (A) 4, New York (N) 1	1966..............Baltimore (A) 4, Los Angeles (N) 0
1914..............Boston (N) 4, Philadelphia (A) 0	1967..............St. Louis (N) 4, Boston (A) 3
1915..............Boston (A) 4, Philadelphia (N) 1	1968..............Detroit (A) 4, St. Louis (N) 3
1916..............Boston (A) 4, Brooklyn (N) 1	1969..............New York (N) 4, Baltimore (A) 1
1917..............Chicago (A) 4, New York (N) 2	1970..............Baltimore (A) 4, Cincinnati (N) 1
1918..............Boston (A) 4, Chicago (N) 2	1971..............Pittsburgh (N) 4, Baltimore (A) 3
1919..............Cincinnati (N) 5, Chicago (A) 3	1972..............Oakland (A) 4, Cincinnati (N) 3
1920..............Cleveland (A) 5, Brooklyn (N) 2	1973..............Oakland (A) 4, New York (N) 3
1921..............New York (N) 5, New York (A) 3	1974..............Oakland (A) 4, Los Angeles (N) 1
1922..............New York (N) 4, New York (A) 0; 1 tie	1975..............Cincinnati (N) 4, Boston (A) 3
1923..............New York (A) 4, New York (N) 2	1976..............Cincinnati (N) 4, New York (A) 0
1924..............Washington (A) 4, New York (N) 3	1977..............New York (A) 4, Los Angeles (N) 2
1925..............Pittsburgh (N) 4, Washington (A) 3	1978..............New York (A) 4, Los Angeles (N) 2
1926..............St. Louis (N) 4, New York (A) 3	1979..............Pittsburgh (N) 4, Baltimore (A) 3
1927..............New York (A) 4, Pittsburgh (N) 0	1980..............Philadelphia (N) 4, Kansas City (A) 2
1928..............New York (A) 4, St. Louis (N) 0	1981..............Los Angeles (N) 4, New York (A) 2
1929..............Philadelphia (A) 4, Chicago (N) 1	1982..............St. Louis (N) 4, Milwaukee (A) 3
1930..............Philadelphia (A) 4, St. Louis (N) 2	1983..............Baltimore (A) 4, Philadelphia (N) 1
1931..............St. Louis (N) 4, Philadelphia (A) 3	1984..............Detroit (A) 4, San Diego (N) 1
1932..............New York (A) 4, Chicago (N) 0	1985..............Kansas City (A) 4, St. Louis (N) 3
1933..............New York (N) 4, Washington (A) 1	1986..............New York (N) 4, Boston (A) 3
1934..............St. Louis (N) 4, Detroit (A) 3	1987..............Minnesota (A) 4, St. Louis (N) 3
1935..............Detroit (A) 4, Chicago (N) 2	1988..............Los Angeles (N) 4, Oakland (A) 1
1936..............New York (A) 4, New York (N) 2	1989..............Oakland (A) 4, San Francisco (N) 0
1937..............New York (A) 4, New York (N) 1	1990..............Cincinnati (N) 4, Oakland (A) 0
1938..............New York (A) 4, Chicago (N) 0	1991..............Minnesota (A) 4, Atlanta (N) 3
1939..............New York (A) 4, Cincinnati (N) 0	1992..............Toronto (A) 4, Atlanta (N) 2
1940..............Cincinnati (N) 4, Detroit (A) 3	1993..............Toronto (A) 4, Philadelphia (N) 2
1941..............New York (A) 4, Brooklyn (N) 1	1994..............Series canceled due to players' strike.
1942..............St. Louis (N) 4, New York (A) 1	1995..............Atlanta (N) 4, Cleveland (A) 2
1943..............New York (A) 4, St. Louis (N) 1	1996..............New York (A) 4, Atlanta (N) 2
1944..............St. Louis (N) 4, St. Louis (A) 2	1997..............Florida (N) 4, Cleveland (A) 3
1945..............Detroit (A) 4, Chicago (N) 3	1998..............New York (A) 4, San Diego (N) 0
1946..............St. Louis (N) 4, Boston (A) 3	1999..............New York (A) 4, Atlanta (N) 0
1947..............New York (A) 4, Brooklyn (N) 3	2000..............New York (A) 4 , New York (N) 1
1948..............Cleveland (A) 4, Boston (N) 2	2001..............Arizona (N) 4, New York (A) 3
1949..............New York (A) 4, Brooklyn (N) 1	2002..............Anaheim (A) 4, San Francisco (N) 3
1950..............New York (A) 4, Philadelphia (N) 0	2003..............Florida (N) 4, New York (A) 2
1951..............New York (A) 4, New York (N) 2	2004..............Boston (A) 4, St. Louis (N) 0
1952..............New York (A) 4, Brooklyn (N) 3	2005..............Chicago (A) 4, Houston (N) 0
1953..............New York (A) 4, Brooklyn (N) 2	2006..............St. Louis (N) 4, Detroit (A) 1
1954..............New York (N) 4, Cleveland (A) 0	2007..............Boston (A) 4, Colorado (N) 0
1955..............Brooklyn (N) 4, New York (A) 3	

Most Valuable Players

1955	Johnny Podres, Bklyn
1956	Don Larsen, NY (A)
1957	Lew Burdette, Mil
1958	Bob Turley, NY (A)
1959	Larry Sherry, LA
1960	Bobby Richardson, NY (A)
1961	Whitey Ford, NY (A)
1962	Ralph Terry, NY (A)
1963	Sandy Koufax, LA
1964	Bob Gibson, StL
1965	Sandy Koufax, LA
1966	Frank Robinson, Balt
1967	Bob Gibson, StL
1968	Mickey Lolich, Det
1969	Donn Clendenon, NY (N)
1970	Brooks Robinson, Balt
1971	Roberto Clemente, Pitt
1972	Gene Tenace, Oak
1973	Reggie Jackson, Oak
1974	Rollie Fingers, Oak
1975	Pete Rose, Cin
1976	Johnny Bench, Cin
1977	Reggie Jackson, NY (A)
1978	Bucky Dent, NY (A)
1979	Willie Stargell, Pitt
1980	Mike Schmidt, Phil
1981	Ron Cey, LA; Steve Yeager, LA; Pedro Guerrero, LA
1982	Darrell Porter, StL
1983	Rick Dempsey, Balt
1984	Alan Trammell, Det
1985	Bret Saberhagen, KC
1986	Ray Knight, NY (N)
1987	Frank Viola, Minn
1988	Orel Hershiser, LA
1989	Dave Stewart, Oak
1990	Jose Rijo, Cin
1991	Jack Morris, Minn
1992	Pat Borders, Tor
1993	Paul Molitor, Tor
1994	Series canceled due to strike.
1995	Tom Glavine, Atl
1996	John Wetteland, NY (A)
1997	Livan Hernandez, Fla
1998	Scott Brosius, NY (A)
1999	Mariano Rivera, NY (A)
2000	Derek Jeter, NY (A)
2001	Randy Johnson, Ariz Curt Schilling, Ariz
2002	Troy Glaus, Ana
2003	Josh Beckett, Fla
2004	Manny Ramirez, Bos
2005	Jermaine Dye, Chi (A)
2006	David Eckstein, StL
2007	Mike Lowell, Bos

Career Batting Leaders (Minimum 40 at bats)

GAMES

Yogi Berra	75
Mickey Mantle	65
Elston Howard	54
Hank Bauer	53
Gil McDougald	53
Phil Rizzuto	52
Joe DiMaggio	51
Frankie Frisch	50
Pee Wee Reese	44
Roger Maris	41
Babe Ruth	41

AT BATS

Yogi Berra	259
Mickey Mantle	230
Joe DiMaggio	199
Frankie Frisch	197
Gil McDougald	190
Hank Bauer	188
Phil Rizzuto	183
Elston Howard	171
Pee Wee Reese	169
Roger Maris	152

HITS

Yogi Berra	71
Mickey Mantle	59
Frankie Frisch	58
Joe DiMaggio	54
Pee Wee Reese	46
Hank Bauer	46
Phil Rizzuto	45
Gil McDougald	45
Lou Gehrig	43
Eddie Collins	42
Babe Ruth	42
Elston Howard	42

BATTING AVERAGE

Bobby Brown	.439
Paul Molitor	.418
Pepper Martin	.418
Hal McRae	.400
Lou Brock	.391
Marquis Grissom	.390
Thurman Munson	.373
George Brett	.373
Pat Borders	.372
Hank Aaron	.364

HOME RUNS

Mickey Mantle	18
Babe Ruth	15
Yogi Berra	12
Duke Snider	11
Reggie Jackson	10
Lou Gehrig	10
Frank Robinson	8
Bill Skowron	8
Joe DiMaggio	8
Goose Goslin	7
Hank Bauer	7
Gil McDougald	7

RUNS BATTED IN

Mickey Mantle	40
Yogi Berra	39
Lou Gehrig	35
Babe Ruth	33
Joe DiMaggio	30
Bill Skowron	29
Duke Snider	26
Reggie Jackson	24
Bill Dickey	24
Hank Bauer	24
Gil McDougald	24

RUNS

Mickey Mantle	42
Yogi Berra	41
Babe Ruth	37
Lou Gehrig	30
Joe DiMaggio	27
Derek Jeter	27
Roger Maris	26
Elston Howard	25
Gil McDougald	23
Jackie Robinson	22

STOLEN BASES

Lou Brock	14
Eddie Collins	14
Frank Chance	10
Davey Lopes	10
Phil Rizzuto	10
Honus Wagner	9
Frankie Frisch	9
Kenny Lofton	9
Johnny Evers	8
Roberto Alomar	7
Joe Tinker	7
Pepper Martin	7
Joe Morgan	7
Rickey Henderson	7

Career Batting Leaders (Cont.)

TOTAL BASES		SLUGGING AVERAGE		STRIKEOUTS	
Mickey Mantle	123	Reggie Jackson	.755	Mickey Mantle	54
Yogi Berra	117	Babe Ruth	.744	Elston Howard	37
Babe Ruth	96	Lou Gehrig	.731	Duke Snider	33
Lou Gehrig	87	Bobby Brown	.707	Derek Jeter	33
Joe DiMaggio	84	Lenny Dykstra	.700	Babe Ruth	30
Duke Snider	79	Al Simmons	.658	David Justice	30
Hank Bauer	75	Lou Brock	.655	Gil McDougald	29
Reggie Jackson	74	Pepper Martin	.636	Bill Skowron	26
Frankie Frisch	74	Paul Molitor	.636	Bernie Williams	26
Gil McDougald	72	Joe Harris	.625	Hank Bauer	25

Career Pitching Leaders

GAMES		LOSSES		COMPLETE GAMES	
Whitey Ford	22	Whitey Ford	8	Christy Mathewson	10
Mariano Rivera	20	Eddie Plank	5	Chief Bender	9
Mike Stanton	19	Schoolboy Rowe	5	Bob Gibson	8
Jeff Nelson	16	Joe Bush	5	Red Ruffing	7
Rollie Fingers	16	Rube Marquard	5	Whitey Ford	7
Allie Reynolds	15	Christy Mathewson	5	George Mullin	6
Bob Turley	15	Andy Pettite	5	Eddie Plank	6
Clay Carroll	14			Art Nehf	6
Clem Labine	13	**SAVES**		Waite Hoyt	6
Mark Wohlers	13	Mariano Rivera	9		
		Rollie Fingers	6		
INNINGS PITCHED		Allie Reynolds	4	**STRIKEOUTS**	
Whitey Ford	146	Johnny Murphy	4	Whitey Ford	94
Christy Mathewson	101⅔	John Wetteland	4	Bob Gibson	92
Red Ruffing	85⅔	Robb Nen	4	Allie Reynolds	62
Chief Bender	85			Sandy Koufax	61
Waite Hoyt	83⅔	***EARNED RUN AVERAGE**		Red Ruffing	61
Bob Gibson	81	Jack Billingham	0.36	Chief Bender	59
Art Nehf	79	Harry Brecheen	0.83	George Earnshaw	56
Allie Reynolds	77	Babe Ruth	0.87	John Smoltz	52
Jim Palmer	65	Sherry Smith	0.89	Waite Hoyt	49
Catfish Hunter	63	Sandy Koufax	0.95	Roger Clemens	49
		Hippo Vaughn	1.00	Christy Mathewson	48
WINS		Monte Pearson	1.01		
Whitey Ford	10	Christy Mathewson	1.06		
Bob Gibson	7	Mariano Rivera	1.16	**BASES ON BALLS**	
Red Ruffing	7	Babe Adams	1.29	Whitey Ford	34
Allie Reynolds	7			Allie Reynolds	32
Lefty Gomez	6	**SHUTOUTS**		Art Nehf	32
Chief Bender	6	Christy Mathewson	4	Jim Palmer	31
Waite Hoyt	6	Three Finger Brown	3	Bob Turley	29
Jack Coombs	5	Whitey Ford	3	Paul Derringer	27
Three Finger Brown	5	Bill Hallahan	2	Red Ruffing	27
Herb Pennock	5	Lew Burdette	2	Don Gullett	26
Christy Mathewson	5	Bill Dinneen	2	Burleigh Grimes	26
Vic Raschi	5	Sandy Koufax	2	Vic Raschi	25
Catfish Hunter	5	Allie Reynolds	2		
		Art Nehf	2		
*Minimum 25 innings pitched.		Bob Gibson	2		

Alltime Team Rankings (by championships)

Team	W	L	Appearances	Pct.	Most Recent	Last Championship
New York Yankees	26	13	39	.666	2003	2000
St. Louis Cardinals	10	7	17	.588	2006	2006
Phila./K.C./Oakland Athletics	9	5	14	.643	1990	1989
Boston Red Sox	7	5	12	.583	2007	2007
Brooklyn/L.A. Dodgers	6	12	18	.333	1988	1988
Pittsburgh Pirates	5	2	7	.714	1979	1979
Cincinnati Reds	5	4	9	.556	1990	1990
New York/San Francisco Giants	5	12	17	.294	2002	1954
Detroit Tigers	4	6	10	.400	2006	1984
Wash. Senators/Minnesota Twins	3	3	6	.500	1991	1991

Alltime Team Rankings (by championships)

Team	W	L	Appearances	Pct.	Most Recent	Last Championship
St. Louis Browns/Baltimore Orioles	3	4	7	.429	1983	1983
Boston/Milwaukee/Atlanta Braves	3	6	9	.333	1999	1995
Florida Marlins	2	0	2	1.000	2003	2003
Toronto Blue Jays	2	0	2	1.000	1993	1993
New York Mets	2	2	4	.500	2000	1986
Chicago White Sox	3	2	5	.600	2005	2005
Cleveland Indians	2	3	5	.400	1997	1948
Chicago Cubs	2	8	10	.200	1945	1908
California/Anaheim/L.A. Angels	1	0	1	1.000	2002	2002
Arizona Diamondbacks	1	0	1	1.000	2001	2001
Kansas City Royals	1	1	2	.500	1985	1985
Philadelphia Phillies	1	4	5	.200	1993	1980
Houston Astros	0	1	1	.000	2005	—
San Diego Padres	0	2	2	.000	1998	—
Seattle Pilots/Milwaukee Brewers	0	1	1	.000	1982	—
Colorado Rockies	0	1	1	.000	2007	—

League Pennant Winners

National League

Year	Team	Manager	W	L	Pct	GA
1900	Brooklyn	Ned Hanlon	82	54	.603	4½
1901	Pittsburgh	Fred Clarke	90	49	.647	7½
1902	Pittsburgh	Fred Clarke	103	36	.741	27½
1903	Pittsburgh	Fred Clarke	91	49	.650	6½
1904	New York	John McGraw	106	47	.693	13
1905	New York	John McGraw	105	48	.686	9
1906	Chicago	Frank Chance	116	36	.763	20
1907	Chicago	Frank Chance	107	45	.704	17
1908	Chicago	Frank Chance	99	55	.643	1
1909	Pittsburgh	Fred Clarke	110	42	.724	6½
1910	Chicago	Frank Chance	104	50	.675	13
1911	New York	John McGraw	99	54	.647	7½
1912	New York	John McGraw	103	48	.682	10
1913	New York	John McGraw	101	51	.664	12½
1914	Boston	George Stallings	94	59	.614	10½
1915	Philadelphia	Pat Moran	90	62	.592	7
1916	Brooklyn	Wilbert Robinson	94	60	.610	2½
1917	New York	John McGraw	98	56	.636	10
1918	Chicago	Fred Mitchell	84	45	.651	10½
1919	Cincinnati	Pat Moran	96	44	.686	9
1920	Brooklyn	Wilbert Robinson	93	61	.604	7
1921	New York	John McGraw	94	59	.614	4
1922	New York	John McGraw	93	61	.604	7
1923	New York	John McGraw	95	58	.621	4½
1924	New York	John McGraw	93	60	.608	1½
1925	Pittsburgh	Bill McKechnie	95	58	.621	8½
1926	St. Louis	Rogers Hornsby	89	65	.578	2
1927	Pittsburgh	Donie Bush	94	60	.610	1½
1928	St. Louis	Bill McKechnie	95	59	.617	2
1929	Chicago	Joe McCarthy	98	54	.645	10½
1930	St. Louis	Gabby Street	92	62	.597	2
1931	St. Louis	Gabby Street	101	53	.656	13
1932	Chicago	Charlie Grimm	90	64	.584	4
1933	New York	Bill Terry	91	61	.599	5
1934	St. Louis	Frankie Frisch	95	58	.621	2
1935	Chicago	Charlie Grimm	100	54	.649	4
1936	New York	Bill Terry	92	62	.597	5
1937	New York	Bill Terry	95	57	.625	3
1938	Chicago	Gabby Hartnett	89	63	.586	2
1939	Cincinnati	Bill McKechnie	97	57	.630	4½
1940	Cincinnati	Bill McKechnie	100	53	.654	12
1941	Brooklyn	Leo Durocher	100	54	.649	2½
1942	St. Louis	Billy Southworth	106	48	.688	2
1943	St. Louis	Billy Southworth	105	49	.682	18
1944	St. Louis	Billy Southworth	105	49	.682	14½

National League (Cont.)

Year	Team	Manager	W	L	Pct	GA
1945	Chicago	Charlie Grimm	98	56	.636	3
1946	St. Louis*	Eddie Dyer	98	58	.628	2
1947	Brooklyn	Burt Shotton	94	60	.610	5
1948	Boston	Billy Southworth	91	62	.595	6½
1949	Brooklyn	Burt Shotton	97	57	.630	1
1950	Philadelphia	Eddie Sawyer	91	63	.591	2
1951	New York†	Leo Durocher	98	59	.624	1
1952	Brooklyn	Chuck Dressen	96	57	.627	4½
1953	Brooklyn	Chuck Dressen	105	49	.682	13
1954	New York	Leo Durocher	97	57	.630	5
1955	Brooklyn	Walter Alston	98	55	.641	13½
1956	Brooklyn	Walter Alston	93	61	.604	1
1957	Milwaukee	Fred Haney	95	59	.617	8
1958	Milwaukee	Fred Haney	92	62	.597	8
1959	Los Angeles‡	Walter Alston	88	68	.564	2
1960	Pittsburgh	Danny Murtaugh	95	59	.617	7
1961	Cincinnati	Fred Hutchinson	93	61	.604	4
1962	San Francisco#	Al Dark	103	62	.624	1
1963	Los Angeles	Walter Alston	99	63	.611	6
1964	St. Louis	Johnny Keane	93	69	.574	1
1965	Los Angeles	Walter Alston	97	65	.599	2
1966	Los Angeles	Walter Alston	95	67	.586	1½
1967	St. Louis	Red Schoendienst	101	60	.627	10½
1968	St. Louis	Red Schoendienst	97	65	.599	9
1969	New York (E)††	Gil Hodges	100	62	.617	8
1970	Cincinnati (W)††	Sparky Anderson	102	60	.630	14½
1971	Pittsburgh (E)††	Danny Murtaugh	97	65	.599	7
1972	Cincinnati (W)††	Sparky Anderson	95	59	.617	10½
1973	New York (E)††	Yogi Berra	82	79	.509	1½
1974	Los Angeles (W)††	Walter Alston	102	60	.630	4
1975	Cincinnati (W)††	Sparky Anderson	108	54	.667	20
1976	Cincinnati (W)††	Sparky Anderson	102	60	.630	10
1977	Los Angeles (W)††	Tommy Lasorda	98	64	.605	10
1978	Los Angeles (W)††	Tommy Lasorda	95	67	.586	2½
1979	Pittsburgh (E)††	Chuck Tanner	98	64	.605	2
1980	Philadelphia (E)††	Dallas Green	91	71	.562	1
1981	Los Angeles (W)††	Tommy Lasorda	63	47	.573	**
1982	St. Louis (E)††	Whitey Herzog	92	70	.568	3
1983	Philadelphia (E)††	Pat Corrales/ Paul Owens	90	72	.556	6
1984	San Diego (W)††	Dick Williams	92	70	.568	12
1985	St. Louis (E)††	Whitey Herzog	101	61	.623	3
1986	New York (E)††	Davey Johnson	108	54	.667	21½
1987	St. Louis (E)††	Whitey Herzog	95	67	.586	3
1988	Los Angeles (W)††	Tommy Lasorda	94	67	.584	7
1989	San Francisco (W)††	Roger Craig	92	70	.568	3
1990	Cincinnati (W)††	Lou Piniella	91	71	.562	5
1991	Atlanta (W)††	Bobby Cox	94	68	.580	1
1992	Atlanta (W)††	Bobby Cox	98	64	.605	8
1993	Philadelphia (E)††	Jim Fregosi	97	65	.599	3
1994	Season ended Aug. 11 due to players' strike.					
1995	Atlanta (E)††	Bobby Cox	90	54	.625	21
1996	Atlanta (E)††	Bobby Cox	96	66	.593	8
1997	Florida (wc)††	Jim Leyland	92	70	.568	-9
1998	San Diego (W)††	Bruce Bochy	98	64	.605	9½
1999	Atlanta (E)††	Bobby Cox	103	59	.636	6½
2000	New York (wc)††	Bobby Valentine	94	68	.580	-6½
2001	Arizona (W)††	Bob Brenly	92	70	.568	2
2002	San Francisco (wc)††	Dusty Baker	95	66	.590	-2½
2003	Florida (wc)††	Jack McKeon	91	71	.562	-10
2004	St. Louis (C)††	Tony LaRussa	105	57	.648	13
2005	Houston (wc)††	Phil Garner	89	73	.549	-11
2006	St. Louis (C)††	Tony LaRussa	83	78	.516	1½
2007	Colorado (wc)††§	Clint Hurdle	89	73	.549	-1

*Defeated Brooklyn, two games to none, in playoff for pennant. †Defeated Brooklyn, two games to one, in playoff for pennant. ‡Defeated Milwaukee, two games to none, in playoff for pennant. #Defeated Los Angeles, two games to one, in playoff for pennant. ††Won Championship Series. **First half 36–21; second half 27–26, in season split by strike; defeated Houston in playoff for Western Division title.

League Pennant Winners *(Cont.)*

American League

Year	Team	Manager	W	L	Pct	GA
1901	Chicago	Clark Griffith	83	53	.610	4
1902	Philadelphia	Connie Mack	83	53	.610	5
1903	Boston	Jimmy Collins	91	47	.659	14½
1904	Boston	Jimmy Collins	95	59	.617	1½
1905	Philadelphia	Connie Mack	92	56	.622	2
1906	Chicago	Fielder Jones	93	58	.616	3
1907	Detroit	Hughie Jennings	92	58	.613	1½
1908	Detroit	Hughie Jennings	90	63	.588	½
1909	Detroit	Hughie Jennings	98	54	.645	3½
1910	Philadelphia	Connie Mack	102	48	.680	14½
1911	Philadelphia	Connie Mack	101	50	.669	13½
1912	Boston	Jake Stahl	105	47	.691	14
1913	Philadelphia	Connie Mack	96	57	.627	6½
1914	Philadelphia	Connie Mack	99	53	.651	8½
1915	Boston	Bill Carrigan	101	50	.669	2½
1916	Boston	Bill Carrigan	91	63	.591	2
1917	Chicago	Pants Rowland	100	54	.649	9
1918	Boston	Ed Barrow	75	51	.595	2½
1919	Chicago	Kid Gleason	88	52	.629	3½
1920	Cleveland	Tris Speaker	98	56	.636	2
1921	New York	Miller Huggins	98	55	.641	4½
1922	New York	Miller Huggins	94	60	.610	1
1923	New York	Miller Huggins	98	54	.645	16
1924	Washington	Bucky Harris	92	62	.597	2
1925	Washington	Bucky Harris	96	55	.636	8½
1926	New York	Miller Huggins	91	63	.591	3
1927	New York	Miller Huggins	110	44	.714	19
1928	New York	Miller Huggins	101	53	.656	2½
1929	Philadelphia	Connie Mack	104	46	.693	18
1930	Philadelphia	Connie Mack	102	52	.662	8
1931	Philadelphia	Connie Mack	107	45	.704	13½
1932	New York	Joe McCarthy	107	47	.695	13
1933	Washington	Joe Cronin	99	53	.651	7
1934	Detroit	Mickey Cochrane	101	53	.656	7
1935	Detroit	Mickey Cochrane	93	58	.616	3
1936	New York	Joe McCarthy	102	51	.667	19½
1937	New York	Joe McCarthy	102	52	.662	13
1938	New York	Joe McCarthy	99	53	.651	9½
1939	New York	Joe McCarthy	106	45	.702	17
1940	Detroit	Del Baker	90	64	.584	1
1941	New York	Joe McCarthy	101	53	.656	17
1942	New York	Joe McCarthy	103	51	.669	9
1943	New York	Joe McCarthy	98	56	.636	13½
1944	St. Louis	Luke Sewell	89	65	.578	1
1945	Detroit	Steve O'Neill	88	65	.575	1½
1946	Boston	Joe Cronin	104	50	.675	12
1947	New York	Bucky Harris	97	57	.630	12
1948	Cleveland†	Lou Boudreau	97	58	.626	1
1949	New York	Casey Stengel	97	57	.630	1
1950	New York	Casey Stengel	98	56	.636	3
1951	New York	Casey Stengel	98	56	.636	5
1952	New York	Casey Stengel	95	59	.617	2
1953	New York	Casey Stengel	99	52	.656	8½
1954	Cleveland	Al Lopez	111	43	.721	8
1955	New York	Casey Stengel	96	58	.623	3
1956	New York	Casey Stengel	97	57	.630	9
1957	New York	Casey Stengel	98	56	.636	8
1958	New York	Casey Stengel	92	62	.597	10
1959	Chicago	Al Lopez	94	60	.610	5
1960	New York	Casey Stengel	97	57	.630	8
1961	New York	Ralph Houk	109	53	.673	8
1962	New York	Ralph Houk	96	66	.593	5
1963	New York	Ralph Houk	104	57	.646	10½
1964	New York	Yogi Berra	99	63	.611	1
1965	Minnesota	Sam Mele	102	60	.630	7
1966	Baltimore	Hank Bauer	97	63	.606	9
1967	Boston	Dick Williams	92	70	.568	1

American League (Cont.)

Year	Team	Manager	W	L	Pct	GA
1968	Detroit	Mayo Smith	103	59	.636	12
1969	Baltimore (E)‡	Earl Weaver	109	53	.673	19
1970	Baltimore (E)‡	Earl Weaver	108	54	.667	15
1971	Baltimore (E)‡	Earl Weaver	101	57	.639	12
1972	Oakland (W)‡	Dick Williams	93	62	.600	5½
1973	Oakland (W)‡	Dick Williams	94	68	.580	6
1974	Oakland (W)‡	Al Dark	90	72	.556	5
1975	Boston (E)‡	Darrell Johnson	95	65	.594	4½
1976	New York (E)‡	Billy Martin	97	62	.610	10½
1977	New York (E)‡	Billy Martin	100	62	.617	2½
1978	New York (E)†‡	Billy Martin, Bob Lemon	100	63	.613	1
1979	Baltimore (E)‡	Earl Weaver	102	57	.642	8
1980	Kansas City (W)‡	Jim Frey	97	65	.599	14
1981	New York (E)‡	Gene Michael/Bob Lemon	59	48	.551	#
1982	Milwaukee (E)‡	Buck Rodgers, Harvey Kuenn	95	67	.586	1
1983	Baltimore (E)‡	Joe Altobelli	98	64	.605	6
1984	Detroit (E)‡	Sparky Anderson	104	58	.642	15
1985	Kansas City (W)‡	Dick Howser	91	71	.562	1
1986	Boston (E)‡	John McNamara	95	66	.590	5½
1987	Minnesota (W)‡	Tom Kelly	85	77	.525	2
1988	Oakland (W)‡	Tony LaRussa	104	58	.642	13
1989	Oakland (W)‡	Tony LaRussa	99	63	.611	7
1990	Oakland (W)‡	Tony LaRussa	103	59	.636	9
1991	Minnesota (W)‡	Tom Kelly	95	67	.586	8
1992	Toronto‡	Cito Gaston	96	66	.593	4
1993	Toronto‡	Cito Gaston	95	67	.586	7
1994	Season ended Aug. 11 due to players' strike.					
1995	Cleveland (C)‡	Mike Hargrove	100	44	.694	30
1996	New York (E)‡	Joe Torre	92	70	.568	4
1997	Cleveland (C)‡	Mike Hargrove	86	75	.534	6
1998	New York (E)‡	Joe Torre	114	48	.704	22
1999	New York (E)‡	Joe Torre	98	64	.605	4
2000	New York (E)‡	Joe Torre	87	74	.540	2½
2001	New York (E)‡	Joe Torre	95	65	.594	13½
2002	Anaheim (wc)	Mike Scioscia	99	63	.611	-4
2003	New York (E)‡	Joe Torre	101	61	.623	6
2004	Boston (wc)‡	Terry Francona	98	64	.605	-3
2005	Chicago (C)‡	Ozzie Guillen	99	63	.611	6
2006	Detroit (wc)‡	Jim Leyland	95	67	.586	-1
2007	Boston (E)‡	Terry Francona	96	66	.593	2

†Defeated Boston in one-game playoff. ‡Won championship series.
#First half 34–22; second half 25–26, in season split by strike; defeated Milwaukee in playoff for Eastern Divison title.

National League | American League

National League	American League
1969 ....New York (E) 3, Atlanta (W) 0	1969 ....Baltimore (E) 3, Minnesota (W) 0
1970 ....Cincinnati (W) 3, Pittsburgh (E) 0	1970 ....Baltimore (E) 3, Minnesota (W) 0
1971 ....Pittsburgh (E) 3, San Francisco (W) 1	1971 ....Baltimore (E) 3, Oakland (W) 0
1972 ....Cincinnati (W) 3, Pittsburgh (E) 2	1972 ....Oakland (W) 3, Detroit (E) 2
1973 ....New York (E) 3, Cincinnati (W) 2	1973 ....Oakland (W) 3, Baltimore (E) 2
1974 ....Los Angeles (W) 3, Pittsburgh (E) 1	1974 ....Oakland (W) 3, Baltimore (E) 1
1975 ....Cincinnati (W) 3, Pittsburgh (E) 0	1975 ....Boston (E) 3, Oakland (W) 0
1976 ....Cincinnati (W) 3, Philadelphia (E) 0	1976 ....New York (E) 3, Kansas City (W) 2
1977 ....Los Angeles (W) 3, Philadelphia (E) 1	1977 ....New York (E) 3, Kansas City (W) 2
1978 ....Los Angeles (W) 3, Philadelphia (E) 1	1978 ....New York (E) 3, Kansas City (W) 1
1979 ....Pittsburgh (E) 3, Cincinnati (W) 0	1979 ....Baltimore (E) 3, California (W) 1
1980 ....Philadelphia (E) 3, Houston (W) 2	1980 ....Kansas City (W) 3, New York (E) 0
1981 ....Los Angeles (W) 3, Montreal (E) 2	1981 ....New York (E) 3, Oakland (W) 0
1982 ....St. Louis (E) 3, Atlanta (W) 0	1982 ....Milwaukee (E) 3, California (W) 2
1983 ....Philadelphia (E) 3, Los Angeles (W) 1	1983 ....Baltimore (E) 3, Chicago (W) 1
1984 ....San Diego (W) 3, Chicago (E) 2	1984 ....Detroit (E) 3, Kansas City (W) 0
1985 ....St. Louis (E) 4, Los Angeles (W) 2	1985 ....Kansas City (W) 4, Toronto (E) 3
1986 ....New York (E) 4, Houston (W) 2	1986 ....Boston (E) 4, California (W) 3
1987 ....St. Louis (E) 4, San Francisco (W) 3	1987 ....Minnesota (W) 4, Detroit (E) 1
1988 ....Los Angeles (W) 4, New York (E) 3	1988 ....Oakland (W) 4, Boston (E) 0
1989 ....San Francisco (W) 4, Chicago (E) 1	1989 ....Oakland (W) 4, Toronto (E) 1
1990 ....Cincinnati (W) 4, Pittsburgh (E) 2	1990 ....Oakland (W) 4, Boston (E) 0
1991 ....Atlanta (W) 4, Pittsburgh (E) 3	1991 ....Minnesota (W) 4, Toronto (E) 1
1992 ....Atlanta (W) 4, Pittsburgh (E) 3	1992 ....Toronto (E) 4, Oakland (W) 2
1993 ....Philadelphia (E) 4, Atlanta (W) 2	1993 ....Toronto (E) 4, Chicago (W) 2
1994 ....Playoffs canceled due to players' strike.	1994 ....Playoffs canceled due to players' strike.
1995 ....Atlanta (E) 4, Cincinnati (C) 0	1995 ....Cleveland (C) 4, Seattle (W) 2
1996 ....Atlanta (E) 4, St. Louis (C) 3	1996 ....New York (E) 4, Baltimore (wc) 1
1997 ....Florida (wc) 4, Atlanta (E) 2	1997 ....Cleveland (C) 4, Baltimore (E) 2
1998 ....San Diego (W) 4, Atlanta (E) 2	1998 ....New York (E) 4, Cleveland (C) 2
1999 ....Atlanta (E) 4, New York (wc) 2	1999 ....New York (E) 4, Boston (wc) 1
2000 ....New York (wc) 4, St. Louis (C) 1	2000 ....New York (E) 4, Seattle (wc) 2
2001 ....Arizona (W) 4, Atlanta (E) 1	2001 ....New York (E) 4, Seattle (W) 1
2002 ....San Francisco (wc) 4, St. Louis (C) 1	2002 ....Anaheim (wc) 4, Minnesota (C) 1
2003 ....Florida (wc) 4, Chicago (C) 3	2003 ....New York (E) 4, Boston (wc) 3
2004 ....St. Louis (C) 4, Houston (wc) 3	2004 ....Boston (wc) 4, New York (E) 3
2005 ....Houston (wc) 4, St. Louis (C) 2	2005 ....Chicago (C) 4, Los Angeles (W) 1
2006 ....St. Louis (C) 4, New York (E) 3	2006 ....Detroit (wc) 4, Oakland (W) 0
2007 ....Colorado (wc) 4, Arizona (W) 0	2007 ....Boston (E) 4, Cleveland (C) 3

NLCS Most Valuable Player

1977........Dusty Baker, LA	1988........Orel Hershiser, LA	1999........Eddie Perez, Atl
1978........Steve Garvey, LA	1989........Will Clark, SF	2000........Mike Hampton, NY
1979........Willie Stargell, Pitt	1990........R. Myers/R. Dibble, Cin	2001........Craig Counsell, Ariz
1980........Manny Trillo, Phi	1991........Steve Avery, Atl	2002........Benito Santiago, SF
1981........Burt Hooton, LA	1992........John Smoltz, Atl	2003........Ivan Rodriguez, Fla
1982........Darrell Porter, StL	1993........Curt Schilling, Phi	2004........Albert Pujols, StL
1983........Gary Matthews, Phi	1994........Playoffs canceled	2005........Roy Oswalt, Hou
1984........Steve Garvey, SD	1995........Mike Devereaux, Atl	2006........Jeff Suppan, StL
1985........Ozzie Smith, StL	1996........Javier Lopez, Atl	2007........Matt Holliday, Col
1986........Mike Scott, Hou	1997........Livan Hernandez, Fla	
1987........Jeffrey Leonard, SF	1998........Sterling Hitchcock, SD	

ALCS Most Valuable Player

1980........Frank White, KC	1990........Dave Stewart, Oak	2000........David Justice, NY
1981........Graig Nettles, NY	1991........Kirby Puckett, Minn	2001........Andy Pettitte, NY
1982........Fred Lynn, Calif	1992........Roberto Alomar, Tor	2002........Adam Kennedy, Ana
1983........Mike Boddicker, Balt	1993........Dave Stewart, Tor	2003........Mariano Rivera, NY
1984........Kirk Gibson, Det	1994........Playoffs canceled	2004........David Ortiz, Bos
1985........George Brett, KC	1995........Orel Hershiser, Clev	2005........Paul Konerko, Chi
1986........Marty Barrett, Bos	1996........Bernie Williams, NY	2006........Placido Polanco, Det
1987........Gary Gaetti, Minn	1997........Marquis Grissom, Clev	2007........Josh Beckett, Bos
1988........Dennis Eckersley, Oak	1998........David Wells, NY	
1989........Rickey Henderson, Oak	1999........Orlando Hernandez, NY	

Divisional Playoffs

National League

1995 ....Atlanta (E) 3, Colorado (wc) 1
    Cincinnati (C) 3, Los Angeles (W) 0
1996 ....St. Louis (C) 3, San Diego (W) 0
    Atlanta (E) 3, Los Angeles (wc) 0
1997 ....Atlanta (E) 3, Houston (C) 0
    Florida (wc) 3, San Francisco (W) 0
1998 ....San Diego (W) 3, Houston (C) 1
    Atlanta (E) 3, Chicago (wc) 0
1999 ....Atlanta (E) 3, Houston (C) 1
    New York (wc) 3, Arizona (W) 1
2000 ....St. Louis (C) 3, Atlanta (E) 0
    New York (wc) 3, San Francisco (W) 1
2001 ....Atlanta (E) 3, Houston (C) 0
    Arizona (W) 3, St. Louis (wc) 2
2002 ....St. Louis (C) 3, Arizona (W) 0
    San Francisco (wc) 3, Atlanta (E) 2
2003 ....Chicago (C) 3, Atlanta (E) 2
    Florida (wc) 3, San Francisco (W) 1
2004 ....St. Louis (C) 3, Los Angeles (W) 1
    Houston (wc) 3, Atlanta (E) 2
2005 ....Houston (wc) 3, Atlanta (E) 1
    St. Louis (C) 3, San Diego (W) 1
2006 ....St. Louis (C) 3, San Diego (W) 1
    New York (E) 3, Los Angeles (wc) 0
2007 ....Colorado (wc) 3, Philadelphia 0
    Arizona (W) 3, Chicago (C) 0

American League

1995 ....Cleveland (C) 3, Boston (E) 0
    Seattle (W) 3, New York (wc) 2
1996 ....Baltimore (wc) 3, Cleveland (C) 1
    New York (E) 3, Texas (W) 1
1997 ....Baltimore (E) 3, Seattle (W) 1
    Cleveland (C) 3, New York (wc) 2
1998 ....New York (E) 3, Texas (W) 0
    Cleveland (C) 3, Boston (wc) 1
1999 ....New York (E) 3, Texas (W) 1
    Boston (wc) 3, Cleveland (C) 2
2000 ....New York (E) 3, Oakland (W) 2
    Seattle (wc) 3, Chicago (C) 0
2001 ....Seattle (W) 3, Cleveland (wc) 2
    New York (E) 3, Oakland (wc) 2
2002 ....Minnesota (C) 3, Oakland (W) 2
    Anaheim (wc) 3, New York (E) 1
2003 ....New York (E) 3, Minnesota (C) 1
    Boston (wc) 3, Oakland (W) 2
2004 ....New York (E) 3, Minnesota (C) 1
    Boston (wc) 3 Anaheim (W) 0
2005 ....Los Angeles (W) 3, New York (E) 2
    Chicago (C) 3, Boston (wc) 0
2006 ....Oakland (W) 3, Minnesota (C) 0
    Detroit (wc) 3, New York (E) 1
2007 ....Boston (E) 3, Los Angeles (W) 0
    Cleveland (C) 3, New York (wc) 1

The All-Star Game

Results

Date	Winner	Score	Site	Date	Winner	Score	Site
7-6-33	American	4–2	Comiskey Park, Chi	7-12-66	National	2–1	Busch Stadium, StL
7-10-34	American	9–7	Polo Grounds, NY	7-11-67	National	2–1	Anaheim Stadium, Cal
7-8-35	American	4–1	Municipal Stadium, Clev	7-9-68	National	1–0	Astrodome, Hou
7-7-36	National	4–3	Braves Field, Bos	7-23-69	National	9–3	R.F.K. Stadium, Wash.
7-7-37	American	8–3	Griffith Stadium, Wash	7-14-70	National	5–4	Riverfront Stadium, Cin
7-6-38	National	4–1	Crosley Field, Cin	7-13-71	American	6–4	Tiger Stadium, Det
7-11-39	American	3–1	Yankee Stadium, NY	7-25-72	National	4–3	Atlanta Stadium, Atl
7-10-40	National	4–0	Sportsman's Park, StL	7-24-73	National	7–1	Royals Stadium, KC
7-8-41	American	7–5	Briggs Stadium, Det	7-23-74	National	7–2	Three Rivers Stadium, Pitt
7-6-42	American	3–1	Polo Grounds, NY	7-15-75	National	6–3	County Stadium, Mil
7-13-43	American	5–3	Shibe Park, Phi	7-13-76	National	7–1	Veterans Stadium, Phi
7-11-44	National	7–1	Forbes Field, Pitt	7-19-77	National	7–5	Yankee Stadium, NY
1945	No game due to wartime travel restrictions.			7-11-78	National	7–3	Jack Murphy Stadium, SD
7-9-46	American	12–0	Fenway Park, Bos	7-17-79	National	7–6	Kingdome, Sea
7-8-47	American	2–1	Wrigley Field, Chi	7-8-80	National	4–2	Dodger Stadium, LA
7-13-48	American	5–2	Sportsman's Park, StL	8-9-81	National	5–4	Municipal Stadium, Clev
7-12-49	American	11–7	Ebbets Field, Bklyn	7-13-82	National	4–1	Olympic Stadium, Mtl
7-11-50	National	4–3	Comiskey Park, Chi	7-6-83	American	13–3	Comiskey Park, Chi
7-10-51	National	8–3	Briggs Stadium, Det	7-10-84	National	3–1	Candlestick Park, SF
7-8-52	National	3–2	Shibe Park, Phi	7-16-85	National	6–1	Metrodome, Minn
7-14-53	National	5–1	Crosley Field, Cin	7-15-86	American	3–2	Astrodome, Hou
7-13-54	American	11–9	Municipal Stadium, Clev	7-14-87	National	2–0	Oakland Coliseum, Oak
7-12-55	National	6–5	County Stadium, Mil	7-12-88	American	2–1	Riverfront Stadium, Cin
7-10-56	National	7–3	Griffith Stadium, Wash	7-11-89	American	5–3	Anaheim Stadium, Cal
7-9-57	American	6–5	Busch Stadium, StL	7-10-90	American	2–0	Wrigley Field, Chi
7-8-58	American	4–3	Memorial Stadium, Balt	7-9-91	American	4–2	SkyDome, Tor
7-7-59	National	5–4	Forbes Field, Pitt	7-14-92	American	13–6	Jack Murphy Stadium, SD
8-3-59	American	5–3	Memorial Coliseum, LA	7-13-93	American	9–3	Camden Yards, Balt
7-11-60	National	5–3	Municipal Stadium, KC	7-12-94	National	8–7	Three Rivers Stadium, Pitt
7-13-60	National	6–0	Yankee Stadium, NY	7-11-95	National	3–2	The Ballpark in Arlington, Tex
7-11-61	National	5–4	Candlestick Park, SF				
7-31-61	Tie*	1–1	Fenway Park, Bos	7-9-96	National	6–0	Veterans Stadium, Phi
7-10-62	National	3–1	D.C. Stadium, Wash	7-8-97	American	3–1	Jacobs Field, Clev
7-30-62	American	9–4	Wrigley Field, Chi	7-7-98	American	13–8	Coors Field, Col
7-9-63	National	5–3	Municipal Stadium, Clev	7-13-99	American	4–1	Fenway Park, Bos
7-7-64	National	7–4	Shea Stadium, NY	7-11-00	American	6–3	Turner Field, Atl
7-13-65	National	6–5	Metro. Stadium, Minn	7-10-01	American	4–1	Safeco Field, Sea

*Game called because of rain after nine innings.

Results *(Cont.)*

Date	Winner	Score	Site	Date	Winner	Score	Site
7-9-02	Tie (11 inn)	7–7	Miller Park, Milwaukee	7-12-05	American	7–5	Comerica Park, Detroit
7-15-03	American	7–6	Comiskey Park, Chicago	7-11-06	American	3–2	PNC Park, Pittsburgh
7-13-04	American	9–4	Minute Maid Park, Houston	7-10-07	American	5–4	AT&T Park, San Francisco

Most Valuable Players

Year	Player	League		Year	Player	League		Year	Player	League
1962	Maury Wills, LA	NL		1976	George Foster, Cin	NL		1992	Ken Griffey Jr., Sea	AL
	Leon Wagner, LA	AL		1977	Don Sutton, LA	NL		1993	Kirby Puckett, Minn	AL
1963	Willie Mays, SF	NL		1978	Steve Garvey, LA	NL		1994	Fred McGriff, Atl	NL
1964	Johnny Callison, Phi	NL		1979	Dave Parker, Pitt	NL		1995	Jeff Conine, Fla	NL
1965	Juan Marichal, SF	NL		1980	Ken Griffey, Cin	NL		1996	Mike Piazza, LA	NL
1966	Brooks Robinson, Balt	AL		1981	Gary Carter, Mtl	NL		1997	Sandy Alomar, Clev	AL
1967	Tony Perez, Cin	NL		1982	Dave Concepcion, Cin	NL		1998	Roberto Alomar, Balt	AL
1968	Willie Mays, SF	NL		1983	Fred Lynn, Calif	AL		1999	Pedro Martinez, Bos	AL
1969	Willie McCovey, SF	NL		1984	Gary Carter, Mtl	NL		2000	Derek Jeter, NY	AL
1970	Carl Yastrzemski, Bos	AL		1985	LaMarr Hoyt, SD	NL		2001	Cal Ripken Jr., Balt	AL
1971	Frank Robinson, Balt	AL		1986	Roger Clemens, Bos	AL		2002	None selected	
1972	Joe Morgan, Cin	NL		1987	Tim Raines, Mtl	NL		2003	Garret Anderson, Ana	AL
1973	Bobby Bonds, SF	NL		1988	Terry Steinbach, Oak	AL		2004	Alfonso Soriano, Tex	AL
1974	Steve Garvey, LA	NL		1989	Bo Jackson, KC	AL		2005	Miguel Tejada, Balt	AL
1975	Bill Madlock, Chi	NL		1990	Julio Franco, Tex	AL		2006	Michael Young, Tex	AL
	Jon Matlack, NY	NL		1991	Cal Ripken Jr., Balt	AL		2007	Ichiro Suzuki, Sea	AL

The Regular Season

Most Valuable Players

NATIONAL LEAGUE

Year	Name and Team	Position	Noteworthy
1911	Wildfire Schulte, Chi	Outfield	21 HR†, 121 RBI†, .300
1912	*Larry Doyle, NY	Second base	10 HR, 90 RBI, .330
1913	Jake Daubert, Bklyn	First base	52 RBI, .350†
1914	*Johnny Evers, Bos	Second base	FA .976†, .279
1915–23	No selection		
1924	Dazzy Vance, Bklyn	Pitcher	28†–6, 2.16 ERA†, 262 K†
1925	Rogers Hornsby, StL	Second base, Manager	39 HR†, 143 RBI†, .403†
1926	*Bob O'Farrell, StL	Catcher	7 HR, 68 RBI, .293
1927	*Paul Waner, Pitt	Outfield	237 hits†, 131 RBI†, .380†
1928	*Jim Bottomley, StL	First base	31 HR†, 136 RBI†, .325
1929	*Rogers Hornsby, Chi	Second base	39 HR, 149 RBI, 156 runs†, .380
1930	No selection		
1931	*Frankie Frisch, StL	Second base	4 HR, 82 RBI, 28 SB†, .311
1932	Chuck Klein, Phi	Outfield	38 HR†, 137 RBI, 226 hits†, .348
1933	*Carl Hubbell, NY	Pitcher	23†–12, 1.66 ERA†, 10 SO†
1934	*Dizzy Dean, StL	Pitcher	30†–7, 2.66 ERA, 195 K†
1935	*Gabby Hartnett, Chi	Catcher	13 HR, 91 RBI, .344
1936	*Carl Hubbell, NY	Pitcher	26†–6, 2.31 ERA†
1937	Joe Medwick, StL	Outfield	31 HR‡, 154 RBI†, 111 runs†, .374†
1938	Ernie Lombardi, Cin	Catcher	19 HR, 95 RBI, .342†
1939	*Bucky Walters, Cin	Pitcher	27†–11, 2.29 ERA†, 137 K‡
1940	*Frank McCormick, Cin	First base	19 HR, 127 RBI, 191 hits†, .309
1941	*Dolph Camilli, Bklyn	First base	34 HR†, 120 RBI†, .285
1942	*Mort Cooper, StL	Pitcher	22†–7, 1.78 ERA†, 10 SO†
1943	*Stan Musial, StL	Outfield	13 HR, 81 RBI, 220 hits†, .357†
1944	*Marty Marion, StL	Shortstop	FA .972†, 63 RBI
1945	*Phil Cavarretta, Chi	First base	6 HR, 97 RBI, .355†
1946	*Stan Musial, StL	First base, Outfield	103 RBI, 124 runs†, 228 hits†, .365†
1947	Bob Elliott, Bos	Third base	22 HR, 113 RBI, .317
1948	Stan Musial, StL	Outfield	39 HR, 131 RBI†, .376†
1949	*Jackie Robinson, Bklyn	Second base	16 HR, 124 RBI, 37 SB†, .342†
1950	*Jim Konstanty, Phi	Pitcher	16–7, 22 saves†, 2.66 ERA
1951	Roy Campanella, Bklyn	Catcher	33 HR, 108 RBI, .325
1952	Hank Sauer, Chi	Outfield	37 HR‡, 121 RBI†, .270

*Played for pennant or, after 1968, division winner. †Led league. ‡Tied for league lead.

Most Valuable Players *(Cont.)*

NATIONAL LEAGUE *(Cont.)*

Year	Name and Team	Position	Noteworthy
1953	*Roy Campanella, Bklyn	Catcher	41 HR, 142 RBI†, .312
1954	*Willie Mays, NY	Outfield	41 HR, 110 RBI, 13 3B†, .345†
1955	*Roy Campanella, Bklyn	Catcher	32 HR, 107 RBI, .318
1956	*Don Newcombe, Bklyn	Pitcher	27†–7, 3.06 ERA
1957	*Hank Aaron, Mil	Outfield	44 HR†, 132 RBI†, .322
1958	Ernie Banks, Chi	Shortstop	47 HR†, 129 RBI, .313
1959	Ernie Banks, Chi	Shortstop	45 HR, 143 RBI†, .304
1960	*Dick Groat, Pitt	Shortstop	2 HR, 50 RBI, .325†
1961	*Frank Robinson, Cin	Outfield	37 HR, 124 RBI, .323
1962	Maury Wills, LA	Shortstop	104 SB†, 208 hits, .299, GG
1963	*Sandy Koufax, LA	Pitcher	25‡–5, 1.88 ERA†, 306 K†
1964	*Ken Boyer, StL	Third Base	24 HR, 119 RBI†, .295
1965	Willie Mays, SF	Outfield	52 HR†, 112 RBI, .317, GG
1966	Roberto Clemente, Pitt	Outfield	29 HR, 119 RBI, 202 hits, .317, GG
1967	*Orlando Cepeda, StL	First base	25 HR, 111 RBI†, .325
1968	*Bob Gibson, StL	Pitcher	22–9, 1.12 ERA†, 268 K†, 13 SO†, GG
1969	Willie McCovey, SF	First base	45 HR†, 126 RBI†, .320
1970	*Johnny Bench, Cin	Catcher	45 HR†, 148 RBI†, .293, GG
1971	Joe Torre, StL	Third base	24 HR, 137 RBI†, .363†
1972	*Johnny Bench, Cin	Catcher	40 HR†, 125 RBI†, .270, GG
1973	*Pete Rose, Cin	Outfield	5 HR, 64 RBI, .338†, 230 hits†
1974	*Steve Garvey, LA	First base	21 HR, 111 RBI, 200 hits, .312, GG
1975	*Joe Morgan, Cin	Second base	17 HR, 94 RBI, 67 SB, .327, GG
1976	*Joe Morgan, Cin	Second base	27 HR, 111 RBI, 60 SB, .320, GG
1977	George Foster, Cin	Outfield	52 HR†, 149 RBI†, .320
1978	Dave Parker, Pitt	Outfield	30 HR, 117 RBI, .334†, GG
1979	Keith Hernandez, StL	First base	11 HR, 105 RBI, 210 hits, .344†, GG
	*Willie Stargell, Pitt	First base	32 HR, 82 RBI, .281
1980	*Mike Schmidt, Phi	Third base	48 HR†, 121 RBI†, .286, GG
1981	Mike Schmidt, Phi	Third base	31 HR†, 91 RBI†, 78 runs†, .316, GG
1982	*Dale Murphy, Atl	Outfield	36 HR, 109 RBI†, .281, GG
1983	Dale Murphy, Atl	Outfield	36 HR, 121 RBI†, .302, GG
1984	*Ryne Sandberg, Chi	Second base	19 HR, 84 RBI, 114 runs†, .314, GG
1985	*Willie McGee, StL	Outfield	10 HR, 82 RBI, 18 3B†, .353†, GG
1986	Mike Schmidt, Phi	Third base	37 HR†, 119 RBI†, .290, GG
1987	Andre Dawson, Chi	Outfield	49 HR†, 137 RBI†, .287, GG
1988	*Kirk Gibson, LA	Outfield	25 HR, 76 RBI, 106 runs, .290
1989	*Kevin Mitchell, SF	Outfield	47 HR†, 125 RBI†, .291
1990	*Barry Bonds, Pitt	Outfield	33 HR, 114 RBI, .301
1991	*Terry Pendleton, Atl	Third base	23 HR, 86 RBI, .319†
1992	Barry Bonds, Pitt	Outfield	34 HR, 103 RBI, .311
1993	Barry Bonds, SF	Outfield	46 HR†, 123 RBI†, .336
1994	Jeff Bagwell, Hou	First base	39 HR, 116 RBI†, .368
1995	*Barry Larkin, Cin	Shortstop	15 HR, 66 RBI, 51 SB, .319
1996	*Ken Caminiti, SD	Third base	40 HR, 130 RBI, .326
1997	Larry Walker, Col	Outfield	49 HR†, 130 RBI, .452 OBA†, .366, GG
1998	Sammy Sosa, Chi	Outfield	66 HR†, 158 RBI†, 134 runs†, 416 TB†, .308
1999	*Chipper Jones, Atl	Third Base	45 HR, 110 RBI, 116 runs, .319
2000	*Jeff Kent, SF	Second Base	33 HR, 125 RBI, 114 runs, .334
2001	Barry Bonds, SF	Outfield	73 HR†, 137 RBI, 177 BB†, .328, .863 SLG†
2002	Barry Bonds, SF	Outfield	46 HR, 110 RBI, .582 OBP, 198 BB†, .370
2003	Barry Bonds, SF	Outfield	45 HR, .341, .529 OBP†, .749 SLG†
2004	Barry Bonds, SF	Outfield	45HR, 101 RBI, .609 OBP, .812 SLG
2005	Albert Pujols, StL	First Base	41 HR, 117 RBI, .330, .430 OBP†, .609 SLG†
2006	Ryan Howard, Phi	First Base	58 HR†, 149 RBI†, .313, .425 OBP, .659 SLG

*Played for pennant or, after 1968, division winner. †Led league. ‡Tied for league lead.

Most Valuable Players (Cont.)

AMERICAN LEAGUE

Year	Name and Team	Position	Noteworthy
1911	Ty Cobb, Det	Outfield	8 HR, 144 RBI†, 24 3B†, .420†
1912	*Tris Speaker, Bos	Outfield	10 HR‡, 98 RBI, 53 2B†, .383
1913	Walter Johnson, Wash	Pitcher	36†–7, 1.09 ERA†, 11 SO†, 243 K†
1914	*Eddie Collins, Phi	Second base	2 HR, 85 RBI, 122 runs†, .344
1915–21	No selection		
1922	George Sisler, StL	First base	8 HR, 105 RBI, 246 hits†, .420†
1923	*Babe Ruth, NY	Outfield	41 HR†, 131 RBI†, .393
1924	*Walter Johnson, Wash	Pitcher	23†–7, 2.72 ERA†, 158 K†
1925	*Roger Peckinpaugh, Wash	Shortstop	4 HR, 64 RBI, .294
1926	George Burns, Clev	First base	114 RBI, 216 hits‡, 64 2B†, .358
1927	*Lou Gehrig, NY	First base	47 HR, 175 RBI†, 52 2B†, .373
1928	Mickey Cochrane, Phi	Catcher	10 HR, 57 RBI, .293
1929	No selection		
1930	No selection		
1931	*Lefty Grove, Phi	Pitcher	31†–4, 2.06 ERA†, 175 K†
1932	Jimmie Foxx, Phi	First base	58 HR†, 169 RBI†, 151 runs†, .364
1933	Jimmie Foxx, Phi	First base	48 HR†, 163 RBI†, .356†
1934	*Mickey Cochrane, Det	Catcher	2 HR, 76 RBI, .320
1935	*Hank Greenberg, Det	First base	36 HR†, 170 RBI†, 203 hits, .328
1936	*Lou Gehrig, NY	First base	49 HR†, 152 RBI, 167 runs†, .354
1937	Charlie Gehringer, Det	Second base	14 HR, 96 RBI, 133 runs, .371†
1938	Jimmie Foxx, Bos	First base	50 HR, 175 RBI†, .349†
1939	*Joe DiMaggio, NY	Outfield	30 HR, 126 RBI, .381†
1940	*Hank Greenberg, Det	Outfield	41 HR†, 150 RBI†, 50 2B†, .340
1941	*Joe DiMaggio, NY	Outfield	30 HR, 125 RBI†, .357
1942	*Joe Gordon, NY	Second base	18 HR, 103 RBI, .322
1943	*Spud Chandler, NY	Pitcher	20†–4, 1.64 ERA†, 5 SO‡
1944	Hal Newhouser, Det	Pitcher	29†–9, 2.22 ERA†, 187 K†
1945	*Hal Newhouser, Det	Pitcher	25†–9, 1.81 ERA†, 8 SO†, 212 K†
1946	*Ted Williams, Bos	Outfield	38 HR, 123 RBI, 142 runs†, .342
1947	*Joe DiMaggio, NY	Outfield	20 HR, 97 RBI, .315
1948	*Lou Boudreau, Clev	Shortstop	18 HR, 106 RBI, .355
1949	Ted Williams, Bos	Outfield	43 HR†, 159 RBI‡, 150 runs†, .343
1950	*Phil Rizzuto, NY	Shortstop	125 runs, 200 hits, .324
1951	*Yogi Berra, NY	Catcher	27 HR, 88 RBI, .294
1952	Bobby Shantz, Phi	Pitcher	24†–7, 2.48 ERA
1953	Al Rosen, Clev	Third base	43 HR†, 145 RBI†, 115 runs†, .336
1954	Yogi Berra, NY	Catcher	22 HR, 125 RBI, .307
1955	*Yogi Berra, NY	Catcher	27 HR, 108 RBI, .272
1956	*Mickey Mantle, NY	Outfield	52 HR†, 130 RBI†, 132 runs†, .353†
1957	*Mickey Mantle, NY	Outfield	34 HR, 94 RBI, 121 runs†, .365
1958	Jackie Jensen, Bos	Outfield	35 HR, 122 RBI†, .286
1959	*Nellie Fox, Chi	Second base	2 HR, 70 RBI, .306, GG
1960	*Roger Maris, NY	Outfield	39 HR, 112 RBI†, .283, GG
1961	*Roger Maris, NY	Outfield	61 HR†, 142 RBI†, .269
1962	*Mickey Mantle, NY	Outfield	30 HR, 89 RBI, .321, GG
1963	*Elston Howard, NY	Catcher	28 HR, 85 RBI, .287, GG
1964	Brooks Robinson, Balt	Third base	28 HR, 118 RBI†, .317, GG
1965	*Zoilo Versalles, Minn	Shortstop	126 runs†, 45 2B†, 12 3B‡, GG
1966	*Frank Robinson, Balt	Outfield	49 HR†, 122 RBI†, 122 runs†, .316†
1967	*Carl Yastrzemski, Bos	Outfield	44 HR†, 121 RBI†, 112 runs†, .326†, GG
1968	*Denny McLain, Det	Pitcher	31†–6, 1.96 ERA, 280 K
1969	*Harmon Killebrew, Minn	Third base, First base	49 HR†, 140 RBI†, .276
1970	*Boog Powell, Balt	First base	35 HR, 114 RBI, .297
1971	*Vida Blue, Oak	Pitcher	24–8, 1.82 ERA†, 8 SO†, 301 K
1972	Dick Allen, Chi	First base	37 HR†, 113 RBI†, .308
1973	*Reggie Jackson, Oak	Outfield	32 HR†, 117 RBI†, 99 runs†, .293
1974	Jeff Burroughs, Tex	Outfield	25 HR, 118 RBI†, .301
1975	*Fred Lynn, Bos	Outfield	21 HR, 105 RBI, 103 runs†, .331, GG
1976	*Thurman Munson, NY	Catcher	17 HR, 105 RBI, .302
1977	Rod Carew, Minn	First base	100 RBI, 128 runs†, 239 hits†, .388†
1978	Jim Rice, Bos	Outfield, DH	46 HR†, 139 RBI†, 213 hits†, .315
1979	*Don Baylor, Calif	Outfield, DH	36 HR, 139 RBI†, 120 runs†, .296
1980	*George Brett, KC	Third base	24 HR, 118 RBI, .390†
1981	*Rollie Fingers, Mil	Pitcher	6–3, 28 saves†, 1.04 ERA

Most Valuable Players *(Cont.)*
AMERICAN LEAGUE *(Cont.)*

Year	Name and Team	Position	Noteworthy
1982	.....*Robin Yount, Mil	Shortstop	29 HR, 114 RBI, 210 hits†, .331, GG
1983	.....*Cal Ripken Jr., Balt	Shortstop	27 HR, 102 RBI, 121 runs†, 211 hits†, .318
1984	.....*Willie Hernandez, Det	Pitcher	9–3, 32 saves, 1.92 ERA
1985	.....Don Mattingly, NY	First base	35 HR, 145 RBI†, 48 2B†, .324, GG
1986	.....*Roger Clemens, Bos	Pitcher	24†–4, 2.48 ERA†, 238 K
1987	.....George Bell, Tor	Outfield	47 HR, 134 RBI†, .308
1988	.....*Jose Canseco, Oak	Outfield	42 HR†, 124 RBI†, 40 SB, .307
1989	.....Robin Yount, Mil	Outfield	21 HR, 103 RBI, 101 runs, .318
1990	.....*Rickey Henderson, Oak	Outfield	28 HR, 119 runs†, 65 SB†, .325
1991	.....Cal Ripken Jr., Balt	Shortstop	34 HR, 114 RBI, .323
1992	.....Dennis Eckersley, Oak	Pitcher	7–1, 1.91 ERA, 51 saves
1993	.....Frank Thomas, Chi	First base	41 HR, 128 RBI, .317
1994	.....Frank Thomas, Chi	First base	38 HR, 101 RBI, .353
1995	.....*Mo Vaughn, Bos	First base	39 HR, 126 RBI, .300
1996	.....*Juan Gonzalez, Tex	Outfield	47 HR, 144 RBI, .314
1997	.....*Ken Griffey Jr., Sea	Outfield	56 HR†, 125 runs†, 393 TB†, 147 RBI†, .304
1998	.....*Juan Gonzalez, Tex	Outfield	45 HR, 157 RBI†, 50 2B†, .318
1999	.....*Ivan Rodriguez, Tex	Catcher	35 HR, 113 RBI, 116 runs, .332, GG
2000	.....*Jason Giambi, Oak	First Base	43 HR, 137 RBI, .333
2001	.....*Ichiro Suzuki, Sea	Outfield	.350†, 242 H†, 127 R, 56 SB†
2002	.....*Miguel Tejada, Oak	Shortstop	34 HR, 131 RBI, .308
2003	.....Alex Rodriguez, Tex	Shortstop	47 HR†, 118 RBI, .600 SLG†
2004	.....*Vladimir Guerrero, Ana	Outfield	39 HR, 126 RBI, .598 SLG
2005	.....*Alex Rodriguez, NYY	Third Base	48 HR†, 130 RBI, .610 SLG†
2006	.....Justin Morneau, Min	First Base	30HR, 130 RBI, .321, 190 hits

*Played for pennant or, after 1968, division winner. †Led league. ‡Tied for league lead.
Notes: 2B=doubles; 3B=triples; FA=fielding average; GG=won Gold Glove, award begun in 1957; K=strikeouts; O=shutouts; SB=stolen bases; TB=total bases.

Rookies of the Year

NATIONAL LEAGUE

1947*	Jackie Robinson, Bklyn (1B)
1948*	Alvin Dark, Bos (SS)
1949	Don Newcombe, Bklyn (P)
1950	Sam Jethroe, Bos (OF)
1951	Willie Mays, NY (OF)
1952	Joe Black, Bklyn (P)
1953	Junior Gilliam, Bklyn (2B)
1954	Wally Moon, StL (OF)
1955	Bill Virdon, StL (OF)
1956	Frank Robinson, Cin (OF)
1957	Jack Sanford, Phi (P)
1958	Orlando Cepeda, SF (1B)
1959	Willie McCovey, SF (1B)
1960	Frank Howard, LA (OF)
1961	Billy Williams, Chi (OF)
1962	Ken Hubbs, Chi (2B)
1963	Pete Rose, Cin (2B)
1964	Dick Allen, Phi (3B)
1965	Jim Lefebvre, LA (2B)
1966	Tommy Helms, Cin (2B)
1967	Tom Seaver, NY (P)
1968	Johnny Bench, Cin (C)
1969	Ted Sizemore, LA (2B)
1970	Carl Morton, Mtl(P)
1971	Earl Williams, Atl (C)
1972	Jon Matlack, NY (P)
1973	Gary Matthews, SF (OF)
1974	Bake McBride, StL (OF)
1975	John Montefusco, SF (P)
1976	Pat Zachry, Cin (P)
	Butch Metzger, SD (P)
1977	Andre Dawson, Mtl (OF)
1978	Bob Horner, Atl (3B)
1979	Rick Sutcliffe, LA (P)
1980	Steve Howe, LA (P)

AMERICAN LEAGUE

1949	Roy Sievers, StL (OF)
1950	Walt Dropo, Bos (1B)
1951	Gil McDougald, NY (3B)
1952	Harry Byrd, Phi (P)
1953	Harvey Kuenn, Det (SS)
1954	Bob Grim, NY (P)
1955	Herb Score, Clev (P)
1956	Luis Aparicio, Chi (SS)
1957	Tony Kubek, NY (OF, SS)
1958	Albie Pearson, Wash (OF)
1959	Bob Allison, Wash (OF)
1960	Ron Hansen, Balt (SS)
1961	Don Schwall, Bos (P)
1962	Tom Tresh, NY (SS)
1963	Gary Peters, Chi (P)
1964	Tony Oliva, Minn (OF)
1965	Curt Blefary, Balt (OF)
1966	Tommie Agee, Chi (OF)
1967	Rod Carew, Minn (2B)
1968	Stan Bahnsen, NY (P)
1969	Lou Piniella, KC (OF)
1970	Thurman Munson, NY (C)
1971	Chris Chambliss, Clev (1B)
1972	Carlton Fisk, Bos (C)
1973	Al Bumbry, Balt (OF)
1974	Mike Hargrove, Tex (1B)
1975	Fred Lynn, Bos (OF)
1976	Mark Fidrych, Det (P)
1977	Eddie Murray, Balt (DH)
1978	Lou Whitaker, Det (2B)
1979	Alfredo Griffin, Tor (SS)
	John Castino, Minn (3B)
1980	Joe Charboneau, Clev (OF)
1981	Dave Righetti, NY (P)
1982	Cal Ripken Jr., Balt (SS)

*Just one selection for both leagues.

Rookies of the Year *(Cont.)*

NATIONAL LEAGUE *(Cont.)*

1981	Fernando Valenzuela, LA (P)
1982	Steve Sax, LA (2B)
1983	Darryl Strawberry, NY (OF)
1984	Dwight Gooden, NY (P)
1985	Vince Coleman, StL (OF)
1986	Todd Worrell, StL (P)
1987	Benito Santiago, SD (C)
1988	Chris Sabo, Cin (3B)
1989	Jerome Walton, Chi (OF)
1990	Dave Justice, Atl (OF)
1991	Jeff Bagwell, Hou (3B)
1992	Eric Karros, LA (1B)
1993	Mike Piazza, LA (C)
1994	Raul Mondesi, LA (OF)
1995	Hideo Nomo, LA (P)
1996	Todd Hollandsworth, LA (OF)
1997	Scott Rolen, Phi (3B)
1998	Kerry Wood, Chi (P)
1999	Scott Williamson, Cin (P)
2000	Rafael Furcal, Atl (SS)
2001	Albert Pujols, StL (OF)
2002	Jason Jennings, Col (P)
2003	Dontrelle Willis, Fla (P)
2004	Jason Bay, Pit (OF)
2005	Ryan Howard, Phi (1B)
2006	Hanley Ramirez, Fla (SS)

AMERICAN LEAGUE *(Cont.)*

1983	Ron Kittle, Chi (OF)
1984	Alvin Davis, Sea (1B)
1985	Ozzie Guillen, Chi (SS)
1986	Jose Canseco, Oak (OF)
1987	Mark McGwire, Oak (1B)
1988	Walt Weiss, Oak (SS)
1989	Gregg Olson, Balt (P)
1990	Sandy Alomar Jr, Clev (C)
1991	Chuck Knoblauch, Minn (2B)
1992	Pat Listach, Mil (SS)
1993	Tim Salmon, Calif (OF)
1994	Bob Hamelin, KC (DH)
1995	Marty Cordova, Minn (OF)
1996	Derek Jeter, NY (SS)
1997	Nomar Garciaparra, Bos (SS)
1998	Ben Grieve, Oak (OF)
1999	Carlos Beltran, KC (OF)
2000	Kazuhiro Sasaki, Sea (P)
2001	Ichiro Suzuki, Sea (OF)
2002	Eric Hinske, Tor (3B)
2003	Angel Berroa, KC (SS)
2004	Bobby Crosby, Oak (SS)
2005	Huston Street, Oak (P)
2006	Justin Verlander, Det (P)

Cy Young Award

Year		W–L	Sv	ERA	Year		W–L	Sv	ERA
1956	*Don Newcombe, Bklyn (NL)	27–7	0	3.06	1962	Don Drysdale, LA (NL)	25–9	1	2.83
1957	Warren Spahn, Mil (NL)	21–11	3	2.69	1963	*Sandy Koufax, LA (NL)	25–5	0	1.88
1958	Bob Turley, NY (AL)	21–7	1	2.97	1964	Dean Chance, LA (AL)	20–9	4	1.65
1959	Early Wynn, Chi (AL)	22–10	0	3.17	1965	Sandy Koufax, LA (NL)	26–8	2	2.04
1960	Vernon Law, Pitt (NL)	20–9	0	3.08	1966	Sandy Koufax, LA (NL)	27–9	0	1.73
1961	Whitey Ford, NY (AL)	25–4	0	3.21					

NATIONAL LEAGUE

Year		W–L	Sv	ERA
1967	Mike McCormick, SF	22–10	0	2.85
1968	*Bob Gibson, StL	22–9	0	1.12
1969	Tom Seaver, NY	25–7	0	2.21
1970	Bob Gibson, StL	23–7	0	3.12
1971	Ferguson Jenkins, Chi	24–13	0	2.77
1972	Steve Carlton, Phi	27–10	0	1.97
1973	Tom Seaver, NY	19–10	0	2.08
1974	Mike Marshall, LA	15–12	21	2.42
1975	Tom Seaver, NY	22–9	0	2.38
1976	Randy Jones, SD	22–14	0	2.74
1977	Steve Carlton, Phi	23–10	0	2.64
1978	Gaylord Perry, SD	21–6	0	2.72
1979	Bruce Sutter, Chi	6–6	37	2.23
1980	Steve Carlton, Phi	24–9	0	2.34
1981	Fernando Valenzuela, LA	13–7	0	2.48
1982	Steve Carlton, Phi	23–11	0	3.10
1983	John Denny, Phi	19–6	0	2.37
1984	†Rick Sutcliffe, Chi	16–1	0	2.69
1985	Dwight Gooden, NY	24–4	0	1.53
1986	Mike Scott, Hou	18–10	0	2.22
1987	Steve Bedrosian, Phi	5–3	40	2.83
1988	Orel Hershiser, LA	23–8	1	2.26
1989	Mark Davis, SD	4–3	44	1.85
1990	Doug Drabek, Pitt	22–6	0	2.76
1991	Tom Glavine, Atl	20–11	0	2.55
1992	Greg Maddux, Chi	20–11	0	2.18
1993	Greg Maddux, Atl	20–10	0	2.36
1994	Greg Maddux, Atl	16–6	0	1.56

AMERICAN LEAGUE

Year		W–L	Sv	ERA
1967	Jim Lonborg, Bos	22–9	0	3.16
1968	*Denny McLain, Det	31–6	0	1.96
1969	Denny McLain, Det	24–9	0	2.80
	Mike Cuellar, Balt	23–11	0	2.38
1970	Jim Perry, Minn	24–12	0	3.03
1971	*Vida Blue, Oak	24–8	0	1.82
1972	Gaylord Perry, Clev	24–16	1	1.92
1973	Jim Palmer, Balt	22–9	1	2.40
1974	Catfish Hunter, Oak	25–12	0	2.49
1975	Jim Palmer, Balt	23–11	1	2.09
1976	Jim Palmer, Balt	22–13	0	2.51
1977	Sparky Lyle, NY	13–5	26	2.17
1978	Ron Guidry, NY	25–3	0	1.74
1979	Mike Flanagan, Balt	23–9	0	3.08
1980	Steve Stone, Balt	25–7	0	3.23
1981	*Rollie Fingers, Mil	6–3	28	1.04
1982	Pete Vuckovich, Mil	18–6	0	3.34
1983	LaMarr Hoyt, Chi	24–10	0	3.66
1984	*Willie Hernandez, Det	9–3	32	1.92
1985	Bret Saberhagen, KC	20–6	0	2.87
1986	*Roger Clemens, Bos	24–4	0	2.48
1987	Roger Clemens, Bos	20–9	0	2.97
1988	Frank Viola, Minn	24–7	0	2.64
1989	Bret Saberhagen, KC	23–6	0	2.16
1990	Bob Welch, Oak	27–6	0	2.95
1991	Roger Clemens, Bos	18–10	0	2.62
1992	*Dennis Eckersley, Oak	7–1	51	1.91
1993	Jack McDowell, Chi	22–10	0	3.37

Cy Young Award

NATIONAL LEAGUE					AMERICAN LEAGUE			
Year	W–L	Sv	ERA		Year	W–L	Sv	ERA
1995.....Greg Maddux, Atl	19–2	0	1.63		1994.....David Cone, KC	16–4	0	2.94
1996.....John Smoltz, Atl	24–8	0	2.94		1995.....Randy Johnson, Sea	18–2	0	2.48
1997.....Pedro Martinez, Mtl	17–8	0	1.90		1996.....Pat Hentgen, Tor	20–10	0	3.22
1998.....Tom Glavine, Atl	20–6	0	2.47		1997.....Roger Clemens, Tor	21–7	0	2.05
1999.....Randy Johnson, Ariz	17–9	0	2.48		1998.....Roger Clemens, Tor	20–6	0	2.65
2000.....Randy Johnson, Ariz	19–7	0	2.64		1999.....Pedro Martinez, Bos	23–4	0	1.55
2001.....Randy Johnson, Ariz	21–6	0	2.49		2000.....Pedro Martinez, Bos	18–6	0	1.74
2002.....Randy Johnson, Ariz	24–5	0	2.32		2001.....Roger Clemens, NY	20–3	0	3.51
2003.....Eric Gagne, LA	2–3	55	1.20		2002.....Barry Zito, Oak	23–5	0	2.75
2004.....Roger Clemens, Hou	18-4	0	2.98		2003.....Roy Halladay, Tor	22–7	0	3.25
2005.....Chris Carpenter, StL	21-5	0	2.83		2004.....Johan Santana, Min	20-6	0	2.61
2006.....Brandon Webb, Ariz	16–8	0	3.10		2005.....Bartolo Colon, LAA	21-8	0	3.48
					2006.....Johan Santana, Min	19–6	0	2.77

*Won the MVP and Cy Young awards in the same season.
†NL games only. Sutcliffe pitched 15 games with Cleveland before being traded to the Cubs.

Career Individual Batting

GAMES

Pete Rose	3562
Carl Yastrzemski	3308
Hank Aaron	3298
Rickey Henderson	3081
Ty Cobb	3034
Eddie Murray	3026
Stan Musial	3026
Cal Ripken Jr.	3001
Willie Mays	2992
*Barry Bonds	2986
Dave Winfield	2973
Rusty Staub	2951
Brooks Robinson	2896
Robin Yount	2856
*Craig Biggio	2850
Al Kaline	2834
Rafael Palmeiro	2831
Harold Baines	2830
Eddie Collins	2826
Reggie Jackson	2820
Frank Robinson	2808
Honus Wagner	2792
Tris Speaker	2789

RUNS

Rickey Henderson	2295
Ty Cobb	2245
*Barry Bonds	2227
Hank Aaron	2174
Babe Ruth	2174
Pete Rose	2165
Willie Mays	2062
Cap Anson	1996
Stan Musial	1949
Lou Gehrig	1888
Tris Speaker	1882
Mel Ott	1859
*Craig Biggio	1834
Frank Robinson	1829
Eddie Collins	1821
Carl Yastrzemski	1816
Ted Williams	1798
Paul Molitor	1782
Charlie Gehringer	1774
Jimmie Foxx	1751
Honus Wagner	1736

HOME RUNS

*Barry Bonds	762
Hank Aaron	755
Babe Ruth	714
Willie Mays	660
*Sammy Sosa	609
*Ken Griffey Jr.	593
Frank Robinson	586
Mark McGwire	583
Harmon Killebrew	573
Rafael Palmeiro	569
Reggie Jackson	563
Mike Schmidt	548
Mickey Mantle	536
Jimmie Foxx	534
Willie McCovey	521
Ted Williams	521
*Alex Rodriguez	518
*Frank Thomas	513
Ernie Banks	512
Eddie Mathews	512
Mel Ott	511
*Jim Thome	507
Eddie Murray	504

BATTING AVERAGE (5,000 AB)

Ty Cobb	.367
Rogers Hornsby	.358
Ed Delahanty	.346
Tris Speaker	.345
Billy Hamilton	.344
Ted Williams	.344
Dan Brouthers	.342
Harry Heilmann	.342
Babe Ruth	.342
Willie Keeler	.341
Bill Terry	.341
Lou Gehrig	.340
George Sisler	.340
Jesse Burkett	.338
Tony Gwynn	.338
Nap Lajoie	.338
Al Simmons	.334
Cap Anson	.333
Eddie Collins	.333
Paul Waner	.333
*Todd Helton	.332

HITS

Pete Rose	4256
Ty Cobb	4189
Hank Aaron	3771
Stan Musial	3630
Tris Speaker	3515
Carl Yastrzemski	3419
Cap Anson	3418
Honus Wagner	3415
Paul Molitor	3319
Eddie Collins	3313
Willie Mays	3283
Eddie Murray	3255
Nap Lajoie	3251
Cal Ripken Jr.	3184
George Brett	3154
Paul Waner	3152
Robin Yount	3142
Tony Gwynn	3141
Dave Winfield	3110
*Craig Biggio	3060
Rickey Henderson	3055
Rod Carew	3053
Lou Brock	3023
Rafael Palmeiro	3020
Wade Boggs	3010
Al Kaline	3007
Roberto Clemente	3000

AT BATS

Pete Rose	14053
Hank Aaron	12364
Carl Yastrzemski	11988
Cal Ripken Jr.	11551
Ty Cobb	11429
Eddie Murray	11336
Robin Yount	11008
Dave Winfield	11003
Stan Musial	10972
Rickey Henderson	10961
Willie Mays	10881
*Craig Biggio	10876
Paul Molitor	10835
Brooks Robinson	10654
Rafael Palmeiro	10472
Honus Wagner	10430
George Brett	10349
Lou Brock	10332

* Active in 2007.

Career Individual Batting *(Cont.)*

DOUBLES

Tris Speaker	792
Pete Rose	746
Stan Musial	725
Ty Cobb	724
*Craig Biggio	668
George Brett	665
Nap Lajoie	657
Carl Yastrzemski	646
Honus Wagner	640
Hank Aaron	624
Paul Molitor	605
Paul Waner	605
Cal Ripken Jr.	603
*Barry Bonds	601
Rafael Palmeiro	585
Robin Yount	583
Cap Anson	581
Wade Boggs	578
Charlie Gehringer	574
*Luis Gonzalez	570

TRIPLES

Sam Crawford	309
Ty Cobb	295
Honus Wagner	252
Jake Beckley	243
Roger Connor	233
Tris Speaker	222
Fred Clarke	220
Dan Brouthers	205
Joe Kelley	194
Paul Waner	191
Bid McPhee	188
Eddie Collins	187
Ed Delahanty	185
Sam Rice	184
Jesse Burkett	182
Ed Konetchy	182
Edd Roush	182
Buck Ewing	178
Rabbit Maranville	177
Stan Musial	177

BASES ON BALLS

*Barry Bonds	2558
Rickey Henderson	2190
Babe Ruth	2062
Ted Williams	2021
Joe Morgan	1865
Carl Yastrzemski	1845
Mickey Mantle	1733
Mel Ott	1708
*Frank Thomas	1628
Eddie Yost	1614
Darrell Evans	1605
Stan Musial	1599
Pete Rose	1566
Harmon Killebrew	1559
Lou Gehrig	1508
Mike Schmidt	1507
Eddie Collins	1499
Willie Mays	1464
*Jim Thome	1459
Jimmie Foxx	1452
Eddie Mathews	1444

RUNS BATTED IN

Hank Aaron	2297
Babe Ruth	2213
Cap Anson	2076
*Barry Bonds	1996
Lou Gehrig	1995
Stan Musial	1951
Ty Cobb	1937
Jimmie Foxx	1922
Eddie Murray	1917
Willie Mays	1903
Mel Ott	1860
Carl Yastrzemski	1844
Ted Williams	1839
Rafael Palmeiro	1835
Dave Winfield	1833
Al Simmons	1827
Frank Robinson	1812
Honus Wagner	1732
Reggie Jackson	1702
*Ken Griffey Jr.	1701
Cal Ripken Jr.	1695

SLUGGING AVERAGE (5,000 AB)

Babe Ruth	.690
Ted Williams	.634
Lou Gehrig	.632
Jimmie Foxx	.609
*Barry Bonds	.607
Hank Greenberg	.605
*Manny Ramirez	.593
Mark McGwire	.588
*Todd Helton	.583
Joe Dimaggio	.579
*Vladimir Guerrero	.579
*Alex Rodriguez	.578
Rogers Hornsby	.577
*Jim Thome	.565
Larry Walker	.565
Albert Belle	.564
Johnny Mize	.562
Juan Gonzalez	.561
*Frank Thomas	.561
Stan Musial	.559

STOLEN BASES

Rickey Henderson	1406
Lou Brock	938
Billy Hamilton	912
Ty Cobb	892
Tim Raines	808
Vince Coleman	752
Eddie Collins	745
Max Carey	738
Honus Wagner	722
Joe Morgan	689
Willie Wilson	668
Bert Campaneris	649
*Kenny Lofton	622
Otis Nixon	620
George Davis	616
Tom Brown	615
Dummy Hoy	594
Maury Wills	586
George Van Haltren	583
Ozzie Smith	580

ON-BASE PERCENTAGE (5,000 AB)

Ted Williams	.482
Babe Ruth	.469
*Barry Bonds	.444
Lou Gehrig	.442
*Todd Helton	.430
Jimmie Foxx	.425
Ty Cobb	.424
Rogers Hornsby	.424
Mickey Mantle	.422
*Frank Thomas	.421
Edgar Martinez	.418
Stan Musial	.417
Tris Speaker	.417
Wade Boggs	.415
*Jason Giambi	.411
Mel Ott	.410
Mickey Cochrane	.409
Hank Greenberg	.409
*Manny Ramirez	.409
*Jim Thome	.409

TOTAL BASES

Hank Aaron	6856
Stan Musial	6134
Willie Mays	6066
*Barry Bonds	5976
Ty Cobb	5859
Babe Ruth	5793
Pete Rose	5752
Carl Yastrzemski	5539
Eddie Murray	5397
Rafael Palmeiro	5388
Frank Robinson	5373
Dave Winfield	5221
Cal Ripken Jr.	5168
Tris Speaker	5101
Lou Gehrig	5060
George Brett	5044
Mel Ott	5041
Jimmie Foxx	4956
*Ken Griffey Jr.	4884
Ted Williams	4884
Honus Wagner	4862

STRIKEOUTS

Reggie Jackson	2597
*Sammy Sosa	2306
*Jim Thome	2043
Andres Galarraga	2003
Jose Canseco	1942
Willie Stargell	1936
Mike Schmidt	1883
Fred McGriff	1882
Tony Perez	1867
Dave Kingman	1816
Bobby Bonds	1757
*Craig Biggio	1753
Dale Murphy	1748
Lou Brock	1730
Mickey Mantle	1710
Harmon Killebrew	1699
Chili Davis	1698
Dwight Evans	1697
Rickey Henderson	1694
Dave Winfield	1686

*Active in 2006.

The 30–30 Club (30 HR, 30 SB in single season)

Year		HR	SB	Year		HR	SB
1922	Kenny Williams, StL	39	37	1996	Dante Bichette, Col	31	31
1956	Willie Mays, NYG	36	40	1997	Larry Walker, Col	49	33
1957	Willie Mays, NYG	35	38	1997	Jeff Bagwell, Hou	43	31
1963	Hank Aaron, Mil	44	31	1997	Raul Mondesi, LA	30	32
1969	Bobby Bonds, SF	32	45	1997	Barry Bonds, SF	40	37
1970	Tommy Harper, Mil	31	38	1998	Alex Rodriguez, Sea	42	46
1973	Bobby Bonds, SF	39	43	1998	Shawn Green, Tor	35	35
1975	Bobby Bonds, NYY	32	30	1999	Jeff Bagwell, Hou	42	30
1977	Bobby Bonds, Cal	37	41	1999	Raul Mondesi, LA	33	36
1978	Bobby Bonds, Chi/Tex	31	43	2000	Preston Wilson, Fla	31	36
1983	Dale Murphy, Atl	36	30	2001	Vladimir Guerrero, Mtl	34	37
1987	Joe Carter, Clev	32	31	2001	Jose Cruz Jr., Tor	34	32
1987	Eric Davis, Cin	37	50	2001	Bobby Abreu, Phi	31	36
1987	Darryl Strawberry, NYM	39	36	2002	Alfonso Soriano, NYY	39	41
1987	Howard Johnson, NYM	36	32	2002	Vladimir Guerrero, Mtl	39	40
1988	Jose Canseco, Oak	42	40	2003	Alfonso Soriano, NYY	38	35
1989	Howard Johnson, NYM	36	41	2004	Carlos Beltran, KC/Hou	38	42
1990	Ron Gant, Atl	32	33	2004	Bobby Abreu, Phi	30	40
1990	Barry Bonds, Pitt	33	52	2005	Alfonso Soriano, Tex	36	30
1991	Ron Gant, Atl	32	34	2006	Alfonso Soriano, Wash	46	41
1991	Howard Johnson, NYM	38	30	2007	Brandon Phillips, Cin	30	32
1992	Barry Bonds, Pitt	34	39	2007	Jimmy Rollins, Phi	30	41
1993 *	Sammy Sosa, ChiC	33	36	2007	David Wright, NYM	30	34
1995	Barry Bonds, SF	33	31				
1995	Sammy Sosa, ChiC	36	34				
1996	Barry Bonds, SF	42	40				
1996	Ellis Burks, Col	40	32				
1996	Barry Larkin, Cin	33	36				

Career Individual Pitching

GAMES		INNINGS PITCHED		WINS	
Jesse Orosco	1251	Cy Young	7356.0	Cy Young	511
*Mike Stanton	1178	Pud Galvin	6003.1	Walter Johnson	417
John Franco	1119	Walter Johnson	5914.1	Grover Alexander	373
Dennis Eckersley	1071	Phil Niekro	5404.1	Christy Mathewson	373
Hoyt Wilhelm	1070	Nolan Ryan	5386.0	Pud Galvin	365
Dan Plesac	1064	Gaylord Perry	5350.1	Warren Spahn	363
Kent Tekulve	1050	Don Sutton	5282.1	Kid Nichols	361
*Jose Mesa	1022	Warren Spahn	5243.1	*Roger Clemens	354
Lee Smith	1022	Steve Carlton	5217.1	*Greg Maddux	347
*Mike Timlin	1011	Grover Alexander	5190.0	Tim Keefe	342
*Roberto Hernandez	1010	Kid Nichols	5056.1	Steve Carlton	329
Mike Jackson	1005	Tim Keefe	5049.2	John Clarkson	328
Goose Gossage	1002	Bert Blyleven	4970.0	Eddie Plank	326
Lindy McDaniel	987	Bobby Mathews	4956.0	Nolan Ryan	324
Rollie Fingers	944	*Roger Clemens	4916.2	Don Sutton	324
*Todd Jones	937	*Greg Maddux	4814.1	Phil Niekro	318
Gene Garber	931	Mickey Welch	4802.0	Gaylord Perry	314
Cy Young	906	Tom Seaver	4782.2	Tom Seaver	311
Sparky Lyle	899	Christy Mathewson	4780.2	Charley Radbourn	309
Jim Kaat	898	Tommy John	4710.1	Mickey Welch	307
Paul Assenmacher	884	Robin Roberts	4688.2	*Tom Glavine	303
*Mike Myers	883	Early Wynn	4564.0	Lefty Grove	300
				Early Wynn	300

* Active in 2007.

Career Individual Pitching *(Cont.)*

LOSSES

Cy Young	316
Pud Galvin	310
Nolan Ryan	292
Walter Johnson	279
Phil Niekro	274
Gaylord Perry	265
Don Sutton	256
Jack Powell	254
Eppa Rixey	251
Bert Blyleven	250
Bobby Mathews	248
Robin Roberts	245
Warren Spahn	245
Steve Carlton	244
Early Wynn	244
Jim Kaat	237
Frank Tanana	236
Gus Weyhing	232
Tommy John	231
Bob Friend	230
Ted Lyons	230

WINNING PERCENTAGE**

Al Spalding	.795
Spud Chandler	.717
*Pedro Martinez	.691
Whitey Ford	.690
Dave Foutz	.690
Bob Caruthers	.688
Don Gullett	.686
Lefty Grove	.680
Joe Wood	.672
Vic Raschi	.667
*Roger Clemens	.667
Larry Corcoran	.665
*Tim Hudson	.665
Christy Mathewson	.665
Sam Leever	.660
Sal Maglie	.657
*Randy Johnson	.656
Dick McBride	.656
Sandy Koufax	.655
Johnny Allen	.654

SAVES

*Trevor Hoffman	524
Lee Smith	478
*Mariano Rivera	443
John Franco	424
Dennis Eckersley	390
Jeff Reardon	367
*Billy Wagner	358
Randy Myers	347
Rollie Fingers	341
John Wetteland	330
*Roberto Hernandez	326
*Troy Percival	324
Jose Mesa	321
Rick Aguilera	318
Robb Nen	314
Tom Henke	311
Goose Gossage	310
Jeff Montgomery	304
Doug Jones	303
*Todd Jones	301
Bruce Sutter	300

EARNED RUN AVERAGE (2,000 IP)

Ed Walsh	1.82
Addie Joss	1.89
Al Spalding	2.04
Three Finger Brown	2.06
John Ward	2.10
Christy Mathewson	2.13
Tommy Bond	2.14
Rube Waddell	2.16
Walter Johnson	2.17
Ed Reulbach	2.28
Will White	2.28
Eddie Plank	2.35
Larry Corcoran	2.36
Eddie Cicotte	2.38
Candy Cummings	2.39
Doc White	2.39
Nap Rucker	2.42
George Bradley	2.43
Jim McCormick	2.43
Chief Bender	2.46

SHUTOUTS

Walter Johnson	110
Grover Alexander	90
Christy Mathewson	79
Cy Young	76
Eddie Plank	69
Warren Spahn	63
Nolan Ryan	61
Tom Seaver	61
Bert Blyleven	60
Don Sutton	58
Pud Galvin	57
Ed Walsh	57
Bob Gibson	56
Three Finger Brown	55
Steve Carlton	55
Jim Palmer	53
Gaylord Perry	53
Juan Marichal	52
Rube Waddell	50
Vic Willis	50

COMPLETE GAMES

Cy Young	749
Pud Galvin	639
Tim Keefe	554
Walter Johnson	531
Kid Nichols	531
Mickey Welch	525
Bobby Mathews	525
Charley Radbourn	489
John Clarkson	485
Tony Mullane	468
Jim McCormick	466
Gus Weyhing	448
Grover Alexander	437
Christy Mathewson	434
Jack Powell	422
Eddie Plank	410
Will White	394
Amos Rusie	392
Vic Willis	388
Tommy Bond	386

STRIKEOUTS

Nolan Ryan	5714
*Roger Clemens	4672
*Randy Johnson	4516
Steve Carlton	4136
Bert Blyleven	3701
Tom Seaver	3640
Don Sutton	3574
Gaylord Perry	3534
Walter Johnson	3509
Phil Niekro	3342
*Greg Maddux	3273
Ferguson Jenkins	3192
Bob Gibson	3117
*Curt Schilling	3116
*Pedro Martinez	3030
*John Smoltz	2975
Jim Bunning	2855
Mickey Lolich	2832
Cy Young	2803
Frank Tanana	2773

BASES ON BALLS

Nolan Ryan	2795
Steve Carlton	1833
Phil Niekro	1809
Early Wynn	1775
Bob Feller	1764
Bobo Newsom	1732
Amos Rusie	1707
Charlie Hough	1665
*Roger Clemens	1580
Gus Weyhing	1566
Red Ruffing	1541
*Tom Glavine	1463
Bump Hadley	1442
Warren Spahn	1434
Earl Whitehill	1431
*Randy Johnson	1422
Tony Mullane	1408
Sad Sam Jones	1396
Jack Morris	1390
Tom Seaver	1390

* Active in 2007.   ** Minumum 100 victories.

Alltime Winningest Managers

CAREER

	W	L	Pct	Yrs		W	L	Pct	Yrs
Connie Mack	3755	3967	.486	53	Casey Stengel	1942	1868	.510	25
John McGraw	2810	1987	.586	33	Gene Mauch	1907	2044	.483	26
*Tony LaRussa	2432	2114	.535	29	Bill McKechnie	1904	1737	.523	25
*Bobby Cox	2321	1828	.559	26	*Lou Piniella	1627	1518	.517	20
Sparky Anderson	2238	1855	.547	26	Ralph Houk	1627	1539	.514	20
Bucky Harris	2168	2228	.493	29	Fred Clarke	1609	1189	.575	19
Joe McCarthy	2155	1346	.616	24	Dick Williams	1592	1474	.519	21
*Joe Torre	2143	1820	.541	26	Tommy Lasorda	1589	1434	.526	20
Walter Alston	2063	1634	.558	23	Earl Weaver	1506	1080	.582	17
Leo Durocher	2015	1717	.540	24	Clark Griffith	1491	1367	.522	20

REGULAR SEASON

	W	L	Pct	Yrs		W	L	Pct	Yrs
Connie Mack	3731	3948	.486	53	Casey Stengel	1905	1842	.508	25
John McGraw	2784	1959	.587	33	Gene Mauch	1902	2037	.483	26
*Tony LaRussa	2375	2070	.534	29	Bill McKechnie	1896	1723	.524	25
*Bobby Cox	2255	1764	.561	26	Ralph Houk	1619	1531	.514	20
Sparky Anderson	2194	1834	.545	26	*Lou Piniella	1604	1497	.517	20
Bucky Harris	2157	2218	.493	29	Fred Clarke	1602	1181	.576	19
Joe McCarthy	2125	1333	.615	24	Dick Williams	1571	1451	.520	21
*Joe Torre	2067	1770	.539	26	Tommy Lasorda	1558	1404	.526	20
Walter Alston	2040	1613	.558	23	Lou Piniella	1519	1420	.523	19
Leo Durocher	2008	1709	.540	24	Clark Griffith	1491	1367	.522	20

WORLD SERIES

	W	L	T	Pct	App	WS		W	L	T	Pct	App	WS
Casey Stengel	37	26	0	.587	10	7	Billy Southworth	11	11	0	.500	4	2
Joe McCarthy	30	13	0	.698	9	7	Earl Weaver	11	13	0	.458	4	1
John McGraw	26	28	2	.482	9	2	*Bobby Cox	11	18	0	.379	5	1
Connie Mack	24	19	0	.558	8	5	Whitey Herzog	10	11	0	.476	3	1
*Joe Torre	21	11	0	.657	6	4	*Tony LaRussa	9	13	0	.409	5	2
Walter Alston	20	20	0	.500	7	4	*Terry Francona	8	0	0	1.000	2	2
Miller Huggins	18	15	1	.544	6	3	Bill Carrigan	8	2	0	.800	2	2
Sparky Anderson	16	12	0	.571	5	3	Cito Gaston	8	4	0	.667	2	2
Tommy Lasorda	12	11	0	.522	4	2	Danny Murtaugh	8	6	0	.571	2	2
Dick Williams	12	14	0	.462	4	2	Tom Kelly	8	6	0	.571	2	2
Frank Chance	11	9	1	.548	4	2	Ralph Houk	8	8	0	.500	3	2
Bucky Harris	11	10	0	.524	3	2	Bill McKechnie	8	14	0	.364	4	2

* Active in 2007.

Individual Batting (Single Season)

HITS

Ichiro Suzuki, 2004 262
George Sisler, 1920 257
Lefty O'Doul, 1929...............254
Bill Terry, 1930 254
Al Simmons, 1925................253
Rogers Hornsby, 1922.........250
Chuck Klein, 1930 250
Ty Cobb, 1911 248
George Sisler, 1922 246
Ichiro Suzuki, 2001 242

BATTING AVERAGE

Levi Meyerle, 1871 .... .492
Hugh Duffy, 1894................ .440
Tip O'Neill, 1887.................. .435
Ross Barnes, 1872............ .432
Cal McVey, 1871................. .431
Ross Barnes, 1876.............. .429
Nap Lajoie, 1901 .... .426
Ross Barnes, 1873............. .425
Willie Keeler, 1897 .... .424
Rogers Hornsby, 1924 .... .424

DOUBLES

Earl Webb, 1931....................67
George Burns, 1926..............64
Joe Medwick, 1936 64
Hank Greenberg, 1934.........63
Paul Waner, 1932..................62
Charlie Gehringer, 1936 60
Tris Speaker, 1923................59
Chuck Klein, 1930 59
Todd Helton, 2000 59
Billy Herman, 1936 57
Billy Herman, 1935 57
Carlos Delgado, 2000 57

TOTAL BASES

Babe Ruth, 1921...................457
Rogers Hornsby, 1922.........450
Lou Gehrig, 1927..................447
Chuck Klein, 1930 445
Jimmie Foxx, 1932................438
Stan Musial, 1948................429
Sammy Sosa, 2001..............425
Hack Wilson, 1930................423
Chuck Klein, 1932................420
Luis Gonzalez, 2001............419
Lou Gehrig, 1930.................419

TRIPLES

Chief Wilson, 1912................36
Dave Orr, 1886 31
Heinie Reitz, 1894 31
Perry Werden, 1893...............29
Harry Davis, 1897.................28
George Davis, 1893 27
Sam Thompson, 1894 27
Jimmy Williams, 1899...........27
Sam Crawford, 1914.............26
Kiki Cuyler, 1925...................26
Joe Jackson, 1912 26
John Reilly,1890....................26
George Treadway...................26

HOME RUNS

Barry Bonds, 2001 73
Mark McGwire, 1998 70
Sammy Sosa, 1998...............66
Mark McGwire, 1999 65
Sammy Sosa, 2001...............64
Sammy Sosa, 1999...............63
Roger Maris, 1961.................61
Babe Ruth, 1927...................60
Babe Ruth, 1921...................59
Jimmie Foxx, 1932................58
Hank Greenberg, 1938.........58
Mark McGwire, 1997 58
Ryan Howard, 2006...............58

RUNS BATTED IN

Hack Wilson, 1930................191
Lou Gehrig, 1931..................184
Hank Greenberg, 1937.........183
Lou Gehrig, 1927..................175
Jimmie Foxx, 1938................175
Lou Gehrig, 1930..................174
Babe Ruth, 1921...................171
Chuck Klein, 1930 170
Hank Greenberg, 1935.........170
Jimmie Foxx, 1932................169

STRIKEOUTS

Ryan Howard, 2007...............199
Adam Dunn, 2004................195
Bobby Bonds, 1970..............189
Jose Hernandez, 2002..........188
Bobby Bonds, 1969..............187
Preston Wilson, 2000...........187
Rob Deer, 1987 186
Jose Hernandez, 2001..........185
Pete Incaviglia, 1986...........185
Jim Thome, 2003..................185
Cecil Fielder, 1990...............182
Jim Thome, 2003..................182

RUNS

Billy Hamilton, 1894.............192
Tom Brown, 1891..................177
Babe Ruth, 1921...................177
Lou Gehrig, 1936..................167
Tip O'Neill, 1887...................167
Billy Hamilton, 1895.............166
Willie Keeler, 1894................165
Joe Kelley, 1894...................165
Lou Gehrig, 1931..................163
Arlie Latham, 1887 163
Babe Ruth, 1928...................163

STOLEN BASES

Hugh Nicol, 1887..................138
Rickey Henderson, 1982.....130
Arlie Latham, 1887 129
Lou Brock, 1974...................118
Charlie Comiskey, 1887......117
Billy Hamilton, 1891.............111
Billy Hamilton, 1889.............111
John Ward, 1887 111
Vince Coleman, 1985 110
Vince Coleman, 1987 109
Arlie Latham, 1888 109

BASES ON BALLS

Barry Bonds, 2004 232
Barry Bonds, 2002 198
Barry Bonds, 2001 177
Babe Ruth, 1923...................170
Ted Williams, 1947...............162
Ted Williams, 1949...............162
Mark McGwire, 1998 162
Ted Williams, 1946...............156
Barry Bonds,1996.................151
Eddie Yost, 1956 151
Babe Ruth, 1920...................150

SLUGGING AVERAGE

Barry Bonds, 2001 .... .863
Babe Ruth, 1920................. .847
Babe Ruth, 1921 .... .846
Barry Bonds, 2004 .... .812
Barry Bonds, 2002 .... .799
Babe Ruth, 1927 .... .772
Lou Gehrig, 1927 .... .765
Babe Ruth, 1923 .... .764
Rogers Hornsby, 1925 ...... .756
Mark McGwire, 1998 .... .752

Individual Pitching (Single Season)

GAME APPEARANCES

Mike Marshall, 1974 106
Kent Tekulve, 1979 94
Salomon Torres, 2006.........94
Mike Marshall, 1973 92
Kent Tekulve, 1978 91
Wayne Granger, 1969............90
Mike Marshall, 1979 90
Kent Tekulve, 1987 90
Steve Kline, 2001....................89
Jim Brower, 2004 89
Mark Eichhorn, 1987 89
Steve Kline, 2001....................89

GAMES STARTED

Will White, 1879 75
Pud Galvin, 1883....................75
Jim McCormick, 1880 74
Charley Radbourn, 1884 73
Guy Hecker, 1884...................73
Jim Galvin, 1884....................72
John Clarkson, 1889...............72
Bill Hutchison, 1892...............71
John Clarkson, 1885...............70
Bobby Mathews, 1875...........70

INNINGS PITCHED

Will White, 1878 ....680.0
Charley Radbourn, 1884 ...678.2
Guy Hecker, 1884.............670.2
Jim McCormick, 1880 ....657.2
Jim Galvin, 1883...............656.1
Jim Galvin, 1884...............636.1
Charley Radbourn, 1883 ...632.1
Bill Hutchison, 1892...........627.0
Bobby Mathews, 1875........626.2
John Clarkson, 1885.........623.0

WINS

Charley Radbourn, 1884 59
Al Spalding, 1875..................55
John Clarkson, 1885...............53
Guy Hecker, 1884...................52
Al Spalding, 1874..................52
John Clarkson, 1889...............49
Charlie Buffinton, 1884 48
Charley Radbourn, 1883 48
Al Spalding, 1876 47
John Ward, 1879 47
Matt Kilroy, 1887...................46

LOSSES

John Coleman, 1883 48
Will White, 1880.....................42
Larry McKeon, 1884...............41
George Bradley, 1879 40
Jim McCormick, 1879 40
Bobby Mathews, 1875...........38
Kid Carsey, 1891 37
George Cobb, 1892 37
Henry Porter, 1888.................37

WINNING PERCENTAGE

Roy Face, 1959 947
Johnny Allen, 1937.............938
Greg Maddux, 1995 905
Randy Johnson, 1995 900
Ron Guidry, 1978 893
Freddie Fitzsimmons, 1940...889
Lefty Grove, 1931...............886
Bob Stanley, 1978 882
Preacher Roe, 1951 880
Fred Goldsmith, 1880.........875
Tom Seaver, 1981 875

SAVES

Bobby Thigpen, 1990............57
Eric Gagne, 2003 55
John Smoltz, 2002.................55
Mariano Rivera, 2004 53
Randy Myers, 1993 53
Trevor Hoffman, 1998 53
Eric Gagne, 2002 52
Rod Beck, 1998......................51
Dennis Eckersley, 1992.........51
Mariano Rivera, 2001 50
Francisco Cordero, 2004.......49

EARNED RUN AVERAGE

Tim Keefe, 1880 ....0.86
Dutch Leonard, 1914..........0.96
Three Finger Brown, 1906 ...1.04
Bob Gibson, 1968 ....1.12
Christy Mathewson, 1909...1.14
Walter Johnson, 1913........1.15
Jack Pfiester, 1907 ....1.15
Addie Joss, 1908................1.16
Carl Lundgren, 1907 ....1.17
Denny Driscoll, 1882..........1.21

SHUTOUTS

Grover Alexander, 1916........16
George Bradley, 1876 16
Jack Coombs, 1910 13
Bob Gibson, 1968 13
Grover Alexander, 1915.........12
Jim Galvin, 1884....................12
Ed Morris, 1886 12
Tommy Bond, 1879.................11
Dean Chance, 1964 11
Dave Foutz, 1886...................11
Walter Johnson, 1913............11
Sandy Koufax, 1963...............11
Christy Mathewson, 1908.......11
Charles Radbourn, 1884 11
Ed Walsh, 1908 11

COMPLETE GAMES

Will White, 1879 75
Charley Radbourn, 1884 73
Pud Galvin, 1883....................72
Guy Hecker, 1884...................72
Jim McCormick,1880..............72
Pud Galvin, 1884....................71
Bobby Mathews, 1875...........69
John Clarkson, 1885...............68
John Clarkson, 1889...............68

STRIKEOUTS

Matt Kilroy, 1886...................513
Toad Ramsey, 1886...............499
Hugh Daily, 1884 483
Dupee Shaw, 1884 451
Charley Radbourn, 1884 441
Charlie Buffinton, 1884 417
Guy Hecker, 1884..................385
Nolan Ryan, 1973..................383
Sandy Koufax, 1965 382

BASES ON BALLS

Amos Rusie, 1890 289
Mark Baldwin, 1889...............274
Amos Rusie, 1892 267
Amos Rusie, 1891 262
Mark Baldwin, 1890...............249
Jack Stivetts, 1891 232
Mark Baldwin, 1891...............227
Phil Knell, 1891.....................226
Bob Barr, 1890 219

Manager of the Year

NATIONAL LEAGUE

1983 ....Tommy Lasorda, LA
1984 ....Jim Frey, Chi
1985 ....Whitey Herzog, StL
1986 ....Hal Lanier, Hou
1987 ....Buck Rodgers, Mtl
1988 ....Tommy Lasorda, LA
1989 ....Don Zimmer, Chi
1990 ....Jim Leyland, Pitt
1991 ....Bobby Cox, Atl
1992 ....Jim Leyland, Pitt
1993 ....Dusty Baker, SF
1994 ....Felipe Alou, Mtl
1995 ....Don Baylor, Col
1996 ....Bruce Bochy, SD
1997 ....Dusty Baker, SF
1998 ....Larry Dierker, Hou

AMERICAN LEAGUE

1983 ....Tony LaRussa, Chi
1984 ....Sparky Anderson, Det
1985 ....Bobby Cox, Tor
1986 ....John McNamara, Bos
1987 ....Sparky Anderson, Det
1988 ....Tony LaRussa, Oak
1989 ....Frank Robinson, Balt
1990 ....Jeff Torborg, Chi
1991 ....Tom Kelly, Minn
1992 ....Tony LaRussa, Oak
1993 ....Gene Lamont, Chi
1994 ....Buck Showalter, NY
1995 ....Lou Piniella, Sea
1996 ....Joe Torre, NY/Johnny Oates, Tex
1997 ....Davey Johnson, Balt
1998 ....Joe Torre, NY

Manager of the Year *(Cont.)*

NATIONAL LEAGUE		AMERICAN LEAGUE	
1999	Jack McKeon, Cin	1999	Jimy Williams, Bos
2000	Dusty Baker, SF	2000	Jerry Manuel, Chi
2001	Larry Bowa, Phi	2001	Lou Piniella, Sea
2002	Tony LaRussa, StL	2002	Mike Scioscia, Ana
2003	Jack McKeon, Fla	2003	Tony Pena, KC
2004	Bobby Cox, Atl	2004	Buck Showalter, Tex
2005	Bobby Cox, Atl	2005	Ozzie Guillen, Chi
2006	Joe Girardi, Fla	2006	Jim Leyland, Det

Individual Batting (Single Game)

MOST RUNS

7 ....Guy Hecker, Lou   Aug 15, 1886

MOST HITS

7 ....Wilbert Robinson, Balt   June 10, 1892
       Rennie Stennett, Pitt   Sept 16, 1975

MOST HOME RUNS

4	Bobby Lowe, Bos (N)	May 30, 1894
	Ed Delahanty, Phi	July 13, 1896
	Lou Gehrig, NY (A)	June 3, 1932
	Gil Hodges, Bklyn	Aug 31, 1950
	Joe Adcock, Mil (N)	July 31, 1954
	Rocky Colavito, Clev	June 10, 1959
	Willie Mays, SF	April 30, 1961
	Mike Schmidt, Phi	April 17, 1976
	Bob Horner, Atl	July 6, 1986
	Mark Whiten, StL	Sept 7, 1993
	Mike Cameron, Sea	May 2, 2002
	Shawn Green, LA	May 23, 2002
	Carlos Delgado, Tor	Sept 25, 2003

Note: All single-game hitting records for a nine-inning game.

MOST GRAND SLAMS

2	Tony Lazzeri, NY (A)	May 24, 1936
	Jim Tabor, Bos (A)	July 4, 1939
	Rudy York, Bos (A)	July 27, 1946
	Jim Gentile, Balt	May 9, 1961
	Tony Cloninger, Atl	July 3, 1966
	Jim Northrup, Det	June 24, 1968
	Frank Robinson, Balt	June 26, 1970
	Robin Ventura, Chi (A)	Sept 4, 1995
	Chris Hoiles, Balt	Aug 14, 1998
	Fernando Tatis, StL	Apr 23, 1999
	N. Garciaparra, Bos	May 10, 1999
	Bill Mueller, Bos	July 29, 2003

MOST RBIs

12	Jim Bottomley, StL	Sept 16, 1924
	Mark Whiten, StL	Sept 7, 1993

Individual Batting (Single Inning)

MOST RUNS

3 ....Tommy Burns, Chi (N) Sept 6, 1883, 7th inning
       Ned Williamson, Chi (N) Sept 6, 1883, 7th inning
       Sammy White, Bos (A)   June 18, 1953, 7th inning

MOST HITS

3 ....Tommy Burns, Chi (N) Sept 6, 1883, 7th inning
       Fred Pfeiffer, Chi (N)   Sept 6, 1883, 7th inning
       Ned Williamson, Chi (N) Sept 6, 1883, 7th inning
       Gene Stephens, Bos (A) June 18, 1953, 7th inning
       Johnny Damon, Bos (A), June 27, 2003, 1st inning

MOST RBIs

8.......Fernando Tatis, StL   Apr 23, 1999, 3rd inning

Individual Pitching (Single Game)

MOST INNINGS PITCHED

26 .....Leon Cadore, Bklyn   May 1, 1920, tie 1–1
      Joe Oeschger, Bos (N) May 1, 1920, tie 1–1

MOST RUNS ALLOWED

24 .....Al Travers, Det   May 18, 1912

MOST HITS ALLOWED

36 .....Jack Wadsworth, Lou   Aug 17, 1894

MOST STRIKEOUTS

20	Roger Clemens, Bos	April 29, 1986
20	Roger Clemens, Bos	Sept 18, 1996
20	Kerry Wood, Chi (N)	May 6, 1998
20	Randy Johnson, Ariz	May 8, 2001

MOST WALKS ALLOWED

16	Bill George, NY (N)	May 30, 1887
	George Van Haltren, Chi (N)	June 27, 1887
	Henry Gruber, Clev	Apr 19, 1890
	Bruno Haas, Phi (A)	June 2, 1915

MOST WILD PITCHES

6	J.R. Richard, Hou	April 10, 1979
	Phil Niekro, Atl	Aug 14, 1979
	Bill Gullickson, Mtl	April 10, 1982

Individual Pitching (Single Inning)

MOST RUNS ALLOWED

13 .....Lefty O'Doul, Bos (A)   July 7, 1923

MOST WALKS ALLOWED

8 ....Dolly Gray, Wash   Aug 28, 1909

MOST WILD PITCHES

4 ....Walter Johnson, Wash	Sept 21, 1914
Phil Niekro, Atl	Aug 14, 1979
Kevin Gregg, Ana	July 25, 2004
Ryan Madson, Phi	July 25, 2006

Miscellaneous

LONGEST GAME, BY INNINGS

26 .....Brooklyn 1, Boston 1   May 1, 1920

LONGEST NINE-INNING GAME, BY TIME

4:45...New York (A) 14, Boston 11   Aug 18, 2006

Baseball Hall of Fame

Players

	Position	Career	Selected		Position	Career	Selected
Hank Aaron	OF	1954–76	1982	Stan Coveleski	P	1912–28	1969
Grover Alexander	P	1911–30	1938	Sam Crawford	OF	1899–1917	1957
Cap Anson	1B	1876–97	1939	Joe Cronin	SS	1926–45	1956
Luis Aparicio	SS	1956–73	1984	Candy Cummings	P	1872–77	1939
Luke Appling	SS	1930–50	1964	Kiki Cuyler	OF	1921–38	1968
Richie Ashburn	OF	1948–62	1995	Ray Dandridge*	3B		1987
Earl Averill	OF	1929–41	1975	George Davis	SS	1890–1909	1998
Jose Mendez Baez*	P	1908–26	2006	Leon Day*	P		1995
Frank Baker	3B	1908–22	1955	Dizzy Dean	P	1930–47	1953
Dave Bancroft	SS	1915–30	1971	Ed Delahanty	OF	1888–1903	1945
Ernie Banks	SS-1B	1953–71	1977	Bill Dickey	C	1928–46	1954
Jake Beckley	1B	1888–1907	1971	Martin Dihigo*	P-OF		1977
Cool Papa Bell*	OF		1974	Joe DiMaggio	OF	1936–51	1955
Johnny Bench	C	1967–83	1989	Larry Doby	OF	1947–59	1998
Chief Bender	P	1903–25	1953	Bobby Doerr	2B	1937–51	1986
Yogi Berra	C	1946–65	1972	Don Drysdale	P	1956–69	1984
Wade Boggs	3B	1982-99	2005	Hugh Duffy	OF	1888–1906	1945
Jim Bottomley	1B	1922–37	1974	Dennis Eckersley	P	1975–98	2004
Lou Boudreau	SS	1938–52	1970	Johnny Evers	2B	1902–29	1939
Roger Bresnahan	C	1897–1915	1945	Buck Ewing	C	1880–97	1946
George Brett	3B	1973–93	1999	Red Faber	P	1914–33	1964
Lou Brock	OF	1961–79	1985	Bob Feller	P	1936–56	1962
Dan Brouthers	1B	1879–1904	1945	Rick Ferrell	C	1929–47	1984
Ray Brown*	P	1930–48	2006	Rollie Fingers	P	1968–85	1992
Three Finger Brown	P	1903–16	1949	Carlton Fisk	C	1969–93	2000
Willard Jesse Brown*	OF	1935–58	2006	Elmer Flick	OF	1898–1910	1963
Jim Bunning	P	1955–71	1996	Whitey Ford	P	1950–67	1974
Jesse Burkett	OF	1890–1905	1946	Bill Foster*	P		1996
Roy Campanella	C	1948–57	1969	Nellie Fox	2B	1947–65	1997
Rod Carew	1B-2B	1967–85	1991	Jimmie Foxx	1B	1925–45	1951
Max Carey	OF	1910–29	1961	Frankie Frisch	2B	1919–37	1947
Steve Carlton	P	1965–88	1994	Pud Galvin	P	1879–92	1965
Gary Carter	C	1974–92	2003	Lou Gehrig	1B	1923–39	1939
Orlando Cepeda	1B	1958–74	1999	Charlie Gehringer	2B	1924–42	1949
Frank Chance	1B	1898–1914	1946	Bob Gibson	P	1959–75	1981
Oscar Charleston*	OF		1976	Josh Gibson*	C		1972
Jack Chesbro	P	1899–1909	1946	Lefty Gomez	P	1930–43	1972
Fred Clarke	OF	1894–1915	1945	Goose Goslin	OF	1921–38	1968
John Clarkson	P	1882–94	1963	Ulysses F. Grant*	2B	1886–1903	2006
Roberto Clemente	OF	1955–72	1973	Hank Greenberg	1B	1930–47	1956
Ty Cobb	OF	1905–28	1936	Burleigh Grimes	P	1916–34	1964
Mickey Cochrane	C	1925–37	1947	Lefty Grove	P	1925–41	1947
Eddie Collins	2B	1906–30	1939	Tony Gwynn	OF	1982–2001	2007
Jimmy Collins	3B	1895–1908	1945	Chick Hafey	OF	1924–37	1971
Earle Combs	OF	1924–35	1970	Jesse Haines	P	1918–37	1970
Roger Connor	1B	1880–97	1976	Billy Hamilton	OF	1888–1901	1961
Andrew Cooper*	P	1920–41	2006	Gabby Hartnett	C	1922–41	1955

Note: Career dates indicate first and last appearances in the majors.
*Elected on the basis of their career in the Negro leagues.

Players *(Cont.)*

Name	Position	Career	Selected
Harry Heilmann	OF	1914–32	1952
Billy Herman	2B	1931–47	1975
Jospeh Hill*	OF	1899–1925	2006
Harry Hooper	OF	1909–25	1971
Rogers Hornsby	2B	1915–37	1942
Waite Hoyt	P	1918–38	1969
Carl Hubbell	P	1928–43	1947
Catfish Hunter	P	1965–79	1987
Monte Irvin*	OF	1949–56	1973
Reggie Jackson	OF	1967–87	1993
Travis Jackson	SS	1922–36	1982
Ferguson Jenkins	P	1965–83	1991
Hugh Jennings	SS	1891–1918	1945
Judy Johnson*	3B		1975
Walter Johnson	P	1907–27	1936
Addie Joss	P	1902–10	1978
Al Kaline	OF	1953–74	1980
Tim Keefe	P	1880–93	1964
Willie Keeler	OF	1892–1910	1939
George Kell	3B	1943–57	1983
Joe Kelley	OF	1891–1908	1971
George Kelly	1B	1915–32	1973
King Kelly	C	1878–93	1945
Harmon Killebrew	1B-3B	1954–75	1984
Ralph Kiner	OF	1946–55	1975
Chuck Klein	OF	1928–44	1980
Sandy Koufax	P	1955–66	1972
Nap Lajoie	2B	1896–1916	1937
Tony Lazzeri	2B	1926–39	1991
Bob Lemon	P	1941–58	1976
Buck Leonard*	1B		1977
Fred Lindstrom	3B	1924–36	1976
Pop Lloyd*	SS-1B		1977
Ernie Lombardi	C	1931–47	1986
Ted Lyons	P	1923–46	1955
James Mackey*	C	1920–47	2006
Mickey Mantle	OF	1951–68	1974
Heinie Manush	OF	1923–39	1964
Rabbit Maranville	SS-2B	1912–35	1954
Juan Marichal	P	1960–75	1983
Rube Marquard	P	1908–25	1971
Eddie Mathews	3B	1952–68	1978
Christy Mathewson	P	1900–16	1936
Willie Mays	OF	1951–73	1979
Bill Mazeroski	2B	1956–72	2001
Tommy McCarthy	OF	1884–96	1946
Willie McCovey	1B	1959–80	1986
Joe McGinnity	P	1899–1908	1946
Bid McPhee	2B	1882–99	2000
Joe Medwick	OF	1932–48	1968
Johnny Mize	1B	1936–53	1981
Paul Molitor	3B	1978–98	2004
Joe Morgan	2B	1963–84	1990
Eddie Murray	1B	1977–97	2003
Stan Musial	OF-1B	1941–63	1969
Hal Newhouser	P	1939–55	1992
Kid Nichols	P	1890–1906	1949
Phil Niekro	P	1964–87	1997
Jim O'Rourke	OF	1876–1904	1945
Mel Ott	OF	1926–47	1951
Satchel Paige*	P	1948–65	1971
Jim Palmer	P	1965–84	1990
Herb Pennock	P	1912–34	1948
Tony Perez	1B	1964–86	2000
Gaylord Perry	P	1962–83	1991
Eddie Plank	P	1901–17	1946
Kirby Puckett	OF	1984–95	2001
Charley Radbourn	P	1880–91	1939
Pee Wee Reese	SS	1940–58	1984
Sam Rice	OF	1915–35	1963
Cal Ripken Jr.	SS	1981–2001	2007
Eppa Rixey	P	1912–33	1963
Phil Rizzuto	SS	1941–56	1994
Robin Roberts	P	1948–66	1976
Brooks Robinson	3B	1955–77	1983
Frank Robinson	OF	1956–76	1982
Jackie Robinson	2B	1947–56	1962
Joe (Bullet) Rogan*	P		1998
Edd Roush	OF	1913–31	1962
Red Ruffing	P	1924–47	1967
Amos Rusie	P	1889–1901	1977
Babe Ruth	OF	1914–35	1936
Nolan Ryan	P	1966–93	1999
Ryne Sandberg	2B	1981–97	2005
Louis Santop*	C	1909–26	2006
Ray Schalk	C	1912–29	1955
Mike Schmidt	3B	1972–89	1995
Red Schoendienst	2B	1945–63	1989
Tom Seaver	P	1967–86	1992
Joe Sewell	SS	1920–33	1977
Al Simmons	OF	1924–44	1953
George Sisler	1B	1915–30	1939
Enos Slaughter	OF	1938–59	1985
Hilton Smith*	P		2001
Ozzie Smith	SS	1978–96	2002
Duke Snider	OF	1947–64	1980
Warren Spahn	P	1942–65	1973
Al Spalding	P	1871–78	1939
Tris Speaker	OF	1907–28	1937
Willie Stargell	OF-1B	1962–82	1988
Turkey Stearns*	CF		2000
Don Sutton	P	1966–88	1998
Bruce Sutter	P	1976–88	2006
George Suttles*	C	1923–44	2006
Benjamin Harrison Taylor*	P-1B	1908–29	2006
Bill Terry	1B	1923–36	1954
Sam Thompson	OF	1885–1906	1974
Joe Tinker	SS	1902–16	1946
Cristóbal Torriente*	OF	1913–32	2006
Pie Traynor	3B	1920–37	1948
Dazzy Vance	P	1915–35	1955
Arky Vaughan	SS	1932–48	1985
Rube Waddell	P	1897–1910	1946
Honus Wagner	SS	1897–1917	1936
Bobby Wallace	SS	1894–1918	1953
Ed Walsh	P	1904–17	1946
Lloyd Waner	OF	1927–45	1967
Paul Waner	OF	1926–45	1952
John Ward	2B-P	1878–94	1964
Mickey Welch	P	1880–92	1973
Willie Wells*	SS	1924–49	1997
Zach Wheat	OF	1909–27	1959
Hoyt Wilhelm	P	1952–72	1985
Billy Williams	OF	1959–76	1987
Ted Williams	OF	1939–60	1966
Vic Willis	P	1898–1910	1995
Ernest Judson Wilson*	3B	1922–45	2006
Hack Wilson	OF	1923–34	1979
Dave Winfield	OF	1973–95	2001
Early Wynn	P	1939–63	1972
Carl Yastrzemski	OF	1961–83	1989
Cy Young	P	1890–1911	1937
Ross Youngs	OF	1917–26	1972
Robin Yount	SS	1974–93	1999

*Elected on the basis of their career in the Negro leagues.

Pioneers/Executives

	Selected
Ed Barrow (manager-executive)	1953
Morgan Bulkeley (executive)	1937
Alexander Cartwright (executive)	1938
Henry Chadwick (writer-executive)	1938
Happy Chandler (commissioner)	1982
Charles Comiskey (manager-executive)	1939
Ford Frick (commissioner-executive)	1970
Warren Giles (executive)	1979
Clark Griffith (executive)	1946
Will Harridge (executive)	1972
William Hulbert (executive)	1995
Ban Johnson (executive)	1937
Kenesaw M. Landis (commissioner)	1944
Larry MacPhail Sr. (executive)	1978
Lee MacPhail Jr. (executive)	1998
Effa Manley (owner)	2006
Alex Pompez (owner-executive)	2006
Cum Posey (player-manager-owner)	2006
Branch Rickey (manager-executive)	1967
Al Spalding (player-executive)	1939
Bill Veeck Jr. (owner)	1991
George Weiss (executive)	1971
Sol White (player-manager)	2006
J.L. Wilkinson (owner)	2006
George Wright (player-manager)	1937
Harry Wright (player-manager-executive)	1953
Tom Yawkey (executive)	1980

Managers

	Managed	Selected
Walter Alston	1954–76	1983
Sparky Anderson	1970–94	2000
Leo Durocher	1939–73	1994
Rube Foster	1907–26	1981
Bucky Harris	1924–56	1975
Ned Hanlon	1899–1907	1996
Miller Huggins	1913–29	1964
Tommy Lasorda	1977–96	1997
Al Lopez	1951–69	1977
Connie Mack	1894–1950	1937
Joe McCarthy	1926–50	1957
John McGraw	1899–1932	1937
Bill McKechnie	1915–46	1962
Wilbert Robinson	1902–31	1945
Frank Selee	1890–1905	1999
Casey Stengel	1934–65	1966
Earl Weaver	1968–82, 85–86	1996

Umpires

	Selected
Al Barlick	1989
Nestor Chylak	1999
Jocko Conlan	1974
Tom Connolly	1953
Billy Evans	1973
Cal Hubbard	1976
Bill Klem	1953
Bill McGowan	1992

Notable Achievements

No-Hit Games, Nine Innings or More
NATIONAL LEAGUE

Date	Pitcher and Game
1876......July 15	George Bradley, StL vs Hart 2–0
1880......June 12	John Richmond, Wor vs Clev 1–0 (perfect game)
June 17	Monte Ward, Prov vs Buff 5–0 (perfect game)
Aug 19	Larry Corcoran, Chi vs Bos 6–0
Aug 20	Pud Galvin, Buff vs Wor 1–0
1882......Sept 20	Larry Corcoran, Chi vs Wor 5–0
Sept 22	Tim Lovett, Bkln vs NY 4–0
1883......July 25	Hoss Radbourn, Prov vs Clev 8–0
Sept 13	Hugh Daily, Clev vs Phi 1–0
1884......June 27	Larry Corcoran, Chi vs Prov 6–0
Aug 4	Pud Galvin, Buff vs Det 18–0
1885......July 27	John Clarkson, Chi vs Prov 4–0
Aug 29	Charles Ferguson, Phi vs Prov 1–0
1891......July 31	Amos Rusie, NY vs Bkln 6–0
June 22	Tom Lovett, Bkln vs NY 4–0
1892......Aug 6	Jack Stivetts, Bos vs Bkln 11–0
Aug 22	Alex Sanders, Lou vs Balt 6–2
1892......Oct 15	Bumpus Jones, Cin vs Pitt 7–1 (first major league game)
1893......Aug 16	Bill Hawke, Balt vs Wash 5–0
1897......Sept 18	Cy Young, Clev vs Cin 6–0
1898......Apr 22	Ted Breitenstein, Cin vs Pitt 11–0
Apr 22	Jim Hughes, Balt vs Bos 8–0
July 8	Frank Donahue, Phi vs Bos 5–0
Aug 21	Walter Thornton, Chi vs Bklyn 2–0
1899......May 25	Deacon Phillippe, Lou vs NY 7–0
Aug 7	Vic Willis, Bos vs Wash 7–1
1900......July 12	Noodles Hahn, Cin vs Phi 4–0
1901......July 15	Christy Mathewson, NY vs StL 5–0
1903......Sept 18	Chick Fraser, Phi vs Chi 10–0
1904......June 11	Bob Wicker, Chi at NY 1–0 (hit in 10th; won in 12th)
1905......June 13	Christy Mathewson, NY vs Chi 1–0
1906......May 1	John Lush, Phi vs Bklyn 6–0
July 20	Mal Eason, Bklyn vs StL 2–0
1906......Aug 1	Harry McIntire, Bklyn vs Pitt 0–1 (hit in 11th; lost in 13th)
1907......May 8	Frank Pfeffer, Bos vs Cin 6–0
Sept 20	Nick Maddox, Pitt vs Bklyn 2–1
1908......July 4	George Wiltse, NY vs Phi 1–0 (10 innings)
Sept 5	Nap Rucker, Bklyn vs Bos 6–0
1909......Apr 15	Leon Ames, NY vs Bklyn 0–3 (hit in 10th; lost in 13th)
1912......Sept 6	Jeff Tesreau, NY vs Phi 3–0
1914......Sept 9	George Davis, Bos vs Phi 7–0
1915......Apr 15	Rube Marquard, NY vs Bklyn 2–0
Aug 31	Jimmy Lavender, Bklyn vs NY 2–0
1916......June 16	Tom Hughes, Bos vs Pitt 2–0
1917......May 2	Jim Vaughn, Chi vs Cin 0–1 (hit in 10th; lost in 10th)
May 2	Fred Toney, Cin vs Chi 1–0 (10 innings)

No-Hit Games, Nine Innings or More *(Cont.)*
NATIONAL LEAGUE *(Cont.)*

1919......May 11	Hod Eller, Cin vs StL 6–0	
1922......May 7	Jesse Barnes, NY vs Phi 6–0	
1924......July 17	Jesse Haines, StL vs Bos 5–0	
1925......Sept 13	Dazzy Vance, Bklyn vs Phi 10–1	
1929......May 8	Carl Hubbell, NY vs Pitt 11–0	
1934......Sept 21	Paul Dean, StL vs Bklyn 3–0	
1938......June 11	Johnny Vander Meer, Cin vs Bos 3–0	
June 15	Johnny Vander Meer, Cin vs Bklyn 6–0	
1940......Apr 30	Tex Carleton, Bklyn vs Cin, 3–0	
1941......Aug 30	Lon Warneke, StL vs Cin 2–0	
1944......Apr 27	Jim Tobin, Bos vs Bklyn 2–0	
May 15	Clyde Shoun, Cin vs Bos 1–0	
1946......Apr 23	Ed Head, Bklyn vs Bos 5–0	
1947......June 18	Ewell Blackwell, Cin vs Bos 6–0	
1948......Sept 9	Rex Barney, Bklyn vs NY 2–0	
1950......Aug 11	Vern Bickford, Bos vs Bklyn 7–0	
1951......May 6	Cliff Chambers, Pitt vs Bos 3–0	
1952......June 19	Carl Erskine, Bklyn vs Chi 5–0	
1954......June 12	Jim Wilson, Mil vs Phi 2–0	
1955......May 12	Sam Jones, Chi vs Pitt 4–0	
1956......May 12	Carl Erskine, Bklyn vs NY 3–0	
Sept 25	Sal Maglie, Bklyn vs Phi 5–0	
1959......May 26	Harvey Haddix, Pitt vs Mil 0–1	
	(hit in 13th; lost in 13th)	
1960......May 15	Don Cardwell, Chi vs StL 4–0	
Aug 18	Lew Burdette, Mil vs Phi 1–0	
Sept 16	Warren Spahn, Mil vs Phi 4–0	
1961......Apr 28	Warren Spahn, Mil vs SF 1–0	
1962......June 30	Sandy Koufax, LA vs NY 5–0	
1963......May 11	Sandy Koufax, LA vs SF 8–0	
May 17	Don Nottebart, Hou vs Phi 4–1	
June 15	Juan Marichal, SF vs Hou 1–0	
1964......Apr 23	Ken Johnson, Hou vs Cin 0–1	
June 4	Sandy Koufax, LA vs Phi 3–0	
June 21	Jim Bunning, Phi vs NY 6–0	
	(perfect game)	
1965......June 14	Jim Maloney, Cin vs NY 0–1	
	(hit in 11th; lost in 11th)	
Aug 19	Jim Maloney, Cin vs Chi 1–0	
	(10 innings)	
Sept 9	Sandy Koufax, LA vs Chi 1–0	
	(perfect game)	
1967......June 18	Don Wilson, Hou vs Atl 2–0	
1968......July 29	George Culver, Cin vs Phi 6–1	
Sept 17	Gaylord Perry, SF vs StL 1–0	
Sept 18	Ray Washburn, StL vs SF 2–0	
1969......Apr 17	Bill Stoneman, Mtl vs Phi 7–0	
Apr 30	Jim Maloney, Cin vs Hou 10–0	
May 1	Don Wilson, Hou vs Cin 4–0	
Aug 19	Ken Holtzman, Chi vs Atl 3–0	
Sept 20	Bob Moose, Pitt vs NY 4–0	
1970......June 12	Dock Ellis, Pitt vs SD 2–0	
July 20	Bill Singer, LA vs Phi 5–0	

1971......June 3	Ken Holtzman, Chi vs Cin 1–0	
June 23	Rick Wise, Phi vs Cin 4–0	
Aug 14	Bob Gibson, StL vs Pitt 11–0	
1972......Apr 16	Burt Hooton, Chi vs Phi 4–0	
Sept 2	Milt Pappas, Chi vs SD 8–0	
Oct 2	Bill Stoneman, Mtl vs NY 7–0	
1973......Aug 5	Phil Niekro, Atl vs SD 9–0	
1975......Aug 24	Ed Halicki, SF vs NY 6–0	
1976......July 9	Larry Dierker, Hou vs Mtl 6–0	
Aug 9	John Candelaria, Pitt vs LA 2–0	
Sept 29	John Montefusco, SF vs Atl 9–0	
1978......Apr 16	Bob Forsch, StL vs Phi 5–0	
June 16	Tom Seaver, Cin vs StL 4–0	
1979......Apr 7	Ken Forsch, Hou vs Atl 6–0	
1980......June 27	Jerry Reuss, LA vs SF 8–0	
1981......May 10	Charlie Lea, Mtl vs SF 4–0	
Sept 26	Nolan Ryan, Hou vs LA 5–0	
1983......Sept 26	Bob Forsch, StL vs Mtl 3–0	
1986......Sept 25	Mike Scott, Hou vs SF 2–0	
1988......Sept 16	Tom Browning, Cin vs LA 1–0	
	(perfect game)	
1990......June 29	Fernando Valenzuela, LA vs StL 6–0	
1990......Aug 15	Terry Mulholland, Phi vs SF 6–0	
1991......May 23	Tommy Greene, Phi vs Mtl 2–0	
July 26	Mark Gardner, Mtl vs LA 0–1	
	(hit in 10th, lost in 10th)	
July 28	Dennis Martinez, Mtl vs LA 2–0	
	(perfect game)	
Sept 11	Kent Mercker (6), Mark Wohlers (2),	
	and Alejandro Pena (1), Atl vs SD 1–0	
1992......Aug 17	Kevin Gross, LA vs SF 2–0	
1993......Sept 8	Darryl Kile, Hou vs NY 7–1	
1994......Apr 8	Kent Mercker, Atl vs LA 6–0	
1995......June 3	Pedro Martinez, Mtl vs SD 1–0	
	(perfect through nine, hit in 10th)	
July 14	Ramon Martinez, LA vs Fla 7–0	
1996......May 11	Al Leiter, Fla vs Col 11–0	
Sept 17	Hideo Nomo, LA vs Col 9–0	
1997......June 10	Kevin Brown, Fla vs SF 9–0	
July 12	Francisco Cordova (9) and	
	Ricardo Rincon (1), Pitt vs Col 3–0	
1999......June 25	Jose Jimenez, StL vs Ariz 1–0	
2001......May 12	A.J. Burnett, Fla vs SD 3–0	
Sept 3	Bud Smith, StL vs SD 4–0	
2003......June 11	R. Oswalt (1), P. Munro (2.2), K.	
	Saarloos (1.1), B. Lidge (2), O. Dotel	
	(1), B. Wagner (1), Hou vs NYY 8–0	
April 27	Kevin Millwood, Phi vs SF 1–0	
2004......May 18	Randy Johnson, Ariz vs Atl 2–0	
	(perfect game)	
2006......Sept 6	Anibal Sanchez, Fla vs Ariz 2–0	

Note: Includes the games struck from the official record book on Sept. 4, 1991, when baseball's committee on statistical accuracy voted to define no-hitters as games of nine innings or more that end with a team getting no hits.

No-Hit Games, Nine Innings or More *(Cont.)*

AMERICAN LEAGUE

Date	Pitcher and Game	Date	Pitcher and Game
1901......May 9	Earl Moore, Clev vs Chi 2–4 (hit in 10th; lost in 10th)	1966......Oct 8	Don Larsen, NY (A) vs Bklyn (N) 2–0 (World Series) (perfect game)
1902......Sept 20	Jimmy Callahan, Chi vs Det 3–0	1957......Aug 20	Bob Keegan, Chi vs Wash 6–0
1904......May 5	Cy Young, Bos vs Phi 3–0 (perfect game)	1958......July 20	Jim Bunning, Det vs Bos 3–0
		Sept 20	Hoyt Wilhelm, Balt vs NY 1–0
Aug 17	Jesse Tannehill, Bos vs Chi 6–0	1962......May 5	Bo Belinsky, LA vs Balt 2–0
1905......July 22	Weldon Henley, Phi vs StL 6–0	June 26	Earl Wilson, Bos vs LA 2–0
Sept 6	Frank Smith, Chi vs Det 15–0	Aug 1	Bill Monbouquette, Bos vs Chi 1–0
Sept 27	Bill Dinneen, Bos vs Chi 2–0	Aug 26	Jack Kralick, Minn vs KC 1–0
1908......June 30	Cy Young, Bos vs NY 8–0	1965......Sept 16	Dave Morehead, Bos vs Clev 2–0
Sept 18	Bob Rhoades, Clev vs Bos 2–1	1966......June 10	Sonny Siebert, Clev vs Wash 2–0
Sept 20	Frank Smith, Chi vs Phi 1–0	1967......Apr 30	Steve Barber (8⅔) and Stu Miller (⅓), Balt vs Det 1–2
1908......Oct 2	Addie Joss, Clev vs Chi 1–0 (perfect game)		
		Aug 25	Dean Chance, Minn vs Clev 2–1
1910......Apr 20	Addie Joss, Clev vs Chi 1–0	Sept 10	Joel Horlen, Chi vs Det 6–0
May 12	Chief Bender, Phi vs Clev 4–0	1968......Apr 27	Tom Phoebus, Balt vs Bos 6–0
Aug 30	Tom Hughes, NY vs Clev 0–5 (hit in 10th; lost in 11th)	May 8	Catfish Hunter, Oak vs Minn 4–0 (perfect game)
1911......July 29	Joe Wood, Bos vs StL 5–0	1969......Aug 13	Jim Palmer, Balt vs Oak 8–0
Aug 27	Ed Walsh, Chi vs Bos 5–0	1970......July 3	Clyde Wright, Cal vs Oak 4–0
1912......July 4	George Mullin, Det vs StL 7–0	Sept 21	Vida Blue, Oak vs Minn 6–0
Aug 30	Earl Hamilton, StL vs Det 5–1	1973......Apr 27	Steve Busby, KC vs Det 3–0
1914......May 14	Jim Scott, Chi vs Wash 0–1 (hit in 10th; lost in 10th)	May 15	Nolan Ryan, Cal vs KC 3–0
		July 15	Nolan Ryan, Cal vs Det 6–0
May 31	Joe Benz, Chi vs Clev 6–1	July 30	Jim Bibby, Tex vs Oak 6–0
1916......June 21	George Foster, Bos vs NY 2–0	1974......June 19	Steve Busby, KC vs Mil 2–0
Aug 26	Joe Bush, Phi vs Clev 5–0	July 19	Dick Bosman, Clev vs Oak 4–0
Aug 30	Dutch Leonard, Bos vs StL 4–0	Sept 28	Nolan Ryan, Cal vs Minn 4–0
1917......Apr 14	Ed Cicotte, Chi vs StL 11–0	1975......June 1	Nolan Ryan, Cal vs Balt 1–0
Apr 24	George Mogridge, NY vs Bos 2–1	Sept 28	Vida Blue (5), Glenn Abbott and Paul Lindblad (1), Rollie Fingers (2), Oak vs Cal 5–0
May 5	Ernie Koob, StL vs Chi 1–0		
May 6	Bob Groom, StL vs Chi 3–0		
June 23	Ernie Shore, Bos vs Wash 4–0 (perfect game)	1976......July 28	John Odom (5) and Francisco Barrios (4), Chi vs Oak 2–1
1918......June 3	Dutch Leonard, Bos vs Det 5–0	1977......May 14	Jim Colborn, KC vs Tex 6–0
1919......Sept 10	Ray Caldwell, Clev vs NY 3–0	May 30	Dennis Eckersley, Clev vs Cal 1–0
1920......July 1	Walter Johnson, Wash vs Bos 1–0		
1922......Apr 30	Charlie Robertson, Chi vs Det 2–0 (perfect game)	Sept 22	Bert Blyleven, Tex vs Cal 6–0
		1981......May 15	Len Barker, Clev vs Tor 3–0 (perfect game)
1923......Sept 4	Sam Jones, NY vs Phi 2–0		
Sept 7	Howard Ehmke, Bos vs Phi 4–0	1983......July 4	Dave Righetti, NY vs Bos 4–0
1926......Aug 21	Ted Lyons, Chi vs Bos 6–0	Sept 29	Mike Warren, Oak vs Chi 3–0
1931......Apr 29	Wes Ferrell, Clev vs StL 9–0	1984......Apr 7	Jack Morris, Det vs Chi 4–0
Aug 8	Bob Burke, Wash vs Bos 5–0	Sept 30	Mike Witt, Cal vs Tex 1–0 (perfect game)
1934......Sept 18	Bobo Newsom, StL vs Bos 1–2 (hit in 10th; lost in 10th)		
		1986......Sept 19	Joe Cowley, Chi vs Cal 7–1
1935......Aug 31	Vern Kennedy, Chi vs Clev 5–0	1987......Apr 15	Juan Nieves, Mil vs Balt 7–0
1937......June 1	Bill Dietrich, Chi vs StL 8–0	1990......Apr 11	Mark Langston (7), Mike Witt (2), Cal vs Sea 1–0
1938......Aug 27	Mtle Pearson, NY vs Clev 13–0		
1940......Apr 16	Bob Feller, Clev vs Chi 1–0 (opening day)	June 2	Randy Johnson, Sea vs Det 2–0
		June 11	Nolan Ryan, Tex vs Oak 5–0
1945......Sept 9	Dick Fowler, Phi vs StL 1–0	June 29	Dave Stewart, Oak vs Tor 5–0
1946......Apr 30	Bob Feller, Clev vs NY 1–0	1990......July 1	Andy Hawkins, NY vs Chi 0–4 (pitched eight of nine–innning game)
1947......July 10	Don Black, Clev vs Phi 3–0		
Sep 3	Bill McCahan, Phi vs Wash 3–0	Sept 2	Dave Stieb, Tor vs Clev 3–0
1948......June 30	Bob Lemon, Clev vs Det 2–0	1991......May 1	Nolan Ryan, Tex vs Tor 3–0
1951......July 1	Bob Feller, Clev vs Det 2–1	July 13	Bob Milacki (6), Mike Flanagan (1), Mark Williamson (1), and Gregg Olson (1), Balt vs Oak 2–0
July 12	Allie Reynolds, NY vs Clev 1–0		
Sept 28	Allie Reynolds, NY vs Bos 8–0		
1952......May 15	Virgil Trucks, Det vs Wash 1–0	Aug 11	Wilson Alvarez, Chi vs Balt 7–0
Aug 25	Virgil Trucks, Det vs NY 1–0	Aug 26	Bret Saberhagen, KC vs Chi 7–0
1953......May 6	Bobo Holloman, StL vs Phi 6–0 (first major league start)	1993......Apr 22	Chris Bosio, Sea vs Bos 7–0
		Sept 4	Jim Abbott, NY vs Clev 4–0
1956......July 14	Mel Parnell, Bos vs Chi 4–0		

No-Hit Games, Nine Innings or More (*Cont.*)

AMERICAN LEAGUE (*Cont.*)

1994......Apr 27	Scott Erickson, Minn vs Mil 6–0
July 28	Kenny Rogers, Texas vs Cal 4–0 (perfect game)
1996......May 14	Dwight Gooden, NY vs Sea 2–0
1998......May 17	David Wells, NY vs Minn 4–0 (perfect game)
1999......July 18	David Cone, NY vs Mtl 6–0 (perfect game)
Sept 11	Eric Milton, Minn vs Ana 7–0
2001......Apr 4	Hideo Nomo, Bos vs Balt 3–0
2002......Apr 27	Derek Lowe, Bos vs TB 10–0
2007......Apr 19	Mark Buehrle, Chi vs Tex, 6–0
June 12	Justin Verlander, Det vs Mil, 4–0
Sep 1	Clay Buchholz, Bos vs Balt, 10–0

Longest Hitting Streaks

NATIONAL LEAGUE

Player and Team	Year	G
Willie Keeler, Balt	1897	44
Pete Rose, Cin	1978	44
Bill Dahlen, Chi	1894	42
Tommy Holmes, Bos	1945	37
Billy Hamilton, Phi	1894	36
Jimmy Rollins, Phi	2005–06	36
Luis Castillo, Fla	2002	35
Fred Clarke, Lou	1895	35
Chase Utley, Phi	2006	35
Benito Santiago, SD	1987	34
George Davis, NY	1893	33
Rogers Hornsby, StL	1922	33

AMERICAN LEAGUE

Player and Team	Year	G
Joe DiMaggio, NY	1941	56
George Sisler, StL	1922	41
Ty Cobb, Det	1911	40
Paul Molitor, Mil	1987	39
Ty Cobb, Det	1917	35
George Sisler, StL	1925	34
George McQuinn, StL	1938	34
Dom DiMaggio, Bos	1949	34
Hal Chase, NY	1907	33
Heinie Manush, Wash	1933	33

Triple Crown Hitters

NATIONAL LEAGUE

Player and Team	Year	HR	RBI	BA
Paul Hines, Prov	1878	4	50	.358
Hugh Duffy, Bos	1894	18	145	.438
Heinie Zimmerman*, Chi	1912	14	103	.372
Rogers Hornsby, StL	1922	42	152	.401
	1925	39	143	.403
Chuck Klein, Phi	1933	28	120	.368
Joe Medwick, StL	1937	31	154	.374

*Zimmerman ranked first in RBIs as calculated by Ernie Lanigan, but only third as calculated by Information Concepts Inc.

AMERICAN LEAGUE

Player and Team	Year	HR	RBI	BA
Nap Lajoie, Phi	1901	14	125	.422
Ty Cobb, Det	1909	9	115	.377
Jimmie Foxx, Phi	1933	48	163	.356
Lou Gehrig, NY	1934	49	165	.363
Ted Williams, Bos	1942	36	137	.356
	1947	32	114	.343
Mickey Mantle, NY	1956	52	130	.353
Frank Robinson, Balt	1966	49	122	.316
Carl Yastrzemski, Bos	1967	44	121	.326

Triple Crown Pitchers

NATIONAL LEAGUE

Player and Team	Year	W	L	SO	ERA
Tommy Bond, Bos	1877	40	17	170	2.11
Hoss Radbourn, Prov	1884	60	12	441	1.38
Tim Keefe, NY	1888	35	12	333	1.74
John Clarkson, Bos	1889	49	19	284	2.73
Amos Rusie, NY	1894	36	13	195	2.78
Christy Mathewson, NY	1905	31	8	206	1.27
	1908	37	11	259	1.43
Grover Alexander, Phi	1915	31	10	241	1.22
	1916	33	12	167	1.55
	1917	30	13	201	1.86
Hippo Vaughn, Chi	1918	22	10	148	1.74
Dazzy Vance, Bklyn	1924	28	6	262	2.16
Bucky Walters, Cin	1939	27	11	137	2.29
Sandy Koufax, LA	1963	25	5	306	1.88
	1965	26	8	382	2.04
	1966	27	9	317	1.73
Steve Carlton, Phi	1972	27	10	310	1.97
Dwight Gooden, NY	1985	24	4	268	1.53
Randy Johnson, Ariz	2002	24	5	334	2.32

AMERICAN LEAGUE

Player and Team	Year	W	L	SO	ERA
Cy Young, Bos	1901	33	10	158	1.62
Rube Waddell, Phi	1905	26	11	287	1.48
Walter Johnson, Wash	1913	36	7	303	1.09
	1918	23	13	162	1.27
	1924	23	7	158	2.72
Lefty Grove, Phi	1930	28	5	209	2.54
	1931	31	4	175	2.06
Lefty Gomez, NY	1934	26	5	158	2.33
	1937	21	11	194	2.33
Hal Newhouser, Det	1945	25	9	212	1.81
Roger Clemens, Tor	1997	21	7	292	2.05
	1998	20	6	271	2.64
Pedro Martinez, Bos	1999	23	4	313	2.07
*Johan Santana, Min	2006	19	6	245	2.77

*Tied with another pitcher for wins

Consecutive Games Played, 500 or More Games

Cal Ripken Jr.	2,632
Lou Gehrig	2,130
Everett Scott	1,307
Steve Garvey	1,207
Miguel Tejada	1,152
Billy Williams	1,117
Joe Sewell	1,103
Stan Musial	895
Eddie Yost	829
Gus Suhr	822
Nellie Fox	798
Pete Rose	745
Dale Murphy	740
Richie Ashburn	730
Ernie Banks	717
Pete Rose	678
Earl Averill	673
Frank McCormick	652
Sandy Alomar Sr.	648
Eddie Brown	618
Roy McMillan	585
George Pinckney	577
Steve Brodie	574
Aaron Ward	565
Alex Rodriguez	546
Candy LaChance	540
Buck Freeman	535
Fred Luderus	533
Hideki Matsui	518
Clyde Milan	511
Charlie Gehringer	511
Vada Pinson	508
Tony Cuccinello	504
Charlie Gehringer	504

Unassisted Triple Plays

Player and Team	Date	Pos	Opp	Opp Batter
Neal Ball, Clev	7-19-09	SS	Bos	Amby McConnell
Bill Wambsganss, Clev	10-10-20	2B	Bklyn	Clarence Mitchell
George Burns, Bos	9-14-23	1B	Clev	Frank Brower
Ernie Padgett, Bos	10-6-23	SS	Phi	Walter Holke
Glenn Wright, Pitt	5-7-25	SS	StL	Jim Bottomley
Jimmy Cooney, Chi	5-30-27	SS	Pitt	Paul Waner
Johnny Neun, Det	5-31-27	1B	Clev	Homer Summa
Ron Hansen, Wash	7-30-68	SS	Clev	Joe Azcue
Mickey Morandini, Phi	9-20-92	2B	Pitt	Jeff King
John Valentin, Bos	7-15-94	SS	Minn	Marc Newfield
Randy Velarde, Oak	5-29-00	2B	NYY	Shane Spencer
Rafael Furcal, Atl	8-10-03	SS	StL	Woody Williams
Troy Tulowitzki, Col	4-29-07	SS	Atl	Chipper Jones

Leading Batsmen

Year	Player and Team	BA	Year	Player and Team	BA
1900	Honus Wagner, Pitt	.381	1954	Willie Mays, NY	.345
1901	Jesse Burkett, StL	.382	1955	Richie Ashburn, Phi	.338
1902	Ginger Beaumtl, Pitt	.357	1956	Hank Aaron, Mil	.328
1903	Honus Wagner, Pitt	.355	1957	Stan Musial, StL	.351
1904	Honus Wagner, Pitt	.349	1958	Richie Ashburn, Phi	.350
1905	Cy Seymour, Cin	.377	1959	Hank Aaron, Mil	.355
1906	Honus Wagner, Pitt	.339	1960	Dick Groat, Pitt	.325
1907	Honus Wagner, Pitt	.350	1961	Roberto Clemente, Pitt	.351
1908	Honus Wagner, Pitt	.354	1962	Tommy Davis, LA	.346
1909	Honus Wagner, Pitt	.339	1963	Tommy Davis, LA	.326
1910	Sherry Magee, Phi	.331	1964	Roberto Clemente, Pitt	.339
1911	Honus Wagner, Pitt	.334	1965	Roberto Clemente, Pitt	.329
1912	Heinie Zimmerman, Chi	.372	1966	Matty Alou, Pitt	.342
1913	Jake Daubert, Bklyn	.350	1967	Roberto Clemente, Pitt	.357
1914	Jake Daubert, Bklyn	.329	1968	Pete Rose, Cin	.335
1915	Larry Doyle, NY	.320	1969	Pete Rose, Cin	.348
1916	Hal Chase, Cin	.339	1970	Rico Carty, Atl	.366
1917	Edd Roush, Cin	.341	1971	Joe Torre, StL	.363
1918	Zach Wheat, Bklyn	.335	1972	Billy Williams, Chi	.333
1919	Edd Roush, Cin	.321	1973	Pete Rose, Cin	.338
1920	Rogers Hornsby, StL	.370	1974	Ralph Garr, Atl	.353
1921	Rogers Hornsby, StL	.397	1975	Bill Madlock, Chi	.354
1922	Rogers Hornsby, StL	.401	1976	Bill Madlock, Chi	.339
1923	Rogers Hornsby, StL	.384	1977	Dave Parker, Pitt	.338
1924	Rogers Hornsby, StL	.424	1978	Dave Parker, Pitt	.334
1925	Rogers Hornsby, StL	.403	1979	Keith Hernandez, StL	.344
1926	Bubbles Hargrave, Cin	.353	1980	Bill Buckner, Chi	.324
1927	Paul Waner, Pitt	.380	1981	Bill Madlock, Pitt	.341
1928	Rogers Hornsby, Bos	.387	1982	Al Oliver, Mtl	.331
1929	Lefty O'Doul, Phi	.398	1983	Bill Madlock, Pitt	.323
1930	Bill Terry, NY	.401	1984	Tony Gwynn, SD	.351
1931	Chick Hafey, StL	.349	1985	Willie McGee, StL	.353
1932	Lefty O'Doul, Bklyn	.368	1986	Tim Raines, Mtl	.334
1933	Chuck Klein, Phi	.368	1987	Tony Gwynn, SD	.370
1934	Paul Waner, Pitt	.362	1988	Tony Gwynn, SD	.313
1935	Arky Vaughan, Pitt	.385	1989	Tony Gwynn, SD	.336
1936	Paul Waner, Pitt	.373	1990	Willie McGee, StL	.335
1937	Joe Medwick, StL	.374	1991	Terry Pendleton, Atl	.319
1938	Ernie Lombardi, Cin	.342	1992	Gary Sheffield, SD	.330
1939	Johnny Mize, StL	.349	1993	Andres Galarraga, Col	.370
1940	Debs Garms, Pitt	.355	1994	Tony Gwynn, SD	.394
1941	Pete Reiser, Bklyn	.343	1995	Tony Gwynn, SD	.368
1942	Ernie Lombardi, Bos	.330	1996	Tony Gwynn, SD	.353
1943	Stan Musial, StL	.357	1997	Tony Gwynn, SD	.372
1944	Dixie Walker, Bklyn	.357	1998	Larry Walker, Col	.363
1945	Phil Cavarretta, Chi	.355	1999	Larry Walker, Col	.379
1946	Stan Musial, StL	.365	2000	Todd Helton, Col	.372
1947	Harry Walker, StL-Phi	.363	2001	Larry Walker, Col	.350
1948	Stan Musial, StL	.376	2002	Barry Bonds, SF	.370
1949	Jackie Robinson, Bklyn	.342	2003	Albert Pujols, StL	.359
1950	Stan Musial, StL	.346	2004	Barry Bonds, SF	.362
1951	Stan Musial, StL	.355	2005	Derrek Lee, Chi	.335
1952	Stan Musial, StL	.336	2006	Freddy Sanchez, Pitt	.334
1953	Carl Furillo, Bklyn	.344	2007	Matt Holliday, Col	.340*

*includes NL Wild Card tiebreaker

Leaders in Runs Scored

Year	Player and Team	Runs	Year	Player and Team	Runs
1900	Roy Thomas, Phi	131	1954	Stan Musial, StL	120
1901	Jesse Burkett, StL	139		Duke Snider, Bklyn	120
1902	Honus Wagner, Pitt	105	1955	Duke Snider, Bklyn	126
1903	Ginger Beaumont, Pitt	137	1956	Frank Robinson, Cin	122
1904	George Browne, NY	99	1957	Hank Aaron, Mil	118
1905	Mike Donlin, NY	124	1958	Willie Mays, SF	121
1906	Honus Wagner, Pitt	103	1959	Vada Pinson, Cin	131
	Frank Chance, Chi	103	1960	Bill Bruton, Mil	112
1907	Spike Shannon, NY	104	1961	Willie Mays, SF	129
1908	Fred Tenney, NY	101	1962	Frank Robinson, Cin	134
1909	Tommy Leach, Pitt	126	1963	Hank Aaron, Mil	121
1910	Sherry Magee, Phi	110	1964	Dick Allen, Phi	125
1911	Jimmy Sheckard, Chi	121	1965	Tommy Harper, Cin	126
1912	Bob Bescher, Cin	120	1966	Felipe Alou, Atl	122
1913	Tommy Leach, Chi	99	1967	Hank Aaron, Atl	113
	Max Carey, Pitt	99		Lou Brock, StL	113
1914	George Burns, NY	100	1968	Glenn Beckert, Chi	98
1915	Gavvy Cravath, Phi	89	1969	Bobby Bonds, SF	120
1916	George Burns, NY	105		Pete Rose, Cin	120
1917	George Burns, NY	103	1970	Billy Williams, Chi	137
1918	Heinie Groh, Cin	88	1971	Lou Brock, StL	126
1919	George Burns, NY	86	1972	Joe Morgan, Cin	122
1920	George Burns, NY	115	1973	Bobby Bonds, SF	131
1921	Rogers Hornsby, StL	131	1974	Pete Rose, Cin	110
1922	Rogers Hornsby, StL	141	1975	Pete Rose, Cin	112
1923	Ross Youngs, NY	121	1976	Pete Rose, Cin	130
1924	Frankie Frisch, NY	121	1977	George Foster, Cin	124
	Rogers Hornsby, StL	121	1978	Ivan DeJesus, Chi	104
1925	Kiki Cuyler, Pitt	144	1979	Keith Hernandez, StL	116
1926	Kiki Cuyler, Pitt	113	1980	Keith Hernandez, StL	111
1927	Lloyd Waner, Pitt	133	1981	Mike Schmidt, Phi	78
	Rogers Hornsby, NY	133	1982	Lonnie Smith, StL	120
1928	Paul Waner, Pitt	142	1983	Tim Raines, Mtl	133
1929	Rogers Hornsby, Chi	156	1984	Ryne Sandberg, Chi	114
1930	Chuck Klein, Phi	158	1985	Dale Murphy, Atl	118
1931	Bill Terry, NY	121	1986	Von Hayes, Phi	107
	Chuck Klein, Phi	121		Tony Gwynn, SD	107
1932	Chuck Klein, Phi	152	1987	Tim Raines, Mtl	123
1933	Pepper Martin, StL	122	1988	Brett Butler, SF	109
1934	Paul Waner, Pitt	122	1989	Howard Johnson, NY	104
1935	Augie Galan, Chi	133		Will Clark, SF	104
1936	Arky Vaughan, Pitt	122		Ryne Sandberg, Chi	104
1937	Joe Medwick, StL	111	1990	Ryne Sandberg, Chi	116
1938	Mel Ott, NY	116	1991	Brett Butler, LA	112
1939	Billy Werber, Cin	115	1992	Barry Bonds, Pitt	109
1940	Arky Vaughan, Pitt	113	1993	Lenny Dykstra, Phi	143
1941	Pete Reiser, Bklyn	117	1994	Jeff Bagwell, Hou	104
1942	Mel Ott, NY	118	1995	Craig Biggio, Hou	123
1943	Arky Vaughan, Bklyn	112	1996	Ellis Burks, Col	142
1944	Bill Nicholson, Chi	116	1997	Craig Biggio, Hou	146
1945	Eddie Stanky, Bklyn	128	1998	Sammy Sosa, Chi	134
1946	Stan Musial, StL	124	1999	Jeff Bagwell, Hou	143
1947	Johnny Mize, NY	137	2000	Jeff Bagwell, Hou	152
1948	Stan Musial, StL	135	2001	Sammy Sosa, Chi	146
1949	Pee Wee Reese, Bklyn	132	2002	Sammy Sosa, Chi	122
1950	Earl Torgeson, Bos	120	2003	Albert Pujols, StL	137
1951	Stan Musial, StL	124	2004	Albert Pujols, StL	133
	Ralph Kiner, Pitt	124	2005	Albert Pujols, StL	129
1952	Stan Musial, StL	105	2006	Chase Utley, Phi	131
	Solly Hemus, StL	105	2007	Jimmy Rollins, Phi	139
1953	Duke Snider, Bklyn	132			

Leaders in Hits

Year	Player and Team	Hits	Year	Player and Team	Hits
1900	Willie Keeler, Bklyn	208	1956	Hank Aaron, Mil	200
1901	Jesse Burkett, StL	228	1957	Red Schoendienst, NY-Mil	200
1902	Ginger Beaumont, Pitt	194	1958	Richie Ashburn, Phi	215
1903	Ginger Beaumont, Pitt	209	1959	Hank Aaron, Mil	223
1904	Ginger Beaumont, Pitt	185	1960	Willie Mays, SF	190
1905	Cy Seymour, Cin	219	1961	Vada Pinson, Cin	208
1906	Harry Steinfeldt, Chi	176	1962	Tommy Davis, LA	230
1907	Ginger Beaumont, Bos	187	1963	Vada Pinson, Cin	204
1908	Honus Wagner, Pitt	201	1964	Roberto Clemente, Pitt	211
1909	Larry Doyle, NY	172		Curt Flood, StL	211
1910	Honus Wagner, Pitt	178	1965	Pete Rose, Cin	209
	Bobby Byrne, Pitt	178	1966	Felipe Alou, Atl	218
1911	Doc Miller, Bos	192	1967	Roberto Clemente, Pitt	209
1912	Heinie Zimmerman, Chi	207	1968	Felipe Alou, Atl	210
1913	Gavvy Cravath, Phi	179		Pete Rose, Cin	210
1914	Sherry Magee, Phi	171	1969	Matty Alou, Pitt	231
1915	Larry Doyle, NY	189	1970	Pete Rose, Cin	205
1916	Hal Chase, Cin	184		Billy Williams, Chi	205
1917	Heinie Groh, Cin	182	1971	Joe Torre, StL	230
1918	Charlie Hollocher, Chi	161	1972	Pete Rose, Cin	198
1919	Ivy Olson, Bklyn	164	1973	Pete Rose, Cin	230
1920	Rogers Hornsby, StL	218	1974	Ralph Garr, Atl	214
1921	Rogers Hornsby, StL	235	1975	Dave Cash, Phi	213
1922	Rogers Hornsby, StL	250	1976	Pete Rose, Cin	215
1923	Frankie Frisch, NY	223	1977	Dave Parker, Pitt	215
1924	Rogers Hornsby, StL	227	1978	Steve Garvey, LA	202
1925	Jim Bottomley, StL	227	1979	Garry Templeton, StL	211
1926	Eddie Brown, Bos	201	1980	Steve Garvey, LA	200
1927	Paul Waner, Pitt	237	1981	Pete Rose, Phi	140
1928	Freddy Lindstrom, NY	231	1982	Al Oliver, Mtl	204
1929	Lefty O'Doul, Phi	254	1983	Jose Cruz, Hou	189
1930	Bill Terry, NY	254		Andre Dawson, Mtl	189
1931	Lloyd Waner, Pitt	214	1984	Tony Gwynn, SD	213
1932	Chuck Klein, Phi	226	1985	Willie McGee, StL	216
1933	Chuck Klein, Phi	223	1986	Tony Gwynn, SD	211
1934	Paul Waner, Pitt	217	1987	Tony Gwynn, SD	218
1935	Billy Herman, Chi	227	1988	Andres Galarraga, Mtl	184
1936	Joe Medwick, StL	223	1989	Tony Gwynn, SD	203
1937	Joe Medwick, StL	237	1990	Brett Butler, SF	192
1938	Frank McCormick, Cin	209		Lenny Dykstra, Phi	192
1939	Frank McCormick, Cin	209	1991	Terry Pendleton, Atl	187
1940	Stan Hack, Chi	191	1992	Terry Pendleton, Atl	199
	Frank McCormick, Cin	191		Andy Van Slyke, Pitt	199
1941	Stan Hack, Chi	186	1993	Lenny Dykstra, Phi	194
1942	Enos Slaughter, StL	188	1994	Tony Gwynn, SD	165
1943	Stan Musial, StL	220	1995	Dante Bichette, Col	197
1944	Stan Musial, StL	197		Tony Gwynn, SD	197
	Phil Cavarretta, Chi	197	1996	Lance Johnson, NY	227
1945	Tommy Holmes, Bos	224	1997	Tony Gwynn, SD	220
1946	Stan Musial, StL	228	1998	Dante Bichette, Col	219
1947	Tommy Holmes, Bos	191	1999	Luis Gonzalez, Ariz	206
1948	Stan Musial, StL	230	2000	Todd Helton, Col	216
1949	Stan Musial, StL	207	2001	Rich Aurilia, SF	206
1950	Duke Snider, Bklyn	199	2002	Vladimir Guerrero	206
1951	Richie Ashburn, Phi	221	2003	Albert Pujols, StL	212
1952	Stan Musial, StL	194	2004	Juan Pierre, Fla	221
1953	Richie Ashburn, Phi	205	2005	Derrek Lee, Chi	199
1954	Don Mueller, NY	212	2006	Juan Pierre, Chi	204
1955	Ted Kluszewski, Cin	192	2007	Matt Holliday, Col	216*

*includes NL Wild Card tiebreaker

Home Run Leaders

Year	Player and Team	HR	Year	Player and Team	HR
1900	Herman Long, Bos	12	1951	Ralph Kiner, Pitt	42
1901	Sam Crawford, Cin	16	1952	Ralph Kiner, Pitt	37
1902	Tommy Leach, Pitt	6		Hank Sauer, Chi	37
1903	Jimmy Sheckard, Bklyn	9	1953	Eddie Mathews, Mil	47
1904	Harry Lumley, Bklyn	9	1954	Ted Kluszewski, Cin	49
1905	Fred Odwell, Cin	9	1955	Willie Mays, NY	51
1906	Tim Jordan, Bklyn	12	1956	Duke Snider, Bklyn	43
1907	Dave Brain, Bos	10	1957	Hank Aaron, Mil	44
1908	Tim Jordan, Bklyn	12	1958	Ernie Banks, Chi	47
1909	Red Murray, NY	7	1959	Eddie Mathews, Mil	46
1910	Fred Beck, Bos	10	1960	Ernie Banks, Chi	41
	Wildfire Schulte, Chi	10	1961	Orlando Cepeda, SF	46
1911	Wildfire Schulte, Chi	21	1962	Willie Mays, SF	49
1912	Heinie Zimmerman, Chi	14	1963	Hank Aaron, Mil	44
1913	Gavvy Cravath, Phi	19		Willie McCovey, SF	44
1914	Gavvy Cravath, Phi	19	1964	Willie Mays, SF	47
1915	Gavvy Cravath, Phi	24	1965	Willie Mays, SF	52
1916	Dave Robertson, NY	12	1966	Hank Aaron, Atl	44
	Cy Williams, Chi	12	1967	Hank Aaron, Atl	39
1917	Dave Robertson, NY	12	1968	Willie McCovey, SF	36
	Gavvy Cravath, Phi	12	1969	Willie McCovey, SF	45
1918	Gavvy Cravath, Phi	8	1970	Johnny Bench, Cin	45
1919	Gavvy Cravath, Phi	12	1971	Willie Stargell, Pitt	48
1920	Cy Williams, Phi	15	1972	Johnny Bench, Cin	40
1921	George Kelly, NY	23	1973	Willie Stargell, Pitt	44
1922	Rogers Hornsby, StL	42	1974	Mike Schmidt, Phi	36
1923	Cy Williams, Phi	41	1975	Mike Schmidt, Phi	38
1924	Jack Fournier, Bklyn	27	1976	Mike Schmidt, Phi	38
1925	Rogers Hornsby, StL	39	1977	George Foster, Cin	52
1926	Hack Wilson, Chi	21	1978	George Foster, Cin	40
1927	Hack Wilson, Chi	30	1979	Dave Kingman, Chi	48
	Cy Williams, Phi	30	1980	Mike Schmidt, Phi	48
1928	Hack Wilson, Chi	31	1981	Mike Schmidt, Phi	31
	Jim Bottomley, StL	31	1982	Dave Kingman, NY	37
1929	Chuck Klein, Phi	43	1983	Mike Schmidt, Phi	40
1930	Hack Wilson, Chi	56	1984	Dale Murphy, Atl	36
1931	Chuck Klein, Phi	31		Mike Schmidt, Phi	36
1932	Chuck Klein, Phi	38	1985	Dale Murphy, Atl	37
	Mel Ott, NY	38	1986	Mike Schmidt, Phi	37
1933	Chuck Klein, Phi	28	1987	Andre Dawson, Chi	49
1934	Ripper Collins, StL	35	1988	Darryl Strawberry, NY	39
	Mel Ott, NY	35	1989	Kevin Mitchell, SF	47
1935	Wally Berger, Bos	34	1990	Ryne Sandberg, Chi	40
1936	Mel Ott, NY	33	1991	Howard Johnson, NY	38
1937	Mel Ott, NY	31	1992	Fred McGriff, SD	35
	Joe Medwick, StL	31	1993	Barry Bonds, SF	46
1938	Mel Ott, NY	36	1994	Matt Williams, SF	43
1939	Johnny Mize, StL	28	1995	Dante Bichette, Col	40
1940	Johnny Mize, StL	43	1996	Andres Galarraga, Col	47
1941	Dolph Camilli, Bklyn	34	1997	Larry Walker, Col	49
1942	Mel Ott, NY	30	1998	Mark McGwire, StL	70
1943	Bill Nicholson, Chi	29	1999	Mark McGwire, StL	65
1944	Bill Nicholson, Chi	33	2000	Sammy Sosa, Chi	50
1945	Tommy Holmes, Bos	28	2001	Barry Bonds, SF	73
1946	Ralph Kiner, Pitt	23	2002	Sammy Sosa, Chi	49
1947	Ralph Kiner, Pitt	51	2003	Jim Thome, Phi	47
	Johnny Mize, NY	51	2004	Adrian Beltre, LA	48
1948	Ralph Kiner, Pitt	40	2005	Andruw Jones, Atl	51
	Johnny Mize, NY	40	2006	Ryan Howard, Phi	58
1949	Ralph Kiner, Pitt	54	2007	Prince Fielder, Mil	50
1950	Ralph Kiner, Pitt	47			

Runs Batted In Leaders

Year	Player and Team	RBI	Year	Player and Team	RBI
1900	Elmer Flick, Phi	110	1955	Duke Snider, Bklyn	136
1901	Honus Wagner, Pitt	126	1956	Stan Musial, StL	109
1902	Honus Wagner, Pitt	91	1957	Hank Aaron, Mil	132
1903	Sam Mertes, NY	104	1958	Ernie Banks, Chi	129
1904	Bill Dahlen, NY	80	1959	Ernie Banks, Chi	143
1905	Cy Seymour, Cin	121	1960	Hank Aaron, Mil	126
1906	Jim Nealon, Pitt	83	1961	Orlando Cepeda, SF	142
	Harry Steinfeldt, Chi	83	1962	Tommy Davis, LA	153
1907	Sherry Magee, Phi	85	1963	Hank Aaron, Mil	130
1908	Honus Wagner, Pitt	109	1964	Ken Boyer, StL	119
1909	Honus Wagner, Pitt	100	1965	Deron Johnson, Cin	130
1910	Sherry Magee, Phi	123	1966	Hank Aaron, Atl	127
1911	Wildfire Schulte, Chi	121	1967	Orlando Cepeda, StL	111
1912	Heinie Zimmerman, Chi	103	1968	Willie McCovey, SF	105
1913	Gavvy Cravath, Phi	128	1969	Willie McCovey, SF	126
1914	Sherry Magee, Phi	103	1970	Johnny Bench, Cin	148
1915	Gavvy Cravath, Phi	115	1971	Joe Torre, StL	137
1916	Heinie Zimmerman, Chi-NY	83	1972	Johnny Bench, Cin	125
1917	Heinie Zimmerman, NY	102	1973	Willie Stargell, Pitt	119
1918	Sherry Magee, Phi	76	1974	Johnny Bench, Cin	129
1919	Hi Myers, Bklyn	73	1975	Greg Luzinski, Phi	120
1920	George Kelly, NY	94	1976	George Foster, Cin	121
	Rogers Hornsby, StL	94	1977	George Foster, Cin	149
1921	Rogers Hornsby, StL	126	1978	George Foster, Cin	120
1922	Rogers Hornsby, StL	152	1979	Dave Winfield, SD	118
1923	Irish Meusel, NY	125	1980	Mike Schmidt, Phi	121
1924	George Kelly, NY	136	1981	Mike Schmidt, Phi	91
1925	Rogers Hornsby, StL	143	1982	Dale Murphy, Atl	109
1926	Jim Bottomley, StL	120		Al Oliver, Mtl	109
1927	Paul Waner, Pitt	131	1983	Dale Murphy, Atl	121
1928	Jim Bottomley, StL	136	1984	Gary Carter, Mtl	106
1929	Hack Wilson, Chi	159		Mike Schmidt, Phi	106
1930	Hack Wilson, Chi	190	1985	Dave Parker, Cin	125
1931	Chuck Klein, Phi	121	1986	Mike Schmidt, Phi	119
1932	Don Hurst, Phi	143	1987	Andre Dawson, Chi	137
1933	Chuck Klein, Phi	120	1988	Will Clark, SF	109
1934	Mel Ott, NY	135	1989	Kevin Mitchell, SF	125
1935	Wally Berger, Bos	130	1990	Matt Williams, SF	122
1936	Joe Medwick, StL	138	1991	Howard Johnson, NY	117
1937	Joe Medwick, StL	154	1992	Darren Daulton, Phi	109
1938	Joe Medwick, StL	122	1993	Barry Bonds, SF	123
1939	Frank McCormick, Cin	128	1994	Jeff Bagwell, Hou	116
1940	Johnny Mize, StL	137	1995	Dante Bichette, Col	128
1941	Dolph Camilli, Bklyn	120	1996	Andres Galarraga, Col	150
1942	Johnny Mize, NY	110	1997	Andres Galarraga, Col	140
1943	Bill Nicholson, Chi	128	1998	Sammy Sosa, Chi	158
1944	Bill Nicholson, Chi	122	1999	Mark McGwire, StL	147
1945	Dixie Walker, Bklyn	124	2000	Todd Helton, Col	147
1946	Enos Slaughter, StL	130	2001	Sammy Sosa, Chi	160
1947	Johnny Mize, NY	138	2002	Lance Berkman, Hou	128
1948	Stan Musial, StL	131	2003	Preston Wilson, Col	141
1949	Ralph Kiner, Pitt	127	2004	Vinny Castilla, Col	131
1950	Del Ennis, Phi	126	2005	Andruw Jones, Atl	128
1951	Monte Irvin, NY	121	2006	Ryan Howard, Phi	149
1952	Hank Sauer, Chi	121	2007	Matt Holliday, Col	137*
1953	Roy Campanella, Bklyn	142			
1954	Ted Kluszewski, Cin	141			

*includes NL Wild Card tiebreaker

Leading Base Stealers

Year	Player and Team	SB	Year	Player and Team	SB
1900	George Van Haltren, NY	45	1953	Bill Bruton, Mil	26
	Patsy Donovan, StL	45	1954	Bill Bruton, Mil	34
1901	Honus Wagner, Pitt	48	1955	Bill Bruton, Mil	35
1902	Honus Wagner, Pitt	43	1956	Willie Mays, NY	40
1903	Jimmy Sheckard, Bklyn	67	1957	Willie Mays, NY	38
	Frank Chance, Chi	67	1958	Willie Mays, SF	31
1904	Honus Wagner, Pitt	53	1959	Willie Mays, SF	27
1905	Billy Maloney, Chi	59	1960	Maury Wills, LA	50
	Art Devlin, NY	59	1961	Maury Wills, LA	35
1906	Frank Chance, Chi	57	1962	Maury Wills, LA	104
1907	Honus Wagner, Pitt	61	1963	Maury Wills, LA	40
1908	Honus Wagner, Pitt	53	1964	Maury Wills, LA	53
1909	Bob Bescher, Cin	54	1965	Maury Wills, LA	94
1910	Bob Bescher, Cin	70	1966	Lou Brock, StL	74
1911	Bob Bescher, Cin	80	1967	Lou Brock, StL	52
1912	Bob Bescher, Cin	67	1968	Lou Brock, StL	62
1913	Max Carey, Pitt	61	1969	Lou Brock, StL	53
1914	George Burns, NY	62	1970	Bobby Tolan, Cin	57
1915	Max Carey, Pitt	36	1971	Lou Brock, StL	64
1916	Max Carey, Pitt	63	1972	Lou Brock, StL	63
1917	Max Carey, Pitt	46	1973	Lou Brock, StL	70
1918	Max Carey, Pitt	58	1974	Lou Brock, StL	118
1919	George Burns, NY	40	1975	Davey Lopes, LA	77
1920	Max Carey, Pitt	52	1976	Davey Lopes, LA	63
1921	Frankie Frisch, NY	49	1977	Frank Taveras, Pitt	70
1922	Max Carey, Pitt	51	1978	Omar Moreno, Pitt	71
1923	Max Carey, Pitt	51	1979	Omar Moreno, Pitt	77
1924	Max Carey, Pitt	49	1980	Ron LeFlore, Mtl	97
1925	Max Carey, Pitt	46	1981	Tim Raines, Mtl	71
1926	Kiki Cuyler, Pitt	35	1982	Tim Raines, Mtl	78
1927	Frankie Frisch, StL	48	1983	Tim Raines, Mtl	90
1928	Kiki Cuyler, Chi	37	1984	Tim Raines, Mtl	75
1929	Kiki Cuyler, Chi	43	1985	Vince Coleman, StL	110
1930	Kiki Cuyler, Chi	37	1986	Vince Coleman, StL	107
1931	Frankie Frisch, StL	28	1987	Vince Coleman, StL	109
1932	Chuck Klein, Phi	20	1988	Vince Coleman, StL	81
1933	Pepper Martin, StL	26	1989	Vince Coleman, StL	65
1934	Pepper Martin, StL	23	1990	Vince Coleman, StL	77
1935	Augie Galan, Chi	22	1991	Marquis Grissom, Mtl	76
1936	Pepper Martin, StL	23	1992	Marquis Grissom, Mtl	78
1937	Augie Galan, Chi	23	1993	Chuck Carr, Fla	58
1938	Stan Hack, Chi	16	1994	Craig Biggio, Hou	39
1939	Stan Hack, Chi	17	1995	Quilvio Veras, Fla	56
	Lee Handley, Pitt	17	1996	Eric Young, Col	53
1940	Lonny Frey, Cin	22	1997	Tony Womack, Pitt	60
1941	Danny Murtaugh, Phi	18	1998	Tony Womack, Pitt	58
1942	Pete Reiser, Bklyn	20	1999	Tony Womack, Ariz	72
1943	Arky Vaughan, Bklyn	20	2000	Luis Castillo, Fla	62
1944	Johnny Barrett, Pitt	28	2001	Juan Pierre, Col	46
1945	Red Schoendienst, StL	26	2002	Luis Castillo, Fla	48
1946	Pete Reiser, Bklyn	34	2003	Juan Pierre, Fla	65
1947	Jackie Robinson, Bklyn	29	2004	Scott Podsednik, Mil	70
1948	Richie Ashburn, Phi	32	2005	Jose Reyes, NY	60
1949	Jackie Robinson, Bklyn	37	2006	Jose Reyes, NY	64
1950	Sam Jethroe, Bos	35	2007	Jose Reyes, NY	78
1951	Sam Jethroe, Bos	35			
1952	Pee Wee Reese, Bklyn	30			

Leading Pitchers—Winning Percentage

Year	Pitcher and Team	W	L	Pct	Year	Pitcher and Team	W	L	Pct
1900	Jesse Tannehill, Pitt	20	6	.769	1955	Don Newcombe, Bklyn	20	5	.800
1901	Jack Chesbro, Pitt	21	10	.677	1956	Don Newcombe, Bklyn	27	7	.794
1902	Jack Chesbro, Pitt	28	6	.824	1957	Bob Buhl, Mil	18	7	.720
1903	Sam Leever, Pitt	25	7	.781	1958	Warren Spahn, Mil	22	11	.667
1904	Joe McGinnity, NY	35	8	.814		Lew Burdette, Mil	20	10	.667
1905	Sam Leever, Pitt	20	5	.800	1959	Roy Face, Pitt	18	1	.947
1906	Ed Reulbach, Chi	19	4	.826	1960	Ernie Broglio, StL	21	9	.700
1907	Ed Reulbach, Chi	17	4	.810	1961	Johnny Podres, LA	18	5	.783
1908	Ed Reulbach, Chi	24	7	.774	1962	Bob Purkey, Cin	23	5	.821
1909	Christy Mathewson, NY	25	6	.806	1963	Ron Perranoski, LA	16	3	.842
	Howie Camnitz, Pitt	25	6	.806	1964	Sandy Koufax, LA	19	5	.792
1910	King Cole, Chi	20	4	.833	1965	Sandy Koufax, LA	26	8	.765
1911	Rube Marquard, NY	24	7	.774	1966	Juan Marichal, SF	25	6	.806
1912	Claude Hendrix, Pitt	24	9	.727	1967	Dick Hughes, StL	16	6	.727
1913	Bert Humphries, Chi	16	4	.800	1968	Steve Blass, Pitt	18	6	.750
1914	Bill James, Bos	26	7	.788	1969	Tom Seaver, NY	25	7	.781
1915	Grover Alexander, Phi	31	10	.756	1970	Bob Gibson, StL	23	7	.767
1916	Tom Hughes, Bos	16	3	.842	1971	Don Gullett, Cin	16	6	.727
1917	Ferdie Schupp, NY	21	7	.750	1972	Gary Nolan, Cin	15	5	.750
1918	Claude Hendrix, Chi	19	7	.731	1973	Tommy John, LA	16	7	.696
1919	Dutch Ruether, Cin	19	6	.760	1974	Andy Messersmith, LA	20	6	.769
1920	Burleigh Grimes, Bklyn	23	11	.676	1975	Don Gullett, Cin	15	4	.789
1921	Bill Doak, StL	15	6	.714	1976	Steve Carlton, Phi	20	7	.741
1922	Pete Donohue, Cin	18	9	.667	1977	John Candelaria, Pitt	20	5	.800
1923	Dolf Luque, Cin	27	8	.771	1978	Gaylord Perry, SD	21	6	.778
1924	Emil Yde, Pitt	16	3	.842	1979	Tom Seaver, Cin	16	6	.727
1925	Bill Sherdel, StL	15	6	.714	1980	Jim Bibby, Pitt	19	6	.760
1926	Ray Kremer, Pitt	20	6	.769	1981*	Tom Seaver, Cin	14	2	.875
1927	Larry Benton, Bos-NY	17	7	.708	1982	Phil Niekro, Atl	17	4	.810
1928	Larry Benton, NY	25	9	.735	1983	John Denny, Phi	19	6	.760
1929	Charlie Root, Chi	19	6	.760	1984	Rick Sutcliffe, Chi	16	1	.941
1930	Freddie Fitzsimmons, NY	19	7	.731	1985	Orel Hershiser, LA	19	3	.864
1931	Paul Derringer, StL	18	8	.692	1986	Bob Ojeda, NY	18	5	.783
1932	Lon Warneke, Chi	22	6	.786	1987	Dwight Gooden, NY	15	7	.682
1933	Ben Cantwell, Bos	20	10	.667	1988	David Cone, NY	20	3	.870
1934	Dizzy Dean, StL	30	7	.811	1989	Mike Bielecki, Chi	18	7	.720
1935	Bill Lee, Chi	20	6	.769	1990	Doug Drabeck, Pitt	22	6	.786
1936	Carl Hubbell, NY	26	6	.813	1991	John Smiley, Pitt	20	8	.714
1937	Carl Hubbell, NY	22	8	.733		Jose Rijo, Cin	15	6	.714
1938	Bill Lee, Chi	22	9	.710	1992	Bob Tewksbury, StL	16	5	.762
1939	Paul Derringer, Cin	25	7	.781	1993	Tom Glavine, Atl	22	6	.786
1940	Freddie Fitzsimmons, Bklyn	16	2	.889	1994	Ken Hill, Mtl	16	5	.762
1941	Elmer Riddle, Cin	19	4	.826	1995	Greg Maddux, Atl	19	2	.905
1942	Larry French, Bklyn	15	4	.789	1996	John Smoltz, Atl	24	8	.750
1943	Mort Cooper, StL	21	8	.724	1997	Denny Neagle, Atl	20	5	.800
1944	Ted Wilks, StL	17	4	.810	1998	John Smoltz, Atl	17	3	.850
1945	Harry Brecheen, StL	15	4	.789	1999	Mike Hampton, Hou	22	4	.846
1946	Murray Dickson, StL	15	6	.714	2000	Randy Johnson, Ariz	19	7	.730
1947	Larry Jansen, NY	21	5	.808	2001	Curt Schilling, Ariz	22	6	.786
1948	Harry Brecheen, StL	20	7	.741	2002	Randy Johnson, Ariz	24	5	.828
1949	Preacher Roe, Bklyn	15	6	.714	2003	Jason Schmidt, SF	17	5	.773
1950	Sal Maglie, NY	18	4	.818	2004	Roger Clemens, Hou	18	4	.818
1951	Preacher Roe, Bklyn	22	3	.880	2005	Chris Carpenter, StL	21	5	.808
1952	Hoyt Wilhelm, NY	15	3	.833	2006	Carlos Zambrano, Chi	16	7	.695
1953	Carl Erskine, Bklyn	20	6	.769	2007	Brad Penny, LAD	16	4	.800
1954	Johnny Antonelli, NY	21	7	.750					

*1981 percentages based on 10 or more victories. Note: Percentages based on 15 or more victories in all other years.

Leading Pitchers—Earned Run Average

Year	Player and Team	ERA	Year	Player and Team	ERA
1900	Rube Waddell, Pitt	2.37	1954	Johnny Antonelli, NY	2.29
1901	Jesse Tannehill, Pitt	2.18	1955	Bob Friend, Pitt	2.84
1902	Jack Taylor, Chi	1.33	1956	Lew Burdette, Mil	2.71
1903	Sam Leever, Pitt	2.06	1957	Johnny Podres, Bklyn	2.66
1904	Joe McGinnity, NY	1.61	1958	Stu Miller, SF	2.47
1905	Christy Mathewson, NY	1.27	1959	Sam Jones, SF	2.82
1906	Three Finger Brown, Chi	1.04	1960	Mike McCormick, SF	2.70
1907	Jack Pfiester, Chi	1.15	1961	Warren Spahn, Mil	3.01
1908	Christy Mathewson, NY	1.43	1962	Sandy Koufax, LA	2.54
1909	Christy Mathewson, NY	1.14	1963	Sandy Koufax, LA	1.88
1910	George McQuillan, Phi	1.60	1964	Sandy Koufax, LA	1.74
1911	Christy Mathewson, NY	1.99	1965	Sandy Koufax, LA	2.04
1912	Jeff Tesreau, NY	1.96	1966	Sandy Koufax, LA	1.73
1913	Christy Mathewson, NY	2.06	1967	Phil Niekro, Atl	1.87
1914	Bill Doak, StL	1.72	1968	Bob Gibson, StL	1.12
1915	Grover Alexander, Phi	1.22	1969	Juan Marichal, SF	2.10
1916	Grover Alexander, Phi	1.55	1970	Tom Seaver, NY	2.81
1917	Grover Alexander, Phi	1.83	1971	Tom Seaver, NY	1.76
1918	Hippo Vaughn, Chi	1.74	1972	Steve Carlton, Phi	1.98
1919	Grover Alexander, Chi	1.72	1973	Tom Seaver, NY	2.08
1920	Grover Alexander, Chi	1.91	1974	Buzz Capra, Atl	2.28
1921	Bill Doak, StL	2.58	1975	Randy Jones, SD	2.24
1922	Rosy Ryan, NY	3.00	1976	John Denny, StL	2.52
1923	Dolf Luque, Cin	1.93	1977	John Candelaria, Pitt	2.34
1924	Dazzy Vance, Bklyn	2.16	1978	Craig Swan, NY	2.43
1925	Dolf Luque, Cin	2.63	1979	J.R. Richard, Hou	2.71
1926	Ray Kremer, Pitt	2.61	1980	Don Sutton, LA	2.21
1927	Ray Kremer, Pitt	2.47	1981	Nolan Ryan, Hou	1.69
1928	Dazzy Vance, Bklyn	2.09	1982	Steve Rogers, Mtl	2.40
1929	Bill Walker, NY	3.08	1983	Atlee Hammaker, SF	2.25
1930	Dazzy Vance, Bklyn	2.61	1984	Alejandro Pena, LA	2.48
1931	Bill Walker, NY	2.26	1985	Dwight Gooden, NY	1.53
1932	Lon Warneke, Chi	2.37	1986	Mike Scott, Hou	2.22
1933	Carl Hubbell, NY	1.66	1987	Nolan Ryan, Hou	2.76
1934	Carl Hubbell, NY	2.30	1988	Joe Magrane, StL	2.18
1935	Cy Blanton, Pitt	2.59	1989	Scott Garrelts, SF	2.28
1936	Carl Hubbell, NY	2.31	1990	Danny Darwin, Hou	2.21
1937	Jim Turner, Bos	2.38	1991	Dennis Martinez, Mtl	2.39
1938	Bill Lee, Chi	2.66	1992	Bill Swift, SF	2.08
1939	Bucky Walters, Cin	2.29	1993	Greg Maddux, Atl	2.36
1940	Bucky Walters, Cin	2.48	1994	Greg Maddux, Atl	1.56
1941	Elmer Riddle, Cin	2.24	1995	Greg Maddux, Atl	1.63
1942	Mort Cooper, StL	1.77	1996	Kevin Brown, Fla	1.89
1943	Howie Pollet, StL	1.75	1997	Pedro Martinez, Mtl	1.90
1944	Ed Heusser, Cin	2.38	1998	Greg Maddux, Atl	1.98
1945	Hank Borowy, Chi	2.14	1999	Randy Johnson, Ariz	2.48
1946	Howie Pollet, StL	2.10	2000	Kevin Brown, LA	2.58
1947	Warren Spahn, Bos	2.33	2001	Randy Johnson, Ariz	2.49
1948	Harry Brecheen, StL	2.24	2002	Randy Johnson, Ariz	2.32
1949	Dave Koslo, NY	2.50	2003	Jason Schmidt, SF	2.34
1950	Jim Hearn, StL-NY	2.49	2004	Jake Peavy, SD	2.27
1951	Chet Nichols, Bos	2.88	2005	Roger Clemens, Hou	1.87
1952	Hoyt Wilhelm, NY	2.43	2006	Roy Oswalt, Hou	2.98
1953	Warren Spahn, Mil	2.10	2007	Jake Peavy, SD	2.54*

*includes NL Wild Card tiebreaker

Note: Based on 10 complete games through 1950, then 154 innings until National League expanded in 1962, when it became 162 innings. In strike-shortened 1981, one inning per game required.

Leading Pitchers—Strikeouts

Year	Player and Team	SO	Year	Player and Team	SO
1900	Rube Waddell, Pitt	133	1953	Robin Roberts, Phi	198
1901	Noodles Hahn, Cin	233	1954	Robin Roberts, Phi	185
1902	Vic Willis, Bos	226	1955	Sam Jones, Chi	198
1903	Christy Mathewson, NY	267	1956	Sam Jones, Chi	176
1904	Christy Mathewson, NY	212	1957	Jack Sanford, Phi	188
1905	Christy Mathewson, NY	206	1958	Sam Jones, StL	225
1906	Fred Beebe, Chi-StL	171	1959	Don Drysdale, LA	242
1907	Christy Mathewson, NY	178	1960	Don Drysdale, LA	246
1908	Christy Mathewson, NY	259	1961	Sandy Koufax, LA	269
1909	Orval Overall, Chi	205	1962	Don Drysdale, LA	232
1910	Christy Mathewson, NY	190	1963	Sandy Koufax, LA	306
1911	Rube Marquard, NY	237	1964	Bob Veale, Pitt	250
1912	Grover Alexander, Phi	195	1965	Sandy Koufax, LA	382
1913	Tom Seaton, Phi	168	1966	Sandy Koufax, LA	317
1914	Grover Alexander, Phi	214	1967	Jim Bunning, Phi	253
1915	Grover Alexander, Phi	241	1968	Bob Gibson, StL	268
1916	Grover Alexander, Phi	167	1969	Ferguson Jenkins, Chi	273
1917	Grover Alexander, Phi	200	1970	Tom Seaver, NY	283
1918	Hippo Vaughn, Chi	148	1971	Tom Seaver, NY	289
1919	Hippo Vaughn, Chi	141	1972	Steve Carlton, Phi	310
1920	Grover Alexander, Chi	173	1973	Tom Seaver, NY	251
1921	Burleigh Grimes, Bklyn	136	1974	Steve Carlton, Phi	240
1922	Dazzy Vance, Bklyn	134	1975	Tom Seaver, NY	243
1923	Dazzy Vance, Bklyn	197	1976	Tom Seaver, NY	235
1924	Dazzy Vance, Bklyn	262	1977	Phil Niekro, Atl	262
1925	Dazzy Vance, Bklyn	221	1978	J.R. Richard, Hou	303
1926	Dazzy Vance, Bklyn	140	1979	J.R. Richard, Hou	313
1927	Dazzy Vance, Bklyn	184	1980	Steve Carlton, Phi	286
1928	Dazzy Vance, Bklyn	200	1981	Fernando Valenzuela, LA	180
1929	Pat Malone, Chi	166	1982	Steve Carlton, Phi	286
1930	Bill Hallahan, StL	177	1983	Steve Carlton, Phi	275
1931	Bill Hallahan, StL	159	1984	Dwight Gooden, NY	276
1932	Dizzy Dean, StL	191	1985	Dwight Gooden, NY	268
1933	Dizzy Dean, StL	199	1986	Mike Scott, Hou	306
1934	Dizzy Dean, StL	195	1987	Nolan Ryan, Hou	270
1935	Dizzy Dean, StL	182	1988	Nolan Ryan, Hou	228
1936	Van Lingle Mungo, Bklyn	238	1989	Jose DeLeon, StL	201
1937	Carl Hubbell, NY	159	1990	David Cone, NY	233
1938	Clay Bryant, Chi	135	1991	David Cone, NY	241
1939	Claude Passeau, Phi-Chi	137	1992	John Smoltz, Atl	215
	Bucky Walters, Cin	137	1993	Jose Rijo, Cin	227
1940	Kirby Higbe, Phi	137	1994	Andy Benes, SD	189
1941	Johnny Vander Meer, Cin	202	1995	Hideo Nomo, LA	236
1942	Johnny Vander Meer, Cin	186	1996	John Smoltz, Atl	276
1943	Johnny Vander Meer, Cin	174	1997	Curt Schilling, Phi	319
1944	Bill Voiselle, NY	161	1998	Curt Schilling, Phi	300
1945	Preacher Roe, Pitt	148	1999	Randy Johnson, Ariz	364
1946	Johnny Schmitz, Chi	135	2000	Randy Johnson, Ariz	347
1947	Ewell Blackwell, Cin	193	2001	Randy Johnson, Ariz	372
1948	Harry Brecheen, StL	149	2002	Randy Johnson, Ariz	334
1949	Warren Spahn, Bos	151	2003	Kerry Wood, Chi	266
1950	Warren Spahn, Bos	191	2004	Randy Johnson, Ariz	290
1951	Warren Spahn, Bos	164	2005	Jake Peavy, SD	216
	Don Newcombe, Bklyn	164	2006	Aaron Harang, Cin	216
1952	Warren Spahn, Bos	183	2007	Jake Peavy, SD	240*

*includes NL Wild Card tiebreaker

Leading Pitchers—Saves

Year	Player and Team	SV	Year	Player and Team	SV
1947	Hugh Casey, Bklyn	18	1977	Rollie Fingers, SD	35
1948	Harry Gumpert, Cin	17	1978	Rollie Fingers, SD	37
1949	Ted Wilks, StL	9	1979	Bruce Sutter, Chi	37
1950	Jim Konstanty, Phi	22	1980	Bruce Sutter, Chi	28
1951	Ted Wilks, StL, Pitt	13	1981	Bruce Sutter, StL	25
1952	Al Brazle, StL	16	1982	Bruce Sutter, StL	36
1953	Al Brazle, StL	18	1983	Lee Smith, Chi	29
1954	Jim Hughes, Bklyn	24	1984	Bruce Sutter, StL	45
1955	Jack Meyer, Phi	16	1985	Jeff Reardon, Mtl	41
1956	Clem Labine, Bklyn	19	1986	Todd Worrell, StL	36
1957	Clem Labine, Bklyn	17	1987	Steve Bedrosian, Phi	40
1958	Roy Face, Pitt	20	1988	John Franco, Cin	39
1959	Lindy McDaniel, StL	15	1989	Mark Davis, SD	44
	Don McMahon, Mil	15	1990	John Franco, NY	33
1960	Lindy McDaniel, StL	26	1991	Lee Smith, StL	47
1961	Stu Miller, SF	17	1992	Lee Smith, StL	42
	Roy Face, Pitt	17	1993	Randy Myers, Chi	53
1962	Roy Face, Pitt	28	1994	John Franco, NY	30
1963	Lindy McDaniel, Chi	22	1995	Randy Myers, Chi	38
1964	Hal Woodeshick, Hou	23	1996	Jeff Brantley, Cin	44
1965	Ted Abernathy, Chi	31		Todd Worrell, LA	44
1966	Phil Regan, LA	21	1997	Jeff Shaw, Cin	42
1967	Ted Abernathy, Cin	28	1998	Trevor Hoffman, SD	53
1968	Phi Regan, Chi,.LA	25	1999	Ugueth Urbina, Mtl	41
1969	Fred Gladding, Hou	29	2000	Antonio Alfonseca, Fla	45
1970	Wayne Granger, Cin	35	2001	Robb Nen, SF	45
1971	Dave Giusti, Pitt	30	2002	John Smoltz, Atl	55
1972	Clay Carroll, Cin	37	2003	Eric Gagne, LA	55
1973	Mike Marshall, Mtl	13	2004	Armando Benitez, Fla	47
1974	Mike Marshall, LA	21		Jason Isringhausen, StL	47
1975	Al Hrabosky, StL	22	2005	Chad Cordero, Wash	47
	Rawly Eastwick, Cin	22	2006	Trevor Hoffman, SD	46
1976	Rawly Eastwick, Cin	26	2007	Jose Valverde, Ariz	47

Leading Batsmen

Year	Player and Team	BA	Year	Player and Team	BA
1901	Nap Lajoie, Phi	.422	1955	Al Kaline, Det	.340
1902	Ed Delahanty, Wash	.376	1956	Mickey Mantle, NY	.353
1903	Nap Lajoie, Clev	.355	1957	Ted Williams, Bos	.388
1904	Nap Lajoie, Clev	.381	1958	Ted Williams, Bos	.328
1905	Elmer Flick, Clev	.306	1959	Harvey Kuenn, Det	.353
1906	George Stone, StL	.358	1960	Pete Runnels, Bos	.320
1907	Ty Cobb, Det	.350	1961	Norm Cash, Det	.361
1908	Ty Cobb, Det	.324	1962	Pete Runnels, Bos	.326
1909	Ty Cobb, Det	.377	1963	Carl Yastrzemski, Bos	.321
1910	Nap Lajoie, Clev*	.383	1964	Tony Oliva, Minn	.323
1911	Ty Cobb, Det	.420	1965	Tony Oliva, Minn	.321
1912	Ty Cobb, Det	.410	1966	Frank Robinson, Balt	.316
1913	Ty Cobb, Det	.390	1967	Carl Yastrzemski, Bos	.326
1914	Ty Cobb, Det	.368	1968	Carl Yastrzemski, Bos	.301
1915	Ty Cobb, Det	.369	1969	Rod Carew, Minn	.332
1916	Tris Speaker, Clev	.386	1970	Alex Johnson, Cal	.329
1917	Ty Cobb, Det	.383	1971	Tony Oliva, Minn	.337
1918	Ty Cobb, Det	.382	1972	Rod Carew, Minn	.318
1919	Ty Cobb, Det	.384	1973	Rod Carew, Minn	.350
1920	George Sisler, StL	.407	1974	Rod Carew, Minn	.364
1921	Harry Heilmann, Det	.394	1975	Rod Carew, Minn	.359
1922	George Sisler, StL	.420	1976	George Brett, KC	.333
1923	Harry Heilmann, Det	.403	1977	Rod Carew, Minn	.388
1924	Babe Ruth, NY	.378	1978	Rod Carew, Minn	.333
1925	Harry Heilmann, Det	.393	1979	Fred Lynn, Bos	.333
1926	Heinie Manush, Det	.378	1980	George Brett, KC	.390
1927	Harry Heilmann, Det	.398	1981	Carney Lansford, Bos	.336
1928	Goose Goslin, Wash	.379	1982	Willie Wilson, KC	.332
1929	Lew Fonseca, Clev	.369	1983	Wade Boggs, Bos	.361
1930	Al Simmons, Phi	.381	1984	Don Mattingly, NY	.343
1931	Al Simmons, Phi	.390	1985	Wade Boggs, Bos	.368
1932	Dale Alexander, Det-Bos	.367	1986	Wade Boggs, Bos	.357
1933	Jimmie Foxx, Phi	.356	1987	Wade Boggs, Bos	.363
1934	Lou Gehrig, NY	.363	1988	Wade Boggs, Bos	.366
1935	Buddy Myer, Wash	.349	1989	Kirby Puckett, Minn	.339
1936	Luke Appling, Chi	.388	1990	George Brett, KC	.329
1937	Charlie Gehringer, Det	.371	1991	Julio Franco, Tex	.341
1938	Jimmie Foxx, Bos	.349	1992	Edgar Martinez, Sea	.343
1939	Joe DiMaggio, NY	.381	1993	John Olerud, Tor	.363
1940	Joe DiMaggio, NY	.352	1994	Paul O'Neill, NY	.359
1941	Ted Williams, Bos	.406	1995	Edgar Martinez, Sea	.356
1942	Ted Williams, Bos	.356	1996	Alex Rodriguez, Sea	.358
1943	Luke Appling, Chi	.328	1997	Frank Thomas, Chi	.347
1944	Lou Boudreau, Clev	.327	1998	Bernie Williams, NY	.339
1945	Snuffy Stirnweiss, NY	.309	1999	Nomar Garciaparra, Bos	.357
1946	Mickey Vernon, Wash	.353	2000	Nomar Garciaparra, Bos	.372
1947	Ted Williams, Bos	.343	2001	Ichiro Suzuki, Sea	.350
1948	Ted Williams, Bos	.369	2002	Manny Ramirez, Bos	.349
1949	George Kell, Det	.343	2003	Bill Mueller, Bos	.326
1950	Billy Goodman, Bos	.354	2004	Ichiro Suzuki, Sea	.372
1951	Ferris Fain, Phi	.344	2005	Michael Young, Tex	.331
1952	Ferris Fain, Phi	.327	2006	Joe Mauer, Minn	.347
1953	Mickey Vernon, Wash	.337	2007	Magglio Ordonez, Det	.363
1954	Bobby Avila, Clev	.341			

*League president Ban Johnson declared Ty Cobb batting champion with a .385 average, beating Lajoie's .384. However, subsequent research has led to the revision of Lajoie's average to .383 and Cobb's to .382.

Leaders in Runs Scored

Year	Player and Team	Runs	Year	Player and Team	Runs
1901	Nap Lajoie, Phi	145	1956	Mickey Mantle, NY	132
1902	Dave Fultz, Phi	110	1957	Mickey Mantle, NY	121
1903	Patsy Dougherty, Bos	108	1958	Mickey Mantle, NY	127
1904	Patsy Dougherty, Bos-NY	113	1959	Eddie Yost, Det	115
1905	Harry Davis, Phi	92	1960	Mickey Mantle, NY	119
1906	Elmer Flick, Clev	98	1961	Mickey Mantle, NY	132
1907	Sam Crawford, Det	102		Roger Maris, NY	132
1908	Matty McIntyre, Det	105	1962	Albie Pearson, LA	115
1909	Ty Cobb, Det	116	1963	Bob Allison, Minn	99
1910	Ty Cobb, Det	106	1964	Tony Oliva, Minn	109
1911	Ty Cobb, Det	147	1965	Zoilo Versalles, Minn	126
1912	Eddie Collins, Phi	137	1966	Frank Robinson, Balt	122
1913	Eddie Collins, Phi	125	1967	Carl Yastrzemski, Bos	112
1914	Eddie Collins, Phi	122	1968	Dick McAuliffe, Det	95
1915	Ty Cobb, Det	144	1969	Reggie Jackson, Oak	123
1916	Ty Cobb, Det	113	1970	Carl Yastrzemski, Bos	125
1917	Donie Bush, Det	112	1971	Don Buford, Balt	99
1918	Ray Chapman, Clev	84	1972	Bobby Murcer, NY	102
1919	Babe Ruth, Bos	103	1973	Reggie Jackson, Oak	99
1920	Babe Ruth, NY	158	1974	Carl Yastrzemski, Bos	93
1921	Babe Ruth, NY	177	1975	Fred Lynn, Bos	103
1922	George Sisler, StL	134	1976	Roy White, NY	104
1923	Babe Ruth, NY	151	1977	Rod Carew, Minn	128
1924	Babe Ruth, NY	143	1978	Ron LeFlore, Det	126
1925	Johnny Mostil, Chi	135	1979	Don Baylor, Cal	120
1926	Babe Ruth, NY	139	1980	Willie Wilson, KC	133
1927	Babe Ruth, NY	158	1981	Rickey Henderson, Oak	89
1928	Babe Ruth, NY	163	1982	Paul Molitor, Mil	136
1929	Charlie Gehringer, Det	131	1983	Cal Ripken, Balt	121
1930	Al Simmons, Phi	152	1984	Dwight Evans, Bos	121
1931	Lou Gehrig, NY	163	1985	Rickey Henderson, NY	146
1932	Jimmie Foxx, Phi	151	1986	Rickey Henderson, NY	130
1933	Lou Gehrig, NY	138	1987	Paul Molitor, Mil	114
1934	Charlie Gehringer, Det	134	1988	Wade Boggs, Bos	128
1935	Lou Gehrig, NY	125	1989	Rickey Henderson, NY-Oak	113
1936	Lou Gehrig, NY	167		Wade Boggs, Bos	113
1937	Joe DiMaggio, NY	151	1990	Rickey Henderson, Oak	119
1938	Hank Greenberg, Det	144	1991	Paul Molitor, Mil	133
1939	Red Rolfe, NY	139	1992	Tony Philips, Det	114
1940	Ted Williams, Bos	134	1993	Rafael Palmeiro, Tex	124
1941	Ted Williams, Bos	135	1994	Frank Thomas, Chi	106
1942	Ted Williams, Bos	141	1995	Albert Belle, Clev	121
1943	George Case, Wash	102		Edgar Martinez, Sea	121
1944	Snuffy Stirnweiss, NY	125	1996	Alex Rodriguez, Sea	141
1945	Snuffy Stirnweiss, NY	107	1997	Ken Griffey Jr., Sea	125
1946	Ted Williams, Bos	142	1998	Derek Jeter, NY	127
1947	Ted Williams, Bos	125	1999	Roberto Alomar, Clev	138
1948	Tommy Henrich, NY	138	2000	Johnny Damon, KC	136
1949	Ted Williams, Bos	150	2001	Alex Rodriguez, Tex	133
1950	Dom DiMaggio, Bos	131	2002	Alfonso Soriano, NY	128
1951	Dom DiMaggio, Bos	113	2003	Alex Rodriguez, Tex	124
1952	Larry Doby, Clev	104	2004	Vladimir Guerrero, Ana	124
1953	Al Rosen, Clev	115	2005	Alex Rodriguez, NY	124
1954	Mickey Mantle, NY	129	2006	Grady Sizemore, Clev	134
1955	Al Smith, Clev	123	2007	Alex Rodriguez, NY	143

Leaders in Hits

Year	Player and Team	Hits	Year	Player and Team	Hits
1901	Nap Lajoie, Phi	229	1954	Nellie Fox, Chi	201
1902	Piano Legs Hickman, Bos-Clev	194		Harvey Kuenn, Det	201
1903	Patsy Dougherty, Bos	195	1955	Al Kaline, Det	200
1904	Nap Lajoie, Clev	211	1956	Harvey Kuenn, Det	196
1905	George Stone, StL	187	1957	Nellie Fox, Chi	196
1906	Nap Lajoie, Clev	214	1958	Nellie Fox, Chi	187
1907	Ty Cobb, Det	212	1959	Harvey Kuenn, Det	198
1908	Ty Cobb, Det	188	1960	Minnie Minoso, Chi	184
1909	Ty Cobb, Det	216	1961	Norm Cash, Det	193
1910	Nap Lajoie, Clev	227	1962	Bobby Richardson, NY	209
1911	Ty Cobb, Det	248	1963	Carl Yastrzemski, Bos	183
1912	Ty Cobb, Det	227	1964	Tony Oliva, Minn	217
1913	Joe Jackson, Clev	197	1965	Tony Oliva, Minn	185
1914	Tris Speaker, Bos	193	1966	Tony Oliva, Minn	191
1915	Ty Cobb, Det	208	1967	Carl Yastrzemski, Bos	189
1916	Tris Speaker, Clev	211	1968	Bert Campaneris, Oak	177
1917	Ty Cobb, Det	225	1969	Tony Oliva, Minn	197
1918	George Burns, Phi	178	1970	Tony Oliva, Minn	204
1919	Ty Cobb, Det	191	1971	Cesar Tovar, Minn	204
	Bobby Veach, Det	191	1972	Joe Rudi, Oak	181
1920	George Sisler, StL	257	1973	Rod Carew, Minn	203
1921	Harry Heilmann, Det	237	1974	Rod Carew, Minn	218
1922	George Sisler, StL	246	1975	George Brett, KC	195
1923	Charlie Jamieson, Clev	222	1976	George Brett, KC	215
1924	Sam Rice, Wash	216	1977	Rod Carew, Minn	239
1925	Al Simmons, Phi	253	1978	Jim Rice, Bos	213
1926	George Burns, Clev	216	1979	George Brett, KC	212
	Sam Rice, Wash	216	1980	Willie Wilson, KC	230
1927	Earle Combs, NY	231	1981	Rickey Henderson, Oak	135
1928	Heinie Manush, StL	241	1982	Robin Yount, Mil	210
1929	Dale Alexander, Det	215	1983	Cal Ripken Jr., Balt	211
	Charlie Gehringer, Det	215	1984	Don Mattingly, NY	207
1930	Johnny Hodapp, Clev	225	1985	Wade Boggs, Bos	240
1931	Lou Gehrig, NY	211	1986	Don Mattingly, NY	238
1932	Al Simmons, Phi	216	1987	Kirby Puckett, Minn	207
1933	Heinie Manush, Wash	221		Kevin Seitzer, KC	207
1934	Charlie Gehringer, Det	214	1988	Kirby Puckett, Minn	234
1935	Joe Vosmik, Clev	216	1989	Kirby Puckett, Minn	215
1936	Earl Averill, Clev	232	1990	Rafael Palmeiro, Tex	191
1937	Beau Bell, StL	218	1991	Paul Molitor, Mil	216
1938	Joe Vosmik, Bos	201	1992	Kirby Puckett, Minn	210
1939	Red Rolfe, NY	213	1993	Paul Molitor, Tor	211
1940	Rip Radcliff, StL	200	1994	Kenny Lofton, Clev	160
	Barney McCosky, Det	200	1995	Lance Johnson, Chi	186
	Doc Cramer, Bos	200	1996	Paul Molitor, Minn	225
1941	Cecil Travis, Wash	218	1997	Nomar Garciaparra, Bos	209
1942	Johnny Pesky, Bos	205	1998	Alex Rodriguez, Sea	213
1943	Dick Wakefield, Det	200	1999	Derek Jeter, NY	219
1944	Snuffy Stirnweiss, NY	205	2000	Darin Erstad, Ana	240
1945	Snuffy Stirnweiss, NY	195	2001	Ichiro Suzuki, Sea	242
1946	Johnny Pesky, Bos	208	2002	Alfonso Soriano, NY	209
1947	Johnny Pesky, Bos	207	2003	Vernon Wells, Tor	215
1948	Bob Dillinger, StL	207	2004	Ichiro Suzuki, Sea	262
1949	Dale Mitchell, Clev	203	2005	Michael Young, Tex	221
1950	George Kell, Det	218	2006	Ichiro Suzuki, Sea	224
1951	George Kell, Det	191	2007	Ichiro Suzuki, Sea	238
1952	Nellie Fox, Chi	192			
1953	Harvey Kuenn, Det	209			

Home Run Leaders

Year	Player and Team	HR	Year	Player and Team	HR
1901	Nap Lajoie, Phi	13	1959	Rocky Colavito, Clev	42
1902	Socks Seybold, Phi	16		Harmon Killebrew, Wash	42
1903	Buck Freeman, Bos	13	1960	Mickey Mantle, NY	40
1904	Harry Davis, Phi	10	1961	Roger Maris, NY	61
1905	Harry Davis, Phi	8	1962	Harmon Killebrew, Minn	48
1906	Harry Davis, Phi	12	1963	Harmon Killebrew, Minn	45
1907	Harry Davis, Phi	8	1964	Harmon Killebrew, Minn	49
1908	Sam Crawford, Det	7	1965	Tony Conigliaro, Bos	32
1909	Ty Cobb, Det	9	1966	Frank Robinson, Balt	49
1910	Jake Stahl, Bos	10	1967	Harmon Killebrew, Minn	44
1911	Frank Baker, Phi	9		Carl Yastrzemski, Bos	44
1912	Frank Baker, Phi	10	1968	Frank Howard, Wash	44
	Tris Speaker, Bos	10	1969	Harmon Killebrew, Minn	49
1913	Frank Baker, Phi	13	1970	Frank Howard, Wash	44
1914	Frank Baker, Phi	9	1971	Bill Melton, Chi	33
1915	Braggo Roth, Chi-Clev	7	1972	Dick Allen, Chi	37
1916	Wally Pipp, NY	12	1973	Reggie Jackson, Oak	32
1917	Wally Pipp, NY	9	1974	Dick Allen, Chi	32
1918	Babe Ruth, Bos	11	1975	Reggie Jackson, Oak	36
	Tilly Walker, NY	11		George Scott, Mil	36
1919	Babe Ruth, Bos	29	1976	Graig Nettles, NY	32
1920	Babe Ruth, NY	54	1977	Jim Rice, Bos	39
1921	Babe Ruth, NY	59	1978	Jim Rice, Bos	46
1922	Ken Williams, StL	39	1979	Gorman Thomas, Mil	45
1923	Babe Ruth, NY	41	1980	Reggie Jackson, NY	41
1924	Babe Ruth, NY	46		Ben Oglivie, Mil	41
1925	Bob Meusel, NY	33	1981	Tony Armas, Oak	22
1926	Babe Ruth, NY	47	1981	Dwight Evans, Bos	22
1927	Babe Ruth, NY	60		Bobby Grich, Cal	22
1928	Babe Ruth, NY	54		Eddie Murray, Balt	22
1929	Babe Ruth, NY	46	1982	Reggie Jackson, Cal	39
1930	Babe Ruth, NY	49		Gorman Thomas, Mil	39
1931	Babe Ruth/ Lou Gehrig NY	46	1983	Jim Rice, Bos	39
1932	Jimmie Foxx, Phi	58	1984	Tony Armas, Bos	43
1933	Jimmie Foxx, Phi	48	1985	Darrell Evans, Det	40
1934	Lou Gehrig, NY	49	1986	Jesse Barfield, Tor	40
1935	Jimmie Foxx, Phi	36	1987	Mark McGwire, Oak	49
	Hank Greenberg, Det	36	1988	Jose Canseco, Oak	42
1936	Lou Gehrig, NY	49	1989	Fred McGriff, Tor	36
1937	Joe DiMaggio, NY	46	1990	Cecil Fielder, Det	51
1938	Hank Greenberg, Det	58	1991	Jose Canseco, Oak	44
1939	Jimmie Foxx, Bos	35		Cecil Fielder, Det	44
1940	Hank Greenberg, Det	41	1992	Juan Gonzalez, Tex	43
1941	Ted Williams, Bos	37	1993	Juan Gonzalez, Tex	46
1942	Ted Williams, Bos	36	1994	Ken Griffey Jr., Sea	40
1943	Rudy York, Det	34	1995	Albert Belle, Clev	50
1944	Nick Etten, NY	22	1996	Mark McGwire, Oak	52
1945	Vern Stephens, StL	24	1997	Ken Griffey Jr., Sea	56
1946	Hank Greenberg, Det	44	1998	Ken Griffey Jr., Sea	56
1947	Ted Williams, Bos	32	1999	Ken Griffey Jr., Sea	48
1948	Joe DiMaggio, NY	39	2000	Troy Glaus, Ana	47
1949	Ted Williams, Bos	43	2001	Alex Rodriguez, Tex	52
1950	Al Rosen, Clev	37	2002	Alex Rodriguez, Tex	57
1951	Gus Zernial, Chi-Phi	33	2003	Alex Rodriguez, Tex	47
1952	Larry Doby, Clev	32	2004	Manny Ramirez, Bos	43
1953	Al Rosen, Clev	43	2005	Alex Rodriguez, NY	48
1954	Larry Doby, Clev	32	2006	David Ortiz, Bos	54
1955	Mickey Mantle, NY	37	2007	Alex Rodriguez, NY	54
1956	Mickey Mantle, NY	52			
1957	Roy Sievers, Wash	42			
1958	Mickey Mantle, NY	42			

Runs Batted In Leaders

Year	Player and Team	RBI	Year	Player and Team	RBI
1907	Ty Cobb, Det	116	1957	Roy Sievers, Wash	114
1908	Ty Cobb, Det	108	1958	Jackie Jensen, Bos	122
1909	Ty Cobb, Det	107	1959	Jackie Jensen, Bos	112
1910	Sam Crawford, Det	120	1960	Roger Maris, NY	112
1911	Ty Cobb, Det	144	1961	Roger Maris, NY	142
1912	Frank Baker, Phi	133	1962	Harmon Killebrew, Minn	126
1913	Frank Baker, Phi	126	1963	Dick Stuart, Bos	118
1914	Sam Crawford, Det	104	1964	Brooks Robinson, Balt	118
1915	Sam Crawford, Det	112	1965	Rocky Colavito, Clev	108
	Bobby Veach, Det	112	1966	Frank Robinson, Balt	122
1916	Del Pratt, StL	103	1967	Carl Yastrzemski, Bos	121
1917	Bobby Veach, Det	103	1968	Ken Harrelson, Bos	109
1918	Bobby Veach, Det	78	1969	Harmon Killebrew, Minn	140
1919	Babe Ruth, Bos	114	1970	Frank Howard, Wash	126
1920	Babe Ruth, NY	137	1971	Harmon Killebrew, Minn	119
1921	Babe Ruth, NY	171	1972	Dick Allen, Chi	113
1922	Ken Williams, StL	155	1973	Reggie Jackson, Oak	117
1923	Babe Ruth, NY	131	1974	Jeff Burroughs, Tex	118
1924	Goose Goslin, Wash	129	1975	George Scott, Mil	109
1925	Bob Meusel, NY	138	1976	Lee May, Balt	109
1926	Babe Ruth, NY	145	1977	Larry Hisle, Minn	119
1927	Lou Gehrig, NY	175	1978	Jim Rice, Bos	139
1928	Babe Ruth/ Lou Gehrig, NY	142	1979	Don Baylor, Cal	139
1929	Al Simmons, Phi	157	1980	Cecil Cooper, Mil	122
1930	Lou Gehrig, NY	174	1981	Eddie Murray, Balt	78
1931	Lou Gehrig, NY	184	1982	Hal McRae, KC	133
1932	Jimmie Foxx, Phi	169	1983	Cecil Cooper, Mil	126
1933	Jimmie Foxx, Phi	163		Jim Rice, Bos	126
1934	Lou Gehrig, NY	165	1984	Tony Armas, Bos	123
1935	Hank Greenberg, Det	170	1985	Don Mattingly, NY	145
1936	Hal Trosky, Clev	162	1986	Joe Carter, Clev	121
1937	Hank Greenberg, Det	183	1987	George Bell, Tor	134
1938	Jimmie Foxx, Bos	175	1988	Jose Canseco, Oak	124
1939	Ted Williams, Bos	145	1989	Ruben Sierra, Tex	119
1940	Hank Greenberg, Det	150	1990	Cecil Fielder, Det	132
1941	Joe DiMaggio, NY	125	1991	Cecil Fielder, Det	133
1942	Ted Williams, Bos	137	1992	Cecil Fielder, Det	124
1943	Rudy York, Det	118	1993	Albert Belle, Clev	129
1944	Vern Stephens, StL	109	1994	Kirby Puckett, Minn	112
1945	Nick Etten, NY	111	1995	Albert Belle, Clev	126
1946	Hank Greenberg, Det	127		Mo Vaughn, Bos	126
1947	Ted Williams, Bos	114	1996	Albert Belle, Clev	148
1948	Joe DiMaggio, NY	155	1997	Ken Griffey Jr., Sea	147
1949	Ted Williams, Bos	159	1998	Juan Gonzales, Tex	157
	Vern Stephens, Bos	159	1999	Manny Ramirez, Clev	165
1950	Walt Dropo, Bos	144	2000	Edgar Martinez, Sea	145
	Vern Stephens, Bos	144	2001	Bret Boone, Sea	141
1951	Gus Zernial, Chi-Phi	129	2002	Alex Rodriguez, Tex	142
1952	Al Rosen, Clev	105	2003	Carlos Delgado, Tor	145
1953	Al Rosen, Clev	145	2004	Miguel Tejada, Balt	150
1954	Larry Doby, Clev	126	2005	David Ortiz, Bos	148
1955	Ray Boone, Det	116	2006	David Ortiz, Bos	137
	Jackie Jensen, Bos	116	2007	Alex Rodriguez, NY	156
1956	Mickey Mantle, NY	130			

Leading Base Stealers

Year	Player and Team	SB	Year	Player and Team	SB
1901	Frank Isbell, Chi	48	1910	Eddie Collins, Phi	81
1902	Topsy Hartsel, Phi	54	1911	Ty Cobb, Det	83
1903	Harry Bay, Clev	46	1912	Clyde Milan, Wash	88
1904	Elmer Flick, Clev	42	1913	Clyde Milan, Wash	75
	Harry Bay, Clev	42	1914	Fritz Maisel, NY	74
1905	Danny Hoffman, Phi	46	1915	Ty Cobb, Det	96
1906	Elmer Flick, Clev	39	1916	Ty Cobb, Det	68
	John Anderson, Wash	39	1917	Ty Cobb, Det	55
1907	Ty Cobb, Det	49	1918	George Sisler, StL	45
1908	Patsy Dougherty, Chi	47	1919	Eddie Collins, Chi	33
1909	Ty Cobb, Det	76	1920	Sam Rice, Wash	63

Note: Runs Batted In not compiled before 1907; officially adopted in 1920.

Leading Base Stealers *(Cont.)*

Year	Player and Team	SB	Year	Player and Team	SB
1921	George Sisler, StL	35	1965	Bert Campaneris, KC	51
1922	George Sisler, StL	51	1966	Bert Campaneris, KC	52
1923	Eddie Collins, Chi	49	1967	Bert Campaneris, KC	55
1924	Eddie Collins, Chi	42	1968	Bert Campaneris, Oak	62
1925	John Mostil, Chi	43	1969	Tommy Harper, Sea	73
1926	John Mostil, Chi	35	1970	Bert Campaneris, Oak	42
1927	George Sisler, StL	27	1971	Amos Otis, KC	52
1928	Buddy Myer, Bos	30	1972	Bert Campaneris, Oak	52
1929	Charlie Gehringer, Det	27	1973	Tommy Harper, Bos	54
1930	Marty McManus, Det	23	1974	Bill North, Oak	54
1931	Ben Chapman, NY	61	1975	Mickey Rivers, Cal	70
1932	Ben Chapman, NY	38	1976	Bill North, Oak	75
1933	Ben Chapman, NY	27	1977	Freddie Patek, KC	53
1934	Bill Werber, Bos	40	1978	Ron LeFlore, Det	68
1935	Bill Werber, Bos	29	1979	Willie Wilson, KC	83
1936	Lyn Lary, StL	37	1980	Rickey Henderson, Oak	100
1937	Bill Werber, Phi	35	1981	Rickey Henderson, Oak	56
	Ben Chapman, Wash-Bos	35	1982	Rickey Henderson, Oak	130
1938	Frank Crosetti, NY	27	1983	Rickey Henderson, Oak	108
1939	George Case, Wash	51	1984	Rickey Henderson, Oak	66
1940	George Case, Wash	35	1985	Rickey Henderson, NY	80
1941	George Case, Wash	33	1986	Rickey Henderson, NY	87
1942	George Case, Wash	44	1987	Harold Reynolds, Sea	60
1943	George Case, Wash	61	1988	Rickey Henderson, NY	93
1944	Snuffy Stirnweiss, NY	55	1989	Rickey Henderson, NY-Oak	77
1945	Snuffy Stirnweiss, NY	33	1990	Rickey Henderson, Oak	65
1946	George Case, Clev	28	1991	Rickey Henderson, Oak	58
1947	Bob Dillinger, StL	34	1992	Kenny Lofton, Clev	66
1948	Bob Dillinger, StL	28	1993	Kenny Lofton, Clev	70
1949	Bob Dillinger, StL	20	1994	Kenny Lofton, Clev	60
1950	Dom DiMaggio, Bos	15	1995	Kenny Lofton, Clev	54
1951	Minnie Minoso, Clev-Chi	31	1996	Kenny Lofton, Clev	75
1952	Minnie Minoso, Chi	22	1997	Brian Hunter, Det	74
1953	Minnie Minoso, Chi	25	1998	Rickey Henderson, Oak	66
1954	Jackie Jensen, Bos	22	1999	Brian Hunter, Sea	44
1955	Jim Rivera, Chi	25	2000	Johnny Damon, KC	46
1956	Luis Aparicio, Chi	21	2001	Ichiro Suzuki, Sea	56
1957	Luis Aparicio, Chi	28	2002	Alfonso Soriano, NY	41
1958	Luis Aparicio, Chi	29	2003	Carl Crawford, TB	55
1959	Luis Aparicio, Chi	56	2004	Carl Crawford, TB	59
1960	Luis Aparicio, Chi	51	2005	Chone Figgins, LA	62
1961	Luis Aparicio, Chi	53	2006	Carl Crawford, TB	58
1962	Luis Aparicio, Chi	31	2007	Carl Crawford, TB	50
1963	Luis Aparicio, Balt	40		Brian Roberts, Balt	50
1964	Luis Aparicio, Balt	57			

Leading Pitchers—Winning Percentage

Year	Pitcher and Team	W	L	Pct	Year	Pitcher and Team	W	L	Pct
1901	Clark Griffith, Chi	24	7	.774	1920	Jim Bagby, Clev	31	12	.721
1902	Bill Bernhard, Phi-Clev	18	5	.783	1921	Carl Mays, NY	27	9	.750
1903	Earl Moore, Clev	22	7	.759	1922	Joe Bush, NY	26	7	.788
1904	Jack Chesbro, NY	41	12	.774	1923	Herb Pennock, NY	19	6	.760
1905	Jess Tannehill, Bos	22	9	.710	1924	Walter Johnson, Wash	23	7	.767
1906	Eddie Plank, Phi	19	6	.760	1925	Stan Coveleski, Wash	20	5	.800
1907	Wild Bill Donovan, Det	25	4	.862	1926	George Uhle, Clev	27	11	.711
1908	Ed Walsh, Chi	40	15	.727	1927	Waite Hoyt, NY	22	7	.759
1909	George Mullin, Det	29	8	.784	1928	General Crowder, StL	21	5	.808
1910	Chief Bender, Phi	23	5	.821	1929	Lefty Grove, Phi	20	6	.769
1911	Chief Bender, Phi	17	5	.773	1930	Lefty Grove, Phi	28	5	.848
1912	Smoky Joe Wood, Bos	34	5	.872	1931	Lefty Grove, Phi	31	4	.886
1913	Walter Johnson, Wash	36	7	.837	1932	Johnny Allen, NY	17	4	.810
1914	Chief Bender, Phi	17	3	.850	1933	Lefty Grove, Phi	24	8	.750
1915	Smoky Joe Wood, Bos	15	5	.750	1934	Lefty Gomez, NY	26	5	.839
1916	Eddie Cicotte, Chi	15	7	.682	1935	Eldon Auker, Det	18	7	.720
1917	Reb Russell, Chi	15	5	.750	1936	Monte Pearson, NY	19	7	.731
1918	Sad Sam Jones, Bos	16	5	.762	1937	Johnny Allen, Clev	15	1	.938
1919	Eddie Cicotte, Chi	29	7	.806	1938	Red Ruffing, NY	21	7	.750

Leading Pitchers—Winning Percentage *(Cont.)*

Year	Pitcher and Team	W	L	Pct	Year	Pitcher and Team	W	L	Pct
1939	Lefty Grove, Bos	15	4	.789	1974	Mike Cuellar, Balt	22	10	.688
1940	Schoolboy Rowe, Det	16	3	.842	1975	Mike Torrez, Balt	20	9	.690
1941	Lefty Gomez, NY	15	5	.750	1976	Bill Campbell, Minn	17	5	.773
1942	Ernie Bonham, NY	21	5	.808	1977	Paul Splittorff, KC	16	6	.727
1943	Spud Chandler, NY	20	4	.833	1978	Ron Guidry, NY	25	3	.893
1944	Tex Hughson, Bos	18	5	.783	1979	Mike Caldwell, Mil	16	6	.727
1945	Hal Newhouser, Det	25	9	.735	1980	Steve Stone, Balt	25	7	.781
1946	Boo Ferriss, Bos	25	6	.806	1981*	Pete Vuckovich, Mil	14	4	.778
1947	Allie Reynolds, NY	19	8	.704	1982	Pete Vuckovich, Mil	18	6	.750
1948	Jack Kramer, Bos	18	5	.783		Jim Palmer, Balt	15	5	.750
1949	Ellis Kinder, Bos	23	6	.793	1983	Richard Dotson, Chi	22	7	.759
1950	Vic Raschi, NY	21	8	.724	1984	Doyle Alexander, Tor	17	6	.739
1951	Bob Feller, Clev	22	8	.733	1985	Ron Guidry, NY	22	6	.786
1952	Bobby Shantz, Phi	24	7	.774	1986	Roger Clemens, Bos	24	4	.857
1953	Ed Lopat, NY	16	4	.800	1987	Roger Clemens, Bos	20	9	.690
1954	Sandy Consuegra, Chi	16	3	.842	1988	Frank Viola, Minn	24	7	.774
1955	Tommy Byrne, NY	16	5	.762	1989	Bret Saberhagen, KC	23	6	.793
1956	Whitey Ford, NY	19	6	.760	1990	Bob Welch, Oak	27	6	.818
1957	Dick Donovan, Chi	16	6	.727	1991	Scott Erickson, Minn	20	8	.714
	Tom Sturdivant, NY	16	6	.727	1992	Mike Mussina, Balt	18	5	.783
1958	Bob Turley, NY	21	7	.750	1993	Jimmy Key, NY	18	6	.750
1959	Bob Shaw, Chi	18	6	.750	1994	Jimmy Key, NY	17	4	.810
1960	Jim Perry, Clev	18	10	.643	1995	Randy Johnson, Sea	18	2	.900
1961	Whitey Ford, NY	25	4	.862	1996	Charles Nagy, Clev	17	5	.773
1962	Ray Herbert, Chi	20	9	.690	1997	Randy Johnson, Sea	20	4	.833
1963	Whitey Ford, NY	24	7	.774	1998	David Wells, NY	18	4	.818
1964	Wally Bunker, Balt	19	5	.792	1999	Pedro Martinez, Bos	23	4	.852
1965	Mudcat Grant, Minn	21	7	.750	2000	Tim Hudson, Oak	20	6	.769
1966	Sonny Siebert, Clev	16	8	.667	2001	Roger Clemens, NY	20	3	.870
1967	Joel Horlen, Chi	19	7	.731	2002	Pedro Martinez, Bos	20	4	.833
1968	Denny McLain, Det	31	6	.838	2003	Roy Halladay, Tor	22	7	.759
1969	Jim Palmer, Balt	16	4	.800	2004	Curt Schilling, Bos	21	6	.778
1970	Mike Cuellar, Balt	24	8	.750	2005	Cliff Lee, Cle	18	5	.783
1971	Dave McNally, Balt	21	5	.808	2006	Roy Halladay, Tor	16	5	.762
1972	Catfish Hunter, Oak	21	7	.750	2007	Justin Verlander, Det	18	6	.750
1973	Catfish Hunter, Oak	21	5	.808					

*1981 percentages based on 10 or more victories. Note: Percentages based on 15 or more victories in all other years.

Leading Pitchers—Earned Run Average

Year	Player and Team	ERA	Year	Player and Team	ERA
1913	Walter Johnson, Wash	1.14	1940	Bob Feller, Clev†	2.62
1914	Dutch Leonard, Bos	1.01	1941	Thornton Lee, Chi	2.37
1915	Smoky Joe Wood, Bos	1.49	1942	Ted Lyons, Chi	2.10
1916	Babe Ruth, Bos	1.75	1943	Spud Chandler, NY	1.64
1917	Eddie Cicotte, Chi	1.53	1944	Dizzy Trout, Det	2.12
1918	Walter Johnson, Wash	1.27	1945	Hal Newhouser, Det	1.81
1919	Walter Johnson, Wash	1.49	1946	Hal Newhouser, Det	1.94
1920	Bob Shawkey, NY	2.46	1947	Spud Chandler, NY	2.46
1921	Red Faber, Chi	2.47	1948	Gene Bearden, Clev	2.43
1922	Red Faber, Chi	2.80	1949	Mel Parnell, Bos	2.78
1923	Stan Coveleski, Clev	2.76	1950	Early Wynn, Clev	3.20
1924	Walter Johnson, Wash	2.72	1951	Saul Rogovin, Det-Chi	2.78
1925	Stan Coveleski, Wash	2.84	1952	Allie Reynolds, NY	2.07
1926	Lefty Grove, Phi	2.51	1953	Ed Lopat, NY	2.43
1927	Wilcy Moore, NY#	2.28	1954	Mike Garcia, Clev	2.64
1928	Garland Braxton, Wash	2.52	1955	Billy Pierce, Chi	1.97
1929	Lefty Grove, Phi	2.81	1956	Whitey Ford, NY	2.47
1930	Lefty Grove, Phi	2.54	1957	Bobby Shantz, NY	2.45
1931	Lefty Grove, Phi	2.06	1958	Whitey Ford, NY	2.01
1932	Lefty Grove, Phi	2.84	1959	Hoyt Wilhelm, Balt	2.19
1933	Monte Pearson, Clev	2.33	1960	Frank Baumann, Chi	2.68
1934	Lefty Gomez, NY	2.33	1961	Dick Donovan, Wash	2.40
1935	Lefty Grove, Bos	2.70	1962	Hank Aguirre, Det	2.21
1936	Lefty Grove, Bos	2.81	1963	Gary Peters, Chi	2.33
1937	Lefty Gomez, NY	2.33	1964	Dean Chance, LA	1.65
1938	Lefty Grove, Bos	3.07	1965	Sam McDowell, Clev	2.18
1939	Lefty Grove, Bos	2.54	1966	Gary Peters, Chi	1.98

American League *(Cont.)*

Leading Pitchers—Earned Run Average *(Cont.)*

Year	Player and Team	ERA	Year	Player and Team	ERA
1967	Joe Horlen, Chi	2.06	1988	Allan Anderson, Minn	2.45
1968	Luis Tiant, Clev	1.60	1989	Bret Saberhagen, KC	2.16
1969	Dick Bosman, Wash	2.19	1990	Roger Clemens, Bos	1.93
1970	Diego Segui, Oak	2.56	1991	Roger Clemens, Bos	2.62
1971	Vida Blue, Oak	1.82	1992	Roger Clemens, Bos	2.41
1972	Luis Tiant, Bos	1.91	1993	Kevin Appier, KC	2.56
1973	Jim Palmer, Balt	2.40	1994	Steve Ontiveros, Oak	2.65
1974	Catfish Hunter, Oak	2.49	1995	Randy Johnson, Sea	2.48
1975	Jim Palmer, Balt	2.09	1996	Juan Guzman, Tor	2.93
1976	Mark Fidrych, Det	2.34	1997	Roger Clemens, Tor	2.05
1977	Frank Tanana, Cal	2.54	1998	Roger Clemens, Tor	2.64
1978	Ron Guidry, NY	1.74	1999	Pedro Martinez, Bos	2.07
1979	Ron Guidry, NY	2.78	2000	Pedro Martinez, Bos	1.74
1980	Rudy May, NY	2.47	2001	Freddy Garcia, Sea	3.05
1981	Steve McCatty, Oak	2.32	2002	Pedro Martinez, Bos	2.26
1982	Rick Sutcliffe, Clev	2.96	2003	Pedro Martinez, Bos	2.22
1983	Rick Honeycutt, Tex	2.42	2004	Johan Santana, Minn	2.61
1984	Mike Boddicker, Balt	2.79	2005	Kevin Millwood, Cle	2.86
1985	Dave Stieb, Tor	2.48	2006	Johan Santana, Minn	2.77
1986	Roger Clemens, Bos	2.48	2007	John Lackey, LA	3.01
1987	Jimmy Key, Tor	2.76			

Note: Based on 10 complete games through 1950, then 154 innings until the American League expanded in 1961, when it became 162 innings. In strike-shortened 1981, one inning per game required. Earned runs not tabulated in American League prior to 1913.

#Wilcy Moore pitched only six complete games—he started 12—in 1927 but was recognized as leader because of 213 innings pitched. †Ernie Bonham, New York, had 1.91 ERA and 10 complete games in 1940 but appeared in only 12 games and 99 innings, and Bob Feller was recognized as leader.

Leading Pitchers—Strikeouts

Year	Player and Team	SO	Year	Player and Team	SO
1901	Cy Young, Bos	159	1939	Bob Feller, Clev	246
1902	Rube Waddell, Phi	210	1940	Bob Feller, Clev	261
1903	Rube Waddell, Phi	301	1941	Bob Feller, Clev	260
1904	Rube Waddell, Phi	349	1942	Bobo Newsom, Wash	
1905	Rube Waddell, Phi	286		Tex Hughson, Bos	113
1906	Rube Waddell, Phi	203	1943	Allie Reynolds, Clev	151
1907	Rube Waddell, Phi	226	1944	Hal Newhouser, Det	187
1908	Ed Walsh, Chi	269	1945	Hal Newhouser, Det	212
1909	Frank Smith, Chi	177	1946	Bob Feller, Clev	348
1910	Walter Johnson, Wash	313	1947	Bob Feller, Clev	196
1911	Ed Walsh, Chi	255	1948	Bob Feller, Clev	164
1912	Walter Johnson, Wash	303	1949	Virgil Trucks, Det	153
1913	Walter Johnson, Wash	243	1950	Bob Lemon, Clev	170
1914	Walter Johnson, Wash	225	1951	Vic Raschi, NY	164
1915	Walter Johnson, Wash	203	1952	Allie Reynolds, NY	160
1916	Walter Johnson, Wash	228	1953	Billy Pierce, Chi	186
1917	Walter Johnson, Wash	188	1954	Bob Turley, Balt	185
1918	Walter Johnson, Wash	162	1955	Herb Score, Clev	245
1919	Walter Johnson, Wash	147	1956	Herb Score, Clev	263
1920	Stan Coveleski, Clev	133	1957	Early Wynn, Clev	184
1921	Walter Johnson, Wash	143	1958	Early Wynn, Chi	179
1922	Urban Shocker, StL	149	1959	Jim Bunning, Det	201
1923	Walter Johnson, Wash	130	1960	Jim Bunning, Det	201
1924	Walter Johnson, Wash	158	1961	Camilo Pascual, Minn	221
1925	Lefty Grove, Phi	116	1962	Camilo Pascual, Minn	206
1926	Lefty Grove, Phi	194	1963	Camilo Pascual, Minn	202
1927	Lefty Grove, Phi	174	1964	Al Downing, NY	217
1928	Lefty Grove, Phi	183	1965	Sam McDowell, Clev	325
1929	Lefty Grove, Phi	170	1966	Sam McDowell, Clev	225
1930	Lefty Grove, Phi	209	1967	Jim Lonborg, Bos	246
1931	Lefty Grove, Phi	175	1968	Sam McDowell, Clev	283
1932	Red Ruffing, NY	190	1969	Sam McDowell, Clev	279
1933	Lefty Gomez, NY	163	1970	Sam McDowell, Clev	304
1934	Lefty Gomez, NY	158	1971	Mickey Lolich, Det	308
1935	Tommy Bridges, Det	163	1972	Nolan Ryan, Cal	329
1936	Tommy Bridges, Det	175	1973	Nolan Ryan, Cal	383
1937	Lefty Gomez, NY	194	1974	Nolan Ryan, Cal	367
1938	Bob Feller, Clev	240	1975	Frank Tanana, Cal	269

Leading Pitchers—Strikeouts *(Cont.)*

Year	Player and Team	SO	Year	Player and Team	SO
1976	Nolan Ryan, Cal	327	1992	Randy Johnson, Sea	241
1977	Nolan Ryan, Cal	341	1993	Randy Johnson, Sea	308
1978	Nolan Ryan, Cal	260	1994	Randy Johnson, Sea	204
1979	Nolan Ryan, Cal	223	1995	Randy Johnson, Sea	294
1980	Len Barker, Clev	187	1996	Roger Clemens, Bos	257
1981	Len Barker, Clev	127	1997	Roger Clemens, Tor	292
1982	Floyd Bannister, Sea	209	1998	Roger Clemens, Tor	271
1983	Jack Morris, Det	232	1999	Pedro Martinez, Bos	313
1984	Mark Langston, Sea	204	2000	Pedro Martinez, Bos	284
1985	Bert Blyleven, Clev-Minn	206	2001	Hideo Nomo, Bos	220
1986	Mark Langston, Sea	245	2002	Pedro Martinez, Bos	239
1987	Mark Langston, Sea	262	2003	Esteban Loaiza, Chi	207
1988	Roger Clemens, Bos	291	2004	Johan Santana, Minn	265
1989	Nolan Ryan, Tex	301	2005	Johan Santana, Minn	238
1990	Nolan Ryan, Tex	232	2006	Johan Santana, Minn	245
1991	Roger Clemens, Bos	241	2007	Scott Kazmir, TB	239

Leading Pitchers—Saves

FYear	Player and Team	SV	Year	Player and Team	SV
1947	Joe Page, NY	17	1978	Goose Gossage, NY	27
1948	Russ Christopher, Clev	17	1979	Mike Marshall, Minn	32
1949	Joe Page, NY	29	1980	Dan Quisenberry, KC	33
1950	Mickey Harris, Wash	15	1981	Rollie Fingers, Mil	28
1951	Ellis Kinder, Bos	14	1982	Dan Quisenberry, KC	35
1952	Harry Dorish, Chi	11	1983	Dan Quisenberry, KC	35
1953	Ellis Kinder, Bos	27	1984	Dan Quisenberry, KC	44
1954	Johnny Sain, NY	22	1985	Dan Quisenberry, KC	37
1955	Ray Narleski, Clev	19	1986	Dave Righetti, NY	46
1956	George Zuverink, Bal	16	1987	Tom Henke, Tor	34
1957	Bob Grim, NY	19	1988	Dennis Eckersley, Oak	45
1958	Ryne Duren, NY	20	1989	Jeff Russell, Tex	38
1959	Turk Lown, Chi	15	1990	Bobby Thigpen, Chi	57
1960	Mike Fornieles, Bos	14	1991	Bryan Harvey, Cal	46
	Johnny Klippstein, Clev	14	1992	Dennis Eckersley, Oak	51
1961	Luis Arroyo, NY	29	1993	Jeff Montgomery, KC	45
1962	Dick Radatz, Bos	24		Duane Ward, Tor	45
1963	Stu Miller, Bal	27	1994	Lee Smith, Bal	33
1964	Dick Radatz, Bos	29	1995	Jose Mesa, Clev	46
1965	Ron Kline, Wash	29	1996	John Wetteland, NY	43
1966	Jack Aker, KC	32	1997	Randy Myers, Balt	45
1967	Minnie Rojas, Cal	27	1998	Tom Gordon, Bos	46
1968	Al Worthington, Minn	18	1999	Mariano Rivera, NY	45
1969	Ron Perranoski, Minn	31	2000	Todd Jones, Det	42
1970	Ron Perranoski, Minn	34	2001	Mariano Rivera, NY	50
1971	Ken Sanders, Mil	31	2002	Eddie Guardado, Minn	45
1972	Sparky Lyle, NY	35	2003	Keith Foulke, Oak	43
1973	John Hiller, Det	38	2004	Mariano Rivera, NY	53
1974	Terry Forster, Chi	24	2005	Francisco Rodríguez, LA	45
1975	Goose Gossage, Chi	26		Bob Wickman, Cle	45
1976	Sparky Lyle, NY	23	2006	Francisco Rodriguez, LA	47
1977	Bill Campbell, Bos	31	2007	Joe Borowski, Cle	45

The Commissioners of Baseball

Kenesaw Mountain Landis	Elected Nov. 12, 1920. Served until his death on Nov. 25, 1944.
Happy Chandler	Elected April 24, 1945. Served until July 15, 1951.
Ford Frick	Elected Sept. 20, 1951. Served until Nov. 16, 1965.
William Eckert	Elected Nov. 17, 1965. Served until Dec. 20, 1968.
Bowie Kuhn	Elected Feb. 8, 1969. Served until Sept. 30, 1984.
Peter Ueberroth	Elected March 3, 1984. Took office Oct. 1, 1984. Served through March 31, 1989.
A. Bartlett Giamatti	Elected Sept. 8, 1988. Took office April 1, 1989. Served until his death on Sept. 1, 1989.
Francis Vincent Jr.	Appointed Acting Commissioner Sept. 2, 1989. Elected Commissioner Sept. 13, 1989. Served through Sept. 7, 1992.
Allan H. (Bud) Selig	Elected chairman of the executive council and given the powers of interim commissioner on Sept. 9, 1992. Unanimously elected Commissioner July 9, 1998.

Pro Football

The Colts' Tony Dungy and the Bears' Lovie Smith (l.) became the first African-American head coaches to reach the Super Bowl

Peyton's Place, Tony's Time

After years of postseason disappointment, Tony Dungy and Peyton Manning silenced the doubters, taking the Colts to pro football's promised land and bringing home a title

BY HANK HERSCH

REALLY, DID YOU BELIEVE HIM? It sounded like a line plucked from any title in the self-help section, a handy way of deflecting the 1,000-watt glare applied by inquisitors demanding to know why he couldn't—*all together now*—win the big one. He was only 30 and in nine NFL campaigns he had done almost everything that could be asked of a quarterback: 144 starts in 144 career games, a couple of MVP awards, second in alltime passer rating, good for 4,000 yards and 30 touchdowns per season. He was in a no-win position that only winning would solve. And yet that's not how Peyton Manning preferred to see his lot after his Indianapolis Colts had defeated the Baltimore Ravens 15–6 in an AFC Divisional playoff showdown. "I'm not into overanalyzing my career," Manning said. "I'm into the journey, not the destination."

Eight days later Manning's journey appeared headed for an all-too-familiar and none-too-appealing destination. This was what he professed to be "into"? A 21–6 deficit in the AFC championship game against the New England Patriots, who had a 6–2 record against Manning's team, including going 2–0 in the play-offs? Another crushing loss to his QB foil, Tom Brady, primed for a fourth Super Bowl title after his upset of the top-seeded San Diego Chargers and MVP running back LaDainian Tomlinson a week earlier? Yet another opportunity for critics to consign Manning's accomplishments to a footnote in the larger story of his failures in the clutch?

Well, yes: This was *exactly* what he was into. As Manning himself might have said in one of his credit card ads, *Chance to exact the sweetest revenge: Priceless.* Picking up on coach Tony Dungy's upbeat halftime message in the RCA Dome locker room: "I'm telling you this is our game. It's our time," Manning rallied the Colts to within 34–31 with 2:17 to play. Taking over on his own 20, he then marched the length of the field; when rookie running back Joseph Addai roared three yards into the end zone, Indy had a 38–34 victory and its first title game berth since the franchise moved from Baltimore in 1984. "I just wanted to do my job and do my job well," said Manning, who completed 27 of 47 passes for 349 yards. "I didn't think I needed to be super. I just needed to be good."

Upon his arrival in Miami for Super

Bowl XLI, Manning's journey took a twist: His counterpart, Rex Grossman of the Chicago Bears, was suddenly the one undergoing more microscopic scrutiny. But then, the past year marked a long, strange trip for a wide range of NFL quarterbacks.

First, there was Ben Roethlisberger, who, after guiding the Steelers to the Super Bowl XL title, suffered a broken jaw, among other injuries, in a June motorcycle crash, then underwent an emergency appendectomy four days before the season opener. Roethlisberger missed only one start but, shaky in the pocket, he was a shadow of his usually accurate self throughout an 8–8 season that ended with the retirement of coach Bill Cowher.

There was Carson Palmer, who made a miraculously rapid recovery from a horrific left knee injury and reached the Pro Bowl; his heroics for the Cincinnati Bengals were undone, however, by off-the-field transgressions by his teammates (no fewer than nine arrests in as many months) and late-season, last-minute losses.

And then there was Michael Vick. On the field, the Falcons QB rushed for a

Tomlinson flew past the alltime NFL single-season records for scoring (186), total touchdowns (31) and rushing touchdowns (28) in 2006.

record 1,039 yards in 2006, at a clip of 8.4 yards per carry, and finished third among all players with 44 runs of 10 yards or more. Alas, Vick completed just 52.6 percent of his passes and the Atlanta Falcons finished 7–9. But the disappointment of missing the playoffs paled in comparison to Vick's off-field problems. In late July 2007, after a months-long federal investigation, Vick was indicted on a number of serious charges related to running an illegal dog-fighting operation on his Virginia property. Not long after, he pleaded guilty to conspiracy charges, which wiped out his 2007 and 2008 seasons and seriously jeopardized his chances of ever returning to play in the NFL again.

Not every QB, of course, had an such a turbulent, unfulfilling odyssey. Under rookie coach Eric Mangini, Chad Pennington showed his former effectiveness following rotator cuff surgery and guided the New York Jets, who were 4–12 in

2005, to a 10–6 record and the playoffs, where they lost to New England. Donovan McNabb suffered a season-ending injury in a November home game for the third straight year (ankles, sports hernia, ACL), but the Philadelphia Eagles found a savior in 36-year-old third-stringer Jeff Garcia, who orchestrated six straight victories, including a 23–20 NFC wild-card victory over the New York Giants.

Another NFC East team uncovered an even more unlikely spark under center. By the fourth week of the season the Dallas Cowboys were being distracted by that most reliable source of turmoil, wide receiver Terrell Owens, who had signed a three-year, $25 million deal in the spring. Owens was whisked to a Dallas emergency room after what police initially classified as a suicide attempt but was later determined to be disorientation after a mixture of pain medication and nutritional supplements. In denying that Owens had tried to harm himself, his publicist infamously asserted that "he has 25 million reasons why he should be alive."

With the team 3–3, Cowboys coach Bill Parcells benched veteran quarterback Drew Bledsoe for Tony Romo, who, four seasons after being signed as a free agent out of Eastern Illinois, had yet to throw a pass. He responded with a 5–1 stretch during which his passer rating of 102.4 eclipsed Peyton Manning's. "What can you not like about Tony?" said Owens. "Student of the game, great athlete, and every receiver out there knows he might get the ball on every play." The unofficial league leader in dropped passes, T.O. wasn't exactly a reliable target, but it was a bobble by Romo that ended the Cowboys' season. With 1:19 left in a wild-card matchup with the Seattle Seahawks, he fumbled the snap on a 19-yard field goal attempt. Dallas lost, 21–20.

No quarterback had a more exciting trajectory than 6'4", 233-pound rookie Vince Young, who flattened the learning curve as thoroughly as a defensive back at the goal line. The No. 3 pick in the draft out of Texas, he wasn't inserted into the Tennessee Titans' starting lineup until Week 4. After settling in, he reeled off six wins in a row and, with four fourth-quarter rallies, nearly lifted a moribund team to the postseason. Along the way he became the first rookie QB to achieve two comebacks of 14 points or more; in a 24–21 defeat of the Giants, he set a rookie record by bringing his team back from 21 points down. He was also the first rook with at least three touchdowns of 20 yards or more both on the ground and through the air.

"When you have a dominant guy like Vince, his confidence becomes contagious," said rookie fullback Ahmard Hall. "Before you know it, everyone starts believing in what we can do as a team."

Young was far from the only newcomer to provide his team a lift; with more colleges playing pro-style offenses and scheduling their work week like the NFL's, and with players putting in more intensive post-school, pre-NFL preparation, the 2006 rookie class produced an unprecedented number of starters and impact players. Among them: Indy's Addai (1,081 yards rushing), Chicago defensive end Mark Anderson (12 sacks) and Bears defensive back Devin Hester out of Miami (Fla.)—"the best rookie in the league by far," according to former Green Bay Packers G.M. Ron Wolf—who had an NFL high six returns for touchdowns: two kickoffs, three punts and a missed field goal for a record-tying 108 yards.

The New Orleans Saints, in particular, rode their rookie class to stunning success. One came from nowhere: wideout Marques Colston, a seventh-round pick out of Hofstra, was so impressive in camp that the team unloaded veteran Donte' Stallworth to the Eagles to make room for him. Despite missing two games, he caught 70 passes for 1,038 yards and eight touchdowns—and still wasn't the most dangerous first-year receiver in the Big Easy. Tailback Reggie Bush, chosen second out of USC, wound up with 88 catches, in addition to rushing for 565 yards. With free-agent signee Drew Brees

at quarterback, the Saints went from 3–13 in 2005 to 10–6, and claimed just their second playoff victory (27–24 over Philly) in the 40-year history of the franchise.

Bush's arrival coincided with the departure of another game-breaking back, the Giants' Tiki Barber. Despite breaking the 1,200-yard mark for the fifth straight year and finishing with 1,662 yards, fourth most in the NFL, he chose to retire at age 31 rather than subject himself to more punishment. Before heading off to a career in broadcasting, Barber explained his decision: "Lie down on the floor 30 times and then get up. Now imagine getting knocked down 30 times and getting up. Every day."

But no player rampaged through the record book in 2006 like San Diego's Tomlinson. One year after Seahawks running back Shaun Alexander set the NFL single-season touchdown record with 28, Tomlinson shattered that mark after just 13 games, scoring 31 (not to mention two more passing TDs). He also led the league with 1,815 yards rushing, and with 186 points, broke Paul Hornung's 46-year-old

Rookies Bush (r.), Colston (l.) and 11-year veteran Joe Horn gave the Saints one of the NFL's most prolific receiving corps.

record by 10. LT's career TD production of 1.05 per game ranks second only to Hall of Famer Jim Brown's 1.07, and at 27 he's just entering his prime. "He's phenomenal," said the St. Louis Rams multipurpose star, Marshall Faulk. "He's the one who blows us all away, because he does everything."

With LT on one side of the ball and Shawne "Lights Out" Merriman on the other—the second-year linebacker had an NFL-high 17 sacks, despite being suspended for four games for testing positive for performance-enhancing drugs—the Chargers roared to a 14–2 record, the best in the league. In their playoff opener, they held an eight-point lead over New England in the fourth quarter, but Brady rallied the Pats to a 24–21 win with a pair of scores over the final 4:30. The loss dropped 63-year-old coach Marty Schottenheimer, whose 200 wins rank fifth alltime, to 5–13 in the postseason. A few weeks later, the Chargers showed him the door.

last 14 games with a knee injury, the Colts became staunch and stingy: They had allowed just 220 rushing yards in three playoff games entering Miami. As rain pelted Dolphin Stadium, the Bears struck first when Hester brought back the opening kickoff return 92 yards, and they scored again with 4:34 left in the first quarter on Grossman's four-yard strike to Muhsin Muhammad. But after that, Indy's D surrendered only a field goal, thanks largely to a pair of picks on poor throws. "We *knew*," said Colts cornerback Nick Harper. "We wanted to put the ball in Grossman's hands. We'd seen the film, and there was no way in hell they were going to beat us in the passing game."

After an early interception Manning settled down, finishing with 25 completions in 38 attempts for 247 yards. He got plenty of help from his rotating backfield of Addai (10 receptions, 143 all-purpose yards) and Dominic Rhodes (21 carries, 113 rushing yards), and the Colts cruised to a 29–17 victory. It was the franchise's first championship in 36 years, and the first in NFL history by a black head coach. But Dungy's acumen (he devised the Tampa Two scheme used by Smith, his former Buccaneers assistant) and his demeanor (never cursing and seldom even raising his voice) had already set him apart. "As much as being the first African-American coach to win a Super Bowl," the 51-year-old Dungy said, "I'm just as proud to represent coaches who don't believe football is the biggest thing in their lives."

Like his quarterback, Dungy was into the journey. But that didn't mean they couldn't enjoy it when they had finally reached their destination.

The Colts derailed Brady & Co. the following week; in the NFC title game the Bears stopped New Orleans 39–14 behind their Tampa Two defense, which relied on he run-stuffing, pass-covering talents of middle linebacker Brian Urlacher. Grossman, a model of inconsistency all season—his passer rating ranged from 148.0 in Week 2 to 1.3 in Week 13—was effective for stretches, but in misfiring on 15 of 26 throws, the 26-year-old's performance raised even more questions. Except, that is, among Bears coach Lovie Smith and his staff. "Nobody, and I mean nobody, has more mental toughness than Rex Grossman," said offensive coordinator Ron Turner. "After the criticism he's taken this year, a few bad throws aren't going to kill him."

In years past, a meeting with the Indianapolis defense would have been a welcome occurrence. But after the return of safety Bob Sanders, who missed 12 of the

2006 NFL Final Standings

American Football Conference

EAST DIVISION

	W	L	T	Pct	Pts	OP
New England	12	4	0	.750	385	237
*NY Jets	10	6	0	.625	316	295
Buffalo	7	9	0	.438	300	311
Miami	6	10	0	.375	260	283

NORTH DIVISION

	W	L	T	Pct	Pts	OP
Baltimore	13	3	0	.812	353	201
Cincinnati	8	8	0	.500	373	331
Pittsburgh	8	8	0	.500	353	315
Cleveland	4	12	0	.250	238	356

SOUTH DIVISION

	W	L	T	Pct	Pts	OP
Indianapolis	12	4	0	.750	427	360
Tennessee	8	8	0	.500	324	400
Jacksonville	8	8	0	.500	371	274
Houston	6	10	0	.375	267	366

WEST DIVISION

	W	L	T	Pct	Pts	OP
San Diego	14	2	0	.875	492	303
*Kansas City	9	7	0	.562	331	315
Denver	9	7	0	.562	319	305
Oakland	2	14	0	.125	168	332

* Wild-card team.

National Football Conference

EAST DIVISION

	W	L	T	Pct	Pts	OP
Philadelphia	10	6	0	.625	398	328
*Dallas	9	7	0	.562	425	350
*NY Giants	8	8	0	.500	355	362
Washington	5	11	0	.312	307	376

NORTH DIVISION

	W	L	T	Pct	Pts	OP
Chicago	13	3	0	.812	427	255
Green Bay	8	8	0	.500	301	366
Minnesota	6	10	0	.375	282	327
Detroit	3	13	0	.188	305	398

SOUTH DIVISION

	W	L	T	Pct	Pts	OP
New Orleans	10	6	0	.625	413	322
Carolina	8	8	0	.500	270	305
Atlanta	7	9	0	.438	292	328
Tampa Bay	4	12	0	.250	211	353

WEST DIVISION

	W	L	T	Pct	Pts	OP
Seattle	9	7	0	.562	335	341
St. Louis	8	8	0	.500	367	381
San Francisco	7	9	0	.438	298	412
Arizona	5	11	0	.312	314	389

* Wild-card team.

2006–07 NFL Playoffs

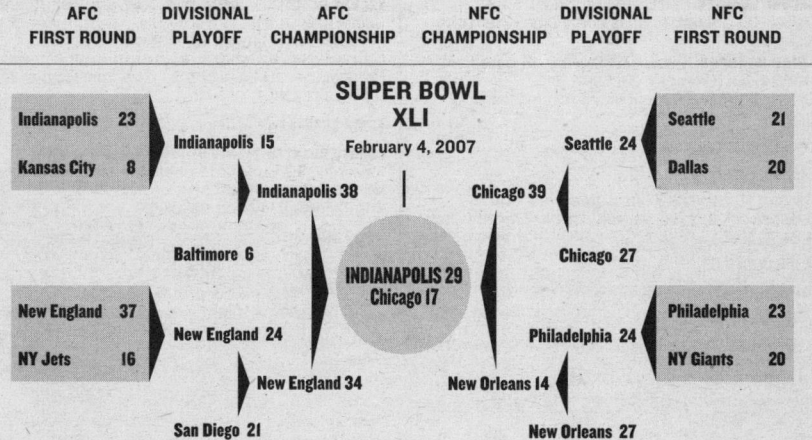

AFC FIRST ROUND	AFC DIVISIONAL PLAYOFF	AFC CHAMPIONSHIP	NFC CHAMPIONSHIP	NFC DIVISIONAL PLAYOFF	NFC FIRST ROUND

SUPER BOWL XLI
February 4, 2007

Indianapolis 23
Kansas City 8

Indianapolis 15

Indianapolis 38

Baltimore 6

New England 37
NY Jets 16

New England 24

New England 34

San Diego 21

INDIANAPOLIS 29
Chicago 17

Chicago 39

Chicago 27

Philadelphia 24

New Orleans 14

New Orleans 27

Seattle 24

Seattle 21
Dallas 20

Philadelphia 23
NY Giants 20

AFC Wild-card Games

Kansas City	...0	0	8	0—8
Indianapolis	...6	3	7	7—23

FIRST QUARTER: Indianapolis: FG Vinatieri 48, 8:41.
Indianapolis: FG Vinatieri 19, 2:09.

SECOND QUARTER: Indianapolis: FG Vinatieri 50, 0:00.

THIRD QUARTER: Indianapolis: TD Addai 6 run
(Vinatieri kick), 4:14.
Kansas City: TD Gonzalez 6 pass from Green (Green
pass to Wilson for 2pt. conversion), 0:08.

FOURTH QUARTER: Indianapolis: TD Wayne 5 pass from
Manning (Vinatieri kick), 10:16.

A: 57,215; 2:42.

NY Jets	...3	7	3	3—16
New England	...7	10	6	14—37

FIRST QUARTER: New England:TD Dillon 11 run
(Gostkowski kick) 11:53.
New York: FG Nugent 28, 2:36.

SECOND QUARTER: New York: TD Cotchery 77 pass
from Pennington (Nugent kick) 14:45.
New England: FG Gostkowski 20, 10:57.
New England TD Graham 1 pass from Brady
(Gostkowski kick) 0:11.

THIRD QUARTER: New York: FG Nugent 21, 8:19.
New England: FG Gostkowski 40, 4:22.
New England: FG Gostkowski 28, 0:04.

FOURTH QUARTER: New York: FG Nugent 37, 11:39.
New England: TD Faulk 7 pass from Brady
(Gostkowski kick) 5:16.
New England: TD Samuel 36 interception return
(Gostkowski kick), 4:54.

A: 68,756; 3:13.

NFC Wild-card Games

Dallas	...3	7	7	3—20
Seattle	...3	3	7	8—21

FIRST QUARTER: Seattle: FG Brown 23, 11:13.
Dallas: FG Gramatica 50, 4:50.

SECOND QUARTER: Seattle: FG Brown 30, 8:23.
Dallas: TD Crayton 13 pass from Romo (Gramatica
kick), 0:11.

THIRD QUARTER: Seattle: TD Stevens 15 pass from
Hasselbeck (Brown kick) 6:08.
Dallas: TD Austin 93 kick return (Gramatica kick),
5:57.

FOURTH QUARTER: Dallas: FG Gramatica 29, 10:15.

Seattle: Safety, 6:32.

Seattle: TD Stevens 37 pass from Hasselbeck
(Hasselbeck 2 pt. conversion pass to Branch failed)
4:24.

A: 68,058; 3:09.

NY Giants	...7	3	0	10—20
Philadelphia	...0	17	3	3—23

FIRST QUARTER: New York: Burress 17 pass from
Manning (Feely kick), 11:44.

SECOND QUARTER: Philadelphia: TD Westbrook 49 run
(Akers kick), 14:11.
Philadelphia: FG Akers 19, 9:34.
New York: FG Feely 20, 4:45.
Philadelphia: TD Stallworth 28 pass from Garcia
(Akers kick), 1:01.

THIRD QUARTER: Philadelphia: FG Akers 48, 2:37.

FOURTH QUARTER: New York: FG Feely 24, 14:50.
New York: TD Burress 11 pass from Manning (Feely
kick), 5:04.
Philadelphia: FG Akers 38, 0:00.

A: 69,094; 3:16.

AFC Divisional Games

Indianapolis	6	3	3	3—15
Baltimore	0	3	0	3—6

FIRST QUARTER: Indianapolis: FG Vinatieri 23, 8:04. Indianapolis: FG Vinatieri 42, 5:36.

SECOND QUARTER: Baltimore: FG Stover 40, 14:56. Indianapolis: FG Vinatieri 51, 3:15.

THIRD QUARTER: Indianapolis: FG Vinatieri 48, 10:57.

FOURTH QUARTER: Baltimore: FG Stover 51, 13:03. Indianapolis: FG Vinatieri 35, 0:23.

A: 71,162; 3:01.

New England	3	7	3	11—24
San Diego	0	14	0	7—21

FIRST QUARTER: New England: FG Gostkowski 50, 0:40.

SECOND QUARTER: San Diego: TD Tomlinson 2 run (Kaeding kick), 7:19.
San Diego: TD Turner 6 run (Kaeding kick), 2:04.
New England: TD Gaffney 6 pass from Brady (Gostkowski kick), 0:08.

THIRD QUARTER: New England: FG Gostkowski 34, 2:11.

FOURTH QUARTER: San Diego: TD Tomlinson 3 run (Kaeding kick), 8:35.
New England: TD Caldwell 4 pass from Brady (Faulk run for 2 pt. conversion), 4:36.
New England: FG Gostkowski 31, 1:10.

A: 68,810; 3:39.

NFC Divisional Games

Philadelphia	0	14	7	3—24
New Orleans	3	10	14	0—27

FIRST QUARTER: New Orleans: FG Carney 33, 9:24.

SECOND QUARTER: New Orleans: FG Carney 23, 14:46.
Philadelphia: TD Stallworth 75 pass from Garcia (Akers kick), 13:38.
New Orleans: TD Bush 4 run (Carney kick), 5:19.
Philadelphia: TD Westbrook 1 run (Akers kick), 0:50.

THIRD QUARTER: Philadelphia: TD Westbrook 62 run (Akers kick), 13:25.
New Orleans: TD McAllister 5 run (Carney kick), 9:36.
New Orleans: TD McAllister 11 pass from Brees (Carney kick), 1:05.

FOURTH QUARTER: Philadelphia: FG Akers 24, 11:08

A: 70,001; 3:06.

Seattle	0	14	10	0	0—24
Chicago	7	14	0	3	3—27

FIRST QUARTER: Chicago: TD Jones 9 run (Gould kick), 8:35.

SECOND QUARTER: Seattle: TD Burleson 16 pass from Hasselbeck (Brown kick), 14:54.
Chicago: TD Berrian 68 pass from Grossman (Gould kick), 14:36.
Seattle: TD Alexander 4 run (Brown kick), 2:29.
Chicago: TD Jones 7 run (Gould kick), 0:48.

THIRD QUARTER: Seattle: FG Brown 40, 9:56.
Seattle: TD Alexander 13 run (Brown kick), 4:57.

FOURTH QUARTER: Chicago: FG Gould 41, 4:24.
Chicago: FG Gould 49, 10:02.

OVERTIME: Chicago: FG Gould 49, 10:02.

A: 62,184; 3:16.

AFC Championship

New England	7	14	7	6—34
Indianapolis	3	3	15	17—38

FIRST QUARTER: New England: TD Mankins 0 fumble return (Gostkowski kick), 7:24.
Indianapolis: FG Vinatieri 42, 0:48.

SECOND QUARTER: New England: TD Dillon 7 run (Gostkowski kick) 10:18.
New England: TD Samuel 39 interception return (Gostkowski kick), 9:25.
Indianapolis: FG Vinatieri 26, 0:07.

THIRD QUARTER: Indianapolis: TD Manning 1 run (Vinatieri kick), 8:13.
Indianapolis: TD Klecko 1 pass from Manning (Manning pass to Harrison for 2 pt conversion) 4:00.
New England: TD Gaffney 6 pass from Brady (Gostkowski kick), 1:25.

FOURTH QUARTER: Indianapolis: TD Saturday 0 fumble return (Vinatieri kick), 13:24.
New England: FG Gostkowski 28 yd, 7:42.
Indianapolis: FG Vinatieri 36, 5:31.
New England: FG Gostkowski 43, 3:49.
Indianapolis: Addai 3 run (Vinatieri kick), 1:00.

A: 57,433; 3:34

NFC Championship

New Orleans	0	7	7	0—14
Chicago	3	13	2	21—39

FIRST QUARTER: Chicago: FG Gould 19, 0:41.

SECOND QUARTER: Chicago: FG Gould 43, 13:40.
Chicago: FG Gould 24, 8:52.
Chicago: TD Jones 2 run (Gould kick), 1:56.
New Orleans: TD Colston 13 pass from Brees (Carney kick), 0:46.

THIRD QUARTER: New Orleans: TD Bush 88 pass from Brees (Carney kick), 12:20.
Chicago: Safety, 5:27.

FOURTH QUARTER: Chicago: TD Berrian 33 pass from Grossman (Gould kick), 14:23.
Chicago: TD Benson 12 run (Gould kick), 11:37.
Chicago: TD Jones 15 run (Gould kick), 4:19.

A: 61,817; 3:10

Super Bowl XLI Recap

Indianapolis	6	10	6	7—29
Chicago	14	0	3	0—17

FIRST QUARTER: Chicago: TD Hester 92 yd kick return (Gould kick)14:46.
Chicago 7-0.
Indianapolis: TD Wayne 53 pass from Manning, 6:50 (Vinatieri kick failed).
Chicago 7-6.
Chicago: TD Muhammad 4 pass from Grossman (Gould kick), 4:34.
Chicago 14-6.

SECOND QUARTER: Indianapolis: FG Vinatieri 29, 11:17.
Chicago 14-9.
Indianapolis: TD Rhodes 1 run (Vinatieri kick), 6:09.
Indianapolis 16-14.

THIRD QUARTER: Indianapolis: FG Vinatieri 24, 7:26.
Indianapolis 19-14.
Indianapolis: FG Vinatieri 20, 3:16.
Indianapolis 22-14.
Chicago: FG Gould 44, 1:14.
Indianapolis 22-17.

FOURTH QUARTER: Indianapolis: TD Hayden 56 interception return (Vinatieri kick) 11:44.
Indianapolis 29-17.

A: 74,512; 3:31

Team Statistics

	Indianapolis	Chicago
FIRST DOWNS	24	11
Rushing	12	3
Passing	11	8
Penalty	1	0
THIRD DOWN EFF	8-18	3-10
FOURTH DOWN EFF	0-1	0-1
TOTAL NET YARDS	430	265
Total plays	81	48
Avg gain	5.3	5.5
NET YARDS RUSHING	191	111
Rushes	42	19
Avg per rush	4.5	5.8
NET YARDS PASSING	239	154
Completed–Att.	25-38	20-28
Yards per pass	6.1	5.3
Sacked–yards lost	1-8	1-11
Had intercepted	1	2
PUNTS–Avg	4-40.5	5-45.2
PENALTIES–Yds	6-40	4-35
FUMBLES–Lost	2-2	4-3

Passing

INDIANAPOLIS

	Comp	Att	Yds	Int	TD
Manning	25	38	247	1	1

CHICAGO

	Comp	Att	Yds	Int	TD
Grossman	20	28	165	2	1

Rushing

INDIANAPOLIS

	No.	Yds	Lg	TD
Rhodes	21	113	36	1
Addai	19	77	14	0
Clark	1	1	1	0
Manning	1	0	0	0

CHICAGO

	No.	Yds	Lg	TD
Jones	15	112	52	0
Grossman	2	0	0	0
Benson	2	-1	4	0

Receiving

INDIANAPOLIS

	No.	Yds	Lg	TD
Addai	10	66	12	0
Wayne	2	61	53	1
Harrison	5	59	22	0
Clark	4	36	17	0
Fletcher	2	9	6	0
Rhodes	1	8	8	0
Utecht	1	8	8	0

CHICAGO

	No.	Yds	Lg	TD
Clark	6	64	18	0
Berrian	4	38	14	0
Muhammad	3	35	22	1
Jones	4	18	14	0
McKie	2	8	4	0
Davis	1	2	2	0

Defense

INDIANAPOLIS

	Tck	Ast	Int	Sack
Brackett	6	2	0	0
June	5	2	0	0
Bethea	4	0	0	0
Hayden	4	1	1	0
Morris	4	0	0	0
Harper	3	0	0	0
David	2	0	0	0
Jackson	2	0	0	0
Mathis	2	1	0	0
McFarland	2	0	0	1
Sanders	2	1	1	0
Boiman	1	0	0	0
Diem	1	0	0	0
Fletcher	1	0	0	0
Keiaho	1	0	0	0
Moorehead	1	0	0	0
Reid	1	0	0	0
Brock	0	1	0	0

CHICAGO

	Tck	Ast	Int	Sack
Briggs	11	2	0	0
Manning	7	1	0	0
Tillman	7	4	0	0
Urlacher	7	3	0	0
Johnson	4	1	0	.5
Scott	4	0	0	0
Vasher	4	2	0	0
Harris	3	1	1	0
Brown	2	0	0	0
Manning	2	0	0	0
Ogunleye	2	0	0	0
Anderson	1	1	0	.5
Ayanbadejo	1	0	0	0
Boone	1	0	0	0
Garza	1	0	0	0
Grossman	1	0	0	0
Hillenmeyer	1	5	0	0
Johnson	1	1	0	0
Jones	1	0	0	0
Peterson	1	0	0	0
Mannelly	0	1	0	0

2006 Associated Press All-Pro Team

OFFENSE

Drew Brees, New Orleans	Quarterback
LaDainian Tomlinson, San Diego	Running Back
Larry Johnson, Kansas City	Running Back
Lorenzo Neal, San Diego	Fullback
Antonio Gates, San Diego	Tight End
Marvin Harrison, Indianapolis	Wide Receiver
Chad Johnson, Cincinnati	Wide Receiver
Jammal Brown, New Orleans	Tackle
Willie Anderson, Cincinnati	Tackle
Shawn Andrews, Philadelphia	Guard
Alan Faneca, Pittsburgh	Guard
Olin Kreutz, Chicago	Center

DEFENSE

Jason Taylor, Miami	Defensive End
Julius Peppers, Carolina	Defensive End
Jamal Williams, San Diego	Defensive Tackle
Kevin Williams, Minnesota	Defensive Tackle
Shawne Merriman, San Diego	Linebacker
Adalius Thomas, Baltimore	Linebacker
Brian Urlacher, Chicago	Linebacker
Zach Thomas, Miami	Linebacker
Rashean Mathis, Jacksonville	Cornerback
Champ Bailey, Denver	Cornerback
Brian Dawkins, Philadelphia	Safety
Ed Reed, Baltimore	Safety

SPECIALISTS

Robbie Gould, Chicago	Kicker
Devin Hester, Chicago	Kick Returner
Brian Moorman, Buffalo	Punter

2006 AFC Team-by-Team Results

BALTIMORE RAVENS (13-3)

27	at Tampa Bay	0
28	OAKLAND	6
15	at Cleveland	14
16	SAN DIEGO	13
3	at Denver	13
21	CAROLINA	23
35	at New Orleans	22
26	CINCINNATI	20
27	at Tennessee	26
24	ATLANTA	10
27	PITTSBURGH	0
7	at Cincinnati	13
20	at Kansas City	10
27	CLEVELAND	17
31	at Pittsburgh	7
19	BUFFALO	7
353		201

BUFFALO BILLS (7-9)

17	at New England	19
16	at Miami	6
20	N.Y. JETS	28
17	MINNESOTA	12
7	at Chicago	40
17	at Detroit	20
6	NEW ENGLAND	28
24	GREEN BAY	10
16	at Indianapolis	17
24	at Houston	21
27	JACKSONVILLE	24
21	SAN DIEGO	24
31	at N.Y. Jets	13
21	MIAMI	0
29	TENNESSEE	30
7	at Baltimore	19
300		311

CINCINNATI BENGALS (8-8)

23	at Kansas City	10
34	CLEVELAND	17
28	at Pittsburgh	20
13	NEW ENGLAND	38
13	at Tampa Bay	14
17	CAROLINA	14
27	ATLANTA	29
20	at Baltimore	26
41	SAN DIEGO	49
31	at New Orleans	16
30	at Cleveland	0
13	BALTIMORE	7
27	OAKLAND	10
16	at Indianapolis	34
23	at Denver	24
17	PITTSBURGH	23
373		331

CLEVELAND BROWNS (4-12)

14	NEW ORLEANS	19	17	at Atlanta	13
17	at Cincinnati	34	20	PITTSBURGH	24
14	BALTIMORE	15	0	CINCINNATI	30
24	at Oakland	21	31	KANSAS CITY	28
12	at Carolina	20	7	at Pittsburgh	27
7	DENVER	17	17	at Baltimore	27
20	NY JETS	13	7	TAMPA BAY	22
25	at San Diego	32	6	at Houston	14
			238		356

DENVER BRONCOS (9-7)

10	at St. Louis	18
9	KANSAS CITY	6
17	at New England	7
13	BALTIMORE	3
13	OAKLAND	3
17	at Cleveland	7
31	INDIANAPOLIS	34
31	at Pittsburgh	20
17	at Oakland	13
27	SAN DIEGO	35
10	at Kansas	19
20	SEATTLE	23
20	at San Diego	48
37	at Arizona	20
24	CINCINNATI	23
23	SAN FRANCISCO	26
319		305

JACKSONVILLE JAGUARS (8-8)

24	DALLAS	17
9	PITTSBURGH	0
14	at Indianapolis	21
30	at Washington	36
41	NY JETS	0
7	at Houston	27
13	at Philadelphia	6
37	TENNESSEE	7
10	HOUSTON	13
26	NY GIANTS	10
24	at Buffalo	27
24	at Miami	10
44	INDIANAPOLIS	17
17	at Tennessee	24
21	NEW ENGLAND	24
30	at Kansas City	35
371		274

NEW ENGLAND PATRIOTS (12-4)

19	BUFFALO	17
24	at NY Jets	17
7	DENVER	17
38	at Cincinnati	13
20	MIAMI	10
28	at Buffalo	6
31	at Minnesota	7
20	INDIANAPOLIS	27
14	NY JETS	17
35	at Green Bay	0
17	CHICAGO	13
28	DETROIT	21
0	at Miami	21
40	HOUSTON	7
24	at Jacksonville	21
40	at Tennessee	23
385		237

HOUSTON TEXANS (6-10)

10	PHILADELPHIA	24
24	at Indianapolis	43
15	WASHINGTON	31
17	MIAMI	15
6	at Dallas	34
27	JACKSONVILLE	7
22	at Tennessee	28
10	at NY Giants	14
13	at Jacksonville	10
21	BUFFALO	24
11	at NY Jets	26
23	at Oakland	14
20	TENNESSEE	26
7	at New England	40
27	INDIANAPOLIS	24
14	CLEVELAND	6
267		366

KANSAS CITY CHIEFS (9-7)

10	CINCINNATI	23
6	at Denver	9
41	SAN FRANCISCO	0
23	at Arizona	20
7	at Pittsburgh	45
30	SAN DIEGO	27
35	SEATTLE	28
31	at St. Louis	17
10	at Miami	13
17	OAKLAND	13
19	DENVER	10
28	at Cleveland	31
10	BALTIMORE	20
9	at San Diego	20
20	at Oakland	9
35	JACKSONVILLE	30
331		315

NEW YORK JETS (10-6)

23	at Tennessee	16
17	NEW ENGLAND	24
28	at Buffalo	20
28	INDIANAPOLIS	31
0	at Jacksonville	41
20	MIAMI	17
31	DETROIT	24
13	at Cleveland	20
17	at New England	14
0	CHICAGO	10
26	HOUSTON	11
38	at Green Bay	10
13	BUFFALO	31
26	at Minnesota	13
13	at Miami	10
23	OAKLAND	3
316		295

INDIANAPOLIS COLTS (12-4)

26	at NY Giants	21
43	HOUSTON	24
21	JACKSONVILLE	14
31	at NY Jets	28
14	TENNESSEE	13
36	WASHINGTON	22
34	at Denver	31
27	at New England	20
17	BUFFALO	16
14	at Dallas	21
45	PHILADELPHIA	21
17	at Tennessee	20
17	at Jacksonville	44
34	CINCINNATI	16
24	at Houston	27
27	MIAMI	22
427		360

MIAMI DOLPHINS (6-10)

17	at Pittsburgh	28
6	BUFFALO	16
13	TENNESSEE	10
15	at Houston	17
10	at New England	20
17	at NY Jets	20
24	GREEN BAY	34
31	at Chicago	13
13	KANSAS CITY	10
24	MINNESOTA	20
27	at Detroit	10
10	JACKSONVILLE	24
21	NEW ENGLAND	0
0	at Buffalo	21
10	NY JETS	13
22	at Indianapolis	27
260		283

OAKLAND RAIDERS (2-14)

0	SAN DIEGO	27
6	at Baltimore	28
21	CLEVELAND	24
20	at San Francisco	34
3	at Denver	13
22	ARIZONA	9
20	PITTSBURGH	13
0	at Seattle	16
13	DENVER	17
13	at Kansas City	17
14	at San Diego	21
14	HOUSTON	23
10	at Cincinnati	27
0	ST. LOUIS	20
9	KANSAS CITY	20
3	at NY Jets	23
168		332

PITTSBURGH STEELERS (8-8)

28	MIAMI	17
0	at Jacksonville	9
20	CINCINNATI	28
13	at San Diego	23
45	KANSAS CITY	7
38	at Atlanta	41
13	at Oakland	20
20	DENVER	31
38	NEW ORLEANS	31
24	at Cleveland	20
0	at Baltimore	27
20	TAMPA BAY	3
27	CLEVELAND	7
37	at Carolina	3
7	BALTIMORE	31
23	at Cincinnati	17
353		315

SAN DIEGO CHARGERS (14-2)

27	at Oakland	0
40	TENNESSEE	7
13	at Baltimore	16
23	PITTSBURGH	13
48	at San Francisco	19
27	at Kansas City	30
38	ST. LOUIS	24
32	CLEVELAND	25
49	at Cincinnati	41
35	at Denver	27
21	OAKLAND	14
24	at Buffalo	21
48	DENVER	20
20	KANSAS CITY	9
20	at Seattle	17
27	ARIZONA	20
492		303

TENNESSEE TITANS (8-8)

16	NY JETS	23
7	at San Diego	40
10	at Miami	13
14	DALLAS	45
13	at Indianapolis	14
25	at Washington	22
28	HOUSTON	22
7	at Jacksonville	37
26	BALTIMORE	27
31	at Philadelphia	13
24	NY GIANTS	21
20	INDIANAPOLIS	17
26	at Houston	20
24	JACKSONVILLE	17
30	at Buffalo	29
23	NEW ENGLAND	40
324		400

ARIZONA CARDINALS (5-11)

34	SAN FRANCISCO	27
10	at Seattle	21
14	ST. LOUIS	16
10	at Atlanta	32
20	KANSAS CITY	23
23	CHICAGO	24
9	at Oakland	22
14	at Green Bay	31
10	DALLAS	27
17	DETROIT	10
26	at Minnesota	31
34	at St. Louis	20
27	SEATTLE	21
20	DENVER	37
26	at San Francisco	20
20	at San Diego	27
314		389

ATLANTA FALCONS (7-9)

20	at Carolina	6
14	TAMPA BAY	3
3	at New Orleans	23
32	ARIZONA	10
14	NY GIANTS	27
41	PITTSBURGH	38
29	at Cincinnati	27
14	at Detroit	30
13	CLEVELAND	17
10	at Baltimore	24
13	NEW ORLEANS	31
24	at Washington	14
17	at Tampa Bay	6
28	DALLAS	38
3	CAROLINA	10
17	at Philadelphia	24
292		328

CAROLINA PANTHERS (8-8)

6	ATLANTA	20
13	at Minnesota	16
26	at Tampa Bay	24
21	NEW ORLEANS	18
20	CLEVELAND	12
23	at Baltimore	21
14	at Cincinnati	17
14	DALLAS	35
24	TAMPA BAY	10
15	ST. LOUIS	0
13	at Washington	17
24	at Philadelphia	27
13	NY GIANTS	27
3	PITTSBURGH	37
10	at Atlanta	3
31	at New Orleans	21
270		305

CHICAGO BEARS (13-3)

26	at Green Bay	0
34	DETROIT	7
19	at Minnesota	16
37	SEATTLE	6
40	BUFFALO	7
24	at Arizona	23
41	SAN FRANCISCO	10
13	MIAMI	31
38	at NY Giants	20
10	at NY Jets	0
13	at New England	17
23	MINNESOTA	13
42	at St. Louis	27
34	TAMPA BAY	31
26	at Detroit	21
7	GREEN BAY	26
427		255

DALLAS COWBOYS (9-7)

17	at Jacksonville	24
27	WASHINGTON	10
45	at Tennessee	14
24	at Philadelphia	38
34	HOUSTON	6
22	NY GIANTS	36
35	at Carolina	14
19	at Washington	22
27	at Arizona	10
21	INDIANAPOLIS	14
38	TAMPA BAY	10
23	at NY Giants	20
17	NEW ORLEANS	42
38	at Atlanta	28
7	PHILADELPHIA	23
31	DETROIT	39
425		350

DETROIT LIONS (3-13)

6	SEATTLE	9
7	at Chicago	34
24	GREEN BAY	31
34	at St. Louis	41
17	at Minnesota	26
20	BUFFALO	17
24	at NY Jets	31
30	ATLANTA	14
13	SAN FRANCISCO	19
10	at Arizona	17
10	MIAMI	27
21	at New England	28
20	MINNESOTA	30
9	at Green Bay	17
21	CHICAGO	26
39	at Dallas	31
305		398

GREEN BAY PACKERS (8-8)

0	CHICAGO	26
27	NEW ORLEANS	34
31	at Detroit	24
9	at Philadelphia	31
20	ST. LOUIS	23
34	at Miami	24
31	ARIZONA	14
10	at Buffalo	24
23	at Minnesota	17
0	NEW ENGLAND	35
24	at Seattle	34
10	NY JETS	38
30	at San Francisco	19
17	DETROIT	9
9	MINNESOTA	7
26	at Chicago	7
301		366

MINNESOTA VIKINGS (6-10)

19	at Washington	16
16	CAROLINA	13
16	CHICAGO	19
12	at Buffalo	17
26	DETROIT	17
31	at Seattle	13
7	NEW ENGLAND	31
3	at San Francisco	9
17	GREEN BAY	23
20	at Miami	24
31	ARIZONA	26
13	at Chicago	23
30	at Detroit	20
13	NY JETS	26
7	at Green Bay	9
21	ST. LOUIS	41
282		327

NEW ORLEANS SAINTS (10-6)

19	at Cleveland	14
34	at Green Bay	27
23	ATLANTA	3
18	at Carolina	21
24	TAMPA BAY	21
27	PHILADELPHIA	24
22	BALTIMORE	35
31	at Tampa Bay	14
31	at Pittsburgh	38
16	CINCINNATI	31
31	at Atlanta	13
34	SAN FRANCISCO	10
42	at Dallas	17
10	WASHINGTON	16
30	at NY Giants	7
21	CAROLINA	31
413		322

NEW YORK GIANTS (8-8)

21	INDIANAPOLIS	26
30	at Philadelphia	24
30	at Seattle	42
19	WASHINGTON	3
27	at Atlanta	14
36	at Dallas	22
17	TAMPA BAY	3
14	HOUSTON	10
20	CHICAGO	38
10	at Jacksonville	26
21	at Tennessee	24
20	DALLAS	23
27	at Carolina	13
22	PHILADELPHIA	36
7	NEW ORLEANS	30
34	at Washington	28
355		362

PHILADELPHIA EAGLES (10-6)

24	at Houston	10
24	NY GIANTS	30
38	at San Francisco	24
31	GREEN BAY	9
38	DALLAS	24
24	at New Orleans	27
21	at Tampa Bay	23
6	JACKSONVILLE	13
27	WASHINGTON	3
13	TENNESSEE	31
21	at Indianapolis	45
27	CAROLINA	24
21	at Washington	19
36	at NY Giants	22
23	at Dallas	7
24	ATLANTA	17
398		328

ST. LOUIS RAMS (8-8)

18	DENVER	10
13	at San Francisco	20
16	at Arizona	14
41	DETROIT	34
23	at Green Bay	20
28	SEATTLE	30
24	at San Diego	38
17	KANSAS CITY	31
22	at Seattle	24
0	at Carolina	15
20	SAN FRANCISCO	17
20	ARIZONA	34
27	CHICAGO	42
20	at Oakland	0
37	WASHINGTON	31
41	at Minnesota	21
367		381

SAN FRANCISCO 49ERS (7-9)

27	at Arizona	34
20	ST. LOUIS	13
24	PHILADELPHIA	38
0	at Kansas City	41
34	OAKLAND	20
19	SAN DIEGO	48
10	at Chicago	41
9	MINNESOTA	3
19	at Detroit	13
20	SEATTLE	14
17	at St. Louis	20
10	at New Orleans	34
19	GREEN BAY	30
24	at Seattle	14
20	ARIZONA	26
26	at Denver	23
298		412

SEATTLE SEAHAWKS (9-7)

9	at Detroit	6
21	ARIZONA	10
42	NY GIANTS	30
6	at Chicago	37
30	at St. Louis	28
13	MINNESOTA	31
28	at Kansas City	35
16	OAKLAND	0
24	ST. LOUIS	22
14	at San Francisco	20
34	GREEN BAY	24
23	at Denver	20
21	at Arizona	27
14	SAN FRANCISCO	24
17	SAN DIEGO	20
23	at Tampa Bay	7
335		341

TAMPA BAY BUCCANEERS (4-12)

0	BALTIMORE	27
3	at Atlanta	14
24	CAROLINA	26
21	at New Orleans	24
14	CINCINNATI	13
23	PHILADELPHIA	21
3	at NY Giants	17
14	NEW ORLEANS	31
10	at Carolina	24
20	WASHINGTON	17
10	at Dallas	38
3	at Pittsburgh	20
6	ATLANTA	17
31	at Chicago	34
22	at Cleveland	7
7	SEATTLE	23
211		353

WASHINGTON REDSKINS (5-11)

16	MINNESOTA	19	17	at Tampa Bay	20
10	at Dallas	27	17	CAROLINA	13
31	at Houston	15	14	ATLANTA	24
36	JACKSONVILLE	30	19	PHILADELPHIA	21
3	at NY Giants	19	16	at New Orleans	10
22	TENNESSEE	25	31	at St. Louis	37
22	at Indianapolis	36	28	NY GIANTS	34
22	DALLAS	19	307		376
3	at Philadelphia	27			

American Football Conference

Scoring

TOUCHDOWNS	TD	Rush	Rec	Ret	2PT	Pts	KICKING	PAT	FG	Pts
Tomlinson, SD	31	28	3	0	0	186	Stover, Balt	37	28	121
L. Johnson, KC	19	17	2	0	0	114	Elam, Den	34	27	115
Jones-Drew, Jac	16	13	2	1	0	96	Mare, Mia	22	26	100
Parker, Pitt	16	13	3	0	0	96	Scobee, Jac	41	26	119
Dillon, NE	13	13	0	0	0	78	Kaeding, SD	58	26	136
Harrison, Ind	12	0	12	0	0	72	Vinatieri, Ind	38	25	113
R. Johnson, Cin	12	12	0	0	0	72	Graham, Cin	42	25	115
Wayne, Ind	9	0	9	0	1	56	Nugent, NYJ	35	24	106
Lewis, Balt	9	9	0	0	0	54	Tynes, KC	36	24	107
Henry, Cin	9	0	9	0	0	54	Lindell, Buff	33	23	102

Passing

	Att	Comp	Yds	TD	Int	Lg	Rating Pts
Manning, Ind	557	362	4397	31	9	68	101.0
Huard, KC	244	148	1878	11	1	78	98.0
Palmer, Cin	520	324	4035	28	13	74	93.9
Rivers, SD	460	284	3388	22	9	57	92.0
Brady, NE	516	319	3529	24	12	62	87.9
Losman, Buff	429	268	3051	19	14	83	84.9
Pennington, NYJ	485	313	3352	17	16	71	82.6
McNair, Balt	468	295	3050	16	12	87	82.5
Carr, Hou	442	302	2767	11	12	53	82.1
Garrard, Jac	241	145	1735	10	9	49	80.5

Pass Receiving

RECEPTIONS	No.	Yds	Avg	Lg	TD	YARDS	Yds	No.	Avg	Lg	TD
A. Johnson, Hou	103	1147	11.1	53	5	C. Johnson, Cin	1369	87	15.7	74	7
Harrison, Ind	95	1366	14.4	68	12	Harrison, Ind	1366	95	14.4	68	12
Coles, NYJ	91	1098	12.1	58	6	Wayne, Ind	1310	86	15.2	51	9
Houshmandzadeh, Cin	90	1081	12.0	40	9	Evans, Buff	1292	82	15.8	83	8
Winslow, Cle	89	875	9.8	40	3	A. Johnson, Hou	1147	103	11.1	53	5
C. Johnson, Cin	87	1369	15.7	74	7	Coles, NYJ	1098	91	12.1	58	6
Wayne, Ind	86	1310	15.2	51	9	Walker, Den	1084	69	15.7	83	8
Evans, Buff	82	1292	15.8	83	8	Houshmandzadeh, Cin	1081	90	12.0	40	9
Cotchery, NYJ	82	961	11.7	71	6	Ward, Pitt	975	74	13.2	70	6
Ward, Pitt	74	975	13.2	70	6	Cotchery, NYJ	961	82	11.7	71	6
Gonazlez, KC	73	900	12.3	57	5	Clayton, Balt	939	67	14.0	87	5

Rushing

	Att	Yds	Avg	Lg	TD
Tomlinson, SD	348	1815	5.2	85	28
L. Johnson, KC	416	1789	4.3	47	17
Parker, Pitt	337	1494	4.4	76	13
R. Johnson, Cin	341	1309	3.8	22	12
Henry, Tenn	270	1211	4.5	70	7
Taylor, Jac	231	1146	5.0	76	5
Lewis, Balt	314	1132	3.6	52	9
Addai, Ind	226	1081	4.8	41	7
Bell, Den	233	1025	4.4	51	2
Brown, Mia	241	1008	4.2	47	5

Interceptions

	No.	Yds	Lg	TD
Samuel, NE	10	120	33	0
Bailey, Den	10	162	70	1
Mathis, Jac	8	146	55	0
Asomugha, Oak	8	59	24	1
McAlister, Balt	6	121	60	2

Sacks

Merriman, SD	17.0
Schobel, Buff	14.0
Taylor, Mia	13.5
Pryce, Balt	13.0
Phillips, SD	11.5

American Football Conference *(Cont.)*

Punting

	No.	Yds	Avg	Net Avg	TB	In 20	Lg	Blk	Ret	Ret Avg
Lechler, Oak	77	3660	47.5	36.4	19	19	67	0	34	12.9
Larson, Cin	77	3428	44.5	38.6	11	26	67	0	42	5.6
Smith, Ind	47	2085	44.4	34.5	5	14	61	0	25	13.1
Colquitt, KC	71	3145	44.3	39.3	5	23	72	0	32	7.9
Graham, NYJ	72	3182	44.2	37.8	11	26	69	0	28	7.3

Punt Returns

	No.	Yds	Avg	Lg	TD
A. Jones, Ten	34	440	12.9	90	3
Parrish, Buff	32	364	11.4	82	1
Northcutt, Cle	28	312	11.1	81	0
Faulk, NE	31	330	10.6	43	0
Sams, Balt	29	307	10.6	65	0

Kickoff Returns

	No.	Yds	Avg	Lg	TD
Miller, NYJ	46	1304	28.3	103	2
Maroney, NE	28	783	28.0	77	0
Jones-Drew, Jac	31	860	27.7	93	1
Turner, SD	36	954	26.5	58	0
McGee, Buff	52	1355	26.1	88	0

National Football Conference

Scoring

TOUCHDOWNS	TD	Rush	Rec	Ret	2PT	Pts
Barber, Dal	16	14	2	0	0	96
S. Jackson, StL	16	13	3	0	0	96
Owens, Dal	13	0	13	0	1	80
Westbrook, Phi	11	7	4	0	0	66
McAllister, NO	11	10	0	0	0	66
D. Jackson, Sea	10	0	10	0	0	60
Burress, NYG	10	0	10	0	0	60
Holt, StL	10	0	10	0	0	60
Jacobs, NYG	9	9	0	0	0	54
Brown, Phi	9	1	8	0	0	54

KICKING	PAT	FG	Pts
Gould, Chi	47	32	143
Wilkins, StL	35	32	131
Hanson, Det	30	29	117
Nedney, SF	29	29	116
Rackers, Ari	32	28	116
Rayner, GB	32	26	109
Brown, Sea	36	25	111
Kasay, Car	28	24	100
Feely, NYG	38	23	107
Carney, NO	47	23	115

Passing

	Att	Comp	Yds	TD	Int	Lg	Rating Pts
Brees, NO	554	356	4418	26	11	86	96.2
McNabb, Phi	316	180	2647	18	6	87	95.5
Romo, Dal	337	220	2903	19	13	56	95.1
Bulger, StL	588	370	4301	24	8	67	92.9
Brunell, Wash	260	162	1789	8	4	74	86.5
Delhomme, Car	431	263	2805	17	11	72	82.6
Kitna, Det	596	372	4208	21	22	60	79.9
Manning, NYG	522	301	3244	24	18	55	77.0
Hasselbeck, Sea	371	210	2442	18	15	72	76.0
Vick, Atl	388	204	2474	20	13	55	75.7

Pass Receiving

RECEPTIONS	No.	Yds	Avg	Lg	TD
Furrey, Det	98	1086	11.1	31	6
Holt, StL	93	1188	12.8	67	10
Driver, GB	92	1295	14.1	82	8
Jackson, StL	90	806	9.0	64	3
Bush, NO	88	742	8.4	74	2
Owens, Dal	85	1180	13.9	56	13
Boldin, Ariz	83	1203	14.5	64	4
Smith, Car	83	1166	14.0	72	8
Williams, Det	82	1310	16.0	60	7
Westbrook, Phi	77	699	9.1	52	4

YARDS	Yds	No.	Avg	Lg	TD
Williams, Det	1310	82	16.0	60	7
Driver, GB	1295	92	14.1	82	8
Boldin, Ariz	1203	83	14.5	64	4
Holt, StL	1188	93	12.8	67	10
Owens, Dal	1180	85	13.9	56	13
Smith, Car	1166	83	14.0	72	8
Bruce, StL	1098	74	14.8	45	3
Furrey, Det	1086	98	11.1	31	6
Galloway, TB	1057	62	17.0	64	7
Glenn, Dal	1047	70	15.0	54	6

National Football Conference *(Cont.)*

Rushing

	Att	Yds	Avg	Lg	TD
Gore, SF	312	1695	5.4	72	8
Barber, NYG	327	1662	5.1	55	5
S. Jackson, StL	346	1528	4.4	59	13
Westbrook, Phi	240	1217	5.1	71	7
Taylor, Minn	303	1216	4.0	95	6
T. Jones, Chi	296	1210	4.1	30	6
James, Ari	337	1159	3.4	18	6
Betts, Wash	245	1154	4.7	26	4
Dunn, Atl	286	1140	4.0	90	4
J. Jones, Dal	267	1084	4.1	77	4

Interceptions

	No.	Yds	Lg	TD
Woodson, GB	8	61	23	1
Harris, SF	8	84	42	1
Sheppard, Phi	6	157	102	1
Williams, Dal	5	33	27	0
Manning, Chi	5	113	54	1
Tillman, Chi	5	32	13	0

Sacks

Kampman, GB	15.5
Peppers, Car	13.0
Little, StL	13.0
Anderson, Chi	12.0
Ware, Dal	11.5

Punting

	No.	Yds	Avg	Net Avg	TB	In 20	Lg	Blk	Ret	Ret Avg
McBriar, Dal	56	2697	48.2	38.6	10	22	75	0	31	10.8
Baker, Car	98	4483	45.7	39.0	12	31	70	0	60	6.4
Plackemeier, Sea	84	3778	45.0	37.3	15	25	72	0	38	9.0
Harris, Det	66	2967	45.0	38.2	9	18	67	0	38	7.0
Player, Ari	66	2965	44.9	34.5	3	18	58	0	44	12.8

Punt Returns

	No.	Yds	Avg	Lg	TD
Hester, Chi	47	600	12.8	84	3
Drummond, Det	28	296	10.6	40	0
Walters, Ari	24	250	10.4	37	0
Newman, Dal	20	202	10.1	56	1
Moore, Minn	36	365	10.1	71	1
Burleson, Sea	34	322	9.5	90	1

Kickoff Returns

	No.	Yds	Avg	Lg	TD
Hester, Chi	20	528	26.4	96	2
Austin, Dal	29	753	26.0	37	0
Thompson, Dal	21	546	26.0	41	0
Hicks, SF	57	1428	25.1	64	0
Burleson, Sea	26	643	24.7	50	0

2006 NFL Team Leaders

AFC Total Offense

	Total Plays	Yds/ Game	Yds/ Play	1st Dwns/ Game	Time of Poss
Indianapolis	1011	379.4	6.0	23.5	29:32
San Diego	1016	365.0	5.7	20.1	31:39
Pittsburgh	1041	357.8	5.5	20.4	31:13
Cincinnati	994	341.4	5.5	19.6	28:34
Jacksonville	989	338.9	5.5	18.3	32:11
New England	1055	335.6	5.1	20.6	31:35
Kansas City	1004	321.4	5.1	19.4	30:06
Baltimore	1017	317.0	5.0	17.6	32:49
Miami	1034	310.0	4.8	17.6	30:01
Denver	973	309.4	5.1	17.8	29:50
NY Jets	1013	305.7	4.8	18.1	31:03
Tennessee	945	300.6	5.1	16.3	27:17
Houston	955	279.1	4.7	17.6	29:14
Buffalo	898	266.9	4.8	14.6	28:04
Cleveland	937	264.6	4.5	15.6	29:21
Oakland	949	246.2	4.2	15.2	28:14

AFC Total Defense

	Opp Total Plays	Opp Yds/ Game	Opp Yds/ Play	Opp Time of Poss
Baltimore	936	264.1	4.5	27:12
Jacksonville	978	283.6	4.6	27:49
Oakland	986	284.8	4.6	31:46
Miami	1005	289.1	4.6	29:59
New England	950	294.4	5.0	28:25
Pittsburgh	976	300.3	4.9	28:47
San Diego	985	301.6	4.9	28:21
Denver	1020	326.4	5.1	30:10
Kansas City	999	328.9	5.3	29:54
Buffalo	1029	329.6	5.1	31:56
NY Jets	1020	331.6	5.2	28:57
Indianapolis	959	332.2	5.5	30:28
Houston	978	337.5	5.5	30:46
Cleveland	1041	344.8	5.3	30:39
Cincinnati	1038	355.1	5.5	31:26
Tennessee	1062	369.7	5.6	32:43

NFC Total Offense

	Total Plays	Yds/ Game	Yds/ Play	1st Dwns/ Game	Time of Poss
New Orleans	1075	391.5	5.8	20.6	31:53
Philadelphia	988	381.4	6.2	19.5	28:38
Dallas	1015	360.8	5.7	21.0	31:02
St. Louis	1065	360.4	5.4	20.8	31:07
Green Bay	1085	341.1	5.0	18.8	30:45
Atlanta	1000	331.9	5.3	17.9	29:48
Washington	979	327.7	5.4	18.4	29:59
NY Giants	1003	325.9	5.2	19.0	29:35
Chicago	1042	324.9	5.0	18.8	30:34
Arizona	999	312.5	5.0	18.6	29:59
Seattle	1045	311.1	4.8	19.5	29:48
Detroit	963	309.3	5.1	18.1	27:41
Minnesota	1025	308.9	4.8	17.0	31:37
Carolina	994	307.7	5.0	17.4	30:12
San Francisco	918	303.8	5.3	15.2	28:37
Tampa Bay	972	270.1	4.4	14.8	28:06

NFC Total Defense

	Opp Total Plays	Opp Yds/ Game	Opp Yds/ Play	Opp Time of Poss
Chicago	1023	294.1	4.6	29:26
Carolina	990	296.1	4.8	29:48
Minnesota	977	300.2	4.9	28:23
New Orleans	930	307.3	5.3	28:07
Green Bay	1002	320.9	5.1	29:15
Dallas	974	322.8	5.3	28:58
Philadelphia	1054	328.1	5.0	31:22
Tampa Bay	1015	329.4	5.2	31:54
Seattle	986	330.3	5.4	30:12
Atlanta	994	332.8	5.4	30:12
St. Louis	962	335.1	5.6	28:53
NY Giants	1057	342.4	5.2	30:25
San Francisco	1025	344.2	5.4	31:23
Detroit	1033	345.6	5.4	32:19
Arizona	1018	349.4	5.5	30:01
Washington	997	355.5	5.7	30:01

Takeaways/Giveaways

American Football Conference

	Takeaways Int	Fum	Total	Giveaways Int	Fum	Total	Net Diff
Baltimore	28	12	40	14	9	23	17
San Diego	16	12	28	9	6	15	13
New England	22	13	35	12	15	27	8
Indianapolis	15	11	26	9	10	19	7
Cincinnati	19	12	31	13	11	24	7
Kansas City	15	15	30	12	14	26	4
Miami	8	19	27	19	6	25	2
Tennessee	17	11	28	19	7	26	2
Jacksonville	20	4	24	14	9	23	1
NY Jets	16	9	25	16	9	25	0
Denver	17	13	30	18	12	30	0
Houston	11	11	22	13	12	25	-3
Buffalo	13	11	24	14	15	29	-5
Pittsburgh	20	9	29	23	14	37	-8
Cleveland	18	9	27	25	17	42	-15
Oakland	18	5	23	24	22	46	-23

National Football Conference

	Takeaways Int	Fum	Total	Giveaways Int	Fum	Total	Net Diff
St. Louis	17	15	32	8	10	18	14
Chicago	24	20	44	22	14	36	8
Atlanta	12	14	26	15	5	20	6
Philadelphia	19	10	29	9	15	24	5
Minnesota	21	15	36	20	12	32	4
Arizona	16	17	33	17	13	30	3
Dallas	18	13	31	21	9	30	1
NY Giants	17	11	28	18	10	28	0
Green Bay	23	10	33	18	15	33	0
New Orleans	11	8	19	13	10	23	-4
Washington	6	6	12	10	7	17	-5
San Francisco	14	13	27	16	16	32	-5
Carolina	14	8	22	17	10	27	-5
Seattle	12	14	26	22	12	34	-8
Detroit	12	18	30	22	17	39	-9
Tampa Bay	11	9	20	18	14	32	-12

Baltimore Ravens

SCORING

SCORING	Rush	Rec	Ret	PAT	FG	S	Pts
Stover	0	0	0	37	28	0	121
Lewis	9	0	0	0	0	0	54
Heap	0	6	0	0	0	0	36
Clayton	0	5	0	0	0	0	30
Wilcox	0	3	0	0	0	0	18
Mason	0	2	0	0	0	0	12

RUSHING	No.	Yds	Avg	Lg	TD
Lewis	314	1132	3.6	52	9
Anderson	39	183	4.7	34	1

PASSING	Att	Comp	Pct Comp	Yds	Avg Gain	TD	Int	Rating Pts
McNair	468	295	63.0	3050	6.5	16	12	82.5
Boller	55	33	60.0	485	8.8	5	2	104.0

RECEIVING	No.	Yds	Avg	Lg	TD
Clayton	67	939	14.0	87	5
Heap	73	765	10.5	30	6
Mason	68	750	11.0	38	2
Wiliams	22	396	18.0	77	2
Mughelli	21	182	8.7	30	2
Wilcox	20	166	8.3	35	3

INTERCEPTIONS: McAlister, 6

PUNTING	No.	Yds	Avg	Net Avg	TB	In 20	Lg	Blk
Koch	86	3695	43.0	37.6	3	30	61	0

SACKS: Pryce, 13

Buffalo Bills

SCORING

SCORING	Rush	Rec	Ret	PAT	FG	S	Pts
Lindell	0	0	0	33	23	0	102
Evans	0	8	0	0	0	0	48
McGahee	6	0	0	0	0	0	36
Price	0	3	0	0	0	0	18
Royal	0	3	0	0	0	0	18
Parrish	0	2	1	0	0	0	18

RUSHING	No.	Yds	Avg	Lg	TD
McGahee	259	990	3.8	57	6
Thomas	107	378	3.5	19	2

PASSING	Att	Comp	Pct Comp	Yds	Avg Gain	TD	Int	Rating Pts
Losman	429	268	62.5	3051	7.1	19	14	84.9
Evans	1	0	0.00	0	0.0	0	0	39.6

RECEIVING	No.	Yds	Avg	Lg	TD
Evans	82	1292	15.8	83	8
Reed	34	410	12.1	52	2
Price	49	402	8.2	25	3
Parrish	23	320	13.9	51	2
Royal	23	233	10.1	33	3

INTERCEPTIONS: Fletcher-Baker, 4

PUNTING	No.	Yds	Avg	Net Avg	TB	In 20	Lg	Blk
Moorman	92	4012	43.6	39.2	7	33	66	0

SACKS: Schobel, 14

Cincinnati Bengals

SCORING

SCORING	Rush	Rec	Ret	PAT	FG	S	Pts
Graham	0	0	0	40	25	0	115
R. Johnson	12	0	0	0	0	0	72
Houshmandzadeh	0	9	0	0	0	0	54
Henry	0	9	0	0	0	0	54
C. Johnson	0	7	0	0	0	0	42
Kelly	0	1	0	0	0	0	6

RUSHING	No.	Yds	Avg	Lg	TD
R. Johnson	341	1309	3.8	22	12
Watson	25	138	5.5	18	1

PASSING	Att	Comp	Pct Comp	Yds	Avg Gain	TD	Int	Rating Pts
Palmer	520	324	62.3	4035	7.8	28	13	93.9

RECEIVING	No.	Yds	Avg	Lg	TD
C. Johnson	87	1369	15.7	74	7
Houshmandzadeh	90	1081	12.0	40	9
Henry	36	605	16.8	71	9
Kelly	21	254	12.1	32	1
Watson	23	213	9.3	46	0
R. Johnson	23	124	5.4	18	0

INTERCEPTIONS: Kaesviharn, 6

PUNTING	No.	Yds	Avg	Net Avg	TB	In 20	Lg	Blk
Larson	77	3428	44.5	38.6	11	26	67	0

SACKS: Geathers, 10.5

Cleveland Browns

SCORING

SCORING	Rush	Rec	Ret	PAT	FG	S	Pts
Dawson	0	0	0	25	21	0	88
Edwards	0	6	0	0	0	0	36
Droughns	4	0	0	0	0	0	24
Jurevicius	0	3	0	0	0	0	18
Winslow	0	3	0	0	0	0	18
Frye	3	0	0	0	0	0	18

RUSHING	No.	Yds	Avg	Lg	TD
Droughns	220	758	3.4	22	4

PASSING	Att	Comp	Pct Comp	Yds	Avg Gain	TD	Int	Rating Pts
Frye	392	252	64.3	2454	6.3	10	17	72.2
Anderson	117	66	56.4	793	6.8	5	8	63.1

RECEIVING	No.	Yds	Avg	Lg	TD
Edwards	61	884	14.5	75	6
Winslow	89	875	9.8	40	3
Jurevicius	40	495	12.4	52	3
Heiden	36	249	6.9	13	2
Northcutt	22	228	10.4	43	0
Droughns	27	169	6.3	24	0
Cribbs	10	91	9.1	14	0

INTERCEPTIONS: Holly, 5; Jones 5

PUNTING	No.	Yds	Avg	Net Avg	TB	In 20	Lg	Blk
Zastudil	81	3563	44.0	38.4	7	28	61	0

SACKS: Wimbley, 11

Denver Broncos

SCORING

| | TD | | | | | | |
	Rush	Rec	Ret	PAT	FG	S	Pts
Elam	0	0	0	34	27	0	115
Walker	1	8	0	0	0	0	54
Bell	8	0	0	0	0	0	48
Scheffler	0	4	0	0	0	0	24
Smith	0	3	0	0	0	0	18

RUSHING

	No.	Yds	Avg	Lg	TD
T. Bell	233	1025	4.4	51	2
M. Bell	157	677	4.3	48	8
Walker	9	123	13.7	72	1

PASSING

	Att	Comp	Pct Comp	Yds	Avg Gain	TD	Int	Rating Pts
Plummer	317	175	55.2	1994	6.3	11	13	68.8

RECEIVING

	No.	Yds	Avg	Lg	TD
Walker	69	1084	15.7	83	8
Smith	52	512	9.8	20	3
Marshall	20	309	15.5	71	2
Scheffler	18	286	15.9	29	4
Kircus	9	187	20.8	45	0
Alexander	18	160	8.9	24	2

INTERCEPTIONS: Bailey, 10

PUNTING

	No.	Yds	Avg	Net Avg	TB	In 20	Lg	Blk
Ernster	80	3338	41.7	36.6	7	23	61	0

SACKS: Dumervil, 8.5

Indianapolis Colts

SCORING

| | TD | | | | | | |
	Rush	Rec	Ret	PAT	FG	S	Pts
Vinatieri	0	0	0	38	25	0	113
Harrison	0	12	0	0	0	0	72
Wayne	0	9	0	0	0	1	56
Addai	7	1	0	0	0	0	48
Rhodes	5	0	0	0	0	0	30
Manning	4	0	0	0	0	1	24

RUSHING

	No.	Yds	Avg	Lg	TD
Addai	226	1081	4.8	41	7
Rhodes	187	641	3.4	17	5

PASSING

	Att	Comp	Pct Comp	Yds	Avg Gain	TD	Int	Rating Pts
Manning	557	362	65.0	4397	7.9	31	9	101.0

RECEIVING

	No.	Yds	Avg	Lg	TD
Harrison	95	1366	14.4	68	12
Wayne	86	1310	15.2	51	9
Utecht	37	377	10.2	26	0
Clark	30	367	12.2	40	4
Addai	40	325	8.1	21	1
Rhodes	36	251	7.0	27	0

INTERCEPTIONS: June, Harper, 3

PUNTING

	No.	Yds	Avg	Net Avg	TB	In 20	Lg	Blk
Smith	47	2085	44.4	34.5	5	14	61	0

SACKS: Mathis, 9.5

Houston Texans

SCORING

| | TD | | | | | | |
	Rush	Rec	Ret	PAT	FG	S	Pts
Brown	0	0	0	26	19	0	83
Dayne	5	0	0	0	0	1	32
Johnson	0	5	0	0	0	0	30
Daniels	0	5	0	0	0	0	30
Lundy	4	0	0	0	0	1	26

RUSHING

	No.	Yds	Avg	Lg	TD
Dayne	151	612	4.1	19	5
Lundy	124	476	3.8	35	4

PASSING

	Att	Comp	Pct Comp	Yds	Avg Gain	TD	Int	Rating Pts
Carr	442	302	68.3	2767	6.3	11	12	82.1

RECEIVING

	No.	Yds	Avg	Lg	TD
Johnson	103	1147	11.1	53	5
Moulds	57	557	9.8	29	1
Daniels	34	352	10.4	33	5
Lundy	33	204	6.2	15	0
Walter	17	160	9.4	15	0
Putzier	13	125	9.6	26	0

INTERCEPTIONS: Faggins, Robinson, 2

PUNTING

	No.	Yds	Avg	Net Avg	TB	In 20	Lg	Blk
Stanley	76	3161	41.6	36.7	5	15	62	0

SACKS: Babin, 5

Jacksonville Jaguars

SCORING

| | TD | | | | | | |
	Rush	Rec	Ret	PAT	FG	S	Pts
Scobee	0	0	0	41	26	0	119
Jones-Drew	13	2	1	0	0	0	96
Taylor	5	1	0	0	0	0	36
Williams	0	4	0	0	0	0	24
Jones	0	4	0	0	0	0	24
Wrighster	0	3	0	0	0	0	18

RUSHING

	No.	Yds	Avg	Lg	TD
Taylor	231	1146	5.0	76	5
Jones-Drew	166	941	5.7	74	13

PASSING

	Att	Comp	Pct Comp	Yds	Avg Gain	TD	Int	Rating Pts
Garrard	241	145	60.2	1735	7.2	10	9	80.5
Leftwich	183	108	59.0	1159	6.3	7	5	79.0

RECEIVING

	No.	Yds	Avg	Lg	TD
Jones	41	643	15.7	49	4
Williams	52	616	11.8	48	4
Wilford	36	524	14.6	41	2
Jones-Drew	46	436	9.5	51	2
Wrighster	39	353	9.1	23	3

INTERCEPTIONS: Mathis, 8

PUNTING

	No.	Yds	Avg	Net Avg	TB	In 20	Lg	Blk
Hanson	72	2920	40.6	33.4	7	20	58	0

SACKS: McCray, 10

Kansas City Chiefs

SCORING	Rush	Rec	Ret	PAT	FG	S	Pts
	TD						
L. Johnson	17	2	0	0	0	0	114
Tynes	0	0	0	35	24	0	107
Gonzalez	0	5	0	0	0	1	32
Kennison	0	5	0	0	0	0	30
Hall	0	2	1	0	0	0	18
Wilson	0	3	0	0	0	0	18

RUSHING	No.	Yds	Avg	Lg	TD
L. Johnson	416	1789	4.3	47	17
Bennett	36	200	5.6	41	0

PASSING	Att	Comp	Pct Comp	Yds	Avg Gain	TD	Int	Rating Pts
Huard	244	148	60.7	1878	7.7	11	1	98.0
T. Green	198	121	61.1	1342	6.8	7	9	74.1

RECEIVING	No.	Yds	Avg	Lg	TD
Gonzalez	73	900	12.3	57	5
Kennison	53	860	16.2	51	5
Parker	41	561	13.7	43	1
L. Johnson	41	410	10.0	78	2
Hall	26	204	7.8	19	2
Wilson	15	132	8.8	19	3

INTERCEPTIONS: Law, 4

PUNTING	No.	Yds	Avg	Net Avg	TB	In 20	Lg	Blk
Colquitt	71	3145	44.3	39.3	5	23	72	0

SACKS: Hali, 8

Miami Dolphins

SCORING	Rush	Rec	Ret	PAT	FG	S	Pts
	TD						
Mare	0	0	0	22	26	0	100
Booker	0	6	0	0	0	2	40
Brown	5	0	0	0	0	0	30
Chambers	0	4	0	0	0	0	24
McMichael	0	3	0	0	0	0	18
Taylor	0	0	2	0	0	0	12

RUSHING	No.	Yds	Avg	Lg	TD
Brown	241	1008	4.2	47	5
Morris	92	400	4.3	55	1

PASSING	Att	Comp	Pct Comp	Yds	Avg Gain	TD	Int	Rating Pts
Harrington	388	223	57.5	2236	5.8	12	15	68.2
Culpepper	134	81	60.4	929	6.9	2	3	77.0

RECEIVING	No.	Yds	Avg	Lg	TD
Booker	55	747	13.6	52	6
Welker	67	687	10.3	38	1
Chambers	59	677	11.5	46	4
McMichael	62	640	10.3	24	3
Brown	33	276	8.4	24	0

INTERCEPTIONS: Taylor, 2; Hill 2

PUNTING	No.	Yds	Avg	Net Avg	TB	In 20	Lg	Blk
Jones	85	3640	42.8	35.7	10	28	64	0

SACKS: Taylor, 13.5

New England Patriots

SCORING	Rush	Rec	Ret	PAT	FG	S	Pts
	TD						
Gostkowski	0	0	0	43	20	0	103
Dillon	13	0	0	0	0	0	78
Maroney	6	1	0	0	0	0	42
Brown	0	4	0	0	0	1	26
Caldwell	0	4	0	0	0	1	26

RUSHING	No.	Yds	Avg	Lg	TD
Dillon	199	812	4.1	50	13
Maroney	175	745	4.3	41	6

PASSING	Att	Comp	Pct Comp	Yds	Avg Gain	TD	Int	Rating Pts
Brady	516	319	61.8	3529	6.8	24	12	87.9

RECEIVING	No.	Yds	Avg	Lg	TD
Caldwell	61	760	12.5	62	4
Watson	49	643	13.1	40	3
Brown	43	384	8.9	23	4
Faulk	43	356	8.3	43	2
Gabriel	25	344	13.8	45	3
Graham	21	235	11.2	29	2

INTERCEPTIONS: Samuel, 10

PUNTING	No.	Yds	Avg	Net Avg	TB	In 20	Lg	Blk
Miller	43	1848	43.0	35.8	7	12	62	0

SACKS: Colvin, 8.5

New York Jets

SCORING	Rush	Rec	Ret	PAT	FG	S	Pts
	TD						
Nugent	0	0	0	34	24	0	106
Coles	0	6	0	0	0	0	36
Barlow	6	0	0	0	0	0	36
Cotchery	0	6	0	0	0	0	36
Houston	5	0	0	0	0	0	30
Baker	0	4	0	0	0	0	24
Washington	4	0	0	0	0	0	24

RUSHING	No.	Yds	Avg	Lg	TD
Washington	151	650	4.3	23	4
Houston	113	374	3.3	31	5

PASSING	Att	Comp	Pct Comp	Yds	Avg Gain	TD	Int	Rating Pts
Pennington	485	313	64.5	3352	6.9	17	16	82.6

RECEIVING	No.	Yds	Avg	Lg	TD
Coles	91	1098	12.1	58	6
Cotchery	82	961	11.7	71	6
McCareins	23	347	15.1	50	1
Baker	31	300	9.7	28	4
Washington	25	270	10.8	64	0

INTERCEPTIONS: Dyson, Rhodes, 4

PUNTING	No.	Yds	Avg	Net Avg	TB	In 20	Lg	Blk
Graham	72	3182	44.2	37.8	11	26	69	0

SACKS: Thomas, 8.5

Oakland Raiders

SCORING	Rush	Rec	Ret	PAT	FG	S	Pts
Janikowski	0	0	0	16	18	0	70
Moss	0	3	0	0	0	0	18
Jordan	2	0	0	0	0	0	12
Lee	2	0	0	0	0	0	12
Anderson	0	2	0	0	0	0	12
Curry	0	1	0	0	0	0	6

RUSHING	No.	Yds	Avg	Lg	TD
Fargas	178	659	3.7	48	1
Jordan	114	434	3.8	59	2

PASSING	Att	Comp	Pct Comp	Yds	Avg Gain	TD	Int	Rating Pts
Walter	276	147	53.3	1677	6.1	3	13	55.8
Brooks	192	110	57.3	1105	5.8	3	8	61.7

RECEIVING	No.	Yds	Avg	Lg	TD
Curry	62	727	11.7	39	1
Moss	42	553	13.2	51	3
Whitted	27	299	11.1	33	0
Williams	28	293	10.5	33	0
Anderson	25	285	11.4	35	2

INTERCEPTIONS: Asomugha, 8

PUNTING	No.	Yds	Avg	Net Avg	TB	In 20	Lg	Blk
Lechler	77	3660	47.5	36.4	19	19	67	0

SACKS: Burgess, 11

San Diego Chargers

SCORING	Rush	Rec	Ret	PAT	FG	S	Pts
Tomlinson	28	3	0	0	0	0	186
Kaeding	0	0	0	58	26	0	136
Gates	0	9	0	0	0	0	54
Jackson	0	6	0	0	0	1	38
Manumaleuna	0	3	0	0	0	0	18
Floyd	0	3	0	0	0	0	18

RUSHING	No.	Yds	Avg	Lg	TD
Tomlinson	348	1815	5.2	85	28
Turner	80	502	6.3	73	2

PASSING	Att	Comp	Pct Comp	Yds	Avg Gain	TD	Int	Rating Pts
Rivers	460	284	61.7	3388	7.4	22	9	92.0

RECEIVING	No.	Yds	Avg	Lg	TD
Gates	71	924	13.0	57	9
Parker	48	659	13.7	38	0
Tomlinson	56	508	9.1	51	3
Jackson	27	453	16.8	55	6
McCardell	36	437	12.1	28	0
Floyd	15	210	14.0	46	3

INTERCEPTIONS: Jammer, 4

PUNTING	No.	Yds	Avg	Net Avg	TB	In 20	Lg	Blk
Scifres	69	2893	41.9	38.2	2	35	71	0

SACKS: Merriman, 17

Pittsburgh Steelers

SCORING	Rush	Rec	Ret	PAT	FG	S	Pts
Reed	0	0	0	41	20	0	101
Parker	13	3	0	0	0	0	96
Ward	0	6	0	0	0	0	36
Miller	0	5	0	0	0	0	30
Washington	0	4	0	0	0	0	24

RUSHING	No.	Yds	Avg	Lg	TD
Parker	337	1494	4.4	76	13
Davenport	60	221	3.7	48	1
Roethlisberger	32	98	3.1	20	2

PASSING	Att	Comp	Pct Comp	Yds	Avg Gain	TD	Int	Rating Pts
Roethlisberger	469	280	59.7	3513	7.5	18	23	75.4
Batch	53	31	58.5	492	9.3	5	0	121.0

RECEIVING	No.	Yds	Avg	Lg	TD
Ward	74	975	13.2	70	6
Holmes	49	824	16.8	67	2
Washington	35	624	17.8	49	4
Wilson	37	504	13.6	38	1
Miller	34	393	11.6	87	5

INTERCEPTIONS: Polamalu, McFadden, 3

PUNTING	No.	Yds	Avg	Net Avg	TB	In 20	Lg	Blk
Gardockl	65	2687	41.3	36.7	4	11	56	0

SACKS: Porter, 7

Tennessee Titans

SCORING	Rush	Rec	Ret	PAT	FG	S	Pts
Bironas	0	0	0	32	22	0	98
Henry	7	0	0	0	0	1	44
Young	7	0	0	0	0	1	44
A. Jones	0	0	4	0	0	0	24

RUSHING	No.	Yds	Avg	Lg	TD
Henry	270	1211	4.5	70	7
Young	83	552	6.7	39	7

PASSING	Att	Comp	Pct Comp	Yds	Avg Gain	TD	Int	Rating Pts
Young	357	184	51.5	2199	6.2	12	13	66.7
Collins	90	42	46.7	549	6.1	1	6	42.3

RECEIVING	No.	Yds	Avg	Lg	TD
Bennett	46	737	16.0	39	3
Wade	33	461	14.0	25	2
Jones	27	384	14.2	53	4
Scaife	29	370	12.8	34	2
Troupe	13	150	11.5	32	2
Hall	15	138	9.2	28	0
Williams	8	121	15.1	20	0
Givens	8	104	13.0	27	0

INTERCEPTIONS: Hope, 5

PUNTING	No.	Yds	Avg	Net Avg	TB	In 20	Lg	Blk
Hentrich	88	3760	42.7	37.3	10	32	73	0

SACKS: Vanden Bosch, 6.5

Arizona Cardinals

SCORING	Rush	Rec	Ret	PAT	FG	S	Pts
Rackers	0	0	0	32	28	0	116
James	6	0	0	0	0	0	36
Fitzgerald	0	6	0	0	0	0	36
Shipp	4	0	0	0	0	0	24
Johnson	0	4	0	0	0	0	24

RUSHING	No.	Yds	Avg	Lg	TD
James	337	1159	3.4	18	6
Leinart	22	49	2.2	14	2

PASSING	Att	Comp	Pct Comp	Yds	Avg Gain	TD	Int	Rating Pts
Leinart	377	214	56.8	2547	6.8	11	12	74.0
Warner	168	108	64.3	1377	8.2	6	5	89.3

RECEIVING	No.	Yds	Avg	Lg	TD
Boldin	83	1203	14.5	64	4
Fitzgerald	69	946	13.7	57	6
Johnson	40	740	18.5	58	4
James	38	217	5.7	14	0
Walters	23	209	9.1	26	2
Pope	16	161	10.1	33	0

INTERCEPTIONS: Wilson, 4

PUNTING	No.	Yds	Avg	Net Avg	TB	In 20	Lg	Blk
Player	66	2965	44.9	34.5	3	18	58	0

SACKS: Okeafor, 8.5

Carolina Panthers

SCORING	Rush	Rec	Ret	PAT	FG	S	Pts
Kasay	0	0	0	28	24	0	100
Smith	1	8	0	0	0	0	54
Johnson	1	4	0	0	0	0	30
Foster	3	0	0	0	0	0	18
Carter	0	3	0	0	0	0	18

RUSHING	No.	Yds	Avg	Lg	TD
Foster	227	897	4.0	43	3
Williams	121	501	4.1	31	1
Hoover	22	73	3.3	17	1

PASSING	Att	Comp	Pct Comp	Yds	Avg Gain	TD	Int	Rating Pts
Delhomme	431	263	61.0	2805	6.5	17	11	82.6

RECEIVING	No.	Yds	Avg	Lg	TD
Smith	83	1166	14.0	72	8
Johnson	70	815	11.6	40	4
Carter	28	357	12.8	42	3
Williams	33	313	9.5	41	1
Mangum	21	170	8.1	19	1

INTERCEPTIONS: Gamble, Marshall, Lucas, 3

PUNTING	No.	Yds	Avg	Net Avg	TB	In 20	Lg	Blk
Baker	98	4483	45.7	39.0	12	31	70	0

SACKS: Peppers, 13

Atlanta Falcons

SCORING	Rush	Rec	Ret	PAT	FG	S	Pts
Andersen	0	0	0	27	20	0	87
Crumpler	0	8	0	0	0	0	48
Jenkins	0	7	0	0	0	1	42
Dunn	0	4	1	0	0	1	30
Griffith	1	3	0	0	0	0	24

RUSHING	No.	Yds	Avg	Lg	TD
Dunn	286	1140	4.0	90	4
Vick	123	1039	8.4	51	2
Norwood	99	633	6.4	78	2

PASSING	Att	Comp	Pct Comp	Yds	Avg Gain	TD	Int	Rating Pts
Vick	388	204	52.6	2474	6.4	20	13	75.7
Schaub	27	18	66.7	208	7.7	1	2	71.2

RECEIVING	No.	Yds	Avg	Lg	TD
Crumpler	56	780	13.9	46	8
White	30	506	16.9	55	0
Jenkins	39	436	11.2	34	7
Lelie	28	430	15.4	51	1
Dunn	22	170	7.7	18	1
Griffith	23	168	7.3	16	3

INTERCEPTIONS: Hall, 4

PUNTING	No.	Yds	Avg	Net Avg	TB	In 20	Lg	Blk
Koenen	76	3199	42.1	35.9	6	25	65	0

SACKS: Coleman, 6

Chicago Bears

SCORING	Rush	Rec	Ret	PAT	FG	S	Pts
Gould	0	0	0	47	32	0	143

Five tied with 36.

RUSHING	No.	Yds	Avg	Lg	TD
Jones	296	1210	4.1	30	6
Benson	157	647	4.1	30	6
Peterson	10	41	4.1	11	2

PASSING	Att	Comp	Pct Comp	Yds	Avg Gain	TD	Int	Rating Pts
Grossman	480	262	54.6	3193	6.7	23	20	73.9
Griese	32	18	56.3	220	6.9	1	2	62.0

RECEIVING	No.	Yds	Avg	Lg	TD
Muhammad	60	863	14.4	40	5
Berrian	51	775	15.2	62	6
Clark	45	626	13.9	33	6
Davis	22	303	13.8	31	2
Bradley	14	282	20.1	75	3

INTERCEPTIONS: Manning, Tillman, 5

PUNTING	No.	Yds	Avg	Net Avg	TB	In 20	Lg	Blk
Maynard	77	3404	44.2	37.6	7	24	65	0

SACKS: Anderson, 12

Dallas Cowboys

SCORING	TD Rush	Rec	Ret	PAT	FG	S	Pts
Barber	14	2	0	0	0	0	96
Owens	0	13	0	0	0	1	80
Vanderjagt	0	0	0	33	13	0	72
Glenn	0	6	0	0	0	0	36
Gramatica	0	0	0	14	6	0	32
Jones	4	0	0	0	0	0	24
Crayton	0	4	0	0	0	0	24

RUSHING	No.	Yds	Avg	Lg	TD
Jones	267	1084	4.1	77	4
Barber	135	654	4.8	25	14

PASSING	Att	Comp	Pct Comp	Yds	Avg Gain	TD	Int	Rating Pts
Romo	337	220	65.3	2903	8.6	19	13	95.1
Bledsoe	169	90	53.3	1164	6.9	7	8	69.2

RECEIVING	No.	Yds	Avg	Lg	TD
Owens	85	1180	13.9	56	13
Glenn	70	1047	15.0	54	6
Witten	64	754	11.8	42	1
Crayton	36	516	14.3	53	4
Barber	23	196	8.5	26	2

INTERCEPTIONS: Williams, 5

PUNTING	No.	Yds	Avg	Net Avg	TB	In 20	Lg	Blk
McBriar	56	2697	48.2	38.6	10	22	75	0

SACKS: Ware, 11.5

Green Bay Packers

SCORING	TD Rush	Rec	Ret	PAT	FG	S	Pts
Rayner	0	0	0	31	26	0	109
Driver	0	8	0	0	0	0	48
Green	5	1	0	0	0	0	36
Herron	1	2	0	0	0	0	18
Jennings	0	3	0	0	0	0	18
Martin	0	2	0	0	0	0	12

RUSHING	No.	Yds	Avg	Lg	TD
Green	266	1059	4.0	70	5
Morency	91	421	4.6	39	2

PASSING	Att	Comp	Pct Comp	Yds	Avg Gain	TD	Int	Rating Pts
Favre	613	343	56.0	3885	6.3	18	18	72.7

RECEIVING	No.	Yds	Avg	Lg	TD
Driver	92	1295	14.1	82	8
Jennings	45	632	14.0	75	3
Green	46	373	8.1	20	1
Martin	21	358	17.0	36	1
Franks	25	232	9.3	19	0
Herron	29	211	7.3	16	2

INTERCEPTIONS: Woodson, 8

PUNTING	No.	Yds	Avg	Net Avg	TB	In 20	Lg	Blk
Ryan	84	3739	44.5	35.7	12	17	66	0

SACKS: Kampman, 15.5

Detroit Lions

SCORING	TD Rush	Rec	Ret	PAT	FG	S	Pts
Hanson	0	0	0	30	29	0	117
Jones	6	2	0	0	0	0	48
Williams	0	7	0	0	0	0	42
Furrey	0	6	0	0	0	0	36
Campbell	0	4	0	0	0	0	24

RUSHING	No.	Yds	Avg	Lg	TD
Jones	181	689	3.8	52	6
Harris	49	158	3.2	20	1
Kitna	34	156	4.6	18	2

PASSING	Att	Comp	Pct Comp	Yds	Avg Gain	TD	Int	Rating Pts
Kitna	596	372	62.4	4208	7.1	21	22	79.9

RECEIVING	No.	Yds	Avg	Lg	TD
R. Williams	82	1310	16.0	60	7
Furrey	98	1086	11.1	31	6
Jones	61	520	8.5	26	2
Campbell	21	308	14.7	30	4
Bradford	14	164	11.7	23	0

INTERCEPTIONS: Bly, Holt, Fletcher, 3

PUNTING	No.	Yds	Avg	Net Avg	TB	In 20	Lg	Blk
Harris	66	2967	45.0	38.2	9	18	67	0

SACKS: Redding, 8

Minnesota Vikings

SCORING	TD Rush	Rec	Ret	PAT	FG	S	Pts
Longwell	0	0	0	27	21	0	90
C. Taylor	6	0	0	0	0	0	36
Robinson	0	4	0	0	0	0	24
T. Taylor	0	3	0	0	0	0	18
McMullen	0	2	1	0	0	0	18
Pinner	3	0	0	0	0	0	18

RUSHING	No.	Yds	Avg	Lg	TD
C. Taylor	303	1216	4.0	95	6
Pinner	43	190	4.4	21	3

PASSING	Att	Comp	Pct Comp	Yds	Avg Gain	TD	Int	Rating Pts
B. Johnson	439	270	61.5	2750	6.3	9	15	72.0
T. Jackson	81	47	58.0	475	5.9	2	4	62.5

RECEIVING	No.	Yds	Avg	Lg	TD
T. Taylor	57	651	11.4	36	3
Moore	46	468	10.2	50	1
Williamson	37	455	12.3	46	0
Wiggins	46	386	8.4	24	1
Robinson	29	381	13.1	40	4
McMullen	23	307	13.3	40	2
C. Taylor	42	288	6.9	24	0

INTERCEPTIONS: Winfield, Smith, Sharper, 4

PUNTING	No.	Yds	Avg	Net Avg	TB	In 20	Lg	Blk
Kluwe	93	3934	42.3	35.6	7	28	68	0

SACKS: Scott, 5.5

New Orleans Saints

SCORING

	TD			PAT	FG	S	Pts
	Rush	Rec	Ret				
Carney	0	0	0	46	23	0	115
McAllister	10	0	1	0	0	0	66
Bush	6	2	1	0	0	0	54
Colston	0	8	0	0	0	0	48
Henderson	1	5	0	0	0	0	36

RUSHING

	No.	Yds	Avg	Lg	TD
McAllister	244	1057	4.3	57	10
Bush	155	565	3.6	18	6
Karney	11	33	3.0	8	1

PASSING

	Att	Comp	Pct Comp	Yds	Avg Gain	TD	Int	Rating Pts
Brees	554	356	64.3	4418	8.0	26	11	96.2

RECEIVING

	No.	Yds	Avg	Lg	TD
Colston	70	1038	14.8	86	8
Henderson	32	745	23.3	76	5
Bush	88	742	8.4	74	2
Horn	37	679	18.4	72	4
Copper	23	385	16.7	48	3
McAllister	30	198	6.6	24	0

INTERCEPTIONS: Four tied with 2

PUNTING

	No.	Yds	Avg	Net Avg	TB	In 20	Lg	Blk
Weatherford	77	3369	43.8	37.5	10	19	59	0

SACKS: Smith, 10.5

New York Giants

SCORING

	TD			PAT	FG	S	Pts
	Rush	Rec	Ret				
Feely	0	0	0	38	23	0	107
Burress	0	10	0	0	0	0	60
Jacobs	9	0	0	0	0	0	54
Shockey	0	7	0	0	0	0	42
Barber	5	0	0	0	0	0	30
Toomer	0	3	0	0	0	0	18

RUSHING

	No.	Yds	Avg	Lg	TD
Barber	327	1662	5.1	55	5
Jacobs	96	423	4.4	16	9
Morton	1	22	22.0	22	0

PASSING

	Att	Comp	Pct Comp	Yds	Avg Gain	TD	Int	Rating Pts
Manning	522	301	57.7	3244	6.2	24	18	77.0

RECEIVING

	No.	Yds	Avg	Lg	TD
Burress	63	988	15.7	55	10
Shockey	66	623	9.4	25	7
Barber	58	465	8.0	28	0
Toomer	32	360	11.3	44	3

INTERCEPTIONS: Seven tied with 2

PUNTING

	No.	Yds	Avg	Net Avg	TB	In 20	Lg	Blk
Feagles	77	3098	40.2	37.0	3	27	54	0

SACKS: Umenyiora, 6

Philadelphia Eagles

SCORING

	TD			PAT	FG	S	Pts
	Rush	Rec	Ret				
Akers	0	0	0	48	18	0	102
Westbrook	7	4	0	0	0	0	66
Brown	1	8	0	0	0	0	54
Smith	0	5	0	0	0	1	32
Stallworth	0	5	0	0	0	0	30

RUSHING

	No.	Yds	Avg	Lg	TD
Westbrook	240	1217	5.1	71	7
Buckhalter	83	345	4.2	20	2

PASSING

	Att	Comp	Pct Comp	Yds	Avg Gain	TD	Int	Rating Pts
McNabb	316	180	57.0	2647	8.4	18	6	95.5
Garcia	188	116	61.7	1309	7.0	10	2	95.8

RECEIVING

	No.	Yds	Avg	Lg	TD
Brown	46	816	17.7	60	8
Stallworth	38	725	19.1	84	5
Westbrook	77	699	9.1	52	4
Smith	50	611	12.2	65	5
Baskett	22	464	21.1	89	2

INTERCEPTIONS: Sheppard, 6

PUNTING

	No.	Yds	Avg	Net Avg	TB	In 20	Lg	Blk
Johnson	78	3326	42.6	34.9	11	21	60	0

SACKS: Cole, 8

St. Louis Rams

SCORING

	TD			PAT	FG	S	Pts
	Rush	Rec	Ret				
Wilkins	0	0	0	35	32	0	131
Jackson	13	3	0	0	0	0	96
Holt	0	10	0	0	0	0	60
Curtis	0	4	0	0	0	0	24
Bruce	0	3	0	0	0	1	20

RUSHING

	No.	Yds	Avg	Lg	TD
Jackson	346	1528	4.4	59	13
Davis	40	177	4.4	16	0

PASSING

	Att	Comp	Pct Comp	Yds	Avg Gain	TD	Int	Rating Pts
Bulger	588	370	62.9	4301	7.3	24	8	92.9

RECEIVING

	No.	Yds	Avg	Lg	TD
Holt	93	1188	12.8	67	10
Bruce	74	1098	14.8	45	3
Jackson	90	806	9.0	64	3
Curtis	40	479	12.0	42	4

INTERCEPTIONS: Four tied with 3

PUNTING

	No.	Yds	Avg	Net Avg	TB	In 20	Lg	Blk
Turk	72	3132	43.5	38.3	5	26	74	0

SACKS: Little, 13

San Francisco 49ers

SCORING

		TD					
SCORING	Rush	Rec	Ret	PAT	FG	S	Pts
Nedney	0	0	0	29	29	0	116
Gore	8	1	0	0	0	0	54
Bryant	0	3	0	0	0	0	18
Battle	0	3	0	0	0	0	18
Davis	0	3	0	0	0	0	18
Norris	0	2	0	0	0	0	12

RUSHING

RUSHING	No.	Yds	Avg	Lg	TD
Gore	312	1695	5.4	72	8
Smith	44	147	3.3	22	2
Robinson	38	116	3.1	33	2

PASSING

PASSING	Att	Comp	Pct Comp	Yds	Avg Gain	TD	Int	Rating Pts
Smith	442	257	58.1	2890	6.5	16	16	74.8

RECEIVING

RECEIVING	No.	Yds	Avg	Lg	TD
Bryant	40	733	18.3	72	3
Battle	59	686	11.6	56	3
Gore	61	485	8.0	39	1
Johnson	34	292	8.6	26	2

INTERCEPTIONS: Harris, 8

PUNTING	No.	Yds	Avg	Net Avg	TB	In 20	Lg	Blk
Lee	81	3625	44.8	36.8	9	22	66	0

SACKS: Moore, 6.5

Seattle Seahawks

SCORING

		TD					
SCORING	Rush	Rec	Ret	PAT	FG	S	Pts
Brown	0	0	0	36	25	0	111
Jackson	0	10	0	0	0	0	60
Alexander	7	0	0	0	0	0	42
Stevens	0	4	0	0	0	1	26
Branch	0	4	0	0	0	0	24
Hackett	0	4	0	0	0	0	24

RUSHING

RUSHING	No.	Yds	Avg	Lg	TD
Alexander	252	896	3.6	43	7
Morris	161	604	3.8	29	0

PASSING

PASSING	Att	Comp	Pct Comp	Yds	Avg Gain	TD	Int	Rating Pts
Hasselbeck	371	210	56.6	2442	6.6	18	15	76.0

RECEIVING

RECEIVING	No.	Yds	Avg	Lg	TD
Jackson	63	956	15.2	72	10
Branch	53	725	13.7	38	4
Hackett	45	610	13.6	47	4
Engram	24	290	12.1	25	1
Stevens	22	231	10.5	26	4
Burleson	18	192	10.7	36	2

INTERCEPTIONS: Hamlin, 3

PUNTING	No.	Yds	Avg	Net Avg	TB	In 20	Lg	Blk
Plackemeier	84	3778	45.0	37.3	15	25	72	0

SACKS: Peterson, 10

Tampa Bay Buccaneers

SCORING

		TD					
SCORING	Rush	Rec	Ret	PAT	FG	S	Pts
Bryant	0	0	0	22	17	0	73
Galloway	0	7	0	0	0	0	42
Alstott	3	0	0	0	0	0	18
Smith	0	3	0	0	0	0	18
Hilliard	0	2	0	0	0	0	12
Barber	0	0	2	0	0	0	12

RUSHING

RUSHING	No.	Yds	Avg	Lg	TD
Williams	225	798	3.5	38	1
Pittman	50	245	4.9	32	1

PASSING

PASSING	Att	Comp	Pct Comp	Yds	Avg Gain	TD	Int	Rating Pts
Gradkowski	328	177	54.0	1661	5.1	9	9	65.9
Rattay	101	61	60.4	748	7.4	4	2	88.2
Simms	106	58	54.7	585	5.5	1	7	46.3

RECEIVING

RECEIVING	No.	Yds	Avg	Lg	TD
Galloway	62	1057	17.0	64	7
Pittman	47	405	8.6	25	0
Clayton	33	356	10.8	27	1
Hilliard	34	339	10.0	44	2
Smith	35	250	7.1	27	3
Williams	30	196	6.5	21	0

INTERCEPTIONS: Barber, Brooks, 3

PUNTING	No.	Yds	Avg	Net Avg	TB	In 20	Lg	Blk
Bidwell	93	4045	43.5	36.8	7	20	59	0

SACKS: Spires, White, Wyms, 5

Washington Redskins

SCORING

		TD					
SCORING	Rush	Rec	Ret	PAT	FG	S	Pts
Portis	7	0	0	0	0	0	42
Moss	0	6	0	0	0	1	38
Cooley	0	6	0	0	0	1	38
Hall	0	0	0	9	9	0	36
Suisham	0	0	0	12	8	0	36
Betts	4	1	0	0	0	0	30

RUSHING

RUSHING	No.	Yds	Avg	Lg	TD
Betts	245	1154	4.7	26	4
Portis	127	523	4.1	38	7
Duckett	38	132	3.5	19	2
Randle El	19	118	6.2	20	0

PASSING

PASSING	Att	Comp	Pct Comp	Yds	Avg Gain	TD	Int	Rating Pts
Brunell	260	162	62.3	1789	6.9	8	4	86.5
Campbell	207	110	53.1	1297	6.3	10	6	76.5

RECEIVING

RECEIVING	No.	Yds	Avg	Lg	TD
Moss	55	790	14.4	68	6
Cooley	57	734	12.9	66	6
Betts	53	445	8.4	34	1
Lloyd	23	365	15.9	52	0

INTERCEPTIONS: Six tied with 1

PUNTING	No.	Yds	Avg	Net Avg	TB	In 20	Lg	Blk
Frost	81	3471	42.9	36.7	7	27	60	0

SACKS: Carter, 6

First two rounds of the 71st annual NFL Draft, held April 28–29, 2007 in New York City.

First Round

	Team	Selection	Position
1.	Oakland	JaMarcus Russell, LSU	QB
2.	Detroit	Calvin Johnson, Ga.Tech	WR
3.	Cleveland	Joe Thomas, Wisconsin	OT
4.	Tampa Bay	Gaines Adams, Clemson	DE
5.	Arizona	Levi Brown, Penn St	OT
6.	Washington	LaRon Landry, LSU	FS
7.	Minnesota	Adrian Peterson, Oklahoma	RB
8.	Atlanta (from Houston)	Jamaal Anderson, Arkansas	DE
9.	Miami	Ted Ginn Jr., Ohio St	WR
10.	Houston (from Atlanta)	Amobi Okoye, Louisville	DT
11.	San Francisco	Patrick Willis, Mississippi	ILB
12.	Buffalo	Marshawn Lynch, California	RB
13.	St. Louis	Adam Carriker, Nebraska	DE
14.	NY Jets (from Carolina)	Darrelle Revis, Pittsburgh	CB
15.	Pittsburgh	Lawrence Timmons, Florida St	OLB
16.	Green Bay	Justin Harrell, Tennessee	DT
17.	Denver (from Jacksonville)	Jarvis Moss, Florida	DE
18.	Cincinnati	Leon Hall, Michigan	CB
19.	Tennessee	Michael Griffin, Texas	FS
20.	NY Giants	Aaron Ross, Texas	CB
21.	Jacksonville (from Denver)	Reggie Nelson, Florida	FS
22.	Cleveland (from Dallas)	Brady Quinn, Notre Dame	QB
23.	Kansas City	Dwayne Bowe, Louisiana	WR
24.	New England (from Seattle)	Brandon Meriweather, Miami (Fla.)	FS
25.	Carolina (from NY Jets)	Jon Beason, Miami (Fla.)	OLB
26.	Dallas (from Philadelphia)	Anthony Spencer, Purdue	DE
27.	New Orleans	Robert Meachem, Tennessee	WR
28.	San Francisco (from New England)	Joe Staley, Central Michigan	OT
29.	Baltimore	Ben Grubbs, Auburn	G
30.	San Diego	Craig Davis, LSU	WR
31.	Chicago	Greg Olsen, Miami (Fla.)	TE
32.	Indianapolis	Anthony Gonzalez, Ohio St	WR

Second Round

	Team	Selection	Position
33.	Arizona (from Oakland)	Alan Branch, Michigan	DT
34.	Buffalo (from Detroit)	Paul Posluszny, Penn St	OLB
35.	Tampa Bay	Arron Sears, Tennessee	OT
36.	Philadelphia (from Cleveland through Dallas)	Kevin Kolb, Houston	QB
37.	San Diego (from Wash. through NY Jets and Chicago)	Eric Weddle, Utah	SS
38.	Oakland (from Arizona)	Zach Miller, Arizona St	TE
39.	Atlanta (from Houston)	Justin Blalock, Texas	OT
40.	Miami	John Beck, BYU	QB
41.	Atlanta (from Minnesota)	Chris Houston, Arkansas	CB
42.	Indianapolis (from San Francisco)	Tony Ugoh, Arkansas	G
43.	Detroit (from Buffalo)	Drew Stanton, Michigan St	QB
44.	Minnesota (from Atlanta)	Sidney Rice, South Carolina	WR
45.	Carolina	Dwayne Jarrett, USC	WR
46.	Pittsburgh	LaMarr Woodley, Michigan	DE
47.	NY Jets (from Green Bay)	David Harris, Michigan	ILB
48.	Jacksonville	Justin Durant, Hampton	ILB
49.	Cincinnati	Kenny Irons, Auburn	RB
50.	Tennessee	Chris Henry, Arizona	RB
51.	NY Giants	Steve Smith, USC	WR
52.	St. Louis	Brian Leonard, Rutgers	FB
53.	Cleveland (from Dallas)	Eric Wright, UNLV	CB
54.	Kansas City	Turk McBride, Tennessee	DT
55.	Seattle	Josh Wilson, Maryland	CB
56.	Denver	Tim Crowder, Texas	DE
57.	Philadelphia	Victor Abiamiri, Notre Dame	DE
58.	Detroit (from New Orleans)	Ikaika Alama-Francis, Hawaii	DE
59.	Carolina (from NY Jets)	Ryan Kalil, USC	C
60.	Miami (from New England)	Samson Satele, Hawaii	C
61.	Detroit (from Baltimore)	Gerald Alexander, Boise State	FS
62.	Chicago (from San Diego)	Dan Bazuin, Central Michigan	DE
63.	Green Bay (from Chicago through NY Jets)	Brandon Jackson, Nebraska	RB
64.	Tampa Bay (from Indianapolis)	Sabby Piscitelli, Oregon State	SS

2007 Final Standings

	W	L	T	Pct	Pts	OP
Hamburg	7	3	0	.700	231	176
Frankfurt	7	3	0	.700	254	179
Cologne	6	4	0	.600	205	172
Rhein	4	6	0	.400	166	212
Amsterdam	4	6	0	.400	194	250
Berlin	2	8	0	.200	146	207

2007 World Bowl

June 23, 2007, in Frankfurt, Germany

Hamburg	13	10	7	7	—37
Frankfurt	0	14	14	0	—28

FIRST QUARTER

Hamburg: J. Jenkins 3 yd. pass from C. Bramlet (kick failed), 8:04

Hamburg 6–0.

Hamburg: M. Maxwell 35 yd. pass from C. Bramlet (S. Andrus kick), 3:28

Hamburg 13–0.

SECOND QUARTER

Frankfurt: B. Middleton 24 yd. pass from J. O'Sullivan (R. Lloyd kick), 12:28

Hamburg 13–7.

SECOND QUARTER *(CONT.)*

Hamburg: J. Allen 33 yd. run (S. Andrus kick), 7:56

Hamburg 20–7.

Frankfurt: D. Birmingham 5 yd. run (R. Lloyd kick), 4:28

Hamburg 20–14.

Hamburg: S. Andrus 24 yd. field goal, 0:03

Hamburg 23–14.

THIRD QUARTER

Frankfurt: R. Ortiz 24 yd. pass from J. O'Sullivan (R. Lloyd kick), 11:35

Hamburg 23–21.

Hamburg: J. Davis 51 yd. pass from C. Bramlet (S. Andrus kick), 4:27

Hamburg 30–21.

Frankfurt: S. Edwards 2 yd. run (R. Lloyd kick), 0:00

Hamburg 30–28.

FOURTH QUARTER

Hamburg: M. Maxwell 10 yd. pass from C. Bramlet (S. Andrus kick), 10:55

Frankfurt 37–28.

A: 48,125. T: 3:02.

NFL Europe Individual Leaders

PASSING

	Att	Comp	Pct Comp	Yds	Avg Gain	TD	Pct TD	Int	Pct Int	Lg	Rating Pts
J.T. O'Sullivan, Fra	235	160	68.1%	1,997	8.50	15	6.4%	7	3.0	65t	103.1
E. Meyer, Col	171	115	67.3%	1,384	8.09	12	7.0%	6	3.5	50	100.6
C. Bramlet, Ham	220	133	60.5%	1,810	8.23	15	6.8%	5	2.3	75t	100.0
C. Pickett, Rhe	197	127	64.5%	1,314	6.67	6	3.0%	6	3.0	46	81.1
D. Olson, Ams	282	154	54.6%	1,724	6.11	11	3.9%	11	3.9	58	69.8

RECEIVING

RECEPTIONS	No.	Yds	Avg	Lg	TD
B. Middleton, Fra	44	532	12.1	44	3
S. Fulton, Ams	42	531	12.6	42	3
C. Brewster, Ber	35	535	15.3	55t	1
B. Blizzard, Col	33	454	13.8	40	5
P.K. Sam, Rhe	32	529	16.5	46	3

YARDS	Yds	No.	Avg	Lg	TD
C. Brewster, Ber	535	35	15.3	55t	1
B. Middleton, Fra	532	44	12.1	44	3
S. Fulton, Ams	531	42	12.6	42	3
P.K. Sam, Rhe	529	32	16.5	46	3
M. Maxwell, Ham	459	27	17.0	51	7

RUSHING

	Att	Yds	Avg	Lg	TD
D. Ross, Col	190	693	3.6	40	4
C. Barclay, Ber	127	668	5.3	52	2
J. Smith, Ams	97	412	4.2	34t	8
C. Anthony, Rhe	81	378	4.7	23t	4
A.J. Harris, Col	95	362	3.8	54t	2

Other Statistical Leaders

Points (TDs)	Smith, Ams	54
Points (Kicking)	Lloyd, Fra	65
Yards from Scrimmage	Barclay, Ber	814
Interceptions	Smith, Col	3
Sacks	Hall, Col	11
Net Punting Avg	Baugher, Rhe	37.4
Punt Return Avg	Kinoshita, Ams	19.2
Kickoff Return Avg	Griffin, Ham	36.9

2006 Canadian Football League

EASTERN DIVISION

	W	L	T	Pts	PF	PA
†Montreal	10	8	0	20	451	431
*Toronto	10	8	0	20	359	343
*Winnipeg	9	9	0	18	362	408
Hamilton	4	14	0	8	292	495

WESTERN DIVISION

	W	L	T	Pts	PF	PA
†British Columbia	13	5	0	26	555	355
*Calgary	10	8	0	20	477	426
*Saskatchewan	9	9	0	18	465	434
Edmonton	7	11	0	14	399	468

†Clinched division title.

*Clinched playoff berth.

2006 Playoff Results

DIVISION SEMI-FINALS

TORONTO 31, Winnipeg 27
Saskatchewan 31, CALGARY 21

DIVISION FINALS

MONTREAL 33, Toronto 24
BRITISH COLUMBIA 45, Saskatchewan 18

Home team in caps.

2006 Grey Cup Championship

November 19, 2006 at Winnipeg, Manitoba

British Columbia Lions	9	10	0	6	25
Montreal Alouettes	0	3	9	2	14

A: 44,786.

2007 Arena Football League

AMERICAN CENTRAL DIVISION

	W	L	T	PF	PA
†Chicago	12	4	0	869	719
*Kansas City	10	6	0	840	776
*Colorado	8	8	0	793	858
Nashville	7	9	0	851	876
Grand Rapids	4	12	0	835	1,014

AMERICAN WESTERN DIVISION

	W	L	T	PF	PA
†San Jose	13	3	0	1,012	761
*Los Angeles	9	7	0	843	848
*Utah	8	8	0	955	933
Arizona	4	12	0	846	915
Las Vegas	2	14	0	701	986

NATIONAL EASTERN DIVISION

	W	L	T	PF	PA
†Dallas	15	1	0	1,016	806
*Philadelphia	8	8	0	900	835
*Columbus	7	9	0	802	793
New York	5	11	0	787	967

NATIONAL SOUTHERN DIVISION

	W	L	T	PF	PA
†Georgia	14	2	0	1,007	836
*Tampa Bay	9	7	0	809	825
*Orlando	8	8	0	814	766
New Orleans	5	11	0	833	928
Austin	4	12	0	879	950

†Clinched division title.

*Clinched playoff berth.

2007 AFL Playoff Results

DIVISIONAL ROUND

SAN JOSE 76, Colorado 67
Columbus 66, DALLAS 59
GEORGIA 65, Philadelphia 39
CHICAGO 52, Los Angeles 20

CONFERENCE CHAMPIONSHIPS

Columbus 66, GEORGIA 56
SAN JOSE 61, Chicago 49

Home team in caps.

Arena Bowl XXI
July 29, 2007 at New Orleans

Columbus	7	7	13	6—33
San Jose	14	13	7	21—55

FIRST QUARTER
SJ: Johnson 4 run (Haglund kick), 11:47 **San Jose 7-0.**
Col: Wells 1 run (Martinez kick, 6:55 **7-7.**
SJ: Roe 7 pass from Grieb (Haglund kick), 3:50 **San Jose 14-7.**

SECOND QUARTER
Col: Hilliard 4 pass from Nagy (Martinez kick), 10:44. **14-14.**
SJ: George 56 kickoff return (Haglund kick failed), 9:50 **San Jose 20-14.**
SJ: Williams 1 pass from Grieb (Haglund kick), 3:17 **San Jose 27-14.**

THIRD QUARTER
Col: Magner 3 pass from Nagy (Martinez kick), 8:44 **San Jose 27-21.**
SJ: Nelson 4 pass from Grieb (Haglund kick), 3:44 **San Jose 34-21.**
Col: Groce 39 pass from Nagy (Martinez kick failed), 0:05 **San Jose 34-27.**

FOURTH QUARTER
SJ: Glover 1 run (Haglund kick), 11:07 **San Jose 41-27.**
SJ: Roe 20 pass from Grieb (Haglund kick), 6:51 **San Jose 48-27.**
Col: Saunders 8 pass from Nagy (Martinez pass failed), 1:29 **San Jose 48-33.**
SJ: Johnson 4 run (Haglund kick), 0:38 **San Jose 55-33.**

A: 17,056.

Season-by-Season NFL Final Standings

1920*

	W	L	T	Pct	Pts	OP
Akron Pros	8	0	3	1.000	95	7
Decatur Staleys	10	1	2	.909	67	14
Buffalo All-Americans	9	1	1	.900	74	19
Chicago Cardinals	6	2	2	.750	34	26
Rock Island Independents	6	2	2	.750	98	35
Dayton Triangles	5	2	2	.714	127	47
Rochester Jeffersons	6	3	2	.667	6	17
Canton Bulldogs	7	4	2	.636	72	44
Detroit Heralds	2	3	3	.400	6	61
Cleveland Tigers	2	4	2	.333	22	63
Chicago Tigers	2	5	1	.286	22	63
Hammond Pros	2	5	0	.286	7	98
Columbus Panhandles	2	6	2	.250	7	107
Muncie Flyers	0	1	0	.000	0	45

*no official standings kept

1921

	W	L	T	Pct	Pts	OP
Chicago Staleys	9	1	1	.900	128	53
Buffalo All-Americans	9	1	2	.900	211	29
Akron Pros	8	3	1	.727	148	31
Canton Bulldogs	5	2	3	.714	106	55
Rock Island Independents	4	2	1	.667	65	30
Evansville Crimson Giants	3	2	0	.600	89	46
Green Bay Packers	3	2	1	.600	70	55
Dayton Triangles	4	4	1	.500	96	67
Chicago Cardinals	3	3	2	.500	54	53
Rochester Jeffersons	2	3	0	.400	85	76
Cleveland Tigers	3	5	0	.375	95	58
Washington Senators	1	2	0	.333	21	43
Cincinnati Celts	1	3	0	.250	14	117
Hammond Pros	1	3	1	.250	17	45
Minneapolis Marines	1	3	0	.250	37	41
Detroit Tigers	1	5	1	.167	19	109
Columbus Panhandles	1	8	0	.111	47	222
Tonawanda Kardex	0	1	0	.000	0	45
Muncie Flyers	0	2	0	.000	0	28
Louisville Brecks	0	2	0	.000	0	27
New York Giants	0	2	0	.000	0	72

1922

	W	L	T	Pct	Pts	OP
Canton Bulldogs	10	0	2	1.000	184	15
Chicago Bears	9	3	0	.750	123	44
Chicago Cardinals	8	3	0	.727	96	50
Toledo Maroons	5	2	2	.714	94	59
Rock Island Independents	4	2	1	.667	154	27
Racine Legion	6	4	1	.600	122	56
Dayton Triangles	4	3	1	.571	80	62
Green Bay Packers	4	3	3	.571	70	54
Buffalo All-Americans	5	4	1	.556	87	41
Akron Pros	3	5	2	.375	146	95
Milwaukee Badgers	2	4	3	.333	51	71
Oorang Indians	3	6	0	.333	69	190
Minneapolis Marines	1	3	0	.250	19	40
Louisville Brecks	1	3	0	.250	13	140
Evansville Crimson Giants	0	3	0	.000	6	88
Rochester Jeffersons	0	4	1	.000	13	76
Hammond Pros	0	5	1	.000	0	69
Columbus Panhandles	0	8	0	.000	24	174

1923

	W	L	T	Pct	Pts	OP
Canton Bulldogs	11	0	1	1.000	246	19
Chicago Bears	9	2	1	.818	123	35
Green Bay Packers	7	2	1	.778	85	34
Milwaukee Badgers	7	2	3	.778	100	49
Cleveland Indians	3	1	3	.750	52	49
Chicago Cardinals	8	4	0	.667	139	37
Duluth Kelleys	4	3	0	.571	35	33
Buffalo All-Americans	5	4	3	.556	94	43
Columbus Tigers	5	4	1	.556	119	35
Racine Legion	4	4	2	.500	86	76
Toledo Maroons	3	3	2	.500	35	66
Rock Island Independents	2	3	2	.400	83	62
Minneapolis Marines	2	5	1	.286	48	80
St. Louis All-Stars	1	4	2	.200	14	32
Hammond Pros	1	5	1	.167	14	59
Dayton Triangles	1	6	1	.143	16	95
Akron Pros	1	6	0	.143	25	74
Oorang Indians	1	10	0	.091	24	235
Louisville Brecks	0	3	0	.000	0	90
Rochester Jeffersons	0	4	0	.000	6	141

1924

	W	L	T	Pct	Pts	OP
Cleveland Bulldogs	7	1	1	.875	229	60
Chicago Bears	6	1	4	.857	136	55
Frankfort Yellow Jackets	11	2	1	.846	326	109
Duluth Kelleys	5	1	0	.833	56	16
Rock Island Independents	5	2	2	.714	81	15
Green Bay Packers	7	4	0	.636	108	38
Racine Legion	4	3	3	.571	69	47
Chicago Cardinals	5	4	1	.556	90	67
Buffalo Bisons	6	5	0	.545	120	140
Columbus Tigers	4	4	0	.500	91	68
Hammond Pros	2	2	1	.500	18	45
Milwaukee Badgers	5	8	0	.385	142	188
Akron Pros	2	6	0	.250	59	132
Dayton Triangles	2	6	0	.250	45	148
Kansas City Blues	2	7	0	.222	46	124
Kenosha Maroons	0	4	1	.000	12	117
Minneapolis Marines	0	6	0	.000	14	108
Rochester Jeffersons	0	7	0	.000	14	179

1925

	W	L	T	Pct	Pts	OP
Chicago Cardinals	11	2	1	.846	230	65
Pottsville Maroons	10	2	0	.833	280	45
Detroit Panthers	8	2	2	.800	118	42
New York Giants	8	4	0	.667	122	67
Akron Pros	4	2	2	.650	65	51
Frankfort Yellow Jackets	13	7	0	.643	196	189
Chicago Bears	9	5	3	.625	158	96
Rock Island Independents	5	3	3	.615	99	58
Green Bay Packers	8	5	0	.545	151	120
Providence Steam Roller	6	5	1	.500	131	108
Canton Bulldogs	4	4	0	.385	50	73
Cleveland Bulldogs	5	8	1	.286	75	134
Kansas City Cowboys	2	5	1	.200	68	106
Hammond Pros	1	4	0	.143	23	87

1925 (Cont.)

	W	L	T	Pct	Pts	OP
Buffalo Bisons	1	6	2	.143	33	113
Duluth Kelleys	0	3	0	.000	6	25
Rochester Jeffersons	0	6	1	.000	26	91
Milwaukee Badgers	0	6	0	.000	7	191
Dayton Triangles	0	7	1	.000	3	84
Columbus Tigers..............	0	9	0	.000	28	124

1926

	W	L	T	Pct	Pts	OP
Frankfort Yellow Jackets	14	1	2	.765	223	43
Chicago Bears	12	1	3	.844	216	63
Pottsville Maroons	10	2	2	.714	155	29
Kansas City Cowboys......	8	3	0	.727	76	54
Green Bay Packers..........	7	3	3	.462	144	68
Los Angeles Buccaneers.	6	3	1	.600	67	57
NY Giants	8	4	1	.583	140	45
Duluth Eskimos	6	5	3	.429	114	81
Buffalo Rangers	4	4	2	.400	53	62
Chicago Cardinals	5	6	1	.417	67	86
Providence Steam Roller.	5	7	1	.417	94	96
Detroit Panthers	4	6	2	.500	115	52
Hartford Blues	3	7	0	.300	57	99
Brooklyn Lions.................	3	8	0	.273	60	150
Milwaukee Badgers	2	7	0	.222	41	66
Akron Indians	1	4	3	.125	23	89
Dayton Triangles	1	4	1	.167	15	82
Racine Tornadoes	1	4	0	.200	8	92
Columbus Tigers..............	1	6	0	.143	26	93
Canton Bulldogs	1	9	3	.077	46	172
Hammond Pros	0	4	0	.000	3	56
Louisville Colonels	0	4	0	.000	0	108

1927

	W	L	T	Pct	Pts	OP
NY Giants	11	1	1	.917	197	20
Green Bay Packers..........	7	2	1	.778	113	43
Chicago Bears	9	3	2	.750	149	98
Cleveland Bulldogs..........	8	4	1	.667	209	107
Providence Steam Roller.	8	5	1	.615	105	88
New York Yankees...........	7	8	1	.467	142	174
Frankfort Yellow Jackets .	6	9	3	.400	152	166
Pottsville Maroons	5	8	0	.385	80	163
Chicago Cardinals	3	7	1	.300	69	134
Dayton Triangles	1	6	1	.143	15	57
Duluth Eskimos	1	8	0	.111	68	134
Buffalo Bisons	0	5	0	.000	8	123

1928

	W	L	T	Pct	Pts	OP
Providence Steam Roller.	8	1	1	.889	128	36
Frankfort Yellow Jackets	11	3	1	.786	169	84
Detroit Wolverines	7	2	1	.778	189	76
Green Bay Packers..........	6	4	3	.600	120	92
Chicago Bears	7	5	1	.583	182	85
NY Giants	4	7	2	.364	79	137
NY Yankees......................	4	8	1	.333	104	179
Pottsville Maroons	2	8	0	.200	74	134
Chicago Cardinals	1	5	0	.167	7	107
Dayton Triangles	0	7	0	.000	9	131

1929

	W	L	T	Pct	Pts	OP
Green Bay Packers.........	12	0	1	1.000	198	22
NY Giants	13	1	1	.929	312	86
Frankfort Yellow Jackets..	10	4	5	.714	139	128
Chicago Cardinals	6	6	1	.500	154	83
Boston Bulldogs...............	4	4	0	.500	98	73
Staten Island Stapletons ..	3	6	3	.429	89	62
Providence Steam Roller.	4	5	2	.400	107	117
Orange Tornadoes	3	6	4	.375	32	90
Chicago Bears	4	9	2	.308	119	227
Buffalo Bisons	1	7	1	.125	48	142
Minneapolis Red Jackets..	1	9	0	.100	48	185
Dayton Triangles	0	6	0	.000	7	136

1930

	W	L	T	Pct	Pts	OP
Green Bay Packers	10	3	1	.769	234	111
NY Giants	13	4	0	.765	308	98
Chicago Bears	9	4	1	.692	169	71
Brooklyn Dodgers	7	4	1	.636	154	59
Providence Steam Roller.	6	4	1	.600	90	125
Staten Island Stapletons .	5	5	2	.500	95	112
Chicago Cardinals	5	6	2	.455	128	132
Portsmouth Spartans	5	6	3	.455	176	161
Frankfort Yellow Jackets..	4	13	1	.222	113	321
Minneapolis Red Jackets.1	1	7	1	.125	27	165
Newark Tornadoes	1	10	1	.091	51	190

1931

	W	L	T	Pct	Pts	OP
Green Bay Packers.........	12	2	0	.857	318	94
Portsmouth Spartans	11	3	0	.786	161	77
Chicago Bears	8	5	0	.615	145	92
Chicago Cardinals	5	4	0	.556	120	128
NY Giants	7	6	1	.538	161	127
Providence Steam Roller..	4	4	3	.500	78	127
Staten Island Stapletons ..	4	6	1	.400	79	118
Cleveland Indians	2	8	0	.200	45	137
Brooklyn Dodgers	2	12	0	.143	64	199
Frankfort Yellow Jackets .	1	6	1	.143	13	85

1932

	W	L	T	Pct	Pts	OP
Chicago Bears	7	1	6	.875	160	44
Green Bay Packers.........	10	3	1	.769	152	63
Portsmouth Spartans	6	2	4	.750	116	71
Boston Braves..................	4	4	2	.500	55	79
NY Giants	4	6	2	.400	93	113
Brooklyn Dodgers	3	9	0	.250	63	131
Chiago Cardinals	2	6	2	.250	72	114
Staten Island Stapletons ..	2	7	3	.222	77	173

1933

EAST	W	L	T	Pct	Pts	OP
NY Giants	11	3	0	.786	244	101
Brooklyn Dodgers	5	4	1	.556	93	54
Boston Redskins	5	5	2	.500	103	97
Philadelphia Eagles	3	5	1	.375	77	158
Pittsburgh Pirates.............	3	6	2	.333	67	208

1933 (Cont.)

WEST

	W	L	T	Pct	Pts	OP
Chicago Bears	10	2	1	.833	133	82
Portsmouth Spartans	6	5	0	.545	128	87
Green Bay Packers	5	7	1	.417	170	107
Cincinnati Reds	3	6	1	.333	38	110
Chicago Cardinals	1	9	1	.100	52	101

1934

EAST

	W	L	T	Pct	Pts	OP
NY Giants	8	5	0	.615	147	107
Boston Redskins	6	6	0	.500	107	93
Brooklyn Dodgers	4	7	0	.364	60	153
Philadelphia Eagles	4	7	0	.364	127	85
Pittsburgh Pirates	2	10	0	.167	51	206

WEST

	W	L	T	Pct	Pts	OP
Chicago Bears	13	0	0	1.000	286	86
Detroit Lions	10	3	0	.769	238	59
Green Bay Packers	7	6	0	.538	156	112
Chicago Cardinals	5	6	0	.455	80	84
St. Louis Gunners	1	2	0	.333	27	61
Cincinnati Reds	0	8	0	.000	10	243

1935

EAST

	W	L	T	Pct	Pts	OP
NY Giants	9	3	0	.750	180	96
Brooklyn Dodgers	5	6	1	.455	90	141
Pittsburgh Pirates	4	8	0	.333	99	209
Boston Redskins	2	8	1	.200	65	122
Philadelphia Eagles	2	9	0	.182	60	179

WEST

	W	L	T	Pct	Pts	OP
Detroit Lions	7	3	-2	.700	191	111
Green Bay Packers	8	4	0	.667	181	96
Chicago Bears	6	4	2	.600	192	106
Chicago Cardinals	6	4	2	.600	99	97

1936

EAST

	W	L	T	Pct	Pts	OP
Boston Redskins	7	5	0	.583	149	110
Pittsburgh Pirates	6	6	0	.500	98	187
NY Giants	5	6	1	.455	115	163
Brooklyn Dodgers	3	8	1	.273	92	161
Philadelphia Eagles	1	11	0	.083	51	206

WEST

	W	L	T	Pct	Pts	OP
Green Bay	10	1	1	.909	248	118
Chicago Bears	9	3	0	.750	222	94
Detroit Lions	8	4	0	.667	235	102
Chicago Cardinals	3	8	1	.273	74	143

1937

EAST

	W	L	T	Pct	Pts	OP
Washington Redskins	8	3	0	.727	195	120
NY Giants	6	3	2	.667	128	109
Pittsburgh Pirates	4	7	0	.364	122	145
Brooklyn Dodgers	3	7	1	.300	82	174
Philadelphia Eagles	2	8	1	.200	86	177

WEST

	W	L	T	Pct	Pts	OP
Chicago Bears	9	1	1	.900	201	100
Green Bay Packers	7	4	0	.636	220	122
Detroit Lions	7	4	0	.636	180	105
Chicago Cardinals	5	5	1	.500	135	165
Cleveland Rams	1	10	0	.091	75	207

1938

EAST

	W	L	T	Pct	Pts	OP
NY Giants	8	2	1	.800	194	79
Washington Redskins	6	3	2	.667	148	154
Brooklyn Dodgers	4	4	3	.500	131	161
Philadelphia Eagles	5	6	0	.455	154	164
Pittsburgh Pirates	2	9	0	.182	79	169

WEST

	W	L	T	Pct	Pts	OP
Green Bay Packers	8	3	0	.727	223	118
Detroit Lions	7	4	0	.636	119	108
Chicago Bears	6	5	0	.545	194	148
Cleveland Rams	4	7	0	.364	131	215
Chicago Cardinals	2	9	0	.182	111	168

1939

EAST

	W	L	T	Pct	Pts	OP
NY Giants	9	1	1	.168	168	85
Washington Redskins	8	2	1	.242	242	94
Brooklyn Dodgers	4	6	1	.108	108	219
Philadelphia Eagles	1	9	1	.105	105	200
Pittsburgh Pirates	1	9	1	.114	114	216

WEST

	W	L	T	Pct	Pts	OP
Green Bay Packers	9	2	0	.818	233	153
Chicago Bears	8	3	0	.727	298	157
Detroit Lions	6	5	0	.545	145	150
Cleveland Rams	5	5	1	.195	195	164
Chicago Cardinals	1	10	0	.091	84	254

1940

EAST

	W	L	T	Pct	Pts	OP
Washington Redskins	9	2	0	.818	245	142
Brooklyn Dodgers	8	2	0	.800	179	110
NY Giants	6	4	1	.545	131	133
Pittsburgh Pirates	2	7	2	.182	67	174
Philadelphia Eagles	1	10	0	.091	121	200

WEST

	W	L	T	Pct	Pts	OP
Chicago Bears	8	3	0	.727	238	152
Green Bay Packers	6	4	1	.600	238	155
Detroit Lions	5	5	1	.500	120	177
Cleveland Rams	4	6	1	.400	181	191
Chicago Cardinals	2	7	2	.222	139	222

1941

EAST

	W	L	T	Pct	Pts	OP
NY Giants	8	3	0	.727	238	114
Brooklyn Dodgers	7	4	0	.636	158	127
Washington	6	5	0	.545	176	174
Philadelphia	2	8	1	.200	119	218
Pittsburgh Steelers	1	9	1	.100	103	276

WEST

	W	L	T	Pct	Pts	OP
Green Bay	10	1	0	.909	258	120
Chicago Bears	10	1	0	.909	396	147
Detroit	4	6	1	.400	121	195
Chicago Cardinals	3	7	1	.300	127	197
Cleveland Rams	2	9	0	.182	116	244

1942

EAST

	W	L	T	Pct	Pts	OP
Washington	10	1	0	.909	227	102
Pittsburgh Steelers	7	4	0	.636	167	119
NY Giants	5	5	1	.500	155	139
Brooklyn Dodgers	3	8	0	.273	100	168
Philadelphia	2	9	0	.182	134	239

WEST

	W	L	T	Pct	Pts	OP
Chicago Bears	11	0	0	1.000	376	84
Green Bay	8	2	1	.800	300	215
Cleveland Rams	5	6	0	.455	150	207
Chicago Cardinals	3	8	0	.273	98	209
Detroit	0	11	0	.000	38	263

1943

EAST

	W	L	T	Pct	Pts	OP
Washington	6	3	1	.667	229	137
NY Giants	6	3	1	.667	197	170
Phi/Pitt Eagles/Steelers	5	4	1	.556	225	230
Brooklyn Dodgers	2	8	0	.200	65	234

WEST

	W	L	T	Pct	Pts	OP
Chicago Bears	8	1	1	.889	303	157
Green Bay	7	2	1	.778	264	172
Detroit	3	6	1	.333	178	218
Chicago Cardinals	0	10	0	.000	95	238

1944

EAST

	W	L	T	Pct	Pts	OP
NY Giants	8	1	1	.889	206	75
Philadelphia	7	1	2	.875	267	131
Washington	6	3	1	.667	169	180
Boston Yanks	2	8	0	.200	82	233
Brooklyn Tigers	0	10	0	.000	69	166

WEST

	W	L	T	Pct	Pts	OP
Green Bay	8	2	0	.800	238	141
Chicago Bears	6	3	1	.667	258	172
Detroit	6	3	1	.667	216	151
Cleveland Rams	4	6	0	.400	188	224
Chi/Pitt Cards/Steelers	0	10	0	.000	116	336

1945

EAST

	W	L	T	Pct	Pts	OP
Washington	8	2	0	.800	209	121
Philadelphia	7	3	0	.700	272	133
NY Giants	3	6	1	.333	179	198
Bos/Bkn Yanks/Tigers	3	6	1	.333	123	211
Pittsburgh	2	8	0	.200	79	220

WEST

	W	L	T	Pct	Pts	OP
Cleveland Rams	9	1	0	.900	244	136
Detroit	7	3	0	.700	195	194
Green Bay	6	4	0	.600	258	173
Chicago Bears	3	7	0	.300	192	235
Chicago Cardinals	1	9	0	.100	98	228

1946

EAST

	W	L	T	Pct	Pts	OP
NY Giants	7	3	1	.700	236	162
Philadelphia	6	5	0	.545	231	220
Washington	5	5	1	.500	171	191
Pittsburgh	5	5	1	.500	136	117
Boston Yanks	2	8	1	.200	189	273

WEST

	W	L	T	Pct	Pts	OP
Chicago Bears	8	2	1	.800	289	193
Los Angeles Rams	6	4	1	.600	277	257
Chicago Cardinals	6	5	0	.545	260	198
Green Bay	6	5	0	.545	148	158
Detroit	1	10	0	.091	142	310

1947

EAST

	W	L	T	Pct	Pts	OP
Pittsburgh	8	4	0	.667	240	259
Philadelphia	8	4	0	.667	308	242
Boston Yanks	4	7	1	.364	168	256
Washington	4	8	0	.333	295	367
NY Giants	2	8	2	.200	190	309

WEST

	W	L	T	Pct	Pts	OP
Chicago Cardinals	9	3	0	.750	306	231
Chicago Bears	8	4	0	.667	363	241
Green Bay	6	5	1	.542	274	210
LA Rams	6	6	0	.500	259	214
Detroit Lions	3	9	0	.250	231	305

1948

EAST

	W	L	T	Pct	Pts	OP
Philadelphia	9	2	1	.818	376	156
Washington	7	5	0	.583	291	287
Pittsburgh	4	8	0	.333	200	243
NY Giants	4	8	0	.333	297	388
Boston Yanks	3	9	0	.250	174	372

WEST

	W	L	T	Pct	Pts	OP
Chicago Cardinals	11	1	0	.917	395	226
Chicago Bears	10	2	0	.833	375	151
LA Rams	6	5	1	.545	327	269
Green Bay	3	9	0	.250	154	290
Detroit Lions	2	10	0	.167	200	407

Season-by-Season NFL Final Standings *(Cont.)*

1949

EAST	W	L	T	Pct	Pts	OP
Philadelphia	11	1	0	.917	364	134
Pittsburgh	6	5	1	.545	224	214
NY Giants	6	6	0	.500	287	298
Washington	4	7	1	.364	268	339
New York Bulldogs	1	10	1	.091	153	368

WEST	W	L	T	Pct	Pts	OP
LA Rams	8	2	2	.800	360	239
Chicago Bears	9	3	0	.750	332	218
Chicago Cardinals	6	5	1	.545	360	301
Detroit Lions	4	8	0	.333	237	259
Green Bay	2	10	0	.167	114	329

1950

EAST	W	L	T	Pct	Pts	OP
Cleveland Browns	10	2	0	.833	310	144
NY Giants	10	2	0	.833	268	150
Philadelphia	6	6	0	.500	254	141
Pittsburgh	6	6	0	.500	180	195
Chicago Cardinals	5	7	0	.417	233	287
Washington	3	9	0	.250	232	326

WEST	W	L	T	Pct	Pts	OP
Chicago Bears	9	3	0	.750	279	207
LA Rams	9	3	0	.750	466	309
New York Yanks	7	5	0	.583	366	367
Detroit	6	6	0	.500	321	300
San Francisco 49ers	3	9	0	.250	213	300
Green Bay	3	9	0	.250	244	406
Baltimore Colts	1	11	0	.067	213	462

1951

AMERICAN	W	L	T	Pct	Pts	OP
Cleveland	11	1	0	.917	331	152
NY Giants	9	2	1	.818	254	161
Washington	5	7	0	.417	183	296
Pittsburgh	4	7	1	.364	183	235
Philadelphia	4	8	0	.333	234	264
Chicago Cardinals	3	9	0	.250	210	287

NATIONAL	W	L	T	Pct	Pts	OP
LA Rams	8	4	0	.667	392	261
Detroit Lions	7	4	1	.636	336	259
San Francisco 49ers	7	4	1	.636	255	205
Chicago Bears	7	5	0	.583	286	282
Green Bay	3	9	0	.250	254	375
New York Yanks	1	9	2	.100	241	382

1952

AMERICAN	W	L	T	Pct	Pts	OP
Cleveland	8	4	0	.667	310	213
Philadelphia	7	5	0	.583	252	271
NY Giants	7	5	0	.583	234	231
Pittsburgh	5	7	0	.417	300	273
Washington	4	8	0	.333	240	287
Chicago Cardinals	4	8	0	.333	172	221

NATIONAL	W	L	T	Pct	Pts	OP
Detroit	9	3	0	.750	344	192
LA Rams	9	3	0	.750	349	234
San Francisco	7	5	0	.583	285	221
Green Bay	6	6	0	.500	295	312
Chicago Bears	5	7	0	.417	245	326
Dallas Texans	1	11	0	.083	182	427

1953

EAST	W	L	T	Pct	Pts	OP
Cleveland	11	1	0	.917	348	162
Philadelphia	7	4	1	.636	352	215
Washington	6	5	1	.545	208	215
Pittsburgh	5	7	0	.417	211	272
NY Giants	4	8	0	.333	188	277
Chicago Cardinals	1	10	1	.091	190	337

WEST	W	L	T	Pct	Pts	OP
Detroit	10	2	0	.833	271	205
San Francisco	9	3	0	.750	372	237
LA Rams	8	3	1	.727	366	236
Chicago Bears	3	8	1	.273	218	262
Baltimore Colts	3	9	0	.250	182	350
Green Bay	2	9	1	.182	200	338

1954

EAST	W	L	T	Pct	Pts	OP
Cleveland	9	3	0	.750	336	162
Philadelphia	7	4	1	.636	284	230
NY Giants	7	5	0	.583	293	184
Pittsburgh	5	7	0	.417	219	263
Washington	3	9	0	.250	207	432
Chicago Cardinals	2	10	0	.167	183	347

WEST	W	L	T	Pct	Pts	OP
Detroit	9	2	1	.818	337	189
Chicago Bears	8	4	0	.667	301	279
San Francisco	7	4	1	.636	313	251
LA Rams	6	5	1	.545	314	285
Green Bay	4	8	0	.333	234	251
Baltimore	3	9	0	.250	131	279

1955

EAST	W	L	T	Pct	Pts	OP
Cleveland	9	2	1	.818	349	218
Washington	8	4	0	.667	246	222
NY Giants	6	5	1	.545	267	223
Philadelphia	4	7	1	.364	248	231
Chicago Cardinals	4	7	1	.364	224	252
Pittsburgh	4	8	0	.333	195	285

WEST	W	L	T	Pct	Pts	OP
LA Rams	8	3	1	.727	260	231
Chicago Bears	8	4	0	.667	294	251
Green Bay	6	6	0	.500	258	276
Baltimore	5	6	1	.455	214	239
San Francisco	4	8	0	.333	216	298
Detroit	3	9	0	.250	230	275

1956

EAST	W	L	T	Pct	Pts	OP
NY Giants	8	3	1	.727	264	197
Chicago Cardinals	7	5	0	.583	240	182
Washington	6	6	0	.500	183	225
Pittsburgh	5	7	0	.417	217	250
Cleveland	5	7	0	.417	167	177
Philadelphia	3	8	1	.273	143	215

WEST	W	L	T	Pct	Pts	OP
Chicago Bears	9	2	1	.818	269	169
Detroit	9	3	0	.750	300	188
San Francisco	5	6	1	.455	233	284
Baltimore	5	7	0	.417	270	322
Green Bay	4	8	0	.333	264	342
LA Rams	4	8	0	.333	291	307

1957

EAST

	W	L	T	Pct	Pts	OP
Cleveland	9	2	1	.818	269	169
NY Giants	7	5	0	.583	251	211
Pittsburgh	6	6	0	.500	155	178
Washington	5	6	1	.455	251	230
Philadelphia	4	8	0	.333	173	224
Chicago Cardinals	3	9	0	.250	200	299

WEST

	W	L	T	Pct	Pts	OP
San Francisco	8	4	0	.667	260	264
Detroit	8	4	0	.667	251	231
Baltimore	7	5	0	.583	303	235
LA Rams	6	6	0	.500	307	278
Chicago Bears	5	7	0	.417	203	211
Green Bay	3	9	0	.250	218	311

1958

EAST

	W	L	T	Pct	Pts	OP
Cleveland	9	3	0	.750	302	217
NY Giants	9	3	0	.750	246	183
Pittsburgh	7	4	1	.636	261	230
Washington	4	7	1	.364	214	268
Chicago Cardinals	2	9	1	.182	261	356
Philadelphia	2	9	1	.182	235	306

WEST

	W	L	T	Pct	Pts	OP
Baltimore	9	3	0	.750	381	203
LA Rams	8	4	0	.667	344	278
Chicago Bears	8	4	0	.667	298	230
San Francisco	6	6	0	.500	257	324
Detroit	4	7	1	.364	261	276
Green Bay	1	10	1	.091	193	382

1959

EAST

	W	L	T	Pct	Pts	OP
NY Giants	10	2	0	.833	284	167
Philadelphia	7	5	0	.583	268	278
Cleveland	7	5	0	.583	270	214
Pittsburgh	6	5	1	.545	257	216
Washington	3	9	0	.250	185	350
Chicago Cardinals	2	10	0	.167	231	324

WEST

	W	L	T	Pct	Pts	OP
Baltimore	9	3	0	.750	374	251
Chicago Bears	8	4	0	.667	246	196
Green Bay	7	5	0	.583	248	240
San Francisco	7	5	0	.583	255	237
Detroit	3	8	1	.273	203	275
LA Rams	2	10	0	.167	242	315

1960

NFL EAST

	W	L	T	Pct	Pts	OP
Philadelphia	10	2	0	.833	321	246
Cleveland	8	3	1	.727	362	217
NY Giants	6	4	2	.600	271	261
St. Louis Cardinals	6	5	1	.545	288	230
Pittsburgh	5	6	1	.455	240	275
Washington	1	9	2	.100	178	309

NFL WEST

	W	L	T	Pct	Pts	OP
Green Bay	8	4	0	.667	332	209
Detroit	7	5	0	.583	239	212
San Francisco	7	5	0	.583	208	205
Baltimore	6	6	0	.500	288	234
Chicago Bears	5	6	1	.455	194	299
LA Rams	4	7	1	.364	265	297
Dallas Cowboys	0	11	1	.000	177	369

AFL EAST

	W	L	T	Pct	Pts	OP
Houston Oilers	10	4	0	.714	379	285
NY Titans	7	7	0	.500	382	399
Buffalo Bills	5	8	1	.385	296	303
Boston Patriots	5	9	0	.357	286	349

AFL WEST

	W	L	T	Pct	Pts	OP
Los Angeles Chargers	10	4	0	.714	373	336
Dallas Texans	8	6	0	.571	361	253
Oakland Raiders	6	8	0	.429	319	388
Denver Broncos	4	9	1	.308	309	393

1961

NFL EAST

	W	L	T	Pct	Pts	OP
NY Giants	10	3	1	.769	368	220
Philadelphia	10	4	0	.714	361	297
Cleveland	8	5	1	.615	319	270
St. Louis Cardinals	7	7	0	.500	279	267
Pittsburgh	6	8	0	.429	295	287
Dallas Cowboys	4	9	1	.308	236	380
Washington	1	12	1	.077	174	392

NFL WEST

	W	L	T	Pct	Pts	OP
Green Bay	11	3	0	.786	391	223
Detroit	8	5	1	.615	270	258
Baltimore	8	6	0	.571	302	307
Chicago	8	6	0	.571	326	302
San Francisco	7	6	1	.538	346	272
LA Rams	4	10	0	.286	263	407
Minnesota Vikings	3	11	0	.214	285	407

AFL EAST

	W	L	T	Pct	Pts	OP
Houston Oilers	10	3	1	.769	513	242
Boston Patriots	9	4	1	.692	413	313
New York Titans	7	7	0	.500	301	390
Buffalo Bills	6	8	0	.429	294	342

AFL WEST

	W	L	T	Pct	Pts	OP
San Diego Chargers	12	2	0	.857	396	219
Dallas Texans	6	8	0	.429	334	343
Denver	3	11	0	.214	251	432
Oakland	2	12	0	.143	237	458

1962

NFL EAST

	W	L	T	Pct	Pts	OP
NY Giants	12	2	0	.857	398	283
Pittsburgh	9	5	0	.642	312	363
Cleveland	7	6	1	.538	291	257
Washington	5	7	2	.417	305	376
Dallas Cowboys	5	8	1	.385	398	402
St. Louis Cardinals	4	9	1	.308	287	361
Philadelphia	3	10	1	.231	282	356

NFL WEST

	W	L	T	Pct	Pts	OP
Green Bay	13	1	0	.929	415	148
Detroit	11	3	0	.786	315	177
Chicago	9	5	0	.643	321	287
Baltimore	7	7	0	.500	293	288
San Francisco	6	8	0	.429	282	331
Minnesota	2	11	1	.154	254	410
LA Rams	1	12	1	.077	220	334

AFL EAST

	W	L	T	Pct	Pts	OP
Houston	11	3	0	.786	387	270
Boston	9	4	1	.692	346	295
Buffalo	7	6	1	.538	309	272
NY Titans	5	9	0	.357	278	423

AFL WEST

	W	L	T	Pct	Pts	OP
Dallas Texans	11	3	0	.786	389	233
Denver	6	7	0	.462	323	313
San Diego	4	9	0	.308	293	362
Oakland	1	13	0	.071	213	370

1963

NFL EAST

	W	L	T	Pct	Pts	OP
NY Giants	11	3	0	.786	448	280
Cleveland	10	4	0	.714	343	262
St. Louis	9	5	0	.643	341	283
Pittsburgh	7	4	3	.636	321	295
Dallas Cowboys	4	10	0	.286	305	378
Washington	3	11	0	.214	279	398
Philadelphia	2	10	2	.214	242	381

NFL WEST

	W	L	T	Pct	Pts	OP
Chicago	11	1	2	.917	301	144
Green Bay	11	2	1	.846	369	206
Baltimore	8	6	0	.571	316	285
Minnesota	5	8	1	.385	309	390
Detroit	5	8	1	.385	32	265
LA Rams	5	9	0	.357	210	350
San Francisco	2	12	0	.143	198	391

AFL EAST

	W	L	T	Pct	Pts	OP
Boston	7	6	1	.538	327	257
Buffalo	7	6	1	.538	304	291
Houston	6	8	0	.429	302	372
NY Jets	5	8	1	.385	249	399

AFL WEST

	W	L	T	Pct	Pts	OP
San Diego	11	3	0	.786	399	255
Oakland	10	4	0	.714	363	282
Kansas City Chiefs	5	7	2	.417	347	263
Denver	2	11	1	.154	301	473

1964

NFL EAST

	W	L	T	Pct	Pts	OP
Cleveland	10	3	1	.769	415	293
St. Louis	9	3	2	.750	357	331
Philadelphia	6	8	0	.429	312	313
Washington	6	8	0	.429	307	305
Dallas	5	8	1	.385	250	289
Pittsburgh	5	9	0	.357	253	315
NY Giants	2	10	2	.167	241	399

NFL WEST

	W	L	T	Pct	Pts	OP
Baltimore	12	2	0	.857	428	225
Green Bay	8	5	1	.615	342	245
Minnesota	8	5	1	.615	355	296
Detroit	7	5	2	.583	280	260
LA Rams	5	7	2	.417	283	339
Chicago	5	9	0	.357	260	379
San Francisco	4	10	0	.286	236	330

AFL EAST

	W	L	T	Pct	Pts	OP
Buffalo	12	2	0	.857	400	242
Boston	10	3	1	.769	365	297
NY Jets	5	8	1	.385	278	315
Houston	4	10	0	.286	310	355

AFL WEST

	W	L	T	Pct	Pts	OP
San Diego	8	5	1	.615	341	300
Kansas City Chiefs	7	7	0	.500	366	306
Oakland	5	7	2	.417	303	350
Denver	2	11	1	.154	240	438

1965

NFL EAST

	W	L	T	Pct	Pts	OP
Cleveland	11	3	0	.786	363	325
NY Giants	7	7	0	.500	270	338
Dallas	7	7	0	.500	325	280
Washington	6	8	0	.429	257	301
St. Louis	5	9	0	.357	296	309
Philadelphia	5	9	0	.357	363	359
Pittsburgh	2	12	0	.143	202	397

NFL WEST

	W	L	T	Pct	Pts	OP
Green Bay	10	3	1	.769	316	224
Baltimore	9	3	1	.769	389	263
Chicago	9	5	0	.643	409	275
San Francisco	7	6	1	.538	421	402
Minnesota	7	6	0	.500	383	362
Detroit	6	7	1	.462	257	295
LA Rams	4	10	0	.286	269	328

AFL EAST

	W	L	T	Pct	Pts	OP
Buffalo	10	3	1	.769	313	226
NY Jets	5	8	1	.385	285	303
Boston	4	8	2	.333	244	302
Houston	4	10	0	.286	298	429

AFL WEST

	W	L	T	Pct	Pts	OP
San Diego	9	2	3	.818	340	227
Oakland	8	5	1	.615	298	239
Kansas City	7	5	2	.583	322	285
Denver	4	10	0	.286	303	392

1966

NFL EAST

	W	L	T	Pct	Pts	OP
Dallas	10	3	1	.769	445	239
Cleveland	9	5	0	.643	403	259
Philadelphia	9	5	0	.643	326	340
St. Louis	8	5	1	.625	264	265
Washington	7	7	0	.500	351	355
Pittsburgh	5	8	1	.385	316	347
Atlanta Falcons	3	11	0	.214	204	437
NY Giants	1	12	1	.077	263	501

NFL WEST

	W	L	T	Pct	Pts	OP
Green Bay	12	2	0	.857	335	163
Baltimore	9	5	0	.643	314	226
LA Rams	8	6	0	.571	289	212
San Francisco	6	6	2	.500	320	325
Chicago	5	7	2	.417	234	272
Detroit	4	9	1	.308	206	317
Minnesota	4	9	1	.308	292	304

AFL EAST

	W	L	T	Pct	Pts	OP
Buffalo	9	4	1	.692	358	255
Boston	8	4	2	.677	315	283
NY Jets	6	6	2	.500	322	312
Houston	3	11	0	.214	335	396
Miami Dolphins	3	11	0	.214	213	362

AFL WEST

	W	L	T	Pct	Pts	OP
Kansas City	11	2	1	.846	448	276
Oakland	8	5	1	.615	315	288
San Diego	7	6	1	.538	335	284
Denver	4	10	0	.286	196	381

1967

NFL CAPITOL

	W	L	T	Pct	Pts	OP
Dallas	9	5	0	.643	342	268
Philadelphia	6	7	1	.462	351	409
Washington	5	6	3	.455	347	353
New Orleans Saints	3	11	0	.214	233	379

NFL CENTURY

	W	L	T	Pct	Pts	OP
Cleveland	9	5	0	.643	334	297
NY Giants	7	7	0	.500	369	379
St. Louis	6	7	1	.462	333	356
Pittsburgh	4	9	1	.308	281	320

NFL COASTAL

	W	L	T	Pct	Pts	OP
LA Rams	11	1	2	.917	398	196
Baltimore	11	1	2	.917	394	198
San Francisco	7	7	0	.500	273	337
Atlanta	1	12	1	.077	175	422

NFL CENTRAL

	W	L	T	Pct	Pts	OP
Green Bay	9	4	1	.692	332	209
Chicago	7	6	1	.538	239	218
Detroit	5	7	2	.417	260	259
Minnesota	3	8	3	.273	233	294

AFL EAST

	W	L	T	Pct	Pts	OP
Houston	9	4	1	.692	258	199
NY Jets	8	5	1	.615	371	329
Buffalo	4	10	0	.286	237	285
Miami	4	10	0	.286	219	407
Boston	3	10	1	.231	280	389

1967 (Cont.)

AFL WEST

	W	L	T	Pct	Pts	OP
Oakland	13	1	0	.929	468	233
Kansas City	9	5	0	.643	408	254
San Diego	8	5	1	.615	360	352
Denver	3	11	0	.214	256	409

1968

NFL CAPITOL

	W	L	T	Pct	Pts	OP
Dallas	12	2	0	.857	431	186
NY Giants	7	7	0	.500	294	325
Washington	5	9	0	.357	249	358
Philadelphia	2	12	0	.143	202	351

NFL CENTURY

	W	L	T	Pct	Pts	OP
Cleveland	10	4	0	.714	394	273
St. Louis	9	4	1	.692	325	289
New Orleans	4	9	1	.308	246	327
Pittsburgh	2	11	1	.154	244	397

NFL COASTAL

	W	L	T	Pct	Pts	OP
Baltimore	13	1	0	.929	402	144
LA Rams	10	3	1	.769	312	200
San Francisco	7	6	1	.538	303	310
Atlanta	2	12	0	.143	202	351

NFL CENTRAL

	W	L	T	Pct	Pts	OP
Minnesota	8	6	0	.571	282	242
Chicago	7	7	0	.500	250	333
Green Bay	6	7	1	.462	281	227
Detroit	4	8	2	.333	207	241

AFL EAST

	W	L	T	Pct	Pts	OP
NY Jets	11	3	0	.786	419	280
Houston	7	7	0	.500	303	248
Miami	5	8	1	.385	276	355
Boston	4	10	0	.286	229	406
Buffalo	1	12	1	.077	199	367

AFL WEST

	W	L	T	Pct	Pts	OP
Oakland	12	2	0	.857	453	233
Kansas City	12	2	0	.857	371	170
San Diego	9	5	0	.643	382	310
Denver	5	9	0	.357	255	404
Cincinnati Bengals	3	11	0	.214	215	329

1969

NFL CAPITOL

	W	L	T	Pct	Pts	OP
Dallas	11	2	1	.846	369	223
Washington	7	5	2	.583	307	319
New Orleans	5	9	0	.357	311	393
Philadelphia	4	9	1	.308	279	377

NFL CENTURY

	W	L	T	Pct	Pts	OP
Cleveland	10	3	1	.769	351	300
NY Giants	6	8	0	.429	264	298
St. Louis	4	9	1	.308	314	389
Pittsburgh	1	13	0	.071	218	404

NFL COASTAL

	W	L	T	Pct	Pts	OP
LA Rams	11	3	0	.786	320	243
Baltimore	7	5	2	.615	307	319
Atlanta	6	8	0	.429	276	268
San Francisco	4	8	2	.333	277	319

1969 (Cont.)

NFL CENTRAL

	W	L	T	Pct	Pts	OP
Minnesota	12	2	0	.857	379	133
Detroit	9	4	1	.692	259	188
Green Bay	8	6	0	.571	269	221
Chicago	1	13	0	.071	210	339

AFL EAST

	W	L	T	Pct	Pts	OP
NY Jets	10	4	0	.714	353	269
Houston	6	6	2	.500	278	279
Buffalo	4	10	0	.286	230	359
Boston	4	10	0	.286	266	316
Miami	3	10	1	.231	233	332

AFL WEST

	W	L	T	Pct	Pts	OP
Oakland	12	1	1	.923	377	242
Kansas City	11	3	0	.786	359	177
San Diego	8	6	0	.571	288	276
Denver	5	8	1	.385	297	344
Cincinnati	4	9	1	.308	280	367

1970

AFC EAST

	W	L	T	Pct	Pts	OP
Baltimore	11	2	1	.846	321	234
Miami	10	4	0	.714	297	228
NY Jets	4	10	0	.286	255	286
Buffalo	3	10	1	.231	204	337
Boston	2	12	0	.143	149	361

AFC CENTRAL

	W	L	T	Pct	Pts	OP
Cincinnati	8	6	0	.571	312	255
Cleveland	7	7	0	.500	286	265
Pittsburgh	5	9	0	.357	210	272
Houston	3	10	1	.231	217	352

AFC WEST

	W	L	T	Pct	Pts	OP
Oakland	8	4	2	.667	300	293
Kansas City	7	5	2	.583	272	244
San Diego	5	6	3	.455	282	278
Denver	5	8	1	.385	253	264

NFC EAST

	W	L	T	Pct	Pts	OP
Dallas	10	4	0	.714	299	221
NY Giants	9	5	0	.643	301	270
St. Louis	8	5	1	.615	325	228
Washington	6	8	0	.429	297	314
Philadelphia	3	10	1	.231	241	332

NFC CENTRAL

	W	L	T	Pct	Pts	OP
Minnesota	12	2	0	.857	335	143
Detroit	10	4	0	.714	347	202
Green Bay	6	8	0	.429	196	293
Chicago	6	8	0	.429	256	261

NFC WEST

	W	L	T	Pct	Pts	OP
San Francisco	10	3	1	.769	352	267
LA Rams	9	4	1	.692	325	202
Atlanta	4	8	2	.333	206	261
New Orleans	2	11	1	.154	172	347

1971

AFC EAST

	W	L	T	Pct	Pts	OP
Miami	10	3	1	.769	315	174
Baltimore	10	4	0	.714	313	140
New England Patriots	6	8	0	.429	238	325
NY Jets	6	8	0	.429	212	299
Buffalo	1	13	0	.071	184	394

AFC CENTRAL

	W	L	T	Pct	Pts	OP
Cleveland	9	5	0	.643	285	273
Pittsburgh	6	8	0	.429	246	292
Houston	4	9	1	.308	251	330
Cincinnati	4	10	0	.286	284	265

AFC WEST

	W	L	T	Pct	Pts	OP
Kansas City	10	3	1	.769	302	208
Oakland	8	4	2	.667	344	278
San Diego	6	8	0	.429	311	341
Denver	4	9	1	.308	203	275

NFC EAST

	W	L	T	Pct	Pts	OP
Dallas	11	3	0	.786	406	222
Washington	9	4	1	.692	276	190
Philadelphia	6	7	1	.462	221	302
St. Louis	4	9	1	.308	231	279
NY Giants	4	10	0	.286	228	362

NFC CENTRAL

	W	L	T	Pct	Pts	OP
Minnesota	11	3	0	.786	245	139
Detroit	7	6	1	.538	341	286
Chicago	6	8	0	.429	185	276
Green Bay	4	8	2	.333	274	298

NFC WEST

	W	L	T	Pct	Pts	OP
San Francisco	9	5	0	.643	300	216
LA Rams	8	5	1	.615	313	260
Atlanta	7	6	1	.538	274	277
New Orleans	4	8	2	.333	266	347

1972

AFC EAST

	W	L	T	Pct	Pts	OP
Miami	14	0	0	1.000	385	171
NY Jets	7	7	0	.500	367	324
Baltimore	5	9	0	.357	235	252
Buffalo	4	9	1	.321	257	377
New England	3	11	0	.214	192	446

AFC CENTRAL

	W	L	T	Pct	Pts	OP
Pittsburgh	11	3	0	.786	343	175
Cleveland	10	4	0	.714	268	249
Cincinnati	8	6	0	.571	299	229
Houston	1	13	0	.071	164	380

AFC WEST

	W	L	T	Pct	Pts	OP
Oakland	10	3	1	.750	365	248
Kansas City	8	6	0	.571	287	254
Denver	5	9	0	.357	325	350
San Diego	4	9	1	.321	264	344

NFC EAST

	W	L	T	Pct	Pts	OP
Washington	11	3	0	.786	336	218
Dallas	10	4	0	.286	319	240
NY Giants	8	6	0	.571	331	247
St. Louis	4	9	1	.321	193	303
Philadelphia	2	11	1	.179	145	352

1972 (Cont.)

NFC CENTRAL

	W	L	T	Pct	Pts	OP
Green Bay	10	4	0	.714	304	226
Detroit	8	5	1	.607	339	290
Minnesota	7	7	0	.500	301	252
Chicago	4	9	1	.321	225	275

NFC WEST

	W	L	T	Pct	Pts	OP
San Francisco	8	5	1	.607	353	249
Atlanta	7	7	0	.500	269	274
LA Rams	6	7	1	.464	291	286
New Orleans	2	11	1	.179	215	361

1973

AFC EAST

	W	L	T	Pct	Pts	OP
Miami	12	2	0	.857	343	150
Buffalo	9	5	0	.643	259	230
New England	5	9	0	.357	258	300
Baltimore	4	10	0	.286	226	341
NY Jets	4	10	0	.286	240	306

AFC CENTRAL

	W	L	T	Pct	Pts	OP
Pittsburgh	10	4	0	.714	347	210
Cincinnati	10	4	0	.714	286	231
Cleveland	7	5	2	.571	234	255
Houston	1	13	0	.071	199	447

AFC WEST

	W	L	T	Pct	Pts	OP
Oakland	9	4	1	.679	292	175
Kansas City	7	5	2	.571	231	192
Denver	7	5	2	.571	354	296
San Diego	2	11	1	.179	188	386

NFC EAST

	W	L	T	Pct	Pts	OP
Washington	10	4	0	.714	325	198
Dallas	10	4	0	.714	325	198
Philadelphia	5	8	1	.393	310	393
St. Louis	4	9	1	.321	286	365
NY Giants	2	11	1	.179	226	362

NFC CENTRAL

	W	L	T	Pct	Pts	OP
Minnesota	12	2	0	.857	296	168
Detroit	6	7	1	.464	271	247
Green Bay	5	7	2	.429	202	259
Chicago	3	11	0	.214	195	334

NFC WEST

	W	L	T	Pct	Pts	OP
LA Rams	12	2	0	.857	388	178
Atlanta	9	5	0	.643	318	224
New Orleans	5	9	0	.357	163	312
San Francisco	5	9	0	.357	262	319

1974

AFC EAST

	W	L	T	Pct	Pts	OP
Miami	11	3	0	.786	327	216
Buffalo	9	5	0	.643	264	244
NY Jets	7	7	0	.500	279	300
New England	7	7	0	.500	348	289
Baltimore	2	12	0	.143	190	329

AFC CENTRAL

	W	L	T	Pct	Pts	OP
Pittsburgh	10	3	1	.750	305	189
Houston	7	7	0	.500	236	282
Cincinnati	7	7	0	.500	283	259
Cleveland	4	10	0	.283	251	344

1974 (Cont.)

AFC WEST

	W	L	T	Pct	Pts	OP
Oakland	12	2	0	.857	355	228
Denver	7	6	1	.536	302	294
Kansas City	5	9	0	.357	233	293
San Diego	5	9	0	.357	212	285

NFC EAST

	W	L	T	Pct	Pts	OP
Washington	10	4	0	.714	320	196
St. Louis	10	4	0	.714	285	218
Dallas	8	6	0	.571	297	235
Philadelphia	7	7	0	.500	242	217
NY Giants	2	12	0	.143	195	299

NFC CENTRAL

	W	L	T	Pct	Pts	OP
Minnesota	10	4	0	.714	310	195
Detroit	7	7	0	.500	256	270
Green Bay	6	8	0	.429	210	206
Chicago	4	10	0	.286	152	279

NFC WEST

	W	L	T	Pct	Pts	OP
LA Rams	10	4	0	.714	263	181
San Francisco	6	8	0	.429	226	236
New Orleans	5	9	0	.357	166	263
Atlanta	3	11	0	.214	111	271

1975

AFC EAST

	W	L	T	Pct	Pts	OP
Miami	10	4	0	.714	357	222
Baltimore	10	4	0	.714	395	269
Buffalo	8	6	0	.571	420	355
NY Jets	3	11	0	.214	258	433
New England	3	11	0	.214	258	358

AFC CENTRAL

	W	L	T	Pct	Pts	OP
Pittsburgh	12	2	0	.857	373	162
Cincinnati	11	3	0	.786	340	246
Houston	10	4	0	.714	293	226
Cleveland	3	11	0	.214	218	372

AFC WEST

	W	L	T	Pct	Pts	OP
Oakland	11	3	0	.786	375	255
Denver	6	8	0	.429	254	307
Kansas City	5	9	0	.357	282	341
San Diego	2	12	0	.143	189	345

NFC EAST

	W	L	T	Pct	Pts	OP
St. Louis	11	3	0	.786	356	276
Dallas	10	4	0	.714	350	268
Washington	8	6	0	.571	325	276
NY Giants	5	9	0	.357	216	306
Philadelphia	4	10	0	.286	225	302

NFC CENTRAL

	W	L	T	Pct	Pts	OP
Minnesota	12	2	0	.857	377	180
Detroit	7	7	0	.500	245	262
Green Bay	4	10	0	.286	226	285
Chicago	4	10	0	.286	191	379

NFC WEST

	W	L	T	Pct	Pts	OP
LA Rams	12	2	0	.857	312	135
San Francisco	5	9	0	.357	255	286
Atlanta	4	10	0	.286	240	289
New Orleans	2	12	0	.143	165	360

1976

AFC EAST
	W	L	T	Pct	Pts	OP
Baltimore	11	3	0	.786	417	246
New England	11	3	0	.786	376	236
Miami	6	8	0	.429	263	264
NY Jets	3	11	0	.214	169	383
Buffalo	2	12	0	.143	246	363

AFC CENTRAL
	W	L	T	Pct	Pts	OP
Cincinnati	10	4	0	.714	335	210
Pittsburgh	10	4	0	.714	342	138
Cleveland	9	5	0	.643	267	287
Houston	5	9	0	.357	222	273

AFC WEST
	W	L	T	Pct	Pts	OP
Oakland	13	1	0	.929	350	237
Denver	9	5	0	.643	315	206
San Diego	6	8	0	.429	248	285
Kansas City	5	9	0	.357	290	376
Tampa Bay Buccaneers	0	14	0	.000	125	412

NFC EAST
	W	L	T	Pct	Pts	OP
Dallas	11	3	0	.786	296	194
Washington	10	4	0	.714	291	217
St. Louis	10	4	0	.714	309	267
Philadelphia	4	10	0	.286	165	286
NY Giants	3	11	0	.214	170	250

NFC CENTRAL
	W	L	T	Pct	Pts	OP
Minnesota	11	2	1	.821	305	176
Chicago	7	7	0	.500	253	216
Detroit	6	8	0	.429	218	299
Green Bay	5	9	0	.357	218	299

NFC WEST
	W	L	T	Pct	Pts	OP
LA Rams	10	3	1	.750	351	190
San Francisco	8	6	0	.571	270	190
Atlanta	4	10	0	.286	172	312
New Orleans	4	10	0	.286	253	346
Seattle Seahawks	2	12	0	.143	229	429

1977

AFC EAST
	W	L	T	Pct	Pts	OP
Miami	10	4	0	.714	313	197
Baltimore	10	4	0	.714	295	221
New England	9	5	0	.643	279	217
Buffalo	3	11	0	.214	160	313
NY Jets	3	11	0	.214	191	313

AFC CENTRAL
	W	L	T	Pct	Pts	OP
Pittsburgh	9	5	0	.643	283	243
Houston	8	6	0	.571	299	230
Cincinnati	8	6	0	.571	238	235
Cleveland	6	8	0	.429	269	267

AFC WEST
	W	L	T	Pct	Pts	OP
Denver	12	2	0	.857	274	148
Oakland	11	3	0	.786	351	230
San Diego	7	7	0	.500	222	205
Seattle	5	9	0	.357	282	373
Kansas City	2	12	0	.143	225	349

1977 (Cont.)

NFC EAST
	W	L	T	Pct	Pts	OP
Dallas	12	2	0	.857	345	212
Washington	9	5	0	.643	196	189
St. Louis	7	7	0	.500	272	287
NY Giants	5	9	0	.357	181	265
Philadelphia	5	9	0	.357	220	207

NFC CENTRAL
	W	L	T	Pct	Pts	OP
Chicago	9	5	0	.643	255	253
Minnesota	9	5	0	.643	231	227
Detroit	6	8	0	.429	183	252
Green Bay	4	10	0	.286	134	219
Tampa Bay	2	12	0	.143	103	223

NFC WEST
	W	L	T	Pct	Pts	OP
LA Rams	10	4	0	.714	302	146
Atlanta	7	7	0	.500	179	129
San Francisco	5	9	0	.357	220	260
New Orleans	3	11	0	.214	232	336

1978

AFC EAST
	W	L	T	Pct	Pts	OP
New England	11	5	0	.688	358	286
Miami	11	5	0	.688	372	254
NY Jets	8	8	0	.500	359	364
Buffalo	5	11	0	.313	302	354
Baltimore	5	11	0	.313	239	421

AFC CENTRAL
	W	L	T	Pct	Pts	OP
Pittsburgh	14	2	0	.875	356	195
Houston	10	6	0	.625	283	298
Cleveland	8	8	0	.500	334	356
Cincinnati	4	12	0	.250	252	284

AFC WEST
	W	L	T	Pct	Pts	OP
Denver	10	6	0	.625	282	198
Seattle	9	7	0	.563	345	358
Oakland	9	7	0	.563	311	283
San Diego	9	7	0	.563	355	309
Kansas City	4	12	0	.250	243	327

NFC EAST
	W	L	T	Pct	Pts	OP
Dallas	12	4	0	.750	384	208
Philadelphia	9	7	0	.563	270	250
Washington	8	8	0	.500	273	283
St. Louis	6	10	0	.375	248	296
NY Giants	6	10	0	.375	264	298

NFC CENTRAL
	W	L	T	Pct	Pts	OP
Green Bay	8	7	1	.531	249	269
Minnesota	8	7	1	.531	294	306
Detroit	7	9	0	.438	290	300
Chicago	7	9	0	.438	253	274
Tampa Bay	5	11	0	.313	241	259

NFC WEST
	W	L	T	Pct	Pts	OP
LA Rams	12	4	0	.750	316	245
Atlanta	9	7	0	.563	240	290
New Orleans	7	9	0	.438	281	298
San Francisco	2	14	0	.125	219	350

1979

AFC EAST

	W	L	T	Pct	Pts	OP
Miami	10	6	0	.625	341	257
New England	9	7	0	.563	411	326
NY Jets	8	8	0	.500	337	383
Buffalo	7	9	0	.438	268	279
Baltimore	5	11	0	.313	271	351

AFC CENTRAL

	W	L	T	Pct	Pts	OP
Pittsburgh	12	4	0	.750	416	262
Houston	11	5	0	.688	362	331
Cleveland	9	7	0	.563	359	352
Cincinnati	4	12	0	.250	337	421

AFC WEST

	W	L	T	Pct	Pts	OP
San Diego	12	4	0	.750	411	246
Denver	10	6	0	.625	289	262
Seattle	9	7	0	.563	378	372
Oakland	9	7	0	.563	365	337
Kansas City	7	9	0	.438	238	262

NFC EAST

	W	L	T	Pct	Pts	OP
Dallas	11	5	0	.688	371	313
Philadelphia	11	5	0	.688	339	282
Washington	10	6	0	.625	348	295
NY Giants	6	10	0	.375	237	323
St. Louis	5	11	0	.313	307	358

NFC CENTRAL

	W	L	T	Pct	Pts	OP
Chicago	10	6	0	.625	306	249
Tampa Bay	10	6	0	.625	273	237
Minnesota	7	9	0	.438	259	337
Green Bay	5	11	0	.313	246	316
Detroit	2	14	0	.125	219	365

NFC WEST

	W	L	T	Pct	Pts	OP
LA Rams	9	7	0	.563	323	309
New Orleans	8	8	0	.500	370	360
Atlanta	6	10	0	.375	300	388
San Francisco	2	14	0	.125	308	416

1980

AFC EAST

	W	L	T	Pct	Pts	OP
Buffalo	11	5	0	.688	320	260
New England	10	6	0	.625	441	325
Miami	8	8	0	.500	266	305
Baltimore	7	9	0	.438	355	387
NY Jets	4	12	0	.250	302	395

AFC CENTRAL

	W	L	T	Pct	Pts	OP
Cleveland	11	5	0	.688	357	310
Houston	11	5	0	.688	295	251
Pittsburgh	9	7	0	.563	352	313
Cincinnati	6	10	0	.375	244	312

AFC WEST

	W	L	T	Pct	Pts	OP
San Diego	11	5	0	.688	418	327
Oakland	11	5	0	.688	364	306
Denver	8	8	0	.500	310	323
Kansas City	8	8	0	.500	319	336
Seattle	4	12	0	.250	291	408

NFC EAST

	W	L	T	Pct	Pts	OP
Dallas	12	4	0	.750	454	311
Philadelphia	12	4	0	.750	384	222
Washington	6	10	0	.375	261	293
St. Louis	5	11	0	.313	299	350
NY Giants	4	12	0	.250	249	425

1980 (Cont.)

NFC CENTRAL

	W	L	T	Pct	Pts	OP
Detroit	9	7	0	.563	334	272
Minnesota	9	7	0	.563	317	308
Chicago	7	9	0	.438	304	264
Tampa Bay	5	10	1	.344	271	341
Green Bay	5	10	1	.344	231	371

NFC WEST

	W	L	T	Pct	Pts	OP
Atlanta	12	4	0	.750	405	272
LA Rams	11	5	0	.688	424	289
San Francisco	6	10	0	.375	320	415
New Orleans	1	15	0	.063	291	487

1981

AFC EAST

	W	L	T	Pct	Pts	OP
Miami	11	4	1	.719	345	275
NY Jets	10	5	1	.656	355	287
Buffalo	10	6	0	.625	311	276
Baltimore	2	14	0	.125	259	533
New England	2	14	0	.125	322	370

AFC CENTRAL

	W	L	T	Pct	Pts	OP
Cincinnati	12	4	0	.750	421	304
Pittsburgh	8	8	0	.500	356	297
Houston	7	9	0	.438	281	355
Cleveland	5	11	0	.313	276	375

AFC WEST

	W	L	T	Pct	Pts	OP
Denver	10	6	0	.625	321	289
San Diego	10	6	0	.625	478	390
Kansas City	9	7	0	.563	343	290
Oakland	7	9	0	.438	273	343
Seattle	6	10	0	.375	322	388

NFC EAST

	W	L	T	Pct	Pts	OP
Dallas	12	4	0	.750	367	277
Philadelphia	10	6	0	.625	368	221
NY Giants	9	7	0	.563	295	257
Washington	8	8	0	.500	347	349
St. Louis	7	9	0	.438	315	407

NFC CENTRAL

	W	L	T	Pct	Pts	OP
Tampa Bay	9	7	0	.563	315	268
Detroit	8	8	0	.500	397	322
Green Bay	8	8	0	.500	324	361
Minnesota	7	9	0	.438	325	369
Chicago	6	10	0	.375	253	324

NFC WEST

	W	L	T	Pct	Pts	OP
San Francisco	13	3	0	.813	357	250
Atlanta	7	9	0	.438	426	355
LA Rams	6	10	0	.375	303	351
New Orleans	4	12	0	.250	207	378

1982

AFC EAST

	W	L	T	Pct	Pts	OP
Miami	7	2	0	.778	198	131
NY Jets	6	3	0	.667	245	166
New England	5	4	0	.556	143	157
Buffalo	4	5	0	.444	150	154
Baltimore	0	8	1	.056	113	236

1982 (Cont.)

AFC CENTRAL

	W	L	T	Pct	Pts	OP
Cincinnati	7	2	0	.778	232	177
Pittsburgh	6	3	0	.667	204	146
Cleveland	4	5	0	.444	140	182
Houston	1	8	0	.111	136	245

AFC WEST

	W	L	T	Pct	Pts	OP
Los Angeles Raiders	8	1	0	.889	260	200
San Diego	6	3	0	.667	288	221
Seattle	4	5	0	.444	127	147
Kansas City	3	6	0	.333	176	184
Denver	2	7	0	.222	148	226

NFC EAST

	W	L	T	Pct	Pts	OP
Washington	8	1	0	.889	190	128
Dallas	6	3	0	.667	226	145
St. Louis	5	4	0	.556	135	170
NY Giants	4	5	0	.444	164	160
Philadelphia	3	6	0	.333	191	195

NFC CENTRAL

	W	L	T	Pct	Pts	OP
Green Bay	5	3	1	.611	226	169
Tampa Bay	5	4	0	.556	158	178
Minnesota	5	4	0	.556	187	198
Detroit	4	5	0	.444	181	176
Chicago	3	6	0	.333	141	174

NFC WEST

	W	L	T	Pct	Pts	OP
Atlanta	5	4	0	.556	183	199
New Orleans	4	5	0	.444	129	160
San Francisco	3	6	0	.333	209	206
Los Angeles Rams	2	7	0	.222	200	250

1983

AFC EAST

	W	L	T	Pct	Pts	OP
Miami	12	4	0	.750	389	250
Buffalo	8	8	0	.500	283	351
New England	8	8	0	.500	274	289
Baltimore	7	9	0	.438	264	354
NY Jets	7	9	0	.438	313	331

AFC CENTRAL

	W	L	T	Pct	Pts	OP
Pittsburgh	10	6	0	.625	355	303
Cleveland	9	7	0	.563	356	342
Cincinnati	7	9	0	.438	346	302
Houston	2	14	0	.125	288	460

AFC WEST

	W	L	T	Pct	Pts	OP
LA Raiders	12	4	0	.750	442	338
Seattle	9	7	0	.563	403	397
Denver	9	7	0	.563	302	327
San Diego	6	10	0	.375	358	462
Kansas City	6	10	0	.375	386	367

NFC EAST

	W	L	T	Pct	Pts	OP
Washington	14	2	0	.875	541	332
Dallas	12	4	0	.750	479	360
St. Louis	8	7	1	.531	374	428
Philadelphia	5	11	0	.313	233	322
NY Giants	3	12	1	.219	267	347

NFC CENTRAL

	W	L	T	Pct	Pts	OP
Detroit	9	7	0	.563	47	286
Minnesota	8	8	0	.500	316	348
Chicago	8	8	0	.500	311	301
Green Bay	8	8	0	.500	429	439
Tampa Bay	2	14	0	.125	241	380

1983 (Cont.)

NFC WEST

	W	L	T	Pct	Pts	OP
San Francisco	10	6	0	.625	432	293
LA Rams	9	7	0	.563	361	344
New Orleans	8	8	0	.500	319	337
Atlanta	7	9	0	.438	370	389

1984

AFC EAST

	W	L	T	Pct	Pts	OP
Miami	14	2	0	.875	513	298
New England	9	7	0	.563	362	352
NY Jets	7	9	0	.438	332	364
Indianapolis Colts	4	12	0	.250	239	414
Buffalo	2	14	0	.125	250	454

AFC CENTRAL

	W	L	T	Pct	Pts	OP
Pittsburgh	9	7	0	.563	387	310
Cincinnati	8	8	0	.500	339	339
Cleveland	5	11	0	.313	250	297
Houston	3	13	0	.188	240	437

AFC WEST

	W	L	T	Pct	Pts	OP
Denver	13	3	0	.813	353	241
Seattle	12	4	0	.750	418	282
LA Raiders	11	5	0	.313	368	278
Kansas City	8	8	0	.500	314	324
San Diego	7	9	0	.438	394	413

NFC EAST

	W	L	T	Pct	Pts	OP
Washington	11	5	0	.688	426	310
NY Giants	9	7	0	.563	299	301
Dallas	9	7	0	.563	308	308
St. Louis	9	7	0	.563	423	345
Philadelphia	6	9	1	.406	278	320

NFC CENTRAL

	W	L	T	Pct	Pts	OP
Chicago	10	6	0	.625	325	248
Green Bay	8	8	0	.500	390	309
Tampa Bay	6	10	0	.375	335	380
Detroit	4	11	1	.281	283	408
Minnesota	3	13	0	.188	276	484

	W	L	T	Pct	Pts	OP
San Francisco	15	1	0	.938	475	227
LA Rams	10	6	0	.625	346	316
New Orleans	7	9	0	.438	298	361
Atlanta	4	12	0	.20	281	382

1985

AFC EAST

	W	L	T	Pct	Pts	OP
Miami	12	4	0	.750	428	320
New England	11	5	0	.688	362	290
NY Jets	11	5	0	.688	393	264
Indianapolis	5	11	0	.313	320	386
Buffalo	2	14	0	.125	200	381

AFC CENTRAL

	W	L	T	Pct	Pts	OP
Cleveland	8	8	0	.500	287	294
Cincinnati	7	9	0	.438	441	437
Pittsburgh	7	9	0	.438	379	355
Houston	5	11	0	.313	284	412

AFC WEST

	W	L	T	Pct	Pts	OP
LA Raiders	12	4	0	.750	354	308
Denver	11	5	0	.688	380	329
Seattle	8	8	0	.500	349	303
San Diego	8	8	0	.500	467	435
Kansas City	6	10	0	.375	317	360

NFC EAST

	W	L	T	Pct	Pts	OP
Washington	10	6	0	.625	297	312
NY Giants	10	6	0	.625	399	283
Dallas	10	6	0	.625	357	333
Philadelphia	7	9	0	.438	286	310
St. Louis	5	11	0	.313	278	414

NFC CENTRAL

	W	L	T	Pct	Pts	OP
Chicago	15	1	0	.938	456	198
Green Bay	8	8	0	.500	337	355
Detroit	7	9	0	.438	307	366
Minnesota	7	9	0	.438	346	359
Tampa Bay	2	14	0	.125	294	448

NFC WEST

	W	L	T	Pct	Pts	OP
LA Rams	11	5	0	.688	340	277
San Francisco	10	6	0	.625	411	263
New Orleans	5	11	0	.313	294	401
Atlanta	4	12	0	.250	282	452

1986

AFC EAST

	W	L	T	Pct	Pts	OP
New England	11	5	0	.688	412	307
NY Jets	10	6	0	.625	364	386
Miami	8	8	0	.500	430	405
Buffalo	4	12	0	.250	287	348
Indianapolis	3	13	0	.188	299	400

AFC CENTRAL

	W	L	T	Pct	Pts	OP
Cleveland	12	4	0	.750	391	310
Cincinnati	10	6	0	.625	409	394
Pittsburgh	6	10	0	.375	307	336
Houston	5	11	0	.313	274	329

AFC WEST

	W	L	T	Pct	Pts	OP
Denver	11	5	0	.688	378	327
Kansas City	10	6	0	.625	358	326
Seattle	10	6	0	.625	366	293
LA Raiders	8	8	0	.500	323	346
San Diego	4	12	0	.250	335	396

NFC EAST

	W	L	T	Pct	Pts	OP
NY Giants	14	2	0	.875	371	236
Washington	12	4	0	.750	368	296
Dallas	7	9	0	.438	346	337
Philadelphia	5	10	1	.344	256	312
St. Louis	4	11	1	.281	518	351

1986 (Cont.)

NFC CENTRAL

	W	L	T	Pct	Pts	OP
Chicago	14	2	0	.875	352	187
Minnesota	9	7	0	.563	398	276
Detroit	5	11	0	.313	277	326
Green Bay	4	12	0	.250	254	418
Tampa Bay	2	14	0	.125	239	473

NFC WEST

	W	L	T	Pct	Pts	OP
San Francisco	10	5	1	.656	374	247
LA Rams	10	6	0	.625	309	267
Atlanta	7	8	1	.469	280	280
New Orleans	7	9	0	.438	288	287

1987

AFC EAST

	W	L	T	Pct	Pts	OP
Indianapolis	9	6	0	.643	300	238
Miami	8	7	0	.533	362	335
New England	8	7	0	.533	320	293
Buffalo	7	8	0	.467	320	293
NY Jets	6	9	0	.400	334	360

AFC CENTRAL

	W	L	T	Pct	Pts	OP
Cleveland	10	5	0	.700	390	239
Houston	9	6	0	.600	345	349
Pittsburgh	8	7	0	.533	285	299
Cincinnati	4	11	0	.267	285	370

AFC WEST

	W	L	T	Pct	Pts	OP
Denver	10	4	1	.667	379	288
Seattle	9	6	0	.600	371	314
San Diego	8	7	0	.563	253	317
LA Raiders	5	10	0	.333	301	289
Kansas City	4	11	0	.267	276	388

NFC EAST

	W	L	T	Pct	Pts	OP
Washington	11	4	0	.733	379	285
Dallas	7	8	0	.467	340	348
St. Louis	7	8	0	.467	362	368
Philadelphia	7	8	0	.467	337	380
NY Giants	6	9	0	.400	280	312

NFC CENTRAL

	W	L	T	Pct	Pts	OP
Chicago	11	4	0	.733	356	282
Minnesota	8	7	0	.533	336	335
Green Bay	5	9	1	.367	255	300
Tampa Bay	4	11	0	.267	286	360
Detroit	4	11	0	.267	269	384

NFC WEST

	W	L	T	Pct	Pts	OP
San Francisco	13	2	0	.867	459	253
New Orleans	12	3	0	.800	422	283
LA Rams	6	9	0	.400	317	361
Atlanta	3	12	0	.200	205	436

Season-by-Season NFL Final Standings *(Cont.)*

1988

AFC EAST
	W	L	T	Pct	Pts	OP
Buffalo	12	4	0	.750	329	237
New England	9	7	0	.563	250	284
Indianapolis	9	7	0	.563	354	315
NY Jets	8	7	1	.531	372	354
Miami	6	10	0	.375	319	380

AFC CENTRAL
	W	L	T	Pct	Pts	OP
Cincinnati	12	4	0	.750	448	329
Cleveland	10	6	0	.625	304	288
Houston	10	6	0	.625	424	365
Pittsburgh	5	1	0	.313	336	421

AFC WEST
	W	L	T	Pct	Pts	OP
Seattle	9	7	0	.563	339	329
Denver	8	8	0	.500	327	352
LA Raiders	7	9	0	.438	325	369
San Diego	6	10	0	.375	231	332
Kansas City	4	11	1	.281	254	320

NFC EAST
	W	L	T	Pct	Pts	OP
NY Giants	10	6	0	.625	359	304
Philadelphia	10	6	0	.625	379	319
Phoenix Cardinals	7	9	0	.438	344	398
Washington	7	9	0	.438	345	387
Dallas	3	13	0	.188	265	381

NFC CENTRAL
	W	L	T	Pct	Pts	OP
Chicago	12	4	0	.750	312	215
Minnesota	11	5	0	.688	406	233
Tampa Bay	5	11	0	.313	261	350
Detroit	4	12	0	.250	220	313
Green Bay	4	12	0	.250	240	315

NFC WEST
	W	L	T	Pct	Pts	OP
New Orleans	10	6	0	.625	312	283
San Francisco	10	6	0	.625	369	294
LA Rams	10	6	0	.625	407	293
Atlanta	5	11	0	.313	244	315

1989

AFC EAST
	W	L	T	Pct	Pts	OP
Buffalo	9	7	0	.563	407	317
Miami	8	8	0	.500	331	379
Indianapolis	8	8	0	.500	298	301
New England	5	11	0	.313	297	391
NY Jets	4	12	0	.250	253	411

AFC CENTRAL
	W	L	T	Pct	Pts	OP
Cleveland	9	6	1	.594	334	254
Houston	9	7	0	.563	365	412
Pittsburgh	9	7	0	.563	265	326
Cincinnati	8	8	0	.500	404	285

AFC WEST
	W	L	T	Pct	Pts	OP
Denver	11	5	0	.688	362	226
Kansas City	8	7	1	.531	318	286
LA Raiders	8	8	0	.500	315	297
Seattle	7	9	0	.438	241	327
San Diego	6	10	0	.375	266	290

1989 (Cont.)

NFC EAST
	W	L	T	Pct	Pts	OP
NY Giants	12	4	0	.750	348	252
Philadelphia	11	5	0	.688	342	274
Washington	10	6	0	.625	386	308
Phoenix	5	11	0	.313	258	377
Dallas	1	15	0	.063	204	393

NFC CENTRAL
	W	L	T	Pct	Pts	OP
Green Bay	10	6	0	.625	362	356
Minnesota	10	6	0	.625	351	275
Detroit	7	9	0	.438	312	364
Chicago	6	10	0	.375	358	377
Tampa Bay	5	11	0	.313	320	419

NFC WEST
	W	L	T	Pct	Pts	OP
San Francisco	14	2	0	.875	442	253
LA Rams	11	5	0	.688	426	344
New Orleans	9	7	0	.563	386	301
Atlanta	3	13	0	.188	279	437

1990

AFC EAST
	W	L	T	Pct	Pts	OP
Buffalo	13	3	0	.813	428	263
Miami	12	4	0	.750	336	242
Indianapolis	7	9	0	.438	281	353
NY Jets	6	10	0	.375	295	345
New England	1	15	0	.063	181	446

AFC CENTRAL
	W	L	T	Pct	Pts	OP
Pittsburgh	9	7	0	.563	292	240
Cincinnati	9	7	0	.563	360	352
Houston	9	7	0	.563	405	307
Cleveland	3	13	0	.188	228	462

AFC WEST
	W	L	T	Pct	Pts	OP
LA Raiders	12	4	0	.750	337	268
Kansas City	11	5	0	.688	369	257
Seattle	9	7	0	.563	306	286
San Diego	6	10	0	.375	315	281
Denver	5	11	0	.313	331	374

NFC EAST
	W	L	T	Pct	Pts	OP
NY Giants	13	3	0	.813	335	211
Washington	10	6	0	.625	381	301
Philadelphia	10	6	0	.625	396	299
Dallas	7	9	0	.438	244	308
Phoenix	5	11	0	.313	268	396

NFC CENTRAL
	W	L	T	Pct	Pts	OP
Chicago	11	5	0	.688	348	280
Green Bay	6	10	0	.375	271	347
Minnesota	6	10	0	.375	351	326
Detroit	6	10	0	.375	373	413
Tampa Bay	6	10	0	.375	264	367

NFC WEST
	W	L	T	Pct	Pts	OP
San Francisco	14	2	0	.875	353	239
New Orleans	8	8	0	.500	274	275
LA Rams	5	11	0	.313	345	412
Atlanta	5	11	0	.313	348	365

1991

AFC EAST

	W	L	T	Pct	Pts	OP
Buffalo	13	3	0	.813	458	318
Miami	8	8	0	.500	343	349
NY Jets	8	8	0	.500	314	293
New England	6	10	0	.375	211	305
Indianapolis	1	15	0	.063	143	381

AFC CENTRAL

	W	L	T	Pct	Pts	OP
Houston	11	5	0	.688	386	251
Pittsburgh	7	9	0	.438	292	344
Cleveland	6	10	0	.375	293	298
Cincinnati	3	13	0	.188	263	435

AFC WEST

	W	L	T	Pct	Pts	OP
Denver	12	4	0	.750	304	235
Kansas City	10	6	0	.625	322	252
LA Raiders	9	7	0	.563	298	297
Seattle	7	9	0	.438	276	261
San Diego	4	12	0	.250	274	342

NFC EAST

	W	L	T	Pct	Pts	OP
Washington	14	2	0	.875	485	224
Dallas	11	5	0	.688	342	310
Philadelphia	10	6	0	.625	285	244
NY Giants	8	8	0	.500	281	297
Phoenix	4	12	0	.250	196	344

NFC CENTRAL

	W	L	T	Pct	Pts	OP
Detroit	12	4	0	.750	339	295
Chicago	11	5	0	.688	299	269
Minnesota	8	8	0	.500	301	306
Green Bay	4	12	0	.250	273	313
Tampa Bay	3	13	0	.188	199	365

NFC WEST

	W	L	T	Pct	Pts	OP
New Orleans	11	5	0	.688	341	211
Atlanta	10	6	0	.625	361	338
San Francisco	10	6	0	.625	393	239
LA Rams	3	13	0	.188	234	390

1992

AFC EAST

	W	L	T	Pct	Pts	OP
Buffalo	11	5	0	.688	381	283
Miami	11	5	0	.688	340	281
Indianapolis	9	7	0	.563	216	302
NY Jets	4	12	0	.250	220	315
New England	2	14	0	.125	205	363

AFC CENTRAL

	W	L	T	Pct	Pts	OP
Pittsburgh	11	5	0	.688	299	225
Houston	10	6	0	.625	352	258
Cleveland	7	9	0	.438	272	275
Cincinnati	5	11	0	.313	274	364

AFC WEST

	W	L	T	Pct	Pts	OP
San Diego	11	5	0	.688	335	241
Kansas City	10	6	0	.625	348	282
Denver	8	8	0	.500	262	329
LA Raiders	7	9	0	.438	249	281
Seattle	2	14	0	.125	140	312

1992 (Cont.)

NFC EAST

	W	L	T	Pct	Pts	OP
Dallas	13	3	0	.813	409	243
Philadelphia	11	5	0	.688	354	245
Washington	9	7	0	.563	300	255
NY Giants	6	10	0	.375	306	367
Phoenix	4	12	0	.250	243	332

NFC CENTRAL

	W	L	T	Pct	Pts	OP
Minnesota	11	5	0	.688	374	249
Green Bay	9	7	0	.563	276	296
Tampa Bay	5	11	0	.313	267	365
Detroit	5	11	0	.313	273	332
Chicago	5	11	0	.313	295	361

NFC WEST

	W	L	T	Pct	Pts	OP
San Francisco	14	2	0	.875	431	236
New Orleans	12	4	0	.750	330	202
Atlanta	6	10	0	.375	327	414
LA Rams	6	10	0	.375	313	383

1993

AFC EAST

	W	L	T	Pct	Pts	OP
Buffalo	12	4	0	.750	329	242
Miami	9	7	0	.563	349	351
NY Jets	8	8	0	.500	270	247
New England	5	11	0	.313	238	286
Indianapolis	4	12	0	.250	189	378

AFC CENTRAL

	W	L	T	Pct	Pts	OP
Houston	12	4	0	.750	368	238
Pittsburgh	9	7	0	.563	308	281
Cleveland	7	9	0	.438	304	307
Cincinnati	3	13	0	.188	187	319

AFC WEST

	W	L	T	Pct	Pts	OP
Kansas City	11	5	0	.688	328	291
LA Raiders	10	6	0	.625	306	326
Denver	9	7	0	.563	373	284
San Diego	8	8	0	.500	322	290
Seattle	6	10	0	.375	280	314

NFC EAST

	W	L	T	Pct	Pts	OP
Dallas	12	4	0	.750	376	229
NY Giants	11	5	0	.688	288	205
Philadelphia	8	8	0	.500	293	315
Phoenix	7	9	0	.438	326	269
Washington	4	12	0	.250	230	345

NFC CENTRAL

	W	L	T	Pct	Pts	OP
Detroit	10	6	0	.625	298	292
Green Bay	9	7	0	.563	340	282
Minnesota	9	7	0	.563	277	290
Chicago	7	9	0	.438	234	230
Tampa Bay	5	11	0	.313	237	375

NFC WEST

	W	L	T	Pct	Pts	OP
San Francisco	10	6	0	.625	473	295
New Orleans	8	8	0	.500	317	343
Atlanta	6	10	0	.375	316	385
LA Rams	5	11	0	.313	221	367

1994

AFC EAST

	W	L	T	Pct	Pts	OP
Miami	10	6	0	.625	389	327
New England	10	6	0	.625	351	312
Indianapolis	8	8	0	.500	307	320
Buffalo	7	9	0	.438	340	356
NY Jets	6	10	0	.375	264	320

AFC CENTRAL

	W	L	T	Pct	Pts	OP
Pittsburgh	12	4	0	.750	316	234
Cleveland	11	5	0	.688	340	204
Cincinnati	3	13	0	.188	276	406
Houston	2	14	0	.125	226	352

AFC WEST

	W	L	T	Pct	Pts	OP
San Diego	11	5	0	.688	384	306
LA Raiders	9	7	0	.563	303	327
Kansas City	9	7	0	.563	319	298
Denver	7	9	0	.438	347	396
Seattle	6	10	0	.375	287	323

NFC EAST

	W	L	T	Pct	Pts	OP
Dallas	12	4	0	.750	414	248
NY Giants	9	7	0	.563	279	305
Arizona Cardinals	8	8	0	.500	235	267
Philadelphia	7	9	0	.438	308	308
Washington	3	13	0	.188	320	412

NFC CENTRAL

	W	L	T	Pct	Pts	OP
Minnesota	10	6	0	.625	356	314
Green Bay	9	7	0	.563	382	287
Detroit	9	7	0	.563	357	342
Chicago	9	7	0	.563	271	307
Tampa Bay	6	10	0	.375	251	351

NFC WEST

	W	L	T	Pct	Pts	OP
San Francisco	13	3	0	.813	505	296
New Orleans	7	9	0	.438	348	407
Atlanta	7	9	0	.438	317	385
LA Rams	4	12	0	.250	286	365

1995

AFC EAST

	W	L	T	Pct	Pts	OP
Buffalo	10	6	0	.625	350	335
Miami	9	7	0	.563	398	332
Indianapolis	9	7	0	.563	331	316
New England	6	10	0	.375	294	377
NY Jets	3	13	0	.188	233	384

AFC CENTRAL

	W	L	T	Pct	Pts	OP
Pittsburgh	11	5	0	.688	407	327
Houston	7	9	0	.438	348	324
Cincinnati	7	9	0	.438	349	374
Cleveland	5	11	0	.313	289	356
Jacksonville Jaguars	4	12	0	.250	275	404

AFC WEST

	W	L	T	Pct	Pts	OP
Kansas City	13	3	0	.813	358	241
San Diego	9	7	0	.563	321	323
Oakland Raiders	8	8	0	.500	348	332
Denver	8	8	0	.500	388	345
Seattle	8	8	0	.500	363	366

1995 (Cont.)

NFC EAST

	W	L	T	Pct	Pts	OP
Dallas	12	4	0	.750	435	291
Philadelphia	10	6	0	.625	318	338
Washington	6	10	0	.375	326	359
NY Giants	5	11	0	.313	290	340
Arizona	4	12	0	.250	275	422

NFC CENTRAL

	W	L	T	Pct	Pts	OP
Green Bay	11	5	0	.688	404	314
Detroit	10	6	0	.625	436	336
Chicago	9	7	0	.563	392	360
Minnesota	8	8	0	.500	412	385
Tampa Bay	7	9	0	.438	238	335

NFC WEST

	W	L	T	Pct	Pts	OP
San Francisco	11	5	0	.688	457	258
Atlanta	9	7	0	.563	362	349
St. Louis Rams	7	9	0	.438	309	418
Carolina Panthers	7	9	0	.438	289	325
New Orleans	7	9	0	.438	319	348

1996

AFC EAST

	W	L	T	Pct	Pts	OP
New England	11	5	0	.688	418	313
Buffalo	10	6	0	.625	319	266
Indianapolis	9	7	0	.563	317	334
Miami	8	8	0	.500	339	325
NY Jets	1	15	0	.063	279	454

AFC CENTRAL

	W	L	T	Pct	Pts	OP
Pittsburgh	10	6	0	.625	344	257
Jacksonville	9	7	0	.563	325	334
Houston	8	8	0	.500	345	319
Cincinnati	8	8	0	.500	372	369
Baltimore Ravens	4	12	0	.250	371	441

AFC WEST

	W	L	T	Pct	Pts	OP
Denver	13	3	0	.813	391	275
Kansas City	9	7	0	.563	297	300
San Diego	8	8	0	.500	310	376
Seattle	7	9	0	.438	317	375
Oakland	7	9	0	.438	340	293

NFC EAST

	W	L	T	Pct	Pts	OP
Dallas	10	6	0	.625	286	250
Philadelphia	10	6	0	.625	363	341
Washington	9	7	0	.563	364	312
Arizona	7	9	0	.438	300	397
NY Giants	6	10	0	.375	242	297

NFC CENTRAL

	W	L	T	Pct	Pts	OP
Green Bay	13	3	0	.813	456	210
Minnesota	9	7	0	.563	298	315
Chicago	7	9	0	.438	283	305
Tampa Bay	6	10	0	.375	221	293
Detroit	5	11	0	.313	302	368

NFC WEST

	W	L	T	Pct	Pts	OP
San Francisco	12	4	0	.750	398	257
Carolina	12	4	0	.750	367	218
St. Louis	6	10	0	.375	303	409
New Orleans	3	13	0	.188	229	339
Atlanta	3	13	0	.188	309	461

1997

AFC EAST	W	L	T	Pct	Pts	OP
New England	10	6	0	.625	369	289
Miami	9	7	0	.563	339	327
NY Jets	9	7	0	.563	348	287
Buffalo	6	10	0	.375	255	367
Indianapolis	3	13	0	.188	313	401

AFC CENTRAL	W	L	T	Pct	Pts	OP
Jacksonville	11	5	0	.688	394	318
Pittsburgh	11	5	0	.688	372	307
Tennessee Oilers	8	8	0	.500	333	310
Cincinnati	7	9	0	.438	355	405
Baltimore	6	9	1	.375	326	345

AFC WEST	W	L	T	Pct	Pts	OP
Kansas City	13	3	0	.813	375	232
Denver	12	4	0	.750	472	287
Seattle	8	8	0	.500	365	362
Oakland	4	12	0	.250	324	419
San Diego	4	12	0	.250	266	425

NFC EAST	W	L	T	Pct	Pts	OP
NY Giants	10	5	1	.656	307	265
Washington	8	7	1	.531	327	289
Philadelphia	6	9	1	.406	317	372
Dallas	6	10	0	.375	304	314
Arizona	4	12	0	.250	283	379

NFC CENTRAL	W	L	T	Pct	Pts	OP
Green Bay	13	3	0	.813	422	282
Tampa Bay	10	6	0	.625	299	263
Detroit	9	7	0	.563	379	306
Minnesota	9	7	0	.563	354	359
Chicago	4	12	0	.250	263	421

NFC WEST	W	L	T	Pct	Pts	OP
San Francisco	13	3	0	.813	375	265
Carolina	7	9	0	.438	265	314
Atlanta	7	9	0	.438	320	361
New Orleans	6	10	0	.375	237	327
St. Louis	5	11	0	.313	299	359

1998

AFC EAST	W	L	T	Pct	Pts	OP
NY Jets	12	4	0	.750	416	266
Miami	10	6	0	.625	321	265
Buffalo	10	6	0	.625	400	333
New England	9	7	0	.563	337	329
Indianapolis	3	13	0	.188	310	444

AFC CENTRAL	W	L	T	Pct	Pts	OP
Jacksonville	11	5	0	.688	392	338
Tennessee	8	8	0	.500	330	320
Pittsburgh	7	9	0	.438	263	303
Baltimore	6	10	0	.375	269	335
Cincinnati	3	13	0	.188	268	452

AFC WEST	W	L	T	Pct	Pts	OP
Denver	14	2	0	.875	501	309
Oakland	8	8	0	.500	288	356
Seattle	8	8	0	.500	372	310
Kansas City	7	9	0	.438	327	363
San Diego	5	11	0	.313	241	342

1998 (Cont.)

NFC EAST	W	L	T	Pct	Pts	OP
Dallas	10	6	0	.625	381	275
Arizona	9	7	0	.563	325	378
NY Giants	8	8	0	.500	287	309
Washington	6	10	0	.375	319	421
Philadelphia	3	13	0	.188	161	344

NFC CENTRAL	W	L	T	Pct	Pts	OP
Minnesota	15	1	0	.938	556	296
Green Bay	11	5	0	.688	408	319
Tampa Bay	8	8	0	.500	314	295
Detroit	5	11	0	.313	306	378
Chicago	4	12	0	.250	276	368

NFC WEST	W	L	T	Pct	Pts	OP
Atlanta	14	2	0	.875	442	289
San Francisco	12	4	0	.750	479	328
New Orleans	6	10	0	.375	305	359
Carolina	4	12	0	.250	336	413
St. Louis	4	12	0	.250	285	378

1999

AFC EAST	W	L	T	Pct	Pts	OP
Indianapolis	13	3	0	.813	423	333
Buffalo	11	5	0	.688	320	229
Miami	9	7	0	.563	326	336
NY Jets	8	8	0	.500	309	309
New England	8	8	0	.500	299	284

AFC CENTRAL	W	L	T	Pct	Pts	OP
Jacksonville	14	2	0	.875	396	217
Tennessee Titans	13	3	0	.813	392	324
Baltimore	8	8	0	.500	324	277
Pittsburgh	6	10	0	.375	317	320
Cincinnati	4	12	0	.250	283	460
Cleveland Browns	2	14	0	.125	217	437

AFC WEST	W	L	T	Pct	Pts	OP
Seattle	9	7	0	.563	338	298
Kansas City	9	7	0	.563	390	322
Oakland	8	8	0	.500	390	329
San Diego	8	8	0	.500	269	316
Denver	6	10	0	.375	314	318

NFC EAST	W	L	T	Pct	Pts	OP
Washington	10	6	0	.625	443	377
Dallas	8	8	0	.500	352	276
NY Giants	7	9	0	.438	299	358
Arizona	6	10	0	.375	245	382
Philadelphia	5	11	0	.313	272	357

NFC CENTRAL	W	L	T	Pct	Pts	OP
Tampa Bay	11	5	0	.688	270	235
Minnesota	10	6	0	.625	399	335
Green Bay	8	8	0	.500	357	341
Detroit	8	8	0	.500	322	323
Chicago	6	10	0	.375	272	341

NFC WEST	W	L	T	Pct	Pts	OP
St. Louis	13	3	0	.813	526	242
Carolina	8	8	0	.500	421	381
Atlanta	5	11	0	.313	285	380
San Francisco	4	12	0	.250	295	453
New Orleans	3	13	0	.188	260	434

2000

AFC EAST

	W	L	T	Pct	Pts	OP
Miami	11	5	0	.688	323	226
Indianapolis	10	6	0	.625	429	326
NY Jets	9	7	0	.563	321	321
Buffalo	8	8	0	.500	315	350
New England	5	11	0	.313	276	338

AFC CENTRAL

	W	L	T	Pct	Pts	OP
Tennessee	13	3	0	.813	346	191
Baltimore	12	4	0	.750	333	165
Pittsburgh	9	7	0	.563	321	255
Jacksonville	7	9	0	.438	367	327
Cincinnati	4	12	0	.250	185	359
Cleveland	3	13	0	.188	161	419

AFC WEST

	W	L	T	Pct	Pts	OP
Oakland	12	4	0	.750	479	299
Denver	11	5	0	.688	485	369
Kansas City	7	9	0	.438	355	354
Seattle	6	10	0	.375	320	405
San Diego	1	15	0	.063	269	440

NFC EAST

	W	L	T	Pct	Pts	OP
NY Giants	12	4	0	.750	328	246
Philadelphia	11	5	0	.688	351	245
Washington	8	8	0	.500	281	269
Dallas	5	11	0	.313	294	361
Arizona	3	13	0	.188	210	443

NFC CENTRAL

	W	L	T	Pct	Pts	OP
Minnesota	11	5	0	.688	397	371
Tampa Bay	10	6	0	.625	388	269
Green Bay	9	7	0	.563	353	323
Detroit	9	7	0	.563	307	307
Chicago	5	11	0	.313	216	355

NFC WEST

	W	L	T	Pct	Pts	OP
New Orleans	10	6	0	.625	354	306
St. Louis	10	6	0	.625	540	471
Carolina	7	9	0	.438	310	310
San Francisco	6	10	0	.375	388	422
Atlanta	4	12	0	.250	252	413

2001

AFC EAST

	W	L	T	Pct	Pts	OP
New England	11	5	0	.688	371	272
Miami	11	5	0	.688	344	290
NY Jets	10	6	0	.625	413	486
Indianapolis	6	10	0	.375	413	486
Buffalo	3	13	0	.188	265	420

AFC CENTRAL

	W	L	T	Pct	Pts	OP
Pittsburgh	13	3	0	.813	352	212
Baltimore	10	6	0	.625	303	265
Cleveland	7	9	0	.438	285	319
Tennessee	7	9	0	.438	336	388
Jacksonville	6	10	0	.375	294	286
Cincinnati	6	10	0	.375	226	309

AFC WEST

	W	L	T	Pct	Pts	OP
Oakland	10	6	0	.625	399	327
Seattle	9	7	0	.563	301	324
Denver	8	8	0	.500	340	339
Kansas City	6	10	0	.375	320	344
San Diego	5	11	0	.313	332	321

2001 (Cont.)

NFC EAST

	W	L	T	Pct	Pts	OP
Philadelphia	11	5	0	.688	343	208
Washington	8	8	0	.500	256	303
NY Giants	7	9	0	.438	294	321
Arizona	7	9	0	.438	295	343
Dallas	5	11	0	.313	246	338

NFC CENTRAL

	W	L	T	Pct	Pts	OP
Chicago	13	3	0	.813	338	203
Green Bay	12	4	0	.750	390	266
Tampa Bay	9	7	0	.563	324	280
Minnesota	5	11	0	.313	290	390
Detroit	2	14	0	.125	270	424

NFC WEST

	W	L	T	Pct	Pts	OP
St. Louis	14	2	0	.875	503	273
San Francisco	12	4	0	.750	409	282
Atlanta	7	9	0	.438	291	377
New Orleans	7	9	0	.438	333	409
Carolina	1	15	0	.938	253	410

2002

AFC EAST

	W	L	T	Pct	Pts	OP
New England	9	7	0	.563	384	346
Miami	9	7	0	.563	378	301
NY Jets	9	7	0	.563	359	336
Buffalo	8	8	0	.500	379	397

AFC NORTH

	W	L	T	Pct	Pts	OP
Pittsburgh	10	5	1	.656	390	345
Cleveland	9	7	0	.563	344	320
Baltimore	7	9	0	.438	316	354
Cincinnati	2	14	0	.125	279	456

AFC SOUTH

	W	L	T	Pct	Pts	OP
Tennessee	11	5	0	.688	367	324
Indianapolis	10	6	0	.625	349	313
Jacksonville	6	10	0	.375	328	315
Houston Texans	4	12	0	.250	213	356

AFC WEST

	W	L	T	Pct	Pts	OP
Oakland	11	5	0	.688	450	304
Denver	9	7	0	.563	392	344
Kansas City	8	8	0	.500	467	399
San Diego	8	8	0	.500	333	367

NFC EAST

	W	L	T	Pct	Pts	OP
Philadelphia	12	4	0	.750	415	241
NY Giants	10	6	0	.625	320	279
Washington	7	9	0	.438	307	365
Dallas	5	11	0	.313	217	329

NFC NORTH

	W	L	T	Pct	Pts	OP
Green Bay	12	4	0	.750	398	328
Minnesota	6	10	0	.375	390	442
Chicago	4	12	0	.250	281	379
Detroit	3	13	0	.188	306	451

2002 (Cont.)

NFC SOUTH

	W	L	T	Pct	Pts	OP
Tampa Bay	12	4	0	.750	346	196
Atlanta	9	6	1	.594	402	314
New Orleans	9	7	0	.563	432	388
Carolina	7	9	0	.438	258	302

NFC WEST

	W	L	T	Pct	Pts	OP
San Francisco	10	6	0	.625	367	351
St. Louis	7	9	0	.438	316	367
Seattle	7	9	0	.438	355	369
Arizona	5	11	0	.313	262	417

2003

AFC EAST

	W	L	T	Pct	Pts	OP
New England	14	2	0	.875	348	238
Miami	10	6	0	.625	311	261
Buffalo	6	10	0	.375	243	279
NY Jets	6	10	0	.375	283	299

AFC NORTH

	W	L	T	Pct	Pts	OP
Baltimore	10	6	0	.625	391	281
Cincinnati	8	8	0	.500	346	384
Pittsburgh	6	10	0	.375	300	327
Cleveland	5	11	0	.313	254	322

AFC SOUTH

	W	L	T	Pct	Pts	OP
Indianapolis	12	4	0	.750	447	336
Tennessee	12	4	0	.750	435	324
Houston	5	11	0	.313	255	380
Jacksonville	5	11	0	.313	276	331

AFC WEST

	W	L	T	Pct	Pts	OP
Kansas City	13	3	0	.813	484	332
Denver	10	6	0	.625	381	301
Oakland	4	12	0	.250	270	379
San Diego	4	12	0	.250	313	441

NFC EAST

	W	L	T	Pct	Pts	OP
Philadelphia	12	4	0	.750	374	287
Dallas	10	6	0	.625	289	260
Washington	5	11	0	.313	287	372
NY Giants	4	12	0	.250	243	387

NFC NORTH

	W	L	T	Pct	Pts	OP
Green Bay	10	6	0	.625	442	307
Minnesota	9	7	0	.563	416	353
Chicago	7	9	0	.438	283	346
Detroit	5	11	0	.313	270	379

NFC SOUTH

	W	L	T	Pct	Pts	OP
Carolina	11	5	0	.688	325	304
New Orleans	8	8	0	.500	340	326
Tampa Bay	7	9	0	.438	301	264
Atlanta	5	11	0	.313	299	422

NFC WEST

	W	L	T	Pct	Pts	OP
St. Louis	12	4	0	.750	447	328
Seattle	10	6	0	.625	404	327
San Francisco	7	9	0	.438	384	337
Arizona	4	12	0	.250	225	452

2004

AFC EAST

	W	L	T	Pct	Pts	OP
New England	14	2	0	.875	437	260
NY Jets	10	6	0	.625	333	261
Buffalo	9	7	0	.562	395	284
Miami	4	12	0	.250	275	354

AFC NORTH

	W	L	T	Pct	Pts	OP
Pittsburgh	15	1	0	.938	372	251
Baltimore	9	7	0	.562	317	268
Cincinnati	8	8	0	.500	374	372
Cleveland	4	12	0	.250	275	354

AFC SOUTH

	W	L	T	Pct	Pts	OP
Indianapolis	12	4	0	.750	522	351
Jacksonville	9	7	0	.562	261	280
Houston	7	9	0	.438	309	339
Tennessee	5	11	0	.312	344	439

AFC WEST

	W	L	T	Pct	Pts	OP
San Diego	12	4	0	.750	446	313
Denver	10	6	0	.625	381	304
Kansas City	7	9	0	.438	483	435
Oakland	5	11	0	.312	320	442

NFC EAST

	W	L	T	Pct	Pts	OP
Philadelphia	13	3	0	.812	386	260
NY Giants	6	10	0	.375	303	347
Dallas	6	10	0	.375	293	405
Washington	6	10	0	.375	240	265

NFC NORTH

	W	L	T	Pct	Pts	OP
Green Bay	10	6	0	.625	424	380
Minnesota	8	8	0	.500	405	395
Detroit	6	10	0	.375	296	350
Chicago	5	11	0	.312	231	331

NFC SOUTH

	W	L	T	Pct	Pts	OP
Atlanta	11	5	0	.688	340	337
New Orleans	8	8	0	.500	348	405
Carolina	7	9	0	.438	355	339
Tampa Bay	5	11	0	.312	301	304

NFC WEST

	W	L	T	Pct	Pts	OP
Seattle	9	7	0	.562	371	373
St. Louis	8	8	0	.500	319	392
Arizona	6	10	0	.375	284	322
San Francisco	2	14	0	.125	259	452

2005

AFC EAST

	W	L	T	Pct	Pts	OP
New England	14	2	0	.875	437	260
NY Jets	10	6	0	.625	333	261
Buffalo	9	7	0	.562	395	284
Miami	4	12	0	.250	275	354

AFC NORTH

	W	L	T	Pct	Pts	OP
Pittsburgh	15	1	0	.938	372	251
Baltimore	9	7	0	.562	317	268
Cincinnati	8	8	0	.500	374	372
Cleveland	4	12	0	.250	275	354

AFC SOUTH

	W	L	T	Pct	Pts	OP
Indianapolis	12	4	0	.750	522	351
Jacksonville	9	7	0	.562	261	280
Houston	7	9	0	.438	309	339
Tennessee	5	11	0	.312	344	439

AFC WEST

	W	L	T	Pct	Pts	OP
San Diego	12	4	0	.750	446	313
Denver	10	6	0	.625	381	304
Kansas City	7	9	0	.438	483	435
Oakland	5	11	0	.312	320	442

NFC EAST

	W	L	T	Pct	Pts	OP
Philadelphia	13	3	0	.812	386	260
NY Giants	6	10	0	.375	303	347
Dallas	6	10	0	.375	293	405
Washington	6	10	0	.375	240	265

NFC NORTH

	W	L	T	Pct	Pts	OP
Green Bay	10	6	0	.625	424	380
Minnesota	8	8	0	.500	405	395
Detroit	6	10	0	.375	296	350
Chicago	5	11	0	.312	231	331

NFC SOUTH

	W	L	T	Pct	Pts	OP
Atlanta	11	5	0	.688	340	337
New Orleans	8	8	0	.500	348	405
Carolina	7	9	0	.438	355	339
Tampa Bay	5	11	0	.312	301	304

NFC WEST

	W	L	T	Pct	Pts	OP
Seattle	9	7	0	.562	371	373
St. Louis	8	8	0	.500	319	392
Arizona	6	10	0	.375	284	322
San Francisco	2	14	0	.125	259	452

2006

AFC EAST

	W	L	T	Pct	Pts	OP
New England	12	4	0	.750	385	237
NY Jets	10	6	0	.625	316	295
Buffalo	7	9	0	.438	300	311
Miami	6	10	0	.375	260	283

AFC NORTH

	W	L	T	Pct	Pts	OP
Baltimore	13	3	0	.812	353	201
Cincinnati	8	8	0	.500	373	331
Pittsburgh	8	8	0	.500	353	315
Cleveland	4	12	0	.250	238	356

AFC SOUTH

	W	L	T	Pct	Pts	OP
Indianapolis	12	4	0	.750	427	360
Tennessee	8	8	0	.500	324	400
Jacksonville	8	8	0	.500	371	274
Houston	6	10	0	.375	267	366

AFC WEST

	W	L	T	Pct	Pts	OP
San Diego	14	2	0	.875	492	303
Kansas City	9	7	0	.562	331	315
Denver	9	7	0	.562	319	305
Oakland	2	14	0	.125	168	332

NFC EAST

	W	L	T	Pct	Pts	OP
Philadelphia	10	6	0	.625	398	328
Dallas	9	7	0	.562	425	350
NY Giants	8	8	0	.500	355	362
Washington	5	11	0	.312	307	376

NFC NORTH

	W	L	T	Pct	Pts	OP
Chicago	13	3	0	.812	427	255
Green Bay	8	8	0	.500	301	366
Minnesota	6	10	0	.375	282	327
Detroit	3	13	0	.188	305	398

NFC SOUTH

	W	L	T	Pct	Pts	OP
New Orleans	10	6	0	.625	413	322
Carolina	8	8	0	.500	270	305
Atlanta	7	9	0	.438	292	328
Tampa Bay	4	12	0	.250	211	353

NFC WEST

	W	L	T	Pct	Pts	OP
Seattle	9	7	0	.562	335	341
St. Louis	8	8	0	.500	367	381
San Francisco	7	9	0	.438	298	412
Arizona	5	11	0	.312	314	389

Results

	Date	Winner (Share)	Loser (Share)	Score	Site (Attendance)
I	1-15-67	Green Bay ($15,000)	Kansas City ($7,500)	35–10	Los Angeles (61,946)
II	1-14-68	Green Bay ($15,000)	Oakland ($7,500)	33–14	Miami (75,546)
III	1-12-69	NY Jets ($15,000)	Baltimore ($7,500)	16–7	Miami (75,389)
IV	1-11-70	Kansas City ($15,000)	Minnesota ($7,500)	23–7	New Orleans (80,562)
V	1-17-71	Baltimore ($15,000)	Dallas ($7,500)	16–13	Miami (79,204)
VI	1-16-72	Dallas ($15,000)	Miami ($7,500)	24–3	New Orleans (81,023)
VII	1-14-73	Miami ($15,000)	Washington ($7,500)	14–7	Los Angeles (90,182)
VIII	1-13-74	Miami ($15,000)	Minnesota ($7,500)	24–7	Houston (71,882)
IX	1-12-75	Pittsburgh ($15,000)	Minnesota ($7,500)	16–6	New Orleans (80,997)
X	1-18-76	Pittsburgh ($15,000)	Dallas ($7,500)	21–17	Miami (80,187)
XI	1-9-77	Oakland ($15,000)	Minnesota ($7,500)	32–14	Pasadena (103,438)
XII	1-15-78	Dallas ($18,000)	Denver ($9,000)	27–10	New Orleans (76,400)
XIII	1-21-79	Pittsburgh ($18,000)	Dallas ($9,000)	35–31	Miami (79,484)
XIV	1-20-80	Pittsburgh ($18,000)	Los Angeles ($9,000)	31–19	Pasadena (103,985)
XV	1-25-81	Oakland ($18,000)	Philadelphia ($9,000)	27–10	New Orleans (76,135)
XVI	1-24-82	San Francisco ($18,000)	Cincinnati ($9,000)	26–21	Pontiac, Mich. (81,270)
XVII	1-30-83	Washington ($36,000)	Miami ($18,000)	27–17	Pasadena (103,667)
XVIII	1-22-84	LA Raiders ($36,000)	Washington ($18,000)	38–9	Tampa (72,920)
XIX	1-20-85	San Francisco ($36,000)	Miami ($18,000)	38–16	Stanford, Calif. (84,059)
XX	1-26-86	Chicago ($36,000)	New England ($18,000)	46–10	New Orleans (73,818)
XXI	1-25-87	NY Giants ($36,000)	Denver ($18,000)	39–20	Pasadena (101,063)
XXII	1-31-88	Washington ($36,000)	Denver ($18,000)	42–10	San Diego (73,302)
XXIII	1-22-89	San Francisco ($36,000)	Cincinnati ($18,000)	20–16	Miami (75,129)
XXIV	1-28-90	San Francisco ($36,000)	Denver ($18,000)	55–10	New Orleans (72,919)
XXV	1-27-91	NY Giants ($36,000)	Buffalo ($18,000)	20–19	Tampa (73,813)
XXVI	1-26-92	Washington ($36,000)	Buffalo ($18,000)	37–24	Minneapolis (63,130)
XXVII	1-31-93	Dallas ($36,000)	Buffalo ($18,000)	52–17	Pasadena (98,374)
XXVIII	1-30-94	Dallas ($38,000)	Buffalo ($23,500)	30–13	Atlanta (72,817)
XXIX	1-29-95	San Francisco ($42,000)	San Diego ($26,000)	49–26	Miami (74,107)
XXX	1-28-96	Dallas ($42,000)	Pittsburgh ($27,000)	27–17	Tempe, Ariz. (76,347)
XXXI	1-26-97	Green Bay ($48,000)	New England ($29,000)	35–21	New Orleans (72,301)
XXXII	1-25-98	Denver ($48,000)	Green Bay ($27,500)	31–24	San Diego (68,912)
XXXIII	1-31-99	Denver ($53,000)	Atlanta ($32,500)	34–19	Miami (74,803)
XXXIV	1-30-00	St. Louis ($58,000)	Tennessee ($33,000)	23–16	Atlanta (72,625)
XXXV	1-28-01	Baltimore ($58,000)	NY Giants ($34,500)	34–7	Tampa (71,921)
XXXVI	2-3-02	New England ($63,000)	St. Louis ($34,500)	20–17	New Orleans (72,922)
XXXVII	1-26-03	Tampa Bay ($64,000)	Oakland ($35,000)	48–21	San Diego (67,603)
XXXVIII	2-1-04	New England ($64,000)	Carolina ($35,000)	32–29	Houston (71,525)
XXXIX	2-6-05	New England ($68,000)	Philadelphia ($36,500)	24–21	Jacksonville (78,125)
XL	2-5-06	Pittsburgh ($73,000)	Seattle ($38,000)	21–10	Detroit (68,206)
XLI	2-4-07	Indianapolis ($78,000)	Chicago ($40,000)	29–17	Miami (74,512)

Most Valuable Players

Super Bowl	Player/ Team	Position	Super Bowl	Player/ Team	Position
I	Bart Starr, GB	QB	XXI	Phil Simms, NYG	QB
II	Bart Starr, GB	QB	XXII	Doug Williams, Wash	QB
III	Joe Namath, NYJ	QB	XXIII	Jerry Rice, SF	WR
IV	Len Dawson, KC	QB	XXIV	Joe Montana, SF	QB
V	Chuck Howley, Dal	LB	XXV	Ottis Anderson, NYG	RB
VI	Roger Staubach, Dal	QB	XXVI	Mark Rypien, Wash	QB
VII	Jake Scott, Mia	S	XXVII	Troy Aikman, Dal	QB
VIII	Larry Csonka, Mia	RB	XXVIII	Emmitt Smith, Dal	RB
IX	Franco Harris, Pitt	RB	XXIX	Steve Young, SF	QB
X	Lynn Swann, Pitt	WR	XXX	Larry Brown, Dal	CB
XI	Fred Biletnikoff, Oak	WR	XXXI	Desmond Howard, GB	KR
XII	Randy White, Dal	DT	XXXII	Terrell Davis, Den	RB
	Harvey Martin, Dal	DE	XXXIII	John Elway, Den	QB
XIII	Terry Bradshaw, Pitt	QB	XXXIV	Kurt Warner, StL	QB
XIV	Terry Bradshaw, Pitt	QB	XXXV	Ray Lewis, Balt	LB
XV	Jim Plunkett, Oak	QB	XXXVI	Tom Brady, NE	QB
XVI	Joe Montana, SF	QB	XXXVII	Dexter Jackson, TB	S
XVII	John Riggins, Wash	RB	XXXVIII	Tom Brady, NE	QB
XVIII	Marcus Allen, LA Rai	RB	XXXIX	Deion Branch, NE	WR
XIX	Joe Montana, SF	QB	XL	Hines Ward, Pitt	WR
XX	Richard Dent, Chi	DE	XLI	Peyton Manning, Ind	QB

Composite Standings

	W	L	Pct	Pts	Opp Pts
San Francisco 49ers	5	0	1.000	188	89
Baltimore Ravens	1	0	1.000	34	7
New York Jets	1	0	1.000	16	7
Tampa Bay Buccaneers	1	0	1.000	48	21
Pittsburgh Steelers	5	1	.833	141	110
Green Bay Packers	3	1	.750	127	76
Baltimore/Indianapolis Colts	2	1	.667	52	46
New York Giants	2	1	.667	66	73
Dallas Cowboys	5	3	.625	221	132
New England Patriots	3	2	.600	107	148
Oakland/LA Raiders	3	2	.600	132	114
Washington Redskins	3	2	.600	122	103
Chicago Bears	1	1	.500	63	39
Kansas City Chiefs	1	1	.500	33	42
Miami Dolphins	2	3	.400	74	103
Denver Broncos	2	4	.333	115	206
Los Angeles/St. Louis Rams	1	2	.333	59	67
Atlanta Falcons	0	1	.000	19	34
Carolina Panthers	0	1	.000	29	32
San Diego Chargers	0	1	.000	26	49
Seattle Seahawks	0	1	.000	10	21
Tennessee Titans	0	1	.000	16	23
Cincinnati Bengals	0	2	.000	37	46
Philadelphia Eagles	0	2	.000	31	51
Buffalo Bills	0	4	.000	73	139
Minnesota Vikings	0	4	.000	34	95

Career Leaders

Passing

	GP	Att	Comp	Pct Comp	Yds	Avg Gain	TD	Pct TD	Int	Pct Int	Lg	Rating Pts
Joe Montana, SF	4	122	83	68.0	1142	9.36	11	9.0	0	0.0	44	127.8
Jim Plunkett, Oak/LA Rai	2	46	29	63.0	433	9.41	4	8.7	0	0.0	t80	122.8
Terry Bradshaw, Pitt	4	84	49	58.3	932	11.10	9	10.7	4	4.8	t75	112.8
Troy Aikman, Dal	3	80	56	70.0	689	8.61	5	6.3	1	1.3	t56	111.9
Bart Starr, GB	2	47	29	61.7	452	9.62	3	6.4	1	2.1	t62	106.0
Tom Brady, NE	3	108	71	65.7	735	6.81	6	5.5	1	0.9	52	99.9
Brett Favre, GB	2	69	39	56.5	502	7.28	5	7.2	1	1.4	t81	97.7
Roger Staubach, Dal	4	98	61	62.2	734	7.49	8	8.2	4	4.1	t45	95.4
Kurt Warner, StL	2	89	52	58.4	779	8.75	3	3.4	2	1.1	t73	93.8
Len Dawson, KC	2	44	28	63.6	353	8.02	2	4.5	2	4.5	t46	84.8

Note: Minimum 40 attempts.

Rushing

	GP	Yds	Att	Avg	Lg	TD
Franco Harris, Pitt	4	354	101	3.5	25	4
Larry Csonka, Mia	3	297	57	5.2	49	2
Emmitt Smith, Dal	3	289	70	4.1	38	5
Terrell Davis, Den	2	259	55	4.7	27	3
John Riggins, Wash	2	230	64	3.6	43	2
Timmy Smith, Wash	1	204	22	9.3	58	2
Thurman Thomas, Buff	4	204	52	3.9	31	4
Roger Craig, SF	3	217	44	4.9	20	3
Marcus Allen, LA Rai	1	191	20	9.6	t74	2
Antowain Smith, NE	2	175	44	4.0	17	1

Receiving

	GP	No.	Yds	Avg	Lg	TD
Jerry Rice, SF	4	33	589	17.9	t48	8
Andre Reed, Buff	4	27	323	12.0	40	0
Deion Branch, NE	2	21	276	13.1	52	1
Roger Craig, SF	3	20	212	10.6	40	2
Thurman Thomas, Buff	4	20	144	7.2	24	0
Jay Novacek, Dal	3	17	148	8.7	23	2
Lynn Swann, Pitt	4	16	364	22.8	t74	3
Michael Irvin, Dal	3	16	256	16.0	25	2
Troy Brown, NE	3	16	182	11.4	23	0
Chuck Foreman, Minn	3	15	139	9.3	26	0

t-scored touchdown

Single-Game Leaders

Scoring

	Pts
Roger Craig: XIX, San Francisco vs Miami (1 rush, 2 rec)	18
Jerry Rice: XXIV, San Francisco vs Denver (3 rec); XXIX, SF vs San Diego (3 rec)	18
Ricky Watters: XXIX, San Francisco vs San Diego (1 rush, 2 rec)	18
Terrell Davis: XXXII, Denver vs Green Bay (3 rec)	18

Rushing Yards

	Yds
Timmy Smith: XXII, Washington vs Denver	204
Marcus Allen: XVIII, LA Raiders vs Washington	191
John Riggins: XVII, Washington vs Miami	166
Franco Harris: IX, Pittsburgh vs Minnesota	158
Terrell Davis: XXXII, Denver vs Green Bay	157
Larry Csonka: VIII, Miami vs Minnesota	145
Clarence Davis: XI, Oakland vs Minnesota	137
Thurman Thomas: XXV, Buffalo vs NY Giants	135
Emmitt Smith: XXVIII, Dallas vs Buffalo	132
Michael Pittman: XXXVII, Tampa Bay vs Oakland	124

Receptions

	No.
Deion Branch: XXXIX, New England vs Phila.	11
Jerry Rice: XXIII, San Francisco vs Cincinnati	11
Dan Ross: XVI, Cincinnati vs San Francisco	11
Joseph Addai: XLI, Indianapolis vs Chicago	10
Deion Branch: XXXVIII, New England vs Carolina	10
Andre Hastings: XXX, Pittsburgh vs Dallas	10
Tony Nathan: XIX, Miami vs San Francisco	10
Jerry Rice: XXIX, San Francisco vs San Diego	10
Antonio Freeman: XXXII, Green Bay vs Denver	9
Terrell Owens: XXXIX, Philadelphia vs New England	9
Ricky Sanders: XXII, Washington vs Denver	9
Seven tied with eight.	

Touchdown Passes

	No.
Steve Young: XXIX, San Francisco vs San Diego	6
Joe Montana: XXIV, San Francisco vs Denver	5
Terry Bradshaw: XIII, Pittsburgh vs Dallas	4
Doug Williams: XXII, Washington vs Denver	4
Troy Aikman: XXVII, Dallas vs Buffalo	4
Seven tied with three.	

Passing Yards

	Yds
Kurt Warner: XXXIV, St. Louis vs Tennessee	414
Kurt Warner: XXXVI, St. Louis vs New England	365
Donovan McNabb: XXXIX, Phila vs. New England	357
Joe Montana: XXIII, San Francisco vs Cincinnati	357
Tom Brady: XXXVIII, New England vs. Carolina	354
Doug Williams: XXII, Washington vs Denver	340
John Elway: XXXIII, Denver vs Atlanta	336
Joe Montana: XIX, San Francisco vs Miami	331
Steve Young: XXIX, San Francisco vs San Diego	325
Jake Delhomme: XXXVIII, Carolina vs New England	323
Terry Bradshaw: XIII, Pittsburgh vs Dallas	318
Dan Marino: XIX, Miami vs San Francisco	318

Receiving Yards

	Yds
Jerry Rice: XXIII, San Francisco vs Cincinnati	215
Ricky Sanders: XXII, Washington vs Denver	193
Isaac Bruce: XXXIV, St. Louis vs Tennessee	162
Lynn Swann: X, Pittsburgh vs Dallas	161
Andre Reed: XXVII, Buffalo vs Dallas	152
Rod Smith: XXXIII, Denver vs Atlanta	152
Jerry Rice: XXIX, San Francisco vs San Diego	149
Jerry Rice: XXIV, San Francisco vs Denver	148
Deion Branch: XXXVIII, New England vs Carolina	143

I - 1967

Green Bay	7	7	14	7—35
Kansas City	0	10	0	0—10

FIRST QUARTER: GB: McGee 37 pass from Starr (Chandler kick), 8:56. **Green Bay 7-0.**

SECOND QUARTER: KC: McClinton 7 pass from Dawson (Mercer kick), 4:20. **7-7.**
GB: Taylor 14 run (Chandler kick), 10:23. **Green Bay 14-7.**
KC: FG Mercer 31, 14:06. **Green Bay 14-10.**

THIRD QUARTER: GB: Pitts 5 run (Chandler kick), 2:27. **Green Bay 21-10.**
GB: McGee 13 pass from Starr (Chandler kick), 14:09. **Green Bay 28-10.**

FOURTH QUARTER: GB: Pitts 1 run (Chandler kick), 8:25. **Green Bay 35-10.**

A: 61,946

II - 1968

Green Bay	3	13	10	7—33
Oakland	0	7	0	7—14

FIRST QUARTER: GB: FG Chandler 39 5:07. **Green Bay 3-0.**

SECOND QUARTER: GB: FG Chandler, 20, 3:08. **Green Bay 6-0.**
GB: Dowler 62 pass from Starr (Chandler kick), 4:10. **Green Bay 13-0.**
Oak: Miller 23 pass from Lamonica (Blanda kick), 8:45. **Green Bay 13-7.**
GB: FG Chandler 43, 14:59. **Green Bay 16-7.**

THIRD QUARTER: GB: Anderson 2 run (Chandler kick), 9:06. **Green Bay 23-7.**
GB: FG Chandler 31, 14:58. **Green Bay 26-7.**

FOURTH QUARTER:
GB: Adderley 60 int return (Chandler kick), 3:57. **Green Bay 33-7.**
Oak: Miller 23 pass from Lamonica (Blanda kick), 5:47. **Green Bay 33-14.**

A: 75,546

III - 1969

NY Jets	0	7	6	3—16
Baltimore	0	0	0	7—7

SECOND QUARTER: Jets: Snell 4 run (Turner kick), 5:57. **Jets: 7-0.**

THIRD QUARTER: Jets: FG Turner 32, 4:52. **Jets: 10-0.**
Jets: FG Turner 30, 11:02. **Jets: 13-0.**

FOURTH QUARTER: Jets: FG Turner 9, 1:34. **Jets: 16-0.**
Balt: Hill 1 run (Michaels kick), 11:41. **Jets: 16-7.**

A: 75,389

IV - 1970

Kansas City	3	13	7	0—23
Minnesota	0	0	7	0—7

FIRST QUARTER: KC: FG Stenerud 48, 8:08. **Kansas City 3-0.**

SECOND QUARTER: KC: FG Stenerud 32, 1:40. **Kansas City 6-0.**
KC: FG Stenerud 25, 7:08. **Kansas City 9-0.**
KC: Garrett 5 run (Stenerud kick), 9:26. **Kansas City 16-0.**

THIRD QUARTER: Minn: Osborn 4 run (Cox kick), 10:28. **Kansas City 16-7.**
KC: Taylor 46 pass from Dawson (Stenerud kick), 13:38. **Kansas City 23-7.**

A: 80,562

V - 1971

Baltimore	0	6	0	10—16
Dallas	3	10	0	0—13

FIRST QUARTER: Dal (9:28): FG Clark 14, 9:28. **Dallas 3-0.**

SECOND QUARTER: Dal: FG Clark 30, 0:08. **Dallas 6-0.**
Balt: Mackey 75 pass from Unitas (kick blocked). 0:50. **6-6.**
Dal: Thomas 7 pass from Morton (Clark kick), 7:07. **Dallas 13-6.**

FOURTH QUARTER: Balt: Nowatzke 2 run (O'Brien kick), 7:25. **13-13.**
Balt: FG O'Brien 32, 14:55. **Baltimore 16-13.**

A: 79,204

VI - 1972

Dallas	3	7	7	7—24
Miami	0	3	0	0—3

FIRST QUARTER: Dal: FG Clark 9, 13:37. **Dallas 3-0.**

SECOND QUARTER: Dal: Alworth 7 pass from Staubach (Clark kick), 13:45. **Dallas 10-0.**
Mia: FG Yepremian, 31, 14:56. **Dallas 10-3.**

THIRD QUARTER: Dal: D. Thomas 3 run (Clark kick), 5:17. **Dallas 17-3.**

FOURTH QUARTER: Dal: Ditka 7 pass from Staubach (Clark kick), 3:18. **Dallas 24-3.**

A: 81,023

VII - 1973

Miami	7	7	0	0—14
Washington	0	0	0	7—7

FIRST QUARTER: Mia: Twilley 28 pass from Griese (Yepremian kick), 14:59. **Miami 7-0.**

SECOND QUARTER: Mia: Kiick 1 run (Yepremian kick), 14:42. **Miami 14-0.**

FOURTH QUARTER: Wash: Bass 49 fumble recovery return (Knight kick), 12:53. **Miami 14-7.**

A: 90,182

*-From 1967 to 1999, Super Bowl scoring times indicate the time elapsed in each quarter. Starting in 2000, times listed give the time remaining in each quarter.

VIII - 1974

Miami	14	3	7	0—24
Minnesota	0	0	0	7—7

FIRST QUARTER: Mia: Csonka 5 run (Yepremian kick), 5:27. **Miami 7-0.**
Mia: Kiick 1 run (Yepremian kick), 13:38. **Miami 14-0.**
SECOND QUARTER: Mia: FG Yepremian 28, 8:58. **Miami 17-0.**
THIRD QUARTER: Mia: Csonka 2 run (Yepremian kick), 6:16. **Miami 24-0.**
FOURTH QUARTER: Minn: Tarkenton 4 run (Cox kick), 1:35. **Miami 24-7.**

A: 71,882

IX - 1975

Pittsburgh	0	2	7	7—16
Minnesota	0	0	0	6—6

SECOND QUARTER: Pit: White tackled Tarkenton for safety, 7:49. **Pittsburgh 2-0.**
THIRD QUARTER: Pit: Harris 9 run (Gerela kick), 1:35. **Pittsburgh 9-0.**
FOURTH QUARTER: Minn: T. Brown recovered blocked punt in end zone (kick failed), 4:27. **Pittsburgh 9-6.**
Pit: L. Brown 4 pass from Bradshaw (Gerela kick), 11:29. **Pittsburgh 16-6.**

A: 80,997

X - 1976

Pittsburgh	7	0	0	14—21
Dallas	7	3	0	7—17

FIRST QUARTER: Dal: D. Pearson 29 pass from Staubach (Fritsch kick), 4:36. **Dallas 7-0.**
Pit: Grossman 7 pass from Bradshaw (Gerela kick), 9:03. **7-7.**
SECOND QUARTER: Dal: FG Fritsch 36, 0:15. **Dallas 10-7.**
FOURTH QUARTER: Pit: Harrison blocked Hoopes's punt for safety, 3:32. **Dallas 10-9.**
Pit: FG Gerela 36, 6:19. **Pittsburgh 12-10.**
Pit: FG Gerela 18, 8:32. **Pittsburgh 15-10.**
Pit: Swann 64 pass from Bradshaw (kick failed), 11:58. **Pittsburgh 21-10.**
Dal: P. Howard 34 pass from Staubach (Fritsch kick), 13:12. **Pittsburgh 21-17.**

A: 80,187

XI - 1977

Oakland	0	16	3	13—32
Minnesota	0	0	7	7—14

SECOND QUARTER: Oak: FG Mann, 24, 0:48. **Oakland 3-0.**
Oak: Casper 1 pass from Stabler (Mann kick), 7:50. **Oakland 10-0.**
Oak: Banaszak 1 run (kick failed), 11:27. **Oakland 16-0.**
THIRD QUARTER: Oak: FG Mann, 40, 9:44. **Oakland 19-0.**
Min: S..White 8 pass from Tarkenton (Cox kick), 14:13. **Oakland 19-7.**
FOURTH QUARTER: Oak: Banaszak 2 run (Mann kick), 7:21. **Oakland 26-7.**
Oak: Brown 75 int return (kick failed), 9:17. **Oakland 32-7.**
Min: Voigt 13 pass from Lee (Cox kick), 14:35. **Oakland 32-14.**

A: 103,438

XII - 1978

Dallas	10	3	7	7—27
Denver	0	0	10	0—10

FIRST QUARTER: FIRST QUARTER: Dal: Dorsett 3 run (Herrera kick), 10:31. **Dallas 7-0.**
Dal: FG Herrera 35, 13:29. **Dallas 10-0.**
SECOND QUARTER: Dal: FG Herrera 43, 3:44. **Dallas 13-0.**
THIRD QUARTER: Den: FG Turner 47, 2:28. **Dallas 13-3.**
Dal: Johnson 45 pass from Staubach (Herrera kick), 8:01. **Dallas 20-3.**
Den: Lytle 1 run (Turner kick), 9:21. **Dallas 20-10.**
FOURTH QUARTER: Dal: Richards 29 pass from Newhouse (Herrera kick), 7:56. **Dallas 27-10.**

A: 76,400

XIII - 1979

Pittsburgh	7	14	0	14—35
Dallas	7	7	3	14—31

FIRST QUARTER: Pit: Stallworth 28 pass from Bradshaw (Gerela kick), 5:13. **Pittsburgh 7-0.**
Dal: Hill 39 pass from Staubach (Septien kick), 15:00. **7-7.**
SECOND QUARTER: Dal: Hegman 37 fumble recovery return (Septien kick), 2:52. **Dallas 14-7.**
Pit: Stallworth 75 pass from Bradshaw (Gerela kick), 4:35. **14-14.**
Pit: Bleier 7 pass from Bradshaw (Gerela kick), 14:34. **Pittsburgh 21-14.**
THIRD QUARTER: Dal: FG Septien 27, 12:24. **Pittsburgh 21-17.**
FOURTH QUARTER: Pit: Harris 22 run (Gerela kick), 7:50. **Pittsburgh 28-17.**
Pit: Swann 18 pass from Bradshaw (Gerela kick), 8:09. **Pittsburgh 35-17.**
Dal: DuPree 7 pass from Staubach (Septien kick), 12:33. **Pittsburgh 35-24.**
Dal: B. Johnson 4 pass from Staubach (Septien kick), 14:38. **Pittsburgh 35-31.**

A: 79,484

XIV - 1980

Pittsburgh	3	7	7	14—31
LA Rams	7	6	6	0—19

FIRST QUARTER: Pit: FG Bahr, 41, 7:29. **Pittsburgh 3-0.** LA: Bryant 1 run (Corral kick), 12:16. **LA Rams 7-3.**

SECOND QUARTER: Pit: Harris 1 run (Bahr kick), 2:08. **Pittsburgh 10-7.** LA: FG Corral 31, 7:39. **10-10.** LA: FG Corral 45, 14:46. **LA Rams 13-10.**

THIRD QUARTER: Pit: Swann 47 pass from Bradshaw (Bahr kick), 2:48. **Pittsburgh 17-13.** LA: Smith 24 pass from McCutcheon (kick failed), 4:45. **LA Rams 19-17.**

FOURTH QUARTER: Pit: Stallworth 73 pass from Bradshaw (Bahr kick), 2:56. **Pittsburgh 24-19.** Pit: Harris 1 run (Bahr kick), 13:11. **Pittsburgh 31-19.**

A: 103,985

XV - 1981

Oakland	14	0	10	3—27
Philadelphia	0	3	0	7—10

FIRST QUARTER: Oak: Branch 2 pass from Plunkett (Bahr kick), 6:04. **Oakland 7-0.** Oak: King 80 pass from Plunkett (Bahr kick), 14:51. **Oakland 14-0.**

SECOND QUARTER: Phi: FG Franklin 30, 4:32. **Oakland 14-3.**

THIRD QUARTER: Oak: Branch 29 pass from Plunkett (Bahr kick), 2:36. **Oakland 21-3.** Oak: FG Bahr 46, 10:25. **Oakland 24-3.**

FOURTH QUARTER: Phi: Krepfle 8 pass from Jaworski (Franklin kick), 1:01. **Oakland 24-10.** Oak: FG Bahr, 35, 6:31. **Oakland 27-10.**

A: 76,135

XVI - 1982

San Francisco	7	13	0	6—26
Cincinnati	0	0	7	14—21

FIRST QUARTER: SF: Montana 1 run (Wersching kick), 9:08. **San Francisco 7-0.**

SECOND QUARTER: SF: E. Cooper 11 pass from Montana (Wersching kick), 8:07. **San Francisco 14-0.** SF: FG Wersching 22, 14:45. **San Francisco 17-0.** SF: FG Wersching 26, 14:58. **San Francisco 20-0.**

THIRD QUARTER: Cin: Anderson 5 run (Breech kick), 3:35. **San Francisco 20-7.**

FOURTH QUARTER: Cin: Ross 4 pass from Anderson (Breech kick), 4:54. **San Francisco 20-14.** SF: FG Wersching 40, 9:35. **San Francisco 23-14.** SF: FG Wersching 23, 13:03. **San Francisco 26-14.** Cin: Ross 3 pass from Anderson (Breech kick), 14:44. **San Francisco 26-21.**

A: 81,270

XVII - 1983

Washington	0	10	3	14—27
Miami	7	10	0	0—17

FIRST QUARTER: Mia: Cefalo 76 pass from Woodley (Von Schamann kick), 6:49. **Miami 7-0.**

SECOND QUARTER: Wash: FG Moseley 31, 0:21. **Miami 7-3.** Mia: FG Von Schamann 20, 9:00. **Miami 10-3.** Wash: Garrett 4 pass from Theismann (Moseley kick), 13:09. **10-10.** Mia: Walker 98 kick return (Von Schamann kick), 13:22. **Miami 17-10.**

THIRD QUARTER: Wash: FG Moseley 20, 6:51. **Miami 17-13.**

FOURTH QUARTER: Wash: Riggins 43 run (Moseley kick), 4:59. **Washington 20-17.** Wash: Brown 6 pass from Theismann (Moseley kick), 13:05. **Washington 27-17.**

A: 103,667

XVIII - 1984

LA Raiders	7	14	14	3—38
Washington	0	3	6	0—9

FIRST QUARTER: LA: Jensen 0 blocked punt return (Bahr kick), 4:52. **LA Raiders 7-0.**

SECOND QUARTER: LA: Branch 12 pass from Plunkett (Bahr kick), 5:46. **LA Raiders 14-0.** Wash: FG Moseley 24, 11:55. **LA Raiders 14-3.** LA: Squirek 5 int return (Bahr kick), 14:53. **LA Raiders 21-3.**

THIRD QUARTER: Wash: Riggins 1 run (kick blocked), 4:08. **LA Raiders 21-9.** LA: Allen 5 run (Bahr kick), 7:54. **LA Raiders 28-9.** LA: Allen 74 run (Bahr kick), 15:00. **LA Raiders 35-9.**

FOURTH QUARTER: LA: FG Bahr 21, 12:36. **LA Raiders 38-9.**

A: 72,920

XIX - 1985

San Francisco	7	21	10	0—38
Miami	10	6	0	0—16

FIRST QUARTER: Mia: FG Von Schamann 37, 7:36.
Miami 3-0.
SF: Monroe 33 pass from Montana (Wersching kick), 11:48. **San Francisco 7-3.**
Mia: D. Johnson 2 pass from Marino (Von Schamann kick), 14:15. **Miami 10-7.**
SECOND QUARTER: SF: Craig 8 pass from Montana (Wersching kick), 3:26. **San Francisco 14-10.**
SF: Montana 6 run (Wersching kick), 8:02.
San Francisco 21-10.
SF: Craig 2 run (Wersching kick), 12:55.
San Francisco 28-10.
Mia: FG Von Schamann 31, 14:48.
San Francisco 28-13.
Mia: FG Von Schamann 30, 15:00.
San Francisco 28-16.
THIRD QUARTER: SF: FG Wersching 27, 4:48.
San Francisco 31-16.
SF: Craig 16 pass from Montana (Wershing kick), 8:42. **San Francisco 38-16.**

A: 84,059

XX - 1986

Chicago	13	10	21	2—46
New England	3	0	0	7—10

FIRST QUARTER: NE: FG Franklin 36, 1:19.
New England 3-0.
Chi: FG Butler 28, 5:40. **3-3.**
Chi: FG Butler 24, 13:34. **Chicago 6-3.**
Chi: Suhey 11 run (Butler kick), 14:37. **Chicago 13-3.**
SECOND QUARTER: Chi: McMahon 2 run (Butler kick), 7:36. **Chicago 20-3.**
Chi: FG Butler 24, 15:00. **Chicago 23-3.**
THIRD QUARTER: Chi: McMahon 1 run (Butler kick), 7:38. **Chicago 30-3.**
Chi: Phillips 28 int return (Butler kick), 8:44. **Chicago 37-3.**
Chi: Perry 1 run (Butler kick), 11:38. **Chicago 44-3.**
FOURTH QUARTER: NE: Fryar 8 pass from Grogan (Franklin kick), 1:46. **Chicago 44-10.**
Chi: Waechter safety, 9:24. **Chicago 46-10.**

A: 73,818

XXI - 1987

NY Giants	7	2	17	13—39
Denver	10	0	0	10—20

FIRST QUARTER: Den: FG Karlis 48, 4:09. **Denver 3-0.**
NYG: Mowatt 6 pass from Simms (Allegre kick), 9:33.
NY Giants 7-3.
Den: Elway 4 run (Karlis kick), 12:54. **Denver 10-7.**
SECOND QUARTER: NYG: Martin safety, 12:14.
Denver 10-9.
THIRD QUARTER: NYG: Bavaro 13 pass from Simms (Allegre kick), 4:52. **NY Giants 16-10.**
NYG: FG Allegre 21, 11:06. **NY Giants 19-10.**
NYG: Morris 1 run (Allegre kick), 14:36.
NY Giants 26-10.
FOURTH QUARTER: NYG: McConkey 6 pass from Simms (Allegre kick), 4:04. **NY Giants 33-10.**
Den: FG Karlis 28, 8:59. **Denver 33-13.**
NYG: Anderson 2 run (kick failed), 11:42.
NY Giants 39-13.
Den: Johnson 47 pass from Elway (Karlis kick), 12:54. **NY Giants 39-20.**

A: 101,063

XXII - 1988

Washington	0	35	0	7—42
Denver	10	0	0	0—10

FIRST QUARTER: Den: Nattiel 56 pass from Elway (Karlis kick), 1:57. **Denver 7-0.**
Den: FG Karlis 24, 5:51. **Denver 10-0.**
SECOND QUARTER: Wash: Sanders 80 pass from D. Williams (Haji-Sheikh kick), 0:53. **Denver 10-7.**
Wash: Clark 27 pass from D. Williams (Haji-Sheikh kick), 4:45. **Washington 14-10.**
Wash: Smith 58 run (Haji-Sheikh kick), 8:33.
Washington 21-10.
Wash: Sanders 50 pass from D. Williams (Haji-Sheikh kick), 11:18. **Washington 28-10.**
Wash: Didier 8 pass from D. Williams (Haji-Sheikh kick), 13:56. **Washington 35-10.**
FOURTH QUARTER: Wash: Smith 4 run (Haji-Sheikh kick), 1:51. **Washington 42-10.**

A: 73,302

XXIII - 1989

San Francisco	3	0	3	14—20
Cincinnati	0	3	10	3—16

FIRST QUARTER: SF: FG Cofer 41, 11:46.
San Francisco 3-0.
SECOND QUARTER: Cin: FG Breech 34, 13:41. **3-3.**
THIRD QUARTER: Cin: FG Breech 43, 9:15.
Cincinnati 6-3.
SF: FG Cofer 32, 14:10. **6-6.**
Cin: Jennings 93 kick return (Breech kick), 14:26.
Cincinnati 13-6.
FOURTH QUARTER: SF: Rice 14 pass from Montana (Cofer kick), 0:57. **13-13.**
Cin: FG Breech 40, 11:40. **Cincinnati 16-13.**
SF: Taylor 10 pass from Montana (Cofer kick), 14:26.
San Francisco 20-16.

A: 75,129

XXIV - 1990

San Francisco	13	14	14	14—55
Denver	3	0	7	0—10

FIRST QUARTER: SF: Rice 20 pass from Montana (Cofer kick), 4:54. **San Francisco 7-0.**
Den: FG Treadwell 42, 8:13. **San Francisco 7-3.**
SF: Jones 7 pass from Montana (kick failed), 14:57. **San Francisco 13-3.**

SECOND QUARTER: SF: Rathman 1 run (Cofer kick), 7:45. **San Francisco 20-3.**
SF: Rice 38 pass from Montana (Cofer kick), 14:26. **San Francisco 27-3.**

THIRD QUARTER: SF: Rice 28 pass from Montana (Cofer kick), 2:12. **San Francisco 34-3.**
SF: Taylor 35 pass from Montana (Cofer kick), 5:16. **San Francisco 41-3.**
Den: Elway 3 run (Treadwell kick), 8:07. **San Francisco 41-10.**

FOURTH QUARTER: SF: Rathman 3 run (Cofer kick), 0:03. **San Francisco 48-10.**
SF: Craig 1 run (Cofer kick), 1:13. **San Francisco 55-10.**

A: 72,919

XXV - 1991

NY Giants	3	7	7	3—20
Buffalo	3	9	0	7—19

FIRST QUARTER: NYG: FG Bahr 28, 7:46. **NY Giants 3-0.**
Buff: FG Norwood 23, 9:09. **3-3.**

SECOND QUARTER: Buff: D. Smith 1 run (Norwood kick), 2:30. **Buffalo 10-3.**
Buff: B. Smith safety 0, 6:33. **Buffalo 12-3.**
NYG: Baker 14 pass from Hostetler (Bahr kick), 14:35. **Buffalo 12-10.**

THIRD QUARTER: NYG: Anderson 1 run (Bahr kick), 9:29. **NY Giants 17-12.**

FOURTH QUARTER: Buff: Thomas 31 run (Norwood kick), 0:08. **Buffalo 19-17.**
NYG: FG Bahr 21, 7:40. **NY Giants 20-19.**

A: 73,813

XXVI - 1992

Washington	0	17	14	6—37
Buffalo	0	0	10	14—24

SECOND QUARTER: Wash: FG Lohmiller 34, 1:58. **Washington 3-0.**
Wash: Byner 10 pass from Rypien (Lohmiller kick), 5:06. **Washington 10-0.**
Wash: Riggs 1 run (Lohmiller kick), 7:43. **Washington 17-0.**

THIRD QUARTER: Wash: Riggs 2 run (Lohmiller kick), 0:16. **Washington 24-0.**
Buff: FG Norwood 21, 3:01. **Washington 24-3.**
Buff: Thomas 1 run (Norwood kick), 9:02. **Washington 24-10.**
Wash: Clark 30 pass from Rypien (Lohmiller kick), 13:36. **Washington 31-10.**

FOURTH QUARTER: Wash: FG Lohmiller 25, 0:06. **Washington 34-10.**
Wash: FG Lohmiller 39, 3:24. **Washington 37-10.**
Buff: Metzelaars 2 pass from Kelly (Norwood kick), 9:01. **Washington 37-17.**
Buff: Beebe 4 pass from Kelly (Norwood kick), 11:05. **Washington 37-24.**

A: 63,130.

XXVII - 1993

Dallas	14	14	3	21—52
Buffalo	7	3	7	0—17

FIRST QUARTER: Buff: Thomas 2 run (Christie kick), 5:00. **Buffalo 7-0.**
Dal: Novacek 23 pass from Aikman (Elliott kick), 13:24. **7-7.**
Dal: J.Jones 2 fumble return (Elliott kick), 13:39. **Dallas 14-7.**

SECOND QUARTER: Buff: FG Christie 21, 11:36. **Dallas 14-10.**
Dal: Irvin 19 pass from Aikman (Elliott kick)13:06. **Dallas 21-10.**
Dal: Irvin 18 pass from Aikman (Elliott kick), 13:24. **Dallas 28-10.**

THIRD QUARTER: Dal: FG Elliott 20, 6:39. **Dallas 31-10.**
Buff: Beebe 40 pass from Reich (Christie kick), 15:00. **Dallas 31-17.**

FOURTH QUARTER: Dal: Harper 45 pass from Aikman (Elliott kick), 4:56. **Dallas 38-17.**
Dal: E. Smith 10 run (Elliott kick), 6:48. **Dallas 45-17.**
Dal: Norton 9 fumble return (Elliott kick), 7:29. **Dallas 52-17.**

A: 98,374

XXVIII - 1994

Dallas	6	0	14	10—30
Buffalo	3	10	0	0—13

FIRST QUARTER: Dal: FG Murray 41, 2:19. **Dallas 3-0.**
Buff: FG Christie 54: 4:41. **3-3.**
Dal: FG Murray 24, 11:05. **Dallas 6-3.**

SECOND QUARTER: Buff: Thomas 4 run (Christie kick), 2:34. **Buffalo 10-6.**
Buff: FG Christie 28, 15:00. **Buffalo 13-6.**

THIRD QUARTER: Dal: Washington fumble return (Murray kick), 0:55. **13-13.**
Dal: Smith15 run (Murray kick), 0:55. **Dallas 20-13.**

FOURTH QUARTER: Dal: Smith1 run (Murray kick), 5:10. **Dallas 27-13.**
Dal: FG Murray 20, 12:10. **Dallas 30-13.**

A: 72,817

XXIX - 1995

San Francisco	14	14	14	7—49
San Diego	7	3	8	8—26

FIRST QUARTER: SF: Rice 44 pass from Young (Brien kick), 1:24.
San Francisco 7-0.
SF: Watters 51 pass from Young (Brien kick, 4:55.
San Francisco 14-0.
SD: Means 1 run (Carney kick), 12:16.
San Francisco 14-7.

SECOND QUARTER: SF: Floyd 5 pass from Young (Brien kick), 1:58.
San Francisco 21-7.
SF: Watters 8 pass from Young (Brien kick), 10:16.
San Francisco 28-7.
SD: FG Carney 31, 13:16. **San Francisco 28-10.**

THIRD QUARTER: SF: Watters 9 run (Brien kick), 5:25.
San Francisco 35-10.
SF: Rice 15 pass from Young (Brien kick), 11:42.
San Francisco 42-10.
SD: Coleman 98 kickoff return (Humphries 2-pt conv pass to Seay), 11:59. **San Francisco 42-18.**

FOURTH QUARTER: SF: Rice 7 pass from Young (Brien kick), 1:11.
San Francisco 49-18.
SD: Martin 30 pass from Humphries (Humphries 2 pt-conv pass to Pupunu), 12:35. **San Francisco 49-26.**

A: 74,107.

XXX - 1996

Dallas	10	3	7	7—27
Pittsburgh	0	7	0	10—17

FIRST QUARTER: Dal: FG Boniol 42, 2:55. **Dallas 3-0.**
Dal: Novacek 3 pass from Aikman (Boniol kick), 9:37.
Dallas 10-0.

SECOND QUARTER: Dal: FG Boniol 35, 8:57.
Dallas 13-0.
Pitt: Thigpen 6 pass from O'Donnell (N. Johnson kick), 14:47. **Dallas 13-7.**

THIRD QUARTER: Dal: E. Smith 1 run (Boniol kick), 8:18.
Dallas 20-7.

FOURTH QUARTER: Pitt: FG N. Johnson 46, 3:40.
Dallas 20-10.
Pitt: Morris 1 run (N. Johnson kick), 8:24. **Dallas 20-17.**
Dal: E. Smith 4 run (Boniol kick), 11:17. **Dallas 27-17.**

A: 76,347.

XXXI - 1997

Green Bay	10	17	8	0—35
New England	14	0	7	0—21

FIRST QUARTER: GB: Rison 54 pass from Favre (Jacke kick), 3:32. **Green Bay 7-0.**
GB: FG Jacke 37, 6:18. **Green Bay 10-0.**
NE: Byars 1 pass from Bledsoe (Vinatieri kick), 8:25. **Green Bay 10-7.**
NE: Coates 4 pass from Bledsoe (Vinatieri kick), 12:27. **New England 14-10.**

SECOND QUARTER: GB: Freeman 81 pass from Favre (Jacke kick), 0:56. **Green Bay 17-14.**
GB: FG Jacke 31, 6:45. **Green Bay 20-14.**
GB: Favre 2 run (Jacke kick), 13:49. **Green Bay 27-14.**

THIRD QUARTER: NE: Martin 18 run (Vinatieri kick), 11:33.
Green Bay 27-21.
GB: Howard 99 kickoff return (Favre 2 pt conv pass to Chmura), 11:50. **Green Bay 35-21.**

A: 72,301.

XXXII - 1998

Denver	7	10	7	7—31
Green Bay	7	7	3	7—24

FIRST QUARTER: GB: Freeman 22 pass from Favre (Longwell kick), 4:02. **Green Bay 7-0.**
Den: Davis 1 run (Elam kick), 9:21. **7-7.**

SECOND QUARTER: Den: Elway 1 run (Elam kick), 0:05.
Denver 14-7.
Den: FG Elam 51, 2:39. **Denver 17-7.**
GB: Chmura 6 pass from Favre (Longwell kick), 14:48. **Denver 17-14.**

THIRD QUARTER: GB: FG Longwell 27, 3:01. **17-17.**
Den: Davis 1 run (Elam kick), 14:26. **Denver 24-17.**

FOURTH QUARTER: GB: Freeman 13 pass from Favre (Longwell kick), 1:28. **24-24.**
Den: Davis 1 run (Elam kick), 13:15. **Denver 31-24.**

A: 68,912

XXXIII - 1999

Denver	7	10	0	17—34
Atlanta	3	3	0	13—19

FIRST QUARTER: Atl: FG Andersen 32, 5:25.
Atlanta 3-0.
Den: Griffith 1 run (Elam kick), 11:05. **Denver 7-3.**

SECOND QUARTER: Den: FG Elam 26, 5:43.
Denver 10-3.
Den: Smith 80 pass from Elway (Elam kick), 10:06.
Denver 17-3.
Atl: FG Andersen 28, 12:35. **Denver 17-6.**

FOURTH QUARTER: Den: Griffith 1 run (Elam kick), 0:04.
Denver 24-6.
Den: Elway 3 run (Elam kick), 3:40. **Denver 31-6.**
Atl: Dwight 94 kickoff return (Andersen kick), 3:59.
Denver 31-13.
Den: FG Elam 37, 7:52. **Denver 34-13.**
Atl: Mathis 3 pass from Chandler (2-pt conv failed),
12:56. **Denver 34-19.**

A: 74,803

XXXIV - 2000

St. Louis	3	6	7	7—23
Tennessee	0	0	6	10—16

FIRST QUARTER: StL: FG Wilkins 27, 3:00.
St. Louis 3-0.

SECOND QUARTER: StL: FG Wilkins 29, 4:16.
St. Louis 6-0.
StL: FG Wilkins 28, 0:15. **St. Louis 9-0.**

THIRD QUARTER: StL: Holt 9 pass from Warner (Wilkins
kick), 7:20. **St. Louis 16-0.**
Tenn: George 1 run (2-pt conv failed), 0:14.
St. Louis 16-6.

FOURTH QUARTER: Tenn: George 2 run (Del Greco kick),
7:21. **St. Louis 16-13.**
Tenn: FG Del Greco 43, 2:15. **16-16.**
StL: : Bruce 73 pass from Warner, 1:54. **St. Louis 23-16.**

A: 72,265

XXXV - 2001

Baltimore	7	3	14	10—34
NY Giants	0	0	7	0—7

FIRST QUARTER: Balt: Stokely 38 pass from Dilfer
(Stover kick), 6:50. **Baltimore 7-0.**

SECOND QUARTER: Balt: FG Stover 47, 1:41.
Baltimore 10-0.

THIRD QUARTER: Balt: Starks 49 int return (Stover kick),
3:49. **Baltimore 17-0.**
NYG: Dixon 97 kickoff return (Daluiso kick), 3:31.
Baltimore 17-7.
Balt: Je. Lewis 84 kickoff return (Stover kick), 3:13.
Baltimore 24-7.

FOURTH QUARTER: Balt: Ja. Lewis 3 run (Stover kick),
8:45. **Baltimore 31-7.**
Balt: FG Stover 34, 5:28. **Baltimore 34-7.**

A: 71,921

XXXVI - 2002

New England	0	14	3	3—20
St. Louis	3	0	0	14—17

FIRST QUARTER: StL: FG Wilkins 50, 3:50.
St. Louis 3-0.

SECOND QUARTER: NE: Law 47 int return (Vinatieri kick),
8:49. **New England 7-3.**
NE: Patten 8 pass from Brady (Vinatieri kick), 0:31.
New England 14-3.

THIRD QUARTER: NE: FG Vinatieri 37, 1:18.
New England 17-3.

FOURTH QUARTER: StL: Warner 2 run (Wilkins kick), 9:31.
New England 17-10.
StL: Proehl 26 pass from Warner (Wilkins kick),
1:30. **17-17.**
NE: FG Vinatieri 48, 0:00. **New England 20-17.**

A: 72,922

XXXVII - 2003

Tampa Bay	3	17	14	14—48
Oakland	3	0	6	12—21

FIRST QUARTER: Oak: FG Janikowski 40, 10:20.
Oakland 3-0.
TB: FG Gramatica 31, 7:51. **3-3.**

SECOND QUARTER: TB: FG Gramatica 43, 11:16.
Tampa Bay 6-3.
TB: Alstott 2 run (Gramatica kick), 6:24.
Tampa Bay 13-3.
TB: McCardell 5 pass from B. Johnson (Gramatica
kick), 0:30. **Tampa Bay 20-3.**

THIRD QUARTER: TB: McCardell 8 pass from B. Johnson
(Gramatica kick), 5:30. **Tampa Bay 27-3.**
TB: Smith 44 int. return (Gramatica kick), 4:47.
Tampa Bay 34-3.
Oak: Porter 39 pass from Gannon (2-pt conv failed),
2:14. **Tampa Bay 34-9.**

FOURTH QUARTER: Oak: Johnson 13 return of blocked
punt (two-pt. conversion failed), 14:14.
Tampa Bay 34-15.
Oak: Rice 48 pass from Gannon (2-pt conv failed),
6:06. **Tampa Bay 34-21.**
TB: Brooks 44 int. return (Gramatica kick), 1:18.
Tampa Bay 41-21.
TB: Smith 50 int. return (Gramatica kick), 0:02.
Tampa Bay 48-21.

A: 67,603

XXXVIII - 2004

New England	0	14	0	18—32
Carolina	0	10	0	19—29

SECOND QUARTER: NE: Branch 5 pass from Brady (Vinatieri kick), 3:11. **New England 7-0.**

Car: Smith 39 pass from Delhomme (Kasay kick), 1:17. **7-7.**

NE: Givens 5 pass from Brady (Vinatieri kick), 0:28. **New England 14-7.**

Car: FG Kasay 50, 0:00. **New England 14-10.**

FOURTH QUARTER: NE: Smith 2 run (Vinatieri kick), 14:49. **New England 21-10.**

Car: Foster 33 run (2-pt conv failed), 12:49. **New England 21-16.**

Car: Muhammad 85 pass from Delhomme (2-pt conv failed), 7:13. **Carolina 22-21.**

NE: Vrabel 1 pass from Brady (Faulk ran for 2-pt conv), 2:51. **New England 29-22.**

Car: Proehl 12 pass from Delhomme (Kasay kick), 1:18. **29-29.**

NE: FG Vinatieri 41, 0:04. **New England 32-29.**

A: 71,525

XXXIX - 2005

New England	0	7	7	10—24
Philadelphia	0	7	7	7—21

SECOND QUARTER: Phil: Smith 6 pass from McNabb (Akers kick), 10:05. **Philadelphia 7-0.**
NE: Givens 4 pass from Brady (Vinatieri kick), 1:10. **7-7.**

THIRD QUARTER: NE: Vrabel 2 pass from Brady (Vinatieri kick), 11:04. **New England 14-7.**
Phil: Westbrook 10 pass from McNabb (Akers kick), 3:45. **14-14.**

FOURTH QUARTER: NE: Dillon 2 run (Vinatieri kick), 13:44. **New England 21-14.**

NE: FG Vinatieri 22, 9:40. **New England 24-14.**
Phil: Lewis 30 pass from McNabb (Akers kick), 13:12. **New England 24-21.**

A: 78,125

XL - 2006

Pittsburgh	0	7	7	7—21
Seattle	3	0	7	0—10

FIRST QUARTER: Sea: FG Brown 47, 0:22. **Seattle 3-0.**

SECOND QUARTER: Pit: Roethlisberger 1 run (Reed kick), 1:55. **Pittsburgh 7-3.**

THIRD QUARTER: Pit: Parker 75 run (Reed kick), 14:38. **Pittsburgh 14-3.**
Sea: Stevens 16 pass from Hasselbeck (Brown kick), 6:45. **Pittsburgh 14-10.**

FOURTH QUARTER: Pit: Ward 43 pass from Randle El (Reed kick), 8:56. **Pittsburgh 21-10.**

A: 68,206

XLI - 2007

Indianapolis	6	10	6	7—29
Chicago	14	0	3	0—17

FIRST QUARTER: Chicago: TD Hester 92 yd kick return (Gould kick)14:46. **Chicago 7-0.**
Indianapolis: TD Wayne 53 pass from Manning, 6:50 (Vinatieri kick failed). **Chicago 7-6.**
Chicago: TD Muhammad 4 pass from Grossman (Gould kick), 4:34. **Chicago 14-6.**

SECOND QUARTER: Indianapolis: FG Vinatieri 29, 11:17. **Chicago 14-9.**
Indianapolis: TD Rhodes 1 run (Vinatieri kick), 6:09. **Indianapolis 16-14.**

THIRD QUARTER: Indianapolis: FG Vinatieri 24, 7:26. **Indianapolis 19-14.**
Indianapolis: FG Vinatieri 20, 3:16. **Indianapolis 22-14.**
Chicago: FG Gould 44, 1:14. **Indianapolis 22-17.**

FOURTH QUARTER: Indianapolis: TD Hayden 56 interception return (Vinatieri kick) 11:44. **Indianapolis 29-17.**

A: 74,512

1933
NFL championship Chicago Bears 23, NY Giants 21

1934
NFL championship NY Giants 30, Chicago Bears 13

1935
NFL championship Detroit 26, NY Giants 7

1936
NFL championship Green Bay 21, Boston 6

1937
NFL championship Washington 28, Chicago Bears 21

1938
NFL championship NY Giants 23, Green Bay 17

1939
NFL championship Green Bay 27, NY Giants 0

1940
NFL championship Chicago Bears 73, Washington 0

1941
W. div. playoff Chicago Bears 33, Green Bay 14
NFL championship Chicago Bears 37, NY Giants 9

1942
NFL championship Washington 14, Chicago Bears 6

1943
E. div. playoff Washington 28, NY Giants 0
NFL championship Chicago Bears 41, Washington 21

1944
NFL championship Green Bay 14, NY Giants 7

1945
NFL championship Cleveland 15, Washington 14

1946
NFL championship Chicago Bears 24, NY Giants 14

1947
E. div. playoff Philadelphia 21, Pittsburgh 0
NFL championship Chi Cardinals 28, Philadelphia 21

1948
NFL championship Philadelphia 7, Chi Cardinals 0

1949
NFL championship Philadelphia 14, Los Angeles 0

1950
Am. Conf. playoff Cleveland 8, NY Giants 3
Nat. Conf. playoff Los Angeles 24, Chicago Bears 14
NFL championship Cleveland 30, Los Angeles 28

1951
NFL championship Los Angeles 24, Cleveland 17

1952
Nat. Conf. playoff Detroit 31, Los Angeles 21
NFL championship Detroit 17, Cleveland 7

1953
NFL championship Detroit 17, Cleveland 16

1954
NFL championship Cleveland 56, Detroit 10

1955
NFL championship Cleveland 38, Los Angeles 14

1956
NFL championship NY Giants 47, Chicago Bears 7

1957
W. Conf. playoff Detroit 31, San Francisco 27
NFL championship Detroit 59, Cleveland 14

1958
E. Conf. playoff NY Giants 10, Cleveland 0
NFL championship Baltimore 23, NY Giants 17

1959
NFL championship Baltimore 31, NY Giants 16

1960
NFL championship Philadelphia 17, Green Bay 13
AFL championship Houston 24, LA Chargers 16

1961
NFL championship Green Bay 37, NY Giants 0
AFL championship Houston 10, San Diego 3

1962
NFL championship Green Bay 16, NY Giants 7
AFL championship Dallas Texans 20, Houston 17

1963
NFL championship Chicago 14, NY Giants 10
AFL E. div. playoff Boston 26, Buffalo 8
AFL championship San Diego 51, Boston 10

1964
NFL championship Cleveland 27, Baltimore 0
AFL championship Buffalo 20, San Diego 7

1965
NFL W. Conf. Green Bay 13, Baltimore 10
playoff
NFL championship Green Bay 23, Cleveland 12
AFL championship Buffalo 23, San Diego 0

1966
NFL championship Green Bay 34, Dallas 27
AFL championship Kansas City 31, Buffalo 7

1967
NFL E. Conf. Dallas 52, Cleveland 14
championship
NFL W. Conf. Green Bay 28, Los Angeles 7
championship
NFL championship Green Bay 21, Dallas 17
AFL championship Oakland 40, Houston 7

1968
NFL E. Conf. Cleveland 31, Dallas 20
championship
NFL W. Conf. Baltimore 24, Minnesota 14
championship
NFL championship Baltimore 34, Cleveland 0
AFL W. div. playoff Oakland 41, Kansas City 6
AFL championship NY Jets 27, Oakland 23

1969
NFL E. Conf. Cleveland 38, Dallas 14
championship
NFL W. Conf. Minnesota 23, Los Angeles 20
championship
NFL championship Minnesota 27, Cleveland 7
AFL div. playoffs Kansas City 13, NY Jets 6
                   Oakland 56, Houston 7
AFL championship Kansas City 17, Oakland 7

1970

AFC div. playoffs	Baltimore 17, Cincinnati 0
	Oakland 21, Miami 14
AFC championship	Baltimore 27, Oakland 17
NFC div. playoffs	Dallas 5, Detroit 0
	San Francisco 17, Minnesota 14
NFC championship	Dallas 17, San Francisco 10

1971

AFC div. playoffs	Miami 27, Kansas City 24
	Baltimore 20, Cleveland 3
AFC championship	Miami 21, Baltimore 0
NFC div. playoffs	Dallas 20, Minnesota 12
	San Francisco 24, Washington 20
NFC championship	Dallas 14, San Francisco 3

1972

AFC div. playoffs	Pittsburgh 13, Oakland 7
	Miami 20, Cleveland 14
AFC championship	Miami 21, Pittsburgh 17
NFC div. playoffs	Dallas 30, San Francisco 28
	Washington 16, Green Bay 3
NFC championship	Washington 26, Dallas 3

1973

AFC div. playoffs	Oakland 33, Pittsburgh 14
	Miami 34, Cincinnati 16
AFC championship	Miami 27, Oakland 10
NFC div. playoffs	Minnesota 27, Washington 20
	Dallas 27, Los Angeles 16
NFC championship	Minnesota 27, Dallas 10

1974

AFC div. playoffs	Oakland 28, Miami 26
	Pittsburgh 32, Buffalo 14
AFC championship	Pittsburgh 24, Oakland 13
NFC div. playoffs	Minnesota 30, St Louis 14
	Los Angeles 19, Washington 10
NFC championship	Minnesota 14, Los Angeles 10

1975

AFC div. playoffs	Pittsburgh 28, Baltimore 10
	Oakland 31, Cincinnati 28
AFC championship	Pittsburgh 16, Oakland 10
NFC div. playoffs	Los Angeles 35, St Louis 23
	Dallas 17, Minnesota 14
NFC championship	Dallas 37, Los Angeles 7

1976

AFC div. playoffs	Oakland 24, New England 21
	Pittsburgh 40, Baltimore 14
AFC championship	Oakland 24, Pittsburgh 7
NFC div. playoffs	Minnesota 35, Washington 20
	Los Angeles 14, Dallas 12
NFC championship	Minnesota 24, Los Angeles 13

1977

AFC div. playoffs	Denver 34, Pittsburgh 21
	Oakland 37, Baltimore 31
AFC championship	Denver 20, Oakland 17
NFC div. playoffs	Dallas 37, Chicago 7
	Minnesota 14, Los Angeles 7
NFC championship	Dallas 23, Minnesota 6

1978

AFC 1st-rd. playoff	Houston 17, Miami 9
AFC div. playoffs	Houston 31, New England 14
	Pittsburgh 33, Denver 10
AFC championship	Pittsburgh 34, Houston 5
NFC 1st-rd. playoff	Atlanta 14, Philadelphia 13
NFC div. playoffs	Dallas 27, Atlanta 20
	Los Angeles 34, Minnesota 10
NFC championship	Dallas 28, Los Angeles 0

1979

AFC 1st-rd. playoff	Houston 13, Denver 7
AFC div. playoffs	Houston 17, San Diego 14
	Pittsburgh 34, Miami 14
AFC championship	Pittsburgh 27, Houston 13
NFC 1st-rd. playoff	Philadelphia 27, Chicago 17
NFC div. playoffs	Tampa Bay 24, Philadelphia 17
	Los Angeles 21, Dallas 19
NFC championship	Los Angeles 9, Tampa Bay 0

1980

AFC 1st-rd. playoff	Oakland 27, Houston 7
AFC div. playoffs	San Diego 20, Buffalo 14
	Oakland 14, Cleveland 12
AFC championship	Oakland 34, San Diego 27
NFC 1st-rd. playoff	Dallas 34, Los Angeles 13
NFC div. playoffs	Philadelphia 31, Minnesota 16
	Dallas 30, Atlanta 27
NFC championship	Philadelphia 20, Dallas 7

1981

AFC 1st-rd. playoff	Buffalo 31, NY Jets 27
AFC div. playoffs	San Diego 41, Miami 38
	Cincinnati 28, Buffalo 21
AFC championship	Cincinnati 27, San Diego 7
NFC 1st-rd. playoff	NY Giants 27, Philadelphia 21
NFC div. playoffs	Dallas 38, Tampa Bay 0
	San Francisco 38, NY Giants 24
NFC championship	San Francisco 28, Dallas 27

1982

AFC 1st-rd. playoffs	Miami 28, New England 13
	LA Raiders 27, Cleveland 10
	NY Jets 44, Cincinnati 17
	San Diego 31, Pittsburgh 28
AFC div. playoffs	NY Jets 17, LA Raiders 14
	Miami 34, San Diego 13
AFC championship	Miami 14, NY Jets 0
NFC 1st-rd. playoffs	Washington 31, Detroit 7
	Green Bay 41, St Louis 16
	Minnesota 30, Atlanta 24
	Dallas 30, Tampa Bay 17
NFC div. playoffs	Washington 21, Minnesota 7
	Dallas 37, Green Bay 26
NFC championship	Washington 31, Dallas 17

1983

AFC 1st-rd. playoff	Seattle 31, Denver 7
AFC div. playoffs	Seattle 27, Miami 20
	LA Raiders 38, Pittsburgh 10
AFC championship	LA Raiders 30, Seattle 14
NFC 1st-rd. playoff	LA Rams 24, Dallas 17
NFC div. playoffs	San Francisco 24, Detroit 23
	Washington 51, LA Rams 7
NFC championship	Washington 24, San Francisco 21

1984

AFC 1st-rd. playoff	Seattle 13, LA Raiders 7
AFC div. playoffs	Miami 31, Seattle 10
	Pittsburgh 24, Denver 17
AFC championship	Miami 45, Pittsburgh 28
NFC 1st-rd. playoff	NY Giants 16, LA Rams 13
NFC div. playoffs	San Francisco 21, NY Giants 10
	Chicago 23, Washington 19
NFC championship	San Francisco 23, Chicago 0

1985

AFC 1st-rd. playoff	New England 26, NY Jets 14
AFC div. playoffs	Miami 24, Cleveland 21
	New England 27, LA Raiders 20
AFC championship	New England 31, Miami 14
NFC 1st-rd. playoff	NY Giants 17, San Francisco 3
NFC div. playoffs	LA Rams 20, Dallas 0
	Chicago 21, NY Giants 0
NFC championship	Chicago 24, LA Rams 0

1986

AFC 1st-rd. playoff	NY Jets 35, Kansas City 15
AFC div. playoffs	Cleveland 23, NY Jets 20
	Denver 22, New England 17
AFC championship	Denver 23, Cleveland 20
NFC 1st-rd. playoff	Washington 19, LA Rams 7
NFC div playoffs	Washington 27, Chicago 13
	NY Giants 49, San Francisco 3
NFC championship	NY Giants 17, Washington 0

1987

AFC 1st-rd. playoff	Houston 23, Seattle 20
AFC div. playoffs	Cleveland 38, Indianapolis 21
	Denver 34, Houston 10
AFC championship	Denver 38, Cleveland 33
NFC 1st-rd. playoff	Minnesota 44, New Orleans 10
NFC div playoffs	Minnesota 36, San Francisco 24
	Washington 21, Chicago 17
NFC championship	Washington 17, Minnesota 10

1988

AFC 1st-rd. playoff	Houston 24, Cleveland 23
AFC div. playoffs	Cincinnati 21, Seattle 13
	Buffalo 17, Houston 10
AFC championship	Cincinnati 21, Buffalo 10
NFC 1st-rd. playoff	Minnesota 28, LA Rams 17
NFC div. playoffs	Chicago 20, Philadelphia 12
	San Francisco 34, Minnesota 9
NFC championship	San Francisco 28, Chicago 3

1989

AFC 1st-rd. playoff	Pittsburgh 26, Houston 23
AFC div. playoffs	Cleveland 34, Buffalo 30
	Denver 24, Pittsburgh 23
AFC championship	Denver 37, Cleveland 21
NFC 1st-rd. playoff	LA Rams 21, Philadelphia 7
NFC div. playoffs	LA Rams 19, NY Giants 13
	San Francisco 41, Minnesota 13
NFC championship	San Francisco 30, LA Rams 3

1990

AFC 1st-rd. playoffs	Miami 17, Kansas City 16
	Cincinnati 41, Houston 14
AFC div. playoffs	Buffalo 44, Miami 34
	LA Raiders 20, Cincinnati 10
AFC championship	Buffalo 51, LA Raiders 3
NFC 1st-rd. playoffs	Chicago 16, New Orleans 6
NFC 1st-rd playoffs	Washington 20, Philadelphia 6
NFC div. playoffs	NY Giants 31, Chicago 3
	San Francisco 28, Washington 10
NFC championship	NY Giants 15, San Francisco 13

1991

AFC 1st-rd. playoffs	Houston 17, NY Jets 10
	Kansas City 10, LA Raiders 6
AFC div. playoffs	Denver 26, Houston 24
	Buffalo 37, Kansas City 14
AFC championship	Buffalo 10, Denver 7
NFC 1st-rd. playoffs	Atlanta 27, New Orleans 20
	Dallas 17, Chicago 13
NFC div. playoffs	Washington 24, Atlanta 7
	Detroit 38, Dallas 6
NFC championship	Washington 41, Detroit 10

1992

AFC 1st-rd. playoffs	San Diego 17, Kansas City 0
	Buffalo 41, Houston 38 (OT)
AFC div. playoffs	Buffalo 24, Pittsburgh 3
	Miami 31, San Diego 0
AFC championship	Buffalo 29, Miami 10
NFC 1st-rd. playoffs	Washington 24, Minnesota 7
	Philadelphia 36, New Orleans 20
NFC div. playoffs	San Francisco 20, Washington 13
	Dallas 34, Philadelphia 10
NFC championship	Dallas 30, San Francisco 20

1993

AFC 1st-rd. playoffs	LA Raiders 42, Denver 24
	Kansas City 27, Pittsburgh 24 (OT)
AFC div. playoffs	Buffalo 29, LA Raiders 23
	Kansas City 28, Houston 20
AFC championship	Buffalo 30, Kansas City 13
NFC 1st-rd. playoffs	NY Giants 17, Minnesota 10
	Green Bay 28, Detroit 24
NFC div. playoffs	San Francisco 44, NY Giants 3
	Dallas 27, Green Bay 17
NFC championship	Dallas 38, San Francisco 21

1994

AFC 1st-rd. playoffs	Miami 27, Kansas City 17
	Cleveland 20, New England 13
AFC div. playoffs	San Diego 22, Miami 21
	Pittsburgh 29, Cleveland 9
AFC championship	San Diego 17, Pittsburgh 13
NFC 1st-rd. playoffs	Green Bay 16, Detroit 12
	Chicago 35, Minnesota 18
NFC div. playoffs	Dallas 35, Green Bay 9
	San Francisco 44, Chicago 15
NFC championship	San Francisco 38, Dallas 28

1995

AFC 1st-rd. playoffs	Buffalo 37, Miami 22
	Indianapolis 35, San Diego 20
AFC div. playoffs	Pittsburgh 40, Buffalo 21
	Indianapolis 10, Kansas City 7
AFC championship	Pittsburgh 20, Indianapolis 16
NFC 1st-rd. playoffs	Philadelphia 58, Detroit 37
	Green Bay 37, Atlanta 20
NFC div. playoffs	Dallas 30, Philadelphia 11
	Green Bay 27, San Francisco 17
NFC championship	Dallas 38, Green Bay 27

1996

AFC 1st-rd. playoffs	Jacksonville 30, Buffalo 27
	Pittsburgh 42, Indianapolis 14
AFC div. playoffs	Jacksonville 30, Denver 27
	New England 28, Pittsburgh 3
AFC championship	New England 20, Jacksonville 6
NFC 1st-rd. playoffs	Dallas 40, Minnesota 15
	San Francisco 14, Philadelphia 0
NFC div. playoffs	Green Bay 35, San Francisco 14
	Carolina 26, Dallas 17
NFC championship	Green Bay 30, Carolina 13

1997

AFC 1st-rd. playoffs	Denver 42, Jacksonville 17
	New England 17, Miami 3
AFC div. playoffs	Denver 14, Kansas City 0
	Pittsburgh 7, New England 6
AFC championship	Denver 24, Pittsburgh 21
NFC 1st-rd. playoffs	Minnesota 23, NY Giants 22
	Tampa Bay 20, Detroit 10
NFC div. playoffs	Green Bay 21, Tampa Bay 7
	San Francisco 38, Minnesota 22
NFC championship	Green Bay 23, San Francisco 10

1998

AFC 1st-rd. playoffs	Miami 24, Buffalo 17
	Jacksonville 25, New England 10
AFC div. playoffs	Denver 38, Miami 3
	NY Jets 34, Jacksonville 24
AFC championship	Denver 23, NY Jets 10
NFC 1st-rd. playoffs	Arizona 20, Dallas 7
	San Francisco 30, Green Bay 27
NFC div. playoffs	Atlanta 20, San Francisco 18
	Minnesota 41, Arizona 21
NFC championship	Atlanta 30, Minnesota 27 (OT)

1999

AFC 1st-rd. playoffs	Tennessee 22, Buffalo 16
	Miami 20, Seattle 17
AFC div. playoffs	Jacksonville 62, Miami 7
	Tennessee 19, Indianapolis 16
AFC championship	Tennessee 33, Jacksonville 14
NFC 1st-rd. playoffs	Washington 27, Detroit 13
	Minnesota 27, Dallas 10
NFC div. playoffs	Tampa Bay 14, Washington 13
	St Louis 49, Minnesota 37
NFC championship	St Louis 11, Tampa Bay 6

2000

AFC 1st-rd. playoffs	Baltimore 21, Denver 3
	Miami 23, Indianapolis 17 (OT)
AFC div. playoffs	Baltimore 24, Tennessee 10
	Oakland 27, Miami 0
AFC championship	Baltimore 16, Oakland 3
NFC 1st-rd. playoffs	New Orleans 31, St. Louis 28
	Philadelphia 21, Tampa Bay 3
NFC div. playoffs	NY Giants 20, Philadelphia 10
	Minnesota 34, New Orleans 16
NFC championship	NY Giants 41, Minnesota 0

2001

AFC 1st-rd. playoffs	Oakland 38, NY Jets 24
	Baltimore 20, Miami 3
AFC div. playoffs	New England 16, Oakland 13(OT)
	Pittsburgh 27, Baltimore 10
AFC championship	New England 24, Pittsburgh 17
NFC 1st-rd. playoffs	Philadelphia 31, Tampa Bay 9
	Green Bay 25, San Francisco 15
NFC div. playoffs	Philadelphia 33, Chicago 19
	St. Louis 45, Green Bay 17
NFC championship	St. Louis 29, Philadelphia 24

2002

AFC 1st-rd. playoffs	NY Jets 41, Indianapolis 0
	Pittsburgh 36, Cleveland 33
AFC div. playoffs	Tennessee 34, Pittsburgh 31 (OT)
	Oakland 30, NY Jets 10
AFC championship	Oakland 41, Tennessee 24
NFC 1st-rd. playoffs	Atlanta 27, Green Bay 7
	San Francisco 39, NY Giants 38
NFC div. playoffs	Philadelphia 20, Atlanta 6
	Tampa Bay 31, San Francisco 6
NFC championship	Tampa Bay 27, Philadelphia 10

2003

AFC 1st-rd. playoffs	Tennessee 20, Baltimore 17
	Indianapolis 41, Denver 10
AFC div. playoffs	New England 17, Tennessee 14
	Indianapolis 38, Kansas City 31
AFC championship	New England 24, Indianapolis 14
NFC 1st-rd. playoffs	Carolina 29, Dallas 10
	Green Bay 37, Seattle 31 (OT)
NFC div. playoffs	Carolina 29, St. Louis 23
	Philadelphia 20, Green Bay 17 (OT)
NFC championship	Carolina 14, Philadelphia 3

2004

AFC 1st-rd. playoffs	Indianapolis 49, Denver 24
	NY Jets 20, San Diego 17
AFC div. playoffs	New England 20, Indianapolis 3
	Pittsburgh 20, NY Jets 17
AFC championship	New England 41, Pittsburgh 27
NFC 1st-rd. playoffs	Minnesota 31, Green Bay 17
	St. Louis 27, Seattle 20
NFC div. playoffs	Atlanta 47, St. Louis 17
	Philadelphia 27, Minnesota 14
NFC championship	Philadelphia 27, Atlanta 10

2005

AFC 1st-rd. playoffs	Pittsburgh 31, Cincinnati 17
	New England 28, Jacksonville 3
AFC div. playoffs	Pittsburgh 21, Indianapolis 18
	Denver 27, New England 13
AFC championship	Pittsburgh 34, Denver 17
NFC 1st-rd. playoffs	Washington 17, Tampa Bay 10
	Carolina 23, NY Giants 0
NFC div. playoffs	Seattle 20, Washington 10
	Carolina 29, Chicago 21
NFC championship	Seattle 34, Carolina 14

2006

AFC 1st-rd. playoffs	Indianapolis 23, Kansas City 8
	New England 37, NY Jets 16
AFC div. playoffs	Indianapolis 15, Baltimore 6
	New England 24, San Diego 21
AFC championship	Indianapolis 38, New England 34
NFC 1st-rd. playoffs	Seattle 21, Dallas 20
	Philadelphia 23, NY Giants 20
NFC div. playoffs	Chicago 27, Seattle 24
	New Orleans 27, Philadelphia 24
NFC championship	Chicago 39, New Orleans 14

Career Leaders

Scoring

	Yrs	TD	FG	PAT	Pts
†Morten Andersen	25	0	540	825	2,445
Gary Anderson	23	0	538	820	2,434
George Blanda	26	9	335	943	2,002
†John Carney	17	0	413	510	1,749
Norm Johnson	18	0	366	638	1,736
†Matt Stover	17	0	408	491	1,715
Nick Lowery	18	0	383	562	1,711
Jan Stenerud	19	0	373	580	1,699
†Jason Elam	14	0	368	568	1,672
Eddie Murray	19	0	352	538	1,594
Al Del Greco	17	0	347	543	1,584
†Jason Hanson	15	0	356	469	1,537
Steve Christie	15	0	336	468	1,476
Pat Leahy	18	0	304	558	1,470
Jim Turner	16	1	304	521	1,439

Rushing

	Yrs	Att	Yds	Avg	Lg	TD
Emmitt Smith	15	4,409	18,355	4.2	75	164
Walter Payton	13	3,838	16,726	4.4	76	110
Barry Sanders	10	3,062	15,269	5.0	85	99
Curtis Martin	11	3,518	14,101	4.0	70	90
Jerome Bettis	13	3,479	13,662	3.9	71	91
Eric Dickerson	11	2,996	13,259	4.4	85	90
Tony Dorsett	12	2,936	12,739	4.3	99	77
Jim Brown	9	2,359	12,312	5.2	80	106
Marshall Faulk	12	2,836	12,279	4.3	71	100
Marcus Allen	16	3,022	12,243	4.1	61	123
Franco Harris	13	2,949	12,120	4.1	75	91
Thurman Thomas	13	2,877	12,074	4.2	80	66
John Riggins	14	2,916	11,352	3.9	66	104
†Corey Dillon	10	2,618	11,241	4.3	96	82
O.J. Simpson	11	2,404	11,236	4.7	94	61

Touchdowns

	Yrs	Rush	Rec	Ret	Total TD
Jerry Rice	20	10	197	1	208
Emmitt Smith	15	164	11	0	175
Marcus Allen	16	123	21	1	145
Marshall Faulk	12	100	36	0	136
Cris Carter	16	0	130	0	130
Jim Brown	9	106	20	0	126
Walter Payton	13	110	15	0	125
†Marvin Harrison	11	0	122	0	122
†Terrell Owens	11	2	114	0	116

	Yrs	Rush	Rec	Ret	Total TD
John Riggins	14	104	12	0	116
Lenny Moore	12	63	48	2	113
†LaDainian Tomlinson	6	100	11	0	111
Barry Sanders	10	99	10	0	109
†Shaun Alexander	7	96	11	0	107
Don Hutson	11	3	99	1	103
Tim Brown	17	1	100	0	101
Steve Largent	14	1	100	0	101
Randy Moss	9	0	101	0	101

Combined Yards Gained

	Yrs	Total	Rush	Rec	Int Ret	Punt Ret	Kickoff Ret	Fum Ret
Jerry Rice	20	23,546	645	22,895	0	0	6	0
Brian Mitchell	14	23,330	1,967	2,336	0	4,999	14,014	14
Walter Payton	13	21,803	16,726	4,538	0	0	539	0
Emmitt Smith	15	21,564	18,355	3,224	0	0	0	-15
Tim Brown	17	19,682	190	14,934	0	3,320	1,235	3
Marshall Faulk	12	19,154	12,279	6,875	0	0	18	18
Barry Sanders	10	18,308	15,269	2,921	0	0	118	0
Herschel Walker	12	18,168	8,225	4,859	0	0	5,084	0
Marcus Allen	16	17,648	12,243	5,411	0	0	0	-6
Curtis Martin	11	17,430	14,101	3,329	0	0	0	-9
Eric Metcalf	13	17,230	2,392	5,572	0	3,453	5,813	0
Thurman Thomas	13	16,532	12,074	4,458	0	0	0	0
Tony Dorsett	12	16,326	12,739	3,554	0	0	0	33

†-active player in 2006.

Career Leaders *(Cont.)*

Passing

PASSER RATING*

	Yrs	Att	Comp	Pct Comp	Yds	Avg Gain	TD	Pct TD	Int	Pct Int	Rating Pts
Steve Young	15	4,149	2,667	64.3	33,124	8.0	232	5.6	107	2.6	96.8
†Peyton Manning	9	4,890	3,131	64.0	37,586	7.7	275	5.6	139	3.2	94.4
†Kurt Warner	9	2,508	1,645	65.6	20,591	8.2	125	5.0	83	3.3	93.8
Joe Montana	15	5,391	3,409	63.2	40,551	7.5	273	5.2	139	2.6	92.3
†Marc Bulger	6	2,106	1,357	64.4	16,233	7.7	95	4.5	59	2.8	91.3
†Daunte Culpepper	8	2,741	1,759	64.2	21,091	7.7	137	5.0	89	3.2	90.8
†Chad Pennington	7	1,659	1,080	65.1	11,973	7.2	72	4.3	46	2.8	89.3
†Tom Brady	7	3,064	1,896	61.9	21,564	7.1	147	4.8	78	2.5	88.4
†Trent Green	14	3,527	2,143	60.8	26,963	7.6	157	4.4	101	2.9	87.5
†Drew Brees	6	2,363	1,481	62.7	16,766	7.1	106	4.4	64	2.9	87.5
†Jeff Garcia	8	2,973	1,811	60.9	20,385	6.9	136	4.6	73	2.5	86.4
†Donovan McNabb	8	3,259	1,898	58.2	22,080	6.8	152	4.7	72	2.2	85.2
Dan Marino	17	8,358	4,967	59.4	61,361	7.3	420	5.0	252	3.0	85.1
†Brett Favre	16	8,223	5,021	61.1	57,500	7.0	414.	5.0	273	3.3	85.1
†Matt Hasselbeck	8	2,576	1,552	60.2	18,367	7.1	114	4.4	72	2.8	85.1
Rich Gannon	18	4,206	2,533	60.2	28,743	6.8	180	4.3	104	2.3	84.7
†Brian Griese	9	2,350	1,481	63.0	16,564	7.0	104	4.4	80	3.4	84.5
Jim Kelly	11	4,779	2,874	60.1	35,467	7.4	237	5.0	175	3.7	84.4
†Mark Brunell	14	4,594	2,738	59.6	31,826	6.9	182	4.0	106	2.3	84.2
†Jake Delhomme	9	1,934	1,151	59.5	13,965	7.2	92	4.8	63	3.3	84.0
Roger Staubach	11	2,958	1,685	57.0	22,700	7.7	153	5.2	109	3.7	83.4
†Steve McNair	12	4,339	2,600	59.9	30,191	7.0	172	4.0	115	2.7	83.2
†Brad Johnson	15	4,237	2,620	61.8	28,548	6.7	164	4.1	117	2.7	83.1

*1,500 or more attempts. The passer ratings are based on performance standards established for completion percentage, interception percentage, touchdown percentage and average gain. Passers are allocated points according to how their marks compare with those standards.

YARDS

	Yrs	Att	Comp	Pct Comp	Yds
Dan Marino	17	8,358	4,967	59.4	61,361
†Brett Favre	16	8,223	5,021	61.1	57,500
John Elway	16	7,250	4,123	56.9	51,475
Warren Moon	17	6,823	3,988	58.5	49,325
Fran Tarkenton	18	6,467	3,686	57.0	47,003
†Vinny Testaverde	20	6,529	3,693	56.6	45,281
†Drew Bledsoe	14	6,717	3,839	57.2	44,611
Dan Fouts	15	5,604	3,297	58.8	43,040
Joe Montana	15	5,391	3,409	63.2	40,551
Johnny Unitas	18	5,186	2,830	54.6	40,239
Dave Krieg	19	5,311	3,105	58.5	38,147

	Yrs	Att	Comp	Pct Comp	Yds
Boomer Esiason	14	5,205	2,969	57.0	37,920
†Peyton Manning	9	4,890	3,131	64.0	37,586
Jim Kelly	11	4,779	2,874	60.1	35,467
Jim Everett	12	4,923	2,841	57.7	34,837
Jim Hart	19	5,076	2,593	51.1	34,665
Steve DeBerg	17	4,746	2,924	61.6	34,241
†Kerry Collins	12	5,172	2,868	55.5	34,186
John Hadl	16	4,687	2,363	50.4	33,503
Phil Simms	14	4,647	2,576	55.4	33,462
Steve Young	15	4,149	2,667	64.3	33,124
Troy Aikman	12	4,715	2,898	61.5	32,942

TOUCHDOWNS

	No.
Dan Marino	420
†Brett Favre	414
Fran Tarkenton	342
John Elway	300
Warren Moon	291
Johnny Unitas	290
†Peyton Manning	275
Joe Montana	273
†Vinny Testaverde	270
Dave Krieg	261

	No.
Sonny Jurgensen	255
Dan Fouts	254
†Drew Bledsoe	251
Boomer Esiason	247
John Hadl	244
Len Dawson	239
Jim Kelly	237
George Blanda	236
Steve Young	232
John Brodie	214

	No.
Terry Bradshaw	212
Y.A. Tittle	212
Jim Hart	209
Randall Cunningham	207
Jim Everett	203
Roman Gabriel	201
Phil Simms	199
Ken Anderson	197
Joe Ferguson	196
Bobby Layne	196

† Active in 2006.

Career Leaders *(Cont.)*

Receiving

RECEPTIONS

	Yrs	No.	Yds	Avg	Lg	TD		Yrs	No.	Yds	Avg	Lg	TD
Jerry Rice	20	1,549	22,895	14.8	96	197	Shannon Sharpe	15	815	10,060	12.3	82	62
Cris Carter	16	1,101	13,899	12.6	80	130	Henry Ellard	16	814	13,777	16.9	81	65
Tim Brown	17	1,094	14,934	13.7	80	100	†Keyshawn Johnson	11	814	10,571	13.0	76	64
†Marvin Harrison	11	1,022	13,697	13.4	80	122	†Terrell Owens	11	801	11,715	14.6	91	114
Andre Reed	16	951	13,198	13.9	83	87	Marshall Faulk	11	767	6,875	9.0	85	36
Art Monk	16	940	12,721	13.5	79	68	James Lofton	16	764	14,004	18.3	80	75
†Isaac Bruce	13	887	13,376	15.1	80	80	Michael Irvin	12	750	11,904	15.9	87	65
Jimmy Smith	13	862	12,287	14.3	75	67	Charlie Joiner	18	750	12,146	16.2	87	65
†Keenan McCardell	15	861	11,117	12.9	76	62	Andre Rison	12	743	10,205	13.7	80	84
Irving Fryar	17	851	12,785	15.0	80	84	†Eric Moulds	11	732	9,648	13.2	84	49
†Rod Smith	12	849	11,389	13.4	85	68	†Tony Gonzalez	10	721	8,710	12.1	73	61
Larry Centers	14	826	6,797	8.2	54	28	Gary Clark	11	699	10,856	15.5	84	65
Steve Largent	14	819	13,089	16.0	74	100	Terance Mathis	13	689	8,809	12.8	81	63

YARDS

Jerry Rice	22,895	Andre Reed	13,198	Don Maynard	11,834
Tim Brown	14,934	Steve Largent	13,089	†Terrell Owens	11,715
James Lofton	14,004	Irving Fryar	12,785	†Rod Smith	11,389
Cris Carter	13,899	Art Monk	12,721	†Keenan McCardell	11,117
Henry Ellard	13,777	Jimmy Smith	12,287	Gary Clark	10,856
†Marvin Harrison	13,697	Charlie Joiner	12,146	Stanley Morgan	10,716
†Isaac Bruce	13,376	Michael Irvin	11,904	†Randy Moss	10,700

SACKS

Bruce Smith	200.0	Chris Doleman	150.5
Reggie White	198.0	John Randle	137.5
Kevin Greene	160.0	Richard Dent	137.5

Note: Officially compiled since 1982.

Interceptions

	Yrs	No.	Yds	Avg	Lg	TD
Paul Krause	16	81	1185	14.6	81	3
Emlen Tunnell	14	79	1282	16.2	55	4
Rod Woodson	17	71	1483	20.9	98	17
Dick (Night Train) Lane	14	68	1207	17.8	80	5
Ken Riley	15	65	596	9.2	66	5

Punting

	Yrs	No.	Yds	Avg	Lg	Blk
†Shane Lechler	7	519	23,926	46.1	73	0
Sammy Baugh	16	338	15,245	45.1	85	9
Tommy Davis	11	511	22,833	44.7	82	2
Yale Lary	11	503	22,279	44.3	74	4
†Todd Sauerbrun	12	842	37,008	44.0	73	0

Note: 250 or more punts.

Punt Returns

	Yrs	No.	Yds	Avg	Lg	TD
George McAfee	8	112	1,431	12.8	74	2
Jack Christiansen	8	85	1,084	12.8	89	8
Claude Gibson	5	110	1,381	12.6	85	3
Bill Dudley	9	124	1,515	12.2	96	3
Rick Upchurch	9	248	3,008	12.1	92	8
Desmond Howard	11	244	2,895	11.9	95	8

Note: 75 or more returns.

Kickoff Returns

	Yrs	No.	Yds	Avg	Lg	TD
Gale Sayers	7	91	2,781	30.6	103	6
Lynn Chandnois	7	92	2,720	29.6	93	3
Abe Woodson	9	193	5,538	28.7	105	5
Claude (Buddy) Young	6	90	2,514	27.9	104	2
Travis Williams	5	102	2,801	27.5	105	6

Note: 75 or more returns.

† Active in 2006.

Single-Season Leaders
Scoring

POINTS

	Year	TD	PAT	FG	Pts
†LaDainian Tomlinson,SD	2006	31	0	0	186
Paul Hornung, GB	1960	15	41	15	176
†Shaun Alexander, Sea	2005	28	0	0	168
Gary Anderson, Minn	1998	0	59	35	164
†Jeff Wilkins, StL	2003	0	46	39	163
†Priest Holmes, KC	2003	27	0	0	162
Mark Moseley, Wash	1983	0	62	33	161
†Mike Vanderjagt, Ind	2003	0	46	37	157
†Marshall Faulk, StL	2000	26	0	0	156
Gino Cappelletti, Bos	1964	7	38	25	155
Emmitt Smith, Dal	1995	25	0	0	150
Chip Lohmiller, Wash	1991	0	56	31	149
†Jay Feely, NYG	2005	0	43	35	148

Note: Cappelletti's total includes a two-point conversion.

TOUCHDOWNS

	Year	Rush	Rec	Ret	Total
†LaDainian Tomlinson, SD.	2006	28	3	0	31
†Shaun Alexander, Sea	2005	27	1	0	28
†Priest Holmes, KC	2003	27	0	0	27
†Marshall Faulk, StL	2000	18	8	0	26
Emmitt Smith, Dal	1995	25	0	0	25
John Riggins, Wash	1983	24	0	0	24
†Priest Holmes, KC	2002	21	3	0	24
O.J. Simpson, Buff	1975	16	7	0	23
Jerry Rice, SF	1987	1	22	0	23
Terrell Davis, Den	1998	21	2	0	23

FIELD GOALS

	Year	Att	No.
†Neil Rackers, Ari	2005	42	40
†Olindo Mare, Mia	1999	46	39
†Jeff Wilkins, StL	2003	42	39
†John Kasay, Car	1996	45	37
†Mike Vanderjagt, Ind	2003	37	37
Cary Blanchard, Ind	1996	40	36
Al Del Greco, Tenn	1998	39	36

Rushing

YARDS GAINED

	Year	Att	Yds	Avg
Eric Dickerson, LA Rams	1984	379	2,105	5.6
†Jamal Lewis, Balt	2003	387	2,066	5.3
Barry Sanders, Det	1997	335	2,053	6.1
Terrell Davis, Den	1998	392	2,008	5.1
O.J. Simpson, Buff	1973	332	2,003	6.0
Earl Campbell, Hou	1980	373	1,980	5.2
†Ahman Green, GB	2003	355	1,883	5.3
Barry Sanders, Det	1994	331	1,883	5.7
†Shaun Alexander, Sea	2005	370	1,880	5.1
Jim Brown, Clev	1963	291	1,863	6.4
†Tiki Barber, NYG	2005	357	1,860	5.2
Ricky Williams, Mia	2002	383	1,853	4.8

AVERAGE GAIN

	Year	Avg
Beattie Feathers, Chi	1934	8.44
Randall Cunningham, Phil	1990	7.98
†Michael Vick, Atl	2004	7.50
†Michael Vick, Atl	2002	6.88
Bobby Douglass, Chi	1972	6.87

Minimum 100 attempts.

TOUCHDOWNS

	Year	No.
†LaDainian Tomlinson, SD	2006	28
†Shaun Alexander, Sea	2005	27
†Priest Holmes, KC	2003	27
Emmitt Smith, Dal	1995	25
John Riggins, Wash	1983	24
†Priest Holmes, KC	2002	24
Emmitt Smith, Dal	1994	21
Joe Morris, NYG	1985	21
Terry Allen, Wash	1996	21
Terrell Davis, Den	1998	21

Passing

YARDS GAINED

	Year	Att	Comp	Pct	Yds
Dan Marino, Mia	1984	564	362	64.2	5,084
†Kurt Warner, StL Rams	2001	546	375	68.7	4,830
Dan Fouts, SD	1981	609	360	59.1	4,802
Dan Marino, Mia	1986	623	378	60.7	4,746
†Daunte Culpepper	2004	548	379	69.2	4,717
Dan Fouts, SD	1980	589	348	59.1	4,715
Warren Moon, Hou	1991	655	404	61.7	4,690
Warren Moon, Hou	1990	584	362	62.0	4,689
Rich Gannon, Oak	2002	618	418	67.6	4,689
Neil Lomax, StL Cards	1984	560	345	61.6	4,614
†Trent Green, StL Rams	2004	556	369	66.4	4,591
†Peyton Manning, Ind.	2004	497	336	67.6	4,557
†Drew Bledsoe, NE	1994	691	400	57.9	4,555

PASSER RATING

	Year	Rat.
†Peyton Manning, Colts	2004	121.1
Steve Young, SF	1994	112.8
Joe Montana, SF	1989	112.4
†Daunte Culpepper, Minn	2004	110.9
Milt Plum, Clev	1960	110.4
Sammy Baugh, Wash	1945	109.9
†Kurt Warner, Rams	1999	109.2

TOUCHDOWNS

	Year	No.
†Peyton Manning, Ind	2004	49
Dan Marino, Mia	1984	48
Dan Marino, Mia	1986	44
†Kurt Warner, Rams	1999	41
†Daunte Culpepper, Minn	2004	39
†Brett Favre, GB	1995	38

Five tied with 36.

† Active in 2006.

Single-Season Leaders *(Cont.)*

Receiving

RECEPTIONS

	Year	No.	Yds
†Marvin Harrison, Ind	2002	143	1,722
Herman Moore, Det	1995	123	1,686
Cris Carter, Minn	1994	122	1,256
Jerry Rice, SF	1995	122	1,848
Cris Carter, Minn	1995	122	1,371
†Isaac Bruce, Rams	1995	119	1,781
†Torry Holt, StL	2003	117	1,696
Jimmy Smith, Jac	1999	116	1,636
†Marvin Harrison, Ind	1999	115	1,663
†Rod Smith, Den	2001	113	1,343

YARDS GAINED

	Year	Yds
Jerry Rice, SF	1995	1,848
†Isaac Bruce, Rams	1995	1,781
Charley Hennigan, Hou	1961	1,746
†Marvin Harrison, Ind	2002	1,722
†Torry Holt, StL	2003	1,696

TOUCHDOWNS

	Year	No.
Jerry Rice, SF	1987	22
Mark Clayton, Mia	1984	18
Sterling Sharpe, GB	1994	18
Seven tied with 17.		

All-Purpose Yards

	Year	Run	Rec	Ret	Total
Derrick Mason, Tenn	2000	1		895	1794
Michael Lewis, NO	2002	15	200	2432	2647
Lionel James, SD	1985	516	1027	992	2535
Terry Metcalf, StL Cards	1975	816	378	1268	2462
Mack Herron, NE	1974	824	474	1146	2444
Gale Sayers, Chi	1966	1231	447	762	2440
Marshall Faulk, Rams	1999	1381	1048	0	2429
Timmy Brown, Phil	1963	841	487	1100	2428
†Tiki Barber, NYG	2005	1860	530	0	2390
Barry Sanders, Det	1997	2053	305	0	2358
Tim Brown, LA Rai	1988	50	725	1542	2317
Marcus Allen, LA Rai	1985	1759	555	−6	2308

Punting

	Year	No.	Yds	Avg
Sammy Baugh, Wash,	1940	35	1,799	51.4
Yale Lary, Det	1963	35	1,713	48.9
Sammy Baugh, Wash	1941	30	1,462	48.7
Yale Lary, Det	1961	52	2,519	48.4
Sammy Baugh, Wash	1942	37	1,785	48.2

Interceptions

	Year	No.
Dick (Night Train) Lane, LA Rams	1952	14
Dan Sandifer, Wash	1948	13
Spec Sanders, NY Yanks	1950	13
Lester Hayes, Oak	1980	13
Nine tied with 12.		

Sacks

	Year	No.
†Michael Strahan, NYG	2001	22.5
Mark Gastineau, NYJ	1984	22
Reggie White, Phil	1987	21
Chris Doleman, Minn	1989	21
Lawrence Taylor, NYG	1986	20.5

Kickoff Returns

	Year	Avg
Travis Williams, GB	1967	41.1
Gale Sayers, Chi	1967	37.7
Ollie Matson, Chi Cards	1958	35.5
Jim Duncan, Balt Colts	1970	35.4
Lynn Chandnois, Pitt	1952	35.2

Punt Returns

	Year	Avg
Herb Rich, Balt Colts	1950	23.0
Jack Christiansen, Det	1952	21.5
Dick Christy, NY Titans	1961	21.3
Bob Hayes, Dal	1968	20.8

Single-Game Leaders

Scoring

POINTS

	Date	Pts
Ernie Nevers, Chi Cards vs Chi	11-28-29	40
Dub Jones, Clev vs Chi	11-25-51	36
Gale Sayers, Chi vs SF	12-12-65	36
Paul Hornung, GB vs Balt Colts	10-8-61	33

On Thanksgiving Day, 1929, Nevers scored all the Cardinals' points on six rushing TDs and four PATs. The Cards defeated Red Grange and the Bears, 40–6. Jones and Sayers each rushed for four touchdowns and scored two more on returns in their teams' victories. Hornung scored four touchdowns and kicked 6 PATs and a field goal in a 45-7 win over the Colts.

FIELD GOALS

	Date	No.
Jim Bakken, StL Cards vs Pitt	9-24-67	7
Rich Karlis, Minn vs Rams	11-5-89	7
Chris Boniol, Dal vs GB	11-18-96	7
†Billy Cundiff, Dal vs NYG	9-15-03	7

Bakken was 7 for 9; Cundiff was 7 for 8; and Karlis and Boniol 7 for 7.

† Active in 2006.

Single-Game Leaders *(Cont.)*

Scoring *(Cont.)*

TOUCHDOWNS

	Date	No.
Ernie Nevers, Chi Cards vs Chi	11-28-29	6
Dub Jones, Clev vs Chi	11-25-51	6
Gale Sayers, Chi vs SF	12-12-65	6
Bob Shaw, Chi Cards vs Balt Colts	10-2-50	5
Jim Brown, Clev vs Balt Colts	11-1-59	5
Abner Haynes, Dal Texans vs Oak	11-26-61	5
Billy Cannon, Hou vs NY Titans	12-10-61	5
Cookie Gilchrist, Buff vs NYJ	12-8-63	5
Paul Hornung, GB vs Balt Colts	12-12-65	5
Kellen Winslow, SD vs Oak	11-22-81	5
Jerry Rice, SF vs Atl	10-14-90	5
James Stewart, Jax vs Phil	10-12-97	5
†Shaun Alexander, Sea vs Minn	9-29-02	5

Rushing

YARDS GAINED

	Date	Yds
†Jamal Lewis, Balt vs Clev	9-14-03	295
†Corey Dillon, Cin vs Den	10-22-00	278
Walter Payton, Chi vs Minn	11-20-77	275
O.J. Simpson, Buff vs Det	11-25-76	273
†Shaun Alexander, Sea vs Oak	11-11-01	266

TOUCHDOWNS

	Date	No.
Ernie Nevers, Chi Cards vs Chi	11-28-29	6
Jim Brown, Clev vs Balt Colts	11-1-59	5
Cookie Gilchrist, Buff vs NYJ	12-8-63	5
James Stewart, Jac vs Phil	10-12-97	5
†Clinton Portis, Den vs KC	12-7-03	5

CARRIES

	Date	No.
Jamie Morris, Wash vs Cin	12-17-88	45
Butch Woolfolk, NYG vs Phil	11-20-83	43
James Wilder, TB vs GB	9-30-84	43
†Rudi Johnson, Cin vs Hou	11-9-03	43
James Wilder, TB vs Pitt	10-30-83	42
Terrell Davis, Den vs Buff	10-26-97	42
Ricky Williams, Mia vs Buff	9-21-03	42

Passing

YARDS GAINED

	Date	Yds
N. Van Brocklin, Rams vs NY Yanks	9-28-51	554
Warren Moon, Hou vs KC	12-16-90	527
Boomer Esiason, Ariz vs Wash	11-10-96	522
Dan Marino, Mia vs NYJ	10-23-88	521
Phil Simms, NYG vs Cin	10-13-85	513

TOUCHDOWNS

	Date	No.
Sid Luckman, Chi vs NYG	11-14-43	7
Adrian Burk, Phil vs Wash	10-17-54	7
George Blanda, Hou vs NY Titans	11-19-61	7
Y. A. Tittle, NYG vs Wash	10-28-62	7
Joe Kapp, Minn vs Balt Colts	9-28-69	7

COMPLETIONS

	Date	No.
†Drew Bledsoe, NE vs Minn	11-13-94	45
Rich Gannon, Oak vs Pitt	9-15-02	43
Richard Todd, NYJ vs SF	9-21-80	42
†Vinny Testaverde, NYJ vs Sea	12-6-98	42
Warren Moon, Hou vs Dal	11-10-91	41
Ken Anderson, Cin vs SD	12-20-82	40
Phil Simms, NYG vs Cin	10-13-85	40
†Brad Johnson, TB vs Chi	11-18-01	40
†Marc Bulger, StL Rams vs. NYG	10-02-05	40

Receiving

YARDS GAINED

	Date	Yds
Flipper Anderson, Rams vs NO	11-26-89	336
Stephone Paige, KC vs SD	12-22-85	309
Jim Benton, Clev vs Det	11-22-45	303
Cloyce Box, Det vs Balt Colts	12-3-50	302
Jimmy Smith, Jax vs Balt Ravens	9-10-00	291

RECEPTIONS

	Date	No.
†Terrell Owens, SF vs Chi	12-17-00	20
Tom Fears, Rams vs GB	12-3-50	18
Clark Gaines, NYJ vs SF	9-21-80	17
Sonny Randle, StL Cards vs NYG	11-4-62	16
Jerry Rice, SF vs Rams	11-20-94	16
†Keenan McCardell, Jax vs Rams	10-20-96	16
†Troy Brown, NE vs KC	9-22-02	16

Six tied with 15.

† Active in 2006.

Single-Game Leaders *(Cont.)*

Receiving *(Cont.)*
TOUCHDOWNS

	Date	No.
Bob Shaw, Chi Cards vs Balt Colts	10-2-50	5
Kellen Winslow, SD vs Oak	11-22-81	5
Jerry Rice, SF vs Atl	10-14-90	5

All-Purpose Yards

	Date	Yds
Glyn Milburn, Den vs Sea	12-10-95	404
Billy Cannon, Hou vs NY Titans	12-10-61	373
Tyrone Hughes, NO vs LA Rams	10-23-94	347
Lionel James, SD vs LA Rai	11-10-85	345
Timmy Brown, Phil vs StL Cards	12-16-62	341

Longest Plays

RUSHING

	Opponent	Year	Yds
Tony Dorsett, Dal	Minn	1983	99
Ahman Green, GB	Den	2003	98
Andy Uram, GB	Chi Cards	1939	97
Bob Gage, Pitt	Chi	1949	97
Jim Spavital, Balt Colts	GB	1950	96
Bob Hoernschemeyer, Det	NY Yanks	1950	96
Garrison Hearst, SF	NYJ	1998	96
Corey Dillon, Cin	Det	2001	96

PASSING

	Opponent	Year	Yds
Frank Filchock to Andy Farkas, Wash	Pitt	1939	99
George Izo to Bobby Mitchell, Wash	Clev	1963	99
Karl Sweetan to Pat Studstill, Det	Balt Colts	1966	99
Sonny Jurgensen to Gerry Allen, Wash	Chi	1968	99
Jim Plunkett to Cliff Branch, LA Rai	Wash	1983	99
Ron Jaworski to Mike Quick, Phil	Atl	1985	99
Stan Humphries to Tony Martin, SD	Sea	1994	99
Brett Favre to Robert Brooks, GB	Chi	1995	99
Trent Green to Marc Boerigter, KC	SD	2002	99
Jeff Garcia to Andre Davis, Cle	Cin	2004	99

FIELD GOALS

	Opponent	Year	Yds
Tom Dempsey, NO	Det	1970	63
Jason Elam, Den	Jax	1998	63
Steve Cox, Clev	Cin	1984	60
Morten Andersen, NO	Chi	1991	60

PUNTS

	Opponent	Year	Yds
Steve O'Neal, NYJ	Den	1969	98
Joe Lintzenich, Chi	NYG	1931	94
Shawn McCarthy, NE	Buff	1991	93
Randall Cunningham, Phil	NYG	1989	91

INTERCEPTION RETURNS

	Opponent	Year	Yds
Ed Reed, Balt	Clev	2004	106
Vencie Glenn, SD	Den	1987	103
Louis Oliver, Mia	Buff	1992	103
Eight players tied at 102.			

KICKOFF RETURNS

	Opponent	Year	Yds
Al Carmichael, GB	Chi	1956	106
Noland Smith, KC	Den	1967	106
Roy Green, StL Cards	Dal	1979	106

PUNT RETURNS

	Opponent	Year	Yds
Robert Bailey, LA Rams	NO	1994	103
Gil LeFebvre, Cin	Brooklyn	1933	98
Charlie West, Minn	Wash	1968	98
Dennis Morgan, Dal	StL Cards	1974	98
Terance Mathis, NYJ	Dal	1990	98

MISSED FIELD GOAL RETURNS

	Opponent	Year	Yds
Devin Hester, Chi	NYG	2006	108
Nathan Vasher, Chi	SF	2005	108
Chris McAllister, Balt	Den	2002	107
Aaron Glenn, NYJ	Ind	1998	104

Rushing

Year	Player, Team	Att	Yards	Avg	TD
1932	Cliff Battles, Bos	148	576	3.9	3
1933	Jim Musick, Bos	173	809	4.7	5
1934	Beattie Feathers, Chi	119	1,004	8.4	8
1935	Doug Russell, Chi Cards	140	499	3.6	0
1936	Alphonse Leemans, NY	206	830	4.0	2
1937	Cliff Battles, Wash	216	874	4.0	5
1938	Byron White, Pitt	152	567	3.7	4
1939	Bill Osmanski, Chi	121	699	5.8	7
1940	Byron White, Det	146	514	3.5	5
1941	Clarence Manders, Bklyn	111	486	4.4	5
1942	Bill Dudley, Pitt	162	696	4.3	5
1943	Bill Paschal, NY	147	572	3.9	10
1944	Bill Paschal, NY	196	737	3.8	9
1945	Steve Van Buren, Phil	143	832	5.8	15
1946	Bill Dudley, Pitt	146	604	4.1	3
1947	Steve Van Buren, Phil	217	1,008	4.6	13
1948	Steve Van Buren, Phil	201	945	4.7	10
1949	Steve Van Buren, Phil	263	1,146	4.4	11
1950	Marion Motley, Clev	140	810	5.8	3
1951	Eddie Price, NY	271	971	3.6	7
1952	Dan Towler, LA	156	894	5.7	10
1953	Joe Perry, SF	192	1,018	5.3	10
1954	Joe Perry, SF	173	1,049	6.1	8
1955	Alan Ameche, Balt	213	961	4.5	9
1956	Rick Casares, Chi	234	1,126	4.8	12
1957	Jim Brown, Clev	202	942	4.7	9
1958	Jim Brown, Clev	257	1,527	5.9	17
1959	Jim Brown, Clev	290	1,329	4.6	14
1960	Jim Brown, Clev, NFL	215	1,257	5.8	9
	Abner Haynes, Dallas Texans, AFL	156	875	5.6	9
1961	Jim Brown, Clev, NFL	305	1,408	4.6	8
	Billy Cannon, Hou, AFL	200	948	4.7	6
1962	Jim Taylor, GB, NFL	272	1,474	5.4	19
	Cookie Gilchrist, Buff, AFL	214	1,096	5.1	13
1963	Jim Brown, Clev, NFL	291	1,863	6.4	12
	Clem Daniels, Oak, AFL	215	1,099	5.1	3
1964	Jim Brown, Clev, NFL	280	1,446	5.2	7
	Cookie Gilchrist, Buff, AFL	230	981	4.3	6
1965	Jim Brown, Clev, NFL	289	1,544	5.3	17
	Paul Lowe, SD, AFL	222	1,121	5.0	7
1966	Jim Nance, Bos, AFL	299	1,458	4.9	11
	Gale Sayers, Chi, NFL	229	1,231	5.4	8
1967	Jim Nance, Bos, AFL	269	1,216	4.5	7
	Leroy Kelly, Clev, NFL	235	1,205	5.1	11
1968	Leroy Kelly, Clev, NFL	248	1,239	5.0	16
	Paul Robinson, Cin, AFL	238	1,023	4.3	8
1969	Gale Sayers, Chi, NFL	236	1,032	4.4	8
	Dickie Post, SD, AFL	182	873	4.8	6
1970	Larry Brown, Wash, NFC	237	1,125	4.7	5
	Floyd Little, Den, AFC	209	901	4.3	3
1971	Floyd Little, Den, AFC	284	1,133	4.0	6
	John Brockington, GB, NFC	216	1,105	5.1	4
1972	O.J. Simpson, Buff, AFC	292	1,251	4.3	6
	Larry Brown, Wash, NFC	285	1,216	4.3	8
1973	O.J. Simpson, Buff, AFC	332	2,003	6.0	12
	John Brockington, GB, NFC	265	1,144	4.3	3
1974	Otis Armstrong, Den, AFC	263	1,407	5.3	9
	Lawrence McCutcheon, LA, NFC	236	1,109	4.7	3
1975	O.J. Simpson, Buff, AFC	329	1,817	5.5	16
	Jim Otis, StL, NFC	269	1,076	4.0	5
1976	O.J. Simpson, Buff, AFC	290	1,503	5.2	8
	Walter Payton, Chi, NFC	311	1,390	4.5	13
1977	Walter Payton, Chi, NFC	339	1,852	5.5	14
	Mark van Eeghen, Oak, AFC	324	1,273	3.9	7
1978	Earl Campbell, Hou, AFC	302	1,450	4.8	13
	Walter Payton, Chi, NFC	333	1,395	4.2	11
1979	Earl Campbell, Hou, AFC	368	1,697	4.6	19
	Walter Payton, Chi, NFC	369	1,610	4.4	14
1980	Earl Campbell, Hou, AFC	373	1,934	5.2	13
	Walter Payton, Chi, NFC	317	1,460	4.6	6
1981	George Rogers, NO, NFC	378	1,674	4.4	13
	Earl Campbell, Hou, AFC	361	1,376	3.8	10
1982	Freeman McNeil, NYJ, AFC	151	786	5.2	6
	Tony Dorsett, Dal, NFC	177	745	4.2	5
1983	Eric Dickerson, LA, NFC	390	1,808	4.6	18
	Curt Warner, Sea, AFC	335	1,449	4.3	13
1984	Eric Dickerson, LA, NFC	379	2,105	5.6	14
	Earnest Jackson, SD, AFC	296	1,179	4.0	8
1985	Marcus Allen, LA, AFC	380	1,759	4.6	11
	Gerald Riggs, Atl, NFC	397	1,719	4.3	10
1986	Eric Dickerson, LA, NFC	404	1,821	4.5	11
	Curt Warner, Sea, AFC	319	1,481	4.6	13
1987	Charles White, LA, NFC	324	1,374	4.2	11
	Eric Dickerson, Ind, AFC	223	1,011	4.5	5
1988	Eric Dickerson, Ind, AFC	388	1,659	4.3	14
	Herschel Walker, Dal, NFC	361	1,514	4.2	5
1989	Christian Okoye, KC, AFC	370	1,480	4.0	12
	Barry Sanders, Det, NFC	280	1,470	5.3	14
1990	Barry Sanders, Det, NFC	255	1,304	5.1	13
	Thurman Thomas, Buff, AFC	271	1,297	4.8	11
1991	Emmitt Smith, Dal, NFC	365	1,563	4.3	12
	Thurman Thomas, Buff, AFC	288	1,407	4.9	7
1992	Emmitt Smith, Dal, NFC	373	1,713	4.6	18
	Barry Foster, Pitt, AFC	390	1,690	4.3	11
1993	Emmitt Smith, Dal, NFC	283	1,486	5.3	9
	Thurman Thomas, Buff, AFC	355	1,315	3.7	6

Rushing *(Cont.)*

Year	Player, Team	Att	Yards	Avg	TD
1994	Barry Sanders, Det, NFC ..331		1,883	5.7	7
	Chris Warren, Sea, AFC ...333		1,545	4.6	9
1995	Emmitt Smith, Dal, NFC....377		1,773	4.7	25
	Curtis Martin, NE, AFC.....368		1,487	4.0	14
1996	Barry Sanders, Det, NFC .307		1,553	5.1	11
	Terrell Davis, Den, AFC 345		1,538	4.5	13
1997	Barry Sanders, Det, NFC .335		2,053	6.1	11
	Terrell Davis, Den, AFC 369		1,750	4.7	15
1998	Terrell Davis, Den, AFC 392		2,008	5.1	21
	Jamal Anderson, Atl, NFC ..410		1,846	4.5	14
1999	Edgerrin James, Ind, AFC ..369		1,553	4.2	13
	Stephen Davis, Wash, NFC...290		1,405	4.8	17
2000	Edgerrin James, Ind, AFC ..387		1,709	4.4	13
	Robert Smith, Minn, NFC ..295		1,521	5.2	7
2001	Priest Holmes, Kan, AFC...327		1,555	4.8	8
	Stephen Davis, Wash, NFC..356		1,432	4.0	5
2002	Ricky Williams, Mia, AFC ..383		1,853	4.8	16
	Deuce McAllister,				
	NO, NFC 325		1,388	4.3	13
2003	Jamal Lewis, Balt, AFC 387		2,066	5.3	14
	Ahman Green, GB, NFC ..355		1,883	5.3	15
2004	Curtis Martin				
	NY Jets, AFC 371		1,697	4.6	12
	Shaun Alexander,				
	Sea, NFC.....................353		1,696	4.8	16
2005	Shaun Alexander,				
	Sea, NFC.....................370		1,880	5.1	27
	Larry Johnson, KC, AFC ..336		1,750	5.2	20
2006	LaDainian Tomlinson,				
	SD, AFC 348		1,815	5.2	28
	Frank Gore, SF, NFC 312		1,695	5.4	8

Passing

Year	Player, Team	Att	Comp	Yards	TD	Int
1932	Arnie Herber, GB...........101		37	639	9	9
1933	Harry Newman, NYG.....136		53	973	11	17
1934	Arnie Herber, GB...........115		42	799	8	12
1935	Ed Danowski, NYG........113		57	794	10	9
1936	Arnie Herber, GB...........173		77	1,239	11	13
1937	Sammy Baugh, Wash....171		81	1,127	8	14
1938	Ed Danowski, NYG........129		70	848	7	8
1939	Parker Hall, Clev 208		106	1,227	9	13
1940	Sammy Baugh, Wash....177		111	1,367	12	10
1941	Cecil Isbell, GB 206		117	1,479	15	11
1942	Cecil Isbell, GB 268		146	2,021	24	14
1943	Sammy Baugh, Wash....239		133	1,754	23	19
1944	Frank Filchock, Wash....147		84	1,139	13	9
1945	Sammy Baugh, Wash....182		128	1,669	11	4
	Sid Luckman, Chi..........217		117	1,725	14	10
1946	Bob Waterfield, LA 251		127	1,747	18	17
1947	Sammy Baugh, Wash....354		210	2,938	25	15
1948	Tommy Thompson, Phil...246		141	1,965	25	11
1949	Sammy Baugh, Wash....255		145	1,903	18	14
1950	Norm Van Brocklin, LA....233		127	2,061	18	14
1951	Bob Waterfield, LA 176		88	1,566	13	10
1952	Norm Van Brocklin, LA....205		113	1,736	14	17
1953	Otto Graham, Clev 258		167	2,722	11	9
1954	Norm Van Brocklin, LA....260		139	2,637	13	21
1955	Otto Graham, Clev 185		98	1,721	15	8
1956	Ed Brown, Chi 168		96	1,667	11	12
1957	Tommy O'Connell, Clev ...110		63	1,229	9	8
1958	Eddie LeBaron, Wash ...145		79	1,365	11	10
1959	Charlie Conerly, NYG 194		113	1,706	14	4
1960	Milt Plum, Clev, NFL......250		151	2,297	21	5
	Jack Kemp, LA, AFL 406		211	3,018	20	25
1961	George Blanda,					
	Hou, AFL....................362		187	3,330	36	22
	Milt Plum, Clev, NFL......302		177	2,416	18	10
1962	Len Dawson, Dal, AFL ...310		189	2,759	29	17
	Bart Starr, GB, NFL 285		178	2,438	12	9
1963	Y.A. Tittle, NY, NFL 367		221	3,145	36	14
	Tobin Rote, SD, AFL......286		170	2,510	20	17
1964	Len Dawson, KC, AFL....354		199	2,879	30	18
	Bart Starr, GB, NFL 272		163	2,144	15	4
1965	Rudy Bukich, Chi, NFL...312		176	2,641	20	9
	John Hadl, SD, AFL 348		174	2,798	20	21
1966	Bart Starr, GB, NFL 251		156	2,257	14	3
	Len Dawson, KC, AFL...284		159	2,527	26	10
1967	Sonny Jurgensen,					
	Wash, NFL 508		288	3,747	31	16
	Daryle Lamonica,					
	Oak, AFL....................425		220	3,228	30	20
1968	Len Dawson, KC, AFL....224		131	2,109	17	9
	Earl Morrall, Balt, NFL....317		182	2,909	26	17
1969	S. Jurgensen, Wash, NFL..442		274	3,102	22	15
	Greg Cook, Cin, AFL.....197		106	1,854	15	11
1970	John Brodie, SF, NFC....378		223	2,941	24	10
	Daryle Lamonica,					
	Oak, AFC 356		179	2,516	22	15
1971	Roger Staubach,					
	Dal, NFC 211		126	1,882	15	4
	Bob Griese, Mia, AFC ...263		145	2,089	19	9
1972	Norm Snead, NY, NFC...325		196	2,307	17	12
	Earl Morrall, Mia, AFC ...150		83	1,360	11	7

Passing* *(Cont.)*

*Since 1973, the annual passing NFL leaders have been determined by a passer rating system that compares individual performances to a fixed performance standard. Before 1973, total passing yards gained was used.

Year	Player, Team	Comp%	Yds	TD	Int	Rating	Year	Player, Team	Comp%	Yds	TD	Int	Rating
1973	Roger Staubach, Dal, NFC	62.6	2,428	23	15	94.6	1988	Boomer Esiason, Cin, AFC	57.5	3,572	28	14	97.4
	Ken Stabler, Oak, AFC	62.7	1,997	14	10	88.3		Wade Wilson, Minn, NFC	61.4	2,746	15	9	91.5
1974	Ken Anderson, Cin, AFC	64.9	2,667	18	10	95.7	1989	Joe Montana, SF, NFC	70.2	3,521	26	8	112.4
	Sonny Jurgensen, Wash, NFC	64.1	1,185	11	5	94.5		Boomer Esiason, Cin, AFC	56.7	3,525	28	11	92.1
1975	Ken Anderson, Cin, AFC	60.5	3,169	21	11	93.9	1990	Jim Kelly, Buffalo, AFC	63.3	2,829	24	9	101.2
	Fran Tarkenton, Minn, NFC	64.2	2,994	25	13	91.8		Phil Simms, NY, NFC	59.2	2,284	15	4	92.7
1976	Ken Stabler, Oak, AFC	66.7	2,737	27	17	103.4	1991	Steve Young, SF, NFC	64.5	2,517	17	8	101.8
	James Harris, LA, NFC	57.6	1,460	8	6	89.6		Jim Kelly, Buff, AFC	64.1	3,844	33	17	97.6
1977	Bob Griese, Mia, AFC	58.6	2,252	22	13	87.8	1992	Steve Young, SF, NFC	66.7	3,465	25	7	107.0
	Roger Staubach, Dal, NFC	58.2	2,620	18	9	87.0		Warren Moon, Hou, AFC	64.7	2,521	18	12	89.3
1978	Roger Staubach, Dal, NFC	55.9	3,190	25	16	84.9	1993	Steve Young, SF, NFC	68.0	4,023	29	16	101.5
	Terry Bradshaw, Pitt, AFC	56.3	2,915	28	20	84.7		John Elway, Den, AFC	63.2	4,030	25	10	92.8
1979	Roger Staubach, Dal, NFC	57.9	3,586	27	11	92.3	1994	Steve Young, SF, NFC	70.3	3,969	35	10	112.8
	Dan Fouts, SD, AFC	62.6	4,082	24	24	82.6		Dan Marino, Mia, AFC	62.0	4,453	30	17	89.2
1980	Brian Sipe, Clev, AFC	60.8	4,132	30	14	91.4	1995	Brett Favre, GB, NFC	62.9	4,413	38	13	99.5
	Ron Jaworski, Phi, NFC	57.0	3,529	27	12	91.0		Jim Harbaugh, Ind, AFC	61.2	2,575	17	5	100.7
1981	Ken Anderson, Cin, AFC	62.6	3,754	29	10	98.4	1996	John Elway, Den, AFC	61.6	3,328	26	14	89.2
	Joe Montana, SF, NFC	63.7	3,565	19	12	88.4		Steve Young, SF, NFC	67.7	2,410	14	6	97.2
1982	Ken Anderson, Cin, AFC	70.6	2,495	12	9	95.3	1997	Steve Young, SF, NFC	67.7	3,029	19	6	104.7
	Joe Theismann, Wash, NFC	63.9	2,033	13	9	91.3		Mark Brunell, Jax, AFC	60.7	3,281	18	7	91.2
1983	Steve Bartkowski, Atl, NFC	63.4	3,167	22	5	97.6	1998	Randall Cunningham, Minn, NFC	60.9	3,704	34	10	106.0
	Dan Marino, Mia AFC	58.4	2,210	20	6	96.0		Vinny Testaverde, NYJ, AFC	61.5	3,256	29	7	101.6
1984	Dan Marino, Mia, AFC	64.2	5,084	48	17	108.9	1999	Kurt Warner, StL, NFC	65.1	4,353	41	13	109.2
	Joe Montana, SF, NFC	64.6	3,630	28	10	102.9		Peyton Manning, Ind, AFC	62.1	4,135	26	15	90.7
1985	Ken O'Brien, NY, AFC	60.9	3,888	25	8	96.2	2000	Trent Green, StL, NFC	60.4	2,063	16	5	101.8
	Joe Montana, SF, NFC	61.3	3,653	27	13	91.3		Brian Griese, Den, AFC	64.3	2,688	19	4	102.9
1986	Tommy Kramer, Minn, NFC	55.9	3,000	24	10	92.6	2001	Kurt Warner, StL, NFC	68.7	4,830	36	22	101.4
	Dan Marino, Mia, AFC	60.7	4,746	44	23	92.5		Rich Gannon, Oak, AFC	65.8	3,828	27	9	95.5
1987	Joe Montana, SF, NFC	66.8	3,054	31	13	102.1	2002	Brad Johnson, TB, NFC	62.3	3,049	22	6	92.9
	Bernie Kosar, Clev, AFC	61.9	3,033	22	9	95.4		Chad Pennington, NY, AFC	68.9	3,120	22	6	104.2

Passing *(Cont.)*

Year	Player, Team	Comp%	Yds	TD	Int	Rating
2003	Steve McNair, Tenn, AFC	62.5	3,215	24	7	100.4
	Daunte Culpepper, Minn, NFC	65.0	3,479	25	11	96.4
2004	Peyton Manning, Ind, AFC	67.6	4,557	49	10	121.1
	Daunte Culpepper, Minn, NFC	69.2	4,717	39	11	110.9
2005	Peyton Manning, Ind, AFC	67.3	3,747	28	10	104.1
	Matt Hasselbeck, GB, NFC	65.5	3,459	24	9	98.2
2006	Peyton Manning, Ind, AFC	65.0	4,397	31	9	101.0
	Drew Brees, NO, NFC	64.3	4,418	26	11	96.2

Pass Receiving†

Year	Player, Team	No.	Yds	Avg	TD
1932	Ray Flaherty, NY	21	350	16.7	3
1933	John Kelly, Brooklyn	22	246	11.2	3
1934	Joe Carter, Phil	16	238	14.9	4
	Morris Badgro, NY	16	206	12.9	1
1935	Tod Goodwin, NY	26	432	16.6	4
1936	Don Hutson, GB	34	536	15.8	8
1937	Don Hutson, GB	41	552	13.5	7
1938	Gaynell Tinsley, Chi Cards	41	516	12.6	1
1939	Don Hutson, GB	34	846	24.9	6
1940	Don Looney, Phil	58	707	12.2	4
1941	Don Hutson, GB	58	738	12.7	10
1942	Don Hutson, GB	74	1,211	16.4	17
1943	Don Hutson, GB	47	776	16.5	11
1944	Don Hutson, GB	58	866	14.9	9
1945	Don Hutson, GB	47	834	17.7	9
1946	Jim Benton, LA	63	981	15.6	6
1947	Jim Keane, Chi	64	910	14.2	10
1948	Tom Fears, LA	51	698	13.7	4
1949	Tom Fears, LA	77	1,013	13.2	9
1950	Tom Fears, LA	84	1,116	13.3	7
1951	Elroy Hirsch, LA	66	1,495	22.7	17
1952	Mac Speedie, Clev	62	911	14.7	5
1953	Pete Pihos, Phil	63	1,049	16.7	10
1954	Pete Pihos, Phil	60	872	14.5	10
	Billy Wilson, SF	60	830	13.8	5
1955	Pete Pihos, Phil	62	864	13.9	7
1956	Billy Wilson, SF	60	889	14.8	5
1957	Billy Wilson, SF	52	757	14.6	6
1958	Raymond Berry, Balt	56	794	14.2	9
	Pete Retzlaff, Phil	56	766	13.7	2
1959	Raymond Berry, Balt	66	959	14.5	14
1960	Lionel Taylor, Den, AFL	92	1,235	13.4	12
	Raymond Berry, Balt, NFL	74	1,298	17.5	10
1961	Lionel Taylor, Den, AFL	100	1,176	11.8	4
	Jim Phillips, LA, NFL	78	1,092	14.0	5
1962	Lionel Taylor, Den, AFL	77	908	11.8	4
	Bobby Mitchell, Wash, NFL	72	1,384	19.2	11
1963	Lionel Taylor, Den, AFL	78	1,101	14.1	10
	Bobby Joe Conrad, St. Louis, NFL	73	967	13.2	10
1964	Charley Hennigan, Houston, AFL	101	1,546	15.3	8
	Johnny Morris, Chi, NFL	93	1,200	12.9	10
1965	Lionel Taylor, Den, AFL	85	1,131	13.3	6
	Dave Parks, SF, NFL	80	1,344	16.8	12
1966	Lance Alworth, SD, AFL	73	1,383	18.9	13
	Charley Taylor, Wash, NFL	72	1,119	15.5	12
1967	George Sauer, NY, AFL	75	1,189	15.9	6
	Charley Taylor, Wash, NFL	70	990	14.1	9
1968	Clifton McNeil, SF, NFL	71	994	14.0	7
	Lance Alworth, SD, AFL	68	1,312	19.3	10
1969	Dan Abramowicz, NO, NFL	73	1,015	13.9	7
	Lance Alworth, SD, AFL	64	1,003	15.7	4
1970	Dick Gordon, Chi, NFC	71	1,026	14.5	13
	Marlin Briscoe, Buff, AFC	57	1,036	18.2	8
1971	Fred Biletnikoff, Oak, AFC	61	929	15.2	9
	Bob Tucker, NY, NFC	59	791	13.4	4
1972	Harold Jackson, Phil, NFC	62	1,048	16.9	4
	Fred Biletnikoff, Oak, AFC	58	802	13.8	7
1973	Harold Carmichael, Phil, NFC	67	1,116	16.7	9
	Fred Willis, Hou, AFC	57	371	6.5	1
1974	Lydell Mitchell, Balt, AFC	72	544	7.6	2
	Charles Young, Phil, NFC	63	696	11.0	3
1975	Chuck Foreman, Minn, NFC	73	691	9.5	9
	Reggie Rucker, Clev, AFC	60	770	12.8	3
	Lydell Mitchell, Balt, AFC	60	544	9.1	4
1976	MacArthur Lane, KC, AFC	66	686	10.4	1
	Drew Pearson, Dal, NFC	58	806	13.9	6
1977	Lydell Mitchell, Balt, AFC	71	620	8.7	4
	Ahmad Rashad, Minn, NFC	51	681	13.4	2
1978	Rickey Young, Minn, NFC	88	704	8.0	5
	Steve Largent, Sea, AFC	71	1,168	16.5	8
1979	Joe Washington, Balt, AFC	82	750	9.1	3
	Ahmad Rashad, Minn, NFC	80	1,156	14.5	9
1980	Kellen Winslow, SD, AFC	89	1,290	14.5	9
	Earl Cooper, SF, NFC	83	567	6.8	4
1981	Kellen Winslow, SD, AFC	88	1,075	12.2	10
	Dwight Clark, SF, NFC	85	1,105	13.0	4
1982	Dwight Clark, SF, NFC	60	913	15.2	5
	Kellen Winslow, SD, AFC	54	721	13.4	6

†Most catches.

Pass Receiving† *(Cont.)*

Year	Player, Team	No.	Yds	Avg	TD
1983	Todd Christensen, LA, AFC	92	1,247	13.6	12
	Roy Green, StL, NFC	78	1,227	15.7	14
	Charlie Brown, Wash, NFC	78	1,225	15.7	8
	Earnest Gray, NY, NFC	78	1,139	14.6	5
1984	Art Monk, Wash, NFC	106	1,372	12.9	7
	Ozzie Newsome, Clev, AFC	89	1,001	11.2	5
1985	Roger Craig, SF, NFC	92	1,016	11.0	6
	Lionel James, SD, AFC	86	1,027	11.9	6
1986	Todd Christensen, LA, AFC	95	1,153	12.1	8
	Jerry Rice, SF, NFC	86	1,570	18.3	15
1987	J.T. Smith, StL Card, NFC	91	1,117	12.3	8
	Al Toon, NY, AFC	68	976	14.4	5
1988	Al Toon, NY, AFC	93	1,067	11.5	5
	Henry Ellard, LA, NFC	86	1,414	16.4	10
1989	Sterling Sharpe, GB, NFC	90	1,423	15.8	12
	Andre Reed, Buff, AFC	88	1,312	14.9	9
1990	Jerry Rice, SF, NFC	100	1,502	15.0	13
	Haywood Jeffires, Hou, AFC	74	1,048	14.2	8
	Drew Hill, Hou, AFC	74	1,019	13.8	5
1991	Haywood Jeffires, Hou, AFC	100	1,181	11.8	7
	Michael Irvin, Dal, NFC	93	1,523	16.4	8
1992	Sterling Sharpe, GB, NFC	108	1,461	13.5	13
	Haywood Jeffires, Hou, AFC	90	913	10.1	9
1993	Sterling Sharpe, GB, NFC	112	1,274	11.4	11
	Reggie Langhorne, Ind, AFC	85	1,038	12.2	3
1994	Cris Carter, Minn, NFC	122	1,256	10.3	7
	Ben Coates, NE, AFC	96	1,174	12.2	7
1995	Herman Moore, Det, NFC	123	1,686	13.7	14
	Carl Pickens, Cin, AFC	99	1,234	12.5	17
1996	Jerry Rice, SF, NFC	108	1,254	11.6	8
	Carl Pickens, Cin, AFC	100	1,180	11.8	12
1997	Herman Moore, Det, NFC	104	1,293	12.4	8
	Tim Brown, Oak, AFC	104	1,408	13.5	5
1998	Frank Sanders, Ariz, NFC	89	1,145	12.9	3
	O.J. McDuffie, Mia, AFC	90	1,050	11.7	7
1999	Muhsin Muhammad, Car, NFC	96	1,253	13.1	8
	Jimmy Smith, Jax, AFC	116	1,636	14.1	6
2000	Mushin Muhammad, Car, NFC	102	1,183	11.6	6
	Marvin Harrison, Ind, AFC	102	1,413	13.9	14
2001	Rod Smith, Den, AFC	113	1,343	11.9	11
	Keyshawn Johnson, TB, NFC	106	1,266	11.9	1
2002	Marvin Harrison, Ind, AFC	143	1,722	12.0	11
	Randy Moss, Minn, NFC	106	1,347	12.7	7
2003	LaDainian Tomlinson, SD, AFC	100	725	7.3	4
	Torry Holt, StL, NFC	117	1,696	14.5	12
2004	Tony Gonzalez, KC, AFC	102	1,258	12.3	7
	Joe Horn, NO, NFC	94	1,399	14.9	11
2005	Chad Johnson, Cin, AFC	97	1,432	14.8	9
	Steve Smith, Car, NFC	103	1,563	15.2	12
2006	Chad Johnson, Cin, AFC	87	1,369	15.7	7
	Roy Williams, Det, NFC	82	1,310	16.0	7

†Most catches.

Scoring

Year	Player, Team	TD	FG	PAT	TP
1932	Earl Clark, Portsmouth	6	3	10	55
1933	Ken Strong, NY	6	5	13	64
	Glenn Presnell, Ports	6	6	10	64
1934	Jack Manders, Chi	3	10	31	79
1935	Earl Clark, Det	6	1	16	55
1936	Earl Clark, Det	7	4	19	73
1937	Jack Manders, Chi	5	18	15	69
1938	Clarke Hinkle, GB	7	3	7	58
1939	Andy Farkas, Wash	11	0	2	68
1940	Don Hutson, GB	7	0	15	57
1941	Don Hutson, GB	12	1	20	95
1942	Don Hutson, GB	17	1	33	138
1943	Don Hutson, GB	12	3	36	117
1944	Don Hutson, GB	9	0	31	85
1945	Steve Van Buren, Phil	18	0	2	110
1946	Ted Fritsch, GB	10	9	13	100
1947	Pat Harder, Chicago Cards	7	7	39	102
1948	Pat Harder, Chicago Cards	6	7	53	110
1949	Pat Harder, Chicago Cards	8	3	45	102
	Gene Roberts, NY	17	0	0	102
1950	Doak Walker, Det	11	8	38	128
1951	Elroy Hirsch, LA	17	0	0	102
1952	Gordy Soltau, SF	7	6	34	94
1953	Gordy Soltau, SF	6	10	48	114
1954	Bobby Walston, Phil	11	4	36	114
1955	Doak Walker, Det	7	9	27	96
1956	Bobby Layne, Det	5	12	33	99
1957	Sam Baker, Wash	1	14	29	77
	Lou Groza, Clev	0	15	32	77
1958	Jim Brown, Clev	18	0	0	108
1959	Paul Hornung, GB	7	7	31	94
1960	Paul Hornung, GB, NFL	15	15	41	176
	Gene Mingo, Den, AFL	6	18	33	123
1961	Gino Cappelletti, Bos, AFL	8	17	48	147
	Paul Hornung, GB, NFL	10	15	41	146
1962	Gene Mingo, Den, AFL	4	27	32	137
	Jim Taylor, GB, NFL	19	0	0	114
1963	Gino Cappelletti, Bos, AFL	2	22	35	113
	Don Chandler, NY, NFL	0	18	52	106

Scoring *(Cont.)*

Year	Player, Team	TD	FG	PAT	TP
1964	Gino Cappelletti, Bos, AFL.....7	25	36	155
	Lenny Moore, Balt, NFL........20	0	0	120
1965	Gale Sayers, Chi, NFL..........22	0	0	132
	Gino Cappelletti, Bos, AFL.....9	17	27	132
1966	Gino Cappelletti, Bos, AFL.....6	16	35	119
	Bruce Gossett, LA, NFL 0	28	29	113
1967	Jim Bakken, StL, NFL 0	27	36	117
	George Blanda, Oak, AFL......0	20	56	116
1968	Jim Turner, NY, AFL 0	34	43	145
	Leroy Kelly, Clev, NFL 20	0	0	120
1969	Jim Turner, NY, AFL 0	32	33	129
	Fred Cox, Minn, NFL 0	26	43	121
1970	Fred Cox, Minn, NFC...............0	30	35	*125
	Jan Stenerud, KC, AFC 0	30	26	116
1971	Garo Yepremian, Mia, AFC.....0	28	33	117
	Curt Knight, Wash, NFC 0	29	27	114
1972	Chester Marcol, GB, NFC 0	33	29	128
	Bobby Howfield, NY AFC 0	27	40	121
1973	David Ray, LA, NFC................0	30	40	130
	Roy Gerela, Pitt, AFC 0	29	36	123
1974	Chester Marcol, GB, NFC 0	25	19	94
	Roy Gerela, Pitt, AFC 0	20	33	93
1975	O.J. Simpson, Buff, AFC 23	0	0	138
	Chuck Foreman, Minn, NFC ..22	0	0	132
1976	Toni Linhart, Balt, AFC............0	20	49	109
	Mark Moseley, Wash, NFC 0	22	31	97
1977	Errol Mann, Oak, AFC 0	20	39	99
	Walter Payton, Chi, NFC.......16	0	0	96
1978	Frank Corral, LA, NFC.............0	29	31	118
	Pat Leahy, NY, AFC 0	22	41	107
1979	John Smith, NE, AFC...............0	23	46	115
	Mark Moseley, Wash, NFC 0	25	39	114
1980	John Smith, NE, AFC...............0	26	51	129
	Ed Murray, Det, NFC 0	27	35	116
1981	Ed Murray, Det, NFC 0	25	46	121
	Rafael Septien, Dal, NFC 0	27	40	121
	Jim Breech, Cin, AFC 0	22	49	115
	Nick Lowery, KC, AFC............0	26	37	115
1982	Marcus Allen, LA, AFC 14	0	0	84
	Wendell Tyler, LA, NFC.........13	0	0	78
1983	Mark Moseley, Wash, NFC 0	33	62	161
	Gary Anderson, Pitt, AFC.......0	27	38	119
1984	Ray Wersching, SF, NFC 0	25	56	131
	Gary Anderson, Pitt, AFC.......0	24	45	117
1985	Kevin Butler, Chi, NFC............0	31	51	144
	Gary Anderson, Pitt, AFC.......0	33	40	139
1986	Tony Franklin, NE, AFC...........0	32	44	140
	Kevin Butler, Chi, NFC............0	28	36	120
1987	Jerry Rice, SF, NFC 23	0	0	138
	Jim Breech, Cin, AFC 0	24	25	97
1988	Scott Norwood, Buff, AFC 0	32	33	129
	Mike Cofer, SF, NFC 0	27	40	121
1989	Mike Cofer, SF, NFC 0	29	49	136
	David Treadwell, Den, AFC 0	27	39	120
1990	Nick Lowery, KC, AFC............0	34	37	139
	Chip Lohmiller, Wash, NFC 0	30	41	131
1991	Chip Lohmiller, Wash, NFC 0	31	56	149
	Pete Stoyanovich, Mia, AFC...0	31	28	121
1992	Pete Stoyanovich, Mia, AFC...0	30	34	124
	Morten Anderson, NO, NFC...0	29	33	120
	Chip Lohmiller, Wash, NFC 0	30	30	120
1993	Jeff Jaeger, Rai, AFC..............0	35	27	132
	Jason Hanson, Det, NFC........0	34	28	130
1994	John Carney, SD, AFC 0	34	33	135
	Fuad Reveiz, Minn, NFC 0	34	30	132
	Emmitt Smith, Dal, NFC.........22	0	0	132
1995	Emmitt Smith, Dal, NFC.........25	0	0	150
	Norm Johnson, Pitt, AFC........0	34	39	141
1996	John Kasay, Car, NFC 0	37	34	145
	Cary Blanchard, Ind, AFC 0	36	27	135
1997	Richie Cunningham,			
	Dal, NFC..............................0	34	24	126
	Mike Hollis, Jax, AFC 0	41	31	134
1998	Gary Anderson, Minn, NFC....0	35	59	164
	Steve Christie, Buff, AFC........0	33	41	140
1999	Jeff Wilkins, StL, NFC.............0	20	64	124
	Mike Vanderjagt, Ind, AFC 0	34	43	145
2000	Marshall Faulk, StL, NFC.......26	0	0	160
	Matt Stover, Balt, AFC 0	35	30	135
2001	Marshall Faulk, StL, NFC.......21	0	0	128
	Mike Vanderjagt, Ind, AFC 0	28	41	125
2002	Jay Feely. Atl, NFC 0	32	42	138
	Priest Holmes, KC, AFC 24	0	0	144
2003	Jeff Wilkins StL, NFC 0	39	46	163
	Priest Holmes, KC, AFC 27	0	0	162
2004	Adam Vinatieri, NE, AFC 0	31	48	141
	David Akers, Phil, NFC............0	27	41	122
2005	Shayne Graham, Cin, AFC 0	28	47	131
	Shaun Alexander, Sea, NFC ...28	0	0	168
2006	LaDainian Tomlinson. SD, AFC..31	0	0	186
	Robbie Gould, Chi, NFC...........0	32	47	143

Interceptions

Year	Player, Team	Int	Yds
1940	Clarence Parker, Brooklyn	6	146
	Kent Ryan, Det	6	65
	Don Hutson, GB	6	24
1941	Marshall Goldberg, Chicago Card	7	54
	Art Jones, Pitt	7	*35
1942	Clyde Turner, Chicago Bears	8	96
1943	Sammy Baugh, Wash	11	112
1944	Howard Livingston, NYG	9	172
1945	Ray Zimmerman, Phil	7	90
1946	Bill Dudley, Pittsburgh	10	242
1947	Frank Reagan, NYG	10	203
	Frank Seno, Bos	10	100
1948	Dan Sandifer, Wash	13	258
1949	Bob Nussbaumer, Chicago Car	12	157
1950	Orban Sanders, NY Yanks	13	199
1951	Otto Schnellbacher, NYG	11	194
1952	Dick Lane, LA	14	298
1953	Jack Christiansen, Det	12	238
1954	Dick Lane, Chicago Card	10	181
1955	Will Sherman, LA	11	101
1956	Lindon Crow, Chicago Card	11	170
1957	Milt Davis, Balt	10	219
	Jack Christiansen, Det	10	137
	Jack Butler, Pitt	10	85
1958	Jim Patton, NYG	11	183
1959	Dean Derby, Pitt	7	127
	Milt Davis, Balt	7	119
	Don Shinnick, Balt	7	70
1960	Goose Gonsoulin, Den, AFL	11	98
	Dave Baker, SF, NFL	10	96
	Jerry Norton, StL, NFL	10	96
1961	Billy Atkins, Buff, AFL	10	158
	Dick Lynch, NYG, NFL	9	60
1962	Lee Riley, NY Titans, AFL	11	122
	Willie Wood, GB, NFL	9	132
1963	Fred Glick, Hous, AFL	12	180
	Dick Lynch, NYG, NFL	9	251
	Roosevelt Taylor, Chi, NFL	9	172
1964	Dainard Paulson, NYJ, AFL	12	157
	Paul Krause, Wash, NFL	12	140
1965	W. K. Hicks, Hous, AFL	9	156
	Bobby Boyd, Balt, NFL	9	78
1966	Larry Wilson, StL, NFL	10	180
	Johnny Robinson, KC, AFL	10	136
	Bobby Hunt, KC, AFL	10	113
1967	Lem Barney, Det, NFL	10	232
	Dave Whitsell, NO, NFL	10	178
	Miller Farr, Hous, AFL	10	264
	Tom Janik, Buff, AFL	10	222
	Dick Westmoreland, Mia, AFL	10	127
1968	Dave Grayson, Oak, AFL	10	195
	Willie Williams, NYG, NFL	10	103
1969	Mel Renfro, Dal, NFL	10	118
	Emmitt Thomas, KC, AFL	9	146
1970	Johnny Robinson, KC, AFC	10	155
	Dick LeBeau, Det, NFC	9	96
1971	Bill Bradley, Phil, NFC	11	248
	Ken Houston, Hou, AFC	9	220
1972	Bill Bradley, Phil, NFC	9	73
	Mike Sensibaugh, KC, AFC	8	65
1973	Dick Anderson, Mia, AFC	8	163
	Mike Wagner, Pitt, AFC	8	134
	Bobby Bryant, Minn, NFC	7	105
1974	Emmitt Thomas, KC, AFC	12	214
	Ray Brown, Atl, NFC	8	164
1975	Mel Blount, Pitt, AFC	11	121
	Paul Krause, Minn, NFC	10	201
1976	Monte Jackson, LA, NFC	10	173
	Ken Riley, Cin, AFC	9	141
1977	Lyle Blackwood, Balt, AFC	10	163
	Rolland Lawrence, Atl, NFC	7	138
1978	Thom Darden, Clev, AFC	10	200
	Ken Stone, StL, NFC	9	139
	Willie Buchanon, GB, NFC	9	93
1979	Mike Reinfeldt, Hou, AFC	12	205
	Lemar Parrish, Wash, NFC	9	65
1980	Lester Hayes, Oak, AFC	13	273
	Nolan Cromwell, LA, NFC	8	140
1981	Everson Walls, Dal, NFC	11	133
	John Harris, Sea, AFC	10	155
1982	Everson Walls, Dal, NFC	7	61
	Ken Riley, Cin, AFC	5	88
	Bobby Jackson, NYJ, AFC	5	84
	Dwayne Woodruff, Pitt, AFC	5	53
	Donnie Shell, Pitt, AFC	5	27
1983	Mark Murphy, Wash, NFC	9	127
	Ken Riley, Cin, AFC	8	89
	Vann McElroy, LA, AFC	8	68
1984	Ken Easley, Sea, AFC	10	126
	Tom Flynn, GB, NFC	9	106
1985	Everson Walls, Dal, NFC	9	31
	Albert Lewis, KC, AFC	8	59
	Eugene Daniel, Ind, AFC	8	53
1986	Ronnie Lott, SF, NFC	10	134
	Deron Cherry, KC, AFC	9	150
1987	Barry Wilburn, Wash, NFC	9	135
	Mike Prior, Ind, AFC	6	57
	Mark Kelso, Buff, AFC	6	25
	Keith Bostic, Hou, AFC	6	-14
1988	Scott Case, Atl, NFC	10	47
	Erik McMillan, NYJ, AFC	8	168
1989	Felix Wright, Clev, AFC	9	91
	Eric Allen, Phil, NFC	8	38
1990	Mark Carrier, Chi, NFC	10	39
	Richard Johnson, Hou, AFC	8	100
1991	Ronnie Lott, LA, AFC	8	52
	Ray Crockett, Det, NFC	6	141
	Deion Sanders, Atl, NFC	6	119
	Aeneas Williams, Phoenix, NFC	6	60
	Tim McKyer, Atl, NFC	6	24
1992	Henry Jones, Buff, AFC	8	263
	Audray McMillian, Minn, NFC	8	157
1993	Eugene Robinson, Sea, AFC	9	80
	Nate Odomes, Buff, AFC	9	65
	Deion Sanders, Atl, NFC	7	91
1994	Eric Turner, Clev, AFC	9	199
	Aeneas Williams, Ariz, NFC	9	89

Interceptions *(Cont.)*

Year	Player, Team	Int	Yds	Year	Player, Team	Int	Yds
1995	Orlando Thomas, Minn, NFC	9	108	2001	Ronde Barber, TB, NFC	10	86
	Willie Williams, Pitt, AFC	7	122		Anthony Henry, Clev, AFC	10	177
1996	Tyrone Braxton, Den, AFC	9	128	2002	Rod Woodson, Oak, AFC	8	225
	Keith Lyle, StL, NFC	9	152		Brian Kelly, TB, NFC	8	68
1997	Ryan McNeil, StL, NFC	9	127	2003	Brian Russell, Minn, NFC	9	185
	Mark McMillian, KC, AFC	8	274		Tony Parrish, SFo, NFC	9	202
	Darryl Williams, Sea, AFC	8	172		Patrick Surtain, Mia, AFC	7	59
1998	Ty Law, NE, AFC	9	133		Ed Reed, Balt, AFC	7	132
	Kwamie Lassiter, Ariz, NFC	8	80		Marcus Coleman, Hou, AFC	7	95
1999	Rod Woodson, Balt, AFC	7	195	2004	Ed Reed, Balt, AFC	9	358
	Sam Madison, Mia, AFC	7	164		Chris Gamble, Car, NFC	6	15
	James Hasty, KC, AFC	7	98		Ken Lucas, Sea, NFC	6	46
	Donnie Abraham, TB, NFC	7	115	2005	Ty Law, NYJ, AFC	10	195
	Troy Vincent, Phil, NFC	7	91		Deltha O'Neal, Cin, AFC	10	103
2000	Darren Sharper, GB, NFC	9	109		Darren Sharper, Minn, NFC	9	276
	Samari Rolle, Tenn, AFC	7	140	2006	Champ Bailey, Den, AFC	10	162
	Brian Walker, Mia, AFC	7	80		Asante Samuel, NE, AFC	10	120
					Walt Harris, SF, NFC	8	84
					Charles Woodson, GB, NFC	8	61

Sacks*

Year	Player, Team	Sacks	Year	Player, Team	Int	Yds
1982	Doug Martin, Minn, NFC	11.5	1995	Bryce Paup, Buff, AFC		17.5
	Jesse Baker, Hou, AFC	7.5		William Fuller, Phil, NFC		13.0
1983	Mark Gastineau, NYJ, AFC	19.0		Wayne Martin, NO, NFC		13.0
	Fred Dean, SF, NFC	17.5	1996	Kevin Greene, Car, NFC		14.5
1984	Mark Gastineau, NYJ, AFC	22.0		Michael McCrary, Sea, AFC		13.5
	Richard Dent, Chi, NFC	17.5		Bruce Smith, Buff, AFC		13.5
1985	Richard Dent, Chi, NFC	17.0	1997	John Randle, Minn, NFC		15.5
	Andre Tippett, NE, AFC	16.5		Bruce Smith, Buff, AFC		14.0
1986	Lawrence Taylor, NYG, NFC	20.5	1998	Michael Sinclair, Sea, AFC		16.5
	Sean Jones, LA, AFC	15.5		Reggie White, GB, NFC		16.0
1987	Reggie White, Phil, NFC	21.0	1999	Kevin Carter, StL, NFC		17.0
	Andre Tippett, NE, AFC	12.5		Jevon Kearse, Tenn, AFC		14.5
1988	Reggie White, Phil, NFC	18.0	2000	La'Roi Glover, NO, NFC		17.0
	G. Townsend, LA, AFC	11.5		Trace Armstrong, Mia, AFC		16.5
1989	Chris Doleman, Minn, NFC	21.0	2001	Michael Strahan, NYG, NFC		22.5
	Lee Williams, SD, AFC	14.0		Peter Boulware, Balt, AFC		15.0
1990	Derrick Thomas, KC, AFC	20.0	2002	Jason Taylor, Mia, AFC		18.5
	Charles Haley, SF, NFC	16.0		Simeon Rice, TB, NFC		15.5
1991	Pat Swilling, NO, NFC	17.0	2003	Michael Strahan, NYG, NFC		18.5
	William Fuller, Hou, AFC	15.0		Adewale Ogunleye, Mia, AFC		15.0
1992	Clyde Simmons, Phil, NFC	19.0	2004	Dwight Freeney, Ind, AFC		16.0
	Leslie O'Neal, SD, AFC	17.0		Bertrand Berry, Ariz, NFC		14.5
1993	Neil Smith, KC, AFC	15.0	2005	Derrick Burgess, Oak, AFC		16.0
	Renaldo Turnbull, NO, NFC	13.0		Osi Umenyiora, NYG, NFC		14.5
	Reggie White, GB, NFC	13.0	2006	Shawne Merriman, SD, AFC		17.0
1994	Kevin Greene, Pitt, AFC	14.0		Aaron Kampman, GB, NFC		15.5
	Ken Harvey, Wash, NFC	13.5				
	John Randle, Minn, NFC	13.5				

*Sacks were not kept as an official NFL statistic until 1982.

Pro Bowl Alltime Results

Date	Result	Date	Result	Date	Result
1-15-39	NY Giants 13, Pro All-Stars 10	1-19-64	AFL West 27, East 24	2-6-83	NFC 20, AFC 19
1-14-40	Green Bay 16, NFL All-Stars 7	1-10-65	NFL West 34, East 14	1-29-84	NFC 45, AFC 3
12-29-40	Chi Bears 28, NFL All-Stars 14	1-16-65	AFL West 38, East 14	1-27-85	AFC 22, NFC 14
1-4-42	Chi Bears 35, NFL All-Stars 24	1-15-66	AFL All-Stars 30, Buffalo 19	2-2-86	NFC 28, AFC 24
12-27-42	NFL All-Stars 17, Washington 14	1-15-66	NFL East 36, West 7	2-1-87	AFC 10, NFC 6
1-14-51	A. Conf. 28, N. Conf. 27	1-21-67	AFL East 30, West 23	2-7-88	AFC 15, NFC 6
1-12-52	N. Conf. 30, A. Conf. 13	1-22-67	NFL East 20, West 10	1-29-89	NFC 34, AFC 3
1-10-53	N. Conf. 27, A. Conf. 7	1-21-68	AFL East 25, West 24	2-4-90	NFC 27, AFC 21
1-17-54	East 20, West 9	1-21-68	NFL West 38, East 20	2-3-91	AFC 23, NFC 21
1-16-55	West 26, East 19	1-19-69	AFL West 38, East 25	2-2-92	NFC 21, AFC 15
1-15-56	East 31, West 30	1-19-69	NFL West 10, East 7	2-7-93	AFC 23, NFC 20
1-13-57	West 19, East 10	1-17-70	AFL West 26, East 3	2-6-94	NFC 17, AFC 3
1-12-58	West 26, East 7	1-18-70	NFL West 16, East 13	2-5-95	AFC 41, NFC 13
1-11-59	East 28, West 21	1-24-71	NFC 27, AFC 6	2-4-96	NFC 20, AFC 13
1-17-60	West 38, East 21	1-23-72	AFC 26, NFC 13	2-2-97	AFC 26, NFC 23
1-15-61	West 35, East 31	1-21-73	AFC 33, NFC 28	2-1-98	AFC 29, NFC 24
1-7-62	AFL West 47, East 27	1-20-74	AFC 15, NFC 13	2-7-99	AFC 23, NFC 10
1-14-62	NFL West 31, East 30	1-20-75	NFC 17, AFC 10	2-6-00	NFC 51, AFC 31
1-13-63	AFL West 21, East 14	1-26-76	NFC 23, AFC 20	2-4-01	AFC 38, NFC 17
1-13-63	NFL East 30, West 20	1-17-77	AFC 24, NFC 14	2-10-02	AFC 38, NFC 30
1-12-64	NFL West 31, East 17	1-23-78	NFC 14, AFC 13	2-2-03	AFC 45, NFC 20
		1-29-79	NFC 13, AFC 7	2-8-04	NFC 55, AFC 52
		1-27-80	NFC 37, AFC 27	2-13-05	AFC 38, NFC 27
		2-1-81	NFC 21, AFC 7	2-12-06	NFC 23, AFC 17
		1-31-82	AFC 16, NFC 13	2-10-07	AFC 31, NFC 28

Chicago All-Star Game* Results

Date	Result (Attendance)	Date	Result (Attendance)
8-31-34	Chi Bears 0, All-Stars 0 (79,432)	8-10-56	Cleveland 26, All-Stars 0 (75,000)
8-29-35	Chi Bears 5, All-Stars 0 (77,450)	8-9-57	NY Giants 22, All-Stars 12 (75,000)
9-2-36	All-Stars 7, Detroit 7 (76,000)	8-15-58	All-Stars 35, Detroit 19 (70,000)
9-1-37	All-Stars 6, Green Bay 0 (84,560)	8-14-59	Baltimore 29, All-Stars 0 (70,000)
8-31-38	All-Stars 28, Washington 16 (74,250)	8-12-60	Baltimore 32, All-Stars 7 (70,000)
8-30-39	NY Giants 9, All-Stars 0 (81,456)	8-4-61	Philadelphia 28, All-Stars 14 (66,000)
8-29-40	Green Bay 45, All-Stars 28 (84,567)	8-3-62	Green Bay 42, All-Stars 20 (65,000)
8-28-41	Chi Bears 37, All-Stars 13 (98,203)	8-2-63	All-Stars 20, Green Bay 17 (65,000)
8-28-42	Chi Bears 21, All-Stars 0 (101,100)	8-7-64	Chicago 28, All-Stars 17 (65,000)
8-25-43	All-Stars 27, Washington 7 (48,471)	8-6-65	Cleveland 24, All-Stars 16 (68,000)
8-30-44	Chi Bears 24, All-Stars 21 (48,769)	8-5-66	Green Bay 38, All-Stars 0 (72,000)
8-30-45	Green Bay 19, All-Stars 7 (92,753)	8-4-67	Green Bay 27, All-Stars 0 (70,934)
8-23-46	All-Stars 16, Los Angeles 0 (97,380)	8-2-68	Green Bay 34, All-Stars 17 (69,917)
8-22-47	All-Stars 16, Chi Bears 0 (105,840)	8-1-69	NY Jets 26, All-Stars 24 (74,208)
8-20-48	Chi Cardinals 28, All-Stars 0 (101,220)	7-31-70	Kansas City 24, All-Stars 3 (69,940)
8-12-49	Philadelphia 38, All-Stars 0 (93,780)	7-30-71	Baltimore 24, All-Stars 17 (52,289)
8-11-50	All-Stars 17, Philadelphia 7 (88,885)	7-28-72	Dallas 20, All-Stars 7 (54,162)
8-17-51	Cleveland 33, All-Stars 0 (92,180)	7-27-73	Miami 14, All-Stars 3 (54,103)
8-15-52	Los Angeles 10, All-Stars 7 (88,316)	1974	No game
8-14-53	Detroit 24, All-Stars 10 (93,818)	8-1-75	Pittsburgh 21, All-Stars 14 (54,562)
8-13-54	Detroit 31, All-Stars 6 (93,470)	7-23-76	Pittsburgh 24, All-Stars 0 (52,895)
8-12-55	All-Stars 30, Cleveland 27 (75,000)		

*Discontinued.

Most Career Wins

Coach	Yrs	Teams	Regular Season				Career			
			W	L	T	Pct	W	L	T	Pct
Don Shula 33		Colts, Dolphins	328	156	6	.676	347	173	6	.665
George Halas..........40		Bears	318	148	31	.671	324	151	31	.671
Tom Landry 29		Cowboys	250	162	6	.605	270	178	6	.601
Curly Lambeau 33		Packers, Cardinals, Redskins	226	132	22	.624	229	134	22	.623
Chuck Noll 23		Steelers	193	148	1	.566	209	156	1	.572
†M. Schottenheimer...20		Browns, Chiefs, Redskins, Chargers	200	126	1	.613	205	139	1	.596
Dan Reeves 23		Broncos, Giants, Falcons	190	165	2	.535	201	174	2	.536
Chuck Knox 22		Rams, Bills, Seahawks	186	147	1	.558	193	158	1	.550
†Bill Parcells 18		Giants, Patriots, Jets, Cowboys	172	130	1	.569	183	138	1	.570
Paul Brown..............21		Browns, Bengals	166	100	6	.621	170	108	6	.609
Bud Grant 18		Vikings	158	96	5	.620	168	108	5	.607
†Joe Gibbs 14		Redskins	145	87	0	.625	162	93	0	.635
†Bill Cowher............14		Steelers	149	90	1	.623	161	99	1	.619
†Mike Holmgren......14		Packers, Seahawks	147	93	0	.613	159	103	0	.607
Marv Levy 17		Chiefs, Bills	143	112	0	.561	154	120	0	.562
Steve Owen.............23		Giants	151	100	17	.595	153	108	17	.581
Hank Stram 17		Chiefs, Saints	131	97	10	.571	136	100	10	.573
Weeb Ewbank........20		Colts, Jets	130	129	7	.502	134	130	7	.507
Mike Ditka 14		Bears, Saints	121	95	0	.560	127	101	0	.557
Jim Mora 15		Saints, Colts	125	106	0	.541	125	112	0	.527

Top Winning Percentages

	W	L	T	Pct		W	L	T	Pct
Vince Lombardi 105		35	6	.740	George Seifert.................124		67	0	.650
John Madden 112		39	7	.731	†Joe Gibbs.....................162		93	0	.635
George Allen 118		54	5	.681	Curly Lambeau................229		134	22	.623
George Halas.................324		151	31	.671	†Bill Cowher 161		99	1	.619
Don Shula.....................347		173	6	.665	Paul Brown 170		108	6	.609

Note: Minimum 100 victories.

†Active in 2006.

Year	Player/ Team	Position	Year	Player/ Team	Position
1938	Mel Hein, NYG (NFL)	C	1955	Otto Graham, Clev (UP, TSN)	QB
1939	Parker Hall, Clev (NFL)	HB		Harlon Hill, Chi Bears (NEA)	E
1940	Ace Parker, Brooklyn (NFL)	QB	1956	Frank Gifford, NYG (UP, NEA, TSN)	HB
1941	Don Hutson, GB (NFL)	E	1957	Y.A. Tittle, SF (UP)	QB
1942	Don Hutson, GB (NFL)	E		Jim Brown, Clev (AP, TSN)	FB
1943	Sid Luckman, Chi Bears (NFL)	QB		John Unitas, Balt (NEA)	QB
1944	Frank Sinkwich, Det (NFL)	HB	1958	Jim Brown, Clev (UP, AP, NEA, TSN)	FB
1945	Bob Waterfield, Clev (NFL)	HB	1959	John Unitas, Balt (UP, MCP, TSN)	QB
1946	Bill Dudley, Pitt (NFL)	HB		Charley Conerly, NYG (AP, NEA)	QB
	Glenn Dobbs, Brooklyn (AAFC)	HB	1960	Norm Van Brocklin, Phil, NFL (UP, AP, NEA, TSN, MCP)	QB
1947	No Selection (NFL)			Joe Schmidt, Det, NFL (UP- tie)	LB
	Otto Graham, Clev (AAFC)	QB		Abner Haynes, Dal Texans, AFL (UP, TSN)	HB
1948	No Selection (NFL)		1961	Paul Hornung, GB, NFL (UP, AP, TSN, MCP)	HB
	Otto Graham, Clev (AAFC-tie)	QB		Y.A. Tittle, NYG, NFL (NEA)	QB
	Frankie Albert, SF (AAFC-tie)	QB		George Blanda, Hous, AFL (UP, TSN)	QB
1949	No Selection (NFL)		1962	Y.A. Tittle, NYG, NFL (UP, TSN)	QB
1950	No Selection (NFL)			Jim Taylor, GB, NFL (AP, NEA)	FB
1951	Otto Graham, Clev (UP)	QB		Andy Robustelli, NYG, NFL (MCP)	DE
1952	No Selection (NFL)			Cookie Gilchrist, Buff, AFL (UP)	FB
1953	Otto Graham, Clev (UP)	QB		Len Dawson, Dal Texans, AFL (TSN)	QB
1954	Joe Perry, SF (UP)	FB	1963	Jim Brown, Clev, NFL (UP, NEA tie, MCP)	FB
	Lou Groza, Clev (TSN)	OT/K		Y.A. Tittle, NYG, NFL (AP, NEA tie, TSN)	QB
				Lance Alworth, SD, AFL (UP)	WR
				Clem Daniels, Oak, AFL (TSN)	HB

Year	Player/ Team	Position	Year	Player/ Team	Position
1964	Johnny Unitas, Balt, NFL (UP, AP, TSN, MCP)	QB		Eric Dickerson, LA Rams (TSN)	RB
	Lenny Moore, Balt, NFL (NEA)	HB		John Riggins, Washington (MCP)	RB
	Gino Cappelletti, Boston, AFL (UP, TSN)	WR	1984	Dan Marino, Miami (PFWAA, AP, NEA, MCP, TSN)	QB
1965	Jim Brown, Clev, NFL (UP, AP, TSN, NEA)	FB	1985	Marcus Allen, LA Raiders (PFWAA, AP, TSN)	RB
	Pete Retzlaff, Phil, NFL (MCP)	TE		Walter Payton, Chi Bears (NEA, MCP)	RB
	Jack Kemp, Buff, AFL (UP)	QB	1986	Lawrence Taylor, NYG (PFWAA, AP, MCP, TSN)	LB
	Paul Lowe, SD, AFL (TSN)	RB		Phil Simms, NYG (NEA)	QB
1966	Bart Starr, GB, NFL (UP, AP, NEA, TSN)	QB	1987	Jerry Rice, SF (PFWAA, NEA, MCP, TSN)	WR
	Don Meredith, Dal, NFL (MCP)	QB		John Elway, Den (AP)	QB
	Jim Nance, Boston, AFL (UP, AP, TSN)	FB	1988	Boomer Esiason, Cin (PFWAA, AP, TSN)	QB
1967	Johnny Unitas, Balt, NFL (UP, AP, NEA, TSN, MCP)	QB		Roger Craig, SF (NEA)	RB
	Daryl Lamonica, Oak, AFL (UP, AP, TSN)	QB		Randall Cunningham, Phil (MCP)	QB
1968	Earl Morrall, Balt, NFL (UP, AP, NEA, TSN, PFW)	QB	1989	Joe Montana, SF (PFWAA, AP, NEA, MCP, TSN)	QB
	Leroy Kelly, Clev, AFL (MCP)	HB	1990	Randall Cunningham, Phil (PFWAA)	QB
	Joe Namath, NY Jets, AFL (UP, TSN, PFW)	QB		Joe Montana, SF (AP)	QB
1969	Roman Gabriel, LA Rams, NFL (UP, AP, NEA, MCP, TSN, PFW)	QB		Jerry Rice, SF (TSN)	WR
	Daryle Lamonica, Oak, AFL (UP, TSN, PFW)	QB	1991	Thurman Thomas, Buff (PFWAA, AP, TSN)	RB
	Joe Namath, NY Jets, AFL (AP)	QB		Barry Sanders, Det (MCP)	RB
1970	John Brodie, SF (AP, NEA)	QB	1992	Steve Young, SF (PFWAA, AP, MCP, TSN)	QB
	George Blanda, Oak (MCP)	QB/K	1993	Emmitt Smith, Dal (PFWAA, AP, MCP, TSN)	RB
1971	Alan Page, Minn (AP)	DT	1994	Steve Young, SF (PFWAA, AP, MCP, TSN)	QB
	Bob Griese, Miami (NEA)	QB	1995	Brett Favre, GB (PFWAA, AP, MCP, TSN)	QB
	Roger Staubach, Dal (MCP)	QB	1996	Brett Favre, GB (PFWAA, AP, MCP, TSN)	QB
1972	Larry Brown, Washington (AP, NEA, MCP)	RB	1997	Brett Favre, GB (AP – tie)	QB
1973	O.J. Simpson, Buff (AP, NEA, MCP)	RB		Barry Sanders, Det (PFWAA, AP (tie), MCP, TSN)	RB
1974	Ken Stabler, Oak (AP, NEA)	QB	1998	Terrell Davis, Den (PFWAA, AP, TSN)	RB
	Merlin Olsen, LA Rams (MCP)	DT		Randall Cunningham, Minn (MCP)	QB
1975	Fran Tarkenton, Minn (PFWA, AP, NEA, MCP)	QB	1999	Kurt Warner, StL (AP, PFWAA, MCP)	QB
1976	Bert Jones, Balt (PFWA, AP, NEA)	QB	2000	Marshall Faulk, StL (AP, PFWAA)	RB
	Ken Stabler, Oak (MCP)	QB		Rich Gannon, Oak (MCP)	QB
1977	Walter Payton, Chi (PFWA, AP, NEA)	RB	2001	Kurt Warner, StL (AP)	QB
	Bob Griese, Miami (MCP)	QB		Marshall Faulk, StL (PFWAA, MCP, TSN)	RB
1978	Earl Campbell, Hous (PFWA, NEA)	RB	2002	Rich Gannon, Oak (AP)	QB
	Terry Bradshaw, Pitt (AP, MCP)	QB	2003	Peyton Manning, Ind (AP - tie)	QB
1979	Earl Campbell, Hous (PFWA, AP, NEA, MCP)	RB		Steve McNair, Tenn (AP - tie)	QB
1980	Brian Sipe, Clev (PFWA, AP, TSN)	QB	2004	Peyton Manning, Ind (AP)	QB
	Earl Campbell, Hous (NEA)	RB	2005	Shaun Alexander, Sea (AP)	RB
	Ron Jaworski, Phil (MCP)	QB	2006	LaDainian Tomlinson, SD (AP)	RB
1981	Ken Anderson, Cin (PFWA, AP, NEA, TSN, MCP)	QB			
1982	Dan Fouts, SD (PFWA, NEA)	QB			
	Mark Moseley, Washington (AP, TSN)	K			
	Joe Theismann, Washington (MCP)	QB			
1983	Joe Theismann, Washington (PFWAA, AP, NEA)	QB			

NOTE: AP-Associated Press, UP-United Press, PFW-*Pro Football Weekly*, TSN-*The Sporting News*, PFWAA-Pro Football Writers Association of America, PFWA-Pro Football Writers of America, MCP-Maxwell Club of Philadelphia, NEA-Newspaper Enterprise Association.

The NFL began awarding its MVP award, the Joe F. Carr Trophy (Carr was league president from 1921-39), in 1938, and continued to do so until 1946. Since that time, the NFL's Most Valuable Players and Players of the Year have been named by a variety of sources, among them, the United Press, the Associated Press, the Maxwell Club of Philadelphia, and the Pro Football Writers Association of America as well as magazines such as *Pro Football Weekly* and *The Sporting News.*

Year	Player/ Team	Position
1955	Alan Ameche, Balt (UP, TSN)	FB
1956	Lenny Moore, Balt (UP)	HB
	J.C. Caroline, Chi Bears (TSN)	DB
1957	Jim Brown, Clev (UP, AP, TSN)	FB
1958	Jimmy Orr, Pitt (UP, AP)	OE
	Bobby Mitchell, Cleveland (TSN)	HB
1959	Nick Pietrosante, Det (AP, TSN)	FB
	Boyd Dowler, GB (UP)	OE
1960	Gail Cogdill, Det, NFL (AP, UP, TSN)	OE
	Abner Haynes, Dal Texans, AFL (UP, TSN)	HB
1961	Mike Ditka, Chi Bears, NFL (AP, UP, TSN)	OE
	Earl Faison, SD, AFL (UP, TSN)	DE
1962	Ronnie Bull, Chi Bears, NFL (AP, UP, TSN)	HB
	Curtis McClinton, Dal, AFL (UP, TSN)	FB
1963	Paul Flatley, Minn, NFL (AP, UP, TSN)	OE
	Billy Joe, Den, AFL (UP, TSN)	FB
1964	Charley Taylor, Wash, NFL (AP, UP, TSN, NEA)	HB
	Matt Snell, NYJ, AFL (UP, TSN)	FB
1965	Gale Sayers, Chi, NFL (AP, UP, TSN, NEA)	HB
	Joe Namath, NYJ, AFL (UP, TSN)	QB
1966	Johnny Roland, StL, NFL (UP)	HB
	Tommy Nobis, Atl, NFL (AP, TSN, NEA)	LB
	Bobby Burnett, Buff, AFL (UP, TSN)	HB
1967	Mel Farr, Det, NFL (AP-Off, UP, TSN, NEA)	HB
	Lem Barney, Det NFL (AP-Def)	CB
	George Webster, Hous, AFL (UP)	LB
	Dickie Post, SD, AFL (TSN)	HB
1968	Earl McCullouch, Det, NFL (AP-Off, UP, TSN, NEA)	OE
	Claude Humphrey NFL (AP-Def)	DE
	Paul Robinson, Cin, AFL (UP, TSN)	HB
1969	Calvin Hill, Dal, NFL (AP-Off, UP, TSN, NEA)	HB
	Joe Greene NFL (AP-Def)	DT
	Greg Cook, Cin, AFL (UP)	QB
	Carl Garrett, Boston, AFL (TSN)	HB
1970	Raymond Chester, Oak (NEA)	TE
	Dennis Shaw Buff (AP-Off, UP-AFC)	QB
	Bruce Taylor, DB SF (AP-Def, UP-NFC)	DB
1971	Jim Plunkett NE (UP-AFC)	QB
	John Brockington GB (AP-Off, UP-NFC)	RB
	Isiah Robertson, SF (AP-Def)	LB
1972	Franco Harris, Pitt (AP-Off, PFW, UP-AFC)	RB
	Chester Marcol, GB (UP-NFC)	PK
	Willie Buchanan, GB (AP-Def)	CB
1973	Chuck Foreman, Minn (AP-Off, PFW)	RB
	Wally Chambers, Chi (AP-Def)	DT
	Bobbie Clark, Cin (UP-AFC)	RB
	Charle Young Phil (UP-NFC)	TE
1974	Don Woods, SD (AP-Off, PFW, UP-AFC)	RB
	John Hicks, NYG (UP-NFC)	G
	Jack Lambert, Pitt (AP-Def)	LB
1975	Steve Bartkowski, Atl (PFW)	QB
	Robert Brazile, Hous (AP-Def, UP-AFC)	LB
	Mike Thomas, Wash (AP-Off, UP-NFC)	RB
1976	Mike Haynes, DB NE (AP-Def, UP-AFC)	DB
	Sammy White, Minn (AP-Off, UP-NFC)	WR
1977	Tony Dorsett, Dal (NEA, AP-Off, UP-NFC)	RB
	A.J. Duhe, Mia (AP-Def, UP-AFC)	DE
1978	Earl Campbell, Hous Oilers (NEA, PFWA, AP-Off, UP-AFC)	RB
	Al "Bubba" Baker, Det (AP-Def, UP-NFC)	DE
1979	Ottis Anderson, StL Card (NEA, PFWA, AP-Off, UP-NFC)	RB
	Jerry Butler, Buff (UP-AFC)	WR
	Jim Haslett, Buff (AP-Def)	LB
1980	Billy Sims, Det (NEA, TSN, PFWA, AP-Off, UP-NFC)	RB
	Joe Cribbs Buff (UP-AFC)	RB
	Buddy Curry, Atl (AP-Def tie)	LB
	Al Richardson, Atl (AP-Def tie)	LB
1981	Lawrence Taylor, NYG (NEA, AP-Def)	LB
	George Rogers, NO (TSN, PFWA, AP-Off, UP-NFC)	RB
	Joe Delaney, KC (UP-AFC)	RB
1982	Marcus Allen, LA Raiders (NEA, TSN, PFWA, AP-Off, UP-AFC)	RB
	Jim McMahon, Chi (UP-NFC)	QB
	Chip Banks, Cle (AP-Def)	LB
1983	Eric Dickerson, LA Rams (NEA, PFWA, AP-Off, UP-NFC)	RB
	Dan Marino, Mia (TSN)	QB
	Curt Warner, Sea (UP-AFC)	RB
	Vernon Maxwell, Balt (AP-Def)	LB
1984	Louis Lipps, Pitt (NEA, TSN, PFWA, AP-Off, UP-AFC)	WR
	Paul McFadden, Phil (UP-NFC)	PK
	Bill Maas, KC (AP-Def)	DT
1985	Eddie Brown, Cin (NEA, TSN, AP-Off, PFWA)	WR
	Kevin Mack, Clev (UP-AFC)	RB
	Jerry Rice, SF (UP-NFC)	WR
	Duane Bickett, Ind (AP-Def)	LB
1986	Reuben Mayes, NO (NEA, TSN, PFWA, AP-Off, UP-NFC)	RB
	Leslie O'Neal, SD (AP-Def, UP-AFC)	DE
1987	Shane Conlan, Buff (PFWA, AP-Def, UP-AFC)	LB
	Bo Jackson, LA Raiders (NEA)	RB
	Robert Awalt, StL Card (TSN, UP-NFC)	TE
	Troy Stradford, Mia (AP-Off)	RB
1988	John Stephens, NE (NEA, AP-Off, PFWA)	RB
	Keith Jackson, Phil (TSN, UP-NFC)	TE
	Eric McMillan, NYJ (AP-Def)	S
1989	Barry Sanders, Det (NEA, TSN, PFWA, AP-Off, UP-NFC)	RB
	Derrick Thomas KC (AP-Def, UP-AFC)	LB
1990	Mark Carrier, Chi (PFWA, UP-NFC, AP-Def)	S
	Emmitt Smith, Dal (AP-Off)	RB
	Richmond Webb, Mia (TSN, UP-AFC)	OT
1991	Mike Croel, Den (PFWA, TSN, AP-Def, UP-AFC)	LB
	Lawrence Dawsey TB (UP-NFC)	WR
	Leonard Russell, NE (AP-Off)	RB
1992	Dale Carter, KC (PFWA, AP-Def, UP-AFC)	CB
	Carl Pickens, Cin (AP-Off)	WR
	Santana Dotson, TB (TSN)	DE
	Robert Jones, Dal (UP-NFC)	LB
1993	Jerome Bettis, LA Rams (PFWA, TSN, AP-Off, UP-NFC)	RB
	Rick Mirer, Sea (UP-AFC)	QB
	Dana Stubblefield, SF (AP-Def)	DT
1994	Marshall Faulk, Ind (PFWA, TSN, AP-Off, UP-AFC)	RB
	Bryant Young, SF (UP-NFC)	DT
	Tim Bowens, Mia (AP-Def)	DT

Year	Player/ Team	Position
1995	Curtis Martin, NE (PFWA, TSN, AP-Off, UP-AFC)	RB
	Rashaan Salaam Chi (UP-NFC)	RB
	Hugh Douglas, NYJ (AP-Def)	DE
1996	Eddie George, Tenn (AP, PFWA, AP-Off, TSN)	RB
	Terry Glenn, NE (UP-AFC)	WR
	Simeon Rice, Ariz (AP-Def, UP-NFC)	DE
1997	Warrick Dunn, TB (PFWA, AP-Off, TSN)	RB
	Peter Boulware, Balt (AP-Def)	LB
1998	Randy Moss, Minn (PFWA, AP-Off, TSN)	WR
	Charles Woodson LA Raiders (AP-Def)	CB
1999	Edgerrin James, Ind (AP-Off, TSN)	RB
	Jevon Kearse, Tenn (AP-Def)	DE
2000	Mike Anderson, Den (AP-Off, TSN)	RB
	Brian Urlacher, Chi (AP-Def)	LB

Year	Player/ Team	Position
2001	Anthony Thomas, Chi (AP-Off)	RB
	Kendrell Bell, Pitt (AP-Def)	LB
2002	Clinton Ports, Den (AP-Off)	RB
	Julius Peppers, Car (AP-Def)	DE
2003	Anquan Boldin, Ariz (AP-Off)	WR
	Terrell Suggs, Bal (AP-Def)	LB
2004	Ben Roethlisberger, Pitt (AP-Off)	QB
	Jonathan Vilma, NYJ (AP-Def)	LB
2005	Carnell Williams, TB (AP-Off)	RB
	Shawne Merriman, SD (AP-Def)	LB
2006	Vince Young, Tenn (AP-Off)	QB
	DeMeco Ryans, Hou (AP-Def)	LB

NOTE: AP-Associated Press, UP-United Press, PFW-*Pro Football Weekly*, TSN-*The Sporting News*, PFWAA-Pro Football Writers Association of America, PFWA-Pro Football Writers of America, MCP-Maxwell Club of Philadelphia, NEA-Newspaper Enterprise Association

Starting in 1960, the United Press annually awarded two Rookie of the Year awards, one to an AFL player and one to a NFL player. After the AFL-NFL merger, the UP kept the two-award format for the AFC and NFC. The UP stopped awarding RoY awards after the 1996 season.

Starting in 1967, the Associated Press began announcing two annual Rookie of the Year awards, as well. One went to the best offensive rookie in the NFL, the other to the best defensive rookie.

Alltime Number-One Draft Choices

Year	Team	Selection	Position
1936	Philadelphia	Jay Berwanger, Chicago	HB
1937	Philadelphia	Sam Francis, Nebraska	FB
1938	Cleveland	Corbett Davis, Indiana	FB
1939	Chicago Cardinals	Ki Aldrich, Texas Christian	C
1940	Chicago Cardinals	George Cafego, Tennessee	HB
1941	Chicago Bears	Tom Harmon, Michigan	HB
1942	Pittsburgh	Bill Dudley, Virginia	HB
1943	Detroit	Frank Sinkwich, Georgia	HB
1944	Boston	Angelo Bertelli, Notre Dame	QB
1945	Chicago Cardinals	Charley Trippi, Georgia	HB
1946	Boston	Frank Dancewicz, Notre Dame	QB
1947	Chicago Bears	Bob Fenimore, Oklahoma A&M	HB
1948	Washington	Harry Gilmer, Alabama	QB
1949	Philadelphia	Chuck Bednarik, Pennsylvania	C
1950	Detroit	Leon Hart, Notre Dame	E
1951	New York Giants	Kyle Rote, SMU	HB
1952	Los Angeles	Bill Wade, Vanderbilt	QB
1953	San Francisco	Harry Babcock, Georgia	E
1954	Cleveland	Bobby Garrett, Stanford	QB
1955	Baltimore	George Shaw, Oregon	QB
1956	Pittsburgh	Gary Glick, Colorado A&M	DB
1957	Green Bay	Paul Hornung, Notre Dame	HB
1958	Chicago Cardinals	King Hill, Rice	QB
1959	Green Bay	Randy Duncan, Iowa	QB
1960	Los Angeles	Billy Cannon, LSU	RB
1961	Minnesota	Tommy Mason, Tulane	RB
	Buffalo (AFL)	Ken Rice, Auburn	G
1962	Washington	Ernie Davis, Syracuse	RB
	Oakland (AFL)	Roman Gabriel, North Carolina St	QB
1963	LA Rams	Terry Baker, Oregon St	QB
	Kansas City (AFL)	Buck Buchanan, Grambling	DT
1964	San Francisco	Dave Parks, Texas Tech	E
	Boston (AFL)	Jack Concannon, Boston College	QB
1965	NY Giants	Tucker Frederickson, Auburn	RB
	Houston (AFL)	Lawrence Elkins, Baylor	E
1966	Atlanta	Tommy Nobis, Texas	LB
	Miami (AFL)	Jim Grabowski, Illinois	RB

Year	Team	Selection	Position
1967	Baltimore	Bubba Smith, Michigan St	DT
1968	Minnesota	Ron Yary, USC	T
1969	Buffalo (AFL)	O.J. Simpson, USC	RB
1970	Pittsburgh	Terry Bradshaw, Louisiana Tech	QB
1971	New England	Jim Plunkett, Stanford	QB
1972	Buffalo	Walt Patulski, Notre Dame	DE
1973	Houston	John Matuszak, Tampa	DE
1974	Dallas	Ed Jones, Tennessee St	DE
1975	Atlanta	Steve Bartkowski, California	QB
1976	Tampa Bay	Lee Roy Selmon, Oklahoma	DE
1977	Tampa Bay	Ricky Bell, USC	RB
1978	Houston	Earl Campbell, Texas	RB
1979	Buffalo	Tom Cousineau, Ohio St	LB
1980	Detroit	Billy Sims, Oklahoma	RB
1981	New Orleans	George Rogers, South Carolina	RB
1982	New England	Kenneth Sims, Texas	DT
1983	Baltimore	John Elway, Stanford	QB
1984	New England	Irving Fryar, Nebraska	WR
1985	Buffalo	Bruce Smith, Virginia Tech	DE
1986	Tampa Bay	Bo Jackson, Auburn	RB
1987	Tampa Bay	Vinny Testaverde, Miami (Fla.)	QB
1988	Atlanta	Aundray Bruce, Auburn	LB
1989	Dallas	Troy Aikman, UCLA	QB
1990	Indianapolis	Jeff George, Illinois	QB
1991	Dallas	Russell Maryland, Miami (Fla.)	DT
1992	Indianapolis	Steve Emtman, Washington	DT
1993	New England	Drew Bledsoe, Washington St	QB
1994	Cincinnati	Dan Wilkinson, Ohio St	DT
1995	Cincinnati	Ki-Jana Carter, Penn St	RB
1996	New York Jets	Keyshawn Johnson, USC	WR
1997	St Louis	Orlando Pace, Ohio St	OT
1998	Indianapolis	Peyton Manning, Tennessee	QB
1999	Cleveland	Tim Couch, Kentucky	QB
2000	Cleveland	Courtney Brown, Penn St	DE
2001	Atlanta	Michael Vick, Virginia Tech	QB
2002	Houston	David Carr, Fresno St	QB
2003	Cincinnati	Carson Palmer, USC	QB
2004	San Diego	Eli Manning, Mississippi	QB
2005	San Francisco	Alex Smith, Utah	QB
2006	Houston	Mario Williams, North Carolina St	DE
2007	Oakland	JaMarcus Russell, LSU	QB

From 1947 through 1958, the first selection in the draft was a bonus pick, awarded to the winner of a random draw. That club, in turn, forfeited its last-round draft choice. The winner of the bonus choice was eliminated from future draws. The system was abolished after 1958, by which time all clubs had received a bonus choice.

Herb Adderley
Troy Aikman
George Allen
Marcus Allen
Lance Alworth
Doug Atkins
Morris (Red) Badgro
Lem Barney
Cliff Battles
Sammy Baugh
Chuck Bednarik
Bert Bell
Bobby Bell
Raymond Berry
Elvin Bethea
Charles W. Bidwill Sr.
Fred Biletnikoff
George Blanda
Mel Blount
Terry Bradshaw
Bob (the Boomer) Brown
Jim Brown
Paul Brown
Roosevelt Brown
Willie Brown
Junios (Buck) Buchanan
Nick Buoniconti
Dick Butkus
Earl Campbell
Tony Canadeo
Joe Carr
Harry Carson
Dave Casper
Guy Chamberlin
Jack Christiansen
Earl (Dutch) Clark
George Connor
Jimmy Conzelman
Lou Creekmur
Larry Csonka
Al Davis
Willie Davis
Len Dawson
Joe DeLamielleure
Eric Dickerson
Dan Dierdorf
Mike Ditka
Art Donovan
Tony Dorsett
John (Paddy) Driscoll
Bill Dudley
Albert Glen (Turk) Edwards
Carl Eller
John Elway
Weeb Ewbank
Tom Fears
Jim Finks
Ray Flaherty
Len Ford
Dan Fortmann
Dan Fouts
Benny Friedman
Frank Gatski
Bill George
Joe Gibbs

Frank Gifford
Sid Gillman
Otto Graham
Harold (Red) Grange
Bud Grant
Joe Greene
Forrest Gregg
Bob Griese
Lou Groza
Joe Guyon
George Halas
Jack Ham
Dan Hampton
John Hannah
Franco Harris
Mike Haynes
Ed Healey
Mel Hein
Ted Hendricks
Wilbur (Pete) Henry
Arnie Herber
Bill Hewitt
Gene Hickerson
Clarke Hinkle
Elroy (Crazylegs) Hirsch
Paul Hornung
Ken Houston
Robert (Cal) Hubbard
Sam Huff
Lamar Hunt
Don Hutson
Michael Irvin
Jimmy Johnson
John Henry Johnson
Charlie Joiner
David (Deacon) Jones
Stan Jones
Henry Jordan
Sonny Jurgensen
Jim Kelly
Leroy Kelly
Walt Kiesling
Frank (Bruiser) Kinard
Paul Krause
Earl (Curly) Lambeau
Jack Lambert
Tom Landry
Dick (Night Train) Lane
Jim Langer
Willie Lanier
Steve Largent
Yale Lary
Dante Lavelli
Bobby Layne
Alphonse (Tuffy) Leemans
Marv Levy
Bob Lilly
Larry Little
James Lofton
Vince Lombardi
Howie Long
Ronnie Lott
Sid Luckman
William Roy (Link) Lyman
Tom Mack

John Mackey
John Madden
Tim Mara
Wellington Mara
Gino Marchetti
Dan Marino
George Preston Marshall
Ollie Matson
Bruce Matthews
Don Maynard
George McAfee
Mike McCormack
Tommy McDonald
Hugh McElhenny
John (Blood) McNally
Mike Michalske
Wayne Millner
Bobby Mitchell
Ron Mix
Joe Montana
Warren Moon
Lenny Moore
Marion Motley
Mike Munchak
Anthony Munoz
George Musso
Bronko Nagurski
Joe Namath
Earle (Greasy) Neale
Ernie Nevers
Ozzie Newsome
Ray Nitschke
Chuck Noll
Leo Nomellini
Merlin Olsen
Jim Otto
Steve Owen
Alan Page
Clarence (Ace) Parker
Jim Parker
Walter Payton
Joe Perry
Pete Pihos
Fritz Pollard
Hugh (Shorty) Ray
Dan Reeves
Mel Renfro
John Riggins
Jim Ringo
Andy Robustelli
Art Rooney
Dan Rooney
Pete Rozelle
Bob St. Clair
Barry Sanders
Charlie Sanders
Gale Sayers
Joe Schmidt
Tex Schramm
Lee Roy Selmon
Billy Shaw
Art Shell
Don Shula
O.J. Simpson
Mike Singletary

Jackie Slater
Jackie Smith
John Stallworth
Bart Starr
Roger Staubach
Ernie Stautner
Jan Stenerud
Dwight Stephenson
Hank Stram
Ken Strong
Joe Stydahar
Lynn Swann
Fran Tarkenton
Charley Taylor
Jim Taylor
Lawrence Taylor
Thurman Thomas
Jim Thorpe
Y.A. Tittle
George Trafton
Charley Trippi
Emlen Tunnell
Clyde (Bulldog) Turner
Johnny Unitas
Gene Upshaw
Norm Van Brocklin
Steve Van Buren
Doak Walker
Bill Walsh
Paul Warfield
Bob Waterfield
Mike Webster
Roger Wehrli
Arnie Weinmeister
Randy White
Reggie White
Dave Wilcox
Bill Willis
Larry Wilson
Kellen Winslow
Alex Wojciechowicz
Willie Wood
Rayfield Wright
Ron Yary
Steve Young
Jack Youngblood

Canadian Football League Grey Cup

Year	Results	Site	Attendance
1909	U of Toronto 26, Parkdale 6	Toronto	3,807
1910	U of Toronto 16, Hamilton Tigers 7	Hamilton	12,000
1911	U of Toronto 14, Toronto 7	Toronto	13,687
1912	Hamilton Alerts 11, Toronto 4	Hamilton	5,337
1913	Hamilton Tigers 44, Parkdale 2	Hamilton	2,100
1914	Toronto 14, U of Toronto 2	Toronto	10,500
1915	Hamilton Tigers 13, Toronto RAA 7	Toronto	2,808
1916–19	No game	—	—
1920	U of Toronto 16, Toronto 3	Toronto	10,088
1921	Toronto 23, Edmonton 0	Toronto	9,558
1922	Queen's U 13, Edmonton 1	Kingston	4,700
1923	Queen's U 54, Regina 0	Toronto	8,629
1924	Queen's U 11, Balmy Beach 3	Toronto	5,978
1925	Ottawa Senators 24, Winnipeg 1	Ottawa	6,900
1926	Ottawa Senators 10, Toronto U 7	Toronto	8,276
1927	Balmy Beach 9, Hamilton Tigers 6	Toronto	13,676
1928	Hamilton Tigers 30, Regina 0	Hamilton	4,767
1929	Hamilton Tigers 14, Regina 3	Hamilton	1,906
1930	Balmy Beach 11, Regina 6	Toronto	3,914
1931	Montreal AAA 22, Regina 0	Montreal	5,112
1932	Hamilton Tigers 25, Regina 6	Hamilton	4,806
1933	Toronto 4, Sarnia 3	Sarnia	2,751
1934	Sarnia 20, Regina 12	Toronto	8,900
1935	Winnipeg 18, Hamilton Tigers 12	Hamilton	6,405
1936	Sarnia 26, Ottawa RR 20	Toronto	5,883
1937	Toronto 4, Winnipeg 3	Toronto	11,522
1938	Toronto 30, Winnipeg 7	Toronto	18,778
1939	Winnipeg 8, Ottawa 7	Ottawa	11,738
1940	Ottawa 8, Balmy Beach 2	Toronto	4,998
1940	Ottawa 12, Balmy Beach 5	Ottawa	1,700
1941	Winnipeg 18, Ottawa 16	Toronto	19,065
1942	Toronto RCAF 8, Winnipeg RCAF 5	Toronto	12,455
1943	Hamilton F Wild 23, Winnipeg RCAF 14	Toronto	16,423
1944	Montreal St H-D Navy 7, Hamilton F Wild 6	Hamilton	3,871
1945	Toronto 35, Winnipeg 0	Toronto	18,660
1946	Toronto 28, Winnipeg 6	Toronto	18,960
1947	Toronto 10, Winnipeg 9	Toronto	18,885
1948	Calgary 12, Ottawa 7	Toronto	20,013
1949	Montreal Als 28, Calgary 15	Toronto	20,087
1950	Toronto 13, Winnipeg 0	Toronto	27,101
1951	Ottawa 21, Saskatchewan 14	Toronto	27,341
1952	Toronto 21, Edmonton 11	Toronto	27,391
1953	Hamilton Ticats 12, Winnipeg 6	Toronto	27,313
1954	Edmonton 26, Montreal 25	Toronto	27,321
1955	Edmonton 34, Montreal 19	Vancouver	39,417
1956	Edmonton 50, Montreal 27	Toronto	27,425
1957	Hamilton 32, Winnipeg 7	Toronto	27,051
1958	Winnipeg 35, Hamilton 28	Vancouver	36,567
1959	Winnipeg 21, Hamilton 7	Toronto	33,133
1960	Ottawa 16, Edmonton 6	Vancouver	38,102
1961	Winnipeg 21, Hamilton 14	Toronto	32,651
1962	Winnipeg 28, Hamilton 27	Toronto	32,655
1963	Hamilton 21, British Columbia 10	Vancouver	36,545
1964	British Columbia 34, Hamilton 24	Toronto	32,655
1965	Hamilton 22, Winnipeg 16	Toronto	32,655
1966	Saskatchewan 29, Ottawa 14	Vancouver	36,553
1967	Hamilton 24, Saskatchewan 1	Ottawa	31,358
1968	Ottawa 24, Calgary 21	Toronto	32,655
1969	Ottawa 29, Saskatchewan 11	Montreal	33,172
1970	Montreal 23, Calgary 10	Toronto	32,669
1971	Calgary 14, Toronto 11	Vancouver	34,484
1972	Hamilton 13, Saskatchewan 10	Hamilton	33,993
1973	Ottawa 22, Edmonton 18	Toronto	36,653
1974	Montreal 20, Edmonton 7	Vancouver	34,450
1975	Edmonton 9, Montreal 8	Calgary	32,454
1976	Ottawa 23, Saskatchewan 20	Toronto	53,467
1977	Montreal 41, Edmonton 6	Montreal	68,318

Canadian Football League Grey Cup

Year	Results	Site	Attendance
1978	Edmonton 20, Montreal 13	Toronto	54,695
1979	Edmonton 17, Montreal 9	Montreal	65,113
1980	Edmonton 48, Hamilton 10	Toronto	54,661
1981	Edmonton 26, Ottawa 23	Montreal	52,478
1982	Edmonton 32, Toronto 16	Toronto	54,741
1983	Toronto 18, British Columbia 17	Vancouver	59,345
1984	Winnipeg 47, Hamilton 17	Edmonton	60,081
1985	British Columbia 37, Hamilton 24	Montreal	56,723
1986	Hamilton 39, Edmonton 15	Vancouver	59,621
1987	Edmonton 38, Toronto 36	Vancouver	59,478
1988	Winnipeg 22, British Columbia 21	Ottawa	50,604
1989	Saskatchewan 43, Hamilton 40	Toronto	54,088
1990	Winnipeg 50, Edmonton 11	Vancouver	46,968
1991	Toronto 36, Calgary 21	Winnipeg	51,985
1992	Calgary 24, Winnipeg 10	Toronto	45,863
1993	Edmonton 33, Winnipeg 23	Calgary	50,035
1994	British Columbia 26, Baltimore 23	Vancouver	55,097
1995	Baltimore 37, Calgary 20	Regina, Saskatchewan	52,564
1996	Toronto 43, Edmonton 37	Hamilton, Ontario	38,595
1997	Toronto 47, Saskatchewan 23	Edmonton	60,431
1998	Calgary 26, Hamilton 24	Winnipeg	34,157
1999	Hamilton 32, Calgary 21	Vancouver	45,118
2000	British Columbia 28, Montreal 26	Calgary	43,822
2001	Calgary 27, Winnipeg 19	Montreal	65,255
2002	Montreal 25, Edmonton 16	Edmonton	62,531
2003	Edmonton 34, Montreal 22	Regina, Saskatchewan	50,909
2004	Toronto 27, British Columbia 19	Ottawa	51,242
2005	Edmonton 38, Montreal 35 (OT)	Vancouver	59,157
2006	British Columbia 25, Montreal 14	Winnipeg	44,786

In 1909, Earl Grey, the Governor-General of Canada, donated a trophy for the Rugby Football Championship of Canada. The trophy, which subsequently became known as the Grey Cup, was originally open only to teams registered with the Canada Rugby Union. Since 1954, it has been awarded to the winner of the Canadian Football League's championship game.

AMERICAN FOOTBALL LEAGUE I

Year	Champion	Record
1926	Philadelphia Quakers	7-2

AMERICAN FOOTBALL LEAGUE II

Year	Champion	Record
1936	Boston Shamrocks	8-3
1937	LA Bulldogs	8-0

AMERICAN FOOTBALL LEAGUE III

Year	Champion	Record
1940	Columbus Bullies	8-1-1
1941	Columbus Bullies	5-1-2

ALL-AMERICAN FOOTBALL CONFERENCE

Year	Championship Game
1946	Cleveland 14, NY Yankees 9
1947	Cleveland 14, NY Yankees 3
1948	Cleveland 49, Buffalo 7
1949	Cleveland 21, San Francisco 7

WORLD FOOTBALL LEAGUE

Year	World Bowl Championship
1974	Birmingham 22, Florida 21
1975	Disbanded midseason

UNITED STATES FOOTBALL LEAGUE

Year	Championship Game
1983	Michigan 24, Philadelphia 22
1984	Philadelphia 23, Arizona 3
1985	Baltimore 28, Oakland 24

X FOOTBALL LEAGUE

Year	Championship Game
2001	Los Angeles 38, San Francisco 6

NFL EUROPE

Year Record	Champion	
1991	London	9-1-0
1992	Sacramento	8-2-0
1995	Frankfurt	6-4-0
1996	Scotland	7-3-0
1997	Barcelona	5-5-0
1998	Rhein	7-3-0
1999	Frankfurt	6-4-0
2000	Rhein	7-3-0
2001	Berlin	6-4-0
2002	Berlin	6-4-0
2003	Frankfurt	6-4-0
2004	Berlin	9-1-0
2005	Amsterdam	6-4-0
2006	Frankfurt	7-3-0
2007	Hamburg	7-3-0

Known as World League of American Football until 1998.

Results

Date	Winner	Loser	Score	Site (Attendance)
I 8-1-87	Denver	Pittsburgh	45–16	Pittsburgh (13,232)
II 7-30-88	Detroit	Chicago	24–13	Chicago (15,018)
III 8-18-89	Detroit	Pittsburgh	39–26	Detroit (12,046)
IV 8-11-90	Detroit	Dallas	51–27	Detroit (19,875)
V 8-17-91	Tampa Bay	Detroit	48–42	Detroit (20,357)
VI 8-22-92	Detroit	Orlando	56–38	Orlando (13,680)
VII 8-21-93	Tampa Bay	Detroit	51–31	Detroit (12,989)
VIII 9-2-94	Arizona	Orlando	36–31	Orlando (14,368)
IX 9-1-95	Tampa Bay	Orlando	48–35	St. Petersburg (25,087)
X 8-26-96	Tampa Bay	Iowa	42–38	Des Moines (11,411)
XI 8-25-97	Arizona	Iowa	55–33	Phoenix (17,436)
XII 8-23-98	Orlando	Tampa Bay	62–31	Tampa (17,222)
XIII 8-21-99	Albany	Orlando	59–48	Albany, N.Y. (13,652)
XIV 8-20-00	Orlando	Nashville	41–38	Orlando (15,989)
XV 8-19-01	Grand Rapids	Nashville	64–42	Grand Rapids (11,217)
XVI 8-18-02	San Jose	Arizona	52–14	San Jose (16,942)
XVII 6-22-03	Tampa Bay	Arizona	43–29	Tampa (20,496)
XVIII 6-27-04	San Jose	Arizona	69–62	Phoenix (17,391)
XIX 6-12-05	Colorado	Georgia	51–48	Las Vegas (10,822)
XX 6-11-06	Chicago	Orlando	69–61	Las Vegas (13,476)
XXI 7-29-07	San Jose	Columbus	55–33	New Orleans (17,056)

Arena Bowl Recaps*

I - 1987

Denver Dynamite 12	6	14	13—45	
Pittsburgh Gladiators.....0	0	0	16—16	

FIRST QUARTER: Den: Forte fumble recovery (Morales kick), 8:27. **Denver 6–0.**
Den: Prather 2 run (pass failed), 9:37. **Denver 12–0.**
SECOND QUARTER: Den: Mullen 26 pass from W. Taylor (pass failed), 4:38. **Denver 18–0.**
THIRD QUARTER: Den: Rodgers 32 pass from W. Taylor (Morales kick), 9:48. **Denver 25–0.**
Den: Trimble 47 int return (Morales kick), 15:00. **Denver 32–0.**
FOURTH QUARTER: Pitt: Hairston 11 pass from Hohensee (two-point conversion), 3:43. **Denver 32–8.**
Den: Mullen 5 pass from W. Taylor (Morales kick), 6:13. **Denver 39–8.**
Den: Mullen 19 pass from W. Taylor (kick blocked), 11:49. **Denver 45–8.**
Pitt: Richmond 14 pass from Folmar (two-point conversion), 14:28. **Denver 45–16.**

A: 13,232

II - 1988

Detroit Drive 7	14	0	3—24	
Chicago Bruisers 7	0	0	6—13	

FIRST QUARTER: Det: Ingold 1 run (Bojovic kick), 3:15. **Detroit 7–0.**
Chi: McDade 3 pass from Bennett (Morales kick), 9:20. **7–7.**
SECOND QUARTER: Det: Holman 8 run (Bojovic kick), 0:49. **Detroit 14–7.**
Det: Browne 2 run (Bojovic kick), 14:19. **Detroit 21–7.**
FOURTH QUARTER: Chi: Stone 10 run (kick failed), 2:42. **Detroit 21–13.**
Det: FG Bojovic 17, 13:51. **Detroit 24–13.**

A: 15,018

III - 1989

Detroit Drive 16	10	13	0—39	
Pittsburgh Gladiators.....3	9	14	0—26	

FIRST QUARTER: Det: Safety, fumble through endzone, 1:07. **Detroit 2–0.**
Det: Burris 1 run (Bojovic kick), 7:35. **Detroit 9–0.**
Pitt: FG Fricke 55, 9:58. **Detroit 9–3.**
Det: Bradford 17 run (Bojovic kick), 13:29. **Detroit 16–3.**
SECOND QUARTER: Det: FG Bojovic 50, 3:09. **Detroit 19–3.**
Pitt: FG Fricke 30, 5:41. **Detroit 19–6.**
Det: Bradford 2 run (Bojovic kick), 12:53. **Detroit 26–6.**
Pitt: Powell 2 run (pass failed), 14:50. **Detroit 26–12.**
THIRD QUARTER: Pitt: Ross 23 fumble return (Fricke kick), 0:42. **Detroit 26–19.**
Det: LaFrance 32 pass from Burris (kick failed), 7:05. **Detroit 32–19.**
Det: Mullen 12 pass from Burris (Bojovic kick), 8:53. **Detroit 39–19.**
Pitt: Gardner 19 pass from Totten (Fricke kick), 13:56. **Detroit 39–26.**

A: 12,046

IV - 1990

Detroit Drive 14	17	13	7—51	
Dallas Texans 0	14	0	13—27	

FIRST QUARTER: Det: Schlichter 2 run (Bojovic kick), 5:52. **Detroit 7–0.**
Det: Schlichter 5 run (Bojovic kick), 7:00. **Detroit 14–0.**
SECOND QUARTER: Det: Rettig 1 run (Bojovic kick), 3:08. **Detroit 21–0.**
Det: Rettig 11 pass from Schlichter (Bojovic kick), 5:24. **Detroit 28–0.**
Dal: Ward 1 run (Morales kick), 10:00. **Detroit 28–7.**
Dal: Kenney 6 pass from Bennett (Morales kick), 14:49. **Detroit 28–14.**
Det: FG Bojovic 42, 15:00. **Detroit 31–14.**

*-From 1987 to 1992, scoring times listed indicate time elapsed in each quarter. After 1992, scoring times listed indicate time remaining.

IV - 1990 *(Cont.)*

THIRD QUARTER: Det: Schlichter 1 run (Bojovic kick), 2:20. **Detroit 38–14.**
Det: Mullen 37 pass from Schlichter (kick failed), 8:58. **Detroit 44–14.**
FOURTH QUARTER: Dal: Ward 1 run (Morales kick), 2:13. **Detroit 44–21.**
Dal: Blackmon 3 run (pass failed), 12:19. **Detroit 44–27.**
Det: Schlichter 2 run (Bojovic kick), 14:25. **Detroit 51–27.**

A: 19,875

V - 1991

Tampa Bay Storm	7	21	14	6—48
Detroit Drive	14	7	9	12—42

FIRST QUARTER: TB: Gruden 1 run (Hickert kick), 5:15. **Tampa Bay 7–0.**
Det: Mullen 10 pass from Schlichter (Bojovic kick), 7:42. **7–7.**
Det: LaFrance 32 pass from Schlichter (Bojovic kick), 14:38. **Detroit 14–7.**
SECOND QUARTER: TB: Thomas 13 pass from Gruden (Hickert kick), 4:53. **14–14.**
Det: Rettig 2 run (Bojovic kick), 8:10. **Detroit 21–14.**
TB: Bradford 3 run (Hickert kick), 14:20. **21–21.**
TB: Thomas 42 pass from Gruden (Hickert kick), 15:00. **Tampa Bay 28–21.**
THIRD QUARTER: Det: McClay 13 pass from Schlichter (kick failed), 3:14. **Tampa Bay 28–27.**
TB: Willis 37 pass from Gruden (Hickert kick), 5:58. **Tampa Bay 35–27.**
Det: FG Bojovic 46, 9:30. **Tampa Bay 35–30.**
TB: Thomas 17 pass from Gruden (Hickert kick), 14:08. **Tampa Bay 42–30.**
FOURTH QUARTER: Det: Mullen 23 pass from Schlichter (kick failed), 0:50. **Tampa Bay 42–36.**
Det: Anderson 1 run (pass failed), 13:40. **42–42.**
TB: Thomas 35 pass from Gruden (kick failed), 14:21. **Tampa Bay 48–42.**

A: 20,357

VI - 1992

Detroit Drive	7	21	14	14—56
Orlando Predators	6	17	0	15—38

FIRST QUARTER: Orl: FG Cimadevilla 48, 8:41. **Orlando 3–0.**
Det: Sargent 1 run (Langeloh kick), 5:14. **Detroit 7–3.**
Orl: FG Cimadevilla 36, 1:44. **Detroit 7–6.**
SECOND QUARTER: Orl: FG Cimadevilla 26, 5:50. **Orlando 9–7.**
Det: Langley 6 pass from Renfroe (Langeloh kick), 3:28. **Detroit 14–9.**
Det: McSwain fumble recovery (Langeloh kick), 3:03. **Detroit 21–9.**
Orl: Drakes 8 pass from Bennett (Cimadevilla kick), 0:51. **Detroit 21–16.**
Det: LaFrance 57 kickoff return (Langeloh kick), 0:45. **Detroit 28–16.**
Orl: Aikens 8 pass from Bennett (Cimadevilla kick), 0:15. **Detroit 28–23.**

---

*-From 1987 to 1992, scoring times listed indicate time elapsed in each quarter. After 1992, scoring times listed indicate time remaining.

VI - 1992 *(Cont.)*

THIRD QUARTER: Det: Fleming 1 run (Langeloh kick), 10:25. **Detroit 35–23.**
Det: LaFrance 24 pass from Renfroe (Langeloh kick), 4:12. **Detroit 42–23.**
FOURTH QUARTER: Orl: FG Cimadevilla 31, 14:51. **Detroit 42–26.**
Det: Langley 15 pass from Renfroe (Langeloh kick), 11:08. **Detroit 49–26.**
Orl: Walls 20 pass from Bennett (kick failed), 6:38. **Detroit 49–32.**
Det : Mullen 17 pass from Renfroe (Langeloh kick), 4:02. **Detroit 56–32.**
Orl: Moore 7 pass from Bennett (conversion failed), 1:00. **Detroit 56–38.**

A: 13,680

VII - 1993

Tampa Bay Storm	10	20	7	14—51
Detroit Drive	0	17	7	7—31

FIRST QUARTER: TB: FG Czyzewski 24, 6:35. **Tampa Bay 3–0.**
TB: Thomas 15 pass from Gruden (Czyzewski kick), 4:04. **Tampa Bay 10–0.**
SECOND QUARTER: Det: FG Langeloh 21, 14:14. **Tampa Bay 10–3.**
TB: FG Czyzewski 47, 11:05. **Tampa Bay 13–3.**
TB: Browner fumble recovery (Czyzewski kick), 9:11. **Tampa Bay 20–3.**
Det: LaFrance 27 pass from Renfroe (Langeloh kick), 7:22. **Tampa Bay 20–10.**
TB: Field 18 pass from Gruden (Czyzewski kick), 2:22. **Tampa Bay 27–10.**
Det: Goode 2 pass from Renfroe (Langeloh kick), 0:57. **Tampa Bay 27–17.**
TB: FG Czyzewski 26, 0:04. **Tampa Bay 30–17.**
THIRD QUARTER: TB: Browner 9 pass from Byrd (Czyzewski kick), 6:05. **Tampa Bay 37–17.**
Det: Bell 34 pass from Renfroe (Langeloh kick), 4:35. **Tampa Bay 37–24.**
FOURTH QUARTER: TB: Brown 7 pass from Gruden (Czyzewski kick), 13:31. **Tampa Bay 44–24.**
Det: Burse 1 run (Langeloh kick), 10:36. **Tampa Bay 44–31.**
TB: Barley 4 run (Czyzewski kick), 3:48. **Tampa Bay 51–31.**

A: 12,989

VIII - 1994

Arizona Rattlers	7	13	7	9—36
Orlando Predators	10	7	7	7—31

FIRST QUARTER: Orl: Shell 5 pass from Bennett (Cimadevilla kick), 10:51. **Orlando 7–0.**
Ariz: Tillman 33 pass from Bonner (Zendejas kick), 7:54. **7–7.**
Orl: FG Cimadevilla 24, 3:41. **Orlando 10–7.**
SECOND QUARTER: Ariz: Schexnaer 6 pass from Bonner (Zendejas kick), 11:25. **Arizona 14–10.**
Orl: Shell 42 pass from Bennett (Cimadevilla kick), 9:53. **Orlando 17–14.**
Ariz: FG Zendejas 23, 0:53. **17–17.**
Ariz: FG Zendejas 40, 0:00. **Arizona 20–17.**
THIRD QUARTER: Ariz: Vaughn 2 pass from Bonner (Zendejas kick), 2:45. **Arizona 27–17.**
Orl: Walls 38 pass from Bennett (Cimadevilla kick), 0:47. **Arizona 27–24.**

VIII - 1994 *(Cont.)*

FOURTH QUARTER: Ariz: FG Zendejas 21, 11:49.
Arizona 30–24.
Orl: Wagner 3 run (Cimadevilla kick), 6:55. **Orlando 31–30.**
Ariz: Schexnaer 24 pass from Bonner (dropkick failed), 0:31. **Arizona 36–31.**

A: 14,368

IX - 1995

Tampa Bay Storm	15	14	6	13—48
Orlando Predators	15	0	7	13—35

FIRST QUARTER: Orl: Wagner 2 run (two-point conversion), 13:14. **Orlando 8–0.**
TB: Thomas 10 pass from Gruden (two-point conversion), 8:39. **8–8.**
Orl: Shell 4 pass from O'Hara (Bennett kick), 3:23. **Orlando 15–8.**
TB: LaFrance 57 kickoff return (Cimadevilla kick), 2:23. **15–15.**
SECOND QUARTER: TB: LaFrance 3 pass from Gruden (Cimadevilla kick), 9:03. **Tampa Bay 22–15.**
TB: LaFrance 1 pass from Gruden (Cimadevilla kick), 0:03. **Tampa Bay 29–15.**
THIRD QUARTER: Orl: Wagner 3 MFG return (Bennett kick), 9:42. **Tampa Bay 29–22.**
TB: Thomas 35 pass from Gruden (kick failed), 7:43. **Tampa Bay 35–22.**
FOURTH QUARTER: Orl: Fleming 14 run (Bennett kick), 11:16. **Tampa Bay 35–29.**
TB: Gruden 1 run (pass failed), 6:30. **Tampa Bay 41–29.**
TB: Sanders 47 int return (Cimadevilla kick), 2:15. **Tampa Bay 48–29.**
Orl: Wagner 3 pass from O'Hara (pass failed), 1:00. **Tampa Bay 48–35.**

A: 25,087

X - 1996

Tampa Bay Storm	13	15	7	7—42
Iowa Barnstormers	14	14	3	7—38

FIRST QUARTER: TB: Rowland 12 pass from Gruden (Cimadevilla kick), 9:32. **Tampa Bay 7–0.**
Iowa: Spencer 16 pass from Warner (Black kick), 6:48. **7–7.**
Iowa: Cooper 30 pass from Warner (Black kick), 2:02. **Iowa 14–7.**
TB: LaFrance 30 pass from Gruden (kick failed), 0:00. **Iowa 14–13.**
SECOND QUARTER: Iowa: Jacox 9 pass from Warner (Black kick), 10:46. **Iowa 21–13.**
TB: Thomas 35 pass from Gruden (two-point conversion), 0:59. **21–21.**
TB: Thomas 9 int return (Cimadevilla kick), 0:36. **Tampa Bay 28–21.**
Iowa: Moran 1 run (Black kick), 0:09. **28–28.**
THIRD QUARTER: TB: Caesar 21 pass from Gruden (Cimadevilla kick), 5:46. **Tampa Bay 35–28.**
Iowa: FG Black 32, 0:03. **Tampa Bay 35–31.**
FOURTH QUARTER: TB: Thomas 7 pass from Gruden (Cimadevilla kick), 11:55. **Tampa Bay 42–31.**
Iowa: Spencer 4 pass from Warner (Black kick), 8:22. **Tampa Bay 42–38.**

A: 11,411

XI - 1997

Arizona Rattlers	3	21	21	10—55
Iowa Barnstormers	7	6	7	13—33

FIRST QUARTER: Ariz: FG Brenner 19, 6:19.
Arizona 3–0.
Iowa: L. Cooper 30 pass from Warner (Black kick), 4:59. **Iowa 7–3.**
SECOND QUARTER: Ariz: McMillen 1 run (Brenner kick), 14:57. **Arizona 10–7.**
Iowa: FG Black 25, 9:44. **10–10.**
Ariz: H. Cooper 4 pass from Davis (Brenner kick), 4:33. **Arizona 17–10.**
Iowa: FG Black 20, 0:28. **Arizona 17–13.**
Ariz: H. Cooper 56 kickoff return (Brenner kick), 0:21. **Arizona 24–13.**
THIRD QUARTER: Ariz: Davis 1 run (Brenner kick), 9:09. **Arizona 31–13.**
Ariz: H. Cooper 30 int return (Brenner kick), 7:22. **Arizona 38–13.**
Iowa: L. Cooper 30 pass from Warner (Black kick), 4:33. **Arizona 38–20.**
Ariz: Schexnaer 49 pass from Davis (Brenner kick), 3:47. **Arizona 45–20.**
FOURTH QUARTER: Iowa: Jacox 1 run (Black kick), 14:56. **Arizona 45–27.**
Ariz: Schexnaer 28 pass from Davis (Brenner kick), 9:01. **Arizona 52–27.**
Ariz: FG Brenner 44, 3:43. **Arizona 55–27.**
Iowa: Conley 9 pass from Warner (conversion failed), 0:21. **Arizona 55–33.**

A: 17,436

XII - 1998

Orlando Predators	10	14	26	12—62
Tampa Bay Storm	14	3	8	6—31

FIRST QUARTER: Orl: FG Cool 23, 10:52.
Orlando 3–0.
TB: LaFrance 12 pass from Willis (Nittmo kick), 7:34. **Tampa Bay 7–3.**
Orl : Gordon 23 pass from O'Hara (Cool kick), 4:16. **Orlando 10–7.**
TB: LaFrance 9 pass from Willis (Nittmo kick), 0:31. **Tampa Bay 14–10.**
SECOND QUARTER: Orl: Maynor 3 run (Cool kick), 7:47. **Orlando 17–14.**
TB: FG Nittmo 44, 4:34. **17–17.**
Orl: Hamilton 36 run (Cool kick), 2:31. **Orlando 24–17.**
THIRD QUARTER: Orl: Hamilton 5 run (Cool kick), 14:03. **Orlando 31–17.**
Orl: Burnett safety, 13:12. **Orlando 33–17.**
Orl: Hamilton 10 run (Cool kick), 10:02. **Orlando 40–17.**
Orl: Wagner 48 MFG return (Cool kick), 5:25. **Orlando 47–17.**
TB: LaFrance 7 pass from Willis (two-point conversion), 4:01. **Orlando 47–25.**
Orl: FG Cool 20, 0:24. **Orlando 50–25.**
FOURTH QUARTER: Orl: Mason 22 int return (kick failed), 14:22. **Orlando 56–25.**
TB: Thomas 8 pass from Willis (pass failed), 11:34. **Orlando 56–31.**
Orl: Gordon 8 kickoff return (kick failed), 10:46. **Orlando 62–31.**

A: 17,222

XIII - 1999

Albany Firebirds	21	17	0	21—59
Orlando Predators	14	7	13	14—48

FIRST QUARTER: Alb: Brown 12 pass from Pawlawski (Silvestri kick), 13:18. **Albany 7-0.**
Orl: Wagner 22 pass from Maynor (Cool kick), 11:38. **7-7.**
Alb: Krick 1 run (Silvestri kick), 8:50. **Albany 14-7.**
Orl: Law 37 pass from Maynor (Cool kick), 7:09. **14-14.**
Alb: Johnson 2 pass from Pawlawski (Silvestri kick), 2:14. **Albany 21-14.**
SECOND QUARTER: Orl: Wagner 22 pass from Maynor (Cool kick), 13:21. **21-21.**
Alb: Hopkins 6 pass from Pawlawski (Silvestri kick), 10:34. **Albany 28-21.**
Alb: Brown 29 pass from Pawlawski (Silvestri kick), 3:59. **Albany 35-21.**
Alb: FG Silvestri 18, 0:00. **Albany 38-21.**
THIRD QUARTER: Orl: Jackson 33 pass from Maynor (Cool kick), 7:24. **Albany 38-28.**
Orl: Jackson 34 pass from Maynor (kick failed), 2:00. **Albany 38-34.**
FOURTH QUARTER: Alb: Brown 14 pass from Pawlawski (Silvestri kick), 12:35. **Albany 45-34.**
Orl: Dorsey 4 run (two-point conversion), 4:35. **Albany 45-42.**
Alb: Brown 5 pass from Pawlawski (Silvestri kick), 0:54. **Albany 52-42.**
Orl: Jackson 39 pass from Maynor (kick failed), 0:26. **Albany 52-48.**
Alb: Krick 6 pass from Pawlawski (Silvestri kick), 0:10. **Albany 59-48.**

A: 13,652

XIV - 2000

Orlando Predators	15	14	3	9—41
Nashville Kats	7	16	7	8—38

FIRST QUARTER: Orl: Allen safety, 14:01. **Orlando 2-0.**
Orl: Dell 16 pass from Maynor (Cool kick), 10:13. **Orlando 9-0.**
Orl: Douglass 3 run (kick failed), 4:08. **Orlando 15-0.**
Nash: Russell 33 pass from Kelly (McLaughlin kick), 1:40. **Orlando 15-7.**
SECOND QUARTER: Orl: Hamilton 18 pass from Maynor (Cool kick), 14:04. **Orlando 22-7.**
Orl: Douglass 5 pass from Maynor (Cool kick), 10:45. **Orlando 29-7.**
Nash: Gaines safety, 2:50. **Orlando 29-9.**
Nash: Fleming 1 pass from Kelly (McLaughlin kick), 0:39. **Orlando 29-16.**
Nash: Hammond 5 pass from Kelly (McLaughlin kick), 0:00. **Orlando 29-23.**
THIRD QUARTER: Nash: Baron 28 pass from Kelly (McLaughlin kick), 9:43. **Nashville 30-29.**
Orl: FG Cool 38, 3:20. **Orlando 32-30.**
FOURTH QUARTER: Orl: Cool 15 pass from Maynor (McLaughlin miss), 12:23. **Orlando 39-30.**
Nash: Hammond 45 pass from Brown (Fleming pass), 6:26. **Orlando 39-38.**
Orl: FG Cool 19, 0:00. **Orlando 41-38.**

A: 15,989

XV -2001

Grand Rapids Rampage	14	23	14	13—64
Nashville Kats	14	7	14	7—42

FIRST QUARTER: GR: Shaw 6 pass from Dolezel (Gowins kick), 10:08. **Grand Rapids 7-0.**
Nash: Jones 17 pass from Kelly (McLaughlin kick), 7:10. **7-7.**
GR: Shaw 6 pass from Dolezel (Gowins kick), 2:21. **Grand Rapids 14-7.**
Nash: Grant 1 run (McLaughlin kick), 0:00. **14-14.**
SECOND QUARTER: GR: Shaw 41 pass from Dolezel (Gowins kick), 13:34. **Grand Rapids 21-14.**
GR: Odems 14 pass from Dolezel (kick failed), 9:23. **Grand Rapids 27-14.**
Nash: Jones 34 pass from Kelly (McLaughlin kick), 4:54. **Grand Rapids 27-21.**
GR: Avery 1 run (Gowins kick), 1:00. **Grand Rapids 34-21.**
GR: FG Gowins 36, 0:03. **Grand Rapids 37-21.**
THIRD QUARTER: Nash: Reece 1 run (McLaughlin kick), 11:45. **Grand Rapids 37-28.**
GR: Shaw 31 pass from Dolezel (Gowins kick), 9:33. **Grand Rapids 44-28.**
Nash: Hillery 33 pass from Kelly (McLaughlin kick), 6:44. **Grand Rapids 44-35.**
GR: H. Shaw 1 run (Gowins kick), 0:41. **Grand Rapids 51-35.**
FOURTH QUARTER: Nash: Baron 28 pass from Fleming (McLaughlin kick), 14:24. **Grand Rapids 51-42.**
GR: Shaw 15 pass from Dolezel (Gowins kick), 8:11. **Grand Rapids 58-42.**
GR: Odems 17 pass from Dolezel (kick failed), 2:05. **Grand Rapids 64-42.**

A: 11,217

XVI - 2002

San Jose SaberCats	7	17	14	14—52
Arizona Rattlers	0	0	0	14—14

FIRST QUARTER: SJ: Hundon 28 pass from Dutton (Alcorn kick), 9:17. **San Jose 7-0.**
SECOND QUARTER: SJ: Hundon 2 pass from Dutton (Alcorn kick), 14:18. **San Jose 14-0.**
SJ: FG Alcorn 31, 0:50. **San Jose 17-0.**
SJ: Wagner 2 run (Alcorn kick), 0:11. **San Jose 24-0.**
THIRD QUARTER: SJ: Roe 12 pass from Dutton (Alcorn kick), 12:38. **San Jose 31-0.**
SJ: Reese 32 pass from Dutton (Alcorn kick), 6:55. **San Jose 38-0.**
FOURTH QUARTER: SJ: McMillen 1 run (Alcorn kick), 12:05. **San Jose 45-0.**
Ariz: M. Bryant 30 pass from Bonner (Cooper pass), 9:24. **San Jose 45-8.**
SJ: Hundon 2 pass from Dutton (Alcorn kick), 6:01. **San Jose 52-8.**
Ariz: Kelly 3 run (Cooper pass failed), 2:30. **San Jose 52-14.**

A: 16,942

XVII - 2003

Tampa Bay Storm	14	9	7	13—43
Arizona Rattlers	10	6	6	7—29

FIRST QUARTER: Ariz: FG Garner 36, 11:02. **Arizona 3–0.**
TB: Samuels 33 pass from Kaleo (Stucker kick failed), 7:43. **Tampa Bay 7–3.**
Ariz: Bonner 1 run (Garner kick), 5:07. **Arizona 10–7.**
TB: Proctor 1 run (Dell pass), 1:24. **Tampa Bay 14–10.**
SECOND QUARTER: TB: Kinney 26 fumble recovery (Stucker kick failed), 12:34. **Tampa Bay 20–10.**
Ariz: Kelly 8 run (Garner kick failed), 7:53. **Tampa Bay 20–16.**
TB: FG Stucker 23, 0:00. **Tampa Bay 23–16.**
THIRD QUARTER: TB: Samuels 9 pass from O'Hara (Stucker kick), 7:24. **Tampa Bay 30–16.**
Ariz: Bryant 3 pass from Bonner (Garner kick failed), 2:38. **Tampa Bay 30–22.**
FOURTH QUARTER: TB: Samuels 43 pass from O'Hara (Stucker kick), 14:54. **Tampa Bay 37–22.**
TB: O'Hara 3 run (Stucker kick failed), 10:39. **Tampa Bay 43–22.**
Ariz: Gatewood 3 pass from Bonner (Garner kick), 8:02. **Tampa Bay 43–29.**

A: 20,496

XVIII - 2004

San Jose SaberCats	14	21	7	27—69
Arizona Rattlers	14	14	14	20—62

FIRST QUARTER: Ariz: Burley 29 pass from Bonner (Garner kick), 10:13. **Arizona 7–0.**
SJ: Roe 8 pass from Grieb (Frantz kick), 6:59. **7–7.**
Ariz: Bryant 33 pass from Bonner (Garner kick), 5:18. **Arizona 14–7.**
SJ: Coleman 22 pass from Grieb (Frantz kick), 1:27. **14–14.**
SECOND QUARTER: SJ: Roe 11 pass from Grieb (Frantz kick), 8:34. **San Jose 21–14.**
Ariz: Burley 26 pass from Bonner (Garner kick), 4:33. **21–21.**
SJ: Roe 3 pass from Grieb (Frantz kick), 0:52. **San Jose 28–21.**
Ariz: Cooper 4 run (Garner kick), 0:07. **28–28.**
SJ: Roe 38 pass from Grieb (Frantz kick), 0:00. **San Jose 35–28.**
THIRD QUARTER: Ariz: Kelly 6 run (Garner kick), 11:35. **35–35.**
SJ: Roe 38 pass from Grieb (Frantz kick), 8:42. **San Jose 42–35.**
Ariz: Bryant 21 pass from Bonner (Garner kick), 3:51. **San Jose 42–42.**
FOURTH QUARTER SJ: Wagner 1 run (Frantz kick), 14:50. **San Jose 49–42.**
Ariz: Bryant 7 pass from Bonner (Garner kick), 11:31. **49–49.**
SJ: Hundon 33 pass from Grieb (Frantz kick), 8:36. **San Jose 56–42.**
Ariz: Burley 5 pass from Bonner (Garner kick), 6:03. **56–56.**
SJ: Coleman 2 pass from Grieb (Frantz kick), 3:44. **San Jose 63–56.**
Ariz: Burley 9 from Bonner (Bonner pass failed), 0:31. **San Jose 63–62.**
SJ: Reed 7 kickoff return (Frantz kick failed), 0:30. **San Jose 69–62.**

A: 17,391

XIX - 2005

Colorado Crush	10	14	7	20—51
Georgia Force	7	13	7	21—48

FIRST QUARTER: Col: Marshall 1 run (Rush kick), 12:18. **Colorado 7–0.**
Col: FG Rush 20, 4:42. **Colorado 10–0.**
Geo: Nagy 1 run (Garner kick), 0:42. **Colorado 10–7.**
SECOND QUARTER: Col: Marshall 4 run (Rush kick), 11:56. **Colorado 17–7.**
Geo: Aldridge 27 run (Garner kick failed), 5:42. **Colorado 17–13.**
Col: Marshall 3 run (Rush kick), 0:52. **Colorado 24–13.**
Geo: Thomas 2 run (Garner kick), 0:29. **Colorado 24–20.**
THIRD QUARTER: Col: Harrell 12 pass from Dutton (Rush kick), 7:53. **Colorado 31–20.**
Geo: Lee 2 pass from Nagy (Garner kick), 3:01. **Colorado 31–27.**
FOURTH QUARTER: Col: FG Rush 26, 12:03. **Colorado 34–27.**
Geo: Lee 34 pass from Nagy (Garner kick), 9:19. **34–34.**
Col: Marshall 45 pass from Dutton (Rush kick), 7:57. **Colorado 41–34.**
Geo: Lee 27 pass from Nagy (Garner kick), 4:47. **41–41.**
Col: Harrell 30 pass from Dutton (Rush kick), 3:36. **Colorado 48–41.**
Geo: Jackson 20 pass from Nagy (Garner kick), 0:18. **48–48.**
Col: FG Rush 20, 0:00. **Colorado 51–48.**

A: 10,822

XX - 2006

Chicago Rush	10	24	14	21—69
Orlando Predators	0	28	6	27—61

FIRST QUARTER: Chi: Matt D'Orazio 1 run (Dan Frantz kick), 12:00. **Chicago 7–0.**
Chi: FG Frantz 23, 1:49. **Chicago 10–0.**
SECOND QUARTER: Orl: Dudley 4 pass from Hamilton (Taylor kick), 14:22. **Chicago 10–7.**
Orl: Dudley 7 pass from Hamilton (Taylor kick), 11:56. **Orlando 14–10.**
Chi: Molden 24 pass from D'Orazio (Frantz kick), 10:38. **Chicago 17–14.**
Orl: Carter 36 run (Taylor kick), 8:39. **Orlando 21–17.**
Chi: Sippio 3 pass from D'Orazio (Frantz kick), 4:39. **Chicago 24–21.**
Orl: Rubin 30 pass from Hamilton (Taylor kick), 2:10. **Orlando 28–24.**
Chi: Sippio 8 pass from D'Orazio (Frantz kick), 0:06. **Chicago 31–28.**
Chi: FG Frantz 51, 0:00. **Chicago 34–28.**
THIRD QUARTER: Chi: D'Orazio 5 run (Frantz kick), 14:31. **Chicago 41–28.**
Chi: Robinson 44 int return (Frantz kick), 9:07. **Chicago 48–28.**
Orl: Dudley 45 pass from Hamilton (Taylor kick missed), 7:18. **Chicago 48–34.**
FOURTH QUARTER: Chi: Sippio 31 pass from D'Orazio (Frantz kick), 13:09. **Chicago 55–34.**
Orl: Fryzel 11 pass from Eaton (Taylor kick), 9:00. **Chicago 55–41.**
Orl: Hamilton 5 run (Taylor kick missed), 4:04. **Chicago 55–47.**

XX - 2006 *(Cont.)*

Chi: Molden 2 pass from D'Orazio (Frantz kick), 1:58.
Chicago 62–47.
Orl: Dudley 1 pass from Hamilton (Taylor kick), 0:33.
Chicago 62–54.
Chi: Alfonzo 15 pass from D'Orazio (Frantz kick),
0:27. **Chicago 69–54.**
Orl: Davidson 29 pass from Hamilton (Taylor), 0:13.
Chicago 69–6l.

A: 13,476

XXI - 2007

Columbus Destroyers	7	7	13	6—33
San Jose SaberCats	14	l3	7	21—55

FIRST QUARTER
SJ: Johnson 4 run (Haglund kick), 11:47 **San Jose 7–0.**
Col: Wells 1 run (Martinez kick), 6:55 **7–7.**
SJ: Roe 7 pass from Grieb (Haglund kick), 3:50
San Jose l4–7.

SECOND QUARTER
Col: Hilliard 4 pass from Nagy (Martinez kick), 10:44.
l4–14.
SJ: George 56 kickoff return (Haglund kick failed), 9:50
San Jose 20–14.
SJ: Williams 1 pass from Grieb (Haglund kick), 3:17
San Jose 27–14.

THIRD QUARTER
Col: Magner 3 pass from Nagy (Martinez kick), 8:44
San Jose 27–2l.
SJ: Nelson 4 pass from Grieb (Haglund kick), 3:44
San Jose 34–2l.
Col: Groce 39 pass from Nagy (Martinez kick failed),
0:05 **San Jose 34–27.**

FOURTH QUARTER
SJ: Glover 1 run (Haglund kick), 11:07 **San Jose 4l–27.**
SJ: Roe 20 pass from Grieb (Haglund kick), 6:51
San Jose 48–27.
Col: Saunders 8 pass from Nagy (Martinez pass failed),
1:29 **San Jose 48–33.**
SJ: Johnson 4 run (Haglund kick), 0:38 **San Jose 55–33.**

A: 17,056.

College Football

QB Chris Leak led Florida to its second national championship

Swamped!

A funny thing happened on the way to Ohio State's coronation in the desert—a faster Florida team ran away with the championship in a stunning upset

BY B.J. SCHECTER

THERE'S NO SUBSTITUTE FOR SPEED. When Urban Meyer took over at Florida prior to the 2005 season, critics proclaimed that Meyer wouldn't be able to use the trickery and misdirection he used to propel Utah into the national spotlight. Those smoke and mirrors, people said, wouldn't work in the powerful SEC. Meyer chuckled to himself when he heard that; after all, it's commonly known that the best athletes hail from the Southeastern Conference and Meyer was going to take full advantage of them.

It took a little while for Meyers' Gators to get going. Lead-footed quarterback Chris Leak wasn't the best person to run the spread-option offense, but Meyer was determined to stick with him. And the coach was committed to surrounding Leak with the fastest and most explosive players on both sides of the ball. The strategy worked and now—after much politicking to the pollsters—Florida was faced with its biggest test.

Winning the nation's toughest conference enabled Florida to baffle the BCS (more on that later) and earn a trip to Glendale, Ariz., to face Ohio State in the national title game. Not many people gave the Gators much of a chance against the big, bad Buckeyes, who were No. 1 all season and boasted a Heisman Trophy-winning quarterback and the nation's best defense. Ohio State

was bigger and stronger than Florida and many predicted that the Buckeyes would dominate the Gators and show that Michigan or USC would have been a more worthy opponent for Ohio State.

But Meyer had other ideas. He knew if he could spread Ohio State out, get the ball in the hands of his playmakers and make the Buckeyes chase the Gators, top-ranked Ohio State wouldn't know what hit them. They sure don't see this kind of speed in the Big Ten, he reasoned.

Said Florida receiver Andre Caldwell before the game: "We're going to run them up and down the field, and see if they can keep up with us. If they try to match up with us man-to-man, it's going to be a long day for them."

It was a long day (or night) indeed. It didn't start off well for Florida as Ohio State's Ted Ginn Jr. returned the opening kickoff 93 yards for a touchdown. But the Gators didn't get rattled and calmly marched down the field for the equalizer and took back control of the game. Before the Buckeyes knew it, Florida had stormed to a 21–7 lead. And the Gators would never look back, cruising to a 41–14 victory that was never in doubt.

From sensational (and super fast) freshman Percy Harvin to the unflappable Leak, bruising backup quarterback Tim Tebow and a deep stable of receivers, Florida frustrated Ohio State with an array of bubble screens, direct snaps, criss-crossing routes, option and misdirection. But it was the Florida defense that provided the biggest surprise. Ohio State's offensive line was big and strong, but they couldn't handle the speed and athleticism of Florida.

Defensive ends Jarvis Moss and Derrick Harvey combined for five sacks and spent more time in Ohio State's backfield on this night than Paris Hilton in a club. Normally poised Buckeyes quarterback Troy Smith was clearly flustered and had nowhere to turn. He completed just 4 of 14 passes for 35 yards with an interception and a fumble. And even more impressive, Florida held Ohio State to just 82 yards. The result was a stunning victory, leaving no doubt that Florida was the undisputed No. 1 team.

Said Florida linebacker Brian Crum: "This is a fast-ass team."

Fast indeed. In the midst of the celebration on the field, no one was

BOB ROSATO/SPORTS ILLUSTRATED

In 2006, Ohio State's QB Smith ruled the regular season and became the sixth Buckeye to win the Heisman Trophy.

quicker to hug Leak than Meyer. Though he entered the game with more than 11,000 passing yards and 87 touchdowns, Leak was one of the most maligned players in Florida history. A decorated high school star out of Charlotte, N.C., Leak vowed to lead Florida to multiple national championships, but prior to the 2006 season he had failed to win even one. Worse, his inconsistent play and introverted personality angered fans (and teammates) and many called for Tebow to take over full-time during this season. During one home game, Florida fans loudly booed Leak when he replaced Tebow after one series.

But Meyer stuck with Leak, encouraged

him to bond with his teammates and altered the offense to fit Leak. Now, after completing 25 of 36 passes for 213 yards, a touchdown and no interceptions, Leak looked like the Heisman Trophy winner. More importantly, he had brought home the coveted national title when nobody (not even Gators fans) expected him to do so.

"He is officially one of the top two quarterbacks ever to play at the University of Florida," Meyer said (Danny Wuerffel was the other). "We made this comment two years ago: [winning championships] is the way you're judged at Florida. There's been two quarterbacks to win a national championship, and Chris Leak is one of them."

Boise State may not have won the national championship, but the Broncos captured the hearts of the nation by using a variety of brilliantly executed trick plays to pull off a stunning overtime victory over Oklahoma in the Fiesta Bowl (on the same field that Florida pulled off its upset a week later). Boise's thrilling 43–42 win was one of the best—and wackiest—college football games since Cal's lateral-through-the-band win over Stanford in 1982. And if watching the Broncos' pull off three meticulously intricate plays as part of their unbelievable comeback wasn't enough, add in a storybook marriage proposal from the star running back to the captain of the cheerleading squad just after time expired.

From the opening kickoff, Boise State proved it belonged with the big boys, storming out to leads of 21–10 at the half and 28–10 with 5:16 remaining in the third quarter. But Oklahoma came back and scored 25 unanswered points to take the lead with just over a minute left after Marcus Walker picked off a Jared Zabransky pass and took it 33 yards to the house.

Clearly rattled, it appeared as if Boise State's Cinderella run was about to end when it faced a fourth-and-18 from midfield with 18 seconds remaining. Then, a play called "Circus" was signaled in and the drama began. "Circus" is a play that the Broncos run every week at the end of practice to lighten things up. "It's like a basketball team practicing a half-court shot," said reserve quarterback Bush Hamdan. "It's a screw-around play."

This time it was for real, though, and it worked to perfection. Drisan James caught Zabransky's pass at the Oklahoma 43 and with five Sooners defenders converging on him he pitched the ball to Jerad Raab, who took it down the left sideline for a touchdown. As it turned out, "Circus" was code for the old hook-and-lateral play.

On the first play in overtime, Oklahoma star running back Adrian Peterson burst through the line and went virtually untouched for a touchdown. At that moment, Boise State coach Chris Peterson decided that if the Broncos scored a touchdown they would go for two. But first they had to score. To do so, the Broncos would need another trick play.

This time it would be a halfback pass. Facing a fourth-and-2 from the five, 5'9" reserve Vinny Perretta threw a perfect spiral to Derek Schouman, who fully extended to catch the pass in the end zone for the score. Now, it was gut-check time. When Boise State came out for the two-point conversion attempt, Oklahoma called timeout, but Coach Peterson didn't lose his nerve. He called "Statue" and while the Broncos were stunned at first, they had the utmost confidence in the play. When Boise State came back out onto the field, receiver Legedu Naanee said, "We just won this game."

The play worked to perfection. Zabransky faked a pass to the right, froze the defense and brought the ball behind his back with his left hand and gave it to Ian Johnson, who had nothing but open field and took the ball into the end zone untouched. Boise State won the game and the Sooners—along with college football fans everywhere—stood in stunned silence trying to comprehend what they had just witnessed. Then, in a moment made for Hollywood, Johnson proposed to his girlfriend, Boise State cheerleader Chrissy Popadics, in the euphoric celebration. Of course, she said yes.

In the end, Boise State finished as the nation's only undefeated team at 13–0, making the ultimate case for a playoff: Why shouldn't the Broncos get a shot at facing Florida for the national title?

During the last few weeks of the season, a number of teams were wondering why they were being left out of the national championship discussion. After narrowly losing to Ohio State in Columbus, many had penciled Michigan in to face the Buckeyes in a rematch for the national title. But its game with Ohio State the Saturday before Thanksgiving was Michigan's regular-season finale, and while the Wolverines were home in Ann Arbor waiting, USC and Florida were busy making their cases.

Florida's Meyer was an outspoken critic of the BCS and challenged the voters to consider the Gators' schedule. Could Ohio State

or Michigan have done the same thing in the brutal SEC? USC, meanwhile, overtook Michigan in the polls by thrashing Notre Dame and appeared headed to Glendale. But when the Trojans were unexpectedly upended by UCLA, the door opened for Florida. Later that same day, the Gators beat Arkansas in the SEC championship game, and—*presto!*—Florida was in.

But was it fair? What about one-loss Michigan and Louisville? What about undefeated Boise State? A playoff seemed like the only reasonable solution to the arcane BCS and, increasingly, the idea is beginning to gain favor among coaches. Meyer called it the only fair way to determine things, and this was after the Gators had already clinched a spot in the title game.

"From a competitive standpoint, you can't make an argument against it," noted Auburn coach Tommy Tuberville. "Let's just go to a playoff and be done with it."

From the time that Ohio State went into Austin and knocked off defending national champion Texas in September, it appeared as if Ohio State might roll straight on to the national title. With the seasoned Smith, a pair of big-play receivers and a rebuilt and powerful defense, the Buckeyes had all the

Johnson's trick-play, two-point conversion in overtime capped off an improbable Fiesta Bowl comeback for Boise State.

ingredients of a championship team. And when Ohio State hosted Michigan in late November, many were calling it the *de facto* national title game.

The game was being hyped like a national championship matchup when tragedy stuck. Legendary coach Bo Schembechler, who made the Michigan program what it was, died suddenly of a heart attack the day before the game. Bo had held a presence over the Michigan program long after he had retired as coach and athletic director—the school's coaching offices (along with the football team's meeting rooms) are housed in Schembechler Hall.

The news shocked the entire college football community, including Ohio State. When news of Schembechler's death spread on Friday afternoon, Buckeyes coach Jim Tressel told his team. "I wanted to emphasize to them that Bo was a Buckeye," Tressel said. "He was born in this state, coached here under Woody [Hayes] and got his master's degree here. I wanted them to fully understand his ties [to Ohio State]."

Coach Schiano led Rutgers to its first bowl win, first 11-win season and first top-15 final ranking in 2006.

atmosphere never seen before on the Piscataway, N.J. campus, Rutgers proved it had turned the corner, beating Louisville 28–25 on a Jeremy Ito field goal with 13 seconds remaining.

"I don't usually do this, but right before kickoff I took off my headset, looked around and said, "Wow, this is really something," Schiano said. "It's everything you could ever hope for in a college football game. The atmosphere, you just knew it would be, you just didn't know when."

Though Rutgers would lose at Cincinnati the following week and fell in triple overtime to West Virginia in December, the Scarlet Knights won their first bowl game in school history by beating Kansas State in the Texas Bowl to finish 11–2. A remarkable turnaround. Wake Forest also engineered quite a turnaround by coming out of nowhere to win the ACC, but the year belonged to Florida.

The Gators not only won the national title, but also established themselves as the program of the future. Even while Florida was winning games, Meyer was personally recruiting, text messaging prospects (even while attending the Super Bowl) and visiting them when permissible. For the second straight year Meyer landed a top recruiting class, and like his team had at the end of the season, Florida finished No. 1. With a wealth of new talent coming to Gainesville, the Gators sent a message that they will be tough to beat for years to come.

"Florida is the place to be right now," said *SuperPrep* publisher Allen Wallace. "They're the new USC."

During the game, one had to wonder if Schembechler was covering his eyes in heaven. Schembechler's teams were known for their grit and defense, but in this one Ohio State and Michigan were marching up and down the field with ease. Defense was an afterthought. In the end, Ohio State pulled out a 42–39 victory, but despite the fireworks, Bo would have been proud of the fact that Michigan never gave up.

Greg Schiano brought that same never-say-die mentality to a downtrodden Rutgers program when he took over as head coach in 2000. The Scarlet Knights were the laughingstock of college football when Schiano was hired, but as a Jersey guy the young coach knew what it would take to win: keep the best players in the state and build the program with a Jersey edge.

It wasn't easy, as Rutgers routinely got drilled in Schiano's first few years, but the coach never lost faith and finally, in 2006, his vision became a reality. After storming out to an 8–0 start, many wondered how good Rutgers really was. A home game against No. 3 Louisville in October would provide the answer. In an electric

Final Polls

Associated Press

	Record	Pts	Head Coach	SI Preseason Rank
1. Florida (64)	13-1	1624	Urban Meyer	2
2. Ohio St	12-1	1492	Jim Tressel	1
3. LSU	11-2	1452	Les Miles	4
4. USC	11-2	1389	Pete Carroll	8
5. Boise St (1)	13-0	1383	Chris Petersen	9
6. Louisville	12-1	1338	Steve Kragthorpe	5
7. Wisconsin	12-1	1288	Bret Bielema	6
8. Michigan	11-2	1145	Lloyd Carr	3
9. Auburn	11-2	1112	Tommy Tuberville	10
10. West Virginia	11-2	1035	Rich Rodriguez	13
11. Oklahoma	11-3	933	Bob Stoops	7
12. Rutgers	11-2	884	Greg Schiano	16
13. Texas	10-3	772	Mack Brown	18
14. California	10-3	697	Jeff Tedford	20
15. Arkansas	10-4	677	Houston Nutt	12
16. BYU	11-2	673	Bronco Mendenhall	19
17. Notre Dame	10-3	553	Charlie Weis	11
18. Wake Forest	11-3	551	Jim Grobe	15
19. Virginia Tech	10-3	407	Frank Beamer	14
20. Boston College	10-3	353	Jeff Jagodzinski	23
21. Oregon St	10-4	291	Mike Riley	24
22. TCU	11-2	279	Gary Patterson	25
23. Georgia	9-4	204	Mark Richt	26
24. Penn St	9-4	183	Joe Paterno	30
25. Tennessee	9-4	181	Phillip Fulmer	17

Note: As voted by a panel of 65 sportswriters and broadcasters following bowl games (1st place votes in parentheses).

USA Today/ESPN

	Pts	SI Preseason Rank		Pts	SI Preseason Rank
1. Florida (63)	1575	2	13. Texas	791	16
2. Ohio St	1435	1	14. California	716	19
3. LSU	1418	4	15. BYU	615	20
4. USC	1345	7	16. Arkansas	592	13
5. Wisconsin	1328	5	17. Wake Forest	535	15
6. Boise St	1275	9	18. Virginia Tech	494	14
7. Louisville	1270	6	19. Notre Dame	485	11
8. Auburn	1119	10	20. Boston College	388	23
9. Michigan	1092	3	21. TCU	339	24
10. West Virginia	1012	12	22. Oregon St	206	25
11. Oklahoma	849	8	23. Tennessee	202	18
12. Rutgers	841	17	24. Hawaii	152	NR
			25. Penn St	142	NR

Note: Voted by a panel of 63 Div. I-A head coaches; 25 points for 1st, 24 for 2nd, etc. (First place votes in parentheses).

Bowls and Playoffs

NCAA Division I-A Bowl Results

Date	Bowl	Result	Payout/Team ($)	Attendance
12-19-06	Poinsettia	TCU 37, Northern Illinois 7	750,000	29,709
12-21-06	Las Vegas	BYU 38, Oregon 8	950,000	44,615
12-22-06	New Orleans	Troy 41, Rice 17	325,000	24,791
12-23-06	PapaJohns.com	South Florida 24, East Carolina 7	300,000	32,023
12-23-06	New Mexico	San Jose St 20, New Mexico 12	750,000	34,111
12-23-06	Armed Forces	Utah 25, Tulsa 13	600,000	32,412
12-24-06	Hawaii	Hawaii 41, Arizona St 24	398,000	40,623
12-26-06	Motor City	Central Michigan 31, Middle Tenn St 14	750,000	54,113
12-27-06	Emerald	Florida St 44, UCLA 27	850,000	40,331
12-28-06	Independence	Oklahoma St 34, Alabama 31	1.1 million	45,054

NCAA Division I-A Bowl Results *(Cont.)*

Date	Bowl	Result	Payout/Team($)	Attendance
12-28-06	Holiday	California 45, Texas A&M 10	2.2 million	62,395
12-28-06	Texas	Rutgers 37, Kansas St 10	750,000 (Big 12)	52,210
			500,000 (Big East)	
12-29-06	Music City	Kentucky 28, Clemson 20	1.6 million	68,024
12-29-06	Sun	Oregon St 39, Missouri 38	1.9 million	48,732
12-29-06	Liberty	South Carolina 44, Houston 36	1.5 million	56,103
12-29-06	Insight	Texas Tech 44, Minnesota 41	1.2 million	48,391
12-29-06	Champs	Maryland 24, Purdue 7	2.25 million	40,168
12-30-06	Meineke Car Care	Boston College 25, Navy 24	750,000	52,303
12-30-06	Alamo	Texas 26, Iowa 24	2.2 million	65,875
12-30-06	Chick-fil-A	Georgia 31, Virginia Tech 24	3.25 million (ACC)	75,406
			2.4 million (SEC)	
12-31-06	MPC Computers	Miami (Fla.) 21, Nevada 20	250,000	28,652
01-01-07	Outback	Penn St 20, Tennessee 10	3 million	65,601
01-01-07	Cotton	Auburn 17, Nebraska 14	3 million	66,777
01-01-07	Gator	West Virginia 38, Georgia Tech 35	2.25 million	67,714
01-01-07	Capital One	Wisconsin 17, Arkansas 14	4.25 million	60,774
01-01-07	Rose	USC 32, Michigan 18	17 million	93,852
01-01-07	Fiesta	Boise St 43, Oklahoma 42	17 million	73,719
01-02-07	Orange	Louisville 24, Wake Forest 13	17 million	74,470
01-03-07	Sugar	LSU 41, Notre Dame 14	17 million	77,781
01-06-07	International	Cincinnati 27, Western Michigan 24	750,000	26,717
01-07-07	GMAC	Southern Mississippi 28, Ohio 7	750,000	38,751
01-08-07	BCS Nat'l Championship	Florida 41, Ohio St 14	17 million	74,628

NCAA Division I-AA Championship Box Score

Appalachian State	7	7	0	14—28
Massachusetts	7	0	7	3—17

FIRST QUARTER
Massachusetts: Lawrence 1 run (Koepplin kick), 11:49.
Appalachian St: Richardson 45 run (Rauch kick), 1:15.

SECOND QUARTER
Appalachian St: Richardson 6 run (Rauch kick) 0:49.

THIRD QUARTER
Massachusetts: Coen to Listorti 17 pass (Koepplin kick), 4:22.

FOURTH QUARTER
Appalachian St: Richardson 4 run (Rauch kick), 13:22
Massachusetts: FG Koepplin 42 yarder, 8:46.
Appalachian St: Richardson 2 run (Rauch kick), 1:51.

	APPALACHIAN ST	MASSACHUSETTS
First downs	24	19
Rushes–yards	53-285	32-151
Passing yards	146	221
Comp/Att/Int	12-19-1	20-33-2
Punts	4-31.5	4-44.8
Fumbles-lost	0-0	0-0
Penalties-yards	3-15	2-25
Time of possession	33:10	26:50

12-15-06, Chattanooga, Tennessee; Att: 22,808.

Small College Championship Summaries

NCAA DIVISION II

First round: South Dakota 31, Northwood 28 (OT); North Dakota 42, Winona St 0; Delta St 17, Elizabeth City St 10; Newberry 34, Albany St 28; Merrimack 28, Southern Connecticut 26; West Chester 31, Bryant 29; Midwestern St 28, Missouri Western 26; West Texas A&M 30, Abilene Christian 27 (OT).
Second Round: Grand Valley St 35, South Dakota 17; North Dakota 38, Nebraska-Omaha 35; Delta St 24, North Carolina Central 17; North Alabama 38, Newberry 20; Shepherd 31, Merrimack 7; Bloomsburg 21, West Chester 20; NW Missouri St 27, Midwestern St 0; Chadron St 43, West Texas A&M 17.
Quarterfinals: Grand Valley St 30, North Dakota 20; Delta State 27, North Alabama 10; Bloomsburg 24, Shepherd 21; NW Missouri St 28, Chadron St 21.
Semifinals: NW Missouri St 33, Bloomsburg 3; Grand Valley St 49, Delta St 30.

NCAA DIVISION II

Championship: 12-16-06, Florence, Alabama

Grand Valley St (Mich.)	0	10	0	7—17
NW Missouri St	0	7	7	0—14

NCAA DIVISION III

First round: Mt. Union 49, Hope 0; Wheaton 42, Mt. St. Joseph 28; North Central 35, Concordia 6; Capital 32, Wittenberg 14; Wilkes 42, Washington & Lee 0; Rowan 20, Hobart 18; St. John Fisher 49, Union 21; Springfield 42, Curry 14; Wesley 49, Dickinson 21; Carnegie Mellon 21, Millsaps 0; Washington & Jefferson 27, Christopher Newport 23; Mary Hardin-Baylor 33, Hardin-Simmons 21; UW-Whitewater 59, St. Norbert 17; UW-La Crosse 28, Bethel 21; Whitworth 27, Occidental 23; St. John's 21, Central 13.

NCAA DIVISION III *(CONT.)*

Second Round: Mt. Union 35, Wheaton 3; Capital 41, North Central 13; Rowan 21, Wilkes 14; St. John Fisher 27, Springfield 21; Wesley 37, Carnegie Mellon 0; Mary Hardin-Baylor 30, Washington & Jefferson 27; UW-Whitewater 24, UW-La Crosse 21; St. John's 21, Whitworth 3.

Quarterfinals: Mt. Union 17, Capital 14; St. John Fisher 31, Rowan 0; Wesley 34, Mary Hardin-Baylor 20; UW-Whitewater 17, St. John's 14.

NCAA DIVISION III

Semifinals: Mt. Union 26, St. John Fisher 14; UW-Whitewater 44, Wesley 7.

Championship: 12-16-06, Salem, Virginia

Mt. Union	0	14	14	7—35
UW-Whitewater	3	10	0	3—16

NAIA CHAMPIONSHIP

12-16-06, Savannah, Tennessee

Sioux Falls (S.D.)	13	0	10	0—23
St. Francis (Ind.)	13	0	0	6—19

Awards

Heisman Memorial Trophy

Player, School	Class	Pos	1st	2nd	3rd	Total
Troy Smith, Ohio St	Sr.	QB	801	62	13	2540
Darren McFadden, Arkansas	So.	RB	45	298	147	878
Brady Quinn, Notre Dame	Sr.	QB	13	276	191	782
Steve Slaton, West Virginia	So.	RB	6	51	94	214
Mike Hart, Michigan	Sr.	RB	5	58	79	210

Note: Former Heisman winners and the media vote, with ballots allowing for three names (3 points for 1st, 2 for 2nd, 1 for 3rd).

Other Awards

Maxwell Award (Player)	Brady Quinn, Notre Dame, QB
Sporting News Player of the Year	Troy Smith, Ohio St, QB
Walter Camp Player of the Year	Troy Smith, Ohio St, QB
Chuck Bednarik Award (Defense)	Paul Posluszny, Penn St, LB
Vince Lombardi/Rotary Award (Lineman/LB)	LaMarr Woodley, Michigan, DE
Outland Trophy (Interior Lineman)	Joe Thomas, Wisconsin, OL
Davey O'Brien Award (QB)	Troy Smith, Ohio St, QB
Unitas Golden Arm Award (Senior QB)	Brady Quinn, Notre Dame, QB
Doak Walker Award (RB)	Darren McFadden, Arkansas, RB
Biletnikoff Award (WR)	Calvin Johnson, Geogia Tech, WR
Butkus Award (Linebacker)	Patrick Willis, Mississippi, LB
Jim Thorpe Award (Defensive Back)	Aaron Ross, Texas, CB
Associated Press Player of the Year	Troy Smith, Ohio St, QB
Walter Payton Award (Div I-AA Player)	Ricky Santos, New Hampshire, QB
Harlon Hill Trophy (Div II Player)	Danny Woodhead, Chadron St, RB
Gagliardi Trophy (Div III Player)	Josh Brehm, Alma, QB

Coaches' Awards

Walter Camp Award	Greg Schiano, Rutgers
Eddie Robinson Award (Div I-AA)	Jerry Moore, Appalachian St
Bobby Dodd Award	Jim Grobe, Wake Forest
Bear Bryant Award	Chris Petersen, Boise St

AFCA COACHES OF THE YEAR

Division I-A	Jim Grobe, Wake Forest
Division I-AA	Jerry Moore, Appalachian St
Division II	Chuck Martin, Grand Valley St
Division III	Larry Kehres, Mt. Union

Football Writers Association of America All-America Team

OFFENSE

QB .... Troy Smith, Ohio St, Sr.
RB .... Darren McFadden, Arkansas, So.
RB .... Steve Slaton, West Virginia, So.
WR ...... Calvin Johnson, Georgia Tech, Jr.
WR ...... Dwayne Jarrett, USC, Jr.
TE .... Matt Spaeth, Minnesota, Sr.
T .... Jake Long, Michigan, Sr.
T .... Joe Thomas, Wisconsin, Sr.
G .... Josh Beekman, Boston College, Sr.
G .... Justin Blalock, Texas, Sr.
C .... Dan Mozes, West Virginia, Sr.
K .... Justin Medlock, UCLA, Sr.
KR .... DeSean Jackson, California, So.

DEFENSE

E .... LaMarr Woodley, Michigan, Sr.
E .... Gaines Adams, Clemson, Sr.
T .... Glenn Dorsey, LSU, Jr.
T .... Quinn Pitcock, Ohio St, Sr.
LB .... Paul Posluszny, Penn St, Sr.
LB .... Patrick Willis, Mississippi, Sr.
LB .... James Laurinaitis, Ohio St, So.
CB .... Leon Hall, Michigan, Sr.
CB .... Daymeion Hughes, California, Sr.
S .... LaRon Landry, LSU, Sr.
S .... Reggie Nelson, Florida, Jr.
P .... Daniel Sepulveda, Baylor, Sr.

Division I-A

ATLANTIC COAST CONFERENCE

| | Conference | | Full Season | | |
	W	L	W	L	Pct
Wake Forest	6	2	11	3	.786
Boston College	5	3	10	3	.769
Virginia Tech	6	2	10	3	.769
Maryland	5	3	9	4	.692
Georgia Tech	7	1	9	5	.643
Clemson	5	3	8	5	.615
Florida State	3	5	7	6	.538
Miami (Fla.)	3	5	7	6	.538
Virginia	4	4	5	7	.417
North Carolina State	2	6	3	9	.250
North Carolina	2	6	3	9	.250
Duke	0	8	0	12	.000

BIG EAST CONFERENCE

| | Conference | | Full Season | | |
	W	L	W	L	Pct
Louisville	6	1	12	1	.923
West Virginia	5	2	11	2	.846
Rutgers	5	2	11	2	.846
South Florida	4	3	9	4	.692
Cincinnati	4	3	8	5	.615
Pittsburgh	2	5	6	6	.500
Connecticut	1	6	4	8	.333
Syracuse	1	6	4	8	.333

BIG TEN CONFERENCE

| | Conference | | Full Season | | |
	W	L	W	L	Pct
Ohio State	8	0	12	1	.923
Wisconsin	7	1	12	1	.923
Michigan	7	1	11	2	.846
Penn State	5	3	9	4	.692
Purdue	5	3	8	6	.571
Minnesota	3	5	6	7	.462
Iowa	2	6	6	7	.462
Indiana	3	5	5	7	.417
Northwestern	2	6	4	8	.333
Michigan State	1	7	4	8	.333
Illinois	1	7	2	10	.167

BIG 12 CONFERENCE

| | Conference | | Full Season | | |
NORTH	W	L	W	L	Pct
Nebraska	6	2	9	5	.643
Missouri	4	4	8	5	.615
Kansas State	4	4	7	6	.538
Kansas	3	5	6	6	.500
Colorado	2	6	2	10	.167
Iowa State	1	7	4	8	.333
SOUTH					
Oklahoma	7	1	11	3	.786
Texas	6	2	10	3	.769
Texas A&M	5	3	9	4	.692
Texas Tech	4	4	8	5	.615
Oklahoma State	3	5	7	6	.538
Baylor	3	5	4	8	.333

Division I-A *(Cont.)*

CONFERENCE USA

| | Conference | | Full Season | | |
	W	L	W	L	Pct
Houston	7	1	10	4	.714
Southern Mississippi	6	2	9	5	.643
Tulsa	5	3	8	5	.615
Rice	6	2	7	6	.538
East Carolina	5	3	7	6	.538
SMU	4	4	6	6	.500
Marshall	4	4	5	7	.417
UTEP	3	5	5	7	.417
Central Florida	3	5	4	8	.333
Tulane	2	6	4	8	.333
Ala.-Birmingham	2	6	3	9	.250
Memphis	1	7	2	10	.167

MID-AMERICAN ATHLETIC CONFERENCE

| | Conference | | Full Season | | |
EAST	W	L	W	L	Pct
Ohio U	7	1	9	5	.643
Kent State	5	3	6	6	.500
Akron	3	5	5	7	.417
Bowling Green	3	5	4	8	.333
Miami (Ohio)	2	6	2	10	.167
Buffalo	1	7	2	10	.167
WEST					
Central Michigan	7	1	10	4	.714
Western Michigan	6	2	8	5	.615
Northern Illinois	5	3	7	6	.538
Ball State	5	3	5	7	.417
Toledo	3	5	5	7	.417
Eastern Michigan	1	7	1	11	.083

MOUNTAIN WEST CONFERENCE

| | Conference | | Full Season | | |
	W	L	W	L	Pct
BYU	8	0	11	2	.846
TCU	6	2	11	2	.846
Utah	5	3	8	5	.615
Wyoming	5	3	6	6	.500
New Mexico	4	4	6	7	.462
Air Force	3	5	4	8	.333
Colorado State	1	7	4	8	.333
San Diego State	3	5	3	9	.250
UNLV	1	7	2	10	.167

PACIFIC 10 CONFERENCE

| | Conference | | Full Season | | |
	W	L	W	L	Pct
USC	7	2	11	2	.846
California	7	2	10	3	.769
Oregon State	6	3	10	4	.714
UCLA	5	4	7	6	.538
Oregon	4	5	7	6	.538
Arizona State	4	5	7	6	.538
Washington State	4	5	6	6	.500
Arizona	4	5	6	6	.500
Washington	3	6	5	7	.417
Stanford	1	8	1	11	.083

Division I-A *(Cont.)*

SOUTHEASTERN CONFERENCE

EAST	Conference		Full Season		
	W	L	W	L	Pct
Florida	7	1	13	1	.929
Tennessee	5	3	9	4	.692
Georgia	4	4	9	4	.692
Kentucky	4	4	8	5	.615
South Carolina	3	5	8	5	.615
Vanderbilt	1	7	4	8	.333
WEST					
Arkansas	7	1	10	4	.714
LSU	6	2	11	2	.846
Auburn	6	2	11	2	.846
Alabama	2	6	6	7	.462
Mississippi	2	6	4	8	.333
Mississippi State	1	7	3	9	.250

SUN BELT CONFERENCE

	Conference		Full Season		
	W	L	W	L	Pct
Troy	6	1	8	5	.615
Middle Tennessee St	6	1	7	6	.538
Arkansas State	4	3	6	6	.500
La.-Lafayette	3	4	6	6	.500
Florida Atlantic	4	3	5	7	.417
La.-Monroe	3	4	4	8	.333
North Texas	2	5	3	9	.250
Florida International	0	7	0	12	.000

WESTERN ATHLETIC CONFERENCE

	Conference		Full Season		
	W	L	W	L	Pct
Boise State	8	0	13	0	1.00
Hawaii	7	1	11	3	.786
San Jose State	5	3	9	4	.692
Nevada	5	3	8	5	.615
Fresno State	4	4	4	8	.333
Idaho	3	5	4	8	.333
New Mexico State	2	6	4	8	.333
Louisiana Tech	1	7	3	10	.231
Utah State	1	7	1	11	.083

INDEPENDENTS

	Full Season		
	W	L	Pct
Notre Dame	10	3	.769
Navy	9	4	.692
Army	3	9	.250
Temple	1	11	.083

Division I-AA

ATLANTIC 10 CONFERENCE

	Conference		Full Season		
	W	L	W	L	Pct
Massachusetts	8	0	13	2	.867
James Madison	7	1	9	3	.750
New Hampshire	5	3	9	4	.692
Towson	4	4	7	4	.636
Maine	5	3	6	5	.545
Villanova	5	3	6	5	.545
Richmond	3	5	6	5	.545
Northeastern	4	4	5	6	.455
Delaware	3	5	5	6	.455
Rhode Island	2	6	4	7	.364
William & Mary	1	7	3	8	.273
Hofstra	1	7	2	9	.182

BIG SKY CONFERENCE

	Conference		Full Season		
	W	L	W	L	Pct
Montana	8	0	12	2	.857
Montana State	6	2	8	5	.615
Portland State	6	2	7	4	.636
Northern Arizona	5	3	6	5	.545
Sacramento State	4	4	4	7	.364
Weber State	3	5	4	7	.364
Eastern Washington	3	5	3	8	.273
Idaho State	1	7	2	9	.182
Northern Colorado	0	8	1	10	.091

BIG SOUTH CONFERENCE

	Conference		Full Season		
	W	L	W	L	Pct
Coastal Carolina	4	0	9	3	.750
Charleston Southern	2	2	9	2	.818
Gardner-Webb	2	2	6	5	.545
Liberty	2	2	6	5	.545
Va. Military Inst	0	4	1	10	.091

GATEWAY COLLEGIATE ATHLETIC CONFERENCE

	Conference		Full Season		
	W	L	W	L	Pct
Youngstown State	6	1	11	3	.786
Illinois State	5	2	9	4	.692
Southern Illinois	4	3	9	4	.692
Northern Iowa	5	2	7	4	.636
Western Kentucky	4	3	6	5	.545
Western Illinois	2	5	5	6	.455
Missouri State	1	6	2	9	.182
Indiana State	1	6	1	10	.091

IVY LEAGUE

	Conference		Full Season		
	W	L	W	L	Pct
Princeton	6	1	9	1	.900
Yale	6	1	8	2	.800
Harvard	4	3	7	3	.700
Penn	3	4	5	5	.500
Cornell	3	4	5	5	.500
Columbia	2	5	5	5	.500
Brown	2	5	3	7	.300
Dartmouth	2	5	2	8	.200

Division I-AA *(Cont.)*

METRO ATLANTIC ATHLETIC CONFERENCE

	Conference		Full Season		
	W	L	W	L	Pct
Duquesne	3	1	7	3	.700
Marist	3	1	4	7	.364
Iona	2	2	3	7	.300
LaSalle	1	3	3	7	.300
St. Peters	1	3	2	8	.200

MID-EASTERN ATHLETIC CONFERENCE

	Conference		Full Season		
	W	L	W	L	Pct
Hampton	7	1	10	2	.833
Delaware State	6	2	8	3	.727
South Carolina State	6	2	7	4	.636
Florida A&M	5	3	7	4	.636
Morgan State	4	4	5	6	.455
Howard	4	4	5	6	.455
Bethune-Cookman	3	5	5	6	.455
Norfolk State	1	7	4	7	.364
North Carolina A&T	0	8	0	11	.000

NORTHEAST CONFERENCE

	Conference		Full Season		
	W	L	W	L	Pct
Monmouth (N.J.)	6	1	10	2	.833
Central Connecticut St	4	3	8	3	.727
Robert Morris	5	2	7	4	.636
Albany	5	2	7	4	.636
Stony Brook	5	2	5	6	.455
Wagner	0	7	4	7	.364
St. Francis (Pa.)	2	5	3	8	.273
Sacred Heart	1	6	2	9	.182

OHIO VALLEY CONFERENCE

	Conference		Full Season		
	W	L	W	L	Pct
Tenn.-Martin	6	1	9	3	.750
Eastern Illinois	7	1	8	5	.615
Tennessee State	5	2	6	5	.545
Jacksonville State	5	3	6	5	.545
Eastern Kentucky	5	3	6	5	.545
Tennessee Tech	4	4	4	7	.364
SE Missouri State	2	6	4	7	.364
Samford	1	7	3	8	.273
Murray State	0	8	1	10	.091

PATRIOT LEAGUE

	Conference		Full Season		
	W	L	W	L	Pct
Holy Cross	4	2	7	4	.636
Lehigh	5	1	6	5	.545
Bucknell	3	3	6	5	.545
Lafayette	5	1	6	6	.500
Colgate	3	3	4	7	.364
Fordham	1	5	3	8	.273
Georgetown	0	6	2	9	.182

Division I-AA *(Cont.)*

PIONEER LEAGUE

	Conference		Full Season		
	W	L	W	L	Pct
San Diego	7	0	11	1	.917
Drake	6	1	9	2	.818
Davidson	5	2	6	4	.600
Jacksonville	4	3	4	6	.400
Dayton	1	6	4	6	.400
Butler	2	5	3	8	.273
Valparaiso	1	6	3	8	.273
Morehead St	2	5	2	9	.182

SOUTHERN CONFERENCE

	Conference		Full Season		
	W	L	W	L	Pct
Appalachian State	7	0	14	1	.933
Furman	6	1	8	4	.667
Wofford	5	2	7	4	.636
Citadel	4	3	5	6	.455
Elon	2	5	5	6	.455
Georgia Southern	2	5	3	8	.273
Chattanooga	2	5	3	8	.273
Western Carolina	0	7	2	9	.182

SOUTHLAND CONFERENCE

	Conference		Full Season		
	W	L	W	L	Pct
McNeese State	5	1	7	5	.583
Sam Houston State	4	2	6	5	.545
Texas State	3	3	5	6	.455
Stephen F. Austin	4	2	4	7	.364
Nicholls State	2	4	4	7	.364
Northwestern State	2	4	4	7	.364
SE Louisiana	1	5	2	9	.182

SOUTHWESTERN ATHLETIC CONFERENCE

	Conference		Full Season		
	W	L	W	L	Pct
EASTERN					
Alabama A&M	6	3	9	3	.750
Jackson State	5	4	6	5	.545
Alcorn State	5	4	6	5	.545
Mississippi Valley St	5	4	6	5	.545
Alabama State	5	4	5	6	.455
WESTERN					
Ark.-Pine Bluff	7	2	8	4	.667
Southern Univ.	4	5	5	6	.455
Prairie View A&M	2	7	3	7	.300
Grambling State	3	6	3	8	.273
Texas Southern	3	6	3	8	.273

INDEPENDENTS

	Full Season		
	W	L	Pct
Central Arkansas	8	3	.727
Winston-Salem State	4	7	.364
Austin Peay	3	8	.273
Savannah State	2	9	.182

Division I-A

SCORING

	Class	GP	TD	XP	FG	Pts	Pts/Game
Ian Johnson, Boise St	So.	12	25	0	0	152	12.67
Ahmad Bradshaw, Marshall	Jr.	12	21	0	0	126	10.50
Jarett Dillard, Rice	Jr.	13	21	0	0	126	9.69
Arthur Carmody, Louisville	Jr.	13	0	0	21	123	9.46
Ray Rice, Rutgers	So.	13	20	0	0	120	9.23
Patrick White, West Virginia	So.	12	18	0	0	108	9.00
Garrett Wolfe, Northern Illinois	Sr.	13	19	0	0	116	8.92
Jorvorskie Lane, Texas A&M	So.	13	19	0	0	114	8.77
Pat McAfee, West Virginia	Jr.	13	0	0	17	113	8.69
Justin Medlock, UCLA	Sr.	13	0	0	28	113	8.69

FIELD GOALS

	Class	GP	FGA	FG	Pct	FG/Game
Justin Medlock, UCLA	Sr.	13	32	28	.875	2.15
Jeremy Ito, Rutgers	Jr.	13	29	22	.759	1.69
Kevin Kelly, Penn State	So.	13	34	22	.647	1.69
Sam Swank, Wake Forest	So.	14	31	23	.742	1.64
Arthur Carmody, Louisville	Jr.	13	25	21	.840	1.62

TOTAL OFFENSE

			Rushing		Passing			Total Offense	
	Class	GP	Car	Net	Att	Yds	Yds	Yds/Play	Yds/Game
Colt Brennan, Hawaii	Jr.	14	86	366	517	5549	5915	9.9	422.5
Chase Holbrook, New Mexico St	So.	12	80	-78	566	4619	4541	8.2	378.4
Graham Harrell, Texas Tech	So.	13	33	-78	562	4555	4477	7.4	344.4
John Beck, BYU	Sr.	12	50	-8	494	3885	3877	9.5	323.1
Chase Daniel, Missouri	So.	13	147	379	429	3527	3906	7.8	300.5
Jordan Palmer, UTEP	Sr.	12	47	-86	371	3595	3509	8.4	292.4
Curtis Painter, Purdue	So.	14	76	107	393	3985	4092	7.5	292.3
Kevin Kolb, Houston	Sr.	14	111	154	432	3809	3963	8.8	283.1
Brian Brohm, Louisville	Jr.	11	47	45	391	3049	3094	9.7	281.3
Shawn Bell, Baylor	Sr.	9	27	-137	423	2582	2445	6.7	271.7

RUSHING

	Class	GP	Car	Yds	TD	Avg	Yds/Game
Garrett Wolfe, Northern Illinois	Sr.	13	309	1928	18	6.24	148.31
Ian Johnson, Boise St	So.	12	276	1714	25	6.21	142.83
Ray Rice, Rutgers	So.	13	335	1794	20	5.36	138.00
Steve Slaton, West Virginia	So.	13	248	1744	16	7.03	134.15
Ahmad Bradshaw, Marshall	Jr.	12	249	1523	19	6.12	126.92
Dwayne Wright, Fresno St	Jr.	12	261	1462	11	5.60	121.83
Jon Cornish, Kansas	Sr.	12	250	1457	8	5.83	121.42
P.J. Hill, Wisconsin	Fr.	13	311	1569	15	5.05	120.69
Mike Hart, Michigan	Jr.	13	318	1562	14	4.91	120.15
Darren McFadden, Arkansas	So.	14	284	1647	14	5.80	117.64

PASSING EFFICIENCY

	Class	GP	Att	Comp	Pct Comp	Yds	Yds/Att	TD	Int	Rating Pts
Colt Brennan, Hawaii	Jr.	14	559	406	72.6	5549	9.9	58	12	186.0
John Beck, BYU	Sr.	12	417	289	69.3	3885	9.3	32	8	169.1
JaMarcus Russell, LSU	Jr.	13	342	232	67.8	3129	9.1	28	8	167.0
Tyler Palko, Pittsburgh	Sr.	12	322	220	68.3	2871	8.9	25	9	163.2
Kevin Kolb, Houston	Sr.	14	432	292	67.6	3809	8.8	30	4	162.7
Jared Zabransky, Boise St	Sr.	13	288	191	66.3	2587	9.0	23	8	162.6
Troy Smith, Ohio St	Sr.	13	311	203	65.3	2542	8.2	30	6	161.9
Colt McCoy, Texas	Fr.	13	318	217	68.2	2570	8.1	29	7	161.8
Brian Brohm, Louisville	Sr.	11	313	199	63.6	3049	9.7	16	5	159.1
Justin Willis, SMU	Fr.	11	270	182	67.4	2047	7.6	26	6	158.4

Note: Minimum 15 attempts per game.

Division I-A *(Cont.)*

RECEPTIONS PER GAME

	Class	GP	No.	Yds	TD	R/Game
Chris Williams, New Mexico St	So.	12	92	1415	12	7.67
Ryne Robinson, Miami (Ohio)	Sr.	12	91	1178	8	7.58
Mike Walker, Central Florida	Sr.	12	90	1178	7	7.50
Robert Johnson, Texas Tech	Sr.	12	89	871	11	7.42
Jarett Dillard, Rice	Jr.	13	91	1247	21	7.00
Joel Filani, Texas Tech	Sr.	13	91	1300	13	7.00

RECEIVING YARDS PER GAME

	Class	GP	No.	Yds	TD	Yds/Game
Chris Williams, New Mexico St	So.	12	92	1415	12	117.92
Johnnie Lee Higgins, Jr., UTEP	Sr.	12	82	1319	13	109.92
Joel Filani, Texas Tech	Sr.	13	91	1300	13	100.00
Robert Meachem, Tennessee	Jr.	13	71	1298	11	99.85
Ryne Robinson, Miami (Ohio)	Sr.	12	91	1178	8	98.17
Mike Walker, Central Florida	Sr.	12	90	1178	7	98.17

ALL-PURPOSE RUNNERS

	Class	GP	Rush	Rec	PR	KOR	Yds	Yds/Game
Garrett Wolfe, Northern Illinois	Sr.	13	1928	249	0	0	2177	167.46
Steve Slaton, West Virginia	So.	13	1744	360	0	0	2104	161.85
Johnnie Lee Higgins, Jr., UTEP	Sr.	12	-2	1319	281	275	1873	156.08
Chris Williams, New Mexico St	So.	12	53	1415	92	301	1861	155.08
Ian Johnson, Boise State	So.	12	1714	55	0	0	1769	147.42

INTERCEPTIONS

	Class	GP	No.	Int/Game
Stanley Franks, Idaho	Jr.	12	9	.75
Dwight Lowery, San Jose St	Jr.	13	9	.69
Daymeion Hughes, California	Sr.	13	8	.62
Aqib Talib, Kansas	So.	10	6	.60
John Talley, Duke	Jr.	12	7	.58
Quintin Demps, UTEP	Jr.	12	7	.58

PUNT RETURNS

	Class	No.	Yds	TD	Avg
DeSean Jackson, California	Jr.	25	455	4	18.20
Jeremy Trimble, Army	Jr.	18	325	2	18.06
Sammie Stroughter, Oregon St	Jr.	30	470	3	15.67
Ean Randolph, South Florida	So.	25	370	1	14.80
Yamon Figurs, Kansas St	Sr.	22	323	2	14.68

Note: Minimum 1.2 per game.

PUNTING

	Class	No.	Avg
Daniel Sepulveda, Baylor	Sr.	66	46.48
Chris Miller, Ball State	So.	57	46.26
Kody Bliss, Auburn	Sr.	47	45.72
Durant Brooks, Georgia Tech	Sr.	79	45.52
Geoffrey Price, Notre Dame	Sr.	50	45.44

Note: Minimum of 3.6 per game.

KICKOFF RETURNS

	Class	No.	Yds	TD	Avg
Marcus Thigpen, Indiana	So.	24	723	3	30.13
David Harvey, Akron	Fr.	17	510	0	30.00
Lionell Singleton, Florida Int'l	Jr.	12	354	1	29.50
Darrell Blackman, NC State	Jr.	21	605	2	28.81

Note: Minimum of 1.2 per game.

Division I-A Team Single-Game Highs

RUSHING AND PASSING

Rushing and passing yards: 559—Colt Brennan, Hawaii, QB, Dec 24, 2006 (vs Arizona St)
Rushing and passing plays: 64—Colt Brennan, Hawaii, QB, Dec. 2, 2006 (vs Oregon St)
Rushing plays: 43—Donald Brown II, Connecticut, RB, Nov. 11, 2006 (vs Pittsburgh)
Net rushing yards: 364—Garrett Wolfe, Northern Illinois, RB, Sept 30, 2006 (vs Ball St)
Passes attempted: 73—Chase Holbrook, New Mexico St, QB, Sept 30, 2006 (vs UTEP)
Passes completed: 50—Chase Holbrook, New Mexico St, QB, Oct 15, 2006 (vs Boise St)
Passing yards: 574—Colt Brennan, Hawaii, QB, Dec 24, 2006 (vs Arizona St)

RECEIVING AND RETURNS

Passes caught: 15—Robert Johnson, Texas Tech, WR, Sept 2, 2006 (vs SMU)
Receiving yards: 308—Jason Rivers, Hawaii, WR, Dec 24, 2006 (vs Arizona St)
Punt return Yards: 155—Brandon James, Florida. Nov 18, 2006 (vs Western Carolina)
Kickoff return yards: 213—Jeff Smith, Boston College, Sept 9, 2006 (vs Clemson)

Division I-AA

SCORING

	Class	GP	TD	XP	FG	Pts	Pts/Game
Clifton Dawson, Harvard	Sr.	10	22	0	0	132	13.20
Kevin Richardson, Appalachian St	Jr.	15	31	0	0	186	12.40
Mike McLeod, Yale	So.	10	20	0	0	120	12.00
Jerome Felton, Furman	Jr.	12	23	0	0	140	11.67
Arkee Whitlock, Southern Illinois	Sr.	13	25	0	0	150	11.54

FIELD GOALS

	Class	GP	FGA	FG	Pct	FG/Game
Dan Carpenter, Montana	Jr.	14	30	24	.800	1.71
Rob Zarrilli, Hofstra	So.	11	21	18	.857	1.64
Robert Weeks, Northwestern St	So.	11	24	18	.750	1.64
Brian Wingert, Northern Iowa	Sr.	11	23	17	.739	1.55
Blake Bercegeay, McNeese St	So.	12	20	18	.900	1.50

TOTAL OFFENSE

			Rushing		Passing		Total Offense		
	Class	GP	Car	Net	Att	Yds	Yds	Yds/Play	Yds/Game
Josh Johnson, San Diego	Jr.	12	107	720	371	3320	4040	8.9	336.7
Tyler Thigpen, Coastal Carolina	Jr.	12	113	656	339	3296	3952	9.7	329.3
Sean Schaefer, Towson	So.	10	61	-60	380	3033	2973	8.0	297.3
Collin Drafts, Charleston So.	Sr.	11	130	513	319	2665	3178	8.4	288.9
Scott Knapp, Duquesne	So.	10	40	-44	351	2853	2809	8.1	280.9

RUSHING

	Class	GP	Car	Yds	Avg	TD	Yds/Game
Justise Hairston, Central Connecticut St	Sr.	11	277	1847	6.7	20	167.9
Marcus Mason, Youngstown St	Sr.	12	302	1847	6.1	23	153.9
Scott Phaydavong, Drake	So.	11	277	1613	5.8	10	146.6
Arkee Whitlock, Southern Illinois	Sr.	13	317	1828	5.8	25	140.6
Steve Baylark, Massachusetts	Sr.	14	338	1960	5.8	15	140.0

PASSING EFFICIENCY

	Class	GP	Att	Comp	Pct Comp	Yds	Yds/Att	TD	Int	Rating Pts
Josh Johnson, San Diego	Jr.	12	371	246	66.3	3320	8.9	34	5	169.0
Jason Murrietta, Northern Arizona	Sr.	11	329	214	65.0	2827	8.6	34	5	168.3
Tyler Thigpen, Coastal Carolina	Sr.	12	339	217	64.0	3296	9.7	29	11	167.4
Chris Wallace, Ark.-Pine Bluff	Sr.	12	211	129	61.1	2023	9.6	20	9	164.4
Justin Rascati, James Madison	Sr.	12	231	153	66.2	2045	8.9	20	6	164.0

Note: Minimum 15 attempts per game.

RECEPTIONS PER GAME

	Class	GP	No.	Yds	TD	R/G
Maurice Price, Charleston Southern	Jr.	11	103	985	10	9.36
Alex Watson, Northern Arizona	Jr.	11	82	1017	15	7.45
Jaleel Kindell, St. Peter's	So.	10	74	855	3	7.40
David Ball, New Hampshire	Sr.	13	93	1114	13	7.15
Lou Russo, La Salle	Sr.	10	70	744	5	7.00

RECEIVING YARDS PER GAME

	Class	GP	No.	Yds	TD	Yds/G
Terrell Hudgins, Elon	Fr.	9	69	1027	8	114.1
Bruce Hocker, Duquesne	Jr.	10	61	1070	16	107.0
Alex Roberson, Duquesne	Jr.	1	3	105	0	105.0
Lanis Frederick, Austin Peay	So.	11	77	1101	7	100.1
Nick Ruhe, Dayton	Sr.	10	49	977	3	97.7

INTERCEPTIONS

	Class	GP	No.	Yds	TD	Int/G
Dre Dokes, Northern Iowa	Sr.	11	7	116	1	.64
B. Webber, Sacramento St	Jr.	10	6	23	0	.60
Chris Parsons, Northern Iowa	Jr.	11	6	34	0	.55
D. Rodgers-Cromartie, Tenn. St.	Jr.	11	6	70	0	.55
J. Marshall, Miss. Valley St.	Jr.	11	6	2	0	.55
B. Williams, Bethune-Cookman	Jr.	11	6	25	0	.55

PUNTING

	Class	No.	Avg
Jonathan Dudley, Georgia Southern	Sr.	1	58.0
Rafael Revuelta, Prairie View A&M	So.	1	53.0
Brian Dandrige, Morgan State	Fr.	1	50.0
Kevin McCants, Alabama A&M	Fr.	1	50.0
Andrew Wilcox, Elon	So.	3	48.0

Division I-AA (Cont.)

ALL-PURPOSE RUNNERS

	Class	GP	Rush	Rec	PR	KOR	Yds	Yds/Game
Josh Johnson, San Diego	Jr.	12	720	27	0	0	747	336.7
Tyler Thigpen, Coastal Carolina	Sr.	12	656	0	0	0	656	329.3
Sean Schaefer, Towson	So.	10	-60	0	0	0	-60	297.3
Collin Drafts, Charleston Southern	Sr.	11	513	0	0	0	513	288.9
Scott Knapp, Duquesne	So.	10	-44	0	0	0	-44	280.9

Division II

SCORING

	Class	GP	TD	XP	FG	Pts	Pts/Game
Danny Woodhead, Chadron St	So.	13	38	0	0	228	17.5
Germaine Race, Pittsburg St	Sr.	13	31	0	0	188	15.7
Joique Bell, Wayne St (Mich.)	So.	11	23	0	0	138	12.5
Lorenzo Perry, Bryant	Jr.	11	21	0	0	126	11.5
Zach Miller, Nebraska-Omaha	Jr.	10	19	0	0	114	11.4

FIELD GOALS

	Class	GP	FGA	FG	Pct	FG/Game
Sean Sehnem, Western New Mexico	So.	10	20	15	.750	1.5
Dustin Strickler, Missouri Western St	So.	12	23	17	.739	1.4
Geoff Carnahan, Nebraska-Kearney	So.	10	22	14	.636	1.4
Paul Williams, Tarleton State	Sr.	10	16	13	.812	1.3
David Chudzinski, Wayne St (Mich.)	Jr.	11	16	14	.875	1.3
Jon Gutierrez, St. Cloud State	So.	11	20	14	.700	1.3

TOTAL OFFENSE

	Class	GP	Yds	Yds/Game
Joe Winters, Missouri-Rolla	Sr.	11	3731	339.2
Jimmy Terwilliger, East Stroudsburg	Sr.	11	3470	315.5
Dalton Bell, West Texas A&M	Sr.	13	3878	298.3
Ben King, Minnesota St-Mankato	Sr.	10	2931	293.1
Billy Malone, Abilene Christian	So.	11	3107	282.5

RUSHING

	Class	GP	Car	Yds	TD	Yds/Game
Danny Woodhead, Chadron St	So.	13	344	2756	34	212.0
Joique Bell, Wayne State (Mich.)	So.	11	348	2065	22	187.7
Lorenzo Perry, Bryant	Jr.	11	291	1924	20	174.9
Brandon Toles, Southern Connecticut St	Jr.	11	305	1899	16	172.6
Germaine Race, Pittsburg St	Sr.	12	310	1944	31	162.0

PASSING EFFICIENCY

	Class	GP	Att	Comp	TD	Int	Rating Pts
Cullen Finnerty, Grand Valley St (Mich.)	Sr.	15	343	195	41	10	169.3
Charles Granatell, Bryant	Jr.	11	212	134	21	7	167.5
Jimmy Terwilliger, East Stroudsburg	Sr.	11	346	222	35	7	165.5
Bill Zwaan Jr., West Chester	Jr.	13	223	136	22	10	164.1
Daniel Latorre, Bloomsburg	Fr.	14	239	144	20	10	163.8

RECEPTIONS PER GAME

	Class	GP	No.	Yds	TD	R/G
Colin Bado, Missouri Southern St	Fr.	11	88	953	4	8.0
Brian Jark, Northern State	Sr.	11	84	925	9	7.6
Dan Paulsen, St. Joseph's (Ind.)	Jr.	11	82	1121	9	7.5
Ashton Gronewold, Missouri-Rolla	Jr.	11	78	1120	15	7.1
Weston Dressler, North Dakota		13	90	1215	16	6.9

RECEIVING YARDS PER GAME

	Class	GP	No.	Yds	TD	Yds/G
Eric Fowler, Grand Valley St (Mich.)	Sr.	15	83	1694	22	112.9
Evan Prall, East Stroudsburg	Sr.	11	76	1174	17	106.7
Dan Paulsen, St. Joseph's (Ind.)	Jr.	11	82	1121	9	101.9
Ashton Gronewold, Missouri-Rolla	Jr.	11	78	1120	15	101.8
Almonzo Banks, West Liberty St	Jr.	10	67	977	8	97.7

Division II *(Cont.)*

INTERCEPTIONS

	Class	GP	No.	Yds	Int/Game
Dan Peters, Shepherd	Sr.	12	14	219	1.2
Darren Banks, West Liberty St	Jr.	11	10	68	0.9
Josh Jones, Minn St-Moorhead	So.	11	10	138	0.9
Christopher Anzano, Pace	Sr.	10	9	64	0.9
Quincy Skinner, Arkansas Tech	Jr.	10	8	95	0.8
Robert Towns, Harding	Sr.	10	8	83	0.8

PUNTING

	Class	No.	Avg
Curtis Lilly, East Central	Sr.	46	45.2
Wayne Durham, Adams St	Jr.	59	44.0
George Villa, New Mexico Highlands	Sr.	57	43.0
Jason Davis, Western State	Jr.	63	42.3
Josh Vanlue, Western Oregon	So.	41	41.9

Note: Minimum 3.6 per game.

Division III

SCORING

	Class	GP	TD	XP	FG	Pts	Pts/Game
Chris Sharpe, Springfield	Jr.	12	35	0	0	212	17.7
Matthew Andersen, Occidental	Jr.	9	18	0	0	108	12.0
Tom Arcidiacono, Union (N.Y.)	Jr.	10	20	0	0	120	12.0
Rory Lee, Puget Sound	Sr.	10	20	0	0	120	12.0
Nate Kmic, Mt. Union	So.	15	28	0	0	168	11.2

FIELD GOALS

	Class	GP	FGA	FG	Pct	FG/Game
Chris Kemmerer, Buena Vista	So.	10	22	16	.727	1.6
Connor Pearce, Cal. Lutheran	Jr.	9	17	14	.823	1.6
Ben Scott, Johns Hopkins	Jr.	10	19	13	.684	1.3
Steve Hauschka, Middlebury	Sr.	8	12	10	.833	1.3
Vincent Doffont, Montclair State	Sr.	10	17	12	.705	1.2
Jeff Schebler, UW-Whitewater	Sr.	15	21	18	.857	1.2

TOTAL OFFENSE

	Class	GP	Yds	Yds/Game
Josh Brehm, Alma	Sr.	10	4084	408.4
Josh Vogelbach, Guilford	So.	10	3472	347.2
Dustin Huff, Wabash	Sr.	10	3287	328.7
Jason Vrable, Marietta	Sr.	10	3123	312.3
Zach Sweers, Luther	Sr.	10	2960	296.0

RUSHING

	Class	GP	Car	Yds	TD	Yds/Game
Chris Sharpe, Springfield	Jr.	12	261	1941	35	161.8
Nate Kmic, Mount Union	So.	15	336	2365	26	157.7
Dante Daniels, Monmouth (Ill.)	Sr.	10	271	1557	16	155.7
Peter Ereg, MacMurray	Sr.	10	288	1510	14	151.0
Tristan Murray, Wittenburg	Sr.	11	290	1517	17	137.9

PASSING EFFICIENCY

	Class	GP	Att	Comp	Pct Comp	Yds	TD	Int	Rating Pts
Dustin Huff, Wabash	Sr.	10	318	215	.676	2961	29	8	170.9
Jordan Neal, Hardin-Simmons	Sr.	10	280	185	.660	2605	29	8	170.3
Bobby Swallow, Washington & Jefferson	So.	12	229	159	.694	2022	20	5	168.1
Rob Kramer, St. John Fisher	Jr.	13	233	151	.648	2019	22	1	167.9
Patrick Lucey, Williams	Jr.	8	168	112	.666	1528	14	4	165.8

Note: Minimum 15 attempts per game.

RECEPTIONS PER GAME

	Class	GP	No.	Yds	TD	Rec/Game
Joe Cline, Alma	Jr.	10	98	1256	17	9.8
Chris Barnette, Guilford	Sr.	10	94	900	9	9.4
Kyle Pearson, Luther	So.	10	89	1068	5	8.9
Brandon Zerr-Smith, Lewis & Clark	Sr.	9	70	545	1	7.8
Jay Jay Vanderstyne, Rochester (N.Y.)	Jr.	11	85	1128	11	7.7

RECEIVING YARDS PER GAME

	Class	GP	No.	Yds	TD	Yds/Game
Joe Cline, Alma	Jr.	10	98	1256	17	125.6
Matt Frank, Carleton	So.	10	74	1120	8	112.0
Adam Brossman, Lebanon Valley	Jr.	10	62	1107	15	110.7
Kyle Pearson, Luther	So.	10	89	1068	5	106.8
Michael Russell, Wabash	Jr.	10	60	1052	13	105.2

Division III (Cont.)

INTERCEPTIONS	Class	GP	No.	Yds	Int/G
Craig Haywood, King's (Pa.)	Sr.	10	12	209	1.2
Steve Arguelles, Coast Guard	Fr.	11	11	132	1.0
Chad Otte, Wilmington (Ohio)	Sr.	10	9	69	0.9
Phil Schroer, Nebraska Wesleyan	So.	10	9	117	0.9
Joe Harasymiak, Springfield	Jr.	12	10	137	0.8

PUNTING	Class	No.	Avg
Kevin Soflkiancs, Baldwin-Wallace	Jr.	44	42.6
Ken Alvord, Lawrence	Sr.	43	42.4
Ben Scott, Johns Hopkins	Jr.	53	41.6
Jesse Harms, Coast Guard	Jr.	52	41.6
Dom Ancona, Hobart	So.	44	41.3

Note: Minimum 3.6 per game.

2006 NCAA Division I-A Team Leaders

Offense

SCORING

	GP	Pts	Avg
Hawaii	14	656	46.86
Boise St	13	516	39.69
West Virginia	13	505	38.85
Louisville	13	491	37.77
BYU	13	478	36.77
Texas	13	467	35.92
Oklahoma St	13	458	35.23
Ohio State	13	450	34.62
LSU	13	438	33.69
Houston	14	462	33.00

RUSHING

	GP	Car	Yds	Avg	TD	Yds/Game
Navy	13	764	4251	5.56	39	327.00
West Virginia	13	590	3939	6.68	48	303.00
Air Force	12	660	2753	4.17	22	229.42
Arkansas	14	539	3199	5.94	26	228.50
Clemson	13	495	2832	5.72	31	217.85
Boise St	13	551	2784	5.05	39	214.15
Oklahoma St	13	522	2704	5.18	28	208.00
Texas A&M	13	540	2689	4.98	32	206.85
TCU	13	557	2530	4.54	28	194.62
Illinois	12	434	2266	5.22	15	188.83

TOTAL OFFENSE

	GP	Plays	Yds	Avg	TD	Yds/Game
Hawaii	14	913	7829	8.58	89	559.21
Louisville	13	867	6179	7.13	61	475.31
New Mexico St	12	930	5702	6.13	53	475.17
BYU	13	889	6051	6.81	63	465.46
West Virginia	13	823	5998	7.29	65	461.38
Texas Tech	13	875	5822	6.65	54	447.85
Houston	14	935	6245	6.68	60	446.07
Missouri	13	922	5533	6.00	48	425.62
Oregon	13	958	5497	5.74	48	422.85
Boise St	13	857	5468	6.38	68	420.62

PASSING

	GP	Att	Comp	Int	Pct Comp	Yds	Yds/Gm	TD
Hawaii	14	615	444	12	72.20	6178	441.3	62
New Mexico St	12	607	421	12	69.36	4792	399.3	34
Texas Tech	13	655	438	11	66.87	4803	369.5	39
BYU	13	452	311	9	68.81	4206	323.5	33
UTEP	12	447	290	17	64.88	3754	312.8	29
Purdue	14	541	322	20	59.52	4082	291.6	24
Louisville	13	384	245	7	63.80	3770	290.0	22
Houston	14	445	300	5	67.42	3889	277.8	30
Kentucky	13	436	273	7	62.61	3597	276.7	31
Missouri	13	465	291	11	62.58	3590	276.2	29

Single-Game Highs

Points Scored: 68—Hawaii, Oct 14, 2006 (vs Fresno St)
68—Hawaii, Oct 28, 2006 (vs Idaho)
Net Rushing Yards: 476—San Jose St, Oct 28, 2006 (vs Louisiana Tech)
Passing Yards: 559—Hawaii, Dec 24, 2006 (vs Arizona St)
Rushing and Passing Yards: 682—Texas Tech, Nov 4, 2006 (vs Baylor)
Fewest Rushing and Passing Yards Allowed: 32—Arizona, Oct 14, 2006 (vs. Stanford)

Defense

SCORING

	GP	Pts	Avg
Virginia Tech	13	143	11.0
Wisconsin	13	157	12.1
TCU	13	160	12.3
LSU	13	164	12.6
Ohio St.	13	166	12.8
Florida	14	189	13.5
Auburn	13	181	13.9
Rutgers	13	186	14.3
Penn State	13	187	14.4
BYU	13	191	14.7

TOTAL DEFENSE

	GP	Plays	Yds	Avg Y/Play	Avg Y/G
Virginia Tech	13	743	2853	3.84	219.46
TCU	13	753	3054	4.06	234.92
LSU	13	764	3156	4.13	242.77
Rutgers	13	759	3279	4.32	252.23
Wisconsin	13	775	3290	4.25	253.08
Florida	14	828	3576	4.32	255.43
Miami (Fla.)	13	753	3322	4.41	255.54
Georgia	13	775	3357	4.33	258.23
Wyoming	12	723	3155	4.36	262.92
Michigan	13	789	3488	4.42	268.31

RUSHING

	GP	Car	Yds	Avg	TD	Yds/Game
Michigan	13	301	564	1.87	5	43.4
TCU	13	367	791	2.16	8	60.8
Texas	13	345	795	2.30	8	61.2
Miami (Fla.)	13	391	882	2.26	12	67.8
Florida	14	370	1015	2.74	8	72.5
Western Michigan	13	380	989	2.60	11	76.1
Penn State	13	400	1137	2.84	8	87.5
Boise State	13	361	1158	3.21	7	89.1
UCLA	13	419	1184	2.83	9	91.1
USC	13	399	1184	2.97	6	91.1

TURNOVER MARGIN

		Turnovers Gained			Turnovers Lost			
	GP	Fum	Int	Total	Fum	Int	Total	Mar/Gm
Minnesota	13	15	17	32	3	11	14	1.38
Boston College	13	16	21	37	11	11	22	1.15
Kentucky	13	18	14	32	10	7	17	1.15
BYU	13	9	18	27	4	9	13	1.08
Michigan	13	14	12	26	4	8	12	1.08
Wake Forest	14	9	22	31	12	6	18	.93
Nevada	13	17	20	37	13	12	25	.92
W. Michigan	13	10	24	34	9	13	22	.92
Syracuse	12	11	17	28	12	5	17	.92
Boise St	13	11	20	31	11	9	20	.85

PASSING EFFICIENCY

	GP	Att	Comp	Pct Comp	Int	Pct Int	Yds	Yds/Att	TD	Pct TD	Rating Pts
Hawaii	14	615	444	72.20	12	1.95	6178	10.05	62	10.08	185.95
BYU	13	452	311	68.81	9	1.99	4206	9.31	33	7.30	167.08
Pittsburgh	12	332	228	68.67	9	2.71	2991	9.01	28	8.43	163.30
LSU	13	368	245	66.58	9	2.45	3272	8.89	30	8.15	163.30
Louisville	13	384	245	63.80	7	1.82	3770	9.82	22	5.73	161.53
Boise St	13	306	204	66.67	9	2.94	2684	8.77	25	8.17	161.46
Houston	14	445	300	67.42	5	1.12	3889	8.74	30	6.74	160.81
Ohio St	13	340	221	65.00	6	1.76	2791	8.21	31	9.12	160.51
Texas	13	371	244	65.77	9	2.43	2975	8.02	31	8.36	155.88
West Virginia	13	233	149	63.95	8	3.43	2059	8.84	15	6.44	152.51

NCAA Football Bowl Subdivision* National Champions

Year	Champion	Record	Bowl Game	Head Coach
1883	Yale	8-0-0	No bowl	Ray Tompkins (Captain)
1884	Yale	9-0-0	No bowl	Eugene L. Richards (Captain)
1885	Princeton	9-0-0	No bowl	Charles DeCamp (Captain)
1886	Yale	9-0-1	No bowl	Robert N. Corwin (Captain)
1887	Yale	9-0-0	No bowl	Harry W. Beecher (Captain)
1888	Yale	13-0-0	No bowl	Walter Camp
1889	Princeton	10-0-0	No bowl	Edgar Poe (Captain)
1890	Harvard	11-0-0	No bowl	George A. Stewart/George C. Adams
1891	Yale	13-0-0	No bowl	Walter Camp
1892	Yale	13-0-0	No bowl	Walter Camp
1893	Princeton	11-0-0	No bowl	Tom Trenchard (Captain)
1894	Yale	16-0-0	No bowl	William C. Rhodes
1895	Pennsylvania	14-0-0	No bowl	George Woodruff
1896	Princeton	10-0-1	No bowl	Garrett Cochran
1897	Pennsylvania	15-0-0	No bowl	George Woodruff
1898	Harvard	11-0-0	No bowl	W. Cameron Forbes
1899	Harvard	10-0-1	No bowl	Benjamin H. Dibblee
1900	Yale	12-0-0	No bowl	Malcolm McBride
1901	Michigan	11-0-0	Won Rose	Fielding Yost
1902	Michigan	11-0-0	No bowl	Fielding Yost
1903	Princeton	11-0-0	No bowl	Art Hillebrand
1904	Pennsylvania	12-0-0	No bowl	Carl Williams
1905	Chicago	11-0-0	No bowl	Amos Alonzo Stagg
1906	Princeton	9-0-1	No bowl	Bill Roper
1907	Yale	9-0-1	No bowl	Bill Knox
1908	Pennsylvania	11-0-1	No bowl	Sol Metzger
1909	Yale	10-0-0	No bowl	Howard Jones
1910	Harvard	8-0-1	No bowl	Percy Houghton
1911	Princeton	8-0-2	No bowl	Bill Roper
1912	Harvard	9-0-0	No bowl	Percy Houghton
1913	Harvard	9-0-0	No bowl	Percy Houghton
1914	Army	9-0-0	No bowl	Charley Daly
1915	Cornell	9-0-0	No bowl	Al Sharpe
1916	Pittsburgh	8-0-0	No bowl	Pop Warner
1917	Georgia Tech	9-0-0	No bowl	John Heisman
1918	Pittsburgh	4-1-0	No bowl	Pop Warner
1919	Harvard	9-0-1	Won Rose	Bob Fisher
1920	California	9-0-0	Won Rose	Andy Smith
1921	Cornell	8-0-0	No bowl	Gil Dobie
1922	Cornell	8-0-0	No bowl	Gil Dobie
1923	Illinois	8-0-0	No bowl	Bob Zuppke
1924	Notre Dame	10-0-0	Won Rose	Knute Rockne
1925	Alabama (H)	10-0-0	Won Rose	Wallace Wade
	Dartmouth (D)	8-0-0	No bowl	Jesse Hawley
1926	Alabama (H)	9-0-1	Tied Rose	Wallace Wade
	Stanford (D)(H)	10-0-1	Tied Rose	Pop Warner
1927	Illinois	7-0-1	No bowl	Bob Zuppke
1928	Georgia Tech (H)	10-0-0	Won Rose	Bill Alexander
	USC (D)	9-0-1	No bowl	Howard Jones
1929	Notre Dame	9-0-0	No bowl	Knute Rockne
1930	Notre Dame	10-0-0	No bowl	Knute Rockne
1931	USC	10-1-0	Won Rose	Howard Jones
1932	USC (H)	10-0-0	Won Rose	Howard Jones
	Michigan (D)	8-0-0	No bowl	Harry Kipke
1933	Michigan	7-0-1	No bowl	Harry Kipke
1934	Minnesota	8-0-0	No bowl	Bernie Bierman
1935	Minnesota (H)	8-0-0	No bowl	Bernie Bierman
	SMU (D)	12-1-0	Lost Rose	Matty Bell
1936	Minnesota	7-1-0	No bowl	Bernie Bierman
1937	Pittsburgh	9-0-1	No bowl	Jock Sutherland
1938	TCU (AP)	11-0-0	Won Sugar	Dutch Meyer
	Notre Dame (D)	8-1-0	No bowl	Elmer Layden

*In 2007, the NCAA renamed division I-A as the "Football Bowl Subdivision" and divisions I-AA through III as "Football Championship Subdivisions."

Year	Champion	Record	Bowl Game	Head Coach
1939	USC (D)	8-0-2	Won Rose	Howard Jones
	Texas A&M (AP)	11-0-0	Won Sugar	Homer Norton
1940	Minnesota	8-0-0	No bowl	Bernie Bierman
1941	Minnesota	8-0-0	No bowl	Bernie Bierman
1942	Ohio St	9-1-0	No bowl	Paul Brown
1943	Notre Dame	9-1-0	No bowl	Frank Leahy
1944	Army	9-0-0	No bowl	Red Blaik
1945	Army	9-0-0	No bowl	Red Blaik
1946	Notre Dame	8-0-1	No bowl	Frank Leahy
1947	Notre Dame	9-0-0	No bowl	Frank Leahy
	Michigan*	10-0-0	Won Rose	Fritz Crisler
1948	Michigan	9-0-0	No bowl	Bennie Oosterbaan
1949	Notre Dame	10-0-0	No bowl	Frank Leahy
1950	Oklahoma	10-1-0	Lost Sugar	Bud Wilkinson
1951	Tennessee	10-1-0	Lost Sugar	Bob Neyland
1952	Michigan St	9-0-0	No bowl	Biggie Munn
1953	Maryland	10-1-0	Lost Orange	Jim Tatum
1954	Ohio St	10-0-0	Won Rose	Woody Hayes
	UCLA (UPI)	9-0-0	No bowl	Red Sanders
1955	Oklahoma	11-0-0	Won Orange	Bud Wilkinson
1956	Oklahoma	10-0-0	No bowl	Bud Wilkinson
1957	Auburn	10-0-0	No bowl	Shug Jordan
	Ohio St (UPI)	9-1-0	Won Rose	Woody Hayes
1958	LSU	11-0-0	Won Sugar	Paul Dietzel
1959	Syracuse	11-0-0	Won Cotton	Ben Schwartzwalder
1960	Minnesota	8-2-0	Lost Rose	Murray Warmath
1961	Alabama	11-0-0	Won Sugar	Bear Bryant
1962	USC	11-0-0	Won Rose	John McKay
1963	Texas	11-0-0	Won Cotton	Darrell Royal
1964	Alabama	10-1-0	Lost Orange	Bear Bryant
1965	Alabama	9-1-1	Won Orange	Bear Bryant
	Michigan St (UPI)	10-1-0	Lost Rose	Duffy Daugherty
1966	Notre Dame	9-0-1	No bowl	Ara Parseghian
1967	USC	10-1-0	Won Rose	John McKay
1968	Ohio St	10-0-0	Won Rose	Woody Hayes
1969	Texas	11-0-0	Won Cotton	Darrell Royal
1970	Nebraska	11-0-1	Won Orange	Bob Devaney
	Texas (UPI)	10-1-0	Lost Cotton	Darrell Royal
1971	Nebraska	13-0-0	Won Orange	Bob Devaney
1972	USC	12-0-0	Won Rose	John McKay
1973	Notre Dame	11-0-0	Won Sugar	Ara Parseghian
	Alabama (UPI)	11-1-0	Lost Sugar	Bear Bryant
1974	Oklahoma	11-0-0	No bowl	Barry Switzer
	USC (UPI)	10-1-1	Won Rose	John McKay
1975	Oklahoma	11-1-0	Won Orange	Barry Switzer
1976	Pittsburgh	12-0-0	Won Sugar	Johnny Majors
1977	Notre Dame	11-1-0	Won Cotton	Dan Devine
1978	Alabama	11-1-0	Won Sugar	Bear Bryant
	USC (UPI)	12-1-0	Won Rose	John Robinson
1979	Alabama	12-0-0	Won Sugar	Bear Bryant
1980	Georgia	12-0-0	Won Sugar	Vince Dooley
1981	Clemson	12-0-0	Won Orange	Danny Ford
1982	Penn St	11-1-0	Won Sugar	Joe Paterno
1983	Miami (Fla.)	11-1-0	Won Orange	Howard Schnellenberger
1984	BYU	13-0-0	Won Holiday	LaVell Edwards
1985	Oklahoma	11-1-0	Won Orange	Barry Switzer
1986	Penn St	12-0-0	Won Fiesta	Joe Paterno
1987	Miami (Fla.)	12-0-0	Won Orange	Jimmy Johnson
1988	Notre Dame	12-0-0	Won Fiesta	Lou Holtz
1989	Miami (Fla.)	11-1-0	Won Sugar	Dennis Erickson
1990	Colorado	11-1-1	Won Orange	Bill McCartney
	Georgia Tech (UPI)	11-0-1	Won Citrus	Bobby Ross
1991	Miami (Fla.)	12-0-0	Won Orange	Dennis Erickson
	Washington (CNN)	12-0-0	Won Rose	Don James
1992	Alabama	13-0-0	Won Sugar	Gene Stallings
1993	Florida St	12-1-0	Won Orange	Bobby Bowden
1994	Nebraska	13-0-0	Won Orange	Tom Osborne
1995	Nebraska	12-0-0	Won Fiesta	Tom Osborne
†1996	Florida	12–1	Won Sugar	Steve Spurrier

Year	Champion	Record	Bowl Game	Head Coach
1997	Michigan	12–0	Won Rose	Lloyd Carr
	Nebraska (ESPN)	13–0	Won Orange	Tom Osborne
1998	Tennessee	13–0	Won Fiesta	Phillip Fulmer
1999	Florida St	12–0	Won Sugar	Bobby Bowden
2000	Oklahoma	13–0	Won Orange	Bob Stoops
2001	Miami (Fla.)	12–0	Won Rose	Larry Coker
2002	Ohio St	14–0	Won Fiesta	Jim Tressel
2003	LSU	13–1	Won Sugar	Nick Saban
	USC	12–1	Won Rose	Pete Carroll
2004	USC	13–0	Won Orange	Pete Carroll
2005	Texas	13–0	Won Rose	Mack Brown
‡2006	Florida	13–1	Won BCS Nat'l Championship	Urban Meyer

*The AP, which had voted Notre Dame No. 1, took a second vote, giving the national title to Michigan after its 49–0 win over USC in the Rose Bowl.   Note: Selectors: Helms Athletic Foundation (H) 1883–1935, The Dickinson System (D) 1924–40, The Associated Press (AP) 1936–present, United Press International (UPI) 1958–90, *USA Today*/CNN (CNN) 1991–96, and *USA Today*/ESPN (ESPN) 1997–present. †In 1996 the NCAA introduced overtime to break ties. ‡In 2006, the BCS established a separate national championship game in addition to its existing four-bowl structure.¶

Results of Major Bowl Games

Rose Bowl

1-1-02	Michigan 49, Stanford 0		1-1-53	USC 7, Wisconsin 0
1-1-16	Washington St 14, Brown 0		1-1-54	Michigan St 28, UCLA 20
1-1-17	Oregon 14, Pennsylvania 0		1-1-55	Ohio St 20, USC 7
1-1-18	Mare Island 19, Camp Lewis 7		1-2-56	Michigan St 17, UCLA 14
1-1-19	Great Lakes 17, Mare Island 0		1-1-57	Iowa 35, Oregon St 19
1-1-20	Harvard 7, Oregon 6		1-1-58	Ohio St 10, Oregon 7
1-1-21	California 28, Ohio St 0		1-1-59	Iowa 38, California 12
1-2-22	Washington & Jefferson 0, California 0		1-1-60	Washington 44, Wisconsin 8
1-1-23	USC 14, Penn St 3		1-2-61	Washington 17, Minnesota 7
1-1-24	Navy 14, Washington 14		1-1-62	Minnesota 21, UCLA 3
1-1-25	Notre Dame 27, Stanford 10		1-1-63	USC 42, Wisconsin 37
1-1-26	Alabama 20, Washington 19		1-1-64	Illinois 17, Washington 7
1-1-27	Alabama 7, Stanford 7		1-1-65	Michigan 34, Oregon St 7
1-2-28	Stanford 7, Pittsburgh 6		1-1-66	UCLA 14, Michigan St 12
1-1-29	Georgia Tech 8, California 7		1-2-67	Purdue 14, USC 13
1-1-30	USC 47, Pittsburgh 14		1-1-68	USC 14, Indiana 3
1-1-31	Alabama 24, Washington St 0		1-1-69	Ohio St 27, USC 16
1-1-32	USC 21, Tulane 12		1-1-70	USC 10, Michigan 3
1-2-33	USC 35, Pittsburgh 0		1-1-71	Stanford 27, Ohio St 17
1-1-34	Columbia 7, Stanford 0		1-1-72	Stanford 13, Michigan 12
1-1-35	Alabama 29, Stanford 13		1-1-73	USC 42, Ohio St 17
1-1-36	Stanford 7, Southern Methodist 0		1-1-74	Ohio St 42, USC 21
1-1-37	Pittsburgh 21, Washington 0		1-1-75	USC 18, Ohio St 17
1-1-38	California 13, Alabama 0		1-1-76	UCLA 23, Ohio St 10
1-2-39	USC 7, Duke 3		1-1-77	USC 14, Michigan 6
1-1-40	USC 14, Tennessee 0		1-2-78	Washington 27, Michigan 20
1-1-41	Stanford 21, Nebraska 13		1-1-79	USC 17, Michigan 10
1-1-42	Oregon St 20, Duke 16		1-1-80	USC 17, Ohio St 16
1-1-43	Georgia 9, UCLA 0		1-1-81	Michigan 23, Washington 6
1-1-44	USC 29, Washington 0		1-1-82	Washington 28, Iowa 0
1-1-45	USC 25, Tennessee 0		1-1-83	UCLA 24, Michigan 14
1-1-46	Alabama 34, USC 14		1-2-84	UCLA 45, Illinois 9
1-1-47	Illinois 45, UCLA 14		1-1-85	USC 20, Ohio St 17
1-1-48	Michigan 49, USC 0		1-1-86	UCLA 45, Iowa 28
1-1-49	Northwestern 20, California 14		1-1-87	Arizona St 22, Michigan 15
1-2-50	Ohio St 17, California 14		1-1-88	Michigan St 20, USC 17
1-1-51	Michigan 14, California 6		1-2-89	Michigan 22, USC 14
1-1-52	Illinois 40, Stanford 7		1-1-90	USC 17, Michigan 10

Note: The Fiesta, Orange, Rose and Sugar Bowls constitute the Bowl Alliance, formed in 1995 and running through the 2009 regular season and 2010 bowl season. Starting in January 2007, it will include a separate BCS National Championship game as well. The four other BCS Bowls will host the following conference champions with consideration for the following conference tie-ins: the ACC or Big East champion in the FedEx Orange Bowl, the SEC champion in the Allstate Sugar Bowl, the Big Ten and the Pac-10 champions in the Rose Bowl and the Big 12 champion in the Tostitos Fiesta Bowl. rankings. There are also four at-large positions in the BCS that are open to any Division I-A team. This allows any Division I-A school in the nation the opportunity to play in a BCS bowl game.

Results of Major Bowl Games *(Cont.)*

Rose Bowl *(Cont.)*

1-1-91..............Washington 46, Iowa 34
1-1-92..............Washington 34, Michigan 14
1-1-93..............Michigan 38, Washington 31
1-1-94..............Wisconsin 21, UCLA 16
1-2-95..............Penn St 38, Oregon 20
1-1-96..............USC 41, Northwestern 32
1-1-97..............Ohio St 20, Arizona St 17
1-1-98..............Michigan 21, Washington St 16
1-1-99..............Wisconsin 38, UCLA 31
1-1-2000.........Wisconsin 17, Stanford 9
1-1-2001.........Washington 34, Purdue 24
1-3-2002.........Miami 37, Nebraska 14
1-1-2003.........Oklahoma 34, Washington St 14
1-1-2004.........USC 28, Michigan 14
1-1-2005.........Texas 38, Michigan 37
1-4-2006.........Texas 41, USC 38
1-1-2007.........USC 32, Michigan 18

City: Pasadena. Stadium: Rose Bowl, capacity 96,576.
Playing Sites: Tournament Park (1902, 1916–22), Rose Bowl
(1923–41, since 1943), Duke Stadium, Durham, NC (1942).

Orange Bowl

1-1-35..............Bucknell 26, Miami (Fla.) 0
1-1-36..............Catholic 20, Mississippi 19
1-1-37..............Duquesne 13, Mississippi St 12
1-1-38..............Auburn 6, Michigan St 0
1-2-39..............Tennessee 17, Oklahoma 0
1-1-40..............Georgia Tech 21, Missouri 7
1-1-41..............Mississippi St 14, Georgetown 7
1-1-42..............Georgia 40, TCU 26
1-1-43..............Alabama 37, Boston College 21
1-1-44..............LSU 19, Texas A&M 14
1-1-45..............Tulsa 26, Georgia Tech 12
1-1-46..............Miami (Fla.) 13, Holy Cross 6
1-1-47..............Rice 8, Tennessee 0
1-1-48..............Georgia Tech 20, Kansas 14
1-1-49..............Texas 41, Georgia 28
1-2-50..............Santa Clara 21, Kentucky 13
1-1-51..............Clemson 15, Miami (Fla.) 14
1-1-52..............Georgia Tech 17, Baylor 14
1-1-53..............Alabama 61, Syracuse 6
1-1-54..............Oklahoma 7, Maryland 0
1-1-55..............Duke 34, Nebraska 7
1-2-56..............Oklahoma 20, Maryland 6
1-1-57..............Colorado 27, Clemson 21
1-1-58..............Oklahoma 48, Duke 21
1-1-59..............Oklahoma 21, Syracuse 6
1-1-60..............Georgia 14, Missouri 0
1-2-61..............Missouri 21, Navy 14
1-1-62..............LSU 25, Colorado 7
1-1-63..............Alabama 17, Oklahoma 0
1-1-64..............Nebraska 13, Auburn 7
1-1-65..............Texas 21, Alabama 17
1-1-66..............Alabama 39, Nebraska 28
1-2-67..............Florida 27, Georgia Tech 12
1-1-68..............Oklahoma 26, Tennessee 24
1-1-69..............Penn St 15, Kansas 14
1-1-70..............Penn St 10, Missouri 3
1-1-71..............Nebraska 17, LSU 12
1-1-72..............Nebraska 38, Alabama 6
1-1-73..............Nebraska 40, Notre Dame 6
1-1-74..............Penn St 16, LSU 9
1-1-75..............Notre Dame 13, Alabama 11
1-1-76..............Oklahoma 14, Michigan 6
1-1-77..............Ohio St 27, Colorado 10
1-2-78..............Arkansas 31, Oklahoma 6

Orange Bowl *(Cont.)*

1-1-79..............Oklahoma 31, Nebraska 24
1-1-80..............Oklahoma 24, Florida St 7
1-1-81..............Oklahoma 18, Florida St 17
1-1-82..............Clemson 22, Nebraska 15
1-1-83..............Nebraska 21, LSU 20
1-2-84..............Miami (Fla.) 31, Nebraska 30
1-1-85..............Washington 28, Oklahoma 17
1-1-86..............Oklahoma 25, Penn St 10
1-1-87..............Oklahoma 42, Arkansas 8
1-1-88..............Miami (Fla.) 20, Oklahoma 14
1-2-89..............Miami (Fla.) 23, Nebraska 3
1-1-90..............Notre Dame 21, Colorado 6
1-1-91..............Colorado 10, Notre Dame 9
1-1-92..............Miami (Fla.) 22, Nebraska 0
1-1-93..............Florida St 27, Nebraska 14
1-1-94..............Florida St 18, Nebraska 16
1-1-95..............Nebraska 24, Miami (Fla.) 17
1-1-96..............Florida St 31, Notre Dame 26
12-31-96.........Nebraska 41, Virginia Tech 21
1-2-98..............Nebraska 42, Tennessee 17
1-2-99..............Florida 31, Syracuse 10
1-1-00..............Michigan 35, Alabama 34 (ot)
1-3-01..............Oklahoma 13, Florida St 2
1-2-02..............Florida 56, Maryland 23
1-2-03..............USC 38, Iowa 17
1-1-04..............Miami (Fla.) 16, Florida St 15
1-4-05..............USC 55, Oklahoma 19
1-3-06..............Penn State 26, Florida State 23 (3OT)
1-2-07..............Louisville 24, Wake Forest 13

City: Miami. Stadium: Pro Player Stadium, capacity
75,192. Playing Sites: Orange Bowl (1935–96), Pro
Player Stadium (since 1996).

Sugar Bowl

1-1-35..............Tulane 20, Temple 14
1-1-36..............TCU 3, LSU 2
1-1-37..............Santa Clara 21, LSU 14
1-1-38..............Santa Clara 6, LSU 0
1-2-39..............TCU 15, Carnegie Tech 7
1-1-40..............Texas A&M 14, Tulane 13
1-1-41..............Boston Col 19, Tennessee 13
1-1-42..............Fordham 2, Missouri 0
1-1-43..............Tennessee 14, Tulsa 7
1-1-44..............Georgia Tech 20, Tulsa 18
1-1-45..............Duke 29, Alabama 26
1-1-46..............Oklahoma St 33, St. Mary's (Ca.) 13
1-1-47..............Georgia 20, North Carolina 10
1-1-48..............Texas 27, Alabama 7
1-1-49..............Oklahoma 14, North Carolina 6
1-2-50..............Oklahoma 35, LSU 0
1-1-51..............Kentucky 13, Oklahoma 7
1-1-52..............Maryland 28, Tennessee 13
1-1-53..............Georgia Tech 24, Mississippi 7
1-1-54..............Georgia Tech 42, W Virginia 19
1-1-55..............Navy 21, Mississippi 0
1-2-56..............Georgia Tech 7, Pittsburgh 0
1-1-57..............Baylor 13, Tennessee 7
1-1-58..............Mississippi 39, Texas 7
1-1-59..............LSU 7, Clemson 0
1-1-60..............Mississippi 21, LSU 0
1-2-61..............Mississippi 40, Rice 6
1-1-62..............Alabama 10, Arkansas 3
1-1-63..............Mississippi 17, Arkansas 13
1-1-64..............Alabama 12, Mississippi 7
1-1-65..............LSU 13, Syracuse 10
1-1-66..............Missouri 20, Florida 18

COLLEGE FOOTBALL
239

Sugar Bowl *(Cont.)*

1-2-67 .... Alabama 34, Nebraska 7
1-1-68 .... LSU 20, Wyoming 13
1-1-69 .... Arkansas 16, Georgia 2
1-1-70 .... Mississippi 27, Arkansas 22
1-1-71 .... Tennessee 34, Air Force 13
1-1-72 .... Oklahoma 40, Auburn 22
12-31-72 .... Oklahoma 14, Penn St 0
12-31-73 .... Notre Dame 24, Alabama 23
12-31-74 .... Nebraska 13, Florida 10
12-31-75 .... Alabama 13, Penn St 6
1-1-77 .... Pittsburgh 27, Georgia 3
1-2-78 .... Alabama 35, Ohio St 6
1-1-79 .... Alabama 14, Penn St 7
1-1-80 .... Alabama 24, Arkansas 9
1-1-81 .... Georgia 17, Notre Dame 10
1-1-82 .... Pittsburgh 24, Georgia 20
1-1-83 .... Penn St 27, Georgia 23
1-2-84 .... Auburn 9, Michigan 7
1-1-85 .... Nebraska 28, LSU 10
1-1-86 .... Tennessee 35, Miami (Fla.) 7
1-1-87 .... Nebraska 30, LSU 15
1-1-88 .... Syracuse 16, Auburn 16
1-2-89 .... Florida St 13, Auburn 7
1-1-90 .... Miami (Fla.) 33, Alabama 25
1-1-91 .... Tennessee 23, Virginia 22
1-1-92 .... Notre Dame 39, Florida 28
1-1-93 .... Alabama 34, Miami (Fla.) 13
1-1-94 .... Florida 41, West Virginia 7
1-2-95 .... Florida St 23, Florida 17
12-31-95 .... Virginia Tech 28, Texas 10
1-2-97 .... Florida 52, Florida St 20
1-1-98 .... Florida St 31, Ohio St 14
1-1-99 .... Ohio St 24, Texas A&M 14
1-4-00 .... Florida St 46, Virginia Tech 29
1-2-01 .... Miami (Fla.) 37, Florida 20
1-1-02 .... LSU 47, Illinois 34
1-1-03 .... Georgia 26, Florida St 13
1-4-04 .... LSU 21, Oklahoma 14
1-3-05 .... Auburn 16, Virginia Tech 13
1-2-06 .... West Virginia 38, Georgia 35
1-3-07 .... LSU 41, Notre Dame 14

City: New Orleans. Stadium: Louisiana Superdome, capacity 76,791. Playing Sites: Tulane Stadium (1935–74), Louisiana Superdome (since 1975). Due to Hurricane Katrina, 2006 Sugar Bowl played in Atlanta's Georgia Dome.

Cotton Bowl

1-1-37 .... TCU 16, Marquette 6
1-1-38 .... Rice 28, Colorado 14
1-2-39 .... St. Mary's (Ca.) 20, Texas Tech 13
1-1-40 .... Clemson 6, Boston Col 3
1-1-41 .... Texas A&M 13, Fordham 12
1-1-42 .... Alabama 29, Texas A&M 21
1-1-43 .... Texas 14, Georgia Tech 7
1-1-44 .... Texas 7, Randolph Field 7
1-1-45 .... Oklahoma St 34, TCU 0
1-1-46 .... Texas 40, Missouri 27
1-1-47 .... Arkansas 0, LSU 0
1-1-48 .... Southern Methodist 13, Penn St 13
1-1-49 .... Southern Methodist 21, Oregon 13
1-2-50 .... Rice 27, North Carolina 13
1-1-51 .... Tennessee 20, Texas 14
1-1-52 .... Kentucky 20, TCU 7
1-1-53 .... Texas 16, Tennessee 0
1-1-54 .... Rice 28, Alabama 6

Cotton Bowl *(Cont.)*

1-1-55 .... Georgia Tech 14, Arkansas 6
1-2-56 .... Mississippi 14, TCU 13
1-1-57 .... TCU 28, Syracuse 27
1-1-58 .... Navy 20, Rice 7
1-1-59 .... TCU 0, Air Force 0
1-1-60 .... Syracuse 23, Texas 14
1-2-61 .... Duke 7, Arkansas 6
1-1-62 .... Texas 12, Mississippi 7
1-1-63 .... LSU 13, Texas 0
1-1-64 .... Texas 28, Navy 6
1-1-65 .... Arkansas 10, Nebraska 7
1-1-66 .... LSU 14, Arkansas 7
12-31-66 .... Georgia 24, Southern Methodist 9
1-1-68 .... Texas A&M 20, Alabama 16
1-1-69 .... Texas 36, Tennessee 13
1-1-70 .... Texas 21, Notre Dame 17
1-1-71 .... Notre Dame 24, Texas 11
1-1-72 .... Penn St 30, Texas 6
1-1-73 .... Texas 17, Alabama 13
1-1-74 .... Nebraska 19, Texas 3
1-1-75 .... Penn St 41, Baylor 20
1-1-76 .... Arkansas 31, Georgia 10
1-1-77 .... Houston 30, Maryland 21
1-2-78 .... Notre Dame 38, Texas 10
1-1-79 .... Notre Dame 35, Houston 34
1-1-80 .... Houston 17, Nebraska 14
1-1-81 .... Alabama 30, Baylor 2
1-1-82 .... Texas 14, Alabama 12
1-1-83 .... SMU 7, Pittsburgh 3
1-2-84 .... Georgia 10, Texas 9
1-1-85 .... Boston Col 45, Houston 28
1-1-86 .... Texas A&M 36, Auburn 16
1-1-87 .... Ohio St 28, Texas A&M 12
1-1-88 .... Texas A&M 35, Notre Dame 10
1-2-89 .... UCLA 17, Arkansas 3
1-1-90 .... Tennessee 31, Arkansas 27
1-1-91 .... Miami (Fla.) 46, Texas 3
1-1-92 .... Florida St 10, Texas A&M 2
1-1-93 .... Notre Dame 28, Texas A&M 3
1-1-94 .... Notre Dame 24, Texas A&M 21
1-2-95 .... USC 55, Texas Tech 14
1-1-96 .... Colorado 38, Oregon 6
1-1-97 .... BYU 19, Kansas St 15
1-1-98 .... UCLA 29, Texas A&M 23
1-1-99 .... Texas 38, Mississippi St 11
1-1-00 .... Arkansas 27, Texas 6
1-1-01 .... Kansas St 35, Tennessee 21
1-1-02 .... Oklahoma 10, Arkansas 3
1-1-03 .... Texas 35, LSU 20
1-2-04 .... Mississippi 31, Oklahoma St 28
1-1-05 .... Tennessee 38, Texas A&M 7
1-2-06 .... Alabama 13, Texas Tech 10
1-1-07 .... Auburn 17, Nebraska 14

City: Dallas. Stadium: Cotton Bowl, capacity 68,252.

Sun Bowl

1-1-36	Hardin-Simmons 14, New Mexico St 14
1-1-37	Hardin-Simmons 34, UTEP 6
1-1-38	W Virginia 7, Texas Tech 6
1-2-39	Utah 26, New Mexico 0
1-1-40	Catholic 0, Arizona St 0
1-1-41	Case Reserve 26, Arizona St 13
1-1-42	Tulsa 6, Texas Tech 0
1-1-43	2nd Air Force 13, Hardin-Simmons 7
1-1-44	Southwestern (Tex.) 7, New Mexico 0
1-1-45	Southwestern (Tex.) 35, New Mexico 0
1-1-46	New Mexico 34, Denver 24
1-1-47	Cincinnati 18, Virginia Tech 6
1-1-48	Miami (OH) 13, Texas Tech 12
1-1-49	W Virginia 21, UTEP 12
1-2-50	UTEP 33, Georgetown 20
1-1-51	W Texas St 14, Cincinnati 13
1-1-52	Texas Tech 25, Pacific 14
1-1-53	Pacific 26, Southern Miss 7
1-1-54	UTEP 37, Southern Miss 14
1-1-55	UTEP 47, Florida St 20
1-2-56	Wyoming 21, Texas Tech 14
1-1-57	George Washington 13, UTEP 0
1-1-58	Louisville 34, Drake 20
12-31-58	Wyoming 14, Hardin-Simmons 6
12-31-59	New Mexico St 28, N Texas 8
12-31-60	New Mexico St 20, Utah St 13
12-30-61	Villanova 17, Wichita St 9
12-31-62	W Texas St 15, Ohio 14
12-31-63	Oregon 21, Southern Methodist 14
12-26-64	Georgia 7, Texas Tech 0
12-31-65	UTEP 13, TCU 12
12-24-66	Wyoming 28, Florida St 20
12-30-67	UTEP 14, Mississippi 7
12-28-68	Auburn 34, Arizona 10
12-20-69	Nebraska 45, Georgia 6
12-19-70	Georgia Tech 17, Texas Tech 9
12-18-71	LSU 33, Iowa St 15
12-30-72	North Carolina 32, Texas Tech 28
12-29-73	Missouri 34, Auburn 17
12-28-74	Mississippi St 26, North Carolina 24
12-26-75	Pittsburgh 33, Kansas 19
1-2-77	Texas A&M 37, Florida 14
12-31-77	Stanford 24, LSU 14
12-23-78	Texas 42, Maryland 0
12-22-79	Washington 14, Texas 7
12-27-80	Nebraska 31, Mississippi St 17
12-26-81	Oklahoma 40, Houston 14
12-25-82	North Carolina 26, Texas 10
12-24-83	Alabama 28, Southern Methodist 7
12-22-84	Maryland 28, Tennessee 27
12-28-85	Georgia 13, Arizona 13
12-25-86	Alabama 28, Washington 6
12-25-87	Oklahoma St 35, W Virginia 33
12-24-88	Alabama 29, Army 28
12-30-89	Pittsburgh 31, Texas A&M 28
12-31-90	Michigan St 17, USC 16
12-31-91	UCLA 6, Illinois 3
12-31-92	Baylor 20, Arizona 15
12-24-93	Oklahoma 41, Texas Tech 10
12-30-94	Texas 35, North Carolina 31
12-29-95	Iowa 38, Washington 18
12-31-96	Stanford 38, Michigan St 0
12-31-97	Arizona St 17, Iowa 7
12-31-98	TCU 28, USC 19
12-31-99	Oregon 24, Minnesota 20
12-29-00	Wisconsin 21, UCLA 20

Sun Bowl

12-31-01	Washington St 33, Purdue 27
12-31-02	Purdue 34, Washington 24
12-31-03	Minnesota 31, Oregon 30
12-31-04	Arizona State 27, Purdue 23
12-30-05	UCLA 50, Northwestern 39
12-29-06	Oregon State 39, Missouri 38

City: El Paso. Stadium: Sun Bowl, capacity 51,270. Name Changes: Sun Bowl (1936–86; 94–), John Hancock Sun Bowl (1987–88), John Hancock Bowl (1989–93). Playing Sites: Kidd Field (1936–62), Sun Bowl (since 1963).

Gator Bowl

1-1-46	Wake Forest 26, South Carolina 14
1-1-47	Oklahoma 34, North Carolina St 13
1-1-48	Maryland 20, Georgia 20
1-1-49	Clemson 24, Missouri 23
1-2-50	Maryland 20, Missouri 7
1-1-51	Wyoming 20, Washington & Lee 7
1-1-52	Miami (Fla.) 14, Clemson 0
1-1-53	Florida 14, Tulsa 13
1-1-54	Texas Tech 35, Auburn 13
12-31-54	Auburn 33, Baylor 13
12-31-55	Vanderbilt 25, Auburn 13
12-29-56	Georgia Tech 21, Pittsburgh 14
12-28-57	Tennessee 3, Texas A&M 0
12-27-58	Mississippi 7, Florida 3
1-2-60	Arkansas 14, Georgia Tech 7
12-31-60	Florida 13, Baylor 12
12-30-61	Penn St 30, Georgia Tech 15
12-29-62	Florida 17, Penn St 7
12-28-63	North Carolina 35, Air Force 0
1-2-65	Florida St 36, Oklahoma 19
12-31-65	Georgia Tech 31, Texas Tech 21
12-31-66	Tennessee 18, Syracuse 12
12-30-67	Penn St 17, Florida St 17
12-28-68	Missouri 35, Alabama 10
12-27-69	Florida 14, Tennessee 13
1-2-71	Auburn 35, Mississippi 28
12-31-71	Georgia 7, North Carolina 3
12-30-72	Auburn 24, Colorado 3
12-29-73	Texas Tech 28, Tennessee 19
12-30-74	Auburn 27, Texas 3
12-29-75	Maryland 13, Florida 0
12-27-76	Notre Dame 20, Penn St 9
12-30-77	Pittsburgh 34, Clemson 3
12-29-78	Clemson 17, Ohio St 15
12-28-79	North Carolina 17, Michigan 15
12-29-80	Pittsburgh 37, South Carolina 9
12-28-81	North Carolina 31, Arkansas 27
12-30-82	Florida St 31, W Virginia 12
12-30-83	Florida 14, Iowa 6
12-28-84	Oklahoma St 21, South Carolina 14
12-30-85	Florida St 34, Oklahoma St 23
12-27-86	Clemson 27, Stanford 21
12-31-87	LSU 30, South Carolina 13
1-1-89	Georgia 34, Michigan St 27
12-30-89	Clemson 27, W Virginia 7
1-1-91	Michigan 35, Mississippi 3
12-29-91	Oklahoma 48, Virginia 14
12-31-92	Florida 27, North Carolina St 10
12-31-93	Alabama 24, North Carolina 10
12-30-94	Tennessee 45, Virginia Tech 23
1-1-96	Syracuse 41, Clemson 0
1-1-97	North Carolina 20, W Virginia 13

Gator Bowl *(Cont.)*

1-1-98..............North Carolina 42, Viginia Tech 13
1-1-99..............Georgia Tech 35, Notre Dame 28
1-1-00..............Miami 27, Georgia Tech 13
1-1-01..............Virginia Tech 41, Clemson 20
1-1-02..............Florida St 30, Virginia Tech 17
1-1-03..............North Carolina 28, Notre Dame 6
1-1-04..............Maryland 41, W Virginia 7
1-1-05..............Florida State 30, West Virginia 18
1-2-06..............Virginia Tech 35, Louisville 24
1-1-07..............West Virginia 38, Georgia Tech 35

City: Jacksonville, FL. Stadium: Alltel Stadium, capacity 76,976.

Florida Citrus Bowl

1-1-47..............Catawba 31, Maryville (Tenn.) 6
1-1-48..............Catawba 7, Marshall 0
1-1-49..............Murray St 21, Sul Ross St 21
1-2-50..............St. Vincent 7, Emory & Henry 6
1-1-51..............Morris Harvey 35, Emory & Henry 14
1-1-52..............Stetson 35, Arkansas St 20
1-1-53..............E Texas St 33, Tennessee Tech 0
1-1-54..............E Texas St 7, Arkansas St 7
1-1-55..............NE-Omaha 7, Eastern Kentucky 6
1-2-56..............Juniata 6, Missouri Valley 6
1-1-57..............W Texas St 20, Southern Miss 13
1-1-58..............E Texas St 10, Southern Miss 9
12-27-58..........E Texas St 26, Missouri Valley 7
1-1-60..............Middle Tennessee St 21, Presbyterian 12
12-30-60..........Citadel 27, Tennessee Tech 0
12-29-61..........Lamar 21, Middle Tennessee St 14
12-22-62..........Houston 49, Miami (Ohio) 21
12-28-63..........Western Kentucky 27, Coast Guard 0
12-12-64..........E Carolina 14, Massachusetts 13
12-11-65..........E Carolina 31, Maine 0
12-10-66..........Morgan St 14, W Chester 6
12-16-67..........TN-Martin 25, W Chester 8
12-27-68..........Richmond 49, Ohio 42
12-26-69..........Toledo 56, Davidson 33
12-28-70..........Toledo 40, William & Mary 12
12-28-71..........Toledo 28, Richmond 3
12-29-72..........Tampa 21, Kent St 18
12-22-73..........Miami (Ohio) 16, Florida 7
12-21-74..........Miami (Ohio) 21, Georgia 10
12-20-75..........Miami (Ohio) 20, South Carolina 7
12-18-76..........Oklahoma St 49, BYU 21
12-23-77..........Florida St 40, Texas Tech 17
12-23-78..........North Carolina St 30, Pittsburgh 17
12-22-79..........LSU 34, Wake Forest 10
12-20-80..........Florida 35, Maryland 20
12-19-81..........Missouri 19, Southern Miss 17
12-18-82..........Auburn 33, Boston Col 26
12-17-83..........Tennessee 30, Maryland 23
12-22-84..........Georgia 17, Florida St 17
12-28-85..........Ohio St 10, BYU 7
1-1-87..............Auburn 16, USC 7
1-1-88..............Clemson 35, Penn St 10
1-2-89..............Clemson 13, Oklahoma 6
1-1-90..............Illinois 31, Virginia 21
1-1-91..............Georgia Tech 45, Nebraska 21
1-1-92..............California 37, Clemson 13
1-1-93..............Georgia 21, Ohio State 14
1-1-94..............Penn State 31, Tennessee 13
1-2-95..............Alabama 24, Ohio St 17
1-1-96..............Tennessee 20, Ohio St 14

Florida Citrus Bowl *(Cont.)*

1-1-97..............Tennessee 48, Northwestern 28
1-1-98..............Florida 21, Penn St 6
1-1-99..............Michigan 45, Arkansas 31
1-1-00..............Michigan St 37, Florida 34
1-1-01..............Michigan 31, Auburn 28
1-1-02..............Tennessee 45, Michigan 17
1-1-03..............Auburn 13, Penn St 9
1-1-04..............Georgia 34, Purdue 27 (OT)
1-1-05..............Iowa 30, LSU 25
1-2-06..............Wisconsin 24, Auburn 10
1-1-07..............Wisconsin 17, Arkansas 14

City: Orlando, FL. Stadium: Florida Citrus Bowl, capacity 70,000. Name Change: Tangerine Bowl (1947–82). Playing Sites: Tangerine Bowl (1947–72, 1974–82); Florida Field, Gainesville (1973); Orlando Stadium/Florida Citrus Bowl-Orlando (since 1983).

Liberty Bowl

12-19-59..........Penn St 7, Alabama 0
12-17-60..........Penn St 41, Oregon 12
12-16-61..........Syracuse 15, Miami (Fla.) 14
12-15-62..........Oregon St 6, Villanova 0
12-21-63..........Mississippi St 16, North Carolina St 12
12-19-64..........Utah 32, W Virginia 6
12-18-65..........Mississippi 13, Auburn 7
12-10-66..........Miami (Fla.) 14, Virginia Tech 7
12-16-67..........North Carolina St 14, Georgia 7
12-14-68..........Mississippi 34, Virginia Tech 17
12-13-69..........Colorado 47, Alabama 33
12-12-70..........Tulane 17, Colorado 3
12-20-71..........Tennessee 14, Arkansas 13
12-18-72..........Georgia Tech 31, Iowa St 30
12-17-73..........North Carolina St 31, Kansas 18
12-16-74..........Tennessee 7, Maryland 3
12-22-75..........USC 20, Texas A&M 0
12-20-76..........Alabama 36, UCLA 6
12-19-77..........Nebraska 21, North Carolina 17
12-23-78..........Missouri 20, LSU 15
12-22-79..........Penn St 9, Tulane 6
12-27-80..........Purdue 28, Missouri 25
12-30-81..........Ohio St 31, Navy 28
12-29-82..........Alabama 21, Illinois 15
12-29-83..........Notre Dame 19, Boston Col 18
12-27-84..........Auburn 21, Arkansas 15
12-27-85..........Baylor 21, LSU 7
12-29-86..........Tennessee 21, Minnesota 14
12-29-87..........Georgia 20, Arkansas 17
12-28-88..........Indiana 34, South Carolina 10
12-28-89..........Mississippi 42, Air Force 29
12-27-90..........Air Force 23, Ohio St 11
12-29-91..........Air Force 38, Mississippi St 15
12-31-92..........Mississippi 13, Air Force 0
12-28-93..........Louisville 18, Michigan St 7
12-31-94..........Illinois 30, E Carolina 0
12-30-95..........East Carolina 19, Stanford 13
12-27-96..........Syracuse 30, Houston 17
12-31-97..........Southern Miss 41, Pittsburgh 7
12-31-98..........Tulane 41, BYU 27
12-31-99..........Southern Miss 23, Colorado St 17
12-29-01..........Colorado St 22, Louisville 17
12-31-01..........Louisville 28, BYU 10
12-31-02..........TCU 17, Colorado St 3
12-31-03..........Utah 17, Southern Mississippi 0

Liberty Bowl *(Cont.)*

12-31-04 ....Louisville 44, Boise State 40
12-31-05 ....Tulsa 31, Fresno State 24
12-29-06 ....South Carolina 44, Houston 36

City: Memphis (since 1965). Stadium: Liberty Bowl
Memorial Stadium, capacity 62,921.
Playing Sites: Philadelphia (Municipal Stadium, 1959–63),
Atlantic City (Convention Center, 1964).

Bluebonnet Bowl

12-19-59 ....Clemson 23, TCU 7
12-17-60 ....Texas 3, Alabama 3
12-16-61 ....Kansas 33, Rice 7
12-22-62 ....Missouri 14, Georgia Tech 10
12-21-63 ....Baylor 14, LSU 7
12-19-64 ....Tulsa 14, Mississippi 7
12-18-65 ....Tennessee 27, Tulsa 6
12-17-66 ....Texas 19, Mississippi 0
12-23-67 ....Colorado 31, Miami (Fla.) 21
12-31-68 ....Southern Methodist 28, Oklahoma 27
12-31-69 ....Houston 36, Auburn 7
12-31-70 ....Alabama 24, Oklahoma 24
12-31-71 ....Colorado 29, Houston 17
12-30-72 ....Tennessee 24, LSU 17
12-29-73 ....Houston 47, Tulane 7
12-23-74 ....North Carolina St 31, Houston 31
12-27-75 ....Texas 38, Colorado 21
12-31-76 ....Nebraska 27, Texas Tech 24
12-31-77 ....USC 47, Texas A&M 28
12-31-78 ....Stanford 25, Georgia 22
12-31-79 ....Purdue 27, Tennessee 22
12-31-80 ....North Carolina 16, Texas 7
12-31-81 ....Michigan 33, UCLA 14
12-31-82 ....Arkansas 28, Florida 24
12-31-83 ....Oklahoma St 24, Baylor 14
12-31-84 ....W Virginia 31, TCU 14
12-31-85 ....Air Force 24, Texas 16
12-31-86 ....Baylor 21, Colorado 9
12-31-87 ....Texas 32, Pittsburgh 27

City: Houston. Playing sites: Rice Stadium (1959–67;
1985–86), Astrodome (1968–84, 1987).
Name change: Astro-Bluebonnet Bowl (1968–76). Bowl
was discontinued after 1987.

Peach Bowl

12-30-68 ....LSU 31, Florida St 27
12-30-69 ....W Virginia 14, South Carolina 3
12-30-70 ....Arizona St 48, North Carolina 26
12-30-71 ....Mississippi 41, Georgia Tech 18
12-29-72 ....North Carolina St 49, W Virginia 13
12-28-73 ....Georgia 17, Maryland 16
12-28-74 ....Vanderbilt 6, Texas Tech 6
12-31-75 ....W Virginia 13, North Carolina St 10
12-31-76 ....Kentucky 21, North Carolina 0
12-31-77 ....North Carolina St 24, Iowa St 14
12-25-78 ....Purdue 41, Georgia Tech 21
12-31-79 ....Baylor 24, Clemson 18
1-2-81 ....Miami (Fla.) 20, Virginia Tech 10
12-31-81 ....W Virginia 26, Florida 6
12-31-82 ....Iowa 28, Tennessee 22
12-30-83 ....Florida St 28, North Carolina 3
12-31-84 ....Virginia 27, Purdue 24
12-31-85 ....Army 31, Illinois 29
12-31-86 ....Virginia Tech 25, North Carolina St 24

Peach Bowl *(Cont.)*

1-2-88 ....Tennessee 27, Indiana 22
12-31-88 ....North Carolina St 28, Iowa 23
12-30-89 ....Syracuse 19, Georgia 18
12-29-90 ....Auburn 27, Indiana 23
1-1-92 ....E Carolina 37, North Carolina St 34
1-2-93 ....North Carolina 21, Mississippi St 17
12-31-93 ....Clemson 14, Kentucky 13
1-1-95 ....North Carolina St 28, Mississippi St 24
12-30-95 ....Virginia 34, Georgia 27
12-28-96 ....LSU 10, Clemson 7
1-2-98 ....Auburn 21, Clemson 17
12-31-98 ....Georgia 35, Virginia 33
12-30-99 ....Mississippi St 17, Clemson 7
12-29-00 ....LSU 28, Georgia Tech 14
12-31-01 ....North Carolina 16, Auburn 10
12-31-02 ....Maryland 30, Tennessee 3
1-2-04 ....Clemson 27, Tennessee 14
12-31-04 ....Miami (Fla.) 27, Florida 10
12-30-05 ....LSU 40, Miami (Fla.) 3
12-30-06 ....Georgia 31, Virginia Tech 24

City: Atlanta. Stadium: Georgia Dome, capacity 71,500.
Playing Sites: Grant Field (1968–70), Atlanta–Fulton
County Stadium (1971–92), Georgia Dome (since 1993).
Name change: Chick-fil-A Bowl (2006–).

Fiesta Bowl

12-27-71 ....Arizona St 45, Florida St 38
12-23-72 ....Arizona St 49, Missouri 35
12-21-73 ....Arizona St 28, Pittsburgh 7
12-28-74 ....Oklahoma St 16, BYU 6
12-26-75 ....Arizona St 17, Nebraska 14
12-25-76 ....Oklahoma 41, Wyoming 7
12-25-77 ....Penn St 42, Arizona St 30
12-25-78 ....Arkansas 10, UCLA 10
12-25-79 ....Pittsburgh 16, Arizona 10
12-26-80 ....Penn St 31, Ohio St 19
1-1-82 ....Penn St 26, USC 10
1-1-83 ....Arizona St 32, Oklahoma 21
1-2-84 ....Ohio St 28, Pittsburgh 23
1-1-85 ....UCLA 39, Miami (Fla.) 37
1-1-86 ....Michigan 27, Nebraska 23
1-2-87 ....Penn St 14, Miami (Fla.) 10
1-1-88 ....Florida St 31, Nebraska 28
1-2-89 ....Notre Dame 34, W Virginia 21
1-1-90 ....Florida St 41, Nebraska 17
1-1-91 ....Louisville 34, Alabama 7
1-1-92 ....Penn St 42, Tennessee 17
1-1-93 ....Syracuse 26, Colorado 22
1-1-94 ....Arizona 29, Miami (Fla.) 0
1-1-95 ....Colorado 41, Notre Dame 24
1-1-96 ....Nebraska 62, Florida 24
1-1-97 ....Penn St 38, Texas 15
12-31-97 ....Kansas St 35, Syracuse 18
1-4-99 ....Tennessee 23, Florida St 16
1-2-00 ....Nebraska 31, Tennessee 21
1-1-01 ....Oregon St 41, Notre Dame 9
1-1-02 ....Oregon 38, Colorado 16
1-3-03 ....Ohio St 31, Miami (Fla.) 24 [2 OT]
1-2-04 ....Ohio St 35, Kansas St 28
1-1-05 ....Utah 35, Pittsburgh 7
1-2-06 ....Ohio State 34, Notre Dame 20
1-1-07 ....Boise State 43, Oklahoma 42

City: Tempe, AZ. Stadium: Sun Devil Stadium,
capacity 73,471.

Independence Bowl

12-13-76..........McNeese St 20, Tulsa 16
12-17-77..........Louisiana Tech 24, Louisville 14
12-16-78..........E Carolina 35, Louisiana Tech 13
12-15-79..........Syracuse 31, McNeese St 7
12-13-80..........Southern Miss 16, McNeese St 14
12-12-81..........Texas A&M 33, Oklahoma St 16
12-11-82..........Wisconsin 14, Kansas St 3
12-10-83..........Air Force 9, Mississippi 3
12-15-84..........Air Force 23, Virginia Tech 7
12-21-85..........Minnesota 20, Clemson 13
12-20-86..........Mississippi 20, Texas Tech 17
12-19-87..........Washington 24, Tulane 12
12-23-88..........Southern Miss 38, UTEP 18
12-16-89..........Oregon 27, Tulsa 24
12-15-90..........Louisiana Tech 34, Maryland 34
12-29-91..........Georgia 24, Arkansas 15
12-31-92..........Wake Forest 39, Oregon 35
12-31-93..........Virginia Tech 45, Indiana 20
12-28-94..........Virginia 20, TCU 10
12-29-95..........LSU 45, Michigan St 26
12-31-96..........Auburn 32, Army 29
12-28-97..........LSU 27, Notre Dame 9
12-31-98..........Mississippi 35, Texas Tech 18
12-31-99..........Mississippi 27, Oklahoma 25
12-31-00..........Mississippi St 43, Texas A&M 41
12-27-01..........Alabama 14, Iowa St 13
12-27-02..........Mississippi 27, Nebraska 23
12-31-03..........Arkansas 27, Missouri 14
12-28-04..........Iowa State 17, Miami (Ohio) 13
12-30-05..........Missouri 38, South Carolina 31
12-28-06..........Oklahoma State 34, Alabama 31

City: Shreveport, LA. Stadium: Independence Stadium, capacity 50,459.

All-American Bowl

12-22-77..........Maryland 17, Minnesota 7
12-20-78..........Texas A&M 28, Iowa St 12
12-29-79..........Missouri 24, South Carolina 14
12-27-80..........Arkansas 34, Tulane 15
12-31-81..........Mississippi St 10, Kansas 0
12-31-82..........Air Force 36, Vanderbilt 28
12-22-83..........W Virginia 20, Kentucky 16
12-29-84..........Kentucky 20, Wisconsin 19
12-31-85..........Georgia Tech 17, Michigan St 14
12-31-86..........Florida St 27, Indiana 13
12-22-87..........Virginia 22, BYU 16
12-29-88..........Florida 14, Illinois 10
12-28-89..........Texas Tech 49, Duke 21
12-28-90..........North Carolina St 31, Southern Miss 27

City: Birmingham, AL. Stadium: Legion Field.
Name Change: Hall of Fame Classic (1977–84). Bowl was discontinued after 1990.

Holiday Bowl

12-22-78..........Navy 23, BYU 16
12-21-79..........Indiana 38, BYU 37
12-19-80..........BYU 46, SMU 45
12-18-81..........BYU 38, Washington St 36
12-17-82..........Ohio St 47, BYU 17
12-23-83..........BYU 21, Missouri 17
12-21-84..........BYU 24, Michigan 17
12-22-85..........Arkansas 18, Arizona St 17
12-30-86..........Iowa 39, San Diego St 38
12-30-87..........Iowa 20, Wyoming 19
12-30-88..........Oklahoma St 62, Wyoming 14
12-29-89..........Penn St 50, BYU 39
12-29-90..........Texas A&M 65, BYU 14
12-30-91..........Iowa 13, BYU 13
12-30-92..........Hawaii 27, Illinois 17
12-30-93..........Ohio St 28, BYU 21
12-30-94..........Michigan 24, Colorado St 14
12-29-95..........Kansas St 54, Colorado St 21
12-30-96..........Colorado 33, Washington 21
12-29-97..........Colorado St 35, Missouri 24
12-30-98..........Arizona 23, Nebraska 20
12-29-99..........Kansas St 24, Washington 20
12-29-00..........Oregon 35, Texas 30
12-28-01..........Texas 47, Washington 43
12-27-02..........Kansas St 34, Arizona St 27
12-30-03..........Washington St 28, Texas 20
12-30-04..........Texas Tech 45, California 31
12-29-05..........*Oklahoma 17, Oregon 14
12-28-06..........California 45, Texas A&M 10
*victory vacated in 2007

City: San Diego. Stadium: Qualcomm Stadium, capacity 70,000.

Las Vegas Bowl

12-19-81..........Toledo 27, San Jose St 25
12-18-82..........Fresno St 29, Bowling Green 28
12-17-83..........Northern Illinois 20, Cal St–Fullerton 13
12-15-84..........UNLV 30, Toledo 13*
12-14-85..........Fresno St 51, Bowling Green 7
12-13-86..........San Jose St 37, Miami (Ohio) 7
12-12-87..........Eastern Michigan 30, San Jose St 27
12-10-88..........Fresno St 35, Western Michigan 30
12-9-89............Fresno St 27, Ball St 6
12-8-90............San Jose St 48, Central Michigan 24
12-14-91..........Bowling Green 28, Fresno St 21
12-18-92..........Bowling Green 35, Nevada 34
12-17-93..........Utah St 42, Ball St 33
12-15-94..........UNLV 52, Central Michigan 24
12-14-95..........Toledo 40, Nevada 37
12-19-96..........Nevada 18, Ball St 15
12-19-97..........Oregon 41, Air Force 13
12-19-98..........North Carolina 20, San Diego St 13
12-18-99..........Utah 17, Fresno St 16
12-21-00..........UNLV 31, Arkansas 14
12-25-01..........Utah 10, USC 6
12-25-02..........UCLA 27, New Mexico 13
12-24-03..........Oregon St 55, New Mexico 14
12-23-04..........Wyoming 24, UCLA, 21
12-22-05..........California 35, BYU 28
12-21-06..........BYU 38, Oregon 8

* Toledo won later by forfeit. City: Las Vegas (since 1992). Stadium: Sam Boyd Silver Bowl Stadium, capacity 40,000. Name change: California Bowl (1981–91).
Playing sites: Fresno, CA (Bulldog Stadium, 1981–91), Las Vegas.

Aloha Bowl

12-25-82 ....Washington 21, Maryland 20
12-26-83 ....Penn St 13, Washington 10
12-29-84 ....Southern Methodist 27, Notre Dame 20
12-28-85 ....Alabama 24, USC 3
12-27-86 ....Arizona 30, North Carolina 21
12-25-87 ....UCLA 20, Florida 16
12-25-88 ....Washington St 24, Houston 22
12-25-89 ....Michigan St 33, Hawaii 13
12-25-90 ....Syracuse 28, Arizona 0
12-25-91 ....Georgia Tech 18, Stanford 17
12-25-92 ....Kansas 23, BYU 20
12-25-93 ....Colorado 41, Fresno St 30
12-25-94 ....Boston College 12, Kansas St 7
12-25-95 ....Kansas 51, UCLA 30
12-25-96 ....Navy 42, California 38
12-25-97 ....Washington 51, Michigan St 23
12-25-98 ....Colorado 51, Oregon 43
12-25-99 ....Wake Forest 23, Arizona St 3
12-25-00 ....Boston College 31, Arizona St 17

City: Honolulu. Stadium: Aloha Stadium. Bowl was discontinued after 2000.

Freedom Bowl

12-16-84 ....Iowa 55, Texas 17
12-30-85 ....Washington 20, Colorado 17
12-30-86 ....UCLA 31, BYU 10
12-30-87 ....Arizona St 33, Air Force 28
12-29-88 ....BYU 20, Colorado 17
12-30-89 ....Washington 34, Florida 7
12-29-90 ....Colorado St 32, Oregon 31
12-30-91 ....Tulsa 28, San Diego St 17
12-29-92 ....Fresno St 24, USC 7
12-30-93 ....USC 28, Utah 21
12-29-94 ....Utah 16, Arizona 13

City: Anaheim. Stadium: Anaheim Stadium. Bowl was discontinued after 1994.

Outback Bowl

12-23-86 ....Boston College 27, Georgia 24
1-2-88 ....Michigan 28, Alabama 24
1-2-89 ....Syracuse 23, LSU 10
1-1-90 ....Auburn 31, Ohio St 14
1-1-91 ....Clemson 30, Illinois 0
1-1-92 ....Syracuse 24, Ohio St 17
1-1-93 ....Tennessee 38, Boston College 23
1-1-94 ....Michigan 42, North Carolina St 7
1-2-95 ....Wisconsin 34, Duke 20
1-1-96 ....Penn St 43, Auburn 14
1-1-97 ....Alabama 17, Michigan 14
1-1-98 ....Georgia 33, Wisconsin 6
1-1-99 ....Penn St 26, Kentucky 14
1-1-00 ....Georgia 28, Purdue 25
1-1-01 ....South Carolina 24, Ohio St 7
1-1-02 ....South Carolina 31, Ohio St 28
1-1-03 ....Michigan 38, Florida 30
1-1-04 ....Iowa 37, Florida 17
1-1-05 ....Georgia 24, Wisconsin 21
1-2-06 ....Florida 31, Iowa 24
1-1-07 ....Penn State 20, Tennessee 10

City: Tampa. Stadium: Raymond James Stadium, capacity 75,000. Name change: Hall of Fame Bowl (1986–95).

Insight.com Bowl

12-31-89 ....Arizona 17, North Carolina St 10
12-31-90 ....California 17, Wyoming 15
12-31-91 ....Indiana 24, Baylor 0
12-29-92 ....Washington St 31, Utah 28
12-29-93 ....Kansas St 52, Wyoming 17
12-29-94 ....BYU 31, Oklahoma 6
12-27-95 ....Texas Tech 55, Air Force 41
12-27-96 ....Wisconsin 38, Utah 10
12-27-97 ....Arizona 20, New Mexico 14
12-26-98 ....Missouri 34, W Virginia 31
12-31-99 ....Colorado 62, Boston College 28
12-28-00 ....Iowa St 37, Pittsburgh 29
12-29-01 ....Syracuse 26, Kansas St 3
12-26-02 ....Pittsburgh 38, Oregon St 13
12-26-03 ....California 52, Virginia Tech 49
12-28-04 ....Oregon State 38, Notre Dame 21
12-27-05 ....Arizona State 45, Rutgers 40
12-29-06 ....Texas Tech 44, Minnesota 41

City: Tucson. Stadium: Arizona Stadium, capacity 55,883. Name change: Copper Bowl 1989–97.

Tangerine Bowl

12-28-90 ....Florida St 24, Penn St 17
12-28-91 ....Alabama 30, Colorado 25
1-1-93 ....Stanford 24, Penn St 3
1-1-94 ....Boston College 31, Virginia 13
1-2-95 ....South Carolina 24, W Virginia 21
12-30-95 ....North Carolina 20, Arkansas 10
12-27-96 ....Miami (Fla.) 31, Virginia 21
12-29-97 ....Georgia Tech 35, W Virginia 30
12-29-98 ....Miami (Fla.) 46, North Carolina St 23
12-30-99 ....Illinois 62, Virginia 21
12-28-00 ....North Carolina 38, Minnesota 30
12-20-01 ....Pittsburgh 34, North Carolina St 19
12-23-02 ....Texas Tech 55, Clemson 15
12-22-03 ....North Carolina 56, Kansas 26

City: Miami. Stadium: Pro Player Stadium, capacity 75,192. Name change: Blockbuster Bowl (1990–93), Carquest Bowl (1994–97), Micron PC Bowl (1998–01). Discontinued after 2003.

Alamo Bowl

12-31-93 ....California 37, Iowa 3
12-31-94 ....Washington St 10, Baylor 3
12-28-95 ....Texas A&M 22, Michigan 20
12-29-96 ....Iowa 27, Texas Tech 0
12-30-97 ....Purdue 33, Oklahoma St 20
12-29-98 ....Purdue 37, Kansas St 34
12-28-99 ....Penn St 24, Texas A&M 0
12-30-00 ....Nebraska 66, Northwestern 17
12-29-01 ....Iowa 16, Texas Tech 13
12-28-02 ....Wisconsin 31, Colorado 28 (OT)
12-29-03 ....Nebraska 17, Michigan St 3
12-29-04 ....Ohio State 33, Oklahoma State 7
12-28-05 ....Nebraska 32, Michigan 28
12-30-06 ....Texas 26, Iowa 24

City: San Antonio, TX. Stadium: Alamodome, capaciity 67,000.

1936

		Record	Coach
1.	Minnesota	7-1-0	Bernie Bierman
2.	LSU	9-0-1	Bernie Moore
3.	Pittsburgh	7-1-1	Jack Sutherland
4.	Alabama	8-0-1	Frank Thomas
5.	Washington	7-1-1	Jimmy Phelan
6.	Santa Clara	7-1-0	Buck Shaw
7.	Northwestern	7-1-0	Pappy Waldorf
8.	Notre Dame	6-2-1	Elmer Layden
9.	Nebraska	7-2-0	Dana X. Bible
10.	Pennsylvania	7-1-0	Harvey Harman
11.	Duke	9-1-0	Wallace Wade
12.	Yale	7-1-0	Ducky Pond
13.	Dartmouth	7-1-1	Red Blaik
14.	Duquesne	7-2-0	John Smith
15.	Fordham	5-1-2	Jim Crowley
16.	TCU	8-2-2	Dutch Meyer
17.	Tennessee	6-2-2	Bob Neyland
18.	Arkansas	7-3-0	Fred Thomsen
19.	Navy	6-3-0	Tom Hamilton
20.	Marquette	7-1-0	Frank Murray

1937

		Record	Coach
1.	Pittsburgh	9-0-1	Jack Sutherland
2.	California	9-0-1	Stub Allison
3.	Fordham	7-0-1	Jim Crowley
4.	Alabama	9-0-0	Frank Thomas
5.	Minnesota	6-2-0	Bernie Bierman
6.	Villanova	8-0-1	Clipper Smith
7.	Dartmouth	7-0-2	Red Blaik
8.	LSU	9-1-0	Bernie Moore
9.	Notre Dame	6-2-1	Elmer Layden
	Santa Clara	8-0-0	Buck Shaw
11.	Nebraska	6-1-2	Biff Jones
12.	Yale	6-1-1	Ducky Pond
13.	Ohio St	6-2-0	Francis Schmidt
14.	Holy Cross	8-0-2	Eddie Anderson
	Arkansas	6-2-2	Fred Thomsen
16.	TCU	4-2-2	Dutch Meyer
17.	Colorado	8-0-0	Bunnie Oakes
18.	Rice	5-3-2	Jimmy Kitts
19.	North Carolina	7-1-1	Ray Wolf
20.	Duke	7-2-1	Wallace Wade

1938

		Record	Coach
1.	TCU	10-0-0	Dutch Meyer
2.	Tennessee	10-0-0	Bob Neyland
3.	Duke	9-0-0	Wallace Wade
4.	Oklahoma	10-0-0	Tom Stidham
5.	#Notre Dame	8-1-0	Elmer Layden
6.	Carnegie Tech	7-1-0	Bill Kern
7.	USC	8-2-0	Howard Jones
8.	Pittsburgh	8-2-0	Jack Sutherland
9.	Holy Cross	8-1-0	Eddie Anderson
10.	Minnesota	6-2-0	Bernie Bierman
11.	Texas Tech	10-0-0	Pete Cawthon
12.	Cornell	5-1-1	Carl Snavely
13.	Alabama	7-1-1	Frank Thomas
14.	California	10-1-0	Stub Allison
15.	Fordham	6-1-2	Jim Crowley
16.	Michigan	6-1-1	Fritz Crisler
17.	Northwestern	4-2-2	Pappy Waldorf

1938 (Cont.)

		Record	Coach
18.	Villanova	8-0-1	Clipper Smith
19.	Tulane	7-2-1	Red Dawson
20.	Dartmouth	7-2-0	Red Blaik

#Selected No. 1 by the Dickinson System.

1939

		Record	Coach
1.	Texas A&M	10-0-0	Homer Norton
2.	Tennessee	10-0-0	Bob Neyland
3.	#USC	7-0-2	Howard Jones
4.	Cornell	8-0-0	Carl Snavely
5.	Tulane	8-0-1	Red Dawson
6.	Missouri	8-1-0	Don Faurot
7.	UCLA	6-0-4	Babe Horrell
8.	Duke	8-1-0	Wallace Wade
9.	Iowa	6-1-1	Eddie Anderson
10.	Duquesne	8-0-1	Buff Donelli
11.	Boston College	9-1-0	Frank Leahy
12.	Clemson	8-1-0	Jess Neely
13.	Notre Dame	7-2-0	Elmer Layden
14.	Santa Clara	5-1-3	Buck Shaw
15.	Ohio St	6-2-0	Francis Schmidt
16.	Georgia Tech	7-2-0	Bill Alexander
17.	Fordham	6-2-0	Jim Crowley
18.	Nebraska	7-1-1	Biff Jones
19.	Oklahoma	6-2-1	Tom Stidham
20.	Michigan	6-2-0	Fritz Crisler

#Selected No. 1 by the Dickinson System.

1940

		Record	Coach
1.	Minnesota	8-0-0	Bernie Bierman
2.	Stanford	9-0-0	C. Shaughnessy
3.	Michigan	7-1-0	Fritz Crisler
4.	Tennessee	10-0-0	Bob Neyland
5.	Boston College	10-0-0	Frank Leahy
6.	Texas A&M	8-1-0	Homer Norton
7.	Nebraska	8-1-0	Biff Jones
8.	Northwestern	6-2-0	Pappy Waldorf
9.	Mississippi St	9-0-1	Allyn McKeen
10.	Washington	7-2-0	Jimmy Phelan
11.	Santa Clara	6-1-1	Buck Shaw
12.	Fordham	7-1-0	Jim Crowley
13.	Georgetown	8-1-0	Jack Hagerty
14.	Pennsylvania	6-1-1	George Munger
15.	Cornell	6-2-0	Carl Snavely
16.	SMU	8-1-1	Matty Bell
17.	Hard.-Simmons	9-0-0	Abe Woodson
18.	Duke	7-2-0	Wallace Wade
19.	Lafayette	9-0-0	Hooks Mylin
20.	—		

Only 19 teams selected.

1941

		Record	Coach
1.	Minnesota	8-0-0	Bernie Bierman
2.	Duke	9-0-0	Wallace Wade
3.	Notre Dame	8-0-1	Frank Leahy
4.	Texas	8-1-1	Dana X. Bible
5.	Michigan	6-1-1	Fritz Crisler

Note: Except where indicated with an asterisk, the polls from 1936 through 1964 were taken before the bowl games and those from 1965 through the present were taken after the bowl games.

1941 *(Cont.)*

		Record	Coach
6.	Fordham	7-1-0	Jim Crowley
7.	Missouri	8-1-0	Don Faurot
8.	Duquesne	8-0-0	Buff Donelli
9.	Texas A&M	9-1-0	Homer Norton
10.	Navy	7-1-1	Swede Larson
11.	Northwestern	5-3-0	Pappy Waldorf
12.	Oregon St	7-2-0	Lon Stiner
13.	Ohio St	6-1-1	Paul Brown
14.	Georgia	8-1-1	Wally Butts
15.	Pennsylvania	7-1-1	George Munger
16.	Mississippi St	8-1-1	Allyn McKeen
17.	Mississippi	6-2-1	Harry Mehre
18.	Tennessee	8-2-0	John Barnhill
19.	Washington St	6-4-0	Babe Hollingbery
20.	Alabama	8-2-0	Frank Thomas

1942

		Record	Coach
1.	Ohio St	9-1-0	Paul Brown
2.	Georgia	10-1-0	Wally Butts
3.	Wisconsin	8-1-1	H. Stuhldreher
4.	Tulsa	10-0-0	Henry Frnka
5.	Georgia Tech	9-1-0	Bill Alexander
6.	Notre Dame	7-2-2	Frank Leahy
7.	Tennessee	8-1-1	John Barnhill
8.	Boston College	8-1-0	Denny Myers
9.	Michigan	7-3-0	Fritz Crisler
10.	Alabama	7-3-0	Frank Thomas
11.	Texas	8-2-0	Dana X. Bible
12.	Stanford	6-4-0	Marchie Schwartz
13.	UCLA	7-3-0	Babe Horrell
14.	William & Mary	9-1-1	Carl Voyles
15.	Santa Clara	7-2-0	Buck Shaw
16.	Auburn	6-4-1	Jack Meagher
17.	Washington St	6-2-2	Babe Hollingbery
18.	Mississippi St	8-2-0	Allyn McKeen
19.	Minnesota	5-4-0	George Hauser
	Holy Cross	5-4-1	Ank Scanlon
	Penn St	6-1-1	Bob Higgins

1943

		Record	Coach
1.	Notre Dame	9-1-0	Frank Leahy
2.	Iowa Pre-Flight	9-1-0	Don Faurot
3.	Michigan	8-1-0	Fritz Crisler
4.	Navy	8-1-0	Billick Whelchel
5.	Purdue	9-0-0	Elmer Burnham
6.	Great Lakes	10-2-0	Tony Hinkle
7.	Duke	8-1-0	Eddie Cameron
8.	Del Monte P-F	7-1-0	Bill Kern
9.	Northwestern	6-2-0	Pappy Waldorf
10.	March Field	9-1-0	Paul Schissler
11.	Army	7-2-1	Red Blaik
12.	Washington	4-0-0	Ralph Welch
13.	Georgia Tech	7-3-0	Bill Alexander
14.	Texas	7-1-0	Dana X. Bible
15.	Tulsa	6-0-1	Henry Frnka
16.	Dartmouth	6-1-0	Earl Brown
17.	Bainbridge NTS	7-0-0	Joe Maniaci
18.	Colorado College	7-0-0	Hal White
19.	Pacific	7-2-0	Amos A. Stagg
20.	Pennsylvania	6-2-1	George Munger

1944

		Record	Coach
1.	Army	9-0-0	Red Blaik
2.	Ohio St	9-0-0	Carroll Widdoes
3.	Randolph Field	11-0-0	Frank Tritico
4.	Navy	6-3-0	Oscar Hagberg
5.	Bainbridge NTS	9-0-0	Joe Maniaci
6.	Iowa Pre-Flight	10-1-0	Jack Meagher
7.	USC	7-0-2	Jeff Cravath
8.	Michigan	8-2-0	Fritz Crisler
9.	Notre Dame	8-2-0	Ed McKeever
10.	March Field	7-1-2	Paul Schissler
11.	Duke	5-4-0	Eddie Cameron
12.	Tennessee	8-0-1	John Barnhill
13.	Georgia Tech	8-2-0	Bill Alexander
	Norman P-F	6-0-0	John Gregg
15.	Illinois	5-4-1	Ray Eliot
16.	El Toro Marines	8-1-0	Dick Hanley
17.	Great Lakes	9-2-1	Paul Brown
18.	Fort Pierce	9-0-0	Hamp Pool
19.	St. Mary's P-F	4-4-0	Jules Sikes
20.	2nd Air Force	7-2-1	Bill Reese

1945

		Record	Coach
1.	Army	9-0-0	Red Blaik
2.	Alabama	9-0-0	Frank Thomas
3.	Navy	7-1-1	Oscar Hagberg
4.	Indiana	9-0-1	Bo McMillan
5.	Oklahoma A&M	8-0-0	Jim Lookabaugh
6.	Michigan	7-3-0	Fritz Crisler
7.	St. Mary's (CA)	7-1-0	Jimmy Phelan
8.	Pennsylvania	6-2-0	George Munger
9.	Notre Dame	7-2-1	Hugh Devore
10.	Texas	9-1-0	Dana X. Bible
11.	USC	7-3-0	Jeff Cravath
12.	Ohio St	7-2-0	Carroll Widdoes
13.	Duke	6-2-0	Eddie Cameron
14.	Tennessee	8-1-0	John Barnhill
15.	LSU	7-2-0	Bernie Moore
16.	Holy Cross	8-1-0	John DeGrosa
17.	Tulsa	8-2-0	Henry Frnka
18.	Georgia	8-2-0	Wally Butts
19.	Wake Forest	4-3-1	Peahead Walker
20.	Columbia	8-1-0	Lou Little

1946

		Record	Coach
1.	Notre Dame	8-0-1	Frank Leahy
2.	Army	9-0-1	Red Blaik
3.	Georgia	10-0-0	Wally Butts
4.	UCLA	10-0-0	B. LaBrucherie
5.	Illinois	7-2-0	Ray Eliot
6.	Michigan	6-2-1	Fritz Crisler
7.	Tennessee	9-1-0	Bob Neyland
8.	LSU	9-1-0	Bernie Moore
9.	North Carolina	8-1-1	Carl Snavely
10.	Rice	8-2-0	Jess Neely
11.	Georgia Tech	8-2-0	Bobby Dodd
12.	Yale	7-1-1	Howard Odell
13.	Pennsylvania	6-2-0	George Munger
14.	Oklahoma	7-3-0	Jim Tatum
15.	Texas	8-2-0	Dana X. Bible
16.	Arkansas	6-3-1	John Barnhill
17.	Tulsa	9-1-0	J.O. Brothers
18.	North Carolina St	8-2-0	Beattie Feathers
19.	Delaware	9-0-0	Bill Murray
20.	Indiana	6-3-0	Bo McMillan

1947

		Record	Coach
1.	Notre Dame	9-0-0	Frank Leahy
2.	#Michigan	9-0-0	Fritz Crisler
3.	SMU	9-0-1	Matty Bell
4.	Penn St	9-0-0	Bob Higgins
5.	Texas	9-1-0	Blair Cherry
6.	Alabama	8-2-0	Red Drew
7.	Pennsylvania	7-0-1	George Munger
8.	USC	7-1-1	Jeff Cravath
9.	North Carolina	8-2-0	Carl Snavely
10.	Georgia Tech	9-1-0	Bobby Dodd
11.	Army	5-2-2	Red Blaik
12.	Kansas	8-0-2	George Sauer
13.	Mississippi	8-2-0	Johnny Vaught
14.	William & Mary	9-1-0	Rube McCray
15.	California	9-1-0	Pappy Waldorf
16.	Oklahoma	7-2-1	Bud Wilkinson
17.	North Carolina St	5-3-1	Beattie Feathers
18.	Rice	6-3-1	Jess Neely
19.	Duke	4-3-2	Wallace Wade
20.	Columbia	7-2-0	Lou Little

#The AP, which had voted Notre Dame No. 1 before the bowl games, took a second vote, giving the title to Michigan after its 49–0 win over USC in the Rose Bowl.

1948

		Record	Coach
1.	Michigan	9-0-0	Bennie Oosterbaan
2.	Notre Dame	9-0-1	Frank Leahy
3.	North Carolina	9-0-1	Carl Snavely
4.	California	10-0-0	Pappy Waldorf
5.	Oklahoma	9-1-0	Bud Wilkinson
6.	Army	8-0-1	Red Blaik
7.	Northwestern	7-2-0	Bob Voigts
8.	Georgia	9-1-0	Wally Butts
9.	Oregon	9-1-0	Jim Aiken
10.	SMU	8-1-1	Matty Bell
11.	Clemson	10-0-0	Frank Howard
12.	Vanderbilt	8-2-1	Red Sanders
13.	Tulane	9-1-0	Henry Frnka
14.	Michigan St	6-2-2	Biggie Munn
15.	Mississippi	8-1-0	Johnny Vaught
16.	Minnesota	7-2-0	Bernie Bierman
17.	William & Mary	6-2-2	Rube McCray
18.	Penn St	7-1-1	Bob Higgins
19.	Cornell	8-1-0	Lefty James
20.	Wake Forest	6-3-0	Peahead Walker

1949

		Record	Coach
1.	Notre Dame	10-0-0	Frank Leahy
2.	Oklahoma	10-0-0	Bud Wilkinson
3.	California	10-0-0	Pappy Waldorf
4.	Army	9-0-0	Red Blaik
5.	Rice	9-1-0	Jess Neely
6.	Ohio St	6-1-2	Wes Fesler
7.	Michigan	6-2-1	Bennie Oosterbaan
8.	Minnesota	7-2-0	Bernie Bierman
9.	LSU	8-2-0	Gaynell Tinsley
10.	Pacific	11-0-0	Larry Siemering
11.	Kentucky	9-2-0	Bear Bryant
12.	Cornell	8-1-0	Lefty James
13.	Villanova	8-1-0	Jim Leonard
14.	Maryland	8-1-0	Jim Tatum

1949 *(Cont.)*

		Record	Coach
15.	Santa Clara	7-2-1	Len Casanova
16.	North Carolina	7-3-0	Carl Snavely
17.	Tennessee	7-2-1	Bob Neyland
18.	Princeton	6-3-0	Charlie Caldwell
19.	Michigan St	6-3-0	Biggie Munn
20.	Missouri	7-3-0	Don Faurot
	Baylor	8-2-0	Bob Woodruff

1950

		Record	Coach
1.	Oklahoma	10-0-0	Bud Wilkinson
2.	Army	8-1-0	Red Blaik
3.	Texas	9-1-0	Blair Cherry
4.	Tennessee	10-1-0	Bob Neyland
5.	California	9-0-1	Pappy Waldorf
6.	Princeton	9-0-0	Charlie Caldwell
7.	Kentucky	10-1-0	Bear Bryant
8.	Michigan St	8-1-0	Biggie Munn
9.	Michigan	5-3-1	Bennie Oosterhaan
10.	Clemson	8-0-1	Frank Howard
11.	Washington	8-2-0	Howard Odell
12.	Wyoming	9-0-0	Bowden Wyatt
13.	Illinois	7-2-0	Ray Eliot
14.	Ohio St	6-3-0	Wes Fesler
15.	Miami (FL)	9-0-1	Andy Gustafson
16.	Alabama	9-2-0	Red Drew
17.	Nebraska	6-2-1	Bill Glassford
18.	Washington & Lee	8-2-0	George Barclay
19.	Tulsa	9-1-1	J.O. Brothers
20.	Tulane	6-2-1	Henry Frnka

1951

		Record	Coach
1.	Tennessee	10-0-0	Bob Neyland
2.	Michigan St	9-0-0	Biggie Munn
3.	Maryland	9-0-0	Jim Tatum
4.	Illinois	8-0-1	Ray Eliot
5.	Georgia Tech	10-0-1	Bobby Dodd
6.	Princeton	9-0-0	Charlie Caldwell
7.	Stanford	9-1-0	Chuck Taylor
8.	Wisconsin	7-1-1	Ivy Williamson
9.	Baylor	8-1-1	George Sauer
10.	Oklahoma	8-2-0	Bud Wilkinson
11.	TCU	6-4-0	Dutch Meyer
12.	California	8-2-0	Pappy Waldorf
13.	Virginia	8-1-0	Art Guepe
14.	San Francisco	9-0-0	Joe Kuharich
15.	Kentucky	7-4-0	Bear Bryant
16.	Boston University	6-4-0	Buff Donelli
17.	UCLA	5-3-1	Red Sanders
18.	Washington St	7-3-0	Forest Evashevski
19.	Holy Cross	8-2-0	Eddie Anderson
20.	Clemson	7-2-0	Frank Howard

1952

		Record	Coach
1.	Michigan St	9-0-0	Biggie Munn
2.	Georgia Tech	11-0-0	Bobby Dodd
3.	Notre Dame	7-2-1	Frank Leahy
4.	Oklahoma	8-1-1	Bud Wilkinson
5.	USC	9-1-0	Jess Hill
6.	UCLA	8-1-0	Red Sanders
7.	Mississippi	8-0-2	Johnny Vaught

1952 (Cont.)

		Record	Coach
8.	Tennessee	8-1-1	Bob Neyland
9.	Alabama	9-2-0	Red Drew
10.	Texas	8-2-0	Ed Price
11.	Wisconsin	6-2-1	Ivy Williamson
12.	Tulsa	8-1-1	J.O. Brothers
13.	Maryland	7-2-0	Jim Tatum
14.	Syracuse	7-2-0	Ben Schwartzwalder
15.	Florida	7-3-0	Bob Woodruff
16.	Duke	8-2-0	Bill Murray
17.	Ohio St	6-3-0	Woody Hayes
18.	Purdue	4-3-2	Stu Holcomb
19.	Princeton	8-1-0	Charlie Caldwell
20.	Kentucky	5-4-2	Bear Bryant

1953

		Record	Coach
1.	Maryland	10-0-0	Jim Tatum
2.	Notre Dame	9-0-1	Frank Leahy
3.	Michigan St	8-1-0	Biggie Munn
4.	Oklahoma	8-1-1	Bud Wilkinson
5.	UCLA	8-1-0	Red Sanders
6.	Rice	8-2-0	Jess Neely
7.	Illinois	7-1-1	Ray Eliot
8.	Georgia Tech	8-2-1	Bobby Dodd
9.	Iowa	5-3-1	Forest Evashevski
10.	W Virginia	8-1-0	Art Lewis
11.	Texas	7-3-0	Ed Price
12.	Texas Tech	10-1-0	DeWitt Weaver
13.	Alabama	6-2-3	Red Drew
14.	Army	7-1-1	Red Blaik
15.	Wisconsin	6-2-1	Ivy Williamson
16.	Kentucky	7-2-1	Bear Bryant
17.	Auburn	7-2-1	Shug Jordan
18.	Duke	7-2-1	Bill Murray
19.	Stanford	6-3-1	Chuck Taylor
20.	Michigan	6-3-0	Bennie Oosterbaan

1954

		Record	Coach
1.	Ohio St	9-0-0	Woody Hayes
2.	#UCLA	9-0-0	Red Sanders
3.	Oklahoma	10-0-0	Bud Wilkinson
4.	Notre Dame	9-1-0	Terry Brennan
5.	Navy	7-2-0	Eddie Erdelatz
6.	Mississippi	9-1-0	Johnny Vaught
7.	Army	7-2-0	Red Blaik
8.	Maryland	7-2-1	Jim Tatum
9.	Wisconsin	7-2-0	Ivy Williamson
10.	Arkansas	8-2-0	Bowden Wyatt
11.	Miami (FL)	8-1-0	Andy Gustafson
12.	W Virginia	8-1-0	Art Lewis
13.	Auburn	7-3-0	Shug Jordan
14.	Duke	7-2-1	Bill Murray
15.	Michigan	6-3-0	Bennie Oosterbaan
16.	Virginia Tech	8-0-1	Frank Moseley
17.	USC	8-3-0	Jess Hill
18.	Baylor	7-3-0	George Sauer
19.	Rice	7-3-0	Jess Neely
20.	Penn St	7-2-0	Rip Engle

#Selected No. 1 by UP.

1955

		Record	Coach
1.	Oklahoma	10-0-0	Bud Wilkinson
2.	Michigan St	8-1-0	Duffy Daugherty
3.	Maryland	10-0-0	Jim Tatum
4.	UCLA	9-1-0	Red Sanders
5.	Ohio St	7-2-0	Woody Hayes
6.	TCU	9-1-0	Abe Martin
7.	Georgia Tech	8-1-1	Bobby Dodd
8.	Auburn	8-1-1	Shug Jordan
9.	Notre Dame	8-2-0	Terry Brennan
10.	Mississippi	9-1-0	Johnny Vaught
11.	Pittsburgh	7-3-0	John Michelosen
12.	Michigan	7-2-0	Bennie Oosterbaan
13.	USC	6-4-0	Jess Hill
14.	Miami (FL)	6-3-0	Andy Gustafson
15.	Miami (OH)	9-0-0	Ara Parseghian
16.	Stanford	6-3-1	Chuck Taylor
17.	Texas A&M	7-2-1	Bear Bryant
18.	Navy	6-2-1	Eddie Erdelatz
19.	W Virginia	8-2-0	Art Lewis
20.	Army	6-3-0	Red Blaik

1956

		Record	Coach
1.	Oklahoma	10-0-0	Bud Wilkinson
2.	Tennessee	10-0-0	Bowden Wyatt
3.	Iowa	8-1-0	Forest Evashevski
4.	Georgia Tech	9-1-0	Bobby Dodd
5.	Texas A&M	9-0-1	Bear Bryant
6.	Miami (FL)	8-1-1	Andy Gustafson
7.	Michigan	7-2-0	Bennie Oosterbaan
8.	Syracuse	7-1-0	Ben Schwartzwalder
9.	Michigan St	7-2-0	Duffy Daugherty
10.	Oregon St	7-2-1	Tommy Prothro
11.	Baylor	8-2-0	Sam Boyd
12.	Minnesota	6-1-2	Murray Warmath
13.	Pittsburgh	7-2-1	John Michelosen
14.	TCU	7-3-0	Abe Martin
15.	Ohio St	6-3-0	Woody Hayes
16.	Navy	6-1-2	Eddie Erdelatz
17.	Geo Washington	7-1-1	Gene Sherman
18.	USC	8-2-0	Jess Hill
19.	Clemson	7-1-2	Frank Howard
20.	Colorado	7-2-1	Dallas Ward
	Penn St	6-2-1	Rip Engle

1957

		Record	Coach
1.	Auburn	10-0-0	Shug Jordan
2.	#Ohio St	8-1-0	Woody Hayes
3.	Michigan St	8-1-0	Duffy Daugherty
4.	Oklahoma	9-1-0	Bud Wilkinson
5.	Navy	8-1-1	Eddie Erdelatz
6.	Iowa	7-1-1	Forest Evashevski
7.	Mississippi	8-1-1	Johnny Vaught
8.	Rice	7-3-0	Jess Neely
9.	Texas A&M	8-2-0	Bear Bryant
10.	Notre Dame	7-3-0	Terry Brennan
11.	Texas	6-3-1	Darrell Royal
12.	Arizona St	10-0-0	Dan Devine
13.	Tennessee	7-3-0	Bowden Wyatt
14.	Mississippi St	6-2-1	Wade Walker
15.	North Carolina St	7-1-2	Earle Edwards
16.	Duke	6-2-2	Bill Murray

1957 *(Cont.)*

		Record	Coach
17.	Florida	6-2-1	Bob Woodruff
18.	Army	7-2-0	Red Blaik
19.	Wisconsin	6-3-0	Milt Brunt
20.	VMI	9-0-1	John McKenna

#Selected No. 1 by UP.

1958

		Record	Coach
1.	LSU	10-0-0	Paul Dietzel
2.	Iowa	7-1-1	Forest Evashevski
3.	Army	8-0-1	Red Blaik
4.	Auburn	9-0-1	Shug Jordan
5.	Oklahoma	9-1-0	Bud Wilkinson
6.	Air Force	9-0-1	Ben Martin
7.	Wisconsin	7-1-1	Milt Bruhn
8.	Ohio St	6-1-2	Woody Hayes
9.	Syracuse	8-1-0	Ben Schwartzwalder
10.	TCU	8-2-0	Abe Martin
11.	Mississippi	8-2-0	Johnny Vaught
12.	Clemson	8-2-0	Frank Howard
13.	Purdue	6-1-2	Jack Mollenkopf
14.	Florida	6-3-1	Bob Woodruff
15.	South Carolina	7-3-0	Warren Giese
16.	California	7-3-0	Pete Elliott
17.	Notre Dame	6-4-0	Terry Brennan
18.	SMU	6-4-0	Bill Meek
19.	Oklahoma St	7-3-0	Cliff Speegle
20.	Rutgers	8-1-0	John Stiegman

1959

		Record	Coach
1.	Syracuse	10-0-0	Ben Schwartzwalder
2.	Mississippi	9-1-0	Johnny Vaught
3.	LSU	9-1-0	Paul Dietzel
4.	Texas	9-1-0	Darrell Royal
5.	Georgia	9-1-0	Wally Butts
6.	Wisconsin	7-2-0	Milt Bruhn
7.	TCU	8-2-0	Abe Martin
8.	Washington	9-1-0	Jim Owens
9.	Arkansas	8-2-0	Frank Broyles
10.	Alabama	7-1-2	Bear Bryant
11.	Clemson	8-2-0	Frank Howard
12.	Penn St	8-2-0	Rip Engle
13.	Illinois	5-3-1	Ray Eliot
14.	USC	8-2-0	Don Clark
15.	Oklahoma	7-3-0	Bud Wilkinson
16.	Wyoming	9-1-0	Bob Devaney
17.	Notre Dame	5-5-0	Joe Kuharich
18.	Missouri	6-4-0	Dan Devine
19.	Florida	5-4-1	Bob Woodruff
20.	Pittsburgh	6-4-0	John Michelosen

1960

		Record	Coach
1.	Minnesota	8-1-0	Murray Warmath
2.	Mississippi	9-0-1	Johnny Vaught
3.	Iowa	8-1-0	Forest Evashevski
4.	Navy	9-1-0	Wayne Hardin
5.	Missouri	9-1-0	Dan Devine
6.	Washington	9-1-0	Jim Owens
7.	Arkansas	8-2-0	Frank Broyles
8.	Ohio St	7-2-0	Woody Hayes
9.	Alabama	8-1-1	Bear Bryant

1960 *(Cont.)*

		Record	Coach
10.	Duke	7-3-0	Bill Murray
11.	Kansas	7-2-1	Jack Mitchell
12.	Baylor	8-2-0	John Bridgers
13.	Auburn	8-2-0	Shug Jordan
14.	Yale	9-0-0	Jordan Oliver
15.	Michigan St	6-2-1	Duffy Daugherty
16.	Penn St	6-3-0	Rip Engle
17.	New Mexico St	10-0-0	Warren Woodson
18.	Florida	8-2-0	Ray Graves
19.	Syracuse	7-2-0	Ben Schwartzwalder
	Purdue	4-4-1	Jack Mollenkopf

1961

		Record	Coach
1.	Alabama	10-0-0	Bear Bryant
2.	Ohio St	8-0-1	Woody Hayes
3.	Texas	9-1-0	Darrell Royal
4.	LSU	9-1-0	Paul Dietzel
5.	Mississippi	9-1-0	Johnny Vaught
6.	Minnesota	7-2-0	Murray Warmath
7.	Colorado	9-1-0	Sonny Grandelius
8.	Michigan St	7-2-0	Duffy Daugherty
9.	Arkansas	8-2-0	Frank Broyles
10.	Utah St	9-0-1	John Ralston
11.	Missouri	7-2-1	Dan Devine
12.	Purdue	6-3-0	Jack Mollenkopf
13.	Georgia Tech	7-3-0	Bobby Dodd
14.	Syracuse	7-3-0	Ben Schwartzwalder
15.	Rutgers	9-0-0	John Bateman
16.	UCLA	7-3-0	Bill Barnes
17.	Rice	7-3-0	Jess Neely
	Penn St	7-3-0	Rip Engle
	Arizona	8-1-1	Jim LaRue
20.	Duke	7-3-0	Bill Murray

1962

		Record	Coach
1.	USC	10-0-0	John McKay
2.	Wisconsin	8-1-0	Milt Bruhn
3.	Mississippi	9-0-0	Johnny Vaught
4.	Texas	9-0-1	Darrell Royal
5.	Alabama	9-1-0	Bear Bryant
6.	Arkansas	9-1-0	Frank Broyles
7.	LSU	8-1-1	Charlie McClendon
8.	Oklahoma	8-2-0	Bud Wilkinson
9.	Penn St	9-1-0	Rip Engle
10.	Minnesota	6-2-1	Murray Warmath
11-20: UPI			
11.	Georgia Tech	7-2-1	Bobby Dodd
12.	Missouri	7-1-2	Dan Devine
13.	Ohio St	6-3-0	Woody Hayes
14.	Duke	8-2-0	Bill Murray
	Washington	7-1-2	Jim Owens
16.	Northwestern	7-2-0	Ara Parseghian
	Oregon St	8-2-0	Tommy Prothro
18.	Arizona St	7-2-1	Frank Kush
	Miami (FL)	7-3-0	Andy Gustafson
	Illinois	2-7-0	Pete Elliott

1963

		Record	Coach
1.	Texas	10-0-0	Darrell Royal
2.	Navy	9-1-0	Wayne Hardin
3.	Illinois	7-1-1	Pete Elliott

1963 *(Cont.)*

		Record	Coach
4.	Pittsburgh	9-1-0	John Michelosen
5.	Auburn	9-1-0	Shug Jordan
6.	Nebraska	9-1-0	Bob Devaney
7.	Mississippi	7-0-2	Johnny Vaught
8.	Alabama	8-2-0	Bear Bryant
9.	Oklahoma	8-2-0	Bud Wilkinson
10.	Michigan St	6-2-1	Duffy Daugherty
11–20: UPI			
11.	Mississippi St	6-2-2	Paul Davis
12.	Syracuse	8-2-0	Ben Schwartzwalder
13.	Arizona St	8-1-0	Frank Kush
14.	Memphis St	9-0-1	Billy J. Murphy
15.	Washington	6-4-0	Jim Owens
16.	Penn St	7-3-0	Rip Engle
	USC	7-3-0	John McKay
	Missouri	7-3-0	Dan Devine
19.	North Carolina	8-2-0	Jim Hickey
20.	Baylor	7-3-0	John Bridgers

1964

		Record	Coach
1.	Alabama	10-0-0	Bear Bryant
2.	Arkansas	10-0-0	Frank Broyles
3.	Notre Dame	9-1-0	Ara Parseghian
4.	Michigan	8-1-0	Bump Elliott
5.	Texas	9-1-0	Darrell Royal
6.	Nebraska	9-1-0	Bob Devaney
7.	LSU	7-2-1	Charlie McClendon
8.	Oregon St	8-2-0	Tommy Prothro
9.	Ohio St	7-2-0	Woody Hayes
10.	USC	7-3-0	John McKay
11–20: UPI			
11.	Florida St	8-1-1	Bill Peterson
12.	Syracuse	7-3-0	Ben Schwartzwalder
13.	Princeton	9-0-0	Dick Colman
14.	Penn St	6-4-0	Rip Engle
	Utah	8-2-0	Ray Nagel
16.	Illinois	6-3-0	Pete Elliott
	New Mexico	9-2-0	Bill Weeks
18.	Tulsa	8-2-0	Glenn Dobbs
19.	Missouri	6-3-1	Dan Devine
20.	Mississippi	5-4-1	Johnny Vaught
	Michigan St	4-5-1	Duffy Daugherty

1965

		Record	Coach
1.	Alabama	9-1-1	Bear Bryant
2.	#Michigan St	10-1-0	Duffy Daugherty
3.	Arkansas	10-1-0	Frank Broyles
4.	UCLA	8-2-1	Tommy Prothro
5.	Nebraska	10-1-0	Bob Devaney
6.	Missouri	8-2-1	Dan Devine
7.	Tennessee	8-1-2	Doug Dickey
8.	LSU	8-3-0	Charlie McClendon
9.	Notre Dame	7-2-1	Ara Parseghian
10.	USC	7-2-1	John McKay
11–20: UPI			
11.	Texas Tech	8-2-0	J.T. King
12.	Ohio St	7-2-0	Woody Hayes
13.	Florida	7-3-0	Ray Graves
14.	Purdue	7-2-1	Jack Mollenkopf
15.	Georgia	6-4-0	Vince Dooley
16.	Tulsa	8-2-0	Glenn Dobbs
17.	Mississippi	6-4-0	Johnny Vaught

1965 *(Cont.)*

		Record	Coach
18.	Kentucky	6-4-0	Charlie Bradshaw
19	Syracuse	7-3-0	Ben Schwartzwalder
20.	Colorado	6-2-2	Eddie Crowder
#Selected No. 1 by UPI.			

1966*

		Record	Coach
1.	Notre Dame	9-0-1	Ara Parseghian
2.	Michigan St	9-0-1	Duffy Daugherty
3.	Alabama	10-0-0	Bear Bryant
4.	Georgia	9-1-0	Vince Dooley
5.	UCLA	9-1-0	Tommy Prothro
6.	Nebraska	9-1-0	Bob Devaney
7.	Purdue	8-2-0	Jack Mollenkopf
8.	Georgia Tech	9-1-0	Bobby Dodd
9.	Miami (FL)	7-2-1	Charlie Tate
10.	SMU	8-2-0	Hayden Fry
11–20: UPI			
11.	Florida	8-2-0	Ray Graves
12.	Mississippi	8-2-0	Johnny Vaught
13.	Arkansas	8-2-0	Frank Broyles
14.	Tennessee	7-3-0	Doug Dickey
15.	Wyoming	9-1-0	Lloyd Eaton
16.	Syracuse	8-2-0	Ben Schwartzwalder
17.	Houston	8-2-0	Bill Yeoman
18.	USC	7-3-0	John McKay
19.	Oregon St	7-3-0	Dee Andros
20.	Virginia Tech	8-1-1	Jerry Claiborne

1967*

		Record	Coach
1.	USC	9-1-0	John McKay
2.	Tennessee	9-1-0	Doug Dickey
3.	Oklahoma	9-1-0	Chuck Fairbanks
4.	Indiana	9-1-0	John Pont
5.	Notre Dame	8-2-0	Ara Parseghian
6.	Wyoming	10-0-0	Lloyd Eaton
7.	Oregon St	7-2-1	Dee Andros
8.	Alabama	8-1-1	Bear Bryant
9.	Purdue	8-2-0	Jack Mollenkopf
10.	Penn St	8-2-0	Joe Paterno
11–20: UPI†			
11.	UCLA	7-2-1	Tommy Prothro
12.	Syracuse	8-2-0	Ben Schwartzwalder
13.	Colorado	8-2-0	Eddie Crowder
14.	Minnesota	8-2-0	Murray Warmath
15.	Florida St	7-2-1	Bill Peterson
16.	Miami (FL)	7-3-0	Charlie Tate
17.	North Carolina St	8-2-0	Earle Edwards
18.	Georgia	7-3-0	Vince Dooley
19.	Houston	9-2-0	Bill Yeoman
20.	Arizona St	8-2-0	Frank Kush

†UPI ranked Penn St 11th and did not rank Alabama, which was on probation.

1968

		Record	Coach
1.	Ohio St	10-0-0	Woody Hayes
2.	Penn St	11-0-0	Joe Paterno
3.	Texas	9-1-1	Darrell Royal
4.	USC	9-1-1	John McKay
5.	Notre Dame	7-2-1	Ara Parseghian

1968 *(Cont.)*

		Record	Coach
6.	Arkansas	10-1-0	Frank Broyles
7.	Kansas	9-2-0	Pepper Rodgers
8.	Georgia	8-1-2	Vince Dooley
9.	Missouri	8-3-0	Dan Devine
10.	Purdue	8-2-0	Jack Mollenkopf
11.	Oklahoma	7-4-0	Chuck Fairbanks
12.	Michigan	8-2-0	Bump Elliott
13.	Tennessee	8-2-1	Doug Dickey
14.	SMU	8-3-0	Hayden Fry
15.	Oregon St	7-3-0	Dee Andros
16.	Auburn	7-4-0	Shug Jordan
17.	Alabama	8-3-0	Bear Bryant
18.	Houston	6-2-2	Bill Yeoman
19.	LSU	8-3-0	Charlie McClendon
20.	Ohio	10-1-0	Bill Hess

1969

		Record	Coach
1.	Texas	11-0-0	Darrell Royal
2.	Penn St	11-0-0	Joe Paterno
3.	USC	10-0-1	John McKay
4.	Ohio St	8-1-0	Woody Hayes
5.	Notre Dame	8-2-1	Ara Parseghian
6.	Missouri	9-2-0	Dan Devine
7.	Arkansas	9-2-0	Frank Broyles
8.	Mississippi	8-3-0	Johnny Vaught
9.	Michigan	8-3-0	Bo Schembechler
10.	LSU	9-1-0	Charlie McClendon
11.	Nebraska	9-2-0	Bob Devaney
12.	Houston	9-2-0	Bill Yeoman
13.	UCLA	8-1-1	Tommy Prothro
14.	Florida	9-1-1	Ray Graves
15.	Tennessee	9-2-0	Doug Dickey
16.	Colorado	8-3-0	Eddie Crowder
17.	W Virginia	10-0-1	Jim Carlen
18.	Purdue	8-2-0	Jack Mollenkopf
19.	Stanford	7-2-1	John Ralston
20.	Auburn	8-3-0	Shug Jordan

1970

		Record	Coach
1.	Nebraska	11-0-1	Bob Devaney
2.	Notre Dame	10-1-0	Ara Parseghian
3.	#Texas	10-1-0	Darrell Royal
4.	Tennessee	11-0-1	Bill Battle
5.	Ohio St	9-1-0	Woody Hayes
6.	Arizona St	11-0-0	Frank Kush
7.	LSU	9-3-0	Charlie McClendon
8.	Stanford	9-3-0	John Ralston
9.	Michigan	9-1-0	Bo Schembechler
10.	Auburn	9-2-0	Shug Jordan
11.	Arkansas	9-2-0	Frank Broyles
12.	Toledo	12-0-0	Frank Lauterbur
13.	Georgia Tech	9-3-0	Bud Carson
14.	Dartmouth	9-0-0	Bob Blackman
15.	USC	6-4-1	John McKay
16.	Air Force	9-3-0	Ben Martin
17.	Tulane	8-4-0	Jim Pittman
18.	Penn St	7-3-0	Joe Paterno
19.	Houston	8-3-0	Bill Yeoman
20.	Oklahoma	7-4-1	Chuck Fairbanks
	Mississippi	7-4-0	Johnny Vaught

#Selected No. 1 by UPI.

1971

		Record	Coach
1.	Nebraska	13-0-0	Bob Devaney
2.	Oklahoma	11-1-0	Chuck Fairbanks
3.	Colorado	10-2-0	Eddie Crowder
4.	Alabama	11-1-0	Bear Bryant
5.	Penn St	11-1-0	Joe Paterno
6.	Michigan	11-1-0	Bo Schembechler
7.	Georgia	11-1-0	Vince Dooley
8.	Arizona St	11-1-0	Frank Kush
9.	Tennessee	10-2-0	Bill Battle
10.	Stanford	9-3-0	John Ralston
11.	LSU	9-3-0	Charlie McClendon
12.	Auburn	9-2-0	Shug Jordan
13.	Notre Dame	8-2-0	Ara Parseghian
14.	Toledo	12-0-0	John Murphy
15.	Mississippi	10-2-0	Billy Kinard
16.	Arkansas	8-3-1	Frank Broyles
17.	Houston	9-3-0	Bill Yeoman
18.	Texas	8-3-0	Darrell Royal
19.	Washington	8-3-0	Jim Owens
20.	USC	6-4-1	John McKay

1972

		Record	Coach
1.	USC	12-0-0	John McKay
2.	Oklahoma	11-1-0	Chuck Fairbanks
3.	Texas	10-1-0	Darrell Royal
4.	Nebraska	9-2-1	Bob Devaney
5.	Auburn	10-1-0	Shug Jordan
6.	Michigan	10-1-0	Bo Schembechler
7.	Alabama	10-2-0	Bear Bryant
8.	Tennessee	10-2-0	Bill Battle
9.	Ohio St	9-2-0	Woody Hayes
10.	Penn St	10-2-0	Joe Paterno
11.	LSU	9-2-1	Charlie McClendon
12.	North Carolina	11-1-0	Bill Dooley
13.	Arizona St	10-2-0	Frank Kush
14.	Notre Dame	8-3-0	Ara Parseghian
15.	UCLA	8-3-0	Pepper Rodgers
16.	Colorado	8-4-0	Eddie Crowder
17.	North Carolina St	8-3-1	Lou Holtz
18.	Louisville	9-1-0	Lee Corso
19.	Washington St	7-4-0	Jim Sweeney
20.	Georgia Tech	7-4-1	Bill Fulch

1973

		Record	Coach
1.	Notre Dame	11-0-0	Ara Parseghian
2.	Ohio St	10-0-1	Woody Hayes
3.	Oklahoma	10-0-1	Barry Switzer
4.	#Alabama	11-1-0	Bear Bryant
5.	Penn St	12-0-0	Joe Paterno
6.	Michigan	10-0-1	Bo Schembechler
7.	Nebraska	9-2-1	Tom Osborne
8.	USC	9-2-1	John McKay
9.	Arizona St	11-1-0	Frank Kush
	Houston	11-1-0	Bill Yeoman
11.	Texas Tech	11-1-0	Jim Carlen
12.	UCLA	9-2-0	Pepper Rodgers
13.	LSU	9-3-0	Charlie McClendon
14.	Texas	8-3-0	Darrell Royal
15.	Miami (OH)	11-0-0	Bill Mallory
16.	North Carolina St	9-3-0	Lou Holtz
17.	Missouri	8-4-0	Al Onofrio
18.	Kansas	7-4-1	Don Fambrough

1973 *(Cont.)*

		Record	Coach
19.	Tennessee	8-4-0	Bill Battle
20.	Maryland	8-4-0	Jerry Claiborne
	Tulane	9-3-0	Bennie Ellender

#Selected No. 1 by UPI.

1974

		Record	Coach
1.	Oklahoma	11-0-0	Barry Switzer
2.	#USC	10-1-1	John McKay
3.	Michigan	10-1-0	Bo Schembechler
4.	Ohio St	10-2-0	Woody Hayes
5.	Alabama	11-1-0	Bear Bryant
6.	Notre Dame	10-2-0	Ara Parseghian
7.	Penn St	10-2-0	Joe Paterno
8.	Auburn	10-2-0	Shug Jordan
9.	Nebraska	9-3-0	Tom Osborne
10.	Miami (Ohio)	10-0-1	Dick Crum
11.	North Carolina St	9-2-1	Lou Holtz
12.	Michigan St	7-3-1	Denny Stolz
13.	Maryland	8-4-0	Jerry Claiborne
14.	Baylor	8-4-0	Grant Teaff
15.	Florida	8-4-0	Doug Dickey
·16.	Texas A&M	8-3-0	Emory Ballard
17.	Mississippi St	9-3-0	Bob Tyler
	Texas	8-4-0	Darrell Royal
19.	Houston	8-3-1	Bill Yeoman
20.	Tennessee	7-3-2	Bill Battle

#Selected No. 1 by UPI

1975

		Record	Coach
1.	Oklahoma	11-1-0	Barry Switzer
2.	Arizona St	12-0-0	Frank Kush
3.	Alabama	11-1-0	Bear Bryant
4.	Ohio St	11-1-0	Woody Hayes
5.	UCLA	9-2-1	Dick Vermeil
6.	Texas	10-2-0	Darrell Royal
7.	Arkansas	10-2-0	Frank Broyles
8.	Michigan	8-2-2	Bo Schembechler
9.	Nebraska	10-2-0	Tom Osborne
10.	Penn St	9-3-0	Joe Paterno
11.	Texas A&M	10-2-0	Emory Bellard
12.	Miami (OH)	11-1-0	Dick Crum
13.	Maryland	9-2-1	Jerry Claiborne
14.	California	8-3-0	Mike White
15.	Pittsburgh	8-4-0	Johnny Majors
16.	Colorado	9-3-0	Bill Mallory
17.	USC	8-4-0	John McKay
18.	Arizona	9-2-0	Jim Young
19.	Georgia	9-3-0	Vince Dooley
20.	W Virginia	9-3-0	Bobby Bowden

1976

		Record	Coach
1.	Pittsburgh	12-0-0	Johnny Majors
2.	USC	11-1-0	John Robinson
3.	Michigan	10-2-0	Bo Schembechler
4.	Houston	10-2-0	Bill Yeoman
5.	Oklahoma	9-2-1	Barry Switzer
6.	Ohio St	9-2-1	Woody Hayes
7.	Texas A&M	10-2-0	Emory Bellard
8.	Maryland	11-1-0	Jerry Claiborne

1976 *(Cont.)*

		Record	Coach
9.	Nebraska	9-3-1	Tom Osborne
10.	Georgia	10-2-0	Vince Dooley
11.	Alabama	9-3-0	Bear Bryant
12.	Notre Dame	9-3-0	Dan Devine
13.	Texas Tech	10-2-0	Steve Sloan
14.	Oklahoma St	9-3-0	Jim Stanley
15.	UCLA	9-2-1	Terry Donahue
16.	Colorado	8-4-0	Bill Mallory
17.	Rutgers	11-0-0	Frank Burns
18.	Kentucky	9-3-0	Fran Curci
19.	Iowa St	8-3-0	Earle Bruce
20.	Mississippi St	9-2-0	Bob Tyler

1977

		Record	Coach
1.	Notre Dame	11-1-0	Dan Devine
2.	Alabama	11-1-0	Bear Bryant
3.	Arkansas	11-1-0	Lou Holtz
4.	Texas	11-1-0	Fred Akers
5.	Penn St	11-1-0	Joe Paterno
6.	Kentucky	10-1-0	Fran Curci
7.	Oklahoma	10-2-0	Barry Switzer
8.	Pittsburgh	9-2-1	Jackie Sherrill
9.	Michigan	10-2-0	Bo Schembechler
10.	Washington	10-2-0	Don James
11.	Ohio St	9-3-0	Woody Hayes
12.	Nebraska	9-3-0	Tom Osborne
13.	USC	8-4-0	John Robinson
14.	Florida St	10-2-0	Bobby Bowden
15.	Stanford	9-3-0	Bill Walsh
16.	San Diego St	10-1-0	Claude Gilbert
17.	North Carolina	8-3-1	Bill Dooley
18.	Arizona St	9-3-0	Frank Kush
19.	Clemson	8-3-1	Charley Pell
20.	BYU	9-2-0	LaVell Edwards

1978

		Record	Coach
1.	Alabama	11-1-0	Bear Bryant
2.	#USC	12-1-0	John Robinson
3.	Oklahoma	11-1-0	Barry Switzer
4.	Penn St	11-1-0	Joe Paterno
5.	Michigan	10-2-0	Bo Schembechler
6.	Clemson	11-1-0	Charley Pell
7.	Notre Dame	9-3-0	Dan Devine
8.	Nebraska	9-3-0	Tom Osborne
9.	Texas	9-3-0	Fred Akers
10.	Houston	9-3-0	Bill Yeoman
11.	Arkansas	9-2-1	Lou Holtz
12.	Michigan St	8-3-0	Darryl Rogers
13.	Purdue	9-2-1	Jim Young
14.	UCLA	8-3-1	Terry Donahue
15.	Missouri	8-4-0	Warren Powers
16.	Georgia	9-2-1	Vince Dooley
17.	Stanford	8-4-0	Bill Walsh
18.	North Carolina St	9-3-0	Bo Rein
19.	Texas A&M	8-4-0	Emory Bellard (4–2)
			Tom Wilson (4–2)
20.	Maryland	9-3-0	Jerry Claiborne

#Selected No. 1 by UPI.

1979

		Record	Coach
1.	Alabama	12-0-0	Bear Bryant
2.	USC	11-0-1	John Robinson
3.	Oklahoma	11-1-0	Barry Switzer
4.	Ohio St	11-1-0	Earle Bruce
5.	Houston	11-1-0	Bill Yeoman
6.	Florida St	11-1-0	Bobby Bowden
7.	Pittsburgh	11-1-0	Jackie Sherrill
8.	Arkansas	10-2-0	Lou Holtz
9.	Nebraska	10-2-0	Tom Osborne
10.	Purdue	10-2-0	Jim Young
11.	Washington	10-1-0	Don James
12.	Texas	9-3-0	Fred Akers
13.	BYU	11-1-0	LaVell Edwards
14.	Baylor	8-4-0	Grant Teaff
15.	North Carolina	8-3-1	Dick Crum
16.	Auburn	8-3-0	Doug Barfield
17.	Temple	10-2-0	Wayne Hardin
18.	Michigan	8-4-0	Bo Schembechler
19.	Indiana	8-4-0	Lee Corso
20.	Penn St	8-4-0	Joe Paterno

1980

		Record	Coach
1.	Georgia	12-0-0	Vince Dooley
2.	Pittsburgh	11-1-0	Jackie Sherrill
3.	Oklahoma	10-2-0	Barry Switzer
4.	Michigan	10-2-0	Bo Schembechler
5.	Florida St	10-2-0	Bobby Bowden
6.	Alabama	10-2-0	Bear Bryant
7.	Nebraska	10-2-0	Tom Osborne
8.	Penn St	10-2-0	Joe Paterno
9.	Notre Dame	9-2-1	Dan Devine
10.	North Carolina	11-1-0	Dick Crum
11.	USC	8-2-1	John Robinson
12.	BYU	12-1-0	LaVell Edwards
13.	UCLA	9-2-0	Terry Donahue
14.	Baylor	10-2-0	Grant Teaff
15.	Ohio St	9-3-0	Earle Bruce
16.	Washington	9-3-0	Don James
17.	Purdue	9-3-0	Jim Young
18.	Miami (FL)	9-3-0	H. Schnellenberger
19.	Mississippi St	9-3-0	Emory Bellard
20.	SMU	8-4-0	Ron Meyer

1981

		Record	Coach
1.	Clemson	12-0-0	Danny Ford
2.	Texas	10-1-1	Fred Akers
3.	Penn St	10-2-0	Joe Paterno
4.	Pittsburgh	11-1-0	Jackie Sherrill
5.	SMU	10-1-0	Ron Meyer
6.	Georgia	10-2-0	Vince Dooley
7.	Alabama	9-2-1	Bear Bryant
8.	Miami (FL)	9-2-0	H. Schnellenberger
9.	North Carolina	10-2-0	Dick Crum
10.	Washington	10-2-0	Don James
11.	Nebraska	9-3-0	Tom Osborne
12.	Michigan	9-3-0	Bo Schembechler
13.	BYU	11-2-0	LaVell Edwards
14.	USC	9-3-0	John Robinson
15.	Ohio St	9-3-0	Earle Bruce
16.	Arizona St	9-2-0	Darryl Rogers
17.	W Virginia	9-3-0	Don Nehlen

1981 *(Cont.)*

		Record	Coach
18.	Iowa	8-4-0	Hayden Fry
19.	Missouri	8-4-0	Warren Powers
20.	Oklahoma	7-4-1	Barry Switzer

1982

		Record	Coach
1.	Penn St	11-1-0	Joe Paterno
2.	SMU	11-0-1	Bobby Collins
3.	Nebraska	12-1-0	Tom Osborne
4.	Georgia	11-1-0	Vince Dooley
5.	UCLA	10-1-1	Terry Donahue
6.	Arizona St	10-2-0	Darryl Rogers
7.	Washington	10-2-0	Don James
8.	Clemson	9-1-1	Danny Ford
9.	Arkansas	9-2-1	Lou Holtz
10.	Pittsburgh	9-3-0	Foge Fazio
11.	LSU	8-3-1	Jerry Stovall
12.	Ohio St	9-3-0	Earle Bruce
13.	Florida St	9-3-0	Bobby Bowden
14.	Auburn	9-3-0	Pat Dye
15.	USC	8-3-0	John Robinson
16.	Oklahoma	8-4-0	Barry Switzer
17.	Texas	9-3-0	Fred Akers
18.	North Carolina	8-4-0	Dick Crum
19.	W Virginia	9-3-0	Don Nehlen
20.	Maryland	8-4-0	Bobby Ross

1983

		Record	Coach
1.	Miami (Fla.)	11-1-0	H. Schnellenberger
2.	Nebraska	12-1-0	Tom Osborne
3.	Auburn	11-1-0	Pat Dye
4.	Georgia	10-1-1	Vince Dooley
5.	Texas	11-1-0	Fred Akers
6.	Florida	9-2-1	Charlie Pell
7.	BYU	11-1-0	LaVell Edwards
8.	Michigan	9-3-0	Bo Schembechler
9.	Ohio St	9-3-0	Earle Bruce
10.	Illinois	10-2-0	Mike White
11.	Clemson	9-1-1	Danny Ford
12.	SMU	10-2-0	Bobby Collins
13.	Air Force	10-2-0	Ken Hatfield
14.	Iowa	9-3-0	Hayden Fry
15.	Alabama	8-4-0	Ray Perkins
16.	W Virginia	9-3-0	Don Nehlen
17.	UCLA	7-4-1	Terry Donahue
18.	Pittsburgh	8-3-1	Foge Fazio
19.	Boston College	9-3-0	Jack Bicknell
20.	E Carolina	8-3-0	Ed Emory

1984

		Record	Coach
1.	BYU	13-0-0	LaVell Edwards
2.	Washington	11-1-0	Don James
3.	Florida	9-1-1	Chas Pell (0-1-1) Galen Hall (9-0)
4.	Nebraska	10-2-0	Tom Osborne
5.	Boston College	10-2-0	Jack Bicknell
6.	Oklahoma	9-2-1	Barry Switzer
7.	Oklahoma St	10-2-0	Pat Jones
8.	SMU	10-2-0	Bobby Collins
9.	UCLA	9-3-0	Terry Donahue

1984 *(Cont.)*

	Record	Coach
10. USC	10-3-0	Ted Tollner
11. South Carolina	10-2-0	Joe Morrison
12. Maryland	9-3-0	Bobby Ross
13. Ohio St	9-3-0	Earle Bruce
14. Auburn	9-4-0	Pat Dye
15. LSU	8-3-1	Bill Arnsparger
16. Iowa	8-4-1	Hayden Fry
17. Florida St	7-3-2	Bobby Bowden
18. Miami (Fla.)	8-5-0	Jimmy Johnson
19. Kentucky	9-3-0	Jerry Claiborne
20. Virginia	8-2-2	George Welsh

1985

	Record	Coach
1. Oklahoma	11-1-0	Barry Switzer
2. Michigan	10-1-1	Bo Schembechler
3. Penn St	11-1-0	Joe Paterno
4. Tennessee	9-1-2	Johnny Majors
5. Florida	9-1-1	Galen Hall
6. Texas A&M	10-2-0	Jackie Sherrill
7. UCLA	9-2-1	Terry Donahue
8. Air Force	12-1-0	Fisher DeBerry
9. Miami (Fla.)	10-2-0	Jimmy Johnson
10. Iowa	10-2-0	Hayden Fry
11. Nebraska	9-3-0	Tom Osborne
12. Arkansas	10-2-0	Ken Hatfield
13. Alabama	9-2-1	Ray Perkins
14. Ohio St	9-3-0	Earle Bruce
15. Florida St	9-3-0	Bobby Bowden
16. BYU	11-3-0	LaVell Edwards
17. Baylor	9-3-0	Grant Teaff
18. Maryland	9-3-0	Bobby Ross
19. Georgia Tech.	9-2-1	Bill Curry
20. LSU	9-2-1	Bill Arnsparger

1986

	Record	Coach
1. Penn St	12-0-0	Joe Paterno
2. Miami (Fla.)	11-1-0	Jimmy Johnson
3. Oklahoma	11-1-0	Barry Switzer
4. Arizona St	10-1-1	John Cooper
5. Nebraska	10-2-0	Tom Osborne
6. Auburn	10-2-0	Pat Dye
7. Ohio St	10-3-0	Earle Bruce
8. Michigan	11-2-0	Bo Schembechler
9. Alabama	10-3-0	Ray Perkins
10. LSU	9-3-0	Bill Arnsparger
11. Arizona	9-3-0	Larry Smith
12. Baylor	9-3-0	Grant Teaff
13. Texas A&M	9-3-0	Jackie Sherrill
14. UCLA	8-3-1	Terry Donahue
15. Arkansas	9-3-0	Ken Hatfield
16. Iowa	9-3-0	Hayden Fry
17. Clemson	8-2-2	Danny Ford
18. Washington	8-3-1	Don James
19. Boston College	9-3-0	Jack Bicknell
20. Virginia Tech.	9-2-1	Bill Dooley

1987

	Record	Coach
1. Miami (Fla.)	12-0-0	Jimmy Johnson
2. Florida St	11-1-0	Bobby Bowden
3. Oklahoma	11-1-0	Barry Switzer
4. Syracuse	11-0-1	Dick MacPherson
5. LSU	10-1-1	Mike Archer
6. Nebraska	10-2-0	Tom Osborne
7. Auburn	9-1-2	Pat Dye
8. Michigan St	9-2-1	George Perles
9. UCLA	10-2-0	Terry Donahue
10. Texas A&M	10-2-0	Jackie Sherrill
11. Oklahoma St	10-2-0	Pat Jones
12. Clemson	10-2-0	Danny Ford
13. Georgia	9-3-0	Vince Dooley
14. Tennessee	10-2-1	Johnny Majors
15. South Carolina	8-4-0	Joe Morrison
16. Iowa	10-3-0	Hayden Fry
17. Notre Dame	8-4-0	Lou Holtz
18. USC	8-4-0	Larry Smith
19. Michigan	8-4-0	Bo Schembechler
20. Arizona St	7-4-1	John Cooper

1988

	Record	Coach
1. Notre Dame	12-0-0	Lou Holtz
2. Miami (Fla.)	11-1-0	Jimmy Johnson
3. Florida St	11-1-0	Bobby Bowden
4. Michigan	9-2-1	Bo Schembechler
5. West Virginia	11-1-0	Don Nehlen
6. UCLA	10-2-0	Terry Donahue
7. USC	10-2-0	Larry Smith
8. Auburn	10-2-0	Pat Dye
9. Clemson	10-2-0	Danny Ford
10. Nebraska	11-2-0	Tom Osborne
11. Oklahoma St	10-2-0	Pat Jones
12. Arkansas	10-2-0	Ken Hatfield
13. Syracuse	10-2-0	Dick MacPherson
14. Oklahoma	9-3-0	Barry Switzer
15. Georgia	9-3-0	Vince Dooley
16. Washington St	9-3-0	Dennis Erickson
17. Alabama	9-3-0	Bill Curry
18. Houston	9-3-0	Jack Pardee
19. LSU	8-4-0	Mike Archer
20. Indiana	8-3-1	Bill Mallor

†1989

	Record	Coach
1. Miami (Fla.)	11-1-0	Dennis Erickson
2. Notre Dame	12-1-0	Lou Holtz
3. Florida St	10-2-0	Bobby Bowden
4. Colorado	11-1-0	Bill McCartney
5. Tennessee	11-1-0	Johnny Majors
6. Auburn	10-2-0	Pat Dye
7. Michigan	10-2-0	Bo Schembechler
8. USC	9-2-1	Larry Smith
9. Alabama	10-2-0	Bill Curry
10. Illinois	10-2-0	John Mackovic
11. Nebraska	10-2-0	Tom Osborne
12. Clemson	10-2-0	Danny Ford
13. Arkansas	10-2-0	Ken Hatfield
14. Houston	9-2-0	Jack Pardee
15. Penn St	8-3-1	Joe Paterno
16. Michigan St	8-4-0	George Perles
17. Pittsburgh	8-3-1	Mike Gottfried
18. Virginia	10-3-0	George Welsh

†In 1989 the AP expanded its final poll to 25 teams.

†1989 *(Cont.)*

		Record	Coach
19.	Texas Tech	9-3-0	Spike Dykes
20.	Texas A&M	8-4-0	R.C. Slocum
21.	W Virginia	8-3-1	Don Nehlen
22.	BYU	10-3-0	LaVell Edwards
23.	Washington	8-4-0	Don James
24.	Ohio St	8-4-0	John Cooper
25.	Arizona	8-4-0	Dick Tomey

1990

		Record	Coach
1.	Colorado	11-1-1	Bill McCartney
2.	#Ga. Tech (UPI)	11-0-1	Bobby Ross
3.	Miami (Fla.)	10-2-0	Dennis Erickson
4.	Florida St	10-2-0	Bobby Bowden
5.	Washington	10-2-0	Don James
6.	Notre Dame	9-3-0	Lou Holtz
7.	Michigan	9-3-0	Gary Moeller
8.	Tennessee	9-2-2	Johnny Majors
9.	Clemson	10-2-0	Ken Hatfield
10.	Houston	10-1-0	John Jenkins
11.	Penn St	9-3-0	Joe Paterno
12.	Texas	10-2-0	David McWilliams
13.	Florida	9-2-0	Steve Spurrier
14.	Louisville	10-1-1	H. Schnellenberger
15.	Texas A&M	9-3-1	R.C. Slocum
16.	Michigan St	8-3-1	George Perles
17.	Oklahoma	8-3-0	Gary Gibbs
18.	Iowa	8-4-0	Hayden Fry
19.	Auburn	8-3-1	Pat Dye
20.	USC I	8-4-1	Larry Smith
21.	Mississippi	9-3-0	Billy Brewer
22.	BYU	10-3-0	LaVell Edwards
23.	Virginia	8-4-0	George Welsh
24.	Nebraska	9-3-0	Tom Osborne
25.	Illinois	8-4-0	John Mackovic

1991

		Record	Coach
1.	Miami (Fla.)	12-0-0	Dennis Erickson
2.	#Washington	12-0-0	Don James
3.	Penn St	11-2-0	Joe Paterno
4.	Florida St	11-2-0	Bobby Bowden
5.	Alabama	11-1-0	Gene Stallings
6.	Michigan	10-2-0	Gary Moeller
7.	Florida	10-2-0	Steve Spurrier
8.	California	10-2-0	Bruce Snyder
9.	E Carolina	11-1-0	Bill Lewis
10.	Iowa	10-1-1	Hayden Fry
11.	Syracuse	10-2-0	Paul Pasquàloni
12.	Texas A&M	10-2-0	R.C. Slocum
13.	Notre Dame	10-3-0	Lou Holtz
14.	Tennessee	9-3-0	Johnny Majors
15.	Nebraska	9-2-1	Tom Osborne
16.	Oklahoma	9-3-0	Gary Gibbs
17.	Georgia	9-3-0	Ray Goff
18.	Clemson	9-2-1	Ken Hatfield
19.	UCLA	9-3-0	Terry Donahue
20.	Colorado	8-3-1	Bill McCartney
21.	Tulsa	10-2-0	David Rader
22.	Stanford	8-4-0	Dennis Green
23.	BYU	8-3-2	LaVell Edwards
24.	North Carolina St	9-3-0	Dick Sheridan
25.	Air Force	10-3-0	Fisher DeBerry

#Selected No. 1 by *USA Today*/CNN.

1992

		Record	Coach
1.	Alabama	13-0-0	Gene Stallings
2.	Florida St	11-1-0	Bobby Bowden
3.	Miami	11-1-0	Dennis Erickson
4.	Notre Dame	10-1-1	Lou Holtz
5.	Michigan	9-0-3	Gary Moeller
6.	Syracuse	10-2-0	Paul Pasqualoni
7.	Texas A&M	12-1-0	R.C. Slocum
8.	Georgia	10-2-0	Ray Goff
9.	Stanford	10-3-0	Bill Walsh
10.	Florida	9-4-0	Steve Spurrier
11.	Washington	9-3-0	Don James
12.	Tennessee	9-3-0	Johnny Majors
13.	Colorado	9-2-1	Bill McCartney
14.	Nebraska	9-3-0	Tom Osborne
15.	Washington St	9-3-0	Mike Price
16.	Mississippi	9-3-0	Billy Brewer
17.	North Carolina St	9-3-1	Dick Sheridan
18.	Ohio St	8-3-1	John Cooper
19.	North Carolina	9-3-0	Mack Brown
20.	Hawaii	11-2-0	Bob Wagner
21.	Boston College	8-3-1	Tom Coughlin
22.	Kansas	8-4-0	Glen Mason
23.	Mississippi St	7-5-0	Jackie Sherrill
24.	Fresno St	9-4-0	Jim Sweeney
25.	Wake Forest	8-4-0	Bill Dooley

1993

		Record	Coach
1.	Florida St	12-1-0	Bobby Bowden
2.	Notre Dame	11-1-0	Lou Holtz
3.	Nebraska	11-1-0	Tom Osborne
4.	Auburn	11-0-0	Terry Bowden
5.	Florida	11-2-0	Steve Spurrier
6.	Wisconsin	10-1-1	Barry Alvarez
7.	W Virginia	11-1-0	Don Nehlen
8.	Penn St	10-2-0	Joe Paterno
9.	Texas A&M	10-2-0	R.C. Slocum
10.	Arizona	10-2-0	Dick Tomey
11.	Ohio St	10-1-1	John Cooper
12.	Tennessee	9-2-1	Phil Fulmer
13.	Boston College	9-3-0	Tom Coughlin
14.	Alabama	9-3-1	Gene Stallings
15.	Miami	9-3-0	Dennis Erickson
16.	Colorado	8-3-1	Bill McCartney
17.	Oklahoma	9-3-0	Gary Gibbs
18.	UCLA	8-4-0	Terry Donahue
19.	North Carolina	10-3-0	Mack Brown
20.	Kansas St	9-2-1	Bill Snyder
21.	Michigan	8-4-0	Gary Moeller
22.	Virginia Tech	9-3-0	Frank Beamer
23.	Clemson	9-3-0	Ken Hatfield
24.	Louisville	9-3-0	H. Schnellenberger
25.	California	9-4-0	Keith Gilbertson

1994

		Record	Coach
1.	Nebraska	13-0-0	Tom Osborne
2.	Penn St	12-0-0	Joe Paterno
3.	Colorado	11-1-0	Bill McCartney
4.	Florida St	10-1-1	Bobby Bowden
5.	Alabama	12-1-0	Gene Stallings
6.	Miami (Fla.)	10-2-0	Dennis Erickson
7.	Florida	10-2-1	Steve Spurrier
8.	Texas A&M	10-0-1	R.C. Slocum

†In 1989 the AP expanded its final poll to 25 teams.

1994 *(Cont.)*

		Record	Coach
9.	Auburn	9-1-1	Terry Bowden
10.	Utah	10-2-0	Ron McBride
11.	Oregon	9-4-0	Rich Brooks
12.	Michigan	8-4-0	Gary Moeller
13.	USC	8-3-1	John Robinson
14.	Ohio St	9-4-0	John Cooper
15.	Virginia	9-3-0	George Welsh
16.	Colorado St	10-2-0	Sonny Lubick
17.	North Carolina St	9-3-0	Mike O'Cain
18.	BYU	10-3-0	LaVell Edwards
19.	Kansas St	9-3-0	Bill Snyder
20.	Arizona	8-4-0	Dick Tomey
21.	Washington St	8-4-0	Mike Price
22.	Tennessee	8-4-0	Phillip Fulmer
23.	Boston College	7-4-1	Dan Henning
24.	Mississippi St	8-4-0	Jackie Sherrill
25.	Texas	8-4-0	John Mackovic

1995

		Record	Coach
1.	Nebraska	12-0-0	Tom Osborne
2.	Florida	12-1-0	Steve Spurrier
3.	Tennessee	11-1-0	Phillip Fulmer
4.	Florida St.	10-2-0	Bobby Bowden
5.	Colorado	10-2-0	Rick Neuheisel
6.	Ohio St	11-2-0	John Cooper
7.	Kansas St	10-2-0	Bill Snyder
8.	Northwestern	10-2-0	Gary Barnett
9.	Kansas	10-2-0	Glen Mason •
10.	Virginia Tech	10-2-0	Frank Beamer
11.	Notre Dame	9-3-0	Lou Holtz
12.	USC	9-2-1	John Robinson
13.	Penn St	9-3-0	Joe Paterno
14.	Texas	10-2-1	John Mackovic
15.	Texas A&M	9-3-0	S.C. Slocum
16.	Virginia	9-4-0	George Welsh
17.	Michigan	9-4-0	Lloyd Carr
18.	Oregon	9-3-0	Mike Bellotti
19.	Syracuse	9-3-0	Paul Pasqualoni
20.	Miami (Fla.)	8-3-0	Butch Davis
21.	Alabama	8-3-0	Gene Stallings
22.	Auburn	8-4-0	Terry Bowden
23.	Texas Tech	9-3-0	Spike Dykes
24.	Toledo	11-0-1	Gary Pinkel
25.	Iowa	8-4-0	Hayden Fry

1996

		Record*	Coach
1.	Florida	12–1	Steve Spurrier
2.	Ohio St	11–1	John Cooper
3.	Florida St	11–1	Bobby Bowden
4.	Arizona St	11–1	Bruce Snyder
5.	BYU	14–1	LaVell Edwards
6.	Nebraska	11–2	Tom Osborne
7.	Penn St	11–2	Joe Paterno
8.	Colorado	10–2	Rick Neuheisel
9.	Tennessee	10–2	Phillip Fulmer
10.	North Carolina	10–2	Mack Brown
11.	Alabama	10–3	Gene Stallings
12.	LSU	10–2	Gerry DiNardo
13.	Virginia Tech	10–2	Frank Beamer

*In 1996 the NCAA introduced overtime to break ties.

1996 *(Cont.)*

		Record*	Coach
14.	Miami (Fla.)	9–3	Butch Davis
15.	Northwestern	9–3	Gary Barnett
16.	Washington	9–3	Jim Lambright
17.	Kansas St	9–3	Bill Snyder
18.	Iowa	9–3	Hayden Fry
19.	Notre Dame	8–3	Lou Holtz
20.	Michigan	8–4	Lloyd Carr
21.	Syracuse	9–3	Paul Pasqualoni
22.	Wyoming	10–2	Joe Tiller
23.	Texas	8–5	John Mackovic
24.	Auburn	8–4	Terry Bowden
25.	Army	10–2	Bob Sutton

1997

		Record	Coach
1.	Michigan	12–0	Lloyd Carr
2.	Nebraska	13–0	Tom Osborne
3.	Florida St	11–1	Bobby Bowden
4.	Florida	10–2	Steve Spurrier
5.	UCLA	10–2	Bob Toledo
6.	North Carolina	11–1	Mack Brown
7.	Tennessee	11–2	Phillip Fulmer
8.	Kansas St	11–1	Bill Snyder
9.	Washington St	10–2	Mike Price
10.	Georgia	10–2	Jim Donnan
11.	Auburn	10–3	Terry Bowden
12.	Ohio St	10–3	John Cooper
13.	LSU	9–3	Gerry DiNardo
14.	Arizona St	8–3	Bruce Snyder
15.	Purdue	9–3	Joe Tiller
16.	Penn St	9–3	Joe Paterno
17.	Colorado St	11–2	Sonny Lubick
18.	Washington	8–4	Jim Lambright
19.	Southern Mississippi	9–3	Jeff Bower
20.	Texas A&M	9–4	R. C. Slocum
21.	Syracuse	9–4	Paul Pasqualoni
22.	Mississippi	8–4	Tommy Tuberville
23.	Missouri	7–5	Larry Smith
24.	Oklahoma St	8–4	Bob Simmons
25.	Georgia Tech	7–5	George O'Leary

1998

		Record	Coach
1.	Tennessee	13–0	Phillip Fulmer
2.	Ohio St	11–1	John Cooper
3.	Florida St	11–2	Bobby Bowden
4.	Arizona	12–1	Dick Tomey
5.	Florida	10–2	Steve Spurrier
6.	Wisconsin	11–1	Barry Alvarez
7.	Tulane	12–0	Tommy Bowden
8.	UCLA	10–2	Bob Toledo
9.	Georgia Tech	10–2	George O'Leary
10.	Kansas St	11–2	Bill Snyder
11.	Texas A&M	11–3	R.C. Slocum
12.	Michigan	10–3	Lloyd Carr
13.	Air Force	12–1	Fisher DeBerry
14.	Georgia	9–3	Jim Donnan
15.	Texas	9–3	Mack Brown
16.	Arkansas	9–3	Houston Nutt
17.	Penn St	9–3	Joe Paterno
18.	Virginia	9–3	George Welsh
19.	Nebraska	9–4	Frank Solich
20.	Miami (Fla.)	9–3	Butch Davis

1998 *(Cont.)*

	Record	Coach
21. Missouri	8–4	Larry Smith
22. Notre Dame	9–3	Bob Davie
23. Virginia Tech	9–3	Frank Beamer
24. Purdue	9–4	Joe Tiller
25. Syracuse	8–4	Paul Pasqualoni

1999

	Record	Coach
1. Florida St	12–0	Bobby Bowden
2. Virginia Tech	11–1	Frank Beamer
3. Nebraska	12–1	Frank Solich
4. Wisconsin	10–2	Barry Alvarez
5. Michigan	10–2	Lloyd Carr
6. Kansas St	11–1	Bill Snyder
7. Michigan St	10–2	Nick Saban
8. Alabama	10–3	Mike DuBose
9. Tennessee	9–3	Phillip Fulmer
10. Marshall	13–0	Bob Pruett
11. Penn St	10–3	Joe Paterno
12. Florida.	9–4	Steve Spurrier
13. Mississippi St	10–2	Jackie Sherrill
14. Southern Miss	9–3	Jeff Bower
15. Miami (Fla.)	9–4	Butch Davis
16. Georgia	8–4	Jim Donnan
17. Arkansas	8–4	Houston Nutt
18. Minnesota	8–4	Glen Mason
19. Oregon	9–3	Mike Bellotti
20. Georgia Tech	8–4	Goerge O'Leary
21. Texas	9–5	Mack Brown
22. Mississippi	8–4	David Cutcliffe
23. Texas A&M	8–4	R.C. Slocum
24. Illinois	8–4	Ron Turner
25. Purdue	7–5	Joe Tiller

2000

	Record	Coach
1. Oklahoma	13–0	Bob Stoops
2. Miami (Fla.)	11–1	Butch Davis
3. Washington	11–1	Rick Neuheisel
4. Oregon St	11–1	Dennis Erickson
5. Florida St	11–2	Bobby Bowden
6. Virginia Tech	11–1	Frank Beamer
7. Oregon	10–2	Mike Belotti
8. Nebraska	10–2	Frank Solich
9. Kansas St	11–3	Bill Snyder
10. Florida	10–3	Steve Spurrier
11. Michigan	9–3	Lloyd Carr
12. Texas	9–3	Mack Brown
13. Purdue	8–4	Joe Tiller
14. Colorado St	10–2	Sonny Lubeck
15. Notre Dame	9–3	Bob Davie
16. Clemson	9–3	Tommy Bowden
17. Georgia Tech	9–3	George O'Leary
18. Auburn	9–4	Tommy Tuberville
19. South Carolina	8–4	Lou Holtz
20. Georgia	8–4	Jim Donnan
21. TCU	10–2	Dennis Franchione
22. LSU	8–4	Nick Saban
23. Wisconsin	9–4	Barry Alvarez
24. Mississippi St	8–4	Jackie Sherrill
25. Iowa St	9–3	Dan McCarney

2001

	Record	Coach
1. Miami (Fla.)	12–0	Larry Coker
2. Oregon	11–1	Mike Belotti
3. Florida	10–2	Steve Spurrier
4. Tennessee	11–2	Phillip Fulmer
5. Texas	11–2	Mack Brown
6. Oklahoma	11–2	Bob Stoops
7. LSU	10–3	Nick Saban
8. Nebraska	11–2	Frank Solich
9. Colorado	10–3	Gary Barnett
10. Washington St	10–2	Mike Price
11. Maryland	10–2	Ralph Friedgen
12. Illinois	10–2	Ron Turner
13. South Carolina	9–3	Lou Holtz
14. Syracuse	10–3	Paul Pasqualoni
15. Florida St	8–4	Bobby Bowden
16. Stanford	9–3	Tyrone Willingham
17. Louisville	11–2	John Smith
18. Virginia Tech	8–4	Frank Beamer
19. Washington	8–4	Rick Neuheisel
20. Michigan	8–4	Lloyd Carr
21. Boston College	8–4	Tom O'Brien
22. Georgia	8–4	Mark Richt
23. Toledo	10–2	Tom Amstutz
24. Georgia Tech	8–5	George O'Leary
25. BYU	12–2	Gary Crowton

2002

	Record	Coach
1. Ohio St	14–0	Jim Tressel
2. Miami (Fla.)	12–1	Larry Coker
3. Georgia	13–1	Mark Richt
4. USC	11–2	Pete Carroll
5. Oklahoma	12–2	Bob Stoops
6. Texas	11–2	Mack Brown
7. Kansas St	11–2	Bill Snyder
8. Iowa	11–2	Kirk Ferentz
9. Michigan	10–3	Lloyd Carr
10. Washington St	10–3	Mike Price
11. Alabama	10–3	Dennis Franchione
12. North Carolina St	11–3	Chuck Amato
13. Maryland	11–3	Ralph Friedgen
14. Auburn	9–4	Tommy Tuberville
15. Boise St	12–1	Dan Hawkins
16. Penn St	9–4	Joe Paterno
17. Notre Dame	10–3	Tyrone Willingham
18. Virginia Tech	10–4	Frank Beamer
19. Pittsburgh	9–4	Walt Harris
20. Colorado	9–5	Gary Barnett
21. Florida St	9–5	Bobby Bowden
22. Virginia	9–5	Al Groh
23. TCU	10–2	Gary Patterson
24. Marshall	11–2	Bob Pruett
25. W Virginia	9–4	Rich Rodriguez

2003

		Record	Coach
1.	USC	12–1	Pete Carroll
2.	LSU*	13–1	Nick Saban
3.	Oklahoma	12–2	Bob Stoops
4.	Ohio St.	11–2	Jim Tressel
5.	Miami (Fla.)	11–2	Larry Coker
6.	Michigan	10–3	Lloyd Carr
7.	Georgia	11–3	Mark Richt
8.	Iowa	10–3	Kirk Ferentz
9.	Washington St	10–3	Bill Doba
10.	Miami (Ohio)	13–1	Terry Hoeppner
11.	Florida St	10–3	Bobby Bowden
12.	Texas	10–3	Mack Brown
13.	Kansas St	11–4	Bill Snyder
	Mississippi	10–3	David Cutcliffe
15.	Tennessee	10–3	Phillip Fulmer
16.	Boise St	13–1	Dan Hawkins
17.	Maryland	10–3	Ralph Friedgen
18.	Nebraska	10–3	Frank Solich/Bo Pelini
	Purdue	9–4	Joe Tiller
20.	Minnesota	10–3	Glen Mason
21.	Utah	10–2	Urban Meyer
22.	Clemson	9–4	Tommy Bowden
23.	Bowling Green	11–3	Gregg Brandon
24.	Florida	8–5	Ron Zook
25.	TCU	11–2	Gary Patterson

*Ranked No. 1 in *USAToday*/ESPN Poll.

2005

		Record	Coach
1.	Texas	13-0	Mack Brown
2.	USC	12-1	Pete Carroll
3.	Penn St	11-1	Joe Paterno
4.	Ohio State	10-2	Jim Tressel
5.	Texas	11-1	Mack Brown
6.	LSU	11-2	Les Miles
7.	Virginia Tech	10-3	Frank Beamer
8.	Alabama	10-2	Mike Shula
9.	Notre Dame	9-3	Charlie Weis
10.	Georgia	10-3	Mark Richt
11.	TCU	11-1	Gary Patterson
12.	Florida	9-3	Urban Meyer
12.	Oregon	10-2	Mike Bellotti
14.	Auburn	9-3	Tommy Tuberville
15.	Wisconsin	9-3	Barry Alvarez
15.	Michigan	9-3	Lloyd Carr
16.	UCLA	10-2	Karl Dorrell
17.	Miami (Fla.)	9-3	Larry Coker
18.	Boston College	9-3	Tom O'Brien
19.	Louisville	9-3	Bobby Petrino
20.	Texas Tech	9-3	Mike Leach
21.	Clemson	8-4	Tommy Bowden
22.	Oklahoma	8-4	Bob Stoops
23.	Florida St	8-5	Bobby Bowden
24.	Nebraska	8-4	Bill Callahan
25.	California	8-4	Jeff Tedford

2004

		Record	Coach
1.	USC	13-0	Pete Carroll
2.	Auburn	13-0	Tommy Tuberville
3.	Oklahoma	12-1	Bob Stoops
4.	Utah	12-0	Kyle Whittingham
5.	Texas	11-1	Mack Brown
6.	Louisville	11-1	Bobby Petrino
7.	Georgia	10-2	Mark Richt
8.	Iowa	10-2	Kirk Ferentz
9.	California	10-2	Jeff Tedford
10.	Virginia Tech	10-3	Frank Beamer
11.	Miami	9-3	Larry Coker
12.	Tennessee	10-3	Phillip Fulmer
13.	Michigan	9-3	Lloyd Carr
14.	Florida	8-5	Ron Zook
15.	Michigan	9-3	Lloyd Carr
16.	LSU	9-3	Les Miles
17.	Wisconsin	9-3	Barry Alvarez
18.	Texas Tech	8-4	Mike Leach
19.	Arizona State	9-3	Dirk Koetter
20.	Ohio State	8-4	Jim Tressel
21.	Boston College	9-3	Tom O'Brien
22.	Fresno State	9-3	Pat Hill
23.	Virginia	8-4	Al Groh
24.	Navy	10-2	Paul Johnson
25.	Pittsburgh	8-4	Walt Harris

2006

		Record	Coach
1.	Florida	13-1	Urban Meyer
2.	Ohio State	12-1	Jim Tressel
3.	LSU	11-2	Les Miles
4.	USC	11-2	Pete Carroll
5.	Boise State	13-0	Chris Petersen
6.	Louisville	12-1	Steve Kragthorpe
7.	Wisconsin	12-1	Bret Bielema
8.	Michigan	11-2	Lloyd Carr
9.	Auburn	11-2	Tommy Tuberville
10.	West Virginia	11-2	Rich Rodriguez
11.	Oklahoma	11-3	Bob Stoops
12.	Rutgers	11-2	Greg Schiano
13.	Texas	10-3	Mack Brown
14.	California	10-3	Jeff Tedford
15.	Arkansas	10-4	Houston Nutt
16.	BYU	11-2	Bronco Mendenhall
17.	Notre Dame	10-3	Charlie Weis
18.	Wake Forest	11-3	Jim Grobe
19.	Virginia Tech	10-3	Frank Beamer
20.	Boston College	10-3	Jeff Jagodzinski
21.	Oregon State	10-4	Mike Riley
22.	TCU	11-2	Gary Patterson
23.	Georgia	9-4	Mark Richt
24.	Penn State	9-4	Joe Paterno
25.	Tennessee	9-4	Phillip Fulmer

Football Championship Subdivision (Div. I-AA)

Year	Winner	Runner-Up	Score
1978	Florida A&M	Massachusetts	35–28
1979	Eastern Kentucky	Lehigh	30–7
1980	Boise St	Eastern Kentucky	31–29
1981	Idaho St	Eastern Kentucky	34–23
1982	Eastern Kentucky	Delaware	17–14
1983	Southern Illinois	Western Carolina	43–7
1984	Montana St	Louisiana Tech	19–6
1985	Georgia Southern	Furman	44–42
1986	Georgia Southern	Arkansas St	48–21
1987	NE Louisiana	Marshall	43–42
1988	Furman	Georgia Southern	17–12
1989	Georgia Southern	Stephen F. Austin St	37–34
1990	Georgia Southern	Nevada-Reno	36–13
1991	Youngstown St	Marshall	25–17
1992	Marshall	Youngstown St	31–28
1993	Youngstown St	Marshall	17–5
1994	Youngstown St	Boise St	28–14
1995	Montana	Marshall	22–20
1996	Marshall	Montana	49–29
1997	Youngstown St	McNesse St	10–9
1998	Massachusetts	Georgia Southern	55–43
1999	Georgia Southern	Youngstown St	59–24
2000	Georgia Southern	Montana	27–25
2001	Montana	Furman	13–6
2002	Western Kentucky	McNeese St	34–14
2003	Delaware	Colgate	40–0
2004	James Madison	Montana	31–21
2005	Appalachian State	Northern Iowa	21–16
2006	Appalachian State	Massachusetts	28–17

Division II

Year	Winner	Runner-Up	Score
1973	Louisiana Tech	Western Kentucky	34–0
1974	Central Michigan	Delaware	54–14
1975	Northern Michigan	Western Kentucky	16–14
1976	Montana St	Akron	24–13
1977	Lehigh	Jacksonville St	33–0
1978	Eastern Illinois	Delaware	10–9
1979	Delaware	Youngstown St	38–21
1980	Cal Poly SLO	Eastern Illinois	21–13
1981	SW Texas St	North Dakota St	42–13
1982	SW Texas St	UC-Davis	34–9
1983	North Dakota St	Central St (Ohio)	41–21
1984	Troy St	North Dakota St	18–17
1985	North Dakota St	North Alabama	35–7
1986	North Dakota St	South Dakota	27–7
1987	Troy St	Portland St	31–17
1988	North Dakota St	Portland St	35–21
1989	Mississippi College	Jacksonville St	3–0
1990	N Dakota St	Indiana (Pa.)	51–11
1991	Pittsburg St	Jacksonville St	23–6
1992	Jacksonville St	Pittsburg St	17–13
1993	North Alabama	Indiana (Pa.)	41–34
1994	North Alabama	Texas A&M–Kingsville	16–10
1995	North Alabama	Pittsburg St	27–7
1996	Northern Colorado	Carson-Newman	23–14
1997	Northern Colorado	New Haven	51–0
1998	NW Missouri St	Carson-Newman	24–6
1999	NW Missouri St	Carson-Newman	58–52 (OT)
2000	Delta St	Bloomsburg	63–34
2001	Grand Valley St	North Dakota	17–14
2002	Grand Valley St	Valdosta St	31–24
2003	Grand Valley St	North Dakota	10–3
2004	Valdosta State	Pittsburg State	36–31
2005	Grand Valley St	NW Missouri St	21–17
2006	Grand Valley St	NW Missouri St	17–14

Division III

Year	Winner	Runner-Up	Score
1973	Wittenberg	Juniata	41–0
1974	Central (Iowa)	Ithaca	10–8
1975	Wittenberg	Ithaca	28–0
1976	St. John's (Minn.)	Towson St	31–28
1977	Widener	Wabash	39–36
1978	Baldwin-Wallace	Wittenberg	24–10
1979	Ithaca	Wittenberg	14–10
1980	Dayton	Ithaca	63–0
1981	Widener	Dayton	17–10
1982	W Georgia	Augustana (Ill.)	14–0
1983	Augustana (Ill.)	Union (N.Y.)	21–17
1984	Augustana (Ill.)	Central (Iowa)	21–12
1985	Augustana (Ill.)	Ithaca	20–7
1986	Augustana (Ill.)	Salisbury St	31–3
1987	Wagner	Dayton	19–3
1988	Ithaca	Central (Iowa)	39–24
1989	Dayton	Union (N.Y.)	17–7
1990	Allegheny	Lycoming	21–14 (OT)
1991	Ithaca	Dayton	34–20
1992	WI-LaCrosse	Washington & Jefferson	16–12
1993	Mount Union	Rowan	34–24
1994	Albion	Washington & Jefferson	38–15
1995	WI-LaCrosse	Rowan	36–7
1996	Mount Union	Rowan	56–24
1997	Mount Union	Lycoming	61–12
1998	Mount Union	Rowan	44–24
1999	Pacific Lutheran	Rowan	42–13
2000	Mount Union	St. John's (Minn.)	10–7
2001	Mount Union	Bridgewater	30–27
2002	Mount Union	Trinity (Tex.)	48–7
2003	St. John's (Minn.)	Mount Union	24–6
2004	Linfield	Mary Hardin-Baylor	28–21
2005	Mount Union	UW-Whitewater	35–28
2006	Mount Union	UW-Whitewater	35–16

NAIA Divisional Championships

Division I

Year	Winner	Runner-Up	Score
1956	St. Joseph's (Ind.)/Montana St		0–0
1957	Pittsburg St (Kan.)	Hillsdale	27–26
1958	NE Oklahoma	Northern Arizona	19–13
1959	Texas A&I	Lenoir-Rhyne	20–7
1960	Lenoir-Rhyne	Humboldt St	15–14
1961	Pittsburg St (Kan.)	Linfield	12–7
1962	Central St (Okla.)	Lenoir-Rhyne	28–13
1963	St. John's (Minn.)	Prairie View	33–27
1964	Concordia-Moorhead/ Sam Houston St		7–7
1965	St. John's (Minn.)	Linfield	33–0
1966	Waynesburg	UW-Whitewater	42–21
1967	Fairmont St	Eastern Washington	28–21
1968	Troy St (Mich.)	Texas A&I	43–35
1969	Texas A&I	Concordia-Moorhead (Minn.)	32–7
1970	Texas A&I	Wofford	48–7
1971	Livingston (Ala.)	Arkansas Tech	14–12
1972	E Texas St	Carson-Newman	21–18
1973	Abilene Christian	Elon	42–14
1974	Texas A&I	Henderson St	34–23
1975	Texas A&I	Salem (W.V.)	37–0
1976	Texas A&I	Central Arkansas	26–0
1977	Abilene Christian	SW Oklahoma	24–7
1978	Angelo St	Elon	34–14
1979	Texas A&I	Central St (Okla.)	20–14

Division I *(Cont.)*

Year	Winner	Runner-Up	Score
1980	Elon	NE Oklahoma	17–10
1981	Elon	Pittsburg St	3–0
1982	Central St (Okla.)	Mesa	14–11
1983	Carson-Newman	Mesa	36–28
1984	Carson-Newman/Central Arkansas		19–19
1985	Central Arkansas/Hillsdale		10–10
1986	Carson-Newman	Cameron	17–0
1987	Cameron	Carson-Newman	30–2
1988	Carson-Newman	Adams St (Col.)	56–21
1989	Carson-Newman	Emporia St	34–20
1990	Central St (Ohio)	Mesa St	38–16
1991	Central Arkansas	Central St (Ohio)	19–16
1992	Central St (Ohio)	Gardner-Webb	19–16
1993	E Central (Okla.)	Glenville St	49–35
1994	Northeastern St (Okla.)	Arkansas–Pine Bluff	13–12
1995	Central St (Ohio)	Northeastern St (Okla.)	37–7
1996	SW Oklahoma St	Montana Tech	33–31
1997	Findlay	Willamette	14–7
1998	Azusa Pacific	Olivet Nazarene	17–14
1999	Northwestern Oklahoma St	Georgetown (Ky.)	34–26
2000	Georgetown (Ken.)	Northwestern Oklahoma St	20–0
2001	Georgetown (Ken.)	Sioux Falls	49–27
2002	Carroll (Minn.)	Georgetown (Ky.)	28–7
2003	Carroll (Minn.)	Northwestern Oklahoma St	41–28
2004	Carroll (Minn.)	St. Francis (Ind.)	15–13
2005	Carroll (Minn.)	St. Francis (Ind.)	27–10
2006	Sioux Falls (S.D.)	St. Francis (Ind.)	23–19

Division II†

Year	Winner	Runner-Up	Score
1970	Westminster (Pa.)	Anderson	21–16
1971	California Lutheran	Westminster (Pa.)	30–14
1972	Missouri Southern	Northwestern (Iowa)	21–14
1973	Northwestern (Iowa)	Glenville St	10–3
1974	Texas Lutheran	Missouri Valley	42–0
1975	Texas Lutheran	California Lutheran	34–8
1976	Westminster (Pa.)	Redlands	20–13
1977	Westminster (Pa.)	California Lutheran	17–9
1978	Concordia-Moorhead (Minn.)	Findlay	7–0
1979	Findlay	Northwestern (Iowa)	51–6
1980	Pacific Lutheran	Wilmington (Ohio)	38–10
1981	Austin Coll./Conc.-Moorhead (Minn.)		24–24
1982	Linfield	William Jewell	33–15
1983	Northwestern (Iowa)	Pacific Lutheran	25–21
1984	Linfield	Northwestern (Iowa)	33–22
1985	WI-La Crosse	Pacific Lutheran	24–7
1986	Linfield	Baker	17–0
1987	Pacific Lutheran	UW-Stevens Point*	16–16
1988	Westminster (Pa.)	UW-La Crosse	21–14
1989	Westminster (Pa.)	UW-La Crosse	51–30
1990	Peru St	Westminster (Pa.)	17–7
1991	Georgetown (Ky.)	Pacific Lutheran	28–20
1992	Findlay	Linfield	26–13
1993	Pacific Lutheran	Westminster (Pa.)	50–20
1994	Westminster (Pa.)	Pacific Lutheran	27–7
1995	Findlay	Central Washington	21–21
1996	Sioux Falls (S.D.)	Western Washington	47–25

*Forfeited 1987 season due to use of an ineligible player.   †In 1997 the NAIA consolidated its two divisions into one.

Awards

Heisman Memorial Trophy

Awarded to the best college player by the Downtown Athletic Club of New York City. The trophy is named after John W. Heisman, who coached Georgia Tech to the national championship in 1917 and later served as DAC athletic director.

Year	Winner, College, Position	Winner's Season Statistics	Runner-Up, College
1935	Jay Berwanger, Chicago, HB	Rush: 119 Yds: 577 TD: 6	Monk Meyer, Army
1936	Larry Kelley, Yale, E	Rec: 17 Yds: 372 TD: 6	Sam Francis, Nebraska
1937	Clint Frank, Yale, HB	Rush: 157 Yds: 667 TD: 11	Byron White, Colorado
1938	†Davey O'Brien, TCU, QB	Att/Comp: 194/110 Yds: 1733 TD: 19	Marshall Goldberg, Pittsburgh
1939	Nile Kinnick, Iowa, HB	Rush: 106 Yds: 374 TD: 5	Tom Harmon, Michigan
1940	Tom Harmon, Michigan, HB	Rush: 191 Yds: 852 TD: 16	John Kimbrough, Texas A&M
1941	†Bruce Smith, Minnesota, HB	Rush: 98 Yds: 480 TD: 6	Angelo Bertelli, Notre Dame
1942	Frank Sinkwich, Georgia, HB	Att/Comp: 166/84 Yds: 1392 TD: 10	Paul Governali, Columbia
1943	Angelo Bertelli, Notre Dame, QB	Att/Comp: 36/25 Yds: 511 TD: 10	Bob Odell, Pennsylvania
1944	Les Horvath, Ohio State, QB	Rush: 163 Yds: 924 TD: 12	Glenn Davis, Army
1945	*†Doc Blanchard, Army, FB	Rush: 101 Yds: 718 TD: 13	Glenn Davis, Army
1946	Glenn Davis, Army, HB	Rush: 123 Yds: 712 TD: 7	Charley Trippi, Georgia
1947	†John Lujack, Notre Dame, QB	Att/Comp: 109/61 Yds: 777 TD: 9	Bob Chappius, Michigan
1948	*Doak Walker, SMU, HB	Rush: 108 Yds: 532 TD: 8	Charlie Justice, North Carolina
1949	†Leon Hart, Notre Dame, E	Rec: 19 Yds: 257 TD: 5	Charlie Justice, North Carolina
1950	*Vic Janowicz, Ohio St, HB	Att/Comp: 77/32 Yds: 561 TD: 12	Kyle Rote, SMU
1951	Dick Kazmaier, Princeton, HB	Rush: 149 Yds: 861 TD: 9	Hank Lauricella, Tennessee
1952	Billy Vessels, Oklahoma, HB	Rush: 167 Yds: 1072 TD: 17	Jack Scarbath, Maryland
1953	John Lattner, Notre Dame, HB	Rush: 134 Yds: 651 TD: 6	Paul Giel, Minnesota
1954	Alan Ameche, Wisconsin, FB	Rush: 146 Yds: 641 TD: 9	Kurt Burris, Oklahoma
1955	Howard Cassady, Ohio St, HB	Rush: 161 Yds: 958 TD: 15	Jim Swink, TCU
1956	Paul Hornung, Notre Dame, QB	Att/Comp: 111/59 Yds: 917 TD: 3	Johnny Majors, Tennessee
1957	John David Crow, Texas A&M, HB	Rush: 129 Yds: 562 TD: 10	Alex Karras, Iowa
1958	Pete Dawkins, Army, HB	Rush: 78 Yds: 428 TD: 6	Randy Duncan, Iowa
1959	Billy Cannon, LSU, HB	Rush: 139 Yds: 598 TD: 6	Rich Lucas, Penn St
1960	Joe Bellino, Navy, HB	Rush: 168 Yds: 834 TD: 18	Tom Brown, Minnesota
1961	Ernie Davis, Syracuse, HB	Rush: 150 Yds: 823 TD: 15	Bob Ferguson, Ohio St
1962	Terry Baker, Oregon St, QB	Att/Comp: 203/112 Yds: 1738 TD: 15	Jerry Stovall, LSU
1963	*Roger Staubach, Navy, QB	Att/Comp: 161/107 Yds: 1474 TD: 7	Billy Lothridge, Georgia Tech
1964	John Huarte, Notre Dame, QB	Att/Comp: 205/114 Yds: 2062 TD: 16	Jerry Rhome, Tulsa
1965	Mike Garrett, USC, HB	Rush: 267 Yds: 1440 TD: 16	Howard Twilley, Tulsa
1966	Steve Spurrier, Florida, QB	Att/Comp: 291/179 Yds: 2012 TD: 16	Bob Griese, Purdue
1967	Gary Beban, UCLA, QB	Att/Comp: 156/87 Yds: 1359 TD: 8	O.J. Simpson, USC
1968	O.J. Simpson, USC, HB	Rush: 383 Yds: 1880 TD: 23	Leroy Keyes, Purdue
1969	Steve Owens, Oklahoma, FB	Rush: 358 Yds: 1523 TD: 23	Mike Phipps, Purdue
1970	Jim Plunkett, Stanford, QB	Att/Comp: 358/191 Yds: 2715 TD: 18	Joe Theismann, Notre Dame
1971	Pat Sullivan, Auburn, QB	Att/Comp: 281/162 Yds: 2012; 20 TD	Ed Marinaro, Cornell
1972	Johnny Rodgers, Nebraska, FL	Rec: 55 Yds: 942 TD: 17	Greg Pruitt, Oklahoma
1973	John Cappelletti, Penn St, HB	Rush: 286 Yds: 1522 TD: 17	John Hicks, Ohio St
1974	*Archie Griffin, Ohio St, HB	Rush: 256 Yds: 1695 TD: 12	Anthony Davis, USC
1975	Archie Griffin, Ohio St, HB	Rush: 262 Yds: 1450 TD: 4	Chuck Muncie, California
1976	†Tony Dorsett, Pittsburgh, HB	Rush: 370 Yds: 2150 TD: 23	Ricky Bell, USC
1977	Earl Campbell, Texas, FB	Rush: 267 Yds: 1744 TD: 19	Terry Miller, Oklahoma St
1978	*Billy Sims, Oklahoma, HB	Rush: 231 Yds: 1762 TD: 20	Chuck Fusina, Penn St
1979	Charles White, USC, HB	Rush: 332 Yds: 1803 TD: 19	Billy Sims, Oklahoma
1980	George Rogers, South Carolina, HB	Rush: 324 Yds: 1894 TD: 14	Hugh Green, Pittsburgh
1981	Marcus Allen, USC, HB	Rush: 433 Yds: 2427 TD: 23	Herschel Walker, Georgia
1982	*Herschel Walker, Georgia, HB	Rush: 335 Yds: 1752 TD: 17	John Elway, Stanford
1983	Mike Rozier, Nebraska, HB	Rush: 275 Yds: 2148 TD: 29	Steve Young, BYU
1984	Doug Flutie, Boston College, QB	Att/Comp: 396/233 Yds: 3454 TD: 27	Keith Byars, Ohio St
1985	Bo Jackson, Auburn, HB	Rush: 278 Yds: 1786 TD: 17	Chuck Long, Iowa
1986	Vinny Testaverde, Miami (Fla.), QB	Att/Comp: 276/175 Yds: 2557 TD: 26	Paul Palmer, Temple

Heisman Memorial Trophy *(Cont.)*

Year	Winner, College, Position	Winner's Season Statistics	Runner-Up, College
1987	...Tim Brown, Notre Dame, WR	Rec: 39 Yds: 846 TD: 7	Don McPherson, Syracuse
1988	...*Barry Sanders, Oklahoma St, RB	Rush: 344 Yds: 2628 TD: 39	Rodney Peete, USC
1989	...*Andre Ware, Houston, QB	Att/Comp: 578/365 Yds: 4699 TD: 46	Anthony Thompson, Indiana
1990	...*Ty Detmer, BYU, QB	Att/Comp: 562/361 Yds: 5188 TD: 41	Raghib Ismail, Notre Dame
1991	...*Desmond Howard, Michigan, WR	Rec: 61 Yds: 950 TD: 23	Casey Weldon, Florida St
1992	...Gino Torretta, Miami (FL), QB	Att/Comp: 402/228 Yds: 3060 TD: 19	Marshall Faulk, San Diego St
1993	...†Charlie Ward, Florida St, QB	Att/Comp: 380/264 Yds: 3032 TD: 27	Heath Shuler, Tennessee
1994	...Rashaan Salaam, Colorado, RB	Rush: 298 Yds: 2055 TD: 24	Ki-Jana Carter, Penn St
1995	...Eddie George, Ohio State, RB	Rush: 303 Yds: 1826 TD: 23	Tommie Frazier, Nebraska
1996	...†Danny Wuerffel, Florida, QB	Att/Comp: 360/207 Yds: 3625 TD: 39	Troy Davis, Iowa St
1997	...†Charles Woodson, Michigan, CB/WR	7 interceptions; Rec: 11 Yds: 231 TD: 4	Peyton Manning, Tennessee
1998	...Ricky Williams, Texas, RB	Rush: 361 Yds: 2124 TD: 28	Michael Bishop, Kansas St
1999	...Ron Dayne, Wisconsin, RB	Rush: 303 Yds: 1834 TD: 19	Joe Hamilton, Georgia Tech
2000	...Chris Weinke, Florida St, QB	Att/Comp: 431/266 Yds: 4167 TD: 33	Josh Heupel, Oklahoma
2001	...Eric Crouch, Nebraska, QB	Att/Comp: 189/105 Yds: 1510 TD: 7; Rush: 1115 Yds, 18 TD	Rex Grossman, Florida
2002	...Carson Palmer, USC, QB	Att/Comp: 450/228 Yds: 3639 TD: 32	Brad Banks, Iowa
2003	...Jason White, Oklahoma, QB	Pct. Comp: 64; 3744 Yds; TD: 40	Larry Fitzgerald, Pittsburgh
2004	...*†Matt Leinart, USC, QB	Att/Comp: 269/412 Yds: 2990 TD: 28	Adrian Peterson, Oklahoma
2005	...*Reggie Bush, USC, RB	Rush: 200 Yds:1,740 TD: 16	Vince Young, Texas
2006	...Troy Smith, Ohio State, QB	Att/Comp: 311/203 Yds: 2542 TD: 30	Darren McFadden, Arkansas

*Juniors (all others seniors). †Winners who played for national championship teams the same year. Note: Former Heisman winners and national media cast votes, with ballots allowing for three names (3 points for first, 2 for second and 1 for third).

Maxwell Award

Given to the nation's outstanding college football player by the Maxwell Football Club of Philadelphia.

Year	Player, College, Position	Year	Player, College, Position
1937	Clint Frank, Yale, HB	1964	Glenn Ressler, Penn St, C
1938	Davey O'Brien, TCU, QB	1965	Tommy Nobis, Texas, LB
1939	Nile Kinnick, Iowa, HB	1966	Jim Lynch, Notre Dame, LB
1940	Tom Harmon, Michigan, HB	1967	Gary Beban, UCLA, QB
1941	Bill Dudley, Virginia, HB	1968	O.J. Simpson, USC, RB
1942	Paul Governali, Columbia, QB	1969	Mike Reid, Penn St, DT
1943	Bob Odell, Pennsylvania, HB	1970	Jim Plunkett, Stanford, QB
1944	Glenn Davis, Army, HB	1971	Ed Marinaro, Cornell, RB
1945	Doc Blanchard, Army, FB	1972	Brad Van Pelt, Michigan St, DB
1946	Charley Trippi, Georgia, HB	1973	John Cappelletti, Penn St, RB
1947	Doak Walker, SMU, HB	1974	Steve Joachim, Temple, QB
1948	Chuck Bednarik, Pennsylvania, C.	1975	Archie Griffin, Ohio St, RB
1949	Leon Hart, Notre Dame, E	1976	Tony Dorsett, Pittsburgh, RB
1950	Reds Bagnell, Pennsylvania, HB	1977	Ross Browner, Notre Dame, DE
1951	Dick Kazmaier, Princeton, HB	1978	Chuck Fusina, Penn St, QB
1952	John Lattner, Notre Dame, HB	1979	Charles White, USC, RB
1953	John Lattner, Notre Dame, HB	1980	Hugh Green, Pittsburgh, DE
1954	Ron Beagle, Navy, E	1981	Marcus Allen, USC, RB
1955	Howard Cassady, Ohio St, HB	1982	Herschel Walker, Georgia, RB
1956	Tommy McDonald, Oklahoma, HB	1983	Mike Rozier, Nebraska, RB
1957	Bob Reifsnyder, Navy, T	1984	Doug Flutie, Boston College, QB
1958	Pete Dawkins, Army, HB	1985	Chuck Long, Iowa, QB
1959	Rich Lucas, Penn St, QB	1986	Vinny Testaverde, Miami (Fla.), QB
1960	Joe Bellino, Navy, HB	1987	Don McPherson, Syracuse, QB
1961	Bob Ferguson, Ohio St, FB	1988	Barry Sanders, Oklahoma St, RB
1962	Terry Baker, Oregon St, QB	1989	Anthony Thompson, Indiana, RB
1963	Roger Staubach, Navy, QB	1990	Ty Detmer, BYU, QB

Maxwell Award (Cont.)

Year	Player, College, Position	Year	Player, College, Position
1991	Desmond Howard, Michigan, WR	1999	Ron Dayne, Wisconsin, RB
1992	Gino Torretta, Miami (Fla.), QB	2000	Drew Brees, Purdue, QB
1993	Charlie Ward, Florida St, QB	2001	Ken Dorsey, Miami (Fla.), QB
1994	Kerry Collins, Penn St, QB	2002	Larry Johnson, Penn St, RB
1995	Eddie George, Ohio St, RB	2003	Eli Manning, Mississippi, QB
1996	Danny Wuerffel, Florida, QB	2004	Jason White, Oklahoma, QB
1997	Peyton Manning, Tennessee, QB	2005	Vince Young, Texas, QB
1998	Ricky Williams, Texas, RB	2006	Brady Quinn, Notre Dame, QB

Davey O'Brien National Quarterback Award

Given to the top quarterback in the nation by the Davey O'Brien Educational and Charitable Trust of Fort Worth. Named for TCU Hall of Fame quarterback Davey O'Brien (1936–38).

Year	Player, College	Year	Player, College
1981	Jim McMahon, BYU	1994	Kerry Collins, Penn St
1982	Todd Blackledge, Penn St	1995	Danny Wuerffel, Florida
1983	Steve Young, BYU	1996	Danny Wuerffel, Florida
1984	Doug Flutie, Boston College	1997	Peyton Manning, Tennessee
1985	Chuck Long, Iowa	1998	Michael Bishop, Kansas St
1986	Vinny Testaverde, Miami (Fla.)	1999	Joe Hamilton, Georgia Tech
1987	Don McPherson, Syracuse	2000	Chris Weinke, Florida St
1988	Troy Aikman, UCLA	2001	Eric Crouch, Nebraska
1989	Andre Ware, Houston	2002	Brad Banks, Iowa
1990	Ty Detmer, BYU	2003	Jason White, Oklahoma
1991	Ty Detmer, BYU	2004	Jason White, Oklahoma
1992	Gino Torretta, Miami (Fla.)	2005	Vince Young, Texas
1993	Charlie Ward, Florida St	2006	Troy Smith, Ohio St

Note: Originally honored the outstanding football player in the Southwest as follows: 1977—Earl Campbell, Texas, RB; 1978—Billy Sims, Oklahoma, RB; 1979—Mike Singletary, Baylor, LB; 1980—Mike Singletary, Baylor, LB.

Vince Lombardi/Rotary Award

Given to the outstanding college lineman of the year, the award is sponsored by the Rotary Club of Houston.

Year	Player, College, Position	Year	Player, College, Position
1970	Jim Stillwagon, Ohio St, MG	1989	Percy Snow, Michigan St, LB
1971	Walt Patulski, Notre Dame, DE	1990	Chris Zorich, Notre Dame, NG
1972	Rich Glover, Nebraska, MG	1991	Steve Emtman, Washington, DT
1973	John Hicks, Ohio St, OT	1992	Marvin Jones, Florida St, LB
1974	Randy White, Maryland, DT	1993	Aaron Taylor, Notre Dame, OT
1975	Lee Roy Selmon, Oklahoma, DT	1994	Warren Sapp, Miami (Fla.), DT
1976	Wilson Whitley, Houston, DT	1995	Orlando Pace, Ohio St, OT
1977	Ross Browner, Notre Dame, DE	1996	Orlando Pace, Ohio St, OT
1978	Bruce Clark, Penn St, DT	1997	Grant Wistrom, Nebraska, DE
1979	Brad Budde, USC, G	1998	Dat Nguyen, Texas A&M, LB
1980	Hugh Green, Pittsburgh, DE	1999	Corey Moore, Virginia Tech, DE
1981	Kenneth Sims, Texas, DT	2000	Jamal Reynolds, Florida St, DE
1982	Dave Rimington, Nebraska, C	2001	Julius Peppers, North Carolina, DE
1983	Dean Steinkuhler, Nebraska, G	2002	Terrell Suggs, Arizona St, DL
1984	Tony Degrate, Texas, DT	2003	Tommie Harris, Oklahoma, DT
1985	Tony Casillas, Oklahoma, NG	2004	David Pollack, Georgia, DE
1986	Cornelius Bennett, Alabama, LB	2005	A.J. Hawk, Ohio St, LB
1987	Chris Spielman, Ohio St, LB	2006	LaMarr Woodley, Michigan, DE
1988	Tracy Rocker, Auburn, DT		

Outland Trophy

Given to the outstanding interior lineman, selected by the Football Writers Association of America.

Year	Player, College, Position	Year	Player, College, Position
1946	George Connor, Notre Dame, T	1954	Bill Brooks, Arkansas, G
1947	Joe Steffy, Army, G	1955	Calvin Jones, Iowa, G
1948	Bill Fischer, Notre Dame, G	1956	Jim Parker, Ohio St, G
1949	Ed Bagdon, Michigan St, G	1957	Alex Karras, Iowa, T
1950	Bob Gain, Kentucky, T	1958	Zeke Smith, Auburn, G
1951	Jim Weatherall, Oklahoma, T	1959	Mike McGee, Duke, T
1952	Dick Modzelewski, Maryland, T	1960	Tom Brown, Minnesota, G
1953	J.D. Roberts, Oklahoma, G	1961	Merlin Olsen, Utah St, T

Outland Trophy *(Cont.)*

Year	Player, College, Position
1962	Bobby Bell, Minnesota, T
1963	Scott Appleton, Texas, T
1964	Steve DeLong, Tennessee, T
1965	Tommy Nobis, Texas, G
1966	Loyd Phillips, Arkansas, T
1967	Ron Yary, USC, T
1968	Bill Stanfill, Georgia, T
1969	Mike Reid, Penn St, DT
1970	Jim Stillwagon, Ohio St, MG
1971	Larry Jacobson, Nebraska, DT
1972	Rich Glover, Nebraska, MG
1973	John Hicks, Ohio St, OT
1974	Randy White, Maryland, DE
1975	Lee Roy Selmon, Oklahoma, DT
1976	Ross Browner, Notre Dame, DE
1977	Brad Shearer, Texas, DT
1978	Greg Roberts, Oklahoma, G
1979	Jim Ritcher, North Carolina St, C
1980	Mark May, Pittsburgh, OT
1981	Dave Rimington, Nebraska, C
1982	Dave Rimington, Nebraska, C
1983	Dean Steinkuhler, Nebraska, G
1984	Bruce Smith, Virginia Tech, DT
1985	Mike Ruth, Boston College, NG
1986	Jason Buck, BYU; DT
1987	Chad Hennings, Air Force, DT
1988	Tracy Rocker, Auburn, DT
1989	Mohammed Elewonibi, BYU, G
1990	Russell Maryland, Miami (Fla.), DT
1991	Steve Emtman, Washington, DT
1992	Will Shields, Nebraska, G
1993	Rob Waldrop, Arizona, NG
1994	Zach Wiegert, Nebraska, G
1995	Jonathan Ogden, UCLA, OT
1996	Orlando Pace, Ohio St, OT
1997	Aaron Taylor, Nebraska, G
1998	Kris Farris, UCLA, OL
1999	Chris Samuels, Alabama, OL
2000	John Henderson, Tennessee, DT
2001	Bryant McKinnie, Miami (Fla.), OT
2002	Rien Long, Washington St, DL
2003	Robert Gallery, Iowa, OT
2004	Jammal Brown, Oklahoma, OT
2005	Greg Eslinger, Minnesota, LB
2006	Joe Thomas, Wisconsin, OT

Butkus Award

Given to the top collegiate linebacker, the award was established by the Downtown Athletic Club of Orlando and named for college Hall of Famer Dick Butkus of Illinois.

Year	Player, College
1985	Brian Bosworth, Oklahoma
1986	Brian Bosworth, Oklahoma
1987	Paul McGowan, Florida St
1988	Derrick Thomas, Alabama
1989	Percy Snow, Michigan St
1990	Alfred Williams, Colorado
1991	Erick Anderson, Michigan
1992	Marvin Jones, Florida St
1993	Trev Alberts, Nebraska
1994	Dana Howard, Illinois
1995	Kevin Hardy, Illinois
1996	Matt Russell, Colorado
1997	Andy Katzenmoyer, Ohio St
1998	Chris Claiborne, USC
1999	LaVar Arrington, Penn St
2000	Dan Morgan, Miami (Fla.)
2001	Rocky Calmus, Oklahoma
2002	E.J. Henderson, Maryland
2003	Teddy Lehman, Oklahoma
2004	Derrick Johnson, Texas
2005	Paul Posluszny, Penn State
2006	Patrick Willis, Mississippi

Jim Thorpe Award

Given to the best defensive back of the year, the award is presented by the Jim Thorpe Athletic Club of Oklahoma City.

Year	Player, College
1986	Thomas Everett, Baylor
1987	Bennie Blades, Miami (Fla.)
	Rickey Dixon, Oklahoma
1988	Deion Sanders, Florida St
1989	Mark Carrier, USC
1990	Darryl Lewis, Arizona
1991	Terrell Buckley, Florida St
1992	Deon Figures, Colorado
1993	Antonio Langham, Alabama
1994	Chris Hudson, Colorado
1995	Greg Myers, Colorado St
1996	Lawrence Wright, Florida
1997	Charles Woodson, Michigan
1998	Antoine Winfield, Ohio St
1999	Tyrone Carter, Minnesota
2000	Jamar Fletcher, Wisconsin
2001	Roy Williams, Oklahoma
2002	Terence Newman, Kansas St
2003	Derrick Strait, Oklahoma
2004	Carlos Rogers, Auburn
2005	Michael Huff, Texas
2006	Aaron Ross, Texas

Walter Payton Player of the Year Award

Given to the top FCS (I-AA) player, voted by Div. I-AA sports information directors. Sponsored by Sports Network.

Year	Player, College, Position	Year	Player, College, Position
1987	Kenny Gamble, Colgate, RB	1997	Brian Finneran, Villanova, WR
1988	Dave Meggett, Towson St, RB	1998	Jerry Azumah, New Hampshire, RB
1989	John Friesz, Idaho, QB	1999	Adrian Peterson, Georgia Southern, RB
1990	Walter Dean, Grambling, RB	2000	Louis Ivory, Furman, RB
1991	Jamie Martin, Weber St, QB	2001	Brian Westbrook, Villanova, RB
1992	Michael Payton, Marshall, QB	2002	Tony Romo, Eastern Ilinois, QB
1993	Doug Nussmeier, Idaho, QB	2003	Jamaal Branch, Colgate, RB
1994	Steve McNair, Alcorn St, QB	2004	Lang Campbell, William & Mary, QB
1995	Dave Dickenson, Montana, QB	2005	Erik Meyer, Eastern Washington, QB
1996	Archie Amerson, Northern Arizona, RB	2006	Ricky Santos, New Hampshire, QB

NCAA Football Bowl Subdivision (I-A) Individual Records

Career

SCORING

Most Points Scored: 468—Travis Prentice, Miami (OH), 1996–99
Most Points Scored per Game: 12.1—Marshall Faulk, San Diego St, 1991–93
Most Touchdowns Scored: 78—Travis Prentice, Miami (OH), 1996–99
Most Touchdowns Scored per Game: 2.0—Marshall Faulk, San Diego St, 1991–93
Most Touchdowns Scored, Rushing: 73—Travis Prentice, Miami (OH), 1996–99
Most Touchdowns Scored, Passing: 121—Ty Detmer, BYU, 1988–91
Most Touchdowns Scored, Receiving: 50—Troy Edwards, Louisiana Tech, 1996–98
Most Touchdowns Scored, Interception Returns: 5—Ken Thomas, San Jose St, 1979–82; Jackie Walker, Tennessee, 1969–71; Deltha O'Neal, California, 1996–99; Darrent Williams, Okla St 2001–04
Most Touchdowns Scored, Punt Returns: 8—Wes Walker, Texas Tech, 2000–03; Antonio Perkins, Oklahoma, 2001–04
Most Touchdowns Scored, Kickoff Returns: 6—Anthony Davis, USC, 1972–74

TOTAL OFFENSE

Most Plays: 2,587—Timmy Chang, Hawaii, 2000–04
Most Plays per Game: 50.1—Kliff Kingsbury, Texas Tech, 1999–2002
Most Yards Gained: 16,910—Timmy Chang, Hawaii, 2000–04 (17,072 passing, -162 rushing)
Most Yards Gained per Game: 382.4—Tim Rattay, Louisiana Tech, 1997–99
Most 300+ Yard Games: 33 —Ty Detmer, BYU, 1988–91

RUSHING

Most Rushes: 1,215—Steve Bartalo, Colorado St, 1983–86 (4813 yds)
Most Rushes per Game: 34.0—Ed Marinaro, Cornell, 1969–71
Most Yards Gained: 6,397—Ron Dayne, Wisconsin, 1996–99
Most Yards Gained per Game: 174.6—Ed Marinaro, Cornell, 1969–71
Most I00+ Yard Games: 34—DeAngelo Williams, Memphis, 2002–05
Most 200+ Yard Games: 11—Marcus Allen, USC, 1978–81; Ricky Williams, Texas, 1995–98; Ron Dayne, Wisconsin, 1996–99

PASSING

Highest Passing Efficiency Rating: 168.9—Ryan Dinwiddie, Boise St, 2000–03
Most Passes Attempted: 2,436—Timmy Chang, Hawaii, 2000–04
Most Passes Attempted per Game: 47.0—Tim Rattay, Louisiana Tech, 1997–99
Most Passes Completed: 1,388—Timmy Chang, Hawaii, 2000–04
Most Passes Completed per Game: 30.8—Tim Rattay, Louisiana Tech, 1997–99
*Highest Completion Percentage: 68.2—Bruce Gradkowski, Toledo, 2002–05
Most Yards Gained: 17,072—Timmy Chang, Hawaii, 2000–04
Most Yards Gained per Game: 386.2—Tim Rattay, Louisiana Tech, 1997–99 (3 years); 326.8—Ty Detmer, BYU, 1988–91 (4 years)

RECEIVING

Most Passes Caught: 316—Taylor Stubblefield, Purdue, 2001–04
Most Passes Caught per Game: 10.5—Emmanuel Hazard, Houston, 1989–90
Most Yards Gained: 5,005—Trevor Insley, Nevada, 1996–99
Most Yards Gained per Game: 140.9—Alex Van Dyke, Nevada, 1994–95
†Highest Average Gain per Reception: 22.0—Herman Moore, Virginia, 198–90

ALL-PURPOSE RUNNING

Most Plays: 1,347—Steve Bartalo, Colorado St, 1983-86 (1,215 rushes, 132 receptions)
Most Yards Gained: 7,573—DeAngelo Williams, Memphis, 2002–05 (6,026 rushing, 723 receiving, 824 KO retrurns)
Most Yards Gained per Game: 237.8—Ryan Benjamin, Pacific, 1990–92
Highest Average Gain per Play: 17.4—Anthony Carter, Michigan, 1979–82

*Minimum 1,000 attempts.
†Minimum 105 receptions.

Career *(Cont.)*

INTERCEPTIONS

Most Passes Intercepted: 29—Al Brosky, Illinois, 1950–52
Most Passes Intercepted per Game: 1.1—Al Brosky, Illinois, 1950–52
Most Yards on Interception Returns: 501—Terrell Buckley, Florida St, 1989–91
Highest Average Gain per Interception: 26.5—Tom Pridemore, West Virginia, 1975–77

SPECIAL TEAMS

Highest Punt Return Average: 23.6—Jack Mitchell, Oklahoma, 1946–48
Highest Kickoff Return Average: 36.2—Forrest Hall, San Francisco, 1946–47
Highest Average Yards per Punt: 46.3—Todd Sauerbrun, West Virginia, 1991–93 (150–199 punts). 45.3—Ryan Plackemeier, Wake Forest, 2002–05 (200-250 punts). 45.2—Daniel Sepulved, Baylor, 2003–06 (250+ punts).

Single Season

SCORING

Most Points Scored: 234—Barry Sanders, Oklahoma St, 1988
Most Points Scored per Game: 21.3—Barry Sanders, Oklahoma St, 1988
Most Touchdowns Scored: 39—Barry Sanders, Oklahoma St, 1988
Most Touchdowns Scored, Rushing: 37—Barry Sanders, Oklahoma St, 1988
Most Touchdowns Scored, Passing: 58—Colt Brennan, Hawaii, 2006
Most Touchdowns Scored, Receiving: 27—Troy Edwards, Louisiana Tech, 1998
Most Touchdowns Scored, Interception Returns: 4—Deltha O'Neal, California, 1999
Most Touchdowns Scored, Punt Returns: 5—Chad Owens, Hawaii, 2004
Most Touchdowns Scored, Kickoff Returns: 5—Ashlan Davis, Tulsa, 2004

TOTAL OFFENSE

Most Plays: 814—Kliff Kingsbury, Texas Tech, 2002
Most Yards Gained: 5,976—B.J. Symons, Texas Tech, 2003
Most Yards Gained per Game: 474.6—David Klingler, Houston, 1990
Most 300+ Yard Games: 12—Ty Detmer, BYU, 1990

RUSHING

Most Rushes: 403—Marcus Allen, USC, 1981
Most Rushes per Game: 39.6—Ed Marinaro, Cornell, 1971
Most Yards Gained: 2,628—Barry Sanders, Oklahoma St, 1988
Most Yards Gained per Game: 238.9—Barry Sanders, Oklahoma St, 1988
Most 100+ Yard Games: 12—Quentin Griffin, Oklahoma, 2002

PASSING

Highest Passing Efficiency Rating: 186.0—Colt Brennan, Hawaii, 2006
Most Passes Attempted: 719—B.J. Symons, Texas Tech, 2003
Most Passes Attempted per Game: 58.5—David Klingler, Houston, 1990
Most Passes Completed: 479—Kliff Kingsbury, Texas Tech, 2002

PASSING *(Cont.)*

Most Passes Completed per Game: 36.4—Tim Couch, Kentucky, 1998
Highest Completion Percentage: 73.6—Daunte Culpepper, Central Florida, 1998
Most Yards Gained: 5,833—B.J. Symons, Texas Tech, 2003
Most Yards Gained per Game: 467.3—David Klingler, Houston, 1990

RECEIVING

Most Passes Caught: 142—Emmanuel Hazard, Houston, 1989
Most Passes Caught per Game: 13.4—Howard Twilley, Tulsa, 1965
Most Yards Gained: 2,060—Trevor Insley, Nevada, 1999
Most Yards Gained per Game: 187.3—Trevor Insley, Nevada, 1999
Highest Average Gain per Reception: 27.9—Elmo Wright, Houston, 1968 (min. 30 receptions)

ALL-PURPOSE RUNNING

Most Plays: 432—Marcus Allen, USC, 1981
Most Yards Gained: 3,250—Barry Sanders, Oklahoma St, 1988
Most Yards Gained per Game: 295.5—Barry Sanders, Oklahoma St, 1988
Highest Average Gain per Play: 18.5—Henry Bailey, UNLV, 1992

INTERCEPTIONS

Most Passes Intercepted: 14 — Al Worley, Washington, 1968
Most Yards on Interception Returns: 302 — Charles Phillips, USC, 1974
Highest Average Gain per Interception: 50.6 — Norm Thompson, Utah, 1969

SPECIAL TEAMS

Highest Punt Return Average: 28.5—Maurice Drew, UCLA, 2005
Highest Kickoff Return Average: 40.1 — Paul Allen, BYU, 1961
Highest Average Yards per Punt: 50.3 — Chad Kessler, LSU, 1997

*Minimum 1,000 attempts.

Single Game

SCORING

Most Points Scored: 48—Howard Griffith, Illinois, 1990 (vs Southern Illinois)
Most Field Goals: 7—Dale Klein, Nebraska, 1985 (vs Missouri); Mike Prindle, Western Michigan, 1984 (vs Marshall)
Most Extra Points (Kick): 13—Derek Mahoney, Fresno St, 1991 (vs New Mexico); Terry Leiweke, Houston, 1968 (vs Tulsa)
Most Extra Points (2-Pts): 6—Jim Pilot, New Mexico St, 1961 (vs Hardin-Simmons)

TOTAL OFFENSE

Most Yards Gained: 732—David Klingler, Houston, 1990 (vs Arizona St)

RUSHING

Most Yards Gained: 406—LaDainian Tomlinson, TCU, 1999 (vs UTEP)
Most Touchdowns Rushed: 8—Howard Griffith, Illinois, 1990 (vs Southern Illinois)

PASSING

Most Passes Completed: 55—Rusty LaRue, Wake Forest, 1995 (vs Duke); Drew Brees, Purdue, 1998 (vs Wisconsin)
Most Yards Gained: 716—David Klingler, Houston, 1990 (vs Arizona St)
Most Touchdown Passes: 11—David Klingler, Houston, 1990 [vs Eastern Washington (I-AA)]

RECEIVING

Most Passes Caught: 23—Randy Gatewood, UNLV, 1994 (vs Idaho)
Most Yards Gained: 405—Troy Edwards, Louisiana Tech, 1998 (vs Nebraska)
Most Touchdown Catches: 7—Rashaun Woods, Oklahoma St, 2003 (vs SMU)

NCAA Football Championship Subdivision (I-AA) Ind. Records

Career

SCORING

Most Points Scored: 544—Brian Westbrook, Villanova, 1998-2001
Most Touchdowns Scored: 89—Brian Westbrook, Villanova, 1998-2001
Most Touchdowns Scored, Rushing: 84—Adrian Peterson, Georgia Southern, 1998–2001
Most Touchdowns Scored, Passing: 140—Bruce Eugene, Grambling St, 2002–05
Most Touchdowns Scored, Receiving: 50—Jerry Rice, Mississippi Valley St, 1981–84

RUSHING

Most Rushes: 1,124—Charles Roberts, Cal St–Sacramento, 1997–2000
Most Rushes per Game: 38.2—Arnold Mickens, Butler, 1994–95
Most Yards Gained: 6,559—Adrian Peterson, Georgia Southern, 1998–2001
Most Yards Gained per Game: 190.7—Arnold Mickens, Butler, 1994–95 (2 years); 164.5—Adrian Peterson, Georgia Southern, 1998–2000 (3 years); 156.2—Adrian Peterson, Georgia Southern, 1998–2001 (4 years)

PASSING

Highest Passing Efficiency Rating: 170.8—Shawn Knight, William & Mary, 1991–94 (3 years); 166.3—Dave Dickenson, Montana, 1992–95 (4 years)
Most Passes Attempted: 1,680—Marcus Brady, Cal St–Northridge, 1998–2001; Steve McNair, Alcorn St, 1991–94
Most Passes Completed: 1,039—Marcus Brady, Cal St–Northridge, 1998–2001
Most Passes Completed per Game: 26.5—Chris Sanders, Chattanooga, 1999–2000
Highest Completion Percentage: 67.3—Dave Dickenson, Montana, 1992–95
Most Yards Gained: 14,496—Steve McNair, Alcorn St, 1991–94
Most Yards Gained per Game: 350.0—Neil Lomax, Portland St, 1978–80

RECEIVING

Most Passes Caught: 317—Jacquay Nunnally, Florida A&M, 1997–2000
Most Yards Gained: 4,693—Jerry Rice, Mississippi Valley St, 1981–84
Most Yards Gained per Game: 114.5—Jerry Rice, Mississippi Valley St, 1981–84 (min. 3,000 yds)
Highest Average Gain per Reception: 22.0—Dedric Ward, Northern Iowa, 1993–96 (min. 125 rec.)

Single Season

SCORING

Most Points Scored: 186—Kevin Richardson, Appalachian State, 2006
Most Touchdowns Scored: 31—Kevin Richardson, Appalachian State, 2006
Most Touchdowns Scored, Rushing: 30—Kevin Richardson, Appalachian State, 2006
Most Touchdowns Scored, Passing: 56—Willie Totten, Mississippi Valley St, 1984; Bruce Eugene, Grambling St, 2005
Most Touchdowns Scored, Receiving: 27—Jerry Rice, Mississippi Valley St, 1984

RUSHING

Most Rushes: 450—Jamaal Branch, Colgate, 2003
Most Rushes per Game: 40.9—Arnold Mickens, Butler, 1994
Most Yards Gained: 2,326—Jamaal Branch, Colgate, 2003
Most Yards Gained per Game: 225.5—Arnold Mickens, Butler, 1994

Single Season *(Cont.)*

PASSING

Highest Passing Efficiency Rating: 204.6—Shawn Knight, William & Mary, 1993

Most Passes Attempted: 592—Martin Hankins, SE Louisiana, 2003

Most Passes Completed: 405—Brett Gordon, Villanova, 2002

Most Passes Completed per Game: 32.4—Willie Totten, Mississippi Valley St, 1984

Highest Completion Percentage: 70.6—Giovanni Carmazzi, Hofstra, 1997

Most Yards Gained: 4,863—Steve McNair, Alcorn St, 1994

Most Yards Gained per Game: 455.7—Willie Totten, Mississippi Valley St, 1984

RECEIVING

Most Passes Caught: 120—Stephen Campbell, Brown, 2000

Most Yards Gained: 1,712—Eddie Conti, Delaware, 1998

Most Yards Gained per Game: 168.2—Jerry Rice, Mississippi Valley St, 1984

Highest Average Gain per Reception: 28.9—Mikhael Ricks, Stephen F. Austin, 1997; (min. 35 receptions)

Single Game

SCORING

Most Points Scored: 42—Jesse Burton, McNeese St, 1998 (vs Southern Utah); Archie Amerson, Northern Arizona, 1996 (vs Weber St)

Most Field Goals: 8—Goran Lingmerth, Northern Arizona, 1986 (vs Idaho)

RUSHING

Most Yards Gained: 437—Maurice Hicks, North Carolina A&T, 2001 (vs Morgan St)

Most Touchdowns Rushed: 7—Archie Amerson, Northern Arizona, 1996 (vs Weber St)

PASSING

Most Passes Completed: 50—Martin Hankins, SE Louisiana, 2004, (vs. Jacksonville)

Most Yards Gained: 624—Jamie Martin, Weber St, 1991 (vs Idaho St)

Most Touchdown Passes: 9—Willie Totten, Mississippi Valley St, 1984 (vs Kentucky St)

RECEIVING

Most Passes Caught: 24—Chas Gessner, Brown, 2002, (vs Rhode Island); Jerry Rice, Mississippi Valley, 1983 (vs Southern–Birmingham)

Most Yards Gained: 376—Kassim Osgood, Cal Poly, 2000 (vs Northern Iowa)

Most Touchdown Catches: 6—Cos DeMatteo, Chattanooga, 2000 (vs Mississippi Valley St)

NCAA Division II Individual Records

Career

SCORING

Most Points Scored: 656—Germaine Rice, Pittsburg St, 2003–06

Most Touchdowns Scored: 109—Germaine Rice, Pittsburg St, 2003–06

Most Touchdowns Scored, Rushing: 107—Germaine Rice, Pittsburg St, 2003–06

Most Touchdowns Scored, Passing: 148—Jimmy Terwilliger, East Stroudsburg, 2003–06

Most Touchdowns Scored, Receiving: 78—Dallas Mall, Bentley, 2001–04

RUSHING

Most Rushes: 1,131—Josh Ranek, S Dakota St, 1997–01

Most Rushes per Game: 29.8—Bernie Peeters, Luther, 1968–71

Most Yards Gained: 6,985—Germaine Rice, Pittsburg St, 2003–06

Most Yards Gained per Game: 183.4—Anthony Gray, Western NM, 1997–98

PASSING

Highest Passing Efficiency Rating: 170.7—Jimmy Terwilliger, East Stroudsburg, 2003–06 (Min. 750 comp.)

Most Passes Attempted: 1,898—Andrew Webb, Fort Lewis, 2000–03

PASSING *(Cont.)*

Most Passes Completed: 1,007—Andrew Webb, Fort Lewis, 2000–03

Most Passes Completed per Game: 25.9—Evan Gray, Missouri-Rolla, 2003–05

Highest Completion Percentage: 69.0—Chris Hatcher, Valdosta St, 1991–94 (Min. 1,000 att.)

Most Yards Gained: 14,350—Jimmy Terwilliger, East Stroudsburg, 2003–06

Most Yards Gained per Game: 323.7—Dusty Bonner, Valdosta St, 2000–01

RECEIVING

Most Passes Caught: 323—Clarence Coleman, Ferris St, 1998–2001

Most Yards Gained: 4,983—Clarence Coleman, Ferris St, 1998–2001

Most Yards Gained per Game: 160.8—Chris George, Glenville St, 1993–94

Highest Average Gain per Reception: 23.2—Romar Crenshaw, SE Oklahoma, 2000–03

NCAA Division II Individual Records *(Cont.)*

Single Season

SCORING

Most Points Scored: 228—Danny Woodhead, Chadron State, 2006
Most Touchdowns Scored: 38—Danny Woodhead, Chadron St, 2006
Most Touchdowns Scored, Rushing: 34—Danny Woodhead, Chadron St, 2006
Most Touchdowns Scored, Passing: 54—Dusty Bonner, Valdosta St, 2000
Most Touchdowns Scored, Receiving: 35—David Kircus, Grand Valley St, 2002

RUSHING

Most Rushes: 385—Joe Gough, Wayne St (Mich.), 1994
Most Rushes per Game: 38.6—Mark Perkins, Hobart, 1968
Most Yards Gained: 2,756—Danny Woodhead, Chadron St, 2006
Most Yards Gained per Game: 222.0—Anthony Gray, Western New Mexico, 1997

PASSING

Highest Passing Efficiency Rating: 221.63—Curt Anes, Grand Valley St, 2001
Most Passes Attempted: 583—Dalton Bell, West Texas A&M 2006
Most Passes Completed: 386—Dalton Bell, West Texas A&M 2006
Most Passes Completed per Game: 32.4—Lance Funderburk, Valdosta St, 1995
Highest Completion Percentage: 74.7—Chris Hatcher, Valdosta St, 1994
Most Yards Gained: 4,646—Chad Friehauf, Colorado Mines 2004
Most Yards Gained per Game: 393.4—Grady Benton, West Texas A&M, 1994

RECEIVING

Most Passes Caught: 119—Brad Bailey, W Texas A&M, 1994
Most Yards Gained: 1,876—Chris George, Glenville St, 1993
Most Yards Gained per Game: 187.6—Chris George, Glenville St, 1993
Highest Average Gain per Reception: 32.5—Tyrone Johnson, Western St, 1991 (min. 30 receptions)

Single Game

SCORING

Most Points Scored: 48—Paul Zaeske, N Park, 1968 (vs N Central); Junior Wolf, Panhandle St, 1958 (vs St. Mary [Ks.])
Most Field Goals: 6—Steve Huff, Central Missouri St, 1985 (vs SE Missouri St); Austin Wellock, Ashland, 2002 (vs. Wayne St)

RUSHING

Most Yards Gained: 410—Andrew Terry, Ferris St, 2004 (vs Findlay)
Most Touchdowns Rushed: 8—Junior Wolf, Panhandle St, 1958 (vs St. Mary [Ks.])

PASSING

Most Passes Completed: 56—Jarrod DeGeorgia, Wayne St (Neb.),1996 (vs Drake)
Most Yards Gained: 645—Matt Kohn, Indianapolis, 2003 (vs Michigan Tech)
Most Touchdowns Passed: 10—Bruce Swanson, N Park, 1968 (vs N Central)

RECEIVING

Most Passes Caught: 23—Chris George, Glenville St, 1994 (vs WV Wesleyan); Barry Wagner, Alabama A&M, 1989 (vs Clark Atlanta)
Most Yards Gained: 401—Kevin Ingram, W Chester, 1998 (vs Clarion)
Most Touchdown Catches: 8—Paul Zaeske, N Park, 1968 (vs N Central)

NCAA Division III Individual Records

Career

SCORING

Most Points Scored: 562—R.J. Bowers, Grove City, 1997–00
Most Touchdowns Scored: 92—R.J. Bowers, Grove City, 1997–00
Most Touchdowns Scored, Rushing: 91—R.J. Bowers, Grove City, 1997–00
Most Touchdowns Scored, Passing: 148—Justin Peery, Westminster (Mo.), 1996–99
Most Touchdowns Scored, Receiving: 75—Scott Pingel, Westminster (Mo.), 1996–99

RUSHING

Most Rushes: 1,190—Steve Tardif, Maine Maritime, 1996–99
Most Rushes per Game: 32.7—Chris Sizemore, Bridgewater (Va.), 1972–74

RUSHING *(Cont.)*

Most Yards Gained: 7,353—R.J. Bowers, Grove City, 1997–00
Most Yards Gained per Game: 187.1—Tony Sutton, Wooster, 2002–04

PASSING

Highest Passing Efficiency Rating: 194.2—Bill Borchert, Mount Union, 1994–97
Most Passes Attempted: 1,696—Kirk Baumgartner, UW–Stevens Point, 1986–89
Most Passes Completed: 1,012—Justin Peery, Westminster (Mo.), 1996–99
Most Passes Completed per Game: 25.9—Justin Peery, Westminster (Mo.), 1996–99
Highest Completion Percentage: 66.5—Bill Borchert, Mount Union, 1994–97 (Min. 1,000 att.)

Career (Cont.)

PASSING (Cont.)

Most Yards Gained: 13,262—Justin Peery, Westminster (Mo.), 1996–99
Most Yards Gained per Game: 340.1—Justin Peery, Westminster (Mo.), 1996–99

RECEIVING

Most Passes Caught: 436—Scott Pingel, Westminster (Mo.), 1996–99
Most Yards Gained: 6,108—Scott Pingel, Westminster (Mo.), 1996–99
Most Yards Gained per Game: 156.6—Scott Pingel, Westminster (Mo.), 1996–99
Highest Average Gain per Reception: 23.4—Michael Coleman, Widener, 1998–2001

Single Season

SCORING

Most Points Scored: 248—Dan Pugh, Mount Union, 2002
Most Points Scored per Game: 20.8—James Regan, Pomona-Pitzer, 1997
Most Touchdowns Scored: 41—Dan Pugh Mount Union, 2002
Most Touchdowns Scored, Rushing: 35—Chris Sharpe, Springfield, 2006; Dan Pugh, Mount Union, 2002
Most Touchdowns Scored, Passing: 61—Brett Elliott, Linfield, 2004
Most Touchdowns Scored, Receiving: 26—Scott Pingel, Westminster (Mo.), 1998

RUSHING

Most Rushes: 463—Dante Washington, Carthage, 2004
Most Rushes per Game: 38.0—Mike Birosak, Dickinson, 1989
Most Yards Gained: 2,420—Justin Beaver, UW–Whitewater, 2005

PASSING

Highest Passing Efficiency Rating: 225.0—Mike Simpson, Eureka, 1994
Most Passes Attempted: 575—Brett Dietz, Hanover, 2003
Most Passes Completed: 360—Brett Dietz, Hanover, 2003
Most Passes Completed per Game: 32.9—Justin Peery, Westminster (Mo.), 1999
Highest Completion Percentage: 73.6—Mitch Tanney, Monmouth (Ill.), 2005
Most Yards Gained: 4,595—Brett Elliott, Linfield, 2004
Most Yards Gained per Game: 450.1—Justin Peery, Westminster (Mo.), 1998

RECEIVING

Most Passes Caught: 136—Scott Pingel, Westminster (Mo.), 1999
Most Yards Gained: 2,157—Scott Pingel, Westminster, (Mo.), 1998
Most Yards Gained per Game: 215.7—Scott Pingel, Westminster, (Mo.), 1998
Highest Average Gain per Reception: 26.9—Marty Redlawsk, Concordia (Ill.), 1985

Single Game

SCORING

Most Field Goals: 6—Jim Hever, Rhodes, 1984 (vs Millsaps)

PASSING

Most Passes Completed: 51—Scott Kello, Sul Ross St, 2002 (vs Howard Payne)
Most Yards Gained: 731—Zamir Amin, Menlo, 2000 (vs California Lutheran)
Most Touchdown Passes: 9—Joe Zarlinga, Ohio Northern, 1998 (vs Capital)

RUSHING

Most Yards Gained: 441—Dante Brown, Marietta, 1996 (vs Baldwin-Wallace)
Most Touchdowns Rushed: 8—Carey Bender, Coe, 1994 (vs Beloit)

RECEIVING

Most Passes Caught: 23—Sean Munroe, Mass-Boston, 1992 (vs Mass-Maritime)
Most Yards Gained: 418—Lewis Howes, Principia, 2002 (vs Martin Luther)
Most Touchdown Catches: 7—Matt Perceval, Wesleyan (Conn.), 1998 (vs Middlebury)

Career

Scoring

POINTS (KICKERS)

	Years	Pts
Roman Anderson, Houston	1988–91	423
Billy Bennett, Georgia	2000–03	409
Carlos Huerta, Miami (Fla.)	1988–91	397
Jason Elam, Hawaii	1988–92	395
Derek Schmidt, Florida St	1984–87	393
Nick Novak, Maryland	2001–04	393

POINTS (NON-KICKERS)

	Years	Pts
Travis Prentice, Miami (Ohio)	1996–99	468
Ricky Williams, Texas	1995–98	452
Taurean Henderson, Texas Tech	2002–05	414
Brock Forsey, Boise St	1999–02	408
Cedric Benson, Texas	2001–04	404

POINTS PER GAME (NON-KICKERS)

	Years	Pts/Game
Marshall Faulk, San Diego St	1991–93	12.1
Ed Marinaro, Cornell	1969–71	11.8
Bill Burnett, Arkansas	1968–70	11.3
Steve Owens, Oklahoma	1967–69	11.2
Eddie Talboom, Wyoming	1948–50	10.8

Total Offense

YARDS GAINED

	Years	Yds
Timmy Chang, Hawaii	2000–04	16,910
Ty Detmer, BYU	1988–91	14,665
Kevin Kolb, Houston	2003–06	13,715
Philip Rivers, North Carolina St	2000–03	13,582
Brad Smith, Missouri	2002–05	13,088

YARDS PER GAME

	Years	Yds/Game
Tim Rattay, Louisiana Tech	1997–99	382.4
Chris Vargas, Nevada	1992–93	320.9
Timmy Chang, Hawaii	2000–04	319.1
Ty Detmer, BYU	1988–91	318.8
Daunte Culpepper, Central Florida	1993–96	313.5

Rushing

YARDS GAINED

	Years	Yds
Ron Dayne, Wisconsin	1996–99	6,397
Ricky Williams, Texas	1995–98	6,279
Tony Dorsett, Pittsburgh	1973–76	6,082
DeAngelo Williams, Memphis	2002–05	6,026
Charles White, USC	1976–79	5,598
Travis Prentice, Miami (Ohio)	1996–99	5,596

YARDS PER GAME

	Years	Yds/Game
Ed Marinaro, Cornell	1969–71	174.6
O.J. Simpson, USC	1967–68	164.4
Herschel Walker, Georgia	1980–82	159.4
Garrett Wolfe, Northern Illinois	2004-06	156.6
LeShon Johnson, Northern Illinois	1992–93	150.6

TOUCHDOWNS RUSHING

	Years	TD
Travis Prentice, Miami (Ohio)	1996–99	73
Ricky Williams, Texas	1995–98	72
Anthony Thompson, Indiana	1986–89	64
Cedric Benson, Texas	2001–04	64
Ron Dayne, Wisconsin	1996–99	63

Passing

PASSING EFFICIENCY

	Years	Rating
Ryan Dinwiddie, Boise St	2000–03	168.4
Danny Wuerffel, Florida	1993–96	163.6
Omar Jacobs, Bowling Green	2003–05	163.5
Ty Detmer, BYU	1988–91	162.7
Steve Sarkisian, BYU	1995–96	162.0

Note: Minimum 500 completions.

YARDS GAINED

	Years	Yds
Timmy Chang, Hawaii	2000–04	17,072
Ty Detmer, BYU	1988–91	15,031
Philip Rivers, North Carolina St	2000–03	13,484
Kevin Kolb, Houston	2003-06	12,964
Tim Rattay, Louisiana Tech	1997–99	12,746

COMPLETIONS

	Years	Comp
Timmy Chang, Hawaii	2000–04	1,388
Kliff Kingsbury, Texas Tech	1999–02	1,231
Philip Rivers, North Carolina St	2000–03	1,147
Luke McCown, Louisiana Tech	2000–03	1,063
Chris Redman, Louisville	1996–99	1,031
Tim Rattay, Louisiana Tech	1997–99	1,015

TOUCHDOWNS PASSING

	Years	TD
Ty Detmer, BYU	1988–91	121
Timmy Chang, Hawaii	2000–04	117
Tim Rattay, Louisiana Tech	1997–99	115
Danny Wuerffel, Florida	1993–96	114
Chad Pennington, Marshall	1997–99	100
Matt Leinart, USC	2002–05	99

Receiving

CATCHES

	Years	No.
Taylor Stubblefield, Purdue	2001–04	316
Josh Davis, Marshall	2001–04	306
Taurean Henderson, Texas Tech	2002–05	303
Arnold Jackson, Louisville	1997–00	300
Trevor Insley, Nevada	1996–99	298

CATCHES PER GAME

	Years	No./Game
Emmanuel Hazard, Houston	1989–90	10.5
Alex Van Dyke, Nevada	1994–95	10.3
Howard Twilley, Tulsa	1963–65	10.0
Jason Phillips, Houston	1987–88	9.4
Troy Edwards, Louisiana Tech	1996–98	8.2
Bryan Reeves, Nevada	1992–93	8.2

YARDS GAINED

	Years	Yds
Trevor Insley, Nevada	1996–99	5,005
Marcus Harris, Wyoming	1993–96	4,518
Rashaun Woods, Oklahoma St	2000–03	4,412
Ryan Yarborough, Wyoming	1990–93	4,357
Troy Edwards, Louisiana Tech	1996–98	4,352

TOUCHDOWN CATCHES

	Years	TD
Troy Edwards, Louisiana Tech	1996–98	50
Darius Watts, Marshall	2000–03	47
Aaron Turner, Pacific	1989–92	43
Ryan Yarborough, Wyoming	1990–93	42
Rashaun Woods, Oklahoma St	2000–03	42
Dwayne Jarrett, South California	2004-06	41
Braylon Edwards, Michigan	2001–04	39
Greg Jennings, Western Michigan	2002–05	39

Career *(Cont.)*

All-Purpose Running

YARDS GAINED	Years	Yds
DeAngelo Williams, Memphis	2002–05	7,573
Ricky Williams, Texas	1996–98	7,206
Napoleon McCallum, Navy	1981–85	7,172
Darrin Nelson, Stanford	1977–78, 80–81	6,885
Kevin Faulk, LSU	1995–98	6,833

YARDS PER GAME	Years	Yds/Game
Ryan Benjamin, Pacific	1990–92	237.8
Sheldon Canley, San Jose St	1988–90	205.8
Howard Stevens, Louisville	1971–72	193.7
O.J. Simpson, USC	1967–68	192.9
Alex Van Dyke, Nevada	1994–95	188.5

Interceptions

PLAYER/SCHOOL	Years	Int
Al Brosky, Illinois	1950–52	29
John Provost, Holy Cross	1972–74	27
Martin Bayless, Bowling Green	1980–83	27
Tom Curtis, Michigan	1967–69	25
Tony Thurman, Boston College	1981–84	25
Tracy Saul, Texas Tech	1989–92	25

Punting Average

PLAYER/SCHOOL	Years	Avg
Daniel Sepulveda, Baylor	2003–06	45.2
Shane Lechler, Texas A&M	1996–99	44.7
Bill Smith, Mississippi	1983–88	44.3
Jim Arnold, Vanderbilt	1979–82	43.9
Ralk Mojsiejenko, Michigan St	1981–84	43.6

Note: 250+ punts.

Punt Return Average

PLAYER/SCHOOL	Years	Avg
Jack Mitchell, Oklahoma	1946–48	23.6
Gene Gibson, Cincinnati	1949–50	20.5
Eddie Macon, Pacific	1949–51	18.9
Jackie Robinson, UCLA	1939–40	18.8
Dan Shelton, Illinois	2001–04	17.9

Note: Minimum 30 returns.

Kickoff Return Average

PLAYER/SCHOOL	Years	Avg
Anthony Davis, USC	1972–74	35.1
Eric Booth, Southern Miss	1994–97	32.4
Overton Curtis, Utah St	1957–58	31.0
Fred Montgomery, New Mexico St	1991–92	30.5
Alfie Taylor, Utah St	1966–68	29.3

Note: Minimum 30 returns.

Single Season

Scoring

POINTS	Year	Pts
Barry Sanders, Oklahoma St	1988	234
Brock Forsey, Boise St	2002	192
Troy Edwards, Louisiana Tech	1998	186
Mike Rozier, Nebraska	1983	174
Lydell Mitchell, Penn St	1971	174

FIELD GOALS	Year	FG
Billy Bennett, Georgia	2003	31
John Lee, UCLA	1984	29
Paul Woodside, W Virginia	1982	28
Luis Zendejas, Arizona St	1983	28
Nick Browne, TCU	2003	28

Three tied with 27.

All-Purpose Running

YARDS GAINED	Year	Yds
Barry Sanders, Oklahoma St	1988	3,250
Ryan Benjamin, Pacific	1991	2,995
Reggie Bush, USC	2005	2,890
Troy Edwards, Louisiana Tech	1998	2,784
Darren Sproles, Kansas St	2003	2,735

YARDS PER GAME	Year	Yds/Game
Barry Sanders, Oklahoma St	1988	295.5
Ryan Benjamin, Pacific	1991	249.6
Byron (Whizzer) White, Colorado	1937	246.3
Mike Pringle, Fullerton St	1989	244.6
Paul Palmer, Temple	1986	239.4

Total Offense

YARDS GAINED	Year	Yds
B.J. Symons, Texas Tech	2003	5,976
Colt Brennan, Hawaii	2006	5,915
David Klingler, Houston	1990	5,221
Ty Detmer, BYU	1990	5,022
Kliff Kingsbury, Texas Tech	2002	4,903

YARDS PER GAME	Year	Yds/Game
David Klingler, Houston	1990	474.6
B.J. Symons, Texas Tech	2003	459.7
Andre Ware, Houston	1989	423.7
Colt Brennan, Hawaii	2006	422.5
Ty Detmer, BYU	1990	418.5

Rushing

YARDS GAINED	Year	Yds
Barry Sanders, Oklahoma St	1988	2,628
Marcus Allen, USC	1981	2,342
Troy Davis, Iowa St	1996	2,185
LaDainian Tomlinson, TCU	2000	2,158
Mike Rozier, Nebraska	1983	2,148

YARDS PER GAME	Year	Yds/Game
Barry Sanders, Oklahoma St	1988	238.9
Marcus Allen, USC	1981	212.9
Ed Marinaro, Cornell	1971	209.0
Troy Davis, Iowa St	1996	198.6
LaDainian Tomlinson, TCU	2000	196.2

Single Season *(Cont.)*

Rushing *(Cont.)*

TOUCHDOWNS RUSHING

	Year	TD
Barry Sanders, Oklahoma St	1988	37
Mike Rozier, Nebraska	1983	29
Willis McGahee, Miami (Fla.)	2002	28
Ricky Williams, Texas	1998	27
Lee Suggs, Virginia Tech	2000	27

Passing

PASSING EFFICIENCY

	Year	Rating
Colt Brennan, Hawaii	2006	186.0
Shaun King, Tulane	1998	183.3
Stefan Lefors, Louisville	2004	181.7
Michael Vick, Virginia Tech	1999	180.4
Danny Wuerffel, Florida	1995	178.4

YARDS GAINED

	Year	Yds
B.J. Symons, Texas Tech	2003	5,833
Colt Brennan, Hawaii	2006	5,549
Ty Detmer, BYU	1990	5,188
David Klingler, Houston	1990	5,140
Kliff Kingsbury, Texas Tech	2002	5,017

COMPLETIONS

	Year	Att	Comp
Kliff Kingsbury, Texas Tech	2002	712	479
B.J. Symons, Texas Tech	2003	719	470
Sonny Cumbie, Texas Tech	2004	642	421
Colt Brennan, Hawaii	2006	559	406
Tim Couch, Kentucky	1998	553	400

TOUCHDOWNS PASSING

	Year	TD
Colt Brennan, Hawaii	2006	58
David Klingler, Houston	1990	54
B.J. Symons, Texas Tech	2003	52
Jim McMahon, BYU	1980	47
Andre Ware, Houston	1989	46
Tim Rattay, Louisiana Tech	1998	46

Receiving

CATCHES

	Year	GP	No.
Emmanuel Hazard, Houston	1989	11	142
Troy Edwards, Louisiana Tech	1998	12	140
Nate Burleson, Nevada	2002	12	138
Howard Twilley, Tulsa	1965	10	134
Trevor Insley, Nevada	1999	11	134

CATCHES PER GAME

	Year	No.	No./Game
Howard Twilley, Tulsa	1965	134	13.4
Emmanuel Hazard, Houston	1989	142	12.9
Trevor Insley, Nevada	1999	134	12.2
Troy Edwards, Louisiana Tech	1998	140	11.7
Alex Van Dyke, Nevada	1995	129	11.7

YARDS GAINED

	Year	Yds
Trevor Insley, Nevada	1999	2,060
Troy Edwards, Louisiana Tech	1998	1,996
Alex Van Dyke, Nevada	1995	1,854
J.R. Tolver, San Diego St	2002	1,785
Howard Twilley, Tulsa	1965	1,779

TOUCHDOWN CATCHES

	Year	TD
Troy Edwards, Louisiana Tech	1998	27
Randy Moss, Marshall	1997	25
Emmanuel Hazard, Houston	1989	22
Larry Fitzgerald, Pittsburgh	2003	22
Jarett Dillard, Rice	2006	21

Single Game

Scoring

POINTS

	Opponent	Year	Pts
Howard Griffith, Illinois	Southern Illinois	1990	48
Marshall Faulk, San Diego St	Pacific	1991	44
Jim Brown, Syracuse	Colgate	1956	43
Fred Wendt, UTEP*	New Mexico St	1948	42
Arnold "Showboat" Boykin, Mississippi	Mississippi St	1951	42
Rashaun Woods, Oklahoma St	SMU	2003	42

*UTEP was Texas Mines in 1948.

FIELD GOALS

	Opponent	Year	FG
Dale Klein, Nebraska	Missouri	1985	7
Mike Prindle, Western Michigan	Marshall	1984	7

Note: 17 tied with 6.

Klein's distances were 32-22-43-44-29-43-43.
Prindle's distances were 32-44-42-23-48-41-27.

Total Offense

YARDS GAINED

	Opponent	Year	Yds
David Klingler, Houston	Arizona St	1990	732
Matt Vogler, TCU	Houston	1990	696
B.J. Symons, Texas Tech	Mississippi	2003	681
Brian Lindgren, Idaho	Middle Tenn St	2001	657

Total Offense *(Cont.)*

YARDS GAINED

	Opponent	Year	Yds
David Klingler, Houston	TCU	1990	625
Scott Mitchell, Utah	Air Force	1988	625

Passing

YARDS GAINED

	Opponent	Year	Yds
David Klingler, Houston	Arizona St	1990	716
Matt Vogler, TCU	Houston	1990	690
B.J. Symons, Texas Tech	Mississippi	2003	661
Cody Hodges, Texas Tech	Kansas St	2005	643
Brian Lindgren, Idaho	Middle Tenn St	2001	637

COMPLETIONS

	Opponent	Year	Comp
Drew Brees, Purdue	Wisconsin	1998	55
Rusty LaRue, Wake Forest	Duke	1995	55
Rusty LaRue, Wake Forest	NC St	1995	50
C. Holbrook, New Mexico St.	Boise St	2006	49
Brian Lindgren, Idaho	Middle Tenn St	2001	49
Kliff Kingsbury, Texas Tech	Missouri	2002	49
Kliff Kingsbury, Texas Tech	Texas A&M	2002	49
Bruce Gradkowski, Toledo	Pittsburgh	2003	49

TOUCHDOWNS PASSING

	Opponent	Year	TD
David Klingler, Houston	E Wash	1990	11

Note: Klingler's TD passes were 5-48-29-7-3-7-40-10-7-8-51.

Single Game *(Cont.)*

Rushing

YARDS GAINED	Opponent	Year	Yds
LaDainian Tomlinson, TCU	...UTEP	1999	406
Tony Sands, Kansas	........Missouri	1991	396
Marshall Faulk, San Diego St	....................Pacific	1991	386
Troy Davis, Iowa St	...........Missouri	1996	378
Anthony Thompson, Indiana	...........Wisconsin	1989	377
Robbie Mixon, Central Michigan	..............Eastern Mich	2002	377

TOUCHDOWNS RUSHING	Opponent	Year	TD
Howard Griffith, Illinois	.....Southern Illinois	1990	8

Note: Griffith's TD runs were 5-51-7-41-5-18-5-3.

Receiving

CATCHES	Opponent	Year	No.
Randy Gatewood, UNLV	.....Idaho	1994	23
Jay Miller, BYU	....................New Mexico	1973	22
Troy Edwards, La. Tech	......Nebraska	1998	21
Chris Daniels, Purdue	.........Michigan St	1999	21
Rick Eber, Tulsa	..................Idaho St	1967	20
Kenny Christian, Eastern Michigan	...............Temple	2000	20

YARDS GAINED	Opponent	Year	Yds
Troy Edwards, Louisiana Tech	...Nebraska	1998	405
Randy Gatewood, UNLV	.........Idaho	1994	363
Chuck Hughes, UTEP*	............N Texas St	1965	349
Nate Burleson, Nevada	...........San Jose St	2001	326
Rick Eber, Tulsa	.......................Idaho St	1967	322

*UTEP was Texas Western in 1965.

TOUCHDOWN CATCHES	Opponent	Year	TD
Rashaun Woods, Okla. St	.....SMU	2003	7
Tim Delaney, San Diego St	....New Mex. St	1969	6

Longest Plays (since 1941)

PASSING	Opponent	Year	Yds
Fred Owens to Jack Ford, Portland	...................St. Mary's (Ca.)	1947	99
Bo Burris to Warren McVea, Houston	...................Washington St	1966	99
Colin Clapton to Eddie Jenkins, Holy Cross	...........................Boston U	1970	99
Terry Peel to Robert Ford, Houston	...........................Syracuse	1970	99
Terry Peel to Robert Ford, Houston	...........................San Diego St	1972	99
Cris Collinsworth to Derrick Gaffney, Florida	....................................Rice	1977	99
Scott Ankrom to James Maness, TCU	....................................Rice	1984	99
Gino Toretta to Horace Copeland, Miami (Fla.)	..........................Arkansas	1991	99
John Paci to Thomas Lewis, Indiana	...................................Penn St	1993	99
Troy DeGar to Wes Caswell, Tulsa	...................................Oklahoma	1996	99
Drew Brees to Vinny Sutherland, Purdue	............................Northwestern	1999	99
Dan Urban to Justin McCariens, Northern Illinois	.....................Ball St	2000	99
Jason Johnson to Brandon Marshall, Arizona	...................................Idaho	2001	99
Dondrial Pinkins to Troy Williamson, South Carolina	......................Virginia	2003	99
Jim Sorgi to Lee Evans, Wisconsin	................................Akron	2003	99

RUSHING	Opponent	Year	Yd
Gale Sayers, Kansas	............Nebraska	1963	99
Max Anderson, Arizona St	....Wyoming	1967	99
Ralph Thompson, West Texas St	.......................Wichita St	1970	99
Kelsey Finch, Tennessee	......Florida	1977	99
Eric Vann, Kansas	................Oklahoma	1997	99
Terry Caulley, Connecticut	....Army	2006	99

FIELD GOALS	Opponent	Year	Yds
Steve Little, Arkansas	............Texas	1977	67
Russell Erxleben, Texas	.........Rice	1977	67
Joe Williams, Wichita St	........Southern IL	1978	67
Martin Gramatica, Kansas St	...Northern IL	1998	65
Tony Franklin, Texas A&M	.....Baylor	1976	65

PUNTS	Opponent	Year	Yds
Pat Brady, Nevada*	...............Loyola (Ca.)	1950	99
George O'Brien, Wisconsin	...Iowa	1952	96
John Hadl, Kansas	.................Oklahoma	1959	94
Carl Knox, TCU	.....................Oklahoma St	1947	94
Preston Johnson, SMU	..........Pittsburgh	1940	94

*Nevada was Nevada-Reno in 1950.

FOOTBALL BOWL SUBDIVISION (DIV. I-A) WINNINGEST TEAMS

Alltime Winning Percentage

	Yrs	W	L	T	Pct	GP	Bowl Record
Michigan	127	860	282	36	.745	1,178	18-20-0
Notre Dame	118	821	269	42	.744	1,132	13-15-0
Texas	114	810	313	33	.715	1,156	23-21-2
Oklahoma	112	768	292	53	.714	1,113	24-15-1
Ohio St	117	786	301	53	.713	1,140	18-20-0
Alabama	112	780	308	43	.709	1,131	30-21-3
Nebraska	117	803	326	40	.704	1,169	22-22-0
USC	114	743	300	54	.702	1,097	29-16-0
Tennessee	110	761	316	53	.697	1,130	24-22-0
Boise St	39	317	140	2	.693	459	5-2-0
Penn St	119	780	343	41	.688	1,164	25-12-2
Florida St	60	443	211	17	.673	671	20-13-2
Georgia	113	702	379	54	.642	1,135	23-16-3
Miami (Fla.)	80	532	297	19	.639	848	18-13-0
LSU	113	680	376	47	.638	1,103	19-18-1
Miami (Ohio)	118	641	362	44	.633	1,047	6-3-0
Auburn	114	667	384	47	.629	1,098	18-13-2
Washington	117	646	379	50	.624	1,075	14-14-1
Florida	100	619	368	40	.622	1,027	16-18-0
South Florida	10	70	43	0	.619	113	1-1-0
Arizona St	94	530	324	24	.617	878	12-10-1
Colorado	117	652	412	36	.609	1,100	12-15-0
Central Michigan	106	542	342	36	.609	920	1-2-0
Texas A&M	112	648	419	48	.603	1,15	13-16-0
UCLA	88	528	344	37	.601	909	14-14-1

Note: Includes bowl games.

Alltime Victories

Michigan	860	
Notre Dame	821	
Texas	810	
Nebraska	803	
Ohio St	786	
Alabama	780	
Penn St	780	
Oklahoma	768	
Tennessee	761	
USC	743	

Georgia	702
LSU	680
Syracuse	669
Auburn	667
West Virginia	653
Colorado	652
Texas A&M	648
Washington	646
Georgia Tech	646
Miami (Ohio)	641

Pittsburgh	639
Arkansas	638
Virginia Tech	636
Army	631
Minnesota	629
North Carolina	627
Florida	619
Clemson	616
Navy	616
California	598

NUMBER ONE VS NUMBER TWO

The No. 1 and No. 2 teams, according to the Associated Press Poll, have met 33 times, including 13 bowl games, since the poll's inception in 1936. The No. 1 teams have a 20-11-2 record in these matchups. Notre Dame (4-3-2) has played in nine of the games.

Date	Results	Stadium
10-9-43	No. 1 Notre Dame 35, No. 2 Michigan 12	Michigan (Ann Arbor)
11-20-43	No. 1 Notre Dame 14, No. 2 Iowa Pre-Flight 13	Notre Dame (South Bend)
12-2-44	No. 1 Army 23, No. 2 Navy 7	Municipal (Baltimore)
11-10-45	No. 1 Army 48, No. 2 Notre Dame 0	Yankee (New York)
12-1-45	No. 1 Army 32, No. 2 Navy 13	Municipal (Philadelphia)
11-9-46	No. 1 Army 0, No. 2 Notre Dame 0	Yankee (New York)
1-1-63	No. 1 USC 42, No. 2 Wisconsin 37 (Rose Bowl)	Rose Bowl (Pasadena)
10-12-63	No. 2 Texas 28, No. 1 Oklahoma 7	Cotton Bowl (Dallas)
1-1-64	No. 1 Texas 28, No. 2 Navy 6 (Cotton Bowl)	Cotton Bowl (Dallas)
11-19-66	No. 1 Notre Dame 10, No. 2 Michigan St 10	Spartan (East Lansing)
9-28-68	No. 1 Purdue 37, No. 2 Notre Dame 22	Notre Dame (South Bend)
1-1-69	No. 1 Ohio St 27, No. 2 USC 16 (Rose Bowl)	Rose Bowl (Pasadena)
12-6-69	No. 1 Texas 15, No. 2 Arkansas 14	Razorback (Fayetteville)
11-25-71	No. 1 Nebraska 35, No. 2 Oklahoma 31	Owen Field (Norman)
1-1-72	No. 1 Nebraska 38, No. 2 Alabama 6 (Orange Bowl)	Orange Bowl (Miami)
1-1-79	No. 2 Alabama 14, No. 1 Penn St 7 (Sugar Bowl)	Sugar Bowl (New Orleans)
9-26-81	No. 1 USC 28, No. 2 Oklahoma 24	Coliseum (Los Angeles)
1-1-83	No. 2 Penn St 27, No. 1 Georgia 23 (Sugar Bowl)	Sugar Bowl (New Orleans)
10-19-85	No. 1 Iowa 12, No. 2 Michigan 10	Kinnick (Iowa City)

NUMBER ONE VS NUMBER TWO *(Cont.)*

Date	Results	Stadium
9-27-86	No. 2 Miami (Fla.) 28, No. 1 Oklahoma 16	Orange Bowl (Miami)
1-2-87	No. 2 Penn St 14, No. 1 Miami (FL) 10 (Fiesta Bowl)	Sun Devil (Tempe)
11-21-87	No. 2 Oklahoma 17, No. 1 Nebraska 7	Memorial (Lincoln)
1-1-88	No. 2 Miami (Fla.) 20, No. 1 Oklahoma 14 (Orange Bowl)	Orange Bowl (Miami)
11-26-88	No. 1 Notre Dame 27, No. 2 USC 10	Coliseum (Los Angeles)
9-16-89	No. 1 Notre Dame 24, No. 2 Michigan 19	Michigan (Ann Arbor)
11-16-91	No. 2 Miami (Fla.) 17, No. 1 Florida St 16	Campbell (Tallahassee)
1-1-93	No. 2 Alabama 34, No. 1 Miami (Fla.) 13 (Sugar Bowl)	Superdome (New Orleans)
11-13-93	No. 2 Notre Dame 31, No. 1 Florida St 24	Notre Dame (South Bend)
1-1-94	No. 1 Florida St 18, No. 2 Nebraska 16 (Orange Bowl)	Orange Bowl (Miami)
1-2-96	No. 1 Nebraska 62, No. 2 Florida 24 (Fiesta Bowl)	Sun Devil (Tempe)
11-30-96	No. 2 Florida St 24, No. 1 Florida 21	Campbell (Tallahassee)
1-4-99	No. 1 Tennessee 23, No. 2 Florida St 16 (Fiesta Bowl)	Sun Devil (Tempe)
1-4-00	No. 1 Florida St 46, No. 2 Virginia Tech 29 (Sugar Bowl)	Superdome (New Orleans)
1-3-03	No. 2 Ohio St 31, No. 1 Miami (Fla.) 24 [2OT] (Fiesta Bowl)	Sun Devil (Tempe)
1-4-05	No. 1 USC 55, No. 2 Oklahoma 19 (Orange Bowl)	Pro Player Stadium (Miami)
1-5-06	No. 2 Texas 41, No. 1 USC 38 (Rose Bowl)	Rose Bowl (Pasadena)
9-9-06	No. 1 Ohio St 24, No. 2 Texas 7	Texas Memorial (Austin)
11-18-06	No. 1 Ohio St 42, No. 2 Michigan 39	Ohio (Columbus)
1-8-07	No. 2 Florida 41, No. 1 Ohio St 14 (BCS Championship)	Univ. of Phoenix (Glendale)

LONGEST FBS (DIV. I-A) WINNING STREAKS

Wins	Team	Yrs	Ended by	Score
47	Oklahoma	1953–57	Notre Dame	7–0
39	Washington	1908–14	Oregon St	0–0
37	Yale	1890–93	Princeton	6–0
37	Yale	1887–89	Princeton	10–0
35	Toledo	1969–71	Tampa	21–0
34	USC	2003–05	Texas	41–38
34	Miami	2000–03	Ohio St	31–24 (2ot)
34	Pennsylvania	1894–96	Lafayette	6–4
31	Oklahoma	1948–50	Kentucky	13–7
31	Pittsburgh	1914–18	Cleveland Naval Reserve	10–9
31	Pennsylvania	1896–98	Harvard	10–0

LONGEST FBS (DIV. I-A) UNBEATEN STREAKS

No.	W	T	Team	Yrs	Ended by	Score
63	59	4	Washington	1907–17	California	27–0
56	55	1	Michigan	1901–05	Chicago	2–0
50	46	4	California	1920–25	Olympic Club	15–0
48	47	1	Oklahoma	1953–57	Notre Dame	7–0
48	47	1	Yale	1885–89	Princeton	10–0
47	42	5	Yale	1879–85	Princeton	6–5
44	42	2	Yale	1894–96	Princeton	24–6
42	39	3	Yale	1904–08	Harvard	4–0
39	37	2	Notre Dame	1946–50	Purdue	28–14
37	36	1	Oklahoma	1972–75	Kansas	23–3
37	37	0	Yale	1890–93	Princeton	6–0
35	35	0	Toledo	1969–71	Tampa	21–0
35	34	1	Minnesota	1903–05	Wisconsin	16–12
34	34	0	USC	2003–05	Texas	41–38
34	34	0	Miami	2000–03	Ohio St	31–24 (2ot)
34	33	1	Nebraska	1912–16	Kansas	7–3
34	34	0	Pennsylvania	1894–96	Lafayette	6–4
34	32	2	Princeton	1884–87	Harvard	12–0
34	29	5	Princeton	1877–82	Harvard	1–0
33	30	3	Tennessee	1926–30	Alabama	18–6
33	31	2	Georgia Tech	1914–18	Pittsburgh	32–0
33	30	3	Harvard	1911–15	Cornell	10–0
32	31	1	Nebraska	1969–71	UCLA	20–17
32	30	2	Army	1944–47	Columbia	21–20
32	31	1	Harvard	1898–1900	Yale	28–0

Note: Includes bowl games.

LONGEST DIVISION I-A LOSING STREAKS

Losses		Seasons	Ended Against	Score
34	Northwestern	1979–82	Northern Illinois	31–6
28	Virginia	1958–61	William & Mary	21–6
28	Kansas St	1945–48	Arkansas St	37–6
27	New Mexico St	1988–90	Cal St–Fullerton	43–9
27	Eastern Michigan	1980–82	Kent St	9–7

MOST-PLAYED DIVISION I-A RIVALRIES

GP	Opponents (Series Leader Listed First)	Record	First Game	GP	Opponents (Series Leader Listed First)	Record	First Game
116	Minnesota–Wisconsin	59-49-8	1890	104	Clemson–South Carolina	63-37-4	1896
115	Kansas–Missouri	53-53-9	1891	104	Kansas–Kansas St	63-36-5	1902
113	Nebraska-Kansas	88-22-3	1892	103	Michigan–Ohio St	57-40-6	1897
113	Texas–Texas A&M	73-35-5	1894	103	Mississippi–Miss St	59-38-6	1901
111	Miami (Ohio)–Cincinnati	59-45-7	1888	102	N Carolina–Wake Forest	67-33-2	1897
111	North Carolina–Virginia	†57-50-4	1892	102	Tennessee–Kentucky	70-23-9	1893
110	Auburn–Georgia	53-49-8	1892	101	Georgia–Georgia Tech	58-38-5	1893
110	Oregon–Oregon St	55-45-10	1894	101	Nebraska–Iowa St	83-16-2	1896
109	Purdue–Indiana	68-35-6	1891	101	Texas–Oklahoma	57-39-5	1900
109	Stanford–California	54-44-11	1892	101	Oklahoma–Oklahoma St	78-16-7	1904
107	Navy–Army	51-49-7	1890				
106	Utah–Utah St	74-28-4	1892				
104	Baylor–TCU*	49-48-7	1899				

*Have not met since 1995.

†Disputed series record: Virginia claims North Carolina leads series 55-51-4 based on a forfeited game in 1956.

ALLTIME WINNINGEST FBS (DIV. I-A) COACHES

By Percentage

Coach (Alma Mater)	Colleges Coached	Yrs	W	L	T	Pct
Knute Rockne (Notre Dame '14)†	Notre Dame 1918–30	13	105	12	5	.881
Frank W. Leahy (Notre Dame '31)†	Boston College 1939–40; Notre Dame 1941–43, 1946–53	13	107	13	9	.864
George W. Woodruff (Yale 1889)†	Pennsylvania 1892–01; Illinois 1903; Carlisle 1905	12	142	25	2	.846
Barry Switzer (Arkansas '60)	Oklahoma 1973–88	16	157	29	4	.837
Tom Osborne (Hastings '59)†	Nebraska 1973–97	25	255	49	3	.836
Percy D. Haughton (Harvard 1899)†	Cornell 1899–1900; Harvard 1908–16; Columbia 1923–24	13	96	17	6	.832
Bob Neyland (Army '16)†	Tennessee 1926–34, 1936–40, 1946–52	21	173	31	12	.829
Fielding Yost (West Virginia 1895)†	Ohio Wesleyan 1897; Nebraska 1898; Kansas 1899; Stanford 1900; Michigan 1901–23, 1925–26	29	196	36	12	.828
Bud Wilkinson (Minnesota '37)†	Oklahoma 1947–63	17	145	29	4	.826
Jock Sutherland (Pittsburgh '18)†	Lafayette 1919–23; Pittsburgh 1924–38	20	144	28	14	.812
Bob Devaney (Alma [Mich] '39)†	Wyoming 1957–61; Nebraska 1962–72	16	136	30	7	.806
Frank W. Thomas (Notre Dame '23)†	Tenn.-Chattanooga 1925–28; Alabama 1931–42, 1944–46	19	141	33	9	.795
Henry L. Williams (Yale 1891)†	Army 1891; Minnesota 1900–21	23	141	34	12	.786
Gil Dobie (Minnesota '02)†	North Dakota St 1906–07; Washington 1908-16; Navy 1917–19; Cornell 1920–35; Boston College 1936–38	33	180	45	15	.781
Bear Bryant (Alabama '36)†	Maryland 1945, Kentucky 1946–53,	38	323	85	17	.780
Fred Folsom (Dartmouth 1895)	Colorado 1895–99, 1901–02; Dartmouth 1903–06; Colorado 1908–15	19	106	28	6	.779
Bo Schembechler (Miami [Ohio] '51)	Miami (Ohio) 1963–68; Michigan 1969–89	27	234	65	8	.775
*Phillip Fulmer (Tennessee '72)	Tennessee 1992–	15	137	41	0	.770

*Active in 2006. †Hall of Fame member.

Note: Minimum 10 years as head coach at Division I institutions; record at four-year colleges only; bowl games included; ranked by percentage, ties computed as half won, half lost.

ALLTIME WINNINGEST FBS (DIV. I-A) COACHES *(Cont.)*
By Victories

	Yrs	W	L	T	Pct		Yrs	W	L	T	Pct
*Bobby Bowden	41	366	113	4	.762	Bo Schembechler	27	234	65	8	.775
*Joe Paterno	41	363	121	3	.748	Hayden Fry	37	232	178	10	.564
Paul (Bear) Bryant	38	323	85	17	.780	Jess Neely	40	207	176	19	.539
Glenn (Pop) Warner	44	319	106	32	.733	Warren Woodson	31	203	95	14	.673
Amos Alonzo Stagg	57	314	199	35	.605	Don Nehlen	30	202	128	8	.609
LaVell Edwards	29	257	100	3	.718	Vince Dooley	25	201	77	10	.715
Tom Osborne	25	255	49	3	.836	Eddie Anderson	39	201	128	15	.606
Lou Holtz	33	249	132	7	.651	Jim Sweeney	32	200	154	4	.564
Woody Hayes	33	238	72	10	.759						

*Active in 2006.

Most Bowl Victories

	W	L	T		W	L	T
*Joe Paterno	22	10	1	Barry Switzer	8	5	0
*Bobby Bowden	20	9	1	Jackie Sherrill	8	6	0
Paul (Bear) Bryant	15	12	2	Darrell Royal	8	7	1
Lou Holtz	12	8	2	Vince Dooley	8	10	2
Tom Osborne	12	13	0	Pat Dye	7	2	1
Don James	10	5	0	Bob Devaney	7	3	0
John Vaught	10	8	0	Dan Devine	7	3	0
Bobby Dodd	9	4	0	Earle Bruce	7	5	0
*Mack Brown	9	6	0	Charlie McClendon	7	6	0
Johnny Majors	9	7	0	*Philip Fulmer	7	7	0
John Robinson	8	1	0	*Steve Spurrier	7	7	0
Barry Alvarez	8	3	0	Hayden Fry	7	9	1
Terry Donahue	8	4	1	LaVell Edwards	7	14	1

*Active in 2006.

WINNINGEST ACTIVE FBS (DIV. I-A) COACHES
By Percentage

Coach, College	Yrs	W	L	T	Pct.	Bowls W	L	T
Pete Carroll, USC	6	65	12	0	.844	4	2	0
Urban Meyer, Florida	6	61	12	0	.836	4	0	0
*Bob Stoops, Oklahoma	8	78	19	0	.804	4	3	0
Mark Richt, Georgia	6	61	17	0	.782	4	2	0
Phillip Fulmer, Tennessee	15	137	41	0	.770	7	7	0
Bobby Bowden, Florida St.	41	366	113	4	.762	20	9	1
Lloyd Carr, Michigan	12	113	36	0	.758	5	7	0
Steve Spurrier, South Carolina	17	157	50	2	.756	7	7	0
Joe Paterno, Penn St	41	363	121	3	.748	22	10	1
Paul Johnson, Navy	10	99	35	0	.739	2	2	0
Dan Hawkins, Colorado	11	94	33	1	.738	2	2	0
Jim Tressel, Ohio State	21	197	71	1	.733	4	1	0
Gary Patterson, TCU	6	54	20	0	.730	3	3	0
Butch Davis, North Carolina	6	51	20	0	.718	4	0	0
Chris Ault, Nevada	22	185	78	1	.703	1	3	0
Dennis Erickson, Arizona St	18	149	64	1	.699	5	5	0
Frank Solich, Ohio	8	71	64	0	.696	2	3	0
Nick Saban, Alabama	11	91	42	1	.683	3	5	0
Jeff Tedford, California	5	43	20	0	.683	3	1	0
Ralph Friedgen, Maryland	6	50	24	0	.676	3	1	0

#Bowl games included. Ties computed as half win, half loss. Note: Min. five years as Div. I-A head coach at four-year collges only. *Seven regular season wins and one bowl victory from Stoops' 2005 season at Oklahoma were vacated in 2007 due to NCAA rules violations.

By Victories

Bobby Bowden, Florida St	366	Steve Spurrier, South Carolina	157
Joe Paterno, Penn St	363	Mike Price, UTEP	150
Frank Beamer, Virginia Tech	198	Dennis Erickson, Arizona St	149
Jim Tressel, Ohio State	197	Phillip Fulmer, Tennessee	137
Chris Ault, Nevada	185	Howard Schellenberger, Fla. Atlantic	133
Dennis Franchione, Texas A&M	180	Larry Blakeney, Troy	127
Mack Brown, Texas	179	Sonny Lubick, Colorado St	126
Dick Tomey, San Jose St	170	Mike Bellotti, Oregon	118

WINNINGEST ACTIVE FCS (DIV. I-AA) COACHES
By Percentage

Coach, College	Yrs	W	L	T	Pct*
Mike Kelly, Dayton	26	235	53	1	.815
Al Bagnoli, Pennsylvania	25	190	63	0	.751
K.C. Keeler, Delaware	14	129	43	1	.749
Joe Taylor, Hampton	24	191	71	4	.726
Pete Lembo, Elon	6	49	20	0	.710
Pete Richardson, Southern Univ.	19	155	63	1	.710
Buddy Pough, South Carolina St	5	40	17	0	.702
Bobby Lamb, Furman	5	43	19	0	.694
Mark Farley, Northern Iowa	6	51	24	0	.680
Dan Brown, Massachusetts	10	78	37	0	.678
Dick Biddle, Colgate	11	88	42	0	.677

*Playoff games included.
Note: Minimum five years as a Division I-A and/or Division I-AA head coach; record at four-year colleges only.

By Victories

Mike Kelly, Dayton	235	Walt Hameline, Wagner	179
Bob Ford, Albany St	217	Jimmye Laycock, William & Mary	178
Joe Taylor, Hampton	191	Rob Ash, Montana St	176
Al Bagnoli, Pennsylvania	190	Andy Talley, Villanova	175
Jerry Moore, Appalachian St	181	Pete Richardson, Southern U.	155

WINNINGEST ACTIVE DIVISION II COACHES
By Percentage

Coach, College	Yrs	W	L	T	Pct*
Chuck Broyles, Pittsburg St (Kan.)	17	174	36	2	.825
Ken Sparks, Carson-Newman	27	259	62	2	.805
Bryan Collins, C.W. Post	9	80	120	0	.800
Dale Lennon, North Dakota	10	91	31	0	.746
Danny Hale, Bloomsburg	19	158	54	1	.742
John Luckhardt, California (Pa.)	22	169	58	2	.742
Peter Yetten, Bentley	19	139	51	1	.730
Tom Sawyer, Winona St	11	93	35	0	.727
Mark Hudspeth, North Alabama	5	44	17	0	.721
Mel Tjeerdsma, Northwest Missouri St	23	191	75	4	.715

*Ties computed as half win, half loss. Playoff games included.
Note: Minimum five years as a college head coach; record at four-year colleges only.

By Victories

Ken Sparks, Carson-Newman	259	John Luckhardt, California (Pa.)	169
Willard Bailey, St. Paul's	216	Monte Cater, Shepherd	169
Dennis Douds, East Stroudsburg	206	Danny Hale, Bloomsburg	158
Mel Tjeerdsma, Northwest Missouri St	191	Peter Yetten, Bentley	139
Chuck Broyles, Pittsburg St	174	Rocky Rees, Shippensburg	138

WINNINGEST ACTIVE DIVSION III COACHES
By Percentage

Coach, College	Yrs	W	L	T	Pct*
Larry Kehres, Mount Union	21	246	20	3	.920
Jim Purthill, St. Norbert	8	74	12	0	.860
Joe Fincham, Wittenberg	11	100	23	0	.813
Chris Creighton, Wabash	10	84	20	0	.808
Jay Accorsi, Rowan	5	47	12	0	.797
John Gagliardi, St. John's (Minn.)	58	443	120	11	.781
Jimmie Keeling, Hardin-Simmons	17	143	41	0	.777
Mike Swider, Wheaton (Ill.)	11	88	27	0	.765
Pete Fredenberg, Mary Hardin-Baylor	9	75	25	0	.750
†Dean Paul, Ohio Northern	8	54	18	0	.750

*Ties computed as half won, half lost. Playoff games included. †Dean Paul's 8–2 season with Ohio Northern in 2004 was later vacated.

Note: Minimum five years as a college head coach; record at four-year colleges only.

By Victories

John Gagliardi, St John's (Minn.)	443		Rich Lackner, Carnegie Mellon	148
Frank Girardi, Lycoming	254		Dale Widolff, Occidental	146
Larry Kehres, Mount Union	246		Michael DeLong, Springfield	146
Eric Hamilton, College of New Jersey	179		Jimmie Keeling, Hardin-Simmons	143
Wayne Perry, Hanover	172		Larry Kindham, Wash U.-St. Louis	142
Rick Giancola, Montclair St	164		Larry Streeter, Gettysburg	141

NAIA Coaches' Records

WINNINGEST ACTIVE NAIA COACHES
By Percentage

Coach, College	Yrs	W	L	T	Pct*
Bill Cronin, Georgetown (Ky.)	11	107	18	0	.856
Mike Van Diest, Carroll (Mont.)	9	89	18	0	.832
Mike Cochran, Southern Nazarene (Okla.)	6	53	15	0	.779
Mac Bryan, Pikeville College (Ky.)	6	48	16	1	.746
Hank Biesiot, Dickinson St (N.D.)	32	225	78	1	.742
Carl Poelker, McKendree (Ill.)	26	170	72	1	.702
Orv Otten, Northwestern (Ia.)	13	90	40	0	.692
Patrick Ross, Lindenwood (Mo.)	5	37	18	0	.673
Keith Barefield, Northwestern Oklamoma St.	10	66	33	2	.663
Kevin Donley, St. Francis (Ind.)	29	206	105	1	.662
Steve Ryan, Morningside College (Ia.)	5	37	19	0	.661
Paul Troth, Missouri Valley College	11	71	37	0	.657
Mike Feminis, St. Xavier (Ill.)	9	59	31	0	.656
Larry Wilcox, Benedictine (Kan.)	29	195	103	0	.654
Monty Lewis, Friends (Kan.)	14	85	46	0	.649

*Playoff games included.

Note: Minimum five years as a collegiate head coach and includes record against four-year institutions only.

By Victories

Hank Biesiot, Dickinson St (N.D.)	225		Jim Dennison, Walsh (Ohio)	168
Kevin Donley, St. Francis (Ind.)	206		Fran Schwenk, William Jewll (Mo.)	125
Larry Wilcox, Benedictine (Kan.)	195		Bob Green, Montana Tech	116
Vic Wallace, Lambuth (Tenn.)	172		Bill Cronin, Georgetown (Ky.)	107
Carl Poelker, McKendree (Ill.)	170		Merle Masonholder, Central Methodist (Mo.)	105

Pro Basketball

**Tim Duncan (r.)
of the NBA champion
San Antonio Spurs**

Dynasty with a Capital "D"

Flashy? Not so much. Boring? Maybe. Nonetheless, San Antonio's suffocating defense and selfless play led the Spurs to their fourth NBA title in nine seasons

BY STEPHEN CANNELLA

ON THE DAY BEFORE HIS team took on the Cleveland Cavaliers in Game 1 of the 2006–07 NBA Finals, San Antonio Spurs' coach Gregg Popovich put his squad through a workout that entailed, in the words of one San Antonio assistant, "things that eighth-grade teams do." The Spurs hustled through a shell drill, a four-on-four exercise designed to choreograph defensive rotations. It was the basketball equivalent of Hemingway practicing his penmanship before sitting down to write *The Old Man and the Sea*. The Spurs, the NBA's stingiest team during the regular season (they allowed a league-low 90.1 points per game), were already defensive wizards. Besides, the shell drill is so basic and boring that most NBA teams erase it from their to-do lists the second preseason training camp ends. It's impossible to envision, say, the practice-averse Allen Iverson putting his all into a shell drill on the eve of the Finals.

But there were Popovich's charges, minding their defensive Ps and Qs like the country's most overgrown intramural team. It was a microcosmic moment for the Spurs, a franchise built around an unassuming superstar (Tim Duncan) and upon the principles of teamwork, attention to detail, understated

excellence...and obsessive defense. In San Antonio, even on the eve of a championship series, it's the little things that matter.

To many fans, the Spurs' approach is a formula for—there's no other way to put it—boredom. While it's true that the Spurs' artistry is subtle, there's no denying its effectiveness. San Antonio overwhelmed LeBron James and the Cavaliers in a Finals sweep, giving the franchise its fourth NBA title in nine years. That's one more championship than the New York Yankees, New England Patriots and Detroit Red Wings have won in the same span, making the low-key Spurs the most successful franchise in pro sports over the last decade. As former NBA coach and ESPN analyst Jack Ramsey said after the Finals, "If you're in the basketball business, the Spurs are who you want to be."

That's true as long as on-court success is your main concern; if media attention is what you're after, the Spurs model is useless. The basketball-watching public (to say nothing of casual sports fans) has never fully embraced a group of players who play the game methodically and sublimate their individual talents and personalities to the team's. Never mind that the Spurs are hardly bland once you get to know them. Yes, Duncan is a colorless media personal-

ity, but he's also the best power forward to ever play the game. Argentinian guard Manu Ginobili plays with a controlled and entertaining recklessness that is evident every time he crashes through the lane. And point guard Tony Parker, who averaged 24.5 points against Cleveland and was named the Finals MVP, even brought the Spurs some tabloid glitz: A few weeks after the championship, the Frenchman married *Desperate Housewives* starlet Eva Longoria in a lavish affair outside of his native Paris. "We are kind of the vanilla of the NBA," Ginobili said during the Finals. "It's a good vanilla, not a boring vanilla."

At least in terms of storylines, the Cavaliers were the perfect Finals foil for the staid Spurs. The 22-year-old James, with his $90 million Nike endorsement contract and many commercial appearances, is the anti-Duncan: He's the NBA's most marketed player and a worldwide media personality.

Three-time NBA Finals MVP Tim Duncan (l.) watched teammate Tony Parker take home the MVP hardware at the 2007 Finals.

And while there's little novelty left in an appearance by San Antonio in the Finals, the Cavs were playing for a championship for the first time in the franchise's 37-year history. After the Detroit Pistons were dispatched in the Eastern Conference finals, Cleveland became giddy at the prospect of exorcising the ghosts of the city's tortured pro sports history.

David Stern had to be thrilled at the prospect of James in the Finals as well. The Cavs' ascension and their star's heroics in the Eastern Conference playoffs (before knocking off Detroit in six games, Cleveland eliminated the Washington Wizards and New Jersey Nets) marked the dawn of a new era for the NBA: The reign of King James. When he broke into the league as an

JOHN BIEVER/SPORTS ILLUSTRATED

Criticized for not taking control down the stretch, LeBron James silenced the doubters with a historic 48-point performance in Game 5 of the Eastern Conference Finals.

18-year-old in 2003, James was anointed as the heir to Michael Jordan's throne, a transcendent NBA star for the 21st century. In carrying his team to the Finals in his fourth season—Jordan, it's worth noting, didn't win a conference championship until his seventh—James made it official. His time had come.

Assuming he eventually wins an NBA ring, James's playoff legend will be said to have bloomed in Game 5 of the Eastern Conference finals. After losing the first two games of the series on the road, the Cavs fought back to tie the series on their home court, setting the stage for an epic Game 5 in Detroit. Technically the win was credited

to the Cavaliers (109–107, in double overtime), but James was a one-man team. He finished with 48 points, nine rebounds and seven assists. He scored the Cavs' final 25 points, 18 of which came in the two overtime periods, and by the end the normally combative Pistons seemed dazed by his brilliance. As James displayed his arsenal—power dunks created off the dribble, midrange jumpers, and deadly fadeaways off the post—the Pistons' vaunted defense crumbled, often failing to stop James with double teams or failing to pick him up when he blew by any poor sap who dared try to guard him one-on-one. It was one of the most sublime individual performances in NBA playoff history, instantly ranking next to Magic Johnson's 42-point masterpiece in the 1980 Finals and Jordan's 63-point explosion against the Boston Celtics in '86. Said Cavaliers coach Mike Brown, "That was the single best game I've ever seen at this level in this atmosphere, hands down."

James's performance in Game 6, which Cleveland won 98–82 to clinch the series, was less gaudy but equally impressive. Rather than try to duplicate his Game 5 pyrotechnics, James demonstrated maturity beyond his years, staying calm amid a defensive assault from Detroit and spreading the ball around to unguarded teammates. He finished with 20 points, and rookie Daniel (Boobie) Gibson led the Cavs with a career-high 31, a performance Brown called "LeBronesque." It wasn't quite that, but the comment was a reminder that all revolves around LeBron in Cleveland. The year before he arrived the Cavs won 17 games. Since then they've gone 35–47, 42–40 and 50–32. "Z has been through a lot, been through losing seasons, year after year after year," James said while basking in the Game 6 win, referring to center and 11-year Cleveland veteran Zydrunas Ilgauskas. "I promised him when I got drafted, I was going to try to change it."

But a championship would have to wait. The defense-first Spurs held James to 14 points in a 85–76 win in Game 1, then sprinted to a 29-point lead in Game 2 before winning 103–92. The Cavs made it close in Games 3 and 4 at home but lost each time, by deficits of three and one, respectively. In the series James shot just 35.6 percent and averaged 22 points, well below his overall playoff averages of 41.6 percent and 25.1 points, and even his star power wasn't able to raise interest in the one-sided series among television viewers. The Spurs' sweep drew a Nielsen rating of 6.2 and averaged 9.3 million viewers, record lows for the NBA Finals.

The fizzle of the Finals was in stark contrast to the buzz created earlier in the playoffs by the Golden State Warriors. After sneaking into the postseason as the eighth seed in the Western Conference, the band of outcasts and second-tier players led by coach Don Nelson ambushed the Dallas Mavericks in the first round. The six-game victory, which was sparked by the electric shooting of guard Baron Davis (25.0 points per game) was a stunning upset, and not only because the Mavs, at 67–15, were the league's best regular-season team and Golden State (42–40) didn't clinch a playoff spot until the final day of the schedule. Dallas was the first top seed in NBA history to lose to an eighth seed in a seven-game series. "This is as much fun as I've had coaching," said the 66-year-old Nelson, the second-winningest coach in NBA history. "I've never enjoyed a year more than this one."

Golden State's magic ran out in a second-round loss to the Utah Jazz, who then fell to San Antonio in the Western Conference finals. Still, for a few blissful weeks the NBA overshadowed even Barry Bonds's chase for Hank Aaron's home run record in the Bay Area. Down in Southern California Los Angeles Lakers guard Kobe Bryant surely followed the Warriors' exploits with envy. For the second year in a row, the Lakers failed to advance past the first round of the playoffs; this time L.A. was done in by the Phoenix Suns. Bryant's frustration bubbled over during the summer, when he said he wanted to be traded if the Lakers front office didn't improve the roster during the offseason.

Bryant later backed off the demand, but more than a few teams would be happy to have him. He led the league in scoring (31.6 points per game) and during one memorable stretch in March scored 50 or more points in four straight games. It was the first time in 45 years a player had strung together four straight 50-point performances.

It's telling, perhaps, that Bryant's scoring outburst came after January 1. That's the day the NBA began using its traditional leather ball again after an ill-conceived, two-month experiment with a synthetic model. The new ball was supposed to have an improved grip and wick away moisture, but it was widely panned by players for being too slippery. Shaquille O'Neal complained that it felt like a cheap toy. Bryant more diplomatically said, "I'm old school, so I love the old-school ball."

It was a New Coke moment for the NBA, and Stern finally was persuaded to shelve the synthetic balls and bring leather back starting on New Year's Day. The players were less successful in overturning another

GREG NELSON

Will the Western Conference's dominance continue? The top two 2007 draft picks, Greg Oden and Kevin Durant (above, left), went to Portland and Seattle, respectively.

Stern-directed innovation: The so-called Rasheed Wallace Rule, a crackdown on arguing with referees. Officials were instructed to issue technical fouls for the slightest post-whistle whining, and the zebras followed orders. Overall 1,109 technicals were handed out during the regular season, up from 1,014 in 2005-06.

All those technical fouls took on a more sinister light, however, when veteran NBA referee Tim Donaghy was indicted and eventually pleaded guilty during the off-season to giving gamblers inside information and personally betting on NBA games from 2003 through 2007. (Even after his plea agreement, it was not clear which games he bet on or whether he fixed games or shaved points through his officiating calls.) The allegations rocked the league and left the usually unflappable Stern scrambling to restore the fans' faith in the sport.

Of course, some teams may not have minded handing the opposition the chance to score easy points. The 2007 draft class, led by seven-foot Ohio State center Greg Oden and Texas forward Kevin Durant, was the deepest since at least '03, when James and Carmelo Anthony entered the league.

Late in the season, there were whispers that some teams out of the playoff races were tanking games to improve their chance of winning the top pick in the draft lottery. The Grizzlies ended up with the league's worst record (22-60), but the lottery was won by the Trail Blazers, who made Oden the No. 1 pick. (Durant went to the Seattle SuperSonics at No. 2.) Oden joined a Portland team already stocked with young talent, including 2006-07 Rookie of the Year Brandon Roy, although a microfracture knee injury during the off-season meant that Oden would have to delay his debut until the 2008–09 season.

Alas, even when he does finally start, the Blazers will still be in the Western Conference, where the Spurs rule. San Antonio was due to return virtually intact for the 2007–08 season and had a corps of young players that could continue their success well beyond that. Boring? Maybe, but the Spurs look like a dynasty nonetheless.

NBA Final Standings

Eastern Conference
ATLANTIC DIVISION

Team	W	L	Pct	GB
†Toronto	47	35	.573	—
*New Jersey	41	41	.500	6
Philadelphia	35	47	.427	12
New York	33	49	.402	14
Boston	24	58	.293	23

CENTRAL DIVISION

Team	W	L	Pct	GB
‡Detroit	53	29	.646	—
*Cleveland	50	32	.610	3
*Chicago	49	33	.598	4
Indiana	35	47	.427	18
Milwaukee	28	54	.341	25

SOUTHEAST DIVISION

Team	W	L	Pct	GB
†Miami	44	38	.537	—
*Washington	41	41	.500	3
*Orlando	40	42	.488	4
Charlotte	33	49	.402	11
Atlanta	30	52	.366	14

Western Conference
NORTHWEST DIVISION

Team	W	L	Pct	GB
†Utah	51	31	.622	—
*Denver	45	37	.549	6
Portland	32	50	.390	19
Minnesota	32	50	.390	19
Seattle	31	51	.378	20

PACIFIC DIVISION

Team	W	L	Pct	GB
†Phoenix	61	21	.744	—
*LA Lakers	42	40	.512	19
*Golden State	42	40	.512	19
LA Clippers	40	42	.488	21
Sacramento	33	49	.402	28

SOUTHWEST DIVISION

Team	W	L	Pct	GB
‡Dallas	67	15	.817	—
*San Antonio	58	24	.707	9
*Houston	52	30	.634	15
New Orleans/Okla. City	39	43	.476	28
Memphis	22	60	.268	45

†Clinched division title.   *Clinched playoff berth.   ‡Clinched conference title.

2007 NBA Playoffs

EASTERN CONFERENCE

1st ROUND	SEMIFINALS	FINALS

Detroit
Orlando
Detroit (4-0)
Miami
Chicago
Chicago (4-0)
Detroit (4-2)
Toronto
New Jersey
New Jersey (4-2)
Cleveland (4-2)
Cleveland
Washington
Cleveland (4-0)

NBA FINALS

San Antonio (4-0)

WESTERN CONFERENCE

FINALS	SEMIFINALS	1st ROUND

Dallas
Golden St
Golden St (4-2)
Utah
Houston
Utah (4-3)
Utah (4-1)
San Antonio
Denver
San Antonio (4-1)
San Antonio (4-1)
Phoenix
LA Lakers
Phoenix (4-1)
San Antonio (4-2)

2007 NBA Playoff Results

Eastern Conference First Round

Game 1......Orlando	92	at Detroit	100
Game 2......Orlando	90	at Detroit	98
Game 3......Detroit	93	at Orlando	77
Game 4......Detroit	97	at Orlando	93

Detroit won series 4–0.

Game 1......New Jersey	96	at Toronto	91
Game 2......New Jersey	83	at Toronto	89
Game 3......Toronto	89	at New Jersey	102
Game 4......Toronto	81	at New Jersey	102
Game 5......New Jersey	96	at Toronto	98
Game 6......Toronto	97	at New Jersey	98

New Jersey won series 4–2.

Game 1......Washington	82	at Cleveland	97
Game 2......Washington	102	at Cleveland	109
Game 3......Cleveland	98	at Washington	92
Game 4......Cleveland	97	at Washington	90

Cleveland won series 4–0.

Game 1......Miami	91	at Chicago	96
Game 2......Miami	89	at Chicago	107
Game 3......Chicago	104	at Miami	96
Game 4......Chicago	92	at Miami	79

Chicago won series 4–0.

Western Conference First Round

Game 1......Golden State	97	at Dallas	85
Game 2......Golden State	99	at Dallas	112
Game 3......Dallas	91	at Golden St	109
Game 4......Dallas	99	at Golden St	103
Game 5......Golden State	112	at Dallas	118
Game 6......Dallas	86	at Golden St	111

Golden State won series 4–2.

Game 1......Denver	95	at San Antonio	89
Game 2......Denver	88	at San Antonio	97
Game 3......San Antonio	96	at Denver	91
Game 4......San Antonio	96	at Denver	89
Game 5......Denver	78	at San Antonio	93

San Antonio won series 4–1.

Game 1......LA Lakers	87	at Phoenix	95
Game 2......LA Lakers	98	at Phoenix	126
Game 3......Phoenix	89	at LA Lakers	95
Game 4......Phoenix	113	at LA Lakers	100
Game 5......LA Lakers	110	at Phoenix	119

Phoenix won series 4–1.

Game 1......Utah	75	at Houston	84
Game 2......Utah	90	at Houston	98
Game 3......Houston	67	at Utah	81
Game 4......Houston	85	at Utah	98
Game 5......Utah	92	at Houston	96
Game 6......Houston	82	at Utah	94
Game 7......Utah	103	at Houston	99

Utah won series 4–3.

Eastern Conference Semifinals

Game 1......New Jersey	77	at Cleveland	81
Game 2......New Jersey	92	at Cleveland	102
Game 3......Cleveland	85	at New Jersey	96
Game 4......Cleveland	87	at New Jersey	85
Game 5......New Jersey	83	at Cleveland	72
Game 6......Cleveland	88	at New Jersey	72

Cleveland won series 4–2.

Game 1......Chicago	69	at Detroit	95
Game 2......Chicago	87	at Detroit	108
Game 3......Detroit	81	at Chicago	74
Game 4......Detroit	87	at Chicago	102
Game 5......Chicago	108	at Detroit	92
Game 6......Detroit	95	at Chicago	85

Detroit won series 4–2.

Western Conference Semifinals

Game 1......Golden State	112	at Utah	116
Game 2......Golden State	117	at Utah	127*
Game 3......Utah	105	at Golden State	125
Game 4......Utah	115	at Golden State	101
Game 5......Golden State	87	at Utah	100

Utah won series 4–1

Game 1......San Antonio	111	at Phoenix	106
Game 2......San Antonio	81	at Phoenix	101
Game 3......Phoenix	101	at San Antonio	108
Game 4......Phoenix	104	at San Antonio	98
Game 5......San Antonio	88	at Phoenix	85
Game 6......Phoenix	106	at San Antonio	114

San Antonio won series 4–2.

Eastern Conference Finals

Game 1......Cleveland	76	at Detroit	79
Game 2......Cleveland	76	at Detroit	79
Game 3......Detroit	82	at Cleveland	88
Game 4......Detroit	87	at Cleveland	91
Game 5......Cleveland	109	at Detroit	107†
Game 6......Detroit	82	at Cleveland	98

Cleveland won series 4–2.

Western Conference Finals

Game 1......Utah	100	at San Antonio	108
Game 2......Utah	96	at San Antonio	105
Game 3......San Antonio	83	at Utah	109
Game 4......San Antonio	91	at Utah	79
Game 5......Utah	84	at San Antonio	109

San Antonio won series 4–1.

NBA Finals

Game 1......Cleveland	76	at San Antonio	85
Game 2......Cleveland	92	at San Antonio	103
Game 3......San Antonio	75	at Cleveland	72
Game 4......San Antonio	83	at Cleveland	82

San Antonio won series 4–0.

* Overtime. †Double overtime.

CLEVELAND CAVALIERS

Player	GP	Mpg	FG%	3FG%	FT%	Rebounds Off	Rebounds Total	Apg	Spg	Bpg	TO	Ppg
LeBron James	4	42.5	.356	.200	.690	1.0	7.0	6.8	1.0	0.5	5.8	22.0
Drew Gooden	4	27.5	.500	.000	.875	3.0	8.3	0.3	0.3	0.5	1.3	12.8
Daniel Gibson	4	34.8	.439	.316	1.000	0.3	1.8	2.5	1.5	0.0	0.0	10.8
Aleksandar Pavlovic	4	31.8	.364	.417	.333	1.0	2.5	0.8	0.5	0.0	1.3	9.8
Zydrunas Ilgauskas	4	25.8	.351	.000	.833	4.5	10.3	0.5	0.5	1.0	1.0	7.8
Anderson Varejao	4	24.5	.667	.000	.625	1.5	5.3	0.8	1.3	0.5	0.5	7.5
Damon Jones	4	16.3	.455	.556	1.000	0.3	1.3	1.0	0.0	0.0	0.0	4.5
Donyell Marshall	4	15.3	.313	.182	.750	0.5	2.3	1.3	0.8	0.0	0.5	3.8
Eric Snow	4	10.3	.400	.000	.500	0.3	1.0	2.3	0.3	0.3	0.3	1.3
Larry Hughes	2	22.0	.100	.000	.000	0.0	2.5	1.0	0.5	0.0	1.0	1.0
Ira Newble	1	1.0	.000	.000	.000	0.0	1.0	0.0	0.0	0.0	0.0	0.0
Scot Pollard	1	1.0	.000	.000	.000	0.0	0.0	0.0	0.0	0.0	0.0	0.0
Shannon Brown	1	0.0	.000	.000	.000	0.0	0.0	0.0	0.0	0.0	0.0	0.0
Avg/Total	**4**	**240.0**	**.395**	**.293**	**.693**	**12.3**	**41.0**	**16.5**	**6.2**	**2.8**	**11.8**	**80.5**

SAN ANTONIO SPURS

Player	GP	Mpg	FG%	3FG%	FT%	Rebounds Off	Rebounds Total	Apg	Spg	Bpg	TO	Ppg
Tony Parker	4	37.8	.568	.571	.526	0.8	5.0	3.3	0.8	0.0	3.0	24.5
Tim Duncan	4	37.3	.446	.000	.625	4.0	11.5	3.8	1.3	2.3	2.8	18.3
Manu Ginobili	4	29.3	.367	.435	.833	0.3	5.8	2.5	1.3	0.0	2.3	17.8
Bruce Bowen	4	41.8	.296	.389	.250	0.8	5.5	1.3	0.5	0.3	0.8	6.0
Fabricio Oberto	4	20.8	.471	.000	.333	1.8	4.3	0.5	0.3	0.0	1.0	4.3
Francisco Elson	4	11.5	1.00	.000	.800	1.5	2.5	0.0	0.3	0.0	0.8	4.0
Michael Finley	4	18.5	.261	.083	.667	0.3	2.0	1.25	0.0	0.0	3.8	3.8
Brent Barry	4	10.5	.364	.400	.000	0.3	1.5	0.5	0.3	0.0	0.8	3.0
Robert Horry	4	22.0	.333	.375	.750	1.0	4.5	3.3	0.3	1.3	1.3	3.0
Jacque Vaughn	4	10.3	.571	.000	.000	0.3	1.3	1.0	0.0	0.0	0.0	2.0
Beno Udrih	2	0.5	.000	.000	.000	0.0	0.0	0.0	0.0	0.0	0.0	0.0
Avg/Total	**4**	**240.0**	**.444**	**.372**	**.663**	**10.8**	**43.8**	**16.8**	**6.0**	**3.8**	**13.0**	**86.5**

Game 1

CLEVELAND 76

Player	Min	FG M-A	FT M-A	Reb O-T	A	PF	S	TO	TP
L. Hughes	23	1-5	0-0	0-3	0	2	0	0	2
A. Pavlovic	37	6-12	1-2	2-5	0	2	0	1	13
D. Gooden	26	6-9	2-2	1-4	0	4	1	2	14
L. James	44	4-16	4-4	1-7	4	1	1	6	14
Z. Ilgauskas	23	1-8	0-0	2-6	1	2	1	0	2
A. Varejao	31	3-6	4-7	3-4	0	3	0	1	10
D. Gibson	28	7-9	0-0	0-1	4	1	4	0	14
D. Marshall	16	2-5	0-0	0-2	0	1	1	1	5
D. Jones	12	0-0	0-0	0-0	0	0	0	0	0
E. Snow	1	0-0	0-0	0-0	0	0	0	0	0
Totals	240	30-70	11-15	9-32	9	16	8	11	76

Percentages: FG—.429, FT—.733. 3-pt goals: 5-15, .333 (Hughes 0-1, Pavlovic 0-1, James 2-6, Gibson 2-3, Marshall 1-4). Team rebounds: 7. Blocked shots: 2 (James, Ilgauskas).

SAN ANTONIO 85

Player	Min	FG M-A	FT M-A	Reb O-T	A	PF	S	TO	TP
T. Parker	38	12-23	3-6	1-4	7	1	2	4	27
M. Finley	20	1-7	0-0	0-3	0	1	0	0	2
T. Duncan	39	10-17	4-5	5-13	1	2	2	2	24
B. Bowen	40	2-6	0-0	1-3	1	1	0	1	6
F. Oberto	17	0-2	0-0	2-4	2	3	0	1	0
M. Ginobili	28	5-12	3-4	0-8	0	3	1	2	16
R. Horry	23	1-3	0-0	0-1	6	2	1	3	3
F. Elson	16	2-2	1-1	3-6	0	1	0	0	5
J. Vaughn	10	1-3	0-0	1-1	1	0	0	0	2
B. Barry	8	0-0	0-0	0-0	0	1	0	1	0
B. Udrih	1	0-0	0-0	0-0	0	0	0	0	0
Totals	240	34-75	11-16	13-43	18	15	6	14	85

Percentages: FG—.453, FT—.688. 3-pt goals: 6-16, .375 (Finley 0-4, Bowen 2-4, Ginobili 3-5, Horry 1-3). Team rebounds: 8. Blocked shots: 5 (Duncan 5).

A: 18,797. Officials: Callahan, Javie, Mauer.

Game 2

CLEVELAND 92

Player	Min	FG M-A	FT M-A	Reb O-T	A	PF	S	TO	TP
L. Hughes	20	0-5	0-0	0-2	2	1	1	2	0
A. Pavlovic	27	4-11	0-2	2-4	0	1	1	3	10
D. Gooden	24	6-12	1-1	3-6	0	2	0	0	13
L. James	38	9-21	7-11	3-7	6	3	1	6	25
Z. Ilgauskas	22	3-8	3-3	1-4	0	3	0	0	9
D. Gibson	32	6-12	1-1	0-1	0	3	1	0	15
A. Varejao	28	2-2	4-7	1-10	2	4	0	0	8
D. Marshall	21	1-4	2-2	1-2	3	2	1	0	5
D. Jones	15	2-4	0-0	1-3	0	0	0	0	6
E. Snow	11	0-1	1-2	1-2	2	0	0	0	1
S. Pollard	1	0-0	0-0	0-0	0	0	0	0	0
I. Newble	1	0-1	0-0	0-1	0	0	0	0	0
Totals	240	33-81	19-29	13-42	15	19	5	11	92

Percentages: FG—.407, FT—.655. 3-pt goals: 7-19, .368 (Hughes 0-1, Pavlovic 2-3, Gooden 0-2, Gibson 2-5, Marshall 1-3, Jones 2-3, Newble 0-1). Team rebounds: 12. Blocked shots: 2 (Gooden, Ilgauskas).

SAN ANTONIO 103

Player	Min	FG M-A	FT M-A	Reb O-T	A	PF	S	TO	TP
T. Parker	36	13-20	3-4	1-4	2	2	1	2	30
M. Finley	15	1-4	0-0	1-1	2	2	1	1	2
T. Duncan	36	9-16	5-7	4-9	8	4	0	1	23
B. Bowen	41	1-9	0-0	1-5	0	1	1	1	3
F. Oberto	20	2-3	0-2	1-4	0	3	0	1	4
M. Ginobili	28	5-11	11-11	0-6	2	5	3	3	25
R. Horry	26	1-3	2-2	2-9	4	3	0	0	5
F. Elson	13	3-3	0-0	2-3	0	3	0	1	6
J. Vaughn	12	0-0	0-0	0-3	2	0	0	0	0
B. Barry	12	1-6	0-0	0-2	1	0	0	0	3
B. Udrih	1	0-0	0-0	0-0	0	0	0	0	0
Totals	240	37-77	21-26	12-46	21	23	6	10	103

Percentages: FG—.481, FT—.808. 3-pt goals: 8-24, .333 (Parker 1-1, Finley 0-3, Bowen 1-6, Ginobili 4-6, Horry 1-2, Barry 1-6). Team rebounds: 3. Blocked shots: 6 (Horry 5, Bowen).

A: 18,797. Officials: Bavetta, Clark, DeRosa.

Game 3

SAN ANTONIO 75

Player	Min	FG M-A	FT M-A	Reb O-T	A	PF	S	TO	TP
T. Parker	39	7-17	2-4	1-5	3	0	0	3	17
M. Finley	24	3-17	0-0	0-2	1	1	4	1	7
T. Duncan	34	6-17	2-2	2-9	3	4	1	2	14
B. Bowen	44	4-6	1-4	0-9	1	1	1	3	13
F. Oberto	21	3-7	0-0	1-4	0	3	0	2	6
M. Ginobili	27	0-7	3-4	0-4	5	2	0	3	3
R. Horry	20	1-1	0-0	0-0	5	2	1	0	2
B. Barry	17	3-5	0-0	1-2	0	1	1	1	9
J. Vaughn	9	1-1	0-0	0-0	0	1	0	0	2
F. Elson	6	0-0	1-2	1-1	0	1	0	1	1
Totals	240	28-68	9-16	7-41	15	15	7	14	75

Percentages: FG—.412, FT—.563. 3-pt goals: 10-19, .526 (Parker 1-3, Finley 1-3, Bowen 4-5, Ginobili 0-3, Horry 1-1, Barry 3-4). Team rebounds: 8. Blocked shots: 2 (Duncan 2).

CLEVELAND 72

Player	Min	FG M-A	FT M-A	Reb O-T	A	PF	S	TO	TP
D. Gibson	36	1-10	0-0	0-3	1	0	1	0	2
A. Pavlovic	42	5-15	1-2	0-0	3	3	0	1	13
D. Gooden	33	5-11	3-4	4-12	1	6	0	2	13
L. James	42	9-23	7-8	0-8	7	3	2	5	25
Z. Ilgauskas	32	6-13	0-1	10-18	0	2	1	3	12
D. Jones	18	1-2	0-0	0-1	2	1	0	0	2
E. Snow	17	0-0	0-0	0-1	5	0	1	0	0
A. Varejao	15	2-4	0-0	1-4	0	1	2	1	4
D. Marshall	6	0-1	0-0	0-0	0	1	0	0	1
Totals	240	29-79	11-15	15-48	19	17	7	12	72

Percentages: FG—.367, FT—.733. 3-pt goals: 3-19, .158 (Gibson 0-5, Pavlovic 2-6, James 0-5, Jones 1-2, Marshall 0-1). Team rebounds: 4. Blocked shots: 5 (Varejao 2, Gooden, James, Ilgauskas).

A: 20,562. Officials: Crawford, Delaney, Fryer.

Game 4

SAN ANTONIO 83

Player	Min	FG M-A	FT M-A	Reb O-T	A	PF	S	TO	TP
T. Parker	39	10-14	2-5	0-7	1	2	0	3	24
M. Finley	16	1-5	2-3	0-2	0	0	0	0	4
T. Duncan	40	4-15	4-10	5-15	3	3	2	6	12
B. Bowen	42	1-6	0-0	1-5	3	4	0	0	2
F. Oberto	25	3-5	1-1	3-5	0	2	1	0	7
M. Ginobili	33	8-19	8-11	1-5	3	5	1	1	27
R. Horry	19	0-2	1-2	1-3	1	1	0	2	1
F. Elson	11	1-1	2-2	0-0	0	0	1	1	4
J. Vaughn	9	1-1	0-0	0-1	1	1	0	0	2
B. Barry	5	0-0	0-0	0-2	1	1	0	1	0
Totals	240	29-68	20-34	11-45	13	19	5	14	83

Percentages: FG—.426, FT—.588. 3-pt goals: 5-19, .263 (Parker 2-3, Finley 0-2, Bowen 0-3, Ginobili 3-9, Horry 0-2). Team rebounds: 12. Blocked shots: 2 (Duncan 2).

CLEVELAND 82

Player	Min	FG M-A	FT M-A	Reb O-T	A	PF	S	TO	TP
D. Gibson	44	4-10	0-0	1-2	5	4	0	0	10
A. Pavlovic	21	1-6	0-0	0-1	0	4	1	0	3
D. Gooden	27	5-12	1-1	4-11	0	2	0	1	11
L. James	46	10-30	2-6	0-6	10	1	0	6	24
Z. Ilgauskas	26	3-8	2-2	5-13	1	3	0	1	8
A. Varejao	24	3-3	2-2	1-3	1	4	3	0	8
D. Jones	20	2-5	3-3	0-1	2	1	0	0	9
D. Marshall	19	2-6	1-12	1-4	2	4	1	1	5
E. Snow	13	2-4	0-0	0-1	2	1	0	1	4
S. Brown	1	0-0	0-0	0-0	0	0	0	0	0
Totals	240	32-84	11-16	12-42	23	24	5	10	82

Percentages: FG—.381, FT—.688. 3-pt goals: 7-22, .318 (Gibson 2-6, Pavlovic 1-2, James 2-7, Jones 2-4, Marshall 0-3). Team rebounds: 11. Blocked shots: 2 (Ilgauskas, Snow).

A: 20,562. Officials: Forte, Rush, Salvatore.

2006–07 All-NBA Teams

FIRST TEAM
F Tim Duncan, SA
F Dirk Nowitzki, Dall
C Amare Stoudemire, Phoe
G Steve Nash, Phoe
G Kobe Bryant, LAL

SECOND TEAM
F Chris Bosh, Tor
F LeBron James, Clev
C Yao Ming, Hou
G Gilbert Arenas, Wash
G Tracy McGrady, Hou

THIRD TEAM
F Kevin Garnett, Minn
F Carmelo Anthony, Den
C Dwight Howard, Orl
G Dwyane Wade, Mia
G Chauncey Billups, Det

All-Defensive Team

FIRST TEAM
F Tim Duncan, SA
F Bruce Bowen, SA
C Marcus Camby, Den
G Kobe Bryant, LAL
G Raja Bell, Phoe

SECOND TEAM
F Tayshaun Prince, Det
F Kevin Garnett, Minn
C Ben Wallace, Chi
G Kirk Hinrich, Chi
G Jason Kidd, NJ

All-Rookie Teams

FIRST TEAM
Brandon Roy, Port
Andrea Bargnani, Tor
Randy Foy, Minn
Rudy Gay, Mem
Jorge Garbajosa, Tor
LaMarcus Aldridge, Port

SECOND TEAM
Paul Millsap, Utah
Adam Morrison, Char
Tyrus Thomas, Chi
Craig Smith, Minn
Rajon Rondo, Bost
Walter Herrmann, Char
Marcus Williams, NJ

Scoring

	GP	Pts	Avg
Kobe Bryant LAL	77	2,430	31.6
Carmelo Anthony, Den	65	1,881	28.9
Gilbert Arenas, Wash	74	2,150	28.4
LeBron James, Cle	78	2,132	27.3
Ray Allen, Sea	55	1,454	26.4
Allen Iverson, Den/Phi	65	1,709	26.3
Vince Carter, NJ	82	2,070	25.2
Joe Johnson, Atl	57	1,426	25.0
Tracy McGrady, Hou	71	1,747	24.6
Dirk Nowitzki, Dal	78	1,916	24.6

Rebounds

	GP	Reb	Avg
Kevin Garnett, Minn	76	975	12.8
Tyson Chandler, NO-OC	73	904	12.4
Dwight Howard, Orl	82	1,008	12.3
Carlos Boozer, Utah	74	867	11.7
Marcus Camby, Den	70	816	11.7
Ben Wallace, Chi	77	821	10.7
Tim Duncan, SA	80	845	10.6
Shawn Marion, Phoe	80	785	9.8
Amare Stoudemire, Phoe	82	786	9.6
Elton Brand, LAC	80	744	9.3

Assists

	GP	Assists	Avg
Steve Nash, Phoe	76	884	11.6
Deron Williams, Utah	80	745	9.3
Jason Kidd, NJ	80	736	9.2
Chris Paul, Nor	64	569	8.9
Baron Davis, GS	63	509	8.1
T.J. Ford, Tor	75	595	7.9
Andre Miller, Den/Phi	80	625	7.8
Allen Iverson, Phi/Den	65	468	7.2
Chauncey Billups, Det	70	502	7.2
Raymond Felton, Cha	78	545	7.0

Field-Goal Percentage

	FGA	FGM	Pct
Mikki Moore, NJ	506	308	.609
Dwight Howard, Orl	873	526	.603
Andris Biedrins, GS	581	348	.599
Eddy Curry, NY	1,016	585	.576
Amare Stoudemire, Phoe	1,055	607	.575
Carlos Boozer, Utah	1,154	647	.561
Andrew Bogut, Mil	629	348	.553
Ruben Patterson, Mil	867	475	.548
Tim Duncan, SA	1,131	618	.546
Samuel Dalembert, Phi	658	356	.541

Free-Throw Percentage

	FTA	FTM	Pct
Kyle Korver, Phi	209	191	.914
Matt Carroll, Cha	208	188	.904
Dirk Nowitzki, Dal	551	498	.904
Ray Allen, Sea	309	279	.903
Steve Nash, Phoe	247	222	.899
Earl Boykins, Den/Mil	245	220	.898
Tyronn Lue, Atl	163	144	.883
Chauncey Billups, Det	437	386	.883
Damien Wilkins, Sea	170	150	.882
Sam Cassell, LAC	182	160	.879

Three-Point Field-Goal Percentage

	3FGA	3FGM	Pct
Jason Kapono, Mia	210	108	.514
Steve Nash, Phoe	343	156	.454
Brent Barry, SA	287	128	.446
Luther Head, Hou	401	177	.441
Anthony Parker, Tor	261	115	.441
Jason Terry, Dal	370	162	.438
Leandro Barbosa, Phoe	438	190	.434
Al Harrington, GS/Ind	293	127	.433
Kyle Korver, Phi	307	132	.430
Eddie House, NJ	175	75	.429

Steals

	GP	Steals	Avg
Baron Davis, GS	63	135	2.14
Ron Artest, Sac	70	149	2.13
Caron Butler, Was	63	134	2.13
Andre Iguodala, Phi	76	152	2.00
Gerald Wallace, Cha	72	144	2.00
Shawn Marion, Phoe	80	156	1.95
Allen Iverson, Phi/Den	65	123	1.89
Gilbert Arenas, Was	74	139	1.88
Monta Ellis, GS	77	132	1.71
Rajon Rondo, Bos	78	128	1.64

Blocked Shots

	GP	BS	Avg
Marcus Camby, Den	70	231	3.30
Josh Smith, Atl	72	207	2.88
Jermaine O'Neal, Ind	69	182	2.64
Emeka Okafor, Cha	67	172	2.57
Tim Duncan, SA	80	190	2.38
Alonzo Mourning, Mia	77	178	2.31
Elton Brand, LAC	80	179	2.24
Pau Gasol, Mem	59	126	2.14
Andrei Kirilenko, Utah	70	144	2.06
Ben Wallace, Chi	77	156	2.03

Offense

Team	FG Pct	3FG Pct	FT Pct	Rebound Avg Off	Total	A	TO	Stl	Scoring Avg
Phoenix	49.4	39.9	80.8	9.0	40.5	25.9	14.5	6.7	110.2
Golden State	46.3	35.6	71.7	11.5	41.4	23.8	16.0	9.1	106.5
Denver	46.5	33.6	74.6	12.2	43.4	23.4	16.5	8.3	105.4
Washington	45.0	34.8	76.5	12.2	41.2	20.2	13.8	7.7	104.3
LA Lakers	46.6	35.3	74.7	10.8	41.2	22.6	15.5	7.3	103.3
Memphis	46.5	36.7	76.1	10.6	39.5	20.5	16.4	6.9	101.6
Utah	47.4	33.5	74.3	12.6	42.5	24.7	15.6	7.0	101.5
Sacramento	45.0	35.0	76.5	9.7	38.9	20.3	14.6	8.2	101.3
Dallas	46.7	38.1	80.5	11.2	41.9	19.9	13.9	6.8	100.0
Milwaukee	46.5	35.6	73.3	11.5	39.2	21.6	15.1	7.2	99.7
Toronto	46.3	36.3	78.8	9.2	39.5	22.2	13.5	7.1	99.5
Seattle	46.0	36.2	79.1	11.3	39.6	20.7	15.5	7.7	99.1
Chicago	45.7	38.8	73.4	12.0	43.7	22.3	16.0	7.8	98.8
San Antonio	47.4	38.1	75.1	9.3	40.7	22.1	13.9	7.2	98.5
New Jersey	45.7	36.3	72.7	10.0	40.8	23.9	14.8	6.1	97.6
New York	45.7	34.6	71.5	12.6	43.3	18.7	17.1	6.6	97.5
Houston	44.5	37.2	75.3	10.7	43.3	20.8	14.2	7.1	97.0
Charlotte	44.6	35.7	73.4	11.2	39.8	22.4	14.9	7.8	96.9
Cleveland	44.7	35.2	69.6	12.7	43.5	20.8	14.4	7.6	96.8
Minnesota	46.1	35.3	79.2	10.0	40.1	22.5	14.2	6.5	96.1
Detroit	45.4	34.4	77.4	11.6	40.5	21.6	12.2	7.1	96.0
Boston	44.3	36.7	76.7	11.2	40.4	19.9	16.5	7.2	95.8
LA Clippers	45.6	34.8	78.8	10.8	41.1	21.5	15.1	7.3	95.6
Indiana	43.8	34.6	76.0	12.1	41.8	20.5	16.3	7.3	95.6
New Orleans/Oklahoma City	44.5	36.2	74.0	12.5	43.1	18.7	14.5	6.4	95.5
Philadelphia	45.8	34.5	76.7	11.0	39.7	20.4	15.3	7.2	94.9
Orlando	47.2	35.6	70.2	11.2	40.7	18.6	17.0	6.9	94.8
Miami	46.4	34.3	69.0	10.0	40.8	20.5	14.6	6.9	94.6
Portland	45.0	34.6	76.9	11.3	39.3	18.5	15.1	6.8	94.1
Atlanta	44.4	32.9	76.1	11.9	40.1	19.2	15.9	7.4	93.7

Defense (Opponents' Statistics)

Team	FG Pct	3FG Pct	FT Pct	Rebound Avg. Off	Total	A	TO	Stl	Scoring Avg
San Antonio	44.3	33.4	74.0	10.1	39.1	17.3	14.3	7.1	90.1
Detroit	44.5	33.9	74.0	11.9	41.2	20.1	14.7	6.4	91.8
Houston	42.9	35.1	74.9	9.8	40.8	19.4	14.2	7.0	92.1
Dallas	44.7	34.9	74.6	10.2	38.1	17.9	14.5	6.9	92.8
Cleveland	44.8	32.9	73.4	9.8	39.9	20.1	15.3	6.6	92.9
Chicago	43.5	34.9	73.0	10.9	40.9	20.4	17.4	7.5	93.8
Orlando	44.2	35.3	76.0	10.5	37.6	19.6	15.0	8.3	94.0
Miami	44.4	35.5	74.2	11.2	41.3	20.2	14.5	6.9	95.5
LA Clippers	45.2	33.9	74.8	10.3	39.3	21.0	13.8	7.1	96.1
New Orleans/Oklahoma City	45.7	35.5	75.9	10.4	40.8	20.8	13.6	6.8	97.1
Philadelphia	46.3	35.3	75.4	11.8	41.1	22.3	15.6	7.4	98.0
Indiana	45.7	37.2	75.3	11.2	41.6	20.0	15.7	7.9	98.0
New Jersey	45.0	35.7	76.2	10.6	41.4	22.0	14.5	7.1	98.3
Portland	47.1	36.1	77.8	10.4	39.0	20.8	13.7	6.6	98.4
Atlanta	46.6	37.6	73.4	11.6	40.5	21.1	15.2	7.3	98.4
Toronto	46.3	35.7	75.4	10.3	42.5	21.2	15.1	6.0	98.5
Utah	45.5	35.5	76.7	9.9	37.0	18.9	15.0	7.6	98.6
Boston	46.8	35.4	74.7	10.3	40.5	22.1	15.2	7.4	99.2
Minnesota	46.0	34.8	76.0	11.7	41.4	21.7	14.2	7.1	99.7
New York	46.0	37.6	75.6	10.8	38.8	21.3	13.7	7.5	100.3
Charlotte	46.5	36.3	75.0	11.3	42.6	20.9	15.8	7.4	100.6
Seattle	47.6	36.1	75.1	11.6	41.0	22.8	15.0	7.2	102.0
Phoenix	45.7	36.3	76.7	12.3	42.8	18.9	15.1	6.9	102.9
Sacramento	47.2	36.5	75.7	11.1	43.4	22.4	16.3	7.0	103.1
LA Lakers	46.1	35.8	76.0	11.6	42.2	21.9	14.7	7.9	103.4
Denver	46.0	35.3	73.9	12.3	42.3	24.5	16.4	8.3	103.7
Milwaukee	48.0	36.8	74.2	13.0	43.0	25.3	16.7	7.5	104.0
Washington	47.3	37.7	77.7	11.9	43.0	23.7	15.7	6.3	104.9
Memphis	48.6	38.9	75.9	11.8	42.0	25.1	15.3	8.3	106.7
Golden State	46.2	36.6	75.0	13.1	46.4	24.7	18.6	8.3	106.9

Atlanta Hawks

Player	GP	MPG	FG%	3Pt%	FT%	OFF	DEF	Total	APG	SPG	BPG	TO	PF	PPG
			Field Goals			Rebounds								
Joe Johnson	57	41.4	47.1	38.1	74.8	0.9	3.3	4.2	4.4	1.1	0.2	3.1	2.0	25.0
Josh Smith	72	36.8	43.9	25.0	69.3	2.3	6.3	8.6	3.3	1.4	2.9	3.1	3.3	16.4
Marvin Williams	64	34.0	43.3	24.4	81.5	1.3	4.0	5.3	1.9	0.8	0.5	1.9	3.0	13.1
Josh Childress	55	36.8	50.4	33.8	79.5	2.2	3.9	6.2	2.3	1.1	0.7	1.4	2.1	13.0
Zaza Pachulia	72	28.1	47.4	00.0	78.6	2.8	4.2	6.9	1.5	1.1	0.5	2.2	3.7	12.2
Tyronn Lue	56	26.6	41.6	34.8	88.3	0.3	1.5	1.9	3.6	0.4	0.0	1.5	1.8	11.4
Salim Stoudamire	61	17.0	41.6	36.1	89.7	0.1	1.1	1.2	1.0	0.3	0.0	0.9	1.4	7.7
Anthony Johnson	27	27.4	41.6	31.8	78.1	0.3	1.6	2.0	4.6	0.6	0.1	1.6	1.9	7.5
Shelden Williams	81	18.7	45.5	50.0	76.4	1.6	3.8	5.4	0.5	0.6	0.5	1.2	2.5	5.5
Speedy Claxton	47	25.1	32.7	21.4	55.0	0.3	1.6	1.9	4.4	1.7	0.1	1.8	3.1	5.3
Solomon Jones	58	11.5	50.8	00.0	78.7	0.8	1.5	2.3	0.2	0.2	0.7	0.4	2.1	3.3
Royal Ivey	53	10.2	44.8	31.3	68.6	0.3	0.7	1.0	0.8	0.5	0.1	0.6	1.2	3.0
Slava Medvedenko	14	5.8	41.4	50.0	85.0	0.3	0.7	1.0	0.1	0.0	0.1	0.4	1.1	3.0
Dijon Thompson	6	8.3	40.0	00.0	83.3	0.5	0.8	1.3	0.3	0.0	0.0	0.2	0.3	2.8
Lorenzen Wright	67	15.4	44.8	00.0	28.1	1.3	2.0	3.2	0.6	0.4	0.4	0.6	3.0	2.6
Matt Freije	19	7.7	29.6	13.6	83.3	0.4	0.8	1.3	0.4	0.2	0.1	0.2	0.7	2.1
Jeremy Richardson	5	3.8	50.0	66.7	00.0	0.2	0.2	0.4	0.0	0.2	0.0	0.2	0.4	1.6
Esteban Batista	13	6.2	50.0	00.0	57.1	0.5	1.8	2.3	0.3	0.2	0.0	0.3	1.0	1.5
Cedric Bozeman	23	8.7	28.2	15.4	33.3	0.1	0.9	1.0	0.4	0.2	0.10	0.34	1.4	1.1
Hawks	82	242.4	44.4	32.9	76.1	11.9	28.2	40.1	19.2	7.4	5.4	15.9	24.0	93.7
Opponents	82	242.4	46.6	37.6	73.4	11.6	28.9	40.5	21.1	7.3	5.1	15.2	22.6	98.4

Boston Celtics

Player	GP	MPG	FG%	3Pt%	FT%	OFF	DEF	Total	APG	SPG	BPG	TO	PF	PPG
			Field Goals			Rebounds								
Paul Pierce	47	37.0	43.9	38.9	79.6	0.8	5.1	5.9	4.1	1.0	0.3	3.2	2.6	25.0
Al Jefferson	69	33.6	51.4	00.0	68.1	3.4	7.5	11.0	1.3	0.7	1.5	2.0	3.4	16.0
Wally Szczerbiak	32	28.1	41.5	41.5	89.7	0.5	2.6	3.1	1.7	0.6	0.1	1.7	2.0	15.0
Delonte West	69	32.2	42.7	36.5	85.3	0.5	2.6	3.0	4.4	1.1	0.5	2.0	2.2	12.2
Ryan Gomes	73	31.2	46.7	38.1	81.1	1.7	3.9	5.6	1.6	0.7	0.2	1.4	2.3	12.1
Tony Allen	33	24.4	51.4	24.2	78.4	1.1	2.7	3.8	1.7	1.5	0.4	2.3	2.6	11.5
Gerald Green	81	22.0	41.9	36.8	80.5	0.8	1.7	2.6	1.0	0.5	0.3	1.5	2.4	10.4
Rajon Rondo	78	23.5	41.8	20.7	64.7	0.9	2.8	3.7	3.8	1.6	0.1	1.8	2.3	6.4
Allan Ray	47	15.1	38.6	41.4	76.4	0.4	1.1	1.5	0.9	0.4	0.1	0.9	1.8	6.2
Sebastian Telfair	78	20.2	37.1	28.9	81.8	0.2	1.2	1.4	2.8	0.6	0.1	1.3	2.1	6.1
Kevin Pinkney	6	16.7	44.4	50.0	66.7	1.2	1.3	2.5	0.8	0.5	0.5	0.7	2.0	5.2
Kendrick Perkins	72	21.9	49.1	00.0	60.0	1.6	3.6	5.2	1.3	0.3	1.3	1.6	3.0	4.5
Leon Powe	63	11.4	44.6	00.0	73.6	1.5	1.9	3.4	0.2	0.2	0.4	0.8	1.7	4.2
Brian Scalabrine	54	19.0	40.3	40.0	78.3	0.4	1.5	1.9	1.1	0.4	0.3	0.8	2.4	4.0
Theo Ratliff	2	22.0	33.3	00.0	75.0	1.0	2.5	3.5	0.0	0.5	1.5	0.5	3.0	2.5
M. Olowokandi	24	9.8	41.3	00.0	66.7	0.6	1.4	2.0	0.2	0.3	0.5	0.7	2.0	1.7
Celtics	82	242.1	44.3	36.7	76.7	11.2	29.2	40.4	19.9	7.2	4.7	16.5	24.0	95.8
Opponents	82	242.1	46.8	35.4	74.7	10.3	30.2	40.5	22.1	7.4	5.5	15.2	21.4	99.2

Charlotte Bobcats

Player	GP	MPG	FG%	3Pt%	FT%	OFF	DEF	Total	APG	SPG	BPG	TO	PF	PPG
			Field Goals			Rebounds								
Gerald Wallace	72	36.7	50.2	32.5	69.1	2.0	5.2	7.2	2.6	2.0	1.0	2.2	2.9	18.1
Emeka Okafor	67	34.8	53.2	00.0	59.3	3.9	7.4	11.3	1.2	0.9	2.6	1.7	3.1	14.4
Raymond Felton	78	36.3	38.4	33.0	79.7	0.7	2.8	3.4	7.0	1.5	0.1	2.9	2.3	14.0
Matt Carroll	72	26.1	43.3	41.6	90.4	0.5	2.4	2.9	1.3	0.7	0.1	1.0	2.4	12.1
Sean May	35	23.9	50.0	66.7	76.8	2.1	4.6	6.7	1.9	0.5	0.7	1.6	2.9	11.9
Adam Morrison	78	29.8	37.6	33.7	71.0	0.7	2.3	2.9	2.1	0.4	0.1	1.7	2.3	11.8
Walter Hermann	48	19.5	52.7	46.1	77.4	0.6	2.3	2.9	0.5	0.4	0.2	0.7	1.6	9.2
Brevin Knight	45	28.3	41.9	05.6	80.5	0.3	2.2	2.6	6.6	1.5	0.0	2.1	2.5	9.1
Derek Anderson	50	23.8	42.9	35.5	87.7	0.6	1.7	2.3	2.7	1.0	0.1	1.1	2.3	8.0
Alan Anderson	17	15.1	45.7	25.0	82.6	0.6	1.2	1.9	1.2	0.4	0.0	1.3	1.9	5.8
Primoz Brezec	58	14.4	44.5	33.3	63.2	1.4	1.8	3.2	0.4	0.2	0.4	0.7	2.8	5.0
Jake Voskuhl	73	14.3	47.5	00.0	68.1	1.2	2.4	3.5	0.6	0.4	0.3	0.8	2.7	4.4
Jeff McInnis	38	18.5	39.2	12.5	68.8	0.4	1.3	1.6	3.3	0.4	0.0	1.1	1.9	4.3
Melvin Ely	24	10.2	38.3	00.0	68.6	0.5	1.1	1.6	0.6	0.1	0.2	1.0	1.6	2.9
O. Harrington	26	8.5	44.6	00.0	77.3	0.5	1.0	1.5	0.2	0.0	0.0	0.6	1.9	2.6
Ryan Hollins	27	6.9	55.6	00.0	60.0	0.4	0.7	1.1	0.0	0.3	0.3	0.6	1.5	2.4
Bernard Robinson	21	11.5	29.6	00.0	86.4	0.4	1.6	2.0	0.8	0.6	0.1	0.8	1.3	2.4
Eric Williams	5	6.6	30.8	00.0	57.1	0.4	0.2	0.6	0.2	0.2	0.0	0.4	1.2	2.4
Bobcats	82	244.0	44.6	35.7	73.4	11.2	28.6	39.8	22.4	7.8	4.5	14.9	24.2	96.9
Opponents	82	244.0	46.5	36.3	75.0	11.3	31.2	42.6	20.9	7.4	5.3	15.8	21.8	100.6

Chicago Bulls

Player	GP	MPG	Field Goals FG%	3Pt%	FT%	Rebounds OFF	DEF	Total	APG	SPG	BPG	TO	PF	PPG
Ben Gordon	82	33.0	45.5	41.3	86.4	0.4	2.7	3.1	3.6	0.8	0.2	3.0	3.1	21.4
Luol Deng	82	37.5	51.7	14.3	77.7	1.8	5.3	7.1	2.5	1.2	0.6	1.9	2.0	18.8
Kirk Hinrich	80	35.5	44.8	41.5	83.5	0.4	3.0	3.4	6.3	1.3	0.3	2.4	3.4	16.6
Andres Nocioni	53	26.5	46.7	38.3	84.8	0.8	4.9	5.7	1.1	0.5	0.5	2.0	3.1	14.1
Chris Duhon	78	24.4	40.8	35.9	75.2	0.3	1.9	2.2	4.0	0.9	0.1	1.4	1.9	7.2
Ben Wallace	77	35.0	45.3	20.0	40.8	3.9	6.7	10.7	2.4	1.4	2.0	1.3	2.0	6.4
P.J. Brown	72	20.2	40.7	00.0	78.7	1.8	3.0	4.8	0.7	0.3	0.7	1.2	2.6	6.1
Tyrus Thomas	72	13.4	47.5	00.0	60.6	1.2	2.5	3.7	0.6	0.6	1.1	1.3	2.3	5.2
Malik Allen	60	10.6	41.5	00.0	82.4	0.7	1.3	2.0	0.3	0.3	0.3	0.4	1.4	4.0
Thabo Sefolosha	71	12.2	42.6	35.7	51.1	0.5	1.7	2.2	0.8	0.5	0.2	0.9	1.4	3.6
Michael Sweetney	48	8.0	43.3	00.0	56.1	0.9	1.6	2.5	0.6	0.2	0.2	0.9	1.6	3.2
Adrian Griffin	54	10.8	47.3	00.0	78.9	0.7	1.3	2.0	1.1	0.6	0.1	0.7	1.4	2.5
Viktor Khryapa	33	7.0	38.6	00.0	73.1	0.6	1.1	1.7	0.6	0.3	0.0	0.5	1.6	2.2
Andre Barrett	6	4.8	50.0	00.0	00.0	0.2	0.7	0.8	1.2	0.0	0.0	0.7	0.7	1.3
Bulls	82	241.2	45.7	38.8	73.4	12.0	31.7	43.7	22.3	7.8	5.4	16.0	23.3	98.8
Opponents	82	241.2	43.5	34.9	73.0	10.9	30.0	40.9	20.4	7.5	5.3	17.4	23.2	93.8

Cleveland Cavaliers

Player	GP	MPG	Field Goals FG%	3Pt%	FT%	Rebounds OFF	DEF	Total	APG	SPG	BPG	TO	PF	PPG
LeBron James	78	40.9	47.6	31.9	69.8	1.1	5.7	6.7	6.0	1.6	0.7	3.2	2.2	27.3
Larry Hughes	70	37.1	40.0	33.3	67.6	0.6	3.2	3.8	3.7	1.3	0.4	2.2	2.3	14.9
Z. Ilgauskas	78	27.3	48.5	00.0	80.7	3.1	4.6	7.7	1.6	0.6	1.3	1.8	3.3	11.9
Drew Gooden	80	28.0	47.3	16.7	71.4	3.3	5.2	8.5	1.1	0.9	0.4	1.4	2.6	11.1
A. Pavlovic	67	22.9	45.3	40.5	78.7	0.3	2.0	2.4	1.6	0.8	0.3	1.5	2.2	9.0
Donyell Marshall	81	16.8	42.4	35.1	66.3	1.1	2.9	4.0	0.6	0.5	0.5	0.8	1.6	7.0
Anderson Varejao	81	23.9	47.6	00.0	61.6	2.4	4.4	6.7	0.9	0.9	0.6	0.8	3.3	6.8
Damon Jones	60	19.6	38.6	38.5	82.2	0.0	1.0	1.1	1.6	0.3	0.0	0.6	0.9	6.6
Daniel Gibson	60	16.5	42.4	41.9	71.8	0.5	1.1	1.5	1.2	0.4	0.1	0.7	1.6	4.6
Eric Snow	82	23.5	41.7	00.0	63.7	0.4	1.9	2.3	4.0	0.7	0.2	1.4	2.3	4.2
Shannon Brown	23	8.8	37.8	28.0	71.4	0.3	0.7	0.9	0.9	0.3	0.1	0.6	1.0	3.2
Ira Newble	15	8.6	43.2	53.3	60.0	0.9	1.1	2.0	0.1	0.4	0.0	0.2	1.1	3.1
David Wesley	35	10.1	29.3	23.7	71.4	0.1	0.9	1.0	1.1	0.3	0.1	0.5	0.9	2.1
Scot Pollard	24	4.5	42.3	00.0	50.0	0.6	0.7	1.3	0.1	0.2	0.0	0.2	1.1	1.0
Dwayne Jones	4	4.5	00.0	00.0	50.0	0.3	1.3	1.5	0.0	0.0	0.0	0.5	0.8	0.8
Cavaliers	82	242.4	44.7	35.2	69.5	12.7	30.8	43.5	20.8	7.6	4.3	14.4	21.7	96.8
Opponents	82	242.4	44.8	32.9	73.4	9.8	30.0	39.9	20.1	6.6	4.3	15.3	22.0	92.9

Dallas Mavericks

Player	GP	MPG	Field Goals FG%	3Pt%	FT%	Rebounds OFF	DEF	Total	APG	SPG	BPG	TO	PF	PPG
Dirk Nowitzki	78	36.2	50.2	41.6	90.4	1.6	7.3	8.9	3.4	0.7	0.8	2.1	2.2	24.6
Josh Howard	70	35.1	45.9	38.5	82.7	1.9	4.9	6.8	1.8	1.2	0.8	1.8	2.6	18.9
Jason Terry	81	35.1	48.4	43.8	80.4	0.5	2.3	2.9	5.2	1.0	0.2	1.9	2.1	16.7
Jerry Stackhouse	67	24.1	42.8	38.3	84.7	0.6	1.6	2.2	2.8	0.8	0.2	1.8	1.2	12.0
Devin Harris	80	26.0	49.2	28.0	82.4	0.6	1.9	2.5	3.7	1.2	0.3	1.8	2.0	10.2
Erick Dampier	76	25.2	62.6	00.0	62.3	2.9	4.6	7.4	0.6	0.3	1.1	1.4	3.1	7.1
Devean George	60	21.4	39.5	35.3	75.0	1.0	2.6	3.6	0.6	0.8	0.4	0.9	2.4	6.4
Greg Buckner	76	18.1	41.1	31.1	79.4	0.5	1.6	2.1	0.9	0.6	0.1	0.5	2.0	4.8
Anthony Johnson	40	14.0	41.1	37.9	72.4	0.3	0.9	1.2	2.0	0.4	0.0	0.8	1.7	3.8
Austin Croshere	61	11.9	35.1	28.6	86.5	0.5	2.5	3.0	0.7	0.2	0.1	0.5	1.1	3.7
Jose Barea	33	5.8	35.9	28.6	66.7	0.2	0.5	0.8	0.7	0.0	0.0	0.4	0.6	2.4
Kevin Willis	5	8.6	38.5	00.0	100.0	0.4	1.2	1.6	0.2	0.4	0.2	0.4	2.2	2.4
P. Mensah-Bonsu	12	5.9	64.7	00.0	38.9	0.8	1.0	1.8	0.0	0.1	0.0	0.8	0.7	2.4
DeSagana Diop	81	17.4	47.0	00.0	55.8	2.0	3.4	5.4	0.4	0.5	1.4	0.8	3.0	2.3
Maurice Ager	32	6.7	31.4	33.3	60.6	0.0	0.6	0.7	0.2	0.1	0.1	0.5	0.8	2.2
D. Ilunga-Mbenga	21	3.8	31.3	00.0	87.5	0.1	0.4	0.5	0.3	0.1	0.2	0.2	0.8	0.8
Mavericks	82	240.9	46.7	38.1	80.5	11.2	30.7	41.9	19.9	6.8	5.0	13.9	22.4	100.0
Opponents	82	240.9	44.7	34.9	74.6	10.2	27.9	38.1	17.9	6.9	3.8	14.5	22.1	92.8

Denver Nuggets

Player	GP	MPG	FG%	3Pt%	FT%	OFF	DEF	Total	APG	SPG	BPG	TO	PF	PPG
Carmelo Anthony...65		38.2	47.6	26.8	80.8	2.2	3.8	6.0	3.8	1.2	0.4	3.6	3.1	28.9
Allen Iverson 50		42.4	45.4	34.7	75.9	0.3	2.7	3.0	7.2	1.8	0.2	4.0	1.5	24.8
Earl Boykins 31		28.3	41.3	37.3	90.8	0.7	1.3	2.0	4.3	0.8	0.1	1.7	1.0	15.2
J.R. Smith.............63		23.3	44.1	39.0	81.0	0.5	1.8	2.3	1.4	0.8	0.1	1.4	2.3	13.0
Andre Miller..........23		35.7	47.2	25.0	72.9	1.1	3.4	4.5	9.1	1.6	0.2	3.0	2.5	13.0
Nene...................64		26.8	57.0	00.0	68.9	2.3	4.7	7.0	1.2	1.0	0.9	2.0	3.3	12.2
Marcus Camby....70		33.8	47.3	00.0	72.9	2.3	9.3	11.7	3.2	1.2	3.3	1.7	2.6	11.2
Kenyon Martin........2		31.5	50.0	00.0	25.0	3.0	7.0	10.0	0.5	0.0	0.0	2.5	5.0	9.5
Steve Blake 49		33.5	43.2	34.3	72.7	0.3	2.2	2.5	6.6	1.0	0.1	2.1	1.5	8.3
Linas Kleiza..........79		18.8	42.2	37.6	85.2	1.0	2.4	3.4	0.6	0.4	0.2	1.0	2.5	7.6
Eduardo Najera....75		22.1	57.6	08.3	71.5	1.7	2.4	4.1	0.9	1.0	0.4	0.8	2.8	6.6
Joe Smith 11		13.5	47.9	00.0	83.3	1.2	2.5	3.6	0.3	0.6	0.6	1.2	2.1	5.1
Reggie Evans.......66		17.1	54.4	00.0	49.7	2.4	4.6	7.0	0.7	0.6	0.2	1.4	2.2	4.9
Yakhouba Diawara..64		18.4	34.2	28.8	66.0	0.4	1.3	1.7	0.9	0.5	0.1	0.6	2.1	4.4
DerMarr Johnson..39		10.7	32.5	21.6	76.2	0.3	1.2	1.5	0.4	0.4	0.3	0.7	1.0	3.5
Anthony Carter.......2		18.5	37.5	00.0	00.0	0.0	1.5	1.5	5.5	0.0	0.5	3.0	2.0	3.0
Julius Hodge.........4		9.3	40.0	00.0	100.0	0.3	0.5	0.8	2.5	0.8	0.0	0.3	0.8	1.5
Jamal Sampson...22		5.7	64.3	00.0	42.9	0.7	1.5	2.2	0.2	0.1	0.3	0.5	0.8	1.1
Nuggets............82		**241.2**	**46.5**	**33.6**	**74.6**	**12.2**	**31.2**	**43.4**	**23.4**	**8.3**	**5.3**	**16.5**	**21.4**	**105.4**
Opponets...............82		**241.2**	**46.0**	**35.3**	**73.9**	**12.3**	**30.0**	**42.3**	**24.5**	**8.3**	**5.2**	**16.4**	**23.7**	**103.7**

Detroit Pistons

Player	GP	MPG	FG%	3Pt%	FT%	OFF	DEF	Total	APG	SPG	BPG	TO	PF	PPG
Richard Hamilton...75		36.8	46.8	34.1	86.1	1.0	2.8	3.8	3.8	0.8	0.2	2.1	3.1	19.8
Chauncey Billups..70		36.2	42.7	34.5	88.3	0.3	3.1	3.4	7.2	1.2	0.2	2.0	2.3	17.0
Tayshaun Prince...82		36.6	46.0	38.6	76.8	1.8	3.5	5.2	2.8	0.6	0.7	1.2	1.4	14.3
Rasheed Wallace..75		32.3	42.3	35.1	78.8	1.2	6.0	7.2	1.7	1.0	1.6	1.3	3.0	12.3
Chris Webber.......43		29.7	48.9	33.3	63.6	2.0	4.7	6.7	3.0	1.0	0.6	1.7	2.5	11.3
Antonio McDyess.82		21.1	52.6	00.0	69.1	2.0	4.0	6.0	0.9	0.7	0.8	0.9	2.9	8.1
Ronald Murray 69		21.4	40.4	28.9	72.5	0.4	1.3	1.6	2.7	0.7	0.2	1.3	1.4	6.7
Amir Johnson 8		15.5	54.5	00.0	78.6	1.9	2.8	4.6	0.4	0.6	1.6	1.1	2.4	5.9
Nazr Mohammed...51		15.2	53.2	00.0	61.0	1.7	2.7	4.5	0.2	0.5	0.8	0.8	2.6	5.6
Carlos Delfino 82		16.7	41.5	33.3	78.7	0.8	2.4	3.2	1.1	0.6	0.1	0.7	1.2	5.2
Jason Maxiell 67		14.1	50.0	00.0	52.6	1.3	1.5	2.8	0.2	0.5	0.9	0.8	1.6	5.0
Lindsey Hunter.....52		14.3	38.5	31.9	90.9	0.2	0.7	0.9	1.8	0.7	0.1	0.7	1.1	4.9
Dale Davis...........46		10.1	44.6	00.0	65.4	1.3	1.7	3.0	0.3	0.2	0.7	0.3	1.3	1.8
Will Blalock..........14		11.9	30.0	20.0	100.0	0.4	0.6	1.1	1.2	0.4	0.0	0.9	0.6	1.8
Ronald Dupree....19		4.9	35.5	00.0	33.3	0.3	0.6	0.9	0.3	0.3	0.1	0.2	0.6	1.3
Pistons 82		**242.4**	**45.4**	**34.4**	**77.4**	**11.6**	**29.0**	**40.5**	**21.6**	**7.1**	**5.8**	**12.2**	**20.4**	**96.0**
Opponents...............82		**242.4**	**44.5**	**33.9**	**74.0**	**11.9**	**29.3**	**41.2**	**20.1**	**6.4**	**3.5**	**14.7**	**20.3**	**91.8**

Golden State Warriors

Player	GP	MPG	FG%	3Pt%	FT%	OFF	DEF	Total	APG	SPG	BPG	TO	PF	PPG
Baron Davis..........63		35.3	43.9	30.4	74.5	0.8	3.6	4.4	8.1	2.1	0.5	3.1	2.9	20.1
Al Harrington 42		32.3	45.6	41.7	68.1	1.9	4.5	6.4	2.3	1.0	0.3	1.9	3.6	17.0
Stephen Jackson..38		34.0	44.6	34.1	80.4	1.2	2.2	3.3	4.6	1.3	0.4	2.7	3.0	16.8
Monta Ellis............77		34.3	47.5	27.3	76.3	0.8	2.4	3.2	4.1	1.7	0.3	2.9	2.7	16.5
Jason Richardson..51		32.8	41.7	36.5	65.7	1.4	3.7	5.1	3.4	1.1	0.6	1.6	2.5	16.0
Mike Dunleavy 39		26.9	44.9	34.6	77.2	1.0	3.8	4.8	3.0	1.0	0.3	1.8	2.1	11.4
Mickael Pietrus...72		26.9	48.8	38.8	64.8	1.1	3.4	4.5	0.9	0.7	0.8	1.5	3.1	11.1
Matt Barnes.........76		23.9	43.8	36.6	73.2	1.2	3.4	4.6	2.1	1.0	0.5	1.4	2.5	9.8
Andris Biedrins....82		29.0	59.9	00.0	52.1	3.1	6.2	9.3	1.1	0.8	1.7	1.5	3.7	9.5
Troy Murphy.........26		25.7	45.0	37.3	71.2	1.4	4.6	6.0	2.3	0.8	0.6	1.1	2.4	8.9
Ike Diogu..............17		13.1	53.0	00.0	79.5	1.2	2.5	3.7	0.5	0.2	0.6	1.1	2.1	7.2
Kelenna Azubuike..41		16.3	44.5	43.0	78.2	0.6	1.7	2.3	0.7	0.5	0.2	1.0	1.2	7.1
Anthony Roberson..20		11.4	42.3	38.2	66.7	0.1	1.0	1.1	0.5	0.6	0.0	0.7	1.4	5.6
Keith McLeod.......26		14.6	39.0	39.1	88.7	0.1	0.7	0.8	1.7	0.6	0.1	0.9	0.8	5.3
Renaldo Major........1		27.0	20.0	00.0	50.0	0.0	2.0	2.0	0.0	2.0	0.0	1.0	4.0	5.0
S. Jasikevicius ...26		11.9	36.6	27.3	87.1	0.2	0.6	0.8	2.3	0.5	0.0	1.2	0.8	4.3
Dajuan Wagner 1		7.0	100.0	100.0	50.0	0.0	0.0	0.0	1.0	0.0	0.0	1.0	1.0	4.0
Josh Powell.........30		9.6	52.6	00.0	73.3	0.6	1.7	2.3	0.6	0.2	0.4	0.8	1.4	3.5
Adonal Foyle........48		9.9	56.5	00.0	44.0	1.1	1.6	2.6	0.4	0.2	1.0	0.5	1.3	2.2
Patrick O'Bryant....16		7.4	31.3	00.0	64.7	0.4	0.9	1.3	0.6	0.4	0.5	0.5	1.6	1.9
Warriors 82		**240.9**	**46.3**	**35.6**	**71.7**	**11.5**	**30.0**	**41.4**	**23.8**	**9.2**	**5.7**	**16.0**	**23.6**	**106.5**
Opponents...............82		**240.9**	**46.2**	**36.6**	**75.0**	**13.1**	**33.3**	**46.4**	**24.7**	**8.3**	**4.9**	**18.6**	**22.3**	**106.9**

Houston Rockets

Player	GP	MPG	FG%	3Pt%	FT%	OFF	DEF	Total	APG	SPG	BPG	TO	PF	PPG
Yao Ming	48	33.8	51.6	00.0	86.2	2.1	7.3	9.4	2.0	0.4	2.0	3.5	3.3	25.0
Tracy McGrady	71	35.8	43.1	33.1	70.7	0.8	4.5	5.3	6.5	1.3	0.5	3.0	1.9	24.6
Rafer Alston	82	37.1	37.5	36.3	73.4	0.4	3.1	3.4	5.4	1.6	0.1	2.1	2.4	13.3
Luther Head	80	27.6	43.7	44.1	79.0	0.4	2.8	3.2	2.4	1.0	0.1	1.7	1.7	10.9
Shane Battier	82	36.4	44.6	42.1	77.9	0.8	3.3	4.1	2.1	1.0	0.7	0.9	2.3	10.1
Juwan Howard	80	26.5	46.5	00.0	82.4	1.7	4.2	5.9	1.6	0.4	0.1	1.4	2.6	9.7
Bonzi Wells	28	21.1	44.1	14.3	56.1	0.9	3.4	4.3	1.1	0.9	0.5	2.0	2.2	7.8
Chuck Hayes	78	22.0	57.3	00.0	61.8	2.6	4.1	6.7	0.6	0.9	0.2	0.8	3.6	5.6
Kirk Snyder	39	14.4	45.2	25.0	65.3	0.4	1.7	2.1	1.0	0.3	0.3	0.7	1.3	4.9
John Lucas III	47	8.1	39.7	25.4	78.9	0.2	0.6	0.8	0.7	0.4	0.0	0.3	0.8	3.3
Dikembe Mutombo	75	17.2	55.6	00.0	69.0	2.2	4.3	6.5	0.2	0.3	1.0	0.5	2.1	3.1
Vassilis Spanoulis	31	8.8	31.9	17.2	81.0	0.2	0.5	0.7	0.9	0.2	0.0	0.9	1.1	2.7
Jake Tskalidis	13	10.2	45.9	00.0	80.0	1.4	1.7	3.1	0.2	0.1	0.1	0.2	1.3	2.3
Scott Padgett	24	8.3	30.6	27.6	54.5	0.5	1.4	1.9	0.3	0.2	0.1	0.3	1.4	1.8
Steve Novak	35	5.5	36.0	33.3	100.0	0.1	0.6	0.7	0.2	0.1	0.0	0.1	0.6	1.5
Rockets	**82**	**242.1**	**44.5**	**37.2**	**75.3**	**10.7**	**32.6**	**43.3**	**20.8**	**7.1**	**4.1**	**14.2**	**20.9**	**97.0**
Opponents	**82**	**242.1**	**42.9**	**35.1**	**74.9**	**9.8**	**31.1**	**40.8**	**19.4**	**7.0**	**4.3**	**14.2**	**19.9**	**92.1**

Indiana Pacers

Player	GP	MPG	FG%	3Pt%	FT%	OFF	DEF	Total	APG	SPG	BPG	TO	PF	PPG
Jermaine O'Neal	69	35.6	43.6	00.0	76.7	2.2	7.4	9.6	2.4	0.7	2.6	2.9	3.4	19.4
Al Harrington	36	33.6	45.8	45.8	71.3	2.0	4.3	6.3	1.4	0.7	0.3	2.5	3.2	15.9
Stephen Jackson	37	32.1	41.9	29.7	82.2	0.5	2.1	2.6	3.1	0.9	0.5	2.2	2.4	14.1
Mike Dunleavy	43	35.6	45.4	28.3	79.2	1.0	4.7	5.7	2.6	1.1	0.2	1.8	2.8	14.0
Danny Granger	82	34.0	45.9	38.2	80.3	1.4	3.3	4.6	1.4	0.8	0.7	1.7	3.0	13.9
Jamaal Tinsley	72	31.2	38.9	31.6	72.0	0.8	2.5	3.3	6.9	1.6	0.4	2.8	2.6	12.8
Troy Murphy	42	28.2	46.0	40.9	77.2	1.5	4.6	6.1	1.6	0.6	0.6	1.2	3.2	11.1
S. Jasikevicius	37	17.9	41.2	37.2	92.2	0.3	1.0	1.3	3.0	0.4	0.0	1.6	1.4	7.4
Marquis Daniels	45	17.8	45.9	23.1	70.0	0.6	1.2	1.8	1.3	0.6	0.2	1.2	1.2	7.1
Ike Diogu	42	12.8	45.4	00.0	80.2	1.3	2.0	3.3	0.5	0.1	0.4	1.2	2.1	5.8
Darrell Armstrong	81	15.7	41.4	33.6	78.5	0.4	1.2	1.7	2.4	0.9	0.1	0.9	1.3	5.6
Jeff Foster	75	23.2	46.9	00.0	63.9	3.4	4.7	8.1	0.8	0.8	0.5	0.9	2.7	4.3
Keith McLeod	22	15.4	38.6	31.8	88.0	0.0	1.0	1.0	2.0	0.3	0.1	1.1	1.4	4.2
Shawne Williams	46	12.1	46.9	36.5	55.0	0.7	1.1	1.8	0.5	0.1	0.2	0.5	1.5	3.9
David Harrison	24	7.9	51.7	00.0	50.0	0.4	1.4	1.8	0.3	0.2	0.5	1.1	2.0	3.0
Maceo Baston	47	8.6	64.5	42.9	78.7	0.4	1.1	1.6	0.3	0.3	0.4	0.7	1.4	2.9
Rawle Marshall	40	9.0	36.0	22.2	68.9	0.2	0.5	0.7	0.3	0.3	0.1	0.5	0.6	2.5
Josh Powell	7	9.1	13.3	0.0	66.7	1.0	1.7	2.7	0.4	0.0	0.0	0.7	2.6	1.7
Orien Greene	41	6.2	37.1	18.2	60.0	0.3	0.8	1.1	0.5	0.4	0.1	0.7	0.9	1.5
Pacers	**82**	**241.2**	**43.8**	**34.6**	**76.0**	**12.1**	**29.8**	**41.8**	**20.5**	**7.3**	**5.4**	**16.3**	**23.3**	**95.6**
Opponents	**82**	**241.2**	**45.7**	**37.2**	**75.3**	**11.2**	**30.5**	**41.6**	**20.0**	**7.8**	**5.0**	**15.7**	**23.7**	**98.0**

Los Angeles Clippers

Player	GP	MPG	FG%	3Pt%	FT%	OFF	DEF	Total	APG	SPG	BPG	TO	PF	PPG
Elton Brand	80	38.5	53.3	100.0	76.1	3.4	6.0	9.3	2.9	1.0	2.2	2.5	3.0	20.5
Corey Maggette	75	30.5	45.4	20.0	82.0	1.2	4.7	5.9	2.8	0.9	0.2	2.7	3.3	16.9
Cuttino Mobley	78	36.4	44.0	41.1	83.7	0.7	2.8	3.4	2.5	1.2	0.3	1.9	2.4	13.8
Sam Cassell	58	24.3	41.8	29.4	87.9	0.5	2.4	2.9	4.7	0.5	0.1	1.7	2.2	12.3
Tim Thomas	76	27.0	41.4	38.2	70.8	0.8	4.1	5.0	2.3	0.7	0.4	1.4	3.0	11.0
Chris Kaman	75	29.0	45.1	00.0	74.1	2.1	5.7	7.8	1.1	0.6	1.6	2.0	3.3	10.1
Shaun Livingston	54	29.8	46.3	31.3	70.7	1.0	2.4	3.4	5.1	1.1	0.5	2.0	2.5	9.3
Jason Hart	23	32.4	43.8	17.4	88.9	0.5	3.1	3.6	4.0	1.8	0.0	1.5	2.6	9.0
Quinton Ross	81	21.0	46.7	20.0	78.2	0.7	1.6	2.3	1.1	0.9	0.4	0.4	2.2	5.2
Daniel Ewing	61	11.7	40.4	31.8	77.8	0.1	1.0	1.2	1.5	0.5	0.1	0.8	1.0	2.9
Aaron Williams	38	9.8	54.7	00.0	81.8	0.7	1.5	2.2	0.2	0.2	0.4	0.5	1.5	2.0
Doug Christie	7	11.7	29.4	16.7	66.7	0.4	1.1	1.6	1.1	0.4	0.1	0.7	1.6	1.9
Paul Davis	31	5.8	42.3	00.0	70.0	0.7	0.7	1.4	0.2	0.2	0.2	0.3	0.9	1.6
James Singleton	53	7.1	36.6	21.4	75.9	0.7	1.3	2.0	0.3	0.3	0.3	0.3	0.8	1.6
Yaroslav Korolev	10	4.1	25.0	20.0	50.0	0.1	0.2	0.3	0.4	0.3	0.0	0.1	0.0	1.2
Luke Jackson	3	5.3	12.5	25.0	0.0	0.0	0.3	0.3	1.3	0.0	0.0	0.3	1.0	1.0
Alvin Williams	2	5.0	00.0	00.0	50.0	0.5	0.0	0.5	1.5	1.0	0.0	1.5	0.0	1.0
Will Conroy	4	8.8	00.0	00.0	00.0	0.5	0.8	1.3	2.0	0.0	0.0	0.5	1.5	0.0
Clippers	**82**	**240.6**	**45.6**	**34.8**	**78.8**	**10.8**	**30.3**	**41.1**	**21.5**	**7.3**	**5.8**	**15.1**	**22.7**	**95.6**
Opponents	**82**	**240.6**	**45.2**	**33.9**	**74.8**	**10.3**	**29.0**	**39.3**	**21.0**	**7.1**	**3.9**	**13.8**	**22.3**	**96.1**

Los Angeles Lakers

Player	GP	MPG	FG%	3Pt%	FT%	OFF	DEF	Total	APG	SPG	BPG	TO	PF	PPG
Kobe Bryant	77	40.8	46.3	34.4	86.8	1.0	4.7	5.7	5.4	1.4	0.5	3.3	2.7	31.6
Lamar Odom	56	39.3	46.8	29.7	70.0	1.8	7.9	9.8	4.8	1.0	0.6	2.9	3.3	15.9
Luke Walton	60	33.0	47.4	38.7	74.5	1.5	3.6	5.0	4.3	1.0	0.4	2.0	2.0	11.4
Smush Parker	82	30.0	43.6	36.5	64.6	0.5	2.0	2.5	2.8	1.5	0.1	1.9	2.6	11.1
Kwame Brown	41	27.6	59.1	00.0	44.0	2.0	4.0	6.0	1.8	1.0	1.2	1.9	3.0	8.4
Maurice Evans	76	22.8	43.2	36.1	78.7	1.2	1.7	2.9	1.0	0.5	0.2	0.8	1.7	8.4
Andrew Bynum	82	21.9	55.8	00.0	66.8	1.7	4.2	5.9	1.1	0.2	1.6	1.4	3.0	7.8
Brian Cook	65	15.7	45.3	40.0	72.3	0.9	2.4	3.3	1.0	0.4	0.4	0.8	2.1	6.9
V. Radmanovic	55	17.9	42.4	33.9	72.6	1.0	2.3	3.3	1.2	0.5	0.3	1.3	2.3	6.6
Ronny Turiaf	72	15.1	54.9	00.0	66.4	1.2	2.4	3.6	0.9	0.2	1.1	0.7	2.8	5.3
Jordan Farmar	72	15.1	42.2	32.8	71.1	0.3	1.3	1.7	1.9	0.6	0.1	1.0	1.1	4.4
Sasha Vujacic	73	12.8	39.2	37.3	87.8	0.4	1.1	1.5	0.9	0.6	0.0	0.4	1.4	4.3
Shammond Williams	30	11.5	40.7	40.0	66.7	0.4	1.0	1.3	1.0	0.4	0.0	0.4	0.7	3.1
Aaron McKie	10	13.1	64.7	00.0	00.0	0.1	1.7	1.8	1.3	0.4	0.0	0.8	1.4	2.2
Lakers	82	244.3	46.6	35.3	74.7	10.8	30.4	41.2	22.6	7.3	5.1	15.5	23.0	103.3
Opponents	82	244.3	46.1	35.8	76.0	11.6	30.6	42.2	21.9	7.9	5.0	14.7	23.4	103.4

Memphis Grizzlies

Player	GP	MPG	FG%	3Pt%	FT%	OFF	DEF	Total	APG	SPG	BPG	TO	PF	PPG
Pau Gasol	59	36.2	53.8	27.3	74.8	2.5	7.3	9.8	3.4	0.5	2.1	2.8	2.3	20.8
Mike Miller	70	39.1	46.0	40.6	79.3	0.7	4.7	5.4	4.3	0.8	0.3	2.6	2.0	18.5
Chucky Atkins	75	27.5	43.4	37.9	81.0	0.2	1.6	1.9	4.6	0.7	0.1	1.7	1.8	13.2
Hakim Warrick	82	26.2	52.4	00.0	77.1	1.6	3.5	5.1	0.9	0.5	0.4	2.0	2.8	12.7
Rudy Gay	78	27.0	42.2	36.4	72.7	1.2	3.3	4.5	1.3	0.9	1.0	1.8	2.5	10.8
Stromile Swift	54	19.1	46.5	00.0	72.4	1.6	3.1	4.6	0.3	0.6	1.2	1.3	2.7	7.8
Tarence Kinsey	48	20.1	45.7	28.3	79.6	0.6	1.4	2.0	0.9	1.1	0.0	1.0	1.2	7.7
Dahntay Jones	78	21.4	47.7	41.7	79.3	0.6	1.4	2.0	0.9	0.5	0.3	1.2	2.5	7.5
Damon Stoudamire	62	24.2	39.1	33.7	79.5	0.5	1.7	2.2	4.8	0.8	0.0	1.6	1.5	7.5
Kyle Lowry	10	17.5	36.8	37.5	89.3	1.2	1.9	3.1	3.2	1.4	0.1	1.2	2.0	5.6
Eddie Jones	29	19.3	37.7	29.7	73.5	0.5	1.6	2.1	1.1	0.8	0.5	0.8	1.9	5.6
Lawrence Roberts	54	17.9	45.2	00.0	72.5	1.9	3.0	4.8	0.6	0.7	0.2	0.7	2.5	5.2
Junior Harrington	29	18.7	41.6	26.9	67.4	0.4	1.9	2.3	3.1	0.7	0.2	1.8	2.7	5.2
Brian Cardinal	28	11.2	49.4	40.9	92.6	0.5	1.6	2.1	1.1	0.8	0.0	0.8	1.5	4.5
Alexander Johnson	59	12.8	53.8	00.0	66.1	0.8	2.2	3.1	0.3	0.4	0.6	0.8	2.3	4.4
Jake Tsakalidis	23	11.2	40.0	00.0	58.3	1.0	1.7	2.8	0.1	0.3	0.5	0.9	1.5	2.3
Scott Padgett	7	4.7	14.3	00.0	00.0	0.7	0.6	1.3	0.0	0.1	0.0	0.1	0.3	0.3
Will Conroy	3	5.7	00.0	00.0	00.0	0.3	0.3	0.7	0.3	0.0	0.0	0.0	0.3	0.3
Grizzlies	82	243.7	46.5	36.7	76.1	10.6	29.0	39.5	20.5	6.9	5.0	16.4	22.3	101.6
Opponents	82	243.7	48.6	38.9	75.9	11.8	30.3	42.0	25.1	8.3	5.5	15.3	24.3	106.7

Miami Heat

Player	GP	MPG	FG%	3Pt%	FT%	OFF	DEF	Total	APG	SPG	BPG	TO	PF	PPG
Dwyane Wade	51	37.9	49.1	26.6	80.7	1.0	3.7	4.7	7.5	2.1	1.2	4.2	2.3	27.4
Shaquille O'Neal	40	28.4	59.1	00.0	42.2	2.4	5.0	7.4	2.0	0.2	1.4	2.4	3.5	17.3
Jason Kapono	67	26.4	49.4	51.4	89.2	0.4	2.3	2.7	1.2	0.6	0.0	1.0	2.0	10.9
Jason Williams	61	30.6	41.3	33.9	91.3	0.3	2.0	2.3	5.3	1.0	0.0	1.6	1.1	10.9
Udonis Haslem	79	31.4	49.2	00.0	68.0	2.4	5.9	8.3	1.2	0.6	0.3	1.4	3.0	10.7
Eddie Jones	35	29.5	44.6	37.8	82.9	0.5	3.2	3.7	2.2	1.3	0.2	0.7	2.0	9.5
Alonzo Mourning	77	20.4	56.0	00.0	60.1	1.6	2.9	4.5	0.2	0.2	2.3	1.7	2.8	8.6
Antoine Walker	78	23.3	39.7	27.5	43.8	1.2	3.2	4.3	1.7	0.6	0.2	1.8	2.2	8.5
James Posey	71	27.0	43.1	37.5	82.7	0.9	4.1	5.0	1.3	1.0	0.3	0.8	2.7	7.7
Dorell Wright	66	19.6	44.5	14.7	74.4	0.6	3.5	4.1	1.4	0.6	0.7	1.0	1.7	6.0
Gary Payton	68	22.1	39.3	26.0	66.7	0.3	1.7	1.9	3.0	0.6	0.0	1.0	1.7	5.3
Robert Hite	12	11.3	31.7	21.7	66.7	0.3	1.0	1.3	0.7	0.3	0.2	0.5	0.7	4.3
Michael Doleac	56	12.5	46.9	00.0	87.8	0.8	2.0	2.8	0.4	0.3	0.5	1.7	3.6	3.6
Chris Quinn	42	9.7	36.6	35.1	67.6	0.1	0.6	0.7	1.5	0.4	0.0	0.5	0.8	3.4
Wayne Simien	8	11.6	39.1	00.0	71.4	0.6	0.8	1.4	0.5	0.3	0.0	0.4	1.6	2.9
Earl Barron	28	7.3	28.9	00.0	94.4	0.7	0.8	1.5	0.2	0.2	0.1	0.4	0.8	2.3
Heat	82	242.1	46.4	34.3	69.0	10.0	30.8	40.8	20.5	6.9	5.4	14.6	21.3	94.6
Opponents	82	242.1	44.4	35.5	74.2	11.2	30.1	41.3	20.2	6.8	3.8	14.4	21.8	95.5

Milwaukee Bucks

Player	GP	MPG	FG%	3Pt%	FT%	OFF	DEF	Total	APG	SPG	BPG	TO	PF	PPG
Michael Redd	53	38.4	46.5	38.2	82.9	0.8	2.9	3.7	2.3	1.2	0.2	2.3	1.5	26.7
Maurice Williams	68	36.4	44.6	34.6	85.5	0.8	4.0	4.8	6.1	1.3	0.1	3.0	3.0	17.3
Ruben Patterson	81	31.0	54.8	15.8	64.1	2.3	3.1	5.4	2.9	1.4	0.3	2.5	2.9	14.7
Earl Boykins	35	33.0	42.7	41.9	88.6	0.7	1.4	2.2	4.5	0.9	0.0	1.9	1.7	14.0
Charlie Bell	82	34.7	43.7	35.2	78.0	0.7	2.2	2.9	3.0	1.2	0.1	1.3	2.6	13.5
Andrew Bogut	66	34.2	55.3	20.0	57.7	2.5	6.3	8.8	3.0	0.7	0.5	2.3	3.3	12.3
Charlie Villanueva	39	25.2	47.0	33.7	82.0	1.6	4.3	5.8	0.9	0.6	0.3	1.4	2.8	11.8
Ersan Ilyasova	66	14.7	38.3	36.5	78.7	0.9	2.0	2.9	0.7	0.4	0.3	0.8	2.2	6.1
Dan Gadzuric	54	15.6	47.4	00.0	46.7	1.7	2.8	4.6	0.5	0.4	0.6	0.9	2.6	4.8
Brian Skinner	67	22.7	49.0	00.0	58.2	1.6	4.2	5.7	0.9	0.3	1.0	1.1	2.9	4.4
Lynn Greer	41	10.5	43.3	34.6	84.4	0.0	0.6	0.7	1.3	0.4	0.0	0.4	0.8	4.1
Steve Blake	33	17.7	34.9	27.9	55.0	0.2	1.2	1.4	2.5	0.3	0.1	0.9	1.5	3.6
David Noel	68	11.6	36.7	32.1	86.0	0.6	1.2	1.8	1.0	0.4	0.1	0.6	1.1	2.7
Julius Hodge	5	5.6	57.1	00.0	50.0	0.2	0.8	1.0	0.4	0.2	0.0	0.4	0.6	1.8
Damir Markota	30	5.7	36.5	37.5	63.6	0.4	0.7	1.0	0.2	0.1	0.0	0.5	0.7	1.7
Jared Reiner	27	9.0	34.9	00.0	30.0	0.8	1.9	2.6	0.5	0.2	0.2	0.5	1.7	1.2
Chris McCray	5	2.4	00.0	00.0	00.0	0.0	0.0	0.0	0.0	0.0	0.0	0.4	0.2	0.0
Bucks	82	242.1	46.5	35.6	73.3	11.5	27.7	39.2	21.6	7.2	2.7	15.1	22.2	99.7
Opponents	82	242.1	48.0	36.8	74.2	13.0	30.1	43.0	25.3	7.5	5.3	15.7	21.0	104.0

Minnesota Timberwolves

Player	GP	MPG	FG%	3Pt%	FT%	OFF	DEF	Total	APG	SPG	BPG	TO	PF	PPG
Kevin Garnett	76	39.4	47.6	21.4	83.5	2.4	10.4	12.8	4.1	1.2	1.7	2.7	2.4	22.4
Ricky Davis	81	37.3	46.5	39.7	83.9	0.7	3.2	3.9	4.8	1.0	0.3	2.6	2.3	17.0
Mark Blount	82	31.0	50.9	29.0	75.4	1.7	4.5	6.2	0.8	0.5	0.7	2.0	2.9	12.3
Randy Foye	82	22.9	43.4	36.8	85.4	0.6	2.1	2.7	2.8	0.7	0.3	1.9	2.2	10.1
Mike James	82	25.2	42.2	37.2	83.7	0.3	1.7	2.0	3.6	0.7	0.1	1.6	2.1	10.1
Craig Smith	82	18.7	53.1	00.0	62.4	1.8	3.3	5.1	0.6	0.6	0.2	0.9	2.7	7.4
Trenton Hassell	76	29.3	49.0	24.0	78.3	1.1	2.1	3.2	2.7	0.3	0.3	1.1	1.9	6.7
Troy Hudson	34	16.3	37.9	35.0	81.3	0.2	1.2	1.4	2.1	0.4	0.1	1.2	0.7	5.9
Marko Jaric	70	22.2	41.8	37.6	76.1	0.8	1.9	2.6	2.1	1.1	0.2	1.3	2.5	5.3
Rashad McCants	37	15.0	35.0	26.7	69.0	0.4	0.9	1.3	1.0	0.7	0.2	1.1	1.9	5.0
Bracey Wright	19	10.0	40.0	30.0	72.2	0.4	0.7	1.1	0.8	0.5	0.1	0.3	0.3	3.5
Justin Reed	41	7.8	37.4	00.0	86.7	0.4	0.8	1.1	0.4	0.1	0.1	0.5	1.1	2.6
Eddie Griffin	13	7.1	25.9	00.0	80.0	0.5	1.4	1.9	0.3	0.0	0.5	0.5	0.6	1.4
Mark Madsen	56	8.4	53.5	00.0	51.7	0.6	0.9	1.6	0.2	0.2	0.2	0.4	1.8	1.1
Timberwolves	82	244.0	46.1	35.3	79.2	10.0	30.2	40.2	22.5	6.5	4.0	15.6	21.4	96.1
Opponents	82	244.0	46.0	34.8	76.0	11.7	29.7	41.4	21.7	7.1	4.4	14.2	20.5	99.7

New Jersey Nets

Player	GP	MPG	FG%	3Pt%	FT%	OFF	DEF	Total	APG	SPG	BPG	TO	PF	PPG
Vince Carter	82	38.1	45.4	35.7	80.2	1.4	4.6	6.0	4.8	1.0	0.4	2.7	3.2	25.2
Nenad Krstic	26	32.6	52.6	00.0	71.1	2.0	4.8	6.8	1.8	0.4	0.9	2.0	3.4	16.4
Richard Jefferson	55	35.6	45.6	35.9	73.3	0.9	3.5	4.4	2.7	0.6	0.2	2.2	2.2	16.3
Jason Kidd	80	36.7	40.6	34.3	77.8	1.7	6.5	8.2	9.2	1.6	0.3	2.7	1.8	13.0
Mikki Moore	79	26.4	60.9	00.0	68.1	1.8	3.3	5.1	0.9	0.6	0.8	1.4	3.3	9.8
Bostjan Nachbar	76	20.2	45.7	42.3	80.5	0.4	3.0	3.3	0.8	0.4	0.3	0.9	2.4	9.2
Eddie House	56	16.9	42.8	42.9	91.7	0.3	1.4	1.6	1.2	0.5	0.1	0.5	1.2	8.4
Marcus Williams	79	16.6	39.5	28.2	84.7	0.4	1.7	2.1	3.3	0.4	0.0	1.8	1.2	6.8
Antoine Wright	63	18.0	43.8	32.2	60.3	0.6	2.2	2.8	0.9	0.5	0.2	0.7	1.9	4.5
Josh Boone	61	11.0	57.9	00.0	54.4	1.0	1.8	2.9	0.2	0.2	0.3	0.5	1.5	4.2
Clifford Robinson	50	19.1	37.2	37.9	44.4	0.6	1.8	2.4	1.0	0.2	0.5	0.6	2.0	4.1
Hassan Adams	61	8.1	55.6	00.0	66.7	0.6	0.7	1.3	0.2	0.3	0.1	0.4	0.8	2.9
Jason Collins	80	23.1	36.4	00.0	46.5	1.1	2.8	4.0	0.6	0.5	0.5	0.9	3.4	2.1
Bernard Robinson	10	3.7	37.5	00.0	80.0	0.1	0.5	0.6	0.2	0.4	0.1	0.0	0.4	1.0
Mile Ilic	5	1.2	00.0	00.0	00.0	0.0	0.2	0.2	0.0	0.0	0.6	0.2	0.0	0.0
Nets	82	242.4	45.7	36.3	72.7	10.0	30.8	40.8	23.9	6.1	3.3	14.8	22.8	97.6
Opponents	82	242.4	45.0	35.7	76.2	10.6	30.8	41.4	22.0	7.1	4.5	14.5	23.0	98.3

New Orleans/Oklahoma City Hornets

Player	GP	MPG	FG%	3Pt%	FT%	OFF	DEF	Total	APG	SPG	BPG	TO	PF	PPG
			Field Goals			Rebounds								
David West	52	36.5	47.6	32.0	82.4	2.4	5.7	8.2	2.2	0.8	0.7	1.8	2.8	18.3
Peja Stojakovic	13	32.7	42.3	40.5	81.6	0.8	3.3	4.2	0.8	0.6	0.3	1.5	2.2	17.8
Chris Paul	64	36.8	43.7	35.0	81.8	0.8	3.5	4.4	8.9	1.8	0.1	2.5	2.4	17.3
Desmond Mason	75	34.3	45.2	00.0	66.3	1.7	2.9	4.6	1.5	0.7	0.3	2.6	2.3	13.7
Devin Brown	58	28.7	42.0	35.7	79.4	0.9	3.4	4.3	2.6	0.8	0.2	1.6	2.4	11.6
Bobby Jackson	56	23.8	39.4	32.7	77.4	0.8	2.4	3.2	2.5	0.9	0.1	1.4	1.8	10.6
Rasual Butler	81	27.4	39.8	36.9	64.4	0.5	2.6	3.2	0.8	0.5	0.7	0.8	1.8	10.1
Tyson Chandler	73	34.6	62.4	00.0	52.7	4.4	8.0	12.4	0.9	0.5	1.8	1.7	3.3	9.5
Jannero Pargo	82	20.9	40.9	38.8	85.2	0.2	2.0	2.2	2.5	0.7	0.1	1.5	1.5	9.2
Marc Jackson	56	18.3	41.0	00.0	87.4	1.1	2.3	3.4	1.0	0.4	0.1	1.2	1.6	7.3
Linton Johnson III	54	13.3	48.9	33.3	81.1	1.0	2.1	3.0	0.3	0.6	0.3	0.5	1.9	4.2
Hilton Armstrong	56	11.3	54.4	00.0	59.7	1.0	1.6	2.7	0.2	0.2	0.5	0.6	1.4	3.1
Cedric Simmons	43	12.4	41.7	00.0	48.5	1.0	1.5	2.5	0.3	0.2	0.5	0.5	1.7	2.9
Brandon Bass	21	7.7	34.1	00.0	75.0	0.6	1.4	2.0	0.1	0.1	0.1	0.5	0.8	2.0
Marcus Vinicius	13	7.9	46.7	42.9	71.4	0.2	0.7	0.8	0.4	0.2	0.1	0.5	0.8	1.7
Hornets	82	242.4	44.5	36.2	74.0	12.5	30.6	43.1	18.7	6.4	4.2	14.5	19.8	95.5
Opponents	82	242.4	45.7	35.5	75.9	10.4	30.4	40.8	20.8	6.8	4.8	13.6	21.1	97.1

New York Knicks

Player	GP	MPG	FG%	3Pt%	FT%	OFF	DEF	Total	APG	SPG	BPG	TO	PF	PPG
			Field Goals			Rebounds								
Eddy Curry	81	35.2	57.6	100.0	61.5	2.4	4.6	7.0	0.8	0.4	0.5	3.6	3.3	19.5
Jamal Crawford	59	37.3	40.0	32.0	83.8	0.7	2.5	3.2	4.4	1.0	0.1	2.8	1.9	17.6
Stephon Marbury	74	37.1	41.5	35.7	76.9	0.5	2.4	2.9	5.4	1.0	0.1	2.4	2.5	16.4
Quentin Richardson	49	33.1	41.8	37.6	69.2	1.3	5.9	7.2	2.2	0.7	0.1	1.4	2.7	13.0
Steve Francis	44	28.1	40.8	37.8	82.9	0.8	2.8	3.6	3.9	0.9	0.3	2.3	2.9	11.3
David Lee	58	29.8	60.0	00.0	81.5	3.4	7.0	10.4	1.8	0.8	0.4	1.6	2.7	10.7
Nate Robinson	64	21.2	43.4	39.0	77.7	0.9	1.5	2.4	1.4	0.8	0.1	1.1	2.5	10.1
Channing Frye	72	26.3	43.3	16.7	78.7	1.3	4.2	5.5	0.9	0.5	0.6	1.4	3.0	9.5
Renaldo Balkman	68	15.6	50.5	18.5	56.7	1.4	2.9	4.3	0.6	0.8	0.7	0.7	2.1	4.9
Mardy Collins	52	14.9	38.2	27.7	58.5	0.5	1.5	2.0	1.6	0.6	0.1	1.1	1.4	4.5
Jared Jeffries	55	23.8	46.1	10.0	45.6	2.0	2.3	4.3	1.2	0.8	0.6	1.1	2.7	4.1
Malik Rose	65	12.5	39.8	25.0	80.8	0.7	2.0	2.7	1.0	0.4	0.1	1.0	1.8	3.0
Jerome James	41	6.7	41.8	00.0	55.6	0.5	1.1	1.6	0.1	0.2	0.4	0.6	1.8	1.9
Kelvin Cato	18	5.3	31.8	00.0	66.7	0.7	1.1	1.7	0.0	0.2	0.6	0.3	0.6	1.2
Randolph Morris	5	8.8	16.7	00.0	33.3	0.2	1.6	1.8	0.2	0.4	0.2	0.4	0.8	0.8
Knicks	82	244.0	45.7	34.6	71.5	12.6	30.7	43.3	18.7	6.6	3.2	17.1	23.6	97.5
Opponents	82	244.0	46.0	37.6	75.6	10.8	28.0	38.8	21.3	7.5	5.0	13.7	22.9	100.3

Orlando Magic

Player	GP	MPG	FG%	3Pt%	FT%	OFF	DEF	Total	APG	SPG	BPG	TO	PF	PPG
			Field Goals			Rebounds								
Dwight Howard	82	36.9	60.3	50.0	58.6	3.5	8.8	12.3	1.9	0.9	1.9	3.9	3.0	17.6
Grant Hill	65	30.9	51.8	16.7	74.6	0.8	2.8	3.6	2.1	0.9	0.4	2.2	2.2	14.4
Hedo Turkoglu	73	31.1	41.9	38.8	78.1	0.8	3.2	4.0	3.2	1.0	0.2	2.0	3.0	13.3
Jameer Nelson	77	30.3	43.0	33.5	82.8	0.6	2.4	3.1	4.3	1.0	0.1	2.4	2.9	13.0
Trevor Ariza	57	22.4	43.0	00.0	62.0	1.7	2.6	4.4	1.1	1.0	0.3	1.5	2.4	8.9
Darko Milicic	80	23.9	45.4	00.0	61.3	1.8	3.7	5.5	1.1	0.6	1.8	1.6	2.7	8.0
Keyon Dooling	66	21.7	41.0	32.3	80.9	0.3	1.0	1.3	1.7	0.8	0.2	1.1	1.9	7.9
Carlos Arroyo	72	18.1	42.5	27.5	79.5	0.4	1.4	1.9	2.8	0.5	0.0	1.3	1.8	7.7
Tony Battie	66	23.9	48.9	00.0	67.5	1.4	3.8	5.2	0.5	0.4	0.5	0.9	2.8	6.1
J.J. Redick	42	14.8	41.0	38.8	90.0	0.2	1.0	1.2	0.9	0.3	0.0	0.5	1.2	6.0
Keith Bogans	59	16.8	40.4	38.7	74.6	0.3	1.3	1.6	1.0	0.5	0.0	0.8	1.7	5.1
Travis Diener	26	11.1	42.5	36.0	80.0	0.1	0.6	0.7	1.3	0.2	0.0	0.5	1.0	3.8
Pat Garrity	33	8.4	31.4	34.4	88.9	0.4	1.0	1.3	0.4	0.2	0.0	0.4	1.1	2.2
Bo Outlaw	41	11.2	66.7	00.0	59.1	1.1	1.4	2.6	0.4	0.4	-0.2	0.5	1.4	2.0
James Augustine	2	3.5	33.3	00.0	00.0	0.5	1.0	1.5	1.0	0.0	0.0	1.0	1.0	1.0
Magic	82	241.2	47.2	35.6	70.2	11.2	29.5	40.7	18.6	6.9	5.1	17.0	23.2	94.8
Opponents	82	241.2	44.2	35.3	76.0	10.5	27.0	37.6	19.6	8.3	4.6	15.0	23.4	94.0

Philadelphia 76ers

Player	GP	MPG	Field Goals		FT%	Rebounds		Total	APG	SPG	BPG	TO	PF	PPG
			FG%	3Pt%		OFF	DEF							
Allen Iverson	15	42.7	41.3	22.6	88.5	0.5	2.3	2.7	7.3	2.2	0.1	4.4	1.4	31.2
Andre Iguodala	76	40.3	44.7	31.0	82.0	1.0	4.7	5.7	5.7	2.0	0.4	3.4	2.6	18.2
Kyle Korver	74	30.9	44.0	43.0	91.4	0.4	3.1	3.5	1.4	0.8	0.3	1.6	2.5	14.4
Andre Miller	57	37.6	46.4	05.3	80.8	1.3	3.1	4.4	7.3	1.3	0.1	2.7	2.2	13.6
Willie Green	74	24.9	41.1	32.5	66.7	0.6	1.6	2.1	1.5	0.8	0.1	1.4	1.9	11.3
Chris Webber	18	30.2	38.7	40.0	64.3	2.1	6.2	8.3	3.4	1.0	0.8	1.8	2.0	11.0
Samuel Dalembert	82	30.9	54.1	00.0	74.6	2.9	6.0	8.9	0.8	0.6	1.9	2.0	3.5	10.7
Joe Smith	54	25.1	44.5	00.0	84.6	2.0	4.7	6.7	0.9	0.6	0.4	1.2	2.3	9.2
Rodney Carney	67	17.4	46.4	34.7	60.9	0.6	1.3	1.9	0.4	0.6	0.3	0.6	1.8	6.6
Steven Hunter	70	22.9	57.7	00.0	49.0	1.6	3.2	4.8	0.4	0.2	1.1	0.9	2.0	6.4
Shavlik Randolph	13	13.8	47.9	00.0	54.5	1.5	2.7	4.2	0.3	0.5	0.8	0.7	1.8	4.5
Louis Williams	61	11.3	44.1	32.4	69.6	0.3	0.9	1.1	1.8	0.4	0.0	0.8	0.7	4.3
Kevin Ollie	53	17.3	43.3	00.0	82.2	0.2	1.2	1.4	2.5	0.4	0.0	0.9	1.4	3.8
Alan Henderson	38	11.0	64.2	00.0	70.2	1.3	1.6	2.8	0.3	0.2	0.3	0.3	1.6	3.1
Bobby Jones	44	7.6	46.2	11.1	56.1	0.5	0.8	1.3	0.4	0.3	0.0	0.4	1.3	2.5
Louis Amundson	10	8.7	40.0	00.0	40.0	1.3	1.5	2.8	0.1	0.1	0.8	0.5	1.5	1.6
Ivan McFarlin	11	3.7	38.5	00.0	71.4	0.6	0.4	1.0	0.1	0.0	0.0	0.1	0.7	1.4
Steven Smith	8	3.5	25.0	00.0	50.0	0.1	0.5	0.6	0.0	0.1	0.0	0.3	0.5	0.6
76ers	82	242.4	45.8	34.5	76.7	11.0	28.7	39.7	20.4	7.2	4.8	15.3	20.4	94.9
Opponents	82	242.4	46.3	35.3	75.4	11.8	29.3	41.1	22.3	7.4	3.9	15.6	22.0	98.0

Phoenix Suns

Player	GP	MPG	Field Goals		FT%	Rebounds		Total	APG	SPG	BPG	TO	PF	PPG
			FG%	3Pt%		OFF	DEF							
Amare Stoudemire	82	32.8	57.5	00.0	78.1	2.7	6.9	9.6	1.0	1.0	1.3	2.8	3.6	20.4
Steve Nash	76	35.3	53.2	45.5	89.9	0.4	3.1	3.5	11.6	0.8	0.1	3.8	1.5	18.6
Leandro Barbosa	80	32.7	47.6	43.4	84.5	0.3	2.4	2.7	4.0	1.2	0.2	1.8	2.6	18.1
Shawn Marion	80	37.6	52.4	31.7	81.0	2.2	7.7	9.8	1.7	2.0	1.5	1.4	2.7	17.5
Raja Bell	78	37.4	43.2	41.3	77.6	0.6	2.6	3.2	2.5	0.6	0.3	1.1	3.0	14.7
Boris Diaw	73	31.1	53.8	33.3	68.3	1.2	3.1	4.3	4.8	0.4	0.5	2.1	2.4	9.7
James Jones	76	18.1	36.8	37.8	87.7	0.4	1.9	2.3	0.6	0.4	0.6	0.4	1.5	6.4
Marcus Banks	45	11.2	42.9	17.2	80.0	0.2	0.6	0.8	1.3	0.5	0.1	0.9	1.6	4.9
Kurt Thomas	67	18.0	48.6	00.0	78.9	1.3	4.4	5.7	0.4	0.4	0.4	0.5	2.3	4.6
Jalen Rose	29	8.5	44.2	44.7	91.7	0.1	0.7	0.8	0.6	0.2	0.1	0.3	0.8	3.7
Pat Burke	23	7.1	35.4	27.3	61.5	0.5	1.5	2.0	0.2	0.1	0.1	0.3	0.8	2.6
Eric Piakowski	11	6.6	36.0	38.9	100.0	0.2	0.6	0.8	0.4	0.0	0.1	0.5	0.5	2.5
Jumaine Jones	18	7.7	27.5	31.3	100.0	0.3	0.9	1.3	0.1	0.3	0.1	0.4	1.1	2.2
Sean Marks	3	5.7	33.3	00.0	100.0	0.0	1.0	1.0	0.0	0.0	0.3	0.0	1.3	2.0
Suns	82	242.7	49.4	39.9	80.8	9.0	31.5	40.5	25.9	6.7	4.8	14.5	20.2	110.2
Opponents	82	242.7	45.7	36.3	76.7	12.3	30.5	42.8	18.9	6.9	3.7	15.2	21.5	102.9

Portland Trail Blazers

Player	GP	MPG	Field Goals		FT%	Rebounds		Total	APG	SPG	BPG	TO	PF	PPG
			FG%	3Pt%		OFF	DEF							
Zach Randolph	68	35.7	46.7	29.2	81.9	2.9	7.2	10.1	2.2	0.8	0.2	3.2	2.7	23.6
Brandon Roy	57	35.4	45.6	37.7	83.8	1.0	3.4	4.4	4.0	1.2	0.2	2.0	2.4	16.8
Jarrett Jack	79	33.6	45.4	35.0	87.1	0.2	2.4	2.6	5.3	1.1	0.1	2.4	2.6	12.0
Travis Outlaw	67	22.9	43.4	27.0	79.0	1.0	2.3	3.2	0.8	0.9	1.1	1.0	2.2	9.6
LaMarcus Aldridge	63	22.1	50.3	00.0	72.2	2.3	2.7	5.0	0.4	0.4	1.2	0.7	3.0	9.0
Juan Dixon	55	22.6	42.6	36.4	83.3	0.3	1.3	1.5	1.5	0.9	0.1	1.4	2.0	8.9
Ime Udoka	75	28.6	46.1	40.6	74.2	1.3	2.5	3.7	1.5	1.0	0.2	1.0	2.8	8.4
Martell Webster	82	21.5	39.6	36.4	70.5	0.5	2.4	2.9	0.6	0.4	0.2	0.9	1.5	7.0
Jamaal Magloire	81	21.0	50.4	00.0	54.1	1.9	4.2	6.1	0.4	0.3	0.8	1.6	2.8	6.5
Fred Jones	24	18.7	38.4	25.9	84.6	0.3	1.1	1.4	2.2	0.8	0.2	0.7	1.7	4.8
Raef LaFrentz	27	13.0	38.2	08.7	76.9	0.9	1.7	2.6	0.3	0.3	0.4	0.5	2.1	3.7
Sergio Rodriguez	67	12.9	42.3	28.2	80.8	0.3	1.1	1.4	3.3	0.5	0.0	1.2	1.1	3.7
Dan Dickau	50	8.9	35.8	26.2	79.2	0.1	0.7	0.9	1.4	0.3	0.0	0.5	1.1	3.3
Stephen Graham	14	11.8	42.5	27.3	88.9	0.4	1.1	1.5	0.4	0.3	0.1	0.9	1.8	3.2
Joel Przybilla	43	16.3	47.4	00.0	37.0	1.4	2.5	3.9	0.3	0.2	1.6	0.9	2.9	2.0
Luke Schenscher	11	10.7	30.4	00.0	71.4	0.9	1.4	2.3	0.1	0.2	0.4	0.4	2.3	1.7
Jeremy Richardson	1	1.0	00.0	00.0	00.0	0.0	0.0	0.0	0.0	0.0	0.0	0.0	0.0	0.0
Trail Blazers	82	243.4	45.0	34.6	76.9	11.3	28.0	39.3	18.5	6.8	4.6	15.1	23.5	94.1
Opponents	82	243.4	47.1	36.1	77.8	10.4	28.6	39.0	20.8	6.6	4.6	13.7	21.3	98.4

Sacramento Kings

Player	GP	MPG	FG%	3Pt%	FT%	OFF	DEF	Total	APG	SPG	BPG	TO	PF	PPG
Kevin Martin	80	35.2	47.3	38.1	84.4	0.9	3.4	4.3	2.2	1.2	0.1	1.7	2.3	20.2
Ron Artest	70	37.7	44.0	35.8	74.0	1.5	5.0	6.5	3.4	2.1	0.6	2.1	2.9	18.8
Mike Bibby	82	34.0	40.4	36.0	83.0	0.5	2.7	3.2	4.7	1.1	0.1	2.4	1.7	17.1
S. Abdur-Rahim	80	25.2	47.4	15.0	72.6	1.5	3.5	5.0	1.4	0.7	0.5	1.5	3.0	9.9
Corliss Williamson	68	19.7	51.0	00.0	71.5	0.9	2.3	3.3	0.6	0.4	0.2	1.4	2.7	9.1
Brad Miller	63	28.3	45.3	15.2	77.2	1.3	5.1	6.4	3.6	0.6	0.6	1.7	2.5	9.0
John Salmons	79	27.0	45.6	35.7	77.9	0.6	2.7	3.3	3.2	0.9	0.3	1.5	2.2	8.5
Francisco Garcia	79	17.8	42.9	35.6	83.3	0.7	1.9	2.6	1.1	0.6	0.5	0.9	2.4	6.0
Kenny Thomas	62	22.8	48.2	00.0	51.3	2.2	3.9	6.1	1.2	0.7	0.3	1.5	2.3	5.3
Justin Williams	26	12.8	61.4	00.0	36.5	2.0	2.5	4.4	0.1	0.2	0.6	0.6	2.0	5.0
Ronnie Price	58	9.7	39.0	32.3	67.3	0.3	1.0	1.2	0.8	0.5	0.1	0.6	1.1	3.3
Jason Hart	13	7.7	50.0	50.0	90.9	0.2	1.0	1.2	0.8	0.2	0.0	0.3	1.8	3.3
Quincy Douby	42	8.5	38.1	24.0	73.3	0.3	0.6	0.9	0.4	0.4	0.1	0.4	0.5	2.8
Maurice Taylor	12	8.6	28.6	00.0	61.5	0.8	1.5	2.3	0.4	0.3	0.1	0.5	1.3	2.0
Vitaly Potapenko	3	4.3	00.0	00.0	00.0	0.0	0.7	0.7	0.0	0.0	0.0	0.7	1.0	0.0
Kings	82	241.5	45.0	35.0	76.5	9.7	29.2	38.9	20.3	8.2	3.2	14.6	21.9	101.3
Opponents	82	241.5	47.2	36.5	75.7	11.1	32.3	43.4	22.4	7.0	4.9	16.3	24.3	103.1

San Antonio Spurs

Player	GP	MPG	FG%	3Pt%	FT%	OFF	DEF	Total	APG	SPG	BPG	TO	PF	PPG
Tim Duncan	80	34.1	54.6	11.1	63.7	2.7	7.9	10.6	3.4	0.8	2.4	2.8	2.5	20.0
Tony Parker	77	32.5	52.0	39.5	78.3	0.4	2.8	3.2	5.5	1.1	0.1	2.5	1.8	18.6
Manu Ginobili	75	27.5	46.4	39.6	86.0	0.8	3.6	4.4	3.5	1.5	0.4	2.1	2.1	16.5
Michael Finley	82	22.2	41.2	36.4	91.8	0.4	2.3	2.7	1.3	0.4	0.2	0.6	0.9	9.0
Brent Barry	75	21.7	47.5	44.6	88.0	0.2	1.9	2.1	1.8	0.8	0.2	0.8	1.2	8.5
James White	6	22.8	43.9	28.6	80.0	0.5	2.8	3.3	0.8	0.5	0.2	0.8	1.2	8.3
Bruce Bowen	82	30.0	40.5	38.4	58.9	0.3	2.4	2.7	1.4	0.8	0.3	0.8	2.1	6.2
Francisco Elson	70	19.0	51.1	00.0	71.5	1.2	3.6	4.8	0.8	0.4	0.8	1.2	2.6	5.0
Matt Bonner	56	11.7	44.7	38.3	71.1	1.1	1.6	2.8	0.4	0.3	0.2	0.5	1.2	4.9
Beno Udrih	73	13.0	36.9	28.7	88.3	0.2	1.0	1.1	1.7	0.4	0.0	0.8	1.0	4.7
Fabricio Oberto	79	17.3	56.2	00.0	64.7	1.7	3.0	4.7	0.9	0.3	0.3	0.9	2.7	4.4
Robert Horry	68	16.5	35.9	33.6	59.4	1.1	2.3	3.4	1.1	0.7	0.6	0.7	1.5	3.9
Jackie Butler	11	9.4	45.7	00.0	90.0	0.5	1.5	2.0	0.5	0.2	0.0	0.9	1.5	3.7
Melvin Ely	6	10.8	30.0	00.0	58.3	0.5	1.8	2.3	0.7	0.7	0.3	0.8	2.0	3.2
Jacque Vaughn	64	11.9	42.5	50.0	75.4	0.1	0.9	1.1	2.0	0.4	0.0	0.6	1.2	3.0
Eric Williams	16	5.5	44.1	47.1	57.1	0.1	0.8	0.9	0.4	0.1	0.0	0.3	0.4	2.6
Spurs	82	241.2	47.4	38.1	75.1	9.3	31.4	40.7	22.1	7.2	5.1	13.9	19.4	98.5
Opponents	82	241.2	44.3	33.4	74.0	10.1	29.0	39.1	17.3	7.1	4.1	14.3	21.2	90.1

Seattle SuperSonics

Player	GP	MPG	FG%	3Pt%	FT%	OFF	DEF	Total	APG	SPG	BPG	TO	PF	PPG
Ray Allen	55	40.3	43.8	37.2	90.3	1.0	3.5	4.5	4.1	1.5	0.2	2.8	2.1	26.4
Rashard Lewis	60	39.1	46.1	39.0	84.1	1.5	5.1	6.6	2.4	1.1	0.7	2.0	2.4	22.4
Chris Wilcox	82	31.5	52.9	00.0	68.4	2.2	5.5	7.7	1.0	0.8	0.5	1.5	3.0	13.5
Luke Ridnour	71	29.5	43.3	35.3	80.5	0.4	1.9	2.3	5.2	1.2	0.3	2.2	2.5	11.0
Nick Collison	82	29.0	50.0	00.0	77.4	2.8	5.3	8.1	1.0	0.6	0.8	1.5	3.5	9.6
Earl Watson	77	27.9	38.3	32.9	73.5	0.4	2.0	2.4	5.7	1.3	0.3	2.2	2.0	9.4
Damien Wilkins	82	24.8	43.5	41.0	88.2	1.1	1.7	2.8	1.9	1.1	0.2	1.4	1.9	8.8
Johan Petro	81	18.6	51.6	00.0	64.9	1.1	3.0	4.1	0.6	0.5	0.6	1.0	2.9	6.2
Mickael Gelabale	70	17.7	46.2	23.4	80.5	0.8	1.6	2.5	0.8	0.3	0.3	0.7	1.5	4.6
Mike Wilks	47	11.4	46.8	33.3	78.6	0.3	0.8	1.1	1.7	0.3	0.1	0.7	1.1	3.6
Danny Fortson	14	11.3	50.0	00.0	76.9	0.9	2.1	3.1	0.1	0.1	0.0	1.1	2.7	2.9
Andre Brown	38	7.1	56.8	00.0	60.0	0.7	1.3	1.9	0.1	0.2	0.1	0.8	0.7	2.4
Mouhamed Sene	28	6.0	36.7	00.0	58.6	0.6	1.0	1.6	0.0	0.1	0.4	0.4	1.2	1.9
Desmon Farmer	8	4.0	33.3	25.0	100.0	0.0	0.1	0.1	1.1	0.1	0.0	0.1	0.3	1.6
A. Glyniadakis	13	6.2	47.1	00.0	50.0	0.2	0.5	0.6	0.1	0.0	0.0	0.7	1.5	1.3
Randy Livingston	4	6.5	00.0	00.0	00.0	0.3	0.0	0.3	1.0	0.0	0.0	0.3	0.5	0.0
Sonics	82	241.8	46.0	36.2	79.1	11.3	28.3	39.6	20.7	7.7	3.7	15.5	22.0	99.1
Opponents	82	241.8	47.6	36.1	75.1	11.6	29.4	41.0	22.8	7.2	4.2	15.0	19.9	102.0

Toronto Raptors

Player	GP	MPG	FG%	3Pt%	FT%	OFF	DEF	Total	APG	SPG	BPG	TO	PF	PPG
Chris Bosh 69		38.5	49.6	34.3	78.5	2.7	8.0	10.7	2.5	0.6	1.3	2.6	2.4	22.6
T.J. Ford 75		29.9	43.6	30.4	81.9	0.7	2.4	3.1	7.9	1.4	0.1	3.1	2.5	14.0
Anthony Parker 73		33.4	47.7	44.1	83.5	0.8	3.1	3.9	2.1	1.0	0.2	1.0	1.8	12.4
Andrea Bargnani..65		25.1	42.7	37.3	82.4	0.8	3.1	3.9	0.8	0.5	0.8	1.7	2.8	11.6
Juan Dixon 26		26.3	42.5	32.5	93.2	0.4	2.4	2.8	1.6	1.0	0.1	0.9	2.5	11.1
Morris Peterson....71		21.3	42.9	35.9	68.3	0.5	2.9	3.3	0.7	0.6	0.2	0.8	1.8	8.9
Jose Calderon......77		21.0	52.1	33.3	81.8	0.3	1.5	1.7	5.0	0.8	0.1	1.4	1.8	8.7
Jorge Garbajosa..67		28.5	42.0	34.2	73.1	0.7	4.2	4.9	1.9	1.2	0.2	1.0	1.3	8.5
Fred Jones 39		22.3	38.6	31.7	83.0	0.4	1.7	2.1	1.4	0.8	0.3	1.3	2.1	7.6
Joey Graham 79		16.7	49.5	29.0	84.0	0.7	2.4	3.1	0.6	0.4	0.1	0.6	2.0	6.4
Rasho Nesterovic.80		21.0	54.6	00.0	68.0	1.4	3.1	4.5	0.9	0.5	1.1	0.7	2.4	6.2
Luke Jackson.......10		12.2	51.4	30.8	55.6	0.2	0.7	0.9	0.9	0.5	0.1	0.6	1.2	4.5
Kris Humphries 60		11.2	47.0	00.0	67.1	1.3	1.8	3.1	0.3	0.2	0.4	0.5	1.6	3.8
Darrick Martin 31		7.1	35.1	35.1	71.4	0.1	0.3	0.4	1.4	0.1	0.0	0.4	0.7	3.0
Uros Slokar........20		3.6	53.8	50.0	69.2	0.4	0.4	0.7	0.1	0.1	0.1	0.5	0.6	1.9
P.J. Tucker............17		4.9	50.0	00.0	57.1	0.6	0.7	1.4	0.2	0.1	0.0	0.4	0.7	1.8
Pape Sow 7		4.9	33.3	00.0	66.7	0.9	0.7	1.6	0.3	0.1	0.1	0.1	0.3	1.4
Raptors..................82		240.9	46.3	36.3	78.8	9.2	30.2	39.5	22.2	7.1	3.9	13.5	20.4	99.5
Opponets...............82		240.9	46.3	35.7	75.4	10.3	32.2	42.5	21.2	6.0	3.9	15.1	21.8	98.5

Utah Jazz

Player	GP	MPG	FG%	3Pt%	FT%	OFF	DEF	Total	APG	SPG	BPG	TO	PF	PPG
Carlos Boozer 74		34.6	56.1	00.0	68.5	3.2	8.5	11.7	3.0	1.0	0.3	2.6	2.9	20.9
Mehmet Okur 80		33.3	46.2	38.4	76.5	2.0	5.2	7.2	2.0	0.5	0.5	1.6	3.2	17.6
Deron Williams 80		36.9	45.6	32.2	76.7	0.5	2.8	3.3	9.3	1.0	0.2	3.1	3.2	16.2
Matt Harpring.......77		25.5	49.1	33.3	76.7	1.5	3.1	4.6	1.3	0.7	0.1	1.5	3.0	11.6
Derek Fisher.........82		27.9	38.2	30.8	85.3	0.4	1.5	1.8	3.3	1.0	0.1	1.5	2.9	10.1
Andrei Kirilenko....70		29.3	47.1	21.3	72.8	1.3	3.4	4.7	2.9	1.1	2.1	1.9	2.5	8.3
Gordan Giricek.....61		19.5	46.2	42.6	81.6	0.4	1.7	2.1	1.0	0.5	0.1	1.1	2.0	7.8
Paul Millsap.........82		18.0	52.5	33.3	67.3	2.2	2.9	5.2	0.8	0.8	0.9	1.2	2.9	6.8
Ronnie Brewer......56		12.1	52.8	00.0	67.5	0.7	0.7	1.3	0.4	0.7	0.1	0.4	0.8	4.6
C.J. Miles 37		10.1	34.5	21.9	60.9	0.3	0.6	0.9	0.7	0.3	0.1	0.8	1.6	2.7
Rafael Araujo 28		8.9	41.5	00.0	62.1	0.8	1.6	2.4	0.4	0.2	0.1	0.6	1.4	2.6
Jarron Collins 82		11.1	44.1	00.0	65.1	0.9	1.2	2.1	0.7	0.2	0.1	0.5	1.8	2.5
Dee Brown 49		9.2	32.7	21.4	64.9	0.2	0.7	0.8	1.7	0.5	0.1	0.6	1.0	1.9
Roger Powell 3		4.3	00.0	00.0	100.0	1.0	0.0	1.0	0.0	0.0	0.0	1.0	0.7	0.7
Louis Amundson 1		2.0	00.0	00.0	00.0	0.0	0.0	0.0	0.0	0.0	0.0	0.0	0.0	0.0
Jazz..........................82		241.5	47.4	33.5	74.3	12.6	30.0	42.5	24.7	7.0	4.1	15.6	25.2	101.5
Opponents................82		241.5	45.5	35.5	76.7	9.9	27.1	37.0	18.9	7.6	5.3	15.0	24.5	98.6

Washington Wizards

Player	GP	MPG	FG%	3Pt%	FT%	OFF	DEF	Total	APG	SPG	BPG	TO	PF	PPG
Gilbert Arenas......74		39.8	41.8	35.1	84.4	0.8	3.7	4.6	6.0	1.9	0.2	3.2	3.4	28.4
Antawn Jamison...70		38.0	45.0	36.4	73.6	1.9	6.1	8.0	1.9	1.1	0.5	1.5	2.8	19.8
Caron Butler.........63		39.3	46.3	25.0	86.3	2.3	5.1	7.4	3.7	2.1	0.3	2.9	3.0	19.1
D. Stevenson........82		29.5	46.1	40.4	70.4	0.7	2.0	2.6	2.7	0.8	0.2	1.5	1.9	11.2
Darius Songaila....37		18.9	52.4	00.0	85.2	1.2	2.4	3.6	1.0	0.5	0.3	1.2	2.8	7.6
Jarvis Hayes 81		20.1	41.0	36.1	84.5	0.5	2.1	2.6	1.0	0.6	0.2	0.7	2.0	7.2
Antonio Daniels....80		22.0	44.2	30.2	83.2	0.2	1.7	1.9	3.6	0.5	0.1	0.9	1.0	7.1
Brendan Haywood..77		22.6	55.8	00.0	54.8	2.5	3.7	6.2	0.6	0.4	1.1	1.2	2.7	6.6
Etan Thomas 65		19.2	57.4	00.0	55.8	2.1	3.7	5.8	0.4	0.3	1.4	1.1	2.5	6.1
Andray Blatche 56		12.2	43.7	14.8	61.2	1.4	2.0	3.4	0.7	0.3	0.6	0.9	1.7	3.7
Roger Mason 62		7.9	33.0	32.4	87.5	0.1	0.6	0.7	0.6	0.2	0.1	0.3	1.1	2.7
Donell Taylor 47		7.9	40.0	17.6	52.4	0.3	0.8	1.1	1.0	0.4	0.1	0.5	0.7	2.7
Calvin Booth.........44		8.6	47.0	50.0	60.0	0.6	1.2	1.8	0.4	0.1	0.7	0.2	1.6	1.6
Mike Hall 2		6.5	25.0	00.0	00.0	0.5	0.5	1.0	0.5	0.0	0.0	0.0	0.5	1.0
James Lang 11		5.0	44.4	00.0	60.0	0.5	0.5	1.0	0.2	0.0	0.3	0.2	1.3	1.0
Michael Ruffin 30		9.0	27.8	00.0	36.8	1.2	0.9	2.1	0.2	0.2	0.3	0.4	1.4	0.6
Wizards 82		241.8	45.0	34.8	76.5	12.2	29.0	41.2	20.2	7.7	4.6	13.8	22.2	104.3
Opponents................82		241.8	47.3	37.7	77.7	11.9	31.1	43.0	23.7	6.3	4.6	15.7	23.5	104.9

2007 NBA Draft

The 2007 NBA Draft was held on June 28, 2007 in New York City.

First Round

1. Greg Oden, Portland
2. Kevin Durant, Seattle
3. Al Horford, Atlanta
4. Mike Conley Jr., Memphis
5. Jeff Green, Boston
6. Yi Jianlin, Milwaukee
7. Corey Brewer, Minnesota
8. Brandan Wright, Charlotte
9. Joakim Noah, Chicago
   (from New York)
10. Spencer Hawes, Sacramento
11. Acie Law IV, Atlanta
    (from Indiana)
12. Thaddeus Young, Philadelphia
13. Julian Wright, NO/Okla. City
14. Al Thornton, LA Clippers
15. Rodney Stuckey, Detroit
    (from Orlando)
16. Nick Young, Washington
17. Sean Williams, New Jersey
18. Marco Belinelli, Golden State
19. Javaris Crittenton, LA Lakers
20. Jason Smith, Miami
21. Daequan Cook, Philadelphia
    (from Denver)
22. Jared Dudley, Charlotte
    (from Toronto)
23. Wilson Chandler, New York
    (from Chicago)
24. Rudy Fernandez, Phoenix
    (from Cleveland)
25. Morris Almond, Utah
26. Aaron Brooks, Houston
27. Arron Afflalo, Detroit
28. Tiago Splitter, San Antonio
29. Alando Tucker, Phoenix
30. Petteri Koponen, Philadelphia
    (from Dallas)

Second Round

31. Carl Landry, Seattle
    (from Memphis)
32. Gabe Pruitt, Boston
33. Marcus Williams, San Antonio
    (from Milwaukee)
34. Nick Fazekas, Dallas (from Atl.)
35. Glen Davis, Seattle
36. Jermareo Davidson, G. State
    (from Minnesota)
37. Josh McRoberts, Portland
38. Kyrylo Fesenko, Philadelphia
    (from New York)
39. Stanko Barac, Miami
    (from Sacramento)
40. Sun Yue, LA Lakers
    (from Charlotte)
41. Chris Richard, Minnesota
    (from Philadelphia)
42. Derrick Byars, Portland
    (from Indiana)
43. Adam Haluska, NO/Okla. City
44. Reyshawn Terry, Orlando
45. Jared Jordan, LA Clippers
46. Stephane Lasme, Golden State
    (from New Jersey)
47. Dominic McGuire, Washington
48. Marc Gasol, LA Lakers
49. Aaron Gray, Chicago
    (from Golden State via 3 teams)
50. Renaldas Seibutis, Dallas
    (from Miami via LA Lakers)
51. JamesOn Curry, Chicago
    (from Denver)
52. Taurean Green, Portland
    (from Toronto)
53. Demetris Nichols, Portland
    (from Chicago)
54. Brad Newley, Houston
    (from Cleveland)
55. Herbert Hill, Utah
56. Ramon Sessions, Milwaukee
    (from Houston)
57. Sammy Mejia, Detroit
58. Giorgos Printezis, San Antonio
59. D.J. Strawberry, Phoenix
60. Milovan Rakovic, Dallas

Women's National Basketball Association

2007 Final Standings

EASTERN CONFERENCE

Team	W	L	Pct	GB
†Detroit	24	10	.706	—
*Indiana	21	13	.618	3.0
*Connecticut	18	16	.529	6.0
*New York	16	18	.471	8.0
Washington	16	18	.471	8.0
Chicago	14	20	.412	10.0

WESTERN CONFERENCE

Team	W	L	Pct	GB
†Phoenix	23	11	.676	—
*San Antonio	20	14	.588	3.0
*Sacramento	19	15	.559	4.0
*Seattle	17	17	.500	6.0
Houston	13	21	.382	10.0
Minnesota	10	24	.294	13.0
Los Angeles	10	24	.294	13.0

†Clinched conference title.   *Clinched playoff berth.

2007 Playoffs

FIRST ROUND

EASTERN CONFERENCE

Game 1	Detroit 51	at New York 73
Game 2	New York 73	at Detroit 76
Game 3	New York 70	at Detroit 71 (OT)

Detroit won series 2–1.

Game 1	Indiana 88	at Connecticut 93 (3OT)
Game 2	Connecticut 59	at Indiana 78
Game 2	Connecticut 88	at Indiana 93 (OT)

Indiana won series 2–1.

WESTERN CONFERENCE

Game 1	Phoenix 101	at Seattle 84
Game 2	Seattle 89	at Phoenix 95

Phoenix won series 2–0.

Game 1	San Antonio 65	at Sacramento 86
Game 2	Sacramento 61	at San Antonio 86
Game 2	Sacramento 78	at San Antonio 80

San Antonio won series 2–1.

EASTERN CONFERENCE FINALS

Game 1	Detroit 65	at Indiana 75
Game 2	Indiana 63	at Detroit 77
Game 3	Indiana 65	at Detroit 81

Detroit won series 2–1.

WESTERN CONFERENCE FINALS

Game 1	Phoenix 102	at San Antonio 100
Game 2	San Antonio 92	at Phoenix 98

Phoenix won series 2–0.

WNBA FINALS

Game 1	Phoenix 100	at Detroit 108
Game 2	Phoenix 98	at Detroit 70
Game 3	Detroit 88	at Phoenix 83
Game 4	Detroit 76	at Phoenix 77
Game 5	Phoenix 108	at Detroit 92

Phoenix won series 3–2.

FOR THE RECORD • Year by Year

NBA Champions

Season	Winner	Series	Runner-Up	Winning Coach	Finals MVP
1946–47	Philadelphia	4–1	Chicago	Eddie Gottlieb	—
1947–48	Baltimore	4–2	Philadelphia	Buddy Jeannette	—
1948–49	Minneapolis	4–2	Washington	John Kundla	—
1949–50	Minneapolis	4–2	Syracuse	John Kundla	—
1950–51	Rochester	4–3	New York	Les Harrison	—
1951–52	Minneapolis	4–3	New York	John Kundla	—
1952–53	Minneapolis	4–1	New York	John Kundla	—
1953–54	Minneapolis	4–3	Syracuse	John Kundla	—
1954–55	Syracuse	4–3	Ft Wayne	Al Cervi	—
1955–56	Philadelphia	4–1	Ft Wayne	George Senesky	—
1956–57	Boston	4–3	St Louis	Red Auerbach	—
1957–58	St Louis	4–2	Boston	Alex Hannum	—
1958–59	Boston	4–0	Minneapolis	Red Auerbach	—
1959–60	Boston	4–3	St Louis	Red Auerbach	—
1960–61	Boston	4–1	St Louis	Red Auerbach	—
1961–62	Boston	4–3	LA Lakers	Red Auerbach	—
1962–63	Boston	4–2	LA Lakers	Red Auerbach	—
1963–64	Boston	4–1	San Francisco	Red Auerbach	—
1964–65	Boston	4–1	LA Lakers	Red Auerbach	—
1965–66	Boston	4–3	LA Lakers	Red Auerbach	—
1966–67	Philadelphia	4–2	San Francisco	Alex Hannum	—
1967–68	Boston	4–2	LA Lakers	Bill Russell	—
1968–69	Boston	4–3	LA Lakers	Bill Russell	Jerry West, LA
1969–70	New York	4–3	LA Lakers	Red Holzman	Willis Reed, NY
1970–71	Milwaukee	4–0	Baltimore	Larry Costello	Kareem Abdul-Jabbar, Mil
1971–72	LA Lakers	4–1	New York	Bill Sharman	Wilt Chamberlain, LA
1972–73	New York	4–1	LA Lakers	Red Holzman	Willis Reed, NY
1973–74	Boston	4–3	Milwaukee	Tommy Heinsohn	John Havlicek, Bos
1974–75	Golden State	4–0	Washington	Al Attles	Rick Barry, GS
1975–76	Boston	4–2	Phoenix	Tommy Heinsohn	JoJo White, Bos
1976–77	Portland	4–2	Philadelphia	Jack Ramsay	Bill Walton, Port
1977–78	Washington	4–3	Seattle	Dick Motta	Wes Unseld, Wash
1978–79	Seattle	4–1	Washington	Lenny Wilkens	Dennis Johnson, Sea
1979–80	LA Lakers	4–2	Philadelphia	Paul Westhead	Magic Johnson, LA
1980–81	Boston	4–2	Houston	Bill Fitch	Cedric Maxwell, Bos
1981–82	LA Lakers	4–2	Philadelphia	Pat Riley	Magic Johnson, LA
1982–83	Philadelphia	4–0	LA Lakers	Billy Cunningham	Moses Malone, Phil
1983–84	Boston	4–3	LA Lakers	K.C. Jones	Larry Bird, Bos
1984–85	LA Lakers	4–2	Boston	Pat Riley	Kareem Abdul-Jabbar, LA
1985–86	Boston	4–2	Houston	K.C. Jones	Larry Bird, Bos
1986–87	LA Lakers	4–2	Boston	Pat Riley	Magic Johnson, LA
1987–88	LA Lakers	4–3	Detroit	Pat Riley	James Worthy, LA
1988–89	Detroit	4–0	LA Lakers	Chuck Daly	Joe Dumars, Det
1989–90	Detroit	4–1	Portland	Chuck Daly	Isiah Thomas, Det
1990–91	Chicago	4–1	LA Lakers	Phil Jackson	Michael Jordan, Chi
1991–92	Chicago	4–2	Portland	Phil Jackson	Michael Jordan, Chi
1992–93	Chicago	4–2	Phoenix	Phil Jackson	Michael Jordan, Chi
1993–94	Houston	4–3	New York	Rudy Tomjanovich	Hakeem Olajuwon, Hou
1994–95	Houston	4–0	Orlando	Rudy Tomjanovich	Hakeem Olajuwon, Hou
1995–96	Chicago	4–2	Seattle	Phil Jackson	Michael Jordan, Chi
1996–97	Chicago	4–2	Utah	Phil Jackson	Michael Jordan, Chi
1997–98	Chicago	4–2	Utah	Phil Jackson	Michael Jordan, Chi
1998–99	San Antonio	4–1	New York	Gregg Popovich	Tim Duncan, SA
1999–00	LA Lakers	4–2	Indiana	Phil Jackson	Shaquille O'Neal, LA
2000–01	LA Lakers	4–1	Philadelphia	Phil Jackson	Shaquille O'Neal, LA
2001–02	LA Lakers	4–0	New Jersey	Phil Jackson	Shaquille O'Neal, LA
2002–03	San Antonio	4–2	New Jersey	Gregg Popovich	Tim Duncan, SA
2003–04	Detroit	4–1	LA Lakers	Larry Brown	Chauncey Billups, Det
2004–05	San Antonio	4–3	Detroit	Gregg Popovich	Tim Duncan, SA
2005–06	Miami	4–2	Dallas	Pat Riley	Dwyane Wade, Mia
2006–07	San Antonio	4–0	Cleveland	Gregg Popovich	Tony Parker, SA

Most Valuable Player: Maurice Podoloff Trophy

Season	Player, Team	GP	Field Goals FGM	Pct	3-Pt FG FGM	Pct	Free Throws FTM	Pct	Rebounds Off	Total	A	Stl	BS	Avg
1955–56	Bob Pettit, StL	72	646	42.9	–	–	557	73.6	–	1,164	189	–	–	25.7
1956–57	Bob Cousy, Bos	64	478	37.8	–	–	363	82.1	–	309	478	–	–	20.6
1957–58	Bill Russell, Bos	69	456	44.2	–	–	230	51.9	–	1,564	202	–	–	16.6
1958–59	Bob Pettit, StL	72	719	43.8	–	–	667	75.9	–	1,182	221	–	–	29.2
1959–60	Wilt Chamberlain, Phil	72	1,065	46.1	–	–	577	58.2	–	1,941	168	–	–	37.6
1960–61	Bill Russell, Bos	78	532	42.6	–	–	258	55.0	–	1,868	264	–	–	16.9
1961–62	Bill Russell, Bos	76	575	45.7	–	–	286	59.5	–	1,891	341	–	–	18.9
1962–63	Bill Russell, Bos	78	511	43.2	–	–	287	55.5	–	1,843	348	–	–	16.8
1963–64	Oscar Robertson, Cin	79	840	48.3	–	–	800	85.3	–	783	868	–	–	31.4
1964–65	Bill Russell, Bos	78	429	43.8	–	–	244	57.3	–	1,878	410	–	–	14.1
1965–66	Wilt Chamberlain, Phil	79	1,074	54.0	–	–	501	51.3	–	1,943	414	–	–	33.5
1966–67	Wilt Chamberlain, Phil	81	785	68.3	–	–	386	44.1	–	1,957	630	–	–	24.1
1967–68	Wilt Chamberlain, Phil	82	819	59.5	–	–	354	38.0	–	1,952	702	–	–	24.3
1968–69	Wes Unseld, Balt	82	427	47.6	–	–	277	60.5	–	1,491	213	–	–	13.8
1969–70	Willis Reed, NY	81	702	50.7	–	–	351	75.6	–	1,126	161	–	–	21.7
1970–71	Lew Alcindor*, Mil	82	1,063	57.7	–	–	470	69.0	–	1,311	272	–	–	31.7
1971–72	Kareem Abdul-Jabbar, Mil	81	1,159	57.4	–	–	504	68.9	–	1,346	370	–	–	34.8
1972–73	Dave Cowens, Bos	82	740	45.2	–	–	204	77.9	–	1,329	333	–	–	20.5
1973–74	Kareem Abdul-Jabbar, Mil	81	948	53.9	–	–	295	70.2	287	1,178	386	112	283	27.0
1974–75	Bob McAdoo, Buff	82	1,095	51.2	–	–	641	80.5	307	1,155	179	92	174	34.5
1975–76	Kareem Abdul-Jabbar, LAL	82	914	52.9	–	–	447	70.3	272	1,383	413	119	338	27.7
1976–77	Kareem Abdul-Jabbar, LAL	82	888	57.9	–	–	376	70.1	266	1,090	319	101	261	26.2
1977–78	Bill Walton, Port	58	460	52.2	–	–	177	72.0	118	766	291	60	146	18.9
1978–79	Moses Malone, Hou	82	716	54.0	–	–	599	73.9	587	1,444	147	79	119	24.8
1979–80	Kareem Abdul-Jabbar, LAL	82	835	60.4	0	00.0	364	76.5	190	886	371	81	280	24.8
1980–81	Julius Erving, Phil	82	794	52.1	4	22.2	422	78.7	244	657	364	173	147	24.6
1981–82	Moses Malone, Hou	81	945	51.9	0	00.0	630	76.2	558	1,188	142	76	125	31.1
1982–83	Moses Malone, Phil	78	654	50.1	0	00.0	600	76.1	445	1,194	101	89	157	24.5
1983–84	Larry Bird, Bos	79	758	49.2	18	24.7	374	88.8	181	796	520	144	69	24.2
1984–85	Larry Bird, Bos	80	918	52.2	56	42.7	403	88.2	164	842	531	129	98	28.7
1985–86	Larry Bird, Bos	82	796	49.6	82	42.3	441	89.6	190	805	557	166	51	25.8
1986–87	Magic Johnson, LAL	80	683	52.2	8	20.5	535	84.8	122	504	977	138	36	23.9
1987–88	Michael Jordan, Chi	82	1,069	53.5	7	13.2	723	84.1	139	449	485	259	131	35.0
1988–89	Magic Johnson, LAL	77	579	50.9	59	31.4	513	91.1	111	607	988	138	22	22.5
1989–90	Magic Johnson, LAL	79	546	48.0	106	38.4	567	89.0	128	522	907	132	34	22.3
1990–91	Michael Jordan, Chi	82	990	53.9	29	31.2	571	85.1	118	492	453	223	83	31.5
1991–92	Michael Jordan, Chi	80	943	51.9	27	27.0	491	83.2	91	511	489	182	75	30.1
1992–93	Charles Barkley, Phoe	76	716	52.0	67	30.5	445	76.5	237	928	385	119	74	25.6
1993–94	Hakeem Olajuwon, Hou	80	894	52.8	8	42.1	388	71.6	229	955	287	128	297	27.3
1994–95	David Robinson, SA	81	788	53.0	6	30.0	656	77.4	234	877	236	134	262	27.6
1995–96	Michael Jordan, Chi	82	916	49.5	111	42.7	548	83.4	148	543	352	180	42	30.4
1996–97	Karl Malone, Utah	82	864	55.0	0	00.0	521	75.5	193	809	368	113	48	27.4
1997–98	Michael Jordan, Chi	82	881	46.5	30	23.8	565	78.4	130	475	283	141	45	28.7
1998–99	Karl Malone, Utah	49	393	49.3	0	00.0	378	78.8	107	463	201	62	28	23.8
1999–00	Shaquille O'Neal, LAL	79	956	57.4	0	00.0	432	52.4	336	1078	299	36	239	29.7
2000–01	Allen Iverson, Phil	71	762	42.0	98	32.0	585	81.4	50	273	325	78	20	31.1
2001–02	Tim Duncan, SA	82	764	50.8	1	10.0	560	79.9	268	1042	307	61	203	25.5
2002–03	Tim Duncan, SA	81	714	51.3	6	27.3	450	71.0	260	1045	316	55	237	23.3
2003–04	Kevin Garnett, Minn	82	804	49.9	11	25.6	368	79.1	245	1139	409	120	178	24.2
2004–05	Steve Nash, Phoe	75	430	50.2	94	43.1	211	88.7	80	330	861	74	6	26.0
2005–06	Steve Nash, Phoe	79	541	51.2	150	43.9	257	92.1	47	333	826	61	12	18.8
2006–07	Dirk Nowitzki, Dal	78	673	50.2	72	41.6	498	90.4	122	693	263	52	62	24.6

*Alcindor changed his name to Kareem Abdul-Jabbar after the 1970–71 season.

Coach of the Year: Arnold (Red) Auerbach Trophy

1962–63...Harry Gallatin, StL	1977–78...Hubie Brown, Atl	1992–93...Pat Riley, NY
1963–64...Alex Hannum, SF	1978–79...Cotton Fitzsimmons, KC	1993–94...Lenny Wilkens, Atl
1964–65...Red Auerbach, Bos	1979–80...Bill Fitch, Bos	1994–95...Del Harris, LA Lakers
1965–66...Dolph Schayes, Phil	1980–81...Jack McKinney, Ind	1995–96...Phil Jackson, Chi
1966–67...Johnny Kerr, Chi	1981–82...Gene Shue, Wash	1996–97...Pat Riley, Mia
1967–68...Richie Guerin, StL	1982–83...Don Nelson, Mil	1997–98...Larry Bird, Ind
1968–69...Gene Shue, Balt	1983–84...Frank Layden, Utah	1998–99...Mike Dunleavy, Port
1969–70...Red Holzman, NY	1984–85...Don Nelson, Mil	1999–00 ..Glenn (Doc) Rivers, Orl
1970–71...Dick Motta, Chi	1985–86...Mike Fratello, Atl	2000–01...Larry Brown, Phil
1971–72...Bill Sharman, LA	1986–87...Mike Schuler, Port	2001–02...Rick Carlisle, Det
1972–73...Tom Heinsohn, Bos	1987–88...Doug Moe, Den	2002–03...Gregg Popovich, SA
1973–74...Ray Scott, Det	1988–89...Cotton Fitzsimmons, Phoe	2003–04...Hubie Brown, Mem
1974–75...Phil Johnson, KC-Oma	1989–90...Pat Riley, LAL	2004–05...Mike D'Antoni, Phoe
1975–76...Bill Fitch, Clev	1990–91...Don Chaney, Hou	2005–06...Avery Johnson, Dall
1976–77...Tom Nissalke, Hou	1991–92...Don Nelson, GS	2006–07...Sam Mitchell, Tor

Note: Award named after Auerbach in 1986.

Rookie of the Year: Eddie Gottlieb Trophy

1952–53...Don Meineke, FW	1971–72...Sidney Wicks, Port	1990–91...Derrick Coleman, NJ
1953–54...Ray Felix, Balt	1972–73...Bob McAdoo, Buff	1991–92...Larry Johnson, Char
1954–55...Bob Pettit, Mil	1973–74...Ernie DiGregorio, Buff	1992–93...Shaquille O'Neal, Orl
1955–56...Maurice Stokes, Roch	1974–75...Keith Wilkes, GS	1993–94...Chris Webber, GS
1956–57...Tom Heinsohn, Bos	1975–76...Alvan Adams, Phoe	1994–95...J. Kidd, Dall/G. Hill, Det
1957–58...Woody Sauldsberry, Phil	1976–77...Adrian Dantley, Buff	1995–96...Damon Stoudamire, Tor
1958–59...Elgin Baylor, Minn	1977–78...Walter Davis, Phoe	1996–97...Allen Iverson, Phil
1959–60...Wilt Chamberlain, Phil	1978–79...Phil Ford, KC	1997–98...Tim Duncan, SA
1960–61...Oscar Robertson, Cin	1979–80...Larry Bird, Bos	1998–99...Vince Carter, Tor
1961–62...Walt Bellamy, Chi	1980–81...Darrell Griffith, Utah	1999–00 ..Steve Francis, Hou
1962–63...Terry Dischinger, Chi	1981–82...Buck Williams, NJ	Elton Brand, Chi
1963–64...Jerry Lucas, Cin	1982–83...Terry Cummings, SD	2000–01 ..Mike Miller, Orl
1964–65...Willis Reed, NY	1983–84...Ralph Sampson, Hou	2001–02...Pau Gasol, Mem
1965–66...Rick Barry, SF	1984–85...Michael Jordan, Chi	2002–03 ..Amare Stoudemire, Phoe
1966–67...Dave Bing, Det	1985–86...Patrick Ewing, NY	2003–04 ..LeBron James, Clev
1967–68...Earl Monroe, Balt	1986–87...Chuck Person, Ind	2004–05...Emeka Okafor, Char
1968–69...Wes Unseld, Balt	1987–88...Mark Jackson, NY	2005–06...Chris Paul, NO
1969–70...K. Abdul-Jabbar, Mil	1988–89...Mitch Richmond, GS	2006–07...Brandon Roy, Port
1970–71...Dave Cowens, Bos	1989–90...David Robinson, SA	
Geoff Petrie, Port		

Defensive Player of the Year

1982–83...Sidney Moncrief, Mil	1991–92...David Robinson, SA	2000–01...Dikembe Mutombo, Phi/Atl
1983–84...Sidney Moncrief, Mil	1992–93...Hakeem Olajuwon, Hou	2001–02...Ben Wallace, Det
1984–85...Mark Eaton, Utah	1993–94...Hakeem Olajuwon, Hou	2002–03...Ben Wallace, Det
1985–86...Alvin Robertson, SA	1994–95...Dikembe Mutombo, Den	2003–04...Ron Artest, Ind
1986–87...Michael Cooper, LAL	1995–96...Gary Payton, Sea	2004–05...Ben Wallace, Det
1987–88...Michael Jordan, Chi	1996–97...Dikembe Mutombo, Atl	2005–06...Ben Wallace, Det
1988–89...Mark Eaton, Utah	1997–98...Dikembe Mutombo, Atl	2006–07...Marcus Camby, Den
1989–90...Dennis Rodman, Det	1998–99...Alonzo Mourning, Mia	
1990–91...Dennis Rodman, Det	1999–00...Alonzo Mourning, Mia	

Sixth Man Award

1982–83...Bobby Jones, Phil	1991–92...Detlef Schrempf, Ind	2000–01...Aaron McKie, Phil
1983–84...Kevin McHale, Bos	1992–93...Cliff Robinson, Port	2001–02...Corliss Williamson, Det
1984–85...Kevin McHale, Bos	1993–94...Dell Curry, Char	2002–03...Bobby Jackson, Sac
1985–86...Bill Walton, Bos	1994–95...Anthony Mason, NY	2003–04...Antawn Jamison, Dall
1986–87...Ricky Pierce, Mil	1995–96...Tony Kukoc, Chi	2004–05...Ben Gordon, Chi
1987–88...Roy Tarpley, Dall	1996–97...John Starks, NY	2005–06...Mike Miller, Mem
1988–89...Eddie Johnson, Phoe	1997–98...Danny Manning, Phoe	2006–07...Leandro Barbosa, Phoe
1989–90...Ricky Pierce, Mil	1998–99...Darrell Armstrong, Orl	
1990–91...Detlef Schrempf, Ind	1999–00...Rodney Rogers, Phoe	

J. Walter Kennedy Citizenship Award

1974–75...Wes Unseld, Wash	1985–86...Michael Cooper, LAL	1996–97...P.J. Brown, Mia
1975–76...Slick Watts, Sea	Rory Sparrow, NY	1997–98...Steve Smith, Atl
1976–77...Dave Bing, Wash	1986–87...Isiah Thomas, Det	1998–99...Brian Grant, Port
1977–78...Bob Lanier, Det	1987–88...Alex English, Den	1999–00...Vlade Divac, Sac
1978–79...Calvin Murphy, Hou	1988–89...Thurl Bailey, Utah	2000–01...Dikembe Mutombo, Phil
1979–80...Austin Carr, Clev	1989–90...Glenn (Doc) Rivers, Atl	2001–02...Alonzo Mourning, Mia
1980–81...Mike Glenn, NY	1990–91...Kevin Johnson, Phoe	2002–03...David Robinson, SA
1981–82...Kent Benson, Det	1991–92...Magic Johnson, LAL	2003–04...Reggie Miller, Ind
1982–83...Julius Erving, Phil	1992–93...Terry Porter, Port	2004–05...Eric Snow, Clev
1983–84...Frank Layden, Utah	1993–94...Joe Dumars, Det	2005–06...Kevin Garnett, Minn
1984–85...Dan Issel, Den	1994–95...Joe O'Toole, Atl	2006–07...Luol Deng, Chi
	1995–96...Chris Dudley, Port	

Most Improved Player

1985–86 ....Alvin Robertson, SA	1993–94 ....Don MacLean, Wash	2001–02 ....Jermaine O'Neal, Ind
1986–87 ...Dale Ellis, Sea	1994–95 ....Dana Barros, Phil	2002–03 ....Gilbert Arenas, GS
1987–88 ....Kevin Duckworth, Port	1995–96 ....Gheorghe Muresan, Wash	2003–04 ....Zach Randolph, Port
1988–89 ....Kevin Johnson, Phoe	1996–97 ...Isaac Austin, Mia	2004–05 ....Bobby Simmons, LAC
1989–90 ...Rony Seikaly, Mia	1997–98 ...Alan Henderson, Atl	2005–06 ....Boris Diaw, Phoe
1990–91 ...Scott Skiles, Orl	1998–99 ....Darrell Armstrong, Orl	2006–07 ....Monta Ellis, GS
1991–92 ....Pervis Ellison, Wash	1999–00 ....Jalen Rose, Ind	
1992–93 ....Mahmoud	2000–01 ....Tracy McGrady, Orl	
Abdul-Rauf, Den		

Executive of the Year

1972–73...Joe Axelson, KC-Oma	1984–85...Vince Boryla, Den	1996–97...Bob Bass, Char
1973–74...Eddie Donovan, Buff	1985–86...Stan Kasten, Atl	1997–98...Wayne Embry, Clev
1974–75...Dick Vertlieb, GS	1986–87...Stan Kasten, Atl	1998–99...Geoff Petrie, Sac
1975–76...Jerry Colangelo, Phoe	1987–88...Jerry Krause, Chi	1999–00...John Gabriel, Orl
1976–77...Ray Patterson, Hou	1988–89...Jerry Colangelo, Phoe	2000–01...Geoff Petrie, Sac
1977–78...Angelo Drossos, SA	1989–90...Bob Bass, SA	2001–02...Rod Thorn, NJ
1978–79...Bob Ferry, Wash	1990–91...Bucky Buckwalter, Port	2002–03...Joe Dumars, Det
1979–80...Red Auerbach, Bos	1991–92...Wayne Embry, Clev	2003–04...Jerry West, Mem
1980–81...Jerry Colangelo, Phoe	1992–93...Jerry Colangelo, Phoe	2004–05...Bryan Colangelo, Phoe
1981–82...Bob Ferry, Wash	1993–94...Bob Whitsitt, Sea	2005–06...Elgin Baylor, LAC
1982–83...Zollie Volchok, Sea	1994–95...Jerry West, LAL	2006–07...Bryan Colangelo, Tor
1983–84...Frank Layden, Utah	1995–96...Jerry Krause, Chi	

NBA Alltime Individual Leaders

Scoring

MOST POINTS, CAREER

	Pts	Avg
Kareem Abdul-Jabbar	38,387	24.6
Karl Malone	36,928	25.0
Michael Jordan	32,292	30.1
Wilt Chamberlain	31,419	30.1
Moses Malone	27,409	20.6
Elvin Hayes	27,313	21.0
Hakeem Olajuwon	26,946	21.8
Oscar Robertson	26,710	25.7
Dominique Wilkins	26,668	24.8
John Havlicek	26,395	20.8

HIGHEST SCORING AVERAGE, CAREER

Michael Jordan	30.1	1,072 games	
Wilt Chamberlain	30.1	1,045 games	
Allen Iverson	27.9	747 games	
Elgin Baylor	27.4	846 games	
Jerry West	27.0	932 games	
Bob Pettit	26.4	792 games	
George Gervin	26.2	791 games	
Shaquille O'Neal	25.9	981 games	
Oscar Robertson	25.7	1,040 games	
Karl Malone	25.0	1,476 games	

Note: Minimum 400 games.

MOST POINTS, SEASON

Wilt Chamberlain, Phil	4,029	1961–62
Wilt Chamberlain, SF	3,586	1962–63
Michael Jordan, Chi	3,041	1986–87
Wilt Chamberlain, Phil	3,033	1960–61
Wilt Chamberlain, SF	2,948	1963–64
Michael Jordan, Chi	2,868	1987–88
Kobe Bryant, LA	2,832	2005–06
Bob McAdoo, Buff	2,831	1974–75
Rick Barry, SF	2,775	1966–67
Michael Jordan, Chi	2,753	1989–90

HIGHEST SCORING AVERAGE, SEASON

Wilt Chamberlain, Phil	50.4	1961–62
Wilt Chamberlain, SF	44.8	1962–63
Wilt Chamberlain, Phil	38.4	1960–61
Wilt Chamberlain, Phil	37.6	1959–60
Michael Jordan, Chi	37.1	1986–87
Wilt Chamberlain, SF	36.9	1963–64
Rick Barry, SF	35.6	1966–67
Kobe Bryant, LA	35.4	2005–06
Michael Jordan, Chi	35.0	1987–88
Elgin Baylor, LA	34.8	1960–61

Note: Minimum 70 games.

Scoring *(Cont.)*

MOST POINTS, SINGLE GAME

Player, Team	Opp	Date
100 ....Wilt Chamberlain, Phil	NY	3/2/62
81 ....Kobe Bryant, LAL	Tor	1/22/06
78 ....Wilt Chamberlain, Phil	LAL	12/8/61
73 ....Wilt Chamberlain, Phil	Chi	1/13/62
73 ....Wilt Chamberlain, SF	NY	11/16/62
73 ....David Thompson, Den	Det	4/9/78
72 ....Wilt Chamberlain, SF	LAL	11/3/62
71 ....David Robinson, SA	LAC	4/24/94
71 ....Elgin Baylor, LAL	NY	11/15/60
70 ....Wilt Chamberlain, SF	Syr	3/10/63

Field-Goal Percentage

Highest FG Percentage, Career: .599—Artis Gilmore

Highest FG Percentage, Season: .727—Wilt Chamberlain, LA Lakers, 1972–73 (426/586)

Free Throws

HIGHEST FREE-THROW PERCENTAGE, CAREER

Mark Price............................	.904
Rick Barry	.900
Steve Nash	.896
Peja Stojakovic	.892
Calvin Murphy......................	.892

Note: Minimum 1200 free throws made.

HIGHEST FREE-THROW PERCENTAGE, SEASON

Calvin Murphy, Hou	.958	1980–81
Mahmoud Abdul-Rauf, Den...	.956	1993–94
Jeff Hornacek, Utah.............	.950	1999–00
Mark Price, Clev	.948	1992–93
Mark Price, Clev	.947	1991–92
Rick Barry, Hou...................	.947	1978–79

MOST FREE THROWS MADE, CAREER

	No.	Yrs	Pct
Karl Malone........................	9,787	19	.742
Moses Malone	8,531	19	.769
Oscar Robertson	7,694	14	.838
Michael Jordan..................	7,327	15	.835
Jerry West.........................	7,160	14	.814

Three-Point Field Goals

Most Three-Point Field-Goals, Career: 2,560—Reggie Miller

Highest Three-Point Field-Goal Percentage, Career: .454—Steve Kerr

Most Three-Point Field Goals, Season: 269—Ray Allen, Sea, 2005–06

Highest Three-Point Field-Goal Percentage, Season: .524—Steve Kerr, Chi, 1994–95

Most Three-Point Field Goals, Game: 12—Kobe Bryant, LA Lakers vs Seattle, 1/7/03; Donyell Marshall, Toronto vs. Philadelphia, 3/13/05

Note: First season of three-point field goal: 1979–80.

Steals

Most Steals, Career: 3,265—John Stockton

Most Steals, Season: 301—Alvin Robertson, San Antonio, 1985–86

Most Steals, Game: 11—Kendall Gill, New Jersey vs Miami, 4/3/99; Larry Kenon, San Antonio vs Kansas City, 12/26/76

Rebounds

MOST REBOUNDS, CAREER

	No.	Yrs	Avg
Wilt Chamberlain	23,924	14	22.9
Bill Russell	21,620	13	22.5
Kareem Abdul-Jabbar	17,440	20	11.2
Elvin Hayes........................	16,279	16	12.5
Moses Malone	16,212	19	12.2
Karl Malone	14,968	19	10.1
Robert Parish.....................	14,715	21	9.1
Nate Thurmond..................	14,464	14	15.0
Walt Bellamy	14,241	14	13.7
Wes Unseld	13,769	13	14.0

MOST REBOUNDS, SEASON

Wilt Chamberlain, Phil	2,149	1960–61
Wilt Chamberlain, Phil	2,052	1961–62
Wilt Chamberlain, Phil	1,957	1966–67
Wilt Chamberlain, Phil	1,952	1967–68
Wilt Chamberlain, SF	1,946	1962–63
Wilt Chamberlain, Phil	1,943	1965–66
Wilt Chamberlain, Phil	1,941	1959–60
Bill Russell, Bos	1,930	1963–64
Bill Russell, Bos	1,878	1964–65
Bill Russell, Bos	1,868	1960–61

MOST REBOUNDS, GAME

	Player, Team	Opp	Date
55 ....Wilt Chamberlain, Phil		Bos	11/24/60
51 ....Bill Russell, Bos		Syr	02/05/60
49 ....Bill Russell, Bos		Phil	11/16/57
49 ....Bill Russell, Bos		Det	03/11/65
45 ....Wilt Chamberlain, Phil		Syr	02/06/60
45 ....Wilt Chamberlain, Phil		LA	01/21/61

Assists

MOST ASSISTS, CAREER

John Stockton...................................	15,806
Mark Jackson....................................	10,334
Magic Johnson	10,141
Oscar Robertson	9,887
Isiah Thomas	9,061

MOST ASSISTS, SEASON

John Stockton, Utah..................	1,164	1990–91
John Stockton, Utah..................	1,134	1989–90
John Stockton, Utah..................	1,128	1987–88
John Stockton, Utah..................	1,126	1991–92
Isiah Thomas, Det	1,123	1984–85

MOST ASSISTS, GAME: 30—Scott Skiles, Orlando vs Denver, 12/30/90

Blocked Shots

MOST BLOCKED SHOTS, CAREER

Hakeem Olajuwon	3,830
Dikembe Mutombo	3,230
Kareem Abdul-Jabbar	3,189
Mark Eaton	3,064
David Robinson	2,954

MOST BLOCKED SHOTS, SEASON

Mark Eaton, Utah	456	1984–85
Manute Bol, Wash	397	1985–86
Elmore Smith, LA...........................	393	1973–74

MOST BLOCKED SHOTS, GAME: 17—Elmore Smith, LA Lakers vs Portland, 10/28/73

Scoring

MOST POINTS, CAREER

	Pts	Yrs	Avg
Michael Jordan	5,987	13	33.4
Kareem Abdul-Jabbar	5,762	18	24.3
Shaquille O'Neal	5,045	13	25.5
Karl Malone	4,761	19	24.7
Jerry West	4,457	13	29.1
Larry Bird	3,897	12	23.8
John Havlicek	3,776	13	22.0
Hakeem Olajuwon	3,755	15	25.9
Magic Johnson	3,701	13	19.5
Scottie Pippen	3,642	15	17.7

*HIGHEST SCORING AVERAGE, CAREER

	Avg	Games
Michael Jordan	33.4	179
Allen Iverson	30.0	67
Jerry West	29.1	153
Tracy McGrady	28.8	32
LeBron James	27.3	33
Elgin Baylor	27.0	134
George Gervin	27.0	59
Hakeem Olajuwon	25.9	145
Vince Carter	25.9	42
Shaquille O'Neal	25.5	198
Bob Pettit	25.5	88
Dominique Wilkins	25.4	55
Amare Stoudemire	25.2	31
Dwyane Wade	25.3	54
Dirk Nowitzki	25.2	82

*Minimum of 25 games.

MOST POINTS, GAME

Player, Team		Opp	Date
†63	Michael Jordan, Chi	Bos	4/20/86
61	Elgin Baylor, LA	Bos	4/14/62
56	Wilt Chamberlain, Phil	Syr	3/22/62
56	Michael Jordan, Chi	Mia	4/29/92
56	Charles Barkley, Phoe	GS	5/4/94
55	Rick Barry, SF	Phil	4/18/67
55	Michael Jordan, Chi	Clev	5/1/88
55	Michael Jordan, Chi	Phoe	4/16/95
55	Michael Jordan, Chi	Wash	4/27/97

†Double overtime game.

Rebounds

MOST REBOUNDS, CAREER

	No.	Yrs	Avg
Bill Russell	4,104	13	24.9
Wilt Chamberlain	3,913	13	24.5
Kareem Abdul-Jabbar	2,481	18	10.5
Shaquille O'Neal	2,401	13	12.1
Karl Malone	2,062	19	10.7

MOST REBOUNDS, GAME

Player, Team		Opp	Date
41	Wilt Chamberlain, Phil	Bos	4/5/67
40	Bill Russell, Bos	Phil	3/23/58
40	Bill Russell, Bos	StL	3/29/60
*40	Bill Russell, Bos	LA	4/18/62

Three tied at 39.
*Overtime game.

Assists

MOST ASSISTS, CAREER

	No.	Games
Magic Johnson	2,346	190
John Stockton	1,839	182
Larry Bird	1,062	164
Scottie Pippen	1,048	208
Michael Jordan	1,022	179

MOST ASSISTS, GAME

Player, Team		Opp	Date
24	Magic Johnson, LAL	Phoe	5/15/84
24	John Stockton, Utah	LAL	5/17/88
23	Magic Johnson, LAL	Port	5/3/85
23	John Stockton, Utah	Port	4/25/96
23	Steve Nash, Phoe	LAL	4/24/07

Games played

Kareem Abdul-Jabbar	237
Robert Horry	229
Scottie Pippen	208
Shaquille O'Neal	198
Danny Ainge	193
Karl Malone	193

Appearances

John Stockton	19
Karl Malone	19
Kareem Abdul-Jabbar	18
Robert Parish	16
Scottie Pippen	16
Terry Porter	16
Dolph Schayes	15
Clyde Drexler	15
Tree Rollins	15
Jerome Kersey	15
Hakeem Olajuwon	15

Scoring

1946–47	Joe Fulks, Phil	1389
1947–48	Max Zaslofsky, Chi	1007
1948–49	George Mikan, Minn	1698
1949–50	George Mikan, Minn	1865
1950–51	George Mikan, Minn	1932
1951–52	Paul Arizin, Phil	1674
1952–53	Neil Johnston, Phil	1564
1953–54	Neil Johnston, Phil	1759
1954–55	Neil Johnston, Phil	1631
1955–56	Bob Pettit, StL	1849
1956–57	Paul Arizin, Phil	1817
1957–58	George Yardley, Det	2001
1958–59	Bob Pettit, StL	2105
1959–60	Wilt Chamberlain, Phil	2707
1960–61	Wilt Chamberlain, Phil	3033
1961–62	Wilt Chamberlain, Phil	4029
1962–63	Wilt Chamberlain, SF	3586
1963–64	Wilt Chamberlain, SF	2948
1964–65	Wilt Chamberlain, SF-Phil	2534
1965–66	Wilt Chamberlain, Phil	2649
1966–67	Rick Barry, SF	2775
1967–68	Dave Bing, Det	2142
1968–69	Elvin Hayes, SD	2327
1969–70	Jerry West, LA	*31.2
1970–71	Kareem Abdul-Jabbar, Mil	31.7
1971–72	Kareem Abdul-Jabbar, Mil	34.8
1972–73	Nate Archibald, KC-Oma	34.0
1973–74	Bob McAdoo, Buff	30.6
1974–75	Bob McAdoo, Buff	34.5
1975–76	Bob McAdoo, Buff	31.1
1976–77	Pete Maravich, NO	31.1
1977–78	George Gervin, SA	27.2
1978–79	George Gervin, SA	29.6
1979–80	George Gervin, SA	33.1
1980–81	Adrian Dantley, Utah	30.7
1981–82	George Gervin, SA	32.3
1982–83	Alex English, Den	28.4
1983–84	Adrian Dantley, Utah	30.6
1984–85	Bernard King, NY	32.9
1985–86	Dominique Wilkins, Atl	30.3
1986–87	Michael Jordan, Chi	37.1
1987–88	Michael Jordan, Chi	35.0
1988–89	Michael Jordan, Chi	32.5
1989–90	Michael Jordan, Chi	33.6
1990–91	Michael Jordan, Chi	31.5
1991–92	Michael Jordan, Chi	30.1
1992–93	Michael Jordan, Chi	32.6
1993–94	David Robinson, SA	29.8
1994–95	Shaquille O'Neal, Orl	29.3
1995–96	Michael Jordan, Chi	30.4
1996–97	Michael Jordan, Chi	29.6
1997–98	Michael Jordan, Chi	28.7
1998–99	Allen Iverson, Phil	26.8
1999–00	Shaquille O'Neal, LA Lakers	29.7
2000–01	Allen Iverson, Phil	31.1
2001–02	Allen Iverson, Phil	31.4
2002–03	Tracy McGrady, Orl	32.1
2003–04	Tracy McGrady, Orl	28.0
2004–05	Allen Iverson, Phil	30.7
2005–06	Kobe Bryant, LA Lakers	35.4
2006–07	Kobe Bryant, LA Lakers	31.6

*Based on per game average since 1969–70.

Rebounding

1950–51	Dolph Schayes, Syr	1080
1951–52	Larry Foust, FW	880
	Mel Hutchins, Mil	880
1952–53	George Mikan, Minn	1007
1953–54	Harry Gallatin, NY	1098
1954–55	Neil Johnston, Phil	1085
1955–56	Bob Pettit, StL	1164
1956–57	Maurice Stokes, Roch	1256
1957–58	Bill Russell, Bos	1564
1958–59	Bill Russell, Bos	1612
1959–60	Wilt Chamberlain, Phil	1941
1960–61	Wilt Chamberlain, Phil	2149
1961–62	Wilt Chamberlain, Phil	2052
1962–63	Wilt Chamberlain, SF	1946
1963–64	Bill Russell, Bos	1930
1964–65	Bill Russell, Bos	1878
1965–66	Wilt Chamberlain, Phil	1943
1966–67	Wilt Chamberlain, Phil	1957
1967–68	Wilt Chamberlain, Phil	1952
1968–69	Wilt Chamberlain, LA	1712
1969–70	Elvin Hayes, SD	*16.9
1970–71	Wilt Chamberlain, LA	18.2
1971–72	Wilt Chamberlain, LA	19.2
1972–73	Wilt Chamberlain, LA	18.6
1973–74	Elvin Hayes, Capital	18.1
1974–75	Wes Unseld, Wash	14.8
1975–76	Kareem Abdul-Jabbar, LA	16.9
1976–77	Bill Walton, Port	14.4
1977–78	Len Robinson, NO	15.7
1978–79	Moses Malone, Hou	17.6
1979–80	Swen Nater, SD	15.0
1980–81	Moses Malone, Hou	14.8
1981–82	Moses Malone, Hou	14.7
1982–83	Moses Malone, Phil	15.3
1983–84	Moses Malone, Phil	13.4
1984–85	Moses Malone, Phil	13.1
1985–86	Bill Laimbeer, Det	13.1
1986–87	Charles Barkley, Phil	14.6
1987–88	Michael Cage, LA Clippers	13.0
1988–89	Hakeem Olajuwon, Hou	13.5
1989–90	Hakeem Olajuwon, Hou	14.0
1990–91	David Robinson, SA	13.0
1991–92	Dennis Rodman, Det	18.7
1992–93	Dennis Rodman, Det	18.3
1993–94	Dennis Rodman, SA	17.3
1994–95	Dennis Rodman, SA	16.8
1995–96	Dennis Rodman, Chi	14.9
1996–97	Dennis Rodman, Chi	16.1
1997–98	Dennis Rodman, Chi	15.0
1998–99	Chris Webber, Sac	13.0
1999–00	Dikembe Mutombo, Atl	14.1
2000–01	Dikembe Mutombo, Atl	13.5
2001–02	Ben Wallace, Det	13.0
2002–03	Ben Wallace, Det	15.4
2003–04	Kevin Garnett, Minn	13.9
2004–05	Kevin Garnett, Minn	13.5
2005–06	Kevin Garnett, Minn	12.7
2006–07	Kevin Garnett, Minn	12.8

*Based on per game average since 1969–70.

Assists

1946–47	Ernie Calverly, Prov	202	1978–79	Kevin Porter, Det	13.4
1947–48	Howie Dallmar, Phil	120	1979–80	Micheal Ray Richardson, NY	10.1
1948–49	Bob Davies, Roch	321	1980–81	Kevin Porter, Wash	9.1
1949–50	Dick McGuire, NY	386	1981–82	Johnny Moore, SA	9.6
1950–51	Andy Phillip, Phil	414	1982–83	Magic Johnson, LA	10.5
1951–52	Andy Phillip, Phil	539	1983–84	Magic Johnson, LA	13.1
1952–53	Bob Cousy, Bos	547	1984–85	Isiah Thomas, Det	13.9
1953–54	Bob Cousy, Bos	518	1985–86	Magic Johnson, LA Lakers	12.6
1954–55	Bob Cousy, Bos	557	1986–87	Magic Johnson, LA Lakers	12.2
1955–56	Bob Cousy, Bos	642	1987–88	John Stockton, Utah	13.8
1956–57	Bob Cousy, Bos	478	1988–89	John Stockton, Utah	13.6
1957–58	Bob Cousy, Bos	463	1989–90	John Stockton, Utah	14.5
1958–59	Bob Cousy, Bos	557	1990–91	John Stockton, Utah	14.2
1959–60	Bob Cousy, Bos	715	1991–92	John Stockton, Utah	13.7
1960–61	Oscar Robertson, Cin	690	1992–93	John Stockton, Utah	12.0
1961–62	Oscar Robertson, Cin	899	1993–94	John Stockton, Utah	12.6
1962–63	Guy Rodgers, SF	825	1994–95	John Stockton, Utah	12.3
1963–64	Oscar Robertson, Cin	868	1995–96	John Stockton, Utah	11.2
1964–65	Oscar Robertson, Cin	861	1996–97	Mark Jackson, Ind	11.4
1965–66	Oscar Robertson, Cin	847	1997–98	Rod Strickland, Wash	10.5
1966–67	Guy Rodgers, Chi	908	1998–99	Jason Kidd, Phoe	10.8
1967–68	Wilt Chamberlain, Phil	702	1999–00	Jason Kidd, Phoe	10.1
1968–69	Oscar Robertson, Cin	772	2000–01	Jason Kidd, Phoe	9.8
1969–70	Lenny Wilkens, Sea	*9.1	2001–02	Andre Miller, Clev	10.9
1970–71	Norm Van Lier, Cin	10.1	2002–03	Jason Kidd, NJ	8.9
1971–72	Jerry West, LA	9.7	2003–04	Jason Kidd, NJ	9.2
1972–73	Nate Archibald, KC-Oma	11.4	2004–05	Steve Nash, Phoe	11.5
1973–74	Ernie DiGregorio, Buff	8.2	2005–06	Steve Nash, Phoe	10.5
1974–75	Kevin Porter, Wash	8.0	2006–07	Steve Nash, Phoe	11.6
1975–76	Don Watts, Sea	8.1			
1976–77	Don Buse, Ind	8.5			
1977–78	Kevin Porter, NJ-Det	10.2	*Based on per game average since 1969–70.		

Field-Goal Percentage

1946–47	Bob Feerick, Wash	40.1	1977–78	Bobby Jones, Den	57.8
1947–48	Bob Feerick, Wash	34.0	1978–79	Cedric Maxwell, Bos	58.4
1948–49	Arnie Risen, Roch	42.3	1979–80	Cedric Maxwell, Bos	60.9
1949–50	Alex Groza, Ind	47.8	1980–81	Artis Gilmore, Chi	67.0
1950–51	Alex Groza, Ind	47.0	1981–82	Artis Gilmore, Chi	65.2
1951–52	Paul Arizin, Phil	44.8	1982–83	Artis Gilmore, SA	62.6
1952–53	Neil Johnston, Phil	45.2	1983–84	Artis Gilmore, SA	63.1
1953–54	Ed Macauley, Bos	48.6	1984–85	James Donaldson, LAC	63.7
1954–55	Larry Foust, FW	48.7	1985–86	Steve Johnson, SA	63.2
1955–56	Neil Johnston, Phil	45.7	1986–87	Kevin McHale, Bos	60.4
1956–57	Neil Johnston, Phil	44.7	1987–88	Kevin McHale, Bos	60.4
1957–58	Jack Twyman, Cin	45.2	1988–89	Dennis Rodman, Det	59.5
1958–59	Ken Sears, NY	49.0	1989–90	Mark West, Phoe	62.5
1959–60	Ken Sears, NY	47.7	1990–91	Buck Williams, Port	60.2
1960–61	Wilt Chamberlain, Phil	50.9	1991–92	Buck Williams, Port	60.4
1961–62	Walt Bellamy, Chi	51.9*	1992–93	Cedric Ceballos, Phoe	57.6
1962–63	Wilt Chamberlain, SF	52.8	1993–94	Shaquille O'Neal, Orl	59.9
1963–64	Jerry Lucas, Cin	52.7	1994–95	Chris Gatling, GS	63.3
1964–65	Wilt Chamberlain, SF-Phil	51.0	1995–96	Gheorghe Muresan, Wash	58.4
1965–66	Wilt Chamberlain, Phil	54.0	1996–97	Gheorghe Muresan, Wash	60.4
1966–67	Wilt Chamberlain, Phil	68.3	1997–98	Shaquille O'Neal, LAL	58.4
1967–68	Wilt Chamberlain, Phil	59.5	1998–99	Shaquille O'Neal, LAL	57.6
1968–69	Wilt Chamberlain, LAL	58.3	1999–00	Shaquille O'Neal, LAL	57.4
1969–70	Johnny Green, Cin	55.9	2000–01	Shaquille O'Neal, LAL	57.2
1970–71	Johnny Green, Cin	58.7	2001–02	Shaquille O'Neal, LAL	57.9
1971–72	Wilt Chamberlain, LAL	64.9	2002–03	Eddy Curry, Chi	58.5
1972–73	Wilt Chamberlain, LAL	72.7	2003–04	Shaquille O'Neal, LAL	58.4
1973–74	Bob McAdoo, Buff	54.7	2004–05	Shaquille O'Neal, Mia	60.1
1974–75	Don Nelson, Bos	53.9	2005–06	Shaquille O'Neal, Mia	60.0
1975–76	Wes Unseld, Wash	56.1	2006–07	Mikki Moore, NJ	60.9
1976–77	Kareem Abdul-Jabbar, LAL	57.9			

Free-Throw Percentage

1946–47	Fred Scolari, Wash	81.1	1977–78	Rick Barry, GS	92.4
1947–48	Bob Feerick, Wash	78.8	1978–79	Rick Barry, Hou	94.7
1948–49	Bob Feerick, Wash	85.9	1979–80	Rick Barry, Hou	93.5
1949–50	Max Zaslofsky, Chi	84.3	1980–81	Calvin Murphy, Hou	95.8
1950–51	Joe Fulks, Phil	85.5	1981–82	Kyle Macy, Phoe	89.9
1951–52	Bob Wanzer, Roch	90.4	1982–83	Calvin Murphy, Hou	92.0
1952–53	Bill Sharman, Bos	85.0	1983–84	Larry Bird, Bos	88.8
1953–54	Bill Sharman, Bos	84.4	1984–85	Kyle Macy, Phoe	90.7
1954–55	Bill Sharman, Bos	89.7	1985–86	Larry Bird, Bos	89.6
1955–56	Bill Sharman, Bos	86.7	1986–87	Larry Bird, Bos	91.0
1956–57	Bill Sharman, Bos	90.5	1987–88	Jack Sikma, Mil	92.2
1957–58	Dolph Schayes, Syr	90.4	1988–89	Magic Johnson, LAL	91.1
1958–59	Bill Sharman, Bos	93.2	1989–90	Larry Bird, Bos	93.0
1959–60	Dolph Schayes, Syr	89.3	1990–91	Reggie Miller, Ind	91.8
1960–61	Bill Sharman, Bos	92.1	1991–92	Mark Price, Clev	94.7
1961–62	Dolph Schayes, Syr	89.7	1992–93	Mark Price, Clev	94.8
1962–63	Larry Costello, Syr	88.1	1993–94	Mahmoud Abdul-Rauf, Den	95.6
1963–64	Oscar Robertson, Cin	85.3	1994–95	Spud Webb, Sac	93.4
1964–65	Larry Costello, Phil	87.7	1995–96	Mahmoud Abdul-Rauf, Den	93.0
1965–66	Larry Siegfried, Bos	88.1	1996–97	Mark Price, GS	90.6
1966–67	Adrian Smith, Cin	90.3	1997–98	Chris Mullin, Ind	93.9
1967–68	Oscar Robertson, Cin	87.3	1998–99	Reggie Miller, Ind	91.5
1968–69	Larry Siegfried, Bos	86.4	1999–00	Jeff Hornacek, Utah	95.0
1969–70	Flynn Robinson, Mil	89.8	2000–01	Reggie Miller, Ind	92.8
1970–71	Chet Walker, Chi	85.9	2001–02	Reggie Miller, Ind	91.1
1971–72	Jack Marin, Balt	89.4	2002–03	Allan Houston, NY	91.9
1972–73	Rick Barry, GS	90.2	2003–04	Peja Stojakovic, Sac	92.7
1973–74	Ernie DiGregorio, Buff	90.2	2004–05	Reggie Miller, Ind	93.3
1974–75	Rick Barry, GS	90.4	2005–06	Steve Nash, Phoe	92.1
1975–76	Rick Barry, GS	92.3	2006–07	Kyle Korver, Phi	91.4
1976–77	Ernie DiGregorio, Buff	94.5			

Three-Point Field-Goal Percentage

1979–80	Fred Brown, Sea	44.3	1993–94	Tracy Murray, Por	45.9
1980–81	Brian Taylor, SD	38.3	1994–95	Steve Kerr, Chi	52.4
1981–82	Campy Russell, NY	43.9	1995–96	Tim Legler, Wash	52.2
1982–83	Mike Dunleavy, SA	34.5	1996–97	Glen Rice, Char	47.0
1983–84	Darrell Griffith, Utah	36.1	1997–98	Dale Ellis, Sea	46.0
1984–85	Byron Scott, LAL	43.3	1998–99	Dell Curry, Char	47.6
1985–86	Craig Hodges, Mil	45.1	1999–00	Hubert Davis, Dall	49.1
1986–87	Kiki Vandeweghe, Por	48.1	2000–01	Brent Barry, Sea	47.6
1987–88	Craig Hodges, Mil-Phoe	49.1	2001–02	Steve Smith, SA	47.2
1988–89	Jon Sundvold, Mia	52.2	2002–03	Bruce Bowen, SA	44.1
1989–90	Steve Kerr, Clev	50.7	2003–04	Anthony Peeler, Sac	48.2
1990–91	Jim Les, Sac	46.1	2004–05	Fred Hoiberg, Minn	48.3
1991–92	Dana Barros, Sea	44.6	2005–06	Richard Hamilton, Det	45.8
1992–93	Chris Mullin, GS	45.1	2006–07	Jason Kapono, Mia	51.4

Steals

1973–74	Larry Steele, Por	2.68	1990–91	Alvin Robertson, Mil	3.04
1974–75	Rick Barry, GS	2.85	1991–92	John Stockton, Utah	2.98
1975–76	Don Watts, Sea	3.18	1992–93	Michael Jordan, Chi	2.83
1976–77	Don Buse, Ind	3.47	1993–94	Nate McMillan, Sea	2.96
1977–78	Ron Lee, Phoe	2.74	1994–95	Scottie Pippen, Chi	2.94
1978–79	M.L. Carr, Det	2.46	1995–96	Gary Payton, Sea	2.85
1979–80	Micheal Ray Richardson, NY	3.23	1996–97	Mookie Blaylock, Atl	2.72
1980–81	Magic Johnson, LAL	3.43	1997–98	Mookie Blaylock, Atl	2.61
1981–82	Magic Johnson, LAL	2.67	1998–99	Kendall Gill, NJ	2.68
1982–83	Micheal Ray Richardson, GS-NJ	2.84	1999–00	Eddie Jones, Char	2.67
1983–84	Rickey Green, Utah	2.65	2000–01	Allen Iverson, Phil	2.51
1984–85	Micheal Ray Richardson, NJ	2.96	2001–02	Allen Iverson, Phil	2.80
1985–86	Alvin Robertson, SA	3.67	2002–03	Allen Iverson, Phil	2.74
1986–87	Alvin Robertson, SA	3.21	2003–04	Baron Davis, NO	2.36
1987–88	Michael Jordan, Chi	3.16	2004–05	Larry Hughes, Wash	2.89
1988–89	John Stockton, Utah	3.21	2005–06	Gerald Wallace, Char	2.51
1989–90	Michael Jordan, Chi	2.77	2006–07	Baron Davis, GS	2.14

Blocked Shots

1973–74	Elmore Smith, LAL	4.85	1990–91	Hakeem Olajuwon, Hou	3.95
1974–75	Kareem Abdul-Jabbar, Mil	3.26	1991–92	David Robinson, SA	4.49
1975–76	Kareem Abdul-Jabbar, LAL	4.12	1992–93	Hakeem Olajuwon, Hou	4.17
1976–77	Bill Walton, Port	3.25	1993–94	Dikembe Mutombo, Den	4.10
1977–78	George Johnson, NJ	3.38	1994–95	Dikembe Mutombo, Den	3.91
1978–79	Kareem Abdul-Jabbar, LAL	3.95	1995–96	Dikembe Mutombo, Den	4.49
1979–80	Kareem Abdul-Jabbar, LAL	3.41	1996–97	Shawn Bradley, NJ	3.40
1980–81	George Johnson, SA	3.39	1997–98	Marcus Camby, Tor	3.65
1981–82	George Johnson, SA	3.12	1998–99	Alonzo Mourning, Mia	3.91
1982–83	Wayne Rollins, Atl	4.29	1999–00	Alonzo Mourning, Mia	3.72
1983–84	Mark Eaton, Utah	4.28	2000–01	Theo Ratliff, Phil/Atl	3.74
1984–85	Mark Eaton, Utah	5.56	2001–02	Ben Wallace, Det	3.48
1985–86	Manute Bol, Wash	4.96	2002–03	Theo Ratliff, Atl	3.23
1986–87	Mark Eaton, Utah	4.06	2003–04	Theo Ratliff, Port	3.61
1987–88	Mark Eaton, Utah	3.71	2004–05	Andrei Kirilenko, Utah	3.32
1988–89	Manute Bol, GS	4.31	2005–06	Marcus Camby, Den	3.29
1989–90	Hakeem Olajuwon, Hou	4.59	2006–07	Marcus Camby, Den	3.30

NBA All-Star Game Results

Year	Result	Site	Winning Coach	Most Valuable Player
1951	East 111, West 94	Boston	Joe Lapchick	Ed Macauley, Bos
1952	East 108, West 91	Boston	Al Cervi	Paul Arizin, Phil
1953	West 79, East 75	Ft Wayne	John Kundla	George Mikan, Minn
1954	East 98, West 93 (OT)	New York	Joe Lapchick	Bob Cousy, Bos
1955	East 100, West 91	New York	Al Cervi	Bill Sharman, Bos
1956	West 108, East 94	Rochester	Charley Eckman	Bob Pettit, StL
1957	East 109, West 97	Boston	Red Auerbach	Bob Cousy, Bos
1958	East 130, West 118	St Louis	Red Auerbach	Bob Pettit, StL
1959	West 124, East 108	Detroit	Ed Macauley	B. Pettit, StL/ E. Baylor, Minn
1960	East 125, West 115	Philadelphia	Red Auerbach	Wilt Chamberlain, Phil
1961	West 153, East 131	Syracuse	Paul Seymour	Oscar Robertson, Cin
1962	West 150, East 130	St Louis	Fred Schaus	Bob Pettit, StL
1963	East 115, West 108	Los Angeles	Red Auerbach	Bill Russell, Bos
1964	East 111, West 107	Boston	Red Auerbach	Oscar Robertson, Cin
1965	East 124, West 123	St Louis	Red Auerbach	Jerry Lucas, Cin
1966	East 137, West 94	Cincinnati	Red Auerbach	Adrian Smith, Cin
1967	West 135, East 120	San Francisco	Fred Schaus	Rick Barry, SF
1968	East 144, West 124	New York	Alex Hannum	Hal Greer, Phil
1969	East 123, West 112	Baltimore	Gene Shue	Oscar Robertson, Cin
1970	East 142, West 135	Philadelphia	Red Holzman	Willis Reed, NY
1971	West 108, East 107	San Diego	Larry Costello	Lenny Wilkens, Sea
1972	West 112, East 110	Los Angeles	Bill Sharman	Jerry West, LA
1973	East 104, West 84	Chicago	Tom Heinsohn	Dave Cowens, Bos
1974	West 134, East 123	Seattle	Larry Costello	Bob Lanier, Det
1975	East 108, West 102	Phoenix	K.C. Jones	Walt Frazier, NY
1976	East 123, West 109	Philadelphia	Tom Heinsohn	Dave Bing, Wash
1977	West 125, East 124	Milwaukee	Larry Brown	Julius Erving, Phil
1978	East 133, West 125	Atlanta	Billy Cunningham	Randy Smith, Buff
1979	West 134, East 129	Detroit	Lenny Wilkens	David Thompson, Den
1980	East 144, West 135 (OT)	Washington	Billy Cunningham	George Gervin, SA
1981	East 123, West 120	Cleveland	Billy Cunningham	Nate Archibald, Bos
1982	East 120, West 118	New Jersey	Bill Fitch	Larry Bird, Bos
1983	East 132, West 123	Los Angeles	Billy Cunningham	Julius Erving, Phil
1984	East 154, West 145 (OT)	Denver	K.C. Jones	Isiah Thomas, Det
1985	West 140, East 129	Indiana	Pat Riley	Ralph Sampson, Hou
1986	East 139, West 132	Dallas	K.C. Jones	Isiah Thomas, Det
1987	West 154, East 149 (OT)	Seattle	Pat Riley	Tom Chambers, Sea
1988	East 138, West 133	Chicago	Mike Fratello	Michael Jordan, Chi
1989	West 143, East 134	Houston	Pat Riley	Karl Malone, Utah
1990	East 130, West 113	Miami	Chuck Daly	Magic Johnson, LAL
1991	East 116, West 114	Charlotte	Chris Ford	Charles Barkley, Phil
1992	West 153, East 113	Orlando	Don Nelson	Magic Johnson, LAL
1993	West 135, East 132	Salt Lake City	Paul Westphal	K. Malone/ J. Stockton, Utah
1994	East 127, West 118	Minneapolis	Lenny Wilkens	Scottie Pippen, Chi

Year	Result	Site	Winning Coach	Most Valuable Player
1995	West 139, East 112	Phoenix	Paul Westphal	Mitch Richmond, Sac
1996	East 129, West 118	San Antonio	Phil Jackson	Michael Jordan, Chi
1997	East 132, West 120	Cleveland	Doug Collins	Glen Rice, Char
1998	East 135, West 114	New York	Larry Bird	Michael Jordan, Chi
1999	Cancelled due to lockout.			
2000	West 137, East 126	Oakland	Phil Jackson	O'Neal, Lakers/T. Duncan,SA
2001	East 111, West 110	Washington	Larry Brown	Allen Iverson, Phil
2002	West 135, East 120	Philadelphia	Don Nelson	Kobe Bryant, LAL
2003	West 155, East 145 (2OT)	Atlanta	Rick Adelman	Kevin Garnett, Minn
2004	West 136, East 132	Los Angeles	Flip Saunders	Shaquille O'Neal, LAL
2005	East 125, West 115	Denver	Stan Van Gundy	Allen Iverson, Phil
2006	East 122, West 120	Houston	Flip Saunders	LeBron James, Cle
2007	West 153, East 132	Las Vegas	Mike D'Antoni	Kobe Bryant, LAL

Members of the Basketball Hall of Fame

Contributors

Senda Abbott (1984)
Clair F. Bee (1967)
Danny Biasone (2000)
Hubie Brown (2005)
Walter A. Brown (1965)
John W. Bunn (1964)
Jerry Colangelo (2004)
Bob Douglas (1971)
Al Duer (1981)
Wayne Embry (1999)
Clifford Fagan (1983)
Harry A. Fisher (1973)
Larry Fleisher (1991)
Dave Gavitt (2006)
Edward Gottlieb (1971)
Luther H. Gulick (1959)
Lester Harrison (1979)
Chick Hearn (2003)

Ferenc Hepp (1980)
Edward J. Hickox (1959)
Paul D. (Tony) Hinkle (1965)
Ned Irish (1964)
R. William Jones (1964)
J. Walter Kennedy (1980)
Meadowlark Lemon (2003)
Emil S. Liston (1974)
Earl Lloyd (2003)
Bill Mokray (1965)
Ralph Morgan (1959)
Frank Morgenweck (1962)
James Naismith (1959)
C.M. Newton (2000)
John J. O'Brien (1961)
Larry O'Brien (1991)
Harold G. Olsen (1959)
Maurice Podoloff (1973)

H. V. Porter (1960)
William A. Reid (1963)
Elmer Ripley (1972)
Lynn W. St. John (1962)
Abe Saperstein (1970)
Arthur A. Schabinger (1961)
Amos Alonzo Stagg (1959)
Boris Stankovic (1991)
Edward Steitz (1983)
Chuck Taylor (1968)
Bertha F. Teague (1984)
Oswald Tower (1959)
Arthur L. Trester (1961)
Clifford Wells (1971)
Lou Wilke (1982)
Fred Zollner (1999)

Players

Kareem Abdul-Jabbar (1995)
Nate (Tiny) Archibald (1991)
Paul J. Arizin (1977)
Charles Barkley (2006)
Thomas B. Barlow (1980)
Rick Barry (1987)
Elgin Baylor (1976)
John Beckman (1972)
Walt Bellamy (1993)
Sergei Belov (1992)
Dave Bing (1990)
Larry Bird (1998)
Carol Blazejowski (1994)
Bennie Borgmann (1961)
Bill Bradley (1982)
Joseph Brennan (1974)
Al Cervi (1984)
Wilt Chamberlain (1978)
Charles (Tarzan) Cooper (1976)
Kresimir Cosic (1996)
Bob Cousy (1970)
Dave Cowens (1991)
Joan Crawford (1997)
Billy Cunningham (1986)
Denise Curry (1997)
Drazen Dalipagic (2004)
Bob Davies (1969)
Forrest S. DeBernardi (1961)

Dave DeBusschere (1982)
H.G. (Dutch) Dehnert (1968)
Anne Donovan (1995)
Clyde Drexler (2004)
Joe Dumars (2006)
Paul Endacott (1971)
Alex English (1997)
Julius Erving (1993)
Harold (Bud) Foster (1964)
Walter (Clyde) Frazier (1987)
Max (Marty) Friedman (1971)
Joe Fulks (1977)
Lauren (Laddie) Gale (1976)
Harry (the Horse) Gallatin (1991)
William Gates (1989)
George Gervin (1996)
Tom Gola (1975)
Gail Goodrich (1996)
Hal Greer (1981)
Robert (Ace) Gruenig (1963)
Clifford O. Hagan (1977)
Victor Hanson (1960)
Lusia Harris-Stewart (1992)
John Havlicek (1983)
Connie Hawkins (1992)
Elvin Hayes (1990)
Marques Haynes (1998)
Tom Heinsohn (1986)

Nat Holman (1964)
Robert J. Houbregs (1987)
Bailey Howell (1997)
Chuck Hyatt (1959)
Dan Issel (1993)
Harry (Buddy) Jeannette (1994)
Earvin (Magic) Johnson (2002)
William C. Johnson (1976)
D. Neil Johnston (1990)
K.C. Jones (1989)
Sam Jones (1983)
Edward (Moose) Krause (1975)
Bob Kurland (1961)
Bob Lanier (1992)
Joe Lapchick (1966)
Nancy Lieberman-Cline (1996)
Clyde Lovellette (1988)
Jerry Lucas (1979)
Angelo (Hank) Luisetti (1959)
C. Edward Macauley (1960)
Moses Malone (2001)
Peter P. Maravich (1987)
Hortencia Marcari (2005)
Slater Martin (1981)
Bob McAdoo (2000)
Branch McCracken (1960)
Jack McCracken (1962)
Bobby McDermott (1988)

Players

Dick McGuire (1993)
Kevin McHale (1999)
Dino Meneghin (2003)
Ann Meyers (1993)
George L. Mikan (1959)
Vern Mikkelsen (1995)
Cheryl Miller (1995)
Earl Monroe (1990)
Calvin Murphy (1993)
Charles (Stretch) Murphy (1960)
H. O. (Pat) Page (1962)
Robert Parish (2003)
Drazen Petrovic (2002)
Bob Pettit (1970)
Andy Phillip (1961)
Jim Pollard (1977)
Frank Ramsey (1981)

Willis Reed (1981)
Arnie Risen (1998)
Oscar Robertson (1979)
John S. Roosma (1961)
Bill Russell (1974)
John (Honey) Russell (1964)
Adolph Schayes (1972)
Ernest J. Schmidt (1973)
John J. Schommer (1959)
Barney Sedran (1962)
Uljana Semjonova (1993)
Bill Sharman (1975)
Christian Steinmetz (1961)
Lusia Harris Stewart (1992)
Maurice Stokes (2004)
Isiah Thomas (2000)
David Thompson (1996)

John A. (Cat) Thompson (1962)
Nate Thurmond (1984)
Jack Twyman (1982)
Wes Unseld (1988)
Robert (Fuzzy) Vandivier (1974)
Edward A. Wachter (1961)
Bill Walton (1993)
Robert F. Wanzer (1987)
Jerry West (1979)
Nera White (1992)
Lenny Wilkens (1989)
Dominique Wilkins (2006)
Lynette Woodard (2004)
John R. Wooden (1960)
James Worthy (2003)
George (Bird) Yardley (1996)

Coaches

Forest C. (Phog) Allen (1959)
Harold Anderson (1984)
Red Auerbach (1968)
Geno Auriemma (2006)
Leon Barmore (2003)
Sam Barry (1978)
Ernest A. Blood (1960)
Jim Boeheim (2005)
Larry Brown (2002)
Jim Calhoun (2005)
Howard G. Cann (1967)
H. Clifford Carlson (1959)
Lou Carnesecca (1992)
Ben Carnevale (1969)
Pete Carril (1997)
Everett Case (1981)
Van Chancellor (2007)
John Chaney (2001)
Jody Conradt (1998)
Denny Crum (1994)
Chuck Daly (1994)
Everett S. Dean (1966)
Antonio Diaz-Miguel (1997)
Edgar A. Diddle (1971)
Bruce Drake (1972)
Pedro Ferrandiz (2007)

Sandro Gamba (2006)
Clarence Gaines (1981)
Jack Gardner (1983)
Amory T. (Slats) Gill (1967)
Aleksandr Gomelsky (1995)
Sue Gunter (2005)
Alex Hannum (1998)
Marv Harshman (1984)
Don Haskins (1997)
Edgar S. Hickey (1978)
Howard A. Hobson (1965)
Red Holzman (1986)
Hank Iba (1968)
Phil Jackson (2007)
Alvin F. (Doggie) Julian (1967)
Frank W. Keaney (1960)
George E. Keogan (1961)
Bob Knight (1991)
Mike Krzyzewski (2001)
John Kundla (1995)
Ward L. Lambert (1960)
Harry Litwack (1975)
Kenneth D. Loeffler (1964)
A.C. (Dutch) Lonborg (1972)
John B. McLendon (1978)
Arad A. McCutchan (1980)
Al McGuire (1992)

Frank McGuire (1976)
Walter E. Meanwell (1959)
Raymond J. Meyer (1978)
Ralph Miller (1988)
Billie Moore (1999)
Peter F. Newell (1978)
Aleksandar Nikolic (1998)
Mirko Novosel (2007)
Lute Olson (2002)
Jack Ramsay (1992)
Cesare Rubini (1994)
Adolph F. Rupp (1968)
Leonard D. Sachs (1961)
Bill Sharman (2004)
Everett F. Shelton (1979)
Dean Smith (1982)
Pat Summitt (2000)
Fred R. Taylor (1985)
John Thompson (1999)
Margaret Wade (1984)
Stanley H. Watts (1985)
Lenny Wilkens (1998)
Roy Williams (2007)
John R. Wooden (1972)
Morgan Wooten (2000)
Phil Woolpert (1992)
Kay Yow (2002)

Note: Year of election in parentheses.

Referees

James E. Enright (1978)
George T. Hepbron (1960)
George Hoyt (1961)
Matthew P. Kennedy (1959)
Lloyd Leith (1982)
Zigmund J. Mihalik (1985)
John P. Nucatola (1977)

Ernest C. Quigley (1961)
Marvin Rudolph (2007)
J. Dallas Shirley (1979)
Earl Strom (1995)
David Tobey (1961)
David H. Walsh (1961)

Teams

Buffalo Germans (1961)
First Team (1959)
Harlem Globetrotters (2002)
Original Celtics (1959)
Renaissance (1963)
1966 Texas Western (2007)

ABA Champions

Year	Champion	Series	Runner-up	Winning Coach
1968	Pittsburgh Pipers	4–3	New Orleans Bucs	Vince Cazetta
1969	Oakland Oaks	4–1	Indiana Pacers	Alex Hannum
1970	Indiana Pacers	4–2	Los Angeles Stars	Bob Leonard
1971	Utah Stars	4–3	Kentucky Colonels	Bill Sharman
1972	Indiana Pacers	4–2	New York Nets	Bob Leonard
1973	Indiana Pacers	4–3	Kentucky Colonels	Bob Leonard
1974	New York Nets	4–1	Utah Stars	Kevin Loughery
1975	Kentucky Colonels	4–1	Indiana Pacers	Hubie Brown
1976	New York Nets	4–2	Denver Nuggets	Kevin Loughery

ABA Postseason Awards

Most Valuable Player

1967–68 .... Connie Hawkins, Pitt
1968–69 .... Mel Daniels, Ind
1969–70 .... Spencer Haywood, Den
1970–71 .... Mel Daniels, Ind
1971–72 .... Artis Gilmore, Ken
1972–73 .... Billy Cunningham, Car
1973–74 .... Julius Erving, NY
1974–75 .... Julius Erving, NY
                       George McGinnis, Ind
1975–76 .... Julius Erving, NY

Rookie of the Year

1967–68 .... Mel Daniels, Minn
1968–69 .... Warren Armstrong, Oak
1969–70 .... Spencer Haywood, Den
1970–71 .... Charlie Scott, Vir
                       Dan Issel, Ken
1971–72 .... Artis Gilmore, Ken
1972–73 .... Brian Taylor, NY
1973–74 .... Swen Nater, SA
1974–75 .... Marvin Barnes, StL
1975–76 .... David Thompson, Den

Coach of the Year

1967–68 .... Vince Cazetta, Pitt
1968–69 .... Alex Hannum, Oak
1969–70 .... Bill Sharman, LA
                       Joe Belmont, Den
1970–71 .... Al Bianchi, Vir
1971–72 .... Tom Nissalke, Dall
1972–73 .... Larry Brown, Car
1973–74 .... Babe McCarthy, Ken
                       Joe Mullaney, Utah
1974–75 .... Larry Brown, Den
1975–76 .... Larry Brown, Den

ABA Season Leaders

Scoring

	GP	Pts	Avg
1967–68...Connie Hawkins, Pitt	70	1875	26.8
1968–69...Rick Barry, Oak	35	1190	34.0
1969–70...Spencer Haywood, Den	84	2519	30.0
1970–71...Dan Issel, Ken	83	2480	29.9
1971–72...Charlie Scott, Vir	79	2637	33.4
1972–73...Julius Erving, Vir	71	2268	31.9
1973–74...Julius Erving, NY	84	2299	27.4
1974–75...George McGinnis, Ind	79	2353	29.8
1975–76...Julius Erving, NY	84	2462	29.3

Rebounds

1967–68...............Mel Daniels, Minn	15.6
1968–69................Mel Daniels, Ind	16.5
1969–70...............Spencer Haywood, Den	19.5
1970–71...............Mel Daniels, Ind	18.0
1971–72...............Artis Gilmore, Ken	17.8
1972–73...............Artis Gilmore, Ken	17.6
1973–74...............Artis Gilmore, Ken	18.3
1974–75...............Swen Nater, SA	16.4
1975–76...............Artis Gilmore, Ken	15.5

Assists

1967–68...............Larry Brown, NO	6.5
1968–69...............Larry Brown, Oak	7.1
1969–70...............Larry Brown, Wash	7.1
1970–71...............Bill Melchionni, NY	8.3
1971–72...............Bill Melchionni, NY	8.4
1972–73...............Bill Melchionni, NY	7.4
1973–74...............Al Smith, Den	8.2
1974–75...............Mack Calvin, Den	7.7
1975–76...............Don Buse, Ind	8.2

Steals

1973–74...............Ted McClain, Car	2.98
1974–75...............Brian Taylor, NY	2.80
1975–76...............Don Buse, Ind	4.12

Blocked Shots

1973–74...............Caldwell Jones, SD	4.00
1974–75...............Caldwell Jones, SD	3.24
1975–76...............Billy Paultz, SA	3.05

World Championship of Basketball

Year	Winner	Runner-Up	Score	Site
1950	Argentina	United States	†	Buenos Aires
1954	United States	Brazil	†	Rio de Janeiro
1959	Brazil	United States	†	Santiago, Chile
1963	Brazil	Yugoslavia	†	Rio de Janeiro
1967	Soviet Union	Yugoslavia	†	Montevideo, Uruguay
1970	Yugoslavia	Brazil	†	Ljubljana, Yugoslavia
1974	Soviet Union	Yugoslavia	†	San Juan
1978	Yugoslavia	Soviet Union	82–81 (OT)	Manila
1982	Soviet Union	United States	95–94	Cali, Colombia
1986	United States	Soviet Union	87–85	Madrid
1990	Yugoslavia	Soviet Union	92–75	Buenos Aires
1994*	United States	Russia	137–91	Toronto
1998	Yugoslavia	Russia	64–62	Athens
2002	Yugoslavia	Argentina	84–77 (OT)	Indianapolis
2006	Spain	Greece	70–47	Saitama, Japan

*U.S. professionals began competing in 1994. In 1998, a labor dispute resulted in a boycott of the World Championship by NBA stars; the U.S. roster was filled by members of the CBA and European professional leagues and college players.
†Result determined by overall record in final round of competition.

Corey Brewer, Most Outstanding Player of the Final Four, led the Gators to their second straight title

College Basketball

Second Helpings

Florida captured its second-straight NCAA men's title by emphasizing T-E-A-M, while controversy overshadowed sterling seasons from the women of Rutgers and Tennessee

BY B.J. SCHECTER

COREY BREWER HAD A LITTLE extra bounce in his step. Less than an hour earlier, he had led Florida to back-to-back national titles with a virtuoso performance in the team's 84–75 victory over Ohio State—hitting three-pointers, digging in on defense and sending an emphatic message that the Gators were the team of this generation with a thundering dunk on the break—and now here he was in the bowels of the Georgia Dome, hopping up and down and grinning like a little kid. The fans were long gone and most of his teammates were showered and ready to leave the arena when Brewer, still in full uniform, was asked to explain his sudden killer instinct and proficiency from beyond the arc. "Big stage, baby," he said. "When the bright lights are on, the biggest players step up."

That statement perfectly described Florida's season. When Brewer, Joakim Noah and Al Horford decided to put aside millions of dollars from the NBA and return to school after beating UCLA to win the 2005–06 national title, the Gators were the clear favorites to repeat. Everywhere the Gators went, they were met with the toughest game their opponents had to offer. For the most part, Florida handled it well— thrashing No. 3-ranked Ohio State at home in December and cruising to the SEC regu-

lar season title. After that, there was seemingly little left to play for. Florida lost three straight (to Vanderbilt, LSU and Tennessee) and many wondered if the Gators had lost their swagger.

Such a slide might have rattled a lesser team, but this group was different. Tight-knit and undaunted, the Gators stayed together. While having dinner one evening with Sidney Green (father of point guard Taurean Green) the Oh-Fours—as '04 high school grads Green, Brewer, Horford and Noah were affectionately dubbed—realized they were feeling the pressure, trying to live up to everyone's expectations but their own. After dinner they watched a tape of a 2005 game against Syracuse, during which they dove for loose balls, hit shot after shot and played freely. Suddenly something clicked. "They were jumping up and down, yelling and rewinding [the tape] and playing it back again," said Sidney Green. After that night, Florida played like champions again.

Then the Gators made history, becoming the first team to repeat as national champions since Duke in 1991 and '92. That's when Brewer began talking about Florida as one of the greatest teams of all time. "I feel like we're one of the best teams to ever play the game," said Brewer. "You can argue about it, but I'd put us up against anybody."

A few minutes later, Florida coach Billy Donovan looked up into the chilly night and

Tennessee's Candace Parker helped the Lady Vols win their seventh championship, but the game was quickly overshadowed when the women from runner-up Rutgers were insulted by a radio shock jock .

beamed as he spoke about his team. By winning his second national title at 41, Donovan put himself in elite company (Bob Knight won his second national championship at age 40) and he did it at a football school, whose team, incidentally, was coming off a national title of its own (over Ohio State to boot). Donovan and the Gators also cemented their legacy after overcoming rumors in the days leading up to the title game that Donovan was going to leave Florida for Kentucky after Tubby Smith bolted for Minnesota. (Donovan turned Kentucky down, but in June he accepted a lucrative head coaching offer from the NBA's Orlando Magic, only to have second thoughts and back out of the deal days later.)

On the women's side, Tennessee's Lady Vols established their place in history by winning the school's seventh national title under coach Pat Summit with a 59–46 victory over Rutgers' Scarlet Knights. Led by

Player of the Year Candace Parker, Tennessee overpowered the Cinderella Rutgers team. But it was the Scarlet Knights who were thrown into the media firestorm a few days later when controversial radio personality Don Imus called them "nappy-headed hos" and "rough girls" with tattoos. Imus' sidekick Bernard McGuirk chimed in, saying the game was "the Jigaboos versus the Wannabes."

It took a few days for the story to gain attention, but when it did it quickly spiraled out of control. The Rutgers women acquitted themselves well, speaking eloquently and with perspective, while Imus continued to put his foot in his mouth.

Soon the Revs. Jesse Jackson and Al Sharpton got involved and they were calling for Imus' head. "For 10 days it seemed like we weren't in control of our own lives," said Rutgers junior guard Essence Carson. "It was like we were paper dolls."

Imus was eventually fired, but the Rutgers women came away scarred and jaded. "Where were these major networks when we were making history [on the court] for a prestigious university?" Carson pointedly asked.

And what about Tennessee? With little attention given to the women all year, the spotlight shone on a controversy rather than the Vols' brilliance on the court. It's too bad because these women also showcased tremendous team basketball in 2006–07. But while the Florida men were heralded as the team of this generation for winning back-to-back national titles, the women's champ (and runner-up) were both overshadowed by an ignorant loudmouth.

Any overshadowing on the men's side was courtesy of Florida's starters, all of whom could match any player in the country at their position: A point guard who could run the team and hit the open shot (Green); a sharpshooting two-guard (Lee Humphrey) with deadly range from three-point land; a slasher who could do it all (Brewer) and two dominant big men inside who could block shots, rebound and score in the post (Noah and Horford).

The thing that made Florida such a great team was its ability to play like one. There were no egos and the Gators genuinely liked being together—on and off the court. Noah was just as happy dunking (and letting out primal screams) as he was kicking the ball out to Humphrey and watching him drill a three. "We're close and we all appreciate that we're part of something special," said Humphrey, who became the NCAA tournament's all-time leader in career three-pointers with 47.

After dominating UCLA in the national semifinal, the Florida coaching staff gathered in a meeting room in the Atlanta Marriott downtown. It was in the wee hours when Donovan and his staff started putting together a game plan for Ohio State. The images on the TV monitor in the front of the room scared the coaches: freshman sensation Greg Oden blocking shots and eating up opponents inside, lightning-quick point guard Mike Conley Jr. beating everyone down the floor on the break, and all of the Buckeyes hitting three-pointers. But soon those fears were allayed when the coaching staff remembered what they had. "These guys can handle anything we throw at them," said Florida assistant Larry Shyatt.

Two days later, Florida handled Ohio State with remarkable ease. Sure, Oden showed why he would become the No. 1 pick in the NBA draft a few months later, scoring 25 points and grabbing 12 rebounds, but for the most part the Gators shut down the rest of the Buckeyes. Afterward, fans and coaches alike wondered if we'd ever see a team like this again.

"In all my years of coaching, I've never seen a team mesh together as well as these guys," said Shyatt, who has been in the coaching business for 30 years, including stints as a head coach at Clemson and Wyoming. "You go into a room, whether it's a team meeting or a meal, and no two guys are sitting in the same place. There were no cliques and they legitimately rooted for one another. They became so close that all they really cared about was winning. Team came first and all the personal accolades didn't matter."

Personal accolades never meant much to Ohio State freshman phenom Greg Oden. Growing up, Oden dreamed of becoming a dentist and stuck to that goal through his sophomore year in high school, even as he approached seven feet and towered over everyone in his path on the basketball court. When he was 12, Mike Conley Sr., whose son Mike Jr. was and still is best friends and teammates with Oden, asked the budding star what he wanted to be when he grew up. "He told me he wanted to be a dentist and he stuck to that," said Conley Sr. "Every now and then I'd say, 'You changed your mind yet?' He'd say, 'Nope. Dentist.'"

The new NBA age minimum rule required Oden to attend college for at least

one year and he enjoyed every minute of his time at Ohio State. Though it didn't start out auspiciously as Oden missed the Buckeyes' first seven games after recovering from surgery on his right wrist, he took it all in stride and deferred to his teammates. Ohio State learned to play without its big man and took the pressure off Oden when he returned (his wrist was far from fully healed and he played the first half of the regular season with a cast, forcing him to shoot free throws left-handed).

"We could have become a team that just threw the ball into Greg and stood around watching," said senior forward Ivan Harris. "But we never got a chance to develop that bad habit."

The Buckeyes gelled as a team, winning the Big Ten regular season and tournament titles and it was Oden and Conley Jr. who made them go. Oden was a presence inside, and though his offensive game was unpolished, he drew attention, blocked many shots and altered many more. Meanwhile, Conley improved with every dribble, using his speed and court savvy to stifle opponents, and by the end of the season was

Buckeye center Greg Oden (l.) and fellow freshman guard Mike Conley Jr. (r.) both jumped from the same high school to Ohio State to the NBA in the course of two years.

playing better than any point guard in the nation.

By the time the NCAA tournament rolled around the Buckeyes were a juggernaut, running in transition, drilling three-pointers and, of course, featuring an athletic, shot-blocking 7-foot center in the middle. Ohio State marched to the Final Four, where it faced Georgetown and 7'2" center Roy Hibbert. It would be the first time since his AAU days that Oden faced someone bigger than him. How did Oden prepare for the game? He watched the comedy *I (Heart) Huckabees* in his hotel room. "He's a little nutty, and he doesn't care who knows it," said Conley Jr. "He might look like this mean big man on the court, but he doesn't try to play that part in real life."

In the national semifinal, both Oden and Hibbert were quickly taken out of the action as they each picked up two fouls in the first 10 minutes. But Ohio State had plenty of

GREG NELSON

Another phenomenal freshman, Texas forward Kevin Durant, also left college for the NBA after playing a single, sizzling season.

school. But once he stepped on the floor it was clear that Durant had an NBA-ready game. Early in the season, he established himself as the best player in the nation with a stretch of 30-point games. What made him so difficult to defend was his ability to play every position.

"If I had went into the season knowing we didn't have a point guard and said, 'Kevin, you have to be our point guard,' he could have done that," said Texas coach Rick Barnes. "If I said to him, 'You've got to be a low-post player and stay there,' Kevin would do that. So what we've done this year is let him do all of it. I told him when I recruited him: 'You should want it all. I'm talking about the impact you can have on your sport and on other people. Look at Tiger Woods, Michael Jordan, the great ones. There's more to it than what you see on the court. You're one of those guys.' I'm just not sure he can understand that yet."

It might take a few years for Durant to make an impact off the court, but on it, he made history by becoming the first freshman to be named consensus Player of the Year. Durant was the headliner of a fabulous freshman class and with Oden, Conley Jr., North Carolina's Brandan Wright and Washington's Spencer Hawes, this class was one of the best in history. "I've been in college basketball since 1978," said Tennessee coach Bruce Pearl, "and I've never seen a class that was this good at the top and this deep."

But, in the end, the experienced Gators stood tallest. "I'd like for this team to be remembered as the greatest team that ever played," Donovan said. "I'm not saying that this team would beat the UNLVs [of the early '90s] and the UCLAs [of the John Wooden dynasty]. I'm not talking about wins and losses. I'm talking about the word team."

experience playing without its big man and continually beat Georgetown down the floor and created open looks from three-point range. "Our greatest strength," said Buckeyes coach Thad Matta, "is our ability to adjust."

The battle of the big men had its moments in the second half, but by then Ohio State was in control and the Buckeyes held on for a 67–60 victory. In the end, Hibbert got the better of Oden, outscoring him 19–13 and afterward the normally gentile giant was peeved. "We won the game, but I need 20 or 30 minutes to reflect on how I lost the one-on-one matchup."

One player who rarely loses a one-on-one matchup is Texas' phenomenal freshman Kevin Durant. The 6'9" wing guard came to Austin with a complete game and the ability to score from inside out. Off the court, he looked like a baby-faced freshman—in high

NCAA Men's Championship Game Box Score

Florida 84

	Min	FG M-A	FT M-A	Reb O-T	A	PF	TP
T. Green	38	4–6	5–5	0–3	6	0	16
C. Brewer	36	4–12	2–2	0–8	1	2	13
L. Humphrey	34	5–8	0–0	0–1	1	1	14
A. Horford	34	6–15	6–8	4–12	3	3	18
J. Noah	21	1–3	6–6	0–3	0	4	8
C. Richard	20	3–5	2–3	5–8	0	5	8
W. Hodge	11	2–2	1–1	0–1	0	1	5
M. Speights	6	1–2	0–0	1–2	0	3	2
Totals		26–53	22–25	10–38	11	19	84

Percentages: FG-.490, FT-.880. 3-Point Goals: 10–18, .555 (L. Humphrey 4–7, C. Brewer 3–8, T. Green 3–3). Team Rebounds: 38. Blocked Shots: 3 (C. Brewer 3). Turnovers: 15 (T. Green 6, C. Richard 3, J. Noah 2, A. Horford 2, C. Brewer 1, W. Hodge 1). Steals: 5 (C. Brewer 3, J. Noah 1, W. Hodge 1). Halftime: Florida 44, Ohio St 46.

A: 51,458.

Ohio State 75

	Min	FG M-A	FT M-A	Reb O-T	A	PF	TP
G. Oden	38	10–15	5–8	4–12	1	4	25
J. Butler	36	1–7	0–0	0–2	1	3	3
M. Conley Jr.	34	7–13	5–6	1–3	6	3	20
R. Lewis	34	6–13	0–1	2–3	0	3	12
I. Harris	26	2–8	1–2	1–5	0	2	7
D. Lighty	13	2–3	0–0	0–0	1	1	4
D. Cook	9	1–2	0–0	0–0	1	1	2
M. Terwilliger	5	1–1	0–0	0–0	0	1	2
O. Hunter	5	0–2	0–0	2–2	0	2	0
Totals		30–64	11–17	10–27	10	20	75

Percentages: FG-.468, FT-.647. 3-Point Goals:4–23, .173 (J. Butler 1–6, M. Conley Jr. 1–3, R. Lewis 0–4, I. Harris 2–8, D. Lighty 0–1, D. Cook 0–1). Team Rebounds: 27. Blocked Shots: 4 (G. Oden 4). Turnovers: 7 (G. Oden 2, M. Conley Jr. 2, J. Butler 1, O. Hunter 1). Steals:11 (M. Conley Jr. 4, J. Butler 2, G. Oden 1, R. Lewis 1, I. Harris 1, D. Lighty 1, D. Cook 1).

Officials: Karl Hess, Tony Greene, Edward Corbett

Final Regular Season AP Top 25 Poll

1. Florida	35–5
2. Ohio State	35–4
3. UCLA	30–6
4. Georgetown	30–7
5. Kansas	33–5
5. North Carolina	31–7
7. Memphis	33–4
8. Oregon	29–8
9. Texas A&M	27–7
10. Pittsburgh	29–8
11. Southern Illinois	29–7
11. Wisconsin	30–6
13. Butler	29–7
14. UNLV	30–7
15. USC	25–12
16. Texas	25–10
17. Washington State	26–8
18. Tennessee	24–11
19. Vanderbilt	22–12
20. Louisville	24–10
21. Nevada	29–5
22. Winthrop	29–5
23. Maryland	25–9
24. Virginia	21–11
25. Virginia Tech	22–12

National Invitation Tournament Scores

First round: Mississippi State 82, Mississippi Valley State 63; Michigan 68, Utah St 58; Florida St 77, Toledo 61; West Virginia 74, Delaware St 50; Massachusetts 89, Alabama 87; Drexel 56, North Carolina State 63; Oklahoma St 64, Marist 67; Bradley 90, Providence 78; Air Force 75, Austin Peay 51; Georgia 88, Fresno St 78; DePaul 83, Hofstra 71; Kansas St 59, Vermont 57; Clemson 64, East Tennessee St 57; Mississippi 73, Appalachian St 59; Missouri St 70, San Diego St 74; Syracuse 79, South Alabama 73

Second round: Florida St 87, Michigan 66; West Virginia 90, Massachusetts 77; North Carolina State 69, Marist 52; Mississippi St 101, Bradley 72; Air Force 83, Georgia 52; Kansas 65, DePaul 70; Clemson 89, Mississippi 68; Syracuse 80, San Diego St 64

Quarterfinals: West Virginia 71, North Carolina State 66; Mississippi St 86, Florida St 71; Air Force 52, DePaul 51; Clemson 74, Syracuse 70

Semifinals: West Virginia 63, Mississippi St 62; Clemson 68, Air Force 67

Championship Game: West Virginia 78, Clemson 73

2007 NCAA Basketball Men's Division I Tournament

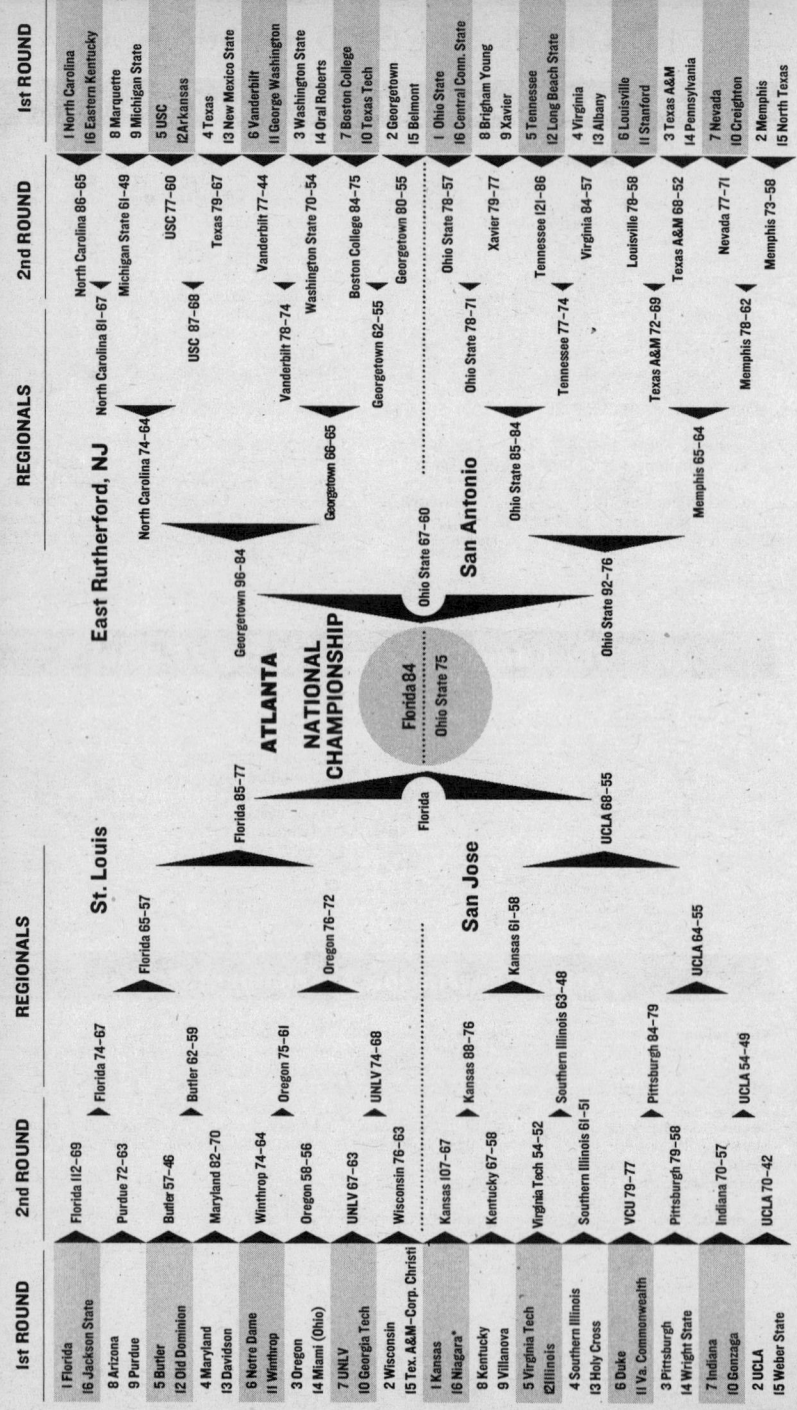

*won 77–69 vs. Florida A&M in opening game at Dayton, Ohio.

America East

	Conference			All Games		
	W	L	Pct	W	L	Pct
Vermont	15	1	.938	25	7	.781
Albany	13	3	.813	23	9	.719
Boston Univ.	8	8	.500	12	18	.400
Maine	7	9	.438	12	18	.400
UMBC	7	9	.438	12	19	.387
Binghamton	6	10	.375	13	16	.448
Hartford	6	10	.375	13	18	.419
New Hampshire	6	10	.375	10	20	.333
Stony Brook	4	12	.250	9	20	.310

Atlantic Coast

	Conference			All Games		
	W	L	Pct	W	L	Pct
North Carolina	11	5	.688	28	6	.824
Virginia	11	5	.688	20	10	.667
Maryland	10	6	.625	24	8	.750
Virginia Tech	10	6	.625	21	11	.656
Boston College	10	6	.625	20	11	.645
Duke	8	8	.500	22	10	.688
Geogia Tech	8	8	.500	20	11	.645
Clemson	7	9	.438	21	10	.677
Florida St	7	9	.438	20	12	.625
North Carolina St	5	11	.313	18	15	.545
Wake Forest	5	11	.313	15	16	.484
Miami (Fla.)	4	12	.250	12	20	.375

Atlantic Sun

	Conference			All Games		
	W	L	Pct	W	L	Pct
East Tennnessee St	16	2	.889	24	9	.727
Belmont	14	4	.778	23	9	.719
Lipscomb	11	7	.611	18	13	.581
Jacksonville	11	7	.611	15	14	.517
Kennesaw St.	9	9	.500	13	18	.419
Mercer	8	10	.444	13	17	.433
Campbell	7	11	.389	14	17	.452
Gardner–Webb	7	11	.389	9	21	.300
Stetson	6	12	.333	11	20	.355
North Florida	1	17	.056	3	26	.103

Atlantic 10

	Conference			All Games		
	W	L	Pct	W	L	Pct
Xavier	13	3	.813	24	8	.750
Massachusetts	13	3	.813	23	8	.742
George Washington	11	5	.688	23	8	.742
Fordham	10	6	.625	18	12	.600
Rhode Island	10	6	.625	19	14	.576
St. Joseph's	9	7	.563	18	14	.563
Dayton	8	8	.500	19	12	.613
St. Louis	8	8	.500	20	13	.606
Charlotte	7	9	.438	14	16	.467
Temple	6	10	.375	12	18	.400
Duquesne	6	10	.375	10	19	.345
Richmond	4	12	.250	8	22	.267
St. Bonaventure	4	12	.250	7	22	.241
La Salle	3	13	.188	10	20	.333

Big East

	Conference			All Games		
	W	L	Pct	W	L	Pct
Georgetown	13	3	.813	26	6	.813
Pittsburgh	12	4	.750	27	7	.794
Louisville	12	4	.750	23	9	.719
Notre Dame	11	5	.688	24	7	.774
Marquette	10	6	.625	24	9	.727
Syracuse	10	6	.625	22	10	.688
West Virginia	9	7	.563	22	9	.710
Villanova	9	7	.563	22	10	.688
DePaul	9	7	.563	18	13	.581
Providence	8	8	.500	18	12	.600
St. John's	7	9	.438	16	15	.516
Connecticut	6	10	.375	17	14	.548
Seton Hall	4	12	.250	13	16	.448
South Florida	3	13	.188	12	18	.400
Rutgers	3	13	.188	10	19	.345
Cincinnati	2	14	.125	11	19	.367

Big Sky

	Conference			All Games		
	W	L	Pct	W	L	Pct
Weber St	11	5	.688	20	11	.645
Northern Arizona	11	5	.688	18	12	.600
Montana	10	6	.625	17	15	.531
Portland St	9	7	.563	19	13	.594
Eastern Washington	8	8	.500	15	14	.517
Idaho St	8	8	.500	13	17	.433
Montana St	8	8	.500	11	19	.367
Sacramento St	5	11	.313	10	19	.345

Big South

	Conference			All Games		
	W	L	Pct	W	L	Pct
Winthrop	14	0	1.00	28	4	.875
High Point	11	3	.786	22	10	.688
Liberty	8	6	.571	14	17	.452
Coastal Carolina	7	7	.500	15	15	.500
UNC-Ashville	6	8	.429	12	19	.387
Virginia Military Inst.	5	9	.357	14	19	.424
Radford	3	11	.214	8	22	.267
Charleston Southern	2	12	.143	8	22	.267

Big 10

	Conference			All Games		
	W	L	Pct	W	L	Pct
Ohio St	15	1	.938	30	3	.909
Wisconsin	13	3	.813	29	5	.853
Indiana	10	6	.625	20	10	.667
Illinois	9	7	.563	23	11	.676
Purdue	9	7	.563	21	11	.656
Iowa	9	7	.563	17	14	.548
Michigan St	8	8	.500	22	11	.667
Michigan	8	8	.500	21	12	.636
Minnesota	3	13	.188	9	22	.290
Northwestern	2	14	.125	13	18	.419
Penn St	2	14	.125	11	19	.367

Note: Standings based on regular-season conference play only; overall records include all tournament play.

Big 12

	Conference			All Games		
	W	L	Pct	W	L	Pct
Kansas	14	2	.875	30	4	.882
Texas A&M	13	3	.813	25	6	.806
Texas	12	4	.750	24	9	.727
Kansas St	10	6	.625	22	11	.667
Texas Tech	9	7	.563	21	12	.636
Missouri	7	9	.438	18	12	.600
Oklahoma St	6	10	.375	22	12	.647
Nebraska	6	10	.375	17	14	.548
Oklahoma	6	10	.375	16	15	.516
Iowa St	6	10	.375	15	16	.484
Baylor	4	12	.250	15	16	.484
Colorado	3	13	.188	7	20	.259

Big West

	Conference			All Games		
	W	L	Pct	W	L	Pct
Long Beach St	12	2	.857	24	7	.774
CSU-Fullerton	9	5	.643	20	10	.667
Cal Poly	9	5	.643	19	11	.633
UC-Santa Barb.	9	5	.643	18	11	.621
UC-Irvine	6	8	.429	15	18	.455
CSU-Northridge	5	9	.357	14	17	.452
Pacific	5	9	.357	12	19	.387
UC-Riverside	1	13	.071	7	24	.226

Colonial

	Conference			All Games		
	W	L	Pct	W	L	Pct
VCU	16	2	.889	27	6	.818
Old Dominion	15	3	.833	24	8	.750
Hofstra	14	4	.778	22	9	.710
Drexel	13	5	.722	23	8	.742
George Mason	9	9	.500	18	15	.545
Northeastern	9	9	.500	13	19	.406
William & Mary	8	10	.444	15	15	.500
Towson	8	10	.444	15	17	.469
Georgia St	5	13	.278	11	20	.355
UNC-Wilmington	4	14	.222	7	22	.241
James Madison	4	14	.222	7	23	.233
Delaware	3	15	.167	5	26	.161

Conference USA

	Conference			All Games		
	W	L	Pct	W	L	Pct
Memphis	16	0	1.00	30	3	.909
UCF	11	5	.688	22	9	.710
Houston	10	6	.625	18	15	.545
Southern Miss	9	7	.563	20	11	.645
Tulsa	9	7	.563	20	11	.645
Tulane	9	7	.563	17	13	.567
Rice	8	8	.500	16	16	.500
UAB	7	9	.438	15	16	.484
Marshall	7	9	.438	13	19	.406
UTEP	6	10	.375	14	17	.452
SMU	3	13	.188	14	17	.452
East Carolina	1	15	.063	6	24	.200

Horizon League

	Conference			All Games		
	W	L	Pct	W	L	Pct
Butler	13	3	.813	27	6	.818
Wright St	13	3	.813	23	9	.719
Loyola (Ill.)	10	6	.625	21	11	.656
UW-Green Bay	7	9	.438	18	15	.545
Youngstown St	7	9	.438	14	17	.452
Ill-Chicago	7	9	.438	14	18	.438
Detroit	6	10	.375	11	19	.367
UW-Milwaukee	6	10	.375	9	22	.290
Cleveland St	3	13	.188	10	21	.323

Ivy League

	Conference			All Games		
	W	L	Pct	W	L	Pct
Pennsylvania	13	1	.929	22	8	.733
Yale	10	4	.714	14	13	.519
Cornell	9	5	.643	16	12	.571
Columbia	7	7	.500	16	12	.571
Brown	6	8	.429	11	18	.379
Harvard	5	9	.357	12	16	.429
Dartmouth	4	10	.286	9	18	.333
Princeton	2	12	.143	11	17	.393

Metro Atlantic

	Conference			All Games		
	W	L	Pct	W	L	Pct
Marist	14	4	.778	24	8	.750
Niagara	13	5	.722	22	11	.667
Siena	12	6	.667	20	12	.625
Loyola (Md.)	12	6	.667	18	13	.581
Manhattan	10	8	.556	13	17	.433
Fairfield	10	8	.556	13	19	.406
Rider	9	9	.500	16	15	.516
Canisius	6	12	.333	12	19	.387
St. Peter's	3	15	.167	5	25	.167
Iona	1	17	.056	2	28	.067

Mid-American

	Conference			All Games		
EAST	W	L	Pct	W	L	Pct
Akron	13	3	.813	26	7	.788
Kent St	12	4	.750	21	11	.656
Miami (Ohio)	10	6	.625	18	14	.563
Ohio	9	7	.563	19	13	.594
Buffalo	4	12	.250	12	19	.387
Bowling Green	3	13	.188	13	18	.419
WEST						
Toledo	14	2	.875	19	12	.613
Western Michigan	9	7	.563	16	16	.500
Central Michigan	7	9	.438	13	18	.419
Eastern Michigan	6	10	.375	13	19	.406
Ball St	5	11	.313	9	22	.290
Northern Illinois	4	12	.250	7	23	.233

Mid-Continent

	Conference			All Games		
	W	L	Pct	W	L	Pct
Oral Roberts	12	2	.857	23	10	.697
Oakland	10	4	.714	19	14	.576
Valparaiso	9	5	.643	16	15	.516
IUPUI	7	7	.500	15	15	.500
Southern Utah	6	8	.429	16	14	.533
UMKC	6	8	.429	12	20	.375
Centenary	3	11	.214	10	21	.323
Western Illinois	3	11	.214	7	23	.233

Mid-Eastern Athletic

	Conference			All Games		
	W	L	Pct	W	L	Pct
Delaware St	16	2	.889	20	11	.645
Florida A&M	12	6	.667	19	13	.594
Hampton	10	8	.556	15	16	.484
North Carolina A&T	10	8	.556	15	16	.484
South Carolina St	10	8	.556	13	17	.433
Morgan St	10	8	.556	13	17	.433
Norfolk St	10	8	.556	11	19	.367
Coppin State	9	9	.500	12	20	.375
Bethune-Cookman	6	12	.333	9	21	.300
Howard	5	13	.278	9	22	.290
Md-Eastern Shore	1	17	.056	4	27	.129

Missouri Valley

	Conference			All Games		
	W	L	Pct	W	L	Pct
Southern Illinois	15	3	.833	27	6	.818
Creighton	13	5	.722	22	10	.688
Missouri St	12	6	.667	22	10	.688
Bradley	10	8	.556	21	12	.636
Northern Iowa	9	9	.500	18	13	.581
Wichita St	8	10	.444	17	14	.548
Drake	6	12	.333	15	17	.531
Illinois St	6	12	.333	15	16	.484
Evansville	6	12	.333	14	17	.452
Indiana St	5	13	.278	13	18	.419

Mountain West

	Conference			All Games		
	W	L	Pct	W	L	Pct
Brigham Young	13	3	.813	25	8	.758
UNLV	12	4	.750	28	6	.824
Air Force	10	6	.625	23	8	.742
San Diego St	10	6	.625	21	10	.677
Wyoming	7	9	.438	17	15	.531
Colorado St	6	10	.375	17	13	.567
Utah	6	10	.375	11	19	.367
New Mexico	4	12	.250	15	17	.469
TCU	4	12	.250	13	17	.433

Northeast

	Conference			All Games		
	W	L	Pct	W	L	Pct
Central Conn. St	16	2	.889	22	11	.667
Sacred Heart	12	6	.667	18	14	.563
Quinnipiac	11	7	.611	14	15	.483
Robert Morris	9	9	.500	17	11	.607
Fairleigh Dickinson	9	9	.500	14	16	.467
Mt. St. Mary's	9	9	.500	11	20	.355
Wagner	8	10	.444	11	19	.367
Monmouth	7	11	.389	12	18	.400
St. Francis (NY)	7	11	.389	9	22	.290
Long Island	6	12	.333	10	19	.345
St. Francis (Pa.)	5	13	.278	8	21	.276

Ohio Valley

	Conference			All Games		
	W	L	Pct	W	L	Pct
Austin Peay	16	4	.800	21	11	.656
Eastern Kentucky	13	7	.650	21	11	.656
Tennessee Tech	13	7	.650	19	13	.594
Murray St	13	7	.650	16	14	.533
Samford	12	8	.600	16	16	.500
SE Missouri St	9	11	.450	11	20	.355
Morehead St	8	12	.400	12	18	.400
Tennessee St	8	12	.400	12	20	.375
Jacksonville St	7	13	.350	9	21	.300
Eastern Illinois	6	14	.300	10	20	.333
Tenn.-Martin	5	15	.250	8	23	.258
UCLA	15	3	.833	26	5	.839

Pac 10

	Conference			All Games		
	W	L	Pct	W	L	Pct
Washington St	13	5	.722	25	7	.781
Oregon	11	7	.611	26	7	.788
USC	11	7	.611	23	11	.676
Arizona	11	7	.611	20	10	.667
Stanford	10	8	.556	18	12	.600
Washington	8	10	.444	19	13	.594
California	6	12	.333	16	17	.485
Oregon St	3	15	.167	11	21	.344
Arizona St	2	16	.111	8	22	.267
Holy Cross	13	1	.929	25	8	.758

Patriot League

	Conference			All Games		
	W	L	Pct	W	L	Pct
Bucknell	13	1	.929	22	9	.710
American	7	7	.500	16	14	.533
Lehigh	7	7	.500	12	19	.387
Colgate	5	9	.357	10	19	.345
Army	4	10	.286	15	16	.484
Navy	4	10	.286	14	16	.467
Lafayette	3	11	.214	9	21	.300

Southeastern

EAST	Conference W	L	Pct	All Games W	L	Pct
Florida	13	3	.813	29	5	.853
Tennessee	10	6	.625	22	10	.688
Vanderbilt	10	6	.625	20	11	.645
Kentucky	9	7	.563	21	11	.656
Geogia	8	8	.500	18	13	.581
South Carolina	4	12	.250	14	16	.467
WEST						
Mississippi	8	8	.500	20	12	.625
Mississippi St	8	8	.500	18	13	.581
Alabama	7	9	.438	20	11	.645
Arkansas	7	9	.438	21	13	.618
Auburn	7	9	.438	17	15	.531
LSU	5	11	.313	17	15	.531

Southern

NORTH	Conference W	L	Pct	All Games W	L	Pct
Appalachian St	15	3	.833	25	7	.781
UNC-Greensboro	12	6	.667	16	14	.533
Western Carolina	7	11	.389	11	20	.355
Chattanooga	6	12	.333	15	18	.455
Elon	5	13	.278	7	23	.233
SOUTH						
Davidson	17	1	.944	29	4	.879
Col. of Charleston	13	5	.722	22	11	.667
Furman	8	10	.444	15	16	.484
Georgia Southern	7	11	.389	15	16	.484
Wofford	5	13	.278	10	20	.333
Citadel	4	14	.222	7	23	.233

Southland

EAST	Conference W	L	Pct	All Games W	L	Pct
Northwestern St	10	6	.625	17	15	.531
McNeese St	9	7	.563	15	17	.469
SE Louisiana	8	8	.500	16	14	.533
Lamar	8	8	.500	15	17	.469
Nicholls St	7	9	.438	8	22	.267
Central Arkansas	4	12	.250	10	20	.333
WEST						
Tex. A&M-Corp. Chrs.	14	2	.875	26	6	.813
Sam Houston St	13	3	.813	21	10	.677
Stephen F. Austin	8	8	.500	15	14	.517
Tex.-Arlington	8	8	.500	13	17	.433
Texas St	4	12	.250	9	20	.310
Tex.-San Antonio	3	13	.188	7	22	.241

Southwestern Athletic

	Conference W	L	Pct	All Games W	L	Pct
Mississippi Valley St	13	5	.722	18	15	.545
Jackson St	12	6	.667	21	13	.618
Grambling St	10	8	.556	12	14	.462
Alcorn St	10	8	.556	11	19	.367
Texas Southern	9	9	.500	14	17	.452
Ark.-Pine Bluff	9	9	.500	12	19	.387
Southern Univ.	9	9	.500	10	21	.323
Alabama St	8	10	.444	10	20	.333
Prairie View A&M	6	12	.333	8	22	.267
Alabama A&M	4	14	.222	10	20	.333

Sun Belt

EAST	Conference W	L	Pct	All Games W	L	Pct
South Alabama	13	5	.722	20	11	.645
Western Kentucky	12	6	.667	22	11	.667
Florida Atlantic	10	8	.556	16	15	.516
Mid. Tennessee St	8	10	.444	15	17	.469
Troy	8	10	.444	13	17	.433
Florida Int'l	7	11	.389	12	17	.414
WEST						
La-Monroe	11	7	.611	18	14	.563
Arkansas St	11	7	.611	18	15	.545
North Texas	10	8	.556	23	10	.697
New Orleans	9	9	.500	14	17	.452
Ark-Little Rock	8	10	.444	13	17	.433
La-Lafayette	7	11	.389	9	21	.300

West Coast

	Conference W	L	Pct	All Games W	L	Pct
Gonzaga	11	3	.786	23	10	.697
Santa Clara	10	4	.714	21	10	.677
St. Mary's (Ca.)	8	6	.571	17	15	.531
San Francisco	8	6	.571	13	18	.419
San Diego	6	8	.429	18	14	.563
Loyola-Marymount	5	9	.357	13	18	.419
Portland	4	10	.286	9	23	.281
Pepperdine	4	10	.286	8	23	.258

Western Athletic

	Conference W	L	Pct	All Games W	L	Pct
Nevada	14	2	.875	28	4	.875
New Mexico St	11	5	.688	25	8	.758
Fresno St	10	6	.625	22	9	.710
Utah St	9	7	.563	23	11	.676
Hawaii	8	8	.500	18	13	.581
Boise St	8	8	.500	17	14	.548
Louisiana Tech	7	9	.438	10	20	.333
San Jose St	4	12	.250	5	25	.167
Idaho	1	15	.063	4	27	.129

Independents

	All Games W	L	Pct
Utah Valley St	22	7	.759
North Dakota St	20	8	.714
Tex.-Pan American	14	5	.483
IPFW	12	7	.414
Savannah St	12	8	.400
Chicago St	9	0	.310
Longwood	9	2	.290
South Dakota St	6	4	.200
UC-Davis	5	3	.179
New Jersey Tech	5	4	.172

Scoring

	Class	GP	FG	3FG	FT	Pts	Avg
Reggie Williams, Virginia Military Inst.	Jr.	33	338	76	176	928	28.1
Trey Johnson, Jackson St	Sr.	34	303	77	239	922	27.1
Morris Almond, Rice	Sr.	32	263	77	241	844	26.4
Kevin Durant, Texas	Fr.	33	289	80	188	846	25.6
Gary Neal, Towson	Sr.	32	267	93	183	810	25.3
Bo McCalebb, New Orleans	Jr.	31	287	26	176	776	25.0
Rodney Stuckey, Eastern Washington	So.	29	227	43	215	712	24.6
Gerald Brown, Loyola (Md.)	Jr.	29	205	58	175	643	22.2
Jaycee Carroll, Utah State	Jr.	34	247	80	150	724	21.3
Stephen Curry, Davidson	Fr.	33	233	117	117	700	21.2
Alex Harris, UC-Santa Barbara	Jr.	29	191	71	158	611	21.1
Adrian Banks, Arkansas St	Jr.	33	232	97	134	695	21.1
Charron Fisher, Niagara	Jr.	25	178	36	133	525	21.0
Arizona 'AZ' Reid, High Point	Jr.	32	285	20	81	671	21.0
Loren Stokes, Hofstra	Sr.	32	236	31	167	670	20.9
Kyle Hines, UNC-Greensboro	Jr.	29	233	1	138	605	20.9
Caleb Green, Oral Roberts	Sr.	33	203	6	273	685	20.8
Chris Lofton, Tennessee	Jr.	28	183	93	117	576	20.6
Adam Haluska, Iowa	Sr.	31	190	90	167	637	20.5
Nick Fazekas, Nevada	Sr.	30	236	27	116	615	20.5
Larry Blair, Liberty	Sr.	31	237	52	105	631	20.4
Bobby Brown, CSU-Fullerton	Sr.	27	188	80	90	546	20.2
Jarrius Jackson, Texas Tech	Sr.	33	220	77	150	667	20.2
Jason Thompson, Rider	Jr.	31	221	6	176	624	20.1
Dionte Chirstmas, Temple	So.	30	192	88	128	600	20.0

FIELD-GOAL PERCENTAGE

	Class	GP	FG	FGA	Pct
Roy Hibbert, Georgetown	Jr.	32	156	225	69.3
Mike Freeman, Hampton	Fr.	30	162	239	67.8
Stuart Creason, Colorado St	Jr.	30	118	176	67.0
Florentino Valencia, Toledo	Sr.	31	159	239	66.5
Vladimir Kuljanin, UNC-Wilmington	Jr.	29	165	249	66.3
Brandan Wright, North Carolina	Fr.	33	208	314	66.2
Calvin Brown, Norfolk St	Sr.	30	152	233	65.2
Rome Sanders, Florida A&M	Sr.	34	168	259	64.9
Greg Dilligard, Illinois St	Sr.	31	128	198	64.6
Zach Andrews, Bradley	Sr.	33	147	228	64.5

Note: Minimum 5 made per game.

FREE-THROW PERCENTAGE

	Class	GP	FT	FTA	Pct
Ryan Toolson, Utah Valley St	So.	29	96	99	97.0
Derek Raivio, Gonzaga	Sr.	33	146	152	96.1
A.J. Graves, Butler	Jr.	32	137	143	95.8
Blake Ahearn, Missouri St	Sr.	32	109	117	93.2
Tristan Blackwood, Central Conn. St	Jr.	33	97	105	92.4
David Kool, Western Michigan	Fr.	29	99	108	91.7
Darren Cooper, Portland	Sr.	23	104	114	91.2
Mike Schachtner, UW-Green Bay	So.	33	104	114	91.2
Arvydas Eitutavicius, American Univ.	Sr.	30	95	105	90.5
Leemire Goldwire, UNC-Charlotte	Jr.	30	95	105	90.5

Note: Minimum 2.5 made per game.

REBOUNDS

	Class	GP	Reb	Avg
R. Jones-Jennings, Ark.-Little Rock	Sr.	30	392	13.1
Chris Holm, Vermont	Sr.	32	387	12.1
Kentrell Gransberry, South Florida	Jr.	23	263	11.4
Kevin Durant, Texas	Fr.	33	373	11.3
Nick Fazekas, Nevada	Sr.	30	336	11.2
Obie Nwadike, Central Conn. St	Sr.	30	326	10.9
Ryvon Covile, Detroit	Sr.	30	317	10.6
Glen Davis, LSU	Jr.	29	303	10.4
Jason Smith, Colorado St	Jr.	30	304	10.1
Jason Thompson, Rider	Jr.	31	312	10.1

ASSISTS

	Class	GP	A	Avg
Jared Jordan, Marist	Jr.	31	274	8.8
Jason Richards, Davidson	Jr.	33	242	7.3
Mustafa Shakur, Arizona	Sr.	30	207	6.9
D.J. Augustin, Texas	Fr.	33	221	6.7
Mike Conley Jr., Ohio St.	Fr.	33	209	6.3
Eric Maynor, VCU	So.	33	208	6.3
Keenan Jones, Northwestern St	Sr.	32	200	6.3
Dwayne Foreman, Georgia So	Jr.	29	176	6.1
Josh Wilson, Northern Arizona	So.	30	181	6.0
Ishmeal Smith, Wake Forest	Fr.	31	186	6.0

*Includes games played in tournaments.

THREE-POINT FIELD-GOAL PERCENTAGE

	Class	GP	FG	FGA	Avg
Josh Carter, Texas A&M	So.	31	83	161	51.6
Jeremy Crouch, Bradley	Jr.	25	77	151	51.0
Stephen Sir, Northern Arizona	Sr.	30	124	253	49.0
Jimmy Baron, Rhode Island	So.	32	97	203	47.8
Josh Washington, A&M-Corpus Christi	Sr.	31	89	187	47.6
Adrian Banks, Arkansas St.	Jr.	33	97	204	47.5
James Parlow, New Orleans	Jr.	27	85	180	47.2
Blake Ahearn, Missouri St	Sr.	32	91	193	47.2
Chad Toppert, New Mexico	So.	32	85	183	46.4
Brian Roberts, Dayton	Jr.	31	82	179	45.8

Note: Minimum 2.5 made per game.

BLOCKED SHOTS

	Class	GP	BS	Avg
Mickell Gladness, Alabama A&M	Jr.	30	188	6.3
Stephane Lasme, Massachusetts	Sr.	31	156	5.0
Hasheem Thabeet, Connecticut	Fr.	31	119	3.8
McHugh Mattis, South Florida	Sr.	30	109	3.6
Dominic McGuire, Fresno St	Jr.	31	110	3.5
Greg Oden, Ohio St	Fr.	26	92	3.5
Scott Vandermeer, Ill-Chicago	So.	32	111	3.5
Darryl Watkins, Syracuse	Sr.	30	102	3.4
Durrell Watkins, Syracuse	Sr.	30	99	3.3
John Bunch, Monmouth	Sr.	29	95	3.3

THREE-POINT FIELD GOALS MADE PER GAME

	Class	G	3FG	Avg
Stephen Sir, Northern Arizona	Sr.	30	124	4.1
Will Whittington, Marist	Sr.	32	127	4.0
Steven Rush, NC A&T	Jr.	30	115	3.8
Tristan Blackwood, Central Conn. St	Jr.	33	118	3.6
Keddric Mays, Chattanooga	Sr.	33	118	3.6
Stephen Curry, Davidson	Fr.	33	117	3.5
Robert McKiver, Houston	Jr.	33	116	3.5
Daryl Cohen, Southeastern La.	Sr.	30	105	3.5
A.J. Abrams, Texas	So.	33	114	3.5
Chavis Holmes, Virginia Military	So.	32	108	3.4

STEALS

	Class	GP	S	Avg
Travis Holmes, Virginia Military	So.	33	111	3.4
Paul Gause, Seton Hall	So.	29	90	3.1
Ledell Eackles, Campbell	Sr.	31	94	3.0
Ibrahim Jaaber, Pennsylvania	Sr.	30	90	3.0
Chavis Holmes, Virginia Military	So.	32	90	2.8
Torey Thomas, Holy Cross	Sr.	33	92	2.8
Tony Lee, Robert Morris	Jr.	28	77	2.8
Derek Johnson, Prairie View A&M	Jr.	30	82	2.7
Jamon Gordon, Virginia Tech	Sr.	32	86	2.7
Carl Elliott, George Washington	Sr.	31	82	2.6

Single-Game Highs

POINTS

49........Trey Johnson, Jackson St., December 22, 2006 (vs UTEP)
47........Bobby Brown, CSU-Fullerton, December 16, 2006 (vs Bethune-Cookman)
45........Al Thornton, Florida St., March 3, 2007 (vs Miami-Fla.)
45........Reggie Williams, Virginia Military Inst., November 15, 2006 (vs Va.-Inter.)

REBOUNDS

25..........Arizona 'AZ' Reid, High Point, February 24, 2007 (vs Virginia Military Inst.)
23........Kentrell Gransberry, South Florida, March 3, 2007 (vs DePaul)
23........Kevin Durant, Texas, January 31, 2007 (vs Texas Tech)

ASSISTS

19........Jason Richards, Davidson, December 15, 2006 (vs Mt. St. Mary (N.Y.)
16........Ryan Evanochko, Wis.-Green Bay, December 12, 2006 (vs Chicago St)
16........Jason Richards, Davidson, November 21, 2006 (vs Colby)
Seven tied with 15

THREE POINT FIELD GOALS

12 ....Michael Jenkins, Winthrop, November 10, 2006 (vs UNC-Greenville)
11........Eric Moore, Buffalo, January 7, 2007 (vs Bowling Green)
11..........Bobby Brown, CSU-Fullerton, December 16, 2006 (vs Bethune-Cookman)

STEALS

11 ....Travis Holmes, Virginia Military Inst., January 18, 2007 (vs Bridgewater [Va.])
10........Ledell Eackles, Campbell, November 11, 2006 (vs UNC-Pembroke)
Five tied with 9

BLOCKED SHOTS

16 ....Mickell Gladness, Alabama A&M, February 24, 2007 (vs Texas Southern)
13........Joel Anthony, UNLV, February 7, 2007 (vs TCU)
13........Sean Williams, Boston College, December 28, 2006 (vs Duquesne)

SCORING OFFENSE

	GP	W	L	Pts	Avg
Virginia Military Institute	33	14	19	3331	100.9
North Carolina	34	28	6	2933	86.3
Eastern Washington	29	15	14	2443	84.2
Northern Arizona	30	18	12	2490	83.0
Texas	33	24	9	2713	82.2
CSU-Fullerton	30	20	10	2462	82.1
Davidson	33	29	4	2695	81.7
Notre Dame	31	24	7	2528	81.5
Long Beach St	31	24	7	2489	80.3
Tex. A&M-Corpus Christi	32	26	6	2552	79.8

SCORING DEFENSE

	GP	W	L	Pts	Avg
Princeton	28	11	17	1493	53.3
Air Force	31	23	8	1738	56.1
Southern Illinois	33	27	6	1863	56.5
Michigan St	33	22	11	1871	56.7
Georgetown	32	26	6	1820	56.9
Illinois	34	23	11	1943	57.1
Butler	33	27	6	1886	57.2
Wisconsin	34	29	5	1946	57.2
Holy Cross	33	25	8	1893	57.4
Miami (Ohio)	32	18	14	1837	57.4

SCORING MARGIN

	Off	Def	Mar
North Carolina	86.3	68.1	18.1
Florida	79.3	61.6	17.8
Kansas	78.4	61.0	17.4
Memphis	79.6	62.3	17.2
Texas A&M	76.3	59.2	17.1
Winthrop	75.3	60.9	14.4
Akron	75.3	61.0	14.3
Notre Dame	81.5	67.8	13.7
Ohio St	73.6	60.2	13.5
Davidson	81.7	68.3	13.4

FIELD-GOAL PERCENTAGE

	FG	FGA	Pct
Florida	971	1843	52.7
Texas A&M-Corpus Christi	892	1701	52.4
Georgetown	784	1548	50.6
North Carolina	1070	2122	50.4
North Dakota St	799	1589	50.3
Texas A&M	837	1672	50.1
Eastern Washington	846	1708	49.5
Northern Arizona	873	1766	49.4
North Carolina St	842	1705	49.4
Pennsylvania	815	1654	49.3

FIELD-GOAL PERCENTAGE DEFENSE

	FG	FGA	Pct
Connecticut	677	1824	37.1
Texas A&M	608	1636	37.2
Syracuse	761	2040	37.3
Kansas	714	1910	37.4
Fresno St	759	1995	38.0
Georgetown	630	1645	38.3
Michigan St	631	1647	38.3
Memphis	691	1793	38.5
Belmont	717	1851	38.7
Maryland	776	1995	38.9

FREE-THROW PERCENTAGE

	FT	FTA	Pct
Villanova	579	741	78.1
Utah St	487	625	77.9
California	419	540	77.6
Florida St	467	608	76.8
Oakland	546	711	76.8
Butler	529	693	76.3
UW-Green Bay	530	697	76.0
Harvard	497	655	75.9
Robert Morris	369	487	75.8
Air Force	424	560	75.7

THREE-POINT FIELD GOALS MADE PER GAME

	GP	FG	Avg
Virginia Military Institute	33	442	13.4
West Virginia	31	321	10.4
Bradley	33	335	10.2
Houston	33	330	10.0
Wofford	30	297	9.9
Pepperdine	31	303	9.8
Davidson	33	318	9.6
Oregon	33	313	9.5
New Mexico	32	299	9.3
Cal Poly	30	280	9.3

REBOUNDING MARGIN

	GP	REB	Opp REB	Margin Avg
Vermont	32	1307	994	9.8
Washington	32	1225	938	9.0
North Carolina	34	1384	1105	8.2
Massachusetts	31	1259	1010	8.0
Michigan St	33	1160	903	7.8
Kansas	34	1373	1117	7.5
Florida	34	1264	1014	7.4
Davidson	33	1343	1102	7.3
Southern Miss	31	1196	972	7.2
Tulsa	31	1230	1007	7.2

2007 NCAA Basketball Women's Division I Tournament

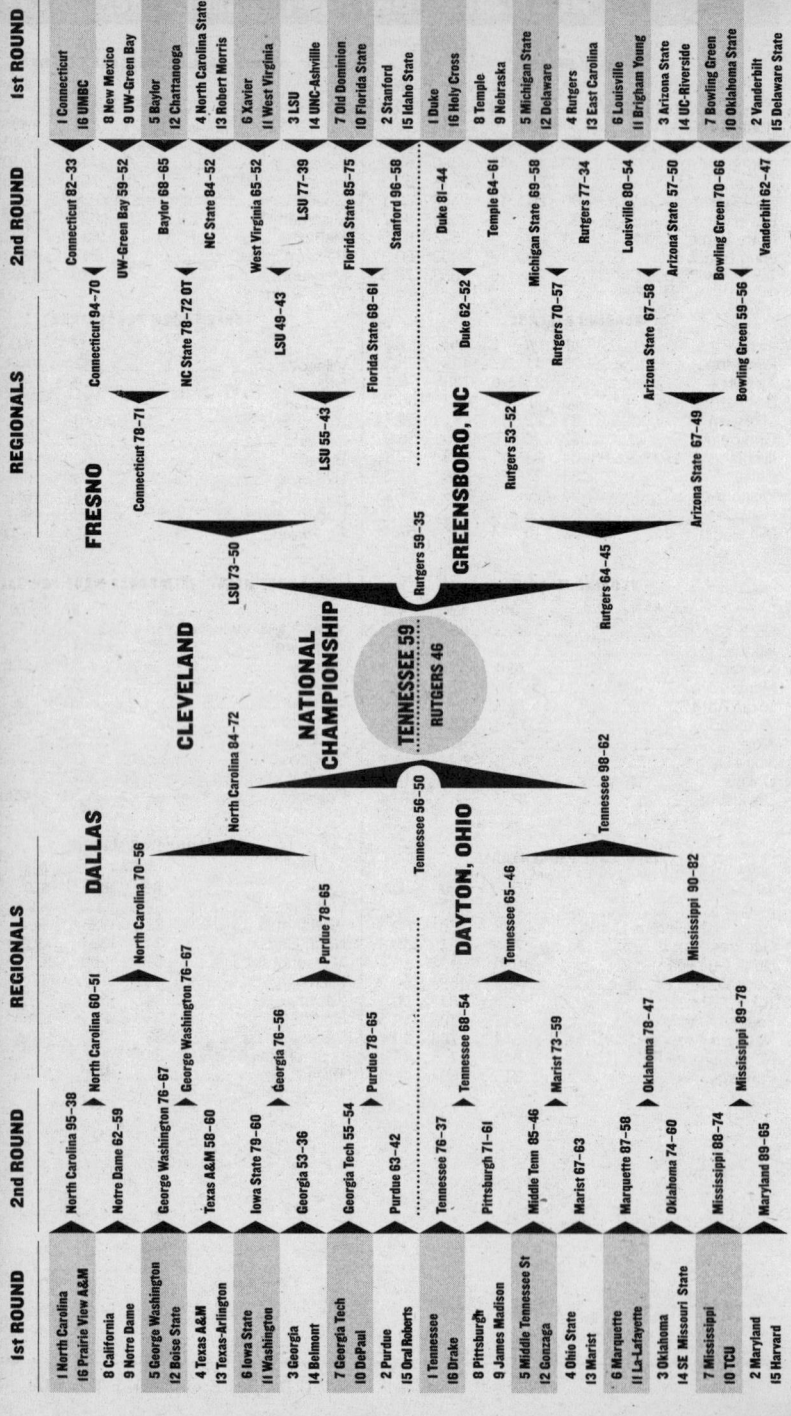

1st ROUND

1 Connecticut
16 UMBC
8 New Mexico
9 UW-Green Bay
5 Baylor
12 Chattanooga
4 North Carolina State
13 Robert Morris
6 Xavier
11 West Virginia
3 LSU
14 UNC-Ashville
7 Old Dominion
10 Florida State
2 Stanford
15 Idaho State
1 Duke
16 Holy Cross
8 Temple
9 Nebraska
5 Michigan State
12 Delaware
4 Rutgers
13 East Carolina
6 Louisville
11 Brigham Young
3 Arizona State
14 UC-Riverside
7 Bowling Green
10 Oklahoma State
2 Vanderbilt
15 Delaware State

2nd ROUND

Connecticut 82–33
UW-Green Bay 59–52
Baylor 68–65
NC State 84–52
West Virginia 65–52
LSU 77–39
Florida State 85–75
Stanford 96–58
Duke 81–44
Temple 64–61
Michigan State 69–58
Rutgers 77–34
Louisville 80–54
Arizona State 57–50
Bowling Green 70–66
Vanderbilt 62–47

REGIONALS

FRESNO

Connecticut 94–70
Connecticut 78–71
NC State 78–72 OT
LSU 49–43
LSU 55–43
Florida State 68–61

GREENSBORO, NC

Duke 62–52
Rutgers 53–52
Rutgers 70–57
Arizona State 67–58
Arizona State 67–49
Bowling Green 59–56

REGIONALS

CLEVELAND

LSU 73–50
North Carolina 84–72

DAYTON, OHIO

Tennessee 56–50
Tennessee 65–46
Tennessee 98–62
Mississippi 90–82

NATIONAL CHAMPIONSHIP

Rutgers 59–35

Rutgers 64–45

TENNESSEE 59
RUTGERS 46

REGIONALS

DALLAS

North Carolina 70–56
George Washington 76–67
Georgia 76–56
Purdue 78–65

2nd ROUND

North Carolina 95–38
North Carolina 60–51
Notre Dame 62–59
George Washington 76–67
Texas A&M 58–60
Iowa State 79–60
Georgia 53–36
Georgia Tech 55–54
Purdue 63–42
Tennessee 76–37
Pittsburgh 71–61
Middle Tenn 85–46
Marist 67–63
Marquette 87–58
Oklahoma 74–60
Mississippi 88–74
Maryland 89–65

George Washington 76–67
Georgia 76–56
Purdue 78–65
Tennessee 68–54
Marist 73–59
Oklahoma 78–47
Mississippi 89–78

1st ROUND

1 North Carolina
16 Prairie View A&M
8 California
9 Notre Dame
5 George Washington
12 Boise State
4 Texas A&M
13 Texas-Arlington
6 Iowa State
11 Washington
3 Georgia
14 Belmont
7 Georgia Tech
10 DePaul
2 Purdue
15 Oral Roberts
1 Tennessee
16 Drake
8 Pittsburgh
9 James Madison
5 Middle Tennessee St
12 Gonzaga
4 Ohio State
13 Marist
6 Marquette
11 La-Lafayette
3 Oklahoma
14 SE Missouri State
7 Mississippi
10 TCU
2 Maryland
15 Harvard

NCAA Women's Championship Game Box Score

Tennessee 59

	Min	FG M-A	FT M-A	Reb O-T	A	PF	TP
C. Parker	39	5-15	7-10	2-7	3	3	17
A. Hornbuckle	37	2-8	0-0	3-7	1	2	4
S. Spencer	36	4-12	2-2	2-2	2	4	11
N. Anosike	34	2-9	0-5	10-16	2	2	4
S. Bobbitt	32	4-9	1-2	2-3	0	1	13
A. Auguste	15	3-5	4-4	4-5	1	1	10
A. Fuller	6	0-0	0-0	0-0	0	0	0
D. Redding	1	0-0	0-0	0-0	0	0	0
Totals		20-58	14-23	23-40	9	13	59

Percentages: FG—34.4, FT—60.8, 3-pt goals: 5-15, .333 (A. Hornbuckle 0-3, S. Spencer 1-4, S. Bobbitt 4-8). Team rebounds: 40. Blocked shots: 0. Turnovers: 12 (C. Parker 2, A. Hornbuckle 7, N. Anosike 1, S. Bobbitt 1, A. Auguste 1). Steals: 7 (A. Hornbuckle 2, N. Anosike 1, S. Bobbitt 3, A. Auguste).
Halftime: Tennessee 30, Rutgers 28

A: 20,704.

Rutgers 46

	Min	FG M-A	FT M-A	Reb O-T	A	PF	TP
E. Carson	40	4-11	0-3	1-6	1	4	8
M. Ajavon	37	3-9	0-0	0-4	1	5	8
K. Vaughn	34	9-15	2-3	7-10	2	2	20
E. Prince	26	0-0	2-4	1-3	.2	4	2
H. Zurich	23	2-6	0-0	0-1	0	3	4
M. McCurdy	17	1-3	0-0	0-1	0	3	2
B. Ray	15	0-3	0-0	1-2	0	0	0
R. Junaid	6	1-2	0-0	1-3	0	1	2
Totals		25-65	22-28	11-36	14	21	75

Percentages: FG—40.8, FT—40.0, 3-pt goals: 2-10, .200 (E. Carson 0-3, M. Ajavon 2-5, B. Ray 0-2). Team rebounds: 30. Blocked shots: 3 (K. Vaughn 1, H. Zurich 1, R. Junaid 1). Turnovers: 17 (E. Carson 2, M. Ajavon 5, K. Vaughn 4, E. Prince 4, M. McCurdy 2). Steals: 6 (M. Ajavon 1, K. Vaughn 3, H. Zurich 1, M. McCurdy 1).

Officials: Lisa Mattingly, Michael Price, Tina Napier

NCAA Women's Division I Individual Leaders

SCORING

Player and Team	Class	GP	TFG	3FG	FT	Pts	Avg
Carrie Moore, Western Michigan	Sr.	32	272	52	217	813	25.4
Crystal Kelly, Western Kentucky	Jr.	28	220	7	220	667	23.8
Courtney Paris, Oklahoma	So.	30	289	0	129	707	23.6
Chrissy Givens, Middle Tennessee St	Sr.	32	285	25	133	728	22.8
Tye Jackson, Houston	Jr.	22	162	54	117	495	22.5
Alisha Dill, Coastal Carolina	Sr.	29	209	62	172	652	22.5
Angel McCoughtry, Louisville	So.	33	274	41	134	723	21.9
Natalie Doma, Idaho St	Jr.	30	248	8	149	653	21.8
Joi Scott, Murray St	Sr.	26	213	6	133	565	21.7
Carmen Guzman, UAB	Sr.	30	220	64	142	646	21.5
Adrianne Davie, Arkansas St	Sr.	32	250	16	153	669	20.9
Alex Anderson, Chattanooga	Jr.	32	265	8	123	661	20.7
Traci Edwards, UW-Milwaukee	So.	30	218	4	175	615	20.5
Jessica Davenport, Ohio St	Sr.	31	218	1	189	626	20.2
Mandy Morales, Montana	So.	30	186	55	175	602	20.1
Casey Nash, Oregon St	Sr.	28	212	14	122	560	20.0
Tyresa Smith, Delaware	Sr.	31	223	0	167	613	19.8
Candace Parker, Tennessee	So.	30	223	6	140	592	19.7
Jessica Dickson, South Florida	Sr.	31	212	40	147	611	19.7
Jillian Robbins, Tulsa	Sr.	30	201	8	180	590	19.7
Amber Bland, North Carolina A&T	So.	30	207	75	100	589	19.6
Amanda Pape, Sacred Heart	Sr.	32	219	24	158	620	19.4
Kamesha Hairston, Temple	Sr.	31	231	17	118	597	19.3
Shavonte Zellous, Pittsburgh	So.	31	207	9	173	596	19.2
Chinata Nesbit, Robert Morris	Jr.	31	218	14	143	593	19.1

FIELD-GOAL PERCENTAGE

Player and Team	Class	GP	FG	FGA	Pct
Crystal Langhorne, Maryland ....Jr.		32	202	280	72.1
Crystal Kelly, Western Ky..........Jr.		28	220	356	61.8
Jackie McFarland, Colorado......Jr.		29	172	285	60.4
Jessica Davenport, Ohio St.......Sr.		31	218	364	59.9
Jenna Real, Loyola (Ill.)............Sr.		28	148	250	59.2
Dani Wright, Brigham Young ....Sr.		32	162	274	59.1
Tina Charles, Connecticut ....Fr.		32	168	286	58.7
Alysha Clark, Belmont ....So.		29	168	286	58.7
Joi Scott, Murray St ....Sr.		26	213	365	58.4
Marcedes Walker, Pittsburgh ....Jr.		30	185	318	58.2

Note: Minimum 5 FG per game.

REBOUNDS

Player and Team	Class	GP	Reb	Avg
Lachelle Lyles, SE Missouri St ......Sr.		30	517	17.2
Courtney Paris, Oklahoma...........So.		30	485	16.2
Sylvia Fowles, LSU ....Jr.		33	423	12.8
Alysha Clark, Belmont..................So.		29	367	12.7
Natalie Doma, Idaho St ....Jr.		30	365	12.2
Meredith Alexis, James Madison ..Sr.		32	376	11.8
Jillian Robbins, Tulsa...................Sr.		30	349	11.6
Stephanie Duda, UC-Irvine ....Jr.		30	332	11.1
LaJoyce King, CSU-Northridge ....Sr.		26	284	10.9
Sherell Neal, New Mexico St ....Jr.		31	335	10.8

FREE-THROW PERCENTAGE

Player and Team	Class	GP	FT	FTA	Pct
Bracey Barker, Maine................Sr.		24	92	100	92.0
Carlynn Savant, Missouri ....Sr.		30	104	114	91.2
Chelsea Marandola, Providence .So.		28	87	96	90.6
Stephanie Raymond, No. Illinois.....Sr.		31	163	181	90.1
Jami Montagnino, Tulane...........Sr.		31	107	119	89.9
Jordan Sykes, Fairleigh Dickinson...Fr.		29	80	89	89.9
Katie Gearlds, Purdue...............Sr.		33	100	112	89.3
Morgan Warburton, Utah...........So.		31	129	145	89.0
Julie Briody, New Mexico ....Sr.		32	163	184	88.6
Laiken Dollente, Portland..............Fr.		30	163	184	88.6

Note: Minimum 2.5 made per game.

ASSISTS

Player and Team	Class	GP	A	Avg
Amanda Rego, San Diego...............Jr.		29	222	7.7
Kristin Chaney, Southern Miss ....Sr.		30	210	7.0
Andrea Benvenuto, James Madison ...Sr.		32	217	6.8
Mandy Morales, Montana ....So.		30	203	6.8
Kelcey Roegiers-Jensen, Georgia St ...Sr.		30	197	6.6
Stephanie Raymond, No. Illinois ....Sr.		31	201	6.5
Mercedes Fox-Griffin, Oregon St........So.		28	180	6.4
Lyndsey Medders, Iowa St..................Sr.		31	197	6.4
Ashley Langford, Tulane ....So.		31	195	6.3
Brooke Wilhoit, East Tennessee St........Sr.		31	188	6.1

THREE-POINT FIELD-GOAL PERCENTAGE

Player and Team	Class	GP	FG	FGA	Pct
Brittany Carfora, Columbia........Jr.		27	55	106	51.9
Caroline Williams, Vanderbilt ....Sr.		32	89	178	50.0
Kristi Toliver, Maryland ....So.		32	66	140	47.1
Kelsey Luna, Indiana St ....Fr.		30	79	171	46.2
Candice Wiggins, Stanford ....Jr.		27	75	168	44.6
Mel Thomas, Connecticut ....Jr.		32	78	181	43.1
Jenna Graber, La Salle ....Sr.		30	62	144	43.1
Chandice Cronk, Santa Clara ...Jr.		30	94	220	42.7
Ashley Davis, TCU ....Sr.		31	74	175	42.3
Leah Phillips, Indiana St ....So.		30	65	154	42.2

Note: Minimum 2.0 made per game.

BLOCKED SHOTS

Player and Team	Class	GP	BS	Avg
Alison Bales, Duke ....Sr.		31	140	4.5
Allyssa DeHaan, Michigan St ....Fr.		31	138	4.5
Amber Harris, Xavier ....Fr.		33	133	4.0
Courtney Paris, Oklahoma ....So.		30	105	3.5
Katja Bavendam, St. Francis (N.Y.)..Jr.		31	98	3.2
LaToya Pringle, North Carolina .....Jr.		33	104	3.2
Hope Foster, Bucknell ....Jr.		30	93	3.1
Lasma Jekabsone, Florida Int'l.....Sr.		30	92	3.1
Lacey Cormier', Grambling ....Sr.		28	85	3.0
Lindsay Wisdom-Hylton, Purdue..Jr.		33	99	3.0
Jessica Bobbitt, Belmont.............So.		31	93	3.0

NCAA Men's Division II Individual Leaders

SCORING

Player and Team	Class	GP	TFG	3FG	FT	Pts	Avg
Ted Scott, West Virginia St ....Jr.		31	292	119	131	834	26.9
Tyrone Anderson, Concord ....Sr.		30	295	17	176	783	26.1
Gil Goodrich, Bowie St...Sr.		25	194	102	160	650	26.0
Nate Newell, Ark.-Monticello ....Sr.		26	186	104	192	668	25.7
Andre Dabney, Bloomfield ....Sr.		27	215	94	139	663	24.6
DeMario Grier, Pfeiffer...Sr.		28	208	102	166	684	24.4
Kris Krzyminski, Wayne St (Mich.) ....Sr.		26	210	83	117	620	23.8
Jontae Vinson, Cal St.-L.A. ....Jr.		26	244	1	129	618	23.8
Bradd Wierzbicki, Queens (N.Y.) ....Sr.		25	195	55	140	585	23.4
Damien Lolar, West Texas A&M ....Sr.		27	225	36	143	629	23.3

REBOUNDS

Player and Team	Class	GP	Reb	Avg
Eric Dawson, Midwestern St	Sr.	28	320	11.4
Christian Burns, Philadelphia Univ.	Sr.	28	315	11.3
Eric Babers, SE Oklahoma St	Sr.	29	314	10.8
John Davis, Tarleton St	Sr.	28	301	10.8
Brandon Bingle, East Central	Sr.	26	276	10.6
Jeff Fahnbulleh, Kentucky Wesleyan	Jr.	26	273	10.5
Brian Stamer, Colorado Chirstian	Jr.	28	293	10.5
Anthony Hilliard, Elizabeth City St	So.	26	272	10.5
Michael Pierrot, Felician	Sr.	27	280	10.4
Tony Cornett, West Virginia St	Sr.	30	311	10.4

ASSISTS

Player and Team	Class	GP	A	Avg
Zack Whiting, Chaminade	Sr.	27	284	10.5
Luke Cooper, AK-Anchorage	Jr.	27	223	8.3
Jonny Reibel, Rollins	Jr.	30	236	7.9
Gil Goodrich, Bowie St	Sr.	25	183	7.3
Shawn Poppie, Limestone	Sr.	26	176	6.8
Ronnie Means, Fairmont St	Fr.	28	189	6.8
Shejdie Childs, GC&SU	Sr.	29	191	6.6
Ryan Webb, Seattle	Sr.	26	171	6.6
Darren Duncan, Merrimack	Fr.	28	183	6.5
Brain Graves, Catawba	Sr.	30	196	6.5

FIELD-GOAL PERCENTAGE

Player and Team	Class	GP	FG	FGA	Pct
Garret Siler, Augusta St	So.	29	153	220	69.5
Dzaflo Larkai, Bellamine	Jr.	27	146	220	66.4
Taylor Mullenax, St. Edward's	So.	29	145	221	65.6
Chirs Gilliam, Pitt.-Johnstown	Jr.	29	189	290	65.2
Kenny Jones, Kentucky St	Jr.	29	220	343	64.1
Elijah Rouse, Mount Olive	Sr.	30	174	273	63.7
Patrick Hannaway, UC-Colo. Springs	Sr.	26	203	319	63.6
Brandon Butler, Regis (Colorado)	Sr.	26	184	291	63.2
Ian Elseth, Colorado Mines	Sr.	21	114	181	63.0
Willie Shaw, Dist. Columbia	Jr.	25	149	237	62.9

Note: Minimum 5 made per game.

FREE-THROW PERCENTAGE

Player and Team	Class	GP	FT	FTA	Pct
Richard Stone, St. Andrews	Sr.	28	101	110	91.8
Lance Den Boer, Cen. Washington	Sr.	27	150	164	91.5
Danley Shank, Shephard	Sr.	25	76	84	90.5
Radayl Richardson, Michigan Tech.	Sr.	28	89	99	89.9
Michael Jenkins, Neb.-Omaha	So.	27	133	148	89.9
Carl Arts, AK-Anchorage	Jr.	27	84	94	89.4
Lukas Henne, Western Washington	Sr.	26	136	153	88.9
Dustin Bremerman, Seattle Pacific	Sr.	27	109	123	88.6
Jake Linton, St. Martin's	So.	27	105	119	88.2
Vahn Knight, Ashland	Sr.	28	127	144	88.2

Note: Minimum 2.5 made per game.

NCAA Women's Division II Individual Leaders

SCORING

Player and Team	Class	GP	TFG	3FG	FT	Pts	Avg
Erika Quigley, St. Cloud St.	Sr.	28	273	1	138	685	24.5
Amber Rall, Ashland	Sr.	25	220	27	117	584	23.4
Johannah Leedham, Franklin Pierce	Fr.	25	187	39	165	578	23.1
Emily Brister, West Texas A&M	So.	33	231	84	209	755	22.9
Leora Juster, UC-San Diego	Sr.	30	239	36	165	679	22.6
Jeannie Sanders, Salem Int'l	Fr.	28	236	60	84	616	22.0
Tiara Good, Lander	Fr.	28	205	81	122	613	21.9
Darcee Schmidt, Lewis	Sr.	32	262	67	104	695	21.7
Cherrise Graham, Goldey-Beacom	Sr.	27	202	27	148	579	21.4
Meg Abele, Philadelphia Univ.	Sr.	31	206	70	176	658	21.2

REBOUNDS

Player and Team	Class	GP	Reb	Avg
Latoya Wily, BYU-Hawaii	Fr.	25	356	14.2
Alisha Ferguson, Philadelphia Univ.	Sr.	31	409	13.2
Angelina Jimenez, Bridgeport	Sr.	28	365	13.0
Celeste Trahan, Elizabeth City St	Jr.	30	389	13.0
Rochelle Bodie, Johnson C. Smith	Jr.	30	358	11.9
Erika Quigley, St. Cloud St.	Sr.	28	324	11.6
Kaneetha Gordon, Armstrong Atlantic	Jr.	29	335	11.6
Marquita Driskell, GC&SU	Jr.	32	365	11.4
Kim Nowakowski, California (Pa.)	Jr.	28	308	11.0
Danielle Edwards, S.C. Upstate	Sr.	24	262	10.9

ASSISTS

Player and Team	Class	GP	A	Avg
Katie LaViolette, Concordia-St. Paul	Jr.	32	297	9.3
Lisa Perry, West Liberty St	Jr.	31	284	9.2
Brooke Underwood, Tusculum	Sr.	29	229	7.9
Tiffany Davis, Missouri Western St	Sr.	34	240	7.1
Jamie Cluesman, Concord	Jr.	29	203	7.0
Keona Corley, Mount Olive	Jr.	28	193	6.9
Jenna Eckleberry, Fairmont St	Sr.	29	193	6.7
Sherrelle Holmes, Wilmington (Del.)	Jr.	28	182	6.5
Shelby Krueger, Winona St.	Jr.	27	173	6.4
Tiara Good, Lander	Fr.	28	177	6.3

FIELD-GOAL PERCENTAGE

Player and Team	Class	GP	FG	FGA	Pct
Michelle Lieber, MSU-Billings ...Sr.		26	147	216	68.1
Katie Schrader, Fla. Gulf Coast ....Sr.		31	190	302	62.9
Vanessa Wilt, CSU-San B'dino......Jr.		28	216	365	59.2
Mattie Jones, Kentucky St............Fr.		21	111	189	58.7
Kierah Kimbrough, North Dakota.....So.		35	226	387	58.4
Shanna Oaddams, Shippensburg....Sr.		28	162	279	58.1
Inga Buzoka, Mo. Western St......Sr.		33	217	378	57.4
Jessica Zapf, Pitt.-Johnstown ....Sr.		29	180	314	57.3
Rachel Pike, Charleston (W.V.)..Sr.		31	169	299	56.5
Ashley Wallace, Pace.................Sr.		33	191	338	56.5

Note: Minimum 5 FG per game.

FREE-THROW PERCENTAGE

Player and Team	Class	GP	FT	FTA	Pct
Amber Rutherford, N. Alabama....So.		26	134	143	93.7
Whitney Sykes, SIU-Edwardsville...Jr.		29	112	120	93.3
Amy Mathis, Nebraska-Kearney ....Jr.		32	91	100	91.0
Jamey Gelhar, St. Martin's ....Fr.		27	116	128	90.6
Karyn Creager, Northern Kentucky .Sr.		29	79	89	88.8
Gemma Gibson, Ark.-Monticello ......Jr.		26	102	115	88.7
Monica Rehmann, Lake Superior St..Sr.		27	90	102	88.2
Erin McCormick, Wayne St. (Neb.)..Sr.		29	165	188	87.8
Jennifer Havens, Nova Southeastern .Sr.		28	129	147	87.8
Katie Wilder, Humboldt St. ....Sr.		27	107	122	87.7

Note: Minimum 2.5 made per game.

NCAA Men's Division III Individual Leaders

SCORING

Player and Team	Class	GP	TFG	3FG	FT	Pts	Avg
Mike Hoyt, Mt. St. Mary (N.Y.) ....Sr.		26	274	121	229	898	34.5
Amir Mazarei, Redlands ....Sr.		23	220	143	75	658	28.6
John Grotberg, Grinnell...............................So.		24	209	112	145	675	28.1
Alex Kuchar, Centenary................................So.		24	195	70	128	588	24.5
Jake Baldwin, Piedmont ....Jr.		26	239	22	126	626	24.1
Ben Strong, Guilford ....Jr.		27	248	0	148	644	23.9
Thomas Baker, Rowan ....Sr.		26	246	21	107	620	23.8
Bryan Rouse, Emerson.................................Fr.		20	171	0	128	470	23.5
Tony Barros, Mass.-Boston...........................Sr.		27	203	84	144	634	23.5
John Murphy, Suffolk ....Sr.		24	170	81	140	561	23.4

REBOUNDS

Player and Team	Class	GP	Reb	Avg
Nick Harrington, Southern Vt. ....Fr.		21	281	13.4
Jeff Prebeck, Coast Guard............:..Jr.		27	333	12.3
Gari Blackett, Staten Island............Jr.		28	345	12.3
Marochee Jean, Hardin-Simmons ..Jr.		28	324	11.6
Jesse Gutekunst, Hood.................Jr.		29	332	11.4
Jose Guitian, Lasell......................So.		28	319	11.4
Kyle Born, Whitman ....So.		23	259	11.3
Antoine Sylvia, New England Col. .Sr.		23	255	11.1
Danny Nawrocki, Johns Hopkins...Sr.		29	319	11.0
Ben Strong, Guilford ....Jr.		27	295	10.9

FIELD-GOAL PERCENTAGE

Player and Team	Class	GP	FG	FGA	Pct
Michael Romes, Mt. St. Joseph...Fr.		22	145	212	68.4
Brandon Adair, Va. Wesleyan ......Sr.		28	216	320	67.5
Mike Kilburg, Coe.......................Sr.		27	187	284	65.8
Brian Schmidt, Heidelberg..........Jr.		20	103	157	65.6
Matt Griffin, Johns Hopkins.........Sr.		29	170	262	64.9
Tori Davis, Baldwin-Wallace........Sr.		27	209	323	64.7
Brian Schmitting, Ripon...............Sr.		23	172	266	64.7
Robert Krauel, Puget Sound ....So.		25	136	213	63.8
David Goode, Chestnut Hill..........Jr.		25	153	241	63.5
Jack Lighthall, Utica ....Sr.		26	146	232	62.9

Note: Minimum 5 made per game.

ASSISTS

Player and Team	Class	GP	A	Avg
David Arseneault, Grinnell ....So.		24	203	8.5
Davon Barton, Chris. Newport ......So.		26	217	8.3
Andrew Olson, Amherst.................Jr.		28	212	7.6
Eddie Ohlson, DeSales.................Jr.		30	225	7.5
Corey Mcadam, Nazareth..............Fr.		25	186	7.4
Sean Wallis, Washington (Mo.).......So.		26	192	7.4
Bryan Williams, Whitworth ....Sr.		27	194	7.2
Josh Winans, Cazenovia ....Sr.		25	164	6.6
Mike Staley, Hiram ....Fr.		24	155	6.5
Jake Green, Piedmont ....Jr.		26	164	6.3

FREE-THROW PERCENTAGE

Player and Team	Class	GP	FT	FTA	Pct
Joseph Chatman, Lesley..............Fr.		27	126	133	94.7
Bryan Schnettler, St. Thomas (Minn.)..Sr.		28	74	80	92.5
Zachary Silas, Albion ....Sr.		25	70	77	90.9
Ryan Dupic, Buena Vista.......Sr.		26	88	97	90.7
Brendan Schuler, Baldwin-Wallace ..Jr.		27	86	95	90.5
Kevin Guyden, Mary Hardin-Baylor.Sr.		28	164	182	90.1
Ryan Burks, Elmhurst......................So.		27	130	145	89.7
Sean Burton, Ithaca......................So.		28	85	95	89.5
Ryan Jaziri, New England Col......Jr.		24	109	122	89.3
Andrew Hippert, Bowdoin..............Jr.		25	100	112	89.3

Note: Minimum 2.5 made per game.

SCORING

Player and Team	Class	GP	TFG	3FG	FT	Pts	Avg
Lindsay Ippel, Millikin	Jr.	26	239	0	196	674	25.9
Staci Humphrey, Greensboro	Sr.	27	240	71	119	670	24.8
Tori Huggins, Hendrix	Sr.	26	184	55	186	609	23.4
Naomi Guise, Aurora	So.	26	247	44	65	603	23.2
Ashley Marble, Southern Maine	Sr.	30	224	28	217	693	23.1
Hannah Wolf, Grinnell	Jr.	23	175	80	83	513	22.3
Meghan DePatsy, Anna Maria	Sr.	25	193	1	167	554	22.2
Amber Bodrick, Thiel	So.	23	204	14	87	509	22.1
Quandra Rodgers, Medgar Evers	Fr.	24	195	46	93	529	22.0
Crystal Hoewisch, Carroll (Wis.)	Jr.	27	198	29	168	593	22.0

REBOUNDS

Player and Team	Class	GP	Reb	Avg
Ashley Yeast, Monmouth (Ill.)	Jr.	23	315	13.7
Lashannen Hogue, John Jay	Jr.	21	286	13.6
Jessica McEntee, NYU	So.	29	368	12.7
Karen Berk, Swarthmore	Jr.	24	299	12.5
Ava Thomas, Utica	Sr.	27	335	12.4
Meghan DePatsy, Anna Maria	Sr.	25	309	12.4
Ashley Marble, Southern Maine	Sr.	30	367	12.2
Mary Rotimi, Lincoln (Pa.)	Sr.	27	329	12.2
Megan Bailey, Anna Maria	So.	24	290	12.1
Andrea Buckham, Hunter	Fr.	26	303	11.7

FIELD-GOAL PERCENTAGE

Player and Team	Class	GP	FG	FGA	Pct
Lindsay Ippel, Millikin	Jr.	26	239	363	65.8
Carly Loehrke, Wooster	Sr.	26	159	265	60.0
Christine Halter, D'Youville	So.	25	126	210	60.0
Bianca White, St. Norbert	Sr.	24	153	258	59.3
Kelsey Duoss, UW-Stout	Sr.	29	169	285	59.3
Andrea Carter, Chestnut Hill	Sr.	26	138	234	59.0
Jenna Boehm, Lakeland	Sr.	26	152	258	58.9
Allie Wilhelm, Maryville (Mo.)	So.	21	106	181	58.6
Hilary Klimowicz, TCNJ	So.	27	136	233	58.4
M. Hageman, Concordia-Moorehead	Jr.	27	155	266	58.3

Note: Minimum 5 made per game.

ASSISTS

Player and Team	Class	GP	A	Avg
Symbri Tuttle, McMurray	Sr.	29	228	7.9
Staci Humphrey, Greensboro	Sr.	27	195	7.2
Sarah Barton, Bates	Jr.	25	172	6.9
Kasey Hicks, Immaculata	So.	26	166	6.4
Beth Reed, Maryville (Tenn.)	Jr.	27	167	6.2
Marlis Graves, La Roche	Jr.	25	154	6.2
Marisa Clark, Medaille	Jr.	28	171	6.1
Lauren Percodani, Mt. St. Vincent	Fr.	27	164	6.1
Karen Tierney, Gwynedd-Mercy	Jr.	29	176	6.1
Chelsea Slater, Rockford	Jr.	25	151	6.0

FREE-THROW PERCENTAGE

Player and Team	Class	GP	FT	FTA	Pct
Korry Schwanz, Chicago	Sr.	25	69	74	93.2
Suzy Carlson, Rose-Hulman	Sr.	26	150	163	92.0
Beth Bergmann, Emory	Sr.	23	69	75	92.0
Melissa Kraft, Drew	Sr.	27	85	94	90.4
Kimberly Ordille, Notre Dame (Md.)	Sr.	25	73	81	90.1
Jess Vadnais, Gust. Adolphus	Jr.	28	169	188	89.9
Elizabeth Fox, Wheaton (Ill.)	Sr.	23	71	79	89.9
Tori Huggins, Hendrix	Sr.	26	186	211	88.2
Danielle Muller, Rochester (N.Y.)	Sr.	26	77	88	87.5
Kennan Killeen, Wash. & Jeff.	Fr.	28	89	102	87.3

Note: Minimum 2.5 made per game.

NCAA Men's Division I Championship Results

NCAA Final Four Results

Year	Winner	Score	Runner-up	Third Place	Fourth Place	Winning Coach
1939	Oregon	46–33	Ohio St	*Oklahoma	*Villanova	Howard Hobson
1940	Indiana	60–42	Kansas	*Duquesne	*USC	Branch McCracken
1941	Wisconsin	39–34	Washington St	*Pittsburgh	*Arkansas	Harold Foster
1942	Stanford	53–38	Dartmouth	*Colorado	*Kentucky	Everett Dean
1943	Wyoming	46–34	Georgetown	*Texas	*DePaul	Everett Shelton
1944	Utah	42–40 (OT)	Dartmouth	*Iowa St	*Ohio St	Vadal Peterson
1945	Oklahoma St	49–45	NYU	*Arkansas	*Ohio St	Hank Iba
1946	Oklahoma St	43–40	North Carolina	Ohio St	California	Hank Iba
1947	Holy Cross	58–47	Oklahoma	Texas	CCNY	Alvin Julian
1948	Kentucky	58–42	Baylor	Holy Cross	Kansas St	Adolph Rupp
1949	Kentucky	46–36	Oklahoma St	Illinois	Oregon St	Adolph Rupp
1950	CCNY	71–68	Bradley	North Carolina St	Baylor	Nat Holman
1951	Kentucky	68–58	Kansas St	Illinois	Oklahoma St	Adolph Rupp
1952	Kansas	80–63	St. John's (N.Y.)	Illinois	Santa Clara	Forrest Allen
1953	Indiana	69–68	Kansas	Washington	LSU	Branch McCracken
1954	La Salle	92–76	Bradley	Penn St	USC	Kenneth Loeffler
1955	San Francisco	77–63	La Salle	Colorado	Iowa	Phil Woolpert
1956	San Francisco	83–71	Iowa	Temple	SMU	Phil Woolpert
1957	North Carolina	54–53 (3OT)	Kansas	San Francisco	Michigan St	Frank McGuire
1958	Kentucky	84–72	Seattle	Temple	Kansas St	Adolph Rupp
1959	California	71–70	West Virginia	Cincinnati	Louisville	Pete Newell
1960	Ohio St	75–55	California	Cincinnati	NYU	Fred Taylor
1961	Cincinnati	70–65 (OT)	Ohio St	Vacated‡	Utah	Edwin Jucker
1962	Cincinnati	71–59	Ohio St	Wake Forest	UCLA	Edwin Jucker
1963	Loyola (Ill.)	60–58 (OT)	Cincinnati	Duke	Oregon St	George Ireland
1964	UCLA	98–83	Duke	Michigan	Kansas St	John Wooden
1965	UCLA	91–80	Michigan	Princeton	Wichita St	John Wooden
1966	UTEP	72–65	Kentucky	Duke	Utah	Don Haskins
1967	UCLA	79–64	Dayton	Houston	North Carolina	John Wooden
1968	UCLA	78–55	North Carolina	Ohio St	Houston	John Wooden
1969	UCLA	92–72	Purdue	Drake	North Carolina	John Wooden
1970	UCLA	80–69	Jacksonville	New Mexico St	St. Bonaventure	John Wooden
1971	UCLA	68–62	Vacated‡	Vacated‡	Kansas	John Wooden
1972	UCLA	81–76	Florida St	North Carolina	Louisville	John Wooden
1973	UCLA	87–66	Memphis St	Indiana	Providence	John Wooden
1974	North Carolina St	76–64	Marquette	UCLA	Kansas	Norm Sloan
1975	UCLA	92–85	Kentucky	Louisville	Syracuse	John Wooden
1976	Indiana	86–68	Michigan	UCLA	Rutgers	Bob Knight
1977	Marquette	67–59	North Carolina	UNLV	UNC-Charlotte	Al McGuire
1978	Kentucky	94–88	Duke	Arkansas	Notre Dame	Joe Hall
1979	Michigan St	75–64	Indiana St	DePaul	Penn	Jud Heathcote
1980	Louisville	59–54	Vacated‡	Purdue	Iowa	Denny Crum
1981	Indiana	63–50	North Carolina	Virginia	LSU	Bob Knight
1982	North Carolina	63–62	Georgetown	*Houston	*Louisville	Dean Smith
1983	North Carolina St	54–52	Houston	*Georgia	*Louisville	Jim Valvano
1984	Georgetown	84–75	Houston	*Kentucky	*Virginia	John Thompson
1985	Villanova	66–64	Georgetown	St. John's (N.Y.)	Vacated‡	Rollie Massimino
1986	Louisville	72–69	Duke	*Kansas	*LSU	Denny Crum
1987	Indiana	74–73	Syracuse	*UNLV	*Providence	Bob Knight
1988	Kansas	83–79	Oklahoma	*Arizona	*Duke	Larry Brown
1989	Michigan	80–79 (OT)	Seton Hall	*Duke	*Illinois	Steve Fisher
1990	UNLV	103–73	Duke	*Arkansas	*Georgia Tech	Jerry Tarkanian
1991	Duke	72–65	Kansas	*UNLV	*North Carolina	Mike Krzyzewski
1992	Duke	71–51	Michigan	*Cincinnati	*Indiana	Mike Krzyzewski
1993	North Carolina	77–71	Michigan	*Kansas	*Kentucky	Dean Smith
1994	Arkansas	76–72	Duke	*Arizona	*Florida	Nolan Richardson
1995	UCLA	89–78	Arkansas	*North Carolina	*Oklahoma St	Jim Harrick
1996	Kentucky	76–67	Syracuse	Vacated‡	Mississippi St	Rick Pitino
1997	Arizona	84–79 (OT)	Kentucky	*Minnesota	*North Carolina	Lute Olson
1998	Kentucky	78–69	Utah	*Stanford	*North Carolina	Tubby Smith
1999	Connecticut	77–74	Duke	*Michigan St	*Ohio St	Jim Calhoun
2000	Michigan St	89–76	Florida	*Wisconsin	*North Carolina	Tom Izzo
2001	Duke	82–72	Arizona	*Maryland	*Michigan St	Mike Krzyzewski

NCAA Final Four Results (Cont.)

Year	Winner	Score	Runner-up	Third Place	Fourth Place	Winning Coach
2002	Maryland	64–52	Indiana	*Kansas	*Oklahoma	Gary Williams
2003	Syracuse	81–78	Kansas	*Marquette	*Texas	Jim Boeheim
2004	Connecticut	82–73	Georgia Tech	*Oklahoma St	*Duke	Jim Calhoun
2005	North Carolina	75-70	Illinois	*Louisville	*Michigan St	Roy Williams
2006	Florida	73-57	UCLA	*George Mason	*LSU	Billy Donovan
2007	Florida	84–75	Ohio St	*UCLA	*Georgetown	Billy Donovan

*Tied for third place. ‡Student-athletes representing St. Joseph's (Pa.) in 1961, Villanova in 1971, Western Kentucky in 1971, UCLA in 1980, Memphis State in 1985 and Massachusetts in 1996 were declared ineligible subsequent to the tournament. Under NCAA rules, the teams' and ineligible student-athletes' records were deleted, and the teams' places in the standings were vacated.

NCAA Final Four Most Outstanding Players

Year	Winner, School	GP	Field Goals		3-Pt FG		Free Throws		Reb	Asst	Stl	BS	Avg
			FGM	Pct	FGA	FGM	FTM	Pct					
1939	None selected												
1940	Marv Huffman, Indiana	2	7	—	—	—	4	—	—	—	—	—	9.0
1941	John Kotz, Wisconsin	2	8	—	—	—	6	—	—	—	—	—	11.0
1942	Howard Dallmar, Stanford	2	8	—	—	—	4	66.7	—	—	—	—	10.0
1943	Ken Sailors, Wyoming	2	10	—	—	—	8	72.7	—	—	—	—	14.0
1944	Arnie Ferrin, Utah	2	11	—	—	—	6	—	—	—	—	—	14.0
1945	Bob Kurland, Oklahoma St	2	16	—	—	—	5	—	—	—	—	—	18.5
1946	Bob Kurland, Oklahoma St	2	21	—	—	—	10	66.7	—	—	—	—	26.0
1947	George Kaftan, Holy Cross	2	18	—	—	—	12	70.6	—	—	—	—	24.0
1948	Alex Groza, Kentucky	2	16	—	—	—	5	—	—	—	—	—	18.5
1949	Alex Groza, Kentucky	2	19	—	—	—	14	—	—	—	—	—	26.0
1950	Irwin Dambrot, CCNY	2	12	42.9	—	—	4	50.0	—	—	—	—	14.0
1951	None selected												
1952	Clyde Lovellette, Kansas	2	24	—	—	—	18	—	—	—	—	—	33.0
1953	*B.H. Horn, Kansas	2	17	—	—	—	17	—	—	—	—	—	25.5
1954	Tom Gola, La Salle	2	12	—	—	—	14	—	—	—	—	—	19.0
1955	Bill Russell, San Francisco	2	19	—	—	—	9	—	—	—	—	—	23.5
1956	*Hal Lear, Temple	2	32	—	—	—	16	—	—	—	—	—	40.0
1957	*Wilt Chamberlain, Kansas	2	18	51.4	—	—	19	70.4	25	—	—	—	32.5
1958	*Elgin Baylor, Seattle	2	18	34.0	—	—	12	75.0	41	—	—	—	24.0
1959	*Jerry West, West Virginia	2	22	66.7	—	—	22	68.8	25	—	—	—	33.0
1960	Jerry Lucas, Ohio St	2	16	66.7	—	—	3	100.0	23	—	—	—	17.5
1961	*Jerry Lucas, Ohio St	2	20	71.4	—	—	16	94.1	25	—	—	—	28.0
1962	Paul Hogue, Cincinnati	2	23	63.9	—	—	12	63.2	38	—	—	—	29.0
1963	Art Heyman, Duke	2	18	41.0	—	—	15	68.2	19	—	—	—	25.5
1964	Walt Hazzard, UCLA	2	11	55.0	—	—	8	66.7	10	—	—	—	15.0
1965	*Bill Bradley, Princeton	2	34	63.0	—	—	19	95.0	24	—	—	—	43.5
1966	*Jerry Chambers, Utah	2	25	53.2	—	—	20	83.3	35	—	—	—	35.0
1967	Lew Alcindor, UCLA	2	14	60.9	—	—	11	45.8	38	—	—	—	19.5
1968	Lew Alcindor, UCLA	2	22	62.9	—	—	9	90.0	34	—	—	—	26.5
1969	Lew Alcindor, UCLA	2	23	67.7	—	—	16	64.0	41	—	—	—	31.0
1970	Sidney Wicks, UCLA	2	15	71.4	—	—	9	60.0	34	—	—	—	19.5
1971	*†Howard Porter, Villanova	2	20	48.8	—	—	7	77.8	24	—	—	—	23.5
1972	Bill Walton, UCLA	2	20	69.0	—	—	17	73.9	41	—	—	—	28.5
1973	Bill Walton, UCLA	2	28	82.4	—	—	2	40.0	30	—	—	—	29.0
1974	David Thompson, N.C. St	2	19	51.4	—	—	11	78.6	17	—	—	—	24.5
1975	Richard Washington, UCLA	2	23	54.8	—	—	8	72.7	20	—	—	—	27.0
1976	Kent Benson, Indiana	2	17	50.0	—	—	7	63.6	18	—	—	—	20.5
1977	Butch Lee, Marquette	2	11	34.4	—	—	8	100.0	6	2	1	1	15.0
1978	Jack Givens, Kentucky	2	28	65.1	—	—	8	66.7	17	4	1	3	32.0
1979	Earvin Johnson, Michigan St	2	17	68.0	—	—	19	86.4	17	3	0	2	26.5
1980	Darrell Griffith, Louisville	2	23	62.2	—	—	11	68.8	7	15	0	2	28.5
1981	Isiah Thomas, Indiana	2	14	56.0	—	—	9	81.8	4	9	3	4	18.5
1982	James Worthy, North Carolina	2	20	74.1	—	—	2	28.6	8	9	0	4	21.0
1983	*Akeem Olajuwon, Houston	2	16	55.2	—	—	9	64.3	40	3	2	5	20.5
1984	Patrick Ewing, Georgetown	2	8	57.1	—	—	2	100.0	18	1	1	15	9.0
1985	Ed Pinckney, Villanova	2	8	57.1	—	—	12	75.0	15	6	3	0	14.0
1986	Pervis Ellison, Louisville	2	15	60.0	—	—	6	75.0	24	2	3	1	18.0
1987	Keith Smart, Indiana	2	14	63.6	1	0	7	77.8	7	7	0	2	17.5
1988	Danny Manning, Kansas	2	25	55.6	1	0	6	66.7	17	4	8	9	28.0

*Not a member of the championship-winning team.   †Record later vacated.

NCAA Final Four MOPs (Cont.)

Year	Winner, School	GP	Field Goals		3-Pt FG		Free Throws		Reb	Asst	Stl	BS	Avg
			FGM	Pct	FGA	FGM	FTM	Pct					
1989	Glen Rice, Michigan	2	24	49.0	16	7	4	100.0	16	1	0	3	29.5
1990	Anderson Hunt, UNLV	2	19	61.3	16	9	2	50.0	4	9	1	1	24.5
1991	Christian Laettner, Duke	2	12	54.5	1	1	21	91.3	17	2	1	2	23.0
1992	Bobby Hurley, Duke	2	10	41.7	12	7	8	80.0	3	11	0	3	17.5
1993	Donald Williams, North Carolina	2	15	65.2	14	10	10	100.0	4	2	2	0	25.0
1994	Corliss Williamson, Arkansas	2	21	50.0	0	0	10	71.4	21	8	4	3	26.0
1995	Ed O'Bannon, UCLA	2	16	45.7	8	3	10	76.9	25	3	7	1	22.5
1996	Tony Delk, Kentucky	2	15	41.7	16	8	6	54.6	9	2	3	2	22.0
1997	Miles Simon, Arizona	2	17	45.9	10	3	17	77.3	8	6	0	1	27.0
1998	Jeff Sheppard, Kentucky	2	16	55.2	10	4	7	77.8	10	7	4	0	21.5
1999	Richard Hamilton, Connecticut	2	20	51.3	7	3	8	72.7	12	4	2	1	25.5
2000	Mateen Cleaves, Michigan St	2	8	44.4	4	3	10	83.3	6	5	2	0	14.5
2001	Shane Battier, Duke	2	13	50.0	12	5	12	70.6	19	8	2	6	21.5
2002	Juan Dixon, Maryland	2	16	59.3	15	7	12	80.0	8	5	7	0	25.5
2003	Carmelo Anthony, Syracuse	2	19	54.3	6	9	9	81.1	24	8	4	0	26.5
2004	Emeka Okafor, Connecticut	2	17	65.4	0	0	8	53.3	22	2	1	4	21.0
2005	Sean May, North Carolina	2	19	65.5	0	0	10	71.4	17	5	1	2	24.0
2006	Joakim Noah, Florida	2	12	60.0	1	0	4	100.0	17	5	2	10	14.0
2007	Corey Brewer, Florida	2	9	47.3	13	7	7	87.5	10	2	3	5	16.0

Best NCAA Tournament Single-Game Scoring Performances

Player and Team	Year	Round	FG	3FG	FT	TP
Austin Carr, Notre Dame vs Ohio	1970	1st	25	—	11	61
Bill Bradley, Princeton vs Wichita St	1965	C*	22	—	14	58
Oscar Robertson, Cincinnati vs Arkansas	1958	C	21	—	14	56
Austin Carr, Notre Dame vs Kentucky	1970	2nd	22	—	8	52
Austin Carr, Notre Dame vs TCU	1971	1st	20	—	12	52
David Robinson, Navy vs Michigan	1987	1st	22	0	6	50
Elvin Hayes, Houston vs Loyola (Ill.)	1968	1st	20	—	9	49
Hal Lear, Temple vs SMU	1956	C*	17	—	14	48
Austin Carr, Notre Dame vs Houston	1971	C	17	—	13	47
Dave Corzine, DePaul vs Louisville	1978	2nd	18	—	10	46

C=regional third place; C*=third-place game.

NIT Championship Results

Year	Winner	Score	Runner-up	Year	Winner	Score	Runner-up
1938	Temple	60–36	Colorado	1965	St. John's (N.Y.)	55–51	Villanova
1939	Long Island U.	44–32	Loyola (Ill.)	1966	BYU	97–84	NYU
1940	Colorado	51–40	Duquesne	1967	Southern Illinois	71–56	Marquette
1941	Long Island U.	56–42	Ohio U	1968	Dayton	61–48	Kansas
1942	West Virginia	47–45	W. Kentucky	1969	Temple	89–76	Boston College
1943	St. John's (N.Y.)	48–27	Toledo	1970	Marquette	65–53	St. John's (N.Y.)
1944	St. John's (N.Y.)	47–39	DePaul	1971	North Carolina	84–66	Georgia Tech
1945	DePaul	71–54	Bowling Green	1972	Maryland	100–69	Niagara
1946	Kentucky	46–45	Rhode Island	1973	Virginia Tech	92–91 (OT)	Notre Dame
1947	Utah	49–45	Kentucky	1974	Purdue	97–81	Utah
1948	St. Louis	65–52	NYU	1975	Princeton	80–69	Providence
1949	San Francisco	48–47	Loyola (Ill.)	1976	Kentucky	71–67	UNC-Charlotte
1950	CCNY	69–61	Bradley	1977	St. Bonaventure	94–91	Houston
1951	BYU	62–43	Dayton	1978	Texas	101–93	North Carolina St
1952	La Salle	75–64	Dayton	1979	Indiana	53–52	Purdue
1953	Seton Hall	58–46	St. John's (N.Y.)	1980	Virginia	58–55	Minnesota
1954	Holy Cross	71–62	Duquesne	1981	Tulsa	86–84 (OT)	Syracuse
1955	Duquesne	70–58	Dayton	1982	Bradley	67–58	Purdue
1956	Louisville	93–80	Dayton	1983	Fresno St	69–60	DePaul
1957	Bradley	84–83	Memphis St	1984	Michigan	83–63	Notre Dame
1958	Xavier (Ohio)	78–74 (OT)	Dayton	1985	UCLA	65–62	Indiana
1959	St. John's (N.Y.)	76–71 (OT)	Bradley	1986	Ohio St	73–63	Wyoming
1960	Bradley	88–72	Providence	1987	Southern Miss	84–80	La Salle
1961	Providence	62–59	St. Louis	1988	Connecticut	72–67	Ohio St
1962	Dayton	73–67	St. John's (N.Y.)	1989	St. John's (N.Y.)	73–65	St. Louis
1963	Providence	81–66	Canisius	1990	Vanderbilt	74–72	St. Louis
1964	Bradley	86–54	New Mexico	1991	Stanford	78–72	Oklahoma

NIT Championship Results (Cont.)

Year	Winner	Score	Runner-up	Year	Winner	Score	Runner-up
1992	Virginia	81–76	Notre Dame	2000	Wake Forest	71–61	Notre Dame
1993	Minnesota	62–61	Georgetown	2001	Tulsa	79–60	Alabama
1994	Villanova	80–73	Vanderbilt	2002	Memphis	72–62	South Carolina
1995	Virginia Tech	65–64 (OT)	Marquette	2003	St. John's	70–67	Georgetown
1996	Nebraska	60–56	St. Joseph's	2004	Michigan	62–55	Rutgers
1997	Michigan	82–73	Florida St	2005	South Carolina	60–57	Saint Joseph's
1998	Minnesota	79–72	Penn St	2006	South Carolina	76–64	Michigan
1999	California	61–60	Clemson	2007	West Virginia	78–73	Clemson

NCAA Men's Division I Season Leaders

Scoring Average

Year	Player and Team	Ht	Class	GP	FG	3FG	FT	Pts	Avg
1948	Murray Wier, Iowa	5-9	Sr.	19	152	—	95	399	21.0
1949	Tony Lavelli, Yale	6-3	Sr.	30	228	—	215	671	22.4
1950	Paul Arizin, Villanova	6-3	Sr.	29	260	—	215	735	25.3
1951	Bill Mlkvy, Temple	6-4	Sr.	25	303	—	125	731	29.2
1952	Clyde Lovellette, Kansas	6-9	Sr.	28	315	—	165	795	28.4
1953	Frank Selvy, Furman	6-3	Jr.	25	272	—	194	738	29.5
1954	Frank Selvy, Furman	6-3	Sr.	29	427	—	355	1209	41.7
1955	Darrell Floyd, Furman	6-1	Jr.	25	344	—	209	897	35.9
1956	Darrell Floyd, Furman	6-1	Sr.	28	339	—	268	946	33.8
1957	Grady Wallace, South Carolina	6-4	Sr.	29	336	—	234	906	31.2
1958	Oscar Robertson, Cincinnati	6-5	So.	28	352	—	280	984	35.1
1959	Oscar Robertson, Cincinnati	6-5	Jr.	30	331	—	316	978	32.6
1960	Oscar Robertson, Cincinnati	6-5	Sr.	30	369	—	273	1011	33.7
1961	Frank Burgess, Gonzaga	6-1	Sr.	26	304	—	234	842	32.4
1962	Billy McGill, Utah	6-9	Sr.	26	394	—	221	1009	38.8
1963	Nick Werkman, Seton Hall	6-3	Jr.	22	221	—	208	650	29.5
1964	Howard Komives, Bowling Green	6-1	Sr.	23	292	—	260	844	36.7
1965	Rick Barry, Miami (Fla.)	6-7	Sr.	26	340	—	293	973	37.4
1966	Dave Schellhase, Purdue	6-4	Sr.	24	284	—	213	781	32.5
1967	Jim Walker, Providence	6-3	Sr.	28	323	—	205	851	30.4
1968	Pete Maravich, LSU	6-5	So.	26	432	—	274	1138	43.8
1969	Pete Maravich, LSU	6-5	Jr.	26	433	—	282	1148	44.2
1970	Pete Maravich, LSU	6-5	Sr.	31	522	—	337	1381	44.5
1971	Johnny Neumann, Mississippi	6-6	So.	23	366	—	191	923	40.1
1972	Dwight Lamar, SW Louisiana	6-1	Jr.	29	429	—	196	1054	36.3
1973	William Averitt, Pepperdine	6-1	Sr.	25	352	—	144	848	33.9
1974	Larry Fogle, Canisius	6-5	So.	25	326	—	183	835	33.4
1975	Bob McCurdy, Richmond	6-7	Sr.	26	321	—	213	855	32.9
1976	Marshall Rodgers, Tex.-Pan American	6-2	Sr.	25	361	—	197	919	36.8
1977	Freeman Williams, Portland St	6-4	Jr.	26	417	—	176	1010	38.8
1978	Freeman Williams, Portland St	6-4	Sr.	27	410	—	149	969	35.9
1979	Lawrence Butler, Idaho St	6-3	Sr.	27	310	—	192	812	30.1
1980	Tony Murphy, Southern-Birmingham	6-3	Sr.	29	377	—	178	932	32.1
1981	Zam Fredrick, South Carolina	6-2	Sr.	27	300	—	181	781	28.9
1982	Harry Kelly, Texas Southern	6-7	Jr.	29	336	—	190	862	29.7
1983	Harry Kelly, Texas Southern	6-7	Sr.	29	333	—	169	835	28.8
1984	Joe Jakubick, Akron	6-5	Sr.	27	304	—	206	814	30.1
1985	Xavier McDaniel, Wichita St	6-8	Sr.	31	351	—	142	844	27.2
1986	Terrance Bailey, Wagner	6-2	Jr.	29	321	—	212	854	29.4
1987	Kevin Houston, Army	5-11	Sr.	29	311	63	268	953	32.9
1988	Hersey Hawkins, Bradley	6-3	Sr.	31	377	87	284	1125	36.3
1989	Hank Gathers, Loyola Marymount	6-7	Jr.	31	419	0	177	1015	32.7
1990	Bo Kimble, Loyola Marymount	6-5	Sr.	32	404	92	231	1131	35.3
1991	Kevin Bradshaw, U.S. Int'l	6-6	Sr.	28	358	60	278	1054	37.6
1992	Brett Roberts, Morehead St	6-8	Sr.	29	278	66	193	815	28.1
1993	Greg Guy, Tex.-Pan American	6-1	Jr.	19	189	67	111	556	29.3
1994	Glenn Robinson, Purdue	6-8	Jr.	34	368	79	215	1030	30.3
1995	Kurt Thomas, TCU	6-9	Sr.	27	288	3	202	781	28.9
1996	Kevin Granger, Texas Southern	6-3	Sr.	24	194	30	230	648	27.0
1997	Charles Jones, LIU-Brooklyn	6-3	Jr.	30	338	109	118	903	30.1
1998	Charles Jones, LIU-Brooklyn	6-3	Sr.	30	326	116	101	869	29.0
1999	Alvin Young, Niagara	6-3	Sr.	29	253	65	157	728	25.1

Scoring Average (Cont.)

Year	Player and Team	Ht	Class	GP	FG	3FG	FT	Pts	Avg
2000	Courtney Alexander, Fresno St	6-6	Sr.	27	252	58	107	669	24.8
2001	Ronnie McCollum, Centenary	6-4	Sr.	27	244	85	214	787	29.1
2002	Jason Conley, Virginia Military	6-5	Fr.	28	285	79	171	820	29.3
2003	Ruben Douglas, New Mexico	6-5	Sr.	28	218	94	253	783	28.0
2004	Keydren Clark, St. Peter's	5-8	So.	29	233	112	197	775	26.7
2005	Keydren Clark, St. Peter's	5-9	Jr.	28	230	109	152	721	25.8
2006	Adam Morrison, Gonzaga	6-8	Jr.	33	306	74	240	926	28.1
2007	Reggie Williams, Virginia Military Institute	6-5	Jr.	33	338	76	176	928	28.1

Rebounds

Year	Player and Team	Ht	Class	GP	Reb	Avg
1951	Ernie Beck, Pennsylvania	6-4	So.	27	556	20.6
1952	Bill Hannon, Army	6-3	So.	17	355	20.9
1953	Ed Conlin, Fordham	6-5	So.	26	612	23.5
1954	Art Quimby, Connecticut	6-5	Jr.	26	588	22.6
1955	Charlie Slack, Marshall	6-5	Jr.	21	538	25.6
1956	Joe Holup, George Washington	6-6	Sr.	26	604	†.256
1957	Elgin Baylor, Seattle	6-6	Jr.	25	508	†.235
1958	Alex Ellis, Niagara	6-5	Sr.	25	536	†.262
1959	Leroy Wright, Pacific	6-8	Jr.	26	652	†.238
1960	Leroy Wright, Pacific	6-8	Sr.	17	380	†.234
1961	Jerry Lucas, Ohio St	6-8	Jr.	27	470	†.198
1962	Jerry Lucas, Ohio St	6-8	Sr.	28	499	†.211
1963	Paul Silas, Creighton	6-7	Sr.	27	557	20.6
1964	Bob Pelkington, Xavier (Ohio)	6-7	Sr.	26	567	21.8
1965	Toby Kimball, Connecticut	6-8	Sr.	23	483	21.0
1966	Jim Ware, Oklahoma City	6-8	Sr.	29	607	20.9
1967	Dick Cunningham, Murray St	6-10	Jr.	22	479	21.8
1968	Neal Walk, Florida	6-10	Jr.	25	494	19.8
1969	Spencer Haywood, Detroit	6-8	So.	22	472	21.5
1970	Artis Gilmore, Jacksonville	7-2	Jr.	28	621	22.2
1971	Artis Gilmore, Jacksonville	7-2	Sr.	26	603	23.2
1972	Kermit Washington, American	6-8	Jr.	23	455	19.8
1973	Kermit Washington, American	6-8	Sr.	22	439	20.0
1974	Marvin Barnes, Providence	6-9	Sr.	32	597	18.7
1975	John Irving, Hofstra	6-9	So.	21	323	15.4
1976	Sam Pellom, Buffalo	6-8	So.	26	420	16.2
1977	Glenn Mosley, Seton Hall	6-8	Sr.	29	473	16.3
1978	Ken Williams, North Texas St	6-7	Sr.	28	411	14.7
1979	Monti Davis, Tennessee St	6-7	Jr.	26	421	16.2
1980	Larry Smith, Alcorn St	6-8	Sr.	26	392	15.1
1981	Darryl Watson, Miss. Valley St	6-7	Sr.	27	379	14.0
1982	LaSalle Thompson, Texas	6-10	Jr.	27	365	13.5
1983	Xavier McDaniel, Wichita St	6-7	So.	28	403	14.4
1984	Akeem Olajuwon, Houston	7-0	Jr.	37	500	13.5
1985	Xavier McDaniel, Wichita St	6-8	Sr	31	460	14.8
1986	David Robinson, Navy	6-11	Jr.	35	455	13.0
1987	Jerome Lane, Pittsburgh	6-6	So.	33	444	13.5
1988	Kenny Miller, Loyola (Ill.)	6-9	Fr.	29	395	13.6
1989	Hank Gathers, Loyola (Calif.)	6-7	Jr.	31	426	13.7
1990	Anthony Bonner, St. Louis	6-8	Sr.	33	456	13.8
1991	Shaquille O'Neal, LSU	7-1	So.	28	411	14.7
1992	Popeye Jones, Murray St	6-8	Sr.	30	431	14.4
1993	Warren Kidd, Middle Tenn. St	6-9	Sr.	26	386	14.8
1994	Jerome Lambert, Baylor	6-8	Jr.	24	355	14.8
1995	Kurt Thomas, TCU	6-9	Sr.	27	393	14.6
1996	Marcus Mann, Miss. Valley St	6-8	Sr.	29	394	13.6
1997	Tim Duncan, Wake Forest	6-11	Sr.	31	457	14.7
1998	Ryan Perryman, Dayton	6-7	Sr.	33	412	12.5
1999	Ian McGinnis, Dartmouth	6-8	So.	26	317	12.2
2000	Darren Phillips, Fairfield	6-7	Sr.	29	405	14.0
2001	Chris Marcus, Western Kentucky	7-1	Jr.	31	374	12.1
2002	Jeremy Bishop, Quinnipiac	6-6	J..	29	347	12.0
2003	Brandon Hunter, Ohio	6-7	Sr.	30	378	12.6
2004	Paul Millsap, Louisiana Tech	6-7	Fr.	30	374	12.5
2005	Paul Millsap, Louisiana Tech	6-8	So.	29	360	12.4
2006	Paul Millsap, Louisiana Tech	6-8	Jr.	33	438	13.3
2007	Rashad Jones-Jennings, Ark.-Little Rock	6-8	Sr.	30	392	13.1

†From 1956–1962, title was based on highest individual recoveries out of total by both teams in all games.

Assists

Year	Player and Team	Class	GP	Ast	Avg
1984	Craig Lathen, Ill.-Chicago	Jr.	29	274	9.45
1985	Rob Weingard, Hofstra	Sr.	24	228	9.50
1986	Mark Jackson, St. John's (N.Y.)	Jr.	36	328	9.11
1987	Avery Johnson, Southern-Birm.	Jr.	31	333	10.74
1988	Avery Johnson, Southern-Birm.	Sr.	30	399	13.30
1989	Glenn Williams, Holy Cross	Sr.	28	278	9.93
1990	Todd Lehmann, Drexel	Sr.	28	260	9.29
1991	Chris Corchiani, North Carolina St	Sr.	31	299	9.65
1992	Van Usher, Tennessee Tech	Sr.	29	254	8.76
1993	Sam Crawford, New Mex. St	Sr.	34	310	9.12
1994	Jason Kidd, California	So.	30	272	9.06
1995	Nelson Haggerty, Baylor	Sr.	28	284	10.10
1996	Raimonds Miglinieks, UC-Irvine	Sr.	27	230	8.52
1997	Kenny Mitchell, Dartmouth	Sr.	26	203	7.81
1998	Ahlon Lewis, Arizona St	Sr.	32	294	9.19
1999	Doug Gottlieb, Oklahoma St	Jr.	34	299	8.79
2000	Mark Dickel, UNLV	Sr.	31	280	9.03
2001	Markus Carr, CSU–Northridge	Jr.	32	286	8.94
2002	T.J. Ford, Texas	Fr.	33	273	8.27
2003	Martell Bailey, Ill.-Chicago	Jr.	30	244	8.13
2004	Greg Davis, Troy St	Sr.	31	256	8.26
2005	Damitrius Coleman, Mercer	Jr.	28	224	8.00
	Will Funn, Portland St	Sr.	28	224	8.00
2006	Jared Jordan, Marist	Jr.	29	247	8.52
2007	Jared Jordan, Marist	Sr.	31	274	8.83

Blocked Shots

Year	Player and Team	Class	GP	BS	Avg
1986	David Robinson, Navy	Jr.	35	207	5.91
1987	David Robinson, Navy	Sr.	32	144	4.50
1988	Rodney Blake, St. Joseph's (Pa.)	Sr.	29	116	4.00
1989	Alonzo Mourning, Georgetown	Fr.	34	169	4.97
1990	Kenny Green, Rhode Island	Sr.	26	124	4.77
1991	Shawn Bradley, BYU	Fr.	34	177	5.21
1992	Shaquille O'Neal, LSU	Jr.	30	157	5.23
1993	Theo Ratliff, Wyoming	Jr.	28	124	4.43
1994	Grady Livingston, Howard	Jr.	26	115	4.42
1995	Keith Closs, Central Conn. St	Fr.	26	139	5.35
1996	Keith Closs, Central Conn. St	So.	28	178	6.36
1997	Adonal Foyle, Colgate	Jr.	28	180	6.43
1998	Jerome James, Florida A&M	Sr.	27	125	4.63
1999	Tarvis Williams, Hampton	Jr.	27	135	5.00
2000	Ken Johnson, Ohio St	Sr.	30	161	5.37
2001	Tarvis Williams, Hampton	Sr	32	147	4.59
2002	Wojciech Myrda, La.-Monroe	Sr.	32	172	5.38
2003	Emeka Okafor, Connecticut	So.	33	156	4.73
2004	Anwar Ferguson, Houston	Sr.	27	111	4.11
2005	Deng Gai, Fairfield	Sr.	30	165	5.50
2006	Shawn James, Northeastern	So.	30	196	6.53
2007	Mickell Gladness, Ala.-A&M	Jr.	30	188	6.26

Steals

Year	Player and Team	Class	GP	Stl	Avg
1986	Darron Brittman, Chicago St	Sr.	28	139	4.96
1987	Tony Fairley, Charleston South.	Sr.	28	114	4.07
1988	Aldwin Ware, Florida A&M	Sr.	29	142	4.90
1989	Kenny Robertson, Cleveland St	Jr.	28	111	3.96
1990	Ronn McMahon, E. Washington	Sr.	29	130	4.48
1991	Van Usher, Tennessee Tech	Jr.	28	104	3.71
1992	Victor Snipes, NE Illinois	So.	25	86	3.44
1993	Jason Kidd, California	Fr.	29	110	3.80
1994	Shawn Griggs, SW Louisiana	Sr.	30	120	4.00
1995	Roderick Anderson, Texas	Sr.	30	101	3.37
1996	Pointer Williams, McNeese St	Sr.	27	118	4.37

Steals (Cont.)

Year	Player and Team	Class	GP	Stl	Avg
1997	Joel Hoover, Md.-Eastern Shore	Fr.	28	90	3.21
1998	Bonzi Wells, Ball St	Sr.	29	103	3.55
1999	Shawnta Rogers, George Wash.	Sr.	29	103	3.55
2000	Carl Williams, Liberty	Sr.	28	107	3.82
2001	Greedy Daniels, TCU	Jr.	25	108	4.32
2002	Desmond Cambridge, Ala. A&M	Sr.	29	160	5.52
2003	Alexis McMillan, Stetson	Sr.	22	87	3.95
2004	Marques Green, St. Bonaventure	Sr.	27	107	3.96
2005	Obie Trotter, Alabama A&M	Jr.	32	125	3.91
2006	Tim Smith, East Tennessee St	Sr.	28	95	3.39
2007	Travis Holmes, Virginia Military Inst.	So..	33	111	3.36

NCAA Men's Division I Alltime Individual Leaders

Single Game Records

SCORING HIGHS VS DIVISION I OPPONENT

Pts	Player and Team vs Opponent	Date
72	Kevin Bradshaw, U.S. Int'l vs Loyola Marymount	1-5-91
69	Pete Maravich, LSU vs Alabama	2-7-70
68	Calvin Murphy, Niagara vs Syracuse	12-7-68
66	Jay Handlan, Washington & Lee vs Furman	2-17-51
66	Pete Maravich, LSU vs Tulane	2-10-69
66	Anthony Roberts, Oral Roberts vs North Carolina A&T	2-19-77
65	Anthony Roberts, Oral Roberts vs Oregon	3-9-77
65	Scott Haffner, Evansville vs Dayton	2-18-89
64	Pete Maravich, LSU vs Kentucky	2-21-70
63	Johnny Neumann, Mississippi vs LSU	1-30-71
63	Hersey Hawkins, Bradley vs Detroit	2-22-88

SCORING HIGHS VS NON-DIVISION I OPPONENT

Pts	Player and Team vs Opponent	Date
100	Frank Selvy, Furman vs Newberry	2-13-54
85	Paul Arizin, Villanova vs Philadelphia NAMC	2-12-49
81	Freeman Williams, Portland St vs Rocky Mountain	2-3-78
73	Bill Mlkvy, Temple vs Wilkes	3-3-51
71	Freeman Williams, Portland St vs S. Oregon	2-9-77

REBOUNDING HIGHS ALL-TIME

Reb	Player and Team vs Opponent	Date
51	Bill Chambers, William & Mary vs Virginia	2-14-53
43	Charlie Slack, Marshall vs Morris Harvey	1-12-54
42	Tom Heinsohn, Holy Cross vs Boston College	3-1-55
40	Art Quimby, Connecticut vs Boston University	1-11-55
39	Maurice Stokes, St. Francis (Pa.) vs John Carroll	1-28-55
39	Dave DeBusschere, Detroit vs C. Michigan	1-30-60
39	Keith Swagerty, Pacific vs UC-Santa Barbara	3-5-65

REBOUNDING HIGHS SINCE 1973*

Reb	Player and Team vs Opponent	Date
35	Larry Abney, Fresno St vs SMU	2-17-00
34	David Vaughn, Oral Roberts vs Brandeis	1-8-73
32	Jervaughn Scales, Southern-Birm. vs Grambling	2-7-94
32	Durand Macklin, LSU vs Tulane	11-26-76
31	Jim Bradley, Northern Illinois vs UW-Milwaukee	2-19-73
31	Calvin Natt, NE Louisiana vs Georgia Southern	12-29-76

ASSISTS

Asst	Player and Team vs Opponent	Date
22	Tony Fairley, Baptist vs Armstrong St	2-9-87
22	Avery Johnson, Southern-Birm. vs Texas Southern	1-25-88
22	Sherman Douglas, Syracuse vs Providence	1-28-89
21	Kelvin Scarborough, New Mexico vs Hawaii	2-13-87
21	Anthony Manuel, Bradley vs UC-Irvine	12-19-87
21	Avery Johnson, Southern-Birm. vs Alabama St	1-16-88

*Freshmen became eligible for varsity play in 1973.

Single Game Records (Cont.)
STEALS

Stl	Player and Team vs Opponent	Date
13	Mookie Blaylock, Oklahoma vs Centenary	12-12-87
13	Mookie Blaylock, Oklahoma vs Loyola Marymount	12-17-88
12	Kenny Robertson, Cleveland St vs Wagner	12-3-88
12	Terry Evans, Oklahoma vs Florida A&M	1-27-93
12	Richard Duncan, Middle Tenn. St vs Eastern Kentucky	2-20-99
12	Greedy Daniels, Texas Christian vs Ark.–Pine Bluff	12-30-00
12	Jehiel Lewis, Navy vs Bucknell	1-12-02
12	Carldell Johnson, Ala.-Birmingham vs. South Carolina St	11-27-05

BLOCKED SHOTS

BS	Player and Team vs Opponent	Date
16	Mickell Gladness, Alabama A&M vs Texas Southern	2-24-07
14	David Robinson, Navy vs UNC–Wilmington	1-4-86
14	Shawn Bradley, BYU vs Eastern Kentucky	12-7-90
14	Roy Rogers, Alabama vs Georgia	2-10-96
14	Loren Woods, Arizona vs Oregon	2-3-00

Ten tied with 13

Single Season Records
POINTS

Player and Team	Year	GP	FG	3FG	FT	Pts
Pete Maravich, LSU	1970	31	522	—	337	1381
Elvin Hayes, Houston	1968	33	519	—	176	1214
Frank Selvy, Furman	1954	29	427	—	355	1209
Pete Maravich, LSU	1969	26	433	—	282	1148
Pete Maravich, LSU	1968	26	432	—	274	1138
Bo Kimble, Loyola Marymount	1990	32	404	92	231	1131
Hersey Hawkins, Bradley	1988	31	377	87	284	1125
Austin Carr, Notre Dame	1970	29	444	—	218	1106
Austin Carr, Notre Dame	1971	29	430	—	241	1101
Otis Birdsong, Houston	1977	36	452	—	186	1090

SCORING AVERAGE

Player and Team	Year	GP	FG	3FG	FT	Pts	
Pete Maravich, LSU	1970	31	522	337	1381	44.5	
Pete Maravich, LSU	1969	26	433	282	1148	44.2	
Pete Maravich, LSU	1968	26	432	274	1138	43.8	
Frank Selvy, Furman	1954	29	427	355	1209	41.7	
Johnny Neumann, Mississippi	1971	23	366	191	923	40.1	
Freeman Williams, Portland St	1977	26	417	176	1010	38.8	
Billy McGill, Utah	1962	26	394	221	1009	38.8	
Calvin Murphy, Niagara	1968	24	337	242	916	38.2	
Austin Carr, Notre Dame	1970	29	444	218	1106	38.1	
Austin Carr, Notre Dame	1971	29	430	241	1101	38.0	

REBOUNDS

Player and Team	Year	GP	Reb	Player and Team	Year	GP	Reb
Walt Dukes, Seton Hall	1953	33	734	Artis Gilmore, Jacksonville	1970	28	621
Leroy Wright, Pacific	1959	26	652	Tom Gola, La Salle	1955	31	618
Tom Gola, La Salle	1954	30	652	Ed Conlin, Fordham	1953	26	612
Charlie Tyra, Louisville	1956	29	645	Art Quimby, Connecticut	1955	25	611
Paul Silas, Creighton	1964	29	631	Bill Russell, San Francisco	1956	29	609
Elvin Hayes, Houston	1968	33	624	Jim Ware, Oklahoma City	1966	29	607

REBOUND AVERAGE ALL-TIME

Player and Team	Year	GP	Reb	Avg
Charlie Slack, Marshall	1955	21	538	25.6
Leroy Wright, Pacific	1959	26	652	25.1
Art Quimby, Connecticut	1955	25	611	24.4
Charlie Slack, Marshall	1956	22	520	23.6
Ed Conlin, Fordham	1953	26	612	23.5

REBOUND AVERAGE SINCE 1973*

Player and Team	Year	GP	Reb	Avg
Kermit Washington, American	1973	22	439	20.0
Marvin Barnes, Providence	1973	30	571	19.0
Marvin Barnes, Providence	1974	32	597	18.7
Pete Padgett, Nev.-Reno	1973	26	462	17.8
Jim Bradley, Northern Illinois	1973	24	426	17.8

Single Season Records (Cont.)

ASSISTS

Player and Team	Year	GP	Asst	Player and Team	Year	GP	Asst
Mark Wade, UNLV	1987	38	406	Sherman Douglas, Syracuse	1989	38	326
Avery Johnson, Southern-Birm.	1988	30	399	Sam Crawford, New Mex. St	1993	34	310
Anthony Manuel, Bradley	1988	31	373	Greg Anthony, UNLV	1991	35	310
Avery Johnson, Southern-Birm.	1987	31	333	Reid Gettys, Houston	1984	37	309
Mark Jackson, St. John's (N.Y.)	1986	32	328	Carl Golston, Loyola (Ill.)	1985	33	305

ASSIST AVERAGE

Player and Team	Year	GP	Asst	Avg	Player and Team	Year	GP	Asst	Avg
Avery Johnson, Southern-Birm.	1988	30	399	13.3	Chris Corchiani, North Carolina St.	1991	31	299	9.6
Anthony Manuel, Bradley	1988	31	373	12.0	Tony Fairley, Charleston South.*	1987	28	270	9.6
Avery Johnson, Southern-Birm.	1987	31	333	10.7	Tyrone Bogues, Wake Forest	1987	29	276	9.5
Mark Wade, UNLV	1987	38	406	10.7	Ron Weingard, Hofstra	1985	24	228	9.5
Nelson Haggerty, Baylor	1995	28	284	10.1	Craig Neal, Georgia Tech	1988	32	303	9.5
Glenn Williams, Holy Cross	1989	28	278	9.9					

FIELD-GOAL PERCENTAGE

Player and Team	Year	GP	FG	FGA	Pct
Steve Johnson, Oregon St	1981	28	235	315	74.6
Dwayne Davis, Florida	1989	33	179	248	72.2
Keith Walker, Utica	1985	27	154	216	71.3
Steve Johnson, Oregon St	1980	30	211	297	71.0
Adam Mark, Belmont	2002	26	150	212	70.8
Oliver Miller, Arkansas	1991	38	254	361	70.4
Alan Williams, Princeton	1987	25	163	232	70.3
Mark McNamara, California	1982	27	231	329	70.2
Warren Kidd, Middle Tennessee St	1991	30	173	247	70.0
Pete Freeman, Akron	1991	28	175	250	70.0

Based on qualifiers for annual championship.

FREE-THROW PERCENTAGE

Player and Team	Year	GP	FT	FTA	Pct
Blake Ahearn SW Missouri St†	2004	33	117	120	97.5
Ryan Toolson, Utah Valley St	2006	29	96	99	97.0
Derek Raivio, Gonzaga	2006	33	146	152	96.1
Craig Collins, Penn St	1985	27	94	98	95.9
A.J. Graves, Butler	2006	32	137	143	95.8
J.J. Redick, Duke	2004	37	143	150	95.3
Steve Drabyn, Belmont	2003	29	78	82	95.1
Rod Foster, UCLA	1982	27	95	100	95.0
Clay McKnight, Pacific	2000	24	74	78	94.9
Matt Logie, Lehigh	2003	28	91	96	94.8
Blake Ahearn, Missouri State	2005	32	90	95	94.7

THREE-POINT FIELD-GOAL PERCENTAGE

Player and Team	Year	GP	3FG	3FGA	Pct
Glenn Tropf, Holy Cross	1988	29	52	82	63.4
Sean Wightman, Western Michigan	1992	30	48	76	63.2
Keith Jennings, East Tennessee St	1991	33	84	142	59.2
Dave Calloway, Monmouth (N.J.)	1989	28	48	82	58.5
Steve Kerr, Arizona	1988	38	114	199	57.3
Reginald Jones, Prairie View	1987	28	64	112	57.1
Jim Cantamessa, Siena	1998	29	66	117	56.4
Joel Tribelhorn, Colorado St	1989	33	76	135	56.3
Mike Joseph, Bucknell	1988	28	65	116	56.0
Brian Jackson, Evansville	1995	27	53	95	55.8

Based on qualifiers for annual championship.

*Formerly Baptist
†Southwest Missouri State changed name to Missouri State after 2004–05 season
Based on qualifiers for annual championship.

Single Season Records (Cont.)

STEALS

Player and Team	Year	GP	Stl
Desmond Cambridge, Alabama A&M	2002	29	160
Mookie Blaylock, Oklahoma	1988	39	150
Aldwin Ware, Florida A&M	1988	29	142
Darron Brittman, Chicago St.	1986	28	139
John Linehan, Providence	2002	31	139

STEAL AVERAGE

Player and Team	Year	GP	Stl	Avg
D. Cambridge, Alabama A&M	2002	29	160	5.52
Darron Brittman, Chicago St	1986	28	139	4.96
Aldwin Ware, Florida A&M	1988	29	142	4.90
John Linehan, Providence	2002	31	139	4.48
Ronn McMahon, E. Washington	1990	29	130	4.48

BLOCKED SHOTS

Player and Team	Year	GP	BS
David Robinson, Navy	1986	35	207
Shawn James, Northeastern	2005	30	196
Mickell Gladness, Alabama A&M	2006	30	188
Adonal Foyle, Colgate	1997	28	180
Keith Closs, Central Conn. St	1996	28	178

BLOCKED-SHOT AVERAGE

Player and Team	Year	GP	BS	Avg
Shawn James, Northeastern	2005	30	196	6.53
Adonal Foyle, Colgate	1997	28	180	6.43
Keith Closs, Central Conn. St.	1996	28	178	6.36
Mickell Gladness, Alabama A&M	2006	30	188	6.26
David Robinson, Navy	1986	35	207	5.91

Career Records

POINTS

Player and Team	Ht	Final Year	GP	FG	3FG*	FT	Pts
Pete Maravich, LSU	6-5	1970	83	1387	—	893	3667
Freeman Williams, Portland St.	6-4	1978	106	1369	—	511	3249
Lionel Simmons, La Salle	6-7	1990	131	1244	56	673	3217
Alphonso Ford, Mississippi Valley St.	6-2	1993	109	1121	333	590	3165
Harry Kelly, Texas Southern	6-7	1983	110	1234	—	598	3066
Keydren Clark, St. Peter's	5-9	2006	118	967	435	689	3058
Hersey Hawkins, Bradley	6-3	1988	125	1100	118	690	3008
Oscar Robertson, Cincinnati	6-5	1960	88	1052	—	869	2973
Danny Manning, Kansas	6-10	1988	147	1216	10	509	2951
Alfredrick Hughes, Loyola (Ill.)	6-5	1985	120	1226	—	462	2914
Elvin Hayes, Houston	6-8	1968	93	1215	—	454	2884
Larry Bird, Indiana St.	6-9	1979	94	1154	—	542	2850
Otis Birdsong, Houston	6-4	1977	116	1176	—	480	2832
Kevin Bradshaw, Bethune-Cookman, U.S. Int'l	6-6	1991	111	1027	132	618	2804
Allan Houston, Tennessee	6-6	1993	128	902	346	651	2801
J.J. Redick, Duke	6-4	2006	139	825	457	662	2769
Hank Gathers, USC, Loyola Marymount	6-7	1990	117	1127	0	469	2723
Reggie Lewis, Northeastern	6-7	1987	122	1043	30 (1)	592	2708
Daren Queenan, Lehigh	6-5	1988	118	1024	29	626	2703
Byron Larkin, Xavier (Ohio)	6-3	1988	121	1022	51	601	2696
David Robinson, Navy	7-1	1987	127	1032	1	604	2669

*Listed is the number of three-pointers scored since it became the national rule in 1987; the number in the parentheses is number scored prior to 1987—these counted as three points in the game but counted as two-pointers in the national rankings. The three-pointers in the parentheses are not included in total points.

SCORING AVERAGE

Player and Team	Final Year	GP	FG	FT	Pts	Avg
Pete Maravich, LSU	1968	83	1387	893	3667	44.2
Austin Carr, Notre Dame	1971	74	1017	526	2560	34.6
Oscar Robertson, Cincinnati	1960	88	1052	869	2973	33.8
Calvin Murphy, Niagara	1970	77	947	654	2548	33.1
Dwight Lamar, SW Louisiana	1973	57	768	326	1862	32.7
Frank Selvy, Furman	1954	78	922	694	2538	32.5
Rick Mount, Purdue	1970	72	910	503	2323	32.3
Darrell Floyd, Furman	1956	71	868	545	2281	32.1
Nick Werkman, Seton Hall	1964	71	812	649	2273	32.0
Willie Humes, Idaho St.	1971	48	565	380	1510	31.5
William Averitt, Pepperdine	1973	49	615	311	1541	31.4
Elgin Baylor, Coll. of Idaho, Seattle	1958	80	956	588	2500	31.3
Elvin Hayes, Houston	1968	93	1215	454	2884	31.0
Freeman Williams, Portland St.	1978	106	1369	511	3249	30.7
Larry Bird, Indiana St.	1979	94	1154	542	2850	30.3

Career Records (Cont.)

REBOUNDS ALL-TIME

Player and Team	Final Year	GP	Reb
Tom Gola, La Salle	1955	118	2201
Joe Holup, George Washington	1956	104	2030
Charlie Slack, Marshall	1956	88	1916
Ed Conlin, Fordham	1955	102	1884
Dickie Hemric, Wake Forest	1955	104	1802

REBOUNDS SINCE 1973*

Player and Team	Final Year	GP	Reb
Tim Duncan, Wake Forest	1997	128	1570
Derrick Coleman, Syracuse	1990	143	1537
Malik Rose, Drexel	1996	120	1514
Ralph Sampson, Virginia	1983	132	1511
Pete Padgett, Nev.-Reno	1976	104	1464

ASSISTS

Player and Team	Final Year	GP	Asst
Bobby Hurley, Duke	1993	140	1076
Chris Corchiani, North Carolina St	1991	124	1038
Ed Cota, North Carolina	2000	138	1030
Keith Jennings, East Tennessee St	1991	127	983
Steve Blake, Maryland	2003	138	972

FIELD-GOAL PERCENTAGE

Player and Team	Final Year	FG	FGA	Pct
Steve Johnson, Oregon St	1981	828	1222	67.8
Michael Bradley, Kentucky/Villanova	2001	441	651	67.7
Murray Brown, Florida St	1980	566	847	66.8
Lee Campbell, SW Missouri St	1990	411	618	66.5
Warren Kidd, Middle Tennessee St	1993	496	747	66.4

Note: Minimum 400 field goals and 4 FG made per game.

FREE-THROW PERCENTAGE

Player and Team	Final Year	FT	FTA	Pct
Blake Ahearn, Missouri St	2007	435	460	94.6
Derek Raivio, Gonzaga	2007	343	370	92.7
Gary Buchanan, Villanova	2003	324	355	91.3
J.J. Redick, Duke	2006	662	726	91.2
Greg Starrick, Kentucky/Southern Illinois	1972	341	375	90.9

Note: Minimum 300 free throws made.
*Freshmen became eligible for varsity play in 1973.

THREE-POINT FIELD GOALS MADE

Player and Team	Final Year	GP	3FG
J.J. Redick, Duke	2006	139	457
Keydren Clark, St. Peter's	2006	118	435
Curtis Staples, Virginia	1998	122	413
Keith Veney, Lamar/Marshall	1997	111	409
Doug Day, Radford	1993	117	401

THREE-POINT FIELD-GOAL PERCENTAGE

Player and Team	Final Year	3FG	3FGA	Pct
Tony Bennett, UW–Green Bay	1992	290	584	49.7
Stephen Sir, San Diego St/Northern Ariz	2007	323	689	46.9
David Olson, Eastern Illinois	1992	262	562	46.6
Ross Land, Northern Arizona	2000	308	664	46.4
Dan Dickau, Washington/Gonzaga	2002	215	465	46.2

Note: Minimum 200 3-point field goals and 2.0 3FG/G.

NCAA Men's Division I Alltime Individual Leaders (Cont.)

Career Records (Cont.)

STEALS

Player and Team	Final Year	GP	Stl
John Linehan, Providence	2002	122	385
Eric Murdock, Providence	1991	117	376
Pepe Sanchez, Temple	2000	116	365
Cookie Belcher, Nebraska	2001	131	353
Kevin Braswell, Georgetown	2002	128	349

BLOCKED SHOTS

Player and Team	Final Year	GP	BS
Wojciech Myrda, La.-Monroe	2002	115	535
Adonal Foyle, Colgate	1997	87	492
Tim Duncan, Wake Forest	1997	128	481
Alonzo Mourning, Georgetown	1992	120	453

NCAA Men's Division I Team Leaders

Division I Team Alltime Wins

Team	First Year	Yrs	W	L	T
Kentucky	1903	104	1948	608	1
North Carolina	1911	97	1914	696	0
Kansas	1899	109	1906	782	0
Duke	1906	102	1818	802	0
Syracuse	1901	106	1704	782	0
Temple	1895	111	1668	935	0
St. John's (N.Y.)	1908	100	1659	831	0
Pennsylvania	1897	107	1634	913	2
UCLA	1920	88	1611	713	0
Indiana	1901	107	1610	876	0
Notre Dame	1898	102	1605	885	1
Utah	1909	99	1595	833	0
Oregon St	1902	106	1570	1137	0
Illinois	1906	102	1569	824	0
Western Kentucky	1915	88	1548	764	0

Division I Alltime Winning Percentage

Team	First Year	Yrs	W	L	T	Pct
Kentucky	1903	104	1948	608	1	.762
North Carolina	1911	97	1914	696	0	.733
UNLV	1959	49	1010	410	0	.711
Kansas	1899	109	1906	782	0	.709
Duke	1906	102	1818	802	0	.694
UCLA	1920	89	1611	713	0	.693
Syracuse	1901	106	1704	782	0	.685
Western Kentucky	1915	88	1548	764	0	.670
St. John's (N.Y.)	1908	96	1659	831	0	.666
Utah	1909	98	1595	833	0	.657
Illinois	1906	102	1569	824	0	.656
Louisville	1912	93	1529	816	0	.652
Missouri St	1909	95	1470	797	0	.648
Arizona	1905	102	1528	829	1	.648
Indiana	1901	107	1610	876	0	.648

Note: Minimum of 25 years in Division I.

NCAA Men's Division I Winning Streaks

Longest—Full Season

Team	Games	Years	Ended by
UCLA	88	1971–74	Notre Dame (71–70)
San Francisco	60	1955–57	Illinois (62–33)
UCLA	47	1966–68	Houston (71–69)
UNLV	45	1990–91	Duke (79–77)
Texas	44	1913–17	Rice (24–18)
Seton Hall	43	1939–41	LIU-Brooklyn (49–26)
LIU-Brooklyn	43	1935–37	Stanford (45–31)
UCLA	41	1968–69	USC (46–44)
Marquette	39	1970–71	Ohio St (60–59)
Cincinnati	37	1962–63	Wichita St (65–64)
North Carolina	37	1957–58	W Virginia (75–64)

Longest—Regular Season

Team	Games	Years	Ended by
UCLA	76	1971–74	Notre Dame (71–70)
Indiana	57	1975–77	Toledo (59–57)
Marquette	56	1970–72	Detroit (70–49)
Kentucky	54	1952–55	Georgia Tech (59–58)
San Francisco	51	1955–57	Illinois (62–33)
Pennsylvania	48	1970–72	Temple (57–52)
Ohio State	47	1960–62	Wisconsin (86–67)
Texas	44	1913–17	Rice (24–18)
UCLA	43	1966–68	Houston (71–69)
LIU-Brooklyn	43	1935–37	Stanford (45–31)
Seton Hall	42	1939–41	LIU-Brooklyn (49–26)

Longest—Home Court

Team	Games	Years	Team	Games	Years
Kentucky	129	1943–55	Lamar	80	1978–84
St. Bonaventure	99	1948–61	Long Beach St	75	1968–74
UCLA	98	1970–76	UNLV	72	1974–78
Cincinnati	86	1957–64	Arizona	71	1987–92
Marquette	81	1967–73	Cincinnati	68	1972–78
Arizona	81	1945–51	Western Kentucky	67	1949–55

NCAA Men's Division I Winningest Coaches

Active Coaches*

WINS

Coach and Team	W
Bob Knight, Texas Tech	880
Lute Olson, Arizona	780
Mike Krzyzewski, Duke	775
Jim Boeheim, Syracuse	750
Jim Calhoun, Connecticut	750
Bob Huggins, West Virginia	590
Gary Williams, Maryland	585
Tom Penders, Houston	584
Homer Drew, Valparaiso	574
Ben Braun, California	539

WINNING PERCENTAGE

Coach and Team	Yrs	W	L	Pct
Mark Few, Gonzaga	8	211	50	.802
Roy Williams, North Carolina	19	524	131	.800
Bruce Pearl, Tennessee	15	363	103	.779
Thad Matta, Ohio St	7	183	53	.775
Bo Ryan, Wisconsin	23	525	158	.769
Mike Krzyzewski, Duke	32	775	261	.748
Jim Boeheim, Syracuse	31	750	264	.740
Bob Huggins, West Virginia	25	590	211	.737
Lute Olson, Arizona	34	780	280	.736
John Calipari, Memphis	15	370	133	.736

Note: Minimum 5 years as a Division I head coach; includes record at 4-year colleges only.

Note: Minimum 5 years as a Division I head coach; includes record at 4-year colleges only.

Alltime Winningest Men's Division I Coaches

	W
*Bob Knight (Army, Indiana, Texas Tech)	890
Dean Smith (North Carolina)	879
Adolph Rupp (Kentucky)	876
Jim Phelan (Mt. St. Mary's)	830
Eddie Sutton (Creighton, Arkansas, Kentucky, Oklahoma St)	798
Lefty Driesell (Davidson, Maryland, James Madison, Georgia St)	786
*Lute Olson (Long Beach St, Iowa, Arizona)	780
Lou Henson (Hardin-Simmons, New Mexico St, Illinois, New Mexico St)	779
*Mike Krzyzewski (Army, Duke)	775
Henry Iba (NW Missouri St, Colorado, Oklahoma St)	764
Ed Diddle (Western Kentucky)	759
*Jim Boeheim (Syracuse)	750
*Jim Calhoun (Northeastern, Connecticut)	750
Phog Allen (Baker, Kansas, Haskell, Central Missouri St, Kansas)	746
John Chaney (Cheyney St, Temple)	741
Jerry Tarkanian (Long Beach St, UNLV, Fresno St)	729
Norm Stewart (Northern Iowa, Missouri)	728
Ray Meyer (DePaul)	724
Don Haskins (Oklahoma St, UTEP)	719
Denny Crum (UCLA, Louisville)	675
John Wooden (Purdue, Indiana St, UCLA)	664
Ralph Miller (Wichita St, Iowa, Oregon St)	657
Gene Bartow (C. Missouri St, Valparaiso, Memphis, Illinois, UCLA, UAB)	647
Billy Tubbs (Lamar, Southwestern [Tex.], Oklahoma, TCU)	641
Marv Harshman (Pacific Lutheran, Washington St, Washington)	637

Note: Minimum 10 head coaching seasons in Division I.

*Active in 2006–07.

Alltime Winningest Men's Division I Coaches (Cont.)

WINNING PERCENTAGE

Coach (Team, Years)	Yrs	W	L	Pct
Clair Bee (Rider 1929–31, LIU-Brooklyn 1932–45, 1946–51)	21	412	87	.826
Adolph Rupp (Kentucky 1931–72)	41	876	190	.822
John Wooden (Indiana St 1947–48, UCLA 1949–75)	29	664	162	.804
*Roy Williams (Kansas 1989–2003, North Carolina 2003–)	19	524	131	.800
John Kresse (College of Charleston 1980–2002)	23	560	143	.797
Jerry Tarkanian (Long Beach St 1969–73, UNLV 1974–92, Fresno St 1995–2002)	31	729	201	.784
Francis Schmidt (Tulsa 1916–17, Arkansas 1924–29, TCU 1930–34)	17	258	72	.782
Dean Smith (North Carolina 1962–97)	36	879	254	.776
Jack Ramsay (St. Joseph's [Pa.] 1956–66)	11	231	71	.765
Frank Keaney (Rhode Island 1921–48)	28	401	124	.764
George Keogan (St. Louis 1916, Allegheny 1919, Valparaiso 1920–21, Notre Dame 1924–43)	27	414	127	.764
Vic Bubas (Duke 1960–69)	10	213	67	.761
Harry Fisher (Columbia 1907–16, Army 1922–23, 1925)	16	189	60	.759
Fred Bennion (Brigham Young 1909–10, Utah 1911-14, Montana St 1915-19)	11	95	32	.748
Charles (Chick) Davies (Duquesne 1925–43, 1947–48)	21	314	106	.748
*Mike Krzyzewski (Army 1976–80, Duke 1981–)	32	775	261	.748
Ray Mears (Wittenberg 1957–62, Tennessee 1963–77)	21	399	135	.747
Edward McNichol (Penn 1921-30)	10	186	63	.747
Rick Majerus (Marquette 1984–86, Ball St 1988–89, Utah 1990–2004, St. Louis 2007–)	20	422	147	.742
Al McGuire (Belmont Abbey 1958–64, Marquette 1965–77)	20	406	142	.741
*Jim Boeheim (Syracuse 1977–)	31	750	264	.740
Phog Allen (Baker 1906–08, Haskell 1909, C. Mo. St 1913–19, Kansas 1908–09, 1920–56)	50	746	264	.739
Everett Case (North Carolina St 1947–65)	19	377	134	.738
*Bob Huggins (Walsh 1980–83, Akron 1984–89, Cinn. 1989–2005, Kan. St 2006–07, W.V. 2007–)	25	590	211	.737
*Lute Olson (Long Beach St 1973–74, Iowa 1974–83, Arizona 1983–)	34	780	280	.736

Note: Minimum 10 head coaching seasons in Division I.

*Active in 2006–07.

Alltime Winningest Women's Division I Coaches

WINNING PERCENTAGE

Coach (Team, Years)	Yrs	W	L	Pct
Leon Barmore (Louisiana Tech 1983–02)	20	576	87	.869
*Pat Summitt (Tennessee 1975–)	33	947	180	.840
*Geno Auriemma (Connecticut 1986–)	22	621	120	.838
*Gail Goestenkors (Duke 1993–07, Texas 2007–)	15	396	99	.800
*Tara VanDerveer (Idaho 1979-80, Ohio St 1981–85, Stanford 1986–95, 97–)	28	689	184	.789
Bill Sheahan (Mt. St. Mary's 1982–98)	17	372	104	.782
*Robin Selvig (Montana 1979–)	29	672	192	.778
*Andy Landers (Georgia 1980–)	28	684	215	.761
Marsha Sharp (Texas Tech 1983–06)	24	571	189	.751
*C. Vivian Stringer (Cheyney St 1972–83, Iowa 1984–95, Rutgers 1996–)	36	777	260	.749

Note: Minimum 10 head coaching seasons in Division I.

*Active in 2006–07.

Alltime Winningest Women's Division I Coaches

	W
*Pat Summitt (Tennessee)	947
*Jody Conradt (Sam Houston St, Tex.-Arlington, Texas)	900
*C. Vivian Stringer (Cheyney St, Iowa, Rutgers)	777
*Sylvia Rhyne Hatchell (Francis Marison, North Carolina)	751
Sue Gunter (Stephen F. Austin, LSU)	708
*Kay Yow (Elon, North Carolina St)	708
*Rene Portland (St. Joseph's, Colorado, Penn St)	693
*Tara VanDerveer (Idaho, Ohio St, Stanford)	689
*Andy Landers (Georgia)	684
*Robin Selvig (Montana)	672
*Theresa Grentz (St. Joseph's, Rutgers, Illinois)	671

Note: Minimum 10 head coaching seasons in Division I.

*Active in 2006–07.

NCAA Women's Division I Championship Results

Year	Winner	Score	Runner-up	Winning Coach
1982	Louisiana Tech	76–62	Cheyney	Sonja Hogg/Leon Barmore
1983	USC	69–67	Louisiana Tech	Linda Sharp
1984	USC	72–61	Tennessee	Linda Sharp
1985	Old Dominion	70–65	Georgia	Marianne Stanley
1986	Texas	97–81	USC	Jody Conradt
1987	Tennessee	67–44	Louisiana Tech	Pat Summitt
1988	Louisiana Tech	56–54	Auburn	Leon Barmore
1989	Tennessee	76–60	Auburn	Pat Summitt
1990	Stanford	88–81	Auburn	Tara VanDerveer
1991	Tennessee	70–67 (OT)	Virginia	Pat Summitt
1992	Stanford	78–62	Western Kentucky	Tara VanDerveer
1993	Texas Tech	84–82	Ohio State	Marsha Sharp
1994	North Carolina	60–59	Louisiana Tech	Sylvia Hatchell
1995	Connecticut	70–64	Tennessee	Geno Auriemma
1996	Tennessee	83–65	Georgia	Pat Summitt
1997	Tennessee	68–59	Old Dominion	Pat Summitt
1998	Tennessee	93–75	Louisiana Tech	Pat Summitt
1999	Purdue	62–45	Duke	Carolyn Peck
2000	Connecticut	71–52	Tennessee	Geno Auriemma
2001	Notre Dame	68–66	Purdue	Muffet McGraw
2002	Connecticut	82–70	Oklahoma	Geno Auriemma
2003	Connecticut	73–68	Tennessee	Geno Auriemma
2004	Connecticut	70–61	Tennessee	Geno Auriemma
2005	Baylor	84–62	Michigan St	Kim Mulkey-Robinson
2006	Maryland	78–75	Duke	Brenda Frese
2007	Tennessee	59-46	Rutgers	Pat Summitt

NCAA Women's Division I Alltime Individual Leaders

Single-Game Records

SCORING HIGHS

Pts	Player and Team vs Opponent	Year
60	Cindy Brown, Long Beach St vs San Jose St	1987
58	Kim Perrot, SW Louisiana vs SE Louisiana	1990
58	Lorri Bauman, Drake vs SW Missouri St*	1984
56	Jackie Stiles, SW Missouri St vs Evansville	2000
55	Patricia Hoskins, Mississippi Valley St vs Southern-Birm.	1989
55	Patricia Hoskins, Mississippi Valley St vs Alabama St	1989
54	Anjinea Hopson, Grambling vs Jackson St	1994
54	Mary Lowry, Baylor vs Texas	1994
54	Wanda Ford, Drake vs SW Missouri St*	1986

Three tied with 53.

REBOUNDS

Reb	Player and Team vs Opponent	Year
40	Deborah Temple, Delta St vs UAB	1983
37	Rosina Pearson, Bethune-Cookman vs Florida Memorial	1985
33	Maureen Formico, Pepperdine vs Loyola (Calif.)	1985
32	Lachelle Lyles, Southeast Mo. St. vs Tennessee St.	2006
31	Darlene Beale, Howard vs South Carolina St	1987
30	Cindy Bonforte, Wagner vs Queens (N.Y.)	1983
30	Kayone Hankins, New Orleans vs. Nicholls St	1994
30	Wanda Ford, Drake vs Eastern Illinois	1985
30	Jennifer Butler, Massachusetts vs Florida	2003

Three tied with 29.

ASSISTS

Asst	Player and Team vs Opponent	Year
23	Michelle Burden, Kent St vs Ball St	1991
22	Shawn Monday, Tennessee Tech vs Morehead St	1988
22	Veronica Pettry, Loyola (Ill.) vs Detroit	1989
22	Tine Freil, Pacific vs Wichita St	1991
21	Tine Freil, Pacific vs Fresno St	1992
21	Amy Bauer, Wisconsin vs Detroit	1989
21	Neacole Hall, Alabama St vs Southern-Birm.	1989

Six tied with 20.

*school changed name to Missouri State after 2004–05 season

Single Season Records

POINTS

Player and Team	Year	GP	FG	3FG	FT	Pts
Jackie Stiles, SW Missouri St*	2001	35	365	65	267	1062
Cindy Brown, Long Beach St	1987	35	362	—	250	974
Genia Miller, CSU-Fullerton	1991	33	376	0	217	969
Sheryl Swoopes, Texas Tech	1993	34	356	32	211	955
Andrea Congreaves, Mercer	1992	28	353	77	142	925
Wanda Ford, Drake	1986	30	390	—	139	919
Chamique Holdsclaw, Tennessee	1998	39	370	9	166	915
Barbara Kennedy, Clemson	1982	31	392	—	124	908
Patricia Hoskins, Mississippi Valley St	1989	27	345	13	205	908
LaTaunya Pollard, Long Beach St	1983	31	376	—	155	907

SEASON SCORING AVERAGE

Player and Team	Year	GP	FG	3FG	FT	Pts	Avg
Patricia Hoskins, Mississippi Valley St	1989	27	345	13	205	908	33.6
Andrea Congreaves, Mercer	1992	28	353	77	142	925	33.0
Deborah Temple, Delta St	1984	28	373	—	127	873	31.2
Andrea Congreaves, Mercer	1993	26	302	51	150	805	31.0
Wanda Ford, Drake	1986	30	390	—	139	919	30.6
Anucha Browne, Northwestern	1985	28	341	—	173	855	30.5
LeChandra LeDay, Grambling	1988	28	334	36	146	850	30.4
Jackie Stiles, SW MIssouri St*	2001	35	365	65	267	1062	30.3
Kim Perrot, SW Louisiana	1990	28	308	95	128	839	30.0
Tina Hutchinson, San Diego St	1984	30	383	—	132	898	29.9
Jan Jensen, Drake	1991	30	358	6	166	888	29.6
Genia Miller, CSU-Fullerton	1991	33	376	0	217	969	29.4
Barbara Kennedy, Clemson	1982	31	392	—	124	908	29.3
LaTaunya Pollard, Long Beach St	1983	31	376	—	155	907	29.3
Lisa McMullen, Alabama St	1991	28	285	126	119	815	29.1

REBOUNDS

Player and Team	Year	GP	Reb	Player and Team	Year	GP	Reb
Courtney Paris, Oklahoma	2006	36	539	Darlene Jones, Miss Valley St	1983	31	487
Wanda Ford, Drake	1985	30	534	Melanie Simpson, Okla. City	1982	37	481
Lachelle Lyles, SE Missouri St	2006	30	517	R. Pearson, Beth.-Cookman	1985	26	480
Wanda Ford, Drake	1986	30	506	Patricia Hoskins, Miss. Valley St	1987	28	476
Anne Donovan, Old Dominion	1983	35	504	Cheryl Miller, USC	1985	30	474

REBOUND AVERAGE

Player and Team	Year	GP	Reb	Avg
Rosina Pearson, Bethune-Cookman	1985	26	480	18.5
Wanda Ford, Drake	1985	30	534	17.8
Katie Beck, East Tennessee St	1988	25	441	17.6
DeShawne Blocker, East Tennessee St	1994	26	450	17.3
Lachelle Lyles, SE Missouri St.	2006	30	517	17.2
Patricia Hoskins, Mississippi Valley St	1987	28	476	17.0
Wanda Ford, Drake	1986	30	506	16.9
Patricia Hoskins, Mississippi Valley St	1989	27	440	16.3
Joy Kellogg, Oklahoma City	1984	23	373	16.2
Courtney Paris, Oklahoma	2006	30	485	16.2
Deborah Mitchell, Mississippi Coll.	1983	28	447	16.0
Cheryl Miller, USC	1985	30	474	15.8

*school changed name to Missouri State after 2004–05 season

Single Season Records (Cont.)

FIELD-GOAL PERCENTAGE

Player and Team	Year	GP	FG	FGA	Pct
Myndee Larsen, Southern Utah	1998	28	249	344	72.4
Chantelle Anderson, Vanderbilt	2001	34	292	404	72.3
Deneka Knowles, SE Louisiana	1996	26	199	276	72.1
Crystal Langhorne, Maryland	2006	32	202	280	72.1
Barbara Farris, Tulane	1998	27	151	210	71.9
Renay Adams, Tennessee Tech	1991	30	185	258	71.7
Regina Days, Georgia Southern	1986	27	234	332	70.5
Kim Wood, UW-Green Bay	1994	27	188	271	69.4
Kelly Lyons, Old Dominion	1990	31	308	444	69.4
Alisha Hill, Howard	1995	28	194	281	69.0

Based on qualifiers for annual championship.

FREE-THROW PERCENTAGE

Player and Team	Year	GP	FT	FTA	Pct
Adrienne Squire, Penn St	2006	29	80	83	96.4
Shanna Zolman, Tennessee	2004	35	88	92	95.7
Ginny Doyle, Richmond	1992	29	96	101	95.0
Jill Marano, La Salle	2003	29	88	93	94.6
Sue Bird, Connecticut	2002	39	98	104	94.2
Paula Corder-King, SE Missouri St	1999	28	111	118	94.1
Kandi Brown, Morehead St	2003	28	104	111	93.7
Linda Cyborski, Delaware	1991	29	74	79	93.7
Kandi Brown, Morehead St	2002	29	74	79	93.7
Kristin Iwanaga, California	2005	29	85	91	93.4

Based on qualifiers for annual championship.

Career Records

POINTS

Player and Team	Yrs	GP	Pts
Jackie Stiles, SW Missouri St*	1997–01	129	3393
Patricia Hoskins, Mississippi Valley St	1985–89	110	3122
Lorri Bauman, Drake	1981–84	120	3115
Chamique Holdsclaw, Tennessee	1995–99	148	3025
Cheryl Miller, USC	1983–86	128	3018
Cindy Blodgett, Maine	1994–98	118	3005
LaToya Thomas, Mississippi St	1999–2003	125	2981
Valorie Whiteside, Appalachian St	1984–88	116	2944
Kelly Mazzante, Penn St	2000–04	133	2919
Joyce Walker, LSU	1981–84	117	2906

SCORING AVERAGE

Player and Team	Yrs	GP	FG	3FG	FT	Pts	Avg
Patricia Hoskins, Mississippi Valley St	1985–89	110	1196	24	706	3122	28.4
Sandra Hodge, New Orleans	1981–84	107	1194	—	472	2860	26.7
Jackie Stiles, SW Missouri St*	1997–01	129	1160	221	852	3393	26.3
Lorri Bauman, Drake	1981–84	120	1104	—	907	3115	26.0
Andrea Congreaves, Mercer	1989–93	108	1107	153	429	2796	25.9
Cindy Blodgett, Maine	1994–98	118	1055	219	676	3005	25.5
Valorie Whiteside, Appalachian St	1984–88	116	1153	0	638	2944	25.4
Joyce Walker, LSU	1981–84	117	1259	—	388	2906	24.8
Tarcha Hollis, Grambling	1988–91	85	904	3	247	2058	24.2
Korie Hlede, Duquesne	1994–98	109	1045	162	379	2631	24.1

*school changed name to Missouri State after 2004–05 season

Year	Winner	Score	Runner-up	Third Place	Fourth Place
1957	Wheaton (Ill.)	89–65	Kentucky Wesleyan	Mt. St. Mary's (Md.)	CSU-Los Angeles
1958	South Dakota	75–53	St. Michael's	Evansville	Wheaton (Ill.)
1959	Evansville	83–67	SW Missouri St	North Carolina A&T	CSU-Los Angeles
1960	Evansville	90–69	Chapman	Kentucky Wesleyan	Cornell College
1961	Wittenberg	42–38	SE Missouri St	South Dakota St	Mt. St. Mary's (Md.)
1962	Mt. St. Mary's (Md.)	58–57 (OT)	CSU-Sacramento	Southern Illinois	Nebraska Wesleyan
1963	South Dakota St	44–42	Wittenberg	Oglethorpe	Southern Illinois
1964	Evansville	72–59	Akron	North Carolina A&T	Northern Iowa
1965	Evansville	85–82 (OT)	Southern Illinois	North Dakota	St. Michael's
1966	Kentucky Wesleyan	54–51	Southern Illinois	Akron	North Dakota
1967	Winston-Salem	77–74	SW Missouri St	Kentucky Wesleyan	Illinois St
1968	Kentucky Wesleyan	63–52	Indiana St	Trinity (Tex.)	Ashland
1969	Kentucky Wesleyan	75–71	SW Missouri St	†Vacated	Ashland
1970	Philadelphia Textile	76–65	Tennessee St	UC-Riverside	Buffalo St
1971	Evansville	97–82	Old Dominion	†Vacated	Kentucky Wesleyan
1972	Roanoke	84–72	Akron	Tennessee St	Eastern Mich
1973	Kentucky Wesleyan	78–76 (OT)	Tennessee St	Assumption	Brockport St
1974	Morgan St	67–52	SW Missouri St	Assumption	New Orleans
1975	Old Dominion	76–74	New Orleans	Assumption	Tenn.-Chattanooga
1976	Puget Sound	83–74	Tenn.-Chattanooga	Eastern Illinois	Old Dominion
1977	Tenn.-Chattanooga	71–62	Randolph-Macon	North Alabama	Sacred Heart
1978	Cheyney	47–40	UW-Green Bay	Eastern Illinois	Central Florida
1979	North Alabama	64–50	UW-Green Bay	Cheyney	Bridgeport
1980	Virginia Union	80–74	New York Tech	Florida Southern	North Alabama
1981	Florida Southern	73–68	Mt. St. Mary's (Md.)	Cal Poly-SLO	UW-Green Bay
1982	District of Columbia	73–63	Florida Southern	Kentucky Wesleyan	CSU-Bakersfield
1983	Wright St	92–73	District of Columbia	*CSU-Bakersfield	*Morningside
1984	Central Missouri St	81–77	St. Augustine's	*Kentucky Wesleyan	*N Alabama
1985	Jacksonville St	74–73	South Dakota St	*Kentucky Wesleyan	*Mt. St. Mary's (Md.)
1986	Sacred Heart	93–87	SE Missouri St	*Cheyney	*Florida Southern
1987	Kentucky Wesleyan	92–74	Gannon	*Delta St	*Eastern Montana
1988	Lowell	75–72	Ak.-Anchorage	Florida Southern	Troy St
1989	North Carolina Central	73–46	SE Missouri St	UC-Riverside	Jacksonville St
1990	Kentucky Wesleyan	93–79	CSU-Bakersfield	North Dakota	Morehouse
1991	North Alabama	79–72	Bridgeport (Conn.)	*CSU-Bakersfield	*Virginia Union
1992	Virginia Union	100–75	Bridgeport (Conn.)	*CSU-Bakersfield	*California (Pa.)
1993	CSU-Bakersfield	85–72	Troy St (Ala.)	*New Hampshire Coll	*Wayne St (Mich.)
1994	CSU-Bakersfield	92–86	Southern Indiana	*New Hampshire Coll	*Washburn
1995	Southern Indiana	71–63	UC-Riverside	*Norfolk St	*Indiana (Pa.)
1996	Fort Hays St	70–63	Northern Kentucky	*California (Pa.)	*Virginia Union
1997	CSU-Bakersfield	57–56	Northern Kentucky	*Lynn	*Salem-Teikyo
1998	UC-Davis	83–77	Kentucky Wesleyan	*St. Rose	*Virginia Union
1999	Kentucky Wesleyan	75–60	Metropolitan St	*Truman St	*Florida Southern
2000	Metropolitan St	97–79	Kentucky Wesleyan	*Missouri Southern	*Seattle Pacific
2001	Kentucky Wesleyan	72–63	Washburn	*Western Washington	*Tampa
2002	Metropolitan St	80–72	Kentucky Wesleyan	*Shaw	*Indiana (Pa.)
2003	Northeastern St (Okla.)	75–64	†Vacated	*Bowie St	*Queens (N.Y.)
2004	Kennesaw St	84–59	Southern Indiana	*Humboldt St	*Metropolitan St
2005	Virginia Union	63–58	Bryant	*Lynn	*Tarleton St
2006	Winona St (Minn.)	73–61	Virginia Union	*Seattle Pacific	*Stonehill
2007	Barton	77–75	Winona St (Minn.)	*CSU-San Bernardino	*Central Missouri

*tied for third place

*Indicates tied for third. †Student-athletes representing American International in 1969, Southwestern Louisiana in 1971, and Kentucky Wesleyan in 2003 were declared ineligible subsequent to the tournament. Under NCAA rules, the teams' and ineligible student-athletes' records were deleted, and the teams' places in the final standings were vacated.

SINGLE-GAME SCORING HIGHS

Pts	Player and Team vs Opponent	Date
113	Bevo Francis, Rio Grande vs Hillsdale	1954
84	Bevo Francis, Rio Grande vs Alliance	1954
82	Bevo Francis, Rio Grande vs Bluffton	1954
80	Paul Crissman, USC vs Pacific Christian	1966
77	William English, Winston-Salem vs Fayetteville St	1968

Single Season Records

SCORING AVERAGE

Player and Team	Year	GP	FG	FT	Pts	Avg
Bevo Francis, Rio Grande	1954	27	444	367	1255	46.5
Earl Glass, Mississippi Industrial	1963	19	322	171	815	42.9
Earl Monroe, Winston-Salem	1967	32	509	311	1329	41.5
John Rinka, Kenyon	1970	23	354	234	942	41.0
Willie Shaw, Lane	1964	18	303	121	727	40.4

REBOUND AVERAGE

Player and Team	Year	GP	Reb	Avg
Tom Hart, Middlebury	1956	21	620	29.5
Tom Hart, Middlebury	1955	22	649	29.5
Frank Stronczek, American Int'l	1966	26	717	27.6
R.C. Owens, College of Idaho	1954	25	677	27.1
Maurice Stokes, St. Francis (Pa.)	1954	26	689	26.5

ASSISTS

Player and Team	Year	GP	Asst
Steve Ray, Bridgeport	1989	32	400
Steve Ray, Bridgeport	1990	33	385
Tony Smith, Pfeiffer	1992	35	349
Jim Ferrer, Bentley	1989	31	309
Rob Paternostro, New Hamp. Coll.	1995	33	309

ASSIST AVERAGE

Player and Team	Year	GP	Asst	Avg
Steve Ray, Bridgeport	1989	32	400	12.5
Steve Ray, Bridgeport	1990	33	385	11.7
Demetri Beekman, Assumption	1993	23	264	11.5
Ernest Jenkins, N.M.-Highlands	1995	27	291	10.8
Brian Gregory, Oakland	1989	28	300	10.7

FIELD-GOAL PERCENTAGE

Player and Team	Year	Pct
Todd Linder, Tampa	1987	75.2
Maurice Stafford, North Alabama	1984	75.0
Matthew Cornegay, Tuskegee	1982	74.8
Callistus Eziukwu, Grand Valley St	2005	73.7
Brian Moten, W. Georgia	1992	73.4

FREE-THROW PERCENTAGE

Player and Team	Year	Pct
Paul Cluxton, Northern Kentucky	1997	100.0
Tomas Rimkus, Pace	1997	95.6
C.J. Cowgill, Chaminade	2001	95.0
Billy Newton, Morgan St	1976	94.4
Kent Andrews, McNeese St	1968	94.4

Career Records

POINTS

Player and Team	Yrs	Pts
Travis Grant, Kentucky St	1969–72	4045
Bob Hopkins, Grambling	1953–56	3759
Tony Smith, Pfeiffer	1989–92	3350
Earnest Lee, Clark Atlanta	1984–87	3298
Joe Miller, Alderson-Broaddus	1954–57	3294

CAREER SCORING AVERAGE

Player and Team	Yrs	GP	Pts	Avg
Travis Grant, Kentucky St	1969–72	121	4045	33.4
John Rinka, Kenyon	1967–70	99	3251	32.8
Florindo Vieira, Quinnipiac	1954–57	69	2263	32.8
Willie Shaw, Lane	1961–64	76	2379	31.3
Mike Davis, Virginia Union	1966–69	89	2758	31.0

REBOUND AVERAGE

Player and Team	Yrs	GP	Reb	Avg
Tom Hart, Middlebury	1953, 55–56	63	1738	27.6
Maurice Stokes, St. Francis (Pa.)	1953–55	72	1812	25.2
Frank Stronczek, American Int'l	1965–67	62	1549	25.0
Bill Thieben, Hofstra	1954–56	76	1837	24.2
Hank Brown, Lowell Tech	1965–67	49	1129	23.0

Career Records (Cont.)

ASSISTS

Player and Team	Yrs	Asst
Demetri Beekman, Assumption	1990–93	1044
Adam Kaufman, Edinboro	1998–01	936
Rob Paternostro, New Hamp. Coll.	1992–95	919
Tony Smith, Pfeiffer	1989–92	828
Jamie Stevens, MSU-Billings	1996–99	805

ASSIST AVERAGE

Player and Team	Yrs	GP	Asst	Avg
Steve Ray, Bridgeport	1989-90	65	785	12.1
Demetri Beekman, Assumption	1990–93	119	1044	8.8
Ernest Jenkins, N.M.-Highlands	1992-95	84	699	8.3
Zack Whiting, Chaminade	2004–07	86	703	8.2
Adam Kaufman, Edinboro	1998-01	116	936	8.1

Note: Minimum 550 Assists.

FIELD-GOAL PERCENTAGE

Player and Team	Yrs	Pct
Todd Linder, Tampa	1984–87	70.8
Tom Schurfranz, Bellarmine	1989–92	70.2
Chad Scott, California (Pa.)	1991–94	70.0
Ed Phillips, Alabama A&M	1968–71	68.9
Ulysses Hackett, SC-Spartanburg	1990–92	67.9

Note: Minimum 400 FGM.

FREE-THROW PERCENTAGE

Player and Team	Yrs	Pct
Paul Cluxton, Northern Kentucky	1994-97	93.5
Kent Andrews, McNeese St	1967-69	91.6
Jon Hagen, Minnesota St–Mankato	1963-65	90.0
Lance Den Boer, Central Wash.	2005–07	89.4
Dave Reynolds, Davis & Elkins	1986-89	89.3

Note: Minimum 250 FTM.

NCAA Men's Division III Championship Results

Year	Winner	Score	Runner-up	Third Place	Fourth Place
1975	LeMoyne-Owen	57–54	Glassboro St	Augustana (Ill.)	Brockport St
1976	Scranton	60–57	Wittenberg	Augustana (Ill.)	Plattsburgh St
1977	Wittenberg	79–66	Oneonta St	Scranton	Hamline
1978	North Park	69–57	Widener	Albion	Stony Brook
1979	North Park	66–62	Potsdam St	Franklin & Marshall	Centre
1980	North Park	83–76	Upsala	Wittenberg	Longwood
1981	Potsdam St	67–65 (OT)	Augustana (Ill.)	Ursinus	Otterbein
1982	Wabash	83–62	Potsdam St	Brooklyn	CSU-Stanislaus
1983	Scranton	64–63	Wittenberg	Roanoke	UW–Whitewater
1984	UW–Whitewater	103–86	Clark (Mass.)	DePauw	Upsala
1985	North Park	72–71	Potsdam St	Nebraska Wesleyan	Widener
1986	Potsdam St	76–73	LeMoyne-Owen	Nebraska Wesleyan	Jersey City St
1987	North Park	106–100	Clark (Mass.)	Wittenberg	Stockton St
1988	Ohio Wesleyan	92–70	Scranton	Nebraska Wesleyan	Hartwick
1989	UW–Whitewater	94–86	Trenton St	Southern Maine	Centre
1990	Rochester	43–42	DePauw	Washington (Md.)	Calvin
1991	UW–Platteville	81–74	Franklin & Marshall	Otterbein	Ramapo (N.J.)
1992	Calvin	62–49	Rochester	UW–Platteville	Jersey City St
1993	Ohio Northern	71–68	Augustana	Mass.–Dartmouth	Rowan
1994	Lebanon Valley Coll	66–59 (OT)	NYU	Wittenberg	St Thomas (Minn.)
1995	UW–Platteville	69–55	Manchester	Rowan	Trinity (Conn.)
1996	Rowan	100–93	Hope (Mich.)	Illinois Wesleyan	Franklin & Marshall
1997	Illinois Wesleyan	89–86	Nebraska Wesleyan	Williams	Alvernia
1998	UW–Platteville	69–56	Hope (Mich.)	Williams	Wilkes
1999	UW–Platteville	76–75 (2 OT)	Hampden-Sydney	William Paterson	Connecticut Coll.
2000	Calvin	79–74	UW-Eau Claire	Salem St	Franklin & Marshall
2001	Catholic	76–62	William Paterson	Illinois Wesleyan	Ohio Northern
2002	Otterbein	102–83	Elizabethtown	Carthage	Rochester
2003	Williams	67–65	Gustavus Adolphus	Wooster	Hampden Sydney
2004	UW–Stevens Point	84–82	Williams	John Carroll	Amherst
2005	UW–Stevens Point	73–49	Rochester	Calvin	York
2006	Virginia Wesleyan	59–56	Wittenberg	Illinois Wesleyan	Amherst
2007	Amherst	80–67	Virginia Wesleyan	Washington (Mo.)	Wooster

SINGLE-GAME SCORING HIGHS

Pts	Player and Team vs Opponent	Year
77	Jeff Clement, Grinnell vs Illinois College	1998
69	Steve Diekmann, Grinnell vs Simpson	1995
64	Tim Russell, Albertus Magnus	2005
63	Ryan Hodges, Cal-Lutheran	2005
63	Joe DeRoche, Thomas vs St. Joseph's (Me.)	1988
62	Kyle Myrick, Lincoln (Pa.) vs. Penn St.-Abington	2006
62	Nick Pelotte, Plymouth St	2005
62	Shannon Lilly, Bishop vs Southwest Assembly of God	1983
61	Steve Honderd, Calvin vs Kalamazoo	1993
61	Dana Wilson, Husson vs Ricker	1974

Single Season Records

SCORING AVERAGE

Player and Team	Year	GP	FG	FT	Pts	Avg
Steve Diekmann, Grinnell	1995	20	223	162	745	37.3
Rickey Sutton, Lyndon St	1976	14	207	93	507	36.2
Shannon Lilly, Bishop	1983	26	345	218	908	34.9
Dana Wilson, Husson	1974	20	288	122	698	34.9
Rickey Sutton, Lyndon St	1977	16	223	112	558	34.9

REBOUND AVERAGE

Player and Team	Year	GP	Reb	Avg
Joe Manley, Bowie St	1976	29	579	20.0
Fred Petty, New Hampshire Coll.	1974	22	436	19.8
Larry Williams, Pratt	1977	24	457	19.0
Charles Greer, Thomas	1977	17	318	18.7
Larry Parker, Plattsburgh St	1975	23	430	18.7

ASSISTS

Player and Team	Year	GP	Asst
Robert James, Kean	1989	29	391
Tennyson Whitted, Ramapo	2002	29	319
Ricky Spicer, UW-Whitewater	1989	31	295
Joe Marcotte, New Jersey Tech	1995	30	292
Andre Bolton, Chris. Newport	1996	30	289

ASSIST AVERAGE

Player and Team	Year	GP	Asst	Avg
Robert James, Kean	1989	29	391	13.5
Albert Kirchner, Mt. St. Vincent	1990	24	267	11.1
Tennyson Whitted, Ramapo	2002	29	319	11.0
Ron Torgalski, Hamilton	1989	26	275	10.6
Louis Adams, Rust	1989	22	227	10.3

FIELD-GOAL PERCENTAGE

Player and Team	Year	Pct
Travis Weiss, St. John's (Minn.)	1994	76.6
Brian Schmitting, Ripon	2006	76.3
Pete Metzelaars, Wabash	1982	75.3
Tony Rychlec, Mass. Maritime	1981	74.9
Tony Rychlec, Mass. Maritime	1982	73.1

FREE-THROW PERCENTAGE

Player and Team	Year	Pct
Korey Coon, Illinois Wesleyan	2000	96.3
Chanse Young, Manchester	1998	95.6
Andy Enfield, Johns Hopkins	1991	95.3
Nick Wilkins, Coe	2003	95.7
Chris Carideo, Widener	1992	95.2

Career Records

POINTS

Player and Team	Yrs	Pts
Andre Foreman, Salisbury St	1989–92	2940
Willie Chandler, Misericordia	2000–03	2898
Lamont Strothers, Chris. Newport	1988–91	2709
Matt Hancock, Colby	1987–90	2678
Scott Fitch, Geneseo St	1990–94	2634

SCORING AVERAGE

Player and Team	Yrs	GP	Avg
Dwain Govan, Bishop	1974–75	55	32.8
Dave Russell, Shepherd	1974–75	60	30.6
Kyle Myrick, Lincoln (Pa.)	2005–06	57	30.2
Rickey Sutton, Lyndon St	1976–79	80	29.7
John Atkins, Knoxville	1976–78	70	28.7

REBOUND AVERAGE

Player and Team	Yrs	GP	Reb	Avg
Larry Parker, Plattsburgh St.	1975–78	85	1482	17.4
Charles Greer, Thomas	1975–77	58	926	16.0
Willie Parr, LeMoyne-Owen	1974–76	76	1182	15.6
Michael Smith, Hamilton	1989–92	107	1632	15.2
Dave Kufeld, Yeshiva	1977–80	81	1222	15.1

ASSIST AVERAGE

Player and Team	Yrs	Avg
Phil Dixon, Shenandoah	1993–96	8.6
Tennyson Whitted, Ramapo	2000–03	8.5
Steve Artis, Chris. Newport	1990–93	8.1
David Genovese, Mt. St. Vincent	1992–95	7.5
Kevin Root, Eureka	1989–91	7.1

Hockey

Brothers Rob (l.) and Scott
Niedermayer of the
Stanley Cup champion
Anaheim Ducks

Old-School Cool

As part of the NHL's continued resurgence, a throwback Anaheim Ducks team cruised to the Cup title and made hockey hip in Hollywood. So why wasn't anyone watching?

BY B.J. SCHECTER

PITY THE NHL. THE LEAGUE had one of the worst work stoppages in the history of professional sports, during which the season was canceled and few in the United States seemed to care. But somehow the NHL recovered from that and came back in 2005–06 stronger than ever with a financially sound business model and an exciting brand of hockey. To a man, the game continued to grow a season later with full arenas (if you believe the inflated attendance figures), thrilling hockey (for those who watched it) and emerging young stars. But to the average American sports fan (not to mention television executives), the game remained irrelevant.

It's too bad; watch any NHL playoff game or venture up to Canada for a regular-season Ottawa Senators-Toronto Maple Leafs blood war and you'll come away entertained. But if a thrilling game takes place in the middle of a pond in Quebec with nobody around, does it count? Or if a major television network cuts away from a conference final with the score tied at the end of regulation for a horse-racing pre-show, is it important?

The latter happened during Game 5 of the Eastern Conference finals between the Ottawa Senators and Buffalo Sabres. With the score tied at 2–2 heading into overtime, NBC decided to switch to its pre-Preakness coverage just before 6 p.m. in the East. The network claimed that it kept the game on in Buffalo and made it clear that the overtime would be shown on Versus, the NHL's cable-television partner. Problem was, not many households got Versus and the abrupt switch was a huge slap in the face to a league that tried to fashion itself as a major player in American sports. (For the record, Ottawa captain Daniel Alfredsson fired home the game-winner at 9:32 of overtime to lift the Senators to a series-clinching 3–2 victory.)

It's hard to blame NBC. Ratings are king in the television business and the NHL simply wasn't pulling its weight. Case in point: the abysmal viewership for the Stanley Cup Final on NBC. The series-ending game received a 1.8 rating, which translates into just over 2 million households. By comparison, a soccer game, the CONCACAF Gold Cup final between the United States and Mexico drew a 2.5 rating or 2.83 million households—on Spanish-language station Univision. And if you didn't see the games on television, you weren't likely to read much about the games other than a wire story. Many major newspapers, including the *Washington Post*, *Dallas Morning News*,

Chicago Tribune and *Detroit News* (where hockey is extremely popular) chose not to send writers to the Finals.

Those who didn't pay attention to the Final (or the playoffs for that matter) missed out on quite a team. On the surface, the name Anaheim Ducks doesn't exactly strike fear into opponents (the team dropped the "Mighty" from their name before the start of the season). But beneath those ducky sweaters was the toughest team in the NHL and one that bear some resemblance to the New York Islanders dynasty of the 1980s. Rugged, not afraid to take penalties (many senseless) and possessing the ability to score goals in bunches or win ugly, the Ducks were an extremely difficult matchup.

"Those Islanders teams [of the '80s] could skate with you, play offense or defense, beat you in an alley, beat you 1–0 or 5–4," said Ducks defenseman Sean O'Donnell. "I'd never compare us to a dynasty, but I think the styles or play are similar."

Despite scoring a league-high 14 goals and 22 points in the playoffs, Ottawa Senators captain Daniel Alfredsson still wasn't able to bring the Stanley Cup back to Canada.

That style included using size and intimidation to control play. Led by captain Scott Niedermayer, whose punishing playing style helped the New Jersey Devils win three Cups in nine years, and hard-hitting 6'6" bruiser Chris Pronger, Anaheim bullied its way to the top of the hockey world. "This is the toughest team I've ever played on, up and down the lineup," said Pronger, a 13-year veteran.

The Ducks dominated the playoffs and turned back the red-hot Senators in the Final in five games. In becoming the first California team to win the Cup and denying Canada a silver chalice once again (the last Canadian team to win a Stanley Cup was the Montreal Canadiens in 1993) Anaheim brought hockey to Hollywood.

Celebrities, including Academy Award-winner Cuba Gooding Jr., Jerry Bruckheimer, Kevin James, Snoop Dogg and Jerry O'Connell, flocked to the games in California. Gooding Jr. attended all three games in Anaheim, and after the Game 5 clincher sprayed champagne in the locker room with the players. "This is intense," Gooding Jr. said. "It doesn't get any better than this. It's awesome. I predicted they'd win in five games and they did. I love that the Cup is in California."

Even Governor Arnold Schwarzenegger made it to Game 1, making a grand entrance during which security shoved aside NHL Commissioner Gary Bettman and NBC Sports Chairman Dick Ebersol to make way for the Governator. When all was said and done, the Ducks had made it cool for fans and celebrities alike from Tinseltown make the trek down to Orange County.

"This is amazing," said O'Connell, before echoing a truly Hollywood sentiment. "I know this is going to make me sound like I have awful loyalty, but in Southern California you really can't be a Kings fan anymore. You have to cheer for the Ducks. They're the most exciting team in hockey and there's nothing like watching a championship team."

There's also nothing like watching a pair of brothers fulfill their lifelong dream by hoisting the Stanley Cup together. Scott and Rob Niedermayer grew up in Cranbrook, B.C., in a hockey family. Their mother, Carol, taught power skating at a local rink, and in lieu of salary she was paid in ice time. The Niedermayers have always been good skaters, but once they reached the NHL the brother's careers went in different directions.

Scott, who is 16 months older than Rob, won three Cups with the New Jersey Devils, beating the Dallas Stars in the 2003 Finals. The brothers were reunited in 2005 with Scott assuming the Captain's role and Rob being named an Alternate. When the Ducks finally won the Cup, teammates and fans were ecstatic for the Niedermayers. As Anaheim celebrated on the ice many wondered what Scott would do once he was handed the Cup from Bettman.

Protocol dictates that the Captain hand the Cup to the most senior Alternate, which in this case was Pronger. But nobody was expecting it to happen and it didn't. The most decorated cup in North America was passed from one Niedermayer to another and soon the brothers were hoisting the hardware together to a raucous ovation.

"Obviously it seemed like the right thing," Scott Niedermayer, who won the Conn Smythe Trophy as the MVP of the playoffs. "I didn't stop to check who had played more games, but I didn't think anyone would hold this against me. I was using Captain's prerogative.

"People sometimes ask you to rate [Cups]. I've never done that, and I'm not going to start now. But you can only dream of passing it to your brother. And to be able to do that is definitely a highlight of my career. It was tough to enjoy the Cup [in Cranbrook] when one has won it and the other hasn't. Now we'll get to keep it for two days...maybe three."

What did Rob Niedermayer say to his older brother when he handed him the Cup? Rob was at a loss for words. "It was tough coming up with something," said Rob Niedermayer. "I think I said, 'Thanks for winning the Cup for me.' And I know I told him that I love him."

In two seasons, hockey fans have fallen in love with phenom Sidney Crosby. Labeled as the next Gretzky and hockey's savior since Juniors, Crosby delivered, and with each smooth stride down the ice he became the face of the sport. Drafted to an abysmal Pittsburgh Penguins club in 2005, Crosby helped turn around the franchise.

Crosby led the Penguins to a 47–24–11 record and a No. 5 seed in the Eastern Conference playoffs in 2006–07 with a record-setting season. The 19-year-old wunderkind became the youngest scoring champion in major professional sports history with 120 points (36 goals, 84 assists) and became the second-youngest player behind Gretzky to win the Hart Trophy as the league's MVP.

More importantly, he earned the respect of veteran players. "He's going to make this game better for a lot of years like Wayne

LOU CAPOZZOLA

19-year-old Sidney Crosby continued to live up to high expectations, leading the NHL in scoring, and winning his first Hart Trophy.

Gretzky did," said New Jersey's Martin Brodeur, who won the Vezina Trophy as the league's top goaltender.

Crosby's first foray into the playoffs was a learning experience. Matched up against the rugged Senators, Crosby and the Penguins were embarrassed 6–3 in Game 1, but Crosby was already thinking ahead counseling the team in the game's final moments. "The first game was average," said Crosby, "and I don't accept being average. I have to be one play ahead. And at times I wasn't. No doubt I have better in me."

He did, dishing out an assist and scoring the game-winner in Game 2, and following that up with another goal and assist in a 4–2 Game 3 loss. But alas, it wasn't meant to be as the Penguins were overwhelmed and elimated in five games. For Crosby, who later admitted that he played the last 2½ weeks of the regular season and the playoffs with a broken left foot, it was humbling.

"We had two games where I think we were trying to get our feet wet, and we got caught watching," said Crosby. "That's not going to happen again. We had a good regular season. It was a tough ending, but I think we exceeded a lot of expectations. We'll have to learn from this."

As Crosby matures and carries the Penguins into a new era, the NHL will have to learn how to become a major player in American sports again. With the feisty and perpetually upbeat Bettman leading the charge, the league is in good hands, but still has a long way to go. On one hand, Bettman said NHL revenue increased seven percent in 2006–07 and the salary cap will probably

Despite a modest revenue increase and packed arenas, NHL Commissioner Gary Bettman saw the league's TV ratings sink lower in 2007.

game, don't watch it as much on TV in the United States as we'd all like. We don't need to apologize to anybody for who we are. We like who we are. We think we're special."

If the NHL is to carry Bettman's vision, riding the likes of Crosby and a healthy group of young stars, it needs to define itself as more than a niche sport. Yes, the game is as strong as ever in Canada and moving a team or two north of the border wouldn't hurt. But it needs to find more of a television presence. The occasional appearance on NBC and a deal with the unknown and hard-to-find Versus network won't cut it. The league does have the advantage of much more tradition than up-and-coming sports like NASCAR and Ultimate Fighting, but to survive in today's marketplace it needs to grow, not just financially, but also in the minds of American sports fans.

"This isn't a 60-minute game," Bettman said. "This game gets played year after year and generation after generation. We've been around since 1917. We'll be around for hundreds of years. I'm not concerned. In fact, I'm optimistic."

Back in Anaheim, Ducks fans share the commissioner's optimism. With their first Cup in hand, the Ducks, despite the name change, were indeed mighty. And with several stars embracing hockey, the sport was in the spotlight for a Hollywood minute. But like many things in Los Angeles, stars tend to fade quickly. And if the NHL is to remain relevant in the mainstream American sports culture, it must find a way to shine bright from coast to coast.

rise from $44 million to $50.3 million for the 2007–08 season. That's the good news, but when tradition-rich areas like Detroit can't sell out a single playoff game and you're relying on places like Atlanta, Nashville and Columbus (hockey hotbeds not) to boost the bottom line, you have your work cut out for you.

Hard work has never fazed Bettman, and if you ask the commissioner, the horrible TV ratings are explainable. "We are what we are, and we think we're pretty good," he said. "This is a business that will close with close to $2.4 billion in revenue. We play to virtually 100-percent capacity in the playoffs. Research shows that we have somewhere around 50 million fans. Our visits to NHL.com are growing dramatically. Nielsen TV ratings are but one measure. It doesn't define us. What it tells you is people who follow this game, who are passionate about the

2007 NHL Final Standings

Eastern Conference

NORTHEAST DIVISION

	GP	W	L	OTL	Pts	GF	GA
Buffalo	82	53	22	7	113	308	242
*Ottawa	82	48	25	9	105	288	222
Toronto	82	40	31	11	91	258	269
Montreal	82	42	34	6	90	245	256
Boston	82	35	41	6	76	219	289

ATLANTIC DIVISION

	GP	W	L	OTL	Pts	GF	GA
New Jersey	82	49	24	9	107	216	210
*Pittsburgh	82	47	24	11	105	277	246
*NY Rangers	82	42	30	10	94	242	216
*NY Islanders	82	40	30	12	92	248	240
Philadelphia	82	22	48	12	56	214	303

SOUTHEAST DIVISION

	GP	W	L	OTL	Pts	GF	GA
Atlanta	82	43	28	11	97	246	245
*Tampa Bay	82	44	33	5	93	253	261
Carolina	82	40	34	8	88	241	253
Florida	82	35	31	16	86	247	257
Washington	82	28	40	14	70	235	286

*Wild Card

Western Conference

CENTRAL DIVISION

	GP	W	L	OTL	Pts	GF	GA
Detroit	82	50	19	13	113	254	199
*Nashville	82	51	23	8	110	272	212
St. Louis	82	34	35	13	81	214	254
Columbus	82	33	42	7	73	201	249
Chicago	82	31	42	9	71	201	258

NORTHWEST DIVISION

	GP	W	L	OTL	Pts	GF	GA
Vancouver	82	49	26	7	105	222	201
*Minnesota	82	48	26	8	104	235	191
*Calgary	82	43	29	10	96	258	226
Colorado	82	44	31	7	95	272	251
Edmonton	82	32	43	7	71	195	248

PACIFIC DIVISION

	GP	W	L	OTL	Pts	GF	GA
Anaheim	82	48	20	14	110	258	208
*San Jose	82	51	26	5	107	258	199
*Dallas	82	50	25	7	107	226	197
Los Angeles	82	27	41	14	68	227	283
Phoenix	82	31	46	5	67	216	284

OTL=overtime loss; worth 1 pt.

2007 Stanley Cup Playoffs

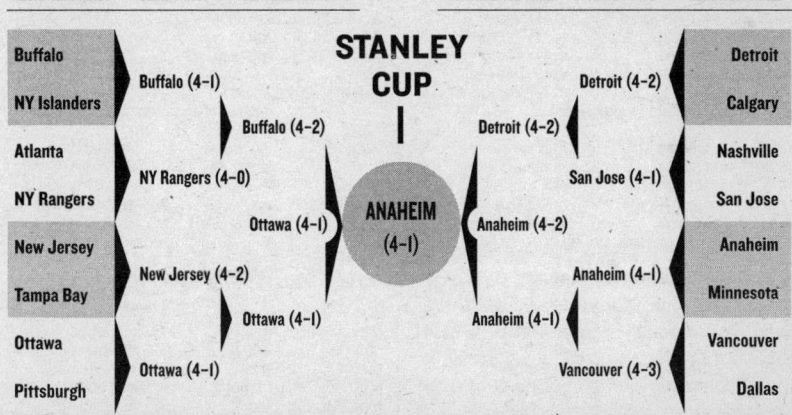

EASTERN CONFERENCE					WESTERN CONFERENCE			
QUARTERFINALS	SEMIFINALS	CONFERENCE FINAL			CONFERENCE FINAL	SEMIFINALS	QUARTERFINALS	

STANLEY CUP

ANAHEIM (4–1)

Buffalo — Buffalo (4–1) — Buffalo (4–2) — Ottawa (4–1)
NY Islanders
Atlanta — NY Rangers (4–0)
NY Rangers
New Jersey — New Jersey (4–2) — Ottawa (4–1) — Ottawa (4–1)
Tampa Bay
Ottawa — Ottawa (4–1)
Pittsburgh

Detroit — Detroit (4–2) — Detroit (4–2) — Anaheim (4–2)
Calgary
Nashville — San Jose (4–1)
San Jose
Anaheim — Anaheim (4–1) — Anaheim (4–1)
Minnesota
Vancouver — Vancouver (4–3)
Dallas

Stanley Cup Playoff Results

Conference Quarterfinals

EASTERN CONFERENCE

April 12	NY Rangers	4	at Atlanta	3		April 18	Atlanta	2	at NY Rangers	4
April 14	NY Rangers	2	at Atlanta	1			NY Rangers won series 4–0.		
April 17	Atlanta	0	at NY Rangers	7					

Conference Quarterfinals *(Cont.)*

EASTERN CONFERENCE *(CONT.)*

April 12	NY Islanders	1	at Buffalo	4	April 17	Ottawa	2	at Pittsburgh	1
April 14	NY Islanders	3	at Buffalo	2	April 19	Pittsburgh	0	at Ottawa	3

April 12 ....NY Islanders 1 at Buffalo 4
April 14 ....NY Islanders 3 at Buffalo 2
April 16 ....Buffalo 3 at NY Islanders 2
April 18 ....Buffalo 4 at NY Islanders 2
April 20 ....NY Islanders 3 at Buffalo 4
Buffalo won series 4–1.

April 17.........Ottawa 2 at Pittsburgh 1
April 19.........Pittsburgh 0 at Ottawa 3
Ottawa won series 4–1.

April 11.........Pittsburgh 3 at Ottawa 6
April 14.........Pittsburgh 4 at Ottawa 3
April 15.........Ottawa 4 at Pittsburgh 2

April 12.........Tampa Bay 3 at New Jersey 5
April 14.........Tampa Bay 3 at New Jersey 2
April 16.........New Jersey 2 at Tampa Bay 3
April 18.........New Jersey 4 at Tampa Bay 3*
April 20.........Tampa Bay 0 at New Jersey 3
April 22.........New Jersey 3 at Tampa Bay 2
New Jersey won series 4–2.

WESTERN CONFERENCE

April 12.........Calgary 1 at Detroit 4
April 15.........Calgary 1 at Detroit 3
April 17.........Detroit 2 at Calgary 3
April 19.........Detroit 2 at Calgary 3
April 21.........Calgary 1 at Detroit 5
April 22.........Detroit 2 at Calgary 1†
Detroit won series 4–2.

April 11 ....Dallas 4 at Vancouver 5‡
April 13 ....Dallas 2 at Vancouver 0
April 15 ....Vancouver 2 at Dallas 1*
April 17 ....Vancouver 2 at Dallas 1
April 19 ....Dallas 1 at Vancouver 0*
April 21 ....Vancouver 0 at Dallas 2
April 23 ....Dallas 1 at Vancouver 4
Vancouver won series 4–3.

April 11 ....San Jose 5 at Nashville 4†
April 13 ....San Jose 2 at Nashville 5
April 16 ....Nashville 1 at San Jose 3
April 18 ....Nashville 2 at San Jose 3
April 20 ....San Jose 3 at Nashville 2
San Jose won series 4–1.

April 11 ....Minnesota 1 at Anaheim 2
April 13 ....Minnesota 1 at Anaheim 3
April 15 ....Anaheim 2 at Minnesota 1*
April 17 ....Anaheim 1 at Minnesota 4
April 19 ....Minnesota 1 at Anaheim 4
Anaheim won series 4–1.

Conference Semifinals

EASTERN CONFERENCE

April 25 ....NY Rangers 2 at Buffalo 5
April 27 ....NY Rangers 2 at Buffalo 3
April 29 ....Buffalo 1 at NY Rangers 2†
May 1 ....Buffalo 1 at NY Rangers 2
May 4 ....NY Rangers 1 at Buffalo 2*
May 6 ....Buffalo 5 at NY Rangers 4
Buffalo won series 4–2.

April 26 ....Ottawa 5 at New Jersey 4
April 28 ....Ottawa 2 at New Jersey 3†
April 30 ....New Jersey 0 at Ottawa 3
May 2 ....New Jersey 2 at Ottawa 3
May 5 ....Ottawa 3 at New Jersey 2
Ottawa won series 4–1.

WESTERN CONFERENCE

April 26 ....San Jose 2 at Detroit 0
April 28 ....San Jose 2 at Detroit 3
April 30 ....Detroit 1 at San Jose 2
May 2 ....Detroit 3 at San Jose 2*
May 5 ....San Jose 1 at Detroit 4
May 7 ....Detroit 2 at San Jose 0
Detroit won series 4–2.

April 25 ....Vancouver 1 at Anaheim 5
April 27 ....Vancouver 2 at Anaheim 1†
April 29 ....Anaheim 3 at Vancouver 2
May 1 ....Anaheim 3 at Vancouver 2*
May 3 ....Vancouver 1 at Anaheim 2†
Anaheim won series 4–1.

Eastern Finals

May 10 ....Buffalo 2 at Ottawa 5
May 12 ....Buffalo 3 at Ottawa 4†
May 14 ....Ottawa 1 at Buffalo 0
May 16 ....Ottawa 2 at Buffalo 3
May 19 ....Buffalo 2 at Ottawa 3*
Ottawa won series 4–1.

Western Finals

May 11 ....Anaheim 1 at Detroit 2
May 13 ....Anaheim 4 at Detroit 3*
May 15 ....Detroit 5 at Anaheim 0
May 17 ....Detroit 3 at Anaheim 5
May 20 ....Anaheim 2 at Detroit 1*
May 22 ....Detroit 3 at Anaheim 4
Anaheim won series 4–2.

Stanley Cup Finals

May 28 ....Ottawa 2 at Anaheim 3
May 30 ....Ottawa 0 at Anaheim 1
June 2 ....Anaheim 3 at Ottawa 5
June 4 ....Anaheim 3 at Ottawa 2

June 6 ....Anaheim 6 at Ottawa 2
Anaheim won series 4–1.

*Overtime game. †Double overtime game. **Triple overtime game. ‡Quadruple overtime game.

Game 1

Ottawa	1	1	0	2
Anaheim	1	0	2	3

FIRST PERIOD

Scoring: 1, Ottawa, M Fisher 4 (power play) (A Meszaros, M Comrie), 1:38. 2, Anaheim, A McDonald 6 (T Selanne), 10:55. Penalties: S Niedermayer, Ana (high-sticking), 0:53; D Heatley, Ott (tripping), 2:34; R Jackman, Ana (roughing), 14:14.

SECOND PERIOD

Scoring: 3, Ottawa, W Redden 3 (power play) (D Alfredsson, J Spezza), 4:36. Penalties: W Redden, Ott (hooking), 0:59; R Getzlaf, Ana (cross-checking), 3:52; F Beauchemin, Ana (tripping), 6:34; S Pahlsson, Ana (slashing), 6:59.

THIRD PERIOD

Scoring: 4, Anaheim, R Getzlaf 6 (C Perry, R Jackman), 5:44. 5, Anaheim, T Moen 5 (R Niedermayer, S Niedermayer), 17:09. Penalties: C Schubert, Ott (slashing), 6:37; A Meszaros, Ott (interference), 10:03; S Niedermayer, Ana (hooking), 13:08; C Pronger, Ana (holding the stick), 19:16.

Shots on goal: OTT 3-10-7—20; ANA 8-10-14—32

Power-play opportunities: OTT 2-7, ANA 0-4.

Goalies: Ott, R Emery (32 shots, 29 saves). Ana, J Giguere (20 shots, 18 saves).

Referees: Devorski, O'Halloran. Linesmen: Morin, Heyer. A: 17.274.

Game 2

Ottawa	0	0	0	0
Anaheim	0	0	1	1

FIRST PERIOD

Scoring: None. Penalties: M Comrie, Ott (boarding), 2:17; A Miller, Ana (interference), 5:40; A Volchenkov, Ott (boarding), 8:05; S Thornton, Ana (charging), 12:31; C Pronger, Ana (slashing), 13:24; M Fisher, Ott (roughing), 18:07.

SECOND PERIOD

Scoring: None. Penalties: T Preissing, Ott (tripping), 18:04; A McDonald, Ana (hooking), 19:36.

THIRD PERIOD

Scoring: 1, Anaheim, S Pahlsson 3 (Unassisted), 14:16. Penalties: None

Shots on goal: OTT 7-4-5—16; ANA 12-14-5—31

Power-play opportunities: OTT 0-4, ANN 0-4.

Goalies: Ott, R Emery (31 shots, 30 saves). Ana, J Giguere (16 shots, 16 saves).

Referees: McCreary, Watson. Linesmen: Driscoll, Sharrers. A: 17,258.

Game 3

Anaheim	1	2	0	3
Ottawa	1	3	1	5

FIRST PERIOD

Scoring: 1, Anaheim, A McDonald 7 (power play) (T Selanne), 5:39. 2, Ottawa, C Neil 2 (C Kelly, A Meszaros), 16:10. Penalties: W Redden, Ott (interference), 3:51; B May, Ana (interference), 6:01; T Moen, Ana (diving), 11:29; M Fisher, Ott (roughing), 11:29.

SECOND PERIOD

Scoring: 3, Anaheim, C Perry 5 (D Penner, R Getzlaf), 5:20. 4, Ottawa, M Fisher 5 (A Volchenkov), 5:47. 5, Anaheim, R Getzlaf 7 (D Penner, C Perry), 7:38. 6, Ottawa, D Alfredsson 11 (power play) (W Redden, J Corvo), 16:14. 7, Ottawa, D McAmmond 5 (O Saprykin, C Schubert), 18:34. Penalties: S Pahlsson, Ana (roughing), 2:04; M Comrie, Ott (holding), 2:04; S Niedermayer, Ana (hooking), 13:44; S O'Donnell, Ana (cross checking), 15:39.

THIRD PERIOD

Scoring: 8, Ottawa, A Volchenkov 2 (A Vermette, C Kelly), 8:22. Penalties: C Neil, Ott (roughing), 2:55; R Getzlaf, Ana (roughing), 2:55; D. Penner, Ana (roughing), 2:55; C Perry, Ana (roughing), 2:55; M Fisher, Ott (roughing), 2:55; P Schaefer, Ott (roughing), 2:55; C Perry, Ana (roughing), 2:55; B May, Ana (tripping), 5:43; P Schaefer, Ott (interference), 10:41; R Getzlaf, Ana (holding), 11:05; A McDonald, Ana (interference-goalkeeper), 15:29; C Phillips, Ott (roughing), 19:49.

Shots on goal: ANA 8-11-3—22; OTT 10-12-7—29

Power-play opportunities: ANA 1-3, OTT 1-7.

Goalies: Ana, J Giguere (29 shots, 24 saves). Ott, R Emery (22 shots, 19 saves).

Referees: Devorski, O' Halloran. Linesmen: Morin, Heyer. A: 20,500.

Game 4

Anaheim 0	2	1——3
Ottawa........................I	I	0——2

FIRST PERIOD

Scoring: 1, Ottawa, D Alfredsson12 (power play) (P Schaefer, M Fisher), 19:59. Penalties: F Beauchemin, Ana (slashing) 0:58; C Perry, Ana (cross checking), 3:54; C Neil, Ott (interference-goalkeeper), 6:13; C Perry, Ana (roughing), 17:11; P Eaves, Ott (holding), 17:11; R Getzlaf, Ana (interference-goalkeeper), 18:16.

SECOND PERIOD

Scoring: 2, Anaheim, A McDonald 8 (T Marchant, C Perry), 10:06. 3, Anaheim, A McDonald 8 (R Niedermayer, S O'Donnell), 11:06. 4, Ottawa, D Heatley 7 (P Eaves, J Spezza), 18:00. Penalties: C

SECOND PERIOD *(CONT.)*

Neil, Ott (interference), 4:29; C Phillips, Ott (hooking), 8:02; M Fisher, Ott (roughing), 20:00; S Pahlsson, Ana (roughing), 20:00.

THIRD PERIOD

Scoring: 5, Anaheim, D Penner 3 (T Selanne, A McDonald), 4:07. Penalties: F Beauchemin, Ana (holding), 1:02.

Shots on goal: ANA 2-13-6—21; OTT 13-4-6—23. Power-play opportunities: ANA 0-3, OTT 1-4.

Goalies: Ana, J Giguere (23 shots, 21 saves). Ott, R Emery (21 shots, 18 saves).

Referees: McCreary, Watson. Linesmen: Driscoll, Sharrers. A: 20,500.

Game 5

Ottawa 0	2	0——2
Anaheim 2	2	2——6

FIRST PERIOD

Scoring: 1, Anaheim, A McDonald 10 (power play) (R Getzlaf, C Pronger), 3:41. 2, Anaheim, R Niedermayer 5 (C Perry), 17:41. Penalties: T Preissing, Ott (interference), 1:40; A Volchenkov, Ott (hooking), 3:25; J Spezza, Ott (holding the stick), 5:39; S Pahlsson, Ana (elbowing), 10:14; C Perry, Ana (roughing), 15:31; T Selanne, Ana (holding), 18:10.

SECOND PERIOD

Scoring: 3, Ottawa, D Alfredsson 13 (P Schaefer, M Fisher), 11:27. 4, Anaheim, T Moen 6 (Unassisted), 15:44. 5, Ottawa, D Alfredsson 13 (shorthanded) (Unassisted), 17:38. 6, Anaheim, F Beauchemin 4 (power play) (A McDonald), 18:28. Penalties: C Schubert, Ott (elbowing), 16:46.

THIRD PERIOD

Scoring: 7, Anaheim, T Moen 6 (S Niedermayer, S Pahlsson), 4:01. 8, Anaheim, C Perry 6, (Unassisted), 17:00. Penalties: C Schubert, Ott (slashing), 5:48; A Volchenkov, Ott (slashing), 12:27.

Shots on goal: OTT 3-5-5—13; ANA 5-7-6—18

Power-play Opportunities: OTT 0-3, ANA 2-6.

Goalies : Ott, R Emery (18 shots, 12 saves). Ana, J Giguere (13 shots, 11 saves).

Referees: Devorski, O' Halloran. Linesmen: Morin, Heyer. A: 17,372.

Individual Playoff Leaders

Scoring

POINTS

Player and Team	GP	G	A	Pts	+/-	PM	Player and Team	GP	G	A	Pts	+/-	PM
Daniel Alfredsson, Ott	20	14	8	22	4	10	Scott Gomez, NJ	11	4	10	14	6	14
Dany Heatley, Ott	20	7	15	22	4	14	Chris Drury, Buff	16	8	5	13	3	2
Jason Spezza, Ott	20	7	15	22	5-	10	Michael Nylander, NYR	10	6	7	13	9	0
Nicklas Lidstrom, Det	18	4	14	18	0	6	Travis Moen, Ana	21	7	5	12	5	22
Ryan Getzlaf, Ana	21	7	10	17	1	32	Daniel Cleary, Det	18	4	8	12	2	30
Pavel Datsyuk, Det	18	8	8	16	2	8	Samuel Pahlsson, Ana	21	3	9	12	10	20
Corey Perry, Ana	21	6	9	15	5	37	Jaromir Jagr, NYR	10	5	6	11	6	12
Teemu Selanne, Ana	21	5	10	15	1	10	Scott Niedermayer, Ana	21	3	8	11	2	26
Daniel Briere, Buff	16	3	12	15	3	16	Mikael Samuelsson, Det	18	3	8	11	2	14
Chris Pronger, Ana	19	3	12	15	10	26	Joe Thornton, SJ	11	1	10	11	2	10
Andy McDonald, Ana	21	10	4	14	6	10	Zach Parise, NJ	11	7	3	10	4	8
Henrik Zetterberg, Det	18	6	8	14	1	12							

GOALS

Player and Team	GP	G
Daniel Alfredsson, Ott	20	14
Andy McDonald, Ana	21	10
Pavel Datsyuk, Det	18	8
Chris Drury, Buff	16	8
Brian Gionta, NJ	11	8
Dany Heatley, Ott	20	7
Jason Spezza, Ott	20	7
Ryan Getzlaf, Ana	21	7

SHORT-HANDED GOALS

Player and Team	GP	SH
Daniel Cleary, Det	18	2

POWER PLAY GOALS

Player and Team	GP	PP
Daniel Alfredsson, Ott	20	6
Andy McDonald, Ana	21	5
Nicklas Lidstrom, Det	18	4
Tomas Holmstrom, Det	15	4

ASSISTS

Player and Team	GP	A
Dany Heatley, Ott	20	15
Jason Spezza, Ott	20	15
Nicklas Lidstrom, Det	18	14
Daniel Briere, Buff	16	12
Chris Pronger, Ana	19	12

PLUS/MINUS

Player and Team	GP	+/-
Chris Pronger, Ana	19	10
Teppo Numminen, Buf	16	10
Samuel Pahlsson, Ana	21	10
Michael Nylander, NYR	10	9
Dmitri Kalinin, Buff	16	9
Rob Niedermayer, Ana	21	9
Johan Franzen, Det	18	8
Sean O'Donnell, Ana	21	8
Chris Chelios, Det	18	7
Michael Rozsival, NYR	10	6
Jaromir Jagr, NYR	10	6

Goaltending (Minimum 420 minutes)

GOALS AGAINST AVERAGE

Player and Team	GP	W-L	Avg
Marty Turco, Dal	7	3-4	1.30
Roberto Luongo, Van	12	5-7	1.77
Dominik Hasek, Det	18	10-8	1.79
Jean-Sebastien Giguere, Ana	18	13-4	1.97
Henrik Lundqvist, NYR	10	6-4	2.07
Ryan Miller, Buff	16	9-7	2.22

SAVE PERCENTAGE

Player and Team	GP	W-L	GAA	GA	SV	SV%	SA
Marty Turco, Dal	7	3-4	1.30	11	218	.952	229
R. Luongo, Van	12	5-7	1.77	25	402	.942	427
M. Kiprusoff, Cgy	6	2-4	2.81	18	237	.929	255
H. Lundqvist, NYR	10	6-4	2.07	22	269	.924	291
D. Hasek, Det	18	10-8	1.79	34	410	.923	444
J. Giguere, Ana	18	13-4	1.97	35	416	.922	451

NHL Awards

Award	Player and Team
Hart Trophy (MVP)	Sidney Crosby, Pitt
Calder Trophy (top rookie)	Evgeni Malkin, Pitt
Vezina Trophy (top goaltender)	Martin Brodeur, NJ
Norris Trophy (top defenseman)	Nicklas Lidstrom, Det
Lady Byng Trophy (for gentlemanly play)	Pavel Datsyuk, Det
Adams Award (top coach)	Alain Vigneault, Van
Selke Trophy (top defensive forward)	Rod Brind'Amour, Car
Jennings Trophy (goaltender on club allowing fewest goals)	Niklas Backstrom/ Manny Fernandez, Min
Conn Smythe Trophy (playoff MVP)	Scott Niedermayer, Ana

Individual Regular Season Leaders

Scoring

POINTS

Player and Team	GP	G	A	Pts	+/-	PM	Player and Team	GP	G	A	Pts	+/-	PM
Sidney Crosby, Pitt	79	36	84	120	10	60	Daniel Briere, Buff	81	32	63	95	17	89
Joe Thornton, SJ	82	22	92	114	24	44	Teemu Selanne, Ana	82	48	46	94	26	82
Vincent Lecavalier, TB	82	52	56	108	2	44	Jarome Iginla, Cgy	70	39	55	94	12	40
Dany Heatley, Ott	82	50	55	105	31	74	A. Ovechkin, Wash	82	46	46	92	-19	52
Martin St. Louis, TB	82	43	59	102	7	28	Olli Jokinen, Fla	82	39	52	91	18	78
Marian Hossa, Atl	82	43	57	100	.18	49	Jason Spezza, Ott	67	34	53	87	19	45
Joe Sakic, Col	82	36	64	100	2	46	Daniel Alfredsson, Ott	77	29	58	87	42	42
Jaromir Jagr, NYR	82	30	66	96	26	78	Pavel Datsyuk, Det	79	27	60	87	36	20
Marc Savard, Bos	82	22	74	96	-19	96	Evgeni Malkin, Pitt	78	33	52	85	2	80

Scoring *(Cont.)*

GOALS

Player and Team	GP	G
Vincent Lecavalier, TB	82	52
Dany Heatley, Ott	82	50
Teemu Selanne, Ana	82	48
A. Ovechkin, Wash	82	46
Martin St. Louis, TB	82	43
Marian Hossa, Atl	82	43
Thomas Vanek, Buff	82	43
Ilya Kovalchuk, Atl	82	42
Simon Gagne, Phil	76	41
Jason Blake, NYI	82	40

POWER PLAY GOALS

Player and Team	GP	PP
Teemu Selanne, Ana	82	25
Sheldon Souray, Mtl	81	19
Ilya Kovalchuk, Atl	82	18
Marian Hossa, Atl	82	17
Dany Heatley, Ott	82	17

ASSISTS

Player and Team	GP	A
Joe Thornton, SJ	82	92
Sidney Crosby, Pitt	79	84
Marc Savard, Bos	82	74
Henrik Sedin, Van	82	71
Jaromir Jagr, NYR	82	66
Joe Sakic, Col	82	64
Daniel Briere, Buff	81	63
Pavel Datsyuk, Det	79	60

SHORT-HANDED GOALS

Player and Team	GP	SHG
Jordan Staal, Pitt	81	7
Martin St. Louis, TB	82	5
Vincent Lecavalier, TB	82	5
Kris Draper, Det	81	5

5 tied with 4.

GAME-WINNING GOALS

Player and Team	GP	GW
Dany Heatley, Ott	82	10
Teemu Selanne, Ana	82	10
Henrik Zetterberg, Det	63	10
Chris Drury, Buff	77	9
Patrick Marleau, SJ	77	9
Milan Michalek, SJ	78	9

PLUS/MINUS

Player and Team	GP	+/–
Thomas Vanek, Buff	82	47
Daniel Alfredsson, Ott	77	42
Nicklas Lidstrom, Det	80	40
Tom Preissing, Ott	80	40
Derek Roy, Buff	75	37
Anton Volchenkov, Ott	78	37
Pavel Datsyuk, Det	79	36
Chris Phillips, Ott	82	36
Marek Malik, NYR	69	32

Goaltending
(Minimum 25 games)

GOALS AGAINST AVERAGE

Player and Team	GP	W-L	GAA	GA
N. Backstrom, Min	41	23-8	1.97	73
Dominik Hasek, Det	56	38-11	2.05	114
Martin Brodeur, NJ	78	48-23	2.18	171
Marty Turco, Dal	67	38-20	2.23	140
J. Giguere, Ana	56	36-10	2.26	122
Roberto Luongo, Van	76	47-22	2.29	171
Evgeni Nabokov, SJ	50	25-16	2.29	106

SAVE PERCENTAGE

Player and Team	GP	W-L	GA	SA	Pct
N. Backstrom, Min	41	23-8	73	1028	.929
Chris Mason, Nash	40	24-11	93	1244	.925
Martin Brodeur, NJ	78	48-23	171	2182	.922
R. Luongo, Van	76	47-22	171	2169	.921
T. Vokoun, Nash	44	27-12	104	1299	.920
Rick Dipietro, NYI	62	32-19	156	1917	.919
Ray Emery, Ott	58	33-16	138	1691	.918

WINS

Player and Team	GP	GAA	W	L
Martin Brodeur, NJ	78	2.18	48	23
Roberto Luongo, Van	76	2.29	47	22
Marc-Andre Fleury, Pitt	67	2.83	40	16
Ryan Miller, Buff	63	2.73	40	16
Miikka Kiprusoff, Cgy	74	2.46	40	24

SHUTOUTS

Player and Team	GP	W	L	SO
Martin Brodeur, NJ	78	48	23	12
Dominik Hasek, Det	56	38	11	8
Miikka Kiprusoff, Cgy	74	40	24	7
Evgeni Nabokov, SJ	50	25	16	7
Marty Turco, Dal	67	38	20	6

NHL Team-by-Team Statistical Leaders

Anaheim Ducks

SCORING

Player	GP	G	A	Pts	+/–	PM
Teemu Selanne, RW	82	48	46	94	26	82
Andy McDonald, C	82	27	51	78	16	46
Scott Niedermayer, D	79	15	54	69	6	86
Chris Kunitz, LW	81	25	35	60	23	81
Chris Pronger, D	66	13	46	59	27	69
Ryan Getzlaf, C	82	25	33	58	17	66
Dustin Penner, RW	82	29	16	45	-2	58
Corey Perry, RW	82	17	27	44	12	55
F. Beauchemin, D	71	7	21	28	7	49
Samuel Pahlsson, C	82	8	18	26	-4	42
Todd Marchant, C	56	8	15	23	7	44
Travis Moen, LW	82	11	10	21	-4	101
Sean O'Donnell, D	79	2	15	17	9	92
Rob Niedermayer, C	82	5	11	16	-8	77
Shane O'Brien, D	62	2	12	14	5	140
Ric Jackman, D	24	1	10	11	3	10

SCORING *(CONT.)*

Player	GP	G	A	Pts	+/–	PM
Ryan Shannon, RW	53	2	9	11	-2	10
Shawn Thornton, LW	48	2	7	9	3	88
Joe DiPenta, D	76	2	6	8	1	48
Todd Fedoruk, LW	10	0	3	3	2	36
Kent Huskins, D	33	0	3	3	-3	14
Travis Green, C	7	1	1	2	3	6
Brad May, LW	14	0	1	1	-1	13
Tim Brent, C	15	1	0	1	-5	6
George Parros, RW	32	1	0	1	-2	102
Curtis Glencross, LW	2	1	0	1	1	2

GOALTENDING

Player	GP	Mins	W	L	TGA	GAA	SO
J. Giguere	56	3244	36	10	122	2.26	4
Ilya Bryzgalov	27	1508	10	8	62	2.47	1

Atlanta Thrashers

SCORING

Player	GP	G	A	Pts	+/-	PM
Marian Hossa, RW	82	43	57	100	18	49
Slava Kozlov, LW	81	28	52	80	9	36
Ilya Kovalchuk, LW	82	42	34	76	-2	66
Scott Mellanby, RW	69	12	24	36	-9	63
Bobby Holik, C	82	11	18	29	-3	86
Jon Sim, LW	77	17	12	29	-1	60
Glen Metropolit, C	57	12	16	28	9	20
Greg de Vries, D	82	3	21	24	-3	66
Niclas Havelid, D	77	3	18	21	-2	52
Steve Rucchin, C	47	5	16	21	-4	14
Jim Slater, C	74	5	14	19	8	62
Steve McCarthy, D	46	4	12	16	4	24
Andy Sutton, D	55	2	14	16	6	76
Eric Belanger, C	24	9	6	15	0	12
Keith Tzachuk, LW	18	7	8	15	8	34
Alexei Zhitnik, D	18	2	12	14	4	14
Brad Larsen, LW	72	7	6	13	-11	39
Jean-Pierre Vigier, RW	72	5	8	13	0	27
Niko Kapanen, C	60	4	9	13	-12	20
Shane Hnidy, D	72	5	7	12	15	63
Vitaly Vishnevski, D	52	3	9	12	-5	31
Garnet Exelby, D	58	2	8	10	2	56
Eric Boulton, LW	45	3	4	7	2	49
Pascal Dupuis, LW	17	3	2	5	-6	4
Jason Krog, C	14	1	3	4	3	6
Braydon Coburn, D	29	0	4	4	1	30
Denis Hamel, LW	3	1	0	1	0	0

GOALTENDING

Player	GP	Mins	W	L	TGA	GAA	SO
Kari Lehtonen	68	3934	34	24	183	2.79	4
Johan Hedberg	21	1057	9	4	51	2.89	0

Boston Bruins

SCORING

Player	GP	G	A	Pts	+/-	PM
Marc Savard, C	82	22	74	96	-19	96
Patrice Bergeron, C	77	22	48	70	-28	26
Glen Murray, RW	59	28	17	45	-12	44
Marco Sturm, LW	76	27	17	44	-24	46
Zdeno Chara, D	80	11	32	43	-21	100
Brad Boyes, C	62	13	21	34	-17	25
Phil Kessel, C	70	11	18	29	-12	12
P.J. Axelsson, LW	55	11	16	27	-10	52
B. Bochenski, RW	31	11	11	22	3	14
Paul Mara, D	59	3	15	18	-22	95
Shean Donovan, RW	76	6	11	17	-13	56
Mark Mowers, RW	78	5	12	17	-10	26
Brad Stuart, D	48	7	10	17	-22	26
Wayne Primeau, C	51	7	8	15	-15	75
Petr, Tenkrat, RW	64	9	5	14	-16	34
Stanislav Chistov, RW	60	5	8	13	-8	36
Andrew Alberts, D	76	0	10	10	-15	124
Jason York, D	49	1	7	8	-14	32
Petr Kalus, RW	9	4	1	5	0	6
Andrew Ference, D	26	1	2	3	-2	31
Aaron Ward, D	20	1	2	3	-8	18
Bobby Allen, D	31	0	3	3	-1	10
Milan Jurcina, D	40	2	1	3	-5	20
Dennis Wideman, D	20	1	2	3	-3	27
Chuck Kobasew, RW	10	1	1	2	-6	25
Yan Stastny, C	21	0	2	2	-3	19
Jeff Hoggan, RW	46	0	2	2	-8	33

GOALTENDING

Player	GP	Mins	W	L	TGA	GAA	SO
Tim Thomas	66	3619	30	29	183	3.13	3
Hannu Toivonen	18	893	3	9	63	4.23	0

Buffalo Sabres

SCORING

Player	GP	G	A	Pts	+/-	PM
Daniel Briere, C	81	32	63	95	17	88
Thomas Vanek, LW	82	43	41	84	47	40
Chris Drury, C	77	37	32	69	1	30
Jason Pominville, RW	82	34	34	68	25	30
Derek Roy, C	75	21	42	63	37	60
Maxim Afinogenov, RW	56	23	38	61	19	66
Jochen Hecht, C	76	19	37	56	19	39
Brian Campbell, D	82	6	42	48	28	35
Ales Kotalik, RW	66	16	22	38	-5	46
Dmitri Kalinin, D	82	7	22	29	19	36
Teppo Numminen, D	79	2	27	29	17	32
Drew Stafford, RW	41	13	14	27	5	33
Nathan Paetsch, D	63	2	22	24	10	50
Paul Gaustad, C	54	9	13	22	11	74
Jaroslav Spacek, D	65	5	16	21	20	62
Toni Lydman, D	67	2	17	19	10	55

SCORING (CONT.)

Player	GP	G	A	Pts	+/-	PM
Henrik Tallinder, D	47	4	10	14	19	34
Jiri Novotny, C	50	6	7	13	-2	26
Adam Mair, C	82	2	9	11	-1	128
Daniel Paille, LW	29	3	8	11	5	18
Dainius Zubrus, RW	19	4	4	8	-3	12
Clarke MacArthur, LW	19	3	4	7	4	4
Michael Ryan, C	19	3	2	5	-8	2
Andrew Peters, LW	58	1	1	2	-1	125
Michael Funk, D	5	0	2	2	2	0
Patrick Kaleta, RW	7	0	2	2	3	21
Tim Connolly, C	2	1	0	1	1	2
Mark Mancari, RW	3	0	1	1	-1	2

GOALTENDING

Player	GP	Mins	W	L	TGA	GAA	SO
Ryan Miller	63	3692	40	16	168	2.73	2
Martin Biron	19	1066	12	4	54	3.04	0

Calgary Flames

SCORING

Player	GP	G	A	Pts	+/–	PM
Jarome Iginla, RW	70	39	55	94	12	40
Alex Tanquay, LW	81	22	59	81	12	44
Daymond Langkow, C	81	33	44	77	23	44
Kristian Huselius, LW	81	34	43	77	21	26
Dion Phaneuf, D	79	17	33	50	10	98
Matthew Lombardi, C	81	20	26	46	10	48
Roman Hamrlik, D	75	7	31	38	22	88
Tony Amonte, RW	81	10	20	30	-4	40
Stephane Yelle, C	56	10	14	24	5	32
Craig Conroy, C	28	8	13	21	10	18
Robyn Regehr, D	78	2	19	21	27	75
David Moss, LW	41	10	8	18	5	12
Brad Stuart, D	48	7	10	17	-22	26
Marcus Nilson, D	63	5	10	15	7	27
Wayne Primeau, C	51	7	8	15	-15	75
Mark Giordano, D	48	7	8	15	7	36
Byron Ritchie, C	64	8	6	14	3	68
Jeff Friesen, LW	72	6	6	12	-2	34
Rhett Warrener, D	62	4	6	10	6	67
Andrei Zyuzin, D	49	1	5	6	-2	30
Jamie Lundmark, C	39	0	4	4	-4	31
Dustin Boyd, C	13	2	2	4	5	4
Andrew Ference, D	26	1	2	3	-2	31
Richie Regehr, D	6	1	1	2	-1	0

GOALTENDING

Player	GP	Mins	W	L	TGA	GAA	SO
Miikka Kiprusoff	74	4419	40	24	181	2.46	7
Jamie McLennan	9	532	3	5	32	3.60	0

Carolina Hurricanes

SCORING

Player	GP	G	A	Pts	+/–	PM
Ray Whitney, LW	81	32	51	83	-5	46
Rod Brind'Amour, C	78	26	56	82	7	46
Eric Staal, C	82	30	40	70	-6	68
Justin Williams, RW	82	33	34	67	-11	73
Erik Cole, LW	71	29	32	61	2	76
Scott Walker, RW	81	21	30	51	-10	45
Mike Commodore, D	82	7	22	29	0	113
Cory Stillman, LW	43	5	22	27	-8	24
Andrew Ladd, LW	65	11	10	21	1	46
Eric Belanger, C	56	8	12	20	-2	14
Chad LaRose, RW	80	6	12	18	-2	10
David Tanabe, D	60	5	12	17	5	44
Craig Adams, RW	82	7	7	14	-9	54
Anton Babchuk, D	52	2	12	14	-6	30
Andrew Hutchinson, D	41	3	11	14	0	30
Glen Wesley, D	68	1	12	13	11	56
Bret Hedican, D	50	0	10	10	-8	36
Niclas Wallin, D	67	2	8	10	-2	48
Josef Vasicek, C	25	2	7	9	-6	22
Frantisek Kaberle, D	27	2	6	8	8	20
Trevor Letowski, RW	61	2	6	8	-8	18
Tim Gleason, D	57	2	4	6	-10	57
Dennis Seidenberg, D	20	1	5	6	-12	2
Kevyn Adams, C	35	2	2	4	-10	17

GOALTENDING

Player	GP	Mins	W	L	TGA	GAA	SO
Cam Ward	60	3422	30	21	167	2.93	2
John Grahame	28	1514	10	13	72	2.85	0

Chicago Blackhawks

SCORING

Player	GP	G	A	Pts	+/–	PM
Martin Havlat, RW	56	25	32	57	15	28
Radim Vrbata, RW	77	14	27	41	-4	26
Jeff Hamilton, C	70	18	21	39	-4	22
Tuomo Ruutu, C	71	17	21	38	4	95
Bryan Smolinski, C	62	14	23	37	10	29
Patrick Sharp, RW	80	20	15	35	-15	74
Duncan Keith, D	82	2	29	31	0	76
Denis Arkhipov, C	79	10	17	27	-13	54
Martin Lapointe, RW	82	13	11	24	-14	98
Brent Seabrook, D	81	4	20	24	-6	104
Tony Salmelainen, LW	57	6	11	17	-3	26
Rene Bourque, LW	44	7	10	17	-4	38
Adrian Aucoin, D	59	4	12	16	-22	50
Peter Bondra, RW	37	5	9	14	2	26
Lasse Kukkonen, D	54	5	9	14	5	30

SCORING *(CONT.)*

Player	GP	G	A	Pts	+/–	PM
Mikael Holmqvist, C	63	6	7	13	-5	31
James Wisniewski, D	50	2	8	10	3	39
Michal Handzus, C	8	3	5	8	4	6
Cam Barker, D	35	1	7	8	-12	44
Jassen Cullimore, D	65	1	6	7	-6	64
Jim Vandermeer, D	46	1	6	7	-3	53
Jason Wiliams, C	20	4	2	6	-6	20
Craig MacDonald, C	25	3	2	5	-2	14
Karl Stewart, LW	37	2	3	5	-2	43
Martin St. Pierre, C	14	1	3	4	-3	8
Dustin Byfuglien, D	9	1	2	3	-2	10

GOALTENDING

Player	GP	Mins	W	L	TGA	GAA	SO
Nikolai Khabibulin	60	3424	25	26	163	2.86	1
Brian Boucher	15	826	1	10	45	3.27	1

Colorado Avalanche

SCORING

Player	GP	G	A	Pts	+/-	PM
Joe Sakic, C	82	36	64	100	2	46
Andrew Brunette, LW	82	27	56	83	-8	36
Paul Stastny, C	82	28	50	78	4	42
Milan Hejduk, RW	80	35	35	70	10	44
Wojtek Wolski, LW	76	22	28	50	2	14
Tyler Arnason, C	82	16	33	49	-8	26
John-Michael Liles, D	71	14	30	44	0	24
Brett Clark, D	82	10	29	39	5	50
Brett McLean, C	78	15	20	35	8	36
Marek Svatos, RW	66	15	15	30	1	46
Ian Laperriere, C	81	8	21	29	5	133
Brad Richardson, RW	73	14	8	22	4	28
Ken Klee, D	81	3	16	19	18	68
Mark Rycroft, RW	66	6	6	12	3	31
Patrice Brisebois, D	33	1	10	11	-5	22
Karlis Skrastins, S	68	0	11	11	0	30
Ben Guite, RW	39	3	8	11	-4	16
Ossi Vaananen, D	74	2	6	8	6	69
Pierre Turgeon, C	17	4	3	7	-1	10
Kurt Sauer, D	48	0	6	6	-3	24
Jordan Leopold, D	15	2	3	5	-4	14
Jeff Finger, D	22	1	4	5	10	11
Antti Laaksonen, LW	41	3	1	4	-3	16

GOALTENDING

Player	GP	Mins	W	L	TGA	GAA	SO
Peter Budaj	57	3198	31	16	143	2.68	3
Jose Theodore	33	1748	13	15	95	3.26	0

Columbus Blue Jackets

SCORING

Player	GP	G	A	Pts	+/-	PM
David Vyborny, RW	82	16	48	64	6	60
Rick Nash, LW	75	27	30	57	-8	73
Sergei Fedorov, C	73	18	24	42	-7	56
Fredrik Modin, LW	79	22	20	42	-3	50
Jason Chimera, LW	82	15	21	36	2	91
Ron Hainsey, D	80	9	25	34	-19	69
Nikolai Zherdev, RW	71	10	22	32	-19	26
Anson Carter, RW	54	10	17	27	-1	16
Dan Fritsche, C	59	12	15	27	3	35
Manny Malhotra, C	82	9	16	25	-8	76
Anders Eriksson, D	79	0	23	23	12	46
Rostislav Klesla, D	75	9	13	22	-13	105
Gilbert Brule, C	78	9	10	19	-21	28
Alexander Svitov, C	76	7	11	18	-10	145
Adam Foote, D	59	3	9	12	-17	71
Duvie Westcott, D	23	4	6	10	-13	18
Aaron Johnson, D	61	3	7	10	-9	38
Geoff Platt, C	26	4	5	9	1	10
Ole-Kristian Tollefsen, D	70	2	3	5	2	123
Marc Methot, D	20	0	4	4	5	12
Bryan Berard, D	11	0	3	3	-4	8
Mark Hartigan, C	6	1	2	3	2	2
Jody Shelley, LW	72	1	1	2	-6	125

GOALTENDING

Player	GP	Mins	W	L	TGA	GAA	SO
Fredrik Norrena	55	2952	24	23	137	2.78	3
Pascal Leclaire	24	1315	6	15	65	2.97	1

Dallas Stars

SCORING

Player	GP	G	A	Pts	+/-	PM
Mike Ribeiro, C	81	18	41	59	3	22
Sergei Zubov, D	78	12	42	54	0	26
Philippe Boucher, D	76	19	32	51	2	104
Jussi Jokinen, LW	82	14	34	48	8	18
Jere Lehtinen, RW	73	26	17	43	5	16
Mike Modano, C	59	22	21	43	9	34
Brenden Morrow, LW	40	16	15	31	-2	33
Niklas Hagman, LW	82	17	12	29	3	34
Eric Lindros, C	49	5	21	26	-1	70
Stu Barnes, C	82	13	12	25	-2	40
Jeff Halpern, C	76	8	17	25	-7	78
Antti Miettinen, RW	74	11	14	25	-5	38
Darryl Sydor, D	74	5	16	21	-4	36
Loui Eriksson, LW	59	6	13	19	-3	18
Stephane Robidas, D	75	0	17	17	-1	86
Ladislav Nagy, LW	25	4	10	14	-3	6
Trevor Daley, D	74	4	8	12	2	63
Patrik Stefan, C	41	5	6	11	5	10
Jaroslav Modry, D	57	1	9	10	10	32
Mattias Nordstrom, D	62	2	7	9	-20	40
Matthew Barnaby, RW	39	1	6	7	5	127
Joel Lundqvist, C	36	3	3	6	-5	14
Krys Barch, RW	26	3	2	5	2	107
Mathias Tjarnqvist, LW	18	1	3	4	-3	4
Steve Ott, C	38	1	2	3	0	24

GOALTENDING

Player	GP	Mins	W	L	TGA	GAA	SO
Marty Turco	67	3763	38	20	140	2.23	6
Mike Smith	23	1213	12	5	45	2.23	3

Detroit Red Wings

SCORING

Player	GP	G	A	Pts	+/-	PM
Pavel Datsyuk, C	79	27	60	87	36	20
Henrik Zetterberg, LW	63	33	35	68	26	36
Nicklas Lidstrom, D	80	13	49	62	40	46
Tomas Holmstrom, LW	77	30	22	52	13	58
Robert Lang, C	81	19	33	52	12	66
Mathieu Schneider, D	68	11	41	52	12	66
Daniel Cleary, RW	71	20	20	40	6	24
Mikael Samuelsson, RW	53	14	20	34	1	28
Johan Franzen, C	69	10	20	30	20	37
Kris Draper, C	81	14	15	29	7	58
Jason Williams, C	58	11	15	26	7	24
Jiri Hudler, C	76	15	10	25	16	36
Niklas Kronwall, D	68	1	21	22	0	54
Brett Lebda, D	74	5	13	18	16	61
Valtteri Filppula, C	73	10	7	17	8	20
Danny Markov, D	66	4	12	16	25	59
Kyle Calder, LW	19	5	9	14	6	22
Chris Chelios, D	71	0	11	11	11	34
Kirk Maltby, LW	82	6	5	11	-9	50
Andreas Lilja, D	57	0	5	5	6	54
Todd Bertuzzi, RW	8	2	2	4	3	6
Josh Langfeld, RW	33	0	2	2	2	12
Brad Norton, D	6	0	1	1	2	20
Tomas Kopecky, RW	26	1	0	1	-2	22
Kyle Quincey, D	6	1	0	1	0	0

GOALTENDING

Player	GP	Mins	W	L	TGA	GAA	SO
Dominik Hasek	56	3340	38	11	114	2.05	8
Chris Osgood	21	1161	11	3	46	2.38	0

Edmonton Oilers

SCORING

Player	GP	G	A	Pts	+/-	PM
Ryan Smyth, LW	53	31	22	53	2	38
Petr Sykora, C	82	22	31	53	-20	40
Ales Hemsky, RW	64	13	40	53	-7	40
Shawn Horcoff, C	80	16	35	51	-22	56
Jarret Stoll, C	51	13	26	39	2	48
Raffi Torres, LW	82	15	19	34	-7	88
Joffrey Lupul, RW	81	16	12	28	-29	45
Fernando Pisani, RW	77	14	14	28	-1	40
Marc-Andre Bergeron, D	55	8	17	25	-9	28
Marty Reasoner, C	72	6	14	20	-15	60
Steve Staios, D	58	2	15	17	-5	97
Patrick Thoresen, LW	68	4	12	16	-1	52
Toby Petersen, C	64	6	9	15	-18	4
Daniel Tjarnqvist, D	37	3	12	15	3	30
Jason Smith, D	82	2	9	11	-13	103
Marc-Antoine Pouliot, C	46	4	7	11	-2	18
Matt Greene, D	78	1	9	10	-22	109
Ladislav Smid, D	77	3	7	10	-16	37
Brad Winchester, LW	59	4	5	9	-10	86
Jan Hejda, D	39	1	8	9	-6	20
Tom Gilbert, D	12	1	5	6	-1	0
Petr Nedved, C	19	1	4	5	-5	10
Mathieu Roy, D	16	2	0	2	-7	30
Ethan Moreau, LW	7	1	0	1	-4	12
Kyle Brodziak, C	6	1	0	1	0	2
Zack Sortini, RW	29	1	0	1	-7	105
Danny Syvret, D	16	0	1	1	-10	6

GOALTENDING

Player	GP	Mins	W	L	TGA	GAA	SO
Dwayne Roloson	68	3931	27	34	180	2.75	4
Jussi Markkanen	22	992	5	9	52	3.14	0

Florida Panthers

SCORING

Player	GP	G	A	Pts	+/-	PM
Olli Jokinen, C	82	39	52	91	18	78
Nathan Horton, C	82	31	62	15	61
Jozef Stumpel, C	73	23	34	57	2	22
Stephen Weiss, C	74	20	28	48	-1	28
Martin Gelinas, LW	82	14	30	44	7	36
Jay Bouwmeester, D	82	12	30	42	23	66
Ville Peltonen, LW	72	17	20	87	7	28
Chris Gratton, C	81	13	22	35	1	94
Ruslan Salei, D	82	6	26	32	-13	102
Rostislav Olesz, C	75	11	19	30	2	28
Gary Roberts, LW	50	13	16	29	5	71
Mike Van Ryn, D	78	4	25	29	-5	64
Juraj Kolnik, RW	64	11	14	25	2	18
Bryan Allen, D	82	4	21	25	7	112
Joel Kwiatkowski, D	41	5	5	10	-5	20
David Booth, LW	48	3	7	10	0	12
Steve Montador, D	72	1	8	9	1	119
Gregory Campbell, C	79	6	3	9	-10	66
Joe Nieuwendyk, C	15	5	3	8	-4	4
Todd Bertuzzi, RW	7	1	6	7	-4	13
Alexei Semenov, D	23	0	5	5	9	28
Branislav Mezei, D	45	0	3	3	5	55
Janis Sprukts, C	13	1	2	3	1	2
Kamil Kreps, C	14	1	1	2	-1	6
Drew Larman, C	16	2	0	2	-3	2
Ric Jackman, D	7	1	0	1	-3	10
Anthony Stewart, C	10	0	1	1	1	2

GOALTENDING

Player	GP	Mins	W	L	TGA	GAA	SO
Ed Belfour	58	3289	27	17	152	2.77	1
Alex Auld	27	1470	7	13	82	3.35	1

Los Angeles Kings

SCORING

Player	GP	G	A	Pts	+/-	PM
Michael Cammalleri, C	81	34	46	80	5	48
Alexander Frolov, LW	82	35	36	71	-8	34
Anze Kopitar, C	72	20	41	61	-12	24
Lubomir Visnovsky, D	69	18	40	58	1	26
Dustin Brown, LW	81	17	29	46	-21	54
Derek Armstrong, C	67	11	33	44	13	62
Rob Blake, D	72	14	20	34	-26	82
Sean Avery, LW	55	10	18	28	-10	116
Brent Sopel, D	44	4	19	23	2	14
Tom Kostopoulos, RW	76	7	15	22	-2	73
Brian Willsie, RW	81	11	10	21	-20	49
Patrick O'Sullivan, C	44	5	14	19	-6	14
Craig Conroy, C	52	5	11	16	-13	38
Scott Thornton, LW	58	7	6	13	-15	85
Kevin Dallman, D	53	1	9	10	-13	12
Mattias Norstrom, D	62	2	7	9	-20	40

SCORING *(CONT.)*

Player	GP	G	A	Pts	+/-	PM
Mike Weaver, D	39	3	6	9	-4	16
Jamie Lundmark, C	29	7	2	9	-8	25
Jamie Heward, D	19	2	6	8	-2	20
Aaron Miller, D	82	0	8	8	-14	60
Jaroslav Modry, D	19	0	8	8	1	22
Raitis Ivanans, LW	66	4	4	8	-12	140
Oleg Tverdovsky, D	26	0	4	4	-10	10
K. Pushkarev, RW	16	2	2	4	-2	8
John Zeiler, RW	23	1	2	3	-2	22

GOALTENDING

Player	GP	Mins	W	L	TGA	GAA	SO
Mathieu Garon	32	1778	13	10	79	2.66	2
Dan Cloutier	24	1281	6	14	85	3.98	0
Sean Burke	23	1309	6	10	68	3.12	1

Minnesota Wild

SCORING

Player	GP	G	A	Pts	+/-	PM
Pavol Demitra, RW	71	25	39	64	0	28
Brian Rolston, RW	78	31	33	64	6	46
Marian Gaborik, RW	48	30	27	57	12	40
Pierre-Marc Bouchard, C	82	20	37	57	13	14
Mikko Koivu, C	82	20	34	54	6	58
Todd White, C	77	13	31	44	8	24
Mark Parrish, RW	76	19	20	39	9	18
Brent Burns, D	77	7	18	25	16	26
Wes Walz, C	62	9	15	24	3	30
B. Radivojevic, RW	82	11	13	24	-9	21
Kurtis Foster, D	57	3	20	23	-3	52
Kim Johnsson, D	76	3	19	22	-4	64
Petteri Nummelin, D	51	3	17	20	-15	22
Stephane Veilleux, LW	75	7	11	18	3	47
Keith Carney, D	80	4	13	17	22	58
Martin Skoula, D	81	0	15	15	9	36
Pascal Dupuis, LW	48	10	3	13	-7	38
Nick Schultz, D	82	2	10	12	0	42
Adam Hall, RW	49	4	8	12	-13	18
Wyatt Smith, C	61	3	3	6	-8	16
Mattias Weinhandl, RW	12	1	1	2	-2	10
Derek Boogaard, LW	48	0	1	1	0	120

GOALTENDING

Player	GP	Mins	W	L	TGA	GAA	SO
Manny Fernandez	44	2421	22	16	103	2.55	2
Niklas Backstrom	41	2226	23	8	73	1.97	5
Josh Harding	7	360	3	2	7	1.16	1

Montreal Canadiens

SCORING

Player	GP	G	A	Pts	+/-	PM
Saku Koivu, C	81	22	53	75	-21	74
Sheldon Souray, D	81	26	38	64	-28	135
Michael Ryder, RW	82	30	28	58	-25	60
Andrei Markov, D	77	6	43	49	2	56
Alexei Kovalev, RW	73	18	29	47	-19	78
Tomas Plekanec, C	81	20	27	47	10	36
Christopher Higgins, C	61	22	16	38	-11	26
Mark Streit, D	76	10	26	36	-5	14
Mike Johnson, RW	80	11	20	31	6	40
G. Latendresse, RW	80	16	13	29	-20	47
Sergei Samsonov, LW	63	9	17	26	-4	10
Radek Bonk, C	74	13	10	23	0	54
Mike Komisarek, D	82	4	15	19	7	96
Craig Rivet, D	54	6	10	16	-7	57
A. Perezhogin, RW	61	6	9	15	11	48
Francis Bouillon, D	62	3	11	14	-10	52
Maxim Lapierre, C	46	6	6	12	-7	24
Andrei Kostitsyn, LW	22	1	10	11	3	6
Steve Begin, LW	52	5	5	10	-6	46
Mathieu Dandenault, D	68	2	6	8	-8	40
Janne Niinimaa, D	41	0	3	3	-13	36
Garth Murray, LW	43	2	1	3	-10	32

GOALTENDING

Player	GP	Mins	W	L	TGA	GAA	SO
Cristobal Huet	42	2286	19	16	107	2.81	2
David Aebischer	32	1760	13	12	93	3.17	0
Jaroslav Halak	16	912	10	6	44	2.89	2

Nashville Predators

SCORING

Player	GP	G	A	Pts	+/-	PM
Paul Kariya, LW	82	24	52	76	6	36
J.P. Dumont, RW	82	21	45	66	14	28
David Legwand, C	78	27	36	63	-23	44
Steve Sullivan, RW	57	22	38	60	16	20
Martin Erat, LW	68	16	41	57	13	50
Kimmo Timonen, D	80	13	42	55	20	42
Jason Arnott, C	68	27	27	54	15	48
Shea Weber, D	79	17	23	40	13	60
Scott Hartnell, LW	64	22	17	39	19	96
Alexander Radulov, RW	64	18	19	37	19	26
Marek Zidlicky, D	79	4	26	30	8	72
Vernon Fiddler, C	72	11	16	26	11	40
Ryan Suter, D	82	8	15	24	10	54
Dan Hamhuis, D	81	6	14	20	8	66
Peter Forsberg, C	17	2	13	15	5	16
Josef Vasicek, C	38	4	9	13	1	29
Scott Nichol, C	59	7	6	13	7	79
Jerred Smithson, C	64	5	7	12	-8	42
Jordin Tootoo, RW	65	3	6	9	-11	116
Greg Zanon, D	66	3	5	8	16	32
Ramzi Abid, LW	13	1	4	5	-3	13
Darcy Hordichuk, LW	53	1	3	4	-2	90
Scottie Upshall, RW	14	2	1	3	-1	18
Mikko Lehtonen, D	15	1	2	3	0	8

GOALTENDING

Player	GP	Mins	W	L	TGA	GAA	SO
Tomas Vokoun	44	2601	27	12	104	2.40	5
Chris Mason	40	2341	24	11	93	2.38	5

New Jersey Devils

SCORING

Player	GP	G	A	Pts	+/-	PM
Patrik Elias, C	75	21	48	69	1	38
Zach Parise, LW	82	31	31	62	-3	30
Scott Gomez, C	72	13	47	60	7	42
J. Langenbrunner, RW	82	23	37	60	-10	64
Brian Rafalski, D	82	8	47	55	4	34
Brian Gionta, RW	62	25	20	45	-3	36
Travis Zajac, C	80	17	25	42	1	16
Sergei Brylin, C	82	16	24	40	-5	35
John Madden, C	74	12	20	32	-7	14
Jay Pandolfo, LW	82	13	14	27	-5	8
Paul Martin, D	82	3	23	26	-9	18
Brad Lukowich, D	75	4	8	12	1	36
Johnny Oduya, D	76	2	9	11	-5	61
Erik Rasmussen, C	71	3	7	10	-2	25
Michael Rupp, RW	76	6	3	9	-10	92
Jim Dowd, C	66	4	4	8	-5	20
Collin White, D	69	0	8	8	-8	69
Andy Greene, D	23	1	5	6	-1	6
David Clarkson, RW	7	3	1	4	-1	6
Alex Broks, D	19	0	1	1	-1	4
Jim Fahey, D	13	0	1	1	0	2
David Hale, D	43	0	1	1	2	26
Cam Janssen, RW	48	1	0	1	-2	114

GOALTENDING

Player	GP	Mins	W	L	TGA	GAA	SO
Martin Brodeur	78	4696	48	23	171	2.18	12
S. Clemmensen	6	305	1	1	16	3.14	0

New York Islanders

SCORING

Player	GP	G	A	Pts	+/-	PM
Jason Blake, LW	82	40	29	69	1	34
Miroslav Satan, RW	81	27	32	59	-12	46
Mike Sillinger, C	82	26	33	59	5	46
Viktor Kozlov, C	81	25	26	51	12	28
Alexei Yashin, C	58	18	32	50	6	44
Tom Poti, D	78	6	38	44	-1	74
Trent Hunter, RW	77	20	15	35	5	22
Andy Hilbert, C	81	8	20	28	10	34
Chris Simon, LW	67	10	17	27	17	75
Richard Park, RW	82	10	16	26	4	33
Sean Hill, D	81	1	24	25	6	110
Arron Asham, RW	80	11	12	23	3	63
Randy Robitaille, C	50	6	17	23	-2	22
Marc-Andre Bergeron, D	23	6	15	21	5	10
Radek Martinek, D	43	2	15	17	19	40
Ryan Smyth, LW	18	5	10	15	0	14
Brendan Witt, D	81	1	13	14	14	131
Chris Campoli, D	51	1	13	14	-3	23
Mike York, LW	32	6	7	13	-9	14
Alexei Zhitnik, D	30	2	9	11	13	40
Shawn Bates, C	48	4	6	10	13	34
Jeff Tambellini, LW	23	2	7	9	6	6

GOALTENDING

Player	GP	Mins	W	L	TGA	GAA	SO
Rick DiPietro, G	62	3626	32	19	156	2.58	5
Mike Dunham	19	979	4	10	61	3.74	0
Wade Dubielewicz	8	378	4	1	13	2.06	0

New York Rangers

SCORING

Player	GP	G	A	Pts	+/-	PM
Jaromir Jagr, RW	82	30	66	96	26	78
Michael Nylander, C	79	26	57	83	12	42
Martin Straka, LW	77	29	41	70	16	24
Brendan Shanahan, LW	67	29	33	62	2	47
Matt Cullen, C	80	16	25	41	0	52
Michal Rozsival, D	80	10	30	40	10	52
Petr Prucha, C	79	22	18	40	-7	30
Karel Rachunek, D	66	6	20	26	-9	38
Marek Malik, D	69	2	19	21	32	70
Sean Avery, LW	29	8	12	20	11	58
Marcel Hossa, LW	64	10	8	18	-4	26
Fedor Tyutin, D	66	2	12	14	-8	44
Aaron Ward, D	60	3	10	13	-3	57
Blair Betts, C	82	9	4	13	-4	24
Adam Hall, RW	49	4	8	12	-13	18
Jed Ortmeyer, RW	41	2	9	11	7	22
Jason Ward	46	4	6	10	-3	26
Thomas Pock	44	4	4	8	4	16
Jarkko Immonen, C	14	1	5	6	-2	4
Ryan Callahan, RW	14	4	2	6	5	9
Daniel Girardi, D	34	0	6	6	7	8

GOALTENDING

Player	GP	Mins	W	L	TGA	GAA	SO
Henrik Lundqvist	70	4108	37	22	160	2.34	5
Kevin Weekes	14	761	4	6	43	3.39	0
Stephen Valiquette	3	114	1	2	6	3.14	0

Ottawa Senators

SCORING

Player	GP	G	A	Pts	+/-	PM
Dany Heatley, LW	82	50	55	105	31	74
Daniel Alfredsson, RW	77	29	58	87	42	42
Jason Spezza, C	67	34	53	87	19	45
Mike Fisher, C	68	22	26	48	15	41
Peter Schaefer, LW	77	12	34	46	7	32
Antoine Vermette, C	77	19	20	39	-2	52
Chris Kelly, C	82	15	23	38	28	40
Tom Preissing, D	80	7	31	38	40	18
Joe Corvo, D	76	8	29	37	8	42
Wade Redden, D	64	7	29	36	1	50
Andrej Meszaros, D	82	7	28	35	-15	102
Patrick Eaves, RW	73	14	18	32	1	36
Dean McAmmond, LW	81	14	15	29	11	28
Chris Neil, RW	82	12	16	28	6	177
Chris Phillips, D	82	8	18	26	36	80
Mike Comrie, C	41	13	12	25	-1	24
Christoph Schubert, D	80	8	17	25	30	56
Anton Volchenkov, D	78	1	18	19	37	67
Denis Hamel, LW	43	4	3	7	4	10
Oleg Saprykin, LW	12	1	1	2	-3	4
Brian McGrattan, RW	45	0	2	2	-1	100
Josh Hennessy, C	10	1	0	1	0	4
Alexei Kaigorodov, C	6	0	1	1	1	0

GOALTENDING

Player	GP	Mins	W	L	TGA	GAA	SO
Ray Emery	58	3351	33	16	138	2.47	5
Martin Gerber	29	1598	15	9	74	2.78	1

Philadelphia Flyers

SCORING

Player	GP	G	A	Pts	+/-	PM
Simon Gagne, LW	76	41	27	68	2	30
Mike Knuble, RW	64	24	30	54	2	56
Joni Pitkanen, D	77	4	39	43	-25	88
Peter Forsberg, C	40	11	29	40	2	72
Jeff Carter, C	62	14	23	37	-17	48
Mike Richards, C	59	10	22	32	-12	52
Geoff Sanderson, LW	58	11	18	29	-16	44
R.J. Umberger, C	81	16	12	28	-32	41
Sami Kapanen, RW	77	11	14	25	-21	22
Randy Jones, D	66	4	18	22	-14	38
Alexandre Picard, D	62	3	19	22	-19	17
Kyle Calder, LW	59	9	12	21	-31	36
Randy Robitaille, C	28	5	12	17	-4	22
Dmitry Afanasenkov, LW	41	8	7	15	-19	12
Alexei Zhitnik, D	31	3	10	13	-16	38
Scottie Upshall, RW	18	6	7	13	4	8
Stefan Ruzicka, RW	40	3	10	13	-6	18
Ryan Potulny, C	35	7	5	12	1	22
Todd Fedoruk, LW	48	3	8	11	-11	84
Ben Eager, LW	63	6	5	11	-13	233
Derian Hatcher, D	82	3	6	9	-24	67
Mike York, LW	34	4	4	8	-9	8

GOALTENDING

Player	GP	Mins	W	L	TGA	GAA	SO
Antero Niittymaki	52	2942	9	29	166	3.38	0
Robert Esche	18	860	5	9	62	4.32	1
Martin Biron	16	935	6	8	47	3.01	0

Phoenix Coyotes

SCORING

Player	GP	G	A	Pts	+/–	PM
Shane Doan, LW	73	27	28	55	-14	73
Ladislav Nagy, LW	55	8	33	41	-2	48
Owen Nolan, RW	76	16	24	40	-2	56
Oleg Saprykin, LW	59	14	20	34	8	54
Yanic Perreault, C	49	19	14	33	-2	30
Steve Reinprecht, C	49	9	24	33	-3	28
Ed Jovanovski, D	54	11	18	29	-6	63
Jeremy Roenick, C	70	11	17	28	-18	32
Zbynek Michalek, D	82	4	24	28	-20	34
Keith Ballard, D	70	5	22	27	-7	59
Derek Morris, D	82	6	19	25	-18	115
Mike Zigomanis, C	75	14	9	23	-8	46
Georges Laraque, RW	56	5	17	22	7	52
Mike Comrie, C	24	7	13	20	1	20
Travis Roche, D	50	6	13	19	2	22
Fredrik Sjostrom, RW	78	9	9	18	-11	48
Bill Thomas, RW	24	8	6	14	-6	2
Nick Boynton, D	59	2	9	11	-13	138
Patrick Fischer, C	27	4	6	10	0	24
Niko Kapanen, C	19	2	7	9	-11	8
Mathias Tjarnqvist, LW	26	5	4	9	-2	2
Kevyn Adams, C	33	1	7	8	-10	8
Dave Scatchard, C	46	3	5	8	-18	72

GOALTENDING

Player	GP	Mins	W	L	TGA	GAA	SO
Curtis Joseph	55	2993	18	31	159	3.19	4
Mikael Tellqvist	30	1591	11	11	90	3.39	2

Pittsburgh Penguins

SCORING

Player	GP	G	A	Pts	+/–	PM
Sidney Crosby, C	79	36	84	120	10	60
Evgeni Malkin, LW	78	33	52	85	2	80
Mark Recchi, RW	82	24	44	68	1	62
Sergei Gonchar, D	82	13	54	67	-5	72
Ryan Whitney, D	81	14	45	59	9	77
Michel Ouellet, RW	73	19	29	48	-3	30
Jordan Staal, C	81	29	13	42	16	24
Colby Armstrong, RW	80	12	22	34	2	67
Erik Christensen, C	61	18	15	33	-3	26
Ryan Malone, LW	64	16	15	31	4	71
Maxime Talbot, C	75	13	11	24	-2	53
Jarkko Ruutu, LW	81	7	9	16	0	125
Nils Ekman, RW	34	6	9	15	-14	24
Dominic Moore, C	59	6	9	15	1	46
Gary Roberts, LW	19	7	6	13	-5	26
Josef Melichar, D	70	1	11	12	1	44
Robert Scuderi, D	78	1	10	11	3	28
John LeClair, LW	21	2	5	7	-2	12
Ronald Petrovicky, RW	31	3	3	6	4	28
Brooks Orpik, D	70	0	6	6	4	82
Alain Nasreddine, D	44	1	4	5	12	18
Chris Thorburn, C	39	3	2	5	1	69
Mark Eaton, D	35	0	3	3	-6	16

GOALTENDING

Player	GP	Mins	W	L	TGA	GAA	SO
Marc-Andre Fleury	67	3905	40	16	184	2.83	5
Jocelyn Thibault	22	1101	7	8	52	2.83	1

San Jose Sharks

SCORING

Player	GP	G	A	Pts	+/–	PM
Joe Thornton, C	82	22	92	114	24	44
Patrick Marleau, C	77	32	46	78	9	33
Jonathan Cheechoo, RW	76	37	32	69	11	69
Milan Michalek, RW	78	26	40	66	17	36
Matt Carle, D	77	11	31	42	9	30
Ryane Clowe, LW	58	16	18	34	4	78
Mike Grier, RW	81	16	17	33	-5	43
Christian Ehrhoff, D	82	10	23	33	8	63
Steve Bernier, RW	62	15	16	31	5	29
Joe Pavelski, C	46	14	14	28	4	18
Marc-Edouard Vlasic, D	81	3	23	26	13	18
Scott Hannan, D	79	4	20	24	1	38
Patrick Rissmiller, C	79	7	15	22	1	22
Mark Bell, LW	71	11	10	21	-9	83
Curtis Brown, C	78	8	12	20	-2	56

SCORING *(CONT.)*

Player	GP	G	A	Pts	+/–	PM
Kyle McLaren, D	67	5	12	17	10	61
Mark Smith, C	41	3	10	13	-4	42
Marcel Goc, C	78	5	8	13	-2	24
Bill Guerin, RW	16	8	1	9	2	14
Craig Rivet, D	17	1	7	8	8	12
Josh Gorges, D	47	1	3	4	-3	26
Doug Murray, D	35	0	3	3	0	31
Ville Nieminen, LW	30	1	1	2	-7	14
Rob Davison, D	22	0	2	2	-2	27

GOALTENDING

Player	GP	Mins	W	L	TGA	GAA	SO
Evgeni Nabokov	50	2777	25	16	106	2.29	7
Vesa Toskala	38	2141	26	10	84	2.35	4

St. Louis Blues

SCORING

Player	GP	G	A	Pts	+/-	PM
Doug Weight, C	82	16	43	59	10	56
Lee Stempniak, RW	82	27	25	52	-2	33
Petr Cajanek, C	77	15	33	48	9	54
Bill Guerin, RW	61	28	19	47	8	52
Keith Tkachuk, LW	61	20	23	43	3	92
Radek Dvorak, RW	82	10	27	37	-6	48
Jay McClement, C	81	8	28	36	3	55
Martin Rucinsky, LW	52	12	21	33	-3	48
Eric Brewer, D	82	6	23	29	-10	69
Barret Jackman, D	70	3	24	27	20	82
David Backes, C	49	10	13	23	6	37
Jamal Mayers, RW	80	8	14	22	-19	89
Dennis Wideman, D	55	5	17	22	-7	44
Christian Backman, D	61	7	11	18	13	36
Dallas Drake, RW	60	6	6	12	-14	38
Brad Boyes, C	19	4	8	12	0	4
Ryan Johnson, C	59	7	4	11	-7	47
Dan Hinote, RW	41	5	5	10	-8	23
Jeff Woywitka, D	34	1	6	7	4	12
Bryce Salvador, D	64	2	5	7	-5	55
Glen Metropolit, C	20	2	3	5	0	14
Matt Walker, D	48	0	5	5	7	72
Jamie Rivers, D	31	1	3	4	-7	36
Peter Sejna, LW	22	3	1	4	2	4
D.J. King, LW	27	1	1	2	-3	52

GOALTENDING

Player	GP	Mins	W	L	TGA	GAA	SO
Manny Legace	45	2521	23	15	109	2.59	5
Curtis Sanford	31	1491	8	12	79	3.18	0

Tampa Bay Lightning

SCORING

Player	GP	G	A	Pts	+/-	PM
Vincent Lecavalier, C	82	52	56	108	2	44
Martin St. Louis, RW	82	43	59	102	7	28
Brad Richards, C	82	25	45	70	-19	23
Dan Boyle, D	82	20	43	63	-5	62
Vaclav Prospal, C	82	14	41	55	-24	36
Filip Kuba, D	81	15	22	37	-9	36
Eric Perrin, C	82	13	23	36	-7	30
Ruslan Fedotenko, LW	80	12	20	32	-3	52
Paul Ranger, D	72	4	24	28	5	42
Ryan Craig, C	72	14	13	27	-11	55
Nikita Alexeev, RW	63	10	11	21	10	12
Cory Sarich, D	82	0	15	15	-6	70
Doug Janik, D	75	2	9	11	-11	53
Andreas Karlsson, C	53	3	6	9	-4	12
Nick Tarnasky, C	77	5	4	9	-6	80
Nolan Pratt, D	81	1	7	8	0	44
Jason Ward, RW	17	4	4	8	-11	10
Tim Taylor, C	71	1	5	6	-5	16
Dmitry Afanasenkov, LW	33	3	3	6	-6	8
Luke Richardson, D	27	0	3	3	3	16
Andre Roy, RW	51	1	2	3	-3	116
Blair Jones, C	20	1	2	3	0	2
Shane O'Brien, D	18	0	2	2	-8	36
Kyle Wanvig, RW	4	0	0	0	0	0
Karl Stewart, LW	7	0	0	0	-2	2

GOALTENDING

Player	GP	Mins	W	L	TGA	GAA	SO
Johan Holmqvist	48	2547	27	15	121	2.85	1
Marc Denis	44	2352	17	18	125	3.19	1

Toronto Maple Leafs

SCORING

Player	GP	G	A	Pts	+/-	PM
Mats Sundin, C	75	27	49	76	-2	48
Tomas Kaberle, D	74	11	47	58	3	20
Bryan McCabe, D	82	15	42	57	3	115
Alexei Ponikarovsky, LW	71	21	24	45	8	63
Darcy Tucker, RW	56	24	19	43	-11	81
Jeff O'Neill, C	74	20	22	42	1	54
Kyle Wellwood, C	48	12	30	42	3	0
Matthew Stajan, C	82	10	29	39	3	44
Alexander Steen, C	82	15	20	35	5	26
Nik Antropov, C	54	18	15	33	8	44
Bates Battaglia, LW	82	12	19	31	9	45
Johnny Pohl, C	74	13	16	29	-4	10
Chad Kilger, LW	82	14	14	28	-5	58
Ian White, D	76	3	23	26	8	40
Pavel Kubina, D	61	7	14	21	7	48

SCORING *(CONT.)*

Player	GP	G	A	Pts	+/-	PM
Hal Gill, D	82	6	14	20	11	91
Boyd Devereaux, C	33	8	11	19	4	12
Carlo Colaiacovo, D	48	8	9	17	5	22
Michael Peca, C	35	4	11	15	2	60
Yanic Perreault, C	17	2	3	5	1	4
Brendan Bell, D	31	1	4	5	-3	19
Kris Newbury, C	15	2	2	4	4	26
Wade Belak, D	65	0	3	3	-8	110
Ben Ondrus, RW	16	0	2	2	-5	20
Andy Wozniewski, D	15	0	2	2	-1	14
Jeremy Williams, RW	1	1	0	1	1	0

GOALTENDING

Player	GP	Mins	W	L	TGA	GAA	SO
Andrew Raycroft	72	4108	37	25	205	2.99	2
J. Aubin	20	804	3	5	46	3.43	0

Vancouver Canucks

SCORING

Player	GP	G	A	Pts	+/-	PM
Daniel Sedin, LW	81	36	48	84	19	36
Henrik Sedin, C	82	10	71	81	19	66
Markus Naslund, RW	82	24	36	60	3	54
Brendan Morrison, C	82	20	31	51	-9	60
Kevin Bieksa, D	81	12	30	42	1	134
Taylor Pyatt, LW	76	23	14	37	5	42
Sami Salo, D	67	14	23	37	21	26
Mattias Ohlund, D	77	11	20	31	-3	80
Matt Cooke, LW	81	10	20	30	0	64
Trevor Linden, C	80	12	13	25	-6	34
Jan Bulis, C	79	12	11	23	-8	70
Lukas Krajicek, D	78	3	13	16	-4	64
Ryan Kesler, C	48	6	10	16	1	40
Willie Mitchell, D	62	1	10	11	1	45
Jeff Cowan, LW	42	7	3	10	4	93
Alex Burrows, LW	81	3	6	9	-7	93

SCORING

Player	GP	G	A	Pts	+/-	PM
Rory Fitzpatrick, D	58	1	6	7	12	46
Josh Green, C	57	2	5	7	0	25
Bryan Smolinski, C	20	4	3	7	-3	8
Tommi Santala, C	30	1	5	6	0	24
Brent Sopel, D	20	1	4	5	0	10
Marc Chouinard, C	42	2	2	4	-2	10
Yannick Tremblay, D	12	1	2	3	-6	12
Alexander Edler, D	22	1	2	3	3	6
Brad Moran, C	3	0	1	1	0	2
Patrick Coulombe, D	7	0	1	1	-6	4

GOALTENDING

Player	GP	Mins	W	L	TGA	GAA	SO
Roberto Luongo	76	4490	47	22	171	2.28	5
Dany Sabourin	9	479	2	4	21	2.63	0

Washington Capitals

SCORING

Player	GP	G	A	Pts	+/-	PM
Alexander Ovechkin, LW	82	46	46	92	-19	52
Alexander Semin, LW	77	38	35	73	-7	90
Chris Clark, RW	74	30	24	54	-10	66
Dainius Zubrus, RW	60	20	32	52	-16	50
Matt Pettinger, LW	64	16	16	32	-13	22
Boyd Gordon, RW	71	7	22	29	10	14
Brian Pothier, D	72	3	25	28	-11	44
Kris Beech, C	64	8	18	26	-11	46
Ben Clymer, D	66	7	13	20	-17	44
Richard Zednik, LW	32	6	12	18	-4	16
Brooks Laich, C	73	8	10	18	-2	29
Brian Sutherby, C	69	7	10	17	-9	78
Steve Eminger, D	68	1	16	17	-14	63
Jamie Heward, D	53	4	12	16	4	27
Matt Bradley, RW	57	4	9	13	-5	47
Donald Brashear, LW	77	4	9	13	1	156

SCORING

Player	GP	G	A	Pts	+/-	PM
Shaone Morrisonn, D	78	3	10	13	3	106
Mike Green, D	70	2	10	12	-10	36
Jakub Klepis, C	41	3	7	10	-2	28
Milan Jurcina, D	30	2	7	9	5	24
Lawrence Nycholat, D	18	2	6	8	-3	12
Tomas Fleischmann, C	29	4	4	8	-6	8
Bryan Muir, D	26	3	4	7	3	42
John Erskine, D	29	1	6	7	-13	69
Jiri Novotny, C	18	0	6	6	-2	2
Alexandre Giroux, C	9	2	2	4	-4	2

GOALTENDING

Player	GP	Mins	W	L	TGA	GAA	SO
Olaf Kolzig	54	3184	22	24	159	3.00	1
Brent Johnson	30	1644	6	15	99	3.61	0

2007 NHL Draft

First Round

The opening round of the 2007 NHL draft was held on June 22 in Columbus, Ohio.

	Team	Selection	Position
1	Chicago	Patrick Kane	F
2	Philadelphia	James vanRiemsdyk	F
3	Phoenix	Kyle Turris	C
4	Los Angeles	Thomas Hickey	D
5	Washington	Kurt Alzner	D
6	Edmonton	Sam Gagner	C
7	Columbus	Jakub Voracek	F
8	Boston	Zach Hamill	C
9	San Jose	Logan Couture	C
10	Florida	Keaton Ellerby	D
11	Carolina	Brandon Sutter	F
12	Montreal	Ryan McDonagh	D
13	St. Louis	Lars Eller	C
14	Colorado	Kevin Shattenkirk	D
15	Edmonton	Alex Plante	D
16	Minnesota	Colton Gillies	C
17	N.Y. Rangers	Alexei Cherepanov	F
18	St. Louis	Ian Cole	D
19	Anaheim	Logan MacMillan	C
20	Pittsburgh	Angelo Esposito	C
21	Edmonton	Riley Nash	C
22	Montreal	Max Pacioretty	F
23	Nashville	Jon Blum	D
24	Calgary	Mikael Backlund	C
25	Vancouver	Patrick White	C
26	St. Louis	David Perron	F
27	Detroit	Brendan Smith	D
28	San Jose	Nick Petrecki	D
29	Ottawa	James O'Brien	C
30	Phoenix	Nick Ross	D

The Stanley Cup

Awarded annually to the team that wins the NHL's best-of-seven final-round playoffs. The Stanley Cup is the oldest trophy competed for by professional athletes in North America. It was donated in 1893 by Frederick Arthur, Lord Stanley of Preston.

Results

1892–93	Montreal A.A.A.
1893–94	Montreal A.A.A.
1894–95	Montreal Victorias
1895–96	Winnipeg Victorias (Feb)
1895–96	Montreal Victorias (Dec)
1896–97	Montreal Victorias
1897–98	Montreal Victorias
1898–99	Montreal Victorias (Feb)
1898–99	Montreal Shamrocks (Mar)
1899–1900	Montreal Shamrocks
1900–01	Winnipeg Victorias
1901–02	Winnipeg Victorias (Jan)
1901–02	Montreal A.A.A. (Mar)
1902–03	Montreal A.A.A. (Feb)
1902–03	Ottawa Silver Seven (Mar)
1903–04	Ottawa Silver Seven
1904–05	Ottawa Silver Seven
1905–06	Ottawa Silver Seven (Feb)
1905–06	Montreal Wanderers (Mar)
1906–07	Kenora Thistles (Jan)
1906–07	Montreal Wanderers (Mar)
1907–08	Montreal Wanderers
1908–09	Ottawa Senators
1909–10	Montreal Wanderers
1910–11	Ottawa Senators
1911–12	Quebec Bulldogs
1912–13	Quebec Bulldogs
1913–14	Toronto Blueshirts
1914–15	Vancouver Millionaires
1915–16	Montreal Canadiens
1916–17	Seattle Metropolitans

NHL WINNERS AND FINALISTS

Season	Champion	Finalist	GP in Final
1917–18	Toronto Arenas	Vancouver Millionaires	5
1918–19	No decision*	No decision*	5
1919–20	Ottawa Senators	Seattle Metropolitans	5
1920–21	Ottawa Senators	Vancouver Millionaires	5
1921–22	Toronto St. Pats	Vancouver Millionaires	5
1922–23	Ottawa Senators	Vancouver Maroons, Edmonton Eskimos	2, 4
1923–24	Montreal Canadiens	Vancouver Maroons, Calgary Tigers	2, 2
1924–25	Victoria Cougars	Montreal Canadiens	4
1925–26	Montreal Maroons	Victoria Cougars	4
1926–27	Ottawa Senators	Boston Bruins	4
1927–28	New York Rangers	Montreal Maroons	5
1928–29	Boston Bruins	New York Rangers	2
1929–30	Montreal Canadiens	Boston Bruins	2
1930–31	Montreal Canadiens	Chicago Black Hawks	5
1931–32	Toronto Maple Leafs	New York Rangers	3
1932–33	New York Rangers	Toronto Maple Leafs	4
1933–34	Chicago Black Hawks	Detroit Red Wings	4
1934–35	Montreal Maroons	Toronto Maple Leafs	3
1935–36	Detroit Red Wings	Toronto Maple Leafs	4
1936–37	Detroit Red Wings	New York Rangers	5
1937–38	Chicago Black Hawks	Toronto Maple Leafs	4
1938–39	Boston Bruins	Toronto Maple Leafs	5
1939–40	New York Rangers	Toronto Maple Leafs	6
1940–41	Boston Bruins	Detroit Red Wings	4
1941–42	Toronto Maple Leafs	Detroit Red Wings	7
1942–43	Detroit Red Wings	Boston Bruins	4
1943–44	Montreal Canadiens	Chicago Black Hawks	4
1944–45	Toronto Maple Leafs	Detroit Red Wings	7
1945–46	Montreal Canadiens	Boston Bruins	5
1946–47	Toronto Maple Leafs	Montreal Canadiens	6
1947–48	Toronto Maple Leafs	Detroit Red Wings	4
1948–49	Toronto Maple Leafs	Detroit Red Wings	4
1949–50	Detroit Red Wings	New York Rangers	7
1950–51	Toronto Maple Leafs	Montreal Canadiens	5
1951–52	Detroit Red Wings	Montreal Canadiens	4
1952–53	Montreal Canadiens	Boston Bruins	5
1953–54	Detroit Red Wings	Montreal Canadiens	7
1954–55	Detroit Red Wings	Montreal Canadiens	7

The Stanley Cup *(Cont.)*

NHL WINNERS AND FINALISTS

Season	Champion	Finalist	GP in Final
1955–56	Montreal Canadiens	Detroit Red Wings	5
1956–57	Montreal Canadiens	Boston Bruins	5
1957–58	Montreal Canadiens	Boston Bruins	6
1958–59	Montreal Canadiens	Toronto Maple Leafs	5
1959–60	Montreal Canadiens	Toronto Maple Leafs	4
1960–61	Chicago Blackhawks	Detroit Red Wings	6
1961–62	Toronto Maple Leafs	Chicago Blackhawks	6
1962–63	Toronto Maple Leafs	Detroit Red Wings	5
1963–64	Toronto Maple Leafs	Detroit Red Wings	7
1964–65	Montreal Canadiens	Chicago Blackhawks	7
1965–66	Montreal Canadiens	Detroit Red Wings	6
1966–67	Toronto Maple Leafs	Montreal Canadiens	6
1967–68	Montreal Canadiens	St. Louis Blues	4
1968–69	Montreal Canadiens	St. Louis Blues	4
1969–70	Boston Bruins	St. Louis Blues	4
1970–71	Montreal Canadiens	Chicago Blackhawks	7
1971–72	Boston Bruins	New York Rangers	6
1972–73	Montreal Canadiens	Chicago Blackhawks	6
1973–74	Philadelphia Flyers	Boston Bruins	6
1974–75	Philadelphia Flyers	Buffalo Sabres	6
1975–76	Montreal Canadiens	Philadelphia Flyers	4
1976–77	Montreal Canadiens	Boston Bruins	4
1977–78	Montreal Canadiens	Boston Bruins	6
1978–79	Montreal Canadiens	New York Rangers	5
1979–80	New York Islanders	Philadelphia Flyers	6
1980–81	New York Islanders	Minnesota North Stars	5
1981–82	New York Islanders	Vancouver Canucks	4
1982–83	New York Islanders	Edmonton Oilers	4
1983–84	Edmonton Oilers	New York Islanders	5
1984–85	Edmonton Oilers	Philadelphia Flyers	5
1985–86	Montreal Canadiens	Calgary Flames	5
1986–87	Edmonton Oilers	Philadelphia Flyers	7
1987–88	Edmonton Oilers	Boston Bruins	4
1988–89	Calgary Flames	Montreal Canadiens	6
1989–90	Edmonton Oilers	Boston Bruins	5
1990–91	Pittsburgh Penguins	Minnesota North Stars	6
1991–92	Pittsburgh Penguins	Chicago Blackhawks	4
1992–93	Montreal Canadiens	Los Angeles Kings	5
1993–94	New York Rangers	Vancouver Canucks	7
1994–95	New Jersey Devils	Detroit Red Wings	4
1995–96	Colorado Avalanche	Florida Panthers	4
1996–97	Detroit Red Wings	Philadelphia Flyers	4
1997–98	Detroit Red Wings	Washington Capitals	4
1998–99	Dallas Stars	Buffalo Sabres	6
1999–2000	New Jersey Devils	Dallas Stars	6
2000–01	Colorado Avalanche	New Jersey Devils	7
2001–02	Detroit Red Wings	Carolina Hurricanes	5
2002–03	New Jersey Devils	Anaheim Mighty Ducks	7
2003–04	Tampa Bay Lightning	Calgary Flames	7
2004–05	No Stanley Cup due to season lockout		
2005–06	Carolina Hurricanes	Edmonton Oilers	7
2006–07	Anaheim Ducks	Ottawa Senators	5

*In 1919 the Montreal Canadiens traveled to meet Seattle, the PCHL champions. After five games had been played—the teams were tied at two wins and one tie—the series was called off by the local Department of Health because of the influenza epidemic and the death of Canadiens defenseman Joe Hall from influenza.

Conn Smythe Trophy

Awarded to the Most Valuable Player of the Stanley Cup playoffs, as selected by the Professional Hockey Writers Association. The trophy is named after the former coach, general manager, president and owner of the Toronto Maple Leafs.

1965	Jean Beliveau, Mtl
1966	Roger Crozier, Det
1967	Dave Keon, Tor
1968	Glenn Hall, StL
1969	Serge Savard, Mtl
1970	Bobby Orr, Bos
1971	Ken Dryden, Mtl
1972	Bobby Orr, Bos
1973	Yvan Cournoyer, Mtl
1974	Bernie Parent, Phil
1975	Bernie Parent, Phil
1976	Reggie Leach, Phil
1977	Guy Lafleur, Mtl
1978	Larry Robinson, Mtl
1979	Bob Gainey, Mtl
1980	Bryan Trottier, NYI
1981	Butch Goring, NYI
1982	Mike Bossy, NYI
1983	Bill Smith, NYI
1984	Mark Messier, Edm
1985	Wayne Gretzky, Edm
1986	Patrick Roy, Mtl
1987	Ron Hextall, Phil
1988	Wayne Gretzky, Edm
1989	Al MacInnis, Cgy
1990	Bill Ranford, Edm
1991	Mario Lemieux, Pitt
1992	Mario Lemieux, Pitt
1993	Patrick Roy, Mtl
1994	Brian Leetch, NYR
1995	Claude Lemieux, NJ
1996	Joe Sakic, Col
1997	Mike Vernon, Det
1998	Steve Yzerman, Det
1999	Joe Nieuwendyk, Dall
2000	Scott Stevens, NJ
2001	Patrick Roy, Col
2002	Nicklas Lidstrom, Det
2003	J.-S. Giguere, Ana
2004	Brad Richards, TB
2005	No Award–No Season
2006	Cam Ward, Car
2007	Scott Niedermayer, Ana

Alltime Stanley Cup Playoff Leaders

Points

	Yrs	GP	G	A	Pts		Yrs	GP	G	A	Pts
Wayne Gretzky, four teams	16	208	122	260	382	Jean Beliveau, Mtl	17	162	79	97	176
Mark Messier, Edm, Van, NYR	18	236	109	186	295	Denis Savard, Chi, Mtl	16	169	66	109	175
Jari Kurri, four teams	15	200	106	127	233	Mario Lemieux, Pitt	8	107	76	96	172
Glenn Anderson, four teams	15	225	93	121	214	*Peter Forsberg, Que, Col, Phil	12	144	63	103	166
Paul Coffey, six teams	16	194	59	137	196	Denis Potvin, NYI	14	185	56	108	164
Brett Hull, four teams	19	202	103	87	190	*Sergei Fedorov, Det, Ana	13	162	50	113	163
Doug Gilmour, seven teams	18	182	60	128	188	Mike Bossy, NYI	10	129	85	75	160
Steve Yzerman, Det	20	196	70	115	185	Gordie Howe, Det, Hart	20	157	68	92	160
Bryan Trottier, NYI, Pitt	17	221	71	113	184	Bobby Smith, Minn, Mtl	13	184	64	96	160
Ray Bourque, Bos, Col	21	214	41	139	180	Al MacInnis, Cgy, StL	19	177	39	121	160
*Joe Sakic, Que, Col	12	162	82	96	178						

*Active in 2006–07.

Goals

	Yrs	GP	G			Yrs	GP	G
Wayne Gretzky, four teams	16	208	122					
Mark Messier, Edm, NYR	18	236	109					
Jari Kurri, five teams	15	200	106					
Brett Hull, Cgy, StL, Dall, Det	19	202	103					
Glenn Anderson, four teams	15	225	93					
Mike Bossy, NYI	10	129	85					
*Joe Sakic, Que, Col	12	162	82					
Maurice Richard, Mtl	15	133	82					
Claude Lemieux, six teams	17	233	80					
Jean Beliveau, Mtl	17	162	79					
*Mario Lemieux, Pitt	8	107	76					

*Active in 2006–07.

Assists

	Yrs	GP	A
Wayne Gretzky, four teams	16	208	260
Mark Messier, Edm, NYR	18	236	186
Ray Bourque, Bos, Col	21	214	139
Paul Coffey, six teams	16	194	137
Doug Gilmour, seven teams	18	182	128
Jari Kurri, five teams	15	200	127
Glenn Anderson, four teams	15	225	121
Al MacInnis, Cgy, StL	19	177	121
Larry Robinson, Mtl, LA	20	227	116
Larry Murphy, six teams	15	215	115
Steve Yzerman, Det	20	196	115

*Active in 2006–07.

Alltime Stanley Cup Playoff Goaltending Leaders

WINS	W	L	Pct
Patrick Roy, Mtl, Col	151	94	.616
*Martin Brodeur, NJ	94	70	.573
Grant Fuhr, five teams	92	50	.648
Billy Smith, LA, NYI	88	36	.710
*Ed Belfour, four teams	88	68	.564
Ken Dryden, Mtl	80	32	.714
Mike Vernon, four teams	77	56	.579
Jacques Plante, five teams	71	36	.663
Andy Moog, four teams	68	57	.544
*Curtis Joseph, four teams	62	66	.484

*Active in 2006–07.

SHUTOUTS	GP	W	SO
Patrick Roy, Mtl, Col	247	151	23
*Martin Brodeur, NJ	164	94	22
*Curtis Joseph, four teams	131	62	16
*Ed Belfour, four teams	161	88	14
Jacques Plante, five teams	112	71	14

GOALS AGAINST AVG		Avg
*Martin Brodeur, NJ		1.93
George Hainsworth, Mtl, Tor		1.93
Turk Broda, Tor		1.98
*Dominik Hasek, Chi, Buff, Det		1.99
*Ed Belfour, four teams		2.17

Note: At least 50 games played.
*Active in 2006–07.

Alltime Stanley Cup Playoff Wins

TEAM	W	L	Pct	TEAM	W	L	Pct
Montreal	393	266	.596	New Jersey†	117	96	.549
Detroit	269	248	.520	Calgary*	89	106	.456
Toronto	251	269	.483	Vancouver	71	96	.425
Boston	242	264	.478	Washington	69	85	.448
NY Rangers	189	203	.482	Los Angeles	65	105	.382
Chicago	188	218	.463	Carolina§	51	58	.468
Pittsburgh	181	170	.516	San Jose	51	55	.481
Philadelphia	180	166	.520	Ottawa	49	50	.495
Edmonton	152	99	.606	Anaheim	44	29	.603
Dallas#	138	141	.495	Phoenix††	29	63	.315
St. Louis	138	165	.455	Tampa Bay	26	25	.551
NY Islanders	131	102	.562	Florida	13	18	.419
Colorado**	126	107	.541	Minnesota	8	10	.444
Buffalo	119	124	.490	Nashville	3	8	.273

*Atlanta Flames 1972–80. †Colorado Rockies 1976–82. #Minnesota North Stars 1967–93. **Quebec Nordiques 1979–95. ††Winnipeg Jets 1979–96. §Hartford Whalers 1979–97. Note: Teams ranked by playoff victories.

Stanley Cup Playoff Coaching Records

Coach	Team	Yrs	Series W	Series L	Games	Games W	Games L	T	Cups	Pct
Glen Sather	Edm	10	27	21	6	*126	89	37	0	4	.706
Toe Blake	Mtl	13	23	18	5	119	82	37	0	8	.689
Scott Bowman	Five teams	28	68	49	19	353	223	130	0	9	.632
Hap Day	Tor	9	14	10	4	80	49	31	0	5	.613
Al Arbour	StL, NYI	16	42	30	12	209	123	86	0	4	.589
†Bob Hartley	Col, Atl	5	14	10	4	84	49	35	0	1	.583
Fred Shero	Phil, NYR	8	21	15	6	110	63	47	0	2	.573
Mike Keenan	five teams	11	28	18	10	160	91	69	0	1	.569
†Ken Hitchcock	Dall, Phil	8	20	13	7	117	66	51	0	1	.564
†Jacques Lemaire	Mtl, NJ, Minn	8	19	12	7	106	58	50	0	1	.547

*Does not include suspended game, May 24, 1988. †Active in 2006–07.
Note: Coaches ranked by winning percentage. Minimum: 65 games.

The 10 Longest Overtime Games

Date	Result	OT	Scorer	Series	Series Winner
3-24-36	Det 1 vs Mtl M 0	116:30	Mud Bruneteau	SF	Det
4-3-33	Tor 1 vs Bos 0	104:46	Ken Doraty	SF	Tor
5-4-00	Phil 2 vs Pitt 1	92:01	Keith Primeau	CSF	Phil
4-24-03	Ana 4 vs Dall 3	80:48	Petr Sykora	CSF	Ana
4-24-96	Pitt 3 vs Wash 2	79:15	Petr Nedved	CQF	Pitt
3-23-43	Tor 3 vs Det 2	70:18	Jack McLean	SF	Det
3-28-30	Mtl 2 vs NYR 1	68:52	Gus Rivers	SF	Mtl
4-18-87	NYI 3 vs Wash 2	68:47	Pat LaFontaine	DSF	NYI
4-27-94	Buff 1 vs NJ 0	65:43	Dave Hannan	CQF	NJ
3-27-51	Mtl 3 vs Det 2	61:09	Maurice Richard	SF	Mtl

NHL Awards

Hart Memorial Trophy

Awarded annually "to the player adjudged to be the most valuable to his team." The original trophy was donated by Dr. David A. Hart, father of Cecil Hart, former manager-coach of the Montreal Canadiens. In the 1980s Wayne Gretzky won the award nine times.

Year	Winner	Key Statistics	Runner-Up
1924	Frank Nighbor, Ott	10 goals, 3 assists in 20 games	Sprague Cleghorn, Mtl
1925	Billy Burch, Ham	20 goals, 4 assists in 27 games	Howie Morenz, Mtl
1926	Nels Stewart, Mtl M	42 points in 36 games	Sprague Cleghorn, Mtl
1927	Herb Gardiner, Mtl	12 points in 44 games as defenseman	Bill Cook, NYR
1928	Howie Morenz, Mtl	33 goals, 18 assists	Roy Worters, Pitt
1929	Roy Worters, NYA	1.21 goals against, 13 shutouts	Ace Bailey, Tor
1930	Nels Stewart, Mtl M	39 goals, 16 assists	Lionel Hitchman, Bos
1931	Howie Morenz, Mtl	28 goals, 23 assists	Eddie Shore, Bos
1932	Howie Morenz, Mtl	24 goals, 25 assists	Ching Johnson, NYR
1933	Eddie Shore, Bos	27 assists in 48 games as defenseman	Bill Cook, NYR
1934	Aurel Joliat, Mtl	27 points	Lionel Conacher, Chi
1935	Eddie Shore, Bos	26 assists in 48 games as defenseman	Charlie Conacher, Tor
1936	Eddie Shore, Bos	16 assists in 46 games as defenseman	Hooley Smith, Mtl M
1937	Babe Siebert, Mtl	28 points	Lionel Conacher, Mtl M
1938	Eddie Shore, Bos	17 points in 47 games as defenseman	Paul Thompson, Chi
1939	Toe Blake, Mtl	led NHL in points (47)	Syl Apps, Tor
1940	Ebbie Goodfellow, Det	28 points	Syl Apps, Tor
1941	Bill Cowley, Bos	led NHL in assists (45) and points (62)	Dit Clapper, Bos
1942	Tom Anderson, Bos	41 points	Syl Apps, Tor
1943	Bill Cowley, Bos	led NHL in assists (45)	Doug Bentley, Chi
1944	Babe Pratt, Tor	57 points in 50 games	Bill Cowley, Bos
1945	Elmer Lach, Mtl	led NHL in assists (54) and points (80)	Maurice Richard, Mtl
1946	Max Bentley, Chi	61 points in 47 games	Gaye Stewart, Tor
1947	Maurice Richard, Mtl	led NHL in goals (45); 26 assists	Milt Schmidt, Bos
1948	Buddy O'Connor, NYR	60 points in 60 games	Frank Brimsek, Bos
1949	Sid Abel, Det	28 goals, 26 assists	Bill Durnan, Mtl
1950	Charlie Rayner, NYR	6 shutouts	Ted Kennedy, Tor
1951	Milt Schmidt, Bos	61 points in 62 games	Maurice Richard, Mtl
1952	Gordie Howe, Det	led NHL in goals (47) and points (86)	Elmer Lach, Mtl
1953	Gordie Howe, Det	led NHL in goals (49) and points (95)	Al Rollins, Chi
1954	Al Rollins, Chi	5 shutouts	Red Kelly, Det
1955	Ted Kennedy, Tor	52 points	Harry Lumley, Tor
1956	Jean Beliveau, Mtl	led NHL in goals (47) and points (88)	Tod Sloan, Tor
1957	Gordie Howe, Det	led NHL in goals (44) and points (89)	Jean Beliveau, Mtl
1959	Andy Bathgate, NYR	74 points in 70 games	Gordie Howe, Det
1960	Gordie Howe, Det	45 assists, 73 points	Bobby Hull, Chi
1961	Bernie Geoffrion, Mtl	50 goals, 95 points	Johnny Bower, Tor
1962	Jacques Plante, Mtl	42 wins, 2.37 goals against avg.	Doug Harvey, NYR
1963	Gordie Howe, Det	47 assists, 73 points	Stan Mikita, Chi
1964	Jean Beliveau, Mtl	50 assists, 78 points	Bobby Hull, Chi
1965	Bobby Hull, Chi	39 goals, 32 assists	Norm Ullman, Det
1966	Bobby Hull, Chi	led NHL in goals (54) and points (97)	Jean Beliveau, Mtl
1967	Stan Mikita, Chi	led NHL in assists (62) and points (97)	Ed Giacomin, NYR
1968	Stan Mikita, Chi	40 goals, 47 assists	Jean Beliveau, Mtl
1969	Phil Esposito, Bos	led NHL in assists (77) and points (126)	Jean Beliveau, Mtl
1970	Bobby Orr, Bos	led NHL in assists (87) and points (120)	Tony Esposito, Chi
1971	Bobby Orr, Bos	102 assists, 139 points	Phil Esposito, Bos
1972	Bobby Orr, Bos	80 assists, 117 points	Ken Dryden, Mtl
1973	Bobby Clarke, Phil	67 assists, 104 points	Phil Esposito, Bos
1974	Phil Esposito, Bos	led NHL in goals (68) and points (145)	Bernie Parent, Phil
1975	Bobby Clarke, Phil	89 assists, 116 points	Rogatien Vachon, LA
1976	Bobby Clarke, Phil	89 assists, 119 points	Denis Potvin, NYI
1977	Guy Lafleur, Mtl	led NHL in assists (80) and points (136)	Bobby Clarke, Phil
1978	Guy Lafleur, Mtl	led NHL in goals (60) and points (132)	Bryan Trottier, NYI
1979	Bryan Trottier, NYI	led NHL in assists (87) and points (134)	Guy Lafleur, Mtl
1980	Wayne Gretzky, Edm	51 goals, 86 points	Marcel Dionne, LA
1981	Wayne Gretzky, Edm	led NHL in assists (109) and points (164)	Mike Liut, StL
1982	Wayne Gretzky, Edm	NHL-record 92 goals and 212 points	Bryan Trottier, NYI
1983	Wayne Gretzky, Edm	led NHL in goals (71) and points (196)	Pete Peeters, Bos
1984	Wayne Gretzky, Edm	led NHL in goals (87) and points (205)	Rod Langway, Wash
1985	Wayne Gretzky, Edm	led NHL in goals (73) and points (208)	Dale Hawerchuk, Winn
1986	Wayne Gretzky, Edm	NHL-record 163 assists and 215 points	Mario Lemieux, Pitt
1987	Wayne Gretzky, Edm	led NHL in assists (121) and points (183)	Ray Bourque, Bos

Hart Memorial Trophy (Cont.)

Year	Winner	Key Statistics	Runner-Up
1988	Mario Lemieux, Pitt	led NHL in goals (70) and points (168)	Grant Fuhr, Edm
1989	Wayne Gretzky, LA	114 assists, 168 points	Mario Lemieux, Pitt
1990	Mark Messier, Edm	84 assists, 129 points	Ray Bourque, Bos
1991	Brett Hull, StL	led NHL in goals (86); 131 points	Wayne Gretzky, LA
1992	Mark Messier, NYR	72 assists, 107 points	Patrick Roy, Mtl
1993	Mario Lemieux, Pitt	69 goals, 91 assists in 60 games	Doug Gilmour, Tor
1994	Sergei Fedorov, Det	56 goals, 64 assists	Dominik Hasek, Buff
1995	Eric Lindros, Phil	29 goals, 41 assists in 46 games	Jaromir Jagr, Pitt
1996	Mario Lemieux, Pitt	led NHL in goals (69) and points (161)	Mark Messier, NYR
1997	Dominik Hasek, Buff	5 shutouts, 2.27 goals against avg.	Paul Kariya, Ana
1998	Dominik Hasek, Buff	13 shutouts, 2.09 goals against avg.	Jaromir Jagr, Pitt
1999	Jaromir Jagr, Pitt	44 goals, 127 points	Alexei Yashin, Ott
2000	Chris Pronger, StL	62 points, +52 plus/minus rating	Jaromir Jagr, Pitt
2001	Joe Sakic, Col	118 points, +45 plus/minus rating	Mario Lemieux, Pitt
2002	Jose Theodore, Mtl	2.11 goals against avg./7 shutouts	Jarome Iginla, Cal
2003	Peter Forsberg, Col	77 assists, +52 plus/minus rating	Markus Naslund, Van
2004	Martin St. Louis, TB	94 points, +35 plus/minus rating	Jarome Iginla, Cal
2005	No Award		
2006	Joe Thornton, Bos/SJ	29 goals, 96 assists; 125 points	Jaromir Jagr, NYR
2007	Sidney Crosby, Pitt	36 goals, 84 assists; 120 points	Roberto Luongo, Van

Art Ross Trophy

Awarded annually "to the player who leads the league in scoring points at the end of the regular season." The trophy was presented to the NHL in 1947 by Arthur Howie Ross, former manager-coach of the Boston Bruins. The tie-breakers, in order, are as follows: (1) player with most goals, (2) player with fewer games played, (3) player scoring first goal of the season. Bobby Orr is the only defenseman in NHL history to win this trophy, and he won it twice (1970 and 1975).

Year	Winner	Pts	Year	Winner	Pts
1919	Newsy Lalonde, Mtl	44	1958	Dickie Moore, Mtl	84
1920	Joe Malone, Que	30	1959	Dickie Moore, Mtl	96
1921	Newsy Lalonde, Mtl	48	1960	Bobby Hull, Chi	81
1922	Punch Broadbent, Ott	41	1961	Bernie Geoffrion, Mtl	95
1923	Babe Dye, Tor	46	1962	Bobby Hull, Chi	84
1924	Cy Denneny, Ott	37	1963	Gordie Howe, Det	86
1925	Babe Dye, Tor	23	1964	Stan Mikita, Chi	89
1926	Nels Stewart, Mtl M	44	1965	Stan Mikita, Chi	87
1927	Bill Cook, NYR	42	1966	Bobby Hull, Chi	97
1928	Howie Morenz, Mtl	37	1967	Stan Mikita, Chi	97
1929	Ace Bailey, Tor	51	1968	Stan Mikita, Chi	87
1930	Cooney Weiland, Bos	32	1969	Phil Esposito, Bos	126
1931	Howie Morenz, Mtl	73	1970	Bobby Orr, Bos	120
1932	Harvey Jackson, Tor	51	1971	Phil Esposito, Bos	152
1933	Bill Cook, NYR	53	1972	Phil Esposito, Bos	133
1934	Charlie Conacher, Tor	50	1973	Phil Esposito, Bos	130
1935	Charlie Conacher, Tor	57	1974	Phil Esposito, Bos	145
1936	Sweeney Schriner, NYA	45	1975	Bobby Orr, Bos	135
1937	Sweeney Schriner, NYA	46	1976	Guy Lafleur, Mtl	125
1938	Gordie Drillon, Tor	52	1977	Guy Lafleur, Mtl	136
1939	Toe Blake, Mtl	47	1978	Guy Lafleur, Mtl	132
1940	Milt Schmidt, Bos	52	1979	Bryan Trottier, NYI	134
1941	Bill Cowley, Bos	62	1980	Marcel Dionne, LA	137
1942	Bryan Hextall, NYR	56	1981	Wayne Gretzky, Edm	164
1943	Doug Bentley, Chi	73	1982	Wayne Gretzky, Edm	212
1944	Herb Cain, Bos	82	1983	Wayne Gretzky, Edm	196
1945	Elmer Lach, Mtl	80	1984	Wayne Gretzky, Edm	205
1946	Max Bentley, Chi	61	1985	Wayne Gretzky, Edm	208
1947	*Max Bentley, Chi	72	1986	Wayne Gretzky, Edm	215
1948	Elmer Lach, Mtl	61	1987	Wayne Gretzky, Edm	183
1949	Roy Conacher, Chi	68	1988	Mario Lemieux, Pitt	168
1950	Ted Lindsay, Det	78	1989	Mario Lemieux, Pitt	199
1951	Gordie Howe, Det	86	1990	Wayne Gretzky, LA	142
1952	Gordie Howe, Det	86	1991	Wayne Gretzky, LA	163
1953	Gordie Howe, Det	95	1992	Mario Lemieux, Pitt	131
1954	Gordie Howe, Det	81	1993	Mario Lemieux, Pitt	160
1955	Bernie Geoffrion, Mtl	75	1994	Wayne Gretzky, LA	130
1956	Jean Beliveau, Mtl	88	1995	Jaromir Jagr, Pitt	70
1957	Gordie Howe, Det	89	1996	Mario Lemieux, Pitt	161

Art Ross Trophy *(Cont.)*

Year	Winner	Pts	Year	Winner	Pts
1997	Mario Lemieux, Pitt	122	2003	Peter Forsberg, Col	106
1998	Jaromir Jagr, Pitt	102	2004	Martin St. Louis, TB	94
1999	Jaromir Jagr, Pitt	127	2005	No Award	
2000	Jaromir Jagr, Pitt	96	2006	Joe Thornton, Bos/SJ	125
2001	Jaromir Jagr, Pitt	121	2007	Sidney Crosby, Pitt	120
2002	Jarome Iginla, Cgy	96			

Note: Listing includes scoring leaders prior to inception of Art Ross Trophy in 1947–48.

Lady Byng Memorial Trophy

Awarded annually "to the player adjudged to have exhibited the best type of sportsmanship and gentlemanly conduct combined with a high standard of playing ability." Lady Byng, who first presented the trophy in 1925, was the wife of Canada's Governor-General. She donated a second trophy in 1936 after the first was given permanently to Frank Boucher of the New York Rangers, who won it seven times in eight seasons. Stan Mikita, one of the league's most penalized players during his early years in the NHL, won the trophy twice late in his career (1967 and 1968).

1925 .... Frank Nighbor, Ott	1953 .... Red Kelly, Det	1981 .... Rick Kehoe, Pitt
1926 .... Frank Nighbor, Ott	1954 .... Red Kelly, Det	1982 .... Rick Middleton, Bos
1927 .... Billy Burch, NYA	1955 .... Sid Smith, Tor	1983 .... Mike Bossy, NYI
1928 .... Frank Boucher, NYR	1956 .... Earl Reibel, Det	1984 .... Mike Bossy, NYI
1929 .... Frank Boucher, NYR	1957 .... Andy Hebenton, NYR	1985 .... Jari Kurri, Edm
1930 .... Frank Boucher, NYR	1958 .... Camille Henry, NYR	1986 .... Mike Bossy, NYI
1931 .... Frank Boucher, NYR	1959 .... Alex Delvecchio, Det	1987 .... Joe Mullen, Cgy
1932 .... Joe Primeau, Tor	1960 .... Don McKenney, Bos	1988 .... Mats Naslund, Mtl
1933 .... Frank Boucher, NYR	1961 .... Red Kelly, Tor	1989 .... Joe Mullen, Cgy
1934 .... Frank Boucher, NYR	1962 .... Dave Keon, Tor	1990 .... Brett Hull, StL
1935 .... Frank Boucher, NYR	1963 .... Dave Keon, Tor	1991 .... Wayne Gretzky, LA
1936 .... Doc Romnes, Chi	1964 .... Ken Wharram, Chi	1992 .... Wayne Gretzky, LA
1937 .... Marty Barry, Det	1965 .... Bobby Hull, Chi	1993 .... Pierre Turgeon, NY
1938 .... Gordie Drillon, Tor	1966 .... Alex Delvecchio, Det	1994 .... Wayne Gretzky, LA
1939 .... Clint Smith, NYR	1967 .... Stan Mikita, Chi	1995 .... Ron Francis, Pitt
1940 .... Bobby Bauer, Bos	1968 .... Stan Mikita, Chi	1996 .... Paul Kariya, Ana
1941 .... Bobby Bauer, Bos	1969 .... Alex Delvecchio, Det	1997 .... Paul Kariya, Ana
1942 .... Syl Apps, Tor	1970 .... Phil Goyette, StL	1998 .... Ron Francis, Pitt
1943 .... Max Bentley, Chi	1971 .... John Bucyk, Bos	1999 .... Wayne Gretzky, NYR
1944 .... Clint Smith, Chi	1972 .... Jean Ratelle, NYR	2000 .... Pavol Demitra, StL
1945 .... Billy Mosienko, Chi	1973 .... Gilbert Perreault, Buff	2001 .... Joe Sakic, Col
1946 .... Toe Blake, Mtl	1974 .... John Bucyk, Bos	2002 .... Ron Francis, Car
1947 .... Bobby Bauer, Bos	1975 .... Marcel Dionne, Det	2003 .... Alexander Mogilny, Det
1948 .... Buddy O'Connor, NYR	1976 .... Jean Ratelle, NYR-Bos	2004 .... Brad Richards, TB
1949 .... Bill Quackenbush, Det	1977 .... Marcel Dionne, LA	2005 .... No Award
1950 .... Edgar Laprade, NYR	1978 .... Butch Goring, LA	2006 .... Pavel Datsyuk, Det
1951 .... Red Kelly, Det	1979 .... Bob MacMillan, Atl	2007 .... Pavel Datsyuk, Det
1952 .... Sid Smith, Tor	1980 .... Wayne Gretzky, Edm	

James Norris Memorial Trophy

Awarded annually "to the defense player who demonstrates throughout the season the greatest all-around ability in the position." James Norris was the former owner-president of the Detroit Red Wings. Bobby Orr holds the record for most consecutive times winning the award (eight, 1968–1975).

1954 .... Red Kelly, Det	1972 .... Bobby Orr, Bos	1990 .... Ray Bourque, Bos
1955 .... Doug Harvey, Mtl	1973 .... Bobby Orr, Bos	1991 .... Ray Bourque, Bos
1956 .... Doug Harvey, Mtl	1974 .... Bobby Orr, Bos	1992 .... Brian Leetch, NYR
1957 .... Doug Harvey, Mtl	1975 .... Bobby Orr, Bos	1993 .... Chris Chelios, Chi
1958 .... Doug Harvey, Mtl	1976 .... Denis Potvin, NYI	1994 .... Ray Bourque, Bos
1959 .... Tom Johnson, Mtl	1977 .... Larry Robinson, Mtl	1995 .... Paul Coffey, Det
1960 .... Doug Harvey, Mtl	1978 .... Denis Potvin, NYI	1996 .... Chris Chelios, Chi
1961 .... Doug Harvey, Mtl	1979 .... Denis Potvin, NYI	1997 .... Brian Leetch, NYR
1962 .... Doug Harvey, NYR	1980 .... Larry Robinson, Mtl	1998 .... Rob Blake, LA
1963 .... Pierre Pilote, Chi	1981 .... Randy Carlyle, Pitt	1999 .... Al MacInnis, StL
1964 .... Pierre Pilote, Chi	1982 .... Doug Wilson, Chi	2000 .... Chris Pronger, StL
1965 .... Pierre Pilote, Chi	1983 .... Rod Langway, Wash	2001 .... Nicklas Lidstrom, Det
1966 .... Jacques Laperriere, Mtl	1984 .... Rod Langway, Wash	2002 .... Nicklas Lidstrom, Det
1967 .... Harry Howell, NYR	1985 .... Paul Coffey, Edm	2003 .... Nicklas Lidstrom, Det
1968 .... Bobby Orr, Bos	1986 .... Paul Coffey, Edm	2004 .... Scott Niedermayer, NJ
1969 .... Bobby Orr, Bos	1987 .... Ray Bourque, Bos	2005 .... No Award
1970 .... Bobby Orr, Bos	1988 .... Ray Bourque, Bos	2006 .... Nicklas Lidstrom, Det
1971 .... Bobby Orr, Bos	1989 .... Chris Chelios, Mtl	2007 .... Nicklas Lidstrom, Det

Calder Memorial Trophy

Awarded annually "to the player selected as the most proficient in his first year of competition in the National Hockey League." Frank Calder was a former NHL president. Sergei Makarov, who won the award in 1989–90, was the oldest recipient of the trophy, at 31. Players are no longer eligible for the award if they are 26 or older as of September 15th of the season in question.

1933 ....Carl Voss, Det	1958 ....Frank Mahovlich, Tor	1983 ....Steve Larmer, Chi
1934 ....Russ Blinko, Mtl M	1959 ....Ralph Backstrom, Mtl	1984 ....Tom Barrasso, Buff
1935 ....Dave Schriner, NYA	1960 ....Bill Hay, Chi	1985 ....Mario Lemieux, Pitt
1936 ....Mike Karakas, Chi	1961 ....Dave Keon, Tor	1986 ....Gary Suter, Cgy
1937 ....Syl Apps, Tor	1962 ....Bobby Rousseau, Mtl	1987 ......Luc Robitaille, LA
1938 ....Cully Dahlstrom, Chi	1963 ....Kent Douglas, Tor	1988 ....Joe Nieuwendyk, Cgy
1939 ....Frank Brimsek, Bos	1964 ....Jacques Laperriere, Mtl	1989 ....Brian Leetch, NYR
1940 ....Kilby MacDonald, NYR	1965 ....Roger Crozier, Det	1990 ......Sergei Makarov, Cgy
1941 ....Johnny Quilty, Mtl	1966 ....Brit Selby, Tor	1991 ......Ed Belfour, Chi
1942 ....Grant Warwick, NYR	1967 ....Bobby Orr, Bos	1992 ....Pavel Bure, Van
1943 ....Gaye Stewart, Tor	1968 ....Derek Sanderson, Bos	1993 ....Teemu Selanne, Winn
1944 ....Gus Bodnar, Tor	1969 ....Danny Grant, Minn	1994 ....Martin Brodeur, NJ
1945 ....Frank McCool, Tor	1970 ....Tony Esposito, Chi	1995 ....Peter Forsberg, Que
1946 ....Edgar Laprade, NYR	1971 ....Gilbert Perreault, Buff	1996 ....Daniel Alfredsson, Ott
1947 ....Howie Meeker, Tor	1972 ....Ken Dryden, Mtl	1997 ....Bryan Berard, NYI
1948 ....Jim McFadden, Det	1973 ....Steve Vickers, NYR	1998 ......Sergei Samsonov, Bos
1949 ....Pentti Lund, NYR	1974 ....Denis Potvin, NYI	1999 ....Chris Drury, Col
1950 ....Jack Gelineau, Bos	1975 ....Eric Vail, Atl	2000 ....Scott Gomez, NJ
1951 ....Terry Sawchuk, Det	1976 ....Bryan Trottier, NYI	2001 ....Evgeni Nabokov, SJ
1952 ....Bernie Geoffrion, Mtl	1977 ....Willi Plett, Atl	2002 ....Dany Heatley, Atl
1953 ....Gump Worsley, NYR	1978 ....Mike Bossy, NYI	2003 ....Barret Jackman, StL
1954 ....Camille Henry, NYR	1979 ....Bobby Smith, Minn	2004 ....Andrew Raycroft, Bos
1955 ....Ed Litzenberger, Chi	1980 ....Ray Bourque, Bos	2005 ....No Award
1956 ....Glenn Hall, Det	1981 ....Peter Stastny, Que	2006.......Alexander Ovechkin, Wash
1957 ....Larry Regan, Bos	1982 ....Dale Hawerchuk, Winn	2007.........Evgeni Malkin, Pitt

Vezina Trophy

Awarded annually "to the goalkeeper adjudged to be the best at his position." The trophy is named after Georges Vezina, an outstanding goalie for the Montreal Canadiens who collapsed during a game on November 28, 1925, and died four months later of tuberculosis. The general managers of the NHL teams vote on the award.

1927 ....George Hainsworth, Mtl	1959 ....Jacques Plante, Mtl	Don Edwards, Buff
1928 ....George Hainsworth, Mtl	1960 ....Jacques Plante, Mtl	1981 ....Richard Sevigny, Mtl
1929 ....George Hainsworth, Mtl	1961 ....Johnny Bower, Tor	Michel Larocque, Mtl
1930 ....Tiny Thompson, Bos	1962 ....Jacques Plante, Mtl	1982 ....Billy Smith, NYI
1931 ....Roy Worters, NYA	1963 ....Glenn Hall, Chi	Denis Herron, Mtl
1932 ....Charlie Gardiner, Chi	1964 ....Charlie Hodge, Mtl	1983 ....Pete Peeters, Bos
1933 ....Tiny Thompson, Bos	1965 ....Terry Sawchuk, Tor	1984 ....Tom Barrasso, Buff
1934 ....Charlie Gardiner, Chi	Johnny Bower, Tor	1985 ....Pelle Lindbergh, Phil
1935 ....Lorne Chabot, Chi	1966 ....Gump Worsley, Mtl	1986 ....John Vanbiesbrouck, NYR
1936 ....Tiny Thompson, Bos	Charlie Hodge, Mtl	
1937 ....Normie Smith, Det	1967 ....Glenn Hall, Chi	1987 ....Ron Hextall, Phil
1938 ....Tiny Thompson, Bos	Denis DeJordy, Chi	1988 ....Grant Fuhr, Edm
1939 ....Frank Brimsek, Bos	1968 ....Lorne Worsley, Mtl	1989 ....Patrick Roy, Mtl
1940 ......Dave Kerr, NYR	1969 ....Jacques Plante, StL	1990 ....Patrick Roy, Mtl
1941 ....Turk Broda, Tor	Glenn Hall, StL	1991 ....Ed Belfour, Chi
1942 ....Frank Brimsek, Bos	1970 ....Tony Esposito, Chi	1992 ....Patrick Roy, Mtl
1943 ....Johnny Mowers, Det	1971 ....Ed Giacomin, NYR	1993 ....Ed Belfour, Chi
1944 ....Bill Durnan, Mtl	Gilles Villemure, NYR	1994 ....Dominik Hasek, Buff
1945 ....Bill Durnan, Mtl	1972 ....Tony Esposito, Chi	1995 ....Dominik Hasek, Buff
1946 ....Bill Durnan, Mtl	Gary Smith, Chi	1996 ....Jim Carey, Wash
1947 ....Bill Durnan, Mtl	1973 ....Ken Dryden, Mtl	1997 ....Dominik Hasek, Buff
1948 ....Turk Broda, Tor	1974 ....Bernie Parent, Phil	1998 ....Dominik Hasek, Buff
1949 ....Bill Durnan, Mtl	Tony Esposito, Chi	1999 ....Dominik Hasek, Buff
1950 ....Bill Durnan, Mtl	1975 ....Bernie Parent, Phil	2000 ....Olaf Kolzig, Wash
1951 ....Al Rollins, Tor	1976 ....Ken Dryden, Mtl	2001 ....Dominik Hasek, Buff
1952 ....Terry Sawchuk, Det	1977 ....Ken Dryden, Mtl	2002 ....Jose Theodore, Mtl
1953 ....Terry Sawchuk, Det	Michel Larocque, Mtl	2003 ....Martin Brodeur, NJ
1954 ....Harry Lumley, Tor	1978 ....Ken Dryden, Mtl	2004 ....Martin Brodeur, NJ
1955 ....Terry Sawchuk, Det	Michel Larocque, Mtl	2005 ....No Award
1956 ....Jacques Plante, Mtl	1979 ....Ken Dryden, Mtl	2006 ....Miikka Kiprusoff, Cgy
1957 ....Jacques Plante, Mtl	Michel Larocque, Mtl	2007 ....Martin Brodeur, NJ
1958 ....Jacques Plante, Mtl	1980 ....Bob Sauve, Buff	

NHL Awards *(Cont.)*

Selke Trophy

Awarded annually "to the forward who best excels in the defensive aspects of the game." The trophy is named after Frank J. Selke, the architect of the Montreal Canadians dynasty that won five consecutive Stanley Cups in the late '50s. The winner is selected by a vote of the Professional Hockey Writers Association.

1978........Bob Gainey, Mtl	1989........Guy Carbonneau, Mtl	1999........Jere Lehtinen, Dall
1979........Bob Gainey, Mtl	1990........Rick Meagher, StL	2000........Steve Yzerman, Det
1980........Bob Gainey, Mtl	1991........Dirk Graham, Chi	2001........John Madden, NJ
1981........Bob Gainey, Mtl	1992........Guy Carbonneau, Mtl	2002........Michael Peca, NYI
1982........Steve Kasper, Bos	1993........Doug Gilmour, Tor	2003........Jere Lehtinen, Dall
1983........Bobby Clarke, Phil	1994........Sergei Fedorov, Det	2004........Kris Draper, Det
1984........Doug Jarvis, Wash	1995........Ron Francis, Pitt	2005........No Award
1985........Craig Ramsay, Buff	1996........Sergei Fedorov, Det	2006........Rod Brind'Amour, Car
1986........Troy Murray, Chi	1997........Michael Peca, Buff	2007........Rod Brind'Amour, Car
1987........Dave Poulin, Phil	1998........Jere Lehtinen, Dall	
1988........Guy Carbonneau, Mtl		

Adams Award

Awarded annually "to the NHL coach adjudged to have contributed the most to his team's success." The trophy is named in honor of Jack Adams, longtime coach and general manager of the Detroit Red Wings. The winner is selected by a vote of the National Hockey League Broadcasters' Association.

1974.....Fred Shero, Phil	1986.....Glen Sather, Edm	1998.....Pat Burns, Bos
1975.....Bob Pulford, LA	1987.....Jacques Demers, Det	1999.....Jacques Martin, Ott
1976.....Don Cherry, Bos	1988.....Jacques Demers, Det	2000.....Joel Quenneville, StL
1977.....Scott Bowman, Mtl	1989.....Pat Burns, Mtl	2001.....Bill Barber, Phil
1978.....Bobby Kromm, Det	1990.....Bob Murdoch, Winn	2002.....Bob Francis, Phoe
1979.....Al Arbour, NYI	1991.....Brian Sutter, StL	2003.....Jacques Lemaire, Minn
1980.....Pat Quinn, Phil	1992.....Pat Quinn, Van	2004.....John Tortorella, TB
1981.....Red Berenson, StL	1993.....Pat Burns, Tor	2005.....No Award
1982.....Tom Watt, Winn	1994.....Jacques Lemaire, NJ	2006.....Lindy Ruff, Buff
1983.....Orval Tessier, Chi	1995.....Marc Crawford, Que	2007.....Alain Vigneault, Van
1984.....Bryan Murray, Wash	1996.....Scotty Bowman, Det	
1985.....Mike Keenan, Phil	1997.....Ted Nolan, Buff	

Career Records

Alltime Point Leaders

Player	Yrs	GP	G	A	Pts	Pts/game
Wayne Gretzky, Edm, LA, StL, NYR	20	1487	894	1963	2857	1.921
Mark Messier, Edm, NYR, Van	25	1756	694	1193	1887	1.074
Gordie Howe, Det, Hart	26	1767	801	1049	1850	1.047
Ron Francis, four teams	23	1731	549	1249	1798	1.039
Marcel Dionne, Det, LA, NYR	18	1348	731	1040	1771	1.314
Steve Yzerman, Det	22	1514	692	1063	1755	1.159
Mario Lemieux, Pitt	17	915	690	1033	1723	1.883
Phil Esposito, Chi, Bos, NYR	18	1282	717	873	1590	1.240
*Joe Sakic, Que, Col	18	1319	610	979	1589	1.205
Ray Bourque, Bos, Col	22	1612	410	1169	1579	.980
Paul Coffey, eight teams	21	1409	396	1135	1531	1.087
*Jaromir Jagr, Pitt, Wash, NYR	16	1191	621	907	1528	1.283
Stan Mikita, Chi	22	1394	541	926	1467	1.052
Bryan Trottier, NYI, Pitt	18	1279	524	901	1425	1.114
Adam Oates, seven teams	19	1337	341	1079	1420	1.062

*Active in 2006–07.

Alltime Goal-Scoring Leaders

Player	Yrs	GP	G	G/game
Wayne Gretzky, Edm, LA, StL, NYR	20	1487	894	.601
Gordie Howe, Det, Hart	26	1767	801	.453
Brett Hull, Cal, StL, Dall, Det	19	1269	741	.584
Marcel Dionne, Det, LA, NYR	18	1348	731	.542
Phil Esposito, Chi, Bos, NYR	18	1282	717	.559
Mike Gartner, Wash, Minn, NYR, Tor, Phoe	19	1432	708	.494
Mark Messier, Edm, NYR, Van	25	1756	694	.395
Steve Yzerman, Det	22	1514	692	.457
Mario Lemieux, Pitt	17	915	690	.754
Luc Robitaille, LA, Pitt, NYR, Det	19	1431	668	.467

Alltime Assist Leaders

Player	Yrs	GP	A	A/game
Wayne Gretzky, Edm, LA, StL, NYR	20	1487	1963	1.320
Ron Francis, Hart, Pitt, Car	23	1731	1249	.722
Mark Messier, Edm, NYR, Van	25	1756	1193	.679
Ray Bourque, Bos, Col	22	1612	1169	.725
Paul Coffey, eight teams	21	1409	1135	.806
Adam Oates, seven teams	22	1337	1079	.807
Steve Yzerman, Det	22	1514	1063	.702
Gordie Howe, Det, Hart	26	1767	1049	.594
Marcel Dionne, Det, LA, NYR	18	1348	1040	.772
Mario Lemieux, Pitt	17	915	1033	1.129

Alltime Penalty Minutes Leaders

Player	Yrs	GP	PIM	Min/game
Dave Williams, Tor, Van, Det, LA, Hart	14	962	3966	4.12
Dale Hunter, Que, Wash, Col	19	1407	3565	2.53
Tie Domi, Tor, NYR, Winn	16	1020	3515	3.45
Marty McSorley, Pitt, Edm, LA, NYR, SJ, Bos	17	961	3381	3.52
Bob Probert, Det, Chi	16	935	3300	3.53
Rob Ray, Buff, Ott	15	900	3207	3.56
Craig Berube, Phil, Tor, Cgy, Wash, NYI	17	1054	3149	2.99
Tim Hunter, Cgy, Que, Van, SJ	16	815	3142	3.86
Chris Nilan, Mtl, NYR, Bos	13	688	3043	4.42
Rick Tocchet, Phil, Pitt, LA, Bos, Wash, Phoe	18	1144	2972	2.60

Goaltending Records

ALLTIME GOALTENDING LEADERS, BY WINS

Goaltender	W	L	T	Pct
Patrick Roy, Mtl, Col	551	315	131	.618
*Martin Brodeur, NJ	494	263	105	.634
*Ed Belfour, five teams	484	320	111	.590
Terry Sawchuk, five teams	447	330	172	.562
*Curtis Joseph, five teams	446	341	90	.560
Jacques Plante, five teams	437	246	145	.615
Tony Esposito, Mtl, Chi	423	306	151	.566
Glenn Hall, Det, Chi, StL	407	326	163	.545
Grant Fuhr, six teams	403	295	114	.567
Mike Vernon, Cgy, Det, SJ, Fla	385	273	92	.575

*Active in 2006–07.

ACTIVE GOALTENDING LEADERS, BY PERCENTAGE

Goaltender	W	L	T	Pct
Marty Turco, Dall	175	82	26	.664
Martin Brodeur, NJ	494	263	105	.634
Chris Osgood, Det, NYI, StL	336	186	66	.628
Dominik Hasek, Chi, Buff, Det, Ott	362	213	82	.613
Ed Belfour, five teams	484	320	111	.590
Curtis Joseph, five teams	446	341	90	.560
Patrick Lalime, Pitt, Ott, StL	175	136	32	.557
Evgeni Nabokov, SJ	162	129	29	.552
Nikolai Khabibulin, Phoe, TB, Chi	251	239	58	.511
Olaf Kolzig, Wash	276	272	63	.503

Note: Ranked by winning percentage; minimum 250 games played. All players active in 2006–07.

ALLTIME SHUTOUT LEADERS

Goaltender	Team	Yrs	GP	SO
Terry Sawchuk	Det, Bos, Tor, LA, NYR	21	971	103
George Hainsworth	Mtl, Tor	11	465	94
*Martin Brodeur	NJ	14	891	92
Glenn Hall	Det, Chi, StL	18	906	84
Jacques Plante	Mtl, NYR, StL, Tor, Bos	18	837	82
Tiny Thompson	Bos, Det	12	553	81
Alex Connell	Ott, Det, NYA, Mtl M	12	417	81
Tony Esposito	Mtl, Chi	16	886	76
*Ed Belfour	Chi, SJ, Dall, Tor	17	963	76
Lorne Chabot	NYR, Tor, Mtl, Chi, Mtl M, NYA	11	411	72

*Active in 2006–07.

ALLTIME GOALS AGAINST AVERAGE LEADERS (PRE-1950)

Goaltender	Team	Yrs	GP	GA	GAA
Alec Connell	Ott, Det, NYA, Mtl M	12	417	830	1.91
George Hainsworth	Mtl, Tor	11	465	937	1.93
Chuck Gardiner	Chi	7	316	664	2.02
Lorne Chabot	NYR, Tor, Mtl, Chi, Mtl M, NYA	11	411	860	2.04
Tiny Thompson	Bos, Det	12	553	1183	2.08

ALLTIME GOALS AGAINST AVERAGE LEADERS (POST-1950)

Goaltender	Team	Yrs	GP	GA	GAA
*Martin Brodeur	NJ	14	891	1931	2.20
*Dominik Hasek	Chi, Buff, Det, Ott	15	694	1488	2.21
Ken Dryden	Mtl	8	397	870	2.24
Roman Turek	Dall, StL, Cgy	8	328	734	2.31
Jacques Plante	Mtl, NYR, StL, Tor, Bos	19	837	1964	2.38

*Active in 2006–07.

Note: Minimum 250 games played. Goals against average equals goals against per 60 minutes played.

Alltime Coaching Leaders

Coach	Team	Seasons	W	L	T/OTL	Pct
Scott Bowman	five teams	1967–87, 91–2002	1244	584	313	.654
Toe Blake	Mtl	1955–68	500	255	159	.634
*Marc Crawford	Que, Col, Van, LA	1994–	438	342	125	.622
Fred Shero	Phil, NYR	1971–81	390	225	119	.612
Glen Sather	Edm, NYR	1979-89, 93-94, 2003-04	497	314	121	.598
*Ken Hitchcock	Dall, Phil	1995–	436	278	127	.594
Emile Francis	NYR, StL	1965–77, 81–83	388	273	117	.574
Billy Reay	Tor, Chi	1957–59, 63–77	542	385	175	.571
Pat Burns	Mtl, Tor, Bos, NJ	1988–2001, 2002–05	501	367	151	.566
Al Arbour	StL, NYI	1970–94	781	577	248	.564
Pat Quinn	Phil, LA, Van, Tor	1978–2006	657	499	162	.560

Note: Minimum 600 regular-season games. Ranked by percentage. *Active in 2006–07.

Single-Season Records

Goals

Player	Season	GP	G	Player	Season	GP	G
Wayne Gretzky, Edm	1981–82	80	92	Wayne Gretzky, Edm	1982–83	80	71
Wayne Gretzky, Edm	1983–84	74	87	Brett Hull, StL	1991–92	73	70
Brett Hull, StL	1990–91	78	86	Mario Lemieux, Pitt	1987–88	77	70
Mario Lemieux, Pitt	1988–89	76	85	Bernie Nicholls, LA	1988–89	79	70
Alexander Mogilny, Buff	1992–93	77	76	Mario Lemieux, Pitt	1992–93	60	69
Phil Esposito, Bos	1970–71	78	76	Mario Lemieux, Pitt	1995–96	70	69
Teemu Selanne, Winn	1992–93	84	76	Mike Bossy, NYI	1978–79	80	69
Wayne Gretzky, Edm	1984–85	80	73	Phil Esposito, Bos	1973–74	78	68
Brett Hull, StL	1989–90	80	72	Jari Kurri, Edm	1985–86	78	68
Jari Kurri, Edm	1984–85	73	71	Mike Bossy, NYI	1980–81	79	68

Assists

Player	Season	GP	Asst	Player	Season	GP	Asst
Wayne Gretzky, Edm	1985–86	80	163	Bobby Orr, Bos	1970–71	78	102
Wayne Gretzky, Edm	1984–85	80	135	Mario Lemieux, Pitt	1987–88	77	98
Wayne Gretzky, Edm	1982–83	80	125	Adam Oates, Bos	1992–93	84	97
Wayne Gretzky, LA	1990–91	78	122	Joe Thornton, SJ	2005-06	81	96
Wayne Gretzky, Edm	1986–87	79	121	Doug Gilmour, Tor	1992–93	83	95
Wayne Gretzky, Edm	1981–82	80	120	Pat LaFontaine, Buff	1992–93	84	95
Wayne Gretzky, Edm	1983–84	74	118	Mario Lemieux, Pitt	1985–86	79	93
Mario Lemieux, Pitt	1988–89	76	114	Peter Stastny, Que	1981–82	80	93
Wayne Gretzky, LA	1988–89	78	114	Wayne Gretzky, LA	1993–94	81	92
Wayne Gretzky, Edm	1987–88	64	109	Mario Lemieux, Pitt	1995–96	70	92
Wayne Gretzky, Edm	1980–81	80	109	Ron Francis, Pitt	1995–96	77	92
Wayne Gretzky, LA	1989–90	73	102	Joe Thornton, SJ	2006-07	82	92

Points

Player	Season	G	Asst	Pts	Player	Season	G	Asst	Pts
Wayne Gretzky, Edm	1985–86	52	163	215	Wayne Gretzky, LA	1990–91	41	122	163
Wayne Gretzky, Edm	1981–82	92	120	212	Mario Lemieux, Pitt	1995–96	69	92	161
Wayne Gretzky, Edm	1984–85	73	135	208	Mario Lemieux, Pitt	1992–93	69	91	160
Wayne Gretzky, Edm	1983–84	87	118	205	Steve Yzerman, Det	1988–89	65	90	155
Mario Lemieux, Pitt	1988–89	85	114	199	Phil Esposito, Bos	1970–71	76	76	152
Wayne Gretzky, Edm	1982–83	71	125	196	Bernie Nicholls, LA	1988–89	70	80	150
Wayne Gretzky, Edm	1986–87	62	121	183	Wayne Gretzky, Edm	1987–88	40	109	149
Mario Lemieux, Pitt	1987–88	70	98	168	Pat LaFontaine, Buff	1992–93	53	95	148
Wayne Gretzky, LA	1988–89	54	114	168	Mike Bossy, NYI	1981–82	64	83	147
Wayne Gretzky, Edm	1980–81	55	109	164	Phil Esposito, Bos	1973–74	68	77	145

Points per Game

Player	Season	GP	Pts	Avg
Wayne Gretzky, Edm	1983–84	74	205	2.77
Wayne Gretzky, Edm	1985–86	80	215	2.69
Mario Lemieux, Pitt	1992–93	60	160	2.67
Wayne Gretzky, Edm	1981–82	80	212	2.65
Mario Lemieux, Pitt	1988–89	76	199	2.62
Wayne Gretzky, Edm	1984–85	80	208	2.60
Wayne Gretzky, Edm	1982–83	80	196	2.45
Wayne Gretzky, Edm	1987–88	64	149	2.33
Wayne Gretzky, Edm	1986–87	79	183	2.32
Mario Lemieux, Pitt	1995–96	70	161	2.30
Mario Lemieux, Pitt	1987–88	77	168	2.18
Wayne Gretzky, LA	1988–89	78	168	2.15
Wayne Gretzky, LA	1990–91	78	163	2.09
Mario Lemieux, Pitt	1989–90	59	123	2.08
Wayne Gretzky, Edm	1980–81	80	164	2.05
Mario Lemieux, Pitt	1991–92	64	131	2.05
Bill Cowley, Bos	1943–44	36	71	1.97
Phil Esposito, Bos	1970–71	78	152	1.95
Wayne Gretzky, LA	1989–90	73	142	1.95
Steve Yzerman, Det	1988–89	80	155	1.94

Note: Minimum 50 points in one season.

Goals per Game

Player	Season	GP	G	Avg
Joe Malone, Mtl	1917–18	20	44	2.20
Cy Denneny, Ott	1917–18	20	36	1.80
Newsy Lalonde, Mtl	1917–18	14	23	1.64
Joe Malone, Que	1919–20	24	39	1.63
Newsy Lalonde, Mtl	1919–20	23	36	1.57
Reg Noble, Tor	1917–18	20	30	1.50
Babe Dye, Ham-Tor	1920–21	24	35	1.46
Cy Denneny, Ott	1920–21	24	34	1.42
Joe Malone, Ham	1920–21	20	28	1.40
Newsy Lalonde, Mtl	1920–21	24	33	1.38

Note: Minimum 20 goals in one season.

Assists per Game

Player	Season	GP	Asst	Avg
Wayne Gretzky, Edm	1985–86	80	163	2.04
Wayne Gretzky, Edm	1987–88	64	109	1.70
Wayne Gretzky, Edm	1984–85	80	135	1.69
Wayne Gretzky, Edm	1983–84	74	118	1.59
Wayne Gretzky, Edm	1982–83	80	125	1.56
Wayne Gretzky, LA	1990–91	78	122	1.56
Wayne Gretzky, Edm	1986–87	79	121	1.53
Mario Lemieux, Pitt	1992–93	60	91	1.52
Wayne Gretzky, Edm	1981–82	80	120	1.50
Mario Lemieux, Pitt	1988–89	76	114	1.50

Note: Minimum 35 assists in one season.

Shutout Leaders

	Season	SO	Length of Schedule
George Hainsworth, Mtl	1928–29	22	44
Alec Connell, Ott	1925–26	15	36
Alec Connell, Ott	1927–28	15	44
Hal Winkler, Bos	1927–28	15	44
Tony Esposito, Chi	1969–70	15	76
George Hainsworth, Mtl	1926–27	14	44
Clint Benedict, Mtl M	1926–27	13	44
Alec Connell, Ott	1926–27	13	44
George Hainsworth, Mtl	1927–28	13	44
John Roach, NYR	1928–29	13	44
Roy Worters, NYA	1928–29	13	44
Harry Lumley, Tor	1953–54	13	70
Dominik Hasek, Buff	1997–98	13	82
Tiny Thompson, Bos	1928–29	12	44
Chuck Gardiner, Chi	1930–31	12	44
Terry Sawchuk, Det	1951–52	12	70
Terry Sawchuk, Det	1953–54	12	70
Terry Sawchuk, Det	1954–55	12	70
Glenn Hall, Det	1955–56	12	70
Bernie Parent, Phil	1973–74	12	78
Bernie Parent, Phil	1974–75	12	80
Martin Brodeur, NJ	2006-07	12	82
Lorne Chabot, NYR	1927–28	11	44
Harry Holmes, Det	1927–28	11	44
Roy Worters, Pitt Pirates	1927–28	11	44
Lorne Chabot, Tor	1928–29	11	44
Clint Benedict, Mtl M	1928–29	11	44
Joe Miller, Pitt Pirates	1928–29	11	44
Tiny Thompson, Bos	1932–33	11	48
Terry Sawchuck, Det	1950–51	11	70
Dominik Hasek, Buff	2000–01	11	82
Martin Brodeur, NJ	2003–04	11	82
Lorne Chabot, NYR	1926–27	10	44
Clarence Dolson, Det	1928–29	10	44
John Roach, Det	1932–33	10	48
Chuck Gardiner, Chi	1933–34	10	48
Tiny Thompson, Bos	1935–36	10	48
Frank Brimsek, Bos	1938–39	10	48
Bill Durnan, Mtl	1948–49	10	60
Gerry McNeil, Mtl	1952–53	10	70
Harry Lumley, Tor	1952–53	10	70
Tony Esposito, Chi	1973–74	10	78
Ken Dryden, Mtl	1976–77	10	80
Martin Brodeur, NJ	1996–97	10	82
Martin Brodeur, NJ	1997–98	10	82
Roman Cechmanek, Phil	2000–01	10	82
Byron Dafoe, Bos	1998–99	10	82
Ed Belfour, Tor	2003–04	10	82
Miikka Kiprusoff, Cgy	2005–06	10	82

Wins

	Season	Record*
Martin Brodeur, NJ	2006-07	48-23
Roberto Luongo, Van	2006-07	47-22
Bernie Parent, Phil	1973–74	47-13-12
Bernie Parent, Phil	1974–75	44-14-9
Terry Sawchuk, Det	1950–51	44-13-13
Terry Sawchuk, Det	1951–52	44-14-12
Tom Barrasso, Pitt	1992–93	43-14-5
Ed Belfour, Chi	1990–91	43-19-7
Martin Brodeur, NJ	1997–98	43-17-8
Martin Brodeur, NJ	1999–00	43-20-8
Martin Brodeur, NJ	2005-06	43-23
Jacques Plante, Mtl	1955–56	42-12-10
Jacques Plante, Mtl	1961–62	42-14-14
Ken Dryden, Mtl	1975–76	42-10-8
Mike Richter, NYR	1993–94	42-12-6
Roman Turek, StL	1999–00	42-15-9
Martin Brodeur, NJ	2000–01	42-17-11
Miikka Kiprusoff, Cgy	2005–06	42-20

*Starting in the 2005-06 season, ties were eliminated.

Goals Against Average

(PRE-1950)	Season	GP	GAA	(POST-1950)	Season	GP	GAA
George Hainsworth, Mtl	1928–29	44	0.92	Miika Kiprusoff, Cal	2003–04	38	1.69
George Hainsworth, Mtl	1927–28	44	1.05	Marty Turco, Dall	2002–03	55	1.73
Alec Connell, Ott	1925–26	36	1.12	Tony Esposito, Chi	1971–72	48	1.7698
Tiny Thompson, Bos	1928–29	44	1.15	Al Rollins, Tor	1950–51	40	1.7744
Roy Worters, NYA	1928–29	38	1.15	Ron Tugnutt, Ott	1998–99	43	1.79

Single-Game Records

Goals

	Date	G
Joe Malone, Que vs Tor	1-31-20	7
Newsy Lalonde, Mtl vs Tor	1-10-20	6
Joe Malone, Que vs Ott	3-10-20	6
Corb Denneny, Tor vs Ham	1-26-21	6
Cy Denneny, Ott vs Ham	3-7-21	6
Syd Howe, Det vs NYR	2-3-44	6
Red Berenson, StL vs Phil	11-7-68	6
Darryl Sittler, Tor vs Bos	2-7-76	6

Assists

	Date	A
Billy Taylor, Det vs Chi	3-16-47	7
Wayne Gretzky, Edm vs Wash	2-15-80	7
Wayne Gretzky, Edm vs Chi	12-11-85	7
Wayne Gretzky, Edm vs Que	2-14-86	7

Note: 24 tied with 6.

Points

	Date	G	A	Pts
Darryl Sittler, Tor vs Bos	2-7-76	6	4	10
Maurice Richard, Mtl vs Det	12-28-44	5	3	8
Bert Olmstead, Mtl vs Chi	1-9-54	4	4	8
Tom Bladon, Phil vs Clev	12-11-77	4	4	8
Bryan Trottier, NYI vs NYR	12-23-78	5	3	8
Peter Stastny, Que vs Wash	2-22-81	4	4	8
Anton Stastny, Que vs Wash	2-22-81	3	5	8
Wayne Gretzky, Edm vs NJ	11-19-83	3	5	8
Wayne Gretzky, Edm vs Minn	1-4-84	4	4	8
Paul Coffey, Edm vs Det	3-14-86	2	6	8
Mario Lemieux, Pitt vs StL	10-15-88	2	6	8
Bernie Nicholls, LA vs Tor	12-1-88	2	6	8
Mario Lemieux, Pitt vs NJ	12-31-88	5	3	8

NHL Season Leaders

Points

Season	Player and Club	Pts	Season	Player and Club	Pts
1917–18	Joe Malone, Mtl	44	1950–51	Gordie Howe, Det	86
1918–19	Newsy Lalonde, Mtl	30	1951–52	Gordie Howe, Det	86
1919–20	Joe Malone, Que	48	1952–53	Gordie Howe, Det	95
1920–21	Newsy Lalonde, Mtl	41	1953–54	Gordie Howe, Det	81
1921–22	Punch Broadbent, Ott	46	1954–55	Bernie Geoffrion, Mtl	75
1922–23	Babe Dye, Tor	37	1955–56	Jean Beliveau, Mtl	88
1923–24	Cy Denneny, Ott	23	1956–57	Gordie Howe, Det	89
1924–25	Babe Dye, Tor	44	1957–58	Dickie Moore, Mtl	84
1925–26	Nels Stewart, Mtl M	42	1958–59	Dickie Moore, Mtl	96
1926–27	Bill Cook, NY	37	1959–60	Bobby Hull, Chi	81
1927–28	Howie Morenz, Mtl	51	1960–61	Bernie Geoffrion, Mtl	95
1928–29	Ace Bailey, Tor	32	1961–62	Andy Bathgate, NY	84
1929–30	Cooney Weiland, Bos	73		Bobby Hull, Chi	84
1930–31	Howie Morenz, Mtl	51	1962–63	Gordie Howe, Det	86
1931–32	Harvey Jackson, Tor	53	1963–64	Stan Mikita, Chi	89
1932–33	Bill Cook, NY	50	1964–65	Stan Mikita, Chi	87
1933–34	Charlie Conacher, Tor	52	1965–66	Bobby Hull, Chi	97
1934–35	Charlie Conacher, Tor	57	1966–67	Stan Mikita, Chi	97
1935–36	Sweeney Schriner, NYA	45	1967–68	Stan Mikita, Chi	87
1936–37	Sweeney Schriner, NYA	46	1968–69	Phil Esposito, Bos	126
1937–38	Gord Drillon, Tor	52	1969–70	Bobby Orr, Bos	120
1938–39	Hector Blake, Mtl	47	1970–71	Phil Esposito, Bos	152
1939–40	Milt Schmidt, Bos	52	1971–72	Phil Esposito, Bos	133
1940–41	Bill Cowley, Bos	62	1972–73	Phil Esposito, Bos	130
1941–42	Bryan Hextall, NY	54	1973–74	Phil Esposito, Bos	145
1942–43	Doug Bentley, Chi	73	1974–75	Bobby Orr, Bos	135
1943–44	Herb Cain, Bos	82	1975–76	Guy Lafleur, Mtl	125
1944–45	Elmer Lach, Mtl	80	1976–77	Guy Lafleur, Mtl	136
1945–46	Max Bentley, Chi	61	1977–78	Guy Lafleur, Mtl	132
1946–47	Max Bentley, Chi	72	1978–79	Bryan Trottier, NYI	134
1947–48	Elmer Lach, Mtl	61	1979–80	Marcel Dionne, LA	137
1948–49	Roy Conacher, Chi	68		Wayne Gretzky, Edm	137
1949–50	Ted Lindsay, Det	78	1980–81	Wayne Gretzky, Edm	164

Points *(Cont.)*

Season	Player and Club	Pts	Season	Player and Club	Pts
1981–82	Wayne Gretzky, Edm	212	1994–95	Jaromir Jagr, Pitt	70
1982–83	Wayne Gretzky, Edm	196	1995–96	Mario Lemieux, Pitt	161
1983–84	Wayne Gretzky, Edm	205	1996–97	Mario Lemieux, Pitt	122
1984–85	Wayne Gretzky, Edm	208	1997–98	Jaromir Jagr, Pitt	102
1985–86	Wayne Gretzky, Edm	215	1998–99	Jaromir Jagr, Pitt	127
1986–87	Wayne Gretzky, Edm	183	1999–00	Jaromir Jagr, Pitt	96
1987–88	Mario Lemieux, Pitt	168	2000–01	Jaromir Jagr, Pitt	121
1988–89	Mario Lemieux, Pitt	199	2001–02	Jarome Iginla, Cgy	96
1989–90	Wayne Gretzky, LA	142	2002–03	Peter Forsberg, Col	106
1990–91	Wayne Gretzky, LA	163	2003–04	Martin St. Louis, TB	94
1991–92	Mario Lemieux, Pitt	131	2004-05	No season	
1992–93	Mario Lemieux, Pitt	160	2005-06	Joe Thornton, Bos/SJ	125
1993–94	Wayne Gretzky, LA	130	2006-07	Sidney Crosby, Pitt	120

Goals

Season	Player and Club	G	Season	Player and Club	G
1917–18	Joe Malone, Mtl	44	1962–63	Gordie Howe, Det	38
1918–19	Odie Cleghorn, Mtl	23	1963–64	Bobby Hull, Chi	43
1919–20	Joe Malone, Que	39	1964–65	Norm Ullman, Det	42
1920–21	Babe Dye, Ham-Tor	35	1965–66	Bobby Hull, Chi	54
1921–22	Punch Broadbent, Ott	32	1966–67	Bobby Hull, Chi	52
1922–23	Babe Dye, Tor	26	1967–68	Bobby Hull, Chi	44
1923–24	Cy Denney, Ott	22	1968–69	Bobby Hull, Chi	58
1924–25	Babe Dye, Tor	38	1969–70	Phil Esposito, Bos	43
1925–26	Nels Stewart, Mtl	34	1970–71	Phil Esposito, Bos	76
1926–27	Bill Cook, NY	33	1971–72	Phil Esposito, Bos	66
1927–28	Howie Morenz, Mtl	33	1972–73	Phil Esposito, Bos	55
1928–29	Ace Bailey, Tor	22	1973–74	Phil Esposito, Bos	68
1929–30	Cooney Weiland, Bos	43	1974–75	Phil Esposito, Bos	61
1930–31	Charlie Lonacher, Tor	31	1975–76	Guy Lafleur, Mtl	56
1931–32	Charlie Conacher, Tor	34	1976–77	Steve Shutt, Mtl	60
	Bill Cook, NY	34	1977–78	Guy Lafleur, Mtl	60
1932–33	Bill Cook, NY	28	1978–79	Mike Bossy, NYI	69
1933–34	Charlie Conacher, Tor	32	1979–80	Charlie Simmer, LA	56
1934–35	Charlie Conacher, Tor	36		Blaine Stoughton, Hart	56
1935–36	Charlie Conacher, Tor	23	1980–81	Mike Bossy, NYI	68
	Bill Thoms, Tor	23	1981–82	Wayne Gretzky, Edm	92
1936–37	Larry Aurie, Det	23	1982–83	Wayne Gretzky, Edm	71
	Nels Stewart, Bos-NYA	23	1983–84	Wayne Gretzky, Edm	87
1937–38	Gord Drillon, Tor	26	1984–85	Wayne Gretzky, Edm	73
1938–39	Roy Conacher, Bos	26	1985–86	Jari Kurri, Edm	68
1939–40	Bryan Hextall, NY	24	1986–87	Wayne Gretzky, Edm	62
1940–41	Bryan Hextall, NY	26	1987–88	Mario Lemieux, Pitt	70
1941–42	Lynn Patrick, NY	32	1988–89	Mario Lemieux, Pitt	85
1942–43	Doug Bentley, Chi	33	1989–90	Brett Hull, StL	72
1943–44	Doug Bentley, Chi	38	1990–91	Brett Hull, StL	86
1944–45	Maurice Richard, Mtl	50	1991–92	Brett Hull, StL	70
1945–46	Gaye Stewart, Tor	37	1992–93	Alexander Mogilny, Buff	76
1946–47	Maurice Richard, Mtl	45		Teemu Selanne, Winn	76
1947–48	Ted Lindsay, Det	33	1993–94	Pavel Bure, Van	60
1948–49	Sid Abel, Det	28	1994–95	Peter Bondra, Wash	34
1949–50	Maurice Richard, Mtl	43	1995–96	Mario Lemieux, Pitt	69
1950–51	Gordie Howe, Det	43	1996–97	Keith Tkachuk, Phoe	52
1951–52	Gordie Howe, Det	47	1997–98	Teemu Selanne, Ana	52
1952–53	Gordie Howe, Det	49		Peter Bondra, Wash	52
1953–54	Maurice Richard, Mtl	37	1998–99	Teemu Selanne, Ana	47
1954–55	Bernie Geoffrion, Mtl	38	1999–00	Pavel Bure, Fla	58
	Maurice Richard, Mtl	38	2000–01	Pavel Bure, Fla	59
1955–56	Jean Beliveau, Mtl	47	2001–02	Jarome Iginla, Cgy	52
1956–57	Gordie Howe, Det	44	2002–03	Milan Hejduk, Col	50
1957–58	Dickie Moore, Mtl	36	2003–04	Jarome Iginla, Cgy	41
1958–59	Jean Beliveau, Mtl	45		Rick Nash, Clb	41
1959–60	Bobby Hull, Chi	39		Ilya Kovalchuk, Atl	41
	Bronco Horvath, Bos	39	2004–05	No season	
1960–61	Bernie Geoffrion, Mtl	50	2005–06	Jonathan Cheechoo, SJ	56
1961–62	Bobby Hull, Chi	50	2006–07	Vincent Lecavalier, TB	52

Assists

Season	Player and Club	Asst	Season	Player and Club	Asst
1917–18	statistic not kept		1965–66	Stan Mikita, Chi	48
1918–19	Newsy Lalonde, Mtl	9		Bobby Rousseau, Mtl	48
1919–20	Corbett Denneny, Tor	12		Jean Beliveau, Mtl	48
1920–21	Louis Berlinquette, Mtl	9	1966–67	Stan Mikita, Chi	62
1921–22	Punch Broadbench, Ott	14	1967–68	Phil Esposito, Bos	49
1922–23	Babe Dye, Tor	11	1968–69	Phil Esposito, Bos	77
1923–24	Billy Boucher, Mtl	6	1969–70	Bobby Orr, Bos	87
1924–25	Cy Denneny, Ott	15	1970–71	Bobby Orr, Bos	102
1925–26	Frank Nighbor, Ott	13	1971–72	Bobby Orr, Bos	80
1926–27	Dick Irvin, Chi	18	1972–73	Phil Esposito, Bos	75
1927–28	Howie Morenz, Mtl	18	1973–74	Bobby Orr, Bos	90
1928–29	Frank Boucher, NY	16	1974–75	Bobby Clarke, Phil	89
1929–30	Frank Boucher, NY	36		Bobby Orr, Bos	89
1930–31	Joe Primeau, Tor	32	1975–76	Bobby Clarke, Phil	89
1931–32	Joe Primeau, Tor	37	1976–77	Guy Lafleur, Mtl	80
1932–33	Frank Boucher, NY	28	1977–78	Bryan Trottier, NYI	77
1933–34	Joe Primeau, Tor	32	1978–79	Bryan Trottier, NYI	87
1934–35	Art Chapman, NYA	34	1979–80	Wayne Gretzky, Edm	86
1935–36	Art Chapman, NYA	28	1980–81	Wayne Gretzky, Edm	109
1936–37	Syl Apps, Tor	29	1981–82	Wayne Gretzky, Edm	120
1937–38	Syl Apps, Tor	29	1982–83	Wayne Gretzky, Edm	125
1938–39	Bill Cowley, Bos	34	1983–84	Wayne Gretzky, Edm	118
1939–40	Milt Schmidt, Bos	30	1984–85	Wayne Gretzky, Edm	135
1940–41	Bill Cowley, Bos	45	1985–86	Wayne Gretzky, Edm	163
1941–42	Phil Watson, NY	37	1986–87	Wayne Gretzky, Edm	121
1942–43	Bill Cowley, Bos	45	1987–88	Wayne Gretzky, Edm	109
1943–44	Clint Smith, Chi	49	1988–89	Wayne Gretzky, LA	114
1944–45	Elmer Lach, Mtl	54		Mario Lemieux, Pitt	114
1945–46	Elmer Lach, Mtl	34	1989–90	Wayne Gretzky, LA	102
1946–47	Billy Taylor, Det	46	1990–91	Wayne Gretzky, LA	122
1947–48	Doug Bentley, Chi	37	1991–92	Wayne Gretzky, LA	90
1948–49	Doug Bentley, Chi	43	1992–93	Adam Oates, Bos	97
1949–50	Ted Lindsay, Det	55	1993–94	Wayne Gretzky, LA	92
1950–51	Gordie Howe, Det	43	1994–95	Ron Francis, Pitt	48
	Ted Kennedy, Tor	43	1995–96	Mario Lemieux, Pitt	92
1951–52	Elmer Lach, Mtl	50		Ron Francis, Pitt	92
1952–53	Gordie Howe, Det	46	1996–97	Mario Lemieux, Pitt	72
1953–54	Gordie Howe, Det	48	1997–98	Jaromir Jagr, Pitt	67
1954–55	Bert Olmstead, Mtl	48		Wayne Gretzky, NYR	67
1955–56	Bert Olmstead, Mtl	56	1998–99	Jaromir Jagr, Pitt	83
1956–57	Ted Lindsay, Det	55	1999–00	Mark Recchi, Phil	63
1957–58	Henri Richard, Mtl	52	2000–01	Jaromir Jagr, Pitt	69
1958–59	Dickie Moore, Mtl	55		Adam Oates, Wash	69
1959–60	Bobby Hull, Chi	42	2001–02	Adam Oates, Wash	64
1960–61	Jean Beliveau, Mtl	58	2002–03	Peter Forsberg, Col	77
1961–62	Andy Bathgate, NY	56	2003–04	Scott Gomez, NJ	56
1962–63	Henri Richard, Mtl	50		Martin St. Louis, TB	56
1963–64	Andy Bathgate, NY-Tor	58	2004–05	No season	
1964–65	Stan Mikita, Chi	59	2005–06	Joe Thornton, Bos/SJ	96
			2006–07	Joe Thornton, SJ	92

Goals Against Average

Season	Goaltender and Club	GP	Min	GA	SO	Avg
1917–18	Georges Vezina, Mtl	21	1282	84	1	3.93
1918–19	Clint Benedict, Ott	18	1113	53	2	2.86
1919–20	Clint Benedict, Ott	24	1444	64	5	2.66
1920–21	Clint Benedict, Ott	24	1457	75	2	3.09
1921–22	Clint Benedict, Ott	24	1508	84	2	3.34
1922–23	Clint Benedict, Ott	24	1478	54	4	2.18
1923–24	Georges Vezina, Mtl	24	1459	48	3	1.97
1924–25	Georges Vezina, Mtl	30	1860	56	5	1.81
1925–26	Alec Connell, Ott	36	2251	42	15	1.12
1926–27	Clint Benedict, Mtl M	43	2748	65	13	1.42
1927–28	George Hainsworth, Mtl	44	2730	48	13	1.05
1928–29	George Hainsworth, Mtl	44	2800	43	22	0.92
1929–30	Tiny Thompson, Bos	44	2680	98	3	2.19

Goals Against Average *(Cont.)*

Season	Goaltender and Club	GP	Min	GA	SO	Avg
1930–31	Roy Worters, NYA	44	2760	74	8	1.61
1931–32	Chuck Gardiner, Chi	48	2989	92	4	1.85
1932–33	Tiny Thompson, Bos	48	3000	88	11	1.76
1933–34	Wilf Cude, Det-Mtl	30	1920	47	5	1.47
1934–35	Lorne Chabot, Chi	48	2940	88	8	1.80
1935–36	Tiny Thompson, Bos	48	2930	82	10	1.68
1936–37	Normie Smith, Det	48	2980	102	6	2.05
1937–38	Tiny Thompson, Bos	48	2970	89	7	1.80.
1938–39	Frank Brimsek, Bos	43	2610	68	10	1.56
1939–40	Dave Kerr, NYR	48	3000	77	8	1.54
1940–41	Turk Broda, Tor	48	2970	99	5	2.00
1941–42	Frank Brimsek, Bos	47	2930	115	3	2.35
1942–43	Johnny Mowers, Det	50	3010	124	6	2.47
1943–44	Bill Durnan, Mtl	50	3000	109	2	2.18
1944–45	Bill Durnan, Mtl	50	3000	121	1	2.42
1945–46	Bill Durnan, Mtl	40	2400	104	4	2.60
1946–47	Bill Durnan, Mtl	60	3600	138	4	2.30
1947–48	Turk Broda, Tor	60	3600	143	5	2.38
1948–49	Bill Durnan, Mtl	60	3600	126	10	2.10
1949–50	Bill Durnan, Mtl	64	3840	141	8	2.20
1950–51	Al Rollins, Tor	40	2367	70	5	1.77
1951–52	Terry Sawchuk, Det	70	4200	133	12	1.90
1952–53	Terry Sawchuk, Det	63	3780	120	9	1.90
1953–54	Harry Lumley, Tor	69	4140	128	13	1.86
1954–55	Harry Lumley, Tor	69	4140	134	8	1.94
1955–56	Jacques Plante, Mtl	64	3840	119	7	1.86
1956–57	Jacques Plante, Mtl	61	3660	122	9	2.00
1957–58	Jacques Plante, Mtl	57	3386	119	9	2.11
1958–59	Jacques Plante, Mtl	67	4000	144	9	2.16
1959–60	Jacques Plante, Mtl	69	4140	175	3	2.54
1960–61	Charlie Hodge, Mtl	30	1800	74	4	2.47
1961–62	Jacques Plante, Mtl	70	4200	166	4	2.37
1962–63	Don Simmons, Tor	28	1680	69	1	2.46
1963–64	Johnny Bower, Tor	51	3009	106	5	2.11
1964–65	Johnny Bower, Tor	34	2040	81	3	2.38
1965–66	Johnny Bower, Tor	35	1998	75	3	2.25
1966–67	Glenn Hall, Chi	32	1664	66	2	2.38
1967–68	Gump Worsley, Mtl	40	2213	73	6	1.98
1968–69	Jacques Plante, StL	37	2139	70	5	1.96
1969–70	Ernie Wakely, StL	30	1651	58	4	2.11
1970–71	Jacques Plante, Tor	40	2329	73	4	1.88
1971–72	Tony Esposito, Chi	48	2780	82	9	1.77
1972–73	Ken Dryden, Mtl	54	3165	119	6	2.26
1973–74	Bernie Parent, Phil	73	4314	136	12	1.89
1974–75	Bernie Parent, Phil	68	4041	137	12	2.03
1975–76	Ken Dryden, Mtl	62	3580	121	8	2.03
1976–77	Michel Larocque, Mtl	26	1525	53	4	2.09
1977–78	Ken Dryden, Mtl	52	3071	105	5	2.05
1978–79	Ken Dryden, Mtl	47	2814	108	5	2.30
1979–80	Bob Sauve, Buff	32	1880	74	4	2.36
1980–81	Richard Sevigny, Mtl	33	1777	71	2	2.40
1981–82	Denis Herron, Mtl	27	1547	68	3	2.64
1982–83	Pete Peeters, Bos	62	3611	142	8	2.36
1983–84	Pat Riggin, Wash	41	2299	102	4	2.66
1984–85	Tom Barrasso, Buff	54	3248	144	5	2.66
1985–86	Bob Froese, Phil	51	2728	116	5	2.55
1986–87	Brian Hayward, Mtl	37	2178	102	1	2.81
1987–88	Pete Peeters, Wash	35	1896	88	2	2.78
1988–89	Patrick Roy, Mtl	48	2744	113	4	2.47
1989–90	Patrick Roy, Mtl	54	3173	134	3	2.53
	Mike Liut, Hart-Wash	37	2161	91	4	2.53
1990–91	Ed Belfour, Chi	74	4127	170	4	2.47
1991–92	Patrick Roy, Mtl	67	3935	155	5	2.36
1992–93	Felix Potvin, Tor	48	2781	116	2	2.50
1993–94	Dominik Hasek, Buff	58	3358	109	7	1.95
1994–95	Dominik Hasek, Buff	41	2416	85	5	2.11

Goals Against Average *(Cont.)*

Season	Goaltender and Club	GP	Min	GA	SO	Avg
1995–96	Ron Hextall, Phil	53	3102	112	4	2.17
	Chris Osgood, Det	50	2932	106	5	2.17
1996–97	Martin Brodeur, NJ	67	3838	120	10	1.88
1997–98	Ed Belfour, Dall	61	3581	112	9	1.88
1998–99	Ron Tugnutt, Ott	43	2508	75	3	1.79
1999–00	Brian Boucher, Phil	35	2038	65	4	1.91
2000–01	Marty Turco, Dall	26	1266	40	3	1.90
2001–02	Patrick Roy, Col	63	3773	122	9	1.94
2002–03	Marty Turco, Dall	55	3202	92	7	1.72
2003–04	Miikka Kiprusoff, Cgy	38	2301	65	4	1.69
2004–05	No season					
2005–06	Miikka Kiprusoff, Cgy	74	4379	151	10	2.07
2006–07	Niklas Backstrom, Minn	41	2226	73	5	1.97

Penalty Minutes

Season	Player and Club	GP	PIM	Season	Player and Club	GP	PIM
1918–19	Joe Hall, Mtl	17	135	1963–64	Vic Hadfield, NYR	69	151
1919–20	Cully Wilson, Tor	23	79	1964–65	Carl Brewer, Tor	70	177
1920–21	Bert Corbeau, Mtl	24	86	1965–66	Reggie Fleming, Bos-NYR	69	166
1921–22	Sprague Cleghorn, Mtl	24	63	1966–67	John Ferguson, Mtl	67	177
1922–23	Billy Boucher, Mtl	24	55	1967–68	Barclay Plager, StL	49	153
1923–24	Bert Corbeau, Tor	24	55	1968–69	Forbes Kennedy, Phil-Tor	77	219
1924–25	Billy Boucher, Mtl	30	92	1969–70	Keith Magnuson, Chi	76	213
1925–26	Bert Corbeau, Tor	36	121	1970–71	Keith Magnuson, Chi	76	291
1926–27	Nels Stewart, Mtl M	44	133	1971–72	Brian Watson, Pitt	75	212
1927–28	Eddie Shore, Bos	44	165	1972–73	Dave Schultz, Phil	76	259
1928–29	Red Dutton, Mtl M	44	139	1973–74	Dave Schultz, Phil	73	348
1929–30	Joe Lamb, Ott	44	119	1974–75	Dave Schultz, Phil	76	472
1930–31	Harvey Rockburn, Det	42	118	1975–76	Steve Durbano, Pitt-KC	69	370
1931–32	Red Dutton, NYA	47	107	1976–77	Dave Williams, Tor	77	338
1932–33	Red Horner, Tor	48	144	1977–78	Dave Schultz, LA-Pitt	74	405
1933–34	Red Horner, Tor	42	126	1978–79	Dave Williams, Tor	77	298
1934–35	Red Horner, Tor	46	125	1979–80	Jimmy Mann, Winn	72	287
1935–36	Red Horner, Tor	43	167	1980–81	Dave Williams, Van	77	343
1936–37	Red Horner, Tor	48	124	1981–82	Paul Baxter, Pitt	76	409
1937–38	Red Horner, Tor	47	82	1982–83	Randy Holt, Wash	70	275
1938–39	Red Horner, Tor	48	85	1983–84	Chris Nilan, Mtl	76	338
1939–40	Red Horner, Tor	30	87	1984–85	Chris Nilan, Mtl	77	358
1940–41	Jimmy Orlando, Det	48	99	1985–86	Joey Kocur, Det	59	377
1941–42	Pat Egan, Bklyn	48	124	1986–87	Tim Hunter, Cgy	73	361
1942–43	Jimmy Orlando, Det	40	89	1987–88	Bob Probert, Det	74	398
1943–44	Mike McMahon, Mtl	42	98	1988–89	Tim Hunter, Cgy	75	375
1944–45	Pat Egan, Bos	48	86	1989–90	Basil McRae, Minn	66	351
1945–46	Jack Stewart, Det	47	73	1990–91	Rob Ray, Buff	66	350
1946–47	Gus Mortson, Tor	60	133	1991–92	Mike Peluso, Chi	63	408
1947–48	Bill Barilko, Tor	57	147	1992–93	Marty McSorley, LA	81	399
1948–49	Bill Ezinicki, Tor	52	145	1993–94	Tie Domi, Winn	81	347
1949–50	Bill Ezinicki, Tor	67	144	1994–95	Enrico Ciccone, TB	41	225
1950–51	Gus Mortson, Tor	60	142	1995–96	Matthew Barnaby, Buff	73	335
1951–52	Gus Kyle, Bos	69	127	1996–97	Gino Odjick, Van	70	371
1952–53	Maurice Richard, Mtl	70	112	1997–98	Donald Brashear, Van	77	372
1953–54	Gus Mortson, Chi	68	132	1998–99	Rob Ray, Buff	76	261
1954–55	Fern Flaman, Bos	70	150	1999–00	Denny Lambert, Atl	73	219
1955–56	Lou Fontinato, NYR	70	202	2000–01	Matthew Barnaby, TB	76	265
1956–57	Gus Mortson, Chi	70	147	2001–02	Peter Worrell, Fla	79	354
1957–58	Lou Fontinato, NYR	70	152	2002–03	Jody Shelley, Clb	68	249
1958–59	Ted Lindsay, Chi	70	184	2003–04	Sean Avery, LA	76	261
1959–60	Carl Brewer, Tor	67	150	2004–05	No season		
1960–61	Pierre Pilote, Chi	70	165	2005–06	Sean Avery, LA	75	257
1961–62	Lou Fontinato, Mtl	54	167	2006–07	Ben Eager, Phil	63	233
1962–63	Howie Young, Det	64	273				

First played in 1947, this game was scheduled before the start of the regular season and used to match the defending Stanley Cup champions against a squad made up of the league All-Stars from other teams. In 1966 the game was moved to midseason, although there was no game that year. The format changed to a conference versus conference showdown in 1969.

Results

Year	Site	Score	MVP	Attendance
1947	Toronto	All-Stars 4, Toronto 3	None named	14,169
1948	Chicago	All-Stars 3, Toronto 1	None named	12,794
1949	Toronto	All-Stars 3, Toronto 1	None named	13,541
1950	Detroit	Detroit 7, All-Stars 1	None named	9,166
1951	Toronto	1st team 2, 2nd team 2	None named	11,469
1952	Detroit	1st team 1, 2nd team 1	None named	10,680
1953	Montreal	All-Stars 3, Montreal 1	None named	14,153
1954	Detroit	All-Stars 2, Detroit 2	None named	10,689
1955	Detroit	Detroit 3, All-Stars 1	None named	10,111
1956	Montreal	All-Stars 1, Montreal 1	None named	13,095
1957	Montreal	All-Stars 5, Montreal 3	None named	13,003
1958	Montreal	Montreal 6, All-Stars 3	None named	13,989
1959	Montreal	Montreal 6, All-Stars 1	None named	13,818
1960	Montreal	All-Stars 2, Montreal 1	None named	13,949
1961	Chicago	All-Stars 3, Chicago 1	None named	14,534
1962	Toronto	Toronto 4, All-Stars 1	Eddie Shack, Tor	14,236
1963	Toronto	All-Stars 3, Toronto 3	Frank Mahovlich, Tor	14,034
1964	Toronto	All-Stars 3, Toronto 2	Jean Beliveau, Mtl	14,232
1965	Montreal	All-Stars 5, Montreal 2	Gordie Howe, Det	13,529
1967	Montreal	Montreal 3, All-Stars 0	Henri Richard, Mtl	14,284
1968	Toronto	Toronto 4, All-Stars 3	Bruce Gamble, Tor	15,753
1969	Montreal	East 3, West 3	Frank Mahovlich, Det	16,260
1970	St. Louis	East 4, West 1	Bobby Hull, Chi	16,587
1971	Boston	West 2, East 1	Bobby Hull, Chi	14,790
1972	Minnesota	East 3, West 2	Bobby Orr, Bos	15,423
1973	NY Rangers	East 5, West 4	Greg Polis, Pitt	16,986
1974	Chicago	West 6, East 4	Garry Unger, StL	16,426
1975	Montreal	Wales 7, Campbell 1	Syl Apps Jr, Pitt	16,080
1976	Philadelphia	Wales 7, Campbell 5	Pete Mahovlich, Mtl	16,436
1977	Vancouver	Wales 4, Campbell 3	Rick Martin, Buff	15,607
1978	Buffalo	Wales 3, Campbell 2 (OT)	Billy Smith, NYI	16,433
1980	Detroit	Wales 6, Campbell 3	Reg Leach, Phil	21,002
1981	Los Angeles	Campbell 4, Wales 1	Mike Liut, StL	15,761
1982	Washington	Wales 4, Campbell 2	Mike Bossy, NYI	18,130
1983	NY Islanders	Campbell 9, Wales 3	Wayne Gretzky, Edm	15,230
1984	New Jersey	Wales 7, Campbell 6	Don Maloney, NYR	18,939
1985	Calgary	Wales 6, Campbell 4	Mario Lemieux, Pitt	16,825
1986	Hartford	Wales 4, Campbell 3 (OT)	Grant Fuhr, Edm	15,100
1988	St. Louis	Wales 6, Campbell 5 (OT)	Mario Lemieux, Pitt	17,878
1989	Edmonton	Campbell 9, Wales 5	Wayne Gretzky, LA	17,503
1990	Pittsburgh	Wales 12, Campbell 7	Mario Lemieux, Pitt	16,236
1991	Chicago	Campbell 11, Wales 5	Vince Damphousse, Tor	18,472
1992	Philadelphia	Campbell 10, Wales 6	Brett Hull, StL	17,380
1993	Montreal	Wales 16, Campbell 6	Mike Gartner, NYR	17,137
1994	NY Rangers	East 9, West 8	Mike Richter, NYR	18,200
1996	Boston	East 5, West 4	Ray Bourque, Bos	17,565
1997	San Jose	East 11, West 7	Mark Recchi, Mtl	17,422
1998	Vancouver	N America 8, World 7	Teemu Selanne, Ana (World)	18,422
1999	Tampa Bay	N America 8, World 6	Wayne Gretzky, NYR (N America)	19,758
2000	Toronto	World 9, N America 4	Pavel Bure, Fla (World)	19,300
2001	Denver	N America 14, World 12	Bill Guerin, Bos (N America)	18,646
2002	Los Angeles	World 8, N America 5	Eric Daze, Chi (N America)	18,118
2003	Sunrise, Fla.	West 6, East 5 (shootout)	Dany Heatley, Atl (East)	19,250
2004	St. Paul, Minn.	East 6, West 4	Joe Sakic, Col (West)	19,434
2005	No game played			
2006	No game played due to Winter Olympics			
2007	Dallas	West 12, East 9	Daniel Briere, Buff (East)	18,532

Note: The Challenge Cup, a series between the NHL All-Stars and the Soviet Union, was played instead of the All-Star Game in 1979. Eight years later, Rendez-Vous '87, a two-game series matching the Soviet Union and the NHL All-Stars, replaced the All-Star Game. The 1995 NHL All-Star game was cancelled due to a labor dispute. The 1998 NHL All-Star game, billed as a preview to the 1998 Winter Olympics in Nagano, Japan, matched North Amercian–born All-Stars and All-Stars born elsewhere. In 2005, no game was played due to season-long lockout.

Located in Toronto, the Hockey Hall of Fame was officially opened on August 26, 1961. The current chairman is William C. Hay. There are, at present, 306 members of the Hockey Hall of Fame—209 players, 84 "builders," and 14 on-ice officials. (One member, Alan Eagleson, resigned from the Hall March 25, 1998.) To be eligible, player and referee/linesman candidates should have been out of the game for three years, but the Hall's Board of Directors can make exceptions.

Players

Sid Abel (1969)
Jack Adams (1959)
Charles (Syl) Apps (1961)
George Armstrong (1975)
Irvine (Ace) Bailey (1975)
Donald H. (Dan) Bain (1945)
Hobey Baker (1945)
Bill Barber (1990)
Marty Barry (1965)
Andy Bathgate (1978)
Bobby Bauer (1996)
Jean Beliveau (1972)
Clint Benedict (1965)
Douglas Bentley (1964)
Max Bentley (1966)
Hector (Toe) Blake (1966)
Leo Boivin (1986)
Dickie Boon (1952)
Mike Bossy (1991)
Emile (Butch) Bouchard (1966)
Frank Boucher (1958)
George (Buck) Boucher (1960)
Ray Bourque (2004)
Johnny Bower (1976)
Russell Bowie (1945)
Frank Brimsek (1966)
Harry L. (Punch) Broadbent (1962)
Walter (Turk) Broda (1967)
John Bucyk (1981)
Billy Burch (1974)
Harry Cameron (1962)
Gerry Cheevers (1985)
Francis (King) Clancy (1958)
Aubrey (Dit) Clapper (1947)
Bobby Clarke (1987)
Sprague Cleghorn (1958)
Paul Coffey (2004)
Neil Colville (1967)
Charlie Conacher (1961)
Lionel Conacher (1994)
Roy Conacher (1998)
Alex Connell (1958)
Bill Cook (1952)
Fred (Bun) Cook (1995)
Arthur Coulter (1974)
Yvan Cournoyer (1982)
Bill Cowley (1968)
Samuel (Rusty) Crawford (1962)
Jack Darragh (1962)
Allan M. (Scotty) Davidson (1950)
Clarence (Hap) Day (1961)
Alex Delvecchio (1977)
Cy Denneny (1959)
Marcel Dionne (1992)
Gordie Drillon (1975)
Charles Drinkwater (1950)
Ken Dryden (1983)
Terrance (Dick) Duff (2006)
Woody Dumart (1992)

Thomas Dunderdale (1974)
Bill Durnan (1964)
Mervyn A. (Red) Dutton (1958)
Cecil (Babe) Dye (1970)
Phil Esposito (1984)
Tony Esposito (1988)
Arthur F. Farrell (1965)
Bernie Federko (2002)
Viacheslav Fetisov (2001)
Ferdinand (Fern) Flaman (1990)
Frank Foyston (1958)
Ron Francis (2007)
Frank Frederickson (1958)
Grant Fuhr (2003)
Bill Gadsby (1970)
Bob Gainey (1992)
Chuck Gardiner (1945)
Herb Gardiner (1958)
Jimmy Gardner (1962)
Mike Gartner (2001)
Bernie (Boom Boom) Geoffrion (1972)
Eddie Gerard (1945)
Ed Giacomin (1987)
Rod Gilbert (1982)
Clark Gillies (2002)
Hamilton (Billy) Gilmour (1962)
Frank (Moose) Goheen (1952)
Ebenezer R. (Ebbie) Goodfellow (1963)
Michel Goulet (1998)
Mike Grant (1950)
Wilfred (Shorty) Green (1962)
Jim Gregory (2007)
Wayne Gretzky (1999)
Si Griffis (1950)
George Hainsworth (1961)
Glenn Hall (1975)
Joe Hall (1961)
Doug Harvey (1973)
Dale Hawerchuk (2001)
George Hay (1958)
William (Riley) Hern (1962)
Bryan Hextall (1969)
Harry (Hap) Holmes (1972)
Tom Hooper (1962)
George (Red) Horner (1965)
Miles (Tim) Horton (1977)
Gordie Howe (1972)
Syd Howe (1965)
Harry Howell (1979)
Bobby Hull (1983)
John (Bouse) Hutton (1962)
Harry M. Hyland (1962)
James (Dick) Irvin (1958)
Harvey (Busher) Jackson (1971)
Ernest (Moose) Johnson (1952)
Ivan (Ching) Johnson (1958)
Tom Johnson (1970)

Players *(Cont.)*

Aurel Joliat (1947)
Gordon (Duke) Keats (1958)
Leonard (Red) Kelly (1969)
Ted (Teeder) Kennedy (1966)
Dave Keon (1986)
Valeri Kharlamov (2005)
Jari Kurri (2001)
Elmer Lach (1966)
Guy Lafleur (1988)
Pat LaFontaine (2003)
Edouard (Newsy) Lalonde (1950)
Rod Langway (2002)
Jacques Laperriere (1987)
Guy Lapointe (1993)
Edgar Laprade (1993)
Jean (Jack) Laviolette (1962)
Hugh Lehman (1958)
Jacques Lemaire (1984)
Mario Lemieux (1997)
Percy LeSueur (1961)
Herbert A. Lewis (1989)
Ted Lindsay (1966)
Harry Lumley (1980)
Lanny McDonald (1992)
Frank McGee (1945)
Billy McGimsie (1962)
George McNamara (1958)
Al MacInnis (2007)
Duncan (Mickey) MacKay (1952)
Frank Mahovlich (1981)
Joe Malone (1950)
Sylvio Mantha (1960)
Jack Marshall (1965)
Fred G. (Steamer) Maxwell (1962)
Mark Messier (2007)
Stan Mikita (1983)
Dicky Moore (1974)
Patrick (Paddy) Moran (1958)
Howie Morenz (1945)
Billy Mosienko (1965)
Joe Mullen (2000)
Larry Murphy (2004)
Cam Neely (2005)
Frank Nighbor (1947)
Reg Noble (1962)
Herbert (Buddy) O'Connor (1988)
Harry Oliver (1967)
Bert Olmstead (1985)
Bobby Orr (1979)
Bernie Parent (1984)
Brad Park (1988)
Lester Patrick (1947)
Lynn Patrick (1980)
Gilbert Perreault (1990)
Tommy Phillips (1945)
Pierre Pilote (1975)
Didier (Pit) Pitre (1962)
Jacques Plante (1978)
Denis Potvin (1991)
Walter (Babe) Pratt (1966)
Joe Primeau (1963)
Marcel Pronovost (1978)
Bob Pulford (1991)

Harvey Pulford (1945)
Hubert (Bill) Quackenbush (1976)
Frank Rankin (1961)
Jean Ratelle (1985)
Claude (Chuck) Rayner (1973)
Kenneth Reardon (1966)
Henri Richard (1979)
Maurice (Rocket) Richard (1961)
George Richardson (1950)
Gordon Roberts (1971)
Larry Robinson (1995)
Art Ross (1945)
Patrick Roy (2006)
Blair Russel (1965)
Ernest Russell (1965)
Jack Ruttan (1962)
Borje Salming (1996)
Denis Savard (2000)
Serge Savard (1986)
Terry Sawchuk (1971)
Fred Scanlan (1965)
Milt Schmidt (1961)
Dave (Sweeney) Schriner (1962)
Earl Seibert (1963)
Oliver Seibert (1961)
Eddie Shore (1947)
Steve Shutt (1993)
Albert C. (Babe) Siebert (1964)
Harold (Bullet Joe) Simpson (1962)
Daryl Sittler (1989)
Alfred E. Smith (1962)
Billy Smith (1993)
Clint Smith (1991)
Reginald (Hooley) Smith (1972)
Thomas Smith (1973)
Allan Stanley (1981)
Russell (Barney) Stanley (1962)
Peter Stastny (1998)
Scott Stevens (2007)
John (Black Jack) Stewart (1964)
Nels Stewart (1962)
Bruce Stuart (1961)
Hod Stuart (1945)
Frederic (Cyclone) (O.B.E.)
  Taylor (1947)
Cecil R. (Tiny) Thompson (1959)
Vladislav Tretiak (1989)
Harry J. Trihey (1950)
Bryan Trottier (1997)
Norm Ullman (1982)
Georges Vezina (1945)
Jack Walker (1960)
Marty Walsh (1962)
Harry Watson (1994)
Harry E. Watson (1962)
Ralph (Cooney) Weiland (1971)
Harry Westwick (1962)
Fred Whitcroft (1962)
Gordon (Phat) Wilson (1962)
Lorne (Gump) Worsley (1980)
Roy Worters (1969)

Note: Year of election to the Hall of Fame is in parentheses after the member's name.

Builders

Charles Adams (1960)
Weston W. Adams (1972)
Thomas (Frank) Ahearn (1962)
John (Bunny) Ahearne (1977)
Montagu Allan (C.V.O.) (1945)
Keith Allen (1992)
Al Arbour (1996)
Harold Ballard (1977)
David Bauer (1989)
John Bickell (1978)
Scott Bowman (1991)
Herb Brooks (2006)
George V. Brown (1961)
Walter A. Brown (1962)
Frank Buckland (1975)
Walter L. Bush (2000)
Jack Butterfield (1980)
Frank Calder (1947)
Angus D. Campbell (1964)
Clarence Campbell (1966)
Joe Cattarinich (1977)
Bob Cole (1996, Media)
Murray Costello (2005)
Joseph (Leo) Dandurand (1963)
Francis Dilio (1964)
George S. Dudley (1958)
James A. Dunn (1968)
*Robert Alan Eagleson (1989–98)
Cliff Fletcher (2004)
Emile Francis (1982)
Jack Gibson (1976)
Tommy Gorman (1963)
Frank Griffiths (1993)
William Hanley (1986)
Charles Hay (1974)
James C. Hendy (1968)
Foster Hewitt (1965)
William Hewitt (1947)
Harley Hotchkiss (2006)
Fred J. Hume (1962)
Mike Ilitch (2003)
George (Punch) Imlach (1984)
Tommy Ivan (1974)
William M. Jennings (1975)
Bob Johnson (1992)
Gordon W. Juckes (1979)
John Kilpatrick (1960)
Brian Kilrea (2003)
Seymour Knox III (1993)

George Leader (1969)
Robert LeBel (1970)
Thomas F. Lockhart (1965)
Paul Loicq (1961)
Frederic McLaughlin (1963)
John Mariucci (1985)
Frank Mathers (1992)
John (Jake) Milford (1984)
Hartland Molson (1973)
Scotty Morrison (1999)
Mngr. Athol (Pere) Murray (1998)
Roger Neilson (2002)
Francis Nelson (1947)
Bruce A. Norris (1969)
James Norris, Sr. (1958)
James D. Norris (1962)
William M. Northey (1947)
John O'Brien (1962)
Brian O'Neill (1994)
Fred Page (1993)
Craig Patrick (1996)
Frank Patrick (1958)
Allan W. Pickard (1958)
Rudy Pilous (1985)
Norman (Bud) Poile (1990)
Samuel Pollock (1978)
Donat Raymond (1958)
John Robertson (1947)
Claude C. Robinson (1947)
Philip D. Ross (1976)
Gunther Sabetzki (1995)
Glen Sather (1997)
Frank J. Selke (1960)
Harry Sinden (1983)
Frank D. Smith (1962)
Conn Smythe (1958)
Edward M. Snider (1988)
Lord Stanley of Preston (1945)
James T. Sutherland (1947)
Anatoli V. Tarasov (1974)
Bill Torrey (1995)
Lloyd Turner (1958)
William Tutt (1978)
Carl Potter Voss (1974)
Fred C. Waghorn (1961)
Arthur Wirtz (1971)
Bill Wirtz (1976)
John A. Ziegler, Jr. (1987)

Referees/Linesmen

Neil Armstrong (1991)
John Ashley (1981)
William L. Chadwick (1964)
John D'Amico (1993)
Chaucer Elliott (1961)
George Hayes (1988)
Robert W. Hewitson (1963)
Fred J. (Mickey) Ion (1961)

Matt Pavelich (1987)
Mike Rodden (1962)
J. Cooper Smeaton (1961)
Roy (Red) Storey (1967)
Frank Udvari (1973)
Andy Van Hellemond (1999)

*Eagleson resigned from Hall March 25, 1998.

Tennis

Roger Federer won
three Grand Slam
events in 2007

... Winner and Still Champion...

In 2007, the Williams sisters made a comeback while Roger Federer made history

BY B.J. SCHECTER

IT WAS A FITTING END TO another dominating year—methodical, precise and lacking drama. We have come to expect tears, emotional sendoffs and unexpected performances at the U.S. Open, but not this year. The men's champion played so well that not only was he the King of Queens, he was King of the Court nearly everywhere. Day after day and night after night, A-listers trudged out to Queens to watch the world's best players try to dethrone Roger Federer at the U.S. Open. But to beat Federer is to rise to another level, and as runner-up Novak Djokovic astutely pointed out when he called Federer "The Untouchable One," Federer is simply several notches above the rest.

Federer makes things look effortless and often barely breaks a sweat. The precision with which he hits his shots is at times scary, and to watch him stand at the baseline and calmly hit winner after winner is a thing of beauty. In claiming his fourth straight U.S. Open, fifth consecutive Wimbledon and 12th overall Grand Slam title, Federer capped another remarkable year in which he won three out of the four Slams and made it to the final of the other (the French Open, where he lost to his nemesis, Spaniard Rafael Nadal).

"A lot of times you don't understand how can do it," said Justine Henin, who won two Slams in '07, the French and U.S. Opens. "The way he covers the court, it's like he's never forcing his game. He's everywhere. His attitude never changes—winning, losing, if he doesn't play well—he's very calm. He's going to be the best ever. I don't see anyone who can stop him now."

Because Federer often plays without emotion and doesn't have a booming personality like Andy Roddick, James Blake, Nadal or Djokovic, he doesn't get the adulation he deserves. Tiger Woods is universally considered the world's best golfer, Michael Jordan is known as the best basketball player of all time, but Federer's greatness isn't as appreciated, especially when you consider his legacy is growing exponentially. After all, he's just 26 years old, has 12 Slams and will likely obliterate Pete Sampras' career record of 14 by the time he is done.

People are starting to appreciate Federer for his tennis, but it's much more in awe and admiration of his game (he won the Australian Open without dropping a set) than his personality. Fans still don't cheer for him the way they do Roddick and Nadal, and often they pull for him to lose, something that has bothered Federer. "It's important that people respect what I do, and I think over the past couple years that has happened," said Federer.

BOB MARTIN

"There were times I felt people were like...," he said, shrugging. "It was a bit strange. But now I almost have the feeling [they know] they're watching greatness. Especially after that fifth Wimbledon, that really put me in a different league. That Wimbledon and this U.S. Open are going to change a lot of things."

Even more impressive is that Federer's run has come without a coach. While former tennis great Jimmy Connors has helped retool Roddick's game and other top players change coaches as often as they do rackets, Federer's dominance has come with little council other than his own. "I don't need to sit down and talk about an opponent for an hour," said Federer. "Takes me basically 15 seconds [to come up with a game plan]. I know everything I need to know."

The Williams sisters feel the same way. Venus and Serena infuriate the tennis establishment because they do what they please. They practice when they want to practice, play the tournaments they want to play, bask in the spotlight away from the game and still find a way to win—when they want to. It may not always be pretty, but when the stakes are the highest the Williams sisters reach down and pull out their competitive greatness, rankings be damned.

Serena Williams entered the Australian Open ranked 81st in the world and few expected her to make a run at the title. In

Venus Williams, like her sister Serena, began the year ranked outside the top 40 before climbing back into the top 10.

fact, just before the Australian she lost to an unknown Austrian and looked like she would flame out in the first round. But as it turned out, it was all the motivation she would need. After the match, Serena ran wind sprints in a park. "It was like Rocky," she said. "I was so mad I lost the match, and I just did the ultimate workout. I think it paid off."

It did indeed. Serena got her groove back and rediscovered her competitive edge. She found a way to win when she was on the brink of losing, and more importantly she again intimidated her opponents. She may have won her fourth-round match against Jelena Jankovic, who entered the match as one of the hottest players on the Tour, before it began. "I was thinking what would happen if [her serve] came too close to my body, and I couldn't get out of the way and it him me in the stomach," Jankovic said after losing to Williams. "Would it go through me?"

Williams seemingly went through everyone before thoroughly dominating top-seeded Maria Sharapova in the final. She again beat the world's best in extreme heat, throwing her title into the faces of critics who questioned her stamina and physique.

"I'm definitely in better shape than I get credit for," said Williams. "[It's] just because

BOB MARTIN

but she was awfully good at times. She averaged 115 mph on her serve for the tournament, an impressive feat when you consider that only seven female players even managed to reach that speed once. And when she needed it the most, she reached down and came up with the big shot. Venus marched to the final, where she dispatched France's Marion Bartoli to capture her fourth Wimbledon title and became the lowest-seeded player to win the women's singles championship.

"I was really motivated because no one picked me to win," said Venus. "They didn't even say, 'She can't win.' They weren't even talking about me. "I never would doubt myself that way.

"As long as we're fit, we just have so much to give on the court," Williams said, referring to her sister as well. "Obviously, I feel fantastic. My sixth Slam. I want some more."

While the Williams sisters won two of the four women's Grand Slam titles, Henin took the other two to give her seven overall. Petite and not overpowering like Venus and Serena, Henin dominated with precision and resolve. Mentally strong from her difficult childhood (her mother died when she was young and she is estranged from her father, who was also her coach), Henin overcame breathing problems to win the French and had to go through both Williams sisters to take the U.S. Open title without losing a set. "It's just a great feeling because I had a tough draw and I had a lot of things to prove to myself—not to anyone else, just to myself," said Henin. "And I did it."

Henin may have proven that she can beat the Williams sisters and maintain her No. 1 ranking, but on the men's side nobody has demonstrated that they're in the same universe as Federer. Until someone comes along and shows he can consistently beat him in a Slam other than the French, Federer will be the undisputed best player in the game and will move closer to the best of all time. And the scary thing is, the gap for the former is widening while the latter is closing quickly.

I have large bosoms and I have a big ass.... I was just in the locker room staring at my body, and I'm like, 'Am I really not fit? Or is it just because I have all these extra assets that I look not fit?' I think if I were not to eat for two years, I still wouldn't be a size two. We're living in a Mary-Kate Olsen world. I'm just not built that way. I'm bootylicious, and that's how it's always going to be."

Venus Williams may not be bootylicious like her sister—she's an exceptional athlete and built like one—but she's just as aloof. Her dedication to the game has been questioned and even her father said she might as well retire given that she had played so poorly entering Wimbledon. Venus came into the hallowed tournament ranked 31st and only received a No. 23 seed because of her past Wimbledon success.

But like her younger sister, Venus entered Wimbledon armed with confidence and proved that sometimes talent and self-belief can overcome all. "No matter where I'm ranked, I think the other players feel at a disadvantage," Venus said. "They feel like they have to play their best, and I have to play not my best."

Venus didn't play her best at Wimbledon,

2007 Grand Slam Champions

Australian Open

Men's Singles

	Winner	Runner-up	Score
Quarterfinals	Roger Federer	Tommy Robredo	6-3, 7-6 (7-2), 7-5
	Andy Roddick	Mardy Fish	6-2, 6-2, 6-2
	Tommy Haas	Nikolay Davydenko	6-3, 2-6, 1-6, 6-1, 7-5
	Fernando Gonzalez	Rafael Nadal	6-2, 6-4, 6-3
Semifinals	Roger Federer	Andy Roddick	6-4, 6-0, 6-2
	Fernando Gonzalez	Tommy Haas	6-1, 6-3, 6-1
Final	Roger Federer	Fernando Gonzalez	7-6 (7-2), 6-4, 6-4

Women's Singles

	Winner	Runner-up	Score
Quarterfinals	Maria Sharapova	Anna Chakvetadze	7-6 (7-5), 7-5
	Kim Clijsters	Martina Hingis	3-6, 6-4, 6-3
	Serena Williams	Shahar Peer	3-6, 6-2, 8-6
	Nicole Vaidisova	Lucie Safarova	6-1, 6-4
Semifinals	Maria Sharapova	Kim Clijsters	6-4, 6-2
	Serena Williams	Nicole Vaidisova	7-6 (7-5), 6-4
Final	Serena Williams	Maria Sharapova	6-1, 6-2

Doubles

	Winner	Runner-up	Score
Men's Final	Bob Bryan/ Mike Bryan	Jonas Bjorkman/ Max Mirnyi	7-5, 7-5
Women's Final	Cara Black/ Liezel Huber	Yung-Jan Chan/ Chia-Jung Chuang	6-4, 6-7 (4-7), 6-1
Mixed Final	Daniel Nestor/ Elena Likhovtseva	Max Mirnyi/ Victoria Azarenka	6-4, 6-4

French Open

Men's Singles

	Winner	Runner-up	Score
Quarterfinals	Roger Federer	Tommy Robredo	7-5, 1-6, 6-1, 6-2
	Nikolay Davydenko	Guillermo Canas	7-5, 6-4, 6-4
	Novak Djokovic	Igor Andreev	6-3, 6-3, 6-3
	Rafael Nadal	Carlos Moya	6-4, 6-3, 6-0
Semifinals	Roger Federer	Nikolay Davydenko	7-5, 7-6 (7-5), 7-6 (9-7)
	Rafael Nadal	Novak Djokovic	7-5, 6-4, 6-2
Final	Rafael Nadal	Roger Federer	6-3, 4-6, 6-3, 6-4

Women's Singles

	Winner	Runner-up	Score
Quarterfinals	Justine Henin	Serena Williams	6-2, 6-4
	Jelena Jankovic	Nicole Vaidisova	6-3, 7-5
	Ana Ivanovic	Svetlana Kuznetsova	6-0, 3-6, 6-1
	Maria Sharapova	Anna Chakvetadze	6-3, 6-4
Semifinals	Justine Henin	Jelena Jankovic	6-2, 6-2
	Ana Ivanovic	Maria Sharapova	6-2, 6-1
Final	Justine Henin	Ana Ivanovic	6-1, 6-2

Doubles

	Winner	Runner-Up	Score
Men's Final	Daniel Nestor/ Mark Knowles	Lukas Dlouhy/ Pavel Vizner	2-6, 6-3, 6-4
Women's Final	Alicia Molik/ Mara Santangelo	Katarina Srebotnik/ Ai Sugiyama	7-6 (7-5), 6-4
Mixed Final	Andy Ram/ Nathalie Dechy	Nenad Zimonjic/ Katarina Srebotnik	7-5, 6-3

Wimbledon

Men's Singles

	Winner	Runner-Up	Score
Quarterfinals	Roger Federer	Juan Carlos Ferrero	7-6 (7-2),3-6,6-1,6-3
	Richard Gasquet	Andy Roddick	4-6, 4-6, 7-6 (7-2), 7-6 (7-3),8-6
	Novak Djokovic	Marcos Baghdatis	7-6 (7-4), 7-6 (11-9),6-7(3-7), 4-6, 7-5
	Rafael Nadal	Tomas Berdych	7-6 (7-1), 6-4, 6-2
Semifinals	Roger Federer	Richard Gasquet	7-5, 6-3, 6-4
	Rafael Nadal	Novak Djokovic	3-6, 6-1, 4-1 ret.
Final	Roger Federer	Rafael Nadal	7-6 (9-7), 4-6, 7-6 (7-3), 2-6, 6-2

Women's Singles

	Winner	Runner-Up	Score
Quarterfinals	Justine Henin	Serena Williams	6-4, 3-6, 6-3
	Marion Bartoli	Michaella Krajicek	3-6, 6-3, 6-2
	Ana Ivanovic	Nicole Vaidisova	4-6, 6-2, 7-5
	Venus Williams	Svetlana Kuznetsova	6-3, 6-4
Semifinals	Marion Bartoli	Justine Henin	1-6, 7-5, 6-1
	Venus William	Ana Ivanovic	6-2, 6-4
Final	Venus Williams	Marion Bartoli	6-4, 6-1

Doubles

	Winner	Runner-Up	Score
Men's Final	Arnaud Clement/ Michael Llodra	Bob Bryan/ Mike Bryan	6-7 (5-7), 6-3, 6-4, 6-4
Women's Final	Cara Black/ Liezel Huber	Katarina Srebotnik/ Ai Sugiyama	3-6, 6-3, 6-2
Mixed Final	Jamie Murray/ Jelena Jankovic	Jonas Bjorkman/ Alicia Molik	6-4, 3-6, 6-1

U.S. Open

Men's Singles

	Winner	Runner-Up	Score
Quarterfinals	Roger Federer	Andy Roddick	7-6 (7-5), 7-6 (7-4), 6-2
	Nikolay Davydenko	Tommy Haas	6-3, 6-3, 6-4
	Novak Djokovic	Carlos Moya	6-4, 7-6 (9-7), 6-1
	David Ferrer	Juan Ignacio Chela	6-2, 6-3, 7-5
Semifinals	Roger Federer	Nikolay Davydenko	7-5, 6-1, 7-5
	Novak Djokovic	David Ferrer	6-4, 6-4, 6-3
Final	Roger Federer	Novak Djokovic	7-6 (7-4), 7-6 (7-2), 6-4

Women's Singles

	Winner	Runner-Up	Score
Quarterfinals	Justine Henin	Serena Williams	7-6 (7-3), 6-1
	Venus Williams	Jelena Jankovic	4-6, 6-1, 7-6 (7-4)
	Svetlana Kuznetsova	Agnes Szavay	6-1, 6-4
	Anna Chakvetadze	Shahar Peer	6-4, 6-1
Semifinals	Justine Henin	Venus Williams	7-6 (7-2), 6-4
	Svetlana Kuznetsova	Anna Chakvetadze	3-6, 6-1, 6-1
Final	Justine Henin	Svetlana Kuznetsova	6-1, 6-3

Doubles

	Winner	Runner-Up	Score
Men's Final	Simon Aspelin/ Julian Knowle	Lukas Dlouhy/ Pavel Vizner	7-5, 6-4
Women's Final	Nathalie Dechy/ Dinara Safina	Yung-Jan Chan/ Chia-Jung Chuang	6-4, 6-2
Mixed Final	Max Mirnyi/ Victoria Azarenka	Leander Paes/ Meghann Shaughnessy	6-4, 7-6 (8-6)

Men's Tour (late 2006 through Sept. 10, 2007)

Date	Tournament	Site	Singles Winner	Surface	Prize Money ($)
Sep 25	Thailand Open	Bangkok, Thailand	James Blake	Indoor Hard	76,500
Oct 2	AIG Open	Tokyo, Japan	Roger Federer	Outdoor Hard	145,000
Oct 9	Kremlin Cup	Moscow, Russia	Nikolay Davydenko	Indoor Carpet	142,000
Oct 16	Madrid Masters	Madrid, Spain	Roger Federer	Outdoor Hard	450,000
Oct 23	Swiss Indoor	Basel, Switzerland	Roger Federer	Indoor Carpet	145,000
Oct 23	Lyon Grand Prix	Lyon, France	Richard Gasquet	Indoor Carpet	115,000
Oct 23	St. Petersburg Open	St. Petersburg, Russia	Mario Ancic	Indoor Carpet	142,000
Oct 30	Paris Masters	Paris, France	Nikolay Davydenko	Indoor Carpet	447,000
Nov 12	China Masters	Shanghai, China	Roger Federer	Indoor Hard	1,400,000
Jan 1	Qatar Open	Doha, Qatar	Ivan Ljubicic	Outdoor Hard	142,000
Jan 16	Australian Open	Melbourne, Australia	Roger Federer	Outdoor Hard	1,281,560
Feb 12	Marseille Open	Marseille, France	Gilles Simon	Indoor Hard	85,300
Feb 19	ABM/Amro	Rotterdam, Netherlands	Mikhail Youzhny	Indoor Hard	174,000
Feb 27	Dubai Open	Dubai, U.A.E.	Roger Federer	Outdoor Hard	300,000
Mar 9	Pacific Life Open	Indian Wells, California	Rafael Nadal	Outdoor Hard	500,000
Mar 21	Sony Ericsson Open	Miami, Fla.	Novak Djokovic	Outdoor Hard	533,350
Apr 16	Monte Carlo Masters	Monte Carlo, Monaco	Rafael Nadal	Outdoor Clay	418,778
Apr 23	Open SEAT Godó	Barcelona, Spain	Rafael Nadal	Outdoor Clay	164,000
Apr 29	Estoril Open	Estoril, Portugal	Novak Djokovic	Outdoor Clay	95,500
Apr 30	BMW Open	Munich, Germany	Philipp Kohlschreiber	Outdoor Clay	56,100
May 14	Hamburg Masters	Hamburg, Germany	Roger Federer	Outdoor Clay	340,000
May 28	French Open	Paris, France	Rafael Nadal	Outdoor Clay	1,180,000
June 11	Gerry Weber Open	Halle, Germany	Tomas Berdych	Outdoor Grass	120,000
June 18	Ordina Open	Hertog'bosch, Netherlands	Ivan Ljubicic	Outdoor Grass	55,820
June 25	Wimbledon	Wimbledon, England	Roger Federer	Outdoor Grass	1,212,244
July 9	Allianz Suisse Open	Gstaad, Switzerland	Paul-Henri Mathieu	Outdoor Clay	74,200
July 16	Dutch Open	Amersfoort, Netherlands	Steve Darcis	Outdoor Clay	56,000
July 16	Mercedes Cup	Stuttgart, Germany	Rafael Nadal	Outdoor Clay	127,000
July 23	RCA Championship	Indianapolis, Indiana	Dmitiry Tursunov	Outdoor Hard	73,000
July 23	Austrian Open	Kitzbuhel, Austria	Juan Monaco	Outdoor Clay	110,000
July 29	Legg Mason Classic	Wash., D.C.	Andy Roddick	Outdoor Hard	74,250
Aug 5	Rogers Cup	Montreal, Canada	Novak Djokovic	Outdoor Hard	400,500
Aug 13	Western & Southern	Cincinnati, Ohio	Roger Federer	Outdoor Hard	400,000
Aug 27	U.S. Open	New York City	Roger Federer	Outdoor Hard	1,200,000
Sept 10	China Open	Beijing, China	Fernando Gonzalez	Outdoor Hard	69,200

Women's Tour (Late 2006 through September 10, 2007)

Date	Tournament	Site	Winner	Runner-Up	Score
Sept 30	Porsche Grand Prix	Stuttgart, Germany	Nadia Petrova	Tatiana Golovin	6–3, 7-6 (7-4)
Oct 7	Ladies Kremlin Cup	Moscow, Russia	Anna Chakvetadze	Nadia Petrova	6–4, 6–4
Oct 7	Bangkok Open	Bangkok, Thailand	Vania King	Tamarine Tanasugarn	7-5, 2-6, 7-5
Oct 14	Zurich Open	Zurich, Switzerland	Maria Sharapova	Daniela Hantuchova	6–1, 4-6, 6-3
Oct 21	Generali Ladies Open	Linz, Austria	Maria Sharapova	Nadia Petrova	7–5, 6–2
Jan 7	Medibank Int'l	Sydney, Australia	Kim Clijsters	Jelena Jankovic	4-6, 7-6 (7-1) 6-4
Jan 15	Australian Open	Melbourne	Serena Williams	Maria Sharapova	6-1, 6-2
Jan 29	Pan Pacific Open	Tokyo, Japan	Martina Hingis	Ana Ivanovic	6-4, 6-2
Feb 26	Qatar Open	Doha, Qatar	Justine Henin	Svetlana Kuznetsova	6-4, 6-2
Mar 5	Pacific Life Open	Indian Wells, California	Daniela Hantuchova	Svetlana Kuznetsova	6-3, 6-4
Mar 19	Sony Ericsson Open	Key Biscayne, Florida	Serena Williams	Justine Henin	0-6, 7-5, 6-3
Apr 2	Bausch & Lomb Championships	Amelia Island, Florida	Tatiana Golovin	Nadia Petrova	6-2, 6-1
Apr 9	Family Circle Cup	Charleston, South Carolina	Jelena Jankovic	Dinara Safina	6-2, 6-2
Apr 30	J&S Cup	Warsaw, Poland	Justine Henin	Alona Bondarenko	6-1, 6-3
May 7	German Open	Berlin	Ana Ivanovic	Sevetlana Kuznetsova	3-6, 6-4, 7-6 (7-4)
May 14	Italia Masters	Rome, Italy	Jelena Jankovic	Sevtlana Kuznetsova	7-5, 6-1
May 21	Int'l de Strasbourg	Strasbourg, France	Anabel Medina Garrigues	Amelie Mauresmo	6-4, 4-6, 6-4
May 28	French Open	Paris France	Justine Henin	Ana Ivanovic	6-1, 6-2
June 18	Hastings Direct Int'l Championships	Eastbourne, England	Justine Henin	Amelie Mauresmo	7-5, 6-7 (7-4), 7-6 (7-2)
Jun 25	Wimbledon	Wimbledon, England	Venus Williams	Marion Bartoli	6-4, 6-1
July 23	Bank of the West	Stanford, Calif.	Anna Chakvetadze	Sania Mirza	6-3, 6-2
July 30	Acura Classic	San Diego, California	Maria Sharpova	Patty Schnyder	6-2, 3-6, 6-0
Aug 6	East West Bank Classic	Los Angeles, California	Ana Ivanovic	Nadia Petrova	7-5, 6-4
Aug 13	Rogers Cup	Toronto, Canada	Justine Henin	Jelena Jankovic	7-6 (7-3), 7-5
Aug 19	Pilot Pen Int'l	New Haven, Connecticut	Svetlana Kuznetsova	Agnes Szavay	4-6, 3-0, ret.
Aug 28	U.S. Open	New York City	Justine Henin	Svetlana Kuznetsova	6-1, 6-3
Sept 10	Wismilak International	Bali, Indonesia	Lindsay Davenport	Daniela Hantuchova	6-4, 3-6, 6-2

2006 Singles Leaders

Men

Rank	Player	Country	Points	Events
1.	Roger Federer	SUI	8370	19
2.	Rafael Nadal	ESP	4470	19
3.	Nikolay Davydenko	RUS	2825	32
4.	James Blake	USA	2530	26
5.	Ivan Ljubicic	CRO	2495	22
6.	Andy Roddick	USA	2415	21
7.	Tommy Robredo	ESP	2375	27
8.	David Nalbandian	ARG	2295	17
9.	Mario Ancic	CRO	2060	24
10.	Fernando Gonzalez	CHI	2015	20

Note: Compiled by the ATP Tour, through the 2006 season.

Women

Rank	Player	Country	Points
1.	Justine Henin-Hardenne	BEL	3998
2.	Maria Sharapova	RUS	3532
3.	Amelie Mauresmo	FRA	3391
4.	Svetlana Kuznetsova	RUS	2523
5.	Kim Clijsters	BEL	2215
6.	Nadia Petrova	RUS	2189
7.	Martina Hingis	SUI	2018
8.	Elena Dementieva	RUS	1875
9.	Patty Schnyder	SUI	1578
10.	Nicole Vaidisova	CZE	1391

Note: Compiled by the WTA, through the 2006 season.

National Team Competition

2006 Davis Cup World Group Final
Russia def. Argentina 3–2, Dec 1-3, 2006, in Moscow, Russia
Nikolay Davydenko (RUS) def. Juan Ignacio Chela (ARG), 6-1, 6-2, 5-7, 6-4
David Nalbandian (ARG) def. Marat Safin (RUS), 6-4, 6-4, 6-4
Marat Safin/Dmitry Tursunov (RUS) def. Augustin Calleri/David Nalbandian (ARG), 6-2, 6-3, 6-4
David Nalbandian (ARG) def. Nikolay Davydenko (RUS), 6-2, 6-2, 4-6, 6-4
Marat Safin (CRO) def. Jose Acasuso (ARG), 6-3, 3-6, 6-3, 7-6 (7-5)

2007 Davis Cup World Group Tournament

FIRST ROUND
Russia def. Chile 3-2
France def. Romania 4-1
Germany def. Croatia 3-2
Belgium def. Australia 3-2
USA def. Czech Republic 4-1
Spain def. Switzerland 3-2
Sweden def. Belarus 3-2
Argentina def. Austria 4-1

QUARTERFINAL ROUND
Russia def. France 3-2
Germany def. Belgium 3-2
USA def. Spain 4-1
Sweden def. Argentina 4-1

SEMIFINALS

Russia def. Germany 3-2
Igor Andreev (RUS) def. Tommy Haas (Ger) 6-2, 6-2, 6-2
Philipp Kohlschreiber (GER) def. Nikolay Davydenko (RUS) 6-7 (5-7), 6-2, 6-2, 4-6, 7-5
P. Petzschner/A. Waske (GER) def. D. Tursunov/M. Youzhny (RUS) 6-3, 3-6, 7-6 (7-4), 7-6 (7-5)
Mikhail Youzhny (RUS) def. Philipp Petzschner (GER) 6-4, 6-4, 3-6, 6-3
Igor Andreev (RUS) def. Philipp Kohlschreiber (GER) 6-3, 3-6, 6-0, 6-3

USA def. Sweden 4-1
Andy Roddick (USA) def. Joachim Johansson (SWE) 7-6 (7-4), 7-6 (7-3), 6-3
Thomas Johansson (SWE) def. James Blake (USA) 6-4 6-2, 3-6, 6-3
B. Bryan/M. Bryan (USA) def. S. Aspelin/J.Bjorkman (SWE) 7-6 (13-11), 6-2, 6-3
Andy Roddick (USA) def. Jonas Bjorkman (SWE) 6-2, 7-6 (7-3), 6-4
James Blake (USA) def. Simon Aspelin (SWE) 6-1, 6-3

FINAL: Russia versus USA to be held Nov. 30-Dec. 2, 2007.

2007 Fed Cup World Group Tournament

QUARTERFINALS
USA def. Belgium 5-0
Russia def. Spain 5-0
France def. Japan 5-0
Italy def. China, P.R. 2-0

SEMIFINALS
Russia def. USA 3-2
Italy def. France 3-2

FINALS
Russia def. Italy 4-0

Note: Finals were held Sept. 15-16, 2007, in Moscow, Russia.

Grand Slam Tournaments

MEN

Australian Championships

Year	Winner	Finalist	Score
1905	Rodney Heath	A. H. Curtis	4–6, 6–3, 6–4, 6–4
1906	Tony Wilding	H. A. Parker	6–0, 6–4, 6–4
1907	Horace M. Rice	H. A. Parker	6–3, 6–4, 6–4
1908	Fred Alexander	A. W. Dunlop	3–6, 3–6, 6–0, 6–2, 6–3
1909	Tony Wilding	E. F. Parker	6–1, 7–5, 6–2
1910	Rodney Heath	Horace M. Rice	6–4, 6–3, 6–2
1911	Norman Brookes	Horace M. Rice	6–1, 6–2, 6–3
1912	J. Cecil Parke	A. E. Beamish	3–6, 6–3, 1–6, 6–1, 7–5
1913	E. F. Parker	H. A. Parker	2–6, 6–1, 6–2, 6–3
1914	Pat O'Hara Wood	G. L. Patterson	6–4, 6–3, 5–7, 6–1
1915	Francis G. Lowe	Horace M. Rice	4–6, 6–1, 6–1, 6–4
1916–18	No tournament		
1919	A. R. F. Kingscote	E. O. Pockley	6–4, 6–0, 6–3
1920	Pat O'Hara Wood	Ron Thomas	6–3, 4–6, 6–8, 6–1, 6–3
1921	Rhys H. Gemmell	A. Hedeman	7–5, 6–1, 6–4
1922	Pat O'Hara Wood	Gerald Patterson	6–0, 3–6, 3–6, 6–3, 6–2
1923	Pat O'Hara Wood	C. B. St John	6–1, 6–1, 6–3
1924	James Anderson	R. E. Schlesinger	6–3, 6–4, 3–6, 5–7, 6–3
1925	James Anderson	Gerald Patterson	11–9, 2–6, 6–2, 6–3
1926	John Hawkes	J. Willard	6–1, 6–3, 6–1
1927	Gerald Patterson	John Hawkes	3–6, 6–4, 3–6, 18–16, 6–3
1928	Jean Borotra	R. O. Cummings	6–4, 6–1, 4–6, 5–7, 6–3
1929	John C. Gregory	R. E. Schlesinger	6–2, 6–2, 5–7, 7–5
1930	Gar Moon	Harry C. Hopman	6–3, 6–1, 6–3
1931	Jack Crawford	Harry C. Hopman	6–4, 6–2, 2–6, 6–1
1932	Jack Crawford	Harry C. Hopman	4–6, 6–3, 3–6, 6–3, 6–1
1933	Jack Crawford	Keith Gledhill	2–6, 7–5, 6–3, 6–2
1934	Fred Perry	Jack Crawford	6–3, 7–5, 6–1
1935	Jack Crawford	Fred Perry	2–6, 6–4, 6–4, 6–4
1936	Adrian Quist	Jack Crawford	6–2, 6–3, 4–6, 3–6, 9–7
1937	Vivian B. McGrath	John Bromwich	6–3, 1–6, 6–0, 2–6, 6–1
1938	Don Budge	John Bromwich	6–4, 6–2, 6–1
1939	John Bromwich	Adrian Quist	6–4, 6–1, 6–3
1940	Adrian Quist	Jack Crawford	6–3, 6–1, 6–2
1941–45	No tournament		
1946	John Bromwich	Dinny Pails	5–7, 6–3, 7–5, 3–6, 6–2
1947	Dinny Pails	John Bromwich	4–6, 6–4, 3–6, 7–5, 8–6
1948	Adrian Quist	John Bromwich	6–4, 3–6, 6–3, 2–6, 6–3
1949	Frank Sedgman	Ken McGregor	6–3, 6–3, 6–2
1950	Frank Sedgman	Ken McGregor	6–3, 6–4, 4–6, 6–1
1951	Richard Savitt	Ken McGregor	6–3, 2–6, 6–3, 6–1
1952	Ken McGregor	Frank Sedgman	7–5, 12–10, 2–6, 6–2
1953	Ken Rosewall	Mervyn Rose	6–0, 6–3, 6–4
1954	Mervyn Rose	Rex Hartwig	6–2, 0–6, 6–4, 6–2
1955	Ken Rosewall	Lew Hoad	9–7, 6–4, 6–4
1956	Lew Hoad	Ken Rosewall	6–4, 3–6, 6–4, 7–5
1957	Ashley Cooper	Neale Fraser	6–3, 9–11, 6–4, 6–2
1958	Ashley Cooper	Mal Anderson	7–5, 6–3, 6–4
1959	Alex Olmedo	Neale Fraser	6–1, 6–2, 3–6, 6–3
1960	Rod Laver	Neale Fraser	5–7, 3–6, 6–3, 8–6, 8–6
1961	Roy Emerson	Rod Laver	1–6, 6–3, 7–5, 6–4
1962	Rod Laver	Roy Emerson	8–6, 0–6, 6–4, 6–4
1963	Roy Emerson	Ken Fletcher	6–3, 6–3, 6–1
1964	Roy Emerson	Fred Stolle	6–3, 6–4, 6–2
1965	Roy Emerson	Fred Stolle	7–9, 2–6, 6–4, 7–5, 6–1
1966	Roy Emerson	Arthur Ashe	6–4, 6–8, 6–2, 6–3
1967	Roy Emerson	Arthur Ashe	6–4, 6–1, 6–1
1968	Bill Bowrey	Juan Gisbert	7–5, 2–6, 9–7, 6–4
1969*	Rod Laver	Andres Gimeno	6–3, 6–4, 7–5

*Became Open (amateur and professional) in 1969.

MEN *(Cont.)*

Australian Championships *(Cont.)*

Year	Winner	Finalist	Score
1970	Arthur Ashe	Dick Crealy	6–4, 9–7, 6–2
1971	Ken Rosewall	Arthur Ashe	6–1, 7–5, 6–3
1972	Ken Rosewall	Mal Anderson	7–6, 6–3, 7–5
1973	John Newcombe	Onny Parun	6–3, 6–7, 7–5, 6–1
1974	Jimmy Connors	Phil Dent	7–6, 6–4, 4–6, 6–3
1975	John Newcombe	Jimmy Connors	7–5, 3–6, 6–4, 7–5
1976	Mark Edmondson	John Newcombe	6–7, 6–3, 7–6, 6–1
1977 (Jan)	Roscoe Tanner	Guillermo Vilas	6–3, 6–3, 6–3
1977 (Dec)	Vitas Gerulaitis	John Lloyd	6–3, 7–6, 5–7, 3–6, 6–2
1978	Guillermo Vilas	John Marks	6–4, 6–4, 3–6, 6–3
1979	Guillermo Vilas	John Sadri	7–6, 6–3, 6–2
1980	Brian Teacher	Kim Warwick	7–5, 7–6, 6–3
1981	Johan Kriek	Steve Denton	6–2, 7–6, 6–7, 6–4
1982	Johan Kriek	Steve Denton	6–3, 6–3, 6–2
1983	Mats Wilander	Ivan Lendl	6–1, 6–4, 6–4
1984	Mats Wilander	Kevin Curren	6–7, 6–4, 7–6, 6–2
1985 (Dec)	Stefan Edberg	Mats Wilander	6–4, 6–3, 6–3
1987 (Jan)	Stefan Edberg	Pat Cash	6–3, 6–4, 3–6, 5–7, 6–3
1988	Mats Wilander	Pat Cash	6–3, 6–7, 3–6, 6–1, 8–6
1989	Ivan Lendl	Miloslav Mecir	6–2, 6–2, 6–2
1990	Ivan Lendl	Stefan Edberg	4–6, 7–6, 5–2, ret.
1991	Boris Becker	Ivan Lendl	1–6, 6–4, 6–4, 6–4
1992	Jim Courier	Stefan Edberg	6–3, 3–6, 6–4, 6–2
1993	Jim Courier	Stefan Edberg	6–2, 6–1, 2–6, 7–5
1994	Pete Sampras	Todd Martin	7–6, 6–4, 6–4
1995	Andre Agassi	Pete Sampras	4–6, 6–1, 7–6, 6–4
1996	Boris Becker	Michael Chang	6–2, 6–4, 2–6, 6–2
1997	Pete Sampras	Carlos Moya	6–2, 6–3, 6–3
1998	Petr Korda	Marcelo Rios	6–2, 6–2, 6–2
1999	Yevgeny Kafelnikov	Thomas Enqvist	4–6, 6–0, 6–3, 7–6
2000	Andre Agassi	Yevgeny Kafelnikov	3–6, 6–3, 6–2, 6–4
2001	Andre Agassi	Arnaud Clement	6–4, 6–2, 6–2
2002	Thomas Johansson	Marat Safin	3–6, 6–4, 6–4, 7–6 (7-4)
2003	Andre Agassi	Rainer Schuettler	6–2, 6–2, 6–1
2004	Roger Federer	Marat Safin	7–6 (7–3), 6–4, 6–2
2005	Marat Safin	Lleyton Hewitt	1–6, 6–3, 6–4, 6–4
2006	Roger Federer	Marcos Baghdatis	5–7, 7–5, 6–0, 6–2
2007	Roger Federer	Fernando Gonzalez	7–6 (7–2), 6–4, 6–4

French Championships

Year	Winner	Finalist	Score
1925†	Rene Lacoste	Jean Borotra	7–5, 6–1, 6–4
1926	Henri Cochet	Rene Lacoste	6–2, 6–4, 6–3
1927	Rene Lacoste	Bill Tilden	6–4, 4–6, 5–7, 6–3, 11–9
1928	Henri Cochet	Rene Lacoste	5–7, 6–3, 6–1, 6–3
1929	Rene Lacoste	Jean Borotra	6–3, 2–6, 6–0, 2–6, 8–6
1930	Henri Cochet	Bill Tilden	3–6, 8–6, 6–3, 6–1
1931	Jean Borotra	Claude Boussus	2–6, 6–4, 7–5, 6–4
1932	Henri Cochet	Giorgio de Stefani	6–0, 6–4, 4–6, 6–3
1933	Jack Crawford	Henri Cochet	8–6, 6–1, 6–3
1934	Gottfried von Cramm	Jack Crawford	6–4, 7–9, 3–6, 7–5, 6–3
1935	Fred Perry	Gottfried von Cramm	6–3, 3–6, 6–1, 6–3
1936	Gottfried von Cramm	Fred Perry	6–0, 2–6, 6–2, 2–6, 6–0
1937	Henner Henkel	Henry Austin	6–1, 6–4, 6–3
1938	Don Budge	Roderick Menzel	6–3, 6–2, 6–4
1939	Don McNeill	Bobby Riggs	7–5, 6–0, 6–3
1940	No tournament		
1941‡	Bernard Destremau	n/a	n/a
1942‡	Bernard Destremau	n/a	n/a
1943‡	Yvon Petra	n/a	n/a
1944‡	Yvon Petra	n/a	n/a
1945‡	Yvon Petra	Bernard Destremau	7–5, 6–4, 6–2

†1925 was the first year that entries were accepted from all countries.
‡From 1941 to 1945 the event was called Tournoi de France and was closed to all foreigners.

MEN *(Cont.)*

French Championships *(Cont.)*

Year	Winner	Finalist	Score
1946	Marcel Bernard	Jaroslav Drobny	3–6, 2–6, 6–1, 6–4, 6–3
1947	Joseph Asboth	Eric Sturgess	8–6, 7–5, 6–4
1948	Frank Parker	Jaroslav Drobny	6–4, 7–5, 5–7, 8–6
1949	Frank Parker	Budge Patty	6–3, 1–6, 6–1, 6–4
1950	Budge Patty	Jaroslav Drobny	6–1, 6–2, 3–6, 5–7, 7–5
1951	Jaroslav Drobny	Eric Sturgess	6–3, 6–3, 6–3
1952	Jaroslav Drobny	Frank Sedgman	6–2, 6–0, 3–6, 6–4
1953	Ken Rosewall	Vic Seixas	6–3, 6–4, 1–6, 6–2
1954	Tony Trabert	Arthur Larsen	6–4, 7–5, 6–1
1955	Tony Trabert	Sven Davidson	2–6, 6–1, 6–4, 6–2
1956	Lew Hoad	Sven Davidson	6–4, 8–6, 6–3
1957	Sven Davidson	Herbie Flam	6–3, 6–4, 6–4
1958	Mervyn Rose	Luis Ayala	6–3, 6–4, 6–4
1959	Nicola Pietrangeli	Ian Vermaak	3–6, 6–3, 6–4, 6–1
1960	Nicola Pietrangeli	Luis Ayala	3–6, 6–3, 6–4, 4–6, 6–3
1961	Manuel Santana	Nicola Pietrangeli	4–6, 6–1, 3–6, 6–0, 6–2
1962	Rod Laver	Roy Emerson	3–6, 2–6, 6–3, 9–7, 6–2
1963	Roy Emerson	Pierre Darmon	3–6, 6–1, 6–4, 6–4
1964	Manuel Santana	Nicola Pietrangeli	6–3, 6–1, 4–6, 7–5
1965	Fred Stolle	Tony Roche	3–6, 6–0, 6–2, 6–3
1966	Tony Roche	Istvan Gulyas	6–1, 6–4, 7–5
1967	Roy Emerson	Tony Roche	6–1, 6–4, 2–6, 6–2
1968*	Ken Rosewall	Rod Laver	6–3, 6–1, 2–6, 6–2
1969	Rod Laver	Ken Rosewall	6–4, 6–3, 6–4
1970	Jan Kodes	Zeljko Franulovic	6–2, 6–4, 6–0
1971	Jan Kodes	Ilie Nastase	8–6, 6–2, 2–6, 7–5
1972	Andres Gimeno	Patrick Proisy	4–6, 6–3, 6–1, 6–1
1973	Ilie Nastase	Nikki Pilic	6–3, 6–3, 6–0
1974	Bjorn Borg	Manuel Orantes	6–7, 6–0, 6–1, 6–1
1975	Bjorn Borg	Guillermo Vilas	6–2, 6–3, 6–4
1976	Adriano Panatta	Harold Solomon	6–1, 6–4, 4–6, 7–6
1977	Guillermo Vilas	Brian Gottfried	6–0, 6–3, 6–0
1978	Bjorn Borg	Guillermo Vilas	6–1, 6–1, 6–3
1979	Bjorn Borg	Victor Pecci	6–3, 6–1, 6–7, 6–4
1980	Bjorn Borg	Vitas Gerulaitis	6–4, 6–1, 6–2
1981	Bjorn Borg	Ivan Lendl	6–1, 4–6, 6–2, 3–6, 6–1
1982	Mats Wilander	Guillermo Vilas	1–6, 7–6, 6–0, 6–4
1983	Yannick Noah	Mats Wilander	6–2, 7–5, 7–6
1984	Ivan Lendl	John McEnroe	3–6, 2–6, 6–4, 7–5, 7–5
1985	Mats Wilander	Ivan Lendl	3–6, 6–4, 6–2, 6–2
1986	Ivan Lendl	Mikael Pernfors	6–3, 6–2, 6–4
1987	Ivan Lendl	Mats Wilander	7–5, 6–2, 3–6, 7–6
1988	Mats Wilander	Henri Leconte	7–5, 6–2, 6–1
1989	Michael Chang	Stefan Edberg	6–1, 3–6, 4–6, 6–4, 6–2
1990	Andres Gomez	Andre Agassi	6–3, 2–6, 6–4, 6–4
1991	Jim Courier	Andre Agassi	3–6, 6–4, 2–6, 6–1, 6–4
1992	Jim Courier	Petr Korda	7–5, 6–2, 6–1
1993	Sergi Bruguera	Jim Courier	6–4, 2–6, 6–2, 3–6, 6–3
1994	Sergi Bruguera	Alberto Berasategui	6–3, 7–5, 2–6, 6–1
1995	Thomas Muster	Michael Chang	7–5, 6–2, 6–4
1996	Yevgeny Kafelnikov	Michael Stich	7–6, 7–5, 7–6
1997	Gustavo Kuerten	Sergi Bruguera	6–3, 6–4, 6–2
1998	Carlos Moya	Alex Corretja	6–3, 7–5, 6–3
1999	Andre Agassi	Andrei Medvedev	1–6, 2–6, 6–4, 6–3, 6–4
2000	Gustavo Kuerten	Magnus Norman	6–2, 6–3, 2–6, 7–6
2001	Gustavo Kuerten	Alex Corretja	6–7, 7–5, 6–2, 6–0
2002	Albert Costa	Juan Carlos Ferrero	6–1, 6–0, 4–6, 6–3
2003	Juan Carlos Ferrero	Martin Verkerk	6–1, 6–3, 6–2
2004	Gaston Gaudio	Guillermo Coria	0–6, 3–6, 6–4, 6–1, 8–6
2005	Rafael Nadal	Mariano Puerta	6–7, 6–3, 6–1, 7–5
2006	Rafael Nadal	Roger Federer	1–6, 6–1, 6–4, 7–6
2007	Rafael Nadal	Roger Federer	6–3, 4–6, 6–3, 6–4

*Became Open (amateur and professional) in 1968, but restricted to only contract professionals in 1972.

MEN *(Cont.)*

Wimbledon Championships

Year	Winner	Finalist	Score
1877	Spencer W. Gore	William C. Marshall	6–1, 6–2, 6–4
1878	P. Frank Hadow	Spencer W. Gore	7–5, 6–1, 9–7
1879	John T. Hartley	V. St Leger Gould	6–2, 6–4, 6–2
1880	John T. Hartley	Herbert F. Lawford	6–0, 6–2, 2–6, 6–3
1881	William Renshaw	John T. Hartley	6–0, 6–2, 6–1
1882	William Renshaw	Ernest Renshaw	6–1, 2–6, 4–6, 6–2, 6–2
1883	William Renshaw	Ernest Renshaw	2–6, 6–3, 6–3, 4–6, 6–3
1884	William Renshaw	Herbert F. Lawford	6–0, 6–4, 9–7
1885	William Renshaw	Herbert F. Lawford	7–5, 6–2, 4–6, 7–5
1886	William Renshaw	Herbert F. Lawford	6–0, 5–7, 6–3, 6–4
1887	Herbert F. Lawford	Ernest Renshaw	1–6, 6–3, 3–6, 6–4, 6–4
1888	Ernest Renshaw	Herbert F. Lawford	6–3, 7–5, 6–0
1889	William Renshaw	Ernest Renshaw	6–4, 6–1, 3–6, 6–0
1890	William J. Hamilton	William Renshaw	6–8, 6–2, 3–6, 6–1, 6–1
1891	Wilfred Baddeley	Joshua Pim	6–4, 1–6, 7–5, 6–0
1892	Wilfred Baddeley	Joshua Pim	4–6, 6–3, 6–3, 6–2
1893	Joshua Pim	Wilfred Baddeley	3–6, 6–1, 6–3, 6–2
1894	Joshua Pim	Wilfred Baddeley	10–8, 6–2, 8–6
1895	Wilfred Baddeley	Wilberforce V. Eaves	4–6, 2–6, 8–6, 6–2, 6–3
1896	Harold S. Mahoney	Wilfred Baddeley	6–2, 6–8, 5–7, 8–6, 6–3
1897	Reggie F. Doherty	Harold S. Mahoney	6–4, 6–4, 6–3
1898	Reggie F. Doherty	H. Laurie Doherty	6–3, 6–3, 2–6, 5–7, 6–1
1899	Reggie F. Doherty	Arthur W. Gore	1–6, 4–6, 6–2, 6–3, 6–3
1900	Reggie F. Doherty	Sidney H. Smith	6–8, 6–3, 6–1, 6–2
1901	Arthur W. Gore	Reggie F. Doherty	4–6, 7–5, 6–4, 6–4
1902	H. Laurie Doherty	Arthur W. Gore	6–4, 6–3, 3–6, 6–0
1903	H. Laurie Doherty	Frank L. Riseley	7–5, 6–3, 6–0
1904	H. Laurie Doherty	Frank L. Riseley	6–1, 7–5, 8–6
1905	H. Laurie Doherty	Norman E. Brookes	8–6, 6–2, 6–4
1906	H. Laurie Doherty	Frank L. Riseley	6–4, 4–6, 6–2, 6–3
1907	Norman E. Brookes	Arthur W. Gore	6–4, 6–2, 6–2
1908	Arthur W. Gore	H. Roper Barrett	6–3, 6–2, 4–6, 3–6, 6–4
1909	Arthur W. Gore	M. J. G. Ritchie	6–8, 1–6, 6–2, 6–2, 6–2
1910	Anthony F. Wilding	Arthur W. Gore	6–4, 7–5, 4–6, 6–2
1911	Anthony F. Wilding	H. Roper Barrett	6–4, 4–6, 2–6, 6–2, ret.
1912	Anthony F. Wilding	Arthur W. Gore	6–4, 6–4, 4–6, 6–4
1913	Anthony F. Wilding	Maurice E. McLoughlin	8–6, 6–3, 10–8
1914	Norman E. Brookes	Anthony F. Wilding	6–4, 6–4, 7–5
1915–18	No tournament		
1919	Gerald L. Patterson	Norman E. Brookes	6–3, 7–5, 6–2
1920	Bill Tilden	Gerald L. Patterson	2–6, 6–3, 6–2, 6–4
1921	Bill Tilden	Brian I. C. Norton	4–6, 2–6, 6–1, 6–0, 7–5
1922	Gerald L. Patterson	Randolph Lycett	6–3, 6–4, 6–2
1923	Bill Johnston	Francis T. Hunter	6–0, 6–3, 6–1
1924	Jean Borotra	Rene Lacoste	6–1, 3–6, 6–1, 3–6, 6–4
1925	Rene Lacoste	Jean Borotra	6–3, 6–3, 4–6, 8–6
1926	Jean Borotra	Howard Kinsey	8–6, 6–1, 6–3
1927	Henri Cochet	Jean Borotra	4–6, 4–6, 6–3, 6–4, 7–5
1928	Rene Lacoste	Henri Cochet	6–1, 4–6, 6–4, 6–2
1929	Henri Cochet	Jean Borotra	6–4, 6–3, 6–4
1930	Bill Tilden	Wilmer Allison	6–3, 9–7, 6–4
1931	Sidney B. Wood Jr	Francis X. Shields	walkover
1932	Ellsworth Vines	Henry Austin	6–4, 6–2, 6–0
1933	Jack Crawford	Ellsworth Vines	4–6, 11–9, 6–2, 2–6, 6–4
1934	Fred Perry	Jack Crawford	6–3, 6–0, 7–5
1935	Fred Perry	Gottfried von Cramm	6–2, 6–4, 6–4
1936	Fred Perry	Gottfried von Cramm	6–1, 6–1, 6–0
1937	Don Budge	Gottfried von Cramm	6–3, 6–4, 6–2
1938	Don Budge	Henry Austin	6–1, 6–0, 6–3
1939	Bobby Riggs	Elwood Cooke	2–6, 8–6, 3–6, 6–3, 6–2
1940–45	No tournament		
1946	Yvon Petra	Geoff E. Brown	6–2, 6–4, 6–7 (7–9), 5–7, 6–4
1947	Jack Kramer	Tom P. Brown	6–1, 6–3, 6–2
1948	Bob Falkenburg	John Bromwich	7–5, 0–6, 6–2, 3–6, 7–5
1949	Ted Schroeder	Jaroslav Drobny	3–6, 6–0, 6–3, 4–6, 6–4

Note: Prior to 1922 the tournament was run on a challenge-round system. The previous year's winner "stood out" of an All Comers event, which produced a challenger to play him for the title.

MEN *(Cont.)*

Wimbledon Championships *(Cont.)*

Year	Winner	Finalist	Score
1950	Budge Patty	Frank Sedgman	6–1, 6–7 (8–10), 6–2, 6–3
1951	Dick Savitt	Ken McGregor	6–4, 6–4, 6–4
1952	Frank Sedgman	Jaroslav Drobny	4–6, 6–3, 6–2, 6–3
1953	Vic Seixas	Kurt Nielsen	9–7, 6–3, 6–4
1954	Jaroslav Drobny	Ken Rosewall	13–11, 4–6, 6–2, 9–7
1955	Tony Trabert	Kurt Nielsen	6–3, 7–5, 6–1
1956	Lew Hoad	Ken Rosewall	6–2, 4–6, 7–5, 6–4
1957	Lew Hoad	Ashley Cooper	6–2, 6–1, 6–2
1958	Ashley Cooper	Neale Fraser	3–6, 6–3, 6–4, 13–11
1959	Alex Olmedo	Rod Laver	6–4, 6–3, 6–4
1960	Neale Fraser	Rod Laver	6–4, 3–6, 9–7, 7–5
1961	Rod Laver	Chuck McKinley	6–3, 6–1, 6–4
1962	Rod Laver	Martin Mulligan	6–2, 6–2, 6–1
1963	Chuck McKinley	Fred Stolle	9–7, 6–1, 6–4
1964	Roy Emerson	Fred Stolle	6–4, 12–10, 4–6, 6–3
1965	Roy Emerson	Fred Stolle	6–2, 6–4, 6–4
1966	Manuel Santana	Dennis Ralston	6–4, 11–9, 6–4
1967	John Newcombe	Wilhelm Bungert	6–3, 6–1, 6–1
1968*	Rod Laver	Tony Roche	6–3, 6–4, 6–2
1969	Rod Laver	John Newcombe	6–4, 5–7, 6–4, 6–4
1970	John Newcombe	Ken Rosewall	5–7, 6–3, 6–2, 3–6, 6–1
1971	John Newcombe	Stan Smith	6–3, 5–7, 2–6, 6–4, 6–4
1972	Stan Smith	Ilie Nastase	4–6, 6–3, 6–3, 4–6, 7–5
1973	Jan Kodes	Alex Metreveli	6–1, 9–8, 6–3
1974	Jimmy Connors	Ken Rosewall	6–1, 6–1, 6–4
1975	Arthur Ashe	Jimmy Connors	6–1, 6–1, 5–7, 6–4
1976	Bjorn Borg	Ilie Nastase	6–4, 6–2, 9–7
1977	Bjorn Borg	Jimmy Connors	3–6, 6–2, 6–1, 5–7, 6–4
1978	Bjorn Borg	Jimmy Connors	6–2, 6–2, 6–3
1979	Bjorn Borg	Roscoe Tanner	6–7, 6–1, 3–6, 6–3, 6–4
1980	Bjorn Borg	John McEnroe	1–6, 7–5, 6–3, 6–7, 8–6
1981	John McEnroe	Bjorn Borg	4–6, 7–6, 7–6, 6–4
1982	Jimmy Connors	John McEnroe	3–6, 6–3, 6–7, 7–6, 6–4
1983	John McEnroe	Chris Lewis	6–2, 6–2, 6–2
1984	John McEnroe	Jimmy Connors	6–1, 6–1, 6–2
1985	Boris Becker	Kevin Curren	6–3, 6–7, 7–6, 6–4
1986	Boris Becker	Ivan Lendl	6–4, 6–3, 7–5
1987	Pat Cash	Ivan Lendl	7–6, 6–2, 7–5
1988	Stefan Edberg	Boris Becker	4–6, 7–6, 6–4, 6–2
1989	Boris Becker	Stefan Edberg	6–0, 7–6, 6–4
1990	Stefan Edberg	Boris Becker	6–2, 6–2, 3–6, 3–6, 6–4
1991	Michael Stich	Boris Becker	6–4, 7–6, 6–4
1992	Andre Agassi	Goran Ivanisevic	6–7, 6–4, 6–4, 1–6, 6–4
1993	Pete Sampras	Jim Courier	7–6, 7–6, 3–6, 6–3
1994	Pete Sampras	Goran Ivanisevic	7–6, 7–6, 6–0
1995	Pete Sampras	Boris Becker	6–7, 6–2, 6–4, 6–2
1996	Richard Krajicek	MaliVai Washington	6–3, 6–4, 6–3
1997	Pete Sampras	Cedric Pioline	6–4, 6–2, 6–4
1998	Pete Sampras	Goran Ivanisevic	6–7, 7–6, 6–4, 3–6, 6–2
1999	Pete Sampras	Andre Agassi	6–3, 6–4, 7–5
2000	Pete Sampras	Patrick Rafter	6–7, 7–6, 6–4, 6–2
2001	Goran Ivanisevic	Patrick Rafter	6–3, 3–6, 6–3, 2–6, 9–7
2002	Lleyton Hewitt	David Nalbandian	6–1, 6–3, 6–2
2003	Roger Federer	Mark Philippoussis	7–6 (7–5), 6–2, 7–6 (7–3)
2004	Roger Federer	Andy Roddick	4–6, 7–5, 7–6 (7–3), 6–4
2005	Roger Federer	Andy Roddick	6–2, 7–6 (7–2), 6–4
2006	Roger Federer	Rafael Nadal	6–0, 7–6, (7–5), 6–7 (2–7), 6–3
2007	Roger Federer	Rafael Nadal	7–6 (9–7), 4–6, 7–6 (7–3), 2–6, 6–2

*Became Open (amateur and professional) in 1968, but restricted to only contract professionals in 1972.

MEN *(Cont.)*
United States Championships

Year	Winner	Finalist	Score
1881	Richard D. Sears	W.E. Glyn	6–0, 6–3, 6–2
1882	Richard D. Sears	C.M. Clark	6–1, 6–4, 6–0
1883	Richard D. Sears	James Dwight	6–2, 6–0, 9–7
1884	Richard D. Sears	H.A. Taylor	6–0, 1–6, 6–0, 6–2
1885	Richard D. Sears	G.M. Brinley	6–3, 4–6, 6–0, 6–3
1886	Richard D. Sears	R.L. Beeckman	4–6, 6–1, 6–3, 6–4
1887	Richard D. Sears	H.W. Slocum Jr	6–1, 6–3, 6–2
1888†	H. W. Slocum Jr	H.A. Taylor	6–4, 6–1, 6–0
1889	H. W. Slocum Jr	Q.A. Shaw	6–3, 6–1, 4–6, 6–2
1890	Oliver S. Campbell	H.W. Slocum Jr	6–2, 4–6, 6–3, 6–1
1891	Oliver S. Campbell	Clarence Hobart	2–6, 7–5, 7–9, 6–1, 6–2
1892	Oliver S. Campbell	Frederick H. Hovey	7–5, 3–6, 6–3, 7–5
1893†	Robert D. Wrenn	Frederick H. Hovey	6–4, 3–6, 6–4, 6–4
1894	Robert D. Wrenn	M.F. Goodbody	6–8, 6–1, 6–4, 6–4
1895	Frederick H. Hovey	Robert D. Wrenn	6–3, 6–2, 6–4
1896	Robert D. Wrenn	Frederick H. Hovey	7–5, 3–6, 6–0, 1–6, 6–1
1897	Robert D. Wrenn	Wilberforce V. Eaves	4–6, 8–6, 6–3, 2–6, 6–2
1898†	Malcolm D. Whitman	Dwight F. Davis	3–6, 6–2, 6–2, 6–1
1899	Malcolm D. Whitman	J. Parmly Paret	6–1, 6–2, 3–6, 7–5
1900	Malcolm D. Whitman	William A. Larned	6–4, 1–6, 6–2, 6–2
1901†	William A. Larned	Beals C. Wright	6–2, 6–8, 6–4, 6–4
1902	William A. Larned	Reggie F. Doherty	4–6, 6–2, 6–4, 8–6
1903	H. Laurie Doherty	William A. Larned	6–0, 6–3, 10–8
1904†	Holcombe Ward	William J. Clothier	10–8, 6–4, 9–7
1905	Beals C. Wright	Holcombe Ward	6–2, 6–1, 11–9
1906	William J. Clothier	Beals C. Wright	6–3, 6–0, 6–4
1907†	William A. Larned	Robert LeRoy	6–2, 6–2, 6–4
1908	William A. Larned	Beals C. Wright	6–1, 6–2, 8–6
1909	William A. Larned	William J. Clothier	6–1, 6–2, 5–7, 1–6, 6–1
1910	William A. Larned	Thomas C. Bundy	6–1, 5–7, 6–0, 6–8, 6–1
1911	William A. Larned	Maurice E. McLoughlin	6–4, 6–4, 6–2
1912‡	Maurice E. McLoughlin	Bill Johnson	3–6, 2–6, 6–2, 6–4, 6–2
1913	Maurice E. McLoughlin	Richard N. Williams	6–4, 5–7, 6–3, 6–1
1914	Richard N. Williams	Maurice E. McLoughlin	6–3, 8–6, 10–8
1915	Bill Johnston	Maurice E. McLoughlin	1–6, 6–0, 7–5, 10–8
1916	Richard N. Williams	Bill Johnston	4–6, 6–4, 0–6, 6–2, 6–4
1917#	R.L. Murray	N. W. Niles	5–7, 8–6, 6–3, 6–3
1918	R.L. Murray	Bill Tilden	6–3, 6–1, 7–5
1919	Bill Johnston	Bill Tilden	6–4, 6–4, 6–3
1920	Bill Tilden	Bill Johnston	6–1, 1–6, 7–5, 5–7, 6–3
1921	Bill Tilden	Wallace F. Johnson	6–1, 6–3, 6–1
1922	Bill Tilden	Bill Johnston	4–6, 3–6, 6–2, 6–3, 6–4
1923	Bill Tilden	Bill Johnston	6–4, 6–1, 6–4
1924	Bill Tilden	Bill Johnston	6–1, 9–7, 6–2
1925	Bill Tilden	Bill Johnston	4–6, 11–9, 6–3, 4–6, 6–3
1926	Rene Lacoste	Jean Borotra	6–4, 6–0, 6–4
1927	Rene Lacoste	Bill Tilden	11–9, 6–3, 11–9
1928	Henri Cochet	Francis T. Hunter	4–6, 6–4, 3–6, 7–5, 6–3
1929	Bill Tilden	Francis T. Hunter	3–6, 6–3, 4–6, 6–2, 6–4
1930	John H. Doeg	Francis X. Shields	10–8, 1–6, 6–4, 16–14
1931	Ellsworth Vines	George M. Lott Jr	7–9, 6–3, 9–7, 7–5
1932	Ellsworth Vines	Henri Cochet	6–4, 6–4, 6–4
1933	Fred Perry	Jack Crawford	6–3, 11–13, 4–6, 6–0, 6–1
1934	Fred Perry	Wilmer L. Allison	6–4, 6–3, 1–6, 8–6
1935	Wilmer L. Allison	Sidney B. Wood Jr	6–2, 6–2, 6–3
1936	Fred Perry	Don Budge	2–6, 6–2, 8–6, 1–6, 10–8
1937	Don Budge	Gottfried von Cramm	6–1, 7–9, 6–1, 3–6, 6–1
1938	Don Budge	Gene Mako	6–3, 6–8, 6–2, 6–1
1939	Bobby Riggs	Welby Van Horn	6–4, 6–2, 6–4
1940	Don McNeill	Bobby Riggs	4–6, 6–8, 6–3, 6–3, 7–5
1941	Bobby Riggs	Francis Kovacs II	5–7, 6–1, 6–3, 6–3
1942	Ted Schroeder	Frank Parker	8–6, 7–5, 3–6, 4–6, 6–2
1943	Joseph R. Hunt	Jack Kramer	6–3, 6–8, 10–8, 6–0
1944	Frank Parker	William F. Talbert	6–4, 3–6, 6–3, 6–3

†No challenge round played. ‡Challenge round abolished. #National Patriotic Tournament.

MEN *(Cont.)*
United States Championships *(Cont.)*

Year	Winner	Finalist	Score
1945	Frank Parker	William F. Talbert	14–12, 6–1, 6–2
1946	Jack Kramer	Tom P. Brown	9–7, 6–3, 6–0
1947	Jack Kramer	Frank Parker	4–6, 2–6, 6–1, 6–0, 6–3
1948	Pancho Gonzales	Eric W. Sturgess	6–2, 6–3, 14–12
1949	Pancho Gonzales	Ted Schroeder	16–18, 2–6, 6–1, 6–2, 6–4
1950	Arthur Larsen	Herbie Flam	6–3, 4–6, 5–7, 6–4, 6–3
1951	Frank Sedgman	Vic Seixas	6–4, 6–1, 6–1
1952	Frank Sedgman	Gardnar Mulloy	6–1, 6–2, 6–3
1953	Tony Trabert	Vic Seixas	6–3, 6–2, 6–3
1954	Vic Seixas	Rex Hartwig	3–6, 6–2, 6–4, 6–4
1955	Tony Trabert	Ken Rosewall	9–7, 6–3, 6–3
1956	Ken Rosewall	Lew Hoad	4–6, 6–2, 6–3, 6–3
1957	Mal Anderson	Ashley J. Cooper	10–8, 7–5, 6–4
1958	Ashley J. Cooper	Mal Anderson	6–2, 3–6, 4–6, 10–8, 8–6
1959	Neale Fraser	Alex Olmedo	6–3, 5–7, 6–2, 6–4
1960	Neale Fraser	Rod Laver	6–4, 6–4, 9–7
1961	Roy Emerson	Rod Laver	7–5, 6–3, 6–2
1962	Rod Laver	Roy Emerson	6–2, 6–4, 5–7, 6–4
1963	Rafael Osuna	Frank Froehling III	7–5, 6–4, 6–2
1964	Roy Emerson	Fred Stolle	6–4, 6–2, 6–4
1965	Manuel Santana	Cliff Drysdale	6–2, 7–9, 7–5, 6–1
1966	Fred Stolle	John Newcombe	4–6, 12–10, 6–3, 6–4
1967	John Newcombe	Clark Graebner	6–4, 6–4, 8–6
1968*	Arthur Ashe	Tom Okker	14–12, 5–7, 6–3, 3–6, 6–3
1968**	Arthur Ashe	Bob Lutz	4–6, 6–3, 8–10, 6–0, 6–4
1969	Rod Laver	Tony Roche	7–9, 6–1, 6–3, 6–2
1969**	Stan Smith	Bob Lutz	9–7, 6–3, 6–1
1970	Ken Rosewall	Tony Roche	2–6, 6–4, 7–6, 6–3
1971	Stan Smith	Jan Kodes	3–6, 6–3, 6–2, 7–6
1972	Ilie Nastase	Arthur Ashe	3–6, 6–3, 6–7, 6–4, 6–3
1973	John Newcombe	Jan Kodes	6–4, 1–6, 4–6, 6–2, 6–3
1974	Jimmy Connors	Ken Rosewall	6–1, 6–0, 6–1
1975	Manuel Orantes	Jimmy Connors	6–4, 6–3, 6–3
1976	Jimmy Connors	Bjorn Borg	6–4, 3–6, 7–6, 6–4
1977	Guillermo Vilas	Jimmy Connors	2–6, 6–3, 7–6, 6–0
1978	Jimmy Connors	Bjorn Borg	6–4, 6–2, 6–2
1979	John McEnroe	Vitas Gerulaitis	7–5, 6–3, 6–3
1980	John McEnroe	Bjorn Borg	7–6, 6–1, 6–7, 5–7, 6–4
1981	John McEnroe	Bjorn Borg	4–6, 6–2, 6–4, 6–3
1982	Jimmy Connors	Ivan Lendl	6–3, 6–2, 4–6, 6–4
1983	Jimmy Connors	Ivan Lendl	6–3, 6–7, 7–5, 6–0
1984	John McEnroe	Ivan Lendl	6–3, 6–4, 6–1
1985	Ivan Lendl	John McEnroe	7–6, 6–3, 6–4
1986	Ivan Lendl	Miloslav Mecir	6–4, 6–2, 6–0
1987	Ivan Lendl	Mats Wilander	6–7, 6–0, 7–6, 6–4
1988	Mats Wilander	Ivan Lendl	6–4, 4–6, 6–3, 5–7, 6–4
1989	Boris Becker	Ivan Lendl	7–6, 1–6, 6–3, 7–6
1990	Pete Sampras	Andre Agassi	6–4, 6–3, 6–2
1991	Stefan Edberg	Jim Courier	6–2, 6–4, 6–0
1992	Stefan Edberg	Pete Sampras	3–6, 6–4, 7–6, 6–2
1993	Pete Sampras	Cedric Pioline	6–4, 6–4, 6–3
1994	Andre Agassi	Michael Stich	6–1, 7–6, 7–5
1995	Pete Sampras	Andre Agassi	6–4, 6–3, 4–6, 7–5
1996	Pete Sampras	Michael Chang	6–1, 6–4, 7–6
1997	Patrick Rafter	Greg Rusedski	6–3, 6–2, 4–6, 7–5
1998	Patrick Rafter	Mark Philippoussis	6–3, 3–6, 6–2, 6–0
1999	Andre Agassi	Todd Martin	6–4, 6–7, 6–7, 6–3, 6–2
2000	Marat Safin	Pete Sampras	6–4, 6–3, 6–3
2001	Lleyton Hewitt	Pete Sampras	7–6, 6–1, 6–1
2002	Pete Sampras	Andre Agassi	6–3, 6–4, 5–7, 6–4
2003	Andy Roddick	Juan Carlos Ferrero	6–3, 7–6 (7–2), 6–3
2004	Roger Federer	Lleyton Hewitt	6–0, 7–6 (7–3), 6–0
2005	Roger Federer	Andre Agassi	6–3, 2–6, 7–6 (7–1), 6–1
2006	Roger Federer	Andy Roddick	6–2, 4–6, 7–5, 6–1
2007	Roger Federer	Novak Djokovic	7–6 (7–4), 7–6 (7–2), 6–4

*Became Open (amateur and professional) in 1968. **Amateur event held.

WOMEN
Australian Championships

Year	Winner	Finalist	Score
1922	Margaret Molesworth	Esna Boyd	6–3, 10–8
1923	Margaret Molesworth	Esna Boyd	6–1, 7–5
1924	Sylvia Lance	Esna Boyd	6–3, 3–6, 6–4
1925	Daphne Akhurst	Esna Boyd	1–6, 8–6, 6–4
1926	Daphne Akhurst	Esna Boyd	6–1, 6–3
1927	Esna Boyd	Sylvia Harper	5–7, 6–1, 6–2
1928	Daphne Akhurst	Esna Boyd	7–5, 6–2
1929	Daphne Akhurst	Louise Bickerton	6–1, 5–7, 6–2
1930	Daphne Akhurst	Sylvia Harper	10–8, 2–6, 7–5
1931	Coral Buttsworth	Margorie Crawford	1–6, 6–3, 6–4
1932	Coral Buttsworth	Kathrine Le Messurier	9–7, 6–4
1933	Joan Hartigan	Coral Buttsworth	6–4, 6–3
1934	Joan Hartigan	Margaret Molesworth	6–1, 6–4
1935	Dorothy Round	Nancye Wynne Bolton	1–6, 6–1, 6–3
1936	Joan Hartigan	Nancye Wynne Bolton	6–4, 6–4
1937	Nancye Wynne Bolton	Emily Westacott	6–3, 5–7, 6–4
1938	Dorothy Bundy	D. Stevenson	6–3, 6–2
1939	Emily Westacott	Nell Hopman	6–1, 6–2
1940	Nancye Wynne Bolton	Thelma Coyne	5–7, 6–4, 6–0
1941–45	No tournament		
1946	Nancye Wynne Bolton	Joyce Fitch	6–4, 6–4
1947	Nancye Wynne Bolton	Nell Hopman	6–3, 6–2
1948	Nancye Wynne Bolton	Marie Toomey	6–3, 6–1
1949	Doris Hart	Nancye Wynne Bolton	6–3, 6–4
1950	Louise Brough	Doris Hart	6–4, 3–6, 6–4
1951	Nancye Wynne Bolton	Thelma Long	6–1, 7–5
1952	Thelma Long	H. Angwin	6–2, 6–3
1953	Maureen Connolly	Julia Sampson	6–3, 6–2
1954	Thelma Long	J. Staley	6–3, 6–4
1955	Beryl Penrose	Thelma Long	6–4, 6–3
1956	Mary Carter	Thelma Long	3–6, 6–2, 9–7
1957	Shirley Fry	Althea Gibson	6–3, 6–4
1958	Angela Mortimer	Lorraine Coghlan	6–3, 6–4
1959	Mary Carter-Reitano	Renee Schuurman	6–2, 6–3
1960	Margaret Smith	Jan Lehane	7–5, 6–2
1961	Margaret Smith	Jan Lehane	6–1, 6–4
1962	Margaret Smith	Jan Lehane	6–0, 6–2
1963	Margaret Smith	Jan Lehane	6–2, 6–2
1964	Margaret Smith	Lesley Turner	6–3, 6–2
1965	Margaret Smith	Maria Bueno	5–7, 6–4, 5–2, ret.
1966	Margaret Smith	Nancy Richey	Default
1967	Nancy Richey	Lesley Turner	6–1, 6–4
1968	Billie Jean King	Margaret Smith	6–1, 6–2
1969*	Margaret Smith Court	Billie Jean King	6–4, 6–1
1970	Margaret Smith Court	Kerry Melville Reid	6–3, 6–1
1971	Margaret Smith Court	Evonne Goolagong	2–6, 7–6, 7–5
1972	Virginia Wade	Evonne Goolagong	6–4, 6–4
1973	Margaret Smith Court	Evonne Goolagong	6–4, 7–5
1974	Evonne Goolagong	Chris Evert	7–6, 4–6, 6–0
1975	Evonne Goolagong	Martina Navratilova	6–3, 6–2
1976	Evonne Goolagong Cawley	Renata Tomanova	6–2, 6–2
1977 (Jan)	Kerry Melville Reid	Dianne Balestrat	7–5, 6–2
1977 (Dec)	Evonne Goolagong Cawley	Helen Gourlay	6–3, 6–0
1978	Chris O'Neil	Betsy Nagelsen	6–3, 7–6
1979	Barbara Jordan	Sharon Walsh	6–3, 6–3
1980	Hana Mandlikova	Wendy Turnbull	6–0, 7–5
1981	Martina Navratilova	Chris Evert Lloyd	6–7, 6–4, 7–5
1982	Chris Evert Lloyd	Martina Navratilova	6–3, 2–6, 6–3
1983	Martina Navratilova	Kathy Jordan	6–2, 7–6
1984	Chris Evert Lloyd	Helena Sukova	6–7, 6–1, 6–3
1985 (Dec)	Martina Navratilova	Chris Evert Lloyd	6–2, 4–6, 6–2
1987 (Jan)	Hana Mandlikova	Martina Navratilova	7–5, 7–6
1988	Steffi Graf	Chris Evert	6–1, 7–6
1989	Steffi Graf	Helena Sukova	6–4, 6–4
1990	Steffi Graf	Mary Joe Fernandez	6–3, 6–4
1991	Monica Seles	Jana Novotna	5–7, 6–3, 6–1

*Became Open (amateur and professional) in 1969.

WOMEN *(Cont.)*

Australian Championships *(Cont.)*

Year	Winner	Finalist	Score
1992	Monica Seles	Mary Joe Fernandez	6–2, 6–3
1993	Monica Seles	Steffi Graf	4–6, 6–3, 6–2
1994	Steffi Graf	Arantxa Sánchez Vicario	6–0, 6–2
1995	Mary Pierce	Arantxa Sánchez Vicario	6–3, 6–2
1996	Monica Seles	Anke Huber	6–4, 6–1
1997	Martina Hingis	Mary Pierce	6–2, 6–2
1998	Martina Hingis	Conchita Martinez	6–3, 6–3
1999	Martina Hingis	Amelie Mauresmo	6–2, 6–3
2000	Lindsay Davenport	Martina Hingis	6–1, 7–5
2001	Jennifer Capriati	Martina Hingis	6–4, 6–3
2002	Jennifer Capriati	Martina Hingis	4–6, 7–6 (9–7), 6–2
2003	Serena Williams	Venus Williams	7–6 (7-4), 3–6, 6–4
2004	Justine Henin-Hardenne	Kim Clijsters	6–3, 4–6, 6–3
2005	Serena Williams	Lindsay Davenport	2–6, 6–3, 6–0
2006	Amelie Mauresmo	Justine Henin-Hardenne	6–1, 2–0, ret.
2007	Serena Williams	Maria Sharapova	6–1, 6–2

French Championships

Year	Winner	Finalist	Score
1925†	Suzanne Lenglen	Kathleen McKane	6–1, 6–2
1926	Suzanne Lenglen	Mary K. Browne	6–1, 6–0
1927	Kea Bouman	Irene Peacock	6–2, 6–4
1928	Helen Wills	Eileen Bennett	6–1, 6–2
1929	Helen Wills	Simone Mathieu	6–3, 6–4
1930	Helen Wills Moody	Helen Jacobs	6–2, 6–1
1931	Cilly Aussem	Betty Nuthall	8–6, 6–1
1932	Helen Wills Moody	Simone Mathieu	7–5, 6–1
1933	Margaret Scriven	Simone Mathieu	6–2, 4–6, 6–4
1934	Margaret Scriven	Helen Jacobs	7–5, 4–6, 6–1
1935	Hilde Sperling	Simone Mathieu	6–2, 6–1
1936	Hilde Sperling	Simone Mathieu	6–3, 6–4
1937	Hilde Sperling	Simone Mathieu	6–2, 6–4
1938	Simone Mathieu	Nelly Landry	6–0, 6–3
1939	Simone Mathieu	Jadwiga Jedrzejowska	6–3, 8–6
1940–45	No tournament		
1946	Margaret Osborne	Pauline Betz	1–6, 8–6, 7–5
1947	Patricia Todd	Doris Hart	6–3, 3–6, 6–4
1948	Nelly Landry	Shirley Fry	6–2, 0–6, 6–0
1949	Margaret Osborne duPont	Nelly Adamson	7–5, 6–2
1950	Doris Hart	Patricia Todd	6–4, 4–6, 6–2
1951	Shirley Fry	Doris Hart	6–3, 3–6, 6–3
1952	Doris Hart	Shirley Fry	6–4, 6–4
1953	Maureen Connolly	Doris Hart	6–2, 6–4
1954	Maureen Connolly	Ginette Bucaille	6–4, 6–1
1955	Angela Mortimer	Dorothy Knode	2–6, 7–5, 10–8
1956	Althea Gibson	Angela Mortimer	6–0, 12–10
1957	Shirley Bloomer	Dorothy Knode	6–1, 6–3
1958	Zsuzsi Kormoczi	Shirley Bloomer	6–4, 1–6, 6–2
1959	Christine Truman	Zsuzsi Kormoczi	6–4, 7–5
1960	Darlene Hard	Yola Ramirez	6–3, 6–4
1961	Ann Haydon	Yola Ramirez	6–2, 6–1
1962	Margaret Smith	Lesley Turner	6–3, 3–6, 7–5
1963	Lesley Turner	Ann Haydon Jones	2–6, 6–3, 7–5
1964	Margaret Smith	Maria Bueno	5–7, 6–1, 6–2
1965	Lesley Turner	Margaret Smith	6–3, 6–4
1966	Ann Jones	Nancy Richey	6–3, 6–1
1967	Francoise Durr	Lesley Turner	4–6, 6–3, 6–4
1968*	Nancy Richey	Ann Jones	5–7, 6–4, 6–1
1969	Margaret Smith Court	Ann Jones	6–1, 4–6, 6–3
1970	Margaret Smith Court	Helga Niessen	6–2, 6–4

†1925 was the first year that entries were accepted from all countries. *Became Open (amateur and professional) in 1968, but restricted to only contract professionals in 1972.

WOMEN *(Cont.)*

French Championships *(Cont.)*

Year.	Winner	Finalist	Score
1971	Evonne Goolagong	Helen Gourlay	6–3, 7–5
1972	Billie Jean King	Evonne Goolagong	6–3, 6–3
1973	Margaret Smith Court	Chris Evert	6–7, 7–6, 6–4
1974	Chris Evert	Olga Morozova	6–1, 6–2
1975	Chris Evert	Martina Navratilova	2–6, 6–2, 6–1
1976	Sue Barker	Renata Tomanova	6–2, 0–6, 6–2
1977	Mima Jausovec	Florenza Mihai	6–2, 6–7, 6–1
1978	Virginia Ruzici	Mima Jausovec	6–2, 6–2
1979	Chris Evert Lloyd	Wendy Turnbull	6–2, 6–0
1980	Chris Evert Lloyd	Virginia Ruzici	6–0, 6–3
1981	Hana Mandlikova	Sylvia Hanika	6–2, 6–4
1982	Martina Navratilova	Andrea Jaeger	7–6, 6–1
1983	Chris Evert Lloyd	Mima Jausovec	6–1, 6–2
1984	Martina Navratilova	Chris Evert Lloyd	6–3, 6–1
1985	Chris Evert Lloyd	Martina Navratilova	6–3, 6–7, 7–5
1986	Chris Evert Lloyd	Martina Navratilova	2–6, 6–3, 6–3
1987	Steffi Graf	Martina Navratilova	6–4, 4–6, 8–6
1988	Steffi Graf	Natalia Zvereva	6–0, 6–0
1989	Arantxa Sánchez Vicario	Steffi Graf	7–6, 3–6, 7–5
1990	Monica Seles	Steffi Graf	7–6, 6–4
1991	Monica Seles	Arantxa Sánchez Vicario	6–3, 6–4
1992	Monica Seles	Steffi Graf	6–2, 3–6, 10–8
1993	Steffi Graf	Mary Joe Fernandez	4–6, 6–2, 6–4
1994	Arantxa Sánchez Vicario	Mary Pierce	6–4, 6–4
1995	Steffi Graf	Arantxa Sánchez Vicario	7–5, 4–6, 6–0
1996	Steffi Graf	Arantxa Sánchez Vicario	6–3, 6–7 (4–7), 10–8
1997	Iva Majoli	Martina Hingis	6–4, 6–2
1998	Arantxa Sánchez Vicario	Monica Seles	7–6 (7–5), 0–6, 6–2
1999	Steffi Graf	Martina Hingis	4–6, 7–5, 6–2
2000	Mary Pierce	Conchita Martinez	6–2, 7–5
2001	Jennifer Capriati	Kim Clijsters	1–6, 6–4, 12–10
2002	Serena Williams	Venus Williams	7–5, 6–3
2003	Justine Henin-Hardenne	Kim Clijsters	6–0, 6–4
2004	Anastasia Myskina	Elena Dementieva	6–1, 6–2
2005	Justine Henin-Hardenne	Mary Pierce	6–1, 6–1
2006	Justine Henin-Hardenne	Svetlana Kuznetsova	6–4, 6–4
2007	Justine Henin	Ana Ivanovic	6–1, 6–2

Wimbledon Championships

Year	Winner	Finalist	Score
1884	Maud Watson	Lilian Watson	6–8, 6–3, 6–3
1885	Maud Watson	Blanche Bingley	6–1, 7–5
1886	Blanche Bingley	Maud Watson	6–3, 6–3
1887	Charlotte Dod	Blanche Bingley	6–2, 6–0
1888	Charlotte Dod	Blanche Bingley Hillyard	6–3, 6–3
1889	Blanche Bingley Hillyard	n/a	n/a
1890	Lena Rice	n/a	n/a
1891	Charlotte Dod	n/a	n/a
1892	Charlotte Dod	Blanche Bingley Hillyard	6–1, 6–1
1893	Charlotte Dod	Blanche Bingley Hillyard	6–8, 6–1, 6–4
1894	Blanche Bingley Hillyard	n/a	n/a
1895	Charlotte Cooper	n/a	
1896	Charlotte Cooper	Mrs. W. H. Pickering	6–2, 6–3
1897	Blanche Bingley Hillyard	Charlotte Cooper	5–7, 7–5, 6–2
1898	Charlotte Cooper	n/a	n/a
1899	Blanche Bingley Hillyard	Charlotte Cooper	6–2, 6–3
1900	Blanche Bingley Hillyard	Charlotte Cooper	4–6, 6–4, 6–4
1901	Charlotte Cooper Sterry	Blanche Bingley Hillyard	6–2, 6–2
1902	Muriel Robb	Charlotte Cooper Sterry	7–5, 6–1
1903	Dorothea Douglass	n/a	n/a
1904	Dorothea Douglass	Charlotte Cooper Sterry	6–0, 6–3
1905	May Sutton	Dorothea Douglass	6–3, 6–4
1906	Dorothea Douglass	May Sutton	6–3, 9–7

WOMEN *(Cont.)*
Wimbledon Championships *(Cont.)*

Year	Winner	Finalist	Score
1907	May Sutton	Dorothea Douglass Lambert Chambers	6–1, 6–4
1908	Charlotte Cooper Sterry	n/a	n/a
1909	Dora Boothby	n/a	n/a
1910	Dorothea Douglass Lambert Chambers	Dora Boothby	6–2, 6–2
1911	Dorothea Douglass Lambert Chambers	Dora Boothby	6–0, 6–0
1912	Ethel Larcombe	n/a	n/a
1913	Dorothea Douglass Lambert Chambers		
1914	Dorothea Douglass Lambert Chambers	Ethel Larcombe	7–5, 6–4
1915–18	No tournament		
1919	Suzanne Lenglen	Dorothea Douglass Lambert Chambers	10–8, 4–6, 9–7
1920	Suzanne Lenglen	Dorothea Douglass Lambert Chambers	6–3, 6–0
1921	Suzanne Lenglen	Elizabeth Ryan	6–2, 6–0
1922	Suzanne Lenglen	Molla Mallory	6–2, 6–0
1923	Suzanne Lenglen	Kathleen McKane	6–2, 6–2
1924	Kathleen McKane	Helen Wills	4–6, 6–4, 6–2
1925	Suzanne Lenglen	Joan Fry	6–2, 6–0
1926	Kathleen McKane Godfree	Lili de Alvarez	6–2, 4–6, 6–3
1927	Helen Wills	Lili de Alvarez	6–2, 6–4
1928	Helen Wills	Lili de Alvarez	6–2, 6–3
1929	Helen Wills	Helen Jacobs	6–1, 6–2
1930	Helen Wills Moody	Elizabeth Ryan	6–2, 6–2
1931	Cilly Aussem	Hilde Kranwinkel	7–5, 7–5
1932	Helen Wills Moody	Helen Jacobs	6–3, 6–1
1933	Helen Wills Moody	Dorothy Round	6–4, 6–8, 6–3
1934	Dorothy Round	Helen Jacobs	6–2, 5–7, 6–3
1935	Helen Wills Moody	Helen Jacobs	6–3, 3–6, 7–5
1936	Helen Jacobs	Hilde Kranwinkel Sperling	6–2, 4–6, 7–5
1937	Dorothy Round	Jadwiga Jedrzejowska	6–2, 2–6, 7–5
1938	Helen Wills Moody	Helen Jacobs	6–4, 6–0
1939	Alice Marble	Kay Stammers	6–2, 6–0
1940–45	No tournament		
1946	Pauline Betz	Louise Brough	6–2, 6–4
1947	Margaret Osborne	Doris Hart	6–2, 6–4
1948	Louise Brough	Doris Hart	6–3, 8–6
1949	Louise Brough	Margaret Osborne duPont	10–8, 1–6, 10–8
1950	Louise Brough	Margaret Osborne duPont	6–1, 3–6, 6–1
1951	Doris Hart	Shirley Fry	6–1, 6–0
1952	Maureen Connolly	Louise Brough	6–4, 6–3
1953	Maureen Connolly	Doris Hart	8–6, 7–5
1954	Maureen Connolly	Louise Brough	6–2, 7–5
1955	Louise Brough	Beverly Fleitz	7–5, 8–6
1956	Shirley Fry	Angela Buxton	6–3, 6–1
1957	Althea Gibson	Darlene Hard	6–3, 6–2
1958	Althea Gibson	Angela Mortimer	8–6, 6–2
1959	Maria Bueno	Darlene Hard	6–4, 6–3
1960	Maria Bueno	Sandra Reynolds	8–6, 6–0
1961	Angela Mortimer	Christine Truman	4–6, 6–4, 7–5
1962	Karen Hantze Susman	Vera Sukova	6–4, 6–4
1963	Margaret Smith	Billie Jean Moffitt	6–3, 6–4
1964	Maria Bueno	Margaret Smith	6–4, 7–9, 6–3
1965	Margaret Smith	Maria Bueno	6–4, 7–5
1966	Billie Jean King	Maria Bueno	6–3, 3–6, 6–1
1967	Billie Jean King	Ann Haydon Jones	6–3, 6–4
1968*	Billie Jean King	Judy Tegart	9–7, 7–5
1969	Ann Haydon Jones	Billie Jean King	3–6, 6–3, 6–2

Note: Prior to 1922 the tournament was run on a challenge-round system. The previous year's winner "stood out" of an All-Comers event, which produced a challenger to play her for the title.

*Became Open (amateur and professional) in 1968, but restricted to only contract professionals in 1972.

WOMEN *(Cont.)*
Wimbledon Championships *(Cont.)*

Year	Winner	Finalist	Score
1970	Margaret Smith Court	Billie Jean King	14–12, 11–9
1971	Evonne Goolagong	Margaret Smith Court	6–4, 6–1
1972	Billie Jean King	Evonne Goolagong	6–3, 6–3
1973	Billie Jean King	Chris Evert	6–0, 7–5
1974	Chris Evert	Olga Morozova	6–0, 6–4
1975	Billie Jean King	Evonne Goolagong Cawley	6–0, 6–1
1976	Chris Evert	Evonne Goolagong Cawley	6–3, 4–6, 8–6
1977	Virginia Wade	Betty Stove	4–6, 6–3, 6–1
1978	Martina Navratilova	Chris Evert	2–6, 6–4, 7–5
1979	Martina Navratilova	Chris Evert Lloyd	6–4, 6–4
1980	Evonne Goolagong Cawley	Chris Evert Lloyd	6–1, 7–6
1981	Chris Evert Lloyd	Hana Mandlikova	6–2, 6–2
1982	Martina Navratilova	Chris Evert Lloyd	6–1, 3–6, 6–2
1983	Martina Navratilova	Andrea Jaeger	6–0, 6–3
1984	Martina Navratilova	Chris Evert Lloyd	7–6, 6–2
1985	Martina Navratilova	Chris Evert Lloyd	4–6, 6–3, 6–2
1986	Martina Navratilova	Hana Mandlikova	7–6, 6–3
1987	Martina Navratilova	Steffi Graf	7–5, 6–3
1988	Steffi Graf	Martina Navratilova	5–7, 6–2, 6–1
1989	Steffi Graf	Martina Navratilova	6–2, 6–7, 6–1
1990	Martina Navratilova	Zina Garrison	6–4, 6–1
1991	Steffi Graf	Gabriela Sabatini	6–4, 3–6, 8–6
1992	Steffi Graf	Monica Seles	6–2, 6–1
1993	Steffi Graf	Jana Novotna	7–6, 1–6, 6–4
1994	Conchita Martinez	Martina Navratilova	6–4, 3–6, 6–3
1995	Steffi Graf	Arantxa Sánchez Vicario	4–6, 6–1, 7–5
1996	Steffi Graf	Arantxa Sánchez Vicario	6–3, 7–5
1997	Martina Hingis	Jana Novotna	2–6, 6–3, 6–3
1998	Jana Novotna	Nathalie Tauziat	6–4, 7–6
1999	Lindsay Davenport	Steffi Graf	6–4, 7–5
2000	Venus Williams	Lindsay Davenport	6–3, 7–6
2001	Venus Williams	Justine Henin	6–1, 3–6, 6–0
2002	Serena Williams	Venus Williams	7–6 (7–4), 6–3
2003	Serena Williams	Venus Williams	4–6, 6–4, 6–2
2004	Maria Sharapova	Serena Williams	6–1, 6–4
2005	Venus Williams	Lindsay Davenport	4–6, 7–6 (7–4), 7–6 (9–7)
2006	Amelie Mauresmo	Justine Henin-Hardenne	2–6, 6–3, 6–4
2007	Venus Williams	Marion Bartoli	6–4, 6–1

United States Championships

Year	Winner	Finalist	Score
1887	Ellen Hansell	Laura Knight	6–1, 6–0
1888	Bertha L. Townsend	Ellen Hansell	6–3, 6–5
1889	Bertha L. Townsend	Louise Voorhes	7–5, 6–2
1890	Ellen C. Roosevelt	Bertha L. Townsend	6–2, 6–2
1891	Mabel Cahill	Ellen C. Roosevelt	6–4, 6–1, 4–6, 6–3
1892	Mabel Cahill	Elisabeth Moore	5–7, 6–3, 6–4, 4–6, 6–2
1893	Aline Terry	Alice Schultze	6–1, 6–3
1894	Helen Hellwig	Aline Terry	7–5, 3–6, 6–0, 3–6, 6–3
1895	Juliette Atkinson	Helen Hellwig	6–4, 6–2, 6–1
1896	Elisabeth Moore	Juliette Atkinson	6–4, 4–6, 6–2, 6–2
1897	Juliette Atkinson	Elisabeth Moore	6–3, 6–3, 4–6, 3–6, 6–3
1898	Juliette Atkinson	Marion Jones	6–3, 5–7, 6–4, 2–6, 7–5
1899	Marion Jones	Maud Banks	6–1, 6–1, 7–5
1900	Myrtle McAteer	Edith Parker	6–2, 6–2, 6–0
1901	Elisabeth Moore	Myrtle McAteer	6–4, 3–6, 7–5, 2–6, 6–2
1902*	Marion Jones	Elisabeth Moore	6–1, 1–0, ret.
1903	Elisabeth Moore	Marion Jones	7–5, 8–6
1904	May Sutton	Elisabeth Moore	6–1, 6–2
1905	Elisabeth Moore	Helen Homans	6–4, 5–7, 6–1
1906	Helen Homans	Maud Barger-Wallach	6–4, 6–3
1907	Evelyn Sears	Carrie Neely	6–3, 6–2
1908	Maud Barger–Wallach	Evelyn Sears	6–3, 1–6, 6–3
1909	Hazel Hotchkiss	Maud Barger–Wallach	6–0, 6–1

*Five-set final abolished;

WOMEN *(Cont.)*

United States Championships *(Cont.)*

Year	Winner	Finalist	Score
1910	Hazel Hotchkiss	Louise Hammond	6–4, 6–2
1911	Hazel Hotchkiss	Florence Sutton	8–10, 6–1, 9–7
1912†	Mary K. Browne	Eleanora Sears	6–4, 6–2
1913	Mary K. Browne	Dorothy Green	6–2, 7–5
1914	Mary K. Browne	Marie Wagner	6–2, 1–6, 6–1
1915	Molla Bjurstedt	Hazel Hotchkiss Wightman	4–6, 6–2, 6–0
1916	Molla Bjurstedt	Louise Hammond Raymond	6–0, 6–1
1917‡	Molla Bjurstedt	Marion Vanderhoef	4–6, 6–0, 6–2
1918	Molla Bjurstedt	Eleanor Goss	6–4, 6–3
1919	Hazel Hotchkiss Wightman	Marion Zinderstein	6–1, 6–2
1920	Molla Bjurstedt Mallory	Marion Zinderstein	6–3, 6–1
1921	Molla Bjurstedt Mallory	Mary K. Browne	4–6, 6–4, 6–2
1922	Molla Bjurstedt Mallory	Helen Wills	6–3, 6–1
1923	Helen Wills	Molla Bjurstedt Mallory	6–2, 6–1
1924	Helen Wills	Molla Bjurstedt Mallory	6–1, 6–3
1925	Helen Wills	Kathleen McKane	3–6, 6–0, 6–2
1926	Molla Bjurstedt Mallory	Elizabeth Ryan	4–6, 6–4, 9–7
1927	Helen Wills	Betty Nuthall	6–1, 6–4
1928	Helen Wills	Helen Jacobs	6–2, 6–1
1929	Helen Wills	Phoebe Holcroft Watson	6–4, 6–2
1930	Betty Nuthall	Anna McCune Harper	6–1, 6–4
1931	Helen Wills Moody	Eileen Whitingstall	6–4, 6–1
1932	Helen Jacobs	Carolin Babcock	6–2, 6–2
1933	Helen Jacobs	Helen Wills Moody	8–6, 3–6, 3–0, ret.
1934	Helen Jacobs	Sarah Palfrey	6–1, 6–4
1935	Helen Jacobs	Sarah Palfrey Fabyan	6–2, 6–4
1936	Alice Marble	Helen Jacobs	4–6, 6–3, 6–2
1937	Anita Lizane	Jadwiga Jedrzèjowska	6–4, 6–2
1938	Alice Marble	Nancye Wynne	6–0, 6–3
1939	Alice Marble	Helen Jacobs	6–0, 8–10, 6–4
1940	Alice Marble	Helen Jacobs	6–2, 6–3
1941	Sarah Palfrey Cooke	Pauline Betz	7–5, 6–2
1942	Pauline Betz	Louise Brough	4–6, 6–1, 6–4
1943	Pauline Betz	Louise Brough	6–3, 5–7, 6–3
1944	Pauline Betz	Margaret Osborne	6–3, 8–6
1945	Sarah Palfrey Cooke	Pauline Betz	3–6, 8–6, 6–4
1946	Pauline Betz	Patricia Canning	11–9, 6–3
1947	Louise Brough	Margaret Osborne	8–6, 4–6, 6–1
1948	Margaret Osborne duPont	Louise Brough	4–6, 6–4, 15–13
1949	Margaret Osborne duPont	Doris Hart	6–4, 6–1
1950	Margaret Osborne duPont	Doris Hart	6–4, 6–3
1951	Maureen Connolly	Shirley Fry	6–3, 1–6, 6–4
1952	Maureen Connolly	Doris Hart	6–3, 7–5
1953	Maureen Connolly	Doris Hart	6–2, 6–4
1954	Doris Hart	Louise Brough	6–8, 6–1, 8–6
1955	Doris Hart	Patricia Ward	6–4, 6–2
1956	Shirley Fry	Althea Gibson	6–3, 6–4
1957	Althea Gibson	Louise Brough	6–3, 6–2
1958	Althea Gibson	Darlene Hard	3–6, 6–1, 6–2
1959	Maria Bueno	Christine Truman	6–1, 6–4
1960	Darlene Hard	Maria Bueno	6–4, 10–12, 6–4
1961	Darlene Hard	Ann Haydon	6–3, 6–4
1962	Margaret Smith	Darlene Hard	9–7, 6–4
1963	Maria Bueno	Margaret Smith	7–5, 6–4
1964	Maria Bueno	Carole Graebner	6–1, 6–0
1965	Margaret Smith	Billie Jean Moffitt	8–6, 7–5
1966	Maria Bueno	Nancy Richey	6–3, 6–1
1967	Billie Jean King	Ann Haydon Jones	11–9, 6–4
1968**	Virginia Wade	Billie Jean King	6–4, 6–4
1968#	Margaret Smith Court	Maria Bueno	6–2, 6–2
1969	Margaret Smith Court	Nancy Richey	6–2, 6–2
1969#	Margaret Smith Court	Virginia Wade	4–6, 6–3, 6–0

†Challenge round abolished. ‡National Patriotic Tournament.
**Became Open (amateur and professional) in 1968. #Amateur event held.

WOMEN (Cont.)

United States Championships (Cont.)

Year	Winner	Finalist	Score
1970	Margaret Smith Court	Rosie Casals	6–2, 2–6, 6–1
1971	Billie Jean King	Rosie Casals	6–4, 7–6
1972	Billie Jean King	Kerry Melville	6–3, 7–5
1973	Margaret Smith Court	Evonne Goolagong	7–6, 5–7, 6–2
1974	Billie Jean King	Evonne Goolagong	3–6, 6–3, 7–5
1975	Chris Evert	Evonne Goolagong Cawley	5–7, 6–4, 6–2
1976	Chris Evert	Evonne Goolagong Cawley	6–3, 6–0
1977	Chris Evert	Wendy Turnbull	7–6, 6–2
1978	Chris Evert	Pam Shriver	7–6, 6–4
1979	Tracy Austin	Chris Evert Lloyd	6–4, 6–3
1980	Chris Evert Lloyd	Hana Mandlikova	5–7, 6–1, 6–1
1981	Tracy Austin	Martina Navratilova	1–6, 7–6, 7–6
1982	Chris Evert Lloyd	Hana Mandlikova	6–3, 6–1
1983	Martina Navratilova	Chris Evert Lloyd	6–1, 6–3
1984	Martina Navratilova	Chris Evert Lloyd	4–6, 6–4, 6–4
1985	Hana Mandlikova	Martina Navratilova	7–6, 1–6, 7–6
1986	Martina Navratilova	Helena Sukova	6–3, 6–2
1987	Martina Navratilova	Steffi Graf	7–6, 6–1
1988	Steffi Graf	Gabriela Sabatini	6–3, 3–6, 6–1
1989	Steffi Graf	Martina Navratilova	3–6, 6–4, 6–2
1990	Gabriela Sabatini	Steffi Graf	6–2, 7–6
1991	Monica Seles	Martina Navratilova	7–6, 6–1
1992	Monica Seles	Arantxa Sánchez Vicario	6–3, 6–2
1993	Steffi Graf	Helena Sukova	6–3, 6–3
1994	Arantxa Sánchez Vicario	Steffi Graf	1–6, 7–6, 6–4
1995	Steffi Graf	Monica Seles	7–6, 0–6, 6–3
1996	Steffi Graf	Monica Seles	7–5, 7–4
1997	Martina Hingis	Venus Williams	6–0, 6–4
1998	Lindsay Davenport	Martina Hingis	6–3, 7–5
1999	Serena Williams	Martina Hingis	6–3, 7–6
2000	Venus Williams	Lindsay Davenport	6–4, 7–5
2001	Venus Williams	Serena Williams	6–2, 6–4
2002	Serena Williams	Venus Williams	6–4, 6–3
2003	Justine Henin-Hardenne	Kim Clijsters	7–5, 6–1
2004	Svetlana Kuznetsova	Elena Dementieva	6–3, 7–5
2005	Kim Clijsters	Mary Pierce	6–3, 6–1
2006	Maria Sharapova	Justine Henin-Hardenne	6–4, 6–4
2007	Justine Henin	Svetlana Kuznetsova	6–1, 6–3

Single-Year Grand Slam Winners

Singles	Doubles	Mixed Doubles
Don Budge, 1938	Frank Sedgman and Ken McGregor, 1951	Margaret Smith and Ken Fletcher, 1963
Maureen Connolly, 1953	Martina Navratilova and Pam Shriver, 1984	Owen Davidson and two partners, 1967
Rod Laver, 1962, 1969	Maria Bueno and two partners, 1960	Lesley Turner (Australian),
Margaret Smith Court, 1970	Christine Truman (Australian), Darlene Hard (French, Wimbledon and U.S.)	Billie Jean King (French, Wimbledon and U.S.)
Steffi Graf, 1988	Martina Hingis and two partners, 1998 Mirjana Lucic (Australian), Jana Novotna (French, Wimbledon and U.S.)	

Alltime Grand Slam Champions (Singles, Doubles, Mixed Doubles)

MEN

Player	Aus. S-D-M	French S-D-M	Wim. S-D-M	U.S. S-D-M	Total
Roy Emerson	6-3-0	2-6-0	2-3-0	2-4-0	28
John Newcombe	2-5-0	0-3-0	3-6-0	2-3-1	25
Frank Sedgman	2-2-2	0-3-2	1-2-2	2-2-2	22
Todd Woodbridge	0-3-1	0-1-1	0-9-1	0-3-3	22
Bill Tilden	†	0-0-1	3-1-0	7-5-4	21
Rod Laver	3-4-0	2-1-1	4-1-2	2-0-0	20
John Bromwich	2-8-1	0-0-0	0-2-2	0-3-1	19
Jean Borotra	1-1-1	1-5-2	2-3-1	0-0-1	18
Fred Stolle	0-3-1	1-2-0	0-2-3	1-3-2	18
Ken Rosewall	4-3-0	2-2-0	0-2-0	2-2-1	18
Neale Fraser	0-3-1	0-3-0	1-2-0	2-3-3	18
Adrian Quist	3-10-0	0-1-0	0-2-0	0-1-0	17
John McEnroe	0-0-0	0-0-1	3-4-0	4-5-0	17
Jack Crawford	4-4-3	1-1-1	1-1-1	0-0-0	17
Mark Woodforde	0-2-2	0-1-1	0-6-1	0-3-1	17

†Did not compete.

WOMEN

Player	Aus. S-D-M	French S-D-M	Wim. S-D-M	U.S. S-D-M	Total
Margaret Smith Court	11-8-2	5-4-4	3-2-5	5-5-8	62
Martina Navratilova	3-8-1	2-7-2	9-7-4	4-9-3	59
Billie Jean King	1-0-1	1-1-2	6-10-4	4-5-4	39
Doris Hart	1-1-2	2-5-3	1-4-5	2-4-5	35
Helen Wills Moody	†	4-2-0	8-3-1	7-4-2	31
Louise Brough	1-1-0	0-3-0	4-5-4	1-8-3	30**
Margaret Osborne duPont	†	2-3-0	1-5-1	3-8-6	29**
Elizabeth Ryan	†	0-4-0	0-12-7	0-1-2	26
Steffi Graf	4-0-0	6-0-0	7-1-0	5-0-0	23
Pam Shriver	0-7-0	0-4-1	0-5-0	0-5-0	22
Chris Evert	2-0-0	7-2-0	3-1-0	6-0-0	21
Darlene Hard	†	1-3-2	0-4-3	2-6-0	21
Suzanne Lenglen	†	2-2-2#	6-6-3	0-0-0	21
Nancye Wynne Bolton	6-10-4	0-0-0	0-0-0	0-0-0	20
Maria Bueno	0-1-0	0-1-1	3-5-0	4-4-0	19
Thelma Coyne Long	2-12-4	0-0-0	0-0-0	0-0-0	19

*Active player in 2007. †Did not compete. #Suzanne Lenglen also won four singles titles at the French Championships before 1925, when competition was first opened to entries from all nations.**From 1940–45, with competition in the U.S. Championships thinned due to wartime constraints, Louise Brough Clapp also won four doubles titles (1942–45) and one mixed doubles title (1942); and Margaret Osborne duPont won five doubles titles (1941–45) and three mixed doubles titles (1943–45).

Alltime Grand Slam Singles Champions

MEN Player	Aus.	French	Wim.	U.S.	Total	WOMEN Player	Aus.	French	Wim.	U.S.	Total
Pete Sampras	2	0	7	5	14	Margaret Smith Court	11	5	3	5	24
Roy Emerson	6	2	2	2	12	Steffi Graf	4	6	7	5	22
*Roger Federer	3	0	5	4	12	Helen Wills Moody	†	4	8	7	19
Bjorn Borg	0	6	5	0	11	Chris Evert	2	7	3	6	18
Rod Laver	3	2	4	2	11	Martina Navratilova	3	2	9	4	18
Bill Tilden	†	0	3	7	10	Billie Jean King	1	1	6	4	12
Jimmy Connors	1	0	2	5	8	Maureen Connolly	1	2	3	3	9
Ivan Lendl	2	3	0	3	8	*Monica Seles	4	3	0	2	9
Fred Perry	1	1	3	3	8	Suzanne Lenglen	†	2#	6	0	8
Ken Rosewall	4	2	0	2	8	Molla Bjurstedt Mallory	†	†	0	8	8
Andre Agassi	4	1	1	2	8	*Serena Williams	3	1	2	2	8
Henri Cochet	†	4	2	1	7	Maria Bueno	0	0	3	4	7
Rene Lacoste	†	3	2	2	7	Evonne Goolagong	4	1	2	0	7
Bill Larned	†	†	0	7	7	Dorothea D.L. Chambers	†	†	7	0	7
John McEnroe	0	0	3	4	7	*Justine Henin	1	4	0	2	7
John Newcombe	2	0	3	2	7						
Willie Renshaw	†	†	7	†	7						
Dick Sears	†	†	0	7	7						

*Active player in 2007. †Did not compete.
#Suzanne Lenglen also won four singles titles at the French Championships before 1925, when competition was first opened to entries from all nations.

Davis Cup

Started in 1900 as the International Lawn Tennis Challenge Trophy by America's Dwight Davis, the runner up in the 1898 U.S. Championships. A Davis Cup meeting between two countries is known as a tie and is a three-day event consisting of two singles matches, followed by one doubles match and then two more singles matches. The United States boasts the greatest number of wins (40), followed by Australia (22).

Year	Winner	Finalist	Site	Score
1900	United States	Great Britain	Boston	3–0
1901	No tournament			
1902	United States	Great Britain	New York	3–2
1903	Great Britain	United States	Boston	4–1
1904	Great Britain	Belgium	Wimbledon	5–0
1905	Great Britain	United States	Wimbledon	5–0
1906	Great Britain	United States	Wimbledon	5–0
1907	Australasia	Great Britain	Wimbledon	3–2
1908	Australasia	United States	Melbourne	3–2
1909	Australasia	United States	Sydney	5–0
1910	No tournament			
1911	Australasia	United States	Christchurch, NZ	5–0
1912	Great Britain	Australasia	Melbourne	3–2
1913	United States	Great Britain	Wimbledon	3–2
1914	Australasia	United States	New York	3–2
1915–18	No tournament			
1919	Australasia	Great Britain	Sydney	4–1
1920	United States	Australasia	Auckland, N.Z.	5–0
1921	United States	Japan	New York	5–0
1922	United States	Australasia	New York	4–1
1923	United States	Australasia	New York	4–1
1924	United States	Australia	Philadelphia	5–0
1925	United States	France	Philadelphia	5–0
1926	United States	France	Philadelphia	4–1
1927	France	United States	Philadelphia	3–2
1928	France	United States	Paris	4–1
1929	France	United States	Paris	3–2
1930	France	United States	Paris	4–1
1931	France	Great Britain	Paris	3–2
1932	France	United States	Paris	3–2
1933	Great Britain	France	Paris	3–2
1934	Great Britain	United States	Wimbledon	4–1
1935	Great Britain	United States	Wimbledon	5–0
1936	Great Britain	Australia	Wimbledon	3–2
1937	United States	Great Britain	Wimbledon	4–1
1938	United States	Australia	Philadelphia	3–2
1939	Australia	United States	Philadelphia	3–2
1940–45	No tournament			
1946	United States	Australia	Melbourne	5–0
1947	United States	Australia	New York	4–1
1948	United States	Australia	New York	5–0
1949	United States	Australia	New York	4–1
1950	Australia	United States	New York	4–1
1951	Australia	United States	Sydney	3–2
1952	Australia	United States	Adelaide	4–1
1953	Australia	United States	Melbourne	3–2
1954	United States	Australia	Sydney	3–2
1955	Australia	United States	New York	5–0
1956	Australia	United States	Adelaide	5–0
1957	Australia	United States	Melbourne	3–2
1958	United States	Australia	Brisbane	3–2
1959	Australia	United States	New York	3–2
1960	Australia	Italy	Sydney	4–1
1961	Australia	Italy	Melbourne	5–0
1962	Australia	Mexico	Brisbane	5–0
1963	United States	Australia	Adelaide	3–2
1964	Australia	United States	Cleveland	3–2
1965	Australia	Spain	Sydney	4–1
1966	Australia	India	Melbourne	4–1
1967	Australia	Spain	Brisbane	4–1
1968	United States	Australia	Adelaide	4–1
1969	United States	Romania	Cleveland	5–0
1970	United States	West Germany	Cleveland	5–0

Davis Cup *(Cont.)*

Year	Winner	Finalist	Site	Score
1971	United States	Romania	Charlotte, N.C.	3–2
1972	United States	Romania	Bucharest, Rom.	3–2
1973	Australia	United States	Cleveland	5–0
1974	South Africa	India	*	walkover
1975	Sweden	Czechoslovakia	Stockholm	3–2
1976	Italy	Chile	Santiago	4–1
1977	Australia	Italy	Sydney	3–1
1978	United States	Great Britain	Palm Springs	4–1
1979	United States	Italy	San Francisco	5–0
1980	Czechoslovakia	Italy	Prague	4–1
1981	United States	Argentina	Cincinnati	3–1
1982	United States	France	Grenoble, France	4–1
1983	Australia	Sweden	Melbourne	3–2
1984	Sweden	United States	Goteborg, Sweden	4–1
1985	Sweden	West Germany	Munich	3–2
1986	Australia	Sweden	Melbourne	3–2
1987	Sweden	India	Goteborg, Sweden	5–0
1988	West Germany	Sweden	Goteborg, Sweden	4–1
1989	West Germany	Sweden	Stuttgart	3–2
1990	United States	Australia	St. Petersburg	3–2
1991	France	United States	Lyon	3–1
1992	United States	Switzerland	Fort Worth, Tex.	3–1
1993	Germany	Australia	Dusseldorf	4–1
1994	Sweden	Russia	Moscow	4–1
1995	United States	Russia	Moscow	3–2
1996	France	Sweden	Malmo, Sweden	3–2
1997	Sweden	United States	Goteborg, Sweden	5–0
1998	Sweden	Italy	Milan	4–1
1999	Australia	France	Nice, France	3–2
2000	Spain	Australia	Barcelona	3–1
2001	France	Australia	Melbourne	3–2
2002	Russia	France	Paris	3–2
2003	Australia	Spain	Melbourne	3–1
2004	Spain	United States	Seville, Spain	3–2
2005	Croatia	Slovakia	Bratislava, Slovakia	3–2
2006	Russia	Argentina	Moscow, Russia	3–2

*India refused to play the final in protest over South Africa's governmental policy of apartheid.
Note: Prior to 1972 the challenge-round system was in effect, with the previous year's winner "standing out" of the competition until the finals. A straight 16-nation tournament has been held since 1981.

Federation Cup

The Federation Cup was started in 1963 by the International Lawn Tennis Federation (now the ITF). Until 1991 all entrants gathered at one site at one time for a tournament that was concluded within one week. Since 1995 the Fed Cup, as it is now called, has been contested in three rounds by a World Group of eight nations. A meeting between two countries now consists of five matches: four singles and one doubles. The United States has the most wins (17), followed by Australia (7).

Year	Winner	Finalist	Site	Score
1963	United States	Australia	London	2–1
1964	Australia	United States	Philadelphia	2–1
1965	Australia	United States	Melbourne	2–1
1966	United States	West Germany	Turin	3–0
1967	United States	Great Britain	W Berlin	2–0
1968	Australia	Netherlands	Paris	3–0
1969	United States	Australia	Athens	2–1
1970	Australia	Great Britain	Freiburg	3–0
1971	Australia	Great Britain	Perth	3–0
1972	South Africa	Great Britain	Johannesburg	2–1
1973	Australia	South Africa	Bad Homburg	3–0
1974	Australia	United States	Naples	2–1
1975	Czechoslovakia	Australia	Aix-en-Provence	3–0

Federation Cup (Cont.)

Year	Winner	Finalist	Site	Score
1976	United States	Australia	Philadelphia	2–1
1977	United States	Australia	Eastbourne, Eng.	2–1
1978	United States	Australia	Melbourne	2–1
1979	United States	Australia	Madrid	3–0
1980	United States	Australia	West Berlin	3–0
1981	United States	Great Britain	Nagoya	3–0
1982	United States	West Germany	Santa Clara, Calif.	3–0
1983	Czechoslovakia	West Germany	Zürich	2–1
1984	Czechoslovakia	Australia	Sao Paulo	2–1
1985	Czechoslovakia	United States	Tokyo	2–1
1986	United States	Czechoslovakia	Prague	3–0
1987	West Germany	United States	Vancouver	2–1
1988	Czechoslovakia	USSR	Melbourne	2–1
1989	United States	Spain	Tokyo	3–0
1990	United States	USSR	Atlanta	2–1
1991	Spain	United States	Nottingham	2–1
1992	Germany	Spain	Frankfurt	2–1
1993	Spain	Australia	Frankfurt	3–0
1994	Spain	United States	Frankfurt	3–0
1995	Spain	United States	Valencia, Spain	3–2
1996	United States	Spain	Atlantic City	5–0
1997	France	Netherlands	Hertogenbosch, Neth.	4–1
1998	Spain	Switzerland	Geneva	3–2
1999	United States	Russia	Palo Alto, Calif.	4–1
2000	United States	Spain	Las Vegas	5–0
2001	Belgium	Russia	Barcelona	2–1
2002	Slovak Republic	Spain	Maspalomas, Canary Isl.	3–1
2003	France	United States	Moscow	4–1
2004	Russia	France	Moscow	3–2
2005	Russia	France	Paris	3–2
2006	Italy	Belgium	Charleroi, Belgium	3–2
2007	Russia	Italy	Moscow	4–0

Rankings

ATP Computer Year-End Top 10 — Men

1973
1. Ilie Nastase
2. John Newcombe
3. Jimmy Connors
4. Tom Okker
5. Stan Smith
6. Ken Rosewall
7. Manuel Orantes
8. Rod Laver
9. Jan Kodes
10. Arthur Ashe

1974
1. Jimmy Connors
2. John Newcombe
3. Bjorn Borg
4. Rod Laver
5. Guillermo Vilas
6. Tom Okker
7. Arthur Ashe
8. Ken Rosewall
9. Stan Smith
10. Ilie Nastase

1975
1. Jimmy Connors
2. Guillermo Vilas
3. Bjorn Borg
4. Arthur Ashe
5. Manuel Orantes
6. Ken Rosewall
7. Ilie Nastase
8. John Alexander
9. Roscoe Tanner
10. Rod Laver

1976
1. Jimmy Connors
2. Bjorn Borg
3. Ilie Nastase
4. Manuel Orantes
5. Raul Ramirez
6. Guillermo Vilas
7. Adriano Panatta
8. Harold Solomon
9. Eddie Dibbs
10. Brian Gottfried

1977
1. Jimmy Connors
2. Guillermo Vilas
3. Bjorn Borg
4. Vitas Gerulaitis
5. Brian Gottfried
6. Eddie Dibbs
7. Manuel Orantes
8. Raul Ramirez
9. Ilie Nastase
10. Dick Stockton

1978
1. Jimmy Connors
2. Bjorn Borg
3. Guillermo Vilas
4. John McEnroe
5. Vitas Gerulaitis
6. Eddie Dibbs
7. Brian Gottfried
8. Raul Ramirez
9. Harold Solomon
10. Corrado Barazzutti

1979
1. Bjorn Borg
2. Jimmy Connors
3. John McEnroe
4. Vitas Gerulaitis
5. Roscoe Tanner
6. Guillermo Vilas
7. Arthur Ashe
8. Harold Solomon
9. Jose Higueras
10. Eddie Dibbs

1980
1. Bjorn Borg
2. John McEnroe
3. Jimmy Connors
4. Gene Mayer
5. Guillermo Vilas
6. Ivan Lendl
7. Harold Solomon
8. Jose–Luis Clerc
9. Vitas Gerulaitis
10. Eliot Teltscher

1981
1. John McEnroe
2. Ivan Lendl
3. Jimmy Connors
4. Bjorn Borg
5. Jose–Luis Clerc
6. Guillermo Vilas
7. Gene Mayer
8. Eliot Teltscher
9. Vitas Gerulaitis
10. Peter McNamara

1982
1. John McEnroe
2. Jimmy Connors
3. Ivan Lendl
4. Guillermo Vilas
5. Vitas Gerulaitis
6. Jose–Luis Clerc
7. Mats Wilander
8. Gene Mayer
9. Yannick Noah
10. Peter McNamara

ATP Computer Year-End Top 10 — Men *(Cont.)*

1983	1988	1993	1998	2003
1 John McEnroe	1 Mats Wilander	1 Pete Sampras	1 Pete Sampras	1 Andy Roddick
2 Ivan Lendl	2 Ivan Lendl	2 Michael Stich	2 Marcelo Rios	2 Roger Federer
3 Jimmy Connors	3 Andre Agassi	3 Jim Courier	3 Alex Corretja	3 Juan Carlos Ferrero
4 Mats Wilander	4 Boris Becker	4 Sergi Bruguera	4 Patrick Rafter	4 Andre Agassi
5 Yannick Noah	5 Stefan Edberg	5 Stefan Edberg	5 Carlos Moya	5 Guillermo Coria
6 Jimmy Arias	6 Kent Carlsson	6 Andrei Medvedev	6 Andre Agassi	6 Rainer Schuettler
7 Jose Higueras	7 Jimmy Connors	7 Goran Ivanisevic	7 Tim Henman	7 Carlos Moya
8 Jose–Luis Clerc	8 Jakob Hlasek	8 Michael Chang	8 Karol Kucera	8 David Nalbandian
9 Kevin Curren	9 Henri Leconte	9 Thomas Muster	9 Greg Rusedski	9 Mark Philippoussis
10 Gene Mayer	10 Tim Mayotte	10 Cedric Pioline	10 Richard Krajicek	10 Sebastien Grosjean
1984	**1989**	**1994**	**1999**	**2004**
1 John McEnroe	1 Ivan Lendl	1 Pete Sampras	1 Andre Agassi	1 Roger Federer
2 Jimmy Connors	2 Boris Becker	2 Andre Agassi	2 Yevgeny Kafelnikov	2 Andy Roddick
3 Ivan Lendl	3 Stefan Edberg	3 Boris Becker	3 Pete Sampras	3 Lleyton Hewitt
4 Mats Wilander	4 John McEnroe	4 Sergi Bruguera	4 Thomas Enqvist	4 Marat Safin
5 Andres Gomez	5 Michael Chang	5 Goran Ivanisevic	5 Gustavo Kuerten	5 Carlos Moya
6 Anders Jarryd	6 Brad Gilbert	6 Michael Chang	6 Nicolas Kiefer	6 Tim Henman
7 Henrik Sundstrom	7 Andre Agassi	7 Stefan Edberg	7 Todd Martin	7 Guillermo Coria
8 Pat Cash	8 Aaron Krickstein	8 Alberto Berasategui	8 Nicolas Lapentti	8 Andre Agassi
9 Eliot Teltscher	9 Alberto Mancini	9 Michael Stich	9 Marcelo Rios	9 David Nalbandian
10 Yannick Noah	10 Jay Berger	10 Todd Martin	10 Richard Krajicek	10 Gaston Gaudio
1985	**1990**	**1995**	**2000**	**2005**
1 Ivan Lendl	1 Stefan Edberg	1 Pete Sampras	1 Gustavo Kuerten	1 Roger Federer
2 John McEnroe	2 Boris Becker	2 Andre Agassi	2 Marat Safin	2 Rafael Nadal
3 Mats Wilander	3 Ivan Lendl	3 Thomas Muster	3 Pete Sampras	3 Andy Roddick
4 Jimmy Connors	4 Andre Agassi	4 Boris Becker	4 Magnus Norman	4 Lleyton Hewitt
5 Stefan Edberg	5 Pete Sampras	5 Michael Chang	5 Yevgeny Kafelnikov	5 Nikolay Davydenko
6 Boris Becker	6 Andres Gomez	6 Yevgeny Kafelnikov	6 Andre Agassi	6 David Nalbandian
7 Yannick Noah	7 Thomas Muster	7 Thomas Enqvist	7 Lleyton Hewitt	7 Andre Agassi
8 Anders Jarryd	8 Emilio Sanchez	8 Jim Courier	8 Alex Corretja	8 Guillermo Coria
9 Miloslav Mecir	9 Goran Ivanisevic	9 Wayne Ferreira	9 Thomas Enqvist	9 Ivan Ljubicic
10 Kevin Curren	10 Brad Gilbert	10 Goran Ivanisevic	10 Tim Henman	10 Gaston Gaudio
1986	**1991**	**1996**	**2001**	**2006**
1 Ivan Lendl	1 Stefan Edberg	1 Pete Sampras	1 Lleyton Hewitt	1 Roger Federer
2 Boris Becker	2 Jim Courier	2 Michael Chang	2 Gustavo Kuerten	2 Rafael Nadal
3 Mats Wilander	3 Boris Becker	3 Yevgeny Kafelnikov	3 Andre Agassi	3 Nikolay Davydenko
4 Yannick Noah	4 Michael Stich	4 Goran Ivanisevic	4 Yevgeny Kafelnikov	4 James Blake
5 Stefan Edberg	5 Ivan Lendl	5 Thomas Muster	5 Juan Carlos Ferrero	5 Ivan Ljubicic
6 Henri Leconte	6 Pete Sampras	6 Boris Becker	6 Sebastien Grosjean	6 Andy Roddick
7 Joakim Nystrom	7 Guy Forget	7 Richard Krajicek	7 Patrick Rafter	7 Tommy Robredo
8 Jimmy Connors	8 Karel Novacek	8 Andre Agassi	8 Tommy Haas	8 David Nalbandian
9 Miloslav Mecir	9 Petr Korda	9 Thomas Enqvist	9 Tim Henman	9 Mario Ancic
10 Andres Gomez	10 Andre Agassi	10 Wayne Ferreira	10 Pete Sampras	10 Fernando Gonzalez
1987	**1992**	**1997**	**2002**	
1 Ivan Lendl	1 Jim Courier	1 Pete Sampras	1 Lleyton Hewitt	
2 Stefan Edberg	2 Stefan Edberg	2 Patrick Rafter	2 Andre Agassi	
3 Mats Wilander	3 Pete Sampras	3 Michael Chang	3 Marat Safin	
4 Jimmy Connors	4 Goran Ivanisevic	4 Jonas Björkman	4 Juan Carlos Ferrero	
5 Boris Becker	5 Boris Becker	5 Yevgeny Kafelnikov	5 Carlos Moya	
6 Miloslav Mecir	6 Michael Chang	6 Greg Rusedski	6 Roger Federer	
7 Pat Cash	7 Petr Korda	7 Carlos Moya	7 Jiri Novak	
8 Yannick Noah	8 Ivan Lendl	8 Sergei Bruguera	8 Tim Henman	
9 Tim Mayotte	9 Andre Agassi	9 Thomas Muster	9 Albert Costa	
10 John McEnroe	10 Richard Krajicek	10 Marcelo Ríos	10 Andy Roddick	

WTA Computer Year-End Top 10 — Women

1973
1 Margaret Smith Court
2 Billie Jean King
3 Evonne Goolagong
4 Chris Evert
5 Rosie Casals
6 Virginia Wade
7 Kerry Reid
8 Nancy Gunter
9 Julie Heldman
10 Helga Masthoff

1974
1 Billie Jean King
2 Evonne Goolagong
3 Chris Evert
4 Virginia Wade
5 Julie Heldman
6 Rosie Casals
7 Kerry Reid
8 Olga Morozova
9 Lesley Hunt
10 Francoise Durr

1975
1 Chris Evert
2 Billie Jean King
3 Evonne Goolagong Cawley
4 Martina Navratilova
5 Virginia Wade
6 Margaret Smith Court
7 Olga Morozova
8 Nancy Gunter
9 Francoise Durr
10 Rosie Casals

1976
1 Chris Evert
2 Evonne Goolagong Cawley
3 Virginia Wade
4 Martina Navratilova
5 Sue Barker
6 Betty Stove
7 Dianne Balestrat
8 Mima Jausovec
9 Rosie Casals
10 Francoise Durr

1977
1 Chris Evert
2 Billie Jean King
3 Martina Navratilova
4 Virginia Wade
5 Sue Barker
6 Rosie Casals
7 Betty Stove
8 Dianne Balestrat
9 Wendy Turnbull
10 Kerry Reid

1978
1 Martina Navratilova
2 Chris Evert
3 Evonne Goolagong Cawley
4 Virginia Wade
5 Billie Jean King
6 Tracy Austin
7 Wendy Turnbull
8 Kerry Reid
9 Betty Stove
10 Dianne Balestrat

1979
1 Martina Navratilova
2 Chris Evert Lloyd
3 Tracy Austin
4 Evonne Goolagong Cawley
5 Billie Jean King
6 Dianne Balestrat
7 Wendy Turnbull
8 Virginia Wade
9 Kerry Reid
10 Sue Barker

1980
1 Chris Evert Lloyd
2 Tracy Austin
3 Martina Navratilova
4 Hana Mandlikova
5 Evonne Goolagong Cawley
6 Billie Jean King
7 Andrea Jaeger
8 Wendy Turnbull
9 Pam Shriver
10 Greer Stevens

1981
1 Chris Evert Lloyd
2 Tracy Austin
3 Martina Navratilova
4 Andrea Jaeger
5 Hana Mandlikova
6 Sylvia Hanika
7 Pam Shriver
8 Wendy Turnbull
9 Bettina Bunge
10 Barbara Potter

1982
1 Martina Navratilova
2 Chris Evert Lloyd
3 Andrea Jaeger
4 Tracy Austin
5 Wendy Turnbull
6 Pam Shriver
7 Hana Mandlikova
8 Barbara Potter
9 Bettina Bunge
10 Sylvia Hanika

1983
1 Martina Navratilova
2 Chris Evert Lloyd
3 Andrea Jaeger
4 Pam Shriver
5 Sylvia Hanika
6 Jo Durie
7 Bettina Bunge
8 Wendy Turnbull
9 Tracy Austin
10 Zina Garrison

1984
1 Martina Navratilova
2 Chris Evert Lloyd
3 Hana Mandlikova
4 Pam Shriver
5 Wendy Turnbull
6 Manuela Maleeva
7 Helena Sukova
8 Claudia Kohde-Kilsch
9 Zina Garrison
10 Kathy Jordan

1985
1 Martina Navratilova
2 Chris Evert Lloyd
3 Hana Mandlikova
4 Pam Shriver
5 Claudia Kohde-Kilsch
6 Steffi Graf
7 Manuela Maleeva
8 Zina Garrison
9 Helena Sukova
10 Bonnie Gadusek

1986
1 Martina Navratilova
2 Chris Evert Lloyd
3 Pam Shriver
4 Hana Mandlikova
5 Helena Sukova
6 Pam Shriver
7 Claudia Kohde-Kilsch
8 Manuela Maleeva
9 Kathy Rinaldi
10 Gabriela Sabatini

1987
1 Steffi Graf
2 Martina Navratilova
3 Chris Evert
4 Pam Shriver
5 Hana Mandlikova
6 Gabriela Sabatini
7 Helena Sukova
8 Manuela Maleeva
9 Zina Garrison
10 Claudia Kohde-Kilsch

1988
1 Steffi Graf
2 Martina Navratilova
3 Chris Evert
4 Gabriela Sabatini
5 Pam Shriver
6 Manuela Maleeva-Fragniere
7 Natalia Zvereva
8 Helena Sukova
9 Zina Garrison
10 Barbara Potter

1989
1 Steffi Graf
2 Martina Navratilova
3 Gabriela Sabatini
4 Zina Garrison
5 Arantxa Sánchez Vicario
6 Monica Seles
7 Conchita Martinez
8 Helena Sukova
9 Manuela Maleeva-Fragniere
10 Chris Evert*

1990
1 Steffi Graf
2 Monica Seles
3 Martina Navratilova
4 Mary Joe Fernandez
5 Gabriela Sabatini
6 Katerina Maleeva
7 Arantxa Sánchez Vicario
8 Jennifer Capriati
9 Manuela Maleeva-Fragniere
10 Zina Garrison

1991
1 Monica Seles
2 Steffi Graf
3 Gabriela Sabatini
4 Martina Navratilova
5 Arantxa Sánchez Vicario
6 Jennifer Capriati
7 Jana Novotna
8 Mary Joe Fernandez
9 Conchita Martinez
10 Manuela Maleeva-Fragniere

1992
1 Monica Seles
2 Steffi Graf
3 Gabriela Sabatini
4 Arantxa Sánchez Vicario
5 Martina Navratilova
6 Mary Joe Fernandez
7 Jennifer Capriati
8 Conchita Martinez
9 M. Maleeva-Fragniere
10 Jana Novotna

1993
1 Steffi Graf
2 Arantxa Sánchez Vicario
3 Martina Navratilova
4 Conchita Martinez
5 Gabriela Sabatini
6 Jana Novotna
7 Mary Joe Fernandez
8 Monica Seles
9 Jennifer Capriati
10 Anke Huber

1994
1 Steffi Graf
2 Arantxa Sánchez Vicario
3 Conchita Martinez
4 Jana Novotna
5 Mary Pierce
6 Lindsay Davenport
7 Gabriela Sabatini
8 Martina Navratilova
9 Kimiko Date
10 Natasha Zvereva

1995
1 Steffi Graf (co-No.1)
1 Monica Seles(co-No.1)
2 Conchita Martinez
3 A. S.Vicario
4 Kimiko Date
5 Mary Pierce
6 Magdalena Maleeva
7 Gabriela Sabatini
8 Mary Joe Fernandez
9 Iva Majoli
10 Anke Huber

1996
1 Steffi Graf
2 Monica Seles
3 Jana Novotna
4 Lindsay Davenport
5 Martina Hingis
6 Stephanie de Ville
7 Tamarine Tanasugarn
8 Anke Huber
9 Conchita Martinez
10 Julie Halard-Decugis

*When Chris Evert announced her retirement at the 1989 United States Open, she was ranked fourth in the world. That was her last official series tournament.

WTA Computer Year-End Top 10 — Women *(Cont.)*

1997
1 Martina Hingis
2 Jana Novotna
3 Lindsay Davenport
4 Amanda Coetzer
5 Monica Seles
6 Iva Majoli
7 Mary Pierce
8 Irina Spirlea
9 Arantxa Sánchez Vicario
10 Mary Joe Fernandez

1998
1 Lindsay Davenport
2 Martina Hingis
3 Jana Novotna
4 A.S. Vicario
5 Venus Williams
6 Monica Seles
7 Mary Pierce
8 Conchita Martinez
9 Steffi Graf
10 Nathalie Tauziat

1999
1 Martina Hingis
2 Lindsay Davenport
3 Venus Williams
4 Serena Williams
5 Mary Pierce
6 Monica Seles
7 Nathalie Tauziat
8 Barbara Schett
9 J. Halard-Decugis
10 Amelie Mauresmo

2000
1 Martina Hingis
2 Lindsay Davenport
3 Venus Williams
4 Monica Seles
5 Conchita Martinez
6 Serena Williams
7 Mary Pierce
8 Anna Kournikova
9 Arantxa Sánchez Vicario
10 Nathalie Tauziat

2001
1 Lindsay Davenport
2 Jennifer Capriati
3 Venus Williams
4 Martina Hingis
5 Kim Clijsters
6 Serena Williams
7 Justine Henin
8 Jelena Dokic
9 Amelie Mauresmo
10 Monica Seles

2002
1 Serena Williams
2 Venus Williams
3 Jennifer Capriati
4 Kim Clijsters
5 Justine Henin
6 Amelie Mauresmo
7. Monica Seles
8 Daniela Hantuchova
9 Jelena Dokic
10 Martina Hingis

2003
1 Justine Henin-Hardenne
2 Kim Clijsters
3 Serena Williams
4 Amelie Mauresmo
5 Lindsay Davenport
6 Jennifer Capriati
7 Anastasia Myskina
8 Elena Dementieva
9 Chandra Rubin
10 Ai Sugiyama

2004
1 Lindsay Davenport
2 Amelie Mauresmo
3 Anastasia Myskina
4 Maria Sharapova
5 Svetlana Kuznetsova
6 Elena Dementieva
7 Serena Williams
8 Justine Henin-Hardenne
9 Venus Williams
10 Jennifer Capriati

2005
1. Lindsay Davenport
2. Maria Sharapova
3. Amelie Mauresmo
4. Serena Williams
5. Elena Dementieva
6. Anastasia Myskina
7. Svetlana Kuznetsova
8. Alicia Molik
9. Venus Williams
10. Vera Zvonareva

2006
1 Justine Henin-Hardenne
2 Maria Sharapova
3 Amelie Mauresmo
4 Svetlana Kuznetsova
5 Kim Clijsters
6 Nadia Petrova
7 Martina Hingis
8 Elena Dementieva
9 Patty Schnyder
10 Nicole Vaidisova

Prize Money

Top 25 Men's Career Prize Money Leaders

Note: From arrival of Open tennis in 1968 through September 10, 2007.

	Earnings ($)
Pete Sampras	43,280,489
Roger Federer	35,640,078
Andre Agassi	31,152,975
Boris Becker	25,080,956
Yevgeny Kafelnikov	23,883,797
Ivan Lendl	21,262,417
Stefan Edberg	20,630,941
Goran Ivanisevic	19,876,579
Michael Chang	19,145,632
Lleyton Hewitt	17,242,512
Gustavo Kuerten	14,609,954
Jim Courier	14,033,132
Jonas Bjorkman	13,917,509
Andy Roddick	12,984,526
Carlos Moya	12,827,944
Rafael Nadal	12,681,374
Michael Stich	12,592,483
John McEnroe	12,539,622
Thomas Muster	12,224,410
Tim Henman	11,635,542
Sergi Bruguera	11,632,199
Patrick Rafter	11,127,058
Petr Korda	10,448,450
Alex Corretja	10,338,209
Thomas Enqvist	10,290,743

Top 25 Women's Career Prize Money Leaders

Note: From arrival of Open tennis in 1968 through September 10, 2007.

	Earnings ($)
Steffi Graf	21,895,277
Lindsay Davenport	21,798,237
Martina Navratilova	21,626,089
Martina Hingis	20,123,427
Venus Williams	18,096,031
Serena Williams	17,953,083
Justine Henin	17,665,995
Arantxa Sánchez Vicario	16,942,640
Monica Seles	14,891,762
Kim Clijsters	14,764,296
Amelie Mauresmo	13,541,766
Conchita Martinez	11,527,977
Jana Novotna	11,249,284
Jennifer Capriati	10,206,639
Maria Sharapova	9,716,272
Mary Pierce	9,793,119
Chris Evert	8,896,195
Gabriela Sabatini	8,785,850
Elena Dementieva	8,289,362
Svetlana Kuznetsova	7,935,454
Natasha Zvereva	7,792,503
Lisa Raymond	6,851,566
Ai Sugiyama	6,792,631
Nathalie Tauziat	6,650,093
Helena Sukova	6,391,245

Men's Career Leaders—Singles Titles Won

The top tournament-winning men from the institution of Open tennis in 1968 through September 10, 2007..

	W		W
Jimmy Connors	109	Thomas Muster	44
Ivan Lendl	94	Stefan Edberg	41
John McEnroe	77	Stan Smith	39
Pete Sampras	64	Michael Chang	34
Bjorn Borg	62	Arthur Ashe	33
Guillermo Vilas	62	Mats Wilander	33
Andre Agassi	60	John Newcombe	32
Ilie Nastase	57	Manuel Orantes	32
Roger Federer	51	Ken Rosewall	32
Boris Becker	49	Tom Okker	31
Rod Laver	47		

Women's Career Leaders—Singles Titles Won

The top tournament-winning women from the institution of Open tennis in 1968 through September 10, 2007.

	W		W
Martina Navratilova	167	Helga Masthoff	37
Chris Evert	157	Venus Williams	35
Steffi Graf	107	Kim Clijsters	34
Margaret Smith Court	92	Conchita Martinez	33
Evonne Goolagong Cawley	88	Olga Morozova	31
Billie Jean King	67	Tracy Austin	29
Maria Bueno	63	Arantxa Sánchez Vicario	29
Virginia Wade	55	Serena Williams	28
Monica Seles	53	Hana Mandlikova	27
Lindsay Davenport	52	Gabriela Sabatini	27
Martina Hingis	43	Francoise Durr-Browning	26

Annual ATP/WTA Champions

Men—Tennis Masters Cup*

Year	Player	Year	Player	Year	Player
1970	Stan Smith	1983	Ivan Lendl	1995	Boris Becker
1971	Ilie Nastase	1984	John McEnroe	1996	Pete Sampras
1972	Ilie Nastase	1985	John McEnroe	1997	Pete Sampras
1973	Ilie Nastase	1986 (Jan)	Ivan Lendl	1998	Alex Corretja
1974	Guillermo Vilas	1986 (Dec)	Ivan Lendl	1999	Pete Sampras
1975	Ilie Nastase	1987	Ivan Lendl	2000	Gustavo Kuerten
1976	Manuel Orantes	1988	Boris Becker	2001	Lleyton Hewitt
1977	Not held	1989	Stefan Edberg	2002	Lleyton Hewitt
1978	Jimmy Connors	1990	Andre Agassi	2003	Roger Federer
1979	John McEnroe	1991	Pete Sampras	2004	Roger Federer
1980	Bjorn Borg	1992	Boris Becker	2005	David Nalbandian
1981	Bjorn Borg	1993	Michael Stich	2006	Roger Federer
1982	Ivan Lendl	1994	Pete Sampras		

Women—WTA Tour Championships

Year	Player	Year	Player	Year	Player
1972	Chris Evert	1984*	Martina Navratilova	1996	Steffi Graf
1973	Chris Evert	1985	Martina Navratilova	1997	Jana Novotna
1974	Evonne Goolagong	1986 (Mar)	Martina Navratilova	1998	Martina Hingis
1975	Chris Evert	1986 (Nov)	Martina Navratilova	1999	Lindsay Davenport
1976	Evonne Goolagong Cawley	1987	Steffi Graf	2000	Martina Hingis
1977	Chris Evert	1988	Gabriela Sabatini	2001	Serena Williams
1978	Martina Navratilova	1989	Steffi Graf	2002	Kim Clijsters
1979	Martina Navratilova	1990	Monica Seles	2003	Kim Clijsters
1980	Tracy Austin	1991	Monica Seles	2004	Maria Sharapova
1981	Martina Navratilova	1992	Monica Seles	2005	Amelie Mauresmo
1982	Sylvia Hanika	1993	Steffi Graf	2006	Justine Henin-Hardenne
1983	Martina Navratilova	1994	Gabriela Sabatini		
		1995	Steffi Graf		

*From 1970 to 1989, tournament was known as the The Masters, from1990 to 1999, tournament was known as the ATP Tour World Championship.

Russ Adams (2007)
Pauline Betz Addie (1965)
George T. Adee (1964)
Fred B. Alexander (1961)
Wilmer L. Allison (1963)
Manuel Alonso (1977)
Malcolm Anderson (2000)
Arthur Ashe (1985)
Juliette Atkinson (1974)
H.W. Bunny Austin (1997)
Tracy Austin (1992)
Lawrence A. Baker Sr. (1975)
Maud Barger–Wallach (1958)
Angela Mortimer Barrett (1993)
Boris Becker (2003)
Karl Behr (1969)
Nancy Wynne Bolton (2006)
Bjorn Borg (1987)
Jean Borotra (1976)
Lesley Turner Bowrey (1997)
Maureen Connolly Brinker (1968)
John Bromwich (1984)
Norman Everard Brookes (1977)
Mary K. Browne (1957)
Jacques Brugnon (1976)
Butch Buchholz (2005)
J. Donald Budge (1964)
Maria E. Bueno (1978)
May Sutton Bundy (1956)
Mabel E. Cahill (1976)
Rosie Casals (1996)
Oliver S. Campbell (1955)
Malcolm Chace (1961)
Dorothy (Dodo) Cheney (2004)
Dorothea Douglass Chambers (1981)
Philippe Chatrier (1992)
Louise Brough Clapp (1967)
Clarence Clark (1983)
Joseph S. Clark (1955)
Gianni Clerici (2006)
William J. Clothier (1956)
Henri Cochet (1976)
Arthur W. (Bud) Collins Jr. (1994)
Jimmy Connors (1998)
Ashley Cooper (1991)
Jim Courier (2004)
Margaret Smith Court (1979)
Gottfried von Cramm (1977)
Jack Crawford (1979)
Joseph F. Cullman III (1990)
Allison Danzig (1968)
Sarah Palfrey Danzig (1963)
Hermán David (1998)
Sven Davidson (2007)
Dwight F. Davis (1956)
Charlotte Dod (1983)
John H. Doeg (1962)
Lawrence Doherty (1980)
Reginald Doherty (1980)
Jaroslav Drobny (1983)
Margaret Osborne duPont (1967)
Francoise Durr (2003)
James Dwight (1955)
Stefan Edberg (2004)
Roy Emerson (1982)
Pierre Etchebaster (1978)
Chris Evert (1995)
Robert Falkenburg (1974)
Marion Jones Farquhar (2006)

Neale Fraser (1984)
Shirley Fry-Irvin (1970)
Charles S. Garland (1969)
Althea Gibson (1971)
Kathleen McKane Godfree (1978)
Richard A. Gonzales (1968)
Evonne Goolagong Cawley (1988)
Arthur Gore (2006)
Steffi Graf (2004)
Bryan M. Grant Jr. (1972)
David Gray (1985)
Clarence Griffin (1970)
King Gustaf V of Sweden (1980)
Harold H. Hackett (1961)
Ellen Forde Hansell (1965)
Darlene R. Hard (1973)
Doris J. Hart (1969)
Gladys M. Heldman (1979)
W.E. (Slew) Hester Jr. (1981)
Bob Hewitt (1992)
Lew Hoad (1980)
Harry Hopman (1978)
Fred Hovey (1974)
Joseph R. Hunt (1966)
Lamar Hunt (1993)
Francis T. Hunter (1961)
Helen Hull Jacobs (1962)
William Johnston (1958)
Ann Haydon Jones (1985)
Perry Jones (1970)
Robert Kelleher (2000)
Billie Jean King (1987)
Jan Kodes (1990)
Karel Kozeluh (2006)
John A. Kramer (1968)
Rene Lacoste (1976)
Al Laney (1979)
William A. Larned (1956)
Arthur D. Larsen (1969)
Rod G. Laver (1981)
Herbert Lawford (2006)
Ivan Lendl (2001)
Suzanne Lenglen (1978)
Dorothy Round Little (1986)
George M. Lott Jr. (1964)
Gene Mako (1973)
Molla Bjurstedt Mallory (1958)
Hana Mandlikova (1994)
Alice Marble (1964)
Alastair B. Martin (1973)
William McChesney Martin (1982)
Dan Maskell (1996)
Simonne Mathieu (2006)
John McEnroe (1999)
Ken McGregor (1999)
Chuck McKinley (1986)
Maurice McLoughlin (1957)
Frew McMillan (1992)
W. Donald McNeill (1965)
Elisabeth H. Moore (1971)
Gardnar Mulloy (1972)
R. Lindley Murray (1958)
Julian S. Myrick (1963)
Ilie Nastase (1991)
Martina Navratilova (2000)
John D. Newcombe (1986)
Arthur C. Nielsen Sr (1971)
Yannick Noah (2005)
Jana Novotna (2005)

Hans Nusslein (2006)
Alex Olmedo (1987)
Rafael Osuna (1979)
Mary Ewing Outerbridge (1981)
Frank A. Parker (1966)
Gerald Patterson (1989)
Budge Patty (1977)
Theodore R. Pell (1966)
Fred Perry (1975)
Tom Pettitt (1982)
Nicola Pietrangeli (1986)
Adrian Quist (1984)
Patrick Rafter (2006)
Dennis Ralston (1987)
Ernest Renshaw (1983)
William Renshaw (1983)
Vincent Richards (1961)
Nancy Richey (2003)
Bobby Riggs (1967)
Helen Wills Moody Roark (1959)
Anthony D. Roche (1986)
Ellen C. Roosevelt (1975)
Mervyn Rose (2001)
Ken Rosewall (1980)
Elizabeth Ryan (1972)
Gabriela Sabatini (2006)
Pete Sampras (2007)
Arantxa Sanchez-Vicario (2007)
Manuel Santana (1984)
Richard Savitt (1976)
Frederick R. Schroeder (1966)
Eleonora Sears (1968)
Richard D. Sears (1955)
Frank Sedgman (1979)
Pancho Segura (1984)
Vic Seixas Jr. (1971)
Francis X. Shields (1964)
Betty Nuthall Shoemaker (1977)
Pam Shriver (2002)
Henry W. Slocum Jr. (1955)
Stan Smith (1987)
Fred Stolle (1985)
William F. Talbert (1967)
Bill Tilden (1959)
Lance Tingay (1982)
Ted Tinling (1986)
Brian Tobin (2003)
Bertha Townsend Toulmin (1974)
Tony Trabert (1970)
James H. Van Alen (1965)
John Van Ryn (1963)
Guillermo Vilas (1991)
Ellsworth Vines (1962)
Virginia Wade (1989)
Marie Wagner (1969)
Holcombe Ward (1956)
Watson Washburn (1965)
Malcolm D. Whitman (1955)
Hazel Hotchkiss Wightman (1957)
Mats Wilander (2002)
Anthony Wilding (1978)
Richard Norris Williams II (1957)
Mjr Walter Clopton Wingfield (1997)
Sidney B. Wood (1964)
Robert D. Wrenn (1955)
Beals C. Wright (1956)

Golf

Tiger Woods won his
13th career major in 2007
as well as the inaugural
PGA Tour playoff

New Format, Same Result

After coming up just short in the year's first three majors, Tiger Woods won the PGA and the Tour's new FedEx Cup

BY STEPHEN CANNELLA

HOW LONG DOES IT TAKE to reinvigorate a sport? In the case of the PGA Tour, the answer appears to be about 10 months, the time that elapsed between Adam Scott's victory at the 2006 season-ending Tour Championship at East Lake Golf Club in Atlanta and Tiger Woods's triumph at the same event and course on Sept. 16, 2007. When Scott hoisted his trophy in '06, Woods (officially) and the Tour (effectively) were well into their winter vacations. Few of the game's top players bothered to show up in Atlanta (both Woods and Phil Mickelson blew it off) and, with the year's major championships distant memories and Woods having long since locked up 2006 Player of the Year honors and the top spot on the money list, the event lacked meaning for fans and incentive for players. The PGA Tour, as usual, ended its year with a whimper, not a bang.

Fast forward to September of '07: Thanks to the inaugural Fedex Cup playoff, drama—and competitive golf—were still alive and well long after the year's final major, the PGA Championship, had been played. The outcome of the FedEx Cup was predictable; Woods locked down the title, and an $11.26 million payday, with an eight-stroke victory at East Lake. But the four-event FedEx playoff was a shot in the arm for a Tour that had traditionally begun drifting toward hibernation immediately after the year's final major. "I think, overall, the FedEx was a success," said Woods, whose four-round total of 257 at East Lake was the third-lowest in Tour history. "I think there needs to be some tweaks, but overall it provided a lot of drama toward the end of the season, especially post-PGA when most of the guys [used to] shut it down."

Despite varied complaints about logistics, the points system used to tabulate FedEx rankings and the way prize money was disbursed (most of it was deposited, tax free, into players' retirement accounts), most players echoed Woods's sentiment that the Cup added sizzle to the Tour's stretch run. The rank-and-file reaction to the Cup might have been more enthusiastic if Woods hadn't turned the playoff into little more than a race for second place. Woods blitzed the rest of the Tour with a 2007 finish spectacular even by his standards. In August he won the Bridgestone Invitational by eight strokes and followed with an efficient victory at the PGA Championship. (His second-round 63, shot in scorching heat at Southern Hills Country Club in Tulsa, Okla., tied the lowest score in major-championship history.) A few weeks later

No. 1-ranked Lorena Ochoa claimed her first career major in 2007, winning the Women's British Open on the Old Course at St. Andrew's.

Woods shot another 63 en route to a run-away win at the BMW Championship, the third of the four FedEx Cup events.

Woods's Tour Championship title the following week gave him 61 career victories, one short of Arnold Palmer on the career list, a feat even more impressive once it's placed in proper perspective. Palmer was 44 and had played more than 450 events when he won his 62nd tournament. Woods notched his 61st in his 216th start, at age 31. In his 10th season as a pro, Woods shattered any conceivable doubts that he is the greatest golfer of all time—and left his contemporaries equal parts amazed and demoralized. "You sit back and think to yourself, How does that happen?" Woods's final-round playing partner, Steve Stricker, said after seeing Tiger's magic firsthand at the Championship. "It gets to you after a while."

Still, before Woods's blistering finish to 2007, there were whispers that there might be chinks in his armor. They started at the Masters, where Woods finished second, two shots behind first-time major winner Zach Johnson. While Woods shot even-par on a blustery Masters Sunday, Johnson shot three-under and coolly manipulated a course that had stumped most of his opponents. (In the first round there were 12 rounds shot in the 80s and just nine under par, and a mere two eagles were made all day.) Unseasonably cold weather left the Augusta National course dry and its greens rock-hard throughout the tournament, conditions that benefited Johnson, a 31-year-old PGA Tour grinder from Cedar Rapids, Iowa, with a masterful short game. Johnson's conservative style and skill on the greens helped him finish the final round with a 69 and a two-stroke lead over Woods, who had two holes to play. As Woods, who had briefly held the lead earlier in the round, walked to his ball on the 17th fairway, Johnson chatted in the locker room with tennis great Boris Becker. "My legs are numb," Johnson told him. "I'm not sure

RICHARD MARTIN-ROBERTS/GETTY IMAGES

they're still attached to my body."

Woods missed an approach on 18 that would have given him an eagle and forced a playoff, and Johnson's wobbly legs were soon taking him to be fitted for a green jacket. It was the start of a career year for Johnson, who finished seventh in the FedEx Cup standings and eighth on the Tour money list. After clinching the green jacket, the humble Johnson—his 289 was the highest winning score in Masters history—said he was "very privileged, very honored," to have survived one of the most difficult Masters ever. It was, he said, "very surreal."

Johnson's victory was a surprise, but not as surreal as Woods's frittering away of a second straight major two months later, at the U.S. Open at Oakmont Country Club.

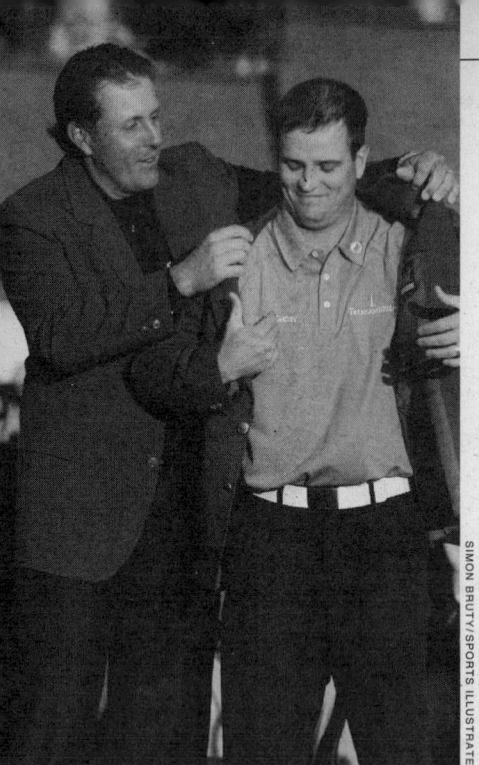

SIMON BRUTY/SPORTS ILLUSTRATED

pointed. Before the Open, one of Woods's rivals, Rory Sabbatini, said he liked the "new Tiger" because "he's more beatable now than ever." Woods's second straight Sunday fall in a major suggested Sabbatini might be on to something.

Woods's major struggles continued at the British Open at Carnoustie (he finished tied for 12th), but the tournament will be remembered for another, more spectacular final-round collapse. Spain's Sergio Garcia dominated the first three rounds of the Open, leading after each day and carrying a three-stroke advantage into Sunday. Ireland's Padraig Harrington—like Garcia, a contender for the unenviable title of Best Golfer Never to Win a Major—entered the final round as an afterthought, six shots back. But Garcia let the field back into the tournament with three bogeys in four holes on the front nine. He continued to struggle, but could have clinched the claret jug with a 10-foot putt on the final hole of the tournament, which Harrington had double-bogeyed. Instead Garcia whiffed on his putt, forcing a playoff which the Irishman won by a stroke. It was an excruciating loss for Garcia, reminiscent of the collapse by France's Jean Van de Velde on the same course at the 1999 British Open.

Woods rebounded to win the PGA Championship, his 13th Grand Slam championship, tying him with Bobby Jones on the career list and leaving him just five short of Jack Nicklaus's mark of 18. Woods followed his FedEx Cup rampage with a solid performance in the Presidents Cup, helping the U.S. to a convincing win over the International team at Royal Montreal Golf Club. The Americans were captained by Nicklaus, a fact that solidified Woods's link to the greats that came before him. "It's always great to see him, great to have him around," Woods said. "He's the greatest player of all time." Despite his struggles early in 2007, Woods may have the better claim to that throne.

The beneficiary this time was Argentina's Angel Cabrera, a 37-year-old veteran of the European Tour who entered the Open without a victory in a major. Cabrera shot a sizzling 69 in the final round, but this Open will be remembered most as one that Woods let get away. He was tied for the lead entering the third hole on Sunday, but a double bogey on No. 3 sent him spiraling into eighth place. He had regained a share of the lead by the eight hole, but a bogey on 11, a missed birdie opportunity on the par-3 13th and pars on 17 and 18 left him tied for second place with Jim Furyk, a stroke behind Cabrera.

The questions for the fun-loving Cabrera afterward centered on what he would drink to toast his first win in the U.S. and the first U.S. Open title by a South American. "Everything," said his lifelong friend and agent Manuel Tagle. "Beer, wine, his favorite Italian liqueur, Fernet Blanca...." The questions for Woods, once the sport's most feared Sunday closer, were more

Men's Majors

The Masters
Augusta National GC (par 72; 7,445 yds);
Augusta, Ga., April 5–8, 2007

Player	Score	Earnings ($)
Zach Johnson	71-73-76-69--289	1,305,000
Tiger Woods	73-74-72-72--291	541,333
Retief Goosen	76-76-70-69--291	541,333
Rory Sabbatini	73-76-73-69--291	541,333
Justin Rose	69-75-75-73--292	275,500
Jerry Kelly	75-69-78-70--292	275,500
Stuart Appleby	75-70-73-75--293	233,812
Padraig Harrington	77-68-75-73--293	233,812
David Toms	70-78-74-72--294	210,250
Vaughn Taylor	71-72-77-75--295	181,250
Luke Donald	73-74-75-73--295	181,250
Paul Casey	79-68-77-71--295	181,250
Jim Furyk	75-71-76-74--296	135,937
Tim Clark	71-71-80-74--296	135,937
Vijay Singh	73-82-79-73--296	135,937
Ian Poulter	75-75-76-70--296	135,937
Henrik Stenson	72-76-77-72--297	108,750
Tom Pernice Jr.	75-72-79-71--297	108,750
Stewart Cink	77-75-75-70--297	108,750
Lucas Glove	74-71-79-74--298	84,462
Mark Calcavecchia	76-71-78-73--298	84,462
John Rollins	77-74-76-71--298	84,462
Mike Weir	75-72-80-71--298	84,462

U.S. Open
Oakmont CC (par 70; 7,355 yds);
Oakmont, Pa., June 14–17, 2007

Player	Score	Earnings ($)
Angel Cabrera	69-71-76-69--285	1,260,000
Jim Furyk	71-75-70-70--286	611,336
Tiger Woods	71-74-69-72--286	611,336
Niclas Fasth	71-71-75-70--287	325,923
David Toms	72-72-73-72--289	248,948
Bubba Watson	70-71-74-74--289	248,948
Nick Dougherty	68-77-74-71--290	194,245
Jerry Kelly	74-71-73-72--290	194,245
Scott Verplank	73-71-74-72--290	194,245
Stephen Ames	73-69-73-76--291	154,093
Paul Casey	77-66-72-76--291	154,093
Justin Rose	71-71-73-76--291	154,093
Aaron Baddeley	72-70-70-80--292	124,706
Lee Janzen	73-73-73-73--292	124,706
Hunter Mahan	73-74-72-73--292	124,706
Steve Stricker	75-73-68-76--292	124,706
Jeff Brehaut	73-75-70-75--293	102,536
Tim Clark	72-76-71-74--293	102,536
Carl Pettersson	72-72-75-74--293	102,536
Anthony Kim	74-73-80-67--294	86,200
Vijay Singh	71-77-70-76--294	86,200
Mike Weir	74-72-73-75--294	86,200

British Open
Carnoustie GC (par 71; 7,112 yds);
Carnoustie, Scotland, July 19–22, 2007

Player	Score	Earnings ($)
*Padraig Harrington	69-73-68-67--277	1,542,450
Sergio Garcia	65-71-68-73--277	925,470
Andres Romero	71-70-70-67--278	596,414
Ernie Els	72-70-68-69--279	411,320
Richard Green	72-73-70-64--279	411,320
Stewart Cink	69-73-68-70--280	299,235
Hunter Mahan	73-73-69-65--280	299,235
K. J. Choi	69-69-72-71--281	194,863
Ben Curtis	72-74-70-65--281	194,863
Steve Stricker	71-72-64-74--281	194,863
Mike Weir	71-68-72-70--281	194,863
Markus Brier	68-75-70-69--282	120,458
Paul Broadhurst	71-71-68-72--282	120,458
Pelle Edberg	72-73-67-70--282	120,458
Jim Furyk	70-70-71-71--282	120,458
Miguel Jimenez	69-70-72-71--282	120,458
Justin Rose	75-70-67-70--282	120,458
Tiger Woods	69-74-69-70--282	120,458
Paul McGinley	67-75-68-73--283	94,603
Rich Beem	70-73-69-72--284	86,377
Zach Johnson	73-73-68-70--284	86,377
Pat Perez	73-70-71-70--284	86,377

PGA Championship
Southern Hills CC (par 70; 7,131 yds)
Tulsa, Okla., August 9–12, 2007

Player	Score	Earnings ($)
Tiger Woods	73-63-69-69--272	1,260,000
Woody Austin	68-70-69-67--274	756,000
Ernie Els	72-68-69-66--275	476,000
Arron Oberholser	68-72-70-69--279	308,000
John Senden	69-70-69-71--279	308,000
Simon Dyson	73-71-72-64--280	227,500
Trevor Immelman	75-70-66-69--280	227,500
Geoff Ogilvy	69-68-74-69--280	227,500
Scott Verplank	70-66-74-71--281	170,333
Kevin Sutherland	73-69-68-71--281	170,333
Boo Weekley	76-69-65-71--281	170,333
Stuart Appleby	72-70-70-69--282	119,833
Anders Hansen	71-71-71-69--282	119,833
Stephen Ames	71-71-68-72--282	119,833
K.J. Choi	71-71-68-72--282	119,833
Justin Rose	70-73-70-69--282	119,833
Adam Scott	72-68-70-72--282	119,833
Ken Duke	73-71-69-71--284	81,600
Joe Durant	71-73-70-70--284	81,600
Hunter Mahan	71-73-72-68--284	81,600
Pat Perez	70-69-77-68--284	81,600
Brandt Snedeker	74-71-69-70--284	81,600

*won in playoff

Late 2006 PGA Tour Events

Tournament	Final Round	Winner	Score/ Under Par	Earnings ($)
Chrysler Classic of Greensboro	Oct 8	Davis Love II	272/-16	900,000
Frys.com Open	Oct 15	Troy Matteson	265/-22	720,000
Funai Classic at Walt Disney World	Oct 22	Joe Durant	263/-25	828,000
Chrysler Championship	Oct 29	K.J. Choi	271/-13	954,000
The Tour Championship	Nov 5	Adam Scott	269/-11	1,170,000

2007 PGA Tour Events

Tournament	Final Round	Winner	Score/ Under Par	Earnings ($)
Mercedes Championships	Jan 7	Vijay Singh	278/-14	1,100,000
Sony Open in Hawaii	Jan 14	Paul Goydos	266/-14	936,000
Bob Hope Chrysler Classic	Jan 21	Charley Hoffman	343/-17†	900,000
Buick Invitational	Jan 28	Tiger Woods	273/-15	936,000
FBR Open	Feb 4	Aaron Baddeley	263/-21	1,080,000
AT&T Pebble Beach National Pro-Am	Feb 11	Phil Mickelson	268/-20	990,000
Nissan Open	Feb 18	Charles Howell III	268/-16	936,000
WGC Match Play Championship	Feb 25	Henrik Stenson	2&1	1,350,000
Mayakoba Classic at Riviera Maya	Feb 25	Fred Funk	266/-14	630,000
Honda Classic	Mar 4	Mark Wilson	275/-5	990,000
PODS Championship	Mar 11	Mark Calcavecchia	274/-10	954,000
Arnold Palmer Invitational	Mar 18	Vijay Singh	272/-8	990,000
WGC-CA Championship	Mar 25	Tiger Woods	278/-10	1,350,000
Shell Houston Open	Apr 1	Adam Scott	271/-17	990,000
The Masters	Apr 8	Zach Johnson	289/+1	1,305,000
Verizon Heritage	Apr 15	Boo Weekley	270/-14	972,000
Zurich Classic of New Orleans	Apr 22	Nick Watney	273/-15	1,098,000
EDS Byron Nelson Classic	Apr 29	Scott Verplank	267/-13	1,134,000
Wachovia Championship	May 6	Tiger Woods	275/-13	1,134,000
The Players Championship	May 13	Phil Mickelson	277/-11	1,620,000
AT&T Classic	May 20	Zach Johnson	273/-15	972,000
Crowne Plaza Invitational at Colonial	May 27	Rory Sabbatini	266/-14	1,080,000
Memorial Tournament	June 3	K.J. Choi	271/-17	1,080,000
St. Jude Championship	June 10	Woody Austin	267/-13	1,080,000
U.S. Open Championship	June 17	Angel Cabrera	285/+5	1,260,000
Travelers Championship	June 24	Hunter Mahan	265/-15	1,080,000
Buick Open	July 1	Brian Bateman	273/-15	882,000
AT&T National	July 8	K.J. Choi	271/-9	1,080,000
John Deere Classic	July 15	Jonathan Byrd	266/-18	738,000
British Open	July 22	Padraig Harrington	277/-7	1,542,000
U.S. Bank Championship	July 22	Joe Ogilvie	266/-14	720,000
Canadian Open	July 29	Jim Furyk	268/-16	900,000
WGC Bridgestone Invitational	Aug 5	Tiger Woods	272/-8	1,350,000
Reno-Tahoe Open	Aug 5	Steve Flesch	273/-15	540,000
PGA Championship	Aug 12	Tiger Woods	272/-8	1,260,000
*Wyndham Championship	Aug 19	Brandt Snedeker	266/-22	900,000
*Barclays Classic	Aug 26	Steve Stricker	268/-16	1,260,000
*Deutsche Bank Championship	Sept 3	Phil Mickelson	268/-16	1,260,000
*BMW Championship	Sept 9	Tiger Woods	260/-20	1,260,000
*TOUR Championship	Sept 16	Tiger Woods	257/-23	1,260,000
Turning Stone Championship	Sept 23	Steve Flesch	270/-18	1,080,000
Viking Classic	Sept 30	Chad Campbell	275/-13	630,000

† Five-round tournament.

*Events part of five-week FedEx Cup, the PGA Tour's playoff format.

Kraft Nabisco Championship

Mission Hills CC; (par 72; 6,673 yds)
Rancho Mirage, Calif., March 29–April 1, 2007

Player	Score	Earnings ($)
Morgan Pressel	74-72-70-69--285	300,000
Catriona Matthew	70-73-72-71--286	140,945
Brittany Lincicome	72-71-71-72--286	140,945
Suzann Pettersen	72-69-71-74--286	140,945
†Stacy Lewis	71-73-73-70--287	N/A
Shi Hyun Ahn	68-73-74-72--287	69,688
Stacy Prammanasudh	76-70-70-71--287	69,688
Meaghan Francella	72-72-69-74--287	69,688
Maria Hjorth	70-73-72-73--288	50,114
Angela Stanford	72-75-73-69--289	41,340
Lorena Ochoa	69-71-77-72--289	41,340
Se Ri Pak	72-70-70-77--289	41,340
Jee Young Lee	70-77-71-72--290	34,321
Sarah Lee	72-74-70-74--290	34,321
Ji-Yai Shin	76-72-71-72--291	28,651
Brittany Lang	71-73-75-72--291	28,651
Ai Miyazato	76-73-69-73--291	28,651
Paula Creamer	73-67-73-78--291	28,651
Moira Dunn	76-73-72-71--292	25,108
Karrie Webb	70-77-73-73--293	22,881
Cristie Kerr	75-73-72-73--293	22,881
Laura Davies	74-73-73-73--293	22,881
Sherri Steinhauer	71-78-70-74--293	22,881

†Amateur.

U.S. Women's Open

Pine Needles Glof Club; (par 71; 6,664 yds)
Southern Pines, N.C., June 28-July 1, 2007

Player	Score	Earnings ($)
Cristie Kerr	71-72-66-70--279	560,000
Angela Park	68-69-74-70--281	271,022
Lorena Ochoa	71-71-68-71--281	271,022
Se Ri Pak	74-72-68-68--282	130,549
In-Bee Park	69-73-71-69--282	130,549
Ji-Yai Shin	70-69-71-74--284	103,581
Jee Young Lee	72-71-71-71--285	93,031
Mi Hyun Kim	71-75-70-70--286	82,464
Jeong Jang	72-71-70-73--286	82,464
Ai Miyazato	73-73-72-69--287	66,177
Kyeong Bee	74-71-72-70--287	66,177
Julieta Granada	70-69-75-73--287	66,177
Morgan Pressel	71-70-69-77--287	66,177
Brittany Lincicome	71-74-71-72--288	55,032
Joo Mi Kim	70-73-70-75--288	55,032
Jimin Kang	73-73-73-70--289	44,129
Paula Creamer	72-74-71-72--289	44,129
Angela Stanford	72-71-73-73--289	44,129
Catriona Matthew	75-67-74-73--289	44,129
Birdie Kim	73-70-71-75--289	44,129
Amy Hung	70-69-75-75--289	44,129

LPGA Championship

Bulle Rock GC; (par 72; 6,596 yds)
Havre de Grace, Md., June 7-10, 2007

Player	Score	Earnings ($)
Suzann Pettersen	69-67-71-67--274	300,000
Karrie Webb	68-69-71-67--275	179,038
Na On Min	71-70-65-70--276	129,880
Lindsey Wright	71-70-71-66--278	100,473
Angela Park	67-73-68-71--279	80,869
Paula Creamer	71-68-73-68--280	53,422
Sophie Gustafson	70-71-71-68--280	53,422
Brittany Lincicome	69-69-73-69--280	53,422
Lorena Ochoa	71-71-69-69--280	53,422
Catriona Matthew	71-69-74-67--281	57,464
Sarah Lee	71-69-72-69--281	35,730
Jee Young Lee	71-72-68-70--281	35,730
Nicole Castrale	70-73-68-70--281	35,730
Morgan Pressel	68-71-70-73--282	30,192
Mi Hyun Kim	70-73-71-69--283	26,925
Annika Sorenstam	70-69-73-71--283	26,925
Stacy Prammanasudh	68-74-71-70--283	26,925
Cristie Kerr	75-70-73-66--284	23,396
Mhairi McKay	71-69-74-70--284	23,396
Siew-Ai Lim	72-69-70-73--284	23,396
Juli Inkster	73-73-73-66--285	20,585
Shi Hyun Ahn	71-73-71-70--285	20,585
Meaghan Francella	72-75-68-70--285	20,585
In-Kyung Klm	73-70-71-71--285	20,585

Women's British Open

Old Courses, St. Andrews; (par 73; 6,638 yds)
St. Andrews, Scotland, August 2-5, 2007

Player	Score	Earnings ($)
Lorena Ochoa	67-73-73-74--287	320,512
Maria Hjorth	72-73-75-71--291	170,272
Jee Young Lee	75-73-72-71--291	170,272
Reilley Rankin	73-74-74-71--292	110,176
Eun-Hee Ji	73-71-77-72--293	84,135
Se Ri Pak	73-73-75-72--293	84,135
Miki Saiki	76-70-81-67--294	61,098
Paula Creamer	73-75-74-72--294	61,098
Catriona Matthew	73-68-80-73--294	61,098
Linda Wessberg	74-73-72-75--295	40,665
Mhairi McKay	75-74-79-67--295	40,665
Yuri Fudoh	74-69-81-71--295	40,665
In-Bee Park	69-79-76-71--295	40,665
Na On Min	72-75-75-73--295	40,665
Brittany Lincicome	71-76-75-73--295	40,665
Gloria Park	74-75-76-71--296	28,128
†Melissa Reid	73-75-76-72--296	N/A
V. Lagoutte-Clement	72-73-78-73--296	28,128
Becky Brewerton	74-75-74-73--296	28,128
Stacy Prammanasudh	74-76-72-74--296	28,128
Annika Sorenstam	72-71-77-76--296	28,128
Karine Icher	72-71-77-76--296	28,128

†Amateur.

Late 2006 LPGA Tour Events

Tournament	Final Round	Winner	Score/ Under Par	Earnings ($)
Longs Drug Challenge	Sept 24	Karrie Webb	273/-15	165,000
Corona Morelia Championship	Oct 8	Lorena Ochoa	272/-20	150,000
Samsung World Championship	Oct 15	Lorena Ochoa	272/-16	218,750
Honda LPGA Thailand	Oct 22	Hee-Won Han	202/-14	195,000
Hana Bank Championship	Oct 29	Jin Joo Hong	205/-11	202,500
Mizuno Classic	Nov 5	Karrie Webb	202/-14	180,000
LPGA Tournament of Champions	Nov 12	Lorena Ochoa	267/-21	150,000
ADT Championship	Nov 19	Julieta Granada	276/-4	1,000,000

2007 LPGA Tour Events

Tournament	Final Round	Winner	Score/ Under Par	Earnings ($)
SBS Open	Feb 17	Paula Creamer	207/-19	165,000
Fields Open	Feb. 24	Stacy Prammanasudh	202/-14	180,000
MasterCard Classic	Mar 11	Megan Francella	205/-11	180,000
Safeway International	Mar 25	Lorena Ochoa	270/-18	225,000
Kraft Nabisco Championship	Apr 1	Morgan Pressel	285/-3	300,000
Ginn Open	Apr 15	Brittany Lincicome	278/-10	390,000
Corona Morelia Championship	Apr 29	Silvia Cavalleri	272/-20	195,000
SemGroup Championship	May 6	Mi Hyun Kim	210/-3	210,000
Michelob Ultra Open	May 13	Suzann Pettersen	274/-10	330,000
Sybase Classic	May 20	Lorena Ochoa	270/-18	210,000
LPGA Corning Classic	May 27	Young Kim	268/-20	195,000
GINN Tribute	June 3	Nicole Castrale	279/-9	390,000
McDonald's LPGA Championship	June 10	Suzann Pettersen	274/-14	300,000
Wegman's Rochester LPGA	June 24	Lorena Ochoa	280/-8	270,000
U.S. Women's Open	July 1	Cristie Kerr	279/-5	560,000
Jamie Farr Owens Corning	July 15	Se Rik Pak	267/-17	195,000
HSBC Women's World Match Play	July 22	Seon Hwa Lee	2&1	500,000
Evian Masters	July 29	Natalie Gulbis*	284/-4	450,000
Ricoh Women's British Open.	Aug 5	Lorena Ochoa	287/-5	320,080
Canadian Women's Open	Aug 19	Lorena Ochoa	268/-16	337,500
Safeway Classic	Aug 26	Lorena Ochoa	204/-12	255,000
State Farm Classic	Sept 2	Sherri Steinhauer	271/-17	195,000
†NW Arkansas Classic	Sept 9	Stacy Lewis	65/-7	
Navistar Classic	Sept 30	Maria Hjorth	274/-14	195,000

* Won playoff.
† Due to rain, tournament was shortened to 18 holes and stats and earnings will not count toward season total.

Late 2006 Champions Tour Events

Tournament	Final Round	Winner	Score/ Under Par	Earnings ($)
SAS Championship	Oct 8	Tom Jenkins	134/-10	300,000
Administaff Small Business Classic	Oct 15	Jay Haas	128/-16	240,000
AT&T Championship	Oct 22	Fred Funk	201/-12	240,000
Charles Schwab Cup Championship	Oct 29	Jim Thorpe	271/-17	440,000

2007 Champions Tour Events

Tournament	Final Round	Winner	Score/ Under Par	Earnings ($)
MasterCard Championship	Jan 21	Hale Irwin	193/-23	290,000
Turtle Bay Championship	Jan 28	Fred Funk	193/-23	240,000
Allianz Championship	Feb 11	Mark James	201/-15	240,000
Outback Steakhouse Pro-Am	Feb 18	Tom Watson	209/-4	240,000
ACE Group Classic	Feb 25	Bobby Wadkins	201/-15	240,000
Toshiba Senior Classic	Mar 11	Jay Haas	213/-9	247,000
AT&T Classic	Mar 18	Tom Purtzer*	194/-19	240,000
Ginn Championship	Apr 1	Keith Fergus	204/-12	375,000
Liberty Mutual Legends of Golf	April 22	Jay Haas*	207/-9	395,000
FedEx Kinko's Classic	May 7	Scott Hoch	201/-15	240,000
Regions Charity Classic	May 20	Brad Bryant*	204/-12	240,000
Senior PGA Championship	May 27	Denis Watson	279/-9	360,000
The Boeing Championship	June 3	Loren Roberts	197/-16	247,000
Principal Charity Classic	June 10	Jay Haas	201/-12	240,000
Bank of America Championship	June 24	Jay Haas	203/-13	247,500
Commerce Bank Championship	July 1	Lonnie Nielsen	199/-14	225,000
U.S. Senior Open	July 8	Brad Bryant	282/-6	470,000
Dick's Sporting Goods Open	July 15	R.W. Eaks	199/-17	240,000
Senior British Open	July 29	Tom Watson	284/E	320,176
3M Championship	Aug 5	D.A. Weibring	198/-18	262,500
Jeld-Wen Tradition	Aug 19	Mark McNulty	272/-16	390,000
Boeing Greater Seattle Classic	Aug 26	Denis Watson*	207/-9	240,000
First Tee Open at Pebble Beach	Sept 2	Gil Morgan	202/-14	300,000
Greater Hickory Classic	Sept 16	R.W. Eaks	199/-17	240,000
SAS Championship	Sept 23	Mark Wiebe	198/-18	300,000

*Won playoff.

Tournament	Final Round	Winner	Score	Runner-Up
Women's Amateur Public Links	June 23	Mina Harigae	4 & 3	Stephanie Fleet
Men's Amateur Public Links	July 14	Colt Knost	6 & 4	Cody Paladino
Girls' Junior Amateur	July 28	Kristen Park	4 & 3	Ayaka Kaneko
Boys' Junior Amateur	July 28	Corey Whitsett	8 & 7	Anthony Paolucci
Women's Amateur	Aug 12	Maria Uribe	1 up	Amanda Blumenhurst
Men's Amateur	Aug 26	Colt Knost	2 & 1	Michael Thompson
Men's Mid-Amateur	Sep 6	Stan Lee	4 & 3	Sam Farlow

*Results through 10/01/07.

International Results

Tournament	Final Round	Winner	Score	Runner-Up
Walker Cup	Sept 9	United States	12½–11½	Great Britain/Ireland
Presidents Cup	Sept 30	United States	19½–14½	International

PGA Tour Final 2006 Money Leaders

Name	Events	Best Finish	Scoring Average*	Money ($)
Tiger Woods	15	1 (8)	68.11	9,941,563
Jim Furyk	24	1 (2)	68.86	7,213,316
Adam Scott	19	1 (1)	68.95	4,978,858
Vijay Singh	27	1 (1)	69.62	4,602,416
Geoff Ogilvy	20	1 (1)	70.29	4,354,969
Phil Mickelson	19	1 (2)	69.50	4,256,505
Trevor Immelman	24	1 (1)	69.51	3,844,189
Stuart Appleby	23	1 (2)	70.25	3,470,457
Luke Donald	18	1 (1)	69.17	3,177,408
Brett Wetterich	25	1 (1)	70.72	3,023,185

*Adjusted for average score of field in each tournament entered.

LPGA Tour Final 2006 Money Leaders

Name	Events	Best Finish	Scoring Average	Money ($)
Lorena Ochoa	25	1 (6)	69.24	2,592,872
Karrie Webb	21	1 (5)	70.11	2,090,113
Annika Sorenstam	20	1 (3)	69.82	1,971,741
Julieta Granada	30	1 (1)	71.33	1,633,586
Cristie Kerr	26	1 (3)	70.07	1,578,362
Mi Hyun Kim	30	1 (2)	71.02	1,332,274
Juli Inkster	21	1 (1)	70.48	1,326,442
Jeong Jang	27	1 (1)	70.81	1,151,070
Hee-Won Han	27	1 (2)	70.78	1,147,651
Pat Hurst	24	1 (1)	71.20	1,128,662

Champions Tour Final 2006 Money Leaders

Name	Events	Best Finish	Scoring Average	Money ($)
Jay Haas	21	1 (4)	69.07	2,420,227
Loren Roberts	21	1 (4)	69.01	2,365,395
Brad Bryant	20	1 (2)	69.71	1,692,417
Tom Kite	25	1 (2)	70.29	1,643,348
Gil Morgan	27	1 (1)	69.99	1,525,050
Scott Simpson	27	1 (1)	70.64	1,340,676
Jim Thorpe	26	1 (1)	70.56	1,296,784
Tom Jenkins	27	1 (1)	70.38	1,287,666
Bobby Wadkins	25	1 (2)	71.26	1,193,173
David Edwards	20	1 (1)	69.94	1,191,086

Men's Golf

THE MAJOR TOURNAMENTS
The Masters

Year	Winner	Score	Runner-Up
1934	Horton Smith	284	Craig Wood
1935	Gene Sarazen* (144) (only 36-hole playoff)	282	Craig Wood (149)
1936	Horton Smith	285	Harry Cooper
1937	Byron Nelson	283	Ralph Guldahl
1938	Henry Picard	285	Ralph Guldahl / Harry Cooper
1939	Ralph Guldahl	279	Sam Snead
1940	Jimmy Demaret	280	Lloyd Mangrum
1941	Craig Wood	280	Byron Nelson
1942	Byron Nelson* (69)	280	Ben Hogan (70)
1943–45	No tournament		
1946	Herman Keiser	282	Ben Hogan
1947	Jimmy Demaret	281	Byron Nelson / Frank Stranahan
1948	Claude Harmon	279	Cary Middlecoff
1949	Sam Snead	282	Johnny Bulla / Lloyd Mangrum
1950	Jimmy Demaret	283	Jim Ferrier
1951	Ben Hogan	280	Skee Riegel
1952	Sam Snead	286	Jack Burke Jr.
1953	Ben Hogan	274	Ed Oliver Jr.
1954	Sam Snead* (70)	289	Ben Hogan (71)
1955	Cary Middlecoff	279	Ben Hogan
1956	Jack Burke Jr.	289	Ken Venturi
1957	Doug Ford	282	Sam Snead
1958	Arnold Palmer	284	Doug Ford / Fred Hawkins
1959	Art Wall Jr.	284	Cary Middlecoff
1960	Arnold Palmer	282	Ken Venturi
1961	Gary Player	280	Charles R. Coe / Arnold Palmer
1962	Arnold Palmer* (68)	280	Gary Player (71) / D. Finsterwald (77)
1963	Jack Nicklaus	286	Tony Lema
1964	Arnold Palmer	276	Dave Marr / Jack Nicklaus
1965	Jack Nicklaus	271	Arnold Palmer / Gary Player
1966	Jack Nicklaus* (70)	288	Tommy Jacobs (72) / Gay Brewer Jr. (78)
1967	Gay Brewer Jr.	280	Bobby Nichols
1968	Bob Goalby	277	Roberto DeVicenzo
1969	George Archer	281	Billy Casper / George Knudson / Tom Weiskopf
1970	Billy Casper* (69)	279	Gene Littler (74)
1971	Charles Coody	279	Johnny Miller / Jack Nicklaus
1972	Jack Nicklaus	286	Bruce Crampton / Bobby Mitchell / Tom Weiskopf
1973	Tommy Aaron	283	J.C. Snead
1974	Gary Player	278	Tom Weiskopf / Dave Stockton
1975	Jack Nicklaus	276	Johnny Miller / Tom Weiskopf
1976	Ray Floyd	271	Ben Crenshaw
1977	Tom Watson	276	Jack Nicklaus
1978	Gary Player	277	Hubert Green / Rod Funseth / Tom Watson
1979	Fuzzy Zoeller* (4–3)†	280	Ed Sneed (4–4) / Tom Watson (4–4)
1980	Seve Ballesteros	275	Gibby Gilbert / Jack Newton
1981	Tom Watson	280	Johnny Miller / Jack Nicklaus
1982	Craig Stadler* (4)	284	Dan Pohl (5)
1983	Seve Ballesteros	280	Ben Crenshaw / Tom Kite
1984	Ben Crenshaw	277	Tom Watson
1985	Bernhard Langer	282	Curtis Strange / Seve Ballesteros / Ray Floyd
1986	Jack Nicklaus	279	Greg Norman / Tom Kite
1987	Larry Mize* (4–3)	285	Seve Ballesteros (5) / Greg Norman (4–4)
1988	Sandy Lyle	281	Mark Calcavecchia
1989	Nick Faldo* (5–3)	283	Scott Hoch (5–4)
1990	Nick Faldo* (4–4)	278	Ray Floyd (4–x)
1991	Ian Woosnam	277	José María Olazábal
1992	Fred Couples	275	Ray Floyd
1993	Bernhard Langer	277	Chip Beck
1994	José María Olazábal	279	Tom Lehman
1995	Ben Crenshaw	274	Davis Love III
1996	Nick Faldo	276	Greg Norman
1997	Tiger Woods	270	Tom Kite
1998	Mark O'Meara	279	David Duval / Fred Couples
1999	José María Olazábal	280	Davis Love III
2000	Vijay Singh	278	Ernie Els
2001	Tiger Woods	272	David Duval
2002	Tiger Woods	276	Retief Goosen
2003	Mike Weir	281	Len Mattiace
2004	Phil Mickelson	279	Ernie Els
2005	Tiger Woods	276	Chris DiMarco
2006	Phil Mickelson	281	Tim Clark
2007	Zach Johnson	289	Tiger Woods / Retief Goosen / Rory Sabbatini

*Winner in playoff. Playoff scores are in parentheses. †Playoff cut from 18 holes to sudden death.
Note: Played at Augusta National Golf Club, Augusta, GA.

United States Open Championship

Year	Winner	Score	Runner-Up	Site
1895	Horace Rawlins	†173	Willie Dunn	Newport GC, Newport, RI
1896	James Foulis	†152	Horace Rawlins	Shinnecock Hills GC, Southampton, NY
1897	Joe Lloyd	†162	Willie Anderson	Chicago GC, Wheaton, IL
1898	Fred Herd	328	Alex Smith	Myopia Hunt Club, Hamilton, MA
1899	Willie Smith	315	George Low Val Fitzjohn W.H. Way	Baltimore CC, Baltimore
1900	Harry Vardon	313	John H. Taylor	Chicago GC, Wheaton, IL
1901	Willie Anderson* (85)	331	Alex Smith (86)	Myopia Hunt Club, Hamilton, MA
1902	Laurie Auchterlonie	307	Stewart Gardner	Garden City GC, Garden City, NY
1903	Willie Anderson* (82)	307	David Brown (84)	Baltusrol GC, Springfield, NJ
1904	Willie Anderson	303	Gil Nicholls	Glen View Club, Golf, IL
1905	Willie Anderson	314	Alex Smith	Myopia Hunt Club, Hamilton, MA
1906	Alex Smith	295	Willie Smith	Onwentsia Club, Lake Forest, IL
1907	Alex Ross	302	Gil Nicholls	Philadelphia Cricket Club, Chestnut Hill, PA
1908	Fred McLeod* (77)	322	Willie Smith (83)	Myopia Hunt Club, Hamilton, MA
1909	George Sargent	290	Tom McNamara	Englewood GC, Englewood, NJ
1910	Alex Smith* (71)	298	John McDermott (75) Macdonald Smith (77)	Philadelphia Cricket Club, Chestnut Hill, PA
1911	John McDermott* (80)	307	Mike Brady (82) George Simpson (85)	Chicago GC, Wheaton, IL
1912	John McDermott	294	Tom McNamara	CC of Buffalo, Buffalo
1913	Francis Ouimet* (72)	304	Harry Vardon (77) Edward Ray (78)	The Country Club, Brookline, MA
1914	Walter Hagen	290	Chick Evans	Midlothian CC, Blue Island, IL
1915	Jerry Travers	297	Tom McNamara	Baltusrol GC, Springfield, NJ
1916	Chick Evans	286	Jock Hutchison	Minikahda Club, Minneapolis
1917–18	No tournament			
1919	Walter Hagen* (77)	301	Mike Brady (78)	Brae Burn CC, West Newton, MA
1920	Edward Ray	295	Harry Vardon Jack Burke Leo Diegel Jock Hutchison	Inverness CC, Toledo
1921	Jim Barnes	289	Walter Hagen Fred McLeod	Columbia CC, Chevy Chase, MD
1922	Gene Sarazen	288	John L. Black Bobby Jones	Skokie CC, Glencoe, IL
1923	Bobby Jones* (76)	296	Bobby Cruickshank (78)	Inwood CC, Inwood, NY
1924	Cyril Walker	297	Bobby Jones	Oakland Hills CC, Birmingham, MI
1925	W. MacFarlane* (75–72)	291	Bobby Jones (75–73)	Worcester CC, Worcester, MA
1926	Bobby Jones	293	Joe Turnesa	Scioto CC, Columbus, OH
1927	Tommy Armour* (76)	301	Harry Cooper (79)	Oakmont CC, Oakmont, PA
1928	Johnny Farrell* (143)	294	Bobby Jones (144)	Olympia Fields CC, Matteson, IL
1929	Bobby Jones* (141)	294	Al Espinosa (164)	Winged Foot GC, Mamaroneck, NY
1930	Bobby Jones	287	Macdonald Smith	Interlachen CC, Hopkins, MN
1931	Billy Burke* (149–148)	292	George Von Elm (149–149)	Inverness Club, Toledo
1932	Gene Sarazen	286	Phil Perkins Bobby Cruickshank	Fresh Meadows CC, Flushing, NY
1933	Johnny Goodman	287	Ralph Guldahl	North Shore CC, Glenview, IL
1934	Olin Dutra	293	Gene Sarazen	Merion Cricket Club, Ardmore, PA
1935	Sam Parks Jr.	299	Jimmy Thompson	Oakmont CC, Oakmont, PA
1936	Tony Manero	282	Harry Cooper	Baltusrol GC (Upper Course), Springfield, NJ
1937	Ralph Guldahl	281	Sam Snead	Oakland Hills CC, Birmingham, MI
1938	Ralph Guldahl	284	Dick Metz	Cherry Hills CC, Denver
1939	Byron Nelson* (68–70)	284	Craig Wood (68–73) Denny Shute (76)	Philadelphia CC, Philadelphia
1940	Lawson Little* (70)	287	Gene Sarazen (73)	Canterbury GC, Cleveland
1941	Craig Wood	284	Denny Shute	Colonial Club, Fort Worth
1942–45	No tournament			
1946	Lloyd Mangrum* (72–72)	284	Vic Ghezzi (72–73) Byron Nelson (72–73)	Canterbury GC, Cleveland
1947	Lew Worsham* (69)	282	Sam Snead (70)	St. Louis CC, Clayton, MO
1948	Ben Hogan	276	Jimmy Demaret	Riviera CC, Los Angeles
1949	Cary Middlecoff	286	Sam Snead Clayton Heafner	Medinah CC, Medinah, IL

United States Open Championship *(Cont.)*

Year	Winner	Score	Runner-Up	Site
1950	Ben Hogan* (69)	287	Lloyd Mangrum (73) George Fazio (75)	Merion GC, Ardmore, PA
1951	Ben Hogan	287	Clayton Heafner	Oakland Hills CC, Birmingham, MI
1952	Julius Boros	281	Ed Oliver	Northwood CC, Dallas
1953	Ben Hogan	283	Sam Snead	Oakmont CC, Oakmont, PA
1954	Ed Furgol	284	Gene Littler	Baltusrol GC (Lower Course), Springfield, NJ
1955	Jack Fleck* (69)	287	Ben Hogan (72)	Olympic Club (Lake Course), San Francisco
1956	Cary Middlecoff	281	Ben Hogan Julius Boros	Oak Hill CC, Rochester, NY
1957	Dick Mayer* (72)	282	Cary Middlecoff (79)	Inverness Club, Toledo
1958	Tommy Bolt	283	Gary Player	Southern Hills CC, Tulsa
1959	Billy Casper	282	Bob Rosburg	Winged Foot GC, Mamaroneck, NY
1960	Arnold Palmer	280	Jack Nicklaus	Cherry Hills CC, Denver
1961	Gene Littler	281	Bob Goalby Doug Sanders	Oakland Hills CC, Birmingham, MI
1962	Jack Nicklaus* (71)	283	Arnold Palmer (74)	Oakmont CC, Oakmont, PA
1963	Julius Boros* (70)	293	Jacky Cupit (73) Arnold Palmer (76)	The Country Club, Brookline, MA
1964	Ken Venturi	278	Tommy Jacobs	Congressional CC, Bethesda, MD
1965	Gary Player* (71)	282	Kel Nagle (74)	Bellerive CC, St. Louis
1966	Billy Casper* (69)	278	Arnold Palmer (73)	Olympic Club (Lake Course), San Francisco
1967	Jack Nicklaus	275	Arnold Palmer	Baltusrol GC (Lower Course), Springfield, NJ
1968	Lee Trevino	275	Jack Nicklaus	Oak Hill CC, Rochester, NY
1969	Orville Moody	281	Deane Beman Al Geiberger Bob Rosburg	Champions GC (Cypress Creek Course), Houston
1970	Tony Jacklin	281	Dave Hill	Hazeltine GC, Chaska, MN
1971	Lee Trevino* (68)	280	Jack Nicklaus (71)	Merion GC (East Course), Ardmore, PA
1972	Jack Nicklaus	290	Bruce Crampton	Pebble Beach GL, Pebble Beach, CA
1973	Johnny Miller	279	John Schlee	Oakmont CC, Oakmont, PA
1974	Hale Irwin	287	Forrest Fezler	Winged Foot GC, Mamaroneck, NY
1975	Lou Graham* (71)	287	John Mahaffey (73)	Medinah CC, Medinah, IL
1976	Jerry Pate	277	Tom Weiskopf Al Geiberger	Atlanta Athletic Club, Duluth, GA
1977	Hubert Green	278	Lou Graham	Southern Hills CC, Tulsa
1978	Andy North	285	Dave Stockton J.C. Snead	Cherry Hills CC, Denver
1979	Hale Irwin	284	Gary Player Jerry Pate	Inverness Club, Toledo
1980	Jack Nicklaus	272	Isao Aoki	Baltusrol GC (Lower Course), Springfield, NJ
1981	David Graham	273	George Burns Bill Rogers	Merion GC, Ardmore, PA
1982	Tom Watson	282	Jack Nicklaus	Pebble Beach GL, Pebble Beach, CA
1983	Larry Nelson	280	Tom Watson	Oakmont CC, Oakmont, PA
1984	Fuzzy Zoeller* (67)	276	Greg Norman (75)	Winged Foot GC, Mamaroneck, NY
1985	Andy North	279	Dave Barr T.C. Chen Denis Watson	Oakland Hills CC, Birmingham, MI
1986	Ray Floyd	279	Lanny Wadkins Chip Beck	Shinnecock Hills GC, Southampton, NY
1987	Scott Simpson	277	Tom Watson	Olympic Club (Lake Course), San Francisco
1988	Curtis Strange* (71)	278	Nick Faldo (75)	The Country Club, Brookline, MA
1989	Curtis Strange	278	Chip Beck Mark McCumber Ian Woosnam	Oak Hill CC, Rochester, NY
1990	Hale Irwin* (74) (3)	280	Mike Donald (74) (4)	Medinah CC, Medinah, IL
1991	Payne Stewart* (75)	282	Scott Simpson (77)	Hazeltine GC, Chaska, MN
1992	Tom Kite	285	Jeff Sluman	Pebble Beach GL, Pebble Beach, CA
1993	Lee Janzen	272	Payne Stewart	Baltusrol GC, Springfield, NJ
1994	Ernie Els*	279	Loren Roberts Colin Montgomerie	Oakmont CC, Oakmont, PA
1995	Corey Pavin	280	Greg Norman	Shinnecock Hills GC, Southampton, NY
1996	Steve Jones	278	Davis Love III Tom Lehman	Oakland Hills CC, Birmingham, MI
1997	Ernie Els	276	Colin Montgomerie	Congressional CC, Bethesda, MD
1998	Lee Janzen	280	Payne Stewart	The Olympic Club, San Francisco
1999	Payne Stewart	279	Phil Mickelson	Pinehurst Resort and CC, Pinehurst, NC

United States Open Championship (Cont.)

Year	Winner	Score	Runner-Up	Site
2000	Tiger Woods	272	Miguel Angel Jiménez	Pebble Beach GL, Pebble Beach, CA
			Ernie Els	
2001	Retief Goosen* (70)	276	Mark Brooks (72)	Southern Hills CC, Tulsa
2002	Tiger Woods	277	Phil Mickelson	Bethpage Black Course, Bethpage, NY
2003	Jim Furyk	272	Stephen Leaney	Olympia Fields CC, Olympia Fields, IL
2004	Retief Goosen	276	Phil Mickelson	Shinnecock Hills GC, Southampton, NY
2005	Michael Campbell	280	Tiger Woods	Pinehurst Resort and CC, Pinehurst, NC
2006	Geoff Ogilvy	285	Jim Furyk	Winged Foot GC, Mamaroneck, NY
			Colin Montgomerie	
			Phil Mickelson	
2007	Angel Cabrera	285	Jim Furyk	Oakmont CC, Oakmont, PA
			Tiger Woods	

*Winner in playoff. Playoff scores are in parentheses. The 1990 playoff went to one hole of sudden death after an 18-hole playoff. In the 1994 playoff, Montgomerie was eliminated after 18 playoff holes, and Els beat Roberts on the 20th.
†Before 1898, 36 holes. From 1898 on, 72 holes.

British Open

Year	Winner	Score	Runner-Up	Site
1860†	Willie Park	174	Tom Morris Sr.	Prestwick, Scotland
1861‡	Tom Morris Sr.	163	Willie Park	Prestwick, Scotland
1862	Tom Morris Sr.	163	Willie Park	Prestwick, Scotland
1863	Willie Park	168	Tom Morris Sr.	Prestwick, Scotland
1864	Tom Morris, Sr.	160	Andrew Strath	Prestwick, Scotland
1865	Andrew Strath	162	Willie Park	Prestwick, Scotland
1866	Willie Park	169	David Park	Prestwick, Scotland
1867	Tom Morris Sr.	170	Willie Park	Prestwick, Scotland
1868	Tom Morris Jr.	154	Tom Morris Sr.	Prestwick, Scotland
1869	Tom Morris Jr.	157	Tom Morris Sr.	Prestwick, Scotland
1870	Tom Morris Jr.	149	David Strath	Prestwick, Scotland
			Bob Kirk	
1871	No tournament			
1872	Tom Morris Jr.	166	David Strath	Prestwick, Scotland
1873	Tom Kidd	179	Jamie Anderson	St. Andrews, Scotland
1874	Mungo Park	159	No record	Musselburgh, Scotland
1875	Willie Park	166	Bob Martin	Prestwick, Scotland
1876	Bob Martin#	176	David Strath	St. Andrews, Scotland
1877	Jamie Anderson	160	Bob Pringle	Musselburgh, Scotland
1878	Jamie Anderson	157	Robert Kirk	Prestwick, Scotland
1879	Jamie Anderson	169	Andrew Kirkaldy	St. Andrews, Scotland
			James Allan	
1880	Robert Ferguson	162	No record	Musselburgh, Scotland
1881	Robert Ferguson	170	Jamie Anderson	Prestwick, Scotland
1882	Robert Ferguson	171	Willie Fernie	St. Andrews, Scotland
1883	Willie Fernie*	159	Robert Ferguson	Musselburgh, Scotland
1884	Jack Simpson	160	Douglas Rolland	Prestwick, Scotland
			Willie Fernie	
1885	Bob Martin	171	Archie Simpson	St. Andrews, Scotland
1886	David Brown	157	Willie Campbell	Musselburgh, Scotland
1887	Willie Park Jr.	161	Bob Martin	Prestwick, Scotland
1888	Jack Burns	171	Bernard Sayers	St. Andrews, Scotland
			David Anderson	
1889	Willie Park Jr.* (158)	155	Andrew Kirkaldy (163)	Musselburgh, Scotland
1890	John Ball	164	Willie Fernie	Prestwick, Scotland
1891	Hugh Kirkaldy	166	Andrew Kirkaldy	St. Andrews, Scotland
			Willie Fernie	
1892	Harold Hilton	**305	John Ball	Muirfield, Scotland
			Hugh Kirkaldy	
1893	William Auchterlonie	322	John E. Laidlay	Prestwick, Scotland
1894	John H. Taylor	326	Douglas Rolland	Royal St. George's, England
1895	John H. Taylor	322	Alexander Herd	St. Andrews, Scotland
1896	Harry Vardon* (157)	316	John H. Taylor (161)	Muirfield, Scotland
1897	Harold Hilton	314	James Braid	Hoylake, England
1898	Harry Vardon	307	Willie Park Jr.	Prestwick, Scotland
1899	Harry Vardon	310	Jack White	Royal St. George's, England
1900	John H. Taylor	309	Harry Vardon	St. Andrews, Scotland
1901	James Braid	309	Harry Vardon	Muirfield, Scotland
1902	Alexander Herd	307	Harry Vardon	Hoylake, England
1903	Harry Vardon	300	Tom Vardon	Prestwick, Scotland

British Open *(Cont.)*

Year	Winner	Score	Runner-Up	Site
1904	Jack White	296	John H. Taylor	Royal St. George's, England
1905	James Braid	318	John H. Taylor	St. Andrews, Scotland
			Rolland Jones	
1906	James Braid	300	John H. Taylor	Muirfield, Scotland
1907	Arnaud Massy	312	John H. Taylor	Hoylake, England
1908	James Braid	291	Tom Ball	Prestwick, Scotland
1909	John H. Taylor	295	James Braid	Deal, England
			Tom Ball	
1910	James Braid	299	Alexander Herd	St. Andrews, Scotland
1911	Harry Vardon	303	Arnaud Massy	Royal St. George's, England
1912	Ted Ray	295	Harry Vardon	Muirfield, Scotland
1913	John H. Taylor	304	Ted Ray	Hoylake, England
1914	Harry Vardon	306	John H. Taylor	Prestwick, Scotland
1915–19	No tournament			
1920	George Duncan	303	Alexander Herd	Deal, England
1921	Jock Hutchison* (150)	296	Roger Wethered (159)	St. Andrews, Scotland
1922	Walter Hagen	300	George Duncan	Royal St. George's, England
			Jim Barnes	
1923	Arthur G. Havers	295	Walter Hagen	Troon, Scotland
1924	Walter Hagen	301	Ernest Whitcombe	Hoylake, England
1925	Jim Barnes	300	Archie Compston	Prestwick, Scotland
			Ted Ray	
1926	Bobby Jones	291	Al Watrous	Royal Lytham & St. Annes, England
1927	Bobby Jones	285	Aubrey Boomer	St. Andrews, Scotland
1928	Walter Hagen	292	Gene Sarazen	Royal St. George's, England
1929	Walter Hagen	292	Johnny Farrell	Muirfield, Scotland
1930	Bobby Jones	291	Macdonald Smith	Hoylake, England
			Leo Diegel	
1931	Tommy Armour	296	Jose Jurado	Carnoustie, Scotland
1932	Gene Sarazen	283	Macdonald Smith	Prince's, England
1933	Denny Shute* (149)	292	Craig Wood (154)	St. Andrews, Scotland
1934	Henry Cotton	283	Sidney F. Brews	Royal St. George's, England
1935	Alfred Perry	283	Alfred Padgham	Muirfield, Scotland
1936	Alfred Padgham	287	James Adams	Hoylake, England
1937	Henry Cotton	290	Reginald A. Whitcombe	Carnoustie, Scotland
1938	Reginald A. Whitcombe	295	James Adams	Royal St. George's, England
1939	Richard Burton	290	Johnny Bulla	St. Andrews, Scotland
1940–45	No tournament			
1946	Sam Snead	290	Bobby Locke	St. Andrews, Scotland
			Johnny Bulla	
1947	Fred Daly	293	Reginald W. Horne	Hoylake, England
			Frank Stranahan	
1948	Henry Cotton	294	Fred Daly	Muirfield, Scotland
1949	Bobby Locke* (135)	283	Harry Bradshaw (147)	Royal St. George's, England
1950	Bobby Locke	279	Roberto DeVicenzo	Troon, Scotland
1951	Max Faulkner	285	Tony Cerda	Portrush, Ireland
1952	Bobby Locke	287	Peter Thomson	Royal Lytham & St. Annes, England
1953	Ben Hogan	282	Frank Stranahan	Carnoustie, Scotland
			Dai Rees	
			Peter Thomson	
			Tony Cerda	
1954	Peter Thomson	283	Sidney S. Scott	Royal Birkdale, England
			Dai Rees	
			Bobby Locke	
1955	Peter Thomson	281	John Fallon	St. Andrews, Scotland
1956	Peter Thomson	286	Flory Van Donck	Hoylake, England
1957	Bobby Locke	279	Peter Thomson	St. Andrews, Scotland
1958	Peter Thomson* (139)	278	Dave Thomas (143)	Royal Lytham & St. Annes, England
1959	Gary Player	284	Fred Bullock	Muirfield, Scotland
			Flory Van Donck	
1960	Kel Nagle	278	Arnold Palmer	St. Andrews, Scotland
1961	Arnold Palmer	284	Dai Rees	Royal Birkdale, England
1962	Arnold Palmer	276	Kel Nagle	Troon, Scotland
1963	Bob Charles* (140)	277	Phil Rodgers (148)	Royal Lytham & St. Annes, England
1964	Tony Lema	279	Jack Nicklaus	St. Andrews, Scotland
1965	Peter Thomson	285	Brian Huggett	Southport, England
			Christy O'Connor	

British Open *(Cont.)*

Year	Winner	Score	Runner-Up	Site
1966	Jack Nicklaus	282	Doug Sanders Dave Thomas	Muirfield, Scotland
1967	Robert DeVicenzo	278	Jack Nicklaus	Hoylake, England
1968	Gary Player	289	Jack Nicklaus Bob Charles	Carnoustie, Scotland
1969	Tony Jacklin	280	Bob Charles	Royal Lytham & St. Annes, England
1970	Jack Nicklaus* (72)	283	Doug Sanders (73)	St. Andrews, Scotland
1971	Lee Trevino	278	Lu Liang Huan	Royal Birkdale, England
1972	Lee Trevino	278	Jack Nicklaus	Muirfield, Scotland
1973	Tom Weiskopf	276	Johnny Miller	Troon, Scotland
1974	Gary Player	282	Peter Oosterhuis	Royal Lytham & St. Annes, England
1975	Tom Watson* (71)	279	Jack Newton (72)	Carnoustie, Scotland
1976	Johnny Miller	279	Jack Nicklaus Seve Ballesteros	Royal Birkdale, England
1977	Tom Watson	268	Jack Nicklaus	Turnberry, Scotland
1978	Jack Nicklaus	281	Ben Crenshaw Tom Kite Ray Floyd Simon Owen	St. Andrews, Scotland
1979	Seve Ballesteros	283	Ben Crenshaw Jack Nicklaus	Royal Lytham & St. Annes, England
1980	Tom Watson	271	Lee Trevino	Muirfield, Scotland
1981	Bill Rogers	276	Bernhard Langer	Royal St. George's, England
1982	Tom Watson	284	Nick Price Peter Oosterhuis	Troon, Scotland
1983	Tom Watson	275	Andy Bean	Royal Birkdale, England
1984	Seve Ballesteros	276	Tom Watson Bernhard Langer	St. Andrews, Scotland
1985	Sandy Lyle	282	Payne Stewart	Royal St. George's, England
1986	Greg Norman	280	Gordon Brand	Turnberry, Scotland
1987	Nick Faldo	279	Paul Azinger Rodger Davis	Muirfield, Scotland
1988	Seve Ballesteros	273	Nick Price	Royal Lytham & St. Annes, England
1989††	Mark Calcavecchia* (4-3-3-3)	275	Wayne Grady (4-4-4-4) Greg Norman (3-3-4-x)	Troon, Scotland
1990	Nick Faldo	270	Payne Stewart Mark McNulty	St. Andrews, Scotland
1991	Ian Baker-Finch	272	Mike Harwood	Royal Birkdale, England
1992	Nick Faldo	272	John Cook	Muirfield, Scotland
1993	Greg Norman	267	Nick Faldo	Royal St. George's, England
1994	Nick Price	268	Jesper Parnevik	Turnberry, Scotland
1995	John Daly* (4-3-4-4)	282	C. Rocca (5-4-7-3)	St. Andrews, Scotland
1996	Tom Lehman	271	Mark McCumber Ernie Els	Royal Lytham & St. Annes, England
1997	Justin Leonard	272	Jesper Parnevik Darren Clarke	Troon, Scotland
1998	Mark O'Meara* (4-4-5-4)	280	Brian Watts (5-4-5-5)	Southport, England
1999	Paul Lawrie* (5-4-3-3)	290	Jean Van de Velde (6-4-3-5) Justin Leonard (5-4-4-5)	Carnoustie GC, Carnoustie, Scotland
2000	Tiger Woods	269	Thomas Bjorn Ernie Els	St. Andrews, Scotland
2001	David Duval	274	Niclas Fasth	Royal Lytham & St. Annes, England
2002	Ernie Els*	278	Stuart Appleby	Muirfield, Scotland
2003	Ben Curtis	283	Vijay Singh	Royal St. George's, England
2004	Todd Hamilton*	274	Ernie Els	Troon, Scotland
2005	Tiger Woods	274	Colin Montgomerie	St. Andrews, Scotland
2006	Tiger Woods	270	Chris DiMarco	Hoylake, England
2007	Padraig Harrington*	277	Sergio Garcia	Carnoustie, Scotland

*Winner in playoff. †The first event was open only to professional golfers.
‡The second annual open was open to amateurs and pros. #Tied, but refused playoff.
**Championship extended from 36 to 72 holes. ††Playoff cut from 18 holes to 4 holes.

PGA Championship

Year	Winner	Score	Runner-Up	Site
1916	Jim Barnes	1 up	Jock Hutchison	Siwanoy CC, Bronxville, NY
1917–18	No tournament			
1919	Jim Barnes	6 & 5	Fred McLeod	Engineers CC, Roslyn, NY
1920	Jock Hutchison	1 up	J. Douglas Edgar	Flossmoor CC, Flossmoor, IL
1921	Walter Hagen	3 & 2	Jim Barnes	Inwood CC, Far Rockaway, NY
1922	Gene Sarazen	4 & 3	Emmet French	Oakmont CC, Oakmont, PA
1923	Gene Sarazen	1 up 38 holes	Walter Hagen	Pelham CC, Pelham, NY
1924	Walter Hagen	2 up	Jim Barnes	French Lick CC, French Lick, IN
1925	Walter Hagen	6 & 5	William Mehlhorn	Olympia Fields CC, Olympia Fields, IL
1926	Walter Hagen	5 & 3	Leo Diegel	Salisbury GC, Westbury, NY
1927	Walter Hagen	1 up	Joe Turnesa	Cedar Crest CC, Dallas
1928	Leo Diegel	6 & 5	Al Espinosa	Five Farms CC, Baltimore
1929	Leo Diegel	6 & 4	Johnny Farrell	Hillcrest CC, Los Angeles
1930	Tommy Armour	1 up	Gene Sarazen	Fresh Meadow CC, Flushing, NY
1931	Tom Creavy	2 & 1	Denny Shute	Wannamoisett CC, Rumford, RI
1932	Olin Dutra	4 & 3	Frank Walsh	Keller GC, St. Paul
1933	Gene Sarazen	5 & 4	Willie Goggin	Blue Mound CC, Milwaukee
1934	Paul Runyan	1 up	Craig Wood	Park CC, Williamsville, NY
1935	Johnny Revolta	5 & 4 38 holes	Tommy Armour	Twin Hills CC, Oklahoma City
1936	Denny Shute	3 & 2	Jimmy Thomson	Pinehurst CC, Pinehurst, NC
1937	Denny Shute	1 up 37 holes	Harold McSpaden	Pittsburgh FC, Aspinwall, PA
1938	Paul Runyan	8 & 7	Sam Snead	Shawnee CC, Shawnee-on-Delaware, PA
1939	Henry Picard	1 up 37 holes	Byron Nelson	Pomonok CC, Flushing, NY
1940	Byron Nelson	1 up	Sam Snead	Hershey CC, Hershey, PA
1941	Vic Ghezzi	1 up 38 holes	Byron Nelson	Cherry Hills CC, Denver
1942	Sam Snead	2 & 1	Jim Turnesa	Seaview CC, Atlantic City
1943	No tournament			
1944	Bob Hamilton	1 up	Byron Nelson	Manito G & CC, Spokane, WA
1945	Byron Nelson	4 & 3	Sam Byrd	Morraine CC, Dayton
1946	Ben Hogan	6 & 4	Ed Oliver	Portland GC, Portland, OR
1947	Jim Ferrier	2 & 1	Chick Harbert	Plum Hollow CC, Detroit
1948	Ben Hogan	7 & 6	Mike Turnesa	Norwood Hills CC, St. Louis
1949	Sam Snead	3 & 2	Johnny Palmer	Hermitage CC, Richmond
1950	Chandler Harper	4 & 3	Henry Williams Jr.	Scioto CC, Columbus, OH
1951	Sam Snead	7 & 6	Walter Burkemo	Oakmont CC, Oakmont, PA
1952	Jim Turnesa	1 up	Chick Harbert	Big Spring CC, Louisville
1953	Walter Burkemo	2 & 1	Felice Torza	Birmingham CC, Birmingham, MI
1954	Chick Harbert	4 & 3	Walter Burkemo	Keller GC, St. Paul
1955	Doug Ford	4 & 3	Cary Middlecoff	Meadowbrook CC, Detroit
1956	Jack Burke	3 & 2	Ted Kroll	Blue Hill CC, Boston
1957	Lionel Hebert	2 & 1	Dow Finsterwald	Miami Valley CC, Dayton
1958	Dow Finsterwald	276	Billy Casper	Llanerch CC, Havertown, PA
1959	Bob Rosburg	277	Jerry Barber Doug Sanders	Minneapolis GC, St. Louis Park, MN
1960	Jay Hebert	281	Jim Ferrier	Firestone CC, Akron
1961	Jerry Barber* (67)	277	Don January (68)	Olympia Fields CC, Olympia Fields, IL
1962	Gary Player	278	Bob Goalby	Aronimink GC, Newton Square, PA
1963	Jack Nicklaus	279	Dave Ragan Jr.	Dallas Athletic Club, Dallas
1964	Bobby Nichols	271	Jack Nicklaus Arnold Palmer	Columbus CC, Columbus, OH
1965	Dave Marr	280	Billy Casper Jack Nicklaus	Laurel Valley CC, Ligonier, PA
1966	Al Geiberger	280	Dudley Wysong	Firestone CC, Akron
1967	Don January* (69)	281	Don Massengale (71)	Columbine CC, Littleton, CO
1968	Julius Boros	281	Bob Charles Arnold Palmer	Pecan Valley CC, San Antonio
1969	Ray Floyd	276	Gary Player	NCR CC, Dayton
1970	Dave Stockton	279	Arnold Palmer Bob Murphy	Southern Hills CC, Tulsa
1971	Jack Nicklaus	281	Billy Casper	PGA Nat'l GC, Palm Beach Gardens, FL

PGA Championship (Cont.)

Year	Winner	Score	Runner-Up	Site
1972	Gary Player	281	Tommy Aaron	Oakland Hills CC, Birmingham, MI
			Jim Jamieson	
1973	Jack Nicklaus	277	Bruce Crampton	Canterbury GC, Cleveland
1974	Lee Trevino	276	Jack Nicklaus	Tanglewood GC, Winston-Salem, NC
1975	Jack Nicklaus	276	Bruce Crampton	Firestone CC, Akron
1976	Dave Stockton	281	Ray Floyd	Congressional CC, Bethesda, MD
			Don January	
1977†	Lanny Wadkins* (4-4-4)	282	Gene Littler (4-4-5)	Pebble Beach GL, Pebble Beach, CA
1978	John Mahaffey* (4–3)	276	Jerry Pate (4–4)	Oakmont CC, Oakmont, PA
			Tom Watson (4–5)	
1979	David Graham* (4-4-2)	272	Ben Crenshaw (4-4-4)	Oakland Hills CC, Birmingham, MI
1980	Jack Nicklaus	274	Andy Bean	Oak Hill CC, Rochester, NY
1981	Larry Nelson	273	Fuzzy Zoeller	Atlanta Athletic Club, Duluth, GA
1982	Raymond Floyd	272	Lanny Wadkins	Southern Hills CC, Tulsa
1983	Hal Sutton	274	Jack Nicklaus	Riviera CC, Pacific Palisades, CA
1984	Lee Trevino	273	Gary Player	Shoal Creek, Birmingham, AL
			Lanny Wadkins	
1985	Hubert Green	278	Lee Trevino	Cherry Hills CC, Denver
1986	Bob Tway	276	Greg Norman	Inverness CC, Toledo
1987	Larry Nelson* (4)	287	Lanny Wadkins (5)	PGA Natl GC, Palm Beach Gardens, FL
1988	Jeff Sluman	272	Paul Azinger	Oak Tree GC, Edmond, OK
1989	Payne Stewart	276	Mike Reid	Kemper Lakes GC, Hawthorn Woods, IL
1990	Wayne Grady	282	Fred Couples	Shoal Creek, Birmingham, AL
1991	John Daly	276	Bruce Lietzke	Crooked Stick GC, Carmel, IN
1992	Nick Price	278	Jim Gallagher Jr.	Bellerive CC, St. Louis
1993	Paul Azinger* (4–4)	272	Greg Norman (4–5)	Inverness CC, Toledo
1994	Nick Price	269	Corey Pavin	Southern Hills CC, Tulsa
1995	Steve Elkington* (3)	267	Colin Montgomerie (4)	Riviera CC, Pacific Palisades, CA
1996	Mark Brooks* (3)	277	Kenny Perry (x)	Valhalla GC, Louisville
1997	Davis Love III	269	Justin Leonard	Winged Foot GC, Mamaroneck, NY
1998	Vijay Singh	271	Steve Stricker	Sahalee CC, Redmond, WA
1999	Tiger Woods	277	Sergio Garcia	Medinah CC, Medinah, IL
2000	Tiger Woods* (3-4-5)	270	Bob May (4-4-x)	Valhalla GC, Louisville
2001	David Toms	265	Phil Mickelson	Atlanta AC, Duluth, GA
2002	Rich Beem	278	Tiger Woods	Hazeltine National GC, Shaska, MN
2003	Shaun Micheel	276	Chad Campbell	Oak Hill CC, Rochester, NY
2004	Vijay Singh*	280	Chris DiMarco	Whistling Straits GC, Kohler, WI
2005	Phil Mickelson	276	Steve Elkington	Baltusrol GC, Springfield, NJ
2006	Tiger Woods	270	Shaun Micheel	Medinah CC, Medinah, IL
2007	Tiger Woods	272	Woody Austin	Southern Hills CC, Tulsa, OK

*Winner in playoff. †Playoff changed from 18 holes to sudden death.

Alltime Major Championship Winners

	Masters	U.S. Open	British Open	PGA Champ.	U.S. Amateur	British Amateur	Total
Jack Nicklaus	6	4	3	5	2	0	20
*Tiger Woods	4	2	3	4	3	0	16
Bobby Jones	0	4	3	0	5	1	13
Walter Hagen	0	2	4	5	0	0	11
Ben Hogan	2	4	1	2	0	0	9
Gary Player	3	1	3	2	0	0	9
John Ball	0	0	1	0	0	8	9
Arnold Palmer	4	1	2	0	1	0	8
Tom Watson	2	1	5	0	0	0	8
Harold Hilton	0	0	2	0	1	4	7
Gene Sarazen	1	2	1	3	0	0	7
Sam Snead	3	0	1	3	0	0	7
Harry Vardon	0	1	6	0	0	0	7

*Active PGA Tour player.

Alltime Multiple Professional Major Winners

MASTERS		U.S. OPEN *(Cont.)*		BRITISH OPEN *(Cont.)*		PGA CHAMPIONSHIP	
Jack Nicklaus	6	Hale Irwin	3	Peter Thomson	5	Walter Hagen	5
Arnold Palmer	4	Julius Boros	2	Tom Watson	5	Jack Nicklaus	5
Tiger Woods	4	Billy Casper	2	Walter Hagen	4	Tiger Woods	4
Jimmy Demaret	3	Ernie Els	2	Bobby Locke	4	Gene Sarazen	3
Nick Faldo	3	Retief Goosen	2	Tom Morris Sr.	4	Sam Snead	3
Gary Player	3	Ralph Guldahl	2	Tom Morris Jr.	4	Jim Barnes	2
Sam Snead	3	Walter Hagen	2	Willie Park	4	Leo Diegel	2
Seve Ballesteros	2	Lee Janzen	2	Jamie Anderson	3	Raymond Floyd	2
Ben Crenshaw	2	John McDermott	2	Seve Ballesteros	3	Ben Hogan	2
Ben Hogan	2	Cary Middlecoff	2	Henry Cotton	3	Byron Nelson	2
Bernhard Langer	2	Andy North	2	Nick Faldo	3	Larry Nelson	2
Phil Mickelson	2	Gene Sarazen	2	Robert Ferguson	3	Gary Player	2
Byron Nelson	2	Alex Smith	2	Bobby Jones	3	Paul Runyan	2
José María Olazábal	2	Payne Stewart	2	Jack Nicklaus	3	Denny Shute	2
Horton Smith	2	Curtis Strange	2	Gary Player	3	Dave Stockton	2
Tom Watson	2	Lee Trevino	2	Tiger Woods	3	Lee Trevino	2
		Tiger Woods	2	Harold Hilton	2	Vijay Singh	2
U.S. OPEN				Bob Martin	2		
Willie Anderson	4	**BRITISH OPEN**		Greg Norman	2		
Ben Hogan	4	Harry Vardon	6	Arnold Palmer	2		
Bobby Jones	4	James Braid	5	Willie Park Jr.	2		
Jack Nicklaus	4	J.H. Taylor	5	Lee Trevino	2		

THE PGA TOUR

Most Career Wins*

	Wins		Wins		Wins
Sam Snead	82	Billy Casper	51	Phil Mickelson	32
Jack Nicklaus	73	Walter Hagen	44	Horton Smith	32
Ben Hogan	64	Cary Middlecoff	40	Harry Cooper	31
Arnold Palmer	62	Gene Sarazen	39	Jimmy Demaret	31
Tiger Woods	61	Tom Watson	39	Vijay Singh	31
Byron Nelson	52	Lloyd Mangrum	36	Leo Diegel	30

* Through 10/1/07

Season Money Leaders

	Earnings ($)		Earnings ($)		Earnings ($)
1934 ...Paul Runyan	6,767.00	1959 ...Art Wall	53,167.60	1984 ...Tom Watson	476,260.00
1935 ...Johnny Revolta	9,543.00	1960 ...Arnold Palmer	75,262.85	1985 ...Curtis Strange	542,321.00
1936 ...Horton Smith	7,682.00	1961 ...Gary Player	64,540.45	1986 ...Greg Norman	653,296.00
1937 ...Harry Cooper	14,138.69	1962 ...Arnold Palmer	81,448.33	1987 ...Curtis Strange	925,941.00
1938 ...Sam Snead	19,534.49	1963 ...Arnold Palmer	128,230.00	1988 ...Curtis Strange	1,147,644.00
1939 ...Henry Picard	10,303.00	1964 ...Jack Nicklaus	113,284.50	1989 ...Tom Kite	1,395,278.00
1940 ...Ben Hogan	10,655.00	1965 ...Jack Nicklaus	140,752.14	1990 ...Greg Norman	1,165,477.00
1941 ...Ben Hogan	18,358.00	1966 ...Billy Casper	121,944.92	1991 ...Corey Pavin	979,430.00
1942 ...Ben Hogan	13,143.00	1967 ...Jack Nicklaus	188,998.08	1992 ...Fred Couples	1,344,188.00
1943 ...No statistics compiled		1968 ...Billy Casper	205,168.67	1993 ...Nick Price	1,478,557.00
1944 ...Byron Nelson*	37,967.69	1969 ...Frank Beard	164,707.11	1994 ...Nick Price	1,499,927.00
1945 ...Byron Nelson*	63,335.66	1970 ...Lee Trevino	157,037.63	1995 ...Greg Norman	1,654,959.00
1946 ...Ben Hogan	42,556.16	1971 ...Jack Nicklaus	244,490.50	1996 ...Tom Lehman	1,780,159.00
1947 ...Jimmy Demaret	27,936.83	1972 ...Jack Nicklaus	320,542.26	1997 ...Tiger Woods	2,066,833.00
1948 ...Ben Hogan	32,112.00	1973 ...Jack Nicklaus	308,362.10	1998 ...David Duval	2,591,031.00
1949 ...Sam Snead	31,593.83	1974 ...Johnny Miller	353,021.59	1999 ...Tiger Woods	6,616,585.00
1950 ...Sam Snead	35,758.83	1975 ...Jack Nicklaus	298,149.17	2000 ...Tiger Woods	9,188,321.00
1951 ...Lloyd Mangrum	26,088.83	1976 ...Jack Nicklaus	266,438.57	2001 ...Tiger Woods	5,687,777.00
1952 ...Julius Boros	37,032.97	1977 ...Tom Watson	310,653.16	2002 ...Tiger Woods	6,912,625.00
1953 ...Lew Worsham	34,002.00	1978 ...Tom Watson	362,428.93	2003 ...Vijay Singh	7,573,907.00
1954 ...Bob Toski	65,819.81	1979 ...Tom Watson	462,636.00	2004 ...Vijay Singh	10,905,166.00
1955 ...Julius Boros	63,121.55	1980 ...Tom Watson	530,808.33	2005 ...Tiger Woods	10,628,024.00
1956 ...Ted Kroll	72,835.83	1981 ...Tom Kite	375,698.84	2006 ...Tiger Woods	9,941,563.00
1957 ...Dick Mayer	65,835.00	1982 ...Craig Stadler	446,462.00		
1958 ...Arnold Palmer	42,607.50	1983 ...Hal Sutton	426,668.00		

* War bonds. Note: Total money listed from 1968 through 1974. Official money listed from 1975 on.

Career Money Leaders*

#	Player	Earnings ($)	#	Player	Earnings ($)	#	Player	Earnings ($)
1	Tiger Woods	$76,579,376	18	Chris DiMarco	$19,660,264	35	Charles Howell III	$15,218,876
2	Vijay Singh	$54,108,218	19	Sergio Garcia	$19,540,777	36	Loren Roberts	$15,103,540
3	Phil Mickelson	$45,334,026	20	Fred Couples	$19,172,199	37	Bob Tway	$14,908,615
4	Davis Love III	$35,630,313	21	Scott Hoch	$18,487,114	38	Steve Stricker	$14,705,580
5	Jim Furyk	$35,534,112	22	Retief Goosen	$18,275,403	39	Jay Haas	$14,440,317
6	Ernie Els	$31,126,111	23	Jeff Sluman	$18,114,866	40	Paul Azinger	$14,404,620
7	David Toms	$27,911,952	24	Brad Faxon	$17,656,554	41	Tim Herron	$14,395,101
8	Mark Calcavecchia	$22,228,419	25	David Duval	$16,743,323	42	John Houston	$14,205,791
9	Justin Leonard	$21,910,092	26	Adam Scott	$16,390,401	43	Mark O'Meara	$14,125,097
10	Kenny Perry	$21,532,649	27	Jerry Kelly	$16,280,934	44	Gerg Norman	$13,963,611
11	Stewart Cink	$20,984,693	28	Bob Estes	$16,207,613	45	Steve Flesch	$13,938,230
12	Scott Verplank	$20,831,472	29	K.J. Choi	$16,118,197	46	Jesper Parnevik	$13,871,206
13	Stuart Appleby	$20,636,826	30	Rory Sabbatini	$16,056,986	47	Corey Pavin	$13,657,870
14	Fred Funk	$20,624,835	31	Robert Allenby	$15,632,654	48	Kirk Triplett	$13,470,066
15	Nick Price	$20,551,208	32	Billy Mayfair	$15,496,156	49	Chad Campbell	$13,457,393
16	Mike Weir	$19,843,988	33	Hal Sutton	$15,267,685	50	Lee Janzen	$13,431,312
17	Tom Lehman	$19,701,862	34	Jeff Maggert	$15,239,249			

*Through 10/1/07.

Year by Year Statistical Leaders

SCORING AVERAGE

Year	Player	Avg
1980	Lee Trevino	69.73
1981	Tom Kite	69.80
1982	Tom Kite	70.21
1983	Raymond Floyd	70.61
1984	Calvin Peete	70.56
1985	Don Pooley	70.36
1986	Scott Hoch	70.08
1987	David Frost	70.09
1988	Greg Norman	69.38
1989	Payne Stewart	69.485†
1990	Greg Norman	69.10
1991	Fred Couples	69.59
1992	Fred Couples	69.38
1993	Greg Norman	68.90
1994	Greg Norman	68.81
1995	Greg Norman	69.06
1996	Tom Lehman	69.32
1997	Nick Price	68.98
1998	David Duval	69.13
1999	Tiger Woods	68.43
2000	Tiger Woods	67.79
2001	Tiger Woods	68.81
2002	Tiger Woods	68.13
2003	Tiger Woods	68.41
2004	Vijay Singh	69.19
2005	Tiger Woods	68.66
2006	Tiger Woods	68.11

Note: Scoring average per round, with adjustments made at each round for the field's course scoring average.

DRIVING DISTANCE

Year	Player	Yds
1980	Dan Pohl	274.3
1981	Dan Pohl	280.1
1982	Bill Calfee	275.3
1983	John McComish	277.4
1984	Bill Glasson	276.5
1985	Andy Bean	278.2
1986	Davis Love III	285.7
1987	John McComish	283.9
1988	Steve Thomas	284.6
1989	Ed Humenik	280.9
1990	Tom Purtzer	279.6
1991	John Daly	288.9

DRIVING DISTANCE *(Cont.)*

Year	Player	Yds
1992	John Daly	283.4
1993	John Daly	288.9
1994	Davis Love III	283.8
1995	John Daly	289.0
1996	John Daly	288.8
1997	John Daly	302.0
1998	John Daly	299.4
1999	John Daly	305.6
2000	John Daly	301.4
2001	John Daly	306.7
2002	John Daly	306.8
2003	Hank Kuehne	321.4
2004	Hank Kuehne	314.4
2005	Scott Hend	318.9
2006	Bubba Watson	319.6

Note: Average computed by charting distance of two tee shots on a predetermined par-four or par-five hole (one on front nine, one on back nine).

DRIVING ACCURACY

Year	Player	%
1980	Mike Reid	79.5
1981	Calvin Peete	81.9
1982	Calvin Peete	84.6
1983	Calvin Peete	81.3
1984	Calvin Peete	77.5
1985	Calvin Peete	80.6
1986	Calvin Peete	81.7
1987	Calvin Peete	83.0
1988	Calvin Peete	82.5
1989	Calvin Peete	82.6
1990	Calvin Peete	83.7
1991	Hale Irwin	78.3
1992	Doug Tewell	82.3
1993	Doug Tewell	82.5
1994	David Edwards	81.6
1995	Fred Funk	81.3
1996	Fred Funk	78.7
1997	Allen Doyle	80.8
1998	Bruce Fleisher	81.4
1999	Fred Funk	80.2
2000	Fred Funk	79.7
2001	Joe Durant	81.1
2002	Fred Funk	81.2

DRIVING ACCURACY *(Cont.)*

Year	Player	%
2003	Fred Funk	77.9
2004	Fred Funk	77.2
2005	Jeff Hart	76.0
2006	Joe Durant	78.4

Note: Percentage of fairways hit on number of par-four and par-five holes played; par-three holes excluded.

GREENS IN REGULATION

Year	Player	%
1980	Jack Nicklaus	72.1
1981	Calvin Peete	73.1
1982	Calvin Peete	72.4
1983	Calvin Peete	71.4
1984	Andy Bean	72.1
1985	John Mahaffey	71.9
1986	John Mahaffey	72.0
1987	Gil Morgan	73.3
1988	John Adams	73.9
1989	Bruce Lietzke	72.6
1990	Doug Tewell	70.9
1991	Bruce Lietzke	73.3
1992	Tim Simpson	74.0
1993	Fuzzy Zoeller	73.6
1994	Bill Glasson	73.0
1995	Lenny Clements	72.3
1996	Fred Couples	71.8
	Mark O'Meara	71.8
1997	Tom Lehman	72.7
1998	Hal Sutton	71.3
1999	Tiger Woods	71.4
2000	Tiger Woods	75.2
2001	Tom Lehman	74.5
2002	Tiger Woods	74.0
2003	Joe Durant	72.9
2004	Joe Durant	73.3
2005	Sergio Garcia	71.8
2006	Tiger Woods	74.2

Note: Average of greens reached in regulation out of total holes played; hole is considered hit in regulation if any part of the ball rests on the putting surface in two shots less than the hole's par—a par-5 hit in two shots is one green in regulation.

† Number had to be carried to extra decimal place to determine winner.

Year by Year Statistical Leaders (Cont.)

PUTTING

1980	Jerry Pate	28.81
1981	Alan Tapie	28.70
1982	Ben Crenshaw	28.65
1983	Morris Hatalsky	27.96
1984	Gary McCord	28.57
1985	Craig Stadler	28.627†
1986	Greg Norman	1.736
1987	Ben Crenshaw	1.743
1988	Don Pooley	1.729
1989	Steve Jones	1.734
1990	Larry Rinker	1.7467†
1991	Jay Don Blake	1.7326†
1992	Mark O'Meara	1.731
1993	David Frost	1.739
1994	Loren Roberts	1.737
1995	Jim Furyk	1.708
1996	Brad Faxon	1.709
1997	Don Pooley	1.718
1998	Rick Fehr	1.722
1999	Brad Faxon	1.723
2000	Brad Faxon	1.704
2001	David Frost	1.708
2002	Bob Heintz	1.682
2003	John Huston	1.713
2004	Stewart Cink	1.723
2005	Arjun Atwal	1.710
2006	Daniel Chopra	1.712

Note: Average number of putts taken on greens reached in regulation; prior to 1986, based on average number of putts per 18 holes.

SAND SAVES

1980	Bob Eastwood	65.4
1981	Tom Watson	60.1
1982	Isao Aoki	60.2
1983	Isao Aoki	62.3
1984	Peter Oosterhuis *	64.7
1985	Tom Purtzer	60.8
1986	Paul Azinger	63.8
1987	Paul Azinger	63.2
1988	Greg Powers	63.5
1989	Mike Sullivan	66.0
1990	Paul Azinger	67.2
1991	Ben Crenshaw	64.9
1992	Mitch Adcock	66.9
1993	Ken Green	64.4
1994	Corey Pavin	65.4
1995	Billy Mayfair	68.6
1996	Gary Rusnak	64.0
1997	Bob Estes	70.3
1998	Keith Fergus	71.0
1999	Jeff Sluman	67.3
2000	Fred Couples	67.0
2001	Franklin Langham	68.9
2002	J. Olazabal	64.9
2003	Stuart Appleby	62.1
2004	Dan Forsman	62.3
2005	Pat Perez	63.0
2006	Luke Donald	63.6

Note: Percentage of up-and-down efforts from greenside sand traps only—fairway bunkers excluded.

PAR BREAKERS

1980	Tom Watson	.213
1981	Bruce Lietzke	.225
1982	Tom Kite	.2154†
1983	Tom Watson	.211
1984	Craig Stadler	.220
1985	Craig Stadler	.218
1986	Greg Norman	.248
1987	Mark Calcavecchia	.221
1988	Ken Green	.236
1989	Greg Norman	.224
1990	Greg Norman	.219

Note: Average based on total birdies and eagles scored out of total holes played. Discontinued as an official category after 1990.

EAGLES

1980	Dave Eichelberger	16
1981	Bruce Lietzke	12
1982	Tom Weiskopf	10
	J.C. Snead	10
	Andy Bean	10
1983	Chip Beck	15
1984	Gary Hallberg	15
1985	Larry Rinker	14
1986	Joey Sindelar	16
1987	Phil Blackmar	20
1988	Ken Green	21
1989	Lon Hinkle	14
	Duffy Waldorf	14
1990	Paul Azinger	14
1991	Andy Bean	15
1992	Dan Forsman	18
1993	Davis Love III	15
1994	Davis Love III	18
1995	Kelly Gibson	16
1996	Tom Watson	97.2
1997	Tiger Woods	104.1
1998	Davis Love III	83.3
1999	Vijay Singh	104.8
2000	Tiger Woods	72.0
2001	Phil Mickelson	73.8
2002	John Daly	78.4
2003	Tiger Woods	76.5
2004	Nick Price	90.0
2005	Brenden Pappas	70.6
2006	J.B. Holmes	72.9

Note: Total of eagles scored 1980–1995. Since 1996 winner determined by number of holes played per eagle.

BIRDIES

1980	Andy Bean	388
1981	Vance Heafner	388
1982	Andy Bean	392
1983	Hal Sutton	399
1984	Mark O'Meara	419
1985	Joey Sindelar	411
1986	Joey Sindelar	415
1987	Dan Forsman	409
1988	Dan Forsman	465
1989	Ted Schulz	415
1990	Mike Donald	401
1991	Scott Hoch	446
1992	Jeff Sluman	417

BIRDIES (Cont.)

1993	John Huston	426
1994	Brad Bryant	397
1995	Steve Lowery	410
1996	Fred Couples	4.20
1997	Tiger Woods	4.25
1998	David Duval	4.29
1999	Tiger Woods	4.46
2000	Tiger Woods	4.92
2001	Phil Mickelson	4.49
2002	Tiger Woods	4.47
2003	Vijay Singh	4.41
2004	Vijay Singh	4.40
2005	Tiger Woods	4.57
2006	Tiger Woods	4.65

Note: Total of birdies scored 1980–95. Since 1996, winner determined by average number of birdies per round.

ALL-AROUND

1987	Dan Pohl	170
1988	Payne Stewart	170
1989	Paul Azinger	250
1990	Paul Azinger	162
1991	Scott Hoch	283
1992	Fred Couples	256
1993	Gil Morgan	252
1994	Bob Estes	227
1995	Justin Leonard	323
1996	Fred Couples	214
1997	Bill Glasson	282
1998	John Huston	151
1999	Tiger Woods	120
2000	Tiger Woods	113
2001	Phil Mickelson	174
2002	Phil Mickelson	259
2003	Tiger Woods	206
2004	Jeff Ogilvy	268
2005	Tiger Woods	265
2006	Tiger Woods	216

Note: Sum of the places of standing from the other statistical categories; the player with the number closest to zero leads.

† Number had to be carried to extra decimal place to determine winner.

PGA Player of the Year Award

1948 ....Ben Hogan	1968 ....Not awarded	1988 ....Curtis Strange
1949 ....Sam Snead	1969 ....Orville Moody	1989 ....Tom Kite
1950 ....Ben Hogan	1970 ....Billy Casper	1990 ....Wayne Levi
1951 ....Ben Hogan	1971 ....Lee Trevino	1991 ....Fred Couples
1952 ....Julius Boros	1972 ....Jack Nicklaus	1992 ....Fred Couples
1953 ....Ben Hogan	1973 ....Jack Nicklaus	1993 ....Nick Price
1954 ....Ed Furgol	1974 ....Johnny Miller	1994 ....Nick Price
1955 ....Doug Ford	1975 ....Jack Nicklaus	1995 ....Greg Norman
1956 ....Jack Burke	1976 ....Jack Nicklaus	1996 ....Tom Lehman
1957 ....Dick Mayer	1977 ....Tom Watson	1997 ....Tiger Woods
1958 ....Dow Finsterwald	1978 ....Tom Watson	1998 ....David Duval
1959 ....Art Wall	1979 ....Tom Watson	1999 ....Tiger Woods
1960 ....Arnold Palmer	1980 ....Tom Watson	2000 ....Tiger Woods
1961 ....Jerry Barber	1981 ....Bill Rogers	2001 ....Tiger Woods
1962 ....Arnold Palmer	1982 ....Tom Watson	2002 ....Tiger Woods
1963 ....Julius Boros	1983 ....Hal Sutton	2003 ....Tiger Woods
1964 ....Ken Venturi	1984 ....Tom Watson	2004 ....Vijay Singh
1965 ....Dave Marr	1985 ....Lanny Wadkins	2005 ....Tiger Woods
1966 ....Billy Casper	1986 ....Bob Tway	2006 ....Tiger Woods
1967 ....Jack Nicklaus	1987 ....Paul Azinger	

Vardon Trophy: Scoring Average

Year	Winner	Avg	Year	Winner	Avg	Year	Winner	Avg
1937	Harry Cooper	*500	1963	Billy Casper	70.58	1985	Don Pooley	70.36
1938	Sam Snead	520	1964	Arnold Palmer	70.01	1986	Scott Hoch	70.08
1939	Byron Nelson	473	1965	Billy Casper	70.85	1987	Don Pohl	70.25
1940	Ben Hogan	423	1966	Billy Casper	70.27	1988	Chip Beck	69.46
1941	Ben Hogan	494	1967	Arnold Palmer	70.18	1989	Greg Norman	69.49
1942–46	No award		1968	Billy Casper	69.82	1990	Greg Norman	69.10
1947	Jimmy Demaret	69.90	1969	Dave Hill	70.34	1991	Fred Couples	69.59
1948	Ben Hogan	69.30	1970	Lee Trevino	70.64	1992	Fred Couples	69.38
1949	Sam Snead	69.37	1971	Lee Trevino	70.27	1993	Nick Price	69.11
1950	Sam Snead	69.23	1972	Lee Trevino	70.89	1994	Greg Norman	68.81
1951	Lloyd Mangrum	70.05	1973	Bruce Crampton	70.57	1995	Steve Elkington	69.62
1952	Jack Burke	70.54	1974	Lee Trevino	70.53	1996	Tom Lehman	69.32
1953	Lloyd Mangrum	70.22	1975	Bruce Crampton	70.51	1997	Nick Price	68.98
1954	E.J. Harrison	70.41	1976	Don January	70.56	1998	David Duval	69.13
1955	Sam Snead	69.86	1977	Tom Watson	70.32	1999	Tiger Woods	68.43
1956	Cary Middlecoff	70.35	1978	Tom Watson	70.16	2000	Tiger Woods	67.79
1957	Dow Finsterwald	70.30	1979	Tom Watson	70.27	2001	Tiger Woods	68.81
1958	Bob Rosburg	70.11	1980	Lee Trevino	69.73	2002	Tiger Woods	68.13
1959	Art Wall	70.35	1981	Tom Kite	69.80	2003	Tiger Woods	68.41
1960	Billy Casper	69.95	1982	Tom Kite	70.21	2004	Vijay Singh	68.84
1961	Arnold Palmer	69.85	1983	Raymond Floyd	70.61	2005	Tiger Woods	68.66
1962	Arnold Palmer	70.27	1984	Calvin Peete	70.56	2006	Jim Furyk	68.86

*Point system used, 1937–41. NOTE: As of 1988, based on minimum of 60 rounds per year. Adjusted for average score of field in tournaments entered.

Alltime PGA Tour Records*
Scoring

90 HOLES

324—(65-61-67-66-65) by Joe Durant, at four courses, La Quinta, CA, to win the 2001 Bob Hope Classic (36 under par).

72 HOLES, TOTAL STROKES

254—(64-62-63-65) by Tommy Armour III, at LaCantera GC, San Antonio, TX, to win the 2003 Valero Texas Open (26 under par).

72 HOLES, TO PAR

-31—(64-65-65-67) by Ernie Els, at Kapalua Resort GC Kapalua, HI, to win the 2003 Mercedes Championship (261 total, par 73).

54 HOLES, OPENING ROUNDS

189—(64-62-63) by John Cook, at the TPC at Southwind, Memphis, en route to winning the 1996 St. Jude Classic.

54 HOLES, OPENING ROUNDS *(CONT.)*

189—(65-60-64) Mark Calcavecchia, at the TPC at Scottsdale, Scottsdale, AZ, en route to winning the 2001 Phoenix Open.

189—(64-62-63) by Tommy Armour III, at LaCantera GC, San Antonio, TX, en route to winning the 2003 Valero Texas Open.

54 HOLES, CONSECUTIVE ROUNDS

189—(63-63-63) by Chandler Harper in the last three rounds to win the 1954 Texas Open at Brackenridge Park GC, San Antonio.

189—(64-62-63) by John Cook, at the TPC at Southwind, Memphis, in the first three rounds en route to winning the 1996 St. Jude Classic.

Alltime PGA Tour Records (Cont.)*

Scoring (Cont.)

54 HOLES, CONSECUTIVE ROUNDS (Cont.)

189—(65-60-64) Mark Calcavecchia, at the TPC at Scottsdale, Scottsdale, AZ, in the first three rounds en route to winning the 2001 Phoenix Open.

189—(64-62-63) by Tommy Armour III, at LaCantera GC, San Antonio, TX, in the first three rounds en route to winning the 2003 Valero Texas Open.

36 HOLES, OPENING ROUNDS

125—(64-61) by Tiger Woods, in the 2000 World Golf Championships/ NEC Invitational, which he won, at Firestone CC, Akron.

125—(65-60) by Mark Calcavecchia, in the 2001 Phoenix Open, which he won, at TPC at Scottsdale, Scottsdale, AZ.

36 HOLES, CONSECUTIVE ROUNDS

124—(60-64) by Mark Calcavecchia, in the middle rounds of the 2001 Phoenix Open, which he won, at TPC of Scottsdale, Scottsdale, AZ.

18 HOLES

59—by Al Geiberger, at Colonial Country Club, Memphis, in second round in winning the 1977 Memphis Classic.

59—by Chip Beck, at Sunrise Golf Club, Las Vegas, in third round of the 1991 Las Vegas Invitational.

59—by David Duval, on the Palmer Course at PGA West, La Quinta, CA, in the fifth round of the 1999 Bob Hope Chrysler Classic.

9 HOLES

26—by Corey Pavin, at Brown Deer Park GC, Milwaukee, WI, on par-34 front nine during the first round of the 2006 US Bank Championship.

MOST CONSECUTIVE ROUNDS UNDER 70

19—Byron Nelson in 1945.

MOST BIRDIES IN A ROW

8—Bob Goalby, at Pasadena GC, St. Petersburg, FL, during fourth round in winning the 1961 St Petersburg Open.

8—Fuzzy Zoeller, at Oakwood CC, Coal Valley, IL, during first round of 1976 Quad Cities Open.

8—Dewey Arnette, at Warwick Hills GC, Grand Blanc, MI, during first round of the 1987 Buick Open.

8—Edward Fryatt, at the Blue Course of the Doral Resort and Spa, Miami, during second round of the 2000 Doral-Ryder Open.

8—J.P. Hayes, at Palmer Private Course, Palm Springs, CA, during first round of the 2002 Bob Hope Chrysler Classic.

8—Jerry Kelly, at TPC at Summerlin, Las Vegas, NV, during third round of the 2003 Las Vegas Invitational.

MOST BIRDIES IN ONE TOURNAMENT

32—Mark Calcavecchia, at TPC at Scottsdale, Scottsdale, AZ, en route to winning the 2001 Phoenix Open.

32—Paul Gow, at the En-Joie GC, Endicott, NY, en route to second place finish at the 2001 B.C. Open.

MOST BIRDIES IN A ROW TO WIN

6—Mike Souchak, to win 1956 St. Paul Open (last 6 holes).

5—Jack Nicklaus, to win 1978 Jackie Gleason Inverrary Classic (last 5 holes).

LOWEST SCORING AVERAGE OVER ONE SEASON

68.17—Tiger Woods, in 2000.

Wins

MOST CONSECUTIVE YEARS WINNING AT LEAST ONE TOURNAMENT

17—Jack Nicklaus, 1962–78.

17—Arnold Palmer, 1955–71.

16—Billy Casper, 1956–71.

MOST CONSECUTIVE YEARS WINNING AT LEAST ONE TOURNAMENT, ACTIVE PLAYER

12—Tiger Woods, 1996–2007.

MOST CONSECUTIVE WINS IN ENTERED TOURNAMENTS

11—Byron Nelson, from Miami Four Ball, March 8–11, 1945, through Canadian Open, August 2–4, 1945.

7—Tiger Woods, from British Open, July 20–23, 2006, through Buick Invitational, January 25–28, 2007.

MOST WINS IN A SINGLE EVENT

8—Sam Snead, Greater Greensboro Open, 1938, 1946, 1949, 1950, 1955, 1956, 1960, and 1965.

MOST CONSECUTIVE WINS IN A SINGLE EVENT

4—Walter Hagen, PGA Championships, 1924–27.

4—Gene Sarazen, Miami Open, 1926, (schedule change) 1928–30.

4—Tiger Woods, Bay Hill Invitational, 2000–03.

MOST WINS IN A CALENDAR YEAR

18—Byron Nelson, 1945.

13—Ben Hogan, 1946.

MOST YEARS BETWEEN WINS

15 yrs, 6 mos—Robert Gamez, March 15, 1990 to September 25, 2005.

MOST YEARS FROM FIRST WIN TO LAST

28 yrs, 11 mos, 20 days—Raymond Floyd, 1963–92.

YOUNGEST WINNER

19 yrs, 10 mos—John McDermott, 1911 U.S. Open.

OLDEST WINNER

52 yrs, 10 mos—Sam Snead, 1965 Greater Greensboro Open.

WIDEST WINNING MARGIN: STROKES

16—Bobby Locke, 1948 Chicago Victory National Championship.

WIDEST WINNING MARGIN AT A MAJOR: STROKES

15—Tiger Woods, 2000 U.S. Open.

*Through 10/1/07

THE MAJOR TOURNAMENTS
LPGA Championship

Year	Winner	Score	Runner-Up	Site
1955	Beverly Hanson† (4 & 3)	220	Louise Suggs	Orchard Ridge CC, Ft Wayne, IN
1956	Marlene Hagge*	291	Patty Berg	Forest Lake CC, Detroit
1957	Louise Suggs	285	Wiffi Smith	Churchill Valley CC, Pittsburgh
1958	Mickey Wright	288	Fay Crocker	Churchill Valley CC, Pittsburgh
1959	Betsy Rawls	288	Patty Berg	Sheraton Hotel CC, French Lick, IN
1960	Mickey Wright	292	Louise Suggs	Sheraton Hotel CC, French Lick, IN
1961	Mickey Wright	287	Louise Suggs	Stardust CC, Las Vegas
1962	Judy Kimball	282	Shirley Spork	Stardust CC, Las Vegas
1963	Mickey Wright	294	Mary Lena Faulk Mary Mills Louise Suggs	Stardust CC, Las Vegas
1964	Mary Mills	278	Mickey Wright	Stardust CC, Las Vegas
1965	Sandra Haynie	279	Clifford A. Creed	Stardust CC, Las Vegas
1966	Gloria Ehret	282	Mickey Wright	Stardust CC, Las Vegas
1967	Kathy Whitworth	284	Shirley Englehorn	Pleasant Valley CC, Sutton, MA
1968	Sandra Post*	294	Kathy Whitworth (75)	Pleasant Valley CC, Sutton, MA
1969	Betsy Rawls	293	Susie Berning Carol Mann	Concord GC, Kiameshia Lake, NY
1970	Shirley Englehorn*	285	Kathy Whitworth (78)	Pleasant Valley CC, Sutton, MA
1971	Kathy Whitworth	288	Kathy Ahern	Pleasant Valley CC, Sutton, MA
1972	Kathy Ahern	293	Jane Blalock	Pleasant Valley CC, Sutton, MA
1973	Mary Mills	288	Betty Burfeindt	Pleasant Valley CC, Sutton, MA
1974	Sandra Haynie	288	JoAnne Carner	Pleasant Valley CC, Sutton, MA
1975	Kathy Whitworth	288	Sandra Haynie	Pine Ridge GC, Baltimore
1976	Betty Burfeindt	287	Judy Rankin	Pine Ridge GC, Baltimore
1977	Chako Higuchi	279	Pat Bradley Sandra Post Judy Rankin	Bay Tree Golf Plantation, N Myrtle Beach, SC
1978	Nancy Lopez	275	Amy Alcott	Jack Nicklaus GC, Kings Island, OH
1979	Donna Caponi	279	Jerilyn Britz	Jack Nicklaus GC, Kings Island, OH
1980	Sally Little	285	Jane Blalock	Jack Nicklaus GC, Kings Island, OH
1981	Donna Caponi	280	Jerilyn Britz Pat Meyers	Jack Nicklaus GC, Kings Island, OH
1982	Jan Stephenson	279	JoAnne Carner	Jack Nicklaus GC, Kings Island, OH
1983	Patty Sheehan	279	Sandra Haynie	Jack Nicklaus GC, Kings Island, OH
1984	Patty Sheehan	272	Beth Daniel Pat Bradley	Jack Nicklaus GC, Kings Island, OH
1985	Nancy Lopez	273	Alice Miller	Jack Nicklaus GC, Kings Island, OH
1986	Pat Bradley	277	Patty Sheehan	Jack Nicklaus GC, Kings Island, OH
1987	Jane Geddes	275	Betsy King	Jack Nicklaus GC, Kings Island, OH
1988	Sherri Turner	281	Amy Alcott	Jack Nicklaus GC, Kings Island, OH
1989	Nancy Lopez	274	Ayako Okamoto	Jack Nicklaus GC, Kings Island, OH
1990	Beth Daniel	280	Rosie Jones	Bethesda CC, Bethesda, MD
1991	Meg Mallon	274	Pat Bradley Ayako Okamoto	Bethesda CC, Bethesda, MD
1992	Betsy King	267	Karen Noble	Bethesda CC, Bethesda, MD
1993	Patty Sheehan	275	Lauri Merten	Bethesda CC, Bethesda, MD
1994	Laura Davies	279	Alice Ritzman	DuPont CC, Wilmington, DE
1995	Kelly Robbins	274	Laura Davies	DuPont CC, Wilmington, DE
1996	Laura Davies	213†	Julie Piers	DuPont CC, Wilmington, DE
1997	Chris Johnson*	281	Leta Lindley	DuPont CC, Wilmington, DE
1998	Se Ri Pak	273	Donna Andrews	DuPont CC, Wilmington, DE
1999	Juli Inkster	268	Liselotte Neumann	DuPont CC, Wilmington, DE
2000	Juli Inkster*	281	Stefania Croce	DuPont CC, Wilmington, DE
2001	Karrie Webb	270	Laura Diaz	DuPont CC, Wilmington, DE
2002	Se Ri Pak	279	Beth Daniel	DuPont CC, Wilmington, DE
2003	Annika Sorenstam*	278	Grace Park	DuPont CC, Wilmington, DE
2004	Annika Sorenstam	271	Shi Hyun Ahn	DuPont CC, Wilmington, DE
2005	Annika Sorenstam	277	Michelle Wie	Bulle Rock GC, Havre de Grace, MD
2006	Se Ri Pak*	280	Karrie Webb	Bulle Rock GC, Havre de Grace, MD
2007	Suzann Pettersen	274	Karrie Webb	Bulle Rock GC, Havre de Grace, MD

*Won playoff. †Won match-play final. #Shortened due to rain.

U.S. Women's Open

Year	Winner	Score	Runner-Up	Site
1946	Patty Berg	5 & 4	Betty Jameson	Spokane CC, Spokane, WA
1947	Betty Jameson	295	Sally Sessions	Starmount Forest CC, Greensboro, NC
			Polly Riley	
1948	Babe Zaharias	300	Betty Hicks	Atlantic City CC, Northfield, NJ
1949	Louise Suggs	291	Babe Zaharias	Prince George's G & CC, Landover, MD
1950	Babe Zaharias	291	Betsy Rawls	Rolling Hills CC, Wichita, KS
1951	Betsy Rawls	293	Louise Suggs	Druid Hills GC, Atlanta
1952	Louise Suggs	284	Marlene Bauer	Bala GC, Philadelphia
			Betty Jameson	
1953	Betsy Rawls* (71)	302	Jackie Pung (77)	CC of Rochester, Rochester, NY
1954	Babe Zaharias	291	Betty Hicks	Salem CC, Peabody, MA
1955	Fay Crocker	299	Mary Lena Faulk	Wichita CC, Wichita, KS
			Louise Suggs	
1956	Kathy Cornelius* (75)	302	Barbara McIntire (82)	Northland CC, Duluth, MN
1957	Betsy Rawls	299	Patty Berg	Winged Foot GC, Mamaroneck, NY
1958	Mickey Wright	290	Louise Suggs	Forest Lake CC, Detroit
1959	Mickey Wright	287	Louise Suggs	Churchill Valley CC, Pittsburgh
1960	Betsy Rawls	292	Joyce Ziske	Worcester CC, Worcester, MA
1961	Mickey Wright	293	Betsy Rawls	Baltusrol GC (Lower Course), Springfield, NJ
1962	Murle Breer	301	Jo Ann Prentice	Dunes GC, Myrtle Beach, SC
			Ruth Jessen	
1963	Mary Mills	289	Sandra Haynie	Kenwood CC, Cincinnati
			Louise Suggs	
1964	Mickey Wright* (70)	290	Ruth Jessen (72)	San Diego CC, Chula Vista, CA
1965	Carol Mann	290	Kathy Cornelius	Atlantic City CC, Northfield, NJ
1966	Sandra Spuzich	297	Carol Mann	Hazeltine Natl GC, Chaska, MN
1967	Catherine LaCoste	294	Susie Berning	Hot Springs GC (Cascades Course),
			Beth Stone	Hot Springs, VA
1968	Susie Berning	289	Mickey Wright	Moslem Springs GC, Fleetwood, PA
1969	Donna Caponi	294	Peggy Wilson	Scenic Hills CC, Pensacola, FL
1970	Donna Caponi	287	Sandra Haynie	Muskogee CC, Muskogee, OK
			Sandra Spuzich	
1971	JoAnne Carner	288	Kathy Whitworth	Kahkwa CC, Erie, PA
1972	Susie Berning	299	Kathy Ahern	Winged Foot GC, Mamaroneck, NY
			Pam Barnett	
			Judy Rankin	
1973	Susie Berning	290	Gloria Ehret	CC of Rochester, Rochester, NY
			Shelley Hamlin	
1974	Sandra Haynie	295	Carol Mann	La Grange CC, La Grange, IL
			Beth Stone	
1975	Sandra Palmer	295	JoAnne Carner	Atlantic City CC, Northfield, NJ
			Sandra Post	
			Nancy Lopez	
1976	JoAnne Carner* (76)	292	Sandra Palmer (78)	Rolling Green CC, Springfield, PA
1977	Hollis Stacy	292	Nancy Lopez	Hazeltine Natl GC, Chaska, MN
1978	Hollis Stacy	289	JoAnne Carner	CC of Indianapolis, Indianapolis
			Sally Little	
1979	Jerilyn Britz	284	Debbie Massey	Brooklawn CC, Fairfield, CT
			Sandra Palmer	
1980	Amy Alcott	280	Hollis Stacy	Richland CC, Nashville
1981	Pat Bradley	279	Beth Daniel	La Grange CC, La Grange, IL
1982	Janet Anderson	283	Beth Daniel	Del Paso CC, Sacramento
			Sandra Haynie	
			Donna White	
			JoAnne Carner	
1983	Jan Stephenson	290	JoAnne Carner	Cedar Ridge CC, Tulsa
			Patty Sheehan	
1984	Hollis Stacy	290	Rosie Jones	Salem CC, Peabody, MA
1985	Kathy Baker	280	Judy Dickinson	Baltusrol GC (Upper Course), Springfield, NJ
1986	Jane Geddes* (71)	287	Sally Little (73)	NCR GC, Dayton
1987	Laura Davies* (71)	285	Ayako Okamoto (73)	Plainfield CC, Plainfield, NJ
			JoAnne Carner (74)	
1988	Liselotte Neumann	277	Patty Sheehan	Baltimore CC, Baltimore
1989	Betsy King	278	Nancy Lopez	Indianwood G & CC, Lake Orion, MI
1990	Betsy King	284	Patty Sheehan	Atlanta Athletic Club, Duluth, GA
1991	Meg Mallon	283	Pat Bradley	Colonial Club, Fort Worth
1992	Patty Sheehan* (72)	280	Juli Inkster	Oakmont CC, Oakmont, PA
1993	Lauri Merten	280	Donna Andrew	Crooked Stick, Carmel, IN
			Helen Alfredsson	

U.S. Women's Open *(Cont.)*

Year	Winner	Score	Runner-Up	Site
1994	Patty Sheehan	277	Tammie Green	Indianwood G & CC, Lake Orion, MI
1995	Annika Sorenstam	278	Meg Mallon	The Broadmoor GC, Colorado Springs, CO
1996	Annika Sorenstam	272	Kris Tschetter	Pine Needles GC, Southern Pines, NC
1997	Alison Nicholas	274	Nancy Lopez	Pumpkin Ridge CC, North Plains, OR
1998	Se Ri Pak†	290	Jenny Chuasiriporn	Blackwolf Run Golf Resort, Kohler, WI
1999	Juli Inkster	272	Sherri Turner	Old Waverly GC, West Point, MS
2000	Karrie Webb	282	Cristie Kerr/ Meg Mallon	Merit GC, Libertyville, IL
2001	Karrie Webb	273	Se Ri Pak	Pine Needles GC, Southern Pines, NC
2002	Juli Inkster	276	Annika Sorenstam	Prairie Dunes CC, Hutchinson, KS
2003	Hilary Lunke*	283	Kelly Robbins	Pumpkin Ridge CC, North Plains, OR
2004	Meg Mallon	274	Annika Sorenstam	The Orchards GC, South Hadley, MA
2005	Birdie Kim	287	Brittany Lang Morgan Pressel	Cherry Hills CC, Cherry Hills Village, CO
2006	Annika Sorenstam*	284	Pat Hurst	Newport CC, Newport, RI
2007	Cristie Kerr	279	Angela Park Lorena Ochoa	Pine Needles GC, Southern Pines, NC

* Winner in playoff. † Winner on second hole of sudden death after 18-hole playoff ended in a tie.

Nabisco Championship

Year	Winner	Score	Runner-Up	Year	Winner	Score	Runner-Up
1972	Jane Blalock	213	Carol Mann Judy Rankin	1990	Betsy King	283	Kathy Postlewait Shirley Furlong
1973	Mickey Wright	284	Joyce Kazmierski	1991	Amy Alcott	273	Dottie Mochrie
1974	Jo Ann Prentice*	289	Jane Blalock Sandra Haynie	1992	Dottie Mochrie*	279	Juli Inkster Amy Benz
1975	Sandra Palmer	283	Kathy McMullen	1993	Helen Alfredsson	284	Tina Barrett
1976	Judy Rankin	285	Betty Burfeindt				Betsy King
1977	Kathy Whitworth	289	JoAnne Carner Sally Little	1994	Donna Andrews	276	Laura Davies
				1995	Nanci Bowen	285	Susie Redman
1978	Sandra Post*	283	Penny Pulz	1996	Patti Sheehan	281	Kelly Robbins
1979	Sandra Post	276	Nancy Lopez				Meg Mallon
1980	Donna Caponi	275	Amy Alcott				Annika Sorenstam
1981	Nancy Lopez	277	Carolyn Hill	1997	Betsy King	276	Kris Tschetter
1982	Sally Little	278	Hollis Stacy Sandra Haynie	1998	Pat Hurst	281	Helen Dobson
				1999	Dottie Pepper	269	Meg Mallon
1983	Amy Alcott	282	Beth Daniel Kathy Whitworth	2000	Karrie Webb	274	Dottie Pepper
				2001	Annika Sorenstam	281	five players
1984	Juli Inkster*	280	Pat Bradley	2002	Annika Sorenstam	280	Liselotte Neumann
1985	Alice Miller	275	Jan Stephenson	2003	P. Meunier-Lebouc	281	Annika Sorenstam
1986	Pat Bradley	280	Val Skinner	2004	Grace Park	277	Aree Song
1987	Betsy King*	283	Patty Sheehan	2005	Anika Sorenstam	273	Rosie Jones
1988	Amy Alcott	274	Colleen Walker	2006	Karrie Webb*	279	Lorena Ochoa
1989	Juli Inkster	279	Tammie Green JoAnne Carner	2007	Morgan Pressel	285	Catriona Matthew Brittany Lincicome Suzann Pettersen

*Winner in sudden-death playoff. Note: Designated fourth major in 1983; played at Mission Hills CC, Rancho Mirage, CA.

du Maurier Classic

Year	Winner	Score	Runner-Up	Site
1973	Jocelyne Bourassa*	214	Sandra Haynie Judy Rankin	Montreal GC, Montreal
1974	Carole Jo Callison	208	JoAnne Carner	Candiac GC, Montreal
1975	JoAnne Carner*	214	Carol Mann	St. George's CC, Toronto
1976	Donna Caponi*	212	Judy Rankin	Cedar Brae G & CC, Toronto
1977	Judy Rankin	214	Pat Meyers Sandra Palmer	Lachute G & CC, Montreal
1978	JoAnne Carner	– 278	Hollis Stacy	St. George's CC, Toronto
1979	Amy Alcott	285	Nancy Lopez	Richelieu Valley CC, Montreal
1980	Pat Bradley	277	JoAnne Carner	St. George's CC, Toronto
1981	Jan Stephenson	278	Nancy Lopez Pat Bradley	Summerlea CC, Dorion, Quebec
1982	Sandra Haynie	280	Beth Daniel	St. George's CC, Toronto
1983	Hollis Stacy	277	JoAnne Carner Alice Miller	Beaconsfield GC, Montreal
1984	Juli Inkster	279	Ayako Okamoto	St. George's G & CC, Toronto
1985	Pat Bradley	278	Jane Geddes	Beaconsfield CC, Montreal
1986	Pat Bradley*	276	Ayako Okamoto	Board of Trade CC, Toronto
1987	Jody Rosenthal	272	Ayako Okamoto	Islesmere GC, Laval, Quebec

du Maurier Classic (Cont.)

Year	Winner	Score	Runner-Up	Site
1988	Sally Little	279	Laura Davies	Vancouver GC, Coquitlam, British Columbia
1989	Tammie Green	279	Pat Bradley	Beaconsfield GC, Montreal
			Betsy King	
1990	Cathy Johnston	276	Patty Sheehan	Westmount G & CC, Kitchener, Ontario
1991	Nancy Scranton	279	Debbie Massey	Vancouver GC, Coquitlam, British Columbia
1992	Sherri Steinhauer	277	Judy Dickinson	St. Charles CC, Winnipeg, Manitoba
1993	Brandie Burton	277	Betsy King	London Hunt and CC, London, Ontario
1994	Martha Nause	279	Michelle McGann	Ottawa Hunt and GC, Ottawa, Ont.
1995	Jenny Lidback	280	Liselotte Neumann	Beaconsfield GC, Pointe-Claire, Quebec
1996	Laura Davies	277	Nancy Lopez	Edmonton CC, Edmonton, Alberta
			Karrie Webb	
1997	Colleen Walker	278	Liselotte Neumann	Glen Abbey GC, Oakville, Ontario
1998	Brandie Burton	270	Annika Sorenstam	Essex G & CC, Windsor, Ontario
1999	Karrie Webb	277	Laura Davies	Priddis Greens G & CC, Calgary, Alberta
2000	Meg Mallon	282	Rosie Jones	Royal Ottawa GC, Aylmer, Quebec

*Winner in sudden-death playoff. Note: Designated third major in 1979; discontinued in 2001.

Women's British Open

Year	Winner	Score	Runner-Up	Site
2001	Se Ri Pak	277	Mi Hyun Kim	Sunningdale GC, Berkshire, England
2002	Karrie Webb	273	Michelle Ellis	Turnberry GC, Ailsa, Scotland
			Paula Marti	
2003	Annika Sorenstam	278	Se Ri Pak	Royal Lytham & St. Annes, England
2004	Karen Stupples	269	Rachel Teske	Sunningdale GC, Berjshire, England
2005	Jeong Jang	272	Sophie Gustafson	Royal Birkdale CC, Merseyside, England
2006	Sherri Steinhauer	281	Cristie Kerr	Royal Lytham & St. Anne's, England
2007	Lorena Ochoa	287	Jee Young Lee	Old Course, St. Andrew's, Scotland
			Maria Hjorth	

Note: Designated fourth major in 2001.

Alltime Major Championship Winners

	LPGA	U.S. Open	Nabisco	Brit. Open	‡du Maurier	#Titleholders	†Western	U.S. Am	Brit. Am	Total
Patty Berg	0	1	0	0	0	7	7	1	0	16
Mickey Wright	4	4	0	0	0	2	3	0	0	13
Louise Suggs	1	2	0	0	0	4	4	1	1	13
Babe Zaharias	0	3	0	0	0	3	4	1	1	12
*Juli Inkster	2	2	2	0	1	0	0	3	0	10
*Annika Sorenstam	3	3	3	1	0	0	0	0	0	10
Betsy Rawls	2	4	0	0	0	0	2	0	0	8
JoAnne Carner	0	2	0	0	0	0	0	5	0	7
*Karrie Webb	1	2	2	1	1	0	0	0	0	7
Kathy Whitworth	3	0	0	0	0	2	1	0	0	6
Pat Bradley	1	1	1	0	3	0	0	0	0	6
*Patty Sheehan	3	2	1	0	0	0	0	0	0	6
Glenna Vare	0	0	0	0	0	0	0	6	0	6
*Betsy King	1	2	3	0	0	0	0	0	0	6

*Active LPGA player.
#Major from 1937–1972. †Major from 1937–1967. ‡Major from 1979–2000.

Alltime Multiple Professional Major Winners

LPGA	U.S. OPEN	NABISCO/DINAH SHORE	WESTERN OPEN
Mickey Wright.........4	Betsy Rawls.........4	Amy Alcott.........3	Patty Berg.........7
Nancy Lopez.........3	Mickey Wright.........4	Betsy King.........3	Louise Suggs.........4
Se Ri Pak.........3	Susie Maxwell Berning..3	Annika Sorenstam.......3	Babe Zaharias.........4
Patty Sheehan.........3	Hollis Stacy.........3	Juli Inkster.........2	Mickey Wright.........3
Annika Sorenstam.......3	Babe Zaharias.........3	Karrie Webb.........2	June Beebe.........2
Kathy Whitworth.......3	Annika Sorenstam.......3		Opal Hill.........2
Donna Caponi.........2	JoAnne Carner.........2	**TITLEHOLDERS**	Betty Jameson.........2
Sandra Haynie.........2	Donna Caponi.........2	Patty Berg.........7	Betsy Rawls.........2
Mary Mills.........2	Betsy King.........2	Louise Suggs.........4	
Betsy Rawls.........2	Meg Mallon.........2	Babe Zaharias.........3	**DU MAURIER**
Laura Davies.........2	Patty Sheehan.........2	Dorothy Kirby.........2	Pat Bradley.........3
Juli Inkster.........2	Louise Suggs.........2	Marilynn Smith.........2	Brandie Burton.........2
	Karrie Webb.........2	Kathy Whitworth.........2	JoAnne Carner.........2
	Juli Inkster.........2	Mickey Wright.........2	

THE LPGA TOUR

Most Career Wins†

	Wins		Wins		Wins
Kathy Whitworth	88	JoAnne Carner	43	Beth Daniel*	33
Mickey Wright	82	Sandra Haynie	42	Pat Bradley	31
Annika Sorenstam*	69	Babe Zaharias	41	Juli Inkster*	31
Patty Berg	60	Carol Mann	38	Amy Alcott*	29
Louise Suggs	58	Patty Sheehan	35	Jane Blalock	29
Betsy Rawls	55	Karrie Webb*	35	Judy Rankin	26
Nancy Lopez	48	Betsy King	34	Marlene Hagge	26

*Active player.

Season Money Leaders

	Earnings ($)		Earnings ($)		Earnings ($)
1950...Babe Zaharias	14,800	1969...Carol Mann	49,152	1988...Sherri Turner	350,851
1951...Babe Zaharias	15,087	1970...Kathy Whitworth	30,235	1989...Betsy King	654,132
1952...Betsy Rawls	14,505	1971...Kathy Whitworth	41,181	1990...Beth Daniel	863,578
1953...Louise Suggs	19,816	1972...Kathy Whitworth	65,063	1991...Pat Bradley	763,118
1954...Patty Berg	16,011	1973...Kathy Whitworth	82,864	1992...Dottie Mochrie	693,335
1955...Patty Berg	16,492	1974...JoAnne Carner	87,094	1993...Betsy King	595,992
1956...Marlene Hagge	20,235	1975...Sandra Palmer	76,374	1994...Laura Davies	687,201
1957...Patty Berg	16,272	1976...Judy Rankin	150,734	1995...Annika Sorenstam	666,533
1958...Beverly Hanson	12,639	1977...Judy Rankin	122,890	1996...Karrie Webb	1,002,000
1959...Betsy Rawls	26,774	1978...Nancy Lopez	189,814	1997...Annika Sorenstam	1,236,789
1960...Louise Suggs	16,892	1979...Nancy Lopez	197,489	1998...Annika Sorenstam	1,092,748
1961...Mickey Wright	22,236	1980...Beth Daniel	231,000	1999...Karrie Webb	1,591,959
1962...Mickey Wright	21,641	1981...Beth Daniel	206,998	2000...Karrie Webb	1,876,853
1963...Mickey Wright	31,269	1982...JoAnne Carner	310,400	2001...Annika Sorenstam	2,105,868
1964...Mickey Wright	29,800	1983...JoAnne Carner	291,404	2002...Annika Sorenstam	2,863.904
1965...Kathy Whitworth	28,658	1984...Betsy King	266,771	2003...Annika Sorenstam	2,029,506
1966...Kathy Whitworth	33,517	1985...Nancy Lopez	416,472	2004...Annika Sorenstam	2,544,707
1967...Kathy Whitworth	32,937	1986...Pat Bradley	492,021	2005...Annika Sorenstam	2,588,240
1968...Kathy Whitworth	48,379	1987...Ayako Okamoto	466,034	2006...Lorena Ochoa	2,592,872

Career Money Leaders†

	Earnings ($)		Earnings ($)		Earnings ($)
1. Annika Sorenstam	20,718,680	11. Betsy King	7,637,621	21. Nancy Lopez	5,320,877
2. Karrie Webb	13,436,187	12. Mi-Hyun Kim	7,612,628	22. Rachel Hetherington	5,315,943
3. Juli Inkster	11,671,175	13. Dottie Pepper	6,827,284	23. Grace Park	5,228,650
4. Se Ri Pak	9,736,140	14. Lorie Kane	6,635,611	24. Catriona Matthew	4,976,116
5. Lorena Ochoa	9,137,643	15. Pat Hurst	5,847,181	25. Michelle Redman	4,917,030
6. Meg Mallon	8,871,495	16. Pat Bradley	5,755,951	26. Jeong Jang	4,828,409
7. Beth Daniel	8,755,733	17. Liselotte Neumann	5,721,425	27. Hee-Won Han	4,772,330
8. Rosie Jones	8,355,068	18. Kelly Robbins	5,621,742	28. Brandie Burton	4,326,921
9. Laura Davies	7,975,664	19. Sherri Steinhauer	5,599,964	29. Tammie Green	4,099,696
10. Cristie Kerr	7,765,401	20. Patty Sheehan	5,513,409	30. Laura Diaz	4,064,024

LPGA Player of the Year

1966	Kathy Whitworth	1980	Beth Daniel	1994	Beth Daniel
1967	Kathy Whitworth	1981	JoAnne Carner	1995	Annika Sörenstam
1968	Kathy Whitworth	1982	JoAnne Carner	1996	Laura Davies
1969	Kathy Whitworth	1983	Patty Sheehan	1997	Annika Sorenstam
1970	Sandra Haynie	1984	Betsy King	1998	Annika Sorenstam
1971	Kathy Whitworth	1985	Nancy Lopez	1999	Karrie Webb
1972	Kathy Whitworth	1986	Pat Bradley	2000	Karrie Webb
1973	Kathy Whitworth	1987	Ayako Okamoto	2001	Annika Sorenstam
1974	JoAnne Carner	1988	Nancy Lopez	2002	Annika Sorenstam
1975	Sandra Palmer	1989	Betsy King	2003	Annika Sorenstam
1976	Judy Rankin	1990	Beth Daniel	2004	Annika Sorenstam
1977	Judy Rankin	1991	Pat Bradley	2005	Annika Sorenstam
1978	Nancy Lopez	1992	Dottie Mochrie	2006	Lorena Ochoa
1979	Nancy Lopez	1993	Betsy King		

†Through 10/1/07.

Vare Trophy: Best Scoring Average*

	Avg		Avg		Avg
1953......Patty Berg	75.00	1971......Kathy Whitworth	72.88	1989......Beth Daniel	70.38
1954......Babe Zaharias	75.48	1972......Kathy Whitworth	72.38	1990......Beth Daniel	70.54
1955......Patty Berg	74.47	1973......Judy Rankin	73.08	1991......Pat Bradley	70.76
1956......Patty Berg	74.57	1974......JoAnne Carner	72.87	1992......Dottie Mochrie	70.80
1957......Louise Suggs	74.64	1975......JoAnne Carner	72.40	1993......Nancy Lopez	70.83
1958......Beverly Hanson	74.92	1976......Judy Rankin	72.25	1994......Beth Daniel	70.90
1959......Betsy Rawls	74.03	1977......Judy Rankin	72.16	1995......Annika Sorenstam	71.00
1960......Mickey Wright	73.25	1978......Nancy Lopez	71.76	1996......Annika Sorenstam	70.47
1961......Mickey Wright	73.55	1979......Nancy Lopez	71.20	1997......Karrie Webb	70.00
1962......Mickey Wright	73.67	1980......Amy Alcott	71.51	1998......Karrie Webb	69.99
1963......Mickey Wright	72.81	1981......JoAnne Carner	71.75	1999......Karrie Webb	69.43
1964......Mickey Wright	72.46	1982......JoAnne Carner	71.49	2000......Karrie Webb	70.05
1965......Kathy Whitworth	72.61	1983......JoAnne Carner	71.41	2001......Annika Sorenstam	69.42
1966......Kathy Whitworth	72.60	1984......Patty Sheehan	71.40	2002......Annika Sorenstam	68.70
1967......Kathy Whitworth	72.74	1985......Nancy Lopez	70.73	2003......Se Ri Pak	70.03
1968......Carol Mann	72.04	1986......Pat Bradley	71.10	2004......Grace Park	69.99
1969......Kathy Whitworth	72.38	1987......Betsy King	71.14	2005......Annika Sorenstam	69.33
1970......Kathy Whitworth	72.26	1988......Colleen Walker	71.26	2006......Lorena Ochoa	69.23

Alltime LPGA Tour Records†

Scoring

72 HOLES, TOTAL STROKES

258—(63-66-66-63) by Karen Stupples to win at the Dell Urich GC, Tucson, AZ, in the 2004 Welch's/Fry's Champ. (22 under par).

259—(65-62-67-65) by Wendy Doolan to win at the Dell Urich GC, Tucson, AZ, in the 2003 Welch's/Fry's Champ. (21 under par).

72 HOLES, TO PAR

-27—(65-59-69-68) by Annika Sorenstam to win at the 2001 Standard Register PING Invitational in Moon Valley CC, Phoenix (par 72).

-26—(63-67-64-68) by Karrie Webb to win at the 1999 Australian Ladies Masters at the Royal Pines Resort, Ashmore, Australia (par 72).

54 HOLES

192—(63-63-66) by Annika Sorenstam to win at the Seta GC, Otsu-shi, Shiga, Japan in the 2003 Mizuno Classic (24 under par).

193—(66-61-66) by Karrie Webb to lead at the Walnut Hills CC, East Lansing, MI, in the 2000 Oldsmobile Classic (23 under par).

193—(65-59-69) by Annika Sorenstam to lead at the Moon Valley CC, Phoenix, in the 2001 Standard Register PING (23 under par).

36 HOLES

124—(65-59) by Annika Sorenstam to lead at the Moon Valley CC, Phoenix, in the 2001 Standard Register PING (20 under par).

124—(65-60) by Meg Mallong to lead at the Dell Urich GC, Tucson, AZ, in the 2003 Wendy's Fry's Champ. (16 under par).

18 HOLES

59—by Annika Sorenstam at the Moon Valley CC, Phoenix, in the second round in winning the 2001 Standard Register PING (13 under par).

9 HOLES

27—by Jimin Kang at Seaview Marriott Resort & Spa, Bay Course, 2005 ShopRite LPGA Classic, Galloway Twp, N.J., (par 35). Kang shot 62.

Scoring *(Cont.)*

MOST CONSECUTIVE ROUNDS UNDER 70

14—Annika Sorenstam, in 2005.

11—Annika Sorenstam, in 2002.

10—Lorena Ochoa, in 2004.

MOST BIRDIES IN A ROW

9—Beth Daniel at Onion Creek Club in Austin, TX in the second round of the 1999 Philips Invitational. Daniel shot 62 (8 under par).

MOST BIRDIES IN ONE ROUND

13—Annika Sorenstam at Moon Valley CC in Phoenix, AZ, in the second round of the 2001 Standard Register PING Invitational. Sorenstam shot 59 (13 under par).

LOWEST SCORING AVERAGE OVER ONE SEASON

68.696—Annika Sorenstam, in 2004.

Wins

MOST CONSECUTIVE WINS IN SCHEDULED EVENTS

4—Mickey Wright, in 1962.

4—Mickey Wright, in 1963.

4—Kathy Whitworth, in 1969.

4—Annika Sorenstam, in 2001.

MOST CONSECUTIVE WINS IN ENTERED TOURNAMENTS

5—Nancy Lopez, in 1978.

5—Annika Sorenstam, in 2004–05.

MOST CONSECUTIVE WINS AT SAME TOURNAMENT

5—Annika Sorenstam, Mizuno Classic, 2001–05.

4—Laura Davies, Standard Register PING, 1994–97.

MOST CONSECUTIVE YEARS WITH A TOURNAMENT WIN

17—Kathy Whitworth, from 1962–78.

MOST WINS IN A CALENDAR YEAR

13—Mickey Wright, in 1963.

11—Mickey Wright, in 1964.

11—Annika Sorenstam, in 2002.

WIDEST WINNING MARGIN, STROKES

14—Louise Suggs, 1949 U.S. Women's Open.

14—Cindy Mackey, 1986 MasterCard Int'l Pro-Am.

†Through 10/1/07. *Must play 70 rounds in order to qualify; Annika Sorenstam compiled an average of 69.02 in 60 rounds in 2003.

U.S. Senior Open

Year	Winner	Score	Runner-Up	Site
1980	Roberto DeVicenzo	285	William C. Campbell	Winged Foot GC, Mamaroneck, NY
1981	Arnold Palmer* (70)	289	Bob Stone (74)	Oakland Hills CC, Birmingham, MI
			Billy Casper (77)	
1982	Miller Barber	282	Gene Littler, Dan Sikes, Jr.	Portland GC, Portland, OR
1983	Billy Casper* (75) (3)	288	Rod Funseth (75) (4)	Hazeltine GC, Chaska, MN
1984	Miller Barber	286	Arnold Palmer	Oak Hill CC, Rochester, NY
1985	Miller Barber	285	Roberto DeVicenzo	Edgewood Tahoe GC, Stateline, NV
1986	Dale Douglass	279	Gary Player	Scioto CC, Columbus, OH
1987	Gary Player	270	Doug Sanders	Brooklawn CC, Fairfield, CT
1988	Gary Player* (68)	288	Bob Charles (70)	Medinah CC, Medinah, IL
1989	Orville Moody	279	Frank Beard	Laurel Valley GC, Ligonier, PA
1990	Lee Trevino	275	Jack Nicklaus	Ridgewood CC, Paramus, NJ
1991	Jack Nicklaus* (65)	282	Chi Chi Rodriguez (69)	Oakland Hills CC, Birmingham, MI
1992	Larry Laoretti	275	Jim Colbert	Saucon Valley CC, Bethlehem, PA
1993	Jack Nicklaus	278	Tom Weiskopf	Cherry Hills CC, Englewood, CO
1994	Simon Hobday	274	Jim Albus	Pinehurst Resort & CC, Pinehurst, NC
1995	Tom Weiskopf	275	Jack Nicklaus	Congressional CC, Bethesda, MD
1996	Dave Stockton	277	Hale Irwin	Canterbury GC, Beachwood, OH
1997	Graham Marsh	280	Hale Irwin	Olympia Fields CC, Olympia Fields, IL
1998	Hale Irwin	285	Vicente Fernandez	Riviera CC, Pacific Palisades, CA
1999	Dave Eichelberger	281	Ed Dougherty	Des Moines G & CC, Des Moines, IA
2000	Hale Irwin	267	Bruce Fleisher	Saucon Valley CC, Bethlehem, PA
2001	Bruce Fleisher	280	Isao Aoki, Gil Morgan	Salem CC, Peabody, MA
2002	Don Pooley* (19) (5)	274	Tom Watson (18)	Caves Valley GC, Owings Mill, MD
2003	Bruce Lietzke	277	Tom Watson	Inverness GC, Toledo, OH
2004	Peter Jacobsen	272	Hale Irwin	Bellerive CC, St. Louis, MO
2005	Allen Doyle	274	D.A. Weibring	NCR GC, Kettering, OH
			Loren Roberts	
2006	Allen Doyle	272	Tom Watson	Prairie Dunes CC, Hutchinson, KS
2007	Brad Bryant	282	Ben Crenshaw	Whistling Straits GC, Kohler, WI

*Winner in playoff. Playoff scores are in parentheses. The 1983 playoff went to one hole of sudden death after an 18-hole playoff.

CHAMPIONS TOUR
Season Money Leaders

Year	Winner	Earnings ($)	Year	Winner	Earnings ($)	Year	Winner	Earnings ($)
1980	Don January	44,100	1989	Bob Charles	725,887	1998	Hale Irwin	2,861,945
1981	Miller Barber	83,136	1990	Lee Trevino	1,190,518	1999	Bruce Fleisher	2,515,705
1982	Miller Barber	106,890	1991	Mike Hill	1,065,657	2000	Larry Nelson	2,708,005
1983	Don January	237,571	1992	Lee Trevino	1,027,002	2001	Allen Doyle	2,553,582
1984	Don January	328,597	1993	Dave Stockton	1,175,944	2002	Hale Irwin	3,028,304
1985	Peter Thomson	386,724	1994	Dave Stockton	1,402,519	2003	Tom Watson	1,853,108
1986	Bruce Crampton	454,299	1995	Jim Colbert	1,444,386	2004	Craig Stadler	2,306,066
1987	Chi Chi Rodriguez	509,145	1996	Jim Colbert	1,627,890	2005	Dana Quigley	2,170,258
1988	Bob Charles	533,929	1997	Hale Irwin	2,449,420	2006	Jay Haas	2,420,227

Career Money Leaders†

	Earnings ($)		Earnings ($)		Earnings ($)
1. Hale Irwin	24,544,691	11. Dave Stockton	10,926,788	21. Bob Gilder	8,729,362
2. Gil Morgan	18,314,934	12. Tom Watson	10,015,484	22. John Jacobs	8,401,179
3. Dana Quigley	13,915,250	13. Lee Trevino	9,837,242	23. Mike Hill	8,383,104
4. Burce Fleischer	13,497,906	14. Raymond Floyd	9,449,519	24. Vicente Fernandez	8,254,543
5. Larry Nelson	13,047,507	15. Jay Sigel	9,340,917	25. Tom Wargo	7,717,720
6. Allen Doyle	12,587,170	16. Isao Aoki	9,295,043	26. Doug Tewell	7,707,695
7. Jim Thorpe	12,007,651	17. Graham Marsh	9,059,607	27. John Bland	7,493,787
8. Jim Colbert	11,620,231	18. Bob Charles	9,032,001	28. J.C. Snead	7,349,716
9. Tom Kite	11,281,176	19. Jim Dent	8,966,279	29. Bob Murphy	7,191,996
10. Tom Jenkins	11,165,946	20. Bruce Summerhays	8,861,135	30. Jose Maria Canizares	7,177,792

Most Career Wins†

	Wins		Wins
Hale Irwin	45	Jim Colbert	20
Lee Trevino	29	Bruce Crampton	20
Gil Morgan	25	George Archer	19
Miller Barber	24	Gary Player	19
Bob Charles	23	Larry Nelson	19
Don January	22	Bruce Fleischer	18
Chi Chi Rodriguez	22	Mike Hill	18

†Through 10/1/07

MAJOR MEN'S AMATEUR CHAMPIONSHIPS

U.S. Amateur

Year	Winner	Score	Runner-Up	Site
1895	Charles B. Macdonald	12 & 11	Charles E. Sands	Newport GC, Newport, RI
1896	H.J. Whigham	8 & 7	J.G Thorp	Shinnecock Hills GC, Southampton, NY
1897	H.J. Whigham	8 & 6	W. Rossiter Betts	Chicago GC, Wheaton, IL
1898	Findlay S. Douglas	5 & 3	Walter B. Smith	Morris County GC, Morristown, NJ
1899	H.M. Harriman	3 & 2	Findlay S. Douglas	Onwentsia Club, Lake Forest, IL
1900	Walter Travis	2 up	Findlay S. Douglas	Garden City GC, Garden City, NY
1901	Walter Travis	5 & 4	Walter E. Egan	CC of Atlantic City, NJ
1902	Louis N. James	4 & 2	Eben M. Byers	Glen View Club, Golf, IL
1903	Walter Travis	5 & 4	Eben M. Byers	Nassau CC, Glen Cove, NY
1904	H. Chandler Egan	8 & 6	Fred Herreshoff	Baltusrol GC, Springfield, NJ
1905	H. Chandler Egan	6 & 5	D.E. Sawyer	Chicago GC, Wheaton, IL
1906	Eben M. Byers	2 up	George S. Lyon	Englewood GC, Englewood, NJ
1907	Jerry Travers	6 & 5	Archibald Graham	Euclid Club, Cleveland, OH
1908	Jerry Travers	8 & 7	Max H. Behr	Garden City GC, Garden City, NY
1909	Robert A. Gardner	4 & 3	H. Chandler Egan	Chicago GC, Wheaton, IL
1910	William C. Fownes Jr.	4 & 3	Warren K. Wood	The Country Club, Brookline, MA
1911	Harold Hilton	1 up	Fred Herreshoff	The Apawamis Club, Rye, NY
1912	Jerry Travers	7 & 6	Charles Evans Jr.	Chicago GC, Wheaton, IL
1913	Jerry Travers	5 & 4	John G. Anderson	Garden City GC, Garden City, NY
1914	Francis Ouimet	6 & 5	Jerry Travers	Ekwanok CC, Manchester, VT
1915	Robert A. Gardner	5 & 4	John G. Anderson	CC of Detroit, Grosse Pt. Farms, MI
1916	Chick Evans	4 & 3	Robert A. Gardner	Merion Cricket Club, Haverford, PA
1917–18	No tournament			
1919	S. Davidson Herron	5 & 4	Bobby Jones	Oakmont CC, Oakmont, PA
1920	Chick Evans	7 & 6	Francis Ouimet	Engineers' CC, Roslyn, NY
1921	Jesse P. Guilford	7 & 6	Robert A. Gardner	St. Louis CC, Clayton, MO
1922	Jess W. Sweetser	3 & 2	Chick Evans	The Country Club, Brookline, MA
1923	Max R. Marston	1 up	Jess W. Sweetser	Flossmoor CC, Flossmoor, IL
1924	Bobby Jones	9 & 8	George Von Elm	Merion Cricket Club, Ardmore, PA
1925	Bobby Jones	8 & 7	Watts Gunn	Oakmont CC, Oakmont, PA
1926	George Von Elm	2 & 1	Bobby Jones	Baltusrol GC, Springfield, NJ
1927	Bobby Jones	8 & 7	Chick Evans	Minikahda Club, Minneapolis
1928	Bobby Jones	10 & 9	T. Phillip Perkins	Brae Burn CC, West Newton, MA
1929	Harrison R. Johnston	4 & 3	Dr. O.F. Willing	Del Monte G & CC, Pebble Beach, CA
1930	Bobby Jones	8 & 7	Eugene V. Homans	Merion Cricket Club, Ardmore, PA
1931	Francis Ouimet	6 & 5	Jack Westland	Beverly CC, Chicago, IL
1932	C. Ross Somerville	2 & 1	John Goodman	Baltimore CC, Timonium, MD
1933	George T. Dunlap Jr.	6 & 5	Max R. Marston	Kenwood CC, Cincinnati, OH
1934	Lawson Little	8 & 7	David Goldman	The Country Club, Brookline, MA
1935	Lawson Little	4 & 2	Walter Emery	The Country Club, Cleveland, OH
1936	John W. Fischer	1 up	Jack McLean	Garden City GC, Garden City, NY
1937	John Goodman	2 up	Raymond E. Billows	Alderwood CC, Portland, OR
1938	William P. Turnesa	8 & 7	B. Patrick Abbott	Oakmont CC, Oakmont, PA
1939	Marvin H. Ward	7 & 5	Raymond E. Billows	North Shore CC, Glenview, IL
1940	Richard D. Chapman	11 & 9	W. McCullough Jr.	Winged Foot GC, Mamaroneck, NY
1941	Marvin H. Ward	4 & 3	B. Patrick Abbott	Omaha Field Club, Omaha, NE
1942–45	No tournament			
1946	Ted Bishop	1 up	Smiley L. Quick	Baltusrol GC, Springfield, NJ
1947	Skee Riegel	2 & 1	John W. Dawson	Del Monte G & CC, Pebble Beach, CA
1948	William P. Turnesa	2 & 1	Raymond E. Billows	Memphis CC, Memphis, TN
1949	Charles R. Coe	11 & 10	Rufus King	Oak Hill CC, Rochester, NY
1950	Sam Urzetta	1 up	Frank Stranahan	Minneapolis GC, Minneapolis, MN
1951	Billy Maxwell	4 & 3	Joseph F. Gagliardi	Saucon Valley CC, Bethlehem, PA
1952	Jack Westland	3 & 2	Al Mengert	Seattle GC, Seattle, WA
1953	Gene Littler	1 up	Dale Morey	Oklahoma City G & CC, Oklahoma City
1954	Arnold Palmer	1 up	Robert Sweeny	CC of Detroit, Grosse Pt. Farms, MI
1955	E. Harvie Ward Jr.	9 & 8	William Hyndman III	CC of Virginia, Richmond, VA
1956	E. Harvie Ward Jr.	5 & 4	Charles Kocsis	Knollwood Club, Lake Forest, IL
1957	Hillman Robbins Jr.	5 & 4	Dr. Frank M. Taylor	The Country Club, Brookline, MA
1958	Charles R. Coe	5 & 4	Tommy Aaron	Olympic Club, San Francisco, CA
1959	Jack Nicklaus	1 up	Charles R. Coe	Broadmoor GC, Colorado Springs, CO
1960	Deane Beman	6 & 4	Robert W. Gardner	St. Louis CC, Clayton, MO
1961	Jack Nicklaus	8 & 6	H. Dudley Wysong	Pebble Beach GL, Pebble Beach, CA
1962	Labron E. Harris Jr.	1 up	Downing Gray	Pinehurst CC, Pinehurst, NC

U.S. Amateur *(Cont.)*

Year	Winner	Score	Runner-Up	Site
1963	Deane Beman	2 & 1	Richard H. Sikes	Wakonda Club, Des Moines, IA
1964	William C. Campbell	1 up	Edgar M. Tutwiler	Canterbury GC, Cleveland, OH
1965	Robert J. Murphy Jr.	291	Robert B. Dickson	Southern Hills, CC, Tulsa
1966	Gary Cowan	285-75	Deane Beman	Merion GC, Ardmore, PA
1967	Robert B. Dickson	285	Marvin Giles III	Broadmoor GC, Colorado Springs
1968	Bruce Fleisher	284	Marvin Giles III	Scioto CC, Columbus, OH
1969	Steven N. Melnyk	286	Marvin Giles III	Oakmont CC, Oakmont, PA
1970	Lanny Wadkins	279	Tom Kite	Waverley CC, Portland, OR
1971	Gary Cowan	280	Eddie Pearce	Wilmington CC, Wilmington DE
1972	Marvin Giles III	285	two tied	Charlotte CC, Charlotte, NC
1973	Craig Stadler	6 & 5	David Strawn	Inverness Club, Toledo
1974	Jerry Pate	2 & 1	John P. Grace	Ridgewood CC, Ridgewood, NJ
1975	Fred Ridley	2 up	Keith Fergus	CC of Virginia, Richmond
1976	Bill Sander	8 & 6	C. Parker Moore Jr.	Bel Air CC, Los Angeles
1977	John Fought	9 & 8	Doug Fischesser	Aronimink GC, Newton Square, PA
1978	John Cook	5 & 4	Scott Hoch	Plainfield CC, Plainfield, NJ
1979	Mark O'Meara	8 & 7	John Cook	Canterbury GC, Cleveland
1980	Hal Sutton	9 & 8	Bob Lewis	CC of North Carolina, Pinehurst, NC
1981	Nathaniel Crosby	1 up	Brian Lindley	Olympic Club, San Francisco
1982	Jay Sigel	8 & 7	David Tolley	The Country Club, Brookline, MA
1983	Jay Sigel	8 & 7	Chris Perry	North Shore CC, Glenview, IL
1984	Scott Verplank	4 & 3	Sam Randolph	Oak Tree GC, Edmond, OK
1985	Sam Randolph	1 up	Peter Persons	Montclair GC, West Orange, NJ
1986	Buddy Alexander	5 & 3	Chris Kite	Shoal Creek, Shoal Creek, AL
1987	Bill Mayfair	4 & 3	Eric Rebmann	Jupiter Hills Club, Jupiter, FL
1988	Eric Meeks	7 & 6	Danny Yates	Va. Hot Springs G & CC, VA
1989	Chris Patton	3 & 1	Danny Green	Merion GC, Ardmore, PA
1990	Phil Mickelson	5 & 4	Manny Zerman	Cherry Hills CC, Englewood, CO
1991	Mitch Voges	7 & 6	Manny Zerman	The Honors Course, Ooltewah, TN
1992	Justin Leonard	8 & 7	Tom Scherrer	Muirfield Village GC, Dublin, OH
1993	John Harris	5 & 3	Danny Ellis	Champions GC, Houston
1994	Tiger Woods	2 up	Trip Kuehne	TPC-Sawgrass, Ponte Vedre, FL
1995	Tiger Woods	2 up	Buddy Marucci	Newport Country Club, Newport, RI
1996	Tiger Woods	38 holes	Steve Scott	Pumpkin Ridge GC, Cornelius, OR
1997	Matthew Kuchar	2 & 1	Joel Kribel	Cog Hill G & CC, Lemont, IL
1998	Hank Kuehne	2 & 1	Tom McKnight	Oak Hill CC, Rochester, NY
1999	David Gossett	9 & 8	Sung Yoon Kim	Pebble Beach GL, Pebble Beach, CA
2000	Jeff Quinney	39 holes	James Driscoll	Baltusrol GC, Upper Springfield, NJ
2001	Bubba Dickerson	1 up	Robert Hamilton	East Lake CC, Atlanta
2002	Ricky Barnes	2 & 1	Hunter Mahan	Oakland Hills CC, Bloomfield Hills, MI
2003	Nick Flanagan	37 holes	Frank Abbott	East Lake CC, Atlanta
2004	Ryan Moore	2 & 1	Luke List	Winged Foot GC, Mamaroneck, NY
2005	Edoardo Molinari	4 & 3	Dillon Dougherty	Merion GC, Ardmore, PA
2006	Richie Ramsay	3 & 2	John Kelly	Hazeltine National GC, Chaska, MN
2007	Colt Knost	2 & 1	Michael Thompson	Olympic Club, San Francisco, CA

Note: All stroke play from 1965 to 1972.

U.S. Junior Amateur

1948...Dean Lind	1963...Gregg McHatton	1978...Don Hurter	1993...Tiger Woods
1949...Gay Brewer	1964...Johnny Miller	1979...Jack Larkin	1994...Terry Noe
1950...Mason Rudolph	1965...James Masserio	1980...Eric Johnson	1995...D. Scott Hailes
1951...Tommy Jacobs	1966...Gary Sanders	1981...Scott Erickson	1996...Shane McMenamy
1952...Don Bisplinghoff	1967...John Crooks	1982...Rich Marik	1997...Jason Allred
1953...Rex Baxter	1968...Eddie Pearce	1983...Tim Straub	1998...James Oh
1954...Foster Bradley	1969...Aly Trompas	1984...Doug Martin	1999...Hunter Mahan
1955...William Dunn	1970...Gary Koch	1985...Charles Rymer	2000...Matthew Rosenfeld
1956...Harlan Stevenson	1971...Mike Brannan	1986...Brian Montgomery	2001...Henry Liaw
1957...Larry Beck	1972...Bob Byman	1987...Brett Quigley	2002...Charlie Beljan
1958...Buddy Baker	1973...Jack Renner	1988...Jason Widener	2003...Brian Harman
1959...Larry Lee	1974...David Nevatt	1989...David Duval	2004...Sihwan Kim
1960...Bill Tindall	1975...Brett Mullin	1990...Mathew Todd	2005...Kevin Tway
1961...Charles McDowell	1976...Madden Hatcher III	1991...Tiger Woods	2006...Phillip Francis
1962...Jim Wiechers	1977...Willie Wood Jr.	1992...Tiger Woods	2007...Cory Whitsett

Mid-Amateur Championship

1981...Jim Holtgrieve	1988...David Eger	1995...Jerry Courville Jr.	2002...George Zahringer
1982...William Hoffer	1989...James Taylor	1996...John Miller	2003...Nathan Smith
1983...Jay Sigel	1990...Jim Stuart	1997...Ken Bakst	2004...Austin Eaton III
1984...Mike Podolak	1991...Jim Stuart	1998...John Miller	2005...Kevin Marsh
1985...Jay Sigel	1992...Danny Yates	1999...Danny Green	2006...Dave Womack
1986...Bill Loeffler	1993...Jeff Thomas	2000...Greg Puga	2007...Trip Kuehne
1987...Jay Sigel	1994...Tim Jackson	2001...Tim Jackson	

British Amateur

1887 ....H. G. Hutchinson	1929 ..............C.J.H. Tolley	1972 ....Trevor Homer
1888 ....John Ball	1930 ....Robert T. Jones Jr	1973 ....R. Siderowf
1889 .............J.E. Laidlay	1931 ....E. Martin Smith	1974 ....Trevor Homer
1890 ....John Ball	1932 ....J. DeForest	1975 ....M. Giles
1891 .............J.E. Laidlay	1933 ....M. Scott	1976 ....R. Siderowf
1892 ....John Ball	1934 ....W. Lawson Little	1977 ....P. McEvoy
1893 ....Peter Anderson	1935 ....W. Lawson Little	1978 ....P. McEvoy
1894 ....John Ball	1936 ....H. Thomson	1979 ....J. Sigel
1895 .............L.M.B. Melville	1937 ....R. Sweeney Jr	1980 ....D. Evans
1896 .............F.G. Tait	1938 .............C.R. Yates	1981 ....P. Ploujoux
1897 .............A.J.T. Allan	1939 .............A.T. Kyle	1982 ....M. Thompson
1898 .............F.G. Tait	1940–45 ......not held	1983 ....A. Parkin
1899 ....John Ball	1946 ....J. Bruen	1984 .............J.M. Olazabal
1900 .............H.H. Hilton	1947 ....Willie D. Turnesa	1985 ....G. McGimpsey
1901 .............H.H. Hilton	1948 ....Frank R. Stranahan	1986 ....D. Curry
1902 ....C. Hutchings	1949 ....:S.M. McReady	1987 ....P. Mayo
1903 ....R. Maxwell	1950 ....Frank R. Stranahan	1988 ....C. Hardin
1904 .............W.J. Travis	1951 ....Richard D. Chapman	1989 ....S. Dodd
1905 .............A.G. Barry	1952 .............E.H. Ward	1990 ....R. Muntz
1906 ....James Robb	1953 .............J.B. Carr	1991 ....G. Wolstenholme
1907 ....John Ball	1954 .............D.W. Bachli	1992 ....S. Dundas
1908 .............E.A. Lassen	1955 .............J.W. Conrad	1993 ....I. Pyman
1909 ....R. Maxwell	1956 .............J.C. Beharrel	1994 ....L. James
1910 ....John Ball	1957 ....R. Reid Jack	1995 ....G. Sherry
1911 .............H.H. Hilton	1958 .............J.B. Carr	1996 ....W. Bladon
1912 ....John Ball	1959 ....Deane Beman	1997 ....C. Watson
1913 .............H.H. Hilton	1960 .............J.B. Carr	1998 ....Sergio Garcia
1914 .............J.L.C. Jenkins	1961 ....M. Bonallack	1999 ....Graeme Storm
1915–19 ....not held	1962 ....R. Davies	2000 ....Mikko Ilonen
1920 .............C.J.H. Tolley	1963 ....M. Lunt	2001 ....Michael Hoey
1921 .............W.I. Hunter	1964 ....C. Clark	2002 ....Alejandro Larrazabal
1922 .............E.W.E. Holderness	1965 ....M. Bonallack	2003 ....Gary Wolstenholme
1923 .............R.H. Wethered	1966 .............C.R. Cole	2004 ....Stuart Wilson
1924 .............E.W.E. Holderness	1967 ....R. Dickson	2005 ....Brian McElhinney
1925 ....R. Harris	1968 ....M. Bonallack	2006 ....Julien Guerrier
1926 ....Jess Sweetser	1969 ....M. Bonallack	2007 ....Drew Weaver
1927 ....Dr. W. Tweddell	1970 ....M. Bonallack	
1928 .............T.P. Perkins	1971 ....Steve Melnyk	

Amateur Public Links

1922 ....Edmund R. Held	1938 ....Al Leach	1959 ....William A. Wright
1923 ....Richard J. Walsh	1939 ....Andrew Szwedko	1960 ....Verne Callison
1924 ....Joseph Coble	1940 ....Robert C. Clark	1961 ....Richard H. Sikes
1925 ....Raymond J.	1941 ....William M. Welch Jr	1962 ....Richard H. Sikes
McAuliffe	1942–45 ....not held	1963 ....Robert Lunn
1926 ....Lester Bolstad	1946 ....Smiley L. Quick	1964 ....William McDonald
1927 ....Carl F. Kauffmann	1947 ....Wilfred Crossley	1965 ....Arne Dokka
1928 ....Carl F. Kauffmann	1948 ....Michael R. Ferentz	1966 ....Lamont Kaser
1929 ....Carl F. Kauffmann	1949 ....Kenneth J. Towns	1967 ....Verne Callison
1930 ....Robert E. Wingate	1950 ....Stanley Bielat	1968 ....Gene Towry
1931 ....Charles Ferrera	1951 ....Dave Stanley	1969 ....John M. Jackson Jr
1932 .............R.L. Miller	1952 ....Omer L. Bogan	1970 ....Robert Risch
1933 ....Charles Ferrera	1953 ....Ted Richards Jr	1971 ....Fred Haney
1934 ....David A. Mitchell	1954 ....Gene Andrews	1972 ....Bob Allard
1935 ....Frank Strafaci	1955 ....Sam D. Kocsis	1973 ....Stan Stopa
1936 ....B. Patrick Abbott	1956 ....James H. Buxbaum	1974 ....Charles Barenaba
1937 ....Bruce N.	1957 ....Don Essig III	1975 ....Randy Barenaba
McCormick	1958 ....Daniel D. Sikes Jr	1976 ,............Eddie Mudd

Amateur Public Links *(Cont.)*

1977 ....Jerry Vidovic	1988 ....Ralph Howe III	1999 ....Hunter Haas
1978 ....Dean Prince	1989 ....Tim Hobby	2000 ............D.J. Trahan
1979 ....Dennis Walsh	1990 ....Michael Combs	2001 ....Chez Reavie
1980 ....Jodie Mudd	1991 ....David Berganio Jr	2002 ....Ryan Moore
1981 ....Jodie Mudd	1992 ....Warren Schulte	2003 ....Brandt Snedeker
1982 ....Billy Tuten	1993 ....David Berganio Jr	2004 ....Ryan Moore
1983 ....Billy Tuten	1994 ....Guy Yamamoto	2005 ....Clay Ogden
1984 ....Bill Malley	1995 ....Chris Wollmann	2006 ....Casey Watabu
1985 ....Jim Sorenson	1996 ....Tim Hogarth	2007 ....Colt Knost
1986 ....Bill Mayfair	1997 ....Tim Clark	
1987 ....Kevin Johnson	1998 ....Trevor Immelman	

U.S. Senior Men's Amateur

1955 ....J. Wood Platt	1973 ....William Hyndman III	1991 ....Bill Bosshard
1956 ....Frederick J. Wright	1974 ....Dale Morey	1992 ....Clarence Moore
1957 ....J. Clark Espie	1975 ....William F. Colm	1993 ....Joe Ungvary
1958 ....Thomas C. Robbins	1976 ....Lewis W. Oehmig	1994 ....O. Gordon Brewer
1959 ....J. Clark Espie	1977 ....Dale Morey	1995 ....James Stahl Jr.
1960 ....Michael Cestone	1978 ..........K.K. Compton	1996 ....O. Gordon Brewer
1961 ....Dexter H. Daniels	1979 ....William C. Campbell	1997 ....Cliff Cunningham
1962 ....Merrill L. Carlsmith	1980 ....William C. Campbell	1998 ....Bill Shean Jr.
1963 ....Merrill L. Carlsmith	1981 ....Ed Updegraff	1999 ....Bill Ploeger
1964 ....William D. Higgins	1982 ....Alton Duhon	2000 ....Bill Shean Jr.
1965 ....Robert B. Kiersky	1983 ....William Hyndman III	2001 ....Kemp Richardson
1966 ....Dexter H. Daniels	1984 ....Bob Rawlins	2002 ....Greg Reynolds
1967 ....Ray Palmer	1985 ....Lewis W. Oehmig	2003 ....Kemp Richardson
1968 ....Curtis Person Sr.	1986 ....Bo Williams	2004 ....Mark Bemowski
1969 ....Curtis Person Sr.	1987 ....John Richardson	2005 ....Mike Rice
1970 ....Gene Andrews	1988 ....Clarence Moore	2006 ....Mike Bell
1971 ....Tom Draper	1989 ....Bo Williams	2007 ....Stan Lee
1972 ....Lewis W. Oehmig	1990 ....Jackie Cummings	

Note: Event is for amateur golfers at least 55 years of age.

MAJOR WOMEN'S AMATEUR CHAMPIONSHIPS

U.S. Women's Amateur

Year	Winner	Score	Runner-Up	Site
1895 ....Mrs. Charles S. Brown		132	Nellie Sargent	Meadow Brook Club, Hempstead, NY
1896 ....Beatrix Hoyt		2 & 1	Mrs. Arthur Turnure	Morris Couty GC, Morristown, NJ
1897 ....Beatrix Hoyt		5 & 4	Nellie Sargent	Essex County Club, Manchester, MA
1898 ....Beatrix Hoyt		5 &3	Maude Wetmore	Ardsley Club, Ardsley-on-Hudson, NY
1899 ....Ruth Underhill		2 & 1	Margaret Fox	Philadelphia CC, Philadelphia, PA
1900 ....Frances C. Griscom		6 & 5	Margaret Curtis	Shinnecock Hills GC, Shinnecock Hills, NY
1901 ....Genevieve Hecker		5 & 3	Lucy Herron	Baltusrol GC, Springfield, NJ
1902 ....Genevieve Hecker		4 & 3	Louisa A. Wells	The Country Club, Brookline, MA
1903 ....Bessie Anthony		7 & 6	J. Anna Carpenter	Chicago GC, Wheaton, IL
1904 ....Georgianna M. Bishop		5 & 3	Mrs. E.F. Sanford	Merion Cricket Club, Haverford, PA
1905 ....Pauline Mackay		1 up	Margaret Curtis	Morris County GC, Convent, NJ
1906 ....Harriot S. Curtis		2 & 1	Mary B. Adams	Brae Burn CC, West Newton, MA
1907 ....Margaret Curtis		7 & 6	Harriot S. Curtis	Midlothian CC, Blue Island, IL
1908 ....Katherine C. Harley		6 & 5	Mrs. T.H. Polhemus	Chevy Chase Club, Chevy Chase, MD
1909 ....Dorothy I. Campbell		3 & 2	Nonna Barlow	Merion Cricket Club, Haverford, PA
1910 ....Dorothy I. Campbell		2 & 1	Mrs. G.M. Martin	Homewood CC, Flossmoor, IL
1911 ....Margaret Curtis		5 & 3	Lillian B. Hyde	Baltusrol GC, Springfield, NJ
1912 ....Margaret Curtis		3 & 2	Nonna Barlow	Essex County Club, Manchester, MA
1913 ....Gladys Ravenscroft		2 up	Marion Hollins	Wilmington CC, Wilmington, DE
1914 ....Katherine Harley		1 up	Elaine V. Rosenthal	Nassau CC, Glen Cove, NY
1915 ....Florence Vanderbeck		3 & 2	Margaret Gavin	Onwentsia Club, Lake Forest, IL
1916 ....Alexa Stirling		2 & 1	Mildred Caverly	Belmont Springs CC, Waverley, MA
1917–18 ....No tournament				
1919 ....Alexa Stirling		6 & 5	Margaret Gavin	Shawnee CC, Shawnee-on-Delaware, PA
1920 ....Alexa Stirling		5 & 4	Dorothy Campbell	Mayfield CC, Cleveland
1921 ....Marion Hollins		5 & 4	Alexa Stirling	Hollywood GC, Deal, NJ
1922 ....Glenna Collett		5 & 4	Margaret Gavin	Greenbriar GC, White Sulphur Springs, WV
1923 ....Edith Cummings		3 & 2	Alexa Stirling	Westchester-Biltmore CC, Rye, NY
1924 ....Dorothy Campbell		7 & 6	Mary K. Browne	Rhode Island CC, Nyatt, RI

U.S. Women's Amateur *(Cont.)*

Year	Winner	Score	Runner-Up	Site
1925	Glenna Collett	9 & 8	Alexa Stirling	St. Louis CC, Clayton, MO
1926	Helen Stetson	3 & 1	Elizabeth Goss	Merion Cricket Club, Ardmore, PA
1927	Miiriam Burns Horn	5 & 4	Maureen Orcutt	Cherry Valley Club, Garden City, NY
1928	Glenna Collett	13 & 12	Virginia Van Wie	Va. Hot Springs G & TC, Hot Springs, VA
1929	Glenna Collett	4 & 3	Leona Pressler	Oakland Hills CC, Birmingham, MI
1930	Glenna Collett	6 & 5	Virginia Van Wie	Los Angeles CC, Beverly Hills, CA
1931	Helen Hicks	2 & 1	Glenna Collet Vare	CC of Buffalo, Williamsville, NY
1932	Virginia Van Wie	10 & 8	Glenna Collet Vare	Salem CC, Peabody, MA
1933	Virginia Van Wie	4 & 3	Helen Hicks	Exmoor CC, Highland Park, IL
1934	Virginia Van Wie	2 & 1	Dorothy Traung	Whitemarsh Valley CC, Chestnut Hill, PA
1935	Glenna Collett Vare	3 & 2	Patty Berg	Interlachen CC, Hopkins, MN
1936	Pamela Barton	4 & 3	Maureen Orcutt	Canoe Brook CC, Summit, NJ
1937	Estelle Lawson	7 & 6	Patty Berg	Memphis CC, Memphis, TN
1938	Patty Berg	6 & 5	Estelle Lawson	Westmoreland CC, Wilmette, IL
1939	Betty Jameson	3 & 2	Dorothy Kirby	Wee Burn Club, Darien, CT
1940	Betty Jameson	6 & 5	Jane S. Cothran	Del Monte G & CC, Pebble Beach, CA
1941	Elizabeth Hicks	5 & 3	Helen Sigel	The Country Club, Brookline, MA
1942–45	No tournament			
1946	Babe Zaharias	11 & 9	Clara Sherman	Southern Hills CC, Tulsa
1947	Louise Suggs	2 up	Dorothy Kirby	Franklin Hills CC, Franklin, MI
1948	Grace S. Lenczyk	4 & 3	Helen Sigel	Del Monte G & CC, Pebble Beach, CA
1949	Dorothy Porter	3 & 2	Dorothy Kielty	Merion GC, Ardmore, PA
1950	Beverly Hanson	6 & 4	Mae Murray	Atlanta AC, Atlanta
1951	Dorothy Kirby	2 & 1	Claire Doran	Town & CC, St. Paul
1952	Jacqueline Pung	2 & 1	Shirley McFedters	Waverley CC, Portland, OR
1953	Mary Lena Faulk	3 & 2	Polly Riley	Rhode Island CC, West Barrington, RI
1954	Barbara Romack	4 & 2	Mickey Wright	Allegheny CC, Sewickley, PA
1955	Patricia A. Lesser	7 & 6	Jane Nelson	Myers Park CC, Charlotte
1956	Marlene Stewart	2 & 1	JoAnne Gunderson	Meridian Hills CC, Indianapolis
1957	JoAnne Gunderson	8 & 6	Ann Casey Johnstone	Del Paso CC, SacramentoA
1958	Anne Quast	3 & 2	Barbara Romack	Wee Burn CC, Darien, CT
1959	Barbara McIntire	4 & 3	Joanne Goodwin	Congressional CC, Washington, D.C.
1960	JoAnne Gunderson	6 & 5	Jean Ashley	Tulsa CC, Tulsa
1961	Anne Quast Decker	14 & 13	Phyllis Preuss	Tacoma G & CC, Tacoma, WA
1962	JoAnne Gunderson	9 & 8	Anne Baker	CC of Rochester, Rochester, NY
1963	Anne Quast Decker	2 & 1	Peggy Conley	Taconic GC, Williamstown, MA
1964	Barbara McIntire	3 & 2	JoAnne Gunderson	Prairie Dunes CC, Hutchinson, KS
1965	Jean Ashley	5 & 4	Anne Quast Decker	Lakewood CC, Denver
1966	JoAnne Gunderson	1 up	Marlene Stewart Streit	Sewickley Heights GC, Sewickley, PA
1967	Mary Lou Dill	5 & 4	Jean Ashley	Annandale GC, Pasadena
1968	JoAnne Gunderson Carner	5 & 4	Anne Quast Decker	Birmingham CC, Birmingham, MI
1969	Catherine Lacoste	3 & 2	Shelley Hamling	Las Colinas CC, Irving, TX
1970	Martha Wilkinson	3 & 2	Cynthia Hall	Wee Burn CC, Darien, CT
1971	Laura Baugh	1 up	Beth Barry	Atlanta CC, Atlanta
1972	Mary Budke	5 & 4	Cynthia Hill	St. Louis CC, St. Louis
1973	Carol Semple	1 up	Anne Quast Decker	Montclair CC, Montclair, NJ
1974	Cynthia Hill	5 & 4	Carol Semple	Broadmoor GC, Seattle
1975	Beth Daniel	3 & 2	Donna Horton	Brae Burn CC, West Newton, MA
1976	Donna Horton	2 & 1	Marianne Bretton	Del Paso CC, Sacramento
1977	Beth Daniel	3 & 1	Cathy Sherk	Cincinnati CC, Cincinnati
1978	Cathy Sherk	4 & 3	Judith Oliver	Sunnybrook GC, Plymouth Meeting, PA
1979	Carolyn Hill	7 & 6	Patty Sheehan	Memphis CC, Memphis
1980	Juli Inkster	2 up	Patti Rizzo	Prairie Dunes CC, Hutchinson, KS
1981	Juli Inkster	1 up	Lindy Goggin	Waverley CC, Portland, OR
1982	Juli Inkster	4 & 3	Cathy Hanlon	Broadmoor CC, Colorado Springs, CO
1983	Joanne Pacillo	2 & 1	Sally Quinlan	Canoe Brook CC, Summit, NJ
1984	Deb Richard	1 up	Kimberly Williams	Broadmoor GC, Seattle
1985	Michiko Hattori	5 & 4	Cheryl Stacy	Fox Chapel CC, Pittsburgh
1986	Kay Cockerill	9 & 7	Kathleen McCarthy	Pasatiempo GC, Santa Cruz, CA
1987	Kay Cockerill	3 & 2	Tracy Kerdyk	Rhode Island CC, Barrington, RI
1988	Pearl Sinn	6 & 5	Karen Noble	Minikahda Club, Minneapolis
1989	Vicki Goetze	4 & 3	Brandie Burton	Pinehurst CC (No. 2), Pinehurst, NC
1990	Pat Hurst	37 holes	Stephanie Davis	Canoe Brook CC, Summit, NJ
1991	Amy Fruhwirth	5 & 4	Heidi Voorhees	Prairie Dunes CC, Hutchinson, KN
1992	Vicki Goetz	1 up	Annika Sorenstaem	Kemper Lakes GC, Hawthorne Hills, IL
1993	Jill McGill	1 up	Sarah Ingram	San Diego CC, Chula Vista, CA

U.S. Women's Amateur *(Cont.)*

Year	Winner	Score	Runner-Up	Site
1994	Wendy Ward	2 & 1	Jill McGill	The Homestead, Hot Springs, WV
1995	Kelli Kuehne	4 & 3	Anne-Marie Knight	The Country Club, Brookline, MA
1996	Kelli Kuehne	2 & 1	Marisa Baena	Firethorn GC, Lincoln, NE
1997	Silvia Cavalleri	5 & 4	Robin Burke	Brae Burn CC, West Newton, MA
1998	Grace Park	7 & 6	Jenny Chuasiriporn	Barton Hills CC, Ann Arbor, MI
1999	Dorothy Delasin	4 & 3	Jimin Kang	Biltmore Forest CC, Asheville, NC
2000	Marcy Newton	8 & 7	Laura Myerscough	Waverley CC, Portland, OR
2001	Meredith Duncan	37 holes	Nicole Perrot	Flint Hills GC, Wichita, KA
2002	Becky Lucidi	3 & 2	Brandi Jackson	Sleepy Hollow CC, Scarborough, NY
2003	Virada Nirapathpongporn	2 & 1	Jane Park	Philadelphia CC, Gladwyne, PA
2004	Jane Park	1 up	Amanda McCurdy	Kahkwa Club, Erie, PA
2005	Morgan Pressel	9 & 8	Maru Martinez	Ansley GC, Roswell, GA
2006	Kimberly Kim	1 up	Katharina Schallenberg	Pumpkin Ridge, North Plains, OR
2007	Maria Uribe	1 up	Amanda Blumenhurst	Crooked Stick Golf Club, Carmel, IN

U.S. Girls' Junior Amateur

Year	Winner	Year	Winner	Year	Winner
1949	Marlene Bauer	1970	Hollis Stacy	1991	Emilee Klein
1950	Patricia Lesser	1971	Hollis Stacy	1992	Jamie Koizumi
1951	Arlene Brooks	1972	Nancy Lopez	1993	Kellee Booth
1952	Mickey Wright	1973	Amy Alcott	1962	Maureen Orcutt
1953	Millie Meyerson	1974	Nancy Lopez	1963	Sis Choate
1954	Margaret Smith	1975	Dayna Benson	1994	Kelli Kuehne
1955	Carole Jo Kabler	1976	Pilar Dorado	1995	Marcy Newton
1956	JoAnne Gunderson	1977	Althea Torne	1996	Dorothy Delasin
1957	Judy Eller	1978	Lori Castillo	1997	Beth Bauer
1958	Judy Eller	1979	Penny Hammel	1998	Leigh Anne Hardin
1959	Judy Rand	1980	Laurie Rinker	1999	Aree Wongluekiet
1960	Carol Sorenson	1981	Kay Cornelius	2000	Lisa Ferrero
1961	Mary Lowell	1982	Heather Farr	2001	Nicole Perrot
1962	Mary Lou Daniel	1983	Kim Saiki	2002	In-Bee Park
1963	Janis Ferraris	1984	Cathy Mockett	2003	Sukjin-Lee Wuesthoff
1964	Peggy Conley	1985	Dana Lofland	2004	J. Granada
1965	Gail Sykes	1986	Pat Hurst	2005	In-Kyung Kim
1966	Claudia Mayhew	1987	Michelle McGann	2006	Jenny Shin
1967	Elizabeth Story	1988	Jamille Jose	2007	Kristen Park
1968	Peggy Harmon	1989	Brandie Burton		
1969	Hollis Stacy	1990	Sandrine Mendiburu		

Women's British Open Amateur

Year	Winner	Year	Winner	Year	Winner
1893	Lady Margaret Scott	1921	Miss C. Leitch	1949	F. Stephens
1894	Lady Margaret Scott	1922	Miss J. Wethered	1950	Vicomtesse de Saint Sauveur
1895	Lady Margaret Scott	1923	Miss D. Chambers		
1896	Miss Pascoe	1924	Miss J. Wethered	1951	P.J. MacCann
1897	Miss E.C. Orr	1925	Miss J. Wethered	1952	M. Paterson
1898	Miss L. Thomson	1926	Miss C. Leitch	1953	M. Stewart
1899	Miss M. Hezlet	1927	Miss Thion de la Chaume	1954	F. Stephens
1900	Miss Adair			1955	J. Valentine
1901	Miss Graham	1928	Miss N. Le Blan	1956	M. Smith
1902	Miss M. Hezlet	1929	Miss J. Wethered	1957	P. Garvey
1903	Miss Adair	1930	Miss D. Fishwick	1958	J. Valentine
1904	Miss L. Dod	1931	Miss E. Wilson	1959	E. Price
1905	Miss B. Thompson	1932	Miss E. Wilson	1960	B. McIntyre
1906	Mrs. Kennon	1933	Miss E. Wilson	1961	M. Spearman
1907	Miss M. Hezlet	1934	Mrs. A.M. Holm	1962	M. Spearman
1908	Miss M. Titterton	1935	Miss W. Morgan	1963	B. Varangot
1909	Miss D. Campbell	1936	Miss P. Barton	1964	C. Sorenson
1910	Miss Grant Suttie	1937	Miss J. Anderson	1965	B. Varangot
1911	Miss D. Campbell	1938	Mrs. A.M. Holm	1966	E. Chadwick
1912	Miss G. Ravenscroft	1939	Miss P. Barton	1967	E. Chadwick
1913	Miss M. Dodd	1940–45	not held	1968	B. Varangot
1914	Miss C. Leitch	1946	G.W. Hetherington	1975	C. Lacoste
1915–19	not held	1947	B. Zaharias	1976	D. Oxley
1920	Miss C. Leitch	1948	L. Suggs	1977	A. Uzielli

Women's British Open Amateur *(Cont.)*

1978 ....E. Kennedy	1989 ....H. Dobson	2000 ....Rebecca Hudson
1979 ....M. Madill	1990 ....J. Hall	2001 ....Rebecca Hudson
1980 ....A. Quast	1991 ....V. Michaud	2002 ....Rebecca Hudson
1981 .............I.C. Robertson	1992 ....P. Pedersen	2003 ....Elisa Serramia
1982 ....K. Douglas	1993 ....Catriona Lambert	2004 ....Louise Stahle
1983 ....J. Thornhill	1994 ....Emma Duggleby	2005 ....Heather MacRae
1984 ....J. Rosenthal	1995 ....Julie Hall	2006 ....Belen Mozo
1985 ....L. Beman	1996 ....Kelli Kuehne	2007 ....Carlota Ciganda
1986 ....M. McGuire	1997 ....Alison Rose	
1987 ....J. Collingham	1998 ....K. Rostron	
1988 ....J. Furby	1999 ....Marine Monnet	

Women's Amateur Public Links

1977 ....Kelly Fuiks	1987 ....Tracy Kerdyk	1998 ....Amy Spooner
1978 ....Kelly Fuiks	1988 ....Pearl Sinn	1999 ....Jody Niemann
1979 ....Lori Castillo	1989 ....Pearl Sinn	2000 ....Catherine Cartwright
1980 ....Lori Castillo	1990 ....Cathy Mockett	2001 ....Candie Kung
1981 ....Mary Enright	1991 ....Tracy Hanson	2002 ....Annie Thurman
1982 ....Nancy Taylor	1992 ....Amy Fruhwirth	2003 ....Michelle Wie
1983 ....Kelli Antolock	1993 ....Connie Masterson	2004 ....Ya-Ni Tseng
1984 ....Heather Farr	1994 ....Jill McGill	2005 ....Eun Jung Lee
1985 ....Danielle	1995 ....Jo Jo Robertson	2006 ....Tiffany Joh
Ammaccapane	1996 ....Heather Graff	2007 ....Mina Harigae
1986 ....Cindy Schreyer	1997 ....Jo Jo Robertson	

U.S. Senior Women's Amateur

1964 ....Loma Smith	1979 ....Alice Dye	1994 ....Marlene Streit
1965 ....Loma Smith	1980 ....Dorothy Porter	1995 ....Jean Smith
1966 ....Maureen Orcutt	1981 ....Dorothy Porter	1996 ....Gayle Borthwick
1967 ....Marge Mason	1982 ....Edean Ihlanfeldt	1997 ....Nancy Fitzgerald
1968 ....Carolyn Cudone	1983 ....Dorothy Porter	1998 ....Gayle Borthwick
1969 ....Carolyn Cudone	1984 ....Constance Guthrie	1999 ....C. Semple Thompson
1970 ....Carolyn Cudone	1985 ....Marlene Streit	2000 ....C. Semple Thompson
1971 ....Carolyn Cudone	1986 ....Connie Guthrie	2001 ....C. Semple Thompson
1972 ....Carolyn Cudone	1987 ....Anne Sander	2002 ....C. Semple Thompson
1973 ....Gwen Hibbs	1988 ....Lois Hodge	2003 ....Marlene Streit
1974 ....Justine Cushing	1989 ....Anne Sander	2004 ....Carolyn Creekmore
1975 ....Alberta Bower	1990 ....Anne Sander	2005 ....Diane Lang
1976 ....Cecile H. Maclaurin	1991 ....Phyllis Preuss	2006 ....Diane Lang
1977 ....Dorothy Porter	1992 ....Rosemary Thompson	2007 ....Anna Schultz
1978 ....Alice Dye	1993 ....Anne Sander	

Women's Mid-Amateur Championship

1987 ....Cindy Scholefield	1995 ....Ellen Port	2002 ....Kathy Hartwiger
1988 ....Martha Lang	1996 ....Ellen Port	2003 ....Amber Marsh
1989 ....Robin Weiss	1997 ....C. Semple Thompson	2004 ....Corey Weworski
1990 ....C. Semple Thompson	1998 ....Virginia Derby	2005 ....Mary Anne Lapointe
1991 ....Sarah LeBrun Ingram	Grimes	2006 ....Meghan Bolger
1992 ....M. Mamey-McInerney	1999 ....Alissa Herron	
1993 ....Sarah Ingram	2000 ....Ellen Port	
1994 ....Sarah Ingram	2001 ....Laura Shanahan	

Ryder Cup Matches

Year	Results	Site
1927	United States 9½, Great Britain 2½	Worcester CC, Worcester, MA
1929	Great Britain 7, United States 5	Moortown GC, Leeds, England
1931	United States 9, Great Britain 3	Scioto CC, Columbus, OH
1933	Great Britain 6½, United States 5½	Southport and Ainsdale Courses, Southport, England
1935	United States 9, Great Britain 3	Ridgewood CC, Ridgewood, NJ
1937	United States 8, Great Britain 4	Southport and Ainsdale Courses, Southport, England
1939–1945	No tournament	
1947	United States 11, Great Britain 1	Portland GC, Portland, OR
1949	United States 7, Great Britain 5	Ganton GC, Scarborough, England
1951	United States 9½, Great Britain 2½	Pinehurst CC, Pinehurst, NC
1953	United States 6½, Great Britain 5½	Wentworth Club, Surrey, England
1955	United States 8, Great Britain 4	Thunderbird Ranch & CC, Palm Springs, CA
1957	Great Britain 7½, United States 4½	Lindrick GC, Yorkshire, England
1959	United States 8½, Great Britain 3½	Eldorado CC, Palm Desert, CA
1961	United States 14½, Great Britain 9½	Royal Lytham & St. Annes GC, St Anne's-on-the-Sea, England
1963	United States 23, Great Britain 9	East Lake CC, Atlanta
1965	United States 19½, Great Britain 12½	Royal Birkdale GC, Southport, England
1967	United States 23½, Great Britain 8½	Champions GC, Houston
1969	United States 16, Great Britain 16	Royal Birkdale GC, Southport, England
1971	United States 18½, Great Britain 13½	Old Warson CC, St. Louis
1973	United States 19, Great Britain 13	Hon Co of Edinburgh Golfers, Muirfield, Scotland
1975	United States 21, Great Britain 11	Laurel Valley GC, Ligonier, PA
1977	United States 12½, Great Britain 7½	Royal Lytham & St. Annes GC, St. Annes-on-the-Sea, Eng.
1979	United States 17, Europe 11	Greenbrier, White Sulphur Springs, WV
1981	United States 18½, Europe 9½	Walton Heath GC, Surrey, England
1983	United States 14½, Europe 13½	PGA National GC, Palm Beach Gardens, FL
1985	Europe 16½, United States 11½	Belfry GC, Sutton Coldfield, England
1987	Europe 15, United States 13	Muirfield GC, Dublin, OH
1989	Europe 14, United States 14	Belfry GC, Sutton Coldfield, England
1991	United States 14½, Europe 13½	Ocean Course, Kiawah Island, SC
1993	United States 15, Europe 13	Belfry GC, Sutton Coldfield, England
1995	Europe 14½, United States 13½	Oak Hill CC, Rochester, NY
1997	Europe 14½, United States 13½	Valderrama GC, Sotogrande, Spain
1999	United States 14½, Europe 13½	The Country Club, Brookline, MA
2002	Europe 15½, Unites States 12½	Belfry GC, Sutton Coldfield, England
2004	Europe 18½, United States 9½	Oakland Hills CC, Bloomfield Hills, MI
2006	Europe 18½, United States 9½	The K Club, County Kildare, Ireland

Team matches held every odd year between U.S. professionals and those of Great Britain/Europe. Team members selected on basis of finishes in PGA and European tour events. Match in 2001 canceled due to 9/11 terrorist attacks.

Walker Cup Matches

Year	Results	Site
1922	United States 8, Great Britain 4	Nat'l Golf Links of America, Southampton, NY
1923	United States 6, Great Britain 5	St. Andrews, Scotland
1924	United States 9, Great Britain 3	Garden City GC, Garden City, NY
1926	United States 6, Great Britain 5	St. Andrews, Scotland
1928	United States 11, Great Britain 1	Chicago GC, Wheaton, IL
1930	United States 10, Great Britain 2	Royal St. George GC, Sandwich, England
1932	United States 8, Great Britain 1	The Country Club, Brookline, MA
1934	United States 9, Great Britain 2	St. Andrews, Scotland
1936	United States 9, Great Britain 0	Pine Valley GC, Clementon, NJ
1938	Great Britain 7, United States 4	St. Andrews, Scotland
1940–46	No tournament	
1947	United States 8, Great Britain 4	St. Andrews, Scotland
1949	United States 10, Great Britain 2	Winged Foot GC, Mamaroneck, NY
1951	United States 6, Great Britain 3	Birkdale GC, Southport, England
1953	United States 9, Great Britain 3	The Kittansett Club, Marion, MA
1955	United States 10, Great Britain 2	St. Andrews, Scotland
1957	United States 8, Great Britain 3	Minikahda Club, Minneapolis
1959	United States 9, Great Britain 3	Muirfield, Scotland
1961	United States 11, Great Britain 1	Seattle GC, Seattle
1963	United States 12, Great Britain 8	Ailsa Course, Turnberry, Scotland
1965	Great Britain 11, United States 11	Baltimore CC, Five Farms, Baltimore, MD
1967	United States 13, Great Britain 7	Royal St. George's GC, Sandwich, England
1969	United States 10, Great Britain 8	Milwaukee CC, Milwaukee, WI
1971	Great Britain 13, United States 11	St. Andrews, Scotland
1973	United States 14, Great Britain 10	The Country Club, Brookline, MA
1975	United States 15½, Great Britain 8½	St. Andrews, Scotland
1977	United States 16, Great Britain 8	Shinnecock Hills GC, Southampton, NY
1979	United States 15½, Great Britain 8½	Muirfield, Scotland
1981	United States 15, Great Britain 9	Cypress Point Club, Pebble Beach, CA
1983	United States 13½, Great Britain 10½	Royal Liverpool GC, Hoylake, England
1985	United States 13, Great Britain 11	Pine Valley GC, Pine Valley, NJ
1987	United States 16½, Great Britain 7½	Sunningdale GC, Berkshire, England
1989	Great Britain 12½, United States 11½	Peachtree Golf Club, Atlanta
1991	United States 14, Great Britain 10	Portmarnock GC, Dublin, Ireland
1993	United States 19, Great Britain 5	Interlachen CC, Edina, MN
1995	Great Britain/Ireland 14, United States 10	Royal Porthcawl, Porthcawl, Wales
1997	United States 18, Great Britain/Ireland 6	Quaker Ridge GC, Scarsdale, NY
1999	Great Britain/Ireland 15, United States 9	Nairn GC, Nairn, Scotland
2001	Great Britain/Ireland 15, United States 9	Ocean Forest GC, Sea Island, GA
2003	Great Britain/Ireland 12½, United States 11½	Ganton GC, Ganton, England
2005	United States 12½, Great Britain/Ireland 11½	Chicago GC, Wheaton IL
2007	United States 12½, Great Britain/Ireland 11½	Royal County Down, Newcastle, N. Ireland

Men's amateur team competition every other year between United States and Great Britain/Ireland. U.S. team members selected by USGA.

Solheim Cup Matches

Year	Results	Site
1990	United States 11½, Europe 4½	Lake Nona GC, Orlando, FL
1992	Europe 11½, United States 6½	Dalmahoy Hotel GC, Edinburgh
1994	United States 13, Europe 7	The Greenbriar, White Sulpher Springs, WV
1996	United States 17, Europe 11	Marriot St Pierre Hotel & CC, Chepstow, Wales
1998	United States 16, Europe 12	Muirfield Village GC, Dublin, OH
2000	Europe 14½, United States, 11 ½	Loch Lomond GC, Luss, Scotand
2002	United States 15½, Europe 12 ½	Interlachen CC, Minneapolis, MN
2003	Europe 17½, United States 10 ½	Barseback G&CC, Malmo, Sweden
2005	United States 15½, Europe 12 ½	Crooked Stick GC, Carmel IN
2007	United States 16, Europe 12	Halmstad GC, Halmstad, Sweden

Women's team matches held every other year between U.S. professionals and those of Europe. Team members selected on the basis of finishes in LPGA and European tour events.

Curtis Cup Matches

Year	Results	Site
1932	United States 5½, British Isles 3½	Wentworth GC, Wentworth, England
1934	United States 6½, British Isles 2½	Chevy Chase Club, Chevy Chase, MD
1936	United States 4½ British Isles 4½	King's Course, Gleneagles, Scotland
1938	United States 5½, British Isles 3½	Essex CC, Manchester, MA
1940–46	No tournament	
1948	United States 6½, British Isles 2½	Birkdale GC, Southport, England
1950	United States 7½, British Isles 1½	CC of Buffalo, Williamsville, NY
1952	British Isles 5, United States 4	Muirfield, Scotland
1954	United States 6, British Isles 3	Merion GC, Ardmore, PA
1956	British Isles 5, United States 4	Prince's GC, Sandwich Bay, England
1958	British Isles 4½, United States 4½	Brae Burn CC, West Newton, Mass.
1960	United States 6½, British Isles 2½	Lindrick GC, Worksop, England
1962	United States 8, British Isles 1	Broadmoor CG, Colorado Springs,CO
1964	United States 10½, British Isles 7½	Royal Porthcawl GC, Porthcawl, South Wales
1966	United States 13, British Isles 5	Va. Hot Springs G & TC, Hot Springs, VA
1968	United States 10½, British Isles 7½	Royal County Down GC, Newcastle, N. Ire.
1970	United States 11½, British Isles 6½	Brae Burn CC, West Newton, MA
1972	United States 10, British Isles 8	Western Gailes, Ayrshire, Scotland
1974	United States 13, British Isles 5	San Francisco GC, San Francisco
1976	United States 11½, British Isles 6½	Royal Lytham & St. Annes GC, England
1978	United States 12, British Isles 6	Apawamis Club, Rye, NY
1980	United States 13, British Isles 5	St. Pierre G & CC, Chepstow, Wales
1982	United States 14½, British Isles 3½	Denver CC, Denver
1984	United States 9½ British Isles 8½	Muirfield, Scotland
1986	British Isles 13, United States 5	Prairie Dunes CC, Hutchinson, KS
1988	British Isles 11, United States 7	Royal St. George's GC, Sandwich, England
1990	United States 14, British Isles 4	Somerset Hills CC, Bernardsville, NJ
1992	Great Britain/Ireland 10, United States 8	Royal Liverpool GC, Hoylake, England
1994	Great Britain/Ireland 9, United States 9	The Honors Course, Ooltewah, TN
1996	Great Britain/Ireland 11½, United States 6½	Killarney Golf & Fishing Club, Killarney, Ireland
1998	United States 10, Great Britain/Ireland 8	The Minikahda Club, Minneapolis
2000	United States 10, Great Britain/Ireland 8	Ganton GC, North Yorkshire, England
2002	United States 11, Great Britain/Ireland 7	Fox Chapel GC, Pittsburgh, PA
2004	United States 10, Great Britain/Ireland 8	Formby GC, Merseyside, England
2006	United States 11½, Great Britain/Ireland 6½	Bandon Dunes GC, Bandon, OR

Women's amateur team competition every other year between the United States and Great Britain/Ireland. U.S. team members selected by USGA.

Presidents Cup Matches

Year	Results	Site
1994	United States 20, International 12	Robert Trent Jones GC, Lake Manassas, VA
1996	United States 16½, International 15½	Robert Trent Jones GC, Lake Manassas, VA
1998	International 20½ United States 11½	Royal Melbourne GC, Melbourne, Australia
2000	United States 21½, International 10½	Robert Trent Jones GC, Lake Manassas, VA
2003	International 17, United States 17	Fan Court Hotel CC, George, South Africa
2005	United States 18½, International 15½	Robert Trent Jones GC, Lake Manassas, VA
2005	United States 19½, International 14½	Royal Montreal Golf Club, Bizard, Quebec

A biennial event played in non-Ryder Cup years designed to provide non-European players with international team and match play.

Boxing

ROBERT BECK

Oscar DeLa Hoya versus
Floyd Mayweather Jr. was hailed
as the "Fight to Save Boxing"

Saving the Sweet Science?

Though the De La Hoya-Mayweather Jr. fight was a pay-per-view smash, it looked unlikely that it would revive a sport whose heavyweights are still nobodies

BY STEPHEN CANNELLA

FOR FANS AND JOURNALISTS old enough to have followed boxing in the glory days of the 1970s and '80s, strolling into Las Vegas's MGM Grand Hotel on May 5, 2007, must have been like entering a time machine. For one night, the American sports landscape was transported back to an era when, to be blunt, boxing mattered. A time when marquee bouts were cultural happenings, not merely sports page fodder. A time when megafights grabbed the attention of even those puzzled by the difference between a left jab from a right cross. A time when celebrities certified their importance simply by taking a ringside seat. A time when no one foresaw a day when boxing would be considered little more than a niche sport.

The main event on boxing's throwback night was the WBC super welterweight title bout between Oscar De La Hoya, 38–4 and a champion of six divisions, and Floyd Mayweather Jr., 37–0 and the champ in four weight classes. It was a dream matchup by the standards of any era. De La Hoya, the Golden Boy, was the sport's most popular athlete. Mayweather was its best pound-for-pound athlete, and the two had dominated boxing's lower weight classes for more than a decade. There were storylines galore, too. The 34-year-old De La Hoya, having put most of his effort in recent years into promotion and other lucrative business ventures, was preparing to retire and was looking to cap his Hall of Fame career with one last victory. (Not to mention one last monstrous purse.) Mayweather, 30, perhaps to stave off boredom after conquering every opponent and weight class he'd encountered, had agreed to move up to 154 pounds to take on De La Hoya; a victory against the Golden Boy would further enhance his credentials as one of the greatest pure fighters in history. There were personal entanglements, too. Mayweather's father, Floyd Sr., with whom Floyd the younger had long had a fractious relationship, was De La Hoya's trainer until they had a falling out over money four months before the fight. Floyd Sr. then tried to return to his son's camp—where his younger brother Roger was training his son. But after only a few chaotic weeks, Floyd Jr. banished his father from his camp.

Fortunately for fans who had trouble keeping track of the Mayweather clan's squabbles, the saga was captured on "24/7", the four-part HBO reality series

Though they garnered scant attention, Marquez and Vazquez (l.) fought two of the year's most electrifying bouts.

that followed the combatants' preparations for the bout. (To maximize exposure, HBO aired the show on Sunday nights, immediately after "The Sopranos.") The show was part of a prefight hype onslaught—*Sports Illustrated* billed it as "The Fight to Save Boxing"—that bordered on hysterical. "Somewhere along the way, [boxing] lost the average fan," said HBO Sports president Ross Greenburg, whose network televised the fight on pay-per-view. "But I think we're earmarking this as the fight that can bring him back. In many ways this is the Super Bowl of boxing. We can get that viewer back once again, to create the beauty and drama of this sport."

Certainly, the bout restored the element of spectacle that once was as much a part of boxing as sweat and blood. The sellout crowd of 16,200 at the MGM teemed with megawatt celebrities: Jack Nicholson and Leonardo DiCaprio graced the first row; Will Ferrell strained to see over Jim Carrey in the seat in front of him; Jennifer Lopez

drew stares wherever she roamed. The gate was $19 million, a boxing record. Another $120 million was generated by the 2.15 million pay-per-views buys for the fight, both records. When all was said and done, De La Hoya pocketed nearly $50 million. Mayweather, who had boasted on "24/7" that he never left the house with less than $10,000 in his pocket, took home $30 million.

Whether or not the fight equalled all the buildup was—like most things in boxing—open to debate. De La Hoya won the early rounds, using his size advantage to bully Mayweather into the ropes and attack him with body blows. But Mayweather seemed unhurt by De La Hoya's assaults, and he was able to interrupt them with his quicker hands and vicious counterpunching. By the sixth round, it was clear that De La Hoya was tiring, and Mayweather began to land combinations. (On a few occasions, Mayweather even smiled at his weakening opponent.) De La Hoya rallied in the final round though, performing well enough to win the round on two of the three judges' cards.

The final round scoring turned out to be crucial. If De La Hoya had swept all three judges, he would have earned a draw. Instead, Mayweather earned a split decision victory, the first win of his career that wasn't unanimous. Mayweather was now a champion in his fifth different weight class, and he took to the title with characteristic humility. "It was easy work for me," he said. "[De La Hoya] was rough and tough. But he couldn't beat the best.... That's what you call a masterpiece of boxing. He's one of the best fighters of our era and I showed what I can do to one of the best fighters of our era." Without directly criticizing the judges, De La Hoya suggested that he felt the outcome should have been different. "I don't feel like a loser," he said. "I'm satisfied."

Alas, many in the boxing community weren't. They complained that the in-ring fireworks weren't worthy of all the hype. There was also a sense that the bout may have been the last great moment for boxing. Mayweather announced immediately that he was retiring, scotching any talk of a rematch. (Later in the year he backed off of that claim, however.) De la Hoya, it was clear, was slipping; the loss to Mayweather was his fifth defeat in 12 bouts. Where else could fans look for a fighter with the talent and charisma to excite the masses?

Certainly not the heavyweight division, which remained in disarray in 2007. Identifying the heavyweight champion was a matter of choosing one's favorite sanctioning body. By most accounts the class of the division was Wladimir Klitschko, the Ukrainian Ph.D. and brother of former heavyweight champ Vitali Klitschko. Wladimir won his belt in April 2006 and defended it twice in '07, both times in convincing fashion. In March, he took care of Ray Austin with a second-round knockout in Mannheim, Germany. Four months later, in Cologne, he defeated Lamont Brewster,

whose corner asked for the fight to be stopped in the sixth round. Later it was revealed that Klitschko had beaten Brewster with a broken finger on his left hand, instantly branding himself as the most courageous heavyweight in the world.

Of course, that could be seen as faint praise. The rest of the heavyweight class remained anonymous to all but the most serious fight fans and readers of newspapers in former Soviet republics. In April, Ruslan Chagaev of Uzbekistan ended Nikolai Valuev's reign as WBA champion with a split decision victory. Chagaev, known to his supporters as "White Tyson," then was scheduled for an October bout against Russia's Sultan Ibragimov. The fight would bring some welcome order to the division by unifying the WBA and WBO titles, but it was not to be. In August, Chagaev pulled out and Ibragimov was forced to quickly schedule another title defense. And his new opponent—44-year-old Evander Holyfield—spoke volumes about the state of the division. There was another anticipated bout on the schedule for October as well: WBC champ Oleg Maskaev, the world's second-best known Kazakh after Borat, was scheduled to put his title on the line against hard-punching Nigerian Samuel Peter.

Fans could only hope that either of those title fights would produce the ring magic of the Israel Vazquez-Rafael Marquez WBC super bantamweight battle in March. It was an epic, with Marquez taking Vazquez's belt after seven rounds of brutal give and take. Vazquez, who finished the fight with blood streaming down his face, underwent reconstructive nasal surgery afterward; after he recovered he took back his belt with a TKO of Marquez in August. The two bouts were boxing's gold standards for ring action in 2007, and a rubber match was eagerly anticipated for '08. Still, regardless of the skill of the two fighters, a rematch between Mayweather and De La Hoya would overshadow all else in the sport. As 2007 ended, fight fans hoped the next year would bring yet another "Fight to Save Boxing."

FOR THE RECORD • 2006—2007

Current Champions

Division	Weight Limit	WBA Champion	WBC Champion	IBF Champion
Heavyweight	None	Ruslan Chagaev	Oleg Maskaev	Wladimir Klitschko
Cruiserweight	200	Jean-Marc Mormeck	Jean-Marc Mormeck	Steve Cunningham
Light Heavyweight	175	Stipe Drews	Chad Dawson	Clinton Woods
Super Middleweight	168	Mikkel Kessler	Mikkel Kessler	Alejandro Berrio
Middleweight	160	Felix Sturm	Jermain Taylor	Arhur Abraham
Super Welterweight	154	Joachim Alcine	Floyd Mayweather Jr.	Cory Spinks
Welterweight	147	Miguel Cotto	Floyd Mayweather Jr.	Kermit Cintron
Super Lightweight	140	Gavin Rees	Junior Witter	Paulie Malignaggi
Lightweight	135	Juan Diaz	David Diaz	Julio Diaz
Super Featherweight	130	Edwin Valero	Juan Manuel Marquez	Mzonke Fana
Featherweight	126	Cris John	In-Jin Chi	Robert Guerrero
Super Bantamweight	122	Celestino Caballero	Rafael Marquez	Steve Molitor
Bantamweight	118	Wladimir Sidorenko	Hozumi Hasegawa	Rafael Marquez
Super Flyweight	115	Alexander Munoz	Christian Mijares	Dmitri Kirilov
Flyweight	112	Takefumi Sakata	Daisuke Naito	Nonito Donaire
Light Flyweight	108	Juan Carlos Reveco	Edgar Sosa	Ulises Solis
Strawweight	105	Yukata Niida	Eagle Kyowa	Florante Condes

Note: WBC=World Boxing Council; WBA=World Boxing Association; IBF=International Boxing Federation.
Champions as of October 20, 2007.

Championship and Major Fights of 2006 and 2007

Abbreviations: WBC=World Boxing Council; WBA= World Boxing Association; IBF=International Boxing Federation; KO=knockout; TKO=technical knockout; UD=unanimous decision; SD=split decision; DQ=disqualification; MD=majority decision; TD=technical decision. Bouts from Sept. 1, 2005 to Sept. 1, 2006.

Heavyweight

Date	Winner	Loser	Result	Title/Org.	Site
Jan 20	Nikolay Valuev	Jameel McCline	TKO 3	WBA	Basel, Switzerland
Mar 10	Wladimir Klitschko	Ray Austin	TKO 2	IBF	Mannheim, Germany
April 14	Ruslan Chagaev	Nikolay Valuev	MD	WBA	Stuttgart, Germany
July 7	Wladimir Klitschko	Lamon Brewster	TKO	IBF	Cologne, Germany

Cruiserweight

Date	Winner	Loser	Result	Title/Org.	Site
Mar 17	Jean-Marc Mormeck	O'Neil Bell	UD	WBC/WBA	Paris
May 26	Steve Cunningham	Krzysztof Wlodarczyk	MD	IBF	Katowice, Poland
June 16	Firat Arslan	Valery Brudov	SD	Interim WBA	Budapest, Hungary

Light Heavyweight

Date	Winner	Loser	Result	Title/Org.	Site
Feb 3	Chad Dawson	Tomasz Adamek	UD	WBC	Kissimmee, Florida
April 28	Stipe Drews	Silvio Branco	UD	WBA	Oberhausen, Germany
June 9	Chad Dawson	Jesus Ruiz	TKO 6	WBC	Hartford, Connecticut
Sept 29	Clinton Woods	Julio C. Gonzalez	UD	IBF	Sheffield, England
Sept 29	Chad Dawson	Epifanio Mendoza	TKO 4	WBC	Sacramento, California

Super Middleweight

Date	Winner	Loser	Result	Title/Org.	Site
Mar 7	Anthony Mundine	Sam Soliman	TKO 9	Vacant WBA	Sydney
Mar 24	Mikel Kessler	Librado Andrade	UD	WBC/WBA	Copenhagen
June 27	Anthony Mundine	Pablo Daniel Zamora	UD	WBA	Broadbeach, Australia

*non-title bouts

Middleweight

Date	Winner	Loser	Result	Title/Org.	Site
April 28	Felix Sturm	Javier Castillejos	UD	WBA	Oberhausen, Germany
May 19	Jermain Taylor	Cory Spinks	SD	WBC	Memphis, Tennessee
May 26	Arthur Abraham	Sebastien Demers	TKO 3	IBF	Bamberg, Germany
June 30	Felix Sturm	Noe Tulio Gonzalez	UD	WBA	Stuttgart, Germany

Junior Middleweight (Super Welterweight)

Date	Winner	Loser	Result	Title/Org.	Site
Jan 6	Travis Simms	Jose A. Rivera	TKO 9	WBA	Hollywood, Florida
Feb 3	Cory Spinks	Rodney Jones	UD	IBF	Kissimmee, Florida
May 5	Floyd Mayweather	Oscar de la Hoya	SD	WBC	Las Vegas
June 16	Paulie Malignaggi	Lovemore N'dou	UD	IBF	Uncasville, Connecticut
July 7	Joachim Alcine	Travis Simms	UD	WBA	Bridgeport, Connecticut
July 28	Vernon Forrest	Carlos Baldomir	UD	Vacant WBC	Tacoma, Washington

Welterweight

Date	Winner	Loser	Result	Title/Org.	Site
Feb 10	Shane Mosley	Luis Collazo	UD	Vacant Interim WBC	Las Vegas
Mar 3	Miguel Cotto	Oktay Urkal	TKO 11	WBA	San Juan, Puerto Rico
June 9	Miguel Cotto	Zab Judah	TKO 11	WBA	New York City
July 14	Kermit Cintron	Walter Matthyse	KO 2	IBF	Atlantic City

Super Lightweight (Junior Welterweight)

Date	Winner	Loser	Result	Title/Org.	Site
Jan 20	Ricky Hatton	Juan Urango	UD	IBF	Las Vegas
Jan 20	Junior Witter	Arturo Morua	TKO 9	WBC	London
Mar 10	Souleymane M'Baye	Andres Kotelnik	Draw	WBA	Liverpool, England
June 16	Paulie Malignaggi	Lovemore N'dou	UD	IBF	Uncasville, Connecticut
July 21	Gavin Rees	Souleymane M'Baye	UD	WBA	Cardiff, Wales

Lightweight

Date	Winner	Loser	Result	Title/Org.	Site
Feb 3	Julio Diaz	Jesus Chavez	KO 3	IBF	Kissimmee, Florida
April 28	Juan Diaz	Acelino Freitas	TKO 8	WBA	Mashantucket, Connecticut
May 11	*Prawet Singwangcha	Jose Miguel Cotto	Draw	Vacant WBA	Salinas, Puerto Rico
Aug 4	David Diaz	Erik Morales	UD	WBC	Rosemont, Illinois

Super Featherweight (Junior Lightweight)

Date	Winner	Loser	Result	Title/Org.	Site
Jan 3	Edwin Valero	Michael Lozada	TKO 1	WBA	Tokyo
Mar 17	Juan Manuel Marquez	Marco Antonio Marrera	UD	WBC	Las Vegas
April 20	Mzonke Fana	Malcolm Klassen	SD	IBF	Khayelitsha, S. Africa
May 3	Edwin Valero	Nobuhito Honmo	TKO 8	WBA	Tokyo

Featherweight

Date	Winner	Loser	Result	Title/Org.	Site
Mar 3	Chris John	Jose Rojas	UD	WBA	Jakarta, Indonesia
July 21	Jorge Linares	Oscar Larios	TKO 10	Vacant WBC	Las Vegas
Aug 19	Chris John	Zaiki Takemoto	TKO 9	WBA	Kobè, Japan

*non-title bouts

Super Bantamweight (Junior Featherweight)

Date	Winner	Loser	Result	Title/Org.	Site
Mar 3	Rafael Marquez	Israel Vazquez	TKO 7	WBC	Carson, California
Mar 16	Celestino Caballero	Ricardo Castillo	TKO 9	WBA	Hollywood, Florida
July 14	Steve Molitor	Takalani Ndlovu	TKO 9	IBF	Orillia, Ontario, Canada
Aug 4	Celestino Caballero	Jorge Lacierva	UD	WBA	Hidalgo, Texas
Aug 4	Israel Vazquez	Rafael Marquez *	TKO 6	WBC	Hidalgo, Texas

Bantamweight

Date	Winner	Loser	Result	Title/Org.	Site
Mar 17	Wladimir Sidorenko	Ricardo Cordoba	Draw	WBA	Stuttgart, Germany
May 3	Hozumi Hasegawa	Simpiwe Vetyeka	UD	WBC	Tokyo
June 29	Wladimir Sidorenko	Jerome Arnould	KO 7	WBA	Marseille, France
July 7	Luis Alberto Perez	Genaro Garcia	TKO 7	IBF	Bridgeport, Connecticut
Sept 29	Joseph Agbeko	Luis A. Perez	TKO 7	IBF	Sacramento, California

Super Flyweight (Junior Bantamweight)

Date	Winner	Loser	Result	Title/Org.	Site
Jan 3	Cristian Mijares	Katsushige Kawashima	TKO 10	WBC	Tokyo
April 14	Cristian Mijares	Jorge Arce	UD	WBC	San Antonio, Texas
May 3	Alexander Munoz	Nobua Nashiro	UD	WBA	Tokyo
July 13	Cristian Mijares	Teppei Kikui	TKO 10	WBC	Durango, Mexico
Sept 7	Junior Witter	Vivian Harris	KO 7	WBC	Doncaster, England
Sept 24	Alexander Munoz	Kuniyuki Aizawa	UN	WBA	Tokyo

Flyweight

Date	Winner	Loser	Result	Title/Org.	Site
Mar 3	Vic Darchinyan	Victor Burgos	TKO 12	IBF	Carson, California
Mar 19	Takefumi Sakata	Lorenzo Parra	TKO 3	WBA	Tokyo
April 6	Pongsaklek Wonjongkam	Tomonobu Shimizu	TKO 7	WBC	Saraburi, Thailand
July 1	Takefumi Sakata	Roberto Vasquez	UD	WBA	Tokyo
July 7	Nonito Donaire	Vic Darchinyan	TKO 5	IBF	Bridgeport, Connecticut
July 18	Daisuke Naito	Pongsaklek Wonjongkam	UD	WBC	Tokyo

Light Flyweight (Junior Flyweight)

Date	Winner	Loser	Result	Title/Org.	Site
Jan 25	Ulises Solis	Will Grigsby	TKO 8	IBF	Las Vegas
April 14	Edgar Sosa	Brian Viloria	MD	Vacant WBC	San Antonio, Texas
May 19	Ulises Solis	Jose Antonio Aguirre	TKO 9	IBF	Jalisco, Mexico
June 22	Juan Carlos Reveco	Nethra Sasiprapa	KO 8	Vacant WBA	Mendoza, Argentino
July 28	Edgar Sosa	Luis Alberto Lazarte	DQ 10	WBC	Cancun, Mexico
Aug 4	Ulises Solis	Rodel Mayol	TKO 8	IBF	Rosemont, Illinois
Sept 16	Edgar Sosa	Lorenzo Trejo	TKO 9	WBC	Las Vegas

Strawweight (Mini Flyweight) (Minimum Weight)

Date	Winner	Loser	Result	Title/Org.	Site
June 4	Eagle Kyowa	Akira Yaegashi	UD	WBC	Yokohama, Japan
July 7	Florante Condes	Muhammad Rachman	SD	IBF	Jakarta, Indonesia
April 7	Yutaka Niida	Katsunari Takayama	SD	WBA	Tokyo
Sept1	Yutaka Niida	Eriberto Gejon	UD	WBA	Tokyo

*non-title bouts

World Champions

Sanctioning bodies: the National Boxing Association (NBA), the New York State Athletic Commission (NY), the World Boxing Association (WBA), the World Boxing Council (WBC), and the International Boxing Federation (IBF).

Heavyweights
(Weight: Unlimited)

Champion	Reign	Champion	Reign	Champion	Reign
John L. Sullivan*	1885–92	Jimmy Ellis WBA	1968–70	Riddick Bowe*	1992–93
James J. Corbett*	1892–97	Joe Frazier*	1970–73	Evander Holyfield*	1993–94
Bob Fitzsimmons*	1897–99	George Foreman*	1973–74	Michael Moorer*	1994
James J. Jeffries*	1899–05†	Muhammad Ali*	1974–78	George Foreman*	1994–95
Marvin Hart*	1905–06	Leon Spinks*	1978	Oliver McCall WBC	1995
Tommy Burns*	1906–08	Ken Norton WBC	1978	Frank Bruno WBC	1995–96
Jack Johnson*	1908–15	Larry Holmes WBC	1978–80	Bruce Seldon WBA	1995–96
Jess Willard*	1915–19	Muhammad Ali*	1978–79†	Mike Tyson WBA	1996
Jack Dempsey*	1919–26	John Tate WBA	1979–80	Michael Moorer IBF	1996–97
Gene Tunney*	1926–28†	Mike Weaver WBA	1980–82	Shannon Briggs*	1997–98
Max Schmeling*	1930–32	Larry Holmes*	1980–85	Lennox Lewis* WBC	1997–01
Jack Sharkey*	1932–33	Michael Dokes WBA	1982–83	E. Holyfield WBA, IBF	1996–99
Primo Carnera*	1933–34	Gerrie Coetzee WBA	1983–84	Lennox Lewis	1999–01
Max Baer*	1934–35	Tim Witherspoon WBC	1984	E. Holyfield WBA	2000–01
James J. Braddock*	1935–37	Pinklon Thomas WBC	1984–86	John Ruiz WBA	2001–03
Joe Louis*	1937–49†	Greg Page WBA	1984–85	Hasim Rahman* WBC, IBF	2001–05
Ezzard Charles*	1949–51	Michael Spinks*	1985–87	Chris Byrd IBF	2002–06
Jersey Joe Walcott*	1951–52	Tim Witherspoon WBA	1986	Roy Jones Jr. WBA	2003–05
Rocky Marciano*	1952–56†	Trevor Berbick WBC	1986	Lennox Lewis* WBC	2001–04
Floyd Patterson*	1956–59	Mike Tyson WBC	1986–87	John Ruiz, WBA	2003–05
Ingemar Johansson*	1959–60	James Smith WBA	1986–87	Vitali Klitschko WBC	2004–05
Floyd Patterson*	1960–62	Tony Tucker IBF	1987	Hasim Rahman WBC	2005–06
Sonny Liston*	1962–64	Mike Tyson*	1987–90	Nikolay Valuev WBA	2005–07
Muhammad Ali*	1964–70†	Buster Douglas*	1990	Oleg Maskaev WBC	2006–
Ernie Terrell WBA	1965–67	Evander Holyfield*	1990–92	Wladimir Klitschko IBF	2006–
Joe Frazier* NY	1968–70	Lennox Lewis WBC	1993–95	Ruslan Chagaev WBA	2007–

Cruiserweights
(Weight Limit: 200 pounds)

Champion	Reign	Champion	Reign	Champion	Reign
Marvin Camel* WBC	1980	Toufik Belbouli WBA	1989	Imamu Mayfield IBF	1997–98
Carlos De Leon* WBC	1980–82	Robert Daniels WBA	1989–91	Fabrice Tiozzo WBA	1997–00
Ossie Ocasio WBA	1982–84	Carlos De Leon* WBC	1989–90	J.C. Gomez* WBC	1998–02†
S.T. Gordon* WBC	1982–83	Glenn McCrory IBF	1989–90	Arthur Williams IBF	1998–99
Carlos De Leon* WBC	1983–85	Jeff Lampkin IBF	1990	Vassiliy Girov* IBF	1999–03
Marvin Camel IBF	1983–84	M. Duran* WBA	1990–91	James Toney* IBF	2003
Lee Roy Murphy IBF	1984–86	Bobby Czyz WBA	1991–92†	Virgil Hill WBA	2000–02
Piet Crous WBA	1984–85	Anaclet Wamba* WBC	1991–95†	Wayne Braithwaite WBC	2002–05
Alfonso Ratliff* WBC	1985	James Pritchard IBF	1991	J.M. Mormeck WBA	2002–06
Dwight Braxton WBA	1985–86	James Warring IBF	1991–92	J.M. Mormeck WBC	2005–06
Bernard Benton* WBC	1985–86	Alfred Cole IBF	1992–96	Melvin Davis IBF	2004–05
Carlos De Leon* WBC	1986–88	Orlin Norris WBA	1993–95	O'Neil Bell IBF	2005–06
Evander Holyfield* WBA	1986–88	Nate Miller WBA	1995–97	O'Neil Bell WBC/WBA	2006–07
Ricky Parkey IBF	1986–87	M. Dominguez* WBC	1996–98	J.M.Mormeck WBC/A	2007–
E. Holyfield* WBA, IBF	1987–88	A. Washington IBF	1996–97	Steve Cunningham IBF	2006–
Evander Holyfield*	1988†	Uriah Grant IBF	1997		

Light Heavyweights
(Weight Limit: 175 pounds)

Champion	Reign	Champion	Reign	Champion	Reign
Jack Root*	1903	Georges Carpentier*	1920–22	Tommy Loughran*	1927–29†
George Gardner*	1903	Battling Siki*	1922–23	Maxie Rosenbloom*	1930–34
Bob Fitzsimmons*	1903–05	Mike McTigue*	1923–25	George Nichols NBA	1932
Jack O'Brien*	1905–12†	Paul Berlenbach*	1925–26	Bob Godwin NBA	1933
Jack Dillon*	1914–16	Jack Delaney*	1926–27†	Bob Olin*	1934–35
Battling Levinsky*	1916–20	Jimmy Slattery NBA	1927	John Henry Lewis*	1935–38†

*Lineal champion.
†Champion relinquished title to retire or switch weight classes, or had title stripped by boxing organization.

Light Heavyweights *(Cont.)*

Champion	Reign
Melio Bettina	1939
Billy Conn*	1939–40†
Anton Christoforidis	1941
Gus Lesnevich*	1941–48
Freddie Mills*	1948–50
Joey Maxim*	1950–52
Archie Moore*	1952–62†
Harold Johnson NBA	1961
Harold Johnson*	1962–63
Willie Pastrano*	1963–65
Jose Torres*	1965–66
Dick Tiger*	1966–68
Bob Foster*	1968–74†
Vicente Rondon WBA	1971–72
John Conteh WBC	1974–77
Victor Galindez* WBA	1974–78
Miguel A. Cuello WBC	1977–78
Mate Parlov WBC	1978
Mike Rossman* WBA	1978–79
Victor Galindez* WBA	1979
Marvin Johnson* WBC	1978–79
M.S. Muhammad* WBC	1979–81

Champion	Reign
Marvin Johnson WBA	1979–80
E.M. Muhammad* WBA	1980–81
Michael Spinks* WBA	1981–83
Dwight Qawi WBC	1981–83
Michael Spinks*	1983–85†
J. B. Williamson WBC	1985–86
Slobodan Kacar IBF	1985–86
Marvin Johnson* WBA	1986–87
Dennis Andries WBC	1986–87
Bobby Czyz IBF	1986–87
Leslie Stewart WBA	1987
Virgil Hill* WBA	1987–91
Pr Charles Williams IBF	1987–93
Thomas Hearns WBC	1987†
Donny Lalonde WBC	1987–88
Sugar Ray Leonard WBC	1988
Dennis Andries WBC	1989
Jeff Harding WBC	1989–90
Dennis Andries WBC	1990–91
Thomas Hearns* WBA	1991–92
Jeff Harding WBC	1991–94
Iran Barkley* WBA	1992

Champion	Reign
Virgil Hill* WBA	1992–97
Henry Maske IBF	1993–96
Mike McCallum WBC	1994–95
Fabrice Tiozzo WBC	1995–96
D. Michalczewski IBF	1997†
Roy Jones Jr. WBC, WBA	1997–03
William Guthrie IBF	1997–98
Reggie Johnson IBF	1998–99
Roy Jones Jr.*	1999–03
Bruno Girard WBA	2001–03
Mehdi Sahnoune WBA	2003
Silvio Branco WBA	2003–04
Antonio Tarver WBC, IBF	2003
Roy Jones Jr. WBC	2003
Glencoffe Johnson IBF	2004–05
Fabrice Tiozzo WBC	2004–5
Antonio Tarver* WBC	2004–05
Silvio Branco WBA	2005–07
Clinton Woods IBF	2005–
Tomasz Adamek WBC	2005–07
Stipe Drews WBA	2007–
Chad Dawson WBC	2007–

Super Middleweights
(Weight Limit: 168 pounds)

Champion	Reign
Murray Sutherland* IBF	1984
Chong-Pal Park* IBF	1984–87
Chong-Pal Park* WBA	1987–88
G. Rocchigiani IBF	1988–89
F. Obelmejias* WBA	1988–89
Sugar Ray Leonard WBC	1988–90†
In-Chul Baek* WBA	1989–90
Lindell Holmes IBF	1990–91
Chris Tiozzo* WBA	1990–91
Mauro Galvano WBC	1990–92
Victor Cordova* WBA	1991
Darrin Van Horn IBF	1991–92
Iran Barkley IBF	1992
Nigel Benn WBC	1992–96
James Toney IBF	1992–94

Champion	Reign
Michael Nunn* WBA	1992–94
Steve Little* WBA	1994
Frank Liles* WBA	1994–99
Roy Jones Jr. IBF	1994–96
Thulane Malinga WBC	1996
V. Nardiello WBC	1996
Robin Reid WBC	1996–97
Charles Brewer IBF	1997–98
Thulane Malinga WBC	1997–98
Richie Woodhall WBC	1998–99
Sven Ottke IBF	1998–03
Byron Mitchell* WBA	1999–00
Markus Beyer WBC	1999–00
Bruno Girard* WBA	2000–01†
Glenn Catley WBC	2000–01

Champion	Reign
Eric Lucas WBC	2000–03
Byron Mitchell WBA	2000–03
Sven Ottke WBA	2003†
Anthony Mundine WBA	2003
Markus Beyer WBC	2003–04
Sven Ottke, IBF	2003–05
Cristian Sanavia WBC	2004
Manny Siaca, WBA	2004–05
Mikel Kessler WBA	2005–
Markus Beyer WBC	2004–06
Jeff Lacy IBF	2005
Joe Calzaghe IBF	2006–07
Mikkel Kessler WBC	2006–
Robert Stieglitz IBF	2007
Alejandro Berrio IBF	2007–

Middleweights
(Weight Limit: 160 pounds)

Champion	Reign
Jack Dempsey*	1884–91
Bob Fitzsimmons*	1891–97†
Kid McCoy*	1897–98
Tommy Ryan*	1898–07†
Stanley Ketchel*	1908
Billy Papke*	1908
Stanley Ketchel*	1908–10†
Frank Klaus*	1913
George Chip*	1913–14
Al McCoy*	1914–17
Mike O'Dowd*	1917–20
Johnny Wilson*	1920–23
Harry Greb*	1923–26
Tiger Flowers*	1926
Mickey Walker*	1926–31†
Gorilla Jones*	1931–32
Marcel Thil*	1932–37
Fred Apostoli*	1937–39
Al Hostak NBA	1938

Champion	Reign
Solly Krieger NBA	1938–39
Al Hostak NBA	1939–40
Ceferino Garcia*	1939–40
Ken Overlin*	1940–41
Tony Zale NBA	1940–41
Billy Soose*	1941
Tony Zale*	1941–47
Rocky Graziano*	1947–48
Tony Zale*	1948
Marcel Cerdan*	1948–49
Jake La Motta*	1949–51
Sugar Ray Robinson*	1951
Randy Turpin*	1951
Sugar Ray Robinson*	1951–52†
Bobo Olson*	1953–55
Sugar Ray Robinson*	1955–57
Gene Fullmer*	1957
Sugar Ray Robinson*	1957
Carmen Basilio*	1957–58

Champion	Reign
Sugar Ray Robinson*	1958–60
Gene Fullmer NBA	1959–62
Paul Pender*	1960–61
Terry Downes*	1961–62
Paul Pender*	1962–63†
Dick Tiger WBA	1962–63
Dick Tiger*	1963
Joey Giardello*	1963–65
Dick Tiger*	1965–66
Emile Griffith*	1966–67
Nino Benvenuti*	1967
Emile Griffith*	1967–68
Nino Benvenuti*	1968–70
Carlos Monzon*	1970–77†
Rodrigo Valdez WBC	1974–76
Rodrigo Valdez*	1977–78
Hugo Corro*	1978–79
Vito Antuofermo*	1979–80
Alan Minter*	1980

*Lineal champion. †Champion retired or relinquished title.

Middleweights *(Cont.)*

Champion	Reign
Marvin Hagler*	1980–87
Sugar Ray Leonard*	1987†
Frank Tate IBF	1987–88
Sumbu Kalambay WBA	1987–89
Thomas Hearns* WBC	1987–88
Iran Barkley* WBC	1988–89
Michael Nunn IBF	1988–91
Roberto Duran* WBC	1989–90†
Michael Nunn* IBF	1991
Mike McCallum WBA	1989–91
Julian Jackson WBC	1990–93
James Toney* IBF	1991–93†

Champion	Reign
Reggie Johnson WBA	1992–94
Roy Jones Jr.* IBF	1993–95†
G. McClellan WBC	1993–95†
Jorge Castro WBA	1994–95
Shinji Takehara WBA	1995–96
Jullian Jackson WBC	1995
Quincy Taylor WBC	1995–96
Bernard Hopkins* IBF	1994–
Keith Holmes WBC	1996–98
William Joppy WBA	1996–97
J.C. Green WBA	1997
William Joppy WBA	1998–01
Hassine Cherifi WBC	1998–99

Champion	Reign
Keith Holmes WBC	1999–00
Felix Trinidad WBA	2001
William Joppy WBA	2001–03
Bernard Hopkins* WBC/IBF	2001–05
Bernard Hopkins WBA	2003–05
Jermain Taylor WBA	2005–06
Jermain Taylor WBC/IBF	2005
Kelly Pavlik WBC	2005–
Arthur Abraham IBF	2005–
Felix Sturm WBA	2006
Javier Castillejo WBA	2006–07
Felix Sturm WBA	2007–

Junior Middleweights
(Weight Limit: 154 pounds)

Champion	Reign
Emile Griffith (EBU)	1962–63
Dennis Moyer*	1962–63
Ralph Dupas*	1963
Sandro Mazzinghi*	1963–65
Nino Benvenuti*	1965–66
Ki-Soo Kim*	1966–68
Sandro Mazzinghi*	1968
Freddie Little*	1969–70
Carmelo Bossi*	1970–71
Koichi Wajima*	1971–74
Oscar Albarado*	1974–75
Koichi Wajima*	1975
Miguel de Oliveira WBC	1975–76
Jae-Do Yuh*	1975–76
Elisha Obed WBC	1975–76
Koichi Wajima*	1976
Jose Duran*	1976
Eckhard Dagge WBC	1976–77
Miguel Angel Castellini*	1976–77
Eddie Gazo*	1977–78
Rocky Mattioli WBC	1977–79
Masashi Kudo*	1978–79
Maurice Hope WBC	1979–81
Ayub Kalule*	1979–81
Wilfred Benitez WBC	1981–82
Sugar Ray Leonard*	1981–82†
Tadashi Mihara WBA	1981–82
Davey Moore WBA	1982–83
Thomas Hearns* WBC	1982–84

Champion	Reign
Roberto Duran WBA	1983–84
Mark Medal IBF	1984
Thomas Hearns*	1984–86†
Mike McCallum* WBA	1984–87†
Carlos Santos IBF	1984–86
Buster Drayton IBF	1986–87
Duane Thomas WBC	1986–87
Matthew Hilton IBF	1987–88
Lupe Aquino WBC	1987
Gianfranco Rosi WBC	1987–88
Julian Jackson WBA	1987–90
Donald Curry WBC	1988–89
Robert Hines IBF	1988–89
Darrin Van Horn IBF	1989
Rene Jacquot WBC	1989
John Mugabi* WBC	1989–90
Gianfranco Rosi IBF	1989–94
Terry Norris* WBC	1990–93
Gilbert Dele WBA	1991
Vinny Pazienza WBA	1991–92
Julio C. Vasquez WBA	1992–95
Simon Brown* WBC	1993–94
Terry Norris* WBC	1994
Luis Santana* WBC	1995–95
Vincent Pettway IBF	1994–95
Paul Vaden IBF	1995
Carl Daniels WBA	1995
Terry Norris* WBC	1995–97
Terry Norris* IBF	1995–96†

Champion	Reign
L. Boudouani WBA	1996–99
Raul Marquez IBF	1997
Keith Mullings* WBC	1997–99
Yori Boy Campas IBF	1997–98
Fernando Vargas IBF	1998–00
F. Javier Castillejo* WBC	1999–01
David Reid WBA	1999–00
Felix Trinidad WBA	2000–01
Felix Trinidad WBA, IBF	2001†
Oscar De La Hoya* WBC	2001–03
Fernando Vargas WBA	2001–02
Ronald Wright IBF†	2001–04
Oscar De La Hoya* WBC/WBA	2002–03
Shane Mosley* WBC	2003–04
Alejandro Garcia WBA	2003–05
Ronald Wright WBA, WBC	2004–05
Verno Phillips IBF	2004–05
Ricardo Mayora WBC	2005–06
Alex T. Garcia WBA	2005–06
Roman Karmazin IBF	2005–06
Jose A. Rivera WBA	2006–07
Oscar De La Hoya WBC	2006–07
Cory Spinks IBF	2006–
Travis Simms WBA	2007
Joachim Alcine WBA	2007–
F. Mayweather Jr. WBC	2007–

Welterweights
(Weight Limit: 147 pounds)

Champion	Reign
Paddy Duffy*	1888–90†
Mysterious Billy Smith*	1892–94
Tommy Ryan*	1894–98†
Mysterious Billy Smith*	1898–1900
Rube Ferns*	1900
Matty Matthews*	1900–01
Rube Ferns*	1901
Joe Walcott*	1901–04
The Dixie Kid*	1904–05†
Honey Mellody*	1906–07
Mike Sullivan*	1907–08†
Jimmy Gardner*	1908†
Jimmy Clabby*	1910–1†
Waldemar Holberg*	1914

Champion	Reign
Tom McCormick*	1914
Matt Wells*	1914–15
Mike Glover*	1915
Jack Britton*	1915
Ted "Kid" Lewis*	1915–16
Jack Britton*	1916–17
Ted "Kid" Lewis*	1917–19
Jack Britton*	1919–22
Mickey Walker*	1922–26
Pete Latzo*	1926–27
Joe Dundee*	1927–29
Jackie Fields*	1929–30
Young Jack Thompson*	1930
Tommy Freeman*	1930–31

Champion	Reign
Young Jack Thompson*	1931
Lou Brouillard*	1931–32
Jackie Fields*	1932–33
Young Corbett III*	1933
Jimmy McLarnin*	1933–34
Barney Ross*	1934
Jimmy McLarnin*	1934–35
Barney Ross*	1935–38
Henry Armstrong*	1938–40
Fritzie Zivic*	1940–41
Red Cochrane*	1941–46
Marty Servo*	1946
Sugar Ray Robinson*	1946–51†
Johnny Bratton	1951

*Lineal champion. †Champion relinquished title to retire or switch weight classes, or had title stripped by boxing organization.

Welterweights *(Cont.)*

Champion	Reign	Champion	Reign	Champion	Reign
Kid Gavilan*	1951–54	Sugar Ray Leonard*	1979–80	Ike Quartey WBA	1994–97†
Johnny Saxton*	1954–55	Roberto Duran*	1980	Oscar De La Hoya* WBC	1997–99
Tony DeMarco*	1955	Thomas Hearns WBA	1980–81	James Page WBA	1998–01
Carmen Basilio*	1955–56	Sugar Ray Leonard*	1980–82†	Felix Trinidad* IBF, WBC	1999–00†
Johnny Saxton*	1956	Donald Curry* WBA	1983–85	Shane Mosley* WBC	2000–02
Carmen Basilio*	1956–57†	Milton McCrory WBC	1983–85	Andrew Lewis WBA	2001–02
Virgil Akins*	1958	Donald Curry*	1985–86	Vernon Forrest IBF	2001
Don Jordan*	1958–60	Lloyd Honeyghan*	1986–87	Vernon Forrest* WBC	2001–03
Kid Paret*	1960–61	Jorge Vaca* WBC	1987–88	Ricardo Mayorga WBA	2002
Emile Griffith*	1961	Lloyd Honeyghan* WBC	1988–89	Ricardo Mayorga* WBC	2003–05
Kid Paret*	1961–62	Mark Breland WBA	1987	Michele Piccirillo IBF	2002–03
Emile Griffith*	1962–63	Marlon Starling WBA	1987–88	Jose Rivera WBA	2003
Luis Rodriguez*	1963	Tomas Molinares WBA	1988–89	Cory Spinks IBF,	
Emile Griffith*	1963–66†	Simon Brown IBF	1988–91	WBC, WBA	2003–05
Curtis Cokes*	1966–69	Mark Breland WBA	1989–90	Zab Judah WBA/WBC/IBF..	2005–06
Jose Napoles*	1969–70	Marlon Starling* WBC	1989–90	Luis Collazo WBA	2006
Billy Backus*	1970–71	Aaron Davis WBA	1990–91	Ricky Hatton WBA	2006
Jose Napoles*	1971–75	Maurice Blocker* WBC	1990–91	Carlos Baldomir WBC	2006
Hedgemon Lewis NY	1972–73	Meldrick Taylor WBA	1991–92	F. Mayweather, Jr. IBF	2006
Angel Espada WBA	1975–76	Simon Brown* WBC	1991	Miguel Cotto WBA	2006–
John H. Stracey*	1975–76	Buddy McGirt* WBC	1991–93	F. Mayweather Jr. WBC	2006–
Carlos Palomino*	1976–79	Felix Trinidad IBF	1993–00	Kermit Cintron IBF	2006–
Pipino Cuevas WBA	1976–80	Pernell Whitaker* WBC	1993–97'		
Wilfredo Benitez*	1979	Crisanto Espana WBA	1992–94		

Super Lightweights (Weight Limit: 140 pounds)

Champion	Reign	Champion	Reign	Champion	Reign
Pinkey Mitchell*	1922–25	Sang-Hyun Kim WBC	1978–80	Jake Rodriguez IBF	1994–95
Red Herring	1925	Saoul Mamby WBC	1980–82	Juan Coggi WBA	1993–94
Mushy Callahan*	1926–30	Aaron Pryor* WBA	1980–83	Frankie Randall* WBC	1994
Jack (Kid) Berg*	1930–31	Leroy Haley WBC	1982–83	Frankie Randall WBA	1994–96
Tony Canzoneri*	1931–32	Aaron Pryor* IBF	1983–85†	Juan Coggi WBA	1996
Johnny Jadick*	1932–33	Bruce Curry WBC	1983–84	Julio César Chávez* WBC	1994–96
Sammy Fuller	1932–33	Johnny Bumphus WBA	1984	Kostya Tszyu IBF	1995–97
Battling Shaw*	1933	Bill Costello WBC	1984–85	Frankie Randall WBA	1996–97
Tony Canzoneri*	1933	Gene Hatcher WBA	1984–85	Oscar De La Hoya* WBC	1996–97†
Barney Ross*	1933–35†	Ubaldo Sacco WBA	1985–86	Khalid Rahilou WBA	1997–98
Tippy Larkin*	1946	Lonnie Smith* WBC	1985–86	Vincent Phillips* IBF	1997–99
Carlos Ortiz*	1959–60	Patrizio Oliva WBA	1986–87	Sharmba Mitchell WBA	1998–01
Duilio Loi*	1960–62	Gary Hinton IBF	1986	Kostya Tszyu WBC	1998–
Eddie Perkins*	1962	Rene Arredondo* WBC	1986	Terronn Millett* IBF	1999–00
Duilio Loi*	1962–63†	Tsuyoshi Hamada WBC	1986–87	Zab Judah* IBF	2000–01
Roberto Cruz WBA	1963	Joe Louis Manley IBF	1986–87	Kostya Tszyu*	
Eddie Perkins*	1963–65	Terry Marsh IBF	1987	WBA/WBC	2001–03
Carlos Hernandez*	1965–66	Juan Coggi WBA	1987–90	Kostya Tszyu* IBF	2003–05
Sandro Lopopolo*	1966–67	Rene Arredondo WBC	1987	Vivian Harris WBA	2003–05
Paul Fujii*	1967–68	R. Mayweather* WBC	1987–89	Arturo Gatti WBC	2004–05
Nicolino Loche*	1968–72	James McGirt IBF	1988	F. Mayweather Jr. WBC..	2005–06
Pedro Adigue WBC	1968–70	Meldrick Taylor IBF	1988–90	Carlos Maussa WBA	2005–06
Bruno Arcari WBC	1970–74	Julio César Chávez* WBC	1989–94	Ricky Hatton IBF	2005–06
Alfonso Frazer*	1972	Julio César Chávez* IBF	1990–91	Souleymane M'baye WBA..	2006–07
Antonio Cervantes*	1972–76	Loreto Garza WBA	1990–91	Juan Urango IBF	2006–07
Perico Fernandez WBC	1974–75	Juan Coggi WBA	1991	Junior Wltter WBC	2006–
S. Muangsurin WBC	1975–76	Edwin Rosario WBA	1991–92	Gavin Rees WBA	2007–
Wilfred Benitez*	1976–79†	Rafael Pineda IBF	1991–92	Ricky Hatton IBF	2007
M. Velasquez WBC	1976	Akinobu Hiranaka WBA	1992	Lovemore N'Dou IBF	2007
S. Muangsurin WBC	1976–78	Pernell Whitaker IBF	1992–93†	Paul Malignaggo IBF	2007–
A. Cervantes WBA	1977–80	Charles Murray IBF	1993–94		

Lightweights (Weight Limit: 135 pounds)

Champion	Reign	Champion	Reign	Champion	Reign
Jack McAuliffe*	1886–94†	Joe Gans*	1906–08	Jimmy Goodrich*	1925
Kid Lavigne*	1896–99	Battling Nelson*	1908–10	Rocky Kansas*	1925–26
Frank Erne*	1899–1902	Ad Wolgast*	1910–12	Sammy Mandell*	1926–30
Joe Gans*	1902–04	Willie Ritchie*	1912–14	Al Singer*	1930
Jimmy Britt*	1904–05	Freddie Welsh*	1915–17	Tony Canzoneri*	1930–33
Battling Nelson*	1905–06	Benny Leonard*	1917–25†	Barney Ross*	1933–35†

Lightweights *(Cont.)*

Champion	Reign	Champion	Reign	Champion	Reign
Tony Canzoneri*	1935–36	Jim Watt WBC*	1979–81	Dingaan Thobela WBA	1993
Lou Ambers*	1936–38	Ernesto Espana WBA	1979–80	Fred Pendleton* IBF	1993–94
Henry Armstrong*	1938–39	Hilmer Kenty WBA	1980–81	Orzubek Nazarov WBA	1993–98
Lou Ambers*	1939–40	Sean O'Grady WBA	1981	Rafael Ruelas* IBF	1994–95
Sammy Angott NBA	1940–41	Claude Noel WBA	1981	Oscar De La Hoya* IBF	1995†
Lew Jenkins*	1940–41	Alexis Arguello* WBC	1981–82†	Phillip Holiday IBF	1995–97
Sammy Angott*	1941–42†	Arturo Frias WBA	1981–82	Jean B. Mendy* WBC	1996–97
Beau Jack* NY	1942–43	Ray Mancini* WBA	1982–84	Steve Johnston* WBC	1997–98
Bob Montgomery* NY	1943	Alexis Arguello	1982–83	Shane Mosley IBF	1997–99†
Sammy Angott NBA	1943–44	Edwin Rosario WBC	1983–84	Jean B. Mendy WBA	1998–99
Beau Jack* NY	1943–44	Choo Choo Brown IBF	1984	Cesar Bazan* WBC	1998–99
Bob Montgomery* NY	1944–47	L. Bramble* WBA	1984–86	Steve Johnston* WBC	1999–00
Juan Zurita NBA	1944–45	Jose Luis Ramirez WBC	1984–85	Julien Lorcy WBA	1999
Ike Williams*	1947–51	Harry Arroyo IBF	1984–85	Stefano Zoff WBA	1999
James Carter*	1951–52	Jimmy Paul IBF	1985–86	Paul Spadafora IBF	1999–03
Lauro Salas*	1952	Hector Camacho WBC	1985–86	Gilbert Serrano WBA	1999–00
James Carter*	1952–54	Greg Haugen IBF	1986–87	T. Hatakeyama WBA	2000–01
Paddy DeMarco*	1954	Edwin Rosario* WBA	1986–87	Jose Luis Castillo* WBC	2000–02
James Carter*	1954–55	Julio César Chávez* WBA	1987–88	Julien Lorcy WBA	2001
Wallace Smith*	1955–56	Jose Luis Ramirez WBC	1987–88	Raul Balbi WBA	2001
Joe Brown*	1956–62	Julio César Chávez*	1988–89†	F. Mayweather* WBC	2002–03
Carlos Ortiz*	1962–65	Vinny Pazienza IBF	1987–88	Leonard Dorin WBA	2002–03
Ismael Laguna*	1965	Greg Haugen IBF	1988–89	Javier Jauregui IBF	2003–04
Carlos Ortiz*	1965–68	P. Whitaker* WBC, IBF	1989–90	Julio Diaz IBF	2004–05
Carlos Teo Cruz*	1968–69	Edwin Rosario WBA	1989–90	Lakva Sim WBA	2004
Mando Ramos*	1969–70	Juan Nazario WBA	1990	Juan Diaz WBA	2004–
Ismael Laguna*	1970	P. Whitaker* WBA, WBC	1990–92†	Jose Luis Castillo WBC	2004–05
Ken Buchanan*	1970–72	Pernell Whitaker* IBF	1991–92†	Diego Corrales WBC	2005–06
Roberto Duran*	1972–79†	Julio César Chávez IBF	1990–91	Jesus Chavez IBF	2005–07
Chango Carmona WBC	1972	Edwin Rosario WBA	1991–92	Joel Casamayor WBC	2006–
Rodolfo Gonzalez WBC	1972–74	Julio César Chávez WBC	1990–92	Julio Diaz IBF	2007–
Ishimatsu Suzuki WBC	1974–76	Miguel Gonzalez WBC	1992–95		
Estaban DeJesus WBC	1976–78	Joey Gamache WBA	1992–93		

Super Featherweights (Weight Limit: 130 pounds)

Champion	Reign	Champion	Reign	Champion	Reign
Johnny Dundee*	1921–23	Samuel Serrano*	1981–83	Choi Yong-Soo WBA	1995–98
Jack Bernstein*	1923	R. Navarrete WBC	1981–82	Arturo Gatti IBF	1995–98†
Johnny Dundee*	1923–24	Rafael Limon WBC	1982	Genaro Hernandez* WBC	1997–98
Steve (Kid) Sullivan*	1924–25	Bobby Chacon WBC	1982–83	Roberto Garcia IBF	1998–99
Mike Ballerino*	1925	Roger Mayweather*	1983–84	Floyd Mayweather* WBC	1998–01†
Tod Morgan*	1925–29	Hector Camacho WBC	1983–84	T. Hatakeyama WBA	1998–99
Benny Bass*	1929–31	Rocky Lockridge*	1984–85	Lakva Sim WBA	1999
Kid Chocolate*	1931–33	Hwan-Kil Yuh IBF	1984–85	Diego Corrales IBF	1999–01
Frankie Klick*	1933–34†	Julio César Chávez WBC	1984–87	Jong Kwon Baek WBA	1999–00
Sandy Saddler*	1949–50†	Lester Ellis IBF	1985	Joel Casamayor WBA	2000–02
Harold Gomes*	1959–60	Wilfredo Gomez*	1985–86	Steve Forbes IBF	2000–02†
Gabriel (Flash) Elorde*	1960–67	Barry Michael IBF	1985–87	Acelino Freitas* WBA	2002–04
Yoshiaki Numata*	1967	Alfredo Layne* WBA	1986	Y. Nantchachai WBA	2002–05
Hiroshi Kobayashi*	1967–71	Brian Mitchell* WBA	1986–91†	S. Singmanassak WBC	2002–03
Rene Barrientos WBC	1969–70	Rocky Lockridge IBF	1987–88	Jesus Chavez WBC	2003–04
Yoshiaki Numata WBC	1970–71	Azumah Nelson* WBC	1988–94	Carlos Hernandez IBF	2003–04
Alfredo Marcano*	1971–72	Tony Lopez IBF	1988–89	Erik Morales WBC/IBF	2004–05
R. Arredondo WBC	1971–74	Juan Molina IBF	1989–90	Erik Morales IBF	2004–05
Ben Villaflor*	1972–73	Tony Lopez IBF	1990–91	Marco A. Barrera WBC	2005–07
Kuniaki Shibata*	1973	Joey Gamache WBA	1991	Vicente Mosquera WBA	2005–06
Ben Villaflor*	1973–76	Brian Mitchell IBF	1991	Robbie Peden, IBF	2005
Kuniaki Shibata WBC	1974–75	Genaro Hernandez WBA	1991–95	Marco A. Barrera, IBF	2005–06
Alfredo Escalera WBC	1975–78	James Leija* WBC	1994	Cassius Baloyi, IBF	2006
Samuel Serrano*	1976–80	Juan Molina IBF	1991–95	Edwin Valero, WBA	2006–
Alexis Arguello WBC	1978–80	Gabriel Ruelas* WBC	1994–95	Gairy St. Clair IBF	2006
Yasutsune Uehara*	1980–81	Eddie Hopson IBF	1995	Malcolm Klassen IBF	2006–07
Rafael Limon WBC	1980–81	Tracy Patterson IBF	1995	Mzonke Fana IBF	2007–
C. Boza-Edwards WBC	1981	Azumah Nelson* WBC	1995–97	Juan Marquez WBC	2007–

Featherweights (Weight Limit: 126 pounds)

Champion	Reign
Torpedo Billy Murphy*...1890	
Young Griffo*	1890–92†
George Dixon*	1892–97
Solly Smith*	1897–98
Dave Sullivan*	1898
George Dixon*	1898–1900
Terry McGovern*	1900–01
Young Corbett II*	1901–03†
Abe Attell*	1903–04
Tommy Sullivan*	1904–05†
Abe Attell*	1906–12
Johnny Kilbane*	1912–23
Eugene Criqui*	1923
Johnny Dundee*	1923–24†
"Kid" Kaplan*	1925–26†
Tony Canzoneri*	1927–28
Andre Routis*	1928–29
Battling Battalino*	1929–32†
Tommy Paul NBA	1932–33
Kid Chocolate NY	1932–33†
Freddie Miller NBA	1933–36
Mike Beloise NY	1936–37
Petey Sarron NBA	1936–37
Maurice Holtzer	1937–38
Henry Armstrong*	1937–38†
Joey Archibald* NY	1938–39
Leo Rodak NBA	1938–39
Joey Archibald	1939–40
Petey Scalzo NBA	1940–41
Harry Jeffra*	1940–41
Joey Archibald*	1941
Richie Lamos NBA	1941
Chalky Wright*	1941–42
Jackie Wilson NBA	1941–43
Willie Pep*	1942–48
Jackie Callura NBA	1943
Phil Terranova NBA	1943–44
Sal Bartolo NBA	1944–46
Sandy Saddler*	1948–49
Willie Pep*	1949–50
Sandy Saddler*	1950–57†

Champion	Reign
Kid Bassey*	1957–59
Davey Moore*	1959–63
Sugar Ramos*	1963–64
Vicente Saldivar*	1964–67†
Paul Rojas WBA	1968
Jose Legra WBC	1968–69
Shozo Saijyo WBA	1968–71
J. Famechon* WBC	1969–70
Vicente Saldivar* WBC	1970
Kuniaki Shibata* WBC	1970–72
Antonio Gomez WBA	1971–72
C. Sanchez* WBC	1972
Ernesto Marcel WBA	1972–74
Jose Legra* WBC	1972–73
Eder Jofre* WBC	1973–74†
Ruben Olivares WBA	1974
Bobby Chacon WBC	1974–75
Alexis Arguello* WBA	1974–76†
Ruben Olivares WBC	1975
Poison Kotey WBC	1975–76
Danny Lopez* WBC	1976–80
Rafael Ortega WBA	1977
Cecilio Lastra WBA	1977–78
Eusebio Pedroza* WBA	1978–85
S. Sanchez* WBC	1980–82†
Juan LaPorte WBC	1982–84
Wilfredo Gomez WBC	1984
Min-Keun Oh IBF	1984–85
Azumah Nelson WBC	1984–88
Barry McGuigan* WBA	1985–86
Ki Young Chung IBF	1985–86
Steve Cruz* WBA	1986–87
Antonio Rivera IBF	1986–88
A. Esparragoza* WBA	1987–91
Calvin Grove IBF	1988
Jorge Paez IBF	1988–91
Jeff Fenech WBC	1988–90†
Marcos Villasana WBC	1990–91
Paul Hodkinson WBC	1991–93
Troy Dorsey IBF	1991

Champion	Reign
Manuel Medina IBF	1991–93
Yung Kyun Park* WBA	1991–93
Gregorio Vargas WBC	1993
Tom Johnson IBF	1993–97†
Eloy Rojas* WBA	1993–96
Kevin Kelley WBC	1993–95
A. Gonzalez WBC	1995
Manuel Medina WBC	1995–95
Luisito Espinosa WBC	1995–99
Wilfredo Vazquez* WBA	1996–98
Hector Lizarraga IBF	1997–98
Naseem Hamed* WBA	1998†
Naseem Hamed*	1998–01
Freddy Norwood WBA	1998
Manuel Medina IBF	1998–99
Antonio Cermeno WBA	1998–99
Cesar Soto WBC	1999
Freddy Norwood WBA	1999–00
Naseem Hamed* WBC	1999†
Paul Ingle IBF	1999–00
Guty Espadas WBC	2000–01
Erik Morales WBC	2000–02
Derrick Gainer WBA	2000–03
Mbulelo Botile IBF	2001
Frankie Toledo IBF	2001
Manuel Medina IBF	2001–02
Marco A. Barrera* WBA/WBC	2001–03
Johnny Tapia IBF	2002
Marco A. Barrera* WBC	2002†
Erik Morales WBC	2002–03
Juan Marquez IBF	2003–06
Chris John WBA	2005–
In Jin Chi WBC	2004–06
Valdemir Pereira, IBF	2006
Eric Aiken IBF	2006
T. Koshimoto, WBC	2006
Rudolfo Lopez WBC	2006
In Jin Chi WBC	2006–07
Robert Guerrero IBF	2006–
Jorge Linares WBC	2007–

Super Bantamweights (Weight Limit: 122 pounds)

Champion	Reign
Jack (Kid) Wolfe*	1922–23
Carl Duane*	1923–24
Rigoberto Riasco* WBC	1976
R. Kobayashi* WBC	1976
Dong-Kyun Yum* WBC	1976–77
Wilfredo Gomez* WBC	1977–83†
Soo-Hwan Hong WBA	1977–78
Ricardo Cardona WBA	1978–80
Leo Randolph WBA	1980
Sergio Palma WBA	1980–82
Leonardo Cruz WBA	1982–84
Jaime Garza* WBC	1983
Bobby Berna IBF	1983–84
Loris Stecca WBA	1984
Seung-Il Suh IBF	1984–85
Victor Callejas WBA	1984–86
Juan Meza* WBC	1984–85
Ji-Won Kim IBF	1985–86
Lupe Pintor* WBC	1985–86
S. Payakaroon* WBC	1986–87
Seung-Hoon Lee IBF	1987–88
Louie Espinosa WBA	1987

Champion	Reign
Jeff Fenech* WBC	1987†
Julio Gervacio WBA	1987–88
Daniel Zaragoza* WBC	1988–90
Jose Sanabria IBF	1988–89
B. Pinango WBA	1988
J.J. Estrada WBA	1988–89
Fabrice Benichou IBF	1989–90
Jesus Salud WBA	1989–90
Welcome Ncita IBF	1990–92
Paul Banke* WBC	1990
Luis Mendoza WBA	1990–91
Raul Perez WBA	1992
Pedro Decima* WBC	1990–91
K. Hatanaka* WBC	1991
Daniel Zaragoza* WBC	1991–92
Thiery Jacob* WBC	1992
Tracy Patterson* WBC	1992–94
Kennedy McKinney IBF	1993–94
Wilfredo Vasquez WBA	1992–95
Vuyani Bungu IBF	1994–99†
H. Acero* Sanchez WBC	1994–95
Antonio Cermeno WBA	1995–98†

Champion	Reign
Daniel Zaragoza* WBC	1995–97
Erik Morales* WBC	1997–00†
Enrique Sanchez WBA	1998
Nestor Garza WBA	1998–00
Benedict Ledwaba IBF	1999–01
Clarence Adams WBA	2000–01†
Willie Jorrin WBC	2000–02
Manny Pacquiao IBF	2001–04
Yober Ortega WBA	2001–02
Y. Sithyodthong WBA	2002
Osamu Sato WBA	2002
Salim Medjkoune WBA	2002–03
Mahyar Monshipour WBA	2003–06
Oscar Larios WBC	2002–05
Israel Vazquez IBF	2004–05
S. Sithchatchawal WBA	2006
Israel Vazquez WBC	2005–07
C. Caballero WBA	2006–
Michael Hunter IBF	2006
Steve Molitor IBF	2006–
Rafael Marquez WBC	2007
Israel Vazquez WBC	2007

*Lineal champion. †Champion relinquished title to retire or switch weight classes, or had title stripped by boxing organization.

Bantamweights
(Weight Limit: 118 pounds)

Champion	Reign
Spider Kelly	1887
Hughey Boyle	1887–88
Spider Kelly	1889
Chappie Moran	1889–90
George Dixon	1890–91
Pedlar Palmer	1895–99
Terry McGovern*	1899–00†
Harry Harris	1901
Harry Forbes*	1901–03
Frankie Neil*	1903–04
Joe Bowker*	1904–05†
Jimmy Walsh*	1905–06†
Owen Moran	1907–08
Monte Attell	1909–10
Frankie Conley	1910–11
Johnny Coulon*	1910–14
Kid Williams*	1914–17
Kewpie Ertle	1915
Pete Herman*	1917–20
Joe Lynch*	1920–21
Pete Herman*	1921
Johnny Buff*	1921–22
Joe Lynch*	1922–24
Abe Goldstein*	1924
Cannonball Martin*	1924–25
Phil Rosenberg*	1925–27†
Bud Taylor NBA	1927–28
Bushy Graham NY	1928–29
Panama Al Brown*	1929–35
Sixto Escobar NBA	1934–35
Baltazar Sangchilli*	1935–36
Lou Salica NBA	1935
Sixto Escobar NBA	1935–36
Tony Marino*	1936
Sixto Escobar*	1936–37
Harry Jeffra*	1937–38
Sixto Escobar*	1938–39†
Georgie Pace NBA	1939–40

Champion	Reign
Lou Salica*	1940–42
Manuel Ortiz*	1942–47
Harold Dade*	1947
Manuel Ortiz*	1947–50
Vic Toweel*	1950–52
Jimmy Carruthers*	1952–54†
Robert Cohen*	1954–56
Paul Macias NBA	1955–57
Mario D'Agata*	1956–57
Alphonse Halimi*	1957–59
Joe Becerra*	1959–60†
Eder Jofre*	1961–65
Fighting Harada*	1965–68
Lionel Rose*	1968–69
Ruben Olivares*	1969–70
Chucho Castillo*	1970–71
Ruben Olivares*	1971–72
Rafael Herrera*	1972
Enrique Pinder*	1972–73
Romeo Anaya*	1973
Arnold Taylor*	1973–74
Rafael Herrera WBC	1973–74
Soo-Hwan Hong*	1974–75
Rodolfo Martinez WBC	1974–76
Alfonso Zamora*	1975–77
Carlos Zarate* WBC	1976–79
Jorge Lujan	1977–80
Lupe Pintor* WBC	1979–83†
Julian Solis	1980
Jeff Chandler*	1980–84
Albert Davila WBC	1983–85
Richard Sandoval*	1984–86
Satoshi Shingaki IBF	1984–85
Jeff Fenech IBF	1985
Daniel Zaragoza WBC	1985
Miguel Lora WBC	1985–88
Gaby Canizales*	1986
Bernardo Pinango*	1986–87†

Champion	Reign
W. Vasquez WBA	1987–88
Kevin Seabrooks* IBF	1987–88
Kaokor Galaxy WBA	1988
Moon Sung-Kil WBA	1988–89
Kaokor Galaxy WBA	1989
Raul Perez WBC	1988–91
O. Canizales* IBF	1988–95†
Luisito Espinosa WBA	1989–91
Israel Contreras WBA	1991–92
Eddie Cook WBA	1992–93
Greg Richardson WBC	1991
J. Tatsuyoshi, WBC	1991–92
Victor Rabanales WBC	1992–93
Jung-Il Byun WBC	1993
Jorge Julio WBA	1993
Yasuei Yakushiji WBC	1993–95
Junior Jones WBA	1994
John M. Johnson WBA	1994
D. Chuvatana WBA	1994–95
V. Sahaprom* WBA	1995–96
W. McCullough WBC	1995–96
Harold Mestre IBF	1995
Mbulelo Botile IBF	1995–97
Nana Konadu* WBA	1996–98
S. Singmanassak WBC	1996–97
Tim Austin IBF	1997–03
J.Tatsuyoshi WBC	1997–98
Johnny Tapia* WBA	1998–99
V. Sahaprom* WBC	1998–05
Paulie Ayala* WBA	1999–01†
Eidy Moya WBA	2001–02
Johnny Bredahl WBA	2002–05
Rafael Marquez IBF	2003–07
H. Hasegawa WBC	2005–
W. Sidorenko WBA	2005–
Luis Perez IBF	2007
Joseph Agbeko IBF	2007–

Super Flyweights
(Weight Limit: 115 pounds)

Champion	Reign
Rafael Orono* WBC	1980–81
Chul-Ho Kim* WBC	1981–82
Gustavo Ballas WBA	1981
Rafael Pedroza WBA	1981–82
Jiro Watanabe WBA	1982–84
Rafael Orono* WBC	1982–83
Payao Poontarat* WBC	1983–84
Joo-Do Chun IBF	1983–85
Jiro Watanabe*	1984–86
Kaosai Galaxy WBA	1984
Ellyas Pica IBF	1985–86
Cesar Polanco IBF	1986
Gilberto Roman* WBC	1986–87
Ellyas Pical IBF	1986
Santos Laciar* WBC	1987
Tae-Il Chang IBF	1987
Sugar Rojas* WBC	1987–88
Ellyas Pical IBF	1987–89
Giberto Roman* WBC	1988–89

Champion	Reign
Juan Polo Perez IBF	1989–90
Nana Konadu* WBC	1989–90
Sung-Kil Moon* WBC	1990–93
Robert Quiroga IBF	1990–93
Julio Borboa IBF	1993–94
Katsuya Onizuka WBA	1993–94
Lee Hyung-Chul WBA	1994–95
Jose Luis Bueno* WBC	1993–94
H. Kawashima* WBC	1994–97
Harold Grey IBF	1994–95
Alimi Goitia WBA	1995–96
Yokthai Sith-Oar WBA	1996–97
Carlos Salazar IBF	1995–96
Harold Grey IBF	1996
Danny Romero IBF	1996–97
Gerry Penalosa* WBC	1997–98
Johnny Tapia IBF	1997–99†
Satoshi Iida WBA	1997–98
In-Joo Cho* WBC	1998–00

Champion	Reign
Jesus Rojas WBA	1998–99
Mark Johnson IBF	1999–00
Hideki Todaka WBA	1999–00
Felix Machado IBF	2000–03
M. Tokuyama* WBC	2000–04
Leo Gamez WBA	2000–01
Celes Kobayashi WBA	2001–02
Alexander Munoz WBA	2002–05
Luis Alberto Perez IBF	2003–06
Katsushige Kawashima WBC	2004–05
M. Tokuyama WBC	2005–06
Jose M. Castillo WBA	2005–06
Nobuo Nashiro WBA	2006–07
Cristian Mijares WBC	2006–
Alexander Munoz WBA	2007–
Dmitri Kirilov IBF	2007–

*Lineal champion.
†Champion relinquished title to retire or switch weight classes, or had title stripped by boxing organization.

Flyweights (Weight Limit: 112 pounds)

Champion	Reign
Sid Smith*	1913
Bill Ladbury*	1913–14
Percy Jones*	1914†
Joe Symonds*	1914–16
Jimmy Wilde*	1916–23
Pancho Villa*	1923–25†
Fidel La Barba*	1925–27†
Frenchy Belanger* NBA	1927–28
Izzy Schwartz NY	1927–29
Frankie Genaro* NBA	1928–29
Spider Pladner* NBA	1929
Frankie Genaro* NBA	1929–31
Midget Wolgast NY	1930–35
Young Perez* NBA	1931–32
Jackie Brown* NBA	1932–35
Benny Lynch*	1935–38†
Small Montana NY	1935–37
Peter Kane*	1938–43
Little Dado NY	1938–40
Jackie Paterson*	1943–48
Rinty Monaghan*	1948–50†
Terry Allen*	1950
Dado Marino*	1950–52
Yoshio Shirai*	1952–54
Pascual Perez*	1954–60
Pone Kingpetch*	1960–62
Masahiko Harada*	1962–63
Pone Kingpetch*	1963
Hiroyuki Ebihara*	1963–64
Pone Kingpetch*	1964–65
Salvatore Burrini*	1965–66
H. Accavallo WBA	1966–68
Walter McGowan*	1966
Chartchai Chionoi*	1966–69
Efren Torres*	1969–70
Hiroyuki Ebihara WBA	1969
B. Villacampo WBA	1969–70
Chartchai Chionoi*	1970
B. Chartvanchai WBA	1970
Masao Ohba WBA	1970–73
Erbito Salavarria*	1970–73†
B. Gonzalez WBA	1972
V. Borkorsor WBC	1972–73†
Venice Borkorsor*	1973†
Chartchai Chionoi WBA	1973–74
B. Gonzalez* WBA	1973–74
Shoji Oguma* WBC	1974–75
S. Hanagata WBA	1974–75
Miguel Canto* WBC	1975–79
Erbito Salavarria WBA	1975–76
Alfonso Lopez WBA	1976
G. Espadas WBA	1976–78
B. Gonzalez WBA	1978–79
Chan-Hee Park* WBC	1979–80
Luis Ibarra WBA	1979–80
Tae-Shik Kim WBA	1980
Shoji Oguma* WBC	1980–81
Peter Mathebula WBA	1980–81
Santos Laciar WBA	1981
Antonio Avelar* WBC	1981–82
Luis Ibarra WBA	1981
Juan Herrera WBA	1981–82
P. Cardona* WBC	1982
Santos Laciar WBA	1982–85
Freddie Castillo* WBC	1982
E. Mercedes* WBC	1982–83
Charlie Magri* WBC	1983
Frank Cedeno* WBC	1983–84
Soon-Chun Kwon IBF	1983–85
Koji Kobayashi* WBC	1984
Gabriel Bernal* WBC	1984
Sot Chitalada* WBC	1984–88
Hilario Zapate WBA	1985–87
Chong-Kwan Chung IBF	1985–86
Bi-Won Chung IBF	1986
Hi-Sup Shin IBF	1986–87
Dodie Penalosa IBF	1987
Fidel Bassa WBA	1987–89
Choi-Chang Ho IBF	1987–88
Rolando Bohol IBF	1988
Yong-Kang Kim* WBC	1988–89
Duke McKenzie IBF	1988–89
Sot Chitalada* WBC	1989–91
Dave McAuley IBF	1989–92
Jesus Rojas WBA	1989–90
Yul-Woo Lee WBA	1990
L. Tamakuma WBA	1990–91
M. Kittikasem* WBC	1991–92
Yuri Arbachakov* WBC	1992–97
Yong Kang Kim WBA	1991–92
Rodolfo Blanco IBF	1992–93
P. Sithbangprachan IBF	1993–95
David Griman IBF	1992–94
S.S. Ploenchit WBA	1994–96
Francisco Tejedor IBF	1995
Danny Romero IBF	1995–96
Mark Johnson IBF	1996–99†
Jose Bonilla WBA	1996–98
Chatchai Sasakul* WBC	1997–98
Hugo Soto WBA	1998–99
Manny Pacquiao* WBC	1998–99
Leo Gamez WBA	1999
Irene Pacheco IBF	1999–05
S. Pisnurachan WBA	1999–00
M. Sinsurat* WBC	1999–00
Malcolm Tunacao* WBC	2000–01
Eric Morel WBA	2000–03
P. Wonjongkam* WBC	2001–07
Lorenzo Parra WBA	2003–07
Vic Darchinyan IBF	2005–07
Takefumi Sakata WBA	2007–
Daisuke Naito WBC	2007–
Nonito Donaire IBF	2007–

Light Flyweights (Weight Limit: 108 pounds)

Champion	Reign
Franco Udella WBC	1975
Jaime Rios WBA	1975–76
Luis Estaba* WBC	1975–78
Juan Guzman WBA	1976
Yoko Gushiken WBA	1976–81
Freddy Castillo* WBC	1978
Sor Vorasingh* WBC	1978
Sung-Jun Kim* WBC	1978–80
Shigeo Nakajima* WBC	1980
Hilario Zapata* WBC	1980–82
Pedro Flores WBA	1981
Hwan-Jin Kim WBA	1981
Katsuo Tokashiki WBA	1981–83
Amado Urzua* WBC	1982
Tadashi Tomori* WBC	1982
Hilario Zapata* WBC	1982–83
Jung-Koo Chang* WBC	1983–88†
Lupe Madera WBA	1983–84
Dodie Penalosa IBF	1983–86
Francisco Quiroz WBA	1984–85
Joey Olivo WBA	1985
Myung-Woo Yuh* WBA	1985–91
Jum-Hwan Choi IBF	1986–88
Tacy Macalos IBF	1988–89
German Torres WBC	1988–89
Yul-Woo Lee WBC	1989
M. Kittikasem IBF	1989–90
H. Gonzalez WBC	1989–90
Michael Carbajal IBF	1990–94
R. Pascua WBC	1990
M. C. Castro WBC	1991
H. Gonzalez WBC	1991–93
Hirokia Ioka* WBA	1991–92
Myung-Woo Yuh* WBA	1993†
Michael Carbajal* WBC	1993–94
Leo Gamez WBA	1993–95
H. Gonzalez* WBC, IBF	1994–95
Choi Hi-Yong WBA	1995–96
S. Sor Jaturong WBC, IBF	1995–96
Carlos Murillo WBA	1996
Keiji Yamaguchi WBA	1996
Michael Carbajal IBF	1996–97
Saman Jaturong* WBC	1995–99
Phichitchor Siriwat WBA	1996–00
Mauricio Pastrana IBF	1997–98†
Will Grigsby IBF	1998–99
Ricardo Lopez IBF	1999–02
Yo-Sam Choi* WBC	1999–02
Beibis Mendoza WBA	2000–01
Rosendo Alvarez WBA	2001–05
Jorge Arce* WBC	2002–05
Jose Burgos IBF	2003–05
Brian Viloria WBC	2005–06
R. Vasquez WBA	2005–06
Will Grigsby IBF	2005–06
Koki Kameda WBA	2006–07
Omar Nino Rivero WBC	2006–07
Ulises Solis IBF	2006–
J. C. Reveco WBA	2007–
Edgar Sosa WBC	2007–

*Lineal champion.
†Champion relinquished title to retire or switch weight classes, or had title stripped by boxing organization.

Strawweights (Weight Limit: I05 pounds)

Champion	Reign	Champion	Reign	Champion	Reign
Kyung-Yun Lee* IBF	1987	Manny Melchor IBF	1992	Keitaro Hoshino WBA	2000–01
Hiroki Ioka* WBC	1987–88	Hideyuki Ohashi WBA	1992–93	Chana Porpaoin WBA	2001
Leo Gamez WBA	1988–89	R.S. Voraphin IBF	1992–96	Roberto Leyva IBF	2001–02
S. Sithnaruepol IBF	1988–89	Chana Porpaoin WBA	1993–95	Yutaka Niida WBA	2001†
N. Kiatwanchai* WBC	1988–89	Rosendo Alvarez WBA	1995–98	Miguel Barrera IBF	2002–03
Bong-Jun Kim WBA	1989–91	R. Sor Vorapin IBF	1996–97	Edgar Cardenas IBF	2003
Nico Thomas IBF	1989	Zolani Petelo* IBF	1997–00†	Noel Arambulet WBA	2002–04
Eric Chavez IBF	1989–90	W. Chor Charoen WBC	1998–00	Daniel Reyes IBF	2003–05
Jum-Hwan Choi* WBC	1989–90	R. Lopez* WBA, WBC	1998–99†	Eagle Kyowa WBC	2004–
Hideyuki Ohashi* WBC	1990	Songkram Popaoin WBA	1999	Yukata Niida WBA	2004–
F. Lookmingkwan IBF	1990–92	Noel Arambulet IBF	1999–00	M. Rachman IBF	2005–07
Ricardo Lopez* WBC	1990–98†	Jose Aguirre* WBC	2000–04	Florante Condes IBF	2007–
Hi-Yong Choi WBA	1991–92	Joma Gamboa WBA	2000		

*Lineal champion. †Champion relinquished title to retire or switch weight classes, or had title stripped by boxing organization.

Alltime Career Leaders

Total Bouts

Name	Years Active	Bouts	Name	Years Active	Bouts
Len Wickwar	1928–47	463	Maxie Rosenbloom	1923–39	299
Jack Britton	1905–30	350	Harry Greb	1913–26	298
Johnny Dundee	1910–32	333	Young Stribling	1921–33	286
Billy Bird	1920–48	318	Battling Levinsky	1910–29	282
George Marsden	1928–46	311	Ted (Kid) Lewis	1909–29	279

Note: Based on records in The Ring Record Book and Boxing Encyclopedia.

Most Knockouts

Name	Years Active	KOs	Name	Years Active	KOs
Archie Moore	1936–63	130	Sandy Saddler	1944–56	103
Young Stribling	1921–33	126	Sam Langford	1902–26	102
Billy Bird	1920–48	125	Henry Armstrong	1931–45	100
George Odwell	1930–45	114	Jimmy Wilde	1911–23	98
Sugar Ray Robinson	1940–65	110	Len Wickwar	1928–47	93

Note: Based on records in The Ring Record Book and Boxing Encyclopedia.

World Heavyweight Championship Fights

Date	Winner	Wgt	Loser	Wgt	Result	Site
Sept 7, 1892	James J. Corbett*	178	John L. Sullivan	212	KO 21	New Orleans
Jan 25, 1894	James J. Corbett*	184	Charley Mitchell	158	KO 3	Jacksonville
Mar 17, 1897	Bob Fitzsimmons*	167	James J. Corbett	183	KO 14	Carson City, Nev.
June 9, 1899	James J. Jeffries*	206	Bob Fitzsimmons	167	KO 11	Coney Island, N.Y.
Nov 3, 1899	James J. Jeffries*	215	Tom Sharkey	183	Ref 25	Coney Island, N.Y.
Apr 6, 1900	James J. Jeffries*	n/a	Jack Finnegan	n/a	KO 1	Detroit
May 11, 1900	James J. Jeffries*	218	James J. Corbett	188	KO 23	Coney Island, N.Y.
Nov 15, 1901	James J. Jeffries*	211	Gus Ruhlin	194	TKO 6	San Francisco
July 25, 1902	James J. Jeffries*	219	Bob Fitzsimmons	172	KO 8	San Francisco
Aug 14, 1903	James J. Jeffries*	220	James J. Corbett	190	KO 10	San Francisco
Aug 25, 1904	James J. Jeffries*	219	Jack Munroe	186	TKO 2	San Francisco
July 3, 1905	Marvin Hart*	190	Jack Root	171	KO 12	Reno
Feb 23, 1906	Tommy Burns*	180	Marvin Hart	188	Ref 20	Los Angeles
Oct 2, 1899	Tommy Burns*	n/a	Jim Flynn	n/a	KO 15	Los Angeles
Nov 28, 1906	Tommy Burns*	172	Jack O'Brien	163½	Draw 20	Los Angeles
May 8, 1907	Tommy Burns*	180	Jack O'Brien	167	Ref 20	Los Angeles
Jul 4, 1907	Tommy Burns*	181	Bill Squires	180	KO 1	Colma, Calif.
Dec 2, 1907	Tommy Burns*	177	Gunner Moir	204	KO 10	London
Feb 10, 1908	Tommy Burns*	n/a	Jack Palmer	n/a	KO 4	London
Mar 17, 1908	Tommy Burns*	n/a	Jem Roche	n/a	KO 1	Dublin
Apr 18, 1908	Tommy Burns*	n/a	Jewey Smith	n/a	KO 5	Paris
June 13, 1908	Tommy Burns*	184	Bill Squires	183	KO 8	Paris

Date	Winner	Wgt	Loser	Wgt	Result	Site
Aug 24, 1908	Tommy Burns*	181	Bill Squires	184	KO 13	Sydney
Sept 2, 1908	Tommy Burns*	183	Bill Lang	187	KO 6	Melbourne
Dec 26, 1908	Jack Johnson*	192	Tommy Burns	168	TKO 14	Sydney
Mar 10, 1909	Jack Johnson*	n/a	Victor McLaglen	n/a	ND 6	Vancouver
May 19, 1909	Jack Johnson*	205	Jack O'Brien	161	ND 6	Philadelphia
June 30, 1909	Jack Johnson*	207	Tony Ross	214	ND 6	Pittsburgh
Sept 9, 1909	Jack Johnson*	209	Al Kaufman	191	ND 10	San Francisco
Oct 16, 1909	Jack Johnson*	205½	Stanley Ketchel	170¼	KO 12	Colma, Calif.
July 4, 1910	Jack Johnson*	208	James J. Jeffries	227	KO 15	Reno
July 4, 1912	Jack Johnson*	195½	Jim Flynn	175	TKO 9	Las Vegas
Dec 19, 1913	Jack Johnson*	n/a	Jim Johnson	n/a	Draw 10	Paris
June 27, 1914	Jack Johnson*	221	Frank Moran	203	Ref 20	Paris
Apr 5, 1915	Jess Willard*	230	Jack Johnson	205½	KO 26	Havana
Mar 25, 1916	Jess Willard*	225	Frank Moran	203	ND 10	New York City
July 4, 1919	Jack Dempsey*	187	Jess Willard	245	TKO 4	Toledo, Ohio
Sept 6, 1920	Jack Dempsey*	185	Billy Miske	187	KO 3	Benton Harbor, Mich.
Dec 14, 1920	Jack Dempsey*	188¼	Bill Brennan	197	KO 12	New York City
July 2, 1921	Jack Dempsey*	188	Georges Carpentier	172	KO 4	Jersey City
July 4, 1923	Jack Dempsey*	188	Tommy Givvons	175½	Ref 15	Shelby, Mont.
Sept 14, 1923	Jack Dempsey*	192½	Luis Firpo	216½	KO 2	New York City
Sept 23, 1926	Gene Tunney*	189½	Jack Dempsey	190	UD 10	Philadelphia
Sept 22, 1927	Gene Tunney*	189½	Jack Dempsey	192½	UD 10	Chicago
July 26, 1928	Gene Tunney*	192	Tom Heeney	203½	TKO 11	New York City
June 12, 1930	Max Schmeling*	188	Jack Sharkey	197	DQ 4	New York City
July 3, 1931	Max Schmeling*	189	Young Stribling	186½	TKO 15	Cleveland
June 21, 1932	Jack Sharkey*	205	Max Schmeling	188	Split 15	Long Island City
June 29, 1933	Primo Carnera*	260½	Jack Sharkey	201	KO 6	Long Island City
Oct 22, 1933	Primo Carnera*	259½	Paulino Uzcudun	229¼	UD 15	Rome
Mar 1, 1934	Primo Carnera*	270	Tommy Loughran	184	UD 15	Miami
June 14, 1934	Max Baer*	209½	Primo Carnera	263¼	TKO 11	Long Island City
June 13, 1935	James J. Braddock*	193¾	Max Baer	209½	UD 15	Long Island City
June 22, 1937	Joe Louis*	197¼	James J. Braddock	197	KO 8	Chicago
Aug 30, 1937	Joe Louis*	197	Tommy Farr	204¼	UD 15	New York City
Feb 23, 1938	Joe Louis*	200	Nathan Mann	193½	KO 3	New York City
Apr 1, 1938	Joe Louis*	202½	Harry Thomas	196	KO 5	Chicago
June 22, 1938	Joe Louis*	198¼	Max Schmeling	193	KO 1	New York City
Jan 25, 1939	Joe Louis*	200¼	John Henry Lewis	180¾	KO 1	New York City
Apr 17, 1939	Joe Louis*	201¼	Jack Roper	204¾	KO 1	Los Angeles
June 28, 1939	Joe Louis*	200¾	Tony Galento	233¾	TKO 4	New York City
Sept 20, 1939	Joe Louis*	200	Bob Pastor	183	KO 11	Detroit
Feb 9, 1940	Joe Louis*	203	Arturo Godoy	202	Split 15	New York City
Mar 29, 1940	Joe Louis*	201½	Johnny Paychek	187½	KO 2	New York City
June 20, 1940	Joe Louis*	199	Arturo Godoy	201¼	TKO 8	New York City
Dec 16, 1940	Joe Louis*	202¼	Al McCoy	180¾	TKO 6	Boston
Jan 31, 1941	Joe Louis*	202½	Red Burman	188	KO 5	New York City
Feb 17, 1941	Joe Louis*	203½	Gus Dorazio	193½	KO 2	Philadelphia
Mar 21, 1941	Joe Louis*	202	Abe Simon	254½	TKO 13	Detroit
Apr 8, 1941	Joe Louis*	203½	Tony Musto	199½	TKO 9	St Louis
May 23, 1941	Joe Louis*	201½	Buddy Baer	237½	DQ 7	Washington, D.C.
June 18, 1941	Joe Louis*	199½	Billy Conn	174	KO 13	New York City
Sept 29, 1941	Joe Louis*	202¼	Lou Nova	202½	TKO 6	New York City
Jan 9, 1942	Joe Louis*	206¾	Buddy Baer	250	KO 1	New York City
Mar 27, 1942	Joe Louis*	207½	Abe Simon	255½	KO 6	New York City
June 9, 1946	Joe Louis*	207	Billy Conn	187	KO 8	New York City
Sept 18, 1946	Joe Louis*	211	Tami Mauriello	198½	KO 1	New York City
Dec 5, 1947	Joe Louis*	211½	Jersey Joe Walcott	194½	Split 15	New York City
June 25, 1948	Joe Louis*	213½	Jersey Joe Walcott	194¾	KO 11	New York City
June 22, 1949	Ezzard Charles*	181¾	Jersey Joe Walcott	195½	UD 15	Chicago
Aug 10, 1949	Ezzard Charles*	180	Gus Lesnevich	182	TKO 8	New York City
Oct 14, 1949	Ezzard Charles*	182	Pat Valentino	188½	KO 8	San Francisco
Aug 15, 1950	Ezzard Charles*	183¼	Freddie Beshore	184½	TKO 14	Buffalo
Sept 27, 1950	Ezzard Charles*	184½	Joe Louis	218	UD 15	New York City
Dec 5, 1950	Ezzard Charles*	185	Nick Barone	178½	KO 11	Cincinnati
Jan 12, 1951	Ezzard Charles*	185	Lee Oma	193	TKO 10	New York City
Mar 7, 1951	Ezzard Charles*	186	Jersey Joe Walcott	193	UD 15	Detroit
May 30, 1951	Ezzard Charles*	182	Joey Maxim	181½	UD 15	Chicago
July 18, 1951	Jersey Joe Walcott*	194	Ezzard Charles	182	KO 7	Pittsburgh
June 5, 1952	Jersey Joe Walcott*	196	Ezzard Charles	191½	UD 15	Philadelphia
Sept 23, 1952	Rocky Marciano*	184	Jersey Joe Walcott	196	KO 13	Philadelphia

Date	Winner	Wgt	Loser	Wgt	Result	Site
May 15, 1953	....Rocky Marciano*	184½	Jersey Joe Walcott	197¾	KO 1	Chicago
Sept 24, 1953	....Rocky Marciano*	185	Roland LaStarza	184¾	TKO 11	New York City
June 17, 1954	...Rocky Marciano*	187½	Ezzard Charles	185½	UD 15	New York City
Sept 17, 1954	....Rocky Marciano*	187	Ezzard Charles	192½	KO 8	New York City
May 16, 1955	....Rocky Marciano*	189	Don Cockell	205	TKO 9	San Francisco
Sept 21, 1955	....Rocky Marciano*	188¼	Archie Moore	188	KO 9	New York City
Nov 30, 1956	.....Floyd Patterson*	182¼	Archie Moore	187¾	KO 5	Chicago
July 29, 1957	.....Floyd Patterson*	184	Tommy Jackson	192½	TKO 10	New York City
Aug 22, 1957	.....Floyd Patterson*	187¼	Pete Rademacher	202	KO 6	Seattle
Aug 18, 1958	.....Floyd Patterson*	184½	Roy Harris	194	TKO 13	Los Angeles
May 1, 1959	......Floyd Patterson*	182½	Brian London	206	KO 11	Indianapolis
June 26, 1959	...Ingemar Johansson*	196	Floyd Patterson	182	TKO 3	New York City
June 20, 1960	...Floyd Patterson*	190	Ingemar Johansson	194¾	KO 5	New York City
Mar 13, 1961	.....Floyd Patterson*	194¾	Ingemar Johansson	206½	KO 6	Miami Beach
Dec 4, 1961	.......Floyd Patterson*	188½	Tom McNeeley	197	KO 4	Toronto
Sept 25, 1962	.....Sonny Liston*	214	Floyd Patterson	189	KO 1	Chicago
July 22, 1963	.....Sonny Liston*	215	Floyd Patterson	194½	KO 1	Las Vegas
Feb 25, 1964	.....Cassius Clay*	210½	Sonny Liston	218	TKO 7	Miami Beach
Mar 5, 1965	.......Ernie Terrell	199	Eddie Machen	192	UD 15	Chicago
May 25, 1965	....Muhammad Ali*	206	Sonny Liston	215¼	KO 1	Lewiston, Me.
Nov 1, 1965	.....Ernie Terrell	206	George Chuvalo	209	UD 15	Toronto
Nov 22, 1965	....Muhammad Ali*	210	Floyd Patterson	196¾	TKO 12	Las Vegas
Mar 29, 1966	....Muhammad Ali*	214½	George Chuvalo	216	UD 15	Toronto
May 21, 1966	....Muhammad Ali*	201½	Henry Cooper	188	TKO 6	London
June 28, 1966	....Ernie Terrell	209½	Doug Jones	187½	UD 15	Houston
Aug 6, 1966	.......Muhammad Ali*	209½	Brian London	201½	KO 3	London
Sept 10, 1966	....Muhammad Ali*	203½	Karl Mildenberger	194¼	TKO 12	Frankfurt
Nov 14, 1966	....Muhammad Ali*	212¾	Cleveland Williams	210½	TKO 3	Houston
Feb 6, 1967	.......Muhammad Ali*	212¼	Ernie Terrell	212½	UD 15	Houston
Mar 22, 1967	....Muhammad Ali*	211½	Zora Folley	202½	KO 7	New York City
Mar 4, 1968	.......Joe Frazier	204½	Buster Mathis	243½	TKO 11	New York City
Apr 27, 1968	....Jimmy Ellis	197	Jerry Quarry	195	Maj 15	Oakland
June 24, 1968	...Joe Frazier NY	203½	Manuel Ramos	208	TKO 2	New York City
Aug 14, 1968	....Jimmy Ellis	198	Floyd Patterson	188	Ref 15	Stockholm
Dec 10, 1968	....Joe Frazier NY	203	Oscar Bonavena	207	UD 15	Philadelphia
Apr 22, 1969	.....Joe Frazier NY	204½	Dave Zyglewicz	190½	KO 1	Houston
June 23, 1969	...Joe Frazier NY	203½	Jerry Quarry	198½	TKO 8	New York City
Feb 16, 1970	....Joe Frazier NY	205	Jimmy Ellis	201	TKO 5	New York City
Nov 18, 1970	.....Joe Frazier	209	Bob Foster	188	KO 2	Detroit
Mar 8, 1971	.......Joe Frazier*	205½	Muhammad Ali	215	UD 15	New York City
Jan 15, 1972	.....Joe Frazier*	215½	Terry Daniels	195	TKO 4	New Orleans
May 26, 1972	....Joe Frazier*	217½	Ron Stander	218	TKO 5	Omaha
Jan 22, 1973	.....George Foreman*	217½	Joe Frazier	214	TKO 2	Kingston, Jam.
Sept 1, 1973	....George Foreman*	219½	Jose Roman	196½	KO 1	Tokyo
Mar 26, 1974	.....George Foreman*	224¼	Ken Norton	212¼	TKO 2	Caracas
Oct 30, 1974	....Muhammad Ali*.	216½	George Foreman	220	KO 8	Kinshasa, Zaire
Mar 24, 1975	....Muhammad Ali*	223½	Chuck Wepner	225	TKO 15	Cleveland
May 16, 1975	....Muhammad Ali*	224½	Ron Lyle	219	TKO 11	Las Vegas
July 1, 1975	.......Muhammad Ali*	224½	Joe Bugner	230	UD 15	Kuala Lumpur, Malay.
Oct 1, 1975	....Muhammad Ali*	224½	Joe Frazier	215	TKO 15	Manila
Feb 20, 1976	.....Muhammad Ali*	226	Jean Pierre Coopman	206	KO 5	San Juan
Apr 30, 1976	....Muhammad Ali*	230	Jimmy Young	209	UD 15	Landover, Md.
May 24, 1976	....Muhammad Ali*	230	Richard Dunn	206½	TKO 5	Munich
Sept 28, 1976	....Muhammad Ali*	221	Ken Norton	217½	UD 15	New York City
May 16, 1977	....Muhammad Ali*	221¼	Alfredo Evangelista	209¼	UD 15	Landover, Md.
Sept 29, 1977	....Muhammad Ali*	225	Earnie Shavers	211¼	UD 15	New York City
Feb 15, 1978	.....Leon Spinks*	197¼	Muhammad Ali	224¼	Split 15	Las Vegas
June 9, 1978	.....Larry Holmes	209	Ken Norton	220	Split 15	Las Vegas
Sept 15, 1978	....Muhammad Ali*	221	Leon Spinks	201	UD 15	New Orleans
Nov 10, 1978	.....Larry Holmes*	214	Alfredo Evangelista	208¼	KO 7	Las Vegas
Mar 23, 1979	.....Larry Holmes*	214	Osvaldo Ocasio	207	TKO 7	Las Vegas
June 22, 1979	.....Larry Holmes*	215	Mike Weaver	202	TKO 12	New York City
Sept 28, 1979	.....Larry Holmes*	210	Earnie Shavers	211	TKO 11	Las Vegas
Oct 20, 1979	.....John Tate	240	Gerrie Coetzee	222	UD 15	Pretoria
Feb 3, 1980	.....Larry Holmes *	213½	Lorenzo Zanon	215	TKO 6	Las Vegas
Mar 31, 1980	.....Mike Weaver	232	John Tate	232	KO 15	Knoxville
Mar 31, 1980	.....Larry Holmes*	211	Leroy Jones	254½	TKO 8	Las Vegas
July 7, 1980	.....Larry Holmes*	214¼	Scott LeDoux	226	TKO 7	Minneapolis
Oct 2, 1980	.......Larry Holmes*	211¼	Muhammad Ali	217½	TKO 11	Las Vegas

World Heavyweight Championship Fights *(Cont.)*

Date	Winner	Wgt	Loser	Wgt	Result	Site
Oct 25, 1980	Mike Weaver	210	Gerrie Coetzee	226½	KO 13	Sun City, S. Africa
Apr 11, 1981	Larry Holmes*	215	Trevor Berbick	215½	UD 15	Las Vegas
June 12, 1981	Larry Holmes*	212¼	Leon Spinks	200¼	TKO 3	Detroit
Oct 3, 1981	Mike Weaver	215	James Quick Tillis	209	UD 15	Rosemont, Ill.
Nov 6, 1981	Larry Holmes*	213¼	Renaldo Snipes	215¾	TKO 11	Pittsburgh
June 11, 1982	Larry Holmes*	212½	Gerry Cooney	225½	TKO 13	Las Vegas
Nov 26, 1982	Larry Holmes*	217½	Tex Cobb	234¼	UD 15	Houston
Dec 10, 1982	Michael Dokes	216	Mike Weaver	209¾	TKO 1	Las Vegas
Mar 27, 1983	Larry Holmes*	221	Lucien Rodriguez	209	UD 12	Scranton, Pa.
May 20, 1983	Michael Dokes	223	Mike Weaver	218½	Draw 15	Las Vegas
May 20, 1983	Larry Holmes*	213	Tim Witherspoon	219½	Split 12	Las Vegas
Sept 10, 1983	Larry Holmes*	223	Scott Frank	211¼	TKO 5	Atlantic City
Sept 23, 1983	Gerrie Coetzee	215	Michael Dokes	217	KO 10	Richfield, Ohio
Nov 25, 1983	Larry Holmes*	219	Marvis Frazier	200	TKO 1	Las Vegas
Mar 9, 1984	Tim Witherspoon	220¼	Greg Page	239½	Maj 12	Las Vegas
Aug 31, 1984	Pinklon Thomas	216	Tim Witherspoon	217	Maj 12	Las Vegas
Nov 9, 1984	Larry Holmes* IBF	221½	James Smith	227	TKO 12	Las Vegas
Dec 1, 1984	Greg Page	236½	Gerrie Coetzee	218	KO 8	Sun City, S. Africa
Mar 15, 1985	Larry Holmes*	223½	David Bey	233¼	TKO 10	Las Vegas
Apr 29, 1985	Tony Tubbs	229	Greg Page	239½	UD 15	Buffalo
May 20, 1985	Larry Holmes*	224¼	Carl Williams	215	UD 15	Las Vegas
June 15, 1985	Pinklon Thomas	220¼	Mike Weaver	221¼	KO 8	Las Vegas
Sept 21, 1985	Michael Spinks*	200	Larry Holmes	221½	UD 15	Las Vegas
Jan 17, 1986	Tim Witherspoon	227	Tony Tubbs	229	Maj 15	Atlanta
Mar 22, 1986	Trevor Berbick	218½	Pinklon Thomas	222¾	UD 15	Las Vegas
Apr 19, 1986	Michael Spinks*	205	Larry Holmes	223	Split 15	Las Vegas
July 19, 1986	Tim Witherspoon	234¾	Frank Bruno	228	TKO 11	Wembley, Eng.
Sept 6, 1986	Michael Spinks*	201	Steffen Tangstad	214¾	TKO 4	Las Vegas
Nov 22, 1986	Mike Tyson	221¼	Trevor Berbick	218½	TKO 2	Las Vegas
Dec 12, 1986	James Smith	228½	Tim Witherspoon	233½	TKO 1	New York City
Mar 7, 1987	Mike Tyson	219	James Smith	233	UD 12	Las Vegas
May 30, 1987	Mike Tyson	218¾	Pinklon Thomas	217¾	TKO 6	Las Vegas
May 30, 1987	Tony Tucker	222¼	Buster Douglas	227¼	TKO 10	Las Vegas
June 15, 1987	Michael Spinks*	208¾	Gerry Cooney	238	TKO 5	Atlantic City
Aug 1, 1987	Mike Tyson	221	Tony Tucker	221	UD 12	Las Vegas
Oct 16, 1987	Mike Tyson	216	Tyrell Biggs	228¾	TKO 7	Atlantic City
Jan 22, 1988	Mike Tyson	215¾	Larry Holmes	225¾	TKO 4	Atlantic City
Mar 20, 1988	Mike Tyson	216¼	Tony Tubbs	238¼	KO 2	Tokyo
June 27, 1988	Mike Tyson*	218¼	Michael Spinks	212¼	KO 1	Atlantic City
Feb 25, 1989	Mike Tyson*	218	Frank Bruno	228	TKO 5	Las Vegas
July 21, 1989	Mike Tyson*	219¼	Carl Williams	218	TKO 1	Atlantic City
Feb 10, 1990	Buster Douglas*	231½	Mike Tyson	220½	KO 10	Tokyo
Oct 25, 1990	Evander Holyfield*	208	Buster Douglas	246	KO 3	Las Vegas
Apr 19, 1991	Evander Holyfield*	212	George Foreman	257	UD 12	Atlantic City
Nov 23, 1991	Evander Holyfield*	210	Bert Cooper	215	TKO 7	Atlanta
June 19, 1992	Evander Holyfield*	210	Larry Holmes	233	UD 12	Las Vegas
Nov 13, 1992	Riddick Bowe*	235	Evander Holyfield	205	UD 12	Las Vegas
Feb 6, 1993	Riddick Bowe*	243	Michael Dokes	244	KO 1	New York City
May 8, 1993	Lennox Lewis	235	Tony Tucker	235	UD 12	Las Vegas
May 22, 1993	Riddick Bowe*	244	Jesse Ferguson	224	KO 2	Washington, D.C.
Oct 2, 1993	Lennox Lewis	229	Frank Bruno	233	KO 7	London
Nov 6, 1993	Evander Holyfield*	217	Riddick Bowe	246	Split 12	Las Vegas
Apr 22, 1994	Michael Moorer*	214	Evander Holyfield	214	Split 12	Las Vegas
May 6, 1994	Lennox Lewis	235	Phil Jackson	218	TKO 8	Atlantic City
Nov 6, 1994	George Foreman*	250	Michael Moorer	222	KO 10	Las Vegas
Mar 11, 1995	Riddick Bowe	241	Herbie Hide	214	KO 6	Las Vegas
Apr 8, 1995	Oliver McCall	231	Larry Holmes	236	UD 12	Las Vegas
Apr 8, 1995	Bruce Seldon	236	Tony Tucker	243	TKO 7	Las Vegas
Apr 22, 1995	George Foreman*	256	Axel Schulz	221	Split 12	Las Vegas
Jun 17, 1995	Riddick Bowe	243	Jorge Luis Gonzalez	237	KO 6	Las Vegas
Aug 19, 1995	Bruce Seldon	234	Joe Hipp	233	TKO 10	Las Vegas
Sept 2, 1995	Frank Bruno	247¾	Oliver McCall	234¾	UD 12	London
Dec 9, 1995	Frans Botha	237	Axel Shulz	223	Split 12	Stuttgart
Mar 16, 1996	Mike Tyson	220	Frank Bruno	247	TKO 3	Las Vegas
June 22, 1996	Michael Moorer	222¼	Axel Shulz	222¾	Split 12	Dortmund, Germ.
Sept 7, 1996	Mike Tyson	219	Bruce Seldon	229	TKO 1	Las Vegas
Nov 3, 1996	George Foreman*	253	Crawford Grimsley		UD 12	Tokyo
Nov 9, 1996	Evander Holyfied	215	Mike Tyson	222	TKO 11	Las Vegas
Feb 7, 1997	Lennox Lewis	251	Oliver McCall	237	TKO 5	Las Vegas

Date	Winner	Wgt	Loser	Wgt	Result	Site
Apr 26, 1997	George Foreman*	253	Lou Savarese		Split 12	Atlantic City
June 28, 1997	Evander Holyfied	218	Mike Tyson	218	DQ 4	Las Vegas
Oct 4, 1997	Lennox Lewis	244	Andrew Golota	244	TKO 1	Atlantic City
Nov 8, 1997	Evander Holyfield	214	Michael Moorer	223	TKO 8	Las Vegas
Nov 22, 1997	Shannon Briggs*		George Foreman		MD 12	Atlantic City
Mar 28, 1998	Lennox Lewis*	243	Shannon Briggs	228	TKO 5	Atlantic City
Mar 13, 1999	Evander Holyfield	215	Lennox Lewis*	246	Draw 12	New York City
Nov 13, 1999	Lennox Lewis*	242	Evander Holyfield	217	UD 12	Las Vegas
Apr 29, 2000	Lennox Lewis*	247	Michael Grant	250	KO 2	New York
July 15, 2000	Lennox Lewis*	250	Frans Botha	236	TKO 2	London
Aug 12, 2000	Evander Holyfield	221	John Ruiz	224	UD 12	Las Vegas
Nov 11, 2000	Lennox Lewis*	249	David Tua	245	UD 12	Las Vegas
Mar 3, 2001	John Ruiz	227	Evander Holyfield	217	UD 12	Las Vegas
Apr 22, 2001	Hasim Rahman*	238	Lennox Lewis	253½	KO 5	Brakpan, S. Africa
Nov 17, 2001	Lennox Lewis*	246½	Hasim Rahman	236	KO 4	Las Vegas
Dec 15, 2001	John Ruiz	232	Evander Holyfield	219	Draw 12	Mashantucket, Conn.
June 8, 2002	Lennox Lewis*	249¼	Mike Tyson	234½	KO 8	Memphis, Tenn.
July 27, 2002	John Ruiz	233	Kirk Johnson	238	DQ 10	Las Vegas
Dec 14, 2002	Chris Byrd	214	Evander Holyfield	220	UD 12	Atlantic City
Mar 1, 2003	Roy Jones Jr.	193	John Ruiz	226	UD 12	Las Vegas
June 21, 2003	Lennox Lewis*	256½	Vitali Klitschko	248	TKO 6	Los Angeles
Sept 20, 2003	Chris Byrd	211½	Fres Oquendo	224	UD 12	Uncasville, Conn.
April 17, 2004	Chris Byrd	210½	Andrew Golota	237½	Draw 12	New York City
April 17, 2004	John Ruiz	240	Fres Oquendo	225	TKO 11	New York City
April 24, 2004	Vitali Klitschko	245	Corrie Sanders	235	TKO 8	Los Angeles
Nov 13, 2004	John Ruiz	239	Andrew Golota	238	UD	New York City
Nov 13, 2004	Chris Byrd	214	Jameel McCline	270	Split 12	New York City
Dec 11, 2004	Vitali Klitschko	250	Danny Williams	270	TKO 8	Las Vegas
April 30, 2005	James Toney	231	John Ruiz	244	ND	New York City
Aug 13, 2005	Hasim Rahman	236	Monte Barrett	224	UD	Chicago, Ill.
Dec 17, 2005	Nikolay Valuev	324	John Ruiz	237	MD	Berlin
Oct 1, 2005	Chris Byrd	213	DaVarryl Williamson	225	UD	Reno, Nev.
Mar 18, 2006	Hasim Rahman	238	James Toney	237	MD	Atlantic City
Apr 22, 2006	Wladimir Klitschko	241	Chris Byrd	213	TKO 7	Mannheim, Germ.
June 3, 2006	Nikolay Valuev	320	Owen Beck	242	TKO 3	Hanover, Germ.
Aug 12, 2006	Oleg Maskaev	238	Hasim Rahman	235	TKO 12	Las Vegas
Jan 20, 2007	Nikolai Valuev	322½	Jameel McCline	268½	TKO 3	Basel, Switz.
Mar 10, 2007	Wladimir Klitschko	246½	Ray Austin	247	TKO 2	Mannheim, Germ.
Apr 14, 2007	Ruslan Chagaev	228¼	Nikolay Valuev	319	MD	Stuttgart, Germ.
July 7, 2007	Wladimir Klitschko	243½	Lamon Brewster	228¼	TKO 6	Cologne, Germ.

*Lineal champion. KO=knockout; TKO=technical knockout; UD=unanimous decision; Split=split decision; Ref=referee's decision; MD=majority decision; DQ=disqualification; ND=no decision.

Ring Magazine Fighter and Fight of the Year

Year	Fighter	Year	Fighter	Year	Fighter
1928	Gene Tunney	1935	Barney Ross	1940	Billy Conn
1929	Tommy Loughran	1936	Joe Louis	1941	Joe Louis
1930	Max Schmeling	1937	Henry Armstrong	1942	Ray Robinson
1932	Jack Sharkey	1938	Joe Louis	1943	Fred Apostoli
1934	T. Canzoneri/B. Ross	1939	Joe Louis	1944	Beau Jack

Note: No award in 1933; no fight of the year named until 1945

Year	Fighter	Fight	Winner	Site
1945	Willie Pep	Rocky Graziano–Freddie Cochrane	Rocky Graziano	New York City
1946	Tony Zale	Tony Zale–Rocky Graziano	Tony Zale	New York City
1947	Gus Lesnevich	Rocky Graziano–Tony Zale	Rocky Graziano	Chicago
1948	Ike Williams	Marcel Cerdan–Tony Zale	Marcel Cerdan	Jersey City
1949	Ezzard Charles	Willie Pep–Sandy Saddler	Willie Pep	New York City
1950	Ezzard Charles	Jake LaMotta–Laurent Dauthuille	Jake LaMotta	Detroit
1951	Ray Robinson	Jersey Joe Walcott–Ezzard Charles	Jersey Joe Walcott	Pittsburgh
1952	Rocky Marciano	Rocky Marciano–Jersey Joe Walcott	Rocky Marciano	Philadelphia
1953	Carl Olson	Rocky Marciano–Roland LaStarza	Rocky Marciano	New York City
1954	Rocky Marciano	Rocky Marciano–Ezzard Charles	Rocky Marciano	New York City
1955	Rocky Marciano	Carmen Basilio–Tony DeMarco	Carmen Basilio	Boston
1956	Floyd Patterson	Carmen Basilio–Johnny Saxton	Carmen Basilio	Syracuse
1957	Carmen Basilio	Carmen Basilio–Ray Robinson	Carmen Basilio	New York City
1958	Ingemar Johansson	Ray Robinson–Carmen Basilio	Ray Robinson	Chicago

Year	Fighter	Fight	Winner	Site
1959	Ingemar Johansson	Gene Fullmer–Carmen Basilio	Gene Fullmer	San Francisco
1960	Floyd Patterson	Floyd Patterson–Ingemar Johansson	Floyd Patterson	New York City
1961	Joe Brown	Joe Brown–Dave Charnley	Joe Brown	London
1962	Dick Tiger	Joey Giardello–Henry Hank	Joey Giardello	Philadelphia
1963	Cassius Clay	Cassius Clay–Doug Jones	Cassius Clay	New York City
1964	Emile Griffith	Cassius Clay–Sonny Liston	Cassius Clay	Miami Beach
1965	Dick Tiger	Floyd Patterson–George Chuvalo	Floyd Patterson	New York City
1966	No award	Jose Torres–Eddie Cotton	Jose Torres	Las Vegas
1967	Joe Frazier	Nino Benvenuti–Emile Griffith	Nino Benvenuti	New York City
1968	Nino Benvenuti	Dick Tiger–Frank DePaula	Dick Tiger	New York City
1969	Jose Napoles	Joe Frazier–Jerry Quarry	Joe Frazier	New York City
1970	Joe Frazier	Carlos Monzon–Nino Benvenuti	Carlos Monzon	Rome
1971	Joe Frazier	Joe Frazier–Muhammad Ali	Joe Frazier	New York City
1972	Muhammad Ali Carlos Monzon	Bob Foster–Chris Finnegan	Bob Foster	London
1973	George Foreman	George Foreman–Joe Frazier	George Foreman	Kingston, Jam.
1974	Muhammad Ali	Muhammad Ali–George Foreman	Muhammad Ali	Kinshasa, Zaire
1975	Muhammad Ali	Muhammad Ali–Joe Frazier	Muhammad Ali	Manila
1976	George Foreman	George Foreman–Ron Lyle	George Foreman	Las Vegas
1977	Carlos Zarate	Joe Young–George Foreman	Joe Young	San Juan
1978	Muhammad Ali	Leon Spinks–Muhammad Ali	Leon Spinks	Las Vegas
1979	Ray Leonard	Danny Lopez–Mike Ayala	Danny Lopez	San Antonio
1980	Thomas Hearns	Saad Muhammad–Yaqui Lopez	Saad Muhammad	McAfee, N.J.
1981	Ray Leonard Salvador Sanchez	Ray Leonard–Tommy Hearns	Ray Leonard	Las Vegas
1982	Larry Holmes	Bobby Chacon–Rafael Limon	Bobby Chacon	Sacramento
1983	Marvin Hagler	Bobby Chacon–Cornelius Boza-Edwards	Bobby Chacon	Las Vegas
1984	Thomas Hearns	Jose Luis Ramirez–Edwin Rosario	Jose Luis Ramirez	San Juan
1985	Donald Curry Marvin Hagler	Marvin Hagler–Tommy Hearns	Marvin Hagler	Las Vegas
1986	Mike Tyson	Stevie Cruz–Barry McGuigan	Stevie Cruz	Las Vegas
1987	Evander Holyfield	Ray Leonard–Marvin Hagler	Ray Leonard	Las Vegas
1988	Mike Tyson	Tony Lopez–Rocky Lockridge	Tony Lopez	Inglewood, Calif.
1989	Pernell Whitaker	Roberto Duran–Iran Barkley	Roberto Duran	Atlantic City
1990	Julio César Chávez	Julio César Chávez–Meldrick Taylor	Julio César Chávez	Las Vegas
1991	James Toney	Robert Quiroga–Kid Akeem Anifowoshe	Robert Quiroga	San Antonio
1992	Riddick Bowe	Riddick Bowe–Evander Holyfield	Riddick Bowe	Las Vegas
1993	Michael Carbajal	Michael Carbajal–Humberto Gonzalez	Michael Carbajal	Las Vegas
1994	Roy Jones	Jorge Castro–John David Jackson	Jorge Castro	Monterrey, Mex.
1995	Oscar De La Hoya	Saman Sor Jaturong–Chiquita Gonzalez	Saman Sor Jaturong	Inglewood, Calif.
1996	Evander Holyfield	Evander Holyfield–Mike Tyson	Evander Holyfield	Las Vegas
1997	Evander Holyfield	Arturo Gatti–Gabriel Ruelas	Arturo Gatti	Atlantic City
1998	Floyd Mayweather	Ivan Robinson–Arturo Gatti	Ivan Robinson	Atlantic City
1999	Paulie Ayala	Paulie Ayala–Johnny Tapia	Paulie Ayala	Las Vegas
2000	Felix Trinidad	Erik Morales–Marco Antonio Barrera	Erik Morales	Las Vegas
2001	Bernard Hopkins	Micky Ward–Emanuel Burton	Micky Ward	Las Vegas
2002	Vernon Forrest	Micky Ward–Arturo Gatti	Micky Ward	Uncasville, Conn.
2003	James Toney	Micky Ward–Arturo Gatti	Arturo Gatti	Atlantic City
2004	Glen Johnson	Marco Antonio Barrera–Erik Morales	Marco Barrera	Las Vegas
2005	Ricky Hatton	Diego Corrales–Jose Luis Castillo	Diego Corrales	Las Vegas
2006	Manny Pacquiao	S. Sithchatchawal–Mahyar Monshipour	S. Sithchatchawal	Levallois-Perret, France

U.S. Olympic Gold Medalists

LIGHT FLYWEIGHT

1984	Paul Gonzales

FLYWEIGHT

1904	George Finnegan
1920	Frank Di Gennara
1024	Fidel LaBarba
1952	Nathan Brooks
1976	Leo Randolph
1984	Steve McCrory

BANTAMWEIGHT

1904	Oliver Kirk
1988	Kennedy McKinney

FEATHERWEIGHT

1904	Oliver Kirk
1924	John Fields
1984	Meldrick Taylor

LIGHTWEIGHT

1904	Harry Spanger
1920	Samuel Mosberg
1968	Ronald W. Harris
1976	Howard Davis
1984	Pernell Whitaker
1992	Oscar De La Hoya

LIGHT WELTERWEIGHT

1952	Charles Adkins
1972	Ray Seales
1976	Ray Leonard
1984	Jerry Page

WELTERWEIGHT

1904	Albert Young
1932	Edward Flynn
1984	Mark Breland

LIGHT MIDDLEWEIGHT

1960 .... Wilbert McClure
1984 .... Frank Tate
1996 .... David Reid

MIDDLEWEIGHT

1904 .... Charles Mayer
1932 .... Carmen Bath
1952 .... Floyd Patterson
1960 .... Edward Crook
1976 .... Michael Spinks

LIGHT HEAVYWEIGHT

1920 .... Eddie Eagan
1952 .... Norvel Lee
1956 .... James Boyd
1960 .... Cassius Clay
1976 .... Leon Spinks
1988 .... Andrew Maynard
2004 .... Andre Ward

HEAVYWEIGHT

1984 .... Henry Tillman
1988 .... Ray Mercer

SUPER HEAVYWEIGHT

1904 .... Samuel Berger
1952 .... H. Edward Sanders
1956 .... T. Peter Rademacher
1964 .... Joe Frazier
1968 .... George Foreman
1984 .... Tyrell Biggs

Lineal Heavyweight Champions

Champion	Reign	Age*	Career	W-L-D (KO)	Successful Defenses
John L. Sullivan	1885–92	26	1878–92	38-1-3 (33)	0
James J. Corbett	1892–97	26	1884–03	11-4-2 (7)	1
Bob Fitzsimmons	1897–99	33	1880–16	74-8-3 (67)	0
James J. Jeffries†	1899–05	24	1896–10	18-1-2 (15)	7
Marvin Hart	1905–06	28	1899–10	28-7-4 (19)	0
Tommy Burns	1906–08	24	1900–20	46-5-8 (37)	11
Jack Johnson	1908–15	30	1894–28	77-13-14 (48)	9
Jess Willard	1915–19	33	1911–23	23-6-1 (20)	1
Jack Dempsey	1919–26	24	1914–27	60-6-8 (50)	5
Gene Tunney†	1926–28	29	1915–28	61-1-1 (45)	2
Max Schmeling	1930–32	24	1924–48	56-10-4 (39)	1
Jack Sharkey	1932–33	29	1924–36	38-13-3 (14)	0
Primo Carnera	1933–34	26	1928–37	88-14-0 (69)	2
Max Baer	1934–35	25	1929–41	72-12-0 (53)	0
James J. Braddock	1935–37	29	1926–38	51-26-7 (26)	0
Joe Louis†	1937–49	23	1934–51	68-3-0 (54)	25
Ezzard Charles	1949–51	27	1940–59	96-25-1 (59)	8
Jersey Joe Walcott	1951–52	37	1930–53	53-18-1 (33)	1
Rocky Marciano†	1952–56	29	1947–56	49-0-0 (43)	6
Floyd Patterson	1956–59	21	1952–72	55-8-1 (40)	4
Ingemar Johansson	1959–60	26	1952–63	26-2-0 (17)	0
Floyd Patterson	1960–62	25	1952–72	55-8-1 (40)	2
Sonny Liston	1962–64	30	1953–70	50-4-0 (39)	1
Muhammad Ali	1964–71	22	1960–81	56-5-0 (37)	9
Joe Frazier	1971–73	27	1965–81	32-4-1 (27)	2
George Foreman	1973–74	24	1969–97	76-5-0 (68)	2
Muhammad Ali	1974–78	32	1960–81	56-5-0 (37)	10
Leon Spinks	1978	24	1977–95	26-17-3 (14)	0
Muhammad Ali†	1978–79	36	1960–81	56-5-0 (37)	0
Larry Holmes	1980–85	29	1973–2002	69-6-0 (44)	20
Michael Spinks	1985–88	29	1977–88	32-1-0 (21)	3
Mike Tyson	1988–90	21	1985–2005	49-4-0 (43)	2
Buster Douglas	1990	29	1981–99	38-6-1 (25)	0
Evander Holyfield	1990–92	28	1984–	38-5-2 (26)	3
Riddick Bowe	1992–93	25	1989–96	40-1-0 (32)	2
Evander Holyfield	1993–94	31	1984–	38-5-2 (26)	0
Michael Moorer	1994	26	1988–97	39-2-0 (31)	0
George Foreman	1994–97	45	1969–97	76-5-0 (68)	3
Shannon Briggs	1997–98	25	1992–00	32-3-1 (25)	0
Lennox Lewis	1998–01	32	1989–2004	40-2-1 (31)	5
Hasim Rahman	2001	28	1994–	35-4-0 (29)	0
Lennox Lewis†	2001–04	36	1989–2004	41-2-1 (32)	2
Chris Byrd	2002–06	35	1993–	38-2-1 (20)	3
John Ruiz	2001–03	31	1992–	38-5-1 (28)	2
Roy Jones, Jr.	2003	34	1989–	49-3-0 (38)	0
John Ruiz	2003–05	33	1992–	41-6-1 (28)	2
Vitali Klitschko†	2004–05	34	1996–2005	34-2-0 (33)	1
Hasim Rahman	2005-06	33	1994–	41-5-2 (33)	1
Oleg Maskaev	2006–	37	1993–	32-5-0 (26)	0
Wladimir Klitschko	2006–	30	1996–	46-3-0 (41)	0
Nikolay Valuev	2005–	32	1993–	44-0-0 (32)	1

*Age when boxer won world championship. † Boxer retired or relinquished world title.

Horse Racing

2007 Kentucky Derby winner Street Sense

Homestretch Heroics

Despite the demise of fan favorite and cult icon Barbaro, the fantastic and record-setting Triple Crown finishes offered railbirds plenty of exciting reasons to smile

BY MARK BECHTEL

A S THE GENERATION OF FANS that has grown deep into adulthood without bearing witness to a Triple Crown winner knows well, the racing gods can be cruel. Almost three decades of near misses, stunning upsets and one tragic accident have produced the longest Triple Crown drought since Sir Barton won thoroughbred racing's first trifecta in 1919. It has now been 29 years since Affirmed swept the Kentucky Derby, Preakness and Belmont. For serious railbirds and casual fans alike, the wait continues.

But 2007 was a reminder that there is more to racing than the pursuit of the Crown. Greatness can be attained by other means. History can be made in the most unexpected ways. And sometimes the sport's athletes—the horses—demonstrate their most admirable grace and strike the greatest chords with fans far from the track.

Past Triple Crown winners like Affirmed and Seattle Slew weren't the only ghosts that three-year-olds were chasing in 2007. In January, after a valiant eight-month fight for his life, 2006 Kentucky Derby winner Barbaro finally succumbed to complications from the horrific leg injury he suffered while running the '06 Preakness. Barbaro shattered several bones in his right rear leg that day, and during his recovery he was afflicted with various maladies including an abscess in his injured hoof and laminitis in his left rear hoof. After a risky surgical operation in January, Barbaro developed laminitis in both front hooves. It was then that doctors at the University of Pennsylvania's New Bolton Center, Barbaro's home since his accident, and the horse's owners decided to euthanize him. "He has been an exceptionally quiet, calm and relaxed horse," said Dr. Dean Richardson. "We meant what we said, if we couldn't control his discomfort, we wouldn't go on."

Despite—or perhaps because of—his unfulfilled greatness, Barbaro, who was unbeaten when he broke down at Pimlico Racecourse, struck a nerve with sports fans. During his struggle for survival he became horse racing's most transcendent star, gaining a popularity greater than that of any horse in recent memory. Before and after his death the Internet buzzed with tributes to him, and as Triple Crown season began in the spring Barbaro's legacy was still one of racing's top storylines. But on the first Saturday in May all eyes at Churchill Downs

BILL FRAKES

At the 2007 Preakness, Curlin (l.) nosed out Kentucky Derby champ Street Sense for the win and tied the track record of 1:53.46.

were on trainer Todd Pletcher. As the winner of the three previous Eclipse Awards for best trainer, Pletcher had dominated the sport; in 2006 he won a record 100 stakes races and took home $26.8 million in purses, smashing the record of $20.9 million he had set in '05. But there was a gap in Pletcher's resume: He had saddled 21 horses in Triple Crown races (14 in the Derby, one in the Preakness and six in the Belmont) but had never won.

The odds of Pletcher's drought ending seemed to be good at the Kentucky Derby—he had five entries in the Run for the Roses,

a quarter of the field. But when the bell went off, Street Sense, the nation's champion as a two-year-old, was the 9-to-2 betting favorite, and the dark bay colt did not disappoint. Before the third-largest crowd (156,635) in Derby history, Street Sense started slow, falling to 19th place after a half mile and lingering in 17th a quarter mile later. But his rider, Calvin Borel, wasn't worried. He had guided Street Sense to the rail, and on the far turn he finally asked is mount for speed. Street Sense took off like a shot and, with Borel guiding him as expertly as a New York cabbie weaving through rush-hour traffic, raced past pacesetter Hard Spun just inside the eight pole. Said Edgar Prado, who was riding Pletcher's Scat Daddy, "He went by me so fast, I wasn't sure what horse it was."

Street Sense roared to a 2¼-length victory over Hard Spun. Borel, 40, an unacclaimed Cajun jockey who nonetheless had more then 4,300 career wins, had pulled off one of the most breathtaking rides in Derby history. Street Sense had barely crossed the finish line when talk of his Triple Crown potential began. "Now, I suppose, everyone is going to want to know if he can... run back and do it again in two weeks," trainer Carl Nafzger said after the race. "I'll just say this: What a horse."

By the morning of the Preakness, the Crown buzz had grown to a roar. Rival trainer D. Wayne Lukas had gushed that if Street Sense could win at Pimlico he could "run all day at the Belmont," and the sport braced itself for another run at history. Those dreams were dashed, however, when Curlin, the third-place finisher in the Derby, nipped Street Sense in the closest Preakness finish in a decade. Street Sense ran a commendable race. With an eighth of a mile to go Borel had guided him to a 1½-length lead, bringing a Preakness record crowd of 121,263 to its feet. "You take a lead in a horse race, you're expected to finish it off," said Nafzger afterward.

Street Sense's handlers could find some solace in the fact that it took a historic performance to beat their horse. Curlin's time of 1:53.46 tied the Preakness record set by Tank's Prospect in 1985 and matched by Louis Quatorze in '96. Curlin's race was as precocious as it was brilliant. The horse, prepped by successful trainer Steve Asmussen, had sat out his two-year-old season with sore shins, and the first win of his life had come just three months before the Preakness, a 12¾-length romp at Gulfstream Park. The next day, while the rest of the country was fixated on the Super Bowl,

Curlin's owners, who had bought him for $57,000, sold an 80-percent stake in the horse to a group headed by by Kendall-Jackson wine impresario Jess Jackson for around $3.5 million. "We hoped that Curlin would be good," said Jackson. "But we never dreamed he would develop this explosively."

Even with no Triple Crown on the line, racing fans looked forward to a Curlin-Street Sense rematch in the Belmont. It was not to be: Street Sense was held out of the race so he could head for the breeding shed. His absence softened the Belmont field—or so it was thought before the gun went off. Street Sense's hole in the starting gate was filled by Rags to Riches, a filly trained by Pletcher. She was a talented horse, having breezed to a win in the Kentucky Oaks on the day before the Derby, but little more than a Belmont throw-in. Pletcher didn't even decide to enter her until four days before the race. "She is such a magnificent filly," said jockey Garrett Gomez, who had ridden her in the past but was committed to riding Hard Spun in the Belmont. "I just knew we would see a great display from her."

Gomez was right. Rags to Riches turned out to be a horse for the ages: She became the Belmont's first filly champion in 102 years. Her victory was no soft-field fluke, either. After stumbling out of the gate Rags to Riches, ridden by John Velazquez, took the lead on the stretch and held off Curlin with a brilliant and courageous drive to the finish. Twice she appeared to have a comfortable lead, and twice Curlin rallied. But it was Rags to Riches who led when the 1½-mile marathon was over. Together, Rags to Riches and Curlin ran the final two furlongs in 23.83 seconds, the fastest final quarter in a Belmont since 1934.

It was a historic performance, a much-needed dose of drama in a race that had felt diminished heading in. It was also a sweet triumph for Pletcher, who broke his 0-for-28 Triple Crown winless streak. Racing's wait for a transcendent champion goes on. But as Rags to Riches reminded fans, there is still greatness to be found on the track.

THOROUGHBRED RACING

The Triple Crown

133rd Kentucky Derby

May 5, 2007. Grade I, 3-year-olds; 10th race, Churchill Downs, Louisville. All 126 lbs. Distance: 1¼ miles. Purse: $2,000,000 guaranteed. Track: Fast. Off: 6:16 p.m. Winner: Street Sense (By Street Cry out of Bedazzle by Dixieland Band); Times: 0:22.96, 0:46.26, 1:11.13, 1:37.04, 2:02.17. Won: Driving. Breeder: James B. Tafel

Horse	Finish-PP	Margin	Jockey/Trainer
Street Sense	1–7	2¼	Calvin Borel/Carl Nafzger
Hard Spun	2–8	5¾	Mario Pino/Larry Jones
Curlin	3–2	½	Robby Albarado/Steve Asmussen
Imawildandcrazyguy	4–5	½	Mark Guidry/William Kaplan
Sedgefield	5–1	neck	Julien Leparoux/Darrin Miller
Circular Quay	6–16	¾	John Velazquez/Todd Pletcher
Tiago	7–15	½	Mike Smith/John Shirreffs
Any Given Saturday	8–18	2½	Garrett Gomez/Todd Pletcher
Sam P.	9–13	1¾	Ramon Dominguez/Todd Pletcher
Nobiz Like Shobiz	10–12	3	Cornelio Velasquez/Barclay Tagg
Dominican	11–19	neck	Rafael Bejarno/Darrin Miller
Zanjero	12–3	2¾	Shaun Bridgmohan/Steve Asmussen
Great Hunter	13–20	1¾	Corey Nakatani/Doug O'Neill
Liquidity	14–9	¾	David Flores/Doug O'Neill
Bwana Bull	15–11	1	Javier Castellano/Jerry Hollendorfer
Storm in May	16–4	11½	Juan Leyva/William Kaplan
Teuflesberg	17–10	2¾	Stewart Elliott/Jamie Sanders
Scat Daddy	18–14	6¼	Edgar Prado/Todd Pletcher
Stormello	19–17	7¼	Kent Desormeaux/William Currin
Cowtown Cat	20–6	—	Fernando Jara/Todd Pletcher

132nd Preakness Stakes

May 19, 2007. Grade I, 3-year-olds; 12th race, Pimlico Race Course, Baltimore. All 126 lbs. Distance: 1³⁄₁₆ miles; Stakes value: $1,000,000. Track: Fast. Off: 6:18 p.m. Winner: Curlin (By Smart Strike out of Sherriff's Deputy by Deputy Minister); Times: 0:22.83, 0:45.75, 1:09.80, 1:34.68, 1:53.46. Won: Driving. Breeder: Fares Farm Inc.

Horse	Finish-PP	Margin	Jockey/Trainer
Curlin	1–4	Head	Robby Albarado/Steve Asmussen
Street Sense	2–8	4	Calvin Borel/Carl Nafzger
Hard Spun	3–7	1½	Mario Pino/Larry Jones
C P West	4–9	1¼	Edgar Prado/Nick Zito
Circular Quay	5–3	3³⁄₄	John Velazquez/Todd Pletcher
King of the Roxy	6–5	6½	Garrett Gomez/Todd Pletcher
Mint Slewlep	7–1	8½	Alan Garcia/Larry Jones
Xchanger	8–2	4¼	Ramon Dominguez/Carl Nafzger
Flying First Class	9–6	—	Mark Guidry/D. Wayne Lukas

139th Belmont Stakes

June 9, 2007. Grade I, 3-year-olds; 11th race, Belmont Park, Elmont, NY. All 126 lbs. Distance: 1½ miles. Stakes value: $1,000,000. Track: Fast. Off: 6:29 p.m. Winner: Rags to Riches (By A.P. Indy out of Better Than Honour by Deputy Minister); Times: 0:24.74, 50.14, 1:15.32, 1:40.23, 2:04.91, 2:28.74. Won: Driving. Breeder: Skara Glen Stables

Horse	Finish-PP	Margin	Jockey/Trainer
Rags to Riches	1–7	head	John Velazquez/Todd Pletcher
Curlin	2–3	5½	Robby Albarado/Steve Asmussen
Tiago	3–2	5½	Mike Smith/John Shirreffs
Hard Spun	4–6	4¼	Garrett Gomez/Larry Jones
C P West	5–4	1¾	Edgar Prado/Nick Zito
Imawildandcrazyguy	6–1	17	Mark Guidry/Bill Kaplan
Slew's Tizzy	7–5	—	Rafael Bejarano/Greg Fox

Late 2006

Date	Race	Track	Distance	Winner	Trainer/Jockey	Purse ($)
Sept 2	Woodward Stakes	Saratoga	1⅛ miles	Premium Tap	J. Kimmel/ K. Desormeaux	500,000
Sept 17	Woodbine Mile Stakes	Woodbine	1 mile	Becrux	N. Drysdale/ P. Valenzuela	896,456
Sept 23	Super Derby XXVI	Louisiana Downs	1⅛ miles	Strong Contender	J. Ward/ R. Albarado	486,500
Sept 30	Hawthorne Gold Cup	Hawthorne	1¼ miles	It's No Joke	R. Maker/ E. Razo Jr.	500,000
Sept 30	Yellow Ribon Stakes	Keeneland	1¼ miles	Wait a Minute	T. Pletcher/ G. Gomez	400,000
Oct 6	Darley Alcibiades Stakes	Keeneland	1¹⁄₁₆ miles	Bel Air Beauty	F. Brothers/ F. Jara	400,000
Oct 7	Jockey Club Gold Cup	Belmont	1¼ miles	Bernardini	T. Albertrani/ J. Castellano	712,500
Oct 7	Hirsch Turf Classic Invitational	Belmont	1½ miles	English Channel	T. Pletcher/ J. Velazquez	600,000
Oct 7	Vosburgh Stakes	Belmont	6 furlongs	Henny Hughes	K. McLaughlin/ J. Velazquez	392,000
Oct 7	Flower Bowl Invitational	Belmont	1¼ miles	Honey Ryder	T. Pletcher/ J. Velazquez	588,000
Oct 7	Goodwood B.C.	Santa Anita	1⅛ miles	Lava Man	D. O'Neil/ C. Nakatani	500,000
Oct 7	Indiana B.C. Oaks	Hoosier	1¹⁄₁₆ miles	Baghdaria	T. Amoss/ R. Bejarano	405,100
Oct 7	Beldame Stakes	Belmont	1⅛ miles	Fleet Indian	T. Pletcher/ J. Santos	600,000
Oct 7	Shadwell Turf Mile	Keeneland	1 mile	Aussie Rules	A. O'Brien/ G. Gomez	600,000
Oct 8	Juddmonte Spinster Stakes	Keeneland	1⅛ miles	Asi Siempre	P. Biancone/ J. Leparoux	500,000
Oct 8	Indiana Derby	Hoosier	1¹⁄₁₆ miles	Star Dabbler	M. Hushion/ R. Migliore	513,200
				Cielo Gold	H. Wiggins/ B. Hernandez	513,200
Oct 8	Lane's End B. Futurity	Keeneland	1¹⁄₁₆ miles	Great Hunter	D. O'Neil/ V. Espinoza	500,000
Oct 13	Meadowlands B.C. Stakes	Meadowlands	1⅛ miles	Master Command	T. Pletcher/ J. Velazquez	499,000
Oct 14	Champagne Stakes	Belmont	1 mile	Scat Daddy	T. Pletcher/ J. Velazquez	400,000
Oct 14	Frizette	Belmont	1 mile	Sutra	M. Stidham/ M. Luzzi	400,000
Oct 14	First Lady Stakes	Keeneland	1⅛ miles	Gorella	P. Biancone/ J. Leparoux	400,000
Oct 14	Queen Elizabeth II Challenge Cup	Keeneland	1⅛ miles	Vacare	C. Block/ C. Marquez Jr.	500,000
Oct 21	Pattison Canadian International	Woodbine	1½ miles	Collier Hill	A. Swinbank/ D. McKeown	1,779,300
Oct 21	E.P. Taylor Stakes	Woodbine	1¼ miles	Arravale	M. Benson/ J. Valdivia	890,580
Nov 4	Breeders Cup Classic Stakes	Belmont	1¼ mile	Invasor	K. McLaughlin/ J. Fernando	5,000,000
Nov 4	Breeders Cup Turf Stakes	Belmont	1½ miles	Red Rocks	B. Meehan/ L. Dettori	2,748,000
Nov 4	Breeders Cup Distaff	Belmont	1⅛ mile	Round Pound	M. Matz/ E. Prado	2,070,160
Nov 4	Breeders Cup Mile Stakes	Belmont	1 mile	Miesque's Approval	M. Wolfson/ E. Castro	1,987,720
Nov 4	Breeders Cup Juvenile Stakes	Belmont	1¹⁄₁₆ miles	Street Sense	C. Nafzger/ C. Borel	1,832,000
Nov 4	Breeders Cup Juvenile Fillies	Belmont	1¹⁄₁₆ miles	Dreaming of Anna	W. Catalano/ R. Douglas	1,832,000
Nov 4	Breeders Cup Filly & Mare	Belmont	1⅜ miles	Ouija Board	E. Dunlop/ L. Dettori	2,015,200
Nov 4	Breeders Cup Sprint Stakes	Belmont	6 furlongs	Thor's Echo	D. O'Neil/ C. Nakatani	1,951,080
Nov 24	Clark Handicap	Churchill Downs	1⅛ miles	Premium Tap	J. Kimmel/ K. Desormeaux	572,000

Major Stakes Races (*Cont.*)

2007 (through September 29)

Date	Race	Track	Distance	Winner	Trainer/Jockey	Purse ($)
Jan 27	Sunshine Millions Classic	Santa Anita	1⅛ miles	McCann's Mojave	S. Specht/ F. Alvarado	1,000,000
Jan 27	Sunshine Millions Turf	Gulfstream	1⅛ miles	Lava Man	D. O'Neill/ C. Nakatani	500,000
Jan 27	Sunshine Millions Distaff	Gulfstream	1¹⁄₁₆ miles	Joint Effort	D. Romans/ E. Castro	500,000
Jan 27	Sunshine Milions Sprint	Gulfstream	6 furlongs	Smokey Stover	G. Gilchrist/ A. Gryder	300,000
Jan 27	Sunshine Millions F&M Turf	Santa Anita	1⅛ miles	Miss Shop	H. A. Jerkens/ J. Castellano	500,000
Feb 3	Donn Handicap	Gulfstream	1⅛ miles	Invasor	K. McLaughlin/ F. Jara	500,000
Mar 3	Santa Anita Handicap	Santa Anita	1¼ miles	Lava Man	D. O'Neill/ C. Nakatani	1,000,000
Mar 18	Winstar Derby	Sunland	1⅛ miles	Song of Navarone	H. Dominguez/ V. Espinoza	600,000
Mar 24	Lane's End Stakes	Turfway	1⅛ miles	Hard Spun	J. L. Jones/ M. Pino	500,000
Mar 31	Dubai World Cup	Nad al Sheba	1½ miles	Invasor	K. McLaughlin/ F. Jara	6,000,000
Mar 31	Dubai Duty Free	Nad al Sheba	1⅛ miles	Admire Moon	H. Matsuda/ Y. Take	5,000,000
Mar 31	Dubai Golden Shaheen	Nad al Sheba	6 furlongs	Kelly's Landing	E. Kenneally/ F. Dettori	2,000,000
Mar 31	UAE Derby	Nad al Sheba	1⅛ miles	Asiatic Boy	M. Kock/ W. Marwing/	2,000,000
Mar 31	Florida Derby	Gulfstream	1⅛ miles	Scat Daddy	T. Pletcher/ E. Prado	1,000,000
Apr 7	Wood Memorial Stakes	Aqueduct	1⅛ miles	Nobiz Like Shobiz	B. Tagg/ C. Velasquez	750,000
Apr 7	Santa Anita Derby	Santa Anita	1⅛ miles	Tiago	J. Shirreffs/ M. Smith	750,000
Apr 7	Ashland Stakes	Keeneland	1¹⁄₁₆ miles	Christmas Kid	J. Jerkens/ R. Douglas	500,000
Apr 7	Apple Blossom Handicap	Oaklawn	1¹⁄₁₆ miles	Ermine	R. Werner/ E. Castro	500,000
Apr 7	Illinois Derby	Hawthorne	1⅛ miles	Cowtown Cat	T. Pletcher/ F. Jara	500,000
Apr 7	Oaklawn Handicap	Oaklawn	1⅛ miles	Lawyer Ron	T. Pletcher/ E. Prado	500,000
Apr 14	Toyota Blue Grass	Keeneland	1⅛ miles	Dominican	D. Miller/ R. Bejarno	750,000
Apr 14	Arkansas Derby	Belmont Park	1⅛ miles	Curlin	S. Asmussen/ R. Albarado	1,000,000
May 4	Kentucky Oaks	Churchill Downs	1⅛ miles	Rags to Riches	T. Pletcher/ G. Gomez	589,200
May 5	Kentucky Derby	Churchill Downs	1¼ miles	Street Sense	C. Nafzger/ C. Borel	2,210,000
May 5	Woodford Reserve Classic	Churchill Downs	1⅛ miles	Sky Conqueror	D. Banach/ J. Castellano	561,000
May 12	Lone Star Derby	Lone Star Park	1¹⁄₁₆ miles	Slew's Tizzy	G. Fox/ R. Albarado	300,000
May 19	Preakness Stakes	Pimlico	1³⁄₁₆ miles	Curlin	S. Asmussen/ R. Albarado	1,000,000
May 28	Metropolitan Handicap	Belmont Park	1 mile	Corinthian	J. A. Perkins/ K. Desormeaux	600,000
May 28	Shoemaker B.C. Mile	Hollywood Park	1 mile	The Tin Man	R. Mandella/ V. Espinoza	370,200
May 28	Lone Star Park Handicap	Lone Star	1¹⁄₁₆ miles	Bob and John	B. Baffert/ G. Gomez	388,000
June 9	Belmont Stakes	Belmont	1½ miles	Rags to Riches	T. Pletcher/ J. Velazquez	1,000,000
June 9	Manhattan Handicap	Belmont	1¼ miles	Better Talk Now	G. Motion/ R. Dominguez	400,000
June 16	Stephen Foster Handicap	Churchill Downs	1⅛ miles	Flashy Bull	C. Borel/ R. Moquett	829,500

Major Stakes Races *(Cont.)*

2007 (through September 29) *(Cont.)*

Date	Race	Track	Distance	Winner	Jockey/Trainer	Purse ($)
June 24	Queen's Plate Stakes	Woodbine	1¼ miles	Mike Fox	I. Black/ E. Wilson	936,022
June 30	Suburban Handicap	Belmont	1¼ miles	Political Force	H. A. Jerkens/ C. Velasquez	400,000
June 30	Hollywood Gold Cup	Hollywood	1¼ miles	Lava Man	D. O'Neill/ C. Nakatani	750,000
July 7	United Nations Stakes	Monmouth	1⅜ miles	English Channel	T. Pletcher J. Velazquez	750,000
July 7	Princess Rooney Handicap	Calder	6 furlongs	River's Prayer	P. Capresto/ C. Potts	500,000
July 7	Smile Sprint Handicap	Calder	6 furlongs	Mach Ride	S. Standridge/ E. Trujillo	500,000
July 14	Delaware Oaks	Delaware	1¹⁄₁₆ miles	Moon Catcher	T. Ritchey/ C. Marquez Jr.	505,600
July 21	Virginia Derby	Colonial Downs	1¼ miles	Red Giant	T. Pletcher/ H. Karamanos	1,000,000
July 21	San Diego Handicap	Del Mar	1¹⁄₁₆ miles	Sun Boat	M. Mitchell/ M. Baze	300,000
July 21	American Oaks	Belmont	1¼ miles	Octave	T. Pletcher/ J. Velazquez	300,000
July 22	N. Dancer Handicap	Woodbine	1½ miles	Sky Conqueror	D. Banach/ E. Prado	666,014
July 28	Diana Stakes	Saratoga	1⅛ miles	My Typhoon	W. Mott/ E. Castro	520,000
July 29	Jim Dandy Stakes	Saratoga	1⅛ miles	Street Sense	C. Nafzger/ C. Borrel	500,000
July 28	Whitney Handicap	Saratoga	1⅛ miles	Lawyer Ron	T. Pletcher/ J. Velazquez	810,000
Aug 4	West Virginia Derby	Mountaineer	1⅛ miles	Zanjero	S. Asmussen/ S. Bridgmohan	750,000
Aug 4	John C. Mabee Handicap	Del Mar	1⅛ miles	Precious Kitten	R. Frankel/ R. Bejarno	400,000
Aug 5	Haskell Handicap	Monmouth	1⅛ miles	Any Given Sunday	T. Pletcher/ G. Gomez	1,060,000
Aug 11	Arlington Million Stakes	Arlington	1¼ miles	Jumbalaya	C. D. Phillips/ R. Albarado	1,000,000
Aug 11	Beverly D. Stakes	Arlington	1³⁄₁₆ miles	Royal Highness	C. Clement/ R. Douglas	750,000
Aug 11	Secretariat Stakes	Arlington	1¼ miles	Shamdinan	D. O'Neill/ J. Leparoux	400,000
Aug 11	Sword Dancer Invitational	Saratoga	1½ miles	Grand Couturier	R. Ribaudo/ C. Borel	500,000
Aug 19	Alabama Stakes	Saratoga	1¼ miles	Lady Joanne	C. Nafzger/ C. Borel	600,000
Aug 19	Pacific Classic	Del Mar	1¼ miles	Student Council	V. Cerin/ R. Migliore	1,000,000
Aug 26	Travers Stakes	Saratoga	1¼ miles	Street Sense	C. Nafzger/ C. Borel	1,000,000
Sept 2	Woodward Stakes	Saratoga	1⅛ miles	Premium Tap	K. Desormeaux/ J. Kimmel	500,000
Sept 3	Del Mar Derby	Del Mar	1⅛ miles	Lawyer Ron	T. Pletcher/ J. Velazquez	500,000
Sept 9	Man O'War Stakes	Belmont	1⅜ miles	Doctor Dino	R. Gibson/ O. Peslier	500,000
Sept 17	Woodbine Mile	Woodbine	1 mile	Shakespeare	W. Mott/ G. Gomez	973,892
Sept 22	Super Derby	Louisiana Downs	1⅛ miles	Going Ballistic	D. V. Hemel/ M. Berry	515,000
Sept 29	Yellow Ribbon Stakes	Santa Anita	1¼ miles	Nashoba's Key	C. Gaines/ J. Talamo	400,000
Sept 29	Hawthorne Gold Cup	Hawthorne	1¼ miles	Student Council	S. Asmussen/ R. Migliore	500,000

Horses

Horse	Starts	1st	2nd	3rd	Purses ($)
Invasor	4	4	0	0	3,690,000
Bernardini	8	6	1	0	3,060,480
Lava Man	8	7	0	0	2,770,000
Barbaro	5	4	0	0	2,203,200
Miesque's Approval	7	5	1	0	1,906,405

Horse	Starts	1st	2nd	3rd	Purses ($)
Red Rocks	1	1	0	0	1,620,000
Showing Up	9	7	0	1	1,610,500
Bluegrass Cat	7	2	4	0	1,547,500
English Channel	7	4	0	1	1,507,937
Fleet Indian	7	6	0	0	1,473,720

Jockeys

Jockey	Mounts	1st	2nd	3rd	Purses ($)	Win Pct	$ Pct*
Garrett Gomez	1270	261	230	202	20,122,592	.21	.55
Edgar Prado	1303	248	218	190	19,762,813	.19	.50
Victor Espinoza	1285	259	174	191	16,138,004	.20	.49
John Velazquez	944	218	164	112	15,562,828	.23	.52
Ramon Dominguez	1417	385	284	223	14,410,463	.27	.63
Corey Nakatani	735	145	117	109	13,604,210	.20	.50
Eibar Coa	1612	321	265	214	12,743,612	.20	.50
Julien Leparoux	1740	403	282	210	12,491,316	.23	.51
Cornelio Velasquez	1519	237	216	230	12,393,715	.16	.45
Rafael Bejarno	1481	275	273	228	12,369,078	.19	.52

*Percentage in the Money (1st, 2nd, and 3rd).

Trainers

Trainer	Starts	1st	2nd	3rd	Purses ($)	Win Pct	$ Pct*
Todd Pletcher	1168	294	238	140	26,820,243	.25	.58
Doug O'Neill	968	163	131	129	11,247,756	.17	.44
Robert Frankel	585	139	98	96	9,786,673	.24	.57
Scott Lake	2158	528	383	306	9,565,656	.24	.57
Kiaran McLaughlin	406	80	74	44	8,499,166	.20	.49
Bob Baffert	392	91	75	51	8,136,567	.23	.55
Richard Dutrow Jr.	686	156	124	101	7,842,357	.23	.56
William Mott	640	120	88	76	7,831,106	.19	.44
Steven Asmussen	1141	241	198	171	7,715,373	.21	.53
Scott Blasi	998	198	171	158	6,719,236	.20	.53

*Percentage in the Money (1st, 2nd, and 3rd).

Owners

Owner	Starts	1st	2nd	3rd	Purses ($)
Darley Stable	293	63	60	39	6,449,822
Live Oak Plantation	244	59	43	34	5,263,594
Shadwell Stable	133	22	16	15	5,084,218
Stronach Stables	470	114	70	67	4,765,089
Lael Stables	109	28	19	16	4,333,045
Maggi Moss	756	211	127	97	3,956,619
Melnyk Racing Stables	389	87	50	44	3,809,389
J. Paul Reddam	155	28	28	26	3,793,967
Frank Carl Calabrese	388	128	80	51	3,227,507
Robert L. Cole Jr.	456	190	94	50	3,143,922

HARNESS RACING

Major Stakes Races

Late 2006

Date	Race	Location	Winner	Driver/Trainer	Purse ($)
Oct 28	Breeders Crown Two-year-old Filly Trot	Woodbine	Possess The Magic	Ron Pierce/ Jim Takter	516.800
Oct 28	Breeders Crown Two-year-old Filly Pace	Woodbine	Calgary Hanover	Ron Pierce/ Brendan Johnson	500,000
Oct 28	Breeders Crown Two-year-old Colt Trot	Woodbine	Donato Hanover	Ron Pierce/ Steve Elliott	600,000
Oct 28	Breeders Crown Two-year-old Colt Pace	Woodbine	Charley Barley	Mike Lachance/ Doug Miller	600,000
Oct 28	Breeders Crown Three-year-old Filly Trot	Woodbine	Susie's Magic	David S. Miller/ Anthony O'Sullivan	500,000
Oct 28	Breeders Crown Three-year-old Filly Pace	Woodbine	My Little Dragon	Ron Pierce/ Robert McIntosh	500,000
Oct 28	Breeders Crown Three-year-old Colt Trot	Woodbine	Majestic Son	Brian Sears/ Trond Smedshammer	610,000
Oct 28	Breeders Crown Three-year-old Colt Pace	Woodbine	Shark Gesture	Brian Sears/ Brett Pelling	555,000
Dec 2	Goldsmith Maid	Meadowlands	Falls For You	George Brennan/ Mario Zuanetti	410,000
Dec 2	Governor's Cup	Meadowlands	Sutter Hanover	David S. Miller/ Mark Harder	450,000
Dec 2	Valley Victory	Meadowlands	Ogham	David S. Miller/ Blair Burgess	432,700
Dec 2	Three Diamonds	Meadowlands	Isabella Blue Chip	David S. Miller/ George Teague Jr.	439,000

2007 (through September 20)

Date	Race	Location	Winner	Driver/Trainer	Purse ($)
June 16	North America Cup	Mohawk	Tell All	Jody Jamieson/ Blair Burgess	1,410,000
July 7	WR Haughton Memorial	Meadowlands	Mister Big	David Miller/ Virgil Morgan Jr.	650,000
July 14	Meadowlands Pace	Meadowlands	Southwind Lynx	Tim Tetrick/ George Teague Jr.	1,000,000
July 15	Stanley Dancer Trot	Meadowlands	Donato Hanover	Ron Pierce/ Steve Elliott	400,000
Aug 2	Peter Haughton	Meadowlands	Blue York Yankee	Brian Sears/ Trond Smedshammer	467,000
Aug 2	Merrie Annabelle	Meadowlands	Muscovite	Mike Lachance/ Ron Gurfein	458,550
Aug 3	Woodrow Wilson	Meadowlands	Dali	Luc Ouellette/ Duane Marfisi	415,000
Aug 3	Sweetheart	Meadowlands	McArts N Crafts	Stephen Smith/ Haralabos Giannoulis	441,750
Aug 4	Hambletonian	Meadowlands	Donato Hanover	Ron Pierce/ Steve Elliott	1,500,000
Aug 4	Hambletonian Oaks	Meadowlands	Danae	Tim Tetrick/ George Teague Jr.	750,000
Aug 19	Confederation Cup	Flamboro	Laughing Art	Jody Jamieson/ Bill Elliott	510,105
Sept 1	Breeders Crown Open Trot	Mohawk	Equinox Bi	Trevor Ritchie/ Jan Nordin	726,000
Sept 1	Breeders Crown Open Pace	Mohawk	Artistic Fella	Tim Tetric/ Steve Elliott	500,000
Sept 1	Breeders Crown Mare Pace	Mohawk	Moving Pictures	Mark MacDonald/ Casie Coleman	363,000
Sept 1	Breeders Crown Mare Trot	Mohawk	Mystical Sunshine	Daniel Dube/ Christopher Ryder	250,000
Sept 15	Canadian Trotting Classic	Mohawk	Donato Hanover	Ron Pierce/ Steve Elliott	970,000
Sept 20	Little Brown Jug	Delaware, Ohio	Tell All	Jody Jamieson/ Blair Burgess	480,000

The Hambletonian

Raced at The Meadowlands, East Rutherford, N.J., on August 4, 2007

Horse	Driver	PP	¼	½	¾	Stretch	Finish
Donato Hanover..........R. Pierce		2	3o/1H	1/1H	1/NS	1/2	1/1Q
Adrian Chip..............R. Bergh		3	1/1Q	2/1H	3/2Q	2/2	2/1Q
Laddie.....................P. MacDonnel		7	8o/7H	7o/4H	4o/4H	4/4T	3/5T
Please Poppy...........B. Sears		9	9o/9	9o/5T	70/6Q	5/6	4/5T
Great Success........M. Lachance		6	7/7Q	8/5H	8/8	8/8Q	6P5/7H
Pampered Princess..T. Tetrick		4	4/3T	3o/1H	2o/NS	3X/2	X7XP6/8
Too Salty..................D. Miller		5	5/5H	6/4	6/5T	6X/6T	X5XP7/6H
Don't Blink Twice......C. Manzi		1	2/1Q	4/2T	5/4H	X7X/7H	X8X/28H
Xactly Hanover....... A. Miller		8	6o/6Q	5o/3	X9oX/12	DIS	DIS
Flirtin Man.................J. Campbell		X10X/14	DIS	DIS	DIS	DIS	DIS

Times: 0:28.2, 0:58.2, 1:26.0, 1:53.2

The Little Brown Jug

Raced at the Delaware County Fairgrounds, in Delaware, Ohio, on September 20, 2007

Horse	Driver	PP	¼	½	¾	Stretch	Finish
Tell All...............................J. Jamieson		1	1/1Q	1/1	1/T	1/H	1/H
Hot Rod Mindale...........................D. Miller		3	4/4	2o/1	2o/T	2/H	2/H
Always A Virgin..............................B. Sears		2	2/1Q	3/1H	3/2	3/1T	3/T
Won The West.............................G. Grismore		6	3/2T	5/3	5/3H	4/3Q	4/1Q
Southwind Lynx.............................T. Tetrick		4	X5o/4T	4o/2H	4o/2H	5/4H	5/6H
Artist's View ....Y. Gingras		5	6/5Q	7/4H	7/5H	6/6	6/6T
May June Character....................G. Brennan		7	7o/6Q	6o/4	6Xo/4	7X/13	7BE/32
Western Ace ....B. Sears		8	9	9	8	8-8¾	8-12
Charley Baley................................SCR		JG	—	—	—	—	SCR

Times: 0:27.0, 0:56.2, 1:24.4, 1:52.0

2006 Statistical Leaders

2006 Leading Moneywinners by Age, Sex and Gait

Division	Horse	Starts	1st	2nd	3rd	Earnings ($)
2-Year-Old Pacing Colts ....Yankee Skyscraper		9	4	2	0	545,500
2-Year-Old Pacing Fillies.............................Isabella Blue Chip		15	8	3	2	658,583
3-Year-Old Pacing Colts ....Total Truth		19	8	3	4	1,494,222
3-Year-Old Pacing Fillies.............................Darlin's Delight		15	10	3	1	940,352
Older Pacing Horses ....Lis Mara		17	10	5	1	967,485
Older Pacing Mares.....................................Burning Point		28	5	10	10	782,415
2-Year-Old Trotting Colts ....Donato Hanover		9	8	0	1	662,587
2-Year-Old Trotting Fillies...........................Possess The Magic		13	9	3	0	697,540
3-Year-Old Trotting Colts ....Glidemaster		15	8	7	0	1,918,701
3-Year-Old Trotting Fillies ....Passionate Glide		15	13	1	1	1,087,900
Older Trotting Horses...................................Sand Vic		18	10	3	1	1,130,380
Older Trotting Mares ....Peaceful Way		11	5	1	1	709,763

Drivers

Driver	Earnings ($)	Driver	Earnings ($)
Ron Pierce 14,439,087		Jody Jamieson......................................9,005,804	
Brian Sears 12,053,789		John Campbell 8,790,864	
David Miller......................................10,225,938		Tony Morgan...8,478,313	
Mark MacDonald 10,182,217		Cat Manzi...7,977,729	
George Brennan 9,094,354		Yannick Gingras..................................7,187,013	

FOR THE RECORD • Year by Year

THOROUGHBRED RACING

Kentucky Derby

Run at Churchill Downs, Louisville, KY, on the first Saturday in May.

Year	Winner (Margin)	Jockey	Second	Third	Time
1875	Aristides (1)	Oliver Lewis	Volcano	Verdigris	2:37¾
1876	Vagrant (2)	Bobby Swim	Creedmoor	Harry Hill	2:38¼
1877	Baden-Baden (2)	William Walker	Leonard	King William	2:38
1878	Day Star (2)	Jimmie Carter	Himyar	Leveler	2:37¼
1879	Lord Murphy (1)	Charlie Shauer	Falsetto	Strathmore	2:37
1880	Fonso (1)	George Lewis	Kimball	Bancroft	2:37½
1881	Hindoo (4)	Jimmy McLaughin	Lelex	Alfambra	2:40
1882	Apollo (½)	Babe Hurd	Runnymede	Bengal	2:40¼
1883	Leonatus (3)	Billy Donohue	Drake Carter	Lord Raglan	2:43
1884	Buchanan (2)	Isaac Murphy	Loftin	Audrain	2:40¼
1885	Joe Cotton (Neck)	Erskine Henderson	Bersan	Ten Booker	2:37¼
1886	Ben Ali (½)	Paul Duffy	Blue Wing	Free Knight	2:36½
1887	Montrose (2)	Isaac Lewis	Jim Gore	Jacobin	2:39¼
1888	MacBeth II (1)	George Covington	Gallifet	White	2:38¼
1889	Spokane (Nose)	Thomas Kiley	Proctor Knott	Once Again	2:34½
1890	Riley (2)	Isaac Murphy	Bill Letcher	Robespierre	2:45
1891	Kingman (1)	Isaac Murphy	Balgowan	High Tariff	2:52¼
1892	Azra (Nose)	Alonzo Clayton	Huron	Phil Dwyer	2:41½
1893	Lookout (5)	Eddie Kunze	Plutus	Boundless	2:39¼
1894	Chant (2)	Frank Goodale	Pearl Song	Sigurd	2:41
1895	Halma (3)	Soup Perkins	Basso	Laureate	2:37½
1896	Ben Brush (Nose)	Willie Simms	Ben Eder	Semper Ego	2:07¼
1897	Typhoon II (Head)	Buttons Garner	Ornament	Dr. Catlett	2:12½
1898	Plaudit (Neck)	Willie Simms	Lieber Karl	Isabey	2:09
1899	Manuel (2)	Fred Taral	Corsini	Mazo	2:12
1900	Lieut. Gibson (4)	Jimmy Boland	Florizar	Thrive	2:06¼
1901	His Eminence (2)	Jimmy Winkfield	Sannazarro	Driscoll	2:07¾
1902	Alan-a-Dale (Nose)	Jimmy Winkfield	Inventor	The Rival	2:08¾
1903	Judge Himes (¾)	Hal Booker	Early	Bourbon	2:09
1904	Elwood (½)	Frankie Prior	Ed Tierney	Brancas	2:08½
1905	Agile (3)	Jack Martin	Ram's Horn	Layson	2:10¾
1906	Sir Huon (2)	Roscoe Troxler	Lady Navarre	James Reddick	2:08⅕
1907	Pink Star (2)	Andy Minder	Zal	Ovelando	2:12⅗
1908	Stone Street (1)	Arthur Pickens	Sir Cleges	Dunvegan	2:15⅕
1909	Wintergreen (4)	Vincent Powers	Miami	Dr. Barkley	2:08⅕
1910	Donau (½)	Fred Herbert	Joe Morris	Fighting Bob	2:06⅖
1911	Meridian (¾)	George Archibald	Governor Gray	Colston	2:05
1912	Worth (Neck)	Carroll H. Schilling	Duval	Flamma	2:09⅖
1913	Donerail (½)	Roscoe Goose	Ten Point	Gowell	2:04⅘
1914	Old Rosebud (8)	John McCabe	Hodge	Bronzewing	2:03⅖
1915	Regret (2)	Joe Notter	Pebbles	Sharpshooter	2:05⅖
1916	George Smith (Neck)	Johnny Loftus	Star Hawk	Franklin	2:04
1917	Omar Khayyam (2)	Charles Borel	Ticket	Midway	2:04⅗
1918	Exterminator (1)	William Knapp	Escoba	Viva America	2:10⅘
1919	Sir Barton (5)	Johnny Loftus	Billy Kelly	Under Fire	2:09⅘
1920	Paul Jones (Head)	Ted Rice	Upset	On Watch	2:09
1921	Behave Yourself (Head)	Charles Thompson	Black Servant	Prudery	2:04⅕
1922	Morvich (½)	Albert Johnson	Bet Mosie	John Finn	2:04⅗
1923	Zev (1½)	Earl Sande	Martingale	Vigil	2:05⅖
1924	Black Gold (½)	John Mooney	Chilhowee	Beau Butler	2:05⅕
1925	Flying Ebony (1½)	Earl Sande	Captain Hal	Son of John	2:07⅗
1926	Bubbling Over (5)	Albert Johnson	Bagenbaggage	Rock Man	2:03⅘
1927	Whiskery (Head)	Linus McAtee	Osmond	Jock	2:06
1928	Reigh Count (3)	Chick Lang	Misstep	Toro	2:10⅖
1929	Clyde Van Dusen (2)	Linus McAtee	Naishapur	Panchio	2:10⅘
1930	Gallant Fox (2)	Earl Sande	Gallant Knight	Ned O.	2:07⅗
1931	Twenty Grand (4)	Charles Kurtsinger	Sweep All	Mate	2:01⅘

Kentucky Derby *(Cont.)*

Year	Winner (Margin)	Jockey	Second	Third	Time
1932	Burgoo King (5)	Eugene James	Economic	Stepenfetchit	2:05⅕
1933	Brokers Tip (Nose)	Don Meade	Head Play	Charley O.	2:06⅘
1934	Cavalcade (2½)	Mack Garner	Discovery	Agrarian	2:04
1935	Omaha (1½)	Willie Saunders	Roman Soldier	Whiskolo	2:05
1936	Bold Venture (Head)	Ira Hanford	Brevity	Indian Broom	2:03⅗
1937	War Admiral (1¾)	Charles Kurtsinger	Pompoon	Reaping Reward	2:03⅕
1938	Lawrin (1)	Eddie Arcaro	Dauber	Can't Wait	2:04⅘
1939	Johnstown (8)	James Stout	Challedon	Heather Broom	2:03⅗
1940	Gallahadion (1½)	Carroll Bierman	Bimelech	Dit	2:05
1941	Whirlaway (8)	Eddie Arcaro	Staretor	Market Wise	2:01⅖
1942	Shut Out (2½)	Wayne Wright	Alsab	Valdina Orphan	2:04⅖
1943	Count Fleet (3)	John Longden	Blue Swords	Slide Rule	2:04
1944	Pensive (4½)	Conn McCreary	Broadcloth	Stir Up	2:04⅕
1945	Hoop Jr. (6)	Eddie Arcaro	Pot o' Luck	Darby Dieppe	2:07
1946	Assault (8)	Warren Mehrtens	Spy Song	Hampden	2:06⅗
1947	Jet Pilot (Head)	Eric Guerin	Phalanx	Faultless	2:06⅘
1948	Citation (3½)	Eddie Arcaro	Coaltown	My Request	2:05⅖
1949	Ponder (3)	Steve Brooks	Capot	Palestinian	2:04⅕
1950	Middleground (1¼)	William Boland	Hill Prince	Mr. Trouble	2:01⅗
1951	Count Turf (4)	Conn McCreary	Royal Mustang	Ruhe	2:02⅗
1952	Hill Gail (2)	Eddie Arcaro	Sub Fleet	Blue Man	2:01⅗
1953	Dark Star (Head)	Hank Moreno	Native Dancer	Invigorator	2:02
1954	Determine (1½)	Ray York	Hasty Road	Hasseyampa	2:03
1955	Swaps (1½)	Bill Shoemaker	Nashua	Summer Tan	2:01⅘
1956	Needles (¾)	Dave Erb	Fabius	Come On Red	2:03⅖
1957	Iron Liege (Nose)	Bill Hartack	Gallant Man	Round Table	2:02⅕
1958	Tim Tam (½)	Ismael Valenzuela	Lincoln Road	Noureddin	2:05
1959	Tomy Lee (Nose)	Bill Shoemaker	Sword Dancer	First Landing	2:02⅕
1960	Venetian Way (3½)	Bill Hartack	Bally Ache	Victoria Park	2:02⅖
1961	Carry Back (¾)	John Sellers	Crozier	Bass Clef	2:04
1962	Decidedly (2¼)	Bill Hartack	Roman Line	Ridan	2:00⅖
1963	Chateaugay (1¼)	Braulio Baeza	Never Bend	Candy Spots	2:01⅘
1964	Northern Dancer (Neck)	Bill Hartack	Hill Rise	The Scoundrel	2:00
1965	Lucky Debonair (Neck)	Bill Shoemaker	Dapper Dan	Tom Rolfe	2:01⅕
1966	Kauai King (½)	Don Brumfield	Advocator	Blue Skyer	2:02
1967	Proud Clarion (1)	Bobby Ussery	Barbs Delight	Damascus	2:00⅗
1968	Forward Pass (Disq.)	Ismael Valenzuela	Francie's Hat	T.V. Commercial	2:02⅕
1969	Majestic Prince (Neck)	Bill Hartack	Arts and Letters	Dike	2:01⅘
1970	Dust Commander (5)	Mike Manganello	My Dad George	High Echelon	2:03⅖
1971	Canonero II (3¾)	Gustavo Avila	Jim French	Bold Reason	2:03⅕
1972	Riva Ridge (3¼)	Ron Turcotte	No Le Hace	Hold Your Peace	2:01⅘
1973	Secretariat (2½)	Ron Turcotte	Sham	Our Native	1:59⅖
1974	Cannonade (2¼)	Angel Cordero Jr.	Hudson County	Agitate	2:04
1975	Foolish Pleasure (1¾)	Jacinto Vasquez	Avatar	Diabolo	2:02
1976	Bold Forbes (1)	Angel Cordero Jr.	Honest Pleasure	Elocutionist	2:01⅗
1977	Seattle Slew (1¾)	Jean Cruguet	Run Dusty Run	Sanhedrin	2:02⅕
1978	Affirmed (1¼)	Steve Cauthen	Alydar	Believe It	2:01⅕
1979	Spectacular Bid (2¾)	Ronald J. Franklin	General Assembly	Golden Act	2:02⅖
1980	Genuine Risk (1)	Jacinto Vasquez	Rumbo	Jaklin Klugman	2:02
1981	Pleasant Colony (¾)	Jorge Velasquez	Woodchopper	Partez	2:02
1982	Gato Del Sol (2½)	Eddie Delahoussaye	Laser Light	Reinvested	2:02⅕
1983	Sunny's Halo (2)	Eddie Delahoussaye	Desert Wine	Caveat	2:02⅕
1984	Swale (3¼)	Laffit Pincay Jr.	Coax Me Chad	At the Threshold	2:02⅖
1985	Spend A Buck (5)	Angel Cordero Jr.	Stephan's Odyssey	Chief's Crown	2:00⅕
1986	Ferdinand (2¼)	Bill Shoemaker	Bold Arrangement	Broad Brush	2:02⅘
1987	Alysheba (¾)	Chris McCarron	Bet Twice	Avies Copy	2:03⅖
1988	Winning Colors (Neck)	Gary Stevens	Forty Niner	Risen Star	2:02⅕
1989	Sunday Silence (2½)	Pat Valenzuela	Easy Goer	Awe Inspiring	2:05
1990	Unbridled (3½)	Craig Perret	Summer Squall	Pleasant Tap	2:02
1991	Strike the Gold (1¾)	Chris Antley	Best Pal	Mane Minister	2:03
1992	Lil E. Tee (1)	Pat Day	Casual Lies	Dance Floor	2:03
1993	Sea Hero (2½)	Jerry Bailey	Prairie Bayou	Wild Gale	2:02⅖
1994	Go for Gin (2½)	Chris McCarron	Strodes Creek	Blumin Affair	2:03⅗
1995	Thunder Gulch (2¼)	Gary Stevens	Tejano Run	Timber Country	2:01⅕
1996	Grindstone (Nose)	Jerry Bailey	Cavonnier	Prince of Thieves	2:01
1997	Silver Charm (Head)	Gary Stevens	Captain Bodgit	Free House	2:02⅖

Kentucky Derby *(Cont.)*

Year	Winner (Margin)	Jockey	Second	Third	Time
1998	Real Quiet (½)	Kent Desormeaux	Victory Gallop	Indian Charlie	2:02⅒
1999	Charismatic (Neck)	Chris Antley	Menifee	Cat Thief	2:03⅕
2000	Fusaichi Pegasus (1½)	Kent Desormeaux	Aptitude	Impeachment	2:01.12
2001	Monarchos (4¾)	Jorge Chavez	Invisible Ink	Congaree	1:59.97
2002	War Emblem (4)	Victor Espinoza	Proud Citizen	Perfect Drift	2:01.13
2003	Funny Cide (1¾)	Jose Santos	Empire Maker	Peace Rules	2:01.19
2004	Smarty Jones (2¾)	Stewart Elliott	Lion Heart	Imperialism	2:04.06
2005	Giacomo (½)	Mike Smith	Closing Argument	Afleet Alex	2:02.75
2006	Barbaro (1½)	Edgar Prado	Bluegrass Cat	Steppenwolfer	2:01.36
2007	Street Sense (2¼)	Calvin Borel	Hard Spun	Curlin	2:02.17

Note: Distance: 1½ miles (1875–95), 1¼ miles (1896–present).

Preakness

Run at Pimlico Race Course, Baltimore, Md., two weeks after the Kentucky Derby.

Year	Winner (Margin)	Jockey	Second	Third	Time
1873	Survivor (10)	G. Barbee	John Boulger	Artist	2:43
1874	Culpepper (¾)	W. Donohue	King Amadeus	Scratch	2:56½
1875	Tom Ochiltree (2)	L. Hughes	Viator	Bay Final	2:43½
1876	Shirley (4)	G. Barbee	Rappahannock	Algerine	2:44¾
1877	Cloverbrook (4)	C. Holloway	Bombast	Lucifer	2:45½
1878	Duke of Magenta (6)	C. Holloway	Bayard	Albert	2:41¾
1879	Harold (3)	L. Hughes	Jericho	Rochester	2:40½
1880	Grenada (¾)	L. Hughes	Oden	Emily F.	2:40½
1881	Saunterer (½)	T. Costello	Compensation	Baltic	2:40½
1882	Vanguard (Neck)	T. Costello	Heck	Col Watson	2:44½
1883*	Jacobus (4)	G. Barbee	Parnell		2:42½
1884*	Knight of Ellerslie (2)	S. Fisher	Welcher		2:39½
1885	Tecumseh (2)	Jim McLaughlin	Wickham	John C.	2:49
1886	The Bard (3)	S. Fisher	Eurus	Elkwood	2:45
1887	Dunboyne (1)	W. Donohue	Mahoney	Raymond	2:39½
1888	Refund (3)	F. Littlefield	Judge Murray	Glendale	2:49
1889*	Buddhist (8)	W. Anderson	Japhet	*	2:17½
1890*	Montague (3)	W. Martin	Philosophy	Barrister	2:36¾
1894	Assignee (3)	Fred Taral	Potentate	Ed Kearney	1:49¼
1895	Belmar (1)	Fred Taral	April Fool	Sue Kittie	1:50½
1896	Margrave (1)	H. Griffin	Hamilton II	Intermission	1:51
1897	Paul Kauvar (1½)	C. Thorpe	Elkins	On Deck	1:51¼
1898	Sly Fox (2)	C. W. Simms	The Huguenot	Nuto	1:49⅗
1899	Half Time (1)	R. Clawson	Filigrane	Lackland	1:47
1900	Hindus (Head)	H. Spencer	Sarmation	Ten Candles	1:48⅖
1901	The Parader (2)	F. Landry	Sadie S.	Dr. Barlow	1:47⅕
1902	Old England (Nose)	L. Jackson	Major Daingerfield	Namtor	1:45⅘
1903	Flocarline (½)	W. Gannon	Mackey Dwyer	Rightful	1:44⅘
1904	Bryn Mawr (1)	E. Hildebrand	Wotan	Dolly Spanker	1:44⅕
1905	Cairngorm (Head)	W. Davis	Kiamesha	Coy Maid	1:45⅘
1906	Whimsical (4)	Walter Miller	Content	Larabie	1:45
1907	Don Enrique (1)	G. Mountain	Ethon	Zambesi	1:45⅖
1908	Royal Tourist (4)	E. Dugan	Live Wire	Robert Cooper	1:46⅖
1909	Effendi (1)	Willie Doyle	Fashion Plate	Hilltop	1:39⅘
1910	Layminster (½)	R. Estep	Dalhousie	Sager	1:40⅗
1911	Watervale (1)	E. Dugan	Zeus	The Nigger	1:51
1912	Colonel Holloway (5)	C. Turner	Bwana Tumbo	Tipsand	1:56⅗
1913	Buskin (Neck)	J. Butwell	Kleburne	Barnegat	1:53⅖
1914	Holiday (¾)	A. Schuttinger	Brave Cunarder	Defendum	1:53⅘
1915	Rhine Maiden (1½)	Douglas Hoffman	Half Rock	Runes	1:58
1916	Damrosch (1½)	Linus McAtee	Greenwood	Achievement	1:54⅘
1917	Kalitan (2)	E. Haynes	Al M. Dick	Kentucky Boy	1:54⅖
1918*	War Cloud (¾)	Johnny Loftus	Sunny Slope	Lanius	1:53⅗
1918*	Jack Hare, Jr (2)	C. Peak	The Porter	Kate Bright	1:53⅖
1919	Sir Barton (4)	Johnny Loftus	Eternal	Sweep On	1:53
1920	Man o' War (1½)	Clarence Kummer	Upset	Wildair	1:51⅗

Preakness (*Cont.*)

Year	Winner (Margin)	Jockey	Second	Third	Time
1921	Broomspun (¾)	F. Coltiletti	Polly Ann	Jeg	1:54⅕
1922	Pillory (Head)	L. Morris	Hea	June Grass	1:51⅗
1923	Vigil (1¼)	B. Marinelli	General Thatcher	Rialto	1:53⅗
1924	Nellie Morse (1½)	J. Merimee	Transmute	Mad Play	1:57⅕
1925	Coventry (4)	Clarence Kummer	Backbone	Almadel	1:59
1926	Display (Head)	J. Maiben	Blondin	Mars	1:59⅘
1927	Bostonian (½)	A. Abel	Sir Harry	Whiskery	2:01⅗
1928	Victorian (Nose)	Sonny Workman	Toro	Solace	2:00⅕
1929	Dr. Freeland (1)	Louis Schaefer	Minotaur	African	2:01⅗
1930	Gallant Fox (¾)	Earl Sande	Crack Brigade	Snowflake	2:00⅗
1931	Mate (1½)	G. Ellis	Twenty Grand	Ladder	1:59
1932	Burgoo King (Head)	E. James	Tick On	Boatswain	1:59⅘
1933	Head Play (4)	Charles Kurtsinger	Ladysman	Utopian	2:02
1934	High Quest (Nose)	R. Jones	Cavalcade	Discovery	1:58⅕
1935	Omaha (6)	Willie Saunders	Firethorn	Psychic Bid	1:58⅖
1936	Bold Venture (Nose)	George Woolf	Granville	Jean Bart	1:59
1937	War Admiral (Head)	Charles Kurtsinger	Pompoon	Flying Scot	1:58⅖
1938	Dauber (7)	M. Peters	Cravat	Menow	1:59⅘
1939	Challedon (1¼)	George Seabo	Gilded Knight	Volitant	1:59⅘
1940	Bimelech (3)	F. A. Smith	Mioland	Gallahadion	1:58⅗
1941	Whirlaway (5½)	Eddie Arcaro	King Cole	Our Boots	1:58⅘
1942	Alsab (1)	B. James	Requested Sun Again	(dead heat for second)	1:57
1943	Count Fleet (8)	Johnny Longden	Blue Swords	Vincentive	1:57⅖
1944	Pensive (¾)	Conn McCreary	Platter	Stir Up	1:59⅕
1945	Polynesian (2½)	W. D. Wright	Hoop Jr.	Darby Dieppe	1:58⅘
1946	Assault (Neck)	Warren Mehrtens	Lord Boswell	Hampden	2:01⅖
1947	Faultless (1¼)	Doug Dodson	On Trust	Phalanx	1:59
1948	Citation (5½)	Eddie Arcaro	Vulcan's Forge	Boyard	2:02⅖
1949	Capot (Head)	Ted Atkinson	Palestinian	Noble Impulse	1:56
1950	Hill Prince (5)	Eddie Arcaro	Middleground	Dooley	1:59⅕
1951	Bold (7)	Eddie Arcaro	Counterpoint	Alerted	1:56⅖
1952	Blue Man (3½)	Conn McCreary	Jampol	One Count	1:57⅖
1953	Native Dancer (Neck)	Eric Guerin	Jamie K.	Royal Bay Gem	1:57⅘
1954	Hasty Road (Neck)	Johnny Adams	Correlation	Hasseyampa	1:57⅖
1955	Nashua (1)	Eddie Arcaro	Saratoga	Traffic Judge	1:54⅗
1956	Fabius (¾)	Bill Hartack	Needles	No Regrets	1:58⅖
1957	Bold Ruler (2)	Eddie Arcaro	Iron Liege	Inside Tract	1:56⅕
1958	Tim Tam (1½)	I. Valenzuela	Lincoln Road	Gone Fishin'	1:57⅕
1959	Royal Orbit (4)	William Harmatz	Sword Dancer	Dunce	1:57
1960	Bally Ache (4)	Bobby Ussery	Victoria Park	Celtic Ash	1:57⅗
1961	Carry Back (¾)	Johnny Sellers	Globemaster	Crozier	1:57⅗
1962	Greek Money (Nose)	John Rotz	Ridan	Roman Line	1:56⅕
1963	Candy Spots (3½)	Bill Shoemaker	Chateaugay	Never Bend	1:56⅕
1964	Northern Dancer (2¼)	Bill Hartack	The Scoundrel	Hill Rise	1:56⅘
1965	Tom Rolfe (Neck)	Ron Turcotte	Dapper Dan	Hail to All	1:56⅕
1966	Kauai King (1¾)	Don Brumfield	Stupendous	Amberoid	1:55⅖
1967	Damascus (2¼)	Bill Shoemaker	In Reality	Proud Clarion	1:55⅕
1968	Forward Pass (6)	I. Valenzuela	Out of the Way	Nodouble	1:56⅘
1969	Majestic Prince (Head)	Bill Hartack	Arts and Letters	Jay Ray	1:55⅗
1970	Personality (Neck)	Eddie Belmonte	My Dad George	Silent Screen	1:56⅕
1971	Canonero II (1½)	Gustavo Avila	Eastern Fleet	Jim French	1:54
1972	Bee Bee Bee (1¼)	Eldon Nelson	No Le Hace	Key to the Mint	1:55⅗
1973	Secretariat (2½)	Ron Turcotte	Sham	Our Native	1:54⅖
1974	Little Current (7)	Miguel Rivera	Neapolitan Way	Cannonade	1:54⅗
1975	Master Derby (1)	Darrel McHargue	Foolish Pleasure	Diabolo	1:56⅖
1976	Elocutionist (3)	John Lively	Play the Red	Bold Forbes	1:55
1977	Seattle Slew (1½)	Jean Cruguet	Iron Constitution	Run Dusty Run	1:54⅖
1978	Affirmed (Neck)	Steve Cauthen	Alydar	Believe It	1:54⅖
1979	Spectacular Bid (5½)	Ron Franklin	Golden Act	Screen King	1:54⅕
1980	Codex (4¾)	Angel Cordero Jr.	Genuine Risk	Colonel Moran	1:54⅕
1981	Pleasant Colony (1)	Jorge Velasquez	Bold Ego	Paristo	1:54⅗
1982	Aloma's Ruler (½)	Jack Kaenel	Linkage	Cut Away	1:55⅖
1983	Deputed Testamony (2¾)	Donald Miller Jr.	Desert Wine	High Honors	1:55⅖
1984	Gate Dancer (1½)	Angel Cordero Jr.	Play On	Fight Over	1:53⅗
1985	Tank's Prospect (Head)	Pat Day	Chief's Crown	Eternal Prince	1:53⅖
1986	Snow Chief (4)	Alex Solis	Ferdinand	Broad Brush	1:54⅘
1987	Alysheba (½)	Chris McCarron	Bet Twice	Cryptoclearance	1:55⅘

Preakness (Cont.)

Year	Winner (Margin)	Jockey	Second	Third	Time
1988	Risen Star (1¼)	E. Delahoussaye	Brian's Time	Winning Colors	1:56⅕
1989	Sunday Silence (Nose)	Pat Valenzuela	Easy Goer	Rock Point	1:53⅘
1990	Summer Squall (2¼)	Pat Day	Unbridled	Mister Frisky	1:53⅗
1991	Hansel (Head)	Jerry Bailey	Corporate Report	Mane Minister	1:54
1992	Pine Bluff (¾)	Chris McCarron	Alydeed	Casual Lies	1:55⅗
1993	Prairie Bayou (½)	Mike Smith	Cherokee Run	El Bakan	1:56⅗
1994	Tabasco Cat (¾)	Pat Day	Go For Gin	Concern	1:56⅖
1995	Timber Country (½)	Pat Day	Oliver's Twist	Thunder Gulch	1:54⅖
1996	Louis Quatorze (3¼)	Pat Day	Skip Away	Editor's Note	1:53⅖
1997	Silver Charm (Head)	Gary Stevens	Free House	Captain Bodgit	1:54⅖
1998	Real Quiet (2¼)	Kent Desormeaux	Victory Gallop	Classic Cat	1:54⅗
1999	Charismatic (1½)	Chris Antley	Menifee	Badge	1:55⅕
2000	Red Bullet (3¾)	Jerry Bailey	Fusaichi Pegasus	Impeachment	1:56.04
2001	Point Given (2¼)	Gary Stevens	A P Valentine	Congaree	1:55.51
2002	War Emblem (¾)	Victor Espinoza	Magic Weisner	Proud Citizen	1:56.36
2003	Funny Cide (9¾)	Jose Santos	Midway Road	Scrimshaw	1:55.61
2004	Smarty Jones (11½)	Stewart Elliott	Rock Hard Ten	Eddington	1:55.59
2005	Afleet Alex (7)	Jeremy Rose	Scrappy T	Giacomo	1:55.04
2006	Bernardini (5¼)	Javier Castellano	Sweetnorthernsaint	Hemingway's Key	1:54.65
2007	Curlin (Head)	Robby Albarado	Street Sense	Hard Spun	1:53.46

*Preakness was a two-horse race in 1883, '84 and '89. It was not run 1891–1893; and in 1918, it was run in two divisions.

Note: Distance: 1½ miles (1873–88), 1¼ miles (1889), 1½ miles (1890), 1 1/16 miles (1894–1900), 1 mile and 70 yards (1901–1907), 1 1/16 miles (1908), 1 mile (1909–10), 1⅛ miles (1911–24), 1 3/16 miles (1925–present).

Belmont

Run at Belmont Park, Elmont, NY, three weeks after the Preakness Stakes. Held previously at two locations in the Bronx (NY): Jerome Park (1867–1889) and Morris Park (1890–1904).

Year	Winner (Margin)	Jockey	Second	Third	Time
1867	Ruthless (Head)	J. Gilpatrick	De Courcy	Rivoli	3:05
1868	General Duke (2)	R. Swim	Northumberland	Fannie Ludlow	3:02
1869	Fenian (Unknown)	C. Miller	Glenelg	Invercauld	3:04¼
1870	Kingfisher (½)	E. Brown	Foster	Midday	2:59½
1871	Harry Bassett (3)	W. Miller	Stockwood	By-the-Sea	2:56
1872	Joe Daniels (¾)	James Rowe	Meteor	Shylock	2:58¼
1873	Springbok (4)	James Rowe	Count d'Orsay	Strachino	3:01¾
1874	Saxon (Neck)	G. Barbee	Grinstead	Aaron Pennington	2:39½
1875	Calvin (2)	R. Swim	Aristides	Milner	2:40¼
1876	Algerine (Head)	W. Donahue	Fiddlestick	Barricade	2:40½
1877	Cloverbrook (1)	C. Holloway	Loiterer	Baden-Baden	2:46
1878	Duke of Magenta (2)	L. Hughes	Bramble	Sparta	2:43½
1879	Spendthrift (5)	S. Evans	Monitor	Jericho	2:42¾
1880	Grenada (½)	L. Hughes	Ferncliffe	Turenne	2:47
1881	Saunterer (Neck)	T. Costello	Eole	Baltic	2:47
1882	Forester (5)	James McLaughlin	Babcock	Wyoming	2:43
1883	George Kinney (2)	James McLaughlin	Trombone	Renegade	2:42½
1884	Panique (½)	James McLaughlin	Knight of Ellerslie	Himalaya	2:42
1885	Tyrant (3½)	Paul Duffy	St. Augustine	Tecumseh	2:43
1886	Inspector B (1)	James McLaughlin	The Bard	Linden	2:41
1887*	Hanover (28-32)	James McLaughlin	Oneko		2:43½
1888*	Sir Dixon (12)	James McLaughlin	Prince Royal		2:40¼
1889	Eric (Head)	W. Hayward	Diable	Zephyrus	2:47
1890	Burlington (1)	S. Barnes	Devotee	Padishah	2:07¾
1891	Foxford (Neck)	E. Garrison	Montana	Laurestan	2:08¾
1892*	Patron (Unknown)	W. Hayward	Shellbark		2:17
1893	Comanche (Head)	Willie Simms	Dr. Rice	Rainbow	1:53¼
1894	Henry of Navarre (2-4)	Willie Simms	Prig	Assignee	1:56½
1895	Belmar (Head)	Fred Taral	Counter Tenor	Nanki Pooh	2:11½
1896	Hastings (Neck)	H. Griffin	Handspring	Hamilton II	2:24½
1897	Scottish Chieftain (1)	J. Scherrer	On Deck	Octagon	2:23¼
1898	Bowling Brook (8)	P. Littlefield	Previous	Hamburg	2:32
1899	Jean Bereaud (Head)	R. R. Clawson	Half Time	Glengar	2:23

Belmont *(Cont.)*

Year	Winner (Margin)	Jockey	Second	Third	Time
1900	Ildrim (Head)	N. Turner	Petrucio	Missionary	2:21½
1901	Commando (½)	H. Spencer	The Parader	All Green	2:21
1902	Masterman (2)	John Bullmann	Ranald	King Hanover	2:22½
1903	Africander (2)	John Bullmann	Whorler	Red Knight	2:23⅕
1904	Delhi (3½)	George Odom	Graziallo	Rapid Water	2:06⅗
1905	Tanya (1/2)	E. Hildebrand	Blandy	Hot Shot	2:08
1906	Burgomaster (4)	L. Lyne	The Quail	Accountant	2:20
1907	Peter Pan (1)	G. Mountain	Superman	Frank Gill	Unknown
1908	Colin (Head)	Joe Notter	Fair Play	King James	Unknown
1909	Joe Madden (8)	E. Dugan	Wise Mason	Donald MacDonald	2:21⅗
1910*	Sweep (6)	J. Butwell	Duke of Ormonde		2:22
1913	Prince Eugene (½)	Roscoe Troxler	Rock View	Flying Fairy	2:18
1914	Luke McLuke (8)	M. Buxton	Gainer	Charlestonian	2:20
1915	The Finn (4)	G. Byrne	Half Rock	Pebbles	2:18⅖
1916	Friar Rock (3)	E. Haynes	Spur	Churchill	2:22
1917	Hourless (10)	J. Butwell	Skeptic	Wonderful	2:17⅘
1918	Johren (2)	Frank Robinson	War Cloud	Cum Sah	2:20⅖
1919	Sir Barton (5)	Johnny Loftus	Sweep On	Natural Bridge	2:17⅖
1920*	Man o' War (20)	Clarence Kummer	Donnacona		2:14⅕
1921	Grey Lag (3)	Earl Sande	Sporting Blood	Leonardo II	2:16⅘
1922	Pillory (2)	C. H. Miller	Snob II	Hea	2:18⅘
1923	Zev (1½)	Earl Sande	Chickvale	Rialto	2:19
1924	Mad Play (2)	Earl Sande	Mr. Mutt	Modest	2:18⅘
1925	American Flag (8)	Albert Johnson	Dangerous	Swope	2:16⅘
1926	Crusader (1)	Albert Johnson	Espino	Haste	2:32⅕
1927	Chance Shot (1½)	Earl Sande	Bois de Rose	Flambino	2:32⅖
1928	Vito (3)	Clarence Kummer	Genie	Diavolo	2:33⅕
1929	Blue Larkspur (¾)	Mack Garner	African	Jack High	2:32⅘
1930	Gallant Fox (3)	Earl Sande	Whichone	Questionnaire	2:31⅗
1931	Twenty Grand (10)	Charles Kurtsinger	Sun Meadow	Jamestown	2:29⅗
1932	Faireno (1½)	T. Malley	Osculator	Flag Pole	2:32⅘
1933	Hurryoff (1½)	Mack Garner	Nimbus	Union	2:32⅗
1934	Peace Chançe (6)	W. D. Wright	High Quest	Good Goods	2:29⅕
1935	Omaha (1½)	Willie Saunders	Firethorn	Rosemont	2:30⅗
1936	Granville (Nose)	James Stout	Mr. Bones	Hollyrood	2:30
1937	War Admiral (3)	Charles Kurtsinger	Sceneshifter	Vamoose	2:28⅗
1938	Pasteurized (Neck)	James Stout	Dauber	Cravat	2:29⅖
1939	Johnstown (5)	James Stout	Belay	Gilded Knight	2:29⅗
1940	Bimelech (¾)	F. A. Smith	Your Chance	Andy K	2:29⅗
1941	Whirlaway (2½)	Eddie Arcaro	Robert Morris	Yankee Chance	2:31
1942	Shut Out (2)	Eddie Arcaro	Alsab	Lochinvar	2:29⅕
1943	Count Fleet (25)	Johnny Longden	Fairy Manhurst	Deseronto	2:28⅕
1944	Bounding Home (½)	G. L. Smith	Pensive	Bull Dandy	2:32⅕
1945	Pavot (5)	Eddie Arcaro	Wildlife	Jeep	2:30⅕
1946	Assault (3)	Warren Mehrtens	Natchez	Cable	2:30⅘
1947	Phalanx (5)	R. Donoso	Tide Rips	Tailspin	2:29⅖
1948	Citation (8)	Eddie Arcaro	Better Self	Escadru	2:28⅕
1949	Capot (½)	Ted Atkinson	Ponder	Palestinian	2:30⅕
1950	Middleground (1)	William Boland	Lights Up	Mr. Trouble	2:28⅗
1951	Counterpoint (4)	D. Gorman	Battlefield	Battle Morn	2:29
1952	One Count (2½)	Eddie Arcaro	Blue Man	Armageddon	2:30⅕
1953	Native Dancer (Neck)	Eric Guerin	Jamie K.	Royal Bay Gem	2:38⅗
1954	High Gun (Neck)	Eric Guerin	Fisherman	Limelight	2:30⅘
1955	Nashua (9)	Eddie Arcaro	Blazing Count	Portersville	2:29
1956	Needles (Neck)	David Erb	Career Boy	Fabius	2:29⅘
1957	Gallant Man (8)	Bill Shoemaker	Inside Tract	Bold Ruler	2:26⅗
1958	Cavan (6)	Pete Anderson	Tim Tam	Flamingo	2:30⅕
1959	Sword Dancer (¾)	Bill Shoemaker	Bagdad	Royal Orbit	2:28⅖
1960	Celtic Ash (5½)	Bill Hartack	Venetian Way	Disperse	2:29⅗
1961	Sherluck (2¼)	Braulio Baeza	Globemaster	Guadalcanal	2:29⅕
1962	Jaipur (Nose)	Bill Shoemaker	Admiral's Voyage	Crimson Satan	2:28⅘
1963	Châteaugay (2½)	Braulio Baeza	Candy Spots	Choker	2:30⅕
1964	Quadrangle (2)	Manuel Ycaza	Roman Brother	Northern Dancer	2:28⅖
1965	Hail to All (Neck)	John Sellers	Tom Rolfe	First Family	2:28⅖
1966	Amberold (2½)	William Boland	Buffle	Advocator	2:29⅗
1967	Damascus (2½)	Bill Shoemaker	Cool Reception	Gentleman	2:28⅘

Belmont (Cont.)

Year	Winner (Margin)	Jockey	Second	Third	Time
1968	Stage Door Johnny (1¼)	Hellodoro Gustines	Forward Pass	James Call Me Prince	2:27⅕
1969	Arts and Letters (5½)	Braulio Baeza	Majestic Prince	Dike	2:28⅘
1970	High Echelon (¾)	John L. Rotz	Needles N Pins	Naskra	2:34
1971	Pass Catcher (¾)	Walter Blum	Jim French	Bold Reason	2:30⅖
1972	Riva Ridge (7)	Ron Turcotte	Ruritania	Cloudy Dawn	2:28
1973	Secretariat (31)	Ron Turcotte	Twice a Prince	My Gallant	2:24
1974	Little Current (7)	Miguel A. Rivera	Jolly Johu	Cannonade	2:29⅕
1975	Avatar (Neck)	Bill Shoemaker	Foolish Pleasure	Master Derby	2:28⅕
1976	Bold Forbes (Neck)	Angel Cordero Jr.	McKenzie Bridge	Great Contractor	2:29
1977	Seattle Slew (4)	Jean Cruguet	Run Dusty Run	Sanhedrin	2:29⅗
1978	Affirmed (Head)	Steve Cauthen	Alydar	Darby Creek Road	2:26⅘
1979	Coastal (3¼)	Ruben Hernandez	Golden Act	Spectacular Bid	2:28⅗
1980	Temperence Hill (2)	Eddie Maple	Genuine Risk	Rockhill Native	2:29⅘
1981	Summing (Neck)	George Martens	Highland Blade	Pleasant Colony	2:29
1982	Conquistador Cielo (14½)	Laffit Pincay, Jr.	Gato Del Sol	Illuminate	2:28⅕
1983	Caveat (3½)	Laffit Pincay Jr.	Slew o'Gold	Barberstown	2:27⅘
1984	Swale (4)	Laffit Pincay Jr.	Pine Circle	Morning Bob	2:27⅕
1985	Creme Fraiche (½)	Eddie Maple	Stephan's Odyssey	Chief's Crown	2:27
1986	Danzig Connection (1¼)	Chris McCarron	Johns Treasure	Ferdinand	2:29⅘
1987	Bet Twice (14)	Craig Perret	Cryptoclearance	Gulch	2:28⅕
1988	Risen Star (14¾)	Eddie Delahoussaye	Kingpost	Brian's Time	2:26⅖
1989	Easy Goer (8)	Pat Day	Sunday Silence	Le Voyageur	2:26
1990	Go and Go (8¼)	Michael Kinane	Thirty Six Red	Baron de Vaux	2:27⅕
1991	Hansel (Head)	Jerry Bailey	Strike the Gold	Mane Minister	2:28
1992	A.P. Indy (¾)	Eddie Delahoussaye	My Memoirs	Pine Bluff	2:26
1993	Colonial Affair (2¼)	Julie Krone	Kissin Kris	Wild Gale	2:29⅘
1994	Tabasco Cat (2)	Pat Day	Go For Gin	Strodes Creek	2:26⅘
1995	Thunder Gulch (2)	Gary Stevens	Star Standard	Citadeed	2:32
1996	Editor's Note (1)	Rene Douglas	Skip Away	My Flag	2:28⅘
1997	Touch Gold (¾)	Chris McCarron	Silver Charm	Free House	2:28⅘
1998	Victory Gallop (Nose)	Gary Stevens	Real Quiet	Thomas Jo	2:28⅘
1999	Lemon Drop Kid (Head)	Jose Santos	Vision and Verse	Charismatic	2:27⅘
2000	Commendable (1½)	Pat Day	Aptitude	Unshaded	2:31.19
2001	Point Given (12¼)	Gary Stevens	A P Valentine	Monarchos	2:26.56
2002	Sarava (½)	Edgar Prado	Medaglia d'Oro	Sunday Break	2:29.71
2003	Empire Maker (¾)	Jerry Bailey	Ten Most Wanted	Funny Cide	2:28.26
2004	Birdstone (1)	Edgar Prado	Smarty Jones	Royal Assault	2:27.59
2005	Afleet Alex(4¾)	Jeremy Rose	Andromeda's Hero	Nolan's Cat	2:28.75
2006	Jazil (1¼)	Fernando Jara	Bluegrass Cat	Sunriver	2:27.86
2007	Rags to Riches (Head)	John Velazquez	Curlin	Tiago	2:28.74

*Belmont was a two-horse race in 1887, '88, '92, 1910 and '20; and was not held in 1911–1912.
Note: Distance: 1 mile 5 furlongs (1867–89), 1¼ miles (1890–1905), 1⅜ miles (1906–25), 1½ miles (1926–present).

Triple Crown Winners

Year	Horse	Jockey	Owner	Trainer
1919	Sir Barton	John Loftus	J. K. L. Ross	H. G. Bedwell
1930	Gallant Fox	Earle Sande	Belair Stud	James Fitzsimmons
1935	Omaha	William Saunders	Belair Stud	James Fitzsimmons
1937	War Admiral	Charles Kurtsinger	Samuel D. Riddle	George Conway
1941	Whirlaway	Eddie Arcaro	Calumet Farm	Ben Jones
1943	Count Fleet	John Longden	Mrs J. D. Hertz	Don Cameron
1946	Assault	Warren Mehrtens	King Ranch	Max Hirsch
1948	Citation	Eddie Arcaro	Calumet Farm	Jimmy Jones
1973	Secretariat	Ron Turcotte	Meadow Stable	Lucien Laurin
1977	Seattle Slew	Jean Cruguet	Karen L. Taylor	William H. Turner Jr.
1978	Affirmed	Steve Cauthen	Harbor View Farm	Laz Barrera

Awards

Horse of the Year

Year	Horse	Owner	Trainer	Breeder
1936	Granville	Belair Stud	James Fitzsimmons	Belair Stud
1937	War Admiral	Samuel D. Riddle	George Conway	Mrs. Samuel D. Riddle
1938	Seabiscuit	Charles S. Howard	Tom Smith	Wheatley Stable
1939	Challedon	William L. Brann	Louis J. Schaefer	Branncastle Farm
1940	Challedon	William L. Brann	Louis J. Schaefer	Branncastle Farm
1941	Whirlaway	Calumet Farm	Ben Jones	Calumet Farm
1942	Whirlaway	Calumet Farm	Ben Jones	Calumet Farm
1943	Count Fleet	Mrs. John D. Hertz	Don Cameron	Mrs. John D. Hertz
1944	Twilight Tear	Calumet Farm	Ben Jones	Calumet Farm
1945	Busher	Louis B. Mayer	George Odom	Idle Hour Stock Farm
1946	Assault	King Ranch	Max Hirsch	King Ranch
1947	Armed	Calumet Farm	Jimmy Jones	Calumet Farm
1948	Citation	Calumet Farm	Jimmy Jones	Calumet Farm
1949	Capot	Greentree Stable	John M. Gaver Sr.	Greentree Stable
1950	Hill Prince	C.T. Chenery	Casey Hayes	C.T. Chenery
1951	Counterpoint	C.V. Whitney	Syl Veitch	C.V. Whitney
1952	One Count	Mrs. W. M. Jeffords	O. White	W M. Jeffords
1953	Tom Fool	Greentree Stable	John M. Gaver Sr.	D.A. Headley
1954	Native Dancer	A.G. Vanderbilt	Bill Winfrey	A.G. Vanderbilt
1955	Nashua	Belair Stud	James Fitzsimmons	Belair Stud
1956	Swaps	Ellsworth-Galbreath	Mesh Tenney	R. Ellsworth
1957	Bold Ruler	Wheatley Stable	James Fitzsimmons	Wheatley Stable
1958	Round Table	Kerr Stables	Willy Molter	Claiborne Farm
1959	Sword Dancer	Brookmeade Stable	Elliott Burch	Brookmeade Stable
1960	Kelso	Bohemia Stable	C. Hanford	Mrs. R.C. duPont
1961	Kelso	Bohemia Stable	C. Hanford	Mrs. R.C. duPont
1962	Kelso	Bohemia Stable	C. Hanford	Mrs. R.C. duPont
1963	Kelso	Bohemia Stable	C. Hanford	Mrs. R.C. duPont
1964	Kelso	Bohemia Stable	C. Hanford	Mrs. R.C. duPont
1965	Roman Brother	Harbor View Stable	Burley Parke	Ocala Stud
1966	Buckpasser	Ogden Phipps	Eddie Neloy	Ogden Phipps
1967	Damascus	Mrs. E. W. Bancroft	Frank Y. Whiteley Jr.	Mrs. E. W. Bancroft
1968	Dr. Fager	Tartan Stable	John A. Nerud	Tartan Farms
1969	Arts and Letters	Rokeby Stable	Elliott Burch	Paul Mellon
1970	Fort Marcy	Rokeby Stable	Elliott Burch	Paul Mellon
1971	Ack Ack	E.E. Fogelson	Charlie Whittingham	H.F. Guggenheim
1972	Secretariat	Meadow Stable	Lucien Laurin	Meadow Stud
1973	Secretariat	Meadow Stable	Lucien Laurin	Meadow Stud
1974	Forego	Lazy F Ranch	Sherrill W. Ward	Lazy F Ranch
1975	Forego	Lazy F Ranch	Sherrill W. Ward	Lazy F Ranch
1976	Forego	Lazy F Ranch	Frank Y. Whiteley Jr.	Lazy F Ranch
1977	Seattle Slew	Karen L. Taylor	Billy Turner Jr.	B.S. Castleman
1978	Affirmed	Harbor View Farm	Laz Barrera	Harbor View Farm
1979	Affirmed	Harbor View Farm	Laz Barrera	Harbor View Farm
1980	Spectacular Bid	Hawksworth Farm	Bud Delp	Mmes. Gilmore & Jason
1981	John Henry	Dotsam Stable	Ron McAnally and Lefty Nickerson	Golden Chance Farm
1982	Conquistador Cielo	H. de Kwiatkowski	Woody Stephens	L.E. Landoli
1983	All Along	Daniel Wildenstein	P.L. Biancone	Dayton
1984	John Henry	Dotsam Stable	Ron McAnally	Golden Chance Farm
1985	Spend a Buck	Hunter Farm	Cam Gambolati	Irish Hill & R.W. Harper
1986	Lady's Secret	Mr. & Mrs. Eugene Klein	D. Wayne Lukas	R.H. Spreen
1987	Ferdinand	Mrs. H.B. Keck	Charlie Whittingham	H.B. Keck
1988	Alysheba	D. & P. Scharbauer	Jack Van Berg	Preston Madden
1989	Sunday Silence	Gaillard, Hancock, & Whittingham	Charlie Whittingham	Oak Cliff Thoroughbreds
1990	Criminal Type	Calumet Farm	D. Wayne Lukas	Calumet Farm
1991	Black Tie Affair	Jeffrey Sullivan	Ernie Poulos	Stephen D. Peskoff
1992	A.P. Indy	Tomonori Tsurumaki	Neil Drysdale	W.S. Farish & W.S. Kilroy
1993	Kotashaan	La Presle Farm	Richard Mandella	La Presle Farm
1994	Holy Bull	Jimmy Croll	Jimmy Croll	Pelican Stable
1995	Cigar	Allen E. Paulson	William Mott	Allen E. Paulson
1996	Cigar	Allen E. Paulson	William Mott	Allen E. Paulson
1997	Favorite Trick	Joseph LaCombe	William Mott	Mr. & Mrs. M.L. Wood
1998	Skip Away	Carolyn Hine	Hubert Hine	Anna Marie Barnhart
1999	Charismatic	Robert & Beverly Lewis	D. Wayne Lukas	William Farish/Partners
2000	Tiznow	Michael Cooper and Cecilia Straub-Rubens	Jay M. Robbins	Cecilia Straub-Rubens

Horse of the Year (Cont.)

Year	Horse	Owner	Trainer	Breeder
2001	Point Given	The Thoroughbred Corp.	Bob Baffert	The Thoroughbred Corp.
2002	Azeri	Allen Paulson Living Trust	Laura de Seroux	Allen Paulson
2003	Mineshaft	William Farish	Neil Howard	William Farish
2004	Ghostzapper	Frank Stronach	Bobby Frankel	Frank Stronach
2005	Saint Liam	William & Susan Warren Jr.	Richard Dutrow Jr.	Edward P. Evans
2006	Invasor	Shadwell Stable	Kiarin McLaughlin	Haras Clausan

Note: From 1936 to 1970, the *Daily Racing Form* annually selected a "Horse of the Year." In 1971 the *Daily Racing Form*, with the Thoroughbred Racing Association and the National Turf Writers Association, jointly created the Eclipse Awards.

Eclipse Award Winners

2-YEAR-OLD COLT

1971	Riva Ridge
1972	Secretariat
1973	Protagonist
1974	Foolish Pleasure
1975	Honest Pleasure
1976	Seattle Slew
1977	Affirmed
1978	Spectacular Bid
1979	Rockhill Native
1980	Lord Avie
1981	Deputy Minister
1982	Roving Boy
1983	Devil's Bag
1984	Chief's Crown
1985	Tasso
1986	Capote
1987	Forty Niner
1988	Easy Goer
1989	Rhythm
1990	Fly So Free
1991	Arazi
1992	Gilded Time
1993	Dehere
1994	Timber Country
1995	Maria's Mon
1996	Boston Harbor
1997	Favorite Trick
1998	Answer Lively
1999	Anees
2000	Macho Uno
2001	Johannesburg
2002	Vindication
2003	Action This Day
2004	Declan's Moon
2005	Stevie Wonderboy
2006	Street Sense

2-YEAR-OLD FILLY

1971	Numbered Account
1972	La Prevoyante
1973	Talking Picture
1974	Ruffian
1975	Dearly Precious
1976	Sensational
1977	Lakeville Miss
1978	Candy Eclair, It's in the Air
1979	Smart Angle
1980	Heavenly Cause
1981	Before Dawn
1982	Landaluce
1983	Althea
1984	Outstandingly
1985	Family Style
1986	Brave Raj
1987	Epitome
1988	Open Mind

2-YEAR-OLD FILLY (CONT.)

1989	Go for Wand
1990	Meadow Star
1991	Pleasant Stage
1992	Eliza
1993	Phone Chatter
1994	Flanders
1995	Golden Attraction
1996	Storm Song
1997	Countess Diana
1998	Silverbulletday
1999	Chilukki
2000	Caressing
2001	Tempera
2002	Storm Flag Flying
2003	Halfbridled
2004	Sweet Catomine
2005	Folklore
2006	Dreaming of Anna

3-YEAR-OLD COLT

1971	Canonero II
1972	Key to the Mint
1973	Secretariat
1974	Little Current
1975	Wajima
1976	Bold Forbes
1977	Seattle Slew
1978	Affirmed
1979	Spectacular Bid
1980	Temperence Hill
1981	Pleasant Colony
1982	Conquistador Cielo
1983	Slew o' Gold
1984	Swale
1985	Spend A Buck
1986	Snow Chief
1987	Alysheba
1988	Risen Star
1989	Sunday Silence
1990	Unbridled
1991	Hansel
1992	A.P. Indy
1993	Prairie Bayou
1994	Holy Bull
1995	Thunder Gulch
1996	Skip Away
1997	Silver Charm
1998	Real Quiet
1999	Charismatic
2000	Tiznow
2001	Point Given
2002	War Emblem
2003	Funny Cide
2004	Smarty Jones
2005	Afleet Alex
2006	Bernardini

CHAMPION TURF HORSE

1971	Run the Gantlet (3)
1972	Cougar II (6)
1973	Secretariat (3)
1974	Dahlia (4)
1975	Snow Knight (4)
1976	Youth (3)
1977	Johnny D (3)
1978	Mac Diarmida (3)

CHAMPION MALE TURF HORSE

1979	Bowl Game (5)
1980	John Henry (5)
1981	John Henry (6)
1982	Perrault (5)
1983	John Henry (8)
1984	John Henry (9)
1985	Cozzene (4)
1986	Manila (3)
1987	Theatrical (5)
1988	Sunshine Forever (3)
1989	Steinlen (5)
1990	Itsallgreektome (3)
1991	Tight Spot (4)
1992	Sky Classic (5)
1993	Kotashaan (5)
1994	Paradise Creek (5)
1995	Northern Spur (4)
1996	Singspiel (4)
1997	Chief Bearhart (4)
1998	Buck's Boy (5)
1999	Daylami (5)
2000	Kalanisi (4)
2001	Fantastic Light (5)
2002	High Chaparral (3)
2003	High Chaparral (4)
2004	Kitten's Joy
2005	Leroidesanimaux
2006	Miesque's Approval

CHAMPION FEMALE TURF HORSE

1979	Trillion (5)
1980	Just a Game II (4)
1981	De La Rose (3)
1982	April Run (4)
1983	All Along (4)
1984	Royal Heroine (4)
1985	Pebbles (4)
1986	Estrapade (6)
1987	Miesque (3)
1988	Miesque (4)
1989	Brown Bess (7)
1990	Laugh and Be Merry (5)
1991	Miss Alleged (4)
1992	Flawlessly (4)
1993	Flawlessly (5)

Eclipse Award Winners *(Cont.)*

CHAMPION FEM. TURF HORSE *(CONT.)*

1994 ....Hatoof (5)
1995 ....Possibly Perfect (5)
1996 ....Wandesta (5)
1997 ....Ryafan (3)
1998 ....Fiji (4)
1999 ....Soaring Softly (4)
2000 ....Perfect Sting (4)
2001 ....Banks Hill (3)
2002 ....Golden Apples (4)
2003 ....Islington (4)
2004 ....Ouija Board
2005 ....Intercontinental
2006 ....Ouija Board

3-YEAR-OLD FILLY

1971 ....Turkish Trousers
1972 ....Susan's Girl
1973 ....Desert Vixen
1974 ....Chris Evert
1975 ....Ruffian
1976 ....Revidere
1977 ....Our Mims
1978 ....Tempest Queen
1979 ....Davona Dale
1980 ....Genuine Risk
1981 ....Wayward Lass
1982 ....Christmas Past
1983 ....Heartlight No. One
1984 ....Life's Magic
1985 ....Mom's Command
1986 ....Tiffany Lass
1987 ....Sacahuaista
1988 ....Winning Colors
1989 ....Open Mind
1990 ....Go for Wand
1991 ....Dance Smartly
1992 ....Saratoga Dew
1993 ....Hollywood Wildcat
1994 ....Heavenly Prize
1995 ....Serena's Song
1996 ....Yank's Music
1997 ....Ajina
1998 ....Banshee Breeze
1999 ....Silverbulletday
2000 ....Surfside
2001 ....Xtra Heat
2002 ....Farda Amiga
2003 ....Bird Town
2004 ....Ashado
2005 ....Smuggler
2006 ....Wait a While

OLDER COLT, HORSE OR GELDING

1971 ....Ack Ack (5)
1972 ....Autobiography (4)
1973 ....Riva Ridge (4)
1974 ....Forego (4)
1975 ....Forego (5)
1976 ....Forego (6)
1977 ....Forego (7)
1978 ....Seattle Slew (4)
1979 ....Affirmed (4)
1980 ....Spectacular Bid (4)
1981 ....John Henry (6)
1982 ....Lemhi Gold (4)
1983 ....Bates Motel (4)

OLD. COLT, HORSE OR GELD. *(CONT.)*

1984 ....Slew o'Gold (4)
1985 ....Vanlandingham (4)
1986 ....Turkoman (4)
1987 ....Ferdinand (4)
1988 ....Alysheba (4)
1989 ....Blushing John (4)
1990 ....Criminal Type (5)
1991 ....Black Tie Affair (5)
1992 ....Pleasant Tap (5)
1993 ....Bertrando (4)
1994 ....The Wicked North (5)
1995 ....Cigar (5)
1996 ....Cigar (6)
1997 ....Skip Away (4)
1998 ....Skip Away (5)
1999 ....Victory Gallop (4)
2000 ....Lemon Drop Kid (4)
2001 ....Tiznow (4)
2002 ....Left Bank (5)
2003 ....Mineshaft (4)
2004 ....Ghostzapper (4)
2005 ....Saint Liam
2006 ....Invasor

OLDER FILLY OR MARE

1971 ....Shuvee (5)
1972 ....Typecast (6)
1973 ....Susan's Girl (4)
1974 ....Desert Vixen (4)
1975 ....Susan's Girl (6)
1976 ....Proud Delta (4)
1977 ....Cascapedia (4)
1978 ....Late Bloomer (4)
1979 ....Waya (5)
1980 ....Glorious Song (4)
1981 ....Relaxing (5)
1982 ....Track Robbery (6)
1983 ....Ambassador of Luck (4)
1984 ....Princess Rooney (4)
1985 ....Life's Magic (4)
1986 ....Lady's Secret (4)
1987 ....North Sider (5)
1988 ....Personal Ensign (4)
1989 ....Bayakoa (5)
1990 ....Bayakoa (6)
1991 ....Queena (5)
1992 ....Paseana (5)
1993 ....Paseana (6)
1994 ....Sky Beauty (4)
1995 ....Inside Information (4)
1996 ....Jewel Princess (4)
1997 ....Hidden Lake (4)
1998 ....Escena (5)
1999 ....Beautiful Pleasure (4)
2000 ....Riboletta (6)
2001 ....Gourmet Girl (6)
2002 ....Azeri (4)
2003 ....Azeri (5)
2004 ....Azeri (6)
2005 ....Ashado
2006 ....Fleet Indian

STEEPLECHASE OR HURDLE HORSE

1971 ....Shadow Brook (7)
1972 ....Soothsayer (5)
1973 ....Athenian Idol (5)

STEEPLECHASE OR HURDLE HORSE *(CONT.)*

1974 .....Gran Kan (8)
1975 .....Life's Illusion (4)
1976 .....Straight & True (6)
1977 .....Cafe Prince (7)
1978 .....Cafe Prince (8)
1979 ....Martie's Anger (4)
1980 .....Zaccio (4)
1981 .....Zaccio (5)
1982 .....Zaccio (6)
1983 .....Flatterer (4)
1984 .....Flatterer (5)
1985 .....Flatterer (6)
1986 .....Flatterer (7)
1987 .....Inlander (6)
1988 .....Jimmy Lorenzo (6)
1989 .....Highland Bud (4)
1990 .....Morley Street (7)
1991 .....Morley Street (8)
1992 .....Lonesome Glory (4)
1993 .....Lonesome Glory (5)
1994 .....Warn Spell (6)
1995 .....Lonesome Glory (7)
1996 .....Correggio (5)
1997 .....Lonesome Glory (9)
1998 .....Flat Top (5)
1999 .....Lonesome Glory (11)
2000 .....All Gong (6)
2001 .....Pompeyo (7)
2002 .....Flat Top (9)
2003 .....McDynamo (6)
2004 .....Hirapour (8)
2005 .....McDynamo
2006 .....McDynamo

SPRINTER

1971 ....Ack Ack (5)
1972 ....Chou Croute (4)
1973 ....Shecky Greene (3)
1974 ....Forego (4)
1975 ....Gallant Bob (3)
1976 ....My Juliet (4)
1977 ....What a Summer (4)
1978 ....Dr. Patches (4)
              J.O. Tobin (4)
1979 ....Star de Naskra (4)
1980 ....Plugged Nickel (3)
1981 ....Guilty Conscience (5)
1982 ....Gold Beauty (3)
1983 ....Chinook Pass (4)
1984 ....Eillo (4)
1985 ....Precisionist (4)
1986 ....Smile (4)
1987 ....Groovy (4)
1988 ....Gulch (4)
1989 ....Safely Kept (4)
1990 ....Housebuster (3)
1991 ....Housebuster (4)
1992 ....Rubiano (5)
1993 ....Cardmania (7)
1994 ....Cherokee Run (4)
1995 ....Not Surprising (4)
1996 ....Lit de Justice (6)
1997 ....Smoke Glacken (3)
1998 ....Reraise (3)
1999 ....Artax (4)
2000 .....Kone Gold (6)

Note: Number in parentheses is horse's age.

Eclipse Award Winners (Cont.)

SPRINTER (CONT.)
2001.....Squirtle Squirt (3)
2002.....Orientate (4)
2003.....Aldebaran (5)
2004.....Speightstown (6)
2005.....Lost in the Fog
2006.....Thor's Echo

OUTSTANDING OWNER
1971.....Mr. & Mrs. E. E. Fogleson
1974.....Dan Lasater
1975.....Dan Lasater
1976.....Dan Lasater
1977.....Maxwell Gluck
1978.....Harbor View Farm
1979.....Harbor View Farm
1980.....Mr. & Mrs. Bertram
1981.....Dotsam Stable
1982.....Viola Sommer
1983.....John Franks
1984.....John Franks
1985.....Mr. & Mrs. Eugene Klein
1986.....Mr. & Mrs. Eugene Klein
1987.....Mr. & Mrs. Eugene Klein
1988.....Ogden Phipps
1989.....Ogden Phipps
1990.....Frances Genter
1991.....Sam-Son Farm
1992.....Juddmonte Farms
1993.....John Franks
1994.....John Franks
1995.....Allen E. Paulson
1996.....Allen E. Paulson
1997.....Carolyn Hine
1998.....Frank Stronach
1999.....Frank Stronach
2000.....Frank Stronach
2001.....Richard Englander
2002.....Richard Englander
2003.....Juddmonte Farms
2004.....Frank Stronach
2005.....Michael Gill
2006.....Darley Stable/Lael Stables

OUTSTANDING TRAINER
1971.....Charlie Whittingham
1972.....Lucien Laurin
1973.....H. Allen Jerkens
1974.....Sherrill Ward
1975.....Steve DiMauro
1976.....Lazaro Barrera
1977.....Lazaro Barrera
1978.....Lazaro Barrera
1979.....Lazaro Barrera
1980.....Bud Delp
1981.....Ron McAnally
1982.....Charlie Whittingham
1983.....Woody Stephens
1984.....Jack Van Berg
1985.....D. Wayne Lukas
1986.....D. Wayne Lukas
1987.....D. Wayne Lukas
1988.....Claude R. McGaughey III
1989.....Charlie Whittingham
1990.....Carl Nafzger
1991.....Ron McAnally
1992.....Ron McAnally

OUTSTANDING TRAINER (CONT.)
1993.....Bobby Frankel
1994.....D. Wayne Lukas
1995.....William Mott
1996.....William Mott
1997.....Bob Baffert
1998.....Bob Baffert
1999.....Bob Baffert
2000.....Robert Frankel
2001.....Robert Frankel
2002.....Robert Frankel
2003.....Robert Frankel
2004.....Todd Pletcher
2005.....Todd Pletcher
2006.....Todd Pletcher

OUTSTANDING JOCKEY
1971.....Laffit Pincay Jr.
1972.....Braulio Baeza
1973.....Laffit Pincay Jr
1974.....Laffit Pincay Jr
1975.....Braulio Baeza
1976.....Sandy Hawley
1977.....Steve Cauthen
1978.....Darrel McHargue
1979.....Laffit Pincay Jr
1980.....Chris McCarron
1981.....Bill Shoemaker
1982.....Angel Cordero Jr
1983.....Angel Cordero Jr
1984.....Pat Day
1985.....Laffit Pincay Jr
1986.....Pat Day
1987.....Pat Day
1988.....Jose Santos
1989.....Kent Desormeaux
1990.....Craig Perret
1991.....Pat Day
1992.....Kent Desormeaux
1993.....Mike Smith
1994.....Mike Smith
1995.....Jerry Bailey
1996.....Jerry Bailey
1997.....Jerry Bailey
1998.....Gary Stevens
1999.....Jorge Chavez
2000.....Jerry Bailey
2001.....Jerry Bailey
2002.....Jerry Bailey
2003.....Jerry Bailey
2004.....John Velasquez
2005.....John Velasquez
2006.....Edgar Prado

OUTSTANDING APPRENTICE JOCKEY
1971.....Gene St. Leon
1972.....Thomas Wallis
1973.....Steve Valdez
1974.....Chris McCarron
1975.....Jimmy Edwards
1976.....George Martens
1977.....Steve Cauthen
1978.....Ron Franklin
1979.....Cash Asmussen
1980.....Frank Lovato Jr.
1981.....Richard Migliore

OUTSTANDING APPRENTICE JOCKEY (CONT.)
1982.....Alberto Delgado
1983.....Declan Murphy
1984.....Wesley Ward
1985.....Art Madrid Jr.
1986.....Allen Stacy
1987.....Kent Desormeaux
1988.....Steve Capanas
1989.....Michael Luzzi
1990.....Mark Johnston
1991.....Mickey Walls
1992.....Jesus A. Bracho
1993.....Juan Umana
1994.....Dale Beckner
1995.....Ramon Perez
1996.....Neil Pozansky
1997.....Phil Teator
         Roberto Rosado
1998.....Shaun Bridgmohan
1999.....Ariel Smith
2000.....Tyler Baze
2001.....Jeremy Rose
2002.....Ryan Fogelsonger
2003.....Eddie Castro
2004.....Brian Hernandez
2005.....Emma-Jayne Wilson
2006.....Julien Leparoux

OUTSTANDING BREEDER
1974.....John W. Galbreath
1975.....Fred W. Hooper
1976.....Nelson Bunker Hunt
1977.....Edward Plunket Taylor
1978.....Harbor View Farm
1979.....Claiborne Farm
1980.....Mrs. Henry D. Paxson
1981.....Golden Chance Farm
1982.....Fred W. Hooper
1983.....Edward Plunket Taylor
1984.....Claiborne Farm
1985.....Nelson Bunker Hunt
1986.....Paul Mellon
1987.....Nelson Bunker Hunt
1988.....Ogden Phipps
1989.....North Ridge Farm
1990.....Calumet Farm
1991.....John and Betty Mabee
1992.....William S. Farish III
1993.....Allen Paulson
1994.....William T. Young
1995.....Juddmonte Farms
1996.....Fansworth Farms
1997.....Golden Eagle Farm
1998.....John and Betty Mabee
1999.....William Farish/Partners
2000.....Frank Stronach/Adena
         Springs
2001.....Juddmonte Farms
2002.....Juddmonte Farms
2003.....Juddmonte Farms
2004.....Frank Stronach/Adena
         Springs
2005.....Adena Springs Farms
2006.....Adena Springs Farms

Awards (*Cont.*)

Eclipse Award Winners (*Cont.*)

AWARD OF MERIT

1976.....Jack J. Dreyfus
1977.....Steve Cauthen
1978.....Ogden Phipps
1979.....Frank E. Kilroe
1980.....John D. Schapiro
1981.....Bill Shoemaker
1984.....John Gaines
1985.....Keene Daingerfield
1986.....Herman Cohen
1987.....J. B. Faulconer
1988.....John Forsythe
1989.....Michael P. Sandler

AWARD OF MERIT (*CONT.*)

1991.....Fred W. Hooper
1994.....Alfred G. Vanderbilt
1996.....Allen E. Paulson
2002.....Howard Battle
Ogden Phipps

SPECIAL AWARD

1971.....Robert J. Kleberg
1974.....Charles Hatton
1976.....Bill Shoemaker
1980.....John T. Landry
Pierre E. Bellocq (Peb)

SPECIAL AWARD (*CONT.*)

1984.....C. V. Whitney
1985.....Arlington Park
1987.....Anheuser-Busch
1988.....Edward J. DeBartolo Sr.
1989.....Richard Duchossois
1994.....John Longden
Edward Arcaro
1998.....Oak Tree Racing Association
2002.....Keeneland Library

Note: Special Award and Award of Merit, for long-term and/or outstanding service to the industry, not presented annually.

Breeders' Cup

Location: Hollywood 1984, '87, '97; Aqueduct 1985; Santa Anita 1986, '93, '03; Churchill Downs 1988, '91, '98,'00; Gulfstream (FL) 1989, '92, '99; Belmont 1990, '95, '01; Woodbine (Toronto) 1996; Arlington 2002.

Juveniles

Year	Winner (Margin)	Jockey	Second	Third	Time
1984	Chief's Crown (¾)	Don MacBeth	Tank's Prospect	Spend a Buck	1:36⅕
1985	Tasso (Nose)	Laffit Pincay Jr.	Storm Cat	Scat Dancer	1:36⅕
1986	Capote (1¼)	Laffit Pincay Jr.	Qualify	Alysheba	1:43⅘
1987	Success Express (1¾)	Jose Santos	Regal Classic	Tejano	1:35⅕
1988	Is It True (1¼)	Laffit Pincay Jr.	Easy Goer	Tagel	1:46⅗
1989	Rhythm (2)	Craig Perret	Grand Canyon	Slavic	1:43⅗
1990	Fly So Free (3)	Jose Santos	Take Me Out	Lost Mountain	1:43⅖
1991	Arazi (4¾)	Pat Valenzuela	Bertrando	Snappy Landing	1:44⅗
1992	Gilded Time (¾)	Chris McCarron	It'sali'lknownfact	River Special	1:43⅖
1993	Brocco (5)	Gary Stevens	Blumin Affair	Tabasco Cat	1:42⅘
1994	Timber Country (½)	Pat Day	Eltish	Tejano Run	1:44⅖
1995	Unbridled's Song (Neck)	Mike Smith	Hennessy	Editor's Note	1:41⅗
1996	Boston Harbor (Neck)	Jerry Bailey	Acceptable	Ordway	1:43⅖
1997	Favorite Trick (5½)	Pat Day	Dawson's Legacy	Nationalore	1:41⅗
1998	Answer Lively (Head)	Jerry Bailey	Aly's Alley	Cat Thief	1:44
1999	Anees (2½)	Gary Stevens	Chief Seattle	High Yield	1:42.29
2000	Macho Uno (Nose)	Jerry Bailey	Point Given	Street Cry	1:42.05
2001	Johannesburg (1¼)	Michael Kinane	Repent	Siphonic	1:42.27
2002	Vindication (2¾)	Mike Smith	Kafwain	Hold That Tiger	1:49.61
2003	Action This Day (2¼)	David Flores	Minister Eric	Chapel Royal	1:43.62
2004	Wilko (¾)	Frankie Dettori	Afleet Alex	Sun King	1:42.09
2005	Stevie Wonderboy(1¼)	Garrett Gomez	Henny Hughes	First Samuria	1:41.64
2006	Street Sense (10)	Calvin Borel	Circular Quay	Great Hunter	1:42.59

Note: One mile (1984–85, '87), 1¹⁄₁₆ miles (1986 and 1988–2001, '03), 1⅛ miles (2002).

Juvenile Fillies

Year	Winner (Margin)	Jockey	Second	Third	Time
1984	Outstandingly*	Walter Guerra	Dusty Heart	Fine Spirit	1:37⅘
1985	Twilight Ridge (1)	Jorge Velasquez	Family Style	Steal a Kiss	1:35⅘
1986	Brave Raj (5½)	Pat Valenzuela	Tappiano	Saros Brig	1:43⅕
1987	Epitome (Nose)	Pat Day	Jeanne Jones	Dream Team	1:36⅖
1988	Open Mind (1¾)	Angel Cordero Jr.	Darby Shuffle	Lea Lucinda	1:46⅗
1989	Go for Wand (2¾)	Randy Romero	Sweet Roberta	Stella Madrid	1:44⅕
1990	Meadow Star (5)	Jose Santos	Private Treasure	Dance Smartly	1:44
1991	Pleasant Stage (Neck)	Eddie Delahoussaye	La Spia	Cadillac Women	1:46⅖
1992	Eliza (1½)	Pat Valenzuela	Educated Risk	Boots 'n Jackie	1:42⅘
1993	Phone Chatter (Head)	Laffit Pincay	Sardula	Heavenly Prize	1:43
1994	Flanders (Head)	Pat Day	Serena's Song	Stormy Blues	1:45⅕
1995	My Flag (½)	Jerry Bailey	Cara Rafaela	Golden Attraction	1:42⅖
1996	Storm Song (4½)	Craig Perret	Love That Jazz	Critical Factor	1:43⅗
1997	Countess Diana (8½)	Shane Sellers	Career Collection	Primaly	1:42⅕

*In 1984, winner Fran's Valentine dq'd.

Juvenile Fillies *(Cont.)*

Year	Winner (Margin)	Jockey	Second	Third	Time
1998	Silverbulletday (½)	Gary Stevens	Excellent Meeting	Three Ring	1:43⅗
1999	Cash Run (1¼)	Jerry Bailey	Chilukki	Surfside	1:43.31
2000	Caressing (½)	John Velazquez	Platinum Tiara	Shes a Devil Due	1:42.72
2001	Tempera (1½)	David Flores	Imperial Gesture	Bella Bellucci	1:41.49
2002	Storm Flag Flying (½)	John Velazquez	Composure	Santa Catarina	1:49.60
2003	Halfbridled (2½)	Julie Krone	Ashado	Victory U.S.A.	1:42.75
2004	Sweet Catomine (3¾)	Corey Nakatani	Balleto	Runway Model	1:41.65
2005	Folklore (1¼)	Edgar Prado	Wild Fit	Original Spin	1:42.75
2006	Dreaming of Anna (1½)	Rene Douglas	Octave	Cotton Blossom	1:43.81

Note: One mile (1984-85, '87), 1¹⁄₁₆ miles (1986 and 1988-01, '03), 1⅛ miles ('02).

Sprint

Year	Winner (Margin)	Jockey	Second	Third	Time
1984	Eillo (Nose)	Craig Perret	Commemorate	Fighting Fit	1:10⅕
1985	Precisionist (¾)	Chris McCarron	Smile	Mt. Livermore	1:08⅖
1986	Smile (1¼)	Jacinto Vasquez	Pine Tree Lane	Bedside Promise	1:08⅖
1987	Very Subtle (4)	Pat Valenzuela	Groovy	Exclusive Enough	1:08⅘
1988	Gulch (¾)	Angel Cordero Jr	Play the King	Afleet	1:10⅖
1989	Dancing Spree (Neck)	Angel Cordero Jr	Safely Kept	Dispersal	1:09
1990	Safely Kept (Neck)	Craig Perret	Dayjur	Black Tie Affair	1:09⅗
1991	Sheikh Albadou (Neck)	Pat Eddery	Pleasant Tap	Robyn Dancer	1:09⅕
1992	Thirty Slews (Neck)	Eddie Delahoussaye	Meafara	Rubiano	1:08⅕
1993	Cardmania (Neck)	Eddie Delahoussaye	Meafara	Gilded Time	1:08⅗
1994	Cherokee Run (Head)	Mike Smith	Soviet Problem	Cardmania	1:09⅖
1995	Desert Stormer (Neck)	Kent Desormeaux	Mr. Greeley	Lit de Justice	1:09
1996	Lit de Justice (1¼)	Corey Nakatani	Paying Dues	Honour and Glory	1:08⅗
1997	Elmhurst (½)	Corey Nakatani	Hesabull	Bet on Sunshine	1:08
1998	Reraise (2)	Corey Nakatani	Grand Slam	Kona Gold	1:09
1999	Artax (½)	Jorge Chavez	Kona Gold	Big Jag	1:07.89
2000	Kona Gold (½)	Alex Solis	Honest Lady	Bet on Sunshine	1:07.77
2001	Squirtle Squirt (½)	Jerry Bailey	Xtra Heat	Caller One	1:08.41
2002	Orientate (½)	Jerry Bailey	Thunderello	Crafty C.T.	1:08.89
2003	Cajun Beat (2¼)	Cornelio Velasquez	Bluesthestandard	Shake You Down	1:07.95
2004	Speightstown (1¼)	John Velasquez	Kela	My Cousin Matt	1:08.11
2005	Silver Train (Head)	Edgar Prado	Taste of Paradise	Lion Tamer	1:08.86
2006	Thor's Echo (4)	Corey Nakatani	Friendly Island	Nightmare Affair	1:08.80

Note: Six furlongs (since 1984).

Mile

Year	Winner (Margin)	Jockey	Second	Third	Time
1984	Royal Heroine (1½)	Fernando Toro	Star Choice	Cozzene	1:32⅗
1985	Cozzene (2¼)	Walter Guerra	Al Mamoon*	Shadeed	1:35
1986	Last Tycoon (Head)	Yves St-Martin	Palace Music	Fred Astaire	1:35⅕
1987	Miesque (3½)	Freddie Head	Show Dancer	Sonic Lady	1:32⅘
1988	Miesque (4)	Freddie Head	Steinlen	Simply Majestic	1:38⅗
1989	Steinlen (¾)	Jose Santos	Sabona	Most Welcome	1:37⅕
1990	Royal Academy (Neck)	Lester Piggott	Itsallgreektome	Priolo	1:35⅕
1991	Opening Verse (2¼)	Pat Valenzuela	Val de Bois	Star of Cozzene	1:37⅖
1992	Lure (3)	Mike Smith	Paradise Creek	Brief Truce	1:32⅘
1993	Lure (2¼)	Mike Smith	Ski Paradise	Fourstars Allstar	1:33⅖
1994	Barathea (Head)	Frankie Dettori	Johann Quatz	Unfinished Symph	1:34⅖
1995	Ridgewood Pearl (2)	John Murtagh	Fastness	Sayyedati	1:43⅗
1996	Da Hoss (1½)	Gary Stevens	Spinning World	Same Old Wish	1:35⅘
1997	Spinning World (2)	Cash Asmussen	Geri	Decorated Hero	1:32⅘
1998	Da Hoss (Head)	John Velazquez	Hawksley Hill	Labeeb	1:35⅕
1999	Silic (Neck)	Corey Nakatani	Tuzla	Docksider	1:34.26
2000	War Chant (Neck)	Gary Stevens	North East Bound	Dansili	1:34.67
2001	Val Royal (1¾)	Jose Valdivia	Forbidden Apple	Bach	1:32.05
2002	Domedriver (¾)	Thierry Thulliez	Rock of Gibraltar	Good Journey	1:36.92
2003	Six Perfections (¾)	Jerry Bailey	Touch of the Blues	Century City	1:33.86
2004	Singletary (½)	David Flores	Antonius Pius	Six Perfections	1:36.90
2005	Artie Schiller (¾)	Garrett Gomez	Leroidesanimaux	Gorella	1:36:10
2006	Miesque's Approval (2¾)	Eddie Castro	Aragorn	Badge of Silver	1:34.75

*2nd place finisher Palace Music was disqualified for interference and placed 9th.

Breeders' Cup *(Cont.)*

Distaff

Year	Winner (Margin)	Jockey	Second	Third	Time
1984	Princess Rooney (7)	Eddie Delahoussaye	Life's Magic	Adored	2:02⅖
1985	Life's Magic (6¼)	Angel Cordero Jr.	Lady's Secret	Dontstop themusic	2:02
1986	Lady's Secret (2½)	Pat Day	Fran's Valentine	Outstandingly	2:01⅕
1987	Sacahuista (2¼)	Randy Romero	Clabber Girl	Oueee Bebe	2:02⅘
1988	Personal Ensign (Nose)	Randy Romero	Winning Colors	Goodbye Halo	1:52
1989	Bayakoa (1½)	Laffit Pincay Jr.	Gorgeous	Open Mind	1:47⅖
1990	Bayakoa (6¾)	Laffit Pincay Jr.	Colonial Waters	Valay Maid	1:49⅕
1991	Dance Smarty (½)	Pat Day	Versailles Treaty	Brought to Mind	1:50⅘
1992	Paseana (4)	Chris McCarron	Versailles Treaty	Magical Maiden	1:48
1993	Hollywood Wildcat (Nose)	Eddie Delahoussaye	Paseana	Re Toss	1:48⅕
1994	One Dreamer (Neck)	Gary Stevens	Heavenly Prize	Miss Dominique	1:50⅗
1995	Inside Information (13½)	Mike Smith	Heavenly Prize	Lakeway	1:46
1996	Jewel Princess (1½)	Corey Nakatani	Serena's Song	Different	1:48⅖
1997	Ajina (2)	Mike Smith	Sharp Cat	Escena	1:47⅕
1998	Escena (Nose)	Gary Stevens	Banshee Breeze	Keeper Hill	1:49⅘
1999	Beautiful Pleasure (¾)	Jorge Chavez	Banshee Breeze	Heritage of Gold	1:47.56
2000	Spain (1½)	Victor Espinoza	Surfside	Heritage of Gold	1:47.66
2001	Unbridled Elaine (head)	Pat Day	Spain	Too Item Limit	1:49.21
2002	Azeri (5)	Mike Smith	Farda Amiga	Imperial Gesture	1:48.64
2003	Adoration (4½)	Pat Valenzuela	Elloluv	Got Koko	1:49.17
2004	Ashado (1¼)	J. Velasquez	Storm Flag Flying	Stellar Jane	1:48.26
2005	Pleasant Home (9¼)	Cornelio Velasquez	Society Selection	Ashado	1:48.34
2006	Round Pond (4¼)	Edgar Prado	Happy Ticket	Balletto	1:50.50

Note: 1¼ miles (1984–87), 1⅛ miles (since 1988).

Turf

Year	Winner (Margin)	Jockey	Second	Third	Time
1984	Lashkari (Neck)	Yves St. Martin	All Along	Raami	2:25⅕
1985	Pebbles (Neck)	Pat Eddery	Strawberry Rd II	Mourjane	2:27
1986	Manila (Neck)	Jose Santos	Theatrical	Estrapade	2:25⅖
1987	Theatrical (½)	Pat Day	Trempolino	Village Star II	2:24⅖
1988	Great Communicator (½)	Ray Sibille	Sunshine Forever	Indian Skimmer	2:35⅕
1989	Prized (Head)	Eddie Delahoussaye	Sierra Roberta	Star Lift	2:28
1990	In the Wings (½)	Gary Stevens	With Approval	El Senor	2:29⅗
1991	Miss Alleged (2)	Eric Legrix	Itsallgreektome	Quest for Fame	2:30⅘
1992	Fraise (Nose)	Pat Valenzuela	Sky Classic	Quest For Fame	2:24
1993	Kotashaan (½)	Kent Desormeaux	Bien Bien	Luazar	2:25
1994	Tikkanen (1½)	Mike Smith	Hatoof	Paradise Creek	2:26⅖
1995	Northern Spur (Neck)	Chris McCarron	Freedom Cry	Carnegie	2:42
1996	Pilsudski (1¼)	Walter Swinburn	Singspiel	Swain	2:30⅕
1997	Chief Bearhart (¾)	Jose Santos	Borgia	Flag Down	2:23⅘
1998	Buck's Boy (1¼)	Shane Sellers	Yagli	Dushyantor	2:28⅘
1999	Daylami (2½)	Frankie Dettori	Royal Anthem	Buck's Boy	2:24.73
2000	Kalanisi (½)	John Murtagh	Quiet Resolve	John's Call	2:26.96
2001	Fantastic Light (¾)	Frankie Dettori	Milan	Timboroa	2:24.36
2002	High Chaparral (1¼)	Michael Kinane	With Anticipation	Falcon Flight	2:30.14
2003	High Chaparral/Johar	Michael Kinane/Alex Solis		Falbrav	2:24.24
2004	Better Talk Now (1¼)	R. Dominguez	Kitten's Joy	Powerscourt	2:29.15
2005	Intercontinental (1¼)	Rafael Bejarano	Ouija Board	Film Maker	2:02.34
2006	Red Rocks (½)	Frankie Dettori	Better Talk Now	English Channel	2:27.32

Note: 1½ miles.

Classic

Year	Winner (Margin)	Jockey	Second	Third	Time
1984	Wild Again (Head)	Pat Day	Slew o' Gold*	Gate Dancer	2:03⅖
1985	Proud Truth (Head)	Jorge Velasquez	Gate Dancer	Turkoman	2:00⅘
1986	Skywalker (1¼)	Laffit Pincay Jr.	Turkoman	Precisionist	2:00⅖
1987	Ferdinand (Nose)	Bill Shoemaker	Alysheba	Judge Angelucci	2:01⅖
1988	Alysheba (Nose)	Chris McCarron	Seeking the Gold	Waquoit	2:04⅘
1989	Sunday Silence (½)	Chris McCarron	Easy Goer	Blushing John	2:00⅕
1990	Unbridled (1)	Pat Day	Ibn Bey	Thirty Six Red	2:02⅕
1991	Black Tie Affair (1¼)	Jerry Bailey	Twilight Agenda	Unbridled	2:02⅘
1992	A.P. Indy (2)	Eddie Delahoussaye	Pleasant Tap	Jolypha	2:00⅕
1993	Arcangues (2)	Jerry Bailey	Bertrando	Kissin Kris	2:00⅘
1994	Concern (Neck)	Jerry Bailey	Tabasco Cat	Dramatic Gold	2:02⅖
1995	Cigar (2½)	Jerry Bailey	L'Carriere	Unaccounted For	1:59⅖
1996	Alphabet Soup (Nose)	Chris McCarron	Louis Quatorze	Cigar	2:01

Classic *(Cont.)*

Year	Winner (Margin)	Jockey	Second	Third	Time
1997	Skip Away (6)	Mike Smith	Deputy Commander	Dowty	1:59½
1998	Awesome Again (¾)	Pat Day	Silver Charm	Swain	2:02
1999	Cat Thief (1¼)	Pat Day	Budroyale	Golden Missile	1:59.52
2000	Tiznow (Neck)	Chris McCarron	Giant's Causeway	Captain Steve	2:00.75
2001	Tiznow (Nose)	Chris McCarron	Sakhee	Albert the Great	2:00.62
2002	Volponi (6½)	Jose Santos	Medaglia d'Oro	Milwaukee Brew	2:01.39
2003	Pleasantly Perfect (1½)	Alex Solis	Medaglia d'Oro	Dynever	1:59.88
2004	Ghostzapper (3)	J. Castellano	Roses in May	Perfectly	1:59.02
2005	Saint Liam (1)	Jerry Bailey	Flower Alley	Perfect	2:01.49
2006	Invasor (1)	Fernando Jara	Bernardini	Castellano	2:02.18

*2nd place finisher Gate Dancer was disqualified for interference and placed 3rd. Note: 1¼ miles.

England's Triple Crown Winners

England's Triple Crown consists of the Two Thousand Guineas, held at Newmarket; the Epsom Derby, held at Epsom Downs; and the St. Leger Stakes, held at Doncaster.

Year	Horse	Owner	Year	Horse	Owner
1853	West Australian	Mr. Bowes	1900	Diamond Jubilee	Prince of Wales
1865	Gladiateur	F. DeLagrange	1903	*Rock Sand	J. Miller
1866	Lord Lyon	R. Sutton	1915	Pommern	S. Joel
1886	*Ormonde	Duke of Westminster	1917	Gay Crusader	Mr. Fairie
1891	Common	†F. Johnstone	1918	Gainsborough	Lady James
1893	Isinglass	H. McCalmont			Douglas
1897	Galtee More	J. Gubbins	1935	*Bahram	Aga Khan
1899	Flying Fox	Duke of Westminster	1970	‡Nijinsky II	C. W. Engelhard

*Imported into United States. †Raced in name of Lord Alington in Two Thousand Guineas. ‡Canadian-bred.

Annual Leaders

Horse—Money Won

Year	Horse	Age	Starts	1st	2nd	3rd	Winnings ($)
1919	Sir Barton	3	13	8	3	2	88,250
1920	Man o' War	3	11	11	0	0	166,140
1921	Morvich	2	11	11	0	0	115,234
1922	Pillory	3	7	4	1	1	95,654
1923	Zev	3	14	12	1	0	272,008
1924	Sarzen	3	12	8	1	1	95,640
1925	Pompey	2	10	7	2	0	121,630
1926	Crusader	3	15	9	4	0	166,033
1927	Anita Peabody	2	7	6	0	1	111,905
1928	High Strung	2	6	5	0	0	153,590
1929	Blue Larkspur	3	6	4	1	0	153,450
1930	Gallant Fox	3	10	9	1	0	308,275
1931	Gallant Flight	2	7	7	0	0	219,000
1932	Gusto	3	16	4	3	2	145,940
1933	Singing Wood	2	9	3	2	2	88,050
1934	Cavalcade	3	7	6	1	0	111,235
1935	Omaha	3	9	6	1	0	142,255
1936	Granville	3	11	7	3	0	110,295
1937	Seabiscuit	4	15	11	2	2	168,580
1938	Stagehand	3	15	8	2	3	189,710
1939	Challedon	3	15	9	2	3	184,535
1940	Bimelech	3	7	4	2	1	110,005
1941	Whirlaway	3	20	13	5	2	272,386
1942	Shut Out	3	12	8	2	0	238,872
1943	Count Fleet	3	6	6	0	0	174,055
1944	Pavot	2	8	8	0	0	179,040
1945	Busher	3	13	10	2	1	273,735

Horse—Money Won *(Cont.)*

Year	Horse	Age	Starts	1st	2nd	3rd	Winnings ($)
1946	Assault	3	15	8	2	3	424,195
1947	Armed	6	17	11	4	1	376,325
1948	Citation	3	20	19	1	0	709,470
1949	Ponder	3	21	9	5	2	321,825
1950	Noor	5	12	7	4	1	346,940
1951	Counterpoint	3	15	7	2	1	250,525
1952	Crafty Admiral	4	16	9	4	1	277,225
1953	Native Dancer	3	10	9	1	0	513,425
1954	Determine	3	15	10	3	2	328,700
1955	Nashua	3	12	10	1	1	752,550
1956	Needles	3	8	4	2	0	440,850
1957	Round Table	3	22	15	1	3	600,383
1958	Round Table	4	20	14	4	0	662,780
1959	Sword Dancer	3	13	8	4	0	537,004
1960	Bally Ache	3	15	10	3	1	445,045
1961	Carry Back	3	16	9	1	3	565,349
1962	Never Bend	2	10	7	1	2	402,969
1963	Candy Spots	3	12	7	2	1	604,481
1964	Gun Bow	4	16	8	4	2	580,100
1965	Buckpasser	2	11	9	1	0	568,096
1966	Buckpasser	3	14	13	1	0	669,078
1967	Damascus	3	16	12	3	1	817,941
1968	Forward Pass	3	13	7	2	0	546,674
1969	Arts and Letters	3	14	8	5	1	555,604
1970	Personality	3	18	8	2	1	444,049
1971	Riva Ridge	2	9	7	0	0	503,263
1972	Droll Role	4	19	7	3	4	471,633
1973	Secretariat	3	12	9	2	1	860,404
1974	Chris Evert	3	8	5	1	2	551,063
1975	Foolish Pleasure	3	11	5	4	1	716,278
1976	Forego	6	8	6	1	1	401,701
1977	Seattle Slew	3	7	6	0	1	641,370
1978	Affirmed	3	11	8	2	0	901,541
1979	Spectacular Bid	3	12	10	1	1	1,279,334
1980	Temperence Hill	3	17	8	3	1	1,130,452
1981	John Henry	6	10	8	0	0	1,798,030
1982	Perrault	5	8	4	1	2	1,197,400
1983	All Along	4	7	4	1	1	2,138,963
1984	Slew o'Gold	4	6	5	1	0	2,627,944
1985	Spend A Buck	3	7	5	1	1	3,552,704
1986	Snow Chief	3	9	6	1	1	1,875,200
1987	Alysheba	3	10	3	3	1	2,511,156
1988	Alysheba	4	9	7	1	0	3,808,600
1989	Sunday Silence	3	9	7	2	0	4,578,454
1990	Unbridled	3	11	4	3	2	3,718,149
1991	Dance Smartly	3	8	8	0	0	2,876,821
1992	A.P. Indy	3	7	5	0	1	2,622,560
1993	Kotashaan	3	10	6	3	0	2,619,014
1994	Paradise Creek	5	11	8	2	1	2,610,187
1995	Cigar	5	10	10	0	0	4,819,800
1996	Cigar	6	8	5	2	1	4,910,000
1997	Skip Away	4	11	4	5	2	4,089,000
1998	Silver Charm	4	9	6	2	0	4,696,506
1999	Almutawakel	4	4	1	1	1	3,290,000
2000	Dubai Millennium	4	1	1	0	0	3,600,000
2001	Captain Steve	4	6	2	1	1	4,201,200
2002	War Emblem	4	10	5	0	0	3,455,000
2003	Pleasantly Perfect	5	4	2	0	1	2,470,000
2004	Smarty Jones	3	7	6	1	0	7,563,535
2005	Saint Liam	5	6	4	1	0	3,696,960
2006	Invasor	4	4	4	0	0	3,690,000

Trainer—Money Won

Year	Trainer	Wins	Winnings ($)	Year	Trainer	Wins	Winnings ($)
1908	James Rowe, Sr.	50	284,335	1958	Willie Molter	69	1,116,544
1909	Sam Hildreth	73	123,942	1959	Willie Molter	71	847,290
1910	Sam Hildreth	84	148,010	1960	Hirsch Jacobs	97	748,349
1911	Sam Hildreth	67	49,418	1961	Jimmy Jones	62	759,856
1912	John F. Schorr	63	58,110	1962	Mesh Tenney	58	1,099,474
1913	James Rowe, Sr.	18	45,936	1963	Mesh Tenney	40	860,703
1914	R. C. Benson	45	59,315	1964	Bill Winfrey	61	1,350,534
1915	James Rowe, Sr.	19	75,596	1965	Hirsch Jacobs	91	1,331,628
1916	Sam Hildreth	39	70,950	1966	Eddie Neloy	93	2,456,250
1917	Sam Hildreth	23	61,698	1967	Eddie Neloy	72	1,776,089
1918	H. Guy Bedwell	53	80,296	1968	Eddie Neloy	52	1,233,101
1919	H. Guy Bedwell	63	208,728	1969	Elliott Burch	26	1,067,936
1920	L. Feustal	22	186,087	1970	Charlie Whittingham	82	1,302,354
1921	Sam Hildreth	85	262,768	1971	Charlie Whittingham	77	1,737,115
1922	Sam Hildreth	74	247,014	1972	Charlie Whittingham	79	1,734,020
1923	Sam Hildreth	75	392,124	1973	Charlie Whittingham	85	1,865,385
1924	Sam Hildreth	77	255,608	1974	Pancho Martin	166	2,408,419
1925	G. R. Tompkins	30	199,245	1975	Charlie Whittingham	93	2,437,244
1926	Scott P. Harlan	21	205,681	1976	Jack Van Berg	496	2,976,196
1927	W. H. Bringloe	63	216,563	1977	Laz Barrera	127	2,715,848
1928	John F. Schorr	65	258,425	1978	Laz Barrera	100	3,307,164
1929	James Rowe, Jr.	25	314,881	1979	Laz Barrera	98	3,608,517
1930	Sunny Jim Fitzsimmons	47	397,355	1980	Laz Barrera	99	2,969,151
1931	Big Jim Healey	33	297,300	1981	Charlie Whittingham	74	3,993,300
1932	Sunny Jim Fitzsimmons	68	266,650	1982	Charlie Whittingham	63	4,587,457
1933	Humming Bob Smith	53	135,720	1983	D. Wayne Lukas	78	4,267,261
1934	Humming Bob Smith	43	249,938	1984	D. Wayne Lukas	131	5,835,921
1935	Bud Stotler	87	303,005	1985	D. Wayne Lukas	218	11,155,188
1936	Sunny Jim Fitzsimmons	42	193,415	1986	D. Wayne Lukas	259	12,345,180
1937	Robert McGarvey	46	209,925	1987	D. Wayne Lukas	343	17,502,110
1938	Earl Sande	15	226,495	1988	D. Wayne Lukas	318	17,842,358
1939	Sunny Jim Fitzsimmons	45	266,205	1989	D. Wayne Lukas	305	16,103,998
1940	Silent Tom Smith	14	269,200	1990	D. Wayne Lukas	267	14,508,871
1941	Plain Ben Jones	70	475,318	1991	D. Wayne Lukas	289	15,942,223
1942	John M. Gaver Sr.	48	406,547	1992	D. Wayne Lukas	230	9,806,436
1943	Plain Ben Jones	73	267,915	1993	Robert Frankel	79	8,883,252
1944	Plain Ben Jones	60	601,660	1994	D. Wayne Lukas	147	9,247,457
1945	Silent Tom Smith	52	510,655	1995	D. Wayne Lukas	194	12,842,865
1946	Hirsch Jacobs	99	560,077	1996	D. Wayne Lukas	192	15,966,344
1947	Jimmy Jones	85	1,334,805	1997	D. Wayne Lukas	175	10,338,957
1948	Jimmy Jones	81	1,118,670	1998	Bob Baffert	139	15,000,870
1949	Jimmy Jones	76	978,587	1999	Bob Baffert	169	16,934,607
1950	Preston Burch	96	637,754	2000	Bob Baffert	146	11,831,605
1951	John M. Gaver Sr.	42	616,392	2001	Bob Baffert	138	16,354,996
1952	Plain Ben Jones	29	662,137	2002	Robert Frankel	117	17,748,340
1953	Harry Trotsek	54	1,028,873	2003	Robert Frankel	114	19,143,289
1954	Willie Molter	136	1,107,860	2004	Todd A. Pletcher	240	17,511,923
1955	Sunny Jim Fitzsimmons	66	1,270,055	2005	Todd A. Pletcher	257	20,867,842
1956	Willie Molter	142	1,227,402	2006	Todd A. Pletcher	294	26,820,243
1957	Jimmy Jones	70	1,150,910				

Jockey—Money Won

Year	Jockey	Mts	1st	2nd	3rd	Pct	Winnings ($)
1919	John Loftus	177	65	36	24	.37	252,707
1920	Clarence Kummer	353	87	79	48	.25	292,376
1921	Earl Sande	340	112	69	59	.33	263,043
1922	Albert Johnson	297	43	57	40	.14	345,054
1923	Earl Sande	430	122	89	79	.28	569,394
1924	Ivan Parke	844	205	175	121	.24	290,395
1925	Laverne Fator	315	81	54	44	.26	305,775
1926	Laverne Fator	511	143	90	86	.28	361,435
1927	Earl Sande	179	49	33	19	.27	277,877
1928	Pony McAtee	235	55	43	25	.23	301,295
1929	Mack Garner	274	57	39	33	.21	314,975
1930	Sonny Workman	571	152	88	79	.27	420,438
1931	Charles Kurtsinger	519	93	82	79	.18	392,095

Jockey—Money Won *(Cont.)*

Year	Jockey	Mts	1st	2nd	3rd	Pct	Winnings ($)
1932	Sonny Workman	378	87	48	55	.23	385,070
1933	Robert Jones	471	63	57	70	.13	226,285
1934	Wayne D. Wright	919	174	154	114	.19	287,185
1935	Silvio Coucci	749	141	125	103	.19	319,760
1936	Wayne D. Wright	670	100	102	73	.15	264,000
1937	Charles Kurtsinger	765	120	94	106	.16	384,202
1938	Nick Wall	658	97	94	82	.15	385,161
1939	Basil James	904	191	165	105	.21	353,333
1940	Eddie Arcaro	783	132	143	112	.17	343,661
1941	Don Meade	1,164	210	185	158	.18	398,627
1942	Eddie Arcaro	687	123	97	89	.18	481,949
1943	John Longden	871	173	140	121	.20	573,276
1944	Ted Atkinson	1,539	287	231	213	.19	899,101
1945	John Longden	778	180	112	100	.23	981,977
1946	Ted Atkinson	1,377	233	213	173	.17	1,036,825
1947	Douglas Dodson	646	141	100	75	.22	1,429,949
1948	Eddie Arcaro	726	188	108	98	.26	1,686,230
1949	Steve Brooks	906	209	172	110	.23	1,316,817
1950	Eddie Arcaro	888	195	153	144	.22	1,410,160
1951	Bill Shoemaker	1,161	257	197	161	.22	1,329,890
1952	Eddie Arcaro	807	188	122	109	.23	1,859,591
1953	Bill Shoemaker	1,683	485	302	210	.29	1,784,187
1954	Bill Shoemaker	1,251	380	221	142	.30	1,876,760
1955	Eddie Arcaro	820	158	126	108	.19	1,864,796
1956	Bill Hartack	1,387	347	252	184	.25	2,343,955
1957	Bill Hartack	1,238	341	208	178	.28	3,060,501
1958	Bill Shoemaker	1,133	300	185	137	.26	2,961,693
1959	Bill Shoemaker	1,285	347	230	159	.27	2,843,133
1960	Bill Shoemaker	1,227	274	196	158	.22	2,123,961
1961	Bill Shoemaker	1,256	304	186	175	.24	2,690,819
1962	Bill Shoemaker	1,126	311	156	128	.28	2,916,844
1963	Bill Shoemaker	1,203	271	193	137	.22	2,526,925
1964	Bill Shoemaker	1,056	246	147	133	.23	2,649,553
1965	Braulio Baeza	1,245	270	200	201	.22	2,582,702
1966	Braulio Baeza	1,341	298	222	190	.22	2,951,022
1967	Braulio Baeza	1,064	256	184	127	.24	3,088,888
1968	Braulio Baeza	1,089	201	184	145	.18	2,835,108
1969	Jorge Velasquez	1,442	258	230	204	.18	2,542,315
1970	Laffit Pincay Jr.	1,328	269	208	187	.20	2,626,526
1971	Laffit Pincay Jr.	1,627	380	288	214	.23	3,784,377
1972	Laffit Pincay Jr.	1,388	289	215	205	.21	3,225,827
1973	Laffit Pincay Jr.	1,444	350	254	209	.24	4,093,492
1974	Laffit Pincay Jr.	1,278	341	227	180	.27	4,251,060
1975	Braulio Baeza	1,190	196	208	180	.16	3,674,398
1976	Angel Cordero Jr.	1,534	274	273	235	.18	4,709,500
1977	Steve Cauthen	2,075	487	345	304	.23	6,151,750
1978	Darrel McHargue	1,762	375	294	263	.21	6,188,353
1979	Laffit Pincay Jr.	1,708	420	302	261	.25	8,183,535
1980	Chris McCarron	1,964	405	318	282	.20	7,666,100
1981	Chris McCarron	1,494	326	251	207	.22	8,397,604
1982	Angel Cordero Jr.	1,838	397	338	227	.22	9,702,520
1983	Angel Cordero Jr.	1,792	362	296	237	.20	10,116,807
1984	Chris McCarron	1,565	356	276	218	.23	12,038,213
1985	Laffit Pincay Jr.	1,409	289	246	183	.21	13,415,049
1986	Jose Santos	1,636	329	237	222	.20	11,329,297
1987	Jose Santos	1,639	305	268	208	.19	12,407,355
1988	Jose Santos	1,867	370	287	265	.20	14,877,298
1989	Jose Santos	1,459	285	238	220	.20	13,847,003
1990	Gary Stevens	1,504	283	245	202	.19	13,881,198
1991	Chris McCarron	1,440	265	228	206	.18	14,441,083
1992	Kent Desormeaux	1,568	361	260	208	.23	14,193,006
1993	Mike Smith	1,510	343	235	214	.23	14,008,148
1994	Mike Smith	1,484	317	250	196	.21	15,979,820
1995	Jerry Bailey	1,265	287	193	144	.23	16,308,230
1996	Jerry Bailey	1,187	298	189	165	.25	19,465,376
1997	Jerry Bailey	1,143	272	186	178	.26	18,260,553
1998	Gary Stevens	869	178	145	122	.20	19,358,840

Jockey—Money Won *(Cont.)*

Year	Jockey	Mts	1st	2nd	3rd	Pct	Winnings ($)
1999	Pat Day	1,265	254	209	209	.20	18,092,845
2000	Pat Day	1,219	267	206	186	.22	17,479,838
2001	Jerry Bailey	912	227	194	137	.25	22,597,720
2002	Jerry Bailey	832	213	139	118	.26	19,271,814
2003	Jerry Bailey	776	206	149	97	.27	23,354,960
2004	John R. Velazquez	1,327	335	222	181	.25	22,248,661
2005	John R. Velazquez	1,148	251	177	146	.21	20,799,923
2006	Garrett Gomez	1,270	261	230	202	.21	20,122,592

Jockey—Races Won

Year	Jockey	Mts	1st	2nd	3rd	Pct
1895	J. Perkins	762	192	177	129	.25
1896	J. Scherrer	1,093	271	227	172	.24
1897	H. Martin	803	173	152	116	.21
1898	T. Burns	973	277	213	149	.28
1899	T. Burns	1,064	273	173	266	.26
1900	C. Mitchell	874	195	140	139	.23
1901	W. O'Connor	1,047	253	221	192	.24
1902	J. Ranch	1,069	276	205	181	.26
1903	G.C. Fuller	918	229	152	122	.25
1904	E. Hildebrand	1,169	297	230	171	.25
1905	D. Nicol	861	221	143	136	.26
1906	W. Miller	1,384	388	300	199	.28
1907	W. Miller	1,194	334	226	170	.28
1908	V. Powers	1,260	324	204	185	.26
1909	V. Powers	704	173	121	114	.25
1910	G. Garner	947	200	188	153	.20
1911	T. Koerner	813	162	133	112	.20
1912	P. Hill	967	168	141	129	.17
1913	M. Buxton	887	146	131	136	.16
1914	J. McTaggart	787	157	132	106	.20
1915	M. Garner	775	151	118	90	.19
1916	F. Robinson	791	178	131	124	.23
1917	W. Crump	803	151	140	101	.19
1918	F. Robinson	864	185	140	108	.21
1919	C. Robinson	896	190	140	126	.21
1920	J. Butwell	721	152	129	139	.21
1921	C. Lang	696	135	110	105	.19
1922	M. Fator	859	188	153	116	.22
1923	I. Parke	718	173	105	95	.24
1924	I. Parke	844	205	175	121	.24
1925	A. Mortensen	987	187	145	138	.19
1926	R. Jones	1,172	190	163	152	.16
1927	L. Hardy	1,130	207	192	151	.18
1928	J. Inzelone	1,052	155	152	135	.15
1929	M. Knight	871	149	132	133	.17
1930	H.R. Riley	861	177	145	123	.21
1931	H. Roble	1,174	173	173	155	.15
1932	J. Gilbert	1,050	212	144	160	.20
1933	J. Westrope	1,224	301	235	166	.25
1934	M. Peters	1,045	221	179	147	.21
1935	C. Stevenson	1,099	206	169	146	.19
1936	B. James	1,106	245	195	161	.22
1937	J. Adams	1,265	260	186	177	.21
1938	J. Longden	1,150	236	168	171	.21
1939	D. Meade	1,284	255	221	180	.20
1940	E. Dew	1,377	287	201	180	.21
1941	D. Meade	1,164	210	185	158	.18
1942	J. Adams	1,120	245	185	150	.22
1943	J. Adams	1,069	228	159	171	.21
1944	T. Atkinson	1,539	287	231	213	.19
1945	J.D. Jessop	1,085	290	182	168	.27
1946	T. Atkinson	1,377	233	213	173	.17

Jockey—Races Won (Cont.)

Year	Jockey	Mts	1st	2nd	3rd	Pct
1947	J. Longden	1,327	316	250	195	.24
1948	J. Longden	1,197	319	233	161	.27
1949	G. Glisson	1,347	270	217	181	.20
1950	W. Shoemaker	1,640	388	266	230	.24
1951	C. Burr	1,319	310	232	192	.24
1952	A. DeSpirito	1,482	390	247	212	.26
1953	W. Shoemaker	1,683	485	302	210	.29
1954	W. Shoemaker	1,251	380	221	142	.30
1955	W. Hartack	1,702	417	298	215	.25
1956	W. Hartack	1,387	347	252	184	.25
1957	W. Hartack	1,238	341	208	178	.28
1958	W. Shoemaker	1,133	300	185	137	.26
1959	W. Shoemaker	1,285	347	230	159	.27
1960	W. Hartack	1,402	307	247	190	.22
1961	J. Sellers	1,394	328	212	227	.24
1962	R. Ferraro	1,755	352	252	226	.20
1963	W. Blum	1,704	360	286	215	.21
1964	W. Blum	1,577	324	274	170	.21
1965	J. Davidson	1,582	319	228	190	.20
1966	A. Gomez	996	318	173	142	.32
1967	J. Velasquez	1,939	438	315	270	.23
1968	A. Cordero Jr.	1,662	345	278	219	.21
1969	L. Snyder	1,645	352	290	243	.21
1970	S. Hawley	1,908	452	313	265	.24
1971	L Pincay Jr.	1,627	380	288	214	.23
1972	S. Hawley	1,381	367	269	200	.27
1973	S. Hawley	1,925	515	336	292	.27
1974	C.J. McCarron	2,199	546	392	297	.25
1975	C.J. McCarron	2,194	458	389	305	.21
1976	S. Hawley	1,637	413	245	201	.25
1977	S. Cauthen	2,075	487	345	304	.23
1978	E. Delahoussaye	1,666	384	285	238	.23
1979	D. Gall	2,146	479	396	326	.22
1980	C.J. McCarron	1,964	405	318	282	.20
1981	D. Gall	1,917	376	305	297	.20
1982	Pat Day	1,870	399	326	255	.21
1983	Pat Day	1,725	454	321	251	.26
1984	Pat Day	1,694	399	296	259	.24
1985	C.W. Antley	2,335	469	371	288	.20
1986	Pat Day	1,417	429	246	202	.30
1987	Kent Desormeaux	2,207	450	370	294	.28
1988	Kent Desormeaux	1,897	474	295	276	.25
1989	Kent Desormeaux	2,312	598	385	309	.25
1990	Pat Day	1,421	364	265	222	.26
1991	Pat Day	1,405	430	256	213	.31
1992	Russell Baze	1,691	433	296	237	.25
1993	Russell Baze	1,579	410	297	225	.26
1994	Russell Baze	1,588	415	301	266	.26
1995	Russell Baze	1,531	445	310	232	.29
1996	Russell Baze	1,482	415	297	200	.28
1997	Edgar S. Prado	2,037	533	384	308	.26
1998	Edgar S. Prado	1,969	470	377	285	.23
1999	Edgar S. Prado	1,902	402	307	276	.21
2000	Ramon Dominguez	1,586	361	293	238	.23
2001	Ramon Dominguez	1,864	431	368	278	.23
2002	Russell Baze	1,508	431	302	219	.29
2003	Ramon Dominguez	1,627	453	316	252	.28
2004	Rafael Bejarano	1,922	455	355	280	.24
2005	Russell Baze	1,216	364	242	171	.29
2006	Julien Leparoux	1,740	403	282	210	.23

Leading Jockeys—Career Records

Jockey	Years Riding	Mts	Ist	2nd	3rd	Win Pct	Winnings ($)
*Russell Baze	34	43,550	9,851	7,496	6,242	.226	150,142,060
Laffit Pincay Jr. (2003)	39	48,486	9,530	7,784	6,650	.197	237,120,625
Bill Shoemaker (1990)	42	40,350	8,833	6,136	4,987	.219	123,375,524
Pat Day (2004)	33	40,298	8,803	6,860	5,687	.218	297,912,019
David Gall (1999)	41	41,775	7,396	6,525	6,131	.177	24,972,821
Chris McCarron (2002)	28	34,239	7,141	5,670	4,672	.209	263,985,505
Angel Cordero Jr. (1992)	31	38,657	7,057	6,136	5,359	.183	164,570,227
Jorge Velasquez (1998)	35	40,852	6,795	6,178	5,755	.166	125,544,379
Sandy Hawley (1998)	31	31,455	6,449	4,825	4,159	.205	88,681,292
*Earlie Fires	43	44,775	6,428	5,543	5,352	.144	85,307,754
Larry Snyder (1994)	35	35,681	6,388	5,030	3,440	.179	47,207,289
Eddie Delahoussaye (2002)	32	39,213	6,384	5,676	5,586	.163	195,884,940
Carl Gambardella (1994)	39	39,018	6,349	5,953	5,353	.163	29,389,041
John Longden (1966)	40	32,413	6,032	4,914	4,273	.186	24,665,800
*Mario Pino	28	36,503	5,976	5,445	5,042	.164	103,875,237
*Edgar Prado	24	31,050	5,952	5,055	4,399	.192	199,566,285
Jerry Bailey (2006)	32	30,855	5,893	4,553	3,925	.191	296,104,129
Jacinto Vasquez (1998)	38	37,337	5,228	4,714	4,510	.140	85,754,115
Ron Ardoin (2003)	31	32,335	5,226	4,298	3,793	.162	58,908,059
*Anthony Black	31	32,991	5,080	4,378	4,252	.154	59,320,387

*Active jockeys. Note: Jockeys ranked by wins. Records go through October 1, 2007, and include available statistics for races ridden in foreign countries. Figures in parentheses after jockey's name indicate last year in which they rode.

Leading jockeys courtesy of Equibase company and *National Thoroughbred Racing Association.*

HORSES

Ack Ack (1986, 1966)
Affectionately (1989, 1960)
Affirmed (1980, 1975)
All Along (1990, 1979)
Alsab (1976, 1939)
Alydar (1989, 1975)
Alysheba (1993, 1984)
American Eclipse (1970, 1814)
A.P. Indy (2000, 1989)
Armed (1963, 1941)
Artful (1956, 1902)
Arts and Letters (1994, 1966)
Assault (1964, 1943)
Battleship (1969, 1927)
Bayakoa (1998, 1984)
Bed o' Roses (1976, 1947)
Beldame (1956, 1901)
Ben Brush (1955, 1893)
Bewitch (1977, 1945)
Bimelech (1990, 1937)
Black Gold (1989, 1921)
Black Helen (1991, 1932)
Blue Larkspur (1957, 1926)
Bold 'n.Determined (1997, 1977)
Bold Ruler (1973, 1954)
Bon Nouvel (1976, 1960)
Boston (1955, 1833)
Bowl of Flowers (2004, 1988)
Broomstick (1956, 1901)
Buckpasser (1970, 1963)
Busher (1964, 1942)
Bushranger (1967, 1930)
Cafe Prince (1985, 1970)
Carry Back (1975, 1958)
Cavalcade (1993, 1931)
Challedon (1977, 1936)
Chris Evert (1988, 1971)
Cicada (1967, 1959)
Cigar (2002, 1990)
Citation (1959, 1945)
Coaltown (1983, 1945)
Colin (1956, 1905)
Commando (1956, 1898)
Cougar II (2006, 1966)
Count Fleet (1961, 1940)
Crusader (1995, 1923)
Dahlia (1981, 1970)
Damascus (1974, 1964)
Dance Smartly (2003, 1988)
Dark Mirage (1974, 1965)
Davona Dale (1985, 1976)
Desert Vixen (1979, 1970)
Devil Diver (1980, 1939)
Discovery (1969, 1931)
Domino (1955, 1891)
Dr. Fager (1971, 1964)
Easy Goer (1997, 1986)
Eight Thirty (1994, 1936)

Elkridge (1966, 1938)
Emperor of Norfolk (1988, 1885)
Equipoise (1957, 1928)
Exceller (1999, 1973)
Exterminator (1957, 1915)
Fairmount (1985, 1921)
Fair Play (1956, 1905)
Fashion (1980, 1837)
Firenze (1981, 1884)
Flatterer (1994, 1979)
Flawlessly (2004, 1988)
Foolish Pleasure (1995, 1972)
Forego (1979, 1970)
Fort Marcy (1998, 1964)
Gallant Bloom (1977, 1966)
Gallant Fox (1957, 1927)
Gallant Man (1987, 1954)
Gallorette (1962, 1942)
Gamely (1980, 1964)
Genuine Risk (1986, 1977)
Go For Wand (1996, 1987)
Good and Plenty (1956, 1900)
Grandville (1997, 1933)
Grey Lag (1957, 1918)
Gun Bow (1999, 1960)
Hamburg (1986, 1895)
Hanover (1955, 1884)
Henry of Navarre (1985, 1891)
Hill Prince (1991, 1947)
Hindoo (1955, 1878)
Holy Bull (2001, 1991)
Imp (1965, 1894)
Jay Trump (1971, 1957)
John Henry (1990, 1975)
Johnstown (1992, 1936)
Jolly Roger (1965, 1922)
Kelso (1967, 1957)
Kentucky (1983, 1861)
Kingston (1955, 1884)
Lady's Secret (1992, 1982)
La Prevoyante (1995, 1970)
L'Escargot (1977, 1963)
Lexington (1955, 1850)
Lonesome Glory (2005, 1988)
Longfellow (1971, 1867)
Luke Blackburn (1956, 1877)
Majestic Prince (1988, 1966)
Man o' War (1957, 1917)
Maskette (2001, 1908)
Miesque (1999, 1984)
Miss Woodford (1967, 1880)
Myrtlewood (1979, 1932)
Nashua (1965, 1952)
Native Dancer (1963, 1950)
Native Diver (1978, 1959)
Needles (2000, 1953)
Neji (1966, 1950)
Noor (2002, 1945)

Northern Dancer (1976, 1961)
Oedipus (1978, 1946)
Old Rosebud (1968, 1911)
Omaha (1965, 1932)
Pan Zareta (1972, 1910)
Parole (1984, 1873)
Paseana (2001, 1987)
Personal Ensign (1993, 1984)
Peter Pan (1956, 1904)
Precisionist (2003, 1981)
Princess Doreen (1982, 1921)
Princess Rooney (1991, 1980)
Real Delight (1987, 1949)
Regret (1957, 1912)
Reigh Count (1978, 1923)
Riva Ridge (1998, 1969)
Roamer (1981, 1911)
Roseben (1956, 1901)
Round Table (1972, 1954)
Ruffian (1976, 1972)
Ruthless (1975, 1864)
Salvator (1955, 1886)
Sarazen (1957, 1921)
Seabiscuit (1958, 1933)
Searching (1978, 1952)
Seattle Slew (1981, 1974)
Secretariat (1974, 1970)
Serena's Song (2002, 1992)
Shuvee (1975, 1966)
Silver Spoon (1978, 1956)
Sir Archy (1955, 1805)
Sir Barton (1957, 1916)
Skip Away (2004, 1993)
Slew o'.Gold (1992, 1980)
Spectacular Bid (1982, 1976)
Stymie (1975, 1941)
Sun Beau (1996, 1925)
Sunday Silence (1996, 1986)
Susan's Girl (1976, 1969)
Swaps (1966, 1952)
Sword Dancer (1977, 1956)
Sysonby (1956, 1902)
Ta Wee (1994, 1967)
Ten Broeck (1982, 1872)
Tim Tam (1985, 1955)
Tom Fool (1960, 1949)
Top Flight (1966, 1929)
Tosmah (1984, 1961)
Twenty Grand (1957, 1928)
Twilight Tear (1963, 1941)
Two Lea (1982, 1946)
War Admiral (1958, 1934)
Whirlaway (1959, 1938)
Whisk Broom II (1979, 1907)
Winning Colors (2000, 1985)
Zaccio (1990, 1976)
Zev (1983, 1920)

Note: Years of election and foaling in parentheses.

HARNESS RACING

Hambletonian

Year	Winner	Driver	Year	Winner	Driver
1926	Guy McKinney	Nat Ray	1967	Speedy Streak	Del Cameron
1927	Iosola's Worthy	Marvin Childs	1968	Nevele Pride	Stanley Dancer
1928	Spenser	W. H. Leese	1969	Lindy's Pride	H. Beissinger
1929	Walter Dear	Walter Cox	1970	Timothy T.	J. Simpson Jr.
1930	Hanover's Bertha	Tom Berry	1971	Speedy Crown	H. Beissinger
1931	Calumet Butler	R. D. McMahon	1972	Super Bowl	Stanley Dancer
1932	The Marchioness	William Caton	1973	Flirth	Ralph Baldwin
1933	Mary Reynolds	Ben White	1974	Christopher T.	Bill Haughton
1934	Lord Jim	Doc Parshall	1975	Bonefish	Stanley Dancer
1935	Greyhound	Sep Palin	1976	Steve Lobell	Bill Haughton
1936	Rosalind	Ben White	1977	Green Speed	Bill Haughton
1937	Shirley Hanover	Henry Thomas	1978	Speedy Somolli	H. Beissinger
1938	McLin Hanover	Henry Thomas	1979	Legend Hanover	George Sholty
1939	Peter Astra	Doc Parshall	1980	Burgomeister	Bill Haughton
1940	Spencer Scott	Fred Egan	1981	Shiaway St. Pat	Ray Remmen
1941	Bill Gallon	Lee Smith	1982	Speed Bowl	Tom Haughton
1942	The Ambassador	Ben White	1983	Duenna	Stanley Dancer
1943	Volo Song	Ben White	1984	Historic Freight	Ben Webster
1944	Yankee Maid	Henry Thomas	1985	Prakas	Bill O'Donnell
1945	Titan Hanover	H. Pownall Sr.	1986	Nuclear Kosmos	Ulf Thoresen
1946	Chestertown	Thomas Berry	1987	Mack Lobell	John Campbell
1947	Hoot Mon	Sep Palin	1988	Armbro Goal	John Campbell
1948	Demon Hanover	Harrison Hoyt	1989	Park Ave. Joe/Probe*	R. Waples/B. Fahy
1949	Miss Tilly	Fred Egan	1990	Harmonious	John Campbell
1950	Lusty Song	Del Miller	1991	Giant Victory	Jack Moiseyev
1951	Mainliner	Guy Crippen	1992	Alf Palema	Mickey McNichol
1952	Sharp Note	Bion Shively	1993	American Winner	Ron Pierce
1953	Helicopter	Harry Harvey	1994	Victory Dream	Michel Lachance
1954	Newport Dream	Del Cameron	1995	Tagliabue	John Campbell
1955	Scott Frost	Joe O'Brien	1996	Continentalvictory	Michel Lachance
1956	The Intruder	Ned Bower	1997	Malabar Man	Mal Burroughs
1957	Hickory Smoke	J. Simpson Sr.	1998	Muscles Yankee	John Campbell
1958	Emily's Pride	Flave Nipe	1999	Self Possessed	Michel Lachance
1959	Diller Hanover	Frank Ervin	2000	Yankee Paco	T.J. Ritchie
1960	Blaze Hanover	Joe O'Brien	2001	Scarlet Knight	Stefan Melander
1961	Harlan Dean	James Arthur	2002	Chip Chip Hooray	Eric Ledford
1962	A. C.'s Viking	Sanders Russell	2003	Amigo Hall	Mike Lachance
1963	Speedy Scot	Ralph Baldwin	2004	Windsong's Legacy	T. Smedshammer
1964	Ayres	J. Simpson Sr.	2005	P-Forty-Seven	Dave Palone
1965	Egyptian Candor	Del Cameron	2006	Glidemaster	John Campbell
1966	Kerry Way	Frank Ervin	2007	Donato Hanover	Ronald Pierce

*Park Avenue Joe and Probe dead-heated for win. Park Avenue finished first in the summary 2-1-1 to Probe's 1-9-1 finish.
Note: Run at 1 mile since 1947.

Little Brown Jug

Year	Winner	Driver	Year	Winner	Driver
1946	Ensign Hanover	Wayne Smart	1977	Governor Skipper	John Chapman
1947	Forbes Chief	Del Cameron	1978	Happy Escort	William Popfinger
1948	Knight Dream	Frank Safford	1979	Hot Hitter	Herve Filion
1949	Good Time	Frank Ervin	1980	Niatross	Clint Galbraith
1950	Dudley Hanover	Del Miller	1981	Fan Hanover	Glen Garnsey
1951	Tar Heel	Del Cameron	1982	Merger	John Campbell
1952	Meadow Rice	Wayne Smart	1983	Ralph Hanover	Ron Waples
1953	Keystoner	Frank Ervin	1984	Colt Fortysix	Chris Boring
1954	Adios Harry	Morris MacDonald	1985	Nihilator	Bill O'Donnell
1955	Quick Chief	Bill Haughton	1986	Barberry Spur	Bill O'Donnell
1956	Noble Adios	John Simpson Sr.	1987	Jaguar Spur	Dick Stillings
1957	Torpid	John Simpso Sr.	1988	B. J. Scoot	Michel Lachance
1958	Shadow Wave	Joe O'Brien	1989	Goalie Jeff	Michel Lachance
1959	Adios Butler	Clint Hodgins	1990	Beach Towel	Ray Remmen
1960	Bullet Hanover	John Simpson Sr.	1991	Precious Bunny	Jack Moiseye
1961	Henry T. Adios	Stanley Dancer	1992	Fake Left	Ron.Waples
1962	Lehigh Hanover	Stanley Dancer	1993	Life Sign	John Campbell
1963	Overtrick	John Patterson	1994	Magical Mike	Michel Lachance
1964	Vicar Hanover	Bill Haughton	1995	Nick's Fantasy	John Campbell
1965	Bret Hanover	Frank Ervin	1996	Armbro Operative	Jack Moiseyev
1966	Romeo Hanover	George Sholty	1997	Western Dreamer	Michel Lachance
1967	Best of All	James Hackett	1998	Shady Character	Ron Pierce
1968	Rum Customer	Bill Haughton	1999	Blissful Hall	Ron Pierce
1969	Laverne Hanover	Bill Haughton	2000	Astreos	Chris Christoforou
1970	Most Happy Fella	Stanley Dancer	2001	Bettor's Delight	Michel Lachance
1971	Nansemond	Herve Filion	2002	Million Dollar Cam	Luc Ouellette
1972	Strike Out	Keith Waples	2003	No Pan Intended	David S. Miller
1973	Melvin's Woe	Joe O'Brien	2004	Timesareachanging	Ron Pierce
1974	Armbro Omaha	Bill Haughton	2005	Vivid Photo	Roger Hammer
1975	Seatrain	Ben Webster	2006	Mr. Feelgood	Mark MacDonald
1976	Keystone Ore	Stanley Dancer	2007	Tell All	Jody Jamieson

Breeders' Crown

1984

Div	Winner	Driver
2PC	Dragon's Lair	Jeff Mallet
2PF	Amneris	John Campbell
3PC	Troublemaker	Bill O'Donnell
3PF	Naughty But Nice	Tommy Haughton
2TC	Workaholic	Berndt Lindstedt
2TF	Conifer	George Sholty
3TC	Baltic Speed	Jan Nordin
3TF	Fancy Crown	Bill O'Donnell

1985

Div	Winner	Driver
2PC	Robust Hanover	John Campbell
2PF	Caressable	Herve Filion
3PC	Nihilator	Bill O'Donnell
3PF	Stienam	Buddy Gilmour
2TC	Express Ride	John Campbell
2TF	JEF's Spice	Mickey McNichol
3TC	Prakas	John Campbell
3TF	Armbro Devona	Bill O'Donnell
AP	Division Street	Michel Lachance
AT	Sandy Bowl	John Campbell

1986

Div	Winner	Driver
2PC	Sunset Warrior	Bill Gale
2PF	Halcyon	Ray Remmen
3PC	Masquerade	Richard Silverman
3PF	Glow Softly	Ron Waples
2TC	Mack Lobell	John Campbell
2TF	Super Flora	Ron Waples
3TC	Sugarcane Hanover	Ron Waples
3TF	JEF's Spice	Bill O'Donnell
APM	Samshu Bluegrass	Michel Lachance
ATM	Grades Singing	Herve Filion
APH	Forrest Skipper	Lucien Fontaine
ATH	Nearly Perfect	Mickey McNichol

1987

Div	Winner	Driver
2PC	Camtastic	Bill O'Donnell
2PF	Leah Almahurst	Bill Fahy
3PC	Call For Rain	Clint Galbraith
3PF	Pacific	Tom Harmer
2TC	Defiant One	Howard Beissinger
2TF	Nan's Catch	Berndt Lindstedt
3TC	Mack Lobell	John Campbell
3TF	Armbro Fling	George Sholty
APM	Follow My Star	John Campbell
ATM	Grades Singing	Olle Goop
APH	Armbro Emerson	Walter Whelan
ATH	Sugarcane Hanover	Ron Waples

Breeders' Crown

1988

Div	Winner	Driver
2PC	Kentucky Spur	Dick Stillings
2PF	Central Park West	John Campbell
3PC	Camtastic	Bill O'Donnell
3PF	Sweet Reflection	Bill O'Donnell
2TC	Valley Victory	Bill O'Donnell
2TF	Peace Corps	John Campbell
3TC	Firm Tribute	Mark O'Mara
3TF	Nalda Hanover	Mickey McNichol
APM	Anniecrombie	Dave Magee
ATM	Armbro Flori	Larry Walker
APH	Call For Rain	Clint Galbraith
ATH	Mack Lobell	John Campbell

1989

Div	Winner	Driver
2PC	Till We Meet Again	Mickey McNichol
2PF	Town Pro	Doug Brown
3PC	Goalie Jeff	Michel Lachance
3PF	Cheery Hello	John Campbell
2TC	Royal Troubador	Carl Allen
2TF	Delphi's Lobell	Ron Waples
3TC	Esquire Spur	Dick Stillings
3TF	Pace Corps	John Campbell
APM	Armbro Feather	John Kopas
ATM	Grades Singing	Olle Goop
APH	Matt's Scooter	Michel Lachance
ATH	Delray Lobell	John Campbell

1990

Div	Winner	Driver
2PC	Artsplace	John Campbell
2PF	Miss Easy	John Campbell
3PC	Beach Towel	Ray Remmen
3PF	Town Pro	Doug Brown
2TC	Crysta's Best	Dick Richardson Jr.
2TF	Jean Bi	Jan Nordin
3TC	Embassy Lobell	Michel Lachance
3TF	Me Maggie	Berndt Lindstedt
APM	Caesar's Jackpot	Bill Fahy
ATM	Peace Corps	Stig Johansson
APH	Bay's Fella	Paul MacDonell
ATH	No Sex Please	Ron Waples

1991

Div	Winner	Driver
2PC	Digger Almahurst	Doug Brown
2PF	Hazleton Kay	John Campbell
3PC	Three Wizzards	Bill Gale
3PF	Miss Easy	John Campbell
2TC	King Conch	Bill Gale
2TF	Armbro Keepsake	John Campbell
3TC	Giant Victory	Ron Pierce
3TF	Twelve Speed	Ron Waples
APM	Delinquent Account	Bill O'Donnell
ATM	Me Maggie	Berndt Lindstedt
APH	Camluck	Michel Lachance
ATH	Billyjojimbob	Paul MacDonell

1992

Div	Winner	Driver
2PC	Village Jiffy	Ron Waples
2PF	Immortality	John Campbell
3PC	Kingsbridge	Roger Mayotte
3PF	So Fresh	John Campbell
2TC	Giant Chill	John Patterson Jr.
2TF	Winky's Goal	Cat Manzi
3TC	Baltic Striker	Michel Lachance
3TF	Imperfection	Michel Lachance
APM	Shady Daisy	Ron Pierce
ATM	Peace Corps	Torbjorn Jansson
APH	Artsplace	John Campbell
ATH	No Sex Please	Ron Waples

1993

Div	Winner	Driver
2PC	Expensive Scooter	Jack Moiseyev
2PF	Electric Scooter	Mike Lachance
3PC	Life Sign	John Campbell
3PF	Immortality	John Campbell
2TC	Westgate Crown	John Campbell
2TF	Gleam	Jimmy Takter
3TC	Pine Chip	John Campbell
3TF	Expressway Hanover	Per Henriksen
APM	Swing Back	Kelly Sheppard
ATM	Lifetime Dream	Paul MacDonnell
APH	Staying Together	Bill O'Donnell
ATH	Earl	Chris Christoforou Jr.

1994

Div	Winner	Driver
2PC	Jenna's Beach Boy	Bill Fahy
2PF	Yankee Cashmere	Peter Wrenn
3PC	Magical Mike	Michel Lachance
3PF	Hardie Hanover	Tim Twaddle
2TC	Eager Seelster	Teddy Jacobs
2TF	Lookout Victory	John Patterson
3TC	Incredible Abe	Italo Tamborrino
3TF	Imageofa Clear Day	Bill O'Donnell
APM	Shady Daisy	Michel Lachance
ATM	Armbro Keepsake	Stig Johansson
APH	Village Jiffy	Paul MacDonell
ATH	Pine Chip	John Campbell

1995

Div	Winner	Driver
2PC	John Street North	Jack Moiseyev
2PF	Paige Nicole Q	John Campbell
3PC	Jenna's Beach Boy	Bill Fahy
3PF	Headline Hanover	Doug Brown
2TC	Armbro Officer	Steve Condren
2TF	Continentalvictory	Michel Lachance
3TC	Abundance	Bill O'Donnell
3TF	Lookout Victory	Sonny Patterson
APM	Ellamony	Mike Saftic
ATM	CR Kay Suzie	Rod Allen
APH	That'll Be Me	Roger Mayotte
ATH	Panifesto	Luc Ouellette

Note: 2=Two-year-old; T=Trotter; C=Colt; 3=Three-year-old; P=Pacer; F=Filly; A=Aged; H=Horse; M=Mare.

Breeders' Crown *(Cont.)*

1996

Div	Winner	Driver
2PC	His Mattjesty	Doug Brown
2PF	Before Sunrise	Steve Condren
3PC	Armbro Operative	Michel Lachance
3PF	Mystical Maddy	Michel Lachance
2TC	Malabar Man	Mal Burroughs
2TF	Armbro Prowess	Jimmy Takter
3TC	Running Sea	Wally Hennessey
3TF	Personal Banner	Peter Wrenn
APM	She's A Great Lady	John Campbell
APH	Jenna's Beach Boy	Bill Fahy
AT	CR Kay Suzie	Rod Allen

1997

Div	Winner	Driver
2PC	Artiscape	Michel Lachance
2PF	Take Flight	Luc Ouellette
3PC	Village Jasper	Paul McDonnell
3PF	Stienam's Place	Jack Moiseyev
2TC	Catch As Catch Can	Wally Hennessey
2TF	My Dolly	Wally Hennessey
3TC	Malabar Man	Malvern Burroughs
3TF	No Nonsense Woman	Jim Doherty
APM	Jay's Table	John Campbell
APH	Red Bow Tie	Luc Ouellette
AT	Moni Maker	Wally Hennessey

1998

Div	Winner	Driver
2PC	Badlands Hanover	Ron Pierce
2PF	Juliet's Fate	George Brennan
3PC	Artiscape	Michel Lachance
3PF	Galleria	George Brennan
2TC	CR Commando	Carl Allen
2TF	Musical Victory	Luc Ouellette
3TC	Muscles Yankee	John Campbell
3TF	Lassie's Goal	Mark O'Mara
APM	Shore By Five	Daniel Dube
APH	Red Bow Tie	Luc Ouellette
AT	Supergrit	Ron Pierce

1999

Div	Winner	Driver
2PC	Tyberwood	Richard Silverman
2PF	Eternal Camnation	Eric Ledford
3PC	Grinfromeartoear	Chris Christoforou
3PF	Odies Fame	David Wall
2TC	Master Lavec	Daniel Daley
2TF	Dream of Joy	James Meittinis
3TC	CR Renegade	Rodney Allen
3TF	Oolong	Ronald Pierce
APM	Shore By Five	Daniel Dube
APH	Red Bow Tie	Luc Ouellette
AT	Supergrit	Ronald Pierce

2000

Div	Winner	Driver
2PC	Bettor's Delight	Michel Lachance
2PF	Lady MacBeach	Luc Ouellette
3PC	Gallo Blue Chip	Daniel Dube
3PF	Popcorn Penny	Ryan Anderson
2TC	Banker Hall	Trevor Ritchie
2TF	Syrinx Hanover	Trevor Ritchie
3TC	Fast Photo	Michel Lachance
3TF	Aviano	Trevor Ritchie
APM	Ron's Girl	Michel Lachance
APH	Western Ideal	Michel Lachance
AT	Magician	David Miller

2001

Div	Winner	Driver
2PC	Western Shooter	John Campbell
2PF	Cam Swifty	Jim Meittinis
3PC	Real Desire	John Campbell
3PF	Bunny Lake	John Stark Jr.
2TC	Duke Of York	Paul MacDonnell
2TF	Cameron Hall	Michel Lachance
3TC	Liberty Balance	Randall Waples
3TF	Syrinx Hanover	John Campbell
APM	Eternal Camnation	Eric Ledford
APH	Goliath Bayama	Sylvain Filion
AT	Varenne	G. Minnucci

2002

Div	Winner	Driver
2PC	Totally Western	Mario Baillargeon
2PF	Armbro Amoretto	Luc Ouellette
3PC	Art Major	John Campbell
3PF	Allamerican Nadia	Chris Christoforou
2TC	Broadway Hall	John Campbell
2TF	Pick Me Up	Luc Ouellette
3TC	Kadabra	David S. Miller
3TF	Cameron Hall	Trevor Ritchie
APM	Molly Can Do It	Jack Moiseyev
APH	Real Desire	John Campbell
AT	Fool's Goal	Jack Moiseyev

2003

Div	Winner	Driver
2PC	I Am A Fool	Ron Pierce
2PF	Pans Culottes	Daniel Dube
3PC	No Pan Intended	David Miller
3PF	Burning Point	Kevin Wallis
2TC	Cantab Hall	Michel Lachance
2TF	Forever Starlet	David Miller
3TC	Mr. Muscleman	Ron Pierce
3TF	Stroke Play	Brian Sears
APM	Eternal Camnation	Eric Ledford
APH	Art Major	John Campbell
AT	Fool's Goal	Jack Moiseyev

2004

Div	Winner	Driver
2PC	Village Jolt	Ron Pierce
2PH	Restive Hanover	Andy Miller
3PC	Western Terror	Brian Sears
3PF	Rainbow Blue	Ron Pierce
2TC	Ken Warkentin	David Miller
2TF	Flirtin Miss	John Campbell
3TC	Yankee Slide	Brian Sears
3TF	Housethatruthbuilt	Brian Sears
APM	Always Cam	David Miller
APH	Boulder Creek	Ron Pierce
AT	Ambro Affair	Ron Pierce

2005

Div	Winner	Driver
2PC	Jereme's Jet	Paul MacDonell
2PH	My Little Dragon	Ron Pierce
3PC	Rocknroll Hanover	Brian Sears
3PF	Belovedangel	Ron Pierce
2TC	Chocolatier	D.R. Ackerman
2TF	Passionate Glide	Ron Pierce
3TC	Strong Yankee	Brian Sears
3TF	Blur	Brian Sears
APM	Loyal Opposition	George Brennan
APH	Boulder Creek	Brian Sears
AT	Mr. Muscleman	Ron Pierce

Breeders' Crown *(Cont.)*

2006

Div	Winner	Driver
2PC	Charley Barley	Mike Lachance
2PH	Artistic Fella	Tim Tetrick
3PC	Shark Gesture	Brian Sears
3PF	My Little Dragon	Ron Pierce
2TC	Donato Hanover	Ron Pierce
2TF	Possess the Magic	Ron Pierce
3TC	Majestic Son	Brian Sears
3TF	Susie's Magic	David Miller
APM	Moving Pictures	Mark MacDonald
APH	Artistic Fella	Tim Tetrick
AT	Equinox Bi	Trevor Ritchie

Note: 2=Two-year-old; T=Trotter; C=Colt; 3=Three-year-old; P=Pacer; F=Filly; A=Aged; H=Horse; M=Mare.

Triple Crown Winners

Trotting

Trotting's Triple Crown consists of the Hambletonian (first run in 1926), the Kentucky Futurity (first run in 1893) and the Yonkers Trot (known as the Yonkers Futurity when it began in 1955).

Year	Horse	Owner	Breeder	Trainer & Driver
1955	Scott Frost	S.A. Camp Farms	Est of W.N. Reynolds	Joe O'Brien
1963	Speedy Scot	Castleton Farms	Castleton Farms	Ralph Baldwin
1964	Ayres	Charlotte Sheppard	Charlotte Sheppard	John Simpson Sr
1968	Nevele Pride	Nevele Acres & Lou Resnick	Mr & Mrs E.C. Quin	Stanley Dancer
1969	Lindy's Pride	Lindy Farm	Hanover Shoe Farms	Howard Beissinger
1972	Super Bowl	Rachel Dancer & Rose Hild Breeding Farm	Stoner Creek Stud	Stanley Dancer
2006	Glidemaster	Robert Burgess, Karin Olsson Burgess & Marsha Cohen	Brittany Farms	John Campbell

Pacing

Pacing's Triple Crown consists of the Cane Pace (called the Cane Futurity when it began in 1955), the Little Brown Jug (first run in 1946) and the Messenger Stakes (first run in 1956).

Year	Horse	Owner	Breeder	Trainer/Driver
1959	Adios Butler	Paige West &	R.C. Carpenter	Paige West/Clint Hodgins Angelo Pellillo
1965	Bret Hanover	Richard Downing	Hanover Shoe Farms	Frank Ervin
1966	Romeo Hanover	Lucky Star Stables & Morton Finder	Hanover Shoe Farms	Jerry Silverman/ William Meyer (Cane) & George Sholty (Jug & Messenger)
1968	Rum Customer	Kennilworth Farms & L. C. Mancuso	Mr. & Mrs. R.C. Larkin	Bill Haughton
1970	Most Happy Fella	Egyptian Acres Stable	Stoner Creek Stud	Stanley Dancer
1980	Niatross	Niagara Acres, C. Galbraith & Niatross Stables	Niagara Acres	Clint Galbraith
1983	Ralph Hanover	Waples Stable, Pointsetta Stable, Grant's Direct Stable & P. J. Baugh	Hanover Shoe Farms	Stew Firlotte/Ron Waples
1997	Western Dreamer	Daniel and Matthew Daly and Patrick Daly Jr.	Kentuckiana Farms	Bill Robinson/Michel Lachance
1999	Blissful Hall	Daniel Plouffe	Walnut Hall Limited	Ben Wallace/Ron Pierce
2003	No Pan Intended	Peter Pan Stables, Inc.	Winbak Farm	Ivan Sugg/David Miller

Horse of the Year

Year	Horse	Gait	Owner
1947	Victory Song	T	Castleton Farm
1948	Rodney	T	R.H. Johnston
1949	Good Time	P	William Cane
1950	Proximity	T	Ralph and Gordon Verhurst
1951	Pronto Don	T	Hayes Fair Acres Stable
1952	Good Time	P	William Cane
1953	Hi Lo's Forbes	P	Mr. and Mrs. Earl Wagner
1954	Stenographer	T	Max Hempt
1955	Scott Frost	T	S.A. Camp Farms
1956	Scott Frost	T	S.A. Camp Farms
1957	Torpid	P	Sherwood Farm
1958	Emily's Pride	T	Walnut Hall and Castleton Farms
1959	Bye Bye Byrd	P	Mr. and Mrs. Rex Larkin
1960	Adios Butler	P	Adios Butler Syndicate
1961	Adios Butler	P	Adios Butler Syndicate
1962	Su Mac Lad	T	I.W. Berkemeyer
1963	Speedy Scot	T	Castleton Farm
1964	Bret Hanover	P	Richard Downing
1965	Bret Hanover	P	Richard Downing
1966	Bret Hanover	P	Richard Downing
1967	Nevele Pride	T	Nevele Acres
1968	Nevele Pride	T	Nevele Acres, Louis Resnick
1969	Nevele Pride	T	Nevele Acres, Louis Resnick
1970	Fresh Yankee	T	Duncan MacDonald
1971	Albatross	P	Albatross Stable
1972	Albatross	P	Amicable Stable
1973	Sir Dalrae	P	A La Carte Racing Stable
1974	Delmonica Hanover	T	Delvin Miller, W. Arnold Hanger
1975	Savoir	T	Allwood Stable
1976	Keystone Ore	P	Mr. and Mrs. Stanley Dancer, Rose Hild Farms, Robert Jones
1977	Green Speed	T	Beverly Lloyds
1978	Abercrombie	P	Shirley Mitchell, L. Keith Bulen
1979	Niatross	P	Niagara Acres, Clint Galbraith
1980	Niatross	P	Niatross Syndicate, Niagara Acres, Clint Galbraith
1981	Fan Hanover	P	Dr. J. Glen Brown
1982	Cam Fella	P	Norm Clements, Norm Faulkner
1983	Cam Fella	P	JEF's Standardbred, Norm Clements, Norm Faulkner
1984	Fancy Crown	T	Fancy Crown Stable
1985	Nihilator	P	Wall Street-Nihilator Syndicate
1986	Forrest Skipper	P	Forrest L. Bartlett
1987	Mack Lobell	T	One More Time Stable and Fair Wind Farm
1988	Mack Lobell	T	John Erik Magnusson
1989	Matt's Scooter	P	Gordon and Illa Rumpel, Charles Jurasvinski
1990	Beach Towel	P	Uptown Stables
1991	Precious Bunny	P	R. Peter Heffering
1992	Artsplace	P	George Segal
1993	Staying Together	P	Robert Hamather
1994	Cam's Card Shark	P	Jeffrey S. Snyder
1995	CR Kay Suzie	T	Carl & Rod Allen Stable, Inc.
1996	Continental-victory	T	Continentalvictory Stables
1997	Malabar Man	T	Malvern Burroughs
1998	Moni Maker	T	Moni Maker Stable
1999	Moni Maker	T	Moni Maker Stable
2000	Gallo Blue Chip	P	Dan Gernatt Farms
2001	Bunny Lake	P	W. Springtime Racing Stable
2002	Real Desire	P	Brittany Farms
2003	No Pan Intended	P	Peter Pan Stables, Inc.
2004	Rainbow Blue	P	George Teague Jr
2005	Rocknroll Hanover	P	Jeffrey Snyder, Lothlorien Equestrian Centre & Perretti Racing Stb LLC
2006	Glidemaster	T	Robert Burgess, Karin Olsson Burgess, Marsha

Driver of the Year

Year	Driver
1968	Stanley Dancer
1969	Herve Filion
1970	Herve Filion
1971	Herve Filion
1972	Herve Filion
1973	Herve Filion
1974	Herve Filion
1975	Joe O'Brien
1976	Herve Filion
1977	Donald Dancer
1978	Carmine Abbatiello, Herve Filion
1979	Ron Waples
1980	Ron Waples
1981	Herve Filion
1982	Bill O'Donnell
1983	John Campbell
1984	Bill O'Donnell
1985	Michel Lachance
1986	Michel Lachance
1987	Michel Lachance
1988	John Campbell
1989	Herve Filion
1990	John Campbell
1991	Walter Case Jr.
1992	Walter Case Jr.
1993	Jack Moiseyev
1994	Dave Magee
1995	Luc Ouellette
1996	Tony Morgan, Luc Ouellette
1997	Tony Morgan
1998	Walter Case Jr.
1999	Dave Palone
2000	Dave Palone
2001	Stephane Bouchard
2002	Tony Morgan
2003	Dave Palone
2004	Dave Palone
2005	Catello Manzi
2006	Anthony Morgan

Note: Balloting is conducted by the U.S Trotting Association for the U.S. Harness Writers Association.

Leading Drivers—Money Won

Year	Driver	Winnings ($)	Year	Driver	Winnings ($)
1946	Thomas Berry	121,933	1977	Herve Filion	2,551,058
1947	H.C. Fitzpatrick	133,675	1978	Carmine Abbatiello	3,344,457
1948	Ralph Baldwin	153,222	1979	John Campbell	3,308,984
1949	Clint Hodgins	184,108	1980	John Campbell	3,732,306
1950	Del Miller	306,813	1981	Bill O'Donnell	4,065,608
1951	John Simpson Sr.	333,316	1982	Bill O'Donnell	5,755,067
1952	Bill Haughton	311,728	1983	John Campbell	6,104,082
1953	Bill Haughton	374,527	1984	Bill O'Donnell	9,059,184
1954	Bill Haughton	415,577	1985	Bill O'Donnell	10,207,372
1955	Bill Haughton	599,455	1986	John Campbell	9,515,055
1956	Bill Haughton	572,945	1987	John Campbell	10,186,495
1957	Bill Haughton	586,950	1988	John Campbell	11,148,565
1958	Bill Haughton	816,659	1989	John Campbell	9,738,450
1959	Bill Haughton	771,435	1990	John Campbell	11,620,878
1960	Del Miller	567,282	1991	Jack Moiseyev	9,568,468
1961	Stanley Dancer	674,723	1992	John Campbell	8,202,108
1962	Stanley Dancer	760,343	1993	John Campbell	9,926,482
1963	Bill Haughton	790,086	1994	John Campbell	9,834,139
1964	Stanley Dancer	1,051,538	1995	John Campbell	9,469,797
1965	Bill Haughton	889,943	1996	Michel Lachance	8,408,231
1966	Stanley Dancer	1,218,403	1997	Michel Lachance	9,215,388
1967	Bill Haughton	1,305,773	1998	John Campbell	10,768,771
1968	Bill Haughton	1,654,463	1999	Luc Ouellette	10,841,495
1969	Del Insko	1,635,463	2000	John Campbell	11,160,462
1970	Herve Filion	1,647,837	2001	John Campbell	14,184,863
1971	Herve Filion	1,915,945	2002	John Campbell	11,967,597
1972	Herve Filion	2,473,265	2003	David Miller	11,490,590
1973	Herve Filion	2,233,303	2004	Ron Pierce	12,327,863
1974	Herve Filion	3,474,315	2005	Brian Sears	15,085,992
1975	Carmine Abbatiello	2,275,093	2006	Ron Pierce	14,439,087
1976	Herve Filion	2,278,634			

Motor Sports

Kevin Harvick pulled off a razor-thin victory at the 2007 Daytona 500

Last Laps, Checkered Pasts

The 2007 racing season will be remembered for its long goodbyes, dueling teammates, and cheating scandals

BY MARK BECHTEL

WHEN HE NAMED HIS newly formed race team in 1980, Dale Earnhardt chose his own name—one he shared with his five-year-old son. It was a fortuitous decision, because when the boy grew up and embarked on a racing career of his own, the elder Earnhardt envisioned him one day running the company that bore his name.

Earnhardt's sudden death in 2001 changed those plans. Dale Junior was in just his third year in Nextel Cup and was in no position to take over a mammoth operation like Dale Earnhardt Incorporated. The reins were taken over by Earnhardt's widow, Teresa, setting off a chain of events that culminated in the biggest American auto racing story of 2007: Junior's departure from DEI.

Junior and his stepmother have never been close, and their already distant relationship was strained further when Teresa, who married Dale Sr. in 1982, sent the hell-raising Junior to military school. "Sure as hell wasn't my decision," Junior said this year. "It wasn't fun, I'll tell you that." When Earnhardt Sr. died, the one bond Junior and Teresa, who was named co-owner of DEI in 1996, shared was gone. Teresa rarely came to the track—driver Kevin Harvick, who assumed Earnhardt's ride when he died,

once referred to her as a "deadbeat owner." She and Junior seldom appeared together. "Me and Teresa do not see eye to eye," Junior said. "I wish we did, but we don't."

Junior, who was represented by his sister Kelley, began talks on a contract extension, but the sides were unable to agree on how much control Junior, who had matured into a savvy businessman, would have over the day-to-day operations at DEI. So in May Junior announced he was leaving, making himself the most sought-after free agent in the history of the sport.

He found his new home at Hendrick Motorsports, where he will team with Jimmie Johnson and Jeff Gordon to form a juggernaut. Junior had turned down plenty of other offers—despite the fact that he missed the Chase for the Nextel Cup for the second time in three years. A slew of mechanical problems doomed him to 13th place when the 12-car field was set. "If Dale Jr. and I just had a little bit of luck, we'd probably be fourth and fifth in the standings," said Martin Truex Jr., Earnhardt's DEI teammate. "But for whatever reason, Junior's had some blown motors that have really hurt him this year."

Big-name, big-money signings find themselves under the microscope in every sport, but Junior insisted he'd feel no pressure. "To me, pressure was having to go to Rockingham the week after my dad died and racing that whole year," he said. "That was pressure. Next year will be fun, man, a whole lot of fun."

He may be right. He'll be in some of the best equipment in the sport. Johnson and Gordon dominated the season, heading into the Chase ranked 1-2. They each did it despite lengthy absences from their crew chiefs. Both Chad Knaus, Johnson's crew chief, and Steve Letarte (Gordon's) were suspended for six weeks for cheating.

Now, cheating has been a part of stock car racing since the first left turn. At the inaugural "strictly stock" race, in 1949, Glenn Dunnaway was stripped of the win when he was found to have used illegal springs. Drivers and crew chiefs have been pushing the envelope ever since. For the most part, violators were simply told to make their cars comply with the regulations and maybe assessed light penalties. But in 2007 NASCAR launched a serious crackdown on rule bending.

In an effort to make the sport cheaper, safer and more balanced, NASCAR introduced the "Car of Tomorrow," which featured some radical changes—such as a rear wing instead of a spoiler—and templates that allowed for very little difference between the makes. The CoT was run at selected tracks in '07, and NASCAR warned the teams that no tinkering would be tolerated. Earnhardt's team was the first to feel NASCAR's wrath. After Junior's car at Darlington was found to have illegal mounting brackets on the rear wing, his crew chief, Tony Eury, was fined $100,000 and suspended for six races. Then Knaus and Letarte were busted for having front fenders that were an inch too wide.

In a move that rocked the racing world, Dale Earnhardt Jr. announced that he would leave his namesake team to race for Hendrick Motorsports in 2008.

They were the kind of violations that NASCAR would have tolerated in the past. "With the old car, a fender violation may not even have raised an eyebrow," said Nextel Cup director John Darby. "It would have been, 'Go fix this, bring it back when you've got it fixed, and we'll move on down the road.'"

The first sign that cheating was going to be a big story in 2007 came at the season-opening Daytona 500. Michael Waltrip, who was the focal point of Toyota's entry into NASCAR, was caught with an illegal fuel additive during qualifying. His crew chief, David Hyder, was fined and suspended, and his competition director, Bobby Kennedy, were booted out of the track and suspended. That was just the beginning—by the end of Speed Week, NASCAR had handed out five suspensions and fined participants a total of $250,000. The 500 was won by Harvick—in the elder Earnhardt's old car—in a wild and controversial finish. A massive crash led officials to red flag the race with three laps left, setting up a 7.5-mile shootout. Mark Martin, who was looking for his first win in the Great American Race in his 22nd attempt, was the leader on the restart. On the last lap he went low to block Kyle Busch, opening up the high line for Harvick, who had been in seventh place on the restart. With Busch behind him providing drafting help, Martin thought he had the race wrapped up, even as Harvick pulled even. Said Martin, "I thought, 'Hey, this is a no-brainer. I've got the inside line. I've got Kyle back here, he's fast as all get-out. We're going to zoom back.' But we never picked that speed up."

So Harvick and Martin zoomed toward the checkered flag door-to-door. Then things got really interesting. Busch side-swiped Matt Kenseth, setting off a chain reaction that ultimately saw Clint Bowyer's car catch fire and slide on its roof. Under NASCAR rules, the moment a caution flag is flown, the field is frozen. Officials decided to wait to throw the flag until Bowyer's car began to tumble, which didn't happen until after Harvick and Martin crossed the finish line, with Harvick .02 of a second—roughly a bumper and a front fender—ahead. After the race, NASCAR took some heat for not throwing the yellow flag sooner, but Martin refused to complain. "Nobody wants to hear a grown man cry, all right?" he said. "That's what it is. And I'm not going to cry about it. They made their decision, and that's what we're going to live with."

The 48-year-old Martin had planned to retire after the 2005 season, but owner Jack Roush persuaded him to race one final season because he couldn't find an adequate replacement. When the field for the Chase was finally set, Martin was in 26th place—though with his points per race average he would have been comfortably in the top 12 had he run a full slate. "I have got such a good thing going right now," Martin said. "I keep thinking I'm going to wake up. This is certainly the happiest time of my life."

The story of the year in Formula One was the McLaren team, with drivers Fernando Alonso and Lewis Hamilton. Alonso entered the season as the defending world champion, but he soon found himself being outrun by his teammate, a British rookie who made history by becoming F1's first black driver. While team officials did their best to convince reporters that the two drivers were regular pals, it quickly became apparent that a true rivalry existed between the two. After Hamilton finished second—ahead of Alonso—on the Spaniard's home track, Autosport, a British weekly, ran a headline touting a "civil war" in the McLaren camp.

But a little internecine fighting was nothing compared to the bombshell that emerged later in the summer. In July, McLaren designer Mike Coughlan was found to be in possession of a 780-page technical dossier on Ferrari's cars, which he received from Nigel Stepney, a Ferrari engineer. The subsequent investigation revealed that Coughlan had passed critical information along to Alonso and McLaren test driver Pedro de la Rosa. De la Rosa also testified that Stepney gave him details of Ferrari's in-race pit stop strategies. The Italian police were ultimately involved in the case; they told F1 officials that they had traced 288 text messages, 35 phone calls and 23 e-mails between Stepney and Coughlan.

Stepney was fired and Coughlan was suspended, but when the extent of the espionage became evident, the World Motor Sport Council lowered the boom on McLaren, stripping them of all of their constructors' points and fining the team a whopping $100 million. The drivers, however, were not punished, though FIA president Max Mosley said that were it up to him, the two McLaren drivers would have been tossed from the world championship race. "I would have taken all the points away from Hamilton and Alonso, on the grounds that there is a suspicion they had an advantage they shouldn't have had," Mosley said. "That they had an advantage is almost beyond dispute. I feel when people look back in 10 or 15 years' time when all the emotions are gone, they will say 'hang on a minute, we just don't know what would have happened.'" That allowed Alonso to make a late run at Hamilton in the standings, insuring that in a season dominated by off-track news, the world's most sought-after driving prize would be decided where it should be: on the track.

Indy Racing League

Indianapolis 500

Results of the 91st running of the Indianapolis 500 and fifth race of the 2007 Indy Racing League season. Held Sunday, May 27, 2006, at the 2.5-mile Indianapolis Motor Speedway in Indianapolis.

Distance, 500 miles; starters, 33; winning time of race, 2 hours, 44 mins., 3.5608 seconds; average speed, 151.774 mph; margin of victory, 0.3610 seconds; caution flags, 11 for 55 laps; lead 23 among nine drivers.

TOP 10 FINISHERS

Pos.	Driver (start pos.)	C/E/T	Qual. Speed	Laps	Status
1	Dario Franchitti (3)	D/H/F	225.191	166	running
2	Scott Dixon (4)	D/H/F	225.122	166	running
3	Helio Castroneves (1)	D/H/F	225.817	166	running
4	Sam Hornish Jr. (5)	D/H/F	225.109	166	running
5	Ryan Briscoe (7)	D/H/F	224.410	166	running
6	Scott Sharp (12)	D/H/F	223.875	166	running
7	Tomas Scheckter (10)	D/H/F	222.877	166	running
8	Danica Patrick (8)	P/H/F	224.076	166	running
9	Davey Hamilton (20)	D/H/F	222.327	166	running
10	Vitor Meira (19)	D/H/F	222.333	166	running

2007 Indy Racing League Results

Date	Race	Winner (start pos.)	C/E/T	Qual. Speed
Mar 24	Miami 300	Dan Wheldon (1)	D/H/F	214.322
Apr 1	Grand Prix of St. Petersburg	Helio Castroneves (1)	D/H/F	105.052
Apr 21	Japan 300	Tony Kanaan (3)	D/H/F	204.777
Apr 29	Kansas 300	Dan Wheldon(4)	D/H/F	213.812
May 27	Indianapolis 500	Dario Franchitti (3)	D/H/F	225.191
June 3	Milwaukee 225	Tony Kanaan (3)	D/H/F	169.158
June 9	Texas 550	Sam Hornish Jr. (2)	D/H/F	214.518
June 24	Iowa 250	Dario Franchitti (3)	D/H/F	182.043
June 30	Richmond 250*	Dario Franchitti (1)	D/H/F	0.000†
July 8	Grand Prix of Watkins Glen	Scott Dixon (2)	D/H/F	135.449
July 15	Nashville 200	Scott Dixon (1)	D/H/F	204.414
July 22	Mid-Ohio 200	Scott Dixon (6)	D/H/F	120.473
Aug 5	Michigan 400	Tony Kanaan (8)	D/H/F	217.192
Aug 12	Kentucky 300	Tony Kanaan (1)	D/H/F	218.086
Aug 26	Sonoma Grand Prix	Scott Dixon (5)	D/H/F	107.063
Sept 2	Grand Prix of Belle Isle	Tony Kanaan (4)	D/H/F	102.299
Sept 9	Chicago 300	Dario Franchitti (1)	D/H/F	214.646

Note: Distances are in miles unless followed by * (laps). †Qualification round rained out.

2007 Final Championship Standings

Driver	Pts
Dario Franchitti	637
Scott Dixon	624
Tony Kanaan	576
Dan Wheldon	466
Sam Hornish Jr.	465
Helio Castroneves	446
Danica Patrick	424
Scott Sharp	412
Buddy Rice	360
Tomas Scheckter	357

2007 Champ Car Series Results†

Date	Event	Winner (start pos.)	Chassis-Engine	Avg Speed
April 8	Grand Prix of Las Vegas	Will Power (1)	Panoz DP01-Cosworth	93.056
April 15	Grand Prix of Long Beach	Sebastian Bourdais (1)	Panoz DP01-Cosworth	91.432
April 22	Grand Prix of Houston	Sebastian Bourdais (1)	Panoz DP01-Cosworth	89.356
June 10	Grand Prix of Portland	Sebastian Bourdais (3)	Panoz DP01-Cosworth	114.816
June 24	Grand Prix of Cleveland	Paul Tracy (7)	Panoz DP01-Cosworth	106.921
July 1	Grand Prix of Quebec	Robert Doornbos (5)	Panoz DP01-Cosworth	93.265
July 8	Grand Prix of Toronto	Will Power (7)	Panoz DP01-Cosworth	72.534
July 22	Grand Prix of Edmonton	Sebastian Bourdais (2)	Panoz DP01-Cosworth	107.517
July 29	Grand Prix of San Jose	Robert Doornbos (5)	Panoz DP01-Cosworth	88.428
Aug 12	Milwaukee Road America	Sebastian Bourdais (1)	Panoz DP01-Cosworth	127.481
Aug 26	Grand Prix of Belgium	Sebastian Bourdais (1)	Panoz DP01-Cosworth	106.008
Sept 2	Grand Prix of Mexico City	Justin Wilson (2)	Panoz DP01-Cosworth	110.491

† Through October 7, 2007.

2006 Championship Standings

Driver	Overall	Road	Oval
Sebastian Bourdais	387	353	34
Justin Wilson	298	270	28
A.J. Allmendinger	285	261	24
Nelson Philippe	231	205	26
Bruno Junqueira	219	213	6
Will Power	213	203	10
Paul Tracy	209	204	5
Alex Tagliani	205	205	0
Mario Dominguez	202	202	0
Andrew Ranger	200	183	17

National Association for Stock Car Auto Racing

Daytona 500

Results of the 49th Daytona 500, the opening round of the 2007 Nextel Cup series. Held Sunday, February 18, 2007, at the 2.5-mile high-banked Daytona International Speedway.

Distance, 500 miles; starters, 43; winning time of race, 3:22:54; average speed, 149.335 mph; margin of victory, 0.20 seconds; caution flags, 6 for 24 laps; lead changes, 13.

TOP 10 FINISHERS

Pos.	Driver (start pos.)	Car	Laps	Winnings ($)
1	Kevin Harvick (34)	Chevrolet	202	1,510,470
2	Mark Martin (26)	Chevrolet	202	1,120,420
3	Jeff Burton (7)	Chevrolet	202	819,216
4	Mike Wallace (22)	Chevrolet	202	615,658
5	†David Ragan (35)	Ford	202	529,350
6	Elliott Sadler (30)	Dodge	202	407,153
7	Kasey Kahne (28)	Dodge	202	386,074
8	David Gilliland (1)	Ford	202	374,764
9	Joe Nemechek (18)	Chevrolet	202	302,008
10	Jeff Gordon (42)	Chevrolet	202	371,679

†-denotes rookie driver

2006 Nextel Cup* Final Standings

Driver	Pts	Starts	Wins	Top 5	Top 10
Jimmie Johnson	6475	36	5	13	24
Matt Kenseth	6419	36	4	15	21
Denny Hamlin	6407	36	2	8	20
Kevin Harvick	6397	36	5	15	20
Dale Earnhardt Jr.	6328	36	1	10	17
Jeff Gordon	6256	36	2	14	18
Jeff Burton	6228	36	1	7	20
Kasey Kahne	6183	36	6	12	19
Mark Martin	6168	36	0	7	15
Kyle Busch	6027	36	1	10	18

2006 Nextel Cup* Driver Winnings

Driver	Winnings ($)
Jimmie Johnson	8,909,140
Tony Stewart	7,285,280
Matt Kenseth	6,608,920
Kasey Kahne	6,204,220
Kevin Harvick	6,201,580
Jeff Gordon	5,975,870
Dale Earnhardt Jr.	5,466,100
Casey Mears	5,413,340
Ryan Newman	5,364,550
Kurt Busch	5,026,140

*Series name changed from Winston Cup after 2003 season.

Late 2006 Nextel Cup Series Results

Date	Track/Distance	Winner (start pos.)	Car	Laps	Winnings ($)
Oct 14	Charlotte 500	Kasey Kahne (2)	Dodge	334	305,889
Oct 22	Martinsville 500	Jimmie Johnson (9)	Chevrolet	500	191,886
Oct 29	Atlanta 500	Tony Stewart (11)	Chevrolet	325	373,286
Nov 5	Texas 500	Tony Stewart (8)	Chevrolet	339	521,361
Nov 12	Phoenix 500	Kevin Harvick (2)	Chevrolet	312	245,761
Nov 19	Homestead/Miami 400	Greg Biffle (22)	Ford	268	323,800

2007 Nextel Cup Series Results†

Date	Track/Distance	Winner (start pos.)	Car	Laps	Winnings ($)
Feb 18	Daytona 500	Kevin Harvick (34)	Chevrolet	202	1,510,470
Feb 25	Fontana 500	Matt Kenseth (25)	Ford	250	342,216
Mar 11	Las Vegas 400	Jimmie Johnson (23)	Chevrolet	267	415,386
Mar 18	Atlanta 500	Jimmie Johnson (3)	Chevrolet	325	233,261
Mar 25	Bristol 500	Kyle Busch (20)	Chevrolet	504	179,400
Apr 1	Martinsville 500	Jimmie Johnson (20)	Chevrolet	500	198,736
Apr 15	Texas 500	Jeff Burton (2)	Chevrolet	334	526,766
Apr 21	Phoenix 500	Jeff Gordon (1)	Chevrolet	312	251,411
Apr 29	Talladega 499	Jeff Gordon (1)	Chevrolet	192	355,511
May 6	Richmond 400	Jimmie Johnson (4)	Chevrolet	400	244,286
May 13	Darlington 500	Jeff Gordon (10)	Chevrolet	367	323,286
May 27	Charlotte 600	Casey Mears (16)	Chevrolet	400	377,425
June 4	Dover 400	Martin Truex Jr. (26)	Chevrolet	400	295,045
June 10	Pocono 500	Jeff Gordon (18)	Chevrolet	106	238,286
June 17	Michigan 400	Carl Edwards (12)	Ford	200	177,850
June 25	Sonoma 350	Juan Pablo Montoya (32)	Dodge	110	310,660
July 1	New Hampshire 300	Denny Hamlin (11)	Chevrolet	300	235,775
July 7	Daytona 400	Jamie McMurray (15)	Ford	160	302,500
July 15	Chicagoland 400	Tony Stewart (19)	Chevrolet	267	342,161
July 29	Brickyard 400	Tony Stewart (14)	Chevrolet	160	488,111
Aug 5	Pocono 500	Kurt Busch (2)	Chevrolet	200	206,008
Aug 12	Watkins Glen 220	Tony Stewart (5)	Chevrolet	90	239,286
Aug 21	Michigan 400	Kurt Busch (15)	Dodge	203	190,108
Aug 25	Bristol 500	Carl Edwards (6)	Ford	500	297,050
Sept 2	California 500	Jimmie Johnson (2)	Chevrolet	250	289,411
Sept 8	Richmond 400	Jimmie Johnson (1)	Chevrolet	400	249,836
Sept 16	New Hampshire 300	Clint Bowyer (1)	Chevrolet	300	259,175
Sept 23	Dover 400	Carl Edwards (15)	Ford	400	229,250
Sept 30	Kansas 400	Greg Biffle (7)	Ford	210	316,225
Oct 7	Talladega 500	Jeff Gordon (34)	Chevrolet	193	246,036

† Through October 7, 2007.

Formula One Grand Prix Racing

2007 Formula One Results†

Grand Prix	Date	Winner	Car	Laps	Time
Australia	Mar 18	Kimi Räikkönen	Ferrari	58	1:25:28.770
Malaysia	Apr 8	Fernando Alonso	McLaren-Mercedes	56	1:32:14.930
Bahrain	Apr 15	Felipe Massa	Ferrari	57	1:33:27.515
Spain	May 13	Felipe Massa	Ferrari	65	1:31:36.230
Monaco	May 27	Fernando Alonso	McLaren-Mercedes	78	1:40:29.329
Canada	June 10	Lewis Hamilton	McLaren-Mercedes	70	1:44:11.292
United States	June 17	Lewis Hamilton	McLaren-Mercedes	73	1:31:09.965
France	July 1	Kimi Räikkönen	Ferrari	70	1:30:54.200
Britain	July 8	Kimi Räikkönen	Ferrari	59	1:21:43.074
Europe	July 22	Fernando Alonso	McLaren-Mercedes	60	2:06:26.358
Hungary	Aug 5	Lewis Hamilton	McLaren-Mercedes	70	1:35:52.991
Turkey	Aug 26	Felipe Massa	Ferrari	58	1:26:42.161
Italy	Sept 9	Fernando Alonso	McLaren-Mercedes	53	1:18:37.806
Belgium	Sept 16	Kimi Räikkönen	Ferrari	44	1:20:39.066
Japan	Sept 30	Lewis Hamilton	McLaren-Mercedes	67	2:00:34.579
China	Oct 7	Kimi Räikkönen	Ferrari	56	1:37:58.395

† Through October 7, 2007.

2006 World Championship Final Standings

Drivers compete in Grand Prix races for the title of World Driving Champion. Below are the top 10 drivers from the 2005 season. Points are awarded for places 1–6 as follows: 10-6-4-3-2-1.

Driver	Country	Team	Pts
Fernando Alonso	Spain	Renault	134
Michaèl Schumacher	Germany	Ferrari	121
Felipe Massa	Brazil	Ferrari	80
Giancarlo Fisichella	Italy	Renault	72
Kimi Räikkönen	Finland	McLaren- Mercedes	65
Jenson Button	Great Britain	Honda	56
Rubens Barrichello	Brazil	Honda	30
Juan Pablo Montoya	Colombia	McLaren- Mercedes	26
Nick Heidfeld	Germany	BMW Sauber	23
Ralf Schumacher	Germany	Toyota	20

Professional Sports Car Racing

The 24 Hours of Daytona

Held at the Daytona International Speedway on Jan 27–28, 2007, the 24 Hours of Daytona serves as the opening round of the Grand American Road Racing Association's season.

Place	Drivers	Car (Class)	Distance
1	S. Pruett, S. Duran, J. Montoya	Lexus Riley	668 laps (99.02 mph)
2	M. Duno, P. Carpentier, D. Manning, R. Dalziel,	Pontiac Riley	668
3	W. Taylor, M. Angelelli, J. Gordon, J. Magnussen	Pontiac Riley	666
4	H. Haywood, J.C. France, J. Barbosa, R. Moreno	Porsche Riley	662
5	M. Wilkins, D. Empringham, Br. Frisselle, Bu. Frisselle	Lexus Riley	657

2007 American Le Mans Series—Prototype Class†

Date	Race	Winners	Car
Mar 17	12 Hours of Sebring	E. Pirro, M. Werner, F. Biela	Audi R10 TDI
Mar 31	St. Petersburg Challenge	R. Capello, A. McNish	Audi R10 TDI
April 14	Grand Prix of Long Beach	R. Capello, A. McNish	Audi R10 TDI
April 21	Lone Star Grand Prix	R. Capello, A. McNish	Audi R10 TDI
May 19	Utah Grand Prix	R. Capello, A. McNish	Audi R10 TDI
July 7	Northeast Grand Prix	R. Capello, A. McNish	Audi R10 TDI
July 21	Mid Ohio	E. Pirro, M. Werner	Audi R10 TDI
Aug 11	Road America 500	R. Capello, A. McNish	Audi R10 TDI
Aug 26	Grand Prix of Mosport	R. Capello, A. McNish	Audi R10 TDI
Sept 1	Detroit Challenge	E. Pirro, M. Werner	Audi R10 TDI
Oct 6	Petie Le Mans	R. Capello, A. McNish	Audi R10 TDI

2007 American Le Mans Series—GTS Class†

Date	Race	Winners	Car
Mar 17	12 Hours of Sebring	O. Beretta, O. Gavin, M. Papis	Corvette C6.R
Mar 31	St. Petersburg Challenge	O. Beretta, O. Gavin	Corvette C6.R
April 14	Grand Prix of Long Beach	O. Beretta, O. Gavin	Corvette C6.R

2007 American Le Mans Series—GTS Class *(Cont.)*

Date	Race	Winners	Car
April 21	Lone Star Grand Prix	O. Beretta, O. Gavin	Corvette C6.R
May 19	Utah Grand Prix	O. Beretta, O. Gavin	Corvette C6.R
July 7	Northeast Grand Prix	O. Beretta, O. Gavin	Corvette C6.R
July 21	Mid Ohio	O. Beretta, O. Gavin	Corvette C6.R
Aug 11	Road America 500	O. Beretta, O. Gavin	Corvette C6.R
Aug 26	Grand Prix of Mosport	J. O'Connell, J. Magnussen	Corvette C6.R
Sept1	Detroit Challenge	J. O'Connell, J. Magnussen	Corvette C6.R
Oct 6	Petie Le Mans	O. Beretta, O. Gavin, M. Papis	Corvette C6.R

2007 American Le Mans Series—GT Class†

Date	Race	Winners	Car
Mar 17	12 Hours of Sebring	M. Salo, J. Melo, J. Mowlem	Ferrari F430GT
Mar 31	St. Petersburg Challenge	J. van Overbeek, J. Bergmeister	Porsche 911 GT3
April 14	Grand Prix of Long Beach	M. Salo, J. Melo	Ferrari F430GT
April 21	Lone Star Grand Prix	M. Salo, J. Melo	Ferrari F430GT
May 19	Utah Grand Prix	T. Enge, D. Turner	Ferrari F430GT
July 7	Northeast Grand Prix	J. van Overbeek, J. Bergmeister	Porsche 911 GT3
July 21	Mid Ohio	J. van Overbeek, J. Bergmeister	Porsche 911 GT3
Aug 11	Road America 500	M. Salo, J. Melo	Ferrari F430GT
Aug 26	Grand Prix of Mosport	M. Salo, J. Melo	Ferrari F430GT
Sept1	Detroit Challenge	M. Salo, J. Melo	Ferrari F430GT
Oct 6	Petie Le Mans	J. van Overbeek, J. Bergmeister, M. Lieb	Porsche 911 GT3

† Through October 7, 2007.

2006 American Le Mans Series Championship Final Standings

PROTOTYPE CLASS	Pts	GTS CLASS	Pts	GT CLASS	Pts
Rinaldo Capiello	204	Olivier Beretta	176	Jörg Bergmeister	147
Allan McNish	204	Oliver Gavin	176	Johannes van Overbeek	141
James Weaver	119	Stephane Sarrazin	163	Patrick Long	137
Butch Leitzinger	106	Tomas Enge	159	Wolf Henzler	114
Frank Biela	99	Ron Fellows	152	Scott Maxwell	86
Emanuele Pirro	99	Johnny O'Connell	152	David Brabham	86

24 Hours of Le Mans

Held at Le Mans, France, on June 16–17, 2006, the 24 Hours of Le Mans is the most prestigious international event in endurance racing.

Place	Drivers	Car	Laps
1	F. Biela, E. Pirro, M. Werner	Audi R10	369
2	P. Lamy, S. Sarrazin,	Pescarolo Judd	359
3	E. Collard, J. Boullion, S. Bourdais	Peugeot	357
3	J. Barbosa, S. Hall, M. Short	Pescarolo Judd	347
4	D. Brabham, R. Rydell, D. Turner	Aston Martin	342

National Hot Rod Association

2007 Results†

TOP FUEL

Date	Race, Site	Winner
Feb 8–11	Winter Nationals, Pomona, Calif.	J.R. Todd
Feb 23–25	Kragen Nationals, Phoenix	Rod Fuller
Mar 15–18	Gatornationals, Gainesville, Fla.	Tony Schumacher
Mar 30–Apr 1	Spring Nationals, Houston	J.R. Todd
Apr 12–15	Las Vegas Nationals, Las Vegas	Brandon Bernstein
Apr 26–29	Southern Nationals, Atlanta	Brandon Bernstein
May 4–6	Midwest Nationals, Madison, Ill.	Melanie Troxel
June 1–3	Summer Nationals, Topeka, Kan.	Brandon Bernstein
June 7–10	Route 66 Nationals, Chicago, Ill.	Larry Dixon
June 21–24	Super Nationals, Englishtown, N.J.	Larry Dixon
June 28–July 1	Summit Nationals, Norwalk, Ohio	Tony Schumacher
July 6–8	Thunder Valley Nationals, Bristol, Tenn.	Brandon Bernstein
July 13–15	Mile High Nationals, Denver	Rod Fuller

† Through October 7, 2007.

2007 Results† *(Cont.)*

TOP FUEL *(CONT.)*

Date	Race, Site	Winner
July 21-23	Schuck's Nationals, Seattle	Tony Schumacher
July 27–29	Autolite Nationals, Sonoma, Calif.	Tony Schumacher
Aug 9–12	Lucas Oil Nationals, Brainerd, Minn.	Brandon Bernstein
Aug 16–19	Toyo Tires Nationals, Reading, Pa.	Doug Herbert
Aug 29–Sept 3	U.S. Nationals, Indianapolis	Tony Schumacher
Sept 14–16	Mid-South Nationals, Memphis	Melanie Troxel
Sept 20–23	Fall Nationals, Ennis, Tex.	Larry Dixon
Oct 5–7	Torco Racing Fuels Nationals, Richmond, Va.	Doug Kalitta

FUNNY CAR

Date	Race, Site	Winner
Feb 8–11	Winter Nationals, Pomona, Calif.	Gary Scelzi
Feb 23–25	Kragen Nationals, Phoenix	Tony Pedregon
Mar 15–18	Gatornationals, Gainesville, Fla.	Ron Capps
Mar 31–Apr 2	Spring Nationals, Houston	Ron Capps
Apr 12–15	Las Vegas Nationals, Las Vegas	Robert Hight
Apr 26–29	Southern Nationals, Atlanta	Robert Hight
May 4–6	Midwest Nationals, Madison, Ill.	Ron Capps
June 1–3	Summer Nationals, Topeka, Kan.	Mike Ashley
June 7–10	Route 66 Nationals, Chicago, Ill.	Gary Scelzi
June 21–24	Super Nationals, Englishtown, N.J.	Tommy Johnson Jr.
June 28–July 1	Summit Nationals, Norwalk, Ohio	Mike Ashley
July 6–8	Thunder Valley Nationals, Bristol, Tenn.	John Force
July 13–15	Mile High Nationals, Denver	Jack Beckman
July 21-23	Schuck's Nationals, Seattle	Jack Beckman
July 27–29	Autolite Nationals, Sonoma, Calif.	John Force
Aug 9–12	Lucas Oil Nationals, Brainerd, Minn.	John Force
Aug 16–19	Toyo Tires Nationals, Reading, Pa.	Tony Pedregon
Aug 29–Sept 3	U.S. Nationals, Indianapolis	Mike Ashley
Sept 14–16	Mid-South Nationals, Memphis	Gary Scelzi
Sept 20–23	Fall Nationals, Ennis, Tex.	Tony Pedregon
Oct 5–7	Torco Racing Fuels Nationals, Richmond, Va.	Gary Scelzi

PRO STOCK

Date	Race, Site	Winner
Feb 8–11	Winter Nationals, Pomona, Calif.	Greg Anderson
Feb 23–25	Kragen Nationals, Phoenix	Kurt Johnson
Mar 15–18	Gatornationals, Gainesville, Fla.	Greg Anderson
Mar 30–Apr 1	Spring Nationals, Houston	Jason Line
Apr 12–15	Las Vegas Nationals, Las Vegas	Greg Anderson
Apr 26–29	Southern Nationals, Atlanta	Greg Anderson
May 4–6	Midwest Nationals, Madison, Ill.	Dave Connolly
June 1–3	Summer Nationals, Topeka, Kan.	Greg Anderson
June 7–10	Route 66 Nationals, Chicago, Ill.	Jeg Coughlin
June 21–24	Super Nationals, Englishtown, N.J.	Greg Anderson
June 28–July 1	Summit Nationals, Norwalk, Ohio	Dave Connolly
July 6–8	Thunder Valley Nationals, Bristol, Tenn.	Jeg Coughlin
July 13–15	Mile High Nationals, Denver	Allen Johnson
July 21-23	Schuck's Nationals, Seattle	Dave Connolly
July 27–29	Autolite Nationals, Sonoma, Calif.	Greg Anderson
Aug 9–12	Lucas Oil Nationals, Brainerd, Minn.	Jeg Coughlin
Aug 16–19	Toyo Tires Nationals, Reading, Pa.	Dave Connolly
Aug 29–Sept 3	U.S. Nationals, Indianapolis	Dave Connolly
Sept 14–16	Mid-South Nationals, Memphis	Dave Connolly
Sept 20–23	Fall Nationals, Ennis, Tex.	Dave Connolly
Oct 5–7	Torco Racing Fuels Nationals, Richmond, Va.	Dave Connolly

† Through October 7, 2007.

2006 NHRA Final Standings

TOP FUEL		FUNNY CAR		PRO STOCK	
Driver	Pts	Driver	Pts	Driver	Pts
Tony Schumacher	1681	John Force	1636	Jason Line	1787
Doug Kalitta	1667	Robert Hight	1524	Greg Anderson	1664
Brandon Bernstein	1565	Ron Capps	1503	Dave Connolly	1451
Melanie Troxel	1471	Eric Medlen	1407	Mike Edwards	1265
Rod Fuller	1384	Tony Pedregon	1370	Kurt Johnson Jr.	1230

Indianapolis 500

First held in 1911, the Indianapolis 500—200 laps of the 2.5-mile Indianapolis Motor Speedway Track (called the Brickyard in honor of its original pavement)—grew to become the most famous auto race in the world. Though the Memorial Day weekend event lost participants and prestige in the mid-1990s due to feuding in the world of U.S. open-wheel racing, it annually attracts crowds of over 100,000.

Year	Winner (start pos.)	Chassis-Engine	Avg Speed	Pole Winner	Speed
1911	Ray Harroun (28)	Marmon-Marmon	74.590	Lewis Strang	First entered
1912	Joe Dawson (7)	National-National	78.720	Gil Anderson	First entered
1913	Jules Goux (7)	Peugeot-Peugeot	75.930	Caleb Bragg	Drew pole
1914	Rene Thomas (15)	Delage-Delage	82.470	Jean Chassagne	Drew pole
1915	Ralph DePalma (2)	Mercedes-Mercedes	89.840	Howard Wilcox	98.90
1916	Dario Resta (4)	Peugeot-Peugeot	84.000	John Aitken	96.69
1917–18	No race				
1919	Howard Wilcox (2)	Peugeot-Peugeot	88.050	Rene Thomas	104.78
1920	Gaston Chevrolet (6)	Frontenac-Frontenac	88.620	Ralph DePalma	99.15
1921	Tommy Milton (20)	Frontenac-Frontenac	89.620	Ralph DePalma	100.75
1922	Jimmy Murphy (1)	Duesenberg-Miller	94.480	Jimmy Murphy	100.50
1923	Tommy Milton (1)	Miller-Miller	90.950	Tommy Milton	108.17
1924	L.L. Corum / Joe Boyer (21)	Duesenberg-Duesenberg	98.230	Jimmy Murphy	108.037
1925	Peter DePaolo (2)	Duesenberg-Duesenberg	101.130	Leon Duray	113.196
1926	Frank Lockhart (20)	Miller-Miller	95.904	Earl Cooper	111.735
1927	George Souders (22)	Duesenberg-Duesenberg	97.545	Frank Lockhart	120.100
1928	Louis Meyer (13)	Miller-Miller	99.482	Leon Duray	122.391
1929	Ray Keech (6)	Miller-Miller	97.585	Cliff Woodbury	120.599
1930	Billy Arnold (1)	Summers-Miller	100.448	Billy Arnold	113.268
1931	Louis Schneider (13)	Stevens-Miller	96.629	Russ Snowberger	112.796
1932	Fred Frame (27)	Wetteroth-Miller	104.144	Lou Moore	117.363
1933	Louis Meyer (6)	Miller-Miller	104.162	Bill Cummings	118.524
1934	Bill Cummings (10)	Miller-Miller	104.863	Kelly Petillo	119.329
1935	Kelly Petillo (22)	Wetteroth-Offy	106.240	Rex Mays	120.736
1936	Louis Meyer (28)	Stevens-Miller	109.069	Rex Mays	119.664
1937	Wilbur Shaw (2)	Shaw-Offy	113.580	Bill Cummings	123.343
1938	Floyd Roberts (1)	Wetteroth-Miller	117.200	Floyd Roberts	125.681
1939	Wilbur Shaw (3)	Maserati-Maserati	115.035	Jimmy Snyder	130.138
1940	Wilbur Shaw (2)	Maserati-Maserati	114.277	Rex Mays	127.850
1941	Floyd Davis / Mauri Rose (17)	Wetteroth-Offy	115.117	Mauri Rose	128.691
1942–45	No race				
1946	George Robson (15)	Adams-Sparks	114.820	Cliff Bergere	126.471
1947	Mauri Rose (3)	Deidt-Offy	116.338	Ted Horn	126.564
1948	Mauri Rose (3)	Deidt-Offy	119.814	Rex Mays	130.577
1949	Bill Holland (4)	Deidt-Offy	121.327	Duke Nalon	132.939
1950	Johnnie Parsons (5)	Kurtis-Offy	124.002	Walt Faulkner	134.343
1951	Lee Wallard (2)	Kurtis-Offy	126.244	Duke Nalon	136.498
1952	Troy Ruttman (7)	Kuzma-Offy	128.922	Fred Agabashian	138.010
1953	Bill Vukovich (1)	KK500A-Offy	128.740	Bill Vukovich	138.392
1954	Bill Vukovich (19)	KK500A-Offy	130.840	Jack McGrath	141.033
1955	Bob Sweikert (14)	KK500C-Offy	128.209	Jerry Hoyt	140.045
1956	Pat Flaherty (1)	Watson-Offy	128.490	Pat Flaherty	145.596
1957	Sam Hanks (13)	Salih-Offy	135.601	Pat O'Connor	143.948
1958	Jim Bryan (7)	Salih-Offy	133.791	Dick Rathmann	145.974
1959	Rodger Ward (6)	Watson-Offy	135.857	Johnny Thomson	145.908
1960	Jim Rathmann (2)	Watson-Offy	138.767	Eddie Sachs	146.592
1961	A.J. Foyt (7)	Trevis-Offy	139.130	Eddie Sachs	147.481
1962	Rodger Ward (2)	Watson-Offy	140.293	Parnelli Jones	150.370
1963	Parnelli Jones (1)	Watson-Offy	143.137	Parnelli Jones	151.153
1964	A.J. Foyt (5)	Watson-Offy	147.350	Jim Clark	158.828
1965	Jim Clark (2)	Lotus-Ford	150.686	A.J. Foyt	161.233
1966	Graham Hill (15)	Lola-Ford	144.317	Mario Andretti	165.899
1967	A.J. Foyt (4)	Coyote-Ford	151.207	Mario Andretti	168.982
1968	Bobby Unser (3)	Eagle-Offy	152.882	Joe Leonard	171.559
1969	Mario Andretti (2)	Hawk-Ford	156.867	A.J. Foyt	170.568
1970	Al Unser (1)	PJ Colt-Ford	155.749	Al Unser	170.221
1971	Al Unser (5)	PJ Colt-Ford	157.735	Peter Revson	178.696
1972	Mark Donohue (3)	McLaren-Offy	162.962	Bobby Unser	195.940

Year	Winner (start pos.)	Chassis-Engine	Avg speed	Pole Winner	Speed
1973	Gordon Johncock (11)	Eagle-Offy	159.036	Johnny Rutherford	198.413
1974	Johnny Rutherford (25)	McLaren-Offy	158.589	A.J. Foyt	191.632
1975	Bobby Unser (3)	Racers Eagle-Offy	149.213	A.J. Foyt	193.976
1976	Johnny Rutherford (1)	McLaren-Offy	148.725	Johnny Rutherford	188.957
1977	A.J. Foyt (4)	Coyote-Ford	161.331	Tom Sneva	198.884
1978	Al Unser (5)	Lola-Cosworth	161.361	Tom Sneva	202.156
1979	Rick Mears (1)	Penske-Cosworth	158.899	Rick Mears	193.736
1980	Johnny Rutherford (1)	Chaparral-Cosworth	142.862	Johnny Rutherford	192.256
1981	Bobby Unser (1)	Penske-Cosworth	139.084	Bobby Unser	200.546
1982	Gordon Johncock (5)	Wildcat-Cosworth	162.026	Rick Mears	207.004
1983	Tom Sneva (4)	March-Cosworth	162.117	Teo Fabi	207.395
1984	Rick Mears (3)	March-Cosworth	163.612	Tom Sneva	210.029
1985	Danny Sullivan (8)	March-Cosworth	152.982	Pancho Carter	212.583
1986	Bobby Rahal (4)	March-Cosworth	170.722	Rick Mears	216.828
1987	Al Unser (20)	March-Cosworth	162.175	Mario Andretti	215.390
1988	Rick Mears (1)	Penske-Chevrolet	144.809	Rick Mears	219.198
1989	Emerson Fittipaldi (3)	Penske-Chevrolet	167.581	Rick Mears	223.885
1990	Arie Luyendyk (3)	Lola-Chevrolet	185.981*	Emerson Fittipaldi	225.301
1991	Rick Mears (1)	Penske-Chevrolet	176.457	Rick Mears	224.113
1992	Al Unser Jr. (12)	Galmer-Chevrolet	134.477	Roberto Guerrero	232.482
1993	Emerson Fittipaldi (9)	Penske-Chevrolet	157.207	Arie Luyendyk	223.967
1994	Al Unser Jr. (1)	Penske-Mercedes	160.872	Al Unser Jr.	228.011
1995	Jacques Villeneuve (5)	Reynard-Ford	153.616	Scott Brayton	231.616
1996	Buddy Lazier (5)	Reynard-Ford	147.956	Tony Stewart	233.100†
1997	Arie Luyendyk (3)	G Force-Oldsmobile	145.827	Arie Luyendyk	231.468
1998	Eddie Cheever (17)	Dallara-Oldsmobile	145.155	Billy Boat	223.503
1999	Kenny Brack (8)	Dallara-Oldsmobile	153.176	Arie Luyendyk	225.179
2000	Juan Montoya (2)	G Force-Oldsmobile	167.607	Greg Ray	223.471
2001	Helio Castroneves (11)	Dallara-Oldsmobile	153.601	Scott Sharp	226.037
2002	Helio Castroneves (13)	Dallara-Chevrolet	166.499	Bruno Junqueira	231.342
2003	Gil de Ferran	Panoz-Toyota	156.291	Helio Castroneves	231.725
2004	Buddy Rice (1)	G Force-Honda	138.518	Buddy Rice	222.024
2005	Dan Wheldon	Dallara-Honda	157.603	Tony Kanaan	227.566
2006	Sam Hornish Jr.(1)	Dallara-Honda	157.085	Sam Hornish Jr.	228.985
2007	Dario Franchitti (3)	Dallara-Honda	151.744	Helio Castroneves	225.817

Indianapolis 500 Rookie of the Year Award

*Track record, winning speed.
†Track record, qualifying speed.

1952 Art Cross	1971 Denny Zimmerman	1990 Eddie Cheever*
1953 Jimmy Daywalt	1972 Mike Hiss	1991 Jeff Andretti
1954 Larry Crockett	1973 Graham McRae	1992 Lyn St. James
1955 Al Herman	1974 Pancho Carter	1993 Nigel Mansell
1956 Bob Veith	1975 Bill Puterbaugh	1994 Jacques Villeneuve*
1957 Don Edmunds	1976 Vern Schuppan	1995 Gil de Ferran*
1958 George Amick	1977 Jerry Sneva	1996 Tony Stewart
1959 Bobby Grim	1978 Rick Mears*	1997 Jeff Ward
1960 Jim Hurtubise	Larry Rice	1998 Steve Knapp
1961 Parnelli Jones*	1979 Howdy Holmes	1999 Robby McGehee
Bobby Marshman	1980 Tim Richmond	2000 Juan Montoya*
1962 Jimmy McElreath	1981 Josele Garza	2001 Helio Castroneves*
1963 Jim Clark*	1982 Jim Hickman	2002 Alex Barron
1964 Johnny White	1983 Teo Fabi	Tomas Scheckter
1965 Mario Andretti*	1984 Michael Andretti	2003 Tora Tagaki
1966 Jackie Stewart	Roberto Guerrero	2004 Kosuke Matsuura
1967 Denis Hulme	1985 Arie Luyendyk*	2005 Danica Patrick
1968 Billy Vukovich	1986 Randy Lanier	2006 Marco Andretti
1969 Mark Donohue*	1987 Fabrizio Barbazza	2007 Phil Giebler
1970 Donnie Allison	1988 Billy Vukovich III	
	1989 Bernard Jourdain	
	Scott Pruett	

*Future winner of Indy 500.

Champ Car World Series Champions

From 1909 to 1955, this championship was awarded by the American Automobile Association (AAA), and from 1956 to 1979 by the United States Auto Club (USAC). Since 1979, Championship Auto Racing Teams (CART) has conducted the championship. Known as PPG CART World Series until 1998. Series name changed to Champ Car World Series for 2005 racing season.

1909 ....George Robertson	1942–45 ....No racing	1978 ....Tom Sneva
1910 ....Ray Harroun	1946 ....Ted Horn	1979 .............A.J. Foyt
1911 ....Ralph Mulford	1947 ....Ted Horn	1979 ....Rick Mears
1912 ....Ralph DePalma	1948 ....Ted Horn	1980 ....Johnny Rutherford
1913 ....Earl Cooper	1949 ....Johnnie Parsons	1981 ....Rick Mears
1914 ....Ralph DePalma	1950 ....Henry Banks	1982 ....Rick Mears
1915 ....Earl Cooper	1951 ....Tony Bettenhausen	1983 ....Al Unser
1916 ....Dario Resta	1952 ....Chuck Stevenson	1984 ....Mario Andretti
1917 ....Earl Cooper	1953 ....Sam Hanks	1985 ....Al Unser
1918 ....Ralph Mulford	1954 ....Jimmy Bryan	1986 ....Bobby Rahal
1919 ....Howard Wilcox	1955 ....Bob Sweikert	1987 ....Bobby Rahal
1920 ....Tommy Milton	1956 ....Jimmy Bryan	1988 ....Danny Sullivan
1921 ....Tommy Milton	1957 ....Jimmy Bryan	1989 ....Emerson Fittipaldi
1922 ....Jimmy Murphy	1958 ....Tony Bettenhausen	1990 ....Al Unser Jr.
1923 ....Eddie Hearne	1959 ....Rodger Ward	1991 ....Michael Andretti
1924 ....Jimmy Murphy	1960 .............A.J. Foyt	1992 ....Bobby Rahal
1925 ....Peter DePaolo	1961 .............A.J. Foyt	1993 ....Nigel Mansell
1926 ....Harry Hartz	1962 ....Rodger Ward	1994 ....Al Unser Jr.
1927 ....Peter DePaolo	1963 .............A.J. Foyt	1995 ....Jacques Villeneuve
1928 ....Louis Meyer	1964 .............A.J. Foyt	1996 ....Jimmy Vasser
1929 ....Louis Meyer	1965 ....Mario Andretti	1997 ....Alex Zanardi
1930 ....Billy Arnold	1966 ....Mario Andretti	1998 ....Alex Zanardi
1931 ....Louis Schneider	1967 .............A.J. Foyt	1999 ....Juan Montoya
1932 ....Bob Carey	1968 ....Bobby Unser	2000 ....Gil de Ferran
1933 ....Louis Meyer	1969 ....Mario Andretti	2001 ....Gil de Ferran
1934 ....Bill Cummings	1970 ....Al Unser	2002 ....Cristiano da Matta
1935 ....Kelly Petillo	1971 ....Joe Leonard	2003 ....Paul Tracy
1936 ....Mauri Rose	1972 ....Joe Leonard	2004 ....Sebastian Bourdais
1937 ....Wilbur Shaw	1973 ....Roger McCluskey	2005 ....Sebastian Bourdais
1938 ....Floyd Roberts	1974 ....Bobby Unser	2006 ....Sebastian Bourdais
1939 ....Wilbur Shaw	1975 .............A.J. Foyt	
1940 ....Rex Mays	1976 ....Gordon Johncock	
1941 ....Rex Mays	1977 ....Tom Sneva	

Alltime Champ Car* Leaders

WINS		POLE POSITIONS	
A.J. Foyt	67	Mario Andretti	67
Mario Andretti	52	A.J. Foyt	53
Michael Andretti	42	Bobby Unser	49
Al Unser	39	Rick Mears	40
Bobby Unser	35	Michael Andretti	32
Al Unser Jr	31	†Sebastian Bourdais	28
†Paul Tracy	31	Al Unser	27
Rick Mears	29	†Paul Tracy	25
†Sebastian Bourdais	29	Johnny Rutherford	23
Johnny Rutherford	27	Gordon Johncock	20
Rodger Ward	26	Rex Mays	19
Gordon Johncock	25	Danny Sullivan	19
Bobby Rahal	24	Bobby Rahal	18
Ralph DePalma	24	Emerson Fittipaldi	17
Tommy Milton	23	Gil de Ferran	16
Tony Bettenhausen	22	Tony Bettenhausen	14
Emerson Fittipaldi	22	Juan Montoya	14
Earl Cooper	20	Don Branson	14
Jimmy Bryan	19	Tom Sneva	14
Jimmy Murphy	19	Parnelli Jones	12
Danny Sullivan	17		
Ralph Mulford	17		

*Series known as CART prior to 2003 season
†Active driver. Note: Leaders through September 2007.

Stock Car Racing's Major Events

In 1985, Winston began offering a $1 million bonus to any driver to win three of the top four NASCAR events in the same season. A fifth event, the Brickyard 400 (in Indianapolis) was added in 1994. As of 1998 the Winston million was awarded to any driver who won three of the five events. The other four races are the richest (Daytona 500), the fastest (Talladega 500), the longest (Charlotte 600) and the oldest (Southern 500 at Darlington). Only five drivers, Lee Roy Yarbrough (1969), David Pearson (1976), Bill Elliott (1985), Dale Jarrett (1996) and Jeff Gordon (1997, '98) have scored the three-track hat trick.

Daytona 500

Year	Winner (start pos.)	Chassis-Engine	Avg speed	Pole Winner	Qual. speed
1959	Lee Petty	Oldsmobile	135.520	Cotton Owens	143.198
1960	Junior Johnson	Chevrolet	124.740	Fireball Roberts	151.556
1961	Marvin Panch	Pontiac	149.601	Fireball Roberts	155.709
1962	Fireball Roberts	Pontiac	152.529	Fireball Roberts	156.995
1963	Tiny Lund	Ford	151.566	Johnny Rutherford	165.183
1964	Richard Petty	Plymouth	154.345	Paul Goldsmith	174.910
1965	Fred Lorenzen	Ford	141.539	Darel Dieringer	171.151
1966	Richard Petty	Plymouth	160.627	Richard Petty	175.165
1967	Mario Andretti	Ford	149.926	Curtis Turner	180.831
1968	Cale Yarborough	Mercury	143.251	Cale Yarborough	189.222
1969	Lee Roy Yarbrough	Ford	157.950	David Pearson	190.029
1970	Pete Hamilton	Plymouth	149.601	Cale Yarborough	194.015
1971	Richard Petty	Plymouth	144.462	A.J. Foyt	182.744
1972	A.J. Foyt	Mercury	161.550	Bobby Isaac	186.632
1973	Richard Petty	Dodge	157.205	Buddy Baker	185.662
1974	Richard Petty	Dodge	140.894	David Pearson	185.017
1975	Benny Parsons	Chevrolet	153.649	Donnie Allison	185.827
1976	David Pearson	Mercury	152.181	A.J. Foyt	185.943
1977	Cale Yarborough	Chevrolet	153.218	Donnie Allison	188.048
1978	Bobby Allison	Ford	159.730	Cale Yarborough	187.536
1979	Richard Petty	Oldsmobile	143.977	Buddy Baker	196.049
1980	Buddy Baker	Oldsmobile	177.602*	A.J. Foyt	195.020
1981	Richard Petty	Buick	169.651	Bobby Allison	194.624
1982	Bobby Allison	Buick	153.991	Benny Parsons	196.317
1983	Cale Yarborough	Pontiac	155.979	Ricky Rudd	198.864
1984	Cale Yarborough	Chevrolet	150.994	Cale Yarborough	201.848
1985	Bill Elliott	Ford	172.265	Bill Elliott	205.114
1986	Geoff Bodine	Chevrolet	148.124	Bill Elliott	205.039
1987	Bill Elliott	Ford	176.263	Bill Elliott	210.364†
1988	Bobby Allison	Buick	137.531	Ken Schrader	193.823
1989	Darrell Waltrip	Chevrolet	148.466	Ken Schrader	196.996
1990	Derrike Cope	Chevrolet	165.761	Ken Schrader	196.515
1991	Ernie Irvan	Chevrolet	148.148	Davey Allison	195.955
1992	Davey Allison	Ford	160.256	Sterling Marlin	192.213
1993	Dale Jarrett	Chevrolet	154.972	Kyle Petty	189.426
1994	Sterling Marlin	Chevrolet	156.931	Loy Allen Jr	190.158
1995	Sterling Marlin	Chevrolet	141.710	Dale Jarrett	193.498
1996	Dale Jarrett	Ford	154.308	Dale Earnhardt	189.510
1997	Jeff Gordon	Chevrolet	148.295	Mike Skinner	189.813
1998	Dale Earnhardt	Chevrolet	172.712	Bobby Labonte	192.415
1999	Jeff Gordon	Chevrolet	161.551	Jeff Gordon	195.067
2000	Dale Jarrett	Ford	155.669	Dale Jarrett	191.091
2001	Michael Waltrip	Chevrolet	161.783	Bill Elliott	183.570
2002	Ward Burton	Dodge	142.971	Jimmie Johnson	185.831
2003	Michael Waltrip	Chevrolet	133.870	Jeff Green	186.606
2004	Dale Earnhardt Jr.	Chevrolet	156.345	Greg Biffle	188.387
2005	Jeff Gordon	Chevrolet	135.173	Dale Jarrett	188.312
2006	Jimmie Johnson	Chevrolet	142.667	Jeff Burton	188.887
2007	Kevin Harvick	Chevrolet	149.335	David Gilliland	186.320

Note: The Daytona 500, held annually in February, now opens the NASCAR season with 200 laps around the 2.5-mile high-banked Daytona International Speedway. Starting in 1988, cars racing at Daytona have used restrictor plates that lower power and acceleration.

*Track record, winning speed. †Track record, qualifying speed.

Brickyard 400

Year	Winner	Car	Avg Speed	Pole Winner	Speed
1994	Jeff Gordon	Chevrolet	131.977	Rick Mast	172.414
1995	Dale Earnhardt	Chevrolet	155.206	Jeff Gordon	172.536
1996	Dale Jarrett	Ford	139.508	Jeff Gordon	176.419
1997	Ricky Rudd	Ford	130.814	Ernie Irvan	177.736
1998	Jeff Gordon	Chevrolet	126.772	Ernie Irvan	179.394
1999	Dale Jarrett	Ford	148.194	Jeff Gordon	179.612
2000	Bobby Labonte	Pontiac	155.912*	Ricky Rudd	181.068
2001	Jeff Gordon	Chevrolet	130.790	Jimmy Spencer	179.666
2002	Bill Elliott	Dodge	125.033	Tony Stewart	182.960
2003	Kevin Harvick	Chevrolet	134.554	Kevin Harvick	184.343
2004	Jeff Gordon	Chevrolet	115.037	Casey Mears	186.293†
2005	Tony Stewart	Chevrolet	148.782	Elliott Sadler	184.117
2006	Jimmie Johnson	Chevrolet	137.182	Jeff Burton	182.778
2007	Tony Stewart	Chevrolet	117.379	Reed Sorenson	184.207

Note: Held at the 2.5-mile Indianapolis Motor Speedway
*Track record, winning speed. †Track record, qualifying speed

Talladega 500

Year	Winner	Car	Avg Speed	Pole Winner	Speed
1970	Pete Hamilton	Plymouth	152.321	Bobby Isaac	199.658
1971	Donnie Allison	Mercury	147.419	Donnie Allison	185.869
1972	David Pearson	Mercury	134.400	Bobby Isaac	192.428
1973	David Pearson	Mercury	131.956	Buddy Baker	193.435
1974	David Pearson	Mercury	130.220	David Pearson	186.086
1975	Buddy Baker	Ford	144.94	Buddy Baker	189.947
1976	Buddy Baker	Ford	169.887	Dave Marcis	189.197
1977	Darrell Waltrip	Chevrolet	164.887	A.J. Foyt	192.424
1978	Cale Yarborough	Oldsmobile	155.699	Cale Yarborough	191.904
1979	Bobby Allison	Ford	154.770	Darrell Waltrip	195.644
1980	Buddy Baker	Oldsmobile	170.481	David Pearson	197.704
1981	Bobby Allison	Buick	149.376	Bobby Allison	195.864
1982	Darrell Waltrip	Buick	156.697	Benny Parsons	200.176
1983	Richard Petty	Pontiac	135.936	Cale Yarborough	202.650
1984	Cale Yarborough	Chevrolet	172.988	Cale Yarborough	202.692
1985	Bill Elliott	Ford	186.288	Bill Elliott	209.398
1986	Bobby Allison	Buick	157.698	Bill Elliott	212.229
1987	Davey Allison	Ford	154.228	Bill Elliott	221.809†
1988	Phil Parsons	Oldsmobile	156.547	Davey Allison	198.969
1989	Davey Allison	Ford	155.869	Mark Martin	193.061
1990	Dale Earnhardt	Chevrolet	159.571	Bill Elliott	199.388
1991	Harry Gant	Oldsmobile	165.620	Ernie Irvan	195.186
1992	Davey Allison	Ford	167.609	Ernie Irvan	192.831
1993	Ernie Irvan	Chevrolet	155.412	Dale Earnhardt	192.355
1994	Dale Earnhardt	Chevrolet	157.478	Ernie Irvan	193.298
1995	Mark Martin	Ford	178.902	Terry Labonte	196.532
1996	Sterling Marlin	Chevrolet	149.999	Ernie Irvan	192.855
1997	Mark Martin	Ford	188.354*	John Andretti	193.627
1998	Dale Jarrett	Ford	159.318	Ken Schrader	196.153
1999	Dale Earnhardt	Chevrolet	166.632	Joe Nemechek	198.331
2000	Dale Earnhardt	Chevrolet	165.681	Joe Nemechek	190.279
2001	Dale Earnhardt Jr.	Chevrolet	164.185	Stacy Compton	185.240
2002	Dale Earnhardt Jr.	Chevrolet	183.665	qualifying cancelled	—
2003	Michael Waltrip	Chevrolet	156.045	Elliott Sadler	189.943
2004	Jeff Gordon	Chevrolet	129.396	Ricky Rudd	191.180
2005	Dale Jarrett	Ford	143.818	Elliott Sadler	189.260
2006	Brian Vickers	Chevrolet	157.602	David Gilliland	191.712
2007	Jeff Gordon	Chevrolet	143.438	Michael Waltrip	189.070

*Track record, winning speed. †Track record, qualifying speed.

Charlotte 600

Year	Winner	Car	Avg Speed	Pole Winner
1960	Joe Lee Johnson	Chevrolet	107.752	Joe Lee Johnson
1961	David Pearson	Pontiac	111.634	Richard Petty
1962	Nelson Stacy	Ford	125.552	Fireball Roberts
1963	Fred Lorenzen	Ford	132.418	Junior Johnson
1964	Jim Paschal	Plymouth	125.772	Junior Johnson
1965	Fred Lorenzen	Ford	121.772	Fred Lorenzon
1966	Marvin Panch	Plymouth	135.042	Paul Goldsmith
1967	Jim Paschal	Plymouth	135.832	Cale Yarborough
1968	Buddy Baker	Dodge	104.207	Donnie Allison
1969	Lee Roy Yarbrough	Mercury	134.631	Donnie Allison
1970	Donnie Allison	Ford	129.680	Bobby Isaac
1971	Bobby Allison	Mercury	140.442	Charlie Glotzbach
1972	Buddy Baker	Dodge	142.255	Bobby Allison
1973	Buddy Baker	Dodge	134.890	Buddy Baker
1974	David Pearson	Mercury	135.720	David Pearson
1975	Richard Petty	Dodge	145.327	David Pearson
1976	David Pearson	Mercury	137.352	David Pearson
1977	Richard Petty	Dodge	137.636	David Pearson
1978	Darrell Waltrip	Chevrolet	138.355	David Pearson
1979	Darrell Waltrip	Chevrolet	136.674	Neil Bonnet
1980	Benny Parsons	Chevrolet	119.265	Cale Yarborough
1981	Bobby Allison	Buick	129.326	Neil Bonnett
1982	Neil Bonnett	Ford	130.508	David Pearson
1983	Neil Bonnett	Chevrolet	140.406	Buddy Baker
1984	Bobby Allison	Buick	129.233	Harry Gant
1985	Darrell Waltrip	Chevrolet	141.807	Bill Elliott
1986	Dale Earnhardt	Chevrolet	140.406	Geoff Bodine
1987	Kyle Petty	Ford	131.483	Bill Elliott
1988	Darrell Waltrip	Chevrolet	124.460	Davey Allison
1989	Darrell Waltrip	Chevrolet	144.077	Alan Kulwicki
1990	Rusty Wallace	Pontiac	137.650	Ken Schrader
1991	Davey Allison	Ford	138.951	Mark Martin
1992	Dale Earnhardt	Chevrolet	132.980	Bill Elliott
1993	Dale Earnhardt	Chevrolet	145.504	Ken Schrader
1994	Jeff Gordon	Chevrolet	139.445	Jeff Gordon
1995	Bobby Labonte	Chevrolet	151.952*	Jeff Gordon
1996	Dale Jarrett	Ford	147.581	Jeff Gordon
1997	Jeff Gordon	Chevrolet	136.745	Jeff Gordon
1998	Jeff Gordon	Chevrolet	136.424	Jeff Gordon
1999	Jeff Burton	Ford	151.367	Bobby Labonte
2000	Matt Kenseth	Ford	142.640	Dale Earnhardt Jr
2001	Jeff Burton	Ford	138.107	Ryan Newman
2002	Mark Martin	Ford	137.729	Jimmie Johnson
2003	Jimmie Johnson	Chevrolet	126.198	Ryan Newman
2004	Jimmie Johnson	Chevrolet	142.763	Jimmie Johnson
2005	Jimmie Johnson	Chevrolet	114.698	Ryan Newman
2006	Kasey Kahne	Dodge	128.840	Scott Riggs
2007	Casey Mears	Chevrolet	130.222	Ryan Newman

Note: Held at the 1.5 mile high-banked Lowe's Motor Speedway in Charlotte on Memorial Day weekend.

*Track record, winning speed.

Darlington 500

Note: Formerly the Winston 500, held at the 2.66-mile Talladega Superspeedway. Starting in 1988, cars racing at Talladega have used restrictor plates that lower power and acceleration.

Year	Winner	Car	Avg Speed	Pole Winner
1950	Johnny Mantz	Plymouth	76.260	Wally Campbell
1951	Herb Thomas	Hudson	76.900	Marshall Teague
1952	Fonty Flock	Oldsmobile	74.510	Dick Rathman
1953	Buck Baker	Oldsmobile	92.780	Fonty Flock
1954	Herb Thomas	Hudson	94.930	Buck Baker
1955	Herb Thomas	Chevrolet	92.281	Tim Flock
1956	Curtis Turner	Ford	95.067	Buck Baker
1957	Speedy Thompson	Chevrolet	100.100	Paul Goldsmith
1958	Fireball Roberts	Chevrolet	102.590	Fireball Roberts
1959	Jim Reed	Chevrolet	111.836	Fireball Roberts
1960	Buck Baker	Pontiac	105.901	Cotton Owens
1961	Nelson Stacy	Ford	117.880	Fireball Roberts
1962	Larry Frank	Ford	117.965	Fireball Roberts
1963	Fireball Roberts	Ford	129.784	Fireball Roberts
1964	Buck Baker	Dodge	117.757	Richard Petty
1965	Ned Jarrett	Ford	115.924	Junior Johnson
1966	Darel Dieringer	Mercury	114.830	Lee Yarborough
1967	Richard Petty	Plymouth	131.933	David Pearson
1968	Cale Yarborough	Mercury	126.132	Charlie Glotzbach
1969	Lee Roy Yarbrough	Ford	105.612	Cale Yarborough
1970	Buddy Baker	Dodge	128.817	David Pearson
1971	Bobby Allison	Mercury	131.398	Bobby Allison
1972	Bobby Allison	Chevrolet	128.124	David Pearson
1973	Cale Yarborough	Chevrolet	134.033	David Pearson
1974	Cale Yarborough	Chevrolet	111.075	Richard Petty
1975	Bobby Allison	Matador	116.825	David Pearson
1976	David Pearson	Mercury	120.534	David Pearson
1977	David Pearson	Mercury	106.797	Darrell Waltrip
1978	Cale Yarborough	Oldsmobile	116.828	David Pearson
1979	David Pearson	Chevrolet	126.259	Bobby Allison
1980	Terry Labonte	Chevrolet	115.210	Darrell Waltrip
1981	Neil Bonnett	Ford	126.410	Harry Gant
1982	Cale Yarborough	Buick	126.703	David Pearson
1983	Bobby Allison	Buick	123.343	Neil Bonnett
1984	Harry Gant	Chevrolet	128.270	Harry Gant
1985	Bill Elliott	Ford	121.254	Bill Elliott
1986	Tim Richmond	Chevrolet	121.068	Tim Richmond
1987	Dale Earnhardt	Chevrolet	115.520	Davey Allison
1988	Bill Elliott	Ford	128.297	Bill Elliott
1989	Dale Earnhardt	Chevrolet	135.462	Alan Kulwicki
1990	Dale Earnhardt	Chevrolet	123.141	Dale Earnhardt
1991	Harry Gant	Oldsmobile	133.508	Davey Allison
1992	Darrell Waltrip	Chevrolet	129.114	Sterling Marlin
1993	Mark Martin	Ford	137.932	Ken Schrader
1994	Bill Elliott	Ford	127.915	Geoff Bodine
1995	Jeff Gordon	Chevrolet	121.231	John Andretti
1996	Jeff Gordon	Chevrolet	135.757	Dale Jarrett
1997	Jeff Gordon	Chevrolet	121.149	Bobby Labonte
1998	Jeff Gordon	Chevrolet	139.031*	Dale Jarrett
1999	Jeff Burton	Ford	100.816	Kenny Irwin
2000	Bobby Labonte	Pontiac	108.275	Jeremy Mayfield
2001	Ward Burton	Dodge	122.773	Kurt Busch
2002	Jeff Gordon	Chevrolet	118.617	Sterling Marlin
2003	Terry Labonte	Chevrolet	120.744	Ryan Newman
2004	Jimmie Johnson	Chevrolet	125.044	Kurt Busch
2005	Greg Biffle	Ford	135.127	Kasey Kahne
2006	Greg Biffle	Ford	123.031	Kasey Kahne
2007	Jeff Gordon	Chevrolet	124.372	Clint Bowyer

Through 2004, results listed were for the Southern 500, traditionally the second race of the year at the 1.366-mile Darlington (S.C.) Raceway. Starting in 2005, Darlington only hosted one race a year, in May.

*Track record, winning speed.

Nextel Cup* NASCAR Champions

Year	Driver	Car	Wins	Poles	Winnings ($)
1949	Red Byron	Oldsmobile	2	1	5,800
1950	Bill Rexford	Oldsmobile	1	0	6,175
1951	Herb Thomas	Hudson	7	4	18,200
1952	Tim Flock	Hudson	8	4	20,210
1953	Herb Thomas	Hudson	11	10	27,300
1954	Lee Petty	Dodge	7	3	26,706
1955	Tim Flock	Chrysler	18	19	33,750
1956	Buck Baker	Chrysler	14	12	29,790
1957	Buck Baker	Chevrolet	10	5	24,712
1958	Lee Petty	Oldsmobile	7	4	20,600
1959	Lee Petty	Plymouth	10	2	45,570
1960	Rex White	Chevrolet	6	3	45,260
1961	Ned Jarrett	Chevrolet	1	4	27,285
1962	Joe Weatherly	Pontiac	9	6	56,110
1963	Joe Weatherly	Mercury	3	6	58,110
1964	Richard Petty	Plymouth	9	8	98,810
1965	Ned Jarrett	Ford	13	9	77,966
1966	David Pearson	Dodge	14	7	59,205
1967	Richard Petty	Plymouth	27	18	130,275
1968	David Pearson	Ford	16	12	118,824
1969	David Pearson	Ford	11	14	183,700
1970	Bobby Isaac	Dodge	11	13	121,470
1971	Richard Petty	Plymouth	21	9	309,225
1972	Richard Petty	Plymouth	8	3	227,015
1973	Benny Parsons	Chevrolet	1	0	114,345
1974	Richard Petty	Dodge	10	7	299,175
1975	Richard Petty	Dodge	13	3	378,865
1976	Cale Yarborough	Chevrolet	9	2	387,173
1977	Cale Yarborough	Chevrolet	9	3	477,499
1978	Cale Yarborough	Oldsmobile	10	8	530,751
1979	Richard Petty	Chevrolet	5	1	531,292
1980	Dale Earnhardt	Chevrolet	5	0	588,926
1981	Darrell Waltrip	Buick	12	11	693,342
1982	Darrell Waltrip	Buick	12	7	873,118
1983	Bobby Allison	Buick	6	0	828,355
1984	Terry Labonte	Chevrolet	2	2	713,010
1985	Darrell Waltrip	Chevrolet	3	4	1,318,735
1986	Dale Earnhardt	Chevrolet	5	1	1,783,880
1987	Dale Earnhardt	Chevrolet	11	1	2,099,243
1988	Bill Elliott	Ford	6	6	1,574,639
1989	Rusty Wallace	Pontiac	6	4	2,247,950
1990	Dale Earnhardt	Chevrolet	9	4	3,083,056
1991	Dale Earnhardt	Chevrolet	4	0	2,396,685
1992	Alan Kulwicki	Ford	2	6	2,322,561
1993	Dale Earnhardt	Chevrolet	6	2	3,353,789
1994	Dale Earnhardt	Chevrolet	4	2	3,400,733
1995	Jeff Gordon	Chevrolet	7	9	4,347,343
1996	Terry Labonte	Chevrolet	2	4	4,030,648
1997	Jeff Gordon	Chevrolet	10	1	4,201,227
1998	Jeff Gordon	Chevrolet	13	7	6,175,867
1999	Dale Jarrett	Ford	4	0	3,608,829
2000	Bobby Labonte	Pontiac	4	2	4,041,750
2001	Jeff Gordon	Chevrolet	6	8	6,649,076
2002	Tony Stewart	Pontiac	3	4	4,695,150
2003	Matt Kenseth	Ford	1	2	4,038,120
2004	Kurt Busch	Ford	3	1	4,200,330
2005	Tony Stewart	Chevrolet	5	3	6,987,530
2006	Jimmie Johnson	Chevrolet	5	1	8,909,140

*Series name changed from Winston Cup after 2003 season.

Alltime NASCAR Leaders

WINS		POLE POSITIONS	
Richard Petty	200	Richard Petty	126
David Pearson	105	David Pearson	113
Bobby Allison	84	Cale Yarborough	70
Darrell Waltrip	84	*Jeff Gordon	64
Cale Yarborough	83	Darrell Waltrip	59
*Jeff Gordon	80	Bobby Allison	57
Dale Earnhardt	76	Bill Elliott	54
Rusty Wallace	55	Bobby Isaac	51
Lee Petty	54	Junior Johnson	47
Ned Jarrett	50	Buck Baker	44
Junior Johnson	50	*Mark Martin	43
Herb Thomas	48	*Ryan Newman	41
Buck Baker	46	Buddy Baker	40
Bill Elliott	44	Tim Flock	39
Tim Flock	40	Herb Thomas	39

*Active drivers. Note: NASCAR wins leaders and pole position leaders through Oct 7, 2007.

Formula One Grand Prix Racing

World Driving Champions

Year	Winner	Car	Year	Winner	Car
1950	Guiseppe Farina, Italy	Alfa Romeo	1976	James Hunt, Grt Britain	McLaren-Ford
1951	Juan-Manuel Fangio, Argentina	Alfa Romeo	1977	Niki Lauda, Austria	Ferrari
			1978	Mario Andretti, U.S.	Lotus-Ford
1952	Alberto Ascari, Italy	Ferrari	1979	Jody Scheckter, S Africa	Ferrari
1953	Alberto Ascari, Italy	Ferrari	1980	Alan Jones, Australia	Williams-Ford
1954	Juan-Manuel Fangio, Argentina	Maserati-Mercedes	1981	Nelson Piquet, Brazil	Brabham-Ford
			1982	Keke Rosberg, Finland	Williams-Ford
1955	Juan-Manuel Fangio, Argentina	Mercedes	1983	Nelson Piquet, Brazil	Brabham-BMW
			1984	Niki Lauda, Austria	McLaren-Porsche
1956	Juan-Manuel Fangio, Argentina	Ferrari	1985	Alain Prost, France	McLaren-Porsche
			1986	Alain Prost, France	McLaren-Porsche
1957	Juan-Manuel Fangio, Argentina	Maserati	1987	Nelson Piquet, Brazil	Williams-Honda
			1988	Ayrton Senna, Brazil	McLaren-Honda
1958	Mike Hawthorn, Grt Britain	Ferrari	1989	Alain Prost, France	McLaren-Honda
1959	Jack Brabham, Australia	Cooper-Climax	1990	Ayrton Senna, Brazil	McLaren-Honda
1960	Jack Brabham, Australia	Cooper-Climax	1991	Ayrton Senna, Brazil	McLaren-Honda
1961	Phil Hill, U.S.	Ferrari	1992	Nigel Mansell, Grt Britain	Williams-Renault
1962	Graham Hill, Grt Britain	BRM	1993	Alain Prost, France	Williams-Renault
1963	Jim Clark, Scotland	Lotus-Climax	1994	Michael Schumacher, Ger	Benetton-Ford
1964	John Surtees, Grt Britain	Ferrari	1995	Michael Schumacher, Ger	Benetton-Renault
1965	Jim Clark, Scotland	Lotus-Climax	1996	Damon Hill, Grt Britain	Williams-Renault
1966	Jack Brabham, Australia	Brabham-Repco	1997	Jacques Villeneuve, Can	Williams-Renault
1967	Denny Hulme, New Zealand	Brabham-Repco	1998	Mika Hakkinen, Finland	McLaren-Mercedes
			1999	Mika Hakkinen, Finland	McLaren-Mercedes
1968	Graham Hill, Grt Britain	Lotus-Ford	2000	Michael Schumacher, Ger	Ferrari
1969	Jackie Stewart, Scotland	Matra-Ford	2001	Michael Schumacher, Ger	Ferrari
1970	Jochen Rindt, Austria*	Lotus-Ford	2002	Michael Schumacher, Ger	Ferrari
1971	Jackie Stewart, Scotland	Tyrell-Ford	2003	Michael Schumacher, Ger	Ferrari
1972	Emerson Fittipaldi, Brazil	Lotus-Ford	2004	Michael Schumacher, Ger	Ferrari
1973	Jackie Stewart, Scotland	Tyrell-Ford	2005	Fernando Alonso, Spain	Renault
1974	Emerson Fittipaldi, Brazil	McLaren-Ford	2006	Fernando Alonso, Spain	Renault
1975	Niki Lauda, Austria	Ferrari			

*The championship was awarded posthumously, after Rindt was killed during practice for the Italian Grand Prix.

Alltime Grand Prix Winners

Driver	Wins	Driver	Wins
Michael Schumacher, Germany	91	Jim Clark, Great Britain	25
Alain Prost, France	51	Niki Lauda, Austria	25
Ayrton Senna, Brazil	41	Juan Manuel Fangio, Argentina	24
Nigel Mansell, Great Britain	31	Nelson Piquet, Brazil	23
Jackie Stewart, Great Britain	27	Damon Hill, Great Britain	22

*Active driver in 2007. Note: Grand Prix winners through Oct 7, 2007.

Alltime Grand Prix Pole Winners

Driver	Poles	Driver	Poles
Michael Schumacher, Germany	68	Juan Manuel Fangio, Argentina	29
Ayrton Senna, Brazil	65	Mika Hakkinen, Finland	26
Alain Prost, France	33	Niki Lauda, Austria	24
Jim Clark, Great Britain	33	Nelson Piquet, Brazil	24
Nigel Mansell, Great Britain	31	Damon Hill, Great Britain	20

*Active driver in 2007. Note: Grand Prix winners through Oct 7, 2007.

Professional Sports Car Racing

The 24 Hours of Daytona

Year	Winner	Car	Avg Speed	Distance
1962	Dan Gurney	Lotus 19-Class SP11	104.101 mph	3 hrs (312.42 mi)
1963	Pedro Rodriguez	Ferrari-Class 12	102.074 mph	3 hrs (308.61 mi)
1964	Pedro Rodriguez/Phil Hill	Ferrari 250 LM	98.230 mph	2,000 km
1965	Ken Miles/Lloyd Ruby	Ford	99.944 mph	2,000 km
1966	Ken Miles/Lloyd Ruby	Ford Mark II	108.020 mph	24 hrs (2,570.63 mi)
1967	Lorenzo Bandini/Chris Amon	Ferrari 330 P4	105.688 mph	24 hrs (2,537.46 mi)
1968	Vic Elford/Jochen Neerpasch	Porsche 907	106.697 mph	24 hrs (2,565.69 mi)
1969	Mark Donohue/Chuck Parsons	Chevy Lola	99.268 mph	24 hrs (2,383.75 mi)
1970	Pedro Rodriguez/Leo Kinnunen	Porsche 917	114.866 mph	24 hrs (2,758.44 mi)
1971	Pedro Rodriguez/Jackie Oliver	Porsche 917K	109.203 mph	24 hrs (2,621.28 mi)
1972*	Mario Andretti/Jacky Ickx	Ferrari 312/P	122.573 mph	6 hrs (738.24 mi)
1973	Peter Gregg/Hurley Haywood	Porsche Carrera	106.225 mph	24 hrs (2,552.7 mi)
1974	(No race)			
1975	Peter Gregg/Hurley Haywood	Porsche Carrera	108.531 mph	24 hrs (2,606.04 mi)
1976†	Peter Gregg/Brian Redman/ John Fitzpatrick	BMW CSL	104.040 mph	24 hrs (2,092.8 mi)
1977	John Graves/Hurley Haywood/ Dave Helmick	Porsche Carrera	108.801 mph	24 hrs (2,615 mi)
1978	Rolf Stommelen/ Antoine Hezemans/Peter Gregg	Porsche Turbo	108.743 mph	24 hrs (2,611.2 mi)
1979	Ted Field/Danny Ongais/ Hurley Haywood	Porsche Turbo	109.249 mph	24 hrs (2,626.56 mi)
1980	Volkert Meri/Rolf Stommelen/ Reinhold Joest	Porsche Turbo	114.303 mph	24 hrs
1981	Bob Garretson/Bobby Rahal/ Brian Redman	Porsche Turbo	113.153 mph	24 hrs
1982	John Paul Jr/John Paul Sr/ Rolf Stommelen	Porsche Turbo	114.794 mph	24 hrs
1983	Preston Henn/Bob Wollek/ Claude Ballot-Lena/A.J. Foyt	Porsche Turbo	98.781 mph	24 hrs
1984	Sarel van der Merwe/ Graham Duxbury/Tony Martin	Porsche March	103.119 mph	24 hrs (2,476.8 mi)
1985	A.J. Foyt/Bob Wollek/ Al Unser/Thierry Boutsen	Porsche 962	104.162 mph	24 hrs (2,502.68 mi)
1986	Al Holbert/Derek Bell/Al Unser Jr.	Porsche 962	105.484 mph	24 hrs (2,534.72 mi)
1987	Chip Robinson/Derek Bell/ Al Holbert/Al Unser Jr.	Porsche 962	111.599 mph	24 hrs (2,680.68 mi)
1988	Martin Brundle/John Nielsen/ Raul Boesel	Jaguar XJR-9	107.943 mph	24 hrs (2,591.68 mi)
1989	John Andretti/Derek Bell/ Bob Wollek	Porsche 962	92.009 mph	24 hrs (2,210.76 mi)
1990	Davy Jones/ Jan Lammers/ Andy Wallace	Jaguar XJR-12	112.857 mph	24 hrs (2,709.16 mi)

The 24 Hours of Daytona *(Cont.)*

1991	Hurley Haywood/ John Winter/ Frank Jelinski/ Henri Pescarolo/ Bob Wollek	Porsche 962C	106.633 mph	24 hrs (2,559.64 mi)
1992	Massahiro Hasemi/ Kazuoyshi Hoshino/ Toshio Suzuki/ Anders Olofsson	Nissan R91CP	112.987 mph	24 hrs (2,712.72 mi)
1993	P.J. Jones/Mark Dismore/ Rocky Moran	Toyota Eagle MK III	103.537 mph	24 hrs (2,484.88 mi)
1994	Paul Gentilozzi/ Scott Pruett/ Butch Leitzinger/ Steve Millen	Nissan 300 ZX	104.80 mph	24 hrs (2,693.67 mi)
1995	Jurgen Lassig/ Christophe Buochut/ Giovanni Lavaggi/ Marco Werner	Porsche Spyder K8	102.28 mph	690 laps (2,456.4 mi)
1996	Wayne Taylor/ Scott Sharp/ Jim Pace	Oldsmobile Mark III	103.32 mph	697 laps (2,481.32 mi)
1997	Elliot Forbes-Robinson/ John Schneider/Rob Dyson/ John Paul Jr/Butch Leitzinger/James Weaver/Andy Wallace	Ford R & S MK III	102.292 mph	690 laps (2,456.4 mi)
1998	Arie Luyendyk/Didier Theys/ Mauro Baldi	Ferrari 333 SP	105.565 mph	711 laps (2,531.16 mi)
1999	Elliott Forbes-Robinson/ Butch Leitzinger/ Andy Wallace	Ford R & S MK III	104.9 mph	708 laps (2,520.48 mi)
2000	Olivier Beretta/Karl Wendlinger/ Dominique Dupuy	Dodge Viper	107.207 mph	723 laps (2,573.88 m)
2001	Ron Fellows/Chris Kneifel/Franck Freon/Johnny O'Connell	Corvette	97.293 mph	656 laps (2,335.360 mi)
2002	Didier Theys/Fredy Lienhard/ Max Papis/Mauro Baldi	Dallara-Judd (SRP)	106.143 mph	716 laps (2,548.96 mi)
2003	Kevin Buckler/Michael Schrom Timo Bernhard/Jorg Bergmeister	Porsche GT3 RS	114.068† mph	694 laps (2,470.64 mi)
2004	Forest Barber/Terry Borcheller Andy Pilgrim/Christian Fittipaldi	Pontiac Doran	117.651 mph	526 laps (1,872.56 mi)
2005	Wayne Taylor, Max Angelelli, Emmanuel Collard	Pontiac Riley	119.397 mph	710 laps (2,527.60 mi)
2006	Scott Dixon/Dan Wheldon Casey Mears	Lexus Riley	108.826 mph	734 laps (2,613.04 mi)
2007	Scott Pruett/Salvador Duran Juan Pablo Montoya	Lexus Riley	99.020 mph	668 laps (2,378.08 mi)

*Race shortened due to fuel crisis. †Course lengthened from 3.81 miles to 3.84 miles. † Top speed.

World SportsCar Champions*

Year	Winner	Car	Year	Winner	Car
1978	Peter Gregg	Porsche 935	1989	Geoff Brabham	Nissan GTP
1979	Peter Gregg	Porsche 935	1990	Geoff Brabham	Nissan GTP
1980	John Fitzpatrick	Porsche 935	1991	Geoff Brabham	Nissan NPT
1981	Brian Redman	Chevy Lola	1992	Juan Fangio II	Toyota EGL MKIII
1982	John Paul Jr	Chevy Lola	1993	Juan Fangio II	Toyota EGL MKIII
1983	Al Holbert	Chevy March	1994	Wayne Taylor	Mazda Kudzu
1984	Randy Lanier	Chevy March	1995	Fermin Velez	Ferrari 333 SP
1985	Al Holbert	Porsche 962	1996	Wayne Taylor	Mazda Kudzu
1986	Al Holbert	Porsche 962	1997	Butch Leitzinger	Ford R&S MKIII
1987	Chip Robinson	Porsche 962	1998	Butch Leitzinger	Ford R&S MKIII
1988	Geoff Brabham	Nissan GTP			

Year	Prototype	GTS	GT
1999	Elliott Forbes-Robinson	Olivier Beretta	Cort Wagner
2000	Allan McNish	Olivier Beretta	Sascha Maassen
2001	Emanuele Pirro	Terry Borcheller	Jörg Müller
2002	Tom Kristensen	Ron Fellows	Lucas Luhr
2003	Frank Biela/Marco Werner	Ron Fellows/John O'Connell	Sascha Maassen/L. Luhr
2004	Frank Biela/Emanuele Pirro	Oliver Gavin/Olivier Beretta	Patrick Long/Jorg Bergmeister
2005	Frank Biela/Emanuele Pirro	Oliver Gavin/Olivier Beretta	Patrick Long/Jorg Bergmeister
2006	R. Capiello/A. McNish	Oliver Gavin/Olivier Beretta	Johannes van Overbeek

*1978–93 champions raced in the GT series, which in 1994 was replaced by the World SportsCar series. Beginning in 1999, racing was reclassified according to the American Le Mans Series. The Series is comprised of two different types of race cars divided into two categories and five separate classes. The Prototype category features open-cockpit prototype as well as Grand Touring Prototype (GTP) class cars. The Grand Touring category features the Grand Touring S (GTS) class cars, formerly known as GT2, and Grand Touring (GT) cars, formerly known as GT3. Both classes feature purpose-built race cars with an emphasis on spectator car identification.

Alltime SportsCar Leaders

PROTOTYPE WINS

*Rinaldo Capello	30
*Frank Biela	22
*Allan McNish	23
J.J. Lehto	19
*Emanuele Pirro	18
*Marco Werner	17
James Weaver	16
*Butch Leitzinger	15

GTS AND GT WINS

Al Holbert	49
Peter Gregg	41
*Olivier Beretta	36
Hurley Haywood	31
*Oliver Gavin	27
*Johnny O'Connell	27
Geoff Brabham	26
Parker Johnstone	25
Ron Fellows	25

* Active driver in 2007. Note: Leaders through Oct 7, 2007.

24 Hours of Le Mans

Year	Winning Drivers	Car
1923	André Lagache/René Léonard	Chenard & Walker
1924	John Duff/Francis Clement	Bentley
1925	Gérard de Courcelles/André Rossignol	La Lorraine
1926	Robert Bloch/André Rossignol	La Lorraine
1927	J. Dudley Benjafield/Sammy Davis	Bentley
1928	Woolf Barnato/Bernard Rubin	Bentley
1929	Woolf Barnato/Sir Henry Birkin	Bentley Speed 6
1930	Woolf Barnato/Glen Kidston	Bentley Speed 6
1931	Earl Howe/Sir Henry Birkin	Alfa Romeo 8C-2300 sc
1932	Raymond Sommer/Luigi Chinetti	Alfa Romeo 8C-2300 sc
1933	Raymond Sommer/Tazio Nuvolari	Alfa Romeo 8C-2300 sc
1934	Luigi Chinetti/Philippe Etancelin	Alfa Romeo 8C-2300 sc
1935	John Hindmarsh/Louis Fontés	Lagonda M45R
1936	Race cancelled	
1937	Jean-Pierre Wimille/Robert Benoist	Bugatti 57G sc
1938	Eugene Chaboud/Jean Tremoulet	Delahaye 135M
1939	Jean-Pierre Wimille/Pierre Veyron	Bugatti 57G sc
1940–48	Races cancelled	
1949	Luigi Chinetti/Lord Selsdon	Ferrari 166MM
1950	Louis Rosier/Jean-Louis Rosier	Talbot-Lago
1951	Peter Walker/Peter Whitehead	Jaguar C
1952	Hermann Lang/Fritz Reiss	Mercedes-Benz 300 SL
1953	Tony Rolt/Duncan Hamilton	Jaguar C
1954	Froilan Gonzales/Maurice Trintignant	Ferrari 375
1955	Mike Hawthorn/Ivor Bueb	Jaguar D
1956	Ron Flockhart/Ninian Sanderson	Jaguar D
1957	Ron Flockhart/Ivor Bueb	Jaguar D
1958	Olivier Gendebien/Phil Hill	Ferrari 250 TR58
1959	Carroll Shelby/Roy Salvadori	Aston Martin DBR1
1960	Olivier Gendebien/Paul Frère	Ferrari 250 TR59/60
1961	Olivier Gendebien/Phil Hill	Ferrari 250 TR61

Year	Winning Drivers	Car
1962	Olivier Gendebien/Phil Hill	Ferrari 250P
1963	Lodovico Scarfiotti/Lorenzo Bandini	Ferrari 250P
1964	Jean Guichel/Nino Vaccarella	Ferrari 275P
1965	Jochen Rindt/Masten Gregory	Ferrari 250LM
1966	Chris Amon/Bruce McLaren	Ford Mk2
1967	Dan Gurney/A.J. Foyt	Ford Mk4
1968	Pedro Rodriguez/Lucien Bianchi	Ford GT40
1969	Jacky Ickx/Jackie Oliver	Ford GT40
1970	Hans Herrmann/Richard Attwood	Porsche 917
1971	Helmut Marko/Gijs van Lennep	Porsche 917
1972	Henri Pescarolo/Graham Hill	Matra-Simca MS670
1973	Henri Pescarolo/Gérard Larrousse	Matra-Simca MS670B
1974	Henri Pescarolo/Gérard Larrousse	Matra-Simca MS670B
1975	Jacky Ickx/Derek Bell	Mirage-Ford MB
1976	Jacky Ickx/Gijs van Lennep	Porsche 936
1977	Jacky Ickx/Jurgen Barth/Hurley Haywood	Porsche 936
1978	Jean-Pierre Jaussaud/Didier Pironi	Renault-Alpine A442
1979	Klaus Ludwig/Bill Whittington/Don Whittington	Porsche 935
1980	Jean-Pierre Jaussaud/Jean Rondeau	Rondeau-Ford M379B
1981	Jacky Ickx/Derek Bell	Porsche 936-81
1982	Jacky Ickx/Derek Bell	Porsche 956
1983	Vern Schuppan/Hurley Haywood/Al Holbert	Porsche 956-83
1984	Klaus Ludwig/Henri Pescarolo	Porsche 956B
1985	Klaus Ludwig/Paolo Barilla/John Winter	Porsche 956B
1986	Derek Bell/Hans-Joachim Stuck/Al Holbert	Porsche 962C
1987	Derek Bell/Hans-Joachim Stuck/Al Holbert	Porsche 962C
1988	Jan Lammers/Johnny Dumfries/Andy Wallace	Jaguar XJR9LM
1989	Jochen Mass/Manuel Reuter/Stanley Dickens	Sauber-Mercedes C9-88
1990	John Nielsen/Price Cobb/Martin Brundle	TWR Jaguar XJR-12
1991	Volker Weidler/Johnny Herbert/Bertrand Gachof	Mazda 787B
1992	Derek Warwick/Yannick Dalmas/Mark Blundell	Peugeot 905B
1993	Geoff Brabham/Christophe Bouchut/Eric Helary	Peugeot 905
1994	Yannick Dalmas/Hurley Haywood/Mauro Baldi	Porsche 962
1995	Yannick Dalmas/J.J. Lehto/Masanori Sekiya	McLaren BMW
1996	Manuel Reuter/Davy Jones/Alexander Wurz	TWR Porsche
1997	Michele Alboreto/Stefan Johansson/Tom Kristensen	TWR Porsche
1998	Allan McNish/Laurent Aiello/Stephane Ortelli	Porsche GT One
1999	Yannick Dalmas/Joachim Winkelhock/Pierluigi Martini	BMW V12 LMR
2000	Frank Biela/Tom Kristensen/Emanuele Pirro	Audi R8
2001	Frank Biela/Tom Kristensen/Emanuele Pirro	Audi R8
2002	Frank Biela/Tom Kristensen/Emanuele Pirro	Audi R8
2003	Rinaldo Capello/Tom Kristensen/Guy Smith	Bentley EXP Speed 8
2004	Rinaldo Capello/Seiji Ara/Tom Kristensen	Audi R8
2005	J.J. Lehto/Marco Werner/Tom Kristensen	Audi R8
2006	Frank Biela/Emanuele Pirro/Marco Werner	Audi R10
2007	Frank Biela/Emanuele Pirro/Marco Werner	Audi R10

Top Fuel

ELAPSED TIME

Time (Sec.)	Driver	Date	Site
9.00	Jack Chrisman	Feb 18, 1961	Pomona, Calif.
8.97	Jack Chrisman	May 20, 1961	Empona, Va.
7.96	Bobby Vodnick	May 16, 1964	Bayview, Md.
6.97	Don Johnson	May 7, 1967	Carlsbad, Calif.
5.97	Mike Snively	Nov 17, 1972	Ontario, Calif.
5.78	Don Garlits	Nov 18, 1973	Ontario, Calif.
5.698	Gary Beck	Oct 10, 1975	Ontario, Calif.
5.573	Gary Beck	Oct 18, 1981	Irvine, Calif.
5.484	Gary Beck	Sept 6, 1982	Clermont, Ind.
5.391	Gary Beck	Oct 1, 1983	Fremont, Calif.
5.280	Darrell Gwynn	Sept 25, 1986	Ennis, Tex.
5.176	Darrell Gwynn	April 4, 1987	Ennis, Tex.
5.090	Joe Amato	Oct 1, 1987	Ennis, Tex.
4.990	Eddie Hill	April 9, 1988	Ennis, Tex.
4.881	Gary Ormsby	Sept 28, 1990	Topeka, Kan.
4.799	Cory McClenathan	Sept 19, 1992	Mohnton, Pa.
4.762	Cory McClenathan	Oct 3, 1993	Topeka, Kan.
4.690	Michael Brotherton	May 20, 1994	Englishtown, N.J.
4.595	Joe Amato	July 5,1996	Topeka, Kan.
4.539	Joe Amato	Mar 21, 1998	Baytown, Tex.
4.525	Gary Scelzi	Oct 23, 1998	Ennis, Tex.
4.503	Mike Dunn	Feb 5, 1999	Pomona, Calif.
4.486	Larry Dixon	Apr 9, 1999	Houston
4.480	Gary Scelzi	Oct 31, 1999	Houston
4.477	Kenny Bernstein	June 2, 2001	Joliet, Ill.
4.441	Tony Schumacher	Oct 4, 2003	Reading, Pa.
4.420	Doug Kalitta	May 23, 2004	Chicago, Ill.

SPEED

MPH	Driver	Date	Site
180.36	Connie Kalitta	Sept 3, 1962	Indianapolis
190.26	Don Garlits	Sept 21, 1963	East Haddam, Conn.
201.34	Don Garlits	Aug 1, 1964	Great Meadows, N.J.
211.26	Donny Milani	May 15, 1965	Sacramento, Calif.
223.32	Don Cook	Apr 24, 1965	Fremont, Calif.
230.17	James Warren	Apr 10, 1967	Fresno, Calif.
243.24	Don Garlits	Mar 18, 1973	Gainesville, Fla.
250.69	Don Garlits	Oct 11, 1975	Ontario, Calif.
260.11	Joe Amato	Mar 18, 1984	Gainesville, Fla.
272.56	Don Garlits	Mar 23, 1986	Gainesville, Fla.
282.13	Joe Amato	Sept 5, 1987	Clermont, Ind.
291.54	Connie Kalitta	Feb 11, 1989	Pomona, Calif.
301.70	Kenny Bernstein	Mar 20, 1992	Gainesville, Fla.
311.86	Kenny Bernstein	Oct 30, 1994	Pomona, Calif.
319.82	Joe Amato	Mar 21, 1998	Baytown, Tex.
323.50	Joe Amato	May 17, 1998	Englishtown, N.J.
326.44	Gary Scelzi	Nov 2, 1998	Houston
326.91	Tony Schumacher	Oct 22, 1999	Dallas
330.55	Mike Dunn	June 2, 2001	Joliet, Ill.
332.18	Kenny Bernstein	Oct. 7, 2001	Richardson, Tex.
332.75	Larry Dixon	Apr 3, 2003	Las Vegas
333.41	Brandon Bernstein	May 22, 2004	Joliet, Ill.
336.15	Tony Schumacher	May 25, 2005	Hebron, Ohio
337.58	Tony Schumacher	Aug 13, 2005	Brainerd, Minn.

Funny Car

ELAPSED TIME

Time (sec.)	Driver	Date	Site
6.92	Leroy Goldstein	Sept 3, 1970	Clermont, Ind.
5.987	Don Prudhomme	Oct 12, 1975	Ontario, Calif.
5.868	Raymond Beadle	July 16, 1981	Englishtown, N.J.
5.799	Tom Anderson	Sept 3, 1982	Clermont, Ind.
5.637	Don Prudhomme	Sept 4, 1982	Clermont, Ind.
5.588	Rick Johnson	Feb 3, 1985	Pomona, Calif.
5.425	Kenny Bernstein	Sept 26, 1986	Ennis, Tex.
5.397	Kenny Bernstein	April 5, 1987	Ennis, Tex.
5.255	Ed McCulloch	April 17, 1988	Ennis, Tex.
5.193	Don Prudhomme	Mar 2, 1989	Baytown, Tex.
5.077	Cruz Pedregon	Sept 20, 1992	Mohnton, Pa.
4.987	Chuck Etcholis	Oct 2, 1993	Topeka, Kan.
4.819	Cruz Pedregon	Mar 21, 1998	Baytown, Tex.
4.807	Cruz Pedregon	Nov 1, 1998	Houston
4.788	John Force	Apr 11, 1999	Houston
4.763	John Force	June 2, 2001	Joliet, Ill.
4.750	William Bazemore	Sept 28, 2001	Joliet, Ill.
4.731	John Force	Oct. 7, 2001	Yorba Linda, Calif.
4.713	Whit Bazemore	May 22, 2004	Joliet, Ill.
4.664	John Force	Oct 3, 2004	Joliet, Ill.
4.662	Jack Beckman	Nov. 12, 2006	Pomona, Calif.
4.646	Robert Hight	Feb. 11, 2007	Pomona, Calif.
4.636	Robert Hight	Feb. 23, 2007	Phoenix, Ariz.

SPEED

MPH	Driver	Date	Site
200.44	Gene Snow	Aug, 1968	Houston
250.00	Don Prudhomme	May 23, 1982	Baton Rouge, La.
260.11	Kenny Bernstein	Mar 18, 1984	Gainesville, Fla.
271.41	Kenny Bernstein	Aug 30, 1986	Indianapolis
280.72	Mike Dunn	Oct 2, 1987	Ennis, Tex.
290.13	Jim White	Oct 11, 1991	Ennis, Tex.
291.82	Jim White	Oct 25, 1991	Pomona, Calif.
300.40	Jim Epler	Oct 3, 1993	Topeka, Kan.
303.64	John Force	Sept 2, 1995	Indianapolis
308.74	John Force	Sept 28, 1997	Topeka, Kan.
317.46	John Force	Mar 21, 1998	Baytown, Tex.
323.89	John Force	May 17, 1998	Englishtown, N.J.
324.05	John Force	Mar 19, 1999	Gainesville, Fla.
325.45	William Bazemore	Sept 28, 2001	Joliet, Ill.
326.87	Gary Densham	Feb. 9, 2002	Bellflower, Calif.
330.55	Gary Scelzi	May 22, 2004	Joliet, Ill.
333.58	John Force	Oct 3, 2004	Joliet, Ill.
333.66	Jack Beckman	Nov. 12, 2006	Pomona, Calif.
334.32	Mike Ashley	Mar. 13, 2007	Joliet, Ill.

Pro Stock

ELAPSED TIME

Time (sec.)	Driver	Date	Site
7.778	Lee Shepherd	Mar 12, 1982	Gainesville, Fla.
7.655	Lee Shepherd	Oct 1, 1982	Fremont, Calif.
7.557	Bob Glidden	Feb 2, 1985	Pomona, Calif.
7.497	Bob Glidden	Sep 13, 1985	Maple Grove, Pa.
7.377	Bob Glidden	Aug 28, 1986	Clermont, Ind.
7.294	Frank Sanchez	Oct 7, 1988	Baytown, Tex.
7.184	Darrell Alderman	Oct 12, 1990	Ennis, Tex.
7.099	Scott Geoffrion	Sept 19, 1992	Mohnton, Pa.
6.988	Kurt Johnson	May 20, 1994	Englishtown, N.J.
6.873	Warren Johnson	Mar 14, 1998	Gainesville, Fla.
6.867	Warren Johnson	Oct 23, 1998	Ennis, Tex.
6.866	Warren Johnson	Mar 19, 1999	Gainesville, Fla.
6.843	Warren Johnson	Apr 30, 1999	Dinwiddie, Va.
6.840	Kurt Johnson	May 1, 1999	Dinwiddie, Va.
6.822	Warren Johnson	Oct 23, 1999	Dallas

Pro Stock (Cont.)

ELAPSED TIME

Time (sec.)	Driver	Date	Site
6.801	Kurt Johnson	Sept 29, 2001	Joliet, Ill.
6.750	Jeg Coughlin	Oct. 7, 2001	Delaware, Ohio
6.670	Greg Anderson	May 18, 2003	Englishtown, N.J.
6.633	Greg Anderson	Mar 19, 2005	Gainesville, Fla.
6.631	Greg Anderson	Aug 1, 2006	Sonoma, Calif.
6.575	Mike Edwards	Mar 17, 2007	Gainseville, Fla.
6.566	Larry Morgan	Mar 17, 2007	Gainesville, Fla.
6.553	Jason Line	Mar 17, 2007	Gainesville, Fla.
6.536	Greg Anderson	Mar 17, 2007	Gainesville, Fla.

SPEED

Time (sec.)	Driver	Date	Site
181.08	Warren Johnson	Oct 1, 1982	Fremont, Calif.
190.07	Warren Johnson	Aug 29, 1986	Clermont, Ind.
191.32	Bob Glidden	Sept 4, 1987	Clermont, Ind.
192.18	Warren Johnson	Oct 13, 1990	Ennis, Tex.
193.21	Bob Glidden	July 28, 1991	Sonoma, Calif.
194.51	Warren Johnson	July 31, 1992	Sonoma, Calif.
195.99	Warren Johnson	May 21, 1993	Englishtown, N.J.
196.24	Warren Johnson	Mar 19, 1993	Gainesville, Fla.
197.15	Warren Johnson	Apr 23, 1994	Commerce, Ga.
199.15	Warren Johnson	Mar 10, 1995	Baytown, Tex.
201.20	Warren Johnson	Mar 14, 1998	Gainesville, Fla.
201.34	Warren Johnson	Oct 23, 1998	Ennis, Tex.
201.37	Warren Johnson	Mar 19, 1999	Gainesville, Fla.
202.24	Warren Johnson	Apr 30,1999	Dinwiddie, Va.
202.33	Warren Johnson	Oct 23, 1999	Dallas
202.36	Warren Johnson	Oct 31, 1999	Houston
202.70	Kurt Johnson	Sept 29, 2001	Joliet, Ill.
204.35	Mark Osborne	Oct. 6, 2001	Abdingdon, Va.
207.18	Greg Anderson	May 18, 2003	Englishtown, N.J.
208.23	Greg Anderson	Mar 19, 2005	Gainesville, Fla.
210.18	Mike Edwards	Mar 17, 2007	Gainesville, Fla.
210.31	Larry Morgan	Mar 17, 2007	Gainesville, Fla.
211.49	Greg Anderson	Mar 17, 2007	Gainesville, Fla.
211.69	Jason Line	Mar 18, 2007	Gainesville, Fla.

Alltime Drag Racing Leaders

NHRA CAREER WINS

*John Force	125
*Warren Johnson	96
Bob Glidden	85
*Pat Austin	75
*Frank Manzo	71
Kenny Bernstein	69
David Rampy	62
Joe Amato	52
*Greg Anderson	50
Don Prudhomme	49
Bob Newberry	48

*Active driver in 2007. Note: Leaders through Oct 7, 2007.

Soccer

Despite six goals from
Abby Wambach,
the U.S. fell short
at the 2007 Women's
World Cup in China

Not-So Pitch Perfect

Both Major League Soccer and the U.S. Women's team had high hopes for 2007, but injuries and yet another World Cup collapse left their respective fans disappointed

BY HANK HERSCH

SOCCER IN THE U.S. WOULD catch on at last. By signing the sport's most iconic figure, English midfielder David Beckham, to a (potentially) nine-figure contract, the Los Angeles Galaxy snapped the heads of fans across the planet and drew front-page headlines across the country. Major League Soccer, a solid enterprise after 11 seasons but one that had yet to make a huge splash in the States, let alone overseas, finally had a face. And not just any face: one that teens from Mexico City to Moscow plastered to their bedroom walls, that advertisers used to sell shoes and cologne, that even Buddhists in a Thai monastery kneeled before. With his wife, Victoria (the singer formerly known as Posh Spice), Beckham was a bona fide member of the glitterati whose crossover appeal would make the other football suddenly matter.

Soccer in the U.S. would reign supreme. Entering the fifth Women's World Cup in China, the American team was ranked No. 1 in the world, having gone 35–0–7 under coach Greg Ryan since his appointment in April 2005. True, Germany had hoisted the last Cup, in '03, but

the U.S. had taken gold in the Athens Olympics, reasserting its hegemony. In striker Abby Wambach, the Yanks had 5'11" of brute, goal-scoring force; in Kristine Lilly, a skilled forward who had earned a record 331 caps and appeared in four World Cups; in Hope Solo, a 26-year-old goalkeeper eager to stake her claim as the best in the world. The old guard of Mia Hamm, Julie Foudy and Brandi Chastain had retired, but plenty of firepower remained.

But if 2007 was a lesson in anything, it was this: When it comes to soccer in the American sports landscape, finding a foothold—or keeping it—is no small feat.

First came the Beckham backslide. In the fall of '06, MLS poked a hole in its $2.4 million salary cap so that each team could offer an unlimited amount to one "designated player." Because the reason behind the change was obvious, this soon came to be called the Beckham Rule. The free agent had long made known his interest in moving to the U.S., and in January the Galaxy met his price: a five-year, $32.5 million deal that, with incentives, could exceed $200 million. Here was a soccer star eager to become an ambas-

sador for the sport in the U.S.—the role Pelé had played in the 1970s with the ill-fated North American Soccer League. "I'm not silly enough to think I'm going to change the whole culture, because it's not going to happen," Beckham told *SI*, "but I do have a belief that soccer can go to a different level, and I'd love to be a part of that."

The deal generated enormous buzz in the U.S.—and nasty shots from aficionados abroad who believed Beckham's best days were behind him. He had already

Nagging injuries forced soccer superstar Beckham (r.) to sit out most of his debut season with the Los Angeles Galaxy.

lost his place on the English team, which he had captained for six years; after he signed with MLS his club, Real Madrid, benched him as well, saying he would never play again. "David Beckham will be a B-list actor living in Hollywood," said Real president Ramón Calderón.

Beckham refused to return fire and, over time, not only won back his starting position but also led Real Madrid from fourth place to the Spanish League title, his first significant trophy since his arrival from Manchester United in 2003. He also rejoined the national team and in a pair of games exhibited the passing skills that earned him worldwide renown. Real Madrid even contacted the Galaxy about keeping him—and received a brisk turn-down.

With thousands of jerseys purchased and tickets bought, the Beckham Show was ready to sweep through the country. He made his Galaxy debut on July 21, coming on in the 78th minute in an exhibition against his former ManU rival, Chelsea. He was battling a left ankle injury that day; five weeks later later—after 310 minutes on the pitch for L.A.—he would be sidelined again with a sprained right knee. Furious fans across the league demanded refunds for their Galaxy tickets, and A-list celebrities no longer bothered to come to the Home Depot Center. And while Becks healed quickly and returned to the lineup for the final few matches of the Galaxy's season, his team ended up missing the playoffs and the momentum he had engendered for MLS largely dissipated.

The U.S. women, on the other hand, had nothing but momentum heading into the Women's World Cup in China. They lost some of it in their opener, a 2–2 draw in which North Korea exhibited superior speed and attacking skill and Solo let in a soft goal. "There were times in that game where I felt we were getting outplayed," said Wambach. "That rarely happens." But the team rebounded with a pair of victories over Sweden (2–0) and Nigeria (1–0) to win its group, then defeated England 3–0 in the quarterfinals.

Aside from winning at an impressive clip, Ryan had done little to call attention to himself during his 29-month tenure. But 24 hours before the Yanks would take on Brazil in the semis, he created an unnecessary stir. Ryan chose to replace Solo with 36-year-old Briana Scurry, who had not started in almost three months.

His reason: Scurry had a 12–0 career record against the Brazilians, including eight shutouts, and he had a hunch her quick reflexes would pay off against their high-powered offense. Just when the U.S. players were on a roll, before their most important match they found themselves having to explain why their coach had benched a keeper who hadn't surrendered a goal in three must-win games.

It would be generous to say Ryan's move backfired. Brazil dealt the U.S. the worst loss in its 22-year history, a 4–0 shellacking in which star forward Marta Vieira da Silva, or "Marta" as she is simply known (her outstanding play has earned her the same single-name status as Pelé and Ronaldinho), danced circles around the American defense and Scurry failed to justify her coach's hunch. Asked afterward about not playing, Solo didn't hold back: "It was the wrong decision, and I think anybody that knows anything about the game knows that. There's no doubt in my mind I would have made those saves." Then she took another shot that sailed past the highly decorated Scurry: "You can't live in the past. It doesn't matter what somebody did in an Olympic gold medal game three years ago. Now is what matters."

Solo's unvarnished remarks not only rankled Scurry's current and former teammates; they also made her, rather than Ryan's ill-timed personnel switch, the primary postgame subject. After consulting the players, he banished Solo from even eating with the team, and she was not in uniform the following day for the U.S.'s 4–1 victory over Norway in the third-place game. That kept the Americans' record of never having finished lower than third in a World Cup intact. A few weeks later, Solo did return for the team's season-ending, three-game exhibition series with Mexico, but the scars from the controversy appear unlikely to heal anytime soon. Just who exactly will be on the U.S. team's roster when it returns to China for the 2008 Olympics remains in question.

Women's World Cup 2007

Group Standings

GROUP A Country	GP	W	L	T	GF	GA	Pts	GROUP C Country	GP	W	L	T	GF	GA	Pts
*Germany	3	2	0	1	13	0	7	*Norway	3	2	0	1	10	4	7
*England	3	1	0	2	8	3	5	*Australia	3	1	0	2	7	4	5
Japan	3	1	1	1	3	4	4	Canada	3	1	1	1	7	4	4
Argentina	3	0	3	0	1	18	0	Ghana	3	0	3	0	3	15	0

GROUP B Country	GP	W	L	T	GF	GA	Pts	GROUP D Country	GP	W	L	T	GF	GA	Pts
*United States	3	2	0	1	5	2	7	*Brazil	3	3	0	0	10	0	9
*North Korea	3	1	1	1	5	4	4	*China	3	2	1	0	5	6	6
Sweden	3	1	1	1	3	4	4	Denmark	3	1	2	0	4	4	3
Nigeria	3	0	2	1	1	4	1	New Zealand	3	0	3	0	0	9	0

*Advanced to Quarterfinals.

Note: In group play, teams are awarded three points for a victory, one for a tie. The top two in each group advance to the Quarterfinals. First tiebreaker is cumulative goal differential, second is total goals scored, third is overall points.

First Round Scores

GROUP A
Germany 11, Argentina 0
Japan 2, England 2
Argentina 0, Japan 1
England 0, Germany 0
Germany 2, Japan 0
England 6, Argentina 1

GROUP B
U.S. 2, North Korea 2
Nigeria 1, Sweden 1
Sweden 0, U.S. 2
North Korea 2, Nigeria 0
Nigeria 0, U.S. 1
North Korea 1, Sweden 2

GROUP C
Ghana 1, Australia 4
Norway 2, Canada 1
Canada 4, Ghana 0
Australia 1, Norway 1
Norway 7, Ghana 2
Australia 2, Canada 2

GROUP D
New Zealand 0, Brazil 5
China 3, Denmark 2
Denmark 2, New Zealand 0
Brazil 4, China 0
China 2, New Zealand 0
Brazil 1, Denmark 0

WORLD CUP FINAL

Germany	Germany (2-0-1)		England (I-0-2)		England
Japan		*Germany (3-0)	USA (3-0)		Argentina
North Korea	North Korea (I-I-I)		USA(2-0-I)		USA
Sweden		Germany (3-0)			Nigeria
Norway	Norway(2-0-I)	Germany (2-0)	Brazil (4-0)	Australia (I-0-2)	Australia
Canada		Norway(I-0)			Ghana
China	China (2-I-0)		Brazil (3-2)		Brazil
New Zealand		USA def. Norway (4-1) in cons. game		Brazil (3-0-0)	Denmark

2006 Final Standings

EASTERN CONFERENCE

Team	GP	W	L	T	Pts	GF	GA
†*D.C. United....32	32	15	7	10	55	52	38
*New England...32	32	12	8	12	48	39	35
*Chicago 32	32	13	11	8	47	43	41
*New York.........32	32	9	11	12	39	41	41
Kansas City.......32	32	10	14	8	38	43	45
Columbus..........32	32	8	15	9	33	30	42

WESTERN CONFERENCE

Team	GP	W	L	T	Pts	GF	GA
†*FC Dallas......32	32	16	12	4	52	48	44
*Houston 32	32	11	8	13	46	44	40
*Chivas USA 32	32	10	9	13	43	45	42
*Colorado.........32	32	11	13	8	41	36	49
Los Angeles.....32	32	11	15	6	39	37	37
Real Salt Lake..32	32	10	13	9	39	45	49

Note: Three points for a win. One point for a tie. †Conference champion. *Qualified for playoffs

SCORING LEADERS

Player, Team	GP	G	A	Pts
Jeff Cunningham, RSL 31	31	16	11	43
Christian Gomez, DC 30	30	14	11	39
Ante Razov, CHV 28	28	14	8	35
Jaime Moreno, DC 32	32	11	10	32
Carlos Ruiz, Dal 27	27	13	5	31
Landon Donovan, LA 24	24	12	7	31
Dwayne De Rosario, Hou 30	30	11	5	27
Taylor Twellman, NE.............32	32	11	5	27
Kenny Cooper, Dal...............31	31	11	4	26
Brian Ching, Hou 21	21	11	2	24

ASSISTS LEADERS

Player, Team	GP	A
Terry Cooke, Col 23	23	12
Jeff Cunningham, RSL 31	31	11
Brad Davis, Hou...................28	28	11
Christian Gomez, DC 30	30	11
Ronnie O'Brien, Dal 27	27	11
Andy Dorman, NE.................32	32	10
Jaime Moreno, DC 32	32	10
Ivan Guerrero, Chi 29	29	9
Richard Mulrooney, Dal.........25	25	9

GOALS LEADERS

Player, Team	GP	G
Jeff Cunningham, RSL 31	31	16
Christian Gomez, DC 30	30	14
Ante Razov, CHV 28	28	14
Carlos Ruiz, Dal 27	27	13
Landon Donovan, LA 24	24	12
Brian Ching, Hou 21	21	11
Kenny Cooper, Dal................31	31	11
Dwayne De Rosario, Hou 32	32	11

GOALS-AGAINST-AVERAGE LEADERS

Player, Team	GAA
Jon Conway, NY 1.00	1.00
Matt Reis, NE....................1.09	1.09
Troy Perkins, DC................1.13	1.13
Kevin Hartman, LA..............1.14	1.14
Preston Burpo, CHV 1.21	1.21
Dario Sala, Dal 1.24	1.24
Pat Onstad, Hou 1.25	1.25
Zach Thornton, Chi 1.25	1.25

2006 PLAYOFFS

MLS CUP 2006

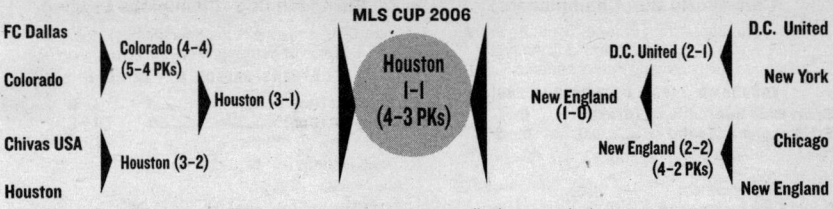

FC Dallas	Colorado (4–4) (5–4 PKs)				D.C. United
Colorado		Houston (3–1)	Houston 1–1 (4–3 PKs)	D.C. United (2–1)	New York
Chivas USA	Houston (3–2)			New England (1–0)	Chicago
Houston				New England (2–2) (4–2 PKs)	New England

Note: Scores for conference semifinals are two-game aggregates, all others are single games.

MLS Cup 2006
FRISCO, TEXAS, NOVEMBER 12, 2006

Houston..	0	0	1
New England....................................	0	0	1

Houston won 4–3 on penalty kicks.
Goals: Twellman 113, Ching 114

Houston— Onstad, Robinson, Cochrane 102, Dalglish 81, Mullan, DeRosario, Waibel, Barrett, Ching, Serioux 114

New England—Reis, Hernandez, John, Heaps, Franchino, Noonan, Ralston, Parkhurst, Twellman, Joseph, Dorman 62
Att: 22,427

International Competition

2007 U.S. Men's National Team Results

Date	Opponent	Result	U.S. Goals	Site
Jan. 20	Denmark	3–1 W	Donovan, Bornstein, Cooper	Carson, Calif.
Feb. 7	Mexico	2–0 W	Conrad, Donovan	Glendale, Ariz.
March 25	Ecuador	3–1 W	Donovan (3)	Tampa, Fla.
March 28	Guatemala	0–0 T	—	Frisco, Tex.
June 2	China	4–1 W	Beasley, Feilhaber, Dempsey, Onyewu	San Jose, Calif.
June 7	Guatemala*	1–0 W	Dempsey	Carson, Calif.
June 9	T&T*	2–0 W	Ching, Johnson	Carson, Calif.
June 12	El Salvador*	4–0 W	Beasley (2), Donovan, Twellman	Foxborough, Mass.
June 16	Panama*	2–1 W	Donovan, Bocanegra	Foxborough, Mass.
June 21	Canada*	2–1 W	Hejduk, Donovan	Chicago, Ill.
June 24	Mexico*	2–1 W	Donovan, Feilhaber	Chicago, Ill.
June 28	Argentina	1–4 L	Johnson	Maracaibo, Venezuela
July 2	Paraguay	1–3 L	Clark	Barinas, Venezuela
July 5	Colombia	0–1 L	—	Barquisimeto, Venezuela
Aug. 22	Sweden	0–1 L	—	Goteborg, Sweden

*CONCACAF tournament play

2007 U.S. Women's National Team Results

Date	Opponent	Result	U.S. Goals	Site
Jan. 26	Germany #	0–0 T	—	Guangzhou, China
Jan. 28	England #	1–1 T	O'Reilly	Guangzhou, China
Jan. 30	China #	2–0 W	Chalupny, Kai	Guangzhou, China
March 7	China @	2–1 W	Lilly, Lloyd	Guangzhou, China
March 9	Finland @	1–0 W	Lloyd	Quarteira, Portugal
March 12	Sweden @	3–2 W	Wambach (2), Lloyd	Faro, Portugal
March 14	Denmark @	2–0 W	Lilly, Lloyd	Guangzhou, China
April 14	Mexico	5–0 W	Wambach, Tarpley, Lilly (2), Cheney	Kumamoto, Japan
May 12	Canada	6–2 W	Wambach (2), Tarpley, Chalupny, Lilly, O'Reilly	Osaka, Japan
June 16	China	2–0 W	Wambach (2)	Blaine, Minn.
Sept. 11	North Korea†	2–2 T	Wambach, O'Reilly	Chengdu, China
Sept. 14	Sweden†	2–0 W	Wambach (2)	Chengdu, China
Sept. 18	Nigeria†	1–0 W	Chalupny	Shanghai, China
Sept. 22	England†	3–0 W	Wambach, Boxx, Lilly	Tianjin, China
Sept. 27	Brazil†	0–4 L	—	Hangzhou, China
Sept. 30	Norway†	4–1 W	Wambach (2), Chalupny, O'Reilly	Shanghai, China

#Four Nations tournament play; @ Algarve Cup tournament play; †-World Cup tournament play

Club World Cup Championship

Club champions from Europe, South America, Oceania, Asia, Africa and North America compete (was formerly Intercontinental Cup).

YOKOHAMA, JAPAN: DECEMBER 17, 2006

Sport Club International (Braz)..1	0—1	
FC Barcelona (Spain)..................0	0—0	

Goals: Carlos Adriano de Souza Vieira 82

Att: 67,128

Sport Club International: Clemer, Ceara, Eller, Indio, Cardoso, Alex (Vargas 47), Edinho, Monteiro, Fernando (Vieira Adriano 76), Iarley, Pato (Luiz Adriano 61).

FC Barcelona: Valdes, Marquez, Puyol, Bronckhorst, Ronaldinho, Deco, Iniesta, Motta (Hernandez 59), Zambrotta (Belletti 46), Giuly, Gudjohnsen (Ezquerro 88).

UEFA Cup

Competition between teams other than league champions and cup-winners from UEFA.

GLASGOW, SCOTLAND: MAY 16, 2007

FC Sevilla (Spain) 1	0	1—2
Espanyol (Spain) 1	0	1—2

FC Sevilla won 3-1 on penalty kicks.

Goals: Riera 28, Jonatas 115, Adriano 18, Kanoute 105

Att: 50,670

FC Sevilla: Palop, Alves, Dragutinovic, Navarro, Adriano (Dirnei 76), Maresca (Navas 46), Soler, Poulsen, Puerta, Fabiano (Kerzhakov 64), Kanoute.

Espanyol: Iraizoz, David Garcia, Jarque, Moises, Torrejon, Pena (Jonatas 87), Zabaleta, Fernandez Garcia, Riera, Rufete (Pandiani 56), Tamudo (Lacruz 72).

European Cup (Champions League)

League champions of the countries belonging to UEFA (Union of European Football Associations).

ATHENS, GREECE: MAY 23, 2007

AC Milan (Italy) 1	1—2	
Liverpool (Eng) 0	1—1	

Goals: Inzaghi 45; 82, Kuyt, 89

Att: 74,000.

AC Milan: Dida, Maldini, Nesta, Oddo, Ambrosini, Gattuso, Kaka, Jankulovski (Kaladze 80), Pirlo, Seedorf (Favalli 90), Inzaghi (Gilardino 89).

Liverpool: Reina, Agger, Carragher, Finnan (Arbeloa 88), Riise, Alonso, Gerrard, Mascherano (Crouch 78), Pennant, Zenden (Kewell 59), Kuyt.

Libertadores Cup

Competition between champion clubs and runners-up of 10 South American National Associations.

(1ST LEG) BUENOS AIRES, ARGENTINA: JUNE 13, 2007

Boca Juniors (Arg) 1	2—3	
Gremio (Braz)..............................0	0—0	

(2ND LEG) PORTO ALEGRE, BRAZIL: JUNE 20, 2007

Boca Juniors (Arg) 0	2—2	
Gremio (Braz)..............................0	0—0	

Boca Juniors wins, two-game aggregate score: 5-0.

(1ST LEG)

Goals: Palacio 19, Riquelme 74, Patricio og 90

Att: 39,993

Boca Juniors: Caranta, Diaz, Ibarra, Claudio Rodriguez, Clemente Rodriguez, Banega (Battaglia 82), Ledesma, Riquelme, Cardozo (Datolo 68), Palacio, Palermo.

Gremio: Saja, Lucio, Patricio, Teco, William, Eduardo, Diego, Sandro, Tcheco (Douglas 81), Gavilan, Tuta (Lucas 77).

(2ND LEG)

Goals: Riquelme 69; 81

Att: 43,952

Boca Juniors: Caranta, Diaz, Ibarra, Claudio Rodriguez, Clemente Rodriguez, Banega (Orteman 83), Ledesma, Riquelme, Cardozo (Battaglia 60), Palacio, Palermo (Boselli 88).

Gremio: Saja, Lucio, Patricio, Teco (Schiavi 35), William, Eduardo, Diego, Lucas, Tcheco (Amoroso 45), Gavilan, Tuta (Everton 71).

Country	League Champion	League Scoring Leader, Club	Cup Winner
Albania	Partizani Tirane	Vioresin Sinani, Tirana	Besa Kavaje
Andorra	Ranger's FC	n/a	Santa Coloma
Armenia	Pyunik Yerevan*	Aram Hakobyan*	Banants Yerevan
Austria	Austria Wien	Sanel Kuljic, Reid; Roland Linz, Austria Wien	Austria Wien
Azerbaijan	FK Baki	Yacouba Bamba, Karvan Yevlax	Qarabag Agdam
Belarus	Shakhtsyor Salihorsk*	Valery Stipeikis, Naftan Navapolatsk*	BATE Barysau
Belgium	Anderlecht	Tosin Dosunmu, Germinal Beerschot	Zulte-Waregem
Bosnia & Herz	Siroki Brijeg	n/a	Orasje
Bulgaria	Levski Sofia	Jose Furtado, Vihren/CSKA Sofia	CSKA Sofia
Channel Islands	Belgrave Wanderers	n/a	Northeners
Croatia	Dinamo Zagreb	n/a	Rijeka/Varteks Varazdin
Cyprus	Apollon Limasol	Lukasz Sosin, Apollon Limasol	APOEL Nicosia
Czech Republic	FC Slovan Liberec	Milan Ivana, Slovacko	AC Sparta Praha
Denmark	FC København	Steffen Højer, Viborg	Randers FC
England	Chelsea	Thierry Henry, Arsenal	Liverpool
Estonia	TVMK Tallinn*	Tarmo Neemelo, TVMK Tallinn*	TVMK Tallinn
Faroe Islands	B36*	Christian Hogni Jacbosen, NSI*	GI Gøta*
Finland	MyPa Anjalankoski*	Juho Mäkela, HJK Helsinki*	Haka Valkeakoski*
France	Olympique Lyonnais	Pedro Pauleta, Paris Saint-Germain	Paris Saint-Germain FC
Georgia	Sioni Bolnisi	Jaba Dvali, Dinamo Tbilisi	Ameri Tblisi
Germany	Bayern München	Miroslav Klose, SV Werder Bremen	Bayern München
Greece	Olympiakos Piraeus	n/a	Olympiakos Piraeus
Hungary	Debreceni Vasutas	Peter Rajczi, Ujpest	Fehervar
Iceland	FH Hafnarfjörour	Marel Johann Baldvinsson, Breidablik	Valur*
Ireland	Cork City*	Jason Byrne, Shelbourne*	Drogheda United*
Israel	Maccabi Haifa	Shai Holtzman, Ashdod SC	Hapoel Tel Aviv
Italy	FC Internazionale †	Luca Toni, Fiorentina	FC Internazionale
Kazakhstan	Aktobe LenTo*	Murat Tleshev, Irtysh Pavlodar	Zhenis Astana
Latvia	Liepajas Metalurgs*	Viktor Dobrecovs, Metalurgs* Igors Slesarcuks, Venta/Ventspils*	FK Ventspils*
Lithuania	Ekranas Panevezys*	Mantas Savenas, Ekranas Panevezys*	FBK Kaunas*
Luxembourg	F 91 Dudelange	Fatih Sozen, Grevenmacher	F91 Dudelange
Macedonia	Rabotniki Kometal Skopje	Stevica Ristic, Sileks	Makedonija Skopje
Malta	Birkirkara	n/a	Hibernians
Moldova	Sheriff Tiraspol	Alexei Kuckiuk, Sheriff Tiraspol	Sheriff Tiraspol
Netherlands	PSV Eindhoven	Klass Jan Huntelaar, SC Heerenveen	Ajax Amsterdam
Northern Ireland	Linfield FC	Peter Thompson, Linfield FC	Linfield FC
Norway	Vålerenga IF*	Ole Martin Ärst, Tromsø*	Molde FK*
Poland	Legia Warszawa	n/a	Wisla Plock
Portugal	FC Porto	Albert Meyong Zé, CF "Os Belenenses"	FC Porto
Romania	Steaua Bucharesti	n/a	Rapid Bucharesti
Russia	CSKA Moskva*	Dmitriy Kirichenko, FK Moskva*	CSKA Moskva*
San Marino	SS Murata	n/a	Libertas
Scotland	Celtic	n/a	Heart of Midlothian
Serbia and Montenegro	Crvena zvevda Beograd	Srdjan Radonjic, Partizan	Crvena zvevda Beograd
Slovakia	MFK Ruzomberok	Robert Rak, FC Nitra Erik Jendrisek, Ruzomberok	MFK Ruzomberok
Slovenia	NK Rudar	Miran Burgic, HIT Gorica	Koper
Spain	FC Barcelona	Samuel Eto'o, FC Barcelona	RC Español
Sweden	Djurgårdens IF*	Gunnar Thorvaldsson, Halmstads BK*	Djurgårdens IF*
Switzerland	FC Zürich	Keita Alhassane, FC Zürich	FC Sion
Turkey	Galatasaray Istanbul	n/a	Besiktas Istanbul
Ukraine	Shakhtar Donetsk	Brandao, Shakhtar Donetsk Emmanuel Okoduwa, Arsenal Kiev	Dynamo Kiev
Wales	TNS Llansantffraid	Marc Lloyd-Williams, TNS Llant.	Rhyl FC

Note: Results are from 2007 unless followed by *.

†-Juventus had its title retroactively revoked for 2005–06 and 2004–05 due to player use of performance enhancing drugs.

The World Cup

Results

Year	Champion	Score	Runner-Up	Winning Coach
1930	Uruguay	4–2	Argentina	Alberto Supicci
1934	Italy	2–1	Czechoslovakia	Vittorio Pozzo
1938	Italy	4–2	Hungary	Vittorio Pozzo
1950	Uruguay	2–1	Brazil	Juan Lopez
1954	W Germany	3–2	Hungary	Sepp Herberger
1958	Brazil	5–2	Sweden	Vicente Feola
1962	Brazil	3–1	Czechoslovakia	Aymore Moreira
1966	England	4–2	W Germany	Alf Ramsey
1970	Brazil	4–1	Italy	Mario Zagalo
1974	W Germany	2–1	Netherlands	Helmut Schoen
1978	Argentina	3–1	Netherlands	César Menotti
1982	Italy	3–1	W Germany	Enzo Bearzot
1986	Argentina	3–2	W Germany	Carlos Bilardo
1990	W Germany	1–0	Argentina	Franz Beckenbauer
1994	Brazil	0–0 (3–2)	Italy	Carlos Alberto Parreira
1998	France	3–0	Brazil	Aime Jacquet
2002	Brazil	2–0	Germany	Luis Felipe Scolari
2006	Italy	1–1 (5–3)	France	Marcello Lippi

Alltime World Cup Participation

Nation	Matches	W	T	L	Goals For	Goals Against
Brazil	92	64	14	14	201	84
*Germany	92	55	19	18	190	112
Italy	77	44	19	14	122	69
Argentina	65	33	13	19	113	73
England	55	25	17	13	74	47
France	51	25	10	16	95	64
Spain	49	22	12	15	80	60
†Russia	37	17	6	14	64	44
Yugoslavia	37	17	6	14	60	46
Netherlands	35	16	10	9	58	36
Poland	31	15	5	11	44	40
Hungary	32	15	3	14	87	57
Uruguay	40	15	10	15	65	57
Sweden	45	15	11	19	70	69
Austria	29	12	4	13	42	48
Czech Republic	33	12	5	16	47	49
Portugal	19	11	1	7	32	21
Mexico	45	11	12	22	48	84
Belgium	36	10	9	17	46	63
Romania	21	8	5	8	30	32
Switzerland	26	8	5	13	37	51
Denmark	13	7	2	4	24	18
Chile	25	7	6	12	31	40
Paraguay	22	6	7	9	27	36
United States	25	6	3	16	27	51
Turkey	10	5	1	4	20	17
Croatia	12	5	2	5	13	10
Nigeria	11	4	1	6	14	16
Cameroon	17	4	7	6	16	28
Peru	15	4	3	8	19	31
Scotland	23	4	7	12	25	41
S. Korea	24	4	7	13	21	53
Ecuador	7	3	0	4	7	8
Northern Ireland	13	3	5	5	13	23
Costa Rica	10	3	1	6	12	21
Colombia	13	3	2	8	14	23
Bulgaria	25	3	8	14	22	49
Wales	5	2	6	1	10	7
Senegal	5	2	2	1	7	6
Ukraine	5	2	1	1	5	7
E Germany	6	2	2	2	5	5
Ghana	4	2	0	2	4	6
Norway	8	2	3	3	7	8
Algeria	6	2	1	3	6	10
Morocco	10	2	4	4	10	13
Japan	10	2	2	6	8	14
Saudi Arabia	13	2	2	9	9	32
Cuba	3	1	1	1	5	12
S Africa	6	1	3	2	8	11
N Korea	4	1	1	2	5	9
Ivory Coast	3	1	0	2	5	6
Jamaica	3	1	0	2	3	9
Israel	3	1	0	2	1	3
Republic of Ireland	13	2	7	4	10	10
Australia	7	1	2	4	5	11
Iran	9	1	2	6	6	18
Tunisia	12	1	4	7	8	17
Honduras	3	0	2	1	2	3
Angola	3	0	2	1	1	2
Dutch East Indies	1	0	0	1	0	6
Egypt	4	0	2	2	3	6
Kuwait	3	0	1	2	2	6
Trinidad and Tobago	3	0	1	2	0	4
Slovenia	3	0	0	3	2	7
Serbia & Montenegro	3	0	0	3	2	10
United Arab Emirates	3	0	0	3	2	11
New Zealand	3	0	0	3	2	12
Haiti	3	0	0	3	2	14
Iraq	3	0	0	3	1	4
Togo	3	0	0	3	1	6
Canada	3	0	0	3	0	5
Greece	3	0	0	3	0	8
China	3	0	0	3	0	9
Zaire	3	0	0	3	0	14
Bolivia	6	0	1	5	1	20
El Salvador	6	0	0	6	1	22

*Includes West Germany 1950–90. †Includes USSR 1930–1990.
Note: Matches decided by penalty kicks are shown as drawn games.

World Cup Final Box Scores

URUGUAY 1930

Uruguay..................I	3	——4
Argentina.............2	0	——2

FIRST HALF

Scoring: 1, Uruguay, Dorado (12); 2, Argentina, Peucelle (20); 3, Argentina, Stabile (37).

SECOND HALF

Scoring: 4, Uruguay, Cea (57); 5, Uruguay, Iriarte (68); 6, Uruguay, Castro (89).

Argentina: Botosso, Della Toree, Paternoster, J. Evaristo, Monti, Suarez, Peucelle, Varallo, Stabile, Ferreira, M. Evaristo.

Uruguay: Ballesteros, Nasazzi, Mascheroni, Andrade, Fernandez, Gestido, Dorado, Scarone, Castro, Cea, Iriarte.

Referee: Langenus (Belgium).

ITALY 1934

Italy.....................0	I	I——2
Czechoslovakia..........0	I	0——I

SECOND HALF

Scoring: 1, Czech., Puc (70); 2, Italy, Orsi (80).

OVERTIME

Scoring: 3, Italy, Schiavio (95).

Italy: Combi, Monzeglio, Allemandi, Ferraris Monti, Monti, Bertolini, Guaita, Meazza, Schiavio, Ferrari, Orsi.

Czechoslovakia: Planicka, Zenisek, Ctyroky, Kostalek, Cambal, Cambal, Krcil, Junek, Svoboda, Sobotka, Nejedly, Puc.

Referee: Eklind (Sweden).

FRANCE 1938

Italy......................3	I	——4
Hungary.................I	I	——2

FIRST HALF

Scoring: 1, Italy, Colaussi (5); 2, Hungary, Titkos (7); 3, Italy, Piola (16); 4, Italy, Piola (35).

SECOND HALF

Scoring: 5, Hungary, Sarosi (70); 6, Italy, Colaussi (82).

Italy: Olivieri, Foni, Rava, Serantoni, Andreolo, Locatelli, Biavati, Meazza, Piola, Ferrari, Colaussi.

Hungary: Szabo, Polger, Biro, Szalay, Szucs, Lazar, Sas, Vincze, Sarosi, Zsengeller, Titkos.

Referee: Capdeville (France).

BRAZIL 1950

Uruguay................0	2	——2
Brazil 0	I	——I

SECOND HALF

Scoring: 1, Brazil, Friaca (47); 2, Uruguay, Schiaffino (66); 3, Uruguay, Ghiggia (79).

Uruguay: Maspoli, Gonzales, Tejera, Gambretta, Varela, Andrade, Ghiggia, Perez, Miguez, Schiffiano, Moran.

Brazil: Barbosa, Augusto, Juvenal, Bauer, Banilo, Bigode, Friaca, Zizinho, Ademir, Jair, Chico.

Referee: Reader (England).

SWITZERLAND 1954

W Germany............2	I	——3
Hungary.................2	0	——2

FIRST HALF

Scoring: 1, Hungary, Puskas (6); 2, Hungary, Czibor (8); 3, W Germ., Morlock (10); 4, W Germ., Rahn (18).

SECOND HALF

Scoring: 5, W Germany, Rahn (84).

W Germany: Turek, Posipal, Kohlmeyer, Eckel, Liebrich, Mai, Rahn, Morlock, O.Walter, F. Walter, Schaefer.

Hungary: Grosics, Buzansky, Lantos, Bozsik, Lorant, Zakarias, Czibor, Kocsis, Hidegkuti, Puskas, Toth.

Referee: Ling (England).

SWEDEN 1958

Brazil.....................2	3	——5
Sweden...................I	I	——2

FIRST HALF

Scoring:1, Sweden, Liedholm (3); 2, Brazil, Vava (9); 3, Brazil, Vava (32).

SECOND HALF

Scoring: 4, Brazil, Pelé (55); 5, Brazil, Zagalo (68); 6, Sweden Simonsson (80); 7, Brazil, Pelé (90).

Brazil: Glymar, D. Santos, N. Santos, Zito, Bellini, Orlando, Garrincha, Didi, Vava, Pelé, Zagalo.

Sweden: Svensson, Bergmark, Axbom, Boerjesson, Gustavsson, Parling, Hamrin, Gren, Simonsson, Liedholm, Skoglund.

Referee: Guigue (France).

CHILE 1962

Brazil I	2	——3
Czechoslovakia I	0	——I

FIRST HALF

Scoring: 1, Czech., Masopust (15); 2, Brazil, Amarildo (17).

SECOND HALF

Scoring: 3, Brazil, Zito (68); 4, Brazil, Vava (77).

Brazil: Glymar, D. Santos, N. Santos, Zito, Mauro, Zozimo, Garrincha, Didi, Vava, Amarildo, Zagalo.

Czechoslovakia: Schroiff, Tichy, Novak, Pluskal, Popluhar, Masopust, Pospichal, Scherer, Kvasnak, Kadraba, Jelinek.

Referee: Latychev (USSR).

World Cup Final Box Scores *(Cont.)*

ENGLAND 1966

England	l	l	2 ——4
W Germany	l	l	0 ——2

FIRST HALF
Scoring: 1, W Germany, Haller (12); 2, England, Hurst (18).

SECOND HALF
Scoring: 3, England, Peters (78); 4, W. Germany, Weber (90).

OVERTIME
Scoring: 5, England, Hurst (101); 6, England, Hurst (120).

England: Banks, Cohen, Wilson, Stiles, J. Charlton, Moore, Ball, Hurst, Hunt, R. Charlton, Peters.

W Germany: Tilkowski, Hottges, Schmellinger, Beckenbauer, Schulz, Weber, Held, Haller, Seeler, Overath, Emmerich.

Referee: Dienst (Switzerland).

MEXICO 1970

Brazil	l	3 ——4
Italy	l	0 ——l

FIRST HALF
Scoring: 1, Brazil, Pelé (18); 2, Italy, Boninsegna (32).

SECOND HALF
Scoring: 3, Brazil, Gerson (65); 4, Brazil, Jairzinho (70); 5, Brazil, Alberto (86).

Brazil: Feliz, Alberto, Brito, Wilson, Piazza, Everaldo, Clodoaldo, Gerson, Jairzinho, Tostao, Pelé, Rivelino.

Italy: Albertosi, Burgnich, Cera, Rosato, Facchetti, Bertini (Juliano), Mazzola, De Sisti, Domenghini, Boninsegna (Rivera), Riva.

Referee: Glockner (E Germany).

W GERMANY 1974

W Germany	2	0 ——2
Netherlands	l	0 ——l

FIRST HALF
Scoring: 1, Netherlands, Neeskens, PK (1); 2, W Germany, Breitner, PK (26); 3, W Germany, Müller (44).

W Germany: Maier, Vogts, Beckenbauer, Schwarzenbeck, Breitner, Hoeness, Bonhof, Overath, Grabowski, Müller, Holzenbein.

Netherlands: Jongbloed, Suurbier, Rijsbergen (de Jong), Haan, Krol, Jansen, Neeskens, van Hanagem, Cruyff, Rensenbrink (van der Kerkhof).

Referee: Taylor (England).

ARGENTINA 1978

Argentina	l	0	2 ——3
Netherlands	0	l	0 ——l

FIRST HALF
Scoring: 1, Argentina, Kempes (38).

SECOND HALF
Scoring: 2, Netherlands, Nanninga (81).

OVERTIME
Scoring: 3, Arg., Kempes (104); 4, Arg., Bertoni (114).

ARGENTINA 1978 *(Cont.)*

Argentina: Fillol, Olguin, Galvan, Passarella, Tarantini, Ardiles (Larrosa), Gallego, Kempes, Bertoni, Luque, Ortiz (Houseman).

Netherlands: Jongbloed, Jansen (Suurbier), Krol, Brandts, Poortvliet, Neeskens, Haan, W. van der Kerkhoff, R. van der Kerkhoff, Rep (Nanninga), Rensenbrink.

Referee: Gonella (Italy).

ITALY 1982

Italy	0	3 ——3
W Germany	0	l ——l

SECOND HALF
Scoring: 1, Italy, Rossi (57); 2, Italy, Tardelli (68); 3, Italy, Altobelli (81); 4, W Germany, Breitner (83).

Italy: Zoff, Bergomi, Scirea, Collovati, Cabrini, Oriali, Gentile, Tardelli, Conti, Rossi, Graziani (Altobelli), Causio).

W Germany: Schumacher, Kaltz, Stielike, K. Foerster, B. Foerster, Dremmler (Hrubesch), Breitner, Briegel, Rummenigge (Müller), Fishcher (Littbarski).

Referee: Coelho (Brazil).

MEXICO 1986

Argentina	l	2 ——3
W Germany	0	2 ——2

FIRST HALF
Scoring: 1, Argentina, Brown (22).

SECOND HALF
Scoring: 2, Arg., Valdano (55); 3, W Germ., Rummenigge (73); 4, W Germ., Voller (81); 5, Arg., Burruchaga (83).

Argentina: Pumpido, Brown, Cuciuffo, Ruggeri, Olarticoecha, Bastista, Giusti, Burruchaga (Trobbiani 90), Enrique, Maradona, Valdona.

W Germany: Schumacher, Jakobs, Forster, Eder, Brehme, Matthaus, Berthold, Magath (Hoeness 62), Briegel, Rummenigge, Allofs (Voller 46).

Referee: Filho (Brazil).

ITALY 1990

W Germany	0	l —— l
Argentina	0	0 ——0

SECOND HALF
Scoring: 1, W Germany, Brehme, PK (84).

W Germany: Illgner, Brehme, Kohler, Augenthaler, Buchwald, Berthold (Reuter), Littbarski, Haessler, Mattaeus, Voeller, Klinsmann.

Argentina: Goychoechea, Lorenzo, Serrizuela; Sensini, Ruggeri (Monzon), Simon, Basualdo, Burruchag (Calderon), Maradona, Troglio, Dezottir.

Referee: Coelho (Brazil).

UNITED STATES 1994

Italy	0	0	0——0
Brazil	0	0	0——0

Scoring: None. Shootout goals: Italy—2: Albertini, Evani; Brazil—3: Romario, Branco, Dunga.

Italy: Pagliuca, Benarrivo, Maldini, Baresi, Mussi

World Cup Final Box Scores *(Cont.)*

UNITED STATES 1994 *(Cont.)*

(Apolloni 35), Albertini, D. Baggio (Evani 95), Berti, Donadoni, Baggio, Massaro.

Brazil: Taffarel, Jorginho (Cafu 21), Branco, Aldair, Santos, Silva, Dunga, Zinho (Viola 106), Mazinho, Bebeto, Romario.

Referee: Puhl (Hungary).

FRANCE 1998

Brazil	0	0——0
France	2	1——3

FIRST HALF

Scoring: 1, France, Zidane (27); 2, France, Zidane (45).

SECOND HALF

Scoring: 3, France, Petit (90).

Brazil: Taffarel, Cafu, Aldair, Baiano, Carlos, Sampaio (Edmundo 74), Dunga, Rivaldo, Leonardo, (Denilson 46), Bebeto, Ronaldo.

France: Barthez, Lizarazu, Desailly, Thuram, Leboeuf, Djorkaeff (Vieira 75) Deschamps, Zidane, Petit, Karembeu (Boghossian 57), Guivarc'h (Dugarry 66).

Referee: Belqola (Morocco).

KOREA/JAPAN 2002

Brazil	0	2——2
Germany	0	0——0

SECOND HALF

Scoring: 1, Brazil, Ronaldo (67); 2, Brazil, Ronaldo (79).

Brazil: Marcos, Cafu, Lucio, Roque Junior, Edmilson, Carlos, Silva, Ronaldo (Denilson, 90), Rivaldo, Ronaldinho (Juninho, 85), Kleberson.

Germany: Kahn, Linke, Ramelow, Neuville, Hamann, Klose (Bierhoff, 74), Jeremies (Asamoah, 77), Bode (Ziege, 84), Schneider, Metzelder, Frings.

Referee: Collina (Italy).

GERMANY 2006

Italy	1	0	0——1
France	1	0	0——1

Italy won on penalty kicks, 5–3.

FIRST HALF

Scoring: 1, France, Zidane (7); 1, Italy, Materazzi (19).

Shootout Goals: Italy—Pirlo, Materazzi, De Rossi, Del Piero, Grosso; France—Wiltord, Abidal, Sagnol.

Italy: Buffon, Zambrotta, Cannavaro, Materazzi, Grosso, Camoranesi (Del Piero 86), Pirlo, Gattuso, Perrotta (Iaquinta 61), Totti (De Rossi 61), Toni.

France: Barthez, Sagnol, Thuram, Gallas, Abidal, Ribery (Trezeguet 100), Vieira (Diarra 56), Makelele, Zidane, Malouda, Henry (Wiltord 107).

Referee: Elizondo (Argentina).

Alltime Leaders

GOALS

Player, Nation	Tournaments	Goals	Player, Nation	Tournaments	Goals
Ronaldo, Brazil	1998, 2002, '04, '06	15	Miroslav Klose, Germany	2002, '04	10
Gerd Müller, W Germany	1970, '74	14	Ademir, Brazil	1950	9
Just Fontaine, France	1958	13	Eusebio, Portugal	1966	9
Pelé, Brazil	1958, '62, '66, '70	12	Jairzinho, Brazil	1970, '74	9
Sandor Kocsis, Hungary	1954	11	Paolo Rossi, Italy	1982, '86	9
Teofilo Cubillas, Peru	1970, '78	10	K.H. Rummenigge, W Ger	1978, '82, '86	9
Gregorz Lato, Poland	1974, '78, '82	10	Uwe Seeler, W Germany	1958, '62, '66, '70	9
Helmut Rahn, W Germany	1954, '58	10	Vava, Brazil	1958, '62	9
Gary Lineker, England	1986, '90	10			

LEADING SCORER, CUP BY CUP

Year	Player, Nation	Goals	Year	Player, Nation	Goals
1930	Guillermo Stabile, Argentina	8	1970	Gerd Müller, W Germany	10
1934	Oldrich Nejedly, Czechoslovakia	5	1974	Gregorz Lato, Poland	7
1938	Leonidas da Silva, Brazil	8	1978	Mario Kempes, Argentina	6
1950	Ademir de Menezes, Brazil	9	1982	Paolo Rossi, Italy	6
1954	Sandor Kocsis, Hungary	11	1986	Gary Lineker, England	6
1958	Just Fontaine, France	13	1990	Salvatore Schillaci, Italy	6
1962	Florian Albert, Hungary	4	1994	Hristo Stoichkov, Bulgaria	6
	Valentin Ivanov, USSR, Garrincha, Brazil,			Oleg Salenko, Russia	
	Vava, Brazil, Drazan Jerkovic, Yugoslavia		1998	Davor Suker, Croatia	6
	Leonel Sanchez, Chile		2002	Ronaldo, Brazil	8
1966	Eusebio Ferreira, Portugal	9	2006	Miroslav Klose, Germany	5

Most Goals, Individual, One Game

Goals	Player, Nation	Score	Date
5	Oleg Salenko, Russia	Russia–Cameroon, 6–1	6-28-94
4	Leonidas, Brazil	Brazil–Poland, 6–5	6-5-38
4	Ernest Willimowski, Poland	Brazil–Poland, 6–5	6-5-38
4	Gustav Wetterström, Sweden	Sweden–Cuba, 8–0	6-12-38
4	Juan Alberto Schiaffino, Uruguay	Uruguay–Bolivia, 8–0	7-2-50
4	Ademir, Brazil	Brazil–Sweden, 7–1	7-9-50

Most Goals, Individual, One Game *(Cont.)*

Goals	Player, Nation	Score	Date
4	Sandor Kocsis, Hungary	Hungary–W Germany, 8–3	6-20-54
4	Just Fontaine, France	France–W Germany, 6–3	6-28-58
4	Eusebio, Portugal	Portugal–N Korea, 5–3	7-23-66
4	Emilio Butragueño, Spain	Spain–Denmark, 5–1	6-18-86

Note: 31 players have scored 32 World Cup hat tricks. Gerd Müller of West Germany is the only man to have two World Cup hat tricks, both in 1970. The last hat tricks were 6-1-02, Miroslav Klose (Ger) vs. Saudi Arabia; 6-21-98, Gabriel Batistuta (Arg) vs. Jamaica; 6-23-90, Tomas Skuhravy (Czech) vs. Costa Rica; and 6-17-90, Michel (Spain) vs. S Korea.

Attendance and Goal Scoring, Year by Year

Year	Site	No. of Games	Goals	Goals/Game	Attendance	Avg Att
1930	Uruguay	18	70	3.89	434,500	24,139
1934	Italy	17	70	4.12	395,000	23,235
1938	France	18	84	4.67	483,000	26,833
1950	Brazil	22	88	4.00	1,337,000	60,773
1954	Switzerland	26	140	5.38	943,000	36,269
1958	Sweden	35	126	3.60	868,000	24,800
1962	Chile	32	89	2.78	776,000	24,250
1966	England	32	89	2.78	1,614,677	50,459
1970	Mexico	32	95	2.97	1,673,975	52,312
1974	W Germany	38	97	2.55	1,774,022	46,685
1978	Argentina	38	102	2.68	1,610,215	42,374
1982	Spain	52	146	2.80	1,856,277	35,698
1986	Mexico	52	132	2.54	2,441,731	46,956
1990	Italy	52	115	2.21	2,514,443	48,354
1994	United States	52	140	2.69	3,567,415	68,604
1998	France	64	171	2.67	2,775,400	43,366
2002	Korea/Japan	64	161	2.52	2,705,216	42,269
2006	Germany	64	147	2.23	3,353,655	52,401
Totals		644	1,901	2.95	28,418,310	44,128

The United States in the World Cup

Date	Opponent	Result	Scoring
URUGUAY 1930: FINAL COMPETITION			
7-13-30	Belgium	3–0 W	U.S.: McGhee 2, Patenaude
7-17-30	Paraguay	3–0 W	U.S.: Patenaude 2, Florie
7-26-30	Argentina	1–6 L	Arg.: Monti 2, Scopelli 2, Stabile 2 U.S.: Brown.
ITALY 1934: FINAL COMPETITION			
5-27-34	Italy	1–7 L	U.S.: Donelli Italy: Schiavio 3, Orsi 2, Meazza, Ferrari
BRAZIL 1950: FINAL COMPETITION			
6-25-50	Spain	1–3 L	U.S.: Pariani Spain: Igoa, Basora, Zarra
6-29-50	England	1–0 W	U.S.: Gaetjens.
7-2-50	Chile	2–5 L	U.S.: Wallace, Maca Chile: Robledo, Cremaschi 3, Prieto
ITALY 1990: FINAL COMPETITION			
6-10-90	Czechoslovakia	1–5 L	U.S.: Caligiuri Czech.: Skuhravy 2, Hasek, Bilek, Luhovy
6-14-90	Italy	0–1 L	Italy: Giannini
6-19-90	Austria	1–2 L	U.S.: Murray Austria: Rodax, Ogris

Date	Opponent	Result	Scoring
UNITED STATES 1994: FINAL COMPETITION			
6-18-94	Switzerland	1–1 T	U.S.: Wynalda Switz.: Bregy
6-22-94	Colombia	2–1 W	U.S.: Escobar (own goal), Stewart Colombia: Valencia
6-26-94	Romania	1–0 L	Romania: Petrescu
7-4-94	Brazil	1–0 L	Brazil: Bebeto
FRANCE 1998: FINAL COMPETITION			
6-15-98	Germany	2–0 L	Germany: Möller, Klinsmann
6-21-98	Iran	2–1 L	U.S.: McBride Iran: Estili, Mahdavikia
6-25-98	Yugoslavia	1–0 L	Yugoslavia: Komljenovic
KOREA/JAPAN 2002: FINAL COMPETITION			
6-5-02	Portugal	3–2 W	U.S.: O'Brien, Costa (own goal), McBride Portugal: Beto, Agoos (own goal)
6-10-02	S Korea	1–1 T	U.S.: Mathis S Korea: Ahn
6-14-02	Poland	3–1 L	Poland: Olisadebe, Kryszalowicz, Zewlakow U.S.: Donovan
6-17-02	Mexico	2–0 W	U.S.: McBride, Donovan
6-21-02	Germany	1–0 L	Germany: Ballack

The United States in the World Cup *(Cont.)*

Date	Opponent	Result	Scoring
2006: FINAL COMPETITION			
6-12-06	Czech Rep.	0–3 L	Czech Rep: Koller, Rosicky (2)
6-17-06	Italy	1–1 T	U.S.: Zaccardo (own goal)
			Italy: Giardino
6-22-06	Ghana	1–2 L	U.S.: Dempsey
			Ghana: Draman, Appiah

European Championship

Official name: the European Football Championship. Held every four years since 1960.

Year	Champion	Score	Runner-up
1960	USSR	2–1	Yugoslavia
1964	Spain	2–1	USSR
1968	Italy	2–0	Yugoslavia
1972	W Germany	3–0	USSR
1976	Czechoslovakia*	2–2	W Germany
1980	W Germany	2–1	Belgium
1984	France	2–0	Spain
1988	Holland	2–0	USSR
1992	Denmark	2–0	Germany
1996	Germany†	2–1	Czech Republic
2000	France†	2–1	Italy
2004	Greece	1–0	Portugal

*Won on penalty kicks. †Won in sudden-death overtime.

Under-20 World Championship

Year	Host	Champion	Runner-Up
1977	Tunisia	USSR	Mexico
1979	Japan	Argentina	USSR
1981	Australia	W Germany	Qatar
1983	Mexico	Brazil	Argentina
1985	USSR	Brazil	Spain
1987	Chile	Yugoslavia	W Germany
1989	Saudi Arabia	Portugal	Nigeria
1991	Portugal	Portugal	Brazil
1993	Australia	Brazil	Ghana
1995	Qatar	Argentina	Brazil
1997	Malaysia	Argentina	Uruguay
1999	Nigeria	Spain	Japan
2001	Argentina	Argentina	Ghana
2003	UAE	Brazil	Spain
2005	Netherlands	Argentina	Nigeria
2007	Canada	Argentina	Czech Rep.

Under-17 World Championship

Year	Champion
1985	Nigeria
1987	USSR
1989	Saudi Arabia
1991	Ghana
1993	Nigeria
1995	Ghana
1997	Brazil
1999	Brazil
2001	France
2003	Brazil
2005	Mexico
2007	Nigeria

Pan American Games

Year	Champion
1951	Argentina
1955	Argentina
1959	Argentina
1963	Brazil
1967	Mexico

Pan American Games *(Cont.)*

Year	Champion
1971	Argentina
1975	Brazil/Mexico (tie)
1979	Brazil
1983	Uruguay
1987	Brazil
1991	United States
1995	Argentina
1999	Mexico
2003	Argentina
2007	Ecuador

South American Championship (Copa America)

Year	Champion	Host
1916	Uruguay	Argentina
1917	Uruguay	Uruguay
1919	Brazil	Brazil
1920	Uruguay	Chile
1921	Argentina	Argentina
1922	Brazil	Brazil
1923	Uruguay	Uruguay
1924	Uruguay	Uruguay
1925	Argentina	Argentina
1926	Uruguay	Chile
1927	Argentina	Peru
1929	Argentina	Argentina
1935	Uruguay	Peru
1937	Argentina	Argentina
1939	Peru	Peru
1941	Argentina	Chile
1942	Uruguay	Uruguay
1945	Argentina	Chile
1946	Argentina	Argentina
1947	Argentina	Ecuador
1949	Brazil	Brazil
1953	Paraguay	Peru
1955	Argentina	Chile
1956	Uruguay	Uruguay
1957	Argentina	Peru
1958	Argentina	Argentina
1959	Uruguay	Ecuador
1963	Bolivia	Bolivia
1967	Uruguay	Urugua
1975	Peru	Various sites
1979	Paraguay	Various sites
1983	Uruguay	Various sites
1987	Uruguay	Argentina
1989	Brazil	Brazil
1990	Brazil	Argentina
1991	Argentina	Chile
1993	Argentina	Ecuador
1995	Uruguay	Uruguay
1997	Brazil	Bolivia
1999	Brazil	Paraguay
2001	Colombia	Colombia
2004	Brazil	Peru
2007	Brazil	Venezuela

Awards

European Footballer of the Year

Year	Player	Club	Year	Player	Club
1956	Stanley Matthews	Blackpool	1982	Paolo Rossi	Juventus
1957	Alfredo Di Stefano	Real Madrid	1983	Michel Platini	Juventus
1958	Raymond Kopa	Real Madrid	1984	Michel Platini	Juventus
1959	Alfredo Di Stefano	Real Madrid	1985	Michel Platini	Juventus
1960	Luis Suarez	Barcelona	1986	Igor Belanov	Dynamo Kiev
1961	Omar Sivori	Juventus	1987	Ruud Gullit	AC Milan
1962	Josef Masopust	Dukla Prague	1988	Marco Van Basten	AC Milan
1963	Lev Yashin	Moscow Dynamo	1989	Marco Van Basten	AC Milan
1964	Denis Law	Manchester United	1990	Lothar Matthaeus	Inter Milan
1965	Eusebio	Benfica	1991	Jean-Pierre Papin	Olympique Marseille
1966	Bobby Charlton	Manchester United	1992	Marco Van Basten	AC Milan
1967	Florian Albert	Ferencvaros	1993	Roberto Baggio	Juventus
1968	George Best	Manchester United	1994	Hristo Stoichkov	Barcelona
1969	Gianni Rivera	AC Milan	1995	George Weah	AC Milan
1970	Gerd Mueller	Bayern Munich	1996	Matthias Sammer	Borussia Dortmund
1971	Johan Cruyff	Ajax	1997	Ronaldo	Inter Milan
1972	Franz Beckenbauer	Bayern Munich	1998	Zinedine Zidane	Juventus
1973	Johan Cruyff	Barcelona	1999	Rivaldo	Barcelona
1974	Johan Cruyff	Barcelona	2000	Luis Figo	Real Madrid
1975	Oleg Blokhin	Dynamo Kiev	2001	Michael Owen	Liverpool
1976	Franz Beckenbauer	Bayern Munich	2002	Ronaldo	Real Madrid
1977	Allan Simonsen	Borussia M'gladbach	2003	Pavel Nedved	Juventus
1978	Kevin Keegan	SV Hamburg	2004	Andriy Shevchenko	AC Milan
1979	Kevin Keegan	SV Hamburg	2005	Ronaldinho	FC Barcelona
1980	Karl-Heinz Rummenigge	Bayern Munich	2006	Fabio Cannavaro	FC Juventus/Real Madrid
1981	Karl-Heinz Rummenigge	Bayern Munich			

African Footballer of the Year

Year	Player	Club	Year	Player	Club
1970	Salif Keita	St. Etienne	1989	George Weah	Monaco
1971	Ibrahim Sunday	Asante Kotoko	1990	Roger Milla	St. Denis
1972	Chérif Soueymane	Hafia	1991	Abedi Pèle Ayew	Marseille
1973	Tshimen Bwanga	TP Mazembe	1992	Abedi Pele Ayew	Marseille
1974	Paul Moukila	CARA Brazzaville	1993	Rashidi Yekini	FC Zurich
1975	Ahmed Faras	Mohammedia	1994	George Weah	Paris St. Germain
1976	Roger Milla	Canon Yaounde	1995	George Weah	AC Milan
1977	Tarak Dhiab	Esperance	1996	Nwankwo Kanu	Inter Milan
1978	Karim Abdul Razak	Asante Kotoko	1997	Victor Ikpeba	Monaco
1979	Thomas Nkono	Canon Yaounde	1998	Mustapha Hadji	Deportivo Coruna
1980	Jean Manga Onguene	Canon Yaounde	1999	Nwankwo Kanu	Arsenal
1981	Lakhdar Belloumi	GCR Mascara	2000	Patrick Mboma	Parma
1982	Thomas Nkono	Espanol	2001	El Hadji Diouf	Lens
1983	Mahmoud Al-Khatib	Al Ahli	2002	El Hadji Diouf	Lens
1984	Theophile Abega	Toulouse	2003	Samuel Eto'o	Real Mallorca
1985	Mohamed Timoumi	Royal Armed Forces	2004	Samuel Eto'o	FC Barcelona
1986	Badou Ezaki	Real Mallorca	2005	Samuel Eto'o	FC Barcelona
1987	Rabah Madjer	FC Porto	2006	Didier Drogba	Chelsea
1988	Kalusha Bwalya	Cercle Bruges			

South American Player of the Year

Year	Player	Club	Year	Player	Club
1971	Tostao	Cruzeiro	1989	Bebeto	Vasco da Gama
1972	Teofilo Cubillas	Alianza Lima	1990	Raul Amarilla	Olimpia
1973	Pelé	Santos	1991	Oscar Ruggeri	Velez Sarsfield
1974	Elias Figueroa	Internacional	1992	Rai	São Paulo
1975	Elias Figueroa	Internacional	1993	Carlos Valderrama	Junior Barranquilla
1976	Elias Figueroa	Internacional	1994	Cafu	São Paulo
1977	Zico	Flamengo	1995	Enzo Francescoli	River Plate
1978	Mario Kempes	Valencia	1996	Jose-Luis Chilavert	Velez Sarsfield
1979	Diego Maradona	Argentinos Juniors	1997	Marcelo Salas	River Plate
1980	Diego Maradona	Boca Juniors	1998	Martin Palermo	Boca Juniors
1981	Zico	Flamengo	1999	Javier Saviola	River Plate
1982	Zico	Flamengo	2000	Romario	Vasco da Gama
1983	Socrates	Corinthians	2001	Juan Riquelme	Boca Juniors
1984	Enzo Francescoli	River Plate	2002	Jose Cardozo	Toluca
1985	Julio Cesar Romero	Fluminense	2003	Carlos Tevez	Boca Juniors
1986	Antonio Alzamendi	River Plate	2004	Carlos Tevez	Boca Juniors
1987	Carlos Valderrama	Deportivo Cali	2005	Carlos Tevez	Corinthians
1988	Ruben Paz	Racing Buenos Aires	2006	Matias Fernandez	Colo-Colo

Club World Cup*

*Formerly the Intercontinental Cup. Competition between winners of European Cup and Libertadores Cup.

1960...Real Madrid, Spain	1978...No tournament	1996...Juventus, Italy
1961...Penarol, Uruguay	1979...Olimpia, Paraguay	1997...Borussia Dortmund, Ger.
1962...Santos, Brazil	1980...Nacional, Uruguay	1998...Real Madrid, Spain
1963...Santos, Brazil	1981...Flamengo, Brazil	1999...Manchester United,
1964...Inter, Italy	1982...Penarol, Uruguay	England
1965...Inter, Italy	1983...Gremio, Brazil	2000...Boca Juniors, Argentina
1966...Penarol, Uruguay	1984...Independiente, Argentina	2001...Bayern Munich, Germany
1967...Racing Club, Argentina	1985...Juventus, Italy	2002...Real Madrid, Spain
1968...Estudiantes, Argentina	1986...River Plate, Argentina	2003...Boca Juniors, Argentina
1969...Milan, Italy	1987...Porto, Portugal	2004...FC Porto, Portugal
1970...Feyenoord, Netherlands	1988...Nacional, Uruguay	2005...São Paulo, Brazil
1971...Nacional, Uruguay	1989...Milan, Italy	2006...Sport Club International, Brazil
1972...Ajax Amsterdam,	1990...Milan, Italy	
Netherlands	1991...Red Star Belgrade, Yugos.	
1973...Independiente, Argentina	1992...São Paulo, Brazil	
1974...Atletico de Madrid, Spain	1993...São Paulo, Brazil	
1975...No tournament	1994...Velez Sarsfield, Argentina	
1976...Bayern Munich	1995...Ajax Amsterdam,	
1977...Boca Juniors, Argentina	Netherlands	

Note: Until 1968 a best-of-three-games format decided the winner. From 1968 to '79: two-game/total-goal format. One-game championship since 1980. The European Cup runner-up substituted for the winner in 1971, 1973, 1974, and 1979.

European Cup (Champions League)

1956...Real Madrid, Spain	1974...Bayern Munich,	1989...AC Milan, Italy
1957...Real Madrid, Spain	W Germany	1990...AC Milan, Italy
1958...Real Madrid, Spain	1975...Bayern Munich,	1991...Red Star Belgrade, Yugoslav.
1959...Real Madrid, Spain	W Germany	1992...Barcelona, Spain
1960...Real Madrid, Spain	1976...Bayern Munich,	1993...Olympique Marseille, France
1961...Benfica, Portugal	W Germany	1994...AC Milan, Italy
1962...Benfica, Portugal	1977...Liverpool, England	1995...Ajax Amsterdam,
1963...AC Milan, Italy	1978...Liverpool, England	Netherlands
1964...Inter-Milan, Italy	1979...Nottingham Forest,	1996...Juventus, Italy
1965...Inter-Milan, Italy	England	1997...Borussia Dortmund, Ger.
1966...Real Madrid, Spain	1980...Nottingham Forest,	1998...Real Madrid, Spain
1967...Celtic, Scotland	England	1999...Manchester United,
1968...Manchester United,	1981...Liverpool, England	England
England	1982...Aston Villa, England	2000...Real Madrid, Spain
1969...AC Milan, Italy	1983...SV Hamburg,	2001...Bayern Munich, Germany
1970...Feyenoord, Netherlands	W Germany	2002...Real Madrid, Spain
1971...Ajax Amsterdam,	1984...Liverpool, England	2003...AC Milan, Italy
Netherlands	1985...Juventus, Italy	2004...FC Porto, Portugal
1972...Ajax Amsterdam,	1986...Steaua Bucharest,	2005...Liverpool, England
Netherlands	Romania	2006...FC Barcelona, Spain
1973...Ajax Amsterdam,	1987...Porto, Portugal	2007...AC Milan, Italy
Netherlands	1988...PSV Eindhoven,	
	Netherlands	

Note: On four occasions the European Cup winner has refused to play in the Intercontinental Cup and has been replaced by the runner-up: Panathinaikos (Greece) in 1971, Juventus (Italy) in 1973, Atletico Madrid (Spain) in 1974, and Malmo (Sweden) in 1979.

Libertadores Cup

Competition between champion clubs and runners-up of 10 South American National Associations.

1960...Penarol, Uruguay	1968...Estudiantes, Argentina	1976...Cruzeiro, Brazil
1961...Penarol, Uruguay	1969...Estudiantes, Argentina	1977...Boca Juniors, Argentina
1962...Santos, Brazil	1970...Estudiantes, Argentina	1978...Boca Juniors, Argentina
1963...Santos, Brazil	1971...Nacional, Uruguay	1979...Olimpia, Paraguay
1964...Independiente, Argentina	1972...Independiente, Argentina	1980...Nacional, Uruguay
1965...Independiente, Argentina	1973...Independiente, Argentina	1981...Flamengo, Brazil
1966...Penarol, Uruguay	1974...Independiente, Argentina	1982...Penarol, Uruguay
1967...Racing Club, Argentina	1975...Independiente, Argentina	1983...Gremio, Brazil

Libertadores Cup *(Cont.)*

1984...Independiente, Argentina
1985...Argentinos Juniors, Arg
1986...River Plate, Argentina
1987...Penarol, Uruguay
1988...Nacional, Uruguay
1989...Atletico Nacional, Colombia
1990...Olimpia, Paraguay
1991...Colo Colo, Chile
1992...São Paulo, Brazil

1993...São Paulo, Brazil
1994...Velez Sarsfield, Argentina
1995...Gremio, Brazil
1996...River Plate, Argentina
1997...Cruzeiro, Brazil
1998...Vasco da Gama, Brazil
1999...Palmeiras, Brazil
2000...Boca Juniors, Argentina
2001...Boca Juniors, Argentina

2002...Olimpia, Paraguay
2003...Boca Juniors, Argentina
2004...Once Caldas, Colombia
2005...São Paulo, Brazil
2006...Internacional, Brazil
2007...Boca Juniors, Argentina

UEFA Cup

1958...Barcelona, Spain
1959...No tournament
1960...Barcelona, Spain
1961...AS Roma, Italy
1962...Valencia, Spain
1963...Valencia, Spain
1964...Real Zaragoza, Spain
1965...Ferencvaros, Hungary
1966...Barcelona, Spain
1967...Dynamo Zagreb, Yugoslav.
1968...Leeds United, England
1969...Newcastle United, England
1970...Arsenal, England
1971...Leeds United, England
1972...Tottenham Hotspur, England
1973...Liverpool, England
1974...Feyenoord, Netherlands
1975...Borussia Monchengladbach,
    W Germany

1976...Liverpool, England
1977...Juventus, Italy
1978...PSV Eindhoven, Netherl.
1979...Borussia Monchengladbach,
    W Germany
1980...Eintracht Frankfurt,
    W Germany
1981...Ipswich Town, England
1982...IFK Gothenburg, Sweden
1983...Anderlecht, Belgium
1984...Tottenham Hotspur, England
1985...Real Madrid, Spain
1986...Real Madrid, Spain
1987...IFK Gothenburg, Sweden
1988...Bayer Leverkusen,
    W Germany
1989...Naples, Italy
1990...Juventus, Italy
1991...Inter-Milan, Italy

1992...Torino, Italy
1993...Juventus, Italy
1994...Internazionale, Italy
1995...Parma, Italy
1996...Bayern Munich, Germany
1997...Schalke 04, Germany
1998...Inter Milan, Italy
1999...Parma, Italy
2000...Galatasaray, Turkey
2001...Liverpool, England
2002...Feyenoord, Netherlands
2003...FC Porto, Portugal
2004...Valencia, Spain
2005...CSKA Moskva, Russia
2006...FC Sevilla, Spain
2007...FC Sevilla, Spain

European Cup-Winners' Cup

1961...AC Fiorentina, Italy
1962...Atletico Madrid, Spain
1963...Tottenham Hotspur, England
1964...Sporting Lisbon, Portugal
1965...West Ham United, England
1966...Borussia Dortmund, W Ger
1967...Bayern Munich, W Germ.
1968...AC Milan, Italy
1969...Slovan Bratislava, Czech.
1970...Manchester City, England
1971...Chelsea, England
1972...Glasgow Rangers, Scotland
1973...AC Milan, Italy

1974...Magdeburg, E Germany
1975...Dynamo Kiev, USSR
1976...Anderlecht, Belgium
1977...SV Hamburg, W Germ.
1978...Anderlecht, Belgium
1979...Barcelona, Spain
1980...Valencia, Spain
1981...Dynamo Tbilisi, USSR
1982...Barcelona, Spain
1983...Aberdeen, Scotland
1984...Juventus, Italy
1985...Everton, England
1986...Dynamo Kiev, USSR

1987...Ajax Amsterdam, Neth.
1988...Mechelen, Belgium
1989...Barcelona, Spain
1990...Sampdoria, Italy
1991...Manchester United, England
1992...Werder Bremen, Germany
1993...Parma, Italy
1994...Arsenal, England
1995...Real Zaragoza, Spain
1996...Paris St. Germain, France
1997...Barcelona, Spain
1998...Chelsea, England
1999...Lazio, Italy

Note: the Cup-Winners Cup was discontinued after 1999.

Major League Soccer

MLS Cup Results

Year	Champion	Score	Runner-up	Regular Season MVP
1996	D.C. United	3–2 (ot)	Los Angeles	Carlos Valderrama, TB
1997	D.C. United	2–1	Colorado	Preki, Kansas City
1998	Chicago	2–0	D.C. United	Marco Etcheverry, D.C.
1999	D.C. United	2–0	Los Angeles	Jason Kreis, Dallas
2000	Kansas City	1–0	Chicago	Tony Meola, Kansas City
2001	San Jose	2–1 (ot)	Los Angeles	Alex Pineda Chacon, Miami
2002	Los Angeles	1–0 (ot)	New England	Carlos Ruiz, Los Angeles
2003	San Jose	4–2	Chicago	Preki, Kansas City
2004	D.C. United	3–2	Kansas City	Amado Guevara, MetroStars
2005	Los Angeles	1–0 (ot)	New England	Taylor Twellman, NE
2006	Houston	1–1 (ot, 4-3 PKs)	New England	Christian Gomez, D.C.

Year	Champion	Score	Runner-Up	Regular Season MVP
1991	San Francisco	1–3, 2–0 (1–0 on PKs)	Albany	Jean Harbor, Maryland
1992	Colorado	1–0	Tampa Bay	Taifour Diane, Colorado
1993	Colorado	3–1 (OT)	Los Angeles	Taifour Diane, Colorado
1994	Montreal	1–0	Colorado	Paulinho, Los Angeles
1995	Seattle	1–2 (SO), 3–0, 2–1 (SO)	Atlanta	Peter Hattrup, Seattle
1996	Seattle	2–0	Rochester	Wolde Harris, Colorado
1997	Milwaukee	2–1 (SO)	Carolina	Doug Miller, Rochester
1998	Rochester	3–1	Minnesota	Mark Baena, Seattle
1999	Minnesota	2–1	Rochester	John Swallen, Minnesota
2000	Rochester	3–1	Minnesota	Vitalis Takawira, Mil
2001	Rochester	2–0	Vancouver	Paul Conway, Charleston
2002	Milwaukee	2–1 (2 OT)	Richmond	Leighton O'Brien, Seattle
2003	Charleston	3–0	Minnesota	Thiago Martins, Pittsburgh
2004	Montreal	2–0	Seattle	Greg Sutton, Montreal
2005	Seattle	1–1 (4–3 on PKs)	Richmond	Jason Jordan, Vancouver
2006	Vancouver	3–0	Rochester	Joey Gjertsen, Vancouver
2007	Seattle	4–0	Atlanta	Sebastien Le Toux, Seattle

United Soccer Leagues includes several former U.S. professional soccer leagues, including the A-League.

Women's United Soccer Association

Founders Cup Results

Year	Champion	Score	Runner-up	Regular Season MVP
2001	Bay Area	3–3 (4–2 PKs)	Atlanta	Tiffeny Milbrett, New York
2002	Carolina	3–2	Washington	Marinette Pichon, Philadelphia
2003	Washington	2–1 (OT)	Atlanta	Maren Meinert, Boston

Note: WUSA suspended operations after the 2003 season.

U.S. Open Cup

Open to all amateur and professional teams in the United States, the annual U.S. Open Cup is the oldest cup competition in the country and among the oldest in the world. The tournament is a single-elimination event running concurrent to the MLS season. The winner advances to the CONCACAF Cup, a tournament of the top club teams from North and Central America and the Caribbean.

Year	Champion	Year	Champion
1914	Brooklyn Field Club (NYC)	1941	Pawtucket FC (RI)
1915	Bethlehem Steel FC (PA)	1942	Gallatin SC (PA)
1916	Bethlehem Steel FC (PA)	1943	Brooklyn Hispano SC (NYC)
1917	Fall River Rovers (MA)	1944	Brooklyn Hispano SC (NYC)
1918	Bethlehem Steel FC (PA)	1945	Brookhattan FC (NYC)
1919	Bethlehem Steel FC (PA)	1946	Chicago Viking FC (IL)
1920	Ben Miller FC (St. Louis)	1947	Ponta Delgada SC (Fall River, MA)
1921	Robbins Dry Dock FC (Brooklyn)		
1922	Scullin Steel FC (St. Louis)	1948	Simpkins-Ford SC (St. Louis)
1923	Paterson FC (NJ)	1949	Morgan SC (PA)
1924	Fall River FC (MA)	1950	Simpkins-Ford SC (St. Louis)
1925	Shawsheen FC (Andover, MA)	1951	German Hungarian SC (NYC)
1926	Bethlehem Steel FC (PA)	1952	Harmarville SC (PA)
1927	Fall River FC (MA)	1953	Falcons SC (Chicago)
1928	New York National FC (NYC)	1954	New York Americans (NYC)
1929	Hakoah All Star SC (NYC)	1955	Eintracht Sport Club (NYC)
1930	Fall River FC (MA)	1956	Harmarville SC (PA)
1931	Fall River FC (MA)	1957	Kutis SC (St. Louis)
1932	New Bedford FC (MA)	1958	Los Angeles Kickers (CA)
1933	Stix, Baer and Fuller FC (St. Louis)	1959	McIlvaine Canvasbacks (Los Angeles)
1934	Stix, Baer and Fuller FC (St. Louis)	1960	Ukrainian Nationals (Philadelphia)
1935	Central Breweries FC (Chicago)	1961	Ukrainian Nationals (Philadelphia)
1936	German-Americans (Philadelphia)	1962	New York Hungaria (NYC)
1937	New York American FC (NYC)	1963	Ukrainian Nationals (Philadelphia)
1938	Sparta A and BA (Chicago)		
1939	St. Mary's Celtic SC (Brooklyn)	1964	Los Angeles Kickers (CA)
1940	Baltimore SC/Sparta A and BA	1965	New York Hungaria (NYC)

Year	Champion	Year	Champion
1966	Ukrainian Nationals (Philadelphia)	1987	Club Espana (Washington, D.C.)
1967	Greek American AA (NYC)	1988	Busch SC (St. Louis)
1968	Greek American AA (NYC)	1989	HRC Kickers (St. Petersburg, FL)
1969	Greek American AA (NYC)	1990	AAC Eagles (Chicago)
1970	Elizabeth SC (Union, NJ)	1991	Brooklyn Italians SC (East NY)
1971	Hota SC (NYC)	1992	San Jose Oaks (CA)
1972	Elizabeth SC (Union, NJ)	1993	Club Deportivo Mexico (San Francisco)
1973	Maccabee SC (Los Angeles)	1994	Greek American AC (San Francisco)
1974	Greek American AA (NYC)		
1975	Maccabee SC (Los Angeles)	1995	Richmond Kickers (VA)
1976	San Francisco AC (CA)	1996	D.C. United (MLS)
1977	Maccabee SC (Los Angeles)	1997	Dallas Burn (MLS)
1978	Maccabee SC (Los Angeles)	1998	Chicago Fire (MLS)
1979	Brooklyn Dodgers SC (NYC)	1999	Rochester Rhinos (A-League)
1980	NY Pancyprian-Freedoms (NYC)	2000	Chicago Fire (MLS)
1981	Maccabee SC (Los Angeles)	2001	Los Angeles Galaxy (MLS)
1982	NY Pancyprian-Freedoms (NYC)	2002	Columbus Crew (MLS)
1983	NY Pancyprian-Freedoms (NYC)	2003	Chicago Fire (MLS)
1984	AO Krete (NYC)	2004	Kansas City Wizards (MLS)
1985	Greek American AC (San Francisco)	2005	Los Angeles Galaxy (MLS)
		2006	Chicago Fire (MLS)
1986	Kutis SC (St. Louis)	2007	New England Revolution (MLS)

North American Soccer League

Formed in 1968 by the merger of the National Professional Soccer League and the USA League, both of which had begun operations a year earlier. The NPSL's lone champion was the Oakland Clippers. The USA League, which brought entire teams in from Europe, was won in 1967 by the L.A. Wolves, who were the English League's Wolverhampton Wanderers.

Year	Champion	Score	Runner-Up	Regular Season MVP
1968	Atlanta	0–0, 3–0	San Diego	John Kowalik, Chi
1969	Kansas City	No game	Atlanta	Cirilio Fernandez, KC
1970	Rochester	3–0,1–3	Washington	Carlos Metidieri, Roch
1971	Dallas	1–2, 4–1, 2–0	Atlanta	Carlos Metidieri, Roch
1972	New York	2–1	St. Louis	Randy Horton, NY
1973	Philadelphia	2–0	Dallas	Warren Archibald, Mia
1974	Los Angeles	4–3*	Miami	Peter Silvester, Balt
1975	Tampa Bay	2–0	Portland	Steve David, Mia
1976	Toronto	3–0	Minnesota	Pelé, NY
1977	New York	2–1	Seattle	Franz Beckenbauer, NY
1978	New York	3–1	Tampa Bay	Mike Flanagan, NE
1979	Vancouver	2–1	Tampa Bay	Johan Cruyff, LA
1980	New York	3–0	Ft. Lauderdale	Roger Davies, Sea
1981	Chicago	1–0*	New York	Giorgio Chinaglia, NY
1982	New York	1–0	Seattle	Peter Ward, Sea
1983	Tulsa	2–0	Toronto	Roberto Cabanas, NY
1984	Chicago	2–1, 3–2	Toronto	Steve Zungul, SJ

*Shootout.

Championship Format: 1968 and 1970: Two games/total goals. 1971 and 1984: Best-of-three series. 1972–1983: One-game championship. Title in 1969 went to the regular-season champion.

Statistical Leaders

SCORING

Year	Player/Team	Pts	Year	Player/Team	Pts
1968	John Kowalik, Chi	69	1977	Steven David, LA	58
1969	Kaiser Motaung, Atl	36	1978	Giorgio Chinaglia, NY	79
1970	Kirk Apostolidis, Dall	35	1979	Oscar Fabbiani, Tampa Bay	58
1971	Carlos Metidieri, Roch	46	1980	Giorgio Chinaglia, NY	77
1972	Randy Horton, NY	22	1981	Giorgio Chinaglia, NY	74
1973	Kyle Rote, Dall	30	1982	Giorgio Chinaglia, NY	55
1974	Paul Child, San Jose	36	1983	Roberto Cabanas, NY	66
1975	Steven David, Miami	52	1984	Slavisa Zungul, Golden Bay	50
1976	Giorgio Chinaglia, NY	49			

NCAA Sports

TIM PARKER/ICON SMI

Men's NCAA Div. I hockey champion Michigan State University

Margins of Victory

A few twists of fate led to some white-knuckle finishes at this year's NCAA championships

BY HANK HERSCH

ONE WAS OUTNUMBERED 99–1 in championship hardware. Another barely squeezed into the 16-team field. A third lost 75 percent of its starting lineup and had to fight for an atlarge berth. What do they have in common? In 2007, these three schools overcame obstacles—not to mention high-caliber finalists—to win NCAA titles.

MEN'S SOCCER

It was mid-October, and UC-Santa Barbara was going nowhere—literally. After a painful 1–0 loss at Riverside, the Gauchos' bus broke down, leaving them stranded for four hours and exposed to passing hecklers. Two years removed from an NCAA finals appearance, without more than five losses in a season since 2000, UCSB stood 7–6, and many players were on the verge of surrender—as was their coach. "We were done," recalled Tim Von Steeg. "We were officially done."

Instead, Von Steeg turned up the heat on his seniors, the seniors responded and the Gauchos (unlike their bus) rolled: They finished by winning five of six to qualify for the NCAA tournament. At the semifinals in St. Louis, unseeded UCSB nearly stalled again against No. 2 Wake Forest, finally advancing 4–3 on

penalty kicks after 110 scoreless minutes. Less than 24 hours later, the Gauchos battled heavily favored UCLA for the College Cup.

In their four previous tournament matches, the eighth-seeded Bruins had scored at least three goals, including a 4–0 wipeout of No. 4 Virginia in the semis. When they last faced UCSB, on Oct. 5, they prevailed 3–1, running their advantage in the series to 30–1–2, with the lone loss coming in 1982. And UCLA was gunning not merely for its fifth soccer title, but the 100th in school history as well. The Gauchos had won only one: the 1979 men's water polo championship.

Despite the short turnaround, the frigid temperatures (24 degrees at game time, with a wind chill of 11) and the lopsided ledgers, UCSB took almost immediate control of the match and never let go. When sophomore striker Nick Perera drove home a cross from Tyler Rosenlund in the third minute, the Gauchos had all the confidence they needed: Entering the final, they were 14–1 when scoring first. Perera helped double the lead in the 60th minute, sending sophomore midfielder Eric Avila through on the counter. The Bruins finally beat goalkeeper Kyle Renish in the 79th minute, but All-America defender Andy Iro and the Gauchos hung on for a 2–1 victory.

"People can talk about a national title, but

SCOTT BALES/ICON SMI

Perera (r.) and the unseeded UCSB Gauchos defeated heavily favored UCLA in the NCAA tournament for the soccer title.

you don't realize what it's like until you're out there," Von Steeg said. "It was thrilling for a lot of reasons, but more than anything, I just love the way we played."

MEN'S HOCKEY

In all the excitement, you can forget. Especially when your asthmatic, 5'6" goaltender stops a key third-period shot and you score in the final seconds and you seize your first hockey title since 1986 by beating a team that has won 13 straight. After all the hugging and yelling on the Scottrade Center ice in St. Louis, amid the upheaval of gloves and sticks, a team could easily repair to the locker room without something important—like the championship trophy.

"That sums us up," said Michigan State junior forward Chris Mueller. "We're just a bunch of kids who love the game of hockey and are having fun."

The fun was hard-won for the Spartans, an up-and-down-and-up team lacking all-America—or even all-league—talent. Michigan State was 7–8–1 in December, finally grasped coach Rick Comley's trapping system to go 12–2–1, then had a season-ending 1–4–1 slump that prompted 25-year-old captain Chris Lawrence to deliver hand-written notes to his teammates spelling out each one's importance. The Spartans entered the tournament as a No. 3 regional seed, but by the time they reached the Frozen Four they weren't feeling like underdogs: Before every practice they did 21 pushups, one for every year since their last title.

In the final against Boston College, the 2006 national runners-up, though, they *were* underdogs. Michigan State's slim chances took a huge hit when BC took a 1–0 advantage into the third period: The Eagles, who had averaged 4.6 goals during a 13-game winning streak, were 23–1 when ahead after two. When BC captain Brian Boyle bore down on the Michigan State goal with 15 minutes left, it seemed likely that the lead would double. But sophomore goalie Jeff Lerg—who uses an oxygen mask

DAMIAN STROHMEYER

anybody to win anything," said Comley. "But what a great group of kids. They deserve this."

BASEBALL

A year earlier, Oregon State had been the embraceable underdog, fighting off elimination six times to become the first Northern team to take the title in four decades. But the departure of six everyday players, two-thirds of the rotation and a closer; the near-departure of coach Pat Casey to Notre Dame; and the constant pressure of being the reigning champ proved onerous for the Beavers, who finished 10–14 in the Pac-10. Only by winning two of three at UCLA at the end of the season did they wrangle an invitation to the 64-team field; only by winning three elimination games in Charlottesville, Va., did they make it out of their regional.

But once Oregon State returned to Rosenblatt Stadium field in Omaha, so did its mojo. "It was something strange that happened and our club felt it," said Casey. "It was some type of energy and it never went away. It followed us on the plane, it followed us to the hotel, it followed us to the yard."

Consider: At the College World Series, the Beavers became the first team to win four games by at least six runs, trailed for only one of their 45 innings and swept the best-of-three final against third-seeded North Carolina. After battling Oregon State for the championship in '06, the Tar Heels put up only token resistance this time, going 2-for-20 with runners in scoring position in losing 11–4 and 9–3. Freshman righthander Jorge Reyes, who beat Cal State-Fullerton 3–2 in the Beavers' CWS opener and got the first victory over North Carolina, was named the Most Outstanding Player.

In taking the title, Oregon State became the first champion with a losing conference record—and the first champion to repeat since LSU in 1996 and '97. "This was different," said Casey. "This was magic.'"

before games and practices because of severe allergies and asthma—gloved the puck on his stomach while reaching above his head. The 60-year-old Comley called it, simply, "the greatest save I'd ever seen in my life."

Inspired, the Spartans tied it five minutes later on a goal by sophomore forward Tim Kennedy. Over the final 10 minutes they outshot Boston College 9–3, scoring the game-winner with 18.9 seconds left. After sophomore forward Justin Abdelkader hit the post from the right circle, Kennedy retrieved the puck behind the net and threaded a pass between two defensemen into the slot, where Abdelkader slammed it home.

Any empty-netter made the final score 3–1, though in the on-ice chaos some Spartans had no idea they had scored again. "We know we're not fancy and we're not picked by

NCAA Team Champions

Fall 2006

			Champion	Runner-Up
Cross-Country	MEN	Division I:	Colorado	Wisconsin
		Division II:	Abilene Christian	Adams St
		Division III:	Calvin College	NYU
	WOMEN	Division I:	Stanford	Colorado
		Division II:	Adams St	Western St
		Division III:	Middlebury	Amherst
Field Hockey	WOMEN	Division I:	Maryland	Wake Forest
		Division II	Bloomsburg	Bentley
		Division III	Ursinus	Messiah
Football	MEN	Division I-AA:	Appalachian	Massachusetts
		Division II:	Grand Valley	NW Missouri St
		Division III:	Mt. Union	UW-Whitewater
Soccer	MEN	Division I:	UC-Santa Barbara	UCLA
		Division II:	Dowling	Fort Lewis
		Division III:	Messiah	Wheaton (Ill.)
	WOMEN	Division I:	North Carolina	Notre Dame
		Division II:	Metro St	Grand Valley St
		Division III:	Wheaton (Ill.)	College of New Jersey
Volleyball	WOMEN	Division I:	Nebraska	Stanford
		Division II:	Tampa	North Alabama
		Division III:	Juniata	Washington (Mo.)
Water Polo	MEN		California	USC

Winter 2006-2007

Basketball	MEN	Division I:	Florida	Ohio St
		Division II:	Barton	Winona
		Division III:	Amherst	Virginia Wesleyan
	WOMEN	Division I:	Tennessee	Rutgers
		Division II:	So. Connecticut St	Florida Gulf Coast
		Division III:	DePauw	Washington (Mo.)
Fencing			Penn St	St. John's
Gymnastics	MEN		Penn St	Oklahoma
	WOMEN		Georgia	Utah
Ice Hockey	MEN	Division I:	Michigan St	Boston College
		Division III:	Oswego St	Middlebury
	WOMEN	Division I:	Wisconsin	Minn.-Duluth
		Division III:	Plattsburgh St	Middlebury
Rifle			AK-Fairbanks	Army
Skiing			Dartmouth	Denver
Swimming and Diving	MEN	Division I:	Auburn	Stanford
		Division II:	Drury	North Dakota
		Division III:	Kenyon	Denison
	WOMEN	Division I:	Auburn	Arizona
		Division II:	Drury	Truman St
		Division III:	Kenyon	Amherst
Wrestling	MEN	Division I:	Minnesota	Iowa St
		Division II:	Central Oklahoma	Neb.-Kearney
		Division III:	Augsburg	Wartburg

Winter 2006-2007 *(Cont.)*

			Champion	Runner-Up
Indoor Track	**MEN**	Division I:	Wisconsin	Florida St
and Field		Division II:	St. Augustine's	Abilene Christian
		Division III:	Lincoln (Pa.)	UW-La Crosse
	WOMEN	Division I:	Arizona St	LSU
		Division II:	St. Augustine's	Lincoln (Pa.)
		Division III:	Williams	City College NY

Spring 2007

Baseball		Division I:	Oregon St	North Carolina
		Division II:	Tampa	Columbus St
		Division III:	Kean	Emory
Golf	**MEN**	Division I:	Stanford	Georgia
		Division II:	Barry	S.C.-Upstate
		Division III:	St. John's (Minn.)	LaVerne
	WOMEN			
		Division I:	Duke	Purdue
		Division II:	Florida Southern	Rollins
		Division III	Methodist	De Paw
Lacrosse	**MEN**	Division I:	Johns Hopkins	Duke
		Division II:	Le Moyne	Mercyhurst
		Division III:	Salisbury	Cortland St
	WOMEN	Division I:	Northwestern	Virginia
		Division II	C.W. Post	West Chester
		Division III:	Franklin & Marshall	Salisbury
Rowing	**WOMEN**	Division I:	Brown	Virginia
		Division II	Western Washington	UC-San Diego
		Division III:	Williams	Trinity
Softball		Division I:	Arizona	Tennessee
		Division II:	SIU-Edwardsville	Lock Haven
		Division III:	Linfield	Washington (Mo.)
Tennis	**MEN**	Division I:	Georgia	Illinois
		Division II:	Lynn	Valdosta St
		Division III:	UC-Santa Cruz	Emory
	WOMEN	Division I:	Georgia Tech	UCLA
		Division II:	BYU-Hawaii	West Florida
		Division III:	Washington & Lee	Amherst
Outdoor Track	**MEN**	Division I:	Florida St	LSU
and Field		Division II:	Abilene Christian	St. Augustine's
		Division III:	UW-La Crosse	SUNY-Cortland
	WOMEN	Division I:	Arizona State	LSU
		Division II:	Lincoln (Mo.)	Abilene Christian
		Division III:	UW-Oshkosh	Calvin
Volleyball	**MEN**		UC-Irvine	IPFW
Water Polo	**WOMEN**		UCLA	Stanford

Fall 2006
Cross Country

MEN
Champion
Josh Rohatinsky, BYU

Runner-Up
Neftalem Araia, Stanford

WOMEN
Champion
Sally Kipyego, Texas Tech

Runner-Up
Jenny Barringer, Colorado

Winter 2006–2007
Fencing

MEN

	Champion	Runner-Up
Sabre	Timothy Hagaman, Harvard	Patrick Ghattas, Notre Dame
Foil	Andras Horanyi, Ohio St	Ronald Berkowsky, Pennsylvania
Épée	Slava Zingerman, Wayne St	Benjamin Bratton, St. John's

WOMEN

Sabre	Daria Schneider, Barnard	Caitlin Thompson, Penn St
Foil	Doris Willette, Penn St	Monika Golebiewski, St. John's
Épée	Anna Garina, Waynse St	Kelley Hurley, Notre Dame

Gymnastics

MEN

	Champion	Runner-Up
All-around	Taqiy Abdullah-Simmons, Okla.	Jonathan Horton, Oklahoma
Vault	David Sender, Stanford	Pejman Ebrahimi, Ohio St
Parallel bars	Tim McNeill, California	DJ Bucher, Ohio St
Horizontal bar	Jonathan Horton, Oklahoma	Tommy Ramos, Penn St Colin Christ, California
Floor exercise	Jonathan Horton, Oklahoma	Adam Reichow, Minnesota
Pommel horse	Timothy McNeill, California	Casey Sandy, Penn St
Rings	Alex Schorsch, Stanford	Tommy Ramos, Penn St

WOMEN

All-around	Courtney Kupets, Georgia	Amanda Castillo, Florida
Balance beam	Ashley Postell, Utah	Grace Taylor, Georgia
Uneven bars	Terin Humphrey, Alabama	Tasha Schwikert, UCLA Courtney Kupets, Georgia
Floor exercise	Morgan Dennis, Alabama	Courtney Kupets, Georgia
Vault	Courtney Kupets, Georgia	Annie DiLuzio, Utah

Skiing

MEN

	Champion	Runner-Up
Slalom	Adam Cole, Denver	David Chodunsky, Dartmouth
Giant slalom	Adam Cole, Denver	Evan Weiss, Dartmouth
10-kilometer classic	Rene Reisshauer, Denver	Snorri Einarsson, Utah
20-kilometer free	Snorri Einarsson, Utah	Rene Reisshauer, Denver

WOMEN

Slalom	Malin Hemmingson, New Mexico	Lucie Zikova, Colorado
Giant slalom	Sarah Schaedler, West'n Colorado	Jenny Tank, Denver
5-kilometer classic	Lindsey Williams, Northern Mich.	Morgan Smyth, Northern Mich.
15-kilometer free	Lindsey Weier, Northern Mich.	Lindsey Williams, Northern Mich.

Wrestling

	Champion	Runner-Up
125 lb	Paul Donahoe, Nebraska	Sam Hazewinkel, Oklahoma
133 lb	Matthew Valenti, Penn	Coleman Scott, Oklahoma
141 lb	Derek Moore, UC-Davis	Ryan Lang, Northwestern
149 lb	Gregor Gillespie, Edinboro	Joshua Churella, Michigan
157 lb	Trent Paulson, Iowa St	Craig Henning, Wisconsin
165 lb	Mark Perry, Iowa	Johny Hendricks, Oklahoma St
174 lb	Ben Askren, Missouri	Keith Gavin, Pittsburgh
184 lb	Jake Herbert, Northwestern	Jake Varner, Iowa St
197 lb	Joshua Glenn, American Univ.	Kurt Backes, Iowa St
285 lb	Cole Konrad, Minnesota	Aaron Anspach, Penn St

Swimming and Diving — Men

	Champion	Time	Runner-Up	Time
50-yd freestyle	Cesar Cielo, Auburn	18.69	Matt Targett, Auburn	19.08
100-yd freestyle	Cesar Cielo, Auburn	41.17	Ben Wildman-Tobriner, Stanford	41.90
200-yd freestyle	Darian Townsend, Arizona	1:33.29	Dominik Meichtry, California	1:33.45
500-yd freestyle	Larsen Jensen, USC	4:09.80	Shaun Phillips, Stanford	4:13.07
1650-yd freestyle	Larsen Jensen, USC	14:26.70	Shaun Phillips, Stanford	14:37.62
100-yd backstroke	Albert Subirats, Arizona	44.83*	Ben Hesen, Indiana	45.45
200-yd backstroke	Matt Grevers, Northwestern	1:38.71	Hongzhe Sun, Stanford	1:40.78

#American record. *NCAA record.

Winter 2006-2007 *(Cont.)*
Swimming and Diving — Men *(Cont.)*

	Champion	Time/Pts	Runner-Up	Time/Pts
100-yd breaststroke	Mike Alexandrov, Northwestern	51.56	Paul Kornfeld, Stanford	52.19
200-yd breaststroke	Vladislav Polyakovi, Alabama	1:52.71	Nate Cass, Stanford	1:53.36
100-yd butterfly	Albert Subirats, Arizona	44.57*	Ben Wildman-Tobriner, Stanford	45.36
200-yd butterfly	Patrick O'Neil, California	1:42.98	John Scott, Auburn	1:43.47
200-yd IM	Adam Ritter, Arizona	1:44.40	Matt Grevers, Northwestern	1:44.95
400-yd IM	Alex Vanderkaay, Michigan	3:40.89	Lucas Salatta, Florida	3:41.08
1-meter diving	Terry Horner, Florida St	399.35	Magnus Frick, Hawaii	395.05
3-meter diving	Steven Segerlin, Auburn	415.80	Kellen Harkness, Ohio St	407.15
Platform	Steven Segerlin, Auburn	414.90	Michele Benedetti, Arizona	412.10

Swimming and Diving — Women

	Champion	Time/Pts	Runner-Up	Time/Pts
50-yd freestyle	Kara Lynn Joyce, Georgia	21.71	Lara Jackson, Arizona	21.73
100-yd freestyle	Kara Lynn Joyce, Georgia	47.24*	Lacey Nymeyer, Arizona	47.37
200-yd freestyle	Lacey Nymeyer, Arizona	1:43.49	Emily Kukors, Auburn	1:43.72
500-yd freestyle	Adrienne Binder, Auburn	4:36.96	Caroline Burckle, Florida	4:38.28
1650-yd freestyle	Hayley Peirsol, Auburn	15:45.92	Adrienne Binder, Auburn	15:53.44
100-yd backstroke	Rachel Goh, Auburn	51.97	Hailey Degolia, Arizona	52.60
200-yd backstroke	Gemma Spofforth, Florida	1:52.96	Julia Smit, Stanford	1:53.39
100-yd breaststroke	Jessica Hardy, California	59.43	Annie Chandler, Arizona	1:00.03
200-yd breaststroke	Rebecca Soni, USC	2:08.23	YI Ting Siow, Wisconsin	2:10.42
100-yd butterfly	Dana Vollmer, California	51.33	Elaine Breeden, Stanford	51.72
200-yd butterfly	Elaine Breeden, Stanford	1:53.02*	Whitney Meyers, Arizona	1:53.75
200-yd IM	Whitney Myers, Arizona	1:54.89	Ava Ohlegren, Auburn	1:55.67
400-yd IM	Ava Ohlgren, Auburn	4:04.08	Alicia Aemisegger, Princeton	4:04.80
1-meter diving	Cassidy Krug, Stanford	361.55	Christina Loukas, Indiana	360.35
3-meter diving	Cassidy Krug, Stanford	420.90	Nasti Podniakova, Houston	407.10
Platform	Jessica Livingston, Texas	357.85	Lindsay Weigle, Indiana	356.55

Indoor Track and Field — Men

	Champion	Time/Mark	Runner-Up	Time/Mark
60-meter dash	Travis Padgett, Clemson	6.56	Demi Omole, Wisconsin	6.57
60-meter hurdles	Jeff Porter, Michigan	7.64	Alleyne Lett, LSU	7.70
200-meter dash	Walter Dix, Florida St	20.32	Rubin Williams, Tennessee	20.63
400-meter dash	Ricardo Chambers, Florida St	45.65	Aaron Buzard, Minnesota	45.86
800-meter run	Ryan Brown, Washington	1:48.40	Andrew Ellerton, Michigan	1:48.55
Mile run	Leonel Manzano, Texas	3:59.90	Russel Brown, Stanford	4:00.84
3,000-meter run	Lopez Lomong, Northern Arizona	7:49.74	Chris Solinsky, Wisconsin	7:51.69
5,000-meter run	Chris Solinsky, Wisconsin	13:38.61	Peter Kosgei, Arkansas	13:39.88
High jump	Donald Thomas, Auburn	2.33m	Dusty Jonas, Nebraska	2.25m
Pole Vault	Brad Gebauer, McNeese St	5.50m	Rory Quiller, SUNY-Binghamton	5.50m
Long jump	Tone Belt, Louisville	7.97m	Trey Hardee, Texas	7.83m
Triple jump	Andre Black, Louisville	16.29m	Muhammad Halim, Cornell	16.24m
Shot put	Noah Bryant, USC	20.55m	Russ Winger, Idaho	20.52m
35-pound wt throw	Egor Agafonov, Kansas	23.60m	Cory Martin, Auburn	23.27m

Indoor Track and Field — Women

	Champion	Time/Mark	Runner-Up	Time/Mark
60-meter dash	Kerron Stewart, Auburn	7.15	Courtney Champion, Tennessee	7.15
60-meter hurdles	Shantia Moss, Georgia Tech	7.98	Jessica Phanaja, LSU	8.00
200-meter dash	Kerron Stewart, Auburn	22.57	Kelly Ann Baptiste, LSU	22.90
400-meter dash	Natasha Hastings, South Carolina	50.80*	Kineke Alexander, Iowa	51.48
800-meter run	Alysia Johnson, California	2:03.47	Rebekah Noble, Oregon	2:04:70
Mile run	Shannon Rowbury, Duke	4:42.17	Allie Bohannon, UCLA	4:43.36
3,000-meter run	Sally Kipyego, Texas Tech	9:02.05	Shannon Rowbury, Duke	9.02.73
5,000-meter run	Sally Kipyego, Texas Tech	15:27.42	Arianna Lambie, Stanford	15:37.42
High jump	Patty Sylvester, Georgia	1.89m	Levern Sylvester, Georgia	1.89m
Pole vault	Elouise Rudy, Montana St	4.30m	Natalie Moser, Florida	4.30m
Long jump	Rhonda Watkins, UCLA	6.57m	Brenda Faluade, Miami	6.48m
Triple jump	Erica McLain, Stanford	13.91m	Michelle Vuaghn, Auburn	13.21m
Shot Put	Sarah Stevens, Arizona St	18.16m	Michelle Carter, Texas	18.12m
20-pound wt throw	Brittany Riley, Southern Illinois	25.56m	Jenny Dahlgren, Georgia	22.53m

Rifle

	Champion	Pts	Runner-Up	Pts
Smallbore	Josh Albright, Navy	96.5	Kirsten Weiss, Nebraska	97.6
Air rifle	Michael Dickinson, Jacksonville	96.5	Matthias Dierolf, AK-Fairbanks	98.4

† World record. #American record. *NCAA record.

Spring 2007

Golf

MEN	Champion	Score	Runners-Up	Score
MEN	Jamie Lovemark, USC	271	Kyle Stanley, Clemson	273
WOMEN	Stacy Lewis, Arkansas	282	Christel Boeljon, Purdue	286
			Paola Moreno, USC	286

Outdoor Track and Field

MEN

	Champion	Mark	Runner-Up	Mark
100-meter dash	Walter Dix, Florida St	9.93	Trindon Holliday, LSU	10.06
200-meter dash	Walter Dix, Florida St	20.32	Rubin Williams, Tennessee	20.72
400-meter dash	Ricardo Chambers, Florida St	44.66	Lionel Larry, USC	44.68
800-meter run	Andrew Ellerton, Michigan	1:47.48	Elias Koech, UTEP	1:47.70
1,500-meter run	Lopez Lomong, Northern Arizona	3:37.07	Leonel Manzano, Texas	3:37.48
5,000-meter run	Chris Solinksy, Wisconsin	13:35.12	Bobby Curtis, Villanova	13:39.88
10,000-meter run	Shadrack Songok, Texas A&M-CC	28:55.83	Galen Rupp, Oregon	28:56.19
110-meter hurdles	Tyron Akins, Auburn	13.42	John Yarbrough, Mississippi	13.57
400-meter hurdles	Isa Phillips, LSU	48.51	Brandon Johnson, UCLA	49.02
3,000-meter steeple	Barnabas Kirui, Mississippi	8:20.36	Andrew Lemoncello, Florida St	8:27.29
High jump	Scott Sellers, Kansas St	2.32m	Andrew Manson, Texas	2.29m
Pole vault	Thomas Skipper, Oregon	5.50m	Chip Heuser, Oklahoma	5.45m
Long jump	Dashalle Andrews, CSU-Northridge	7.68m	Tone Belt, Louisville	7.68m
Triple jump	Ray Taylor, Cornell	16.37m	Andre Black, Louisville	16.15m
Shot put	Noah Bryant, USC	20.04m	Mitchell Pope, North Carolina St	19.75m
Discus throw	Niklas Arrhenius, BYU	62.84m	Michael Robertson, Stanford	62.08m
Hammer throw	Jake Dunkleberger, Auburn	71.87m	Nick Owens, North Carolina	71.20m
Javelin throw	Justin Ryncavage, North Carolina	73.58m	Adam Montague, North Carolina	71.96m
Decathlon	Jake Arnold, Arizona	8,215 pts	Joe Detmer, Wisconsin	7,963 pts

WOMEN

	Champion	Mark	Runner-Up	Mark
100-meter dash	Sherry Fletcher, LSU	11.20	Ebonie Floyd, Houston	11.28
200-meter dash	Kerron Stewart, Auburn	22.42	Simone Facey, Texas A&M	22.64
400-meter dash	Natasha Hastings, South Carolina	50.15	Shana Cox, Penn St	51.27
800-meter run	Alysia Johnson, California	1:59.29	Katie Erdman, Michigan	1:59.35
1,500-meter run	Brie Felnagle, North Carolina	4:09.93	Susan Kuijken, Florida St	4:11.34
5,000-meter run	Michelle Sikes, Wake Forest	15:16.76*	Sally Kipyego, Texas Tech	15:24.22
10,000-meter run	Sally Kipyego, Texas Tech	32:55.71	Melissa Grelli, Georgetown	33:01.56
100-meter hurdles	Tiffany Ofili, Michigan	12.80	Candice Davis, USC	12.90
400-meter hurdles	Nicole Leach, UCLA	54.32*	Nickiesha Wilson, LSU	55.68
3,000-meter steeple	Anna Willard, Michigan	9:38.08	Lindsey Anderson, Weber St	9:46.48
High jump	Destinee Hooker, Texas	1.92m	Miruna Mataoanu, Alabama	1.92m
Pole vault	April Kubishta, Arizona St	4.25m	Jodi Unger, Arkansas	4.25m
Long jump	Brittney Reese, Mississippi	6.60m	Natasha Harvey, Jacksonville	6.49m
Triple jump	Yvette Lewis, Hampton	13.73m	Erica McLain, Stanford	13.67m
Shot put	Jessica Pressley, Arizona St	18.00m	Abigail Ruston, Texas St	17.44m
Discus throw	Kelechi Anyanwu, California	57.58m	Tai Battle, Arizona St	54.79m
Hammer throw	Jenny Dahlgren, Georgia	70.72m*	Brittany Riley, Southern Illinois	69.29m
Javelin throw	Lindsey Blaine, Purdue	55.56m	Erma Gene Evans, UTEP	54.78m
Heptathlon	Jacquelyn Johnson, Arizona St	5,984 pts	Julie Pickler, Washington St	5,831 pts

Tennis

MEN		Champion	Score	Runner-Up
MEN	Singles	Somdev Devvarman, Virginia	.7-6(7),4-6,7-6(2)	John Isner, Georgia
	Doubles	M. Born/A. Siljestrom Middle Tennessee St	4-6,7-6(6),7-6(4)	Kevin Anderson/Ryan Rowe, Illinois
WOMEN	Singles	Audra Cohen, Miami (Fla.)	7-5, 6-2	Lindsey Nelson, USC
	Doubles	Sara Anundsen/Jenna Long North Carolina	1-6, 6-2, 6-2	Megan Moulton-Levy/Katarina Zoricic William & Mary

---

*NCAA record.

Baseball

DIVISION I

Year	Champion	Coach	Score	Runner-Up	Most Outstanding Player
1947	California*	Clint Evans	8–7	Yale	No award
1948	USC	Sam Barry	9–2	Yale	No award
1949	Texas*	Bibb Falk	10–3	Wake Forest	Charles Teague, Wake Forest, 2B
1950	Texas	Bibb Falk	3–0	Washington St	Ray VanCleef, Rutgers, CF
1951	Oklahoma*	Jack Baer	3–2	Tennessee	Sidney Hatfield, Tennessee, P-1B
1952	Holy Cross	Jack Barry	8–4	Missouri	James O'Neill, Holy Cross, P
1953	Michigan	Ray Fisher	7–5	Texas	J.L. Smith, Texas, P
1954	Missouri	John (Hi) Simmons	4–1	Rollins	Tom Yewcic, Michigan St, C
1955	Wake Forest	Taylor Sanford	7–6	Western Michigan	Tom Borland, Oklahoma St, P
1956	Minnesota	Dick Siebert	12–1	Arizona	Jerry Thomas, Minnesota, P
1957	California*	George Wolfman	1–0	Penn St	Cal Emery, Penn St, P-1B
1958	USC	Rod Dedeaux	8–7†	Missouri	Bill Thom, USC, P
1959	Oklahoma St	Toby Greene	5–3	Arizona	Jim Dobson, Oklahoma St, 3B
1960	Minnesota	Dick Siebert	2–1‡	USC	John Erickson, Minnesota, 2B
1961	USC*	Rod Dedeaux	1–0	Oklahoma St	Littleton Fowler, Oklahoma St, P
1962	Michigan	Don Lund	5–4	Santa Clara	Bob Garibaldi, Santa Clara, P
1963	USC	Rod Dedeaux	5–2	Arizona	Bud Hollowell, USC, C
1964	Minnesota	Dick Siebert	5–1	Missouri	Joe Ferris, Maine, P
1965	Arizona St	Bobby Winkles	2–1#	Ohio St	Sal Bando, Arizona St, 3B
1966	Ohio St	Marty Karow	8–2	Oklahoma St	Steve Arlin, Ohio St, P
1967	Arizona St	Bobby Winkles	11–2	Houston	Ron Davini, Arizona St, C
1968	USC*	Rod Dedeaux	4–3	Southern Illinois	Bill Seinsoth, USC, 1B
1969	Arizona St	Bobby Winkles	10–1	Tulsa	John Dolinsek, Arizona St, LF
1970	USC	Rod Dedeaux	2–1	Florida St	Gene Ammann, Florida St, P
1971	USC	Rod Dedeaux	7–2	Southern Illinois	Jerry Tabb, Tulsa, 1B
1972	USC	Rod Dedeaux	1–0	Arizona St	Russ McQueen, USC, P
1973	USC*	Rod Dedeaux	4–3	Arizona St	Dave Winfield, Minnesota, P-OF
1974	USC	Rod Dedeaux	7–3	Miami (Fla.)	George Milke, USC, P
1975	Texas	Cliff Gustafson	5–1	S Carolina	Mickey Reichenbach, Texas, 1B
1976	Arizona	Jerry Kindall	7–1	Eastern Michigan	Steve Powers, Arizona, P-DH
1977	Arizona St	Jim Brock	2–1	S Carolina	Bob Horner, Arizona St, 3B
1978	USC*	Rod Dedeaux	10–3	Arizona St	Rod Boxberger, USC, P
1979	CSU–Fullerton	Augie Garrido	2–1	Arkansas	Tony Hudson, CSU–Fullerton, P
1980	Arizona	Jerry Kindall	5–3	Hawaii	Terry Francona, Arizona, LF
1981	Arizona St	Jim Brock	7–4	Oklahoma St	Stan Holmes, Arizona St, LF
1982	Miami (Fla.)*	Ron Fraser	9–3	Wichita St	Dan Smith, Miami (Fla.), P
1983	Texas*	Cliff Gustafson	4–3	Alabama	Calvin Schiraldi, Texas, P
1984	CSU–Fullerton	Augie Garrido	3–1	Texas	John Fishel, CSU–Fullerton, LF
1985	Miami (Fla.)	Ron Fraser	10–6	Texas	Greg Ellena, Miami (Fla.), DH
1986	Arizona	Jerry Kindall	10–2	Florida St	Mike Senne, Arizona, LF
1987	Stanford	Mark Marquess	9–5	Oklahoma St	Paul Carey, Stanford, RF
1988	Stanford	Mark Marquess	9–4	Arizona St	Lee Plemel, Stanford, P
1989	Wichita St	Gene Stephenson	5–3	Texas	Greg Brummett, Wichita St, P
1990	Georgia	Steve Webber	2–1	Oklahoma St	Mike Rebhan, Georgia, P
1991	LSU	Skip Bertman	6–3	Wichita St	Gary Hymel, LSU, C
1992	Pepperdine	Andy Lopez	3–2	CSU–Fullerton	Phil Nevin, CSU–Fullerton, 3B
1993	LSU	Skip Bertman	8–0	Wichita St	Todd Walker, LSU, 2B
1994	Oklahoma	Larry Cochell	13–5	Georgia Tech	Chip Glass, Oklahoma, CF
1995	CSU–Fullerton*	Augie Garrido	11–5	USC	Mark Kotsay, CSU–Fullerton, CF-P
1996	LSU*	Skip Bertman	9–8	Miami (Fla.)	Pat Burrell, Miami (Fla.), 3B
1997	LSU*	Skip Bertman	13–6	Alabama	Brandon Larson, LSU, SS
1998	USC	Mike Gillespie	21–14	Arizona St	Wes Rachels, USC, 2B
1999	Miami (Fla.)	Jim Morris	6–5	Florida St	Marshall McDougall, FSU 3B/2B
2000	LSU*	Skip Bertman	6–5	Stanford	Trey Hodges, LSU, P
2001	Miami (Fla.)*	Jim Morris	12–1	Stanford	Charlton Jimerson, Miami (Fla.), OF
2002	Texas	Augie Garrido	12–6	South Carolina	Huston Street, Texas, P
2003	Rice	Wayne Graham	14–2^	Stanford	John Hudgins, Stanford, P
2004	CSU–Fullerton	George Horton	3–2^	Texas	Jason Windsor, CSU–Fullerton
2005	Texas	Augie Garrido	6–2^	Florida	David Maroul, Texas
2006	Oregon St	Pat Casey	3–2^	North Carolina	Jonah Nickerson, Oregon St, P
2007	Oregon St	Pat Casey	9–3^	North Carolina	Jorge Reyes, Oregon St, P

*Undefeated teams in College World Series play. †12 innings. ‡10 innings. #15 innings. ^Score of decisive game of best-of-three series.

DIVISION II

Year	Champion	Year	Champion	Year	Champion
1968	Chapman*	1982	UC–Riverside*	1996	Kennesaw St*
1969	Illinois St*	1983	Cal Poly–Pomona*	1997	CSU–Chico*
1970	CSU–Northridge	1984	CSU–Northridge	1998	Tampa*
1971	Florida Southern	1985	Florida Southern*	1999	CSU–Chico
1972	Florida Southern	1986	Troy St	2000	SE Oklahoma St
1973	UC–Irvine*	1987	Troy St*	2001	St. Mary's (Tex.)
1974	UC–Irvine	1988	Florida Southern*	2002	Columbus St
1975	Florida Southern	1989	Cal Poly–SLO	2003	Central Missouri St
1976	Cal Poly–Pomona	1990	Jacksonville St	2004	Kennesaw St
1977	UC–Riverside	1991	Jacksonville St	2005	Florida Southern
1978	Florida Southern	1992	Tampa*	2006	Tampa
1979	Valdosta St	1993	Tampa	2007	Tampa
1980	Cal Poly–Pomona*	1994	Central Missouri St		
1981	Florida Southern*	1995	Florida Southern*		

DIVISION III

Year	Champion	Year	Champion	Year	Champion
1976	CSU-Stanislaus	1987	Montclair St	1998	Eastern Connecticut St
1977	CSU-Stanislaus	1988	Ithaca	1999	N.Carolina Wesleyan
1978	Glassboro St	1989	N. Carolina Wesleyan	2000	Montclair St
1979	Glassboro St	1990	Eastern Connecticut St	2001	St. Thomas (Minn.)
1980	Ithaca	1991	Southern Maine	2002	Eastern Connecticut St
1981	Marietta	1992	William Paterson	2003	Chapman
1982	Eastern Connecticut St	1993	Montclair St	2004	UW-Stevens Pt
1983	Marietta	1994	UW-Oshkosh	2005	Wisconsin
1984	Ramapo	1995	La Verne	2006	Marietta
1985	UW-Oshkosh	1996	William Paterson	2007	Kean
1986	Marietta	1997	Southern Maine		

*Undefeated teams in final series.

Cross-Country

Men
DIVISION I

Year	Champion	Coach	Pts	Runner-Up	Pts	Individual Champion	Time
1938	Indiana	Earle Hayes	51	Notre Dame	61	Greg Rice, Notre Dame	20:12.9
1939	Michigan St	Lauren Brown	54	Wisconsin	57	Walter Mehl, Wisconsin	20:30.9
1940	Indiana	Earle Hayes	65	Eastern Michigan	68	Gilbert Dodds, Ashland	20:30.2
1941	Rhode Island	Fred Tootell	83	Penn St	110	Fred Wilt, Indiana	20:30.1
1942	Indiana	Earle Hayes	57			Oliver Hunter, Notre Dame	20:18.0
	Penn St	Charles Werner	57				
1943	No meet						
1944	Drake	Bill Easton	25	Notre Dame	64	Fred Feiler, Drake	21:04.2
1945	Drake	Bill Easton	50	Notre Dame	65	Fred Feiler, Drake	21:14.2
1946	Drake	Bill Easton	42	NYU	98	Quentin Brelsford, Ohio Wesleyan	20:22.9
1947	Penn St	Charles Werner	60	Syracuse	72	Jack Milne, North Carolina	20:41.1
1948	Michigan St	Karl Schlademan	41	Wisconsin	69	Robert Black, Rhode Island	19:52.3
1949	Michigan St	Karl Schlademan	59	Syracuse	81	Robert Black, Rhode Island	20:25.7
1950	Penn St	Charles Werner	53	Michigan St	55	Herb Semper Jr, Kansas	20:31.7
1951	Syracuse	Robert Grieve	80	Kansas	118	Herb Semper Jr, Kansas	20:09.5
1952	Michigan St	Karl Schlademan	65	Indiana	68	Charles Capozzoli, Georgetown	19:36.7
1953	Kansas	Bill Easton	70	Indiana	82	Wes Santee, Kansas	19:43.5
1954	Oklahoma St	Ralph Higgins	61	Syracuse	118	Allen Frame, Kansas	19:54.2
1955	Michigan St	Karl Schlademan	46	Kansas	68	Charles Jones, Iowa	19:57.4
1956	Michigan St	Karl Schlademan	28	Kansas	88	Walter McNew, Texas	19:55.7
1957	Notre Dame	Alex Wilson	121	Michigan St	127	Max Truex, USC	19:12.3
1958	Michigan St	Francis Dittrich	79	Western Michigan	104	Crawford Kennedy, Michigan St	20:07.1
1959	Michigan St	Francis Dittrich	44	Houston	120	Al Lawrence, Houston	20:35.7
1960	Houston	John Morriss	54	Michigan St	80	Al Lawrence, Houston	19:28.2
1961	Oregon St	Sam Bell	68	San Jose St	82	Dale Story, Oregon St	19:46.6

Men *(Cont.)*

DIVISION I *(Cont.)*

Year	Champion	Coach	Pts	Runner-Up	Pts	Individual Champion	Time
1962	San Jose St	Dean Miller	58	Villanova	69	Tom O'Hara, Loyola (Ill.)	19:20.3
1963	San Jose St	Dean Miller	53	Oregon	68	Victor Zwolak, Villanova	19:35.0
1964	W. Michigan	George Dales	86	Oregon	116	Elmore Banton, Ohio	20:07.5
1965	W. Michigan	George Dales	81	Northwestern	114	John Lawson, Kansas	29:24.0
1966	Villanova	James Elliott	79	Kansas St	155	Gerry Lindgren, Wash. St	29:01.4
1967	Villanova	James Elliott	91	Air Force	96	Gerry Lindgren, Wash. St	30:45.6
1968	Villanova	James Elliott	78	Stanford	100	Michael Ryan, Air Force	29:16.8
1969	UTEP	Wayne Vandenburg	74	Villanova	88	Gerry Lindgren, Wash. St	28:59.2
1970	Villanova	James Elliott	85	Oregon	86	Steve Prefontaine, Oregon	28:00.2
1971	Oregon	Bill Dellinger	83	Washington St	122	Steve Prefontaine, Oregon	29:14.0
1972	Tennessee	Stan Huntsman	134	East Tennessee St	148	Neil Cusack, E Tenn St	28:23.0
1973	Oregon	Bill Dellinger	89	UTEP	157	Steve Prefontaine, Oregon	28:14.0
1974	Oregon	Bill Dellinger	77	Western Kentucky	110	Nick Rose, W. Kentucky	29:22.0
1975	UTEP	Ted Banks	88	Washington St	92	Craig Virgin, Illinois	28:23.3
1976	UTEP	Ted Banks	62	Oregon	117	Henry Rono, Washington St	28:06.6
1977	Oregon	Bill Dellinger	100	UTEP	105	Henry Rono, Washington St	28:33.5
1978	UTEP	Ted Banks	56	Oregon	72	Alberto Salazar, Oregon	29:29.7
1979	UTEP	Ted Banks	86	Oregon	93	Henry Rono, Washington St	28:19.6
1980	UTEP	Ted Banks	58	Arkansas	152	Suleiman Nyambui, UTEP	29:04.0
1981	UTEP	Ted Banks	17	Providence	109	Mathews Motshwarateu,UTEP	28:45.6
1982	Wisconsin	Dan McClimon	59	Providence	138	Mark Scrutton, Colorado	30:12.6
1983	Vacated			Wisconsin	164	Zakarie Barie,UTEP	29:20.0
1984	Arkansas	John McDonnell	101	Arizona	111	Ed Eyestone, BYU	29:28.8
1985	Wisconsin	Martin Smith	67	Arkansas	104	Timothy Hacker, Wisconsin	29:17.88
1986	Arkansas	John McDonnell	69	Dartmouth	141	Aaron Ramirez, Arizona	30:27.53
1987	Arkansas	John McDonnell	87	Dartmouth	119	Joe Falcon, Arkansas	29:14.97
1988	Wisconsin	Martin Smith	105	Northern Arizona	160	Robert Kennedy, Indiana	29:20.0
1989	Iowa St	Bill Bergan	54	Oregon	72	John Nuttall, Iowa St	29:30.55
1990	Arkansas	John McDonnell	68	Iowa St	96	Jonah Koech, Iowa St	29:05.0
1991	Arkansas	John McDonnell	52	Iowa St	114	Sean Dollman, W. Kentucky	30:17.1
1992	Arkansas	John McDonnell	46	Wisconsin	87	Bob Kennedy, Indiana	30:15.3
1993	Arkansas	John McDonnell	31	BYU	153	Josephat Kapkory, Wash. St	29:32.4
1994	Iowa St	Bill Bergan	65	Colorado	88	Martin Keino, Arizona	30:08.7
1995	Arkansas	John McDonnell	100	Northern Arizona	142	Godfrey Siamusiye, Arkansas	30:09
1996	Stanford	Vin Lananna	46	Arkansas	74	Godfrey Siamusiye, Arkansas	29:49
1997	Stanford	Vin Lananna	53	Arkansas	56	Mebrahtom Keflezighi, UCLA	28:54
1998	Arkansas	John McDonnell	97	Stanford	114	Adam Goucher, Colorado	29:26
1999	Arkansas	John McDonnell	58	Wisconsin	185	David Kimani, S. Alabama	30:06.6
2000	Arkansas	John McDonnell	83	Colorado	94	Keith Kelly, Providence	30:14.5
2001	Colorado	Mark Wetmore	90	Stanford	91	Boaz Cheboiywo, E. Michigan	28:47
2002	Stanford	Andrew Gerard	47	Wisconsin	107	Jorge Torres, Colorado	29:04.7
2003	Stanford	Andrew Gerard	24	Wisconsin	124	Dathan Ritzenhein, Colorado	29:14.1
2004	Colorado	Mark Wetmore	90	Wisconsin	94	Simon Bairu, Wisconsin	30:37.7
2005	Wisconsin	Jerry Schumacher	37	Arkansas	105	Simon Bairu, Wisconsin	29:15.9
2006	Colorado	Mark Wetmore	94	Wisconsin	142	Josh Rohatinsky, BYU	30:44.9

DIVISION II

Year	Champion	Year	Champion	Year	Champion
1958	Northern Illinois	1974	SW Missouri St	1990	Edinboro
1959	South Dakota St	1975	UC–Irvine	1991	UMass–Lowell
1960	Central St (Ohio)	1976	UC–Irvine	1992	Adams St
1961	South Illinois	1977	Eastern Illinois	1993	Adams St
1962	Central St (Ohio)	1978	Cal Poly–SLO	1994	Adams St
1963	Emporia St	1979	Cal Poly–SLO	1995	Western St
1964	Kentucky St	1980	Humboldt St	1996	South Dakota St
1965	San Diego St	1981	Millersville	1997	South Dakota
1966	San Diego St	1982	Eastern Washington	1998	Adams St
1967	San Diego St	1983	Cal Poly–Pomona	1999	Western St
1968	Eastern Illinois	1984	SE Missouri St	2000	Western St
1969	Eastern Illinois	1985	South Dakota St	2001	Western St
1970	Eastern Michigan	1986	Edinboro	2002	Western St
1971	CSU–Fullerton	1987	Edinboro	2003	Adams St
1972	North Dakota St	1988	Edinboro/ Mankato St	2004	Western St
1973	South Dakota St	1989	South Dakota St	2005	Western St
				2006	Abilene Christian

Men *(Cont.)*
DIVISION III

Year	Champion	Year	Champion	Year	Champion
1973	Ashland	1985	Luther	1997	N. Central
1974	Mount Union	1986	St. Thomas (Minn.)	1998	N. Central
1975	North Central	1987	N Central	1999	N. Central
1976	North Central	1988	UW–Oshkosh	2000	Calvin
1977	Occidental	1989	UW–Oshkosh	2001	UW-La Crosse
1978	N. Central	1990	UW–Oshkosh	2002	UW-Oshkosh
1979	N. Central	1991	Rochester	2003	Calvin College
1980	Carleton	1992	N. Central	2004	Calvin College
1981	N. Central	1993	N. Central	2005	UW-La Crosse
1982	N. Central	1994	Williams	2006	Calvin College
1983	Brandeis	1995	Williams		
1984	St. Thomas (Minn.)	1996	UW–La Crosse		

Women
DIVISION I

Year	Champion	Coach	Pts	Runner-Up	Pts	Individual Champion	Time
1981	Virginia	John Vasvary	36	Oregon	83	Betty Springs, N Carolina St	16:19.0
1982	Virginia	Martin Smith	48	Stanford	91	Lesley Welch, Virginia	16:39.7
1983	Oregon	Tom Heinonen	95	Stanford	98	Betty Springs, N Carolina St	16:30.7
1984	Wisconsin	Peter Tegen	63	Stanford	89	Cathy Branta, Wisconsin	16:15.6
1985	Wisconsin	Peter Tegen	58	Iowa St	98	Suzie Tuffey, N Carolina St	16:22.5
1986	Texas	Terry Crawford	62	Wisconsin	64	Angela Chalmers, N Arizona	16:55.49
1987	Oregon	Tom Heinonen	97	North Carolina St	99	Kimberly Betz, Indiana	16:10.85
1988	Kentucky	Don Weber	75	Oregon	128	Michelle Dekkers, Indiana	16:30.0
1989	Villanova	Marty Stern	99	Kentucky	168	Vicki Huber, Villanova	15:59.86
1990	Villanova	Marty Stern	82	Providence	172	Sonia O'Sullivan, Villanova	16:06.0
1991	Villanova	Marty Stern	85	Arkansas	168	Sonia O'Sullivan, Villanova	16:30.3
1992	Villanova	Marty Stern	123	Arkansas	130	Carole Zajac, Villanova	17:01.9
1993	Villanova	Marty Stern	66	Arkansas	71	Carole Zajac, Villanova	16:40.3
1994	Villanova	John Marshall	75	Michigan	108	Jennifer Rhines, Villanova	16:31.2
1995	Providence	Ray Treacy	88	Colorado	123	Kathy Butler, Wisconsin	16:51
1996	Stanford	Beth Alford-Sullivan	101	Villanova	106	Amy Skieresz, Arizona	17:04
1997	BYU	Patrick Shane	100	Stanford	102	Carrie Tollefson, Villanova	16:58
1998	Villanova	Marcus O'Sullivan	106	BYU	110	Katie McGregor, Michigan	16:47.21
1999	BYU	Patrick Shane	72	Arkansas	125	Erica Palmer, Wisconsin	16:39.50
2000	Colorado	Mark Wetmore	117	BYU	167	Kara Grgas-Wheeler, Colorado	20:30.5
2001	BYU	Patrick Shane	62	North Carolina St	148	Tara Chaplin, Arizona	20:24
2002	BYU	Patrick Shane	85	Stanford	113	Shalane Flanagan	19:36.0
2003	Stanford	Dena Evans	120	BYU	128	Shalane Flanagan	19:30.4
2004	Colorado	Mark Wetmore	63	Duke	144	Kim Smith, Providence	20:08.5
2005	Stanford	Peter Tegen	146	Colorado	181	Johanna Nilsson, N Arizona	19:33.9
2006	Stanford	Peter Tegen	195	Colorado	223	Sally Kipyego, Texas Tech	20:11.1

DIVISION II

Year	Champion	Year	Champion	Year	Champion
1981	S Dakota St	1990	Cal Poly–SLO	1999	Adams St
1982	Cal Poly–SLO	1991	Cal Poly–SLO	2000	Western St
1983	Cal Poly–SLO	1992	Adams St	2001	Western St
1984	Cal Poly–SLO	1993	Adams St	2002	Western St
1985	Cal Poly–SLO	1994	Adams St	2003	Adams St
1986	Cal Poly–SLO	1995	Adams St	2004	Adams St
1987	Cal Poly–SLO	1996	Adams St	2005	Adams St
1988	Cal Poly–SLO	1997	Adams St	2006	Adams St
1989	Cal Poly–SLO	1998	Adams St		

DIVISION III

Year	Champion	Year	Champion	Year	Champion
1981	Central (Iowa)	1989	Cortland St	1998	Calvin
1982	St. Thomas (Minn.)	1990	Cortland St	1999	Calvin
1983	UW–La Crosse	1991	UW–Oshkosh	2000	Middlebury
1984	St. Thomas (Minn.)	1992	Cortland St	2001	Middlebury
1985	Franklin & Marshall	1993	Cortland St	2002	Williams
1986	St. Thomas (Minn.)	1994	Cortland St	2003	Middlebury
1987	St. Thomas (Minn.)	1995	Cortland St	2004	Williams College
	UW–Oshkosh	1996	UW–Oshkosh	2005	Geneseo St
1988	UW–Oshkosh	1997	Cortland St	2006	Middlebury

Men's and Women's Combined
TEAM CHAMPIONS

Year	Champion	Coach	Pts	Runner-Up	Pts
1990	Penn St	Emmanuil Kaidanov	36	Columbia–Barnard	35
1991	Penn St	Emmanuil Kaidanov	4700	Columbia–Barnard	4200
1992	Columbia–Barnard	G. Kolombatovich/A. Kogler	4150	Penn St	3646
1993	Columbia–Barnard	G. Kolombatovich/A. Kogler	4525	Penn St	4500
1994	Notre Dame	Michael DeCicco	4350	Penn St	4075
1995	Penn St	Emmanuil Kaidanov	440	St. John's (N.Y.)	413
1996	Penn St	Emmanuil Kaidanov	1500	Notre Dame	1190
1997	Penn St	Emmanuil Kaidanov	1530	Notre Dame	1470
1998	Penn St	Emmanuil Kaidanov	149	Notre Dame	147
1999	Penn St	Emmanuil Kaidanov	171	Notre Dame	139
2000	Penn St	Emmanuil Kaidanov	175	Notre Dame	171
2001	St. John's (N.Y.)	Yuri Gelman	180	Penn St	172
2002	Penn St	Emmanuil Kaidanov	195	St. John's (N.Y.)	190
2003	Notre Dame	Janusz Bednarski	182	Penn St	179
2004	Ohio St	Vladimir Nazlymov	194	Penn St	160
2005	Notre Dame	Janusz Bednarski	173	Ohio St	171
2006	Harvard	Peter Brand	165	Penn St	159
2007	Penn St	Emmanuil Kaidanov	194	St. John's	176

Men
TEAM CHAMPIONS

Year	Champion	Coach	Pts	Runner-Up	Pts
1941	Northwestern	Henry Zettleman	28½	Illinois	27
1942	Ohio St	Frank Riebel	34	St. John's (N.Y.)	33½
1943–46	No tournament				
1947	NYU	Martinez Castello	72	Chicago	50½
1948	CCNY	James Montague	30	Navy	28
1949	Army/Rutgers	S. Velarde/D. Cetrulo	63		
1950	Navy	Joseph Fiems	67½	NYU/Rutgers	66½
1951	Columbia	Servando Velarde	69	Pennsylvania	64
1952	Columbia	Servando Velarde	71	NYU	69
1953	Pennsylvania	Lajos Csiszar	94	Navy	86
1954	Columbia	Irving DeKoff	61		
	NYU	Hugo Castello	61		
1955	Columbia	Irving DeKoff	62	Cornell	57
1956	Illinois	Maxwell Garret	90	Columbia	88
1957	NYU	Hugo Castello	65	Columbia	64
1958	Illinois	Maxwell Garret	47	Columbia	43
1959	Navy	Andre Deladrier	72	NYU	65
1960	NYU	Hugo Castello	65	Navy	57
1961	NYU	Hugo Castello	79	Princeton	68
1962	Navy	Andre Deladrier	76	NYU	74
1963	Columbia	Irving DeKoff	55	Navy	50
1964	Princeton	Stan Sieja	81	NYU	79
1965	Columbia	Irving DeKoff	76	NYU	74
1966	NYU	Hugo Castello	5–0	Army	5–2
1967	NYU	Hugo Castello	72	Pennsylvania	64
1968	Columbia	Louis Bankuti	92	NYU	87
1969	Pennsylvania	Lajos Csiszar	54	Harvard	43
1970	NYU	Hugo Castello	71	Columbia	63
1971	NYU/Columbia	Hugo Castello/Louis Bankuti	68		
1972	Detroit	Richard Perry	73	NYU	70
1973	NYU	Hugo Castello	76	Pennsylvania	71
1974	NYU	Hugo Castello	92	Wayne St	87
1975	Wayne St	Istvan Danosi	89	Cornell	83
1976	NYU	Herbert Cohen	79	Wayne St	77
1977	Notre Dame	Michael DeCicco	114*	NYU	114
1978	Notre Dame	Michael DeCicco	121	Pennsylvania	110
1979	Wayne St	Istvan Danosi	119	Notre Dame	108
1980	Wayne St	Istvan Danosi	111	Pennsylvania/MIT	106
1981	Pennsylvania	Dave Micahnik	113	Wayne St	111
1982	Wayne St	Istvan Danosi	85	Clemson	77
1983	Wayne St	Aladar Kogler	86	Notre Dame	80
1984	Wayne St	Gil Pezza	69	Penn St	50
1985	Wayne St	Gil Pezza	141	Notre Dame	140

Men

TEAM CHAMPIONS (CONT.)

Year	Champion	Coach	Pts	Runner-Up	Pts
1986	Notre Dame	Michael DeCicco	151	Columbia	141
1987	Columbia	George Kolombatovich	86	Pennsylvania	78
1988	Columbia	G. Kolombatovich/A. Kogler	90	Notre Dame	83
1989	Columbia	G. Kolombatovich/A. Kogler	88	Penn St	85

*Tie broken by a fence-off. Note: Beginning in 1990, men's and women's combined teams competed for the national championship. See p. 598.

INDIVIDUAL CHAMPIONS

	Foil	Sabre	Épée
1941	Edward McNamara, Northwestern	William Meyer, Dartmouth	G.H. Boland, Illinois
1942	Byron Kreiger, Wayne St	Andre Deladrier, St. John's (NY)	Ben Burtt, Ohio St
1943–46	No tournament		
1947	Abraham Balk, NYU	Oscar Parsons, Temple	Abraham Balk, NYU
1948	Albert Axelrod, CCNY	James Day, Navy	William Bryan, Navy
1949	Ralph Tedeschi, Rutgers	Alex Treves, Rutgers	Richard C. Bowman, Army
1950	Robert Nielsen, Columbia	Alex Treves, Rutgers	Thomas Stuart, Navy
1951	Robert Nielsen, Columbia	Chamberless Johnston, Princeton	Daniel Chafetz, Columbia
1952	Harold Goldsmith, CCNY	Frank Zimolzak, Navy	James Wallner, NYU
1953	Ed Nober, Brooklyn	Robert Parmacek, Penn	Jack Tori, Pennsylvania
1954	Robert Goldman, Pennsylvania	Steve Sobel, Columbia	Henry Kolowrat, Princeton
1955	Herman Velasco, Illinois	Barry Pariser, Columbia	Donald Tadrawski, Notre Dame
1956	Ralph DeMarco, Columbia	Gerald Kaufman, Columbia	Kinmont Hoitsma, Princeton
1957	Bruce Davis, Wayne St	Bernie Balaban, NYU	James Margolis, Columbia
1958	Bruce Davis, Wayne St	Art Schankin, Illinois	Roland Wommack, Navy
1959	Joe Paletta, Navy	Al Morales, Navy	Roland Wommack, Navy
1960	Gene Glazer, NYU	Mike Desaro, NYU	Gil Eisner, NYU
1961	Herbert Cohen, NYU	Israel Colon, NYU	Jerry Halpern, NYU
1962	Herbert Cohen, NYU	Barton Nisonson, Columbia	Thane Hawkins, Navy
1963	Jay Lustig, Columbia	Bela Szentivanyi, Wayne St	Larry Crum, Navy
1964	Bill Hicks, Princeton	Craig Bell, Illinois	Paul Pesthy, Rutgers
1965	Joe Nalven, Columbia	Howard Goodman, NYU	Paul Pesthy, Rutgers
1966	Al Davis, NYU	Paul Apostol, NYU	Bernhardt Hermann, Iowa
1967	Mike Gaylor, NYU	Todd Makler, Pennsylvania	George Masin, NYU
1968	Gerard Esponda, San Francisco	Todd Makler, Pennsylvania	Don Sieja, Cornell
1969	Anthony Kestler, Columbia	Norman Braslow, Penn	James Wetzler, Pennsylvania
1970	Walter Krause, NYU	Bruce Soriano, Columbia	John Nadas, Case Reserve
1971	Tyrone Simmons, Detroit	Bruce Soriano, Columbia	George Szunyogh, NYU
1972	Tyrone Simmons, Detroit	Bruce Soriano, Columbia	Ernesto Fernandez, Penn
1973	Brooke Makler, Pennsylvania	Peter Westbrock, NYU	Risto Hurme, NYU
1974	Greg Benko, Wayne St	Steve Danosi, Wayne St	Risto Hurme, NYU
1975	Greg Benko, Wayne St	Yuri Rabinovich, Wayne St	Risto Hurme, NYU
1976	Greg Benko, Wayne St	Brian Smith, Columbia	Randy Eggleton, Pennsylvania
1977	Pat Gerard, Notre Dame	Mike Sullivan, Notre Dame	Hans Wieselgren, NYU
1978	Ernest Simon, Wayne St	Mike Sullivan, Notre Dame	Bjorne Vaggo, Notre Dame
1979	Andrew Bonk, Notre Dame	Yuri Rabinovich, Wayne St	Carlos Songini, Cleveland St
1980	Ernest Simon, Wayne St	Paul Friedberg, Pennsylvania	Gil Pezza, Wayne St
1981	Ernest Simon, Wayne St	Paul Friedberg, Pennsylvania	Gil Pezza, Wayne St
1982	Alexander Flom, George Mason	Neil Hick, Wayne St	Peter Schifrin, San Jose St
1983	Demetrios Valsamis, NYU	John Friedberg, North Carolina	Ola Harstrom, Notre Dame
1984	Charles Higgs-Coulthard, Notre Dame	Michael Lofton, NYU	Ettore Bianchi, Wayne St
1985	Stephan Chauvel, Wayne St	Michael Lofton, NYU	Ettore Bianchi, Wayne St
1986	Adam Feldman, Penn St	Michael Lofton, NYU	Chris O'Loughlin, Pennsylvania
1987	William Mindel, Columbia	Michael Lofton, NYU	James O'Neill, Harvard
1988	Marc Kent, Columbia	Robert Cottingham, Columbia	Jon Normile, Columbia
1989	Edward Mufel, Penn St	Peter Cox, Penn St	Jon Normile, Columbia
1990	Nick Bravin, Stanford	David Mandell, Columbia	Jubba Beshin, Notre Dame
1991	Ben Atkins, Columbia	Vitali Nazlimov, Penn St	Marc Oshima, Columbia
1992	Nick Bravin, Stanford	Tom Strzalkowski, Penn St	Harald Bauder, Wayne St
1993	Nick Bravin, Stanford	Tom Strzalkowski, Penn St	Ben Atkins, Columbia
1994	Kwame van Leeuwen, Harvard	Tom Strzalkowski, Penn St	Harald Winkman, Princeton
1995	Sean McClain, Stanford	Paul Palestis, NYU	Mike Gattner, Lawrence
1996	Thorstein Becker, Wayne St	Maxim Pekarev, Princeton	Jeremy Kahn, Duke
1997	Cliff Bayer, Pennsylvania	Keith Smart, St. John's (N.Y.)	Alden Clarke, Stanford
1998	Ayo Griffin, Yale	Luke LaValle, Notre Dame	George Hentea, St. John's (N.Y.)

Men *(Cont.)*
INDIVIDUAL CHAMPIONS *(Cont.)*

	Foil	Sabre	Épée
1999	Felíx Reichling, Stanford	Keeth Smart, St. John's (N.Y.)	Alex Roytblat St. John's (N.Y.)
2000	Felíx Reichling, Stanford	Gabor Szelle, Notre Dame	Daniel Landgren, Penn St
2001	William Jed Dupree, Columbia	Ivan Lee, St. John's (N.Y.)	Soren Thompson, Princeton
2002	Nontapat Panchan, Penn St	Ivan Lee, St. John's (N.Y.)	Arpád Horváth, St. John's (N.Y.)
2003	Nontapat Panchan, Penn St	Adam Crompton, Ohio St	Weston Kelsey, Air Force
2004	Boaz Ellis, Ohio St	Adam Crompton, Ohio St	Arpád Horváth, St. John's (N.Y.)
2005	Boaz Ellis, Ohio St	Sergey Isayenko, St. John's	Michal Sobieraj, Notre Dame
2006	Boaz Ellis, Ohio St	Adam Crompton, Ohio St	Benji Ungar, Harvard
2007	Andras Horanyi, Ohio St	Timothy Hagaman, Harvard	Slava Zingerman, Wayne St

Women
TEAM CHAMPIONS

Year	Champion	Coach	Rec	Runner-Up	Rec
1982	Wayne St	Istvan Danosi	7–0	San Jose St	6–1
1983	Penn St	Beth Alphin	5–0	Wayne St	3–2
1984	Yale	Henry Harutunian	3–0	Penn St	2–1
1985	Yale	Henry Harutunian	3–0	Pennsylvania	2–1
1986	Pennsylvania	David Micahnik	3–0	Notre Dame	2–1
1987	Notre Dame	Yves Auriol	3–0	Temple	2–1
1988	Wayne St	Gil Pezza	3–0	Notre Dame	2–1
1989	Wayne St	Gil Pezza	3–0	Columbia-Barnard	2–1

Note: Beginning in 1990, men's and women's combined teams competed for the national championship. See p. 598.

INDIVIDUAL CHAMPIONS

Foil	Foil *(Cont.)*	Sabre *(Cont.)*
1982....Joy Ellingson, San Jose St	1998....F. Zimmermann, Stanford	2005....Emily Jacobson, Col.-Barnard
1983....Jana Angelakis, Penn St	1999....Monique DeBruin, Stanford	2006....Mariel Zagunis, Notre Dame
1984....Mary Jane O'Neill, Penn	2000....Eva Petschnigg, Princeton	2007....Daria Schneider, Col.-Barnard
1985....C. Bilodeaux, Columbia-Barn.	2001....Iris Zimmerman, Stanford	**Épée**
1986....M. Sullivan, Notre Dame	2002....Alicja Kryczalo, Notre Dame	1995....Tina Loven, St. John's (N.Y.)
1987....C. Bilodeaux, Columbia-Barn.	2003....Alicja Kryczalo, Notre Dame	1996....N. Dygert, St. John's (N.Y.)
1988....M. Sullivan, Notre Dame	2004....Alicja Kryczalo, Notre Dame	1997....Magda Krol, Notre Dame
1989....Yasemin Topcu, Wayne St	2005....Alicja Kryczalo, Notre Dame	1998....Charlotte Walker, Penn St
1990....Tzu Moy, Columbia-Barn.	2006....Ezsebet Garay, St. John's (N.Y.)	1999....F. Zimmermann, Stanford
1991....Heidi Piper, Notre Dame	2007....Doris Willette, Penn St	2000....Jessica Burke, Penn St
1992....Olga Cheryak, Penn St	**Sabre**	2001....E. Takács, St. John's (N.Y.)
1993....Olga Kalinovskaya, Penn St	2000....Caroline Purcell, MIT	2002....Stephanie Eim, Penn St
1994....Olga Kalinovskaya, Penn St	2001....Sada Jacobson, Yale	2003....Katarzyna Trzopek, Penn St
1995....Olga Kalinovskaya, Penn St	2002....Sada Jacobson, Yale	2004....Anna Garina, Wayne St
1996....Olga Kalinovskaya, Penn St	2003....Alexis Jemal, Rutgers	2005....Anna Garina, Wayne St
1997....Yelena Kalkina, Ohio St	2004....Valerie Providenza, Notre Dame	2006....Katarzyna Trzopek, Penn St
		2007....Anna Garina, Wayne St.

Field Hockey
DIVISION I

Year	Champion	Coach	Score	Runner-Up
1981	Connecticut	Diane Wright	4–1	Massachusetts
1982	Old Dominion	Beth Anders	3–2	Connecticut
1983	Old Dominion	Beth Anders	3–1 (3 OT)	Connecticut
1984	Old Dominion	Beth Anders	5–1	Iowa
1985	Connecticut	Diane Wright	3–2	Old Dominion
1986	Iowa	Judith Davidson	2–1 (2 OT)	New Hampshire
1987	Maryland	Sue Tyler	2–1 (OT)	North Carolina
1988	Old Dominion	Beth Anders	2–1	Iowa
1989	North Carolina	Karen Shelton	2–1 (3 OT)*	Old Dominion
1990	Old Dominion	Beth Anders	5–0	North Carolina
1991	Old Dominion	Beth Anders	2–0	North Carolina
1992	Old Dominion	Beth Anders	4–0	Iowa
1993	Maryland	Missy Meharg	2–1 (3 OT)*	North Carolina
1994	James Madison	Christy Morgan	2–1 (3 OT)*	North Carolina
1995	North Carolina	Karen Shelton-Scroggs	5–1	Maryland
1996	North Carolina	Karen Shelton-Scroggs	3–0	Princeton
1997	North Carolina	Karen Shelton	3–2	Old Dominion
1998	Old Dominion	Beth Anders	3–2	Princeton
1999	Maryland	Missy Meharg	2–1	Michigan
2000	Old Dominion	Beth Anders	3–1	North Carolina

DIVISION I (CONT.)

Year	Champion	Coach	Score	Runner-Up
2001	Michigan	Marcia Pankratz	2–0	Maryland
2002	Wake Forest	Jennifer Averill	2–0	Penn St
2003	Wake Forest	Jennifer Averill	3–1	Duke
2004	Wake Forest	Jennifer Averill	3–0	Duke
2005	Maryland	Missy Meharg	1–0	Duke
2006	Maryland	Missy Meharg	1–0	Wake Forest

*Penalty strokes.

DIVISION II *(Discontinued, then renewed)*

Year	Champion	Coach	Score	Runner-Up
1981	Pfeiffer	Ellen Briggs	5–3	Bentley
1982	Lock Haven	Sharon E. Taylor	4–1	Bloomsburg
1983	Bloomsburg	Jan Hutchinson	1–0	Lock Haven
1992	Lock Haven	Sharon E. Taylor	3–1	Bloomsburg
1993	Bloomsburg	Jan Hutchinson	2–1 (2 OT)	Lock Haven
1994	Lock Haven	Sharon E. Taylor	2–1	Bloomsburg
1995	Lock Haven	Sharon E. Taylor	1–0	Bloomsburg
1996	Bloomsburg	Jan Hutchinson	1–0	Lock Haven
1997	Bloomsburg	Jan Hutchinson	2–0	Kutztown
1998	Bloomsburg	Jan Hutchinson	4–3 (OT)	Lock Haven
1999	Bloomsburg	Jan Hutchinson	2–0	Bentley
2000	Lock Haven	Pat Rudy	2–0	Bentley
2001	Bentley	Kell McGowan	4–2	E Stroudsburg
2002	Bloomsburg	Jan Hutchinson	5–0	Bentley
2003	Bloomsburg	Jan Hutchinson	4–1	Mass.–Lowell
2004	Bloomsburg	Jan Hutchinson	3–2	Bentley
2005	Mass.-Lowell	Shannon Hlebichuk	2–1	Bloomsburg
2006	Bloomsburg	Jan Hutchinson	1–0	Bentley

DIVISION III

Year	Champion	Year	Champion	Year	Champion
1981	Trenton St	1990	Trenton St	1999	College of New Jersey*
1982	Ithaca	1991	Trenton St	2000	William Smith
1983	Trenton St	1992	William Smith	2001	Cortland St
1984	Bloomsburg	1993	Cortland St	2002	Rowan
1985	Trenton St	1994	Cortland St	2003	Salisbury
1986	Salisbury St	1995	Trenton St	2004	Salisbury
1987	Bloomsburg	1996	College of New Jersey*	2005	Salisbury
1988	Trenton St	1997	William Smith	2006	Ursinus (Pa.)
1989	Lock Haven	1998	Middelbury		*Formerly Trenton St

Golf

Men
DIVISION I — Results, 1897–1938

Year	Champion	Site	Individual Champion
1897	Yale	Ardsley Casino	Louis Bayard Jr, Princeton
1898	Harvard (spring)		John Reid Jr, Yale
1898	Yale (fall)		James Curtis, Harvard
1899	Harvard		Percy Pyne, Princeton
1900	No tournament		
1901	Harvard	Atlantic City	H. Lindsley, Harvard
1902	Yale (spring)	Garden City	Charles Hitchcock Jr, Yale
1902	Harvard (fall)	Morris County	Chandler Egan, Harvard
1903	Harvard	Garden City	F.O. Reinhart, Princeton
1904	Harvard	Myopia	A.L. White, Harvard
1905	Yale	Garden City	Robert Abbott, Yale
1906	Yale	Garden City	W.E. Clow Jr, Yale
1907	Yale	Nassau	Ellis Knowles, Yale
1908	Yale	Brae Burn	H.H. Wilder, Harvard
1909	Yale	Apawamis	Albert Seckel, Princeton
1910	Yale	Essex County	Robert Hunter, Yale
1911	Yale	Baltusrol	George Stanley, Yale
1912	Yale	Ekwanok	F.C. Davison, Harvard
1913	Yale	Huntingdon Valley	Nathaniel Wheeler, Yale
1914	Princeton	Garden City	Edward Allis, Harvard
1915	Yale	Greenwich	Francis Blossom, Yale
1916	Princeton	Oakmont	J.W. Hubbell, Harvard

Men
DIVISION I Results, 1897–1938(Cont.)

Year	Champion	Site	Individual Champion
1917–18	No tournament		
1919	Princeton	Merion	A.L. Walker Jr, Columbia
1920	Princeton	Nassau	Jess Sweetster, Yale
1921	Dartmouth	Greenwich	Simpson Dean, Princeton
1922	Princeton	Garden City	Pollack Boyd, Dartmouth
1923	Princeton	Siwanoy	Dexter Cummings, Yale
1924	Yale	Greenwich	Dexter Cummings, Yale
1925	Yale	Montclair	Fred Lamprecht, Tulane
1926	Yale	Merion	Fred Lamprecht, Tulane
1927	Princeton	Garden City	Watts Gunn, Georgia Tech
1928	Princeton	Apawamis	Maurice McCarthy, Georgetown
1929	Princeton	Hollywood	Tom Aycock, Yale
1930	Princeton	Oakmont	G.T. Dunlap Jr, Princeton
1931	Yale	Olympia Fields	G.T. Dunlap Jr, Princeton
1932	Yale	Hot Springs	J.W. Fischer, Michigan
1933	Yale	Buffalo	Walter Emery, Oklahoma
1934	Michigan	Cleveland	Charles Yates, Georgia Tech
1935	Michigan	Congressional	Ed White, Texas
1936	Yale	North Shore	Charles Kocsis, Michigan
1937	Princeton	Oakmont	Fred Haas Jr, LSU
1938	Stanford	Louisville	John Burke, Georgetown

Results, 1939–2007

Year	Champion (Score)	Coach	Runner-Up (Score)	Host or Site	Individual Champion
1939	Stanford (612)	Eddie Twiggs	Northwestern (614) Princeton (614)	Wakonda	Vincent D'Antoni, Tulane
1940	Princeton (601) LSU (601)	Walter Bourne Mike Donahue		Ekwanok	Dixon Brooke, Virginia
1941	Stanford (580)	Eddie Twiggs	LSU (599)	Ohio St	Earl Stewart, LSU
1942	LSU (590) Stanford (590)	Mike Donahue Eddie Twiggs		Notre Dame	Frank Tatum Jr, Stanford
1943	Yale (614)	William Neale Jr	Michigan (618)	Olympia Fields	Wallace Ulrich, Carleton
1944	Notre Dame (311)	George Holderith	Minnesota (312)	Inverness	Louis Lick, Minnesota
1945	Ohio St (602)	Robert Kepler	Northwestern (621)	Ohio St	John Lorms, Ohio St
1946	Stanford (619)	Eddie Twiggs	Michigan (624)	Princeton	George Hamer, Georgia
1947	LSU (606)	T.P. Heard	Duke (614)	Michigan	Dave Barclay, Michigan
1948	San Jose St (579)	Wilbur Hubbard	LSU (588)	Stanford	Bob Harris, San Jose St
1949	North Texas (590)	Fred Cobb	Purdue (600) Texas (600)	Iowa St	Harvie Ward, North Carolina
1950	North Texas (573)	Fred Cobb	Purdue (577)	New Mexico	Fred Wampler, Purdue
1951	North Texas (588)	Fred Cobb	Ohio St (589)	Ohio St	Tom Nieporte, Ohio St
1952	North Texas (587)	Fred Cobb	Michigan (593)	Purdue	Jim Vickers, Oklahoma
1953	Stanford (578)	Charles Finger	North.Carolina (580)	Broadmoor	Earl Moeller, Oklahoma St
1954	SMU (572)	Graham Ross	North Texas (573)	Houston Hillman	Robbins, Memphis St
1955	LSU (574)	Mike Barbato	North Texas (583)	Tennessee	Joe Campbell, Purdue
1956	Houston (601)	Dave Williams	North Texas (602) Purdue (602)	Ohio St	Rick Jones, Ohio St
1957	Houston (602)	Dave Williams	Stanford (603)	Broadmoor	Rex Baxter Jr., Houston
1958	Houston (570)	Dave Williams	Oklahoma St (582)	Williams	Phil Rodgers, Houston
1959	Houston (561)	Dave Williams	Purdue (571)	Oregon	Dick Crawford, Houston
1960	Houston (603)	Dave Williams	Purdue (607) Oklahoma St (607)	Broadmoor	Dick Crawford, Houston
1961	Purdue (584)	Sam Voinoff	Arizona St (595)	Lafayette	Jack Nicklaus, Ohio St
1962	Houston (588)	Dave Williams	Oklahoma St (598)	Duke	Kermit Zarley, Houston
1963	Oklahoma St (581)	Labron Harris	Houston (582)	Wichita St	R.H. Sikes, Arkansas
1964	Houston (580)	Dave Williams	Oklahoma St (587)	Broadmoor	Terry Small, San Jose St
1965	Houston (577)	Dave Williams	CSU–L.A. (587)	Tennessee	Marty Fleckman, Houston
1966	Houston (582)	Dave Williams	San Jose St (586)	Stanford	Bob Murphy, Florida
1967	Houston (585)	Dave Williams	Florida (588)	Shawnee, Pa.	Hale Irwin, Colorado
1968	Florida (1154)	Buster Bishop	Houston (1156)	New Mexico St	Grier Jones, Oklahoma St
1969	Houston (1223)	Dave Williams	Wake Forest (1232)	Broadmoor	Bob Clark, CSU–LA
1970	Houston (1172)	Dave Williams	Wake Forest (1182)	Ohio St	John Mahaffey, Houston
1971	Texas (1144)	George Hannon	Houston (1151)	Arizona	Ben Crenshaw, Texas
1972	Texas (1146)	George Hannon	Houston (1159)	Cape Coral	Ben Crenshaw, Texas Tom Kite, Texas

Men - DIVISION I *(Cont.)*
Results, 1939–2007 *(Cont.)*

Year	Champion (Score)	Coach	Runner-Up (Score)	Host or Site	Individual Champion
1973	Florida (1149)	Buster Bishop	Oklahoma St (1159)	Oklahoma St	Ben Crenshaw, Texas
1974	Wake Forest (1158)	Jess Haddock	Florida (1160)	San Diego St	Curtis Strange, Wake Forest
1975	Wake Forest (1156)	Jess Haddock	Oklahoma St (1189)	Ohio St	Jay Haas, Wake Forest
1976	Oklahoma St (1166)	Mike Holder	BYU (1173)	New Mexico	Scott Simpson, USC
1977	Houston (1197)	Dave Williams	Oklahoma St (1205)	Colgate	Scott Simpson, USC
1978	Oklahoma St (1140)	Mike Holder	Georgia (1157)	Oregon	David Edwards, Oklahoma St
1979	Ohio St (1189)	James Brown	Oklahoma St (1191)	Wake Forest	Gary Hallberg, Wake Forest
1980	Oklahoma St (1173)	Mike Holder	BYU (1177)	Ohio St	Jay Don Blake, Utah St
1981	BYU (1161)	Karl Tucker	Oral Roberts (1163)	Stanford	Ron Commans, USC
1982	Houston (1141)	Dave Williams	Oklahoma St (1151)	Pinehurst	Billy Ray Brown, Houston
1983	Oklahoma St (1161)	Mike Holder	Texas (1168)	Fresno St	Jim Carter, Arizona St
1984	Houston (1145)	Dave Williams	Oklahoma St (1146)	Houston	John Inman, North Carolina
1985	Houston (1172)	Dave Williams	Oklahoma St (1175)	Florida	Clark Burroughs, Ohio St
1986	Wake Forest (1156)	Jess Haddock	Oklahoma St (1160)	Wake Forest	Scott Verplank, Oklahoma St
1987	Oklahoma St (1160)	Mike Holder	Wake Forest (1176)	Ohio St	Brian Watts, Oklahoma St
1988	UCLA (1176)	Eddie Merrins	UTEP (1179) Oklahoma (1179) Oklahoma St (1179)	USC	E.J. Pfister, Oklahoma St
1989	Oklahoma (1139)	Gregg Grost	Texas (1158)	Oklahoma Oklahoma St	Phil Mickelson, Arizona St
1990	Arizona St (1155)	Steve Loy	Florida (1157)	Florida	Phil Mickelson, Arizona St
1991	Oklahoma St (1161)	Mike Holder	North Carolina (1168)	San Jose St	Warren Schutte, UNLV
1992	Arizona (1129)	Rick LaRose	Arizona St (1136)	New Mexico	Phil Mickelson, Arizona St
1993	Florida (1145)	Buddy Alexander	Georgia Tech (1146)	Kentucky	Todd Demsey, Arizona St
1994	Stanford (1129)	Wally Goodwin	Texas (1133)	McKinney, Tex.	Justin Leonard, Texas
1995	Oklahoma St* (1156)	Mike Holder	Stanford (1156)	Ohio St	Chip Spratlin, Auburn
1996	Arizona St (1186)	Randy Lein	UNLV (1189)	Chattanooga	Tiger Woods, Stanford
1997	Pepperdine (1148)	John Geiberger	Wake Forest (1151)	Evanston, Ill.	Charles Warren, Clemson
1998	UNLV (1118)	Dwaine Knight	Clemson (1121)	Albuquerque	James McLean, Minnesota
1999	Georgia (1180)	Chris Haack	Oklahoma St (1183)	Chaska, Minn.	Donald Luke, Northwestern
2000	Oklahoma St* (1116)	Mike Holder	Georgia Tech (1116)	Opelika, Ala.	Charles Howell, Oklahoma St
2001	Florida (1126)	Buddy Alexander	Clemson (1144)	Durham, N.C.	Nick Gilliam, Florida
2002	Minnesota (1134)	Brad James	Georgia Tech	Ohio St	Troy Matteson, Georgia Tech
2003	Clemson (1191)	Larry Penley	Oklahoma St	Oklahoma St	A. Canizares, Arizona St
2004	California (1134)	Steve Desimone	UCLA (1140)	Hot Springs, Va.	Ryan Moore, UNLV
2005	Georgia, (1135)	Chris Haack	Georgia Tech (1145)	Owings Mills, Md.	James Lepp, Washington
2006	Oklahoma St (1143)	Mike McGraw	Florida (1146)	Sunriver, Ore.	Jonathan Moore, Okla. St
2007	Stanford (1109)	Conrad Ray	Georgia (1121)	Williamsburg, Va.	J. Lovemark, USC

*Won sudden death playoff. Notes: Match play, 1897–1964; par-70 tournaments held in 1969, 1973 and 1989; par-71 tournaments held in 1968, 1981 and 1988; all other championships par-72 tournaments. Scores are based on 4 rounds instead of 2 after 1967.

DIVISION II

Year	Champion	Year	Champion	Year	Champion
1963	SW Missouri St	1978	Columbus St	1993	Abilene Christian (Tex.)
1964	Southern Illinois	1979	UC–Davis	1994	Columbus St
1965	Middle Tennessee St	1980	Columbus St	1995	Florida Southern
1966	CSU–Chico	1981	Florida Southern	1996	Florida Southern
1967	Lamar	1982	Florida Southern	1997	Columbus St
1968	Lamar	1983	SW Texas St	1998	Florida Southern
1969	CSU–Northridge	1984	Troy St	1999	Florida Southern
1970	Rollins	1985	Florida Southern	2000	Florida Southern
1971	New Orleans	1986	Florida Southern	2001	West Florida
1972	New Orleans	1987	Tampa	2002	Rollins
1973	CSU–Northridge	1988	Tampa	2003	Francis Marion
1974	CSU–Northridge	1989	Columbus St	2004	South Carolina–Aiken
1975	UC–Irvine	1990	Florida Southern	2005	West Florida
1976	Troy St	1991	Florida Southern	2006	South Carolina–Aiken
1977	Troy St	1992	Columbus St	2007	Barry

Note: Par-71 tournaments held in 1967, 1970, 1976–78, 1985, 1988 and 2001; par-70 tournament held in 1996; all other championships par-72 tournaments.

Men *(Cont.)*
DIVISION III

Year	Champion	Year	Champion	Year	Champion
1975	Wooster	1986	CSU-Stanislaus	1997	Methodist (N.C.)
1976	CSU-Stanislaus	1987	CSU-Stanislaus	1998	Methodist (N.C.)
1977	CSU-Stanislaus	1988	CSU-Stanislaus	1999	Methodist (N.C.)
1978	CSU-Stanislaus	1989	CSU-Stanislaus	2000	Greensboro
1979	CSU-Stanislaus	1990	Methodist (N.C.)	2001	UW-Eau Claire
1980	CSU-Stanislaus	1991	Methodist (N.C.)	2002	Guilford
1981	CSU-Stanislaus	1992	Methodist (N.C.)	2003	Averett
1982	Ramapo	1993	UC-San Diego	2004	Gustavus Adolphus
1983	Allegheny	1994	Methodist (N.C.)	2005	Guilford
1984	CSU-Stanislaus	1995	Methodist (N.C.)	2006	Nebraska Wesleyan
1985	CSU-Stanislaus	1996	Methodist (N.C.)	2006	St. John's (Minn.)

Note: All championships par-72 except for 1986, 1988 and 2001, which were par-71; fourth round of 1975 championships canceled as a result of bad weather; first round of 1988 championships canceled as a result of rain.

Women
DIVISION I

Year	Champion	Coach	Score	Runner-Up	Score	Individual Champion
1982	Tulsa	Dale McNamara	1191	TCU	1227	Kathy Baker, Tulsa
1983	TCU	Fred Warren	1193	Tulsa	1196	Penny Hammel, Miami (Fla.)
1984	Miami (Fla.)	Lela Cannon	1214	Arizona St	1221	Cindy Schreyer, Georgia
1985	Florida	Mimi Ryan	1218	Tulsa	1233	Danielle Ammaccapane, Arizona St
1986	Florida	Mimi Ryan	1180	Miami (Fla.)	1188	Page Dunlap, Florida
1987	San Jose St	Mark Gale	1187	Furman	1188	Caroline Keggi, New Mexico
1988	Tulsa	Dale McNamara	1175	Georgia/Arizona	1182	Melissa McNamara, Tulsa
1989	San Jose St	Mark Gale	1208	Tulsa	1209	Pat Hurst, San Jose St
1990	Arizona St	Linda Vollstedt	1206	UCLA	1222	Susan Slaughter, Arizona
1991	UCLA*	Jackie Steinmann	1197	San Jose St	1197	Annika Sorenstam, Arizona
1992	San Jose St	Mark Gale	1171	Arizona	1175	Vicki Goetze, Georgia
1993	Arizona St	Linda Vollstedt	1187	Texas	1189	Charlotta Sorenstam, Texas
1994	Arizona St	Linda Vollstedt	1189	USC	1205	Emilee Klein, Arizona St
1995	Arizona St	Linda Vollstedt	1155	San Jose St	1181	Kristel Mourgue d'Algue, Arizona St
1996	Arizona*	Rick LaRose	1240	San Jose St	1240	Marisa Baena, Arizona
1997	Arizona St	Linda Vollstedt	1178	San Jose St	1180	Heather Bowie, Texas
1998	Arizona St	Linda Vollstedt	1155	Florida	1173	Jennifer Rosales, USC
1999	Duke	Dan Brooks	895	Arizona St/Georgia	903	Grace Park, Arizona St
2000	Arizona	Todd McCorkle	1175	Stanford	1196	Jenna Daniels, Arizona
2001	Georgia	Todd McCorkle	1176	Duke	1179	Candy Hannemann, Duke
2002	Duke	Dan Brooks	1164	Arizona/Auburn/Texas	1160	Virada Nirapathpongporn, Duke
2003	USC	Andrea Gaston	1197	Pepperdine	1212	Mikaela Parmlid, USC
2004	UCLA	Carrie Forsyth	1148	Oklahoma St	1151	Sarah Huarte, California
2005	Duke	Dan Brooks	1170	UCLA	1175	Anna Grzebien, Duke
2006	Duke	Dan Brooks	1167	USC	1177	Dewi Schreefel, USC
2007	Duke	Dan Brooks	1170	Purdue	1185	Stacy Lewis, Arkansas

*Won sudden death playoff. Note: Par-74 tournaments held in 1983 and 1988; par-72 tournament held in 1990, 2000 and 2001; all other championships par-73 tournaments.

DIVISIONS II AND III

Year	Champion	Year	Champion
1996	Methodist (N.C.)	1998	Methodist (N.C.)
1997	Lynn	1999	Methodist (N.C.)

DIVISION II

Year	Champion
2000	Florida Southern
2001	Florida Southern
2002	Florida Southern
2003	Rollins (Fla.)
2004	Rollins (Fla.)
2005	Rollins (Fla.)
2006	Rollins (Fla.)
2007	Florida Southern

DIVISION III

Year	Champion
2000	Methodist (N.C.)
2001	Methodist (N.C.)
2002	Methodist (N.C.)
2003	Methodist (N.C.)
2004	Methodist (N.C.)
2005	Methodist (N.C.)
2006	Methodist (N.C.)
2007	Methodist (N.C.)

Men
TEAM CHAMPIONS

Year	Champion	Coach	Pts	Runner-Up	Pts
1938	Chicago	Dan Hoffer	22	Illinois	18
1939	Illinois	Hartley Price	21	Army	17
1940	Illinois	Hartley Price	20	Navy	17
1941	Illinois	Hartley Price	68.5	Minnesota	52.5
1942	Illinois	Hartley Price	39	Penn St	30
1943–47	No tournament				
1948	Penn St	Gene Wettstone	55	Temple	34.5
1949	Temple	Max Younger	28	Minnesota	18
1950	Illinois	Charley Pond	26	Temple	25
1951	Florida St	Hartley Price	26	Illinois/ USC	23.5
1952	Florida St	Hartley Price	89.5	USC	75
1953	Penn St	Gene Wettstone	91.5	Illinois	68
1954	Penn St	Gene Wettstone	137	Illinois	68
1955	Illinois	Charley Pond	82	Penn St	69
1956	Illinois	Charley Pond	123.5	Penn St	67.5
1957	Penn St	Gene Wettstone	88.5	Illinois	80
1958	Michigan St	George Szypula	79		
	Illinois	Charley Pond	79		
1959	Penn St	Gene Wettstone	152	Illinois	87.5
1960	Penn St	Gene Wettstone	112.5	USC	65.5
1961	Penn St	Gene Wettstone	88.5	Southern Illinois	80.5
1962	USC	Jack Beckner	95.5	Southern Illinois	75
1963	Michigan	Newton Loken	129	Southern Illinois	73
1964	Southern Illinois	Bill Meade	84.5	USC	69.5
1965	Penn St	Gene Wettstone	68.5	Washington	51.5
1966	Southern Illinois	Bill Meade	187.200	California	185.100
1967	Southern Illinois	Bill Meade	189.550	Michigan	187.400
1968	California	Hal Frey	188.250	Southern Illinois	188.150
1969	Iowa	Mike Jacobson	161.175	Penn St	160.450
	Michigan*	Newton Loken		Colorado St	
1970	Michigan	Newton Loken	164.150	Iowa St	164.050
				New Mexico St	
1971	Iowa St	Ed Gagnier	319.075	Southern Illinois	316.650
1972	Southern Illinois	Bill Meade	315.925	Iowa St	312.325
1973	Iowa St	Ed Gagnier	325.150	Penn St	323.025
1974	Iowa St	Ed Gagnier	326.100	Arizona St	322.050
1975	California	Hal Frey	437.325	LSU	433.700
1976	Penn St	Gene Wettstone	432.075	LSU	425.125
1977	Indiana St	Roger Counsil	434.475		
	Oklahoma	Paul Ziert	434.475		
1978	Oklahoma	Paul Ziert	439.350	Arizona St	437.075
1979	Nebraska	Francis Allen	448.275	Oklahoma	446.625
1980	Nebraska	Francis Allen	563.300	Iowa St	557.650
1981	Nebraska	Francis Allen	284.600	Oklahoma	281.950
1982	Nebraska	Francis Allen	285.500	UCLA	281.050
1983	Nebraska	Francis Allen	287.800	UCLA	283.900
1984	UCLA	Art Shurlock	287.300	Penn St	281.250
1985	Ohio St	Michael Willson	285.350	Nebraska	284.550
1986	Arizona St	Don Robinson	283.900	Nebraska	283.600
1987	UCLA	Art Shurlock	285.300	Nebraska	284.750
1988	Nebraska	Francis Allen	288.150	Illinois	287.150
1989	Illinois	Yoshi Hayasaki	283.400	Nebraska	282.300
1990	Nebraska	Francis Allen	287.400	Minnesota	287.300
1991	Oklahoma	Greg Buwick	288.025	Penn St	285.500
1992	Stanford	Sadao Hamada	289.575	Nebraska	288.950
1993	Stanford	Sadao Hamada	276.500	Nebraska	275.500
1994	Nebraska	Francis Allen	288.250	Stanford	285.925
1995	Stanford	Sadao Hamada	232.400	Nebraska	231.525
1996	Ohio St	Peter Kormann	232.150	California	231.775
1997	California	Barry Weiner	233.825	Oklahoma	232.725
1998	California	Barry Weiner	231.200	Iowa	229.675
1999	Michigan	Kurt Golder	232.550	Ohio St	230.850
2000	Penn St	Randy Jepson	231.975	Michigan	231.850
2001	Ohio St	Miles Avery	218.125	Oklahoma	217.775
2002	Oklahoma	Mark Williams	219.300	Ohio St	218.650
2003	Oklahoma	Mark Williams	222.600	Ohio St	220.700
2004	Penn St	Randy Jepson	223.350	Oklahoma	222.300

*Trampoline.

TEAM CHAMPIONS *(Cont.)*

Year	Champion	Coach	Pts	Runner-Up	Pts
2005	Oklahoma	Mark Williams	225.675	Ohio St	225.450
2006	Oklahoma	Mark Williams	221.400	Illinois	220.975
2007	Penn St	Randy Jepson	221.000	Oklahoma	220.200

INDIVIDUAL CHAMPIONS

ALL-AROUND

1938.....Joe Giallombardo, Illinois
1939.....Joe Giallombardo, Illinois
1940.....Joe Giallombardo, Illinois
     Paul Fina, Illinois
1941.....Courtney Shanken, Chicago
1942.....Newt Loken, Minnesota
1948.....Ray Sorenson, Penn St
1949.....Joe Kotys, Kent
1950.....Joe Kotys, Kent
1951.....Bill Roetzheim, Florida St
1952.....Jack Beckner, USC
1953.....Jean Cronstedt, Penn St
1954.....Jean Cronstedt, Penn St
1955.....Karl Schwenzfeier, Penn St
1956.....Don Tonry, Illlinois
1957.....Armando Vega, Penn St
1958.....Abie Grossfeld, Illinois
1959.....Armando Vega, Penn St
1960.....Jay Werner, Penn St
1961.....Gregor Weiss, Penn St
1962.....Robert Lynn, USC
1963.....Gil Larose, Michigan
1964.....Ron Barak, USC
1965.....Mike Jacobson, Penn St
1966.....Steve Cohen, Penn St
1967.....Steve Cohen, Penn St
1968.....Makoto Sakamoto, USC
1969.....Mauno Nissinen, Wash
1970.....Yoshi Hayasaki, Wash
1971.....Yoshi Hayasaki, Wash
1972.....Steve Hug, Stanford
1973.....Steve Hug, Stanford
     Marshall Avener, Penn St
1974.....Steve Hug, Stanford
1975.....Wayne Young, BYU
1976.....Peter Kormann,
     Southern Conn. St
1977.....Kurt Thomas, Indiana St
1978.....Bart Conner, Oklahoma
1979.....Kurt Thomas, Indiana St
1980.....Jim Hartung, Nebraska
1981.....Jim Hartung, Nebraska
1982.....Peter Vidmar, UCLA
1983.....Peter Vidmar, UCLA
1984.....Mitch Gaylord, UCLA
1985.....Wes Suter, Nebraska
1986.....Jon Louis, Stanford
1987.....Tom Schlesinger, Nebraska
1988.....Vacated†
1989.....Patrick Kirsey, Nebraska
1990.....Mike Racanelli, Ohio St
1991.....John Roethlisberger, Minn
1992.....John Roethlisberger, Minn
1993.....John Roethlisberger, Minn
1994.....Dennis Harrison, Nebraska
1995.....Richard Grace, Nebraska
1996.....Blaine Wilson, Ohio St
1997.....Blaine Wilson, Ohio St
1998.....Travis Romagnoli, Illinois
1999......Justin Hardabura, Nebraska
2000.....Jamie Natalie, Ohio St

ALL-AROUND *(Cont.)*

2001.....Jamie Natalie, Ohio St
2002.....Raj Bhavsar, Ohio St
2003.....Daniel Furney, Oklahoma
2004.....Luis Vargas, Penn St
2005.....Luis Vargas, Penn St
2006.....Jonathan Horton, Oklahoma
2007.....Taqiy Abdullah-Simmons,
     Oklahoma

HORIZONTAL BAR

1938.....Bob Sears, Army
1939.....Adam Walters, Temple
1940.....Norm Boardman, Temple
1941.....Newt Loken, Minnesota
1942.....Norm Boardman, Temple
1948.....Joe Calvetti, Illinois
1949.....Bob Stout, Temple
1950.....Joe Kotys, Kent
1951.....Bill Roetzheim, Florida St
1952.....Charles Simms, USC
1953.....Hal Lewis, Navy
1954.....Jean Cronstedt, Penn St
1955.....Carlton Rintz, Michigan St
1956.....Ronnie Amster, Florida St
1957.....Abie Grossfeld, Illinois
1958.....Abie Grossfeld, Illinois
1959.....Stanley Tarshis, Mich St
1960.....Stanley Tarshis, Mich St
1961.....Bruno Klaus, Southern Ill
1962.....Robert Lynn, USC
1963.....Gil Larose, Michigan
1964.....Ron Barak, USC
1965.....Jim Curzi, Michigan St
     Mike Jacobsen, Penn St
1966.....Rusty Rock, CSU–
     Northridge
1967.....Rich Grigsby, CSU–
     Northridge
1968.....Makoto Sakamoto, USC
1969.....Bob Manna, New Mexico
1970.....Yoshi Hayasaki, Wash
1971.....Brent Simmons, Iowa St
1972.....Tom Lindner, Souhern Ill
1973.....Jon Aitken, New Mexico
1974.....Rick Banley, Indiana St
1975.....Rich Larsen, Iowa St
1976.....Tom Beach, California
1977.....John Hart, UCLA
1978.....Mel Cooley, Washington
1979.....Kurt Thomas, Indiana St
1980.....Philip Cahoy, Nebraska
1981.....Philip Cahoy, Nebraska
1982.....Peter Vidmar, UCLA
1983.....Scott Johnson, Nebraska
1984.....Charles Lakes, Illinois
1985.....Dan Hayden, Arizona St
     Wes Suter, Nebraska
1986.....Dan Hayden, Arizona St
1987.....David Moriel, UCLA
1988.....Vacated†
1989.....Vacated†

HORIZONTAL BAR *(Cont.)*

1990.....Chris Waller, UCLA
1991.....Luis Lopez, New Mexico
1992.....Jair Lynch, Stanford
1993.....Steve McCain, UCLA
1994.....Jim Foody, UCLA
1995.....Rick Kieffer, Nebraska
1996.....Carl Imhauser, Temple
1997.....Marshall Nelson, Nebraska
1998.....Todd Bishop, Oklahoma
1999.....Todd Bishop, Oklahoma
2000.....Michael Ashe, California
2001.....Michael Ashe, California
2002.....Daniel Diaz-Luong, Mich.
2003.....Linas Gaveika, Iowa
2004.....Justin Spring, Illinois
2005.....Ronald Ferris, Ohio St
2006.....Justin Spring, Illinois
2007.....Jonathan Horton,
     Oklahoma

PARALLEL BARS

1938.....Erwin Beyer, Chicago
1939.....Bob Sears, Army
1940.....Bob Hanning, Minnesota
1941.....Caton Cobb, Illinois
1942.....Hal Zimmerman, Penn St
1948.....Ray Sorenson, Penn St
1949.....Joe Kotys, Kent
     Mel Stout, Michigan St
1950.....Joe Kotys, Kent
1951.....Jack Beckner, USC
1952.....Jack Beckner, USC
1953.....Jean Cronstedt, Penn St
1954.....Jean Cronstedt, Penn St
1955.....Carlton Rintz, Michigan St
1956.....Armando Vega, Penn St
1957.....Armando Vega, Penn St
1958.....Tad Muzyczko, Mich St
1959.....Armando Vega, Penn St
1960.....Robert Lynn, USC
1961.....Fred Tijerina, Southern Ill
     Jeff Cardinalli, Springfield
1962.....Robert Lynn, USC
1963.....Arno Lascari, Michigan
1964.....Ron Barak, USC
1965.....Jim Curzi, Michigan St
1966.....Jim Curzi, Michigan St
1967.....Makoto Sakamoto, USC
1968.....Makoto Sakamoto, USC
1969.....Ron Rapper, Michigan
1970.....Ron Rapper, Michigan
1971.....Brent Simmons, Iowa St
     Tom Dunn, Penn St
1972.....Dennis Mazur, Iowa St
1973.....Steve Hug, Stanford
1974.....Steve Hug, Stanford
1975.....Yoichi Tomita,
     Long Beach St
1976.....Gene Whelan, Penn St
1977.....Kurt Thomas, Indiana St
1978.....John Corritore, Michigan

Men *(Cont.)*

INDIVIDUAL CHAMPIONS *(Cont.)*

PARALLEL BARS *(Cont.)*

1979.....Kurt Thomas, Indiana St
1980.....Philip Cahoy, Nebraska
1981.....Philip Cahoy, Nebraska
        Peter Vidmar, UCLA
        Jim Hartung, Nebraska
1982.....Jim Hartung, Nebraska
1983.....Scott Johnson, Nebraska
1984.....Tim Daggett, UCLA
1985.....Dan Hayden, Arizona St
        Noah Riskin, Ohio St
        Seth Riskin, Ohio St
1986.....Dan Hayden, Arizona St
1987.....Kevin Davis, Nebraska
        Tom Schlesinger, Nebraska
1988.....Kevin Davis, Nebraska
1989.....Vacated†
1990.....Patrick Kirksey, Nebraska
1991.....Scott Keswick, UCLA
        John Roethlisberger, Minn
1992.....Dom Minicucci, Temple
1993.....Jair Lynch, Stanford
1994.....Richard Grace, Nebraska
1995.....Richard Grace, Nebraska
1996.....Jamie Ellis, Stanford
        Blaine Wilson, Ohio St
1997.....Marshall Nelson, Nebraska
1998.....Marshall Nelson, Nebraska
1999.....Justin Toman, Michigan
2000.....Kris Zimmerman, Michigan
        Justin Toman, Michigan
2001 ....Raj Bhavsar, Ohio St
2002 ....Cody Moore, California
2003 ....Daniel Furney, Oklahoma
2004 ....Ramon Jackson, Wm & M
2005 ....Justin Springs, Illinois
2006 ....Justin Springs, Illinois
2007.....Tim McNeill, California

VAULT

1938.....Erwin Beyer, Chicago
1939.....Marv Forman, Illinois
1940.....Earl Shanken, Chicago
1941.....Earl Shanken, Chicago
1942.....Earl Shanken, Chicago
1948.....Jim Peterson, Minnesota
1962.....Bruno Klaus, S. Illinois
1963.....Gil Larose, Michigan
1964.....Sidney Oglesby, Syracuse
1965.....Dan Millman, California
1966.....Frank Schmitz, S. Illinois
1967.....Paul Mayer, S. Illinois
1968.....Bruce Colter, CSU–LA
1969.....Dan Bowles, California
        Jack McCarthy, Illinois
1970.....Doug Boger, Arizona
1971.....Pat Mahoney, CSU–N'ridge
1972.....Gary Morava, S. Illinois
1973.....John Crosby, S. Conn St
1974.....Greg Goodhue, Oklahoma
1975.....Tom Beach, California
1976.....Sam Shaw, CSU-Fullerton
1977.....Steve Wejmar, Wash
1978.....Ron Galimore, LSU
1979.....Leslie Moore, Oklahoma
1980.....Ron Galimore, Iowa St
1981.....Ron Galimore, Iowa St

VAULT *(Cont.)*

1982.....Randall Wickstrom, Cal
        Steve Elliott, Nebraska
1983.....Chris Riegel, Nebraska
        Mark Oates, Oklahoma
1984.....Chris Riegel, Nebraska
1985.....Derrick Cornelius, Cort.
1986.....:Chad Fox, New Mexico
1987.....Chad Fox, New Mexico
1988.....Chad Fox, New Mexico
1989.....Chad Fox, New Mexico
1990.....Brad Hayashi, UCLA
1991.....Adam Carton, Penn St
1992.....Jason Hebert, Syracuse
1993.....Steve Wiegel, New Mexico
1994.....Steve McCain, UCLA
1995.....Ian Bachrach, Stanford
1996.....Jay Thornton, Iowa
1997.....Blaine Wilson, Ohio St
1998.....Travis Romagnoli, Illinois
1999.....Guard Young, BYU
2000.....Guard Young, BYU
2001.....Daren Lynch, Ohio St
2002.....Dan Gill, Stanford
2003.....Andrew DiGiore, Michigan
2004.....Graham Ackerman, Cal
2005.....Michael Reavis, Iowa
2006.....David Sender, Stanford
2007.....David Sender, Stanford

POMMEL HORSE

1938.....Erwin Beyer, Chicago
1939.....Erwin Beyer, Chicago
1940......Harry Koehnemann, Illinois
1941.....Caton Cobb, Illinois
1942.....Caton Cobb, Illinois
1948.....Steve Greene, Penn St
1949.....Joe Berenato, Temple
1950.....Gene Rabbitt, Syracuse
1951.....Joe Kotys, Kent
1952.....Frank Bare, Illinois
1953.....Carlton Rintz, Michigan St
1954.....Robert Lawrence, Penn St
1955.....Carlton Rintz, Michigan St
1956.....James Brown, CSU–L.A.
1957.....John Davis, Illinois
1958.....Bill Buck, Iowa
1959.....Art Shurlock, California
1960.....James Fairchild, California
1961.....James Fairchild, California
1962.....Mike Aufrecht, Illinois
1963.....Russ Mills, Yale
1964.....Russ Mills, Yale
1965.....Bob Elsinger, Springfield
1966.....Gary Hoskins, CSU–L.A.
1967.....Keith McCanless, Iowa
1968.....Jack Ryan, Colorado
1969.....Keith McCanless, Iowa
1970.....Russ Hoffman, Iowa St
        John Russo, Wisconsin
1971.....Russ Hoffman, Iowa St
1972.....Russ Hoffman, Iowa St
1973.....Ed Slezak, Indiana St
1974.....Ted Marcy, Stanford
1975.....Ted Marcy, Stanford
1976.....Ted Marcy, Stanford
1977......Chuck Walter, New Mexico

POMMEL HORSE *(Cont.)*

1978.....Mike Burke, N. Illinois
1979.....Mike Burke, N. Illinois
1980 ....David Stoldt, Illinois
1981.....Mark Bergman, California
        Steve Jennings, New Mexico
1982 ....Peter Vidmar, UCLA
        Steve Jennings, New Mexico
1983.....Doug Kieso, N. Illinois
1984.....Tim Daggett, UCLA
1985.....Tony Pineda, UCLA
1986.....Curtis Holdsworth, UCLA
1987.....Li Xiao Ping, CSU-Fullerton
1988.....Vacated†
        Mark Sohn, Penn St
1989.....Mark Sohn, Penn St
        Chris Waller, UCLA
1990.....Mark Sohn, Penn St
1991.....Mark Sohn, Penn St
1992.....Che Bowers, Nebraska
1993.....John Roethlisberger, Minn
1994.....Jason Bertram, California
1995.....Drew Durbin, Ohio St
1996.....Drew Durbin, Ohio St
1997.....Drew Durbin, Ohio St
1998.....Josh Birckelbaw, California
1999.....Brandon Stefaniak, Penn St
2000.....Brandon Stefaniak, Penn St
        Don Jackson, Iowa
2001.....Clay Strother, Minnesota
2002.....Clay Strother, Minnesota
2003.....Josh Landis, Oklahoma
2004.....Bob Rogers, Illinois
2005 ....Luis Vargas, Penn St
2006.....Timothy McNeill, California
2007.....Timothy McNeill, California

FLOOR EXERCISE

1941.....Lou Fina, Illinois
1953.....Bob Sullivan, Illinois
1954.....Jean Cronsted, Penn St
1955.....Don Faber, UCLA
1956.....Jamile Ashmore, Florida St
1957.....Norman Marks, CSU–L.A.
1958.....Abie Grossfeld, Illinois
1959.....Don Tonry, Illinois
1960.....Ray Hadley, Illinois
1961.....Robert Lynn, USC
1962.....Robert Lynn, USC
1963.....Tom Seward, Penn St
        Mike Henderson, Michigan
1964.....Rusty Mitchell, S. Illinois
1965.....Frank Schmitz, S. Illinois
1966.....Frank Schmitz, S. Illinois
1967.....Dave Jacobs, Michigan
1968.....Toby Towson, Michigan St
1969.....Toby Towson, Michigan St
1970.....Tom Proulx, Colorado St
1971......Stormy Eaton, New Mexico
1972.....Odessa Lovin, Oklahoma
1973.....Odessa Lovin, Oklahoma
1974.....Doug Fitzjarrell, Iowa St
1975.....Kent Brown, Arizona St
1976.....Bob Robbins, Colorado St
1977......Ron Galimore, LSU
1978.....Curt Austin, Iowa St
1979 ....Mike Wilson, Oklahoma
        Bart Conner, Oklahoma

Men *(Cont.)*
INDIVIDUAL CHAMPIONS *(Cont.)*

FLOOR EXERCISE *(CONT.)*

1980.....Steve Elliott, Nebraska
1981.....James Yuhashi, Oregon
1982.....Steve Elliott, Nebraska
1983.....Scott Johnson, Nebraska
　　　　David Branch, Arizona St
　　　　Donnie Hinton, Arizona St
1984.....Kevin Ekburg, N. Illinois
1985.....Wes Suter, Nebraska
1986.....Jerry Burrell, Arizona St
　　　　Brian Ginsberg, UCLA
1987.....Chad Fox, New Mexico
1988.....Chris Wyatt, Temple
1989.....Jody Newman, Arizona St
1990.....Mike Racanelli, Ohio St
1991.....Brad Hayashi, UCLA
1992.....Brian Winkler, Michigan
1993.....Richard Grace, Nebraska
1994.....Mark Booth, Stanford
1995.....Jay Thornton, Iowa
1996.....Ian Bachrach, Stanford
1997.....Jeremy Killen, Oklahoma
1998.....Darin Gerlach, Temple
1999.......Jason Hardabura, Nebraska
2000.....Jamie Natalie, Ohio St
2001.....Clay Strother, Minnesota
2002.....Clay Strother, Minnesota
2003.....Josh Landis, Oklahoma
2004.....Graham Ackerman, Cal
2005.....Graham Ackerman, Cal

FLOOR EXERCISE *(CONT.)*

2006.....Jonathan Horton, Okla.
2007.....Jonathan Horton, Okla.

RINGS

1959.....Armando Vega, Penn St
1960.....Sam Garcia, USC
1961.....Fred Orlofsky, S. Illinois
1962.....Dale Cooper, Michigan St
1963.....Dale Cooper, Michigan St
1964.....Chris Evans, Arizona St
1965.....Glenn Gailis, Iowa
1966.....Ed Gunny, Michigan St
1967.....Josh Robison, California
1968.....Pat Arnold, Arizona
1969.....Paul Vexler, Penn St
　　　　Ward Maythaler, Iowa St
1970.....Dave Seal, Indiana St
1971.....Charles Ropiequet, S. Illinois
1972.....Dave Seal, Indiana St
1973.....Bob Mahorney, Indiana St
1974.....Keith Heaver, Iowa St
1975.....Keith Heaver, Iowa St
1976.....Doug Wood, Iowa St
1977.....Doug Wood, Iowa St
1978.....Scott McEldowney, Oregon
1979.....Kirk Mango, N. Illinois
1980.....Jim Hartung, Nebraska
1981.....Jim Hartung, Nebraska
1982.....Jim Hartung, Nebraska
1983.....Alex Schwartz, UCLA

RINGS *(CONT.)*

1984.....Tim Daggett, UCLA
1985.....Mark Diab, Iowa St
1986.....Mark Diab, Iowa St
1987.....Paul O'Neill, Hou. Baptist
1988.....Paul O'Neill, New Mexico
1989.....Vacated†
　　　　Paul O'Neill, New Mexico
1990.....Wayne Cowden, Penn St
1991.....Adam Carton, Penn St
1992.....Scott Keswick, UCLA
1993.....Chris LaMorte, New Mexico
1994.....Chris LaMorte, New Mexico
1995.....Dave Frank, Temple
1996.....Scott McCall, Will. & Mary
　　　　Blaine Wilson, Ohio St
1997.....Blaine Wilson, Ohio St
1998.....Dan Fink, Oklahoma
1999.....Cortney Bramwell, BYU
2000.....Cortney Bramwell, BYU
2001.....Chris Lakeman, Penn St
2002.....Marshall Erwin, Stanford
2003.....Kevin Tan, Penn St
2004.....Kevin Tan, Penn St
2005.....David Henderson, Okla.
2006.....Jonathan Horton, Okla.
2007.....Alex Schorsch, Stanford

†Championships won by Miguel Rubio (All Around, 1988; Horizontal Bar, 1988–89) and Alfonso Rodriguez (Pommel Horse, 1988; Rings, 1989; Parallel Bars, 1989) were vacated by action of the NCAA Committee on Infractions.

DIVISION II *(Discontinued after 1984)*

Year	Champion	Coach	Pts	Runner-Up	Pts
1968	CSU–Northridge	Bill Vincent	179.400	Springfield	178.050
1969	CSU–Northridge	Bill Vincent	151.800	Southern Connecticut St	145.075
1970	NW Louisiana	Armando Vega	160.250	Southern Connecticut St	159.300
1971	CSU–Fullerton	Dick Wolfe	158.150	Springfield	156.987
1972	CSU–Fullerton	Dick Wolfe	160.550	Southern Connecticut St	153.050
1973	Southern Conn. St	Abe Grossfeld	160.750	CSU–Northridge	158.700
1974	CSU–Fullerton	Dick Wolfe	309.800	Southern Connecticut St	309.400
1975	Southern Conn. St	Abe Grossfeld	411.650	Ill.–Chicago	398.800
1976	Southern Conn. St	Abe Grossfeld	419.200	Ill.–Chicago	388.850
1977	Springfield	Frank Wolcott	395.950	CSU–Northridge	381.250
1978	Ill.–Chicago	C. Johnson/A. Gentile	406.850	CSU–Northridge	400.400
1979	Ill.–Chicago	Clarence Johnson	418.550	UW–Oshkosh	385.650
1980	UW–Oshkosh	Ken Allen	260.550	CSU–Chico	256.050
1981	UW–Oshkosh	Ken Allen	209.500	Springfield	201.550
1982	UW–Oshkosh	Ken Allen	216.050	E Stroudsburg	211.200
1983	E. Stroudsburg	Bruno Klaus	258.650	UW–Oshkosh	257.850
1984	E. Stroudsburg	Bruno Klaus	270.800	Cortland St	246.350

Women
TEAM CHAMPIONS

Year	Champion	Coach	Pts	Runner-Up	Pts
1982	Utah	Greg Marsden	148.60	CSU–Fullerton	144.10
1983	Utah	Greg Marsden	184.65	Arizona St	183.30
1984	Utah	Greg Marsden	186.05	UCLA	185.55
1985	Utah	Greg Marsden	188.35	Arizona St	186.60
1986	Utah	Greg Marsden	186.95	Arizona St	186.70
1987	Georgia	Suzanne Yoculan	187.90	Utah	187.55
1988	Alabama	Sarah Patterson	190.05	Utah	189.50
1989	Georgia	Suzanne Yoculan	192.65	UCLA	192.60
1990	Utah	Greg Marsden	194.900	Alabama	194.575
1991	Alabama	Sarah Patterson	195.125	Utah	194.375
1992	Utah	Greg Marsden	195.650	Georgia	194.600

Women *(Cont.)*
TEAM CHAMPIONS

Year	Champion	Coach	Pts	Runner-Up	Pts
1993	Georgia	Suzanne Yoculan	198.000	Alabama	196.825
1994	Utah	Greg Marsden	196.400	Alabama	196.350
1995	Utah	Greg Marsden	196.650	Alabama	196.425
				Michigan	196.425
1996	Alabama	Sarah Patterson	198.025	UCLA	197.475
1997	UCLA	Valorie Kondos	197.150	Arizona St	196.850
1998	Georgia	Suzanne Yoculan	197.725	Florida	196.350
1999	Georgia	Suzanne Yoculan	196.850	Michigan	196.550
2000	UCLA	Valorie Kondos	197.300	Utah	196.875
2001	UCLA	Valorie Kondos	197.575	Georgia	197.400
2002	Alabama	Sarah Patterson	197.575	Georgia	197.250
2003	UCLA	Valorie Kondos Field	197.825	Alabama	197.275
2004	UCLA	Valorie Kondos Field	198.125	Georgia	197.200
2005	Georgia	Suzanne Yoculan	197.825	Alabama	197.400
2006	Georgia	Suzanne Yoculan	197.750	Utah	196.800
2007	Georgia	Suzanne Yoculan	197.850	Utah	197.250

INDIVIDUAL CHAMPIONS

ALL-AROUND
1982.....Sue Stednitz, Utah
1983.....Megan McCunniff, Utah
1984......Megan McCunniff-Marsden, Utah
1985......Penney Hauschild, Alabama
1986......Penney Hauschild, Alabama
       Jackie Brummer, Arizona St
1987.....Kelly Garrison-Steves, Oklahoma
1988.....Kelly Garrison-Steves, Oklahoma
1989....Corrinne Wright, Georgia
1990.....Dee Dee Foster, Alabama
1991.....Hope Spivey, Georgia
1992.....Missy Marlowe, Utah
1993.....Jenny Hansen, Kentucky
1994.....Jenny Hansen, Kentucky
1995.....Jenny Hansen, Kentucky
1996.....Meredith Willard, Alabama
1997.....Kim Arnold, Georgia
1998.....Kim Arnold, Georgia
1999.....Theresa Kulikowski, Utah
2000.:...Mohini Bhardwaj, UCLA
       Heather Brink, Nebraska
2001....Onnis Willis, UCLA
       Elise Ray, Michigan
2002....Jamie Dantzscher, UCLA
2003....Richelle Simpson, Neb.
2004....Jeana Rice, Alabama
2005....Katie Heenan, Georgia
2006.....Courtney Kupets, Georgia
2007.....Courtney Kupets, Georgia

VAULT
1982.....Elaine Alfano, Utah
1983.....Elaine Alfano, Utah
1984.....Megan Marsden, Utah
1985.....Elaine Alfano, Utah
1986.....Kim Neal, Arizona St
       Pam Loree, Penn St
1987.....Yumi Mordre, Washington
1988.....Jill Andrews, UCLA
1989.....Kim Hamilton, UCLA
1990....Michele Bryant, Nebraska
1991.....Anna Basaldva, Arizona
1992.....Tammy Marshall, Mass.
       Heather Stepp, Georgia
       Kristein Kenoyer, Utah

VAULT *(Cont.)*
1993.....Heather Stepp, Georgia
1994.....Jenny Hansen, Kentucky
1995.....Jenny Hansen, Kentucky
1996.....Leah Brown, Georgia
1997.....Susan Hines, Florida
1998.....Susan Hines, Florida
1999.....Heidi Moneymaker, UCLA
2000.....Heather Brink, Nebraska
2001.....Cory Fritzinger, Georgia
2002.....Jamie Dantzscher, UCLA
2003.....Ashley Miles, Alabama
2004.....Ashley Miles, Alabama
2005.....Kristen Maloney, UCLA
2006.....Ashley Miles, Alabama
2007.....Courtney Kupets, Georgia

BALANCE BEAM
1982.....Sue Stednitz, Utah
1983.....Julie Goewey, CSU–Fullerton
1984.....Heidi Anderson, Oregon St
1985.....Lisa Zeis, Arizona St
1986.....Jackie Brummer, Arizona St
1987.....Yumi Mordre, Washington
1988.....Kelly Garrison-Steves, Oklahoma
1989.....Jill Andrews, UCLA
       Joy Selig, Oregon St
1990.....Joy Selig, Oregon St
1991.....Missy Marlowe, Utah
1992.....Missy Marlowe, Utah
1992   Dana Dobransky, Alabama
1993.....Dana Dobransky, Alabama
1994.....Jenny Hansen, Kentucky
1995.....Jenny Hansen, Kentucky
1996.....Summer Reid, UUtah
1997.....Summer Reid, Utah
       Elizabeth Reid, Arizona St
1998   Larissa Fontaine, Stanford
       Susan Hines, Florida
1999.....Theresa Kulikowski, Utah
2000.....Lena Degteva, UCLA
2001.....Theresa Kulikowski, Utah
2002.....Elise Ray, Michigan
2003.....Kate Richardson, UCLA
2004.....Ashley Kelly, Arizona St

BALANCE BEAM *(Cont.)*
2005.....Kristen Maloney, UCLA
2006.....Courtney Kupets, Georgia
2007.....Ashley Postell, Utah

FLOOR EXERCISE
1982.....Mary Ayotte-Law, Oregon St
1983.....Kim Neal, Arizona St
1984.....Maria Anz, Florida
1985.....Lisa Mitzel, Utah
1986.....Lisa Zeis, Arizona St
       P. Hauschild, Alabama
1987.....Kim Hamilton, UCLA
1988.....Kim Hamilton, UCLA
1989.....Corrinne Wright, Georgia
       Kim Hamilton, UCLA
1990.....Joy Selig, Oregon St
1991.....Hope Spivey, Georgia
1992.....Missy Marlowe, Utah
1993.....Heather Stepp, Georgia
       Tammy Marshall, Mass.
       Amy Durham, Oregon St
1994.....Hope Spivey-Sheeley, Georgia
1995.....Jenny Hansen, Kentucky
       Stella Umeh, UCLA
       Leslie Angeles, Georgia
1996.....Heidi Hornbeek, Arizona
       Kim Kelly, Alabama
1997.....Leah Brown, Georgia
1998.....Kim Arnold, Georgia
       Jenni Beathard, Georgia
       Betsy Hamm, Florida
1999.....Marny Oestreng, Bowl. Green
2000.....Suzanne Sears, Georgia
2001.....Mohini Bhardwaj, UCLA
2002.....Jamie Dantzscher, UCLA
       Nicole Arnstad, LSU
2003.....Richelle Simpson, Neb.
2004.....Ashley Miles, Alabama
       Courtney Bumpers, N.Car.
2005.....Courtney Bumpers, N.Car.
2006.....Kate Richardson UCLA
2007.....Morgan Dennis, Alabama

UNEVEN BARS
1982.....Lisa Shirk, Pittsburgh
1983.....Jeri Cameron, Arizona St
1984.....Jackie Brummer, Ariz.St

Women (Cont.)
INDIVIDUAL CHAMPIONS

UNEVEN BARS (Cont.)

1985	Penney Hauschild, Alabama
1986	Lucy Wener, Georgia
1987	Lucy Wener, Georgia
1988	Kelly Garrison-Steves, Oklahoma
1989	Lucy Wener, Georgia
1990	Marie Roethlisberger, Minnesota
1991	Kelly Macy, Georgia
1992	Missy Marlowe, Utah

UNEVEN BARS (Cont.)

1993	Agina Simpkins, Georgia
	Beth Wymer, Michigan
1994	Sandy Woolsey, Utah
	Beth Wymer, Michigan
	Lori Strong, Georgia
1995	Beth Wymer, Michigan
1996	Stephanie Woods, Alabama
1997	Jenni Beathard, Georgia
1998	Karin Lichey, Georgia
	Stella Umeh, UCLA

UNEVEN BARS (Cont.)

1999	Angie Leionard, Utah
2000	Mohini Bhardwaj, UCLA
2001	Yvonne Tousek, UCLA
2002	Andree' Pickens, Alabama
2003	Jamie Dantzscher, UCLA
	Kate Richardson, UCLA
2004	Elise Ray, Michigan
2005	Terin Humphrey, Alabama
2006	Courtney Kupets, Georgia
2007	Terin Humphrey, Alabama

Ice Hockey

Men

DIVISION I

Year	Champion	Coach	Score	Runner-Up	Most Outstanding Player
1948	Michigan	Vic Heyliger	8–4	Dartmouth	Joe Riley, Dartmouth, F
1949	Boston College	John Kelley	4–3	Dartmouth	Dick Desmond, Dartmouth, G
1950	Colorado College	Cheddy Thompson	13–4	Boston University	Ralph Bevins, Boston University, G
1951	Michigan	Vic Heyliger	7–1	Brown	Ed Whiston, Brown, G
1952	Michigan	Vic Heyliger	4–1	Colorado College	Kenneth Kinsley, Colorado Coll, G
1953	Michigan	Vic Heyliger	7–3	Minnesota	John Matchefts, Michigan, F
1954	Rensselaer	Ned Harkness	5–4 (OT)	Minnesota	Abbie Moore, Rensselaer, F
1955	Michigan	Vic Heyliger	5–3	Colorado College	Philip Hilton, Colorado College, D
1956	Michigan	Vic Heyliger	7–5	Michigan Tech	Lorne Howes, Michigan, G
1957	Colorado College	Thomas Bedecki	13–6	Michigan	Bob McCusker, Colorado Coll, F
1958	Denver	Murray Armstrong	6–2	North Dakota	Murray Massier, Denver, F
1959	North Dakota	Bob May	4–3 (OT)	Michigan St	Reg Morelli, North Dakota, F
1960	Denver	Murray Armstrong	5–3	Michigan Tech	Bob Marquis, Boston University, F
1961	Denver	Murray Armstrong	12–2	St. Lawrence	Barry Urbanski, Boston Univ, G
1962	Michigan Tech	John MacInnes	7–1	Clarkson	Louis Angotti, Michigan Tech, F
1963	North Dakota	Barney Thorndycraft	6–5	Denver	Al McLean, North Dakota, F
1964	Michigan	Allen Renfrew	6–3	Denver	Bob Gray, Michigan, G
1965	Michigan Tech	John MacInnes	8–2	Boston College	Gary Milroy, Michigan Tech, F
1966	Michigan St	Amo Bessone	6–1	Clarkson	Gaye Cooley, Michigan St, G
1967	Cornell	Ned Harkness	4–1	Boston University	Walt Stanowski, Cornell, D
1968	Denver	Murray Armstrong	4–0	North Dakota	Gerry Powers, Denver, G
1969	Denver	Murray Armstrong	4–3	Cornell	Keith Magnuson, Denver, D
1970	Cornell	Ned Harkness	6–4	Clarkson	Daniel Lodboa, Cornell, D
1971	Boston University	Jack Kelley	4–2	Minnesota	Dan Brady, Boston University, G
1972	Boston University	Jack Kelley	4–0	Cornell	Tim Regan, Boston University, G
1973	Wisconsin	Bob Johnson	4–2	Vacated	Dean Talafous, Wisconsin, F
1974	Minnesota	Herb Brooks	4–2	Michigan Tech	Brad Shelstad, Minnesota, G
1975	Michigan Tech	John MacInnes	6–1	Minnesota	Jim Warden, Michigan Tech, G
1976	Minnesota	Herb Brooks	6–4	Michigan Tech	Tom Vanelli, Minnesota, F
1977	Wisconsin	Bob Johnson	6–5 (OT)	Michigan	Julian Baretta, Wisconsin, G
1978	Boston University	Jack Parker	5–3	Boston College	Jack O'Callahan, Boston Univ, D
1979	Minnesota	Herb Brooks	4–3	North Dakota	Steve Janaszak, Minnesota, G
1980	North Dakota	John Gasparini	5–2	Northern Michigan	Doug Smail, North Dakota, F
1981	Wisconsin	Bob Johnson	6–3	Minnesota	Marc Behrend, Wisconsin, G
1982	North Dakota	John Gasparini	5–2	Wisconsin	Phil Sykes, North Dakota, F
1983	Wisconsin	Jeff Sauer	6–2	Harvard	Marc Behrend, Wisconsin, G
1984	Bowling Green	Jerry York	5–4 (OT)	Minn.–Duluth	Gary Kruzich, Bowling Green, G
1985	Rensselaer	Mike Addesa	2–1	Providence	Chris Terreri, Providence, G
1986	Michigan St	Ron Mason	6–5	Harvard	Mike Donnelly, Michigan St, F
1987	North Dakota	John Gasparini	5–3	Michigan St	Tony Hrkac, North Dakota, F
1988	Lake Superior St	Frank Anzalone	4–3 (OT)	St. Lawrence	Bruce Hoffort, Lake Superior St, G
1989	Harvard	Bill Cleary	4–3 (OT)	Minnesota	Ted Donato, Harvard, F
1990	Wisconsin	Jeff Sauer	7–3	Colgate	Chris Tancill, Wisconsin, F
1991	Northern Michigan	Rick Comley	8–7 (3OT)	Boston University	Scott Beattie, Northern Michigan, F
1992	Lake Superior St	Jeff Jackson	4–2	Wisconsin	Paul Constantin, Lake Superior St, F
1993	Maine	Shawn Walsh	5–4	Lake Superior St	Jim Montgomery, Maine, F
1994	Lake Superior St	Jeff Jackson	9–1	Boston University	Sean Tallaire, Lake Superior St, F
1995	Boston University	Jack Parker	6–2	Maine	Chris O'Sullivan, Boston Univ, F

Men

DIVISION I (Cont.)

Year	Champion	Coach	Score	Runner-Up	Most Outstanding Player
1996	Michigan	Red Berenson	3–2 (OT)	Colorado College	Brendan Morrison, Michigan, F
1997	North Dakota	Dean Blais	6–4	Boston University	Matt Henderson, North Dakota, F
1998	Michigan	Red Berenson	3–2 (OT)	Boston College	Marty Turco, Michigan, G
1999	Maine	Shawn Walsh	3–2 (OT)	New Hampshire	Alfie Michaud, Maine, G
2000	North Dakota	Dean Blais	4–2	Boston College	Lee Goren, North Dakota, F
2001	Boston College	Jerry York	3–2 (OT)	North Dakota	Chuck Kobasew, Boston Coll, F
2002	Minnesota	Don Lucia	4–3 (OT)	Maine	Grant Potulny, Minnesota, F
2003	Minnesota	Don Lucia	5–1	New Hampshire	Thomas Vanek, Minnesota, F
2004	Denver	George Gwozdecky	1–0	Maine	Adam Berkhoel, Denver, G
2005	Denver	George Gwozdecky	4–1	North Dakota	Peter Mannino, Denver
2006	Wisconsin	Mike Eaves	2–1	Boston College	Robbie Earl, Wisconsin, F
2007	Michigan St	Rick Comley	3–1	Boston College	Justin Abdelkader, Michigan St, F

DIVISION II (Discontinued)

Year	Champion	Coach	Score	Runner-Up
1978	Merrimack	Thom Lawler	12–2	Lake Forest
1979	Lowell	Bill Riley Jr	6–4	Mankato St
1980	Mankato St	Don Brose	5–2	Elmira
1981	Lowell	Bill Riley Jr	5–4	Plattsburgh St
1982	Lowell	Bill Riley Jr	6–1	Plattsburgh St
1983	RIT	Brian Mason	4–2	Bemidji St
1984	Bemidji St	R.H. (Bob) Peters	14–4*	Merrimack
1993	Bemidji St	R.H. (Bob) Peters	15–6*	Mercyhurst
1994	Bemidji St	R.H. (Bob) Peters	7–6*	Ala.–Huntsville
1995	Bemidji St	R.H. (Bob) Peters	11–6*	Mercyhurst
1996	Ala.–Huntsville	Doug Ross	10–1*	Bemidji St
1997	Bemidji St	R.H. (Bob) Peters	7–4*	Ala.–Huntsville
1998	Ala.–Huntsville	Doug Ross	11–4*	Bemidji St
1999	St. Michael's (Vt.)	Lou DiMasi	12–9*	New Hamp. Coll

*Two-game, total-goal series.

DIVISION III

Year	Champion	Coach	Score	Runner-Up
1984	Babson	Bob Riley	8–0	Union (N.Y.)
1985	RIT	Bruce Delventhal	5–1	Bemidji St
1986	Bemidji St	R.H. (Bob) Peters	8–5	Vacated
1987	Vacated			Oswego St
1988	UW-River Falls	Rick Kozuback	7–1, 3–5, 3–0	Elmira
1989	UW-Stevens Point	Mark Mazzoleni	3–3, 3–2	RIT
1990	UW-Stevens Point	Mark Mazzoleni	10–1, 3–6, 1–0	Plattsburgh St
1991	UW-Stevens Point	Mark Mazzoleni	6–2	Mankato St
1992	Plattsburgh St	Bob Emery	7–3	UW-Stevens Point
1993	UW-Stevens Point	Joe Baldarotta	4–3	UW-River Falls
1994	UW-River Falls	Dean Talafous	6–4	UW-Superior
1995	Middlebury	Bill Beaney	1–0	Fredonia St
1996	Middlebury	Bill Beaney	3–2	RIT
1997	Middlebury	Bill Beaney	3–2	UW-Superior
1998	Middlebury	Bill Beaney	2–1	UW-Stevens Point
1999	Middlebury	Bill Beaney	5–0	UW-Superior
2000	Norwich	Michael McShane	2–1	St. Thomas (Minn.)
2001	Plattsburgh	Bob Emery	6–2	RIT
2002	UW-Superior	Dan Stauber	3–2	Norwich
2003	Norwich	Michael McShane	2–1	Oswego St
2004	Middlebury	Bill Beaney	1–0	St. Norbert
2005	Middlebury	Bill Beaney	5–0	St. Thomas (Minn.)
2006	Middlebury	Bill Beaney	3–0	St. Norbert
2007	Oswego	Ed Gosek	4–3	Middlebury

Women – DIVISION I

Year	Champion	Coach	Score	Runner-Up
2001	Minn.-Duluth	Shannon Miller	4–2	St. Lawrence
2002	Minn.-Duluth	Shannon Miller	3–2	Brown
2003	Minn.-Duluth	Shannon Miller	4–3 (2 OT)	Harvard
2004	Minnesota	Laura Holldorson	6–2	Harvard
2005	Minnesota	Laura Holldorson	4–3	Harvard
2006	Wisconsin	Mark Johnson	3–0	Minnesota
2007	Wisconsin	Mark Johnson	4–1	Minnesota

Lacrosse

Men - DIVISION I

Year	Champion	Coach	Score	Runner-Up
1971	Cornell	Richie Moran	12–6	Maryland
1972	Virginia	Glenn Thiel	13–12	Johns Hopkins
1973	Maryland	Bud Beardmore	10–9 (2 OT)	Johns Hopkins
1974	Johns Hopkins	Bob Scott	17–12	Maryland
1975	Maryland	Bud Beardmore	20–13	Navy
1976	Cornell	Richie Moran	16–13 (OT)	Maryland
1977	Cornell	Richie Moran	16–8	Johns Hopkins
1978	Johns Hopkins	Henry Ciccarone	13–8	Cornell
1979	Johns Hopkins	Henry Ciccarone	15–9	Maryland
1980	Johns Hopkins	Henry Ciccarone	9–8 (2 OT)	Virginia
1981	North Carolina	Willie Scroggs	14–13	Johns Hopkins
1982	North Carolina	Willie Scroggs	7–5	Johns Hopkins
1983	Syracuse	Roy Simmons Jr	17–16	Johns Hopkins
1984	Johns Hopkins	Don Zimmerman	13–10	Syracuse
1985	Johns Hopkins	Don Zimmerman	11–4	Syracuse
1986	North Carolina	Willie Scroggs	10–9 (OT)	Virginia
1987	Johns Hopkins	Don Zimmerman	11–10	Cornell
1988	Syracuse	Roy Simmons Jr	13–8	Cornell
1989	Syracuse	Roy Simmons Jr	13–12	Johns Hopkins
1990	Syracuse	Roy Simmons Jr	21–9	Loyola (Md.)
1991	N.Carolina	Dave Klarmann	18–13	Towson St
1992	Princeton	Bill Tierney	10–9	Syracuse
1993	Syracuse	Roy Simmons Jr	13–12	N.Carolina
1994	Princeton	Bill Tierney	9–8 (OT)	Virginia
1995	Syracuse	Roy Simmons Jr	13–9	Maryland
1996	Princeton	Bill Tierney	13–12 (OT)	Virginia
1997	Princeton	Bill Tierney	19–7	Maryland
1998	Princeton	Bill Tierney	15–5	Maryland
1999	Virginia	Dom Starsia	12–10	Syracuse
2000	Syracuse	John Desko	13–7	Princeton
2001	Princeton	Bill Tierney	10–9 (OT)	Syracuse
2002	Syracuse	John Desko	13–12	Princeton
2003	Virginia	Dom Stargia	9–7	Johns Hopkins
2004	Syracuse	John Desko	14–13	Navy
2005	Johns Hopkins	Dave Pietramala	9–8	Duke
2006	Virgina	Dom Stargia	15–7	Massachusetts
2007	Johns Hopkins	Dave Pietramala	12–11	Duke

DIVISION II *(Discontinued, then renewed)*

Year	Champion	Coach	Score	Runner-Up
1974	Towson St	Carl Runk	18–17 (OT)	Hobart
1975	Cortland St	Chuck Winters	12–11	Hobart
1976	Hobart	Jerry Schmidt	18–9	Adelphi
1977	Hobart	Jerry Schmidt	23–13	Washington (Md.)
1978	Roanoke	Paul Griffin	14–13	Hobart
1979	Adelphi	Paul Doherty	17–12	Md.–Baltimore County
1980	Md.–Baltimore County	Dick Watts	23–14	Adelphi
1981	Adelphi	Paul Doherty	17–14	Loyola (Md.)
1993	Adelphi	Kevin Sheehan	11–7	LIU–C.W. Post
1994	Springfield	Keith Bugbee	15–12	New York Tech
1995	Adelphi	Sandy Kapatos	12–10	Springfield
1996	LIU–C.W. Post	Tom Postel	15–10	Adelphi
1997	New York Tech	Jack Kaley	18–11	Adelphi
1998	Adelphi	Sandy Kapatos	18–6	LIU–C.W. Post
1999	Adelphi	Sandy Kapatos	11–8	LIU–C.W. Post
2000	Limestone	Mike Cerino	10–9	LIU–C.W. Post
2001	Adelphi	Sandy Kapatos	14–10	Limestone
2002	Limestone	T.W. Johnson	11–9	New York Tech
2003	New York Tech	Jack Kaley	9–4	Limestone
2004	Le Moyne	Dan Sheehan	11–10 (2OT)	Limestone
2005	NYIT	Jack Kalley	14–13	Limestone
2006	Le Moyne	Dan Sheehan	12–5	Dowling
2007	Le Moyne	Dan Sheehan	6–5	Mercyhurst

DIVISION III

Year	Champion	Coach	Score	Runner-Up
1980	Hobart	Dave Urick	11–8	Cortland St
1981	Hobart	Dave Urick	10–8	Cortland St
1982	Hobart	Dave Urick	9–8 (OT)	Washington (Md.)
1983	Hobart	Dave Urick	13–9	Roanoke

Men *(Cont.)*

DIVISION III *(Cont.)*

Year	Champion	Coach	Score	Runner-Up
1984	Hobart	Dave Urick	12–5	Washington (Md.)
1985	Hobart	Dave Urick	15–8	Washington (Md.)
1986	Hobart	Dave Urick	13–10	Washington (Md.)
1987	Hobart	Dave Urick	9–5	Ohio Wesleyan
1988	Hobart	Dave Urick	18–9	Ohio Wesleyan
1989	Hobart	Dave Urick	11–8	Ohio Wesleyan
1990	Hobart	B.J. O'Hara	18–6	Washington (Md.)
1991	Hobart	B.J. O'Hara	12–11	Salisbury St
1992	Nazareth (NY)	Scott Nelson	13–12	Hobart
1993	Hobart	B.J. O'Hara	16–10	Ohio Wesleyan
1994	Salisbury St	Jim Berkman	15–9	Hobart
1995	Salisbury St	Jim Berkman	22–13	Nazareth
1996	Nazareth	Scott Nelson	11–10 (OT)	Washington (Md.)
1997	Nazareth	Scott Nelson	15–14 (OT)	Washington (Md.)
1998	Washington (Md.)	John Haus	16–10	Nazareth
1999	Salisbury St	Jim Berkman	13–6	Middlebury
2000	Middlebury	Erin Quinn	16–12	Salisbury St
2001	Middlebury	Erin Quinn	15–10	Gettysburg
2002	Middlebury	Erin Quinn	14–9	Gettysburg
2003	Salisbury	Jim Berkman	14–13	Middlebury
2004	Salisbury	Jim Berkman	13–9	Nazareth
2005	Salisbury	Jim Berkman	11–10	Middlebury
2006	Cortland	Rich Barnes	13–12 (OT)	Salisbury
2007	Salisbury	Rich Barnes	15–9	Cortland St

Women

DIVISION I*

Year	Champion	Coach	Score	Runner-Up
2001	Maryland	Cindy Timchal	14–13 (OT)	Georgetown
2002	Princeton	Chris Sailer	12–7	Georgetown
2003	Princeton	Chris Sailer	8–7 (OT)	Virginia
2004	Virginia	Julie Myers	10–4	Princeton
2005	Northwestern	Kelly Amonte	13–10	Virginia
2006	Northwestern	Kelly Amonte Hiller	7–4	Dartmouth
2007	Northwestern	Kelly Amonte Hiller	15–13	Virginia

DIVISION II

Year	Champion	Coach	Score	Runner-Up
2001	LIU–C.W. Post	Karen MacCrate	13–9	West Chester
2002	Westchester	Ginny Martino	11–6	Stonehill
2003	Stonehill	Michael Daly	9–8	Longwood
2004	Adelphi	Jill Lessne	12–11	West Chester
2005	Stonehill	Michael Daly	13–10	West Chester
2006	Adelphi	Jill Lessne-Solomon	16–8	West Chester
2007	LIU–C.W. Post	Karen MacCrate	15-7	West Chester

*Divisions I and II competed for a single championship until 2001.

DIVISIONS I AND II

Year	Champion	Coach	Score	Runner-Up
1982	Massachusetts	Pamela Hixon	9–6	Trenton St
1983	Delaware	Janet Smith	10–7	Temple
1984	Temple	Tina Sloan Green	6–4	Maryland
1985	New Hampshire	Marisa Didio	6–5	Maryland
1986	Maryland	Sue Tyler	11–10	Penn St
1987	Penn St	Susan Scheetz	7–6	Temple
1988	Temple	Tina Sloan Green	15–7	Penn St
1989	Penn St	Susan Scheetz	7–6	Harvard
1990	Harvard	Carole Kleinfelder	8–7	Maryland
1991	Virginia	Jane Miller	8–6	Maryland
1992	Maryland	Cindy Timchal	11–10	Harvard
1993	Virginia	Jane Miller	8–6 (OT)	Princeton
1994	Princeton	Chris Sailer	10–7	Virginia
1995	Maryland	Cindy Timchal	13–5	Princeton
1996	Maryland	Cindy Timchal	10–5	Virginia
1997	Maryland	Cindy Timchal	8–7	Loyola (Md.)
1998	Maryland	Cindy Timchal	11–5	Virginia
1999	Maryland	Cindy Timchal	16–6	Virginia
2000	Maryland	Cindy Timchal	16–8	Princeton

Women

DIVISION III

Year	Champion	Score	Runner-Up	Year	Champion	Score	Runner-Up
1985	Trenton St	7–4	Ursinus	1997	Middlebury	14–9	College of NJ*
1986	Ursinus	12–10	Trenton St	1998	Coll of NJ	14–9	Williams
1987	Trenton St	8–7 (ot)	Ursinus	1999	Middlebury	10–9	Amherst
1988	Trenton St	14–11	William Smith	2000	Coll of NJ	14–8	Williams
1989	Ursinus	8–6	Trenton St	2001	Middlebury	11–10	Amherst
1990	Ursinus	7–6	St. Lawrence	2002	Middlebury	12–6	College of NJ*
1991	Trenton St	7–6	Ursinus	2003	Amherst	11–9	Middlebury
1992	Trenton St	5–3	William Smith	2004	Middlebury	13–11 (OT)	College of NJ*
1993	Trenton St	10–9	William Smith	2005	College of NJ*	9-7	Salisbury
1994	Trenton St	29–11	William Smith	2006	College of NJ*	10-4	Gettysburg
1995	Trenton St	14–13	William Smith	2007	Franklin &	11–8	Salisbury
1996	Trenton St	15–8	Middlebury		Marshall		

*Formerly Trenton St

Rifle

						INDIVIDUAL CHAMPIONS	
Year	Champion	Coach	Score	Runner-Up	Score	Air Rifle	Smallbore
1980	Tennessee Tech	James Newkirk	6201	West Virginia	6150	Rod Fitz-Randolph, Tennessee Tech	Rod Fitz-Randolph, Tennessee Tech
1981	Tennessee Tech	James Newkirk	6139	West Virginia	6136	John Rost, West Virginia	Kurt Fitz-Randolph Tennessee Tech
1982	Tennessee Tech	James Newkirk	6138	West Virginia	6136	John Rost, West Virginia	Kurt Fitz-Randolph, Tennessee Tech
1983	West Virginia	Edward Etzel	6166	Tennessee Tech	6148	Ray Slonena, Tennessee Tech	David Johnson, West Virginia
1984	West Virginia	Edward Etzel	6206	E Tennessee St	6142	Pat Spurgin, Murray St	Bob Broughton, West Virginia
1985	Murray St	Elvis Green	6150	West Virginia	6149	Christian Heller, West Virginia	Pat Spurgin, Murray St
1986	West Virginia	Edward Etzel	6229	Murray St	6163	Marianne Wallace, Murray St	Mike Anti, West Virginia
1987	Murray St	Elvis Green	6205	West Virginia	6203	Rob Harbison, Tenn.–Martin	Web Wright, West Virginia
1988	West Virginia	Greg Perrine	6192	Murray St	6183	Deena Wigger, Murray St	Web Wright, West Virginia
1989	West Virginia	Edward Etzel	6234	South Florida	6180	Michelle Scarborough, South Florida	Deb Sinclair, AK–Fairbanks
1990	West Virginia	Marsha Beasley	6205	Navy	6101	Gary Hardy, West Virginia	M. Scarborough, South Florida
1991	West Virginia	Marsha Beasley	6171	AK–Fairbanks	6110	Ann Pfiffner, West Virginia	Soma Dutta, UTEP
1992	West Virginia	Marsha Beasley	6214	AK–Fairbanks	6166	Ann Pfiffner, West Virginia	Tim Manges, West Virginia
1993	West Virginia	Marsha Beasley	6179	AK–Fairbanks	6169	Trevor Gathman, West Virginia	Eric Uptagrafft, West Virginia
1994	AK–Fairbanks	Randy Pitney	6194	West Virginia	6187	Nancy Napolski, Kentucky	Cory Brunetti, AK–Fairbanks
1995	West Virginia	Marsha Beasley	6241	Air Force	6187	Benji Belden, Murray St	Oleg Selezner, AK–Fairbanks
1996	West Virginia	Marsha Beasley	6179	Air Force	6168	T. Gathman, WVa	Joe Johnson, Navy
1997	West Virginia	Marsha Beasley	6223	Kentucky	6175	Marra Hastings, Murray St	Marcos Scrivner, West Virginia
1998	West Virginia	Marsha Beasley	6214	AK–Fairbanks	6175	Emily Caruso, Norwich	Karen Juzinuk, Xavier
1999	AK-Fairbanks	Randy Pitney	6276	Navy	6168	Kelly Mansfield, AK–Fairbanks	Kelly Mansfield, AK–Fairbanks
2000	AK-Fairbanks	Randy Pitney	6285	Xavier	6156	Kelly Mansfield, AK–Fairbanks	Nicole Allaire, Nebraska
2001	AK-Fairbanks	David Johnson	6283	Kentucky	6175	Matthew Emmons, AK–Fairbanks	Matthew Emmons, AK–Fairbanks
2002	AK-Fairbanks	Randy Pitney	6241	Kentucky	6209	Ryan Tanoue, Nevada	Matthew Emmons AK–Fairbanks

Rifle (Cont.)

INDIVIDUAL CHAMPIONS

Year	Champion	Coach	Score	Runner-Up	Score	Air Rifle	Smallbore
2003	AK-Fairbanks	Glenn Dubis	6287	Xavier	6187	Jamie Beyerle, AK-Fairbanks	Matthew Emmons AK–Fairbanks
2004	AK-Fairbanks	Glenn Dubis	6273	Nevada	6185	Morgan Hicks, Murray St	Matthew Rawlings AK–Fairbanks
2005	...Army	Ron Wigger	4659	Jacksonville	4658	Beth Tidmore, Murr St	Matthew Rawlings
2006	...AK-Fairbanks	Dan Jordan	4682	Nebraska	4666	Kristina Fehlings, Nebraska	Jamie Beyerle, AK-Fairbanks
2007	...AK-Fairbanks	Dan Jordan	4662	Army	4644	Michael Dickinson, AK-Fairbanks	Josh Albright, Navy

Skiing

Year	Champion	Coach	Pts	Runner-Up	Pts	Host or Site
1954	.....Denver	Willy Schaeffler	384.0	Seattle	349.6	Nev.–Reno
1955	.....Denver	Willy Schaeffler	567.05	Dartmouth	558.935	Norwich
1956	.....Denver	Willy Schaeffler	582.01	Dartmouth	541.77	Winter Park
1957	.....Denver	Willy Schaeffler	577.95	Colorado	545.29	Ogden Snow Basin
1958	.....Dartmouth	Al Merrill	561.2	Denver	550.6	Dartmouth
1959	.....Colorado	Bob Beattie	549.4	Denver	543.6	Winter Park
1960	.....Colorado	Bob Beattie	571.4	Denver	568.6	Bridger Bowl
1961	.....Denver	Willy Schaeffler	376.19	Middlebury	366.94	Middlebury
1962	.....Denver	Willy Schaeffler	390.08	Colorado	374.30	Squaw Valley
1963	.....Denver	Willy Schaeffler	384.6	Colorado	381.6	Solitude
1964	.....Denver	Willy Schaeffler	370.2	Dartmouth	368.8	Franconia Notch
1965	.....Denver	Willy Schaeffler	380.5	Utah	378.4	Crystal Mountain
1966	.....Denver	Willy Schaeffler	381.02	Western Colorado	365.92	Crested Butte
1967	.....Denver	Willy Schaeffler	376.7	Wyoming	375.9	Sugarloaf Mountain
1968	.....Wyoming	John Cress	383.9	Denver	376.2	Mount Werner
1969	.....Denver	Willy Schaeffler	388.6	Dartmouth	372.0	Mount Werner
1970	.....Denver	Willy Schaeffler	386.6	Dartmouth	378.8	Cannon Mountain
1971	.....Denver	Peder Pytte	394.7	Colorado	373.1	Terry Peak
1972	.....Colorado	Bill Marolt	385.3	Denver	380.1	Winter Park
1973	.....Colorado	Bill Marolt	381.89	Wyoming	377.83	Middlebury
1974	.....Colorado	Bill Marolt	176	Wyoming	162	Jackson Hole
1975	.....Colorado	Bill Marolt	183	Vermont	115	Fort Lewis
1976	.....Colo/Dart	Bill Marolt/Jim Page	112			Bates
1977	.....Colorado	Bill Marolt	179	Wyoming	154.5	Winter Park
1978	.....Colorado	Bill Marolt	152.5	Wyoming	121.5	Cannon Mountain
1979	.....Colorado	Tim Hinderman	153	Utah	130	Steamboat Springs
1980	.....Vermont	Chip LaCasse	171	Utah	151	Lake Placid and Stowe
1981	.....Utah	Pat Miller	183	Vermont	172	Park City
1982	.....Colorado	Tim Hinderman	461	Vermont	436.5	Lake Placid
1983	.....Utah	Pat Miller	696	Vermont	650	Bozeman
1984	.....Utah	Pat Miller	750.5	Vermont	684	New Hampshire
1985	.....Wyoming	Tim Ameel	764	Utah	744	Bozeman
1986	.....Utah	Pat Miller	612	Vermont	602	Vermont
1987	.....Utah	Pat Miller	710	Vermont	627	Anchorage
1988	.....Utah	Pat Miller	651	Vermont	614	Middlebury
1989	.....Vermont	Chip LaCasse	672	Utah	668	Jackson Hole
1990	.....Vermont	Chip LaCasse	671	Utah	571	Vermont
1991	.....Colorado	Richard Rokos	713	Vermont	682	Park City, Utah
1992	.....Vermont	Chip LaCasse	693.5	New Mexico	642.5	New Hampshire
1993	.....Utah	Pat Miller	783	Vermont	700.5	Steamboat Springs
1994	.....Vermont	Chip LaCasse	688	Utah	667	Sugarloaf, ME
1995	.....Colorado	Richard Rokos	720.5	Utah	711	New Hampshire
1996	.,...Utah	Pat Miller	719	Denver	635.5	Montana St
1997	.....Utah	Pat Miller	686	Vermont	646.5	Vermont
1998	.....Colorado	Richard Rokos	654	Utah	651.5	Montana St
1999	.....Colorado	Richard Rokos	650	Denver	636	Bates College
2000	.....Denver	Kurt Smitz	720	Colorado	621	Park City, Utah
2001	.....Denver	Kurt Smitz	649	Vermont	605	Middlebury, Vt.
2002	.....Denver	Kurt Smitz	656	Colorado	612	Anchorage
2003	.....Utah	Kevin Sweeney	682	Vermont	551	Hanover, N.H.
2004	.....New Mexico	George Brooks	623	Utah	581	Donner Summit, Calif.
2005	.....Denver	Kurt Smitz	622.5	Vermont	575	Stowe, Vt.
2006	.....Colorodo	Richard Rokos	654	New Mexico	556	Steamboat Springs
2007	.....Dartmouth	Peter Dodge	698	Denver	648	New Hampshire

Soccer

Men
DIVISION I

Year	Champion	Coach	Score	Runner-Up
1959	St. Louis	Bob Guelker	5–2	Bridgeport
1960	St. Louis	Bob Guelker	3–2	Maryland
1961	West Chester	Mel Lorback	2–0	St. Louis
1962	St. Louis	Bob Guelker	4–3	Maryland
1963	St. Louis	Bob Guelker	3–0	Navy
1964	Navy	F.H. Warner	1–0	Michigan St
1965	St. Louis	Bob Guelker	1–0	Michigan St
1966	San Francisco	Steve Negoesco	5–2	LIU–Brooklyn
1967	Michigan St	Gene Kenney	0–0	Game called due to
	St. Louis	Harry Keough		inclement weather
1968	Maryland	Doyle Royal	2–2 (2 OT)	
	Michigan St	Gene Kenney		
1969	St. Louis	Harry Keough	4–0	San Francisco
1970	St. Louis	Harry Keough	1–0	UCLA
1971	Vacated		3–2	St. Louis
1972	St. Louis	Harry Keough	4–2	UCLA
1973	St. Louis	Harry Keough	2–1 (OT)	UCLA
1974	Howard	Lincoln Phillips	2–1 (4 OT)	St. Louis
1975	San Francisco	Steve Negoesco	4–0	SIU–Edwardsville
1976	San Francisco	Steve Negoesco	1–0	Indiana
1977	Hartwick	Jim Lennox	2–1	San Francisco
1978	Vacated		2–0	Indiana
1979	SIU–Edwardsville	Bob Guelker	3–2	Clemson
1980	San Francisco	Steve Negoesco	4–3 (OT)	Indiana
1981	Connecticut	Joe Morrone	2–1 (OT)	Alabama A&M
1982	Indiana	Jerry Yeagley	2–1 (8 OT)	Duke
1983	Indiana	Jerry Yeagley	1–0 (2 OT)	Columbia
1984	Clemson	I.M. Ibrahim	2–1	Indiana
1985	UCLA	Sigi Schmid	1–0 (8 OT)	American
1986	Duke	John Rennie	1–0	Akron
1987	Clemson	I.M. Ibrahim	2–0	San Diego St
1988	Indiana	Jerry Yeagley	1–0	Howard
1989	Santa Clara	Steve Sampson	1–1 (2 OT)	
	Virginia	Bruce Arena		
1990	UCLA	Sigi Schmid	1–0 (OT)	Rutgers
1991	Virginia	Bruce Arena	0–0*	Santa Clara
1992	Virginia	Bruce Arena	2–0	San Diego
1993	Virginia	Bruce Arena	2–0	South-Carolina
1994	Virginia	Bruce Arena	1–0	Indiana
1995	Wisconsin	Jim Launder	2–0	Duke
1996	St. John's (N.Y.)	Dave Masur	4–1	Florida International
1997	UCLA	Sigi Schmid	2–1	Virginia
1998	Indiana	Jerry Yeagley	3–1	Stanford
1999	Indiana	Jerry Yeagley	1–0	Santa Clara
2000	Connecticut	Ray Reid	2–0	Creighton
2001	N.Carolina	Elmar Bolowich	2–0	Indiana
2002	UCLA	Tom Fitzgerald	1–0	Stanford
2003	Indiana	Jerry Yeagley	2–1	St. John's (N.Y.)
2004	Indiana	Jerry Yeagley	1–1 (2 OT 3-2)	UC–Santa Barbara
2005	Maryland	Sasho Cirovski	1–0	New Mexico
2006	UC–Santa Barbara	Tim Vom Steeg	2–1	UCLA

*Under a rule passed in 1991, the NCAA determined that when a score is tied after regulation and overtime, and the championship is determined by penalty kicks, the official score will be 0–0.

DIVISION II

Year	Champion	Year	Champion	Year	Champion
1972	SIU–Edwardsville	1982	Florida International	1992	Southern Connecticut St
1973	Missouri–St. Louis	1983	Seattle Pacific	1993	Seattle Pacific
1974	Adelphi	1984	Florida International	1994	Tampa
1975	Baltimore	1985	Seattle Pacific	1995	Southern Connecticut St
1976	Loyola (Md.)	1986	Seattle Pacific	1996	Grand Canyon
1977	Alabama A&M	1987	Southern Connecticut St	1997	CSU–Bakersfield
1978	Seattle Pacific	1988	Florida Tech	1998	Southern Connecticut St
1979	Alabama A&M	1989	New Hampshire College	1999	Southern Connecticut St
1980	Lock Haven	1990	Southern Connecticut St	2000	CSU–Dominguez Hills
1981	Tampa	1991	Florida Tech	2001	Tampa

Men — DIVISION II *(Cont.)*

Year	Champion	Year	Champion	Year	Champion
2002	Sonoma St	2004	Seattle	2006	Dowling (N.Y.)
2003	Lynn	2005	Fort Lewis		

DIVISION III

Year	Champion	Year	Champion	Year	Champion
1974	Brockport St	1985	NC–Greensboro	1996	College of New Jersey*
1975	Babson	1986	NC–Greensboro	1997	Wheaton (Ill.)
1976	Brandeis	1987	NC–Greensboro	1998	Ohio Wesleyan
1977	Lock Haven	1988	UC–San Diego	1999	St. Lawrence
1978	Lock Haven	1989	Elizabethtown	2000	Messiah
1979	Babson	1990	Glassboro St	2001	Richard Stockton
1980	Babson	1991	UC–San Diego	2002	Messiah
1981	Glassboro St	1992	Kean	2003	Trinity (Tex.)
1982	NC–Greensboro	1993	UC–San Diego	2004	Messiah
1983	NC–Greensboro	1994	Bethany (W.V.)	2005	Messiah
1984	Wheaton (Ill.)	1995	Williams	2006	Messiah
					*Formerly Trenton St

Women — DIVISION I

Year	Champion	Coach	Score	Runner-Up
1982	North Carolina	Anson Dorrance	2–0	Central Florida
1983	North Carolina	Anson Dorrance	4–0	George Mason
1984	North Carolina	Anson Dorrance	2–0	Connecticut
1985	George Mason	Hank Leung	2–0	North Carolina
1986	North Carolina	Anson Dorrance	2–0	Colorado College
1987	North Carolina	Anson Dorrance	1–0	Massachusetts
1988	North Carolina	Anson Dorrance	4–1	North Carolina St
1989	North Carolina	Anson Dorrance	2–0	Colorado College
1990	North Carolina	Anson Dorrance	6–0	Connecticut
1991	North Carolina	Anson Dorrance	3–1	Wisconsin
1992	North Carolina	Anson Dorrance	9–1	Duke
1993	North Carolina	Anson Dorrance	6–0	George Mason
1994	North Carolina	Anson Dorrance	5–0	Notre Dame
1995	Notre Dame	Chris Petrucelli	1–0	Portland
1996	North Carolina	Anson Dorrance	1–0	Notre Dame
1997	North Carolina	Anson Dorrance	2–0	Connecticut
1998	Florida	Becky Burleigh	1–0	North Carolina
1999	North Carolina	Anson Dorrance	2–0	Notre Dame
2000	North Carolina	Anson Dorrance	2–1	UCLA
2001	Santa Clara	Jerry Smith	1–0	North Carolina
2002	Portland	Clive Charles	2–1	Santa Clara
2003	North Carolina	Anson Dorrance	6–0	Connecticut
2004	Norte Dame	Randy Waldrum	1-1(OT 4-3)	UCLA
2005	Portland	Garrett Smith	4–0	UCLA
2006	North Carolina	Anson Dorrance	2–1	Notre Dame

DIVISION II

Year	Champion
1988	CSU–Hayward
1989	Barry
1990	Sonoma St
1991	CSU–Dominguez Hills
1992	Barry
1993	Barry
1994	Franklin Pierce
1995	Franklin Pierce
1996	Franklin Pierce
1997	Franklin Pierce
1998	Lynn
1999	Franklin Pierce
2000	UC-San Diego
2001	UC-San Diego
2002	Christian Brothers
2003	Kennesaw St
2004	Metro St
2005	Nebraska-Omaha
2006	Metro St

*Formerly Trenton St

DIVISION III

Year	Champion
1986	Rochester
1987	Rochester
1988	William Smith
1989	UC–San Diego
1990	Ithaca
1991	Ithaca
1992	Cortland St
1993	Trenton St
1994	Trenton St
1995	UC–San Diego
1996	UC–San Diego
1997	UC–San Diego
1998	Macalester
1999	UC–San Diego
2000	College of New Jersey*
2001	Ohio Wesleyan
2002	Ohio Wesleyan
2003	Oneonta St
2004	Wheaton College
2005	Messiah
2006	Wheaton (Ill.)

Softball

DIVISION I

Year	Champion	Coach	Score	Runner-Up
1982	UCLA*	Sharron Backus	2-0†	Fresno St
1983	Texas A&M	Bob Brock	2-0‡	CSU–Fullerton
1984	UCLA	Sharron Backus	1-0#	Texas A&M
1985	UCLA	Sharron Backus	2-1**	Nebraska
1986	CSU–Fullerton*	Judi Garman	3-0	Texas A&M
1987	Texas A&M	Bob Brock	4-1	UCLA
1988	UCLA	Sharron Backus	3-0	Fresno St
1989	UCLA*	Sharron Backus	1-0	Fresno St
1990	UCLA	Sharron Backus	2-0	Fresno St
1991	Arizona	Mike Candrea	5-1	UCLA
1992	UCLA*	Sharron Backus	2-0	Arizona
1993	Arizona	Mike Candrea	1-0	UCLA
1994	Arizona	Mike Candrea	4-0	CSU–Northridge
1995	Vacated	—		Arizona
1996	Arizona*	Mike Candrea	6-4	Washington
1997	Arizona	Mike Candrea	10-2***	UCLA
1998	Fresno St	Margie Wright	1-0	Arizona
1999	UCLA	Sue Enquist	3-2	Washington
2000	Oklahoma	Patty Gasso	3-1	UCLA
2001	Arizona*	Mike Candrea	1-0	UCLA
2002	California	Diane Ninemire	6-0	Arizona
2003	UCLA	Sue Enquist	1-0**	California
2004	UCLA	Sue Enquist	3-1	California
2005	Michigan	Carol Hutchins	4-1	St. Thomas
2006	Arizona	Mike Candrea	5-0	Northwestern
2007	Arizona	Mike Candrea	5-0	Tennessee

*Undefeated teams in final series. †Eight innings. ‡12 innings. #13 innings. **Nine innings. ***Five innings.

DIVISION II

Year	Champion	Year	Champion	Year	Champion
1982	Sam Houston St	1991	Augustana (S.D.)	2000	North Dakota St
1983	CSU–Northridge	1992	Missouri Southern	2001	Nebraska–Omaha
1984	CSU–Northridge	1993	Florida Southern	2002	St. Mary's (Iowa)
1985	CSU–Northridge	1994	Merrimack	2003	UC-Davis
1986	Stephen F. Austin St	1995	Kennesaw St	2004	Angelo St
1987	CSU–Northridge	1996	Kennesaw St	2005	Lynn University
1988	CSU–Bakersfield	1997	California (Pa.)*	2006	Lock Haven
1989	CSU–Bakersfield	1998	California (Pa.)	2007	SIU-Edwardsville
1990	CSU–Bakersfield	1999	Humboldt St		

DIVISION III

Year	Champion	Year	Champion	Year	Champion
1982	Sam Houston St	1990	Eastern Connecticut St	1999	Simpson (Iowa)
1982	Eastern Connecticut St*	1991	Central (Iowa)	2000	St. Mary's
1983	Trenton St	1992	Trenton St	2001	Muskingum*
1984	Buena Vista*	1993	Central (Iowa)	2002	Williams
1985	Eastern Connecticut St	1994	Trenton St	2003	Central (Iowa)
1986	Eastern Connecticut St	1995	Chapman	2004	St. Thomas
1987	Trenton St*	1996	Trenton St*	2005	St. Thomas
1988	Central (Iowa)	1997	Simpson (Iowa)*	2006	Rutgers-Camden
1989	Trenton St*	1998	UW-Stevens Point	2007	Linfield

*Undefeated teams in final series

Swimming and Diving

Men

DIVISION I

Year	Champion	Coach	Pts	Runner-Up	Pts
1937	Michigan	Matt Mann	75	Ohio St	39
1938	Michigan	Matt Mann	46	Ohio St	45
1939	Michigan	Matt Mann	65	Ohio St	58
1940	Michigan	Matt Mann	45	Yale	42
1941	Michigan	Matt Mann	61	Yale	58
1942	Yale	Robert J.H. Kiphuth	71	Michigan	39
1943	Ohio St	Mike Peppe	81	Michigan	47
1944	Yale	Robert J.H. Kiphuth	39	Michigan	38

Men *(Cont.)*
DIVISION I *(Cont.)*

Year	Champion	Coach	Pts	Runner-Up	Pts
1945	Ohio St	Mike Peppe	56	Michigan	48
1946	Ohio St	Mike Peppe	61	Michigan	37
1947	Ohio St	MIke Peppe	66	Michigan	39
1948	Michigan	Matt Mann	44	Ohio St	41
1949	Ohio St	Mike Peppe	49	Iowa	35
1950	Ohio St	Mike Peppe	64	Yale	43
1951	Yale	Robert J.H. Kiphuth	81	Michigan St	60
1952	Ohio St	Mike Peppe	94	Yale	81
1953	Yale	Robert J.H. Kiphuth	96½	Ohio St	73½
1954	Ohio St	Mike Peppe	94	Michigan	67
1955	Ohio St	Mike Peppe	90	Yale/Michigan	51
1956	Ohio St	Mike Peppe	68	Yale	54
1957	Michigan	Gus Stager	69	Yale	61
1958	Michigan	Gus Stager	72	Yale	63
1959	Michigan	Gus Stager	137½	Ohio St	44
1960	USC	Peter Daland	87	Michigan	73
1961	Michigan	Gus Stager	85	USC	62
1962	Ohio St	Mike Peppe	92	USC	46
1963	USC	Peter Daland	81	Yale	77
1964	USC	Peter Daland	96	Indiana	91
1965	USC	Peter Daland	285	Indiana	278½
1966	USC	Peter Daland	302	Indiana	286
1967	Stanford	Jim Gaughran	275	USC	260
1968	Indiana	James Counsilman	346	Yale	253
1969	Indiana	James Counsilman	427	USC	306
1970	Indiana	James Counsilman	332	USC	235
1971	Indiana	James Counsilman	351	USC	260
1972	Indiana	James Counsilman	390	USC	371
1973	Indiana	James Counsilman	358	Tennessee	294
1974	USC	Peter Daland	339	Indiana	338
1975	USC	Peter Daland	344	Indiana	274
1976	USC	Peter Daland	398	Tennessee	237
1977	USC	Peter Daland	385	Alabama	204
1978	Tennessee	Ray Bussard	307	Auburn	185
1979	California	Nort Thornton	287	USC	227
1980	California	Nort Thornton	234	Texas	220
1981	Texas	Eddie Reese	259	UCLA	189
1982	UCLA	Ron Ballatore	219	Texas	210
1983	Florida	Randy Reese	238	SMU	227
1984	Florida	Randy Reese	287½	Texas	277
1985	Stanford	Skip Kenney	403½	Florida	302
1986	Stanford	Skip Kenney	404	California	335
1987	Stanford	Skip Kenney	374	USC	296
1988	Texas	Eddie Reese	424	USC	369½
1989	Texas	Eddie Reese	475	Stanford	396
1990	Texas	Eddie Reese	506	USC	423
1991	Texas	Eddie Reese	476	Stanford	420
1992	Stanford	Skip Kenney	632	Texas	356
1993	Stanford	Skip Kenney	520½	Michigan	396
1994	Stanford	Skip Kenney	566½	Texas	445
1995	Michigan	Jon Urbanchek	561	Stanford	475
1996	Texas	Eddie Reese	479	Auburn	443½
1997	Auburn	David Marsh	496½	Stanford	340
1998	Stanford	Skip Kenney	594	Auburn	394½
1999	Auburn	David Marsh	467½	Stanford	414½
2000	Texas	Eddie Reese	538	Auburn	385
2001	Texas	Eddie Reese	597½	Stanford	457½
2002	Texas	Eddie Reese	512	Stanford	5011
2003	Auburn	David Marsh	609½	Texas	413
2004	Auburn	David Marsh	634	Stanford	377½
2005	Auburn	David Marsh	491	Stanford	414
2006	Auburn	David Marsh	480.5	Arizona	440.5
2007	Auburn	David Marsh	566	Stanford	387

Men (Cont.)

DIVISION II

Year	Champion	Year	Champion	Year	Champion
1963	SW Missouri St	1978	CSU–Northridge	1993	CSU–Bakersfield
1964	Bucknell	1979	CSU–Northridge	1994	Oakland (Mich.)
1965	San Diego St	1980	Oakland (Mich.)	1995	Oakland (Mich.)
1966	San Diego St	1981	CSU–Northridge	1996	Oakland (Mich.)
1967	UC–Santa Barbara	1982	CSU–Northridge	1997	Oakland (Mich.)
1968	Long Beach St	1983	CSU–Northridge	1998	CSU–Bakersfield
1969	UC–Irvine	1984	CSU–Northridge	1999	Drury
1970	UC–Irvine	1985	CSU–Northridge	2000	CSU–Bakersfield
1971	UC–Irvine	1986	CSU–Bakersfield	2001	CSU–Bakersfield
1972	Eastern Michigan	1987	CSU–Bakersfield	2002	CSU–Bakersfield
1973	CSU–Chico	1988	CSU–Bakersfield	2003	Drury
1974	CSU–Chico	1989	CSU–Bakersfield	2004	CSU–Bakersfield
1975	CSU–Northridge	1990	CSU–Bakersfield	2005	Drury
1976	CSU–Chico	1991	CSU–Bakersfield	2006	Drury
1977	CSU–Northridge	1992	CSU–Bakersfield	2007	Drury

DIVISION III

Year	Champion	Year	Champion	Year	Champion
1975	CSU–Chico	1986	Kenyon	1997	Kenyon
1976	St. Lawrence	1987	Kenyon	1998	Kenyon
1977	Johns Hopkins	1988	Kenyon	1999	Kenyon
1978	Johns Hopkins	1989	Kenyon	2000	Kenyon
1979	Johns Hopkins	1990	Kenyon	2001	Kenyon
1980	Kenyon	1991	Kenyon	2002	Kenyon
1981	Kenyon	1992	Kenyon	2003	Kenyon
1982	Kenyon	1993	Kenyon	2004	Kenyon
1983	Kenyon	1994	Kenyon	2005	Kenyon
1984	Kenyon	1995	Kenyon	2006	Kenyon
1985	Kenyon	1996	Kenyon	2007	Kenyon

Women

DIVISION I

Year	Champion	Coach	Pts	Runner-Up	Pts
1982	Florida	Randy Reese	505	Stanford	383
1983	Stanford	George Haines	418½	Florida	389½
1984	Texas	Richard Quick	392	Stanford	324
1985	Texas	Richard Quick	643	Florida	400
1986	Texas	Richard Quick	633	Florida	586
1987	Texas	Richard Quick	648½	Stanford	631½
1988	Texas	Richard Quick	661	Florida	542½
1989	Stanford	Richard Quick	610½	Texas	547
1990	Texas	Mark Schubert	632	Stanford	622½
1991	Texas	Mark Schubert	746	Stanford	653
1992	Stanford	Richard Quick	735½	Texas	651
1993	Stanford	Richard Quick	649½	Florida	421
1994	Stanford	Richard Quick	512	Texas	421
1995	Stanford	Richard Quick	497½	Michigan	478½
1996	Stanford	Richard Quick	478	SMU	397
1997	USC	Mark Schubert	406	Stanford	395
1998	Stanford	Richard Quick	422	Arizona	378
1999	Georgia	Jack Bauerle	504½	Stanford	441
2000	Georgia	Jack Bauerle	490½	Arizona	472
2001	Georgia	Jack Bauerle	389	Stanford	387½
2002	Auburn	David Marsh	474	Georgia	386
2003	Auburn	David Marsh	536	Georgia	373
2004	Auburn	David Marsh	569	Georgia	431
2005	Georgia	Jack Bauerle	609.5	Auburn	492
2006	Auburn	David Marsh	518.5	Georgia	515.5
2007	Auburn	David Marsh	535	Arizona	477

Women
DIVISION II

Year	Champion	Year	Champion	Year	Champion
1982	CSU–Northridge	1991	Oakland (Mich.)	2000	Drury
1983	Clarion	1992	Oakland (Mich.)	2001	Truman St
1984	Clarion	1993	Oakland (Mich.)	2002	Truman St
1985	S Florida	1994	Oakland (Mich.)	2003	Truman St
1986	Clarion	1995	Air Force	2004	Truman St
1987	CSU–Northridge	1996	Air Force	2005	Truman St
1988	CSU–Northridge	1997	Drury	2006	Truman St
1989	CSU–Northridge	1998	Drury	2007	Drury
1990	Oakland (Mich.)	1999	Drury		

DIVISION III

Year	Champion	Year	Champion	Year	Champion
1982	Williams	1991	Kenyon	2000	Kenyon
1983	Williams	1992	Kenyon	2001	Denison
1984	Kenyon	1993	Kenyon	2002	Kenyon
1985	Kenyon	1994	Kenyon	2003	Kenyon
1986	Kenyon	1995	Kenyon	2004	Kenyon
1987	Kenyon	1996	Kenyon	2005	Emory
1988	Kenyon	1997	Kenyon	2006	Emory
1989	Kenyon	1998	Kenyon	2007	Kenyon
1990	Kenyon	1999	Kenyon		

Tennis

Men
INDIVIDUAL CHAMPIONS 1883-1945

Year	Champion	Year	Champion
1883	Joseph Clark, Harvard (spring)	1914	George Church, Princeton
1883	Howard Taylor, Harvard (fall)	1915	Richard Williams II, Harvard
1884	W.P. Knapp, Yale	1916	G. Colket Caner, Harvard
1885	W.P. Knapp, Yale	1917–18	No tournament
1886	G.M. Brinley, Trinity (Conn.)	1919	Charles Garland, Yale
1887	P.S. Sears, Harvard	1920	Lascelles Banks, Yale
1888	P.S. Sears, Harvard	1921	Philip Neer, Stanford
1889	R.P. Huntington Jr, Yale	1922	Lucien Williams, Yale
1890	Fred Hovey, Harvard	1923	Carl Fischer, Philadelphia Osteo
1891	Fred Hovey, Harvard	1924	Wallace Scott, Washington
1892	William Larned, Cornell	1925	Edward Chandler, California
1893	Malcolm Chace, Brown	1926	Edward Chandler, UC-Berkeley
1894	Malcolm Chace, Yale	1927	Wilmer Allison, Texas
1895	Malcolm Chace, Yale	1928	Julius Seligson, Lehigh
1896	Malcolm Whitman, Harvard	1929	Berkeley Bell, Texas
1897	S.G. Thompson, Princeton	1930	Clifford Sutter, Tulane
1898	Leo Ware, Harvard	1931	Keith Gledhill, Stanford
1899	Dwight Davis, Harvard	1932	Clifford Sutter, Tulane
1900	Raymond Little, Princeton	1933	Jack Tidball, UCLA
1901	Fred Alexander, Princeton	1934	Gene Mako, USC
1902	William Clothier, Harvard	1935	Wilbur Hess, Rice
1903	E.B. Dewhurst, Pennsylvania	1936	Ernest Sutter, Tulane
1904	Robert LeRoy, Columbia	1937	Ernest Sutter, Tulane
1905	E.B. Dewhurst, Pennsylvania	1938	Frank Guernsey, Rice
1906	Robert LeRoy, Columbia	1939	Frank Guernsey, Rice
1907	G. Peabody Gardner Jr, Harvard	1940	Donald McNeil, Kenyon
1908	Nat Niles, Harvard	1941	Joseph Hunt, Navy
1909	Wallace Johnson, Pennsylvania	1942	Frederick Schroeder Jr, Stanford
1910	R.A. Holden Jr, Yale	1943	Pancho Segura, Miami (Fla.)
1911	E.H. Whitney, Harvard	1944	Pancho Segura, Miami (Fla.)
1912	George Church, Princeton	1945	Pancho Segura, Miami (Fla.)
1913	Richard Williams II, Harvard		

Men

DIVISION I

Year	Champion	Coach	Pts	Runner-Up	Pts	Individual Champion
1946	USC	William Moyle	9	William & Mary	6	Robert Falkenburg, USC
1947	William & Mary	Sharvey G. Umbeck	10	Rice	4	Gardner Larned, William & Mary
1948	William & Mary	Sharvey G. Umbeck	6	San Francisco	5	Harry Likas, San Francisco
1949	San Francisco	Norman Brooks	7	Rollins/Tulane/ Washington	4	Jack Tuero, Tulane
1950	UCLA	William Ackerman	11	California/ USC	5	Herbert Flam, UCLA
1951	USC	Louis Wheeler	9	Cincinnati	7	Tony Trabert, Cincinnati
1952	UCLA	J.D. Morgan	11	California/USC	5	Hugh Stewart, USC
1953	UCLA	J.D. Morgan	11	California	6	Hamilton Richardson, Tulane
1954	UCLA	J.D. Morgan	15	USC	10	Hamilton Richardson, Tulane
1955	USC	George Toley	12	Texas	7	Jose Aguero, Tulane
1956	UCLA	J.D. Morgan	15	USC	14	Alejandro Olmedo, USC
1957	Michigan	William Murphy	10	Tulane	9	Barry MacKay, Michigan
1958	USC	George Toley	13	Stanford	9	Alejandro Olmedo, USC
1959	Notre Dame	Thomas Fallon	8			Whitney Reed, San Jose St
	Tulane	Emmet Pare	8			
1960	UCLA	J.D. Morgan	18	USC	8	Larry Nagler, UCLA
1961	UCLA	J.D. Morgan	17	USC	16	Allen Fox, UCLA
1962	USC	George Toley	22	UCLA	12	Rafael Osuna, USC
1963	USC	George Toley	27	UCLA	19	Dennis Ralston, USC
1964	USC	George Toley	26	UCLA	25	Dennis Ralston, USC
1965	UCLA	J.D. Morgan	31	Miami (Fla.)	13	Arthur Ashe, UCLA
1966	USC	George Toley	27	UCLA	23	Charles Pasarell, UCLA
1967	USC	George Toley	28	UCLA	23	Bob Lutz, USC
1968	USC	George Toley	31	Rice	23	Stan Smith, USC
1969	USC	George Toley	35	UCLA	23	Joaquin Loyo-Mayo, USC
1970	UCLA	Glenn Bassett	26	Trinity (Tex.)	22	Jeff Borowiak, UCLA
				Rice	22	
1971	UCLA	Glenn Bassett	35	Trinity (Tex.)	27	Jimmy Connors, UCLA
1972	Trinity (Tex.)	Clarence Mabry	36	Stanford	30	Dick Stockton, Trinity (Tex.)
1973	Stanford	Dick Gould	33	USC	28	Alex Mayer, Stanford
1974	Stanford	Dick Gould	30	USC	25	John Whitlinger, Stanford
1975	UCLA	Glenn Bassett	27	Miami (Fla.)	20	Bill Martin, UCLA
1976	USC	George Toley	21			Bill Scanlon, Trinity (Tex.)
	UCLA	Glenn Bassett	21			
1977	Stanford	Dick Gould		Trinity (Tex.)		Matt Mitchell, Stanford
1978	Stanford	Dick Gould		UCLA		John McEnroe, Stanford
1979	UCLA	Glenn Bassett		Trinity (Tex.)		Kevin Curren, Texas
1980	Stanford	Dick Gould		California		Robert Van't Hof, USC
1981	Stanford	Dick Gould		UCLA		Tim Mayotte, Stanford
1982	UCLA	Glenn Bassett		Pepperdine		Mike Leach, Michigan
1983	Stanford	Dick Gould		SMU		Greg Holmes, Utah
1984	UCLA	Glenn Bassett		Stanford		Mikael Pernfors, Georgia
1985	Georgia	Dan Magill		UCLA		Mikael Pernfors, Georgia
1986	Stanford	Dick Gould		Pepperdine		Dan Goldie, Stanford
1987	Georgia	Dan Magill		UCLA		Andrew Burrow, Miami (Fla.)
1988	Stanford	Dick Gould		LSU		Robby Weiss, Pepperdine
1989	Stanford	Dick Gould		Georgia		Donni Leaycraft, LSU
1990	Stanford	Dick Gould		Tennessee		Steve Bryan, Texas
1991	USC	Dick Leach		Georgia		Jared Palmer, Stanford
1992	Stanford	Dick Gould		Notre Dame		Alex O'Brien, Stanford
1993	USC	Dick Leach		Georgia		Chris Woodruff, Tennessee
1994	USC	Dick Leach		Stanford		Mark Merklein, Florida
1995	Stanford	Dick Gould		Mississippi		Sargis Sargsian, Arizona St
1996	Stanford	Dick Gould		UCLA		Cecil Mamiit, USC
1997	Stanford	Dick Gould		Georgia		Luke Smith, UNLV
1998	Stanford	Dick Gould		Georgia		Bob Bryan, Stanford
1999	Georgia	Manuel Diaz		UCLA		Jeff Morrison, Florida
2000	Stanford	Dick Gould		Virginia Comm.		Alex Kim, Stanford
2001	Georgia	Manuel Diaz		Tennessee		Matias Boeker, Georgia
2002	USC	Dick Leach		Georgia		Matias Boeker, Georgia
2003	Illinois	Craig Tiley		Vanderbilt		Amer Delic, Illinois
2004	Baylor	Matt Knoll		UCLA		Benjamin Becker, Baylor
2005	UCLA	Billy Martin		Baylor		Benedikt Dorsch, Baylor
2006	Pepperdine	Adam Steinberg		Georgia		Benjamin Kohlleoffel, UCLA
2007	Georgia	Manuel Diaz		Illinois		Somdev Devvarman, Virginia

Note: Prior to 1977, individual wins counted in the team's total points. In 1977, a dual-match single-elimination team championship was initiated, eliminating the point system.

Men

DIVISION II

Year	Champion	Year	Champion	Year	Champion
1963	CSU–L.A.	1978	SIU–Edwardsville	1993	Lander
1964	CSU–L.A./Southern Illinois	1979	SIU–Edwardsville	1994	Lander
1965	CSU–L.A.	1980	SIU–Edwardsville	1995	Lander
1966	Rollins	1981	SIU–Edwardsville	1996	Lander
1967	Long Beach St	1982	SIU–Edwardsville	1997	Lander
1968	Fresno St	1983	SIU–Edwardsville	1998	Lander
1969	CSU–Northridge	1984	SIU–Edwardsville	1999	Lander
1970	UC–Irvine	1985	Chapman	2000	Lander
1971	UC–Irvine	1986	Cal-Poly–SLO	2001	Rollins
1972	UC–Irvine/ Rollins	1987	Chapman	2002	BYU-Hawaii
1973	UC–Irvine	1988	Chapman	2003	BYU-Hawaii
1974	San Diego	1989	Hampton	2004	W Florida
1975	UC–Irvine/San Diego	1990	Cal-Poly–SLO	2005	W Florida
1976	Hampton	1991	Rollins	2006	Valdosta
1977	UC–Irvine	1992	UC–Davis	2007	Lynn

DIVISION III

Year	Champion	Year	Champion	Year	Champion
1976	Kalamazoo	1986	Kalamazoo	1997	Washington (Md.)
1977	Swarthmore	1987	Kalamazoo	1998	UC–Santa Cruz
1978	Kalamazoo	1988	Washington & Lee	1999	Williams
1979	Redlands	1989	UC–Santa Cruz	2000	Trinity (Tex.)
1980	Gustavus Adolphus	1990	Swarthmore	2001	Williams
1981	Claremont-M-S/ Swarthmore	1991	Kalamazoo	2002	Williams
1982	Gustavus Adolphus	1992	Kalamazoo	2003	Emory
1983	Redlands	1993	Kalamazoo	2004	Middlebury
1984	Redlands	1994	Washington (Md.)	2005	UC–Santa Cruz
1985	Swarthmore	1995	UC–Santa Cruz	2006	Emory
		1996	UC–Santa Cruz	2007	UC–Santa Cruz

Women

DIVISION I

Year	Champion	Coach	Runner-Up	Individual Champion
1982	Stanford	Frank Brennan	UCLA	Alycia Moulton, Stanford
1983	USC	Dave Borelli	Trinity (Tex.)	Beth Herr, USC
1984	Stanford	Frank Brennan	USC	Lisa Spain, Georgia
1985	USC	Dave Borelli	Miami (Fla.)	Linda Gates, Stanford
1986	Stanford	Frank Brennan	USC	Patty Fendick, Stanford
1987	Stanford	Frank Brennan	Georgia	Patty Fendick, Stanford
1988	Stanford	Frank Brennan	Florida	Shaun Stafford, Florida
1989	Stanford	Frank Brennan	UCLA	Sandra Birch, Stanford
1990	Stanford	Frank Brennan	Florida	Debbie Graham, Stanford
1991	Stanford	Frank Brennan	UCLA	Sandra Birch, Stanford
1992	Florida	Andy Brandi	Texas	Lisa Raymond, Florida
1993	Texas	Jeff Moore	Stanford	Lisa Raymond, Florida
1994	Georgia	Jeff Wallace	Stanford	Angela Lettiere, Georgia
1995	Texas	Jeff Moore	Florida	Keri Phebus, UCLA
1996	Florida	Andy Brandi	Stanford	Jill Craybas, Florida
1997	Stanford	Frank Brennan	Florida	Lilia Osterloh, Stanford
1998	Florida	Andy Brandi	Duke	Vanessa Webb, Duke
1999	Stanford	Frank Brennan	Florida	Zuzana Lesenarova, UC–SD
2000	Georgia	Jeff Wallace	Stanford	Laura Granville, Stanford
2001	Stanford	Lele Forood	Vanderbilt	Laura Granville, Stanford
2002	Stanford	Lele Forood	Florida	Bea Bielek, Wake Forest
2003	Florida	Roland Thornqvist	Stanford	Amber Liu, Stanford
2004	Stanford	Lele Forood	UCLA	Amber Liu, Stanford
2005	Stanford	Lele Forood	Texas	Alice Barnes, Stanford
2006	Stanford	Lele Forood	Miami	Suzi Babos, California
2007	Georgia Tech	Bryan Shelton	UCLA	Audra Cohen, Miami (Fla.)

Women (Cont.)
DIVISION II

Year	Champion	Year	Champion	Year	Champion
1982	CSU–Northridge	1991	Cal Poly–Pomona	2000	BYU–Hawaii
1983	Tenn.–Chattanooga	1992	Cal Poly–Pomona	2001	Lynn
1984	Tenn.–Chattanooga	1993	UC–Davis	2002	BYU–Hawaii
1985	Tenn.–Chattanooga	1994	North Florida	2003	BYU–Hawaii
1986	SIU–Edwardsville	1995	Armstrong St	2004	BYU–Hawaii
1987	SIU–Edwardsville	1996	Armstrong St	2005	Armstrong Atlantic
1988	SIU–Edwardsville	1997	Lynn	2006	BYU–Hawaii
1989	SIU–Edwardsville	1998	Lynn	2007	BYU–Hawaii
1990	UC–Davis	1999	BYU–Hawaii		

DIVISION III

Year	Champion	Year	Champion	Year	Champion
1982	Occidental	1991	Mary Washington	2000	Trinity (Tex.)
1983	Principia	1992	Pomona-Pitzer	2001	Williams
1984	Davidson	1993	Kenyon	2002	Williams
1985	UC–San Diego	1994	UC–San Diego	2003	Emory
1986	Trenton St	1995	Kenyon	2004	Emory
1987	UC–San Diego	1996	Emory	2005	Emory
1988	Mary Washington	1997	Kenyon	2006	Emory
1989	UC–San Diego	1998	Kenyon	2007	Washington & Lee
1990	Gustavus Adolphus	1999	Amherst		

Indoor Track and Field

Men
DIVISION I

Year	Champion	Coach	Pts	Runner-Up	Pts
1965	Missouri	Tom Botts	14	Oklahoma St	12
1966	Kansas	Bob Timmons	14	USC	13
1967	USC	Vern Wolfe	26	Oklahoma	17
1968	Villanova	Jim Elliott	35	USC	25
1969	Kansas	Bob Timmons	41½	Villanova	33
1970	Kansas	Bob Timmons	27½	Villanova	26
1971	Villanova	Jim Elliott	22	UTEP	19 4
1972	USC	Vern Wolfe	19	Bowling Green/Mich St	18
1973	Manhattan	Fred Dwyer	18	Kansas/Kent St/UTEP	12
1974	UTEP	Ted Banks	19	Colorado	18
1975	UTEP	Ted Banks	36	Kansas	17 /2
1976	UTEP	Ted Banks	23	Villanova	15
1977	Washington St	John Chaplin	25½	UTEP	25
1978	UTEP	Ted Banks	44	Auburn	38
1979	Villanova	Jim Elliott	52	UTEP	51
1980	UTEP	Ted Banks	76	Villanova	42
1981	UTEP	Ted Banks	76	SMU	51
1982	UTEP	John Wedel	67	Arkansas	30
1983	SMU	Ted McLaughlin	43	Villanova	32
1984	Arkansas	John McDonnell	38	Washington St	28
1985	Arkansas	John McDonnell	70	Tennessee	29
1986	Arkansas	John McDonnell	49	Villanova	22
1987	Arkansas	John McDonnell	39	SMU	31
1988	Arkansas	John McDonnell	34	Illinois	29
1989	Arkansas	John McDonnell	34	Florida	31
1990	Arkansas	John McDonnell	44	Texas A&M	36
1991	Arkansas	John McDonnell	34	Georgetown	27
1992	Arkansas	John McDonnell	53	Clemson	46
1993	Arkansas	John McDonnell	66	Clemson	30
1994	Arkansas	John McDonnell	83	UTEP	45
1995	Arkansas	John McDonnell	59	GMU/Tennessee	26
1996	George Mason	John Cook	39	Nebraska	31½
1997	Arkansas	John McDonnell	59	Auburn	27
1998	Arkansas	John McDonnell	56	Stanford	36½
1999	Arkansas	John McDonnell	65	Stanford	42½
2000	Arkansas	John McDonnell	69½	Stanford	52
2001	LSU	Pat Henry	34	TCU	33

Men *(Cont.)*
DIVISION I *(Cont.)*

Year	Champion	Coach	Pts	Runner-Up	Pts
2002	Tennessee	Bill Webb	62½	LSU	44
2003	Arkansas	John McDonnell	52	Auburn	28
2004	LSU	Pat Henry	45½	Florida	38
2005	Arkansas	John McDonnell	54	Wisconsin	43
2006	Arkansas	John McDonnell	53	LSU	45
2007	Wisconsin	Ed Nuttycombe	40	Florida St	35

DIVISION II

Year	Champion	Year	Champion	Year	Champion
1985	SE Missouri St	1993	Abilene Christian	2001	St. Augustine's
1986	Not held	1994	Abilene Christian	2002	Abilene Christian
1987	St. Augustine's	1995	St. Augustine's	2003	Abilene Christian
1988	Abil. Christian/St. August.	1996	Abilene Christian	2004	Abilene Christian
1989	St. Augustine's	1997	Abilene Christian	2005	Abilene Christian
1990	St. Augustine's	1998	Abilene Christian	2006	St. Augustine's
1991	St. Augustine's	1999	Abilene Christian	2007	St. Augustine's
1992	St. Augustine's	2000	Abilene Christian		

DIVISION III

Year	Champion	Year	Champion	Year	Champion
1985	St. Thomas (Minn.)	1993	UW-La Crosse	2001	UW-La Crosse
1986	Frostburg St	1994	UW-La Crosse	2002	UW-La Crosse
1987	UW-La Crosse	1995	Lincoln (Pa.)	2003	UW-La Crosse
1988	UW-La Crosse	1996	Lincoln (Pa.)	2004	UW-La Crosse
1989	N Central	1997	UW-La Crosse	2005	UW-La Crosse
1990	Lincoln (Pa.)	1998	Lincoln (Pa.)	2006	UW-La Crosse
1991	UW-La Crosse	1999	Lincoln (Pa.)	2007	Lincoln (Pa.)
1992	UW-La Crosse	2000	Lincoln (Pa.)		

Women
DIVISION I

Year	Champion	Coach	Pts	Runner-Up	Pts
1983	Nebraska	Gary Pepin	47	Tennessee	44
1984	Nebraska	Gary Pepin	59	Tennessee	48
1985	Florida St	Gary Winckler	34	Texas	32
1986	Texas	Terry Crawford	31	USC	26
1987	LSU	Loren Seagrave	49	Tennessee	30
1988	Texas	Terry Crawford	71	Villanova	52
1989	LSU	Pat Henry	61	Villanova	34
1990	Texas	Terry Crawford	50	Wisconsin	26
1991	LSU	Pat Henry	48	Texas	39
1992	Florida	Bev Kearney	50	Stanford	26
1993	LSU	Pat Henry	49	Wisconsin	44
1994	LSU	Pat Henry	48	Alabama	29
1995	LSU	Pat Henry	40	UCLA	37
1996	LSU	Pat Henry	52	Georgia	34
1997	LSU	Pat Henry	49	Texas/Wisconsin	39
1998	Texas	Bev Kearney	60	LSU	30
1999	Texas	Bev Kearney	61	LSU	57
2000	UCLA	Jeanette Bolden	51	South Carolina	41
2001	UCLA	Jeanette Bolden	53½	South Carolina	40
2002	LSU	Pat Henry	57	Florida	35
2003	LSU	Pat Henry	62	South Carolina/Florida	44
2004	Lousiana St	Pat Henry	52	Florida	51
2005	Tennessee	J.J. Clark	46	Florida	36
2006	Texas	Bev Kearney	51	Stanford	36
2007	Arizona	Fred Harvey	38	LSU	33

DIVISION II

Year	Champion	Year	Champion	Year	Champion
1985	St. Augustine's	1993	Abilene Christian	2001	St. Augustine's
1986	Not held	1994	Abilene Christian	2002	North Dakota St
1987	St. Augustine's	1995	Abilene Christian	2003	St. Augustine's
1988	Abilene Christian	1996	Abilene Christian	2004	Lincoln
1989	Abilene Christian	1997	Abilene Christian	2005	St. Augustine's
1990	Abilene Christian	1998	Abilene Christian	2006	Lincoln
1991	Abilene Christian	1999	Abilene Christian	2007	St. Augustine's
1992	Alabama A&M	2000	Abilene Christian		

Women (Cont.)
DIVISION III

Year	Champion	Year	Champion	Year	Champion
1985	UMass–Boston	1993	Lincoln (Pa.)	2001	Wheaton (Mass.)
1986	UMass–Boston	1994	UW-Oshkosh	2002	Wheaton (Mass.)
1987	UMass–Boston	1995	UW-Oshkosh	2003	Wheaton (Mass.)
1988	Christopher Newport	1996	UW-Oshkosh	2004	UW-Oshkosh
1989	Christopher Newport	1997	Christopher Newport	2005	UW-Oshkosh
1990	Christopher Newport	1998	Christopher Newport	2006	UW-Oshkosh
1991	Cortland St	1999	Wheaton (Mass.)	2007	Williams
1992	Christopher Newport	2000	Wheaton (Mass.)		

Outdoor Track and Field

Men
DIVISION I

Year	Champion	Coach	Pts	Runner-Up	Pts
1921	Illinois	Harry Gill	20†	Notre Dame	16†
1922	California	Walter Christie	28†	Penn St	19†
1923	Michigan	Stephen Farrell	29†	Mississippi St	16
1924	No meet				
1925	Stanford*	R.L. Templeton	31†		
1926	USC*	Dean Cromwell	27†		
1927	Illinois*	Harry Gill	35†		
1928	Stanford	R.L. Templeton	72	Ohio St	31
1929	Ohio St	Frank Castleman	50	Washington	42
1930	USC	Dean Cromwell	55†	Washington	40
1931	USC	Dean Cromwell	77†	Ohio St	31†
1932	Indiana	Billy Hayes	56	Ohio St	49†
1933	LSU	Bernie Moore	58	USC	54
1934	Stanford	R.L. Templeton	63	USC	54†
1935	USC	Dean Cromwell	74†	Ohio St	40†
1936	USC	Dean Cromwell	103†	Ohio St	73
1937	USC	Dean Cromwell	62	Stanford	50
1938	USC	Dean Cromwell	67†	Stanford	38
1939	USC	Dean Cromwell	86	Stanford	44†
1940	USC	Dean Cromwell	47	Stanford	28†
1941	USC	Dean Cromwell	81†	Indiana	50
1942	USC	Dean Cromwell	85†	Ohio St	44†
1943	USG	Dean Cromwell	46	California	39
1944	Illinois	Leo Johnson	79	Notre Dame	43
1945	Navy	E.J. Thomson	62	Illinois	48†
1946	Illinois	Leo Johnson	78	USC	42†
1947	Illinois	Leo Johnson	59†	USC	34†
1948	Minnesota	James Kelly	46	USC	41†
1949	USC	Jess Hill	55†	UCLA	31
1950	USC	Jess Hill	49†	Stanford	28
1951	USC	Jess Mortenson	56	Cornell	40
1952	USC	Jess Mortenson	66†	San Jose St	24†
1953	USC	Jess Mortenson	80	Illinois	41
1954	USC	Jess Mortenson	66†	Illinois	31†
1955	USC	Jess Mortenson	42	UCLA	34
1956	UCLA	Elvin Drake	55†	Kansas	51
1957	Villanova	James Elliott	47	California	32
1958	USC	Jess Mortenson	48†	Kansas	40†
1959	Kansas	Bill Easton	73	San Jose St	48
1960	Kansas	Bill Easton	50	USC	37
1961	USC	Jess Mortenson	65	Oregon	47
1962	Oregon	William Bowerman	85	Villanova	40†
1963	USC	Vern Wolfe	61	Stanford	42
1964	Oregon	William Bowerman	70	San Jose St	40
1965	Oregon	William Bowerman	32		
	USC	Vern Wolfe	32		
1966	UCLA	Jim Bush	81	BYU	33
1967	USC	Vern Wolfe	86	Oregon	40
1968	USC	Vern Wolfe	58	Washington St	57
1969	San Jose St	Bud Winter	48	Kansas	45

Men — DIVISION I *(Cont.)*

Year	Champion	Coach	Pts	Runner-Up	Pts
1970	BYU	Clarence Robison	35		
	Kansas	Bob Timmons	35		
	Oregon	William Bowerman	35		
1971	UCLA	Jim Bush	52	USC	41
1972	UCLA	Jim Bush	82*	USC	49
1973	UCLA	Jim Bush	56	Oregon	31
1974	Tennessee	Stan Huntsman	60	UCLA	56
1975	UTEP	Ted Banks	55	UCLA	42
1976	USC	Vern Wolfe	64	UTEP	44
1977	Arizona St	Senon Castillo	64	UTEP	50
1978	UCLA/UTEP	Jim Bush/Ted Banks	50		
1979	UTEP	Ted Banks	64	Villanova	48
1980	UTEP	Ted Banks	69	UCLA	46
1981	UTEP	Ted Banks	70	SMU	57
1982	UTEP	John Wedel	105	Tennessee	94
1983	SMU	Ted McLaughlin	104	Tennessee	102
1984	Oregon	Bill Dellinger	113	Washington St	94½
1985	Arkansas	John McDonnell	61	Washington St	46
1986	SMU	Ted McLaughlin	53	Washington St	52
1987	UCLA	Bob Larsen	81	Texas	28
1988	UCLA	Bob Larsen	82	Texas	41
1989	LSU	Pat Henry	53	Texas A&M	51
1990	LSU	Pat Henry	44	Arkansas	36
1991	Tennessee	Doug Brown	51	Washington St	42
1992	Arkansas	John McDonnell	60	Tennessee	46½
1993	Arkansas	John McDonnell	69	LSU/Ohio St	45
1994	Arkansas	John McDonnell	83*	UTEP	45
1995	Arkansas	John McDonnell	61½	UCLA	55
1996	Arkansas	John McDonnell	55	George Mason	40
1997	Arkansas	John McDonnell	55	Texas	42½
1998	Arkansas	John McDonnell	58½	Stanford	51
1999	Arkansas	John McDonnell	59	Stanford	52
2000	Stanford	Vin Lananna	72	Arkansas	59
2001	Tennessee	Bill Webb	50	TCU	49
2002	LSU	Pat Henry	64	Tennessee	57
2003	Arkansas	John McDonnell	59	Auburn	50
2004	Arkansas	John McDonnell	65½	Florida	49
2005	Arkansa	John McDonnell	109	Adams St	84
2006	Florida St	Bob Bramen	67	LSU	51
2007	Florida St	Bob Bramen	54	LSU	48

*Unofficial championship. †Fraction of a point.

DIVISION II

Year	Champion	Year	Champion	Year	Champion
1963	Md.–Eastern Shore	1978	CSU–L.A.	1994	St. Augustine's
1964	Fresno St	1979	Cal Poly–SLO	1995	St. Augustine's
1965	San Diego St	1980	Cal Poly–SLO	1996	Abilene Christian
1966	San Diego St	1981	Cal Poly–SLO	1997	Abilene Christian
1967	Long Beach St	1982	Abilene Christian	1998	St. Augustine's
1968	Cal Poly–SLO	1983	Abilene Christian	1999	Abilene Christian
1969	Cal Poly–SLO	1984	Abilene Christian	2000	Abilene Christian
1970	Cal Poly–SLO	1985	Abilene Christian	2001	St. Augustine's
1971	Kentucky St	1986	Abilene Christian	2002	Abilene Christian
1972	Eastern Michigan	1987	Abilene Christian	2003	Abilene Christian
1973	Norfolk St	1988	Abilene Christian	2004	Abilene Christian
1974	Eastern Illinois	1989	St. Augustine's	2005	Abilene Christian
	Norfolk St	1990	St. Augustine's	2006	Abilene Christian
1975	CSU–Northridge	1991	St. Augustine's	2007	Abilene Christian
1976	UC–Irvine	1992	St. Augustine's		
1977	CSU–Hayward	1993	St. Augustine's		

DIVISION III

Year	Champion	Year	Champion	Year	Champion
1974	Ashland	1979	Slippery Rock	1984	Glassboro St
1975	Southern–N. Orleans	1980	Glassboro St	1985	Lincoln (Pa.)
1976	Southern–N. Orleans	1981	Glassboro St	1986	Frostburg St
1977	Southern–N. Orleans	1982	Glassboro St	1987	Frostburg St
1978	Occidental	1983	Glassboro St	1988	UW–La Crosse

Men *(Cont.)*

DIVISION III *(CONT.)*

Year	Champion	Year	Champion	Year	Champion
1989	N. Central	1996	Lincoln (Pa.)	2003	UW-La Crosse
1990	Lincoln (Pa.)	1997	UW-La Crosse	2004	UW-La Crosse
1991	UW-La Crosse	1998	N. Central	2005	Lincoln (Pa.)
1992	UW-La Crosse	1999	Lincoln (Pa.)	2006	UW-La Crosse
1993	UW-La Crosse	2000	Nebraska Wesleyan	2007	UW-La Crosse
1994	N. Central	2001	UW-La Crosse		
1995	Lincoln (Pa.)	2002	UW-La Crosse		

Women

DIVISION I

Year	Champion	Coach	Pts	Runner-Up	Pts
1982	UCLA	Scott Chisam	153	Tennessee	126
1983	UCLA	Scott Chisam	116 1/2	Florida St	108
1984	Florida St	Gary Winckler	145	Tennessee	124
1985	Oregon	Tom Heinonen	52	Florida St/LSU	46
1986	Texas	Terry Crawford	65	Alabama	55
1987	LSU	Loren Seagrave	62	Alabama	53
1988	LSU	Loren Seagrave	61	UCLA	58
1989	LSU	Pat Henry	86	UCLA	47
1990	LSU	Pat Henry	53	UCLA	46
1991	LSU	Pat Henry	78	Texas	67
1992	LSU	Pat Henry	87	Florida	81
1993	LSU	Pat Henry	93	Wisconsin	44
1994	LSU	Pat Henry	86	Texas	43
1995	LSU	Pat Henry	69	UCLA	58
1996	LSU	Pat Henry	81	Texas	52
1997	LSU	Pat Henry	63	Texas	62
1998	Texas	Bev Kearney	60	UCLA	55
1999	Texas	Bev Kearney	62	UCLA	60
2000	LSU	Pat Henry	59	USC	56
2001	USC	Ron Allice	64	UCLA	55
2002	South Carolina	Curtis Frye	82	UCLA	72
2003	LSU	Pat Henry	64	UCLA	50
2004	UCLA	Jeanette Bolden	69	LSU	68
2005	Texas	Bev Kearney	55	CSU/South Carolina	48
2006	Auburn	Ralph Spry	57	USC	38.5
2007	Arizona St	Greg Kraft	60	LSU	53

DIVISION II

Year	Champion	Year	Champion	Year	Champion
1982	Cal Poly–SLO	1991	Cal Poly–SLO	2000	St. Augustine's
1983	Cal Poly–SLO	1992	Alabama A&M	2001	St. Augustine's
1984	Cal Poly–SLO	1993	Alabama A&M	2002	St. Augustine's
1985	Abilene Christian	1994	Alabama A&M	2003	Lincoln (Mo.)
1986	Abilene Christian	1995	Abilene Christian	2004	Lincoln (Mo.)
1987	Abilene Christian	1996	Abilene Christian	2005	Lincoln (Mo.)
1988	Abilene Christian	1997	St. Augustine's	2006	Lincoln (Mo.)
1989	Cal Poly–SLO	1998	Abilene Christian	2007	Lincoln (Mo.)
1990	Cal Poly–SLO	1999	Abilene Christian		

DIVISION III

Year	Champion	Year	Champion	Year	Champion
1982	Central (Iowa)	1991	UW-Oshkosh	2000	Lincoln (Pa.)
1983	UW-La Crosse	1992	Chris. Newport	2001	Wheaton (Mass.)
1984	UW-La Crosse	1993	Lincoln (Pa.)	2002	Wheaton (Mass.)
1985	Cortland	1994	Chris. Newport	2003	Wheaton (Mass.)
1986	UMass–Boston	1995	UW-Oshkosh	2004	UW-Oshkosh
1987	Chris. Newport	1996	UW-Oshkosh	2005	Wartburg
1988	Chris. Newport	1997	UW-Oshkosh	2006	UW-Oshkosh
1989	Chris. Newport	1998	Chris. Newport	2007	UW-Oshkosh
1990	UW-Oshkosh	1999	Lincoln (Pa.)		

Volleyball

Men

Year	Champion	Coach	Score	Runner-Up	Most Outstanding Player
1970	UCLA	Al Scates	3–0	Long Beach St	Dane Holtzman, UCLA
1971	UCLA	Al Scates	3–0	UC–Santa Barbara	K. Kilgore, UCLA/T. Bonynge, UCSB
1972	UCLA	Al Scates	3–2	San Diego St	Dick Irvin, UCLA
1973	San Diego St	Jack Henn	3–1	Long Beach St	Duncan McFarland, San Diego St
1974	UCLA	Al Scates	3–2	UC–Santa Barbara	Bob Leonard, UCLA
1975	UCLA	Al Scates	3–1	UC–Santa Barbara	John Bekins, UCLA
1976	UCLA	Al Scates	3–0	Pepperdine	Joe Mika, UCLA
1977	USC	Ernie Hix	3–1	Ohio St	Celso Kalache, USC
1978	Pepperdine	Marv Dunphy	3–2	UCLA	Mike Blanchard, Pepperdine
1979	UCLA	Al Scates	3–1	USC	Sinjin Smith, UCLA
1980	USC	Ernie Hix	3–1	UCLA	Dusty Dvorak, USC
1981	UCLA	Al Scates	3–2	USC	Karch Kiraly, UCLA
1982	UCLA	Al Scates	3–0	Penn St	Karch Kiraly, UCLA
1983	UCLA	Al Scates	3–0	Pepperdine	Ricci Luyties, UCLA
1984	UCLA	Al Scates	3–1	Pepperdine	Ricci Luyties, UCLA
1985	Pepperdine	Marv Dunphy	3–1	USC	Bob Ctvrtlik, Pepperdine
1986	Pepperdine	Rod Wilde	3–2	USC	Steve Friedman, Pepperdine
1987	UCLA	Al Scates	3–0	USC	Ozzie Volstad, UCLA
1988	USC	Bob Yoder	3–2	UC–Santa Barbara	Jen-Kai Liu, USC
1989	UCLA	Al Scates	3–1	Stanford	Matt Sonnichsen, UCLA
1990	USC	Jim McLaughlin	3–1	Long Beach St	Bryan Ivie, USC
1991	Long Beach St	Ray Ratelle	3–1	USC	Brent Hilliard, Long Beach St
1992	Pepperdine	Marv Dunphy	3–0	Stanford	Alon Grinberg, Pepperdine
1993	UCLA	Al Scates	3–0	CSU–Northridge	Mike Sealy/Jeff Nygaard, UCLA
1994	Penn St	Tom Peterson	3–2	UCLA	Ramon Hernandez, Penn St
1995	UCLA	Al Scates	3–0	Penn St	Jeff Nygaard, UCLA
1996	UCLA	Al Scates	3–2	Hawaii	Yuval Katz, Hawaii
1997	Stanford	Ruben Nieves	3–2	UCLA	Mike Lambert, Stanford
1998	UCLA	Al Scates	3–2	Pepperdine	George Roumain, Pepperdine
1999	BYU	Carl McGown	3–0	Long Beach St	Ossie Antonetti, BYU
2000	UCLA	Al Scates	3–0	Ohio St	Brandon Taliaferro, UCLA
2001	BYU	Carl McGown	3–0	UCLA	Mike Wall, BYU
2002	Hawaii	Mike Wilton	3–1	Pepperdine	Costas Theochardis, Hawaii
2003	Lewis	Dave Deuser	3–2	BYU	Gustavo Meyer, Lewis
2004	BYU	Tom Peterson	3–2	Long Beach St	Carlos Moreno, BYU
2005	Pepperdine	Marv Dunphy	3–2	UCLA	Sean Rooney, Pepperdine
2006	UCLA	Al Scates	3–0	Penn	Steve Klosterman, UCLA
2007	UC-Irvine	John Speraw	3–1	IPFW	Matt Webber, UC-Irvine

Women

DIVISION I

Year	Champion	Coach	Score	Runner-Up
1981	USC	Chuck Erbe	3–2	UCLA
1982	Hawaii	Dave Shoji	3–2	USC
1983	Hawaii	Dave Shoji	3–0	UCLA
1984	UCLA	Andy Banachowski	3–2	Stanford
1985	Pacific	John Dunning	3–1	Stanford
1986	Pacific	John Dunning	3–0	Nebraska
1987	Hawaii	Dave Shoji	3–1	Stanford
1988	Texas	Mick Haley	3–0	Hawaii
1989	Long Beach St	Brian Gimmillaro	3–0	Nebraska
1990	UCLA	Andy Banachowski	3–0	Pacific
1991	UCLA	Andy Banachowski	3–2	Long Beach St
1992	Stanford	Don Shaw	3–1	UCLA
1993	Long Beach St	Brian Gimmillaro	3–1	Penn St
1994	Stanford	Don Shaw	3–1	UCLA
1995	Nebraska	Terry Pettit	3–1	Texas
1996	Stanford	Don Shaw	3–0	Hawaii
1997	Stanford	Don Shaw	3–2	Penn St
1998	Long Beach St	Brian Gimmillaro	3–2	Penn St
1999	Penn St	Russ Rose	3–0	Stanford
2000	Nebraska	John Cook	3–2	Wisconsin
2001	Stanford	Don Shaw	3–0	Long Beach St
2002	USC	Mick Haley	3–1	Stanford
2003	USC	Mick Haley	3–1	Florida
2004	Stanford	Don Shaw	3-0	Minnesota
2005	Washington	Jim McLaughlin	3-0	Nebraska
2006	Nebraska	John Cook	3-1	Stanford

Women *(Cont.)*

DIVISION II

Year	Champion	Year	Champion	Year	Champion
1981	CSU–Sacramento	1990	West Texas A&M	1999	BYU–Hawaii
1982	UC–Riverside	1991	West Texas A&M	2000	Hawaii Pacific
1983	CSU–Northridge	1992	Portland St	2001	Barry
1984	Portland St	1993	Northern Michigan	2002	BYU–Hawaii
1985	Portland St	1994	Northern Michigan	2003	N. Alabama
1986	UC–Riverside	1995	Barry	2004	Truman St
1987	CSU–Northridge	1996	Nebraska–Omaha	2005	Grand Valley
1988	Portland St	1997	West Texas A&M	2006	Tampa
1989	CSU–Bakersfield	1998	Hawaii Pacific		

DIVISION III

Year	Champion	Year	Champion	Year	Champion	Year	Champion
1981	UC–San Diego	1988	UC–San Diego	1995	Washington (Mo.)	2002	UW–Whitewater
1982	La Verne	1989	Washington (Mo.)	1996	Washington (Mo.)	2003	Washington (Mo.)
1983	Elmhurst	1990	UC–San Diego	1997	UC–San Diego	2004	Juniata
1984	UC–San Diego	1991	Washington (Mo.)	1998	Central (Iowa)	2005	UW–Whitewater
1985	Elmhurst	1992	Washington (Mo.)	1999	Central (Iowa)	2006	Juniata
1986	UC–San Diego	1993	Washington (Mo.)	2000	Central (Iowa)		
1987	UC–San Diego	1994	Washington (Mo.)	2001	La Verne		

Water Polo

Men

Year	Champion	Coach	Score	Runner-Up
1969	UCLA	Bob Horn	5–2	California
1970	UC–Irvine	Ed Newland	7–6 (3 OT)	UCLA
1971	UCLA	Bob Horn	5–3	San Jose St
1972	UCLA	Bob Horn	10–5	UC–Irvine
1973	California	Pete Cutino	8–4	UC–Irvine
1974	California	Pete Cutino	7–6	UC–Irvine
1975	California	Pete Cutino	9–8	UC–Irvine
1976	Stanford	Art Lambert	13–12	UCLA
1977	California	Pete Cutino	8–6	UC–Irvine
1978	Stanford	Dante Dettamanti	7–6 (3 OT)	California
1979	UC–Santa Barbara	Pete Snyder	11–3	UCLA
1980	Stanford	Dante Dettamanti	8–6	California
1981	Stanford	Dante Dettamanti	17–6	Long Beach St
1982	UC–Irvine	Ed Newland	7–4	Stanford
1983	California	Pete Cutino	10–7	USC
1984	California	Pete Cutino	9–8	Stanford
1985	Stanford	Dante Dettamanti	12–11 (2 OT)	UC–Irvine
1986	Stanford	Dante Dettamanti	9–6	California
1987	California	Pete Cutino	9–8 (OT)	USC
1988	California	Pete Cutino	14–11	UCLA
1989	UC–Irvine	Ed Newland	9–8	California
1990	California	Steve Heaston	8–7	Stanford
1991	California	Steve Heaston	7–6	UCLA
1992	California	Steve Heaston	12–11	Stanford
1993	Stanford	Dante Dettamanti	11–9	USC
1994	Stanford	Dante Dettamanti	14–10	USC
1995	UCLA	Guy Baker	10–8	California
1996	UCLA	Guy Baker	8–7	USC
1997	Pepperdine	Terry Schroeder	8–7 (OT)	USC
1998	USC	John Williams	9–8 (2 OT)	Stanford
1999	UCLA	Guy Baker	6–5	Stanford
2000	UCLA	Guy Baker/Adam Krikorian	11–2	UC–San Diego
2001	Stanford	Dante Dettamanti	8–5	UCLA
2002	Stanford	John Vargas	7–6	California
2003	USC	Jovan Vavic	9–7	Stanford
2004	UCLA	Adam Krikorian	10–9	Stanford
2005	USC	Jovan Vavic	3–2	Stanford
2006	California	Kirk Everist	7–6	USC

Women

Year	Champion	Coach	Score	Runner-Up
2001	UCLA	Adam Krikorian	5–4	Stanford
2002	Stanford	John Tanner	8–4	UCLA
2003	UCLA	Adam Krikorian	4–3	Stanford
2004	USC	Jovan Vavic	10–8	Loyola-Marymount
2005	UCLA	Adam Krikorian	3–2	Stanford
2006	UCLA	Adam Krikorian	9–8	USC
2007	UCLA	Adam Krikorian	5–4	Stanford

Wrestling

DIVISION I

Year	Champion	Coach	Pts	Runner-Up	Pts	Most Outstanding Wrestler
1928	Oklahoma St*	E.C. Gallagher				
1929	Oklahoma St	E.C. Gallagher	26	Michigan	18	
1930	Oklahoma St*	E.C. Gallagher	27	Illinois	14	
1931	Oklahoma St*	E.C. Gallagher		Michigan		
1932	Indiana*	W.H. Thom		Oklahoma St		Edwin Belshaw, Indiana
1933	OK St*/Iowa St*	E. Gallagher/H. Otopalik				A. Kelley, OK St/P. Johnson, Harv
1934	Oklahoma St	E.C. Gallagher	29	Indiana	19	Ben Bishop, Lehigh
1935	Oklahoma St	E.C. Gallagher	36	Oklahoma	18	Ross Flood, Oklahoma St
1936	Oklahoma	Paul Keen	14	Central St/ OK St	10	Wayne Martin, Oklahoma
1937	Oklahoma St	E.C. Gallagher	31	Oklahoma	13	Stanley Henson, Oklahoma St
1938	Oklahoma St	E.C. Gallagher	19	Illinois	15	Joe McDaniels, Oklahoma St
1939	Oklahoma St	E.C. Gallagher	33	Lehigh	12	Dale Hanson, Minnesota
1940	Oklahoma St	E.C. Gallagher	24	Indiana	14	Don Nichols, Michigan
1941	Oklahoma St	Art Griffith	37	Michigan St	26	Al Whitehurst, Oklahoma St
1942	Oklahoma St	Art Griffith	31	Michigan St	26	David Arndt, Oklahoma St
1946	Oklahoma St	Art Griffith	25	Northern Iowa	24	Gerald Leeman, Northern Iowa
1947	Cornell	Paul Scott	32	Northern Iowa	19	William Koll, Northern Iowa
1948	Oklahoma St	Art Griffith	33	Michigan St	28	William Koll, Northern Iowa
1949	Oklahoma St	Art Griffith	32	Northern Iowa	27	Charles Hetrick, Oklahoma St
1950	Northern Iowa	David McCuskey	30	Purdue	16	Anthony Gizoni, Waynesburg
1951	Oklahoma	Port Robertson	24	Oklahoma St	23	Walter Romanowski, Cornell
1952	Oklahoma	Port Robertson	22	Northern Iowa	21	Tommy Evans, Oklahoma
1953	Penn St	Charles Speidel	21	Oklahoma	15	Frank Bettucci, Cornell
1954	Oklahoma St	Art Griffith	32	Pittsburgh	17	Tommy Evans, Oklahoma
1955	Oklahoma St	Art Griffith	40	Penn St	31	Edward Eichelberger, Lehigh
1956	Oklahoma St	Art Griffith	65	Oklahoma	62	Dan Hodge, Oklahoma
1957	Oklahoma	Port Robertson	73	Pittsburgh	66	Dan Hodge, Oklahoma
1958	Oklahoma St	Myron Roderick	77	Iowa St	62	Dick Delgado, Oklahoma
1959	Oklahoma St	Myron Roderick	73	Iowa St	51	Ron Gray, Iowa St
1960	Oklahoma	Thomas Evans	59	Iowa St	40	Dave Auble, Cornell
1961	Oklahoma St	Myron Roderick	82	Oklahoma	63	E. Gray Simons, Lock Haven
1962	Oklahoma St	Myron Roderick	82	Oklahoma	45	E. Gray Simons, Lock Haven
1963	Oklahoma	Thomas Evans	48	Iowa St	45	Mickey Martin, Oklahoma
1964	Oklahoma St	Myron Roderick	87	Oklahoma	58	Dean Lahr, Colorado
1965	Iowa St	Harold Nichols	87	Oklahoma St	86	Yojiro Uetake, Oklahoma St
1966	Oklahoma St	Myron Roderick	79	Iowa St	70	Yojiro Uetake, Oklahoma St
1967	Michigan St	Grady Peninger	74	Michigan	63	Rich Sanders, Portland St
1968	Oklahoma St	Myron Roderick	81	Iowa St	78	Dwayne Keller, Oklahoma St
1969	Iowa St	Harold Nichols	104	Oklahoma	69	Dan Gable, Iowa St
1970	Iowa St	Harold Nichols	99	Michigan St	84	Larry Owings, Washington
1971	Oklahoma St	Tommy Chesbro	94	Iowa St	66	Darrell Keller, Oklahoma St
1972	Iowa St	Harold Nichols	103	Michigan St	72½	Wade Schalles, Clarion
1973	Iowa St	Harold Nichols	85	Oregon St	72½	Greg Strobel, Oregon St
1974	Oklahoma	Stan Abel	69½	Michigan	67	Floyd Hitchcock, Bloomsburg
1975	Iowa	Gary Kurdelmeier	102	Oklahoma	77	Mike Frick, Lehigh
1976	Iowa	Gary Kurdelmeier	123½	Iowa St	85¾	Chuck Yagla, Iowa
1977	Iowa St	Harold Nichols	95½	Oklahoma St	88¾	Nick Gallo, Hofstra
1978	Iowa	Dan Gable	94½	Iowa St	94	Mark Churella, Michigan
1979	Iowa	Dan Gable	122½	Iowa St	88	Bruce Kinseth, Iowa
1980	Iowa	Dan Gable	110¾	Oklahoma St	87	Howard Harris, Oregon St
1981	Iowa	Dan Gable	129¾	Oklahoma	100¼	Gene Mills, Syracuse

DIVISION I (Cont.)

Year	Champion	Coach	Pts	Runner-Up	Pts	Most Outstanding Wrestler
1982	Iowa	Dan Gable	131¾	Iowa St	111	Mark Schultz, Oklahoma
1983	Iowa	Dan Gable	155	Oklahoma St	102	Mike Sheets, Oklahoma St
1984	Iowa	Dan Gable	123¾	Oklahoma St	98	Jim Zalesky, Iowa
1985	Iowa	Dan Gable	145¼	Oklahoma	98½	Barry Davis, Iowa
1986	Iowa	Dan Gable	158	Oklahoma	84¼	Marty Kistler, Iowa
1987	Iowa St	Jim Gibbons	133	Iowa	108	John Smith, Oklahoma St
1988	Arizona St	Bobby Douglas	93	Iowa	85½	Scott Turner, N.Carolina St
1989	Oklahoma St	Joe Seay	91¼	Arizona St	70½	Tim Krieger, Iowa St
1990	Oklahoma St	Joe Seay	117¾	Arizona St	104¾	Chris Barnes, Oklahoma St
1991	Iowa	Dan Gable	157	Oklahoma St	108¾	Jeff Prescott, Penn St
1992	Iowa	Dan Gable	149	Oklahoma St	100½	Tom Brands, Iowa
1993	Iowa	Dan Gable	*123¾	Penn St	87½	Terry Steiner, Iowa
1994	Oklahoma St	John Smith	94¾	Iowa	76½	Pat Smith, Oklahoma St
1995	Iowa	Dan Gable	134	Oregon St	77½	T.J. Jaworsky, North Carolina
1996	Iowa	Dan Gable	122½	Iowa St	78½	Les Gutches, Oregon St
1997	Iowa	Dan Gable	170	Oklahoma St	113½	Lincoln McIlravy, Iowa
1998	Iowa	Jim Zalesky	115	Minnesota	102	Joe Williams, Iowa
1999	Iowa	Jim Zalesky	100½	Minnesota	98½	Cael Sanderson, Iowa St
2000	Iowa	Jim Zalesky	116	Iowa St	109½	Cael Sanderson, Iowa St
2001	Minnesota	J Robinson	138½	Iowa	125½	Cael Sanderson, Iowa St
2002	Minnesota	J Robinson	126½	Iowa St	104	Cael Sanderson, Iowa St
2003	Oklahoma St	John Smith	*143	Minnesota	104½	Eric Larkin, Arizona St
2004	Oklahoma St	John Smith	123½	Iowa	82	Jesse Jantzen, Harvard
2005	Oklahoma	John Smith	150	Michigan	83	Ryan Bertin, Michigan
2006	Oklahoma	John Smith	122½	Minnesota	84	Ben Askren, Missouri
2007	Minnesota	J Robinson	98	Iowa St	88½	Corey Murphy, Thiel College

*Unofficial champions.

DIVISION II

Year	Champion	Year	Champion	Year	Champion
1963	Western St (Colo.)	1979	CSU–Bakersfield	1995	Central Oklahoma
1964	Western St (Colo.)	1980	CSU–Bakersfield	1996	Pitt–Johnstown
1965	Mankato St	1981	CSU–Bakersfield	1997	San Francisco St
1966	Cal Poly–SLO	1982	CSU–Bakersfield	1998	North Dakota St
1967	Portland St	1983	CSU–Bakersfield	1999	Pittsburgh–Johnstown
1968	Cal Poly–SLO	1984	SIU–Edwardsville	2000	North Dakota St
1969	Cal Poly–SLO	1985	SIU–Edwardsville	2001	North Dakota St
1970	Cal Poly–SLO	1986	SIU–Edwardsville	2002	Central Oklahoma
1971	Cal Poly–SLO	1987	CSU–Bakersfield	2003	Central Oklahoma
1972	Cal Poly–SLO	1988	North Dakota St	2004	Nebraska–Omaha
1973	Cal Poly–SLO	1989	Portland St	2005	Omaha
1974	Cal Poly–SLO	1990	Portland St	2006	Nebraska–Omaha
1975	Northern Iowa	1991	Nebraska–Omaha	2007	Central Oklahoma
1976	CSU–Bakersfield	1992	Central Oklahoma		
1977	CSU–Bakersfield	1993	Central Oklahoma		
1978	Northern Iowa	1994	Central Oklahoma		

DIVISION III

Year	Champion	Year	Champion	Year	Champion
1974	Wilkes	1986	Montclair St	1998	Augsburg
1975	John Carroll	1987	Trenton St	1999	Wartburg
1976	Montclair St	1988	St. Lawrence	2000	Augsburg
1977	Brockport St	1989	Ithaca	2001	Augsburg
1978	Buffalo	1990	Ithaca	2002	Augsburg
1979	Trenton St	1991	Augsburg	2003	Wartburg
1980	Brockport St	1992	Brockport	2004	Wartburg
1981	Trenton St	1993	Augsburg	2005	Augsburg
1982	Brockport St	1994	Ithaca	2006	Wartburg
1983	Brockport St	1995	Augsburg	2007	Augsburg
1984	Trenton St	1996	Wartburg		
1985	Trenton St	1997	Augsburg		

SWIMMING
Men

Event	Time	Record Holder	Date
50-yard freestyle	18.69	Cesar Cielo, Auburn	3-15-07
100-yard freestyle	41.49	Duje Draganja, California	3-26-05
200-yard freestyle	1:33.03	Matt Biondi, California	4-3-87
500-yard freestyle	4:08.75	Tom Dolan, Michigan	3-23-95
1,650-yard freestyle	14:26.62	Chris Thompson, Michigan	3-24-01
100-yard backstroke	44.83	Albert Subirats, Arizona	3-15-07
200-yard backstroke	1:38.37	Ryan Lochete, Florida	3-26-05
100-yard breaststroke	52.32	Jeremy Linn, Tennessee	3-28-97
200-yard breaststroke	1:52.62	Brendan Hansen, Texas	3-29-03
100-yard butterfly	44.57	Albert Subirats, Arizona	3-15-07
200-yard butterfly	1:41.78	Melvin Stewart, Tennessee	3-30-91
200-yard individual medley	1:41.71	Ryan Lochte, Florida	3-24-05
400-yard individual medley	3:38.18	Tom Dolan, Michigan	3-24-95

Women

Event	Time	Record Holder	Date
50-yard freestyle	21.69	Maritza Correia, Georgia	3-21-02
100-yard freestyle	47.24	Kara Lynn Joyce, Georgia	3-15-07
200-yard freestyle	1:43.08	Martina Moravcova, SMU	3-28-97
500-yard freestyle	4:34.39	Janet Evans, Stanford	3-15-90
1,650-yard freestyle	15:39.14	Janet Evans, Stanford	3-17-90
100-yard backstroke	49.97	Natalie Coughlin, California	3-22-02
200-yard backstroke	1:49.52	Natalie Coughlin, California	3-22-02
100-yard breaststroke	59.05	Kristy Kowal, Georgia	3-20-98
200-yard breaststroke	2:07.36	Tara Kirk, Stanford	3-22-02
100-yard butterfly	50.01	Natalie Coughlin, California	3-22-02
200-yard butterfly	1:53.02	Elaine Breeden, Stanford	3-15-07
200-yard individual medley	1:53.91	Maggie Bowen, Auburn	3-21-02
400-yard individual medley	4:02.28	Summer Sanders, Stanford	3-20-92

INDOOR TRACK AND FIELD
Men

Event	Mark	Record Holder	Date
55-meter dash	6.00	Lee McRae, Pittsburgh	3-14-86
60-meter dash	6.52	Marcus Brunson, Arizona St	3-5-99
55-meter hurdles	7.07	Allen Johnson, North Carolina	3-14-62
60-meter hurdles	7.52	Terrence Trammell, South Carolina	3-5-99
200-meter dash	20.10	Wallace Spearmon, Arkansas	3-12-05
400-meter dash	44.57	Kerron Clement, Florida	3-12-05
800-meter run	1:45.33	Patrick Nduwimana, Arizona	3-10-01
Mile run	3:55.33	Kevin Sullivan, Michigan	3-11-95
3,000-meter run	7:46.03	Adam Goucher, Colorado	3-14-98
5,000-meter run	13:28.93	Alistair Cragg, Arkansas	3-14-03
High jump	7 ft 9¼ in	Hollis Conway, SW Louisiana	3-11-89
Pole vault	19 ft 2¼ in	Jacob Davis, Texas	3-6-99
Long jump	27 ft 10 in	Carl Lewis, Houston	3-13-81
Triple jump	56 ft 9½ in	Keith Connor, SMU	3-13-81
Shot put	70 ft 6¼ in	Carl Myerscough, Nebraska	3-15-03
35-pound weight throw	78 ft 9¾ in	Libor Charfreitag, SMU	3-9-01

Women

Event	Mark	Record Holder	Date
55-meter dash	6.56	Gwen Torrence, Georgia	3-14-87
60-meter dash	7.13	Angela Williams, USC	3-9-02
55-meter hurdles	7.39	Tiffany Lott, BYU	3-7-97
60-meter hurdles	7.90	Perdita Felicien, Illinois	3-8-02
200-meter dash	22.43	Veronica Campbell, Arkansas	3-12-04
400-meter dash	50.82	Sanya Richards, Texas	3-13-04
800-meter run	2:01.77	Hazel Clark, Florida	3-6-99

INDOOR TRACK AND FIELD *(Cont.)*

Women

Event	Mark	Record Holder	Date
Mile run	4:30.63	Suzy Favor, Wisconsin	3-11-89
3,000-meter run	8:49.18	Kim Smith, Providence	3-13-04
5,000-meter run	15:14.18	Kim Smith, Providence	3-13-04
High jump	6 ft 5½ in	Four recordholders	—
Pole vault	14 ft 10 ¼ in	Amy Linnen, Arizona	3-13-02
Long jump	22 ft 4¼ in	Elva Goulbourne, Auburn	3-14-03
Triple jump	46 ft 9 in	Suzette Lee, LSU	3-8-97
Shot put	62 ft 10 in	Laura Gerraughty, North Carolina	3-13-04
20-pound weight throw	79 ft 3³⁄₄ in	Candice Scott, Florida	3-11-05

OUTDOOR TRACK AND FIELD

Men

Event	Mark	Record Holder	Date
100-meter dash	9.92	Ato Bolden, UCLA	6-2-96
200-meter dash	19.87	Lorenzo Daniel, Mississippi St	6-3-88
		John Capel, Florida	6-5-99
400-meter dash	44.00	Quincy Watts, USC	6-6-92
800-meter run	1:44.70	Mark Everett, Florida	6-1-90
1,500-meter run	3:35.30	Sydney Maree, Villanova	6-6-81
3,000-meter steeplechase	8:12.39	Henry Rono, Washington St	6-1-78
5,000-meter run	13:20.63	Sydney Maree, Villanova	6-2-79
10,000-meter run	28:01.30	Suleiman Nyambui, UTEP	6-1-79
110-meter high hurdles	13.21	Aries Merit, Tennessee	6-9-06
400-meter intermediate hurdles	47.56	Kerron Clement, Florida	5-28-05
High jump	7 ft 9¾ in	Hollis Conway, SW Louisiana	6-3-89
Pole vault	19 ft 1 in	Lawrence Johnson, Tennessee	5-29-96
Long jump	28 ft 0 in	Erick Walder, Arkansas	6-3-93
Triple jump	57 ft 7¾ in	Keith Connor, SMU	6-5-82
Shot put	72 ft 2¼ in	John Godina, UCLA	6-3-95
Discus throw	222 ft 0 in	Hannes Hopley, SMU	6-5-92
Hammer throw	265 ft 3 in	Balazs Kiss, USC	5-31-96
Javelin throw (new javelin)	268 ft 7 in	Esko Mikkola, Arizona	6-3-98
Decathlon (new javelin)	8,276 pts	Brian Brophy, Tennessee	6-5/6-92

Women

Event	Mark	Record Holder	Date
100-meter dash	10.78	Dawn Sowell, LSU	6-3-89
200-meter dash	22.04	Dawn Sowell, LSU	6-2-89
400-meter dash	50.10	Monique Henderson, UCLA	6-11-05
800-meter run	1:59.11	Suzy Favor, Wisconsin	6-1-90
1,500-meter run	4:06.75	Tiffany McWilliams, Mississippi St	6-14-03
3,000-meter run	8:47.35	Vicki Huber, Villanova	6-3-88
5,000-meter run	15:24.06	Lauren Fleshman, Stanford	6-14-03
10,000-meter run	32:28.57	Sylvia Mosqueda, Cal St	6-1-88
100-meter hurdles	12.48	Virginia Powell, USC	6-9-06
400-meter hurdles	53.54	Shenna Johnson, UCLA	6-12-04
High jump	6 ft 5 in	Amy Acuff, UCLA	6-3-95
Pole vault	14 ft 5½ in	Becky Holiday, Oregon St	6-14-03
Long jump	22 ft 9¼ in	Sheila Echols, LSU	6-5-87
Triple jump	46 ft 2in	Candice Bauchman, UCLA	6-11-05
Shot put	61 ft 2¼ in	Tressa Thompson, Nebraska	6-4-98
Discus throw	210 ft 10 in	Sheila Sua, UCLA	6-4-99
Hammer throw	229 ft 0 in	Candice Scott, Florida	6-14-03
Javelin throw (new javelin)	202 ft 10 in	Irina Kharun, Cal Poly	6-13-03
Heptathlon (new javelin)	6,061 pts	Austra Skujyte	5-30/31-02

Olympics

Beijing prepares
to host the 2008
Summer Olympics

Fast Track to China

In Beijing, all systems are go to host next year's Olympics, but concerns over air quality, labor laws, and political unrest have already translated into fireworks for the 2008 Games

BY MERRELL NODEN

FROM THE MOMENT BEIJING was selected to host the 2008 Summer Olympics—way back in July of 2001—anyone with even a passing knowledge of Olympic history knew that these Games would be among the most controversial ever held. In the six years that have passed, the decision to hold the Games in China's capital city has become a glass-half-full, glass-half-empty test—though both sides agree that there's a very good chance the water in the glass is going to be polluted.

Olympic optimists see the Games as a catalyst for the democratization of China, a tool for persuading the world's largest country that if it really wants to join the First World, it must do more than pay lip service to democracy and human rights. Pessimists see something entirely different: They see the Games as validation of a brutal country that has little intention of reforming and will return to its repressive ways as soon as the Olympic torch has been passed. Amnesty International called on the International Olympic Committee to monitor Beijing's preparations closely: "The IOC cannot want an Olympics that is tainted with human rights abuses—whether fami-

lies forcibly evicted from their homes to make way for sports arenas or growing numbers of peaceful activists held under house arrest," said Catherine Baber, Amnesty's deputy Asia-Pacific director.

No matter which side you took, you could find evidence to support your view: PlayFair 2008, a watchdog arm of the International Trade Union Confederation, denounced Lekit Stationary, a Beijing-based company commissioned to make official Olympic paper products, for violating workers' rights: by employing 12- and 13-year-old children and paying them just $2.50 a day, making overtime mandatory, and denying maternity leave. But those arguing that the Games will ultimately do more good than harm pointed to the fact that the Beijing Organizing Committee for the Olympic Games (BOCOG) officials shut down the company once the abuses were proven.

Whichever view one takes, there is no doubt that the Chinese leadership, including President Hu Jintao, regards the Games as an aspiring nation's grand Coming Out Party. While organizing committees in Vancouver and London toiled steadily on in their preparations for the Winter Games of 2010 and the Summer Games of 2012, respectively, President Hu Jintao and his

FENG LI/GETTY IMAGES

government showed how determined they were for Beijing to make a good impression on the world. They took extraordinary measures to make sure all went according to plan—even when compared to the feverish activity that usually accompanies Olympic preparations. They weren't just talking about the weather: They were actually doing something about it. This summer they were busy shooting rockets full of silver iodide into the sky in hopes of discovering the best way to disperse clouds and guarantee a sunny, dry Games. To no one's surprise, all venues were on track to be completed by the end of 2007.

"From what we have seen so far, the preparations for Beijing 2008 are truly impressive in every regard," said Jacques Rogge, the president of the International Olympic Committee. "I don't think we have ever seen preparations on this scale."

Ah, say the pessimists, how hard can it be to stay on schedule if you are willing to use your people for slave labor? Human rights

Beijing's "Bird's Nest" National stadium was completed in 2007, right on schedule.

campaigners had no shortage of abuses to point to, including the forced removal of some 1.5 million residents, whose homes were cleared to make way for new construction without, it was claimed, adequate compensation. Yet concessions were made to economic reality in a country where factory workers earn as little as $91 a month: Of the 7 million tickets available to the public, about 75 percent will go to Chinese residents. And 58 percent of all tickets will cost $12 or less. Some, reserved for students, will even go for as little as $1.

There were the usual worries that terrorists would try to hijack the Games. One guesses that no nation will guard against that possibility more determinedly than the Chinese, who named a special police force to counter this threat. But just as alarming was the possibility that the host country's own lax health and environmental standards would do at least as much harm. In 2007 we

were given numerous reminders that this was a real concern. In early summer tubes of counterfeit Colgate toothpaste were found to contain diethylene glycol, a poisonous chemical usually found in anti-freeze. In August the same chemical was found in another Chinese toothpaste popular with hotel chains, and it too had to be recalled. Toy giant Mattel was also forced to recall millions of toys manufactured in China because they contained lead paint (Mattel later publicly apologized to the Chinese, saying the recall was the company's fault).

With the specter of a bird flu epidemic still fresh in people's minds, Chinese authorities were eager to allay any such fears. BOCOG organizers promised to track all food electronically, from the field to the tables in the Olympic Village, and even then, planned to use white mice to test the food 24 hours before it is to be given to the athletes. Despite this, many visiting Olympic teams planned simply to bring and prepare their own food.

To ready the relatively isolated Chinese for an avalanche of foreign visitors, the government launched a broad program of drills and etiquette lessons designed to make the Chinese people more presentable to the 550,000 visitors and 22,000 credentialed

One of the athletes' major concerns involves Beijing's poor air quality, which may hamper performances.

members of the media they expect. "The Olympic Games is not simply a matter of competitive sports—it is also a question of raising the quality of the people," explained Zhang Faquiang, vice chair of the Chinese Olympic Committee.

Among the biggest concerns were cherished local customs such as spitting, swearing, and queue-jumping. An administrative body known as the Beijing Civilization Office spent 1,700 hours studying the spitting habits of its citizens. They posted reminders and had volunteers pass out little spit bags to those who might be having trouble breaking the habit. Repeat offenders were fined about $33. Crazy as all that sounds, it seems to have worked. Officials announced proudly that the incidence of public expectoration had dropped from 8.4 percent (percent of what, exactly?) in 2005 to just 4.9 percent in 2007.

And since Beijingers are known for their impatience while waiting in lines, officials designated the 11th of every month as "queuing day," when they were expected to practice waiting in orderly lines. They also are known for their loud, colorful swearing at soccer matches, and so were taught polite chants to replace what is known as "Beijing swearing." Stray dogs and cats were removed from the streets, and everyone—with the possible exception of dogs and cats—is being expected to learn some English.

The city's horrendous pollution may not be remedied quite so easily. More than a year before the Opening Ceremonies, a number of refineries and steel mills had either been shut down or moved out of the city. Another plan was to close the city to cars with odd numbered license plates for two-day stretches and to cars with even-numbered ones for others. During the 17 days the Games run, roughly a third of the city's 3.3 million cars will be forced off the road.

Even then, Rogge, who is a doctor as well as president of the International Olympic Committee, admitted that the IOC would not rule out the possibility of moving some endurance events to dates outside the Games' scheduled 17 days. "Sports with short durations would not be a problem," Rogge said, "but endurance sports like cycling are examples of competitions that might be postponed or delayed."

No one who's watched the speedy rise of Chinese athletes—in swimming, diving, gymnastics, and figure skating, to name just a few sports—can doubt how seriously this huge nation is taking these Olympics, both on and off the playing field. The budget for new buildings and improving public transportation—including 132 kilometers of new track—is $39 billion.

In a refreshing contrast to Athens' preparations four years ago, when it seemed quite possible that important facilities would not be completed in time for the Opening Ceremonies, Beijing's preparations look to be right on schedule. The main Olympic Stadium, called National Stadium but nicknamed the Bird's Nest for its design of interwoven twig-like steel cables, is complete. Wukesong Stadium, the baseball venue, was finished in time for a tournament in August 2007 (even if the official BOCOG website, which refers to its three baseball "courts," needed some further fine-tuning.)

The greatest test for the BOCOG will be showing restraint during the protests that are sure to come. When the group Reporters Without Borders staged a protest during the one-year countdown festivities, police detained even the reporters who were covering the event. That same week four pro-Tibet protesters managed to hang a banner on the Great Wall, which played off the Games' motto, reading "One World, One Dream: Free Tibet." They were nabbed and deposited in Hong Kong. That sort of snap reaction will hardly make a good impression on Olympic tourists.

One of the biggest headaches for Chinese authorities is sure to be the Torch Parade, which will be much harder to police. There were objections to its going through Tibet and the mostly Muslim province of Xinjiang. Taiwan had originally agreed to participate in the parade, but only if its leg was sandwiched between two sovereign countries, implying its own independence from mainland China. When the proposed route was announced in April and Taiwanese officials saw that they were to hand off to Hong Kong, they balked at taking part.

The Games even led to finger-pointing by celebrities. On March 27, Mia Farrow published in the *Wall Street Journal* an op-ed piece bearing the headline "The 'Genocide Olympics'." The piece criticized China's unwavering support for the Sudanese government, blasting the Chinese for selling weapons to Khartoum and noting that the state-owned China National Petroleum Corporation, which is Sudan's biggest customer, is also an official partner of the Games. Among Farrow's targets were not only corporate sponsors, such as Johnson & Johnson, Coca-Cola, and McDonalds, but also the film director Steven Spielberg, whom the Chinese had recruited to help stage its Opening Ceremonies. "Does Mr. Spielberg really want to go down in history as the Leni Riefenstahl of the Beijing Games?" she asked, referring to the great filmmaker forever linked to Hitler's Berlin Games of 1936.

The question clearly got to Spielberg. In May he sent a later to Hu Jintao threatening

AP PHOTO/KIRSTY WIGGLESWORTH

One question remains unanswered: How will the Chinese authorities deal with attempts at political protests during the Games?

The key difference between the two bids seemed to be the presence in Guatemala City of Russian president Vladimir Putin, who personally lobbied IOC members and vowed to invest $12 billion in capital improvements to link the coastal city with the Caucasus Mountains nearby. "The Games will help Russia's transition as a young democracy," said Sochi's bid chief, Dmitry Chernyshenko.

That sounds great but awfully familiar. Political rehabilitation seems to be the goal of every Olympics held in a controversial city, and it often seems to work, at least within reason. It's hard to imagine it won't have some positive effect on the Chinese.

To rally the people and demonstrate just how ready they will be, the nation staged a huge celebration exactly one year before the Opening Ceremonies. Knowing that staging a truly great Games will require not only hard work and a certain degree of forbearance and flexibility, but luck too, they invoked the lucky number 8 as often as they could in their planning. Thus the festivities began at 8:08 p.m. on August 8, 2007 — precisely one year before the start of the Opening Ceremonies. Atop the Great Wall, 999 schoolchildren played musical instruments, and a huge celebration was staged in Tiananemen Square, with fireworks, pop music, and dancing. China does indeed seem eager and ready to play host to the world.

The Olympics have a history of surprising us, in ways that have been both horrific and deeply moving. We should not be at all surprised if these, the most nervously anticipated Games in years, follow in that tradition.

to withdraw from the project if China didn't take a harder line against Khartoum, and in July was still talking seriously about resigning his post.

As the Opening Ceremonies draw closer, IOC officials are going to have to monitor the political climate carefully. There was other Olympic business, but it paled in comparison to the approach of these sure-to-be-controversial Games. Even as it was announced that the Turin Games had lost some $32 million—believed to be the first Games to run a deficit in decades—the IOC was announcing the creation of a sort of "junior" Olympics, featuring 3,500 athletes from age 14 to 18. The first staging is to take place in 2010. It marked the first time the IOC had created a whole new event since the addition of the Winter Games in 1924.

The other important item of IOC business was the selection of a city to host the Winter Olympics of 2014. Competition was fierce. Sochi, a resort city of 325,000 on the northeastern shore of the Black Sea, became the first Russian city ever to host the Winter Games (only Moscow has hosted the Summer) when it edged Pyeongchang, South Korea, by just four votes in the second round. The secret vote, taken in Guatemala City, set off the usual jubilant celebrations in Sochi and gloom in Pyeonchang, which, for the second time, led the first round of voting but failed to win the big prize.

2006 Winter Games

BIATHLON

Men | **Women**

10 KILOMETERS

1...........Sven Fisher, Germany — 24:11.6
2..........Halvard Hanevold, Norway — 24:19.8
3..........Frode Andresen, Norway — 24:31.3

7.5 KILOMETERS

1...........Florence Baverel-Robert, France — 22:31.4
2..........Anna Carin Olofsson, Sweden — 22:33.8
3..........Lilia Efremova, Ukraine — 22:38.0

12.5 KILOMETERS PURSUIT

1...........Vincent Defrasne, France — 35:20.2
2..........Ole Einar Bjoerndalen, Norway — 35:22.9
3..........Sven Fisher, Germany — 35:35.8

10 KILOMETERS PURSUIT

1...........Kati Wilhelm, Germany — 36:43.6
2..........Martina Glagow, Germany — 37:57.2
3..........Albina Akhatova, Russia — 38:05.0

15 KILOMETERS

1...........Michael Gries, Germany — 47:20.0
2..........Tomasz Sikora, Poland — 47:26.3
3..........Ole Einar Bjoerndalen, Norway — 47:32.3

12.5 KILOMETERS

1...........Anna Carin Olofsson, Sweden — 40:36.5
2..........Kati Wilhelm, Germany — 40:55.3
3..........Uschi Disl, Germany — 41:18.4

20 KILOMETERS

1...........Michael Gries, Germany — 54:23.0
2..........Ole Einar Bjoerndalen, Norway — 54:39.0
3..........Halvard Hanevold, Norway — 55:31.9

15 KILOMETERS

1...........Svetlana Ishmouratova, Russia — 49:24.1
2..........Martina Glagow, Germany — 50:34.9
3..........Albina Akhatova, Russia — 50:55.0

4 X 7.5-KILOMETER RELAY

1...........Germany — 1:21:51.5
2..........Russia — 1:22:12.4
3..........France — 1:22:35.1

4 X 6-KILOMETER RELAY

1...........Russia — 1:16:12.5
2..........Germany — 1:17:03.2
3..........France — 1:18:38.7

BOBSLED

Men | **Women**

TWO-MAN

1......Andre Lange/ Kevin Kuske, Germany I — 3:43.38
2......Pierre Lueders/ Lascelles Brown Canada I — 3:43.59
3......Martin Annen/ Beat Hefti, Switz I — 3:43.73

TWO-PERSON

1......S. Kiriasis/ A. Schneiderheinze, Ger I — 3:49.98
2......Shauna Rohbock/Valerie Fleming, USA I — 3:50.69
3......G. Weissensteiner/J. Isacco, Italy I — 3:51.01

FOUR-MAN

1......Germany I — 3:40.42
2......Russia I — 3:40.55
3......Switzerland I — 3:40.83

CURLING

Men | **Women**

1...........Canada
2...........Finland
3...........United States

1...........Sweden
2...........Switzerland
3...........Canada

FIGURE SKATING

Men — Pts | **Women** — Pts

1......Evgeni Plushenko, Russia — 258.33
2......Stephane Lambiel, Switzerland — 231.21
3......Jeffrey Buttle, Canada — 227.59

1......Shizuka Arakawa, Japan — 191.34
2......Sasha Cohen, United States — 183.36
3......Irina Slutskaya, Russia — 181.44

Pairs — Pts | **Ice Dancing** — Pts

1......Tatiana Totmianina/Maxim Marinin, Russia — 204.48
2......Zhang Dan, Zhang Hao, China — 189.73
3......Hongbo Zhao, Xue Shen, China — 186.91

1......Tatiana Navka/Roman Kostomarov, Russia — 200.64
2......Tanith Belbin, Ben Agosto, United States — 196.06
3......Elena Grushina, Ruslan Goncharov, Ukraine — 195.85

ICE HOCKEY

Men | **Women**

1...........Sweden
2...........Finland
3...........Czech Republic

1...........Canada
2...........Sweden
3...........United States

LUGE

Men

SINGLES

1....Armin Zoeggeler, Italy	3:26.088
2....Albert Demtschenko, Russia	3:26.198
3....Martinus Rubenis, Latvia	3:26.445

DOUBLES

1....Andreas Linger/Wolfgang Linger, Austria	1:34.497
2....A. Florschuetz/T. Wustlich, Germany	1:34.807
3....G. Plankensteiner/O. Haselrieder, Italy	1:34.930

Women

SINGLES

1....Sylke Otto, Germany	3:07.979
2....Silke Kraushaar, Germany	3:08.115
3....Tatjana Huefner, Germany	3:08.460

SKELETON

Men

1.	Duff Gibson, Canada	1:55.88
2.	Jeff Pain, Canada	1:56.14
3.	Gregor Staehli, Switzerland	1:56.80

Women

1.	Maya Pedersen, Switzerland	1:59.83
2.	Shelley Rudman, United Kingdom	2:01.06
3.	Mellisa Hollingsworth-Richards, Canada	2:01.41

SPEED SKATING

Men

500 METERS

1....Joey Cheek, United States	1:09.76
2....Dmitry Dorofeyev, Russia	1:10.41
3....Lee Kang Seok, S Korea	1:10.43

500 METERS SHORT TRACK

1....Apolo Anton Ohno, United States	41.935
2....Francois-Louis Tremblay, France	42.002
3....Hyun-Soo Ahn, S Korea	42.089

1,000 METERS

1....Shani Davis, United States	1:08.89
2....Joey Cheek, United States	1:09.16
3....Erben Wennemars, Netherlands	1:09.32

1,000 METERS SHORT TRACK

1....Hyun-Soo Ahn, S Korea	1:26.739 OR
2....Ho-Suk Lee, S Korea	1:26.764
3....Apolo Anton Ohno, United States	1:26.927

1,500 METERS

1....Enrico Fabris, Italy	1:45.97
2....Shani Davis, United States	1:46.13
3....Chad Hedrick, United States	1:46.22

1,500 METERS SHORT TRACK

1....Hyun-Soo Ahn, S Korea	2:25.341
2....Ho-Suk Lee, S Korea	2:25.600
3....JiaJun Li, China	2:26.005

5,000 METERS

1....Chad Hedrick, United States	6:14.68
2....Sven Kramer, Netherlands	6:16.40
3....Enrico Fabris, Italy	6:18.25

5,000-METER SHORT TRACK RELAY

1....S Korea	6:43.376 OR
2....Canada	6:43.707
3....United States	6:47.990

10,000 METERS

1....Bob de Jong, Netherlands	13:01.57
2....Chad Hedrick, United States	13:05.40
3....Carl Verheijen, Netherlands	13:08.80

TEAM PURSUIT

1....Italy
2....Canada
3....Netherlands

Women

500 METERS

1....Svetlana Zhurova, Russia	1:16.57
2....Manli Wang, China	1:16.78
3....Hui Ren, China	1:16.87

500 METERS SHORT TRACK

1....Meng Wang, China	44.345
2....Evgenia Radanova, Bulgaria	44.374
3....Anouk Leblanc-Boucher, Canada	44.759

1,000 METERS

1....Marianne Timmer, Netherlands	1:16.05
2....Cindy Klassen, Canada	1:16.09
3....Anni Friesinger,Germany	1:16.11

1,000 METERS SHORT TRACK

1....Sun-Yu Jin, S Korea	1:32.859
2....Meng Wang, China	1:33.079
3....Yang A. Yang, China	1:33.937

1,500 METERS

1....Cindy Klassen, Canada	1:55.27
2....Kristina Groves, Canada	1:56.74
3....Ireen Wust, Netherlands	1:56.90

1,500 METERS SHORT TRACK

1....Sun-Yu Jin, S Korea	2:23.494
2....Eun-Kyung Choi, Korea	2:24.069
3....Meng Wang, China	2:24.469

3,000 METERS

1....Ireen Wust, Netherlands	4:02.43
2....Renate Groenewold, Netherlands	4:03.48
3....Cindy Klassen, Canada	4:04.37

3,000-METER SHORT TRACK RELAY

1....S Korea	4:17.040
2....Canada	4:17.336
3....Italy	4:20.030

5,000 METERS

1....Clara Hughes, Canada	6:59.07
2....Claudia Pechstein, Germany	7:00.08
3....Cindy Klassen, Canada	7:00.57

TEAM PURSUIT

1....Germany
2....Canada
3....Russia

Note: OR=Olympic.Record. WR=World Record. EOR=Equals Olympic Record. EWR=Equals World Record. WB=World Best.

FREESTYLE SKIING

Men

MOGULS	Pts
1. ...Dale Begg-Smith, Australia	26.77
2. ...Mikko Ronkainen, Finland	26.62
3. ...Toby Dawson, United States	26.30

AERIALS	Pts
1. ...Han Xiaopeng, China	250.77
2. ...Dmitri Dashinski, Belarus	248.68
3. ...Vladimir Lebedev, Russia	246.76

Women

MOGULS	Pts
1. ...Jennifer Heil, Canada	26.50
2. ...Kari Traa, Norway	25.65
3. ...Sandra Laoura, France	25.37

AERIALS	Pts
1. ...Evelyne Leu, Switzerland	202.55
2. ...Nina Li, China	197.39
3. ...Alisa Camplin, Australia	191.39

ALPINE SKIING

Men

DOWNHILL	
1. ...Antoine Deneriaz, France	1:48.80
2. ...Michael Walchhofer, Austria	1:49.52
3. ...Bruno Kernen, Switzerland	1:49.82

SLALOM	
1. ...Benjamin Raich, Austria	1:43.14
2. ...Reinfried Herbst, Austria	1:43.97
3. ...Rainer Schoenfelder, Austria	1:44.15

GIANT SLALOM	
1. ...Benjamin Raich, Austria	2:35.00
2. ...Joel Chanel, France	2:35.07
3. ...Hermann Maier, Germany	2:35.16

SUPER GIANT SLALOM	
1. ...Kjetil André Aamodt, Norway	1:30.65
2. ...Hermann Maier, Germany	1:30.78
3. ...Ambrosi Hoffman, Switzerland	1:30.98

COMBINED	
1. ...Ted Ligety, United States	3:09.35
2. ...Ivica Kostelic, Croatia	3:09.88
3. ...Rainer Schoenfelder, Austria	3:10.67

Women

DOWNHILL	
1. ...Michaela Dorfmeister, Austria	1:56.49
2. ...Martina Schild, Switzerland	1:56.86
3. ...Anja Paerson, Sweden	1:57.13

SLALOM	
1. ...Anja Paerson, Sweden	1:29.04
2. ...Nicole Hosp, Austria	1:29.33
3. ...Marlies Schild, Austria	1:29.79

GIANT SLALOM	
1. ...Julia Mancuso, United States	2:09.19
2. ...Tanja Poutiainen, Finland	2:09.86
3. ...Anna Ottosson, Sweden	2:10.33

SUPER GIANT SLALOM	
1. ...Michaela Dorfmeister, Austria	1:32.47
2. ...Janica Kostelic, Croatia	1:32.74
3. ...Alexandra Meissnitzer, Austria	1:33.06

COMBINED	
1. ...Janica Kostelic, Croatia	2:51.08
2. ...Marlies Schild, Austria	2:51.58
3. ...Anja Paerson, Sweden	2:51.63

NORDIC SKIING

Men

1.3 KILOMETERS SPRINT	
1. ...Bjoern Lind, Sweden	2:26.5
2. ...Roddy Darragon, France	2:27.1
3. ...Thobias Fredriksson, Sweden	2:27.8

1.3 KILOMETERS TEAM SPRINT	
1. ...Sweden	17:02.9
2. ...Norway	17:03.5
2. ...Russia	17:05.2

15 KILOMETERS CLASSICAL	
1. ...Andrus Veerpalu, Estonia	38:01.3
2. ...Lukas Bauer, Czech Republic	38:15.8
3. ...Tobias Angerer, Germany	38:20.5

30 KILOMETERS PURSUIT	
1. ...Eugeni Dementiev, Russia	1:17:00.8
2. ...Frode Estil, Norway	1:17:01.4
3. ...Pietro Piller Cottrer, Italy	1:17:01.7

50 KILOMETERS CLASSICAL	
1. ...Giorgio di Centa, Italy	2:06:11.8
2. ...Eugeni Dementiev, Russia	2:06:12.6
3. ...Mikhail Botwinov Austria	2:08:12.7

4 X 10-KILOMETER RELAY MIXED	
1. ...Italy	1:43:45.7
2. ...Germany	1:44:01.4
3. ...Sweden	1:44:01.7

90-METER HILL SKI JUMPING	Pts
1. ...Lars Bystoel, Norway	266.5
2. ...Matti Hautamaeki, Finland	265.5
3. ...Roar Ljoekelsoey, Norway	264.5

120-METER HILL SKI JUMPING	Pts
1. ...Thomas Morgenstern, Austria	276.9
2. ...Andreas Kofler, Austria	276.8
3. ...Lars Bystoel, Norway	250.7

120-METER HILL TEAM SKI JUMPING	Pts
1. ...Austria	984.0
2. ...Finland	976.6
3. ...Norway	950.1

INDIVIDUAL COMBINED	
1. ...Georg Hettich, Germany	39:44.6
2. ...Felix Gottwald, Austria	39:54.4
3. ...Magnus Moan, Norway	40:00.8

INDIVIDUAL SPRINT COMBINED	
1. ...Felix Gottwald, Austria	17:35.0
2. ...Magnus Moan, Norway	17:38.4
3. ...Georg Hettich, Germany	18:38.6

TEAM COMBINED	
1. ...Austria	49:52.6
2. ...Germany	50:07.9
3. ...Finland	50:19.4

NORDIC SKIING
Women

1.1 KILOMETERS SPRINT
1. ...Chandra Crawford, Canada 2:12.3
2. ...Claudia Kuenzel, Germany 2:13.0
3. ...Alena Sidko, Russia 2:13.2

1.1 KILOMETERS TEAM SPRINT
1. ...Sweden 16:36.9
2. ...Canada 16:37.5
3. ...Finland 16:39.2

10 KILOMETERS CLASSICAL
1. ...Kristina Smigun, Estonia 27:51.4
2. ...Marit Bjorgen, Norway 28:12.7
3. ...Hilde G. Pedersen, Norway 28:14.0

15 KILOMETERS PURSUIT
1. ...Kristina Smigun, Estonia 42:48.7
2. ...Katerina Neumannova, Czech Rep. 42:50.6
3. ...Evgenia Medvedeva-Abruzova, Russia 43:03.2

30 KILOMETERS FREESTYLE
1. ...Katerina Neumannova, Czech Rep. 1:22:25.4
2. ...Julija Tchepalova, Russia 1:22:26.8
3. ...Justyna Kowalczyk, Poland 1:22:27.5

4 X 5-KILOMETER RELAY MIXED
1. ...Russia 54:47.7
2. ...Germany 54:57.7
3. ...Italy 54:58.7

SNOWBOARDING

Men

PARALLEL GIANT SLALOM
1. ...Philipp Schoch, Switzerland
2. ...Simon Schoch, Switzerland
3. ...Siegfried Grabner, Austria

HALF-PIPE	Pts
1. ...Shaun White, United States	46.8
2. ...Danny Kass, United States	44.0
3. ...Markku Koski, Finland	41.5

SNOWBOARD CROSS
1. ...Seth Wescott, United States
2. ...Radoslav Zidek, Slovakia
3. ...Paul-Henri Delerue, France

Women

PARALLEL GIANT SLALOM
1. ...Daniela Meuli, Switzerland
2. ...Amelie Kober, Germany
3. ...Rosey Fletcher, United States

HALF-PIPE	Pts
1. ...Hannah Teter, United States	46.4
2. ...Gretchen Bleiler, United States	43.4
3. ...Kjersti Buass, Norway	42.0

SNOWBOARD CROSS
1. ...Tanja Frieden, Switzerland
2. ...Lindsey Jacobellis, United States
3. ...Dominique Maltais, Canada

2004 Summer Games

TRACK AND FIELD
Men

100 METERS
1. ...Justin Gatlin, United States 9.85
2. ...Francis Obikwelu, Portugal 9.86
3. ...Maurice Greene, United States 9.87

200 METERS
1. ...Shawn Crawford, United States 19.79
2. ...Bernard Williams, United States 20.01
3. ...Justin Gatlin, United States 20.03

400 METERS
1. ...Jeremy Wariner, United States 44.00
2. ...Otis Harris, United States 44.16
3. ...Derrick Brew, United States 44.42

800 METERS
1. ...Yuriy Borzakovskiy, Russia 1:44.45
2. ...Mbulaeni Mulaudzi, S Africa 1:44.61
3. ...Wilson Kipketer, Denmark 1:44.65

1,500 METERS
1. ...Hicham El Guerrouj, Morocco 3:34.18
2. ...Bernard Lagat, Kenya 3:34.30
3. ...Rui Silva, Portugal 3:34.68

5,000 METERS
1. ...Hicham El Guerrouj, Morocco 13:14.39
2. ...Kenenisa Bekele, Ethiopia 13:14.59
3. ...Eliud Kipchoge, Kenya 13:15.10

10,000 METERS
1. ...Kenenisa Bekele, Ethiopia 27:05.10 OR
2. ...Sileshi Sihine, Ethiopia 27:09.39
3. ...Zersenay Tadesse, Eritrea 27:22.57

MARATHON
1. ...Stefano Baldini, Italy 2:10:55
2. ...Mebrahtom Keflezighi, United States 2:11:29
3. ...Vanderlei de Lima, Brazil 2:12:11

110-METER HURDLES
1. ...Xiang Liu, China 12.91 EWR
2. ...Terrence Trammell, United States 13.18
3. ...Anier García, Cuba 13.20

400-METER HURDLES
1. ...Felix Sanchez, Dominican Republic 47.63
2. ...Danny McFarlane, Jamaica 48.11
3. ...Naman Keita, France 48.26

3,000-METER STEEPLECHASE
1. ...Ezekiel Kemboi, Kenya 8:05.81
2. ...Brimin Kipruto, Kenya 8:06.11
3. ...Paul Kipsiele Koech, Kenya 8:06.64

4 X 100-METER RELAY
1. ...Great Britian: (Jason Gardener 38.07
    Darren Campbell, Marlon Devonish,
    Mark Lewis Francis)
2. ...United States 38.08
3. ...Nigeria 38.23

Note: OR=Olympic Record. WR=World Record. EOR=Equals Olympic Record. EWR=Equals World Record.

TRACK AND FIELD *(Cont.)*
Men

4 X 400-METER RELAY

1. ...United States: (Otis Harris, Derrick Brew, Jeremy Wariner, Darold Williamson) — 2:55.91
2. ...Australia — 3:00.60
3. ...Nigeria — 3:00.90

20-KILOMETER WALK

1. ...Ivano Brugnetti, Italy — 1:19:40
2. ...Francisco Javier Fernandez, Spain — 1:19:45
3. ...Nathan Deakes, Australian — 1:20:02

50-KILOMETER WALK

1. ...Robert Korzeniowski, Poland — 3:38:46
2. ...Denis Nizhegorodov, Russia — 3:42:50
3. ...Aleksey Voyevodin, Russia — 3:43:34

HIGH JUMP

1. ...Stefan Holm, Sweden — 7 ft 8¾ in
2. ...Matthew Hemingway, United States — 7 ft 8 in
3. ...Yaroslav Baba, Czech Republic — 7 ft 8 in

POLE VAULT

1. ...Timothy Mack, United States — 19 ft 6¼ in
2. ...Toby Stevenson, United States — 19 ft 4¼ in
3. ...Giuseppe Gibilisco, Italy — 19 ft 2¼ in

LONG JUMP

1. ...Dwight Phillips, United States — 28 ft 2¼ in
2. ...John Moffitt, United States — 27 ft 9½ in
3. ...Joan Lino Martinez, Spain — 27 ft 3¾ in

TRIPLE JUMP

1. ...Christian Olsson, Sweden — 58 ft 4½ in
2. ...Marian Oprea, Romania — 57 ft 7 in
3. ...Danila Burkenya, Russia — 57 ft 4¼ in

SHOT PUT

1. ...Yuriy Bilonog, Ukraine — 69 ft 5¼ in
2. ...Adam Nelson, United States — 69 ft 5¼ in
3. ...Joachim Olsen, Denmark — 69 ft 1½ in

DISCUS THROW

1. ...Virgilijus Alekna, Lithuania — 229 ft 3 in
2. ...Zoltan Kovago, Hungary — 219 ft 11 in
3. ...Aleksander Tammert, Estonia — 218 ft 8 in

HAMMER THROW

1. ...Adrian Zsolt, Hungary — 272 ft 11 in
2. ...Koji Murofushi, Japan — 272 ft
3. ...Ivan Tikhon, Belarus — 261 ft 10 in

JAVELIN

1. ...Andreas Thorkildsen, Norway — 283 ft 9 in
2. ...Vadims Vasilevskis, Latvia — 278 ft 8 in
3. ...Sergey Makarov, Russia — 278 ft 4 in

DECATHLON

	Pts
1. ...Roman Seberle, Czech Republic	8893 OR
2. ...Bryan Clay, United States	8820
3. ...Dmitriy Karpov, Kazakhstan	8725

TRACK AND FIELD
Women

100 METERS

1. ...Yuliya Nesterenko, Belarus — 10.93
2. ...Lauryn Williams, United States — 10.96
3. ...Veronica Campbell, Jamaica — 10.97

200 METERS

1. ...Veronica Campbell, Jamaica — 22.05
2. ...Allyson Felix, United States — 22.18
3. ...Debbie Ferguson, Bahamas — 22.30

400 METERS

1. ...Tonique Williams-Darling, Bahamas — 49.41
2. ...Ana Guevara, Mexico — 49.56
3. ...Natalya Antyukh, Russia — 49.89

800 METERS

1. ...Kelly Holmes, Great Britain — 1:56.38
2. ...Hasna Benhassi, Morocco — 1:56.43
3. ...Jolanda Ceplak, Slovenia — 1:56.43

1,500 METERS

1. ...Kelly Holmes, Great Britain — 3:57.90
2. ...Tatyana Tomashova, Russia — 3:58.12
3. ...Maria Cioncan, Romania — 3:58.39

5,000 METERS

1. ...Meseret Defar, Ethiopia — 14:45.65
2. ...Isabella Ochichi, Kenya — 14:48.19
3. ...Tirunesh Dibaba, Ethiopia — 14:51.83

10,000 METERS

1. ...Huina Xing, China — 30:24.36
2. ...Ejegayehu Dibaba, Ethiopia — 30:24.98
3. ...Derartu Tulu, Ethiopia — 30:26.42

MARATHON

1. ...Noguchi Mizuki, Japan — 2:26:20
2 ...Nyambura Wincatherine, Kenya — 2:26:32
3. ...Deena Kastor, United States — 2:27:20

100-METER HURDLES

1. ...Joanna Hayes, United States — 12.37 OR
2. ...Olena Krasovska, Ukraine — 12.45
3. ...Melissa Morrison, United States — 12.56

400-METER HURDLES

1. ...Faní Halkiá, Greece — 52.82
2. ...Ionela Tirlea-Manolache, Romania — 53.38
3. ...Tetiana Tereschuk-Antipova, Ukraine — 53.44

4 X 100-METER RELAY

1. ...Jamaica (T. Lawrence, S. Simpson, Aleen Bailey, Veronica Campbell) — 41.73
2. ...Russia — 42.27
3. ...France — 42.54

4 X 400-METER RELAY

1. ...United States (DeeDee Trotter, Monique Henderson, Sanya Richards, Monique Hennagan) — 3:19.01
2. ...Russia — 3:20.16
3. ...Jamaica — 3:22.00

20-KILOMETER WALK

1. ...Athanasía Tsoumeléka, Greece — 1:29:12
2. ...Olimpiada Ivanova, Russia — 1:29:16
3. ...Jane Saville, Australia — 1:29:25

HIGH JUMP

1. ...Yelena Slesarenko, Russia — 6 ft 9 in
2. ...Hestrie Cloete, S Africa — 6 ft 7½ in
3. ...Vita Styopina, Ukraine — 6 ft 7½ in

TRACK AND FIELD *(Cont.)*

Women

POLE VAULT
1. ...Yelena Isinbayeva, Russia	16 ft 1¼ in WR
2. ...Svetlana Feofanova, Russia	15 ft 7 in
3. ...Anna Rogowska, Poland	15 ft 5 in

DISCUS THROW
1. ...Natalya Sadova, Russia	219 ft 10 in
2. ...Anastasia Kelesidou, Greece	218 ft 9 in
3. ...Iryna Yatchenko, Belarus	217 ft 1 in

LONG JUMP
1. ...Tatyana Lebedeva, Russia	23 ft 2½ in
2. ...Irina Simajina, Russia	23 ft 1¾ in
3. ...Tatyana Kotova, Russia	23 ft 1¾ in

JAVELIN
1. ...Osleidys Menendez, Cuba	234 ft 8 in OR
2. ...Steffi Nerius, Germany	215 ft 11 in
3. ...Mirela Manjani, Greece	210 ft 11 in

TRIPLE JUMP
1. ...Frangoise Mbango Etone, Cameroon	50 ft 2½ in
2. ...Chrysopigi Devetzi, Greece	50 ft ½ in
3. ...Tatyana Lebedeva, Russia	49 ft 8¼ in

HEPTATHLON — Pts
1. ...Carolina Kluft, Sweden	6952
2. ...Austra Skujyte, Lithuania	6435
3. ...Kelly Sotherton, Great Britain	6424

SHOT PUT
1. ...Yumileidi Cumba Jay, Cuba	64 ft 3¼ in
2. ...Nadine Kleinert, Germany	64 ft 1¾ in
3. ...Svetlana Krivelyova, Russia	63 ft 11½ in

HAMMER THROW
1. ...Olga Kuzenkova, Russia	246 ft 1½ in OR
2. ...Yipsi Moreno, Cuba	240 ft 8¼ in
3. ...Yunaika Crawford, Cuba	240 ft ½ in

INDIVIDUAL ARCHERY

Men
1. ...Marco Galiazzo, Italy
2. ...Hiroshi Yamamoto, Japan
3. ...Tim Cuddihy, Australia

Women
1. ...Sung Hyun Park, S Korea
2. ...Sung Jin Lee, S Korea
3. ...Alison Williamson, Great Britain

TEAM ARCHERY

Men
1. ....S Korea
2. ....Taiwan
3. ....Ukraine

Women
1. ....S Korea
2. ....China
3. ....Taiwan

BADMINTON

Men
SINGLES
1. ...Taufik Hidayat, Indonesia
2. ...Seung Mo Shon, S Korea
3. ...Soni Dwi Kuncoro, Indonesia

DOUBLES
1. ...Ha Tae Kwon/ Dong Moon Kim, S Korea
2. ...Dong Soo Lee/ Yoo Yong Sung, S Korea
3. ...Eng Hian/ Limpele Flandy, Indonesia

Women
SINGLES
1. ...Ning Zhang, China
2. ...Mia Audina, Netherlands
3. ...Mi Zhou, China

DOUBLES
1. ....Yang Wei/ Jiewen Zhang, China
2. ...Gao Ling/ Sui Huang, China
3. ...Kyung Min Ra/ Lee Kyung Won, S Korea

MIXED DOUBLES
1. ....Jun Zhang/ Gao Ling, China
2. ...Nathan Robertson/ Gail Emms, Great Britain
3. ...Jens Eriksen/ Schjoldager Mette, Denmark

BASEBALL
1. ....Cuba
2. ....Australia
3. ....Japan

BASKETBALL

Men
Final: Argentina 84, Italy 69
United States (3rd)
Argentina: Juan Sanchez, Emanuel Ginobili, Alejandro Montecchia, Fabricio Oberto, Walter Herrmann, Gabriel Fernandez, Hugo Sconochini, Luis Scola, Leonardo Gutierrez, Andres Nocioni, Carlos Delfino, Ruben Wolkowyski.

Women
Final: United States 74, Australia 63
Russia (3rd)
United States: Shannon Johnson, Dawn Staley, Suzanne Bird, Sheryl Swoopes, Ruth Riley, Lisa Leslie, Tamika Catchings, Tina Thompson, Diana Taurasi, Yolanda Griffith, Katie Smith, Swintayla Cash.

Note: OR=Olympic Record. WR=World Record. EOR=Equals Olympic Record. EWR=Equals World Record.

BOXING

LIGHT FLYWEIGHT (106 LB)
1. ....Yan Bhartelemy Varela, Cuba
2. ....Atagun Yal Cinkaya, Turkey
3. ....Shiming Zou, China
3. ....Sergey Kazakov, Russia

FLYWEIGHT (112 LB)
1. ....Yuriokis Gamboa Toledano, Cuba
2. ....Jerome Thomas, France
3. ....Fuad Aslanov, Azerbaijan
3. ....Rustamhodza Rahimov, Germany

BANTAMWEIGHT (119 LB)
1. ....Guillermo Rigondeaux Ortiz, Cuba
2. ....Worapoj Petchkoom, Thailand
3. ....Aghasi Mammadov, Azerbaijan
3. ....Bahodirion Sooltonov, Uzbekistan

FEATHERWEIGHT (125 LB)
1. ....Alexei Tichtchenko, Russia
2. ....Song Guk Kim, N Korea
3. ....Vitali Tajbert, Germany
3. ....Seok Hwan Jo, S Korea

LIGHTWEIGHT (132 LB)
1. ....Mario Kindelan Mesa, Cuba
2. ....Amir Khan, Great Britain
3. ....Serik Yeleuov, Kazakhstan
3. ....Murat Khrachev, Russia

LIGHT WELTERWEIGHT (139 LB)
1. ....Manus Boonjumnong, Thailand
2. ....Yudel Johnson Cedeno, Cuba
3. ....Boris Georgive, Bulgaria
3. ....Ionut Gheorghe, Romania

WELTERWEIGHT (147 LB)
1. ....Bakhtiyar Artayev, Kazakhstan
2. ....Lorenzo Aragon Armenteros, Cuba
3. ....Oleg Saitov, Russia
3. ....Jung Joo Kim, S Korea

MIDDLEWEIGHT (165 LB)
1. ....Gaydarbek Gaydarbekov, Russia
2. ....Gennadiy Golovkin, Kazakhstan
3. ....Suriya Prasathinphimai, Thailand
3. ....Andre Dirrell, United States

LIGHT HEAVYWEIGHT (178 LB)
1. ....Andre Ward, United States
2. ....Magomed Aripgadjiev, Belarus
3. ....Utkirbek Haydarov, Uzbekistan
3. ....Ahmed Ismail, Egypt

HEAVYWEIGHT (201 LB)
1. ....Odlanier Solis Fonte, Cuba
2. ....Viktar Zuyev, Belarus
3. ....Mohamed Elsayed, Egypt
3. ....Naser Al Shami, Syria

SUPERHEAVYWEIGHT (201+ LB)
1. ....Alexander Povetkin, Russia
2. ....Mohamed Aly, Egypt
3. ....Roberto Cammarelle, Italy
3. ....Michel Lopez Nunez, Cuba

CANOE/KAYAK

Men

C-1 FLATWATER 500 METERS
1.	Andreas Dittmer, Germany	1:46.383
2.	David Cal, Spain	1:46.723
3.	Maxim Opalev, Russia	1:47.767

C-1 FLATWATER 1,000 METERS
1.	David Cal, Spain	3:46.201
2.	Andreas Dittmer, Germany	3:46.721
3.	Attila Vajda, Hungary	3:49.025

C-2 FLATWATER 500 METERS
1.	G. Meng/W. Yang, China	1:40.278
2.	I. Blanco/L. Pajon, Cuba	1:40.350
3.	A. Kostoglod/A. Kovalev, Russia	1:40.442

C-2 FLATWATER 1,000 METERS
1.	C. Gille/T. Wylenzek, Germany	3:41.802
2.	A. Kostoglod/A. Kovalev, Russia	3:42.990
3.	G. Kolonics/G. Kozmann, Hungary	3:43.106

C-1 WHITEWATER SLALOM
		Pts
1.	Tony Estanguet, France	189.16
2.	Michal Martikan, Slovakia	189.28
3.	Stefan Pfannmoeller, Germany	191.56

C-2 WHITEWATER SLALOM
		Pts
1.	Pavel/Peter Hochschorner, Slovakia	207.16
2.	M. Becker/S. Henze, Germany	210.98
3.	J. Volf/O. Stepanek, Czech Republic	212.86

Men *(Cont.)*

K-1 FLATWATER 500 METERS
1.	Adam Van Koeverden, Canada	1:37.919
2.	Nathan Baggaley, Australia	1:38.467
3.	Ian Wynne, Great Britain	1:38.547

K-1 FLATWATER 1,000 METERS
1.	Eirik Veraas Larsen, Norway	3:25.897
2.	Ben Fouhy, New Zealand	3:27.413
3.	Adam Van Koeverden, Canada	3:28.218

Women

K-1 FLATWATER 500 METERS
1.	Natasa Janics, Hungary	1:47.741
2.	Josefa Idem Guerrini, Italy	1:49.729
3.	Caroline Brunet, Canada	1:50.601

K-2 FLATWATER 500 METERS
1.	K. Kovacs/N. Janics, Hungary	1:38.101
2.	B. Fischer/C. Leonhardt, Germany	1:39.533
3.	A. Pastuszka/B. Sokoloska, Poland	1:40.077

K-4 FLATWATER 500 METERS
1.	Germany	1:34.340
2.	Hungary	1:34.536
3.	Ukraine	1:36.192

K-1 WHITEWATER SLALOM
		Pts
1.	Elena Kaliska, Slovakia	210.03
2.	Rebecca Giddens, United States	214.62
3.	Helen Reeves, Great Britain	218.77

CYCLING
Men

ROAD RACE
1. ...Paolo Bettini, Italy — 5:41:44
2. ...Sergio Paulinho, Portugal — 5:41:45
3. ...Axel Merckx, Belgium — 5:41:52

INDIVIDUAL TIME TRIAL
1. ...Tyler Hamilton, United States — 57:31.74
2. ...Vyatcheslav Ekimov, Russia — 57:50.58
3. ...Robert Julich, United States — 57:58.19

1KM TIME TRIAL
1. ...Chris Hoy, Great Britain — 1:00.711
2. ...Arnaud Tournant, France — 1:00.896
3. ...Stefan Nimke, Germany — 1:01.186

4,000-METER INDIVIDUAL PURSUIT
1. ...Bradley Wiggins, Great Britain — 4:16.304
2. ...Brad McGee, Australia — 4:20.436
3. ...Sergi Escobar, Spain — 4:17.947

4,000-METER TEAM PURSUIT
1. ...Australia (Graeme Brown, Brett Lancaster, Brad McGee, Luke Roberts) — 3:58.233
2. ...Great Britain — 4:01.760
3. ...Spain — 4:05.523

SPRINT
1. ...Ryan Bayley, Australia — 10.743
2. ...Theo Bos, Netherlands — 10.710
3. ...Rene Wolff, German — 10.612

POINTS RACE
1. ...Mikhail Ignatyev, Russia — 93
2. ...Joan Llaneras, Spain — 82
3. ...Guido Fulst, Germany — 79

KIERIN
1. ...Ryan Bayley, Australia — 10.601
2. ...Jose Escuredo, Spain
3. ...Shane Kelly, Australia

MADISON
1. ...G. Brown/S. O'Grady, Australia — 22
2. ...F. Marvulli/B. Risi, Switzerland — 15
3. ...R. Hayles/B. Wiggins, Great Britain — 12

OLYMPIC SPRINT
1. ...Germany — 43.980
2. ...Japan — 44.246
3. ...France — 44.359

Women

POINTS RACE
1. ...Olga Slyusareva, Russia — 20
2. ...Belem Guerrero Mendez, México — 14
3. ...Erin Mirabella, United States — 9

INDIVIDUAL TIME TRIAL
1. ...L. Zijlaard-van Moorsel, Netherlands — 31:11.53
2. ...Deirdre Demet-Barry, United States — 31:35.62
3. ...Karin Thuerig, Switzerland — 31:54.89

3,000-METER INDIVIDUAL PURSUIT
1. ...Sarah Ulmer, New Zealand — 3:24.537 WR
2. ...Katie Mactier, Australia — 3:27.650
3. ...L. Zijlaard-van Moorsel, Netherlands — 3:27.037

SPRINT
1. ...Lori-Ann Muenzer, Canada — 12.140
2. ...Tamilla Abassova, Russia — —
3. ...Anna Meares, Australia — 11.822

ROAD RACE
1. ...Sara Carrigan, Australia — 3:24:24
2. ...Judith Arndt, Germany — 3:24:31
3. ...Olga Slyusareva, Russia — 3:25:03

500-M TIME TRIAL
1. ...Anna Meares, Australia — 33.952
2. ...Jiang Yonghua, China — 34.112
3. ...Natallia Tsylinskaya, Belarus — 34.167

DIVING

Men
SPRINGBOARD
	Pts
1.....Bo Peng, China	787.38
2.....Alexandre Despatie, Canada	755.97
3.....Dmitry Sautin, Russia	753.27

PLATFORM
	Pts
1.....Jia Hu, China	748.08
2.....Matthew Helm, Australia	730.56
3.....Liang Tian, China	729.66

Women
SPRINGBOARD
	Pts
1.....Jingjing Guo, China	633.15
2.....Minxia Wu, China	612.00
3.....Yulia Pakhalina, Russia	610.62

PLATFORM
	Pts
1.....Chantelle Newbery, Australia	590.31
2.....Lishi Lao, China	576.30
3.....Loudy Tourky, Australia	561.66

EQUESTRIAN

TEAM EVENTING
1. ......France
2. ......Great Britain
3. ......United States

INDIVIDUAL EVENTING	Pts
1. ......Leslie Law, Great Britain	44.40
2. ......Kim Severson, United States	45.20
3. ......Philippa Funnell, Great Britain	46.60

TEAM DRESSAGE
1. ......Germany
2. ......Spain
3. ......United States

INDIVIDUAL DRESSAGE	Pts
1. ......Anky van Grunsven, Netherlands	85.825
2. ......Ulla Salzgeber, Germany	83.450
3. ......Beatriz Ferrer-Salat, Spain	79.575

TEAM JUMPING
1. ......Germany
2. ......United States
3. ......Sweden

INDIVIDUAL JUMPING	Pts
1. ......Cian O'Connor, Ireland	4.00
2. ......Rodrigo Pessoa, Brazil	8.00
3. ......Chris Kappler, United States	8.00

FENCING
Men

FOIL
1. ....Brice Guyart, France
2. ....Salvatore Sanzo, Italy
3. ....Andrea Cassara, Italy

SABRE
1. ....Aldo Montano, Italy
2. ....Zsolt Nemcsik, Hungary
3. ....Vladislav Tretiak, Ukraine

ÉPÉE
1. ....Marcel Fischer, Switzerland
2. ....Lei Wang, China
3. ....Pavel Kolobkov, Russia

TEAM FOIL
1. ....Italy
2. ....China
3. ....Russia

TEAM SABRE
1. ....France
2. ....Italy
3. ....Russia

TEAM ÉPÉE
1. ....France
2. ....Hungary
3. ....Germany

Women

FOIL
1. ....Valentina Vezzali, Italy
2. ....Giovanna Trillini, Italy
3. ....Sylwia Gruchala, Poland

ÉPÉE
1. ....Timea Nagy, Hungary
2. ....Laura Flessel-Colovic, France
3. ....Maureen Nisima, France

SABRE
1. ....Mariel Zagunis, United States
2. ....Xue Tan, China
3. ....Sada Jacobson, United States

TEAM ÉPÉE
1. ....Russia
2. ....Germany
3. ....France

FIELD HOCKEY

Men
1. Australia
2. Netherlands
3. Germany

Women
1. Germany
2. Netherlands
3. Argentina

GYMNASTICS
Men

ALL-AROUND	Pts
1. ....Paul Hamm, United States	57.823
2. ....Dae Eun Kim, S Korea	57.811
3. ....Tae Young Yang, S Korea	57.774

HORIZONTAL BAR	Pts
1. ....Igor Cassina, Italy	9.812
2. ....Paul Hamm, United States	9.812
3. ....Isao Yoneda, Japan	9.787

PARALLEL BARS	Pts
1. ....Valeri Goncharov, Ukraine	9.787
2. ....Hiroyuki Tomita, Japan	9.775
3. ....Xiaopeng Li, China	9.762

VAULT	Pts
1. ....Gervasio Deferr, Spain	9.737
2. ....Evgeni Sapronenko, Latvia	9.706
3. ....Marian Dragulescu, Romania	9.612

POMMEL HORSE	Pts
1. ....Haibin Teng, China	9.837
2. ....Marius Urzica, Romania	9.825
3. ....Takehiro Kashima, Japan	9.787

RINGS	Pts
1. ....Dimosthenis Tampakos, Greece	9.862
2. ....Jordan Jovtchev, Bulgaria	9.850
3. ....Yuri Chechi, Italy	9.812

GYMNASTICS *(Cont.)*

Men *(Cont.)*

FLOOR EXERCISE

	Pts
1. ....Kyle Shewfelt, Canada	9.787
2. ....Marian Dragulescu, Romania	9.787
3. ....Jordan Jovtchev, Bulgaria	9.775

TEAM COMBINED EXERCISES

1. ....Japan
2. ....United States
3. ....Romania

Women

ALL-AROUND

	Pts
1. ....Carly Patterson, United States	38.387
2. ....Svetlana Khorkina, Russia	38.211
3. ....Nan Zhang, China	38.049

BALANCE BEAM

	Pts
1. ....Catalina Ponor, Romania	9.787
2. ....Carly Patterson, United States	9.775
3. ....Alexandra Eremia, Romania	9.700

VAULT

	Pts
1. ....Monica Rosu, Romania	9.656
2. ....Annia Hatch, United States	9.481
3. ....Anna Pavlova, Russia	9.475

FLOOR EXERCISE

	Pts
1. ....Catalina Ponor, Romania	9.750
2. ....Nicoleta Sofronie, Romania	9.562
3. ....Patricia Moreno, Spain	9.487

UNEVEN BARS

	Pts
1. ....Emilie Lepennec, France	9.687
2. ....Terin Humphrey, United States	9.662
2. ....Courtney Kupets, United States	9.637

TEAM COMBINED EXERCISES

1. ....Romania
2. ....United States
3. ....Russia

JUDO

Men

EXTRA-LIGHTWEIGHT

1. ....Tadahiro Nomura, Japan
2. ....Nestor Khergiani, Georgia
3. ....Khashbaatar Tsagaanbaatar, Mongolia
3. ....Choi Min-ho, S Korea

HALF-LIGHTWEIGHT

1. ....Masato Uchishiba, Japan
2. ....Jozef Krnac, Slovakia
3. ....Georgi Georgiev, Bulgaria
3. ....Yordanis Arencibia, Cuba

LIGHTWEIGHT

1. ....Won Hee Lee, S Korea
2. ....Vitaliy Makarov, Russia
3. ....Leandro Guilheiro, Brazil
3. ....James Pedro, United States

HALF-MIDDLEWEIGHT

1. ....Ilias Iliadas, Greece
2. ....Roman Gontyuk, Ukraine
3. ....Flavio Canto, Brazil
3. ....Dmitri Nossov, Russia

MIDDLEWEIGHT

1. ....Zurab Zviadauri, Georgia
2. ....Hiroshi Izumi, Japan
3. ....Mark Huizinga, Netherlands
3. ....Khasanbi Taov, Russia

HALF-HEAVYWEIGHT

1. ....Ihar Makarau, Belarus
2. ....Sung Ho Jang, S Korea
3. ....Michael Jurack, Germany
3. ....Ariel Zeevi, Israel

HEAVYWEIGHT

1. ....Keiji Suzuki, Japan
2. ....Tamerlan Tmenov, Russia
3. ....Indrek Pertelson, Estonia
3. ....Dennis Van Der Geest, Netherlands

Women

EXTRA-LIGHTWEIGHT

1. ....Ryoko Tani, Japan
2. ....Frederique Jossinet, France
3. ....Feng Gao, China
3. ....Julia Matijass, Germany

HALF-LIGHTWEIGHT

1. ....Dongmei Xian, China
2. ....Yuki Yokosawa, Japan
3. ....Ilse Heylen, Belgium
3. ....Amarilis Savon, Cuba

LIGHTWEIGHT

1. ....Yvonne Boenisch, Germany
2. ....Sun-Hi Kye, N Korea
3. ....Deborah Gravenstijn, Netherlands
3. ....Yurisleidy Lupetey, Cuba

HALF-MIDDLEWEIGHT

1. ....Ayumi Tanimoto, Japan
2. ....Claudia Heill, Austria
3. ....Urska Zolnir, Slovenia
3. ....Driulys Gonzalez, Cuba

MIDDLEWEIGHT

1. ....Masae Ueno, Japan
2. ....Edith Bosch, Netherlands
3. ....Dongya Qin, China
3. ....Annett Boehm, Germany

HALF-HEAVYWEIGHT

1. ....Noriko Anno, Japan
2. ....Xia Liu, China
3. ....Lucia Morico, Italy
3. ....Yurisel Laborde, Cuba

HEAVYWEIGHT

1. ....Maki Tsukada, Japan
2. ....Daima Mayelis Beltran, Cuba
3. ....Fuming Sun, China
3. ....Tea Donguzashvili, Russia

MODERN PENTATHLON

Men
1. ......Andrey Moiseev, Russia
2. ......Andrejus Zadneprovskis, Lithuania
3. ......Libor Capalini, Czech Republic

Women
1. ......Zsuzsanna Voros, Hungary
2. ......Jelena Rublevska, Latvia
3. ......Georgina Harland, Great Britain

MOUNTAIN BIKING

Men
1. ......Julien Absalon, France — 2:15.02
2. ......Jose Antonio Hermida, Spain — 2:16.02
3. ......Bart Brentjens, Netherlands — 2:17.05

Women
1. ......Gunn-Rita Dahle, Norway — 1:56.51
2. ......Marie-Helene Premont, Canada — 1:57.50
3. ......Sabine Spitz, Germany — 1:59.21

ROWING

Men

SINGLE SCULLS
1. ...Olaf Tufte, Norway — 6:49.30
2. ...Jueri Jaanson, Estonia — 6:51.42
3. ...Ivo Yanakiev, Bulgaria — 6:52.80

DOUBLE SCULLS
1. ...S. Vieilledent/A. Hardy, France — 6:29.00
2. ...L. Spik/I. Cop, Slovenia — 6:31.72
3. ...R. Galtarossa/A. Sartori, Italy — 6:32.93

LIGHTWEIGHT DOUBLE SCULLS
1. ...T. Kucharski/R. Sycz, Poland — 6:20.93
2. ...F. Dufour/P. Touron, France — 6:21.46
3. ...V. Polymeros/N. Skiathitis, Greece — 6:23.23

QUADRUPLE SCULLS
1. ...Russia — 5:56.85
2. ...Czech Republic — 5:57.43
3. ...Ukraine — 5:58.87

COXLESS PAIR
1. ...D. Jinn/J. Tomkins, Australia — 6:30.76
2. ...S. Skelin/N. Skelin, Croatia — 6:32.64
3. ...D. Cech/R. di Clemente, S Africa — 6:33.40

COXLESS FOUR
1. ...Great Britain — 6:06.98
2. ...Canada — 6:07.06
3. ...Italy — 6:10.41

LIGHTWEIGHT COXLESS FOUR
1. ...Denmark — 6:01.39
2. ...Australia — 6:02.79
3. ...Italy — 6:03.74

EIGHT-OARS
1. ...United States — 5:42.48
2. ...Netherlands — 5:43.75
3. ...Australia — 5:45.38

Women

SINGLE SCULLS
1. ...Katrin Rutschow-Stomporowski, Germany — 7:18.12
2. ...Yekaterina Karsten, Belarus — 7:22.04
3. ...Rumyana Neykova, Bulgaria — 7:23.10

DOUBLE SCULLS
1. ...C. Evers-Swindell/G. Evers-Swindell, NZ — 7:01.79
2. ...B. Oppelt/P. Waleska, Germany — 7:02.78
3. ...E. Laverick/S. Winckless, Great Britain — 7:07.58

LIGHTWEIGHT DOUBLE SCULLS
1. ...C. Burcica/A. Alupei, Romania — 6:56.05
2. ...D. Reimer/C. Blasberg, Germany — 6:57.33
3. ...K. van Der Kolk/M. van Eupen, Neth — 6:58.54

QUADRUPLE SCULLS
1. ...Germany — 6:29.29
2. ...Great Britain — 6:31.26
3. ...Australia — 6:34.73

COXLESS PAIR
1. ...G. Damian/V. Susanu, Romania — 7:06.55
2. ...K. Grainger/C. Bishop, Great Britain — 7:08.66
3. ...Y. Bichyk/N. Helakh, Bulgaria — 7:09.86

EIGHT-OARS
1. ...Romania — 6:17.70
2. ...United States — 6:19.56
3. ...Netherlands — 6:19.85

SHOOTING

Men

RAPID-FIRE PISTOL	Pts
1. ....Ralf Schumann, Germany	694.9
2. ....Sergei Poliakov, Russia	692.7
3. ....Serguie Alifirenko, Russia	692.3

RUNNING TARGET	Pts
1. ....Manfred Kurzer, Germany	682.4
2. ....Alexander Blinov, Russia	678.0
3. ....Dimitri Lykin, Russia	677.1

FREE PISTOL	Pts
1. ....Mikhail Nestruev, Russia	663.3
2. ....Jong Oh Jin, S Korea	661.5
3. ....Jong Su Kim, N Korea	657.7

SMALL-BORE RIFLE, THREE-POSITION	Pts
1. ....Zhanbo Gia, China	1264.5
2. ....Michael Anti, United States	1263.1
3. ....Christian Planer, Austria	1262.8

AIR PISTOL	Pts
1. ....Yifu Wang, China	690.0
2. ....Mikhail Nestruev, Russia	689.8
3. ....Vladimir Isakov, Russia	684.3

SMALL-BORE RIFLE, PRONE	Pts
1. ....Matt Emmons, United States	703.3
2. ....Christian Lusch, Germany	702.2
3. ....Serguei Martynov, Belarus	701.6

SHOOTING *(Cont.)*

Men *(Cont.)*

AIR RIFLE	Pts	DOUBLE TRAP	Pts
1. ....Qinan Zhu, China	702.7	1. ....Ahmed Al Maktoum, UAE	189.0
2. ....Jie Ling, China	701.3	2. ....Rajyavardhan Rathore, India	179.0
3. ....Jozef Gonci, Slovakia	697.4	3. ....Zheng Wang, China	178.0

TRAP	Pts	SKEET	Pts
1. ....Alexei Alipov, Russia	149.0	1. ....Andrea Benelli, Italy	149.0
2. ....Giovanni Pellielo, Italy	146.0	2. ....Marko Kemppainen, Finland	149.0
3. ....Adam Vella, Australia	145.0	3. ....Juan Miguel Rodriguez, Cuba	147.0

Women

SPORT PISTOL	Pts	DOUBLE TRAP	Pts
1......Mariya Grozdeva, Bulgaria	688.2	1.....Kimberly Rhode, United States	146.0
2......Lenka Hykova, Czech Republic	687.8	2.....Bo Na Lee, S Korea	145.0
3......Irada Ashumova, Azerbaijan	687.3	3.....E Gao, China	142.0

AIR PISTOL	Pts	TRAP	Pts
1......Olena Kostevych, Ukraine	483.3	1.....Suzanne Balogh, Australia	88.0
2......Jasna Sekaric, Serbia & Montenegro	483.3	2.....Maria Quintanal, Spain	84.0
3......Mariya Grozdeva, Bulgaria	482.3	3.....Bo Na Lee, S Korea	83.0

SMALL-BORE RIFLE, THREE-POSITION	Pts	SKEET	Pts
1......Lioubov Galkina, Russia	688.4	1......Diana Igaly, Hungary	97.0
2......Valentina Turisini, Italy	685.9	2......Ning Wei, China	93.0
3......Chengyi Wang, China	685.4	3......Zemfina Meftakhetdinova, Azerbaijan	93.0

AIR RIFLE	Pts
1......Li Du, China	502.0
2......Lioubov Galkina, Russia	501.5
3......Katerina Kurkova, Czech Republic	501.1

SOCCER

Men	Women
1. ....Argentina	1. ....United States
2. ....Paraguay	2. ....Brazil
3. ....Italy	3. ....Germany

SOFTBALL

1...............................United States
2...............................Australia
3...............................Japan

SWIMMING

Men

50-METER FREESTYLE		400-METER FREESTYLE	
1. ...Gary Hall Jr., United States	21.93	1. ...Ian Thorpe, Australia	3:43.10
2. ...Duje Draganja, Croatia	21.94	2. ...Grant Hackett, Australia	3:43.36
3. ...Roland Schoeman, S Africa	22.02	3. ...Klete Keller, United States	3:44.11
100-METER FREESTYLE		**1,500-METER FREESTYLE**	
1. ...Pieter van den Hoogenband, Netherlands	48.17	1. ...Grant Hackett, Australia	14:43.40 OR
2. ...Roland Schoeman, S Africa	48.23	2. ...Larsen Jensen, United States	14:45.29
3. ...Ian Thorpe, Australia	48.56	3. ...David Davies, Great Britain	14:45.95
200-METER FREESTYLE		**100-METER BACKSTROKE**	
1. ...Ian Thorpe, Australia	1:44.71 OR	1. ...Aaron Peirsol, United States	54.06
2. ...Pieter van den Hoogenband, Netherlands	1:45.23	2. ...Markus Rogan, Austria	54.35
		3. ...Tomomi Morita, Japan	54.36
3. ...Michael Phelps, United States	1:45.32	**200-METER BACKSTROKE**	
		1. ...Aaron Peirsol, United States	1:54.95 OR
		2. ...Markus Rogan, Austria	1:57.35
		3. ...Razvan Florea, Romania	1:57.56

Note: OR=Olympic record. WR=world record. EOR=equals Olympic record. EWR=equals world record.

SWIMMING (Cont.)
Men (Cont.)

100-METER BREASTSTROKE
1. ...Kosuke Kitajima, Japan — 1:00.08
2. ...Brendan Hansen, United States — 1:00.25
3. ...Hugues Duboscq, France — 1:00.88

200-METER BREASTSTROKE
1. ...Kosuke Kitajima, Japan — 2:09.44 OR
2. ...Daniel Gyurta, Hungary — 2:10.80
3. ...Brendan Hansen, United States — 2:10.87

100-METER BUTTERFLY
1. ...Michael Phelps, United States — 51.25 OR
2. ...Ian Crocker, United States — 51.29
3. ...Andriy Serdinov, Ukraine — 51.36

200-METER BUTTERFLY
1. ...Michael Phelps, United States — 1:54.04 OR
2. ...Takashi Yamamoto, Japan — 1:54.56
3. ...Stephen Parry, Great Britain — 1:55.52

200-METER INDIVIDUAL MEDLEY
1. ...Michael Phelps, United States — 1:57.14 OR
2. ...Ryan Lochte, United States — 1:58.78
3. ...George Bovell, Trinidad & Tobago — 1:58.80

400-METER INDIVIDUAL MEDLEY
1. ...Michael Phelps, United States — 4:08.26 WR
2. ...Eric Vendt, United States — 4:11.81
3. ...Laszlo Cseh, Hungary — 4:12.15

4 X 100-METER MEDLEY RELAY
1. ...United States (Aaron Peirsol, — 3:30.68 WR
Brendan Hanson, Ian Crocker, Jason Lezak)
2. ...Germany — 3:33.62
3. ...Japan — 3:35.22

4 X 100-METER FREESTYLE RELAY
1. ...S Africa (Schoeman, Ferns, — 3:13.17 WR
Townsend, Neethling)
2. ...Netherlands — 3:14.36
3. ...United States — 3:14.62

4 X 200-METER FREESTYLE RELAY
1. ...United States (Phelps, — 7:07.33
Lochte, Vanderkaay, Keller)
2. ...Australia — 7:07.46
3. ...Italy — 7:11.83

Women

50-METER FREESTYLE
1. ...Inge de Bruijn, Netherlands — 24.58
2. ...Malia Metella, France — 24.89
3. ...Lisbeth Lenton, Australia — 24.91

100-METER FREESTYLE
1. ...Jodie Henry, Australia — 53.84
2. ...Inge de Bruijn, Netherlands — 54.16
3. ...Natalie Coughlin, United States — 54.40

200-METER FREESTYLE
1. ...Camelia Potec, Romania — 1:58.03
2. ...Federica Pellegrini, Italy — 1:58.22
3. ...Solenne Figues, France — 1:58.45

400-METER FREESTYLE
1. ...Laure Manaudou, France — 4:05.34
2. ...Otylia Jedrzejczak, Poland — 4:05.84
3. ...Kaitlin Sandeno, United States — 4:06.19

800-METER FREESTYLE
1. ...Ai Shibata, Japan — 8:24.54
2. ...Laure Manaudou, France — 8:24.96
3. ...Diana Munz, United States — 8:26.61

100-METER BACKSTROKE
1. ...Natalie Coughlin, United States — 1:00.37
2. ...Kirsty Coventry, Zimbabwe — 1:00.50
3. ...Laure Manaudou, France — 1:00.88

200-METER BACKSTROKE
1. ...Kirsty Coventry, Zimbabwe — 2:09.19
2. ...Stanislava Komarova, Russia — 2:09.72
3. ...Antie Buschschulte, Germany — 2:09.88

100-METER BREASTSTROKE
1. ...Xuejuan Luo, China — 1:06.64
2. ...Brooke Hanson, Australia — 1:07.15
3. ...Leisel Jones, Australia — 1:07.16

200-METER BREASTSTROKE
1. ...Amanda Beard, United States — 2:23.37 OR
2. ...Leisel Jones, Australia — 2:23.60
3. ...Anne Poleska, Germany — 2:25.82

100-METER BUTTERFLY
1. ...Petria Thomas, Australia — 57.72
2. ...Otylia Jedrzejczak, Poland — 57.84
3. ...Inge de Bruijn, Netherlands — 57.99

200-METER BUTTERFLY
1. ...Otylia Jedrzejczak, Poland — 2:06.05
2. ...Petria Thomas, Australia — 2:06.36
3. ...Yuko Nakanishi, Japan — 2:08.04

200-METER INDIVIDUAL MEDLEY
1. ...Yana Klochkova, Ukraine — 2:11.14
2. ...Amanda Beard, United States — 2:11.70
3. ...Kirsty Coventry, Zimbabwe — 2:12.72

400-METER INDIVIDUAL MEDLEY
1. ...Yana Klochkova, Ukraine — 4:34.83
2. ...Kaitlin Sandeno, United States — 4:34.95
3. ...Georgina Bardach, Argentina — 4:37.51

4 X 100-METER MEDLEY RELAY
1. ...Australia (Giaan Rooney, — 3:57.32 WR
Leisel Jones, Petria Thomas,
Jodie Henry)
2. ...United States — 3:59.12
3. ...Germany — 4:00.72

4 X 100-METER FREESTYLE RELAY
1. ...Australia (Alice Mills, — 3:35.94 WR
Lisbeth Lenton, Petria Thomas,
Jodie Henry)
2. ...United States — 3:36.39
3. ...Netherlands — 3:37.59

4 X 200-METER FREESTYLE RELAY
1. ...United States (Natalie Coughlin, — 7:53.42 WR
Carly Piper, Dana Vollmer,
Kaitlin Sandeno)
2. ...China — 7:55.97
3. ...Germany — 7:57.35

SYNCHRONIZED SWIMMING

DUET
1. ....Russia
2. ....Japan
3. ....United States

TEAM
1. ....Russia
2. ....Japan
3. ....United States

SYNCHRONIZED DIVING

Men

3M SPRINGBOARD

		Pts
1.	.........N. Siranidis/T. Bimis, Greece	353.34
2.	.........A. Wels/T. Schellenberg, Germany	350.01
3.	.........R. Newbery/S. Barnett, Australia	349.59

10M PLATFORM

		Pts
1.	.........L. Tian/J. Yang, China	383.88
2.	.........P. Waterfield/L. Taylor, Great Britain	371.52
3.	.........M. Helm/R. Newbery, Australia	366.84

Women

3M SPRINGBOARD

		Pts
1.	.........J. Guo/M. Wu, China	336.90
2.	.........V. Ilyina/Y. Pakhalina, Russia	330.84
3.	.........I. Lashko/C. Newbery, Australia	309.30

10M PLATFORM

		Pts
1.	.........L. Lao/T. Li, China	352.54
2.	.........N. Goncharova/Y. Koltunova, Russia	340.92
3.	...........B. Hartley/E. Heymans, Canada	327.78

TABLE TENNIS

Men

SINGLES
1. ....Seung Min Ryu, S Korea
2. ....Hao Wang, China
3. ....Ligin Wang, China

DOUBLES
1. ....M. Lin/Q. Chen, China
2. ....L. Chak Ko/L. Ching, Hong Kong
3. ....M. Maze/F. Tugwell, Denmark

Women

SINGLES
1. ....Zhang Yining, China
2. ....Hyang Mi Kim, N Korea
3. ....Kim Kyung Ah, S Korea

DOUBLES
1. ....N. Wang/Z. Yining, China
2. ...................E.-C. Lee/E. M. Seok, S Korea
3. ....N. Jianfeng/Y. Guo, China

TAEKWONDO

Men

FLYWEIGHT
1. ....Mu Yen Chu, Taiwan
2. ....Oscar Blanco, Mexico
3. ....Tamer Bayoumi, Egypt

FEATHERWEIGHT
1. ....Hadi Saeibonehkohal, Iran
2. ....Chih-Hsiung Huang, Taiwan
3. ....Myeong Seob Song, S Korea

WELTERWEIGHT
1. ....Steven Lopez, United States
2. ....Bahri Tanrikulu, Turkey
3. ....Yossef Karami, Iran

HEAVYWEIGHT
1. ....Dae Sung Moon, S Korea
2. ....Alexandros Nikolaidis, Greece
3. ....Pascal Gentil, France

Women

FLYWEIGHT
1. ....Shih Hsin Chen, Taiwan
2. ....Yanelis Diaz, Cuba
3. ....Yaowapa Boorapolchai, Thailand

FEATHERWEIGHT
1. ....Ji Won Jang, S Korea
2. ....Nia Abdallah, United States
3. ....Iridia Blanco, Mexico

WELTERWEIGHT
1. ....Wei Luo, China
2. ....Elisavet Mystakidou, Greece
3. ....Kyung Sun Hwang

HEAVYWEIGHT
1. ....Zhong Chen, China
2. ....Myriam Baverel, France
3. ....Adriana Carmona, Brazil

TEAM HANDBALL

Men
1. ....Croatia
2. ....Germany
3. ....Russia

Women
1. ....Denmark
2. ....S. Korea
3. ....Ukraine

TENNIS

Men
SINGLES
1...........Nicolas Massu, Chile
2..........Mardy Fish, United States
3..........Fernando Gonzalez, Chile

DOUBLES
1..........Fernando Gonzalez/Nicolas Massu, Chile
2..........Rainer Schuettler/Nicolas Kiefer, Germany
3..........Mario Ancic/Ljubicic Ivan, Croatia

Women
SINGLES
1...........Justine Henin-Hardenne, Belgium
2..........Amelie Mauresmo, France
3..........Alicia Molik, Australia

DOUBLES
1..........Ting Li/Tian Tian Sun, China
2..........Conchita Martinez/Virginia Ruano, Spain
3..........Paola Suares/Patricia Tarbabini, Argentina

TRAMPOLINE

Men
1..........Yuri Nikitin, Ukraine   41.50
2..........Alexandre Moskalenko, Russia 41.20
3..........Henrik Stehlik, Germany   40.80

Women
1..........Anna Dogonadze, Germany   39.60
2..........Karen Cockburn, Canada   39.20
3..........Shaohua Huang, China   39.00

TRIATHLON

Men
1..........Hamish Carter, New Zealand   1:51:07
2..........Bevan Docherty, New Zealand   1:51:15
3..........Sven Riederer, Switzerland   1:51:33

Women
1..........Kate Allen, Austria   2:04:43
2..........Loretta Harrop, Australia   2:04:50
3..........Susan Williams, United States 2:05:08

VOLLEYBALL

Men
1..........Brazil
2..........Italy
3..........Russia

Women
1..........China
2..........Russia
3..........Cuba

BEACH VOLLEYBALL

Men
1..........Emanuel Rigo/Ricardo Santos, Brazil
2..........Pablo Herrera/Javier Bosma, Spain
3..........Patrick Heuscher/Stefan Kobel, Switzerland

Women
1..........Misty May/Kerri Walsh, United States
2..........Shelda Bede/Adriana Behar, Brazil
3..........Holly McPeak/Elaine Youngs, United States

WATER POLO

Men
1..........Hungary
2..........Serbia & Montenegro
3..........Russia

Women
1..........Italy
2..........Greece
3..........United States

WEIGHTLIFTING
Men

123 POUNDS
1..........Halil Mutlu, Turkey   649 lb
2..........Meijin Wu, China   632.5 lb
3..........Sedat Artuc, Turkey   616 lb

137 POUNDS
1..........Zhiyong Shi, China   715 lb
2..........Maosheng Le, China   687.5 lb
3..........Jose Israel Rubio, Venezuela 649 lb

152 POUNDS
1..........Guozheng Zhang, China   764.5 lb
2..........Bae Young Lee, S Korea   753.5 lb
3..........Nikolay Pechalov, Croatia 742.5 lb

170 POUNDS
1..........Taner Sagir, Turkey   825 lb OR
2..........Sergei Filimonov, Kazakhstan 819.5 lb
3..........Oleg Perepetchenov, Russia 803 lb

187 POUNDS
1..........George Asanidze, Georgia   841.5 lb
2..........Andrei Rybakou, Belarus   836 lb
3..........Pyrros Dimas, Greece   830.5 lb

207 POUNDS
1..........Milen Dobrev, Bulgaria   896.5 lb
2..........Khadjimourad Akkaev, Russia 891 lb
3..........Eduard Tjukin, Russia   874.5

231 POUNDS
1..........Dmitry Berestov, Russia   935 lb
2..........Igor Razoronov, Ukraine   924 lb
3..........Gleb Pisarevskiy, Russia   924 lb

231+ POUNDS
1..........Hossein Reza Zadeh, Iran   1,039.5 lb
2..........Viktors Scerbatihs, Latvia 1001 lb
3..........Velichko Cholakov, Bulgaria 984.5 lb

WEIGHTLIFTING (Cont.)

Women

106 POUNDS
1. ....Taylan Nurcan, Turkey — 462 lb
2. ....Zhuo Li, China — 451 lb
3. ....Aree Wiratthaworn, Thailand — 440 lb

117 POUNDS
1. ....Udomporn Polsak, Thailand — 490 lb
2. ....Raema Lisa Rumbewas, Indonesia — 462 lb
3. ....Mabel Mosquera, Colombia — 434.4 lb

128 POUNDS
1. ....Yanging Chen, China — 523 lb
2. ....Song Hui Ri, N Korea — 512 lb
3. ....Wandee Kameajm, Thailand — 506 lb

139 POUNDS
1. ....Natalia Skakun, Ukraine — 535 lb
2. ....Hanna Batsiushka, Belarus — 535 lb
3. ....Tatsiana Stukalava, Belarus — 491 lb

152 POUNDS
1. ....Chunhong Liu, China — 606 lb WR
2. ....Eszter Krutzler, Hungary — 579 lb
3. ....Zarema Kasaeva, Russia — 579 lb

165 POUNDS
1. ....Pawina Thongsuk, Thailand — 601 lb
2. ....Natalia Zabolotnaia, Russia — 601 lb WR
3. ....Valentina Popova, Russia — 583 lb

165+ POUNDS
1. ....Gonghong Tang, China — 671 lb
2. ....Mi Ran Jang, S Korea — 666 lb
3. ....Agata Wrobel, Poland — 638

FREESTYLE WRESTLING

121 POUNDS
1. ....Mavlet Batirov, Russia
2. ....Stephen Abas, United States
3. ....Chikara Tanabe, Japan

132 POUNDS
1. ....Yandro Miguel Quintana, Cuba
2. ....Masuod Jokar, Iran
3. ....Kenji Inoue, Japan

145.5 POUNDS
1. ....Elbrus Tedeyev, Ukraine
2. ....Jamill Kelly, United States
3. ....Makhach Murtazaliev, Russia

163 POUNDS
1. ....Buvaysa Saytive, Russia
2. ....Gennadily Laliyev, Kazakhstan
3. ....Ivan Fundora, Cuba

185 POUNDS
1. ....Cael Sanderson, United States
2. ....Evi Jae Moon, S Korea
3. ....Sazhid Sazhidov, Russia

211.5 POUNDS
1. ....Khadjimourat Gatsalov, Russia
2. ....Magomed Ibragimov, Uzbekistan
3. ....Alireza Heidari, Iran

264.5 POUNDS
1. ....Artur Taymazov, Uzbekistan
2. ....Alireza Rezaei, Iran
3. ....Aydin Polatci, Turkey

GRECO-ROMAN WRESTLING

121 POUNDS
1. ....Istvan Majoros, Hungary
2. ....Gueidar Mamedaliev, Russia
3. ....Artiom Kjourejkian, Greece

132 POUNDS
1. ....Ji Hyun Jung, S Korea
2. ....Roberto Monzon, Cuba
3. ....Armen Nazarian, Bulgaria

145.5 POUNDS
1. ....Farid Monsurov, Azerbaijan
2. ....Seref Eroglu, Turkey
3. ....Mkkhitar Manukyan, Kazakhstan

163 POUNDS
1. ....Alexandr Dokturishivili, Uzbekistan
2. ....Marko Yli-Hannuksela, Finland
3. ....Varteres Samourgachev, Russia

185 POUNDS
1. ....Alexei Michine, Russia
2. ....Ara Abrahamian, Sweden
3. ....Viachaslau Makaranka, Belarus

211.5 POUNDS
1. ....Karam Ibrahim, Egypt
2. ....Ramaz Nozadze, Georgia
3. ....Mehmet Ozal, Turkey

264.5 POUNDS
1. ....Khasan Baroev, Russia
2. ....Georgiy Tsurtsumia, Kazakhstan
3. ....Rulon Gardner, United States

YACHTING

Men

470
1. ....United States
2. ....Great Britain
3. ....Japan

FINN
1. ....Great Britain
2. ....Spain
3. ....Poland

Note: OR=Olympic Record. WR=World Record. EOR=Equals Olympic Record. EWR=Equals World Record.

YACHTING *(Cont.)*
Men *(Cont.)*

MISTRAL
1. ....Israel
2. ....Greece
3. ....Great Britain

STAR
1. ....Brazil
2. ....Canada
3. ....France

TORNADO
1. ....Austria
2. ....United States
3. ....Argentina

MISTRAL
1. ....France
2. ....China
3. ....Italy

470
1. ....Greece
2. ....Spain
3. ....Sweden

LASER
1. ....Brazil
2. ....Austria
3. ....Slovenia

49ER
1. ....Spain
2. ....Ukraine
3. ....Great Britain

Women

EUROPE
1. ....Norway
2. ....Czech Republic
3. ....Denmark

KEEL
1. ....Great Britain
2. ....Ukraine
3. ....Denmark

Olympic Games Locations and Dates

Summer

	Year	Site	Dates	Men	Women	Nations	Most Medals	US Medals
				COMPETITORS				
I	1896	Athens, Greece	Apr 6–15	311	0	13	Greece (10-19-18—47)	11-6-2—19 (2nd)
II	1900	Paris, France	May 20–Oct 28	1319	11	22	France (29-41-32—102)	20-14-19—53 (2nd)
III	1904	St Louis, United States	July 1–Nov 23	681	6	12	United States (80-86-72—238)	
—	1906	Athens, Greece	Apr 22–May 28	77	7	20	France (15-9-16—40)	12-6-5—23 (4th)
IV	1908	London, Great Britain	Apr 27–Oct 31	1999	36	23	Britain (56-50-39—145)	23-12-12—47 (2nd)
V	1912	Stockholm, Sweden	May 5–July 22	2490	57	28	Sweden (24-24-17—65)	23-19-19—61 (2nd)
VI	1916	Berlin, Germany	Canceled because of war					
VII	1920	Antwerp, Belgium	Apr 20–Sep 12	2543	64	29	United States (41-27-28—96)	
VIII	1924	Paris, France	May 4–July 27	2956	136	44	United States (45-27-27—99)	
IX	1928	Amsterdam, Netherlands	May 17–Aug 12	2724	290	46	United States (22-18-16—56)	
X	1932	Los Angeles, United States	July 30–Aug 14	1281	127	37	United States (41-32-31—104)	
XI	1936	Berlin, Germany	Aug 1–16	3738	328	49	Germany (33-26-30—89)	24-20-12—56 (2nd)
XII	1940	Tokyo, Japan	Canceled because of war					
XIII	1944	London, Great Britain	Canceled because of war					
XIV	1948	London, Great Britain	July 29–Aug 14	3714	385	59	United States (38-27-19—84)	
XV	1952	Helsinki, Finland	July 19–Aug 3	4407	518	69	United States (40-19-17—76)	
XVI	1956	Melbourne, Australia*	Nov 22–Dec 8	2958	384	67	USSR (37-29-32—98)	32-25-17—74 (2nd)
XVII	1960	Rome, Italy	Aug 25–Sep 11	4738	610	83	USSR (43-29-31—103)	34-21-16—71 (2nd)
XVIII	1964	Tokyo, Japan	Oct 10–24	4457	683	93	United States (36-26-28—90)	
XIX	1968	Mexico City, Mexico	Oct 12–27	4750	781	112	United States (45-28-34—107)	
XX	1972	Munich, W Germany	Aug 26–Sep 10	5848	1299	122	USSR (50-27-22—99)	33-31-30—94 (2nd)
XXI	1976	Montreal, Canada	July 17–Aug 1	4834	1251	92†	USSR (49-41-35—125)	34-35-25—94 (3rd)
XXII	1980	Moscow, USSR	July 19–Aug 3	4265	1088	81‡	USSR (80-69-46—195)	Did not compete
XXIII	1984	Los Angeles, United States	July 28–Aug 12	5458	1620	141#	United States (83-61-30—174)	
XXIV	1988	Seoul, S Korea	Sep 17–Oct 2	7105	2476	160	USSR (55-31-46—132)	36-31-27—94 (3rd)
XXV	1992	Barcelona, Spain	July 25–Aug. 9	7555	3008	172	Unified Team (45-38-29—112)	37-34-37—108 (2nd)

Summer *(Cont.)*

	Year	Site	Dates	COMPETITORS			Most Medals	US Medals
				Men	Women	Nations		
XXVI	1996	Atlanta, United States	July 19–Aug 4	6984	3766	197	United States (44-32-25—101)	
XXVII	2000	Sydney, Australia	Sept 15–Oct 1	6862	4254	199	United States (39-25-33—97)	
XXVIII	2004	Athens, Greece	Aug 11–Aug 29	11099 total		202	United States (35-39-29—103)	

*The equestrian events were held in Stockholm, Sweden, June 10–17, 1956.
†This figure includes Cameroon, Egypt, Morocco, and Tunisia, countries that boycotted the 1976 Olympics after some of their athletes had already competed.
‡The U.S. was among 65 countries that did not participate in the 1980 Summer Games in Moscow.
#The USSR, East Germany, and 14 other countries did not participate in the 1984 Summer Games in Los Angeles.

Winter

	Year	Site	Dates	Competitors			Most Medals	US Medals
				Men	Women	Nations		
I	1924	Chamonix, France	Jan 25–Feb 4	281	13	16	Norway (4-7-6—17)	1-2-1—4 (3rd)
II	1928	St. Moritz, Switzerland	Feb 11–19	366	27	25	Norway (6-4-5—15)	2-2-2—6 (2nd)
III	1932	Lake Placid, United States	Feb 4–13	277	30	17	United States (6-4-2—12)	
IV	1936	Garmisch-Partenkirchen, Germany	Feb 6–16	680	76	28	Norway (7-5-3—15)	1-0-3—4 (T-5th)
—	1940	Garmisch-Partenkirchen, Germany	Canceled because of war					
—	1944	Cortina d'Ampezzo, Italy	Canceled because of war					
V	1948	St. Moritz, Switzerland	Jan 30–Feb 8	636	77	28	Norway (4-3-3—10) Sweden (4-3-3—10) Switzerland (3-4-3—10)	3-4-2—9 (4th)
VI	1952	Oslo, Norway	Feb 14–25	624	108	30	Norway (7-3-6—16)	4-6-1—11 (2nd)
VII	1956	Cortina d'Ampezzo, Italy	Jan 26–Feb 5	687	132	32	USSR (7-3-6—16)	2-3-2—7 (T-4th)
VIII	1960	Squaw Valley, United States	Feb 18–28	502	146	30	USSR (7-5-9—21)	3-4-3—10 (2nd)
IX	1964	Innsbruck, Austria	Jan 29–Feb 9	758	175	36	USSR (11-8-6—25)	1-2-3—6 (7th)
X	1968	Grenoble, France	Feb 6–18	1063	230	37	Norway (6-6-2—14)	1-5-1—7 (T-7th)
XI	1972	Sapporo, Japan	Feb 3–13	927	218	35	USSR (8-5-3—16)	3-2-3—8 (6th)
XII	1976	Innsbruck, Austria	Feb 4–15	1013	248	37	USSR (13-6-8—27)	3-3-4—10 (T-3rd)
XIII	1980	Lake Placid, United States	Feb 13–24	1012	271	37	East Germany (9-7-7—23)	6-4-2—12 (3rd)
XIV	1984	Sarajevo, Yugoslavia	Feb 8–19	1127	283	49	USSR (6-10-9—25)	4-4-0—8 (T-5th)
XV	1988	Calgary, Canada	Feb 13–28	1270	364	57	USSR (11-9-9—29)	2-1-3—6 (T-8th)
XVI	1992	Albertville, France	Feb 8–23	1313	488	65	Germany (10-10-6—26)	5-4-2—11 (6th)

Winter *(Cont.)*

	Year	Site	Dates	Competitors Men	Women	Nations	Most Medals	US Medals
XVII	1994	Lillehammer, Norway	Feb 12–27	1302	542	67	Norway (10-11-5—26)	6-5-2—13 (T-5th)
XVIII	1998	Nagano, Japan Sweden	Feb 7–22	2302 (total)		72	Germany (12-9-8—29)	6-3-4—13 (6th)
XIX	2002	Salt Lake City, United States	Feb 8–24	1513	886	77	Germany (12-16-7—35)	10-13-11—34 (2nd)
XX	2006	Turin, Italy	Feb 10–26	1627	1006	80	Germany (11-12-6—29)	9-9-7—25 (2nd)

Alltime Olympic Medal Winners

Summary

NATIONS

Nation	Gold	Silver	Bronze	Total	Nation	Gold	Silver	Bronze	Total
United States	906	698	615	2219	West Germany (1952–88)	77	104	120	301
USSR (1952–88)	395	319	296	1010	Finland	101	83	114	298
Great Britain	189	242	237	668	China	112	96	78	286
France	199	202	230	631	Romania	82	88	114	284
Italy	189	154	168	511	Poland	59	74	118	251
Germany (1896–1936, 1992–)	152	154	178	484	Russia	86	80	85	251
					Canada	54	87	101	242
Sweden	140	157	179	476	The Netherlands	65	76	94	235
Hungary	158	141	161	460	Bulgaria	50	83	74	207
East Germany (1956–88)	159	150	136	445	Switzerland	48	76	64	188
Australia	119	126	154	399	Denmark	42	63	64	169
Japan	113	106	114	333	Cuba	64	51	49	164

INDIVIDUALS — OVERALL

Men

Athlete, Nation	Sport	G	S	B	Tot	Athlete, Nation	Sport	G	S	B	Tot
Nikolai Andrianov, USSR	Gym	7	5	3	15	Viktor Chukarin, USSR	Gym	7	3	1	11
Boris Shakhlin, USSR	Gym	7	4	2	13	Carl Osburn, United States	Shoot	5	4	2	11
Edoardo Mangiarotti, Italy	Fen	6	5	2	13	Ray Ewry, United States	Track	10	0	0	10
Takashi Ono, Japan	Gym	5	4	4	13	Carl Lewis, United States	Track	9	1	0	10
Paavo Nurmi, Finland	Track	9	3	0	12	Aladár Gerevich, Hungary	Fen	7	1	2	10
Sawao Kato, Japan	Gym	8	3	1	12	Akinori Nakayama, Japan	Gym	6	2	2	10
Alexei Nemov, Russia	Gym	4	2	6	12	Vitaly Scherbo, UT/Belarus	Gym	6	0	4	10
Mark Spitz, United States	Swim	9	1	1	11	Aleksandr Dityatin, USSR	Gym	3	6	1	10
Matt Biondi, United States	Swim	8	2	1	11						

Women

Athlete, Nation	Sport	G	S	B	Tot	Athlete, Nation	Sport	G	S	B	Tot
Larissa Latynina, USSR	Gym	9	5	4	18	Lyudmila Tourischeva, USSR	Gym	4	3	2	9
Jenny Thompson, United States	Swim	8	3	1	12	Kornelia Ender, E Germany	Swim	4	4	0	8
Vera Cáslavská, Czech	Gym	7	4	0	11	Dawn Fraser, Australia	Swim	4	4	0	8
Agnes Keleti, Hungary	Gym	5	3	2	10	Shirley Babashoff, United States	Swim	2	6	0	8
Polina Astaknova, USSR	Gym	5	2	3	10	Sofia Muratova, USSR	Gym	2	2	4	8
Dara Torres, United States	Swim	4	1	4	9	Inge de Bruijn, Netherlands	Swim	4	2	2	8
Nadia Comaneci, Romania	Gym	5	3	1	9	Eight tied with seven.					

Summer *(Cont.)*

INDIVIDUALS — GOLD

Men

Ray Ewry, United States...........10	Sawao Kato, Japan 8	Viktor Chukarin, USSR...............7
Paavo Nurmi, Finland................9	Matt Biondi, United States 8	Aladár Gerevich, Hungary 7
Carl Lewis, United States..........9	Nikolai Andrianov, USSR 7	
Mark Spitz, United States..........9	Boris Shakhlin, USSR 7	

Women

Larissa Latynina, USSR..............9	Krisztina Egerszegi, Hungary....5	Betty Cuthbert, Australia...........4
Jenny Thompson, U.S. 8	Kornelia Ender, E Germany.......4	Pat McCormick, United States ..4
Vera Cáslavská, Czech 7	Dawn Fraser, Australia...............4	Bärbel Eckert Wöckel, E Ger.....4
Kristin Otto, E Germany 6	Lyudmila Tourischeva, USSR.....4	Amy Van Dyken, United States...4
Agnes Keleti, Hungary..............5	Evelyn Ashford, United States...4	Inge de Bruijn, Netherlands.......4
Nadia Comaneci, Romania.......5	Janet Evans, United States 4	Yana Klochkova, Ukraine...........4
Polina Astaknova, USSR............5	Fanny Blankers-Koen, Neth.......4	Dana Torres, United States........4

Winter

NATIONS

Men

Nation	Gold	Silver	Bronze	Total
Norway..............................96	101	82	279
United States....................79	79	58	216
USSR (1956–88)...............78	56	59	193
Austria..............................50	64	72	186
Germany 65	63	43	171

Women

Nation	Gold	Silver	Bronze	Total
Finland..............................41	57	52	150
Canada 37	38	44	119
Sweden 43	30	43	116
Switzerland 37	37	41	115
E Germany (1956-88) 39	37	35	111

INDIVIDUALS — OVERALL

Men

Athlete, Nation	Sport	G	S	B	Tot
Bjørn Dæhlie, Norway................N Ski	8	4	0	12
Sixten Jernberg, Sweden ....N Ski	4	3	2	9

Seven tied with 7.

Women

Athlete, Nation	Sport	G	S	B	Tot
Raisa Smetanina, USSR/UT.......N Ski	4	5	1	10
Lyubov Egorova, UT/Russia ......N Ski	6	3	0	9
Larissa Lazutina, UT/Russia ......N Ski	5	3	1	9
Stefania Belmondo, Italy............N Ski	2	3	4	9

Four tied with 8.

INDIVIDUALS — GOLD

Men

Bjørn Dæhlie, Norway...............................8
A. Clas Thunberg, Finland 5
O. Bjoerndalen, Norway............................5
Eric Heiden, United States.......................5

Nine tied with 4.

Women

Lyubov Egorova, UT/Russia....................6
Lydia Skoblikova, USSR...........................6
Larissa Lazutina, UT/Russia 5
Bonnie Blair, United States 5

Four tied with 4.

TRACK AND FIELD — Men

100 METERS

1896	Thomas Burke, United States	12.0
1900	Frank Jarvis, United States	11.0
1904	Archie Hahn, United States	11.0
1906	Archie Hahn, United States	11.2
1908	Reginald Walker, S Africa	10.8 OR
1912	Ralph Craig, United States	10.8
1920	Charles Paddock, United States	10.8
1924	Harold Abrahams, Great Britain	10.6 OR
1928	Percy Williams, Canada	10.8
1932	Eddie Tolan, United States	10.3 OR
1936	Jesse Owens, United States	10.3
1948	Harrison Dillard, United States	10.3
1952	Lindy Remigino, United States	10.4
1956	Bobby Morrow, United States	10.5
1960	Armin Hary, W Germany	10.2 OR
1964	Bob Hayes, United States	10.0 EWR
1968	Jim Hines, United States	9.95 WR
1972	Valery Borzov, USSR	10.14
1976	Hasely Crawford, Trinidad	10.06
1980	Allan Wells, Great Britain	10.25
1984	Carl Lewis, United States	9.99
1988	Carl Lewis, United States*	9.92 WR
1992	Linford Christie, Great Britain	9.96
1996	Donovan Bailey, Canada	9.84 WR
2000	Maurice Greene, United States	9.87
2004	Justin Gatlin, United States	9.85

*Ben Johnson, Canada, disqualified.

200 METERS

1900	John Walter Tewksbury, United States	22.2
1904	Archie Hahn, United States	21.6 OR
1906	Not held	
1908	Robert Kerr, Canada	22.6
1912	Ralph Craig, United States	21.7
1920	Allen Woodring, United States	22.0
1924	Jackson Scholz, United States	21.6
1928	Percy Williams, Canada	21.8
1932	Eddie Tolan, United States	21.2 OR
1936	Jesse Owens, United States	20.7 OR
1948	Mel Patton, United States	21.1
1952	Andrew Stanfield, United States	20.7
1956	Bobby Morrow, United States	20.6 OR
1960	Livio Berruti, Italy	20.5 EWR
1964	Henry Carr, United States	20.3 OR
1968	Tommie Smith, United States	19.83 WR
1972	Valery Borzov, USSR	20.00
1976	Donald Quarrie, Jamaica	20.23
1980	Pietro Mennea, Italy	20.19
1984	Carl Lewis, United States	19.80 OR
1988	Joe DeLoach, United States	19.75 OR
1992	Mike Marsh, United States	20.01
1996	Michael Johnson, United States	19.32 WR
2000	Konstadinos Kederis, Greece	20.09
2004	Shawn Crawford, United States	19.79

400 METERS

1896	Thomas Burke, United States	54.2
1900	Maxey Long, United States	49.4 OR
1904	Harry Hillman, United States	49.2 OR
1906	Paul Pilgrim, United States	53.2
1908	Wyndham Halswelle, Great Britain	50.0
1912	Charles Reidpath, United States	48.2 OR
1920	Bevil Rudd, South Africa	49.6
1924	Eric Liddell, Great Britain	47.6 OR
1928	Ray Barbuti, United States	47.8
1932	William Carr, United States	46.2 WR
1936	Archie Williams, United States	46.5
1948	Arthur Wint, Jamaica	46.2
1952	George Rhoden, Jamaica	45.9
1956	Charles Jenkins, United States	46.7

400 METERS (Cont.)

1960	Otis Davis, United States	44.9 WR
1964	Michael Larrabee, United States	45.1
1968	Lee Evans, United States	43.86 WR
1972	Vincent Matthews, United States	44.66
1976	Alberto Juantorena, Cuba	44.26
1980	Viktor Markin, USSR	44.60
1984	Alonzo Babers, United States	44.27
1988	Steve Lewis, United States	43.87
1992	Quincy Watts, United States	43.50 OR
1996	Michael Johnson, United States	43.49 OR
2000	Michael Johnson, United States	43.84
2004	Jeremy Wariner, United States	44.00

800 METERS

1896	Edwin Flack, Australia	2:11
1900	Alfred Tysoe, Great Britain	2:01.2
1904	James Lightbody, United States	1:56 OR
1906	Paul Pilgrim, United States	2:01.5
1908	Mel Sheppard, United States	1:52.8 WR
1912	James Meredith, United States	1:51.9 WR
1920	Albert Hill, Great Britain	1:53.4
1924	Douglas Lowe, Great Britain	1:52.4
1928	Douglas Lowe, Great Britain	1:51.8 OR
1932	Thomas Hampson, Great Britain	1:49.8 WR
1936	John Woodruff, United States	1:52.9
1948	Mal Whitfield, United States	1:49.2 OR
1952	Mal Whitfield, United States	1:49.2 EOR
1956	Thomas Courtney, United States	1:47.7 OR
1960	Peter Snell, New Zealand	1:46.3 OR
1964	Peter Snell, New Zealand	1:45.1 OR
1968	Ralph Doubell, Australia	1:44.3 EWR
1972	Dave Wottle, United States	1:45.9
1976	Alberto Juantorena, Cuba	1:43.50 WR
1980	Steve Ovett, Great Britain	1:45.40
1984	Joaquim Cruz, Brazil	1:43.00 OR
1988	Paul Ereng, Kenya	1:43.45
1992	William Tanui, Kenya	1:43.66
1996	Vebjoern Rodal, Norway	1:42.58 OR
2000	Nils Schumann, Germany	1:45.08
2004	Yuriy Borzakovskiy, Russia	1:44.45

1,500 METERS

1896	Edwin Flack, Australia	4:33.2
1900	Charles Bennett, Great Britain	4:06.2 WR
1904	James Lightbody, United States	4:05.4 WR
1906	James Lightbody, United States	4:12.0
1908	Mel Sheppard, United States	4:03.4 OR
1912	Arnold Jackson, Great Britain	3:56.8 OR
1920	Albert Hill, Great Britain	4:01.8
1924	Paavo Nurmi, Finland	3:53.6 OR
1928	Harry Larva, Finland	3:53.2 OR
1932	Luigi Beccali, Italy	3:51.2 OR
1936	Jack Lovelock, New Zealand	3:47.8 WR
1948	Henri Eriksson, Sweden	3:49.8
1952	Josef Barthel, Luxemburg	3:45.1 OR
1956	Ron Delany, Ireland	3:41.2 OR
1960	Herb Elliott, Australia	3:35.6 WR
1964	Peter Snell, New Zealand	3:38.1
1968	Kipchoge Keino, Kenya	3:34.9 OR
1972	Pekkha Vasala, Finland	3:36.3
1976	John Walker, New Zealand	3:39.17
1980	Sebastian Coe, Great Britain	3:38.4
1984	Sebastian Coe, Great Britain	3:32.53 OR
1988	Peter Rono, Kenya	3:35.96
1992	Fermin Cacho, Spain	3:40.12
1996	Noureddine Morceli, Algeria	3:35.78
2000	Noah Ngeni, Kenya	3:32.07 OR
2004	Hicham El Guerrouj, Morocco	3:34.18

5,000 METERS

1912	Hannes Kolehmainen, Finland	14:36.6 WR
1920	Joseph Guillemot, France	14:55.6

Note: OR=Olympic Record. WR=World Record. EOR=Equals Olympic Record. EWR=Equals World Record. WB=World Best.

TRACK AND FIELD — Men *(Cont.)*

5,000 METERS *(Cont.)*

1924	Paavo Nurmi, Finland	14:31.2 OR
1928	Villie Ritola, Finland	14:38
1932	Lauri Lehtinen, Finland	14:30 OR
1936	Gunnar Höckert, Finland	14:22.2 OR
1948	Gaston Reiff, Belgium	14:17.6 OR
1952	Emil Zatopek, Czechoslovakia	14:06.6 OR
1956	Vladimir Kuts, USSR	13:39.6 OR
1960	Murray Halberg, New Zealand	13:43.4
1964	Bob Schul, United States	13:48.8
1968	Mohamed Gammoudi, Tunisia	14:05.0
1972	Lasse Viren, Finland	13:26.4 OR
1976	Lasse Viren, Finland	13:24.76
1980	Miruts Yifter, Ethiopia	13:21.0
1984	Said Aouita, Morocco	13:05.59 OR
1988	John Ngugi, Kenya	13:11.70
1992	Dieter Baumann, Germany	13:12.52
1996	Venuste Niyongabo, Burundi	13:07.96
2000	Millon Wolde, Ethiopia	13:35.49
2004	Hicham El Guerrouj, Morocco	13:14.39

10,000 METERS

1912	Hannes Kolehmainen, Finland	31:20.8
1920	Paavo Nurmi, Finland	31:45.8
1924	Vilho (Ville) Ritola, Finland	30:23.2 WR
1928	Paavo Nurmi, Finland	30:18.8 OR
1932	Janusz Kusocinski, Poland	30:11.4 OR
1936	Ilmari Salminen, Finland	30:15.4
1948	Emil Zatopek, Czechoslovakia	29:59.6 OR
1952	Emil Zatopek, Czechoslovakia	29:17.0 OR
1956	Vladimir Kuts, USSR	28:45.6 OR
1960	Pyotr Bolotnikov, USSR	28:32.2 OR
1964	Billy Mills, United States	28:24.4 OR
1968	Naftali Temu, Kenya	29:27.4
1972	Lasse Viren, Finland	27:38.4 WR
1976	Lasse Viren, Finland	27:40.38
1980	Miruts Yifter, Ethiopia	27:42.7
1984	Alberto Cova, Italy	27:47.54
1988	Brahim Boutaib, Morocco	27:21.46 OR
1992	Khalid Skah, Morocco	27:46.70
1996	Haile Gebrselassie, Ethiopia	27:07.34 OR
2000	Haile Gebrselassie, Ethiopia	27:18.20
2004	Kenenisa Bekele, Ethiopia	27:05.10 OR

MARATHON

1896	Spiridon Louis, Greece	2:58:50
1900	Michel Theato, France	2:59:45
1904	Thomas Hicks, United States	3:28:53
1906	William Sherring, Canada	2:51:23.6
1908	John Hayes, United States	2:55:18.4 OR
1912	Kenneth McArthur, S Africa	2:36:54.8
1920	Hannes Kolehmainen, Finland	2:32:35.8 WB
1924	Albin Stenroos, Finland	2:41:22.6
1928	Boughera El Ouafi, France	2:32:57
1932	Juan Zabala, Argentina	2:31:36 OR
1936	Kijung Son, Japan (Korea)	2:29:19.2 OR
1948	Delfo Cabrera, Argentina	2:34:51.6
1952	Emil Zatopek, Czechoslovakia	2:23:03.2 OR
1956	Alain Mimoun O'Kacha, France	2:25:00.0
1960	Abebe Bikila, Ethiopia	2:15:16.2 WB
1964	Abebe Bikila, Ethiopia	2:12:11.2 WB
1968	Mamo Wolde, Ethiopia	2:20:26.4
1972	Frank Shorter, United States	2:12:19.8
1976	Waldemar Cierpinski, E Germ.	2:09:55 OR
1980	Waldemar Cierpinski, E Germ.	2:11:03.0
1984	Carlos Lopes, Portugal	2:09:21.0 OR
1988	Gelindo Bordin, Italy	2:10:32
1992	Hwang Young-Cho, S Korea	2:13:23
1996	Josia Thugwane, S Africa	2:12:36
2000	Gezahgne Abera, Ethiopia	2:10:11
2004	Stefano Baldini, Italy	2:10:55

110-METER HURDLES

1896	Thomas Curtis, United States	17.6
1900	Alvin Kraenzlein, United States	15.4 OR
1904	Frederick Schule, United States	16.0

110-METER HURDLES *(Cont.)*

1906	Robert Leavitt, United States	16.2
1908	Forrest Smithson, United States	15.0 WR
1912	Frederick Kelly, United States	15.1
1920	Earl Thomson, Canada	14.8 WR
1924	Daniel Kinsey, United States	15.0
1928	Sydney Atkinson, S Africa	14.8
1932	George Saling, United States	14.6
1936	Forrest Towns, United States	14.2
1948	William Porter, United States	13.9 OR
1952	Harrison Dillard, United States	13.7 OR
1956	Lee Calhoun, United States	13.5 OR
1960	Lee Calhoun, United States	13.8
1964	Hayes Jones, United States	13.6
1968	Willie Davenport, United States	13.3 OR
1972	Rod Milburn, United States	13.24 EWR
1976	Guy Drut, France	13.30
1980	Thomas Munkelt, E Germany	13.39
1984	Roger Kingdom, United States	13.20 OR
1988	Roger Kingdom, United States	12.98 OR
1992	Mark McKoy, Canada	13.12
1996	Allen Johnson, United States	12.95 OR
2000	Anier Garcia, Cuba	13.00
2004	Xiang Liu, China	12.91 EWR

400-METER HURDLES

1900	John Walter Tewksbury, U.S.	57.6
1904	Harry Hillman, United States	53.0
1906	Not held	
1908	Charles Bacon, United States	55.0 WR
1912	Not held	
1920	Frank Loomis, United States	54.0 WR
1924	F. Morgan Taylor, United States	52.6
1928	David Burghley, Great Britain	53.4 OR
1932	Robert Tisdall, Ireland	51.7
1936	Glenn Hardin, United States	52.4
1948	Roy Cochran, United States	51.1 OR
1952	Charles Moore, United States	50.8 OR
1956	Glenn Davis, United States	50.1 EOR
1960	Glenn Davis, United States	49.3 EOR
1964	Rex Cawley, United States	49.6
1968	Dave Hemery, Great Britain	48.12 WR
1972	John Akii-Bua, Uganda	47.82 WR
1976	Edwin Moses, United States	47.64 WR
1980	Volker Beck, E Germany	48.70
1984	Edwin Moses, United States	47.75
1988	Andre Phillips, United States	47.19 OR
1992	Kevin Young, United States	46.78 WR
1996	Derrick Adkins, United States	47.54
2000	Angelo Taylor, United States	47.50
2004	Felix Sanchez, Dominican Rep	47.63

3,000-METER STEEPLECHASE

1920	Percy Hodge, Great Britain	10:00.4 OR
1924	Vilho (Ville) Ritola, Finland	9:33.6 OR
1928	Toivo Loukola, Finland	9:21.8 WR
1932	Volmari Iso-Hollo, Finland	10:33.4*
1936	Volmari Iso-Hollo, Finland	9:03.8 WR
1948	Thore Sjöstrand, Sweden	9:04.6
1952	Horace Ashenfelter, U.S.	8:45.4 WR
1956	Chris Brasher, Great Britain	8:41.2 OR
1960	Zdzislaw Krzyszkowiak, Poland	8:34.2 OR
1964	Gaston Roelants, Belgium	8:30.8 OR
1968	Amos Biwott, Kenya	8:51
1972	Kipchoge Keino, Kenya	8:23.6 OR
1976	Anders Gärderud, Sweden	8:08.2 WR
1980	Bronislaw Malinowski, Poland	8:09.7
1984	Julius Korir, Kenya	8:11.8
1988	Julius Kariuki, Kenya	8:05.51 OR
1992	Matthew Birir, Kenya	8:08.84
1996	Joseph Keter, Kenya	8:07.12
2000	Reuben Kosgei, Kenya	8:21.43
2004	Ezekiel Kemboi, Kenya	8:05.81

*About 3,450 meters; extra lap by error.

TRACK AND FIELD — Men *(Cont.)*

4 X 100-METER RELAY

1912	Great Britain	42.4 OR
1920	United States	42.2 WR
1924	United States	41.0 EWR
1928	United States	41.0 EWR
1932	United States	40.0 EWR
1936	United States	39.8 WR
1948	United States	40.6
1952	United States	40.1
1956	United States	39.5 WR
1960	W Germany	39.5 EWR
1964	United States	39.0 WR
1968	United States	38.2 WR
1972	United States	38.19 EWR
1976	United States	38.33
1980	USSR	38.26
1984	United States	37.83 WR
1988	USSR	38.19
1992	United States	37.40 WR
1996	Canada	37.69
2000	United States	37.61
2004	Great Britain	38.07

4 X 400-METER RELAY

1908	United States	3:29.4
1912	United States	3:16.6 WR
1920	Great Britain	3:22.2
1924	United States	3:16.0 WR
1928	United States	3:14.2 WR
1932	United States	3:08.2 WR
1936	Great Britain	3:09.0
1948	United States	3:10.4 WR
1952	Jamaica	3:03.9 WR
1956	United States	3:04.8
1960	United States	3:02.2 WR
1964	United States	3:00.7 WR
1968	United States	2:56.16 WR
1972	Kenya	2:59.8
1976	United States	2:58.65
1980	USSR	3:01.1
1984	United States	2:57.91
1988	United States	2:56.16 EWR
1992	United States	2:55.74 WR
1996	United States	2:55.99
2000	United States	2:56.35
2004	United States	2:55.91

20-KILOMETER WALK

1956	Leonid Spirin, USSR	1:31:27.4
1960	Vladimir Golubnichiy, USSR	1:33:07.2
1964	Kenneth Mathews, Great Britain	1:29:34.0 OR
1968	Vladimir Golubnichiy, USSR	1:33:58.4
1972	Peter Frenkel, E Germany	1:26:42.4 OR
1976	Daniel Bautista, Mexico	1:24:40.6 OR
1980	Maurizio Damilano, Italy	1:23:35.5 OR
1984	Ernesto Canto, Mexico	1:23:13.0 OR
1988	Jozef Pribilinec, Czechoslovakia	1:19:57.0 OR
1992	Daniel Plaza, Spain	1:21:45.0
1996	Jefferson Pérez, Ecuador	1:20:07
2000	Robert Korzeniowski, Poland	1:18:59 OR
2004	Ivano Brugnetti, Italy	1:19:40

50-KILOMETER WALK

1932	Thomas Green, Great Britain	4:50:10
1936	Harold Whitlock, Great Britain	4:30:41.4 OR
1948	John Ljunggren, Sweden	4:41:52
1952	Giuseppe Dordoni, Italy	4:28:07.8 OR
1956	Norman Read, New Zealand	4:30:42.8
1960	Donald Thompson, Great Britain	4:25:30 OR
1964	Abdon Parnich, Italy	4:11:12.4 OR
1968	Christoph Höhne, E Germany	4:20:13.6
1972	Bernd Kannenberg, W Germany	3:56:11.6 OR

50-KILOMETER WALK *(CONT.)*

1980	Hartwig Gauder, E Germany	3:49:24.0 OR
1984	Raul Gonzalez, Mexico	3:47:26.0 OR
1988	Viacheslav Ivanenko, USSR	3:38:29.0 OR
1992	Andrey Perlov, Unified Team	3:50:13
1996	Robert Korzeniowski, Poland	3:43:30
2000	Robert Korzeniowski, Poland	3:42:22 OR
2004	Robert Korzeniowski, Poland	3:38:46

HIGH JUMP

1896	Ellery Clark, United States	5 ft 11¼ in
1900	Irving Baxter, United States	6 ft 2¾ in OR
1904	Samuel Jones, United States	5 ft 11 in
1906	Cornelius Leahy, Great Britain/Ireland	5 ft 10 in
1908	Harry Porter, United States	6 ft 3 in OR
1912	Alma Richards, United States	6 ft 4 in OR
1920	Richmond Landon, United States	6 ft 4 in OR
1924	Harold Osborn, United States	6 ft 6 in OR
1928	Robert W. King, United States	6 ft 4½ in
1932	Duncan McNaughton, Canada	6 ft 5½ in
1936	Cornelius Johnson, United States	6 ft 8 in OR
1948	John L. Winter, Australia	6 ft 6 in
1952	Walter Davis, United States	6 ft 8½ in OR
1956	Charles Dumas, United States	6 ft 11½ in OR
1960	Robert Shavlakadze, USSR	7 ft 1 in OR
1964	Valery Brumel, USSR	7 ft 1¾ in OR
1968	Dick Fosbury, United States	7 ft 4¼ in OR
1972	Yuri Tarmak, USSR	7 ft 3¾ in
1976	Jacek Wszola, Poland	7 ft 4½ in OR
1980	Gerd Wessig, E Germany	7 ft 8¾ in WR
1984	Dietmar Mögenburg, W Ger	7 ft 8½ in
1988	Gennadiy Avdeyenko, USSR	7 ft 9¾ in OR
1992	Javier Sotomayor, Cuba	7 ft 8 in.
1996	Charles Austin, United States	7 ft 10 in OR
2000	Sergey Kliugin, Russia	7 ft 8¼ in
2004	Stefan Holm, Sweden	7 ft 8¾ in

POLE VAULT

1896	William Hoyt, United States	10 ft 10 in
1900	Irving Baxter, United States	10 ft 10 in
1904	Charles Dvorak, United States	11 ft 5¾ in
1906	Fernand Gonder, France	11 ft 5¾ in
1908	Alfred Gilbert, United States; Edward Cooke Jr., United States	12 ft 2 in OR
1912	Harry Babcock, United States	12 ft 11½ in OR
1920	Frank Foss, United States	13 ft 5 in WR
1924	Lee Barnes, United States	12 ft 11½ in
1928	Sabin Carr, United States	13 ft 9¼ in OR
1932	William Miller, United States	14 ft 1¾ in OR
1936	Earle Meadows, United States	14 ft 3¼ in OR
1948	Guinn Smith, United States	14 ft 1¼ in
1952	Robert Richards, United States	14 ft 11 in OR
1956	Robert Richards, United States	14 ft 11½ in OR
1960	Don Bragg, United States	15 ft 5 in OR
1964	Fred Hansen, United States	16 ft 8¾ in OR
1968	Bob Seagren, United States	17 ft 8½ in OR
1972	Wolfgang Nordwig, E Germany	18 ft ½ in OR
1976	Tadeusz Slusarski, Poland	18 ft ½ in EOR
1980	Wladyslaw Kozakiewicz, Pol	18 ft 11½ in WR
1984	Pierre Quinon, France	18 ft 10¼ in
1988	Sergei Bubka, USSR	19 ft 4¼ in OR
1992	Maksim Tarasov, Unified Team	19 ft ¼ in
1996	Jean Galfione, France	19 ft 5 ¼ in OR
2000	Nick Hysong, United States	19 ft 4¼ in
2004	Timothy Mack, United States	19 ft 6¼ in

Note: OR=Olympic Record. WR=World Record. EOR=Equals Olympic Record. EWR=Equals World Record. WB=World Best.

TRACK AND FIELD — Men *(Cont.)*

LONG JUMP

1896...Ellery Clark, United States	20 ft 10 in	
1900...Alvin Kraenzlein, United States	23 ft 6¾ in OR	
1904...Meyer Prinstein, United States	24 ft 1 in OR	
1906...Meyer Prinstein, United States	23 ft 7½ in	
1908...Frank Irons, United States	24 ft 6½ in OR	
1912...Albert Gutterson, United States	24 ft 11¼ in OR	
1920...William Petersson, Sweden	23 ft 5½ in	
1924...DeHart Hubbard, United States	24 ft 5 in	
1928...Edward B. Hamm, United States	25 ft 4½ in OR	
1932...Edward Gordon, United States	25 ft ¾ in	
1936...Jesse Owens, United States	26 ft 5½ in OR	
1948...William Steele, United States	25 ft 8 in	
1952...Jerome Biffle, United States	24 ft 10 in	
1956...Gregory Bell, United States	25 ft 8¼ in	
1960...Ralph Boston, United States	26 ft 7¾ in OR	
1964...Lynn Davies, Great Britain	26 ft 5¾ in	
1968...Bob Beamon, United States	29 ft 2½ in WR	
1972...Randy Williams, United States	27 ft ½ in	
1976...Arnie Robinson, United States	27 ft 4¾ in	
1980...Lutz Dombrowski, E Germany	28 ft ¼ in	
1984...Carl Lewis, United States	28 ft ¼ in	
1988...Carl Lewis, United States	28 ft 7½ in	
1992...Carl Lewis, United States	28 ft 5½ in	
1996...Carl Lewis, United States	27 ft 10¾ in	
2000...Ivan Pedrosa, Cuba	28 ft ¾ in	
2004...Dwight Phillips, United States	28 ft 2¼ in	

TRIPLE JUMP

1896...James Connolly, United States	44 ft 11¾ in	
1900...Meyer Prinstein, United States	47 ft 5¾ in OR	
1904...Meyer Prinstein, United States	47 ft 1 in	
1906...Peter O'Connor, GB/ Ire	46 ft 2¼ in	
1908...Timothy Ahearne, GB/ Ire	48 ft 11¼ in OR	
1912...Gustaf Lindblom, Sweden	48 ft 5¼ in	
1920...Vilho Tuulos, Finland	47 ft 7 in	
1924...Anthony Winter, Australia	50 ft 11¼ in WR	
1928...Mikio Oda, Japan	49 ft 11 in	
1932...Chuhei Nambu, Japan	51 ft.7 in WR	
1936...Naoto Tajima, Japan	52 ft 6 in WR	
1948...Arne Ahman, Sweden	50 ft 6¼ in	
1952...Adhemar da Silva, Brazil	53 ft 2¾ in WR	
1956...Adhemar da Silva, Brazil	53 ft 7¾ in OR	
1960...Jozef Schmidt, Poland	55 ft 2 in	
1964...Jozef Schmidt, Poland	55 ft 3½ in OR	
1968...Viktor Saneyev, USSR	57 ft ¾ in WR	
1972...Viktor Saneyev, USSR	56 ft 11¾ in	
1976...Viktor Saneyev, USSR	56 ft 8¾ in	
1980...Jaak Uudmae, USSR	56 ft 11¼ in	
1984...Al Joyner, United States	56 ft 7½ in	
1988...Khristo Markov, Bulgaria	57 ft 9½ in OR	
1992...Mike Conley, United States	59 ft 7½ in (w)	
1996...Kenny Harrison, United States	59 ft 4¼ in OR	
2000...Jonathon Edwards, G. Britain	58 ft 1¼ in	
2004...Christian Olsson, Sweden	58 ft 4½ in	

SHOT PUT

1896...Robert Garrett, United States	36 ft 9¾ in	
1900...Richard Sheldon, United States	46 ft 3¼ in OR	
1904...Ralph Rose, United States	48 ft 7 in WR	
1906...Martin Sheridan, United States	40 ft 5¼ in	
1908...Ralph Rose, United States	46 ft 7½ in	
1912...Pat McDonald, United States	50 ft 4 in OR	
1920...Ville Porhola, Finland	48 ft 7¼ in	
1924...Clarence Houser, United States	49 ft 2¼ in	
1928...John Kuck, United States	52 ft ¾ in WR	
1932...Leo Sexton, United States	52 ft 6 in OR	
1936...Hans Woellke, Germany	53 ft 1¾ in OR	
1948...Wilbur Thompson, United States	56 ft 2 in OR	

SHOT PUT *(CONT.)*

1952...Parry O'Brien, United States	57 ft ½ in OR	
1956...Parry O'Brien, United States	60 ft 11¼ in OR	
1960...William Nieder, United States	64 ft 6¾ in OR	
1964...Dallas Long, United States	66 ft 8½ in OR	
1968...Randy Matson, United States	67 ft 4¾ in	
1972...Wladyslaw Komar, Poland	69 ft 6 in OR	
1976...Udo Beyer, E Germany	69 ft ¾ in	
1980...Vladimir Kiselyov, USSR	70 ft ½ in OR	
1984...Alessandro Andrei, Italy	69 ft 9 in	
1988...Ulf Timmermann, E Germany	73 ft 8¾ in OR	
1992...Mike Stulce, United States	71 ft 2½ in	
1996...Randy Barnes, United States	70 ft 11 in	
2000...Arsi Harju, Finland	69 ft 10¼ in	
2004...Yuriy Bilonog, Ukraine	69 ft 5¼ in	

DISCUS THROW

1896...Robert Garrett, United States	95 ft 7½ in	
1900...Rudolf Bauer, Hungary	118 ft 3 in OR	
1904...Martin Sheridan, United States	128 ft 10½ in OR	
1906...Martin Sheridan, United States	136 ft	
1908...Martin Sheridan, United States	134 ft 2 in OR	
1912...Armas Taipele, Finland	148 ft 3 in OR	
1920...Elmer Niklander, Finland	146 ft 7 in	
1924...Clarence Houser, United States	151 ft 4 in OR	
1928...Clarence Houser, United States	155 ft 3 in OR	
1932...John Anderson, United States	162 ft 4 in OR	
1936...Ken Carpenter, United States	165 ft 7 in OR	
1948...Adolfo Consolini, Italy	173 ft 2 in OR	
1952...Sim Iness, United States	180 ft 6 in OR	
1956...Al Oerter, United States	184 ft 11 in OR	
1960...Al Oerter, United States	194 ft 2 in OR	
1964...Al Oerter, United States	200 ft 1 in OR	
1968...Al Oerter, United States	212 ft 6 in OR	
1972...Ludvik Danek, Czechoslovakia	211 ft 3 in	
1976...Mac Wilkins, United States	221 ft 5 in OR	
1980...Viktor Rashchupkin, USSR	218 ft 8 in	
1984...Rolf Dannenberg, W Ger	218 ft 6 in	
1988...Jürgen Schult, E Germany	225 ft 9 in OR	
1992...Romas Ubartas, Lithuania	213 ft 8 in	
1996...Lars Riedel, Germany	227 ft 8 in OR	
2000...Virgilijus Alekna, Lithuania	227 ft 4 in	
2004...Virgilijus Alekna, Lithuania	229 ft 3 in	

HAMMER THROW

1900...John Flanagan, United States	163 ft 1 in	
1904...John Flanagan, United States	168 ft 1 in OR	
1906...Not held		
1908...John Flanagan, United States	170 ft 4 in OR	
1912...Matt McGrath, United States	179 ft 7 in OR	
1920...Pat Ryan, United States	173 ft 5 in	
1924...Fred Tootell, United States	174 ft 10 in	
1928...Patrick O'Callaghan, Ireland	168 ft 7 in	
1932...Patrick O'Callaghan, Ireland	176 ft 11 in	
1936...Karl Hein, Germany	185 ft 4 in OR	
1948...Imre Nemeth, Hungary	183 ft 11 in	
1952...Jozsef Csermak, Hungary	197 ft 11 in WR	
1956...Harold Connolly, United States	207 ft 3 in OR	
1960...Vasily Rudenkov, USSR	220 ft 2 in OR	
1964...Romuald Klim, USSR	228 ft 10 in OR	
1968...Gyula Zsivotsky, Hungary	240 ft 8 in OR	
1972...Anatoli Bondarchuk, USSR	247 ft 8 in OR	
1976...Yuri Sedykh, USSR	254 ft 4 in OR	
1980...Yuri Sedykh, USSR	268 ft 4 in WR	
1984...Juha Tiainen, Finland	256 ft 2 in	
1988...Sergei Litvinov, USSR	278 ft 2 in OR	
1992...Andrey Abduvaliyev, Unified T	270 ft 9 in	
1996...Balazs Kiss, Hungary	266 ft 6 in	
2000...Szymon Ziolkowski, Poland	262 ft 6 in	
2004...Adrian Zsolt, Hungary	272 fr 11 in	

(w)-wind aided

TRACK AND FIELD — Men *(Cont.)*

JAVELIN

1908...Erik Lemming, Sweden	179 ft 10 in
1912...Erik Lemming, Sweden	198 ft 11 in WR
1920...Jonni Myyrä, Finland	215 ft 10 in OR
1924...Jonni Myyrä, Finland	206 ft 6 in
1928...Eric Lundkvist, Sweden	218 ft 6 in OR
1932...Matti Jarvinen, Finland	238 ft 6 in OR
1936...Gerhard Stöck, Germany	235 ft 8 in
1948...Kai Rautavaara, Finland	228 ft 10½ in
1952...Cy Young, United States	242 ft 1 in OR
1956...Egil Danielson, Norway	281 ft 2¼ in WR
1960...Viktor Tsibulenko, USSR	277 ft 8 in
1964...Pauli Nevala, Finland	271 ft 2 in
1968...Janis Lusis, USSR	295 ft 7 in OR
1972...Klaus Wolfermann, W Ger	296 ft 10 in OR
1976...Miklos Nemeth, Hungary	310 ft 4 in WR
1980...Dainis Kuta, USSR	299 ft 2⅜ in
1984...Arto Härkönen, Finland	284 ft 8 in
1988...Tapio Korjus, Finland	276 ft 6 in
1992...Jan Zelezny, Czechoslovakia	294 ft 2 in OR
1996...Jan Zelezny, Czech Republic	289 ft 3 in
2000...Jan Zelezny, Czech Republic	295 ft 9½ in OR
2004...Andrea Thorkildsen, Norway	283 ft 9 in

DECATHLON

		Pts
1904 ...Thomas Kiely, Ireland		6036
1912 ...Jim Thorpe, United States*		8412 WR
1920 ...Helge Lövland, Norway		6803
1924 ...Harold Osborn, United States		7711 WR
1928 ...Paavo Yrjölä, Finland		8053.29 WR
1932 ...James Bausch, United States		8462 WR
1936 ...Glenn Morris, United States		7900 WR
1948 ...Robert Mathias, United States		7139
1952 ...Robert Mathias, United States		7887 WR
1956 ...Milton Campbell, United States		7937 OR
1960 ...Rafer Johnson, United States		8392 OR
1964 ...Willi Holdorf, W Germany		7887
1968 ...Bill Toomey, United States		8193 OR
1972 ...Nikolai Avilov, USSR		8454 WR
1976 ...Bruce Jenner, United States		8617 WR
1980 ...Daley Thompson, Great Britain		8495
1984 ...Daley Thompson, Great Britain		8798 EWR
1988 ...Christian Schenk, E Germany		8488
1992 ...Robert Zmelik, Czechoslovakia		8611
1996 ...Dan O'Brien, United States		8824 OR
2000 ...Erki Nool, Estonia		8641
2004 ...Roman Seberle, Czech Rep		8893 OR

*In 1913, Thorpe was disqualified for having played professional baseball in 1910. His record was restored in 1982.

TRACK AND FIELD — Women

100 METERS

1928....Elizabeth Robinson, US	12.2 EWR
1932....Stella Walsh, Poland	11.9 EWR
1936....Helen Stephens, United States	11.5
1948....Francina Blankers-Koen, Neth	11.9
1952....Marjorie Jackson, Australia	11.5 EWR
1956....Betty Cuthbert, Australia	11.5 EWR
1960....Wilma Rudolph, United States	11.0
1964....Wyomia Tyus, United States	11.4
1968....Wyomia Tyus, United States	11.0 WR
1972....Renate Stecher, E Germany	11.07
1976....Annegret Richter, W Germany	11.08
1980....Lyudmila Kondratyeva, USSR	11.06
1984....Evelyn Ashford, United States	10.97 OR
1988....Florence Griffith Joyner, United States	10.54 WR
1992....Gail Devers, United States	10.82
1996....Gail Devers, United States	10.94
2000....Marion Jones, United States	10.75
2004....Yuliya Nesterenko, Belarus	10.93

200 METERS

1948....Francina Blankers-Koen, Neth	24.4
1952....Marjorie Jackson, Australia	23.7
1956....Betty Cuthbert, Australia	23.4 EOR
1960....Wilma Rudolph, United States	24.0
1964....Edith McGuire, United States	23.0 OR
1968....Irena Szewinska, Poland	22.5 WR
1972....Renate Stecher, E Germany	22.40 EWR
1976....Bärbel Eckert, E Germany	22.37 OR
1980....Bärbel Wöckel (Eckert), E Germ.	22.03 OR
1984....Valerie Brisco-Hooks, U.S.	21.81 OR
1988....Florence Griffith Joyner, U.S.	21.34 WR
1992....Gwen Torrence, United States	21.81
1996....Marie-José Pérec, France	22.12
2000....Marion Jones, United States	21.84
2004....Veronica Campbell, Jamaica	22.05

400 METERS

1964....Betty Cuthbert, Australia	52.0 OR
1968....Colette Besson, France	52.0 EOR
1972....Monika Zehrt, E Germany	51.08 OR
1976....Irena Szewinska, Poland	49.29 WR
1980....Marita Koch, E Germany	48.88 OR
1984....Valerie Brisco-Hooks, U.S.	48.83 OR
1988....Olga Bryzgina, USSR	48.65 OR
1992....Marie-José Pérec, France	48.83
1996....Marie-José Pérec, France	48.25 OR
2000....Cathy Freeman, Australia	49.11
2004....T. Williams-Darling, Bahamas	49.41

800 METERS

1928....Lina Radke, Germany	2:16.8 WR
1932-56..Not held	
1960....Lyudmila Shevtsova, USSR	2:04.3 EWR
1964....Ann Packer, Great Britain	2:01.1 OR
1968....Madeline Manning, United States	2:00.9 OR
1972....Hildegard Falck, W Germany	1:58.55 OR
1976....Tatyana Kazankina, USSR	1:54.94 WR
1980....Nadezhda Olizarenko, USSR	1:53.42 WR
1984....Doina Melinte, Romania	1:57.6
1988....Sigrun Wodars, E Germany	1:56.10
1992....Ellen Van Langen, Netherlands	1:55.54
1996....Svetlana Masterkova, Russia	1:57.73
2000....Maria Mutola, Mozambique	1:56.15
2004....Kelly Holmes, Great Britain	1:56.38

1,500 METERS

1972....Lyudmila Bragina, USSR	4:01.4 WR
1976....Tatyana Kazankina, USSR	4:05.48
1980....Tatyana Kazankina, USSR	3:56.6 OR
1984....Gabriella Dorio, Italy	4:03.25
1988....Paula Ivan, Romania	3:53.96 OR
1992....Hassiba Boulmerka, Algeria	3:55.30
1996....Svetlana Masterkova, Russia	4:00.83
2000....Nouria Merah-Benida, Algeria	4:05.10
2004....Kelly Holmes, Great Britain	3:57.90

Note: OR=Olympic Record. WR=World Record. EOR=Equals Olympic Record. EWR=Equals World Record. WB=World Best.

TRACK AND FIELD — Women *(Cont.)*

3,000 METERS

1984	Maricica Puica, Romania	8:35.96 OR
1988	Tatyana Samolenko, USSR	8:26.53 OR
1992	Elena Romanova, Unified Team	8:46.04

5,000 METERS

1996	Wang Junxia, China	14:57.88
2000	Gabriela Szabo, Romania	14:40.79 OR
2004	Meseret Defar, Ethiopia	14:45.65

10,000 METERS

1988	Olga Bondarenko, USSR	31:05.21 OR
1992	Derartu Tulu, Ethiopia	31:06.02
1996	Fernanda Ribeiro, Portugal	31:01.63 OR
2000	Derartu Tulu, Ethiopia	30:17.49 OR
2004	Huina Xing, China	30:24.36

MARATHON

1984	Joan Benoit, United States	2:24:52 OR
1988	Rosa Mota, Portugal	2:25:40
1992	Valentin Yegorova, Unified Team	2:32:41
1996	Fatuma Roba, Ethiopia	2:26:05
2000	Naoko Takahashi, Japan	2:23:14 OR
2004	Noguchi Mizuki, Japan	2:26:20

80-METER HURDLES

1932	Babe Didrikson, United States	11.7 WR
1936	Trebisonda Valla, Italy	11.7
1948	Francina Blankers-Koen, Neth	11.2 OR
1952	Shirley Strickland, Australia	10.9 WR
1956	Shirley Strickland, Australia	10.7 OR
1960	Irina Press, USSR	10.8
1964	Karin Balzer, E Germany	10.5
1968	Maureen Caird, Australia	10.3 OR

100-METER HURDLES

1972	Annelie Ehrhardt, E Germany	12.59 WR
1976	Johanna Schaller, E Germany	12.77
1980	Vera Komisova, USSR	12.56 OR
1984	Benita Fitzgerald-Brown, U.S.	12.84
1988	Yordanka Donkova, Bulgaria	12.38 OR
1992	Paraskevi Patoulidou, Greece	12.64
1996	Lyudmila Engqvist, Sweden	12.58
2000	Olga Shishigina, Kazakhstan	12.65
2004	Joanna Hayes, United States	12.37 OR

400-METER HURDLES

1984	Nawal el Moutawakel, Morocco	54.61 OR
1988	Debra Flintoff-King, Australia	53.17 OR
1992	Sally Gunnell, Great Britain	53.23
1996	Deon Hemmings, Jamaica	52.82 OR
2000	Irina Privalova, Russia	53.02
2004	Faní Halkiá, Greece	52.82

4 X 100-METER RELAY

1928	Canada	48.4 WR
1932	United States	46.9 WR
1936	United States	46.9
1948	Netherlands	47.5
1952	United States	45.9 WR
1956	Australia	44.5 WR
1960	United States	44.5
1964	Poland	43.6
1968	United States	42.8 WR
1972	W Germany	42.81 EWR
1976	E Germany	42.55 OR
1980	E Germany	41.60 WR
1984	United States	41.65
1988	United States	41.98
1992	United States	42.11
1996	United States	41.95

4 X 100-METER RELAY *(Cont.)*

2000	Bahamas	41.95
2004	Jamaica	41.73

4 X 400-METER RELAY

1972	E Germany	3:23 WR
1976	E Germany	3:19.23 WR
1980	USSR	3:20.02
1984	United States	3:18.29 OR
1988	USSR	3:15.18 WR
1992	Unified Team	3:20.20
1996	United States	3:20.91
2000	United States	3:22.62
2004	United States	3:19.01

10-KILOMETER WALK

1992	Chen Yueling, China	44:32
1996	Elena Nikolayeva, Russia	41:49 OR

20-KILOMETER WALK

2000	Liping Wang, China	1:29:05
2004	Athanasía Tsouméléka, Greece	1:29:12

HIGH JUMP

1928	Ethel Catherwood, Canada	5 ft 2½ in
1932	Jean Shiley, United States	5 ft 5¼ in WR
1936	Ibolya Csak, Hungary	5 ft 3 in
1948	Alice Coachman, United States	5 ft 6 in OR
1952	Esther Brand, South Africa	5 ft 5¾ in
1956	Mildred L. McDaniel, U.S.	5 ft 9¼ in WR
1960	Iolanda Balas, Romania	6 ft ¾ in OR
1964	Iolanda Balas, Romania	6 ft 2¾ in OR
1968	Miloslava Reskova, Czech.	5 ft 11½ in
1972	Ulrike Meyfarth, W. Germany	6 ft 3½ in EWR
1976	Rosemarie Ackermann, E Germ	6 ft 4 in OR
1980	Sara Simeoni, Italy	6 ft 5½ in OR
1984	Ulrike Meyfarth, W Germany	6 ft 7½ in OR
1988	Louise Ritter, United States	6 ft 8 in OR
1992	Heike Henkel, Germany	6 ft 7½ in
1996	Stefka Kostadinova, Bulgaria	6 ft 8¾ in OR
2000	Yelena Yelesina, Russia	6 ft 7 in
2004	Yelena Slesarenko, Russia	6 ft 9 in

POLE VAULT

2000	Stacy Dragila, United States	15 ft 1 in OR
2004	Yelena Isinbayeva, Russia	16 ft 1¼ in WR

LONG JUMP

1948	Olga Gyarmati, Hungary	18 ft 8¼ in
1952	Yvette Williams, New Zealand	20 ft 5¾ in OR
1956	Elzbieta Krzeskinska, Poland	20 ft 10 in EWR
1960	Vyera Krepkina, USSR	20 ft 10¾ in OR
1964	Mary Rand, Great Britain	22 ft 2¼ in WR
1968	Viorica Viscopoleanu, Rom	22 ft 4½ in WR
1972	Heidemarie Rosendahl, W Ger	22 ft 3 in
1976	Angela Voigt, E Germany	22 ft ¾ in
1980	Tatyana Kolpakova, USSR	23 ft 2 in OR
1984	Anisoara Stanciu, Romania	22 ft 10 in
1988	Jackie Joyner-Kersee, U.S.	24 ft 3½ in OR
1992	Heike Drechsler, Germany	23 ft 5¼ in
1996	Chioma Ajunwa, Nigeria	23 ft 4½ in
2000	Heike Drechsler, Germany	22 ft 11¼ in
2004	Tatyana Lebedeva, Russia	23 ft 2½ in

TRIPLE JUMP

1996	Inessa Kravets, Ukraine	50 ft 3½ in
2000	Tereza Marinova, Bulgaria	49 ft 10½ in
2004	Frangoise M. Etone, Cameroon	50 ft 2½ in

SHOT PUT

1948	Micheline Ostermeyer, France	45 ft 1½ in
1952	Galina Zybina, USSR	50 ft 1¾ in WR

Note: OR=Olympic Record; WR=World Record; EOR=Equals Olympic Record; EWR=Equals World Record; WB=World Best.
*In 1971, the 100-meter hurdles replaced the 80-meter hurdles, requiring a change in scoring tables.

TRACK AND FIELD — Women (Cont.)

SHOT PUT (Cont.)

1956...Tamara Tyshkevich, USSR	54 ft 5 in OR
1960...Tamara Press, USSR	56 ft 10 in OR
1964...Tamara Press, USSR	59 ft 6¼ in OR
1968...Margitta Gummel, E Germany	64 ft 4 in WR
1972...Nadezhda Chizhova, USSR	69 ft WR
1976...Ivanka Hristova, Bulgaria	69 ft 5¼ in OR
1980...Ilona Slupianek, E Germany	73 ft 6¼ in
1984...Claudia Losch, W Germany	67 ft 2¼ in
1988...Natalya Lisovskaya, USSR	72 ft 11¾ in
1992...Svetlana Kriveleva, Unified Team	69 ft 1¼ in
1996...Astrid Kumbernuss, Germany	67 ft 5½ in
2000...Yanina Korolchik, Belarus	67 ft 5½ in
2004...Yumileidi Cumba Jay, Cuba	64 ft 3¼ in

DISCUS THROW

1928...Helena Konopacka, Poland	129 ft 11¾ in WR
1932...Lillian Copeland, United States	133 ft 2 in OR
1936...Gisela Mauermayer, Germany	156 ft 3 in OR
1948...Micheline Ostermeyer, France	137 ft 6 in
1952...Nina Romaschkova, USSR	168 ft 8 in OR
1956...Olga Fikotova, Czechoslovakia	176 ft 1 in OR
1960...Nina Ponomaryeva, USSR	180 ft 9 in OR
1964...Tamara Press, USSR	187 ft 10 in OR
1968...Lia Manoliu, Romania	191 ft 2 in OR
1972...Faina Melnik, USSR	218 ft 7 in OR
1976...Evelin Schlaak, E Germany	226 ft 4 in OR
1980...Evelin Jahl (Schlaak), E Germ.	229 ft 6 in OR
1984...Ria Stalman, Netherlands	214 ft 5 in
1988...Martina Hellmann, E Germany	237 ft 2 in OR
1992...Maritza Martén, Cuba	229 ft 10 in
1996...Ilke Wyludda, Germany	228 ft 6 in
2000...Ellina Zvereva, Belarus	224 ft 5 in
2004...Natalya Sadova, Russia	219 ft 10 in

HAMMER THROW

2000...Kamila Skolimowska, Russia	233 ft 5 in OR
2004...Olga Kuzenkova, Russia	246 ft 1½ in OR

JAVELIN THROW

1932...Babe Didrikson, United States	143 ft 4 in OR
1936...Tilly Fleischer, Germany	148 ft 3 in OR
1948...Herma Bauma, Austria	149 ft 6 in
1952...Dana Zatopkova, Czechoslovakia	165 ft 7 in
1956...Inese Jaunzeme, USSR	176 ft 8 in
1960...Elvira Ozolina, USSR	183 ft 8 in OR
1964...Mihaela Penes, Romania	198 ft 7 in
1968...Angela Nemeth, Hungary	198 ft
1972...Ruth Fuchs, E Germany	209 ft 7 in OR
1976...Ruth Fuchs, E Germany	216 ft 4 in OR
1980...Maria Colon, Cuba	224 ft 5 in OR
1984...Tessa Sanderson, Great Britain	228 ft 2 in OR
1988...Petra Felke, E Germany	245 ft OR
1992...Silke Renk, Germany	224 ft 2 in
1996...Heli Rantanen, Finland	222 ft 11 in
2000...Trine Hattestad, Norway	226 ft ½ in OR
2004...Osleidys Menendez, Cuba	234 ft 8 in OR

PENTATHLON

	Pts
1964 ...Irina Press, USSR	5246 WR
1968 ...Ingrid Becker, W Germany	5098
1972 ...Mary Peters, Great Britain	4801 WR
1976 ...Siegrun Siegl, E Germany	4745
1980 ...Nadezhda Tkachenko, USSR	5083 WR

HEPTATHLON

	Pts
1984 ...Glynis Nunn, Australia	6390 OR
1988 ...Jackie Joyner-Kersee, U.S.	7291 WR
1992 ...Jackie Joyner-Kersee, U.S.	7044
1996 ...Ghada Shouaa, Syria	6780
2000 ...Denise Lewis, Great Britain	6584
2004 ...Carolina Kluft, Sweden	6952

BASKETBALL — Men

1936
Final: United States 19, Canada 8
United States: Ralph Bishop, Joe Fortenberry, Carl Knowles, Jack Ragland, Carl Shy, William Wheatley, Francis Johnson, Samuel Balter, John Gibbons, Frank Lubin, Arthur Mollner, Donald Piper, Duane Swanson, Willard Schmidt

1948
Final: United States 65, France 21
United States: Cliff Barker, Don Barksdale, Ralph Beard, Lewis Beck, Vince Boryla, Gordon Carpenter, Alex Groza, Wallace Jones, Bob Kurland, Ray Lumpp, Robert Pitts, Jesse Renick, Bob Robinson, Ken Rollins

1952
Final: United States 36, USSR 25
United States: Charles Hoag, Bill Hougland, Melvin Dean Kelley, Bob Kenney, Clyde Lovellette, Marcus Freiberger, Victor Wayne Glasgow, Frank McCabe, Daniel Pippen, Howard Williams, Ronald Bontemps, Bob Kurland, William Lienhard, John Keller

1956
Final: United States 89, USSR 55
United States: Carl Cain, Bill Hougland, K.C. Jones, Bill Russell, James Walsh, William Evans, Burdette Haldorson, Ron Tomsic, Dick Boushka, Gilbert Ford, Bob Jeangerard, Charles Darling

1960
Final: United States 90, Brazil 63
United States: Jay Arnette, Walt Bellamy, Bob Boozer, Terry Dischinger, Jerry Lucas, Oscar Robertson, Adrian Smith, Burdette Haldorson, Darrall Imhoff, Allen Kelley, Lester Lane, Jerry West

1964
Final: United States 73, USSR 59
United States: Jim Barnes, Bill Bradley, Larry Brown, Joe Caldwell, Mel Counts, Richard Davies, Walt Hazzard, Lucius Jackson, John McCaffrey, Jeff Mullins, Jerry Shipp, George Wilson

1968
Final: United States 65, Yugoslavia 50
United States: John Clawson, Ken Spain, Jo-Jo White, Michael Barrett, Spencer Haywood, Charles Scott, William Hosket, Calvin Fowler, Michael Silliman, Glynn Saulters, James King, Donald Dee

1972
Final: USSR 51, United States 50
United States: Kenneth Davis, Doug Collins, Thomas Henderson, Mike Bantom, Bobby Jones, Dwight Jones, James Forbes, James Brewer, Tom Burleson, Tom McMillen, Kevin Joyce, Ed Ratleff

BASKETBALL — Men (Cont.)

1976
Final: United States 95, Yugoslavia 74
United States: Phil Ford, Steve Sheppard, Adrian Dantley, Walter Davis, Quinn Buckner, Ernie Grunfeld, Kenny Carr, Scott May, Michel Armstrong, Tom La Garde, Phil Hubbard, Mitch Kupchak

1980
Final: Yugoslavia 86, Italy 77
U.S. participated in boycott.

1984
Final: United States 96, Spain 65
United States: Steve Alford, Leon Wood, Patrick Ewing, Vern Fleming, Alvin Robertson, Michael Jordan, Joe Kleine, Jon Koncak, Wayman Tisdale, Chris Mullin, Sam Perkins, Jeff Turner

1988
Final: USSR 76, Yugoslavia 63
U.S. (3rd): Mitch Richmond, Charles E. Smith IV, Vernell Coles, Hersey Hawkins, Jeff Grayer, Charles D. Smith, Willie Anderson, Stacey Augmon, Dan Majerle, Danny Manning, J.R. Reid, David Robinson

1992
Final: United States 117, Croatia 85
United States: David Robinson, Christian Laettner,

1992 (Cont.)
Patrick Ewing, Larry Bird, Scottie Pippen, Michael Jordan, Clyde Drexler, Karl Malone, John Stockton, Chris Mullin, Charles Barkley, Earvin Johnson

1996
Final: United States 95, Yugoslavia 69
United States: Charles Barkley, Anfernee Hardaway, Grant Hill, Karl Malone, Reggie Miller, Hakeem Olajuwon, Shaquille O'Neal, Scottie Pippen, Mitch Richmond, John Stockton, David Robinson, Gary Payton

2000
Final: United States 85, France 75
United States: Shareef Abdur-Rahim, Ray Allen, Vin Baker, Vince Carter, Kevin Garnett, Tim Hardaway, Allan Houston, Jason Kidd, Antonio McDyess, Alonzo Mourning, Gary Payton, Steve Smith

2004
Final: Argentina 84, Italy 69
U.S. (3rd): Allen Iverson, LeBron James, Tim Duncan, Carmelo Anthony, Dwyane Wade, Richard Jefferson, Lamar Odom, Stephon Marbury, Carlos Boozer, Emeka Okafor, Amare Stoudemire, Shawn Marion

BASKETBALL — Women

1976
Gold, USSR; Silver, United States*
United States: Cindy Brogdon, Susan Rojcewicz, Ann Meyers, Lusia Harris, Nancy Dunkle, Charlotte Lewis, Nancy Lieberman, Gail Marquis, Patricia Roberts, Mary Anne O'Connor, Patricia Head, Julienne Simpson

*In 1976 the women played a round-robin tournament, with the gold medal going to the team with the best record. The USSR won with a 5–0 record, and the USA, with a 3–2 record, was given the silver by virtue of a 95–79 victory over Bulgaria, which was also 3–2.

1980
Final: USSR 104, Bulgaria 73
U.S. participated in boycott.

1984
Final: United States 85, Korea 55
United States: Teresa Edwards, Lea Henry, Lynette Woodard, Anne Donovan, Cathy Boswell, Cheryl Miller, Janice Lawrence, Cindy Noble, Kim Mulkey, Denise Curry, Pamela McGee, Carol Menken-Schaudt

1988
Final: United States 77, Yugoslavia 70
United States: Teresa Edwards, Mary Ethridge, Cynthia Brown, Anne Donovan, Teresa Weatherspoon, Bridgette Gordon, Victoria Bullett, Andrea Lloyd, Katrina McClain, Jennifer Gillom, Cynthia Cooper, Suzanne McConnell

1992
Final: Unified Team 76, China 66
United States (3rd): Teresa Edwards, Teresa Weatherspoon, Victoria Bullett, Katrina McClain, Cynthia Cooper, Suzanne McConnell, Daedra Charles, Clarissa Davis, Tammy Jackson, Vickie Orr, Carolyn Jones, Medina Dixon

1996
Final: United States 111, Brazil 87
United States: Jennifer Azzi, Ruthie Bolton, Teresa Edwards, Lisa Leslie, Rebecca Lobo, Katrina McClain, Nikki McCray, Carla McGhee, Dawn Staley, Katy Steding, Sheryl Swoopes, Venus Lacey

2000
Final: United States 76, Australia 54
United States: Ruthie Bolton-Holifield, Teresa Edwards, Yolanda Griffith, Chamique Holdsclaw, Lisa Leslie, Nikki McCray, Delisha Milton, Katie Smith, Dawn Staley, Sheryl Swoopes, Natalie Williams, Kara Wolters

2004
Final: United States 74, Australia 63
United States: Dawn Staley, Diana Taurasi, Lisa Leslie, Sheryl Swoopes, Tamika Catchings, Sue Bird, Ruth Riley, Shannon Johnson, Katie Smith, Yolanda Griffith, Swintayla Cash, Tina Thompson

BOXING

LIGHT FLYWEIGHT (106 LB)
1968	Francisco Rodriguez, Venezuela
1972	Gyorgy Gedo, Hungary
1976	Jorge Hernandez, Cuba
1980	Shamil Sabyrov, USSR
1984	Paul Gonzalez, United States

LIGHT FLYWEIGHT (CONT.)
1988	Ivailo Hristov, Bulgaria
1992	Rogelio Marcelo, Cuba
1996	Daniel Petrov, Bulgaria
2000	Brahim Asloum, France
2004	Yan Bhartelemy Varela, Cuba

BOXING *(Cont.)*

FLYWEIGHT (112 LB)

1904	George Finnegan, United States
1920	Frank Di Gennara, United States
1924	Fidel LaBarba, United States
1928	Antal Kocsis, Hungary
1932	Istvan Enekes, Hungary
1936	Willi Kaiser, Germany
1948	Pascual Perez, Argentina
1952	Nathan Brooks, United States
1956	Terence Spinks, Great Britain
1960	Gyula Torok, Hungary
1964	Fernando Atzori, Italy
1968	Ricardo Delgado, Mexico
1972	Georgi Kostadinov, Bulgaria
1976	Leo Randolph, United States
1980	Peter Lessov, Bulgaria
1984	Steve McCrory, United States
1988	Kim Kwang Sun, S Korea
1992	Su Choi Chol, N Korea
1996	Maikro Romero, Cuba
2000	Wijan Ponlid, Thailand
2004	Yuriokis Toledano, Cuba

BANTAMWEIGHT (119 LB)

1904	Oliver Kirk, United States
1908	A. Henry Thomas, Great Britain
1920	Clarence Walker, S Africa
1924	William Smith, S Africa
1928	Vittorio Tamagnini, Italy
1932	Horace Gwynne, Canada
1936	Ulderico Sergo, Italy
1948	Tibor Csik, Hungary
1952	Pentti Hamalainen, Finland
1956	Wolfgang Behrendt, E Germany
1960	Oleg Grigoryev, USSR
1964	Takao Sakurai, Japan
1968	Valery Sokolov, USSR
1972	Orlando Martinez, Cuba
1976	Yong Jo Gu, N Korea
1980	Juan Hernandez, Cuba
1984	Maurizio Stecca, Italy
1988	Kennedy McKinney, United States
1992	Joel Casamayor, Cuba
1996	István Kovács, Hungary
2000	Guillermo Ortiz, Cuba
2004	Guillermo Ortiz, Cuba

FEATHERWEIGHT (125 LB)

1904	Oliver Kirk, United States
1908	Richard Gunn, Great Britain
1920	Paul Fritsch, France
1924	John Fields, United States
1928	Lambertus van Klaveren, Netherlands
1932	Carmelo Robledo, Argentina
1936	Oscar Casanovas, Argentina
1948	Ernesto Formenti, Italy
1952	Jan Zachara, Czechoslovakia
1956	Vladimir Safronov, USSR
1960	Francesco Musso, Italy
1964	Stanislav Stephashkin, USSR
1968	Antonio Roldan, Mexico
1972	Boris Kousnetsov, USSR
1976	Angel Herrera, Cuba
1980	Rudi Fink, E Germany
1984	Meldrick Taylor, United States
1988	Giovanni Parisi, Italy
1992	Andreas Tews, Germany
1996	Somluck Kamsing, Thailand
2000	Bekzat Sattarkhanox, Kazakhsta
2004	Alexei Tichtchenko, Russia

LIGHTWEIGHT (132 LB)

1904	Harry Spanger, United States
1908	Frederick Grace, Great Britain
1920	Samuel Mosberg, United States
1924	Hans Nielsen, Denmark
1928	Carlo Orlandi, Italy
1932	Lawrence Stevens, S Africa
1936	Imre Harangi, Hungary
1948	Gerald Dreyer, S Africa
1952	Aureliano Bolognesi, Italy
1956	Richard McTaggart, Great Britain
1960	Kazimierz Pazdzior, Poland
1964	Jozef Grudzien, Poland
1968	Ronald Harris, United States
1972	Jan Szczepanski, Poland
1976	Howard Davis, United States
1980	Angel Herrera, Cuba
1984	Pernell Whitaker, United States
1988	Andreas Zuelow, E Germany
1992	Oscar De La Hoya, United States
1996	Hocine Soltani, Algeria
2000	Mario Mesa, Cuba
2004	Mario Mesa, Cuba

LIGHT WELTERWEIGHT (139 LB)

1952	Charles Adkins, United States
1956	Vladimir Yengibaryan, USSR
1960	Bohumil Nemecek, Czechoslovakia
1964	Jerzy Kulej, Poland
1968	Jerzy Kulej, Poland
1972	Ray Seales, United States
1976	Ray Leonard, United States
1980	Patrizio Oliva, Italy
1984	Jerry Page, United States
1988	Viatcheslav Janovski, USSR
1992	Hector Vinent, Cuba
1996	Hector Vinent, Cuba
2000	Mahamadkadyz Abdullaev, Uzbekistan
2004	Manus Boonjumnong, Thailand

WELTERWEIGHT (147 LB)

1904	Albert Young, United States
1920	Albert Schneider, Canada
1924	Jean Delarge, Belgium
1928	Edward Morgan, New Zealand
1932	Edward Flynn, United States
1936	Sten Suvio, Finland
1948	Julius Torma, Czechoslovakia
1952	Zygmunt Chychla, Poland
1956	Nicolae Linca, Romania
1960	Giovanni Benvenuti, Italy
1964	Marian Kasprzyk, Poland
1968	Manfred Wolke, E Germany
1972	Emilio Correa, Cuba
1976	Jochen Bachfeld, E Germany
1980	Andres Aldama, Cuba
1984	Mark Breland, United States
1988	Robert Wangila, Kenya
1992	Michael Carruth, Ireland
1996	Oleg Saitov, Russia
2000	Oleg Saitov, Russia
2004	Bakhtiyar Artayev, Kazakhstan

LIGHT MIDDLEWEIGHT (156 LB)

1952	Laszlo Papp, Hungary
1956	Laszlo Papp, Hungary
1960	Wilbert McClure, United States
1964	Boris Lagutin, USSR
1968	Boris Lagutin, USSR
1972	Dieter Kottysch, W Germany
1976	Jerzy Rybicki, Poland
1980	Armando Martinez, Cuba
1984	Frank Tate, United States

BOXING *(Cont.)*

LIGHT MIDDLEWEIGHT *(CONT.)*
1988 ....Park Si-Hun, S Korea
1992 ....Juan Lemus, Cuba
1996 ....David Reid, United States
2000 ....Yermakhan Ibraimov, Kazakhstan

MIDDLEWEIGHT (165 LB)
1904 ....Charles Mayer, United States
1908 ....John Douglas, Great Britain
1920 ....Harry Mallin, Great Britain
1924 ....Harry Mallin, Great Britain
1928 ....Piero Toscani, Italy
1932 ....Carmen Barth, United States
1936 ....Jean Despeaux, France
1948 ....Laszlo Papp, Hungary
1952 ....Floyd Patterson, United States
1956 ....Gennady Schatkov, USSR
1960 ....Edward Crook, United States
1964 ....Valery Popenchenko, USSR
1968 ....Christopher Finnegan, Great Britain
1972 ....Vyacheslav Lemechev, USSR
1976 ....Michael Spinks, United States
1980 ....Jose Gomez, Cuba
1984 ....Shin Joon Sup, S Korea
1988 ....Henry Maske, E Germany
1992 ....Ariel Hernandez, Cuba
1996 ....Ariel Hernandez, Cuba
2000 ....Jorge Gutierrez, Cuba
2004 ....Gaydarbek Gaydarbekov, Russia

LIGHT HEAVYWEIGHT (178 LB)
1920 ....Edward Eagan, United States
1924 ....Harry Mitchell, Great Britain
1928 ....Victor Avendano, Argentina
1932 ....David Carstens, S Africa
1936 ....Roger Michelot, France
1948 ....George Hunter, S Africa
1952 ....Norvel Lee, United States
1956 ....James Boyd, United States
1960 ....Cassius Clay, United States
1964 ....Cosimo Pinto, Italy
1968 ....Dan Poznyak, USSR
1972 ....Mate Parlov, Yugoslavia
1976 ....Leon Spinks, United States

LIGHT HEAVYWEIGHT *(CONT.)*
1980 ....Slobodan Kacer, Yugoslavia
1984 ....Anton Josipovic, Yugoslavia
1988 ....Andrew Maynard, United States
1992 ....Torsten May, Germany
1996 ....Vassili Jirov, Kazakhstan
2000 ....Alexander Lebziak, Russia
2004 ....Andre Ward, United States

HEAVYWEIGHT (OVER 201 LB)
1904 ....Samuel Berger, United States
1908 ....Albert Oldham, Great Britain
1920 ....Ronald Rawson, Great Britain
1924 ....Otto von Porat, Norway
1928 ....Arturo Rodriguez Jurado, Argentina
1932 ....Santiago Lovell, Argentina
1936 ....Herbert Runge, Germany
1948 ....Rafael Inglesias, Argentina
1952 ....H. Edward Sanders, United States
1956 ....T. Peter Rademacher, United States
1960 ....Franco De Piccoli, Italy
1964 ....Joe Frazier, United States
1968 ....George Foreman, United States
1972 ....Teofilo Stevenson, Cuba
1976 ....Teofilo Stevenson, Cuba
1980 ....Teofilo Stevenson, Cuba

HEAVYWEIGHT (201* LB)
1984 ....Henry Tillman, United States
1988 ....Ray Mercer, United States
1992 ....Félix Sávon, Cuba
1996 ....Félix Sávon, Cuba
2000 ....Félix Sávon, Cuba
2004 ....Odlanier Fonte, Cuba

SUPERHEAVYWEIGHT (UNLIMITED)
1984 ....Tyrell Biggs, United States
1988 ....Lennox Lewis, Canada
1992 ....Roberto Balado, Cuba
1996 ....Vladimir Klitchko, Ukraine
2000 ....Audley Harrison, Great Britain
2004 ....Alexander Povetkin, Russia

*Until 1984 the heavyweight division was unlimited. With the addition of the super heavyweight division, a limit of 201 pounds was imposed.

SWIMMING— Men

50-METER FREESTYLE
1904	Zoltan Halmay, Hungary (50 yds)	28.0
1988	Matt Biondi, United States	22.14 WR
1992	Aleksandr Popov, Unified Team	22.30
1996	Aleksandr Popov, Russia	22.13
2000	Anthony Ervin, United States	21.98
	Gary Hall Jr, United States	21.98
2004	Gary Hall Jr, United States	21.93

100-METER FREESTYLE
1896	Alfred Hajos, Hungary	1:22.2 OR
1904	Zoltan Halmay, Hungary (100 yds)	1:02.8
1906	Charles Daniels, United States	1:13.4
1908	Charles Daniels, United States	1:05.6 WR
1912	Duke Kahanamoku, United States	1:03.4
1920	Duke Kahanamoku, United States	1:00.4 WR
1924	John Weissmuller, United States	59.0 OR
1928	John Weissmuller, United States	58.6 OR
1932	Yasuji Miyazaki, Japan	58.2
1936	Ferenc Csik, Hungary	57.6
1948	Wally Ris, United States	57.3 OR
1952	Clarke Scholes, United States	57.4
1956	Jon Henricks, Australia	55.4 OR

100-METER FREESTLYE *(CONT.)*
1960	John Devitt, Australia	55.2 OR
1964	Don Schollander, United States	53.4 OR
1968	Mike Wenden, Australia	52.2 WR
1972	Mark Spitz, United States	51.22 WR
1976	Jim Montgomery, United States	49.99 WR
1980	Jörg Woithe, E Germany	50.40
1984	Rowdy Gaines, United States	49.80 OR
1988	Matt Biondi, United States	48.63 OR
1992	Aleksandr Popov, Unified Team	49.02
1996	Aleksandr Popov, Russia	48.74
2000	P. van den Hoogenband, Neth	48.30
2004	P. van den Hoogenband, Neth	48.17

200-METER FREESTYLE
1900	Frederick Lane, Australia	2:25.2 OR
1904	Charles Daniels, United States	2:44.2
1968	Michael Wenden, Australia	1:55.2 OR
1972	Mark Spitz, United States	1:52.78 WR
1976	Bruce Furniss, United States	1:50.29 WR
1980	Sergei Kopliakov, USSR	1:49.81 OR
1984	Michael Gross, W Germany	1:47.44 WR

SWIMMING— Men *(Cont.)*

200-METER FREESTYLE *(CONT.)*

1988	Duncan Armstrong, Australia	1:47.25 WR
1992	Evgueni Sadovyi, Unified Team	1:46.70 OR
1996	Danyon Loader, New Zealand	1:47.63
2000	Pieter van den Hoogenband, Neth	1:45.35 EWR
2004	Ian Thorpe, Australia	1:44.71 OR

400-METER FREESTYLE

1896	Paul Neumann, Austria (500 yds)	8:12.6
1904	Charles Daniels, U.S. (440 yds)	6:16.2
1906	Otto Scheff, Austria (440 yds),	6:23.8
1908	Henry Taylor, Great Britain	5:36.8
1912	George Hodgson, Canada	5:24.4
1920	Norman Ross, United States	5:26.8
1924	John Weissmuller, United States	5:04.2 OR
1928	Albert Zorilla, Argentina	5:01.6 OR
1932	Buster Crabbe, United States	4:48.4 OR
1936	Jack Medica, United States	4:44.5 OR
1948	William Smith, United States	4:41.0 OR
1952	Jean Boiteux, France	4:30.7 OR
1956	Murray Rose, Australia	4:27.3 OR
1960	Murray Rose, Australia	4:18.3 OR
1964	Don Schollander, United States	4:12.2 WR
1968	Mike Burton, United States	4:09.0 OR
1972	Brad Cooper, Australia	4:00.27 OR
1976	Brian Goodell, United States	3:51.93 WR
1980	Vladimir Salnikov, USSR	3:51.31 OR
1984	George DiCarlo, United States	3:51.23 OR
1988	Uwe Dassler, E Germany	3:46.95 WR
1992	Evgueni Sadovyi, Unified Team	3:45.00 WR
1996	Danyon Loader, New Zealand	3:47.97
2000	Ian Thorpe, Australia	3:40.59 WR
2004	Ian Thorpe, Australia	3:43.10

1,500-METER FREESTYLE

1908	Henry Taylor, Great Britain	22:48.4 WR
1912	George Hodgson, Canada	22:00.0 WR
1920	Norman Ross, United States	22:23.2
1924	Andrew Charlton, Australia	20:06.6 WR
1928	Arne Borg, Sweden	19:51.8 OR
1932	Kusuo Kitamura, Japan	19:12.4 OR
1936	Noboru Terada, Japan	19:13.7
1948	James McLane, United States	19:18.5
1952	Ford Konno, United States	18:30.3 OR
1956	Murray Rose, Australia	17:58.9
1960	John Konrads, Australia	17:19.6 OR
1964	Robert Windle, Australia	17:01.7 OR
1968	Mike Burton, United States	16:38.9 OR
1972	Mike Burton, United States	15:52.58 OR
1976	Brian Goodell, United States	15:02.40 WR
1980	Vladimir Salnikov, USSR	14:58.27 WR
1984	Michael O'Brien, United States	15:05.20
1988	Vladimir Salnikov, USSR	15:00.40
1992	Kieren Perkins, Australia	14:43.48 WR
1996	Kieren Perkins, Australia	14:56.40
2000	Grant Hackett, Australia	14:48.33
2004	Grant Hackett, Australia	14:43.40 OR

100-METER BACKSTROKE

1904	Walter Brack, Germany (100 yds)	1:16.8
1908	Arno Bieberstein, Germany	1:24.6 WR
1912	Harry Hebner, United States	1:21.2
1920	Warren Kealoha, United States	1:15.2
1924	Warren Kealoha, United States	1:13.2 OR
1928	George Kojac, United States	1:08.2 WR
1932	Masaji Kiyokawa, Japan	1:08.6
1936	Adolph Kiefer, United States	1:05.9 OR
1948	Allen Stack, United States	1:06.4
1952	Yoshi Oyakawa, United States	1:05.4 OR

100-METER BACKSTROKE *(CONT.)*

1956	David Thiele, Australia	1:02.2 OR
1960	David Thiele, Australia	1:01.9 OR
1968	Roland Matthes, E Germany	58.7 OR
1972	Roland Matthes, E Germany	56.58 OR
1976	John Naber, United States	55.49 WR
1980	Bengf Baron, Sweden	56.33
1984	Rick Carey, United States	55.79
1988	Daichi Suzuki, Japan	55.05
1992	Mark Tewksbury, Canada	53.98 WR
1996	Jeff Rouse, United States	54.10
2000	Lenny Krayzelburg, United States	53.72 OR
2004	Aaron Peirsol, United States	54.06

200-METER BACKSTROKE

1900	Ernst Hoppenberg, Germany	2:47.0
1964	Jed Graef, United States	2:10.3 WR
1968	Roland Matthes, E Germany	2:09.6 OR
1972	Roland Matthes, E Germany	2:02.82 EWR
1976	John Naber, United States	1:59.19 WR
1980	Sandor Wladar, Hungary	2:01.93
1984	Rick Carey, United States	2:00.23
1988	Igor Polianski, USSR	1:59.37
1992	Martin Lopez-Zubero, Spain	1:58.47 OR
1996	Brad Bridgewater, United States	1:58.54
2000	Lenny Krayzelburg, United States	1:56.76 OR
2004	Aaron Peirsol, United States	1:54.95 OR

100-METER BREASTSTROKE

1968	Don McKenzie, United States	1:07.7 OR
1972	Nobutaka Taguchi, Japan	1:04.94 WR
1976	John Hencken, United States	1:03.11 WR
1980	Duncan Goodhew, Great Britain	1:03.44
1984	Steve Lundquist, United States	1:01.65 WR
1988	Adrian Moorhouse, Great Britain	1:02.04
1992	Nelson Diebel, United States	1:01.50 OR
1996	Fred DeBurghgraeve, Belgium	1:00.65
2000	Domenico Fioravanti, Italy	1:00.46 OR
2004	Kosuke Kitajima, Japan	1:00.08

200-METER BREASTSTROKE

1908	Frederick Holman, Great Britain	3:09.2 WR
1912	Walter Bathe, Germany	3:01.8 OR
1920	Haken Malmroth, Sweden	3:04.4
1924	Robert Skelton, United States	2:56.6
1928	Yoshiyuki Tsuruta, Japan	2:48.8 OR
1932	Yoshiyuki Tsuruta, Japan	2:45.4
1936	Tetsuo Hamuro, Japan	2:41.5 OR
1948	Joseph Verdeur, United States	2:39.3 OR
1952	John Davies, Australia	2:34.4 OR
1956	Masaru Furukawa, Japan	2:34.7 OR
1960	William Mulliken, United States	2:37.4
1964	Ian O'Brien, Australia	2:27.8 WR
1968	Felipe Munoz, Mexico	2:28.7
1972	John Hencken, United States	2:21.55 WR
1976	David Wilkie, Great Britain	2:15.11 WR
1980	Robertas Zhulpa, USSR	2:15.85
1984	Victor Davis, Canada	2:13.34 WR
1988	Jozsef Szabo, Hungary	2:13.52
1992	Mike Barrowman, United States	2:10.16 WR
1996	Norbert Rózsa, Hungary	2:12.57
2000	Domenico Fioravanti, Italy	2:10.87
2004	Kosuke Kitajima, Japan	2:09.44 OR

100-METER BUTTERFLY

1968	Doug Russell, United States	55.9 OR
1972	Mark Spitz, United States	54.27 WR
1976	Matt Vogel, United States	54.35
1980	Pär Arvidsson, Sweden	54.92

Note: OR=Olympic Record. WR=World Record. EOR=Equals Olympic Record. EWR=Equals World Record. WB=World Best.

SWIMMING — Men (Cont.)

100-METER BUTTERFLY (CONT.)

Year	Champion	Time
1984	Michael Gross, W Germany	53.08 WR
1988	Anthony Nesty, Suriname	53.00 OR
1992	Pablo Morales, United States	53.32
1996	Denis Pankratov, Russia	52.27 WR
2000	Lars Froelander, Sweden	52.00
2004	Michael Phelps, United States	51.25 OR

200-METER BUTTERFLY

Year	Champion	Time
1956	William Yorzyk, United States	2:19.3 OR
1960	Michael Troy, United States	2:12.8 WR
1964	Kevin Berry, Australia	2:06.6 WR
1968	Carl Robie, United States	2:08.7
1972	Mark Spitz, United States	2:00.70 WR
1976	Mike Bruner, United States	1:59.23 WR
1980	Sergei Fesenko, USSR	1:59.76
1984	Jon Sieben, Australia	1:57.04 WR
1988	Michael Gross, W Germany	1:56.94 OR
1992	Melvin Stewart, United States	1:56.26 OR
1996	Denis Pankratov, Russia	1:56.51
2000	Tom Malchow, United States	1:55.35 OR
2004	Michael Phelps, United States	1:54.04 OR

200-METER INDIVIDUAL MEDLEY

Year	Champion	Time
1968	Charles Hickcox, United States	2:12.0 OR
1972	Gunnar Larsson, Sweden	2:07.17 WR
1984	Alex Baumann, Canada	2:01.42 WR
1988	Tamas Darnyi, Hungary	2:00.17 WR
1992	Tamas Darnyi, Hungary	2:00.76
1996	Attila Czene, Hungary	1:59.91 OR
2000	Massimiliano Rosolino, Italy	1:58.98 OR
2004	Michael Phelps, United States	1:57.14 OR

400-METER INDIVIDUAL MEDLEY

Year	Champion	Time
1964	Richard Roth, United States	4:45.4 WR
1968	Charles Hickcox, United States	4:48.4
1972	Gunnar Larsson, Sweden	4:31.98 OR
1976	Rod Strachan, United States	4:23.68 WR
1980	Aleksandr Sidorenko, USSR	4:22.89 OR
1984	Alex Baumann, Canada	4:17.41 WR
1988	Tamas Darnyi, Hungary	4:14.75 WR
1992	Tamas Darnyi, Hungary	4:14.23 OR
1996	Tom Dolan United States	4:14.90
2000	Tom Dolan, United States	4:11.76 WR
2004	Michael Phelps, United States	4:08.26 WR

4 X 100-METER MEDLEY RELAY

Year	Champion	Time
1960	United States	4:05.4 WR
1964	United States	3:58.4 WR

4 X 100-METER MEDLEY RELAY (CONT.)

Year	Champion	Time
1968	United States	3:54.9 WR
1972	United States	3:48.16 WR
1976	United States	3:42.22 WR
1980	Australia	3:45.70
1984	United States	3:39.30 WR
1988	United States	3:36.93 WR
1992	United States	3:36.93 EWR
1996	United States	3:34.84 WR
2000	United States	3:33.73 WR
2004	United States	3:30.68 WR

4 X 100-METER FREESTYLE RELAY

Year	Champion	Time
1964	United States	3:32.2 WR
1968	United States	3:31.7 WR
1972	United States	3:26.42 WR
1984	United States	3:19.03 WR
1988	United States	3:16.53 WR
1992	United States	3:16.74
1996	United States	3:15.41 OR
2000	Australia	3:13.67 WR
2004	S Africa	3:13.17 WR

4 X 200-METER FREESTYLE RELAY

Year	Champion	Time
1906	Hungary (1,000 m)	16:52.4
1908	Great Britain	10:55.6
1912	Australia/New Zealand	10:11.6 WR
1920	United States	10:04.4 WR
1924	United States	9:53.4 WR
1928	United States	9:36.2 WR
1932	Japan	8:58.4 WR
1936	Japan	8:51.5 WR
1948	United States	8:46.0 WR
1952	United States	8:31.1 OR
1956	Australia	8:23.6 WR
1960	United States	8:10.2 WR
1964	United States	7:52.1 WR
1968	United States	7:52.33
1972	United States	7:35.78 WR
1976	United States	7:23.22 WR
1980	USSR	7:23.50
1984	United States	7:15.69 WR
1988	United States	7:12.51 WR
1992	Unified Team	7:11.95 WR
1996	United States	7:14.84
2000	Australia	7:07.05 WR
2004	United States	7:07.33

SWIMMING — Women

50-METER FREESTYLE

Year	Champion	Time
1988	Kristin Otto, E Germany	25.49 OR
1992	Yang Wenyi, China	24.79 WR
1996	Amy Van Dyken, United States	24.87
2000	Inge de Bruijn, Netherlands	24.32 WR
2004	Inge de Bruijn, Netherlands	24.58

100-METER FREESTYLE

Year	Champion	Time
1912	Fanny Durack, Australia	1:22.2
1920	Ethelda Bleibtrey, United States	1:13.6 WR
1924	Ethel Lackie, United States	1:12.4
1928	Albina Osipowich, United States	1:11.0 OR
1932	Helene Madison, United States	1:06.8 OR
1936	Hendrika Mastenbroek, Neth	1:05.9 OR
1948	Greta Andersen, Denmark	1:06.3
1952	Katalin Szöke, Hungary	1:06.8
1956	Dawn Fraser, Australia	1:02.0 WR
1960	Dawn Fraser, Australia	1:01.2 OR
1964	Dawn Fraser, Australia	59.5 OR

100-METER FREESTYLE (CONT.)

Year	Champion	Time
1968	Jan Henne, United States	1:00.0
1972	Sandra Neilson, United States	58.59 OR
1976	Kornelia Ender, E Germany	55.65 WR
1980	Barbara Krause, E Germany	54.79 WR
1984	Carrie Steinseifer, United States	55.92
	Nancy Hogshead, United States	55.92
1988	Kristin Otto, E Germany	54.93
1992	Zhuang Yong, China	54.64 OR
1996	Le Jingyi, China	54.50 OR
2000	Inge de Bruijn, Netherlands	53.83 OR
2004	Jodie Henry, Australia	53.84

200-METER FREESTYLE

Year	Champion	Time
1968	Debbie Meyer, United States	2:10.5 OR
1972	Shane Gould, Australia	2:03.56 WR
1976	Kornelia Ender, E Germany	1:59.26 WR
1980	Barbara Krause, E Germany	1:58.33 OR
1984	Mary Wayte, United States	1:59.23
1988	Heike Friedrich, E Germany	1:57.65 OR

Note: OR=Olympic Record. WR=World Record. EOR=Equals Olympic Record. EWR=Equals World Record. WB=World Best.

SWIMMING — Women *(Cont.)*

200-METER FREESTYLE *(CONT.)*

1992....Nicole Haislett, United States	1:57.90
1996....Claudia Poll, Costa Rica	1:58.16
2000....Susie O'Neill, Australia	1:58.24
2004....Camelia Potec, Romania	1:58.03

400-METER FREESTYLE

1924....Martha Norelius, United States	6:02.2 OR
1928....Martha Norelius, United States	5:42.8 WR
1932....Helene Madison, United States	5:28.5 WR
1936....Hendrika Mastenbroek, Neth.	5:26.4 OR
1948....Ann Curtis, United States	5:17.8 OR
1952....Valeria Gyenge, Hungary	5:12.1 OR
1956....Lorraine Crapp, Australia	4:54.6 OR
1960....Chris von Saltza, United States	4:50.6 OR
1964....Virginia Duenkel, United States	4:43.3 OR
1968....Debbie Meyer, United States	4:31.8 OR
1972....Shane Gould, Australia	4:19.44 WR
1976....Petra Thümer, E Germany	4:09.89 WR
1980....Ines Diers, E Germany	4:08.76 WR
1984....Tiffany Cohen, United States	4:07.10 OR
1988....Janet Evans, United States	4:03.85 WR
1992....Dagmar Hase, Germany	4:07.18
1996....Michelle Smith, Ireland	4:07.25
2000....Brooke Bennett, United States	4:05.80
2004....Laure Manaudou, France	4:05.34

800-METER FREESTYLE

1968....Debbie Meyer, United States	9:24.0 OR
1972....Keena Rothhammer, United States	8:53.68 WR
1976....Petra Thümer, E Germany	8:37.14 WR
1980....Michelle Ford, Australia	8:28.90 OR
1984....Tiffany Cohen, United States	8:24.95 OR
1988....Janet Evans, United States	8:20.20 OR
1992....Janet Evans, United States	8:25.52
1996....Brooke Bennett, United States	8:27.89
2000....Brooke Bennett, United States	8:19.67 OR
2004....Ai Shibata, Japan	8:24.54

100-METER BACKSTROKE

1924....Sybil Bauer, United States	1:23.2 OR
1928....Marie Braun, Netherlands	1:22.0
1932....Eleanor Holm, United States	1:19.4
1936....Dina Senff, Netherlands	1:18.9
1948....Karen Harup, Denmark	1:14.4 OR
1952....Joan Harrison, South Africa	1:14.3
1956....Judy Grinham, Great Britain	1:12.9 OR
1960....Lynn Burke, United States	1:09.3 OR
1964....Cathy Ferguson, United States	1:07.7 WR
1968....Kaye Hall, United States	1:06.2 WR
1972....Melissa Belote, United States	1:05.78 OR
1976....Ulrike Richter, E Germany	1:01.83 OR
1980....Rica Reinisch, E Germany	1:00.86 WR
1984....Theresa Andrews, United States	1:02.55
1988....Kristin Otto, E Germany	1:00.89
1992....Krisztina Egerszegi, Hungary	1:00.68 OR
1996....Beth Botsford, United States	1:01.19
2000....Diana Iuliana Mocanu, Romania	1:00.21 OR
2004....Natalie Coughlin, United States	1:00.37

200-METER BACKSTROKE

1968....Pokey Watson, United States	2:24.8 OR
1972....Melissa Belote, United States	2:19.19 WR
1976....Ulrike Richter, E Germany	2:13.43 OR
1980....Rica Reinisch, E Germany	2:11.77 WR
1984....Jolanda De Rover, Netherlands	2:12.38
1988....Krisztina Egerszegi, Hungary	2:09.29 OR
1992....Krisztina Egerszegi, Hungary	2:07.06 OR
1996....Krisztina Egerszegi, Hungary	2:07.83
2000....Diana Iuliana Mocanu, Romania	2:08.16
2004....Kirsty Coventry, Zimbabwe	2:09.19

100-METER BREASTSTROKE

1968....Djurdjica Bjedov, Yugoslavia	1:15.8 OR
1972....Catherine Carr, United States	1:13.58 WR
1976....Hannelore Anke, E Germany	1:11.16
1980....Ute Geweniger, E Germany	1:10.22
1984....Petra Van Staveren, Netherlands	1:09.88 OR
1988....Tania Dangalakova, Bulgaria	1:07.95 OR
1992....Elena Roudkovskaia, Unified Team	1:08.00
1996....Penelope Heyns, S Africa	1:07.73
2000....Megan Quann, United States	1:07.05
2004....Xue Juan Luo, China	1:06.64

200-METER BREASTSTROKE

1924....Lucy Morton, Great Britain	3:33.2 OR
1928....Hilde Schrader, Germany	3:12.6
1932....Clare Dennis, Australia	3:06.3 OR
1936....Hideko Maehata, Japan	3:03.6
1948....Petronella Van Vliet, Netherlands	2:57.2
1952....Eva Szekely, Hungary	2:51.7 OR
1956....Ursula Happe, W Germany	2:53.1 OR
1960....Anita Lonsbrough, Great Britain	2:49.5 WR
1964....Galina Prozumenshikova, USSR	2:46.4 OR
1968....Sharon Wichman, United States	2:44.4 OR
1972....Beverly Whitfield, Australia	2:41.71 OR
1976....Marina Koshevaia, USSR	2:33.35 WR
1980....Lina Kaciusyte, USSR	2:29.54 OR
1984....Anne Ottenbrite, Canada	2:30.38
1988....Silke Hoerner, E Germany	2:26.71 WR
1992....Kyoko Iwasaki, Japan	2:26.65 OR
1996....Penelope Heyns, S Africa	2:25.41 OR
2000....Agnes Kovacs, Hungary	2:24.35 OR
2004....Amanda Beard, United States	2:23.37 OR

100-METER BUTTERFLY

1956....Shelley Mann, United States	1:11.0 OR
1960....Carolyn Schuler, United States	1:09.5 OR
1964....Sharon Stouder, United States	1:04.7 WR
1968....Lynn McClements, Australia	1:05.5
1972....Mayumi Aoki, Japan	1:03.34 WR
1976....Kornelia Ender, E Germany	1:00.13 EWR
1980....Caren Metschuck, E Germany	1:00.42
1984....Mary T. Meagher, United States	59.26
1988....Kristin Otto, E Germany	59.00 OR
1992....Qian Hong, China	58.62 OR
1996....Amy Van Dyken, United States	59.13
2000....Inge de Bruijn, Netherlands	56.61 WR
2004....Petria Thomas, Australia	57.72

200-METER BUTTERFLY

1968....Ada Kok, Netherlands	2:24.7 OR
1972....Karen Moe, United States	2:15.57 WR
1976....Andrea Pollack, E Germany	2:11.41 OR
1980....Ines Geissler, E Germany	2:10.44 OR
1984....Mary T. Meagher, United States	2:06.90 OR
1988....Kathleen Nord, E Germany	2:09.51
1992....Summer Sanders, United States	2:08.67
1996....Susan O'Neill, Australia	2:07.76
2000....Misty Hyman, United States	2:05.88 OR
2004....Otylia Jedrzegczak, Poland	2:06.05

200-METER INDIVIDUAL MEDLEY

1968....Claudia Kolb, United States	2:24.7 OR
1972....Shane Gould, Australia	2:23.07 WR
1984....Tracy Caulkins, United States	2:12.64 OR
1988....Daniela Hunger, E Germany	2:12.59 OR
1992....Lin Li, China	2:11.65 WR
1996....Michelle Smith, Ireland	2:13.93
2000....Yana Klochkova, Ukraine	2:10.68 OR
2004....Yana Klochkova, Ukraine	2:11.14

Note: OR=Olympic Record. WR=World Record. EOR=Equals Olympic Record. EWR=Equals World Record. WB=World Best.

SWIMMING — Women *(Cont.)*

400-METER INDIVIDUAL MEDLEY

1964	Donna de Varona, United States	5:18.7 OR
1968	Claudia Kolb, United States	5:08.5 OR
1972	Gail Neall, Australia	5:02.97 WR
1976	Ulrike Tauber, E Germany	4:42.77 WR
1980	Petra Schneider, E Germany	4:36.29 WR
1984	Tracy Caulkins, United States	4:39.24
1988	Janet Evans, United States	4:37.76
1992	Krisztina Egerszegi, Hungary	4:36.54
1996	Michelle Smith, Ireland	4:39.18
2000	Yana Klochkova, Ukraine	4:33.59 WR
2004	Yana Klochkova, Ukraine	4:34.83

4 X 100-METER MEDLEY RELAY

1960	United States	4:41.1 WR
1964	United States	4:33.9 WR
1968	United States	4:28.3 OR
1972	United States	4:20.75 WR
1976	E Germany	4:07.95 WR
1980	E Germany	4:06.67 WR
1984	United States	4:08.34
1988	E Germany	4:03.74 OR
1992	United States	4:02.54 WR
1996	United States	4:02.88
2000	United States	3:58:30 WR
2004	Australia	3:57.32 WR

4 X 100-METER FREESTYLE RELAY

1912	Great Britain	5:52.8 WR
1920	United States	5:11.6 WR
1924	United States	4:58.8 WR
1928	United States	4:47.6 WR
1932	United States	4:38.0 WR
1936	Netherlands	4:36.0 OR
1948	United States	4:29.2 OR
1952	Hungary	4:24.4 WR
1956	Australia	4:17.1 WR
1960	United States	4:08.9 WR
1964	United States	4:03.8 WR
1968	United States	4:02.5 OR
1972	United States	3:55.19 WR
1976	United States	3:44.82 WR
1980	E Germany	3:42.71 WR
1984	United States.	3:43.43
1988	E Germany	3:40.63 OR
1992	United States	3:39.46 WR
1996	United States	3:39.29 OR
2000	United States	3:36.61 WR
2004	Australia	3:35.94 WR

4 X 200-METER FREESTYLE RELAY

1996	United States	7:59.87
2000	United States	7:57.80 OR
2004	United States	7:53.42 WR

DIVING — Men

	SPRINGBOARD	Pts
1908	Albert Zürner, Germany	85.5
1912	Paul Günther, Germany	79.23
1920	Louis Kuehn, United States	675.40
1924	Albert White, United States	97.46
1928	Pete DesJardins, United States	185.04
1932	Michael Galitzen, United States	161.38
1936	Richard Degener, United States	163.57
1948	Bruce Harlan, United States	163.64
1952	David Browning, United States	205.29
1956	Robert Clotworthy, United States	159.56
1960	Gary Tobian, United States	170.00
1964	Kenneth Sitzberger, United States	159.90
1968	Bernie Wrightson, United States	170.15
1972	Vladimir Vasin, USSR	594.09
1976	Phil Boggs, United States	619.05
1980	Aleksandr Portnov, USSR	905.02
1984	Greg Louganis, United States	754.41
1988	Greg Louganis, United States	730.80
1992	Mark Lenzi, United States	676.53
1996	Xiong Ni, China	701.46
2000	Xiong Ni, China	708.72
2004	Bo Peng, China	787.38

	PLATFORM	Pts
1904	George Sheldon, United States	12.66
1906	Gottlob Walz, Germany	156.0
1908	Hjalmar Johansson, Sweden	83.75
1912	Erik Adlerz, Sweden	73.94
1920	Clarence Pinkston, United States	100.67
1924	Albert White, United States	97.46
1928	Pete DesJardins, United States	98.74
1932	Harold Smith, United States	124.80
1936	Marshall Wayne, United States	113.58
1948	Sammy Lee, United States	130.05
1952	Sammy Lee, United States	156.28
1956	Joaquin Capilla, Mexico	152.44
1960	Robert Webster, United States	165.56
1964	Robert Webster, United States	148.58
1968	Klaus Dibiasi, Italy	164.18
1972	Klaus Dibiasi, Italy	504.12
1976	Klaus Dibiasi, Italy	600.51
1980	Falk Hoffmann, E Germany	835.65
1984	Greg Louganis, United States	710.91
1988	Greg Louganis, United States	638.61
1992	Sun Shuwei, China	677.31
1996	Dmitri Sautin, Russia	692.34
2000	Tian Liang, China	724.53
2004	Jia Hu, China	748.08

DIVING — Women

	SPRINGBOARD	Pts
1920	Aileen Riggin, United States	539.90
1924	Elizabeth Becker, United States	474.50
1928	Helen Meany, United States	78.62
1932	Georgia Coleman, United States	87.52
1936	Marjorie Gestring, United States	89.27
1948	Victoria Draves, United States	108.74
1952	Patricia McCormick, United States	147.30
1956	Patricia McCormick, United States	142.36
1960	Ingrid Krämer, E Germany	155.81
1964	Ingrid Engel Krämer, E Germany	145.00

	SPRINGBOARD *(CONT.)*	Pts
1968	Sue Gossick, United States	150.77
1972	Micki King, United States	450.03
1976	Jennifer Chandler, United States	506.19
1980	Irina Kalinina, USSR	725.91
1984	Sylvie Bernier, Canada	530.70
1988	Gao Min, China	580.23
1992	Gao Min, China	572.40
1996	Fu Mingxia, China	547.68
2000	Fu Mingxia, China	609.42
2004	Jingjing Guo, China	633.15

DIVING — Women *(Cont.)*

	PLATFORM	Pts		PLATFORM	Pts
1912	Greta Johansson, Sweden	39.90	1968	Milena Duchkova, Czechoslovakia	109.59
1920	Stefani Fryland-Clausen, Denmark	34.60	1972	Ulrika Knape, Sweden	390.00
1924	Caroline Smith, United States	33.20	1976	Elena Vaytsekhovskaya, USSR	406.59
1928	Elizabeth B. Pinkston, United States	31.60	1980	Martina Jäschke, E Germany	596.25
1932	Dorothy Poynton, United States	40.26	1984	Zhou Jihong, China	435.51
1936	Dorothy Poynton Hill, United States	33.93	1988	Xu Yanmei, China	445.20
1948	Victoria Draves, United States	68.87	1992	Mingxia Fu, China	461.43
1952	Patricia McCormick, United States	79.37	1996	Mingxia Fu, China	521.58
1956	Patricia McCormick, United States	84.85	2000	Laura Wilkinson, United States	543.75
1960	Ingrid Krämer, E Germany	91.28	2004	Chantelle Newbery, Australia	590.31
1964	Lesley Bush, United States	99.80			

GYMNASTICS — Men

ALL-AROUND	Pts	PARALLEL BARS *(CONT)*	Pts
1900.....Gustave Sandras, France	302	1924.....August Güttinger, Switzerland	21.63
1904.....Julius Lenhart, Austria	69.80	1928.....Ladislav Vacha, Czechoslovakia	18.83
1906.....Pierre Paysse, France	97	1932.....Romeo Neri, Italy	18.97
1908.....Alberto Braglia, Italy	317.0	1936.....Konrad Frey, Germany	19.067
1912.....Alberto Braglia, Italy	135.0	1948.....Michael Reusch, Switzerland	19.75
1920.....Giorgio Zampori, Italy	88.35	1952.....Hans Eugster, Switzerland	19.65
1924.....Leon Stukelj, Yugoslavia	110.340	1956.....Viktor Chukarin, USSR	19.20
1928.....Georges Miez, Switzerland	247.500	1960.....Boris Shakhlin, USSR	19.40
1932.....Romeo Neri, Italy	140.625	1964.....Yukio Endo, Japan	19.675
1936.....Alfred Schwarzmann, Germany	113.100	1968.....Akinori Nakayama, Japan	19.475
1948.....Veikko Huhtanen, Finland	229.70	1972.....Sawao Kato, Japan	19.475
1952.....Viktor Chukarin, USSR	115.70	1976 ....Sawao Kato, Japan	19.675
1956.....Viktor Chukarin, USSR	114.25	1980.....Aleksandr Tkachyov, USSR	19.775
1960.....Boris Shakhlin, USSR	115.95	1984.....Bart Conner, United States	19.95
1964.....Yukio Endo, Japan	115.95	1988.....Vladimir Artemov, USSR	19.925
1968.....Sawao Kato, Japan	115.90	1992.....Vitaly Scherbo, Unified Team	9.900
1972.....Sawao Kato, Japan	114.65	1996.....Rustan Sharipov, Ukraine	9.837
1976.....Nikolai Andrianov, USSR	116.65	2000.....Xiaopeng Li, China	9.825
1980.....Aleksandr Dityatin, USSR	118.65	2004.....Valeri Goncharov, Ukraine	9.787
1984.....Koji Gushiken, Japan	118.70	**VAULT**	**Pts**
1988.....Vladimir Artemov, USSR	119.125	1896.....Karl Schumann, Germany	—
1992.....Vitaly Scherbo, Unified Team	59.025	1904.....George Eyser, United States	36
1996.....Li Xiaoshuang, China	58.423	1924.....Frank Kriz, United States	9.98
2000.....Alexei Nemov, Russia	58.474	1928.....Eugen Mack, Switzerland	9.58
2004.....Paul Hamm, United States	57.823	1932.....Savino Guglielmetti, Italy	18.03
HORIZONTAL BAR	**Pts**	1936.....Alfred Schwarzmann, Germany	19.20
1896.....Hermann Weingärtner, Germany	—	1948.....Paavo Aaltonen, Finland	19.55
1904.....Anton Heida, United States	40	1952.....Viktor Chukarin, USSR	19.20
1924.....Leon Stukelj, Yugoslavia	19.73	1956.....Helmut Bantz, Germany	18.85
1928.....Georges Miez, Switzerland	19.17	1960.....Takashi Ono, Japan	19.35
1932.....Dallas Bixler, United States	18.33	1964.....Haruhiro Yamashita, Japan	19.60
1936.....Aleksanteri Saarvala, Finland	19.367	1968.....Mikhail Voronin, USSR	19.00
1948.....Josef Stalfer, Switzerland	19.85	1972.....Klaus Köste, E Germany	18.85
1952.....Jack Günthard, Switzerland	19.55	1976.....Nikolai Andrianov, USSR	19.45
1956.....Takashi Ono, Japan	19.60	1980.....Nikolai Andrianov, USSR	19.825
1960.....Takashi Ono, Japan	19.60	1984.....Lou Yun, China	19.95
1964.....Boris Shakhlin, USSR	19.625	1988.....Lou Yun, China	19.875
1968.....Akinori Nakayama, Japan	19.55	1992.....Vitaly Scherbo, Unified Team	9.856
1972.....Mitsuo Tsukahara, Japan	19.725	1996.....Alexei Nemov, Russia	9.787
1976.....Mitsuo Tsukahara, Japan	19.675	2000.....Gervasio Deferr, Spain	9.712
1980.....Stoyan Deltchev, Bulgaria	19.825	2004.....Gervasio Deferr, Spain	9.737
1984.....Shinji Morisue, Japan	20.00	**POMMEL HORSE**	**Pts**
1988.....Vladimir Artemov, USSR	19.90	1896.....Louis Zutter, Switzerland	—
1992.....Trent Dimas, United States	9.875	1904.....Anton Heida, United States	42
1996.....Andreas Wecker, Germany	9.850	1924.....Josef Wilhelm, Switzerland	21.23
2000.....Alexei Nemov, Russia	9.787	1928.....Hermann Hänggi, Switzerland	19.75
2004.....Igor Cassina, Italy	9.812	1932.....Istvan Pelle, Hungary	19.07
PARALLEL BARS	**Pts**	1936.....Konrad Frey, Germany	19.333
1896.....Alfred Flatow, Germany	—	1948.....Paavo Aaltonen, Finland	19.35
1904.....George Eyser, United States	44	1952.....Viktor Chukarin, USSR	19.50

GYMNASTICS — Men *(Cont.)*

POMMEL HORSE *(CONT.)*

Year	Champion	Pts
1956	Boris Shakhlin, USSR	19.25
1960	Eugen Ekman, Finland	19.375
1964	Miroslav Cerar, Yugoslavia	19.525
1968	Miroslav Cerar, Yugoslavia	19.325
1972	Viktor Klimenko, USSR	19.125
1976	Zoltan Magyar, Hungary	19.70
1980	Zoltan Magyar, Hungary	19.925
1984	Li Ning, China	19.95
1988	Dmitri Bilozerchev, USSR	19.95
1992	Vitaly Scherbo, Unified Team	9.925
1996	Donghua Li, Switzerland	9.875
2000	Marius Urzica, Romania	9.862
2004	Haibin Teng, China	9.837

RINGS

Year	Champion	Pts
1896	Ioannis Mitropoulos, Greece	—
1904	Hermann Glass, United States	45
1924	Francesco Martino, Italy	21.553
1928	Leon Stukelj, Yugoslavia	19.25
1932	George Gulack, United States	18.97
1936	Alois Hudec, Czechoslovakia	19.433
1948	Karl Frei, Switzerland	19.80
1952	Grant Shaginyan, USSR	19.75
1956	Albert Azaryan, USSR	19.35
1960	Albert Azaryan, USSR	19.725
1964	Takuji Haytta, Japan	19.475
1968	Akinori Nakayama, Japan	19.45
1972	Akinori Nakayama, Japan	19.35
1976	Nikolai Andrianov, USSR	19.65
1980	Aleksandr Dityatin, USSR	19.875
1984	Koji Gushiken, Japan	19.85
1988	Holger Behrendt, E Germany	19.925
1992	Vitaly Scherbo, Unified Team	9.937
1996	Yuri Chechi, Italy	9.887
2000	Szilveszter Csollany, Hungary	9.862
2004	Dimosthenis Tampakos, Greece	9.862

FLOOR EXERCISE

Year	Champion	Pts
1932	Istvan Pelle, Hungary	9.60
1936	Georges Miez, Switzerland	18.666
1948	Ferenc Pataki, Hungary	19.35
1952	K. William Thoresson, Sweden	19.25
1956	Valentin Muratov, USSR	19.20

FLOOR EXERCISE *(CONT.)*

Year	Champion	Pts
1960	Nobuyuki Aihara, Japan	19.45
1964	Franco Menichelli, Italy	19.45
1968	Sawao Kato, Japan	19.475
1972	Nikolai Andrianov, USSR	19.175
1976	Nikolai Andrianov, USSR	19.45
1980	Roland Brückner, E Germany	19.75
1984	Li Ning, China	19.925
1988	Sergei Kharkov, USSR	19.925
1992	Li Xiaoshuang, China	9.925
1996	Ioannis Melissanidis, Greece	9.850
2000	Igors Vihrovs, Latvia	9.812
2004	Kyle Shewfelt, Canada	9.787

TEAM COMBINED EXERCISES

Year	Champion	Pts
1904	Turngemeinde Philadelphia	374.43
1906	Norway	19.00
1908	Sweden	438
1912	Italy	265.75
1920	Italy	359.855
1924	Italy	839.058
1928	Switzerland	1718.625
1932	Italy	541.850
1936	Germany	657.430
1948	Finland	1358.30
1952	USSR	574.40
1956	USSR	568.25
1960	Japan	575.20
1964	Japan	577.95
1968	Japan	575.90
1972	Japan	571.25
1976	Japan	576.85
1980	USSR	598.60
1984	United States	591.40
1988	USSR	593.35
1992	Unified Team	585.45
1996	Russia	576.778
2000	China	231.919
2004	Japan	173.821

GYMNASTICS — Women

ALL-AROUND

Year	Champion	Pts
1952	Maria Gorokhovskaya, USSR	76.78
1956	Larissa Latynina, USSR	74.933
1960	Larissa Latynina, USSR	77.031
1964	Vera Caslavska, Czechoslovakia	77.564
1968	Vera Caslavska, Czechoslovakia	78.25
1972	Lyudmila Tousischeva, USSR	77.025
1976	Nadia Comaneci, Romania	79.275
1980	Yelena Davydova, USSR	79.15
1984	Mary Lou Retton, United States	79.175
1988	Yelena Shushunova, USSR	79.662
1992	Tatiana Gutsu, Unified Team	39.737
1996	Lilia Podkopayeva, Ukraine	39.255
2000	Simona Amanar, Romania	38.642
2004	Carly Patterson, United States	38.387

VAULT

Year	Champion	Pts
1952	Yekaterina Kalinchuk, USSR	19.20
1956	Larissa Latynina, USSR	18.833
1960	Margarita Nikolayeva, USSR	19.316
1964	Vera Caslavska, Czechoslovakia	19.483
1968	Vera Caslavska, Czechoslovakia	19.775
1972	Karin Janz, E Germany	19.525

VAULT *(CONT.)*

Year	Champion	Pts
1976	Nelli Kim, USSR	19.80
1980	Natalya Shaposhnikova, USSR	19.725
1984	Ecaterina Szabo, Romania	19.875
1988	Svetlana Boginskaya, USSR	19.905
1992	Henrietta Onodi, Hungary	9.925
	Lavinia Milosovici, Romania	9.925
1996	Simona Amanar, Romania	9.825
2000	Yelena Zamolodtchikova, Russia	9.731
2004	Monica Rosu, Romania	9.656

UNEVEN BARS

Year	Champion	Pts
1952	Margit Korondi, Hungary	19.40
1956	Agnes Keleti, Hungary	18.966
1960	Polina Astakhova, USSR	19.616
1964	Polina Astakhova, USSR	19.332
1968	Vera Caslavska, Czechoslovakia	19.65
1972	Karin Janz, E Germany	19.675
1976	Nadia Comaneci, Romania	20.00
1980	Maxi Gnauck, E Germany	19.875
1984	Ma Yanhong, China	19.95
1988	Daniela Silivas, Romania	20.00
1992	Lu Li, China	10.00

GYMNASTICS - Women *(Cont.)*
Women *(Cont.)*

UNEVEN BARS *(CONT.)*		Pts	TEAM COMBINED EXERCISES		Pts
1996	Svetlana Khorkina, Russia	9.850	1928	The Netherlands	316.75
2000	Svetlana Khorkina, Russia	9.862	1932	Not held	
2004	Emilie Lepennec, France	9.687	1936	Germany	506.50
BALANCE BEAM		**Pts**	1948	Czechoslovakia	445.45
1952	Nina Bocharova, USSR	19.22	1952	USSR	527.03
1956	Agnes Keleti, Hungary	18.80	1956	USSR	444.800
1960	Eva Bosakova, Czechoslovakia	19.283	1960	USSR	382.320
1964	Vera Caslavska, Czechoslovakia	19.449	1964	USSR	280.890
1968	Natalya Kuchinskaya, USSR	19.65	1968	USSR	382.85
1972	Olga Korbut, USSR	19.40	1972	USSR	380.50
1976	Nadia Comaneci, Romania	19.95	1976	USSR	466.00
1980	Nadia Comaneci, Romania	19.80	1980	USSR	394.90
1984	Simona Pauca, Romania	19.80	1984	Romania	392.02
1988	Daniela Silivas, Romania	19.924	1988	USSR	395.475
1992	Tatiana Lisenko, Unified Team	9.975	1992	Unified Team	395.666
1996	Shannon Miller, United States	9.862	1996	United States	389.225
2000	Xuan Li, China	9.825	2000	Romania	154.608
2004	Catalina Ponor, Romania	9.787	2004	Romania	114.283
FLOOR EXERCISE		**Pts**	**RHYTHMIC ALL-AROUND**		**Pts**
1952	Agnes Keleti, Hungary	19.36	1984	Lori Fung, Canada	57.95
1956	Agnes Keleti, Hungary	18.733	1988	Marina Lobach, USSR	60.00
1960	Larissa Latynina, USSR	19.583	1992	A. Timoshenko, Unified Team	59.037
1964	Larissa Latynina, USSR	19.599	1996	E. Serebrianskaya, Ukraine	39.683
1968	Vera Caslavska, Czechoslovakia	19.675	2000	Yulia Barsukova, Russia	39.632
1972	Olga Korbut, USSR	19.575	2004	Alina Kabaeva, Russia	108.400
1976	Nelli Kim, USSR	19.85	**RHYTHMIC TEAM COMBINED EXERCISES**		**Pts**
1980	Nadia Comaneci, Romania	19.875	1996	Spain	38.933
1984	Ecaterina Szabo, Romania	19.975	2000	Russia	39.500
1988	Daniela Silivas, Romania	19.937	2004	China	249.750
1992	Lavinia Milosovici, Romania	10.00			
1996	Lilia Podkopayeva, Ukraine	9.887			
2000	Yelena Zamolodtchikova, Russia	9.850			
2004	Catalina Ponor, Romania	9.750			

SOCCER

Men

1900	Great Britain	1928	Uruguay	1964	Hungary	1988	USSR
1904	Canada	1936	Italy	1968	Hungary	1992	Spain
1908	Great Britain	1948	Sweden	1972	Poland	1996	Nigeria
1912	Great Britain	1952	Hungary	1976	E Germany	2000	Cameroon
1920	Belgium	1956	USSR	1980	Czechoslovakia	2004	Argentina
1924	Uruguay	1960	Yugoslavia	1984	France		

Women

1996	United States
2000	Norway
2004	United States

BIATHLON
Men

10 KILOMETERS
1980	....Frank Ullrich, E Germany	32:10.69
1984	....Eirik Kvalfoss, Norway	30:53.8
1988	....Frank-Peter Rötsch, W Germany	25:08.1
1992	....Mark Kirchner, Germany	26:02.3
1994	....Sergei Tchepikov, Russia	28:07.0
1998	....Ole Einar Bjorndalen, Norway	27:16.2
2002	....Ole Einar Bjorndalen, Norway	24:51.3
2006	....Sven Fischer, Germany	24:11.6

12.5 KILOMETERS PURSUIT
2002	....Ole Einar Bjorndalen, Norway	24:51.3
2006	....Vincent Defrasne, France	35:20.2

15 KILOMETERS
2006	....Michael Greis, Germany	47:20.0

20 KILOMETERS
1960	....Klas Lestander, Sweden	1:33:21.6
1964	....Vladimir Melyanin, USSR	1:20:26.8
1968	....Magnar Solberg, Norway	1:13:45.9
1972	....Magnar Solberg, Norway	1:15:55.5
1976	....Nikolay Kruglov, USSR	1:14:12.26

20 KILOMETERS (CONT.)
1980	....Anatoliy Alyabiev, USSR	1:08:16.31
1984	....Peter Angerer, W Germany	1:11:52.7
1988	....Frank-Peter Rötsch, W Germany	56:33.3
1992	....Evgueni Redkine, Unified Team	57:34.4
1994	....Sergei Tarasov, Russia	57:25.3
1998	....Halvard Hanevold, Norway	56:16.4
2002	....Ole Einar Bjorndalen, Norway	51:03.3
2006	....Michael Greis, Germany	54:23.0

4 X 7.5-KILOMETER RELAY
1968	...............USSR	2:13:02.4
1972	...............USSR	1:51:44.92
1976	...............USSR	1:57:55.64
1980	...............USSR	1:34:03.27
1984	...............USSR	1:38:51.7
1988	...............USSR	1:22:30.0
1992	...............Germany	1:24:43.5
1994	...............Germany	1:30:22.1
1998	...............Germany	1:19:43.3
2002	...............Norway	1:23:42.3
2006	...............Germany	1:21:51.5

Women

7.5 KILOMETERS
1992	....Antissa Restzova, Unified Team	24:29.2
1994	....Myriam Bedard, Canada	26:08.8
1998	....Galina Koukleva, Russia	23:08.0
2002	....Kati Wilhemn, Germany	20:41.4
2006	....Florence Baverel-Robert, France	22:31.4

10 KILOMETERS PURSUIT
2002	....Olga Pyleva, Russia	31:07.7
2006	....Kati Wilhemn, Germany	36:43.6

12.5 KILOMETERS
2006	....Anna Carin Olofsson, Sweden	40:36.5

15 KILOMETERS
1992	....Antje Misersky, Germany	51:47.2
1994	....Myriam Bedard, Canada	52:06.6
1998	....Ekaterina Dofovska, Bulgaria	54:52.0
2002	....Andrea Henkel, Germany	47:29.1
2006	....Svetlana Ishmouratova, Russia	49:24.1

3 X 7.5-KILOMETER RELAY
1992	....France	1:15:55.6
1994	....Russia	1:47:19.5
1998	....Germany	1:40:13.6
2002	....Germany	1:27:55.0

4 X 6-KILOMETER RELAY
2006	....Russia	1:16:12.5

BOBSLED

4-MAN
1924	....Switzerland (Eduard Scherrer)	5:45.54
1928	....United States (William Fiske) (5-man)	3:20.50
1932	....United States (William Fiske)	7:53.68
1936	....Switzerland (Pierre Musy)	5:19.85
1948	....United States (Francis Tyler)	5:20.10
1952	....Germany (Andreas Ostler)	5:07.84
1956	....Switzerland (Franz Kapus)	5:10.44
1960	....Not held	
1964	....Canada (Victor Emery)	4:14.46
1968	....Italy (Eugenio Monti) (2 runs)	2:17.39
1972	....Switzerland (Jean Wicki)	4:43.07
1976	....E Germany (Meinhard Nehmer)	3:40.43
1980	....E Germany (Meinhard Nehmer)	3:59.92
1984	....E Germany (Wolfgang Hoppe)	3:20.22
1988	....Switzerland (Ekkehard Fasser)	3:47.51
1992	....Austria (Ingo Appelt)	3:53.90
1994	....Germany (Harold Czudaj)	3:27.78
1998	....Germany (Christoph Langen)	2:39.41
2002	....Germany (Andre Lange)	3:10.11
2006	....Germany (Andre Lange)	3:40.42

Note: Driver in parentheses.

2-MAN
1932	....United States (Hubert Stevens)	8:14.74
1936	....United States (Ivan Brown)	5:29.29
1948	....Switzerland (Felix Endrich)	5:29.20
1952	....Germany (Andreas Ostler)	5:24.54
1956	....Italy (Lamberto Dalla Costa)	5:30.14
1960	....Not held	
1964	....Great Britain (Anthony Nash)	4:21.90
1968	....Italy (Eugenio Monti)	4:41.54
1972	....W Germany	4:57.07
	(Wolfgang Zimmerer)	
1976	....E Germany (Meinhard Nehmer)	3:44.42
1980	....Switzerland (Erich Schärer)	4:09.36
1984	....E Germany (Wolfgang Hoppe)	3:25.56
1988	....USSR (Janis Kipours)	3:53.48
1992	....Switzerland (Gustav Weder)	4:03.26
1994	....Switzerland (Gustav Weder)	3:30.81
1998	....Canada (Pierre Lueders)	3:37.24
	Italy (Guenther Huber)	3:37.24
2002	....Germany (Martin Langen)	3:10:11
2006	....Germany (Andre Lange)	3:43.38

2-WOMAN
2002	....United States (Jill Bakken)	1:37:76
2006	....Germany (Sandra Kiriasis)	3:49.98

CURLING

Men
1998 .....Switzerland, Canada, Norway
2002 .....Norway, Canada, Switzerland
2006 .....Canada, Finland, United States
Note: Gold, silver, and bronze medals.

Women
1998 .....Canada, Denmark, Sweden
2002 .....Britain, Switzerland, Canada
2006 .....Sweden, Switzerland, Canada
Note: Gold, silver, and bronze medals.

ICE HOCKEY

Men
1920*....Canada, United States, Czechoslovakia
1924 .....Canada, United States, Great Britain
1928 .....Canada, Sweden, Switzerland
1932 .....Canada, United States, Germany
1936 .....Great Britain, Canada, United States
1948 .....Canada, Czechoslovakia, Switzerland
1952 .....Canada, United States, Sweden
1956 .....USSR, United States, Canada
1960 .....United States, Canada, USSR
1964 .....USSR, Sweden, Czechoslovakia
1968 .....USSR, Czechoslovakia, Canada
1972 .....USSR, United States, Czechoslovakia

1976 .....USSR, Czechoslovakia, W Germany
1980 .....United States, USSR, Sweden
1984 .....USSR, Czechoslovakia, Sweden
1988 .....USSR, Finland, Sweden
1992 .....Unified Team, Canada, Czechoslovakia
1994 .....Sweden, Canada, Finland
1998 .....Czech Republic, Russia, Finland
2002 .....Canada, United States, Russia
2006 .....Sweden, Finland, Czech Republic
*Competition held at Summer Games in Antwerp.
Note: Gold, silver, and bronze medals.

Women
1998 .....United States, Canada, Finland
2002 .....Canada, United States, Sweden

2006 .....Canada, Sweden, United States
Note: Gold, silver, and bronze medals.

LUGE

Men

SINGLES		DOUBLES	
1964 .....Thomas Köhler, East Germany	3:26.77	1964 ....Austria	1:41.62
1968 .....Manfred Schmid, Austria	2:52.48	1968 ....E Germany	1:35.85
1972 .....Wolfgang Scheidel, W Germany	3:27.58	1972 ....E Germany	1:28.35
1976 ....Detlef Guenther, W Germany	3:27.688	1976 ....E Germany	1:25.604
1980 .....Bernhard Glass, W Germany	2:54.796	1980 ....E Germany	1:19.331
1984 .....Paul Hildgartner, Italy	3:04.258	1984 ....W Germany	1:23.620
1988 .....Jens Müller, W Germany	3:05.548	1988 ....E Germany	1:31.940
1992 .....Georg Hackl, Germany	3:02.363	1992 ....Germany	1:32.053
1994 .....Georg Hackl, Germany	3:21.571	1994 ....Italy	1:36.720
1998 .....Georg Hackl, Germany	3:18.44	1998 ....Germany	1:41.105
2002 .:...Armin Zoeggeler, Italy	2:57.941	2002 ....Germany	1:26.082
2006 .....Armin Zoeggeler, Italy	3:26.088	2006 ....Austria	1:34.497

Women

SINGLES		SINGLES (CONT.)	
1964 .....Ortrun Enderlein, Germany	3:24.67	1988 .....Steffi Walter (Martin), E. Germany	3:03.973
1968 .....Erica Lechner, Italy	2:28.66	1992 ....Doris Neuner, Austria	3:06.696
1972 ....Anna-Maria Müller, E Germany	2:59.18	1994 ....Gerda Weissensteiner, Italy	3:15.517
1976 ....Margit Schumann, E Germany	2:50.621	1998 .....Silke Kraushaar, Germany	3:23.779
1980 .....Vera Zozulya, USSR	2:36.537	2002 .....Sylke Otto, Germany	2:52.464
1984 .....Steffi Martin, E Germany	2:46.570	2006 .....Sylke Otto, Germany	3:07.979

FIGURE SKATING

Men
1908*............Ulrich Salchow, Sweden
1920†...........Gillis Grafström, Sweden
1924 ....Gillis Grafström, Sweden
1928 ....Gillis Grafström, Sweden
1932 ....Karl Schäfer, Austria
1936 ....Karl Schäfer, Austria
1948 ....Dick Button, United States
1952 ....Dick Button, United States
1956 ....Hayes Alan Jenkins, United States
1960 ....David Jenkins, United States
1964 ....Manfred Schnelldorfer, W Germany
1968 ....Wolfgang Schwarz, Austria
1972 ....Ondrej Nepela, Czechoslovakia
1976 ....John Curry, Great Britain
1980 ....Robin Cousins, Great Britain
1984 ....Scott Hamilton, United States

Women
1908*..............Madge Syers, Great Britain
1920†.............Magda Julin, Sweden
1924 ....Herma Szabo-Planck, Austria
1928 ....Sonja Henie, Norway
1932 ....Sonja Henie, Norway
1936 ....Sonja Henie, Norway
1948 ....Barbara Ann Scott, Canada
1952 ....Jeanette Altwegg, Great Britain
1956 ....Tenley Albright, United States
1960 ....Carol Heiss, United States
1964 ....Sjoukje Dijkstra, Netherlands
1968 ....Peggy Fleming, United States
1972 ....Beatrix Schuba, Austria
1976 ....Dorothy Hamill, United States
1980 ....Anett Pötzsch, E Germany
1984 ....Katarina Witt, E Germany

FIGURE SKATING *(Cont.)*

Men	Pts	Women	Pts
1988 ....Brian Boitano, United States		1988 ....Katarina Witt, E Germany	
1992 ....Victor Petrenko, Unified Team		1992 ....Kristi Yamaguchi, United States	
1994 ....Alexei Urmanov, Russia		1994 ....Oksana Baiul, Ukraine	
1998 ....Ilia Kulik, Russia		1998 ....Tara Lipinski, United States	
2002 ....Alexei Yagudin, Russia		2002 ....Sarah Hughes, United States	
2006‡ ....Evgeni Plushenko, Russia	258.33	2006‡ ....Shizuka Arakawa, Japan	191.34

*Competition held at Summer Games in London.
†Competition held at Summer Games in Antwerp.
‡In 2004, the ISU adopted a new overall scoring system

*Competition held at Summer Games in London.
†Competition held at Summer Games in Antwerp.
‡In 2004, the ISU adopted a new overall scoring system

Mixed

PAIRS

1908*....Anna Hübler, Heinrich Burger, Germany
1920†...Ludowika, Walter Jakobsson-Eilers, Finland
1924 .....Helene Engelmann, Alfred Berger, Austria
1928 .....Andree Joly, Pierre Brunet, France
1932 .....Andree Brunet (Joly), Pierre Brunet, France
1936 .....Maxi Herber, Ernst Baier, Germany
1948 .....Micheline Lannoy, Pierre Baugniet, Belgium
1952 .....Ria Falk and Paul Falk, W Germany
1956 .....Elisabeth Schwartz, Kurt Oppelt, Austria
1960 .....Barbara Wagner, Robert Paul, Canada
1964 .....Lyudmila Beloussova, Oleg Protopopov, USSR
1968 .....Lyudmila Beloussova, Oleg Protopopov, USSR
1972 .....Irina Rodnina, Alexei Ulanov, USSR
1976 .....Irina Rodnina, Aleksandr Zaitsev, USSR
1980 .....Irina Rodnina, Aleksandr Zaitsev, USSR
1984 .....Elena Valova, Oleg Vasiliev, USSR
1988 .....Ekaterina Gordeeva, Sergei Grinkov, USSR
1992 .....Natalia Michkouteniok, Artour Dmitriev, Unified Team

PAIRS *(CONT.)*   Pts

1994 .....Ekaterina Gordeeva, Sergei Grinkov, Russia
1998 .....Oksana Kazakova, Artur Dmitriev, Russia
2002 .....E. Berezhnaya, A. Sikharulidze, Russia
      J. Sales, D. Pelletier, Canada
2006‡ .....T. Totmianina, M. Marinin, Russia   204.48

ICE DANCING   Pts

1976 .....L. Pakhomova, A. Gorshkov, USSR
1980 .....N. Linichuk, G. Karponosov, USSR
1984 .....Jayne Torvill, Christopher Dean, UK
1988 .....N. Bestemianova, A. Bukin, USSR
1992 .....M. Klimova, S. Ponomarenko, Unified Team
1994 .....Oksana Grishuk, Evgeny Platov, Russia
1998 .....Pasha Grishuk, Evgeny Platov, Russia
2002 .....Marina Anissina, Gwendal Peizerat, France
2006‡ .....T. Navka, R. Kostomarov, Russia   200.64

*Competition held at Summer Games in London.
†Competition held at Summer Games in Antwerp.
‡In 2004, the ISU adopted a new overall point-scoring system

SKELETON

Men		Women	
1928 .....Jennison Heaton, United States	3:01.8	2002 .....Tristan Gale, United States	1:45.11
1948 .....Nino Bibbia, Italy	5:23.2	2006 .....Maya Pedersen, Switzerland	1:59.83
2002 .....Jim Shea Jr., United States	1:41.96		
2006 .....Duff Gibson, Canada	1:55.88		

SPEED SKATING
Men

500 METERS

1924....Charles Jewtraw, United States	44.0
1928....Clas Thunberg, Finland	43.4 OR
Bernt Evensen, Norway	43.4 OR
1932....John Shea, United States	43.4 EOR
1936....Ivar Ballangrud, Norway	43.4 EOR
1948....Finn Helgesen, Norway	43.1 OR
1952....Kenneth Henry, United States	43.2
1956....Yevgeny Grishin, USSR	40.2 EWR
1960....Yevgeny Grishin, USSR	40.2 EWR
1964....Terry McDermott, United States	40.1 OR
1968....Erhard Keller, W Germany	40.3
1972....Erhard Keller, W Germany	39.44 OR
1976....Yevgeny Kulikov, USSR	39.17 OR
1980....Eric Heiden, United States	38.03 OR
1984....Sergei Fokichev, USSR	38.19
1988....Uwe-Jens Mey, E Germany	36.45 WR
1992....Uwe-Jens Mey, E Germany	37.14

500 METERS *(CONT.)*

1994....Aleksandr Golubev, Russia	36.33
1998....Hiroyasu Shimizu, Japan	35.59 OR
(second run)	
2002....Casey FitzRandolph, United States	1:09.23*
2006....Joey Cheek, United States	1:09.76*

1,000 METERS

1976....Peter Mueller, United States	1:19.32
1980....Eric Heiden, United States	1:15.18 OR
1984....Gaetan Boucher, Canada	1:15.80
1988....Nikolai Gulyaev, USSR	1:13.03 OR
1992....Olaf Zinke, Germany	1:14.85
1994....Dan Jansen, United States	1:12.43 WR
1998....Ids Postma, Netherlands	1:10.64 OR
2002....Gerard van Velde, Netherlands	1:07.18
2006....Shani Davis, United States	1:08.89

SPEED SKATING *(Cont.)*
Men *(Cont.)*

1,500 METERS

1924	Clas Thunberg, Finland	2:20.8
1928	Clas Thunberg, Finland	2:21.1
1932	John Shea, United States	2:57.5
1936	Charles Mathisen, Norway	2:19.2 OR
1948	Sverre Farstad, Norway	2:17.6 OR
1952	Hjalmar Andersen, Norway	2:20.4
1956	Yevgeny Grishin, USSR	2:08.6 WR
	Yuri Mikhailov, USSR	2:08.6 WR
1960	Roald Aas, Norway	2:10.4
	Yevgeny Grishin, USSR	2:10.4
1964	Ants Anston, USSR	2:10.3
1968	Cornelis Verkerk, Netherlands	2:03.4 OR
1972	Ard Schenk, Netherlands	2:02.96 OR
1976	Jan Egil Storholt, Norway	1:59.38 OR
1980	Eric Heiden, United States	1:55.44 OR
1984	Gaetan Boucher, Canada	1:58.36
1988	Andre Hoffmann, E Germany	1:52.06 WR
1992	Johann Olav Koss, Norway	1:54.81
1994	Johann Olav Koss, Norway	1:51.29 WR
1998	Aadne Sondral, Norway	1:47.87 WR
2002	Derek Parra, United States	1:43.95
2006	Enrico Fabris, Italy	1:45.97

5,000 METERS

1924	Clas Thunberg, Finland	8:39.0
1928	Ivar Ballangrud, Norway	8:50.5
1932	Irving Jaffee, United States	9:40.8
1936	Ivar Ballangrud, Norway	8:19.6 OR
1948	Reidar Liaklev, Norway	8:29.4
1952	Hjalmar Andersen, Norway	8:10.6 OR
1956	Boris Shilkov, USSR	7:48.7 OR
1960	Viktor Kosichkin, USSR	7:51.3
1964	Knut Johannesen, Norway	7:38.4 OR

5,000 METERS *(CONT.)*

1968	Fred Anton Maier, Norway	7:22.4 WR
1972	Ard Schenk, Netherlands	7:23.61
1976	Sten Stensen, Norway	7:24.48
1980	Eric Heiden, United States	7:02.29 OR
1984	Sven Tomas Gustafson, Sweden	7:12.28
1988	Tomas Gustafson, Sweden	6:44.63 WR
1992	Geir Karlstad, Norway	6:59.97
1994	Johann Olav Koss, Norway	6:34.96 WR
1998	Gianni Romme, Netherlands	6:22.20 WR
2002	Jochem Uytdehaage, Neth.	6:41.66
2006	Chad Hedrick, United States	6:14.68

10,000 METERS

1924	Julius Skutnabb, Finland	18:04.8
1928	Not held due to thawing of ice	
1932	Irving Jaffee, United States	19:13.6
1936	Ivar Ballangrud, Norway	17:24.3 OR
1948	Ake Seyffarth, Sweden	17:26.3
1952	Hjalmar Andersen, Norway	16:45.8 OR
1956	Sigvard Ericsson, Sweden	16:35.9 OR
1960	Knut Johannesen, Norway	15:46.6 WR
1964	Jonny Nilsson, Sweden	15:50.1
1968	Johnny Höglin, Sweden	15:23.6 OR
1972	Ard Schenk, Netherlands	15:01.35 OR
1976	Piet Kleine, Netherlands	14:50.59 OR
1980	Eric Heiden, United States	14:28.13 WR
1984	Igor Malkov, USSR	14:39.90
1988	Tomas Gustafson, Sweden	13:48.20 WR
1992	Bart Veldkamp, Netherlands	14:12.12
1994	Johann Olav Koss, Norway	13:30.55 WR
1998	Gianni Romme, Netherlands	13:15.33 WR
2002	Jochem Uytdehaage, Netherlands	12:58.92 WR
2006	Bob de Jong, Netherlands	13:01.57

Women

500 METERS

1960	Helga Haase, E Germany	45.9
1964	Lydia Skoblikova, USSR	45.0 OR
1968	Lyudmila Titova, USSR	46.1
1972	Anne Henning, United States	43.33 OR
1976	Sheila Young, United States	42.76 OR
1980	Karin Enke, E Germany	41.78 OR
1984	Christa Rothenburger, E Germany	41.02 OR
1988	Bonnie Blair, United States	39.10 WR
1992	Bonnie Blair, United States	40.33
1994	Bonnie Blair, United States	39.25
1998	Catriona LeMay Doan, Canada (second run)	38.21 OR
2002	Catriona LeMay, Canada	1:14.75*
2006	Svetlana Zhurova, Russia	1:16.57*

1,000 METERS

1960	Klara Guseva, USSR	1:34.1
1964	Lydia Skoblikova, USSR	1:33.2 OR
1968	Carolina Geijssen, Netherlands	1:32.6 OR
1972	Monika Pflug, W Germany	1:31.40 OR
1976	Tatiana Averina, USSR	1:28.43 OR
1980	Natalya Petruseva, USSR	1:24.10 OR
1984	Karin Enke, E Germany	1:21.61 OR
1988	Christa Rothenburger, E Germany	1:17.65 WR
1992	Bonnie Blair, United States	1:21.90
1994	Bonnie Blair, United States	1:18.74

1,000 METERS *CONT.)*

1998	Marianne Timmer, Netherlands	1:16.51 OR
2002	Chris Witty, United States	1:13.83
2006	Marianne Timmer, Netherlands	1:16.05

1,500 METERS

1960	Lydia Skoblikova, USSR	2:25.2 WR
1964	Lydia Skoblikova, USSR	2:22.6 OR
1968	Kaija Mustonen, Finland	2:22.4 OR
1972	Dianne Holum, United States	2:20.85 OR
1976	Galina Stepanskaya, USSR	2:16.58 OR
1980	Anne Borckink, Netherlands	2:10.95 OR
1984	Karin Enke, E Germany	2:03.42 WR
1988	Yvonne van Gennip, Netherlands	2:00.68 OR
1992	Jacqueline Boerner, Germany	2:05.87
1994	Emese Hunyady, Austria	2:02.19
1998	Marianne Timmer, Netherlands	1:57.58 WR
2002	Anni Friesinger, Germany	1:54.02
2006	Cindy Klassen, Canada	1:55.27

3,000 METERS

1960	Lydia Skoblikova, USSR	5:14.3
1964	Lydia Skoblikova, USSR	5:14.9
1968	Johanna Schut, Netherlands	4:56.2 OR
1972	Christina Baas-Kaiser, Netherlands	4:52.14 OR
1976	Tatiana Averina, USSR	4:45.19 OR
1980	Bjorg Eva Jensen, Norway	4:32.13 OR
1984	Andrea Schöne, E Germany	4:24.79 OR
1988	Yvonne van Gennip, Netherlands	4:11.94 WR
1992	Gunda Niemann, Germany	4:19.90

Note: OR=Olympic Record; WR=World Record; EOR=Equals Olympic Record; EWR=Equals World Record; WB=World Best.
*Combined time.

SPEED SKATING — Women *(Cont.)*

3,000 METERS *(CONT.)*

1994	Svetlana Bazhanova, Russia	4:17.43
1998	Gunda Niemann-Stirnemann, Germany	4:07.29 OR
2002	Claudia Pechstein, Germany	3:57.70
2006	Ireen Wust, Netherlands	4:02.43

5,000 METERS

1988	Yvonne van Gennip, Netherlands	7:14.13 WR

5,000 METERS *(CONT.)*

1992	Gunda Niemann, Germany	7:31.57
1994	Claudia Pechstein, Germany	7:14.37
1998	Claudia Pechstein, Germany	6:59.61 WR
2002	Claudia Pechstein, Germany	6:46.91 WR
2006	Clara Hughes, Canada	6:59.07

TEAM PURSUIT

2006	Germany

SHORT TRACK SPEED SKATING

Men

500 METERS

1994	Chae Ji-Hoon, S Korea	43.54
1998	Takafumi Nishitani, Japan	42.862
2002	Marc Gagnon, Canada	41.802 OR
2006	Apolo Anton Ohno, United States	41.935

1,000 METERS

1992	Kim Ki-Hoon, S Korea	1:30.76
1994	Kim Ki-Hoon, S Korea	1:34.57
1998	Kim Dong Sung, S Korea	1:32.375
2002	Steve Bradbury, Austrailia	1:29.109
2006	Hyun-Soo Ahn, S Korea	1:26.739 OR

1,500 METERS

2002	Apolo Anton Ohno, United States	2:18.541
2006	Hyun-Soo Ahn, S Korea	2:25.341

5,000-METER RELAY

1992	S Korea	7:14.02
1994	Italy	7:11.74
1998	Canada	7:06.075
2002	Canada	6:51.579
2006	S Korea	6:43.376 OR

Women

500 METERS

1992	Cathy Turner, United States	47.04
1994	Cathy Turner, United States	45.98
1998	Annie Perreault, Canada	46.568
2002	Yang Yang, China	44.187
2006	Meng Wang, China	44.345

1,000 METERS

1994	Chun Lee Kyung, S Korea	1:36.87
1998	Chun Lee Kyung, S Korea	1:42.776
2002	Yang A. Yang, China	1:36.391
2006	Sun-Yu Jin, S Korea	1:32.859

1,500 METERS

2002	Ko Gi-Hyun, S Korea	2:31.581
2006	Sun-Yu Jin, China	2:23.494

3,000-METER RELAY

1992	Canada	4:36.62
1994	S Korea	4:26.64
1998	S Korea	4:16.260
2002	S Korea	4:12.793
2006	S Korea	4:17.040

ALPINE SKIING

Men

DOWNHILL

1948	Henri Oreiller, France	2:55.0
1952	Zeno Colo, Italy	2:30.8
1956	Anton Sailer, Austria	2:52.2
1960	Jean Vuarnet, France	2:06.0
1964	Egon Zimmermann, Austria	2:18.16
1968	Jean-Claude Killy, France	1:59.85
1972	Bernhard Russi, Switzerland	1:51.43
1976	Franz Klammer, Austria	1:45.73
1980	Leonhard Stock, Austria	1:45.50
1984	Bill Johnson, United States	1:45.59
1988	Pirmin Zurbriggen, Switzerland	1:59.63
1992	Patrick Ortlieb, Austria	1:50.37
1994	Tommy Moe, United States	1:45.75
1998	Jean-Luc Crétier, France	1:50.11
2002	Fritz Strobl, Austria	1:39.13
2006	Antoine Deneriaz, France	1:48.80

SLALOM

1948	Edi Reinalter, Switzerland	2:10.3
1952	Othmar Schneider, Austria	2:00.0
1956	Anton Sailer, Austria	3:14.7
1960	Ernst Hinterseer, Austria	2:08.9
1964	Josef Stiegler, Austria	2:11.13
1968	Jean-Claude Killy, France	1:39.73
1972	F. Fernandez Ochoa, Spain	1:49.27
1976	Piero Gros, Italy	2:03.29
1980	Ingemar Stenmark, Sweden	1:44.26
1984	Phil Mahre, United States	1:39.41
1988	Alberto Tomba, Italy	1:39.47
1992	Finn Christian Jagge, Norway	1:44.39
1994	Thomas Stangassinger, Austria	2:02.02

SLALOM *(CONT.)*

1998	Hans-Petter Buraas, Norway	1:49.31
2002	Jean-Pierre Vidal, France	1:41.06
2006	Benjamin Raich, Austria	1:43.14

GIANT SLALOM

1952	Stein Eriksen, Norway	2:25.0
1956	Anton Sailer, Austria	3:00.1
1960	Roger Staub, Switzerland	1:48.3
1964	Francois Bonlieu, France	1:46.71
1968	Jean-Claude Killy, France	3:29.28
1972	Gustav Thöni, Italy	3:09.62
1976	Heini Hemmi, Switzerland	3:26.97
1980	Ingemar Stenmark, Sweden	2:40.74
1984	Max Julen, Switzerland	2:41.18
1988	Alberto Tomba, Italy	2:06.37
1992	Alberto Tomba, Italy	2:06.98
1994	Markus Wasmeier, Germany	2:52.46
1998	Hermann Maier, Austria	2:38.51
2002	Stephan Eberharter, Austria	2:23.28
2006	Benjamin Raich, Austria	2:35.00

SUPER GIANT SLALOM

1988	Franck Piccard, France	1:39.66
1992	Kjetil André Aamodt, Norway	1:13.04
1994	Markus Wasmeier, Germany	1:32.53
1998	Hermann Maier, Austria	1:34.82
2002	Kjetil André Aamodt, Norway	1:21.58
2006	Kjetil André Aamodt, Norway	1:30.65

COMBINED

1936	Franz Pfnür, Germany	99.25
1948	Henri Oreiller, France	3.27

ALPINE SKIING — Men *(Cont.)*

COMBINED* *(CONT.)*		COMBINED* *(CONT.)*	
1988 .....Hubert Strolz, Austria	36.55	2002 .....Kjetil André Aamodt, Norway	3:17.56
1992 .....Josef Polig, Italy	14.58	2006 .....Ted Ligety, United States	3:09.35
1994 .....Lasse Kjus, Norway	3:17.53	*Beginning in 1994, scoring was based on time.	
1998 .....Mario Reiter, Austria	3:08.06		

ALPINE SKIING — Women

DOWNHILL		GIANT SLALOM	
1948....Hedy Schlunegger, Switzerland	2:28.3	1952....Andrea Mead Lawrence, U.S.	2:06.8
1952....Trude Jochum-Beiser, Austria	1:47.1	1956....Ossi Reichert, W Germany	1:56.5
1956....Madeleine Berthod, Switzerland	1:40.7	1960....Yvonne Rüegg, Switzerland	1:39.9
1960....Heidi Biebl, W Germany	1:37.6	1964....Marielle Goitschel, France	1:52.24
1964....Christl Haas, Austria	1:55.39	1968....Nancy Greene, Canada	1:51.97
1968....Olga Pall, Austria	1:40.87	1972....Marie-Theres Nadig, Switzerland	1:29.90
1972....Marie-Theres Nadig, Switzerland	1:36.68	1976....Kathy Kreiner, Canada	1:29.13
1976....Rosi Mittermaier, W Germany	1:46.16	1980....Hanni Wenzel,	2:41.66
1980....Annemarie Moser-Pröll, Austria	1:37.52	Liechtenstein (2 runs)	
1984....Michela Figini, Switzerland	1:13.36	1984....Debbie Armstrong, United States	2:20.98
1988....Marina Kiehl, W Germany	1:25.86	1988....Vreni Schneider, Switzerland	2:06.49
1992....Kerrin Lee-Gartner, Canada	1:52.55	1992....Pernilla Wiberg, Sweden	2:12.74
1994....Katja Seizinger, Germany	1:35.93	1994....Deborah Compagnoni, Italy	2:30.97
1998....Katja Seizinger, Germany	1:28.89	1998....Deborah Compagnoni, Italy	2:50.59
2002....Carole Montillet, France	1:39.56	2002....Janica Kostelic, Croatia	2:30.01
2006....Michaela Dorfmeister, Austria	1:56.49	2006....Julia Mancuso, United States	2:09.19

SLALOM		SUPER GIANT SLALOM	
1948....Gretchen Fraser, United States	1:57.2	1988....Sigrid Wolf, Austria	1:19.03
1952....Andrea Mead Lawrence,	2:10.6	1992....Deborah Compagnoni, Italy	1:21.22
United States		1994....Diann Roffe-Steinrotter, U.S.	1:22.15
1956....Renee Colliard, Switzerland	1:52.3	1998....Picabo Street, United States	1:18.02
1960....Anne Heggtveigt, Canada	1:49.6	2002....Daniela Ceccarelli, Italy	1:13.59
1964....Christine Goitschel, France	1:29.86	2006....Michaela Dorfmeister, Austria	1:32.47
1968....Marielle Goitschel, France	1:25.86		
1972....Barbara Cochran, United States	1:31.24	COMBINED*	
1976....Rosi Mittermaier, W Germany	1:30.54	1988....Anita Wachter, Austria	29.25
1980....Hanni Wenzel, Liechtenstein	1:25.09	1992....Petra Kronberger, Austria	2.55
1984....Paoletta Magoni, Italy	1:36.47	1994....Pernilla Wiberg, Sweden	3:05.16
1988....Vreni Schneider, Switzerland	1:36.69	1998....Katja Seizinger, Germany	2:40.74
1992....Petra Kronberger, Austria	1:32.68	2002....Janica Kostelic, Croatia	2:43.28
1994....Vreni Schneider, Switzerland	1:56.01	2006....Janica Kostelic, Croatia	2:51.08
1998....Hilde Gerg, Germany	1:32.40	*Beginning in 1994, scoring was based on time.	
2002....Janica Kostelic, Croatia	1:46.10		
2006....Anja Paerson, Sweden	1:29.04		

FREESTYLE SKIING

Men MOGULS	Pts	Women MOGULS	Pts
1992....Edgar Grospiron, France	25.81	1992....Donna Weinbrecht, United States	23.69
1994....Jean-Luc Brassard, Canada	27.24	1994....Stine Lise Hattestad, Norway	25.97
1998....Jonny Moseley, United States	26.93	1998....Tae Satoya, Japan	25.06
2002....Janne Lahtela, Finland	27.97	2002....Kari Traa, Norway	25.94
2006....Dale Begg-Smith, Australia	26.77	2006....Jennifer Heil, Canada	26.50

AERIALS	Pts	AERIALS	Pts
1994....Andreas Schoenbaechler, Switz	234.67	1994....Lina Cherjazova, Uzbekistan	166.84
1998....Eric Bergoust, United States	255.64	1998....Nikki Stone, United States	193.00
2002....Ales Valenta, Czech Republic	257.02	2002....Alisa Camplin, Australia	193.47
2006....Han Xiaopeng, China	250.77	2006....Evelyne Leu, Switzerland	202.55

NORDIC SKIING — Men

10 KILOMETERS CLASSICAL		15 KILOMETERS PURSUIT FREESTYLE	
1992	Vegard Ulvang, Norway	27:36.0	1992	Bjørn Dæhlie, Norway	1:05:37.9
1994	Bjørn Dæhlie, Norway	24:20.1	1994	Bjørn Dæhlie, Norway	1:00:08.8
1998	Bjørn Dæhlie, Norway	27:24.5	1998	Thomas Alsgaard, Norway	1:07:01.7

10 KILOMETERS CLASSICAL		30 KILOMETERS CLASSICAL	
1976	Nikolay Bajukov, Unified Team	43:58.47	1956	Veikko Hakulinen, Finland	1:44:06.0
1980	Thomas Wassberg, Sweden	41:57.63	1960	Sixten Jernberg, Sweden	1:51:03.9
1984	Gunde Swan, Sweden	41:25.6	1964	Eero Mantyrănta, Finland	1:30:50.7
1988	Michael Deviatyarov, USSR	41:18.9	1968	Franco Nones, Italy	1:35:39.2
2002	Andrus Veerpalu, Estonia	37:07.4	1972	Viaceslav Vedenine, USSR	1:36:31.2
2006	Andrus Veerpalu, Estonia	38:01.3			

NORDIC SKIING — Men *(Cont.)*

30 KILOMETERS CLASSICAL *(CONT.)*

1976	Sergei Savelyev, USSR	1:30:29.38
1980	Nikolai Simyatov, USSR	1:27:02.80
1984	Nikolai Simyatov, USSR	1:28:56.3
1988	Alexey Prokororov, USSR	1:24:26.3
1992	Vegard Ulvang, Norway	1:22:27.8
1994	Thomas Alsgaard, Norway	1:12:26.4
1998	Mika Myllylae, Finland	1:33:55.8

30 KILOMETERS PURSUIT

2006	Eugeni Dementiev, Russia	1:17:00.8

50 KILOMETERS FREESTYLE

1924	Thorleif Haug, Norway	3:44:32.0
1928	Per Erik Hedlund, Sweden	4:52:03.0
1932	Veli Saarinen, Finland	4:28:00.0
1936	Elis Wiklund, Sweden	3:30:11.0
1948	Nils Karlsson, Sweden	3:47:48.0
1952	Veikko Hakulinen, Finland	3:33:33.0
1956	Sixten Jernberg, Sweden	2:50:27.0
1960	Kalevi Hämäläinen, Finland	2:59:06.3
1964	Sixten Jernberg, Sweden	2:43:52.6
1968	Olle Ellefsaeter, Norway	2:28:45.8
1972	Paal Tyldrum, Norway	2:43:14.75
1976	Ivar Formo, Norway	2:37:30.50
1980	Nikolai Simyatov, USSR	2:27:24.60
1984	Thomas Wassberg, Sweden	2:15:55.8
1988	Gunde Svan, Sweden	2:04:30.9
1992	Bjørn Dæhlie, Norway	2:03:41.5
1994	Vladimir Smirnov, Kazakhstan	2:07:20.3
1998	Bjørn Dæhlie, Norway	2:05:08.2
2002	Mikhail Ivanov, Russia	2:06:20.8
2006	Giorgio di Centa, Italy	2:06:11.8

4 X 10-KILOMETER RELAY MIXED

1936	Finland	2:41:33.0
1948	Sweden	2:32:80.0
1952	Finland	2:20:16.0
1956	USSR	2:15:30.0
1960	Finland	2:18:45.6
1964	Sweden	2:18:34.6
1968	Norway	2:08:33.5
1972	USSR	2:04:47.94
1976	Finland	2:07:59.72
1980	USSR	1:57:03.46
1984	Sweden	1:55:06.3
1988	Sweden	1:43:58.6
1992	Norway	1:39:26.0
1994	Italy	1:41:15.0
1998	Norway	1:40:55.7
2002	Norway	1:32:45.5
2006	Italy	1:43:45.7

TEAM SPRINT

2006	Sweden	17:02.9

INDIVIDUAL SPRINT

2006	Bjoern Lind, Sweden	2:26.5

SKI JUMPING (90-M HILL)

		Pts
1964	Veikko Kankkonen, Finland	229.90
1968	Jiri Raska, Czechoslovakia	216.5
1972	Yukio Kasaya, Japan	244.2
1976	Hans-Georg Aschenbach, E Germany	252.0
1980	Toni Innauer, Austria	266.3
1984	Jens Weissflog, E Germany	215.2
1988	Matti Nykänen, Finland	229.1
1992	Ernst Vettori, Austria	222.8
1994	Espen Bredesen, Norway	282.0
1998	Jani Soininen, Finland	234.5

SKI JUMPING (90-M HILL) *(CONT.)*

		Pts
2002	Simon Ammann, Switzerland	269.0
2006	Lars Bystoel, Norway	266.5

SKI JUMPING (120-M HILL)

		Pts
1924	Jacob Tullin Thams, Norway	18.960
1928	Alf Andersen, Norway	19.208
1932	Birger Ruud, Norway	228.1
1936	Birger Ruud, Norway	232.0
1948	Petter Hugsted, Norway	228.1
1952	Arnfinn Bergmann, Norway	226.0
1956	Antti Hyvärinen, Finland	227.0
1960	Helmut Recknagel, E Germany	227.2
1964	Toralf Engan, Norway	230.70
1968	Vladimir Beloussov, USSR	231.3
1972	Wojciech Fortuna, Poland	219.9
1976	Karl Schnabl, Austria	234.8
1980	Jouko Tormanen, Finland	271.0
1984	Matti Nykänen, Finland	231.2
1988	Matti Nykänen, Finland	224.0
1992	Toni Nieminen, Finland	239.5
1994	Jens Weissflog, Germany	274.5
1998	Kazuyoshi Funaki, Japan	272.3
2002	Simon Amman, Switzerland	281.4
2006	Thomas Morgenstern, Austria	276.9

TEAM 120-M SKI JUMPING

		Pts
1988	Finland	634.4
1992	Finland	644.4
1994	Germany	970.1
1998	Japan	933.0
2002	Germany	974.1
2006	Austria	984.0

NORDIC COMBINED*

		Pts
1924	Thorleif Haug, Norway	18.906
1928	Johan Gröttumsbraaten, Norway	17.833
1932	Johan Gröttumsbraaten, Norway	446.0
1936	Oddbjörn Hagen, Norway	430.30
1948	Heikki Hasu, Finland	448.80
1952	Simon Slattvik, Norway	451.621
1956	Sverre Stenersen, Norway	455.0
1960	Georg Thoma, W Germany	457.952
1964	Tormod Knutsen, Norway	469.28
1968	Frantz Keller, W Germany	449.04
1972	Ulrich Wehling, E Germany	413.34
1976	Ulrich Wehling, E Germany	423.39
1980	Ulrich Wehling, E Germany	432.20
1984	Tom Sandberg, Norway	422.595
1988	Hippolyt Kempf, Switzerland	432.230
1992	Fabrice Guy, France	426.47
1994	Fred B. Lundberg, Norway	457.970
1998	Bjarte Engen Vik, Norway	41:21.1†
2002	Samppa Lajunen, Finland	38:18.7†
2006	Georg Hettich, Norway	39:44.6†

TEAM NORDIC COMBINED

1988	W Germany
1992	Japan
1994	Japan
1998	Norway
2002	Finland
2006	Austria

SPRINT NORDIC COMBINED

2002	Samppa Lajunen, Finland	123.8
2006	Felix Gottwald, Austria	17:35.0†

* Different scoring system; 1924–1952 distance was 18 km; 1952–present, 15 km.
† Times in the cross-country race were not converted into points. According to the Gundersen Method, used since 1988, starting times in the race are staggered in proportion to points earned in the ski jumping segment of the event.

NORDIC SKIING — Women

INDIVIDUAL SPRINT

2002	Julija Tchepalova, Russia	3:10.6
2006	Chandra Crawford, Canada	2:12.3

5 KILOMETERS PURSUIT

2002	Olga Danilova, Russia	24:52.1

5 KILOMETERS CLASSICAL

1964	Klaudia Boyarskikh, USSR	17:50.5
1968	Toini Gustafsson, Sweden	16:45.2
1972	Galina Kulakova, USSR	17:00.50
1976	Helena Takalo, Finland	15:48.69
1980	Raisa Smetanina, USSR	15:06.92
1984	Marja-Liisa Hamalainen, Finland	17:04.0
1988	Marjo Matikainen, Finland	15:04.0
1992	Marjut Lukkarinen, Finland	14:13.8
1994	Lyubova Egorova, Russia	14:08.8
1998	Larissa Lazhutina, Russia	17:37.9

10 KILOMETERS CLASSICAL

1952	Lydia Widemen, Finland	41:40.0
1956	Lyubov Kosyryeva, USSR	38:11.0
1960	Maria Gusakova, USSR	39:46.6
1964	Klaudia Boyarskikh, USSR	40:24.3
1968	Toini Gustafsson, Sweden	36:46.5
1972	Galina Kulakova, USSR	34:17.8
1976	Raisa Smetanina, USSR	30:13.41
1980	Barbara Petzold, E Germany	30:31.54
1984	Marja-Lissa Hamalainen, Finland	31:44.2
1988	Vida Ventsene, USSR	30:08.3
2002	Bante Skari, Norway	28:05.6
2006	Kristina Smigun, Estonia	27:51.4

10 KILOMETERS PURSUIT FREESTYLE

1992	Lyubov Egorova, Unified Team	40:07.7
1994	Lyubov Egorova, Russia	41:38.1
1998	Larissa Lazhutina, Russia	46:06.9

15 KILOMETERS CLASSICAL

1992	Lyubov Egorova, Unified Team	42:20.8
1994	Manuela Di Centa, Italy	39:44.5
1998	Olga Danilova, Russia	46:55.04

15 KILOMETERS FREESTYLE

2002	Stefania Belmondo, Italy	39:54.4

15 KILOMETERS PURSUIT

2006	Kristina Smigun, Estonia	42:48.7

20 KILOMETERS FREESTYLE

1984	Marja-Liisa Hamalainen, Finland	1:01:45.0
1988	Tamara Tikhonova, USSR	55:53.6

30 KILOMETERS FREESTYLE

1992	Stefania Belmondo, Italy	1:22:30.1
1994	Manuela Di Centa, Italy	1:25:41.6
1998	Julija Tchepalova, Russia	1:22:01.5
2002	Gabriela Paruzzi, Italy	1:30:57.1
2006	Katerina Neumannova, Czech Rep.	1:22:25.4

TEAM SPRINT

2006	Sweden	16:36.9

4 X 5-KILOMETER RELAY MIXED

1956	Finland	1:9:01.0
1960	Sweden	1:4:21.4
1964	USSR	59:20.0
1968	Norway	57:30.0
1972	USSR	48:46.15
1976	USSR	1:07:49.75
1980	E Germany	1:02:11.10
1984	Norway	1:06:49.7
1988	USSR	59:51.1
1992	Unified Team	59:34.8
1994	Russia	57:12.5
1998	Russia	55:13.5
2002	Germany	49:30.6
2006	Russia	54:47.7

SNOWBOARDING

Men

GIANT SLALOM

1998	Ross Rebagliati, Canada	2:03.96

PARALLEL GIANT SLALOM

2002	Philipp Schoch, Switzerland
2006	Philipp Schoch, Switzerland

HALF-PIPE

		Pts
1998	Gian Simmen, Switzerland	85.2
2002	Ross Powers, United States	46.1
2006	Shaun White, United States	46.8

SNOWBOARD CROSS

2006	Seth Wescott, United States

Women

GIANT SLALOM

1998	Karine Ruby, France	2:17.34

PARALLEL GIANT SLALOM

2002	Isabella Blanc, France
2006	Daniela Meuli, Switzerland

HALF-PIPE

		Pts
1998	Nicola Thost, Germany	74.6
2002	Kelly Clark, United States	47.9
2006	Hannah Teter, United States	46.4

SNOWBOARD CROSS

2006	Tanja Frieden, Switzerland

Track & Field

Runaway Victory

After an awful 2006, American track and field rebounded, taking home a record 14 gold medals at the 2007 Worlds

BY MERRELL NODEN

THE BELL LAP FOR NEXT summer's highly anticipated Beijing Olympics began in late August, in steamy Osaka, Japan, where the world's top track and field athletes gathered for the 2007 World Championships. Like most final laps, the Osaka meet was a thrilling spectacle, full of jockeying, posturing, and a variety of fades and flameouts. Some reigning Olympic champions, such as 400-meter man Jeremy Wariner, reaffirmed their status as favorites for next summer, while others stamped themselves as such for the first time. In that group was a pair of versatile U.S. sprinters, Tyson Gay and Allyson Felix, who will have some interesting choices to make in Beijing next summer.

And then there was Alan Webb, who spent the first half of the season looking like the best middle distance runner in the world. Ever since smashing Jim Ryun's ancient high school record for the mile six years ago, Webb has tantalized track fans with his obvious talent and then frustrated them with his spotty record in big meets. Lately his only real competition among Americans has been Bernard Lagat, the veteran transplanted Kenyan. For most of this year, it looked as if he had left even Lagat behind.

At the U.S. Nationals in June, Webb kicked powerfully away from Lagat in the homestretch to claim his third national title, in 3:34.82. Webb then went to Europe and reeled off an impressive series of races: In Paris he beat a crack 1500 field in a personal best of 3:30.54. He clocked another personal best, in the 800 (1:43.84), and finally broke Steve Scott's 25-year-old U.S. record in the mile with a 3:46.91 in Brasschaat, Belgium. Over this stretch Webb looked every inch a world-beater. The only question was whether he could maintain that sharp edge through the three rounds of the 1500 he'd have to run at the Osaka world championships in August.

The other big star to emerge from the U.S. Championships was Gay, a versatile sprinter from Kentucky who has spent the last few years quietly maturing in double Olympic champion Justin Gatlin's slipstream. With Gatlin out serving a drug suspension, there seemed to be no shortage of contenders to replace him, including Gay; Xavier Carter, who ran a 19.63 200 in 2006; and first and foremost Asafa Powell, the powerful young Jamaican who three times had run the world record of 9.77.

Gay opened eyes in early June when he clocked a 9.76 in New York City with a tailwind barely exceeding the limit for records. At nationals, he ran what is arguably the best sprint double in history, winning the 100 in 9.84 and the 200 in 19.62 while running into a slight headwind. But with Powell getting a late start to the season due to tendonitis in his knee, the world's two premiere dash men did not race until Osaka.

Adding intrigue to Gay's season was the fact that his coach, Lance Bauman, was spending his summer in prison, on charges of mail fraud, embezzlement, and theft

BILL FRAKES/SPORTS ILLUSTRATED

of the race. She won by five meters in a personal best time of 21.81 seconds. She also ran legs for both victorious U.S. relay teams and now must decide what she will do in Beijing next year.

In the 1500 semis, Webb ran poorly, but survived. But down the stretch of the final, when the other runners accelerated, Webb began to fade. Closing fastest of all was Lagat, who reached the finish first, in 3:34.77. His gold was the first by an American in a major championship 1500 since 1908. Webb finished eighth. "I was doing so well until this week," said a visibly frustrated Webb. "It was a colossal breakdown." Four days later, Lagat won the 5000 in 13:45.87, a mystifyingly slow race in which the entire pack seemed determined to hand the gold to the best kicker, Lagat.

In the end, the U.S. came away from Osaka with 14 gold medals, including a historic sweep of the relays, all by yawning margins. The real interest there came in the contributions of Felix and Wariner. In the 1600-meter relay Felix ran a 48.0 second leg that broke the race wide open, while Wariner clocked a 43.1 anchor leg, which is second only to the 42.97 once run by 400 world record holder Michael Johnson, who just happens to be Wariner's agent.

The season closed with Powell getting some small measure of revenge by setting a new world 100 record of 9.74 in Rieti, Italy.

There is a lot of intrigue surrounding next year's Summer Games. How will the terrible pollution effect distance runners? Will Chinese authorities crack down on protesters? Whatever happens, there are two things you can count on: The Chinese, determined to prove themselves a first world power, will assemble a superb team. And judging by this year's world championships, the rest of the world will give them plenty of competition.

while he was coaching at a small community college in Kansas. In Bauman's absence, Gay was being coached by retired sprinter Jon Drummond, the self-described "clown prince of track and field" whose histrionics could scarcely have been more different from his pupil's laidback modesty.

"He's the evolution of the 100 meters," Drummond was telling everyone, and it sure looked that way in Osaka. Powell looked good in the early rounds, but in the last half of the final it was all Gay. Eyes bulging with fierce determination, he dominated the field, winning easily in 9.85. Powell, perhaps flustered by Gay's presence, was passed in the closing stages by Derrick Atkins of the Bahamas.

Gay won the 200 by an even wider margin, breaking Michael Johnson's meet record by three hundredths of a second, in 19.76. He then ran a great turn on the U.S. 400 relay team and thus joined Carl Lewis and Maurice Greene as the only men to win those three events at a world championship.

Equally impressive was Felix, a beautifully smooth sprinter, who runs with her long braided hair flowing behind her. In the 200, Felix came out of the turn even with 100 winner Veronica Campbell of Jamaica, then simply flowed away over the last half

2007 USATF Outdoor Championships

Indianapolis, June 20–24, 2007
Men

100 METERS

1.	Tyson Gay, adidas	9.84
2.	Trindon Holliday, LSU	10.07
3.	Walter Dix, Florida St.	10.27

200 METERS

1.	Tyson Gay, adidas	19.62
2.	Wallace Spearmon, Nike	19.89
3.	Rodney Martin, Nike	20.18

400 METERS

1.	Angelo Taylor, unattached	44.05
2.	LaShawn Merritt, Nike	44.06
3.	Lionel Larry, USC	44.84

800 METERS

1.	Khadevis Robinson, Nike	1:44.37
2.	Nicholas Symmonds, Oregon TC	1:45.17
3.	Duane Solomon, USC	1:45.69

1,500 METERS

1.	Alan Webb, Nike	3:34.82
2.	Leonel Manzano, Texas	3:35.29
3.	Bernard Lagat, Nike	3:35.55

3,000 M STEEPLECHASE

1.	Joshua McAdams, New Balance	8:24.46
2.	Aaron Aguayo, Arizona St.	8:27.01
3.	Thomas Brooks, Oregon TC	8:27.34

5,000 METERS

1.	Bernard Lagat, Nike	13:30.73
2.	Matt Tegenkamp, Nike	13:31.31
3.	Adam Goucher, Nike	13:31.50

10,000 METERS

1.	Abdi Abdirahman, Nike	28:13.51
2.	Galen Rupp, Oregon	28:23.31
3.	Dathan Ritzenhein, Nike	28:31.88

110-METER HURDLES

1.	Terrence Trammell, Mizuno	13.08
2.	Dominique Arnold, Nike	13.17
3.	David Oliver, Nike	13.18

400-METER HURDLES

1.	James Carter, unattached	47.72
2.	Kerron Clement, Nike	47.80
3.	Derrick Williams, Reebok	48.26

20-KILOMETER RACE WALK

1.	Kevin Eastler, U.S. Air Force	1:26:43.28
2.	Tim Seaman, New York AC	1:28:17.82
3.	Matthew Boyles, Miami Valley	1:28:40.20

HIGH JUMP

1.	Jim Dilling, unattached	2.27m
2.	Jamie Nieto, Nike	2.24m
3.	Adam Shunk, Nike	§2.24m

POLE VAULT

1.	Brad Walker, Nike	5.70m
2.	Jeff Hartwig, Nike	§5.70m
3.	Jacob Pauli, Nike	§5.70m

LONG JUMP

1.	Dwight Phillips, Nike	8.36m
2.	Miguel Pate, Nike	8.24m
3.	Trevell Quinley, unattached	8.24m

TRIPLE JUMP

1.	Aarik Wilson, Nike	17.06m
2.	Lawrence Willis, unattached	16.97m
3.	Marc Kellman, unattached	16.74m

SHOT PUT

1.	Reese Hoffa, New York A.C.	21.47m
2.	Dan Taylor, Nike	21.00m
3.	Adam Nelson, unattached	20.54m

DISCUS THROW

1.	Michael Robertson, Stanford	64.04m
2.	Ian Waltz, Nike	63.60m
3.	Jarred Rome, Nike	63.56m

HAMMER THROW

1.	A.G. Kruger, New York AC	78.10m
2.	Kibwe Johnson, New York AC	75.12m
3.	Thomas Freeman, New York AC	74.39m

JAVELIN THROW

1.	Breaux Greer, adidas	91.29m
2.	Mike Hazle, unattached	75.06m
3.	Justin St. Clair, unattached	74.71m

DECATHLON

1.	Tom Poppas, Nike	8352
2.	Paul Terek, Asics	8064
3.	Robert Arnold, Arizona	7921

MARATHON*

1.	Mykola Antonenko	2:13.54
2.	Joseph Mutinda	2:20.12
3.	Augustus Kavutu Mbusya	2:21.13

*Held October 7 in Minneapolis, Minnesota
§Final place in high jump and pole vault decided by number of successful clearances at final height.

Women

100 METERS
1. ....Torri Edwards, Nike — 11.02
2. ....Lauryn Williams, Nike — 11.16
3. ....Carmelita Jeter, Nike — 11.17

200 METERS
1. ....Allyson Felix, adidas — 22.34
2. ....Sanya Richards, Nike — 22.43
3. ....Torri Edwards, Nike — 22.55

400 METERS
1. ....De' Hashia Trotter, adidas — 49.64
2. ....Natasha Hastings, S. Carolina — 49.84
3. ....Mary Wineberg, Nike — 50.24

800 METERS
1. ....Alysia Johnson, California — 1:59.47
2. ....Hazel Clark, Nike — 1:59.60
3. ....Alice Schmidt, adidas — 1:59.63

1,500 METERS
1. ....Treniere Clement, Nike — 4:07.04
2. ....Christin Wurth, Nike — 4:07.86
3. ....Erin Donohue, Nike — 4:08.22

3,000 M STEEPLECHASE
1. ....Jennifer Barringer, Colorado — 9:34.64
2. ....Anna Willard, Nike — 9:34.72
3. ....Lindsey Anderson, Nike — 9:40.74

5,000 METERS
1. ....Shalane Flanagan, Nike — 14:51.75
2. ....Jennifer Rhines, adidas — 15:08.53
3. ....Michelle Sikes, Nike — 15:09.28

10,000 METERS
1. ....Deena Kastor, Asics — 31:57.00
2. ....Kara Goucher, Nike — 32:33.80
3. ....Katie McGregor, Reebok — 32:44.69

20-KILOMETER RACE WALK
1. ....Teresa Vaill, Walk USA — 1:37:28.70
2. ....Jolene Moore, New York AC — 1:39:24.14
3. ....Sam Cohen, Parkside AC — 1:40:53.22

100-METER HURDLES
1. ....Virginia Powell, Nike — 12.63
2. ....Michelle Perry, Nike — 12.72
3. ....Lolo Jones, Asics — 12.79

400-METER HURDLES
1. ....Tiffany Williams, Reebok — 53.28
2. ....Sheena Johnson, Nike — 53.29
3. ....Nicole Leach, UCLA — 54.49

HIGH JUMP
1. ....Amy Acuff, Asics — 1.89m
2. ....Sharon Day, C.P./L.S.O. — 1.89m
3. ....Destinee Hooker, unattached — 1.86m

POLE VAULT
1. ....Jennifer Stuczynski, adidas — 4.45m
2. ....Nikole McEwan, unattached — 4.45m
3. ....Lacy Janson, Nike — 4.35m

LONG JUMP
1. ....Grace Upshaw, Nike — 6.74m
2. ....Brittney Reese, Mississippi — 6.67m
3. ....Rose Richmond, Nike — 6.60m

TRIPLE JUMP
1. ....Shani Marks, unattached — 14.08m
2. ....Yvette Lewis, unattached — 13.59m
3. ....Erica McLain, Stanford — 13.57m

SHOT PUT
1. ....Kristin Heaston, Nike — 18.74m
2. ....Jillian Camarena, New York AC — 18.50m
3. ....Sarah Stevens, Arizona St — 18.02m

DISCUS THROW
1. ....Suzy Powell, Asics — 60.63m
2. ....Rebecca Breisch, unattached — 59.89m
3. ....Summer Pierson, unattached — 56.79m

HAMMER THROW
1. ....Brittany Riley, S. Illinois — 72.41m
2. ....Kristal Yush, unattached — 68.24m
3. ....Jessica Cosby, Nike — 68.21m

JAVELIN THROW
1. ....Dana Pounds, Air Force Academy — 59.65m
2. ....Kim Kreiner, Nike — 58.17m
3. ....Anna Raynor, unattached — 53.77m

HEPTATHLON
1. ....Hyleas Fountain, Nike — 6090
2. ....Diana D. Pickler, Washington St. — 6029
3. ....Virginia Johnson, unattached — 6002

MARATHON*
1. ....Svetlana Ponomarenko — 2:34.09
2. ....Alena Vinitskaya — 2:38.23
3. ....Sharon Cherop — 2:38.45

*Held October 7 in Minneapolis, Minnesota.

Boston, Feb 24–25, 2007

Men

60 METERS
1. ....Dabryan Blanton, Nike — 6.56
2. ....Marcus Brunson, Nike — 6.58
3. ....Kyle Farmer, Norfolk Real — 6.62

400 METERS
1. ....Greg Nixon, unattached — 46.75
2. ....Fernada Blakely, Asics — 46.97
3. ....Darold Williamson, Nike — 47.21

1 MILE RUN
1. ....Alan Webb, Nike — 4:01.07
2. ....Rob Myers, Reebok — 4:01.78
3. ....Gabriel Jennings, unattached — 4:01.93

800 METERS
1. ....Nicholas Symmonds, Oregon TC — 1:48.73
2. ....Samuel Burley, Nike — 1:49.42
3. ....Tim Ramirez, unattached — 1:49.59

3,000 METERS
1. ....Matt Tegenkamp, Nike — 7:46.08
2. ....Jonathon Riley, Nike — 7:49.73
3. ....Sean Graham, Oregon TC — 7:52.31

5,000-METER RACE WALK
1. ....Tim Seaman, New York A.C. — 19:24.38
2. ....Kevin Eastler, U.S. Air Force — 19:28.63
3. ....Matthew Boyles, Miami V./Asics — 19:47.82

60-METER HURDLES
1. ....Ron Bramlett, unattached — 7.47
2. ....David Payne, unattached — 7.51
3. ....David Oliver, Nike — 7.57

HIGH JUMP
1. ....Tora Harris, Shore AC/Asics — 2.29m
2. ....Jesse Williams, Nike — §2.29m
3. ....Jamie Nieto, Nike — 2.23m

POLE VAULT
1. ....Jeff Hartwig, Nike — 5.80m
2. ....Russ Buller, Asics — 5.60m
3. ....Darren Niedermeyer, unattached — §5.60m

LONG JUMP
1. ....Trevell Quinley, unattached — 8.06m
2. ....Brian Johnson, Nike — 8.03m
3. ....Aarik Wilson, Nike — 8.00m

TRIPLE JUMP
1. ....Aarik Wilson, Nike — 17.28m
2. ....Rafeeq Curry, unattached — 16.54m
3. ....Marc Kellman, unattached — 16.05m

SHOT PUT
1. ....Christian Cantwell, Nike — 21.72m
1. ....Reese Hoffa, New York AC — 21.21m
3. ....Dan Taylor, Nike — 20.32m

WEIGHT THROW
1. ...........A.G. Kruger, Nike — 24.05m
2. ....Thomas Freeman, New York AC — 23.10m
3. ....Michael Mai, U.S. Army — 22.99m

HEPTATHLON*
1. ....Paul Terek, Asics — 5960
2. ....Chris Boyles, C-Bo-Elite — 5702
3. ....Ryan Olkowski, unattached — 5414

Women

60 METERS
1. ....:Hasani Roseby, Nike — 7.16
2. ....Carmelita Jeter, South Bay TC — 7.17
3. ....Marshevet Hooker, adidas — 7.22

400 METERS
1. ....De'Hashia Trotter, adidas — 51.95
2. ....Monica Hargrove, unattached — 52.26
3. ....Mary Wineberg, Nike — 52.31

1 MILE RUN
1. ....Shayne Culpepper, Nike — 4:34.42
2. ....Sarah Schwald, Nike — 4:36.12
3. ....Christin Wurth, Nike — 4:36.78

800 METERS
1. ....Nikeya Green, Reebok — 2:02.68
2. ....Christin Wurth, Nike — 2:03.70
3. ....Mishael Berger, unattached — 2:04.58

3,000 METERS
1. ....Shalane Flanagan, Nike — 8:56.74
2. ....Lisa Galaviz, Nike — 9:10.75
3. ....Emily Field, unattached — 9:11.32

3,000-METER RACE WALK
1. ....Sam Cohen, Parkside Ath — 13:51.29
2. ....Lauren Forgues, unattached — 13:55.90
3. ....Loretta Schuellein, Walk USA — 14:14.95

60-METER HURDLES
1. ....Lolo Jones, unattached — 7.88
2. ....Danielle Carruthers, Nike — 7.92
3. ....Nichole Denby, Nike — 7.93

HIGH JUMP
1. ....Amy Acuff, Asics — 1.92m
2. ....Gwen Wentland, Nike — 1.86m
3. ....Sheena Gordon, unattached — §1.86m

POLE VAULT
1. ....Jennifer Stuczynski, adidas — 4.60m
2. ....Lacy Janson, Nike — §4.60m
3. ....Mary Sauer, Asics — 4.50m

LONG JUMP
1. ....Akiba McKinney, Nike — 6.55m
2. ....Shameka Marshall, unattached — 6.38m
3. ....Brianna Glenn, unattached — 6.35m

TRIPLE JUMP
1. ....Shani Marks, unattached — 13.56m
2. ....Tiombe Hurd, Nike — 13.39m
3. ....Brandy Depland, unattached — 13.17m

SHOT PUT
1. ....Jillian Camarena, New York AC — 18.46m
2. ....Elizabeth Wanless, New York AC — 17.80m
3. ....Robyn Jarocki, unattached — 16.90m

WEIGHT THROW
1. ....Amber Campbell, Mjolnir Thro — 24.54m
2. ....Erin Gilreath, New York AC — 22.40m
3. ....Kristal Yush, unattached — 22.15m

PENTATHLON*
1. ....Fiona Asigbee, unattached — 4098
2. ....Bridgette Ingram, LeMans TC — 4097
3. ....Lela Nelson, Nike — 3976

*Held on March 3-4 in Chapel Hill, North Carolina.
§Final place in high jump and pole vault decided by number of successful attempts at final height.

2007 IAAF World Cross-Country Championships

Mombasa, Kenya, March 24, 2007

MEN (12,000 METERS; 7.5 MILES)
1. ....Zersenay Tadese, Eritrea — 35:50
2. ....Moses Mosop, Kenya — 36:13
3. ....Bernard Kiprop Kipyego, Kenya — 36:37

WOMEN (8,000 METERS; 5 MILES)
1. ....Lornah Kiplagat, Netherlands — 26:23
2. ....Tirunesh Dibaba, Ethiopia — 26:47
3. ....Meselech Melkamu, Ethiopia — 26:48

Major Marathons

Chicago: October 7, 2007

MEN
1. ....Patrick Ivuti, Kenya — 2:11:11.00
2. ....Jaouad Gharib, Morocco — 2:11:11.05
3. ....Daniel Njenga, Kenya — 2:12:45

WOMEN
1. ....Berhane Adere, Ethiopia — 2:33:49
2. ....Adriana Pirtea, Romania — 2:33:52
3. ....Kate O'Neill, USA — 2:36:15

New York City: November 5, 2006

MEN
1. ....M. Gomes dos Santos, Brazil — 2:09:58
2. ....Stephen Kiogora, Kenya — 2:10:06
3. ....Paul Tergat, Kenya — 2:10:10

WOMEN
1. ....Jelena Prokopcuka, Latvia — 2:25:05
2. ....Tatiana Hladyr, Ukraine — 2:26:05
3. ....Catherine Ndereba, Kenya — 2:26:58

Tokyo: November 19, 2006

WOMEN ONLY
1. ....Reiko Tosa, Japan — 2:26:15
2. ....Akemi Ozaki, Japan — 2:28:51
3. ....Naoko Takahashi — 2:31:22

Tokyo: February 18, 2007

MEN ONLY
1. ....Daniel Njenga, Kenya — 2:09:45
2. ....Tomoyuki Sato, Japan — 2:11:22
3. ....Satoshi Irifune, Japan — 2:12:44

Rome: March 18, 2007

MEN
1. ....Chelimo Kemboi, Kenya — 2:09:36
2. ....Jose Manuel Martinez, Spain — 2:10:12
3. ....Jonathan Kosgei, Kenya — 2:10:25

WOMEN
1. ....Souad Ait Salem, Algeria — 2:25:07
2. ....Hellen Kimutai, Kenya — 2:26:45
3. ....Helena Javornik, Slovenia — 2:27:38

Paris: April 15, 2007

MEN
1. ....Mubarak Shami, Qatar — 2:07:19
2. ....Gashaw Melese, Ethiopia — 2:09:53
3. ....Daniel Rono, Kenya — 2:10:28

WOMEN
1. ....Tafa Magarsa, Ethiopia — 2:25:07
2. ....Gulnara Vigovskaya, Russia — 2:28:22
3. ....Christelle Daunay, France — 2:28:54

Boston: April 16, 2007

MEN
1. ....Robert Cheruiyot, Kenya — 2:14:13
2. ....James Kwambai, Kenya — 2:14:33
3. ....Stephen Kiogora, Kenya — 2:14:47

WOMEN
1. ....Lidiya Grigoryeva, Russia — 2:29:18
2. ....Jelena Prokopcuka, Latvia — 2:29:58
3. ....Madai Perez, Mexico — 2:30:16

Rotterdam: April 08, 2007

MEN
1. ....Joshua Chelanga, Kenya — 2:08:21
2. ....Takayuki Matsumiya — 2:10:04
3. ....William Kipsang, Kenya — 2:11:04

WOMEN
1. ....Hiromi Ominami, Japan — 2:26:37
2. ....Helena Kiprop Loshanyang, Kenya — 2:30:11
3 ....Alevtina Biktamirova — 2:31:02

London: April 22, 2007

MEN
1. ....Martin Lel, Kenya — 2:07:41
2. ....Abderrahim Goumri, Morocco — 2:07:44
3. ....Felix Limo, Kenya — 2:07:47

WOMEN
1. ....Chunxiu Zhou, China — 2:20:38
2. ....Gete Wami, Ethiopia — 2:21:45
3. ....Constantina Tomescu-Dita, Romania — 2:23:55

TRACK AND FIELD

World Records

As of October 1, 2007. World outdoor records are recognized by the International Amateur Athletics Federation (IAAF).

Men

Event	Mark	Record Holder	Date	Site
100 meters	9.77	Asafa Powell, Jamaica	8-18-06	Zurich, Switzerland
200 meters	19.32	Michael Johnson, United States	8-1-96	Atlanta
400 meters	43.18	Michael Johnson, United States	8-26-99	Seville, Spain
800 meters	1:41.11	Wilson Kipketer, Denmark	8-24-97	Cologne
1,000 meters	2:11.96	Noah Ngeny, Kenya	9-5-99	Rieti, Italy
1,500 meters	3:26.00	Hicham El Guerrouj, Morocco	7-14-98	Rome
Mile	3:43.13	Hicham El Guerrouj, Morocco	7-7-99	Rome
2,000 meters	4:44.79	Hicham El Guerrouj, Morocco	9-7-99	Berlin
3,000 meters	7:20.67	Daniel Komen, Kenya	9-1-96	Rieti, Italy
Steeplechase	7:53.63	Saif Saaeed Shaheen, Qatar	9-3-04	Brussels
5,000 meters	12:37.35	Kenenisa Bekele, Ethiopia	5-31-04	Hengelo, Netherlands
10,000 meters	26:17.53	Kenenisa Bekele, Ehtiopia	8-26-05	Brussels
20,000 meters	56:26.0	Haile Gebrselassie, Ethiopia	6-27-07	Ostrava, Czech Republic
Hour	21,285 meters	Haile Gebrselassie, Ethiopia	6-27-07	Ostrava, Czech Republic
25,000 meters	1:13:55.8	Toshihiko Seko, Japan	3-22-81	Christchurch, New Zealand
30,000 meters	1:29:18.8	Toshihiko Seko, Japan	3-22-81	Christchurch, New Zealand
Marathon	2:04:55	Paul Tergat, Kenya	9-28-03	Berlin
110-meter hurdles	12.88	Xiang Liu, China	7-11-06	Lausanne, Switzerland
400-meter hurdles	46.78	Kevin Young, United States	8-6-92	Barcelona
20-kilometer walk	1:17:21	Jefferson Perez, Ecuador	8-23-03	Paris
30-kilometer walk	2:01:44.1	Maurizio Damilano, Italy	10-3-92	Cuneo, Italy
50-kilometer walk	3:35:47	Nathan Deakes, Australia	12-2-06	Geelong, Austalia
4 x 100-meter relay	37.40	United States (Mike Marsh, Leroy Burrell, Dennis Mitchell, Carl Lewis)	8-8-92	Barcelona
		United States (Jon Drummond, Andre Cason, Dennis Mitchell, Leroy Burrell)	8-21-93	Stuttgart, Germany
4 x 200-meter relay	1:18.68	Santa Monica TC (Mike Marsh, Leroy Burrell, Floyd Heard, Carl Lewis)	4-17-94	Walnut, Calif.
4 x 400-meter relay	2:54.20	United States (Jerome Young, Antonio Pettigrew, Tyree Washington, Michael Johnson)	7-22-98	New York City
4 x 800-meter relay	7:02.43	Kenya (Wilfred Bungei, William Yiampoy, Joseph Mutua, Ismael Kombich).	8-25-06	Brussels
4 x 1,500-meter relay	14:38.8	W Germany (Thomas Wessinghage, Harald Hudak, Michael Lederer, Karl Fleschen)	8-17-77	Cologne, Germany
High jump	2.45m	Javier Sotomayor, Cuba	7-27-93	Salamanca, Spain
Pole vault	6.14m	Sergei Bubka, Ukraine	7-31-94	Sestriere, Italy
Long jump	8.95m	Mike Powell, United States	8-30-91	Tokyo
Triple jump	18.29m	Jonathan Edwards, Great Britain	8-7-95	Göteborg, Sweden
Shot put	23.12m	Randy Barnes, United States	5-20-90	Westwood, Calif.
Discus throw	74.08	Jürgen Schult, E Germany	6-6-86	Neubrandenburg, Germany
Hammer throw	86.74m	Yuri Syedykh, USSR	8-30-86	Stuttgart, Germany
Javelin throw	98.48m	Jan Zelezny, Czech Republic	5-25-96	Jena, Germany
Decathlon	9026 pts	Roman Sebrle, Czech Republic	5-27-01	Götzis, Austria

Note: The decathlon consists of 10 events: the 100 meters, long jump, shot put, high jump and 400 meters on the first day; the 110-meter hurdles, discus, pole vault, javelin and 1,500 meters on the second.

Women

Event	Mark	Record Holder	Date	Site
100 meters	10.49	Florence Griffith Joyner, United States	7-16-88	Indianapolis
200 meters	21.34	Florence Griffith Joyner, United States	9-29-88	Seoul
400 meters	47.60	Marita Koch, E Germany	10-6-85	Canberra, Australia
800 meters	1:53.28	Jarmila Kratochvílová, Czechoslovakia	7-26-83	Munich
1,000 meters	2:28.98	Svetlana Masterkova, Russia	8-23-96	Brussels
1,500 meters	3:50.46	Yunxia Qu, China	9-11-93	Beijing
Mile	4:12.56	Svetlana Masterkova, Russia	8-14-96	Zurich
2,000 meters	5:25.36	Sonia O'Sullivan, Ireland	7-8-94	Edinburgh
3,000 meters	8:06.11	Junxia Wang, China	9-13-93	Beijing
Steeplechase	9:01.59	Gulnara Samitova, Russia	7-4-04	Iraklio, Greece
5,000 meters	14:16.63	Meseret Defar, Ethiopia	6-15-07	Oslo
10,000 meters	29:31.78	Junxia Wang, China	9-8-93	Beijing
Hour	18,340 meters	Tegla Loroupe, Kenya	8-7-98	Borgholzhausen, Germany
20,000 meters	1:05:26.6	Tegla Loroupe, Kenya	9-3-00	Borgholzhausen, Germany
25,000 meters	1:27:05.9	Tegla Loroupe, Kenya	9-21-02	Mengerskirchen
30,000 meters	1:45:50	Tegla Loroupe, Kenya	6-6-03	Warstein, Germany
Marathon	2:15:25	Paula Radcliffe, Great Britain	4-13-03	London
100-meter hurdles	12.21	Yordanka Donkova, Bulgaria	8-20-88	Stara Zagora, Bulgaria
400-meter hurdles	52.34	Yuliya Nosova, Russia	8-8-03	Tula, Russia
5-kilometer walk	20:02.60	Gillian O'Sullivan, Ireland	7-13-02	Dublin
10-kilometer walk	41:56.23	Nadezhda Ryashkina, URS	7-24-90	Seattle
4 x 100-meter relay	41.37	East Germany (Silke Gladisch, Sabine Reiger, Ingrid Auerswald, Marlies Göhr)	10-6-85	Canberra, Australia
4 x 200-meter relay	1:27.46	United States (LaTasha Jenkins, LaTasha Colander-Richardson, Nanceen Perry, Marion Jones)	4-29-00	Philadelphia
4 x 400-meter relay	3:15.17	USSR (Tatyana Ledovskaya, Olga Nazarova, Maria Pinigina, Olga Bryzgina)	10-1-88	Seoul
4 x 800-meter relay	7:50.17	USSR (Nadezhda Olizarenko, Lyubov Gurina, Lyudmila Borisova, Irina Podyalovskaya)	8-5-84	Moscow
High jump	2.09m	Stefka Kostadinova, Bulgaria	8-30-87	Rome
Pole vault	5.01m	Yelena Isinbayeva, Russia	8-12-05	Brussels
Long jump	7.52m	Galina Chistyakova, USSR	6-11-88	Leningrad
Triple jump	15.50m	Inessa Kravets, Ukraine	8-10-95	Göteborg, Sweden
Shot put	22.63m	Natalya Lisovskaya, USSR	6-7-87	Moscow
Discus throw	76.80m	Gabriele Reinsch, E Germany	7-9-88	Neubrandenburg, Germany
Hammer throw	77.61m†	Tatyana Lysenko, Russia	5-26-07	Sochi, Russia
Javelin throw	71.70m	Osleidys Menéndez, Cuba	8-14-05	Helsinki
Heptathlon	7291 pts	Jackie Joyner-Kersee, United States	9-24-88	Seoul

Note: The heptathlon consists of 7 events: the 100-meter hurdles, high jump, shot put and 200 meters on the first day; the long jump, javelin and 800 meters on the second.

†Pending ratification.

American Records

As of October 1, 2007. American outdoor records are recognized by USA Track and Field (USATF). WR=world record. EWR=equals world record.

Men

Event	Mark	Record Holder	Date	Site
100 meters	9.79	Maurice Greene	6-16-99	Athens Greece
200 meters	19.32 WR	Michael Johnson	8-1-96	Atlanta
400 meters	43.18 WR	Michael Johnson	8-26-99	Seville, Spain
800 meters	1:42.60	Johnny Gray	8-28-85	Koblenz, Germany
1,000 meters	2:13.9	Rick Wohlhuter	7-30-74	Oslo, Norway
1,500 meters	3:29.30	Bernard Lagat	8-28-05	Rieti, Italy
Mile	3:46.91†	Alan Webb	7-21-07	Brasschaat, Belgium

Men (Cont.)

Event	Mark	Record Holder	Date	Site
2,000 meters	4:52.44	Jim Spivey	9-15-87	Lausanne, Switz.
3,000 meters	7:30.84	Bob Kennedy	8-8-98	Monte Carlo
Steeplechase	8:08.82	Daniel Lincoln	7-14-06	Rome, Italy
5,000 meters	12:58.21	Bob Kennedy	8-14-96	Zurich
10,000 meters	27:13.98	Mebrahtom Keflezighi	5-4-01	Palo Alto, Calif.
20,000 meters	58:25.0	Bill Rodgers	8-9-77	Boston
Hour	20,547 meters	Bill Rodgers	8-9-77	Boston
25,000 meters	1:14:11.8	Bill Rodgers	2-21-79	Saratoga, Calif.
30,000 meters	1:31:49	Bill Rodgers	2-21-79	Saratoga, Calif.
Marathon	2:05:38	Khalid Khannouchi	4-14-02	London
110-meter hurdles	12.90	Dominique Arnold	7-11-06	Lausanne, Swtiz.
400-meter hurdles	46.78 WR	Kevin Young	8-6-92	Barcelona
20-kilometer walk	1:23:40	Tim Seaman	8-14-00	La Jolla, Calif.
30-kilometer walk	2:12:53	Kevin Eastler	1-15-07	Chula Vista, Calif.
50-kilometer walk	3:59:41.1	Herman Nelson	6-9-96	Seattle
4x100-meter relay	37.40 WR	United States (Mike Marsh, Leroy Burrell, Dennis Mitchell, Carl Lewis)	8-8-92	Barcelona
		United States (Jon Drummond, Andre Cason, Dennis Mitchell, Leroy Burrell)	8-21-93	Stuttgart, Germany
4x200-meter relay	1:18.68 WR	Santa Monica Track Club (Mike Marsh, Leroy Burrell, Floyd Heard, Carl Lewis)	4-17-94	Walnut, Calif.
4x400-meter relay	2:54.20 WR	United States (Jerome Young, Antonio Pettigrew, Tyree Washington, Michael Johnson)	7-22-98	New York City
4x800-meter relay	7:02.82	United States (Jebreh Harris, Khadevis Robinson, Sam Burley, David Krummenacker)	8-25-06	Brussels
4x1,500-meter relay	14:46.3	National Team (Dan Aldredge, Andy Clifford, Todd Harbour, Tom Duits)	6-24-79	Bourges, France
High jump	2.40m	Charles Austin	8-17-91	Zurich
Pole vault	6.03m	Jeff Hartwig	6-14-00	Jonesboro, Ark.
Long jump	8.95mWR	Mike Powell	8-30-91	Tokyo
Triple jump	18.09m	Kenny Harrison	7-27-96	Atlanta
Shot put	23.12mWR	Randy Barnes	5-20-90	Westwood, Calif.
Discus throw	72.34m	Ben Plucknett	7-7-81	Stockholm
Hammer throw	82.52m	Lance Deal	9-7-96	Milan
Javelin throw	91.29m	Breaux Greer	6-21-07	Indianapolis
Decathlon	8891 pts	Dan O'Brien	9-4/5-92	Talence, France

†Pending ratification.

Women

Event	Mark	Record Holder	Date	Site
100 meters	10.49 WR	Florence Griffith Joyner	7-16-88	Indianapolis
200 meters	21.34 WR	Florence Griffith Joyner	9-29-88	Seoul
400 meters	48.70	Sanya Richards	9-16-06	Athens, Greece
800 meters	1:56.40	Jearl Miles-Clark	8-11-99	Zurich
1,500 meters	3:57.12	Mary Slaney	7-26-83	Stockholm
Mile	4:16.71	Mary Slaney	8-21-85	Zurich
2,000 meters	5:32.7	Mary Slaney	8-3-84	Eugene, Ore.
3,000 meters	8:25.83	Mary Slaney	9-7-85	Rome
Steeplechase	9:29.32	Brianna Shook	7-31-04	Heusen-Zolder, Holland
5,000 meters	14:44.80	Shalane Flanagan	4-14-07	Walnut, Calif.
10,000 meters	30:50.32	Deena Drossin	5-3-02	Palo Alto, Calif.
Marathon	2:19:36	Deena Kastor	4-2-06	Berlin
100-meter hurdles	12.33	Gail Devers	7-23-00	Sacramento, Calif.
400-meter hurdles	52.61	Kim Batten	8-11-95	Göteborg, Sweden
5,000-meter walk	20:56.88	Michelle Rohl	4-27-96	Philadelphia
10,000-meter walk	44:41.87	Michelle Rohl	7-26-94	St. Petersburg, Russia
4 x 100-meter relay	41.47	National Team (Chryste Gaines, Marion Jones, Inger Miller, Gail Devers)	8-9-97	Athens

WR=World Record. †Pending ratification.

Women *(Cont.)*

Event	Mark	Record Holder	Date	Site
4 x 200-meter relay	1:27.46WR	USA Blue (LaTasha Jenkins, LaTasha Colander, Nanceen Perry, Marion Jones)	4-29-00	Philadelphia
4 x 400-meter relay	3:15.51	United States (Denean Howard, Diane Dixon, Valerie Brisco, Florence Griffith Joyner)	10-1-88	Seoul
4 x 800-meter relay	8:19.90	National Team (Robin Campbell, Joetta Clark, Chris Gregorek, Essie Kelley)	6-24-79	Bourges, France
High jump	2.03m	Louise Ritter	7-9-88	Austin
		Louise Ritter	9-30-88	Seoul
Pole vault	4.88m	Jenn Stuczynski	5-20-07	New York City
Long jump	7.49m	Jackie Joyner-Kersee	5-22-94	New York City
			7-31-94	Sestriere, Italy
Triple jump	14.45m	Tiombe Hurd	7-11-04	Sacramento, Calif.
Shot put	20.18m	Ramona Pagel	6-25-88	San Diego
Discus throw	67.67m†	Suzy Powell	3-14-07	Wailuku, Hawaii
Hammer throw	73.87m	Erin Gilreath	6-25-05	Carson, Calif.
Javelin throw	62.44m†	Kim Kreiner	7-6-06	Arhus, Denmark
Heptathlon	7291 pts WR	Jackie Joyner-Kersee	9-23/24-88	Seoul

†Pending ratification. WR=World record.

World and American Indoor Records

As of September 15, 2004. American indoor records are recognized by USA Track and Field. World Indoor records are recognized by the International Amateur Athletics Federation (IAAF). (A) represents an American record, (W) represents a World record.

Men

Event	Mark	Record Holder	Date	Site
50 meters	5.56	Donovan Bailey, Canada (W)	2-9-96	Reno, Nev.
	5.56	Maurice Greene (A)	2-13-99	Los Angeles
55 meters*	5.99	Obadele Thompson, Barbados (W)	2-22-97	Colorado Springs
	6.00	Lee McRae (A)	3-14-86	Oklahoma City
60 meters	6.39	Maurice Greene (W, A)	3-1-98	Madrid
	6.39	Maurice Greene (W, A)	3-3-01	Atlanta
200 meters	19.92	Frankie Fredericks, Namibia (W)	2-18-96	Liévin, France
	20.10	Wallace Spearmon(A)	3-11-05	Fayetteville, Ark.
400 meters	44.57	Kerron Clement (A, W)	3-12-05	Fayetteville, Ark.
800 meters	1:42.67	Wilson Kipketer, Denmark (W)	3-9-97	Paris
	1:45.00	Johnny Gray (A)	3-8-92	Sindelfingen, Germany
1,000 meters	2:14.96	Wilson Kipketer, Denmark (W)	2-20-00	Birmingham, England
	2:17.86	David Krummenacker (A)	1-27-02	Boston
1,500 meters	3:31.18	Hicham El Guerrouj, Morocco (W)	2-02-97	Stuttgart, Germany
	3:33.34	Bernard Lagat (A)	2-11-05	Fayetteville, Ark.
Mile	3:48.45	Hicham El Guerrouj, Morocco (W)	2-12-97	Ghent, Belgium
	3:49.89	Bernard Lagat (A)	2-11-05	Fayetteville, Ark.
3,000 meters	7:24.90	Daniel Komen, Kenya (W)	2-6-98	Budapest, Hungary
	7:32.43	Bernard Lagat (A)	2-17-07	Birmingham, England
5,000 meters	12:49.60	Kenenisa Bekele, Ethiopia (W)	2-20-04	Birmingham, England
	13:20.55	Doug Padilla (A)	2-12-82	New York City
50-meter hurdles	6.25	Mark McKoy, Canada (W)	3-5-86	Kobe, Japan
	6.35	Greg Foster (A)	1-27-85	Rosemont, Illinois
55-meter hurdles*	6.89	Renaldo Nehemiah (A)	1-20-79	New York City
60-meter hurdles	7.30	Colin Jackson, Great Britain (W)	3-6-94	Sindelfingen, Germany
	7.36	Greg Foster (A)	1-16-87	Los Angeles
	7.36	Allen Johnson (A)	3-6-04	Budapest, Hungary
5,000-meter walk	18:07.08	Mikhail Shchennikov, Russia (W)	2-14-95	Moscow
	19:15.88	Tim Seaman (A)	3-7-87	Indianapolis
4 x 200-meter relay	1:22.11	Great Britain (W) (Linford Christie, Darren Braithwaite, Ade Mafe, John Regis)	3-3-91	Glasgow
	1:22.71	National Team (A) (Thomas Jefferson, Raymond Pierre, Antonio McKay Kevin Little)	3-3-91	Glasgow

*No recognized world record.

Men *(Cont.)*

Event	Mark	Record Holder	Date	Site
4 x 400-meter relay	3:01.96	United States (W, A) (Kerron Clement, Wallace Spearmon, Darold Williamson, Jeremy Wariner)	2-11-06	Fayetteville, Ark.
4 x 800-meter relay	7:13.94	Global Athletics & Marketing (W, A) (Rich Kenah, Joel Woody, Karl Paranya, David Krummenacker)	2-6-00	Boston
High jump	2.43m	Javier Sòtomayor, Cuba (W)	3-4-89	Budapest, Hungary
	2.40m	Hollis Conway (A)	3-10-91	Seville
Pole vault	6.15m	Sergei Bubka, Ukraine (W)	2-21-93	Donetsk, Ukraine
	6.02m	Jeff Hartwig (A)	3-10-02	Sindelfingen, Germany
Long jump	8.79m	Carl Lewis (W, A)	1-27-84	New York City
Triple jump	17.83m	Alicier Urrutia, Cuba (W)	3-1-97	Sindelfingen, Germany
	17.83m	Christian Olsson, Sweden (W)	3-7-04	Budapest, Hungary
	17.76m	Mike Conley (A)	2-27-87	New York City
Shot put	22.66m	Randy Barnes (W, A)	1-20-89	Los Angeles
Weight throw*	25.86m	Lance Deal (W, A)	3-4-95	Atlanta
Pentathlon*	4478 pts	Steve Fritz, (W, A)	1-14-95	Lawrence, Kan.
Heptathlon	6476 pts	Dan O'Brien (W, A)	3-13/14-93	Toronto

*No recognized world record.

Women

Event	Mark	Record Holder	Date	Site
50 meters	5.96	Irina Privolova, Russia (W)	2-9-95	Madrid
	6.02	Gail Devers (A)	2-21-99	Liévin, France
55 meters*	6.56	Gwen Torrence (A)	3-14-87	Oklahoma City, Okla.
60 meters	6.92	Irina Privalova, Russia (W)	2-11-93	Madrid
	6.92	Irina Privalova, Russia (W)	2-9-95	Madrid
	6.95	Gail Devers (A)	3-12-93	Toronto
	6.95	Marion Jones (A)	3-7-98	Maebashi, Japan
200 meters	21.87	Merlene Ottey, Jamaica (W)	2-13-93	Liévin, France
	22.18	Michelle Collins (A)	3-15-03	Birmingham, England
400 meters	49.59	Jarmila Kratochvilová, Czech. (W)	3-7-82	Milan
	50.64	Diane Dixon (A)	3-10-91	Seville
800 meters	1:55.82	Jolanda Ceplak, Slovenia (W)	3-3-02	Vienna
	1:58.71	Nicole Teter (A)	3-2-02	New York
1,000 meters	2:30.94	Maria Mutola, Mozambique (W)	2-25-99	Stockholm
	2:34.19	Jennifer Toomey (A)	2-20-04	Birmingham, England
1,500 meters	3:58.28	Yelena Soboleva, Russia (W)	2-18-06	Moscow, Russia
	3:59.98	Regina Jacobs, United States (A)	2-1-03	Boston
Mile	4:17.14	Doina Melinte, Romania (W)	2-9-90	East Rutherford, N.J.
	4:20.5	Mary Slaney (A)	2-19-82	San Diego
3,000 meters	8:23.72†	Meseret Defar, Ethiopia (W)	2-3-07	Stuttgart
	8:33.25†	Shalane Flanagan (A)	1-27-07	Boston
5,000 meters	13:32.93	Tirunesh Dibaba, Ethiopia (W)	1-29-05	Boston
	14:27.42	Tirunesh Dibaba, Ethiopia	1-27-07	Boston
	15:07.44	Marla Runyan (A)	2-18-01	New York
50-meter hurdles	6.58	Cornelia Oschkenat, E Germany (W)	2-20-88	Berlin
	6.67	Jackie Joyner-Kersee (A)	2-10-95	Reno, Nev.
55-meter hurdles*	7.37	Jackie Joyner-Kersee (A)	2-3-89	New York
60-meter hurdles	7.69	Ludmila Narozhilenko, Russia (W)	2-4-90	Chelyabinsk, Russia
	7.74	Gail Devers (A)	3-1-03	Boston
3,000-meter walk	11:40.33	Claudia Stef, Romania	1-30-99	Bucharest, Romania
	12:20.79	Debbi Lawrence (A)	3-12-93	Toronto
4 x 200-meter relay	1:32.41	Russia (Y, Kondratyeva, I. Khabarova, Y.Pechonkina, Y. Gushchina) (W)	1-29-05	Glasgow
	1:33.24	National Team (A) (Flirtisha Harris, Chryste Gaines, Terri Dendy, Michele Collins)	2-12-94	Glasgow
4 x 400-meter relay	3:23.37	Russia (W)	1-28-06	Glasgow
	3:27.59	National Team (A) (Michelle Collins, Monique Hennagan, Zundra Feagin-Alexander, Shanelle Porter)	3-7-99	Maebashi, Japan

*No recognized world record. †Pending ratification.

Women (cont.)

Event	Mark	Record Holder	Date	Site
4 x 800-meter relay	8:18.54†	Moskovskaya Region, Rus	2-11-07	Volgograd, Russia
	8:18.71	Russia (W) (Natalya Zaytseva, Olga Kuvnetsova, Yelena Afanasyeva, Yekaterina Podkopayeva)	2-4-94	Moscow
	8:28.41	Univ of Wisconsin (A) (Sarah Renk, Kim Sherman, Sue Gentes, Amy Wickus)	3-14-92	Indianapolis
High jump	2.08m	Kajsa Bergqvist, Sweden (W)	2-4-06	Arnstadt, Germany
	2.01m	Tisha Waller (A)	2-28-98	Atlanta
Pole vault	4.93m†	Yelena Isinbaeva, Russia (W)	2-10-07	Donetsk, Ukraine
	4.81m	Stacy Dragila (A)	3-6-04	Budapest, Hungary
Long jump	7.37m	Heike Drechsler, E Germany (W)	2-13-88	Vienna
	7.13m	Jackie Joyner-Kersee (A)	3-5-94	Atlanta
Triple jump	15.36m	Tatyana Lebedeva, Russia (W)	3-6-04	Budapest, Hungary
	14.23m	Sheila Hudson-Strudwick (A)	3-4-95	Atlanta
Shot put	22.50m	Helena Fibingerová, Czech. (W)	2-19-77	Jablonec, Czech.
	19.83m	Ramona Pagel (A)	2-20-87	Inglewood, Calif.
Weight throw*	24.57m†	Brittany Riley (A)	1-27-07	Bloomington, Ind.
Pentathlon	4991 pts	Irina Byelova, CIS (W)	2-14/15-92	Berlin
	4753	De Dee Nathan (A)	3-4/5-99	Maebashi, Japan

*No recognized world record. †Pending ratification.

World Track and Field Championships

Men

100 METERS

1983	Carl Lewis, United States	10.07
1987*	Carl Lewis, United States	9.93 WR
1991	Carl Lewis, United States	9.86 WR
1993	Linford Christie, Great Britain	9.87
1995	Donovan Bailey, Canada	9.97
1997	Maurice Greene, United States	9.86
1999	Maurice Greene, United States	9.80
2001	Maurice Greene, United States	9.82
2003	Kim Collins, St. Kitts & Nevis	10.07
2005	Justin Gatlin, United States	9.88
2007	Tyson Gay, United States	9.85

200 METERS

1983	Calvin Smith, United States	20.14
1987	Calvin Smith, United States	20.16
1991	Michael Johnson, United States	20.01
1993	Frank Fredericks, Namibia	19.85
1995	Michael Johnson, United States	19.79
1997	Ato Boldon, Trinidad and Tobago	20.04
1999	Maurice Greene, United States	19.90
2001	Konstadínos Kedéris, Greece	20.04
2003	John Capel, United States	20.30
2005	Justin Gatlin, United States	20.04
2007	Tyson Gay, United States	19.76

400 METERS

1983	Bert Cameron, Jamaica	45.05
1987	Thomas Schoenlebe, E Germany	44.33
1991	Antonio Pettigrew, United States	44.57
1993	Michael Johnson, United States	43.65
1995	Michael Johnson, United States	43.39
1997	Michael Johnson, United States	44.12
1999	Michael Johnson, United States	43.18 WR
2001	Avard Moncur, Bahamas	44.64
2003	Jerome Young, United States	44.50
2005	Jeremy Wariner, United States	43.93
2007	Jeremy Wariner, United States	43.45

800 METERS

1983	Willi Wulbeck, W Germany	1:43.65
1987	Billy Konchellah, Kenya	1:43.06
1991	Billy Konchellah, Kenya	1:43.99
1993	Paul Ruto, Kenya	1:44.71
1995	Wilson Kipketer, Denmark	1:45.08
1997	Wilson Kipketer, Denmark	1:43.38
1999	Wilson Kipketer, Denmark	1:43.30
2001	André Bucher, Switzerland	1:43.70
2003	Djabir Saïd-Guerni, Algeria	1:44.81
2005	Rashid Ramzi, Brunei	1:44.24
2007	Alfred Kirwa Yego	1:47.09

1,500 METERS

1983	Steve Cram, Great Britain	3:41.59
1987	Abdi Bile, Somalia	3:36.80
1991	Noureddine Morceli, Algeria	3:32.84
1993	Noureddine Morceli, Algeria	3:34.24
1995	Noureddine Morceli, Algeria	3:33.73
1997	Hicham El Guerrouj, Morocco	3:35.83
1999	Hicham El Guerrouj, Morocco	3:27.65
2001	Hicham El Guerrouj, Morocco	3:30.68
2003	Hicham El Guerrouj, Morocco	3:31.77
2005	Rashid Ramzi, Brunei	3:37.88
2007	Bernard Lagat, United States	3:34.77

STEEPLECHASE

1983	Patriz Ilg, W Germany	8:15.06
1987	Francesco Panetta, Italy	8:08.57
1991	Moses Kiptanui, Kenya	8:12.59
1993	Moses Kiptanui, Kenya	8:06.36
1995	Moses Kiptanui, Kenya	8:04.16
1997	Wilson Boit Kipketer, Kenya	8:05.84
1999	Christopher Koskei, Kenya	8:11.76
2001	Reuben Kosgei, Kenya	8:15.16
2003	Saif Saaeed Shaheen, Qatar	8:04.39
2005	Saif Saaeed Shaheen, Qatar	8:13.31
2007	Brimin Kipruto, Kenya	8:13.82

WR=World record. *Ben Johnson, Canada, disqualified.

Men *(Cont.)*

5,000 METERS

1983	Eamonn Coghlan, Ireland	13:28.53
1987	Said Aouita, Morocco	13:26.44
1991	Yobes Ondieki, Kenya	13:14.45
1993	Ismael Kirui, Kenya	13:02.75
1995	Ismael Kirui, Kenya	13:16.77
1997	Daniel Komen, Kenya	13:07.38
1999	Salah Hissou, Morocco	12:58.13
2001	Richard Limo, Kenya	13:00.77
2003	Eliud Kipchoge, Kenya	12:52.79
2005	Benjamin Limo, Kenya	13:32.55
2007	Bernard Lagat, United States	13:45.87

10,000 METERS

1983	Alberto Cova, Italy	28:01.04
1987	Paul Kipkoech, Kenya	27:38.63
1991	Moses Tanui, Kenya	27:38.74
1993	Haile Gebrselassie, Ethiopia	27:46.02
1995	Haile Gebrselassie, Ethiopia	27:12.95
1997	Haile Gebrselassie, Ethiopia	27:24.58
1999	Haile Gebrselassie, Ethiopia	27:57.27
2001	Charles Kamathi, Kenya	27:53.25
2003	Kenenisa Bekele, Ethiopia	26:49.57
2005	Kenenisa Bekele, Ethiopia	27:08.33
2007	Kenenisa Bekele, Ethiopia	27:05.90

MARATHON

1983	Rob de Castella, Australia	2:10:03
1987	Douglas Wakiihuri, Kenya	2:11:48
1991	Hiromi Taniguchi, Japan	2:14:57
1993	Mark Plaatjes, United States	2:13:57
1995	Martín Fiz, Spain	2:11:41
1997	Abel Anton, Spain	2:13:16
1999	Abel Anton, Spain	2:13:36
2001	Gezahegne Abera, Ethiopia	2:12:42
2003	Jaouad Gharib, Morocco	2:08:31
2005	Jaouad Gharib, Morocco	2:10:10
2007	Luke Kibet, Kenya	2:15:59

110-METER HURDLES

1983	Greg Foster, United States	13.42
1987	Greg Foster, United States	13.21
1991	Greg Foster, United States	13.06
1993	Colin Jackson, Great Britain	12.91 WR
1995	Allen Johnson, United States	13.00
1997	Allen Johnson, United States	12.93
1999	Colin Jackson, Great Britain	13.04
2001	Allen Johnson, United States	13.04
2003	Allen Johnson, United States	13.12
2005	Ladji Doucoure, France	13.07
2007	Liu Xiang, China	12.95

400-METER HURDLES

1983	Edwin Moses, United States	47.50
1987	Edwin Moses, United States	47.46
1991	Samuel Matete, Zambia	47.64
1993	Kevin Young, United States	47.18
1995	Derrick Adkins, United States	47.98
1997	Stéphane Diagana, France	47.70
1999	Fabrizio Mori, Italy	47.72
2001	Felix Sánchez, Dominican Rep.	47.49
2003	Felix Sánchez, Dominican Rep.	47.25
2005	Bershawn Jackson, United States	47.30
2007	Kerron Clement, United States	47.61

20-KILOMETER WALK

1983	Ernesto Canto, Mexico	1:20:49
1987	Maurizio Damilano, Italy	1:20:45
1991	Maurizio Damilano, Italy	1:19:37
1993	Valentin Massana, Spain	1:22:31
1995	Michele Didoni, Italy	1:19:59

20-KILOMETER WALK *(CONT.)*

1997	Daniel Garcia, Mexico	1:21:43
1999	Ilya Markov, Russia	1:23:34
2001	Roman Rasskazov, Russia	1:20:31
2003	Jefferson Pérez, Ecuador	1:17.21 WR
2005	Jefferson Pérez, Ecuador	1:18:35
2007	Jefferson Pérez, Ecuador	1:22:20

50-KILOMETER WALK

1983	Ronald Weigel, East Germany	3:43:08
1987	Hartwig Gauder, East Germany	3:40:53
1991	Aleksandr Potashov, USSR	3:53:09
1993	Jesus Angel Garcia, Spain	3:41:41
1995	Valentin Kononen, Finland	3:43:42
1997	Robert Korzeniowski, Poland	3:44:46
1999	German Skurygin, Russia	3:44:23
2001	Robert Korzeniowski, Poland	3:42:08
2003	R. Korzeniowski, Poland	3:36:03 WR
2005	S. Kirdyapkin, Russia	3:38:08
2007	Nathan Deakes, Australia	3:43:53

4 X 100-METER RELAY

1983	United States (Emmit King, Willie Gault, Calvin Smith, Carl Lewis)	37.86
1987	United States (Lee McRae, Lee McNeil, Harvey Glance, Carl Lewis)	37.90
1991	United States (A. Cason L. Burrell, D. Mitchell, C. Lewis)	37.50 WR
1993	United States (J. Drummond, A. Cason, D. Mitchell, L. Burrell)	37.48
1995	Canada (Robert Esmie, Glenroy Gilbert, Bruny Surin, Donovan Bailey)	38.31
1997	Canada (Robert Esmie, Glenroy Gilbert, Bruny Surin, Donovan Bailey)	37.86
1999	United States (Jon Drummond, Tim Montgomery, Brian Lewis, Maurice Greene)	37.59
2001	United States (Mickey Grimes, Bernard Williams, Dennis Mitchell, Tim Montgomery)	37.96
2003	United States (J. Capel, B. Williams D.Patton, J. Johnson)	38.06
2005	Trinidad and Tobago (L. Doucoure, R. Pognon, E. De Lepine, Dovy Lueyi)	38.08
2007	United States (D. Patton, W. Spearmon, T. Gay, L. Dixon)	37.78

4 X 400-METER RELAY

1983	USSR (S. Lovachev, A. Troschilo, N. Chernyetski, V. Markin)	3:00.79
1987	United States (Danny Everett Rod Haley, Antonio McKay, Butch Reynolds)	2:57.29
1991	Great Britain (Roger Black Derek Redmond, John Regis, Kriss Akabusi)	2:57.53
1993	United States (Andrew Valmon, Quincy Watts, Butch Reynolds, Michael Johnson)	2:54.29 WR
1995	United States (Marlon Ramsey, Derek Mills, Butch Reynolds, Michael Johnson)	2:57.32
1997	United States (J. Young, A. Pettigrew, C. Jones, T. Washington)	2:56.47
1999	United States (Jerome Davis, Antonio Pettigrew, Angelo Taylor, Michael Johnson)	2:56.45

Men *(Cont.)*

4 X 400-METER RELAY *(CONT.)*

2001..............United States (L. Byrd,   2:57.54
A. Pettigrew, D. Brew, A. Taylor)
2003.....×.......United States (C. Harrison, 2:58.88
T. Washington, D. Brew, J. Young)
2005..............United States (D. Brew,   2:56.91
R. AndrewD. Williamson, B. Wariner)
2007..............United States, (L. Merritt, 2:55:56
A. Taylor, D. Williamson, J. Wariner)

HIGH JUMP

1983	Gennadi Avdeyenko, USSR	2.32m
1987	Patrik Sjoberg, Sweden	2.38m
1991	Charles Austin, United States	2.38m
1993	Javier Sotomayor, Cuba	2.40mWR
1995	Troy Kemp, Bahamas	2.37m
1997	Javier Sotomayor, Cuba	2.37m
1999	Vyacheslav Voronin, Russia	2.37m
2001	Martin Buss, Germany	2.36m
2003	Jacques Freitag, South Africa	2.35m
2005	Yuriy Krymarenko,Ukraine	2.32m
2007	Donald Thoma, Bahamas	2.35m

POLE VAULT

1983	Sergei Bubka, USSR	5.70m
1987	Sergei Bubka, USSR	5.85m
1991	Sergei Bubka, USSR	5.95m
1993	Sergei Bubka, Ukraine	6.00m
1995	Sergei Bubka, Ukraine	5.92m
1997	Sergei Bubka, Ukraine	6.01m
1999	Maksim Tarasov, Russia	6.02m
2001	Dmitri Markov, Australia	6.05mWR
2003	Guiseppe Gibilisco, Italy	5.90m
2005	Rens Blom, Netherlands	5.80m
2007	Brad Walker, United States	5.86m

LONG JUMP

1983	Carl Lewis, United States	8.55m
1987	Carl Lewis, United States	8.67m
1991	Mike Powell, United States	8.95mWR
1993	Mike Powell, United States	8.59m
1995	Iván Pedroso, Cuba	8.71m
1997	Iván Pedroso, Cuba	8.51m
1999	Iván Pedroso, Cuba	8.62m
2001	Iván Pedroso, Cuba	8.43m
2003	Dwight Phillips, United States	8.29m
2005	Dwight Phillips, United States	8.60m
2007	Irving Saladino, Panama	8.57m

TRIPLE JUMP

1983	Zdzislaw Hoffmann, Poland	17.42m
1987	Hristo Markov, Bulgaria	17.92m
1991	Kenny Harrison, United States	17.78m
1993	Mike Conley, United States	17.86m
1995	Jonathan Edwards, G.B.	18.29m WR
1997	Yoelvis Quesada, Cuba	17.85m
1999	Charles Friedek, Germany	17.59m
2001	Jonathan Edwards, G. Britain	17.92m
2003	Christian Olsson, Sweden	17.72m
2005	Walter Davis, United States	17.57m
2007	Nelson Evora, Portugal	17.74m

SHOT PUT

1983	Edward Sarul, Poland	21.39m
1987	Werner Günthör, Switz.	22.23mWR
1991	Werner Günthör, Switz.	21.67m
1993	Werner Günthör, Switz.	21.97m
1995	John Godina, United States	21.47m
1997	John Godina, United States	21.44m
1999	C.J. Hunter, United States	21.79m

SHOT PUT *(CONT.)*

2001	John Godina, United States	21.87m
2003	Andrei Mikahnevic, Bulgaria	21.69m
2005	Adam Nelson, United States	21.73m
2007	Reese Hoffa, United States	22.04m

DISCUS THROW

1983	Imrich Bugar, Czechoslovakia	67.72m
1987	Juergen Schult, E Germany	68.74m
1991	Lars Riedel, Germany	66.20m
1993	Lars Riedel, Germany	67.72m
1995	Lars Riedel, Germany	68.76m
1997	Lars Riedel, Germany	68.54m
1999	Anthony Washington, U.S.	69.08m
2001	Lars Riedel, Germany	69.72m
2003	Virgilijus Alekna, Lithuania	69.69m
2005	Virgilijus Alekna, Lithuania	70.17mWR
2007	Gerd Kanter, Estonia	68.94m

HAMMER THROW

1983	Sergei Litvinov, USSR	82.68m
1987	Sergei Litvinov, USSR	83.06m
1991	Yuriy Sedykh, USSR	81.70m
1993	Andrey Abduvaliyev, Tajikistan	81.64m
1995	Andrey Abduvaliyev, Tajikistan	81.56m
1997	Heinz Weis, Germany	81.78m
1999	Karsten Kobs, Germany	80.24m
2001	Szymon Ziolkowski, Poland	83.38m
2003	Ivan Tikhon, Belarus	83.05m
2005	Ivan Tikhon, Belarus	83.89mWR
2007	Ivan Tsikhan, Belarus	83.63m

JAVELIN

1983	Detlef Michel, East Germany	89.48m
1987	Seppo Räty, Finland	83.54m
1991	Kimmo Kinnunen, Finland	90.82m
1993	Jan Zelezny, Czech Rep.	85.98m
1995	Jan Zelezny, Czech Rep.	89.58m
1997	Marius Corbett, South Africa	88.40m
1999	Aki Parviainen, Finland	89.52m
2001	Jan Zelezny, Czech Rep.	92.80mWR
2003	Sergey Makarov, Russia	85.44m
2005	Andrus Varnik, Estonia	87.17m
2007	Tero Pitkämäki, Finland	90.33

DECATHLON

1983	Daley Thompson, Great Britain	8666 pts
1987	Torsten Voss, East Germany	8680 pts
1991	Dan O'Brien, United States	8812 pts
1993	Dan O'Brien, United States	8817 pts
1995	Dan O'Brien, United States	8695 pts
1997	Tomás Dvorák, Czech Rep.	8837 pts
1999	Tomás Dvorák, Czech Rep.	8744 pts
2001	Tomás Dvorák, Czech Rep.	8902 ptsWR
2003	Tom Pappas, United States	8750 pts
2005	Bryan Clay, United States	8732 pts
2007	Roman Sebrle, Czech Rep.	8676 pts

WR=World record.

Women

100 METERS

1983	Marlies Gohr, East Germany	10.97
1987	Silke Gladisch, East Germany	10.90
1991	Katrin Krabbe, Germany	10.99
1993	Gail Devers, United States	10.82
1995	Gwen Torrence, United States	10.85
1997	Marion Jones, United States	10.83
1999	Marion Jones, United States	10.70
2001	Zhanna Pintusevich-Block, Ukraine	10.82
2003	Kelli White, United States	10.85
2005	Lauryn Williams, United States	10.93
2007	Veronica Campbell, Jamaica	11.01

200 METERS

1983	Marita Koch, East Germany	22.13
1987	Silke Gladisch, East Germany	21.74
1991	Katrin Krabbe, Germany	22.09
1993	Merlene Ottey, Jamaica	21.98
1995	Merlene Ottey, Jamaica	22.12
1997	Zhanna Pintusevich, Ukraine	22.32
1999	Inger Miller, United States	21.77
2001	Marion Jones, United States	22.39
2003	Kelli White, United States	22.05
2005	Allyson Felix, United States	22.16
2007	Allyson Felix, United States	21.81

400 METERS

1983	Jarmila Kratochvilova, Czech.	47.99
1987	Olga Bryzgina, USSR	49.38
1991	Marie-José Pérec, France	49.13
1993	Jearl Miles, United States	49.82
1995	Marie-José Pérec, France	49.28
1997	Cathy Freeman, Australia	49.77
1999	Cathy Freeman, Australia	49.67
2001	Amy Mbacke Thiam, Senegal	49.86
2003	Ana Guevara, Mexico	48.89
2005	Darling Williams, Bahamas	49.55
2007	Christine Ohuruogu, Great Britain	49.61

800 METERS

1983	Jarmila Kratochvilova, Czech.	1:54.68
1987	Sigrun Wodars, East Germany	1:55.26
1991	Lilia Nurutdinova, USSR	1:57.50
1993	Maria Mutola, Mozambique	1:55.43
1995	Ana Quirot, Cuba	1:56.11
1997	Ana Quirot, Cuba	1:57.14
1999	Ludmila Formanová, Czech Rep.	1:56.68
2001	Maria Mutola, Mozambique	1:57.17
2003	Maria Mutola, Mozambique	1:59.89
2005	Zulia Calatayud, Cuba	1:58.82
2007	Janeth Jepkosgei, Kenya	1:56.04

1,500 METERS

1983	Mary Slaney, United States	4:00.90
1987	Tatyana Samolenko, USSR	3:58.56
1991	Hassiba Boulmerka, Algeria	4:02.21
1993	Dong Liu, China	4:00.50
1995	Hassiba Boulmerka, Algeria	4:02.42
1997	Carla Sacramento, Portugal	4:04.24
1999	Svetlana Masterkova, Russia	3:59.53
2001	Gabriela Szabo, Romania	4:00.57
2003	Tatyana Tomashova, Russia	3:58.52
2005	Tatyana Tomashova, Russia	4:00.35
2007	Maryam Yusuf Jamal, Bahrain	3:58.75

3,000 METERS

1983	Mary Slaney, United States	8:34.62
1987	Tatyana Samolenko, USSR	8:38.73
1991	Tatyana Dorovskikh, USSR	8:35.82
1993	Qu Yunxia, China	8:28.71

WR=World Record. EWR=Equals world record.
*400 meters short.

5,000 METERS

1995	Sonia O'Sullivan, Ireland	14:46.47
1997	Gabriela Szabo, Romania	14:57.68
1999	Gabriela Szabo, Romania	14:41.82
2001	Olga Yegorova, Russia	15:03.39
2003	Tirunesh Dibaba, Ethiopia	14:51.72
2005	Tirunesh Dibaba, Ethiopia	14:38.59
2007	Meseret Defar, Ethiopia	14:57.91

10,000 METERS

1987	Ingrid Kristiansen, Norway	31:05.85
1991	Liz McColgan, Great Britain	31:14.31
1993	Wang Junxia, China	30:49:30
1995	Fernanda Ribeiro, Portugal	31:04.99
1997	Sally Barsosio, Kenya	31:32.92
1999	Gete Wami, Ethiopia	30:24.56
2001	Derartu Tulu, Ethiopia	31:48.81
2003	Berhane Adere, Ethiopia	30:04.18
2005	Tirunesh Dibaba, Ethiopia	30:24.02
2007	Tirunesh Dibaba, Ethiopia	31:55.41

MARATHON

1983	Grete Waitz, Norway	2:28:09
1987	Rosa Mota, Portugal	2:25:17
1991	Wanda Panfil, Poland	2:29:53
1993	Junko Asari, Japan	2:30:03
1995	Manuela Machado, Portugal	2:25:39*
1997	Hiromi Suzuki, Japan	2:29:48
1999	Jong Song-Ok, North Korea	2:26:59
2001	Lidia Simon, Romania	2:26.01
2003	Catherine Ndereba, Kenya	2:23:55
2005	Paula Radcliffe, Great Britain	2:20:57
2007	Catherine Ndereba, Kenya	2:30:37

100-METER HURDLES

1983	Bettine Jahn, East Germany	12.35
1987	Ginka Zagorcheva, Bulgaria	12.34
1991	Lyudmila Narozhilenko, USSR	12.59
1993	Gail Devers, United States	12.46
1995	Gail Devers, United States	12.68
1997	Ludmila Engquist, Sweden	12.50
1999	Gail Devers, United States	12.37
2001	Anjanette Kirkland, United States	12.42
2003	Perdita Felicien, Canada	12.53
2005	Michelle Perry, United States	12.66
2007	Michelle Perry, United States	12.46

400-METER HURDLES

1983	Yekaterina Fesenko, USSR	54.14
1987	Sabine Busch, East Germany	53.62
1991	Tatyana Ledovskaya, USSR	53.11
1993	Sally Gunnell, Great Britain	52.74 WR
1995	Kim Batten, United States	52.61
1997	Nezha Bidouane, Morocco	52.97
1999	Daimi Pernia, Cuba	52.89
2001	Nezha Bidouane, Morocco	53.34
2003	Jana Pittman, Australia	53.22
2005	Yuliya Pechonkina, Russia	52.90
2007	Jana Rawlinson, Australia	53.31

10-KILOMETER WALK

1987	Irina Strakhova, USSR	44:12
1991	Alina Ivanova, USSR	42:57
1993	Sari Essayah, Finland	42:59
1995	Irina Stankina, Russia	42:13
1997	Annarita Sidoti, Italy	42:56

20-KILOMETER WALK

1999	Hongyu Liu, China	1:30:50
2001	Olimpiada Ivanova, Russia	1:27:48
2003	Yelena Nikolayeva, Russia	1:26:52
2005	Olimpiada Ivanova, Russia	1:25:41
2007	Olga Kaniskina, Russia	1:30:09

Women *(Cont.)*

4 X 100-METER RELAY

1983	E Germany (S. Gladisch, M. Koch, I. Auerswald, M. Gohr)	41.76
1987	United States (A. Brown, D. Williams, F. Griffith, P. Marshall)	41.58
1991	Jamaica (Dalia Duhaney, Juliet Cuthbert, Beverley McDonald, Merlene Ottey)	41.94
1993	Russia (Olga Bogoslovskaya, Galina Malchugina, Natalya Voronova, Irina Privalova)	41.49
1995	United States (Celena Mondie-Milner, Carlette Guidry, Chryste Gaines, Gwen Torrence)	42.12
1997	United States (C. Gaines, M. Jones, I. Miller, G.Devers)	41.47
1999	Bahamas (S. Fynes, C. Sturrup, P. Davis-Thompson, D. Ferguson)	41.92
2001	United States (Kelli White, Chryste Gaines, Inger Miller, Marion Jones)	41.71
2003	France (P. Girard, M. Hurtis, S. Félix, C. Arron)	41.78
2005	Jamaica, (A. Daigie, M. Lee, M. B.L. Williams	41.78
2007	United States (L. Williams, A. Felix, M. Barber, T. Edwards)	41.98

4 X 400-METER RELAY

1983	East Germany (Kerstin Walther, Sabine Busch, Marita Koch, Dagmar Rubsam)	3:19.73
1987	East Germany (Dagmar Neubauer, Kirsten Emmelmann, Petra Müller, Sabine Busch)	3:18.63
1991	USSR (Tatyana Ledovskaya, Lyudmila Dzhigalova, Olga Nazarova, Olga Bryzgina)	3:18.43
1993	United States (Gwen Torrence, Maicel Malone, Natasha Kaiser-Brown, Jearl Miles)	3:16.71
1995	United States (Kim Graham, Rochelle Stevens, Camara Jones, Jearl Miles)	3:22.39
1997	Germany (A. Feller, U. Rohlander, A. Rucker, G. Breuer)	3:20.92
1999	Russia (Tatyana Chebykina, Svetlana Goncharenko, Olga Kotylarova, Natalya Nazarova)	3:21.98
2001	Jamaica (Sandie Richards, Catherine Scott, Debbie Ann Parris, Lorraine Fenton)	3:20.65
2003	United States (M. Barber, D. Washington, J. Miles-Clark, S. Richards)	3:22.63
2005	Russia (Y. Pechonkina, O. Krasnomovets, N. Antyukh, S. Pospelova)	3:20.95
2007	United States (D. Trotter, A. Felix, M. Wineberg, S.Richards)	3:18.55

HIGH JUMP

1983	Tamara Bykova, USSR	2.01m
1987	Stefka Kostadinova, Bulgaria	2.09mWR
1991	Heike Henkel, Germany	2.05m
1993	Ioamnet Quintero, Cuba	1.99m
1995	Stefka Kostadinova, Bulgaria	2.01m
1997	Hanne Haugland, Norway	1.99m

HIGH JUMP *(CONT.)*

1999	Inga Babakova, Ukraine	1.99m
2001	Hestrie Cloete, South Africa	2.00m
2003	Hestrie Cloete, South Africa	2.06m
2005	Kajsa Bergvist, Sweden	2.02m
2007	Blanka Vlasik, Croatia	2.05m

POLE VAULT

1999	Stacy Dragila, United States	4.06m EWR
2001	Stacy Dragila, United States	4.75m
2003	Svetlana Feofanova, Russia	4.75m
2005	Yelena Isinbayeva, Russia	5.01mWR
2007	Yelena Isinbayeva, Russia	4.80m

LONG JUMP

1983	Heike Daute, E Germany	7.27m
1987	Jackie Joyner-Kersee, U.S.	7.36mWR
1991	Jackie Joyner-Kersee, United States	7.32m
1993	Heike Drechsler, Germany	7.11m
1995	Fiona May, Italy	6.98m
1997	Lyudmila Galkina, Russia	7.05m
1999	Niurka Montalvo, Spain	7.06m
2001	Fiona May, Italy	6.87m
2003	Eunice Barber, France	6.99m
2005	Tianna Madison, United States	6.89m
2007	Tatyana Lebedeva, Russia	7.03m

TRIPLE JUMP

1993	Ana Biryukova, Russia	15.09m
1995	Inessa Kravets, Ukraine	15.50m WR
1997	S. Kasparkova, Czech Rep.	15.20m
1999	Paraskevi Tsiamíta, Greece	14.88m
2001	Tatyana Lebedeva, Russia	15.25m
2003	Tatyana Lebedeva, Russia	15.18m
2005	Trecia Smith, Jamaica	15.11m
2007	Yargelis Savigne, Cuba	15.28m

SHOT PUT

1983	Helena Fibingerova, Czech.	21.05m
1987	Natalya Lisovskaya, USSR	21.24mWR
1991	Zhihong Huang, China	20.83m
1993	Zhihong Huang, China	20.57m
1995	Astrid Kumbernuss, Germany	21.22m
1997	Astrid Kumbernuss, Germany	20.71m
1999	Astrid Kumbernuss, Germany	19.85m
2001	Yanina Korolchik, Belarus	20.61m
2003	Svetlana Krivelyova, Russia	20.63m
2005	Nadezhda Ostapchuk, Russia	20.51m
2007	Valerie Vili, New Zealand	20.54m

HAMMER THROW

1999	Mihaela Melinte, Romania	75.20mWR
2001	Yipsi Moreno, Cuba	70.65m
2003	Yipsi Moreno, Cuba	70.30m
2005	Olga Kuzenkova, Russia	75.10m
2007	Betty Heidler, Germany	74.76m

DISCUS THROW

1983	Martina Opitz, E Germany	68.94m
1987	Martina Hellmann, East Germ.	71.62mWR
1991	Tsvetanka Khristova, Bulgaria	71.02m
1993	Olga Burova, Russia	67.40m
1995	Ellina Zvereva, Belarus	68.64m
1997	Beatrice Faumuina, New Zeal.	66.82m
1999	Franka Dietzsch, Germany	68.14m
2001	Ellina Zvereva,, Belarus	67.10m
2003	Irina Yatchenko, Belarus	67.32m
2005	Franka Dietzsch, Germany	66.56m
2007	Franka Dietzsch, Germany	66.61m

WR=World Record. EWR=Equals world record.

Women *(Cont.)*

JAVELIN			HEPTATHLON		
1983	Tiina Lillak, Finland	70.82m	1983	Ramona Neubert, East Germany	6714 pts
1987	Fatima Whitbread, G. Britain	76.64m	1987	Jackie Joyner-Kersee, U.S.	7128 ptsWR
1991	Xu Demei, China	68.78m	1991	Sabine Braun, Germany	6672 pts
1993	Trine Hattestad, Finland	69.18m	1993	Jackie Joyner-Kersee, U.S.	6837 pts
1995	Natalya Shikolenko, Belarus	67.56m	1995	Ghada Shouaa, Syria	6651 pts
1997	Trine Hattestad, Norway	68.78m	1997	Sabine Braun, Germany	6739 pts
1999	Miréla Manjani-Tzelili, Greece	67.09m	1999	Eunice Barber, France	6861 pts
2001	Osleidys Menéndez, Cuba	69.53m	2001	Yelena Prokhorova, Russia	6694 pts
2003	Miréla Manjani, Greece	66.52m	2003	Carolina Klüft, Sweden	7001 pts
2005	Osleidys Menendez, Cuba	71.70mWR	2005	Carolina Klüft, Sweden	6887 pts
2007	Barbora Spotakova, Czech Rep.	67.07	2007	Carolina Klüft, Sweden	7032 pts

WR=World record. EWR=Equals world record.

Track and Field News Athlete of the Year

Each year (since 1959 for men and 1974 for women) *Track and Field News* has chosen the outstanding athlete in the sport.

	MEN			WOMEN	
Year	Athlete	Event	Year	Athlete	Event
1959	Martin Lauer, West Germany	110H/Decath	1974	Irena Szewinska, Poland	100/200/400
1960	Rafer Johnson, United States	Decathlon	1975	Faina Melnik, USSR	Shot/Discus
1961	Ralph Boston, United States	Long jump	1976	Tatyana Kazankina, USSR	800/1,500
1962	Peter Snell, New Zealand	800/1,500	1977	R. Ackermann, East Germany	High jump
1963	C. K. Yang, Taiwan	Decath/PV	1978	Marita Koch, East Germany	100/200/400
1964	Peter Snell, New Zealand	800/1,500	1979	Marita Koch, East Germany	100/200/400
1965	Ron Clarke, Australia	5K/10K	1980	Ilona Briesenick, East Germany	Shot put
1966	Jim Ryun, United States	800/1,500	1981	Evelyn Ashford, United States	100/200
1967	Jim Ryun, United States	1,500	1982	Marita Koch, East Germany	100/200/400
1968	Bob Beamon, United States	Long jump	1983	J. Kratochvilova, Czechoslovakia	200/400/800
1969	Bill Toomey, United States	Decathlon	1984	Evelyn Ashford, United States	100
1970	Randy Matson, United States	Shot put	1985	Marita Koch, East Germany	100/200/400
1971	Rod Milburn, United States	110H	1986	Jackie Joyner-Kersee, U.S.	LJ/Hept
1972	Lasse Viren, Finland	5K/10K	1987	Jackie Joyner-Kersee, U.S	100H/LJ/Hept
1973	Ben Jipcho, Kenya	1,500/5K/ST	1988	Florence Griffith Joyner, U.S.	100/200
1974	Rick Wohlhuter, United States	800/1,500	1989	Ana Quirot, Cuba	400/800
1975	John Walker, New Zealand	800/1,500	1990	Merlene Ottey, Jamaica	100/200
1976	Alberto Juantorena, Cuba	400/800	1991	Heike Henkel, Germany	High jump
1977	Alberto Juantorena, Cuba	400/800	1992	Heike Drechsler, Germany	Long Jump
1978	Henry Rono, Kenya	5K/10K/ST	1993	Wang Junxia, China	1.5K/3K/10K
1979	Sebastian Coe, Great Britain	800/1,500	1994	Jackie Joyner-Kersee, U.S.	100H/LJ/Hept
1980	Edwin Moses, United States	400H	1995	Sonia O'Sullivan, Ireland	1,500/3K/5K
1981	Sebastian Coe, Great Britain	800/1,500	1996	Svetlana Masterkova, Russia	800/1,500
1982	Carl Lewis, United States	100/200/LJ	1997	Marion Jones, United States	100/200/LJ
1983	Carl Lewis, United States	100/200/LJ	1998	Marion Jones, United States	100/200/LJ
1984	Carl Lewis, United States	100/200/LJ	1999	Gabriela Szabo, Romania	1,500/5,000
1985	Said Aouita, Morocco	1,500/5000	2000	Marion Jones, United States	100/200/LJ
1986	Yuri Syedikh, USSR	Hammer	2001	Stacy Dragila, United States	Pole vault
1987	Ben Johnson, Canada	100	2002	Paula Radcliffe, Great Britain	Marathon
1988	Sergei Bubka, USSR	Pole vault	2003	Maria Mutola, Mozambique	800
1989	Roger Kingdom, United States	110H	2004	Yelena Isinbayeva, Russia	Pole vault
1990	Michael Johnson, United States	200/400	2005	Yelena Isinbayeva, Russia	Pole vault
1991	Sergei Bubka, CIS	Pole vault	2006	Sanya Richards, United States	100m
1992	Kevin Young, United States	400H			
1993	Noureddine Morceli, Algeria	1,500/mile/3K			
1994	Noureddine Morceli, Algeria	1,500/mile/3K			
1995	Haile Gebrselassie, Ethiopia	5K/10K			
1996	Michael Johnson, United States	200/400			
1997	Wilson Kipketer, Denmark	800			
1998	Haile Gebrselassie, Ethiopia	5K/10K			
1999	Hicham El Guerrouj, Morocco	1,500/Mile			
2000	Virgilijus Alekna, Lithuania	Discus			
2001	Hicham El Guerrouj, Morocco	1,500/Mile			
2002	Hicham El Guerrouj, Morocco	1,500/Mile			
2003	Felix Sanchez, Dominican Rep.	400H			
2004	Kenenisa Bekele, Ethiopia	5K/10K			
2005	Kenenisa Bekele, Ethiopia	5K/10K			
2006	Asafa Powell, Jamaica	100m			

Men

Record Holder	Time	Date	Site
John Hayes, United States	2:55:18.4	7-24-08	Shepherd's Bush, London
Robert Fowler, United States	2:52:45.4	1-1-09	Yonkers, NY
James Clark, United States	2:46:52.6	2-12-09	New York City
Albert Raines, United States	2:46:04.6	5-8-09	New York City
Frederick Barrett, Great Britain	2:42:31	5-26-09	Shepherd's Bush, London
Harry Green, Great Britain	2:38:16.2	5-12-13	Shepherd's Bush, London
Alexis Ahlgren, Sweden	2:36:06.6	5-31-13	Shepherd's Bush, London
Johannes Kolehmainen, Finland	2:32:35.8	8-22-20	Antwerp, Belgium
Albert Michelsen, United States	2:29:01.8	10-12-25	Port Chester, NY
Fusashige Suzuki, Japan	2:27:49	3-31-35	Tokyo
Yasuo Ikenaka, Japan	2:26:44	4-3-35	Tokyo
Kitei Son, Japan	2:26:42	11-3-35	Tokyo
Yun Bok Suh, Korea	2:25:39	4-19-47	Boston
James Peters, Great Britain	2:20:42.2	6-14-52	Chiswick, England
James Peters, Great Britain	2:18:40.2	6-13-53	Chiswick, England
James Peters, Great Britain	2:18:34.8	10-4-53	Turku, Finland
James Peters, Great Britain	2:17:39.4	6-26-54	Chiswick, England
Sergei Popov, USSR	2:15:17	8-24-58	Stockholm
Abebe Bikila, Ethiopia	2:15:16.2	9-10-60	Rome
Toru Terasawa, Japan	2:15:15.8	2-17-63	Beppu, Japan
Leonard Edelen, United States	2:14:28	6-15-63	Chiswick, England
Basil Heatley, Great Britain	2:13:55	6-13-64	Chiswick, England
Abebe Bikila, Ethiopia	2:12:11.2	6-21-64	Tokyo
Morio Shigematsu, Japan	2:12:00	6-12-65	Chiswick, England
Derek Clayton, Australia	2:09:36.4	12-3-67	Fukuoka, Japan
Derek Clayton, Australia	2:08:33.6	5-30-69	Antwerp, Belgium
Rob de Castella, Australia	2:08:18	12-6-81	Fukuoka, Japan
Steve Jones, Great Britain	2:08:05	10-21-84	Chicago
Carlos Lopes, Portugal	2:07:12	4-20-85	Rotterdam, Netherlands
Belayneh Dinsamo, Ethiopia	2:06:50	4-17-88	Rotterdam, Netherlands
Ronaldo Da Costa, Brazil	2:06:05	9-20-98	Berlin, Germany
Khalid Khannouchi, Morocco	2:05:42	10-24-99	Chicago
Khalid Khannouchi, United States	2:05:38	4-14-02	London
Paul Tergat, Kenya	2:04:55	9-28-03	Berlin

Women

Record Holder	Time	Date	Site
Dale Greig, Great Britain	3:27:45	5-23-64	Ryde, England
Mildred Simpson, New Zealand	3:19:33	7-21-64	Auckland, New Zealand
Maureen Wilton, Canada	3:15:22	5-6-67	Toronto
Anni Pede-Erdkamp, West Germany	3:07:26	9-16-67	Waldniel, W Germany
Caroline Walker, United States	3:02:53	2-28-70	Seaside, Ore.
Elizabeth Bonner, United States	3:01:42	5-9-71	Philadelphia
Adrienne Beames, Australia	2:46:30	8-31-71	Werribee, Australia
Chantal Langlace, France	2:46:24	10-27-74	Neuf Brisach, France
Jacqueline Hansen, United States	2:43:54.5	12-1-74	Culver City, Calif.
Liane Winter, West Germany	2:42:24	4-21-75	Boston
Christa Vahlensieck, West Germany	2:40:15.8	5-3-75	Dülmen, W Germany
Jacqueline Hansen, United States	2:38:19	10-12-75	Eugene, Ore.
Chantal Langlace, France	2:35:15.4	5-1-77	Oyarzun, France
Christa Vahlensieck, West Germany	2:34:47.5	9-10-77	Berlin, W Germany
Grete Waitz, Norway	2:32:29.9	10-22-78	New York City
Grete Waitz, Norway	2:27:32.6	10-21-79	New York City
Grete Waitz, Norway	2:25:41.3	10-26-80	New York City
Grete Waitz, Norway	2:25:29	4-17-83	London
Joan Benoit Samuelson, United States	2:22:43	4-18-83	Boston
Ingrid Kristiansen, Norway	2:21:06	4-21-85	London
Tegla Loroupe, Kenya	2:20:47	4-19-98	Rotterdam, Netherlands
Tegla Loroupe, Kenya	2:20:43	9-26-99	Berlin
Naoko Takahashi, Japan	2:19:46	9-30-01	Berlin
Catherine Ndereba, Kenya	2:18:47	10-7-01	Chicago
Paula Radcliffe, Great Britain	2:17:18	10-13-02	Chicago
Paula Radcliffe, Great Britain	2:15:25	4-13-03	London

The Boston Marathon began in 1897 as a local Patriot's Day event. Run every year but 1918 since then, it has grown into one of the world's premier marathons.

Men

Year	Winner	Time	Year	Winner	Time
1897	John J. McDermott, United States	2:55:10	1955	Hideo Hamamura, Japan	2:18:22
1898	Ronald J. McDonald, United States	2:42:00	1956	Antti Viskari, Finland	2:14:14
1899	Lawrence J. Brignolia, United States	2:54:38	1957	John J. Kelley, United States	2:20:05
1900	James J. Caffrey, Canada	2:39:44	1958	Franjo Mihalic, Yugoslavia	2:25:54
1901	James J. Caffrey, Canada	2:29:23	1959	Eino Oksanen, Finland	2:22:42
1902	Sammy Mellor, United States	2:43:12	1960	Paavo Kotila, Finland	2:20:54
1903	John C. Lorden, United States	2:41:29	1961	Eino Oksanen, Finland	2:23:39
1904	Michael Spring, United States	2:38:04	1962	Eino Oksanen, Finland	2:23:48
1905	Fred Lorz, United States	2:38:25	1963	Aurele Vandendriessche, Belgium	2:18:58
1906	Timothy Ford, United States	2:45:45	1964	Aurele Vandendriessche, Belgium	2:19:59
1907	Tom Longboat, Canada	2:24:24	1965	Morio Shigematsu, Japan	2:16:33
1908	Thomas Morrissey, United States	2:25:43	1966	Kenji Kimihara, Japan	2:17:11
1909	Henri Renaud, United States	2:53:36	1967	David McKenzie, New Zealand	2:15:45
1910	Fred Cameron, Canada	2:28:52	1968	Amby Burfoot, United States	2:22:17
1911	Clarence H. DeMar, United States	2:21:39	1969	Yoshiaki Unetani, Japan	2:13:49
1912	Mike Ryan, United States	2:21:18	1970	Ron Hill, England	2:10:30
1913	Fritz Carlson, United States	2:25:14	1971	Alvaro Mejia, Colombia	2:18:45
1914	James Duffy, Canada	2:25:01	1972	Olavi Suomalainen, Finland	2:15:39
1915	Edouard Fabre, Canada	2:31:41	1973	Jon Anderson, United States	2:16:03
1916	Arthur Roth, United States	2:27:16	1974	Neil Cusack, Ireland	2:13:39
1917	Bill Kennedy, United States	2:28:37	1975	Bill Rodgers, United States	2:09:55
1919	Carl Linder, United States	2:29:13	1976	Jack Fultz, United States	2:20:19
1920	Peter Trivoulidas, Greece	2:29:31	1977	Jerome Drayton, Canada	2:14:46
1921	Frank Zuna, United States	2:18:57	1978	Bill Rodgers, United States	2:10:13
1922	Clarence H. DeMar, United States	2:18:10	1979	Bill Rodgers, United States	2:09:27
1923	Clarence H. DeMar, United States	2:23:37	1980	Bill Rodgers, United States	2:12:11
1924	Clarence H. DeMar, United States	2:29:40	1981	Toshihiko Seko, Japan	2:09:26
1925	Chuck Mellor, United States	2:33:00	1982	Alberto Salazar, United States	2:08:52
1926	John C. Miles, Canada	2:25:40	1983	Gregory A. Meyer, United States	2:09:00
1927	Clarence H. DeMar, United States	2:40:22	1984	Geoff Smith, England	2:10:34
1928	Clarence H. DeMar, United States	2:37:07	1985	Geoff Smith, England	2:14:05
1929	John C. Miles, Canada	2:33:08	1986	Rob de Castella, Australia	2:07:51
1930	Clarence H. DeMar, United States	2:34:48	1987	Toshihiko Seko, Japan	2:11:50
1931	James (Hinky) Henigan, United States	2:46:45	1988	Ibrahim Hussein, Kenya	2:08:43
1932	Paul de Bruyn, Germany	2:33:36	1989	Abebe Mekonnen, Ethiopia	2:09:06
1933	Leslie Pawson, United States	2:31:01	1990	Gelindo Bordin, Italy	2:08:19
1934	Dave Komonen, Canada	2:32:53	1991	Ibrahim Hussein, Kenya	2:11:06
1935	John A. Kelley, United States	2:32:07	1992	Ibrahim Hussein, Kenya	2:08:14
1936	Ellison M. (Tarzan) Brown, United States	2:33:40	1993	Cosmas N'Deti, Kenya	2:09:33
1937	Walter Young, Canada	2:33:20	1994	Cosmas N'Deti, Kenya	2:07:15
1938	Leslie Pawson, United States	2:35:34	1995	Cosmas N'Deti, Kenya	2:09:22
1939	Ellison M. (Tarzan) Brown, United States	2:28:51	1996	Moses Tanui, Kenya	2:09:16
1940	Gerard Cote, Canada	2:28:28	1997	Lameck Aguta, Kenya	2:10:34
1941	Leslie Pawson, United States	2:30:38	1998	Moses Tanui, Kenya	2:07:34
1942	Bernard Joseph Smith, United States	2:26:51	1999	Joseph Chebet, Kenya	2:09:52
1943	Gerard Cote, Canada	2:28:25	2000	Elijah Lagat, Kenya	2:09:47
1944	Gerard Cote, Canada	2:31:50	2001	Lee Bong-Ju, Korea	2:09:43
1945	John A. Kelley, United States	2:30:40	2002	Rodgers Rop, Kenya	2:09:02
1946	Stylianos Kyriakides, Greece	2:29:27	2003	Robert Cheruiyot, Kenya	2:10:11
1947	Yun Bok Suh, Korea	2:25:39	2004	Timothy Cherigat, Kenya	2:10:37
1948	Gerard Cote, Canada	2:31:02	2005	Hailu Negussie, Ethiopia	2:04.32
1949	Karl Gosta Leandersson, Sweden	2:31:50	2006	Robert Cheruiyot, Kenya	2:07:14
1950	Kee Yong Ham, Korea	2:32:39	2007	Robert Cheruiyot, Kenya	2:14:13
1951	Shigeki Tanaka, Japan	2:27:45			
1952	Doroteo Flores, Guatemala	2:31:53			
1953	Keizo Yamada, Japan	2:18:51			
1954	Veikko Karvonen, Finland	2:20:39			

Note: Over the years the Boston course has varied in length. The distances have been 24 miles, 1,232 yards (1897–1923); 26 miles, 209 yards (1924–1926); 26 miles, 385 yards (1927–1952); and 25 miles, 958 yards (1953–1956). Since 1957, the course has been certified to be the standard marathon distance of 26 miles, 385 yards. (*Unofficial.)

Women

Year	Winner	Time	Year	Winner	Time
1966	Roberta Gibb, United States	3:21:40*	1987	Rosa Mota, Portugal	2:25:21
1967	Roberta Gibb, United States	3:27:17*	1988	Rosa Mota, Portugal	2:24:30
1968	Roberta Gibb, United States	3:30:00*	1989	Ingrid Kristiansen, Norway	2:24:33
1969	Sara Mae Berman, United States	3:22:46*	1990	Rosa Mota, Portugal	2:25:24
1970	Sara Mae Berman, United States	3:05:07*	1991	Wanda Panfil, Poland	2:24:18
1971	Sara Mae Berman, United States	3:08:30*	1992	Olga Markova, Russia	2:23:43
1972	Nina Kuscsik, United States	3:10:36	1993	Olga Markova, Russia	2:25:27
1973	Jacqueline A. Hansen, United States	3:05:59	1994	Uta Pippig, Germany	2:21:45
1974	Miki Gorman, United States	2:47:11	1995	Uta Pippig, Germany	2:25:11
1975	Liane Winter, W Germany	2:42:24	1996	Uta Pippig, Germany	2:27:12
1976	Kim Merritt, United States	2:47:10	1997	Fatuma Roba, Ethiopia	2:26:23
1977	Miki Gorman, United States	2:48:33	1998	Fatuma Roba, Ethiopia	2:23:21
1978	Gayle Barron, United States	2:44:52	1999	Fatuma Roba, Ethiopia	2:23:25
1979	Joan Benoit, United States	2:35:15	2000	Catherine Ndereba, Kenya	2:26:11
1980	Jacqueline Gareau, Canada	2:34:28	2001	Catherine Ndereba, Kenya	2:23:53
1981	Allison Roe, New Zealand	2:26:46	2002	Margaret Okayo, Kenya	2:20:43
1982	Charlotte Teske, W Germany	2:29:33	2003	Svetlana Zakharova, Russia	2:25:20
1983	Joan Benoit, United States	2:22:43	2004	Catherine Ndereba, Kenya	2:24:27
1984	Lorraine Moller, New Zealand	2:29:28	2005	Catherine Ndereba, Kenya	2:17:38
1985	Lisa Larsen Weidenbach, United States	2:34:06	2006	Rita Jeptoo, Kenya	2:07:14
1986	Ingrid Kristiansen, Norway	2:24:55	2007	Lidiya Grigoryeva, Russia	2:29:18

New York City Marathon

	MEN			WOMEN	
Year	Winner	Time	Year	Winner	Time
1970	Gary Muhrcke, United States	2:31:38	1970	No finisher	
1971	Norman Higgins, United States	2:22:54	1971	Beth Bonner, United States	2:55:22
1972	Sheldon Karlin, United States	2:27:52	1972	Nina Kuscsik, United States	3:08:41
1973	Tom Fleming, United States	2:21:54	1973	Nina Kuscsik, United States	2:57:07
1974	Norbert Sander, United States	2:26:30	1974	Katherine Switzer, United States	3:07:29
1975	Tom Fleming, United States	2:19:27	1975	Kim Merritt, United States	2:46:14
1976	Bill Rodgers, United States	2:10:10	1976	Miki Gorman, United States	2:39:11
1977	Bill Rodgers, United States	2:11:28	1977	Miki Gorman, United States	2:43:10
1978	Bill Rodgers, United States	2:12:12	1978	Grete Waitz, Norway	2:32:30
1979	Bill Rodgers, United States	2:11:42	1979	Grete Waitz, Norway	2:27:33
1980	Alberto Salazar, United States	2:09:41	1980	Grete Waitz, Norway	2:25:41
1981	Alberto Salazar, United States	2:08:13	1981	Allison Roe, New Zealand	2:25:29
1982	Alberto Salazar, United States	2:09:29	1982	Grete Waitz, Norway	2:27:14
1983	Rod Dixon, New Zealand	2:08:59	1983	Grete Waitz, Norway	2:27:00
1984	Orlando Pizzolato, Italy	2:14:53	1984	Grete Waitz, Norway	2:29:30
1985	Orlando Pizzolato, Italy	2:11:34	1985	Grete Waitz, Norway	2:28:34
1986	Gianni Poli, Italy	2:11:06	1986	Grete Waitz, Norway	2:28:06
1987	Ibrahim Hussein, Kenya	2:11:01	1987	Priscilla Welch, Great Britain	2:30:17
1988	Steve Jones, Great Britain	2:08:20	1988	Grete Waitz, Norway	2:28:07
1989	Juma Ikangaa, Tanzania	2:08:01	1989	Ingrid Kristiansen, Norway	2:25:30
1990	Douglas Wakiihuri, Kenya	2:12:39	1990	Wanda Panfil, Poland	2:30:45
1991	Salvador Garcia, Mexico	2:09:28	1991	Liz McColgan, Scotland	2:27:23
1992	Willie Mtolo, S Africa	2:09:29	1992	Lisa Ondieki, Australia	2:24:40
1993	Andres Espinosa, Mexico	2:10:04	1993	Uta Pippig, Germany	2:26:24
1994	German Silva, Mexico	2:11:21	1994	Tegla Loroupe, Kenya	2:27:37
1995	German Silva, Mexico	2:11:00	1995	Tegla Loroupe, Kenya	2:28:06
1996	Giacomo Leone, Italy	2:09:54	1996	Anuta Catuna, Romania	2:28:18
1997	John Kagwe, Kenya	2:08:12	1997	Franziska Rochat-Moser, Switzerland	2:28:43
1998	John Kagwe, Kenya	2:08:45	1998	Franca Fiacconi, Italy	2:25:17
1999	Joseph Chebet, Kenya	2:09:14	1999	Adriana Fernandez, Mexico	2:25:06
2000	Abdelkhader El Mouaziz, Morocco	2:10:09	2000	Ludmila Petrova, Russia	2:25:45
2001	Tesfaye Jifar, Ethiopia	2:07:43	2001	Margaret Okayo, Kenya	2:24:21
2002	Rodgers Rop, Kenya	2:08:07	2002	Joyce Chepchumba, Kenya	2:25:56
2003	Martin Lel, Kenya	2:10:30	2003	Margaret Okayo, Kenya	2:22:31
2004	Hendrik Ramaala, South Africa	2:09:28	2004	Paula Radcliffe, England	2:23:10
2005	Paul Tergat, United States	2:09:30	2005	Jelena Prokopcuka, Latvia	2:24:41
2006	M. Gomes dos Santos, Brazil	2:09:58	2006	Jelena Prokopcuka, Latvia	2:25:05

World Cross-Country Championships

Men

Conducted by the International Amateur Athletic Federation (IAAF), this meet draws the best runners in the world at every distance from the mile to the marathon to compete in the same cross-country race.

Year	Winner	Winning Team	Year	Winner	Winning Team
1973	Pekka Paivarinta, Finland	Belgium	1991	Khalid Skah, Morocco	Kenya
1974	Eric DeBeck, Belgium	Belgium	1992	John Ngugi, Kenya	Kenya
1975	Ian Stewart, Scotland	New Zealand	1993	William Sigei, Kenya	Kenya
1976	Carlos Lopes, Portugal	England	1994	William Sigei, Kenya	Kenya
1977	Leon Schots, Belgium	Belgium	1995	Paul Tergat, Kenya	Kenya
1978	John Treacy, Ireland	France	1996	Paul Tergat, Kenya	Kenya
1979	John Treacy, Ireland	England	1997	Paul Tergat, Kenya	Kenya
1980	Craig Virgin, United States	England	1998	Paul Tergat, Kenya	Kenya
1981	Craig Virgin, United States	Ethiopia	1999	Paul Tergat, Kenya	Kenya
1982	Mohammed Kedir, Ethiopia	Ethiopia	2000	Mohammed Mourhit, Belgium	Kenya
1983	Bekele Debele, Ethiopia	Ethiopia	2001	Mohammed Mourhit, Belgium	Kenya
1984	Carlos Lopes, Portugal	Ethiopia	2002	Kenenisa Bekele , Ethiopia	Kenya
1985	Carlos Lopes, Portugal	Ethiopia	2003	Kenenisa Bekele, Ethiopia	Kenya
1987	John Ngugi, Kenya	Kenya	2004	Kenenisa Bekele, Ethiopia	Ethiopia
1988	John Ngugi, Kenya	Kenya	2005	Kenenisa Bekele, Ethiopia	Ethiopia
1989	John Ngugi, Kenya	Kenya	2006	Kenenisa Bekele, Ethiopia	Kenya
1990	Khalid Skah, Morocco	Kenya	2007	Zersenay Tadese, Eritrea	Kenya

Women

Year	Winner	Winning Team	Year	Winner	Winning Team
1973	Paola Cacchi, Italy	England	1991	Lynn Jennings, United States	Kenya
1974	Paola Cacchi, Italy	England	1992	Lynn Jennings, United States	Kenya
1975	Julie Brown, United States	United States	1993	Albertina Dias, Portugal	Kenya
1976	Carmen Valero, Spain	USSR	1994	Helen Chepngeno, Kenya	Portugal
1977	Carmen Valero, Spain	USSR	1995	Derartu Tulu, Ethiopia	Kenya
1978	Grete Waitz, Norway	Romania	1996	Gete Wami, Ethiopia	Kenya
1979	Grete Waitz, Norway	United States	1997	Derartu Tulu, Ethiopia	Ethiopia
1980	Grete Waitz, Norway	USSR	1998	Sonia O'Sullivan, Ireland	Kenya
1981	Grete Waitz, Norway	USSR	1999	Gete Wami, Ethiopia	Ethiopia
1982	Maricica Puica, Romania	USSR	2000	Derartu Tulu, Ethiopia	Ethiopia
1983	Grete Waitz, Norway	United States	2001	Paula Radcliffe, Great Britain	Kenya
1984	Maricica Puica, Romania	United States	2002	Paula Radcliffe, Great Britain	Ethiopia
1985	Zola Budd, England	United States	2003	Werknesh Kidane, Ethiopia	Ethiopia
1986	Zola Budd, England	England	2004	Benita Johnson, Australia	Ethiopia
1987	Annette Sergent, France	United States	2005	Tirunesh Dibaba, Ethiopia	Ethiopia
1988	Ingrid Kristiansen, Norway	USSR	2006	Tirunesh Dibaba, Ethiopia	Ethiopia
1989	Annette Sergent, France	USSR	2007	Lornah Kiplagat, Netherlands	Ethiopia
1990	Lynn Jennings, United States	USSR			

Notable Achievements

Longest Winning Streaks

MEN

Event	Name and Nationality	Streak	Years
100 meters	Bob Hayes, United States	49	1962–64
200 meters	Manfred Gemar, Germany	41	1956–60
400 meters	Michael Johnson, United States	58	1989–97
800 meters	Mal Whitfield, United States	40	1951–54
1,500 meters	Hicham El Guerrouj, Morocco	23	1996–00
1,500 meters/mile	Steve Ovett, Great Britain	45	1977–80
Mile	Herb Elliott, Australia	35	1957–60
Steeplechase	Gaston Roelants, Belgium	45	1961–66
5,000 meters	Emil Zátopek, Czechoslovakia	48	1949–52
10,000 meters	Emil Zátopek, Czechoslovakia	38	1948–54
Marathon	Frank Shorter, United States	6	1971–73
110-meter hurdles	Jack Davis, United States	44	1952–55
400-meter hurdles	Edwin Moses, United States	107	1977–87
High jump	Ernie Shelton, United States	46	1953–55
Pole vault	Bob Richards, United States	50	1950–52
Long jump	Carl Lewis, United States	65	1981–91
Triple jump	Adhemar da Silva, Brazil	60	1950–56
Shot put	Parry O'Brien, United States	116	1952–56
Discus throw	Ricky Bruch, Sweden	54	1972–73

Notable Achievements *(Cont.)*

Longest Winning Streaks *(Cont.)*

MEN

Event	Name and Nationality	Streak	Years
Hammer throw	Imre Nemeth, Hungary	73	1946–50
Javelin throw	Janis Lusis, USSR	41	1967–70
Decathlon	Bob Mathias, United States	11	1948–56

WOMEN

Event	Name and Nationality	Streak	Years
100 meters	Merlene Ottey, Jamaica	56	1987–91
200 meters	Irena Szewinska, Poland	38	1973–75
400 meters	Irena Szewinska, Poland	36	1973–78
800 meters	Ana Fidelia Quirot, Cuba	36	1987–90
1,500 meters	Paula Ivan, Romania	15	1988–91
1,500 meters/mile	Paula Ivan, Romania	19	1988–90
3,000 meters	Mary Slaney, United States	10	1982–84
10,000 meters	Ingrid Kristiansen, Norway	5	1985–87
Marathon	Katrin Dörre, East Germany	10	1982–86
100-meter hurdles	Annelie Ernhardt, East Germany	44	1972–75
400-meter hurdles	Ann-Louise Skoglund, Sweden	18	1981–83
High jump	Iolanda Balas, Romania	140	1956–67
Long jump	Tatyana Shchelkanova, USSR	19	1964–66
Shot put	Nadezhda Chizhova, USSR	57	1969–73
Discus throw	Gisela Mauermeyer, Germany	65	1935–42
Javelin throw	Ruth Fuchs, East Germany	30	1972–73
Multi	Heide Rosendahl, West Germany	15	1969–72

Most Consecutive Years Ranked No. 1 in the World

MEN

No.	Name and Nationality	Event	Years
11	Sergei Bubka, Ukraine	Pole vault	1984–94
9	Viktor Saneyev, USSR	Triple jump	1968–76
8	Bob Richards, United States	Pole vault	1949–56
8	Ralph Boston, United States	Long jump	1960–67

WOMEN

No.	Name and Nationality	Event	Years
9	Iolanda Balas, Romania	High jump	1958–66
8	Ruth Fuchs, East Germany	Javelin	1972–79
7	Faina Melnick, USSR	Discus throw	1971–77

Major Barrier Breakers

MEN

Event	Mark	Name and Nationality	Date	Site
sub 10-second 100 meters	9.95	Jim Hines, United States	Oct. 14, 1968	Mexico City
sub 20-second 200 meters	19.83	Tommie Smith, United States	Oct. 16, 1968	Mexico City
sub 45-second 400 meters	44.9	Otis Davis, United States	Sept. 6, 1960	Rome
sub 1:45 800 meters	1:44.3	Peter Snell, New Zealand	Feb. 3, 1962	Christchurch, New Zealand
sub four minute mile	3:59.4	Roger Bannister, Great Britain	May 6, 1954	Oxford
sub 3:50 mile	3:49.4	John Walker, New Zealand	Aug. 12, 1975	Göteborg, Sweden
sub 13-minute 5,000 meters	12:58.39	Said Aouita, Morocco	July 22, 1986	Rome
sub 27:00 10,000 meters	26:58.38	Yobes Ondieki, Kenya	July 10, 1993	Oslo
sub 13-second 110-meter hurdles	12.93	Renaldo Nehemiah, United States	Aug. 19, 1981	Zurich
sub 50-second 400-meter hurdles	49.5	Glenn Davis, United States	June 29, 1956	Los Angeles
7 ft high jump	7 ft ⅝ in	Charles Dumas, United States	June 29, 1956	Los Angeles
8 ft high jump	8 ft	Javier Sotomayor, Cuba	July 29, 1989	San Juan
60 ft triple jump	60 ft ¼ in	Jonathan Edwards, Great Britain	Aug. 7, 1995	Göteborg, Sweden
20 ft pole vault	20 ft	Sergei Bubka, USSR	March 15, 1991	San Sebastian, Spain
70 ft shot put	70 ft 7¼ in	Randy Matson, United States	May 5, 1965	College Station, Texas
200 ft discus throw	200 ft 5 in	Al Oerter, United States	May 18, 1962	Los Angeles

Major Barrier Breakers *(Cont.)*

MEN *(CONT.)*

Event	Mark	Name and Nationality	Date	Site
300 ft (new) javelin	300 ft 1 in	Steve Backley, Great Britain	Jan. 25, 1992	Auckland, New Zealand
9,000-pt decathlon	9026	Roman Sebrle, Czech Republic	May 27, 2001	Gotzis, Austria

WOMEN

Event	Mark	Name and Nationality	Date	Site
sub 11-second 100 meters	10.88	Marlies Oelsner, East Germany	July 1, 1977	Dresden
sub 22-second 200 meters	21.71	Marita Koch, East Germany	June 10, 1979	Karl Marxstadt, E Germany
sub 50-second 400 meters	49.9	Irena Szewinska, Poland	June 22, 1974	Warsaw
sub 2:00 800 meters	1:59.1	Shin Geum Dan, North Korea	Nov. 12, 1963	Djakarta
sub 4:00 1,500 meters	3:56.0	Tatyana Kazankina, USSR	June 28, 1976	Podolsk, USSR
sub 4:20 mile	4:17.55	Mary Decker, United States	Feb. 16, 1980	Houston
sub 15:00 5,000 meters	14:58.89	Ingrid Kristiansen, Norway	June 28, 1984	Oslo
sub 30:00 10,000 meters	29:31.78	Wang Junxia, China	Sept. 8, 1993	Beijing
sub 2:30 marathon	2:27:33	Grete Waitz, Norway	Oct. 21, 1979	New York City
sub 2:20 marathon	2:19:46	Naoko Takahashi, Japan	Sept. 30, 2001	Berlin
sub 13-second 100-meter hurdles	12.9	Karin Balzer, East Germany	Sept. 5, 1969	Berlin
6 ft high jump	6 ft	Iolanda Balas, Romania	Oct. 18, 1958	Budapest
15 ft pole vault	15 ft ½ in	Emma George, Australia	March 14, 1998	Melbourne
70 ft shot put	70 ft 4½ in	Nadyezhda Chizhova, USSR	Sept. 29, 1973	Varna, Bulgaria
200 ft discus throw	201 ft	Liesel Westermann, W Germany	Nov. 5, 1967	Sao Paulo
200 ft javelin throw	201 ft 4 in	Elvira Ozolina, USSR	Aug. 27, 1964	Kiev
first 7,000-point heptathlon	7,148	Jackie Joyner-Kersee, U.S.	July 6–7, 1986	Moscow

Olympic Accomplishments

Oldest Olympic gold medalist—Patrick (Babe) McDonald, United States, 42 years, 26 days, 56-pound weight throw, 1920.

Oldest Olympic medalist—Tebbs Lloyd Johnson, Great Britain, 48 years, 115 days, 1948 (bronze), 50K walk.

Youngest Olympic gold medalist—Barbara Jones, United States, 15 years 123 days, 1952, 4 x 100 relay.

Youngest gold medalist in individual event—Ulrike Meyfarth, West Germany, 16 years, 123 days, 1972, high jump.

World Record Accomplishments*

Most world records equaled or set in a day—6, Jesse Owens, United States, 5-25-35, (9.4 100 yards; 26' 8¼" long jump; 20.3 200 meters and 220 yards; and 22.6 220-yard hurdles and 200-meter hurdles.

Most records in a year—10, Gunder Hägg, Sweden, 1941–42, 1,500 to 5,000 meters.

Most records in a career—35, Sergei Bubka, 1983–94, pole vault indoors and out.

Longest span of record setting—11 years, 20 days, Irena Szewinska, Poland, 1965–76, 200 meters.

Youngest person to set a set world record—Carolina Gisolf, Holland, 15 years, 5 days, 1928, high jump, 5 ft 3¾ in.

Youngest man to set a world record—John Thomas, United States, 17 years, 355 days, 1959, high jump, 7 ft 1¼ in.

Oldest person to set world record—Carlos Lopes, Portugal, 38 years, 59 days, marathon, 2:07:12.

Greatest percentage improvement—6.59, Bob Beamon, United States, 1968, long jump.

Longest lasting record—long jump, 26 ft 8¼ in, Jesse Owens, United States, 25 years, 79 days (1935–60).

Highest clearance over head, men—23¼ in, Franklin Jacobs, United States (5' 8"), 1978.

Highest clearance over head, woman—12¾ in, Yolanda Henry, United States (5' 6"), 1990.

*Marks sanctioned by the IAAF.

Swimming

**Michael Phelps
of the United States**

Gold Records Down Under

In 2007, Michael Phelps's dominating performances put the swimming world on notice—to win Olympic gold in Beijing will require passing through his wake first

BY MARK BECHTEL

YOU HAVE TO BE PRETTY bold to talk smack to a guy who has just won seven gold medals and set five world records, but Lisbeth Lenton was understandably feeling pretty good about herself. The 22-year-old Aussie won five golds of her own at the 2007 FINA World Championships in Melbourne, Australia. The night after the meet ended, the U.S. and Australia staged an exhibition 4 x 100 mixed freestyle relay, in which Lenton would face Michael Phelps in the first leg. "I was trash talking before the race, asking what he has got and telling him if he is going to bring it tonight," said Lenton. "I think deep down he was really scared of me."

Lenton was kidding, but she backed up her faux taunts with a world-record performance, finishing her leg in 52.99 seconds. It wasn't enough to beat Phelps, but then again, not much was.

Three years after he missed out on his attempt to equal Mark Spitz's mark of seven gold medals (he won six in Athens), Phelps had a realistic shot at topping Spitz's performance in Melbourne. He won seven golds and would have won an eighth, but teammate Ian Crocker left the blocks too soon in the medley relay and the U.S. was disqualified.

It wasn't just how often Phelps was winning, it was how he was doing it. The 21-year-old set five world records, and in the 200-meter butterfly he shaved an astonishing 1.62 seconds off his own world mark. ""I felt like an age-group swimmer," Phelps said after he knocked 1.34 seconds off his personal best to beat Ian Thorpe's world record by .20 seconds. "The last time I dropped my times by whole seconds, I was 12."

The rest of the field was just happy to have a good view of history being made. Bronze medalist Nikolay Skvortsov of Russia said that he was honored to have been in the pool. Runner-up Wu Peng of China admitted that "to secure that [gold] medal is impossible" when competing with the American.

Phelps attributed his performance to having stronger legs. In the year before the Worlds, he undertook a regimen of squats and plyometrics so he'd have more kick left in his legs late in races in Melbourne. "It makes a huge difference being able to have more strength and speed," said Phelps. "It used to kill at the end of races. Now it doesn't hurt as much underwater."

Phelps was so dominant that Lenton had a suggestion for the dual meet: "To be fair, let's have three teams. America, Australia and Michael Phelps." While Phelps was the class of the meet, Lenton was a revelation. "You don't go into a world titles thinking you'll win one gold medal, let alone five, so to come away with five is just indescribable," Lenton said. "I'm just so happy with the results and to be able to focus on myself and enjoy it."

Lenton was able to parlay her performance into a nice little payday. An Australian magazine paid her handsomely (reports ranged from $20,000 to $100,000) for the right to exclusively photograph her wedding, which was held three weeks after the Worlds, when she was still in the news Down Under. She and her husband walked down the aisle while being shielded by security guards holding a white sheet and black umbrellas to keep unauthorized photographers from snapping their picture.

Lenton anchored Australia's world-record-setting 400-meter medley relay team at the 2007 Worlds in Melbourne.

There were other media-savvy swimmers at the worlds, as well. Laure Manaudou of France won the 200- and 400-meter freestyles. The 20-year-old is a regular on magazine covers in Paris, and her love life is a constant source of interest. (After she won the 200, she held up her left hand, which had a message written on it for her boyfriend, Italian swimmer Luca Marin. "I swim better when I'm in love," she explained.)

Her performance showed that Manaudou will be a force to reckoned with in the 2008 Olympics, but it's unlikely she'll be the top story, not as long as Phelps is in the pool. "He is just superhuman," marveled Aussie Grant Hackett. "We won't see anything like this again."

If Phelps has anything to say about it, we will.

2006-2007 Major Competitions

Men

U.S. OPEN

West Lafayette, IN, November 30-December 2, 2006

50 free	Cullen Jones, NC St. Aqua.	22.11
100 free	Michael Phelps, Club Wolverine	49.16
200 free	Michael Phelps, Club Wolverine	1:49.48
400 free	Ous Mellouli, Trojan Swim.	3:53.20
1,500 free	Robert Margalis, St. Petersburg	15:21.17
100 back	Ryan Lochte, Daytona Beach	54.37
200 back	Roland Rudolf, Univ. of Florida	2:02.27
100 breast	Mark Gangloff, Auburn Aquatics	1:01.07
200 breast	Eric Shanteau, Swim Atlanta	2:13.46
100 fly	Ian Crocker, Longhorn Aqua.	52.78
200 fly	Michael Phelps, Club Wolverine	1:55.77
200 IM	Michael Phelps, Club Wolverine	1:59.26
400 IM	Ous Mellouli, Trojan Swim.	4:15.61
400 m relay	Club Wolverine	3:46.75
400 f relay	Scotland A	3:26.40
800 f relay	Club Wolverine	7:23.51

U.S. NATIONAL CHAMPIONSHIPS

Irvine Calif., August 1-5, 2006

50 free	Cullen Jones, NC St. Aqua.	21.94
100 free	Jason Lezak, Irvine Nova.	48.63
200 free	Michael Phelps, Club Wolverine	1:45.63
400 free	Klete Keller, Club Wolverine	3:44.27
1,500 free	Erik Vendt, Club Wolverine	15:05.41
100 back	Aaron Peirsol, Longhorn Aqua.	53.38
200 back	Aaron Peirsol, Longhorn Aqua.	1:56.36
100 breast	Brendan Hansen, Longhorn Aqua.	59.13
200 breast	Brendan Hansen, Longhorn Aqua.	2:08.74
100 fly	Michael Phelps, Club Wolverine	51.51
200 fly	Michael Phelps, Club Wolverine	1:54.32
200 IM	Michael Phelps, Club Wolverine	1:56.50
400 IM	Michael Phelps, Club Wolverine	4:10.16
400 m relay	Club Wolverine	3:41.96
400 f relay	Longhorn Aqua.	3:24.14
800 f relay	Club Wolverine	7:26.35

U.S. vs. AUSTRALIA DUEL IN THE POOL

April 3, 2007

50 free	Cullen Jones, United States	21.99
100 free	Michael Phelps, United States	48.79
200 free	Peter Vanderkaay, United States	1:47.70

U.S. VS. AUSTRALIA DUEL IN THE POOL *(CONT.)*

400 free	Larsen Jensen, United States	3:45.04
100 back	Ryan Lochte, United States	54.03
200 back	Michael Phelps, United States	1:56.29
100 breast	Brendan Hansen, United States	1:00.08
200 breast	Brendan Hansen, United States	2:10.67
100 fly	Ian Crocker, United States	51.53
200 fly	Davis Tarwater, United States	1:57.12
200 IM	Ryan Lochte, United States	1:58.78
400 IM	Erik Vendt, United States	4:14.75
400 m relay	United States	3:38.04
400 f relay	United States	3:19.54

FINA WORLD CHAMPIONSHIPS

Melbourne, Australia, March 25-April 1, 2007

50 free	Benjamin Wildman-Tobriner, U.S.	21.88
100 free	Filippo Magnini, Italy	48.43
	Brent Hayden, Canada	48.43
200 free	Michael Phelps, United States	1:43.86
400 free	Tae Hwan Park, Korea	3:44.30
1,500 free	Mateusz Sawrymowicz, Poland	14:45.94
50 back	Gerhard Zandberg, South Africa	24.98
100 back	Aaron Peirsol, United States	52.98
200 back	Ryan Lochte, United States	1:54.32
50 breast	Oleg Lisogor, Ukraine	27.66
100 breast	Brendan Hansen, United States	59.80
200 breast	Kosuke Kitajima, Japan	2:09.80
50 fly	Roland Schoeman, South Africa	23.18
100 fly	Michael Phelps, United States	50.77
200 fly	Michael Phelps, United States	1:52.09
200 IM	Michael Phelps, United States	1:54.98
400 IM	Michael Phelps, United States	4:06.22
400 m relay	Australia	3:34.93
400 f relay	United Sates	3:12.72
800 f relay	United States	7:03.24

FINA WORLD DIVING CHAMPIONSHIPS

Melbourne, Australia, March 17-April 1, 2007

1-m spgbd	Yutong Luo, China	477.40
3-m spgbd	Kai Qin, China	545.35
Platform	Gleb Galperin, Russia	554.70
3-m sync	Kai Qin/Feng Wang, China	458.76
10-m sync	Liang Huo/Yue Lin, China	489.48

Women

U.S. OPEN

West Lafayette, IN, November 30-December 2, 2006

50 free	Mar Moravcova, Dallas Mustangs	25.65
100 free	Mary Descenza, Athens Bulldogs	56.19
200 free	Mary Descenza, Athens Bulldogs	2:01.05
400 free	Hayley Peirsol, Auburn Univ.	4:13.78
800 free	Katie Hoff, North Baltimore	8:33.35
100 back	Kirs Coventry, Longhorn Aqua.	1:01.34
200 back	Margaret Hoelzer, Auburn Aqua.	2:10.95
100 breast	Megan Jendrick, King Aqua.	1:08.96
200 breast	Caitl Leverenz, El Dorado Aqua.	2:29.53
100 fly	Mary Descenza, Athens Bulldogs	59.47
200 fly	Kaitli Sandeno, Club Wolverine	2:10.10
200 IM	Katie Hoff, North Baltimore	2:11.58
400 IM	Katie Hoff, North Baltimore	4:38.38
400 m relay	Auburn Univ.	4:17.36

U.S. OPEN *(CONT.)*

400 f relay	Auburn Univ.	3:50.02
800 f relay	UBC Dolphins	8:16.40

U.S. NATIONAL CHAMPIONSHIPS

Irvine, Calif., August 1-5, 2006

50 free	Kara Lynn Joyce, Athens Bulldogs	24.97
100 free	Amanda Weir, Swim Atlanta	53.58
200 free	Natalie Coughlin, Calif. Aqua.	1:58.11
400 free	Kate Ziegler, The Fish	4:05.75
800 free	Haley Peirsol, Club Wolverine	8:26.45
100 back	Leila Vaziri, Coral Springs	1:01.69
200 back	Margaret Hoelzer, Auburn Aqua.	2:10.71
100 breast	Megan Jendrick, King Aqua.	1:07.54
200 breast	Tara Kirk, Stanford Swim	2:28.46
100 fly	Natalie Coughlin, Calif. Aqua.	55.78

Women *(Cont.)*

U.S. NATIONAL CHAMPIONSHIPS *(CONT.)*

200 fly	Kim Vandenberg, UCLA	2:08.51
200 IM	Katie Hoff, North Baltimore	2:10.05
400 IM	Katie Hoff, North Baltimore	4:35.82
400 m relay	California Aqua.	4:03.32
400 f relay	Tucson Ford	3:42.90
800 f relay	California Aqua.	8:08.16

U.S. vs. AUSTRALIA DUEL IN THE POOL
April 3, 2007

50 free	Lisbeth Lenton, Australia	24.93
100 free	Lisbeth Lenton, Australia	54.08
200 free	Linda Mackenzie, Australia	1:58.61
400 free	Kate Zeigler, United States	4:06.70
100 back	Natalie Coughlin	59.83
200 back	Margaret Hoelzer, United States	2:10.25
100 breast	Tara Kirk, United States	1:06.72
200 breast	Leisel Jones, Australia	2:23.60
100 fly	Jessicah Schipper, Australia	57.77
200 fly	Jessicah Schipper, Australia	2:06.58
200 IM	Katie Hoff, United States	2:12.12
400 IM	Katie Hoff, United States	4:37.55
400 m relay	Australia	3:58.64
400 f relay	Australia	3:38.25

FINA WORLD CHAMPIONSHIPS
Melbourne, Australia, March 25-April 1, 2007

50 free	Lisbeth Lenton, Australia	24.53
100 free	Lisbeth Lenton, Australia	53.40

FINA WORLD CHAMPIONSHIPS *(CONT.)*

200 free	Laure Manaudou, France	1:55.52
400 free	Laure Manaudou, France	4:02.61
1,500 free	Kate Ziegler, United States	15:53.05
50 back	Leila Vaziri, United States	28.16
100 back	Natalie Coughlin, United States	59.44
200 back	Margaret Hoelzer, United States	2:07.16
50 breast	Jessica Hardy, United States	30.63
100 breast	Leisel Jones, Australia	1:05.72
200 breast	Leisel Jones, Australia	2:21.84
50 fly	Therese Alshammer, Sweden	25.91
100 fly	Lisbeth Lenton, Australia	57.15
200 fly	Jessicah Schipper, Australia	2:06.39
200 IM	Katie Hoff, United States	2:10.13
400 IM	Katie Hoff, United States	4:32.89
400 m relay	Australia	3:55.74
400 f relay	Australia	3:35.48
800 f relay	United States	7:50.09

FINA WORLD DIVING CHAMPIONSHIPS
Melbourne, Australia, March 17-April 1, 2007

1-m spgbd	Zi He, China	316.65
3-m spgbd	Jingjing Guo, China	381.75
Platform	Wang Xin, China	432.85
3-m sync	Minxia Wu/Jingjing Guo, China	355.80
10-m sync	Jia Tong/Chen Ruoling, China	361.32

World and American Records Set in 2007

Men

Event	Mark	Record Holder	Date	Site
200 free	1:43.86	Michael Phelps, United States (W,A)	3-27-07	Melbourne, Aust.
100 back	52.98	Aaron Peirsol, United States (W,A)	3-27-07	Melbourne, Aust.
200 back	1:54.32	Ryan Lochte, United States (W,A)	3-30-07	Melbourne, Aust.
200 fly	1:52.09	Michael Phelps, United States (W,A)	3-28-07	Melbourne, Aust.
200 IM	1:54.98	Michael Phelps, United States (W,A)	3-29-07	Melbourne, Aust.
400 IM	4:06.22	Michael Phelps, United States (W,A)	4-01-07	Melbourne, Aust.
800 free relay	7:03.24	United States (W,A)	3-30-07	Melbourne, Aust.
		(Phelps, Lochte, Keller, and Vanderkaay)		

Women

Event	Mark	Record Holder	Date	Site
100 free	53.40	Natalie Coughlin, United States (A)	3-29-07	Melbourne, Aust.
200 free	1:55.52	Laure Manaudou, France (W)	3-28-07	Melbourne, Aust.
200 free	1:56.43	Natalie Coughlin, United States (A)	3-29-07	Melbourne, Aust.
1,500 free	15:42.54	Kate Ziegler, United States (W,A)	3-17-07	Mission Viejo, Calif.
50 back	28.16	Leila Vaziri, United States (W,A)	3-29-07	Melbourne, Aust.
100 back	59.44	Natalie Coughlin, United States (W,A)	3-27-07	Melbourne, Aust.
200 back	2:07.16	Margaret Hoelzer, United States (A)	3-31-07	Melbourne, Aust.
100 fly	57.34	Natalie Coughlin, United States (A)	3-26-07	Melbourne, Aust.
400 IM	4:32.89	Katie Hoff, United States (W,A)	4-01-07	Melbourne, Aust.
400 m relay	3:55.74	Australia (W)	3-31-07	Melbourne, Aust.
		(Seebohm, Jones, Schipper, and Lenton)		
400 f relay	3:35.68	United States (A)	3-25-07	Melbourne, Aust.
		(Coughlin, Nymeyer, Weir, and Joyce)		
800 f relay	7:50.09	United States (W,A)	3-29-07	Melbourne, Aust.
		(Coughlin, Vollmer, Nymeyer, Hoff)		

Note: Records through Oct 1, 2007.

W= World Record. A= American Record. EW=Equals World Record.

World and American Records

Men

Freestyle

Event	Time	Record Holder	Date	Site
50 meters	21.64	Alexander Popov, Russia (W)	6-16-00	Moscow
	21.76	Gary Hall Jr. (A)	8-15-00	Indianapolis
100 meters	47.84	Pieter van den Hoogenband, Netherlands (W)	9-19-00	Sydney
	48.17	Jason Lezak (A)	7-10-04	Long Beach, Calif.
200 meters	1:43.86	Michael Phelps (W,A)	3-27-07	Melbourne, Aust.
400 meters	3:40.08	Ian Thorpe, Australia (W)	7-30-02	Manchester, Eng.
	3:44.11	Klete Keller (A)	8-14-04	Athens
800 meters	7:38.65	Grant Hackett, Australia (W)	7-27-05	Montreal
	7:45.63	Larsen Jensen (A)	7-25-03	Montreal
1,500 meters	14:34.56	Grant Hackett, Australia (W)	7-30-01	Fukuoka, Japan
	14:45.29	Larsen Jensen (A)	8-21-04	Athens

Backstroke

Event	Time	Record Holder	Date	Site
50 meters	24.80	Thomas Rupprath, Germany (W)	7-27-03	Barcelona
	24.99	Lenny Krayzelburg (A)	8-28-99	Sydney
100 meters	52.98	Aaron Peirsol (W,A)	3-27-07	Melbourne, Aust.
200 meters	1:54.32	Ryan Lochte (W,A)	3-30-07	Melbourne, Aust.

Breaststroke

Event	Time	Record Holder	Date	Site
50 meters	27.18	Oleg Lisogor, Ukraine (W)	8-1-02	Berlin
	27.39	Ed Moses (A)	3-31-01	Austin, Texas
100 meters	59.13	Brendan Hansen (W,A)	8-01-06	Irvine, Calif.
200 meters	2:08.50	Brendan Hansen (W,A)	8-20-06	Victoria, Can.

Butterfly

Event	Time	Record Holder	Date	Site
50 meters	22.96	Roland Schoeman, Russia (W)	7-25-05	Montreal
50 meters	23.30	Ian Crocker (W,A)	2-29-04	Austin, Texas
100 meters	50.40	Ian Crocker (W,A)	7-30-05	Montreal
200 meters	1:52.09	Michael Phelps (W,A)	3-28-07	Melbourne, Calif.

Individual Medley

Event	Time	Record Holder	Date	Site
200 meters	1:54.98	Michael Phelps (W,A)	3-29-07	Melbourne, Aust.
400 meters	4:06.22	Michael Phelps (W,A)	4-01-07	Melbourne, Aust.

Relays

Event	Time	Record Holder	Date	Site
400-meter medley	3:30.68	United States (W,A)	8-21-04	Athens
		(Aaron Peirsol, Brendan Hansen, Ian Crocker, Jason Lezak)		
400-meter freestyle	3:12.46	United States (W,A)	8-19-06	Victoria, Can.
		(Michael Phelps, Neil Walker, Cullen Jones and Jason Lezak)		
800-meter freestyle	7:03.24	United States (W,A)	3-30-07	Melbourne, Aust.
		(Michael Phelps, Ryan Lochte, Klete Keller, and Peter Vanderkaay)		

Note: Records through Oct 1, 2007.

Women
Freestyle

Event	Time	Record Holder	Date	Site
50 meters	24.13	Inge de Bruijn, Netherlands (W)	9-22-00	Sydney
	24.63	Dara Torres (A)	9-23-00	Sydney
100 meters	53.30	Britta Steffen, Germany (W)	8-02-06	Budapest, Hung.
	53.40	Natalie Coughlin (A)	3-29-07	Melbourne, Aust.
200 meters	1:55.52	Laure Manaudou, France (W)	3-28-07	Melbourne, Aust.
	1:56.43	Natalie Coughlin (A)	3-29-07	Melbourne, Aust.
400 meters	4:02.13	Laure Manaudou, France (W)	8-08-06	Budapest, Hung.
800 meters	8:16.22	Janet Evans (W,A)	8-20-89	Tokyo
1,500 meters	15:42.54	Kate Kiegler (W,A)	6-17-07	Mission Viejo, Calif.

Backstroke

Event	Time	Record Holder	Date	Site
50 meters	28.16	Leila Vaziri (W,A)	3-29-07	Melbourne, Aust.
100 meters	59.44	Natalie Coughlin (W,A)	3-27-07	Melbourne, Aust.
200 meters	2:06.62	Krisztina Egerszegi, Hungary (W)	8-25-91	Athens
	2:07.16	Margaret Hoelzer (A)	3-31-07	Melbourne, Aust.

Breaststroke

Event	Time	Record Holder	Date	Site
50 meters	30.31	Jade Edmistone, Australia (W)	1-30-06	Melbourne, Aust.
	30.85	Jessica Hardy (A)	7-25-05	Montreal
100 meters	1:05.09	Leisel Jones, Australia (W)	3-20-06	Melbourne, Aust.
	1:06.20	Jessica Hardy (A)	7-25-05	Montreal
200 meters	2:20.54	Leisel Jones, Australia (W)	2-01-06	Melbourne, Aust.
	2:22.44	Jessica Hardy (A)	7-12-04	Long Beach, Calif.

Butterfly

Event	Time	Record Holder	Date	Site
50 meters	25.57	Anna-Karin Kammerling, Sweden (W)	7-30-02	Berlin
	26.50	Dara Torres (A)	8-9-00	Indianapolis
100 meters	56.61	Inge de Bruijn, Netherlands (W)	9-17-00	Sydney
	57.34	Natalie Coughlin (A)	3-26-07	Melbourne, Aust.
200 meters	2:05.40	Jessicah Schipper (W)	8-17-06	Victoria, Can.
	2:05.88	Misty Hyman (A)	9-20-00	Sydney

Individual Medley

Event	Time	Record Holder	Date	Site
200 meters	2:09.72	Yanyan Wu, China (W)	10-17-97	Shanghai
	2:10.05	Katie Hoff (A)	8-01-06	Irvine, Calif.
400 meters	4:32.89	Katie Hoff (W,A)	4-01-07	Melbourne, Aust.

Relays

Event	Time	Record Holder	Date	Site
400-meter medley	3:55.74	Australia (W)	3-31-07	Melbourne, Aust.
		(Emily Seebohm, Leisel Jones, Jessicah Schipper, Lisbeth Lenton)		
	3:58.30	United States (A)	9-23-00	Sydney
		(BJ Bedford, Megan Quann, Jenny Thompson, Dana Torres)		
400-meter freestyle	3:35.22	Germany (W)	7-31-06	Budapest, Hung.
		(Petra Dallman, Daniela Goetz, Britta Steffen, Annika Liebs)		
	3:35.68	United States (A)	3-25-07	Melbourne, Aust.
		(Natalie Coughlin, Lacey Nymeyer, Amanda Weir, Kara Lynn Joyce)		
800-meter freestyle	7:50.09	United States	3-29-07	Melbourne, Aust.
		(Natalie Coughlin, Dana Vollmer, Lacey Nymeyer, Katie Hoff)		

Men

50-METER FREESTYLE

1986	Tom Jager, United States	22.49‡
1991	Tom Jager, United States	22.16‡
1994	Alexander Popov, Russia	22.17
1998	Bill Pilczuk, United States	22.29
2001	Anthony Ervin, United States	22.09
2003	Alexander Popov, Russia	21.92‡
2005	Roland Schoeman, Russia	21.69
2007	Benjamin Wildman-Tobriner, U.S.	21.88

100-METER FREESTYLE

1973	Jim Montgomery, United States	51:70
1975	Andy Coan, United States	51.25
1978	David McCagg, United States	50.24
1982	Jorg Woithe, E. Germany	50.18
1986	Matt Biondi, United States	48.94
1991	Matt Biondi, United States	49.18
1994	Alexander Popov, Russia	49.12
1998	Alexander Popov, Russia	48.93‡
2001	Anthony Ervin, United States	48.33‡
2003	Alexander Popov, Russia	48.42
2005	Filippo Magnini, Italy	48:12
2007	Filippo Magnini, Italy	48.43

200-METER FREESTYLE

1973	Jim Montgomery, United States	1:53.02
1975	Tim Shaw, United States	1:52.04‡
1978	Billy Forrester, United States	1:51.02‡
1982	Michael Gross, W Germany	1:49.84
1986	Michael Gross, W Germany	1:47.92
1991	Giorgio Lamberti, Italy	1:47.27‡
1994	Antti Kasvio, Finland	1:47.32
1998	Michael Klim, Australia	1:47.41
2001	Ian Thorpe, Australia	1:44.06*
2003	Ian Thorpe, Australia	1:45.14
2005	Michael Phelps, United States	1:45.20
2007	Michael Phelps, United States	1:43.86*

400-METER FREESTYLE

1973	Rick DeMont, United States	3:58.18‡
1975	Tim Shaw, United States	3:54.88‡
1978	Vladimir Salnikov, U.S.S.R.	3:51.94‡
1982	Vladimir Salnikov, U.S.S.R.	3:51.30‡
1986	Rainer Henkel, W Germany	3:50.05
1991	Joerg Hoffman, Germany	3:48.04‡
1994	Kieran Perkins, Australia	3:43.80*
1998	Ian Thorpe, Australia	3:46.29
2001	Ian Thorpe, Australia	3:40.17*
2003	Ian Thorpe, Australia	3:42.58
2005	Grant Hackett, Australia	3:42.91
2007	Tae Hwan Park, Korea	3:44.30

1,500-METER FREESTYLE

1973	Stephen Holland, Australia	15:31.85
1975	Tim Shaw, United States	15:28.92‡
1978	Vladimir Salnikov, U.S.S.R.	15:03.99‡
1982	Vladimir Salnikov, U.S.S.R.	15:01.77‡
1986	Rainer Henkel, W Germany	15:05.31
1991	Joerg Hoffman, Germany	14:50.36*
1994	Kieran Perkins, Australia	14:50.52
1998	Grant Hackett, Australia	14:51.70
2001	Grant Hackett, Australia	14:34.56*
2003	Grant Hackett, Australia	14:43.14
2005	Grant Hackett, Australia	14:42.58
2007	Mateusz Sawrymowicz, Poland	14:45.94

100-METER BACKSTROKE

1973	Roland Matthes, E. Germany	57.47
1973	Roland Matthes, E. Germany	58.15
1978	Bob Jackson, United States	56.36‡
1982	Dirk Richter, E. Germany	55.95
1986	Igor Polianski, U.S.S.R.	55.58‡
1991	Jeff Rouse, United States	55.23‡
1994	Martin Lopez Zubero, Spain	55.17‡
1998	Lenny Krayzelburg, United States	55.00‡
2001	Matt Welsh, Australia	54.31‡
2003	Aaron Peirsol, United States	53.61‡
2005	Aaron Peirsol, United States	53:62
2007	Aaron Peirsol, United States	52.98*

200-METER BACKSTROKE

1973	Roland Matthes, E. Germany	2:01.87‡
1975	Zoltan Varraszto, Hungary	2:05.05
1978	Jesse Vassallo, United States	2:02.16
1982	Rick Carey, United States	2:00.82‡
1986	Igor Polianski, U.S.S.R.	1:58.78‡
1991	Martin Zubero, Spain	1:59.52
1994	Vladimir Selkov, Russia	1:57.42‡
1998	Lenny Krayzelburg, United States	1:58.84
2001	Aaron Peirsol, United States	1:57.13‡
2003	Aaron Peirsol, United States	1:55.92
2005	Aaron Peirsol, United States	1:54.66*
2007	Ryan Lochte, United States	1:54.32*

100-METER BREASTSTROKE

1973	Roland Matthes, E. Germany	2:01.87‡
1973	John Hencken, United States	1:04.02‡
1975	David Wilkie, Great Britain	1:04.26‡
1978	Walter Kusch, W Germany	1:03.56‡
1982	Steve Lundquist, United States	1:02.75‡
1986	Victor Davis, Canada	1:02.71
1991	Norbert Rozsa, Hungary	1:01.45*
1994	Norbert Rozsa, Hungary	1:01.24‡
1998	Frederik Deburghgraeve, Belgium	1:01.34
2001	Roman Sloudnov, Russia	1:00.16
2003	Kosuke Kitajima, Japan	59.78*
2005	Brendan Hansen, United States	59:13*
2007	Brendan Hansen, United States	59.80

200-METER BREASTSTROKE

1973	David Wilkie, Great Britain	2:19.28‡
1975	David Wilkie, Great Britain	2:18.23‡
1978	Nick Nevid, United States	2:18.37
1982	Victor Davis, Canada	2:14.77*
1986	Jozsef Szabo, Hungary	2:14.27‡
1991	Mike Barrowman, United States	2:11.23*
1994	Norbert Rozsa, Hungary	2:12.81
1998	Kurt Grote, United States	2:13.40
2001	Brendan Hansen, United States	2:10.69‡
2003	Kosuke Kitajima, Japan	2:09.42*
2005	Brendan Hansen, United States	2:08.74*
2007	Kosuke Kitajima, Japan	2:09.80

100-METER BUTTERFLY

1973	Bruce Robertson, Canada	55.69
1975	Greg Jagenburg, United States	55.63
1978	Joe Bottom, United States	54.30
1982	Matt Gribble, United States	53.88‡
1986	Pablo Morales, United States	53.54‡
1991	Anthony Nesty, Suriname	53.29‡
1994	Rafal Szukala, Poland	53.51
1998	Michael Klim, Australia	52.25‡
2001	Lars Frolander, Sweden	52.10‡
2003	Ian Crocker, United States	50.98*
2005	Ian Crocker, United States	50:40*
2007	Michael Phelps, United States	50.77

* World record; ‡ Meet record

Men

200-METER BUTTERFLY

1973	Robin Backhaus, United States	2:03.32
1975	Bill Forrester, United States	2:01.95‡
1978	Mike Bruner, United States	1:59.38‡
1982	Michael Gross, E. Germany	1:58.85‡
1986	Michael Gross, E. Germany	1:56.53‡
1991	Melvin Stewart, United States	1:55.69*
1994	Denis Pankratov, Russia	1:56.54
1998	Denys Sylantyev, Ukraine	1:56.61
2001	Michael Phelps, United States	1:54.58*
2003	Michael Phelps, United States	1:54.35
2005	Pawel Korzeniowski, Poland	1:55.02
2007	Michael Phelps, United States	1:52.09*

200-METER INDIVIDUAL MEDLEY

1973	Gunnar Larsson, Sweden	2:08.36
1975	Andras Hargitay, Hungary	2:07.72
1978	Graham Smith, Canada	2:03.65*
1982	Aleksandr Sidorenko, U.S.S.R.	2:03.30‡
1986	Tamás Darnyi, Hungary	2:01.57‡
1991	Tamás Darnyi, Hungary	1:59.36*
1994	Jani Sievin, Finland	1:58.16*
1998	Marcel Wouda, Netherlands	2:01.18
2001	Massimiliano Rosolino, Italy	1:59.71
2003	Michael Phelps, United States	1:56.04*
2005	Ryan Lochte, United States	1:58.06
2007	Michael Phelps, United States	1:54.98*

400-METER INDIVIDUAL MEDLEY

1975	Andras Hargitay, Hungary	4:32.57
1978	Jesse Vassallo, United States	4:20.05*
1982	Ricardo Prado, Brazil	4:19.78*
1986	Tamás Darnyi, Hungary	4:18.98‡
1991	Tamás Darnyi, Hungary	4:12.36*
1994	Tom Dolan, United States	4:12.30*
1998	Tom Dolan, United States	4:14.95
2001	Alessio Boggiatto, Italy	4:13.15
2003	Michael Phelps, United States	4:09.09*
2005	Laszlo Cseh, Hungary	4:09.63
2007	Michael Phelps, United States	4:06.22*

400-METER MEDLEY RELAY

1973	United States (Mike Stamm, John Hencken, Joe Bottom, Jim Montgomery)	3:49.49
1975	United States (John Murphy, Rick Colella, Greg Jagenburg, Andy Coan)	3:49.00
1978	United States (Robert Jackson, Nick Nevid, Joe Bottom, David McCagg)	3:44.63
1982	United States (Rick Carey, Steve Lundquist, Matt Gribble, Rowdy Gaines)	3:40.84*
1986	United States (Dan Veatch, David Lundberg, Pablo Morales, Matt Biondi)	3:41.25
1991	United States (Jeff Rouse, Eric Wunderlich, Mark Henderson Matt Biondi)	3:39.66‡
1994	United States (Jeff Rouse, Eric Wunderlich, Mark Henderson, Gary Hall Jr.)	3:37.74‡
1998	Australia (Matt Welsh, Phil Rogers, Robin Backhaus, Rick Klatt, Jim Montgomery)	3:37.98
2001	Australia (Matt Welsh, Ian Thorpe, Geoff Huegill, Regan Harrison)	3:35.35

400-METER MEDLEY RELAY (CONT.)

2003	United States (Aaron Peirsol Brendan Hansen, Ian Crocker, Jason Lezak)	3:31.54*
2005	United States (Aaron Peirsol Brendan Hansen, Ian Crocker, Jason Lezak)	3:31.85
2007	Australia (Matt Welsh, Brenton Rickard, Andrew Lauterstein, Eamon Sullivan)	3:34.93

400-METER FREESTYLE RELAY

1973	United States (Mel Nash, Joe Bottom, Jim Montgomery, John Murphy)	3:27.18
1975	United States (Bruce Furniss, Jim Montgomery, Andy Coan, John Murphy)	3:24.85
1978	United States (Jack Babashoff, Rowdy Gaines, Jim Montgomery, David McCagg)	3:19.74
1982	United States (Chris Cavanaugh, Robin Leamy, David McCagg, Rowdy Gaines)	3:19.26*
1986	United States (Tom Jager, Mike Heath, Paul Wallace, Matt Biondi)	3:19.89
1991	United States (Tom Jager, Brent Lang, Doug Gjertsen, Matt Biondi)	3:17.15‡
1994	United States (Jon Olsen, Josh Davis, Ugur Taner, Gary Hall Jr.)	3:16.90‡
1998	United States (Bryan Jones, Jon Olsen, Bradley Schumacher, Gary Hall Jr.)	3:16.69‡
2001	Australia (Michael Klim, Ian Thorpe, Todd Pearson, Ashley Callus)	3:14.10‡
2003	Russia (Andrei Kapralov, Ivan Usov, Denis Pimankov Alexander Popov)	3:14.06‡
2005	United States (Michael Phelps, Neil Walker, Nate Dusing, Jason Lezak)	3:13.77
2007	United States (Michael Phelps, Neil Walker, Cullen Jones, Jason Lezak)	3:12.72

800-METER FREESTYLE RELAY

1973	United States (Kurt Krumpholz, Robin Backhaus, Rick Klatt, Jim Montgomery)	7:33.22*
1975	W Germany (Klaus Steinbach, Werner Lampe, Hans Joachim Geisler, Peter Nocke)	7:39.44
1978	United States (Bruce Furniss, Billy Forrester, Bobby Hackett, Rowdy Gaines)	7:20.82
1982	United States (Rich Saeger, Jeff Float, Kyle Miller, Rowdy Gaines)	7:21.09
1986	E. Germany (Lars Hinneburg, Thomas Flemming, Dirk Richter, Sven Lodziewski)	7:15.91‡
1991	Germany (Peter Sitt, Steffan Zesner, Stefan Pfeiffer, Michael Gross)	7:13.50‡
1994	Sweden (Christer Waller, Tommy Werner, Lars Frolander, Anders Holmertz)	7:17.34

Men *(Cont.)*

800-METER FREESTYLE RELAY *(CONT.)*

1998.....Australia (Daniel Kowalski,   7:12.48‡
Grant Hackett, Ian Thorpe,
Anthony Rogis)
2001.....Australia (Michael Klim, Ian Thorpe, 7:04.66*
William Kirby, Grant Hackett)
2003.....Australia (Grant Hackett,   7:08.58
Craig Stevens, Nicholas Springer,
Ian Thorpe)

800-METER FREESTYLE RELAY *(CONT.)*

2005.....United States (Michael Phelps, Ryan 7:06.58
Lochte, Peter Vanderkaay, Klete Keller)
2007.....United States (Michael Phelps, Ryan 7:03.24*
Lochte, Peter Vanderkaay, Klete Keller)

Women

50-METER FREESTYLE

1986	Tamara Costache, Romania	25.28*
1991	Zhuang Yong, China	25.47
1994	Le Jingyi, China	24.51*
1998	Amy Van Dyken, United States	25.15
2001	Inge de Bruijn, Netherlands	24.47
2003	Inge de Bruijn, Netherlands	24.47
2005	Lisbeth Lenton, Australia	24.59
2007	Lisbeth Lenton, Australia	24.53

100-METER FREESTYLE

1973	Kornelia Ender, E. Germany	57.54
1975	Kornelia Ender, E. Germany	56.50
1978	Barbara Krause, E. Germany	55.68‡
1982	Birgit Meineke, E. Germany	55.79
1986	Kristin Otto, E. Germany	55.05‡
1991	Nicole Haislett, United States	55.17
1994	Le Jingyi, China	54.01*
1998	Jenny Thompson, United States	54.95
2001	Inge de Bruijn, Netherlands	54.18
2003	Hanna-Maria Seppälä, Finland	54.37
2005	Britta Steffen, Germany	53.30*
2007	Lisbeth Lenton, Australia	53.40

200-METER FREESTYLE

1973	Keena Rothhammer, United States	2:04.99
1975	Shirley Babashoff, United States	2:02.50
1978	Cynthia Woodhead, United States	1:58.53*
1982	Annemarie Verstappen, Netherlands	1:59.53‡
1986	Heike Friedrich, E. Germany	1:58.26‡
1991	Hayley Lewis, Australia	2:00.48
1994	Franziska Van Almsick, Germany	1:56.78*
1998	Claudia Poll, Costa Rica	1:58.90
2001	Giaan Rooney, Australia	1:58.57
2003	Alena Popchanka, Bulgaria	1:58.32
2005	Solenne Figues, France	1:58.60
2007	Laure Manaudou, France	1:55.52*

400-METER FREESTYLE

1973	Heather Greenwood, United States	4:20.28
1975	Shirley Babashoff, United States	4:22.70
1978	Tracey Wickham, Australia	4:06.28*
1982	Carmela Schmidt, E. Germany	4:08.98
1986	Heike Friedrich, E. Germany	4:07.45
1991	Janet Evans, United States	4:08.63
1994	Yang Aihua, China	4:09.64
1998	Chen Yan, China	4:06.72
2001	Yana Klochkova, Ukraine	4:07.30
2003	Hannah Stockbauer, Germany	4:06.75
2005	Laure Manaudou, France	4:02.13*
2007	Laure Manaudou, France	4:02.61

800-METER FREESTYLE

1973	Novella Calligaris, Italy	8:52.97
1975	Jenny Turrall, Australia	8:44.75‡

800-METER FREESTYLE *(CONT.)*

1978	Tracey Wickham, Australia	8:24.94‡
1982	Kim Linehan, United States	8:27.48
1986	Astrid Strauss, E. Germany	8:28.24
1991	Janet Evans, United States	8:24.05‡
1994	Janet Evans, United States	8:29.85
1998	Brooke Bennett, United States	8:28.71
2001	Hannah Stockbauer, Germany	8:24.66
2003	Hannah Stockbauer, Germany	8:23.66‡
2005	Kate Ziegler, United States	8:25.31
2007	Kate Ziegler, United States	8:18.62

100-METER BACKSTROKE

1973	Ulrike Richter, E. Germany	1:05.42
1975	Ulrike Richter, E. Germany	1:03.30‡
1978	Linda Jezek, United States	1:02.55‡
1982	Kristin Otto, E. Germany	1:01.30‡
1986	Betsy Mitchell, United States	1:01.74
1991	Krisztina Egerszegi, Hungary	1:01.78
1994	He Cihong, China	1:00.57
1998	Lea Maurer, United States	1:01.16
2001	Natalie Coughlin, United States	1:00.37
2003	Antje Buschschulte, Germany	1:00.50
2005	Kirsty Coventry, Zimbabwe	1:00.24
2007	Natalie Coughlin, United States	59.44*

200-METER BACKSTROKE

1973	Melissa Belote, United States	2:20.52
1975	Birgit Treiber, E. Germany	2:15.46*
1978	Linda Jezek, United States	2:11.93*
1982	Cornelia Sirch, E. Germany	2:09.91*
1986	Cornelia Sirch, E. Germany	2:11.37
1991	Krisztina Egerszegi, Hungary	2:09.15‡
1994	He Cihong, China	2:07.40
1998	Roxanna Maracineanu, France	2:11.26
2001	Diana Mocanu, Romania	2:09.94
2003	Katy Sexton, Great Britain	2:08.74
2005	Kirsty Coventry, Zimbabwe	2:08.52
2007	Margaret Hoelzer, United States	2:07.16

100-METER BREASTSTROKE

1973	Renate Vogel, E. Germany	1:13.74
1975	Hannalore Anke, E. Germany	1:12.72
1978	Julia Bogdanova, U.S.S.R.	1:10.31*
1982	Ute Geweniger, E. Germany	1:09.14‡
1986	Sylvia Gerasch, E. Germany	1:08.11*
1991	Linley Frame, Australia	1:08.81
1994	Samantha Riley, Australia	1:07.96*
1998	Kristy Kowal, United States	1:08.42
2001	Xuejuan Luo, China	1:07.18‡
2003	Xuejuan Luo, China	1:06.80
2005	Leisel Jones, Australia	1:05.09*
2007	Leisel Jones, Australia	1:05.72

200-METER BREASTSTROKE

1973	Renate Vogel, E. Germany	2:40.01

* World record; ‡Meet record.

Women *(Cont.)*

200-METER BREASTSTROKE *(CONT.)*

1975	Hannalore Anke, E. Germany	2:37.25‡
1978	Lina Kachushite, U.S.S.R.	2:31.42*
1982	Svetlana Varganova, U.S.S.R.	2:28.82‡
1986	Silke Hoërner, E. Germany	2:27.40*
1991	Elena Volkova, U.S.S.R.	2:29.53
1994	Samantha Riley, Australia	2:26.87‡
1998	Agnes Kovacs, Hungary	2:25.45‡
2001	Agnes Kovacs, Hungary	2:24.90
2003	Amanda Beard, United States	2:22.99*
2005	Leisel Jones, Australia	2:20.54*
2007	Leisel Jones, Australia	2:21.84

100-METER BUTTERFLY

1973	Kornelia Ender, E. Germany	1:02.53
1975	Kornelia Ender, E. Germany	1:01.24*
1978	Joan Pennington, United States	1:00.20‡
1982	Mary T. Meagher, United States	59.41‡
1986	Kornelia Gressler, E. Germany	59.51
1991	Qian Hong, China	59.68
1994	Liu Limin, China	58.98‡
1998	Jenny Thompson, United States	58.46‡
2001	Petria Thomas, Australia	58:27
2003	Jenny Thompson, United States	57.96‡
2005	Jessicah Schipper, Australia	57.23‡
2007	Lisbeth Lenton, Australia	57.15

200-METER BUTTERFLY

1973	Rosemarie Kother, E. Germany	2:13.76‡
1975	Rosemarie Kother, E. Germany	2:15.92
1978	Tracy Caulkins, United States	2:09.87*
1982	Ines Geissler, E. Germany	2:08.66‡
1986	Mary T. Meagher, United States	2:08.41‡
1991	Summer Sanders, United States	2:09.24
1994	Liu Limin, China	2:07.25‡
1998	Susie O'Neill, Australia	2:07.93‡
2001	Petria Thomas, Australia	2:06.73‡
2003	Otylia Jedrzejczak, Poland	2:07.56
2005	Otylia Jedrzejczak, Poland	2:05.61*
2007	Jessicah Schipper, Australia	2:06.39

200-METER INDIVIDUAL MEDLEY

1973	Andrea Huébner, E. Germany	2:20.51
1975	Kathy Heddy, United States	2:19.80
1978	Tracy Caulkins, United States	2:14.07*
1982	Petra Schneider, E. Germany	2:11.79
1986	Kristin Otto, E. Germany	2:15.56
1991	Li Lin, China	2:13.40
1994	Lu Bin, China	2:12.34‡
1998	Wu Yanyan, China	2:10.88
2001	Martha Bowen, United States	2:11.93
2003	Yana Klochkova, Ukraine	2:10.75‡
2005	Katie Hoff, United States	2:10.41‡
2007	Katie Hoff, United States	2:10.13

400-METER INDIVIDUAL MEDLEY

1973	Gudrun Wegner, E. Germany	4:57.71
1975	Ulrike Tauber, E. Germany	4:52.76‡
1978	Tracy Caulkins, United States	4:40.83*
1982	Petra Schneider, E. Germany	4:36.10*
1986	Kathleen Nord, E. Germany	4:43.75
1991	Lin Li, China	4:41.45
1994	Dai Guohong, China	4:39.14
1998	Chen Yan, China	4:36.66
2001	Yana Klochkova, Ukraine	4:36.98
2003	Yana Klochkova, Ukraine	4:36.74
2005	Katie Hoff, United States	4:36.07‡
2007	Katie Hoff, United States	4:32.89*

400-METER MEDLEY RELAY

1973	E. Germany (Ulrike Richter, Renate Vogel, Rosemarie Kother, Kornelia Ender)	4:16.84
1975	E. Germany (Ulrike Richter, Hannelore Anke, Rosemarie Kother, Kornelia Ender)	4:14.74
1978	United States (Linda Jezek, Tracy Caulkins, Joan Pennington, Cynthia Woodhead)	4:08.21‡
1982	E. Germany (Kristin Otto, Ute Gewinger, Ines Geissler, Birgit Meineke)	4:05.8*
1986	E. Germany (Kathrin Zimmermann, Sylvia Gerasch, Kornelia Gressler, Kristin Otto)	4:04.82
1991	United States (Janie Wagstaff, Tracey McFarlane, Crissy Ahmann-Leighton, Nicole Haislett)	4:06.51
1994	China (He Cihong, Dai Guohong, Liu Limin, Lu Bin)	4:01.67*
1998	United States (Kristy Kowal, Lea Maurer, Jenny Thompson, Amy Van Dyken)	4:01.93
2001	Australia (Dyana Calub, Sarah Ryan, Petria Thomas, Leisel Jones)	4:07.30
2003	China (Shu Xhan, Xuejuan Luo Yafei Zhou, Yu Yang)	3:59.89‡
2005	Australia (Sophie Edington, Leisel Jones, J. Schipper, Lisbeth Lenton)	3:56.30*
2007	Australia (Emily Seebohm, Leisel Jones, Jessicah Schipper, Lisbeth Lenton)	3:55.74*

400-METER FREESTYLE RELAY

1973	E. Germany (Kornelia Ender, Andrea Eife, Andrea Huebner, Sylvia Eichner)	3:52.45
1975	E. Germany (Kornelia Ender, Barbara Krause, Claudia Hempel, Ute Bruckner)	3:49.37
1978	United States (Tracy Caulkins, Stephanie Elkins, Joan Pennington, Cynthia Woodhead)	3:43.43*
1982	E. Germany (Birgit Meineke, Susanne Link, Kristin Otto, Caren Metschuk)	3:43.97
1986	E. Germany (Kristin Otto, Manuela Stellmach, Sabine Schulze, Heike Friedrich)	3:40.57*
1991	United States (Nicole Haislett, Julie Cooper, Whitney Hedgepeth, Jenny Thompson)	3:43.26
1994	China (Le Jingyi, Ying Shan, Le Ying, Lu Bin)	3:37.91*
1998	United States (Catherine Fox, Lindsey Farella, Melanie Valerio, B.J. Bedford)	3:42.11
2001	Germany (Petra Dallman, Antje Buschschulte, Katrin Meissner, Sandra Volkner)	3:39.58
2003	United States (Natalie Coughlin, Lindsay Benko, Rhiannon Jeffrey, Jenny Thompson)	3:38.09
2005	Germany (Petra Dallman, Daniela Goetz, Britta Steffen, Annika Liebs)	3:35.22*
2007	Australia (Lisbeth Lenton, Melanie Schlanger, Shayne Reese, Jodie Henry)	3:35.48

* World record; ‡Meet record.

Women *(Cont.)*

800-METER FREESTYLE RELAY *(CONT.)*

1986	E. Germany (Manuela Stellmach, Astrid Strauss, Nadja Bergknecht, Heike Friedrich)	7:59.33*
1991	Germany (Kerstin Kielgass, Manuela Stellmach, Dagmar Hase, Stephanie Ortwig)	8:02.56
1994	China (Le Ying, Yang Alhua, Zhou Guabin, Lu Bin)	7:57.96
1998	Germany (Silvia Szalai, Antje Buschschulte, Janina Goetz, Franziska Van Almsick)	8:02.56

800-METER FREESTYLE RELAY *(CONT.)*

2001	Great Britain (Nicola Jackson, Janine Belton, Karen Legg, Karen Pickering)	7:58.69
2003	United States (Lindsay Benko, Rachel Komisarz, Rhiannon Jeffrey, Diana Munz)	7:55.70‡
2005	Germany (Petra Dallman, Daniela Samulski, Britta Steffen, Annika Liebs)	7:50.82*
2007	United States (Natalie Coughlin, Dana Vollmer, Lacey Nymeyer, Katie Hoff)	7:50.09*

World Diving Championships

Men

1-METER SPRINGBOARD

		Pts
1991	Edwin Jongejans, Netherlands	588.51
1994	Evan Stewart, Zimbabwe	382.14
1998	Yu Zhuocheng, China	417.54
2001	Wang Feng, China	444.03
2003	Xiang Xu, China	431.94
2005	Alexandre Despatie, Canada	489.69
2007	Yutong Luo, China	477.40

3-METER SPRINGBOARD

		Pts
1973	Phil Boggs, United States	618.57
1975	Phil Boggs, United States	597.12
1978	Phil Boggs, United States	913.95
1982	Greg Louganis, United States	752.67
1986	Greg Louganis, United States	750.06
1991	Kent Ferguson, United States	650.25
1994	Wu Zhuocheng, China	655.44
1998	Dmitry Sautin, Russia	746.79
2001	Dmitry Sautin, Russia	725.82
2003	Alexander Dobrosok, Russia	788.37
2005	Alexandre Despatie, Canada	813.60
2007	Kai Qin, China	545.35

PLATFORM

		Pts
1973	Klaus Dibiasi, Italy	559.53
1975	Klaus Dibiasi, Italy	547.98

PLATFORM *(CONT.)*

		Pts
1978	Greg Louganis, United States	844.11
1982	Greg Louganis, United States	634.26
1986	Greg Louganis, United States	668.58
1991	Sun Shuwei, China	626.79
1994	Dmitry Sautin, Russia	634.71
1998	Dmitry Sautin, Russia	750.90
2001	Tian Lang, China	688.77
2003	Alexandre Despatie, Canada	716.91
2005	Jia Hu, China	698.01
2007	Gleb Galperin, Russia	554.70

3-METER SYNCHRONIZED

		Pts
1998	China (Sun Shuwei, Tian Liang)	313.50
2001	China (Bo Peng, Kenan Wang)	342.63
2003	Russia (A. Dobrosok, D. Sautin)	369.18
2005	China (Chong He, Feng Wang)	384.42
2007	China (Kai Qin, Feng Wang)	458.76

10-METER SYNCHRONIZED

		Pts
1998	China (Xu Hao, Yu Zhuocheng)	326.34
2001	China (Jian Tian, Jia Bu)	361.41
2003	Australia (M. Helm, R. Newbery)	384.6
2005	Russia (D. Dobroskok, G. Galperin)	392.88
2007	China (Liang Huo, Yue Lin)	489.48

Women

1-METER SPRINGBOARD

		Pts
1991	Gao Min, China	478.26
1994	Chen Lixia, China	279.30
1998	Irina Lashko, Russia	296.07
2001	Blythe Hartley, Canada	300.81
2003	Irina Lashko, Australia	299.97
2005	Blythe Hartley, Canada	325.65
2007	Zi He, China	316.65

3-METER SPRINGBOARD

		Pts
1973	Christa Koehler, E. Germany	442.17
1975	Irina Kalinina, U.S.S.R.	489.81
1978	Irina Kalinina, U.S.S.R.	691.43
1982	Megan Neyer, United States	501.03
1986	Gao Min, China	582.90
1991	Gao Min, China	539.01
1994	Tan Shuping, China	548.49
1998	Yulia Pakhalina, Russia	544.62

3-METER SPRINGBOARD *(CONT.)*

		Pts
2001	Jingjing Guo, China	596.67
2003	Jingjing Guo, China	617.94
2005	Jingjing Guo, China	645.54
2007	Jingjing Guo, China	381.75

PLATFORM

		Pts
1973	Ulrike Knape, Sweden	406.77
1975	Janet Ely, United States	403.89
1978	Irina Kalinina, U.S.S.R.	412.71
1982	Wendy Wyland, United States	438.79
1986	Chen Lin, China	449.67
1991	Fu Mingxia, China	426.51
1994	Fu Mingxia, China	434.04
1998	Olena Zhupyna, Ukraine	550.41
2001	Mian Xu, China	532.65
2003	Emilie Heymans, Canada	597.45
2005	Laura Ann Wilkinson, United States	564.87
2007	Xin Wang, China	432.85

* World record; ‡ Meet (Olympic) record.

Women *(Cont.)*

3-METER SYNCHRONIZED

	Pts
1998.......Russia (Irina Lashko, Yulia Pakhalina)	282.30
2001 ....China (Minxia Wu, Jingjing Guo)	347.31
2003 ....China (Minxia Wu, Jingjing Guo)	357.30
2005 ....China (Ting Li, Jingjing Guo)	349.80
2007 ....China (Minxia Wu, Jingjing Guo)	355.80

10-METER SYNCHRONIZED

	Pts
1998........Ukraine (O. Zhupyna, S. Serbina)	278.28
2001 ....China (Qing Duan, Xue Sang)	329.94
2003 ....China (Lishi Lao, Ting Li)	344.58
2005 ....China (Tong Jia, Pei Lin Yuan)	351.60
2007 ....China (Tong Jia, Ruolin Chen)	

U.S. Olympic Champions

Men

50-METER FREESTYLE

1988.....Matt Biondi	22.14*
2000.....Gary Hall Jr.	21.98
Anthony Ervin	21.98
2004.....Gary Hall Jr.	21.93

100-METER FREESTLYE

1906.....Charles Daniels	1:13.4
1908.....Charles Daniels	1:05.6*
1912.....Duke Kahanamoku	1:03.4
1920.....Duke Kahanamoku	1:00.4
1924 .....John Weissmuller	59.0‡
1928.....John Weissmuller	58.6‡
1948.....Wally Ris	57.3‡
1952.....Clarke Scholes	57.4
1964.....Don Schollander	53.4‡
1972.....Mark Spitz	51.22*
1976.....Jim Montgomery	49.99*
1984.....Rowdy Gaines	49.80‡
1988.....Matt Biondi	48.63‡

200-METER FREESTYLE

1904.....Charles Daniels	2:44.2
1906–1964 Not held	
1972.....Mark Spitz	1:52.78*
1976.....Bruce Furniss	1:50.29*

400-METER FREESTYLE

1904.....Charles Daniels (440 yds)	6:16.2
1920.....Norman Ross	5:26.8
1924.....John Weissmuller	5:04.2‡
1932.....Buster Crabbe	4:48.4‡
1936.....Jack Medica	4:44.5‡
1948.....William Smith	4:41.0‡
1964.....Don Schollander	4:12.2*
1968.....Mike Burton	4:09.0‡
1976.....Brian Goodell	3:51.93*
1984.....George DiCarlo	3:51.23‡

1,500-METER FREESTYLE

1920.....Norman Ross	22:23.2
1948.....James McLane	19:18.5
1952.....Ford Konno	18:30.3‡
1968.....Mike Burton	16:38.9‡
1972.....Mike Burton	15:52.58‡
1976.....Brian Goodell	15:02.40*
1984.....Michael O'Brien	15:05.20

100-METER BACKSTROKE

1912.....Harry Hebner	1:21.2

100-METER BACKSTROKE *(CONT.)*

1920.....Warren Kealoha	1:15.2
1924.....Warren Kealoha	1:13.2‡
1928.....George Kojac	1:08.2*
1936.....Adolph Kiefer	1:05.9‡
1948.....Allen Stack	1:06.4
1952.....Yoshi Oyakawa	1:05.4‡
1976.....John Naber	55.49*
1984.....Rick Carey	55.79
1996.....Jeff Rouse	54.10
2000.....Lenny Krayzelburg	53.60‡
2004.....Aaron Peirsol	54.06

200-METER BACKSTROKE

1964.....Jed Graef	2:10.3*
1976.....John Naber	1:59.19*
1984.....Rick Carey	2:00.23
1996.....Brad Bridgewater	1:58.54
2000.....Lenny Krayzelburg	1:56.76‡
2004.....Aaron Peirsol	1:54.95‡

100-METER BREASTSTROKE

1968 :....Donald McKenzie	1:07.7‡
1976.....John Hencken	1:03.11*
1984.....Steve Lundquist	1:01.65 *
1992.....Nelson Diebel	1:01.50‡

200-METER BREASTSTROKE

1924.....Robert Skelton	2:56.6
1948.....Joseph Verdeur	2:39.3‡
1960.....William Mulliken	2:37.4
1972.....John Hencken	2:21.55
1992.....Mike Barrowman	2:10.16*

100-METER BUTTERFLY

1968.....Douglas Russell	55.9‡
1972.....Mark Spitz	54.27*
1976.....Matt Vogel	54.35
1992.....Pablo Morales	53.32
2004.....Michael Phelps	51.24‡

200-METER BUTTERFLY

1956.....William Yorzyk	2:19.3‡
1960.....Michael Troy	2:12.8*
1968.....Carl Robie	2:08.7
1972.....Mark Spitz	2:00.70*
1976.....Mike Bruner	1:59.23*
1992.....Melvin Stewart	1:56.26
2000.....Tom Malchow	1:55.35‡
2004.....Michael Phelps	1:54.04‡

* World record; ‡Meet (Olympic) record.

Men (Cont.)

200-METER INDIVIDUAL MEDLEY

1968	Charles Hickcox	2:12.0‡
2004	Michael Phelps	1:57.14‡

400-METER INDIVIDUAL MEDLEY

1964	Richard Roth	4:45.4*
1968	Charles Hickcox	4:48.4
1976	Rod Strachan	4:23.68*
1996	Tom Dolan	4:14.90
2000	Tom Dolan	4:11.76‡
2004	Michael Phelps	4:08.26*

3-METER SPRINGBOARD DIVING

		Pts
1920	Louis Kuehn	675.4
1924	Albert White	696.4
1928	Pete Desjardins	185.04
1932	Michael Galitzen	161.38
1936	Richard Degener	163.57
1948	Bruce Harlan	163.64
1952	David Browning	205.29
1956	Robert Clotworthy	159.56
1960	Gary Tobian	170.00

3-METER SPRINGBOARD DIVING (CONT.)

1964	Kenneth Sitzberger	159.90
1968	Bernard Wrightson	170.15
1976	Philip Boggs	619.05
1984	Greg Louganis	754.41
1988	Greg Louganis	730.80

PLATFORM DIVING

		Pts
1904	George Sheldon	12.66
1920	Clarence Pinkston	100.67
1924	Albert White	97.46
1928	Pete Desjardins	98.74
1932	Harold Smith	124.80
1936	Marshall Wayne	113.58
1948	Sammy Lee	130.05
1952	Sammy Lee	156.28
1960	Robert Webster	165.56
1964	Robert Webster	148.58
1984	Greg Louganis	576.99
1988	Greg Louganis	638.61

Women

50-METER FREESTYLE

1996	Amy Van Dyken	24.87

100-METER FREESTLYE

1920	Ethelda Bleibtrey	1:13.6*
1924	Ethel Lackie	1:12.4
1928	Albina Osipowich	1:11.0‡
1932	Helene Madison	1:06.8‡
1968	Jan Henne	1:00.0
1972	Sandra Neilson	58.59‡
1984	Carrie Steinseifer	55.92 (tie)
	Nancy Hogshead	55.92

200-METER FREESTYLE

1968	Debbie Meyer	2:10.5‡
1984	Mary Wayte	1:59.23
1992	Nicole Haislett	1:57.90

400-METER FREESTYLE

1924	Martha Norelius	6:02.2‡
1928	Martha Norelius	5:42.8*
1932	Helene Madison	5:28.5*
1948	Ann Curtis	5:17.8‡
1960	Chris von Saltza	4:50.6
1964	Virginia Duenkel	4:43.3‡
1968	Debbie Meyer	4:31.8‡
1984	Tiffany Cohen	4:07.10‡
1988	Janet Evans	4:03.85*

800-METER FREESTYLE

1968	Debbie Meyer	9:24.0‡
1972	Keena Rothhammer	8:53.86*
1984	Tiffany Cohen	8:24.95‡
1988	Janet Evans	8:20.20‡
1992	Janet Evans	8:25.52
1996	Brooke Bennett	8:27.89
2000	Brooke Bennett	8:19.67

100-METER BACKSTROKE

1924	Sybil Bauer	1:23.2‡

100-METER BACKSTROKE (CONT.)

1932	Eleanor Holm	1:19.4
1960	Lynn Burke	1:09.3‡
1964	Cathy Ferguson	1:07.7*
1968	Kaye Hall	1:06.2*
1972	Melissa Belote	1:05.78‡
1984	Theresa Andrews	1:02.55
1996	Beth Botsford	1:01.19
2004	Natalie Coughlin	1:00.37

200-METER BACKSTROKE

1968	Pokey Watson	2:24.8‡
1972	Melissa Belote	2:19.19*

100-METER BREASTSTROKE

1972	Catherine Carr	1:13.58*
2000	Megan Quann	1:07.05

200-METER BREASTSTROKE

1968	Sharon Wichman	2:44.4‡
2004	Amanda Beard	2:23.37‡

100-METER BUTTERFLY

1956	Shelley Mann	1:11.0‡
1960	Carolyn Schuler	1:09.5‡
1964	Sharon Stouder	1:04.7*
1984	Mary T. Meagher	59.26
1996	Amy Van Dyken	59.13

200-METER BUTTERFLY

1972	Karen Moe	2:15.57*
1984	Mary T. Meagher	2:06.90‡
1992	Summer Sanders	2:08.67
2000	Misty Hyman	2:05.88‡

200-METER INDIVIDUAL MEDLEY

1968	Sharon Wichman	2:44.4‡
1984	Tracy Caulkins	2:12.64‡

* World record; ‡ Meet (Olympic) record.

Women *(Cont.)*

400-METER INDIVIDUAL MEDLEY

1964	Donna De Varona	5:18.7‡
1968	Claudia Kolb	5:08.5‡
1984	Tracy Caulkins	4:39.24
1988	Janet Evans	4:37.76

3-METER SPRINGBOARD DIVING

		Pts
1920	Aileen Riggin	539.9
1924	Elizabeth Becker	474.5
1928	Helen Meany	78.62
1932	Georgia Coleman	87.52
1936	Marjorie Gestring	89.27
1948	Victoria Draves	108.74
1952	Patricia McCormick	147.30

* World record; ‡Meet (Olympic) record.

3-METER SPRINGBOARD DIVING *(CONT.)*

1956	Patricia McCormick	142.36
1968	Sue Gossick	150.77
1972	Micki King	450.03
1976	Jennifer Chandler	506.19

PLATFORM DIVING

		Pts
1924	Caroline Smith	33.2
1928	Elizabeth Becker Pinkston	31.6
1932	Dorothy Poynton	40.26
1936	Dorothy Poynton Hill	33.93
1948	Victoria Draves	68.87
1952	Patricia McCormick	79.37
1956	Patricia McCormick	84.85
1964	Lesley Bush	99.80
2000	Laura Wilkinson	543.75

Notable Achievements

Barrier Breakers

MEN

Event	Barrier	Athlete and Nation	Time	Date
100 Freestyle	1:00	Johnny Weissmuller, United States	58.6	7-9-22
100 Freestyle	:50	James Montgomery, United States	49.99	7-25-76
200 Freestyle	2:00	Don Schollander, United States	1:58.8	7-27-63
200 Freestyle	1:50	Sergei Kopliakov, U.S.S.R.	1:49.83	4-7-79
200 Freestyle	1:45	Ian Thorpe, Australia	1:44.06	7-25-01
400 Freestyle	4:00	Rick DeMont, United States	3:58.18	9-6-73
400 Freestyle	3:50	Vladimir Salnikov, U.S.S.R.	3:49.57	3-12-82
800 Freestyle	8:00	Vladimir Salnikov, U.S.S.R.	7:56.49	3-23-79
800 Freestyle	7:40	Ian Thorpe, Australia	7:39.16	7-24-01
1500 Freestyle	15:00	Vladimir Salnikov, U.S.S.R.	14:58.27	7-22-80
1500 Freestyle	14:35	Grant Hackett, Australia	14:34.56	7-29-01
100 Backstroke	1:00	Thompson Mann, United States	59.6	10-16-64
200 Backstroke	2:00	John Naber, United States	1:59.19	7-24-76
100 Breaststroke	1:00	Roman Sloudnov, Russia	59.97	6-28-01
200 Breaststroke	2:30	Chester Jastremski, United States	2:29.6	8-19-61
200 Breaststroke	2:10	Kosuke Kitajima, Japan	2:09.42	7-24-03
100 Butterfly	1:00	Lance Larson, United States	59.0	6-29-60
200 Butterfly	2:00	Roger Pyttel, E. Germany	1:59.63	6-3-76

WOMEN

Event	Barrier	Athlete and Nation	Time	Date
100 Freestyle	1:00	Dawn Fraser, Australia	59.9	10-27-62
200 Freestyle	2:00	Kornelia Ender, E. Germany	1:59.78	6-2-76
400 Freestyle	4:30	Debbie Meyer, United States	4:29.0	8-18-67
800 Freestyle	10:00	Jane Cederqvist, Sweden	9:55.6	8-17-60
800 Freestyle	9:00	Ann Simmons, United States	8:59.4	9-10-71
1500 Freestyle	20:00	Ilsa Konrads, Australia	19:25.7	1-14-60
	16:00	Janet Evans, United States	15:52.10	3-26-88
100 Backstroke	1:00	Natalie Coughlin, United States	59.58	8-16-02
200 Backstroke	2:30	Satoko Tanaka, Japan	2:29.6	2-10-63
100 Butterfly	1:00	Christiane Knacke, E. Germany	59.78	8-28-77
400 Individual Medley	5:00	Gudrun Wegner, E. Germany	4:57.51	9-6-73

Olympic Achievements

MOST INDIVIDUAL GOLDS IN SINGLE OLYMPICS

MEN

No.	Athlete and Nation	Olympic Year	Events
4	Mark Spitz, United States	1972	100, 200 free; 100, 200 fly
4	Michael Phelps, United States	2004	100, 200 fly, 200 IM, 400 IM

WOMEN

No.	Athlete and Nation	Olympic Year	Events
4	Kristin Otto, E. Germany	1988	50, 100 free; 100 back; 100 fly
3	Debbie Meyer, United States	1968	200, 400, 800 free
3	Shane Gould, Australia	1972	200, 400 free; 200 IM
3	Kornelia Ender, E. Germany	1976	100, 200 free; 100 fly
3	Janet Evans, United States	1988	400, 800 free; 400 IM
3	Krisztina Egerszegi, Hungary	1992	100, 200 back; 400 IM
3	Michelle Smith, Ireland	1996	400 free; 200, 400 IM
3	Inge de Bruijn, Netherlands	2000	50, 100 free; 100 fly

MOST INDIVIDUAL OLYMPIC GOLD MEDALS, CAREER

MEN

No.	Athlete and Nation	Olympic Years and Events
4	Charles Meldrum Daniels, United States	1904 (220, 440 free); 1906 (100 free) 1908 (100 free)
4	Roland Matthes, E. Germany	1968 (100, 200 back); 1972 (100, 200 back)
4	Mark Spitz, United States	1972 (100, 200 free; 100, 200 fly)
4	Michael Phelps, United States	2004 (100, 200 fly; 200, 400 IM)

WOMEN

No.	Athlete and Nation	Olympic Years and Events
4	Kristin Otto, E. Germany	1988 (50 free; 100 free, back and fly)
4	Janet Evans, United States	1988 (400, 800 free; 400 IM); 1992 (800 free)
4	Krisztina Egerszegi, Hungary	1992 (100, 200 back; 400 IM); 1996 (200 back)
4	Inge de Bruijn, Netherlands	2000 (50, 100 free; 100 fly); 2004 (50 free)
4	Yana Klochkova, Ukraine	2000 (200, 400 IM); 2004 (200, 400 IM)

Most Olympic Gold Medals in a Single Olympics, Men—7, Mark Spitz, United States, 1972: 100, 200 Free; 100, 200 Fly; 4 x 100, 4 x 200 Free Relays; 4 x 100 Medley Relay.

Most Olympic Gold Medals in a Single Olympics, Women—6, Kristin Otto, E. Germany, 1988: 50, 100 Free; 100 Back; 100 Fly; 4 x 100 Free Relay; 4 x 100 Medley Relay.

Most Olympic Medals in a Single Olympics, Men—8, Michael Phelps, United States, 2004: (six gold, two bronze).

Most Olympic Medals in a Single Olympics, Women—5, Natalie Coughlin, United States, 2004: (two gold, two silver, one bronze)

Most Olympic Medals in a Career, Men—11, Matt Biondi, United States: 1984 (one gold), 1988 (five gold, one silver, one bronze), 1992 (two gold, one silver); 11, Mark Spitz, United States: 1968 (two gold, one silver, one bronze), 1972 (seven gold); 10, Gary Hall Jr., United States 1996 (one gold, three silver), 2000 (three gold, one bronze), 2004 (two gold).

Most Olympic Medals in a Career, Women—12, Jenny Thompson, United States: 1992 (two gold, one silver), 1996 (three gold), 2000 (three gold, one bronze), 2004 (two silver); 8, Dawn Fraser, Australia: 1956 (two gold, one silver), 1960 (one gold, two silver), 1964 (one gold, one silver); 8, Kornelia Ender, E. Germany: 1972 (three silver), 1976 (four gold, one silver); 8, Shirley Babashoff, United States: 1972 (one gold, two silver), 1976 (one gold, four silver); 8, Inge de Bruijn, Netherlands: 2000 (three gold, one silver), 2004 (one gold, one silver, two bronze).

Winner, Same Event, Three Consecutive Olympics—Dawn Fraser, Australia, 100 Freestyle, 1956, 1960, 1964; Krisztina Egerszegi, Hungary, 200 backstroke, 1988, 1992, 1996.

Youngest Person to Win an Olympic Diving Gold—Marjorie Gestring, United States, 1936, 13 years, 9 months, springboard diving.

Youngest Person to Win an Olympic Swimming Gold—Krisztina Egerszegi, Hungary, 1988, 14 years, one month, 200 backstroke.

World Record Achievements

Most World Records, Career, Men—32, Arne Borg, Sweden, 1921–29.

Most World Records, Career, Women—42, Ragnhild Hveger, Denmark, 1936–42.

Most Freestyle Records Held Concurrently—5, Helene Madison, United States, 1931–33; 5, Shane Gould, Australia, 1972.

Most Consecutive Lowerings of a Record—10, Kornelia Ender, E. Germany, 100 Freestyle, 7-13-73 to 7-19-76.

Longest Duration of World Record—19 years, 359 days, 1:04.6 in 100 Free, (1936–56) Willy den Ouden, Netherlands.

Miscellaneous Sports

Shaun White won gold at both the Summer and Winter X Games in 2007

Where Do We Go From Here?

In the aftermath of Turin, some U.S. athletes maintained their hectic performance schedule, others simply rested, and a few took the time to dabble in more trivial pursuits

BY MERRELL NODEN

POST-OLYMPIC YEARS ARE crossroads for Olympic athletes, who know they have three more years to wait before finding so grand a stage. Some decide to rest on their laurels and retire, while others ease into retirement by hitting the banquet circuit. Still others find inspiration in their disappointments and return to training with a fiery new focus.

The 12 months that followed the Winter Olympics in Turin showed U.S. athletes making some interesting choices. No one found a better venue for his skills than Apolo Anton Ohno. The short track speed skater showed he had fast feet off the ice, too, when he and partner Julianne Hough won the fourth season of the ABC series "Dancing with the Stars." Indeed, the only athlete who might have put his Olympic stardom to more lucrative use was Shaun White, the flame-haired halfpipe specialist known as the Flying Tomato. In his ubiquitous American Express commercials White was a charming presence, but he also found time to stay in shape, becoming the first athlete to win a gold medal at both the Winter and Summer X Games when he came from behind on his final run to take the gold medal in the skate vert at the Summer Games in Los Angeles.

Some of last year's top stars chose to hibernate, planning to return who knows when. Following arthroscopic surgery to repair an old injury to her right hip, Michelle Kwan took the season off, while insisting that this was not to be seen as the beginning of her retirement. Sasha Cohen, the Olympic silver medalist in Turin, also took time off with the intention of returning at some point. And the woman who beat Cohen in Turin, Shizuka Arakawa, turned professional, joining the Prince Ice World Team.

The departure of that trio opened the door to some bright new faces. At the 2007 World Championships, held March 20–25 in Tokyo, Japanese women shone. Miki Ando, 19, beat out her teammate Mao Asada for the gold. The U.S. champion, Kimmie Meissner, from Bel Air, Maryland, who had stunned skate fans by winning the world title last year at 16, could not get into the medals this year, finishing fourth.

The U.S. men fared even worse at the world championships, with Evan Lysacek finishing fifth and Johnny Weir eighth, behind Brian Joubert of France, who won the gold on the strength of his short program. The free skate was won by the eventual runner-up, Daisuke Takahashi of Japan. In all, these were very disappointing

After winning gold in Turin, Julia Mancuso continued to impress in 2007, finishing third overall in the World Cup standings.

AP PHOTO/ALESSANDRO TROVATI

championships for U.S. skaters, who came away with a single medal, the bronze won by Tanith Belbin and Benjamin Agosto in ice dancing. Still, the U.S. continues to have considerable talent coming up. At the Junior World Figure Skating Championships, Caroline Zhang took the girls title, leading a U.S. sweep.

One of the big worries for World Cup ski events this year was a shortage of good snow. World Cup races in Kitzbühel, Austria, San Moritz, and Val d'Isere were among a number that had to be cancelled. In this snow-deprived winter, Julia Mancuso, Turin's gold medalist in the giant slalom, was the brightest star on the U.S. team, enjoying probably the best overall season by an American woman since 1984. Mancuso, 23, was the model of consistency, scoring top-three finishes in five consecutive World Cup events in January. She finished third overall in the World Cup standings, and earned silver in the super combined at the world championships. Her teammate, Lindsey Kildow, came away with two silvers, in the downhill and Super G, but missed most of the rest of the season with an injured right ACL.

The star of the world championships, held in Are, Sweden, was Sweden's own Anja Paerson, who won the first three events. No woman had ever won four, and Paerson didn't either, as she got sick and won "only" the bronze in the slalom. Still, it was an impressive performance for the 25-year-old, who belongs to the same sports club as Sweden's national ski idol, Ingemar Stenmark.

For Bode Miller, the biggest flameout on the disappointing U.S. Olympic team last winter, the 2006–07 season was an opportunity to make people forget his bizarrely nonchalant approach to the biggest competition of his life. "The Olympics were only several races, several days of my life," explained Miller on his website. "There is [sic] a lot of things that I love to do, and sometimes my skiing gets in the way of those things ... "

If that was seriously meant to convince anyone, it didn't. After finishing seventh in the downhill at the world championships, where he was the defending champion, Miller acknowledged he'd been warned about his behavior by U.S. ski officials. He did win the World Cup Super-G and now stands two shy of Phil Mahre's U.S. career record of 27 overall World Cup wins. Still, it was another perplexing season from Miller.

There are some athletes for whom post-Olympic success is especially sweet. Remember Zach Lund, the heartbreak kid of the Turin Olympics? Weeks before the Opening Ceremonies, the U.S. skeleton racer learned he would not be allowed to compete. He was suspended after testing positive for finasteride, which can be used to mask performance enhancing drugs. Far from denying he'd used it, Lund said he'd been taking the stuff for seven years—in the anti-balding formula Propecia, which had been added to the banned list since he'd last checked it. So when Lund won the World Cup skeleton title this year, it was hard not to smile. No doubt Lund won't mind one bit if, two years from now in Vancouver, his pate is shining—as long as it's matched by the gleam of a gold medal.

Archery

National Men's Champions

1879...Will H. Thompson	1911...Dr. Robert Elmer	1949...Russ Reynolds	1981...Rick McKinney
1880...L.L. Pedinghaus	1912...George Bryant	1950...Stan Overby	1982...Rick McKinney
1881...F.H. Walworth	1913...George Bryant	1951...Russ Reynolds	1983...Rick McKinney
1882...D.H. Nash	1914...Dr. Robert Elmer	1952...Robert Larson	1984...Darrell Pace
1883...Col. Robert Williams	1915...Dr. Robert Elmer	1953...Bill Glackin	1985...Rick McKinney
1884...Col. Robert Williams	1916...Dr. Robert Elmer	1954...Robert Rhode	1986...Rick McKinney
1885...Col. Robert Williams	1919...Dr. Robert Elmer	1955...Joe Fries	1987...Rick McKinney
1886...W.A. Clark	1920...Dr. Robert Elmer	1956...Joe Fries	1988...Jay Barrs
1887...W.A. Clark	1921...James Jiles	1957...Joe Fries	1989...Ed Eliason
1888...Lewis Maxson	1922...Dr. Robert Elmer	1958...Robert Bitner	1990...Ed Eliason
1889...Lewis Maxson	1923...Bill Palmer	1959...Wilbert Vetrovsky	1991...Ed Eliason
1890...Lewis Maxson	1924...James Jiles	1960...Robert Kadlec	1992...Alan Rasor
1891...Lewis Maxson	1925...Dr. Paul Crouch	1961...Clayton Sherman	1993...Jay Barrs
1892...Lewis Maxson	1926...Stanley Spencer	1962...Charles Sandlin	1994...Jay Barrs
1893...Lewis Maxson	1927...Dr. Paul Crouch	1963...Dave Keaggy Jr.	1995...Justin Huish
1894...Lewis Maxson	1928...Bill Palmer	1964...Dave Keaggy Jr.	1996...Richard (Butch)
1895...W.B. Robinson	1929...Dr. E.K. Roberts	1965...George Slinzer	Johnson
1896...Lewis Maxson	1930...Russ Hoogerhyde	1966...Hardy Ward	1997...Richard (Butch)
1897...W.A. Clark	1931...Russ Hoogerhyde	1967...Ray Rogers	Johnson
1898...Lewis Maxson	1932...Russ Hoogerhyde	1968...Hardy Ward	1998...Victor Wunderle
1899...M.C. Howell	1933...Ralph Miller	1969...Ray Rogers	1999...Victor Wunderle
1900...A.R. Clark	1934...Russ Hoogerhyde	1970...Joe Thornton	2000...Richard (Butch)
1901...Will H. Thompson	1935...Gilman Keasey	1971...John Williams	Johnson
1902...Will H. Thompson	1936...Gilman Keasey	1972...Kevin Erlandson	2001...Richard (Butch)
1903...Will H. Thompson	1937...Russ Hoogerhyde	1973...Darrell Pace	Johnson
1904...George Bryant	1938...Pat Chambers	1974...Darrell Pace	2002...Victor Wunderle
1905...George Bryant	1939...Pat Chambers	1975...Darrell Pace	2003...Joseph Bailey
1906...Henry Richardson	1940...Russ Hoogerhyde	1976...Darrell Pace	2004...Sagar Mistry
1907...Henry Richardson	1941...Larry Hughes	1977...Rick McKinney	2005...Guy Krueger
1908...Will H. Thompson	1946...Wayne Thompson	1978...Darrell Pace	2006...Victor Wunderle
1909...George Bryant	1947...Jack Wilson	1979...Rick McKinney	2007...Brady Ellison
1910...Henry Richardson	1948...Larry Hughes	1980...Rick McKinney	

National Women's Champions

1879...Mrs. S. Brown	1911...Mrs. J.S. Taylor	1949...Jean Lee	1979...Lynette Johnson
1880...Mrs. T. Davies	1912...Mrs. Witwer Tayler	1950...Jean Lee	1980...Judi Adams
1881...Mrs. A.H. Gibbes	1913...Mrs. P. Fletcher	1951...Jean Lee	1981...Debra Metzger
1882...Mrs. A.H. Gibbes	1914...Mrs. B.P. Gray	1952...Ann Weber	1982...Luann Ryon
1883...Mrs. M.C. Howell	1915...Cynthia Wesson	1953...Ann Weber	1983...Nancy Myrick
1884...Mrs. H. Hall	1916...Cynthia Wesson	1954...Laurette Young	1984...Ruth Rowe
1885...Mrs. M.C. Howell	1919...Dorothy Smith	1955...Ann Clark	1985...Terri Pesho
1886...Mrs. M.C. Howell	1920...Cynthia Wesson	1956...Carole Meinhart	1986...Debra Ochs
1887...Mrs. A.M. Phillips	1921...Mrs. L.C. Smith	1957...Carole Meinhart	1987...Terry Quinn
1888...Mrs. A.M. Phillips	1922...Dorothy Smith	1958...Carole Meinhart	1988...Debra Ochs
1889...Mrs. A.M. Phillips	1923...Norma Pierce	1959...Carole Meinhart	1989...Debra Ochs
1890...Mrs. M.C. Howell	1924...Dorothy Smith	1960...Ann Clark	1990...Denise Parker
1891...Mrs. M.C. Howell	1925...Dorothy Smith	1961...Victoria Cook	1991...Denise Parker
1892...Mrs. M.C. Howell	1926...Dorothy Smith	1962...Nancy	1992...Sherry Block
1893...Mrs. M.C. Howell	1927...Mrs. R. Johnson	Vonderheide	1993...Denise Parker
1894...Mrs. Albert Kern	1928...Beatrice Hodgson	1963...Nancy	1994...Judy Adams
1895...Mrs. M.C. Howell	1929...Audrey Grubbs	Vonderheide	1995...Jessica Carlson
1896...Mrs. M.C. Howell	1930...Audrey Grubbs	1964...Victoria Cook	1996...Janet Dykman
1897...Mrs. J.S. Baker	1931...DorothyCummings	1965...Nancy Pfeiffer	1997...Janet Dykman
1898...Mrs. M.C. Howell	1932...Ilda Hanchette	1966...Helen Thornton	1998...Janet Dykman
1899...Mrs. M.C. Howell	1933...Madelaine Taylor	1967...Ardelle Mills	1999...Denise Parker
1900...Mrs. M.C. Howell	1934...Desales Mudd	1968...Victoria Cook	2000...Karen Scavatto
1901...Mrs. C.E. Woodruff	1935...Ruth Hodgert	1969...Doreen Wilber	2001...Kathie Loesch
1902...Mrs. M.C. Howell	1936...Gladys Hammer	1970...Nancy Myrick	2002...Jessica Peterson
1903...Mrs. M.C. Howell	1937...Gladys Hammer	1971...Doreen Wilber	2003...Samantha Marino
1904...Mrs. M.C. Howell	1938...Jean Tenney	1972...Ruth Rowe	2004...Khatuna Lorig
1905...Mrs. M.C. Howell	1939...Belvia Carter	1973...Doreen Wilber	2005...Khatuna Lorig
1906...Mrs. E.C. Cook	1940...Ann Weber	1974...Doreen Wilber	2006...Karen Scavatto
1907...Mrs. M.C. Howell	1941...Ree Dillinger	1975...Irene Lorensen	2007...Khatuna Lorig
1908...Harriet Case	1946...Ann Weber	1976...Luann Ryon	
1909...Harriet Case	1947...Ann Weber	1977...Luann Ryon	
1910...J.V. Sullivan	1948...Jean Lee	1978...Luann Ryon	

PBA TOUR RESULTS
2006–07 Tour

Date	Event	Winner	Earnings ($)	Runner-Up
Sept 19–24	Dydo Drinco Japan Cup	Walter Ray Williams, Jr.	50,000	Pete Weber
Oct. 22–29	USBC Masters	Doug Kent	100,000	Jack Jurek
Nov. 1–5	Motor City Classic	Tony Reyes	35,000	Wes Malott
Nov. 8–12	Etonic Championship	Pete Weber	25,000	Doug Kent
Nov 15–19	Lake County Indiana Classic	Norm Duke	25,100	Mika Koivuniemi
Nov 22–26	Discover Card Windy City Classic	Wes Malott	25,000	Chris Barnes
Nov 29–Dec 3	Ace Hardware Championship	Tommy Jones	25,000	Wes Malott
Dec 6–10	Beltway Classic	Sean Rash	25,100	Parker Bohn III
Dec 13–17	Columbia 300 Classic	Norm Duke	25,000	Ryan Shafer
Jan 3–7	H & R Block Classic	Patrick Allen	25,000	Walter Ray Williams, Jr.
Jan 10–14	Earl Anthony Medford Classic	Sean Rash	25,000	Brian Himmler
Jan 16–21	Dick Weber Open	Jason Couch	25,000	Patrick Allen
Jan 24–28	Motel 6 Classic	Jason Couch	25,000	Billy Oatman
Jan 31–Feb 4	Sun City Classic	Mike Koivuniemi	25,000	Chris Barnes
Feb 7–11	GEICO Classic	Chris Barnes	25,100	John May
Feb 14–18	Go RVing Classic	Patrick Allen	25,000	Parker Bohn III
Feb. 21–25	Bayer Classic	Mike Mineman	25,100	Mike Machuga
Feb 27–March 4	64th U.S. Open	Pete Weber	100,000	Wes Malott
March 11–18	Pepsi Championship	Norm Duke	25,000	Ryan Shafer
March 19–25	Denny's World Championship	Doug Kent	50,000	Chris Barnes
March 28–Apr 1	PBA Tournament of Champions	Tommy Jones	60,000	Tony Reyes
Apr 5	Motel 6 Roll to Riches	Doug Kent	150,000	Norm Duke
Jun 14–15	PBA All Star Shootout	Duke & Williams Jr.	50,000	Reyes & Smith

2007 Senior Tour

Date	Event	Winner	Earnings ($)	Runner-Up
April 28–May 1	Manassas Open	David Ozio	8,000	John Petraglia
May 5–10	PBA Hammer Ladies & Legends, presented by the Illinois State BPA	Roger Kossert	7,550	John Petraglia
May 12–16	Northern Illinois Classic	Sam Zurich	8,000	Michael Henry
May 18–22	Dayton Classic	Sam Maccarone	8,000	Rohn morton
June 9–13	Tucson Open	Ross Packard	8,100	Bob Chamberlain
June 17–22	U.S. Open, by the Suncoast	Rick Minier	20,000	David Ozio
June 24–27	Epicenter Classic	Ernie Schlegel	8,000	David Ozio
July 1–4	Northern California Classic	Tom Baker	8,000	Mark Glover
July 8–13	USBC Senior Masters	Tom Baker	16,000	Shannon Starnes
July 30–Au. 2	Council Bluffs Open	Dave Patchen	8,000	Henry Gonzalez
Aug 6–9	Lake County Open	Don Sylvia	8,050	Roger LeClair
Aug 11–14	Decatur Open	Kevin Croucher	8,000	Gary Smith
Aug 17–21	Dick Weber Invitational	Tom Baker	9,000	David Ozio

TOUR LEADERS
PBA: 2006–07

MONEY LEADERS	Events	Earnings ($)	AVERAGE	Events	Average
Doug Kent	20	200,530	Norm Duke	18	228.47
Pete Weber	19	195,430	Wes Malott	20	226.49
Wes Malott	20	148,425	Walter Ray Williams Jr.	19	226.37
Tommy Jones	21	142,482	Jason Couch	21	225.42
Chris Barnes	21	127,407	Parker Bohn III	21	225.22

Seniors: 2007

MONEY LEADERS	Events	Earnings ($)	AVERAGE	Events	Average
Tom Baker	12	53,150	David Ozio	13	226.03
David Ozio	13	45,695	Tom Baker	12	225.72
Sam Zurich	12	24,995	Kevin Croucher	12	221.12
Kevin Croucher	12	22,970	Henry Gonzalez	12	219.75
Rohn Morton	13	21,485	Roger Kossert	11	219.35

Career Earnings

MEN		WOMEN	
Walter Ray Williams Jr.	$3,673,502	Wendy Macpherson	$1,194,535
Pete Weber	$2,976,248	Aleta Sill	$1,071,194
Parker Bohn III	$2,475,524	Tish Johnson	$1,063,062
Norm Duke	$2,364,611	Leanne Barrette	$1,010,343
Brian Voss	$2,336,642	Anne Marie Duggan	$936,421

Note: Leaders through Sept 1, 2006

TOUR LEADERS
PBA: 2006–07
Career Titles

MEN		WOMEN	
Walter Ray Williams Jr.	42	Lisa Wagner	32
Earl Anthony	41	Aleta Sill	31
Mark Roth	34	Leanne Barrette	26
Pete Weber	34	Patty Costello	25
Parker Bohn III	30	Tish Johnson	25

Chess

World Champions

FIDE		FIDE *(CONT.)*	
1866–94	Wilhelm Steinitz, Austria	1969–72	Boris Spassky, USSR
1894–1921	Emanuel Lasker, Germany	1972–75	Bobby Fischer, United States
1921–27	Jose Capablanca, Cuba	1975–85	Anatoly Karpov, USSR
1927–35	Alexander Alekhine, France	1985–93	*Garry Kasparov, USSR
1935–37	Max Euwe, Holland	1994–98	Anatoly Karpov, Russia
1937–47	Alexander Alekhine, France	1999–2000	Alexander Khalifman, Russia
1948–57	Mikhail Botvinnik, USSR	2000–01	Anand Viswanathan, India
1957–58	Vassily Smyslov, USSR	2002–04	Ruslan Ponomariov, Ukraine
1958–59	Mikhail Botvinnik, USSR	2004–05	Rustam Kasimdzhanov, Uzbekistan
1960–61	Mikhail Tal, USSR	2005–07	Veselin Topalov, Bulgaria
1961–63	Mikhail Botvinnik, USSR	2007–	Viswanathan Anand, India
1963–69	Tigran Petrosian, USSR		

United States Champions

1857–71	Paul Morphy	1962–68	Bobby Fischer	1990	Lev Alburt
1871–76	George Mackenzie	1968–69	Larry Evans	1991	Gata Kamski
1876–80	James Mason	1969–72	Samuel Reshevsky	1992	Patrick Wolff
1880–89	George Mackenzie	1972–73	Robert Byrne	1993	Alex Yermolinsky
1889–90	Samuel Lipschutz	1973–74	Lubomir Kavale		A. Shabalov
1890	Jackson Showalter		John Grefe	1994	Boris Gulko
1890–91	Max Judd	1974–77	Walter Browne	1995	Patrick Wolff
1891–92	Jackson Showalter	1978–80	Lubomir Kavalek		Nick DeFirmian
1892–94	Samuel Lipschutz	1980–81	Larry Evans		Alexander Ivanov
1894	Jackson Showalter		Larry Christiansen	1996	Alex Yermolinsky
1894–95	Albert Hodges		Walter Browne	1997	Alex Yermolinsky
1895–97	Jackson Showalter	1981–83	Walter Browne	1998	Alex Yermolinsky
1897–1906	Harry Pillsbury		Yasser Seirawan	1999	Boris Gulko
1906–09	Vacant	1983	R. Dzindzichashvili	2000	Joel Benjamin
1909–36	Frank Marshall	1983	Larry Christiansen	2001	Joel Benjamin
1936–44	Samuel Reshevsky		Walter Browne	2002	Larry Christiansen
1944–46	Arnold Denker	1984–85	Lev Alburt	2003	Alexander Shabalov
1946–48	Samuel Reshevsky	1986	Yasser Seirawan	2004	Hikaru Nakamura
1948–51	Herman Steiner	1987	Joel Benjamin	2005	Hikaru Nakamura
1951–54	Larry Evans		Nick DeFirmian	2006	Alexander Onischuk
1954–57	Arthur Bisguier	1988	Michael Wilder	2007	Alexander Shabalov
1957–61	Bobby Fischer	1989	R. Dzindzichashvili		
1961–62	Larry Evans		Stuart Rachels		
			Yasser Seirawan		

Curling

World Men's Champions

Year	Country, Skip	Year	Country, Skip	Year	Country, Skip
1972	Canada, Crest Melesnuk	1984	Norway, Eigil Ramsfjell	1996	Canada, Jeff Stoughton
1973	Sweden, Kjell Oscarius	1985	Canada, Al Hackner	1997	Sweden, Peter Lindholm
1974	U.S., Bud Somerville	1986	Canada, Ed Luckowich	1998	Canada, Wayne Middaugh
1975	Switzerland, Otto Danieli	1987	Canada, Russ Howard	1999	Scotland, Hammy McMillan
1976	U.S., Bruce Roberts	1988	Norway, Eigil Ramsfjell	2000	Canada, Greg McAulay
1977	Sweden, Ragnar Kamp	1989	Canada, Pat Ryan	2001	Sweden, Peter Lindholm
1978	U.S., Bob Nichols	1990	Canada, Ed Werenich	2002	Canada, Randy Ferbey
1979	Norway, Kristian Soerum	1991	Scotland, David Smith	2003	Canada, Randy Ferbey
1980	Canada, Rich Folk	1992	Switz., Markus Eggler	2004	Sweden, Peja Lindholm
1981	Switzerland, Jurg Tanner	1993	Canada, Russ Howard	2005	Canada, David Nedohin
1982	Canada, Al Hackner	1994	Canada, Rick Folk	2006	Scotland, David Murdoch
1983	Canada, Ed Werenich	1995	Canada, Kerry Burtnyk	2007	Canada, Glenn Howard

World Women's Champions

Year	Country, Skip	Year	Country, Skip	Year	Country, Skip
1979	Switzerland, Gaby Casanova	1987	Canada, Pat Sanders	1998	Sweden, Elisabet Gustafson
1980	Canada, Marj Mitchell	1988	Germany, Andrea Schopp	1999	Sweden, Elisabet Gustafson
1981	Sweden, Elisabeth Hogstrom	1989	Canada, Heather Houston	2000	Canada, Kelley Law
1982	Denmark, Marianne Jorgenson	1990	Norway, Dordi Nordby	2001	Canada, Colleen Jones
		1991	Norway, Dordi Nordby	2002	Scotland, Jackie Lockhart
1983	Switzerland, Erika Mueller	1992	Sweden, Elisabet Johanssen	2003	United States, Debbie McCormick
1984	Canada, Connie Lallberte	1993	Canada, Sandra Peterson	2004	Canada, Colleen Jones
1985	Canada, Linda Moore	1994	Canada, Sandra Peterson	2005	Sweden, Anette Norberg
1986	Canada, Marilyn Darte	1995	Sweden, Elisabet Gustafson	2006	Sweden, Anette Norberg
		1996	Canada, Marilyn Bodogh	2007	Canada, Kelly Scott
		1997	Canada, Sandra Schmirler		

U.S. Men's Champions

Year	Site	Winning Club	Skip
1957	Chicago, Ill.	Hibbing, Minn.	Harold Lauber
1958	Milwaukee, Wisc.	Detroit, Mich.	Douglas Fisk
1959	Green Bay, Wisc.	Hibbing, Minn.	Fran Kleffman
1960	Chicago, Ill.	Grafton, N.D.	Orvil Gilleshammer
1961	Grand Forks, N.D.	Seattle, Wash.	Frank Crealock
1962	Detroit, Mich.	Hibbing, Minn.	Fran Kleffman
1963	Duluth, Minn.	Detroit, Mich.	Mike Slyziuk
1964	Utica, N.Y.	Duluth, Minn.	Robert Magle Jr.
1965	Seattle, Wash.	Superior, Wisc.	Bud Somerville
1966	Hibbing, Minn.	Fargo, N.D.	Joe Zbacnik
1967	Winchester, Mass.	Seattle, Wash.	Bruce Roberts
1968	Madison, Wisc.	Superior, Wisc.	Bud Somerville
1969	Grand Forks, N.D.	Superior, Wisc.	Bud Somerville
1970	Ardsley, N.Y.	Grafton, N.D.	Art Tallackson
1971	Duluth, Minn.	Edmore, N.D.	Dale Dalziel
1972	Wilmette, Ill.	Grafton, N.D.	Robert Labonte
1973	Colorado Springs, Colo.	Winchester, Mass.	Charles Reeves
1974	Schenectady, N.Y.	Superior, Wisc.	Bud Somerville
1975	Detroit, Mich.	Seattle, Wash.	Ed Risling
1976	Wausau, Wisc.	Hibbing, Minn.	Bruce Roberts
1977	Northbrook, Ill.	Hibbing, Minn.	Bruce Roberts
1978	Utica, N.Y.	Superior, Wisc.	Bob Nichols
1979	Superior, Wisc.	Bemidji, Minn.	Scott Baird
1980	Bemidji, Minn.	Hibbing, Minn.	Paul Pustovar
1981	Fairbanks, Ak.	Superior, Wisc.	Bob Nichols
1982	Brookline, Mass.	Madison, Wisc.	Steve Brown
1983	Colorado Springs, Colo.	Colorado Springs, Colo.	Don Cooper
1984	Hibbing, Minn.	Hibbing, Minn.	Bruce Roberts
1985	Mequon, Wisc.	Wilmette, Ill.	Tim Wright
1986	Seattle, Wash.	Madison, Wisc.	Steve Brown
1987	Lake Placid, N.Y.	Seattle, Wash.	Jim Vukich
1988	St. Paul, Minn.	Seattle, Wash.	Doug Jones
1989	Detroit, Mich.	Seattle, Wash.	Jim Vukich
1990	Superior, Wisc.	Seattle, Wash.	Doug Jones
1991	Utica, N.Y.	Madison, Wisc.	Steve Brown
1992	Grafton, N.D.	Seattle, Wash.	Doug Jones
1993	St. Paul, Minn.	Bemidji, Minn.	Scott Baird
1994	Duluth, Minn.	Bemidji, Minn.	Scott Baird
1995	Appleton, Wisc.	Superior, Wisc.	Tim Somerville
1996	Bemidji, Minn.	Superior, Wisc.	Tim Somerville
1997	Seattle, Wash.	Langdon, N.D.	Craig Disher
1998	Bismarck, N.D.	Stevens Pt., Wisc.	Paul Pustovar
1999	Duluth, Minn.	Superior, Wisc.	Tim Somerville
2000	Ogden, Utah	Madison, Wisc.	Craig Brown
2001	Madison, Wisc.	Washington	Jason Larway
2002	Virginia, Minn.	Madison, Wisc.	Paul Pustovar
2003	Utica, N.Y.	Bemidji, Minn.	Pete Fenson
2004	Grand Forks, N.D.	Seattle, Wash.	Jason Larway
2005	Chicago, Ill.	Illinois	Russ Armstrong
2006	Superior, Wisc.	Bemidji, Minn.	Pete Fenson
2007	Utica, NY	Caledonian (Mankato, Minn.)	Todd Birr

U.S. Women's Champions

Year	Site	Winning Club	Skip
1977	Wilmette, Ill.	Hastings, N.Y.	Margaret Smith
1978	Duluth, Minn.	Wausau, Wisc.	Sandy Robarge
1979	Winchester, Mass.	Seattle, Wash.	Nancy Langley
1980	Seattle, Wash.	Seattle, Wash.	Sharon Kozal
1981	Kettle Moraine, Wisc.	Seattle, Wash.	Nancy Langley
1982	Bowling Green, Ohio	Oak Park, Ill.	Ruth Schwenker
1983	Grafton, N.D.	Seattle, Wash.	Nancy Langley
1984	Wauwatosa, Wisc.	Duluth, Minn.	Amy Hatten
1985	Hershey, Pa.	Fairbanks, Ak.	Bev Birklid
1986	Chicago, Ill.	St Paul, Minn.	Gerri Tilden
1987	St Paul, Minn.	Seattle, Wash.	Sharon Good
1988	Darien, Conn.	Seattle, Wash.	Nancy Langley
1989	Detroit, Mich.	Rolla, N.D.	Jan Lagasse
1990	Superior, Wisc.	Denver, Colo.	Bev Behnke
1991	Utica, N.Y.	Houston, Tex.	Maymar Gemmell
1992	Grafton, N.D.	Madison, Wisc.	Lisa Schoeneberg
1993	St Paul, Minn.	Denver, Colo.	Bev Behnke
1994	Duluth, Minn.	Denver, Colo.	Bev Behnke
1995	Appleton, Wisc.	Madison, Wisc.	Lisa Schoeneberg
1996	Bemidji, Minn.	Madison, Wisc.	Lisa Schoeneberg
1997	Seattle, Wash.	Arlington, Wisc.	Patti Lank
1998	Bismarck, N.D.	Wilmette, Ill.	Kari Erickson
1999	Duluth, Minn.	Madison, Wisc.	Patti Lank
2000	Ogden, Utah	Nebraska	Amy Wright
2001	Madison, Wisc.	Illinois	Kari Erickson
2002	Virginia, Minn.	Madison, Wisc.	Patti Lank
2003	Utica, N.Y.	Illinois	Debbie McCormick
2004	Grand Forks, N.D.	Madison, Wisc.	Patti Lank
2005	Chicago, Ill.	Massachusetts	Shelly Dropkin
2006	Superior, Wisc.	Madison, Wisc.	Debbie McCormick
2007	Utica, NY	Madison, Wisc.	Debbie McCormick

Cycling

Professional Road Race World Champions

Year	Champion
1927	Alfred Binda, Italy
1928	George Ronsse, Belgium
1929	George Ronsse, Belgium
1930	Alfred Binda, Italy
1931	Learco Guerra, Italy
1932	Alfred Binda, Italy
1933	George Speicher, France
1934	Karel Kaers, Belgium
1935	Jean Aerts, Belgium
1936	Antonio Magne, France
1937	Elio Meulenberg, Belgium
1938	Marcel Kint, Belgium
1939–45	No competition
1946	Hans Knecht, Switzerland
1947	Theo. Middelkamp, Holland
1948	Alberic Schotte, Belgium
1949	Henri Van Steenbergen, Belgium
1950	Alberic Schotte, Belgium
1951	Ferdinand Kubler, Switzerland
1952	Heinz Mueller, Germany
1953	Fausto Coppi, Italy
1954	Louison Bobet, France
1955	Stan Ockers, Belgium
1956	Rik Van Steenbergen, Belg.
1957	Rik Van Steenbergen, Belgium
1958	Ercole Baldini, Italy
1959	Andre Darrigade, France
1960	Rik van Looy, Belgium
1961	Rik van Looy, Belgium
1962	Jean Stablenski, France
1963	Bennoni Beheyt, Belgium
1964	Jan Janssen, Holland
1965	Tommy Simpson, England
1966	Rudi Altig, West Germany
1967	Eddy Merckx, Belgium
1968	Vittorio Adorni, Italy
1969	Harm Ottenbros, Netherlands
1970	J.P. Monseré, Belgium
1971	Eddy Merckx, Belgium
1972	Marino Basso, Italy
1973	Felice Gimondi, Italy
1974	Eddy Merckx, Belgium
1975	Hennie Kuiper, Holland
1976	Freddy Maertens, Belgium
1977	Francesco Moser, Italy
1978	Gerri Knetemann, Holland
1979	Jan Raas, Holland
1980	Bernard Hinault, France
1981	Freddy Maertens, Belgium
1982	Giuseppe Saronni, Italy
1983	Greg LeMond, United States
1984	Claude Criquielion, Belgium
1985	Joop Zoetemelk, Holland
1986	Moreno Argentin, Italy
1987	Stephen Roche, Ireland
1988	Maurizio Fondriest, Italy
1989	Greg LeMond, United States
1990	Rudy Dhaenene, Belgium
1991	Gianni Bugno, Italy
1992	Gianni Bugno, Italy
1993	Lance Armstrong, United States
1994	Luc LeBlanc, France
1995	Abraham Olano, Spain
1996	Johan Museeuw, Belgium
1997	Laurent Brochard, France
1998	Oskar Camenzind, Switz.
1999	Oscar Gomez Freire, Spain
2000	Romans Vainsteins, Latvia
2001	Oscar Gomez Freire, Spain
2002	Mario Cipollini, Italy
2003	Igor Astraloa, Spain
2004	Oscar Freire Gomez, Spain
2005	Tom Boonen, Belgium
2006	Paolo Bettini, Italy
2007	Paolo Bettini, Italy

Tour DuPont Winners

Year	Winner	Time
1989	Dag Otto Lauritzen, Norway	33 hrs, 28 min, 48 sec
1990	Raul Alcala, Mexico	45 hrs, 20 min, 9 sec
1991	Erik Breukink, Holland	48 hrs, 56 min, 53 sec
1992	Greg LeMond, United States	44 hrs, 27 min, 43 sec
1993	Raul Alcala, Mexico	46 hrs, 42 min, 52 sec
1994	Viatcheslav Ekimov, Russia	47 hrs, 14 min, 29 sec
1995	Lance Armstrong, United States	46 hrs, 31 min, 16 sec
1996	Lance Armstrong, United States	48 hrs, 20 min, 5 sec

Note: Race not held since 1996.

Tour de France Winners

Year	Winner	Time
1903	Maurice Garin, France	94 hrs, 33 min
1904	Henry Cornet, France	96 hrs, 5 min, 56 sec
1905	Louis Trousselier, France	110 hrs, 26 min, 58 sec
1906	Rene Pottier, France	Not available
1907	Lucien Petit-Breton, France	158 hrs, 54 min, 5 sec
1908	Lucien Petit-Breton, France	Not available
1909	Francois Faber, Luxembourg	157 hrs, 1 min, 22 sec
1910	Octave Lapize, France	162 hrs, 41 min, 30 sec
1911	Gustave Garrigou, France	195 hrs, 37 min
1912	Odile Defraye, Belgium	190 hrs, 30 min, 28 sec
1913	Philippe Thys, Belgium	197 hrs, 54 min
1914	Philippe Thys, Belgium	200 hrs, 28 min, 48 sec
1915–18	No race	
1919	Firmin Lambot, Belgium	231 hrs, 7 min, 15 sec
1920	Philippe Thys, Belgium	228 hrs, 36 min, 13 sec
1921	Leon Scieur, Belgium	221 hrs, 50 min, 26 sec
1922	Firmin Lambot, Belgium	222 hrs, 8 min, 6 sec
1923	Henri Pelissier, France	222 hrs, 15 min, 30 sec
1924	Ottavio Bottechia, Italy	226 hrs, 18 min, 21 sec
1925	Ottavio Bottechia, Italy	219 hrs, 10 min, 18 sec
1926	Lucien Buysse, Belgium	238 hrs, 44 min, 25 sec
1927	Nicolas Frantz, Luxembourg	198 hrs, 16 min, 42 sec
1928	Nicolas Frantz, Luxembourg	192 hrs, 48 min, 58 sec
1929	Maurice Dewaele, Belgium	186 hrs, 39 min, 16 sec
1930	Andre Leducq, France	172 hrs, 12 min, 16 sec
1931	Antonin Magne, France	177 hrs, 10 min, 3 sec
1932	Andre Leducq, France	154 hrs, 12 min, 49 sec
1933	Georges Speicher, France	147 hrs, 51 min, 37 sec
1934	Antonin Magne, France	147 hrs, 13 min, 58 sec
1935	Romain Maes, Belgium	141 hrs, 32 min
1936	Sylvere Maes, Belgium	142 hrs, 47 min, 32 sec
1937	Roger Lapebie, France	138 hrs, 58 min, 31 sec
1938	Gino Bartali, Italy	148 hrs, 29 min, 12 sec
1939	Sylvere Maes, Belgium	132 hrs, 3 min, 17 sec
1940–46	No race	
1947	Jean Robic, France	148 hrs, 11 min, 25 sec
1948	Gino Bartali, Italy	147 hrs, 10 min, 36 sec
1949	Fausto Coppi, Italy	149 hrs, 40 min, 49 sec
1950	Ferdi Kubler, Switzerland	145 hrs, 36 min, 56 sec
1951	Hugo Koblet, Switzerland	142 hrs, 20 min, 14 sec
1952	Fausto Coppi, Italy	151 hrs, 57 min, 20 sec
1953	Louison Bobet, France	129 hrs, 23 min, 25 sec
1954	Louison Bobet, France	140 hrs, 6 min, 5 sec
1955	Louison Bobet, France	130 hrs, 29 min, 26 sec
1956	Roger Walkowiak, France	124 hrs, 1 min, 16 sec
1957	Jacques Anquetil, France	129 hrs, 46 min, 11 sec
1958	Charly Gaul, Luxembourg	116 hrs, 59 min, 5 sec
1959	Federico Bahamontes, Spain	123 hrs, 46 min, 45 sec
1960	Gastone Nencini, Italy	112 hrs, 8 min, 42 sec
1961	Jacques Anquetil, France	122 hrs, 1 min, 33 sec
1962	Jacques Anquetil, France	114 hrs, 31 min, 54 sec
1963	Jacques Anquetil, France	113 hrs, 30 min, 5 sec
1964	Jacques Anquetil, France	127 hrs, 9 min, 44 sec
1965	Felice Gimondi, Italy	116 hrs, 42 min, 6 sec
1966	Lucien Aimar, France	117 hrs, 34 min, 21 sec
1967	Roger Pingeon, France	136 hrs, 53 min, 50 sec

Tour de France Winners *(Cont.)*

Year	Winner	Time
1968	Jan Janssen, Netherlands	133 hrs, 49 min, 32 sec
1969	Eddy Merckx, Belgium	116 hrs, 16 min, 2 sec
1970	Eddy Merckx, Belgium	119 hrs, 31 min, 49 sec
1971	Eddy Merckx, Belgium	96 hrs, 45 min, 14 sec
1972	Eddy Merckx, Belgium	108 hrs, 17 min, 18 sec
1973	Luis Ocana, Spain	122 hrs, 25 min, 34 sec
1974	Eddy Merckx, Belgium	116 hrs, 16 min, 58 sec
1975	Bernard Thevenet, France	114 hrs, 35 min, 31 sec
1976	Lucien Van Impe, Belgium	116 hrs, 22 min, 23 sec
1977	Bernard Thevenet, France	115 hrs, 38 min, 30 sec
1978	Bernard Hinault, France	108 hrs, 18 min
1979	Bernard Hinault, France	103 hrs, 6 min, 50 sec
1980	Joop Zoetemelk, Netherlands	109 hrs, 19 min, 14 sec
1981	Bernard Hinault, France	96 hrs, 19 min, 38 sec
1982	Bernard Hinault, France	92 hrs, 8 min, 46 sec
1983	Laurent Fignon, France	105 hrs, 7 min, 52 sec
1984	Laurent Fignon, France	112 hrs, 3 min, 40 sec
1985	Bernard Hinault, France	113 hrs, 24 min, 23 sec
1986	Greg LeMond, United States	110 hrs, 35 min, 19 sec
1987	Stephen Roche, Ireland	115 hrs, 27 min, 42 sec
1988	Pedro Delgado, Spain	84 hrs, 27 min, 53 sec
1989	Greg LeMond, United States	87 hrs, 38 min, 35 sec
1990	Greg LeMond, United States	90 hrs, 43 min, 20 sec
1991	Miguel Induráin, Spain	101 hrs, 1 min, 20 sec
1992	Miguel Induráin, Spain	100 hrs, 49 min, 30 sec
1993	Miguel Induráin, Spain	95 hrs, 57 min, 9 sec
1994	Miguel Induráin, Spain	103 hrs, 38 min, 38 sec
1995	Miguel Induráin, Spain	92 hrs, 44 min, 59 sec
1996	Bjarne Riis, Denmark	95 hrs, 57 min, 16 sec
1997	Jan Ullrich, Germany	100 hrs, 30 min, 35 sec
1998	Marco Pantani, Italy	92 hrs, 49 min, 46 sec
1999	Lance Armstrong, United States	91 hrs, 32 min, 16 sec
2000	Lance Armstrong, United States	92 hrs, 33 min, 8 sec
2001	Lance Armstrong, United States	86 hrs, 17 min, 28 sec
2002	Lance Armstrong, United States	82 hrs, 5 min, 12 sec
2003	Lance Armstrong, United States	83 hrs, 41 min, 12 sec
2004	Lance Armstrong, United States	83 hrs, 36 min, 2 sec
2005	Lance Armstrong, United States	82 hrs, 34 min, 5 sec
2006	Oscar Pereiro, Spain†	82 hrs, 48 min, 30 sec
2007	Alberto Contador, Spain	91 hrs, 26 min

†Floyd Landis, the initial winner, was officially stripped of his title on Sept. 20, 2007 by the ICU after a hearing affirmed that he had tested positive for using banned substances during Stage 17 of the 2006 Tour.

Sled Dog Racing

Iditarod

Year	Winner	Time	Year	Winner	Time
1973	Dick Wilmarth	20 days, 00:49:41	1991	Rick Swenson	12 days, 16:34:39
1974	Carl Huntington	20 days, 15:02:07	1992	Martin Buser	10 days, 19:17:15
1975	Emmitt Peters	14 days, 14:43:45	1993	Jeff King	10 days, 15:38:15
1976	Gerald Riley	18 days, 22:58:17	1994	Martin Buser	10 days, 13:02:39
1977	Rick Swenson	16 days, 16:27:13	1995	Doug Swingley	9 days, 02:42:19
1978	Dick Mackey	14 days, 18:52:24	1996	Jeff King	9 days, 05:43:13
1979	Rick Swenson	15 days, 10:37:47	1997	Martin Buser	9 days, 08:30:45
1980	Joe May	14 days, 07:11:51	1998	Jeff King	9 days, 05:52:26
1981	Rick Swenson	12 days, 08:45:02	1999	Doug Swingley	9 days, 14:31:19
1982	Rick Swenson	16 days, 04:40:10	2000	Doug Swingley	9 days, 00:58:06
1983	Dick Mackey	12 days, 14:10:44	2001	Doug Swingley	9 days, 19:55:50
1984	Dean Osmar	12 days, 15:07:33	2002	Martin Buser	8 days, 22:46:02
1985	Libby Riddles	18 days, 00:20:17	2003	Robert Sorlie	9 days, 15:47:36
1986	Susan Butcher	11 days, 15:06:00	2004	Mitch Seavey	9 days, 12:20:22
1987	Susan Butcher	11 days, 02:05:13	2005	Robert Sorlie	9 days, 18:39:31
1988	Susan Butcher	11 days, 11:41:40	2006	Jeff King	9 days, 11:11:36
1989	Joe Runyan	11 days, 05:24:34	2007	Lance Mackey	9 days, 05:08:41
1990	Susan Butcher	11 days, 01:53:23			

WORLD CHAMPIONS
Women

1906	Madge Sayers-Cave, Great Britain
1907	Madge Sayers-Cave, Great Britain
1908	Lily Kronberger, Hungary
1909	Lily Kronberger, Hungary
1910	Lily Kronberger, Hungary
1911	Lily Kronberger, Hungary
1912	Opika von Meray Horvath, Hungary
1913	Opika von Meray Horvath, Hungary
1914	Opika von Meray Horvath, Hungary
1915–21	No competition
1922	Herma Plank-Szabo, Austria
1923	Herma Plank-Szabo, Austria
1924	Herma Plank-Szabo, Austria
1925	Herma Jaross-Szabo, Austria
1926	Herma Jaross-Szabo, Austria
1927	Sonja Henie, Norway
1928	Sonja Henie, Norway
1929	Sonja Henie, Norway
1930	Sonja Henie, Norway
1931	Sonja Henie, Norway
1932	Sonja Henie, Norway
1933	Sonja Henie, Norway
1934	Sonja Henie, Norway
1935	Sonja Henie, Norway
1936	Sonja Henie, Norway
1937	Cecilia Colledge, Great Britain
1938	Megan Taylor, Great Britain
1939	Megan Taylor, Great Britain
1940–46	No competition
1947	Barbara Ann Scott, Canada
1948	Barbara Ann Scott, Canada
1949	Alena Vrzanova, Czechoslovakia
1950	Alena Vrzanova, Czechoslovakia
1951	Jeannette Altwegg, Great Britain
1952	Jacqueline duBief, France
1953	Tenley Albright, United States
1954	Gundi Busch, W. Germany
1955	Tenley Albright, United States
1956	Carol Heiss, United States
1957	Carol Heiss, United States
1958	Carol Heiss, United States
1959	Carol Heiss, United States
1960	Carol Heiss, United States
1961	No competition
1962	Sjoukje Dijkstra, Netherlands
1963	Sjoukje Dijkstra, Netherlands
1964	Sjoukje Dijkstra, Netherlands
1965	Petra Burka, Canada
1966	Peggy Fleming, United States
1967	Peggy Fleming, United States
1968	Peggy Fleming, United States
1969	Gabriele Seyfert, E. Germany
1970	Gabriele Seyfert, E. Germany
1971	Beatrix Schuba, Austria
1972	Beatrix Schuba, Austria
1973	Karen Magnussen, Canada
1974	Christine Errath, E. Germany
1975	Dianne DeLeeuw, Netherlands
1976	Dorothy Hamill, United States
1977	Linda Fratianne, United States
1978	Annett Poetzsch, E. Germany
1979	Linda Fratianne, United States
1980	Annett Poetzsch, E. Germany
1981	Denise Biellmann, Switzerland
1982	Elaine Zayak, United States
1983	Rosalynn Sumners, United States
1984	Katarina Witt, E. Germany
1985	Katarina Witt, E. Germany
1986	Debi Thomas, United States
1987	Katarina Witt, E. Germany
1988	Katarina Witt, E. Germany
1989	Midori Ito, Japan
1990	Jill Trenary, United States
1991	Kristi Yamaguchi, United States
1992	Kristi Yamaguchi, United States
1993	Oksana Baiul, Ukraine
1994	Yuka Sato, Japan
1995	Chen Lu, China
1996	Michelle Kwan, United States
1997	Tara Lipinski, United States
1998	Michelle Kwan, United States
1999	Maria Butyrskaya, Russia
2000	Michelle Kwan, United States
2001	Michelle Kwan, United States
2002	Irina Slutskaya, Russia
2003	Michelle Kwan, United States
2004	Shizuka Arakawa, Japan
2005	Irina Slutskaya, Russia
2006	Kimmie Meissner, United States
2007	Miki Ando, Japan

Men

1896	Gilbert Fuchs, Germany
1897	Gustav Hugel, Austria
1898	Henning Grenander, Sweden
1899	Gustav Hugel, Austria
1900	Gustav Hugel, Austria
1901	Ulrich Salchow, Sweden
1902	Ulrich Salchow, Sweden
1903	Ulrich Salchow, Sweden
1904	Ulrich Salchow, Sweden
1905	Ulrich Salchow, Sweden
1906	Gilbert Fuchs, Germany
1907	Ulrich Salchow, Sweden
1908	Ulrich Salchow, Sweden
1909	Ulrich Salchow, Sweden
1910	Ulrich Salchow, Sweden
1911	Ulrich Salchow, Sweden
1912	Fritz Kachler, Austria
1913	Fritz Kachler, Austria
1914	Gosta Sandhal, Sweden
1915–21	No competition
1922	Gillis Grafstrom, Sweden
1923	Fritz Kachler, Austria
1924	Gillis Grafstrom, Sweden
1925	Willy Bockl, Austria
1926	Willy Bockl, Austria
1927	Willy Bockl, Austria
1928	Willy Bockl, Austria
1929	Gillis Grafstrom, Sweden
1930	Karl Schafer, Austria
1931	Karl Schafer, Austria
1932	Karl Schafer, Austria
1933	Karl Schafer, Austria
1934	Karl Schafer, Austria
1935	Karl Schafer, Austria
1936	Karl Schafer, Austria
1937	Felix Kaspar, Austria
1938	Felix Kaspar, Austria
1939	Graham Sharp, Great Britain

WORLD CHAMPIONS *(CONT.)*
Men *(Cont.)*

1940–46 ....No competition	1978 ....Charles Tickner, United States
1947 ....Hans Gerschwiler, Switzerland	1979 ....Vladimir Kovalev, USSR
1948 ....Dick Button, United States	1980 ....Jan Hoffmann, E. Germany
1949 ....Dick Button, United States	1981 ....Scott Hamilton, United States
1950 ....Dick Button, United States	1982 ....Scott Hamilton, United States
1951 ....Dick Button, United States	1983 ....Scott Hamilton, United States
1952 ....Dick Button, United States	1984 ....Scott Hamilton, United States
1953 ....Hayes Alan Jenkins, United States	1985 ....Aleksandr Fadeev, USSR
1954 ....Hayes Alan Jenkins, United States	1986 ....Brian Boitano, United States
1955 ....Hayes Alan Jenkins, United States	1987 ....Brian Orser, Canada
1956 ....Hayes Alan Jenkins, United States	1988 ....Brian Boitano, United States
1957 ....David W. Jenkins, United States	1989 ....Kurt Browning, Canada
1958 ....David W. Jenkins, United States	1990 ....Kurt Browning, Canada
1959 ....David W. Jenkins, United States	1991 ....Kurt Browning, Canada
1960 ....Alan Giletti, France	1992 ....Viktor Petrenko, CIS
1961 ....No competition	1993 ....Kurt Browning, Canada
1962 ....Donald Jackson, Canada	1994 ....Elvis Stojko, Canada
1963 ....Donald McPherson, Canada	1995 ....Elvis Stojko, Canada
1964 ....Manfred Schneldorfer, W. Germany	1996 ....Todd Eldredge, United States
1965 ....Alain Calmat, France	1997 ....Elvis Stojko, Canada
1966 ....Emmerich Danzer, Austria	1998 ....Alexei Yagudin, Russia
1967 ....Emmerich Danzer, Austria	1999 ....Alexei Yagudin, Russia
1968 ....Emmerich Danzer, Austria	2000 ....Alexei Yagudin, Russia
1969 ....Tim Wood, United States	2001 ....Evgeni Plushenko, Russia
1970 ....Tim Wood, United States	2002 ....Alexei Yagudin, Russia
1971 ....Andrej Nepela, Czechoslovakia	2003 ....Evgeni Plushenko, Russia
1972 ....Andrej Nepela, Czechoslovakia	2004 ....Evgeni Plushenko, Russia
1973 ....Andrej Nepela, Czechoslovakia	2005 ....Stephane Lambiel, Switzerland
1974 ....Jan Hoffmann, E. Germany	2006 ....Stephane Lambiel, Switzerland
1975 ....Sergei Volkov, USSR	2007 ....Brian Joubert, France
1976 ....John Curry, Great Britain	
1977 ....Vladimir Kovalev, USSR	

Pairs

1908 ......Anna Hubler, Heinrich Burger, Germany	1934 ......Emilie Rotter, Laszlo Szollas, Hungary
1909 ......Phyllis Johnson, James H. Johnson, Great Britain	1935 ......Emilie Rotter, Laszlo Szollas, Hungary
1910 ......Anna Hubler, Heinrich Burger, Germany	1936 ......Maxi Herber, Ernst Bajer, Germany
1911 ......Ludowika Eilers, Walter Jakobsson, Germany/Finland	1937 ......Maxi Herber, Ernst Bajer, Germany
	1938 ......Maxi Herber, Ernst Bajer, Germany
1912 ......Phyllis Johnson, James H. Johnson, Great Britain	1939 ......Maxi Herber, Ernst Bajer, Germany
	1940–46..No competition
1913 ......Helene Engelmann, Karl Majstrik, Germany	1947 ......Micheline Lannoy, Pierre Baugniet, Belgium
1914 ......Ludowika Jakobsson-Eilers, Walter Jakobsson-Eilers, Finland	1948 ......Micheline Lannoy, Pierre Baugniet, Belgium
	1949 ......Andrea Kekessy, Ede Kiraly, Hungary
1915–21..No competition	1950 ......Karol Kennedy, Peter Kennedy, United States
1922 ......Helene Engelmann, Alfred Berger, Germany	1951 ......Ria Baran, Paul Falk, W. Germany
1923 ......Ludowika Jakobsson-Eilers, Walter Jakobsson-Eilers, Finland	1952 ......Ria Baran Falk, Paul Falk, W. Germany
	1953 ......Jennifer Nicks, John Nicks, Great Britain
1924 ......Helene Engelmann, Alfred Berger, Germany	1954 ......Frances Dafoe, Norris Bowden, Canada
	1955 ......Frances Dafoe, Norris Bowden, Canada
1925 ......Herma Jaross-Szabo, Ludwig Wrede, Austria	1956 ......Sissy Schwarz, Kurt Oppelt, Austria
	1957 ......Barbara Wagner, Robert Paul, Canada
1926 ......Andree Joly, Pierre Brunet, France	1958 ......Barbara Wagner, Robert Paul, Canada
1927 ......Herma Jaross-Szabo, Ludwig Wrede, Austria	1959 ......Barbara Wagner, Robert Paul, Canada
	1960 ......Barbara Wagner, Robert Paul, Canada
1928 ......Andree Joly, Pierre Brunet, France	1961 ......No competition
1929 ......Lilly Scholz, Otto Kaiser, Austria	1962 ......Maria Jelinek, Otto Jelinek, Canada
1930 ......Andree Brunet-Joly, Pierre Brunet-Joly, France	1963 ......Marika Kilius, Hans-Jurgen Baumler, W Germany
1931 ......Emilie Rotter, Laszlo Szollas, Hungary	1964 ......Marika Kilius, Hans-Jurgen Baumler, W Germany
1932 ......Andree Brunet-Joly, Pierre Brunet-Joly, France	1965 ......Ljudmila Protopopov, Oleg Protopopov, USSR
	1966 ......Ljudmila Protopopov, Oleg Protopopov, USSR
1933 ......Emilie Rotter, Laszlo Szollas, Hungary	1967 ......Ljudmila Protopopov, Oleg Protopopov, USSR

WORLD CHAMPIONS *(CONT.)*

Pairs *(Cont.)*

1968 ......Ljudmila Protopopov, Oleg Protopopov, USSR	1989 ......Ekaterina Gordeeva, Sergei Grinkov, USSR
1969 ......Irina Rodnina, Aleksey Ulanov, USSR	1990 ......Ekaterina Gordeeva, Sergei Grinkov, USSR
1970 ......Irina Rodnina, Aleksey Ulanov, USSR	1991 ......Natalia Mishkutienok, Artur Dmitriev, USSR
1971 ......Irina Rodnina, Aleksey Ulanov, USSR	1992 ......Natalia Mishkutienok, Artur Dmitriev, CIS
1972 ......Irina Rodnina, Aleksey Ulanov, USSR	1993 ......Isabelle Brasseur, Lloyd Eisler, Canada
1973 ......Irina Rodnina, Aleksandr Zaytsev, USSR	1994 ......Evgenia Shishkova, Vadim Naumov, Russia
1974 ......Irina Rodnina, Aleksandr Zaytsev, USSR	1995 ......Radka Kovarikova, Rene Novotny,
1975 ......Irina Rodnina, Aleksandr Zaytsev, USSR	Czech Republic
1976 ......Irina Rodnina, Aleksandr Zaytsev, USSR	1996 ......Marina Eltsova, Andrey Buskhov, Russia
1977 ......Irina Rodnina, Aleksandr Zaytsev, USSR	1997 ......Mandy Wötzel, Ingo Steuer, Germany
1978 ......Irina Rodnina, Aleksandr Zaytsev, USSR	1998 ......Jenni Meno, Todd Sand, United States
1979 ......Tai Babilonia, Randy Gardner, United States	1999 ......Elena Berezhnaya, Anton Sikharulidze, Russia
1980 ......Maria Cherkasova, Sergei Shakhrai, USSR	2000 ......Maria Petrova, Aleksei Tikhonov, Russia
1981 ......Irina Vorobieva, Igor Lisovsky, USSR	2001 ......Jamie Salé, David Pelletier, Canada
1982 ......Sabine Baess, Tassilio Thierbach, E. Germany	2002 ......Xue Shen, Hongbo Zhao, China
1983 ......Elena Valova, Oleg Vasiliev, USSR	2003 ......Xue Shen, Hongbo Zhao, China
1984 ......Barbara Underhill, Paul Martini, Canada	2004 ......Tatiana Totmianina, Maxim Marinin, Russia
1985 ......Elena Valova, Oleg Vasiliev, USSR	2005 ......Tatiana Totmianina, Maxim Marinin, Russia
1986 ......Ekaterina Gordeeva, Sergei Grinkov, USSR	2006 ......Qing Pang, Jian Tong, China
1987 ......Ekaterina Gordeeva, Sergei Grinkov, USSR	2007 ......Shen Xue, Zhao Hongbo, China
1988 ......Elena Valova, Oleg Vasiliev, USSR	

Dance

1950 ......Lois Waring, Michael McGean, United States	1977 ......Irina Moiseeva, Andreij Minenkov, USSR
1951 ......Jean Westwood, Lawrence Demmy,	1978 ......Natalia Linichuk, Gennadi Karponosov,
Great Britain	USSR
1952 ......Jean Westwood, Lawrence Demmy,	1979 ......Natalia Linichuk, Gennadi Karponosov,
Great Britain	USSR
1953 ......Jean Westwood, Lawrence Demmy,	1980 ......Krisztina Regoeczy, Andras Sallai, Hungary
Great Britain	1981 ......Jayne Torvill, Christopher Dean, Great Britain
1954 ......Jean Westwood, Lawrence Demmy,	1982 ......Jayne Torvill, Christopher Dean, Great Britain
Great Britain	1983 ......Jayne Torvill, Christopher Dean, Great Britain
1955 ......Jean Westwood, Lawrence Demmy,	1984 ......Jayne Torvill, Christopher Dean, Great Britain
Great Britain	1985 ......Natalia Bestemianova, Andrei Bukin, USSR
1956 ......Pamela Wieght, Paul Thomas, Great Britain	1986 ......Natalia Bestemianova, Andrei Bukin, USSR
1957 ......June Markham, Courtney Jones,	1987 ......Natalia Bestemianova, Andrei Bukin, USSR
Great Britain	1988 ......Natalia Bestemianova, Andrei Bukin, USSR
1958 ......June Markham, Courtney Jones,	1989 ......Marina Klimova, Sergei Ponomarenko, USSR
Great Britain	1990 ......Marina Klimova, Sergei Ponomarenko, USSR
1959 ......Doreen D. Denny, Courtney Jones,	1991 ......Isabelle Duchesnay, Paul Duchesnay, France
Great Britain	1992 ......Marina Klimova, Sergei Ponomarenko, CIS
1960 ......Doreen D. Denny, Courtney Jones,	1993 ......Renee Roca, Gorsha Sur, United States
Great Britain	1994 ......Oksana Grishuk, Evgeny Platov, Russia
1961 ......No competition	1995 ......Oksana Grishuk, Evgeny Platov, Russia
1962 ......Eva Romanova, Pavel Roman, Czechoslovakia	1996 ......Oksana Grishuk, Evgeny Platov, Russia
1963 ......Eva Romanova, Pavel Roman, Czechoslovakia	1997 ......Oksana Grishuk, Evgeny Platov, Russia
1964 ......Eva Romanova, Pavel Roman, Czechoslovakia	1998 ......Anjelika Krylova, Oleg Ovsyannikov, Russia
1965 ......Eva Romanova, Pavel Roman, Czechoslovakia	1999 ......Anjelika Krylova, Oleg Ovsyannikov, Russia
1966 ......Diane Towler, Bernard Ford, Great Britain	2000 ......Marina Anissina, Gwendal Peizerat, France
1967 ......Diane Towler, Bernard Ford, Great Britain	2001 ......Barbara Fusar Poli, Maurizio Margaglio, Italy
1968 ......Diane Towler, Bernard Ford, Great Britain	2002 ......Irina Lobacheva, Ilia Averbukh, Russia
1969 ......Diane Towler, Bernard Ford, Great Britain	2003 ......Shae-Lynn Bourne, Victor Kraatz, Canada
1970 ......Ljudmila Pakhomova, Aleksandr Gorshkov,	2004 ......Tatiana Navka, Roman Kostomarov, Russia
USSR	2005 ......Tatiana Navka, Roman Kostomarov, Russia
1971 ......Ljudmila Pakhomova, Aleksandr Gorshkov	2006 ......Albena Denkova, Maxim Staviski, Bulgaria
USSR	2007 ......Albena Denkova ,Maxim Staviski, Bulgaria
1972 ......Ljudmila Pakhomova, Aleksandr Gorshkov	
USSR	
1973 ......Ljudmila Pakhomova, Aleksandr Gorshkov	
USSR	
1974 ......Ljudmila Pakhomova, Aleksandr Gorshkov	
USSR	
1975 ......Irina Moiseeva, Andreij Minenkov, USSR	
1976 ......Ljudmila Pakhomova, Aleksandr Gorshkov	
USSR	

CHAMPIONS OF THE UNITED STATES

The championships held in 1914, 1918, 1920 and 1921 under the auspices of the International Skating Union of America were open to Canadians, although the competitions were considered to be United States championships. Beginning in 1922, the championships have been held under the auspices of the United States Figure Skating Association.

Women

1914 ....Theresa Weld, SC of Boston	1962 ....Barbara Roles Pursley, Arctic Blades FSC
1915–17 .....No competition	1963 ....Lorraine G. Hanlon, SC of Boston
1918...........Rosemary S. Beresford, New York SC	1964 ....Peggy Fleming, Arctic Blades FSC
1919 ....No competition	1965 ....Peggy Fleming, Arctic Blades FSC
1920 ....Theresa Weld, SC of Boston	1966 ....Peggy Fleming, City of Colorado Springs
1921 ....Theresa Weld Blanchard, SC of Boston	1967 ....Peggy Fleming, Broadmoor SC
1922 ....Theresa Weld Blanchard, SC of Boston	1968 ....Peggy Fleming, Broadmoor SC
1923 ....Theresa Weld Blanchard, SC of Boston	1969 ....Janet Lynn, Wagon Wheel FSC
1924 ....Theresa Weld Blanchard, SC of Boston	1970 ....Janet Lynn, Wagon Wheel FSC
1925 ....Beatrix Loughran, New York SC	1971 ....Janet Lynn, Wagon Wheel FSC
1926 ....Beatrix Loughran, New York SC	1972 ....Janet Lynn, Wagon Wheel FSC
1927 ....Beatrix Loughran, New York SC	1973 ....Janet Lynn, Wagon Wheel FSC
1928 ....Maribel Y. Vinson, SC of Boston	1974 ....Dorothy Hamill, SC of New York
1929 ....Maribel Y. Vinson, SC of Boston	1975 ....Dorothy Hamill, SC of New York
1930 ....Maribel Y. Vinson, SC of Boston	1976 ....Dorothy Hamill, SC of New York
1931 ....Maribel Y. Vinson, SC of Boston	1977 ....Linda Fratianne, Los Angeles FSC
1932 ....Maribel Y. Vinson, SC of Boston	1978 ....Linda Fratianne, Los Angeles FSC
1933 ....Maribel Y. Vinson, SC of Boston	1979 ....Linda Fratianne, Los Angeles FSC
1934 ....Suzanne Davis, SC of Boston	1980 ....Linda Fratianne, Los Angeles FSC
1935 ....Maribel Y. Vinson, SC of Boston	1981 ....Elaine Zayak, SC of New York
1936 ....Maribel Y. Vinson, SC of Boston	1982 ....Rosalynn Sumners, Seattle SC
1937 ....Maribel Y. Vinson, SC of Boston	1983 ....Rosalynn Sumners, Seattle SC
1938 ....Joan Tozzer, SC of Boston	1984 ....Rosalynn Sumners, Seattle SC
1939 ....Joan Tozzer, SC of Boston	1985 ....Tiffany Chin, San Diego FSC
1940 ....Joan Tozzer, SC of Boston	1986 ....Debi Thomas, Los Angeles FSC
1941 ....Jane Vaughn, Philadelphia SC & HS	1987 ....Jill Trenary, Broadmoor SC
1942 ....Jane Vaughn Sullivan, Phila. SC & HS	1988 ....Debi Thomas, Los Angeles FSC
1943...........Gretchen Van Zandt Merrill, SC of Boston	1989 ....Jill Trenary, Broadmoor SC
1944...........Gretchen Van Zandt Merrill, SC of Boston	1990 ....Jill Trenary, Broadmoor SC
1945 ....Gretchen Van Zandt Merrill, SC of Boston	1991 ....Tonya Harding, Carousel FSC
1946 ....Gretchen Van Zandt Merrill, SC of Boston	1992 ....Kristi Yamaguchi, St Moritz ISC
1947...........Gretchen Van Zandt Merrill, SC of Boston	1993 ....Nancy Kerrigan, Colonial FSC
1948 ....Gretchen Van Zandt Merrill, SC of Boston	1994 ....Tonya Harding, Portland FSC
1949 ....Yvonne Claire Sherman, SC of New York	1995 ....Nicole Bobek, Los Angeles FSC
1950 ....Yvonne Claire Sherman, SC of New York	1996 ....Michelle Kwan, Los Angeles FSC
1951 ....Sonya Klopfer, Junior SC of New York	1997 ....Tara Lipinski, Detroit SC
1952 ....Tenley E. Albright, SC of Boston	1998 ....Michelle Kwan, Los Angeles FSC
1953 ....Tenley E. Albright, SC of Boston	1999 ....Michelle Kwan, Los Angeles FSC
1954 ....Tenley E. Albright, SC of Boston	2000 ....Michelle Kwan, Los Angeles FSC
1955 ....Tenley E. Albright, SC of Boston	2001 ....Michelle Kwan, Los Angeles FSC
1956 ....Tenley E. Albright, SC of Boston	2002 ....Michelle Kwan, Los Angeles FSC
1957 ....Carol E. Heiss, SC of New York	2003 ....Michelle Kwan, Los Angeles FSC
1958 ....Carol E. Heiss, SC of New York	2004 ....Michelle Kwan, Los Angeles FSC
1959 ....Carol E. Heiss, SC of New York	2005 ....Michelle Kwan, Los Angeles FSC
1960 ....Carol E. Heiss, SC of New York	2006 ....Sasha Cohen, Orange County FSC
1961 ....Laurence R. Owen, SC of Boston	2007.........Kimmie Meissner, Univ. of Delaware FSC

Men

1914 ....Norman M. Scott, WC of Montreal	1930 ....Roger F. Turner, SC of Boston
1915–17 .....No competition	1931 ....Roger F. Turner, SC of Boston
1918 ....Nathaniel W. Niles, SC of Boston	1932 ....Roger F. Turner, SC of Boston
1919 ....No competition	1933 ....Roger F. Turner, SC of Boston
1920 ....Sherwin C. Badger, SC of Boston	1934 ....Roger F. Turner, SC of Boston
1921 ....Sherwin C. Badger, SC of Boston	1935 ....Robin H. Lee, SC of New York
1922 ....Sherwin C. Badger, SC of Boston	1936 ....Robin H. Lee, SC of New York
1923 ....Sherwin C. Badger, SC of Boston	1937 ....Robin H. Lee, SC of New York
1924 ....Sherwin C. Badger, SC of Boston	1938 ....Robin H. Lee, Chicago FSC
1925 ....Nathaniel W. Niles, SC of Boston	1939 ....Robin H. Lee, St Paul FSC
1926 ....Chris I. Christenson, Twin City FSC	1940 ....Eugene Turner, Los Angeles FSC
1927 ....Nathaniel W. Niles, SC of Boston	1941 ....Eugene Turner, Los Angeles FSC
1928 ....Roger F. Turner, SC of Boston	1942 ....Robert Specht, Chicago FSC
1929 ....Roger F. Turner, SC of Boston	1943 ....Arthur R. Vaughn Jr., Phila. SC & HS

CHAMPIONS OF THE UNITED STATES *(CONT.)*
Men *(Cont.)*

1944–45 .....No competition	1977 ....Charles Tickner, Denver FSC
1946 ....Dick Button, Philadelphia SC & HS	1978 ....Charles Tickner, Denver FSC
1947 ....Dick Button, Philadelphia SC & HS	1979 ....Charles Tickner, Denver FSC
1948 ....Dick Button, Philadelphia SC & HS	1980 ....Charles Tickner, Denver FSC
1949 ....Dick Button, Philadelphia SC & HS	1981 ....Scott Hamilton, Philadelphia SC & HS
1950 ....Dick Button, SC of Boston	1982 ....Scott Hamilton, Philadelphia SC & HS
1951 ....Dick Button, SC of Boston	1983 ....Scott Hamilton, Philadelphia SC & HS
1952 ....Dick Button, SC of Boston	1984 ....Scott Hamilton, Philadelphia SC & HS
1953 ....Hayes Alan Jenkins, Cleveland SC	1985 ....Brian Boitano, Peninsula FSC
1954 ....Hayes Alan Jenkins, Broadmoor SC	1986 ....Brian Boitano, Peninsula FSC
1955 ....Hayes Alan Jenkins, Broadmoor SC	1987 ....Brian Boitano, Peninsula FSC
1956 ....Hayes Alan Jenkins, Broadmoor SC	1988 ....Brian Boitano, Peninsula FSC
1957 ....David Jenkins, Broadmoor SC	1989 ....Christopher Bowman, Los Angeles FSC
1958 ....David Jenkins, Broadmoor SC	1990 ....Todd Eldredge, Los Angeles FSC
1959 ....David Jenkins, Broadmoor SC	1991 ....Todd Eldredge, Los Angeles FSC
1960 ....David Jenkins, Broadmoor SC	1992 ....Christopher Bowman, Los Angeles FSC
1961 ....Bradley R. Lord, SC of Boston	1993 ....Scott Davis, Broadmoor SC
1962 ....Monty Hoyt, Broadmoor SC	1994 ....Scott Davis, Broadmoor SC
1963 ....Thomas Litz, Hershey FSC	1995 ....Todd Eldredge, Detroit SC
1964 ....Scott Ethan Allen, SC of New York	1996 ....Rudy Galindo, St Moritz ISC
1965 ....Gary C. Visconti, Detroit SC	1997 ....Todd Eldredge, Detroit SC
1966 ....Scott Ethan Allen, SC of New York	1998 ....Todd Eldredge, Detroit SC
1967 ....Gary C. Visconti, Detroit SC	1999 ....Michael Weiss, Washington FSC
1968 ....Tim Wood, Detroit SC	2000 ....Michael Weiss, Washington FSC
1969 ....Tim Wood, Detroit SC	2001 ....Timothy Goebel, Winterhurst FSC
1970 ....Tim Wood, City of Colorado Springs	2002 ....Todd Eldredge, Los Angeles FSC
1971 ....John Misha Petkevich, Great Falls FSC	2003 ....Michael Weiss, Washington FSC
1972 ....Kenneth Shelley, Arctic Blades FSC	2004 ....Johnny Weir, SC of New York
1973 ....Gordon McKellen Jr., SC of Lake Placid	2005 ....Johnny Weir, SC of New York
1974 ....Gordon McKellen Jr., SC of Lake Placid	2006 ....Johnny Weir, SC of New York
1975 ....Gordon McKellen Jr., SC of Lake Placid	2007 ....Evan Lysacek, DuPage FSC
1976 ....Terry Kubicka, Arctic Blades FSC	

Pairs

1914.....Jeanne Chevalier, Norman M. Scott, WC of Montreal	1933.....Maribel Y. Vinson, George E. B. Hill, SC of Boston
1915–17 No competition	1934.....Grace E. Madden, James L. Madden, SC of Boston
1918.....Theresa Weld, Nathaniel W. Niles, SC of Boston	1935.....Maribel Y. Vinson, George E. B. Hill, SC of Boston
1919.....No competition	1936.....Maribel Y. Vinson, George E. B. Hill, SC of Boston
1920.....Theresa Weld, Nathaniel W. Niles, SC of Boston	1937.....Maribel Y. Vinson, George E. B. Hill, SC of Boston
1921.....Theresa Weld Blanchard, Nathaniel W. Niles, SC of Boston	1938.....Joan Tozzer, M. Bernard Fox, SC of Boston
1922.....Theresa Weld Blanchard, Nathaniel W. Niles, SC of Boston	1939.....Joan Tozzer, M. Bernard Fox, SC of Boston
1923.....Theresa Weld Blanchard, Nathaniel W. Niles, SC of Boston	1940.....Joan Tozzer, M. Bernard Fox, SC of Boston
1924.....Theresa Weld Blanchard, Nathaniel W. Niles, SC of Boston	1941.....Donna Atwood, Eugene Turner, Mercury FSC/Los Angeles FSC
1925.....Theresa Weld Blanchard, Nathaniel W. Niles, SC of Boston	1942.....Doris Schubach, Walter Noffke, Springfield Ice Birds
1926.....Theresa Weld Blanchard, Nathaniel W. Niles, SC of Boston	1943.....Doris Schubach, Walter Noffke, Springfield Ice Birds
1927.....Theresa Weld Blanchard, Nathaniel W. Niles, SC of Boston	1944.....Doris Schubach, Walter Noffke, Springfield Ice Birds
1928.....Maribel Y. Vinson, Thornton L. Coolidge, SC of Boston	1945.....Donna Jeanne Pospisil, Jean-Pierre Brunet, SC of New York
1929.....Maribel Y. Vinson, Thornton L. Coolidge, SC of Boston	1946.....Donna Jeanne Pospisil, Jean-Pierre Brunet, SC of New York
1930.....Beatrix Loughran, Sherwin C. Badger, SC of New York	1947.....Yvonne Claire Sherman, Robert J. Swenning, SC of New York
1931.....Beatrix Loughran, Sherwin C. Badger, SC of New York	1948.....Karol Kennedy, Peter Kennedy, Seattle SC
1932.....Beatrix Loughran, Sherwin C. Badger, SC of New York	1949.....Karol Kennedy, Peter Kennedy, Seattle SC
	1950.....Karol Kennedy, Peter Kennedy, Broadmoor SC

CHAMPIONS OF THE UNITED STATES *(CONT.)*
Pairs *(Cont.)*

1951.....Karol Kennedy, Peter Kennedy,
Broadmoor SC
1952.....Karol Kennedy, Peter Kennedy,
Broadmoor SC
1953.....Carole Ann Ormaca, Robin Greiner,
SC of Fresno
1954.....Carole Ann Ormaca, Robin Greiner,
SC of Fresno
1955.....Carole Ann Ormaca, Robin Greiner,
St Moritz ISC
1956.....Carole Ann Ormaca, Robin Greiner,
St Moritz ISC
1957.....Nancy Rouillard Ludington, Ronald Ludington,
Commonwealth FSC/SC of Boston
1958.....Nancy Rouillard Ludington, Ronald Ludington,
Commonwealth FSC/SC of Boston
1959.....Nancy Rouillard Ludington, Ronald Ludington,
Commonwealth FSC
1960.....Nancy Rouillard Ludington, Ronald Ludington,
Commonwealth FSC
1961.....Maribel Y. Owen, Dudley S. Richards,
SC of Boston
1962.....Dorothyann Nelson, Pieter Kollen,
Village of Lake Placid
1963.....Judianne Fotheringill, Jerry J. Fotheringill,
Broadmoor SC
1964.....Judianne Fotheringill, Jerry J. Fotheringill,
Broadmoor SC
1965.....Vivian Joseph, Ronald Joseph, Chicago FSC
1966.....Cynthia Kauffman, Ronald Kauffman,
Seattle SC
1967.....Cynthia Kauffman, Ronald Kauffman,
Seattle SC
1968.....Cynthia Kauffman, Ronald Kauffman,
Seattle SC
1969.....Cynthia Kauffman, Ronald Kauffman,
Seattle SC
1970.....Jo Jo Starbuck, Kenneth Shelley,
Arctic Blades FSC
1971.....Jo Jo Starbuck, Kenneth Shelley,
Arctic Blades FSC
1972.....Jo Jo Starbuck, Kenneth Shelley,
Arctic Blades FSC
1973.....Melissa Militano, Mark Militano,
SC of New York
1974.....Melissa Militano, Johnny Johns,
SC of New York/Detroit SC
1975.....Melissa Militano, Johnny Johns,
SC of New York/Detroit SC
1976.....Tai Babilonia, Randy Gardner, LA FSC

1977.....Tai Babilonia, Randy Gardner, LA FSC
1978.....Tai Babilonia, Randy Gardner,
Los Angeles FSC/Santa Monica FSC
1979.....Tai Babilonia, Randy Gardner,
Los Angeles FSC/Santa Monica FSC
1980.....Tai Babilonia, Randy Gardner,
Los Angeles FSC/Santa Monica FSC
1981.....Caitlin Carruthers, Peter Carruthers,
SC of Wilmington
1982.....Caitlin Carruthers, Peter Carruthers,
SC of Wilmington
1983.....Caitlin Carruthers, Peter Carruthers,
SC of Wilmington
1984.....Caitlin Carruthers, Peter Carruthers,
SC of Wilmington
1985.....Jill Watson, Peter Oppegard, LA FSC
1986.....Gillian Wachsman, Todd Waggoner,
SC of Wilmington
1987.....Jill Watson, Peter Oppegard, LA FSC
1988.....Jill Watson, Peter Oppegard, LA FSC
1989.....Kristi Yamaguchi, Rudy Galindo, St Mortiz ISC
1990.....Kristi Yamaguchi, Rudy Galindo, St Mortiz ISC
1991.....Natasha Kuchiki, Todd Sand, LA FSC
1992.....Calla Urbanski, Rocky Marval,
U of Delaware FSC/SC of New York
1993.....Calla Urbanski, Rocky Marval,
U of Delaware FSC/SC of New York
1994.....Jenni Meno, Todd Sand,
Winterhurst FSC/Los Angeles FSC
1995.....Jenni Meno, Todd Sand,
Winterhurst FSC/Los Angeles FSC
1996.....Jenni Meno, Todd Sand,
Winterhurst FSC/Los Angeles FSC
1997.....Kyoko Ina, Jason Dungjen, SC of New York
1998.....Kyoko Ina, Jason Dungjen, SC of New York
1999.....Danielle Hartsell, Steve Hartsell, Detroit SC
2000.....Kyoko Ina, John Zimmerman,
SC of New York/Birmingham FSC
2001.....Kyoko Ina, John Zimmerman,
SC of New York/Birmingham FSC
2002.....Kyoko Ina, John Zimmerman,
SC of New York/Birmingham FSC
2003.....Tiffany Scott, Philip Dulebohn, Colonial FSC/
Univ of Delaware FSC
2004.....Rena Inoue, John Baldwin, All Year FSC
2005.....Kathryn Orscher, Garrett Lucash,
Charter Oak FSC
2006.....Rena Inoue, John Baldwin, All Year FSC
2007.....Brooke Castile, Benjamin Okolski, Arctic FSC

Dance

1914......Waltz: Theresa Weld, Nathaniel W. Niles,
SC of Boston
1915–19..No competition
1920......Waltz: Theresa Weld, Nathaniel W. Niles,
SC of Boston
Fourteenstep: Gertrude Cheever Porter,
Irving Brokaw, New York SC
1921......Waltz and Fourteenstep: Theresa Weld
Blanchard, Nathaniel W. Niles, SC of Boston
1922......Waltz: Beatrix Loughran, Edward M.
Howland, New York SC/SC of Boston
Fourteenstep: Theresa Weld Blanchard,
Nathaniel W. Niles, SC of Boston

1923......Waltz: Mr. & Mrs. Henry W. Howe,
New York SC
Fourteenstep: Sydney Goode, James B.
Greene, New York SC
1924......Waltz: Rosaline Dunn, Frederick Gabel,
New York SC
Fourteenstep: Sydney Goode, James B.
Greene, New York SC
1925......Waltz and Fourteenstep: Virginia Slattery,
Ferrier T. Martin, New York SC
1926......Waltz: Rosaline Dunn, Joseph K. Savage,
New York SC
Fourteenstep: Sydney Goode, James B.

CHAMPIONS OF THE UNITED STATES *(CONT.)*

Dance *(Cont.)*

Greene, New York SC

1927 ......Waltz and Fourteenstep: Rosaline Dunn, Joseph K. Savage, New York SC

1928 ......Waltz: Rosaline Dunn, Joseph K. Savage, New York SC
Fourteenstep: Ada Bauman Kelly, George T. Braakman, New York SC

1929 ......Waltz and Original Dance combined: Edith C. Secord, Joseph K. Savage, SC of New York

1930 ......Waltz: Edith C. Secord, Joseph K. Savage, SC of New York
Original: Clara Rotch Frothingham, George E. B. Hill, SC of Boston

1931 ......Waltz: Edith C. Secord, Ferrier T. Martin, SC of New York
Original: Theresa Weld Blanchard, Nathaniel W. Niles, SC of Boston

1932 ......Waltz: Edith C. Secord, Joseph K. Savage, SC of New York
Original: Clara Rotch Frothingham, George E. B. Hill, SC of Boston

1933 ......Waltz: Ilse Twaroschk, Frederick F. Fleishmann, Brooklyn FSC
Original: Suzanne Davis, Frederick Goodridge, SC of Boston

1934 ......Waltz: Nettie C. Prantel, Roy Hunt, SC of New York
Original: Suzanne Davis, Frederick Goodridge, SC of Boston

1935 ......Waltz: Nettie C. Prantel, Roy Hunt, SC of New York

1936 ......Marjorie Parker, Joseph K. Savage, SC of New York

1937 ......Nettie C. Prantel, Harold Hartshorne, SC of New York

1938 ......Nettie C. Prantel, Harold Hartshorne, SC of New York

1939 ......Sandy Macdonald, Harold Hartshorne, SC of New York

1940 ......Sandy Macdonald, Harold Hartshorne, SC of New York

1941 ......Sandy Macdonald, Harold Hartshorne, SCNY

1942 ......Edith B. Whetstone, Alfred N. Richards, Jr, Philadelphia SC & HS

1943 ......Marcella May, James Lochead Jr., Skate & Ski Club

1944 ......Marcella May, James Lochead Jr., Skate & Ski Club

1945 ......Kathe Mehl Williams, Robert J. Swenning, SC of New York

1946 ......Anne Davies, Carleton C. Hoffner Jr., Washington FSC

1947 ......Lois Waring, Walter H. Bainbridge Jr., Baltimore FSC/Washigton FSC

1948 ......Lois Waring, Walter H. Bainbridge Jr., Baltimore FSC/Washington FSC

1949 ......Lois Waring, Walter H. Bainbridge Jr., Baltimore FSC/Washington FSC

1950 ......Lois Waring, Michael McGean, Baltimore FSC

1951 ......Carmel Bodel, Edward L. Bodel, St. Moritz ISC

1952 ......Lois Waring, Michael McGean, Baltimore FSC

1953 ......Carol Ann Peters, Daniel C. Ryan, Washington FSC

1954 ......Carmel Bodel, Edward L. Bodel, St Moritz ISC

1955 ......Carmel Bodel, Edward L. Bodel, St Moritz ISC

1956 ......Joan Zamboni, Roland Junso, Arctic Blades FSC

1957 ......Sharon McKenzie, Bert Wright, Los Angeles FSC

1958 ......Andree Anderson, Donald Jacoby, Buffalo SC

1959 ......Andree Anderson Jacoby, Donald Jacoby, Buffalo SC

1960 ......Margie Ackles, Charles W. Phillips Jr., Los Angeles FSC/Arctic Blades FSC

1961 ......Diane C. Sherbloom, Larry Pierce, Los Angeles FSC/WC of Indianapolis

1962 ......Yvonne N. Littlefield, Peter F. Betts, Arctic Blades FSC/ Paramount, CA

1963 ......Sally Schantz, Stanley Urban, SC of Boston/Buffalo SC

1964 ......Darlene Streich, Charles D. Fetter Jr., WC of Indianapolis

1965 ......Kristin Fortune, Dennis Sveum, Los Angeles FSC

1966 ......Kristin Fortune, Dennis Sveum, Los Angeles FSC

1967 ......Lorna Dyer, John Carrell, Broadmoor SC

1968 ......Judy Schwomeyer, James Sladky, WC of Indianapolis/Genesee FSC

1969 ......Judy Schwomeyer, James Sladky, WC of Indianapolis/Genesee FSC

1970 ......Judy Schwomeyer, James Sladky, WC of Indianapolis/Genesee FSC

1971 ......Judy Schwomeyer, James Sladky, WC of Indianapolis/Genesee FSC

1972 ......Judy Schwomeyer, James Sladky, WC of Indianapolis/Genesee FSC

1973 ......Mary Karen Campbell, Johnny Johns, Lansing SC/Detroit SC

1974 ......Colleen O'Connor, Jim Millns, Broadmoor SC/ City of Colorado Springs

1975 ......Colleen O'Connor, Jim Millns, Broadmoor SC

1976 ......Colleen O'Connor, Jim Millns, Broadmoor SC

1977 ......Judy Genovesi, Kent Weigle, SC of Hartford/Charter Oak FSC

1978 ......Stacey Smith, John Summers, SC of Wilmington

1979 ......Stacey Smith, John Summers, SC of Wilmington

1980 ......Stacey Smith, John Summers, SC of Wilmington

1981 ......Judy Blumberg, Michael Seibert, Broadmoor SC/ISC of Indianapolis

1982 ......Judy Blumberg, Michael Seibert, Broadmoor SC/ISC of Indianapolis

1983 ......Judy Blumberg, Michael Seibert, Pittsburgh FSC

1984 ......Judy Blumberg, Michael Seibert, Pittsburgh FSC

1985 ......Judy Blumberg, Michael Seibert, Pittsburgh FSC

1986 ......Renee Roca, Donald Adair, Genesee FSC/Academy FSC

1987 ......Suzanne Semanick, Scott Gregory, U of Delaware SC

1988 ......Suzanne Semanick, Scott Gregory, U of Delaware SC

1989 ......Susan Wynne, Joseph Druar, Broadmoor SC/Seattle SC

1990 ......Susan Wynne, Joseph Druar, Broadmoor SC/Seattle SC

CHAMPIONS OF THE UNITED STATES (CONT.)
Dance (Cont.)

1991 ....Elizabeth Punsalan, Jerod Swallow, Broadmoor SC
1992 ......April Sargent, Russ Witherby, Ogdensburg FSC/U of Delaware FSC
1993 ......Renee Roca, Gorsha Sur, Broadmoor SC
1994 ......Elizabeth Punsalan, Jerod Swallow, Broadmoor SC/Detroit SC
1995 ......Renee Roca, Gorsha Sur, Broadmoor SC
1996 ......Elizabeth Punsalan, Jerod Swallow, Detroit SC
1997 ......Elizabeth Punsalan, Jerod Swallow, Detroit SC
1998 ......Elizabeth Punsalan, Jerod Swallow, Detroit SC

1999 ......Naomi Lang, Peter Tchernyshev, Detroit SC
2000 ......Naomi Lang, Peter Tchernyshev, Detroit SC
2001 ......Naomi Lang, Peter Tchernyshev, Detroit SC
2002 ......Naomi Lang, Peter Tchernyshev, American Academy FSC
2003 ......Naomi Lang, Peter Tchernyshev, American Academy FSC
2004 ......Tanith Belbin, Ben Agosto, Detroit SC
2005 ......Tanith Belbin, Ben Agosto, Detroit SC
2006 ......Tanith Belbin, Ben Agosto, Arctic FSC
2007 ......Tanith Belbin, Ben Agosto, Arctic FSC

Fishing

Saltwater Fishing Records

Species	Weight	Where Caught	Date	Angler
Albacore	88 lb 2 oz	Gran Canaria, Canary Islands	Nov 19, 1977	Siegfried Dickemann
Amberjack, greater	155 lb 12 oz	Bermuda	Aug 16, 1992	Larry Trott
Amberjack, Pacific	104 lb	Baja California, Mexico	July 4, 1984	Richard Cresswell
Angler	126 lb 12 oz	Sognefjorden Hoyanger, Norway	July 4, 1996	Gunnar Thorsteinsen
Barracuda, great	85 lb	Christmas Island, Kiribati	April 11, 1992	John W. Helfrich
Barracuda, Mexican	22 lb 8 oz	Pinas Bay, Panama	Nov 11, 2005	Frank Ibarra
Barracuda, pickhandle	29 lb 12 oz	Malindi, Kenya	Nov 7, 2002	Paul Gerritsen
Bass, barred sand	13 lb 3 oz	Huntington Beach, California	Aug 29, 1988	Robert Halal
Bass, black sea	10 lb 4 oz	Virginia Beach, Virginia	Jan 1, 2000	Allan P. Paschall
Bass, European	20 lb 14 oz	Cap d'Agde, France	Sept. 8, 1999	Robert Mari
Bass, giant sea	563 lb 8 oz	Anacapa Island, California	Aug 20, 1968	James D. McAdam Jr.
Bass, striped	78 lb 8 oz	Atlantic City, New Jersey	Sept 21, 1982	Albert R. McReynolds
Bluefish	31 lb 12 oz	Hatteras Inlet, North Carolina	Jan 30, 1972	James M. Hussey
Bonefish	19 lb	Zululand, South Africa	May 26, 1962	Brian W. Batchelor
Bonito, Atlantic	18 lb 4 oz	Faial Island, Azores	July 8, 1953	D.G. Higgs
Bonito, Pacific	21 lb 5 oz	181 Spot, California	Oct 10, 2003	Kim Larson
Cabezon	23 lb	Juan De Fuca Strait, Washington	Aug 4, 1990	Wesley S. Hunter
Cobia	135 lb 9 oz	Shark Bay, Australia	July 9, 1985	Peter W. Goulding
Cod, Atlantic	98 lb 12 oz	Isle of Shoals, New Hampshire	June 8, 1969	Alphonse Bielevich
Cod, Pacific	38 lb 9 oz	Hokkaido, Japan	Jan 16, 2005	Atsunori Takahita
Conger	133 lb 4 oz	South Devon, England	June 5, 1995	Vic Evans
Dolphinfish	87 lb	Papagallo Gulf, Costa Rica	Sept 25, 1976	Manuel Salazar
Drum, black	113 lb 1 oz	Lewes, Delaware	Sept 15, 1975	Gerald M. Townsend
Drum, red	94 lb 2 oz	Avon, North Carolina	Nov 7, 1984	David Deuel
Eel, American	9 lb 4 oz	Cape May, New Jersey	Nov 9, 1995	Jeff Pennick
Eel, marbled	36 lb 1 oz	Durban, South Africa	June 10, 1984	Ferdie van Nooten
Flounder, southern	20 lb 9 oz	Nassau Sound, Florida	Dec 23, 1983	Larenza W. Mungin
Flounder, summer	22 lb 7 oz	Montauk, New York	Sept 15, 1975	Charles Nappi
Grouper, Warsaw	436 lb 12 oz	Destin, Florida	Dec 22, 1985	Steve Haeusler
Halibut, Atlantic	418 lb 13 oz	Vannaya Troms, Norway	July 28, 2004	Thomas Nielsen
Halibut, California	58 lb 9 oz	Santa Rosa Island, California	June 26, 1999	Roger W. Borrell
Halibut, Pacific	459 lb	Dutch Harbor, Alaska	June 11, 1996	Jack Tragis
Jack, crevalle	58 lb 6 oz	Barro do Kwanza, Angola	Dec 10, 2000	Nuno A. P. da Silva
Jack, horse-eye	29 lb 8 oz	Ascencion Island, S. Atlantic Ocean	May 28, 1993	Mike Hanson
Jack, Pacific crevalle	39 lb	Playa Zancudo, Costa Rica	Mar 3, 1997	Ingrid Callaghan
Jewfish	680 lb	Fernandina Beach, Florida	May 20, 1961	Lynn Joyner
Kawakawa	29 lb	Isla Clarion, Mexico	Dec 17, 1986	Ronald Nakamura
Lingcod	77 lb 3 oz	Homer, Alaska	July 5, 2006	Kindal Murry
Mackerel, cero	17 lb 2 oz	Islamorada, Florida	Apr 5, 1986	G. Michael Mills
Mackerel, king	93 lb	San Juan, Puerto Rico	Apr 18, 1999	Steve Perez Graulau
Mackerel, narrowbarred	99 lb	Natal, South Africa	Mar 14, 1982	Michael J. Wilkinson
Mackerel, Spanish	13 lb	Ocracoke Inlet, North Carolina	Nov 4, 1987	Robert Cranton
Marlin, Atlantic blue	1,402 lb 2 oz	Vitoria, Brazil	Feb 29, 1992	Paulo R.A. Amorim
Marlin, black	1,560 lb	Cabo Blanco, Peru	Aug 4, 1953	Alfred C. Glassell Jr.
Marlin, Pacific blue	1,376 lb	Kaaiwi Point, Hawaii	May 31, 1982	J.W. de Beaubien
Marlin, striped	494 lb	Tutukaka, New Zealand	Jan 16, 1986	Bill Boniface
Marlin, white	181 lb 14 oz	Vitoria, Brazil	Dec 8, 1979	Evandro Luiz Coser

Saltwater Fishing Records *(Cont.)*

Species	Weight	Where Caught	Date	Angler
Permit	60 lb	Ilha do Mel Paranagua, Brazil	Dec 14, 2002	Renato P. Fiedler
Pollock	50 lb	Salstraumen, Norway	Nov 30, 1995	Thor Magnus-Lékang
Pompano, African	50 lb 8 oz	Daytona Beach, Florida	Apr 21, 1990	Tom Sargent
Roosterfish	114 lb	La Paz, Mexico	June 1, 1960	Abe Sackheim
Runner, blue	11 lb 2 oz	Dauphin Island, Alaska	June 28, 1997	Stacey M. Moiren
Runner, rainbow	37 lb 9 oz	Isla Clarion, Mexico	Nov 21, 1991	Tom Pfleger
Sailfish, Atlantic	141 lb 1 oz	Luanda, Angola	Feb 19, 1994	Alfredo de Sousa Neves
Sailfish, Pacific	221 lb	Santa Cruz Island, Ecuador	Feb 12, 1947	Carl W. Stewart
Seabass, white	83 lb 12 oz	San Felipe, Mexico	Mar 31, 1953	Lyal C. Baumgardner
Seatrout, spotted	17 lb 7 oz	Ft. Pierce, Florida	May 11, 1995	Craig F. Carson
Shark, bigeye thresher	802 lb	Tutukaka, New Zealand	Feb 8, 1981	Dianne North
Shark, blue	528 lb	Montauk Point, New York	Aug 9, 2001	Joe Seidel
Shark, great hammrhd.	1280 lb	Boca Grande, Florida	May 23, 2006	Bucky Dennis
Shark, Greenland	1708 lb 9 oz	Trondheimsfjord, Norway	Oct 18, 1987	Terje Nordtvedt
Shark, porbeagle	507 lb	Caithness, Scotland	Mar 9, 1993	Christopher Bennet
Shark, shortfin mako	1221 lb	Chatham, Massachusetts	July 21, 2001	Luke Sweeney
Shark, tiger	1780 lb	Cherry Grove, South Carolina	June 14, 1964	Walter Maxwell
Shark, tope	72 lb 12 oz	Parengarenga Harbor, N.Z.	Dec 19, 1986	Melanie B. Feldman
Shark, white	2,664 lb	Ceduna, Australia	Apr 21, 1959	Alfred Dean
Skipjack, black	26 lb	Baja California, Mexico	Oct 23, 1991	Clifford K. Hamaishi
Snapper, cubera	124 lb 12 oz	Garden Bank, Louisiana	June 23, 2007	Marion Rose
Snook, common	53 lb 10 oz	Parismina Ranch, Costa Rica	Oct 18, 1978	Gilbert Ponzi
Spearfish, Mediter.	90 lb 13 oz	Madeira Island, Portugal	June 2, 1980	Joseph Larkin
Spearfish, longbill	127 lb 13 oz	Puerto Rico, Gran Canaria, Spain	May 20, 1999	Paul Cashmore
Spearfish, shortbill	81 lb 2 oz	White Island, New Zealand	Feb 2, 2006	Adrian Lewis
Swordfish	1182 lb	Iquique, Chile	May 7, 1953	Louis Marron
Tarpon	286 lb 9 oz	Rubane, Guinea-Bissau	Mar 20, 2003	Max Domecq
Tautog	25 lb	Ocean City, New Jersey	Jan 20, 1998	Anthony Monica
Tilapia, Mozambique	6 lb 13 oz	Loskop Dam, S Africa	Apr 4, 2003	Eugene C. Kruger
Trevally, bigeye	31 lb 8 oz	Poivre Island, Seychelles	Apr 23, 1997	Les Sampson
Trevally, giant	160 lb 7 oz	Kagoshima, Japan	May 22, 2006	Keiki Hamasaiki
Tuna, Atlantic bigeye	392 lb 6 oz	Puerto Rico, Gran Caneria, Spain	July 25, 1996	Dieter Vogel
Tuna, blackfin	49 lb 6 oz	Marathon, Florida	April 6, 2006	Matthew E. Pullen
Tuna, bluefin	1496 lb	Aulds Cove, Nova Scotia	Oct 26, 1979	Ken Fraser
Tuna, longtail	79 lb 2 oz	Montague Island, New South Wales, Australia	Apr 12, 1982	Tim Simpson
Tuna, Pacific bigeye	435 lb	Cabo Blanco, Peru	Apr 17, 1957	Russel Lee
Tuna, skipjack	45 lb 4 oz	Baja California, Mexico	Nov 16, 1996	Brian Evans
Tuna, southern bluefin	348 lb 5 oz	Whakatane, New Zealand	Jan 16, 1981	Rex Wood
Tuna, yellowfin	388 lb 12 oz	San Benedicto Is, Mexico	Apr 1, 1977	Curt Wiesenhutter
Tunny, little	35 lb 2 oz	Cape de Garde, Algeria	Dec 14, 1988	Jean Yves Chatard
Wahoo	184 lb	Cabo San Lucas, Mexico	July 29, 2005	Sara Hayward
Weakfish	19 lb 2 oz	Jones Beach Inlet, New York	Oct 11, 1984	Dennis Rooney
		Delaware Bay, Delaware	May 20, 1989	William E. Thomas
Yellowtail, California	92 lb 1 oz	Guadalupe Island, Mexico	Aug 4, 2004	Kevin Pfeif
Yellowtail, southern	114 lb 10 oz	Tauranga, New Zealand	Feb 5, 1984	Mike Godfrey

Freshwater Fishing Records

Species	Weight	Where Caught	Date	Angler
Barramundi	83 lb 7 oz	Lake Tinaroo, N Queensl'd, Aus.	Sept 23, 1999	David Powell
Bass, largemouth	22 lb 4 oz	Montgomery Lake, Georgia	June 2, 1932	George W. Perry
Bass, rock	3 lb	York River, Ontario	Aug 1, 1974	Peter Gulgin
		Lake Erie, Pennsylvania	June 18, 1998	Herbert Ratner Jr.
Bass, shoal	8 lb 12 oz	Apalatchicola River, Florida	Jan 28, 1995	Carl W. Davis
Bass, smallmouth	11 lb 15 oz	Dale Hollow, Tennessee	July 9, 1955	David Hayes
Bass, Suwannee	3 lb 14 oz	Suwannee River, Florida	Mar 2, 1985	Ronnie Everett
Bass, white	6 lb 13 oz	Orange, Virginia	July 31, 1989	Ronald Sprouse
Bass, whiterock	27 lb 5 oz	Greers Ferry Lake, Arkansas	Apr 24, 1997	Jerald Shaum
Bass, yellow	2 lb 9 oz	Waverly, Tennessee	Feb 27, 1998	John Chappell
Bluegill	4 lb 12 oz	Ketona Lake, Alabama	Apr 9, 1950	T.S. Hudson
Bowfin	21 lb 8 oz	Florence, South Carolina	Jan 29, 1980	Robert Harmon
Buffalo, bigmouth	70 lb 5 oz	Bastrop, Louisiana	Apr 21, 1980	Delbert Sisk
Buffalo, black	63 lb 6 oz	Mississippi River, Iowa	Aug 14, 1999	Jim Winters
Buffalo, smallmouth	82 lb 3 oz	Athens Lake, Georgia	June 6, 1993	Randy Collins
Bullhead, brown	6 lb 5 oz	Lake Mahopac, New York	Sept 8, 2002	Ray Lawrence
Bullhead, yellow	6 lb 6 oz	Drevel, Missouri	May 27, 2006	John R. Irvin
Burbot	18 lb 11 oz	Angenmanalren, Sweden	Oct 22, 1996	Margit Agren

Freshwater Fishing Records *(Cont.)*

Species	Weight	Where Caught	Date	Angler
Carp, common	75 lb 11 oz	Lac de St. Cassien, France	May 21, 1987	Leo van der Gugten
Catfish, blue	124 lb	Mississippi River, Illinois	May 21, 2005	Timothy E. Pruitt
Catfish, channel	58 lb	Santee-Cooper Reservoir, SC	July 7, 1964	W.B. Whaley
Catfish, flathead	123 lb	Elk City Reservoir, Indep., KS	May 14, 1998	Ken Paulie
Catfish, white	19 lb 5 oz	Oakdale, California	May 7, 2005	Russell D. Price
Char, Arctic	32 lb 9 oz	Tree River, Canada	July 30, 1981	Jeffrey Ward
Crappie, white	5 lb 3 oz	Enid Dam, Mississippi	July 31, 1957	Fred L. Bright
Dolly Varden	20 lb 14 oz	Wulik River, Alaska	July 7, 2001	Raz Reid
Dorado	55 lb 11 oz	Concorida, Argentina	Jan 11, 2006	Andre de Botton
Drum, freshwater	54 lb 8 oz	Nickajack Lake, Tennessee	Apr 20, 1972	Benny E. Hull
Gar, alligator	279 lb	Rio Grande River, Texas	Dec 2, 1951	Bill Valverde
Gar, Florida	10 lb	Florida Everglades, Florida	Jan 28, 2002	Herbert Ratner Jr.
Gar, longnose	50 lb 5 oz	Trinity River, Texas	July 30, 1954	Townsend Miller
Gar, shortnose	5 lb 12 oz	Rend Lake, Illinois	July 16, 1995	Donna K. Willmert
Gar, spotted	9 lb 12 oz	Lake Mexia, Texas	Apr 7, 1994	Rick Rivard
Grayling, Arctic	5 lb 15 oz	Katseyedie River, Northwest Territories	Aug 16, 1967	Jeanne P. Branson
Inconnu	53 lb	Pah River, Alaska	Aug 20, 1986	Lawrence Hudnall
Kokanee	9 lb 6 oz	Okanagan Lake, Vernon, B.C.	June 18, 1988	Norm Kuhn
Muskellunge	67 lb 8 oz	Hayward, Wisconsin	July 24, 1949	Cal Johnson
Muskellunge, tiger	51 lb 3 oz	Lac Vieux-Desert, Michigan	July 16, 1919	John Knobla
Peacock, speckled	27 lb	Rio Negro, Brazil	Dec 4, 1994	Gerald (Doc) Lawson
Perch, Nile	230 lb	Lake Nasser, Egypt	Dec 20, 2000	William Toth
Perch, white	3 lb 1 oz	Forest Hill Park, N.J.	May 6, 1989	Edward Tango
Perch, yellow	4 lb 3 oz	Bordentown, New Jersey	May 1, 1865	Dr. C. Abbot
Pickerel, chain	9 lb 6 oz	Homerville, Georgia	Feb 17, 1961	Baxley McQuaig Jr.
Pike, northern	55 lb 1 oz	Lake of Grefeern, West Germany	Oct 16, 1986	Lothar Louis
Redhorse, greater	9 lb 3 oz	Salmon River, Pulaski, New York	May 11, 1985	Jason Wilson
Redhorse, silver	11 lb 7 oz	Plum Creek, Wisconsin	May 29, 1985	Neal Long
Salmon, Atlantic	79 lb 2 oz	Tana River, Norway	1928	Henrik Henriksen
Salmon, Chinook	97 lb 4 oz	Kenai River, Alaska	May 17, 1985	Les Anderson
Salmon, chum	35 lb	Edye Pass, Canada	July 11, 1995	Todd A. Johansson
Salmon, coho	33 lb 4 oz	Pulaski, New York	Sep 27, 1989	Jerry Lifton
Salmon, pink	14 lb 13 oz	Monroe, Washington	Sep 30, 2001	Alexander Minerich
Salmon, sockeye	15 lb 3 oz	Kenai River, Alaska	Aug 9, 1987	Stan Roach
Sauger	8 lb 12 oz	Lake Sakakawea, North Dakota	Oct 6, 1971	Mike Fischer
Shad, American	11 lb 4 oz	Connecticut River, Massachusetts	May 19, 1986	Bob Thibodo
Sturgeon, white	468 lb	Benicia, California	July 9, 1983	Joey Pallotta III
Sunfish, green	2 lb 2 oz	Stockton Lake, Missouri	June 18, 1971	Paul M. Dilley
Sunfish, redbreast	1 lb 12 oz	Suwannee River, Florida	May 29, 1984	Alvin Buchanan
Sunfish, redear	5 lb 7 oz	Diverson Canal, Georgia	Nov 6, 1998	Amos M. Gay
Tigerfish, giant	97 lb	Zaire River, Kinshasa, Zaire	July 9, 1988	Raymond Houtmans
Trout, Apache	5 lb 3 oz	Apache Reservation, Arizona	May 29, 1991	John Baldwin
Trout, brook	14 lb 8 oz	Nipigon River, Ontario	July 1916	W.J. Cook
Trout, brown	40 lb 4 oz	Heber Springs, Arkansas	May 9, 1992	Howard (Rip) Collins
Trout, bull	32 lb	Lake Pond Oreille, Idaho	Oct 27, 1949	N.L. Higgins
Trout, cutthroat	41 lb	Pyramid Lake, Nevada	Dec 1925	John Skimmerhorn
Trout, golden	11 lb	Cook's Lake, Wyoming	Aug 5, 1948	Charles S. Reed
Trout, lake	72 lb	Great Bear Lake, Northwest Territories, Canada	Aug 19, 1995	Lloyd Bull
Trout, rainbow	43 lb 10 oz	Lake Deinfenbaker, Canada	June 5, 2007	Adam Konrad
Trout, tiger	20 lb 13 oz	Lake Michigan, Wisconsin	Aug 12, 1978	Pete M. Friedland
Walleye	25 lb	Old Hickory Lake, Tennessee	Aug 2, 1960	Mabry Harper
Warmouth	2 lb 7 oz	Yellow River, Holt, Florida	Oct 19, 1985	Tony D. Dempsey
Whitefish, lake	14 lb 6 oz	Meaford, Ontario	May 21, 1984	Dennis Laycock
Whitefish, mountain	5 lb 8 oz	Elbow River, Calgary, Alberta	Aug 1, 1995	Randy Woo
Whitefish, broad	9 lb	Tozitna River, Alaska	July 17, 1989	Al Mathews
Whitefish, round	6 lb	Putahow River, Manitoba	June 14, 1984	Allan J. Ristori
Zander	25 lb 2 oz	Trosa, Sweden	June 12, 1986	Harry Lee Tennison

World Champions — Men

All-Around

Year	Champion, Nation
1903	Joseph Martinez, France
1905	Marcel Lalue, France
1907	Joseph Czada, Czechoslovakia
1909	Marcos Torres, France
1911	Ferdinand Steiner, Czechoslovakia
1913	Marcos Torres, France
1922	Peter Sumi, Yugoslavia
	F. Pechacek, Czechoslovakia
1926	Peter Sumi, Yugoslavia
1930	Josip Primozic, Yugoslavia
1934	Eugene Mack, Switzerland
1938	Jan Gajdos, Czechoslovakia
1950	Walter Lehmann, Switzerland
1954	Valentin Mouratov, USSR
	Victor Chukarin, USSR
1958	Boris Shaklin, USSR
1962	Yuri Titov, USSR
1966	Mikhail Voronin, USSR
1970	Eizo Kenmotsu, Japan
1974	Shigeru Kasamatsu, Japan
1978	Nikolai Andrianov, USSR
1979	Alexander Ditiatin, USSR
1981	Yuri Korolev, USSR
1983	Dimitri Bilozertchev, USSR
1985	Yuri Korolev, USSR
1987	Dimitri Bilozertchev, USSR
1989	Igor Korobchinsky, USSR
1991	Grigori Misutin, CIS
1993	Vitaly Scherbo, Belarus
1994	Ivan Ivankov, Belarus
1995	Li Xiaoshuang, China
1997	Ivan Ivankov, Belarus
1999	Nicolae Krukov, Russia
2001	Feng Jing, China
2003	Paul Hamm, United States
2005	Hiroyuki Tomita, Japan
2007	Yang Wei, China

Pommel Horse

Year	Champion, Nation
1930	Josip Primozic, Yugoslavia
1934	Eugene Mack, Switzerland
1938	Michael Reusch, Switzerland
1950	Josef Stalder, Switzerland
1954	Grant Chaguinjan, USSR
1958	Boris Shaklin, USSR
1962	Miroslav Cerar, Yugoslavia
1966	Miroslav Cerar, Yugoslavia
1970	Miroslav Cerar, Yugoslavia
1974	Zoltan Magyar, Hungary
1978	Zoltan Magyar, Hungary
1979	Zoltan Magyar, Hungary
1981	Michael Mikolai, East Germany
1983	Dmitri Bilozertchev, USSR
1985	Valentin Moguilny, USSR
1987	Zsolt Borkai, Hungary
	Dmitri Bilozertchev, USSR
1989	Valentin Moguilny, USSR
1991	Valeri Belenki, USSR
1992	Pae Gil Su, North Korea
	Vitaly Scherbo, CIS
	Li Jing, China

Pommel Horse (Cont.)

Year	Champion, Nation
1993	Pae Gil Su, North Korea
1994	Marius Urzica, Romania
1995	Li Donghua, Switzerland
1996	Pae Gil Su, North Korea
1997	Valeri Belenki, Germany
1999	Alexei Nemov, Russia
2001	Marius Urzica, Romania
2003	Teng Haibin, China
	Takehiro Kashima, Japan
2005	Qin Xiao, China
2007	Qin Xiao, China

Floor Exercise

Year	Champion, Nation
1930	Josip Primozic, Yugoslavia
1934	Georges Miesz, Switzerland
1938	Jan Gajdos, Czechoslovakia
1950	Josef Stalder, Switzerland
1954	Valentin Mouratov, USSR
	Masao Takemoto, Japan
1958	Masao Takemoto, Japan
1962	Nobuyuki Aihara, Japan
	Yukio Endo, Japan
1966	Akinori Nakayama, Japan
1970	Akinori Nakayama, Japan
1974	Shigeru Kasamatsu, Japan
1978	Kurt Thomas, United States
1979	Kurt Thomas, United States
	Roland Brucker, East Germ.
1981	Yuri Korolev, USSR
	Li Yuejui, China
1983	Tong Fei, China
1985	Tong Fei, China
1987	Lou Yun, China
1989	Igor Korobchinsky, USSR
1991	Igor Korobchinsky, USSR
1993	Grigori Misutin, Ukraine
1994	Vitaly Scherbo, Belarus
1995	Vitaly Scherbo, Belarus
1996	Vitaly Scherbo, Belarus
1997	Alexei Nemov, Russia
1999	Alexei Nemov, Russia
2001	Marian Dragulescu, Romania
2003	Paul Hamm, United States
	Jordan Jovtchev, Bulgaria
2005	Diego Hypolito, Brazil
2007	Zou Kai, China

Rings

Year	Champion, Nation
1930	Emanuel Loffler, Czechoslovakia
1934	Alois Hudec, Czechoslovakia
1938	Alois Hudec, Czechoslovakia
1950	Walter Lehmann, Switzerland
1954	Albert Azarian, USSR
1958	Albert Azarian, USSR
1962	Yuri Titov, USSR
1966	Mikhail Voronin, USSR
1970	Akinori Nakayama, Japan
1974	N. Andrianov, USSR
	D. Grecu, Rom.
1978	Nikolai Andrianov, USSR
1979	Alexander Ditiatin, USSR
1981	Alexander Ditiatin, USSR

Rings (Cont.)

Year	Champion, Nation
1983	Dimitri Bilozertchev, USSR
1985	Li Ning, China
	Yuri Korolev, USSR
1987	Yuri Korolev, USSR
1989	Andreas Aguilar, West Germ.
1991	Grigory Misutin, USSR
1992	Vitaly Scherbo, CIS
1993	Yuri Chechi, Italy
1994	Yuri Chechi, Italy
1995	Yuri Chechi, Italy
1996	Yuri Chechi, Italy
1997	Yuri Chechi, Italy
1999	Zhen Dong, China
2001	Jordan Jovtchev, Bulgaria
2003	Jordan Jovtchev, Bulgaria
	Dimosthenis Tampakos, Greece
2005	Yuri Van Gelder, Netherlands
2007	Diego Hypolito, Brazil

Parallel Bars

Year	Champion, Nation
1930	Josip Primozic, Yugoslavia
1934	Eugene Mack, Switzerland
1938	Michael Reusch, Switzerland
1950	Hans Eugster, Switzerland
1954	Victor Chukarin, USSR
1958	Boris Shaklin, USSR
1962	Miroslav Cerar, Yugoslavia
1966	Sergei Diamidov, USSR
1970	Akinori Nakayama, Japan
1974	Eizo Kenmotsu, Japan
1978	Eizo Kenmotsu, Japan
1979	Bart Conner, United States
1981	Koji Gushiken, Japan
	Alexandr Ditiatin, USSR
1983	Vladimir Artemov, USSR
	Lou Yun, China
1985	Sylvio Kroll, East Germany
	Valentin Moguilny, USSR
1987	Vladimir Artemov, USSR
1989	Li Jing, China
	Vladimir Artemov, USSR
1991	Li Jing, China
1992	Li Jin, China
	Alexei Voropaev, CIS
1993	Vitaly Scherbo, Belarus
1994	Huang Liping, China
1995	Vitaly Scherbo, Belarus
1996	Rustam Sharipov, Ukraine
1997	Zhang Jinjing, China
1999	Joo-Hyung Lee, South Korea
2001	Sean Townsend, U.S.
2003	Li Xiao-Peng, China
2005	Mitja Petkovsek, Slovenia
2007	Mitja Petkovsek, Slovenia

High Bar

Year	Champion, Nation
1930	Istvan Pelle, Hungary
1934	Ernst Winter, Germany
1938	Michael Reusch, Switzerland
1950	Paavo Aaltonen, Finland
1954	Valentin Mouratov, USSR
1958	Boris Shaklin, USSR
1962	Takashi Ono, Japan
1966	Akinori Nakayama, Japan

World Champions — Men *(Cont.)*

High Bar *(Cont.)*

Year	Champion, Nation
1970	Eizo Kenmotsu, Japan
1974	Eberhard Gienger, W Germany
1978	Shigeru Kasamatsu, Japan
1979	Kurt Thomas, United States
1981	Alexander Takchev, USSR
1983	Dimitri Bilozertchev, USSR
1985	Tong Fei, China
1987	Dimitri Bilozertchev, USSR
1989	Li Chunyang, China
1991	Li Chunyang, China R. Buechner, Germ
1992	Grigori Misutin, CIS
1993	Sergei Kharkov, Russia
1994	Vitaly Scherbo, Belarus
1995	Andreas Wecker, Germany
1996	Jesús Carballo, Spain
1997	Jani Tanskanen, Finland
1999	Jesus Carballo, Spain
2001	Vlasios Maras, Greece

High Bar *(Cont.)*

Year	Champion, Nation
2003	Takehiro Kashima, Japan
2005	Vlasios Maras, Greece
2007	Fabian Hambuechen, Germ.

Vault

Year	Champion, Nation
1934	Eugene Mack, Switzerland
1938	Eugene Mack, Switzerland
1950	Ernst Gebendinger, Switzerland
1954	Leo Sotornik, Czechoslovakia
1958	Yuri Titov, USSR
1962	Premysel Krbec, Czechoslovakia
1966	Haruhiro Yamashita, Japan
1970	Mitsuo Tsukahara, Japan
1974	Shigeru Kasamatsu, Japan
1978	Junichi Shimizu, Japan
1979	Alexander Ditiatin, USSR
1981	Ralf-Peter Hemmann, East Germany

Vault *(Cont.)*

Year	Champion, Nation
1983	Arthur Akopian, USSR
1985	Yuri Korolev, USSR
1987	Lou Yun, China Sylvio Kroll, East Germany
1989	Joreg Behrend, East Germany
1991	Yoo Ok Youl, South Korea
1992	Yoo Ok Youl, South Korea
1993	Vitaly Scherbo, Belarus
1994	Vitaly Scherbo, Belarus
1995	G. Misutin, Ukraine A. Nemov, Russia
1996	Alexei Nemov, Russia
1997	Sergei Fedorchenko, Kazakhstan
1999	Li Xiao-Peng, China
2001	Marian Dragulescu, Romania
2003	Li Xiao-Peng, China
2005	Eichi Sekiguchi, Japan
2007	Leszek Blanik, Poland

World Champions — Women

All-Around

Year	Champion, Nation
1934	Vlasta Dekanova, Czechoslovakia
1938	Vlasta Dekanova, Czechoslovakia
1950	Helena Rakoczy, Poland
1954	Galina Roudiko, USSR
1958	Larissa Latynina, USSR
1962	Larissa Latynina, USSR
1966	Vera Caslavska, Czechoslovakia
1970	Ludmilla Tourischeva, USSR
1974	Ludmilla Tourischeva, USSR
1978	Elena Mukhina, USSR
1979	Nelli Kim, USSR
1981	Olga Bicherova, USSR
1983	Natalia Yurchenko, USSR
1985	Elena Shoushounova, USSR Oksana Omeliantchik, USSR
1987	Aurelia Dobre, Romania
1989	Svetlana Bouguinskaia, USSR
1991	Kim Zmeskal, United States
1993	Shannon Miller, United States
1994	Shannon Miller, United States
1995	Lilia Podkopayeva, Ukraine
1997	Svetlana Khorkina, Russia
1999	Maria Olaru, Romania
2001	Svetlana Khorkina, Russia
2003	Svetlana Khorkina, Russia
2005	Chellsie Memmel, United States
2007	Shawn Johnson, United States

Floor Exercise

Year	Champion, Nation
1950	Helena Rakoczy, Poland
1954	Tamara Manina, USSR
1958	Eva Bosakava, Czechoslovakia
1962	Larissa Latynina, USSR
1966	Natalia Kuchinskaya, USSR

Floor Exercise *(Cont.)*

Year	Champion, Nation
1970	Ludmilla Tourischeva, USSR
1974	Ludmilla Tourischeva, USSR
1978	Nelli Kim, USSR Elena Mukhina, USSR
1979	Emilia Eberle, Romania
1981	Natalia Ilenko, USSR
1983	Ecaterina Szabo, Romania
1985	Oksana Omeliantchik, USSR
1987	Elena Shoushounova, USSR Daniela Silivas, Romania
1989	Svetlana Bouguinskaia, USSR Daniela Silivas, Romania
1991	Cristina Bontas, Romania Oksana Tchusovitina, USSR
1992	Kim Zmeskal, United States
1993	Shannon Miller, United States
1994	Dina Kochetkova, Russia
1995	Gina Gogean, Romania
1996	Gina Gogean, Romania
1997	Gina Gogean, Romania
1999	Andreea Raducan, Romania
2001	Andreea Raducan, Romania
2003	Daiane Dos Santos, Brazil
2005	Anastasia Liukin, United States
2007	Shawn Johnson, United States

Uneven Bars

Year	Champion, Nation
1950	Gertchen Kolar, Austria Anna Pettersson, Sweden
1954	Agnes Keleti, Hungary
1958	Larissa Latynina, USSR
1962	Irina Pervuschina, USSR
1966	Natalia Kuchinskaya, USSR
1970	Karin Janz, East Germany
1974	Annelore Zinke, East Germany
1978	Marcia Frederick, United States

Uneven Bars *(Cont.)*

Year	Champion, Nation
1979	Ma Yanhong, China Maxi Gnauck, East Germany
1981	Maxi Gnauck, East Germany
1983	Maxi Gnauck, East Germany
1985	Gabriele Fahnrich, East Germany
1987	Daniela Silivas, Romania Doerte Thuemmler, East Germany
1989	Fan Di, China Daniela Silivas, Romania
1991	Gwang Suk Kim, North Korea
1992	Lavinia Milosivici, Romania
1993	Shannon Miller, United States
1994	Luo Li, China
1995	Svetlana Khorkina, Russia
1996	Svetlana Khorkina, Russia
1997	Svetlana Khorkina, Russia
1999	Svetlana Khorkina, Russia
2001	Svetlana Khorkina, Russia
2003	Chellsie Memmel, U.S. Hollie Vise, United States
2005	Anastasia Liukin, United States
2007	Ksenia Semenov, Russia

Balance Beam

Year	Champion, Nation
1950	Helena Rakoczy, Poland
1954	Keiko Tanaka, Japan
1958	Larissa Latynina, USSR
1962	Eva Bosakova, Czech.
1966	Natalia Kuchinskaya, USSR
1970	Erika Zuchold, East Germany
1974	Ludmilla Tourischeva, USSR
1978	Nadia Comaneci, Romania
1979	Vera Cerna, Czechoslovakia
1981	Maxi Gnauck, East Germany
1983	Olga Mostepanova, USSR
1985	Daniela Silivas, Romania

World Champions — Women *(Cont.)*

Balance Beam *(Cont.)*

Year	Champion, Nation
1987	Aurelia Dobre, Romania
1989	Daniela Silivas, Romania
1991	Svetlana Boguinskaia, USSR
1992	Kim Zmeskal, United States
1993	Lavinia Milosovici, Romania
1994	Shannon Miller, United States
1995	Mo Huilan, China
1996	Dina Kochetkova, Russia
1997	Gina Gogean, Romania
1999	E. Zamolodchikova, Russia
2001	Andreea Raducan, Romania
2003	Fan Ye, China
2005	Nan Zhang, China
2007	Anastasia Liukin, United States

Vault

Year	Champion, Nation
1950	Helena Rakoczy, Poland
1954	T. Manina, USSR
	Anna Pettersson, Sweden
1958	Larissa Latynina, USSR
1962	Vera Caslavska, Czech.
1966	Vera Caslavska, Czech.
1970	Erika Zuchold, East Germany
1974	Olga Korbut, USSR
1978	Nelli Kim, USSR
1979	Dumitrita Turner, Romania
1981	Maxi Gnauck, East Germany
1983	Boriana Stoyanova, Bulgaria
1985	Elena Shoushounova, USSR
1987	Elena Shoushounova, USSR
1989	Olesia Durnik, USSR

Vault *(Cont.)*

Year	Champion, Nation
1991	Lavinia Milosovici, Romania
1992	Henrietta Onodi, Hungary
1993	Elena Piskun, Belarus
1994	Gina Gogean, Romania
1995	L. Podkopayeva, Ukraine
	Simona Amanar, Rom.
1996	Gina Gogean, Romania
1997	Simona Amanar, Romania
1999	Jie Ling, China
2001	Svetlana Khorkina, Russia
2003	Oksana Chusovitina, Uzbekistan
2005	Fei Cheng, China
2007	Fei Cheng, China

National Champions — Men

All-Around

Year	Champion
1963	Art Shurlock
1964	Rusty Mitchell
1965	Rusty Mitchell
1966	Rusty Mitchell
1967	Katsuzoki Kanzaki
1968	Yoshi Hayasaki
1969	Steve Hug
1970	Makoto Sakamoto
	Mas Watanabe
1971	Yoshi Takei
1972	Yoshi Takei
1973	Marshall Avener
1974	John Crosby
1975	Tom Beach
	Bart Conner
1976	Kurt Thomas
1977	Kurt Thomas
1978	Kurt Thomas
1979	Bart Conner
1980	Peter Vidmar
1981	Jim Hartung
1982	Peter Vidmar
1983	Mitch Gaylord
1984	Mitch Gaylord
1985	Brian Babcock
1986	Tim Daggett
1987	Scott Johnson
1988	Dan Hayden
1989	Tim Ryan
1990	John Roethlisberger
1991	Chris Waller
1992	John Roethlisberger
1993	John Roethlisberger
1994	Scott Keswick
1995	John Roethlisberger
1996	Blaine Wilson
1997	Blaine Wilson
1998	Blaine Wilson
1999	Blaine Wilson
2000	Blaine Wilson
2001	Sean Townsend
2002	Paul Hamm
2003	Paul Hamm
2004	Paul Hamm
2005	Todd Thornton

All-Around *(Cont.)*

Year	Champion
2006	Alexander Artemev
2007	David Durante

Floor Exercise

Year	Champion
1963	Tom Seward
1964	Rusty Mitchell
1965	Rusty Mitchell
1966	Dan Millman
1967	Katsuzoki Kanzaki
	Ron Aure
1968	Katsuzoki Kanzaki
1969	Steve Hug
	Dave Thor
1970	Makoto Sakamoto
1971	John Crosby
1972	Yoshi Takei
1973	John Crosby
1974	John Crosby
1975	Peter Korman
1977	Ron Galimore
1978	Kurt Thomas
1979	Ron Galimore
1980	Ron Galimore
1981	Jim Hartung
1982	Jim Hartung
1983	Mitch Gaylord
1984	Peter Vidmar
1985	Mark Oates
1986	Robert Sundstrom
1987	John Sweeney
1988	Mark Oates
	Charles Lakes
1989	Mike Racanelli
1990	Bob Stelter
1991	Mike Racanelli
1992	Gregg Curtis
1993	Kerry Huston
1994	Jeremy Killen
1995	Daniel Stover
1996	Jay Thornton
1997	Jason Gatson
1998	Jason Gatson
1999	Jason Gatson
2000	Blaine Wilson

Floor Exercise *(Cont.)*

Year	Champion
2001	Sean Townsend
2002	Morgan Hamm
2003	Morgan Hamm
2004	Paul Hamm
2005	Guillermo Alvarez
2006	Jonathan Horton
2007	Paul Hamm

Pommel Horse

Year	Champion
1963	Larry Spiegel
1964	Sam Bailie
1965	Jack Ryan
1966	Jack Ryan
1967	Paul Mayer/Dave Doty
1968	Katsuoki Kanzaki
1969	Dave Thor
1970	Mas Watanabe
1971	Leonard Caling
1972	Sadao Hamada
1973	Marshall Avener
1974	Marshall Avener
1975	Bart Conner
1977	Gene Whelan
1978	Jim Hartung
1979	Bart Conner
1980	Jim Hartung
1981	Jim Hartung
1982	Jim Hartung
1983	Bart Conner
1984	Tim Daggett
1985	Phil Cahoy
1986	Phil Cahoy
1987	Tim Daggett
1988	Kevin Davis
1989	Kevin Davis
1990	Patrick Kirksey
1991	Chris Waller
1992	Chris Waller
1993	Chris Waller
1994	Mihai Begiu
1995	Mark Sohn
1996	Josh Stein
1997	John Roethlisberger
1998	John Roethlisberger

National Champions — Men (Cont.)

Pommel Horse (Cont.)

Year	Champion
1999	John Roethlisberger
2000	John Roethlisberger
2001	Brett McClure
2002	Paul Hamm
2003	Paul Hamm
2004	Brett McClure
2005	Yewki Tomita
2006	Alexander Artemev
2007	Alexander Artemev

Rings

Year	Champion
1963	Art Shurlock
1964	Glen Gailis
1965	Glen Gailis
1966	Glen Gailis
1967	Fred Dennis
	Don Hatch
1968	Yoshi Hayasaki
1969	Fred Dennis
	Bob Emery
1970	Makoto Sakamoto
1971	Yoshi Takei
1972	Yoshi Takei
1973	Jim Ivicek
1974	Tom Weeder
1975	Tom Beach
1977	Kurt Thomas
1978	Mike Silverstein
1979	Bart Conner
1980	Jim Hartung
1981	Jim Hartung
1982	Jim Hartung
	Peter Vidmar
1983	Mitch Gaylord
1984	Jim Hartung
1985	Dan Hayden
1986	Dan Hayden
1987	Scott Johnson
1988	Dan Hayden
1989	Scott Keswick
1990	Scott Keswick
1991	Scott Keswick
1992	Tim Ryan
1993	John Roethlisberger
1994	Scott Keswick
1995	Paul O'Neill
1996	Kip Simons
1997	Blaine Wilson
1998	Jeff Johnson
1999	Blaine Wilson
2000	Blaine Wilson
2001	Sean Townsend
2002	Blaine Wilson
2003	Blaine Wilson
2004	Raj Bhavsar
2005	Sean Golden
2006	Kevin Tan
2007	Kevin Tan

Vault

Year	Champion
1963	Art Shurlock
1964	Gary Hery
1965	Brent Williams
1966	Dan Millman

Vault (Cont.)

Year	Champion
1967	Jack Kenan
	Sid Jensen
1968	Rich Scorza
1969	Dave Butzman
1970	Makoto Sakamoto
1971	Gary Morava
1972	Mike Kelley
1973	Gary Morava
1974	John Crosby
1975	Tom Beach
1977	Ron Galimore
1978	Jim Hartung
1979	Ron Galimore
1980	Ron Galimore
1981	Ron Galimore
1982	Jim Hartung/Jim Mikus
1983	Chris Reigel
1984	Chris Reigel
1985	Scott Johnson
	Mark Oates
1986	Scott Wilbanks
1987	John Sweeney
1988	John Sweeney/Bill Paul
1989	Bill Roth
1990	Lance Ringnald
1991	Scott Keswick
1992	Trent Dimas
1993	Bill Roth
1994	Keith Wiley
1995	David St. Pierre
1996	Blaine Wilson
1997	Blaine Wilson
1998	Brent Klaus
1999	Guard Young
2000	Blaine Wilson
2001	Jason Furr
2002	Paul Hamm
2003	Raj Bhavsar
2004	David Sender
2005	Sean Golden
2006	David Sender
2007	Sean Golden

Parallel Bars

Year	Champion
1963	Tom Seward
1964	Rusty Mitchell
1965	Glen Gailis
1966	Ray Hadley
1967	Katsuoki Kanzaki
	Tom Goldsborough
1968	Yoshi Hayasaki
1969	Steve Hug
1970	Makoto Sakamoto
1971	Brent Simmons
1972	Yoshi Takei
1973	Marshall Avener
1974	Jim Ivicek
1975	Bart Conner
1977	Kurt Thomas
1978	Bart Conner
1979	Bart Conner
1980	Phil Cahoy/Larry Gerard
1981	Bart Conner
1982	Peter Vidmar

Parallel Bars (Cont.)

Year	Champion
1983	Mitch Gaylord
1984	Peter Vidmar
	Mitch Gaylord
	Tim Daggett
1985	Tim Daggett
1986	Tim Daggett
1987	Scott Johnson
1988	D. Hayden/K. Davis
1989	Conrad Voorsanger
1990	Trent Dimas
1991	Scott Keswick
1992	Jair Lynch
1993	Chainey Umphrey
1994	Steve McCain
1995	John Roethlisberger
1996	Jair Lynch
1997	Blaine Wilson
1998	Blaine Wilson
1999	Jason Gatson
2000	Trent Wells
2001	Sean Townsend
2002	Sean Townsend
2003	Jason Gatson
2004	Alexander Artemev
2005	D.J. Bucher
2006	Alexander Artemev
2007	David Durante

High Bars

Year	Champion
1963	Art Shurlock
1964	Glen Gailis
1965	Rusty Mitchell
1966	Katsuoki Kanzaki
1967	Katsuoki Kanzaki
	Jerry Fontana
1968	Yoshi Hayasaki
1969	Rich Grisby
1970	Makoto Sakamoto
1971	Yoshi Takei
1972	Tom Lindner
1973	John Crosby
1974	Brent Simmons
1975	Tom Beach
1977	Kurt Thomas
1978	Kurt Thomas
1979	Yoichi Tomita
1980	Jim Hartung
1981	Bart Conner
1982	Mitch Gaylord
1983	Mario McCutcheon
1984	Peter Vidmar
	Tim Daggett
	Mitch Gaylord
1985	Dan Hayden
1986	D. Hayden/D. Moriel
1987	David Moriel
1988	Dan Hayden
1989	Tim Ryan
1990	Trent Dimas
	Lance Ringnald
1991	Lance Ringnald
1992	Jair Lynch
1993	Steve McCain
1994	Scott Keswick
1995	John Roethlisberger

National Champions — Men *(Cont.)*

High Bars *(Cont.)*

Year	Champion
1996	Bill Roth
1997	Douglas Stibel
1998	Jason Gatson
1999	Jamie Natalie

High Bars *(Cont.)*

Year	Champion
2000	Trent Wells
	Jamie Natalie
2001	Daniel Diaz-Luong
2002	Blaine Wilson
2003	Paul Hamm

High Bars *(Cont.)*

Year	Champion
2004	Paul Hamm
2005	D.J. Bucher
2006	Chris Brooks
2007	Justin Spring

National Champions — Women

All-Around

Year	Champion
1963	Donna Schanezer
1965	Gail Daley
1966	Donna Schanezer
1968	Linda Scott
1969	Joyce Tanac Schroeder
1970	Cathy Rigby
1971	Joan Moore Gnat Linda Metheny Mulvihill
1972	Joan Moore Gnat Cathy Rigby
1973	Joan Moore Gnat
1974	Joan Moore Gnat
1975	Tammy Manville
1976	Denise Cheshire
1977	Donna Turnbow
1978	Kathy Johnson
1979	Leslie Pyfer
1980	Julianne McNamara
1981	Tracee Talavera
1982	Tracee Talavera
1983	Dianne Durham
1984	Mary Lou Retton
1985	Sabrina Mar
1986	Jennifer Sey
1987	Kristie Phillips
1988	Phoebe Mills
1989	Brandy Johnson
1990	Kim Zmeskal
1991	Kim Zmeskal
1992	Kim Zmeskal
1993	Shannon Miller
1994	Dominique Dawes
1995	Dominique Moceanu
1996	Shannon Miller
1997	V. Adler/ K. Powell
1998	Kristen Maloney
1999	Kristen Maloney
2000	Elise Ray
2001	Tasha Schwikert
2002	Tasha Schwikert
2003	Courtney Kupets
2004	Courtney Kupets/ Carly Patterson
2005	Anastasia Liukin
2006	Anastasia Liukin
2007	Shawn Johnson

Vault

Year	Champion
1963	Donna Schanezer
1965	Gail Daley
1966	Donna Schanezer

Vault *(Cont.)*

Year	Champion
1968	Terry Spencer
1969	Joyce Tanac Schroeder Cleo Carver
1970	Cathy Rigby
1971	Joan Moore Gnat Adele Gleaves
1972	Cindy Eastwood
1973	Roxanne Pierce Mancha
1974	Dianne Dunbar
1975	Kolleen Casey
1976	Debbie Wilcox
1977	Lisa Cawthron
1978	Rhonda Schwandt Sharon Shapiro
1979	Christa Canary
1980	J. McNamara/B. Kline
1981	Kim Neal
1982	Yumi Mordre
1983	Dianne Durham
1984	Mary Lou Retton
1985	Yolanda Mavity
1986	Joyce Wilborn
1987	Rhonda Faehn
1988	Rhonda Faehn
1989	Brandy Johnson
1990	Brandy Johnson
1991	Kerri Strug
1992	Kerri Strug
1993	Dominique Dawes
1994	Dominique Dawes
1995	Shannon Miller
1996	Dominique Dawes
1997	Vanessa Atler
1998	Dominique Moceanu
1999	Vanessa Atler
2000	Kristen Maloney
2001	Mohini Bhardwaj
2002	Elizabeth Tricase
2003	Annia Hatch
2004	Liz Tricase
2005	Alicia Sacramone
2006	Alicia Sacramone
2007	Alicia Sacramone

Uneven Bars

Year	Champion
1963	Donna Schanezer
1965	Irene Haworth
1966	Donna Schanezer
1968	Linda Scott
1969	Joyce Tanac Schroeder Lisa Nelson

Uneven Bars *(Cont.)*

Year	Champion
1970	Roxanne Pierce Mancha
1971	Joan Moore Gnat
1972	Cathy Rigby
1973	Roxanne Pierce Mancha
1974	Diane Dunbar
1975	Leslie Wolfsberger
1976	Leslie Wolfsberger
1977	Donna Turnbow
1978	Marcia Frederick
1979	Marcia Frederick
1980	Marcia Frederick
1981	Julianne McNamara
1982	Marie Roethlisberger
1983	Julianne McNamara
1984	Julianne McNamara
1985	Sabrina Mar
1986	Marie Roethlisberger
1987	Melissa Marlowe
1988	Chelle Stack
1989	Chelle Stack
1990	Sandy Woolsey
1991	Elisabeth Crandall
1992	Dominique Dawes
1993	Shannon Miller
1994	Dominique Dawes
1995	Dominique Dawes
1996	Dominique Dawes
1997	Kristy Powell
1998	Elise Ray
1999	Jamie Dantzscher Jennie Thompson
2000	Elise Ray
2001	Katie Heenan
2002	Tasha Schwikert
2003	Katie Heenan
2004	Courtney Kupets
2005	Anastasia Liukin
2006	Anastasia Liukin
2007	Anastasia Liukin

Balance Beam

Year	Champion
1963	Leissa Krol
1965	Gail Daley
1966	Irene Haworth Linda Scott
1968	Linda Scott
1969	Lonna Woodward
1970	Joyce Tanac Schroeder
1971	Linda Metheny Mulvihill
1972	Kim Chace
1973	Nancy Thies Marshall

National Champions — Women

Balance Beam *(Cont.)*

Year	Champion
1974	Joan Moore Gnat
1975	Kyle Gayner
1976	Carrie Englert
1977	Donna Turnbow
1978	Christa Canary
1979	Heidi Anderson
1980	Kelly Garrison-Steves
1981	Tracee Talavera
1982	Julianne McNamara
1983	Dianne Durham
1984	Pam Bileck
	Tracee Talavera
1986	Angie Denkins
1987	Kristie Phillips
1985	Kelly Garrison-Steves
1988	Kelly Garrison-Steves
1989	Brandy Johnson
1990	Betty Okino
1991	Shannon Miller
1992	Kerri Strug
	Kim Zmeskal
1993	Dominique Dawes
1994	Dominique Dawes
1995	Doni Thompson
	Monica Flammer
1996	Dominique Dawes
1997	Kendall Beck
1998	Dominique Moceanu
1999	Vanessa Atler

Balance Beam *(Cont.)*

Year	Champion
2000	Alyssa Beckerman
	Amy Chow
2001	Tasha Schwikert
2002	Tasha Schwikert
2003	Hollie Vise
2004	Courtney Kupets
2005	Anastasia Liukin
2006	Anastasia Liukin
2007	Shawn Johnson

Floor Exercise

Year	Champion
1963	Donna Schanezer
1965	Gail Daley
1966	Donna Schanezer
1968	Linda Scott
1970	Cathy Rigby
1971	Joan Moore Gnat
	Linda Metheny Mulvihill
1972	Joan Moore Gnat
1973	Joan Moore Gnat
1974	Joan Moore Gnat
1975	Kathy Howard
1976	Carrie Englert
1977	Kathy Johnson
1978	Kathy Johnson
1979	Heidi Anderson
1980	Beth Kline

Floor Exercise *(Cont.)*

Year	Champion
1981	Michelle Goodwin
1982	Amy Koopman
1983	Dianne Durham
1984	Mary Lou Retton
1985	Sabrina Mar
1986	Yolanda Mavity
1987	Kristie Phillips
1988	Phoebe Mills
1989	Brandy Johnson
1990	Brandy Johnson
1991	Kim Zmeskal
	Dominique Dawes
1992	Kim Zmeskal
1993	Shannon Miller
1994	Dominique Dawes
1995	Dominique Dawes
1996	Dominique Dawes
1997	Lindsay Wing
1998	Vanessa Atler
1999	Elise Ray
2000	Kristen Maloney
2001	Tabitha Yim
2002	Tasha Schwikert
2003	Ashley Postell
2004	Carly Patterson
2005	Alicia Sacramone
2006	Alicia Sacramone
	Randi Stageberg
2007	Shawn Johnson

Handball

National Four-Wall Champions

MEN

Year	Champion	Year	Champion	Year	Champion	Year	Champion
1919	Bill Ranft	1946	Angelo Trutio	1973	Terry Muck	2000	David Chapman
1920	Max Gold	1947	Gus Lewis	1974	Fred Lewis	2001	Vince Munoz
1921	Carl Haedge	1948	Gus Lewis	1975	Fred Lewis	2002	David Chapman
1922	Art Shinners	1949	Vic Hershkowitz	1976	Fred Lewis	2003	John Bike
1923	Joe Murray	1950	Ken Schneider	1977	Naty Alvarado	2004	David Chapman
1924	Maynard Laswe	1951	Walter Plakan	1978	Fred Lewis	2005	Paul Brady
1925	Maynard Laswe	1952	Vic Hershkowitz	1979	Naty Alvarado	2006	Paul Brady
1926	Maynard Laswe	1953	Bob Brady	1980	Naty Alvarado	2007	Sean Lenning
1927	George Nelson	1954	Vic Hershkowitz	1981	Fred Lewis		
1928	Joe Griffin	1955	Jimmy Jacobs	1982	Naty Alvarado		
1929	Al Banuet	1956	Jimmy Jacobs	1983	Naty Alvarado		
1930	Al Banuet	1957	Jimmy Jacobs	1984	Naty Alvarado		
1931	Al Banuet	1958	John Sloan	1985	Naty Alvarado		
1932	Angelo Trutio	1959	John Sloan	1986	Naty Alvarado		
1933	Sam Atcheson	1960	Jimmy Jacobs	1987	Naty Alvarado		
1934	Sam Atcheson	1961	John Sloan	1988	Naty Alvarado		
1935	Joe Platak	1962	Oscar Obert	1989	Poncho Monreal		
1936	Joe Platak	1963	Oscar Obert	1990	Naty Alvarado		
1937	Joe Platak	1964	Jimmy Jacobs	1991	John Bike		
1938	Joe Platak	1965	Jimmy Jacobs	1992	Octavio Silveyra		
1939	Joe Platak	1966	Paul Haber	1993	David Chapman		
1940	Joe Platak	1967	Paul Haber	1994	Octavio Silveyra		
1941	Joe Platak	1968	Stuffy Singer	1995	David Chapman		
1942	Jack Clemente	1969	Paul Haber	1996	David Chapman		
1943	Joe Platak	1970	Paul Haber	1997	Octavio Silveyra		
1944	Frank Coyle	1971	Paul Haber	1998	David Chapman		
1945	Joe Platak	1972	Fred Lewis	1999	David Chapman		

National Four-Wall Champions

WOMEN

1980 .....Rosemary Bellini	1987 .....Rosemary Bellini	1994 .....Anna Engele	2001 .....Anna Christoff
1981 .....Rosemary Bellini	1988 .....Rosemary Bellini	1995 .....Anna Engele	2002 .....Priscilla Shumate
1982 .....Rosemary Bellini	1989 .....Anna Engele	1996 .....Anna Engele	2003.....Lisa Gilmore
1983 .....Diane Harmon	1990 .....Anna Engele	1997 .....Lisa Fraser	2004.....Yvonne August
1984 .....Rosemary Bellini	1991 .....Anna Engele	1998 .....Lisa Fraser	2005......Jennifer Schmitt
1985 .....Peanut Motal	1992 .....Lisa Fraser	1999 .....Anna Christoff	2006......Jennifer Schmitt
1986 .....Peanut Motal	1993 .....Anna Engele	2000 .....Priscilla Shumate	2007 .....Lisa Fraser

National Three-Wall Champions

MEN

1950 .....Vic Hershkowitz	1965 .....Carl Obert	1980 .....Lou Russo	1995 .....David Chapman
1951 .....Vic Hershkowitz	1966 .....Marty Decatur	1981 .....Naty Alvarado	1996 .....Vince Munoz
1952 .....Vic Hershkowitz	1967 .....Carl Obert	1982 .....Naty Alvarado	1997 .....Vince Munoz
1953 .....Vic Herskkowitz	1968 .....Marty Decatur	1983 .....Naty Alvarado	1998 .....Vince Munoz
1954 .....Vic Hershkowitz	1969 .....Marty Decatur	1984 .....Naty Alvarado	1999 .....Vince Munoz
1955 .....Vic Hershkowitz	1970 .....Steve August	1985 .....Vern Roberts	2000 .....Vince Munoz
1956 .....Vic Hershkowitz	1971 .....Lou Russo	1986 .....Vern Roberts	2001 .....Vince Munoz
1957 .....Vic Hershkowitz	1972 .....Lou Russo	1987 .....Vern Roberts	2002 .....Vince Munoz
1958 .....Vic Hershkowitz	1973 .....Paul Haber	1988 .....Jon Kendler	2003 .....Vince Munoz
1959 .....Jimmy Jacobs	1974 .....Fred Lewis	1989 .....John Bike	2004 .....Sean Lenning
1960 .....Jimmy Jacobs	1975 .....Lou Russo	1990 .....Vince Munoz	2005 .....Vince Munoz
1961 .....Jimmy Jacobs	1976 .....Lou Russo	1991 .....John Bike	2006 .....Emmett Peixoto
1962 .....Oscar Obert	1977 .....Fred Lewis	1992 .....John Bike	2007 .....Sean Lenning
1963 .....Marty Decatur	1978 .....Fred Lewis	1993 .....Eric Klarman	
1964 .....Marty Decatur	1979 .....Naty Alvarado	1994 .....David Chapman	

WOMEN

1981 .....Allison Roberts	1988 .....Rosemary Bellini	1995 .....Allison Roberts	2002......Priscilla Shumate
1982 .....Allison Roberts	1989 .....Rosemary Bellini	1996 .....Anna Engele	2003.....Lisa Gilmore
1983 .....Allison Roberts	1990 .....Rosemary Bellini	1997 .....Allison Roberts	2004 .....Jennifer Schmitt
1984 .....Rosemary Bellini	1991 .....Rosemary Bellini	1998 .....Anna Christoff	2005 .....Megan Mehilos
1985 .....Rosemary Bellini	1992 .....Anna Engele	1999 .....Anna Christoff	2006 .....Megan Mehilos
1986 .....Rosemary Bellini	1993 .....Anna Engele	2000......Priscilla Shumate	2007 .....Megan Mehilos
1987 .....Rosemary Bellini	1994 .....Anna Engele	2001......Anna Christoff	

World Four-Wall Champions

1984 ....Merv Deckert, Canada	1997 ....John Bike Jr., United States
1986 ....Vern Roberts, United States	2000 ....David Chapman, United States
1988 ....Naty Alvarado, United States	2003 ....Paul Brady, Ireland
1991 ....Pancho Monreal, United States	2006 ....Paul Brady, Ireland
1994 ....David Chapman, United States	

Lacrosse

United States Club Lacrosse Association Champions*

1960 ......Mt. Washington Club	1977 ......Mt. Washington Club	1994 ......LI-Hofstra Lacrosse Club
1961 ......Baltimore Lacrosse Club	1978 ......Long Island Athletic Club	1995 ......Mt. Washington Club
1962 ......Mt. Washington Club	1979 ......Maryland Lacrosse Club	1996 ......LI-Hofstra Lacrosse Club
1963 ......University Club	1980 ......Long Island Athletic Club	1997 ......LI-Hofstra Lacrosse Club
1964 ......Mt. Washington Club	1981 ......Long Island Athletic Club	1998 ......LI-Hofstra Lacrosse Club
1965 ......Mt. Washington Club	1982 ......Maryland Lacrosse Club	1999 ......New York Athletic Club
1966 ......Mt. Washington Club	1983 ......Maryland Lacrosse Club	2000 ......Team Toyota (Baltimore)
1967 ......Mt. Washington Club	1984 ......Maryland Lacrosse Club	2001 ......LI Lacrosse Club
1968 ......Long Island Athletic Club	1985 ......LI-Hofstra Lacrosse Club	2002 ......Single Source Solutions
1969 ......Long Island Athletic Club	1986 ......LI-Hofstra Lacrosse Club	2003 ......Single Source Solutions
1970 ......Long Island Athletic Club	1987 ......LI-Hofstra Lacrosse Club	2004 ......Single Source Solutions
1971 ......Long Island Athletic Club	1988 ......Maryland Lacrosse Club	2005 ......Team Source (Annapolis)
1972 ......Carling	1989 ......LI-Hofstra Lacrosse Club	2006.......MAB Paints (Philadelphia)
1973 ......Long Island Athletic Club	1990 ......Mt. Washington Club	2007.......New York Athletic Club
1974 ......Long Island Athletic Club	1991 ......Mt. Washington Club	
1975 ......Mt. Washington Club	1992 ......Maryland Lacrosse Club	
1976 ......Mt. Washington Club	1993 ......Mt. Washington Club	

*The U.S. Club Lacrosse Association merged with the American Lacrosse League in 2007.

National Lacrosse League Champions*

1987 ......Baltimore Thunder	1994 .....Philadelphia Wings	2001 ......Philadelphia Wings
1988 ......New Jersey Saints	1995 .....Philadelphia Wings	2002 ......Toronto Rock
1989 ......Philadelphia Wings	1996 ......Buffalo Bandits	2003 ......Toronto Rock
1990 .....Philadelphia Wings	1997 ......Rochester Knighthawks	2004 ......Calgary Roughnecks
1991 ......Detroit Turbos	1998 .....Philadelphia Wings	2005 ......Toronto Rock
1992 ......Buffalo Bandits	1999 ......Toronto Rock	2006 ......Colorado Mammoth
1993 ......Buffalo Bandits	2000 ......Toronto Rock	2007.......Rochester Knighthawks

*Indoor league formerly known as the Eagle Pro Box Lacrosse League, and the Major Indoor Lacrosse League.

Major League Lacrosse

2001 .....Long Island Lizards	2004 .....Philadelphia Barrage	2007.......Philadelphia Barrage
2002 .....Baltimore Bayhawks	2005 ....Baltimore Bayhawks	
2003 .....Long Island Lizards	2006 .....Philadelphia Barrage	

Little League Baseball

Little League World Series Champions

Year	Champion	Runner-Up	Score	Year	Champion	Runner-Up	Score
1947	Williamsport, Pa.	Lock Haven, Pa.	16–7	1978	Pin-Tung, Taiwan	Danville, Calif.	11–1
1948	Lock Haven, Pa.	St. Petersburg, Fla.	6–5	1979	Hsien, Taiwan	Campbell, Calif.	2–1
1949	Hammonton, N.J.	Pensacola, Fla.	5–0	1980	Hua Lian, Taiwan	Tampa, Fla.	4–3
1950	Houston, Tex.	Bridgeport, Conn.	2–1	1981	Tai-Chung, Taiwan	Tampa, Fla.	4–2
1951	Stamford, Conn.	Austin, Tex.	3–0	1982	Kirkland, Wash.	Hsien, Taiwan	6–0
1952	Norwalk, Conn.	Monongahela, Pa.	4–3	1983	Marietta, Ga.	Barahona, D.Rep.	3–1
1953	Birmingham, AL	Schenectady, N.Y.	1–0	1984	Seoul, S. Korea	Altamonte Sgs, Fla.	6–2
1954	Schenectady, N.Y.	Colton, Calif.	7–5	1985	Seoul, S. Korea	Mexicali, Mex.	7–1
1955	Morrisville, Pa.	Merchantville, N.J.	4–3	1986	Tainan Park, Taiwan	Tucson, Ariz.	12–0
1956	Roswell, NM	Merchantville, N.J.	3–1	1987	Hua Lian, Taiwan	Irvine, Calif.	21–1
1957	Monterrey, Mex.	LaMesa, Calif.	4–0	1988	Tai-Chung, Taiwan	Pearl City, Hawaii	10–0
1958	Monterrey, Mex.	Kankakee, Ill.	10–1	1989	Trumbull, Conn.	Kaohsiung, Taiwan	5–2
1959	Hamtramck, Mich.	Auburn, Calif.	12–0	1990	Taipei, Taiwan	Shippensburg, Pa.	9–0
1960	Levittown, Pa.	Ft. Worth, Tex.	5–0	1991	Tai-Chung, Taiwan	San Ramon Vly, Calif.	11–0
1961	El Cajon, Calif.	El Campo, Tex.	4–2	1992*	Long Beach, Calif.	Zamboanga, Phil.	6–0
1962	San Jose, Calif.	Kankakee, Ill.	3–0	1993	Long Beach, Calif.	David Chiriqui, Pan.	3–2
1963	Granada Hills, Calif.	Stratford, Conn.	2–1	1994	Maracaibo, Venez.	Northridge, Calif.	4–3
1964	Staten Island, N.Y.	Monterrey, Mex.	4–0	1995	Tainan, Taiwan	Sprint, Tex.	17–3
1965	Windsor Locks, Conn.	Stoney Creek, Can.	3–1	1996	Kao-Hsuing, Taiwan	Cranston, RI	13–3
1966	Houston, Tex.	W. New York, N.J.	8–2	1997	Guadalupe, Mex.	Mission Viejo, Calif.	5–4
1967	West Tokyo, Japan	Chicago, Ill.	4–1	1998	Toms River, N.J.	Kashima, Japan	12–9
1968	Osaka, Japan	Richmond, VA	1–0	1999	Osaka, Japan	Phenix City, AL	5–0
1969	Taipei, Taiwan	Santa Clara, Calif.	5–0	2000	Maracaibo, Venez.	Bellaire, Tex.	3–2
1970	Wayne, N.J.	Campbell, Calif.	2–0	2001	Tokyo, Japan	Apopka, Fla.	2–1
1971	Tainan, Taiwan	Gary, Ind.	12–3	2002	Louisville, Ky.	Sendai, Japan	1–0
1972	Taipei, Taiwan	Hammond, Ind.	6–0	2003	Tokyo, Japan	Boynton Beach, Fla.	10–1
1973	Tainan City, Taiwan	Tucson, Ariz.	12–0	2004	Willemstad, Curacao	Thousand Oaks, Calif.	5–2
1974	Kao-Hsuing, Taiwan	El Cajun, Calif.	7–2	2005	West Oahu, Hawaii	Willemstad, Curacao	7–6
1975	Lakewood, N.J.	Tampa, Fla.	4–3	2006	Columbus, Georgia	Kawaguchi, Japan	2–1
1976	Tokyo, Japan	Campbell, Calif.	10–3	2007	Warner Robins, Ga.	Tokyo, Japan	3–2
1977	Kao-Hsuing, Taiwan	El Cajun, Calif.	7–2				

*Long Beach declared a 6–0 winner after the international tournament committee determined that Zamboanga City had used players that were not within its city limits.

Motor Boat Racing

American Boat Racing Association Gold Cup Champions

Year	Boat	Driver	Avg MPH	Year	Boat	Driver	Avg MPH
1904	Standard (June)	Carl Riotte	23.160	1911	MIT II	J.H. Hayden	37.000
1904	Vingt-et-Un II (Sep)	W. Sharpe Kilmer	24.900	1912	P.D.Q. II.	A.G. Miles	39.462
1905	Chip I	J. Wainwright	15.000	1913	Ankle Deep	Cas Mankowski	42.779
1906	Chip II	J. Wainwright	25.000	1914	Baby Speed Demon II	Jim Blackton & Bob Edgren	48.458
1907	Chip II	J. Wainwright	23.903				
1908	Dixie II	E.J. Schroeder	29.938	1915	Miss Detroit	Johnny Milot & Jack Beebe	37.656
1909	Dixie II	E.J. Schroeder	29.590				
1910	Dixie III	F.K. Burnham	32.473	1916	Miss Minneapolis	Bernard Smith	48.860

American Boat Racing Association Gold Cup Champions

Year	Boat	Driver	Avg MPH	Year	Boat	Driver	Avg MPH
1917	Miss Detroit II	Gar Wood	54.410	1966	Tahoe Miss	Mira Slovak	93.019
1918	Miss Detroit II	Gar Wood	51.619	1967	Miss Bardahl	Bill Shumacher	101.484
1919	Miss Detroit III	Gar Wood	42.748	1968	Miss Bardahl	Bill Shumacher	108.173
1920	Miss America I	Gar Wood	62.022	1969	Miss Budweiser	Bill Sterett	98.504
1921	Miss America I	Gar Wood	52.825	1970	Miss Budweiser	Dean Chenoweth	99.562
1922	Packard Chriscraft	J.G. Vincent	40.253				
1923	Packard Chriscraft	Caleb Bragg	43.867	1971	Miss Madison	Jim McCormick	98.043
1924	Baby Bootlegger	Caleb Bragg	45.302	1972	Atlas Van Lines	Bill Muncey	104.277
1925	Baby Bootlegger	Caleb Bragg	47.240	1973	Miss Budweiser	Dean Chenoweth	99.043
1926	Greenwich Folly	George Townsend	47.984				
				1974	Pay 'n Pak	George Henley	104.428
1927	Greenwich Folly	George Townsend	47.662	1975	Pay 'n Pak	George Henley	108.921
				1976	Miss U.S.	Tom D'Eath	100.412
1928	No race			1977	Atlas Van Lines	Bill Muncey	111.822
1929	Imp	Richard Hoyt	48.662	1978	Atlas Van Lines	Bill Muncey	111.412
1930	Hotsy Totsy	Vic Kliesrath	52.673	1979	Atlas Van Lines	Bill Muncey	100.765
1931	Hotsy Totsy	Vic Kliesrath	53.602	1980	Miss Budweiser	Dean Chenoweth	106.932
1932	Delphine IV	Bill Horn	57.775				
1933	El Lagarto	George Reis	56.260	1981	Miss Budweiser	Dean Chenoweth	116.932
1934	El Lagarto	George Reis	55.000				
1935	El Lagarto	George Reis	55.056	1982	Atlas Van Lines	Chip Hanauer	120.050
1936	Impshi	Kaye Don	45.735	1983	Atlas Van Lines	Chip Hanauer	118.507
1937	Notre Dame	Clell Perry	63.675	1984	Atlas Van Lines	Chip Hanauer	130.175
1938	Alagi	Theo Rossi	64.340	1985	Miller American	Chip Hanauer	120.643
1939	My Sin	Z.G. Simmons Jr.	66.133	1986	Miller American	Chip Hanauer	116.523
1940	Hotsy Totsy III	Sidney Allen	48.295	1987	Miller American	Chip Hanauer	127.620
1941	My Sin	Z.G. Simmons Jr.	52.509	1988	Miss Circus Circus	Chip Hanauer & Jim Prevost	123.756
1942–45	No race		—				
1946	Tempo VI	Guy Lombardo	68.132	1989	Miss Budweiser	Tom D'Eath	131.209
1947	Miss Peps V	Danny Foster	57.000	1990	Miss Budweiser	Tom D'Eath	143.176
1948	Miss Great Lakes	Danny Foster	46.845	1991	Winston Eagle	Mark Tate	137.771
1949	My Sweetie	Bill Cantrell	73.612	1992	Miss Budweiser	Chip Hanauer	136.282
1950	Slo-Mo-Shun IV	Ted Jones	78.216	1993	Miss Budweiser	Chip Hanauer	141.195
1951	Slo-Mo-Shun V	Lou Fageol	90.871	1994	Smokin' Joe Camel	Mark Tate	145.260
1952	Slo-Mo-Shun IV	Stan Dollar	79.923	1995	Miss Budweiser	Chip Hanauer	149.160
1953	Slo-Mo-Shun IV	Joe Taggart & Lou Fageol	99.108	1996	PICO American Dream	Dave Villwock	149.328
				1997	Miss Budweiser	Dave Villwock	129.366
1954	Slo-Mo-Shun IV	Joe Taggart & Lou Fageol	92.613	1998	Miss Budweiser	Dave Villwock	140.309
				1999	Miss PICO	Chip Hanauer	152.591
1955	Gale V	Lee Schoenith	99.552	2000	Miss Budweiser	Dave Villwock	162.850
1956	Miss Thriftaway	Bill Muncey	96.552	2001	Miss Tubby's Subs	Michael Hanson	140.519
1957	Miss Thriftaway	Bill Muncey	101.787	2002	Miss Budweiser	Dave Villwock	143.093
1958	Hawaii Kai III	Jack Regas	103.000	2003	Miss Fox Hills	Mitch Evans	144.152
1959	Maverick	Bill Stead	104.481	2004	Miss Detroit	Nate Brown	141.195
1960	No race	—	—	2005	Miss Al Deeby Dodge	Terry Troxell	142.448
1961	Miss Century 21	Bill Muncey	99.678				
1962	Miss Century 21	Bill Muncey	100.710	2006	Miss Beccon Plumbing	Jean Theoret	142.441
1963	Miss Bardahl	Ron Musson	105.124				
1964	Miss Bardahl	Ron Musson	103.433	2007	Miss Elam Plus	Dave Villwock	162.754
1965	Miss Bardahl	Ron Musson	103.132				

Hydro-Prop* Annual Champion Drivers

Year	Driver	Boat	Wins	Year	Driver	Boat	Wins
1947	Danny Foster	Miss Peps V	6	1960	Bill Muncey	Miss Thriftway	4
1948	Dan Arena	Such Crust	2	1961	Bill Muncey	Miss Century 21	4
1949	Bill Cantrell	My Sweetie	7	1962	Bill Muncey	Miss Century 21	5
1950	Dan Foster	Such Crust/DaphneX	2	1963	Bill Cantrell	Gale V	0
1951	Chuck Thompson	Miss Pepsi	5	1964	Ron Musson	Miss Bardahl	4
1952	Chuck Thompson	Miss Pepsi	3	1965	Ron Musson	Miss Bardahl	4
1953	Lee Schoenith	Gale II	1	1966	Mira Slovak	Tahoe Miss	4
1954	Lee Schoenith	Gale V	4	1967	Bill Schumacher	Miss Bardahl	6
1955	Lee Schoenith	Gale V/Wha Hoppen	1	1968	Bill Schumacher	Miss Bardahl	4
1956	Russ Schleeh	Shanty I	3	1969	Bill Sterett Sr.	Miss Budweiser	4
1957	Jack Regas	Hawaii Kai III	5	1970	Dean Chenoweth	Miss Budweiser	4
1958	Mira Slovak	Bardah/Miss Buren	3	1971	Dean Chenoweth	Miss Budweiser	2
1959	Bill Stead	Maverick	5	1972	Bill Muncey	Atlas Van Lines	6

Hydro-Prop* Annual Champion Drivers

Year	Driver	Boat	Wins	Year	Driver	Boat	Wins
1973	Mickey Remund	Pay 'n Pak	4	1991	Mark Tate	Winston/Oberto	3
1974	George Henley	Pay 'n Pak	7	1992	Chip Hanauer	Miss Budweiser	7
1975	Billy Schumacher	Weisfield's	2	1993	Chip Hanauer	Miss Budweiser	7
1976	Bill Muncey	Atlas Van Lines	5	1994	Mark Tate	Smokin' Joe Camel	2
1977	Mickey Remund	Miss Budweiser	3	1995	Mark Tate	Smokin' Joe Camel	4
1978	Bill Muncey	Atlas Van Lines	6	1996	Dave Villwock	PICO American Dream	6
1979	Bill Muncey	Atlas Van Lines	7	1997	Mark Tate	Close Call	1
1980	Dean Chenoweth	Miss Budweiser	5	1998	Dave Villwock	Miss Budweiser	8
1981	Dean Chenoweth	Miss Budweiser	6	1999	Dave Villwock	Miss Budweiser	8
1982	Chip Hanauer	Atlas Van Lines	5	2000	Dave Villwock	Miss Budweiser	6
1983	Chip Hanauer	Atlas Van Lines	3	2001	Dave Villwock	Miss Budweiser	1
1984	Jim Kropfeld	Miss Budweiser	6	2002	Dave Villwock	Miss Budweiser	3
1985	Chip Hanauer	Miller American	5	2003	Dave Villwock	Miss Budweiser	2
1986	Jim Kropfeld	Miss Budweiser	3	2004	Dave Villwock	Miss Budweiser	2
1987	Jim Kropfeld	Miss Budweiser	5	2005	Steve David	Miss Madison	0
1988	Tom D'Eath	Miss Budweiser	4	2006	Steve David	Miss Madison	1
1989	Chip Hanauer	Miss Circus Circus	3	2007	Dave Villwock	Miss Elam Plus	4
1990	Chip Hanauer	Miss Circus Circus	6				

Hydro-Prop* Annual Champion Boats

Year	Boat	Owner	Wins	Year	Boat	Owner	Wins
1970	Miss Budweiser	Little-Friedkin	4	1989	Miss Budweiser	Bernie Little	4
1971	Miss Budweiser	Little-Friedkin	2	1990	Miss Circus Circus	Bill Bennett	6
1972	Atlas Van Lines	Joe Schoenith	6	1991	Miss Budweiser	Bernie Little	4
1973	Pay 'n Pak	Dave Heerensperger	4	1992	Miss Budweiser	Bernie Little	7
1974	Pay 'n Pak	Dave Heerensperger	7	1993	Miss Budweiser	Bernie Little	7
1975	Pay 'n Pak	Dave Heerensperger	5	1994	Miss Budweiser	Bernie Little	4
1976	Atlas Van Lines	Bill Muncey	5	1995	Miss Budweiser	Bernie Little	5
1977	Miss Budweiser	Bernie Little	3	1996	PICO Amer. Dream	Fred Leland	6
1978	Atlas Van Lines	Bill Muncey	6	1997	Miss Budweiser	Bernie Little	5
1979	Atlas Van Lines	Bill Muncey	7	1998	Miss Budweiser	Bernie Little	8
1980	Miss Budweiser	Bernie Little	5	1999	Miss Budweiser	Bernie Little	8
1981	Miss Budweiser	Bernie Little	6	2000	Miss Budweiser	Bernie Little	6
1982	Atlas Van Lines	Fran Muncey	5	2001	Miss Budweiser	Bernie Little	1
1983	Atlas Van Lines	Muncey-Lucero	3	2002	Miss Budweiser	Bernie Little	3
1984	Miss Budweiser	Bernie Little	6	2003	Miss Budweiser	Joe Little	2
1985	Miller American	Muncey-Lucero	5	2004	Miss Budweiser	Joe Little	2
1986	Miss Budweiser	Bernie Little	3	2005	Miss Elam	Erick Ellstrom	3
1987	Miss Budweiser	Bernie Little	5	2006	FormulaBoats.com II	Ted Porter	1
1988	Miss Budweiser	Bernie Little	4	2007	Miss Elam Plus	Sven Ellstrom	4

*Formerly known as Unlimited Hydroplane Racing Association.

Polo

United States Open Polo Champions

Year	Champion	Year	Champion	Year	Champion	Year	Champion
1904	Wanderers	1927	Sands Point	1949	Hurricanes	1966	Tulsa
1905–09	Not contested	1928	Meadow Brook	1950	Bostwick	1967	Bunntyco–Oak Brook
1910	Ranelagh	1929	Hurricanes	1951	Milwaukee		
1911	Not contested	1930	Hurricanes	1952	Beverly Hills	1968	Midland
1912	Cooperstown	1931	Santa Paula	1953	Meadow Brook	1969	Tulsa Greenhill
1913	Cooperstown	1932	Templeton	1954	C.C.C.–Meadow Brook	1970	Tulsa Greenhill
1914	Meadow Brook Magpies	1933	Aurora			1971	Oak Brook
		1934	Templeton	1955	C.C.C.	1972	Milwaukee
1915	Not contested	1935	Greentree	1956	Brandywine	1973	Oak Brook
1916	Meadow Brook	1936	Greentree	1957	Detroit	1974	Milwaukee
1917–18	Not contested	1937	Old Westbury	1958	Dallas	1975	Milwaukee
1919	Meadow Brook	1938	Old Westbury	1959	Circle F	1976	Willow Bend
1920	Meadow Brook	1939	Bostwick Field	1960	Oak Brook–C.C.C.	1977	Retama
1921	Great Neck	1940	Aknusti	1961	Milwaukee	1978	Abercrombie & Kent
1922	Argentine	1941	Gulf Stream	1962	Santa Barbara		
1923	Meadow Brook	1942–45	Not contested	1963	Tulsa	1979	Retama
1924	Midwick	1946	Mexico	1964	Concar Oak Brook	1980	Southern Hills
1925	Orange County	1947	Old Westbury	1965	Oak Brook–Santa Barbara	1981	Rolex A & K
1926	Hurricanes	1948	Hurricanes			1982	Retama

Polo

United States Open Polo Champions

1983 ...Ft. Lauderdale	1989 ...Les Diables Bleus	1995 ...Outback	2002 ...Team Coca Cola
1984 ...Retama	1990 ...Les Diables Bleus	1996 ...Outback	2003 ...C Spear
1985 ...Carter Ranch	1991 ...Grant's Farm	1997 ...Isla Carroll	2004 ...Isla Carroll
1986 ...Retama II	Manor	1998 ...Esque	2005 ...White Birch
1987 ...Aloha	1992 ...Hanalei Bay	1999 ...Outback	2006 ...Las Monjitas
1988 ...Les Diables	1993 ...Gehache	2000 ...Outback	2007 ....Crab Orohard
Bleus	1994 ...Aspen	2001 ...Outback	

Top-Ranked Players

The United States Polo Association ranks its registered players from minus 2 to plus 10 goals, with 10-Goal players being the game's best. At present, the USPA recognizes eight 10-Goal and twelve 9-Goal outdoor polo players:

10-GOAL

Mariano Aguerre	Agustin Merlos
Miguel Novillo Astrada	Sebastian Merlos
Adolfo Cambiaso	Juan Martin Nero
Matias G. Magrini	Facundo Pieres

9-GOAL

Eduardo Novillo Astrada	Bautista Heguy
Javier Novillo Astrada	Pablo MacDonough
Michael Vincent Azzaro	Juan Ignacio Merlos
Lucas A. Criado	Lucas Monteverde
Francisco de Narvaez	Gonzalo Pieres Jr.
Carlos Gracida	Adam Snow

Rodeo

Professional Rodeo Cowboys Association World Champions

All-Around

1929 ....Earl Thode	1950 ....Bill Linderman	1969 ....Larry Mahan	1988 ....Dave Appleton
1930 ....Clay Carr	1951 ....Casey Tibbs	1970 ....Larry Mahan	1989 ....Ty Murray
1931 ....John Schneider	1952 ....Harry Tompkins	1971 ....Phil Lyne	1990 ....Ty Murray
1932 ....Donald Nesbit	1953 ....Bill Linderman	1972 ....Phil Lyne	1991 ....Ty Murray
1933 ....Clay Carr	1954 ....Buck Rutherford	1973 ....Larry Mahan	1992 ....Ty Murray
1934 ....Leonard Ward	1955 ....Casey Tibbs	1974 ....Tom Ferguson	1993 ....Ty Murray
1935 ....Everett Bowman	1956 ....Jim Shoulders	1975 ....Tom Ferguson	1994 ....Ty Murray
1936 ....John Bowman	1957 ....Jim Shoulders	1976 ....Tom Ferguson	1995 ....Joe Beaver
1937 :...Everett Bowman	1958 ....Jim Shoulders	1977 ....Tom Ferguson	1996 ....Joe Beaver
1938 ....Burel Mulkey	1959 ....Jim Shoulders	1978 ....Tom Ferguson	1997 ....Dan Mortensen
1939 ....Paul Carney	1960 ....Harry Tompkins	1979 ....Tom Ferguson	1998 ....Ty Murray
1940 ....Fritz Truan	1961 ....Benny Reynolds	1980 ....Paul Tierney	1999 ....Fred Whitfield
1941 ....Homer Pettigrew	1962 ....Tom Nesmith	1981 ....Jimmie Cooper	2000 ....Joe Beaver
1942 ....Gerald Roberts	1963 ....Dean Oliver	1982 ....Chris Lybbert	2001 ....Cody Ohl
1943 ....Louis Brooks	1964 ....Dean Oliver	1983 ....Roy Cooper	2002 ....Trevor Brazile
1944 ....Louis Brooks	1965 ....Dean Oliver	1984 ....Dee Picket	2003 ....Trevor Brazile
1947 ....Todd Whatley	1966 ....Larry Mahan	1985 ....Lewis Feild	2004 ....Trevor Brazile
1948 ....Gerald Roberts	1967 ....Larry Mahan	1986 ....Lewis Feild	2005 ....Ryan Jarrett
1949 ....Jim Shoulders	1968 ....Larry Mahan	1987 ....Lewis Feild	2006 ....Trevor Brazile
			2007 ....Trevor Brazile

Saddle Bronc Riding

1929 ....Earl Thode	1951 ....Casey Tibbs	1971 ....Bill Smith	1991 ....Robert Etbauer
1930 ....Clay Carr	1952 ....Casey Tibbs	1972 ....Mel Hyland	1992 ....Billy Etbauer
1931 ....Earl Thode	1953 ....Casey Tibbs	1973 ....Bill Smith	1993 ....Dan Mortensen
1932 ....Peter Knight	1954 ....Casey Tibbs	1974 ....John McBeth	1994 ....Dan Mortensen
1933 ....Peter Knight	1955 ....Deb Copenhaver	1975 ....Monty Henson	1995 ....Dan Mortensen
1934 ....Leonard Ward	1956 ....Deb Copenhaver	1976 ....Monty Henson	1996 ....Billy Etbauer
1935 ....Peter Knight	1957 ....Alvin Nelson	1977 ....Bobby Berger	1997 ....Dan Mortensen
1936 ....Peter Knight	1958 ....Marty Wood	1978 ....Joe Marvel	1998 ....Dan Mortensen
1937 ....Burel Mulkey	1959 ....Casey Tibbs	1979 ....Bobby Berger	1999 ....Billy Etbauer
1938 ....Burel Mulkey	1960 ....Enoch Walker	1980 ....Clint Johnson	2000 ....Billy Etbauer
1939 ....Fritz Truan	1961 ....Winston Bruce	1981 ....B. Gjermundson	2001 ....Tom Reeves
1940 ....Fritz Truan	1962 ....Kenny McLean	1982 ....Monty Henson	2002 ....Glen O'Neil
1941 ....Doff Aber	1963 ....Guy Weeks	1983 ....B. Gjermundson	2003 ....Dan Mortensen
1942 ....Doff Aber	1964 ....Marty Wood	1984 ....B. Gjermundson	2004 ....Billy Etbauer
1943 ....Louis Brooks	1965 ....Shawn Davis	1985 ....B. Gjermundson	2005 ....Jeffery Willert
1944 ....Louis Brooks	1966 ....Marty Wood	1986 ....Bud Munroe	2006 ....Chad Ferley
1947 ....Carl Olson	1967 ....Shawn Davis	1987 ....Clint Johnson	2007 ....Rusty Allen
1948 ....Gene Pruett	1968 ....Shawn Davis	1988 ....Clint Johnson	
1949 ....Casey Tibbs	1969 ....Bill Smith	1989 ....Clint Johnson	
1950 ....Bill Linderman	1970 ....Dennis Reiners	1990 ....Robert Etbauer	

Professional Rodeo Cowboys Association World Champions *(Cont.)*

Bareback Riding

1932....Smoky Snyder	1953....Eddy Akridge	1972....Joe Alexander	1991....Clint Corey
1933....Nate Waldrum	1954....Eddy Akridge	1973....Joe Alexander	1992....Wayne Herman
1934....Leonard Ward	1955....Eddy Akridge	1974....Joe Alexander	1993....Deb Greenough
1935....Frank Schneider	1956....Jim Shoulders	1975....Joe Alexander	1994....Marvin Garrett
1936....Smoky Snyder	1957....Jim Shoulders	1976....Joe Alexander	1995....Marvin Garrett
1937....Paul Carney	1958....Jim Shoulders	1977....Joe Alexander	1996....Mark Garrett
1938....Pete Grubb	1959....Jack Buschbom	1978....Bruce Ford	1997....Eric Mouton
1939....Paul Carney	1960....Jack Buschbom	1979....Bruce Ford	1998....Mark Gomes
1940....Carl Dossey	1961....Eddy Akridge	1980....Bruce Ford	1999....Lan LaJeunesse
1941....George Mills	1962....Ralph Buell	1981....J.C. Trujillo	2000....Jeffrey Collins
1942....Louis Brooks	1963....John Hawkins	1982....Bruce Ford	2001....Lan LaJeunesse
1943....Bill Linderman	1964....Jim Houston	1983....Bruce Ford	2002....Bobby Mote
1944....Louis Brooks	1965....Jim Houston	1984....Larry Peabody	2003....Will Lowe
1947....Larry Finley	1966....Paul Mayo	1985....Lewis Feild	2004....Kelly Timberman
1948....Sonny Tureman	1967....Clyde Vamvoras	1986....Lewis Feild	2005....Will Lowe
1949....Jack Buschbom	1968....Clyde Vamvoras	1987....Bruce Ford	2006....Will Lowe
1950....Jim Shoulders	1969....Gary Tucker	1988....Marvin Garrett	2007....Bobby Mote
1951....Casey Tibbs	1970....Paul Mayo	1989....Marvin Garrett	
1952....Harry Tompkins	1971....Joe Alexander	1990....Chuck Logue	

Bull Riding

1929....John Schneider	1949....Harry Tompkins	1969....Doug Brown	1989....Tuff Hedeman
1930....John Schneider	1950....Harry Tompkins	1970....Gary Leffew	1990....Jim Sharp
1931....Smokey Snyder	1951....Jim Shoulders	1971....Bill Nelson	1991....Tuff Hedeman
1932....John Schneider	1952....Harry Tompkins	1972....John Quintana	1992....Cody Custer
1932....Smokey Snyder	1953....Todd Whatley	1973....Bobby Steiner	1993....Ty Murray
John Schneider	1954....Jim Shoulders	1974....Don Gay	1994....Daryl Mills
1933....Frank Schneider	1955....Jim Shoulders	1975....Don Gay	1995....Jerome Davis
1934....Frank Schneider	1956....Jim Shoulders	1976....Don Gay	1996....Terry West
1935....Smokey Snyder	1957....Jim Shoulders	1977....Don Gay	1997....Scott Mendes
1936....Smokey Snyder	1958....Jim Shoulders	1978....Don Gay	1998....Ty Murray
1937....Smokey Snyder	1959....Jim Shoulders	1979....Don Gay	1999....Mike White
1938....Kid Fletcher	1960....Harry Tompkins	1980....Don Gay	2000....Cody Hancock
1939....Dick Griffith	1961....Ronnie Rossen	1981....Don Gay	2001....Blue Stone
1940....Dick Griffith	1962....Freckles Brown	1982....Charles Sampson	2002....Blue Stone
1941....Dick Griffith	1963....Bill Kornell	1983....Cody Snyder	2003....Terry West
1942....Dick Griffith	1964....Bob Wegner	1984....Don Gay	2004....Dustin Elliott
1943....Ken Roberts	1965....Larry Mahan	1985....Ted Nuce	2005....Matt Austin
1944....Ken Roberts	1966....Ronnie Rossen	1986....Tuff Hedeman	2006....B.J. Schumacher
1947....Wag Blessing	1967....Larry Mahan	1987....Lane Frost	2007....B.J. Schumacher
1948....Harry Tompkins	1968....George Paul	1988....Jim Sharp	

Calf Roping

1929....Everett Bowman	1952....Don McLaughlin	1973....Ernie Taylor	1994....Herbert Theriot
1930....Jake McClure	1953....Don McLaughlin	1974....Tom Ferguson	1995....Fred Whitfield
1931....Herb Meyers	1954....Don McLaughlin	1975....Jeff Copenhaver	1996....Fred Whitfield
1932....Richard Merchant	1955....Dean Oliver	1976....Roy Cooper	1997....Cody Ohl
1933....Bill McFarlane	1956....Ray Wharton	1977....Roy Cooper	1998....Cody Ohl
1934....Irby Mundy	1957....Don McLaughlin	1978....Roy Cooper	1999....Fred Whitfield
1935....Everett Bowman	1958....Dean Oliver	1979....Paul Tierney	2000....Fred Whitfield
1936....Clyde Burk	1959....Jim Bob Altizer	1980....Roy Cooper	2001....Cody Ohl
1937....Everett Bowman	1960....Dean Oliver	1981....Roy Cooper	2002....Fred Whitfield
1938....Burel Mulkey	1961....Dean Oliver	1982....Roy Cooper	2003....Cody Ohl
1939....Toots Mansfield	1962....Dean Oliver	1983....Roy Cooper	2004....Monty Lewis
1940....Toots Mansfield	1963....Dean Oliver	1984....Roy Cooper	2005....Fred Whitfield
1941....Toots Mansfield	1964....Dean Oliver	1985....Joe Beaver	2006....Cody Ohl
1942....Clyde Burk	1965....Glen Franklin	1986....Chris Lybbert	
1943....Toots Mansfield	1966....Junior Garrison	1987....Joe Beaver	
1944....Clyde Burk	1967....Glen Franklin	1988....Joe Beaver	
1947....Troy Fort	1968....Glen Franklin	1989....Rabe Rabon	
1948....Toots Mansfield	1969....Dean Oliver	1990....Troy Pruitt	
1949....Troy Fort	1970....Junior Garrison	1991....Fred Whitfield	
1950....Toots Mansfield	1971....Phil Lyne	1992....Joe Beaver	
1951....Don McLaughlin	1972....Phil Lyne	1993....Joe Beaver	

Professional Rodeo Cowboys Association World Champions (Cont.)

Steer Wrestling

1929....Gene Ross	1951....Dub Phillips	1971....Billy Hale	1991....Ote Berry
1930....Everett Bowman	1952....Harley May	1972....Roy Duvall	1992....Mark Roy
1931....Gene Ross	1953....Ross Dollarhide	1973....Bob Marshall	1993....Steve Duhon
1932....Hugh Bennett	1954....James Bynum	1974....Tommy Puryear	1994....Blaine Pederson
1933....Everett Bowman	1955....Benny Combs	1975....F. Shepperson	1995....Ote Berry
1934....Shorty Ricker	1956....Harley May	1976....Tom Ferguson	1996....Chad Bedell
1935....Everett Bowman	1957....Clark McEntire	1977....Larry Ferguson	1997....Brad Gleason
1936....Jack Kerschner	1958....James Bynum	1978....Byron Walker	1998....Mike Smith
1937....Gene Ross	1959....Harry Charters	1979....Stan Williamson	1999....Mickey Gee
1938....Everett Bowman	1960....Bob A. Robinson	1980....Butch Myers	2000....Frank Thompson
1939....Harry Hart	1961....Jim Bynum	1981....Byron Walker	2001....Rope Myers
1940....Homer Pettigrew	1962....Tom Nesmith	1982....Stan Williamson	2002....Sid Steiner
1941....Hub Whiteman	1963....Jim Bynum	1983....Joel Edmondson	2003....Teddy Johnson
1942....Homer Pettigrew	1964....C.R. Boucher	1984....John W. Jones	2004....Luke Branquinho
1943....Homer Pettigrew	1965....Harley May	1985....Ote Berry	2005....Lee Graves
1944....Homer Pettigrew	1966....Jack Roddy	1986....Steve Duhon	2006....Den Gorsuch
1947....Todd Whatley	1967....Roy Duvall	1987....Steve Duhon	2007....Luke Branquinho
1948....Homer Pettigrew	1968....Jack Roddy	1988....John W. Jones	
1949....Bill McGuire	1969....Roy Duvall	1989....John W. Jones	
1950....Bill Linderman	1970....John W. Jones	1990....Ote Berry	

Team Roping

1929....Charles Maggini	1953....Ben Johnson	1977....Jerold Camarillo	1997....Speed Williams
1930....Norman Cowan	1954....Eddie Schell	1978....Doyle Gellerman	Rich Skelton
1931....Arthur Beloat	1955....Vern Castro	1979....Allen Bach	1998....Speed Williams
1932....Ace Gardner	1956....Dale Smith	1980....Tee Woolman	Rich Skelton
1933....Roy Adams	1957....Dale Smith	1981....Walt Woodard	1999....Speed Williams
1934....Andy Jauregui	1958....Ted Ashworth	1982....Tee Woolman	Rich Skelton
1935....Lawrence Conltk	1959....Jim Rodriguez Jr.	1983....Leo Camarillo	2000....Speed Williams
1936....John Rhodes	1960....Jim Rodriguez Jr.	1984....Dee Pickett	Rich Skelton
1937....Asbury Schell	1961....Al Hooper	1985....Jake Barnes	2001....Speed Williams
1938....John Rhodes	1962....Jim Rodriguez Jr.	1986....Clay O. Cooper	Rich Skelton
1939....Asbury Schell	1963....Les Hirdes	1987....Clay O. Cooper	2002....Speed Williams
1940....Pete Grubb	1964....Bill Hamilton	1988....Jake Barnes	Rich Skelton
1941....Jim Hudson	1965....Jim Rodriguez Jr.	1989....Jake Barnes	2003....Speed Williams
1942....Verne Castro	1966....Ken Luman	1990....Allen Bach	Rich Skelton
Vic Castro	1967....Joe Glenn	1991....Bob Harris	2004....Speed Williams
1943....Mark Hull	1968....Art Arnold	1992....Clay O. Cooper	Rich Skelton
Leonard Block	1969....Jerold Camarillo	1993....Bobby Hurley	2005....Clay Tryan,
1944....Murphy Chaney	1970....John Miller	1994....Jake Barnes	Patrick Smith
1947....Jim Brister	1971....John Miller	Clay O. Cooper	2006....Matt Sherwood,
1948....Joe Glenn	1972....Leo Camarillo	1995....Bobby Hurley	Allen Bach
1949....Ed Yanez	1973....Leo Camarillo	Allen Bach	2007....Chad Masters,
1950....Buck Sorrels	1974....H.P. Evetts	1996....Steve Purcella	Dean Tuftin
1951....Olan Sims	1975....Leo Camarillo	Steve Northcott	
1952....Asbury Schell	1976....Leo Camarillo		

Steer Roping

1929....Charles Maggini	1947....Ike Rude	1965....Sonney Wright	1983....Roy Cooper
1930....Clay Carr	1948....Everett Shaw	1966....Sonny Davis	1984....Guy Allen
1931....Andy Jauregui	1949....Shoat Webster	1967....Jim Bob Altizer	1985....Jim Davis
1932....George Weir	1950....Shoat Webster	1968....Sonny Davis	1986....Jim Davis
1933....John Bowman	1951....Everett Shaw	1969....Walter Arnold	1987....Shaun Burchett
1934....John McEntire	1952....Buddy Neal	1970....Don McLaughlin	1988....Shaun Burchett
1935....Richard Merchant	1953....Ike Rude	1971....Olin Young	1989....Guy Allen
1936....John Bowman	1954....Shoat Webster	1972....Allen Keller	1990....Phil Lyne
1937....Everett Bowman	1955....Shoat Webster	1973....Roy Thompson	1991....Guy Allen
1938....Hugh Bennett	1956....Jim Snively	1974....Olin Young	1992....Guy Allen
1939....Dick Truitt	1957....Clark McEntire	1975....Roy Thompson	1993....Guy Allen
1940....Clay Carr	1958....Clark McEntire	1976....Marvin Cantrell	1994....Guy Allen
1941....Ike Rude	1959....Everett Shaw	1977....Buddy Cockrell	1995....Guy Allen
1942....King Merrit	1960....Don McLaughlin	1978....Sonny Worrell	1996....Guy Allen
1943....Tom Rhodes	1961....Clark McEntire	1979....Gary Good	1997....Guy Allen
1944....Tom Rhodes	1962....Everett Shaw	1980....Guy Allen	1998....Guy Allen
1945....Everett Shaw	1963....Don McLaughlin	1981....Arnold Felts	1999....Guy Allen
1946....Everett Shaw	1964....Sonny Davis	1982....Guy Allen	2000....Guy Allen

Professional Rodeo Cowboys Association World Champions *(Cont.)*
Steer Roping *(Cont.)*

2001....Guy Allen	2003....Guy Allen	2005....Scott Snedecor	2007....Trevor Brazile
2002....Buster Record	2004....Guy Allen	2006....Dean Gorsuch	

Note: In 1945–46 champions were crowned only in Steer Roping.

Rowing

National Collegiate Rowing Champions

MEN

1985 ....Harvard	1993 ....Brown	2001 ....California
1986 ....Wisconsin	1994 ....Brown	2002 ....California
1987 ....Harvard	1995 ....Brown	2003 ....Harvard
1988 ....Harvard	1996 ....Princeton	2004 ....Harvard
1989 ....Harvard	1997 ....Washington	2005 ....Harvard
1990 ....Wisconsin	1998 ....Princeton	2006 ....California
1991 ....Pennsylvania	1999 ....California	2007 ....Washington
1992 ....Harvard	2000 ....California	

WOMEN

1979 ....Yale	1989 ....Cornell	1999 ....Brown
1980 ....California	1990 ....Princeton	2000 ....Brown
1981 ....Washington	1991 ....Boston University	2001 ....Washington
1982 ....Washington	1992 ....Boston University	2002 ....Brown
1983 ....Washington	1993 ....Princeton	2003 ....Harvard
1984 ....Washington	1994 ....Princeton	2004 ....Brown
1985 ....Washington	1995 ....Princeton	2005 ....California
1986 ....Wisconsin	1996 ....Brown	2006 ....California
1987 ....Washington	1997 ....Washington	2007 ....Brown
1988 ....Washington	1998 ....Washington	

Rugby Union

National Men's Club Championship

Year	Winner	Runner-Up	Year	Winner	Runner-Up
1979 ....Old Blues (Calif.)	St. Louis Falcons		1995	Potomac Athletic Club	Old Mission Beach
1980 ....Old Blues (Calif.)	St. Louis Falcons				
1981 ....Old Blues (Calif.)	Old Blue (N.Y.)		1996 ....Old Mission Beach A.C.	Old Blues (Calif.)
1982 ....Old Blues (Calif.)	Denver Barbos		1997 ....Gentlemen of Aspen	Old Blue (N.Y.)
1983 ....Old Blues (Calif.)	Dallas Harlequins		1998 ....Gentlemen of Aspen	Old Blue (N.Y.)
1984 ....Dallas Harlequins	Los Angeles		1999 ....Gentlemen of Aspen	Golden Gate (Calif.)
1985 ....Milwaukee	Denver Barbos				
1986 ....Old Blues (Calif.)	Old Blue (N.Y.)		2000 ....Gentlemen of Aspen	Hayward Griffins
1987 ....Old Blues (Calif.)	Pittsburgh		2001 ....San Mateo	New York A.C.
1988 ....Old Mission Beach A.C.	Milwaukee		2002 ....San Mateo	Austin
1989 ....Old Mission Beach A.C.	Philly/Whitemarsh		2003 ....Boston Irish Wolfhounds	San Mateo
1990 ....Denver Barbos	Old Blues (Calif.)		2004 ....Boston Irish Wolfhounds	Austin
1991 ....Old Mission Beach A.C.	Washington		2005 ....Santa Monica	Back Bay
1992 ....Old Blues (Calif.)	Mystic River (Mass.)		2006 ....Santa Monica	Boston Irish Wolfhounds
1993	Old Mission Beach A.C.	Milwaukee			
1994 ....Old Mission Beach A.C.	Life College (Ga.)		2007 ....Hayward	Austin Blacks

National Men's Collegiate Championship

Year	Winner	Runner-Up	Year	Winner	Runner-Up
1980 ....California	Air Force		1988 ....California	Dartmouth
1981 ....California	Harvard		1989 ....Air Force	Long Beach
1982 ....California	Life College		1990 ....Air Force	Army
1983 ....California	Air Force		1991 ....California	Army
1984 ....Harvard	Colorado		1992 ....California	Army
1985 ....California	Maryland		1993 ....California	Air Force
1986 ....California	Dartmouth		1994 ....California	Navy
1987 ....San Diego State	Air Force		1995 ....California	Air Force

National Men's Collegiate Championship

Year	Winner	Runner-Up	Year	Winner	Runner-Up
1996	California	Penn St	2002	California	Utah
1997	California	Penn St	2003	Air Force	Harvard
1998	California	Stanford	2004	California	Cal Poly SLO
1999	California	Penn St	2005	California	Utah
2000	California	Wyoming	2006	California	BYU
2001	California	Penn St	2007	California	BYU

World Cup Championship

Year	Winner	Runner-Up	Year	Winner	Runner-Up
1987	New Zealand	France	1999	Australia	France
1991	Australia	England	2003	England	Australia
1995	South Africa	New Zealand	2007	South Africa	England

Rugby League

American National Rugby League Champions

Year	Winner	Runner-Up
1998	Glen Mills Bulls	Philadelphia Bulldogs
1999	Glen Mills Bulls	New Jersey Sharks
2000	Glen Mills Bulls	Philadelphia Fight
2001	Glen Mills Bulls	Media Mantarays
2002	New York Knights	Glen Mills Bulls
2003	Connecticut Wildcats	Glen Mills Bulls
2004	Glen Mills Bulls	Connecticut Wildcats
2005	Glen Mills Bulls	Connecticut Wildcats
2006	Glen Mills Bulls	Connecticut Wildcats
2007	Connecticut Wildcats	Glen Mills Bulls

World Cup Championship

Year	Winner	Runner-Up	Host
1954	Great Britain	France	France
1957	Australia	International Team	Australia
1960	Great Britain	International Team	England
1968	Australia	France	Australia–New Zealand
1970	Great Britain	Australia	England
1972	Australia	Great Britain	France
1975	Australia	England	Worldwide
1977	Australia	Great Britain	Australia–New Zealand
1985–88	Australia	New Zealand	Worldwide
1989–92	Australia	Great Britain	Worldwide
1995	Australia	England	Great Britain
2000	Australia	New Zealand	G. Britain-Ireland-France

Sailing

America's Cup Champions
SCHOONERS AND J-CLASS BOATS

Year	Winner	Skipper	Series	Loser	Skipper
1851	America	Richard Brown			
1870	Magic	Andrew Comstock	1–0	Cambria, Great Britain	J. Tannock
1871	Columbia (2–1) Sappho (2–0)	Nelson Comstock Sam Greenwood	4–1	Livonia, Great Britain	J.R. Woods
1876	Madeleine	Josephus Williams	2–0	Countess of Dufferin, Canada	J.E. Ellsworth
1881	Mischief	Nathanael Clock	2–0	Atalanta, Canada	Alexander Cuthbert
1885	Puritan	Aubrey Crocker	2–0	Genesta, Great Britain	John Carter
1886	Mayflower	Martin Stone	2–0	Galatea, Great Britain	Dan Bradford
1887	Volunteer	Henry Haff	2–0	Thistle, Great Britain	John Barr
1893	Vigilant	William Hansen	3–0	Valkyrie II, Great Britain	William Granfield
1895	Defender	Henry Haff	3–0	Valkyrie III, Great Britain	William Granfield
1899	Columbia	Charles Barr	3–0	Shamrock I, Great Britain	Archie Hogarth
1901	Columbia	Charles Barr	3–0	Shamrock II, Great Britain	E.A. Sycamore

America's Cup Champions

SCHOONERS AND J-CLASS BOATS

Year	Winner	Skipper	Series	Loser	Skipper
1903	Reliance	Charles Barr	3–0	Shamrock III, Great Britain	Bob Wringe
1920	Resolute	Charles F. Adams	3–2	Shamrock IV, Great Britain	William Burton
1930	Enterprise	Harold Vanderbilt	4–0	Shamrock V, Great Britain	Ned Heard
1934	Rainbow	Harold Vanderbilt	4–2	Endeavour, Great Britain	T.O.M. Sopwith
1937	Ranger	Harold Vanderbilt	4–0	Endeavour II, Great Britain	T.O.M. Sopwith

12-METER BOATS

Year	Winner	Skipper	Series	Loser	Skipper
1958	Columbia	Briggs Cunningham	4–0	Sceptre, Great Britain	Graham Mann
1962	Weatherly	Bus Mosbacher	4–1	Gretel, Australia	Jock Sturrock
1964	Constellation	Bob Bavier & Eric Ridder	4–0	Sovereign, Australia	Peter Scott
1967	Intrepid	Bus Mosbacher	4–0	Dame Pattie, Australia	Jock Sturrock
1970	Intrepid	Bill Ficker	4–1	Gretel II, Australia	Jim Hardy
1974	Courageous	Ted Hood	4–0	Southern Cross, Australia	John Cuneo
1977	Courageous	Ted Turner	4–0	Australia	Noel Robins
1980	Freedom	Dennis Conner	4–1	Australia	Jim Hardy
1983	Australia II	John Bertrand	4–3	Liberty, United States	Dennis Conner
1987	Stars & Stripes	Dennis Conner	4–0	Kookaburra III, Australia	Iain Murray

60-FOOT CATAMARAN vs 133-FOOT MONOHULL

Year	Winner	Skipper	Series	Loser	Skipper
1988	Stars & Stripes	Dennis Conner	2–0	New Zealand	David Barnes

75-FOOT MONOHULL (IACC)

Year	Winner	Skipper	Series	Loser	Skipper
1992	America[3]	Bill Koch	4–1	Il Moro di Venezia, Italy	Paul Cayard
1995	Black Magic I	Russell Coutts	5–0	Young America, United States	Dennis Conner
2000	New Zealand	Russell Coutts	5–0	Luna Rossa, Italy	Francesco de Angelis
2003	Swiss Alinghi	Russell Coutts	5–0	New Zealand	Dean Barker
2007	Swiss Alinghi	Brad Butterworth	5–2	Emirates New Zealand	Dean Barker

Note: Winning entries have been from the United States every year but four: In 1983 an Australian vessel won, in 1995 and 2000 a vessel from New Zealand won and in 2003 a Swiss vessel won.

Shooting World Champions

Men

50M FREE RIFLE PRONE

1947 ..... O. Sannes, Norway
1949 ..... A.C. Jackson, U.S.
1952 ..... A.C. Jackson, U.S.
1954 ..... G. Boa, Canada
1958 ..... M. Nordquist
1962 ..... K. Wenk, W Germany
1966 ..... D. Boyd, U.S.
1970 ..... M. Fiess, S. Africa
1974 ..... K. Bulan, Czechoslovakia
1978 ..... A. Allan, Great Britain
1982 ..... V. Danilschenko, USSR
1986 ..... S. Bereczky, Hungary
1990 ..... V. Bochkarev, USSR
1994 ..... Venjie Li, China
1998 ..... Thomas Tamas, U.S.
1999 ..... Thomas Tamas, U.S.
2000 ..... Siarhei Martynau, Belarus
2001 ..... Matthew Emmons, U.S.
2002 ..... Matthew Emmons, U.S.
2006 ..... Sergei Martynov, Belarus

AIR RIFLE

1966 ..... G. Kümmet, W Germany
1970 ..... G. Kusterman, W Germ.
1974 ..... E. Pedzisz, Poland
1978 ..... O. Schlipf, W. Germany
1979 ..... K. Hillenbrand
1981 ..... F. Bessy, France

AIR RIFLE *(Cont.)*

1982 ..... F. Rettkowski, E Germ.
1983 ..... P. Heberle, France
1985 ..... P. Heberle, France
1986 ..... H. Riederer, W Germany
1987 ..... K. Ivanov, USSR
1989 ..... J. P. Amet, France
1990 ..... H. Riederer, W Germany
1994 ..... Boris Polak, Israel
1998 ..... Artem Khadjibekov, Russia
1999 ..... Jozef Gonci, Slovakia
2000 ..... Artem Khadjibekov, Russia
2001 ..... Jason Parker, U.S.
2002 ..... Jason Parker, U.S.
2006 ..... Abhinav Bindra, India

MEN'S TRAP

1929 ..... De Lumniczer, Hungary
1930 ..... M. Arie, U.S.
1931 ..... Kiszkurno, Poland
1933 ..... De Lumniczer, Hungary
1934 ..... A. Montagh, Hungary
1935 ..... R. Sack, W Germany
1936 ..... Kiszkurno, Poland
1937 ..... K. Huber, Finland
1938 ..... I. Strassburger, Hungary
1939 ..... De Lumniczer, Hungary
1947 ..... H. Liljedahl, Sweden

MEN'S TRAP *(Cont.)*

1949 ..... F. Rocchi, Argentina
1950 ..... C. Sala, Italy
1952 ..... P.J. Grossi, Argentina
1954 ..... C. Merlo, Italy
1958 ..... F. Eisenlauer, U.S.
1959 ..... H. Badravi, Egypt
1961 ..... E. Mattarelli, Italy
1962 ..... W. Zimenko, USSR
1965 ..... J.E. Lire, Chile
1966 ..... K. Jones, U.S.
1967 ..... G. Rennard, Belgium
1969 ..... E. Mattarelli, Italy
1970 ..... M. Carrega, France
1971 ..... M. Carrega, France
1973 ..... A. Andrushkin, USSR
1974 ..... M. Carrega, France
1975 ..... J. Primrose, Canada
1977 ..... E. Azkue, Spain
1978 ..... E. Vallduvi, Spain
1979 ..... M. Carrega, France
1981 ..... A. Asanov, USSR
1982 ..... L. Giovonnetti, Italy
1983 ..... J. Primrose, Canada
1985 ..... M. Bednarik, Czechoslovakia
1986 ..... M. Bednarik, Czechoslovakia
1987 ..... D. Monakov, USSR

Men *(Cont.)*

MEN'S TRAP *(Cont.)*

1989 .....M. Venturini, Italy
1990 .....J. Damne, E Germany
1994 .....Dmitriy Monakov, Ukraine
1995 .....Giovanni Pellielo, Italy
1998 .....Giovanni Pellielo, Italy
1999 .....Joao Rebelo, Portugal
2000 .....Michael Diamond, Australia
2001.......Michael Diamond, Australia
2002.......Khaled Almudhaf, Kuwait
2005.......Massimo Fabrizzi, Italy
2006.......Manavjit Singh Sandu, India
2007.......Michael Diamond, Australia

THREE POSITION RIFLE

1929 .....O. Ericsson, Sweden
1930 .....Petersen, Denmark
1931 .....Amundson, Norway
1933 .....De Lisle, France
1935 .....Leskinnen, Finland
1937 .....Mazoyer, France
1939 .....Steigelmann, Germany
1947 .....I.H. Erben, Sweden
1949 .....P. Janhonen, Finland
1952 .....Kongshaug, Norway
1954 .....A. Bugdanov, USSR
1958 .....Itkis, USSR
1962 .....G. Anderson, U.S.
1966 .....G. Anderson, U.S.

THREE POSITION RIFLE *(Cont.)*

1970 .....Parkhimovitch, USSR
1974 .....L. Wigger, U.S.
1978 .....E. Svensson, Sweden
1982 .....K. Ivanov, USSR
1986 .....P. Heinz, W Germany
1990 .....E. C. Lee, S Korea
1994 .....P. Kurka, Czech Republic
1998 ......Jozef Gonci, Slovakia
1999 ......Jozef Gonci, Slovakia
2000 .....Jozef Gonci, Slovakia
2001 .....Marcel Bürge, Switz
2002 .....Marcel Bürge, Switz
2006 .....Artem Khadjibekov, Russia

Women

THREE POSITION RIFLE

1966 .....M. Thompson, U.S.
1970 .....M. Thompson Murdock, U.S.
1974 .....A. Pelova, Bulgaria
1978 .....W. Oliver, U.S.
1982 .....M. Helbig, E Germany
1986 .....V. Letcheva, Bulgaria
1990 .....V. Letcheva, Bulgaria
1994 .....A. Maloukhina, Russia
1998 .....Sonja Pfeilschifter, Germany
1999 ....Sonja Pfeilschifter, Germany
2000 .....Hong Shan, China
2001 .....Petra Horneber, Germany
2002 .....Petra Horneber, Germany
2006 .....C. Jakobsen, Denmark

AIR RIFLE

1970 .....V. Cherkasque, USSR
1974 .....T. Ratkinova, USSR
1978 .....W. Oliver, U.S.
1979 .....K. Monez, U.S.
1981 .....S. Romaristova, USSR
1982 .....S. Lang, W Germany
1983 .....M. Helbig, E Germany
1985 .....E. Forian, Hungary
1986 .....V. Letcheva, Bulgaria
1987 .....V. Letcheva, Bulgaria
1989 .....V. Letcheva, Bulgaria

AIR RIFLE *(Cont.)*

1990 .....E. Joc, Hungary
1994 .....Sonja Pfeilschifter, Germany
1998 .....Sonja Pfeilschifter, Germany
1999 .....Sonja Pfeilschifter, Germany
2000 .....Sonja Pfeilschifter, Germany
2001 .....Katerina Kurkova, Czech.
2002 .....Katerina Kurkova, Czech.
2006 .....Du Li, China

SPORT PISTOL

1966 .....N. Rasskazova, USSR
1970 .....N. Stoljarova, USSR
1974 .....N. Stoljarova, USSR
1978 .....K. Dyer, USSR
1982 .....P. Balogh, Hungary
1986 .....M. Dobrantcheva, USSR
1990 .....M. Logvinenko, USSR
1994 .....Soon Hee Boo, S Korea
1998 .....Yleqing Cai, China
1999 .....Soon Hee Boo, S Korea
2000 .....Lalita Vauhleuskaya, Belarus
2001 .....Munkhbayar Dorjsuren, Germany
2002 .....Munkhbayar Dorjsuren, Germany
2006 .....Chen Ying, China

AIR PISTOL

1970 .....S. Carroll, U.S.
1974 .....Z. Simonian, USSR
1978 .....K. Hansson, Sweden
1979 .....R. Fox, U.S.
1981 .....N. Kalinina, USSR
1982 .....M. Dobrantcheva, USSR
1983 .....K. Bodin, Sweden
1985 .....M. Dobrantcheva, USSR
1986 .....A. Völker, E Germany
1987 .....J. Brajkovic, Yugoslavia
1989 .....N. Salukvadse, USSR
1990 .....Jasna Sekaric, Yugoslavia
1994 .....Jasna Sekaric, IOP
1998 .....Dorisuren Munkhbayar, Mongolia
1999 .....Nino Salukvadze, Georgia
2000 .....Luna Tao, China
2001 .....Olena Kostevych, Ukraine
2002 .....Olena Kostevych, Ukraine
2006 .....Natalia Paderina, Russia

World Cup Alpine Racing Final Standings

Men

	Pts
OVERALL Aksel Lund Svindal, Norway	1268
DOWNHILL Didier Cuche, Swiss	652
SLALOM Benjamin Raich, Austria	605
GIANT SLALOM Aksel Lund Svindal, Norway	416
SUPER G Bode Miller, USA	304
COMBINED Aksel Lund Svindal, Norway	232

Women

	Pts
OVERALL Nicole Hosp, Austria	1572
DOWNHILL Renate Gotschl, Austria	705
SLALOM Marlies Schild, Austria	760
GIANT SLALOM Nicole Hosp, Austria	490
SUPER G Renate Gotschl, Austria	540
COMBINED Marlies Schild, Austria	220

World Cup Season Title Holders

Men – OVERALL

1967 ....Jean-Claude Killy, France
1968 ....Jean-Claude Killy, France
1969 ....Karl Schranz, Austria
1970 ....Karl Schranz, Austria

1971 ....Gustavo Thoeni, Italy
1972 ....Gustavo Thoeni, Italy
1973 ....Gustavo Thoeni, Italy
1974 ....Piero Gros, Italy

Men – OVERALL *(CONT.)*

1975 ....Gustavo Thoeni, Italy	1992 ....Paul Accola, Switzerland
1976 ....Ingemar Stenmark; Sweden	1993 ....Marc Girardelli, Luxembourg
1977 ....Ingemar Stenmark, Sweden	1994 ....Kjetil André Aamodt; Norway
1978 ....Ingemar Stenmark, Sweden	1995 ....Alberto Tomba, Italy
1979 ....Peter Lüscher, Switzerland	1996 ....Lasse Kjus, Norway
1980 ....Andreas Wenzel, Liechtenstein	1997 ....Luc Alphand, France
1981 ....Phil Mahre, United States	1998 ....Hermann Maier, Austria
1982 ....Phil Mahre, United States	1999 ....Lasse Kjus, Norway
1983 ....Phil Mahre, United States	2000 ....Hermann Maier, Austria
1984 ....Pirmin Zurbriggen, Switzerland	2001 ....Hermann Maier, Austria
1985 ....Marc Girardelli, Luxembourg	2002 ....Stephan Eberharter, Austria
1986 ....Marc Girardelli, Luxembourg	2003 ....Stephan Eberharter, Austria
1987 ....Pirmin Zurbriggen, Switzerland	2004 ....Hermann Maier, Austria
1988 ....Pirmin Zurbriggen, Switzerland	2005 ....Bode Miller, United States
1989 ....Marc Girardelli, Luxembourg	2006 ....Benjamin Raich, Austria
1990 ....Pirmin Zurbriggen, Switzerland	2007 ....Aksel Lund Svindal, Norway
1991 ....Marc Girardelli, Luxembourg	

World Cup Season Title Holders

Women – OVERALL

1967 ....Nancy Greene, Canada	1988 ....Michela Figini, Switzerland
1968 ....Nancy Greene, Canada	1989 ....Vreni Schneider, Switzerland
1969 ....Gertrud Gabl, Austria	1990 ....Petra Kronberger, Austria
1970 ....Michèle Jacot, France	1991 ....Petra Kronberger, Austria
1971 ....Annemarie Pröll, Austria	1992 ....Petra Kronberger, Austria
1972 ....Annemarie Pröll, Austria	1993 ....Anita Wachter, Austria
1973 ....Annemarie Pröll, Austria	1994 ....Vreni Schneider, Switzerland
1974 ....Annemarie Moser-Proell, Austria	1995 ....Vreni Schneider, Switzerland
1975 ....Annemarie Moser-Proell, Austria	1996 ....Katja Seizinger, Germany
1976 ....Rosi Mitermaier, W Germany	1997 ....Pernilla Wiberg, Sweden
1977 ....Lise-Marie Morerod, Switzerland	1998 ....Katja Seizinger, Germany
1978 ....Hanni Wenzel, Liechtenstein	1999 ....Alexandra Meissnitzer, Austria
1979 ....Annemarie Moser-Proell, Austria	2000 ....Renate Goetschl, Austria
1980 ....Hanni Wenzel, Liechtenstein	2001 ....Janica Kostelic, Croatia
1981 ....Marie-Thérèse Nadig, Switzerland	2002 ....Michaela Dorfmeister, Austria
1982 ....Erika Hess, Switzerland	2003 ....Janica Kostelic, Austria
1983 ....Tamara McKinney, United States	2004 ....Anja Paerson, Sweden
1984 ....Erika Hess, Switzerland	2005 ....Anja Paerson, Sweden
1985 ....Michela Figini, Switzerland	2006 ....Janica Kostelic, Croatia
1986 ....Maria Walliser, Switzerland	2007 ....Nicole Hosp, Austria
1987 ....Maria Walliser, Switzerland	

Softball

U.S. Champions—Men
MAJOR FAST PITCH

1933..........J.L. Gill Boosters, Chicago	1952..........Briggs Beautyware, Detroit
1934..........Ke-Nash-A, Kenosha, Wisc.	1953..........Briggs Beautyware, Detroit
1935..........Crimson Coaches, Toledo, Ohio	1954..........Clearwater (Fla.) Bombers
1936..........Kodak Park, Rochester, N.Y.	1955..........Raybestos Cardinals, Stratford, Conn.
1937..........Briggs Body Team, Detroit	1956..........Clearwater (Fla.) Bombers
1938..........The Pohlers, Cincinnati	1957..........Clearwater (Fla.) Bombers
1939..........Carr's Boosters, Covington, Ky.	1958..........Raybestos Cardinals, Stratford, Conn.
1940..........Kodak Park, Rochester, N.Y.	1959..........Sealmasters, Aurora, Ill.
1941..........Bendix Brakes, South Bend, Ind.	1960..........Clearwater (Fla.) Bombers
1942..........Deep Rock Oilers, Tulsa	1961..........Sealmasters, Aurora, Ill.
1943..........Hammer Air Field, Fresno	1962..........Clearwater (Fla.) Bombers
1944..........Hammer Air Field, Fresno	1963..........Clearwater (Fla.) Bombers
1945..........Zollner Pistons, Fort Wayne, Ind.	1964..........Burch Tool, Detroit
1946..........Zollner Pistons, Fort Wayne, Ind.	1965..........Sealmasters, Aurora, Ill.
1947..........Zollner Pistons, Fort Wayne, Ind.	1966..........Clearwater (Fla.) Bombers
1948..........Briggs Beautyware, Detroit	1967..........Sealmasters, Aurora, Ill.
1949..........Tip Top Tailors, Toronto	1968..........Clearwater (Fla.) Bombers
1950..........Clearwater (Fla.) Bombers	1969..........Raybestos Cardinals, Stratford, Conn.
1951..........Dow Chemical, Midland, Mich.	1970..........Raybestos Cardinals, Stratford, Conn.

U.S. Champions—Men
MAJOR FAST PITCH

1971..........Welty Way, Cedar Rapids, Iowa	1990..........Penn Corp, Sioux City, Iowa
1972..........Raybestos Cardinals, Stratford, Conn.	1991..........Guanella Brothers, Rohnert Park, Calif.
1973..........Clearwater (Fla.) Bombers	1992..........Natl Health Care Disc, Sioux City, Iowa
1974..........Gianella Bros, Santa Rosa, Calif.	1993..........Natl Health Care Disc, Sioux City, Iowa
1975..........Rising Sun Hotel, Reading, Pa.	1994..........Decatur Pride, Decatur, Ill.
1976..........Raybestos Cardinals, Stratford, Conn.	1995..........Decatur Pride, Decatur, Ill.
1977..........Billard Barbell, Reading, Pa.	1996..........Green Bay All-Car, Green Bay, Wisc.
1978..........Billard Barbell, Reading, Pa.	1997..........Green Bay All-Car, Green Bay, Wisc.
1979..........McArdle Pontiac/Cadillac, Midland, Mich.	1998..........Meierhoffer-Fleeman, St. Joseph, Mo.
1980..........Peterbilt Western, Seattle	1999..........Decatur Pride, Decatur, Ill.
1981..........Archer Daniels Midland, Decatur, Ill.	2000..........Meierhoffer, St. Joseph, Mo.
1982..........Peterbilt Western, Seattle	2001..........Frontier Players Casino, St. Joseph, Mo.
1983..........Franklin Cardinals, Stratford, Conn.	2002..........Frontier Players Casino, St. Joseph, Mo.
1984..........California Kings, Merced, Calif.	2003..........Farm Tavern, Madison, Wisc.
1985..........Pay'n Pak, Seattle	2004..........Farm Tavern, Madison, Wisc.
1986..........Pay'n Pak, Seattle	2005..........Tampa Bay Smokers, Tampa Bay, Fla.
1987..........Pay'n Pak, Seattle	2006..........Circle Tap, Green Bay, Wisc.
1988..........TransAire, Elkhart, Ind.	2007..........Patsy's, New York, N.Y.
1989..........Penn Corp, Sioux City, Iowa	

MAJOR SLOW PITCH

1953..........Shields Construction, Newport, Ky.	1982..........Triangle Sports, Minneapolis
1954..........Waldneck's Tavern, Cincinnati	1983..........No. 1 Electric & Heating, Gastonia, N.C.
1955..........Lang Pet Shop, Covington, Ky.	1984..........Lilly Air Systems, Chicago
1956..........Gatliff Auto Sales, Newport, Ky.	1985..........Blanton's, Fayetteville, N.C.
1957..........Gatliff Auto Sales, Newport, Ky.	1986..........Non-Ferrous Metals, Cleveland
1958..........East Side Sports, Detroit	1987..........Starpath, Monticello, Ky.
1959..........Yorkshire Restaurant, Newport, Ky.	1988..........Bell Corp/FAF, Tampa, Fla.
1960..........Hamilton Tailoring, Cincinnati	1989..........Ritch's Salvage, Harrisburg, N.C.
1961..........Hamilton Tailoring, Cincinnati	1990..........New Construction, Shelbyville, Ind.
1962..........Skip Hogan A.C., Pittsburgh	1991..........Riverside Paving, Louisville, Ky.
1963..........Gatliff Auto Sales, Newport, Ky.	1992..........Vernon's, Jacksonville, Fla.
1964..........Skip Hogan A.C., Pittsburgh	1993..........Back Porch/Destin Roofing, Destin, Fla.
1965..........Skip Hogan A.C., Pittsburgh	1994..........Riverside RAM/Taylor Bros., Louisville, Ky.
1966..........Michael's Lounge, Detroit	1995..........Riverside/RAM/Taylor/TPS, Louisville, Ky.
1967..........Jim's Sport Shop, Pittsburgh	1996..........Bell 2/Robert's/Easton, Orlando, Fla.
1968..........County Sports, Levittown, N.Y.	1997..........Long Haul/TPS, Albertville, Minn.
1969..........Copper Hearth, Milwaukee	1998..........Chase Mortgage/Easton, Wilmington, N.C.
1970..........Little Caesar's, Southgate, Mich.	1999..........Gasoline Heaven/Worth, Commack, N.Y.
1971..........Pile Drivers, Virginia Beach, Va.	2000..........Long Haul/TPS, Albertville, Minn.
1972..........Jiffy Club, Louisville, Ky.	2001..........New Construction, Shelbyville, Ind.
1973..........Howard's Furniture, Denver, N.C.	2002..........Twin States/Worth, Montgomery, Ala.
1974..........Howard's Furniture, Denver, N.C.	2003..........New Construction/B&J/Snap-On,
1975..........Pyramid Cafe, Lakewood, Ohio	Metamora, Ill.
1976..........Warren Motors, Jacksonville, Fla.	2004..........U.S. Vinyl/ZWear, Lafayette, Ga.
1977..........Nelson Painting, Oklahoma City	2005..........Vegas/Benfield/Easton, Manassas, Va.
1978..........Campbell Carpets, Concord, Calif.	2006..........Northwest Pipe/Bud Light/3N2/Easton,
1979..........Nelco Mfg Co., Oklahoma City	Westland, Mich.
1980..........Campbell Carpets, Concord, Calif.	2007..........Long Haul Trucking/Miken, of Durand, Wis.
1981..........Elite Coating, Gordon, Calif.	

U.S. Champions—Women
MAJOR FAST PITCH

1933..........Great Northerns, Chicago	1947..........Jax Maids, New Orleans
1934..........Hart Motors, Chicago	1948..........Arizona Ramblers, Phoenix
1935..........Bloomer Girls, Cleveland	1949..........Arizona Ramblers, Phoenix
1936..........Nat'l Screw & Mfg., Cleveland	1950..........Orange (Calif.) Lionettes
1937..........Nat'l Screw & Mfg., Cleveland	1951..........Orange (Calif.) Lionettes
1938..........J.J. Krieg's, Alameda, Calif.	1952..........Orange (Calif.) Lionettes
1939..........J.J. Krieg's, Alameda, Calif.	1953..........Betsy Ross Rockets, Fresno
1940..........Arizona Ramblers, Phoenix	1954..........Leach Motor Rockets, Fresno
1941..........Higgins Midgets, Tulsa	1955..........Orange (Calif.) Lionettes
1942..........Jax Maids, New Orleans	1956..........Orange (Calif.) Lionettes
1943..........Jax Maids, New Orleans	1957..........Hacienda Rockets, Fresno
1944..........Lind & Pomeroy, Portland, Ore.	1958..........Raybestos Brakettes, Stratford, Conn.
1945..........Jax Maids, New Orleans	1959..........Raybestos Brakettes, Stratford, Conn.
1946..........Jax Maids, New Orleans	1960..........Raybestos Brakettes, Stratford, Conn.

U.S. Champions—Women
MAJOR FAST PITCH

1961	Gold Sox, Whittier, Calif.	1985	Hi-Ho Brakettes, Stratford, Conn.
1962	Orange (Calif.) Lionettes	1986	Southern California Invasion, Los Angeles
1963	Raybestos Brakettes, Stratford, Conn.	1987	Orange County Majestics, Anaheim, Calif.
1964	Erv Lind Florists, Portland, Ore.	1988	Hi-Ho Brakettes, Stratford, Conn.
1965	Orange (Calif.) Lionettes	1989	Whittier (Calif.) Raiders
1966	Raybestos Brakettes, Stratford, Conn.	1990	Raybestos Brakettes, Stratford, Conn.
1967	Raybestos Brakettes, Stratford, Conn.	1991	Raybestos Brakettes, Stratford, Conn.
1968	Raybestos Brakettes, Stratford, Conn.	1992	Raybestos Brakettes, Stratford, Conn.
1969	Orange (Calif.) Lionettes	1993	Redding Rebels, Redding, Calif.
1970	Orange (Calif.) Lionettes	1994	Redding Rebels, Redding, Calif.
1971	Raybestos Brakettes, Stratford, Conn.	1995	Redding Rebels, Redding, Calif.
1972	Raybestos Brakettes, Stratford, Conn.	1996	California Commotion, Woodland Hills, Calif.
1973	Raybestos Brakettes, Stratford, Conn.	1997	California Commotion, Woodland Hills, Calif.
1974	Raybestos Brakettes, Stratford, Conn.	1998	California Commotion, Woodland Hills, Calif.
1975	Raybestos Brakettes, Stratford, Conn.	1999	California Commotion, Woodland Hills, Calif.
1976	Raybestos Brakettes, Stratford, Conn.	2000	Phoenix Storm, Phoenix
1977	Raybestos Brakettes, Stratford, Conn.	2001	Phoenix Storm, Phoenix
1978	Raybestos Brakettes, Stratford, Conn.	2002	Stratford Brakettes, Stratford, Conn.
1979	Sun City (Ariz.) Saints	2003	Stratford Brakettes, Stratford, Conn.
1980	Raybestos Brakettes, Stratford, Conn.	2004	Stratford Brakettes, Stratford, Conn.
1981	Orlando (Fla.) Rebels	2005	Schutt Hurricanes, Burbank, Calif.
1982	Raybestos Brakettes, Stratford, Conn.	2006	Stratford Brakettes, Stratford, Conn.
1983	Raybestos Brakettes, Stratford, Conn.	2007	Stratford Brakettes, Stratford, Conn.
1984	Los Angeles Diamonds		

MAJOR SLOW PITCH

1959	Pearl Laundry, Richmond, Va.	1985	Key Ford Mustangs, Pensacola, Fla.
1960	Carolina Rockets, High Pt, N.C.	1986	Sur-Way Tomboys, Tifton, Ga.
1961	Dairy Cottage, Covington, Ky.	1987	Key Ford Mustangs, Pensacola, Fla.
1962	Dana Gardens, Cincinnati	1988	Spooks, Anoka, Minn.
1963	Dana Gardens, Cincinnati	1989	Canaan's Illusions, Houston
1964	Dana Gardens, Cincinnati	1990	Spooks, Anoka, Minn.
1965	Art's Acres, Omaha, Neb.	1991	Kannan's Illusions, San Antonio, Tex.
1966	Dana Gardens, Cincinnati	1992	Universal Plastics, Cookeville, Tenn.
1967	Ridge Maintenance, Cleveland	1993	Universal Plastics, Cookeville, Tenn.
1968	Escue Pontiac, Cincinnati	1994	Universal Plastics, Cookeville, Tenn.
1969	Converse Dots, Hialeah, Fla.	1995	Armed Forces, Sacramento, Calif.
1970	Rutenschruder Floral, Cincinnati	1996	Spooks, Anoka, Minn.
1971	Gators, Ft. Lauderdale, Fla.	1997	Taylor's Major Slow Pitch, Glendale, Md.
1972	Riverside Ford, Cincinnati	1998	Lakerettes, Conneaut Lake, Pa.
1973	Sweeney Chevrolet, Cincinnati	1999	Lakerettes, Conneaut Lake, Pa.
1974	Marks Brothers Dots, Miami, Fla.	2000	Premier Motor Sports, Pittsboro, N.C.
1975	Marks Brothers Dots, Miami, Fla.	2001	Shooters/Nike, Orlando, Fla.
1976	Sorrento's Pizza, Cincinnati	2002	Diamond Queens, Nashville, Tenn.
1977	Fox Valley Lassies, St. Charles, Ill.	2003	Shooters/Worth, Orlando, Fla.
1978	Bob Hoffman's Dots, Miami, Fl.a	2004	Enough Said/Easton, Tallahassee, Fla.
1979	Bob Hoffman's Dots, Miami, Fla.	2005	Armed Forces, San Antonio, Tex.
1980	Howard's Rubi-Otts, Graham, N.C.	2006	Long Haul/Enough Said/Easton, Tallahassee, Fla.
1981	Tifton (Ga.) Tomboys		
1982	Richmond (Va.) Stompers	2007	Armed Forces, Washington, D.C.
1983	Spooks, Anoka, Minn.		
1984	Spooks, Anoka, Minn.		

Beginning in 2003, the ASA combined the Women's Class Major, Class-A and Class-B into 1 'open' class.

Speed Skating
All-Around World Champions
MEN

1891	Joseph F. Donoghue, U.S.	1901	Franz F. Wathan, Finland	1913	Oscar Mathisen, Norway
1893	Jaap Eden, Netherlands	1904	Sigurd Mathisen, Norway	1914	Oscar Mathisen, Norway
1895	Jaap Eden, Netherlands	1905	C. Coen de Koning, Neth.	1922	Harald Strom, Norway
1896	Jaap Eden, Netherlands	1908	Oscar Mathisen, Norway	1923	Klas Thunberg, Finland
1897	Jack K. McCulloch, Can.	1909	Oscar Mathisen, Norway	1924	Roald Larsen, Norway
1898	Peder Ostlund, Norway	1910	Nikolai Strunnikov, Russia	1925	Klas Thunberg, Finland
1899	Peder Ostlund, Norway	1911	Nikolai Strunnikov, Russia	1926	Ivar Ballangrud, Norway
1900	Edvard Engelsaas, Norw.	1912	Oscar Mathisen, Norway	1927	Bernt Evensen, Norway

All-Around World Champions
MEN

1928 .....Klas Thunberg, Finland	1960 .....Boris Stenin, USSR	1984 .....Oleg Bozhev, USSR
1929 .....Klas Thunberg, Finland	1961 .....Henk van der Grift, Neth.	1985......Hein Vergeer, Netherlands
1930 .....Michael Staksrud, Norw.	1962 .....Viktor Kosichkin, USSR	1986......Hein Vergeer, Netherlands
1931 .....Klas Thunberg, Finland	1963 .....Jonny Nilsson, Sweden	1987 .....Nikolai Guliaev, USSR
1932 .....Ivar Ballangrud, Norway	1964 .....Knut Johannesen, Norw.	1988 .....Eric Flaim, U.S.
1933 .....Hans Engnestangen, Norw.	1965 .....Per Ivar Moe, Norway	1989 .....Leo Visser, Netherlands
1934 .....Bernt Evensen, Norway	1966 .....Kees Verkerk, Neth.	1990 .....Johann Olav Koss, Norw.
1935 .....Michael Staksrud, Norw.	1967 .....Kees Verkerk, Neth.	1991 .....Johann Olav Koss, Norw.
1936 .....Ivar Ballangrud, Norway	1968 .....Fred Anton Maier, Norw.	1992 .....Roberto Sighel, Italy
1937 .....Michael Staksrud, Nor.	1969 .....Dag Fornaes, Norway	1993 .....Falko Zandstra, Neth.
1938 .....Ivar Ballangrud, Norway	1970 .....Ard Schenk, Netherlands	1994 .....Johann Olav Koss, Norw.
1939 .....Birger Wasenius, Finland	1971 .....Ard Schenk, Netherlands	1995 .....Rintje Ritsma, Netherlands
1947 .....Lassi Parkkinen, Finland	1972 .....Ard Schenk, Netherlands	1996......Rintje Ritsma, Netherlands
1948 .....Odd Lundberg, Norway	1973 .....Göran Claeson, Sweden	1997 .....Ids Postma, Netherlands
1949 .....Kornel Pajor, Hungary	1974 .....Sten Stensen, Norway	1998 .....Ids Postma, Netherlands
1950 .....Hjalmar Andersen, Norw.	1975 .....Harm Kuipers, Netherlands	1999 .....Rintje Ritsma, Neth.
1951 .....Hjalmar Andersen, Norw.	1976 .....Piet Kleine, Netherlands	2000 .....Gianni Romme, Neth.
1952 .....Hjalmar Andersen, Norw.	1977 .....Eric Heiden, U.S.	2001 .....Rintje Ritsma, Neth.
1953 .....Oleg Goncharenko, USSR	1978 .....Eric Heiden, U.S.	2002 .....Jochem Uytdehaage, Neth.
1954 .....Boris Shilkov, USSR	1979 .....Eric Heiden, U.S.	2003 .....Gianni Romme, Neth.
1955 .....Sigvard Ericsson, Swe.	1980 .....Hilbert van der Duin,	2004 .....Chad Hedrick, United States
1956 .....Oleg Goncharenko, USSR	Neth.	2005 .....Shani Davis, United States
1957 .....Knut Johannesen, Norw.	1981 .....Amund Sjobrand, Norway	2006 .....Shani Davis, United States
1958 .....Oleg Goncharenko, USSR	1982 .....Hilbert van der Duin, Neth.	2007 .....Sven Kramer, Netherlands
1959 .....Juhani Järvinen, Finland	1983 .....Rolf Falk-Larssen, Norw.	

WOMEN

1936 .....Kit Klein, United States	1966 .....Valentina Stenina, USSR	1989 .....Constanze Moser, East Germ.
1937 .....Laila Schou Nilsen, Norw.	1967 .....Stien Kaiser, Netherlands	1990 .....Jacqueline Börner, East Germ.
1938 .....Laila Schou Nilsen, Norw.	1968 .....Stien Kaiser, Netherlands	1991 .....Gunda Kleemann, Germ.
1939 .....Verné Lesche, Finland	1969 .....Lasma Kauniste, USSR	1992 .....Gunda Niemann-
1947 .....Verné Lesche, Finland	1970 .....Atje Keulen-Deelstra, Neth.	Kleemann, Germany
1948 .....Maria Isakova, USSR	1971 .....Nina Statkevich, USSR	1993 .....Gunda Niemann, Germany
1949 .....Maria Isakova, USSR	1972 .....Atje Keulen-Deelstra, Neth.	1994 .....Emese Hunyady, Austria
1950 .....Maria Isakova, USSR	1973 .....Atje Keulen-Deelstra, Neth.	1995 .....Gunda Niemann, Germany
1951 .....Eevi Huttunen, Finland	1974 .....Atje Keulen-Deelstra, Neth.	1996......Gunda Niemann, Germany
1952 .....Lidia Selikhova, USSR	1975 .....Karin Kessow, East Ger.	1997......Gunda Niemann, Germany
1953 ....Khalida Shchegoleeva, USSR	1976 .....Sylvia Burka, Canada	1997 .....Gunda Niemann, Germany
1954 .....Lidia Selikhova, USSR	1977 .....Vera Bryndzej, USSR	1998......Gunda Niemann, Germany
1955 .....Rimma Zhukova, USSR	1978 .....Tatiana Averina, USSR	1999......Gunda Niemann, Germany
1956 .....Sofia Kondakova, USSR	1979 .....Beth Heiden, United States	2000 .....Claudia Pechstein, Germ.
1957 .....Inga Artamonova, USSR	1980 .....Natalia Petruseva, USSR	2001 .....Anni Friesinger, Germany
1958 .....Inga Artamonova, USSR	1981 .....Natalia Petruseva, USSR	2002 .....Anni Friesinger, Germany
1959 .....Tamara Rylova, USSR	1982 .....Karin Busch, East Ger.	2003 .....Cindy Klassen, Canada
1960 .....Valentina Stenina, USSR	1983 .....Andrea Schöne, East Germ.	2004 .....Renate Groenewold, Neth.
1961 .....Valentina Stenina, USSR	1984 .....Karin Enke-Busch, East Germ.	2005 .....Anni Friesinger, Germany
1962 .....Inga Artamonova, USSR	1985 .....Andrea Schöne, East Germ.	2006 .....Cindy Klassen, Canada
1963 .....Lidia Skoblikova, USSR	1986 .....Karin Enke-Busch, East Germ.	2007 .....Ireen Wüst, Netherlands
1964 .....Lidia Skoblikova, USSR	1987 .....Karin Kania, East Gemr.	
1965 .....Inga Artamonova, USSR	1988 .....Karin Kania, East Germ.	

Squash

National Men's Champions
HARD BALL

Year	Champion	Year	Champion	Year	Champion
1907.........John A. Miskey		1915.........Stanley W. Pearson		1924.........Gerald Roberts	
1908.........John A. Miskey		1916.........Stanley W. Pearson		1925.........W. Palmer Dixon	
1909.........William L. Freeland		1917.........Stanley W. Pearson		1926.........W. Palmer Dixon	
1910.........John A. Miskey		1918–19...No tournament		1927.........Myles Baker	
1911.........Francis S. White		1920.........Charles C. Peabody		1928.........Herbert N. Rawlins Jr.	
1912.........Constantine Hutchins		1921.........Stanley W. Pearson		1929.........J. Lawrence Pool	
1913.........Morton L. Newhall		1922.........Stanley W. Pearson		1930.........Herbert N. Rawlins Jr.	
1914.........Constantine Hutchins		1923.........Stanley W. Pearson		1931.........J. Lawrence Pool	

National Men's Champions
HARD BALL *(CONT.)*

Year	Champion	Year	Champion	Year	Champion
1932	Beckman H. Pool	1959	Benjamin H. Heckscher	1983	Kenton Jernigan
1933	Beckman H. Pool	1960	G. Diehl Mateer Jr.	1984	Kenton Jernigan
1934	Neil J. Sullivan II	1961	Henri R. Salaun	1987	Frank J. Stanley IV
1935	Donald Strachan	1962	Samuel P. Howe III	1988	Scott Dulmage
1936	Germain G. Glidden	1963	Benjamin H.	1989	Rodolfo Rodriquez
1937	Germain G. Glidden		Heckscher	1990	Hector Barragan
1938	Germain G. Glidden	1964	Ralph E. Howe	1991	Hector Barragan
1939	Donald Strachan	1965	Stephen T. Vehslage	1992	Hector Barragan
1940	A. Willing Patterson	1966	Victor Niederhoffer	1985	Kenton Jernigan
1941	Charles M.P. Britton	1967	Samuel P. Howe III	1986	Hugh LaBossier
1942	Charles M.P. Britton	1968	Colin Adair	1993	Hector Barragan
1943–45	No tournament	1969	Anil Nayar	1994	Hector Barragan
1946	Charles M.P. Britton	1970	Anil Nayar	1995	W. Keen Butcher
1947	Charles M.P. Britton	1971	Colin Adair	1996	W. Keen Butcher
1948	Stanley W. Pearson Jr.	1972	Victor Niederhoffer	1997	Rob Hill
1949	H. Hunter Lott Jr.	1973	Victor Niederhoffer	1998	Rob Hill
1950	Edward J. Hahn	1974	Victor Niederhoffer	1999	Rob Hill
1951	Edward J. Hahn	1975	Victor Niederhoffer	2000	Thomas Harrity
1952	Harry B. Conlon	1976	Peter Briggs	2001	Rob Hill
1953	Ernest Howard	1977	Thomas E. Page	2002	Gary Waite
1954	G. Diehl Mateer Jr.	1978	Michael Desaulniers	2003	Thomas Harrity
1955	Henri R. Salaun	1979	Mario Sanchez	2004	Thomas Harrity
1956	G. Diehl Mateer Jr.	1980	Michael Desaulniers	2005	Thomas Harrity
1957	Henri R. Salaun	1981	Mark Alger	2006	Thomas Harrity
1958	Henri R. Salaun	1982	John Nimick	2007	Iago Cornes

SOFT BALL

Year	Champion	Year	Champion	Year	Champion
1983	Kenton Jernigan	1992	Phil Yarrow	2001	Damian Walker
1984	Kenton Jernigan	1993	Phil Yarrow	2002	Damian Walker
1985	Kenton Jernigan	1994	Roberto Rosales	2003	Preston Quick
1986	Darius Pandole	1995	A. Martin Clark	2004	Preston Quick
1987	Richard Hashim	1996	Mohsen Mir	2005	Jullian Illingworth
1988	John Phelan	1997	A. Martin Clark	2006	Jonathon Power
1989	Will Carlin	1998	A. Martin Clark	2007	Nick Matthew
1990	Syed Jafry	1999	David McNeely		
1991	Hector Barragan	2000	A. Martin Clark		

National Women's Champions
HARD BALL

Year	Champion	Year	Champion	Year	Champion
1928	Eleanora Sears	1955	Janet Morgan	1978	Gretchen Spruance
1929	Margaret Howe	1956	Betty Howe Constable	1979	Heather McKay
1930	Hazel Wightman	1957	Betty Howe Constable	1980	Barbara Maltby
1931	Ruth Banks	1958	Betty Howe Constable	1981	Barbara Maltby
1932	Margaret Howe	1959	Betty Howe Constable	1982	Alicia McConnell
1933	Susan Noel	1960	Margaret Varner	1983	Alicia McConnell
1934	Margaret Howe	1961	Margaret Varner	1984	Alicia McConnell
1935	Margot Lumb	1962	Margaret Varner	1985	Alicia McConnell
1936	Anne Page	1963	Margaret Varner	1986	Alicia McConnell
1937	Anne Page	1964	Ann Wetzel	1987	Alicia McConnell
1938	Cecile Bowes	1965	Joyce Davenport	1988	Alicia McConnell
1939	Anne Page	1966	Betty Meade	1986	Alicia McConnell
1940	Cecile Bowes	1967	Betty Meade	1987	Alicia McConnell
1941	Cecile Bowes	1968	Betty Meade	1988	Alicia McConnell
1942–46	No tournament	1969	Joyce Davenport	1989	Demer Holleran
1947	Anne Page Homer	1970	Nina Moyer	1990	Demer Holleran
1948	Cecile Bowes	1971	Carol Thesieres	1991	Demer Holleran
1949	Janet Morgan	1972	Nina Moyer	1992	Demer Holleran
1950	Betty Howe	1973	Gretchen Spruance	1993	Demer Holleran
1951	Jane Austin	1974	Gretchen Spruance	1994	Demer Holleran
1952	Margaret Howe	1975	Ginny Akabane		
1953	Margaret Howe	1976	Gretchen Spruance		
1954	Lois Dilks	1977	Gretchen Spruance	Note: Tournament not held since 1994.	

National Women's Champions
SOFT BALL

Year	Champion	Year	Champion	Year	Champion
1983	Alicia McConnell	1991	Ellie Pierce	1999	Demer Holleran
1984	Julie Harris	1992	Demer Holleran	2000	Latasha Khan
1985	Sue Clinch	1993	Demer Holleran	2001	Shabana Khan
1986	Julie Harris	1994	Demer Holleran	2002	Latasha Khan
1987	Diana Staley	1995	Ellie Pierce	2003	Latasha Khan
1988	Sara Luther	1996	Demer Holleran	2004	Latasha Khan
1989	Nancy Gengler	1997	Demer Holleran	2005	Latasha Khan
1990	Joyce Maycock	1998	Latasha Khan	2006	Latasha Khan

Triathlon

Ironman World Championship

	MEN			WOMEN	
Year	Winner	Time	Year	Winner	Time
1978	Gordon Haller	11:46	1978	No finishers	
1979	Tom Warren	11:15:56	1979	Lyn Lemaire	12:55
1980	Dave Scott	9:24:33	1980	Robin Beck	11:21:24
1981	John Howard	9:38:29	1981	Linda Sweeney	12:00:32
1982	Scott Tinley	9:19:41	1982	Kathleen McCartney	11:09:40
1982	Dave Scott	9:08:23	1982	Julie Leach	10:54:08
1983	Dave Scott	9:05:57	1983	Sylviane Puntous	10:43:36
1984	Dave Scott	8:54:20	1984	Sylviane Puntous	10:25:13
1985	Scott Tinley	8:50:54	1985	Joanne Ernst	10:25:22
1986	Dave Scott	8:28:37	1986	Paula Newby-Fraser	9:49:14
1987	Dave Scott	8:34:13	1987	Erin Baker	9:35:25
1988	Scott Molina	8:31:00	1988	Paula Newby-Fraser	9:01:01
1989	Mark Allen	8:09:15	1989	Paula Newby-Fraser	9:00:56
1990	Mark Allen	8:28:17	1990	Erin Baker	9:13:42
1991	Mark Allen	8:18:32	1991	Paula Newby-Fraser	9:07:52
1992	Mark Allen	8:09:09	1992	Paula Newby-Fraser	8:55:29
1993	Mark Allen	8:07:46	1993	Paula Newby-Fraser	8:58:23
1994	Greg Welch	8:20:27	1994	Paula Newby-Fraser	9:20:14
1995	Mark Allen	8:20:34	1995	Karen Smyers	9:16:46
1996	Luc Van Lierde	8:04:08	1996	Paula Newby-Fraser	9:06:49
1997	Thomas Hellriegel	8:33:01	1997	Heather Fuhr	9:31:43
1998	Peter Reid	8:24:20	1998	Natascha Badmann	9:24:16
1999	Luc Van Lierde	8:17:17	1999	Lori Bowden	9:13:02
2000	Peter Reid	8:21:01	2000	Natascha Badmann	9:26:17
2001	Tim DeBoom	8:31:18	2001	Natascha Badmann	9:28:37
2002	Tim DeBoom	8:29:56	2002	Natascha Badmann	9:07:54
2003	Peter Reid	8:22:35	2003	Lori Bowden	9:11:55
2004	Normann Stadler	8:33:20	2004	Natascha Badmann	9:50:04
2005	Faris Al-Sutan	8:14:17	2005	Natascha Badmann	9:09:30
2006	Normann Stadler	8:11:56	2006	Michellie Jones	9:18:31

Note: The Ironman Championship was contested twice in 1982.
Sites: Waikiki Beach (1978–79); Ala Moana Park (1980); Kailua-Kona (since 1981).

U.S. Triathlon National Champions* — MEN

Year	Winner	Year	Winner	Year	Winner	Year	Winner
1984	Scott Molina	1990	Scott Molina	1996	Jeff Devlin	2002	Seth Wealing
1985	Scott Molina	1991	Mike Pigg	1997	C. Wydoff	2003	Hunter Kemper
1986	Scott Molina	1992	Mike Pigg	1998	Hunter Kemper	2004	Matt Reed
1987	Mike Pigg	1993	Bill Braun	1999	Hunter Kemper	2005	Hunter Kemper
1988	Mike Pigg	1994	Scott Molina	2000	Marcel Viffian	2006	M.Bonnet-Eymard
1989	Ken Glah	1995	Jeff Devlin	2001	Hunter Kemper	2007	Ben Collins

U.S. Triathlon National Champions* — WOMEN

Year	Winner	Year	Winner	Year	Winner	Year	Winner
1984	Beth Mitchell	1990	Karen Smyers	1996	Susan Latshaw	2002	Barb Lindquist
1985	L. Buchanan	1991	Karen Smyers	1997	Sian Welch	2003	Laura Reback
1986	K. Hanssen	1992	Karen Smyers	1998	Siri Lindley	2004	Courtney Bennigson
1987	K. Hanssen	1993	Karen Smyers	1999	Barb Lindquist	2005	Becky Lavelle
1988	C. Kaushansky	1994	Karen Smyers	2000	Joanna Zeiger	2006	Jennifer Garrison
1989	Jan Ripple	1995	Karen Smyers	2001	Karen Smyers	2007	Jennifer Garrison

*Olympic distances: 1.5 km swim, 40km bike, 10km run.

World Champions — Men

Year	Winner	Runner-up	Site
1949	Soviet Union	Czechoslovakia	Prague
1952	Soviet Union	Czechoslovakia	Moscow
1956	Czechoslovakia	Soviet Union	Paris
1960	Soviet Union	Czechoslovakia	Rio de Janeiro
1962	Soviet Union	Czechoslovakia	Moscow
1966	Czechoslovakia	Romania	Prague
1970	East Germany	Bulgaria	Sofia, Bulgaria
1974	Poland	Soviet Union	Mexico City
1978	Soviet Union	Italy	Rome
1982	Soviet Union	Brazil	Buenos Aires
1986	United States	Soviet Union	Paris
1990	Italy	Cuba	Rio de Janeiro
1994	Italy	Netherlands	Athens
1998	Italy	Yugoslavia	Tokyo
2002	Brazil	Russia	Buenos Aires
2006	Brazil	Poland	Japan

World Champions — Women

Year	Winner	Runner-up	Site
1952	Soviet Union	Poland	Moscow
1956	Soviet Union	Romania	Paris
1960	Soviet Union	Japan	Rio de Janeiro
1962	Japan	Soviet Union	Moscow
1966	Japan	United States	Prague
1970	Soviet Union	Japan	Sofia, Bulgaria
1974	Japan	Soviet Union	Mexico City
1978	Cuba	Japan	Rome
1982	China	Peru	Lima, Peru
1986	China	Cuba	Prague
1990	Soviet Union	China	Beijing
1994	Cuba	Brazil	Sao Paulo, Brazil
1998	Cuba	China	Osaka, Japan
2002	Italy	United States	Berlin
2006	Russia	Brazil	Japan

U.S. Men's Open Champions—Gold Division

1928	Germantown, Pa. YMCA
1929	Hyde Park YMCA, Ill.
1930	Hyde Park YMCA, Ill.
1931	San Antonio, Tex. YMCA
1932	San Antonio, Tex. YMCA
1933	Houston, Tex. YMCA
1934	Houston, Tex. YMCA
1935	Houston, Tex. YMCA
1936	Houston, Tex. YMCA
1937	Duncan YMCA, Ill.
1938	Houston, Tex. YMCA
1939	Houston, Tex. YMCA
1940	Los Angeles A.C., CA
1941	North Ave. YMCA, Ill.
1942	North Ave. YMCA, Ill.
1943–44	No championships
1945	North Ave. YMCA, Ill.
1946	Pasadena, Calif. YMCA
1947	North Ave. YMCA, Ill.
1948	Hollywood, Calif. YMCA
1949	Downtown YMCA, Calif.
1950	Long Beach, Calif. YMCA
1951	Hollywood, Calif. YMCA
1952	Hollywood, Calif. YMCA
1953	Hollywood, Calif. YMCA
1954	Stockton, Calif. YMCA
1955	Stockton, Calif. YMCA
1956	Hollywood, Calif. YMCA Stars
1957	Hollywood, Calif. YMCA Stars
1958	Hollywood, Calif. YMCA Stars
1959	Hollywood, Calif. YMCA Stars
1960	Westside JCC, Calif.
1961	Hollywood, Calif. YMCA
1962	Hollywood, Calif. YMCA
1963	Hollywood, Calif. YMCA
1964	Hollywood, Calif. YMCA Stars
1965	Westside JCC, Calif.
1966	Sand & Sea Club, Calif.
1967	Fresno, Calif. VBC
1968	Westside JCC, Los Angeles, Calif.
1969	Los Angeles, Calif. YMCA
1970	Chart House, San Diego
1971	Santa Monica, Calif. YMCA
1972	Chart House, San Diego
1973	Chuck's Steak, Los Angeles
1974	UC Santa Barbara, Calif.
1975	Chart House, San Diego
1976	Malibu, Los Angeles
1977	Chuck's, Santa Barbara
1978	Chuck's, Los Angeles
1979	Nautilus, Long Beach Calif.
1980	Olympic Club, San Francisco
1981	Nautilus, Long Beach Calif.
1982	Chuck's, Los Angeles
1983	Nautilus Pacifica, Calif.
1984	Nautilus Pacifica, Calif.
1985	Molten/SSI Torrance, Calif.
1986	Molten, Torrance, Calif.
1987	Molten, Torrance, Calif.
1988	Molten, Torrance, Calif.
1989	Not held
1990	Nike, Carson, Calif.
1991	Offshore, Woodland Hills, Calif.
1992	Creole Six Pack, Elmhurst, N.Y.

U.S. Men's Open Champions—Gold Division *(Cont.)*

1993	Asics, Huntington Beach, Calif.
1994	Asics/Paul Mitchell, Hunt. Beach, Calif.
1995	Shakter, Belagarad, Ukraine
1996	POL-AM-VBC, Brooklyn, N.Y.
1997	Canuck Stuff VBC, Calgary
1998	T-Town, Tulsa, OK
1999	Los Angeles Athletic Club,
2000	Paul Mitchell, Huntington Beach, Calif.
2001	Los Angeles Athletic Club,
2002	Paul Mitchell, Huntington Beach, Calif.
2003	Paul Mitchell, Huntington Beach, Calif.
2004	Bameso-I Dig, Dominican Republic
2005	Bameso-USA, Columbia, S.C.
2006	Paul Mitchell, Los Angeles, Calif.
2007	Paul Mitchell, Los Angeles, Calif.

U.S. Women's Open Champions—Gold Division

1949	Eagles, Houston
1950	Voit #1, Santa Monica, Calif.
1951	Eagles, Houston
1952	Voit #1, Santa Monica, Calif.
1953	Voit #1, Los Angeles
1954	Houstonettes, Houston, Tex.
1955	Mariners, Santa Monica, Calif.
1956	Mariners, Santa Monica, Calif.
1957	Mariners, Santa Monica, Calif.
1958	Mariners, Santa Monica, Calif.
1959	Mariners, Santa Monica, Calif.
1960	Mariners, Santa Monica, Calif.
1961	Breakers, Long Beach, Calif.
1962	Shamrocks, Long Beach, Calif.
1963	Shamrocks, Long Beach, Calif.
1964	Shamrocks, Long Beach, Calif.
1965	Shamrocks, Long Beach, Calif.
1966	Renegades, Los Angeles
1967	Shamrocks, Long Beach, Calif.
1968	Shamrocks, Long Beach, Calif.
1969	Shamrocks, Long Beach, Calif.
1970	Shamrocks, Long Beach, Calif.
1971	Renegades, Los Angeles
1972	E Pluribus Unum, Houston
1973	E Pluribus Unum, Houston
1974	Renegades, Los Angeles
1975	Adidas, Norwalk, Calif.
1976	Pasadena, Tex.
1977	Spoilers, Hermosa, Calif.
1978	Nick's, Los Angeles
1979	Mavericks, Los Angeles
1980	NAVA, Fountain Valley, Calif.
1981	Utah State, Logan, Utah
1982	Monarchs, Hilo, Hawaii
1983	Syntex, Stockton, Calif.
1984	Chrysler, Palo Alto, Calif.
1985	Merrill Lynch, Ariz.
1986	Merrill Lynch, Ariz.
1987	Chrysler, Pleasanton, Calif.
1988	Chrysler, Hayward, Calif.
1989	Plymouth, Hayward, Calif.
1990	Plymouth, Hayward, Calif.
1991	Fitness, Champaign, Ill.
1992	Nick's Kronies, Chicago
1993	Nick's Fishmarket, Chicago
1994	Nick's Fishmarket, Chicago
1995	Kittleman/Branfield's/Nick's, Chicago
1996	Pure Texas Nuts, Austin, Tex.
1997	Kittleman/Branfield's/Nick's, Chi.
1998	The Exterminators, Barrington, Ill.
1999	Dominican Dream Team, Santo Domingo, D.R.
2000	Dominican Dream Team II, Santo Domingo, D.R.
2001	Dominican Dream Team III, Santo Domingo, D.R.
2002	Team Trim, Long Beach, Calif.
2003	The Exterminators, Barrington, Ill.
2004	U.S.A.-A2, Barrington, Ill.
2005	Bameso-USA, Columbia, S.C.
2006	The Exterminators, Barrington, Ill.
2007	Westwood VBC, Los Angeles, Calif.

Wrestling

United States National Champions

1983
FREESTYLE

105.5	Rich Salamone
114.5	Joe Gonzales
125.5	Joe Corso
136.5	Rich Dellagatta*
149.5	Bill Hugent
163	Lee Kemp
180.5	Chris Campbell
198	Pete Bush
220	Greg Gibson
Hvy	Bruce Baumgartner
Team	Sunkist Kids

GRECO-ROMAN

105.5	T.J. Jones
114.5	Mark Fuller
125.5	Rob Hermann
136.5	Dan Mello
149.5	Jim Martinez
163	James Andre

1983 *(Cont.)*
GRECO-ROMAN *(CONT.)*

180.5	Steve Goss
198	Steve Fraser*
220	Dennis Koslowski
Hvy	No champion
Team	Minn. Wrestling Club

1984
FREESTYLE

105.5	Rich Salamone
114.5	Charlie Heard
125.5	Joe Corso
136.5	Rich Dellagatta*
149.5	Andre Metzger
163	Dave Schultz*
180.5	Mark Schultz
198	Steve Fraser
220	Harold Smith
Hvy	Bruce Baumgartner

1984 *(Cont.)*
FREESTYLE *(CONT.)*

Team	Sunkist Kids

GRECO-ROMAN

105.5	T.J. Jones
114.5	Mark Fuller
136.5	Dan Mello
149.5	Jim Martinez*
163	John Matthews
180.5	Tom Press
198	Mike Houck
220	No champion
Hvy	No champion
Team	Adirondack 3-Style, Wash.

1985
FREESTYLE

105.5	Tim Vanni
114.5	Jim Martin
125.5	Charlie Heard

United States National Champions

1985 (Cont.)

FREESTYLE
136.5 ......Darryl Burley
149.5 ......Bill Nugent*
163 ....Kenny Monday
180.5 ......Mike Sheets
198 ....Mark Schultz
220 ....Greg Gibson
286 ....Bruce Baumgartner
Team........Sunkist Kids

GRECO-ROMAN
105.5 ......T.J. Jones
114.5 ......Mark Fuller
125.5 ......Eric Seward*
136.5 ......Buddy Lee
149.5 ......Jim Martinez
163 ....David Butler
180.5 ......Chris Catallo
198 ....Mike Houck
220 ....Greg Gibson
286 ....Dennis Koslowski
Team........U.S. Marine Corps

1986

FREESTYLE
105.5 ......Rich Salamone
114.5 ......Joe Gonzales
125.5 ......Kevin Darkus
136.5 ......John Smith
149.5 ......Andre Metzger*
163 ....Dave Schultz
180.5 ......Mark Schultz
198 ....Jim Scherr
220 ....Dan Severn
286 ....Bruce Baumgartner
Team........Sunkist Kids (Div. I)
                Hawkeye Wrestling
                Club (Div. II)

GRECO-ROMAN
105.5 ......Eric Wetzel
114.5 ......Shawn Sheldon
125.5 ......Anthony Amado
136.5 ......Frank Famiano
149.5 ......Jim Martinez
163 ....David Butler*
180.5 ......Darryl Gholar
198 ....Derrick Waldroup
220 ....Dennis Koslowski
286 ....Duane Koslowski
Team........U.S. Marine Corps (Div. I)
                U.S. Navy (Div. II)

1987

FREESTYLE
105.5 ......Takashi Irie
114.5 ......Mitsuru Sato
125.5 ......Barry Davis
136.5 ......Takumi Adachi
149.5 ......Andre Metzger
163 ....Dave Schultz*
180.5 ......Mark Schultz
198 ....Jim Scherr
220 ....Bill Scherr
286 ....Bruce Baumgartner
Team........Sunkist Kids (Div. I)
                Team Foxcatcher (Div. II)

GRECO-ROMAN
105.5 ......Eric Wetzel

1987 (Cont.)

GRECO-ROMAN (CONT.)
114.5 ......Shawn Sheldon
125.5 ......Eric Seward
136.5 ......Frank Famiano
149.5 ......Jim Martinez
163 ....David Butler
180.5 ......Chris Catallo
198 ....Derrick Waldroup*
220 ....Dennis Koslowski
286 ....Duane Koslowski
Team........U.S. Marine Corp (Div. I)
                U.S. Army (Div. II)

1988

FREESTYLE
105.5 ......Tim Vanni
114.5 ......Joe Gonzales
125.5 ......Kevin Darkus
136.5 ......John Smith*
149.5 ......Nate Carr
163 ....Kenny Monday
180.5 ......Dave Schultz
198 ....Melvin Douglas III
220 ....Bill Scherr
286 ....Bruce Baumgartner
Team........Sunkist Kids (Div. I)
                Team Foxcatcher (Div. II)

GRECO-ROMAN
105.5 ......T.J. Jones
114.5 ......Shawn Sheldon
125.5 ......Gogi Parseghian*
136.5 ......Dalen Wasmund
149.5 ......Craig Pollard
163 ....Tony Thomas
180.5 ......Darryl Gholar
198 ....Mike Carolan
220 ....Dennis Koslowski
286 ....Duane Koslowski
Team........U.S. Marine Corps (Div. I)
                Sunkist Kids (Div. II)

1989

FREESTYLE
105.5 ......Tim Vanni
114.5 ......Zeke Jones
125.5 ......Brad Penrith
136.5 ......John Smith
149.5 ......Nate Carr
163 ....Rob Koll
180.5 ......Rico Chiapparelli
198 ....Jim Scherr*
220 ....Bill Scherr
286 ....Bruce Baumgartner
Team........Sunkist Kids (Div. I)
                Team Foxcatcher (Div. II)

GRECO-ROMAN
105.5 ......Lew Dorrance
114.5 ......Mark Fuller
125.5 ......Gogi Parseghian
136.5 ......Isaac Anderson
149.5 ......Andy Seras*
163 ....David Butler
180.5 ......John Morgan
198 ....Michial Foy
220 ....Steve Lawson
286 ....Craig Pittman
Team........USMC (I) Jets USA (II)

1990

FREESTYLE
105.5 ......Rob Eiter
114.5 ......Zeke Jones
125.5 ......Joe Melchiore
136.5 ......John Smith
149.5 ......Nate Carr
163 ....Rob Koll
180.5 ......Royce Alger
198 ....Chris Campbell*
220 ....Bill Scherr
286 ....Bruce Baumgartner
Team........Sunkist Kids (Div. I)
                Team Foxcatcher (Div. II)

GRECO-ROMAN
105.5 ......Lew Dorrance
114.5 ......Sam Henson
125.5 ......Mark Pustelnik
136.5 ......Isaac Anderson
149.5 ......Andy Seras
163 ....David Butler
180.5 ......Derrick Waldroup
198 ....Randy Couture*
220 ....Chris Tironi
286 ....Matt Ghaffari
Team........Jets USA (Div. I)
                California Jets (Div. II)

1991

FREESTYLE
105.5 ......Tim Vanni
114.5 ......Zeke Jones
125.5 ......Brad Penrith
136.5 ......John Smith*
149.5 ......Townsend Saunders
163 ....Kenny Monday
180.5 ......Kevin Jackson
198 ....Chris Campbell
220 ....Mark Coleman
286 ....Bruce Baumgartner
Team........Sunkist Kids (Div. I)
                Jets USA (Div. II)

GRECO-ROMAN
105.5 ......Eric Wetzel
114.5 ......Shawn Sheldon
125.5 ......Frank Famiano
136.5 ......Buddy Lee
149.5 ......Andy Seras
163 ....Gordy Morgan
180.5 ......John Morgan*
198 ....Michial Foy
220 ....Dennis Koslowski
286 ....Craig Pittman
Team........Jets USA (Div. I)
                Sunkist Kids (Div. II)

1992

FREESTYLE
105.5 ......Rob Eiter
114.5 ......Jack Griffin
125.5 ......Kendall Cross*
136.5 ......John Fisher
149.5 ......Matt Demaray
163 ....Greg Elinsky
180.5 ......Royce Alger
198 ....Dan Chaid
220 ....Bill Scherr
286 ....Bruce Baumgartner

United States National Champions

1992 (Cont.)

FREESTYLE (CONT.)

Team........Sunkist Kids (Div. I)
Team Foxcatcher (Div. II)

GRECO-ROMAN

105.5 ......Eric Wetzel
114.5 ....Mark Fuller
125.5 ......Dennis Hall
136.5 ......Buddy Lee*
149.5 ......Rodney Smith
163 ....Travis West
180.5 ......John Morgan
198 ....Michial Foy
220 ....Dennis Koslowski
286 ....Matt Ghaffari
Team........N.Y. Athletic Club (Div. I)
Sunkist Kids (Div. II)

1993

FREESTYLE

105.5 ......Rob Eiter
114.5 ......Zeke Jones
125.5 ......Brad Penrith
136.5 ......Tom Brands
149.5 ......Matt Demaray
163 ....Dave Schultz*
180.5 ......Kevin Jackson
198 ....Melvin Douglas
220 ....Kirk Trost
286 ....Bruce Baumgartner
Team........Sunkist Kids (Div. I)
Team Foxcatcher (Div. II)

GRECO-ROMAN

105.5 ......Eric Wetzel
114.5 ......Shawn Sheldon
125.5 ......Dennis Hall*
136.5 ......Shon Lewis
149.5 ......Andy Seras
163 ....Gordy Morgan
180.5 ......Dan Henderson
198 ....Randy Couture
220 ....James Johnson
286 ....Matt Ghaffari
Team........N.Y. Athletic Club (Div. I)
Sunkist Kids (Div. II)

1994

FREESTYLE

105.5 ......Tim Vanni
114.5 ......Zeke Jones
125.5 ......Terry Brands
136.5 ......Tom Brands
149.5 ......Matt Demaray
163 ....Dave Schultz
180.5 ......Royce Alger
198 ....Melvin Douglas
220 ....Mark Kerr
286 ....Bruce Baumgartner*
Team........Sunkist Kids (Div. I)
Team Foxcatcher (Div. II)

GRECO-ROMAN

105.5 ......Isaac Ramaswamy
114.5 ......Shawn Sheldon
125.5 ......Dennis Hall
136.5 ......Shon Lewis
149.5 ......Andy Seras*
163 ....Gordy Morgan
180.5 ......Dan Henderson

1994 (Cont.)

GRECO-ROMAN (CONT.)

198 ....Derrick Waldroup
220 ....James Johnson
286 ....Matt Ghaffari
Team..........Armed Forces (Div. I)
N.Y. Athletic Club (Div. II)

1995

FREESTYLE

105.5 ......Tim Vanni
114.5 ......Zeke Jones
125.5 ......Terry Brands
136.5 ......Tom Brands
149.5 ......Matt Demaray
163 ....Dave Schultz
180.5 ......Royce Alger
198 ....Melvin Douglas
220 ....Mark Kerr
286 ....Bruce Baumgartner*
Team........Sunkist Kids (Div. I)
Team Foxcatcher (Div. II)

GRECO-ROMAN

105.5 ......Isaac Ramaswamy
114.5 ......Shawn Sheldon
125.5 ......Dennis Hall
136.5 ......Shon Lewis
149.5 ......Andy Seras*
163 ....Gordy Morgan
180.5 ......Dan Henderson
198 ....Derrick Waldroup
220 ....James Johnson
286 ....Matt Ghaffari
Team........Armed Forces (Div. I)
N.Y. Athletic Club (Div. II)

1996

FREESTYLE

105.5 ......Rob Eiter
114.5 ......Lou Rosselli
125.5 ......Kendall Cross*
136.5 ......Tom Brands
149.5 ......Matt Demaray
163 ....Dave Schultz
180.5 ......Kevin Jackson
198 ....Melvin Douglas
220 ....Kurt Angle
286 ....Bruce Baumgartner
Team........Sunkist Kids (Div. I)
Team Foxcatcher (Div. II)

GRECO-ROMAN

105.5 ......Isaac Ramaswamy
114.5 ......Shawn Sheldon
125.5 ......Dennis Hall*
136.5 ......Van Fronhofer
149.5 ......Heath Sims
163 ....Matt Lindland
180.5 ......Marty Morgan
198 ....Michial Foy
220 ....James Johnson
286 ....Rulon Gardner
Team........Armed Forces (Div. I)
Sunkist Kids (Div. II)

1997

FREESTYLE

110 ....Kanamti Soloman
119 ....Zeke Jones

1997 (Cont.)

FREESTYLE (CONT.)

127.75 .....Terry Brands
138.75 .....Carl Kolat
152 ....Lincoln McIlravy*
167.5 ......Dan St. John
187.25 .....Les Gutches
213.75 .....Melvin Douglas
275.5 ......Tom Erikson
Team........Sunkist Kids (Div. I)
N.Y. Athletic Club (Div. II)

GRECO-ROMAN

110 ....Mark Yanagihara
119 ....Broderick Lee
127.75 .....Dennis Hall
138.75 .....Kevin Bracken
152 ....Chris Saba
167.5 ......Miguel Spencer
187.25 .....Dan Henderson
213.75 ......Randy Couture*
275.5 ......Rulon Gardner
Team........Armed Forces (Div. I)
N.Y. Athletic Club (Div. II)

1998

FREESTYLE

119 ....Sam Henson
127.75 .....Tony Purler
138.75 .....Shawn Charles
152 ....Lincoln McIlravy
167.5 ......Steve Marianetti
187.25 .....Les Gutches*
213.75 .....Melvin Douglas
286 ....Tolly Thompson
Team........Sunkist Kids (Div. I)
N.Y. Athletic Club (Div. II)

GRECO-ROMAN

119 ....Shawn Sheldon
127.75 .....Dennis Hall
138.75 .....Shon Lewis
152 ....Chris Saba
167.5 ......Matt Lindland
187.25 .....Dan Niebuhr*
213.75 .....Jason Klohs
286 ....Matt Ghaffari
Team........Armed Forces (Div. I)
Sunkist Kids (Div. II)

1999

FREESTYLE

119 ....Lou Rosselli
127.75 .....Terry Brands
138.75 .....Cary Kolat
152 ....Lincoln McIlravy
167.5 ......Joe Williams
187.25 .....Les Gutches
213.75 .....Dominic Black
286 ....Stephen Neal*
Team........Sunkist Kids (Div. I)
N.Y. Athletic Club (Div. II)

GRECO-ROMAN

119 ....Steven Mays
127.75 .....Dennis Hall
138.75 .....Glen Nieradka
152 ....David Zuniga
167.5 ......Matt Lindland
187.25 .....Quincey Clark

---

*Outstanding wrestler.

United States National Champions *(Cont.)*

1999 *(Cont.)*
GRECO-ROMAN *(CONT.)*
213.75 .....Randy Couture
286 ....Dremiel Byers*
Team........Minnesota Storm (Div. I)
          Sunkist Kids (Div. II)

2000
FREESTYLE
119 ....Sammie Henson
127.75 .....Keyy Boumans
138.75 .....Cary Kolat
152 ....Lincoln McIlravy
167.5 ....Brandon Slay*
187.25 .....Les Gutches
213.75 .....Melvin Douglas
286 ....Kerry McCoy
Team........Sunkist Kids (Div. I)
          N.Y. Athletic Club (Div. II)

GRECO-ROMAN
119 ....Brandon Paulson
127.75 .....Dennis Hall
138.75 .....Kevin Bracken
152 ....Heath Sims
167.5 ....Matt Lindland
187.25 .....Quincey Clark*
213.75 .....Jason Gleasman
286 ....Rulon Gardner
Team........Armed Forces (Div. I)
          Sunkist Kids (Div. II)

2001
FREESTYLE
119 ....Eric Akin
127.75 .....Eric Guerrero
138.75 .....Bill Zadick
152 ....Ramico Blackmon
167.5 ....Joe Williams
187.25 .....Cael Sanderson*
213.75 .....Dominic Black
286 ....Kerry McCoy
Team........Sunkist Kids (Div. I)
          New York A.C. (Div. II)

GRECO-ROMAN
119 ....Jeff Cervone
127.75 .....Dennis Hall
138.75 .....Kevin Bracken
152 ....Marcel Cooper
167.5 ....Keith Sieracki
187.25 .....Matt Lindland*
213.75 .....Garrett Lowney
286 ....Rulon Gardner
Team........U.S. Army (Div. I)
          Sunkist Kids (Div. II)

2002
FREESTYLE
121 ....Teague Moore
132 ....Eric Guerrero
145.5 ....Bill Zadick
163 ....Joe Williams*
185 ....Cael Sanderson
211.5 ....Tim Hartung
264.5 ....Kerry McCoy
Team........Sunkist Kids (Div. I)
          New York A.C. (Div. II)

2002 *(Cont.)*
GRECO-ROMAN
121 ....Brandon Paulson
132 ....Glenn Nieradka*
145.5 ....Kevin Bracken
163 ....Keith Sieracki
185 ....Ethan Bosch
211.75 .....Garrett Lowney
264.5 ....Dremiel Byers
Team........U.S. Army (Div. I)
          New York A.C. (Div. II)

2003
FREESTYLE
121 ....Stephen Abas
132 ....Eric Guerrero*
145.5 ....Chris Bono
163 ....Joe Williams
185 ....Cael Sanderson
211.5 ....Daniel Cormier
264.5 ....Kerry McCoy
Team........Sunkist Kids (Div. I)
          Gator WC (Div. II)

GRECO-ROMAN
121 ....Brandon Paulson
132 ....James Gruenwald*
145.5 ....Kevin Bracken
163 ....Keith Sieracki
185 ....Brad Vering
211.5 ....Garrett Lowney
264.5 ....Dremiel Byers
Team........U.S. Army (Div. I)
          Air Force (Div. II)

2004
FREESTYLE
121 ....Stephen Abbas
132 ....Eric Guerrero
145.5 ....Jamill Kelly
163 ....Joe Williams
185 ....Lee Fullhart*
211.5 ....Daniel Cormier
264.5 ....Kerry McCoy
Team........Sunkist Kids (Div. I)
          Gator WC (Div. II)

GRECO-ROMAN
121 ....Brandon Paulson
132 ....James Gruenwald
145.5 ....Faruk Sahin
163 ....Darryl Christian
185 ....Brad Vering
211.5 ....Justin Ruiz
264.5 ....Dremiel Byers*
Team........New York A.C. (Div. I)
          Air Force (Div. II)

2005
FREESTYLE
121 ....Sam Henson
132 ....Michael Lightner*
145.5 ....Chris Bono
163 ....Joe Williams
185 ....Mo Lawal
211.5 ....Daniel Cormier
264.5 ....Tolly Thompson
Team........Sunkist Kids (Div. I)
          Gator WC (Div. II)

2005 *(Cont.)*
GRECO-ROMAN *(CONT.)*
121 ....Sam Hazewinkel
132 ....Joseph Warren
145.5 ....Harry Lester
163 ....Darryl Christian
185 ....Brad Vering
211.5 ....Justin Ruiz
264.5 ....Dremiel Byers*
Team........New York A.C. (Div.I)
          Air Force (Div. II)

2006
FREESTYLE
121 ....:....Henry Cejudo
132 ....Zach Roberson
145.5 ....Chris Bono
163 ....Donny Pritzlaff*
185 ....Mo Lawal
211.5 ....Daniel Cormier
264.5 ....Tolly Thompson
Team........Sunkist Kids (Div. I)
          Gator WC (Div. II)

GRECO-ROMAN
121 ....Lindsey Durlacher
132 ....Joseph Warren
145.5 ....Marcel Cooper
163 .........T.C. Dantzler
185 ....Jacob Clark*
211.5 ....Justin Ruiz
264.5 ....Dremiel Byers
Team........U.S. Army (Div. I)
          New York A.C. (Div. II)

2007
FREESTYLE
121 ....Henry Cejudo
132 ....Nate Gallick*
145.5 ....Chris Bono
163 ....Joe Heskett
185 ....Joe Williams
211.5 ....Daniel Cormier
264.5 ....Tommy Rowlands
Team........Sunkist Kids (Div. I)
          Gator WC (Div. II)

GRECO-ROMAN
121 ....Sam Hazewinkel*
132 ....Joseph Warren
145.5 ....Glenn Garrison
163 .........T.C. Dantzler
185 ....Brad Vering
211.5 ....Justin Ruiz
264.5 ....Russ Davie
Team........U.S. Army (Div. I)
          New York A.C. (Div. II)

*Outstanding wrestler.

Sports Illustrated Trivia Quiz

Dodgers pitcher Al Downing
gave up Hank Aaron's
record-breaking
715th career home run

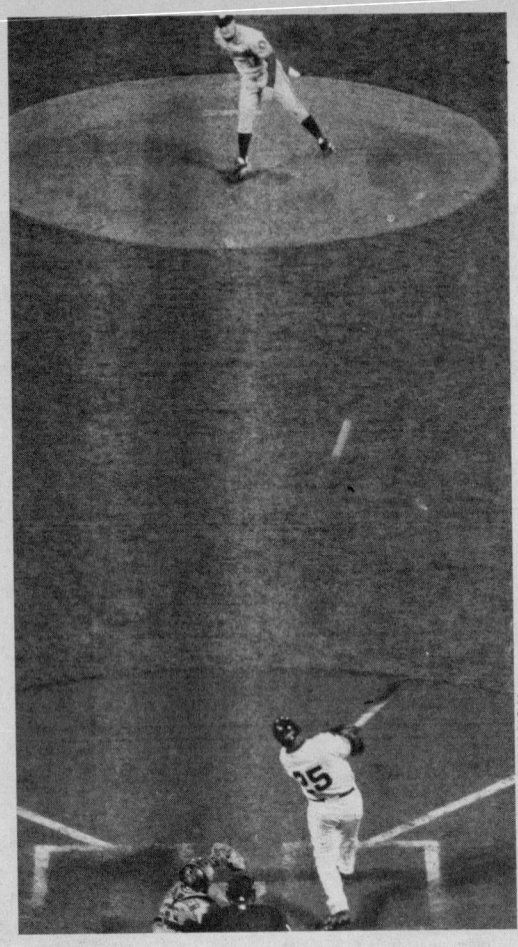

Trivia can be a funny thing. At first, collecting all these arcane dates, names and numbers from the world of sports might not appear to be worth the effort. But we here at *Sports Illustrated* think otherwise. In fact, we believe that sports trivia does fans a service, shining a light into long forgotten corners of the record books and putting into context the great (and not so great) performances of the different eras. And thanks to this abiding passion, this season we were able to appreciate the connections that now link the Nationals' Mike Bacsik Jr. (above, giving up Barry Bonds' 756th career home run) to former major league pitchers like Ralph Branca, Al Downing (previous) and Mike Bacsik Sr.—the current pitcher's father, who happened to face Hank Aaron as a Rangers pitcher in 1976 when Aaron, like Bonds, was sitting on 755 career home runs. As a sports fan, you just can't help but smile at stuff like that, and maybe even say, "Gee, that's funny." And you'd be right. That's why we love sports trivia.

NFL

1. In 2007, Peyton Manning became only the second QB in NFL history to both win a Super Bowl and throw for more than 4,000 yards in the same season. Name the first QB to do this. **HINT:** His 414 passing yards in Super Bowl XXXIV still stands as the single-game record.

2. Since the AFL-NFL merger in 1970, which team has won the most conference championships?

3. Which player holds the alltime NFL record for most consecutive games with a catch by a tight end? **HINT:** Brian and Bernie were his QBs.

4. Which former NFL QB was the first American ever inducted into Canada's Sports Hall of Fame?

5. Kenny Washington was one of two African-American players to break the NFL's color barrier and re-integrate the league when he signed with the Los Angeles Rams in 1946. Name his UCLA college roommate, who also went on to some renown as a pro athlete. **HINT:** He was a four-sport letterman.

6. During the first nine years of his NFL career, how many games had Colts QB Peyton Manning missed due to injury?

7. In NFL history, only five QBs have amassed both 20,000 passing yards and 3,000 rushing yards in their careers. Name four of the five. **HINT:** Only one was active in 2006.

8. Through the 2006–07 postseason, which NFL team had not lost a home playoff game in more than 28 years?

9. With 1:00 left to play in the 2007 AFC Conference Championship, first-year Colts RB Joseph Addai rushed for a three-yard TD, helping Indy beat the Patriots 38–34. Name the only other rookie in NFL history to score a game-winning TD in the final minute of a postseason game.

10. What do the football careers of Antonio Gates, Adam Vinatieri, Kurt Warner, Warren Moon, Marion Motley, and Dick "Night Train" Lane have in common?

ANSWERS
NFL

5. Jackie Robinson—UCLA's first (and only) four-sport letterman, Robinson (right) went on to break major league baseball's color barrier in 1947.

6. Zero. Through 2006, Manning has missed only one play in his career due to injury and his active streak of 144 straight regular-season starts was second only to Brett Favre (232).

7. John Elway (51,475 passing yards, 3,407 rushing yards); Fran Tarkenton (47,003 passing yards, 3,674 rushing yards); Steve Young (33,124 passing yards, 4,239 rushing yards); Randall Cunningham (29,979 passing yards, 4,928 rushing yards); Steve McNair (27,465 passing yards, 3,453 rushing yards).

1. Kurt Warner—In 1999, Warner led the St. Louis Rams over the Tennessee Titans in Super Bowl XXXIV and passed for 4,353 yards during the 1999-2000 regular season. (In the 2006-07 regular season, Peyton Manning had 4,397 passing yards.)

2. Dallas Cowboys—eight. Pittsburgh and Denver are tied for second with six conference titles each.

3. Ozzie Newsome, a favorite target of Browns QBs Brian Sipe and Bernie Kosar, caught a pass in 150 straight games from the 1979 to 1989 seasons.

4. Doug Flutie. Flutie played eight seasons in the CFL and still holds the league's single-season record for passing yards with 6,619 (1991).

8. New England Patriots—Their nine-game home playoff win streak is tied with Buffalo (1988–95) for second-best alltime. Green Bay's 13-game win streak (1939–2001) is first.

9. Pittsburgh's Franco Harris. His 60-yard "Immaculate Reception" TD with 0:05 left beat the Oakland Raiders in the 1972 AFC divisional playoff, 12–7.

10. All six players went undrafted out of college.

QUESTIONS

NFL

11. Through 2007, only three QBs in NFL history have thrown 40 or more TDs during a single season. Name them.

12. During the 2005–06 NFL season, there were two sets of brothers listed as quarterbacks on team rosters. Name these two pairs of brothers.
HINT: One NFC team had one from each set of brothers on their roster.

13. How much was the USFL finally awarded in damages after winning its anti-trust lawsuit against the NFL in 1986?

14. The 2003 AFC Wild Card game between the Colts and the Jets featured, for the first time in NFL history, two teams with African-American head coaches. Name these two head coaches.
EXTRA POINT: One of these two coaches moved to a new team for the start of the 2006–07 NFL season. Name his new team.

15. During the 2007 NFL playoffs, which player set a new league record by scoring in his 21st consecutive playoff game, breaking George Blanda's old record of 19?

16. In 2007, new San Diego Chargers head coach Norv Turner became the first coach in 13 years to inherit a team that had the best record in the NFL the previous year. Name both the incoming and outgoing coaches the last time this happened.
HINT: Hurricane to Sooner.

17. Name the only two NFL franchises, in existence at the time of the 1970 AFL-NFL merger, that have yet to retire a single jersey number.

18. In addition to breaking the NFL single-season scoring record in 2007, LaDainian Tomlinson also set a record for scoring his 100th career TD in just his 89th game. Which two RBs had previously held the record with 100 TDs scored in 93 games?

JOHN IACONO/SPORTS ILLUSTRATED

11. Peyton Manning (49–2004 Indianapolis Colts), Dan Marino (twice: 48—1984 Miami Dolphins, 44—1986 Miami Dolphins) Kurt Warner (41—1999 St. Louis Rams).

12. Mannings (Peyton—Indianapolis Colts, Eli—N.Y. Giants) and Hasselbecks (Matt—Seattle Seahawks, Tim—N.Y. Giants).

13. $1.00—The original judgment was then tripled to $3.00 due to the antitrust nature of the lawsuit.

14. Tony Dungy (Indianapolis Colts) and Herm Edwards (New York Jets) **14 XP.** Herm Edwards' new team for the 2006–07 season was the Kansas City Chiefs.

15. Adam Vinatieri—Vinatieri's (center) streak, which began with New England in the 1996 AFC divisional game against Pittsburgh, remains intact after he scored 11 points with the Indianapolis Colts in Super Bowl XLI.

16. In 1994, Dallas Cowboys head coach Jimmy Johnson (who once coached at the Univ. of Miami [Fla.]) retired, after going 12–4 during 1993 regular season and winning Super Bowl XXVIII. He was replaced by former Oklahoma Univ. head coach Barry Switzer.

17. Dallas Cowboys, Oakland Raiders.

18. Jim Brown and Emmitt Smith.

COLLEGE FOOTBALL

19. Ohio State QB Troy Smith won the 2006 Heisman Trophy voting by 1,662 points, the second-largest margin of victory in history. Name the only player to have won by a more lopsided total.

20. The 2006 Insight Bowl matched up a team enjoying its eighth straight season with a 1,000-yard rusher against a team that had gone eight straight seasons without one. Name these two teams.
HINT: Colorful nicknames

21. Which state sent the most FBS (Div. I-A) teams to a bowl game during the 2006–07 postseason?
a) Ohio   b) Florida
c) California   d) Texas

22. Former Grambling State head coach and college football legend Eddie Robinson passed away in 2007. How old was he when began coaching the Tigers in 1941?
BONUS: How old were future legends Bobby Bowden and Joe Paterno?

23. Through 2006, which college team has played in the most Bowl Championship Series games?
HINT: Its lone win came in 2000.

24. Which two teams compete annually in the most-played rivalry in college football history?

25. Over the past five years, which Div. I-A conference has the best bowl record (minimum of 15 appearances)?

26. As sophomores in 2006, Arkansas RBs Darren McFadden and Felix Jones combined to rush for 2,815 yards, the second-highest total for backfield teammates in Div. I-A history. Which pair of RBs still hold the record (set one year prior)?

27. Which school currently has the longest active bowl streak with 32 straight postseason appearances?

28. Of these four former gunslinging BYU QBs, which one is the only Cougar to have won the Heisman Trophy?
a) Jim McMahon
b) Steve Young
c) Ty Detmer
d) Robbie Bosco

COLLEGE FOOTBALL

22. 22—Robinson, (right) born Feb. 3, 1919, coached the Tigers to 408 wins over 55 seasons. 22 BONUS. Bowden was 11 (born Nov. 8, 1929) and Paterno was 14 (born Dec. 21, 1926) at the start of Robinson's tenure.

AP PHOTO/DAVE MARTIN

19. O.J. Simpson—In 1968, Simpson's margin of victory in the Heisman Trophy voting was 1,750 points.

20. Minnesota Golden Gophers and Texas Tech Red Raiders—The Gophers' 1,000 yard rushers have included Thomas Hamner (1999), Tellis Redmon (2000–01), Terry Jackson II (2002), Marion Barber III (2003–04), Laurence Maroney (2003–05), Gary Russell (2005), and Amir Pinnix (2006). Texas Tech's last 1,000-yard rusher was Ricky Williams (1998).

21. d) Texas—Texas had six bowl teams (TCU, Rice, Houston, Texas A&M, Texas Tech and Texas); California (UCLA, San Jose State, Cal and USC) and Florida (South Florida, Florida State, Miami and Florida) had four each; Ohio had three bowl teams (Cincinnati, Ohio and Ohio State).

23. Florida State—The Seminoles have the most alltime BCS appearances with six. The school's only BCS win came against Virginia Tech in the 2000 Sugar Bowl.

24. Lafayette and Lehigh—Since 1884, the two teams have played a record 142 times. Lafayette leads the alltime series 75–62–5.

25. WAC—11–7 record (.611).

26. Reggie Bush and LenDale White —In 2005, USC's Bush (1,740) and White (1,302) combined for 3,052 rushing yards.

27. Michigan.

28. c) Ty Detmer (1990)—McMahon came in third in Heisman voting ('81), Young placed second ('83) and Bosco reached third in voting twice ('84, '85).

NBA

29.

In the largest-ever swap for one player in NBA history, the Boston-Celtics sent how many players (including first-round draft picks) to the Minnesota Timberwolves in July 2007 for forward Kevin Garnett?

30.

Only one of the NBA's past six regular season MVPs was born inside the continental United States. Name him.

DOUBLE BONUS: Name the birthplaces of the other three MVPs during that same stretch (two won it twice).

31.

Name the only NBA player to have led the league in scoring and assists in the same season.

HINT: Not "big" on nicknames

32.

In 2007, this Western Conference team set a new NBA record by going 14–1 on the road against opponents from outside their conference. Name this team.

AND I: Name the Eastern Conference team from the 1982–83 season that had previously owned the record.

33.

The 2007 Dallas Mavericks –Golden State Warriors first-round playoff was the 20th series in NBA postseason history to feature one team whose regular season record was 25 or more wins greater than their opponent. How many playoff games, *in total*, did those previous 19 underdogs win prior to the Warriors 4–2 series win in 2007?

34.

Name the last two centers to finish the season in the top 10 in scoring?

35.

Which active player holds the alltime record for three-point field goals made in the NBA Finals ?

HINT: He's the only non-Celtic with seven NBA title rings.

36.

Prior to Allen Iverson in '06, name the last time one of the NBA's top 10 scorers was traded mid-season.

NBA

JOHN GICHIGI/GETTY IMAGES

32. Phoenix Suns

32 AND I. Philadelphia 76ers—The Sixers had a 11–1 inter-conference road record that season.

33. Six games—All six of those victories came in series that eventually ended with the underdog team losing the series 4–1.

29. Seven—The Celtics sent five current players (Al Jefferson, Ryan Gomes, Gerald Green, Sebastian Telfair and Theo Ratliff) plus two first-round picks and cash to the T-Wolves for the 10-time All-Star Garnett (above).

30. Kevin Garnett (2003–04)—Garnett was born in Mauldin, South Carolina.
30DB. Germany (Dirk Nowitzki, 2006–07,); Canada (Steve Nash, 2004–06,); U.S. Virgin Islands (Tim Duncan, 2001–03).

31. Nate "Tiny" Archibald—During the 1972–73 season with the Kansas City-Omaha Kings, Archibald led the NBA with averages of 34.0 points per game and 11.4 assists per game.

34. Yao Ming and Amare Stoudemire —Ming finished the 2006–07 season 10th in scoring with 25.0 ppg, while Stoudemire finished 5th in scoring in 2004–05 with 26.0 ppg.

35. Robert Horry—His 53 career 3FGs in the Finals are 11 more than second-place Michael Jordan's alltime total and his seven career NBA titles are eclipsed only by former Boston Celtics Bill Russell (11), Sam Jones (10), K.C. Jones (8), Tommy Heinsohn (8), Satch Sanders (8), and John Havlicek (8).

36. 1994—Dominique Wilkins, who was averaging 24.4 points with the Atlanta Hawks, was traded to the L.A. Clippers on Feb. 24, 1994.

NBA

37. I never played organized basketball before the age of 14, yet I was named a *Parade* All-America player in high school and skipped college to go directly to the NBA where I won Rookie of the Year honors in 2003. In 2007, I scored a Suns franchise record 29 points at the All-Star game. Who am I?

38. Which one of the following basketball accomplishments has Larry Brown *not* achieved during his Hall of Fame career?
a) Won NCAA title as a head coach
b) Won NBA title as a head coach
c) Won Olympic gold as a head coach
d) Won Olympic gold as a player

39. Which player set an NBA record in 2007 by becoming the first non-guard to post at least seven assists over eight straight playoff games? **HINT:** Not Duncan or McGrady.

40. Only three players in NBA history have won the league's Sixth Man Award twice. Name them.

41. When the Spurs swept the Cavaliers to win the 2006–07 NBA title, they were the eighth different team in NBA Finals history to win the series 4–0. Name the only team that has twice been on the *losing* side of an NBA Finals sweep.

42. Name the only player in NBA history to have averaged more than 20 points and 10 rebounds over a season for four different teams?
a) Wilt Chamberlain
b) Moses Malone
c) Dikembe Mutumbo
d) Shaquille O'Neal

43. Name the alltime and active leaders in consecutive games played.

44. How many points per game did league scoring increase during the NBA's first season with a 24-second shot clock?

45. Name the two former ABA franchises that have made it to the NBA Finals but never won the title.

46. Wilt Chamberlain still holds the NBA record for most consecutive field goals made in a season. Between Feb. 17–28, 1967, how many shots in a row did Chamberlain make?

37. Amare Stoudemire (center)—After the 2006–07 season, he was also selected to the All-NBA First Team alongside teammate Steve Nash, marking the first time in team history that two Suns were named to the All-NBA First Team.

38. c)—Brown did win Olympic gold as an assistant coach in 2000, but in his only stint as Olympic head coach in 2004, the U.S. team only claimed the bronze.

39. LeBron James—James finished the 2007 playoffs averaging 25.0 points, 8.0 assists and 8.0 rebounds per game.

40. Kevin McHale (1983–84, '84–85), Ricky Pierce (1986–87, '89–90) and Detlef Schrempf (1990–91, '91–92).

41. Los Angeles Lakers—The Lakers were swept out of the NBA Finals in 1983 (76ers) and 1989 (Pistons).

42. h) Moses Malone—Malone did it with the Houston Rockets (1977–82), Philadelphia 76ers (1982–86), Washington Bullets (1986–88) and Atlanta Hawks (1988–90, '91–92). Chamberlain and O'Neal achieved this feat with three different teams while Mutombo has never averaged over 20 points per game for a season.

43. A.C. Green and Bruce Bowen—Green set the alltime mark with 1,192 straight games, while Bowen's active streak stood at 463 straight games at the end of the 2006–07 season.

AP PHOTO/MATT SLOCUM

44. 13.6 points—During the 1953–54 NBA season, the league averaged just 79.5 points per game. The next year, however, the league's points per game average jumped to 93.1.

45. Indiana Pacers (2000) and New Jersey Nets (2002, '03)—The Spurs are the only former ABA team to have won an NBA title (1999, 2003, '05, '07).

46. 35—Chamberlain also holds the record for most consecutive field goals made in a single game with 18 (March 19, 1967).

COLLEGE BASKETBALL

47. Bobby Knight broke the all-time NCAA record for coaching victories in 2007 —surpassing Dean Smith (879)—and finished the year with a career record of 890–363. How many extra games did it take Knight to get to Smith's mark?

48. Name the only head coach to have achieved college basketball's "Triple Crown," which includes winning an NCAA title, an NIT title, and an Olympic gold medal.

49. For the 2006–07 season, all five starters from Florida's 2005–06 national championship team came back. Name the last NCAA national champion that had all five starters return to play the following year?

50. In 2007, North Carolina received its 11th alltime No. 1 seeding in the Div. I-A men's basketball tournament, making it the most frequently top-seeded team in tourney history. With what college team had the Tar Heels previously shared that honor?

51. What team has received the most No. 1 seeds all-time in the women's NCAA Division I tournament?

52. Who is the only men's head coach to take three different college basketball teams to the Final Four?

53. In the 2007 NCAA men's West regional final, which two teams combined to set a single-game tournament record for combined steals?

54. What year did the NCAA start using the term "Final Four?"

55. What basketball shot was banned by the NCAA in 1968, then reinstated in 1977?
HINT: It can't get much easier.

COLLEGE BASKETBALL

47. 100 games—Smith won his 879 games in just 36 seasons. It wasn't until Knight (right) was in his 41st season, as head coach at Texas Tech, that he reached, and then surpassed, Smith's career wins record.

PETER AIKEN/WIREIMAGE.COM

48. Bobby Knight—Knight won three NCAA titles (1976, '81, '87) and one NIT title (1979) while at Indiana. In 1984, he led the U.S. basketball team to Olympic gold. In addition, Knight is also a four-time National Coach of the Year (1975, '76, '87, '89).

49. Arizona—The Wildcats won the NCAA championship in 1997, but despite having the same five starters, lost in the 1998 West regional final (Elite Eight) to Utah 76–51.

50. Duke—The Blue Devils have had been ranked No. 1 10 times in NCAA men's tournament history.

51. Tennessee—The Lady Vols have been ranked No. 1 in their region 18 times in the NCAA women's tourney's 26-year history.

52. Rick Pitino—Pitino has been to the Final Four with Providence (1987), Kentucky (1993, '96, '97) and Louisville (2005).

53. UCLA and Kansas (32 steals)—The Bruins had 15 steals in their 68–55 win, while the Jayhawks had 17 steals in the loss. The previous tournament record had been 28 steals.

54. 1978—It wasn't until three years later, however, that the NCAA first registered to trademark the term.

55. Slam dunk—As an attempt to prevent injuries, preserve rims and backboards as well as minimize the impact of a new crop of powerful centers like UCLA's Lew Alcindor (Kareem Abdul-Jabbar), the NCAA outlawed the dunk.

BASEBALL

56. Prior to 2007, only two players in major league history had hit 20 doubles, 20 triples and 20 homers and stolen 20 bases in a single season: Willie Mays (1957) and Frank Schulte (1911). Name the *two* players that did it this past year.

57. Which player retired at the start of the 2007 season holding the major league record for most career home runs (315) by a player that never appeared in a postseason game? **HINT:** In 1999, he hit 38 homers and drove in 125 runs for the Brewers.

58. At the 2007 MLB All-Star game, how many AL players were making less than $1 million in annual salary? How about from the NL? Which All-Star was making the lowest overall salary?

59. In 2007, Curt Schilling became just the second 40-year-old pitcher in major league history to win a World Series game. Name the first pitcher to accomplish this feat. **HINT:** He knows when to fold 'em.

60. Rockies SS Troy Tulowitzki hit 24 home runs in 2007, an NL rookie record for shortstops. Whose 53-year-old record did he break?

61. On May 4, 2007, when an NL first baseman hit a homer off of a five-time Cy Young award-winning pitcher, their combined ages equaled 92 years, 125 days, a new MLB record for oldest batter and pitcher involved in a home run. Name both players in this "senior" Senior Circuit combo. **EXTRA BASES:** The previous record (85 years, 159 days) had featured a seven-time MVP going yard against a pitcher with a perfect game on his resume. Name them.

62. In 2007, Manny Ramirez became the fifth alltime player to hit 50 or more home runs against the Yankees in his career. Name the only one of the five that didn't play for the Red Sox at one point.

BASEBALL

JOHN IACONO

56. Curtis Granderson and Jimmy Rollins—Granderson (right) finished the 2007 season with 38 doubles, 23 triples, 23 homers and 26 steals, while Philly's Rollins hit 38 doubles, 20 triples, 30 homers and had 41 steals.

57. Jeromy Burnitz—Burnitz, who played for 14 seasons, is the only player since 1961 to have hit more than 300 career home runs and never played in October.

58. Three, seven and Russell Martin, respectively—The three sub-$1M AL players were Bobby Jenks ($400,000), Jonathan Papelbon ($425,500) and Grady Sizemore ($916,667); the seven from the NL were Martin ($387,500), J.J. Hardy ($400,000),

58. *CONT'D*. Cole Hamels ($400,000), Prince Fielder ($415,000), Brian McCann ($440,000), Dmitri Young ($500,000) and Chris R. Young ($600,000).

59. Kenny Rogers—Pitching for Detroit, Rogers won Game 2 of the 2006 World Series at age 41.

60. Ernie Banks—Banks hit 19 homers as a first-year shortstop with the Chicago Cubs in 1954.

61. Julio Franco (48 years, 254 days) and Randy Johnson (43 years, 236 days) **61EB.** Barry Bonds (42 years, 47 days) hit a home run off of David Wells (43 years, 112 days) on Sept. 9, 2006.

62. Hank Greenberg (53).

BASEBALL

63. In 2007 (my 20th and final season, all of them with the same team), I became the only player in major league history to have recorded more than 3,000 hits, 600 doubles, 250 home runs, and 400 stolen bases in a career. Who am I?

64. Which team had the lowest batting average in MLB history for a seven-game World Series? **HINT:** The team scored just one run total in Games 1 and 2.

65. Name the only pitcher in MLB history to strike out 10 consecutive batters to end a game?

66. Japanese starting pitchers have faced each other four times in MLB history, the latest instance coming on May 9, 2007, when Boston's Daisuke Matsuzaka beat Toronto's Tomo Ohka. Other than Ohka, name the other three Japanese pitchers involved in the previous head-to-head matchups.

67. Name the only player to have hit two home runs in his first two postseason at-bats. **HINT:** For the Twins in the 1987 ALCS.

68. It took Yankees slugger Alex Rodriguez just 7,169 at-bats to reach the 500-home run mark. Name the only three players who reached this same milestone in fewer at-bats than A-Rod.

69. Which future Hall-of-Fame pitcher's bat was Babe Ruth leaning on during his famous 1948 farewell address at Yankee Stadium? **HINT:** In his MLB debut, at just age 17, he struck out 15 St. Louis Browns.

70. Atlanta third baseman Chipper Jones collected the 2,000th hit, 400th double, and 350th home run of his career in 2007. Who are the only two other switch-hitters to reach these same three milestones? **HINT:** Like Chipper, one went by a nickname, rather than his given name: Charles

BASEBALL

JOHN BIEVER

63. Craig Biggio—At the end of his career, Biggio (left) had 3,060 hits, 668 doubles, 291 home runs, and 414 stolen bases.

64. 2001 New York Yankees—The Yanks batted .183 and scored only 14 runs over the seven games, losing to the Arizona Diamondbacks 4–3.

65. Tom Seaver—On April 22, 1970, Seaver, pitching for the Mets, struck out a total of 19 San Diego Padres, including the final 10 batters.

66. Hideki Irabu, Hideo Nomo and Mac Suzuki—Irabu beat Suzuki on May 7, 1999; Nomo beat Suzuki on July 2, 2000; and Ohka beat Suzuki on June 19, 2002.

67. Gary Gaetti—Gaetti hit both home runs off of Detroit starter Doyle Alexander in Game 1.

68. Babe Ruth (5,801 ABs), Harmon Killebrew (6,671 ABs) and Sammy Sosa (7,032 ABs)—Rodriguez was, however, the *youngest* player in history to reach 500 home runs (32 years, 8 days), beating Willie Mays's previous record by 2 years, 122 days.

69. Bob Feller—He amassed 266 career wins and 2,581 strikeouts in 18 seasons with the Cleveland Indians.

70. Eddie Murray (3,026 hits, 560 doubles and 504 home runs) and Charles "Chili" Davis (2,436 hits, 424 doubles and 350 home runs).

BASEBALL

71. During the 2007 regular season, five different NL shortstops equaled or exceeded their age in home runs. Name them.
HINT: Two from the West, one from the Central, two from the East.

72. In 2007, I became major league baseball's active leader in strikeouts with 2,043. In the same season, I also surpassed 2,000 hits and 500 home runs for my career. What's my name?

73. Prior to Boston rookie Daisuke Matsuzaka starting Game 7 of the 2007 ALCS against Cleveland, when was the last time a rookie started a Game 7 in the postseason?

74. What was notable about the Cleveland Indians' 2007 opening homestand against the Mariners?
HINT: Long walk from the parking lot.

75. Who was the only pitcher in major league history to win three Cy Young awards unanimously?
a) Roger Clemens
b) Steve Carlton
c) Jim Palmer
d) Sandy Koufax

76. In the 2007 postseason, the Boston Red Sox set a new major league record by hitting into an incredible 23 double plays. Which team's DP record did they break?

77. Prior to the start of the 2007 World Series, the Colorado Rockies were riding an amazing hot streak, having won 21 of their last 22, including 10 straight victories, seven of which were in the postseason. Name the only other team in major league history to win the first seven games of the MLB playoffs.

78. Which player smacked his 500th career home run in 2007 and currently holds the major league record for most homers as a DH?
HINT: He's one of only seven players with 500 HRs, 1,000 runs, 1,000 RBIs, 1,000 walks and a .300 average.

BASEBALL

FOCUS ON SPORT/GETTY IMAGES

71. Colorado's Troy Tulowitzki (24 HRs, 23 y.o.); San Diego's Khalil Greene (27 HRs, 27 y.o.); Milwaukee's J.J. Hardy (26 HRs, 25 y.o.); Florida's Hanley Ramirez (29 HRs, 23 y.o.); Philadelphia's Jimmy Rollins (30 HRs, 28 y.o.).

72. Jim Thome.

73. Game 7 2002 World Series—Angels rookie John Lackey (win 4–1).

74. Because of snow, the four-game series was played in Milwaukee.

75. d) Sandy Koufax—Koufax (above) won the Cy Young in 1963, '65 and '66.

76. 2006 St. Louis Cardinals—The Cardinals' 17 double plays came in 16 playoff games, while the Red Sox set the new record in just 14 games.

77. 1976 Cincinnati Reds—They swept the Phillies in the NLCS (best-of-five) and the Yankees in the World Series.

78. Frank Thomas—248 career DH HRs.

WILD
CARD

79. Among the four major sports, which pro athlete has won the most regular season games—based on his team's overall win percentage—during the past ten years?

80. Name the three remaining stadiums that still continue to pull double-duty as host to both NFL and MLB teams?

81. Who was the first southpaw in boxing history to be crowned heavyweight champion of the world?

82. Which distance is greater: from the teebox to the center of the island green of the 17th hole at TPC Sawgrass or from home plate to the outfield wall in straightaway centerfield at Yankee Stadium?

83. Which active five-time MLB All-Star slugger was a back-up QB to Heath Shuler and Peyton Manning while at the Univ. of Tennessee?
HINT: Though some say it's artficially *elevated*, his career batting avg. is .332.

84. Which of the following pro athletes did *not* spend the proverbial "cup of coffee" playing with these corresponding teams?
a) Brett Favre–Atlanta Falcons
b) Mike Piazza–Florida Marlins
c) Moses Malone–San Antonio Spurs
d) Brendan Shanahan–Boston Bruins

85. In the 1978 movie *Heaven Can Wait*, Warren Beatty plays Leo Farnsworth, a recently resurrected millionaire who buys the L.A. Rams and, as QB, leads them to a Super Bowl victory over the Pittsburgh Steelers. Just over a year later, these two teams actually met in the Super Bowl. Name the *real* starting QB for the Rams in Super Bowl XIV.
BONUS: What was the *real* final score?

86. Which of Bo Jackson's career statistics is greater: a) his career yards per carry average in the NFL or b) his MLB career hits per at-bat average?

WILD CARD

81. Michael Moorer—The lefthander defeated Evander Holyfield on April 22, 1994 to win both the WBA and IBF heavyweight titles.

82. 17th at TPC Sawgrass —411 feet (137 yards) vs. 408 feet (dead center at Yankee Stadium).

83. Todd Helton—A native of Knoxville, Tenn., Helton played behind Shuler for his freshman and sophomore seasons (1992–94) then briefly backed up Manning as a junior before switching to baseball full-time.

84. d) Shanahan has never played for the Boston Bruins. (Favre appeared in two games with the Falcons, Piazza had five games with the Marlins, and Malone played the final 17 games of his career with San Antonio.)

85. Vince Ferragamo.
85B. Pittsburgh 31, L.A. Rams 19.

86. a) Jackson averaged 5.4 yards per carry (2,782 yards on 515 rushes) while in the NFL, but only 4.0 hits per at-bat (598 hits over 2,393 at-bats) while in the major leagues.

79. Tim Duncan—Since his rookie year (1997–98), Duncan (right) and the Spurs have a .709 win percentage (559 wins, 229 losses).

80. Dolphin Stadium (Miami Dolphins, Florida Marlins), McAfee Coliseum (Oakland Raiders, A's), Hubert H. Humphrey Metrodome (Minnesota Vikings, Twins).

BOB ROSATO/SPORTS ILLUSTRATED

HOCKEY

87. Ontario-born Wayne Gretzky owns the record for alltime career goals scored with 894. His fellow Canadian Gordie Howe comes in second with 801. Name the highest scoring U.S.-born player in NHL history.
HINT: Deep in the heart of Texas

88. Through the 2006–07 season, Red Wings defenseman Chris Chelios had played in 246 career playoff games, one shy of the most all time. Which player still holds the record ?

89. In the 2006–07 season, Avalanche center Paul Stastny set a rookie record by scoring at least one point in how many straight games?

90. In 2007, 19-year-old Penguins center Sidney Crosby won the NHL's regular season scoring award. He was the first teenager to win a scoring award in any major pro sport. How many points did he score in the 2006–07 season?

91. Before the 2006–07 season, the NHL approved a change to the amount of curve on the players' sticks. How much is now allowed?
a) ½"   b) ¾"
c) 1"   d) 1¼"

92. Through 2007, the Detroit Red Wings had played in 16 straight NHL playoffs, the longest active streak of any team. What franchise holds the alltime record for most consecutive playoff appearances?

93. The Philadelphia Flyers gave up a league-worst 303 goals during the 2006–07 season. Which NHL team holds the record for the most goals against in a single season?
HINT: That year, the Flyers won the Cup.

94. Which NHL player in the 2006–07 playoffs was the active leader in career playoff goals scored?

95. Which player accomplished the rare feat, during his career, of winning the Conn Smythe Trophy (playoff MVP) before winning the Calder Trophy (rookie of the year)?

HOCKEY

RONALD MARTINEZ/GETTY IMAGES

87. Mike Modano—In 2007, the Dallas Stars center (above) scored his 500th career goal and finished the season with 507, surpassing Joe Mullen (502) as the highest-scoring American-born player in NHL history.

88. Goaltender Patrick Roy (Montreal Canadiens, Colorado Avalanche) played in 247 career playoff games during his 20-year career.

89. 20—His streak lasted from Feb. 3 to Mar. 18, 2007.

90. 120. Wayne Gretzky holds the record with 215 points scored in the 1985–86 regular season.

91. b) ¾"—Previously, the curve on NHL stick blades was limited to ½".

92. Boston Bruins—From 1968–96, the Bruins appeared in 29 straight postseasons, one more than the Chicago Blackhawks, who made the playoffs every year from 1970–97.

93. Washington Capitals—The Caps' gave up 446 goals in the 1974–75 season.

94. Jaromir Jagr—With 69 career playoff goals, Jagr had six more than Peter Forsberg heading into the '07 playoffs.

95. Ken Dryden—A late season call-up for the Canadiens, Dryden played only six regular season games in 1971 before leading the Habs to that year's Stanley Cup over Chicago in seven games. In his first full season in 1971–72, Dryden posted a 2.24 GAA as an official rookie.

TENNIS

96. By beating Andy Roddick, Rafael Nadal and Roger Federer in consecutive matches at a tournament in Canada, Novak Djokovic became the first man to defeat the top three players in the world in consecutive matches since 1994. Who was the last man to do it?

97. When was the last time an American man or woman won the French Open?

98. From 2005–07, Rafael Nadal won 81 consecutive matches on clay, the longest winning streak on any surface in the history of the men's game. The previous record, 65 wins on carpet, was held by what man?

99. Nadal's win streak on clay is only the longest of any man. What woman holds the record for the most consecutive matches won on the surface?

100. With his fifth straight victory at Wimbledon in 2007, No. 1-ranked Roger Federer tied the record for the most consecutive championships at the All England Club. Whose record did he equal?

101. At a Masters Series event in Indian Wells, Calif., in 2005, then No. 3-ranked Maria Sharapova lost a match 0–6, 0–6. It was the first time a player ranked within the top 3 lost by that score and the first time Maria Sharapova failed to hold serve even once in a match. Which three-time grand slam singles champion and U.S. Olympic gold medalist was responsible for Sharapova's defeat?

102. No. 1-ranked Justine Henin has won every grand slam single's title except Wimbledon, where she has twice been a runner-up. Name one of the two players who have beaten her in the final at Wimbledon.

103. In 2004, Andy Roddick hit the fastest serve in tennis history, clocking in at 155 m.p.h. Which player had previously held the record for the fastest serve?

HINT: Now retired, he was born in Montreal and angered many Canadian fans when he acquired British citizenship in 1995.

ETHAN MILLER / GETTY IMAGES

96. Boris Becker—In 1994; Becker defeated No. 3-ranked Michael Stitch, No. 1-ranked Pete Sampras and No. 2-ranked Goran Ivanisevic in Stockholm, a feat matched by Serbian tennis phenom Novak Djokovic (above) when he defeated the world's top 3 in the Canada Masters in 2007.

97. 2002—Serena Williams defeated her sister Venus, 7–5, 6–3.

98. John McEnroe, who won 65 matches on carpet from 1983–85.

99. Chris Evert—From 1973–79, Evert won 125 consecutive matches on clay, 44 more than Rafael Nadal.

100. Bjorn Borg won five Wimbledon titles from 1976–80.

101. Lindsay Davenport.

102. Venus Williams (2001) and Amelie Mauresmo (2006).

103. Greg Rusedski, with whom Roddick had shared the previous record of 149 m.p.h.

104. For the first time in NBA draft history, three players from the same school were chosen in the first round. Name the school, the players and their new pro teams.

105. Name the most recent No.1 and No. 2 overall NFL draft picks that have been enshrined in the Pro Football Hall of Fame?
HINT: One played college in L.A., one was drafted to play pro in L.A.

106. The first four overall picks of the 1985 MLB draft had also won Olympic gold with the U.S. baseball team in 1984. Name them.
HINT: They started in the big leagues as a Brewer, Giant, Ranger and Red, respectively.

107. In 2007, for the first time in NFL history, one team had two QBs who had been No. 1 overall picks on their active roster at the same time. Name the team and QBs.

108. Put the four major sports in ascending order in terms of the total number of selections in their respective drafts?

109. For the 12th straight year, the No. 1 overall pick in the NFL draft was not a RB. Who was the highest drafted RB in 2007?

110. What was notable about Patrick Kane and James van Riemsdyk being chosen first and second overall in the NHL's 2007 entry draft?
HINT: U.S.A.! U.S.A.! U.S.A.!

111. Since 1994, when the NBA began weighting the lottery selection process for all non-playoff teams based on their regular season record, the teams with the league's worst record have ended up with the No. 1 overall draft pick only twice. Which two years did this happen and who were the players chosen No. 1 overall those two years?

THE DRAFT

JOHN BIEVER

106. B.J. Surhoff (1), Will Clark (2); Bobby Witt (3), and Barry Larkin(4)—Also of note, the sixth overall pick of that year's draft was Barry Bonds.

107. Carolina Panthers; Vinny Testaverde (1987) and David Carr (2002).

108. NBA (two rounds-60 selections); NHL (seven rounds-211 selections); NFL (seven rounds-255 selections); MLB (50 rounds-1,463 selections). [Based on 2007 draft results for each sport.]

104. Florida—The 2006 and 2007 NCAA national champion Gators had three players from that team taken within the first nine picks of the 2007 NBA draft: Al Horford (far left), 3rd pick, to the Atlanta Hawks, Corey Brewer (second from left), 7th pick, to the Minnesota Timberwolves, and Joakim Noah (top), 9th pick, to the Chicago Bulls.

105. Troy Aikman (No. 1 overall-1988) and Eric Dickerson (No. 2 overall-1983) —Aikman, who played college at UCLA and was drafted by the Dallas Cowboys, was enshrined in 2006. Dickerson, who played college ball at SMU, was drafted by the L.A. Rams and voted into the Hall of Fame in 1999.

109. Adrian Peterson—Peterson, from Oklahoma, was drafted 7th overall by the Minnesota Vikings.

110. It was the first time in NHL history that American-born players were chosen first and second overall.

111. 2003 and 2004—LeBron James was chosen No. 1 overall by Cleveland in 2003 and Dwight Howard was chosen No. 1 overall by Orlando in 2004.

GOLF

112.

Through 2007, there are three active Tour players who have gone winless on the PGA Tour since claiming their first major victory at the PGA Championship. Name two of these three golfers. **HINT:** Think double letters.

113.
Which active PGA Tour player is the only Canadian to have ever won a major golf championship? **TAP-IN:** He was also the second leftie to ever win a major. Name the first.

114.
While capturing his first Masters title at a cold and breezy Augusta National in 2007, Zach Johnson tied what tourney record?

115.
Morgan Pressel's victory at the 2007 Kraft Nabisco Championship set a record for the youngest player to win an LPGA major title. How old was she?
a) 17 years, 11 months
b) 18 years, 10 months, 9 days
c) 20 years, 5 months, 1 day
d) 21 years, 2 months, 15 days

116.
In 2007, Alexis Thompson set a U.S.G.A. record by qualifying for the U.S. Women's Open at age 12 years, 4 months, and 1 day. Whose six-year-old record did she break?

117.
The 2007 editions of the U.S. Open and PGA Championship each featured the longest holes in those tournaments' history (No. 12 at Oakmont and No. 5 at Southern Hills, respectively). Within ten yards, guess the combined length of these two monster major holes.

118.
Tiger Woods roared to victory in the PGA Tour's inaugural FedEx Cup playoff system in 2007. Within one stroke, what was his scoring average over the 12 FedEx Cup rounds he played? (Woods only competed in three of the four events.)

GOLF

DAVID CANNON/GETTY IMAGES

112. Mark Brooks (1996), Rich Beem (2002) and Shuan Micheel (2003)—Wayne Grady (1990) has also yet to win another Tour event since winning the PGA Championship, but Grady currently plays on the Champions Tour.

113. Mike Weir—The southpaw Weir won the 2003 Masters with a bogey on the first hole of a sudden death playoff with Len Mattiace. **113 TAP IN.** Bob Charles, who won the 1963 British Open.

114. Highest winning score—Johnson's 1-over-par 289 tied the Masters record set in 1954 (Sam Snead) and 1956 (Jack Burke Jr.).

115. b)—The previous record had been held by Sandra Post, who won the 1968 LPGA Championship at age 20.

116. Morgan Pressel—Pressel (right, celebrating her first major victory at the 2007 Kraft Nabisco Championship) was 12 years, 11 months, 21 days when she qualified for the 2001 U.S. Women's Open. Both Pressel in '01 and Thompson in '07 missed the cut.

117. 1,320 yards (or exactly ¾ of a mile)—Oakmont's No. 12 played to 667 yards and Southern Hills' No. 5 played to 653 yards in their respective 2007 events.

118. 65.75—Woods posted a 72 in the first round of the The Barclays and then reeled off 11 straight sub-70 rounds, including a final round 63 at the BMW Championship and a 64-63-64-66 stretch at the FedEx Cup's finale, The Tour Championship.

Awards

SPORTSMAN OF THE YEAR

Sports Illustrated

Dwyane Wade Plays to Win

By S.L. PRICE

MIAMI 3

DECEMBER 11, 2006 www.SI.com
AOL Keyword: Sports Illustrated

SPORTS ILLUSTRATED'S
**2006 Sportsman of the Year
D w yane Wade**

Athlete Awards

Sports Illustrated Sportsman of the Year

1954	Roger Bannister, Track and Field
1955	Johnny Podres, Baseball
1956	Bobby Morrow, Track and Field
1957	Stan Musial, Baseball
1958	Rafer Johnson, Track and Field
1959	Ingemar Johansson, Boxing
1960	Arnold Palmer, Golf
1961	Jerry Lucas, Basketball
1962	Terry Baker, Football
1963	Pete Rozelle, Pro Football
1964	Ken Venturi, Golf
1965	Sandy Koufax, Baseball
1966	Jim Ryun, Track and Field
1967	Carl Yastrzemski, Baseball
1968	Bill Russell, Pro Basketball
1969	Tom Seaver, Baseball
1970	Bobby Orr, Hockey
1971	Lee Trevino, Golf
1972	B.J. King, Tennis/ J. Wooden, Bask
1973	Jackie Stewart, Auto Racing
1974	Muhammad Ali, Boxing
1975	Pete Rose, Baseball
1976	Chris Evert, Tennis
1977	Steve Cauthen, Horse Racing
1978	Jack Nicklaus, Golf
1979	Terry Bradshaw, Pro Football
	Willie Stargell, Baseball
1980	U.S. Olympic Hockey Team
1981	Sugar Ray Leonard, Boxing
1982	Wayne Gretzky, Hockey
1983	Mary Decker, Track and Field
1984	Mary Lou Retton, Gymnastics
	Edwin Moses, Track and Field
1985	Kareem Abdul-Jabbar, Pro Basketball
1986	Joe Paterno, Football
1987	Athletes Who Care:
	Bob Bourne, Hockey
	Kip Keino, Track and Field
	Judi Brown King, Track and Field
	Dale Murphy, Baseball
	Chip Rives, Football
	Patty Sheehan, Golf
	Rory Sparrow, Pro Basketball
	Reggie Williams, Pro Football
1988	Orel Hershiser, Baseball
1989	Greg LeMond, Cycling
1990	Joe Montana, Pro Football
1991	Michael Jordan, Pro Basketball
1992	Arthur Ashe, Tennis
1993	Don Shula, Pro Football
1994	Bonnie Blair, Speed Skating
	Johann Olav Koss, Speed Skating
1995	Cal Ripken Jr, Baseball
1996	Tiger Woods, Golf
1997	Dean Smith, College Basketball
1998	Mark McGwire, Sammy Sosa, Baseball
1999	U.S. Women's Soccer Team
2000	Tiger Woods, Golf
2001	C. Schilling/ R. Johnson, Baseball
2002	Lance Armstrong, Cycling
2003	Tim Duncan/David Robinson, Basketball
2004	Boston Red Sox, Baseball
2005	Tom Brady, Pro Football
2006	Dwyane Wade, Pro Basketball

Associated Press Athletes of the Year

	MEN	WOMEN
1931	Pepper Martin, Baseball	Helene Madison, Swimming
1932	Gene Sarazen, Golf	Babe Didrikson, Track and Field
1933	Carl Hubbell, Baseball	Helen Jacobs, Tennis
1934	Dizzy Dean, Baseball	Virginia Van Wie, Golf
1935	Joe Louis, Boxing	Helen Wills Moody, Tennis
1936	Jesse Owens, Track and Field	Helen Stephens, Track and Field
1937	Don Budge, Tennis	Katherine Rawls, Swimming
1938	Don Budge, Tennis	Patty Berg, Golf
1939	Nile Kinnick, Football	Alice Marble, Tennis
1940	Tom Harmon, Football	Alice Marble, Tennis
1941	Joe DiMaggio, Baseball	Betty Hicks Newell, Golf
1942	Frank Sinkwich, Football	Gloria Callen, Swimming
1943	Gunder Haegg, Track and Field	Patty Berg, Golf
1944	Byron Nelson, Golf	Ann Curtis, Swimming
1945	Bryon Nelson, Golf	Babe Didrikson Zaharias, Golf
1946	Glenn Davis, Football	Babe Didrikson Zaharias, Golf
1947	Johnny Lujack, Football	Babe Didrikson Zaharias, Golf
1948	Lou Boudreau, Baseball	Fanny Blankers-Koen, Track and Field
1949	Leon Hart, Football	Marlene Bauer, Golf
1950	Jim Konstanty, Baseball	Babe Didrikson Zaharias, Golf
1951	Dick Kazmaier, Football	Maureen Connolly, Tennis
1952	Bob Mathias, Track and Field	Maureen Connolly, Tennis
1953	Ben Hogan, Golf	Maureen Connolly, Tennis
1954	Willie Mays, Baseball	Babe Didrikson Zaharias, Golf
1955	Hopalong Cassidy, Football	Patty Berg, Golf

Associated Press Athletes of the Year (Cont.)

	MEN	WOMEN
1956	Mickey Mantle, Baseball	Pat McCormick, Diving
1957	Ted Williams, Baseball	Althea Gibson, Tennis
1958	Herb Elliott, Track and Field	Althea Gibson, Tennis
1959	Ingemar Johansson, Boxing	Maria Bueno, Tennis
1960	Rafer Johnson, Track and Field	Wilma Rudolph, Track and Field
1961	Roger Maris, Baseball	Wilma Rudolph, Track and Field
1962	Maury Wills, Baseball	Dawn Fraser, Swimming
1963	Sandy Koufax, Baseball	Mickey Wright, Golf
1964	Don Schollander, Swimming	Mickey Wright, Golf
1965	Sandy Koufax, Baseball	Kathy Whitworth, Golf
1966	Frank Robinson, Baseball	Kathy Whitworth, Golf
1967	Carl Yastrzemski, Baseball	Billie Jean King, Tennis
1968	Denny McLain, Baseball	Peggy Fleming, Skating
1969	Tom Seaver, Baseball	Debbie Meyer, Swimming
1970	George Blanda, Pro Football	Chi Cheng, Track and Field
1971	Lee Trevino, Golf	Evonne Goolagong, Tennis
1972	Mark Spitz, Swimming	Olga Korbut, Gymnastics
1973	O.J. Simpson, Pro Football	Billie Jean King, Tennis
1974	Muhammad Ali, Boxing	Chris Evert, Tennis
1975	Fred Lynn, Baseball	Chris Evert, Tennis
1976	Bruce Jenner, Track and Field	Nadia Comaneci, Gymnastics
1977	Steve Cauthen, Horse Racing	Chris Evert, Tennis
1978	Ron Guidry, Baseball	Nancy Lopez, Golf
1979	Willie Stargell, Baseball	Tracy Austin, Tennis
1980	U.S. Olympic Hockey Team	Chris Evert Lloyd, Tennis
1981	John McEnroe, Tennis	Tracy Austin, Tennis
1982	Wayne Gretzky, Hockey	Mary Decker, Track and Field
1983	Carl Lewis, Track and Field	Martina Navratilova, Tennis
1984	Carl Lewis, Track and Field	Mary Lou Retton, Gymnastics
1985	Dwight Gooden, Baseball	Nancy Lopez, Golf
1986	Larry Bird, Pro Basketball	Martina Navratilova, Tennis
1987	Ben Johnson, Track and Field	Jackie Joyner-Kersee, Track and Field
1988	Orel Hershiser, Baseball	Florence Griffith Joyner, Track and Field
1989	Joe Montana, Pro Football	Steffi Graf, Tennis
1990	Joe Montana, Pro Football	Beth Daniel, Golf
1991	Michael Jordan, Pro Basketball	Monica Seles, Tennis
1992	Michael Jordan, Pro Basketball	Monica Seles, Tennis
1993	Michael Jordan, Pro Basketball	Sheryl Swoopes, Basketball
1994	George Foreman, Boxing	Bonnie Blair, Speed Skating
1995	Cal Ripken J r, Baseball	Rebecca Lobo, Basketball
1996	Michael Johnson, Track and Field	Amy Van Dyken, Swimming
1997	Tiger Woods, Golf	Martina Hingis, Tennis
1998	Mark McGwire, Baseball	Se Ri Pak, Golf
1999	Tiger Woods, Golf	U.S. Women's Soccer Team
2000	Tiger Woods, Golf	Marion Jones, Track and Field
2001	Barry Bonds, Baseball	Jennifer Capriati, Tennis
2002	Lance Armstrong, Cycling	Serena Williams, Tennis
2003	Lance Armstrong, Cycling	Annika Sorenstam, Golf
2004	Lance Armstrong, Cycling	Annika Sorenstam, Golf
2005	Lance Armstrong, Cycling	Annika Sorenstam, Golf
2006	Tiger Woods, Golf	Lorena Ochoa, Golf

James E. Sullivan Award

Presented annually by the AAU to the athlete who "by his or her performance, example and influence as an amateur, has done the most during the year to advance the cause of sportsmanship."

1930	Bobby Jones, Golf
1931	Barney Berlinger, Track and Field
1932	Jim Bausch, Track and Field
1933	Glenn Cunningham, Track and Field
1934	Bill Bonthron, Track and Field
1935	Lawson Little, Golf
1936	Glenn Morris, Track and Field
1937	Don Budge, Tennis
1938	Don Lash, Track and Field
1939	Joe Burk, Rowing
1940	Greg Rice, Track and Field
1941	Leslie MacMitchell, Track and Field
1942	Cornelius Warmerdam, Track
1943	Gilbert Dodds, Track and Field
1944	Ann Curtis, Swimming
1945	Doc Blanchard, Football
1946	Arnold Tucker, Football
1947	John B. Kelly Jr, Rowing
1948	Bob Mathias, Track and Field
1949	Dick Button, Skating
1950	Fred Wilt, Track and Field
1951	Bob Richards, Track and Field
1952	Horace Ashenfelter, Track and Field
1953	Sammy Lee, Diving
1954	Mal Whitfield, Track and Field
1955	Harrison Dillard, Track and Field
1956	Pat McCormick, Diving
1957	Bobby Morrow, Track and Field
1958	Glenn Davis, Track and Field
1959	Parry O'Brien, Track and Field
1960	Rafer Johnson, Track and Field
1961	Wilma Rudolph, Track and Field
1962	Jim Beatty, Track and Field
1963	John Pennel, Track and Field
1964	Don Schollander, Swimming
1965	Bill Bradley, Basketball
1966	Jim Ryun, Track and Field
1967	Randy Matson, Track and Field
1968	Debbie Meyer, Swimming
1969	Bill Toomey, Track and Field
1970	John Kinsella, Swimming
1971	Mark Spitz, Swimming
1972	Frank Shorter, Track and Field
1973	Bill Walton, Basketball
1974	Rich Wohlhuter, Track and Field
1975	Tim Shaw, Swimming
1976	Bruce Jenner, Track and Field
1977	John Naber, Swimming
1978	Tracy Caulkins, Swimming
1979	Kurt Thomas, Gymnastics
1980	Eric Heiden, Speed Skating
1981	Carl Lewis, Track and Field
1982	Mary Decker, Track and Field
1983	Edwin Moses, Track and Field
1984	Greg Louganis, Diving
1985	Joan B.-Samuelson, T & F
1986	Jackie Joyner-Kersee, T & F
1987	Jim Abbott, Baseball
1988	Florence Griffith Joyner, Track
1989	Janet Evans, Swimming
1990	John Smith, Wrestling

James E. Sullivan Award (Cont.)

1991	Mike Powell, Track and Field
1992	Bonnie Blair, Speed Skating
1993	Charlie Ward, Football, Basketball
1994	Dan Jansen, Speed Skating
1995	Bruce Baumgartner, Wrestling
1996	Michael Johnson, Track and Field
1997	Peyton Manning, Football
1998	Chamique Holdsclaw, Basketball
1999	Kelly and Coco Miller, Basketball
2000	Rulon Gardner, Wrestling
2001	Michelle Kwan, Figure Skating
2002	Sarah Hughes, Figure Skating
2003	Michael Phelps, Swimming
2004	Paul Hamm, Gymnastics
2005	J. J. Redick, College Basketball
2006	Jessica Long, Paralympic Swimmer

The Sporting News Sportsman of the Year

1968	Denny McLain, Baseball
1969	Tom Seaver, Baseball
1970	John Wooden, Basketball
1971	Lee Trevino, Golf
1972	Charles O. Finley, Baseball
1973	O.J. Simpson, Pro Football
1974	Lou Brock, Baseball
1975	Archie Griffin, Football
1976	Larry O'Brien, Pro Basketball
1977	Steve Cauthen, Horse Racing
1978	Ron Guidry, Baseball
1979	Willie Stargell, Baseball
1980	George Brett, Baseball
1981	Wayne Gretzky, Hockey
1982	Whitey Herzog, Baseball
1983	Bowie Kuhn, Baseball
1984	Peter Ueberroth, LA Olympics
1985	Pete Rose, Baseball
1986	Larry Bird, Pro Basketball
1987	No award
1988	Jackie Joyner-Kersee, T & F
1989	Joe Montana, Pro Football
1990	Nolan Ryan, Baseball
1991	Michael Jordan, Pro Basketball
1992	Mike Krzyzewski, Basketball
1993	Pat Gillick/Cito Gaston, Baseball
1994	Emmitt Smith, Pro Football
1995	Cal Ripken Jr, Baseball
1996	Joe Torre, Baseball
1997	Michael Jordan, Basketball
1998	Mark McGwire, Baseball
1999	New York Yankees, Baseball
2000	Kurt Warner/Marshall Faulk, Pro Football
2001	Curt Schilling, Baseball
2002	Tyrone Willingham, Football
2003	Jack McKeon, Baseball / Dick Vermeil, Pro Football
2004	Tom Brady, Pro Football
2005	Matt Leinart, College Football
2006	LaDainian Tomlinson, Pro Football

United Press International Male and Female Athlete of the Year

	MEN	WOMEN
1974	Muhammad Ali, Boxing	Irena Szewinska, Track and Field
1975	Joao Oliveira, Track and Field	Nadia Comaneci, Gymnastics
1976	Alberto Juantorena, Track and Field	Nadia Comaneci, Gymnastics
1977	Alberto Juantorena, Track and Field	Rosie Ackermann, Track and Field
1978	Henry Rono, Track and Field	Tracy Caulkins, Swimming
1979	Sebastian Coe, Track and Field	Marita Koch, Track and Field
1980	Eric Heiden, Speed Skating	Hanni Wenzel, Alpine Skiing
1981	Sebastian Coe, Track and Field	Chris Evert Lloyd, Tennis
1982	Daley Thompson, Track and Field	Marita Koch, Track and Field
1983	Carl Lewis, Track and Field	Jarmila Kratochvilova, Track and Field
1984	Carl Lewis, Track and Field	Martina Navratilova, Tennis
1985	Steve Cram, Track and Field	Mary Decker Slaney, Track and Field
1986	Diego Maradona, Soccer	Heike Drechsler, Track and Field
1987	Ben Johnson, Track and Field	Steffi Graf, Tennis
1988	Matt Biondi, Swimming	Florence Griffith Joyner, Track and Field
1989	Boris Becker, Tennis	Steffi Graf, Tennis
1990	Stefan Edberg, Tennis	Merlene Ottey, Track and Field
1991	Michael Jordan, Pro Basketball	Monica Seles, Tennis
1992	Mario Lemieux, Hockey	Monica Seles, Tennis
1993	Michael Jordan, Pro Basketball	Steffi Graf, Tennis
1994	Nick Price, Golf	Bonnie Blair, Speed Skating
1995	Cal Ripken Jr, Baseball	Steffi Graf, Tennis

Note: Award not given since 1995.

Dial Award

Presented by the Dial Corporation to the male and female national high school athlete/scholar of the year.

	BOYS	GIRLS
1979	Herschel Walker, Football	No award
1980	Bill Fralic, Football	Carol Lewis, Track and Field
1981	Kevin Willhite, Football	Cheryl Miller, Basketball
1982	Mike Smith, Basketball	Elaine Zayak, Skating
1983	Chris Spielman, Football	Melanie Buddemeyer, Swimming
1984	Hart Lee Dykes, Football	Nora Lewis, Basketball
1985	Jeff George, Football	Gea Johnson, Track and Field
1986	Scott Schaffner, Football	Mya Johnson, Track and Field
1987	Todd Marinovich, Football	Kristi Overton, Water Skiing
1988	Carlton Gray, Football	Courtney Cox, Basketball
1989	Robert Smith, Football	Lisa Leslie, Basketball
1990	Derrick Brooks, Football	Vicki Goetze, Golf
1991	Jeff Buckey, Football, Track and Field	Katie Smith, Basketball, Volleyball, Track
1992	Jacque Vaughn, Basketball	Amanda White, Track and Field, Swimming
1993	Tiger Woods, Golf	Kristin Folkl, Basketball
1994	Taymon Domzalski, Basketball	Shannon Miller, Gymnastics
1995	Brent Abernathy, Baseball	Shea Ralph, Basketball
1996	Grant Irons, Football	Grace Park, Golf
1997	Ronald Curry, Football	Michelle Kwan, Figure Skating

Note: Award not given since 1997.

Obituaries

Red Auerbach
1917–2006

Arnold "Red" Auerbach, 89, NBA coach.
SI writes:

"Auerbach didn't have to wave his rolled-up program from the bench or smoke his victory cigar during another Celtics victory to cut an intimidating (or abrasive) figure at Boston Garden in 1956–57. That season Auerbach coached Boston to the first of 11 NBA championships in 13 years; his larcenous personnel moves as general manager laid the groundwork for five more titles. Auerbach had the foresight to draft Larry Bird prior to his senior year at Indiana State, ensuring that Bird would enter the NBA a year later as a member of the Celtics. Although he lived in Washington, D.C., throughout his career, he remained an executive for the team."

In Washington, D.C., of a heart attack, on October. 28, 2006.

Jack Palance, 87, boxer. *SI writes:*

"Palance attended North Carolina on a football scholarship but dropped out to box under the name Jack Brazzo. 'Then I thought, You must be nuts to get your head beat in for $200 [a fight],' he said in 1995. 'The theater seemed a lot more appealing.' So after a brief stint as a sportswriter following World War II (he received a Purple Heart), Palance gave acting a shot. One of his most notable roles was in '56, when he played a washed-up fighter in a TV production of Requiem for a Heavyweight, for which he won an Emmy."

In Montecito, Calif., of natural causes, on November 10, 2006

Bo Schembechler, 77, college football coach.
SI writes:

"Schembechler learned his trade—pound the ball straight ahead and don't get fancy—from Woody Hayes when he was an assistant coach at Ohio State. In 1969, Schembechler's first season in Ann Arbor, his Wolverines won the Big Ten title by upsetting Hayes's top-ranked Buckeyes, earning a trip to Pasadena. An intense man in the calmest of times, Schembechler suffered a heart attack on the eve of the Rose Bowl. But he was back on the sideline the following fall and for the 20 falls after that. He retired with a dozen more conference championships, 17 bowl appearances and a 5–4–1 record against Hayes in what became known as the Ten-Year War."

In. Southfield, Mich., of heart disease, on November 17, 2006.

Ferenc Puskas, 79, soccer player. *Former Hungarian national team captain. SI writes:*

"One of the giants of international soccer in the 1950s, Puskas, known as the 'Galloping Major' in honor of his rank in the Hungarian army, scored 84 goals in 85 games for the national team and led Hungary to an Olympic gold medal in 1952 and the final of the '54 World Cup. He also starred in one of European soccer's most famous matches, scoring two goals in Hungary's shocking upset of England at Wembley Stadium in 1953. In 1999 Puskas was voted the sixth-best player of the 20th century."

In Budapest, Hungary, of respiratory and circulatory failure, on November, 17, 2006.

Pat Dobson, 64, baseball player. *Former Orioles pitcher was part of the last major league staff with four 20-game winners. SI writes:*

"In 1971 Dobson went 20–8 for the Orioles, whose Dave McNally, Jim Palmer and Mike Cuellar also also hit the milestone. (The only other team with four 20-game winners was the '20 White Sox.) Dobson, who pitched for six teams in his 11-year career, had a record of 122–129. For the past nine years he worked for the Giants as a scout and a special assistant to the general manager. 'He had a great curveball,' said Frank Robinson, a former Baltimore teammate. 'He didn't give in to anybody.'

In San Diego, Calif., of leukemia, on November 22, 2006.

Andra Franklin, 47, football player. *Former Nebraska running back. SI writes:*

"The bruising fullback rushed for 1,738 yards and 10 touchdowns for the Huskers and was taken in the second round of the 1981 draft by the Dolphins. Franklin played four seasons in the NFL. He made the Pro Bowl in 1982, when he was third in the NFL in rushing with 701 yards in a nine-game, strike-shortened season. He was forced to retire at the age 26 due to chronic knee injuries and reportedly had heart problems in recent years.

In. Lincoln, Neb., of heart failure, on December 6, 2006.

Jose Uribe, 47, baseball player. *Former Giants shortstop. SI writes:*

"Dominican Republic police said Uribe crashed his SUV on the highway as he drove toward his hometown of Juan Baron, where he lost a run for mayor in 2006. Uribe played 10 seasons, from 1984 through '93, mostly with the Giants, and had a lifetime .241 average."

In the Dominican Republic, of injuries sustained in an automobile accident, on December 8, 2006.

Gerald R. Ford, 93, college football player and coach. *SI writes:*

"Before becoming the 38th President of the United States, Ford was a genuine big-time athlete. After riding the bench for a couple of very good Michigan football teams, he came into his own as the Wolverines' MVP in 1934 and played center in two All-Star games, going against the Chicago Bears back when college kids played the pro champs. Ford passed up offers from the Green Bay Packers and Detroit Lions, choosing to become an assistant football coach and freshman boxing coach at Yale, where, a few years later, he attended law school. He often mused on the road not taken. 'I've wondered if one year of playing pro ball might have been a good thing,' he told SI's Michael Blamberger in 2005. 'Good for the resume.'"

In Rancho Mirage, Calif., of cerebrovascular disease, on December 26, 2006.

Mario Danelo, 21, college football player. *Former USC kicker and NCAA record-holder. SI writes:*

"Danelo's body was found on the morning of January 6, 2007 after he fell the previous night from a seaside cliff in San Pedro, Calif. Police were unsure what caused the fall but didn't believe it was the result of any criminal behavior. Danelo, a junior and the son of former NFL kicker Joe Danelo, missed only two field goals in two seasons as the Trojans' kicker and set an NCAA record for extra points (83) in 2005."

In San Pedro, Calif., of multiple traumatic injuries sustained from a fall, on January 6.

Bobby Hamilton, 49, NASCAR driver. *SI writes:*

"The Nashville native came into the sport long before the current generation of media-savvy young guns, and he never lost his old school roots or his forthrightness. In 2001, after then rookie Kevin Harvick—who had taken over the car of Hamilton's friend Dale Earnhardt after Earnhardt died—got into a few on-track scrapes, Hamilton said, on live TV, 'He thinks he is Dale Earnardt. But right now he wouldn't be a scab on Dale Earnhardt's butt.'"

"Hamilton won four Nextel Cup races, and in 2004 he won the Craftsman Truck Series championship: He drove the first three races of the 2006 season before turning the seat over to his son Bobby Jr. and beginning treatment for cancer in his neck and head."

In Mt. Juliet, Tenn, of cancer, on January 7.

Maureen Orcutt, 99, golfer/writer. *SI writes:*

"The former amateur golf champion and *New York Times* sportswriter won more than 65 major amateur tournaments and was runner-up for the U.S. Amateur title in 1927 and '36. In 1937 she began covering golf and writing a "Women in Sports" column for the *Times*, where she worked—often as the only woman in the sports department—for 35 years. Throughout her life, Orcutt played exhibitions, including one at Augusta during the 1920s when she was paired with Walter Hagen. 'I would get a lady golfer,' Hagen complained. Years later Orcutt recalled in the *Times*, 'I didn't say anything...But the next day I carried Hagen for nine holes and we won.'"

In Durham, NC., of natural causes, on January 9.

Benny Parsons, 65, NASCAR driver. *SI writes:*

"Ex-Detroit cab driver Parsons raced at local tracks in Michigan before moving up to the ARCA series in 1965. After winning consecutive championships there, he made the jump to the big time, joining NASCAR full time in 1970. Parsons was the Winston Cup (now Nextel Cup) champion in 1973, and in '82 he became the first driver to break the 200-mph barrier in qualifying, at Talladega. In his 21-year career Parsons won 21 races, including the 1975 Daytona 500. His contemporaries swore—only half-jokingly—that he could have won plenty more, but was too friendly to engage in the bumping and paint swapping that his job sometimes required."

In Charlotte, N.C., of lung cancer, on January 16.

Bernie "Schoolboy" Friedkin, 89, boxer. *SI writes:*

"Friedkin got his nickname because of his youthful appearance. (One reason he looked so young: He used his brother's birth certificate to sneak into Brooklyn gyms when he was 14.) The 5'6" lightweigtht and featherweight didn't win many big fights—he was never a world champ—but he didn't lose many either. In the late 1930s and '40s Friedkin, whose record was 48–11–16, fought three former world champs to draws.

In Brooklyn, N.Y., of natural causes, on January 18.

Vern Ruhle, 55, baseball pitcher. *SI writes:*

"In his 13-year career with four teams, Ruhle was 67–88, but in 1980 he played a pivotal role in the Astros' winning their first division title. Ruhle went 12–4 with a 2.37 ERA in 22 starts—many of which came after the team's ace, J.R. Richard, suffered a career-ending stroke that July. After Ruhle retired in 1986, he became a pitching coach for four major league teams."

In Houston, Tex., of cancer, on January 20.

Gump Worsley, 77, hockey player. *SI writes:*

"The colorful Gumper—named after the comic strip character Andy Gump—was old school in every way, down to playing without a mask. He played 21 NHL seasons without one becase, as he was fond of saying,

'My face is my mask.' Worsley's portfolio was impressive —he shared two Vezina trophies as the NHL's best goalie and won four Stanley Cups in the 1960s with his hometown Canadiens."

In. Beloeil, Quebec, Canada, of complications from a heart attack, on January 26.

Hassan Hadi, 42, boxer. *The well-known Iraqi boxer was kidnapped in January. SI writes:*

"The Shiite boxer was abducted from his car on January 22, 2007 on a street in a Sunni stronghold, and his body was found four days later. He had been hanged. His murder was the latest in a spell of attacks aimed at sports figures, which has resulted in the murder of Iraq's Olympic wrestling and cycling coaches. Several other athletes and coaches have been targeted for ransom or retaliation, and approximately 30 members of the country's Olympic committee have been missing since they were kidnapped last July."

In Baghdad, on January 26.

Bing Devine, 90, MLB general manager. *SI writes:*

"Devine, as G.M. of the St. Louis Cardinals, pulled off one of the most lopsided trades in baseball history. In 1964 he swapped sore-shouldered pitcher Ernie Broglio for Cubs outfielder Lou Brock, who went on to a Hall of Fame career in St. Louis. Devine served as the Redbirds' G.M. from 1958 to '64 and from '68 to '78. His teams won two NL pennants and one World Series."

In. St. Louis, Mo., of natural causes; on January 27.

Barbaro, 3, race horse.

Kentucky Derby winner Barbaro was euthanized in January after complications from his breakdown at the Preakness in May 2006. "We just reached a point where it was going to be difficult for him to go on without pain," co-owner Roy Jackson said. "It was the right decision, it was the right thing to do. We said all along if there was a situation where it would become more difficult for him then it would be time.".

In Philadelphia, Penn., January 29.

Steve Barber, 68, baseball player. *SI writes:*

"In 1963 Barber went 20–13 with a 2.75 ERA for the Orioles. Midway through the '67 season, the lefty took part in one of the wildest no-hitters baseball has ever seen. Pitching in Baltimore, he walked 10 Tigers in 8⅔ hitless innings before he was finally pulled with two men on and the score tied 1-1. Detroit then scored the winning run on an error. (Barber also hit two batters, had one wild pitch and made a throwing error that day.) In his 15-year career with seven teams, Barber was 121–106 and made two All-Star teams.

In Henderson, Nev., of complications from pneumonia, on February 4.

Lew Burdette, 80, baseball player. *Former Braves pitcher. SI writes:*

"Burdette knew a thing or two about being crafty. The Nitro, W.V. native—who practiced as a boy by throwing rocks at church windows—relied on a sinker that many insisted was a spitball. But on the field Burdette, who won 203 games, was all business. 'He was a very hard-nosed, tough pitcher when he crossed that white line,' former Braves shortstop Johnny Logan said. 'He was a battler.'"

In Winter Garden, Fla., of lung cancer, on February 6.

Willye White, 67, track and field. *The only track and field athlete to compete in five Olympics for the U.S. SI writes:*

"White won two silver medals in the long jump in 1956 (when she was 16) and in the 4x100-meter relay in 1964. For White, who chopped cotton as a child in the Mississippi delta, the Games were a chance to experience life beyond her hometown of Greenwood, Miss. 'Before my first Olympics, I thought the whole world consisted of cross burnings and lynchings,' she said in 1999."

In Chicago, Ill., of pancreatic cancer, on February 6.

Eddie "The King" Feigner, 81, softball player.
Led the four-man softball team The King and His Court for five decades. SI writes:

"Feigner started his abbreviated squad in 1946 on a dare after his nine-man Walla Walla, Wash., team routed a team from Oregon. Feigner, his catcher, first baseman and shortstop won the rematch 7–0. Over the next 54 years Feigner, whose fastball was once clocked at 104 mph, pitched more than 10,000 games, often throwing between his legs, behind his back or from second base. He also pitched—blindfolded—to celebrities, including Johnny Carson, and in a 1964 exhibition at Dodger Stadium he struck out Willie Mays, Willie McCovey, Maury Wills, Harmon Killebrew, Roberto Clemente and Brooks Robinson in order."

In Huntsville, Ala., from complications of dementia, on February 9.

Hank Bauer, 84, baseball player. *SI writes:*
"After Bauer returned from a 34-month overseas stint in the Marines, he thought his baseball career was over. An outfielder for Oshkosh of the Class D Wisconsin State League, Bauer enlisted in January 1942. He served in nearly every major Pacific invasion and came home with two Bronze Stars, two Purple Hearts and a very sore leg, courtesy of some shrapnel he took in Okinawa. Bauer was ready to take a job as a steamfitter when an old friend persuaded him to give baseball one more chance. Three years later Bauer was in the Yankees' outfield, winning the first of his seven World Series titles with the Bombers. (He won an eighth as the Orioles' manager in 1966.) A three-time All-Star, Bauer hit .277 with 164 homers in 14 seasons. His 17-game World Series hitting streak, set between '56 and '58, is still a record."

In Kansas City, Mo., from lung cancer, on February 9.

Dennis Johnson, 52, basketball player. *Former Celtics guard. SI writes:*
"Johnson depended mainly on his moxie, his mental toughness and his court awareness. But there was a time when the 6'4" guard relied on his athleticism. At Pepperdine, Johnson was so explosive that he—not the Waves' 6'10" center—jumped the opening tip. The Sonics took him in the second round of the 1976 NBA draft, and within three years he had led Seattle to its only NBA title and begun a run of nine straight appearances on the NBA All-Defesive team. The Celtics acquired him in 1983, largely because they needed someone who could stop Philadelphia's Andrew Toney from lighting them up. Johnson also memorably checked Magic Johnson during the last four games of the 1984 NBA Finals; Boston took three of the four to win the series in seven games."

In Austin Tx., from a heart attack, on February 22.

Lamar Lundy, 71, football player. *Former member of the Los Angeles Rams' Fearsome Foursome defensive line of the 1960's. SI writes:*
"The original Fearsome Foursome included Lundy, Hall of Famer Merlin Olsen, Roosevelt Grier and Hall of Famer Deacon Jones. Roger Brown replaced Grier in 1967, and the following season the Rams held opponents to 3,118 yards, the fewest yards ever allowed in a 14-game NFL season. Lundy, who retired in 1969, played his entire 13-year career with the Rams. 'He really was the stabilizing force," said Olsen. 'Mr. Consistency'."

In Richmond, Ind., after a long illness, on February 24.

Damien Nash, 24, football player. *SI writes:*
"Following a charity basketball game in his hometown of St. Louis, Broncos running back Nash was found dead in a suburban residence. The cause of death remains undetermined and was not drug or alcohol-related. Drafted in the fifth round out of Missouri in 2005, Nash ran 18 times for 66 yards in three games in 2006. He helped organized the charity game, which benefited a heart-transplant organization named after his older brother, Darris Nash, the recipient of a heart transplant. 'He looked in great shape [at the game],' said Lee Baker, a teammate of Nash's at Coffeyville (Kan.) Community College. 'He had a big smile on his face. I want to think I'm dreaming.'"

In St. Louis, Mo., on February 24.

Bluffton University baseball players. *SI writes:*
"When their team bus crashed outside Atlanta, five Bluffton University baseball players were killed. The team had been traveling from the small Mennonite-affiliated school 55 miles south of Toledo to Sarasota, Fla., for its season opener. Authorities said the driver apparently mistook an exit ramp for a regular interstate lane and the bus toppled over a barrier, landing on the highway 25 feet below and leaving blood and baseball equipment strewn across the pavement. In addition to the five players who died, the driver and his wife were also killed."

In Atlanta, Ga., on March 2.

Ernie Ladd, 68, football player and professional wrestler. *Ladd has been elected to both the AFL Hall of Fame and the WWE Hall of Fame. SI writes:*
"Ladd was a 6'9" defensive lineman for the Chiefs, Oilers, and Chargers before being lured to the world of pro wrestling by 'Classy' Freddie Blassie. In the early 1960s Blassie was trying to boost attendance in San Diego, so he cast Ladd, who was then with the Chargers, as a bad guy. Ladd gave up football for good in '69 and became one of pro wrestling's biggest stars in the '70s. 'Comparing the two, I would have to say I enjoyed professional wrestling more,' he said in 2000. 'It allowed me to show my gift for gab.'"

In Franklin, La., of cancer, on March 10.

Bowie Kuhn, 80, commissioner of major league baseball.
Bowie Kuhn was baseball's bespectacled Ivy League lawyer and looked the part every day of the tumultuous 15 years (1969–84) he ruled as commissioner. Detractors called him a "stuffed shirt" and "pompous," labels that amused him. Despite his regal bearing, he was as ornery as the owners and players he feuded with over a span that became the second-longest tenure among nine commissioners. "He led our game through a great deal of change and controversy," commissioner Bud Selig said. "Yet, Bowie laid the groundwork for the success we enjoy today."

In Jacksonville, Fla., of respiratory failure, on March 15.

Homer Harris, 90, college football player. *SI writes:*
"Harris was a former defensive lineman at Iowa and the Big Ten's first black football captain. He was a